The Volume Library is user-friendly. The books are organized into six academic disciplines (Mathematics, Science, Social Science, Language, History, and the World), making related subject matter easy to find.

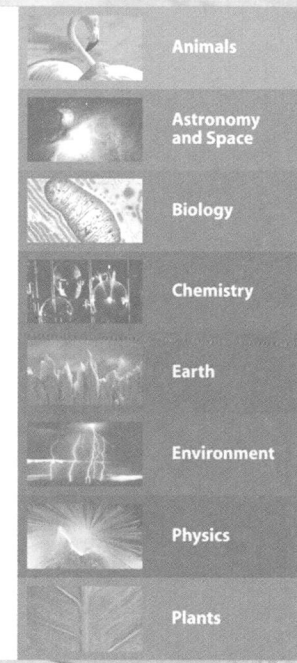

Science

- Animals
- Astronomy and Space
- Biology
- Chemistry
- Earth
- Environment
- Physics
- Plants

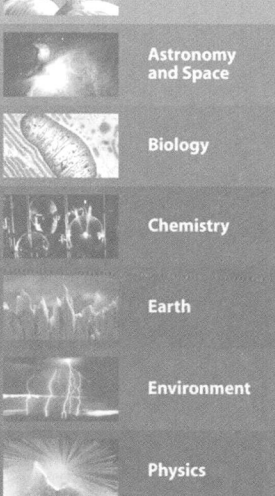

What Is Physics?

Physics may be said to be the story of matter, radiation, and their interaction. Matter appears everywhere in various forms. It has such characteristic properties as mass, temperature, and hardness.

In a similar sense, radiation is omnipresent in the universe. We experience radiation in different forms, for example, as light or heat radiation. Radiation is not matter, although it has some properties of matter. Radiation can be described both as an electromagnetic wave and as a particle called the photon. Bohr was the first to point out that descriptions are complementary: on certain conditions, radiation may behave as a wave or as a particle.

Physics. Physics, once called philosophy, forms the basis of several other sciences. Chemistry may be called the physics of atoms. In chemistry, the physics of atomic physics. The properties of substances and the changes they undergo are determined by properties of the atoms of which they are composed.

Physics is often called the demarcation between physics and engineering now is especially labeled to deal with the matter.

The complex physics, electricity, optics, heat, and nuclear physics...

Mechanics is basic to much of engineering, certainly to structural mechanics. Sir Isaac Newton developed mechanics to the stage where he was able to determine the velocity and energy needed to put a satellite into orbit.

Thermodynamics. Thermodynamics is the study of heat and of the behavior of matter with respect to thermal energy. The laws of thermodynamics include the conservation of energy, the decrease of available energy, the trend in nature that is termed increase of entropy.

Electricity and magnetism. Electricity and magnetism deal with the characteristics of electric charges, currents, electric fields, and magnetic fields. The practical application of this knowledge led to development of electric machinery and of electronics.

Optics. Physical optics deals with light as a form of electromagnetic radiation. Geometrical optics traces the paths of light rays through such devices as lenses and a variety of other optical instruments. Relatively recent developments in optics include lasers and fiber optics.

Acoustics. Acoustics deals with phenomena related to sound and might well have been called the study of elastic waves in solids, liquids, and gases.

Nuclear physics. Radioactivity was the first nuclear phenomenon studied by physicists, and this study established that not all atomic nuclei are stable. Atomic energy, which is more appropriately called nuclear energy, is the practical application of nuclear physics.

Quantum theory. At the beginning of this century, Max Planck introduced to us the theory that energy is quantized, meaning that instead of being able to take on any value, energy comes in little packets, which Einstein dubbed photons. From this realization evolved the field of quantum mechanics. Among the evolution of quantum theory is the uncertainty principle, which states that the precise momentum and position of a particle cannot be known at the same time, not merely due to experimental inaccuracies, but due to the very nature of the particle. Even though many aspects of the theory are very difficult to accept, it is now regarded as the most successful physical theory ever.

Solid-state physics. Engineers and physicists have recently given much attention to the electrical and mechanical properties of solids. Although solids have always been a part of our environment, only recently has it been possible to relate the behavior and characteristics of solids to the properties of the atoms of which solids are composed.

Since 1900, physicists have been aware of a penetrating radiation coming to Earth from outer space. Although called radiation, the primary component that strikes the upper atmosphere is known now to be made up largely, if not completely, of atomic nuclei. Protons, the nuclei of hydrogen atoms, predominate and enter the upper atmosphere with extremely high energies. Their origin and the source of their energy are

Each chapter's pages are individually numbered.

Each chapter's color coding, name, and number are clear and easily accessible.

These blue boxes note the differences between standard British and American spellings.

10 Physics

3

fiber US
fibre Brit.

Milestones in Physics

c 200 B.C.	**Archimedes** observes and formulates laws of levers and pulleys as well as determining weight and volume relationships.
1543	**Nicolaus Copernicus** formulates theory that earth and other planets move in circles around the sun.
1600	**Galileo** builds telescopes for studying the heavens and other planets move in of mechanics.
1687	**Sir Isaac Newton** publishes his laws of motion.
1690	**Christiaan Huygens** publishes the wave theory of light.
1803	**John Dalton** proposes his theory on the atomic structure of matter.
1830s	**Michael Faraday and Joseph Henry** independently produce electricity using magnetism.
1860s	**James Clerk Maxwell** predicts existence of electromagnetic waves.
1895	**Wilhelm Roentgen** discovers x-rays.
1896	**Antoine Bequerel** discovers natural radioactivity.
1898	**Marie and Pierre Curie** isolate radioactive radium.
1900	**Max Planck** publishes his quantum theory.
1912	**Ernest Rutherford** publishes his quantum theory.
	Albert Einstein announces his theory of relativity.
	Paul Dirac predicts existence of positively charged electrons called positrons.
	John Cockcroft and Ernest Walton build first particle accelerator.
	Enrico Fermi achieves first controlled nuclear chain reaction.
	John Bardeen, Walter Brattain, and William Shockley invent the transistor.
	Theodore Maiman builds the first laser.
	Ceramic superconductors are developed.

VOLUME LIBRARY

A Modern, Authoritative Reference for Home and School Use

Clear and Complete • Colorfully Illustrated • Totally Indexed

Slr

SOUTHWESTERN

Nashville, Tennessee

Southwestern/Great American Inc.

Nashville, Tennessee
www.southwestern.com

The Volume Library

Designed, edited, and manufactured
under the direction of FRP™—a division of
Southwestern/Great American Inc.
Nashville, Tennessee

The Volume Library

Editorial

Editorial Director
Mary Cummings

Managing Editor
Judy Jackson

Editors
Georgia L. Brazil
Barbara J. Reed

Volume Editors
Jane Hinshaw
Linda Jones
Susan Larson
Elizabeth Miller
Debbie Van Mol
Tanis Westbrook
Mary Wilson

Research Editors
Ashley Bienvenu
Molly Kempf

Copy Editors
Tammy Binford
Andaleah Freihoefer
Amy Green
Carolyn King

Art

Design Director
Steve Newman

Designers
Mary Jane Huffines
Bill Kersey
Jim Scott

Production Designer
Travis Rader

Illustrators
Laura Goode
Glendo Grider
Richard Jacobson
Paul Trice

Digital Prepress
Donna Bailey

Composition
Jessie Anglin
Sara Anglin
Linda Bennie
Nan Waller

Production

Production Manager
Tom Norvell

Senior Production Coordinator
Powell Ropp

Schedule Coordinator
Wanda Sawyer

Marketing

Vice President and Executive Editor
Dan Moore

Product Manager
Fiona Greenland

Associate Editors
Sharon Dean
Lisa Fairfax

Sales

Sales Director
Roy Loftin

The original *The Volume Library* text, substantial portions of which are included,
was developed by The Hudson Group, Inc., Pleasantville, New York:
Gorton Carruth, Editor-in-Chief, and Eugene Ehrlich, Sponsoring Editor.

iv

Contents

Book 1

7 Chemistry

8 Earth

9 Environment

10 Physics

11 Plants

12 Business and Economics

13 Government and Law

14 People

15 Sociology

Preface

Welcome to *The Volume Library*.

We are pleased to bring you this set of unique, user-friendly family reference books. Their 4,000+ color photographs and illustrations, the organization of subject matter into the familiar educational disciplines, and the addition of a Help Desk for most chapters provide basic information as well as extended enrichment opportunities. (Read more about The Help Desk below.)

Recognizing that language is the mechanism for exchanging information and that English is one of the most widely used languages in the world has led to another unique feature of *The Volume Library*: blue boxes that note differences between standard British and United States spellings. (Read more about this on the next page.)

In the Math and English chapters, you will also note that some text is either highlighted in or printed in one of three different colors. Text highlighted in yellow contains key definitions or concepts; text highlighted in green indicates helpful hints or tips. Blue text is used for worked-out problems and examples.

We are also pleased to offer access to our Web site, www.southwestern.com, where, among other things, you will find listings of additional subject-specific reference materials, post-publication additions and corrections, and notes on using the books effectively. Every effort has been made to ensure that these books are as accurate as possible. If errors or omissions should be discovered, however, we would appreciate hearing from you. Please send comments or suggestions to editor@southwestern.com, or to Editor, Volume Library, P.O. Box 305142, Nashville, Tennessee 37230.

The staff of The Volume Library

THE HELP DESK

➤ **Whether** a regular assignment, extra credit project, or simple curiosity prompts you to seek more information, a focus makes the task easier and more fruitful. We have included in The Help Desks some suggestions for areas of study or exploration that will enable you to define that focus.

➤ **If you** wish to test your own knowledge and understanding, there is no better way than helping a child or friend to master a topic. Some examples and suggestions for that are also included.

➤ **A number** of the suggestions you will find in the Help Desk will help you develop your problem-solving, creative, and interpretive skills.

➤ **Many** Help Desk suggestions are quite broad and lend themselves to numerous more specific areas that allow for projects of varying time, length, and interests. Simply narrowing down a topic can be an interesting adventure.

➤ **Although** some suggestions require a trip to the library or some other interesting location, most will require only time and readily available materials.

➤ **Other** suggestions may be for fun family or group activities that foster sharing and cooperation, while some require purely individual effort and satisfaction.

➤ **Written** reports, directed reading, model building, gathering original data to develop conclusions, oral presentations, and demonstrations—something to meet everyone's needs, talents, and interests.

➤ **Let us** know what works for you so we can share your ideas with others.

Do You Speak English?

If so, you are among the half of the world's population who use English to communicate at least part of the time. The latter part of the 20th century witnessed the rise of English language as the global language. Today communications in business, diplomacy, and science are either conducted in English or translated into English in order to be accessible to the most people in the most readily understood form. Of approximately 6 billion people on Earth, over 30% speak English as their first language. An additional 7% speak English as a second language, having studied it in school. In addition, a sizeable number of people may not be fluent in English but have acquired enough dexterity with it to understand the spoken word through mass communication, radio, and television.

However, is it really the same language? Is the United Kingdom's English the same as that of the United States, or Australia, or Barbados, or Sierra Leone, or Ireland? The answer: a qualified "yes." While the residents of the British Isles have established the basis for the language, various countries and parts of countries have modified it to suit themselves. Such complexity is shown in this partial list of countries where English is considered to be the primary language:

American Samoa	Liberia
Antigua and Barbuda	Montserrat
Australia	New Zealand
Bahamas	Nigeria
Barbados	Northern Marianas
Belize	Papua New Guinea
Bermuda	St. Kitts
Canada	St. Vincent and the
Cayman Islands	Grenadines
Grenada	Sierra Leone
Guyana	Trinidad and Tobago
Ireland	United Kingdom
Jamaica	United States

While all the English-speaking people can presumably watch a television program and enjoy it through the common visual and language bond, the differences are also evident in puzzling words and phrases as well as almost automatic translation adjustments in vocabulary, phrase, and accent. Just as Americans must on occasion strain to filter an unfamiliar New England accent or Southern accent through their own regional ears, the exuberant Australian English must present a challenge to Yorkshire understanding.

The Volume Library has taken the first step in recognizing some of the differences in the magnificent, living, ever-adaptable language we know as English. As a beginning, we have highlighted a few of the spelling variations between British and American English. As you peruse *The Volume Library*, notice the blue boxes in the outside margins of the pages. Those boxes contain words that appear in the text in the standard American spelling. The boxes also contain the preferred British spelling. (Note: In the case of the British spelling, some British dictionaries may show that the American spelling is also

acceptable in British usage and vice versa in American dictionaries.) The first time the word appears on a spread (a spread is the two facing left- and right-hand pages as the volume lies open) in the text, it appears in blue type. The words that have been so treated constitute a select limited lexicon confined to only a few of the spelling variations represented by certain repetitive letter combinations:

The -or/-our group:

color/colour	honor/honour
vigor/vigour	armor/armour
labor/labour	odor/odour
flavor/flavour	endeavor/endeavour
valor/valour	humor/humour
savor/savour	neighbor/neighbour

The -ize/-ise group:
these seem to be in transition but only of recent documentation so all of them on the list will be treated as -ize American for regular text spelling and also appear in the blue box as -ise British.

civilize/civilise
organize/organise
apologize/apologise
analyze/analyse
digitize/digitise
categorize/categorise
emphasize/emphasise
realize/realise/realisation
colonize/colonise/colonisers
colonization for both American/British

The -er/-re group:

center/centre	somber/sombre
fiber/fibre	meager/meagre
liter/litre	specter/spectre
theater/theatre	

The -eo/-oeo group:

esophagus/oesophagus	fetus/foetus
estrogen/oestrogen	fetid/foetid

Other words:

aluminum/aluminium
trapezoid/trapezium
gasoline/petrol
main street/high street
story/storey (of a building)
check/cheque

In coming editions, we intend to increase the scope of British/American linguistic variations. The spelling issue is only one of several we have detected. Some differences are as simple as familiar words for familiar things that are practically synonyms, easily used interchangeably on both sides of the Atlantic, as are the following examples:

British	American
lift	elevator
tube	subway
telly	TV (television)
parcel	package
chemist	drugstore or pharmacist
film	movie
cinema	movie theater
flat	apartment
ring up	call on the phone
bad show	tough luck

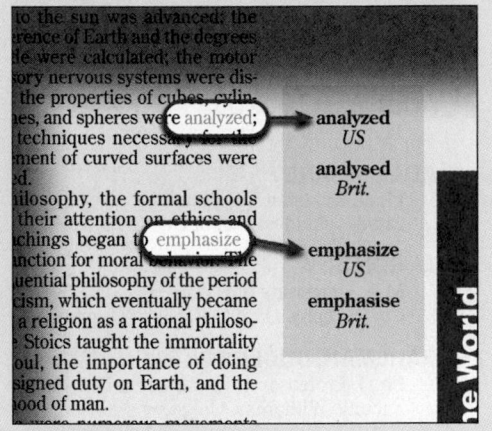

Sample U.S. and British Box Usage

analyzed
US

analysed
Brit.

emphasize
US

emphasise
Brit.

One of the interesting differences between British and American English is the tendency for the British to lengthen words or phrases as in:

I have done   *I have*
departmental store   *department store*

or perhaps it is the Americans who tend to shorten.

While the spoken language and the vocabulary of both spoken and written English accounts for most of the variations, some additional differences appear in the use of written punctuation marks. For more information, refer to pages 122–123 of the ENGLISH WRITING volume.

Some words and phrases can cause great misinterpretation because the British/American meanings may be different—in some cases, totally opposite.

Here is a sampling of the intricacies and color/colour of our glorious language:

If a motion picture or play is dubbed a "bomb," it is a dismal failure in America but a smashing success in England.

An American might want a "cookie," but must ask for a "biscuit" in England.

In England a "casket" is a small box; Americans use casket interchangeably with "coffin."

Americans following the rules of parliamentary procedure might "table" an item to set it aside without further consideration, but in England the item would be submitted for discussion.

Tell your visiting English friend to hang his clothes in the "closet" and he will hang them in the watercloset (bathroom). If you are his guest, he does not expect you to hang your wardrobe in the kitchen when he tells you the "cupboard" is available.

In England, a lady's handbag should never be called a pocketbook—that term is reserved for a gentleman's billfold or notecase.

Can you count to a billion? In England that is 1,000,000,000,000 (called a trillion in the U.S.) but in the U.S. it is only one thousand million (1,000,000,000 and called a milliard in England).

Yes, we speak the same language but the dialects need translation on occasion. We are all the better for our willingness to learn to communicate in our own or an adopted language. For more information on the development of English, see pages 9–14 of the FOREIGN LANGUAGE volume.

Contributors

AARONOVITCH, DAVID
B.A. Manchester University, Chief leader writer, The Independent newspaper, London, England.

ACOCELLA, NICHOLAS
M.A. Political writer and columnist.

ADAMS, JANET
Ph.D. Candidate, Instructor, Rhode Island School of Design.

ANSON. R. W.
M.A. University of Oxford, Principal lecturer, Cartography, Oxford Brookes University.

BAHLMAN, DUDLEY W. R.
Ph.D. Professor of History, and Dean of the Faculty, Williams College.

BARTELMEZ, ERMINNIE H.
Ph.D. Professor of German, Case Western Reserve University.

BARTH, FRANCES F.
Freelance medical writer.

BARZANTI, SERGIO
Ph.D. Associate Professor of Social Sciences, Fairleigh Dickinson University.

BERLAND, LAURA
B.A. Writer and legal aide.

BIRMINGHAM, LLOYD
Freelance educational illustrator.

BOARDMAN, FON W.
A.B. Former Vice President and Marketing Director of Oxford University Press, N.Y.; author of books for young people; freelance writer.

BOCIAN, PHYLLIS R.
B.A. Freelance editor.

BROWN, LEON CARL
Ph.D. Associate Professor of Oriental Studies, Princeton University.

BUNCH, BRYAN H.
B.A. Writer, textbook consultant; former Editor in Chief, American Book Company.

BUSHNELL, DAVID
Ph.D. Associate Professor of History, University of Florida.

BUTTFIELD, HELEN
A.M. Nature writer and photographer.

BYRNES, ROBERT F.
Ph.D. Distinguished Professor of History, Indiana University.

CAREY, GEORGE W.
Ed.D. Associate Professor of Geography, Teachers College, Columbia University.

CARTER, CHARLES H.
Ph.D. Professor of History, Tulane University.

COHN-HAFT, LOUIS
Ph.D. Professor of History, Smith College.

DALLY, EMMA
B.A. Oxon. Editorial director, books. National Magazine Company, London, England.

DANZINGER, ALEX
B.Sc. Freelance writer.

DELURY, GEORGE
M.A. Political science editor.

DICKINSON, RICHARD
M.A. Lecturer and writer on fine arts.

DILLON, JOHN
B.A. Freelance writer.

DIPPEL, JOHN
Ph.D. Freelance writer.

DITTRICK, DIANE K.
M.A. Author and freelance writer on science.

DOWLING, KENNETH W.
Ph.D. Science Supervisor, State of Wisconsin.

DRAPER, EVERETT T.
M.A. Adjunct Lecturer, LaGuardia Community College, City University of New York.

DUPREE, LOUIS
Ph.D. Research Associate in Anthropology, American Museum of Natural History.

ECHERD, ARTHUR R., JR.
Ph.D. Teacher of history, freelance writer.

EHRLICH, HENRY
B.A. Communications specialist, Assistant Vice President, Citibank.

EMBREE, AINSLIE T.
Ph.D. Associate Professor of History, Columbia University.

ENNIS, THOMAS E.
Ph.D. Late Professor of Far Eastern History, West Virginia University.

EPPERT, RAY R.
D.Sc., LL.D. Chairman and Chief Executive Officer, Burroughs Corporation.

FABRICANT, MONA
Ed.D. City University of New York.

FAJARDO, FERNANDO U.
B.S. Chemist, freelance writer.

FELDMAN, ROBERT J.
Freelance writer.

FINAN, JOHN J.
Ph.D. Professor of Latin American Studies, School of International Service, The American University.

FISCHMAN, JEROME
Ph.D. Associate Professor of History, Adelphi University.

FRANKLIN, PAULA
B.A. Writer and editor of school and college texts.

GILBERT, SARA
Freelance writer.

GOLUB, MARCIA H.
B.A. Freelance writer and editor.

GOODMAN, JAMES
B.A. Teacher of maths.

MARCIA H.
B.A. Freelance writer and editor.

GRIFFIN, CHARLES C.
Ph.D. Professor of History Emeritus, Vassar College.

GROTE, DALE A.
Ph.D. Associate Professor of Classics and Director of Main Liberal Studies, University of North Carolina, Charlotte.

HAMBURG, MORRIS
Ph.D. Professor of Statistics and Operations Research, University of Pennsylvania.

HAND, RAYMOND V.
B.A. Writer and editor.

HANNA, FRANCES
B.A. Writer and translator, Acacia House, Toronto, Canada.

HARRINGTON, JOHN P.
Ph.D. Writer and editor of reference works.

HEIMSATH, CHARLES H.
Ph.D. Professor of South Asian Studies, The School of International Service, The American University.

HELLEMANS, ALEXANDER
B.A. Freelance science writer.

HEYL, LAWRENCE, JR.
B.A. Princeton University. Business writer.

HIRSHORN, ARTHUR H.
Ph.D. Teacher, freelance writer.

HOOLIHAN, CHRISTOPHER T.
M.A. Former Professor of French and Latin, St. Meinrad College.

HUERSTER, PATRICIA G.
B.A. Freelance writer.

HYNEK, J. ALLEN
Ph.D. Professor of Astronomy and Department Chairman, Northwestern University; Director, Dearborn Observatory and Lindheimer Astronomical Research Center.

INABA, M.G.
Ph.D. Chairman, Department of Geography, Hofstra University.

ISSAWI, CHARLES
M.A. Ragnar Nurkse Professor of Economics, Columbia University.

JANOWSKY, OSCAR I.
Ph.D. Professor Emeritus of History, City University of New York; Visiting Professor of History, Brandeis University.

KAHKONEN, SHARON
M.S. Freelance science writer.

KISH, GEORGE
Ph.D. Professor of Geography, University of Michigan.

KLINE, HIBBERD V. B., JR.
Ph.D. Professor and Chairman, Department of Geography, University of Pittsburgh.

KREN, GEORGE M.
Ph.D. Associate Professor of History, Kansas State University.

LAGUARDIA, ROBERT
Freelance writer.

LAWRENCE, ROSALIE
B.A. Teacher and freelance writer.

LEITH, JAMES A.
Ph.D. Associate Professor of French History, Queen's University, Ontario.

LEY, WILLY
L.H.D. Late Professor, Long Island University.

LICHTENSTADTER, ILSE
Ph.D., D.Phil.Oxon, Lecturer on Arabic, Center for Middle Eastern Studies, Harvard University.

LINDROTH, DAVID
M.F.A. Cartographer and graphic designer.

LINDSAY, MICHAEL
M.A. Professor of Far Eastern Studies, American University.

LOEWER, H. PETER
B.F.A. Author and illustrator.

LORIMER, DONALD
B.A. Freelance writer.

LORIMER, LAWRENCE T.
M.A. Author, editorial consultant.

MARR, ANNE W.
M.A. Teacher of mathematics and computer science; freelance writer.

McCARTHY, E. JEROME
Ph.D. Professor of Marketing, Michigan State University.

McHUGH, JANET
B.A. Writer and editor of school and college texts.

MELAMID, ALEXANDER
Ph.D. Professor of Economics, New York University.

MERRILL, DAVID G.
M.A. Freelance writer.

MILLER, ELIZABETH
J.D. Freelance editor.

MILLER, PAUL W.
M.B.A. Management Consultant. Department of Management, Western Illinois University.

MILNE, LORUS J.
Ph.D. Professor of Zoology, University of New Hampshire.

MILNE, MARGERY
Ph.D. Lecturer in Nature Recreation and Zoology, University of New Hampshire.

MURPHY, WENDY B.
B.A. Author.

MYERS, ROLLIE J.
Ph.D. Professor of Chemistry Emeritus, University of California, Berkeley.

MYERS, SARAH K.
Ph.D. Geographer and freelance writer.

NOWELL, CHARLES E.
Ph.D. Professor of History, University of Illinois.

O'BRIEN, DENNIS
B.F.A. Illustrator, designer, and author.

O'CONNOR, KIMBERLY
M.A. Freelance writer.

OLIVER, JOHN E.
M.A. Instructor of Geography, Columbia University.

PLUMMER, SAMUEL C.
B.A., M.B.A. Freelance writer and editor.

RANDALL, BERNICE
M.A. Author and editor of educational materials in Spanish and English.

REILLY, E. M.
Ph.D. Curator Emeritus, Zoology, New York State Museum. Author and freelance writer.

ROE, JAMES A.
Ph.D. Associate Professor of Chemistry and Biochemistry, Loyola Marymount University.

ROTBERG, ROBERT I.
D.Phil. Associate Professor of History and Political Science, Massachusetts Institute of Technology.

ROWNEY, DON KARL
Ph.D. Associate Professor of History, Bowling Green State University.

SACERDOTE, MARC
M.A. Teacher of film animation; freelance writer.

SACKS, RICHARD
Ph.D. Assistant Professor of English and Comparative Literature, Columbia University.

SCHUYLER, ERIC B.
B.S. Electrical and Systems Engineer.

SCOTT, FRANKLIN D.
Ph.D. Professor of History, Northwestern University.

SCOTT, FREDERICK
M.S. Chemical engineer; Consulting Editor, International Scientific Communications, Inc.

SEGERBERG, OSBORN, JR.
B.A. Author and journalist.

SHERIDAN, BARBARA
B.Sc. Mathematics and physical sciences writer.

SMITH, DAVID A.
Ph.D. Associate Professor of Georgraphy, State University of New York at Buffalo.

SMYTH, D. McCORMACK
Ph.D. Professor of Administration, Atkinson College, York University, Toronto.

SPELLER, PHILIP W.
B.A. Financial consultant.

TARAPOR, MAHRUKH
Freelance writer.

TESAR, JENNY
M.A. Freelance science and medical writer.

THOMPSON, JOHN M.
Ph.D. Professor of History, Indiana University.

VARCHAVER, MARY
B.A. Freelance writer.

WAGNER, HARRY L.
B.A. Freelance education writer.

WALLACE, PAUL
M.Phil. London School of Economics. Economist, author, and editor.

WEBB, KEMPTON E.
Ph.D. Associate Professor of Geography, and Associate Director of Latin American Studies, Columbia University.

WEISSMAN, GARY A.
Freelance writer.

WERT, THADDEUS
M.E. Teacher of mathematics, freelance writer.

WETTERAU, BRUCE
Freelance writer and editor.

WHITE, DONALD A.
Ph.D. Associate Professor of History, Temple University.

WILLIAMS, L. PEARCE
Ph.D. John Stambaugh Professor of History and Chairman, Department of History, Cornell University.

YARRIS, LYNN
M.A. Science Writer for Lawrence Berkeley Laboratory.

ZOLBERG, VERA L.
B.A. Assistant Professor of Sociology and Anthropology, St. Xavier College.

Photography Credits

How to look up image credits: Each photograph in this volume has been assigned a number which gives the volume number and the spread number (the even page number on the spread) and a letter which indicates the image's position on the spread. The first image on the spread is "a," the second is "b," etc. Positions are determined by the flow of the text. Start at the top left hand corner of the spread, go down the column and then up to the top of the next column, continuing on to the end of the spread. For instance, say a spread has 3 photographs—one at the top of the first column, one at the bottom of the third column, and one in the center of the sixth column. The top left image would be "a," the image at the bottom of the third column would be "b," and the image in the center of the sixth column would be "c."

American Swedish News Exchange: 20:34b

Animals Animals: 27:136b-Johnson

Arensburg Collection, Philadelphia Museum of Art: 19:58b

Arnold, Peter: 28:28c-Heinz Plenge

Art Museum, Princeton University: 20:100a

Art Reference Bureau, Marburg: 19:20c; 19:46b

Art Resource, NY: 19:10b-Erich Lessing; 19:16c-Scala; 19:18b-Scala; 19:26b-Scala; 19:26c-Scala; 19:32a-Scala; 19:32c-Giraudon; 19:34b-Erich Lessing; 19:34c-Erich Lessing; 19:36b-Erich Lessing; 19:40d-Erich Lessing; 19:42c-Scala; 19:44a-Erich Lessing; 19:44b; 19:48b-Erich Lessing; 19:50a-Erich Lessing; 19:60a; 19:76d-Erich Lessing; 20:10c; 20:36a-Giraudon; 21:8a; 21:14c; 21:42b-Giraudon; 21:48a-Giraudon; 24:22c-Scala

Asia Society, Mr. and Mrs. John D. Rockefeller 3rd Collection: 19:66b; 19:66d; 19:70d; 19:72b

Atkins Museum of Fine Arts: 19:64e-William Rockhill Nelson Gallery of Art; 19:66a-William Rockhill Nelson Gallery of Art; 19:68b-William Rockhill Nelson Gallery of Art; 19:68d-William Rockhill Nelson Gallery of Art; 19:70b-William Rockhill Nelson Gallery of Art; 19:70c-William Rockhill Nelson Gallery of Art

Bauer, Jerry: 20:48d

Bettmann Archive: 20:32b; 21:34a; 21:44a; 22:26c; 23:2b-UPI; 23:16a; 23:20c; 23:22b; 23:26b; 23:26d-UPI; 26:38b-UPI; 26:62c-UPI

British Library: 19:18c

British Museum: 19:10a; 20:18a

Brown Brothers: 21:66a; 21:78a

Bruce Coleman, Inc.: 17:126a-David Madison

Canapress Photo Service: 27:186c

Chinese Information Service: 21:60c

Cleveland Museum of Art: 19:68c-Purchase, Leonard C. Hanna Jr. Bequest; 19:72a-Purchase, Edward L. Whittemore Fund

Collection of Mr. and Mrs. Sidney F. Brody, Beverly Hills: 19:6f

Corbis: 17:80a-Dann Tardif; 19:42a-The National Gallery, London; 19:58b-Christie's Images; 19:58d-Francis G. Mayer; 19:58e-Burstein Collection;

19:60b-Angelo Hornak; 19:60c-Patrick Ward; 19:62c-Bettmann; 19:64b-Philadelphia Museum of Art; 19:64c-North Carolina Museum of Art; 19:64d-North Carolina Museum of Art; 19:72c-Bettmann; 19:74a; 19:74b; 19:74c-Bettmann; 19:74d; 19:74e-Bettmann; 19:76a-Roger Ressmeyer; 19:76b-Bettmann; 20:26b-Library of Congress; 20:32a-Robbie Jack; 20:32b-Bettmann; 20:36b-Bettmann; 20:38a-Robbie Jack; 20:38b-Robbie Jack; 20:40a-Bettmann; 20:40b-Peter Turnley; 20:40c-Hulton-Deutsch Collection; 20:40d-Bettmann; 20:40e-Hulton-Deutsch Collection; 20:44a-Library of Congress; 20:46d-Hulton-Deutsch Collection; 20:46e-Library of Congress; 20:48g-Leif Skoogfors; 20:124a-Patrick Ward; 20:124b-Gianni Dagli Orti; 21:72b-Francoise de Mulder; 21:76a-Bettmann; 21:76b-AFP; 21:78a-Shepard Sherbell; 21:78b-Arthur Thévenart; 21:82a-Robert van der Hilst; 21:82b-Michael S. Yamashita; 21:82c-AFP; 21:84a-Reuters; 21:84b-Handout; 21:84c-Patrick Robert; 21:84d-Cheryl Diaz Meyer/Dallas Morning News; 21:86a-Patrick Robert; 21:86b-Thomas Hartwell; 21:86c-Ali Jarekji/Reuters Newmedia Inc; 21:86d-Henny Ray Abrams/Stringer/Reuters Newmedia Inc; 21:86e-Thomas Hartwell; 21:90a; 21:90b-Nicole Duplaix; 21:90c-Bettmann; 21:90d; 21:92a-Austrian Archives; 21:92b-Bettmann; 21:92c; 21:92d-Bettmann; 21:92e-Hulton-Deutsch Collection; 21:94b-Bettmann; 21:94c-Bettmann; 21:94d-Hulton-Deutsch Collection; 23:10c-Charles and Josette Lenars; 23:12a-Hulton-Deutsch Collection; 23:12b-Tom Owen Edmunds; 23:34c-David S. Robbins; 23:36b-Jeremy Horner; 23:36c-Janet Wishnetsky; 23:38b-Wally McNamee; 23:40b-Janet Wishnetsky; 23:40d-Earl Kowall; 23:44c-Erol Gurian; 23:54b-Michael Busselle; 23:56a-Robbie Jack; 23:56c-Jon Spaull; 23:58a-Jon Spaull; 23:60c-David S. Robbins; 23:62c-Owen Fraken; 23:62d-Robert van der Hilst; 23:64a-Francoise de Mulder; 23:70a-Eye Ubiquitous; 23:70b-Michail Maslan Historic Photographs; 24:1a-Jon Hicks; 24:6c-Earl Kowall; 24:8a-Francoise de Mulder; 24:8b-Daniel Laine; 24:12b-Charles and Josette Lenars; 24:12d-Bryn Colton; 24:14a-Heini Schneebeli; 24:16b-Arthur Thevenart; 24:18b-U.S. Department of Defense; 24:18d-Eye Ubiquitous; 24:20a-K.M. Westermann; 24:20b-Vittoriano Rastelli; 24:24b-Caroline Penn; 24:24c-Charles and Josette Lenars; 24:24d-K.M. Westermann; 24:26a-Abbie Enock, Travel Ink; 24:26b-Francoise de Mulder; 24:28b-Richard T. Nowitz; 26:8b-Richard Hamilton Smith; 26:8c-David Lees; 26:10b-Owen Franklin; 26:10c-Jacques M. Chenet; 26:12b-Peter Turnley; 26:14a-O. Alamany and E. Vicens; 26:18a-Caroline Penn; 26:20a-Time Page; 26:34b-Gianni Dagli Orti; 26:42b-Austrian Archives; 26:42c-James L. Amos; 26:44c-Christel Gerstenberg; 26:50a-Bettmann; 26:50b-Bettmann; 26:66b-Dean Conger; 26:68d-Charles and Josette Lenars; 26:74a-Richard T. Nowitz; 26:80b-Peter Wilson; 26:80d-Tiziana and Gianni Baldizzone; 26:84a-Wolfgang Kaehler; 26:84b-Vince Streano; 26:84c-Steve Raymer; 26:86b-The State Russian Museum; 26:86c-The State Russian Museum; 26:86b-Reproduced by permission of The State

Hermitage; 26:90a-Dean Conger; 26:92a-NASA; 26:92c-Owen Franklin; 26:94b-Vittoriano Rastelli; 26:94d-Farrell Grehan; 26:104c-Dean Conger; 26:106a-Tim Graham; 26:108a-Adam Woolfitt; 26:108b-Adam Woolfitt; 26:108c-Bettmann; 26:110b-Adam Woolfitt; 26:112a-Charles and Josette Lenars; 26:112c-Gianni Dagli Orti; 26:114b-Gianni Dagli Orti; 26:116a-Hulton-Deutsch Collection; 26:116b-Leonard de Selva; 26:122b-Historical Picture Archive; 26:124b-Chris/Hellier; 26:124c-Patrick Ward; 26:126a-Hulton-Deutsch Collection; 26:130a-Bettmann; 26:132a; 26:132b-Reuters NewMedia Inc.; 26:134a-Historical Picture Archive; 26:134b-Museum of Flight; 26:136b-Leif Skoogfors; 26:140a-Peter Turnley; 26:140c-Peter Turnley; 26:142b-Patrick Turnley; 26:142c-Charles and Josette Lenars; 26:150a-Adam Woolfitt; 26:150b-Owen Franklin; 26:150c-David Paterson; 26:152b-K.M. Westermann; 26:154a-Gianni Dagli Orti; 26:154b-Nik Wheeler; 26:154c-Charles and Josette Lenars; 26:156a-Macduff Everton; 26:156b-Bob Krist; 26:156c-Vince Streano; 26:158a-Ric Ergenbreit; 26:158b-Roger Ressmeyer; 26:158c-The State Russian Museum; 27:2c-Staffan Widstrand; 27:4a-Sergio Dorantes; 27:4b-Joseph Sohm; ChromoSohm Inc.; 27:4c-Annie Griffiths Belt; 27:6a-Gunter Marx; 27:6b-Morton Beebe-S.F.; 27:6c-David Muench; 27:8a-Annie Griffiths Belt; 27:8b-George Lepp; 27:8c-Joseph Sohm; ChromoSohm Inc.; 27:10b-Phil Schermeister; 27:12b-Kevin Fleming; 27:12c-Annie Griffiths Belt; 27:14c-Library of Congress; 27:16a-Bettmann; 27:16c-Museum of the City of New York; 27:18a-Bettmann; 27:18b-Michael Nicholson; 27:18c-Bettmann; 27:20a-Joseph Sohm; ChromoSohm Inc.; 27:20b-Library of Congress; 27:20c-Bettmann; 27:24c-Bettmann; 27:26a-Bettmann; 27:26c-Bettmann; 27:28a-Bettmann; 27:28b-Eastern National Park and Monument Association; 27:28c-Bettmann; 27:28d-Bettmann; 27:28e-Bettmann; 27:30a-Mark Gibson; 27:30b-Library of Congress; 27:30c-James L. Amos; 27:38a-Library of Congress; 27:38b-Bettmann; 27:44a-Bettmann; 27:46c-Bettmann; 27:48b-Franklin McMahon; 27:48c-Library of Congress; 27:62a-Dean Conger; 27:64b-Owen Franken; 27:66c-Ronald Reagan Library; 27:68c-Ronald Reagan Library; 27:102c-Buddy Mays; 27:122b-W. Cody; 27:128b-Bob Krist; 27:156c-Lowell Georgia; 27:158a-Robert Holmes; 27:158b-Bettmann; 27:162a-Lowell Georgia; 27:162b-National Archives; 27:162c-Richard T. Nowitz; 27:164a-Library of Congress; 27:164b-Lowell Georgia; 27:166b-Bettmann; 27:166c- Paul A. Souders; 27:172a-PEMCO-Webster and Stevens Collection; 27:176a-Hulton-Deutsch Collection; 27:178a-Bettmann; 27:178d-Jan Butchofshy-Houser; 27:180a-Dave Bartruff; 27:182a-Michael Busselle; 27:182c-Richard T. Nowitz; 27:184a-Hulton-Deutsch Collection; 27:190d-Gary Hershorn/Reuters Newmedia Inc.; 27:200a-The Percell Team; 27:202b-George Lepp; 27:204a-Greg Probst; 27:206a-Dave G. Houser; 27:206b-Richard T. Nowitz; 27:208a-Dave G. Houser; 27:208c-Nik

Wheeler; 27:210b-Paul A. Souders; 27:210c-Staffan Widstrand; 27:212a-Ron Sanford; 27:220a-Tim Wright; 27:226a-Charles and Josette Lenars; 27:238b-Leif Skoogfors; 27:246b-Bojan Brecelj; 27:250a-Alastair Shay, Papilio; 27:250b-Bob Krist; 27:252a-Buddy Mays; 27:252b-Stuart Westmorland; 27:252c-Jeremy Horner; 27:252d-Neil Rabinowitz; 27:254a-Paul A. Souders; 27:254b-Kevin Fleming; 27:254c-TSW-Click/Chicago Ltd.-Chad E.; 27:256a-Dave G. Houser; 27:256b-Morton Beebe-S.F.; 27:256d-Richard Bickel; 27:256e-Michael Lewis; 27:258a-Danny Lehman; 27:258c-Nik Wheeler; 27:258d-Jon P. Yeager; 27:260a-Dave G. Houser; 27:260c-Bob Krist; 27:260d-Perry Mastrovito; 27:262a-The Percell Team; 27:262b-Bill Ross; 27:262c-Robert Holmes; 27:262d-Nik Wheeler; 27:262e-Dave G. Houser; 27:264a-Buddy Mays; 27:264b-David Muench; 27:264c-Lee Snider; 27:264d-Tony Arruza; 27:266a-Richard T. Nowitz; 27:266b-Richard T. Nowitz; 27:266c-Wolfgang Kaehler; 27:266d-James P. Blair; 27:266e-First Light; 27:268a-Staffan Widstrand; 27:268b-David Muench; 27:268c-Raymond Gehman; 27:270a-David Muench; 27:270b-George McCarthy; 27:270c-Robert Holmes; 27:272a-Alissa Crandall; 27:272b-Tom Bean; 27:272c-Farrell Grehan; 27:272d-Richard Hamilton Smith; 27:274a-Daniel Laine; 27:274b-Richard T. Nowitz; 27:276a-Library of Congress; 27:276b-MAGELLAN Geographix; 28:16d-Barnabos Bosshart; 28:20a-Charles O'Rear; 28:20c-Sergio Dorantes; 28:26b-Joel Creed; Ecoscene; 28:30b-James L. Amos; 28:30c-Adam Woolfitt; 28:34a-Yann Arthus-Bertrand; 28:34b-Peter Wilson; 28:36b-Roger Ressmeyer; 28:38b-Jeremy Horner

Culver Pictures: 17:108a; 18:2b; 18:8c; 18:10b; 18:12a; 18:12c; 18:14b; 18:22e; 19:6g; 19:14a; 19:14b; 19:14d; 19:14f; 19:20a; 19:22d; 19:46c; 20:4b; 20:4c; 20:14a; 20:22b; 20:22c; 20:38d; 20:42b; 20:46a; 20:46b; 20:46c; 20:48a; 20:52b; 20:52c; 20:54a; 20:54b; 20:56a; 20:56c; 20:58a; 20:60a; 20:66a; 20:66b; 20:68a; 20:68b; 20:68c; 20:70a; 20:74a; 20:76b; 20:82a; 20:84a; 20:84b; 20:86a; 20:86b; 20:88a; 20:88b; 20:90b; 20:90c; 20:94a; 20:94c; 20:94d; 20:102a; 20:102b; 20:104a; 20:106c; 20:108a; 20:108b; 20:110b; 20:114a; 20:114c; 20:116a; 20:116b; 20:118a; 20:118b; 20:118c; 20:122a; 20:122c; 21:8b; 21:50a; 27:180b

Digital Stock: 18:4a; 19:12e; 19:22d; 19:38a; 19:68a; 21:2a; 21:6a; 21:6c; 21:12a; 21:14d; 22:6b; 22:6c; 22:6e; 22:18a; 22:32d; 22:36d; 22:50a; 22:74b; 23:2c; 23:4b; 23:26c; 23:28d; 23:46c; 23:58c; 23:58e; 23:66a 25:6a; 25:6c; 25:8c; 25:10c; 25:14c; 25:16a; 25:16c; 25:16d; 25:20a; 25:20c; 25:20d; 25:22a; 26:2b; 26:14d; 26:18d; 26:20b; 26:24b; 26:24d; 26:26a; 26:26b; 26:26d; 26:32e; 26:34a; 26:34c; 26:34d; 26:36a; 26:38a; 26:38c; 26:42d; 26:44a; 26:44b; 26:46a; 26:48b; 26:48c; 26:58c; 26:60c; 26:62a; 26:62b; 26:62d; 26:74c; 26:88c; 26:98a; 26:102c; 26:102d; 26:106b; 26:112c; 26:126b; 26:136a; 26:138b; 27:56a; 27:56b; 27:56c; 27:58a; 27:58b; 27:58c; 27:130b

Digital Vision: 17:120a; 25:2e; 27:182b

Doubleday: 20:34a

Dwight, Laura: 16:20a

Eagle, Arnold: 20:6b

Earl of Radnor's Collection, Salisbury, England: 19:40c

Embassy of India: 21:68a

EPA: 19:14c-Scala; 19:16a-Alinari; 19:16b-Alinari; 19:20d-Scala; 19:24a-Paula Gerson; 19:24c-Alinari; 19:26d-Alinari-Scala; 19:28a-Alinari-Scala; 19:38b; 19:44c-Alinari; 19:76f-Alinari-Scala; 19:72h

E.P. Dutton, Inc.: 20:122b

Folger Shakespeare Library: 20:78b

FPG International: 16:32c-Ed Lettau; 17:102c-Michael Krasowitz; 17:102d-Michael Krasowitz

Frantz, Allison: 19:10c

Free Library of Philadelphia, Richard Gimbel Collection: 20:72a

French Embassy Press & Information Service: 20:6a; 20:120c; 21:58a; 22:54b

French Government Tourist Office: 19:6b

Gallery Umeda, Osaka, Japan: 19:56

Gamma Liaison: 21:68b-Defense Dept. Photo/F. Lochon; 21:68c; 21:74a-(c) Scott Daniel Peterson; 22:10c-Scott Daniel Peterson; 23:28a-Laurent Maous; 27:70a; 27:188a-Allen McInnis; 27:190c-Pono-Presse

Gibson, Mark E.: 27:124c

Giraudon: 19:22a; 19:24b-Lauros; 19:24d; 19:54c

Goodman Theater of the Art Institute of Chicago: 20:84c-Vories Fisher; 20:90a-Vories Fisher; 20:92b-Vories Fisher; 20:120a-Walter Abel, Geneva Bugbee, Dan Bly: Vories Fisher

Granger Collection: 21:2c; 21:78b; 21:46a; 27:164c

H. Armstrong Roberts: 23:46b-G. Roessler; 26:72a-R. Kord; 26:152a-P. Royer; 27:28f-J. McGrail; 27:186b-R. Krubner; 27:210a-R. Krubner; 27:216c-J. Neubauer; 27:222a-A. Littlejohn; 27:226d-Zefa; 28:6b-Raga/Mauriatius; 28:8a-M. Koene; 28:8b-R. Kord

Harmon Foundation Collection: 21:62b

Harper and Row: 20:62a

Hill-Stead Museum, The: 19:50c

Hirmer Fotoarchiv: 19:8d

Holt, Rinehart & Winston: 20:44b

House of Seven Gables, Salem, Mass.: 20:80b

Illustration by Marguerite Kirmse from Lassie Come Home by Eric Knight: 16:26a

Isabella Stewart Gardner Museum, Boston: 19:34a; 20:74b

Japan National Tourist Organization: 20:96a

John G. Johnson Collection, Philadelphia: 20:64a

Leo Castelli Gallery: 19:58d

Lorimer, Don: 19:8b

Mead/Science Photo Library: 27:106b

Metropolitan Museum of Art: 19:6c-The Cloisters Collection; 19:8e; 19:12a-Rogers Fund; 19:12b-Rogers Fund; 19:46a-Bequest of William K. Vanderbilt; 19:54d-Gift of Miss G. Louise Robinson, 1940; 19:58c-George A. Hearn fund, 1957; 20:24b-Harris Brisbane Dick Fund; 20:112a-Rogers Fund, 1917

Mink, David, Martha Gilpin & Vories Goodman: 20:76a

Monkmeyer: 28:14b-Dunn; 28:28a-Wolf; 28:32b-Rogers

Musee Toulouse Lautrec: 19:54a

Museum of Fine Arts, Boston: 19:6a-Gift of Horace L. Mayor; 19:8c-Harvard Boston Expedition

The Museum of Modern Art, NY: 19:56a-Mrs. Simon Guggengeim; 19:60d

Naturhistorisches Museum, Wien: 19:6d

National Gallery of Art: 19:62a

Newberry Library, Chicago: 20:12b

New York Public Library: 19:14e; 19:30b; 20:10a; 20:12a-Picture Collection; 19:76g; 20:14a; 20:18b; 20:20a; 20:26a; 20:28c; 20:28d; 20:30a; 20:30b; 20:34c; 20:38c; 20:50b; 20:58c-Aster, Lenox & Tilden Foundation; 20:60b; 20:62b; 20:76d; 20:78a; 20:82b; 20:98a; 20:102c; 20:104b; 20:106a; 20:110a; 20:116c; 21:12c-Photo by Andre Held/Museo Nazionale, Rome, Italy; 21:40b; 21:42a; 21:48b-Wood block print by Hiroshige; 21:50c; 22:26b

PhotoDisc (Images 1998 PhotoDisc, Inc.): 17:106a; 17:106b; 18:4b; 19:16a; 21:2d; 21:2e; 21:8c; 21:8d; 21:10a; 21:12d; 21:14a; 21:16a; 21:16b; 21:28a; 21:28b; 21:32a; 21:32c; 21:38a; 21:40a; 21:40c; 21:62a; 21:70c; 22:10a; 22:12a; 22:12b; 22:12c; 22:14c; 22:16a; 22:20a; 22:22b; 22:24b; 22:30c; 22:38c; 22:38d; 22:38e; 22:40b; 22:40d; 22:42b; 22:44c; 22:46c; 22:48c; 22:48d; 22:52b; 22:58a; 22:60a; 22:60b; 22:60d; 22:62b; 22:64a; 22:66b; 22:66c; 22:68c; 22:70c; 22:70d; 22:72a; 22:72c; 22:74a; 22:76a; 23:6a; 23:6b; 23:6c; 23:8a; 23:8b; 23:8c; 23:10a; 23:14d; 23:18a; 23:18b; 23:18c; 23:18d; 23:20b; 23:22a; 23:24b; 23:24c; 23:26a; 23:28c; 23:32a; 23:32c; 23:32d; 23:34a; 23:42a; 23:44d; 23:46a; 23:50b; 23:52b; 23:52c; 23:58d; 23:60a; 23:60b; 23:64h; 23:66h; 23:68a; 23:68b; 23:68c; 23:72a; 24:4a; 24:4b; 24:10b; 24:12a; 24:22b; 24:28a; 25:2b; 25:2c; 25:8a; 25:10a; 25:10b; 25:12b; 25:20b; 25:22b; 25:22c; 26:2a; 26:2c; 26:6a; 26:6b; 26:6c; 26:10a; 26:16a; 26:20a; 26:22b; 26:22c; 26:22d; 26:28a; 26:28c; 26:28d; 26:30b; 26:30c; 26:36d; 26:42a; 26:46b; 26:46c; 26:52a; 26:52c; 26:52d; 26:54a; 26:54b; 26:54c; 26:56c; 26:56d; 26:58b; 26:64a; 26:64c; 26:70c; 26:72c; 26:74b; 26:74e; 26:76b; 26:76c; 26:76d; 26:78b; 26:78c; 26:78d; 26:82b; 26:82c; 26:86a; 26:88a; 26:92b; 26:96a; 26:98b; 26:100c; 26:100d; 26:102a; 26:104a; 26:106c; 26:106d; 26:110a; 26:118a; 26:124a; 26:134c; 26:142a; 26:144a; 26:144b; 26:144c; 26:146a; 26:146b; 26:146c; 26:148a; 26:148b; 26:148c; 27:2a; 27:16b; 27:22b; 27:24b; 27:34c;

27:42b; 27:42c; 27:44c; 27:44d; 27:48a; 27:50a; 27:50c; 27:54a; 27:60c; 27:62b; 27:62c; 27:64d; 27:66a; 27:66b; 27:68a; 27:68b; 27:70b; 27:70c; 27:94a; 27:102c; 27:102d; 27:104a; 27:104b; 27:106c; 27:106d; 27:108a; 27:108b; 27:108c; 27:108d; 27:110b; 27:110c; 27:112a; 27:112b; 27:114a; 27:114b; 27:114c; 27:116a; 27:116b; 27:118a; 27:118b; 27:118c; 27:120a; 27:120b; 27:120c; 27:122c; 27:124d; 27:126a; 27:126b; 27:126c; 27:130a; 27:130c; 27:132a; 27:132b; 27:134c; 27:136c; 27:138a; 27:138b; 27:140a; 27:140c; 27:142a; 27:144a; 27:144b; 27:144c; 27:146a; 27:146b; 27:148a; 27:148b; 27:150a; 27:150b; 27:154a; 27:156a; 27:156b; 27:172c; 27:178b; 27:186a; 27:190a; 27:190b; 27:202a; 27:206c; 27:208b; 27:212b; 27:214a; 27:214b; 27:216a; 27:216d; 27:224a; 27:224b; 27:226c; 27:228a; 27:232a; 27:232b; 27:240a; 27:242a; 27:256c; 27:258a; 27:260a; 28:4a; 28:2b; 28:2c; 28:10c; 28:12b; 28:12c; 28:14d; 28:16a; 28:16b; 28:18b; 28:18c; 28:24c; 28:26a; 28:28b; 28:36c; 28:38a; 28:38c; 28:40b; 28:42a

PhotoEdit: 16:6a-Jeff Greenberg; 16:6g-Mary Kaye Denny; 16:30c-Tony Freeman; 16:30d-David Young-Wolff; 16:32b-David Young-Wolff; 16:32d-Tony Freeman; 16:34a-Robert Brenner; 16:34b-Tony Freeman; 16:34c-Tony Freeman; 16:34d-Tony Freeman; 17:2e-Tom McCarthy; 17:102a-Jeff Greenberg; 17:102b-R. Hutchings; 17:102f-Tony Freeman; 17:104b-Tony Freeman; 17:104c; 17:104d-Michael Newman; 17:106c-Mark Richards; 18:2a-Robert Brenner; 18:2d-David Young-Woolff; 18:6a-Paul Conklin; 18:14c-Michael Newman; 18:14d-Robert Brenner; 26:32c-Ulriche Welsch

Photo Researchers: 16:30b-Renee Lynn; 17:124a-Porterfield.Chickening; 18:2e-George E. Jones III; 18:14e-Katrina Thomas; 18:24a-P. Delarbre/Explorer; 18:32a-Tom McHugh; 19:66c-George Holton; 20:56b-Dick Hanley; 21:6b-c-Scott Peterson; 22:14b-Kazuyashi Nomachi; 22:38b-Victor Englebert; 22:48a-Noboru Komine; 22:62c; 22:74c-Friedman; 25:18b-Jack Fields; 26:58d-Louis Goldman; 26:60b-Judy Poe; 26:76a-Franke Keating; 28:8c-Victor; 28:20b-Victor Englebert; 28:22a-Mathias Oppersdorff

Planet Art: 19:28b; 19:30a; 19:30c; 19:32b; 19:36a; 19:40a; 19:40b; 19:52a; 19:52b; 19:52e; 19:52f; 21:2k; 22:6a; 22:6d; 22:16c; 22:20c; 22:28c; 22:34a; 22:44b; 22:52c; 22:58d; 22:64d; 22:76b; 22:76d; 23:16c; 23:30c; 23:48a; 24:4c; 24:4d; 24:4e; 24:10c; 24:22a; 25:2a; 25:6b; 26:36c; 26:52b-Thomas/Explorer; 26:68b; 26:72b; 26:90b; 26:90c; 26:98d; 26:122a; 26:138b; 27:2b; 27:32a; 27:34c; 27:50b; 27:52b; 27:60a; 27:156d; 27:166a; 27:230a

Private American Collection: 19:6e; 19:52c

Random House: 20:20b; 20:20c

Rooney, Edward: 20:42a

Shooting Star: 27:62a-Martin Mills; 27:72a-Petrie Alexander; 27:236b-Nancy Kaszerman

Siebert, Lisa: 16:30a

SuperStock: 19:48a-Met. Museum of Art, NYC/ET Archive, London; 19:50b-Met. Museum of Art, NYC/A.K.G., Berlin; 19:52d; 19:56c-Museum of Modern Art, New York; 19:58a-Albright Knox Gallery, Buffalo, New York; 19:62b-Met. Museum of Art, NYC; 19:70a-Christie's Images; 19:76e-Pushkin Museum of Fine Arts, Moscow, Russia; 20:26c; 26:16b-The Cummer Museum of Art and Gardens, Jacksonville; 26:32d-Bibliotheque de L'Arsenal, Paris/Explorer; Lascaux Caves II, France/Explorer; 26:98c-Museo del Prado, Madrid/Giraudon, Paris; 26:114a-National Portrait Gallery, London; 26:120a-National Portrait Gallery, London; 26:120b-National Portrait Gallery, London; 26:130b-Maritime Museum, Paris, France/Explorer; 26:152c-Tomb of Leopardi, Tarqina, Italy/Fratelli Allnari; 27:22a-Library of Congress, Washington D.C.; 27:32b-Culver Pictures; 27:32c-Stock Montage; 27:36a-Stock Montage; 27:36b; 27:40a-Stock Montage; 27:40b; 27:42a-Stock Montage; 27:46a; 27:46b; 27:52a-Musee des Deux Guerres/Explorer, Paris; 27:52c; 27:168c-Culver Pictures, Inc.; 27:170b-Library of Congress; 27:216b-Explorer, Paris; 27:226b-Explorer, Paris; 27:234b-Stock Montage

Sygma: 23:24a-J.P. Laffonte

Taurus Photos: 20:120b-Philip Jon Bailey; 21:70a-Eric Kroll

The Louvre, Paris: 19:36c

The Stock Market (TSM): 26:32a-Ted Mahley; 28:14b-Carlos Humberto

TSW-Click/Chicago Ltd.: 22:10b-Brian Seed

Uffizi Gallery, Florence: 19:28c

UN Photo: 17:102e-P. Sudhakaran; 21:2g-P. Sudhakaran; 22:58e-P. Sudhakaran

UPI: 20:48b; 20:48c; 22:76c

Upper Church of San Francisco: 19:26a

U.S. Department of State: 21:62c; 22:32b

Victoria & Albert Museum, London: 19:54b

Wallraf-Richartz Museum, Cologne, Germany: 19:42b

Wide World Photos: 20:48e; 21:60b

Woodfin Camp and Associates: 22:24d-Marc and Evelyn Bernheim; 22:52b; 23:20a-Paula Lerner; 23:36d-Nathan Benn; 26:32b-Adam Woolfitt; 26:40c-Snowdon/Hoyer/Focus; 27:128a-Paul Lerner

Wys, Leo de: 18:2c-Jeff Greenberg; 18:4e-Steve Vidler; 18:38c-Jeff Greenberg; 22:58b-Bob Drist

Today, our students are overwhelmed with information from an amazing number of sources. The *Volume Library* and *Student Handbooks* are a valuable "oasis" from which students can access accurate and reliable information about virtually any academic discipline. These books are outstanding reference guides for all students who wish to excel academically. Additionally, they serve as an excellent resource for students who need a quick review or for students who simply need extra academic help.

Karen C. Tilton, M.A.
Department of English
Maquoketa High School, Maquoketa, Iowa
past recipient of University of Iowa Teacher of the Year award

Having the *Volume Library* and *Student Handbooks* is like having a full-time tutor at home. They are a great learning resource for the entire family.

Daniel H. Durbin, M.A.
Chair, Department of English
Oakland City University, Oakland, Indiana
past recipient of Indiana State Teacher of the Year award

The *Volume Library* and *Student Handbooks* are uniquely designed to provide a student not only with ready access to information but also with problem-solving techniques and study skill guides that enable the student to utilize that information in the most efficient manner. The effective use of boldface type, frequent highlighting, and ample illustrations make the VL and Handbooks extremely user-friendly. Finally, the VL and Handbooks are kept current and topical to an extent that few if any textbooks or other reference books can match.

Art Echerd, Ph.D.
Department of History
Harpeth Hall School, Nashville, Tennessee
past recipient of Presidential Scholar's Inspirational Teacher Award

The *Volume Library* provides coverage of the major topics at Key Stage 1, 2, 3, GCSE, and A-level, allowing students and parents quick and easy access to a wealth of relevant and interesting information.

Many schools are unable to fund textbooks for students to take home, and consequently students and parents are often left with very little to help review for tests or to complete homework. The *Volume Library* provides extensive coverage across all subjects to assist in these areas.

Any student wanting to excel can benefit from the opportunity to increase knowledge beyond the curriculum. The *Volume Library* gives this opportunity by its breadth and depth of content. Students are able to easily discover areas of personal interest that they can research further within the *Volume Library* or elsewhere.

James Goodman
B.A. (Oxon), PGCE
Deputy Head of Maths
Kingsfield Secondary School, Bristol (U.K.)

Designed to put timely and accurate information at the fingertips of people of all ages, the Southwestern Company's *Volume Library* and *Student Handbooks* have quickly become a strategic resource for our entire family. This invaluable compilation of reference material, ranging from a comprehensive review of core curriculum subjects and research skills to a helpful study skills manual and career resource guide, has made our set a series of books that collect no dust. In fact, they are impossible for me to find around our home. If my children don't have them in their rooms, I can assume that they have been loaned to a neighbor or are serving as reference material in my wife's elementary classroom. She has found these texts to be particularly useful as a guide for science fair projects as well as a reliable addition to her modern U.S. and world geography and current affairs lessons. Our college student would not be without them as a desktop encyclopedia resource in his dorm room, while our youngest son continually refers to them for everything from writing his research papers to enhancing his preparations for Advanced Placement exams. If only I had a set to myself! If you're looking for a flexible educational tool that will ensure higher academic performance and increase motivation for learning in your family, the *Volume Library* and *Student Handbooks* belong on an easy-to-reach shelf in your home. Good luck keeping track of where they were last seen!

Stan Johnston, M.A.
Department of English and Assistant Principal
Los Alamos High School, Los Alamos, New Mexico
past recipient of New Mexico State Teacher of the Year award

In math, the *Volume Library* is unique in its combination of content and examples. The VL provides the mathematical content necessary for a student to learn the major topics covered in any math course, from elementary-level arithmetic through Advanced Placement calculus. You would have to purchase at least a dozen regular math textbooks to cover the same amount of material. But the VL doesn't stop with merely the content. In my opinion, its greatest value lies in the multitude of worked-out examples. The VL covers the same types of problems that the typical textbooks cover, but where a textbook might have two or three examples, the VL may have five or six. And every step of every problem is shown; nothing is left out. So, the parent or student doesn't have to waste time wondering "how they got from step C to step D." The quality of the illustrations is top-notch, and the organization of the VL makes it very easy to find a particular topic or problem type.

Obviously, the VL couldn't cover every single topic that a complete math text does, but it does an excellent job of providing help with the topics that tend to give students the most trouble. As a supplement to a student's regular textbook, the VL is invaluable. It is like having a personal tutor, ready whenever you need it. (And math tutors are charging $50 per hour nowadays!)

Tad Wert, M.A.
Chair, Department of Math
Harpeth Hall School, Nashville, Tennessee

Language

English Grammar

English Writing

Foreign Language

Language

What is it that distinguishes humans from the other animals? Until recently, the answer to that question was twofold: the using and making of tools and the development of language. Today we know that a chimpanzee can make a tool by stripping leaves off a twig to insert in termite holes. Thus, written language remains as the dividing line between the animals.

What is language? Defining this oh-so-necessary skill is difficult at

best. It is a means of communication. It must have developed to allow us to exchange information and ideas, so there must be some common ground to permit that exchange. Words must be understood by both the communicator and the communicatee. The pattern in which the words are exchanged must also be commonly understood. It is helpful if more than two people can communicate using this system. There is a story of a husband and wife who had a child and were determined that the child would be multilingual. To that end, the husband spoke only English to the baby, the wife, only French, and the nanny, only German. The child grew up speaking all three languages and was firmly convinced that every person in the world spoke a different language.

Obviously, since you are reading these words, you are one of the millions of people in the world who know the English language. If you are lucky, you may also have a grasp of one or more of the other major languages of the world. Even without having a firm grasp of French, Spanish, or German, you may be able to recognize the language when you hear it spoken just by a few familiar sounding words, the cadence of the sentence structure, or the unique sounds of the language—soft sibilant Spanish, rounded flowing French, or clipped gutteral German. If so, you are on the way to better understanding English, which is a wonderful amalgam of many languages.

To be functional, language must exist on several levels. The first is the spoken language, which is readily adaptable to the needs of the moment. The repetitive sounds that a baby makes—da-da, ma-ma—are the beginnings. Though hardly conversational, the meaning is clear. So must language have developed as people became capable of making and inventing consistent sounds. We will never know how the transition was made from understanding the language used by a small group to many small groups being able to understand each other's language. Probably it was a matter of each group learning the others' languages and melding them together into a more comprehensive language—much in the manner that language today absorbs appropriate words from other sources to enrich us all.

Think about the number of words you use every day that came to us from another language—where would we be without tacos, lasagna, and ice cream parfaits?

Another level of language is the written version. One of the mysteries of language is how long spoken language existed before the idea of writing it down occurred to someone. From pictures on a cave wall to clay tablets and leather scrolls to the invention of paper and the printing

press was only a moment in the history of the world but light-years in the development of humans. What an interesting circle is the story of communications. From the spoken word between two people to the various permutations of the written word to the technological evolution of a device that enables two people to speak to each other over long distances—and the telephone can even let the people see each other while they speak.

What is it that we do with our mastery of language? Now that we can speak and read and write, how do we use that skill? We can impart knowledge. We can entertain with thought-provoking or amusing anecdotes. We can expose others to our philosophies, our politics, and our scientific theories. We can record our memories and dreams. One of

the most wonderful things about language is our ability to leave a bit of ourselves for generations that we will never see. The books that fill our libraries are the result of language.

From the rhymes of childhood to the complex technical treatises that help move the bounds of science and human understanding, language is the key. Use it to enrich your life.

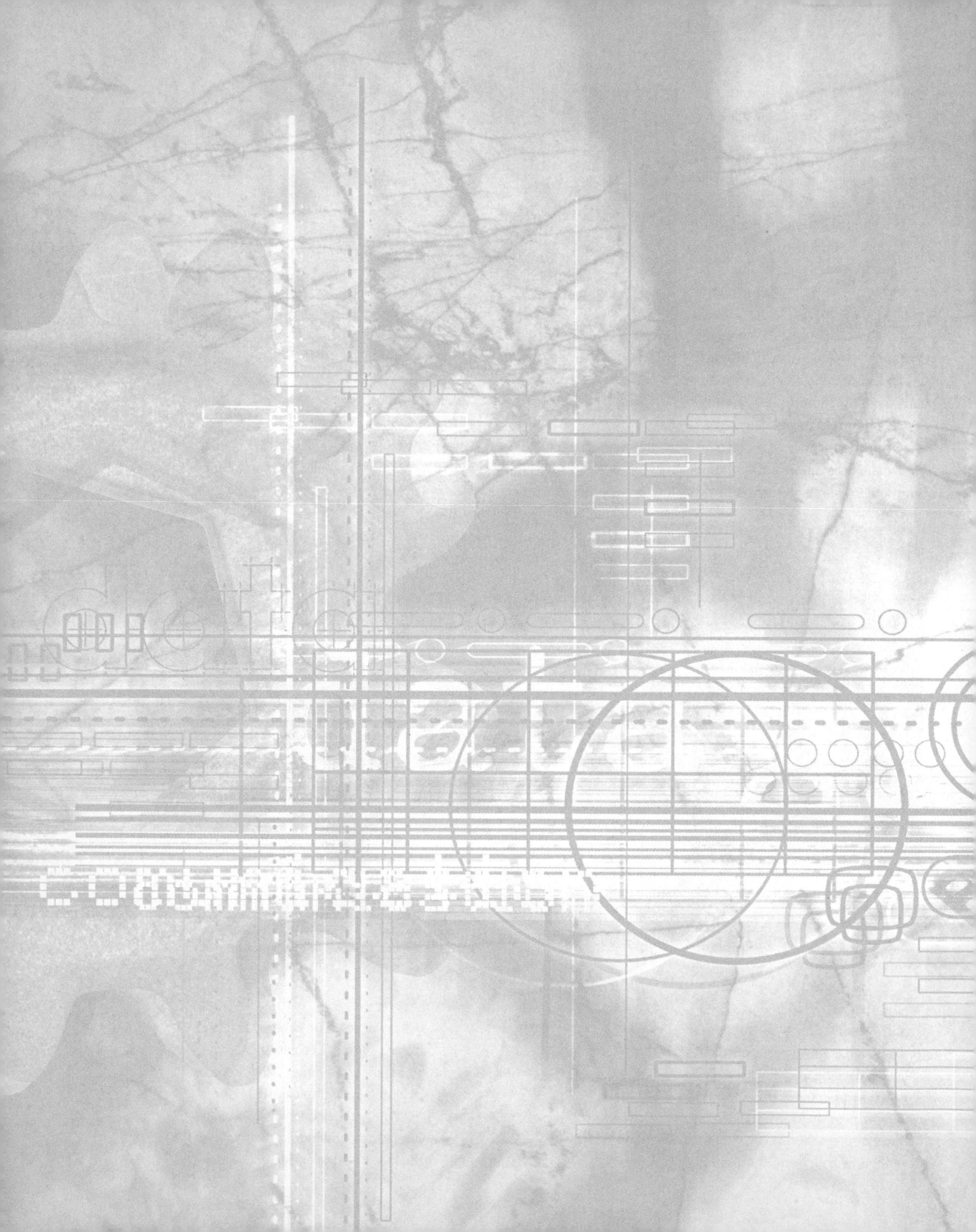

16

English Grammar

16 English Grammar

Overleaf: *Old school desk at Ozark Folk Center in Mountain View, Arkansas*

Elementary Language Skills

Many young children, at one time or another in the growing process, enjoy playing with blocks to construct all kinds of things they have seen and learned about. For example, they use blocks of many different shapes, sizes, and colors to build houses, forts, castles, towers, ships, airplanes, bridges, roads, and automobiles. By trial and error, they learn how to use the blocks correctly, so the things they build will stand on a solid foundation and not wobble or fall down. Often they will knock down what they have built and immediately rebuild it or build something new using the same blocks.

At first, the objects the children build with their blocks are simple, using just a few blocks or pieces. But as the children grow so does their understanding of the physical principles involved in building with blocks, and the things they build become more interesting and complex. They may construct an entire city with schools, roadways, airports, office buildings, hospitals, houses, stores, streets, and parks. They may even use blocks to represent the people who are inhabitants of their city.

In a sense, words are the building blocks of language. The different parts of speech, such as nouns, pronouns, verbs, adverbs, and adjectives, have various uses and functions. When children start to speak, their sentences, like their early block structures, are simple and small and make use of only a few parts of speech. As young people grow, so does their ability to use words

and language, in speaking, writing, and reading. At first they learn by listening to other people speak; later, when they begin to read, they also learn through the experiences of reading and writing. Older children can create sentences that communicate their ideas and experiences in ever more complex, interesting, and varied ways.

For someone who wants to communicate well, learning how to put the different parts of speech together correctly is as important as choosing the right sizes or shapes of building blocks to use. Learning the principal building blocks of language provides a firm foundation for logical thinking and for clear communicating.

LEARNING THE PARTS OF SPEECH and how they work together in sentences can be fun.

Parts of Speech

Words have many different uses and functions. They can be recognized and identified as nouns, verbs, and other parts of speech by these uses and functions. This section explains and defines these parts of speech and illustrates their use in sentences.

Nouns. A noun is a word that names a person, place, or thing: girl, boy, Queen Elizabeth, Manchester, airport, ball, book, pencil, crayon.

There are two types of nouns. A **common noun** refers to any

person, place, or thing: man, woman, street, park, town, city, province, team.

A **proper noun** names a particular person, place, or thing: Thomas Jefferson, Montreal, Hampstead, Windsor Castle, Manchester United, Niagara Falls. Proper nouns always start with capital letters.

The following sentences contain both types of nouns:

Canada (proper noun) and the *United States* (proper noun) are *neighbors* (common noun).

The *Olympic Games* began in *Greece* many *years* ago.

CAT is a common noun; Jack, the cat's name, is a proper noun.

Alexander Graham Bell invented the *telephone*.

A noun is either singular or plural. A **singular noun** names one person, place, or thing: woman, river, hat.

A **plural noun** names more than one person, place, or thing. Most plural nouns are formed by adding -s to the singular form: rivers, hats.

When a singular noun ends in the sound of *ch, sh, s, ss,* or *x,* add -es to form the plural: matches, dishes, circuses, glasses, axes, ibexes.

When a noun ends in *z,* double the *z* and add -es to form the plural: quizzes.

When a noun ends in a consonant followed by *y,* change the *y* to *i* and add -es:

baby	babies
city	cities
party	parties

When a noun ends in a vowel followed by *y,* just add -s:

boy	boys
key	keys
monkey	monkeys
tray	trays

With some singular nouns that end in *f* or *fe,* change *f* or *fe* to *v* and add -es:

calf	calves
knife	knives
leaf	leaves
loaf	loaves
thief	thieves
wife	wives

To form some plural nouns, special forms must be used:

child	children
foot	feet
mouse	mice
ox	oxen
tooth	teeth
woman	women

Some plural forms are the same as the singular:

one deer	ten deer
one moose	three moose
one sheep	two sheep

When in doubt about the plural form of a noun, look it up in a dictionary. Dictionaries give the plural form of nouns that do not simply add -s or -es. For example:

man (măn) *n*
pl men (měn)

Subjects.   Nouns are often used as subjects of verbs. The subject of a verb tells who or what is performing the action described by the verb. For example, consider this sentence:

The *snow* falls.

The noun *snow* is the subject. It tells what is falling. Now consider this sentence:

The *children* laugh.

The noun *children* is the subject. It tells who is laughing.

Verbs.   A verb is a word that usually describes an action: eat, hop, jump, play, run, see, sing, speak, study, swim, throw, write. There are two main types of verbs: transitive and intransitive. **Transitive verbs** need both a subject (someone or something to perform the action) and an object (a person or thing being acted upon):

Susie *hit* the ball.

In this sentence, *Susie* is the subject (the person hitting) and *ball* is the object (the thing being hit). *Hit* is a transitive verb.

An **intransitive verb** does not need an object:

The sun *rose.*
Fish *swim.*
The women *work.*

Some verbs are called **linking verbs.** They show or describe what someone or something is like or how someone is feeling.

An adjective or noun used to complete the meaning of a linking verb is called a **complement.** Complements are commonly referred to as **predicate** or **predicative** (U.K.) **adjectives** or **nouns.** *To be* is the linking verb most often used.

Joan *was* a teacher for many years.

Other common linking verbs are *seem, appear, look, feel,* and *become.*

My mother *seems* sad.
Ants always *appear* busy.
The sky *looks* cloudy.
I continue to *feel* bad.
I still *feel* ill.
A caterpillar *becomes* a butterfly.

To Be

Present

SINGULAR	PLURAL
I am	we are
you are	you are
he/she/it is	they are

She *is* a good student.
Her parents *are* happy.

Past

SINGULAR	PLURAL
I was	we were
you were	you were
he/she/it was	they were

Monday *was* sunny.
We *were* hot and thirsty.

Past Participle

Been is used for all subjects.

SINGULAR	PLURAL
I have been	we have been
you have been	you have been
he/she/it has been	they have been

We have *been* good friends for a long time.
He had *been* ill for a long time.
Have you and Bill *been* busy?

PERSON. The **subject** of a verb—who or what is performing the action—decides the spelling or form of the verb. Most verbs with singular subjects end in s:

A girl (singular) *runs* (singular).
The frog *jumps.*
A dog *barks.*
The bird *sings.*
The child *walks* well.

Verbs with plural subjects drop the *s:*

Girls (plural) *run* (plural).
The frogs *jump.*
Dogs *bark.*
Birds *sing.*

The pronouns *I, he, she, it, you, we,* and *they* can also be used as subjects of verbs.

The pronouns *I* and *we* are in the first person. This means they stand for the person or persons speaking. Notice that the verbs do not end in *s:*

I like soccer.
We like music.

The pronoun *you,* whether singular or plural, is in the second person. This means it stands for the person or persons being spoken to.

You like football.
You (plural) like football.

The pronouns *he, she, it,* and *they* are in the third person. This means they stand for the persons or things being spoken about.

He likes football.
She likes football.
They go to games together.
It bores me.

TENSE. The **tense** of a verb tells when an action takes place. An action happening now is in the **present** *tense:*

Scott *plays* at home today.

An action that has not happened yet is in the **future tense:**

Scott *will play* at home tomorrow.

An action that happened before now is in the **past tense:**

Scott *played* at home yesterday.

Many verbs, called **regular verbs**, form the past tense by adding -ed to the end of the word:

add	added
cook	cooked
open	opened
play	played
wash	washed

Verbs ending in y change the *y* to *i* when adding -es or -ed:

	present	past
copy	copies	copied
cry	cries	cried
fry	fries	fried
hurry	hurries	hurried

Many verbs do not add -ed to form the past tense. Such verbs look quite different and are sometimes called **irregular verbs:**

begin	began
drink	drank
fly	flew
go	went
run	ran
swim	swam
wear	wore

Another form of the past tense uses the helping verbs *have, has,* and *had* plus a form of the verb called the **past participle.** Helping verbs are also called **auxiliary verbs.**

He *has walked* to work every morning.
They *have eaten* in this restaurant many times.
Carla and Bill *had gone* to every meeting.

If unsure about the past tense of a verb, look up the present tense in a dictionary. If it is an irregular verb, all its special forms will be given. For example:

eat (ēt) *v*
ate (āt)
eaten (ēt´n)
eating, eats

The ending -ing can be added to verbs. The resulting form is called the **present participle.** It describes actions that continue over a period of time, took place over a period of time, or are still going on.

I am *writing* letters to all my friends.
They were *having* tea when the phone rang.
We were *flying* our kites in the park.
They have been *wasting* gas (U.K.: petrol) for many weeks.

The -ing form of a verb can be used as a noun. This form is called a *gerund.*

Running is good exercise.
Swimming is too.

FUTURE: The cat *will run.*

PRESENT: The cat *is running.*

PAST: The cat *ran.*

Irregular Verbs

Present	Past	Past Participle	Present	Past	Past Participle	Present	Past	Past Participle
beat	beat	beat, beaten	get	got	got, gotten	see	saw	seen
become	became	become	give	gave	given	sell	sold	sold
begin	began	begun	go	went	gone	send	sent	sent
bend	bent	bent	grow	grew	grown	set	set	set
bet	bet	bet, betted	hang	hung	hung	shake	shook	shaken
bite	bit	bit, bitten	have	had	had	shoot	shot	shot
bleed	bled	bled	hear	heard	heard	shut	shut	shut
blow	blew	blown	hide	hid	hid, hidden	sing	sang	sung
break	broke	broken	hit	hit	hit	sink	sank	sunk
bring	brought	brought	hold	held	held	sit	sat	sat
build	built	built	hurt	hurt	hurt	sleep	slept	slept
buy	bought	bought	keep	kept	kept	slide	slid	slid
catch	caught	caught	know	knew	known	speak	spoke	spoken
choose	chose	chosen	lay	laid	laid	spend	spent	spent
come	came	come	lead	led	led	spread	spread	spread
cost	cost	cost	leave	left	left	spring	sprang	sprung
creep	crept	crept	lend	lent	lent	stand	stood	stood
cut	cut	cut	let	let	let	steal	stole	stolen
dig	dug	dug	lie	lay	lain	stick	stuck	stuck
do	did	done	light	lit	lit, lighted	swear	swore	sworn
draw	drew	drawn	lose	lost	lost	sweep	swept	swept
drink	drank	drunk	make	made	made	swim	swam	swum
drive	drove	driven	mean	meant	meant	take	took	taken
eat	ate	eaten	meet	met	met	teach	taught	taught
fall	fell	fallen	pay	paid	paid	tear	tore	torn
feed	fed	fed	put	put	put	tell	told	told
feel	felt	felt	quit	quit	quit	think	thought	thought
fight	fought	fought	read	read	read	throw	threw	thrown
find	found	found	ride	rode	ridden	understand	understood	understood
fly	flew	flown	ring	rang	rung	wake	woke	waked, woken
forget	forgot	forgotten, forgot	rise	rose	risen	wear	wore	worn
forgive	forgave	forgiven	run	ran	run	win	won	won
freeze	froze	frozen	say	said	said	write	wrote	written

Examples

Present:	I *feel* well today.
Past:	I *felt* well yesterday.
Past Participle:	I *have felt* well all week.
Present:	Our class *writes* letters to pen pals.
Past:	Last week we *wrote* to our pen pals in Mexico.
Past Participle:	We *have written* to them many times.
Present:	She *cut* the grass this morning.
Past:	She also *cut* the grass last week.
Past Participle:	She *has cut* the grass often.

THE CAT has run.
(*Run*, in this sentence, is a past participle.)

Adjectives. Adjectives are words that describe nouns. They may tell about the color, size, shape, feel, taste, smell, age, sound, and number of things. Adjectives add interest, variety, and accuracy to speech and writing.

> The apple grew on a tree.
> The *red* apple grew
> on a tree.
> The *round, red* apple grew
> on a tree.
> The *round, red, juicy* apple
> grew on a tree.

The adjectives *round, red,* and *juicy* help paint a word picture of the noun *apple.*

> A cat sat on the wall.
> A *black* cat sat on the wall.
> A *fat, black* cat sat on
> the wall.
> A *fat, old, black* cat sat on
> the wall.

The adjectives black, fat, and old describe the noun cat.

Articles. There are three articles—*a, an,* and *the.* Because articles tell something about nouns, they act as adjectives. The article *the,* which is called the **definite article**, is used before a specific, or definite, person, place, or thing.

> *The* planes took off from
> *the* airport near my house.

The articles *a* and *an* are called **indefinite articles**. This means they are used before any person, place, or thing rather than a specific person, place, or thing. Notice that *the* can be used before a singular noun or a plural noun. *A* and *an* are used only before singular nouns. Use *a* before words that start with a consonant sound: a show, a plane, a house, a dog, a pen, a man.

> Sue wants *a* dog for
> Christmas.

Use *an* before words that start

THIS CAT is a (article) wet (adjective) cat.

with a vowel *(a, e, i, o, u)* sound: an apple, an igloo, an orange, an umbrella, an hour.

> I ate *an* orange as my snack.

Adverbs. Adverbs are words that describe action words or verbs. They may tell how, when, and where an action takes place. Like adjectives, they add interest and accuracy to speech and writing.

> The baby sleeps.
> The baby sleeps *peacefully.*
> The baby sleeps *peacefully*
> *at night.*
> The baby sleeps *peacefully*
> *at night in his crib.*

The adverbs *peacefully, at night,* and *in his crib* tell how, when, and where the baby sleeps.

> The bells rang.
> The bells rang *loudly.*
> The bells rang *loudly at noon.*
> The bells *in the tower* rang
> *loudly at noon.*

The adverbs *loudly, at noon,* and *in the tower* tell how, when, and where the bells rang. Sometimes adverbs are used to describe other adverbs or adjectives:

> The bells rang *quite loudly.*

Here, *quite* is an adverb describing the adverb *loudly.*

> The *very* loud noise
> scared me.

In this sentence *very* is an adverb describing the adjective *loud.*

NOTE: The words *in his crib, in the tower,* and *at noon* are groups of words that are called phrases. Because these phrases act as adverbs here, they are called **adverbial phrases.** For more about phrases, see the section on Prepositions.

Pronouns. A word that takes the place of, or substitutes for, a noun is called a pronoun.

> Tom ran to school.
> *He* ran to school.
>
> Mom and Dad went out.
> *They* went out.
>
> Jane and I made popcorn.
> *We* made popcorn.

The word that is being replaced by a pronoun is called the **antecedent**.

> Tom ran to school,
> but he was late.

He is replacing *Tom,* so *Tom* is the antecedent.

Pronouns should be used only when the antecedent is clear.

> Tom ran to school with
> *his* dog.
> *He* was late.

A reader might think that the dog was late instead of Tom.

Pronouns are often used to avoid repeating the same noun over and over. For example, in the following paragraph no pronouns are used.

> Lisa and Alec went to
> a party. Lisa and Alec had
> a good time. Lisa and
> Alec ate cake. The cake
> was chocolate. Lisa won
> a prize. Alec won a game.
> The game was
> blindman's buff.

It is easy to see how boring it is to read the same nouns over and over again. Here is the same

color
US

colour
Brit.

paragraph, using the pronouns *they, she, he,* and *it.*

> Lisa and Alec went to
> a party and had a
> good time. *They* ate
> a chocolate cake.
> *She* won a prize,
> and *he* won a game.
> *It* was blindman's buff.

Pronouns are classified as personal, possessive, relative, interrogative, demonstrative, or indefinite.

The **personal pronouns** are *I, you, he, she, it, we,* and *they. Me, him, her, us,* and *them* are also personal pronouns. For more information about using personal pronouns, see the section on Prepositions.

The **possessive pronouns** are *mine, yours, his, hers, its, ours,* and *theirs.* These pronouns may be used in place of possessive nouns:

> Katy's house is blue.
> Tom's house is green.

> Katy's house is blue.
> *His* is green.

In the second sentence, *his* replaces *Tom's house.*

NOTE: Unlike the contraction for *it is*—*it's*—the possessive pronoun *its* does not have an apostrophe.

A **relative pronoun** connects a noun in the main part of the sentence to another group of words, called a **dependent clause.** Such words as who, whom, whose, which, and that are relative pronouns.

> The soldiers *who* are on
> leave seem very cheerful.

> The prize *that* they won was
> not particularly useful.

Interrogative pronouns are used to ask questions. *Who, whom, whose, which,* and *what* are interrogative pronouns.

> *Who* is it? *What* did you say?

Demonstrative pronouns are used to point out a specific person,

place, or thing. The most common demonstratives are *this, that, these,* and *those.* Demonstratives can be used as pronouns and as adjectives.

> *That* (pronoun) is a great car.
> *This* (pronoun) is my house.
> *That* (adjective) film was exciting.
> *This* (adjective) cold is very annoying.

Indefinite pronouns are used to point out persons, places, or things, but less specifically than the demonstratives do. Some common indefinite pronouns are *everybody, nobody, each, either, neither, one, none, some, other, another, few, many, all, several,* and *both.* The indefinites can be used, like the demonstratives, both as pronouns and as adjectives.

> *Many* (adjective) actors have
> stage fright.
> *Many* (adjective) people are
> football fans.
> *Few* (pronoun) of us are successful.

Possessives.   Ownership is shown by possessives—they tell what belongs to someone or something. **Singular possessives** are formed by adding an apostrophe and an -s ('s) to a

singular noun.   Possessives make speech and writing sound more natural.

> The dog that belongs to
> the girl is barking.
> The *girl's* dog is barking.

> The hat that belongs to
> the man blew away.
> The *man's* hat blew away.

Plural possessives are formed by adding an apostrophe (') to a plural noun that already ends in *s.*

> Ears of rabbits are long.
> *Rabbits'* ears are long.

> The names of the brothers
> are Bob and Ed.
> The *brothers'* names are Bob and Ed.

Not all plural nouns end in *s:* for example, men, women, children. If a plural noun does not end in *s,* add 's.

> The *children's* hats are red.

Possessive pronouns also show ownership. They may be used in place of possessive nouns. The possessive pronouns are *mine, yours, his, hers, its, ours,* and *theirs.*

> That book is *Jane's.*
> That book is *hers.*

> The red car is our *neighbors'.*
> The red car is *theirs.*

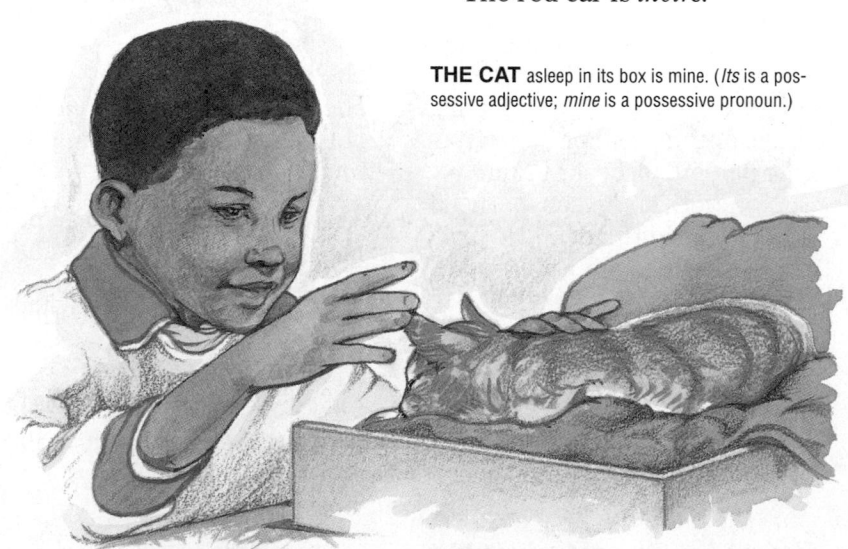

THE CAT asleep in its box is mine. (*Its* is a possessive adjective; *mine* is a possessive pronoun.)

The **possessive adjectives**—*my, your, his, her, its, our,* and *their*—also show ownership. They take the place of possessive nouns that are functioning as adjectives.

> This is *Jack's* dog.
> This is *his* dog.

> *The brothers'* hats are red.
> *Their* hats are red.

NOTE: Do not confuse the possessive pronoun *its* with *it's,* the contraction of *it is.*

Prepositions. A preposition is a word that, combined with a noun, forms a phrase—a small group of words—that usually refers to location, direction, or time. Some common prepositions are *on, in, at, to, by, with, behind, below, over, under, of,* and *for.*

> They walked *to* the store.
> The plane flew *over* the clouds.
> I went home *at* three o'clock.

In the above sentences the prepositional phrases—*to the store, over the clouds,* and *at three o'clock*—act as adverbs, telling where and when the action takes place.

THE CAT is playing *on* the rug, *with* the mouse *and* a ball. (*On* and *with* are prepositions; *and* is a conjunction.)

A prepositional phrase can also act as an adjective, describing a noun.

> The house *with the green shutters* is mine.
> The book *with the torn cover* is Henry's.
> The kitten *in the pet shop* drank milk.

The **subject pronouns** *I, he, she, we,* and *they* cannot be used with prepositions. Instead, use the **object pronouns** *me, him, her, us,* and *them.*

> Give the ball *to me.*
> The postman has some mail *for us.*
> We looked *at them.*

NOTE: The pronouns *it* and *you* are used as subject or object pronouns. For example:

> *It* is a beautiful painting.
> We looked *at it* for a long time.

In the first sentence, *it* is the subject. But in the second sentence, *it* is used as the object of the preposition *at.*

> *You* are my friend.
> I like *you.*

You is the subject of the first sentence. In the second sentence, *you* is the object of the verb *like.*

Conjunctions. Conjunctions are words that join or connect words and phrases. *And, as, but, or, so,* and *when* are common conjunctions.

> Mom *and* Dad are coming to the game.
> I like cake *as* my brother does.
> Will you have tea *or* coffee?

Conjunctions can also be used to connect sentences.

> The test was long *but* it was not very hard.

Prefixes and suffixes. A root word is a base word to which beginnings or endings may be added. For example, the root word *do* can become *undo, redo, doing, doable.* A **prefix** is part of a word added to the beginning of a root word.

Common Prepositions

about	beside	onto
above	between	outside
across	beyond	over
after	by	since
against	down	through
along	except	to
among	for	under
around	from	until
at	in	up
before	inside	upon
behind	into	with
below	of	within
beneath	off	without
	on	

Common Conjunctions

after	if	unless
also	moreover	until
although	nevertheless	when
and	now	where
as	or	wherever
because	since	whether
before	so	which
but	than	while
for	then	yet
how	therefore	
however	though	

A prefix changes the meaning of the word, sometimes to its opposite. The prefix un- means *not*.

happy	unhappy
fair	unfair
cut	uncut
kind	unkind
opened	unopened
used	unused

Cinderella's stepmother was *un*kind.

The prefix dis- also means *not*.

agree	disagree
appear	disappear
like	dislike
obey	disobey
please	displease

The magician made the rabbit *dis*appear.

The prefix re- means *again*.

copy	recopy
do	redo
paint	repaint
read	reread
use	reuse
write	rewrite

We had to *re*copy our stories on white paper.

The prefix mis- means *badly* or *wrongly*.

fit	misfit
inform	misinform
fortune	misfortune
taken	mistaken
use	misuse

Rob could not drive his car because he had *mis*placed his keys.
James is very often *mis*taken for his twin brother John.

A **suffix** is part of a word added to the end of a root or base word. Like prefixes, suffixes change the meanings of words.
The suffixes -ful and -ous mean *full of*.

Leaves are colorful in the fall.
A snake bite can be poison*ous*.

The suffix -less means *without any*.

After Joe struck out, it looked hope*less* for our team.

Many cities have home*less* people.

The suffix -er means *one who*.

A farm*er* is a person who farms.
Someone who paints is a paint*er*.
A baseball team has a pitch*er* and a catch*er*.
A teach*er* is one who teaches.

The suffix -able means *can be*.

The print was small but read*able*.
Water and fruit juice are mix*able*.
That little baby is very lik*able*.

COMPARATIVES.
The suffixes -er and -est are added to adjectives when comparing nouns.
Use -er to compare two nouns. This is called the **comparative form**.

May is warm*er* than January.
Max is tall, but his sister Janet is tall*er*.

Use -est when comparing more than two nouns. This is called the **superlative form**.

May is warmer than January, but July is the warm*est* month of all.

Max is tall, his sister Janet is taller, but his father is the tall*est* person in the family.

NOTE: With longer adjectives, the adverbs *more* and *most* are often used instead of the suffixes -er and -est.

Snow White was *more beautiful* than the queen.
What do you believe is the *most important* academic subject taught in school?

Negatives. A negative is a word that gives a sentence a negative meaning instead of a positive meaning.
Some words that are often used as negatives are *no, not, none, nothing, nowhere, nobody, never*.

We could *not* go to the fair.
We have had *nothing* to eat since breakfast.
Nobody knew how to solve the puzzle.
They *never* see films in daytime.

Remember: Only one negative can be used in a sentence. Two negatives in the same sentence may make a positive statement. For example:

The teacher did *not* assign *no* homework.

If the teacher did *not* assign *no* homework, then some homework must have been given. Substitute *any* for *no*.

The teacher did not assign *any* homework.

There is *not nobody* at home.

If *not nobody* is home, then somebody must be home.

There is *nobody* at home.

They will *not never* scare us again.

If they will *not never* scare us, then they can surely scare us sometime.

They will *never* scare us again.

Ted is *not* going *nowhere*.

If Ted is *not* going *nowhere,* then he is going somewhere.

Ted is not going *anywhere*.

She does *not* know *nothing*.

If she does *not* know *nothing,* then she certainly must know something.

She does not know *anything*.

Punctuation

Punctuation marks are signs that make reading sentences easier. Like traffic signs, they tell the reader when to slow down, go carefully, pause, or stop.

Period.   A period (.) is like a stop sign. A period is used at the end of a sentence that tells or states something. This kind of sentence is called a **telling** or **declarative sentence.**

> Grandfather is old.
> We go to school by bus.

A period is also used at the end of a sentence that gives an order. Such a sentence may be called a **command sentence** or an **imperative.**

> Come here.
> Get on the bus.
> Put away your toys.

In British punctuation, a period is called a **full stop.**

Question mark.   A question mark (?) is used at the end of a sentence that asks something. A sentence that asks a question is called an **asking** or **interrogative sentence.**

> May we go to the party?
> Is it going to rain today?

Exclamation point.   An exclamation point (!) is used at the end of a sentence that expresses strong feelings, such as anger, fear, joy, or surprise. Such a sentence is called an **exclamatory sentence.**

> Watch out! Be careful!
> Stop that!
> Hurray! Our team won!
> Happy birthday!
> This is a great party!

In British punctuation, an exclamation point is called an **exclamation mark.**

Comma.   A comma (,) is a signal to slow down, or pause, but

PUNCTUATION MARKS are like road signs, telling the reader when to pause or stop.

not, like a period, come to a complete stop.

For example, a comma is used to separate items in a series.

> Dad bought milk, bread, eggs, and juice at the store.
> On Thursdays we have gym, art, and science.

A comma is also used to separate two parts of a sentence joined with *and, or, but, yet,* or *for.*

> I like vanilla, *but* my sister likes chocolate.

A comma is used after or before the name of a person being spoken to.

> Lori, please come here.
> We will miss you, Jody.

A comma is used after *yes, no, oh,* and *well* at the beginning of a sentence.

> *Well,* they finally arrived.
> *No,* I haven't cleaned my room yet.

A comma is used to set off or separate nouns that tell about each other.

> Our teacher, Mr. Johnson, often reads us stories.
> The flag, a symbol of Canada, is red and white with a red maple leaf in the center.

A comma is used in a date to separate the day and the year.

> The Declaration of Independence was signed on July 4, 1776.

In British writing, dates are written differently.

> The United States Declaration of Independence was signed on 4 July 1776.

A comma is used to separate the name of a city and state, county, or province.

> Nashville, Tennessee
> Over Wallop, Hampshire

(For other uses of commas, see the following section.)

Quotation marks.   Quotation marks ("/") are used to set off someone's exact words. This is called a **direct quote** or **quotation.** A quotation mark is put before the first word and after the last word of a quote.

When a direct quote comes at the beginning of a declarative sentence, use a comma before the closing quotation mark.

> "I'll help you with your homework," Dad said.

When a direct quote comes at the end of a declarative sentence, use a comma before the opening quotation mark.

> Mother said, "It's time for bed."

When the quote is a question or exclamation, put the question mark or exclamation point before the closing quotation mark.

> "Do you like football?" asked Carlos.
> She shouted, "Stop!"

In British punctuation, a quotation mark is called an **inverted comma.**

> The policeman shouted, 'Stop!'

center
US

centre
Brit.

Two Differences Between American and British Punctuation

	American punctuation	British punctuation
To indicate time	Use a colon (:) between hour and minutes. 3:30 12:45 9:00	Use a full stop (.) between hour and minutes. 3.30 12.45 9.00
To indicate a person's exact words	Use quotation marks ("/"). She said, "I will do my best." "I will do my best," she said.	Use inverted commas ('/'). She said, 'I will do my best'. 'I will do my best', she said.
To indicate a quotation within a quotation	Use double quotation marks ("/") around the entire quotation. Use single quotation marks('/') for a quotation within the quotation. "My exact words", she explained, "were 'I will not go to the dance with you.' " He asked, "Did you hear me when I said, 'Absolutely not'?"	Use inverted commas ('/')—also called single quotes—around the entire quotation. Use double inverted commas ("/")—also called double quotes—for a quotation within a quotation. 'My exact words', she explained, 'were "I shall not go to the dance with you" '. He asked, 'Did you hear me when I said, "Absolutely not" '?

Colon. A colon (:) is a sign to the reader to pay attention to what will follow. For example, a colon is used before a list.

For the first day of school you will need to bring several items: a small pad, a notebook, pencils, and crayons.

A colon is also used in America when showing time.

6:00   2:15   12:30

A colon is used instead of quotation marks before each character's part in a play.

Peter: We'll fly away to Never-Never Land.
Wendy: But, Peter, I can't fly.

Semicolon. A semicolon (;) is used to separate parts of a sentence in order to make the meaning clearer. For instance a semicolon is used to separate words in a series where commas have already been used.

We flew to Salem, Oregon; Seattle, Washington; Calgary, Alberta; and Fairbanks, Alaska.

Capital Letters

Many writers use capital letters when they do not need to. Here are some rules for using capital letters correctly:

The subject pronoun *I* is always capitalized.

I think I'll go to the movies.

A capital letter is always used at the beginning of a sentence.

Do you think I should go?

The first word of a direct quote that is a complete sentence starts with a capital letter.

He said, "Of course I do."

Proper nouns—the names of particular people and places and events—always begin with capital letters.

Edmonton and Winnipeg are cities in Canada. Nancy and David Brown visited Niagara Falls.

The names of the months and the days of the week start with capital letters.

School starts on the first Monday in September.

The names of holidays start with capital letters.

Both Canada and the United States celebrate Thanksgiving Day, but on different dates.

On Easter Sunday we have an egg hunt.

Titles of rank and office are capitalized.

President Lincoln met with General Grant.

The first, last, and all the important words in titles of books, movies, and television shows are capitalized.

In fourth grade we read *Little House on the Prairie.*

My favorite movie is *Home Alone 2: Lost in New York.*

The first letter of the first word in a line of poetry is often capitalized:

I eat my peas with honey;
I've done it all my life.
It makes the peas taste funny,
But it keeps them on the knife.

Spelling

The English language did not grow in an orderly way from one source. It came from many different languages. So English words are often not spelled the way they sound. Such words as *bread* (bred), *guest* (gest), *knight* (nite), *ocean* (oshun), and *some* (sum) are just a few of the examples of words that are not spelled by the sound of their letters.

The strange spelling of these words has to be memorized. A good way to improve spelling skills is to keep a list of your problem words in a notebook. Use a separate page for each letter of the alphabet. Study the words and write sentences that use them.

Reading helps to improve spelling. The more often a word is seen, the easier it becomes to remember its correct spelling.

Though the spelling of many English words does not follow any pattern, there are some basic rules that make it easier to spell correctly.

Spelling rules

1. The rule about when to use *ie* and when to use *ei* is explained in this poem:

> i before e
> except after c,
> or when sounded like a,
> as in sleigh bell and weigh

Words like *friend, believe,* and *receive* follow this rule.

2. Most singular nouns are made plural by adding -s or -es to the end of the word:

pen pens   match matches

When a noun ends with a consonant and *y,* the *y* is changed to *i* and -es is added to form the plural:

baby	babies
candy	candies

But when a noun ends with a vowel (*a, e, i, o, u*) and *y,* an -s is added to form the plural:

bay	bays
boy	boys
day	days
monkey	monkeys

3. When verb endings that begin with a vowel, such as -ing or -ed, are added to verbs that end in silent *e,* the *e* is usually dropped:

bake	+ ed	baked
bake	+ ing	baking
plunge	+ ed	plunged
plunge	+ ing	plunging
salute	+ ed	saluted
salute	+ ing	saluting

The same rule applies when suffixes that begin with a vowel, such as -able, -ical, and -ible, are added to words that end in silent *e*:

live	+ able	livable
sphere	+ ical	spherical
sense	+ ible	sensible

However, most words that end with *ce* and *ge* do not follow this rule. The final silent *e* is needed to show that the soft sounds of *c* and *g* are used when saying these words:

peace	+ able	peaceable
manage	+ able	
		manageable

FYI: A few words may drop the silent *e* before the suffix -ment:

judge	+ ment	judgment
acknowledge	+ ment	
		acknowledgment

4. Many words that end with a short vowel and a consonant, like *hop* and *step,* double the last consonant when a suffix is added that begins with a vowel, such as -ed, -er, or -ing:

hop	hopped
hopper	hopping

If a word consists of or ends in a long vowel and silent *e,*

such as *hope,* the final consonant is not doubled:

hope	hoped
hoper	hoping

Here are some more examples of this rule:

CONSONANT ENDING

bar	barred	barring
pin	pinned	pinning
scrap	scrapped	scrapping
star	starred	starring

SILENT e ENDING

bare	bared	baring
pine	pined	pining
scrape	scraped	scraping
stare	stared	staring

5. There are many words that sound alike, but are spelled differently and have different meanings. They are called **homophones.**

The *two* dogs ran *to* greet us, and the cat did *too.*
We *rode* our bikes along the dirt *road.*

Compound Words

Two words put together form a compound word. Compounds usually originate from words that are said together, such as railroad, combining the words rail and road. Here are some other examples of compound words:

airplane	somebody
mailbox	downtown
airport	someone
mailman	firefighter
barnyard	sunrise
moonlight	football
baseball	sunset
playground	grandfather
bathroom	sunshine
policeman	grandmother
bedroom	teapot
rainbow	however
birthday	teenage
seaport	lunchroom
doorbell	weekend

A bare bear?

A sail sale

Spelling Differences

American	British
acknowledgment	acknowledgement
aluminum	aluminium
anesthetize	anaesthetize
behavior	behaviour
carburetor	carburettor
check (noun)	cheque
color	colour
counselor	counsellor
defense	defence
dishonor	dishonour
encyclopedia	encyclopaedia
favor	favour
favorable	favourable
fulfill	fulfil
furor	furore
honor	honour
jail	gaol
judgment	judgement
labor	labour
laborer	labourer
meager	meagre
mold	mould
offense	offence
practice (verb)	practise
scepter	sceptre
skillful	skilful
tire (noun)	tyre

Homophones

ant	aunt	feat	feet	mail	male	sew	so
ate	eight	fir	fur	meat	meet	some	sum
bare	bear	flea	flee	night	knight	son	sun
be	bee	flour	flower	one	won	stair	stare
beat	beet	great	grate	pail	pale	steal	steel
blew	blue	hair	hare	pain	pane	tail	tale
board	bored	heal	heel	pair	pear	their	there they're
brake	break	hear	here	peace	piece	threw	through
buy	by	heard	herd	plain	plane	to	too two
cell	sell	hole	whole	read	red	toe	tow
cent	sent	hour	our	real	reel	wait	weight
dear	deer	in	inn	right	write	weak	week
dew	do	knew	new	road	rode	whole	hole
die	dye	know	no	sail	sale	wood	would
fair	fare	made	maid	sea	see	your	you're

Contractions

A contraction combines two words, leaving out one or more letters. An apostrophe (') takes the place of the missing letter or letters. Contractions make speech and writing sound more natural.

He is not feeling well.
He *isn't* feeling well.

What is her name?
What's her name?

We are not hungry.
We *aren't* hungry.

I will help you.
I'll help you.

Contractions are considered informal, and it is best to avoid using them in formal writing, as in research reports.

are not	aren't
cannot	can't
could not	couldn't
did not	didn't
does not	doesn't
has not	hasn't
have not	haven't
he has	he's
he is	he's
he will	he'll
he would	he'd
I am	I'm
I have	I've
I will	I'll
I would	I'd
is not	isn't
it has	it's
it is	it's
it will	it'll
must not	mustn't
she has	she's

she is	she's
she will	she'll
she would	she'd
should not	shouldn't
they are	they're
they have	they've
they will	they'll
they would	they'd
was not	wasn't
we have	we've
we will	we'll
we would	we'd
were not	weren't
what is	what's
where is	where's
will not	won't
would not	wouldn't
you are	you're
you have	you've
you will	you'll
you would	you'd

Alphabetical Order

Alphabetical, or ABC, order means putting words in the order of the letters of the alphabet from a to z. Many useful books, or parts of books, are organized in this way. Dictionaries, encyclopedias, telephone books, glossaries, and indexes are in alphabetical order.

Putting words in this order is called **alphabetizing**. Start with the first letter of a name or word. Put the name that begins with *a* first, with *b* second, with *c* third, and so on.

Alice	**Bobby**	**Carol**	**Donald**
Emma	**Fiona**	**George**	**Henry**
Jane	**Ned**	**Peter**	**Vanessa**

If words begin with the same letter, go to the second, third, or fourth letter, and so on.

dill	place	strange
doll	please	string
dull	plum	strong

Synonyms and Antonyms

Synonyms are words that have the same or almost the same meaning. **Antonyms** are words that have opposite meanings. As with pronouns, adjectives, and adverbs, synonyms and antonyms help make speaking and writing more varied and interesting because the same words are not repeated.

Here is a chart of some common synonyms and antonyms:

Synonyms

annoy	bother
beautiful	lovely pretty
begin	start
big	large huge enormous
broad	wide
brook	stream
cap	hat
cold	frigid
cozy	snug
easy	simple
famous	well-known
fast	quick
finish	end
help	aid
hurt	injure
jump	leap
kind	gentle
laugh	giggle
loud	noisy
near	close
polite	courteous
rock	stone
run	jog
same	alike
shiny	bright
shut	close
skinny	thin
small	little tiny
smart	clever
stiff	rigid
story	tale
test	exam
tired	weary
trail	path
troublesome	pesky
ugly	homely
unusual	strange

Antonyms

begin	end
big	little small tiny
clean	dirty
come	go
dangerous	safe
dark	light
day	night
empty	full
far	near
fast	slow
first	last
front	back
give	take
good	bad
happy	sad
hard	soft
heavy	light
high	low
hot	cold
in	out
kind	mean
laugh	cry
late	early
long	short
new	old
over	under
push	pull
quiet	noisy
rich	poor
rough	smooth
smile	frown
stop	go
tall	short
up	down
wet	dry
wild	tame
young	old

Abbreviations

To abbreviate means to make shorter or smaller. An abbreviation is a short form of a word. Most abbreviations end with a period. If a proper noun is abbreviated, it still begins with a capital letter.

Mount Washington
Mt. Washington

Titles of respect, rank, and office can be abbreviated.

Mister Jones	Mr. Jones
Mistress White	Mrs. White
Reverend Smith	Rev. Smith
Doctor Miller	Dr. Miller
President Lund	Pres. Lund
General Young	Gen. Young
Jay Todd, Senior	Jay Todd, Sr.
Jay Todd, Junior	Jay Todd, Jr.

The titles Miss and Ms. cannot be abbreviated.

Names can be shortened, or abbreviated, by using an initial. An initial is the first letter of a name and it is always a capital letter followed by a period.

John Thomas Rogers
J.T. Rogers
Marla Jane Kent
M.J. Kent
Susan Ruth Brown
Susan R. Brown

Words in mailing addresses can be abbreviated.

Apartment	Apt. 5B
Avenue	Park Ave.
Boulevard	Center Blvd.
Circle	Charter Cir.
Court	Tulip Ct.
Drive	Oak Dr.
Lane	Dunn La.
Road	Bedford Rd.
Route	Rte. 100
Street	Main St.
Terrace	Linden Ter.

Direction words in mailing addresses can be abbreviated.

North	120 N. Broadway
South	30 S. Main St.
East	215 E. Post Rd.
West	700 W. Post Rd.

Not all address abbreviations need periods.

Post Office Box   PO Box

Abbreviations

The United States Post Office recommends two-letter capitalized abbreviations for each of the 50 states and the District of Columbia, Guam, Puerto Rico, and the Virgin Islands. No periods are used.

The Canadian Post Office has done the same for its provinces and territories.

U.S. STATES AND TERRITORIES

Alabama	AL
Alaska	AK
Arizona	AZ
Arkansas	AR
California	CA
Colorado	CO
Connecticut	CT
Delaware	DE
District of Columbia	DC
Florida	FL
Georgia	GA
Guam	GU
Hawaii	HI
Idaho	ID
Illinois	IL
Indiana	IN
Iowa	IA
Kansas	KS
Kentucky	KY
Louisiana	LA
Maine	ME
Maryland	MD
Massachusetts	MA
Michigan	MI
Minnesota	MN
Mississippi	MS
Missouri	MO
Montana	MT
Nebraska	NE
Nevada	NV
New Hampshire	NH
New Jersey	NJ
New Mexico	NM
New York	NY
North Carolina	NC
North Dakota	ND
Ohio	OH
Oklahoma	OK
Oregon	OR
Pennsylvania	PA
Puerto Rico	PR
Rhode Island	RI
South Carolina	SC
South Dakota	SD
Tennessee	TN
Texas	TX
Utah	UT
Vermont	VT
Virgin Islands	VI
Virginia	VA
Washington	WA
West Virginia	WV
Wisconsin	WI
Wyoming	WY

CANADIAN PROVINCES AND TERRITORIES

Alberta	AB
British Columbia	BC
Manitoba	MB
New Brunswick	NB
Newfoundland and Labrador	NL
Northern Territories	NT
Nova Scotia	NS
Nunavut	NU
Ontario	ON
Prince Edward Island	PE
Quebec	PQ
Saskatchewan	SK
Yukon	YT

Units of measure can be abbreviated.

inch	in.	ounce	oz.
foot	ft.	pint	pt.
yard	yd.	quart	qt.
mile	mi.	gallon	gal.
millimeter	mm	liter	l
centimeter	cm		
meter	m		
kilometer	km		

Note that abbreviations for metric measurements usually do not have periods.

Days of the week and most of the months of the year can be abbreviated.

Sunday	Sun.	January	Jan.
Monday	Mon.	February	Feb.
Tuesday	Tues.	March	Mar.
Wednesday	Wed.	April	Apr.
Thursday	Thu.	May	May
Friday	Fri.	June	June
Saturday	Sat.	July	July
		August	Aug.
		September	Sept.
		October	Oct.
		November	Nov.
		December	Dec.

COUNTIES OF ENGLAND WITH ABBREVIATIONS IN USE

Avon	
Bedfordshire	Beds.
Berkshire	Berks.
Buckinghamshire	Bucks.
Cambridgeshire	Cambs.
Cheshire	Ches.
Cleveland	
Cornwall	Corn.
Cumbria	
Derbyshire	Derby.
Devon	
Dorset	
Durham	Dur.
East Sussex	
Essex	
Gloucestershire	Glos.
Greater London	
Greater Manchester	
Hampshire	Hants.
Hereford & Worcester	
Hertfordshire	Herts.
Humberside	
Isle of Wight	IOW
Kent	
Lancaster	Lancs.
Leicestershire	Leics.
Lincolnshire	Lincs.
Merseyside	
Norfolk	
Northamptonshire	Northants.
Northumberland	Northumb.
North Yorkshire	
Nottinghamshire	Notts.
Oxfordshire	Oxon.
Shropshire	
Somerset	Som.
South Yorkshire	
Staffordshire	Staffs.
Suffolk	
Surrey	
Tyne and Wear	
Warwickshire	War.
West Midlands	
West Sussex	
West Yorkshire	
Wiltshire	Wilts.

LIKE ANY OTHER SKILL, handwriting takes practice. There are correct ways to play tennis; there are correct ways to write. The photo shows the way to sit, hold a pencil, and angle the paper when writing.

Composition

Like speaking, writing is the act of putting words together to express ideas. To make sense, writing must be orderly and follow certain rules.

Words are joined to make sentences. Sentences that tell the reader about a single idea are grouped together in a paragraph. Sentences and paragraphs are the building blocks of writing. Once a writer has learned to put words together correctly to make sentences, and sentences together properly to make paragraphs, then it is only a short step to putting paragraphs together in order to create stories, letters, or school reports.

Sentences. A sentence is a group of words that states a whole or complete idea. Sentences start with a capital letter and end with a period, or an exclamation point, or a question mark.

Words in a sentence have to be in the right order to make sense. Changing the word order often changes the meaning of a sentence:

The cat caught the mouse.
The mouse caught the cat.

Subject and predicate. A complete sentence has a subject and a predicate. The subject part of a sentence is the naming part. It is either a noun or a pronoun. It tells who or what is doing something.

The *children* play.
The *car* stops.
Steve runs.
I walk.

The predicate part of a sentence is the action part. It is a verb. It tells what the subject is doing.

A fish *swims*.

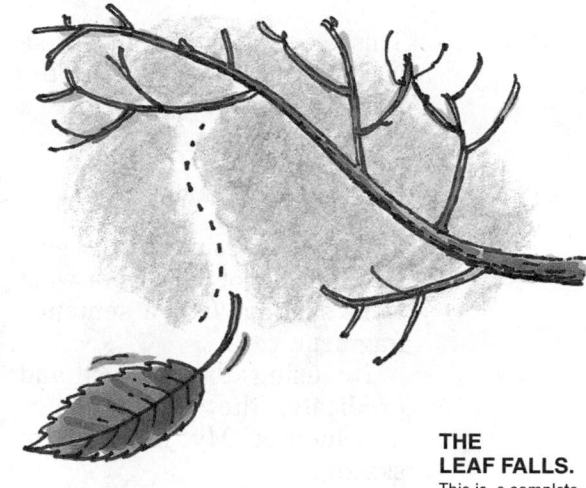

THE LEAF FALLS. This is a complete sentence because it has both a subject (leaf) and a predicate (falls).

Babies *cry*.
We *danced*.

NOTE: The pronoun *I* is always used in the subject part of a sentence. The pronoun *me* is always used in the *predicate* part of a sentence.

I walk to school.
Marie and *I* walk to school.

She walks *me* across the street.
The teacher helped John and *me*.

Sentence fragments. A fragment is a piece of something—not the whole thing. A sentence fragment is not a whole or complete sentence. It lacks either a subject or a predicate.

My friend

HANDWRITING. Neat, readable handwriting helps make writing more understandable. There is a correct way to write each letter. Capital and small letters are often different. Writing printed letters is called *manuscript writing*. Writing connected letters with curving and slanted lines is called *cursive writing*. These two charts show how letters are properly formed.

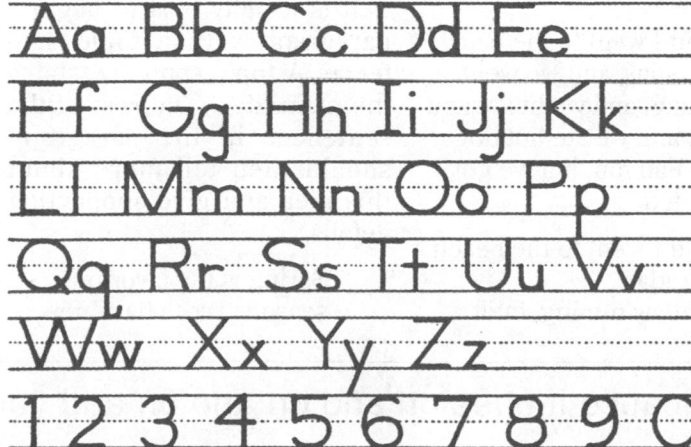

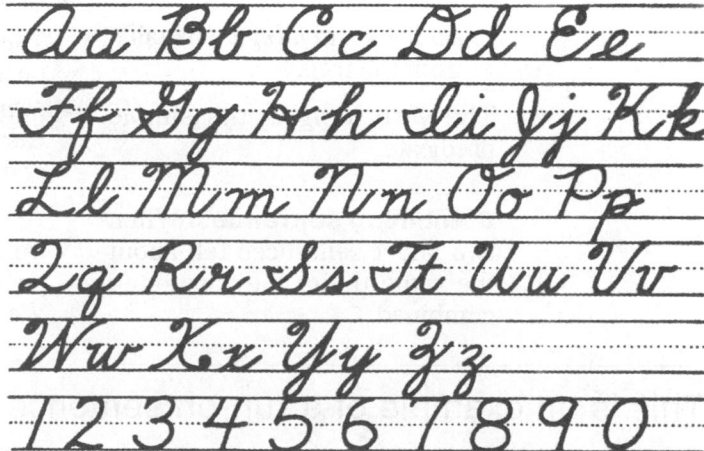

This is a subject without a predicate. It does not tell what the friend does. It is, therefore, a sentence fragment.

went skating

This is a predicate without a subject. It does not tell who or what went skating. It is a sentence fragment.

By using the subject and predicate, the writer makes a sentence: My friend went skating.

Simple subject.   Most sentences are longer than two or three words. In a longer sentence, the main or most important noun or pronoun in the subject part of the sentence is called the simple subject.

The frisky, black and white *puppies* ran around the yard.

In this sentence the noun *puppies* is the simple subject.

After school, all the *children* went to clubs.

The noun *children* is the simple subject.

The main or most important verb in the action or predicate part of a sentence is called the simple predicate.

Meryl and I *ran* happily down the street.

The verb *ran* is the simple predicate.

An opossum *hung* by its tail from the tree.

The verb *hung* is the simple predicate.

Combining sentences. When two short sentences tell about the same thing, they are often combined.

The elephants are big.
The elephants are gray (grey).
The elephants are big and gray (grey).

Longer sentences that tell about the same thing can also be combined by using a comma and the words *and, but,* or *or* (see section on Conjunctions under Parts of Speech).

Canada has many beautiful lakes and rivers. It also has lovely mountains and forests.

Canada has many beautiful lakes and rivers, *and* it also has lovely mountains and forests.

We wanted to visit the Kennedy Space Center on Thursday. It rained so hard we could not go.

We wanted to visit the Kennedy Space Center on Thursday, *but* it rained so hard we could not go.

We could go out to a restaurant for pizza.
We could make it at home.

We could go out to a restaurant for pizza, *or* we could make it at home.

Run-on sentence.   Often, a sentence that is too long has to be separated into shorter sentences. A run-on sentence has too many complete ideas. It can be confusing.

Tom and I went to the beach on Thursday, and we went swimming, and we built sand castles, and we ate hot dogs, and we had fun, but we got sunburned.

Tom and I went to the beach on Thursday.
We went swimming, built

sand castles, and ate hot dogs. We had fun, but we got sunburned.

Many grown-ups think that children watch too much television and they think children do not read or exercise enough and grown-ups worry about this.

Many grown-ups think that children watch too much television. They think children do not read or exercise enough. Grown-ups worry about this.

This is an example of a run-on sentence because it goes on and on and on and you forget what you are reading about and get confused and have to read it over again and again.

To summarize, a sentence should:

1. express a complete thought
2. begin with a capital letter
3. end with a period, question mark, or exclamation point
4. have the words in the correct order
5. have a subject and a predicate
6. not have too many main ideas.

Paragraphs.   A paragraph is a group of sentences that tells about one main idea. The first line of a paragraph is usually indented by moving the first word a few spaces to the right.

It is usually best to begin a paragraph with a topic sentence. A topic sentence states the main idea. The rest of the sentences in the paragraph should then tell more about this idea and give supporting details.

Spring is my favorite season. Trees have new

THE SEQUENCE OF EVENTS is important in any piece of writing. The story told here makes no sense because the events are out of order. A careful writer will always check to make sure that the story makes sense in the order in which he or she is telling it.

green leaves and grass begins to grow. Birds sing and pretty flowers begin to bloom. The air is soft and gentle. Children can play outdoors.

The topic sentence of this paragraph is *Spring is my favorite season.* It states the main idea that is being written about. The other sentences in the paragraph give supporting details, or more information about spring.

American Indians used many different materials to build their homes. Indians of the Plains made tents of buffalo skins. Some Indian tribes of the Southwest made their homes from sunbaked bricks called adobe. Longhouses made of logs were built by Indians who lived in the forests of the Northeast.

The main idea of this paragraph is expressed in the topic sentence *American Indians used many different materials to build their homes.* The rest of the sentences in the paragraph give

more information about this idea.

The topic sentence is not always the first sentence in a paragraph.

In a city there are many interesting things to see and do. There are museums, parks, zoos, theaters, stores, and restaurants. But city streets are often dirty. There is so much traffic that the air is polluted. Many older people are afraid to go out at night because there is a lot of crime. Cities are interesting places, but they have many problems.

In this paragraph the topic sentence is last: *Cities are interesting places, but they have many problems.* The topic sentence at the end sums up or draws a conclusion from the details that come before it. This gives dramatic effect.

Sequence.   When telling a story or giving instructions about how to do something, it is important to write the events or ideas in the correct time order

or sequence. Words like *first, second, next, then, later, last,* or *finally* are often used. The following paragraphs show how time can be put in proper sequence.

In the morning, I get ready for school. *First,* I brush my teeth and wash my face. *Next,* I get dressed. *Then,* I go into the kitchen and eat breakfast. *Last,* I put my homework, schoolbooks, and lunch in my backpack. I am *finally* ready for school.

My dad and I made cookies. *First,* Dad turned on the oven and helped me grease a baking pan. *Second,* we emptied the box of cookie mix into a big bowl. *Next,* we stirred in eggs, oil, and milk. *Then,* we poured the mixture into the pan and put it in the oven. Thirty minutes *later,* Dad carefully lifted the pan out of the oven. *Finally,* after they had cooled, we ate the delicious cookies.

theaters
US

theatres
Brit.

forget what you are reading about and get confused and have to read it over again.

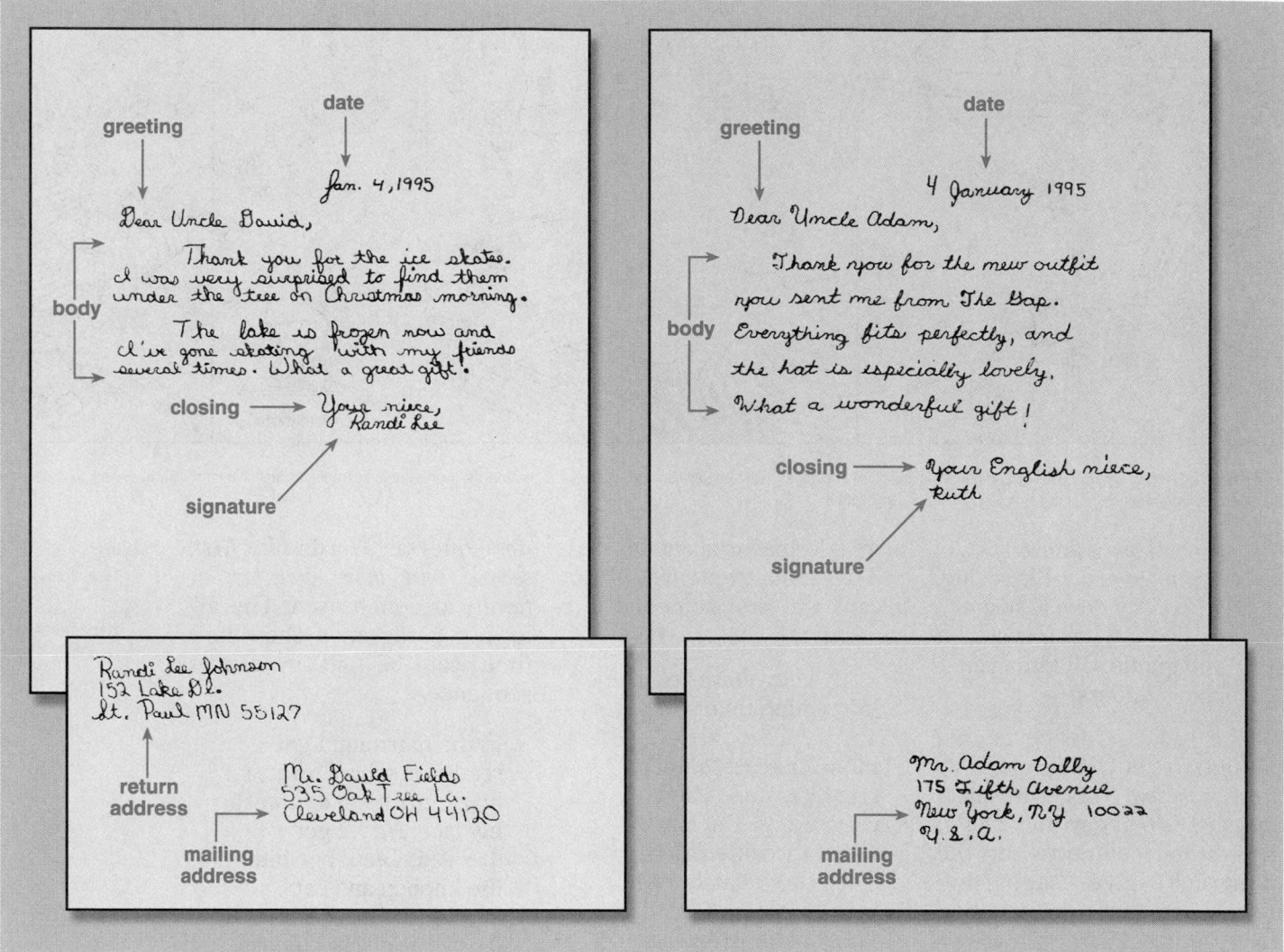

LETTERS AND ENVELOPES should follow the forms shown here. As you can see, there are minor differences between American and British style. You can be assured that your letters will be delivered in either style.

Letter writing. Relatives and friends sometimes move away, go to summer camp, or take long vacations. They may send postcards or gifts for birthdays and holidays. Knowing how to write them friendly letters and notes expressing thanks is important. We must never forget to perform these simple duties.

A friendly letter should include news of what the writer has been doing, but it should also ask about and comment on the reader's activities. Notes expressing thanks need not be long, but should mention the usefulness of a gift and tell how it is being enjoyed.

A letter has five parts:

1. the date

2. the greeting
3. the body
4. the closing
5. the signature.

In the letters above, the parts are labeled.

Note that in the date in America there is a comma between the day and the year. This is not so in Great Britain. A comma is used after the greeting and the closing. All the words in the greeting start with a capital letter. The first word in the closing starts with a capital letter.

Addressing an envelope. Two addresses are written on an envelope: the mailing address and the return address. The mailing address is the address of the person receiving the letter. It is usually written in the middle of the envelope. Be sure to follow the custom of the country of the writer and that of the reader.

The return address is the address of the person sending the letter. It is usually written in the upper left-hand corner. (In Britain it is often not used.)

Because an envelope is a small space, abbreviations are often used (see the section on Abbreviations). Names of people and places are proper nouns and always start with capital letters. Use a comma between an American city and state or a Canadian province. A comma is not needed between a city or town and England, Ireland, or Scotland.

A STORY always has a beginning, a middle, and an end that can be easily identified.

Story writing. Original and imaginative ideas make a story interesting, but in order to be readable, a story should follow certain guidelines.

FORM. A story must always have a beginning, a middle, and an end.

The **beginning** should be interesting enough to make the reader want to find out what happens next.

The **middle** should carry the story along, giving more details in an interesting way.

The **end** should bring the story to a logical and satisfactory conclusion.

CONTENT. A story, whether it is true or made up, has to tell about someone or something. The people, animals, or imaginary creatures in a story are called **characters.**

A story has to take place somewhere. This place is the story's **setting.**

Things have to happen in a story. There has to be action. This is called the **plot.**

In the story shown here these different parts are labeled.

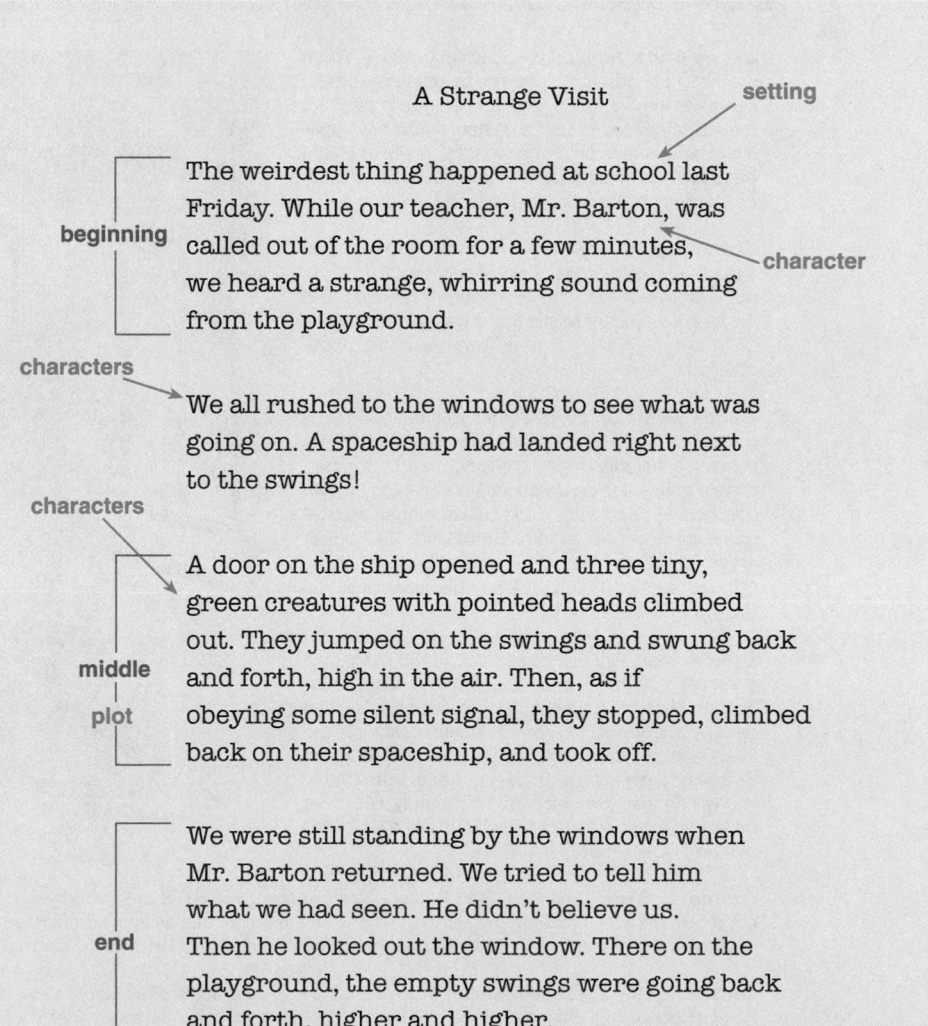

A Strange Visit

setting

beginning

The weirdest thing happened at school last Friday. While our teacher, Mr. Barton, was called out of the room for a few minutes, we heard a strange, whirring sound coming from the playground.

character

characters

We all rushed to the windows to see what was going on. A spaceship had landed right next to the swings!

characters

middle
plot

A door on the ship opened and three tiny, green creatures with pointed heads climbed out. They jumped on the swings and swung back and forth, high in the air. Then, as if obeying some silent signal, they stopped, climbed back on their spaceship, and took off.

end

We were still standing by the windows when Mr. Barton returned. We tried to tell him what we had seen. He didn't believe us. Then he looked out the window. There on the playground, the empty swings were going back and forth, higher and higher.

Book reports. Like a story, a book report should tell the reader about the **setting, plot,** and **characters** in a book.

Only enough of the plot should be related so that someone reading the report will have a general idea of what the book is about. The ending should not be told if knowing it would make reading the book less enjoyable for someone else.

The report should describe a character in detail and give reasons for liking or disliking this character. Was the book interesting or boring? Following is a sample book report:

Sarah, Plain and Tall
by Patricia MacLachlan

Caleb and his papa and his sister, Anna, live on a farm on the prairie. Caleb's mama died the day after he was born. Anna remembers Mama, but Caleb doesn't.

Papa places an ad in a newspaper for a wife. A lady named Sarah from Maine answers the ad. She comes on the train with her cat, Seal, for a visit.

Caleb and Anna like Sarah and hope she will stay, but she misses the sea and her family in Maine.

Sarah is a likable person. She is strong and helps Papa on the farm. She is gentle and kind with the children.

Will Sarah stay or go home? It is certainly worth reading this book to find out. It has a lot to say about families and love.

Titles of Some Modern Classics We All Love

Lassie Come Home, by Eric Knight (1940). When we think of books about great dogs, the name Lassie comes to mind at once. This fine animal is part of a mining family in Yorkshire. When times are especially hard, she is sold to a wealthy family and sent off to live 400 miles away in Scotland. Lassie's arduous journey home to Yorkshire is indeed heroic.

Lad: A Dog, by Albert Payson Terhune (1919). If you already love collie dogs, you will adore Lad. If you do not now love collies, *Lad* will change your mind, and the best thing about *Lad* is that it was merely the first of a series of stories that Terhune wrote about admirable dogs.

Good-bye, Mr. Chips, by James Hilton (1934). Anyone who has known a teacher devoted to his subject, his students, and his school will take immediately to this fine novel about Mr. Chipping, known as Chips. His subject is classical languages, his students all boys, his school Brookfield, an English grammar school. If you have not yet been taught by a great teacher, Hilton's Chips will serve until you meet your own Chips.

Little Women, by Louisa May Alcott (1869). Imagine a 19th-century novel about four sisters and their parents that has been a best seller throughout the 20th century and will surely remain popular well into the 21st century. Here is your chance to meet Meg, Jo, Beth, and Amy March. Once you get to know them, you will be their friend for life. Fortunately, two other novels by Alcott are also available, *Little Men* (1871) and *Jo's Boys* (1886).

Penrod, by Booth Tarkington (1914). If you enjoyed Mark Twain's *Tom Sawyer,* you have another treat in store. Penrod Schofield is a boy's boy. He gets into as many scrapes as one can imagine, has as many cronies as anyone could wish for, and keeps readers turning the pages of this novel and its two sequels, *Penrod and Sam* (1916) and *Penrod Jashber* (1929).

White Fang, by Jack London (1905). Who can fail to enjoy this action-filled story of a wolf cub that learns to live with human beings? White Fang responds to a mining engineer who shows the animal human kindness. After you have read *White Fang,* try Jack London's famous earlier novel, *The Call of the Wild* (1903), about a dog that leaves a tame life with human beings to live in the wilderness of Alaska.

Research reports. When an assignment is given to *research* a particular subject, students must make use of such reference sources as an encyclopedia or books or magazine and newspaper articles. To begin researching a topic it is best to make a trip to the library. Books on a topic can be located by looking up the subject in the card catalog (a set of cards listing all the books in the library arranged alphabetically according to subject, author, and title) or by typing the subject onto the screen of the library's computer system.

Magazine articles can be found by looking up the subject in a guide to periodical literature (a listing of recent magazine and newspaper articles) or searching the library's computer system for articles. Librarians are eager to help people who are not sure how to use the equipment or where to begin their research.

Once material has been gathered, it is important to take careful notes while reading. It is best not to copy the words directly. Instead, the information should be rewritten in the reader's own words. This step helps the reader remember what he or she has read and avoids copying the author's work. Notes should also tell where the information came from (the name of the book or article, the author, and the page number) in case the information is needed again later.

The next step in writing a report is to organize the notes into an outline. An outline briefly states the main topics and subtopics. Each main topic becomes the main idea sentence for a paragraph. The subtopics are used as supporting details.

There is a correct form, as shown here, for writing a good outline:

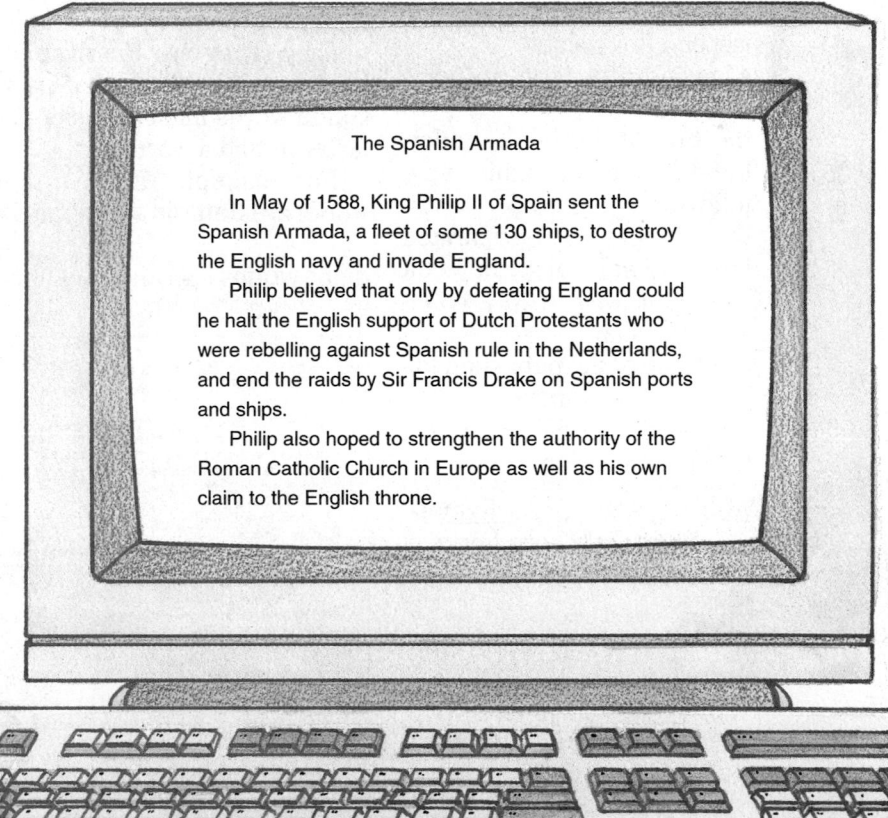

Spanish Armada

King Philip II of Spain sent a fleet against England in May, 1588. English under Queen Elizabeth I had been supporting Dutch rebels against Spanish rule in the Netherlands.

New Encyclopædia Britannica

Spanish Armada

Philip II of Spain was widower of Queen Mary I of England, who ruled before Elizabeth I.

Collier's Encyclopædia, Vol. 2, pg. 659.

Spanish Armada

Dutch rebels prevented an invasion force of Spanish troops in Flanders, from sailing to England.

Academic American Encyclopedia Vol. 18, pg. 151.

Spanish Armada

I. Launched by Spain against England in 1588
  A. King Philip II of Spain (Roman Catholic)
  B. Queen Elizabeth I of England (Protestant)
II. Causes of the Attack
  A. Philip claimed English throne
  B. Philip wanted to defend Catholicism
  C. England supported Dutch against Spain
  D. Sir Francis Drake's raids against Spanish shipping

1. A Roman numeral and a period are put before each main topic.
2. A capital letter and a period are put before each subtopic.
3. The first word of topics and subtopics is capitalized.
4. Subtopics are always indented under main topics.

A report written from this outline might read as follows:

The Spanish Armada

In May of 1588, King Philip II of Spain sent the Spanish Armada, a fleet of some 130 ships, to destroy the English navy and invade England.

Philip believed that only by defeating England could he halt the English support of Dutch Protestants who were rebelling against Spanish rule in the Netherlands, and end the raids by Sir Francis Drake on Spanish ports and ships.

Philip also hoped to strengthen the authority of the Roman Catholic Church in Europe as well as his own claim to the English throne.

Bibliography. A research report usually ends with a list of the books and articles used as sources of information. The sources are arranged in alphabetical order. This list of sources is called a bibliography. Here is the correct way to list encyclopedias, books, and magazine articles:

ENCYCLOPEDIAS

1. the name of the encyclopedia, underlined to indicate italic type, followed by a comma
2. the year of the edition, followed by a comma
3. the volume number or letter, followed by a period
4. the name of the article in quotation marks, with a period before the last quotation mark.

The Volume Library, 1992, 2. "United States History."

BOOKS

1. arranged in alphabetical order by the author's last name, with a comma between the author's last and first names
2. a period after the author's first name
3. the title of the book, underlined to indicate italic type, followed by a period
4. the city and state (separated by a comma) where the book was published, with a colon after the state
5. the name of the publisher, followed by a comma
6. the latest copyright date, followed by a period.

Webster, Alan. Great Explorers. New York, New York: Harper & Row, Publishers, 1988.

MAGAZINE ARTICLES

1. the author's name, with the last name first, followed by a comma
2. the name of the article in quotation marks, with a period before the last quotation mark

3. the name of the magazine, underlined to indicate italic type, followed by a period
4. the month and year of the issue, separated by a comma and followed by a period.

Greene, Ralph, "Columbus and His Journey." Boys' Life. October, 1992.

Dictionary Skills

A dictionary is a book that explains the words of a language. It is an essential tool for finding out how to pronounce, spell, and learn the uses and meanings of words.

The words listed in a dictionary in alphabetical order are called **entry words.** The meaning of each entry word, along with its correct spelling and pronunciation (how to say it), its parts or syllables, its part of speech, and any special forms of the word are given.

Two **guide words** are found at the top of each page of a dictionary. They are the first and last entry words on that page. Guide words make it easier and faster to find a word.

For example, if the guide words are **den/dinosaur**, all the words in alphabetical order between these two guide words would be on that page. Some entry words might be *dentist, desert, detail, different, dig, dime, dinner.*

The entry words *daisy, dare, date, deal,* and *deed,* would be on pages before this page. The entry words *dint, dip, diploma, direct, dirty, disk,* and *distant* would be on pages after the **den/dinosaur** page.

It is sometimes difficult to find a word in a dictionary if the proper spelling of the word is not known. In such a case, list all possible spellings and try to find each one. This will eliminate the misspellings or nonwords.

HELPFUL HINT: When looking up a word in a dictionary, think about whether it would be in the first (*a* to *m*) or the second (*n* to *z*) half of the book. For example, a word starting with *e* would be toward the beginning of the first half. A word starting with *n* would be close to the middle of the book. A word that starts with *w* would be toward the end of the second half. Knowing which part of a big dictionary to open to saves time.

GUIDE WORDS repeat the first and last words on a dictionary page to help the reader find the word he or she is looking for more quickly.

lizard / lock   388

during the day. **living wage,** a wage on which it is possible to live. **within living memory,** within the memory of people who are still alive.
liz·ard (liz-ărd) *n.* a reptile with a rough or scaly hide, four legs, and a long tail.
Lk. *abbr.* Luke.
LL *abbr.* Late Latin.
ll. *abbr.* lines.
lla·ma (lah-mă) *n.* a South American animal related to the camel but with no hump, kept as a beast of burden and for its soft woolly hair. ▷Do not confuse *llama* with *lama*.
lla·no (lah-noh) *n.* (*pl.* **-nos**) any of the treeless grassy plains of Latin America.
LL.B. *abbr.* Bachelor of Laws.
LL.D. *abbr.* Doctor of Laws.
LM *abbr.* lunar module.
LNG *abbr.* liquefied natural gas.
lo (loh) *interj.* (*old use*) see.
loach (lohch) *n.* a small edible freshwater fish of Europe and Asia.
load (lohd) *n.* 1. something carried. 2. the quantity that can be carried, as on a cart. 3. a unit of weight or measure for certain substances. 4. the amount of electric current supplied by a dynamo or generating station. 5. a burden of responsibility or worry or grief. 6. (*informal*) plenty, *loads of time.* **load** *v.* 1. to put a load in or on, to fill with goods or cargo etc., to receive a load. 2. to fill heavily. 3. to weight with something heavy. 4. to put ammunition into (a gun) or film into

(a ball) slowly or in a high arc in tennis etc. **lob** *n.* a lobbed ball in tennis etc.
lo·bar (loh-băr, -bahr) *adj.* of a lobe, especially of the lung, *lobar pneumonia.*
lob·by (lob-ee) *n.* (*pl.* **-bies**) 1. an entrance hall used as a waiting room. 2. a body of people engaged in lobbying for a particular cause. **lobby** *v.* (**lob·bied, lob·by·ing**) to seek to persuade (a legislator) to support one's cause. **lob′by·ist** *n.*
lobe (lohb) *n.* a rounded flattish part or projection (especially of an organ of the body), the lower soft part of the ear.
lobed (lohbd) *adj.* having lobes.
lo·bel·ia (loh-beel-yă) *n.* a low-growing garden plant with blue, red, white, or purple flowers.
lo·bot·o·my (loh-bot-ŏ-mee) *n.* (*pl.* **-mies**) an incision into the frontal lobe of the brain to relieve some cases of mental illness.
lob·ster (lob-stěr) *n.* (*pl.* **-sters, -ster**) 1. a large shellfish with eight legs and two long claws that turns scarlet after being boiled. 2. its flesh as food. □**lobster Newburg,** a dish consisting of pieces of cooked lobster in a rich cream sauce containing brandy or sherry. **lobster pot,** a slatted wooden box for trapping lobsters. **lobster thermidor,** a mixture of lobster meat, mushrooms, cream, egg yolks, and sherry cooked in the lobster shell.
lob·ule (lob-yool) *n.* a small lobe. **lob·u·lar** (lob-yŭ-lăr) *adj.*
lo·cal (loh-kăl) *adj.* 1. belonging to a particular

Each entry in a dictionary may supply the following information about a word:

1. spelling
2. syllable breaks
3. pronunciation
4. part of speech
5. origin
6. definition.

Spelling. The entry word itself is the correct spelling of the word. If there is more than one way to spell a word, all accepted spellings are given.

Syllables. The entry word is usually divided with dots to separate the word into parts or syllables. For example:

heart has one syllable
de·moc·ra·cy has four

Knowing the number of syllables a word has shows where to separate or hyphenate it when writing. For example:

That country is a democ-racy.

British dictionaries do not separate entry words into parts or syllables.

Pronunciation. In most dictionaries, after each entry word is found its phonetic spelling or pronunciation.

co· zy (′kō-zē)

The accent mark shows which part of the word is stressed or emphasized when speaking. Many dictionaries include a small phonetic key on each page.

Parts of speech. After the pronunciation there is an abbreviation telling the word's function or part of speech. These include:

adj   adjective
adv   adverb

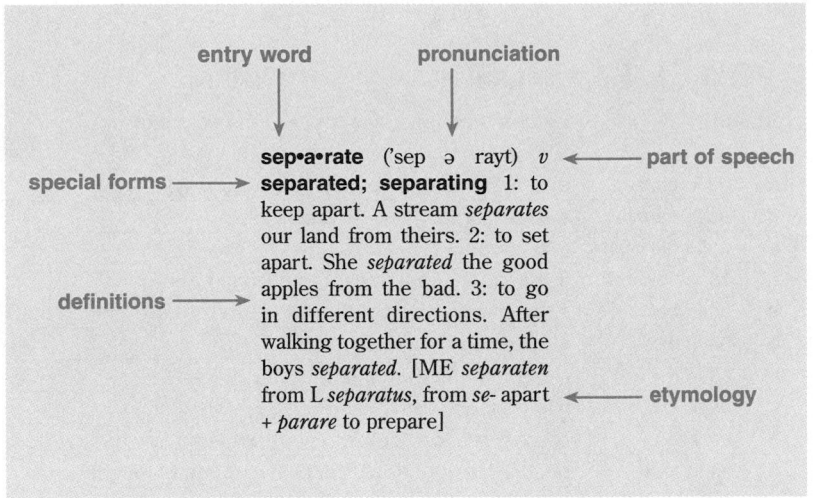

conj   conjunction
n   noun
prep   preposition
pron   pronoun
v or *vb*   verb

For example:

cat (′kăt) *n*
lucky (′lŭk-ē) *adj*
teach (′tēch) *v*

Irregular forms. Next, any irregular forms of a word are listed.

run (′rŭn) *v* **ran, run, running, runs**
man (′măn) *n,*
pl **men** (′měn)

Multiple meanings. When an entry word has more than one meaning, these meanings are usually made clear by supplying sample sentences within their definitions. For example, the noun *batter* can mean a baseball player who bats or it can mean the flour and liquid mixture made for baking. Sentences might be

The *batter* hit the ball.
The baker poured the *batter* into the pans.

Origin. English is derived from many different languages. Some dictionaries tell what language a word came from originally. This part of the dictionary entry is called an etymology.

For example, the word *menu* might have F in its etymology, meaning that it is from French.

Indexes and Glossaries

An index is an alphabetical listing at the end of a book that gives all the main topics included in the book and the page numbers on which they can be found. Using an index is a quick way to find specific information without reading every page.

For example, a book on earth science might include these references to wind:

Wind
    direction, 164
    speed, 143
    surface currents,
        formation of, 201
    waves, formation of, 16

A glossary is an alphabetical list of difficult or special words used in a book. It gives their meanings. For example, the glossary in the same book on earth science might include:

erosion. Wearing away.
solar energy. Energy from the sun.
wind. Movement of air.

—*Rosalie S. Lawrence*

emphasized
US
emphasised
Brit.

VOWEL SOUNDS

Sound		Letters that can make this sound (example)
a	as in cat	a, ai (plaid)
a	as in cake	a, ai (paid), ea (break), ey (obey), ay (say)
a	as in care	a + r, ai + r (fair), ea + r (wear), e + r (there)
a	as in father	a, o (stop)
a	as in saw	a, au (caught), oa (broad), ou (fought)
e	as in bed	e, ea (heavy), ie (friend), ai (said)
e	as in we	e, ei (receive), ey (key), ie (field)
i	as in it	i, ee (been), u (busy), ui (build), y (hymn)
i	as in kite	i, ie (tie), ei (height), ey (eye), uy (buy), y (fly)
o	as in go	o, oa (goat), oe (toe), ou (soul), ew (sew), ow (grow)
oo	as in tool	oo, ue (blue), ui (fruit), ew (threw), ough (through)
oo	as in book	oo, o (wolf), ou (would), u (pull)
ow	as in now	ow, ou (out), ough (bough)
oy	as in boy	oy, oi (toil)
u	as in cuff	u, o (son), oo (flood), oe (does), ou (double)
u	as in hurt	u + r, ea + r (heard), i + r (bird), o + r (worry), ou + r (courage)
u	as in fuse	u, ue (cue), eau (beauty), ew (few), iew (view), yu (yule), you (youth)
ə	(an unaccented uh sound)	a (asleep), e (voted), o (confession), u (focus), etc.

CONSONANT BLENDS

bl	as in black	fl	as in flame	mn	as in mnemonic	tr	as in transfer
cr	as in crush	gl	as in glow	pr	as in prince	wr	as in wrestle
dr	as in drink	kn	as in know	st	as in store		

SOME SHORT, LONG, AND SILENT LETTERS

hăt

hāt̸e

bĕt

lĭt

līgh̸t

sīgn̸

cōne̸

throug̸h̸

sŭm

cūte̸

Improving Reading

Today, the ability to read is considered to be essential for nearly everyone. Adults who cannot read or who read poorly find it difficult to get a good job, find a place to live, buy food or clothing, or even receive medical care. Reading is a basic requirement for nearly all of us.

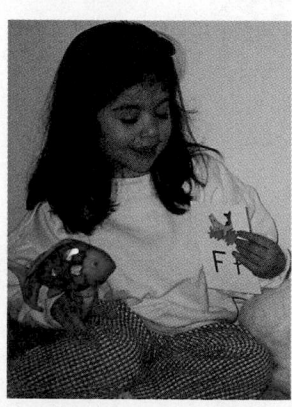

KNOWING YOUR LETTERS and how they sound is the first step toward reading. Knowing how to read is an important and useful skill.

All people, except for those who are burdened by handicaps, learn to speak and learn to understand their native languages. Reading is another matter. This skill ordinarily must be learned over several years of guided instruction, and it is usually taught to children in the elementary grades. In the following sections, you will find help in learning to read to the full extent of your natural ability.

Components of reading. It is helpful to gain some knowledge of three important aspects of reading: word recognition, comprehension, and fusion, which is the process of putting together word recognition and comprehension skills.

WORD RECOGNITION. At the heart of the reading process is the recognition and decoding of printed symbols. This involves translating printed symbols into the sounds we use in speaking. A printed letter represents one or more particular sounds in spoken language, and a combination of letters represents the sounds that make up a word. It is the word that carries meaning. You may not have thought of it this way before, but translating from letters to sound to words to meaning is not easy.

READING FOR ENJOYMENT helps improve reading comprehension, which will help you in later life to paraphrase, or restate, an author's ideas in your own words.

COMPREHENSION. In reading, it is not enough to translate printed symbols into sounds. Readers must also comprehend what is meant by the words they have decoded. For example, take the saying "The early bird catches the worm." Even though a child may have learned to correctly read these words aloud, he or she must also be able to understand what each of the words means, and to understand what the six words mean when they are combined. Therefore, along with symbol decoding skills, readers must know what the words in a language mean (vocabulary) and what they mean when they are put together in various ways (comprehension).

When young readers have learned to do all this, they make rapid progress in increasing their reading skills. And how do they make this progress? By reading and reading and reading. We see some children who seem to devour books. These are the fortunate ones who take pleasure in reading. Aware of the pleasure of reading books they have read before, many children cannot wait to read them again. As time goes by and their interests broaden, most children seek out books they have not read before.

Children who do not enjoy reading are much less likely to read often enough—and widely enough—to bring their skills to high levels of effectiveness. As time goes by, and as these children advance in school, they may find themselves at a disadvantage. But it is never too late to improve reading skills.

Toward better reading. The first goal of reading is *comprehension*. Without comprehension, reading is a meaningless experience. The best single test of your comprehension is to ask yourself whether you can restate the idea presented in a unit of writing—a paragraph, a chapter, or an entire book.

Almost any idea can be expressed in a number of ways, and if you have understood an author's message, you should be able to restate—or **paraphrase**—that message in your own words, words that come naturally to mind, as the original words of the author came to him or her. If you cannot do this, then you have failed to comprehend.

There is much that older children, college students, and adults can do to bring their reading skills to a higher level of proficiency. Usually these people have learned to recognize words, understand what most of them mean, and comprehend sentences. Yet they may find reading tedious and time-consuming. They probably want to read better and faster, that is, with greater comprehension and retention.

As you advance to high school and on to college, you will find that you have to master a variety of reading skills:

- Proficiency in finding an author's main ideas and in drawing conclusions from those ideas;
- Ability to read quickly and thoroughly in order to accomplish the reading required in school;
- Ability to take useful notes on reading material;
- Ability to write and talk about the ideas advanced in the books you read; and
- Ability to read works of all kinds to prepare for tests, write school reports, compose speeches, and solve many problems.

While only a great deal of practice will make you the best reader you can be, an awareness of certain aspects of reading explained below will prove of considerable value.

Eye Movements

Word-by-word reading is slow work, and often confusing.

If put to guess his calling and livelihood, I should have taken him for a country schoolmas-

ter as soon as anything else. He was dressed in a rusty black frock coat and pantaloons,

unbrushed, and worn so faithfully that the suit had adapted itself to the curves and

Reading in phrases speeds up reading and helps comprehension.

If put to guess his calling and livelihood, I should have taken him for a country schoolmas-

ter as soon as anything else. He was dressed in a rusty black frock coat and pantaloons,

unbrushed, and worn so faithfully that the suit had adapted itself to the curves and

OBSERVE the eye movements of another reader to better understand your own.

Most readers believe that their eyes move smoothly and continuously from left to right on a line, except when they have to move on to the next line. This is not so. The truth is that eye movements are not smooth or continuous. Instead, the eyes progress in a series of jumps from point to point along a line, pausing at each point. The pauses, called *fixations*, last for only a fraction of a second. Indeed, it is only during the times when the eyes are at rest during reading that they actually see.

Ideally, readers take in a line of print in three or four fixations, depending on whether the material they are reading is familiar or strange to them. This means that good readers may take in two or more words in each fixation, while less efficient readers must pause at each word—even two or more times with difficult words.

The ability to see two or more words in a single fixation enables good readers to grasp meanings of phrases easily, while less efficient readers have a harder time. To comprehend a full sentence, these readers must try to put together a series of individual words they have struggled with. Instead of easily understanding a logical grouping of words that an author has written for them, sentences become jigsaw puzzles to be assembled slowly and laboriously. When inefficient readers fixate on one word at a time, they eventually get them right. But at the end of a sentence, they have the chore of putting all the words together, remembering what all the words mean—and, finally, understanding what the sentence means.

The process of reading for these people is anything but pleasurable. Small wonder they see reading as a chore rather than something fun to look forward to.

Sometimes, even in good readers, the eyes move backward along a line of type to take a second look. Such a backward movement is called a *regression*.

Inefficient readers, in addition to having to pause at nearly every word in a line, also tend to regress frequently. This is because they not only fail to understand what some of the words mean, they also have trouble in putting all the words together in a way that makes sense. This breaks up a reader's understanding of the meaning of a sentence, as the brain receives information word by word—and often the same word in a line seen again and again.

Good readers, with their ability to see two or more words in a single fixation, thus with fewer fixations on a line, take in information in larger and more meaningful units. Their brains, therefore, are able to process information more quickly and understand it more readily. You can see why good readers, thus, have a considerable advantage in completing their assignments in school and on their jobs.

Learning to read efficiently.

Good readers do not read everything at the same rate. When reading material is easy to understand, they read rapidly. When reading material is more difficult to understand—as in the sciences or in complex or detailed instructions—good readers slow down. But there is more to reading rate than that. For example, when good readers wish to prolong their pleasure in reading stories or novels, or when the stories or novels must be considered with great care, good readers reduce their speed.

The quality that all good readers share is *flexibility*. This means they are able to adjust their reading rate to the difficulty of what they are reading and to their purpose in reading. Less efficient readers lack this flexibility. They tend to read everything at a single speed—from the easiest children's book to the most exciting detective story or suspense novel.

Consider the following techniques that good readers employ in reading, from fastest to slowest rate:

SKIMMING (very rapid) is used for locating desired information, a reference, or an answer to a specific question. It is also a good technique for finding the main idea of a piece of writing, or for going through a book or magazine article before reading it carefully. The technique enables a reader to get a general idea of the contents and style of what is to be read, and refreshes a reader's memory on material that he or she has read before.

NORMAL RATE (as rapid as the reader feels comfortable with) is used in reading material of average difficulty; it is also used to locate answers to broad questions, to identify important details, and to get the overall meaning of writing along with some details.

CAREFUL RATE (slow) is used to master details in a textbook or piece of writing, to evaluate arguments presented by an author, to follow detailed instructions, to read complex or technical material, and to appreciate literary works that demand close attention.

Improving reading rate.

A great deal of emphasis has been placed in recent years on how fast we can read. False claims have appeared in magazines and newspapers telling us of near miracles in which a few hours of instruction can give slow readers the ability to read at great speeds. Students look longingly at these claims and dream of getting through their school assignments in record time. They hear about months of library work being condensed into an afternoon.

Wouldn't it be marvelous to finish a week's assignments in an hour? Think of all the other things you could do in the time saved. Unfortunately, serious reading and study require hard work, and that means steady effort over time.

Most students can increase their reading speed, but only by regular practice. Several techniques are available for bringing your reading rate up to where it should be.

PUSHING YOURSELF.

The most effective method for increasing your reading speed is to push yourself to read a little faster than is comfortable for you. And to keep on doing so—every day, every time you read—until you find that you cannot read any faster.

Here's how to start the process. Mark off the fifth page in a book you are about to read.

READ AT RATES suitable to your purposes: slowly for following recipes, faster for taking notes, and fastest for getting news about friends.

Write the starting time in a notebook. Then begin to read a little faster—only a little faster—than is comfortable for you. When you have finished the fifth page, note the time it took to read the five pages.

Keep in mind that more important than the time it took is whether you were able to comprehend what you read. If you were not, you will have to slow down in the next session of practice reading. If you did comprehend, repeat the timing and reading for five more pages, remembering that the idea is to read at a rate that is slightly uncomfortable for you. About an hour of such practice each day is enough. You soon will read faster.

TACHISTOSCOPE. This device, a replacement for flash cards, enables presentation of words and phrases for brief moments. It is intended to expand a reader's eye span by projecting longer and longer phrases in shorter and shorter times to gradually accomplish the desired result. Slides may be purchased to provide the necessary practice material.

READ QUICKLY through newspaper ads until you find what you are looking for, but read important documents slowly and thoroughly.

PRACTICE READING FASTER by trying to read the screen credits of programs and movies shown on television.

READING PACERS. These small machines move a shade down over the page of a book while a person is reading the page. The reader must read fast enough to keep the shade from covering the line he or she is reading. Because the speed of the shade is controllable, the pacer can be set to move progressively faster. Of course, the reader must read faster to stay ahead of the text.

Challenging yourself. As was stated earlier in this section, practice is the best means of gaining speed and flexibility in reading. Practice is best gained through reading material in which vocabulary and content pose no problem in comprehension. When such material is being read easily and with ever-increasing speed, it is time to move on to material of greater difficulty in content and vocabulary. After a while, you will find that desired levels of speed and comprehension will have been attained.

Throughout this process, the reader must continue to read more and more challenging material and to develop a larger and larger vocabulary.

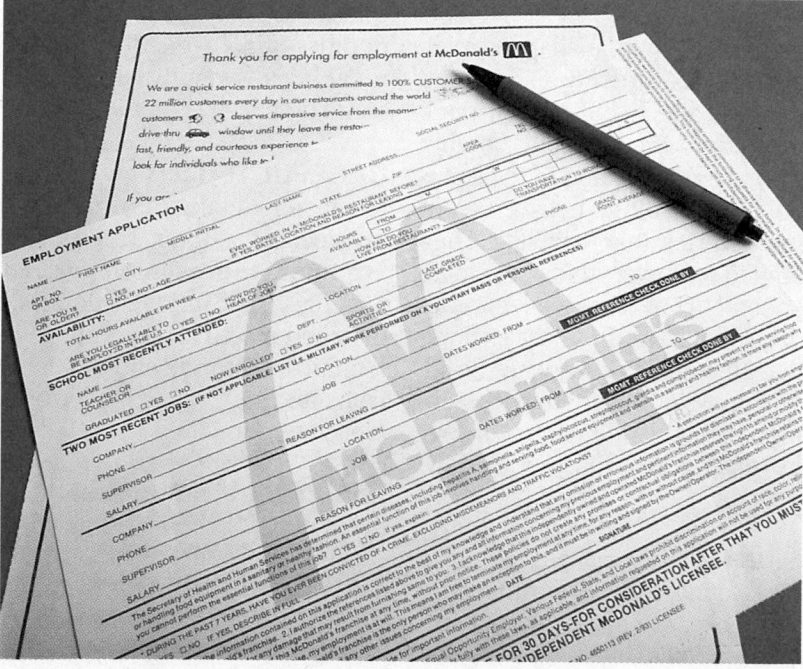

Improving comprehension. There are two principal means to improve one's comprehension of difficult reading material. The first of these is the technique of **prereading**: surveying material that is about to be read to familiarize oneself with its content and organization. This can be done with everything but fiction and poetry.

To preread a book, first run down its table of contents to see what the book contains and how the subjects it covers are organized. Then skim the preface or introduction, which may give further information on the content and structure and on the author's purpose.

Next, skim through the chapters of the book. Read the main headings in the chapters and the introductory and closing paragraphs. Finally, find out whether there is an index at the end of the book that shows the topics that are covered.

Prereading is especially useful for studying high school or college textbooks. The time spent in prereading is only a small fraction of the entire time it will take to read a book.

SUMMARIZING AND OUTLINING. Another valuable technique used by good readers who wish to master what they read is based on the practice known as outlining and summarizing. A **summary** is particularly useful when you are reading from a number of sources—newspapers, magazines, and books. To make a summary, the reader should always take notes carefully while reading, and then briefly summarize all the important points made by the author in the article or book. Summarizing in this manner forces the reader to identify and to concentrate on important ideas.

An **outline** is a schematic organization of material that has been read. It shows the relationship of each idea or important fact to the overall structure of the entire piece. Outlines can be elaborate or can be not much more than a listing of important points, with subordinate details indented and separately listed below the points to which they relate. Outlines are helpful in preparing for tests and for written reports.

Reading and study. For serious readers and for students, reading and study mean almost the same thing. Certainly, anyone who cannot read efficiently cannot hope to go far in any kind of advanced study. In addition to literary works, high school and college reading means using textbooks and challenging books effectively. The task is always to learn what an author has said and to make careful notes for review. The combination of careful initial reading and then review makes for good learning.

It is well known that we learn by repeated exposure to material that is to be learned. Some students consider—mistakenly—that if they somehow pass their eyes over the assigned pages in a book, they have studied their assignment.

ONLINE MENUS provide the same information as tables of contents in books.

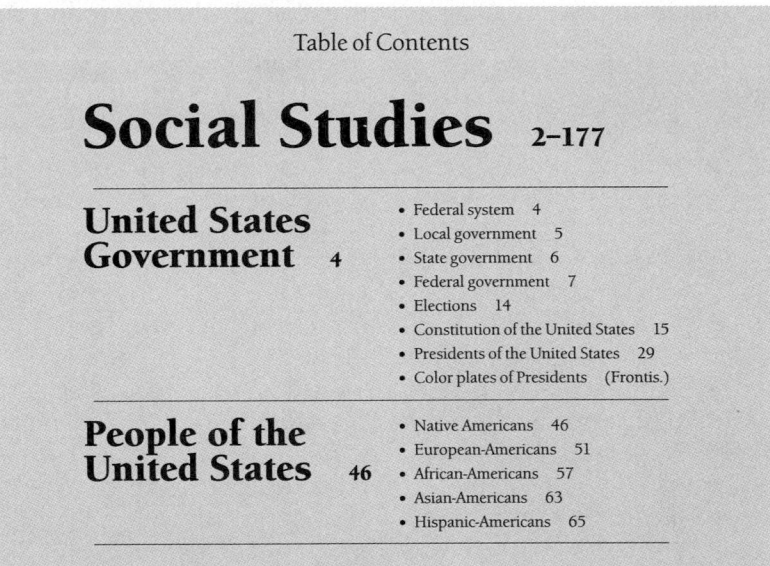

Unfortunately, when these "aimless readers" are asked to discuss the assignment in class, they recall little of what they have read.

By using the suggestions given above for **prereading**, **summarizing**, and **outlining**, you can become a real reader rather than an aimless reader.

Concentration and reading. Good reading of serious books requires an attitude of mental alertness and attention that is hard to manage when your body is relaxed. When your body is relaxed, your brain tends to relax as well. For this reason, take steps to choose surroundings that invite good reading.

You know that most people have no trouble concentrating on reading that is pleasurable—often we hear people say, "I just couldn't put that book down"—but many people find it hard to concentrate on serious reading.

As you advance in your studies, you will have to pay close attention and apply your mental energy in subject areas that may not give you immediate satisfaction. While your mind tells you that you must read well, an inner voice may tell you that you would rather be doing something else. The result is a lack of full concentration. What can you do about this problem?

First, you can address the question of where you do your reading. Whether we like it or not, our minds and thought processes are affected by our physical surroundings. Certain surroundings suggest certain activities. For example, a school gymnasium in which a basketball game is going on suggests physical exercise and your mental involvement—not reading and study. Libraries, on the other hand, suggest quiet reading and study.

To take one more example, a soft armchair suggests relaxation and television viewing, not active reading; a straight, hard chair—with lighting that makes it easy to read—suggests active reading, not passive relaxation. When you attempt to do serious

Sample Reading and Comprehension Test

It might be best to let sleeping sea lions lie. At least this is what Mr. Snow, an explorer, thinks.

One July during the breeding season, he rowed up to an Arctic island through schools of sea lions. They showed no fright and no desire to fight. When he landed he came near the animals and called, "Come on there, you! Come on!"

A sudden roar and a great sea lion was hurtling toward him, his white tusks gleaming. Mr. Snow ran. This big fellow followed. It seemed easy to keep out of reach of the awkward animal. But straight ahead lay a cow with a young one! Mr. Snow knew that he was trapped. He struck frantically at the cow's head with a boat hook. She caught it out of the air and wrenched it from his hand. There was a great crunching and grinding. She was chewing the boat hook to splinters!

Now was Mr. Snow's chance to run. The bull was after him again, but he kept dodging round and round until the sea lion was tired out by the chase. The explorer finally returned to the boat, a wiser man.

1. **The selection is chiefly about** Ⓐ a boat hook Ⓑ a young sea lion Ⓒ a mother Ⓓ an explorer

2. **At first the sea lions were** Ⓐ afraid Ⓑ angry Ⓒ peaceful Ⓓ playful

3. **Which is most probable? The sea lion** Ⓐ did not like the sound of the man's voice Ⓑ was afraid of the man Ⓒ knew he could trap the man Ⓓ liked to fight

4. **Most probably the mother was angry because** Ⓐ she wanted to protect her baby Ⓑ she was a sea lion Ⓒ she lay in the path Ⓓ she did not like the explorer

5. **Sea lions have very strong** Ⓐ tusks Ⓑ tails Ⓒ flippers Ⓓ babies

6. **Sea lions move** Ⓐ gracefully Ⓑ clumsily Ⓒ swiftly Ⓓ crunching and grinding

7. **We may infer from the selection that the mother sea lion** Ⓐ liked to eat wood Ⓑ was playing with the explorer Ⓒ wanted to keep Mr. Snow away Ⓓ was showing one of her tricks

8. **As a result of Mr. Snow's narrow escape he was a** Ⓐ jollier man Ⓑ wiser man Ⓒ more energetic man Ⓓ kinder man

D C A A A B C B

reading in the comfort of an armchair, you are fighting your natural tendency to relax; when you do your serious reading at a table while sitting in a straight, hard chair, you do not have to fight the tendency to relax. You are taking advantage of your physical surroundings, not fighting them.

GOOD STUDY ENVIRONMENTS.

Make use of the power of habit and suggestion so that you are helped, not hindered. To do this, apply yourself to the tasks of learning in a place that suggests learning. Thus, it is a good idea to do your reading and study in the same place each day—whether in your home or in your school library. If you choose your school library, try to sit at the same table each day and begin to work at the same time. That table and that time will suggest learning.

As soon as you sit down, your mind will turn to the serious task you have to perform. Under such conditions, study can begin and flow smoothly, developing its own energy and staying with you until you have completed your day's work. You will have taken advantage of your surroundings to concentrate on your reading—and to learn well.

But not all students have school libraries in which to study, and not all are fortunate enough to have homes that offer the quiet surroundings needed for efficient work. Interruptions by telephones, friends, brothers and sisters, or any of the modern noise sources—usually radios and television sets—will interfere with your ability to concentrate on reading and study.

The best solution for this problem is to do most of your work in a neighborhood public library. Your family and friends are not there. Radios, television sets, and telephones are absent.

In addition, people who use a public library are usually engaged in selecting books or in reading and study. You will find it easy to fit into this environment and get right down to work. Good lighting is almost guaranteed. Interruptions do not occur very often. Noise is reduced to a minimum. And you will probably have all the space you need for your notebook and other school materials. An added bonus is that the library supplies all the possible reference materials you can possibly want.

FIND A GOOD READING PLACE, one that will help you to concentrate on your reading. Avoid noisy distractions, such as loud music or people talking on the telephone, and chairs that are too comfortable (left). Try to find a quiet room with good lighting (right).

17

English
Writing

17

English Writing

Contents

Overleaf: *Paper and quill on a rolltop desk*

Writing

Using language effectively is one of the most valuable skills you will ever learn. Your writing and your speech will make an impression—good or bad—on everyone with whom you interact. Good reading skills will simplify both your school and your business life—and make it more enjoyable, to boot.

This chapter sets out guidelines for writing, as well as the related areas of speaking, vocabulary improvement, and grammar and punctuation.

Writing

Writing is one of our most powerful tools. It can teach, sell, convince, describe, define, narrate, argue, critique, compare, or contrast. However, when faced with a writing assignment, you may feel intimidated, unsure where to start on the daunting task of writing.

If confronting an empty piece of paper or monitor screen with assignment and deadline in hand strikes fear in your heart, relax. Chances are you are already a writer! The computer, Internet, and e-mail have everyone "writing" constantly, communicating with each other about practically everything. Chances are great that you have been caught, on line, in the act of writing.

So, since you already know HOW to write, it will not be hard for you to apply this ability to any kind of written assignment, from personal letters to essays and term papers. Writing is just communication, whether on line or on paper, with another person, whether a friend or a teacher. And anyone, with the right tools and a little work and organization, can do it.

Fortunately, there is one format (the essay) and one system (the Seven-Point System) which work, with variations, for every kind of nonfiction writing you are likely to need to do, regardless of the length or type of assignment.

The Seven-Point System and the Essay Format work for any kind of essay: a term paper, an essay test question or college entrance essay, a personal statement or resumé cover letter, an explication or critique, a business letter or proposal. And they work for every kind of topic from a personal narrative to a detailed biography. In the following, we give you the secrets of how to write any kind of assignment.

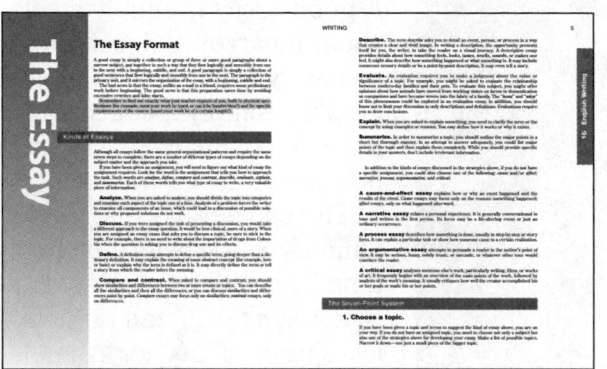

The Writing section is divided into mini-seminars on the essay, taking essay exams, writing about literature, using the library and electronic media, research writing, and business writing.

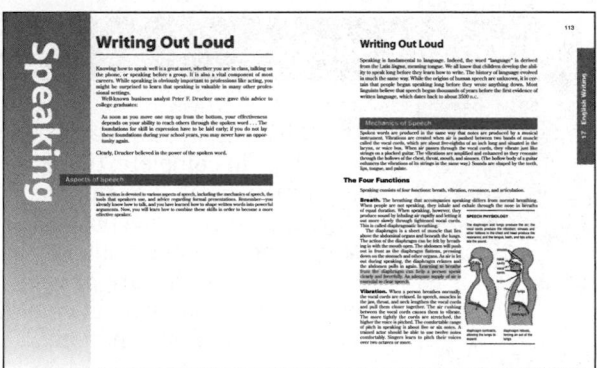

Writing Out Loud covers formal and informal speaking and improving your speaking and vocabulary.

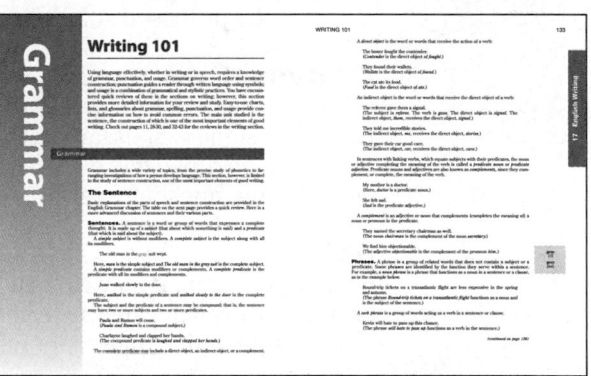

Writing 101 covers grammar, punctuation, and usage.

organization
US

organisation
Brit.

The Seven-Point System

1. **Choose a topic.**
2. **Research or gather details.**
3. **Focus on a main idea or thesis.**
4. **Create an outline.**
5. **Write a first version or draft.**
6. **Revise the draft for structure and style.**
7. **Proofread and correct the draft.**

The Essay Format

A. **The introduction with thesis**
B. **Supporting paragraphs**
C. **The conclusion**

The Essay Format

A good essay is simply a collection or group of three or more good paragraphs about a narrow subject, put together in such a way that they flow logically and smoothly from one to the next with a beginning, middle, and end. A good paragraph is simply a collection of good sentences that flow logically and smoothly from one to the next. The paragraph is the primary unit, and it mirrors the organization of the essay, with a beginning, middle, and end.

The bad news is that the essay, unlike an e-mail to a friend, requires some preliminary work before beginning. The good news is that this preparation saves time by avoiding excessive rewrites and false starts.

Remember to find out exactly what your teacher expects of you, both in physical specifications (for example, must your work be typed, or can it be handwritten?) and the specific requirements of the course (must your work be of a certain length?).

Kinds of Essays

Although all essays follow the same general organizational patterns and require the same seven steps to complete, there are a number of different types of essays depending on the subject matter and the approach you take.

If you have been given an assignment, you will need to figure out what kind of essay the assignment requires. Look for the word in the assignment that tells you how to approach the task. Such words are *analyze, define, discuss, compare* and *contrast, describe, evaluate, explain,* and *summarize.* Each of these words tells you what type of essay to write, a very valuable piece of information.

Analyze. When you are asked to analyze, you should divide the topic into categories and examine each aspect of the topic one at a time. Analysis of a problem forces the writer to examine all components of an issue, which could lead to a discussion of possible solutions or why proposed solutions do not work.

Discuss. If you were assigned the task of presenting a discussion, you would take a different approach to the essay question. It would be less clinical, more of a story. When you are assigned an essay exam that asks you to discuss a topic, be sure to stick to the topic. For example, there is no need to write about the importation of drugs from Colombia when the question is asking you to discuss drug use and its effects.

Define. A definition essay attempts to define a specific term, going deeper than a dictionary definition. It may explain the meaning of some abstract concept (for example, love or hate) or explain why the term is defined as it is. It may directly define the term or tell a story from which the reader infers the meaning.

Compare and contrast. When asked to compare and contrast, you should show similarities and differences between two or more events or topics. You can describe all the similarities and then all the differences, or you can discuss similarities and differences point by point. *Compare* essays may focus only on similarities; *contrast* essays, only on differences.

Describe. The term *describe* asks you to detail an event, person, or process in a way that creates a clear and vivid image. In writing a description, the opportunity presents itself for you, the writer, to take the reader on a visual journey. A descriptive essay provides details about how something feels, looks, tastes, smells, sounds, or makes one feel. It might also describe how something happened or what something is. It may include numerous sensory details or be a point-by-point description. It may even tell a story.

Evaluate. An evaluation requires you to make a judgment about the value or significance of a topic. For example, you might be asked to evaluate the relationship between modern-day families and their pets. To evaluate this subject, you might offer opinions about how animals have moved from working status on farms to domestication as companions and have become woven into the fabric of a family. The "*hows*" and "*whys*" of this phenomenon could be explored in an evaluation essay. In addition, you should know not to limit your discussion to only descriptions and definitions. Evaluations require you to draw conclusions.

Explain. When you are asked to explain something, you need to clarify the term or the concept by using examples or reasons. You may define how it works or why it exists.

Summarize. In order to summarize a topic, you should outline the major points in a short but thorough manner. In an attempt to answer adequately, you could list major points of the topic and then explain them completely. While you should provide specific details in your answers, don't include irrelevant information.

In addition to the kinds of essays discussed in the strategies above, if you do not have a specific assignment, you could also choose one of the following: *cause* and/or *effect; narrative; process; argumentative;* and *critical*.

A cause-and-effect essay explains how or why an event happened and the results of the event. *Cause* essays may focus only on the reasons something happened; *effect* essays, only on what happened afterward.

A narrative essay relates a personal experience. It is generally conversational in tone and written in the first person. Its focus may be a life-altering event or just an ordinary occurrence.

A process essay describes how something is done, usually in step-by-step or story form. It can explain a particular task or show how someone came to a certain realization.

An argumentative essay attempts to persuade a reader to the author's point of view. It may be serious, funny, subtly ironic, or sarcastic, or whatever other tone would convince the reader.

A critical essay analyzes someone else's work, particularly writing, films, or works of art. It frequently begins with an overview of the main points of the work, followed by analysis of the work's meaning. It usually critiques how well the creator accomplished his or her goals or made his or her points.

organization
US

organisation
Brit.

analyze
US

analyse
Brit.

realization
US

realisation
Brit.

17 English Writing

The Seven-Point System

1. Choose a topic.

If you have been given a topic and terms to suggest the kind of essay above, you are on your way. If you do not have an assigned topic, you need to choose not only a subject but also one of the strategies above for developing your essay. Make a list of possible topics. Narrow it down—use just a small piece of the bigger topic.

2. Research details.

Learn as much as you can about your subject from assigned reading, from outside reading (see page 44), by exploring Internet material (see page 48), or by answering these questions:

How would I describe the topic?
To what is it comparable or different?
What are the pieces and parts of the topic and how do they work together?
What are the strengths and weaknesses?
What is the significance of the topic?

3. Focus.

Choose one aspect of the topic, and write down the main point (thesis) you want to make at the top of a page. This does not have to be in final form.

4. Create an outline.

Create a plan for writing about this topic by listing the main ideas you have for supporting the main point.

Now you are ready to write.

5. Write the first draft in essay format.

An essay consists of an **introduction, body paragraphs,** and a **conclusion**. The introduction sets the tone of the entire essay, contains the thesis sentence, and should make your reader want to keep reading. Each of the body paragraphs makes a major point in support of your thesis statement. The conclusion wraps things up and creates a sense of finality.

The Thesis Sentence and Introduction

You probably already know what your first paragraph must do: introduce and incorporate your main point. This is the introduction, and in it will be a thesis sentence. This sentence will summarize what the paper will address, taken from the main point above.
To write a thesis sentence, try writing the subject or topic chosen and add features, results, or point of view.

summarize
US

summarise
Brit.

The Thesis

A marathon runner (subject) + has three physical characteristics (features)

        or + prolongs his life 16 years (results)

        or + may not be really healthy (point of view)

In addition to carrying the thesis sentence, the introduction serves several purposes, but perhaps the most important is to get your reader's attention.
The introduction need not be dramatic or shocking; it simply needs to draw in the reader, telling the reader where the essay is going by clearly expressing its thesis and pointing toward the essay's development. It should unify, or "hold together," the parts of your essay. You can think of it as a road map for your reader.

Create an Introduction

➤ Begin with general lead-in statements to lead your reader up to the main point of the essay, then gradually focus on the specific thesis statement.

➤ Make a striking or astonishing assertion.

➤ Begin a story or anecdote that will be finished in the conclusion.

➤ Give an interesting statistic or quotation.

➤ Ask a provocative question or in some other way pique the reader's interest.

➤ Tell a story or an anecdote.

➤ Identify the main points you will cover.

Choose the best approach and place your thesis sentence near or at the end of the paragraph. The best thesis may be one that seems questionable or unlikely at the outset but becomes persuasive by the end of the essay. The thesis does not necessarily have to be narrow or limited, but it must be focused, interesting, arguable, supportable, and understandable.

The Body

The body of the essay connects the dots by supporting and developing your thesis. The body can be one paragraph or many, depending on the assigned length, but the average is three paragraphs. You can develop or organize the body paragraphs in a number of different ways.

organize
US

organise
Brit.

Types of Body Paragraphs

Explanation. Give examples, facts, and details.

Compare and Contrast. Tell how two things are similar or different. (See page 4.)

Chronological. Arrange paragraphs according to how the events/ideas occur in time sequence.

Spatial. Arrange paragraphs according to how the details occur with regard to location (left to right, front to back, top to bottom).

Emphasis. Arrange paragraphs according to how the ideas are presented in order of importance (least to most important, most important to least).

Cause and Effect. Arrange paragraphs according to how the events/ideas relate in a cause/effect chain (from effect to cause or cause to effect).

Problem/Solution. Arrange paragraphs in an argument essay according to the issue and its solution(s) (also can be arranged in a problem-cause-solution format).

Topical. Arrange paragraphs according to topics discussed (used when one of the other patterns is not appropriate, e.g., discussing the four types of dangerous drivers on the road when they are all equally dangerous).

organized
US

organised
Brit.

summarizes
US

summarises
Brit.

Each paragraph should be organized with a topic sentence that contains or summarizes the main idea of the entire paragraph. The other sentences in the paragraph should support that idea by explaining or giving details about it, very much like the organization of the essay as a whole. Although the topic sentence is generally the first or second sentence in the paragraph, it can be placed in the middle of the paragraph or at the end. It might even be given at the beginning of the paragraph and repeated at its end.

Paragraph Details

➤ giving examples

➤ illustrating your point with a story

➤ discussing a process

➤ comparing and contrasting items

➤ discussing cause-and-effect

➤ defining your terms

This supporting information should be logically organized and smoothly connected. Using more than one supporting method for each paragraph gives variety and interest to the essay. For example, you might define several terms, compare and contrast them, and illustrate the differences with a story. If you use examples to develop your paragraph, keep these ideas in mind:

Examples

➤ Use examples in your essay that are relevant to the reader. An example may work for you, but it may be beyond the experience of your reader.

➤ Be sure the example supports the point you are trying to make. If it doesn't connect the reader to the point of discussion, it adds nothing to your essay or to the value of your argument.

➤ Find examples that are concrete and make only one point. If the reader has to figure out what part of the example is important, he or she may decide to ignore it.

➤ Give enough examples to make your point, but avoid "overkill." Too many examples may tire your reader and cause him or her to lose interest.

Begin a new paragraph to switch to a new idea; highlight an important point; show a change of time or place; emphasize a point; or break up a large amount of text. Each new paragraph encourages the reader to reflect on the preceding ideas and look for their relationship to the new paragraph.

Each paragraph should flow smoothly into the next one. The transitional sentence may come at the end of one paragraph or at the beginning of the next one. It may imply a "building" or "going forward" of an idea, or it may cause the reader to compare ideas or draw conclusions. Choose the right transitional word or phrase based on how the next paragraph is related to the one preceding it.

emphasize
US

emphasise
Brit.

17 English Writing

Transitional Words and Phrases

➤ **To add ideas:** and; again; moreover; furthermore; besides; too; in addition; also

➤ **To compare or contrast:** likewise; similarly; yet; nevertheless; on the other hand; on the contrary; however; although

➤ **To prove:** because; since; obviously; in addition; indeed

➤ **To show exceptions:** yet; however; despite; occasionally; still

➤ **To show time:** thereafter; soon; finally; previously; next; now; then; later

➤ **To show effect:** therefore; consequently; as a result; thus

➤ **To repeat:** as noted; in brief; as stated previously

➤ **To emphasize:** obviously; in fact; unquestionably; certainly; indeed

➤ **To give examples:** for example; for instance; to illustrate; to demonstrate; in another case

➤ **To conclude:** thus; consequently; on the whole; hence; therefore

Other Ways to Achieve Coherence

➤ repetition of a key word or phrase

➤ use of personal pronouns

➤ use of synonyms

➤ use of "pointers" such as *this, that, these, those*

➤ use of parallel construction

The Conclusion

itemization
US

itemisation
Brit.

The conclusion of your essay is at least as important as the rest of it. Unless the essay is quite lengthy, the conclusion should be more than just an itemization of the points you've made earlier. The conclusion must create a sense of finality for the reader. See page 31 for more ideas.

Conclusions

➤ should emphasize a given point

➤ finish the anecdote from the introduction

➤ draw conclusions

➤ encourage the reader to take some sort of action

➤ include your own personal observations

6. Revising the draft.

Your essay is now ready for revision. The plan suggests revising in two stages, once for structure and once for style.

If possible, let your first draft sit for a day or two before you begin polishing it. This will allow you to approach the revision with a more critical eye. Most people, even professional writers, need to edit, revise, and sometimes even rewrite their material to make it as good as it can be. Spending the time to polish your work will be well worth it. Read through your essay and check to see if the road map has been followed. Now is the time to improve and correct any weaknesses by rearranging, adding details or examples, using connective words, etc.

Revising for Structure

➤ Is there a clearly stated focus/thesis?

➤ Does each paragraph support or develop the thesis?

➤ Is each paragraph arranged in a logical sequence (page 7)?

➤ Does each paragraph connect to the one above and below?

➤ Does each paragraph have a topic sentence and points supporting that topic?

➤ Is there a strong conclusion?

Revising for Style

➤ Is the point of view (first, second, or third person) consistent?

➤ Is the tense of the verbs consistent (simple past tense is usual)?

➤ Does each pronoun refer to a specific person or thing that will be obvious to the reader?

➤ Have I used the passive voice (if so, eliminate and reword)?

➤ Look for excess words and phrases, which can clog up your writing and reduce its effectiveness. Cut the fat and make every word work.

➤ Eliminate redundant words. Many word pairs are redundant (for example, *completely finish; past history; terrible tragedy*). Use one word or the other. Some categories are redundant (for example, *round in shape; small in size*). You can probably omit the more general word. Many modifiers are meaningless fillers (for example, *kind of; basically; actually*). "Unique" means one of a kind. Nothing can be "very unique"; it is either unique or it is not. Many phrases can be changed into single words. "The reason for" or "due to the fact that" becomes "because" or "since"; "has the ability to" becomes "can."

➤ Look next for weaker or passive verbs. Most times, the active verb is the better choice. "The binoculars were found last week" conceals, rather than reveals, information. "Jane found the binoculars last week" tells us "who did what to whom."

➤ Check to see if you have overused prepositions. Like the passive voice, too many prepositions drain the action from a sentence. "In this poem is an example of his use of the attitude of scorn toward the reader with which he is usually associated" mercifully becomes "This passage exemplifies his usual scornful attitude toward readers."

➤ Check for and replace imprecise and overused qualifiers, such as *rather, very, little,* and *pretty.*

➤ Check for use of clichés. Avoid them unless you can use them in a new way or to illustrate a point.

7. Proofreading

Check your grammar, spelling, and punctuation. Don't rely solely on your computer's grammar and spell checkers. Use the style book your teacher requires for all grammar and punctuation questions. For more details on structure, style, and proofreading, see pages 28–43.

Congratulations! You have completed the Seven-Point System and now have a polished essay. Read on for how to apply your techniques to all types of writing—the essay exam, essays about literature, and research papers.

Writing Under Pressure

In this section, you will learn how to prepare to take an essay exam. You will learn some note taking and outlining tips that will help you organize your thoughts before the exam, and you will learn to budget your time during the actual exam so that you don't end up with two questions to answer and no time for writing! You will also learn to look for strategy terms—what they are and how they should be used to determine your writing approach.

Preparing for the Essay Exam

As is true for any test you take, you can and should prepare for an essay exam. As is true for any essay, you should follow the Seven-Point System. In the case of a test, you will be given the *topic,* and the question will tell you what kind of essay to write. The *research* step is called STUDYING. The *outline, writing, revision,* and *proofing* are similar—just faster.

Before the test:

- Take good notes during class and from your reading assignments.
- Review and outline your notes periodically.
- When the time for the test approaches, make detailed outlines based on your notes.
- Try to determine which points have been stressed and repeated most often in class.
- Are there any recurring themes?
- Is there a thread that ties all the major points together?
- Write down several possible test questions and try to answer at least one of the questions before the exam to practice your test-taking skills.

Exam Tips

➤ During the exam, take time to prepare each answer.

➤ Begin by reading all of the questions.

➤ If you have several questions from which to choose, answer only the required number.

➤ Devote the appropriate amount of exam time to your answers according to the point value of the questions. For example, on a 100-point exam, a 30-point question should be allotted one-third of the exam time since it is worth approximately one-third of the grade.

Strategy

Essay exams usually require you to recall information, to present it in a logical, orderly fashion, and to draw conclusions. As you read your essay exam question, it is important that you know what you are being asked to do. Look for the strategy term or phrase, which tells you how to approach the task of writing. Words such as *analyze, define, compare* and *contrast, describe, evaluate, explain,* and *summarize* are common strategy terms. See pages 4 and 5 for definitions of these terms.

Caution: Always be sure you are answering the question that is asked. Remember to refer to the question as you write.

Once you have determined the strategy for your essay exam question, you will begin the second component of your exam—content.

Identifying Your Topic

Before you begin to write, examine the question to find your topic. Be sure you understand what you are being asked to define, analyze, discuss, evaluate, or explain.

Planning Your Essay

Once you understand what you are being asked to do, spend about 10% of your time planning your essay. Prepare a quick outline by jotting down important points and sub-points.

Developing Your Outline

One approach to beginning your outline is to make a list of the main points you plan to cover in your essay. Then, fill in this list with supporting examples. The examples you plan to include should be noted in your outline before you begin writing the essay.

Formulating Your Thesis

After you have developed an outline, you can formulate your thesis. This approach is different from the way you normally write an essay, in which you develop your thesis first. Because you are in a time/pressure situation, writing the outline first and developing your thesis from it saves time and keeps you from forgeting a key piece of information.

Writing the Essay

Once you are ready to write, keep the following points in mind.

- Clearly announce your thesis and establish the essay's structure.
- Be direct and to the point.
- Provide examples and clear explanations.
- Avoid digressions and generalizations.
- Do not restate the questions in the essay.
- Follow your outline closely.
- Use transitional phrases to get from one point to another.
- Write neatly and leave room for editing corrections.

Remember to save some time for revising and editing your answers. Follow the same guidelines as you would for any paper. Helpful questions include:

- Does the thesis answer the question on the exam?
- Is the thesis clearly stated?
- Have all the major points been covered?
- Are the details specific?
- Is each sentence complete?
- Are the spelling and grammar correct?
- Is the writing legible and neat—even with cross-outs and inserts?

organize
US

organise
Brit.

analyze
US

analyse
Brit.

summarize
US

summarise
Brit.

generalizations
US

generalisations
Brit.

17 English Writing

Writing About Literature

When you analyze something, you break it down into its parts. By looking at its components, you hope to develop a better understanding of the whole. For example, if you are feeling tired and sluggish, you may go to your family doctor to find out what is wrong. One of the first steps she may take is to order a blood test for you. The lab technician will take a sample of your blood and then analyze it to see which of its components could be impacting your condition. By looking at the lab results, your doctor may have a good idea as to what is causing your tiredness and sluggishness. Thus, by analyzing just a small part of your physical body, the doctor can make some judgment about your overall health.

This same idea holds for writing a literary analysis, except the whole you are looking at is a work of literature, whether a novel, short story, play, or poem. In a literary explication or analysis, your goal is to help your reader achieve a better understanding of a particular work of literature. To achieve this goal, you break down the literary work into its components. Then, by discussing one of these components in depth, you help your reader achieve a greater insight into the work as a whole.

Elements of Literature

Before you can analyze a work of literature, you need to know the elements that go into the making of that work. For example, if you are asked to write a literary analysis of a short story or even a novel, you need to be able to identify the basic components of these genres of literature. Below is a description of these various components of a short story or novel and some suggestions as to how you could approach each in writing a literary analysis.

Plot

The **plot** is the series of events or incidents that occur in the work of fiction. The plot always has a conflict as its basis. The series of events builds this conflict until the opposing forces meet and a resolution results. The point in the literary work where the two forces collide is called the climax.

When you are writing a literary analysis that looks at plot, you are analyzing the conflict. You tell your reader what that conflict is and discuss the major events that illustrate this conflict in the literary work. You point out the climax of the plot and what the resolution of the conflict is. Because your goal is to help your reader understand the whole work, you explain what the conflict and resolution mean for the theme or message of the work.

Types of Conflict in Works of Fiction

➤ human vs. human: one person confronting another person

➤ human vs. society: one person against a group of individuals or against the mores of society

➤ human vs. self: one person facing an internal struggle

➤ human vs. nature or environment: one person confronting some natural element

➤ human vs. animal: one person in a struggle against an animal

➤ human vs. the supernatural: one person against fate, a god, or some miraculous power

analyze
US

analyse
Brit.

17 English Writing

Characters

When you think of **characters,** you think of the people in the literary work. The main character or the person on whom the plot centers is called the protagonist. The literary work may contain one major character or several and some minor characters.

The important aspects of characters in a literary work are personality traits and motivations of the people involved. These traits or motivations cause the conflict that occurs. Is a character naive, suspicious, or aggressive? Does a character behave out of fear, greed, or ambition? Also, you want to look at the growth of a character in the literary work. Is the character static or dynamic? If the character is static, that character's personality or understanding or level of maturity does not change in any way during the series of events that unfolds. If the character is dynamic, however, that character does experience some type of personal growth. Keep in mind that the growth can be positive or negative. Whatever the case, the character at the end of the story is not the same person he or she was at the beginning.

When you write a literary analysis based on character, you look at the personality traits or motivations of that character. You give illustrations from the literary work that show a particular trait and discuss how this trait impacts the conflict. By looking at the climax of the work, you can draw some conclusion about the growth of the character. Does the character undergo a change, or is the character still the same person? Based on this growth factor, you can draw some conclusions as to the message of the story that the author is trying to convey.

Point of View

Closely related to character is **point of view.** Someone tells the story you are reading. That person is called the narrator. There are four main types of narrators: *first-person, third-person limited, third-person objective,* and *third-person omniscient.*

A *first-person* narrator tells his or her story. The events are either happening to that person or being witnessed by that person. The use of the pronoun "I" is the trademark of a first-person narrator. Once in a while, you may find a first-person plural narrator. In this situation, the story will be told from a "we" point of view. With first-person narration, the narrator can relate only the action that occurs when he or she is present and can relate only his or her own thoughts, and not the thoughts of other characters. The narrator can speculate as to what another person may be thinking but can never know another person's thoughts.

With a *third-person* narrator, the story is about someone other than the person telling the story. The use of the third-person pronouns "he" or "she" is an indication of a third-person narrator. There are three types of third-person narrators. A *third-person limited narrator* means the story is being told about someone else but through that person's eyes. It would be like viewing the action while standing behind that person throughout the whole story. Because the narrator is limited, we can know the action only when that character is present, and we can know the thoughts of only that one character.

A *third-person objective narrator* is as the name indicates: a narrator who does not get involved in any way with the telling of the story. The third-person objective narrator tells the story as it unfolds and does not delve into the thoughts and motivations of the characters. The narrator just stands back and relates what happens.

A *third-person omniscient narrator* is an all-knowing narrator. Like the other two third-person narrators, this type of narrator is telling a story about someone else, but can relate the action that happens to any of the characters at any place and at any time. In addition, the third-person omniscient narrator can relate the thoughts of any of the characters.

For a literary analysis, you can analyze the narrator. If the narrator is a key participant in the story as you might have with a first-person narrator, you can analyze the narrator as you would any character. If you feel the type of narrator used has an impact on the telling of the story or is vital to the theme of the work, you can discuss this aspect.

Setting

Setting refers to the location and the time period of the series of events. You may have a story that takes place in one particular location during a relatively short period of time or a story that takes place in multiple locations during an extended period of time. Some stories take place in the past; some, the present; and some, the future. Some stories may shift back and forth between multiple time periods. Shifting to a scene in the past from the present is called a flashback.

Whatever the location or time frame, when you write a literary analysis based on setting, you are discussing how the setting has an impact on the plot or the characters. How does the setting affect the series of events that occurs? How does the setting affect the behavior of the characters?

You can also analyze how the setting reflects the theme of the story. Is the setting reflective of the message of the story? If so, discuss how the locale and atmosphere of the setting reflect the author's views in the story.

Theme

Every literary work will have a **theme.** The theme is the main point or the central idea or the message of the work that the author is trying to convey to the reader. It is important to remember that the theme does not always have to be a message, such as "Crime doesn't pay," or "Honesty is the best policy." The theme may be an illustration of some societal condition, such as "people's inhumanity to others," or "the emptiness of the rich." The theme may present some insight into the human life cycle, such as a boy's transition into manhood or the dissolution of a relationship. The theme may just present a picture of a human characteristic, such as courage or pride.

No matter which elements of a story you decide to analyze, your goal is to help your reader to achieve a better understanding of the theme. You can choose, though, to analyze a story by directly looking at the theme. Let your reader know what the theme of the story is, and then show how that theme is developed in the story. Take excerpts from the story to support your analysis.

Besides these basic components of a short story or novel, you might consider analyzing two other aspects of a work of fiction.

analyzing
US

analysing
Brit.

Language or Style

Language refers to the words an author uses. **Style** refers to the way those words are expressed in sentences. Good writers choose their words carefully. The words not only reflect the background and education of the characters and narrator but also convey the appropriate meaning intended. The words may convey their literal meaning, but they may also have an ironical or satirical meaning. The style of the author is also reflective of the characters and narrator and is appropriate for the theme. The author may use short, simple sentences; long, complicated sentences; or even stream of consciousness.

For your literary analysis, you may want to analyze language and/or style. Tell your reader how the author uses words and style to convey or reinforce the theme of the work. Select key passages from the text that show this use.

Symbols

A **symbol** refers to an object or person that represents an idea or concept. For example, a rose is a flower, but it could represent a person's love. A flag is a piece of cloth, but it could represent a country or the concept of patriotism. Many times an author will use symbols to help convey the theme. If you write a literary analysis based on a symbol, select the object or person that you find to be symbolic and tell what that object or person represents. Of course, you will explain to your reader how you arrived at that interpretation. Finally, show how the symbol relates or conveys the theme of the literary work.

Writing the Explication

Evaluating and judging the places, things, experiences, and even the people you come across are things you do every day. Whether you are choosing a piece of jewelry or selecting a restaurant for dinner, you are evaluating. In an academic context, you may be required to write analyses for classes in the arts and humanities. These subjects don't lend themselves to traditional research formats, so you will need to know how to approach writing assignments in these fields.

The initial steps in writing a research paper involve researching information, formulating a thesis, and organizing data. Sometimes a different approach is appropriate, such as when an element of subjective analysis and evaluation is expected in an assignment.

The **explication** can be seen simply as an explanation. It involves breaking down a work into various elements and analyzing the elements one at a time. In most cases, the explication takes on the form of a typical essay, and the writing is organized around a thesis. Subjects in the arts and humanities, on the other hand, require a modified treatment.

While a research paper gathers existing information on a topic and draws conclusions from the data, an explication is intended to clarify the meaning of a work. This means your thesis will identify the main emotion, message, or statement conveyed in the work. The thesis, then, guides the content of the rest of the explication.

Because an explication is a commentary, you will include your own analysis of the meaning or characteristics of the work. It is important to remain focused on the work you are explicating rather than straying to your own experience or opinions.

Although you will want to stay focused on the work you are explicating, this doesn't mean you will just be paraphrasing or rewording the original piece, nor will you simply summarize the plot. Instead, you will need to determine your overall reaction to the piece by logically analyzing the various elements that contribute to the total effect.

To start, you first need to understand that you can explicate several different types of works.

organizing *US*
organising *Brit.*

Types of Works That You Can Explicate

➤ **Literature**	➤ **Visual Arts**	➤ **Music**
Fiction	Painting	Orchestral
Drama	Sculpture	Vocal
Poetry	Architecture	Musical Theater
	Theater	
	Films	

Each explication will call for a different set of criteria that is appropriate for that specific type of work. For example, music contains rhythm, meter, and harmony, and a fictional story contains plot, setting, and characters. Your thesis sentence will list each of the elements that you will analyze.

One element will be evaluated in each of the body paragraphs. This allows you to include the necessary details to explain how each element contributes to the overall work. It may be tempting to include biographical information or other historical details in the body paragraphs. However, this type of information is valuable only if it contributes to the meaning of the work.

For additional analysis, you could include the comments of a person who is an expert in the field. This could be an artist, a musician, or a writer. As with any paper, you will need to document the sources you use, including personal interviews, in the proper format with a works cited or references list.

In addition to an interview, your explication should include a source that discusses the work you have chosen. You can include the source as a paraphrased statement and as a quote.

With the groundwork laid, you will be ready to express your evaluation and opinion of the work in your concluding paragraph.

To summarize, recommended guidelines for writing the explication include the following:

1. Integrate your viewpoint into the explication while remaining objective.
2. Clarify the meaning of the work.
3. Use relevant source material.
4. Follow the work's organization.

Note: An explication provides commentary and clarifies the meaning of a work. An explication should not:

- paraphrase the work
- summarize the plot
- include biographical or historical data unless it adds to the interpretation

summarize
US

summarise
Brit.

organization
US

organisation
Brit.

analyzing
US

analysing
Brit.

Writing a Literary Analysis Paper

An important consideration before writing a **literary analysis** is the use of secondary sources. Generally, a literary analysis is your own interpretation of a literary work. You read the piece of literature carefully; draw your own conclusions as to the author's intent and message in the work; look at the various elements of the work and determine which element would best help clarify that message for your reader; and then locate the references from the work itself that will justify your conclusions. However, your assignment may require you to use secondary sources to support your contentions. In this case, look for critiques of the work you are analyzing and use these secondary authors to confirm your contentions. You may find a secondary source that contradicts your viewpoint. In this case, present this opposite opinion but then show how you disagree with the author's contention based on the evidence you find in the literary work.

Think about this: Like any essay you write, a literary analysis paper should have an introduction, body, and conclusion. Following are some tips to help you approach each of these sections.

Introduction

There are three components of an Introduction to a literary analysis.

1. The name of the work you are analyzing and its author

2. A brief summary or overview of the work being discussed

3. A thesis statement that fulfills three goals:
   a. Identifies the element of the literary work being analyzed
   b. States the point you are making about that element
   c. Relates your point to the theme or message of the story

Body

In the body of the literary essay, as with any essay, you are supporting your thesis. In this type of essay, though, the majority of the supporting details, if not all of them, are coming directly from the piece of literature you are analyzing. Your goal is to show through direct references from the work that the assertion you made in your thesis is a correct interpretation.

To provide the best support for your thesis and to make sure your reader understands your interpretation, construct your body paragraphs in the following fashion.

1. First, state your topic sentence, identifying the section or part of the work you are going to discuss because it illustrates the point you have established in your thesis.

2. Second, discuss what you feel this section of the work is showing. What is the point you want your reader to grasp about this section you are highlighting?

3. Third, make a direct reference from the literary work that illustrates your assertion. You may quote directly from the literary work, or you may provide an indirect reference to what is found in the work.

4. Fourth, clarify how your reference from the literary work illustrates your point. This clarification is a key componenet of your analysis. You want to make sure your reader understands how the excerpt from the work illustrates your point.

5. Fifth, if your assignment is to include critiques from an outside source, you now, through quoting, paraphrasing, or summarizing, take a reference from your outside source to support or reinforce the point you have made. You are using your outside source to provide an authoritative stamp to your assertion.

Conclusion

The conclusion of your literary analysis should be brief. Because the purpose of your literary analysis is to help your reader develop a better understanding of the work's message or theme, you want to reinforce in your conclusion what that theme is and how the element you just analyzed in your essay conveys that theme.

Some Points to Remember

➤ You are writing your literary analysis to an informed reader. You write from the assumption that your reader is familiar with the work being analyzed. Thus, you do not have to provide your reader with extensive summaries of the work. Your goal is to help your reader interpret the work, so any excerpts from the work are to show where your interpretation can be supported from the work itself.

➤ All references to the literary work should be written in the present tense because a literary work exists throughout time.

➤ Because you generally write a literary analysis for a particular course you are studying, the piece of literature you are analyzing will probably be from a common text. Consequently, you do not need to document the source of the work. However, give the page number from the textual source if it is a short story or novel; the act, scene, and line numbers if a play; and the stanza and/or verse numbers if a poem. Include these numerical references as part of your sentence introducing your textual example, or place them in parentheses after the example. If you are not using a common text, then give the full textual citation for your source on your works cited page. If you are using a secondary source in your paper, however, document this source as you would any source in a research paper, using proper in-text and works cited format.

For explication of poetry, see Solving the Poetry Puzzle, on the next page.

17 English Writing

Solving the Poetry Puzzle

Reading or listening to poetry for fun and pleasure is a familiar thing. We are surrounded by poems almost from birth: lullabies, nursery rhymes, Dr. Seuss and children's stories in rhyme, table graces and bedtime prayers, riddles, memory aids, games, sports cheers, advertisements, and song lyrics—to name a few. We don't find any of these perplexing or hard; in fact, at all ages, we enjoy these poems which fill our lives.

Why, then, does the prospect of studying a thing so familiar as a poem seem so difficult when assigned from a textbook or as the subject of a paper? We feel, it seems, that unlike familiar prose, the poem's meaning is "hidden" within its condensed form, requiring more effort to understand and making poems seem mysterious and difficult.

One reason poetry may appear mysterious is that, in some ways, it actually is and always has been. Poetry is by far the oldest form of literature, predating prose and even the written word. In ancient times, such subjects as history and science were actually discussed in poetry instead of the prose we would use. The creation of a poem seemed beyond the average person, and poets were believed to be divinely or magically inspired. Their poems were thought to hold special powers as well.

Just What Is a Poem Anyway?

Even answering the question of just what is poetry is perplexing. No one seems to be able to define it exactly.

A textbook definition states that "Poetry is a playful, rhythmical composition of words expressing an attitude, designed to surprise and delight and to arouse an emotional response in its reader or hearer."

However, we know that not all poetry is playful. Perhaps a poem does not surprise the reader or arouse an emotional response.

The poet Robert Frost simply said that "Poetry is the kind of things poets do."

No wonder we wonder.

Another definition states that poetry "...seeks to express action, feeling or thought in a concentrated, imaginative way through the use of condensed, arresting, and emotive language that follows a metric or rhythmic pattern."

This definition comes closer, but how does it help us study a poem? It does give us an idea of several elements of a poem that we need to study in order to understand the poem.

Studying Poetry

While reading a poem purely for enjoyment requires only the time to scan it, studying a poem requires more effort. The study of poetry is a mental exercise that decodes the "condensed language" and the "metrical or rhythmic pattern," the methods and techniques the poet has used to express ideas.

> Studying poetry is much like solving a puzzle: analyzing the pieces, fitting them together, and understanding and appreciating the whole.

And while poems can be enjoyed without analysis and analyzed without enjoyment, the analyzed poem, like the completed puzzle, ideally gives us increased understanding, satisfaction, and pleasure.

analyzed
US

analysed
Brit.

meter
US

metre
Brit.

Divide and Conquer

We know that to solve a problem or to do a complex task, the best approach is to divide the job into smaller, easier steps. That method also works on poetry. What you need in order to study poems is a set of tools to use, a logical method to follow, and, above all, the time it takes to look closely at the poem. In order to do a job well, you need the right tools. Analyzing poetry requires such tools also. Doing a task well requires time; studying a poem requires the time to read the poem several times, apply the tools, and unlock the meaning. Once done, the discussion of the poem—in oral or written form—becomes easy; the poem becomes your own. So while such a method and tools are necessary for the study of poems and for analytical writing about them, you may use them with the reading of poems for pleasure. By doing so, you will understand the craft of the poet, enhancing your pleasure even more.

The Poetry Tool Box

Our poetry TOOL BOX contains the techniques poets use and definitions with examples to help explain each one. Some of these tools may be familiar; others may not. All are helpful in explaining the structure and content of poems. The tool box is divided into small items to make understanding and using them easier. Advanced tools are also included in each section, as well as practice exercises for Extra Credit.

1. **SOUND EFFECTS**
   rhyme and sound devices

2. **THE RHYTHM SECTION**
   meter and feet

3. **FORM**
   fixed line patterns in a poem

4. **IMAGERY**
   sensory images and symbols

5. **FIGURES OF SPEECH**
   comparisons

Using the tool box, you can discover the ways in which a poet has given a poem rhythm, musicality, and meaning. Many of the poet's tools are shortcuts—one word suggests many other words unwritten. For these reasons, it will be necessary to read the poem you are studying several times, each time using different poetic tools. It takes a poet a long time to find just the right tools to use: be prepared to spend time figuring them out.

1. Sound Effects

- **Rhyme**—two or more words containing identical vowel and ending consonant sounds (hay/may)
- **End Rhyme**—rhymes occurring at the ends of lines of poems
- **Consonance**—two or more words having the same consonant sounds but different vowel sounds (bake/strike)
- **Alliteration**—repetition of the same consonant sounds at the beginning of consecutive words initially (time/toad/tree) or internally (attic, batter)
- **Assonance**—repetition of the same vowel sounds initially (all/awful) or internally (hush/flutter)

Advanced Sound Effects

Masculine Rhyme—the rhyme of one-syllable words (nail/pail) or of stressed final syllables (cŏm páre/dĕ spáir)

Feminine Rhyme—the stressed rhyming syllables are followed by unstressed syllables (tén dĕr ly/slén dĕr ly)

Onomatopoeia—sounds which imitate meaning (moan/murmur/quack)

2. The Rhythm Section

Rhythm consists of stressed and unstressed syllables repeated in a pattern. The pattern consists of:

- The order in which these syllables are arranged
- The number of syllables put together (2 or 3)
- The number of feet in a line (1 to 10)

Stress—accented syllables, marked in studying poems by the accent marks ´ (acccented) and ˘ (unaccented) (Ó pĕn | ă gaínst | ŭp ón). In English all words, except the articles (a, an, or the) or prepositions, carry one stress, or accent.

Foot—two or three consecutive syllables put together as follows:

iambic–one unaccented plus one accented syllable (ă grée)
anapestic–two unaccented plus one accented syllable (iñ siñ cére)
trochaic–one accented plus one unaccented syllable (dái lў)
dactylic–one accented plus two unaccented syllables (dés pĕr ăte)
spondee–two accented syllables together (this teám)

Meter—repeating of one of the above types of feet throughout the poem in groups as follows:

Advanced Rhythm

To figure out which of the five feet the poem has:

- Mark the accented and unaccented syllables in several lines.
- Count the syllables.
- If the number is divisible by two, the foot is either *iambic* or *trochaic*.
- If the number is divisible by three, the foot is *anapestic* or *dactylic*.
- If the first syllable of each line is unaccented and the last is accented, you have *iambic* or *anapestic*.
- If stressed at first and unstressed at the end, you have *trochaic* or *dactylic*.
- Put a slash between every two syllables. Count the slashes or feet. The type of foot plus the total feet equals meter.

Bŭt íf | thĕ whíle | Ĭ thínk | oñ theé | deăr fríend

ăll lós | sĕs aré | ře stóred | añd sór | rŏws end.

The lines each have 10 syllables, which are divisible by two. Each line begins with an unaccented syllable and ends with an accented syllable (so the meter is iambic). Five is the total number of feet (one unaccented and one accented syllable), which is pentameter. So the meter of this poem is iambic pentameter. **Remember:** Meter is figured by what most of the poem presents, not by the few exceptions there may be.

3. Form

- **Stanza**—group of lines having rhyme and meter
- **Couplet**—two consecutive rhyming lines, usually equal in length
- **Tercet**—three-line stanza
- **Quatrain**—four-line stanza, with lines of varying length
- **Ballad Stanza**—a quatrain that tells a story and has four iambic feet in lines one and three and two iambic feet in lines two and four rhyming abcb
- **Sonnet**—14-line poem in iambic pentameter

Advanced Form

- **Refrain**—repeated lines
- **Terminal Refrain**—repeated lines in a fixed position
- **Rime Royal**—seven-line stanza of iambic pentameter rhyming ababbcc
- **Ottava Rima**—eight-line stanza rhyming abababcc
- **Spenserian Stanza**—eight lines of iambic pentameter and one line of iambic hexameter rhyming ababbcbcc

4. Imagery

Imagery is the use of words to recall a sensory experience.

- **Visual imagery**—words that refer to a sight experience—colors, for example
- **Auditory imagery**—words that refer to a heard experience—moan, screech, etc.
- **Tactile**—words that refer to touch experiences—smooth or rough such as velvety, scratchy (also smell, taste, etc.)
- **Symbol**—a word or words that call to mind any or all imagery associated with a larger idea (flag with stars and stripes symbolizes U.S.A., bread symbolizes food)

Fog

Carl Sandburg

The fog comes
on little cat feet.

It sits looking
over harbor and city
on silent haunches
and then moves on.

5. Figures of Speech

Figures of speech are comparisons, either stated or implied.

- **Personification**—giving human qualities to a non-human object: "The sun smiled."
- **Simile**—comparison of two unrelated objects using like or as: "The wood curved like a snake."
- **Metaphor**—implied comparison using is, are, etc.: "You are a snake."

Advanced Figures of Speech

- **Metonymy**—one word stands for another
- **Synecdoche**—part of a thing stands for the whole
- **Apostrophe**—addressing an inanimate object by name
- **Conceit**—elaborate comparisons
- **Hyperbole**—exaggeration
- **Oxymoron**—contradiction

How to Analyze a Poem, Step by Step

The key to analyzing a poem is to:

- Take your time
- Take one step at a time
- Make a written outline as you go

Tip 1
If you cannot answer all the steps, just go on to the other steps and get help later with the few you do not understand.

Tip 2
If your assignment is to analyze the meter and rhyme only or the figurative language alone, use just the section or steps that you need. Make copies of the study guide and fill out a separate copy for each poem.

Tip 3
Use our study guide to study for tests.

Tip 4
Use the study guide as an outline for an explication or paper explaining the poem.

YOU CAN DO IT!

I. First Things First

- Make copies of the printed poem on which you can make notes. Enlarge the copy if you can to give yourself more room.

or

- Write the numbers of the poem's lines on a piece of paper. Skip a line between each, and draw a line at the end of each verse.

II. See the Obvious

- Look at the title. What does it tell you about the poem?
- Find out a little about the poet—when and where he or she lived.
- Count the number of lines in each verse and in the whole poem. This may tell you what kind of poem it may be (form) (see TOOL BOX).
- Read the poem.
- Look up words you do not know in the dictionary.
- Write a one-sentence summary of what the poem is about (it may be a long sentence).

Now you should know the *subject*, the *time* and *place* context, the *form*, all the *words* and the possible *theme* of the poem.

GREAT!

III. A Second Glance

- Read the poem out loud—listen for sound effects (see TOOL BOX).
- Assign letters to each end rhyme on your copy or beside

the line number. Each word that rhymes gets the same letter; each new sound gets a new letter.

- What form does the rhyme scheme support?
- Circle alliterations.
- Underline consonance.
- Note internal rhymes.
- Is there any onomatopoeia?
- How do sounds support meaning?

IV. It's Got Rhythm

- Count the number of syllables in each line.
- Mark stressed and unstressed syllables.
- Draw a slash between feet.
- Count the feet.
- Note any additional feet such as a double stress or single syllable.
- Name the feet and meter.

V. Trigger the Imagination

- Reread the poem.
- Identify images and figures of speech in each verse.
- Explain what each is comparing.

VI. Explain the Meaning

- Paraphrase each verse or section of the poem in your own words, explaining how the figures of speech and images support the meaning.
- Explain what each is comparing.
- Write a final summary of the theme or overall meaning of the poem.

analyzing *US*

analysing *Brit.*

Writing a Paper Analyzing a Poem

1. Make a *step-by-step outline* and use it as you write the paper. Begin the analysis with an introductory paragraph. This may include the *title*, the *author*, the *author's background*, the *length*, *form*, and, briefly, the *thesis*, which is a statement of the theme or subject. The thesis should indicate or refer to any additional elements of the poem, such as imagery, figures of speech, etc., which add to the theme and which will be discussed in the following paragraphs. ➤ **I. Introduction Thesis**

2. If any of the introductory comments merit *further discussion*, such as the title, author's background, the poem's historic setting, etc., discuss these now. ➤ **II. Introductory Development (optional)**

3. Discuss the overall elements of the poem: the *stanza length* and *form* of the poem; the *rhyme scheme*; the type of *foot* and the *meter*. Note any departures from standard form, such as lines in which the meter changes or sonnets in which the rhyme varies from the standard. *Both 2 and 3 are intended to discuss the overall poem.* ➤ **III. General Analysis**

4. Analyze the poem by section—*sentences, stanzas, thought patterns*. To do this, introduce the paragraph with a topic sentence telling what the poet accomplishes in the section. *Paraphrase the section* to show how this is accomplished, discussing *imagery, figures of speech, sound devices,* etc. Repeat for each segment. ➤ **IV. Line-by-Line Analysis**

5. Conclusion—Discuss the overall theme and how the individual parts and poetic techniques have accomplished this. Reverse order is good here, with a final sentence strongly concluding the results of your analysis, the overall effect of the poem on the reader, and the meaning as you see it. ➤ **V. Conclusion**

YOU DID IT!

Practice Your Analysis Skills

I Wandered Lonely as a Cloud

William Wordsworth

I wandered lonely as a cloud
That floats on high o'er vales and hills,
When all at once I saw a crowd,
A host, of golden daffodils;
Beside the lake, beneath the trees,
Fluttering and dancing in the breeze.

Continuous as the stars that shine
And twinkle on the milky way,
They stretched in never-ending line
Along the margin of a bay:
Ten thousand saw I at a glance,
Tossing their heads in sprightly dance.

The waves beside them danced; but they
Out-did the sparkling waves in glee:
A poet could not but be gay,
In such a jocund company:
I gazed—and gazed—but little thought
What wealth the show to me had brought.

For oft, when on my couch I lie
In vacant or in pensive mood,
They flash upon that inward eye
Which is the bliss of solitude;
And then my heart with pleasure fills,
And dances with the daffodils.

Who Has Seen the Wind?

Christina Rossetti

Who has seen the wind?
    Neither I nor you:
But when the leaves hang trembling,
    The wind is passing through.

Who has seen the wind?
    Neither you nor I:
But when the trees bow down their heads,
    The wind is passing by.

I Never Saw a Moor

Emily Dickinson

I never saw a Moor—
I never saw the Sea—
Yet know I how the Heather looks
And what a Billow be.

I never spoke with God
Nor visited in Heaven—
Yet certain am I of the spot
As if the Checks were given—

My Life Closed Twice Before Its Close

Emily Dickinson

My life closed twice before its close—
It yet remains to see
If Immortality unveil
A third event to me

So huge, so hopeless to conceive
As these that twice befell.
Parting is all we know of heaven,
And all we need of hell.

The Tiger

William Blake

Tiger! Tiger! burning bright
In the forests of the night,
What immortal hand or eye
Could frame thy fearful symmetry?

In what distant deeps or skies
Burnt the fire of thine eyes?
On what wings dare he aspire?
What the hand dare seize the fire?

And what shoulder, & what art,
Could twist the sinews of thy heart?
And when the heart began to beat,
What dread hand? & what dread feet?

What the hammer? what the chain?
In what furnace was thy brain?
What the anvil? what dread grasp
Dare its deadly terrors clasp?

When the stars threw down their spears,
And water'd heaven with their tears,
Did he smile his work to see?
Did he who made the Lamb make thee?

Tiger! Tiger! burning bright
In the forests of the night,
What immortal hand or eye,
Dare frame thy fearful symmetry?

Love

Langston Hughes

Love is a wild wonder
And stars that sing,
Rocks that burst asunder
And mountains that take wing.

John Henry with his hammer
Makes a little spark.
That little spark is love
Dying in the dark.

Hymn

Ralph Waldo Emerson

Sung at the Completion of Concord Monument, April 19, 1836

By the rude bridge that arched the flood,
Their flag to April's breeze unfurled,
Here once the embattled farmers stood,
And fired the shot heard round the world.

The foe long since in silence slept,
Alike the Conqueror silent sleeps,
And Time the ruined bridge has swept
Down the dark stream which seaward
    creeps.

On this green bank, by this soft stream,
We set to-day a votive stone,
That memory may their deed redeem,
When like our sires our sons are gone.

Spirit! who made those freemen dare
To die, or leave their children free,
Bid time and nature gently spare
The shaft we raise to them and Thee.

The Road Not Taken

Robert Frost

Two roads diverged in a yellow wood,
And sorry I could not travel both
And be one traveler, long I stood
And looked down one as far as I could
To where it bent in the undergrowth;

Then took the other, as just as fair,
And having perhaps the better claim,
Because it was grassy and wanted wear;
Though as for that the passing there
Had worn them really about the same,

And both that morning equally lay
In leaves no step had trodden black.
Oh, I kept the first for another day!
Yet knowing how way leads on to way,
I doubted if I should ever come back.

I shall be telling this with a sigh
Somewhere ages and ages hence:
Two roads diverged in a wood, and I—
I took the one less traveled by,
And that has made all the difference.

The Chambered Nautilus

Oliver Wendell Holmes

This is the ship of pearl, which, poets feign,
    Sails the unshadowed main,—
    The venturous bark that flings
On the sweet summer wind its purpled wings
In gulfs enchanted, where the Siren sings,
    And coral reefs lie bare,
Where the cold sea-maids rise to sun their streaming hair.

Its webs of living gauze no more unfurl;
    Wrecked is the ship of pearl!
    And every chambered cell,
Where its dim dreaming life was wont to dwell,
As the frail tenant shaped his growing shell,
    Before thee lies revealed,—
Its irised ceiling rent, its sunless crypt unsealed!

Year after year beheld the silent toil
    That spread his lustrous coil;
    Still, as the spiral grew,
He left the past year's dwelling for the new,
Stole with soft step its shining archway through,
    built up its idle door,
Stretched in his last-found home, and knew the old no more.

Thanks for the heavenly message brought by thee,
    Child of the wandering sea,
    Cast from her lap, forlorn!
From thy dead lips a clearer note is born
Than ever Triton blew from wreathèd horn!
    While on mine ear it rings,
Through the deep caves of thought I hear a voice that sings:—

Build thee more stately mansions, O my soul,
    As the swift seasons roll!
    Leave thy low-vaulted past!
Let each new temple, nobler than the last,
Shut thee from heaven with a dome more vast,
    Till thou at length art free,
Leaving thine outgrown shell by life's unresting sea!

Extra Credit *(see column 1 for answers)*

SOUND EFFECTS

Find examples of end rhyme, consonance, alliteration, assonance, masculine rhyme, and onomatopoeia in the first verse from "The Wind" by Robert Louis Stevenson.

The Wind

I saw you toss the kites on high
And blow the birds about the sky;
And all around I heard you pass,
Like ladies' skirts across the grass—
    O wind, a-blowing all day long
    O wind, that sings so loud a song!

I saw the different things you did,
But always you yourself you hid.
I felt you push, I heard you call,
I could not see yourself at all—
    O wind, a-blowing all day long,
    O wind, that sings so loud a song!

O you that are so strong and cold,
O blower, are you young or old?
Are you a beast of field and tree,
Or just a stronger child than me?
    O wind, a-blowing all day long,
    O wind, that sings so loud a song!

FORM

Identify the form below.

1. Tell me, O Octopus, I begs,
   Is those things arms or is they legs?

2. Love is a wild wonder
   And stars that sing,
   Rocks that burst asunder
   And mountains that take wing.

3. In moving slow he has no Peer.
   You ask him something in his Ear
   He thinks about it for a Year…

4. When to the sessions of sweet silent thought
   I summon up remembrance of things past,
   I sigh the lack of many a thing I sought,
   And with old woes new wail my dear time's waste.
   Then can I drown an eye, unused to flow,
   For precious friends hid in death's dateless night,
   And weep afresh love's long since canceled woe,
   And moan the expense of many a vanished sight.
   Then can I grieve at grievances foregone,
   And heavily from woe to woe tell o'er
   The sad account of fore-bemoanéd moan,
   Which I new pay as if not paid before.

   But if the while I think on thee, dear friend,
   All losses are restored and sorrows end.

THE RHYTHM SECTION

I. Identify the type of foot in each word below:

  1. Adam
  2. never
  3. following
  4. twinkle
  5. see here!
  6. success
  7. in a flash

II. Find the type of foot and the meter of the following:

  1. Adam
    Had 'em
  2. I wandered lonely as a cloud
  3. I never saw a Moor
    I never saw the Sea
  4. Twinkle twinkle
  5. It was many and many a year
  6. Cold sea-maids rise

FIGURES OF SPEECH

Find the figures of speech below and tell what kind they are.

I.
1. The moon has a face like a clock

2. Love is a wild wonder

3. There are sunsets who dance goodbye

II.
1. Give me a hand with this

2. I wandered lonely as a cloud

3. Hideous beauty

4. Her eyes were deep as oceans

5. O Wind!

The Critique

While the explication serves the arts and humanities, another type of essay is best suited for other fields. The type of essay generally written for other fields is the critique. You can expect to write critiques in the following fields:

- Psychology
- Sociology
- Religion
- History
- Political science
- Natural sciences
- Business
- Finance

Your opinion does come across [in a review],
but subtly if you are a good reviewer.

—Elizabeth Lund

Three Types of Critiques

There are three common types of critiques. All three should include your opinions.

Evaluation. Makes a judgment, comments on the value of a piece

Reaction. Summarizes and gives response showing areas where you agree and/or disagree

Review. Summarizes and judges ideas—a consumer piece, as in a book or movie review

Regardless of which type of critique you are assigned, a critique usually begins with an assignment to read a selection, often from a periodical. The paper you write is intended to be an intelligent discussion of the periodical article. The critique should demonstrate your grasp of the topic as well as your judgment of how the topic was handled. The process begins with your first reading of the article as you consider several key questions:

1. Is the article significant?
2. Is it accurate?
3. Has the author defined the different terms carefully?
4. Is the information in the article used and interpreted fairly?

Once you have addressed these questions, you can begin to decide if you agree with the author. Make notes about those items with which you agree with the author, and identify the reasons for your opinion. Also, take time to evaluate the author's assumptions. When this part of the preparation is complete, you are ready to write.

Introduction

The first part of your critique will introduce the article by title and the name of the author or authors. It is also appropriate to identify the intended audience as well as the author's purpose in writing the article. The article's purpose could be any of the following:

- to explain
- to persuade
- to entertain

Because you are laying the foundation for the critique, you will also want to add any background information that your readers might need to help them better understand the article you are reviewing.

Thesis Paragraph

The second part in a critique is to state the author's thesis. You will do this by summarizing the author's main arguments and then noting the author's key assumptions. Then, you can relate the author's assumptions back to the thesis and purpose.

Body

In the third part of the critique, you should identify the specific elements of the topic that the author emphasizes. At this point, you will want to include the ideas, the evidence, and the explanations the author uses to support the thesis of the article. This is also the time to point out whether the author's ideas agree or disagree with other sources.

Since you will need other sources to determine how the author's ideas stack up to others, you will need to rely on your research skills to find the needed sources. As a result of your research, your works cited or reference page will reflect the article you are reviewing, as well as that of at least one other source. Depending on the class and your teacher's wishes, be sure to use the appropriate methodology, such as MLA or APA style.

In the fourth part of your critique, you will identify the criteria you will use to evaluate the article. Possible criteria include:

- the author's purpose
- the method used to achieve that purpose
- the author's assumptions
- the strength and credibility of the author's research

Not all of the above criteria may apply to the article you are reviewing. You will select what is appropriate and analyze the article using these standards.

Conclusion

The fifth and final part of the critique is to express your conclusions about the general value of the selection, reminding your reader of the article's strengths and weaknesses. You might also add how the author's ideas could be used or applied, if appropriate.

Literary Analysis

Clearly, the explication and critique satisfy very specific needs for certain situations in the humanities and sciences, but all well-written papers require you to organize and express yourself clearly. Remember to apply the key steps given here, and you will have what it takes to be a good writer in any field.

---

summarizes
US

summarises
Brit.

organize
US

organise
Brit.

---

17 English Writing

Revising for Structure

Revision takes time and effort, so be sure to give yourself a schedule that allows for revisions before the final paper is due. Ask yourself the questions in the following checklist.

Structure Checklist

➤ Is there a clear, specific thesis for the paper? A thesis is a statement presenting your position on the topic.

➤ Is the paper organized around the thesis?

➤ Does each paragraph have a topic sentence?

➤ Is the order of sentences in each paragraph planned or random?

➤ Do the sentences in the paragraph support the topic sentence?

➤ Do the paragraphs have a logical relationship with one another, or are they isolated blocks of information?

➤ Is the development of ideas adequate?

➤ Will your stance on the subject be apparent to the reader?

➤ Is the wording clear and exact?

➤ Do you have a strong introduction?

➤ Does the draft conclude or just trail off?

Identifying the Problem Areas

Before you jump into the actual process of revising, it is important that you learn how to critique your paper for areas that need work. In addition, you will need to know how to revise before you start this sometimes-daunting task. Once you have identified the problem areas and feel comfortable with the revision process, you will be ready to begin making changes to your paper. These changes are all part of revision.

Even published authors realize the importance of rewriting. Most people can't create a great paper in one sitting. Good writing takes revision, so don't look at revising as an indicator that you didn't write the paper well the first time. It is expected that your paper will go through several revisions before it is complete.

Revision

Revision means:

- Removing words, phrases, sentences, or even entire paragraphs
- Adding words, phrases, sentences, or paragraphs
- Moving words, phrases, sentences, and paragraphs around
- Reworking parts of your paper
- Giving time and attention to the changes needed

Revision is NOT:

- Simply running spell check and grammar check
- Quickly proofreading
- Having a friend glance over the paper

The above three steps are important, but they are not infallible. For example, spell check can't tell whether you meant to use the word "through" or "threw."

Once you have asked all the questions and critiqued your first draft, you will have a better idea of your problem areas. You should also gain a sense of what you are doing well in the writing process. Be sure you have thoroughly critiqued your draft for problem areas before you dive in to the important step of writing the final draft. Also remember that revision—trimming, molding, and rebuilding—is something that should continue until you are fully satisfied with the project.

Revising for Structure

Revising a paper for structure requires looking at the overall picture. To do that, ask yourself these questions:

- How well do my ideas flow one to another?
- How well have I stated my case?
- Will someone new to the subject understand what I am trying to convey?
- Does the paper make sense?
- Do my deductions follow a logical development?

As you begin revising, it is important for you to understand the term *revise*. To revise literally means to "re-see" or "see again." You should read your paper as though you are the intended reader and as if you had never seen it before.

As you take a fresh look at your paper, ask yourself some simple questions:

- Do I understand what I have written?
- Can I follow the stream of information?
- Did I just read a rambling series of disjoined facts?

If you don't follow or understand what you have written, no one else will, either. So, how do you go about correcting errors through revision? First of all, don't worry about problems with spelling and grammar, not yet anyway. For now, you should address the following four elements:

- Paragraph structure
- Paragraph development
- Accuracy
- Polishing your introduction and conclusion

Let us look at each of these elements in more detail.

organized
US

organised
Brit.

realize
US

realise
Brit.

17 English Writing

analyzed
US

analysed
Brit.

Paragraphs

The basics of paragraph structure can be analyzed by reading through your paper and asking yourself if the paper makes sense and if there is a line of reasoning that the reader can follow. If not, how do you correct the problem? This is where understanding paragraph structure will be important.

The body paragraphs of your essay are made up of a topic sentence and several supporting sentences that develop that point. All the other sentences in that paragraph should relate to that topic sentence. This way, you will be sure to make a point. When you stay on point and don't ramble, the next paragraph falls into place much more smoothly.

Development

When addressing the development of your paper, ask yourself if each paragraph has enough material to make sense to a first-time reader. Also ask yourself if any points have been raised that need more support or that should be discussed more fully. If your paper isn't fully developed with supporting evidence and clear details, your reader may not be convinced of what you are trying to argue.

Accuracy

If you read through your first draft and find that you have included contradictory information, you will need to check the accuracy of the sources in question. If you encounter contradiction in your paper, go back through your notes so you can resolve the contradiction. Sometimes a contradiction can't be corrected because the experts themselves may be in disagreement. If that is the case, it is important to point this out so that it doesn't seem as though you simply didn't notice the inconsistency.

Polishing

Your final revisions involve polishing and reworking the introduction and conclusion. These are important elements since the introduction lures the reader into the paper and the conclusion brings home the final impression. As you review the introduction, consider the following:

- Is the thesis expressed actually related to the body of the paper?
- Does the conclusion relate back to your thesis?

Once you have confirmed that your introduction and conclusion have stayed on point, it is time to refine those paragraphs so they become more than statements of intent or summation. Because your introduction and concluding paragraphs are so important to the paper, you will want to breathe some life into them.

As in television promos and magazine articles, your goal when rewriting the introduction is to entice your reader into reading more by presenting your thesis in an intriguing or appealing form. If your introduction is boring, check page 7 for good ways to add interest.

Whichever introductory method you choose, you will limit the effectiveness of the introduction paragraph if you are not aware of the following common pitfalls.

- **Cute or gimmicky introductions.** This type of introduction seems extremely artificial and unnatural.

- **Backing into your thesis.** This occurs when you take forever to get to your point. Beware this pitfall if you begin your paper with an anecdote or story. The key is to remember that the story is meant to set up your thesis, so don't include every detail of the story.

- **Shortcutting the introduction.** While it is important to state your point in the introduction, try to first give the reader a chance to warm up to the topic.

- **Reiterating the argument.** Phrases such as "In this paper I will discuss ..." and "I have been asked to write about ..." are boring to your reader and indicate that you are apparently bored by your subject.

- **Apologetic introductions.** Phrases such as "Some people may not agree with me ..." and "Even though it is difficult to explain and understand ..." are guaranteed to diminish your own credibility to discuss the topic.

- **Indecisive introductions.** Avoid sounding indecisive, especially if your topic is controversial.

Just as the introduction is important to present your thesis, the conclusion is critical to ensuring that your reader takes away a clear view of what you have written. Like the period at the end of a sentence, the final paragraph brings the reader to the logical stopping place or conclusion. See page 10 for more ideas.

There are four basic methods to consider when presenting your conclusion.

- **Restate your thesis.** Try a fresh expression of the thesis idea—don't just recopy it. Avoid phrases such as "As stated in the beginning ..." and "Thus have I shown ...."

- **Return to the introductory anecdote.** Return to the anecdote so that it ties in with the conclusion and thus with the paper.

- **Suggest a course of action.** If your paper exposes a problem, it is reasonable to propose a course of action.

- **Make a prediction.** Making a prediction about an outcome, based on the information in your paper, is also an appropriate way to conclude.

As with the introduction, there are certain problems to avoid with the conclusion.

- Never introduce new information.
- Don't end the paper too suddenly.
- Don't drag out the ending.
- Avoid cute and gimmicky conclusions.

Checklist

➤ Have you read through for coherence?

➤ Have you checked for factual accuracy?

➤ Have you improved descriptions?

➤ Have you written a strong introduction?

➤ Have you written a strong conclusion?

Like a baker making bread, you have taken what looked like a good start, "punched" it down like dough, and given it a more useful form. Because you have taken the steps taught in this section, your finished product will be a more refined representation of your work.

17 English Writing

Revising for Style

Search your own essay for errors in grammar and mechanics. Then, after reading this section, revisit your paper, looking for the types of errors covered here.

You have to be very critical of yourself and cut out all the stuff that is extraneous to the story you are trying to tell.

—LARRY BAKER

Style Checklist

➤ All sentences in a paragraph refer to the topic sentence.

➤ Sentences have logical subjects and verbs.

➤ Subjects and verbs agree in number.

➤ Pronouns match antecedents.

➤ Verb tenses are consistent.

➤ Adjectives and adverbs are close to the words they describe.

Sentence Unity

When you are revising your paper, be sure to check each paragraph for unity. Be sure that every thought is connected to the main idea of the paragraph and that all ideas flow logically. The same holds true for each sentence.

Sample:

The U.S. has a higher infant mortality rate than many other western countries and people are homeless.

Improved:

While the U.S. is one of the richest countries in the world, it has a higher infant mortality rate and a greater problem with homelessness than most western countries.

Sample:

John gave his wife a bracelet for Valentine's Day, and she went shopping with her friend.

Improved:

John gave his wife a bracelet for Valentine's Day, and she was so pleased that she wore it when she went shopping with her friend.

Another way a sentence can be disjointed and lack unity is when it contains too many details.

Sample:

When Linda went on vacation, she flew to Hawaii to go snorkeling on the Big Island where her friend had lived and worked for many years.

Improved:

When Linda went on vacation, she flew to Hawaii to go snorkeling on the Big Island.

Illogical Subject and Predicate

When a sentence's subject and predicate don't fit together logically, the result is a confusing sentence with no unity.

Sample:

One article I read believes that grandparents should have guaranteed visitation rights.

Improved:

The author of one article I read believes that grandparents should have guaranteed visitation rights.

Sample:

The grocery store states that it is an equal opportunity employer.

Improved:

The management of the grocery store states that it is an equal opportunity employer.

Subject-Verb Agreement

Your teacher will want to see that you have subject-verb agreement in your sentences. A verb always agrees in number, singular or plural, with its subject. Even when words or phrases separate the subject and verb, the two must still agree.

Correct Samples:

The motor is running.
The motors are running.
The motor of the car is running.

Errors in agreement:

Sample:

The pounding of the drums make the animals nervous.

Improved:

The pounding of the drums makes the animals nervous.

Sample:

The desert, with its prickly plants and eerie lizards, make Edward yearn for the sidewalks of Seattle.

Improved:

The desert, with its prickly plants and eerie lizards, makes Edward yearn for the sidewalks of Seattle.

Sample:

Revising and editing is important to the process of writing a paper.

Improved:

Revising and editing are important to the process of writing a paper.
The process of revising and editing is important to writing.

Every and each: When two subjects are joined by "and," you generally need to use a plural verb, but there is an exception. If the singular words "every" or "each" precede the subject, the verb needs to be singular. These two words denote one person or a singular unit, so the verb will be singular.

Correct samples:

Every student and instructor has his own ticket to the banquet.
Each male and female is receiving an individual invitation.

Either/or and **neither/nor:** When singular subjects are joined by "or," "either/or," and "neither/nor," you will need a singular verb. With singular and plural subjects within the sentence, choose the verb form based on the word closer to the verb.

Either Judy or Carolyn is the winner.

Sample:

Neither the college or the bus company accept liability for the trip.

Improved:

Neither the college nor the bus company accepts liability for the trip.

Pronouns and Antecedents

As with subjects and verbs, pronouns and antecedents must "match." For example, in the sentence below, "each" doesn't match with "their" since "each" equals one member. Be familiar with the singular pronouns (each, everyone, someone, everybody, somebody, etc.) so that you may avoid this type of error.

Sample:

Each member of the cast was given their own copy of the screenplay.

Improved:

Each member of the cast was given his or her own copy of the screenplay.
All members of the cast were given their own copies of the screenplay.

Sample:

Each of the brides decided to keep their own name.

Improved:

Each of the brides decided to keep her own name.

Sample:

When the director called for volunteers, everyone raised their hand.

Improved:

When the director called for volunteers, everyone raised his or her hand.

Correct samples:

At this clinic, a doctor has his or her own patients.
At this clinic, doctors have their own patients.

Verb Tense Inconsistency

As you write your paper, switching back and forth from past to present tense will distract your reader. Once you choose a tense, be consistent.

Sample:

She drove down the street and turns at the first light.

Improved:

She drove down the street and turned at the first light.
She drives down the street and turns at the first light.

Sample:

He sits down for lunch and ate three helpings.

Improved:

He sits down for lunch and eats three helpings.
He sat down for lunch and ate three helpings.

Misplaced and Dangling Modifiers

Misplaced or dangling modifiers present another problem that needs to be addressed. Modifier problems occur when you separate related parts of sentences. Generally speaking, modifiers should be placed as close as possible to the words they modify or describe.

Sample:

The man spotted a grizzly bear peering through his binoculars.

Improved:

The man, peering through his binoculars, spotted a grizzly bear.

Sample:

Jim made the nachos for the office staff with lots of jalapeño peppers on them.

Improved:

Jim made nachos with jalapeño peppers on them for the office staff.

Sample:

Maria saw the lights go off and panicked in the closet.

Improved:

Maria saw the lights go off in the closet and panicked.

Sample:

Not knowing how to fly, renting a small airplane was a waste of money.

Improved:

Renting a small airplane was a waste of money since he did not know how to fly.

Sample:

She just wanted a salad for dinner.

Improved:

She wanted just a salad for dinner.

Sample:

The car nearly cost $30,000.

Improved:

The car cost nearly $30,000.

Sentence Fragments

A sentence fragment is a phrase that cannot stand by itself. It is not a sentence because it does not contain a subject and/or verb and does not express a complete thought. Look at the following example. The second "sentence" does not express a complete thought.

Sample:

Trey had worked all night. Because his research paper was due the next morning.

When corrected, the first sentence is joined with the second phrase to form one complete sentence.

Corrected:

Trey had worked all night because his research paper was due the next morning. Because his research paper was due the next morning, Trey had worked all night.

Consistency of Person

Another error that can occur is inconsistency of person. As you no doubt recall, you can write papers in either the first, second, or third person.

- First person writing uses "I," "me," "us," etc. Personal essays are written in the first person.
- Second person writing uses "you" and "your." Persuasion or process (how-to) papers are often written in this form.
- Third person writing uses "he," "she," "they," or "it." Description papers are best written in this person.

Once you select a person, you must be consistent. You shouldn't switch back and forth between the forms. Consider the following paragraph.

Sample:

"Perfecting the art of written communication is not an easy task. It is cumbersome because we speak much faster than we write. Because of the passive nature of the printed word, a writer cannot be certain if he has effectively communicated a thought or notion to the reading audience. Bad semantics opens the door to miscommunication. Writing is like a minefield; take one wrong step and you're dead. Words enable us to identify, modify, clarify our day-to-day existence. You name it; we have a word for it. When we speak, we use phrases, idioms, or local colloquialisms to communicate our ideas. When writing, you must be precise."

Do you see how the writer used the first person ("we" and "our") in most of the paragraphs? Note how the awkward switch to second person ("your" and "you") shows inconsistency.

Corrected:

"Perfecting the art of written communication is not an easy task. It is cumbersome because we speak much faster than we write. Because of the passive nature of the printed word, we cannot be certain if we have effectively communicated a thought or notion to the reading audience. Bad semantics opens the door to miscommunication. Writing is like a minefield; if we take one wrong step, we're dead. Words enable us to identify, modify, clarify our day-to-day existence. Name it; we have a word for it. When we speak, we use phrases, idioms, or local colloquialisms to communicate our ideas. When writing, we must be precise."

As you carefully proofread your paper, check for person. Go through it looking for the pronouns "I," "you," and "we." Identify those pronouns that are different, and then change them for consistency.

Besides the mechanics of writing, you should also review your paper for wordiness. Most published writers will tell you that the more you can say with less, the better your writing will be.

17 English Writing

Proofreading

Don't overlook the need for careful proofreading as you check your paper for grammatical and mechanical errors. When you proofread, you will be looking for any remaining typographical errors and corrections you overlooked. There are several proofreading techniques you may consider using.

- Read through the paper line by line, using a ruler to focus your attention on just one line at a time.
- Read the paper backwards, from the last line of the last page through to the beginning.
- Proofread with a partner, who will read every word in the paper.
- Verbally note the beginning of paragraphs as well as punctuation marks.

Although the number of rules to remember may seem overwhelming, and the work is particularly detailed, it is important to remember that if it doesn't sound right, it probably isn't. You will want to refer to a grammar handbook and dictionary throughout the writing process, as you aren't expected to remember every rule without a point reference. By correcting your paper for grammatical and mechanical errors, you will make sure that your readers get the point of your thesis without the distractions and confusion that mistakes can cause. Just as the architect must be skilled at spotting problems with a project's plans, you can fine-tune your paper by learning to identify mistakes and knowing how to correct them.

Things to Check for

Spelling

Proofread your paper for simple errors in spelling. If you are unsure of the correct spelling of a word, check a dictionary. In addition to locating and correcting words that are misspelled, you need to check for words that are misused, such as "weather" and "whether" and "passed" and "past." Errors of this type will not be identified by spell-check options in word processing programs because they represent actual words in the English language. However, words such as these are commonly misused. Even in this electronic age, a paper copy of a grammar handbook and a dictionary will prove useful as you revise your paper.

Capitalizing Words

A number of rules should be followed for capitalization. In the following sample sentence, the writer failed to capitalize the word "English."

capitalization
US

capitalisation
Brit.

17 English Writing

Sample:

The english language is a very expressive language.

Corrected:

The English language is a very expressive language.

Another rule of capitalization applies to proper names. In the following sample sentence, the writer mistakenly capitalized the word "author," which is not a proper name.

Sample:

In writing, the Author may not be able to express thoughts or ideas based on common experiences.

Corrected:

In writing, the author may not be able to express thoughts or ideas based on common experiences.

Evaluating Parallelism

A series of words or phrases should be grammatically equal, or parallel. The following sentence lacks parallelism.

Sample:

We write to instruct, to entertain, to inform, providing a record of passage through life.

To correct this sentence, change *providing* to *provide.* Further, the last item in the series could be preceded by the word *and.* The sentence would then read:

Corrected:

We write to instruct, to entertain, to inform, and to provide a record of passage through life.

Checking for Omissions

Leaving out certain words in a sentence may confuse your reader. In the following sample sentence, the writer omitted the object of the preposition "of."

Sample:

The communication is based on shared experiences and is constantly modified as the listener displays comprehension, or lack of, through facial expression or body language.

The sentence should be corrected to read:

Corrected:

The communication is based on shared experiences and is constantly modified as the listener displays comprehension, or lack of it, through facial expression or body language.

Correcting Punctuation

If the first part of a sentence is restated, specified, listed, or otherwise elaborated upon by the second part, you should separate the two parts with a colon.

Sample:

The American flag consists of three colors: red, white, and blue.

In the following sample sentence, the student used a comma instead of a semicolon.

Sample:

Writing is like a minefield, one wrong step and you're dead.

Corrected:

Writing is like a minefield; one wrong step and you're dead.

Two independent clauses need to be separated by a semicolon, not by a comma.

Sample:

You name it, we have a word for it.

Corrected:

You name it; we have a word for it.

Check your sentences to make sure that you have not separated subjects and verbs by a comma. Notice this error:

Sample:

The body language and facial expressions we take for granted in face-to-face communication, are missing.

Because the comma is unnecessary, it should be deleted.

Corrected:

The body language and facial expressions we take for granted in face-to-face communication are missing.

Unless there is an interrupting word between the subject and verb, don't use a comma between them.

Learning to Use the Library

You have probably used a library catalog before to locate a book, but conducting research requires a working knowledge of reference books, indexes, bibliographies, and computer databases. Without this knowledge, you will be unable to find important sources for your paper. This section will introduce you to the necessary tools for conducting research in a library: a true resource and learning center. You will soon understand the difference between reference and circulating books; use the Library of Congress and Dewey Decimal Classification System to locate print and non-print sources; use various catalogs for locating source material, including computerized versions; use different indexes, both general and specialized, to locate articles in periodicals.

I find television very educational.
The minute somebody turns it on,
I go to the library and read a good book.

—GROUCHO MARX

Two Types of Library Books

Libraries today offer a myriad of sources and services to help you answer virtually any question you might have, from music, to computers, to economics. Whether it's traditional books and magazines or microtext and electronic information, the information you need is literally at your fingertips. Since most people think of books when they think of libraries, let's look at the two types of books found in the library.

Reference Books

These books include encyclopedias, dictionaries, directories, almanacs, and other books that are not meant to be read cover to cover. They cannot be checked out since they are consulted frequently, and most people only use a few pages of information from the whole book.

Dictionary of National Biography
Encyclopedia of Religion

Circulating Books

Most of a library's collection consists of circulating books, which can be checked out. These books could include biographies, anthologies, histories, medical books, or the latest best-seller.

The Bedford Anthology of World Literature
All the King's Men
Chicken Soup for the Soul

Classification Systems

All books in the library are arranged by call number according to one of two classification systems. A classification system works like an address to help you locate a book on the shelves.

Library of Congress Classification System

Many colleges use this system of letters and numbers to arrange books by subject. For example, all books on music are in the "M" section, and all books on education are in the "L" section. These broad categories are further subdivided into narrower two-letter designations. For example, the "N" section contains books on art. "NB" includes sculpture, while "NC" includes drawing. These letters are then followed by numbers to further narrow by specific aspects of the subject, author, and title.

The Art of Illustration would be found under call number NC 960.M413.

Dewey Decimal System

Most public libraries and school libraries and some colleges use this system of dividing books into ten main classes. For example, religion is in the 200s, while social sciences are in the 300s.

Americans with Disabilities Acts Handbook would be found under the class number 346.013 A512.

Of course, you don't need to memorize these classification systems. When you look for a book in the library catalog, it will give you the call number you need to locate the book.

Library Catalog

The library catalog is a directory of all books, audiovisual materials, and periodicals a library owns—arranged by author, title, and subject. The catalog may be on paper cards, but most are computerized.

Library of Congress System

A	General Works
B	Philosophy, Psychology, Religion
C	History
D	Foreign History
E,F	American History
G	Geography, Anthropology
H	Social Science
J	Political Science
K	Law
L	Education
M	Music
N	Fine Arts
P	Language and Literature
Q	Science
R	Medicine
S	Agriculture
T	Technology
U	Military Science
V	Naval Science
Z	Library Science, Bibliography

Dewey Decimal System

000	Generalities
100	Philosophy and Psychology
200	Religion
300	Social Science
400	Language
500	Natural Science and Mathematics
600	Technology (Applied Sciences)
700	Arts
800	Literature
900	Geography and History

Computerized Library Catalogs Offer

➤ keyword searching

➤ ability to search from outside the library

➤ ability to search other library catalogs in addition to your home library

➤ graphical interfaces

➤ easy on-screen instructions

computerized
US
computerised
Brit.

specialized
US
specialised
Brit.

memorize
US
memorise
Brit.

Types of Library Sources

Books—an excellent source for getting in-depth information or a historical perspective on a topic

Periodicals—the best way to find more up-to-date information about a current subject or issue

A periodical is a publication that comes out at regular intervals (daily, weekly, monthly, quarterly, or yearly), such as a newspaper, magazine, or scholarly journal. To find an article in a periodical written on a specific subject, you have to use an index.

Print Periodical Indexes

A printed guide to the contents of various publications

A print index is arranged by general subject and contains citations only to the articles published during the time period covered by that index. The citation includes the title, the periodical in which the article was published, the author, date, volume, page number, and sometimes a brief summary of the article. To find the actual article, you must search your library catalog to see if your library subscribes to that journal. Recent issues will usually be found on the shelves, but older issues may be bound in volumes or on microfiche or microfilm.

Electronic Periodical Indexes

A computerized guide to the contents of various publications

An electronic periodical index makes the process of finding information much easier. Many electronic indexes contain the full text of the article. This way, you can print out the full text without ever having to go to the periodical shelves in the library. Some of the online indexes may even be made available to you for off-campus use. You usually have to enter an identification number in order to access the index from off-campus, so be sure to contact your librarian for assistance.

General Periodical Indexes—If you are writing about a current issue or general topic, such as school violence or rights of birth parents, you will want to use a general index.

> *Reader's Guide to Periodical Literature*
> *Academic Index on Infotrac*
> *ProQuest*
> *WilsonSelect*
> *FirstSearch*

specialized
US

specialised
Brit.

Specific Indexes—If you are writing about a more specialized topic, you will want to use an index designed for that topic. The specialized indexes cover only journals dedicated to their assigned subject and allow you to find more in-depth information.

> ERIC for education
> MLA Bibliography for literature
> MEDLINE for medicine
> ABI Inform for business

Newspapers can be a good way to find regional information. For example, if you wanted to find out your area's latest news on school uniforms, a local newspaper would be a great place to search. If you want to compare what your city or town is doing in relation to another town of comparable size, you may want to check local newspapers of other cities or towns. There are online databases such as Newsbank that index only newspapers and local media. This is an excellent place to look for regional information, and many of the articles can be found full-text online or in microfiche or microfilm.

Audiovisual Material

Audiovisual material may also prove helpful in gathering your research and can be found using the library catalog. Types of audiovisual materials include videotapes, audiotapes, and CD-ROMs.

Starting the Research

Now that you are familiar with what materials are in the library, what is the best way to go about finding what you need? Follow these steps to make your library experience most productive.

Steps to a Productive Library Experience

➤ Start with the librarians at the reference desk. They can be very helpful in getting you started.

➤ Begin learning more about your topic in an encyclopedia or other reference book that will give you a basic overview.

➤ Check the library catalog for books and other material (using the keywords and terminology you learned in the basic overview).

➤ Broaden or narrow your topic depending on how much or how little you find in the catalog.

➤ Find periodical articles on your topic (checking generalized and specific indexes).

While searching the Internet can be helpful, the resources offered by your library should always be your major source for information. In fact, there is a great deal of information on the Web that is not appropriate for a student paper. If you do need to find more information on the Internet, be sure to critically evaluate any Web site that you find for accuracy and reliability.

Using Electronic Information

If you have never written a research paper before, you may be surprised to know how much information is available to you in electronic form. CD-ROMs, DVDs, and the Internet have drastically changed the way many people perform research, inside and outside of the classroom. While there are many strengths to electronic media, you must use electronic sources wisely and scrupulously if you wish to have your paper benefit from their inclusion.

In this section, you will learn to use the advantages of electronic sources and recognize and avoid the disadvantages of electronic information. You will learn how to use Boolean search terms. You will learn to evaluate sources for effectiveness using the five points of accuracy, authority, objectivity, currency, and coverage. You will learn to recognize the strengths and weaknesses of the Web and to judge a Web site by its type (.com, .mil, .gov, etc.).

The new electronic interdependence recreates the world in the image of a global village.

—MARSHALL MCLUHAN

Finding the Information

A writing assignment may require you to do extensive research. During the research stage is when you will find the sources for your argument. These sources will appear on the works cited page of your document. Most research tools are now available on the computer, and in order to research a subject effectively, you need to know how to find information electronically.

Electronic information is found in many formats. They include:

- **CD-ROMs (Compact Disks—Read Only Memory)** A CD-ROM can hold the information of as many as 500 floppy disks and offers searching and interactive capabilities. Periodical indexes on CD-ROM allow the user to quickly find recent articles by simply entering a keyword search.

- **DVD (Digital Video Disk)**—DVDs can hold video, audio, and computer data.

- **Internet**—The Internet is a network of computers that spans the globe. A particular part of the Internet known as the World Wide Web allows you to find information on virtually any topic.

When you find an interesting site on the Web, you can learn more about the site by examining the site address. Most addresses begin with "www," but the last part of the address indicates the type of site.

.com=commercial sites	.org=organization	.gov=government
www.microsoft.com	**www.redcross.org**	**www.whitehouse.gov**
.edu=educational site	.mil=military	
www.utexas.edu	**www.navy.mil**	

recognize
US

recognise
Brit.

organization
US

organisation
Brit.

17 English Writing

Though there are countless wonderful sites of information on the Web, you must be careful about the types of sites you use for research. Almost anyone can put almost anything on the Web, so be sure to check the accuracy of what you find.

Some commercial Web sites charge a fee for use. Your library may purchase subscriptions to some of these Web sites, and you may be able to access the sites for free. Depending on your school, you will either have to access the information from campus computers or enter a username and password from off-campus. The commercial databases can include periodical indexes as well as reference books such as encyclopedias, biographical directories, literary criticisms, and more.

General Web sites can be accessed free and are generally found through a search engine. Search engines are Internet sites that will search the Web for specific terms you enter and then return a list of Web pages that contain those terms. Some popular search engines include *Netscape Navigator, Yahoo, Lycos,* and *Microsoft Explorer.*

If you are using the Internet for research for your paper, the periodical index databases provided by your library should generally be your first stop. You can usually find them on your school or library's Web page. Some of the most popular databases include *FirstSearch, InfoTrac, ProQuest, Lexis/Nexis Academic Universe,* and *Ebsco Academic Search.*

These resources allow you to enter key terms to find articles from well-known journals, magazines, government documents, and other reference works. Using these sources, you can be sure you are getting more reliable and timely information than you will find on most general Web sites.

When searching on the databases, you can make your search much easier by using the Boolean method of searching. This method is named after logician George Boole, who founded the idea of symbolic logic.

Three Major Boolean Search Terms

1. **"AND"**—When you combine two words using AND, you will narrow your search to articles that contain both of these words. For instance, if you searched for "schools," you might get thousands of articles dealing with schools. A second search for "uniforms" would find similar, overwhelming results. However, if you combined the words with AND to search for "uniforms AND schools," your choices would be narrowed down to articles that deal with the idea you wish to explore. The more words you add, the more specific you can make your search. You could search for "uniforms AND schools AND mandatory policies" to get an even more specific search result.

2. **"NOT"**—Adding NOT will narrow your search, too, but by excluding words. For instance, if you found that too many articles for "uniforms AND schools" were about private schools, you might change your search to "uniforms AND schools NOT private."

3. **"OR"**—Using OR in the search will broaden your results if your search finds too few sources. It is best used with terms that have common synonyms, such as "elementary OR primary." OR is usually used in parentheses, so a search might look like this: "uniforms AND schools AND (elementary or primary)."

Keyword Searching on the Web

reocognize
US

recognise
Brit.

organization
US

organisation
Brit.

If you conduct your search on a keyword search engine on the Web, many of the search engines will assume the "OR" when you enter keywords. This results in the search engine finding any site that has any of the words you entered. Your search on "uniforms in public schools" might find every site that mentions any of the words you entered. The result might be hundreds of sites on "public housing" or "schools of business," which obviously aren't relevant. Some search engines recognize the plus sign (+) as a type of Boolean search method. You might type "uniforms + schools + mandatory." This would narrow your results considerably.

If you decide to use Internet sites for your paper, however, you need to be aware of some of the problems that can occur. When you go to the library for information, you know that librarians have carefully selected the books and journals inside. On the Internet, there are no such safeguards. Therefore, it is important that you learn to evaluate information for yourself when searching the Web. To be a critical user of the Internet, you should be aware of the strengths and weaknesses of the Web as a research tool.

Strengths of the Web

- Great place to find basic factual information:
    financial statistics
    the address of a member of Congress
- Tends to be more current than print sources
- Excellent for recent and breaking news stories
    (CNN and *The New York Times* both have their own Web sites
    for offering up-to-the-minute news and information.)
- Offers interesting sites and information when used as a supplement
  to library research

Weaknesses of the Web

- Most copyrighted materials are not available for free.
- Some books and journals do allow access to some but not all of their articles.
- The Web cannot be used as a substitute for the library.
- On many sites, you have no way of knowing if the "facts" given are accurate.

If you decide to use the Web for research, you must learn to judge whether the information you find comes from credible and objective sources. The five criteria that have traditionally been used to evaluate sources are **accuracy, authority, objectivity, currency,** and **coverage.**

These five criteria also work well for evaluating Web sites. Consider what each of the five areas includes.

Accuracy—refers to the level of reliability of the information. Since anyone can put anything on the Web, it is important to double-check the facts you find on a Web page.

Authority—the person or organization providing the information needs to be known as an authority on the subject. If not, try to find another reliable source to verify the information.

Example:

If you get information from *Stephen Hawking's Universe* Web site, you know that the information is put there by Stephen Hawking, a well-known physicist, and the site is sponsored by PBS, a reliable producer. You can feel certain that what you find on this site comes from an authority in the field.

Sometimes, however, the authority of the site won't be so obvious. Authority can be determined by looking for certain information.

- Is the author of the page identified?
- What are his/her credentials?
- Who sponsors the Web site?
- Is it a well-known organization?
- Are they the best known source for the information?

Objectivity—To determine if a site contains objective, unbiased information, you need to learn more about the different types of sites that exist on the Web.

Often, the most trustworthy and objective sites end in .edu (for educational sites) and .gov (for government sites). Their main purpose is to deliver information, and they are held accountable for the information that is disseminated. Sites ending in .org are organizations, and they tend to have a bias on the subject. While an organization is most likely legitimate, you need to be aware of the organization's agenda in providing the information. Sites ending in .com are corporate sites, and their main purpose is to sell their products. The individual home page, created by an individual, should be viewed with a very critical eye, especially since the author is often anonymous.

Currency—This is one of the Web's greatest strengths. However, the date should be clearly noted on the page, and it should indicate whether the date means when the work was produced, when it was first published on the Web, or the last update.

Coverage—To determine coverage, you can look at whether or not the sources of the page's information are cited and whether or not the links on a page work. In addition, ask yourself these questions:

- What topics are included in the work?
- Does the page compare to print sources on the same topic?
- Are the topics explored in-depth?

When you use Web sources in your paper, make sure you don't plagiarize. Web sites are copyrighted just like printed works, so be very careful that you cite the source accurately in the paper and include the source in your works cited list.

Citing Web Pages

The rules of citing Web pages are constantly changing and developing as new technologies emerge, but there are principles that have been established. The major components are the same for most citation styles. These components include:

- name of the author
- title
- place of publication
- publisher's name
- date of publication
- page number

For electronic sources, these components are similar, but they must be translated to make sense in the electronic environment. For example, instead of an author name, you may have only an e-mail address; and instead of page numbers, you may have paragraphs and screen numbers. See pages 87–90 for current MLA and APA bibliography styles.

As mentioned earlier, the system of documenting electronic sources is constantly changing with new technology. The need to completely rethink the way we research and document sources indicates the rapid changes that are taking place in technology. Future changes in online research will likely occur at an increasingly fast pace. The evolution of computers has been exciting and dynamic, and keeping up with this technology has become increasingly important in today's information-based society.

Writing a Research Essay

Writing a research essay involves sifting through information from other sources, reading and understanding the material, and developing a tentative thesis for your essay. Once your tentative thesis is established, you can modify it to become your final thesis, the statement you wish to prove in the essay. In this section you will learn to gather research, develop a thesis, and write a research essay.

Of all those arts in which the wise excel,
Nature's chief masterpiece is writing well.

—DUKE OF BUCKINGHAM SHEFFIELD

Objectives

➤ conduct rudimentary research by gathering information and sifting through it to arrive at a conclusion

➤ quote, paraphrase, and summarize another author's words

➤ develop a working thesis and final thesis for your essay

➤ write a research essay to prepare you before attempting a larger, more involved research paper

Section Preview

Now that you know the basics of essay writing, including the thesis statement, the introduction, the body, and the conclusion, you are in good shape to add research writing to your skills. Instead of depending on personal information for your essay, research writing requires that you deal with topics unfamiliar to you. To write a successful research essay, you will need to learn how to find information from outside sources and incorporate the sources into an essay.

There are more steps to research writing because you are working with information you don't already know. In order to get the information, you have to consult outside sources. When you write a research essay, you start by completing the following steps:

1. sifting through information from other sources
2. reading and understanding the material
3. developing a tentative thesis for your essay

Once you have your tentative thesis, you collect information to support it. To use the sources in your essay, you will paraphrase and organize the information and then reevaluate your thesis to see if it all works. Finally, you will write the paper, paying particular attention to controlling the style of your writing.

Practice Writing Assignments

➤ Find on microfilm the issue of any major national newspaper that was published on your birthday.

➤ Note the stories on the front page, as they would have been considered the most important news stories on that date.

➤ Skim the stories on the front page to see if you can come up with a thesis linking two events reported on this same day.

By completing these three steps, you are covering the first steps of research writing: sifting through the unfamiliar source material, reading it, and processing it. You are trying to come to an understanding about the source content. Do you see any connections between the newspaper stories? Perhaps several of the stories deal with energy-related topics. Or maybe that day's news focused on peace talks and peacekeeping missions overseas. Regardless, you should be able to find some common link between the stories for a working thesis.

For most research papers, you will have to use more than just one source, and for longer papers, keeping track of all the information could be intimidating. To tackle the challenge of keeping up with all the information you find during your research, you must have a system. As you start collecting reliable sources for any research paper, browse for ideas and skim some periodicals and book titles. Let your *thesis* grow as you learn more about the subject. Remember to be flexible; it is expected that your *working thesis* will change as the paper develops.

Working thesis:

A working or tentative thesis is the general, basic statement that you hope to prove in the paper or essay. Because it is a working thesis, it can be changed, expanded, strengthened, and modified during the writing process.

Thesis:

The thesis is a statement, usually appearing in the introduction, giving readers the main topic of a piece of writing. In an argumentative essay, the thesis states the central idea that the paper will prove.

summarize
US

summarise
Brit.

organize
US

organise
Brit.

Once you have a thesis, you will want to think about taking all your source material and writing about it in a good research style. In our newspaper assignment, this calls for turning the newspaper writing style into research writing style. An important skill here is to know when to quote material and when to paraphrase or summarize it.

Paraphrasing involves taking the writer's ideas and putting them into your own words. The catch is that to paraphrase someone's ideas, you must understand them. For example, if you read a chapter in a book and can't summarize it in your own words for someone else, you probably didn't understand it. If you don't understand your source material, neither will your reader. A general guideline to remember is that any time you plan to use more than two words in a row as written in the source, you will need to use quotation marks. So, when using a source, you must make the decision to quote the material, paraphrase it, or summarize it in your own words. Of course statistics, dates, and other specific information will need to be quotes, as you would find it difficult to paraphrase this kind of information.

Quote:

When you record the author's writing word for word from a source, you must place the words in quotation marks when you use them in your own paper.

Paraphrase:

When you read and understand the author's words from a source, you can reword the information for your own paper. This technique of reworking what the author intended is called paraphrasing.

Summary:

Unlike the paraphrase, which rewords the author's writing, the summary condenses the information.

Once you have decided what you will quote and what you will paraphrase, it is time to put it all together. Keep in mind that a research essay is more than a string of paraphrases, summaries, and quotes. As the writer, you will have to draw on the skills you have already practiced in other types of essay writing to make your paper flow smoothly.

As discussed on page 9, use of transitional words and phrases will help connect your thought. In addition, lead-in and signal phrases will help alert the reader to upcoming source material.

Your paper might read,

"In the September 24 edition of *Coastal Daily News*, Allison Reeves professes her beliefs regarding control of boaters in navigable waterways leading to the coast."

By using a signal phrase for the above paraphrase, the writer helped the reader to ease into the material. Some student papers read as if the student wrote out some simple paragraphs and then went back inserting quotes and paraphrases here and there to meet the word count. The result is a choppy, incoherent paper that isn't likely to impress the reader. Making solid connections between sources also helps your reader follow your train of thought in a research essay. Consider again the newspaper assignment. If you want to show how two or more stories relate to one another, you must do more than write a summary of each article. Using examples and specific details from each article to show how they related will make your paper read as a connected, well-thought-out essay. Furthermore, the use of topic sentences helps tie paragraphs together for a unified essay. Remember, any sentence in the body paragraphs that doesn't relate to the main point of the paper needs to be rewritten.

Remembering the basic steps used for the research essay in this newspaper exercise will help you when you are faced with a more complex and challenging research paper. Even in a longer, more involved research essay, the steps are the same. Your sources will just be more varied, and thus there will be more "headlines" from which to choose. The goal is to produce a paper that someone unfamiliar with the news stories can understand on the first reading.

Research

Narrowing the Focus

So far, you have learned how to better communicate your ideas and use the library, and you have had experience with the research essay, which is a precursor to the larger, more formal research paper that will be addressed now. In this section you will be introduced to the nine steps of research writing, and you will learn to complete the first of those two steps: learning to select and narrow a topic by asking focusing questions and working with available resources.

If there is something that you are interested in,
there is no better way to learn about it than to write.

—CLYDE EDGERTON

Objectives

➤ complete the first two stages of your research: selecting and narrowing your topic

➤ choose a topic that interests you

➤ make sure your subject can be adequately covered given the assigned paper length and time

➤ ask focusing questions to limit your scope

➤ work with available resources to narrow your topic

Section Preview

Buying a bicycle or going on vacation are both instances where you would do some research. These real-life examples are very similar to research that you will do for a paper. You communicate the decision you make, and you support your decision through your research.

A research project is simply gathering information and sifting through it to arrive at a conclusion. Then, you communicate your ideas in writing.

What a Research Project Is NOT

➤ A research project is not simply a thesis supported by one source. One source will not be enough information to arrive at a conclusion, nor will it give you enough information to create an accurate picture of your subject.

➤ A research project is not a number of quotes from various sources strung together. The end result would be a paper filled with everyone's ideas except your own.

➤ The point of the project is not to repeat what has been said before, but to demonstrate how what you have learned has shaped your thinking on the topic.

organize
US

organise
Brit.

Now that you know what a research paper is not, you will be relieved to know that there is a simple formula you can use to organize your thoughts and write effectively.

When writing a research paper, follow these steps:

1. Select your topic and narrow your focus.
2. As you research, list your sources and take notes.
3. State the objective of the paper in the form of a thesis.
4. Develop a working outline.
5. Write a first draft.
6. Revise the draft for structure and style.
7. Proofread and correct the draft.

This section will focus on selecting and narrowing your topic. If your teacher doesn't assign a specific topic, it is important to select a subject you are interested in. Keeping in mind that your research project will not be a personal essay, avoid topics that you are already well acquainted with because you will waste time trying to find information that matches what you already know.

Choosing a subject also depends on what information is available and on your deadline. If you choose an obscure topic, you may not find enough information in a library or on line. On the other hand, choosing an overly broad topic such as "Health Issues" will result in more information than any writer could handle. While the word count your teacher assigns may seem daunting at first, a paper of, for example, 2,000 words is relatively short when you consider broad topics like "School Uniforms," "Gun Control," or "Childcare." Depending on the due date and assigned length, you will need to make decisions about how much or how little you can cover in the paper.

Many times you will be given a general subject for an assigned topic, and it will be up to you to narrow it down. You should focus on a specific angle or aspect of the subject to explore in your research project. For example, suppose the assignment is to profile someone who has had a significant impact on society. There are hundreds of possibilities, ranging from political figures to trendsetters to athletes. An assignment such as this one will allow you to write on the given topic while narrowing down to a person who interests you.

After you have selected a topic, it will be time to narrow the subject. Your assignment will probably have a word count minimum and maximum, and you can have too much of a good thing if you don't narrow your focus. When looking at your topic, choose one question to explore. This allows you the luxury of concentrating on one area, not diluting your paper with too many peripheral issues.

As you narrow your topic and begin the process of finding source material, it is imperative that you have more than one source for your paper. The success of your paper is weighed by the quality of your sources, and you must find the middle ground between not enough sources and too many sources.

Working through the process of narrowing your topic involves the following steps:

1. Scan the resources.
2. Generate questions to explore.
3. Review available resources.
4. Focus on one question.

As an example, think back to the bike research example given earlier. If you are looking for a good bike, you probably will not buy the first bicycle you see. You will first consult numerous sources before making a purchase. You might check Consumer Reports, read cycling magazines, and make phone calls to various bike shops. This "research" would help you find a good quality bike within your budget.

Suppose your assignment is to write a research paper of 600 words on services for seniors in your town. After doing some preliminary research, you would need to narrow the focus. Starting with plenty of information allows you the luxury of choice in your topic. The value of narrowing is that you can concentrate on one area and not dilute the paper with too many peripheral issues. Once you have narrowed to one specific aspect, you will begin to gather research that further discusses the more focused topic.

Once you have located some of the articles you plan to use in the research project for your class, you will need to ask yourself the all-important five "W" questions shown at right.

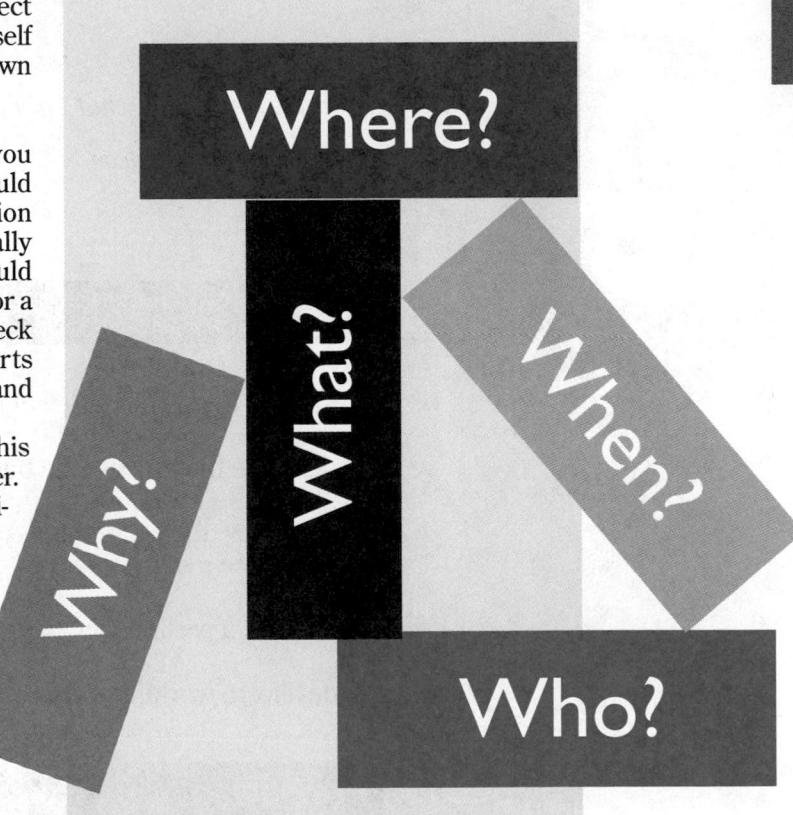

To answer most of these questions, you could go straight to the source. You could interview an employee from the Division of Blind Services for a paper on visually impaired seniors. Another example would be a student interviewing a veterinarian for a paper on animal clinics. As long as you check their credentials, interviews with experts can be as good a source as periodicals and newspapers.

Completing the steps mentioned in this section will help you write a focused paper. The next time you are assigned a multi-source research paper, be sure to follow these steps:

1. Choose a topic that interests you.
2. Make sure your topic can be researched using available resources.
3. Be certain your topic will fit the length of the assignment.
4. Scan your resources to help you narrow your focus.
5. Generate questions and explore those questions (the five "Ws").
6. Focus on one question to further explore.
7. Be flexible.

The final entry in the list, "Be flexible," is an important one since the process of selecting and narrowing a topic is an ongoing task. If you remain flexible, you will avoid being trapped in an unmanageable situation, and you might discover a research paper that is far more interesting than you expected!

Preparing a Bibliography/ Developing a Thesis

Just like other elements of the research paper, you may know more about putting together a bibliography and formulating your thesis than you realize. Whenever you set out to get something done, you put together an informal bibliography. If you were trying to choose a daycare center for a two-year-old child, you would make a list of the centers in your area, how to reach them, and where they are located. You would proceed to research each center until you had found the one most suitable for the child. At work, an address book in a computer is a perfect example of a bibliography of business contacts. Each entry has the name of the person, the address, phone number, and e-mail address. This gathering of information is like a bibliography. In this section you will be introduced to three categories of research: overview, focusing, and supporting materials. You will learn to use what you find in your research to create a bibliography and a working thesis statement.

Basic research is what I am doing when I don't know what I am doing.

—Wernher von Braun

Objectives

➤ identify three categories of research materials: overview, focusing, and supporting

➤ describe the differences between primary and secondary resource materials

➤ recognize the correct MLA (Modern Language Association) format for noting reference materials

➤ prepare a preliminary bibliography with note cards

➤ develop a working thesis statement

Section Preview

In a *bibliography* for a research paper, you start investigating what each book or article says about your topic. You keep careful records of all resources that you find, so that when you go back to look at the information more closely, you will be able to find each source without having to look it up again.

As you collect your material, keep in mind the three basic types of research information: overview material, focusing material, and supporting material.

Overview Material

Overview material can be found in general reference books, like encyclopedias. This kind of information gives you a starting point and helps you establish the boundaries of your search. Include the dictionary and thesaurus in your overview materials, as they help you identify keywords related to your topics. These keywords and synonyms might direct you to related subjects that will narrow your search.

Focusing Material

Focusing material gives you more specific information about your topic, helping you find the books and articles available. Focusing material also helps you narrow down a topic that is too broad. A reference librarian can point you in the direction of specialized sources and search engines for your topic.

Supporting Material

For anyone writing a research paper, the last elements of research information are called *supporting materials.* Specific articles, books, interviews, videos, and brochures are in this category because of the details they provide that help you develop your perspective and support your thesis. There are two types of supporting materials: primary and secondary. *Primary resources* consist of books, articles, and other materials written by the person you are interested in studying. *Secondary resources,* however, include anything written about the subject by another person.

Primary Resources: Books written BY Robert Penn Warren

Secondary Resources: Books written ABOUT Robert Penn Warren, often with excerpts from the primary source

center
US
centre
Brit.
recognize
US
recognise
Brit.
encyclopedias
US
encyclopaedias
Brit.
specialized
US
specialised
Brit.

17 English Writing

Working Bibliography

Simply put, a *working bibliography* is a list of the works you will use in preparing your paper. However, the bibliography is more than just a simple list. It is a crucial compilation of potential sources to get you started on a research paper. A working bibliography should help you:

- narrow the focus of your subject
- adapt the topic to your particular interest
- evaluate whether you have enough information to write a paper
- arrive at a working thesis

As you put your working bibliography together, it is best to use index cards for your notes, rather than notebook paper or little slips of paper. Index cards allow you to:

- order and reorder the arrangement of your notes
- alphabetize your bibliography for the works cited page
- add new resource listings without rewriting

Use one card per source you find on your subject, and then alphabetize your bibliography for the works cited page of your final paper.

As you find a source that looks interesting and relevant to your topic, make a new card for it. Since at this point you are creating a working bibliography, your cards represent any information you might possibly use for further reference. You may not use them all in the final paper, but it is crucial that you write down all possible sources in this early stage of research. Students who keep poor research notes often find themselves in a position where they want to use a source they stumbled upon earlier, only to find out later that they can't find it again. Keeping accurate notes enables you to go directly back to a source, and when writing on a deadline, this is a necessity. A card should contain:

- the author's name (last name first)
- the title
- the publication information (publisher, date)
- the library call number, www. address, or other detailed notes of exactly where the source can be found

Johnson, Charles

The Photography of Martin Luther King, Jr.

Penguin Group.

New York, New York. 2000

E 185.97.

The samples included here follow the *Modern Language Association (MLA)* guidelines, but your teacher may ask you to use the *American Psychological Association (APA)* guidelines, the Chicago Style, or some other specified guideline. Be sure to ask which style he or she wishes you to follow, and be certain you have the most recent edition of the style manual.

No matter where you get your information, or what you choose to ultimately use in the final paper, remember that writing a bibliography is an ongoing process. Even as you begin to read through your supporting material, you may find new sources that will add depth and texture to your paper. In addition, as you read through the information you have assembled, you will begin to form certain opinions on your topic, which will be used to develop a tentative thesis.

Do you remember the definition of a thesis? Thinking back, a thesis is a statement of the main point and central idea of your paper. The vitally important thesis statement, like the bibliography, is also a work in progress. It is expected that your thesis will grow and change as your paper develops, starting as a working thesis and changing over time to become your final thesis.

It is also important to remember that the thesis statement is not simply a statement of fact. Rather, it is a statement about the facts. For example, the statement "Federal employees are not allowed to strike" is a fact. If you wrote, "Federal employees should have the same rights as all other employees, including the right to strike," then you are making a statement about the facts—one you can argue for or against.

analyze
US

analyse
Brit.

Rules to Follow for Creating a Working Thesis

1. A thesis is stated in the form of a declarative sentence, not in the form of a question. A thesis can come from a question, but it should never end with a question mark.
2. The thesis cannot be a statement of fact, but it is rather a statement about the facts.
3. You must be able to prove your thesis with solid facts. Proving your thesis is the basic point of a research paper.
4. A thesis should be precise and to the point. Vague, general, broad language will not work here.
5. Make sure your thesis limits the range of the topics and presents an idea manageable enough to guide the length and scope of your research paper.

Both the working bibliography and the working tentative thesis are important in helping you to form and guide your investigation and the paper that will result. Give yourself enough time to work through the processes of research writing, and the end result will be a paper of which you can be proud.

Research

Gathering Information

When you select a special section of the newspaper to read or decide to watch one TV program instead of another, you are making decisions based on what you think will be the most informative, the most useful, or perhaps the most interesting. You are evaluating your choices and making judgments. Selecting materials for your research paper is done in much the same way. You select sources and collect information based on what you think is important for your research. You may find that some materials are more valuable than others, just as you may discover that the TV program you have selected is not as good as you had expected it to be. In this section, you will be presented with tips and techniques for taking notes, and you will learn the difference between fact and opinion. By following the suggestions in this section, you will learn that taking notes is a manageable process.

If we knew what we were doing, it would not be called research, would it?

—ALBERT EINSTEIN

Objectives

➤ determine if a source is relevant, current, and valuable

➤ differentiate between general and specific source material

➤ recognize highly technical versus consumer-level wording

➤ analyze the credibility of a source and its author(s)

➤ keep note cards for quotes, paraphrases, summaries, and keywords

➤ understand and avoid the serious offense of plagiarism

➤ distinguish opinion from fact

➤ avoid leaping to incorrect conclusions

Section Preview

It is hard to tell in the beginning of the research writing process what kind of material you will include in your final paper. That is where careful note taking can help you evaluate what you have found. In the preceding sections, you have learned to do the following:

1. Choose your topic and narrow it.
2. Search for information on your topic.
3. Prepare a preliminary bibliography.
4. Decide on a tentative thesis.

Now it's time to read through all the resources you have collected on your subject and jot down the main ideas in each. That way, you will be able to prioritize them later on. This is part of step two in the process: *taking notes.*

In any research paper, the proof of your argument will depend heavily on the strength of your research and on how thoroughly you collect your information. Beyond collecting the sources, you must selectively use that information to build your argument. Therefore, it is important to be able to evaluate your sources and to use them effectively. After you have prepared your preliminary bibliography, you will need to skim through your resources to find relevant material for your notes. The goal is to evaluate the author's purpose by asking yourself some questions as you read and review the material.

- Does the thesis/main idea of the article, book, etc., support or aid my thesis?
- Will this information help me make my case?
- Are there any examples, information, statistics that back up my main points?

A "yes" to these questions will help you decide if the information you have gathered is going to serve the purpose of your assignment. You must further ask yourself these questions:

- Is the source *relevant?*
- Is the source *current?*
- Is the information *valuable?*

To know if a source is *relevant,* you must understand your own thesis statement. The best, most relevant sources are the ones which are most closely related to your thesis. To determine the relevancy early in the research process, you might check the preface, table of contents, and index of the reference material. You might also quickly skim the article to look for information that relates to the points you want to make in your paper.

Maybe you are working on a tentative thesis about organ donation and the possibility of financial compensation to the donor. It's easy to see that an article on the success of the first organ transplant is a bit off topic, but an article on pending laws regarding selling organs might hold some promise.

A source may be considered relevant even if it refutes or opposes your points of view. How can this statement be true? In an argumentative/persuasive paper, it is often important to present the opposing viewpoints. In your paper, you can refute the opposition with your own arguments, making your assertions even more valid.

To determine if a source is current, you will need to find out when it was published. Ask yourself these questions:

- How recent is the information?
- Is it current enough to be credible?
- Are there recent publications to help determine if the information is still valid?

To make sure you have the latest information, check magazine and journal articles on the subject first. They are usually the most up-to-date sources of information.

It is important that you understand the changing nature of your topic when deciding if your source is current. Five years may not seem like a long time, but for dynamic topics like managed healthcare and organ donation, you could be overlooking new, relevant information, including laws, court cases, and recent examples, if all the information you use is from years past. Of course, you will probably need to read and understand some background information and history of your topic, but the focus of your argument can't be based on old information.

To determine if a source is *valuable,* you must be able to assess the information in each source. This process calls for some judgment on your part. It is important to remember that not all sources are equal. What you read is written by an author with a specific perspective and goal. Some authors may be better informed than others, and some may have a personal investment in the issue. As you might suspect, some authors may not care what opinion the reader forms as long as the authors make money from what was written. With the advent of the Internet, it is more important than ever that you learn to judge the value of a source. Almost anyone can put almost anything on the Web, so you must be extremely careful that you don't base your work on unreliable sources, either print or electronic forms.

You can determine the value of your source if you start by asking yourself some important questions about the kind of information you have and whether it is credible.

- Is the information *general* or *specialized*?
- Is the information *highly technical?*
- What are the *credentials* of the person who wrote the information?

specialized
US

specialised
Brit.

General or Specialized?

It depends on your thesis, but usually it is easier to find information that gives you a general overview of the topic. Of course, it is not very helpful to have nothing except information of a general nature. By the same token, sources that are too specialized may result in a list of facts that are too narrow to give your reader the big picture—something necessary if you are going to be able to help your readers understand your topic and how it could affect them.

Highly Technical?

You must consider your audience when you answer this question. If you are writing your paper on organ donation, you don't want to get bogged down in technical, scientific, or medical terms that mean nothing to your readers. This is where knowing your audience is key. How much do your readers know about the topic? You don't want to write "over their heads," but you would also be making a mistake if you wrote in an elementary, simplified style.

Credentials?

Ask yourself about the credentials of the person who wrote the information you are considering.

- Is he or she an authority?
- Has he or she studied the issue?
- Has he or she worked in the field?
- Is the author possibly just disgruntled and using the opportunity to vent?

The answers to these questions aren't always obvious. Almost every author has some sort of agenda. This doesn't mean the information isn't credible, but most authors don't publish work for the fun of it. There is always a goal in mind. In assessing the value of the information you find, it is up to you to try to investigate what the author's agenda might be. Then you can decide if there is doubt regarding the credibility of your source. Remember too the importance of closely examining Web sources and their authors.

Four Formats for Note Taking

When you began building your preliminary bibliography, you completed bibliography note cards. As you might guess, you can't build a strong research paper with only a list of facts, regardless of how current and credible the source may be. As you incorporate sourced information into your paper, you will need to use a variety of methods for including outside information. Sometimes you will use the author's exact words as a direct quote. Other times, you will paraphrase and summarize the ideas in the article. Regardless, you must give credit to the source, so keeping careful notes is critical. Following is an explanation of the types of note cards (in addition to your bibliographic cards) you should keep during the research process.

1—Note Cards for Direct Quotation

Using direct quotes ensures that the meaning of the author's words won't be lost. Direct quotes also add credibility to the information you are presenting. If you find a quote you think you may want to use, be sure you copy it down carefully, word for word. Make sure your author, title, and page are accurately recorded as well. Quotes from reliable sources can add emotion, power, and reliability to your writing when used properly. Don't overdo it, though. Too many direct quotes can work against your paper by causing you, the author, to have no voice. The paper is YOUR argument. The sources are there to back up and further your points.

2—Note Cards for Paraphrasing

Paraphrasing puts the information from all sources in the same style. When you paraphrase, you put the author's ideas into your own words. Paraphrasing can be difficult because it forces you to think critically. You must truly understand the source before you can put it into your own words. To check that you have correctly paraphrased an idea, you should:

- double-check the source to see if you have included all the necessary information in your paraphrase
- make sure you have stated the meaning completely in your own words
- check to be certain that you have not included your own comments and reactions
- be careful that you have documented the source for your bibliography or list of references

3—Note Cards for Summarizing

summarizing
US

summarising
Brit.

Summarizing is similar to paraphrasing. However, when you summarize, you condense the information, picking out the basics and leaving out the rest of the detail. This means that an entire paragraph could be summarized in just one sentence. To illustrate, think about how you summarize a movie for a friend who asks. You probably summarize the basics and leave out the details. This is different from paraphrasing, where you would be giving much more detail. Another good example of paraphrasing can often be found in the introduction of a book. The inside jacket of most novels contains a summary (without giving away the ending, of course!). The start of each section on research writing also summarizes the important points.

4—Note Cards for Keywords

Keyword note cards contain words and phrases that give you a shorthand version of the information. The main ideas of your topic will be found on these kinds of note cards. A review of your keyword note cards can reveal where there are gaps in your information. If you have established in your early research on organ donation that "voluntary donations from prison inmates" is a key concept, a review of your keyword cards might remind you that you haven't addressed this issue yet.

Now that we have discussed note taking, this is a good time to address the very serious issue of *plagiarism*. Plagiarism is stealing; it is the theft of someone else's words and ideas and passing them off as your own. Intentional and even accidental plagiarism is a serious offense. Students who use the Internet to buy term papers, use a roommate's paper from last term, copy directly from a source, or keep sloppy notes and accidentally use something in the paper without properly sourcing it are all guilty of the same offense: plagiarism.

Keeping careful, precise notes will eliminate the occurrence of accidental plagiarism, so be sure you follow the methods described for keeping note cards. In addition, remember the following:

1. Keep in mind that just changing a few words in a quote is not paraphrasing.
2. You must significantly restate the idea for it to be a true paraphrase or summary.
3. When you find a passage you want to paraphrase, read over it until you are sure of its meaning.
4. Put the original version of the information away, and then write your version.

If you follow these suggestions, your paraphrase is likely to be changed enough that it is not plagiarism.

Fact vs. Opinion

During the note taking and research phase of writing, it is important that you learn to distinguish *facts* from *opinions*. A person's opinion is not necessarily fact. Even when the person in question is an admired, credible author, you must determine if the information she puts forth is her opinion or fact. A fact is generally accepted as something that has been documented and backed up by reliable, valid research and statistics. An opinion is an individual conclusion formed after a person views and interprets the facts. An article with stated opinions isn't necessarily a bad source, but be careful that you don't mistakenly present (in your paper) the author's opinion as fact.

Fact:

Thursday night, a weapon was found under the gym bleachers at Lee High School.

This statement can be proven. If true, it is a fact.

Opinion:

The weapon found in the gym probably belonged to one of the Lee High School basketball players who practiced Thursday in the gym.

This statement is purely conjecture or a guess about who owned the weapon. This statement is opinion.

Drawing Conclusions

As you read and evaluate data, you are bound to draw some conclusions. How do you avoid leaping to incorrect conclusions? Ask yourself:

- Is there enough information to draw a solid conclusion?
- Is the information up-to-date?
- What is the point of the article, book, Web site, etc.?

Being able to pick out the central idea in any source is crucial to the research process. Just as your thesis statement is the main point you raise in your paper, remember that every source you read also contains a thesis statement. Try not to get sidetracked when reading an article. Go back and skim the source after you have finished reading it to ensure that you have an overview of the main idea. To capture your thoughts after reading a source, write it down in your notes for later.

17 English Writing

Preparing a Tentative Outline

Just as an architect develops a blueprint for building a house, you should prepare an outline before writing your research paper. In the past, you may have scribbled a few notes to yourself before starting to write, but when you undertake a major writing project such as a research paper, you must have a plan from which to work. This written plan is your outline. Although it is difficult to plan a paper completely in advance of actually writing the first draft, an outline will help you order your main points and guide your note card arrangement.

Writing is easy. All you do is stare at a blank sheet of paper until drops of blood form on your forehead.

—GENE FOWLER

Objectives

➤ create a working outline

➤ test your information against your thesis statement

➤ establish an organization for your paper

➤ identify strong areas in your work

➤ recognize and correct weak areas in your research

➤ stay flexible in regard to the working thesis and outline

Section Preview

Using an outline isn't a concept used only when writing a paper. People use "outlines" for many tasks. Architects use a set of blueprints, an outline of a structure, to tell the builder how to put the structure together. Cooks use recipes, an outline of ingredients, to know how to prepare certain foods. An outline, for many purposes, is a plan. It is a rough sketch of what is to happen.

For your research paper, an outline helps you organize your thoughts. Since your ideas may change, you will start with a working outline, one that can and will change. The formal outline presents a condensed treatment of the final product, which is your completed paper. A formal outline is actually put together after the paper is written and presented in a very structured format. It precedes the rest of the paper, like a table of contents would in a book. The formal outline helps your reader understand the content and organization of what he or she is about to read. Your teacher may or may not ask you to complete and submit a formal outline, but you should complete a working outline regardless.

The working outline is an important tool to help you organize all the information you have collected during the research phase of your paper. Outlining is a step in the process of research writing that you do not want to skip.

Best Carrot Cake

2 cups flour
2 teaspoons baking soda
1/2 teaspoon salt
2 teaspoons cinnamon
3 eggs
2 cups sugar
3/4 cup vegetable oil
3/4 cup buttermilk
2 teaspoons vanilla extract
2 cups grated carrots
1 (8-ounce) can crushed pineapple, drained
1 (3-ounce) can flaked coconut
1 cup chopped pecans or walnuts
Buttermilk Glaze (below)
Cream Cheese Frosting (below)

*L*ine three 9-inch cake pans with waxed paper. Lightly grease and flour the waxed paper.

Mix the flour, baking soda, salt, and cinnamon together. Beat the eggs, sugar, oil, buttermilk, and vanilla at medium speed in a mixing bowl until smooth. Add the flour mixture gradually, beating at low speed until blended. Fold in the carrots, pineapple, coconut, and walnuts. Pour into the prepared pans.

Bake at 350 degrees for 25 to 30 minutes or until a wooden pick inserted in the center comes out clean. Drizzle the Buttermilk Glaze evenly over the layers. Cool in the pans on wire racks for 15 minutes. Remove from the pans and cool completely on the wire racks. Spread the Cream Cheese Frosting between the layers and over the top and side of the cake. (You may prepare 1 day ahead.) *Yield: 12 servings.*

recognize
US

recognise
Brit.

organize
US

organise
Brit.

Outlining Helps You

➤ Keep the paper focused

➤ Test information to make sure it fits the thesis

➤ Establish a tentative organization of the paper

➤ Identify the strong and weak areas of information

➤ Guide the direction of the writing

The working outline can help you keep your work focused by ensuring the information you have fits the thesis. It sets up the plan on how your paper will be organized and helps you evaluate the information you have gathered. Perhaps the most helpful aspect of the outline is that it serves as a guide when you get ready to write the paper.

Once you are ready to write the outline, you should begin with these steps:

1. Place all of your note cards out in front of you.
2. Use the headings on the cards to help you group them. (If you used the hints offered earlier on note taking, the outline will be easier to write.)
3. As you sort through the cards, put them in groups, looking for similarities.
4. Next, look for which of the headings have the best and most information.
5. In no particular order, write down those headings so that you can assess what you have and what is missing.

When you are finished, you should find a good list of headings, including, for example, some history of your topic, some examples, and some opposition's points.

If you find that your list contains headings that don't relate well to your thesis, eliminate those cards that will not necessarily help you make your argument. Depending on the length of your assignment, you may need to add to or shorten your list. After coming up with a list that contains all the main points that relate to your thesis and supporting arguments, you need to go back and weed out points that are even slightly off focus or those you won't have time to explore in the paper.

The result of looking carefully over your list according to the steps mentioned before should be a strong, focused list of points to cover in the paper. Once you have revised the list of points, arrange them in some sort of logical order so that the most important points are listed first, and the others follow in descending order of importance.

Depending on what works best for you and your teacher, you may follow a traditional form. If so, your outline will contain:

- Roman numerals (I, II, III, etc.) for your main points
- Capital letters (A, B, C, etc.) for your subheadings
- Numbers for any minor ideas under each subheading (1, 2, 3, etc.)
- Lowercase letters for any supporting details (a, b, c, etc.)

Since you are creating a working outline, it is subject to change. You should look closely at your outline to see what your main points are and what evidence supports them. At this point, you may realize that your thesis is too broad or too limited. If this is the case, you can either rework the outline or rework the thesis. If you find that you must change the outline or thesis at this stage, don't be discouraged. Remember that you wrote a *working* thesis and a *working* outline. You should never assume that the thesis you start with is the one you will end up using in the final paper. You must be flexible, especially if the research you have gathered clearly indicates your thesis is off track.

What if you find there is not enough information to prove your thesis? Note how the following thesis evolves.

Starting Thesis:

The introduction of the weather girl brought on an increased interest in weather-related news.

The writer found there wasn't enough information available to justify the thesis.

Revised Thesis:

It takes a combination of technology and personality to bring the viewers to a newscast.

What if you find new or previously unknown information? This is likely to happen as you begin to read through your source material. An example of a thesis that changed when the writer found new information is included here.

Starting Thesis:

High salaries in television news make it an attractive career to college graduates who study journalism.

Revised Thesis:

College graduates still scramble to get jobs in television news, but they are keeping an eye on a recent trend to cut positions and trim salaries.

Another area to consider while creating and revising your working outline is contradictory sources. What if, while organizing your notes, you find a significant disagreement among your sources? This is likely to happen if you are dealing with a controversial issue. You may find that you have to decide which sources are conflicting facts and which sources contain conflicting opinions. You can integrate conflicting facts, and you may choose to do so in order to refute the opposition, but you can't write a thesis based on conflicting opinions.

It is useful to approach the research and outline process with the understanding that your thesis is unproved and may therefore not be entirely valid. After all, careful examination of any plan for action (the outline) can uncover challenges you didn't anticipate. When looking at your outline, view it as an opportunity for a reality check. The key is flexibility, because the working outline is not your formal outline.

Types of Outlines

Topic outline

Title That Lonely Hawthorne Chamber
   I. Introduction
  II. Early Childhood
       A. The early years
       B. Death of father
          1. Effect on Hawthorne
             a. melancholy
             b. sense of loss
          2. Self-imposed isolation of Hawthorne's mother
          3. Life with relatives
 III. New England School Days
       A. Education
       B. Foot injury and subsequent two-year isolation
       C. Life in Maine
  IV. Bowdoin College Days
       A. Education
       B. Companions
       C. Decision to become a writer
   V. The Lonely Chamber—Learning to Write
       A. Twelve years of isolation
          1. Critics—favorable and unfavorable
          2. Writing apprenticeship
       B. Anguishing through his Puritan ancestry
       C. Emergence from the lonely chamber
  VI. Themes in Hawthorne's Works Showing Early Influences
       A. Isolation of mankind
       B. Evils of Puritanism
 VII. Conclusion

Sentence outline

Theme statement Burial rites among the ancient Greeks, the Egyptians, and the Anglo-Saxons differed in detail, but all three groups used cremation and interment, and both the Egyptians and Anglo-Saxons practiced burial at sea.
Title Ancient Burial Rites
   I. Ancient Greeks usually burned their dead heroes.
       A. The *Iliad* recounts the cremation of Hector and Patroclus.
       B. Frequently the ashes of the dead were placed in urns.
       C. Other sections of the *Iliad* suggest interment.
          1. Erection of a barrow for Patroclus.
          2. Other evidence of the existence of barrows.
  II. Egyptians interred their leaders.
       A. Pyramids are seen in the Nile valley.
       B. Archaeologists have found burial ships.
 III. Anglo-Saxons practiced interment, cremation, and ship burial.
       A. There is evidence of interment in *Beowulf*.
       B. In the same poem, Beowulf is burned on a huge pyre.
       C. The Sutton Hoo find reveals the existence of ship burial.
  IV. Conclusion.

Writing the Argumentative Paper

Whenever you look at an issue critically, rather than just accepting any statement as fact, you are learning to argue. Here, you will learn to write an argumentative paper. To be an effective writer of argumentative prose, you must be able to:

1. Determine if your statement is arguable.
2. Identify the audience.
3. Establish credibility.

If you can accomplish these three things, you will be well on your way to writing an effective argumentative paper.

The first essential is to know what one wishes to say;
the second is to decide whom one wishes to say it to.

—HAROLD NICOLSON

Objectives

➤ determine the difference between an arguable and a non-arguable statement

➤ change a non-arguable statement into an arguable one

➤ address the appropriate reader/audience in argumentative writing

➤ establish credibility and persuade your readers by:

   demonstrating your knowledge of a subject

   establishing a common ground with the reader

   demonstrating fairness to opposing viewpoints

➤ use deductive and/or inductive reasoning to support your thesis

➤ avoid logical fallacies

Section Preview

Writing an argumentative paper involves taking one side of an issue and arguing it. As with all writing, the rules are pretty straightforward. To be effective, you must be able to:

1. Make sure the statement you are arguing is arguable.
2. Identify an audience.
3. Be prepared to establish credibility.

Arguable Statements

Some statements are fact, and thus not arguable. Consider the following examples.

1. The temperatures this year are hotter than they have ever been before.
2. The drought is causing millions of dollars in crops to be lost each year.

By simply changing the above factual statements, you can create your argument.

1. The hot temperatures this year are causing more incidents of road rage and fewer acts of kindness toward others.
2. The loss of millions of dollars in crops each year due to drought could be eliminated if water preservation measures were more strictly enforced.

An arguable statement convinces the reader of something or perhaps changes his or her mind about an issue. An arguable statement addresses a problem for which there is no absolute answer. If there aren't at least two sides to an issue, it isn't arguable.

Audience

As a student in an English class, you will submit your paper to a teacher for grading. When you consider the audience for your paper, you are not simply writing to your teacher! Although he or she may be part of your intended audience, you should envision a specific, targeted group for your argumentative essay. Nowhere in the paper should you use words such as, "My audience is . . ." or "I am writing this paper for people against smoking in restaurants." Instead, this audience will be an intended group to which the paper is directed. Assessing your audience is important in writing, speaking, and everyday interaction. Whenever you present information, spoken or written, you must always consider the recipients. If you make this consideration, you are analyzing your audience.

If you keep in mind those to whom you are writing, your paper will be more successful. Knowing the audience helps you decide what words, phrases, and research may be most suited for your document.

Ask yourself these questions when determining audience:

How sophisticated is my audience about this subject already?

- Do they need to have basic concepts and terms defined?
- Are they experts who require more technical terminology and/or more complex concepts?
- Are they already partly persuaded?
- Do they have no stand at all?
- Are they defiantly opposed to my position?

The answers to these questions help you decide the following:

- what information to include and which deserves special emphasis
- what kind of language to use
- which sources will be most credible
- what type of logical approach will be most effective

Once you have established your audience, you must work to build credibility with them. Using the previous examples (drought and road rage), how could you establish credibility? Did you grow up on a farm that was adversely affected by drought? Have you been accosted by an enraged driver on a sweltering hot day? These experiences may be relevant to your argument, but to truly establish credibility, you must use reliable, relevant sources to support your position. You must be able to support your ideas with evidence through varied research.

analyzing
US

analysing
Brit.

As you work, consider that your audience needs to see that you have done extensive research. This means more than finding a couple of books or journals on your topic and incorporating quotes from these books into your paper. Using only Internet sites will not be sufficient, either. Be careful not to use too many Web sites for your research. Keep in mind also that almost anyone can post almost anything on the Web, so you must determine if a Web site contains reliable, credible information. When using an online document, ask yourself these questions:

- Is there an author listed for this site?
- When was the site last updated?
- Could I verify this information by other means? (book, journal, telephone, face-to-face?)

When using any source as a reference to strengthen your argument in an essay, you should determine the following:

- Does this author have an agenda that might skew the information in the article?
- Does the author have a background that lends credibility to the source?
- Who publishes the magazine, journal, or Web site? Could there be a hidden agenda?

Establish Common Ground

To establish common ground with your audience, you can point out those elements of your argument on which all sides agree. For example, regardless of whether you are for or against mandatory drug testing in the workplace, everyone agrees that drug-related accidents should be minimized. You should further:

- Demonstrate fairness
- Refrain from being one-sided
- Show counterarguments
- Show how the other side's view does not weaken your argument

Inductive Reasoning

organizing
US

organising
Brit.

A good argumentative paper is based on an appeal to logic. As you begin organizing your evidence, you will use reasoning to tie your evidence to the claim in your thesis. The two classical approaches to logic into which all critical reasoning falls are *inductive* and *deductive.*

Inductive reasoning proceeds from the specifics—the facts, data, specific examples— to reach a conclusion. For example, arguing on the basis of a single visit that a certain restaurant has excellent food is less convincing than reaching the conclusion after five or six visits and tasting several different meals. Along with examples, statistics are often used in inductive reasoning. When considering statistics, questions you need to satisfy include:

- Is the sample known?
- Is the sample sufficient?
- Is the sample representative?

Deductive Reasoning

Deductive reasoning, as seen in the form of a syllogism constructed by the Greek philosopher Aristotle over two thousand years ago, moves to a logical conclusion from a generally accepted assumption. Complete deductive syllogisms are constructed in the following manner:

Major Premise:

All real estate representatives who sell one million dollars worth of real estate in one year are invited to join the One Million Club.

Minor Premise:

Maria has sold one million dollars worth of real estate in the past year.

Conclusion:

Therefore, Maria will be invited to join the One Million Club.

Questions about your deductive conclusions include:

- Is the premise true?
- Is the syllogism valid?
- Is the language ambiguous?

Avoiding Logical Fallacies

Clear reasoning requires hard work, time, and careful attention to detail. Some people want quick answers and easy solutions. For the sake of argument, they will jump to conclusions or use shortcuts that actually detract from their positions. There are several logical fallacies or errors to avoid as you frame your argument.

Oversimplification occurs when you fail to investigate an idea thoroughly. Instead of recognizing several causes or effects, oversimplification reduces an event to a single cause or effect. Suppose you saw Dr. Smith hugging another woman, a woman who was not his wife. The syllogism to this situation, though faulty, would look like this:

Major Premise:

Dr. Smith was seen hugging another woman.

Minor Premise:

That woman was not his wife.

Conclusion:

Dr. Smith is having an affair.

This action was not proof that Dr. Smith was unfaithful. The other woman could have been his sister, his cousin, his aunt, or even his best friend. While both the major and minor premises are true, the conclusion resulted from failure to investigate more thoroughly.

Another oversimplification error is called *non sequitur* ("it does not follow"), which arrives at a conclusion based on false or nonexistent assumptions. "Because Joe spends generously on dates, he will make a good husband" is a statement in which the conclusion does not logically follow the premise.

Post hoc ergo propter hoc ("after this therefore because of this") assumes that just because one event occurred before another, the first caused the second. Because Joe received a lawn mower for his birthday he will—not necessarily—have the most beautiful lawn on the block.

Circular reasoning restates the argument itself, with no additional evidence, as a reason for accepting it. For instance, the traffic jam on Main Street is the result of too much traffic. This type of reasoning argues in a circle, with no real reason given. Another example would be to say, "I am sick because I don't feel well." Obviously, if you don't feel well you are possibly sick, and if you are sick you don't feel well, so this statement really doesn't tell your audience much.

Learn to recognize the fallacies above, and don't reduce your argument to oversimplified statements.

Personal attack or *name-calling* (*ad hominem*) is an attempt to discredit the opposing view by attacking the person rather than the issue. At no time does this seem more prevalent than during political campaigns. Have you ever noticed how many advertisements run during election years, focusing almost entirely on how "bad" the opponent is?

Not only is personal attack a digression from the issues, it limits the credibility of the one doing the attacking. As a writer, if you resort to name-calling, you will lose some of your own credibility with the audience. Calling someone a "liberal," a "chauvinist," a "communist," or a "feminist" will alienate the very people you are trying to persuade.

A similar situation—*guilt by association*—occurs when someone tries to ascribe the actions of one group to an individual member of the group. Not all men are chauvinists, nor do all Republicans believe in the same things.

Using ambiguous language is another trap to avoid. Do not use vague terminology and undefined abstractions. Note some of the words in the following sentences from student papers. The terms are almost impossible to define in the context in which they are used.

Many people around the world today admire many different athletes.

It has been said that crime in this day and age is a way of life.

In our society today, some words mean different things to different people.

When you use faulty reasoning and vague language in your paper, you weaken your argument. The successful writer builds an argument slowly and pays careful attention to word choice and concrete evidence. The successful writer is aware that a reasonable tone and solid evidence will result in effective communication.

recognize
US

recognise
Brit.

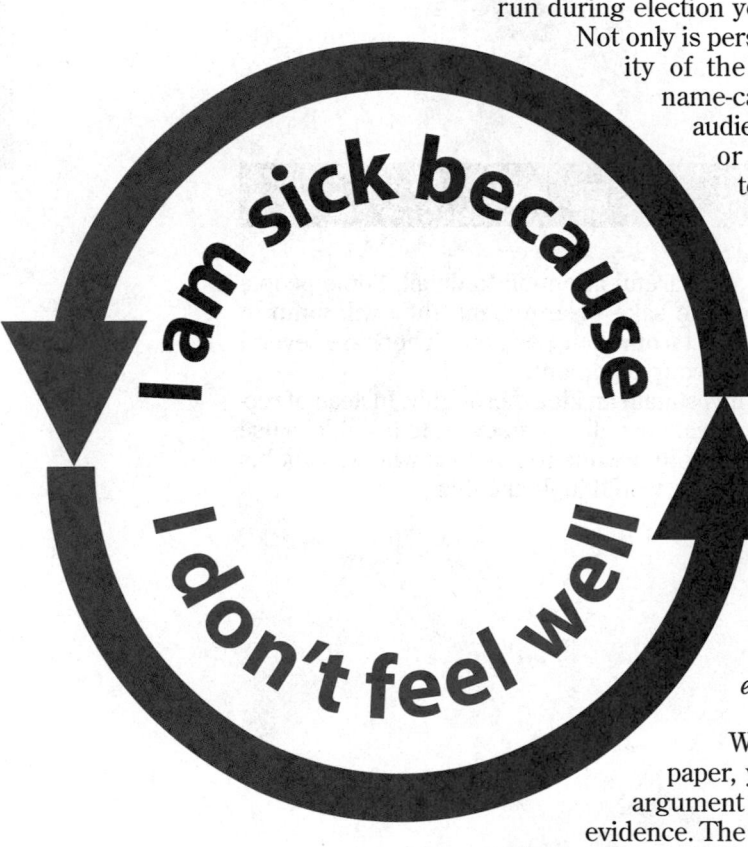

Critiquing the Argumentative Paper

An argumentative paper attempts to convince readers of something, change their minds about an issue, or urge them to take action. When you write in an argumentative style, you should identify and address your audience, establish credibility, and persuade your readers while avoiding logical fallacies. In this section, you will see how to strengthen the thesis statement, recognize the importance of transition, and discuss the importance of a current and varied works cited list.

Creativity is allowing yourself to make mistakes.

—Scott Adams

Objectives

➤ determine if your thesis is arguable

➤ identify the appropriateness of the paper's wording for your audience

➤ establish credibility

➤ use your argumentative skills outside the classroom

➤ recognize weaknesses in your own paper

➤ improve your own argumentative paper by applying some of the principles reviewed

Section Preview

In the previous section, you learned about writing the argumentative paper. This section will go back through the steps of the argumentative paper from a critiquing perspective. After you have written your paper, you will need to critique the most important elements to see if they are solid. As a brief review, take a look at the basic elements of writing an argumentative paper. When you look at your argumentative paper again, are you sure you covered all four areas? Did you:

1. Create an arguable statement? (your thesis)
2. Identify the audience?
3. Establish credibility?
4. Avoid logical fallacies?

An argument is not a statement of belief that cannot be tested. A good argumentative essay will contain a thesis that can be tested. In addition, there will be two sides to the issue, so that a student could write a paper in opposition to your thesis. The following examples of neutral statements turned into arguable statements will illustrate the difference in a statement that can or cannot be argued.

Neutral:

It is hotter today than it was yesterday. (a verifiable fact)

Arguable:

Global warming, caused by hotter temperatures, is destroying the arctic region. (This is not necessarily a fact—some researchers don't believe the changes are significant.)

Neutral:

College freshmen at Valdosta State University are entering with higher SAT scores than ten years ago. (a verifiable fact)

Arguable:

The minimum requirements for admission to Valdosta State University should be raised. (an arguable statement)

Neutral:

Crime statistics show a decrease in robberies and an increase in auto theft. (a verifiable fact)

Arguable:

The "three strikes" law will reduce the number of violent crimes committed in the state. (Opponents don't believe the law will make a noticeable difference.)

By looking at what an argument is not, we can see that an arguable topic is:

- One with two or more defensible sides
- One that can be researched and supported with evidence

defensible
US

defencible
Brit.

Arguable Statements

1. Daylight savings time should become a national standard.
2. Cosmetics manufacturers should not use live animals for product testing.

Not Arguable Statements

1. Daylight savings time provides more hours of daylight after work. (This is true, and therefore not arguable.)
2. Cosmetics manufacturers use live animals for product testing. (Many manufacturers do test products on live animals; this cannot be argued.)

No matter what your thesis statement is, you must consider your purpose. In a good argumentative essay, you seek to discover the truth. Should the minimum admission level for freshmen really be raised? Will the three strikes law really deter crime? To discover the truth, you must convince your audience of the merit of your position and then persuade your audience to act. Look closely at the thesis statement of your argumentative essay to be certain it is an arguable claim. If not, you need to revise it.

Audience Identification

Who is your audience? Is your paper written for a specialized group, one which already has a good deal of knowledge about your topic? If so, you want to make sure you don't write in a style that is too elementary. On the other hand, if your audience isn't as knowledgeable, you will need to avoid using technical language. Any terms that could be unclear should be defined for the less informed audience. Are you wondering who decides on this audience? The answer, for the most part, is you, the writer! You can tailor your paper to fit an audience based on the type of statement you make in the thesis and the direction you take with the argument.

specialized
US

specialised
Brit.

Establishing Credibility

To write a good argument that your audience will believe, you must establish credibility. Have you ever been listening to someone's argument, only later to say, "What does he know about politics (or football, or hockey, etc.)? If that was your feeling, then the speaker didn't establish any credibility with you. You didn't believe that he knew what he was talking about in his argument. When you are writing an argument paper, you must have knowledge of what you are writing about.

Avoiding Logical Fallacies

No matter how strong your thesis is or how well you know your audience, you will have a weak argument if you don't build your paper on an appeal to logic. Whether you choose inductive or deductive reasoning (see pages 72-73), your argument will not stand if you resort to personal attacks, emotionally charged language, or ambiguous language, or if you make an appeal for pity.

Why Do I Need to Learn This Stuff?

Being able to write an effective argument paper has a direct connection to being effective outside the classroom. Attorneys, politicians, salespeople, teachers, parents, and doctors, just to name a few, engage in persuasion all the time. Learning and applying the skills of effective argument relate to more areas than just a class. As you move into college and your professional career, you will find that you need the skills of establishing credibility, speaking or writing appropriately for your audience, and avoiding logical fallacies.

To Check for the Level of Credibility Built into Your Paper, Make Sure You Have

➤ Demonstrated your knowledge—

- used extensive research
- used more than just a few books or periodicals
- didn't rely exclusively on Internet sources
- investigated the credentials of the authors
- looked for objectivity in your sources

➤ Established common ground—

- pointed out elements of your argument on which all sides agree
- worked agreeable areas into your argument to demonstrate a reasonable position

➤ Shown fairness—

- didn't ignore the other positions
- tried to agree or at least sympathize with at least some aspect of the opposition's argument
- supported your argument by refuting other perspectives

realized
US

realised
Brit.

organizing
US

organising
Brit.

Research

Writing the Research Report

By this time, you have spent many hours locating sources, reading your material, taking notes, and developing an outline. If you have narrowed your subject to a workable thesis, you are ready to begin writing the first draft. In this section you will learn some important points to keep in mind as you write the draft of your paper.

Mistakes are the portals of discovery.

—James Joyce

Objectives

➤ expand each thought in the outline with the help of your notes

➤ bridge your ideas and the research together

➤ smoothly incorporate quotes into the text

➤ write the rough draft of the body paragraphs

➤ sketch out the introduction and conclusion paragraphs

Section Preview

During the writing process, you may have realized that writing is a puzzle. This metaphor applies in:

- organizing research
- formulating your outline
- writing the draft

When you assemble a puzzle, you look for similarities, contrasts, and connections among the pieces. You may start assembling the puzzle by putting the border together first and then filling in the middle, or you may put the puzzle together in sections and connect the sections later. There is a similar approach to putting together a first draft. You should have all (or most) of your "pieces" at this point. What you need to do now is fit them all together.

With your note cards and outline, you are already well on your way to organizing your thoughts and developing a solid argument. The outline might be characterized as being like a skeleton. Another way to look at the outline is to consider that the outline is like an architect's blueprint. The blueprint is not the building or house itself, but it is a drawing of what the building will be. This is the role of your outline. The note cards will help you begin the actual construction of the building.

Steps to Writing a Draft

1. Separate note cards by topic heading (which should resemble your outline).
2. Arrange note cards in order of outline.
3. Set deadlines and goals for your writing.
4. Begin writing.

Unlike the order of a puzzle, the arrangement of your outline can change. You can rework your outline (and thus your paper and argument) by rearranging the way you have placed topics in the outline. Keep an open mind and be flexible. You never know when you might find a new article that could change your approach or cause you to see a possibility you never saw before.

Once you start the writing of the paper, it doesn't matter where you begin. You could:

- start at the beginning
- work on individual paragraphs (one paragraph per page)
- start with an area with which you feel comfortable
- start with an area in which you have the most interest

> **summarized**
> *US*
>
> **summarised**
> *Brit.*

Where you start is up to you, but keep in mind that writing is more than just copying summarized and paraphrased notes in some logical order. Your writing has to have its own voice. You can give your paper its own voice by incorporating your own thoughts and ideas. These ideas can provide the direction for all the information on the note cards. Your interpretation of the information will help the reader make sense of it all. Otherwise, your paper will end up as a jumble of miscellaneous ideas lumped together.

Possible Pitfalls

Potential for Plagiarism

Plagiarism is presenting someone else's ideas as if they were your own. When you commit plagiarism, you include someone else's words in your paper without crediting the original author for making those statements. Basically, plagiarism is stealing another person's ideas. You can also commit plagiarism when you change words around and present the information as a summary. Changing words around is still plagiarism if you don't follow the rules of paraphrase, summary, and in-text citations.

Logical Connections

When you transfer your notes into your rough draft, be sure there is a logical connection between the ideas. If you just "cut and paste" all your notes together, the result will be a paper that jumps from one idea to another without smooth transitions. Connective phrases can help bridge ideas together.

Connective Phrases

➤ for example

➤ in contrast

➤ on the other hand

➤ in addition

➤ ironically enough

Use of Source Material

Try to find the middle ground between too many quotations and not enough. Your paper must have a voice. The quotations are meant to strengthen and validate your paper, not take over the content. Properly chosen and placed quotations will help you build credibility. The following list will provide some guidelines for making the decision about when to quote. Use a quote:

- to present an important, significant, or key thought by an authority
- when the material is memorable or unique in its expression

- when an idea conflicts with the mainstream thought
- when presenting specialized or technical information, such as statistics

specialized
US

specialised
Brit

Integrate quotes in the text with lead-in and signal phrases, and never stick a quote in just to fill space or meet the word count!

Look at the following excerpt from a student paper on organ donation. The example shows how you can use lead-in phrases.

> According to Lee Gutkind, author of *Many Sleepless Nights,* "Only one percent, or 25,000 of the 2.5 million people who die in this country each year, die under circumstances suitable to become candidates for organ donation. What is even more unfortunate is that only 15 percent of the possible 25,000 actually become donors" (77).

Now look at the same example with the addition of a phrase that helps ease the reader out of the quoted material and into a related topic.

> According to Lee Gutkind, author of *Many Sleepless Nights,* "Only one percent, or 25,000 of the 2.5 million people who die in this country each year, die under circumstances suitable to become candidates for organ donation. What is even more unfortunate is that only 15 percent of the possible 25,000 actually become donors" (77). According to these statistics, it is obvious that there will always be a shortage of donors using the current methods of procurement. Because of this, researchers are looking into alternative ways of providing viable organs to patients in need of a transplant.

Similarly, paraphrases and summaries need lead-ins as well.

> Giving of organs for the furtherance of life is noble, but there are not enough people donating their organs to keep people from dying every day. According to the United Network for Organ Sharing Web site, Shands Hospital in Jacksonville, Florida, had a waiting list of 117 people for kidney transplant in 1999. One year later, only 38 people had actually received transplants ("Transplant").

Once you have written all the paragraphs in the body of your paper, it will be time to work on the introduction and conclusion. Most writing experts agree that you should write these two paragraphs last, when you know what the body of the paper includes. Following the old rule of "tell your readers what you are going to tell them, tell them, and then remind them of what you told them," you need to know what is actually in the body paragraphs before you can write the introduction and conclusion paragraphs.

Writing the Introduction and Conclusion

The *introduction* and *conclusion* can be fairly sketchy in your first draft, but later on, when you revise the paper, you will want to concentrate on how the introduction and conclusion are developed. Think of the introduction as a short overview to your paper. You want to give your readers an idea of what is to come, but you can't paint the complete picture in the introduction. Otherwise, why would you need all those body paragraphs? Some of the purposes of the introduction are to (1) give your audience a broad view of the topic in general, (2) grab reader attention, and (3) establish the context for the thesis. Here are a few ways to begin your paper:

- Give an anecdote
- Cite an interesting fact
- Use an intriguing quotation
- Pose a rhetorical question
- Give an example

No matter what approach you take, you must introduce the reader to the general topic or problem before you state your position on the issue. Writing "Organ donors' families should be financially compensated for the contribution of life to another human being" is too strong to start your paper. You must ease into the paper and introductory material before announcing your position in the thesis.

When writing your conclusion, you must consider how you want the reader to feel when he has finished reading your paper. Writing "Now I have told you all about organ donation" isn't going to be very inspiring. Instead, consider these ways to conclude your paper:

- Summarize the main points.
- Rephrase the thesis.
- Urge the readers to agree.
- Urge the readers to take action.
- Relate the thesis to larger issues.

The next step in the writing process will be to critique your draft. From that critique will come a revision, and ultimately a final paper. Look back at the deadlines and goals that you set for yourself, and be sure to stick to them. The reward for carefully following the rules of writing, preparing and researching, and using your time wisely will be a final paper of which you can be proud.

Research

Documenting Sources

Just like a credit roll at the end of a movie, a works cited list at the end of your paper gives proper credit to the ideas and research included in your paper. The works cited list lets your readers see the extent of your research—how current it is and what types of sources were consulted—and it helps your readers place your writing within a wider context. Readers familiar with your subject can recognize sources they have encountered before; readers unfamiliar with the topic are given information they can use to locate the source materials themselves.

Although there are several forms or styles for documentation, most classes require documentation according to either the MLA (Modern Language Association) or the APA (American Psychological Association) style. Because MLA is preferred in most English classes, this section will present the MLA format in more detail. Check with your teacher to find out which documentation style is required for your class. Whichever format you use, you must follow it very carefully.

In this section, you will learn to cite different types of sources within the text of your paper. You will also learn how to document your source material for special circumstances, such as using sources without authors, using more than once source by the same author, and including direct quotations. Finally, you will learn how to prepare a works cited or reference list in the appropriate format.

Statistics are like lampposts: they are good to lean on,
but they don't shed much light [alone].

—ROBERT STORM-PETERSON

Objectives

➤ compile an accurate works cited list using MLA or a reference list using APA

➤ properly document sources within the text of your paper

➤ use and record a variety of references

➤ recognize plagiarism in sample sentences and avoid plagiarism in your own papers

Section Preview

As the writer of a research paper, your paper will be judged by the quality of your sources. You will prepare a Works Cited list (MLA) or a Reference list (APA). This is the written record of sources you used to support the information in your research paper. While the list seems to be a relatively small part of the paper, it actually performs several important tasks that ultimately are reflected in the grade assigned to the paper.

As a student, you have many resource materials available for your research. While books and articles will always be important references, you can also get important information from videotapes, radio, television, CDs, audiotapes, and online sources.

The works cited list gives a detailed accounting to the reader of all the sources actually used in a paper. This list is easy to find because it is always the last page of the paper. Your teacher, however, may start evaluating your paper by reviewing the works cited page first. This single page speaks volumes about your research methods.

The Works Cited List Quickly Identifies

➤ how up-to-date your sources are

➤ how many databases you searched

➤ what date you accessed information

➤ the range of sources you used

Your teacher, in looking at your works cited page, will know the value of the publications you have used. In other words, even before the reader reads the opening of your paper, the quality of your paper can be judged by the works cited page.

For example, if you are writing about current economic trends in technology stocks, your first search might have turned up lots of articles in *Time, Newsweek,* and other popular periodicals. A look at these articles might show that the articles focus on the newest technology start-up companies, rather than the economic trends. More business-oriented publications, such as *Forbes, The Economist,* and *Business Week,* would probably offer more analysis addressing the business side of technology. Using more specific sources such as these will show that you put thought into the sources you chose.

Consider the same topic, current economic trends in technology stocks, and the information you might find in a book. A book on technology published in 1999 might be interesting, but it probably won't offer much useful information on the current trends. While 1999 may not seem like that long ago, it is an eternity in terms of changes in technology. Consider your subject when you are deciding whether or not a source is current.

Your teacher will also look at your works cited list to see how thorough your research was. For example, entries for electronic sources give the original publication information. This includes the author, title, periodical, date, and pages. It also includes information about the database name and your access date.

If your works cited page shows that you searched only one particular database for all your sources (as recorded in the entry by name), and that you found them all the same day (as recorded in the entry as the access date), your teacher may conclude that you made a hasty search and spent little time researching the topic.

While the works cited list is a good indicator of the extent of your research, it also:

• provides information to your readers on how to find the source materials used
• lets your reader read more about the subject if he or she wants to
• allows the reader to review the source to see if he or she agrees with your specific interpretation of it.

Plagiarism

This shouldn't be the first time you have read about plagiarism. It is a serious offense, so it is mentioned and explained often in this volume. To avoid plagiarism, you must understand a few of the terms of documentation.

recognizing
US

recognising
Brit.

Crediting your sources	giving credit to and recognizing the ideas and research of others
Plagiarism	using other people's words and ideas, either accidentally or intentionally, as though they were your own
In-text citation	the author's name and page number following the text it references
Works cited entry	the full publication information of the sources you used in the in-text citations

When you accurately credit your sources, you avoid plagiarism. The rule is simple. If the ideas or words are not your own, document them! If you are not sure when to provide the source information, study the following list.

- **Direct quotes:** cite the source
- **Words you have paraphrased:** cite the source
- **Words you have summarized:** cite the source
- **Sentences you have rearranged:** cite the source
- **Ideas you have elaborated on:** cite the source

Do you see a pattern here? You must cite everything that you used from a book, magazine, interview, online database, television show, radio interview, etc.

Once you have included someone else's idea in your paper, you will document the source with an in-text citation. Citations used to take the form of footnotes at the bottom of the page, but new style guides require you to include some information at the point in the paper where you used the source and a detailed citation in a list on the last page of the paper.

Some works won't have an author, or you will have multiple works by the same author. These and other specific cases require different information. What follows here is a set of examples of just a few of the types of sources you may find and use in the text of the paper.

Sample Citations in the Text of the Paper

For a basic entry with author and page number, the reference might look like this:

The author of *The Internet Writer's Handbook* advises, "Although you should write for a target audience, you may still have readers who range from experts to novices" (Sammons 149).

Two Sources by the Same Author

If you cite more than one work by the same author, you will need to identify from which work the information came. Adding a shortened title after the author's name avoids confusion.

"In the inverted pyramid structure, you put the most important information first and details and background last" (Sammons, *Internet Writer's* 168).

Two Authors with the Same Last Name

Sometimes, you will find sources by authors of the same last name. To avoid confusion, use the following method in the text of the paper:

"Net etiquette refers to good Web manners: the do's and don'ts of being a good Internet citizen. Using good 'netiquette' affects the way others perceive you and receive your opinions" (Martha Sammons 277).

No Author Listed

If you use a source with no author listed, it will be entered on the works cited list by title. Therefore, your in-text citations will use the first word or words of the title along with the page number.

"Some of America's largest school districts—New York, Los Angeles, Chicago, Boston, Cleveland, Miami Dade County and most recently Philadelphia—moved to put students in uniforms ("Style and Learning" 11).

The preceding examples follow MLA format guidelines, but be sure to follow the format your teacher assigns.

Regardless of the formatting style you are asked to use, in addition to demonstrating proper use of the in-text citation, you will need to use lead-in and/or signal phrases to smoothly incorporate the quote, summary, or paraphrase into the paper. Notice how the sample below uses a lead-in phrase to alert the reader of a quote. Notice also that identifying the author and/or title of the work shortens and simplifies the parenthetical reference as compared to the previous citation examples on this same source.

The author of *The Internet Writer's Handbook* advises, "Although you should write for a target audience, you may still have readers who range from experts to novices" (Sammons 149).

OR

Martha Sammons, author of *The Internet Writer's Handbook,* advises, "Although you should write for a target audience, you may still have readers who range from experts to novices" (149).

Similarly, you can lead into a paraphrase or summary.

Martha Sammons, author of *The Internet Writer's Handbook,* advises writers to aim for a specific audience, even though experts and novices may read the material (149).

If you follow all of the suggestions given thus far, yet run across some information that you are not sure warrants citing, try to determine if the fact or statistic is widely known or accepted. For example:

Widely known: The United States pulled out of Vietnam in 1975.
Not widely known: In 1975, Pol Pot came to power in Cambodia, and his regime murdered 3 million of the 7.2 million population.

The first example is not a statement you need to cite. The second more detailed and specific fact is probably not common knowledge (or widely known), so you will need to cite the source.

In any case, when you document your source, you are making it clear that you didn't originate the idea. By doing this, you are protecting yourself from plagiarism.

Some points to remember about the works cited list:

- Include only those sources you ultimately used in the paper.
- Follow a specified format.
- Include the list with the paper as the last page.

Don't feel like you should be able to correctly compose the works cited list without a handbook. Graduate students, published authors, and, yes, even English professors need to reference handbooks to be sure they are recording all of their sources exactly as prescribed. There are many rules; you aren't expected to know how to cite without using a handbook as a guide. Be sure you are using the most recent edition of the style handbook/manual, as styles are updated as new technologies emerge.

Your teacher may prefer a particular handbook. In addition, your teacher has probably asked you to follow a specific format, such as MLA (Modern Language Association), APA (American Psychological Association), or maybe the Chicago Style. No matter what style you have been assigned to follow, sources are grouped into categories.

Categories include books, magazine articles, films, audio recordings, interviews, online sources, and many others.

Earlier, you learned about how to use in-text citations in the text of your paper. Once you use a source in the text, it must appear on a works cited list (MLA) or a reference list (APA). The following pages show you the specifics of the MLA and APA bibliographic citation styles. When you compose your own list of sources used, be sure to use the format your teacher has assigned.

Whether you are composing a short research essay or a twenty-page research paper, selecting credible references and documenting your sources will play a large part in the way your work is evaluated. Although preparing your works cited list is time-consuming, meticulous work, it clearly demonstrates that you can identify and acquire a variety of materials and ideas, interpret them, and present them clearly for others to consider. All you need is the right handbook and a little attention to detail.

MLA Style for Preparing the List of Works Cited (bibliography)

The list of works cited appears at the end of the paper and must begin on a new page, each number continuing the page numbers of the text. Center the title, **Works Cited**, one inch from the top of the page. Double-space between the title and the first entry. Each entry must begin justified with the left margin with the second line and any line per entry thereafter indented one-half inch from the left margin. Double-space the entire list, both within and between each entry. (The formats below are single-spaced for space-saving purposes only.) Ignoring A, An, or The, arrange all entries alphabetically on the Works Cited page according to the first word of each entry.

Book by a Single Author

Author's last name, first name. Title of Book. City of publication: publisher's name, date of publication.

Book by Multiple Authors

List authors in order they appear on title page of text.

Author's last name, first name, and second author's first name, last name. Title of Book. City of publication: publisher's name, date of publication.

Book Chapters

Author's last name, first name. "Title of Chapter." Title of Book. City of publication: Name of publisher, year of publication. Inclusive pages.

An Anthology

Editor's last name, first name, ed. Title of Book. City of publication: publisher's name, date of publication.

Information from a Reference Book

"Subject." <u>Name of Reference Book</u>. 1993 ed.(year edition was published). Note: Volume and page numbers are not included if articles are arranged alphabetically.

An Introduction, Preface, Foreword, Afterword

Author's last name, first name. Name of part being cited (intro, preface, etc.). <u>Title of Book</u>. Author's first and last name (if different from author of part being cited). City of publication: publisher's name, date of publication. Page numbers.

Unidentified Author of a Book

<u>Title of Book</u>. City of publication: publisher's name, date of publication.

A Pamphlet

If editor is known:

Editor's last name, first name, ed. <u>Title of Pamphlet</u>. City of publication: publisher's name, date of publication.

An Interview

Interviewee's last name, first name. Personal interview. Date of interview (day month year).

Films and Videotapes

<u>Title of Program</u>. Director's first and last name. Leading actors' or narrators' names. Distributor (film or video company), year.

Television and Radio Programs

<u>Title of Program</u>. Narrator's, writer's, producer's, director's first and last names. Network. Local affiliate, city. Date program aired (day month year).

Computer Software

Writer of program (if known). <u>Title of Program</u>. Version of program, a descriptive label, distributor and year of publication. Operating System of program, number of kilobytes, form of the program.

Example:
Davies, Shirley. <u>Mastermind</u>. Vers. 1.1 Computer software. Viscal, 1996. IBM PC-DOS 2.0, 256KB, disk.

Periodicals (Magazines and Journals)

Author's last name, first name. "Title of Article." <u>Title of Magazine or Journal</u> Date (day month year): page numbers.

Newspaper

Author's last name, first name. "Title of Article." (Headline) <u>Title of Newspaper</u> date of publication (day month year): page number or newspaper section if listed.

Internet Sources from the World Wide Web

<u>Personal Site</u>:

Author's last name, first name. Home page. Date of electronic publication (day month year) <http://website address>.

Example:
Wilcox, Elliot. Home page. 2 March 1999 <http://www.cherro.uquebec.ca:7273/~ell/index.html>.

<u>Professional Site</u>:

<u>Title of Project</u>. Name of University. Date of electronic publication (day month year) <http://website address>.

Example:
<u>Mythical Heroes Page</u>. U of Oregon. 5 April 2001 http://humanities. uoregon.edu/mythology/port/>.

Work from a Subscription Service:

"Name of Topic researched." <u>Title of Online Reference Source</u>. Software version. Internet service. Date (day month year). Keyword(s): (period)

Example:
"U.S. Olympics." <u>Collier's Encyclopedia Online</u>. Vers. 2.0 1998. America Online. 19 May 1998. Keyword: Collier's.

A Letter, A Memo, an E-Mail Communication, or A Public Online Posting

<u>A Letter You Received</u>:

Author's last name, first name. Letter to author. Date (day month year).

<u>Memos and Electronic Mail</u>:

Author's last name, first name. "A description of the document." A description including the recipient. Date (day month year).

Example:
Ellison, Elizabeth. "Lecture Notes." E-mail to Nancy Jaffe. 9 Sept. 1999.

A Map or Chart

Title of the Map or Chart. Map or Chart. City of publication: name of publisher, year published.

Example:
Southwest USA. Map. Chicago: Rand, 1996.

A Lecture, a Speech, or an Address:

Last name, first name of speaker. "Title of the Presentation (if known)." Name of the meeting and the sponsoring organization. Location of meeting. Date.

organization
US

organisation
Brit.

Example:
Mason, Nathaniel. "Eliminating World Hunger." World Bank Forum. WBH Convention. Livingston Hotel, Denver. 2001.

An Article from a Microfiche Collection of Articles

Author's last name, first name. "Title of Article." Title of Source, volume number, year (in parentheses), and microfiche number, grids.

Example:
Nelson, Rayond. "Illegal Aliens." Southwest Regional Demographics Journal, vol. 12, (1997): fiche 4, grids B7-14.

A Review

Reviewer's last name, first name. "Title of the Review." (if given) Rev. of (give the name of the work underlined), author of the work. Title of Publication in which the review is found Date (day month year): page number(s).

APA Style for Preparing the Reference List (bibliography)

Just as the MLA style dictates that the list of works cited appears at the end of the paper, beginning on a new page, and numbered continuing the page numbers of the text, the APA style dictates *that all reference entries be double-spaced within each entry as well as between entries* (the formats below are single-spaced for space-saving purposes only). Unlike the MLA style, however, the APA style dictates that the FIRST line of each entry be indented one-half inch from the left margin with each line thereafter justified with the left margin. In addition, the APA style dictates that the bibliography page be titled "Reference List" as opposed to the MLA's "Works Cited." Each entry included in the reference list must also be cited in the text. Arrange each entry alphabetically according to the first word (ignoring A, An, or The).

Single-Author Book

Author's last name, first initial. (Year). Title of Book. City of publication: Name of publisher.

Note: Include year of publication in parentheses following author's name. Regardless of the entry, capitalize only the first word of a title and any proper nouns in the title.

Book with More than One Author

Author's last name, first initial, & author's last name, first initial. (Year) in parentheses. Title of Book. City of publication: Name of publisher.

Journal Article, One Author

Author's last name, first initial. (Date). Title of article. Name of Journal Publication (underlined), volume number (if known), pages used.

Example: Everett, D. S. (1997). Before the dawn of man. American Psychologist, 24, 111–117.

Magazine Article

Author's last name, first initial. (year published, month and day). Title of article. Title of Magazine, volume number, pages used.

Newsletter Article

Author's last name, first initial. (year published as it appears on the issue). Title of the article. Title of the Publication, volume number, pages used.

Daily Newspaper Article, No Author

Title of article. (year, month day of publication). Title of Newspaper, page number.

Note: Precede page numbers for newspaper article with "p." or "pp." For articles with an author, begin with author's last name, first initial.

17 English Writing

Brochure or Pamphlet

Name of publishing organization. (year of publication). <u>Title of Brochure or Pamphlet</u> (edition number if given) [brochure]. City, state of publication: author (if known).

Note: Include "brochure" or "pamphlet" in brackets following the title.

Encyclopedia Entry

Author's last name, first initials. Headwords used to locate information. <u>Name of Encyclopedia</u> (edition if given, volume number, pages used). City of publication: publisher.

Note: If the author is not provided, begin the reference with the entry title and date of pub.

Technical and Research Reports

Author's last name, first initials. (year of publication). <u>Title of report</u> (numbers identifying the report). City, state of publication: name of publisher.

Report from a University

Author's last name, first initials. (year of publication). <u>Title of Report</u> (numbers identifying the report). City, state of publication: Name of university, name of specific department within university.

Note: If the name of the state is included in the name of the university, do not repeat the name of the state in the publisher location.

Doctoral Dissertation and Master's Theses

Author's last name, first initials. (year of publication). <u>Title of paper</u>. <u>Name of publication, and identifying number</u>. Name of publisher.

Published Proceedings, published Contributions to a Meeting or Symposium, Article or Chapter in an Edited Book

Author's last name, first initials. (year of meeting). Title of talk, article, or chapter in edited book. Editor's name if given followed by (Ed.), <u>Title of Meeting or Symposium: vol. number</u>. (pages used in article or book). City of pub: name of publisher.

Note: Capitalize name of meeting or symposium.

Nonprint Media

Film: Last name, first name (Director). (Year of release). <u>Title of Film</u> [film]. Name of film studio or company.

Television
Broadcast: Last name, first initials (Executive Producer). (year of broadcast, month day). <u>Title of Program</u>. City of broadcast: Name of television network.

Cassette: Last name, first initials of author and speaker (Author and speaker). (year of release). <u>Title of Taped Program</u> [Cassette]. City of publication: publisher.

Musical
Recording: Last <u>name, first initials of writer</u>. (Date of copyright). Title of song [give name of recording artist if different from writer]. <u>Title of Album</u> [Medium of the recording: disk, cassette, etc.]. Location: Label. (Recording date if different from copyright date).

Electronic Resources

Note: Personal communications are cited only within the text and not the reference list as such information is regarded by the APA as personal and not recoverable by others.

<u>On-line Periodical:</u>
Author's last name, first initials. (year of publication). Title of article. <u>Title of Periodical</u>, volume number, pages used. Retrieved month day, year, from source.

<u>Online Document:</u>
Author's last name, first initials. (year of publication). <u>Title of Work</u>, Retrieved month day, year, from source.

<u>Internet Articles Based on a Print Source</u>:
Author's last name, first initials. (year of publication). Title of article [Electronic version]. <u>Title of Publication</u>, volume number, pages used.

<u>Article in an Internet-only Journal</u>:
Author's last name, first initials. (year of publication, month day). Title of article. <u>Title of Publication</u>, volume numbers and other identifying data of article. Retrieved on month day, year, from <http://website address>

Example: Albertson, L. B. (2000, July 6). Health in a health-apathy world. <u>Science Digest</u>, 2, Article 0101a. Retrieved September 8, 2000, from <http://website address>

<u>Document Available on University Program or Department Web Site</u>:
Author's last name, first initials. (year of publication). <u>Title of Document</u>. Retrieved month day, year, from name of university, name of department <http://website address>

For additional information on the APA Reference List format and in-text citations, go to <http://www.apastyle.org>

Sidebar glossary:

organization
US

organisation
Brit.

capitalize
US

capitalise
Brit.

recognize
US

recognise
Brit.

Business

Business Writing

Business writing is the most common form of communication you will encounter in your professional life. At the outset of your career, you will write letters of application and resumés; later you may need to know how to write memos, formal business letters, and business reports. In the business world, "time is money," so it is vital that you learn to communicate in a direct, succinct style. You must get straight to the point with a minimum of descriptive or creative flair. In this section, you will learn tips and guidelines to help you communicate in a business-like manner. You will learn about four types of business writing: resumés and curricula vitae, memos, letters, and reports. A sample memo and resumé are included at the end of this section.

Bureaucrats write memoranda both because they appear to be busy when they are writing and because the memos, once written, immediately become proof that they were busy.

—Charles Peters

Objectives

➤ recognize the components of an effective resumé

➤ write an explicit career objective

➤ understand the components and purpose of memos, letters, and reports

➤ determine and select the appropriate language and style for each form of correspondence

Section Preview

For each type of business writing—resumés, memos, letters, and reports—different kinds of information are required.

Types of Business Writing

➤ *Resumés,* and the application letters that accompany them, are meant to help you get an interview for a potential job. In many countries, employers expect to receive a curriculum vitae, or CV, rather than a resume. In the U.S., the CV is generally used when applying for academic or scientific positions.

➤ A *memo* is for communicating to others within your organization.

➤ *Business letters* are for when you want to write to those outside your organization.

➤ You may also be called upon to write a *business report* that may recommend a product or a course of action.

Each type of writing requires specific language and a different format, and each has its own purpose.

Writing the Resumé

The resumé and letter of application will likely be the first form of written communication you will have with a potential employer. Your resumé should capture your work experience so a potential employer can track your career and determine whether your previous jobs fall in line with his or her company's needs. To write a solid resumé that will make you shine, you should paint an accurate picture of your professional and educational background without embellishing or stretching the truth. You can tailor your resumé for each job interview, but you should never lie. Remember, the purpose of the resumé is to emphasize your strengths and secure an interview.

Your resumé should speak volumes about you, yet resumés usually remain one to two pages in length. A potential employer may receive hundreds of resumés for one opening, so brevity is key if you want your resumé to be read. Each segment of your work or school experience will have its own section with a heading or transitional phrase. The resumé should be well-organized, so don't jump around from your years in school to work and back to school again.

Because resumé formats differ from one profession to another, you may want to find a book containing sample resumés for your profession and follow that format. In the sample provided here, note the placement of the name and address, the specific headings, the concise wording, and the clear format. Include your college address if it is different from your home address. Include your day and evening phone numbers as well.

The Career Objective is a one-sentence statement of your professional goals; it indicates your desired career direction. Think of your career objective as a thesis statement. If you choose to include a career objective section in your resumé, make sure it is not too vague or too limiting. For example, this would be an overly broad, vague career objective: *To manage a retail store.* The more specific career objective is restated here: *To manage a retail establishment that sells quality merchandise in an atmosphere that fosters a loyal clientele while nurturing employees.*

Since the main purpose of the resumé is to secure a job interview, even if you don't include a career objective in your resumé, you might still want to narrow your focus by looking at your goals, experience, and interests. Considering your career objective may help you be better prepared during a job interview. This will help you market yourself, your skills, and your experiences and give you confidence when asked about these areas. A good resumé can get you an interview, and a good interview may get you the job. The more you prepare for the interview, the less likely you will be to fumble while trying to think of an appropriate answer to a direct question. Being prepared and answering questions in a direct, confident (yet not overly confident) fashion is a golden opportunity to make you the leading candidate for a coveted job.

organized
US

organised
Brit.

The next section of your resumé can begin with either your educational background or your work experience—whichever is more relevant to the position you seek. If school has more adequately prepared you for the desired position, list education first; if you don't have any work experience, list the educational experiences that relate to the job.

Under the heading Educational Background, list all the secondary and post-secondary schools you have attended, beginning with the most recent; do not include grammar or elementary schools. For college, include dates of attendance, your major and minor areas of study, and the degrees you received or expect to receive.

Under Work Experience, begin with your current or most recent job and work backward. List the dates of employment, including the month and year you began and left. Include your job title, the name and address of the company, and a brief description of your responsibilities. Each section should be no longer than a paragraph and should contain only truthful, verifiable statements. Use phrases that begin with action verbs to describe your responsibilities. Just as key points in an essay should relate to your thesis, the work experience in your resumé should relate to your career objective.

Under a heading such as Honors and Awards, Organizations, and/or Other, include information you would like potential employers to know. You might also include organizations to which you belong, especially those that relate to your career. As always, this information should be factual and relate to your career objective.

For References, provide the names, titles, affiliations, addresses, and phone numbers of those who can speak for your abilities and potential. Before listing anyone as a reference, contact the person for permission. You may tailor your list of references to each job for which you apply. Some references can give better recommendations for your work experience; others can speak more to your career interests; and still others know more about your academic abilities.

Note: Not all resumés include a references section, and it is acceptable to include "References Available Upon Request" as the last line on a resumé or to leave out any wording about references.

The letter of application (also called a cover letter) accompanies the resumé each time you send your resumé for a potential job. A new, tailored letter should be composed for each job opening, showing knowledge of the company and the position.

The sample in this lesson of a block style letter is a typical letter of application. The style is direct—the writer states the position she is applying for, includes some personal information, and provides information about her availability for interviewing. You may want to research a potential employer to determine how much and what type of information you should provide. Some companies prefer personal information; others do not. When you are unsure of an employer's orientation, simply state the job you are interested in, give a brief summary of your personal background, and indicate briefly how you think your skills would benefit the company.

You can use your letter of application to include relevant information that may not appear in your resumé, or you can use the letter to highlight information. Although your resumé includes dates of employment and a list of awards, you may want to point out the total number of years you have worked in your field or give the number of awards you have received as a way of highlighting that information.

The curriculum vitae and the resumé serve similar purposes, but they are different in several significant ways. There is no set format for a CV, nor a set length. Thus, a resumé will tend toward brevity, while the CV will tend toward completeness. Even so, the CV should generally be held to three pages or less. Since there is no set format, you can choose what to include and how it should look.

The CV itself should set forth your education and qualifications, your relevant work experience, and any outside interests that might bear upon the job for which you are applying. Your covering letter should explain why you're interested in the position and why you're exactly right for the job.

Sample Resumé

Janice Kaiser
1425 Lanier Court
Jacksonville, FL 32211
(904) 744-xxxx (daytime)
(904) 743-xxxx (evenings)

Career Objective: To secure an entry level position in an equipment purchasing division

Work Experience:

4/01-present
T. J. Farris Jewelers
Jacksonville, FL

Bookkeeper—Responsibilities include balancing account books, disbursing cash drawers, making bank deposits, and training personnel on cash registers

4/99-4/01
Ryan's Restaurant
Jacksonville, FL

Cashier—Duties included ringing up customer bills, balancing cash register for every shift, tipping out waiters, and seating customers

Educational Background:

9/99-6/01
University of North Florida
Jacksonville, FL

B.S. Accounting—Major Studies: Accounting and Marketing

9/95-8/99
Florida Community College at Jacksonville
Jacksonville, FL

Major Studies: General Courses

Honors and Awards:
Deans list 3 of 4 years in college
Who's Who Among Students in American Universities and Colleges
Student of the Month—January 2001

Other:
Vice President of Business Club
Board Member—Student Activities
Volunteer—Meals on Wheels

References:
Available upon request

591 Ocean Circle Drive
Honolulu, HI 96822
February 4, 2004

Dr. Steve Brown
Chair, Search Committee
University of Hawaii
Department of Education
120 College Drive
Honolulu, HI 96822

Dear Dr. Brown:

Enclosed please find my resumé in application for the position of Administrative
Assistant to the Director of Distance Learning. I have an Associate of Arts Degree
and over two years of demonstrated successful experience as an administrative
assistant in a community college. My knowledge of distance learning includes
experience with telecourses, Web-based instruction, and interactive television.

I am seeking a change in my current position because I do not see a way to advance
where I am while staying part of instructional technology. The work that is being
done at your university in the areas of distance learning and instructional technology
is widely recognized, and I believe my assets match nicely with the needs of your
organization.

I am available Monday–Thursday afternoons, and I would welcome an opportunity
to talk to you about your plans and the possibility of my involvement.

Sincerely,

Susan Peters

Enclosure

Sample Curriculum Vitae

Personal Details

Name	**RICHMOND**	James Anthony
Date of Birth:	10 July 1976	Address: 12 Downend Road
Sex:	Male	Bristol. BS7 9PF
Marital status:	Married	Telephone: 01111111111
Nationality:	British	E-mail richmond@richmond.co.uk
National insurance:	JE 123456 C	

Education and Qualifications

Education:

September 1986 – July 1994	October 1994 – July 1997	October 1999 – July 2000
Monkton Combe School	Oxford University	Graduate School of Education
Bath, Avon. BA2 7ET	St. Edmund Hall	Bristol University
	Oxford. OX1 4AR	35 Berkeley Square
		Bristol. BS8 1JA

Academic Qualifications:

GCSE Summer 1991/2	Maths A, Co-ordinated Science AA, English A, English Literature A, Geography A, Economics A, Craft Deisgn Technology A, German B.
A-Level Summer 1994	Maths A, Further Maths A, Physics A, Chemistry A.
Degree Summer 1997	Mathematics 2:1 BA(Hons)
Prizes:	Old Monktonians Leadership Prize. Best A-Level Results. All-round Sportsman. Honorary Exhibition of Monkton Combe School - November 1992.

Employment

August 2000 – Present	Teaching Maths at Richmond Secondary School, London Involved in research project into mixed ability teaching Promoted to Deputy Head of department in September 2001.
August 1997 – August 1999	Teaching Maths and Science at a government secondary school in Kenya.
January 1996	Working for Independent Schools Information Service constructing internet pages and processing A-Level and GCSE examination results.

Extra Curricular Activities

Sport:	**Current** Firebrands 2nd XI Hockey
	Social tennis, squash and running
	University 1st XI Hockey – 1995 Tour to Argentina
	College Rugby, Squash, Tennis, Athletics.
	College Ice-Hockey Champions
Interests:	Christianity, Travel, Photography, Bridge.
Activities:	Leading on Easter and Summer camps for 8 – 18 year olds.
Travel:	USA, Canada, West and Eastern Europe, Argentina, Africa.

Non-Academic Qualifications

Life Saving - Award of Merit - July 1994
Driving Licence - December 1993
2* Canoeing - November 1995
Rugby Football Union Coaching Course
Basic Level Hockey Umpire

Writing Memos

Once you have secured a job with your resumé and interview, you may be asked to write memos. Memos are written when you need to communicate with others within your organization. Whether a memo is sent through e-mail or on paper, it is usually short and to the point and structured in the same manner. While the format for memos might differ within each company, the idea of exchanging information in a relatively short period of time is the same.

The memo contains two parts: the heading and the message. Include in your heading the date, the name of the person receiving the memo, your name (the sender), and the subject of the memo. A standard heading like this aids in quick and efficient filing.

> *Date:*
> *To:*
> *From:*
> *Subject:*

Generally, the message section of a memo consists of one or two paragraphs and covers only one major topic. Rarely will the basic memo exceed two pages. If the memo is sent in electronic format (e-mail), you should typically keep the message to one screen. Bullet points can be used to highlight items or ideas, and paragraphs should be written in a clear and direct style. Professional terminology and abbreviations are acceptable in your memo since a memo is meant for in-house use. For example, people who work with computers understand that a "PC" is a personal computer, and health professionals know that "ICU" stands for Intensive Care Unit.

At the end of the memo, you may include the initials of the sender in uppercase and the initials of the typist in lowercase. If others are receiving copies of your memo, you may include "cc" followed by a colon and the name(s) of the person(s) receiving the copy. Depending on your point of reference, "cc" stands for "circulating copy," "carbon copy," or "courtesy copy." Regardless, "cc" always indicates that a copy or copies were sent.

By adding "Enclosure" (or the abbreviation "Encl.") to the wording at the bottom of the memo, you alert the reader to any enclosed information, such as a copy of the annual report or copies of employee surveys. Use these notations ("cc" and "Enclosure") only when appropriate. They do not need to be a part of every memo.

organization
US

organisation
Brit.

17 English Writing

Writing Business Letters

Unlike the memo, the business letter is meant to go outside the company. A business letter is more formal, since it represents you and your employer to those outside your organization. A business letter consists of six major parts.

1. heading
2. inside address
3. salutation
4. body
5. closing
6. notations

As you sit down to compose your letter, remember that there are several style formats that are appropriate for letters.

Formats for Letters

➤ **Block style**—justified left, without indentations (most common format for business letters)

➤ **Modified block style**—heading and closing are indented along with the first line of each paragraph

➤ **Simplified style**—similar to modified style with the omission of the salutation or closing

The common characteristic of all letters is that they inform the reader in some way. Some business letters make requests, while others are meant to persuade. There are also the "good news" and "bad news" letters, but all are meant to make a point. It is likely that you will write your letter on letterhead, which will include the company's name, address, phone and fax numbers, and an e-mail and/or Web address. If you use letterhead, you will start your letter with the date. The inside address consists of the name of the person receiving the letter, his or her title, the name of the business (if applicable), and the complete address.

Next, include the salutation or greeting followed by a colon. While a comma is often used in less formal letters, the colon is appropriate for a business letter. If you don't know whether the contact person is male or female, leave off the title. The examples below show you how you might write the salutation.

Dear Mrs. Amanda Moore:
Dear Mrs. Moore:
Dear Terry Hester:

The body of the letter contains your message. As with all business writing, your message should be short and to the point. The body of the business letter should inform the reader with clear, direct language. Ask yourself, "What does the reader need to know?" Sometimes your sole purpose will be to inform; at other times you may wish to persuade your reader to take some action. Develop the content according to your intent. Toward the end of the letter, sum up your recommended course of action and inform the reader when and how you can be reached for follow-up.

The body of the business letter is followed by your closing. You can use standard closings such as "Sincerely," "Sincerely yours," or "Yours truly." For an alternate closing, you can use "Cordially," "Best regards," or "Respectfully." Leave four spaces for your signature, and then type in your full name followed by your title.

Sincerely,

D. Alex Powers, II
Vice President

Below your name should be any notations that would be appropriate ("cc," "Enclosure," etc.), as in the memo.

Writing a Business Report

In addition to writing memos and letters, you may find yourself writing a business report once you secure a position within a company. (Report writing is covered in more detail in "Technical Writing.") Whether you are asked to write a report about personnel needs in your department or a profit and loss statement, the task will resemble the process for research writing. You will need to gather information from some outside source, compile the information, and prepare a written statement.

To set up the business report, you have to first begin by stating the problem and its significance within the organization. Each problem is unique, and you will have to determine which technique will work best to complete your work. Also provide your readers with some background information, informing them of the necessity of the report. Be sure to state your reasons for the report clearly and succinctly.

In the body of the report, you can either present the information without commentary or you can go one step further and interpret the information for your readers and offer your recommendations. Format depends upon the type of report you have been asked to write. Business reports are sometimes written in narrative form, as in the case of social workers or police investigators. Regardless of field, most employers have specific guidelines for writing a business report. You should closely follow the predetermined guidelines for a business report in your particular workplace.

Whatever your career choice, you will at some time be required to write a resumé, a memo, a business letter, or a business report. No matter what type of writing you are required to produce at work, remember to check the material for spelling errors. Further check that the writing is presented in an easy-to-read, neat format. The tips provided in this section and the guidelines you learn in the business world will combine to make you a successful business writer. If you think of your writing assignments in school as on-the-job training, there is a good chance you will find yourself a well-respected colleague in whatever field you choose.

organization
US

organisation
Brit.

Sample Memorandum

Date: August 12, 2001

To: Hannah Logan
    Trey Douglas

From: Nicole Matthews

Subject: NEW WEEKLY MEETING LOCATION

Due to construction/renovation in the area where we usually meet, the location for our weekly progress meetings has been moved to room A-2157 in the Brookwood building. The day and time for our meetings will remain the same (Wednesday from 12:00-1:00).

If you have any questions or need to contact me for directions to this new location, please do not hesitate to contact me. I can be reached at extension 8195 or by e-mail at nmatthews@shp.com.

cc: Cynthia Williams
    Julie Anne Jefferies

Technical Writing

Your good writing skills will carry over and be well utilized in college and in the business world. Most employees routinely write and draft information as part of their jobs. It is imperative to the company and your success within the company that you produce written information that is clear, concise, easy to follow, and easy to understand. You will likely write information for people within your company and for people outside your company. When the writing you do for your business is industry specific, it is called technical writing. In this section, you will learn the elements of technical writing, and you will learn the details of the elements included in a formal business report.

Report writing, like motor-car driving and love-making, is one of those activities which almost every Englishman thinks he can do well without instruction. The results are of course usually abominable.

—Tom Margerison, from "A Random Walk in Science"

Objectives

- ➤ understand the purpose of technical writing in the workplace

- ➤ determine how to format writing for a specific task

- ➤ use the correct terminology for a piece of technical writing

- ➤ communicate your business message in an effective manner

- ➤ recognize the elements of a formal business report

- ➤ review and edit a report for clarity and conciseness

The purpose of technical writing generally falls into one or more of the following categories:

Technical Writing Categories

➤ **Informative**—Informative technical writing offers fact, not opinion.

➤ **Persuasive**—Persuasive technical communication is designed to convince the reader of the merits of the information presented. It provides facts and evidence.

➤ **Instructive**—Instructive technical information allows the reader to learn a new skill. It teaches new concepts and techniques.

utilized
US

utilised
Brit.

recognize
US

recognise
Brit.

17 English Writing

There is a great deal of written communication in most businesses. Business letters, memos, e-mails, and reports are all common types of writing in the workplace. In addition, businesses often require manuals, documentation of procedures, and instructions for use. No matter the type, all business writing should be clear, concise, and accurate.

Technical writing covers numerous formats. Consider the following examples of technical writing:

- company manuals
- instructions for assembly
- texts used for procedural instruction
- pamphlets on the benefits and side effects of new drugs
- medical reports
- instructions for filling out forms
- a report on a traffic study

It is clear that technical communication touches almost every field. Your job as a technical writer is to determine how to format your writing for your task, use the correct terminology, and communicate your message in an effective manner.

You have probably already dealt with good and bad examples of technical writing. If you have ever bought an item that needed to be assembled, you should have been given a set of instructions with the materials. Sometimes the instructions are too complicated and hard to follow. They may not have been written in a logical manner, making them ineffective. Good technical writing, including instructions, should be direct and simple, following a logical order.

While technical writing varies widely from industry to industry and application to application, it shares an important aspect of writing in general: audience. Who you are writing to is as important as ever when you are writing for business. As you learned in previous sections, audience is an important consideration in any piece of writing.

Another important aspect of technical communication is that it must get right to the point. Your fellow employees and other recipients of your technical documents won't have time to search for your intended message and purpose. Get to the point, and your reader will appreciate it.

Technical writing is meant to present information, and any personal opinion of the writer should be presented separately from the facts. Further, technical writing follows the standard inductive and deductive reasoning that you learned earlier.

As you begin to write a technical document, first ask yourself these questions:

- Who will read this document?
  Employees of the company?
  Retailers?
  Consumers?
  Competitors?

- Considering the audience, how technical will the terminology be in the document?
- What are my goals and objectives? What is my purpose for the document?
- Do I want to persuade, inform, or instruct?
- What about the tone of the document?

A drug company is an example of a business using technical documents. Audience, of course, plays a role in any literature the company distributes. If the drug company plans to market its new medication in general media publications, the tone of the material will be different from what is written for physicians.

Once you know who will read your document, you will need to know your time frame. If a report is to be delivered within a week, the research process will vary greatly from one that is due in 60 days. Also, as mentioned earlier, consider your objective. What do you wish to achieve with the document? Is the objective to sell a new car to potential buyers, or is it to teach personnel how to market the car's features?

Next, you will need to determine how much you, the writer, already know about the issue.

- Is your technical knowledge sufficient to write a proposal?
- Do you need to conduct research?
- Will you need the help of others?

When you have the information you need, you will need to sort through it and retain only the material that will effectively make your point, including visuals and illustrations.

Up to this point, you may have made all the necessary assessments, but at this stage you should determine if this is a project you can write or if you will need collaboration. Collaboration in the workplace is common, especially when you are working on a tight deadline. A group of writers can be quite effective in pooling its resources and creating a completed document in much less time than a single writer.

Whatever the decision at this stage, writing alone or in collaboration, you will need to organize the material you have gathered into the most effective format. You'll also need to create a design that is easy to read and reinforces the information.

Consider the design of a business report. Keep in mind that many of the elements in a report are also applicable to other forms of technical communication.

A report requires that you:

- know your audience
- determine the tone of your report
- establish the appropriate degree of technicality
- decide upon your goals and objectives

As stated earlier, get right to the point as you write your report. Your audience doesn't want to sift through trivial information. However, that doesn't mean that your writing should be dull. Technical writing doesn't need to be dry and boring; indeed, that could defeat the purpose. Technical communication should improve a reader's understanding of a concept and explain unfamiliar ideas in familiar terms. You can use metaphors and analogies, as well as descriptive language.

The parts of a formal report, specifically a recommendation report, are as follows:

- **Title Page**—title of report, the author's name, the recipient, date completed
- **Table of Contents**—lists the report's contents and initial page numbers
- **List of Illustrations**—if there are maps or other supporting materials in the report
- **Summary**—presents an overview of the work without visuals or lengthy discussions
- **Introduction**—includes purpose, scope, and perhaps background or history
- **Body**—contains bulk of the information, discussion, visuals (graphs, tables, and charts)
- **Conclusion**—based on the discussion
- **Recommendation**—presents course of action, positive or negative, free of bias, factual
- **Appendix**—if needed
- **Reference Page**—if outside sources were used

organize
US

organise
Brit.

If you choose to use visuals in the body of your report, be certain that you understand their purpose. The use of visuals helps you demonstrate and explain the points you make in your report. They should be used only when they add to the quality of the information. Consider using visuals in your technical communications if they will:

- add visual clarity to a point you want to make
- help your readers grasp the technical content
- explain how data and other sources of information are tied together

If you use visuals in your report, including diagrams or tables, remember the following:

- Refer to the visual in the text, and include the visual on the same page. Don't make your readers search for the visual in the report.
- Cite all your sources, visuals and otherwise.

If references are to be cited, you will need to add a list of them at the end of your report. Don't forget to include the list in your table of contents. As with all types of writing, be sure to follow the style manual most accepted in your profession or as guided by your instructor or supervisor.

Once you have completed any type of technical communication, whether it is a formal report, procedures for assembly, or directions for medication, your work must go through an edit process. Some companies require written work to be submitted to a department head or co-worker for review. Even if it is not required, have someone else read your work. There is no point in creating a document for presentation only to find out after it has been distributed that the wording was confusing or visuals could not be interpreted.

A thorough review will determine answers to the following questions:

- Is the information accurate?
- Is the language uniform?
- Is the language consistent?
- Is the physical layout appropriate and appealing?
- Do the illustrations follow a logical sequence?
- Are the references noted?
- Is the document grammatically correct?

After a review and edit, the document will go through a final polishing to ensure that it meets company standards and policies.

You have now learned the elements of a formal report, but the workplace also includes informal types of writing. Informal doesn't mean impromptu, however. Any type of technical writing needs to be well-thought-out and planned. As you can guess, audience is an important aspect of informal writing, as it is with all writing.

In today's electronic age, you never know where your report will end up going, so choose your words and tone carefully. If there is a possibility that your report will be read by multiple audiences, do not include any material that can be misconstrued.

There are many advantages to effectively communicating ideas and information in the workplace. It is a core component in many businesses, and client and customer satisfaction may hinge on a well-constructed document. Your professional advancement may even be determined by how well you create and deliver your technical documents. Whatever profession you choose, chances are you will be required at some point to create a technical document. What will set you apart as a successful employee will be your ability to communicate clearly and concisely.

Sample Page from a Technical Report

Table of Contents

Sample Page from a Technical Report *continued*

Executive Summary

This report recommends that the Homeowners Association take action to clean and maintain the lake in the Grayfield neighborhood (see Figure 1 below). It should be brought to the attention of Atlantic Builders that debris from their construction projects is being found in the lake. The home builder should absorb the initial cost of removing all the debris and maintain the lake until all construction is completed.

In addition, the Association should decide on one of the given methods to remove and control the filamentous algae. This pond scum will continue to form until it has consumed the entire water surface. My recommendation is to install a fountain with the use of donated land. This would aerate the water, not allowing the algae to form, and possibly raise resale value.

Introduction

Purpose
This proposal presents the results for the improvement of the common lake area in the Greyfield subdivision. It is recommended that algae and debris be removed from the common area at the expense of the Atlantic Home Builders.

Scope
This report details the problems caused by an excess of algae and debris found in the common area lakes. It then considers solutions to maintain the area. Finally, the report will discuss the issue of cost involved to maintain a clean, healthy, and safe common area. An implementation of photos showing current conditions is included.

Procedure
Information for this research was gathered in several ways. Interviews were conducted with the homeowners adjacent to the lake. Florida Lake Management has viewed the site and provided recommendations. A second opinion by Aquatic Weed Solutions is also provided.

Figure 1

Discussion

Problem

In the past several years, the lake at the front of the Greyfield subdivision has slowly become an eyesore. The problem exists in the large amounts of construction debris floating in the lake and an abundance of algae that has formed. This issue has many of the homeowners adjacent to the lake concerned about the health of the water, the health of their children, and the value of the surrounding property.

Currently, there are two homes under construction by Atlantic Home Builders. They have failed to clean up their construction debris, which is either blowing into the lake by the wind or being tossed in from unconcerned workers. Figures 2 and 3 below show a piece of lumber and a bottle floating in the lake. Interviewing several of the neighbors, it was found that this has been a recurring problem over the past several years while many homes have been under construction.

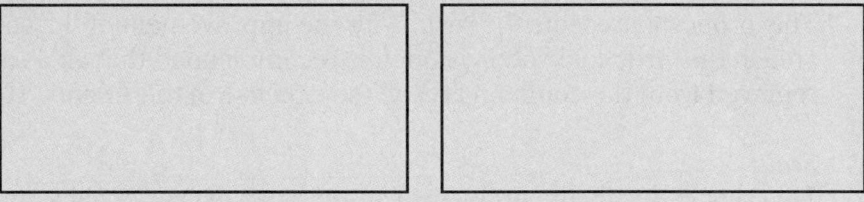

Figure 2   Figure 3

The construction debris has been caught in the pond scum, which is also a problem. Pond scum is a type of floating algae that has formed from an excess of nutrients, fish waste, debris, and stagnant water. According to Mike Landford at the Florida Lake Management Company, the lake contains a type of algae called filamentous algae (more specifically called the Horned Pondweed), which appears as fine green threads forming floating mats (see Figures 4 and 5). Landford agreed that the Horned Pondweed was hindering the pond life to a certain degree. He suggests that the algae need not be removed, but be brought under control by using other methods. I felt it necessary to have a second opinion and contacted John Scott at Aquatic Weed Solutions. Scott said that the Horned Pondweed would eventually take over and cover the entire lake if the nutrients in the lake were not controlled in some manner. Both agreed that some action needs to be taken.

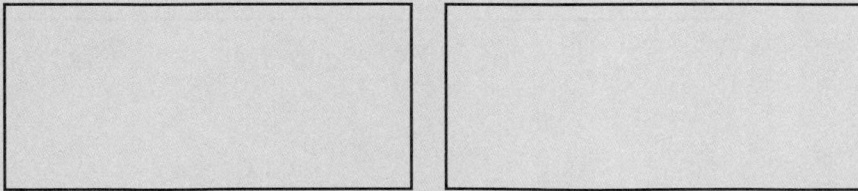

Figure 4   Figure 5

Solution

Landford and Scott both reported that the mats of filamentous algae may be removed with a rake or by dragging a screen wire. According to Scott, the algae would grow back almost as quick as it was removed. Landford said that a small lake such as ours needed some type of plant life in order to provide oxygen to the fish and to remove the carbon dioxide from the stagnant water. His first suggestion was to cover one-third of the lake in floating pond lilies. Pond lilies filter the nutrients before the algae have time to form. This is also a benefit in providing shade for the pond and helping to keep the water temperature down due to the extreme Florida heat. A second way to remove the algae would be to introduce chemicals into the pond in small quantities over a three-week period in order to balance the lake water's ph level. Chemicals provide a risk of endangering the life of fish and swimmers and have a negative effect on lawns if the lake water is used for irrigation. Chemicals need to be closely monitored. The third option is to circulate the water by the use of a water pump or aerator to keep the water flowing. This can be done by installing a fountain or waterfall to oxygenate the water and drive out excess carbon dioxide.

Cost

Understanding that the Homeowners Association only meets quarterly, I have taken the liberty to inquire about the cost associated with the three above items. Please review Table 1 below for a comparison of the cost-effectiveness over the first five years.

Table 1

Cost	Raking Pond	Chemically Treating	Installing Fountain
Year 1	$1,800	$1,200	$4,200
Year 2	$1,800	$1,200	$0
Year 3	$1,800	$1,200	$0
Year 4	$1,800	$1,200	$0
Year 5	$1,800	$1,200	$0
Total at year 5	$9,000	$6,000	$4,200

The cost of raking or screening the lake is based on a bi-monthly rate to remove all trash debris and algae. This is the most costly method and the most time-consuming way to keep the lake clean and in a healthy condition. The second choice is to chemically treat the water, which has many involved risks, but a cost that is within reason over the given period. The most cost-effective way would be to place a fountain in the pond. This would require an extensive initial cost but would be recovered before year four. As you can see, the third method of having a fountain will have no recurring cost other than electricity after the first year. The fountain will require a small 5' × 5' easement and access to the land on which it sits. The cost of this would be approximately $5,000. If we can mutually agree on the terms and conditions, I will donate this 5' × 5' portion of land.

Conclusion

The lake does contain debris and algae that must be removed from the water before any further damage is caused. The Health Department and the Environmental Protection Agency would agree that the conditions are unacceptable.

The major causes of the debris seem to be coming from the construction crews that are working within the area. This gives a very bad impression to anyone who is viewing homes for sale and tends to lower the value of homes within the area. The filamentous algae have been determined to be Horned Pondweed and are known to reproduce if left unattended and untreated. This will eventually cover the lake, suffocating the fish. Controlling the algae is possible with several methods to choose from, ranging in cost from approximately $800 to $1,800 per year.

Recommendation

I called Jim Watson at Atlantic Builders to inform him of the debris issue, and I was assured that he would speak to his area superintendent about the matter. It is my recommendation that the Homeowners Association write a formal letter to the home builder to warn them of the problem and recommend that they place a silt fence at construction areas that are near water or pay the cost to clean the lake on a weekly basis.

The Horned Pondweed is a difficult situation to resolve due to a cost concern. I recommend the installation of a fountain because it is by far the best use of time and money. Savings over a five-year period is $1,800. The initial cost is steep, but would have no costs thereafter, with the exception of electricity. The area homeowners believe that this would add value to their property and an additional incentive to a prospective homeowner. The land would be donated at my cost and installation could start immediately.

Social

Social Writing

Although the use of e-mail for both business and personal correspondence has increased dramatically in recent years, there are still a number of occasions when only "snail mail" will do.

Sincerity is most important in a good personal letter. When you are preparing to write, imagine that the person who will receive your letter is sitting before you. Say aloud what you would like to say to that person. When you finish, write down the words just as you said them. Read them over to see whether you have said what you intended. Then you can just copy your message onto your stationery, and send it on its way.

Some Types of Social Writing

➤ Personal letters

➤ Thank-you notes

➤ Condolence letters

➤ Congratulatory letters

➤ Notes of apology

➤ Wedding invitations

➤ Birth announcements

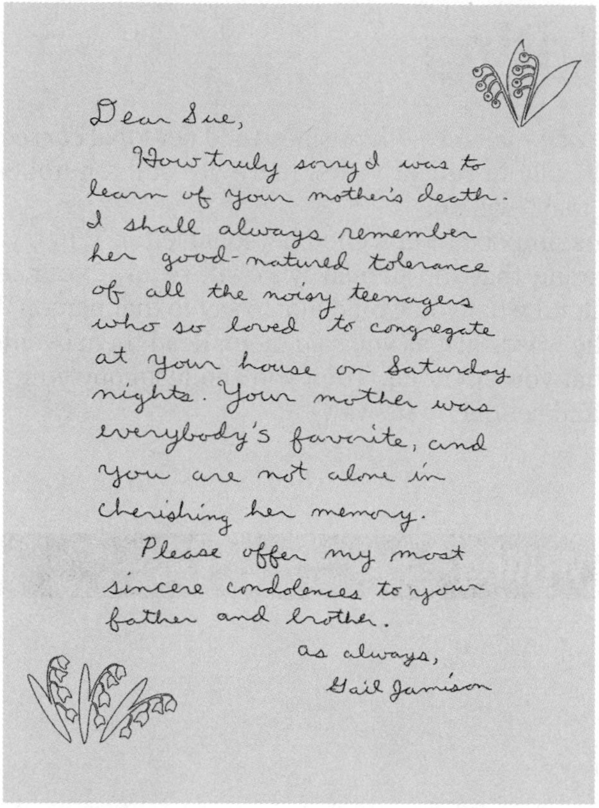

Dear Sue,

How truly sorry I was to learn of your mother's death. I shall always remember her good-natured tolerance of all the noisy teenagers who so loved to congregate at your house on Saturday nights. Your mother was everybody's favorite, and you are not alone in cherishing her memory.

Please offer my most sincere condolences to your father and brother.

as always,
Gail Jamison

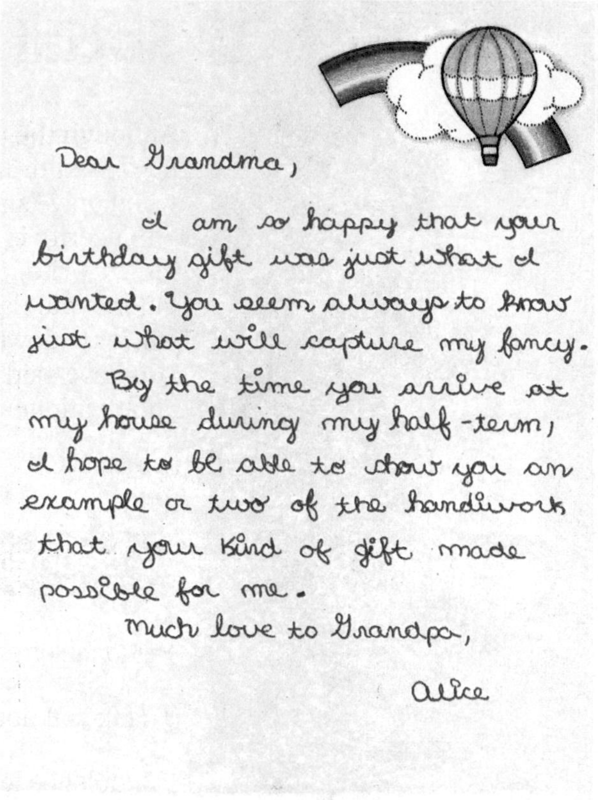

Dear Grandma,

I am so happy that your birthday gift was just what I wanted. You seem always to know just what will capture my fancy.

By the time you arrive at my house during my half-term, I hope to be able to show you an example or two of the handiwork that your kind of gift made possible for me.

Much love to Grandpa,

Alice

SOCIAL LETTERS do not need to have the formal structure that business letters must have. Social letters may be handwritten, particularly if they are short, and they may be written on stationery or any other type of paper.

favor *US*

favour *Brit.*

In general, social letters should be handwritten in ink on light-colored paper. Recent usage, however, has made typing acceptable in many circumstances, especially for long letters between friends.

Certain types of social correspondence, such as wedding invitations, should receive more formal treatment. Some traditional forms and usages are given here, with the caution that in recent years many people have felt free to modify or ignore these forms.

A standard wedding invitation form may read as shown below. The invitation might also give the place of the reception to follow the ceremony. Some people prefer the phrase "the favor of a reply is requested" to the more common RSVP (abbreviation for *Repondez, s'il vous plait,* meaning "Answer, please"). Even in the U.S., the British

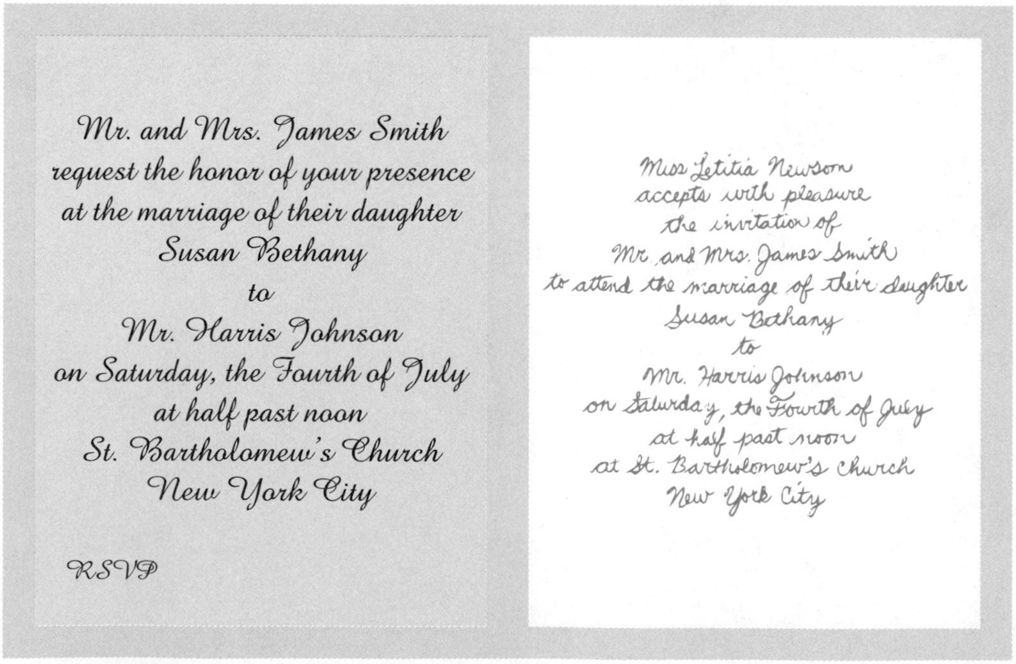

RSVP at the bottom of a wedding invitation is a request for an answer to the invitation. A handwritten formal reply incorporates the exact wording of the invitation.

Mr. and Mrs. James Smith
request the honor of your presence
at the marriage of their daughter
Susan Bethany
to
Mr. Harris Johnson
on Saturday, the Fourth of July
at half past noon
St. Bartholomew's Church
New York City

RSVP

Miss Letitia Newson
accepts with pleasure
the invitation of
Mr. and Mrs. James Smith
to attend the marriage of their daughter
Susan Bethany
to
Mr. Harris Johnson
on Saturday, the Fourth of July
at half past noon
at St. Bartholomew's Church
New York City

spellings such as "honour" and "favour" are frequently used, while others list the hour as "half after noon."

Formal etiquette requires such an invitation to receive a handwritten reply following the exact wording of the invitation. If the invitee will be unable to attend, the same form would follow after an opening line, such as "Miss Letitia Newsom deeply regrets that she will be unable to attend...." A less formal response is increasingly acceptable, but the note of acceptance or regret should still be handwritten. However, many invitations now include self-addressed printed cards on which guests indicate whether or not they plan to attend.

Traditional wedding invitations are engraved in black on white or cream-colored stock with no border. But invitations are now commonly being printed instead, and tinted papers with color-coordinated inks are not at all uncommon.

A similar change has been seen in birth announcements, which were once quite formal. Standard etiquette demanded that the announcement be sent on a white card, perhaps bordered in pink or blue. The child's name and date of birth, along with the parents' names, would appear on this card. Today, birth announcements may be on patterned cards or have brightly colored borders, and they may include the newborn's birth weight as well as his or her siblings' names. They often feature a photograph of the baby.

Traditional usage is still often followed in the writing of condolence notes. A handwritten note on white, cream, or gray personal stationery is the most acceptable. Printed cards purchased at the store are no substitute for a personal letter. A letter of condolence should express sympathy for the bereaved and, if the deceased was well known to the writer, should mention some of the personal qualities that will be particularly missed. The letter need not be long or florid. It should be sincere and brief.

Letters of condolence can be acknowledged by hand or by a printed card on plain white stock. Handwritten acknowledgments should be on plain note paper and be personally addressed. A printed card might read:

> The family of Gertrude Soames
> wishes to acknowledge
> your kind expression of sympathy.

Other personal letters may be long and newsy. These would include letters to someone who lives far away, thank-you notes for gifts or entertainment, congratulatory letters, notes of apology, or notes to someone who is ill or convalescing.

colored	*US*
coloured	*Brit.*

17 English Writing

Writing Out Loud

Knowing how to speak well is a great asset, whether you are in class, talking on the phone, or speaking before a group. It is also a vital component of most careers. While speaking is obviously important to professions like acting, you might be surprised to learn that speaking is valuable in many other professional settings.

Well-known business analyst Peter F. Drucker once gave this advice to college graduates:

> As soon as you move one step up from the bottom, your effectiveness depends on your ability to reach others through the spoken word . . . . The foundations for skill in expression have to be laid early; if you do not lay these foundations during your school years, you may never have an opportunity again.

Clearly, Drucker believed in the power of the spoken word.

Aspects of Speech

This section is devoted to various aspects of speech, including the mechanics of speech, the tools that speakers use, and advice regarding formal presentations. Remember—you already know how to talk, and you have learned how to shape written words into powerful arguments. Now, you will learn how to combine these skills in order to become a more effective speaker.

Writing Out Loud

Speaking is fundamental to language. Indeed, the word "language" is derived from the Latin *lingua*, meaning tongue. We all know that children develop the ability to speak long before they learn how to write. The history of language evolved in much the same way. While the origins of human speech are unknown, it is certain that people began speaking long before they wrote anything down. Most linguists believe that speech began thousands of years before the first evidence of written language, which dates back to about 3500 B.C.

Mechanics of Speech

Spoken words are produced in the same way that notes are produced by a musical instrument. Vibrations are created when air is pushed between two bands of muscle called the vocal cords, which are about five-eighths of an inch long and situated in the larynx, or voice box. When air passes through the vocal cords, they vibrate just like strings on a plucked guitar. The vibrations are amplified and enhanced as they resonate through the hollows of the chest, throat, mouth, and sinuses. (The hollow body of a guitar enhances the vibrations of its strings in the same way.) Sounds are shaped by the teeth, lips, tongue, and palate.

The Four Functions

Speaking consists of four functions: breath, vibration, resonance, and articulation.

Breath. The breathing that accompanies speaking differs from normal breathing. When people are not speaking, they inhale and exhale through the nose in breaths of equal duration. When speaking, however, they produce sound by inhaling air rapidly and letting it out more slowly through tightened vocal cords. This is called diaphragmatic breathing.

The diaphragm is a sheet of muscle that lies above the abdominal organs and beneath the lungs. The action of the diaphragm can be felt by breathing in with the mouth open. The abdomen will push out in front as the diaphragm flattens, pressing down on the stomach and other organs. As air is let out during speaking, the diaphragm relaxes and the abdomen pulls in again. Learning to breathe from the diaphragm can help a person speak clearly and forcefully. An adequate supply of air is essential to clear speech.

Vibration. When a person breathes normally, the vocal cords are relaxed. In speech, muscles in the jaw, throat, and neck lengthen the vocal cords and pull them closer together. The air rushing between the vocal cords causes them to vibrate. The more tightly the cords are stretched, the higher the voice is pitched. The comfortable range of pitch in speaking is about five or six notes. A trained actor should be able to use twelve notes comfortably. Singers learn to pitch their voices over two octaves or more.

SPEECH PHYSIOLOGY

The diaphragm and lungs produce the air; the vocal cords produce the vibration; sinuses and other hollows in the chest and head produce the resonance; and the tongue, teeth, and lips articulate the sound.

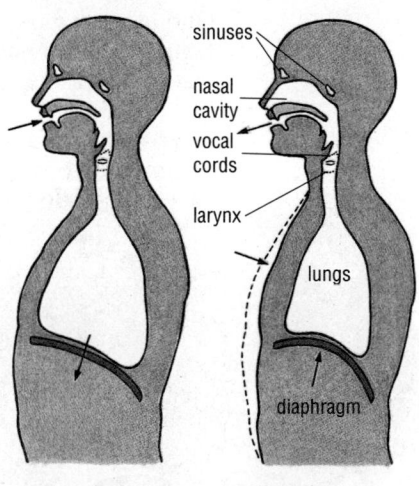

sinuses

nasal cavity

vocal cords

larynx

lungs

diaphragm

diaphragm contracts, allowing the lungs to expand

diaphragm relaxes, forcing air out of the lungs

Resonance. The vocal cords provide only 5 percent of the volume of the voice. Much of the rest is provided by resonators. These are the hollow spaces in the chest and head through which the sound from the vocal cords reverberates. The best way to sense the power of the resonators is to hum loudly. This will produce vibrations that can be felt in the chest and head.

If any of these hollow spaces are tense or filled with fluid, both the volume and tone of the voice will be changed. When someone has a cold, for example, clogged sinuses cause the voice to sound flat. Just as a guitar would sound flat and lifeless if it were filled with water, the voice loses volume and power if the sinuses are filled with fluid.

Articulation. The tongue, the upper surfaces of the mouth, and the lips shape the sounds of the vocal cords into words. By placing these parts of the mouth (called *articulators*) in different positions, one can make an almost unlimited variety of sounds. Some sounds, such as p, t, and s, do not rely on sound from the vocal cords. Others, such as l, m, n, and the vowels, give a different quality to vocal sound. While most people know how to speak, many are sloppy speakers, lazily pronouncing words so that one sound is scarcely different from another. Achieving clear speech requires close attention to articulation.

Speech Disorders

Speech disorders reflect an inability to control one or more parts of the speaking apparatus. Speech therapists help speakers overcome disorders like stuttering, cluttering, and lisping through a variety of techniques. Some speech disorders have psychological as well as physical causes. Even purely physical disorders may cause psychological problems if not corrected, since being unable to communicate effectively is often deeply discouraging. Many speech therapy programs combine physical training and psychological counseling.

Speaker's Tool Box

Speakers use many tools—those of the body and those of the intellect. This section is designed to describe these tools and to suggest ways to sharpen them. The information found here should be useful for all situations that involve speaking, from casual conversation to formal presentations.

Awareness

One of your most valuable tools as a speaker is your awareness of yourself and others. Learning about nonverbal cues and becoming sensitive to your listeners are two excellent ways to improve your speaking skills.

Nonverbal aspects of speech. Communication theorists maintain that people communicate in ways much more subtle than language itself. Such nonverbal aspects of speech include posture, eye contact, and manner of dress. As for speech itself, tone of voice and cadence of speech are often as important as the content of what one says.

Body language. You probably already know that you can convey your attitude toward someone without ever saying a word. Experts have identified bodily gestures that can reveal information like a person's level of confidence, attitude toward others, and purpose. Winks and waves, hand and eye movements, frowns and smiles, posture, scratching, fidgeting, movements of the head and hips, and the distance kept from another person all potentially communicate a person's thoughts. Consciously or unconsciously, everyone is attuned to reading body language. In general, Americans respond most favorably to a strong, confident posture and a firm handshake. That said, interactions can vary considerably from one region to another and from one setting to another. (Consider the differences in acceptable behavior at a pizza party with friends, a family holiday meal, a club meeting, and a team practice session.)

The eyes are a speaker's most important tool after the voice itself. Eyes both send and receive messages. In the U.S. and U.K., looking someone in the eye is a sign of confidence and straightforwardness. Looking someone in the eye also gives a speaker an immediate idea of the effect she is having on the listener. Is the message getting through? Is the listener bored and restless? A speaker who is looking down at the floor or up at the ceiling may not know until it is too late.

Gestures are another important aspect of body language. In the days before television, speakers used their hands and bodies in broad, dramatic movements in order to be visible at great distances. Today, people are more accustomed to subdued gestures. Still, a few gestures can enhance the meaning of words. A speaker's hands can describe things— the shape of a spiral staircase, the length of a fish that was caught, the height of a stack of papers on a desk. To emphasize a dramatic point, a speaker might pound a fist or a table or point a finger at someone or something. At the same time, unconscious gestures— cracking knuckles, rocking back and forth—can be both irritating and distracting.

Whether addressing a friend in conversation or an audience during a formal presentation, make sure that your body language indicates that you are engaged, alert, and confident. Maintain good posture and make frequent eye contact. Otherwise, your body language might distract others from what you are saying.

Pitch, tone, cadence. The sound of a voice is another nonverbal aspect of speech. A speaker with a shrill, nasal, or monotonous voice may have little effect on an audience. By the same token, a skillful speaker can use positive qualities to give a message more impact.

Pitch, or the level of a voice, is partly determined by a person's vocal equipment. Some pitch issues like shrillness can be controlled by relaxation techniques. Tone is the quality of the voice and can be improved. By reading something into a tape recorder or recording a conversation and playing it back, speakers can note what qualities they like (or dislike) about their voices and attempt modifications accordingly. Finally, cadence is the rhythm and inflection of the voice, similar to a melody in music. Good speakers pay close attention to cadence, using it to reflect the mood or message they are communicating.

Audience. In deciding what to say on a given occasion, there are two things a speaker must consider: the listener and the subject of the speech. Aristotle said, "Of the three elements in speech making—speaker, subject, and person addressed—it is the last one, the hearer, that determines the speech's end and object."

Listeners have their own concerns and problems that color and prejudice everything they hear and see. Unless great care is taken, people will not understand everything you say because they will filter it through their own perceptions. Therefore, it is useful to know as much as possible about your audience.

A politician might address a group of landlords on one night and a tenant organization on the next. It would be important to know which was which. The content of the speech might be much the same, but many small adjustments would have to be made in order to present the subject in the best possible light to both groups. Whether talking to strangers or friends, you must constantly make choices in order to present the subject in the best possible light.

What you know about your listeners will help determine what kind of language you use, the mood you adopt, and the approach you take to a subject. As you gain experience as a speaker, you will make these decisions more and more deliberately.

When speaking to a friend, you may be aware of his mood or personality traits. Is he sad or happy, introspective or outgoing? Such information might affect what you say or when you say it. When talking to a stranger, you may not be privy to such information. Instead, you must notice other cues like gender, age, ethnic or regional identity, and political orientation. Every message must be directed to an audience, and different audiences respond to different approaches.

Improving Speech Habits

In informal situations, people usually do not have to be careful about how they speak. Friends can often interpret what we say regardless of grammatical mistakes or poor

---

behavior
US

behaviour
Brit.

color
US

colour
Brit.

organization
US

organisation
Brit.

pronunciation. With strangers or acquaintances, however, bad speech habits can be a serious handicap. People make all sorts of judgments about others from the way they speak. Rooting out these habits can be very difficult, but ultimately rewarding.

Grammar for speech. Grammar for speech need not be as strict as written grammar. Still, you should always make an effort to use good grammar whenever you speak. Grammatical mistakes may lead strangers to misjudge a speaker's intelligence or level of education. Therefore, it is important to pay attention to subject-verb agreement, adjective and adverb use, and tense usage.

Common Grammatical Faults

Wrong	Right
hisself	himself
I ain't	I'm not
I been	I have been, I've been
I done	I did
irregardless	regardless
nowheres	nowhere
out loud	aloud
out of the door	out the door
overly	over
over with	over
supposing	suppose
theirselves	themselves
them people	those people
them things	those things
this here	this
thusly	thus
unawares	unaware
undoubtably	undoubtedly
we ain't	we're not
youse	you

Other common speech faults. Most people are impatient with their speech. Instead of saying what is really on their minds, they habitually use interjections such as "you know" and "umm." This is because many people distrust silence and feel obligated to fill the pauses in their speech. Meaningless mutterings should always be avoided.

People often substitute profanity, jargon, and clichés for vivid, descriptive, original language. Such substitutions often indicate a lack of thought. By using the same words repeatedly, people lose the ability to really express their feelings and their conversation loses meaning.

Some people use offensive language for emphasis. This practice is not only rude, but it also robs those words of any power they might once have had. If people known never to use profanity get angry enough to use it, their listeners understand the depth of the anger being expressed. Those who use profanity in every other sentence make no impression at all no matter how angry they are.

Clichés are words and phrases that have been used so often that they have lost their meaning. Some examples are "fit as a fiddle," "sick as a dog," and "high as a kite." Such expressions usually sound trite and should be avoided. *Jargon* is special language used in a particular field. While jargon is occasionally appropriate, it should never be used with a general audience. Most ideas can be expressed in plain English.

Vocabulary Builder

Perhaps the most important tool of an effective speaker is a well-developed vocabulary. Actually, a sophisticated vocabulary is essential to *all* aspects of communication, including writing, reading, and thinking. An impressive lexicon does not, however, depend on large, obscure words. Instead, having an intelligent vocabulary means using relatively common words so that others will understand you better.

This section describes a number of ways to improve your vocabulary. You may find some of these methods helpful; others may not be useful to you. This is to be expected since we all learn differently. Don't be afraid to try the methods to discover which work best for you. Patience and persistence are the keys to successful vocabulary building. You must be willing to work hard—the result will be well worth your efforts.

Ways to build vocabulary. The single best way to acquire new words is by reading *a lot*. This is the only guaranteed method described in this section. Read everything that you can get your hands on: novels, newspapers, comic books, and magazines. Reading widely exposes you to new words in different contexts, which is the surest way to a solid vocabulary.

It is also important to read *carefully*. Close reading forces you to take notice when you encounter a word that you are not familiar with. You'll find that you can often guess the meaning of an unknown word by examining its context in a sentence. For instance, you might not have known the meaning of "lexicon," a word used in the first paragraph of this section, but you could probably guess that it is closely related to the word "vocabulary" through the clues contained in the sentence.

Ways to Build Your Vocabulary

➤ **Read** as often as you can.

➤ Guess the meaning of a word through its **context** in a sentence.

➤ Look up the word in a **dictionary.**

➤ **Write** the definition.

➤ Study the **etymology** of the word.

➤ **Copy** the sentence the word originally appeared in.

➤ **Devise** your own sentence using the new word.

➤ Make vocabulary **flashcards.**

➤ **Rephrase** the definition in your own words.

➤ Associate a **mental image** with the words.

➤ Try using a **mnemonic device**.

➤ **Use** the new word in your writing and in conversation.

➤ Keep a vocabulary **notebook.**

A word of warning: while contextual clues are often useful in learning new words, they can be misleading. Sometimes the actual definition of a word may differ from your guess. Occasionally, you may even find that the word was misused by the person who wrote it. For these reasons, it is important to verify your guess by **consulting a dictionary**. (If you don't want to put down what you're reading, underline the word and come back to it later.) Read the definition over a few times (to yourself and aloud), and memorize it if you have time. Check the origin, or etymology, of the word. You'll find that many modern words are derived from Latin and Greek. The history of words is interesting in itself and can be a useful tool in learning new words. Read on for more information about etymology.

After looking up a new vocabulary word, many people find it helpful to write the definition. The very act of writing can help to crystallize the word in your memory. You may even want to keep a special vocabulary notebook for this purpose. For example, you can copy the sentence the word originally appeared in; that way, when you review your notebook, you'll be reminded of the word's context. You may also devise your own sentence using the word, or rephrase the definition in your own words.

Flashcards are another useful technique for memorizing new vocabulary. While some people prefer to simply write the word on one side of an index card and the definition on the other side, feel free to let your creative juices flow. Include drawings, paintings, or collages instead of limiting yourself to words. Flashcards can be very convenient—you might run through them during a commercial break as you're watching television, or when you're in the car on the way to school.

There are countless other ways to build your vocabulary. Try associating a mental image with a new word—the more vivid the image, the better. Finally, you should make a point of using new words in your everyday life, including your writing and conversation. The more often you use a word, the easier it will be to remember.

Etymology. The linguistic science of tracing a word's history is known as *etymology*. The derivation of a word presents a concise story about its ancestry. Common vocabulary—those words used every day—comes mainly from the Germanic ancestors of English. Ordinary words like "man," "woman," "boy," and "girl" are Germanic. Most of our intellectual vocabulary (words dealing with thoughts and abstractions) comes from Latin and Greek. Since we already know the meaning of everyday English words, the task of increasing our vocabulary means largely learning the words that have their origins in Latin and Greek.

This job is made easier because many long words from these languages are *combined forms*. Many English words are made up of a **root** and at least one **prefix** or **suffix** that modifies the meaning of the root. Learning to recognize roots, prefixes, and suffixes can go a long way toward building your vocabulary.

For example, consider the word "transportation." The root, *port*, comes from the Latin word that means to carry or bring. *Trans-* is a prefix that means across. Thus, to transport means to carry across. The suffix *-tion* tells us that the word is a noun, so transportation must be something that carries across. It is only a small jump in meaning to the modern use of transportation: a means of getting from one place to another.

Now we will examine roots, prefixes, and suffixes in greater detail.

Roots. A root is the basic part of a word. It suggests its primary idea, or meaning. For example, the Latin root *loqu* is related to speaking. *Loqu* is the base for a number of words: ventr*iloqu*ist (one who talks from the stomach), col*loqu*ial (informal speech), and soli*loquy* (a speech to oneself) are just a few examples.

The spelling of a root is not always the same. One reason for this is that roots come from different forms of the same word in the original language. For example, words with *loqu* come from the present form of a Latin verb meaning talk; those that have the *locut* form come from the past participle meaning talked. Roots may also change their spellings in order to combine more easily with suffixes or prefixes.

Some words do not translate as easily from their root meanings to their modern meanings. This is because they are derived from antiquated customs, myths, or beliefs. Such words usually have the most interesting stories of all attached to them. "Inaugurate," for example, means to begin or to set a person in high office. Literally, it means to practice augury, the reading of omens. In ancient Rome, priests called *augures* interpreted signs around them and told when it was good to start, or inaugurate, an enterprise.

"Candidate" comes from a Latin word, *candidus*, which means white. In ancient Rome, candidates for office would campaign wearing white togas. They were called *candidates*, meaning clothed in white. "Candid" comes from the same word and means honest.

A "maverick" is a dissenter, one who refuses to go along with the group. The word comes from Samuel Maverick, a 19th-century cattleman who refused to brand his calves. "Tantalize" means to tease someone by presenting something desirable but keeping it out of reach. In Greek mythology, Tantalus was condemned to be up to his chin in water that vanished when he tried to drink it, and to have boughs of fruit hanging over him that disappeared when he reached for them.

Common Latin Roots

Root	Meaning	Derivatives	Your Derivatives
acu, acr	sharp	acute, acrimony	*acrid*
aesthe	feel	aesthetic, anesthesia	
ag, act	do, move	agility, activate	
alg	pain	analgesic, nostalgia	
am	love	amorous, amiable	
anim	life, mind, soul	animal, inanimate	
annu, enni	year	annual, bicentennial	
anthropo	humanity	misanthrope	
aqu	water	aquarium, aqualung	
archa, arche	ancient	archaic, archaeology	
aud	hear	auditory, audience	
bel	war	belligerent, bellicose	
bio	life	biology, biopsy	
cad, cid, cas	fall, befall	cadaver, accident, occasion	
cap, cip, cept, ceiv	seize, hold	capture, anticipate, accept, receive	
carn	flesh	carnivore	
chron	time	chronology, synchronize	
clam, claim	shout	clamor, proclaim	
clud, clus, clos	shut	conclude, inclusive, close	
cogn	know	recognize, incognito	
cord	heart	accord, concordance	
corp	body	corpse, corporeal	
cre, cresc	grow	increase, crescendo	
culp	blame	culprit	
cumb, cub	lie down	succumb, incubate	
cur, curs, cours	run	current, cursory, course	
dict	say	dictator	
duc, duct	lead	seduce, induct	
dyna	power	dynamite	
fac, fic	make, do	facile, proficient	
fal, fals	deceive, fail	fallacious, falsify	
fer	carry	transfer, ferry	
flect, flex	bend	reflect, flexible	
flu, flux	flow	influence, influx	
fring, fract, frag	break	infringe, infraction, fragile	
fus, fund, found	melt, pour	fuse, refund, foundry	
gen, genit	produce, birth, race	genealogy, congenital	
gest	produce, action	gesticulate, gesture	
gno	know	agnostic, diagnosis	
grad, gress	step	grade, graduate	
grat	pleasing	gratitude	

Common Latin Roots *continued*

Root	Meaning	Derivatives	Your Derivatives
grav	heavy	gravity	
jac, ject	throw	adjacent, eject	
junct	join	juncture	
jur	swear, right	jury, perjure	
lect	gather, choose	collect	
loqu, locut	speak	eloquent	
mit, miss	send	transmit, emit	
mon, monit	warn, advise	admonition	
mor, mort	death	mortuary, mortal	
mot	move	motion, motor	
mut	change	mutate	
nat	born	native	
neg	deny	negative, negate	
path	feeling, suffering	pathetic	
pel, pell, puls	push	propel, pulse	
pend	hang, weight	pendant, appendage	
pet, petit	go, seek	compete, petition	
plac	please	placate	
ple, plen, plet	fill	complete, plenty	
port	carry	transport	
posit, pound, pose	put, place	position, expound	
pugn	fight	pugnacious, repugnant	
pung, punct	point	pungent, puncture	
quir, quisit, quest	seek	require, inquest	
rog, rogat	ask	arrogance, abrogate	
rupt	burst	corrupt, erupt	
scrib, script	write	scribble, scripture	
sed, sid, sess	sit, settle	sedentary, reside	
spec, spic	look	spectacle, conspicuous	
spir	breath	spirit	
tang, ting, tact	touch	tangible, contingent	
temp, tempor	time	tempo, temporal	
ten, tin, tain	hold	tenant, continue	
tort	twist	contort	
tract	drag	tractor	
trud, trus	push, thrust	protrude, intrusion	
unda	wave	undulate	
ven, vent	come	intervene, invent	
ver	true	veracity, verdant	
vid, vis	see	evident, vision	
viv	life	vivid, vivacious	
voc, vok	voice, call	advocate, revoke	
volv, volut	roll	revolve, evolution	

Such word stories help suggest the fascinations of etymology, but they are less useful for the purposes of vocabulary building. Studying the common roots, however, is an excellent way to enhance your vocabulary. Refer to the Common Roots Table for a list of Latin roots, their basic meanings, and modern derivatives. Many other words that are not listed share the same roots. Fill in your own derivatives as you think of them.

Prefixes. A prefix is found at the beginning of a word, before the root. It can change or add to the meaning of the base word by indicating attitude, number, position, or direction. For example, the root of the word "introvert" is *vert*, which means turn. The prefix *intro-* means into, making the meaning of the word "turned inward." If we changed the prefix to *extro-* the word would become "extrovert," meaning turned outward. Alternatively, changing the prefix to *a-* (meaning away) changes the word to "avert" or turn away.

Many prefixes change spelling depending on the sound that follows. This makes it hard to recognize certain prefixes in some words. Prefixes can also look similar but have different meanings; for example, *ante-* means before (as in antemeridian), and *anti-* means against (as in antiseptic).

recognize
US

recognise
Brit.

17 English Writing

Common Prefixes

Prefix	Meaning	Examples	Your Examples
a-	without	atheism, amoral	*asexual*
ab-, abs-	away, away from	abnormal, aberration, abjure, abrogate	
ad-, a-, ac-, af-, ag-, al-, an-, ap-, -ar, as-, at-	to, toward	admonition, accord, affect, aggravate, appear, assign	
an-	without	anonymous	
ante-	before	antecedent	
anti-	against	antiseptic, antitrust	
auto-	self	automatic, automobile	
bene-	well	beneficial, benign	
circum-	around	circumstantial	
com-, co-, col-, con-, cor-	together	companion, collect, concern, correct	
counter-, contra-, contro-	opposite, against	counterclockwise, contrary, controversy	
de-	down, reversal, away	decay, defect, default, devolve	
dem-	people	democracy, demagogue	
dia-	across, apart, through	diagonal, diagnosis, diagram, diarrhea	
dis-, dif-, di-	not	dislike, differ	
equ-, equi-	equal	equation, equivalent	
eu-	well	euphoria, eulogy	
ex-, e-, ef-	out	exhale, eject	
extra-, extro-	outside of	extraordinary, extrovert	
hyper-	over	hypertension	
hypo-	under	hypodermic, hypocrisy	
in-, em-, en-	in, against	intrude, inspect, embargo, enclave	
in-, ir-, im-	not	inoffensive, irreligious, imbalance	

Common Prefixes *continued*

Prefix	Meaning	Examples	Your Examples
inter-	between	international, interact, interscholastic	
intra-, intro-	within	intravenous, introspective	
macro-	large	macroscopic	
mal-, male-	bad, wrongly	malign, malefactor	
micro-	small	microscope	
multi-	many	multiple, multitude	
neo-	new	neolithic, neocolonialism	
non-	not	nonsense, nonentity	
ob-, oc-, of-, op-	to, against	obtrusive, occlude, occupy, offer, oppose	
omni-	all	omniscient, omnivorous	
para-	alongside	parallel, parody	
per-	through, completely	perfume, perfect	
poly-	many	polygamy, polygon	
post-	after	posterior, postpone	
pre-	before	premature, premise	
pro-	forward, away, in place of	prospectus, proceed, prodigal, pronoun	
pseudo-	false	pseudonym	
re-	again, back	reopen, receive, recall, reaffirm, reinstitute	
recti-	straight, right	rectitude, rectify, rectangle	
sub-, suc-, suf-, sug-, sum-, sup-, sur-, sus-	under, in place of	substitute, suffer, suggest, suppose, surrogate, sustain	
super-	above	superintendent, superhuman	
syn-, syl-, sym-, sys-	together	synchronize, syllable, sympathy, system	
trans-	across, over, through	translate, transcend	
un-	not, reversal	unearthly, unassailable, untie	

Numerical Prefixes

half:	hemisphere, semicircle, demitasse	four:	tetrapod, quadrant, quarter
one:	monologue, universe	five:	pentagon, quintuplet
first:	prototype, primitive	six:	hexagram, sextet
two:	binocular, dilemma, dichotomy, duet	ten: one-tenth:	decade, decennial decimal
both:	ambivalent	one hundred:	centennial
three:	tertiary, triad	one thousand:	millennium

Suffixes. A suffix is found at the end of the word and indicates the root's number, tense, and/or what part of speech it is (i.e., noun, verb, adjective, or adverb). Familiar suffixes like *-ed* or *-ing* tell that a word is a verb in the past or present tense, respectively (e.g., looked or looking). An *-s* or *-es* added at the end of a noun usually means the word is plural (e.g., cat or cats; class or classes).

Other suffixes indicate whether a word is being used as a verb, noun, adjective, or adverb. A word can often be changed from one part of speech to another by altering its suffix. For instance, a common noun suffix like *-ion* can be substituted for the verb suffix *-ate* to change a verb like "motivate" to the noun "motivation." Adding *-al* to the word would produce an adjective, "motivational." A final addition of the suffix *-ly* changes the word to "motivationally," an adverb.

Common Suffixes

Suffix	Meaning	Examples	Your Examples
-able, -ible	able, can do	reliable	*credible*
-ade	result of action	blockade	
-age	state of, collection of	storage, forage	
-al	relating to	natural, artificial	
-an, -ian	native of	African, American	
-ary, -ery, -ory	relating to	visionary, olfactory	
-arch	ruler	matriarch	
-archy	government	anarchy, monarchy	
-cide	murder	genocide	
-cracy	government	democracy	
-cy	action, function	prophecy	
-en	made of, make	frozen, wooden	
-er, -or	one who, that which	diver, doctor	
-escent	in the process of	adolescent	
-et, -ette	small, group	midget, octet	
-fy	make	simplify	
-graph	writing apparatus, writing	autograph, telegraph	
-hood	condition, quality	manhood	
-less	without	thoughtless	
-ment	state of, result	commitment	
-ology	study of	biology, psychology	
-ous	full of, having	gracious	
-nomy	laws governing	astronomy, economy	
-phile	lover	Anglophile	
-tude	state of, condition of	attitude, aptitude	
-ward	in the direction of	eastward, wayward	
-y	inclined to, tend to	sleepy, needy	

17 English Writing

Vocabulary Exercises

These exercises are designed to help you improve your vocabulary. It is important to try to select the correct answers before turning to the answers that are supplied. Feel free to use a dictionary after you've attempted a guess. You may want to write these words on flashcards or in your vocabulary notebook. The correct answers can be found on page 166.

SYNONYMS: Choose the word that is most closely related to the word in bold.

1. His **maladroit** handling of the case caused him to lose the client.

    a. clumsy   d. tentative
    b. competent   e. unjustifiable
    c. skillful

2. Percy's **laconic** reply left Maggie feeling bewildered and hurt.

    a. enthusiastic   d. long-winded
    b. terse   e. befuddled
    c. morose

3. The book was written from an **omnicscient** point-of-view, rather than a limited one.

    a. egalatarian   d. interesting
    b. fictional   e. all-knowing
    c. insightful

4. The president delivered the speech as though it was profound, but it was filled with **platitudes.**

    a. lies   d. clichés
    b. oaths   e. metaphors
    c. solemn remarks

5. The candidate's daughter was his chief advisor, yet he seemed shocked when accused of **nepotism.**

    a. misappropriation   d. favoritism shown
       of public funds   to relatives
    b. indecisiveness   e. cheatng
    c. stubbornness

6. The downtown district was **moribund**, but revived when the new theater opened.

    a. prosperous   d. depressing
    b. boring   f. dying
    c. thriving

7. Despite the thoroughness of the commission's work, the feeling persisted that the public had only an **inchoate** understanding of the new tax system.

    a. confused   d. misleading
    b. distorted   e. superficial
    c. incomplete

8. Mr. Burton cursed Tim's **verbosity** when he turned in another seemingly endless essay.

    a. audacity   d. sense of humor
    b. eloquence   e. intelligence
    c. wordiness

9. A frustrated member of the group dismissed the four-hour discussion as **palaver**.

    a. interesting discourse   d. idle talk
    b. nonsense   e. productive discussion
    c. biased argument

10. **Taciturn** people are often perceived as possessing a quiet, fierce intelligence.

    a. talkative   d. moody
    b. trustworthy   e. depressed
    c. untalkative

ANTONYMS: Draw a line between each word and its antonym.

1. odious		a. unhealthy
2. reticent		b. talkative
3. salubrious		c. goodness
4. scanty		d. aggrevate
5. appease		e. abundant
6. furtive		f. open
7. paucity		g. delightful
8. recalcitrant		h. obedient
9. assuage		i. plethora
10. turpitude		j. provoke

COMPLETIONS: Choose the word that best completes the meaning of the sentence.

1. Rosa had given up her slim figure; her belly was round and her hips were _____.

    a. slender   d. reticent
    b. reliable   e. nefarious
    c. capacious

2. Ben didn't like the _____ tone of the book because he preferred entertainment to instruction.

    a. inept   d. facetious
    b. didactic   e. archaic
    c. querulous

3. Bella admired Winston Churchill and strove to _____ his political career.

    a. infer   d. emulate
    b. ameliorate   e. malign
    c. appease

Vocabulary Exercises *continued*

4. Betty behaved with _____ at tea despite her suspicion that the ladies were putting on airs.

a. decorum
b. temerity
c. ardor
d. remorse
e. duplicity

5. Katie could not abide the _____ attack on her character.

a. frugal
b. ascetic
c. dormant
d. nostalgic
e. truculent

6. Thurston's _____ behavior alarmed his mother; it was unusual for a toddler to be so surly.

a. amiable
b. aberrant
c. affable
d. sagacious
e. pristine

7. Mrs. Rogers' expression was _____; her scowl was permanently fixed.

a. irreverent
b. unchangeable
c. agnostic
d. squalid
e. incompetent

8. Wendy _____ the child for returning her wallet.

a. berated
b. resented
c. vexed
d. extolled
e. forsook

9. Lola's decision to marry the millionaire was _____ upon whether he would include her in his will.

a. contingent
b. squandered
c. engendered
d. proficient
e. beget

10. Carrie's trust fund made her _____, but it ran out quickly and she was forced to work.

a. insipid
b. irate
c. complacent
d. austere
e. orthodox

SYNONYMS: Choose the word that is most closely related to the word in bold.

1. The president's **malapropisms** evoked laughter among most of those present, but his most ardent supporters anguished in silence.

a. misused words
b. transparent exaggerations
c. clever puns
d. outlandish claims
e. hollow promises

2. Alice expected an **opulent** event and dressed accordingly, but the host was shabbily attired in an ill-fitting hat with the price tag still attached.

a. impoverished
b. inadequate
c. ridiculous
d. lavish
e. eccentric

3. The critic insultingly called the work **prosaic** without realizing that it was indeed a novel.

a. poorly written
b. like prose
c. brilliant
d. banal
e. poetic

4. The poet's closet was **replete** with black turtlenecks and berets.

a. replenished
b. subversive
c. filled
d. empty
e. luminous

5. Sally thought that Burt was **impervious** to her insults, but he cried himself to sleep each night.

a. resistant
b. peripatetic
c. unresponsive
d. impartial
e. recalcitrant

6. Stephen's **indolent** lifestyle included sleeping past noon and an abiding love of leisure.

a. active
b. unconventional
c. enviable
d. lazy
e. indignant

7. John was so baffled by Professor Beck's talk that he was unsure whether it was admirably **erudite** or deplorably daft.

a. scholarly
b. elliptical
c. decadent
d. silly
e. circuitous

8. The **nefarious** hen was the bane of Farmer Arbor's existence.

a. angelic
b. docile
c. gregarious
d. cynical
e. wicked

9. After watching Ian kiss his reflection for the seventh time that day, Kay thought that **narcissism** should be punishable by law.

a. murder
b. self-love
c. wrath
d. criminal activity
e. silliness

10. A **dearth** of hairspray caused a riot at the beauty pageant.

a. glut
b. supply
c. bastion
d. shortage
e. anecdote

RELATIONSHIPS: Decide whether each pair of words is synonymous (s), antonymous (a), or unrelated (u).

1. culpable _____ guilty
2. juxtapose _____ irascible
3. appease _____ mollify
4. egregious _____ angelic
5. peruse _____ skim
6. pragmatic _____ profane
7. rudimentary _____ crude
8. salient _____ incipient
9. vernacular _____ idiom
10. largess _____ virulent

Public Speaking

organization
US

organisation
Brit.

emphasize
US

emphasise
Brit.

practicing
US

practising
Brit.

memorize
US

memorise
Brit.

Some people enjoy giving a speech to a group of people. More often, people dread giving a speech. Oral presentations are common classroom assignments. Fortunately, preparation can help ease that dread considerably. Preparing a speech includes research, organization, and rehearsal. This section will provide tips for both writing and delivering a speech.

Writing a Speech

Writing a speech is very similar to writing an essay. (Refer to page 3 to learn the seven point system.) There is, however, one important difference: oral language requires far more elaboration than written language. This is because people generally absorb more information through reading than through listening. In general, you will want to include more examples (or supporting evidence) in a speech than you might in an essay on the same topic. Important points should be stressed through repetition.

Organization. Any talk has three sections, which we can think of as the beginning, the middle, and the end. For a formal address, these sections are called the introduction, the body, and the conclusion. You'll want to consider these sections carefully before you create an outline or write the speech.

Introduction. The beginning of a speech must be calculated to capture the listener's attention. Unless you can capture the listener's attention, the message will not matter.

There is a famous story about the owner of a small New York printing company. For some months he had been visiting the print buyer of a major magazine publisher to ask for a printing contract. Every week, the print buyer replied distantly that his printing needs were taken care of.

One day the printer realized that the buyer did not even remember him from one visit to the next. He set out to make sure that he would not be forgotten again. On his next visit, when the buyer gave his usual refusal, the printer threw his hat on the floor, jumped on it, and left. The buyer came running after him and demanded to know what was wrong. When the printer explained, the buyer gave him his first contract. Word of the printer who made such a scene even reached the chairman of the publishing company. He arranged to meet the printer and eventually lent him money to expand his business.

Most speakers cannot open their talk with a display like the printer's, but they can resolve to find a way to keep the audience from forgetting them. You may try opening with a joke, a dramatic story, or a startling statistic. In any case, you want to make sure to introduce the material you will be talking about in an engaging and informative manner.

Body. The middle of a speech must explain the theme and establish it in the minds of listeners. There are a number of ways to organize the body of your speech. Such a choice is often dictated by the subject matter. For instance, if you are speaking about WWII, you may want to narrate events like battles in chronological order. Alternatively, if you are speaking about inflation, a logical way to organize your speech would be by its economic, social, and political consequences.

Conclusion. The end of a talk leaves the final impression. A speaker wants people to remember the speech and to leave in a certain frame of mind. If the purpose is to entertain, the audience should leave feeling happy. If the message is serious, the speaker wants listeners to feel moved. An effective conclusion will quickly review points discussed and emphasize the importance of the speech.

Script. Some people choose not to prepare a manuscript when they are writing a speech. Instead, they work from an outline and work out the exact content aloud. Other people find it useful to write the speech in its entirety before they ever begin practicing. Refer to the sample speech for an example.

It is extremely important that you never read a speech word-for-word. Reading a speech prevents you from looking out at the audience, which can make it seem boring or insincere. Instead, you should develop note cards that remind you of key points. Also, resist the urge to memorize your speech. You should know it well enough so that you deliver it a little differently each time.

Never read your speech! Instead, use note cards for reference.

Sample Speech

This is an example of a script for a speech that explains how to choose a pet. There are several things you should think about as you read this speech. When are examples used? Is there a clear organizing principle? Is the importance of the speech stated? If so, when?

"When choosing a pet, it seems obvious that there are two sets of considerations that should be dealt with before you ever set foot into a pet shop or the humane society: preference and practicality. The problem is, many people make the mistake of putting their preferences first. In fact, many go so far as to ignore practical considerations altogether. It is easy to see why this happens. When you are faced with a tiny, adorable kitten or a friendly dog, your first impulse is to take it home because it is cute. Today we are going to learn an easy way to make sure that you have thought through all of the practical considerations before you bring your new friend home. All that is necessary is to remember the three 'l's': living space, lifestyle, and lovability.   ← Introduction

[Write the words 'living space' on the board.]   ← Use of brackets for cues

First and foremost, you'll want to think about your living space before you choose a pet. Basically, you want to make sure that your new pet will be comfortable in its new surroundings. The size of your living space will be highly important. For example, I have a cat because I live in a one-bedroom apartment. In my case, unfortunately, it's a rather tight fit because my cat is incredibly obese.   ← Use of humor
Fortunately, cats do not require a large amount of space for physical activity. A dog even half of the size of my cat, by contrast, would need a lot more room to run around in. Another thing you may want to think about is your accessibility to the outdoors. If you live on the 21st floor of an apartment building, you may not   ← Body
want to get a puppy unless you are a patient person who doesn't mind accidents. Finally, if you are a renter, it is very important to speak with your landlord before you get a new pet. Most obviously, you'll want to make sure that pets are allowed in your building. Also, you should check whether there are any pet deposits as to avoid a nasty surprise after you've already brought something home.
After you've thoroughly considered your living space, you'll want to think about your lifestyle   ← Transition

[Write the word 'lifestyle' on the board.]   ← Cue

You need to make sure that your pet's needs are not going to compromise your life in any way, and vice versa. For example, if you work really long hours, you want to be sure that your pet doesn't require a lot of attention so it doesn't get lonely. Also, you should take your finances into account. A starving artist will want to get a low-maintenance pet that does not require vaccinations and frequent trips to the vet, which can be expensive. Finally, don't forget to consider   ← Body
the needs of those you live with. Consider their likes, their dislikes, and most importantly, their allergies. If your spouse or roommate is allergic to fur, you'll need to get a non-furry animal like a bird or a snake. At this point, you really need to ask yourself: Am I the kind of person that can love a bird or snake? I, for one, am not. This question brings us to our final category, lovability.   ← Transition

[Write the word 'lovability' on the board.]   ← Cue

Lovability is pretty self-explanatory. It is also the most fun part of your decision-making process. You have already sorted through the practical considerations, deciding what your living space and lifestyle can accommodate.   ← Body
Now you have time to attend to your preferences, or your heart's desire.
Keeping the balance between practicality and preference is important, and remembering the three 'l's' makes it simple to do. Go through them carefully,   ← Conclusion Last sentence states the importance of the speech.
one at a time. A pet will be your companion for years to come, and your decision shouldn't be made lightly."

Planning Visual Aids

➤ Visual props like posters or slides are an easy way to reframe information for your listeners. They make ideas more understandable and more interesting, and they serve as a memory aid for you. Keep visual aids simple and be sure to practice with them beforehand.

Delivering a Speech

After you've developed the content of your speech, you will need to rehearse and, eventually, deliver it. This section describes how to develop note cards, tips for practicing, and things to keep in mind as you give a speech in front of an audience.

Note cards. Before you ever begin rehearsing your speech, you should develop note cards. These note cards are a form of insurance; even if you do not plan on using them, they will be there in case you forget part of your speech.

Most people prefer placing notes on index cards. Apart from first and last sentences, you should not write in complete sentences. Instead, use key words that will trigger your memory. You may also want to write notes to yourself in brackets (e.g.,[Look at audience]). You should glance at the cards only sparingly; try to look at your audience about 95 percent of the time, reserving only 5 percent for consulting your notes.

There are a few things you can do to make sure that your note cards are as helpful as possible. Limiting each card to one idea or point will make sure that they are easy to read. Write on only one side of the index card. Finally, you should number the cards in case they are shuffled around.

What to Write on Note Cards

➤ Statistics   ➤ Quotations   ➤ Last Sentence

➤ Dates   ➤ Names   ➤ Keywords

➤ Cues   ➤ First Sentence   ➤ Brackets

Sample Note Cards

When choosing a pet, it seems obvious that there are two **1**
sets of considerations that should be dealt with before you
set foot into a pet shop or the humane society: preference
and practicality.

Sample Note Cards

> *2*
>
> *Problem: preference first*
> *—Easy to see why*

Sample Note Cards

> *3*
>
> *Three l's:*
> *living space*
> *lifestyle*
> *lovability*

Sample Note Cards

[*Write the words 'living space' on the board.*]   *4*

Sample Note Cards

Card 5: Living space: ensure comfort of pet
  —Size, accessibility to outdoors, landlord
Card 6: [Write the word 'lifestyle' on the board.]
Card 7: Lifestyle: not compromised
  —For example, long hours, finances, needs
of roommates
Card 8: But could I love a bird or snake?
Card 9: [Write the word 'lovability' on the board.]
  —Easy to see why
Card 10: Lovability: easy and fun

We have combined some points because of space limitations, but it's best for each card to conain only a single point.

Sample Note Cards

> *Keeping the balance between practicality and preference is 11 important, and remembering the three l's makes it simple to do. Go through them carefully, one at a time. A pet will be your companion for years to come, and your decision should not be made lightly.*

Practice. The single best way to make sure that your presentation goes smoothly is to practice it as much as possible. Extensive rehearsal will ensure that you know the material thoroughly and will help ease your fears on the day of the presentation. You may want to devote extra attention to your introduction, since this is probably when you are likely to be most nervous when you deliver your speech.

If possible, you should rehearse your entire speech at least three times. First, practice in front of a mirror. This will help you achieve eye contact and alert you to any distracting gestures you make. Next, deliver your speech into a tape recorder or video camera. Play the tape for yourself and note your strengths and weaknesses. Finally, give your speech in front of a small group of friends or family members. They will probably be able to offer valuable advice, and it will accustom you to speaking in front of a group of people.

As you practice, pay attention to the way that you talk. Your tone, word choice, and cadence should match your everyday speech. Enunciate clearly and speak loudly. Most importantly, time your speech to be sure that you are within the time constraints.

Delivery. It is common to become nervous prior to giving a speech. It is comforting to remember two things: your audience wants you to do well, and you always look better than you feel. If you mess up, continue without acknowledging your mistake. Take a few deep breaths, or pause to collect your thoughts. A blunder that seems large to you is probably unnoticeable to most of the people in your audience.

Luckily, there are many techniques you can use to ensure that you are making a positive impression on your audience. Stand up straight. Speak slowly, even if it seems forced. Make eye contact with people in your audience, or fake it by looking at their foreheads. Pause when you make an important point. Talk loudly and gesticulate to enforce key points. Finally, try to smile as much as possible. You might just trick yourself into having a good time.

Writing 101

Using language effectively, whether in writing or in speech, requires a knowledge of grammar, punctuation, and usage. Grammar governs word order and sentence construction; punctuation guides a reader through written language using symbols; and usage is a combination of grammatical and stylistic practices. You have encountered quick reviews of these in the sections on writing; however, this section provides more detailed information for your review and study. Easy-to-use charts, lists, and glossaries about grammar, spelling, punctuation, and usage provide concise information on how to avoid common errors. The main unit studied is the sentence, the construction of which is one of the most important elements of good writing. Check out pages 11, 28-30, and 32-43 for the reviews in the writing section.

Grammar

Grammar includes a wide variety of topics, from the precise study of phonetics to far-ranging investigations of how a person develops language. This section, however, is limited to the study of sentence construction, one of the most important elements of good writing.

The Sentence

Basic explanations of the parts of speech and sentence construction are provided in the English Grammar chapter. The table on the next page provides a quick review. Here is a more advanced discussion of sentences and their various parts.

Sentences. A sentence is a word or group of words that expresses a complete thought. It is made up of a *subject* (that about which something is said) and a *predicate* (that which is said about the subject).

A *simple subject* is without modifiers. A *complete subject* is the subject along with all its modifiers.

> The old man in the gray suit wept.

Here, *man* is the simple subject and *The old man in the gray suit* is the complete subject.

A *simple predicate* contains modifiers or complements. A *complete predicate* is the predicate with all its modifiers and complements.

> Juan walked slowly to the door.

Here, *walked* is the simple predicate and *walked slowly to the door* is the complete predicate.

The subject and the predicate of a sentence may be compound; that is, the sentence may have two or more subjects and two or more predicates.

> Paula and Ramon will come.
> (*Paula and Ramon* is a compound subject.)

> Charlayne laughed and clapped her hands.
> (The compound predicate is *laughed and clapped her hands.*)

The complete predicate may include a direct object, an indirect object, or a complement.

17 English Writing

A *direct object* is the word or words that receive the action of a verb:

> The boxer fought the contender.
> (*Contender* is the direct object of *fought*.)

> They found their wallets.
> (*Wallets* is the direct object of *found*.)

> The cat ate its food.
> (*Food* is the direct object of *ate*.)

An indirect object is the word or words that receive the direct object of a verb:

> The referee gave them a signal.
> (The subject is *referee*. The verb is *gave*. The direct object is *signal*. The indirect object, *them*, receives the direct object, *signal*.)

> They told me incredible stories.
> (The indirect object, *me*, receives the direct object, *stories*.)

> They gave their car good care.
> (The indirect object, *car*, receives the direct object, *care*.)

In sentences with linking verbs, which equate subjects with their predicates, the noun or adjective completing the meaning of the verb is called a *predicate noun* or *predicate adjective*. Predicate nouns and adjectives are also known as *complements*, since they complement, or complete, the meaning of the verb.

> My mother is a doctor.
> (Here, *doctor* is a predicate noun.)

> She felt sad.
> (*Sad* is the predicate adjective.)

A *complement* is an adjective or noun that complements (completes the meaning of) a noun or pronoun in the predicate.

> They named the secretary chairman as well.
> (The noun *chairman* is the complement of the noun *secretary*.)

> We find him objectionable.
> (The adjective *objectionable* is the complement of the pronoun *him*.)

Phrases. A phrase is a group of related words that does not contain a subject or a predicate. Some phrases are identified by the function they serve within a sentence. For example, a *noun phrase* is a phrase that functions as a noun in a sentence or a clause, as in the example below.

> Round-trip tickets on a transatlantic flight are less expensive in the spring and autumn.
> (The phrase *Round-trip tickets on a transatlantic flight* functions as a noun and is the subject of the sentence.)

A *verb phrase* is a group of words acting as a verb in a sentence or clause.

> Kevin will hate to pass up this chance.
> (The phrase *will hate to pass up* functions as a verb in the sentence.)

gray
US

grey
Brit.

(continued on page 136)

Parts of Speech

The English language has eight basic parts of speech, which are listed here alphabetically. Each part of speech serves a distinct grammatical function, although occasionally one part of speech may be altered to serve a different use. (For example, some verb forms can act as nouns or modifiers.) The table below provides quick definitions and examples of usage for the basic parts of speech.

Adjectives modify nouns or pronouns.

Descriptive adjectives provide additional information about the object or person being described. Degrees of comparison are usually indicated by the suffixes -er for the comparative degree and -est for the superlative (*fat, fatter, fattest*), although some adjectives require the use of more and most (*beautiful, more beautiful, most beautiful*). A few adjectives have special comparative forms (*good, better, best; bad, worse, worst*).

Intensifying adjectives, which emphasize the related noun or pronoun, and *possessive adjectives,* which show ownership, are related to personal pronouns, as can be seen in the chart below:

NUMBER	PERSON	INTENSIFYING ADJECTIVE	POSSESSIVE ADJECTIVE
Singular	first	myself	my
	second	yourself	your
	third	himself	his
		herself	her
		itself	its
Plural	first	ourselves	our
	second	yourselves	your
	third	themselves	their

Demonstrative adjectives (*this, that, etc.*) are used to indicate specific nouns. (Have you read *this* book?)

Adverbs modify verbs, other adverbs, adjectives, phrases, and clauses. Degrees of comparison are usually indicated by the use of *more* and *most* (*quickly, more quickly, most quickly*).

Conjunctions are used to connect individual words or groups of words. When conjunctions are used to connect clauses, either *coordinating* or *subordinating conjunctions* are used.

Coordinating conjunctions (such as *and, but,* and *or*) connect two independent clauses.

Subordinating conjunctions (such as *as, because,* and *until*) connect an independent clause to one that is dependent on it.

Interjections are exclamatory expressions with no grammatical relation to the sentence in which they occur. (*Gosh,* is it really that late?)

Nouns are words that are used to represent a person, animal, place, thing, idea, or quality. Nouns may be *singular* (referring to one) or *plural* (referring to more than one).

Collective nouns refer to groups of people or animals (*family, herd*). When the group is being emphasized, a collective noun is treated as singular, but when the collective noun refers to the members in the group, it is treated as plural.

Common nouns refer to any person, animal, or place (a relative, a pet, a town).

Proper nouns refer to a particular person, animal, or place (Uncle Charlie, Fido, New York City).

Prepositions show the relationship between a noun (or pronoun) and another part of the sentence. Common prepositions include *at, between, for, of,* and *with*. A pronoun following a preposition is always in the objective case.

Pronouns are words that can be used instead of nouns. The noun replaced by a pronoun is called the *antecedent*.

Indefinite pronouns (*each, all, etc.*) do not have a clear antecedent. (*Each* tried to succeed, but **none** did.)

Interrogative pronouns (*who, whom, whose, what, which*) are used to ask questions about unknown nouns. (*Who* came? *What* did she say?)

Personal pronouns are listed in this chart:

Personal Pronouns

NUMBER	PERSON	CASE		
		Nominative	Objective	Possessive
Singular	first	I	me	mine
	second	you	you	yours
	third	he	him	his
		she	her	hers
		it	it	its
Plural	first	we	us	ours
	second	you	you	yours
	third	they	them	theirs

Reflexive pronouns (*myself, yourself, himself, herself, itself, ourselves, yourselves, themselves*) refer back to the person performing an action. (*He* taught *himself*.)

Relative pronouns (*who, whom, whose, that, what, which*) introduce subordinate clauses and replace nouns or pronouns in the main clause. (He is the man *who* tried to help me.)

Verbs are used to express an action or a state of being. There are four types of verbs: *transitive, intransitive, linking,* and *auxiliary.* All verbs have four forms: the *infinitive* (to sing), the *present* (sing), the *past* (sang), and the *past participle* (sung).

Types of Verbs

Transitive verbs show an action that has an effect on an object. (John *sang* the song.)

Intransitive verbs do not have an effect on an object. (John *swam*.)

Linking verbs equate a subject and its predicate. (John *is* good.)

Auxiliary verbs are used with other verbs to indicate tense. (John *has sung* the ballad many times. John *will swim* tomorrow.)

Verbs vary according to tense, mood, and voice.

Tense

The *tense* of a verb indicates time. *Past, present,* and *future* are the three main tenses in English. In addition, English uses the *present perfect,* the *past perfect,* and the *future indicative.* The present and past perfect tenses are used to give more information about the past. The present perfect indicates that something has occurred at some indefinite time in the past, while the past perfect indicates that something has occurred at a particular time in the past. Similarly, the future perfect indicates that something will occur at some particular time in the future. (*She has taken* a nap. By teatime she *had taken* a nap. By dinnertime she *will have taken* her nap.) These tenses are formed by combining auxiliary verbs with the past participle.

Mood

English has three *moods: indicative, imperative,* and *subjunctive.* The indicative is used for statements of fact or questions (*I am coming. Are you coming?*), the imperative to give commands (*Come* here!), and the subjunctive mainly to express wishes (I wish you *were* here) and statements contrary to fact (If you *were* here, I *would be* happy).

Voice

Verbs may either be *active* or *passive.* A verb in the active voice shows that the subject has performed the action, while a verb in the passive voice shows that the subject has received the action. (I *threw* the ball. The ball *was thrown*.)

Other phrases are defined by the part of speech introducing the phrase. *Prepositional phrases* begin with prepositions and may be used as adjectives or adverbs. The noun or pronoun following a preposition is called the *object of the preposition.* Object pronouns (*me, you, him, her, it, us,* and *them*) are the only pronouns used to follow prepositions.

There are no secrets between him and me.

In this sentence, *between* is the preposition introducing the phrase *between him and me; him and me* is the object of the preposition, so both pronouns are in the objective case. (The phrase between you and I is incorrect, no matter how many times you may hear a speaker use it.)

The car sped through the intersection.

Here, the prepositional phrase *through the intersection* is introduced by the preposition through; intersection is the object of the preposition. The entire phrase functions as an adverb modifying *sped.*

Some phrases are introduced by verbals (see pages 137–138 for a more complete discussion of verbals). *Gerund phrases* are introduced by verb forms functioning as nouns.

Seeing Victoria Falls was a wonderful experience, one I'll never forget.

In this example, *Seeing* is a gerund introducing the phrase *Seeing Victoria Falls,* which functions as a noun and is the subject of the sentence.

I hate cleaning my room.

Cleaning is a gerund introducing the phrase *cleaning my room.* The phrase acts like a noun and is the direct object of *hate.*

Infinitive phrases usually function as nouns, but may serve as modifiers.

The object is to win.
(*To win* is an infinitive serving as a predicate noun and complement of is.)

He always finds amusing passages to read aloud.
(*To read* is an infinitive introducing the phrase *to read aloud,* which acts as an adjective modifying the direct object, *passages.*)

Participial phrases begin with the ing or -ed form of a verb and function as adjectives.

The dog barking at me belongs to my neighbor.
(The participial phrase *barking at me* modifies *dog.*)

The boy covered with mud is my brother.
(The participial phrase *covered with mud* modifies *boy.*)

Care must be taken to avoid *dangling participles,* which are misplaced participial phrases.

Walking along the river, many fish were visible.

In this sentence, the phrase *Walking along the river* incorrectly modifies *fish.* The writer clearly meant the phrase to modify an unnamed person. The corrected sentence might read:

Walking along the river, he could see many fish.

An *absolute phrase* is one that is closely related in meaning to the rest of the sentence in which it is found, but is grammatically independent of it and not essential to the sentence. Absolute phrases can occur either before or after an independent clause.

Her marriage over, Jessica set out for the city to start a new life.
(*Her marriage over* is an absolute phrase.)

A DANGLING PARTICIPLE can turn even the simplest thought into nonsense.

Alfred went slowly toward his truck, the rain falling gently on his head and broad shoulders, scarcely wetting him, reminding him only of the approaching winter. (Three absolute phrases follow *Alfred went slowly toward his truck.*)

Clauses. A clause is a group of related words that has a subject and a predicate and that is used as part of a sentence.

If he arrives in time, we can close the deal.

In the first clause, *he* is the subject and *arrives* is the simple predicate. The second clause also has a subject (*we*) and a predicate (*can close*).

Clauses may be independent or they may be dependent. An *independent clause* is a clause that makes sense when it stands alone and is grammatically complete. In the example above, *we can close the deal* is an independent clause and *If he arrives in time* is a dependent clause.

He is too tired to cook, and she is too sick to eat.
(In this sentence *and* connects two independent clauses.)

A *dependent* (sometimes called a subordinate) *clause* usually does not make complete sense when it stands alone, although it contains a subject and a predicate. It is a sentence embedded in another sentence, and it is dependent on another clause to complete its sense. Dependent clauses can be used as different parts of speech in a sentence, playing the role of a noun, an adjective, or an adverb.

He sat down very quietly after he made the statement.

Here, the dependent clause *after he made the statement* functions as an adverb modifying sat.

Conjunctions. Classified as coordinating, conjunctive, subordinating, and correlative, conjunctions often connect clauses.

A *coordinating conjunction* connects two words, two phrases, or two clauses of equal rank. Some common coordinating, or linking, conjunctions are *and, but, for, or,* and *still.*

Some adverbs, known as *conjunctive adverbs,* also are used to connect two independent clauses or two sentences. These include *however, then, therefore,* and *thus.*

It rained all day. *Thus,* the ball game was canceled.

The *subordinating conjunction* is used to connect two clauses of unequal rank. It connects a less important (dependent) clause to the main (independent) clause.

Everyone was happy *until* the telephone rang.

Here, *until* is a subordinating conjunction connecting *the telephone rang* to the main clause, *everyone was happy.*

Correlative conjunctions appear in pairs: *both—and; either—or; neither—nor; not only—but also.*

Neither the meat *nor* the vegetables were cooked properly.
Neither the vegetables *nor* the meat was cooked properly.

Verbals. A *verbal* is a word that is derived from a verb but serves as a different part of speech. There are three types of verbals: gerunds, infinitives, and participles.

A *gerund* is a verbal that ends in -ing and functions as a noun, not as a verb.

Loafing can be productive.

An *infinitive* is a verbal that functions as a noun, an adjective, or an adverb.

She loves *to study.*

A *participle* is a verbal that functions as an adjective.

No one wears a smoking jacket.
You act like a trapped animal.

In these sentences, *smoking* describes the noun *jacket* and *trapped* describes the noun *animal*.

Types of sentences. Sentences are classified as simple, compound, or complex. A *simple sentence* has only one independent clause and no dependent clauses.

The sales figures for May were excellent.

A simple sentence remains simple even though it contains phrases or compound subjects, compound predicates, and compound objects.

A *compound sentence* has two or more independent clauses connected by a coordinating conjunction or by punctuation.

Nathan is a born leader and he will go far.
The roast is burning; the gas must be turned down.

A *complex sentence* contains one independent clause and one or more dependent clauses.

She didn't say anything while I was there.

Here, *while I was there* is the dependent clause and *She didn't say anything* is the independent clause.

Diagramming Sentences

One way to grasp all the parts of a sentence and their relationships to each other is to diagram the sentence, that is, to make a visual representation of it.

Diagram of a simple sentence: *Birds eat.*

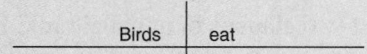

Diagram of a simple sentence with a direct object:

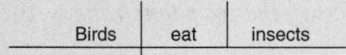

The direct object *insects* is placed above the horizontal line. The line separating *eat* (the verb) from *insects* (the direct object) does not go through the horizontal line.

Expanding the sentence to read *Wild birds usually eat many insects* results in the following diagram:

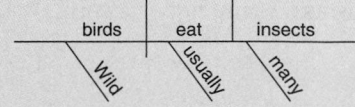

Because the subject *birds* is modified by *Wild*, the modifier *Wild* appears along a slanted line

coming out of the horizontal line before *birds*. The modifiers *usually* and *many* also appear on slanted lines coming out of the horizontal line before the words they modify.

Diagram of a simple sentence with a prepositional phrase used as an adjective and with an adjective as complement: *The lady in the red dress was beautiful.*

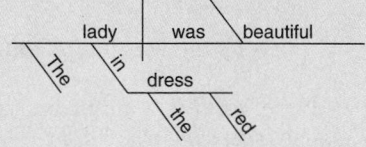

The horizontal line supplies the subject (*lady*), the verb (*was*), and the complement (*beautiful*). The verb and the complement are separated by a slanted line coming down to the horizontal line. This slanted line indicates that *beautiful* is a complement. The subject is modified by a prepositional phrase (*in the red dress*).

Diagram of a simple sentence that contains a predicate noun or complement: *Anne recently became a physician.*

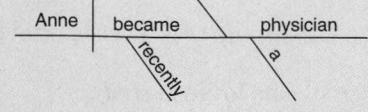

Diagramming Sentences *continued*

The horizontal line now supplies the subject (Anne), the verb (became), and the complement (physician). The verb and the complement are separated by a slanted line coming down to the horizontal line. This slanted line indicates that physician is a complement, not a direct object. The verb and the complement are modified.

Diagram of a simple sentence with a compound subject and a prepositional phrase used as an adverb: *Ray and Bernice sat in the rowboat.*

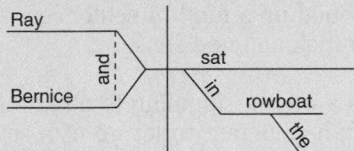

The treatment of subjects, verbs, direct objects, and modifiers has now been demonstrated. The next sentence element to be represented is the indirect object. *Joan sent us a book.*

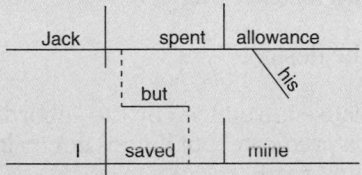

The indirect object us appears on a line below and parallel with the horizontal line on which appear the subject, verb, and direct object. The line for the indirect object is connected to the horizontal line by a slanted line. The fact that *us* is written on a horizontal line shows that it is an indirect object, not a modifier. The direct object *book* is modified by *a*, written on a slanted line.

Diagramming a simple sentence in this way enables the diagramming of other sentence types. For example, the compound sentence *Jack spent his allowance, but I saved mine* may be diagrammed as follows:

Each independent clause has its own horizontal line and the conjunction (*but*) sits between the clauses connected by broken lines to each horizontal line.

When a sentence has more than one word serving as subject, verb, object, or complement, it is diagrammed as follows. *John thoroughly enjoys school and gladly pays his tuition.*

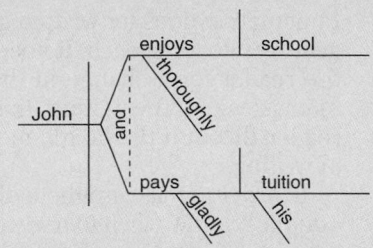

This sentence shows a compound verb (*enjoys, pays*). The conjunction (*and*) is connected to the two horizontal lines by a broken line. Since each verb also has an object, two vertical lines separate the verbs from their objects.

The same system is used with compound subjects and compound objects. *Frank and Jamie pay no attention to me.*

The compound subjects (*Frank, Jamie*) are connected by *and*, shown on the broken line. The object (*attention*) is modified.

Until this point, diagrams of independent clauses have been shown. A few sentences containing dependent clauses follow.

Diagram of a complex sentence: *The programmer will not run the program until she checks the input terminal.*

In this sentence, *until she checks the input terminal* is a dependent clause modifying the verb *will run* in the independent clause.

Diagram of a complex sentence: *That she was a beautiful woman could not be denied.*

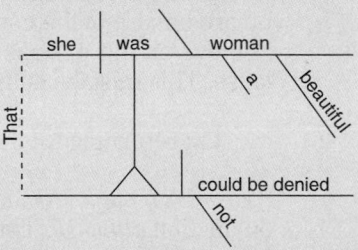

The noun clause *That she was a beautiful woman* is the subject of the sentence.

Diagram of a complex sentence: *I still deny that she gave money to me yesterday.*

In this sentence, the noun clause *that she gave money to me yesterday* is the direct object of *deny*.

Punctuation

Punctuation does for written sentences what facial expression, change of voice tone, and gestures do for speech. It keeps thoughts together, signals a break in continuity, prepares the reader for a change in thought, and keeps incidental comments separate from the mainstream of the writing. In short, punctuation acts like a set of road signs, guiding the reader through the tangle of phrases, sentences, and paragraphs that make up a piece of writing.

In order to master punctuation, you must develop a sense for building logical sentences. You must know when to use words that link clauses of equal rank (*and, but, for,* etc.), when to use words that signal embedded sentences (*when, although, because, while,* etc.), and how to punctuate so that these connective words make sense. If you are having trouble with correct punctuation, practice writing short simple sentences and then combining them into longer compound and complex sentences. As you build up a fund of sentences, you will come to see that punctuation is an important tool for making good sense.

End stops. End-stop or terminal punctuation is a way of signaling to a reader that a sentence has ended. Inexperienced writers are often reluctant to let go of a sentence, stringing it out by using commas or a series of *ands*. They are carried away by the force of an idea. More experienced writers understand that punctuation is most often based on grammatical structure, not on the size of the idea. Big ideas sometimes require many sentences or paragraphs to unfold.

The *period* is the most commonly used end-stop punctuation in English. It is placed after every declarative and imperative sentence, and it is used to punctuate even *elliptical sentences.*

These are sentences in which either the subject or the predicate is not stated because it is understood.

Are you going? Yes.

In this example, Yes is punctuated as a sentence because both the subject and the predicate are understood: "Yes (I am going)."

The period is *not* used to punctuate a declarative or imperative sentence that is embedded parenthetically in another sentence.

The party was attended by Dan Bates (he's the actor) and Charlayne Rogers (she's the congresswoman).

The period has uses other than as end-stop punctuation. It is placed after the initials of a person (T. S. Eliot) and after many abbreviations (B.C., Ph.D.). Accepted practice in punctuating abbreviations, however, varies widely, and you should consult a dictionary if you are unsure of the correct way to write an abbreviation.

Above all, do not use a period to punctuate a clause that is subordinate to another clause. This mistake is known as a *sentence fault* or a *sentence fragment.*

I'm returning the file cases. Although I like the design.

Here, *Although I like the design* is a dependent clause introduced by the subordinating conjunction *although.* The clause has a subject and a predicate, but it does not make complete sense when it stands alone. The example should read,

I'm returning the file cases, although I like the design.

On the other hand, two independent clauses should not be run together without any form of punctuation. This mistake, known as a *run-on sentence,* makes a sentence difficult to read and is a serious grammatical error in written composition.

The sales staff must see the new items they will have to examine all new products carefully.

Here the reader, because there is no sign that a thought has been completed, goes right on to *they will have to . . .* before realizing that there are *two* thoughts expressed. It should read,

> The sales staff must see the new items. They will have to examine all new products carefully.

The *question mark* (?) is the end-stop punctuation for all interrogative sentences. Even though a declarative sentence in parentheses takes no end-stop punctuation, an interrogative sentence in parentheses does retain its question mark.

> Is the theater full?
> At the meeting (you'll be there, won't you?), we'll discuss the matter in full.

The *exclamation mark* or *exclamation point* (!) is used to indicate a sudden or strong emotion or to make a forceful statement. The exclamation mark can go after a word, phrase, expression, or sentence. An exclamatory statement in parentheses retains the exclamation mark.

> Fire! To the barricades! It was horrible!
> Some people still do not see (willful blindness!) that there is an energy problem.

Exclamation marks can be effective when used sparingly. Beware of overuse.

Commas. The comma (,) has a number of important uses in punctuating sentences. Unfortunately, it has become a favorite of inexperienced writers. Some unskilled writers have the mistaken notion that a comma should be used whenever a breath would be taken while speaking. Still others feel that commas should be inserted before every *and* or *but*. Be sparing with commas.

Generally, commas are used to separate the clauses of a compound sentence, to mark off items in a series, to set off nonrestrictive or parenthetical remarks in a sentence, and to set off introductory adverbial phrases.

When separating clauses in a compound sentence, the comma is used only in the case of the clauses being joined by a coordinating conjunction (see Clauses, page 137). The comma does not go before *but* if the subject of the two clauses is the same.

> The train was late in starting, but we got here in time anyway.
> The lorry driver was delayed but had a good excuse.

With *or,* the comma is used when the subject shifts from one clause to another. If the subject remains the same, the comma is not used. With *and,* the comma is used unless the subjects of the two clauses are very closely connected in thought.

> The salesclerk was careless, or we would not have found out.
> The manager looked for help carefully or said he did.

> The executive assistant wrote the memo, and her secretary took it with her when she went to lunch.

> The executive assistant wrote the memo and she did it with great tact.

Under no circumstances should you separate two independent clauses by a comma alone. This mistake is known as a *comma splice* or *comma fault*.

> *Incorrect:*   The personnel office issued the procedures, all the employees are
>   expected to follow them.

> *Correct:*   The personnel office issued the procedures. All the employees
>   are expected to follow them.

Items in a series (words, phrases, and short clauses) are separated by commas.

> Sales on this product will be good in the West, in the Midwest, in the South, and in the Southwest.

> She was angry, she was frightened, she was on the verge of tears.

Commas are used to set off certain phrases and clauses embedded in a sentence. A *nonrestrictive phrase* or *clause* in a sentence is one that is not essential to the meaning of the sentence; it can be omitted and the basic meaning of the main clause will not be changed. Commas are used to set off such nonrestrictive material.

> The accountant, who was chosen just last week, has had years of experience.

When a relative clause is *restrictive,* it is necessary to the meaning of the main clause, and it is not set off by commas.

> The chartered accountant who is out sick was taken to the hospital last night.

Remarks of a parenthetical nature in a sentence can be set off by commas. These include the names of persons addressed and *appositives,* words placed after nouns to explain them.

> Can you do this, Bill? (*person addressed*)
> Ed Bains, our new programmer, seems intelligent. (*appositive*)

A comma is used to set off an introductory adverbial clause. But when such a clause follows the main clause, it is not set off.

> When we get back to the office, we'll confirm the order.
> We'll confirm the order when we get back to the office.

Quotation marks. We use quotation marks ("/") to enclose words, phrases, or sentences that are taken word for word from another source (a *direct quotation*). The quoted material is usually set off from the main clause by a comma and enclosed in quotation marks. (Quoted material printed in indented form uses neither a comma to set it off nor quotation marks.)

In American usage, question marks and exclamation marks are placed inside the quotation marks if they are part of the quote and outside if they apply to the main clause. Periods and commas are always placed inside the quotation marks, while the semicolon is always placed outside. Indirect quotes do not take quotation marks.

> The night manager said, "I want the keys now."
> "Do you have them?" he asked.

> Was it you who said, "Let's go"?
> His comment was, "I don't believe it."

> The manual says, "Stop when red light flashes"; we have no choice.
> The instructor said that we should wait for him.

Quotation marks should not be used to add emphasis or express irony. The choice of words and sentence structure should convey your meaning.

Semicolons. The semicolon (;) is used to stress the closeness or parallelism of thought between two independent clauses. The semicolon is not an end-stop punctuation, but it indicates the end of one complete thought and the beginning of another that is closely related to the first. Semicolons are also used in compound sentences that are joined by words like *therefore, hence, however, nevertheless, accordingly, thus,* and the like. In addition, they are used to separate items in a series when the items themselves have commas.

> The price is high; the quality is not worth it.
> I can't answer your question; however, I will call someone who can.

We must bring handbills for curiosity seekers and new prospects; samples for serious shoppers; and order forms, pens, and receipts for really serious customers.

Colons. The colon (:) ends a statement that leads to a listing, a catalog, an example, a question, a series of statements, or a long quotation. Frequently, the need for a colon is indicated by the expressions as *follows, following, such as,* and *including.*

We would like to order the following: five reams of copier paper, three packages of graph paper, and three boxes of floppy disks.

Colons can also be used to separate sentences when the second sentence provides additional information related to the first sentence.

You were right: John is quite intelligent.

Dashes. The dash (—) is used to indicate a sudden break in thought or change of emphasis in a sentence. It is particularly useful for overcoming the straight-line thrust of a sentence that moves from A to B to C and so on. The dash announces a change of direction or the insertion of a remark.

First the orders must be checked for price, then checked for available stock in inventory, and then—be careful here—copied for shipping labels.

Apostrophes. The apostrophe (') is used for two primary purposes: to indicate missing letters in contractions and to indicate possession. In contractions, the apostrophe is inserted where the missing letter would go. In possessives, the apostrophe and -s are added to the singular of the noun.

can't (cannot)   *Ed's* account
isn't (is not)   *bank's* rules
they're (they are)   *everyone's* problems

British Punctuation

Punctuation of British English is not much different from the practice of punctuation in the United States. (A full discussion of British punctuation follows.) It is important here to note that British writers and editors use single quotation marks ('/') where Americans use double quotation marks ("/"), and double quotation marks where Americans use single quotation marks. Two examples will show this:

UK: 'I consider him the best candidate we can choose', the prime minister said.

US: "I consider him the best candidate we can choose," the president said.

Notice that in British punctuation, the quotation mark after *choose* precedes the comma. In American punctuation, the quotation mark after *choose* follows the comma.

The possessives of singular nouns ending in *s* or *z* are formed by adding an apostrophe and an -s. Some writers prefer to add the apostrophe only.

jazz's interest
business' fascination

The possessive of plural nouns ending in *s* is formed by adding an apostrophe only.

girls' school

If a singular proper name of one syllable ends in *s*, it is customary to add an apostrophe and an -s.

> *James's* debts
> *Keats's* poetry

There are two notable exceptions to the general rule for forming possessives: Jesus and Moses take the apostrophe only.

> *Jesus'* time
> *Moses'* fame

Parentheses. Parentheses ( ) are used to set off material in a sentence that is separate or apart from the main thought. The normal sentence punctuation that would be employed if there were no parentheses should be used after the second or *closing parenthesis* (the first parenthesis is called the *opening parenthesis*).

> As soon as I hear from you (it will be soon, won't it?), I'll call Margaret.

Only when a complete independent sentence is placed within parentheses is the final period placed inside the closing parenthesis.

Italics. Words to be set in *italics* are indicated in typescript or in longhand by an underline. Titles of books, plays, magazines, and newspapers, and the names of ships, aircraft, and all manned spacecraft are always italicized. Shorter works, such as poems and stories, are put in quotation marks.

> Maugham's *Rain* and Shakespeare's *Tempest* are discussed in this Saturday's *Guardian,* which also comments on Hemingway's short story "The Killers."

Words or phrases that are to be considered as words are often italicized to make this obvious to the reader:

> Let us consider the derivation of *dependent*.

Although italics can be used to identify specified words, phrases, or even sentences for special emphasis, the use of italics for this purpose should be limited. When possible, rely on carefully selected words and sentence structures to achieve the desired emphasis.

Basic Usage

Errors in usage may occur when a writer applies the standards for spoken language to written composition. Because most people are able to communicate adequately when speaking, they find the discovery of errors in their written work to be both frustrating and baffling.

The usage problems discussed in this section often appear in the writing of educated adults as well as that of students. There are many fine points of usage, and some usage questions are answered differently by various experts. Here, however, the points of usage discussed are fairly common and enjoy wide agreement.

Cases of pronouns. A pronoun has the attributes of *number* (singular or plural), *gender* (masculine, feminine, or neuter), and *person.*

There are three classes of person: *first person,* denoting the person speaking (*I* am going, *we* are going); *second person,* denoting the person or thing spoken to (*you* may not); and *third person,* denoting the person or thing spoken of (*he* has not arrived, *they* have not arrived).

Pronouns also may be classified by *case.* There are three cases in English: nominative, objective, and possessive. Pronouns often have distinct forms for all the cases. See the chart on page 135 for the forms of personal pronouns for all three cases.

The noun or pronoun *subject* of a verb is in the *nominative case.*

The *fish* were frightened; *they* dove deeper into the pool.

Here, the noun *fish* and the pronoun *they* are in the nominative case because both are the subjects of verbs (*were frightened* and *dove*).

The *object* of a verb or a preposition is in the *objective case.*

Ray would not speak to *her.*

ME AND HIM is always wrong. Use "him and me" as the object of a verb or preposition.

Her is the object of the preposition to and is in the objective case.

The *possessive case* indicates ownership, possession, or some similar relationship. Pronouns have their distinct possessive form; they may stand as nouns or in certain constructions be used as adjectives (sometimes called possessive adjectives).

It is *my* boat; the boat is *mine.* (*adjective, noun*)

Some other pronouns have different forms for adjective and noun uses: *your, yours; her, hers; our, ours; their, theirs.*

One common fault of inexperienced writers is the failure to use the possessive form of the pronoun in cases that call for it. Often, writers feel that closeness is enough to show possession and that no change in form is necessary.

Incorrect:	My friends are happy with *me* goalkeeping.
Correct:	My friends are happy with *my* goalkeeping.

Gerunds frequently require possessive adjectives to make the meaning of a sentence clear. A common error is to use an objective pronoun instead of a possessive adjective:

Incorrect:	His parents are annoyed with *him being late* so frequently.
Correct:	His parents are annoyed with *his being late* so frequently.

Incorrect:	Their mothers like *them playing together.*
Correct:	Their mothers like *their playing together.*

Agreement of pronouns. A pronoun is said to agree with (that is, to conform to or match or be identical with) the number, gender, and person of its antecedent.

The man worked on his project.
All the children are doing their work.

Here, the pronoun *his* is singular, masculine, and in the third person to agree with *man. Children* is plural, so *their* is correct. A common mistake is to think of a singular noun as representing an abstract group.

A young student today must work hard and keep up their attention because of the competition.

Guide to North American Punctuation

Symbol/Name	Use	Example
. period	Placed at end of statements.	Grandfather is old.
	Used after initials.	J. F. K., T. S. Eliot
	Used after abbreviations.	Ph.D.
? question mark	Placed at end of sentences that ask something.	Is your grandfather very old?
	Used in parentheses to express doubt.	Chaucer, born in 1340(?), died in 1400.
! exclamation point	Placed at end of statements that show strong feelings.	Wow! Grandfather is old!
, comma	Used to separate items in a series.	My mom is young, witty, and attractive.
	Used to separate two clauses of a compound sentence joined by a coordinating conjunction.	My dad is old, but he is in good health.
	Used to set off parenthetical information.	Fred, who is quite old, is still in good health.
	Used to set off appositives.	Grandfather, a most generous man, is well regarded in our town.
	Used to set off an introductory modifier.	Despite all her hardships, she remains optimistic.
		Hurt by her taunts, he left abruptly.
		Politically, his future is not rosy.
	Placed after or before the name of someone being addressed.	Jane, please come here.
		We'll miss you, Emma.
	Used before an exact quotation or to conclude a statement in quotation marks.	He said, "We'll miss you."
		"We'll miss you," he said.
	Placed after *yes, no, oh,* and *well,* and also after interjections.	Well, the food finally arrived.
		Yes, food is what we need.
	Used in dates to separate the day and year.	My grandfather was born on May 7, 1910.
	Used to separate the name of a city and state or province.	Duluth, Minnesota Toronto, Ontario
"" quotation marks	Used to set off someone's exact words.	"Grandfather is old," Dad said.

Symbol/Name	Use	Example
' ' single quotation marks	Used for quoted speech within a quoted sentence.	"I use the words attributed to Caesar, *'Et tu, Brute,'* to express my dismay," said John.
; semicolon	Used to separate independent clauses closely related to each other.	Grandfather is old; his face is very wrinkled.
		Grandfather is old; however, I'm not sure when he was born.
	Used to separate items in a series when the items include commas.	He has traveled to London, England; Paris, France; and Munich, Germany.
: colon	Used before a list.	You will need the following items: a pen, a pencil, and an eraser.
	Used to separate independent clauses when the second clause provides additional information about the first.	I now have time to travel: I visit Italy to see Renaissance art and I visit England to see my grandchildren.
	Used before a character's lines in a play.	*Peter:* We'll fly away. *Wendy:* But, Peter, I can't fly.
	Used to separate the hour from the minutes when writing the time.	6:30
— dash	Placed before a sudden break in thought or an interruption.	I want to finish—but first I must tell you how it all began.
	Used to add emphasis to part of a sentence.	Anne was influential in our community—she was the leading physician and an inspiring speaker—and could be counted on to lead us to victory.
' apostrophe	Used to indicate a missing letter in contractions.	He's no friend of mine.
		She's running for office.
	Used to show possession.	Peter's father treats us badly. The Smiths' station wagon was damaged.
( ) parentheses	Used to set off additional information from the rest of a sentence.	He has travelled to two cities (London and Paris) and enjoyed them both.
	Used to set off sentences that are separate from the main sentence.	The president campaigned vigorously. (In fact, he made appearances in all 50 states. According to most reports, he was well received.)
[ ] brackets	Used to set off information inserted to clarify quoted material.	"Nothing was left for him [the president] to do but await word from his ambassador."

Guide to British Punctuation

Symbol/Name	Use	Example
. full stop	Placed at end of statements.	Grandfather is old.
	Used after initials.	T. S. Eliot
	Used after some abbreviations.	Ph.D., but BBC
	Used to separate the hour from the minutes when writing the time.	6.30
? question mark	Placed at end of sentences that ask something.	Is your grandfather very old?
	Used in parentheses to express doubt.	Chaucer, born in 1340(?), died in 1400.
! exclamation mark	Placed at end of statements that show strong feelings.	Grandfather is really old!
, comma	Used to separate items in a series.	My mum is young, witty, and attractive.
	Used to separate two clauses of a compound sentence joined by a coordinating conjunction.	My dad is old, but he is in good health.
	Used to set off parenthetical information.	Fred, who is quite old, still works a full day.
	Used to set off appositives.	Grandfather, a most generous man, is well regarded in our village.
	Used to set off an introductory modifier.	Despite all her hardships, she remains optimistic.
		Hurt by her taunts, he left abruptly.
	Placed after or before the name of someone being addressed.	Jane, please come here.
		We'll miss you, Emma.
	Used before an exact quotation or to conclude a statement in quotation marks.	He said, 'We'll miss you'.
		'We'll miss you', he said.
	Placed after *yes, no, oh,* and *well,* and also after interjections.	Well, the guests finally arrived.
		Gosh, a glass of lager is always welcome.
	Not used in dates to separate the month and year.	My grandfather was born on 7 May 1910.
	Used to separate the name of a city or town and a county or state.	London, England
		Banbury, Oxfordshire
' ' quotation marks or inverted commas	Used to set off someone's exact words.	'Dobbin is old', Dad said.

Symbol/Name	Use	Example
" " double quotation marks	Used for quoted speech within a quoted sentence.	'I use the words attributed to Caesar, *"Et tu, Brute",* to express my dismay', said John.
; semicolon	Used to separate independent clauses closely related to each other.	Grandfather is old; his face is very wrinkled.
		Grandfather is old; however, I'm not sure when he was born.
	Used to separate items in a series when the items include commas.	He has travelled to Madrid, Spain; Paris, France; and Munich, Germany.
: colon	Used before a list.	You will need the following items: a pen, a pencil, and a rubber.
	Used to separate independent clauses when the second clause provides additional information about the first.	I now read only my favorite novelists: the entire group comprises Hardy, Greene, Drabble, and Cary.
	Used before a character's lines in a play.	*Peter:* We'll fly away. *Wendy:* But, Peter, I can't fly.
— dash	Placed before a sudden break in thought or a change of direction in a sentence.	Grandfather is now— What are you doing here?
	Used to add emphasis to part of a sentence.	He said— quite confidently— that everything was fine.
		Anne was influential in our community— she was the leading physician and an inspiring speaker— and could be counted on to lead us to victory in the election.
' apostrophe	Used to indicate a missing letter in contractions.	He's sure to fail.
		My mum's not at home.
	Used to show possession.	Peter's father is quite sick.
		The Smiths' estate car was damaged.
( ) parentheses or round brackets	Used to set off additional information from the rest of a sentence.	He has travelled to two cities (Dublin and Munich) and enjoyed them both.
[ ] or square brackets **{ } or braces**	Used to set off sentences that are separate from the main sentence.	Burton was widely known in his time. [He travelled all over Africa.]
	Used to enclose words or figures.	He supplied the names of eleven (11) candidates. eleven [11] candidates. eleven {11} candidates.

YOU, NOT YOUS, is the plural of the pronoun "you." Always use "you were," not "you was."

Here, the writer sees *student* as the representative of a group (*young students*), hence the incorrect use of the word *their.* The sentence may be rewritten correctly as

> Young students must . . . keep up *their* grades.
> A young student must . . . keep up *his* or *her* grades.

When a pronoun is used after a noun to explain or identify it, the pronoun is termed an *appositive,* and the case of the pronoun must agree with that of the noun.

> The two skaters, she and Alex, glided across the ice.
> (*The two skaters* is the subject of the verb *glided,* so the appositive *she and Alex* must use the nominative pronoun *she.*)

> She gave the book to the brothers, Jay and him.
> (The objective pronoun *him* is used in the appositive *Jay and him* because the noun it is identifying, *brothers,* is the object of the preposition *to.*)

A special group of pronouns, called *indefinite pronouns,* causes trouble with agreement. One group requires plural verbs and complements: *few, some, many, all.*

> *Many are* called but *few are* chosen.

The indefinite singular pronouns include *everybody, everyone, each, either, neither, someone, no one,* and *anyone.* They require singular verbs and complements.

> *Everybody* is happy.
> *No one comes* to see me.

Another problem in pronoun agreement takes place when a writer unnecessarily shifts from one person to another in the same sentence.

> *Incorrect:*   Many young people have heard that if *they* want to succeed and get a good job, *you* have to stay in school.

Here, the writer shifts from the third person (*people, they*) to the second person (*you*). Most likely, the writer is making the mistake of changing perspective while writing. But such shifts are disconcerting to the reader. The corrected sentence should end, . . . *they* have to stay in school.

Subject and predicate agreement. The subject of a sentence must agree with the predicate in number. A plural subject takes a plural verb, and a singular subject takes a singular verb.

> The cats play. A dog runs.

A particularly common subject-predicate error is the wrong use of the contractions *don't* and *doesn't. Don't* is correct for first and second person (I *don't* want to go; you *don't* see the point) and for all plurals (they *don't* care). But for the third person singular, *doesn't* is correct.

> She *doesn't* want to go.

HAVE, the auxiliary verb, requires the past participle "written." Use "I have written."

There are several special rules that help determine whether a subject requires a singular or plural verb and complement.

A subject that is joined to a group of words introduced by *with, together with, accompanied by, as well as, including,* etc., is *not* changed in number.

> The director, together with the department managers, *was* at the meeting.
> The department managers, accompanied by the director, *were* at the meeting.

When two or more singular subjects are joined by *or* or *nor,* the verb is singular. On the other hand, when a singular and a plural subject are joined by *or* or *nor,* the verb must agree in number with the subject nearest it.

Either *Rosita* or *Carmen is* to be in charge.
Neither Roberta nor the *typists are* to be present.
Either the sales representatives or *Daniel is* to handle telephone queries.

A *collective noun* is singular in form but refers to a group. A collective noun is treated as singular when the group is thought of as a unit. A collective noun is treated as plural when the members of the group are considered individually. Some of the most common collective nouns are *audience, cast, choir, flock, majority, minority, opposition, squad, staff,* and *team.*

The minority is too small to make its voice heard.
(The collective noun *minority,* thought of as a unit, is treated as singular.)

The majority in our shop are satisfied with their working conditions.
(The collective noun *majority,* thought of as meaning more than half the number of persons in our shop, is treated as plural.)

When a sentence begins with the words *here* or *there,* the number of the verb must agree with the subject that follows the verb.

Here *is* the *house* I spoke of.
Here *are* the *players* now.

There *is* a great *deal* of grumbling among the staff.
There *are* many *reasons* for this.

In expressions like *one of the strategies that,* the verb agrees in number with the antecedent of the pronoun.

This is one of the strategies that are employed to reduce costs.

Here, the antecedent of *that* is *strategies;* hence the plural verb *are.*

She is the only one of the typists who is capable of doing the job.

Here, the antecedent of *who* is *one* (referring to *she*); hence the singular verb is.

Verb forms. Some of the characteristics of verbs have already been described (see the beginning of the English Grammar chapter). Verbs take many forms to express action or state of being in various times (tense), in ways of acting between subject and object (voice), and in mood.
Tense is used to indicate the time of the action implied or stated in the verb. While there are traditionally six classifications of tenses in English, most simple expository writing concerns itself with two: the present and the past.
The *present tense* is most often used to express action that is going on at present.

The orders *are* ready to ship now.
The canoe *glides* downstream.

However, the present tense can also be used to express future time in certain instances.

The plane *departs* in five minutes.

The *past tense* is used to indicate an action that was completed at a definite time in the past.

Bob *wrote* that letter last week.
The team *played* well in yesterday's match.

All verbs have a present and past tense. Most verbs (sometimes called *weak verbs*) form the past tense by adding -ed or -d to the root.

jump → jumped   *die* → died

Certain common verbs (sometimes called *strong verbs* or *irregular verbs*) change their form in the past tense.

    sing → sang   *write* → wrote

Other tenses of verbs are formed by using *auxiliary verbs.* For example, to show action completed in the past, we use the *perfect tense,* which is formed by using the auxiliary *have* and the past participle of the verb.

Past participles of weak verbs are the same as their simple past.

    I *jumped* over the wall.
    I *have jumped* over the wall.
    She *has jumped* over the wall.

Strong verbs, however, have a separate form when used as past participles.

    She *sang* a song.
    She *has sung* that song before.

The principal parts of a verb are its present form, past form, and past participle form. The forms of the weak verbs are *regular* and easy to predict. In the English Grammar chapter there is a table of strong verbs showing their principal parts.

Though the table includes only a handful of these verbs, it does contain many of the common ones. The most common of all, *to be,* is so irregular that it requires special mention. The present form differs according to person and number, as does the past form.

Present	*Past*
I *am*	I *was*
you, we, they *are*	you, we, they *were*
he, she, it *is*	he, she, it *was*

The present participle of *to be* is *being;* the past participle is *been;* the infinitive form is *(to) be.*

Many people have an ear for the correct form of irregular verbs and automatically use the right form. Those who find themselves using wrong forms should study the table and memorize the correct conjugations. Two special rules may be useful in studying the table:

1. The past form is never used with such auxiliary verbs as *was, were, have,* and *had.* The following expressions are incorrect:

    have *froze*
    has *swam*

THE PRINCIPAL PARTS of the verb *to swim* are present form: *swim* (I *swim* well); past form: *swam* (I *swam* yesterday); and past participle: *swum* (I have *swum* there often).

2. The past participle is always used with these auxiliary verbs. The following expressions are correct:

> have *frozen*
> has *swum*

Mastering the forms of irregular verbs eliminates many writing errors.

There are three forms of the verb with special uses. The *infinitive* consists of the root of the verb often preceded by the word *to*. Infinitives are used in showing intention or desire.

> We plan *to fly* to Los Angeles.
> He wants *to go* to Surrey.

They are also used when reporting what has been said or thought.

> She told him *to be* good.

The infinitive without *to* is also used with the auxiliary verb *will* or *shall* to express future actions or states of being.

> He *will go* to town tomorrow.
> I *shall be angry* if you continue.

Care should be taken to avoid placing adverbs between *to* and the root.

> He wants *to write carefully.*

is preferable to

> He wants *to carefully write.*

The second special form of the verb is the participle. The *past participle* is used with a form of the auxiliary verb *have* to express actions or states of being in the past.

> *Simple past:*   I *ran* fast.
> *Perfect:*   I *have run* fast. (*on past occasions*)
> *Past perfect:*   I was tired because I *had run* fast.
>   (*before becoming tired*)
> *Future perfect:*   By tomorrow at this time *I will have run*
>   the race. (*rarely used*)

The *present participle* is formed by adding -ing to the verb root. It is used with forms of the verb to be to express actions that are continuing or habitual.

> I *am running* three times a week.
> She *was smoking* more than usual.
> They *have been sending* signals all night.

A participle may also be used as an adjective, describing the action or state of the noun it modifies.

> the *broken* doll (*past participle*)
> the *dripping* water pipe (*present participle*)

The third special form of the verb is called the *gerund*. It is the same as the verb's present participle in form, but it is used as a noun.

> *Swimming* is good exercise.
> His hobbies are *singing* and *playing* the piano.

Note in the second example that the gerund can take an object as if it were a verb.

Verbs are usually classified as either transitive or intransitive. *Transitive verbs* show an action of some type that has an effect on an object.

Jack *swung* the bat.

Intransitive verbs have no effect on an object.

They *studied* hard.

Transitive verbs also have *voice*. They use the *active voice* in the most common sentence order.

Jack *hit* the ball hard.

They use the *passive voice* when the receiver of the action is the subject.

The ball *was hit* hard by Jack.

The passive form of a verb is formed by using *to be* as an auxiliary with the past participle of the verb.

The bicycle   *is being stolen.*
                    was stolen.
                    has been stolen.
                    will be stolen.

Mood indicates the manner in which the action of the verb takes place. The *indicative mood* makes a statement or asks a question. The *imperative mood* gives a command or makes a request. The *subjunctive mood* indicates wishfulness, doubt, a condition contrary to fact, or uncertainty about the action of the verb. Verb forms do not change for indicative and imperative mood. The subjunctive mood makes use of auxiliaries such as *would* and *should*.

I *would have loved* a sip of water.

In formal writing, use of the infinitive form of the verb *to be* sometimes shows the subjunctive mood.

If God *be* for us, who can be against us?

The subjunctive may also be recognized by the use of a past form where a present form would otherwise be expected.

I wish you *were* here now.

Today many writers would use an alternative form to express this wish.

I wish you *could* be here now.

When the subjunctive is used in a conditional clause or a clause expressing a condition contrary to fact, a form of the past tense is used rather than a construction employing *would* or *should*.

Incorrect: If I *would have known* that you were home, I would have called.

Correct: If I *had known* that you were home, I would have called.

In the corrected sentence, the clause introduced by *If* uses the past perfect tense of the verb *to know*. This use of the past tense conveys the fact that the speaker did not know that the person addressed had been at home.

Guide to North American Usage

Informal English is the language used most in speaking with friends and family and in writing friendly letters. It is also the language used in many magazines, books, and newspapers meant to be read by the general public. The words of informal English are the familiar, everyday ones.

Formal English is the language used for formal situations—speaking before a town meeting, reporting on research, writing a paper. In these settings, the choice of words should be the best the writer can manage.

Speaking or writing correctly may not guarantee that a message is sound, but correctness does guarantee that an audience will not be distracted by the form of communication.

This guide contains many examples of commonly misused, misspelled, incorrect, and confusing words and phrases. Being aware of them will help you avoid the pitfalls of careless speech or writing.

---

a, an. *A* is the article used before a consonant sound (*a* dog); *an* is used before a vowel sound (*an* ant). This rule is based on the opening sound of the following word, not on its first letter (*a* house, *an* hour).

accept, except. *Accept* is a verb meaning receive or approve. *Except* is a preposition that means excluding. (I *accept* all your comments *except* the last one.)

adapt, adopt. *Adapt* means become accustomed. (Ruth quickly *adapted* to her new home.) *Adapt* also means make suitable to conditions or requirements. (After three trials the engineers were able to *adapt* the engine to meet the requirements of high-speed performance.) *Adopt* means take up or practice, choose to take. (They *adopted* the latest styles as soon as they appeared.)

adjectives. Many overworked and misused adjectives should be avoided in formal writing. Something is *wonderful* if it inspires wonder; otherwise, *wonderful* is an empty adjective. Other adjectives to look out for are *awful, beautiful, incredible, nice, terrible,* and *terrific.* If an adjective tells the reader only that one has vaguely approved or disapproved of something, a better adjective is needed.

advice, advise. *Advice* is a noun; *advise* is a verb. (He *advised* me to take the doctor's *advice*.)

affect, effect. *Affect* is a verb that means influence. (The weather *affects* my moods.) *Effect* is a noun that means result. (She did not consider the *effect* of her action.) *Effect* may also be a verb meaning cause. (The new law *effected* a major change in government.)

aggravate. In formal usage, to *aggravate* means to make worse. (She was told she had *aggravated* her ulcer by worrying about it.) The informal use of *aggravate* to mean annoy, while acceptable in informal speech, is less acceptable in writing.

agree to, agree with. *Agree to* something; *agree with* someone.

ain't. Not acceptable in formal speech or writing.

all of, alongside of. *See* of.

already, all ready. *Already* means by this time. (She was *already* angry when he arrived.) *All ready* means all prepared. (He was *all ready* to leave.)

altogether, all together. *Altogether* means thoroughly or completely. (That is an *altogether* different matter.) *All together* means in a group. (They played cards when they were *all together*.)

among, between. *Among* is most often used for three or more, *between* for two. (*Among* all the applicants; *between* the two brothers.) *Between* is also used to indicate a relationship of any two members of a group of three or more. (Agreements began to arise *between* the nations of Africa.)

amount, number; fewer, less. *Amount* refers to quantity in bulk while *number* refers to separate units. (The *amount* of money; the *number* of dollars.) Likewise, *fewer* refers to *numbered* things while *less* refers to *amount*. (The *number* of pieces in the game was *fewer* than called for; the *amount* of sugar we needed was *less* than we thought.)

an. *See* a.

anxious, eager. In formal writing, *anxious* means apprehensive, worried, while *eager* means looking forward to. (I am *anxious* about the exam; I am *eager* to see you again.)

anybody, anyone, each, everybody, everyone, nobody, none, no one, somebody, someone. These words are all singular and always take a singular verb. (*Everybody is* here.) When a pronoun refers back to these words, *he* and *his* are frequently used. (*Everyone knows* what *he* is supposed to do.) *See also* gender of singular pronouns.

as regards. This expression is a poor substitute for *about* or *concerning*. (I am calling *about* [not *as regards*] the dress I ordered.)

aural. *See* oral.

beautiful. *See* adjectives.

being as, being that. Both these expressions are incorrect replacements for *because* or *since*. (I am quitting *because* [not *being as* or *being that*] you refuse to cooperate.)

beside, besides. *Beside* means by the side of. (They stood *beside* each other.) *Besides* means moreover. (*Besides*, what difference does it make?)

between. *See* among.

between you and me. This is a correct expression. *Between you and I* is grammatically wrong. After prepositions like *between*, use the objective pronouns *me, him, her, us, them*, not the subjective pronouns *I, he, she, we, they*.

burst. Do not confuse this verb with *bust*. (The pipes will *burst* if they are not drained in winter.)

but. *See* double negatives.

can, may. *Can* implies the ability to do something; *may* implies permission or chance. (He *can* drive; his father said he *may* go; she *may* stay or she *may* not.)

capital, capitol. A *capitol* is the main building of a government. (The *Capitol* is open to the public at certain times.) For all other meanings, the correct spelling is *capital*.

censor, censure. To *censor* means to prohibit or cut out objectionable material. (News coverage is strictly *censored* in some countries.) The person whose job it is to examine material for censorship is called a *censor*. To *censure* is to reprimand. (He was *censured* by the principal for cheating.)

childish, childlike. Children can be both lovable and annoying. Someone who is *childish* has some of the annoying traits of children. (His whining and *childish* obstinacy lost him many friends.) Someone who is *childlike* has the innocence and freshness associated with children. (He viewed the most ordinary things with *childlike* wonder.)

cite, sight, site. To *cite* something means to quote or refer to it. (They *cited* the benefits derived from other projects.) *Sight* as a noun means vision. (Her *sight* was improved by wearing glasses.) As a verb, to *sight* something means to see it. (He *sighted* the body floating on the water.) A *site* is a location. (The construction *site* was easily accessible. Her Web *site* is easily navigable.)

Guide to North American Usage *continued*

climactic, climatic. The adjective *climactic,* related to the noun *climax,* refers to decisive acts or events. (The trial was approaching its *climactic* phase.) The adjective *climatic* is related to the noun *climate.* (We have been told we can expect major *climatic* changes in the next five years.)

compare to, compare with. *Compare to* means show the similarities between two things of different classes. (He *compared* Earth *to* a child's ball since they are both spherical.) *Compare with* means show the similarities and differences of two things in the same class. (*Compare* this house *with* the other one and you'll see which is more livable.)

complement, compliment. A *complement* is that which completes; to *complement* means to complete. (The rug *complements* the room; the dessert was the perfect *complement* to a fine meal.) A *compliment* is praise; to *compliment* means to praise. (I *complimented* him on his choice of materials; he returned the *compliment.*)

consensus of opinion. The words *of opinion* are superfluous. *Consensus* means general agreement in belief or opinion. (We were able to reach *consensus.*)

contemptible, contemptuous. Acts worthy of contempt or scorn are contemptible. (We find lying *contemptible.*) People showing contempt are *contemptuous.* (Why are they so *contemptuous* of me?)

continual, continuing, continuous. *Continual* means repeated but frequently interrupted. (She was annoyed by her husband's *continual* snoring.) *Continuing* means existing over a long period. (The designer said she had a *continuing* interest in working for charitable organizations.) *Continuous* means uninterrupted and ongoing. (*Continuous* operation of the television set will lead to serious problems.)

could of. *See* of.

council, counsel, consul. A *council* is a meeting or a group set up to govern or advise. (The *council* voted to accept the proposition.) *Counsel* means advice or, as a verb, to advise. (I offer you my *counsel* in this matter, if you want it; she *counseled* him on which steps to take first.) *Counsel* also means a lawyer. (The *counsel* for the defense called his first witness.) A *consul* is a government official who works in a foreign country.

credible, credulous. *Credible* means believable. (He gave a *credible* excuse for being late.) *Credulous* means gullible. (The *credulous* girl believed every story she heard.) *See also* incredible.

criteria. *Criteria,* meaning standards of judgment, is plural and takes a plural verb. (Their *criteria* for giving her the promotion *were* sound.) The singular is *criterion.*

data. This noun is the plural form of *datum.* The singular, *datum,* is almost never seen except as a modifier in, for example, *datum point.* Careful writers use a plural verb with *data.* (The *data* she collected were sufficient to prove her claim.)

deduce, deduct. To *deduce* is to reach a conclusion through reasoning. (Sherlock Holmes's method was to *deduce* who the criminal was from a few facts surrounding the case.) To *deduct* is to subtract. (Don't forget to *deduct* the amount he owes you.)

dependent. It is a good idea to spell *dependent* with the *-ent* ending. This is acceptable for both the noun and the adjective. *Dependant* is an acceptable spelling for the noun, but is incorrect for the adjective. (Although my son is my only *dependant,* he is not overly *dependent* on me.)

desert, dessert. A *desert* is an arid tract of land. To *desert* means to abandon. (He *deserted* his family when they needed him most.) *Dessert* is a sweet course served at the end of a meal.

desirable, desirous. Desirable objects or people are sought after. (I find some examples of modern art highly *desirable.*) Desirous people yearn for something. (Margie was *desirous* of achieving acceptance.) Even better, *Margie desired wealth.*)

device, devise. *Device* is a noun. (The ingenious *device* had several functions.) *Devise* is a verb. (He *devised* a strategy to get a promotion.)

differ from, differ with. To *differ from* means to be unlike. (Her work methods *differ from* mine.) To *differ with* means to disagree. (He *differs with* me on the best approach to the problem.)

discreet, discrete. *Discreet* means prudent in speech or behavior. (Be *discreet* about our plans if you want us to win.) *Discrete* means separate. (There are five *discrete* steps in the solution of that problem.)

disingenuous. *See* ingenious.

disinterested, uninterested. Use *disinterested* to mean impartial. (A good judge is always *disinterested.*) *Uninterested* means showing lack of interest. (Many students are *uninterested* in mathematics.)

distinctive, distinguished. *Distinctive* means characteristic. (The governor's *distinctive* oratorical style sets him apart from other candidates for national office.) *Distinguished* means eminent or marked by excellence. (My *distinguished* sister is being talked of as a possible recipient of a Nobel Prize.)

double negatives. Double negatives occur in a sentence where two negative words are used. (I *don't* go *nowhere.*) The meaning of such a sentence is unclear. Does it mean that the person does not go anyplace, or that he or she goes everywhere *but* nowhere? Double negatives should be avoided in writing, especially with *but, hardly,* and *scarcely.* (I *don't* have *but* a dollar; I *can't hardly* do it; he *scarcely* knows *nobody.* All three examples are incorrect. Correct usage is I have *but* a dollar; I *can hardly* do it; he *scarcely* knows *anybody.*)

each. *See* anybody.

eager. *See* anxious.

ecology, environment. These two nouns are frequently confused. *Environment* means conditions surrounding a living organism. (Pollution can damage our *environment.*) *Ecology* means the study of the interactions of plants or animals with their environments. (More and more college students are taking courses in *ecology.*)

effect. *See* affect.

e.g. This abbreviation, which is preceded and followed by commas, is usually used in scholarly writing. It means for example. *See also* i.e.

either, neither. *Either* goes with *or; neither* goes with *nor.* (*Either* you go *or* I will; *neither* you *nor* I can go.) *See also* neither.

elicit, illicit. *Elicit* is a verb meaning draw forth. (I hope to *elicit* a positive response to my suggestion.) *Illicit* is an adjective meaning unlawful. (A campaign is under way to eliminate *illicit* drugs from our streets.)

emigrate, immigrate. One *immigrates to* a new country and *emigrates from* an old one. People who move to another country are called *emigrants* in their former country and *immigrants* in their new country. *Migrants* travel from place to place.

eminent, imminent. *Eminent* means distinguished. (The *eminent* scholar lectured at our school.) *Imminent* means about to take place. (The collapse of our government seems *imminent.*)

enormity. The primary meaning of *enormity* is excessive wickedness. (Who can understand the *enormity* of genocide?)

environment. *See* ecology.

epitaph, epithet. An *epitaph* is an inscription on a grave-stone. An *epithet* is a phrase that accompanies or replaces the name of a person. (The Little Tramp is an *epithet* for Charlie Chaplin.) *Epithet* may also mean a word of abuse.

everybody. *See* anybody.

everyone. *See* anybody.

except. *See* accept.

expect. This verb means anticipate. (We *expect* you for lunch.) It does not mean suppose. (I suppose [not *expect*] you know that the next meeting has been canceled.)

feel bad. The correct expression is *feel bad,* not *feel badly;* it means that one does not feel well or happy. *See also* good.

fewer. *See* amount.

flaunt, flout. The verb *flaunt* means show off. (The violinist seemed to want only to *flaunt* his skill.) The verb *flout* means show contempt for. (Too many motorists *flout* traffic regulations.)

former, latter. *Former* refers to the first of two things mentioned; *latter* refers to the second of the two things. (He had to decide between the red tie and the blue, and he chose the *latter.*)

fortuitous, fortunate. These two adjectives are in danger of losing their separate identities. *Fortunate* means lucky. (We are *fortunate* to have a distinguished guest as our speaker tonight.) *Fortuitous* means unplanned, accidental. (The fire at the hospital was entirely *fortuitous.* A *fortuitous* encounter may often turn out to give more pleasure than a thoroughly planned date.)

fulsome. This adjective has nothing to do with full. *Fulsome* means disgustingly insincere. (I found Jane's *fulsome* praise unworthy of so prominent a literary critic.)

gender of singular pronouns. When a pronoun refers back to a singular antecedent, it is often difficult to determine what gender should be used. (The good writer always makes good use of *his* [or *her*] material; *one* must raise *his* [or *her*] hand when *he* [or *she*] wants to be recognized.) Traditionally, the singular pronouns *he* and *his* alone have been used. This may be confusing when the original noun or pronoun is indefinite; furthermore, it is frowned upon in a gender-conscious age. Instead, one may substitute *he or she* and *his or her.* (*One* must raise *his or her* hand when *he or she* wants to be recognized.) This solution is often cumbersome. In many cases, it is best to rewrite the sentence. Often *you* and *your* can be substituted for *one* and *his.* (*You* must raise *your* hand when *you* want to be recognized.) Another solution is to convert to plural forms. (*They* must raise *their* hands when *they* want to be recognized.) Some authorities recommend using the plural pronoun even with a singular noun. This solution has not been widely accepted, however, and should be avoided.

good, well. Good is an adjective; it describes a noun (the *good* child). It also describes nouns when used with verbs of appearance, sound, taste, smell, and feel. (The dress looks *good* on her; the ice cream tastes *good.*) *Well* is the adverbial equivalent of good and is used to describe actions. (He runs *well;* the chorus sings *well.*) *Well* may also be an adjective meaning healthy. (I am not sick; I am *well.*) The following uses of *well* and *good* are incorrect: the dress looks *well* on her; he swims *good.*

got to. This should be changed to *have to.* (I *have to* run; not, I *have got to* run.)

hanged, hung. The past of *hang* is *hung* except when referring to an execution by hanging. (The coat *hung* on the hook; the prisoner was *hanged* at dawn.)

i.e. This abbreviation, usually found in scholarly writing, means that is. It should be set off by commas. (Plato is concerned with the ideal, *i.e.,* the forms in the world of Idea.)

illicit. *See* elicit.

immigrate. *See* emigrate.

imminent. *See* eminent.

imply, infer. To *imply* means to suggest without actually saying so. (You *implied* that I was lying.) To *infer* means to derive a conclusion from evidence, or to surmise. (We *inferred* that she liked him from her tone of voice.)

incidence, incidents. *Incidence* means frequency of occurrence. (The *incidence* of fatal car accidents keeps rising.) *Incidents* is the plural of incident and means events. (The three *incidents* occurred in the same week.)

incredible, incredulous. Something that is *incredible* is hard to believe. Someone who is *incredulous* is hard to convince, or skeptical. *See also* adjectives.

infer. *See* imply.

ingenious, ingenuous. *Ingenious* means able, clever. (Thomas Edison was an *ingenious* inventor.) *Ingenuous* means naive, frank. (Aware that Rebecca was *ingenuous,* her parents seldom confided family secrets when speaking with her.) *Disingenuous,* the antonym of *ingenuous,* means lacking in candor.

inside of. *See* of.

in the event. Use *if* instead. (*If* something should happen to me; not, *in the event . . .*)

irregardless. The correct word is *regardless.* (We will go *regardless* of what you say.)

it's, its. *It's* is the shortened form of it is. (*It's* getting late.) *Its* is the possessive form of it. (Put the toy back in *its* place.)

it's I, it's me. Formal writers prefer *It's I,* which is grammatically correct. But everyday speech insists on *it's me, it's him,* etc. Unless the occasion is formal, use *me, him, her.*

-ize. Verbs made with the *-ize* suffix should be used with caution in writing. Often there is another word that is more precise. For example, use *conceive* instead of *conceptualize;* use *complete* for *finalize;* use *perfect* for *optimize.*

later, latter. *Later* means more late or after some time. (He will not arrive until *later.*) *Latter* refers to the second of two previously mentioned things. (Of the two ideas you mentioned, I am inclined to agree with the *latter.*) *See also* former.

lay, lie. These two verbs are often confused. To *lay* an object down is to put it down; to *lie* down is to recline. *Lay* takes an object while *lie* does not. (I can *lie* down to sleep [no object] or *lay* the pencil on the table [object].) The confusion arises because the past forms of these two verbs overlap. The past forms of *lie* are *lay* and *lain.* (She *lay* back and breathed her last; he had *lain* in that position for nearly an hour.) The past form of *lay* is *laid.* (I *laid* the book down.)

lead, led. *Lead* is the present tense of the verb to *lead.* (She *leads* the class to the auditorium.) *Led* is the past tense of the same verb. (I *led* the class yesterday.) As a noun, *lead* (pronounced led) is a metal.

less. *See* amount.

let's us. *Let's* already means *let us* so *let's us* means let us us. Use *let's* without us.

lie. *See* lay.

literally. *Literally* means in truth, really. Do not use it just to be emphatic. (When he saw me he *literally* fell through the floor is incorrect unless he actually fell through a hole in the floor.)

look good, look well. *See* good.

loose, lose. Something that is loose is slack. (My loose dress is cool in the summer.) If you lose something, you cannot find it. (Did you lose an earring?)

Guide to North American Usage *continued*

may. *See* can.

may of, might of, must of. *See* of.

mean for. In writing, *mean that* is used. (I didn't *mean that* you should go without me, not *mean for* you to go without me.)

migrant. The noun *migrant* means a person who moves from place to place. *Migrant* is also used as an adjective. (*Migrant* workers are essential to American agriculture.) *See also* emigrate.

moral, morale. That which is *moral* is ethical. (He did not think it *moral* to cheat.) It is also the lesson of a tale. (The *moral* of the story was that honesty is the best policy.) *Morale* means mental outlook or spirit. (They blamed the rainy weather for their low *morale*.)

most. *Most* should not be confused with *almost* in formal writing. (I eat *almost* anything, not *most* anything.)

negatives. *See* double negatives.

neither. *Neither* and *nor* are negatives and should not be used with other negatives. Use *either* instead. (She *will not* go to *either* place; or, *will* go to *neither* place.) *See also* double negatives; either.

nice. *See* adjectives.

nobody. *See* anybody.

none, no one. *See* anybody.

number. *See* amount.

of. It is incorrect to use *of* when you mean *have*: could *have*, may *have*, might *have*, must *have*, ought to *have*, should *have*, would *have*, will *have*. (I may *have* done it; not may *of* done it.) *Of* is also often added to expressions where it is not needed with words such as all, alongside, inside, off, and outside. (He took all my money, not he took all *of* my money.)

one. *One* should not be used to replace *I*. (Should *I* raise my hand to answer the question? not should *one* raise *his* hand?) The latter sounds pretentious.

oral, aural. *Oral* refers to the mouth and hence to speaking. An *oral* examination is one in which a student speaks, rather than writes, the answers. *Aural* refers to the ear and hence to sounds. *Aural* is often opposed to *visual*. (Thunder is an *aural* experience, lightning is *visual*.)

persecute, prosecute. To *persecute* means to harass. (The dictatorship *persecuted* those whose views differed from officially sanctioned views.) To *prosecute* means to carry out a legal suit or to perform. (Our lawyer *prosecuted* a claim against the company for negligence; the war was *prosecuted* with ruthlessness on both sides.)

phenomena. This is the plural form of the noun *phenomenon*. (These *phenomena are* strange; this *phenomenon is* strange.)

principal, principle. As an adjective, *principal* means chief. (The *principal* reason for her dismissal was frequent lateness.) *Principal* is also a noun that means capital sum. (She lived off the interest on the *principal* she'd invested.) A head person is often called a *principal*. (He is a school *principal*.) A *principle*, on the other hand, is a general rule or assumption. (He lived by his *principles*, though they differed from the community's; it was the *principle* of the thing, not the small amount of money involved.)

pronouns. *See* gender of singular pronouns.

raise, rise. To *raise* means to lift or grow something. This verb always has an object. (I *raise* my hand; I *raise* corn.) To *rise* means to get up or to increase in size. This verb never has an object. (I *rise* at six each day; the river *rises* in the spring.)

regardless. This word means heedless or unmindful. *See also* irregardless.

respectfully, respectively. *Respectfully* means with respect. (She *respectfully* questioned him.) *Respectively* means in the mentioned order. (The oldest child and the middle child are nine and six *respectively*.)

rise. *See* raise.

scarcely. *See* double negatives.

set, sit. To *set* means to put (something) down. (I'll *set* the book on the table.) To *sit* is to be seated. (You may *sit* anywhere.) *Set* usually takes an object while *sit* does not. Only the sun, the moon, and hens can *set* by themselves. *See also* lay.

should of. *See* of.

sight, site. *See* cite.

sit. *See* set.

somebody, someone. *See* anybody.

stationary, stationery. If an object is *stationary*, it is not moving. *Stationery* means writing paper.

sure and. Use *sure to*. (Be *sure to* bring your family; not, be *sure and* bring your family.)

terrible, terrific. *See* adjectives.

than, then. *Than* means when compared with or except. (He is better equipped for it *than* you; I'd rather be anywhere *than* here.) *Then* means at that time. (*Then* I went to the store.)

their, theirs, there, there's, they're. *Their* and *theirs* mean belonging to them. (*Their* house is red; the book is *theirs*.) *There* means at that place. (The blue house over *there* is mine.) *There* is also used to introduce a sentence. (*There* is nothing left of it.) *There's* is a shortened form of there is. (*There's* nothing left of it.) *They're* is a shortened form of they are. (*They're* going home.)

theirselves. Use *themselves*. (They asked *themselves* the same question, not they asked *theirselves*.)

there is, there are. A singular noun follows *there is;* a plural noun follows *there are*. (*There is* a good reason for bicycle riding; in fact, *there are* several reasons.)

to, too, two. *Too* means also or more than enough. (I want some *too;* they were *too* loud.) *Two* is the number 2. In every other case, the word is *to* (*to* run; give it *to* me; *to*-and-fro; from New York *to* California; dance *to* the music, etc.).

uninterested. *See* disinterested.

unique. This word means the only one of a kind. Therefore, one thing cannot be more unique than another. (The desk that she built was *unique;* not, was most *unique* or was practically *unique*.)

well. *See* good.

which. *Which* does not refer to people; *who* does. (The people *who* own this car are inconsiderate; not *which* own this car.)

who, whom, whoever, whomever. Traditionally, *who* and *whoever* are subjects of verbs; *whom* and *whomever* are objects of verbs. (*Who* is coming? *Whom* do you wish to see?) *Whom* and *whomever* are disappearing, however, and are being replaced by *who* and *whoever*. Many authorities consider it acceptable to write, "*Who* do you wish to see?" Using *whom* where *who* is required is a more serious blunder. *Whom* should be used only when the writer is sure that it is the object of a verb.

who's, whose. *Who's* is the shortened form of who is. (I need to know *who's* going.) *Whose* is the possessive form of who. (*Whose* coat is that?)

-wise. This suffix should be used in formal writing to mean in the manner or direction of, e.g., *clockwise, otherwise, lengthwise*. Do not use it to mean in regard to. (I'm having a bit of trouble *moneywise* is not acceptable. Write instead, I'm having *financial* trouble.)

Guide to British Usage

This compilation owes much to the excellent guidance offered in Robert Burchfield's The Spoken Word, A BBC Guide, published by the British Broadcasting Corporation (1981), and in Bill Bryson's The Penguin Dictionary of Troublesome Words, published by Penguin Books (1987). Mr Burchfield was chief editor of the Oxford English Dictionaries until his retirement in 1986. Mr Bryson, born in the United States, has lived in England since 1977 and writes regularly for newspapers and magazines throughout the English-speaking world.

British usage differs in some respects from American usage but is identical in many others. In the following listing, some items are uniquely British, but others coincide with American usage, so the reader is encouraged to compare the preferences shown here with those shown in the Guide to North American Usage. The American reader would also do well to consult the entries in the Guide to British Usage. In the main, the level of usage shown here represents British practice in formal writing.

---

about. See around.

accrue. This verb means add to bit by bit. Thus, profits may be said to *accrue* from an investment over a period of time, but not from a windfall.

acute, chronic. These adjectives sometimes are confused by careless writers. *Acute* characterises conditions that come to a head suddenly and require immediate attention. (We were faced with an *acute* shortage of funds.) *Chronic* characterises conditions that linger and are generally difficult to overcome except through extended attention. (Her long years of exposure to silica dust resulted in *chronic* difficulty in breathing, and her physician could do little more than ease her problem.)

adverse, averse. These adjectives are regularly confused by careless writers. *Adverse* means contrary, hostile, hurtful, injurious. (The schedule they adopted did not take into account the *adverse* weather that could be expected during winter.) *Averse* means opposed or disinclined. (My father was thought to be *averse* to hard work by those who did not know of his declining health.)

allay, alleviate, assuage. These three verbs all mean relieve in one sense or another. *Allay* means reduce or diminish. (She could do little to *allay* her patient's fears.) *Alleviate* means lessen or make less burdensome. (He tried everything he knew to *alleviate* his parents' suffering.) *Assuage* means calm or soothe. (Nothing he tried could *assuage* his remorse. Surely, you need little more than a biscuit to *assuage* your appetite.)

alleviate. See allay.

all right. This two-word expression is correct. The spelling *alright* is not considered acceptable in formal writing.

allusion, reference. These two nouns and their associated verbs, *allude* and *refer*, are close in meaning but retain an important difference: While the meaning of *refer to* is well understood as mention or direct attention to, *allude* means speak of indirectly. (At the dinner table, do not *refer* to the recent election. If you desire peace at the table, do not even *allude* to it.) Thus, an *allusion* is an indirect reference. (You must bear in mind that any *reference* to his disability—even an *allusion* to it—will not be well received.)

alternate, alternative. When used as adjectives, these two words have different meanings that should be preserved in formal writing, even though careless users treat them as close synonyms. *Alternate* means by turns, first one thing and then the other. (The actor moved his audience to *alternate* groans and peals of laughter.) *Alternative* means serving in place of something else. (The idea of *alternative* schools arose at least two decades ago.) When used as nouns, *alternate* and *alternative* also have different meanings. *Alternate* means deputy or substitute. (The party leaders decided to select and seat two *alternates*, because they knew that a protracted meeting might be too physically demanding for older delegates.) *Alternative* means one of two or more possibilities. (There are only two *alternatives*. Of the several *alternatives* proposed, I prefer the one that causes least discord.)

anticipate. This verb has two meanings that are considered correct. One correct meaning is take action before someone else has had time to do so. (Others may have *anticipated* Columbus in the discovery of America.) A second correct meaning is to notice what needs doing and take action in advance. (A good host *anticipates* every need of his guests. A good boxer *anticipates* his opponent's blows.) A common meaning of *anticipate* that is considered incorrect is expect. (We *anticipate* that it will rain tomorrow.)

anxious, eager. Careless writers use these two adjectives incorrectly as synonyms. *Anxious* means troubled, feeling anxiety, or causing anxiety. (She felt *anxious* about her daughter's appendectomy. The *anxious* moments soon passed, and everyone felt relieved.) By contrast, *eager* means strongly desirous. (As always, they were *eager* to participate in the cricket match.)

appraise, apprise. These two verbs are often confused by careless writers. *Appraise* means evaluate or assess. (It's best to ask a trustworthy jeweller to *appraise* any gems you wish to have insured.) *Apprise* means inform. (We were *apprised* of his stated intention to proceed honourably in the matter.)

approve. See condone.

arbitrate, mediate. These two verbs, along with their related nouns, *arbitrator* and *mediator*, are often confused. An *arbitrator* is appointed to hear arguments and evaluate evidence in order to settle disputes between two parties. Thus, to *arbitrate* is to judge between parties in a dispute. (The chancery appointed a disinterested and highly respected solicitor who could be counted on to *arbitrate* the dispute between the heirs.) A *mediator* is a person who acts as a go-between or peacemaker. *Mediate* means act as mediator in a dispute in an effort to work out a compromise. (The month-long labour dispute was finally *mediated* by a patient minister who skilfully made explicit each party's position and then showed how close to agreement the parties were, enabling them to reach a binding compromise within half an hour.)

around, about. *Around* is considered incorrect as a synonym for *about*, with the meaning of approximately. (We will be home in *about* [not *around*] three hours. *About* 50 people [not *around* 50 people] were present.)

assuage. See allay.

auger, augur. This pair presents a spelling problem for many people. *Auger*, a noun, is a tool used for boring holes in wood or soil. *Augur*, a verb, means foresee, predict, or portend. (Mark's ability to bowl so accurately *augurs* badly for our opponents.) *Augur* is related to the noun *augury*, which means divination.

averse. See adverse.

between you and I. This expression is seen as a gross grammatical error, yet it is often heard. It is not often seen in formal writing, but only because most published writers know better, and sharp-eyed editors correct such lapses before they can appear in print. Why is the form *between you and me* considered correct? Because *you* and *me* are properly in the accusative case as befits pronouns that are objects of a preposition. Just as you would not write *send the present to I*, never write or say *between you and I*.

Guide to British Usage *continued*

bravado, bravery. These two nouns resemble one another but have different meanings. *Bravado* means a display of boldness or daring. (The *bravado* he characteristically displays is intended to obscure his complete abhorrence of conflict.) *Bravery* means courage. (When military decorations are awarded for *bravery*, you can be sure that the recipients have performed admirably under enemy fire.)

chafe, chaff. These two verbs are sometimes confused. The principal meanings of *chafe* are make or become sore or damaged by rubbing, and irritate or fret. (Her new shoes *chafed* at first but soon gave her no cause for complaint. She *chafed* at the unexpected delay in departures from Heathrow.) The verb *chaff* means banter, tease good-naturedly. (I complained many times about the way he persisted in *chaffing* the children, even though his jokes made them uncomfortable.) Both *chafe* and *chaff* are also used as nouns. As a noun *chafe* means a sore made by chafing, and a state of annoyance. As a noun, *chaff* means the husks of grain removed by threshing, hay or straw used as food for cattle, and good-natured teasing or banter.

chronic. *See* acute.

collaboration, collusion. It is worthwhile to observe the differences in meaning of these two synonyms. *Collaboration,* which means co-operation, usually has a positive connotation. (The two scientists worked productively in *collaboration* throughout their long careers.) *Collaboration,* when it is intended to mean traitorous co-operation, is pejorative. (At the end of the war many subjects were tried for *collaboration* [or *collaborating*] with enemy forces.) *Collusion,* always pejorative, means a secret understanding for a fraudulent or deceitful purpose. (The investigators found evidence of *collusion* between the bank manager and some depositors to support a bill of indictment.)

compare to, compare with. Careful writers use *compare to* in showing similarities between people or things, *compare with* in showing differences as well as similarities. (She was overjoyed when reviewers *compared* her latest novel *to* Joyce's *Ulysses*. The unhappy writer *compared* his edited article *with* the manuscript he had submitted to the editors.)

compel, impel. These two verbs are sufficiently distinct in meaning to require close attention. *Compel* means bring about an action by force. (The circumstances are so pressing that we are *compelled* to act at once. The people of our town are completely cut off and starving, *compelling* immediate surrender.) *Impel* means encourage. (Once I realised how desperate the beggar was, I felt *impelled* to give the poor man the three pound notes I had in my pocket.) Thus, *compel* is the stronger of the two verbs, suggesting no alternative but to act, while *impel* suggests willingness to act.

complement, compliment. These two verbs are so close in spelling that some writers fail to use them correctly. *Complement* means complete, fill out, make whole. (A bright red bonnet *complemented* her colourful frock.) *Compliment* means praise. (No matter how often he was *complimented* by his friends, he could never get too much of their praise.)

condone, approve. These two verbs have separate meanings. *Condone* means overlook or forgive. (Nothing they could say about why they acted the way they did could *condone* their behaviour.) *Approve,* of course, means sanction or commend. (Commons *approved* the prompt military response proposed by the government.)

contemptible, contemptuous. These two adjectives are confused even by careful writers, yet the meanings of the two words should be regarded as separate.

Contemptible means despicable, deserving of contempt. (The party leaders decided that her *contemptible* behaviour could not be condoned.) *Contemptuous* means scornful, insolent, showing contempt. (A candidate openly *contemptuous* of ordinary people stands little chance of winning the coming by-election.)

credible, credulous. *Credible* young men are believable, and *credible* excuses should ordinarily be believed. *Credulous* young men are too ready to believe, and excuses are never *credulous*. The antonyms of these adjectives, *incredible* and *incredulous,* also have different meanings. *Incredible* means surprising, unbelievable. (What they did next was almost *incredible*.) *Incredulous* means unbelieving, skeptical. (Voters were predictably *incredulous* when the prime minister promised to balance the national budget while reducing taxes.)

decimate. So many readers mistakenly take *decimate* to mean destroy a large proportion of, and even to mean annihilate, that proper use of this verb is now in mortal danger. *Decimate* is best used to mean reduce by a tenth. (When the attacking force *was decimated,* the assault came to a halt. The outbreak of cholera *decimated* the population.) In the first of these examples, the attacking force was reduced by ten per cent, and in the second example the population was reduced by ten per cent.

deduce, deduct. Careless writers confuse these two verbs. *Deduce* means draw as a conclusion, infer. (Holmes finally *deduced* that the perpetrator he sought was not human.) *Deduct* means take away, put aside, subtract. (So much *was deducted* from my pay-packet that I did not know how I could manage for the rest of the month.)

deprecate, depreciate. These two verbs are confused by careless writers. *Deprecate* means express disapproval of. (It seems that he must invariably *deprecate* every idea his wife advances.) *Depreciate* means diminish in value. (The pound appears to be stabilizing after a long period in which it appeared to *depreciate* every Monday, Wednesday, and Friday.)

diagnosis, prognosis. These two nouns should be properly differentiated. To make a medical *diagnosis,* for example, means identify disease by study of a patient's symptoms. (The clinic was equipped with the latest electronic equipment useful in *diagnosis*.) But *diagnosis* can be used more broadly. (It was necessary to run the engine at full speed to make an accurate *diagnosis* of the cause of mechanical failure.) A *prognosis* is a prediction or forecast of the likely outcome of a problem. (Even when the patient had completed the prescribed chemotherapy, the consultant was not willing to offer a *prognosis*.)

disinterested. This adjective, which means unbiased, should not be used to mean uninterested. (There is no doubt that a fair trial is not possible unless the judge is *disinterested*.)

each and every. This trite three-word substitute for *each* should be avoided. *Each* says everything that is intended by *each and every*.

eager. *See* anxious.

economic, economical. These adjectives make trouble for many writers. *Economic* has multiple meanings, all of them of interest to economics, business affairs, and the like. One meaning of *economic* is designed to yield a profit. (Unless property owners can charge *economic* rents, they will soon have no choice but to sell out.) *Economical* means careful in the spending of money or time, saving, avoiding waste. (Her *economical* ways sustained her family quite admirably during hard times.)

enormity. In careful writing, *enormity* has nothing to do with size, even though more and more people are using it to indicate enormous size. *Enormity* is properly taken to mean great wickedness, serious crime, serious error. (The *enormity* of so-called ethnic cleansing has shocked decent people everywhere.)

epitome. This noun does not mean best of a kind, even though many writers use it to indicate perfection. Rather, it means something that shows on a small scale the characteristics of something much larger, or a person who displays a quality or type. (Patricia is the *epitome* of the modern single mother.)

figuratively. *See* literally.

flounder, founder. These two verbs are frequently confused by writers. *Flounder* in one sense means make mistakes, manage affairs poorly; in another it means flail helplessly in deep water or deep snow. (After making a poor start in addressing his audience, he *floundered* helplessly until the chairman interrupted to call on a different speaker. Because Jack could not swim well, he soon was seen to *flounder* and had to be rescued.) *Founder* means sink in a literal or figurative sense. (Once the hull was pierced, the ship rapidly filled with water and *foundered*. The project, plagued with poor leadership, inevitably *foundered*.)

founder. *See* flounder.

fulsome. This adjective is not related in meaning to the word *full*. *Fulsome,* meaning excessive, insincere, disgusting, odious, is applied to expressions of praise or flattery. (His stock in trade, *fulsome* flattery, soon is perceived as intended only to gain advantage over the unwary.)

historic, historical. These two adjectives maintain separate meanings. *Historic* means famous in history or part of history. (Runnymede, near Windsor, will forever be a *historic* site because of its association with the signing of the Magna Carta.) *Historical* means of history, based on history, belonging to the past. (There is no *historical* basis for your claim to ownership of the west bank of that stream.)

impel. *See* compel.

imply, infer. Many modern authorities warn that these two verbs differ in meaning, leaving the careful writer with no choice but to use them precisely. *Imply* means hint, insinuate, suggest without stating directly. (By saying that I may have been guilty of an oversight, she *implied* I was too foolish for words.) *Infer* means deduce, conclude. (I *infer* from what she said about the weather that I would be foolhardy to attempt to return home tonight.)

infer. *See* imply.

ingenious, ingenuous. These two adjectives have different meanings. *Ingenious* means clever when said of people, skilfully made when said of things. (It takes an *ingenious* mind to produce such an intricate invention. The *ingenious* gadget captivated everyone at the meeting.) *Ingenuous* means frank, open, innocent, artless. (A person so markedly *ingenuous* is well advised to avoid questions from the press.)

just deserts. This common expression is supplied here to warn against the common misspelling *just desserts*. (We believe he will receive his *just deserts*.)

laudable, laudatory. Both these adjectives concern praise. *Laudable* means deserving praise, commendable; *laudatory* means expressing praise, praising. (Her actions were *laudable*. Her evaluation was *laudatory*.)

licence, license. The first of these, *licence,* is a noun; the second, *license,* is a verb. (They were seeking an off-*licence* for their shop. Bookmakers must be *licensed*.)

literally, figuratively. These two adverbs must not be used interchangeably, despite their all-too-frequent confusion by careless writers and speakers. *Literally* means actually. (He found himself *literally* penniless, unable to buy even a crust of bread.) *Figuratively* means metaphorically, not actually. (He exploded with rage, *figuratively,* that is.) Notice that the sentences used as examples can be improved by deleting *literally* and *figuratively*. (He found himself penniless. He exploded with rage.) The discussion presented here is intended to caution writers and speakers against overusing *literally,* especially when *figuratively* is appropriate.

mediate. *See* arbitrate.

militate, mitigate. These two verbs are frequently confused. *Militate* means operate, serve as a strong influence. (Two important groups combined to *militate* against the proposed plan.) *Mitigate* means make less intense, less serious or painful. (Social services too often fail even to *mitigate,* much less cure, the problems of the people they are intended to help.)

obviate. This verb means get rid of, clear away, make unnecessary. *Obviate* does not mean lessen or reduce. (When confirmation of the original diagnosis *obviated* further delay, the planned operation could proceed.)

plethora. This noun means an overabundance, rather than an abundance; an excessive amount, not merely a great deal. (We soon found ourselves overwhelmed by the *plethora* of complaints we received.)

precipitate, precipitous. A *precipitate* action is rash or hasty. (To no one's surprise, his *precipitate* action proved damaging.) *Precipitous* means extremely steep. (The day after I bought shares, they suffered a *precipitous* drop in price.)

prescribe, proscribe. These two verbs are sometimes confused. *Prescribe* means advise or order the use of; lay down as a rule to be followed. (Physicians generally do not *prescribe* drugs that have not been approved for use. Penalties *prescribed* for misdemeanours are relatively mild.) *Proscribe* means forbid, denounce. (Acts dangerous to others are *proscribed* in most civilised societies.)

prognosis. *See* diagnosis.

reference. *See* allusion.

seasonable, seasonal. The first of these adjectives means suitable for the time of year. (The heavy October snowfall was anything but *seasonable*.) *Seasonal* means occurring at a particular season. (Farm work is *seasonal,* so I have long periods of unemployment.)

simplistic. This adjective does not mean simple. It means simpleminded or naive. (My tutor said my reasoning was *simplistic*.)

straitjacket. A spelling problem for too many writers.

supersede. A spelling problem for too many writers.

tortuous, torturous. *Tortuous* in one sense means full of twists and turns. It is not related to *torture*. (The *tortuous* road threatens all but the most experienced motorists.) It also means devious, not straightforward. (We all agreed that his reasoning could best be described as *tortuous,* leaving us no choice but to ask him to resubmit his proposal.) Unfortunately, many writers and speakers use *torturous* incorrectly in place of *tortuous*. *Torturous* is the adjectival form of *torture*.

uninterested. *See* disinterested.

unique. This useful adjective means having no like or equal, being the only one of its kind. Thus, it is incorrect to speak of something or someone as most *unique,* very *unique,* or rather *unique*.

venal, venial. *Venal* means open to bribery. *Venial* means pardonable, as in *venial* sin.

Spelling

SPELLING DIFFICULTIES can even bother sign makers.

"I'm a terrible speller" is a commonly heard remark. Often it is said with mock humility, as if the speaker meant, "Well, I'm too busy to be concerned with something so trivial." Almost no one is willing to admit to being a bad driver. But there is an aura of virtue in being a poor speller.

Poor spelling can be a serious handicap, however. Misspelling words in a letter or a report can cause your reader to think that you did not care enough to be careful. No matter how good the content, a letter or report full of misspellings may be ignored. For this reason alone, it is worth devoting time and energy to improving your spelling skills.

Unfortunately, the spelling of English words is far more erratic than spelling in such phonetic languages as German or Italian. Many English words have long complicated histories, and there are good reasons for their being spelled so many different ways. But this is often of little help in remembering how a certain word is spelled. Through the years, teachers have developed rules to help spellers. Some of these rules have already been explained in the English Grammar chapter. However, since every rule seems inevitably to have a list of exceptions, learning to spell requires a fair amount of memorization.

Keeping a list of your troublesome words is an excellent way to begin. A list of words that you repeatedly spell incorrectly may reveal a pattern (inability to tell whether *i* comes before *e*; not knowing when to drop a final *e*; not knowing when to double a final consonant, etc.).

Once spelling problems have been identified, you can devise ways to go about correcting them. The first step is to study rules covering a particular problem. If rules do not help, memorizing "spelling demons," words difficult to spell, can be of great assistance.

The quickest way to learn to spell a new word or a problem word is to write the word over and over. Then, use each word in a sentence and watch for it when reading. Soon you will be able to see at a glance whether the word looks right.

specialized
US

specialised
Brit.

A dictionary is the best resource when you are trying to improve your spelling. Unless you need to look up specialized words, it need not be a very big dictionary. When in doubt about a word, look it up. Keeping a dictionary by your side when writing and getting comfortable with it is an excellent way to improve your spelling. Once in a while, you may have trouble finding a word because you are not sure of the first letter or two. But, generally, this is not a major problem. With a little practice, your dictionary will become easy to use.

Some dictionaries show the standard pronunciation of words. It is a good idea to practice pronouncing difficult words using the pronunciation guide. Writing words down several times and using them in sentences will help make them familiar. Chances are that these three steps will be enough to fix the correct spelling in mind.

Vocabulary Equivalents

American	British
baby carriage, stroller	pram, perambulator
bookstore	book seller, book shop
bumper (of a car)	fender
can	tin
candy	sweets
candy store	sweet-shop
certified public accountant	chartered accountant
checkers	draughts
closet	cupboard
cookie	sweet biscuit

Vocabulary Equivalents *continued*

American	British
corned beef	salt beef
cracker	biscuit
crib	cot
dentist's office	surgery
diaper	nappy
disbar	strike off
doctor's office	surgery
drugstore	chemist
eggplant	aubergine
elevator	lift
estate tax	solicitor
flashlight	torch
French fries	chips
gasoline	petrol
gripe	whinge
half past twelve	half twelve
hamburger bun	bap
hood (of a car)	bonnet
jelly roll	Swiss roll
jump rope (noun)	skipping-rope
kerosene	paraffin
labor union	trades union
license plate	number plate
loose-leaf notebook	ring book
magnifying glass	reading glass
modeling clay	plasticine
molasses	treacle
pantyhose	tights
paraffin	white wax
perfume	scent
pharmacist	dispenser
potato chips	crisps
potholder	oven glove
prime rate	base rate
pullover sweater	jumper
raincoat	mac (for macintosh)
real estate agent	estate agent
rental car	hire car
sidewalk	pavement
specialist (medical)	consultant
subway	underground, tube
superfine sugar	castor sugar
talk show	chat show
thermos bottle	vacuum flask
thumbtack	push pin, drawing pin
tow truck	breakdown lorry, breakdown van
trash can	dustbin
trial lawyer	barrister
truck	lorry
trunk (of a car)	boot
vending machine	slot machine
wastebasket	waste bin
windbreaker	windcheater
wrench (noun)	spanner

17 English Writing

Frequently Misspelled Words

These words are often misspelled. In some cases, this list indicates suffixes that can be added without other spelling changes. Thus, for example, *anxious, -ly* indicates the correct spellings of two words, *anxious* and *anxiously*.

absence	column	garage	miniature	ridiculous
accident, -ally	committee	gauge	minuscule	roommate
accommodation	compliment	genuine	miscellaneous	sandwich
achieve	confidence	glamour	mischief	satellite
acknowledge	congratulations	government	mischievous	schedule
acquaintance	conscience	governor	misspell	science
acquiesce	conscientious	grammar	necessary	scissors
adjacent	conscious	grateful	neighbor	seize
advice	consensus	grocery	nickel	separate
advise	cooperate	guarantee	niece	siege
all right	courage, -ous	gymnasium	ninety	sieve
a lot	courtesy	handkerchief	nuclear	similar
already	deceive	harass, -ment	nuisance	sincere, -ly
altogether	decision	height	occasion	solemn
among	defense	heroes	occur, -red	sophomore
analyze	definite, -ly	hundredth	omission	specific
ancient	definition	immediate, -ly	ophthalmology	strength
anniversary	descent	independent	pamphlet	strenuous
answer	desert, -ed	indispensable	paradigm	subtlety
anxiety	dessert	innocuous	parallel	subtly
anxious, -ly	develop, -ed, -ment	inoculate	pastime	success
apparel	diamond	interest	peculiar	superintendent
appear, -ance	dilemma	interim	peninsula, -r	supersede
appreciate	disappear	irrelevant	permissible	surprise
arctic	disappoint, -ed	itinerary	perseverance	symbol, -ize
article	disease	jealous	physical	synonym
athlete	ecstasy	jeopardy	picnic, -king	technique
athletic	effect, -ive	jewelry	plagiarism	temperament
audience	eighth	journal, -ism	possession	temperature
auxiliary	either	judgment	precede	theater
basically	electricity	juicy	prefer, -red	therefore
balloon	embarrass, -ing, -ment	khaki	prejudice, -d	though
beginning	entrepreneur	knowledge	privilege	thought
belief	especially	laboratory	probably	threshold
believe	exaggerate	league	proceed	tomorrow
bicycle	exceed, -ed	leisure	pseudonym	tongue
biscuit	excellent, -ly	liable	psychology	truly
bookkeeping	exercise, -d	liaison	publicly	twelfth
boundary	existence	library	pursue, -r	tying
brief	experience	license	pursuit	usage
broccoli	facsimile	lightning	receipt	vaccinate
bureau	familiar	liquefy	questionnaire	vacuum
burglar	fascinating	literature	queue	vegetable
business	February	lonely	raspberry	vicinity
calendar	foreign, -er	loose	receive	villain
campaign	foresee	lose, -r	recommend	Wednesday
candidate	forfeit	machine	reinforce	weight
cemetery	forty	maintenance	religious	weird
census	fourth	maneuver	renaissance	wholly
certain, -ly	freight	mediocre	rescind	wield
changeable	friend	mileage	restaurant	withhold
chief		millennium	rhythm	yield

Mnemonic Devices

A mnemonic (pronounced ni-MON-ik) device is a memory aid that helps one to spell a word correctly. Making up an easily remembered, catchy sentence can give a clue to the correct spelling. For example, *"There is a rat in separate."* The key words *a rat* are a reminder to avoid the common error of spelling the word sep*e*rate.

The following are examples of mnemonic devices:

> *affect* is a verb with *a* for action
> *all right* as one word is all wrong
> *meet:* gr*ee*t those you m*ee*t
> *meat:* we *ea*t meat

Separate yourself from "a rat"; the principal is your "pal"; earn people's respect by being in **earn**est.

➤ separate   →   sep **a rat** e

➤ principal   →   prin ci **pal**

➤ earnest   →   **earn** est

See pages 164–165 for more information on mnemonics.

Paired Words

There are several kinds of paired words in English that may lead to confusion:

Homonyms are spelled and pronounced alike but differ in origin and meaning; for example, *pool* (water) and *pool* (game), or *base* (foundation) and *base* (dishonorable).

Homophones are pronounced alike but differ in spelling, origin, and meaning; for example, *led* (went before) and *lead* (metal), or *pause* (halt temporarily) and *paws* (animal feet).

A list of homophones that often are mistaken for one another is provided in the English Grammar chapter. When unsure about which word is which in a pair, look the words up in a dictionary.

Hyphenation

A common problem in spelling is deciding when to hyphenate words. A good basic rule is that if the words in question are being used as modifiers, they should be hyphenated.

> This easy-to-open can is not opening easily.
> This can is not easy to open.

> Hand-knit sweaters are beautiful.
> Sweaters knit by hand are beautiful.

Consult a dictionary when you are in doubt about hyphenating words, and be aware that British practice is sometimes different from American practice.

Brtish: *n.* come-back, come down;
              adj. hand-picked, home-made
American: *n.* comeback, comedown;
              adj. handpicked, homemade

More About Mnemonics

The rhyme "30 days hath September, April, June, and November" is one that most of us have used to remember how many days there are in each month. We were taught "i before e except after c" in English class. And anyone who has taken music lessons is familiar with the phrase "every good boy does fine," which serves as a reminder of the notes that are on the treble clef. All of these are mnemonic devices.

Mnemonic devices are tools, such as rhymes, phrases, and acronyms, that are designed to assist us in remembering information that otherwise might be difficult to recall. Mnemonics use association to trigger memories. A memory is connected or associated to a particular cue, and when that cue is encountered, it triggers the memory. Mnemonic devices assist us in spelling words, remembering phone numbers, and recalling grocery lists, and they can be particularly helpful in studying for exams.

There are several things that you can do when developing mnemonics to help to make them more memorable. Exaggerate your images, and be creative in making them vivid, colorful, and three-dimensional. Using humor can also be very helpful. A silly rhyme is often easier to remember than a more serious one. Agreeable, upbeat images are also easier to remember than negative images, which we tend to block out.

Some common mnemonics are included here. Feel free to alter them to fit your needs, or use your imagination to create mnemonics that have the most meaning for you.

Biology

To remember the 5 classes of vertebrates in the animal kingdom: **FARM B** (**F**ish, **A**mphibians, **R**eptiles, **M**ammals, **B**irds)

To remember the 5 lobes of the human brain: **F**irst **P**lace **O**ften **T**akes the **T**rophy. (**F**rontal, **P**arietal, **O**ccipital, **T**emporal)

To remember the cranial nerves: **O**n **O**ld **O**lympus' **T**owering **T**ops, **A F**air **A**ngelic **G**irl **V**iewed **S**panish **H**ops (**O**lfactory, **O**ptic, **O**culomotor, **T**rochlear, **T**rigeminal, **A**bducens, **F**acial, **A**uditory, **G**lossopharyngeal, **V**agus, **S**pinal Accessoary, **H**ypoglossal)

To remember the proper ordering of the biological groupings used in taxonomy: **K**ids **P**refer **C**heese **O**ver **F**ried **G**reen **S**pinach (**K**ingdom, **P**hylum, **C**lass, **O**rder, **F**amily, **G**enius, **S**pecies)

To remember that Lichen are made up of Algae and Fungi: She was all gal (ALGAL), and he was a fun guy (FUNGI). They took a likin' (LICHEN) to each other.

Geography

To remember the names of the Great Lakes: **HOMES** (**H**uron, **O**ntario, **M**ichigan, **E**rie, **S**uperior)

To remember the Great Lakes in order of size from largest to smallest: **S**am's **H**orse **M**ust **E**at **O**ats

To remember the 4 oceans: **I** Am **A P**erson (**I**ndian, **A**rctic, **A**tlantic, **P**acific)

To remember the 7 continents: **E**at **A**n **A**spirin **A**fter **A N**ighttime **S**nack (**E**urope, **A**ntarctica, **A**sia, **A**frica, **A**ustralia, **N**orth America, **S**outh America) Note that the second letter in the first 3 words that begin with A serve as a reminder of the "A" continents.

To remember the countries of Central America: **G**o **E**at, **H**oney, **N**ancy **C**an't **P**lay **B**all (**G**uatemala, **E**l Salvador, **H**onduras, **N**icaragua, **C**osta Rica, **P**anama, **B**elize)

Geology

To remember the hardness scale from 1 to 10 for minerals: **T**all **G**irls **C**an **F**lirt **A**nd **O**nly **Q**uit **T**o **C**hase **D**warves (**T**alc, **G**ypsum, **C**alcite, **F**luorite, **A**ppetite, **O**rthoclase, **Q**uartz, **T**opaz, **C**orundum, **D**iamond)

To remember the geological time periods from the oldest to the present: **C**amels **O**ften **S**it **D**own **C**arefully. **P**erhaps **T**heir **J**oints **C**reak. **P**ersistent **E**arly **O**iling **M**ight **P**revent **P**ermanent **R**heumatism. (**C**ambrian, **O**rdovician, **S**ilurian, **D**evonian, **C**arboniferous, **P**ermian, **T**riassic, **J**urassic, **C**retaceous, **P**aleocene, **E**ocene, **O**ligocene, **M**iocene, **P**liocene, **P**leistocene, **R**ecent)

To remember the difference between stalactites and stalagmites: Stala**g**mites and Stala**c**tites = **G**round and **C**eiling (Stalagmites rise up from the ground, and stalactites drop from the ceiling.)

Physics

To remember the colors of the spectrum: **ROY G. BIV** (pronounced as a man's name) or **R**ichard **O**f **Y**ork **G**ave **B**attle **I**n **V**ain (**R**ed, **O**range, **Y**ellow, **G**reen, **B**lue, **I**ndigo, **V**iolet)

From electrochemistry, to remember: **L**ose **E**lectrons **O**xidation and **G**ain **E**lectrons **R**eduction (**LEO** the lion says **GER**)

Math

To remember the Roman numerals in order for 50, 100, 500, and 1,000: **L**ucy **C**an't **D**rink **M**ilk (**LCDM**)

More About Mnemonics *continued*

To remember the order of calculations in algebra: **P**lease **E**xcuse **M**y **D**ear **A**unt **S**ally (**P**arentheses, **E**xponents, **M**ultiplication, **D**ivision, **A**ddition, **S**ubtraction)

When multiplying 2 binomials together such as (a+b) and (c+d), make sure that you have multiplied everything by thinking of: **FOIL**—**F**irst, **O**uter, **I**nner, **L**ast; So that (a+b)*(c+d) = ac(first) + ad(outer) + bc(inner) + bd(last)

To remember trigonometric identities: **T**o **O**il **A** **C**ar **A**lways **H**ave **S**ome **O**il **H**andy (Tangent = **O**pposite/**A**djacent; **C**osine = **A**djacent/**H**ypotenuse; **S**ine = **O**pposite/**H**ypotenuse)

The number of letters in each word in the following rhyme gives the value of pi to the 20th decimal place:

Sir, I send a rhyme excelling
In sacred truth and rigid spelling
Numerical sprites elucidate
For me the lexicon's dull weight
31415926535358979323846

Spelling, Language, and Grammar
Separate is **A RAT** of a word to spell.

Arithmetic—**A R**at **I**n **T**he **H**ouse **M**ight **E**at **T**he **I**ce **C**ream

A de**ss**ert is **s**uper **s**weet; a de**s**ert is **s**andy.

Your **principal** is your **pal**. A principle is a ru**le**.

The word **believe** has a **lie** in it.

Necessary—one **c**ollar, two **s**ocks

Potassium—one **t**ea, two **s**ugars

Mnemonics—**M**nemonics **N**eatly **E**liminate **M**an's **O**nly **N**emesis—**I**nsufficient **C**erebral **S**torage

When two vowels go walking, the first one does the talking (for words like oat and eat).

This rhyme will help you to remember the 8 parts of speech in English grammar:

Every name is called a NOUN,
As *field* and *fountain*, *street* and *town*;
In place of noun the PRONOUN stands,
As *he* and *she* can clap their hands;
The ADJECTIVE describes a thing,
As *magic* wand and *bridal* ring;
The VERB means action, something done—

To *read* and *write*, *jump* and *run*;
How things are done, the ADVERBS tell,
As *quickly*, *slowly*, *badly*, *well*;
The PREPOSITION shows relation,
As *in* the street or *at* the station;
CONJUNCTIONS join, in many ways,
Sentences, words, *or* phrase *and* phrase;
The INTERJECTION cries out, *Hark!*
I need an exclamation mark!

Paragraphing:
Four Ts, a little writing rhyme
Of Topic, Territory, Talker, Time
When there's a change in one of these
Start a new paragraph, if you please

History
In 1492 Columbus sailed the ocean blue.

In 1903 the Wright brothers flew free.

Asked to name the 3 greatest philosophers in history, chances are you will say Aristotle, Socrates, and Plato, but you may not know who influenced whom. By looking at their years of birth (Socrates: 469 BC, Plato: 428 BC, and Aristotle: 384 BC), you could infer that in each case, the older man influenced the younger, and you would be correct. Think of the 3 men sitting in a spa debating philosophy. The word **SPA** (**S**ocrates, **P**lato, **A**ristotle) gives you the order of their influence without your having to remember birth dates.

Astronomy
To remember the names of the planets in order: **M**y **V**ery **E**ducated **M**other **J**ust **S**erved **U**s **N**ine **P**ickles (**M**ercury, **V**enus, **E**arth, **M**ars, **J**upiter, **S**aturn, **U**ranus, **N**eptune, **P**luto)

To remember the order of the phases of the moon and whether the current appearance of the moon indicates waxing or waning, think of this phrase: What's up, **DOC**?

The **D** indicates a (waxing) half-moon with the curve on the right, the **O** indicates a full moon, and the **C** indicates a (waning) crescent moon with the curve on the left, heading toward a new moon.

Answer keys for vocabulary exercises:

Page 116
Synonyms: 1. a, 2. b, 3. e, 4. d, 5. d, 6. f, 7. c, 8. c, 9. d, 10. c
Antonyms: 1. g, 2. b, 3. a, 4. e, 5. j, 6. f, 7. i, 8. h, 9. d, 10. c

Page 117
Completions: 1. c, 2. b, 3. d, 4. a, 5. e, 6. b, 7. b, 8. d, 9. a, 10. c
Synonyms: 1. a, 2. d, 3. b, 4. c, 5. a, 6. d, 7. a, 8. e, 9. b, 10. d
Relationships: 1. s, 2. u, 3. s, 4. a, 5. a, 6. u, 7. s, 8. a, 9. s, 10. u

"Porqué nunca sabe quando lo necesita."

You never know you'll need it.

"Parce que tu ne sais jamais quand tu en besoin."

Because you never know when you'll need it.

UNITED STATES POSTAL SERVICE

"Because you never know wh you nee

Available

18

Foreign Language

18 Foreign Language

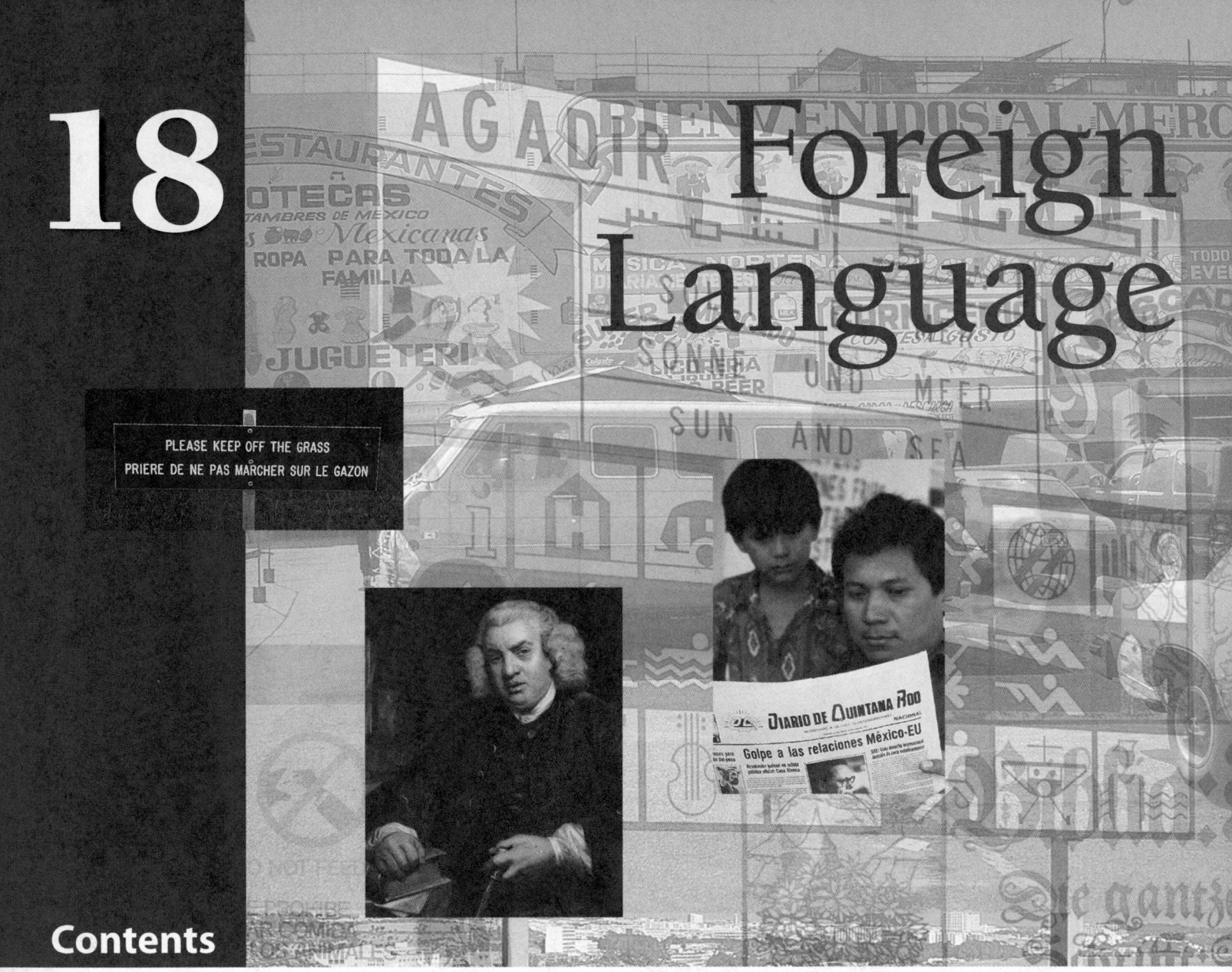

PLEASE KEEP OFF THE GRASS
PRIERE DE NE PAS MARCHER SUR LE GAZON

Contents

Overleaf: *Banners outside NYC post office*

Language Studies

There are many different ways of looking at a language. One person may look at where it comes from or where it is headed. Another may wonder how it differs from other languages. Yet a third may be fascinated by its inner workings or its external written form. A language may be a living language (one still in use) or a dead one (that no one speaks). It may be the language of a familiar culture or it may belong to a culture so different that one is forced to reexamine notions of what language can and cannot express.

WRITTEN LANGUAGES may differ as widely as the cultures in which they were developed. The college fraternity bears Greek letters, the store signs use Chinese characters.

Types of Language Studies

All study of language must ultimately trace back to speech. Students of ancient languages may rely on written materials, but they do so only because writing is a representation of the spoken word. Of the thousands of languages and dialects spoken today, many have no written form. Students of these languages must either invent a written form or rely on what they hear or can record. In cultures where language has had written form for centuries, nearly everyone speaks it. But fewer people can read it, and still fewer can write it. As the spoken language changes, the written language changes as well.

Linguistics. The term used by scholars to describe the study of language in all its various aspects is *linguistics,* also called the science of language. The word linguistics itself is derived from the Latin word *lingua,* meaning both tongue and that which the tongue produces, language.

The first recorded use of the word linguistics in English, according to the *Oxford English Dictionary,* occurred in 1837. There was a surge of interest in the spoken word, and not just in its written form, at about that time. This was a more radical development than it might seem at first glance.

Today the field of linguistics concentrates on the sounds and grammatic structures of language. *Comparative linguistics* compares languages and dialects, and has been able to identify many relationships that exist between languages. For example, two modern languages may be shown to have developed from a common ancient language. *Structural linguistics* seeks basic similarity in *all* languages in order to understand precisely what language is.

Philology. Language study before the mid 1800s was largely the study of the classics, particularly of ancient Greek and Latin. Since ancient Greek and Latin were no longer spoken languages, only their literary form was studied. One term used for such study is *philology.* This word comes from the Greek *phílos* (love) and *lógos* (word), that is, "love of the word." Today scholars use the word philology in relation to the study of older languages. Philology is therefore considered a branch of the broader study of linguistics.

Etymology. A term that sometimes gets confused with linguistics or philology is *etymology.* Etymology is the study of how individual words evolve, both in form and meaning. For example, the Old English version of the Lord's Prayer contains the verb syle, meaning "give." The verb does not survive in Modern English with that meaning, but it is the ancestor of Modern English "sell." Etymological analysis shows how this word changed, both in its form and its meaning; but no word changes in isolation. Words must live within the structure of the language of which they are a part. Etymology, therefore—with its emphasis on individual words—is a branch of linguistics. Interesting and important as it is, it is incomplete by itself.

Semantics. Fascination with meanings has given rise to another branch of linguistics, *semantics.* Semantics is concerned with why and how words signify things. The origin of the word "semantics," the Greek *sēmaínein* (to signify, show by a sign), reflects the object of the field, which considers not only the dictionary meanings of words but their connotative meanings as well—what they connote in a specific situation, both to the speaker or writer and to those who hear or read them. Semantics also considers the historical development of meaning in the words of a language, such as the change in "sell" noted above. In addition, the field deals with larger issues: the theoretical limits and possibilities of meaning in language at any given time. Semantics has attracted the interest of logicians, mathematicians, sociologists, and psychologists. These specialists have brought many new tools and points of view to language study.

Communications theory. This modern elaboration on semantics and linguistics deals with nonverbal as well as

GIVE A HOOT for an example of how some words imitate sounds of nature.

verbal communication. When speaking, people communicate through gestures, tone of voice, facial expressions, and other nonverbal means, as well as through words. A certain tone of voice and facial expression may cause a sentence to have a meaning opposite to its literal meaning. For example, a speaker may say "You're a *wonderful* friend" sarcastically, really meaning, "You're no friend at all." Communications theorists also study the cultural framework in which words exist. To one speaker of English, "I don't care" may mean, "It makes no difference to me." To another, it may mean, "I don't care at all about the issue, and I wish you hadn't asked me."

Grammar. Perhaps the most confusing term we run across—probably because we take it so for granted—is the word "grammar." This word is derived from the Greek *grammatikós* (pertaining to letters), although its modern definitions do not have to do primarily with letters.

In general, grammar refers to the formal side of language, as opposed to the world of meaning, with which etymology and semantics are concerned. Grammar is the study of the elements that make up a sentence, and indeed this is one of the most important things students learn in what is sometimes called grammar school. But the word grammar can also refer to the analysis of individual sounds; this is sometimes called *phonology*. When grammar refers to the prefixes and suffixes that often define a word's function, the study is called *morphology*.

Today, the term *transformational grammar* covers the study of the underlying structure or grammar of a language and the transformations that structure goes through to produce the actual sentences we utter. In contrast, *comparative grammar* is a name for the study of the similarities in form among related languages. The important thing

to bear in mind is that grammar does not just involve the process of labeling nouns, verbs, predicates, subordinate clauses, etc. Rather, its wide range of meanings show just how complex language is and how many elements there are to analyze and understand.

Phonetics. Phonetics is a specialized study of the sounds of different languages. In written form, these sounds are represented by the International Phonetic Alphabet (IPA).

The study of phonetics has been greatly assisted by modern recording techniques. The tape recorder has enabled linguists to collect samples of every spoken language and dialect for study and comparison.

Phonetics may also have practical uses in speech therapy and for speakers or actors who wish to learn a particular accent or dialect.

Dialects. A *dialect* is a variant of a particular language. One dialect of English is spoken in England, another in the United States. Given enough time and distance, two dialects may develop into separate languages.

At any given time, a widely spoken language may exist in dozens of forms. The particular dialect people speak may tell a great deal about them: what region of a country they grew up in; what social status their families had; or how much education they received. In the early 1900s, a dialect specialist in England claimed to be able to tell a person's native town or village, to within 15 miles (24 kilometers), from his or her speech. Dialects in the United States and Canada are generally less distinct than in Great Britain, but most people would have no trouble telling the difference between a Bostonian, a Torontonian, and a Texan after listening to their speech.

Social distinctions are often based on speech. The speaker who says, "Dis chair, dat desk, dem flowers," will be

less well received in an office or school than a person who says, "This, that, those flowers."

Linguists have been able to trace the distinctive sounds of certain dialects to interesting sources. The "oi" sound, generally thought to be characteristic of a New York City native (*foist* for *first, boid* for *bird,* etc.), originated among Cockneys in East London. Large numbers of Cockneys settled in parts of Brooklyn (as well as in New Orleans and Charleston, South Carolina), and the variant pronunciation was established in local speech.

Dialects also tend to have some differences in vocabulary. For example, a bottle of *soda* in most of the Eastern U.S. is a bottle of *pop* in the West.

The English spoken by some African Americans, sometimes called *black English,* is an important and interesting dialect. It shares some characteristics with certain urban and southern dialects, but has many characteristics of its own. For example, the verb *be* is used to make distinctions not possible in standard English. In black English, "She is sick" means that she has a temporary illness, such as a cold. "She be sick" means that she is chronically ill, with a serious physical or emotional ailment.

Recent studies of black English suggest that it may owe some of its differences to the languages spoken by Africans before they were brought to America as slaves. Slaves were often forbidden to speak their native tongues, but the deep structure of those languages may have survived in their English.

Other specialties. There are many other specialties in the study of modern language. For example, *psycholinguistics* analyzes the relationship between the human mind and the way people use language. *Sociolinguistics* focuses on the ways in which the makeup of a society affects the language spoken by that society. One could go on and on listing various branches of language study, but the important thing to keep in mind is that language is a complex phenomenon. Whether students want to analyze a given sentence or the long-term history of a language, there are many factors to be considered. What is the structure of the language being considered? What are the pressures in the society from which it stems? How do individual sounds interact with whole words, and words with sentences, and sentences with groups of sentences, and so on? In other words, every factor—large and small—must be considered. Defining terms helps students focus on each of these factors in their pursuit of understanding language.

Right and wrong. Modern studies of speech differ from earlier language studies in that they tend to concentrate on how the language is spoken, not on how the language ought to be spoken. Proponents of this new

---

analyze
US

analyse
Brit.

kilometers
US

kilometres
Brit.

DIALECTS AND CULTURAL SPEECH PATTERNS
establish variations within a single language: Britons and Americans use different dialects of the same language, English.

approach contend that it is difficult to distinguish between correct and incorrect speech. Too much depends on the setting, the speaker, and the listeners. For example, a speaker at a neighborhood meeting who does not use the local dialect may be considered affected. If the same speaker uses the local dialect on national television, he or she may be considered wrong again.

Most people concerned with practical speech do agree, however, that there is a *standard English* that is widely understood and considered acceptable in the U.K. and U.S.

The Languages of the World

For two centuries, students of language have been seeking to trace the relationship of a given language to other languages. One way of doing this is to look for systematic similarities among languages. In the list of words for the numbers one, two, and three in the following table, English, Old High German, Old Norse, and Gothic present forms that are very like one another. These in turn show some likeness to the forms in Latin, Greek, Old Irish, and Sanskrit (the ancient language of India).

But none of these languages seems to have any similarity to Chinese and Japanese, nor do the last two show forms that are similar to each other. Thus, one may suspect from this evidence that English, German, Norse, and Gothic belong to a single family, that is, that they all come from some common ancestor language, just as brothers and sisters come from the same parents. This ancestor is called Germanic. One may also suspect that this group of languages belongs to a larger family that

includes Latin, Greek, Irish, and Sanskrit. Indeed, all of these languages are thought to belong to a family called Indo-European, which is examined in more detail on the following pages. As for Chinese and Japanese, the evidence suggests that they belong to other language families.

The implication here is that all languages may be organized into different family groupings. Apparently, a particular language may produce "children" in time and die out itself. The family relationships may be shown in a diagram that resembles a family tree. The more distant the common ancestor of two languages, the more remote their similarities become, just as cousins are less likely to resemble each other than are brothers and sisters.

A language creates "children" gradually. At first, its variant forms are enough alike to be mutually understood and are called *dialects*. But if there is little or no contact between two communities with the same language, the language will develop in different directions until, finally, when both the communities can no longer understand one another, they speak two distinct languages. In fact, there is a fine line between a dialect and a true language, and in the end they are simply two stages in a single process.

The Numbers "One," "Two," and "Three" in Selected Languages

Modern English	Old English	Old High German	Old Norse	Gothic	Latin	Greek	Old Irish	Sanskrit	Chinese	Japanese
one	ān	ein	einn	ains	ūnus	heis	ōen	ēkas	i	hitotsu
two	twā	zwei	tveir	twai	duo	dúō	dāu	dvāú	erh	futatsu
three	thrie	driē	thrir	thri	trēs	treis	tri	tráyas	san	mittsu

Major World Languages

Spoken by	Europe and the Americas	Middle East	Indian Subcontinent	Asia	Africa
More than 600 million people				Mandarin	
300–500 million	English Spanish		Hindi		
200–300 million	Russian	Arabic			
100–200 million	Portuguese French German		Bengali	Malay Japanese	
50–100 million	Italian	Turkish	Punjabi Telugu Marathi Tamil	Korean Cantonese Wu Javanese Vietnamese Min	
10–50 million	Ukrainian Polish Romanian Dutch-Flemish Serbo-Croatian Azerbaijan Hungarian Czech Greek Byelorussian	Persian Pashtu Kurdish	Kannada Gujarati Malayalam Oriya Assamese Sindhi Nepali Sinhalese	Thai Tagalog Hakka Burmese Sudanese Zhuang Cebuano Uzbek Madurese	Swahili Hausa Yoruba Amharic Igbo Fula Malagasy Afrikaans Oromo

MODERN LANGUAGES are organized into language families with shared origins.

Language Families

In addition to the Indo-European family, of which English is a member, and which is discussed in more detail below, here is a brief survey of some other major language families.

Sino Tibetan. The Sino-Tibetan languages (formerly known as Indochinese, Tibeto-Chinese, or Sinitic languages) include Chinese, Tibetan, and Burmese. Using a narrow classification system, there are about 300 Sino-Tibetan languages and dialects. These languages have the second largest number of speakers in the world. (The majority of people around the world speak an Indo-European language.)

Even within one branch of the Sino-Tibetan family, such as Chinese, the differences between languages can be so great that speakers of one Chinese language cannot understand speakers of another. What links the various languages is that they have many words that sound alike and have similar meanings. Most of the Sino-Tibetan languages rely on tone to give different meanings to otherwise identical words, and most have vocabularies consisting chiefly of monosyllabic words. The languages use word elements before, within, or after a root to alter the meaning of a word. And many of the languages have a system in which the vowel sounds of words alter with changes in meaning (similar to the vowel changes found in many Indo-European verbs, such as *ring, rang, rung*).

Forms of the Chinese language are spoken throughout mainland China; in Taiwan, Hong Kong, and Singapore; by minority groups throughout Southeast Asia; and in immigrant communities in Oceania, North America, and South America. The most important Sinitic (Chinese) languages are Mandarin (including Modern Standard Chinese, which is based on the dialect of Beijing and spoken in the People's Republic of China, Singapore, and Taiwan), Cantonese (spoken in the province of Canton within the People's Republic and in Hong Kong), Wu (including Shanghaiese), and Min (which includes Taiwanese).

Sinitic languages use a complex system of nonphonetic symbols in their written forms, which date back to at least 1500 B.C. Tibetan and Burmese are more closely related to each other than to Chinese, although both have similarities to the Sinitic languages.

Other language families.

The *Afro-Asiatic* family includes the Semitic languages of the Middle East, among them Hebrew and Arabic, as well as Egyptian and lesser known languages such as Berber (the language of the North African tribe of that name)

and Chad. There is a purely African family known as *Niger-Congo,* which includes languages such as Swahili and Zulu. There is also an extensive grouping in Asia called *Altaic* that derives its name from the Altai Mountains, which stretch from Russia into Mongolia and finally to China. This family includes Turkish in the west and Mongolian in the east. *Malayo-Polynesian* is spoken from Indonesia and Malaysia all the way to Hawaii.

In Europe, two *Uralic* languages—Finnish and Hungarian—are related to one another but are not part of the Indo-European family. In fact, there are languages that seem to defy classification throughout the world. Two examples are Basque, spoken by the people of that name who inhabit the Pyrenees Mountains of France and Spain, and Japanese.

The Americas had several large language families, but many of those languages are no longer spoken. The Europeans conquered most of the two continents, and their languages (especially English, Spanish, Portuguese, and French) replaced the native languages. Those surviving to this day include Eskimo in the far north and Quechua in Peru and Bolivia. Some Native American languages also survive and provide interesting examples of just how different languages can be. For example, Fox—the language of the tribe of that name—does not show the basic differentiation between noun and verb, a difficult concept for a speaker of English to grasp.

But it is English and its history that are primarily discussed here. To be sure, it would be interesting to know how many of the world's language fami-

lies are derived from the same source. Perhaps the families of English and, say, Chinese were once related at some distant moment when language itself first arose. But the evidence does not take us back that far. In fact, the earliest stages of linguistic history will likely remain a mystery. Even for the Indo-European language, there are no written records, and the language must be reconstructed from later evidence. These educated guesses suggest a *prehistory* for languages in the family, including English. One may well begin a study of Indo-European by taking a closer look at the relatives of English.

Indo-European

As can be seen from the corresponding number words (one, two, and three) discussed previously, it is clear English is related to languages spoken as far east as India and throughout much of Europe. Because of this range, this language family has acquired the name Indo-European. Linguistic evidence suggests that there was a people or tribe who spoke a language that is the ancestor of this large language family. But who were these Indo-Europeans? Where and when did they live? Unfortunately, the answers to these questions are unknown and are likely to remain so. But various pieces of evidence enable us to narrow down the possible answers.

For example, the Indo-European languages have no common word for "sea." Nor do they share common words for "olive tree" or "tiger." On the other hand, the descendant languages do have related words for "birch" and "fir"

JUST AS HUMAN FAMILIES have descended from common ancestors, so may the words that name them—mother, father, brother, sister—have come from a single ancestor language.

Most European Languages Are Related to Each Other

Some common words are much alike.
The languages may all have come from a single ancestor language.

English	Old English	German	Latin	Italian	Spanish	French
mother	mōdor	Mutter	mater	madre	madre	mère
father	faeder	Vater	pater	padre	padre	père
brother	brōthor	Bruder	trater	fratello	hermano	frère
sister	sweoster	Schwester	soror	sorella	hermana	soeur

Indo-European Languages

FAMILY (PREHISTORIC)	BRANCH	EARLY HISTORIC LANGUAGES	MODERN LANGUAGES	FAMILY (PREHISTORIC)	BRANCH	EARLY HISTORIC LANGUAGES	MODERN LANGUAGES
Balto-Slavic	Slavic West		Polish Slovak Czech	**Italic** (Romance)	Osco-Umbrian	Oscan Umbrian	
	South	Old Church Slavonic	Slovene Serbo-Croatian Bulgarian		Latino-Feliscan	Feliscan Latin	Portuguese Spanish French
	East		Russian Ukrainian				Italian Romanian (others)
	Baltic	Old Prussian	Latvian Lithuanian	**Greek**		Classical Greek	Modern Greek
Germanic	West	Anglo-Frisian	English Frisian	**Armenian**			Armenian
		Low German	Plattdeutsch Dutch Flemish Afrikaans	**Albanian**			Albanian
				Anatolian		Luvian Palaic Hittite	
		High German	German Yiddish	**Indo-Iranian**	Iranian	Old Persian Avestan	Persian Kurdish (others)
	North	Old Norse	Icelandic Norwegian Danish Swedish		Indic	Sanskrit	Hindi Bengali (others)
	East	Gothic		**Tocharian**		Tocharian	
Celtic	Insular	Gaelic	Irish Scottish Gaelic (Manx)				
		Britannic	Welsh (Cornish) Breton				
	Continental	Gaulish					

and for "bear" and "wolf." The word "snow" is another example of a distinct word shared by all the languages. This type of evidence leads scholars to suspect that the Indo-Europeans did not live on the seacoast and that their homeland was far enough north to have had fir trees, bears, and snow. The best guess is that the Indo-Europeans lived in the steppes of today's Russia and Ukraine.

Scholars have tried to arrive at a date for Indo-European by *glotto-chronology,* the analysis of the rate at which languages change. There are so many variable factors in such a study that the answers are far from certain. But it is estimated that Indo-European was spoken about 4500 B.C.

In the centuries since then, the Indo-European family has spread and grown. A brief tour of the language map in historical times will show just how far. The tour begins in the west of Europe and works its way east.

Celtic. All the way at the western end of Europe there exists, even today, the Celtic family of languages. The Celts originally lived in Europe or western Asia, but a large contingent migrated across the English Channel to England and Ireland. Others remained in Europe. Little survives of Continental Celtic—the language as it developed in Europe. There are a few inscriptions

written in a language called Gaulish, evidently the language spoken by the Celts when the Roman Julius Caesar fought in Gaul (present-day France and Germany). There was also a dialect of this branch spoken in Spain in the 15th century A.D. called Celtiberian (the Celtic of the Iberian peninsula) but little survives of this dialect.

Most of the early forms that remain—and all of the modern Celtic languages—are of the Insular branch, the form that developed in Britain and Ireland. The earliest attested form is the language called Old Irish, the ancestor of Modern Irish or what is sometimes called Gaelic. A rich literature survives in Old Irish. Some speakers of Old Irish moved to the Isle of Man (their language, Manx, was spoken until the early 1900s). Others migrated north to Scotland and their language, Scottish Gaelic, survives to this day in the north and west of Scotland. Welsh, spoken in Wales, in the western part of Great Britain, is another Celtic language that still flourishes. Still another, Cornish, died out in England in the 1600s. Other Celtic speakers moved across the English Channel to Brittany (now a province of France). Their language is called Breton and it survives to the present day.

Italic. Before the time of Christ, several related languages were spoken on the Italian peninsula—Oscan,

Umbrian, Venetic, Feliscan, and Latin. These languages can be grouped into three families: Oscan-Umbrian, Venetic, and Feliscan-Latin. Oscan is believed to have been the most widely spoken language on the peninsula before Latin became the region's major language, probably sometime during the fourth century B.C.

As Rome's power grew, its language, Latin, was introduced to many areas of Europe beyond the Italian peninsula. Throughout the history of the Roman Empire, its armies reached parts of Britain, Germany, France, Spain, North Africa, and the Middle East, and Latin's influence on languages throughout the former Roman Empire was tremendous.

With the fall of Rome in A.D. 476, the empire as such ceased to exist. Although influenced by the Latin spoken by former occupiers, the languages of Europe evolved into distinct languages. Today Latin itself is no longer spoken, although it is the official language of the Roman Catholic Church and continues to be of interest to modern scholars.

The modern-day so-called Romance languages—the most important are French, Italian, Spanish, Portuguese, and Romanian—are direct descendants of Latin. All these languages have closely related vocabularies and grammars. The melodic intonations of the Romance languages stand in contrast to the more guttural Germanic languages. While Latin had a highly complex grammar that depended on suffixes to indicate the function of a word within a sentence, the modern Romance languages have dropped many of the suffixes and rely more heavily on word order to express meaning.

English, while not a Romance language, has many words that are related to Romance vocabularies. This is due in part to the Norman Conquest of England in 1066, when William of Normandy assumed the English Crown and established Norman French as the official language of England. The Normans eventually lost control of the English throne, but their influence on the language remained. Later, in the 18th century, a renewed interest in ancient Greece and Rome encouraged many English scholars to create new English words based on Greek and Latin.

It is interesting to consider the history of the Italic family of languages when imagining what Indo-European might originally have been. When one thinks of the Romance languages, there is a tendency to remember only the vast influence of Latin and the Roman Empire. But several hundred years before the birth of Christ, Latin was simply one of several equally limited languages spoken in Italy, and Italic itself only part of the much larger Indo-European family. In a similar way, Indo-European itself must have once been only a small dialect of a larger family. Thus, one should not be fooled by its vast spread. Like Latin, Indo-European must have started as a language spoken in a limited area that happened to spread out because of events, such as conquest and migration, that are lost to history.

Greek.

Farther to the east there developed the Greek branch of Indo-European. The first evidence of Greek is the so-called Linear B tablets of the 12th century B.C., deciphered in the early 1950s. There are extensive texts in Greek of the eighth century B.C., the date of the famous poems of Homer, the *Iliad* and the *Odyssey.* Though Greek shows clear traces of several distinct dialects from its earliest periods, these dialects were evidently always comprehensible to one another. Indeed, there was always enough contact among the various city-states of the Greek isles to prevent the development of separate languages. Rather, after the classical period of the fifth century B.C., a common dialect became predominant; this gave rise to what we call Modern Greek.

Armenian and Albanian.

Farther east there are two more separate branches. One is Armenian, the earliest form of which shows up before A.D. 1000. Its modern descendant is the official language of Armenia. Some scholars claim that the few traces of the languages called Thracian and Phrygian belong to this family, too. So little

remains of these languages, however, that it is difficult to tell whether this is so. A second branch of Indo-European in this area is Albanian, which first showed up only in 1462 and remains a language unto itself. It has been suggested that another scantily attested language—Illyrian—is related to Albanian, but in this case, too, there is little evidence to go on.

Anatolian.

In Asia Minor one meets Anatolian, the earliest attested branch of Indo-European; its main language is Hittite. It was only in the 20th century that the tablets containing Hittite were deciphered and discovered to be Indo-European. The texts themselves date back almost to 2000 B.C. The contents of these texts range from mythological rituals to bureaucratic lists, and include records of Hittite dealings with Egypt that are also mentioned in the Bible. Other Anatolian languages include Lydian, Lycian, Luvian, and Palaic. None of these languages are spoken today.

Indo-Iranian.

Farther into Asia there is the vast Indo-Iranian branch, of which many languages are still spoken by large numbers of people. The Iranian side of the family includes its oldest form, Avestan, in which the ancient hymns of the prophet Zoroaster were transcribed, and a whole group of modern languages, among which are Kurdish and Persian. Speakers of Indic languages moved even farther east and south into the Indian subcontinent. The oldest version of this family is a form of Sanskrit called Vedic, the language of the Rig Vedic hymns dating before 1000 B.C. These hymns, the central holy text of Hinduism, are recited from memory in their original form to this day. Indeed, it was Vedic Sanskrit—which has many obvious similarities to Greek—that led Sir William Jones, a British jurist, to suggest in 1786 the idea of a prehistoric Indo-European language. Modern languages from this branch include Hindi and Bengali, among many others. One need only compare, for example, English and Hindi to see how different two related languages can become over the course of time.

Tocharian.

There is one other Indo-European language verified in Asia, discovered only in the 20th century. It is called Tocharian, and the only texts date from the seventh and eighth centuries A.D. in the area now part of China's Sinkiang Province. There are no original texts in Tocharian, only translations of Buddhist tracts. One interesting fact about Tocharian is that it seems to belong, according to its linguistic features, to the western branch of Indo-European, even though it was apparently spoken in an isolated area thousands of miles to the east of Europe. Indeed, it is always important to keep in mind that linguistic affinity is not a geographic concept. In a similar way, such

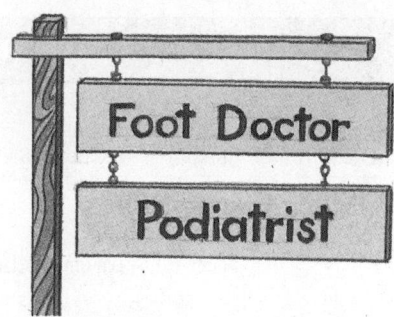

FOOT AND POD come from the same ancient Greek root. Over time the sounds have changed.

non-Indo-European languages as Basque, Finnish, and Hungarian are isolated in a sea of Indo-European languages.

Balto-Slavic.

The tour now heads north and starts circling back toward Western Europe for a look at the Balto-Slavic family of languages. The Baltic side consists of the modern languages Lithuanian and Latvian. Lithuanian is known in an earlier form called Old Lithuanian; there is also an early form of this branch called Old Prussian. The Slavic family falls into three categories. East Slavic is represented primarily by Russian, but it also includes Byelorussian and Ukrainian, the languages of Belarus and Ukraine. South Slavic appears in an early form called Old Church Slavonic, from the 10th and 11th centuries A.D., and in the modern languages Bulgarian, Serbo-Croatian, and Slovene. West Slavic consists primarily of Polish, Czech, and Slovak.

Germanic.

Finally, farther west, comes the Germanic family, of which English is a member.

In the 19th century, the German scholar Jacob Grimm—while working on his stories now known as *Grimm's Fairy Tales*—noticed that what made the Germanic branch of Indo-European so distinctive was a series of consonant shifts. These changes, he pointed out, were shared by all of the Germanic languages, but not by any other Indo-European language. This phenomenon, called Grimm's law, helps explain different forms of many words in English, since English later borrowed words from other Indo-European languages that had not undergone the shift. For example, Grimm noticed that where a *p* appears in Greek, Latin, and other Indo-European languages, an *f* appears in Germanic. Thus, English *father* corresponds to Latin *pater,* English *foot* to Greek *pod-,* and English *fish* to Latin *pisces.* Later on, English borrowed these words from Greek and Latin, but at a time when Grimm's law had stopped functioning. As a result, English is filled with pairs of words such as *fatherly* and *paternal,* and *foot doctor* and *podiatrist.* For example, the sound *d* became *t* in Germanic according to Grimm's law, thus leaving a pair such as native *two* but borrowed *dual.* Similarly, *t* became *th,* giving native *three* but the borrowed prefix tri-.

Germanic also developed a fixed stress. A word like *friend* can be made into *friendly, friendliest,* or *friendship,* and the stress remains on the first syllable. In their oldest forms, the other Indo-European languages had a variable pitch accent. It is, therefore, possible to distinguish native English words from later borrowed words by sound and stress. The *father* in *fatherly* is a native Germanic word, and thus has initial stress. In contrast, *paternal* has a *p* and stress on the second syllable; thus it seems certain that *paternal* is not native to English.

East Germanic. Germanic falls into three groups. The earliest to appear in any text is East Germanic, the language called Gothic, known from the middle of the fourth century A.D. At that time, a local bishop evidently decided that his missionary efforts would have greater success if there were a translation of the Bible in the language of the Goths, whom he was trying to convert. As a result, the one text we have in Gothic is a selection from his translation of the Bible. By the end of the seventh century, Gothic had evidently died out, though a few words of a dialect called Crimean Gothic were recorded in the 1500s.

North Germanic. North and West Germanic survive to this day. North Germanic—which includes all the languages of Scandinavia—appears around the ninth century in a form usually called Old Norse, though this language shows up in several dialects. Old Norse literature has left many sagas and myths that include stories about the Germanic gods after whom some of the days of

Tyr	→	Tuesday
Woden	→	Wednesday
Thor	→	Thursday
Frigg	→	Friday

OLD NORSE settlers in Britain introduced many new words to the English language.

the week are named. For example, the chief god is named Odin (or Woden, as in Wednesday); another important god is Tȳr (Tuesday); and a third is Thor (Thursday). The most important goddess was named Frigg (Friday). There are two main branches of North Germanic. That of the east consists of Danish and Swedish, while the western branch includes Norwegian, Faeroese, and Icelandic. Because of the isolation of Iceland, Icelandic has changed little in the last thousand years. By contrast, English has changed radically and rapidly.

West Germanic. The third branch of Germanic is called West Germanic. One branch of this group is the German branch, consisting of Low and High German. Low German (spoken mainly in the lowlands) survives today in Dutch, Flemish, Afrikaans (the language taken to Africa by the Dutch who settled there), and a language spoken in the northern lowlands of Germany called Plattdeutsch (*platt* means "low," and *Deutsch* is the German word for "German"). High German, or Hochdeutsch

(literally, high German), known from around A.D. 1000, is the ancestor of Modern German as well as of the Yiddish language. At first glance, German does not look as closely related to English as it is, since the consonants of High German went through another series of shifts. The result of this change is that many German words begin with different consonants than their English equivalents. But the differences are systematic. For example, in the Lord's Prayer, the word *thīn* ("thine" in Early Modern English) corresponds to Old High German *dīn.* Another look at the list of numbers reveals that another word beginning with *th* in Old English, *thrīe,* has a *d* in Old High German *drīe.* There are many such pairs in English and German. Other examples include *then* and Ger. *dann; thing* and Ger. *ding; thick* and Ger. *dick; thunder* and Ger. *donner.* The *th* in English is a *d* in German. This kind of systematic and consistent similarity helps establish the close relationship between the two languages.

The other branch of West Germanic is usually called Anglo-Frisian. Frisian is a language that was spoken on the Baltic coast as far back as the A.D. 900s and is still spoken today in the Dutch province of Friesland and in certain areas of the western part of Germany. From this same area along the Baltic, tribes closely related to the Frisians—the Angles, the Saxons, and the Jutes—sailed to England and settled there around A.D. 450. The language spoken by these people, called Anglo-Saxon or Old English, is the earliest form of English proper.

English

When the Angles, Saxons, and Jutes came to England, their dialect of West Germanic must have been quite similar to that of the Germans. Indeed, early Old English was fairly close to Old High German. The striking thing about English in the 1,500 years since its beginning is how much it has changed—far more than any of its related languages.

Why Languages Change

Why has English changed so much? There are two major reasons for a language to change, and both help explain the development of English.

Foreign influence. When two cultures come into contact with each other, their languages reflect this contact. New words—additions to a language's vocabulary—are often the first sign of foreign influence. Traders need common terms for their bartering.

Missionaries often introduce new religious terms. If one people or tribe conquers another, new words having to do with government, law, and social relations are often brought into the language of those conquered.

English has had a rich history on all these fronts. The Anglo-Saxon settlers immediately faced the problem of coexisting with the Celts, particularly the Welsh, who already inhabited England. Indeed, many place-names in England

WORD ADDITIONS from other languages have given English a large and rich vocabulary. Many American words and place-names are from Native American languages.

are Celtic. When Christian missionaries arrived in England, many religious words from Latin entered the language. In the ninth and tenth centuries, Scandinavians settled along the east coast of England and intermingled with the English, who proceeded to borrow many basic words from these immigrants.

The most important event for English, however, was the Norman Conquest of 1066. In the years that followed, hundreds of French words were introduced into English. In fact, for more than a century, it appeared that Norman French might become the language of England. The Normans finally lost their influence, and English reasserted itself. But new influences continued to change it. The European Renaissance, with its emphasis on the art and learning of Classical Greece and Rome, brought new borrowings from ancient Greek and Latin.

In America, borrowing continued. The early American settlers obtained terms from the North American natives whom they met when they arrived. In the Northeast, there were borrowings from the neighboring French, in the Southwest from the Spanish. Immigrants coming to America brought words from many of the languages of the world.

There is, therefore, a remarkable mixture that makes up the word stock of the English language. Indeed, English has as rich and varied a vocabulary as any language in the world, precisely because of an enormous amount of borrowing, while other languages did less borrowing. For example, German took few words from French; but English borrowed many hundreds because of the Norman Conquest.

Structural changes. The second important reason for a language to change is harder to grasp. Changes in the structure of a language are interrelated and seem to have a power of their own, continuing over the course of many centuries.

As already noted, one of the most important changes that occurred in Germanic was the movement to stress on the first syllable of the root in all words. When heavy stress is placed on the beginning of a word or phrase, pronunciation of the rest of the word is weakened. For example, in speech, the phrase *going to* often sounds like *gonna.*

A similar process occurred in Early, or Old, English, which originally had a complex system of endings, or inflections, that conveyed a word's function and meaning within a sentence. For example, if a noun was the subject of a sentence it had one ending; if it was the object of a verb it had another; if it was the indirect object, still another; and so on. Over the course of centuries, these endings became weaker and weaker because of the initial stress, until they finally disappeared. Very few remain in English. For nouns, we still use an -s to signify that a word is plural rather than singular. For verbs, only the -s of the third person singular (for example, *I speak, he speaks*) remains.

Heavy stress on the initial syllable of roots caused a gradual loss of word endings. Loss of these endings made certain sentences hard to understand because the function of some words was not clear. To solve this problem, English came to rely on word order to show word function and developed a different way of showing the tense and mood of verbs through use of *auxiliary* or *function words* such as *have, will, might,* and *could.*

This process illustrates how various structural changes in a language are interrelated and how such changes can alter a language in important ways. In contrast to English, changes in German took place much more slowly. Although endings in German, too, became weaker, many more survived, and the modern language still relies more heavily on the endings of words than English does, and less heavily on word order.

Another good example of structural change concerns the -ed ending of verbs. English had inherited a system from Indo-European in which the past tense of a verb was formed by changing the vowel sound of the root. There are still examples of this process in such forms as *sing sang sung; ride rode ridden; freeze froze;* and *tear tore.* Note that each of these sets presents us with different changes of the vowel sounds.

Originally, all of these verbs had the same pattern of change to show the difference between past and present. But this system began to break down. Many of the vowel sounds in the language began shifting, and the more they changed, the harder it was to tell a verb's past form from its present. In this situation, -ed came to the rescue. It was an ending that showed the past tense in less common verbs. Now it began to be used even in common verbs. Thus, the language was forced to keep this particular ending to avoid confusion. In fact, -ed continues to replace the older way of making past forms of verbs. Today many people are unsure whether to use *dove* (the old form, still used in the U.K.) or *dived* (the new form) for the past of *dive.*

So English is a mixture on many different levels. It has a mixed vocabulary, consisting not only of native Germanic words but also of words borrowed under many circumstances. It also has a mixed set of linguistic changes, some of which seem almost contradictory.

With this overview in mind, one can step back and look at the specific developments—from old to middle to modern times—that created the mixture we call English.

Old English

Old English is the language spoken by the Germanic tribes in England from their arrival before A.D. 500 until after the Norman Conquest in 1066. This is a period of over 600 years. Much can change in such a long stretch of time, and much did. Indeed, many of the changes that began in the Old English period continue even today.

Old English differs from Modern English in several important ways. Chief among these differences is the use of endings to indicate a word's function within a sentence. Modern English preserves only a few such endings, such as the -s added to make a noun plural *(land lands)* or the -s used with a third person singular verb (I *land* he *lands*). In Old English, many forms of nouns, adjectives, and verbs received such endings. Notice the endings on the words for "our" *(ūre)*, "are" *(eart)*, "heaven" *(heofonum)*, "name" *(nama)*, etc., in the Lord's Prayer.

One effect of this feature is that strict patterns of word order, such as those used in Modern English, are not necessary. The endings themselves tell whether a word is a noun, verb, subject, direct object, etc. Again, here is an example from the Old English version of the Lord's Prayer: *ūrnegedaeghwāmlīcan hlāf syle ūs tō daeg* means "give us this day our daily bread." But the order is all wrong from the point of view of Modern

Interesting Origins of English Words

Modern English vocabulary derives from many diverse sources, for example:

Afrikaans: aardvark, apartheid, kraal, trek, veld

American Indian: hickory, moccasin, squash, toboggan

Australian aboriginal: billabong, dingo, kangaroo

Dutch: deck, easel, excise, grab, gruff, hanker, tub

Hindi: nabob, sari, shampoo, sitar, thug, toddy, tom-tom

Italian: allegro, aria, casino, macaroni, soprano

Japanese: honcho, karate, kimono, origami, rickshaw

Malay: amok, gong, ketchup, paddy, rattan, sarong

Mexican: avocado, chocolate, coyote, hoosegow, tomato

English: It says "our daily bread give us today." One may be tempted to assume that *hlāf* (Modern *loaf,* but with the meaning "bread") must be the subject of the sentence. A speaker of Old English would not make this mistake, because the endings of "our" (*ūrne*) and "daily" (*gedaeghwāmlīcan*) tell that person that "bread" is the object of the sentence, regardless of its position in it. Indeed, this system of endings allowed speakers of Old English to use word order for other purposes. For example, "our daily bread"—the central idea of this sentence—is further emphasized by being placed at the beginning. But "our daily bread give us today" is simply awkward and confusing, since it violates the proper word order of Modern English.

As the Old English period progressed, some of these endings became weaker. The weakening process had already begun before English split off from its Germanic relatives. This gradual loss of endings continued through Middle English times and has continued to the present day.

The second major difference between Old and Modern English has to do with vocabulary. When the Angles, Saxons, and Jutes arrived in England in the fifth century, most of their words were from their native Germanic. But just as they found England accessible by sea, so did others throughout the Old English period, in particular Christian missionaries from Rome and the Scandinavian raiders often called Vikings. Many of these missionaries settled in England, establishing monasteries that became famous throughout Europe in the eighth century. Also, increasing numbers of Scandinavians decided to settle down, especially in the ninth and tenth centuries, along the east coast of England.

As is often the case with languages, Old English borrowed many terms from its new speakers. Religious terms such as "devil," "priest," and "presbyter"—most of which are either Greek or Latin in origin—were borrowed. At first, Old English tried to make up words for the new faith with its own vocabulary. In Old English texts we find a native term like *hēahfaeder,* literally "high Father," to refer to the head of Christendom. But we also find its borrowed equivalent *þāpa* (pope), which eventually won out. Most such old native terms were replaced by borrowed words.

The relationship to the Scandinavians was of a different nature. The language of these foreigners, often called Old Norse, was similar to Old English. Over several centuries the two peoples mingled socially until they were indistinguishable, and the changes in Old English reflect this commingling. Many everyday words were borrowed from Old Norse. For example, such basic words as "sister" and "sky," "give" (a new pronunciation) and "take," "skirt" as opposed to its Old English equivalent "shirt," and perhaps even the plural pronouns "they," "them," etc., come from Old Norse.

Gefa, give.
Skil, skill.
Taka, take.
Saga, saga.

OLD NORSE settlers in Britain introduced many new words to the English language.

18 Foreign Language

emphasized
US

emphasised
Brit.

The Lord's Prayer in English

Old English

Fæder ūre
thū the eart on heofonum,
sī thīn nama gehālgod;
tobecume thīn rīce;
gewurthe thīn willa on eorthan swā swā on heofonum;
ūrne gedæghwāmlīcan hlāf syle ūs tō dæg;
and forgyf ūs ūrne gyltas, swā swā wē forgyfath ūrum gyltendum;
and ne gelæd thū ūs on costnunge,
ac ālȳs ūs of yfele. Sōthlīce.

Middle English

Oure fadir
that art in heuenes,
halewid be thi name;
thi kyngdoom come to;
be thi wille don in erthe as in heuene;
gyue to vs this dai oure breed ouer othir substaunce;
and forgyue to vs oure dettis, as we forgyuen to oure dettouris;
and lede vs not in to temptacioun,
but delyuere vs fro yuel. Amen.

Early Modern English

Our father
which art in heaven,
hallowed be thy name;
thy kingdom come;
thy will be done on earth as it is in heaven;
give us this day our daily bread;
and forgive us our debts as we forgive our debtors;
and lead us not into temptation,
but deliver us from evil. Amen.

Modern English

Our Father
in heaven,
hallowed be your Name,
your kingdom come,
your will be done, on earth as in heaven.
Give us today our daily bread.
Forgive us our sins as we forgive those who sin against us.
Save us from the time of trial,
and deliver us from evil. Amen.

Other borrowings during the Old English period are more isolated. From the neighboring Celts came place-names such as Kent, Dover, and Bryn Mawr (from Welsh *bryn* "hill" and *mawr* "great"). There are also nonreligious borrowings from Latin, for example, "cheese," "copper," "mile," and "pound," terms no doubt borrowed as a result of commercial transactions. It is even possible that some of these words may have been adopted by the Anglo-Saxons before they came to England.

Old English reached its height during the eighth and ninth centuries. With the death of the most powerful Old English ruler, King Alfred, in 899, the government became weaker, and the Anglo-Saxon kingdom was besieged by attacks from within and without. With less central government, there was less communication between regions, and so the language began to develop in different directions in different parts of Britain. To the east and north, there were more borrowings from the Scandinavian invaders, for example.

In the middle of the 11th century, there was an invasion of England on a far grander scale. William of Normandy (later known as William the Conqueror) defeated the English king Harold at the Battle of Hastings in 1066, and brought Norman French rule to England. William and his successors brought French-speaking nobles to England, where they became large land-holders. The government and important merchants carried on their business in French. Many native Englishmen learned the new language, and some eventually forgot their mother tongue. The English language did not reassert itself for 150 years after the Norman invasion, and when it did, it was quite a different language.

Middle English

Middle English has its beginnings in the start of French rule at the end of the 11th century. The Old English period came to an abrupt end because of the foreign invasion. This changed the status of the native language. English became a language spoken predominantly by the lower classes. At court, all matters of importance were transacted in French. As a result, groups of words having to do with affairs of state, religion, medicine, etc., were introduced to English speakers during this period. Words like "governor," "councilor," "cardinal," "pastor," "physician," and "surgeon" are typical of such borrowings. Indeed, the words "state," "religion," and "medicine" are themselves French in origin and entered English at this time.

Just how pervasive was this phenomenon can be seen by looking again at the Lord's Prayer. The word *dettis* (debts) instead of the Old English *gyltas, temptacioun* (temptation) instead of the Old English *costnunge,* and *delyuere* (deliver) instead of the Old English *ālȳs* are borrowings from French.

There are other changes to note in the Lord's Prayer between Old and Middle English times that are not the result of borrowing. For example, the Old English word for "kingdom" (*rīce*) became obsolete, but it was replaced by another native word, *kyngdom*. The Old English word for "bread" (*hlāf*) became more restricted in meaning (thus, Modern English "loaf"), but it was nonetheless replaced with the native *breed* (Modern "bread"). Many food words were borrowed from French, including "toast" and "biscuit," but basic bread remained a native word.

There was a tension in the language because of the upper classes' tendency to borrow French terms and the common people's desire to remain with their native English. As the French were gradually driven out of England after 1200, so was the process of borrowing their vocabulary. But many French words had become so familiar that they were probably not recognized as French at all. Today "dinner" and "appetite," and "dress" and "fashion" are used without ever a thought that they were originally French. In fact, the vocabulary of Modern English remains at least one-third French in origin.

English also continued to change structurally. The tendency to weaken word endings, begun in Germanic times and continued in Old English, became even stronger in Middle English. For example, consider the following line of the Middle English version of the Lord's Prayer: *be thi wille don in erthe as in heuene.* When compared with the same line in Old English, it is easy to see that the endings of the words for "earth" and "heaven" have lost their final consonants and that the vowels in those endings, as in the word for "will," have merged into a single sound written *e*. In the present-day version of this line, even this vowel has been lost in Modern English "earth," "heaven," and "will."

This gradual loss of endings led to even greater reliance on word order and on function words. In the Lord's Prayer, in Old English "our daily bread," the direct object of the verb meaning give, preceded that verb. But by Middle English times, the verb comes first, telling us that bread cannot be the subject. Thus, word order gradually took over the function that noun endings previously had filled.

As verb endings disappeared, the English language turned to the use of function words. Helping verbs such as "have," "will," and "may" became important because they helped express the tense and mood of the main verb. English has developed this tendency to such an extent that we can now convey a whole range of meanings through the use of such function words. Consider the differences of meaning in the following verb phrases:

> I am singing
> I do sing
> I have sung
> I have been singing
> I can sing
> I might sing
> I would sing
> I will sing

The range of possibilities is impressive and extends far beyond the capacities of Old English. But again, one should note that this entire system is simply a way of compensating for the loss of verb endings.

Because of this new reliance on word order and function words, and because of the presence of many familiar French words, late Middle English of the London area is fairly easy to read. For example, consider the following lines from the late 1300s, with which Geoffrey Chaucer's famous *Canterbury Tales* begins:

> Whan that Aprille with his shoures soote
> The droghte of March hath perced to the roote
> And bathed every veyne in swich licour
> Of which vertu engendred is the flour,

There is an unfamiliar word or construction every once in a while; for example, in the first line *soote* is a variant form of "sweet," and it follows the noun it modifies rather than precedes it. Also, the spelling often seems odd, since it did not start to become standardized until the introduction of printing to England almost a hundred years later. The lack of standardized spelling points to another important development in Middle English.

Many of the variations in spelling between Middle English and Modern English involve a difference in the use of vowels. Thus, one finds *whan* instead of "when," *shoures* for "showers," *perced* for "pierced," *veyne* for "vine," etc. Yet by

He saugh a mayde walkinge him biforn...

THE MIDDLE ENGLISH of *The Canterbury Tales* is closer to Modern English than to Old English.

Shakespeare's time, only 200 years later, most of these vowels had changed to the ones that are familiar today. The reason for this is that during the 1400s and 1500s, there was a massive shift of the vowels of English, a change that is called the Great Vowel Shift.

Sound changes happen gradually and spellings reflect the changes only after some delay. But right in the middle of this shift in English, the printing press came to England. The advent of printed books was a powerful force for standardized spelling. Unfortunately, the standardization often reflected the old-fashioned pronunciation rather than the new. For example, it seems likely that by 1500 English speakers said *laf,* but the early printers went on spelling the word "laugh."

In Modern English, the spelling of vowels seems particularly confusing. Words such as "great," "late," and "straight" have different spellings but the same vowel sound. Hard as the spellings may be to remember, however, they have preserved an interesting piece of language history: In Middle English, these three words had distinct vowels. On the other hand, the vowel in "great" is spelled the same as that in "breath" or "heath," but all three are pronounced differently. Yet in Middle English, they all had the same vowel, and the spelling reflects that too. Thus, it is an accident of history—the coincidental timing of the Great Vowel Shift and the introduction of the printing press—that produced the written form of English that is recognized as modern. English has one of the more difficult spelling systems among European languages, but to the alert observer, English spelling provides a source of information on the history of the language.

Modern English

By 1600 the English language was already similar to the English of today. In the 200 years after Chaucer's death, the language kept changing, but several factors helped standardize it. In addition to the invention of the printing press, a strong central government under Henry VIII and Elizabeth I tended to impose a single standard—for writing more than for speech. The third factor was the rise of London as a great commercial center. In the Middle English period, regional dialects of English showed considerable differences. But with the rise of London, the city's dialect became the standard for the language; it remained so until the 1800s.

The changes in Early Modern English, though less profound, were of some importance. The growth of interest in the Classical worlds of Greece and Rome brought whole new waves of borrowings as people searched for terms to describe their new interests. Words like "education" and "contemplation" were created from Latin, which was still

SIR FRANCIS DRAKE and other English explorers helped to spread the English language throughout the world.

a principal subject of study in every school. New explorations brought strange new products to England. For example, from explorations of the Americas came "tobacco" and "potato." At the same time, the loss of endings and the spread of auxiliary or function words, discussed previously, continued.

Perhaps the most significant development of Modern English is still another result of losing endings. In Old English, endings could indicate, among other things, whether a word was a noun or a verb. For example, one might select the Old English root *luf* meaning "love": the form *lufu* was a noun meaning "love." But *lufian,* with the ending *ian,* was a verb meaning "to love." By Modern English times, both endings had been lost. Noun and verb now have the same form, "love." Many speakers of the

SAMUEL JOHNSON'S *Dictionary of the English Language* (1745) was a landmark work.

language interpreted this to mean that a noun can be made a verb and a verb can be made a noun. For example, modern businessmen may *target* funds for a given purpose, creating a new verb from the noun "target." Or, when people want to drive around on a Sunday afternoon, they say they are taking *a drive,* making a noun from the verb. Thus, the loss of endings has led to a whole new way to make new words.

At the same time, other procedures for coining new words resulted from different factors. Not only whole words but also many prefixes and suffixes were taken from Greek and Latin. From Greek, for example, English borrowed the suffix -ism, which is used to form nouns. At first, it was attached to words that were Greek in origin, such as "mystic." Thus was coined the word mystic*ism.* Suffixes were also attached to native words, as in tru*ism* though "true" itself is a native Germanic word. The dozens of borrowed prefixes and suffixes have given English still another means of creating new words.

One other historical development was to have great influence on the language. Beginning in the 1600s, the English began to establish a worldwide empire. At one time or another, the empire included most of North America, Australia and New Zealand, large parts of Africa and the Indian subcontinent, and smaller parts of Asia. Wherever the British Empire was established, the English language was planted. It is today the official language of Australia and New Zealand, of Zimbabwe and South Africa (along with Afrikaans), of Jamaica and most of Canada, and of course of the 13 colonies that became the United States of America. English has also gained great importance as a second language. Teaching English to Europeans, Africans, and Asians has become an international business. The language has become the predominant international tongue and is used in every corner of the world for business, trade, and diplomacy. Like Latin, English grew in importance with the parallel growth of an empire.

American English

English came to America with the settlement at Jamestown, Virginia, in 1607. To put this date in perspective, one should note that Shakespeare was still writing his plays in 1607 and the King James translation of the Bible, filled with *thou*s and *ye*s, dates from 1611. The foundations of American English, therefore, lie in the relatively early forms of Modern English. This helps explain what an interesting mixture American English is: On one hand it preserves some of the oldest and most unchanged features of Early Modern English, and on the other hand, it changes more quickly than any dialect in the English-speaking world.

18 Foreign Language

center
US

centre
Brit.

The earliest English settlers of America were conservative in the English they spoke, and as a result all American dialects share certain old features that are rarely found in British English. For example, the Great Vowel Shift in Middle and Early Modern English has been noted already. The sounds of vowels continued to change in English, but the changes were much more rapid in England than in the American colonies. The way Americans pronounce words like "either" and "neither"—with the vowel found in "teeth"—is closer to the Early Modern English pronunciation than the British pronunciation, which uses the vowel in the word "ride." The conservative nature of the early American settlers, or perhaps their isolation, preserved such old features in their brand of English.

Early American English did develop separate, though not very distinct, dialects. The map below shows regional dialects in the mid-1900s. The southern dialects tend to be more conservative. For example, the phenomenon referred to as southern drawl in fact preserves many old features of Early Modern English, particularly with respect to vowels.

In the Northeast, society changed more rapidly. Cities in particular reflected this tumult in their speech patterns, so that distinctive brands of American English are easily noticed in places such as Boston and New York, at least in the speech of local inhabitants of more than a generation. But today these dialect variations seem to be fading. Why is this? The answers to that question provide a clue to this most distinctive feature of American English, its very lack of clear-cut dialect lines.

In England, at least until the 1900s, the great majority of people lived and died within their own small region. Thus, over a long period of time, each region developed certain distinctive speech patterns. By contrast, Americans were restless and mobile. Beginning with the westward expansion and continuing to the present, they move farther and more often than citizens of

NOAH WEBSTER compiled the massive *American Dictionary of the English Language* (1828).

other countries. Naturally, this had its effect on the language. The dialect map shows that the farther west one goes, the more difficult it is to distinguish dialect families. The Midwest and Far West were settled by people from all parts of the eastern United States. Furthermore, as time went on, there was much more north-south, as well as east-west, movement. One can understand what this meant for American English by pausing for a moment to consider again the very notion behind the word *dialect.*

HISPANIC and Latin American cultures are profoundly enriching modern English.

Dialects develop as people speaking the same language lose contact with one another. They may be separated by geography or by social divisions, and the longer they are apart, the more their speech will differ, until they can no longer understand one another and their dialects become separate languages. Conversely, when people speaking different dialects begin to live together, the differences in their speech start to fade.

In the American West, dialect differences tended to fade, and the same thing happened in the East during the 1900s. The immigrants who came to America helped break down dialect barriers. Radio, television, and films have also eroded dialect areas. The evening news, for example, presents an American speech norm, distinctive by its very lack of recognizable dialect. Since the Far West, Deep South, Northeast, and other regions are now in touch with one another via telephone, television, and modern transportation, Americans tend to speak more uniformly now than at any other time in their history.

Groups that remain culturally distinct still show traces of dialectal development. Consider the Chinatowns in many cities. Some communities in Appalachia have remained isolated for over a century, and their residents speak an antique Modern English.

Black English is also the result of social isolation. But one must not think of black—or any other form of—English as "incorrect." It is just the result of changing language, something that has always happened and no doubt always will happen.

The melting pot phenomenon discouraged dialect development, but it encouraged borrowing. Native Americans provided other Americans with words for animals, foods, and other items: "moose" and "skunk," "squash" and "pecan," "canoe" and "moccasin," and many others. Americans also made up new words to describe new ideas, ranging from "backwoodsman" to "statehouse." Immigrants brought still more words. For example, in the realm of food, French colonists gave us "chowder," the Dutch provided "cookies," the Germans brought "noodles," and the Spanish introduced "tortillas."

Will American English ever become a separate language, different from other forms of English? Robert Burchfield, a distinguished British student of language, believes it will. Others, pointing to the increase in international communication and contact, believe it will not.

The residents of Britain in the A.D. 700s would have had no way to predict the future of their language. Although scholars may know more today about how language works, they are not prophets. The development of any language depends on such a rarety of things that it will always remain fascinatingly unpredictable.

—*Richard Sacks*

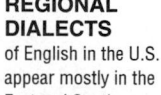

REGIONAL DIALECTS of English in the U.S. appear mostly in the East and South.

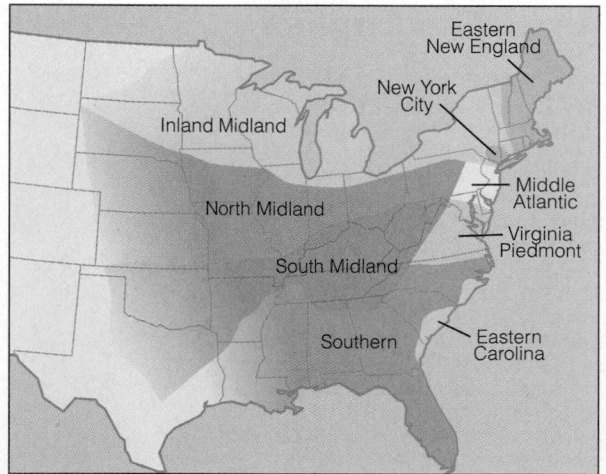

Eastern New England

New York City

Inland Midland

Middle Atlantic

North Midland

Virginia Piedmont

South Midland

Southern

Eastern Carolina

Guide to Other Languages

Most middle and high schools in the United States offer instruction in one or more foreign languages, and many colleges and universities require applicants to have studied a language other than English. German, French, Spanish, and Latin are among the most commonly taught foreign languages. Although most students must study a language for years before they can master its sub-tleties, it is possible to summarize the main points of a new language's grammar. The following section consists of overviews of German, French, Spanish, and Latin grammar that are intended to supplement classroom instruction or to refresh a student's memory about specific points. Only hard work and practice will produce fluency and accuracy in a foreign language.

A SIMPLE REQUEST presented in two different languages, English and French.

German

While German may seem complicated at first, many aspects of the language make it fairly easy to learn. German and English have many cognates (related words) that enable speakers of English to remember some German words quite readily. Another advantage in the learning of German is that all the letters of a German word are pronounced, and pronunciation follows very regular rules. Similarly, once students have memorized the grammatical rules governing German, they discover that the language follows these rules regularly.

Sentence structure. The primary unit of communication is the sentence, which is identified by the intonation pattern at the end. Each of the important sentence types ends with a characteristic intonation pattern. A sentence may consist of a single word, a phrase (a meaningful combination of words without an inflected verb), or a clause (a meaningful combination of words with an inflected verb).

The words that make up sentences are called parts of speech. Some words (nouns, pronouns, adjectives, verbs) are inflected. An inflected word is a word that changes form in some way so that its relationship to other words in a phrase or sentence is made clear, or so that its specific meaning is made clear. The uninflected words (adverbs, prepositions, conjunctions, and interjections) always remain unchanged in form, however they are used.

Nouns and pronouns may be used as the subjects or objects of verbs and as the objects of prepositions. Nouns may also serve as predicate nominatives and as modifiers of other nouns. Adjectives modify nouns, and they may also serve as nouns or pronouns. Adverbs modify verbs, descriptive adjectives, other adverbs, or whole sentences. The verb may be the entire predicate, or it may serve as a link between the subject and the rest of the predicate. Prepositions signal a relationship between a following noun or pronoun and other parts of a phrase or sentence. Conjunctions join words, phrases, or clauses. Interjections usually stand alone as whole utterances. They do not modify other words, and they themselves are not modified by other words.

Word order. Word order is of considerable importance in German sentences. Most rigidly fixed are the positions of verbal elements. Other elements tend to follow patterns; they are subject to variation, however, depending on their importance in the context.

Declarative sentences. Declarative sentences may be simple, compound, or complex. A simple sentence consists of one clause. A compound sentence is made up of two or more main clauses joined by a coordinating conjunction, such as *und* (and), *aber* (but), *denn* (for), *oder* (or).

A complex sentence consists of a main clause and one or more dependent clauses. A dependent clause may have no introductory word at all, or it may be introduced by a subordinating conjunction, such as *da* (since), *wenn* (when, whenever, if), *als* (when, as), *obwohl* (although); it may also be introduced by an interrogative adverb or by a relative pronoun. In a dependent clause introduced by a conjunction or by a relative pronoun, the inflected verb is last, unless the clause contains a double infinitive. A dependent clause that has no introductory word and that follows a verb such as *sagen* (to say) or *wissen* (to know) has the word order of a main clause, in which the inflected verb must be in second place. A dependent clause in which *wenn* is merely implied has its inflected verb in first place. A variant of this word order occurs in a dependent clause of comparison that would usually be introduced by *als ob* or *als wenn* (both meaning as if); the *ob* or *wenn* may be omitted and the inflected verb placed directly after *als*.

Interrogative sentences. An interrogative sentence may be introduced by an interrogative adverb, pronoun, or adjective. The interrogative words introducing the question may be used alone or they may be used with other words. Some common interrogative adverbs are *wann* (when), *warum*

THE GERMAN LANGUAGE has similarities to English in sentence structure as well as in word sounds, as this sign shows.

Fahrrad · Straße · Hammer · Baum · Mann · Frau · Auto · Knabe · Mädchen · Haus · Leiter · Rechen · Hund · Rasen

(why), *wie* (how), *wo* (where), *wohin* (where, to what or which place). When a question employs introductory words, the interrogative word or phrase is placed first and the inflected verb second. When a question employs no introductory words, the inflected verb begins the question.

Imperative sentences. An imperative sentence expresses an order or command and normally implies that some action is anticipated in response to the order or command rather than a verbal reply. The verb of an imperative sentence is placed first, and it is in the imperative mood. In written German an imperative sentence is followed by an exclamation mark.

Articles. Articles function like adjectives, for they agree in case, gender, and number with the nouns that they modify. Articles have their own special set of endings, and their presence or absence affects the endings of descriptive adjectives.

Definite articles. Originally a demonstrative adjective, the definite article still has demonstrative force when stressed. When unstressed, it is equivalent to the English definite article "the."

Because of their similar forms and use, the definite article, the interrogative adjective *welcher* (which), and the demonstrative adjectives make up a group called *der-* words.

Indefinite articles. Originally the numeral "one," the indefinite article still means this when stressed. When unstressed, it is equivalent to the English indefinite article "a" or "an." Its negative *kein* has all the forms of *ein*. It means "not any" or "not a," as in *kein Mann* (not a man). But it also has plural forms that, of course, *ein* lacks.

Because of their similar forms and use, the indefinite article *ein,* the adjective *kein,* and the possessive adjectives make up a group commonly called the *ein-* words.

Nouns. German nouns may be simple or compound (made up of several elements, as a prefix and a noun). The first letter of nouns is capitalized (*das Haus,* the house).

Declension of the Definite Article

	Singular			Plural
	Masc.	Fem.	Neut.	All genders
Nom.	der	die	das	die
Gen.	des	der	des	der
Dat.	dem	der	dem	den
Acc.	den	die	das	die

Declension of the Indefinite Article

	Singular			Plural
	Masc.	Fem.	Neut.	All genders
Nom.	ein	eine	ein	keine
Gen.	eines	einer	eines	keiner
Dat.	einem	einer	einem	keinen
Acc.	einen	eine	ein	keine

Plurals. Nouns are pluralized in various ways. Masculine nouns, for example, may add an -e (*der Freund,* the friend: *die Freunde*) or an -er (*der Leib,* the body: *die Leiber*) or an -er and, over the root vowel, a doubled dot called an umlaut (*der Mann,* the man: *die Männer*); or they may use other endings, or remain unchanged in the plural. Feminine nouns and neuter nouns also vary in the way their plurals are formed. Dictionaries indicate directly after the main entry of a noun how the plural of that noun is formed.

Gender. Nouns are classified as masculine, feminine, or neuter. The gender of most nouns has to be memorized, though nouns denoting animate beings generally have the gender corresponding to their sex. (For suffixes associated with a particular gender, see the noun table.)

Case. As shown in the table on definite articles, the cases used in German are the nominative, genitive, dative, and accusative. Sets of case endings are called declensions. The nominative case is the case form of the subject of a sentence or of a predicate complement. The genitive case shows a possessive relationship or other relationship of one noun to another; it is also used after certain prepositions. The dative case is used for an indirect object, after certain verbs and prepositions, and in some expressions involving adjectives. The accusative case is used for a direct object, after certain verbs and prepositions, and in some expressions of time and space.

The noun table is intended to give a general view of declensional patterns. The dashes in each column stand for the nominative singular form of the noun. The umlaut sign (¨) above the dash indicates that the stem vowel, if *a, o,* or *u,* is umlauted (that is, modified in pronunciation and provided with a written symbol indicating modification). The umlaut sign in parentheses means that not all nouns with the stem vowel *a, o,* or *u* are modified. The sign does not apply to other vowels, for they do not "take an umlaut" and are not modified in the plural. (For the plurals of specific nouns, see a dictionary.)

Pronouns. Pronouns function as subjects of sentences, objects of verbs and prepositions, and as complements of certain adjectives. They may be modified by predicate adjectives, but rarely by other forms. Most personal pronouns have one form when they are used as subjects and another when they are used as objects. The pronoun *du,* along with its plural *ihr,* is used only to address one's family members and close friends; it is the pronoun of familiar address. The capitalized pronoun *Sie* (used with a third person plural verb) is used for both singular and plural; it is the pronoun of formal or polite address. A third person pronoun standing for a noun previously mentioned normally takes its gender and number from that noun. In colloquial speech, however, *er* (masculine) or *sie* (feminine) may replace a neuter noun denoting a person, as in:

Noun Declensions

	PLURAL FORMATION NUMBER	STRONG — Ending zero SING.	PL.	Ending -e SING.	PL.	Ending -er SING.	PL.	WEAK — Ending -(e)n SING.	PL.	MIXED — Ending -(e)n SING.	PL.	OTHER — Ending -s SING.	PL.
masculine CASE nom.		—	(¨)	e	(¨)e	—	¨ er	—	(e)n	—	(e)n	—	⁻s
gen.		⁻s	(¨)	⁻(e)s	(¨)e	⁻(e)s	¨ er	⁻(e)n(s)	⁻(e)n	⁻(e)s	⁻(e)n	⁻s	⁻s
dat.		—	(¨)(n)	⁻(e)	(¨)en	⁻(e)	¨ ern	⁻(e)n	⁻(e)n	⁻(e)	⁻(e)n	—	⁻s
acc.		—	(¨)	—	(¨)e	—	¨ er	⁻(e)n	⁻(e)n	—	⁻(e)n	—	⁻s
neuter nom.		—	(¨)	—	e	—	¨ er	—	en	—	(e)n	—	⁻s
gen.		⁻s	(¨)	⁻(e)s	e	⁻(e)s	¨ er	⁻ens	en	⁻(e)s	⁻(e)n	⁻s	⁻s
dat.		—	(¨)(n)	⁻(e)	en	⁻(e)	¨ ern	⁻en	en	⁻(e)	⁻(e)n	—	⁻s
acc.		—	(¨)	—	e	—	¨ er	⁻en	en	—	⁻(e)n	—	⁻s
feminine nom.		—	¨	—	¨ e			—	⁻(e)n			—	⁻s
gen.		—	¨	—	¨ e			—	⁻(e)n			—	⁻s
dat.		¨ n		—	¨ en			—	⁻(e)n			—	⁻s
acc.		—	¨	—	¨ e			—	⁻(e)n			—	⁻s

explanatory notes

STRONG Ending zero	Ending -e	Ending -er	WEAK Ending -(e)n	MIXED Ending -(e)n	OTHER Ending -s
all have at least two syllables add -n in dative plural, only if nominative singular does not end in -n includes most masculine and all neuter nouns ending in -el, -er, -en *masc:* der Käse *neut:* diminutives ending in -chen, -lein; collectives in Ge—e; infinitives used as nouns *fem:* only two nouns: die Mutter die Tochter	many monosyllables *masc:* many take umlaut *neut:* one takes umlaut: Floß *fem:* all take umlaut some polysyllables, including following suffixes: *masc:* -ig, -ling; most *neut.* and some *fem.* -nis (pl. -nisse); some *neut.* and some *fem.* -sal; *neut.* most in -ment das Hospital das Hospiz	mostly monosyllables; umlaut wherever possible *masc:* less than ten *neut:* many *fem:* none some polysyllables, including suffix -tum (pl. tümer) *masc:* Irrtum, Reichtum *neut:* all others das Regiment das Spital	monosyllables and polysyllables; never umlaut *masc:* nouns denoting live males take only -n (-en) in genitive singular; inanimate masculine nouns add -ns in genitive singular *neut:* only one: das Herz *fem:* almost all feminine nouns except die Mutter, die Tochter. Those ending in -e, -er, -el add only -n for plural; those with suffix -in, add -nen; other *fem.* suffixes: -heit, -keit, -ung, -schaft die Regatta (*pl.* Regatten)	monosyllables and polysyllables; never umlaut *masc:* only a few nouns; those in -or shift stress in plural -óren; others in -r add only -n in plural; irregular. Sporn (*pl.* Sporen) *neut:* those ending in -e add only -s in genitive singular and -n for plural forms; a few substitute -en in plural for a foreign suffix; Museum (*pl.* Museen); Thema (*pl.* Themen); Mineral (*pl.* Mineralien) *fem:* none	nouns of foreign origin that do not fit into regular declensional patterns all surnames *masc:* a few *neut:* a few, including those ending in -o; also, Schema *fem:* Kamera

Wer ist das Mädchen da?
Who is that girl there?

Sie ist meine Schwester.
She is my sister.

The genitive forms of the personal pronouns are rarely used in modern German.

Relative pronouns. The pronouns known as relative pronouns are used to introduce a dependent clause, that is, a clause that describes or limits in some way a noun or pronoun antecedent in another clause. The relative pronoun agrees with its antecedent in gender and number but derives its case from its function in its own clause. It may never be omitted and must be first or be included in the first phrase in the dependent clause in which it appears.

All forms of the interrogative adjective *welcher* except the genitive may be used as relative pronouns. The interrogative pronouns *wer* and *was* are used as relative pronouns if the relative clause itself is subject of the main

Declension of Personal Pronouns

	1st person SINGULAR	PLURAL		2nd familiar SINGULAR	PLURAL	2nd formal SINGULAR AND PLURAL		3rd person SINGULAR MASC.	FEM.	NEUT.	PLURAL ALL GENDERS
Nom.	ich	wir	**Nom.**	du	ihr	Sie	**Nom.**	er	sie	es	sie
Gen.	meiner	unser	**Gen.**	deiner	euer	Ihrer	**Gen.**	seiner	ihrer	seiner	ihrer
Dat.	mir	uns	**Dat.**	dir	euch	Ihnen	**Dat.**	ihm	ihr	ihm	ihnen
Acc.	mich	uns	**Acc.**	dich	euch	Sie	**Acc.**	ihn	sie	es	sie

Declension of the Relative Pronoun

	SINGULAR			PLURAL
	Masc.	Fem.	Neut.	All genders
Nom.	der	die	das	die
Gen.	dessen	deren	dessen	deren
Dat.	dem	der	dem	denen
Acc.	den	die	das	die

Declension of the Interrogative Pronoun

	Animate "who"	Inanimate "what"
Nom.	wer	was
Gen.	wessen	—
Dat.	wem	was
Acc.	wen	was

clause, or if the antecedent is one of the indefinite pronouns, such as *etwas* (something), *nichts* (nothing), or *alles* (everything), as in:

> *Das ist alles, was ich weiss.*
> That is all I know.

Reflexive pronouns. Reflexive pronouns are used as objects that refer back to the subject of the verb. Since they are objects, there are no nominative forms, and the genitive is rare. They are identical with the object pronouns except that a special form, *sich* (himself, herself, itself, etc.), is used in place of all third person object pronouns. The pronoun *sich* (uncapitalized) is also used as the reflexive form of the formal *Sie* and *Ihnen:*

> *Bitte, setzen Sie sich!*
> Please sit down!

> *Der Junge zieht sich an.*
> The boy gets dressed.
> (dresses himself)

A dative reflexive pronoun is used instead of the possessive adjective when parts of the body or articles of clothing associated with the subject of the sentence are involved.

> *Ich putze mir die Zähne.*
> I brush my teeth.

Interrogative pronouns. Interrogative pronouns are used in asking questions and have singular forms only. These pronouns distinguish between living beings and inanimate objects or concepts. There is no genitive form for the inanimate interrogative, and *was* is now often used with prepositions taking the dative. But it may be replaced by special forms like *womit* (with what) or *worauf* (on what). The interrogative adjective *welcher* (which, what) may also be used as an interrogative pronoun.

Demonstrative pronouns. Demonstrative pronouns point out a person or thing without naming the person or thing. They include all the *der-* words except *welcher*—words like *dieser* (this one) and *jener* (that one), along with forms of the definite article (especially *das*). When used as a demonstrative pronoun, the definite article is identical in form with the relative pronoun but

can be distinguished from it by the position of the inflected verb in the sentence. The *ein-* words can also be used as pronouns; as such, these words take the endings -er in the nominative masculine singular and -(e)s in the nominative and accusative neuter singular, but are otherwise declined like the indefinite article.

Adjectives. An adjective limits or qualifies a noun. Descriptive adjectives may be used as attributive or predicate adjectives. An attributive precedes and agrees with the noun modified:

> *ein guter Mann* a good man
> *eine gute Frau* a good woman

A predicate follows a linking verb:

> *Meine Tochter ist jung.*
> My daughter is young.

From the examples given, it is clear that a predicate adjective is invariable, whereas an attributive adjective varies in its endings. Three sets of endings are used for attributive adjectives. If neither a *der-* word nor an *ein-* word precedes the adjective, the adjective takes a so-called "strong" ending (*schwarzer Kaffee,* black coffee); if a *der-* word precedes the adjective,

it takes a so-called "weak" ending (*der schwarze Kaffee,* the black coffee); if an *ein-*word precedes the adjective, it takes a so-called "mixed" ending (*ein schwarzer Kaffee,* a [cup of] black coffee).

Comparison of adjectives and adverbs. German adjectives are compared as to degree by adding suffixes. The comparative is formed by adding -er to the positive or stem form (*heiß,* hot: *heißer*) or just -r (*leise,* soft: *leiser),* the superlative by adding -st- or -est- (*schön,* beautiful: *schönst-; heiß: heißest-*). Adverbs are similarly compared (see comparison chart that follows).

Some adjectives add an umlaut over the stem vowel in the comparative and superlative (kalt, cold: kälter, kältest-). And some have an irregular comparison (gut, good: besser, best-). When used as attributive adjectives, the comparative and superlative forms are declined like any descriptive adjective. However, the comparative may be used without inflection as a predicate adjective or as an adverb, but the superlative always has inflection. When a superlative is used purely as a predicate adjective, it is preceded by the word am (at the) and -en is added to the regular superlative stem (*am schönsten).* The superlative of adverbs is restricted to this am form. The following adjectives are compared irregularly; *gern* is an adverb only, but the others may be adjective or adverb.

Interrogative adjective. The interrogative adjective *welcher* (which, what) is declined like the demonstrative adjective *dieser. Welcher* may also serve as a relative pronoun. The phrase *was für* (what kind of) is often used adjectivally, and a form of *ein* often follows it:

> *Was für ein Buch ist das?*
> What kind of book is that?

Common Words in German

Countries
With few exceptions, the names of countries are not preceded by an article. The exceptions follow.

die Niederlande	the Netherlands
die Schweiz	Switzerland
die Türkei	Turkey
Belgien	Belgium
Dänemark	Denmark
Deutschland	Germany
England	England
Frankreich	France
Polen	Poland
Russland	Russia
Schweden	Sweden
Spanien	Spain

DEUTSCHLAND

Days

Montag	Monday
Dienstag	Tuesday
Mittwoch	Wednesday
Donnerstag	Thursday
Freitag	Friday
Sonnabend	Saturday
Sonntag	Sunday

Months

Januar	January	*Juli*	July
Februar	February	*August*	August
März	March	*September*	
September			
April	April	*Oktober*	October
Mai	May	*November*	November
Juni	June	*Dezember*	December

Seasons

Frühling	spring	*Herbst*	autumn
Sommer	summer	*Winter*	winter

MÄRZ 13 Mittwoch

Comparison of Adjectives and Adverbs

Positive	Comparative	Superlative
groß (large)	größer	größt-
gut (good)	besser	best-
hoch (high)	höher	höchst-
nah (near)	näher	nächst-
viel (much)	mehr	meist-

Attributive Adjective Endings

	Strong				Weak				Mixed			
	Masc.	Fem.	Neut.	Pl.	Masc.	Fem.	Neut.	Pl.	Masc.	Fem.	Neut.	Pl.
Nom.	-er	-e	-es	-e	-e	-e	-e	-en	-er	-e	-es	-en
Gen.	-en	-er	-en	-er	-en	-en	-en	-en	-en	-en	-en	-en
Dat.	-em	-er	-em	-en	-en	-en	-en	-en	-en	-en	-en	-en
Acc.	-en	-e	-es	-e	-en	-e	-e	-en	-en	-e	-es	-en

Demonstrative adjectives. *Dieser* (this), *jeder* (each, every), *jener* (that), *mancher* (many a), and *solcher* (such) are often called demonstrative adjectives. Of these *dieser* occurs most frequently and is often used to contrast with the stressed definite article. In writing it is sometimes used to mean "the latter," in contrast to *jener*, "the former." The declension of *dieser* can serve as a model for all these words.

Possessive adjectives. The possessive adjectives are *mein* (my), *dein* (your, familiar singular), *Ihr* (your, formal, singular and plural), *sein* (his, its), *ihr* (her, their), *unser* (our), and *euer* (your, familiar plural). These adjectives are declined like *(k)ein,* but when endings are added, *unser* is sometimes shortened to *unsr-,* and *euer* to *eur-.*

Numerals. The cardinal numbers (eins, zwei, drei . . .) are used to give a

Declension of *Dieser* "This"

	SINGULAR			PLURAL
	Masc.	Fem.	Neut.	All genders
Nom.	dieser	diese	dieses	diese
Gen.	dieses	dieser	dieses	dieser
Dat.	diesem	dieser	diesem	diesen
Acc.	diesen	diese	dieses	diese

specific count of the members in a collection of objects, and ordinal numbers (erst-, zweit-, dritt-) are used to designate a position in an ordered sequence of numbers. Cardinal numbers must be classed as adjectives when they are used with nouns, although only *ein* (one) regularly shows agreement with the noun it modifies. The numerals above *null* (zero) and through 999,999 are not separated into individual words but are combined into one solid word. The major units above 999,999 are feminine nouns with singular and plural forms that are written as separate words and capitalized. When Arabic numerals are used, German has a period or a space where English requires a comma and a comma where English has a period.

All intermediate numerals can be deduced from the above patterns, for example, 9,876,543,210,123,456 would be read neun Billionen achthundertsechsundsiebzig Milliarden fünfhundertdreiundvierzig Millionen zweihunderzehntausendhundertdrei undzwanzig (Komma) vier fünf sechs.

Ordinal numbers correspond to the cardinal numbers and except for *erst-* (first), *dritt-* (third), and *acht-* (eighth) are regularly derived by adding the suffix -t- to the cardinal numbers through 19 and -st- to those from 20 to 100. The series begins again with 101 (*hundertunderst-,* etc.).

As ordinals these numbers are always inflected and take strong, weak, or mixed endings, depending on what precedes. A period after an Arabic numeral indicates an ordinal number and is used mainly in writing dates, with the word *Tag* understood (*Heute ist der 5. [fünfte] März,* today is the fifth of March; *am 21. [einundzwanzigsten] Mai,* on the twenty-first of May). Ordinals used with names of royalty follow the name and Roman numerals are used (*Wilhelm II, Wilhelm der Zweite; der Sohn Friedrichs III, Friedrichs des Dritten*).

Prepositions. A preposition governs its object, which is put in the appropriate case. Most prepositions make special compounds instead of taking a personal pronoun object if the antecedent is inanimate (*damit,* with it; *darauf,* on it). All prepositions make these compounds except for *außer, bis, ohne, seit* and those prepositions that take the genitive.

Among the common prepositions that take the dative are *aus* (from, of, out of), *außer* (besides, except), *bei* (near, at), *mit* (with), *nach* (after, to), *seit* (since), *von* (of, from, by), and *zu* (to, toward). Contractions of the definite article occur with some prepositions that take the dative. For example, *bei* combines with *dem* to produce *beim; von* and *zu* combine similarly to produce

Cardinal Numbers

Cardinal numbers are not declined.
Zehn is added to the numbers three to nine to form 13 to 19. Note the difference in spelling:

sechs	6	sechzehn	16
sieben	7	siebzehn	17

Zig is added to the numbers three to nine to form 20, etc. Note the differences in spelling:

zwei	2	zwanzig	20
drei	3	dreissig	30
sechs	6	sechzig	60
sieben	7	siebzig	70

The numbers from 20 to 30 and so on up to 99 are formed by using the single numbers first and adding *und* (and).

0	Null	20	zwanzig
1	eins	21	einundzwanzig
2	zwei	22	zweiundzwanzig
3	drei	30	dreissig
4	vier	40	vierzig
5	fünf	50	fünfzig
6	sechs	60	sechzig
7	sieben	70	siebzig
8	acht	80	achtzig
9	neun	90	neunzig
10	zehn	100	hundert
11	elf	101	hunderteins
12	zwölf	200	zweihundert
13	dreizehn	1000	tausend
14	vierzehn	2000	zweitausend
15	fünfzehn	2300	zweitausenddreihundert
16	sechzehn	4002	viertausendzwei
17	siebzehn	10900	zehntausendneunhundert
18	achtzehn	1000000	eine Million
19	neunzehn		

Ordinal Numbers

Ordinal numbers are declined as adjectives. They are usually formed by adding *te* to the cardinal numbers. With ordinal numbers beginning with *zwanzig* (20), add *ste* to form the cardinal number.

erste	first
zweite	second
dritte	third
vierte	fourth
fünfte	fifth
sechste	sixth
siebente	seventh
achte	eighth
neunte	ninth
zehnte	tenth
hundertste	hundredth
tausendste	thousandth
millionste	millionth

Reading a Menu in a German Restaurant

Lunch and dinner　*Mittagessen und Abendessen*

cold cuts	*Aufschnitt*	fish	*Fisch*
sandwich	*belegtes Brot*	codfish	*Cabeljau*
cheese	*Käse*	flounder	*Flunder*
sausage	*Wurst*		
frankfurters	*Würstchen*	potato dumplings	*Kartoffelklösse*
		mashed potatoes	*Kartoffelpüree*
consommé	*Brühe*	boiled potatoes	*Salzkartoffeln*
noodle soup	*Brühe mit Nudeln*		
soup	*Suppe*	vegetables	*Gemüse*
		mushrooms	*Champignons*
salad	*Salat*	peas	*Erbsen*
cucumber salad	*Gurkensalat*	vegetable plate	*Gemüseplatte*
tomato salad	*Tomatensalat*	green beans	*grüne Bohnen*
mixed salad	*Gemischter Salat*	cabbage	*Kohl*
		carrots	*Mohrrüben*
roast beef	*Rinderbraten*		
roast chicken	*Brathuhn*	dessert	*Nachtisch*
roast goose	*Gänsebraten*	ice cream	*Eis*
roast veal	*Kalbsbraten*	stewed fruit	*Kompott*
roast pork	*Schweinebraten*	tarts	*Törtchen*
meatballs	*Klopse*	fruit	*Obst*

vom and *zum. Zu* also combines with *der* to become *zur.*

Among the prepositions that are followed by the accusative are *bis* (up to, until), *durch* (through), *für* (for), *gegen* (toward, against), *ohne* (without), *um* (about), and *wider* (against). *Bis* occurs by itself but is more often paired with other prepositions in phrases such as *bis an* (up to) and *bis auf* (except for). In such phrases the second preposition governs the case of the object. The accusative definite article *das* combines, principally in colloquial speech, with *durch, für,* and *um* to become *durchs, fürs,* and *ums.*

Common prepositions that take the dative or accusative include *an* (to, at), *auf* (on, at, to), *in* (in, to, at), *neben* (beside, near), *über* (over, above), *unter* (under, below, among), *vor* (before, in front of), and *zwischen* (between). These prepositions involve location or motion in space or time with reference to their objects. They take the dative if there is no motion:

> *auf dem Tisch*　on the table
> *im Sommer*　in summer

But if motion is involved or if the usage is nonliteral, they take the accusative:

> *Er legt das Buch auf den Tisch.*
> He puts the book on the table.

> *Er denkt an seinen Vater.*
> He thinks about his father.

An and *in* combine with *das* and *dem* to *ans, ins* and *am, im,* respectively. All the others of this group of prepositions may combine with *das* in colloquial speech.

Of the prepositions that take the genitive, *anstatt* (instead of), *statt* (instead of), *trotz* (in spite of), *während* (during), and *wegen* (because of) occur frequently. *Trotz* is often used with the dative, and the others are sometimes so used, especially in colloquial speech. Most of the less commonly used prepositions (such as *jenseits,* on the other side of, and *oberhalb,* above) and other words used as prepositions (such as *kraft,* by virtue of, and *unweit,* near) take the genitive. When *wegen* is used with personal pronouns, a special form of the pronoun is prefixed to it, as in *meinetwegen* (for my sake).

Verbs.　German verbs consist of stems that carry the central meaning of the verbs and of endings that are attached to the stems. Verbs are inflected for person, number, tense, mood, and voice. Most verbs have three persons (first, second, and third), two numbers (singular and plural), two simple tenses (present and past), four compound tenses (present perfect, past perfect, future, and future perfect), three moods (indicative, subjunctive, and imperative), one simple voice (active), and one compound voice (passive). These forms are collectively called conjugations. Verbs also form nouns (infinitives) and adjectives (present and past participles).

The infinitive form of a verb is the form usually entered in dictionaries or referred to in discussions on grammar. The infinitive form consists of the stem plus a typical, but not exclusive, ending. Most verb stems take the ending -en. A few end in -n, such as the irregular verbs *sein* and *tun* and verbs with stems of two or more syllables that terminate in -el or -er (for example, *wandeln,* to change, and *wandern,* to roam). In many infinitive constructions, *zu* is required, forming an infinitive phrase. But the term "infinitive" is used grammatically for the form without *zu.*

The person and number categories correspond to the personal pronouns and are identified by appropriate endings. The first and second persons, including the formal second person, are used exclusively with personal pronoun subjects (though the subject may be omitted in colloquial speech, especially in the present tense). Since the formal second person is third person plural in form, it is not given separately in the conjugations shown in this section; the term second person applies only to the familiar form, both singular and plural. The subject of a third person verb may be any noun or third person pronoun. In a few constructions (called impersonal constructions), the subject *es* may be omitted if something other than the subject precedes the verb. Thus, *es ist mir kalt,* "I'm cold," may have the equivalent wording *mir ist kalt.*

Verbs occur most frequently in the indicative mood and in the active voice. Unless otherwise stated, verbs in this discussion will be assumed to be indicative and active.

The present and the past (the imperfect) are true tenses, in that the form of the verb that carries basic meaning varies with the tenses. The compound tenses are not true tenses, because the tense indicator is not contained in the basic verb form but is supplied by a tense form of another verb (the auxiliary verb), and the significant verb appears as an infinitive or past participle. The passive voice is also classed as compound, since it is formed with an auxiliary.

The subjunctive mood has one true tense, the present, a tense that has, however, two forms, and two compound tenses, the past and the future, each with two forms. It is used primarily to express speculation; it is also used in most indirect quotations (those in which another person's ideas are quoted without using the exact words). The commonly used subjunctive form, here called general (but also named type II), is, with a few exceptions, based on the past indicative stem. It is the form required in speculative statements that are contrary-to-fact or improbable conditions. The other subjunctive form, here called special (but also named type I), is formed on the infinitive stem. Its use is severely restricted because its forms are often identical with, and indistinguishable from, those of the present indicative. The special third person singular, however, is never identical with the indicative, and it is often used in indirect discourse (indirect quotation).

Weak verbs.　Verbs that form the past stem by adding a suffix to the infinitive stem are known as weak verbs. The suffix is -t, except for stems ending in -d or -t; such stems add -et.

Most German verbs are weak and regular. All their conjugational forms can be derived by adding endings and suffixes, or both, to the infinitive stem.

A few weak verbs form the past stem on a special base that is different from the infinitive stem. These are listed with their principal parts in the table of strong and irregular verbs. The present and past tenses are formed by adding

Weak Verb Endings

1st person	Present Endings		Past Endings	
	SING.	PL.	SING.	PL.
1st person	-e	-en	-e	-en
2nd person	-st	-t	-est	-et
3rd person	-t	-en	-e	-en

appropriate endings to the infinitive and past stems, respectively.

The past endings have no variants. In the present, stems ending in -d, -t, or in certain consonant combinations (such as the *tm* in *atmen,* to breathe) add -e- before the second person singular, the third person singular, and the second person plural endings. Stems ending in -s, -ss, -ß, or -z drop the -s- of the second person singular ending. Two-syllable stems ending in -el (regularly) and -er (optionally) drop the -e- of the stem before the first person singular ending and the -e- of the ending in the first person and third person plural.

The endings for both forms of the subjunctive are identical with the past endings of weak verbs. The present general subjunctive of regular weak verbs is identical with the past indicative. The special subjunctive is formed regularly on the infinitive stem.

Strong verbs. Verbs that form the past stem by changing the vowel of the infinitive stem are known as strong verbs. Both the principal parts and the endings of these verbs must be known in order to derive all their conjugational forms. For most such verbs, the principal parts consist of the infinitive, the third person singular of the past tense, and the past participle. For some of these verbs the third person singular of the present tense (this also provides the stem for the second person singular) is needed; for a few other verbs the general subjunctive stem is needed.

Most strong verbs follow one of the patterns shown in the verb table. Each class is illustrated by two regular verbs. Some common verbs that conform to the classes (except for minor irregularities) are also given, in addition to the unclassified strong verbs and the irregular weak verbs. The examples in the verb table are given in the following order: A is the infinitive; B the third person singular, present tense, indicative; C the third person singular, past tense, indicative; D the past participle.

The present tense endings are the same as for weak verbs. In the first three classes, and in the plural of all classes, the endings vary with the stem terminals, just as for weak verbs. In the remaining classes, where the stem vowel changes in the second and third person singular, stems ending in -d or -t add the regular second person singular ending (-st) but drop the third person singular ending entirely. Verbs of all classes with stems terminating in -s, -ss, -ß, or -z drop the -s- of the second person singular ending.

In the past tense, strong verbs add no ending in the first and third person singular; the second person singular ending is -st (-est if the stem terminates in -s, -ss, -ß); the second person plural ending is -t (-et if the stem terminates in -d or -t); the first and third person plural have the ending -en.

The subjunctive endings are the same as for weak verbs. For most strong verbs the general subjunctive stem is that of the past indicative with umlaut of the stem vowel. A few verbs of class IV and one unclassified verb have the vowel *ü* instead of *ä*. These are *helfen* (to help), *sterben* (to die), *verderben* (to ruin), *werfen* (to throw), and *stehen* (to stand). The special subjunctive of strong verbs is formed regularly on the infinitive stem.

Modal auxiliaries. The six verbs *dürfen* (to be allowed), *können* (to be able),

Strong and Irregular Verbs

CLASSIFIED STRONG VERBS

CLASS I	II	III	IV	V	VI	VII
STEM VOWEL		∫nd ∫nn				
A	ei	ie	i⟨ng i⟩mm e	e	a	a
B	ei	ie	i⟨nk i⟩ (a)i (b)ie	(a)ie (b)i	ä	a
C	(a)ie (b)i	o	a a a	a	u	ie
D	ie i	o	u o o	a	a	a
A	bleiben	bieten	finden	helfen	lesen	wachsen	lassen
B	bleibt	bietet	findet	hilft	liest	wächst	läßt
C	blieb	bot	fand	half	las	wuchs	ließ
D	geblieben	geboten	gefunden	geholfen	gelesen	gewachsen	gelassen
A	greifen	gießen	beginnen	stehlen	messen	fahren	raten
B	greift	gießt	beginnt	stiehlt	mißt	fährt	rät
C	griff	goß	begann	stahl	maß	fuhr	riet
D	gegriffen	gegossen	begonnen	gestohlen	gemessen	gefahren	geraten
A				nehmen		schaffen	
B				nimmt		schafft	
C				nahm		schuf	
D				genommen		geschaffen	

IRREGULAR STRONG VERBS

	I	II	III	IV	V	VI	VII
A	schneiden	ziehen	erlöschen	treten	geben	heißen	laufen
B	schneidet	zieht	erlischt	tritt	gibt	heißt	läuft
C	schnitt	zog	erlosch	trat	gab	hieß	lief
D	geschnitten	gezogen	erloschen	getreten	gegeben	geheißen	gelaufen
A	leiden	heben	saufen	essen	sitzen	stoßen	fangen
B	leidet	hebt	säuft	ißt	sitzt	stößt	fängt
C	litt	hob	soff	aß	saß	stieß	fing
D	gelitten	gehoben	gesoffen	gegessen	gesessen	gestoßen	gefangen
A		schmelzen	betrügen		liegen	hauen	hängen
B		schmilzt	betrügt		liegt	haut	hängt
C		schmolz	brtrog		lag	hieb	hing
D		geschmolzen	betrogen		gelegen	gehauen	gehangen
A		lügen			bitten		rufen
B		lügt			bittet		ruft
C		log			bat		rief
D		gelogen			gebeten		gerufen

UNCLASSIFIED STRONG VERBS

A	kommen	gehen	stehen	tun
B	kommt	geht	steht	tut
C	kam	ging	stand	tat
D	gekommen	gegangen	gestanden	getan

NOTES: **Class I** verb stems ending in a vowel change the vowel of the past tense and of the past participle to *i* before -en.

IRREGULAR WEAK VERBS

A	bringen	denken	kennen	senden
B	bringt	denkt	kennt	sendet
C	brachte	dachte	kannte	sandte
D	gebracht	gedacht	gekannt	gesandt
*	brächt-	dächt-	kennt-	sendet-
			also:	*also:*
			brennen	wenden
			nennen	
			rennen	

*general subjunctive stem

Class IV verbs, *helfen, sterben, verderben,* and *werfen,* have the umlauted vowel *ü* in the general subjunctive. The unclassified verb *stehen* has *ü* for *ä*.

mögen (to like), *müssen* (to be obliged), *sollen* (to be expected), and *wollen* (to want) are called auxiliaries because they are normally used with the infinitive of a verb that carries the basic meaning; they are called modal auxiliaries because they supplement that verb by imparting a shade of meaning akin to mood (and, indeed, they are often used in the subjunctive mood). The verb *wissen* (to know), though not a modal, is included here because its conjugation parallels that of the modals. They are all irregular in the present tense. Their past tense forms are weak, but most are formed on an irregular base.

Auxiliary verbs.   The three auxiliary verbs *haben* (to have), *sein* (to be), and *werden* (to become) have their own explicit meanings, but they also serve as tense indicators for verbs that carry basic meaning (including the auxiliary verbs themselves). *Werden* also serves as the indicator for the passive voice. These verbs form the special subjunctive regularly on the infinitive stem, except that the first person and the third person singular of *sein* lack the ending -e.

Present participle.   The present participle may be formed for any verb by adding the suffix -end (-nd for two-syllable stems terminating in -el or -er) to the infinitive stem. Present participles are never used as predicate adjectives; otherwise, they follow the pattern of descriptive adjectives. The participle retains verbal character to the extent that it shows active voice, may take objects, and may have the same relationship to prepositional phrases and adverbs as the inflected verb.

Past participle: weak and strong verbs.   Past participles are verbal adjectives formed from any verb by the addition of suffixes and, for most verbs, a prefix. The past participle is used mainly to supply the element carrying basic meaning in most compound verbal constructions. It is also used as an adjective in much the same way as the present participle. The past participles of intransitive verbs (those that do not take an accusative object) are not used as predicate adjectives. The past participles of transitive verbs (those that

require an accusative object) have passive force and are used as predicate adjectives in a construction sometimes called the statal passive.

Weak verbs form the past participle by adding the suffix -t (-et to stems terminating in -d or -t) to the infinitive stem or, if irregular, to the special past base. All strong verbs except *tun* (to do) add the suffix -en to the participial stem, and all verbs that stress the first syllable also add the prefix ge-.

Past participle: modals.   The modals (and *wissen*), when used without a dependent infinitive, form weak past participles by prefixing ge- and suffixing -t to the special past base. When the past participle of a modal is used with a dependent infinitive, it takes on the form of its infinitive and follows the dependent infinitive; the construction produced is called a double infinitive. The double infinitive is the only element that follows the inflected verb in a dependent clause.

Certain other verbs (such as *lassen,* to allow) also have a past participle that looks like the infinitive when used with a dependent infinitive.

Compound verb constructions with auxiliaries.   The present perfect, past perfect, future, and future perfect tenses are made up of auxiliaries plus a noninflected form of the basic verb. For the future the noninflected form is the infinitive; for the other tenses it is the past participle.

A synopsis using the third person singular as the inflected verb is given for *machen* (to make, do) and *gehen* (to go) to show the pattern. The relative position of the elements in an independent clause is also shown.

All transitive verbs, the modals, and many intransitive verbs are conjugated in the perfect tenses with *haben.* Verbs conjugated with *sein* are intransitive verbs that express motion, such as *gehen* (to go) and *aufstehen* (to get up); or a change of condition, such as *sterben* (to die), *einschlafen* (to fall asleep), and *werden* (to become). Also conjugated with *sein* are *sein* itself, *bleiben* (to remain), and the impersonal verbs (verbs used only in the third person singular), such as *gelingen* (to succeed) and *geschehen*

Compound Verb Construction

3rd person singular	
Present perfect	er hat gemacht
	er ist gegangen
Past perfect	er hatte gemacht
	er war gegangen
Future	er wird machen
	er wird gehen
Future perfect	er wird gemacht haben
	er wird gegangen sein

(to happen). A few verbs of motion, including *ziehen* (to draw, pull) and *fahren* (to go, drive) may be used transitively or intransitively. When used transitively, they are conjugated with *haben;* when used intransitively, with *sein.*

The past and future tenses of the subjunctive are formed similarly, using the general or special subjunctive of the appropriate auxiliary plus the past participle or infinitive of the basic verb.

The passive voice has the same tenses and moods as the active voice. A synopsis using the third person singular of *machen* is given to show the pattern. The subjunctives use the appropriate subjunctive forms of the auxiliaries. Note that the past participle of *werden* lacks the prefix ge- when it is used as an auxiliary.

Imperative mood.   The imperative is limited to second person familiar forms. The singular is formed by adding -e to the infinitive stem of all weak verbs and strong verbs of classes I, II, III, VI, and VII, the irregulars, *werden,* and *wissen. Sein* uses the infinitive stem but omits the ending. The ending is optional except for verbs with stems ending in -d or -t, two-syllable stems ending in -el (which drop the -e- of the stem) or -er (which may drop the -e- of the stem), and stems ending in a consonant combination not pronounceable in one syllable. For these the ending is mandatory. Strong verbs of classes IV and V form the singular without an ending, using the third person singular present stem. The plural familiar imperative of

Present Tense of Auxiliaries

	haben		sein		werden	
	SING.	PL.	SING.	PL.	SING.	PL.
1st	habe	haben	bin	sind	werde	werden
2nd	hast	habt	bist	seid	wirst	werdet
3rd	hat	haben	ist	sind	wird	werden

Past Tense of Auxiliaries

hatte	hatten	war	waren	wurde	wurden
hattest	hattet	warst	wart	wurdest	wurdet
hatte	hatten	war	waren	wurde	wurden

General Subjunctive Stem

hätt-		wär-		würd-	

Present Tense of Modals and Wissen

	dürfen	können	mögen	müssen	sollen	wollen	wissen
ich	darf	kann	mag	muß	soll	will	weiß
du	darfst	kannst	magst	mußt	sollst	willst	weißt
er	darf	kann	mag	muß	soll	will	weiß
wir	dürfen	können	mögen	müssen	sollen	wollen	wissen
ihr	dürft	könnt	mögt	müßt	sollt	wollt	wißt
sie	dürfen	können	mögen	müssen	sollen	wollen	wissen

Past Stem

	dürft-	konnt-	mocht-	mußt-	sollt-	wollt-	wußt-

General Subjunctive Stem

	dürft-	könnt-	möcht-	müßt-	sollt-	wollt-	wüßt-

Subjunctive

3rd person singular

Present	er wird gemacht
Past	er wurde gemacht
Present perfect	er ist gemacht worden
Past perfect	er war gemacht worden
Future	er wird gemacht werden
Future perfect	er wird gemacht worden sein

Writing Letters

Date
14. August 2003   August 14, 2003

Inside address
The destination is supplied after the name of the addressee. The house number follows the street.

Herrn Max Schulz	Mr. Max Schulz
Hauptstrasse 8	8 Hauptstrasse
Düsseldorf	Düsseldorf

Salutation
(informal)
  Lieber Herr Schulz   Dear Mr. Schulz
(formal)
  Sehr geehrter Herr Schulz   Dear Mr. Schulz

Complimentary close
(informal)
  Mit freundlichen Grüssen
  With kindest regards
(formal)
  Hochachtungsvoll Very truly yours

all verbs is identical with the second person plural present indicative. Except for special emphasis, the personal pronouns are not used with the familiar forms; if used, they follow the verb and are stressed.

When the third person plural is used for the formal second person, it is actually the special subjunctive, but for all verbs except *sein* it looks like the third person plural indicative with the verb and pronoun reversed in position. The pronoun is never omitted. The formal imperative of *sein* is *seien Sie.*

Reflexive verbs. Some verbs are used frequently or exclusively with reflexive pronouns as objects. Many are true reflexives, since the subject acts on itself:

> *Er badet sich.*
> He bathes himself.

But many cannot be taken literally:

> *Das Tor öffnet sich.*
> The gate opens.

Most of these expressions are highly idiomatic and are best studied with the help of a dictionary.

Verbal prefixes. Prefixes may be added to verbs to effect changes in meaning that range from very slight (*zahlen,* to pay; *bezahlen,* to pay) to virtually complete (*kommen,* to come; *bekommen,* to receive). Prefixes are classed as separable or inseparable, depending on how the resulting compound is handled.

Separable prefixes were originally separate adverbial elements that became closely associated with the verb through frequent usage. The prefix may be almost

any part of speech or occur in no other usage. The word *aus* (out) may serve as such an element in addition to its use as a preposition. In the infinitive form the prefix and the verb are written as a single word *ausgehen* (to go out), and the main stress falls on the prefix. When the infinitive is used with the preposition *zu,* the preposition comes between the prefix and the verb and the whole is written as a single word, *auszugehen.* In the past participle the prefix ge- comes between the prefix and the verb:

> *Ich bin ausgegangen.*
> I have gone out.

Separation occurs when these verbs serve as inflected verbs in a main clause; the verb is in second position and the prefix is last:

> *Ich gehe aus.*
> I am going out.

In dependent clauses, when the inflected verb is last, the prefix and verb are again written together:

> *Er weiß, daß ich nicht ausgehe.*
> He knows that I am not going out.

Inseparable prefixes are unstressed elements that never occur as separate words. Though they usually produce a change in meaning in the verb stems to which they are added, the prefixes themselves have no specific meaning. The inseparable prefixes are: be-, ge-, emp-, ent-, er-, miß-, ver-, and zer-. Two examples of their use follow:

kommen	to come
finden	to find
bekommen	to receive
erfinden	to invent

Verbs having inseparable prefixes never add ge- to the past participle, and such a prefix is never stressed.

A few words such as *durch, über, um, unter, voll, wider,* and *wieder* may be used as either separable or inseparable prefixes. The compound verbs in which these prefixes are used vary in stress and meaning, depending on whether such prefixes are being used as separable or inseparable. Thus, the compound *übersetzen* (to transfer), stressed on the first syllable, uses *über* as a separable prefix. However, when this compound is stressed on the third syllable, it means to translate and uses *über* as an inseparable prefix.

—*Erminnie Bartelmez*

18 Foreign Language

GERMAN as a literary language was established by Martin Luther's translation of the Bible in the early 1500s.

French

French is quite easy to read. The words are arranged in sentences very much as they are in English, and many of the words have the same spelling and the same meaning as in English. Some French words are written with special marks called accents. For example, an acute accent is used in *littérature,* a grave accent in *poète,* and a circumflex accent in *câble.* These marks generally show how to pronounce the vowels over which they are

written (*é* sounds like *a* in "late" and *è* like *e* in "let"). Sometimes they merely distinguish one word from another; for example, *a* means "has" but *à* means "to." A small hooklike mark, called a cedilla, is another special mark. It appears under *c,* in words like *garçon* (boy), to show that *c* sounds like *s.* The final vowel of certain short words, like *je* (I), *de* (of), *le* (the), and *la* (the) is replaced by an apostrophe if the following word begins with a vowel (*l'enfant,*

the child), and, often, if the following word begins with an *h* (*l'herbe,* the grass).

Sentence structure. The word order in French is often the same or nearly the same as in English. However, object pronouns (pronouns corresponding to "him," "them," etc.) are usually placed before the verb.

Declarative sentences. A declarative sentence makes a statement:

Elle chante la chanson.
She is singing the song.

To express "not" with a verb, *ne* is put before and *pas* after the verb:

Elle ne chante pas la chanson.
She is not singing the song.

Interrogative sentences. An interrogative sentence asks a question. A declarative sentence can be made a question by beginning the sentence with *Est-ce que* (Is it that):

Est-ce qu'elle chante la chanson?
Is she singing the song?

A declarative sentence can be made a question by adding *n'est-ce pas:*

Elle chante bien, n'est-ce pas?
She sings well, is it not (so)?

A question can also be formed by putting the verb before the subject pronoun. A hyphen then connects the verb with the pronoun:

Il est riche.
He is rich.

Est-il riche?
Is he rich?

In such a question, if the verb and the subject pronoun bring two vowels together, -t- separates the vowels:

Il a la clef.
He has the key.

A-t-il la clef?
Does he have the key?

If the subject of such a question is a noun, the noun begins the question:

Henri, est-il riche?
Is Henry rich?

Imperative sentences. An imperative sentence gives a command:

Chantez la chanson.
Sing the song.

Word order. An object pronoun is usually placed before the verb:

Elle le voit.
She sees him.

The pronoun *lui* means "to him" or "to her"; *leur* means "to them":

Elle lui parle.
She speaks to him.

Vous leur parlez.
You speak to them.

In a negative sentence, *ne* precedes the object pronoun:

Je ne le vois pas.
I don't see him.

If there are two object pronouns, both precede the verb:

Je les lui donne.
I give them to him.

In a positive command, the object pronoun follows the verb:

Parlez-lui.
Speak to him.

If there are two object pronouns, a hyphen connects them:

Donnez-les-lui.
Give them to him.

In a negative command, the object pronouns precede the verb:

Ne le lui dites pas.
Don't say it to him.

Articles. Each noun in French is classified as either masculine or feminine. There is no neuter. Nouns like *père* (father) and *fils* (son) are, of course, masculine. Nouns like *mère* (mother) and *fille* (daughter) are feminine. But the gender of most nouns has to be memorized.

Definite articles. The English definite article (the) is *le* before a masculine noun and *la* before a feminine noun:

le père	the father
la mère	the mother
le livre	the book
la maison	the house

If the nouns are plural, *le* and *la* are changed to *les:*

les pères	the fathers
les mères	the mothers

Before a vowel, and often before *h, le* and *la* become *l':*

l'enfant	the child
l'homme	the man

When *de* (of) precedes *le,* the *de* and the *le* combine into *du:*

du père of the father

But *de* does not combine with *la* or *l':*

de la mère	of the mother
de l'enfant	of the child

When *de* precedes *les,* the combination is *des:*

des pères	of the fathers
des mères	of the mothers

If *à* (to) precedes *le,* the combination is *au:*

au père to the father

But *à* does not combine with *la* or *l':*

à la mère	to the mother
à l'enfant	to the child

When *à* precedes *les,* the combination is *aux:*

aux pères	to the fathers
aux mères	to the mothers

Indefinite articles. The indefinite articles (a, an) are *un* before a masculine noun and *une* before a feminine noun:

un père	a father
une mère	a mother
un livre	a book
une maison	a house

Partitive construction. In an English sentence like "We are eating bread," the word "some" (before bread) is understood and is sometimes expressed. Similarly, in a sentence like "We are not eating bread," the word "any" (before bread) is understood and is sometimes expressed.

Even though "some" and "any" are not always expressed in English, the idea of "some" and "any" is always expressed in French. This is done through the partitive construction, which uses *du, de la, de l',* or *des* to express "some" and *de* alone to express "any":

Nous mangeons du pain.
We are eating (some) bread.

Nous ne mangeons pas de pain.
We are not eating (any) bread.

Noun plurals. In English, most nouns are made plural by the addition of -s. This is also true of most French nouns:

le crayon les crayons	the pencil(s)
la pomme les pommes	the apple(s)

But nouns ending in *s, x,* or *z* remain unchanged in the plural:

le bas les bas	the stocking(s)
la voix les voix	the voice(s)
le gaz les gaz	the gas(es)

Nearly all nouns that end in *au* or *eu* add an -x instead of an -s for the plural:

| le bureau les bureaux | the office(s) |
| le feu les feux | the fire(s) |

Some nouns that end in *ou* add an -x:

| le chou les choux | the cabbage(s) |

Many nouns that end in *al* or *ail* change the ending to *aux*:

| le métal les métaux | the metal(s) |
| le bail les baux | the lease(s) |

Some nouns have irregular plurals:

| l'oeil les yeux | the eye(s) |

Pronouns. Pronouns (I, you, etc.) replace nouns. Like nouns, pronouns may be the subjects or objects of verbs or the objects of prepositions.

Subject pronouns. The subject pronouns are *je* (I), *tu* (you), *il* (he, it), *elle* (she, it), *nous* (we), *vous* (you), *ils* (they), *elles* (they).

The pronoun *tu* is used only within a family, or by very close friends, or in speaking to children, animals, etc. Its plural is *vous*. The pronoun *vous* is both singular and plural. It is the pronoun used whenever *tu* would not be proper, as in formal address.

Object pronouns. The object pronouns are *me* (me), *te* (you), *le* (him, it), *la* (her, it), *nous* (us), *vous* (you), *les* (them); also, *lui* (to him, her, it), *leur* (to them). The pronouns *me, te, nous,* and *vous* may be direct or indirect objects. The pronouns *le, la,* and *les* are direct objects only.

Two of the pronouns, *me* and *te,* change their form when in a positive command:

Répondez-moi.
Answer me.

Lave-toi.
Wash yourself.

Disjunctive pronouns. Disjunctive pronouns follow a preposition or are used alone. The disjunctive pronouns are *moi* (me, I), *toi* (you), *lui* (him, he, it), *elle* (her, she, it), *nous* (us, we), *vous* (you), *eux* (them, they: masculine), *elles* (them, they: feminine):

avec moi with me
avec eux with them

Qui est là? Lui. Who's there? He (is).

The disjunctive pronouns are often used to give emphasis to the subject of a sentence:

Moi, je le crois.
I believe it.

They are also used after *que* in the case of comparisons:

Vous parlez mieux que lui.
You speak better than he (does).

Elle marche plus vite que moi.
She walks more quickly than I.

And they appear after *c'est:*

C'est lui qui l'a dit.
It is he who has said it.

Reflexive pronouns. Reflexive pronouns are used as objects and refer to the subject of the verb. As direct or indirect objects, they are identical with the object pronouns (*me, te,* etc.), except that *se* is used in place of all third person object pronouns (*le, la,* etc.):

Je me lave.
I am washing myself.

Il se lave.
He is washing himself.

The pronoun *se* may also mean "oneself," as in *s'habiller* (to dress oneself).

The reflexive pronoun is always expressed:

Je m'habille.
I am dressing.

A French reflexive verb usually has to be translated into an English phrase that does not include a reflexive pronoun. For example, in English *s'asseoir* means simply "to sit down," *se coucher* means "to go to bed," *se lever* means "to get up," and so on.

Il s'assied.
He sits down.

Couchez-vous.
Go to bed.

Nous nous levons.
We get up.

A sentence like "I am washing my hands" becomes in poor English, "I am washing the hands to myself":

Je me lave les mains.
I wash my hands.

Lavez-vous les mains.
Wash your hands.

Possessive pronouns. The possessive pronouns express possession:

These pronouns agree in gender and number with the noun to which they refer:

Voilà sa mère.
There is his mother.

Où est la mienne?
Where is mine?

The plural of the possessive pronouns is regular: *les miens, les miennes* (mine), *les tiens, les tiennes* (yours), etc.

Voici nos filles.
Here are our daughters.

Où sont les leurs?
Where are theirs?

Possession may also be indicated by use of the preposition *à* followed by a disjunctive pronoun:

Possessive Pronouns

SINGULAR

Masculine	Feminine	
le míen	*la míenne*	mine
le tien	*la tienne*	yours
le sien	*la sienne*	his, hers, its
le nôtre	*la nôtre*	ours
le vôtre	*la vôtre*	yours
le leur	*la leur*	theirs

Le livre est à moi.
The book is mine.

Relative pronouns. In English the relative pronouns are "who," "whom," "whose," "what," "which," and "that." The relative pronouns are always expressed in French, even though they are sometimes omitted in English.

When "who," "which," or "that" is used as a relative pronoun and as a subject, it is expressed in French by *qui:*

L'homme qui est ici est mon ami.
The man who is here is my friend.

Voici un livre qui m'intéresse.
Here is a book that interests me.

To express "whom" or to express "which" and "that" used as direct objects, the relative pronoun *que* is used:

La dame que vous voyez est ma mère.
The lady whom you see is my mother.

Le livre que vous avez est à moi.
The book you have is mine.

The pronoun *dont* may express "whose," "of whom," and "of which":

la dame dont nous parlons
the lady of whom we speak

le livre dont j'ai besoin
the book I need

In a sentence such as "Tell me what happened," the word "what" could be replaced by "that which." Whenever "what" can be replaced by "that which," either *ce qui* or *ce que* is used (*ce qui* if "that which" or "what" is used as a subject; *ce que* if "that which" or "what" is used as an object):

Dites-moi ce qui est arrivé.
Tell me what happened.

Dites-moi ce que vous savez.
Tell me what you know.

Additional relative pronouns include: *lequel* (masculine; plural: *lesquels*); *laquelle* (feminine; plural: *lesquelles*). These pronouns mean "who," "whom," or "which." The prepositions *à* (to) and *de* (of) combine with *lequel, lesquels,* and *lesquelles: auquel, duquel; auxquels,* *desquels; auxquelles, desquelles.* They do not combine with *laquelle:*

une maison dans laquelle
a house in which

une dame à laquelle
a lady to whom

un homme auquel
a man to whom

Phrases like *une dame à laquelle* and *un homme auquel* occur especially in spoken French. In written French *une dame à qui* and *un homme à qui* are more usual, but after a preposition a form of *lequel* is used to refer to things.

Interrogative pronouns. Interrogative pronouns include interrogative words like "who" or "what" when these words are used alone or in independent sentences. Interrogative pronouns do not depend on another word or sentence. The interrogatives "who" and "whom" are both expressed by *qui:*

Qui l'a fait?
Who did it?

Qui?
Who?

Qui vois-tu?
Whom do you see?

A qui écrit-il?
To whom is he writing?

In a sentence, the interrogative "who" is often expressed by *qui est-ce qui* and "whom" by *qui est-ce que:*

Qui est-ce qui chante?
Who is singing?

Qui est-ce que tu vois?
Whom do you see?

When "what" is the direct object of an expressed verb, either *que* or *qu'est-ce que* is used:

Que désirez-vous?
What do you want?

Qu'est-ce que vous désirez?
What do you want?

When "what" is the subject of an expressed verb, *qu'est-ce qui* is used:

Qu'est-ce qui est arrivé?
What happened?

When "what" occurs after a preposition, *quoi* is used:

De quoi parle-t-il?
What is he talking about?

If "what" stands alone, *quoi* is used:

Ça me gêne. Quoi?
That irks me. What (does)?

The phrase *qu'est-ce que c'est que* is used in asking for the definition of something:

Qu'est-ce que c'est que la philosophie?
What is philosophy?

Notice also these questions:

Qu'est-ce que c'est?
What is it?

Qu'est-ce que c'est que cela?
What is that?

The interrogative pronouns used for "which one(s)," referring to a definite object, are *lequel, laquelle, lesquels,* and *lesquelles:*

J'aime ce livre. Lequel?
I like this book. Which one?

Common Words in French

Countries

l'Allemagne	Germany
l'Angleterre	England
l'Autriche	Austria
la Belgique	Belgium
l'Espagne	Spain
la Hongrie	Hungary
l'Irlande	Ireland
l'Italie	Italy
les Pays Bas	Netherlands
la Pologne	Poland
le Portugal	Portugal
la Suisse	Switzerland

Days

lundi	Monday
mardi	Tuesday
mercredi	Wednesday
jeudi	Thursday
vendredi	Friday
samedi	Saturday
dimanche	Sunday

Months

janvier	January	*juillet*	July
février	February	*août*	August
mars	March	*septembre*	September
avril	April	*octobre*	October
mai	May	*novembre*	November
juin	June	*décembre*	December

Seasons

le printemps	spring
l'été	summer
l'automne	autumn
l'hiver	winter

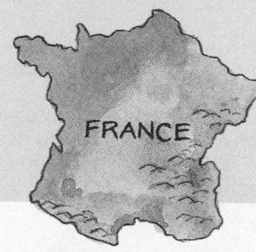

MARS
13
mercredi

FRANCE

Demonstrative pronouns. Demonstrative pronouns are used in pointing out a person or thing without naming the person or thing. When "this" is used in a general sense, it is expressed by *ceci; cela* is used for "that":

> *Ecoutez ceci.*
> Listen to this.

> *Cela me plaît.*
> That pleases me.

Cela is often shortened to ça:

> *Ça vous plaît?*
> Do you like that?

The pronouns used for pointing out an individual person or thing are *celui-ci* (this one: masculine); *celle-ci* (this one: feminine); *ceux-ci* (these: masculine); *celles-ci* (these: feminine); *celui-là, celle-là* (that one); and *ceux-là, celles-là* (those).

> *Voici six complets. Celui-ci est à moi.*
> Here are six suits. This one is mine.

Phrases like "the one who" or "the one that" are expressed by *celui qui, celle qui*, etc. *Celui, celle*, etc. are also used with a following preposition.

> *celui qui arrive*
> the one that arrives

> *mon auto et celle de Jean*
> my car and John's

The pronoun *ce* means "this," "that," or "it" in certain phrases; it sometimes also means "he," "she," or "they":

> *C'est vrai.*
> That's true.

> *C'est mon frère.*
> It's my brother.

> *Ce sont mes amis.*
> They're my friends.

Indefinite pronouns. Indefinite pronouns indicate, without actually pointing out, someone or something understood or already mentioned.

A common indefinite pronoun is *on*. It corresponds to "one" (in the sense of "someone," "anyone," "a person," "people in general"):

> *On ne dit pas ça.*
> People don't say that.

The disjunctive pronoun used with *on* is *soi*. The same pronoun is used with an indefinite pronoun like *chacun*:

> *Chacun pour soi.*
> Everyone for himself.

The pronoun *en* expresses "some" or "any" when the noun is not specified:

> *Voici de l'eau. Buvez-en.*
> Here is some water. Drink some.

In other uses *en* may mean "of it," "of them," "about it," "from there," etc.:

> *J'en ai besoin.*
> I need it.

> *Il en parle.*
> He speaks about it.

> *J'en viens.*
> I come from there.

The pronoun *y* may mean "about it," "on it," "to it," etc.:

> *J'y travaille.*
> I'm working on it.

> *Elle y est fidèle.*
> She's faithful to it.

> *Il y pense.*
> He's thinking about it.

And *y* may mean "there":

> *Nous y allons.*
> We're going there.

Y also occurs in *il y a*:

> *Y a-t-il de l'eau?*
> Is there any water?

> *Oui, il y en a.*
> Yes, there is some.

Adjectives. An adjective is a word that limits or qualifies a noun in some way. English adjectives (such as "wise," "tall," etc.) have the same spelling when they modify a plural noun as they do when they modify a singular one. But French adjectives typically add an ending when they modify a plural noun.

Plurals. Usually the plural of an adjective is shown by adding an -s to the masculine or feminine singular form:

> *le petit garçon*   the little boy
> *les petits garçons* the little boys

Adjectives ending in *s* or *x* in the masculine singular remain unchanged in the plural:

> *un mauvais signe*   a bad sign
> *des mauvais signes* some bad signs
> *le vieux vase*   the old vase
> *les vieux vases*   the old vases

Adjectives whose masculine singular ends in *eau* add an -x instead of an -s in the plural:

> *un beau château*   a beautiful castle
> *six beaux châteaux*   six beautiful castles

Cardinal Numbers

The word *et* is used only in the numbers 21, 31, 41, 51, 61, and 71. In all other compound numbers through 99, the hyphen is used. *Vingt* and *cent* are made plural when multiplied and modifying a noun, but drop the *s* before another number.

> *quatre-vingts garçons*   eighty boys
> *quatre-vingt-deux garçons* eighty-two boys

Cent and *mille* are not preceded by the indefinite article. Numbers, except *un* and *une*, do not show gender.

> *cent bateaux*   a hundred boats
> *six cents bateaux*   six hundred boats

Mille does not change in the plural.

> *mille fois*   a thousand times
> *six mille plantes*   six thousand plants

Periods, not commas, are used with numbers.

> 2.000.000   2,000,000

0	*zero*	20	*vingt*
1	*un, une*	21	*vingt et un*
2	*deux*	22	*vingt-deux*
3	*trois*	30	*trente*
4	*quatre*	40	*quarante*
5	*cinq*	50	*cinquante*
6	*six*	60	*soixante*
7	*sept*	70	*soixante-dix*
8	*huit*	80	*quatre-vingts*
9	*neuf*	90	*quatre-vingt-dix*
10	*dix*	100	*cent*
11	*onze*	101	*cent un*
12	*douze*	122	*cent vingt-deux*
13	*treize*	200	*deux cents*
14	*quatorze*	206	*deux cent-six*
15	*quinze*	1000	*mille*
16	*seize*	1001	*mille un*
17	*dix-sept*	1100	*mille cent*
18	*dix-huit*	3000	*trois mille*
19	*dix-neuf*	1.000.000	*un million*

Ordinal Numbers

Ordinals are formed from cardinals by adding *-ième.*

Silent *e* is dropped before *-ième.*

> *deuxième*   second
> *quatrième*   fourth

Exceptions to this rule:

> *premier, première*   first
> *second, seconde*   second
> *cinquième* (*u* inserted)   fifth
> *neuvième* (*f* changes to *v*) ninth
> *quatre-vingtième* (*s* omitted) eightieth

Fractions are formed by combining cardinal and ordinal numbers. *Quart, moitié,* and *tiers* are irregular. *Moitié* is a noun and must have an article. *Demi,* generally used as an adjective, is connected by a hyphen when it precedes the noun and is invariable. When *demi* follows a noun that it modifies, it agrees with it in gender.

> *la moitié de la bouteille* half the bottle
> *une demi-heure*   half an hour
> *une heure et demie*   an hour and a half

Popular Meals at a French Restaurant

Alose à la provençale
shad baked with garlic, onions, tomatoes, black olives, spinach, and parsley

Blanquette de veau
a stew made of veal and a white sauce, garnished with onions, mushrooms, and parsley

Boeuf bourguignon
a beef dish made with red wine plus braised onions and mushrooms

Bouillabaisse
a fish stew made with fish in season and flavored with thyme, rosemary,
fennel seeds, saffron, onions, fresh tomatoes, orange rind, and olive oil

Moules marinières
mussels cooked in a large kettle with a sauce made of
butter, shallots, pepper, parsley, and white wine

The above are examples of adjectives that precede the noun. Most adjectives, however, follow the noun:

une robe bleue
a blue dress

Adjectives that precede the noun include the following masculine singular forms: *bon* (good), *grand* (big), *jeune* (young), *long* (long), *nouveau* (new).

Gender. An adjective used with a feminine noun must also be feminine. An adjective is made feminine by adding an -e to the masculine singular:

une grande maison
a large house

No -e is added if the masculine form of the adjective already ends in *e*. Thus, *jeune* (young) and *jaune* (yellow) are used to modify both masculine and feminine nouns.

An adjective like *heureux* (happy) becomes *heureuse* in the feminine; *faux* (false) becomes *fausse; doux* (sweet) becomes *douce.*

Here are a few examples of feminines that have to be learned along with the masculine forms of the adjectives: *vieille (vieux,* old); *blanche (blanc,* white); *fraîche (frais,* fresh); *belle (beau,* beautiful); *nouvelle (nouveau,* new); *bonne (bon,* good); *publique (public,* public); *longue (long,* long); *pareille (pareil,* alike).

An adjective like *vif* (lively) changes the *f* to *v* and then adds the -e: *vive.* An adjective like *amer* (bitter), whose masculine form ends in *e* plus a consonant, changes to *amère,* which has a grave accent over this -e as well as the regular feminine -e ending. The feminine of *ancien* (old) is *ancienne; naturel* (natural) becomes *naturelle.*

The forms *bel, nouvel,* and *vieil* are alternative masculine forms of *beau* (beautiful), *nouveau* (new), and *vieux* (old). These other forms are used before masculine nouns that begin with a vowel and before some that begin with

the letter *h:*

un bel enfant   a beautiful child
un vieil homme   an old man

Comparison. The comparative degree of the English adjective "beautiful" is "more beautiful," the superlative degree "most beautiful." Most French adjectives are compared in a similar way: "more" is expressed by *plus,* and "most" is expressed by *le* (or *la) plus.* Thus, the comparative degree of *beau* (beautiful) is *plus beau,* and the superlative degree is *le plus beau; belle,* the feminine of *beau,* becomes *plus belle* and *la plus belle.*

To express "less" and "least" in comparisons, *moins* and *le* (or *la) moins* are used. Thus, "less beautiful" and "least beautiful" become *moins beau* and *le moins beau* (or, for the feminine, *moins belle* and *la moins belle).*

In a phrase like "as beautiful as," the first "as" is expressed by *aussi,* and the second "as" is expressed by *que:*

Ce château-ci est aussi beau que l'autre.
This castle is as beautiful as the other.

The word *que* also expresses "than" in a phrase like "more beautiful than":

Ceux-ci sont plus beaux que ceux-là.
These are more beautiful than those.

Some English adjectives have special comparative forms. Thus, the comparative of "good" is "better." Similarly, certain French adjectives have special comparative forms. The comparative of *bon* (good), for example, is *meilleur* (and of *bonne* it is *meilleure).* The superlative of *bon* is *le meilleur* (of *bonne* the superlative is *la meilleure).*

Possessive adjectives. The possessive adjectives follow:

mon, ma, mes	my
ton, ta, tes	your
son, sa, ses	his (her, its)
notre, nos	our
votre, vos	your
leur, leurs	their

Mon, ton, and *son* modify masculine singular nouns (*mon frère,* my brother); *ma, ta,* and *sa* modify feminine singular nouns (*ma mère,* my mother); *mes, tes,* and *ses* modify all plural nouns, whatever their gender (*mes frères,* my brothers; *mes soeurs,* my sisters).

Notre, votre, and *leur* modify any singular noun, masculine or feminine (*votre père,* your father; *votre mère,* your mother); *nos, vos,* and *leurs* modify all plural nouns, masculine or feminine (*leurs oncles,* their uncles; *leurs tantes,* their aunts).

Demonstrative adjectives. Words like "this" in "this car" or "that" in "that book" are demonstrative adjectives. Before a masculine singular noun *ce* is used to express either "this" or "that" (*ce livre:* this book, that book). To distinguish "this" from "that," -ci is attached to the noun (*ce livre-ci,* this book); to distinguish "that" from "this," -là is attached to the noun (*ce livre-là,* that book).

If the masculine singular noun begins with a vowel (and often if it begins with *h*), the form *cet* is used (*cet enfant:* this child, that child; *cet homme:* this man, that man).

Before a feminine singular noun, *cette* is used (*cette dame:* this lady, that lady).

The form *ces* is used before all plural nouns, masculine or feminine (*ces hommes:* these men, those men; *ces femmes:* these women, those women).

Interrogative adjectives. In a sentence like "Which book do you want?" the word "which" is an interrogative adjective. "What" may be used in the same way. When so used, both "which" and "what" are expressed by *quel* (masculine singular), *quels* (masculine plural), *quelle* (feminine singular), and *quelles* (feminine plural): *Quel étudiant?* (Which student?); *Quelle cravate?* (Which tie?); *Quels étudiants?* (Which students?); *Quelles cravates?* (Which ties?).

These forms are also used in sentences like the following:

Quel est cet animal?
What's that animal?

Quel sera le premier?
Which will be first?

The same forms are used in expressing exclamations:

Quel film!
What a movie!

Adverbs. An adverb is a word that modifies a verb, an adjective, or another adverb.

Formation. An English adverb is often formed by the addition of -ly to an adjective. Similarly, French adverbs are often formed by the addition of -ment to adjectives. Thus, *rapidement* (rapidly) is formed from *rapide* (rapid); *vraiment* (truly) is formed from *vrai* (true).

The -ment can be added only to an adjectival form that ends in a vowel. If an adjective does not end in a vowel, the feminine form of the adjective is used; thus, the adverb *joyeusement* (joyously) is derived from *joyeuse,* the feminine of *joyeux* (joyous), which does not end in a vowel.

Comparison. Adverbs are generally compared just as adjectives are: *plus rapidement* (more rapidly), *moins rapidement* (less rapidly), *aussi rapidement que* (as rapidly as).

Use *le* (never *la*) for the superlative: *le plus rapidement* (most rapidly), *le moins rapidement* (least rapidly).

Certain adverbs have special comparative forms. For example, the comparative of *bien* (well) is *mieux* (better). The superlative of *bien* is *le mieux.*

Negatives. In addition to *ne . . . pas,* other negatives are used. Among the most important are these: *ne . . . jamais, ne . . . personne, ne . . . rien.* The word *jamais* means "never"; *personne* (when used with *ne* or alone) means "no one"; *rien* means "nothing":

> *Je ne le vois jamais.*
> I never see him.

> *Jamais?*
> Never?

> *Tu ne vois personne.*
> You see no one.

> *Personne?*
> No one?

> *Nous n'avons rien.*
> We have nothing.

> *Rien?*
> Nothing?

When *personne* and *rien* are used as subjects, the *ne* follows:

> *Personne n'est ici.*
> No one is here.

> *Rien n'est facile.*
> Nothing is easy.

Jamais means "ever" in a sentence without *ne:*

> *Avez-vous jamais été en France?*
> Have you ever been in France?

Prepositions. Certain verbs are followed by either *à* or *de* before an infinitive that completes the sense of the verbs:

> *Aidez-moi à le faire.*
> Help me do it.

> *Il promet d'écrire.*
> He promises to write.

Other verbs are followed immediately by the infinitive:

> *Je vais étudier.*
> I'm going to study.

> *Nous devons partir.*
> We must leave.

The noun alone follows *de* when this preposition is used after most adverbs of quantity:

> *beaucoup de livres*
> many books

> *trop de voitures*
> too many cars

If the noun is not expressed in a sentence using such expressions, it is replaced by *en* ("of them," "of it," etc.):

> *J'en ai beaucoup.*
> I have many of them.

Verbs. French verbs are grouped into four classes (conjugations). Verbs in the first conjugation have infinitives ending in *er* (*parler,* to speak). Second-conjugation verbs have infinitives ending in *ir* (*finir,* to finish). In the third conjugation the infinitives end in *oir* (*recevoir,* to receive). In the fourth, the ending is *re* (*vendre,* to sell).

Present. The present tense of the English verb "to speak" is "I speak," "you speak," "he speaks," etc. Equivalent forms are "I am speaking" or "I do speak." A form like *je parle* may be translated by whichever form of the English verb fits best.

The present indicative tense of the regular verbs in the four conjugations follow:

je parle	*nous parlons*
tu parles	*vous parlez*
il parle	*ils parlent*

je finis	*nous finissons*
tu finis	*vous finissez*
il finit	*ils finissent*

je reçois	*nous recevons*
tu reçois	*vous recevez*
il reçoit	*ils reçoivent*

je vends	*nous vendons*
tu vends	*vous vendez*
il vend	*ils vendent*

Imperative. The second person formal imperative is formed by the omission of the *vous* of the present tense:

Parlez.	Speak.
Finissez.	Finish.
Recevez.	Receive.
Vendez.	Sell.

First person imperatives ("Let us speak," "Let us finish," etc.) omit the *nous* of the present tense: *parlons, finissons, recevons, vendons.*

Second person *tu* imperatives omit the *tu;* in the first conjugation only, the final *s* is also dropped: *parle, finis, reçois, vends.*

The omitted *s* of a second person imperative such as *parle* is restored before *en* and *y:*

> *Parles-en.*
> Speak of it.

Present perfect. The English present perfect of "to speak" is "I have spoken," "you have spoken," "he has spoken," etc. In the same way, the French present perfect of *parler* (to speak) is formed by combining the present tense of *avoir* (to have) with *parlé,* the past participle of *parler:*

j'ai parlé	*nous avons parlé*
tu as parlé	*vous avez parlé*
il a parlé	*ils ont parlé*

The present perfect of the other three conjugations is formed in the same way as in the first conjugation: *j'ai fini, j'ai reçu, j'ai vendu.*

Any present perfect may be translated by a form using "did" or by a simple past tense. Thus, *j'ai parlé* may be translated as "I have spoken," or "I did speak," or "I spoke."

The past participle of the present perfect (as also of the past perfect and the future perfect) agrees in gender and number with a pronoun as a direct object:

> *Avez-vous vendu les robes?*
> Did you sell the dresses?

> *Oui, nous les avons vendues.*
> Yes, we sold them.

The present perfect of some verbs, such as *entrer,* is formed by combining the present tense of *être* (to be) with the past participle. The past participle of such verbs agrees in gender and number with the subject.

je suis entré	*nous sommes entrés*
tu es entré	*vous êtes entré(s)*
il est entré	*ils sont entrés*

A form like *je suis entré* is translated as "I have entered" (even though *suis* literally means "am").

Because *vous* may be singular or plural, an *s* is shown in parentheses at *vous êtes entré(s).*

If the subject of any part of the present perfect of *entrer* were feminine, an -e would be added after the *é* in the past participle: *je suis entrée; elles sont entrées.*

Reflexive verbs are conjugated in the present perfect in the same way that *entrer* is conjugated. Here is the present perfect of the reflexive verb *se laver* (to wash):

je me suis lavé	*nous nous sommes lavés*
tu t'es lavé	*vous vous êtes lavé(s)*
il s'est lavé	*ils se sont lavés*

Imperfect. The imperfect tense of *parler,* "to speak," is translated as "I was speaking," "you were speaking," etc.

je parlais	*nous parlions*
tu parlais	*vous parliez*
il parlait	*ils parlaient*

Irregular Verbs

Infinitive / Present participle / Past participle	Present	Imperfect	Future	Past definite	Present subjunctive	Imperative
aller (to go) allant allé	vais vas va allons allez vont	allais	irai	allai	aille ailles aille allions alliez aillent	va allons allez
avoir (to have) ayant eu	ai as a avons avez ont	avais	aurai	eus eus eut eûmes eûtes eurent	aie aies ait ayons ayez aient	aie ayons ayez
boire (to drink) buvant bu	bois bois boit buvons buvez boivent	buvais	boirai	bus	boive boives boive buvions buviez boivent	bois buvons buvez
être (to be) étant été	suis es est sommes êtes sont	étais	serai	fus fus fut fûmes fûtes furent	sois sois soit soyons soyez soient	sois soyons soyez
faire (to do, make) faisant fait	fais fais fait faisons faites font	faisais	ferai	fis fis fit fîmes fîtes firent	fasse fasses fasse fassions fassiez fassent	fais faisons faites
pouvoir (to be able) pouvant pu	peux *or* puis puis peux peut pouvons pouvez peuvent	pouvais	pourrai	pus pus put pûmes pûtes purent	puisse puisses puisse puissions puissiez puissent	
savoir (to know) sachant su	sais sais sait savons savez savent	savais	saurai	sus sus sut sûmes sûtes surent	sache saches sache sachions sachiez sachent	sache sachons sachez
venir (to come) venant venu	viens viens vient venons venez viennent	venais	viendrai	vins vins vint vînmes vîntes vinrent	vienne viennes vienne venions veniez viennent	viens venons venez
voir (to see) voyant vu	vois vois voit voyons voyez voient	voyais	verrai	vis vis vit vîmes vîtes virent	voie voies voie voyions voyiez voient	vois voyons voyez
vouloir (to want) voulant voulu	veux veux veut voulons voulez veulent	voulais	voudrai	voulus voulus voulut voulûmes voulûtes voulurent	veuille veuilles veuille voulions vouliez veuillent	veuille veuillons veuillez

je finissais   *nous finissions*
tu finissais   *vous finissiez*
il finissait   *ils finissaient*

je recevais   *nous recevions*
tu recevais   *vous receviez*
il recevait   *ils recevaient*

je vendais   *nous vendions*
tu vendais   *vous vendiez*
il vendait   *ils vendaient*

The imperfect indicates a continued action or condition in the past; so *il parlait,* for example, could be translated as "he was speaking," "he used to speak," "he would speak," or, sometimes, "he spoke."
Past perfect. The past perfect of *parler,* "to speak," is "I had spoken," "you had spoken," etc.

j'avais parlé   *nous avions parlé*
tu avais parlé   *vous aviez parlé*
il avait parlé   *ils avaient parlé*

The form *j'avais* is part of the imperfect tense of *avoir.*

The past perfect of the other three conjugations is formed like the past perfect of *parler: j'avais fini, j'avais reçu, j'avais vendu.*

Verbs like *entrer* combine the imperfect of *être* with the past participle to form the past perfect.

j'étais entré   *nous étions entrés*
tu étais entré   *vous étiez entré(s)*
il était entré   *ils étaient entrés*

Reflexive verbs are conjugated like *entrer: je m'étais lavé, tu t'étais lavé,* etc.
Future perfect. The future perfect of *parler* is "I will have spoken," etc.

j'aurai parlé   *nous aurons parlé*
tu auras parlé   *vous aurez parlé*
il aura parlé   *ils auront parlé*

The form *j'aurai* is part of the future tense of *avoir.*

The future perfect of the other three conjugations is formed like the future perfect of *parler: j'aurai fini,* etc.

Verbs like *entrer* combine the future of *être* with the past participle:

je serai entré   *nous serons entrés*
tu seras entré   *vous serez entré(s)*
il sera entré   *ils seront entrés*

Reflexive verbs are conjugated like *entrer: je me serai lavé, tu te seras lavé,* etc.
Future. The future tense of *parler,* "to speak," is "I will speak," "you will speak."

je parlerai   *nous parlerons*
tu parleras   *vous parlerez*
il parlera   *ils parleront*

je finirai   *nous finirons*
tu finiras   *vous finirez*
il finira   *ils finiront*

je recevrai   *nous recevrons*
tu recevras   *vous recevrez*
il recevra   *ils recevront*

je vendrai	nous vendrons
tu vendras	vous vendrez
il vendra	ils vendront

Present conditional. The present conditional of *parler*, "to speak," is "I would speak," "you would speak," etc. (as in "I would speak if I could").

je parlerais	nous parlerions
tu parlerais	vous parleriez
il parlerait	ils parleraient

je finirais	nous finirions
tu finirais	vous finiriez
il finirait	ils finiraient

je recevrais	nous recevrions
tu recevrais	vous recevriez
il recevrait	ils recevraient

je vendrais	nous vendrions
tu vendrais	vous vendriez
il vendrait	ils vendraient

Past conditional. The past conditional of *parler*, "to speak," is "I would have spoken," "you would have spoken," etc.

j'aurais parlé	nous aurions parlé
tu aurais parlé	vous auriez parlé
il aurait parlé	ils auraient parlé

The form *j'aurais* is part of the present conditional of *avoir*.

The past conditional of the other three conjugations is formed like the past conditional of *parler: j'aurais fini, j'aurais reçu, j'aurais vendu*.

Verbs like *entrer* combine the present conditional of *être* with the past participle:

je serais entré	nous serions entrés
tu serais entré	vous seriez entré(s)
il serait entré	ils seraient entrés

Reflexive verbs are conjugated like *entrer: je me serais lavé, tu te serais lavé,* etc.

Present subjunctive. The subjunctive is used after verbs expressing desire, doubt, emotion, etc.:

Il veut que nous parlions lentement.
He wants us to speak slowly.

The subjunctive is also used after conjunctions like *quoique* (although):

Quoiqu'elle soit ici, je ne l'ai pas vue.
Although she is here, I haven't seen her.

In addition, it is used after an expression like *il faut* (it is necessary):

Il faut que nous finissions vite.
We must finish quickly.

The subjunctive, introduced by *que*, expresses a third person imperative:

Qu'il finisse vite.
Let him finish quickly.

Here is the present subjunctive of the model verbs:

je parle	nous parlions
tu parles	vous parliez
il parle	ils parlent

je finisse	nous finissions
tu finisses	vous finissiez
il finisse	ils finissent

je reçoive	nous recevions
tu reçoives	vous receviez
il reçoive	ils reçoivent

je vende	nous vendions
tu vendes	vous vendiez
il vende	ils vendent

Past subjunctive. The past subjunctive expresses a completed action or a condition, as after a verb of doubt:

Je doute qu'ils aient fini.
I doubt that they have finished.

Here is the past subjunctive of *parler*:

j'aie parlé	nous ayons parlé
tu aies parlé	vous ayez parlé
il ait parlé	ils aient parlé

The form *j'aie* is part of the present subjunctive of *avoir*.

The past subjunctive of the other three conjugations is formed like the past subjunctive of *parler: j'aie fini, j'aie reçu, j'aie vendu*.

Verbs like *entrer* combine the present subjunctive of *être* with the past participle:

je sois entré	nous soyons entrés
tu sois entré	vous soyez entré(s)
il soit entré	ils soient entrés

Reflexive verbs are conjugated like *entrer: je me sois lavé, tu te sois lavé,* etc.

An imperfect subjunctive and a pluperfect subjunctive also occur, but they are relatively infrequent.

Past definite. The past definite is a special past tense used chiefly in written French, as in some kinds of narration. It is translated into English by a simple past tense:

Il parla de toutes ces choses.
He spoke of all these things.

Here is the past definite of the model verbs:

je parlai	nous parlâmes
tu parlas	vous parlâtes
il parla	ils parlèrent

je finis	nous finîmes
tu finis	vous finîtes
il finit	ils finirent

je reçus	nous reçûmes
tu reçus	vous reçûtes
il reçut	ils reçurent

je vendis	nous vendîmes
tu vendis	vous vendîtes
il vendit	ils vendirent

Past anterior. The past anterior expresses an action or condition that precedes what is expressed by the past definite. It is translated into English by the past perfect:

Quand il eut parlé, il s'assit.
When he had spoken, he sat down.

Here is the past anterior of *parler*:

j'eus parlé	nous eûmes parlé
tu eus parlé	vous eûtes parlé
il eut parlé	ils eurent parlé

The form *j'eus* is part of the past definite of *avoir*.

The past anterior of the other three conjugations is formed like the past anterior of *parler: j'eus fini, j'eus reçu, j'eus vendu*.

Babar va dîner chez son amie la vieille dame. Elle le trouve très chic dans son costume neuf. Après le dîner, fatigué, il s'endort vite.

Babar dines with his friend the old lady. She thinks he looks very smart in his new clothes. After dinner, because he is tired, he goes to bed and falls asleep very quickly.

BABAR THE ELEPHANT, created by Frenchman Laurent de Brunhoff, is a favorite both in French and in English.

18 Foreign Language

Verbs like *entrer* combine the past definite of *être* with the past participle:

> *je fus entré* *nous fûmes entrés*
> *tu fus entré* *vous fûtes entré(s)*
> *il fut entré* *ils furent entrés*

Reflexive verbs are conjugated like *entrer: je me fus lavé, tu te fus lavé,* etc.

Present participle. The present participle ends in *ant (parlant,* speaking):

> *parlant   recevant*
> *finissant vendant*

Past participle. The past participle ends in *é* (first conjugation), *i* (second conjugation), and *u* (third and fourth conjugations):

> *parlé reçu*
> *fini   vendu*

Irregular verbs. A sampling of irregular verbs is given on the preceding page. The infinitive, the present participle, and the past participle are shown in the left-hand column. Five tenses of each verb are given next, together with the imperative.

The pronouns (*je, tu,* etc.) are omitted, to save space.

If only a single form is shown (*allais*), *je* (or *j'*) is understood (*j'allais*). The remaining forms use the same stem (as *all-* of *allais*) plus the regular endings of the tense shown (*tu allais, il allait,* etc.).

The present conditional, not shown, can be inferred from the stem of the future (thus, *j'irais* can be inferred from *j'irai,* the future of *aller*).

—*Christopher T. Hoolihan*

Spanish

Although Spanish is spoken on three continents, very few variations of the standard Castilian dialect, which is the main language of Spain, have developed. The main differences between Castilian Spanish and Spanish in other parts of the world have to do with vocabulary (American speakers of Spanish have more loan words from English) and to some extent pronunciation. The grammar, which remains quite consistent from country to country, is reviewed here.

Sentence structure. In Spanish, as in all Indo-European languages, the sentence is the chief unit of communication. Different word orders are used for different types of sentences, and there is some flexibility in word order for some types of sentences.

Declarative sentences. In a simple declarative sentence, the usual word order is article, noun (subject), verb, article, noun (object).

> *El gato toma la leche.*
> The cat drinks the milk.

An adjective ordinarily follows the noun:

> *el gato blanco*
> the white cat

An adverb modifying a verb is placed as close as possible to the verb, usually immediately after it:

El gato come rápidamente.
The cat eats quickly.

A preposition precedes the noun or noun phrase used as its object:

> *en la cocina*
> in the kitchen

A conjunction connects two or more parts of a sentence:

El gato tomó la leche y salió.
The cat drank the milk and went out.

A subject pronoun may replace the subject noun:

> *Él tomó la leche.*
> It drank the milk.

Object pronouns are ordinarily placed before the verb, and the indirect object pronoun precedes the direct:

> *Ella me los dio.*
> She gave them to me.

The elements in a sentence are frequently shifted for syntactic reasons, to indicate a change in meaning or emphasis, or for stylistic effect.

The verb, for example, often precedes the subject:

> *Entró el profesor.*
> The professor came in.

If an adjective stresses a quality inherent in the noun it modifies, rather than simply differentiates the noun from others, the adjective is usually placed first:

la triste verdad the sad truth
la niña triste the child who is sad

A demonstrative or possessive adjective precedes the noun in most instances, as does an adjective indicating quantity or sequence:

esta casa   this house
nuestros amigos our friends
cinco perros   five dogs
la última clase the last class

An adjective modified by an adverb ordinarily follows the noun, as do adjectives joined by a conjunction:

una persona sumamente agradable
a most agreeable person

el árbol alto y verde
the tall, green tree

Although an adverb that indicates manner or degree ordinarily follows the verb, one that indicates place or time is likely to precede the verb:

> *Afuera hace calor.*
> It's hot outside.

An adverb precedes another adverb or an adjective that it modifies:

> *David habla muy claramente.*
> David speaks very clearly.

> *Gloria es menos lista.*
> Gloria is less clever.

Simple negative adverbs such as *no* and *nunca* precede the verb, but adverbs added for negative emphasis follow the verb. (Double negatives are common in Spanish.)

> *Ella no viene.*
> She isn't coming.

> *Ella no viene nunca.*
> She never comes.

Though object pronouns ordinarily precede the verb, they follow the verb and are attached to it if the verb form is an infinitive, an affirmative imperative, or a present participle. To preserve the original verb stress, written accents may be added.

Carlos va a dármelos.
Carlos is going to give them to me.

Démelos, Carlos, por favor.
Give them to me, Carlos, please.

Rosa entró saludándonos.
Rosa came in, saying hello to us.

THE SPANISH in this English/Spanish sign says, "It is prohibited to give food to the animals."

Interrogative sentences. In these sentences, an inverted question mark is placed before a written interrogative sentence or sentence part and a regular question mark after it.

A question can be formed by placing the verb before the subject:

¿Tiene hambre el perro?
Is the dog hungry?

Interrogative adjectives, adverbs, or pronouns may also be used:

¿Cuántas naranjas?
How many oranges?

¿Dónde está Juan?
Where is John?

¿Quién vive aquí?
Who lives here?

¿Cuál prefieres?
Which one do you prefer?

An interrogative clause or phrase may be added to a statement:

¿Usted es americano, no es verdad?
You're an American, right?

Imperative sentences. A command or a request may be formal or familiar. In Spain and the Americas the third person present subjunctive is used for formal commands. If used out of courtesy, *usted* (you: singular) and *ustedes* (you: plural) follow the verb, and *por favor* (please) is often added:

Abra usted la puerta, por favor.
Open the door, please.

Hablen ustedes más despacio.
Speak more slowly.

In Spain and the Americas the true imperative is used for familiar commands (those used with friends, relatives, children, etc.) that are affirmative and singular. Subject pronouns are not ordinarily used:

Abre la ventana, por favor.
Open the window, please.

In Castilian Spanish the true imperative is also used for plural affirmative familiar commands. But in the Americas (as in plural formal commands) the plural third person present subjunctive is used. Thus, in American Spanish, "Open the window" becomes *Abran la ventana*. In Castilian the sentence becomes *Abrid la ventana*.

In both Spain and the Americas, the second person present subjunctive, singular, is used for familiar commands that are negative and singular:

No abras la ventana.
Don't open the window.

In Castilian Spanish the plural, second person present subjunctive is used for plural, negative familiar commands. But in the Americas the plural, third person present subjunctive is used. In American Spanish, "Don't open the window" becomes *No abran la ventana*. In Castilian the sentence becomes *No abráis la ventana*.

Third person imperatives, singular and plural, are expressed in both Spain and the Americas by the corresponding present-subjunctive forms (*¡Que salgan ellos!* Let them leave!), as the first person plural imperatives (*Salgamos.* Let's leave.). The inverted exclamation mark shown in the first example is also used in written exclamations (*¡Qué sorpresa!* What a surprise!).

Articles

Definite articles. The definite article (the) is *el* before a masculine noun and *la* before a feminine noun:

el oro   the gold
la pluma the pen

Before plural nouns, *el* is changed to *los; la* is changed to *las:*

los burros the burros
las niñas the girls

Before a feminine singular noun beginning with a stressed *a* sound, the masculine article *el* is used; but *las* is used before the plural:

el águila   the eagle
las águilas the eagles

A neuter article, *lo,* is occasionally used before adjectives; it gives adjectives the force of nouns: *lo neuvo* (that which is new). When *a* (to) precedes *el,* the *a* and the *el* combine into *al; de* (of) and *el* become *del:*

al teatro   to the theater
del edificio of the building

The definite article is used before clearly identified nouns:

Los maestros llegan a la escuela.
The teachers arrive at the school.

It is also used before nouns taken in a general sense:

Los payasos divierten a la genté.
Clowns amuse people.

Except in direct address, the definite article occurs before most titles:

la señora Chávez Señora Chávez
el coronel Vargas Colonel Vargas

Except after the verb *ser* (to be), it is used before names of days of the week:

Hoy es lunes.
Today is Monday.

Carlos viene el martes.
Carl is coming Tuesday.

It is also used before names of months, seasons, and expressions of time:

el abril   April
la primavera   spring
las diez de la mañana 10 a.m.

The names of certain continents, countries, states, and cities are preceded by the definite article:

la América del Sur South America
los Estados Unidos the United States
la Florida   Florida
la Habana   Havana

18 Foreign Language

theater
US

theatre
Brit.

The definite article is also used before the names of languages:

Me gusta el francés.
I like French.

However, it is not used after the verb *hablar* (to speak) unless there is an intervening word or phrase:

¿Habla usted alemán?
Do you speak German?

¿Habla usted bien el alemán?
Do you speak German well?

Nor is the definite article used before the names of languages when those names are preceded by *en* (in) or *de* (of):

en español in Spanish
de inglés of English

The definite article often replaces the possessive adjective used in English before a noun denoting an article of clothing or a part of the body:

Me quité el abrigo.
I took off my overcoat.

¿Le duele a usted la cabeza?
Your head hurts?

Indefinite articles. The indefinite articles (a, an) are *un* before a masculine noun and *una* before a feminine noun:

un disco   a disk
una palabra   a word

"Some" is expressed by *unos* before a masculine plural and *unas* before a feminine plural:

unos discos   some disks
unas palabras   some words

Before a feminine singular noun beginning with a stressed *a* sound, the masculine article *un* is used; but *unas* is used before the plural:

un alma   a soul
unas almas   some souls

The indefinite article is used before nouns not yet clearly identified:

Una amiga me regaló un libro.
A friend gave me a book.

The indefinite article is ordinarily omitted before a noun of nationality, occupation, rank, or political affiliation when the noun follows the verb *ser:*

Arturo es peruano.
Arthur is a Peruvian.

Mi sobrina es médica.
My niece is a doctor.

But if such a noun is modified, the indefinite article is retained:

Borges es un escritor famoso.
Borges is a famous writer.

The indefinite article is omitted before a qualifying adjective like *mil* (thousand) and *otro* (other):

Pasaron mil soldados.
A thousand soldiers passed by.

¿Vendrás en otra ocasión?
Will you come some other time?

It is also omitted after adjectives like *qué* (what, what a) and *tal* (such, such a) in exclamations:

¡Qué maravilla!
What a marvel!

Nouns

Gender. All but neuter nouns are termed masculine or feminine, for reasons of grammar. The neuter gender is limited to abstract nouns that are ordinarily formed by the combination of *lo* and an adjective. The gender of most nouns has to be memorized.

Nouns like *padre* (father) are, of course, masculine. In general, the following nouns are also masculine: those ending in *o, e, l, r,* (*libro,* book; *juguete,* toy; *sol,* sun; *favor,* favor); those of Greek origin ending in *ma, pa, ta* (*idioma,* language; *mapa,* map; *planeta,* planet); and names of trees and of the days and months (*roble,* oak; *sábado,* Saturday; *enero,* January).

By natural gender, nouns like *madre* (mother) are feminine. The following nouns are also ordinarily feminine: those ending in *a, z, d* (*biblioteca,* library; *paz,* peace; *salud,* health); those ending in *ión* and *umbre* (*canción,* song; *costumbre,* custom); and names of fruits and of letters of the alphabet (*naranja,* orange; *una* c, a *c*).

Most masculine nouns ending in *o* change the *o* to *a* for the feminine

Personal Pronouns

		Subject	Direct object	Indirect object
1st	SING.	yo	me	me
	PL.	nosotros nosotras	nos	nos
2nd	SING.	tú	te	te
	PL.	vosotros vosotras	os	os
3rd	SING.	usted	lo, le, la	le
		él	lo, le	le
		ella	la	le
	PL.	ustedes	los, las	les
		ellos	los	les
		ellas	las	les

(*muchacho,* boy; *muchacha,* girl). Most masculine nouns ending in *ol, or, ón, án,* and *és* add an *a* and, as necessary, drop a written accent (*el español,* Spaniard: *la española; el doctor,* doctor: *la doctora; el patrón,* boss: *la patrona; el alemán,* German: *la alemana; el inglés,* Englishman: *la inglesa,* Englishwoman).

Many nouns denoting persons remain unchanged in the feminine, except for the replacement of *el* by *la (el joven,* the youth: *la joven).*

Some nouns change gender according to their meanings (*el frente,* the front; *la frente,* the forehead). Other nouns can be either masculine or feminine, with no change in meaning (*el mar* or *la mar,* the sea).

Plurals. Nouns ending in an unstressed vowel or in a stressed *e* are made plural by the addition of -s:

la manzana las manzanas the apple(s)
el bebé los bebés the infant(s)

Most nouns ending in a consonant or in a stressed vowel other than *e* add -es:

el mes los meses the month(s)
el cebú los cebúes the zebu(s)

Common Words in Spanish

Countries

Alemania	Germany
Austria	Austria
Bélgica	Belgium
Canadá	Canada
Dinamarca	Denmark
España	Spain
Inglaterra	England
Italia	Italy
Perú	Peru
Rusia	Russia
Suecia	Sweden
Suiza	Switzerland

MARZO
13
el miércoles

ESPANA

Months, days, seasons
The names of the months, days of the week, and seasons are written with small letters.

Days

el lunes	Monday	*el viernes*	Friday
el martes	Tuesday	*el sábado*	Saturday
el miércoles	Wednesday	*el domingo*	Sunday
el jueves	Thursday		

Months

enero	January	*julio*	July
febrero	February	*agosto*	August
marzo	March	*septiembre*	September
abril	April	*octubre*	October
mayo	May	*noviembre*	November
junio	June	*diciembre*	December

Seasons

la primavera	spring	*el otoño*	autumn
el verano	summer	*el invierno*	winter

Nouns ending in *z* change the *z* to *c* and add -es:

el lápiz los lápices the pencil(s)

Nouns ending in unstressed *es* or *is* remain unchanged:

el jueves los jueves   Thursday(s)

Most pluralized nouns retain the same stress as their singular forms, even if written accents must be added or deleted:

el joven los jóvenes   the youth(s)
la ocasión las ocasiones the occasion(s)

Pronouns.   Pronouns (I, you, etc.) replace nouns. Like nouns, pronouns may be the subjects or objects of verbs or the objects of prepositions.

Subject pronouns are frequently implied in the verb but not expressed:

Leemos mucho.
We read a lot.

When subject pronouns are expressed, it is usually for clarity, for emphasis, or out of courtesy.

The pronouns *usted* and *ustedes* are the formal, or polite, pronouns for "you." These pronouns are used with third person verb forms:

Ustedes hablan bien.
You speak well.

The pronoun *tú* is the familiar pronoun for "you" (singular). In Castilian Spanish its plural is *vosotros* and *vosotras,* but the invariable *ustedes* is used in American Spanish.

Because all Spanish nouns are either masculine or feminine, *el* and *ella* mean "it" when referring to a thing.

The pronouns *me, te, le, nos,* and *os* may be direct or indirect objects. The pronouns *lo, la, los,* and *las* are direct objects only.

An additional object pronoun is *les. Les* is the indirect object form of *los* and *las.* The indirect object form of *la* is *le.*

Either *lo* or *le* may be used as the masculine third person singular direct object pronoun; *lo* is more commonly used in the Americas, and *le* is more commonly used in Spain.

Both direct and indirect object pronouns precede most verb forms, but they follow and are attached to others. In either position the indirect object pronoun precedes the direct.

The third person indirect object pronouns *le* and *les* are changed to *se* whenever either one of them immediately precedes a direct object pronoun:

Se lo di.
I gave it to him.

Object pronouns used after a preposition are identical in form with the subject pronouns, except that *mí* is used in place of *yo* and *ti* is used in place of *tú:*

para mí   for me
para ti   for you

When *mí* and *ti* are used with *con* (with), special forms are used:

conmigo   with me
contigo   with you

Relative pronouns.   In English the relative pronouns are "who," "whom," "whose," "what," "which," and "that." The relative pronouns are always expressed in Spanish, even though they are sometimes omitted in English.

The relative pronoun *que* means "who," "whom," "which," or "that." It refers to any subject or object, person or thing.

el libro que   the book which
la alumna que   the pupil who(m)
los libros que   the books which

The relative pronouns *quien* and *quienes* refer only to persons. *Quien* is singular, *quienes* plural.

la muchacha quien   the girl who(m)
los abogados quienes the lawyers
                       who(m)

Other relative pronouns are *el cual, la cual, lo cual, los cuales, las cuales; el que, la que, lo que, los que, las que.* They mean "who," "whom," "which," etc., and refer to persons or things. Their form changes according to the gender and number of the antecedent.

la biblioteca en la cual pienso trabajar
the library in which I think I'll work

The pronouns *cuyo, cuya, cuyos,* and *cuyas* mean "whose" or "of which." They refer to either persons or things and distinguish gender and number.

Raúl, cuya hermana es amiga mía
Ralph, whose sister is my friend

Reflexive pronouns.   Reflexive pronouns are used as objects that refer to the subject of the verb. They may be objects of reflexive verbs or objects in a prepositional phrase. As objects of verbs the reflexive pronouns are *me* (myself), *te* (yourself), *se* (yourself, himself, herself, itself), *nos* (ourselves), *os* (yourselves), and *se* (yourselves, themselves).

Nosotros nos vestimos.
We dressed ourselves.

Even without a reflexive meaning, many verbs take reflexive pronouns:

¿Por qué se fue usted?
Why did you go away?

Cardinal Numbers

The numbers 16 to 19 and 21 to 29 may be written as single words. When used as single words, 16, 22, 23, and 26 carry accent marks on the final syllable.

    16 dieciséis
    22 veintidós

The only numbers that change with gender are *uno* and the compounds of *ciento* from 200 through 900.

    quinientas dos escuelas
    five hundred and two schools

Ciento becomes *cien* before nouns and before the numbers *mil* and *millones.* In all other numbers, the full form *ciento* is used.

    cien soldados   one hundred soldiers

Millón requires the preposition *de* before the noun it multiplies.

    tres millones de pesos   three million pesos

Un is not used before *ciento* or *mil.* It is used before *millón.*

    ciento doce sillas   one hundred twelve chairs
    un millón de pesos   a million pesos

0	*cero*	30	*treinta*
1	*uno, una*	40	*cuarenta*
2	*dos*	50	*cincuenta*
3	*tres*	60	*sesenta*
4	*cuatro*	70	*setenta*
5	*cinco*	80	*ochenta*
6	*seis*	90	*noventa*
7	*siete*	100	*ciento (cien)*
8	*ocho*	101	*ciento uno*
9	*nueve*	200	*doscientos (-as)*
10	*diez*	1,000	*mil*
11	*once*	2,000	*dos mil*
12	*doce*	100,000	*cien mil*
13	*trece*	500,000	*quinientos mil*
14	*catorce*	1,000,000	*un millón*
15	*quince*		
16	*diez y seis (dieciséis)*		
17	*diez y siete (diecisiete)*		
18	*diez y ocho (dieciocho)*		
19	*diez y nueve (diecinueve)*		
20	*veinte*		
21	*veinte y uno (veintiuno)*		

Ordinal Numbers

    22 veinte y dos (veintidós)

Ordinal numbers are generally used only through *tenth;* beyond that, the cardinal numbers are used. An ordinal number agrees in number and gender with the noun it modifies.

    la Quinta Avenida   Fifth Avenue

The ordinal numbers *primero* and *tercero* drop the final *o* before a masculine singular noun.

    el tercer edificio   the third building

primero	first
segundo	second
tercero	third
cuarto	fourth
quinto	fifth
sexto	sixth
séptimo	seventh
octavo	eighth
noveno	ninth
décimo	tenth

18 Foreign Language

Possessive Pronouns

SINGULAR

Masculine	Feminine	
el mío	la mía	mine
el tuyo	la tuya	yours
el suyo	la suya	yours, his, hers, its
el nuestro	la nuestra	ours
el vuestro	la vuestra	yours
el suyo	la suya	yours, theirs

A reflexive construction may be equivalent to the passive voice:

Se habla portugués en el Brasil.
Portuguese is spoken in Brazil.

As objects of prepositions the reflexive pronouns are *mí* (myself), *ti* (yourself), *sí* (yourself, himself, etc.), *nosotros* and *nosotras* (ourselves), *vosotros* and *vosotras* (yourselves), and *sí* (yourselves, themselves). These pronouns frequently take the intensive reflexive *mismo* or one of its variations:

Ellas hablan a sí mismas.
They talk to themselves.

When *sí* is used with *con,* the special form *consigo* is used.

Interrogative pronouns. The principal interrogative pronouns are *qué* (what), *quién, quiénes* (who), *cuál, cuáles* (which, what, which one, which ones), *cuánto, cuánta* (how much), and *cuántos, cuántas* (how many). All but *qué* agree in number with the noun they replace. The various forms of *cuánto* agree in gender as well.

¿Qué es la fecha?
What's the date?

¿Cuál de los dos?
Which of the two?

¿Cuántas vienen?
How many are coming?

Demonstrative pronouns. Demonstrative pronouns point out a person or thing without naming the person or thing. "This" is expressed by *éste, ésta;* "these" by *éstos, éstas:*

De todos los libros, éstos son nuevos.
Of all the books, these are new.

In referring to persons or things not very remote from the speaker, "that" is expressed by *ése, ésa,* and "those" by *ésos, ésas:*

¿Es ése el suyo?
Is that yours?

In referring to persons or things remote from both the speaker and the person addressed, "that" is expressed by *aquél, aquélla,* and "those" by *aquéllos, aquéllas:*

Popular Meals at a Spanish Restaurant

Arroz con pollo
saffron-flavored rice and chicken

Bistec a la parella   *Churrasco*
grilled steak   barbecued steak

Churro
a twist of deep-fried batter, often eaten as a snack with hot chocolate in Spain

Enchilada
a corncake stuffed with meat or chicken, rolled and baked with tomato sauce flavored with chili

Paella
saffron-flavored rice, chicken, and peas

Tortilla
an omelet or cornbread cake

Flan   *Horchata*
custard   a cold drink made of almonds

Me gustan aquéllos.
Those please me.

The forms *esto, eso,* and *aquello* are neuter but, since there are no neuter nouns in Spanish, these refer only to situations, statements, or ideas:

Aquello es lo que me interesa.
That is what interests me.

Possessive pronouns. The possessive pronouns express possession.

The plural of the possessive pronouns is regular: *los míos, las mías* (mine), *los tuyos, las tuyas* (yours), etc.

The possessive pronouns agree in gender and number with the noun to which they refer.

Third person possessive pronouns are often replaced by *de usted, de él,* etc.

After a form of the verb *ser* (to be), the possessive pronoun is usually used without the definite article: *Es mío* (It's mine).

Adjectives. Adjectives agree in gender and number with the nouns they modify.

Gender. The feminine of adjectives ending in *o* is formed by changing the masculine ending *o* to *a: cansado* (tired), *cansada.* To adjectives of nationality ending in a consonant, an -a is added; written accents are dropped as necessary: *francés* (French), *francesa.*

Some adjectives have the same form for both genders: *feliz* (happy), *joven* (young), *pobre* (poor), etc.

Some adjectives drop the final *o* before a masculine singular noun: *un buen amigo,* but *una buena amiga.* The adjective *grande* (big) drops the *de* before all singular nouns: *un gran edificio* (a big building).

Number. Adjectives form the plural in the same way as nouns: *los niños contentos* (the happy children); *los días felices* (the happy days).

Comparison. The regular comparative form is shown by placing *más* (more) or *menos* (less) before the adjective: *alto* (high), *más alto* (higher).

The superlative usually adds the definite article: *el más alto* (highest).

Some adjectives are irregular: *bueno* (good), *mejor* (better), *el* (or *la*) *mejor* (best).

The suffixes -*ísimo(s)* or -*ísima(s)* may be used to express "most" or "very"; *dificilísimo* (most difficult), *grandísimo* (very big).

Demonstrative adjectives. Except for having no written accents and no neuter forms, the demonstrative adjectives are identical with the demonstrative pronouns: *este perro* (this dog); *esa tienda* (that store); *aquellas épocas* (those epochs).

Possessive adjectives. The possessive adjectives follow:

mi, mis	my
tu, tus	your
su, sus	your, his, her, its
nuestro(s), nuestra(s)	our
vuestro(s), vuestra(s)	your
su, sus	your, their

These adjectives precede the noun: *su amigo* (your friend). But emphatic possessive adjectives (*mío, tuyo,* etc., identical with the possessive pronouns except for omission of the definite article) follow: *amigo mío* (my friend).

Interrogative adjectives. The most common interrogative adjectives are *qué* (which, what), *cuál,* and *cuáles* (which); *cuánto, cuánta* (how much); *cuántos, cuántas* (how many).

¿Qué libros?
Which books?

¿Cuántas veces?
How many times?

Adverbs. In Spanish, an adverb is always placed as close as possible to the verb, adjective, or other adverb that it modifies.

Formation of adverbs. Some adverbs, especially those indicating manner or degree, are formed by adding the suffix -*mente* to the singular feminine form of the corresponding adjective or to the invariable form: *solamente* (solely), *ferozmente* (ferociously). If an adjective has a written accent, this accent is retained even though the principal stress shifts to the second-last syllable: *fácil* (easy), *fácilmente* (easily). When two or more adverbs formed with -mente occur together, only the last takes the suffix:

Lola contestó segura y claramente.
Lola answered firmly and clearly.

Some adverbs take the masculine singular form of the adjective, even to indicate manner or degree:

Habla despacio, por favor.
Speak slowly, please.

Some adverbs do not vary in form. This group includes affirmative adverbs like *sí* (yes), *por cierto* (surely), *sin duda* (without doubt), and *de veras* (truly); negative adverbs like *no* (no), *jamás* (never), *nunca* (never), and *tampoco* (neither, nor); and adverbs that express doubt like *tal vez* (perhaps, maybe).

Other adverbs that are fixed in form include adverbs of time such as *ayer* (yesterday), *tarde* (late), *después* (afterward), and *mañana* (tomorrow); adverbs of place like *aquí* (here), *alrededor* (around), *debajo* (beneath, below), and *lejos* (far, far off); adverbs of quantity like *bastante* (enough, quite), *mucho* (much), *muy* (very, much), *demasiado* (too much), *más* (more, plus), and *menos* (less, minus); and a number of interrogative adverbs like *cómo* (how), *cuándo* (when), and *dónde* (where).

¿Cuándo piensa usted volver?
When do you think you will return?

Quizás mañana.
Perhaps tomorrow.

Tarde o temprano llegaremos.
We will arrive sooner or later.

Comparison of adverbs. The comparison of adverbs is generally the same as that of adjectives. Thus, the regular comparative form is shown by placing *más* (more) or *menos* (less) before the adverb:

María maneja más cuidadosamente.
Mary drives more carefully.

¿Escribes menos despacio?
Are you writing less slowly?

The regular superlative of adverbs is shown by placing *lo más* or *lo menos* before the adverb.

Antonio se expresa lo más claramente.
Anthony expresses himself the most clearly.

Some adverbs have irregular forms for the comparative and the superlative:

bien (well), *mejor* (better), *lo mejor* (best); *mucho* (much), *más* (more), *lo más* (the most). To form the absolute superlative the suffix -ísimo or -ísima (very) is added to the stem of adverbs that do not end in *mente: muchísimo* (very much; from *mucho,* much), *tardísimo* (very late; from *tarde,* late). In order to preserve the consonant sound of the stem, a spelling change may be necessary: *cerquísima* (very near; from *cerca,* near).

For adverbs that end in *mente,* the special suffix -ísimamente is used to add the idea of "very": *rarísimamente* (very rarely; from *raramente,* rarely).

Prepositions. A preposition is a word or phrase inserted before a noun, or before a word or phrase used as a noun, to show the relationship between such a noun and the rest of the sentence. Prepositions may be either simple or compound. Simple prepositions consist of just one word. Compound prepositions consist of two or more words.

Common one-word prepositions are *a* (to, toward, at), *ante* (before), *bajo* (under), *de* (of, from), *en* (in, into, at, on), *entre* (among, between), *para* (for, to), *por* (by, through, for), and *sobre* (over, on, about).

Voy a la escuela en una hora.
I'm going to school in an hour.

entre la casa y la biblioteca
between the house and the library

Besides its many other uses, the preposition *a* must be placed before the direct object of a verb when the direct object is a person or a personified thing. This peculiarity of Spanish grammar is known as the personal *a.*

¿Conoce usted a Daniel?
Do you know Daniel?

Él quiere a su gato.
He likes his cat.

Common compound prepositions are *acerca de* (about, concerning), *a causa de* (on account of), *afuera de* (outside), *antes de* (before), *debajo de* (below), *delante de* (before), *dentro de* (inside), *después de* (after), *enfrente de* (opposite, in front of), *en vez de* (instead of), and *lejos de* (far from).

La pelota está debajo de la silla.
The ball is underneath the chair.

Conjunctions. The two most frequently used conjunctions are *y* (and) and *o* (or). The conjunction *y* is changed to *e* before a word beginning with the letters *i* or *hi:*

Juan y Eva son serios e inteligentes.
John and Eva are serious and intelligent.

The conjunction *o* is changed to *u* before a word beginning with the letters *o* or *ho:*

¿Va el avión a Roma o a París?
Is the plane going to Rome or to Paris?

Hay lugar para dos mujeres u hombres.
There is space for two ladies or gentlemen.

Other connecting words used in Spanish include *aunque* (although), *cuando* (when), *como* (as, if, unless), *pero* (but), *porque* (because), *que* (that), and *si.* The connecting word *si* means "if" or "whether." The form written with an accent *(sí)* is an adverb meaning "yes" or a reflexive pronoun meaning "yourself," "himself," etc.

Verbs. Spanish verbs are grouped into three classes (conjugations), according to whether the infinitive ends in *ar* (first conjugation), *er* (second conjugation), or *ir* (third conjugation). Examples of verbs that are conjugated regularly are *mandar* (to send), *beber* (to drink), and *subir* (to climb). Spanish verb forms indicate not only mood and tense but also the number, and frequently the person, of the subject.

In the following sections the principal indicative, conditional, subjunctive, and imperative forms of these three common verbs are shown. These are the forms taken by all regular verbs in each of the three conjugations. In the indicative mood the present, imperfect, and preterit tenses are formed by replacing the infinitive endings with endings that correspond to the person and number of the subject. In the future

18 Foreign Language

Writing Letters

***Carta comercial* Business letter**

ciudad, fecha city, date	
Miami, 8 de mayo de 20____	Miami, May 8, 20____

destinatario, dirreccion inside address
Sr. Juan Encina
Avenida de las Américas 20
Lima, Perú

el saludo	salutation	
Estimado (a) señor (a):		Dear Sir (Madam):

despedida	closing	
Sinceramente,	Sincerely,	

firma	signature	José Antonio Rivera

***Carta personal* Friendly letter**

ciudad, fecha	city, date	
Nueva York, 20 de julio de 20____		
New York, July 20, 20____		

saludo	salutation	
Querido (a) amigo (a),		Dear friend,

despedida	closing	
Recuerdos,	Regards,	

firma	signature	José

Orthographic-Changing Verbs

Infinitive Present participle Past participle	Present	Preterit	Present subjunctive	Imperfect subjunctive	Imperative
alcanzar (to overtake) alcanzando alcanzado		alcancé alcanzaste alcanzó alcanzamos alcanzasteis alcanzaron	alcance alcances alcance alcancemos alcancéis alcancen		
averiguar (to ascertain) averiguando averiguado		averigüé averiguaste averiguó averiguamos averiguasteis averiguaron	averigüe averigües averigüe averigüemos averigüéis averigüen		
convencer (to convince) convenciendo convencido	convenzo convences convence convencemos convencéis convencen		convenza convenzas convenza convenzamos convenzáis convenzan		
distinguir (to distinguish) distinguiendo distinguido	distingo distingues distingue distinguimos distinguís distinguen		distinga distingas distinga distingamos distingáis distingan		
enviar (to send) enviando enviado	envío envías envía enviamos enviáis envían		envíe envíes envíe enviemos enviéis envíen		envía enviad
escoger (to select) escogiendo escogido	escojo escoges escoge escogemos escogéis escogen		escoja escojas escoja escojamos escojáis escojan		
leer (to read) leyendo leído		leí leíste leyó leímos leísteis leyeron		leyera leyeras leyera leyéramos leyerais leyeran	
pagar (to pay) pagando pagado		pagué pagaste pagó pagamos pagasteis pagaron	pague pagues pague paguemos paguéis paguen		
producir (to produce) produciendo producido	produzco produces produce producimos producís producen		produzca produzcas produzca produzcamos produzcáis produzcan		
sacar (to take out) sacando sacado		saqué sacaste sacó sacamos sacasteis sacaron	saque saques saque saquemos saquéis saquen		

indicative and in the conditional mood the inflectional endings are added to the infinitive form.

Present.   Here is the present indicative tense of the regular verbs in the three conjugations:

mando	bebo	subo
mandas	bebes	subes
manda	bebe	sube
mandamos	bebemos	subimos
mandáis	bebéis	subís
mandan	beben	suben

Imperfect.   The imperfect tense indicates a continued action in the past:

mandaba	bebía	subía
mandabas	bebías	subías
mandaba	bebía	subía
mandábamos	bebíamos	subíamos
mandabais	bebíais	subíais
mandaban	bebían	subían

Preterit.   The preterit expresses a simple past action:

mandé	bebí	subí
mandaste	bebiste	subiste
mandó	bebió	subió
mandamos	bebimos	subimos
mandasteis	bebisteis	subisteis
mandaron	bebieron	subieron

Future.   The future tense of *mandar* is translated "I will send," "you will send," etc.

mandaré	beberé	subiré
mandarás	beberás	subirás
mandará	beberá	subirá
mandaremos	beberemos	subiremos
mandaréis	beberéis	subiréis
mandarán	beberán	subirán

Conditional.   The form *mandaría* is equivalent to "I would send" (as in "I would send it if I could").

mandaría	bebería	subiría
mandarías	beberías	subirías
mandaría	bebería	subiría
mandaríamos	beberíamos	subiríamos
mandaríais	beberíais	subiríais
mandarían	beberían	subirían

Present subjunctive.   The present subjunctive is formed by replacing the infinitive ending with special -e endings for *ar* verbs and -a endings for *er* and *ir* verbs.

mande	beba	suba
mandes	bebas	subas
mande	beba	suba
mandemos	bebamos	subamos
mandéis	bebáis	subáis
manden	beban	suban

Imperfect subjunctive.   The basic stem of the imperfect subjunctive is found by dropping the *ron* ending of the third person plural of the preterit indicative, thus: *manda* (from *mandaron*), *bebie* (from *bebieron*), and *subie* (from *subieron*). There are two forms of the imperfect subjunctive. The more common form, having the endings *ra, ras,* etc., is given below. The less frequent form has these alternative endings: -se, -ses, -se, -semos, -seis, -sen; thus: *mandase, mandases,* etc., *bibiese, bibieses,* etc., *subiese, subieses,* etc.

mandara	*bebiera*	*subiera*
mandaras	*bebieras*	*subieras*
mandara	*bebiera*	*subiera*
mandáramos	*bebiéramos*	*subiéramos*
mandarais	*bebierais*	*subierais*
mandaran	*bebieran*	*subieran*

Compound forms. Compound (perfect) tenses, in the indicative, conditional, and subjunctive, are made by combining appropriate forms of the auxiliary verb *haber* (to have) with the past participle of the main verb: *he bebido* (I have drunk).

Present participle. The present participles of the three model verbs are

mandando   bebiendo   subiendo

Past participle. The past participles of the model verbs are

mandado   bebido   subido

Imperative. The imperative mood is used in modern Spanish only to express familiar commands—and then only in the affirmative, never in the negative. Imperative verb forms are thus limited to the second person familiar with the singular subject *tú* or the plural subject *nosotros* either expressed or understood. In the great majority of cases, commands are expressed in the subjunctive; today present subjunctive forms are used for familiar plural commands in American Spanish. The singular forms of the true imperative are

manda   bebe   sube

The plural forms are

mandad   bebed   subid

Irregular verbs. There are three kinds of irregular verbs in Spanish: the orthographic-changing verbs, in which spelling changes are made to preserve the final consonant sound of the stem; the radical-changing verbs, in which the final stem vowel undergoes a phonetic change; and a miscellaneous group that displays other major irregularities in certain moods and tenses.

Orthographic-changing verbs. In orthographic-changing verbs, the final letters of the stem (that is, the letters that immediately precede the *ar, er,* or *ir* infinitive ending) must be changed before certain endings can be added.

Radical-Changing Verbs

Infinitive Present participle Past participle	Present	Preterit	Present subjunctive	Imperfect subjunctive	Imperative
consentir	consiento	consentí	consienta	consintiera	consiente
(to permit)	consientes	consentiste	consientas	consintieras	consentid
consintiendo	consiente	consintio	consienta	consintiera	
consentido	consentimos	consentimos	consintamos	consintiéramos	
	consentís	consentisteis	consintáis	consintierais	
	consienten	consintieron	consientan	consintieran	
contar	cuento		cuente		cuenta
(to count)	cuentas		cuentes		contad
contando	cuenta		cuente		
contado	contamos		contemos		
	contáis		contéis		
	cuentan		cuenten		
dormir	duermo	dormí	duerma	durmiera	duerme
(to sleep)	duermes	dormiste	duermas	durmieras	dormid
durmiendo	duerme	durmió	duerma	durmiera	
dormido	dormimos	dormimos	durmamos	durmiéramos	
	dormís	dormisteis	durmáis	durmierais	
	duermen	durmieron	duerman	durmieran	
medir	mido	medí	mida	midiera	mide
(to measure)	mides	mediste	midas	midieras	medid
midiendo	mide	midió	mida	midiera	
medido	medimos	medimos	midamos	midiéramos	
	medis	medisteis	midáis	midierais	
	miden	midieron	midan	midieran	
perder	pierdo		pierda		pierde
(to lose)	pierdes		pierdas		perded
perdiendo	pierde		pierda		
perdido	perdemos		perdamos		
	perdéis		perdáis		
	pierden		pierdan		

Otherwise, according to the rules of Spanish spelling, the final consonant sound of the stem would be lost.

In *ar* verbs, these changes are made before the letter *e* in the first person singular of the preterit indicative and in all persons of the present subjunctive: the final *c* of the stem becomes *qu; g* becomes *gu; gu* becomes *gü;* and *z* becomes *c.* (For some examples of such changes see *alcanzar, averiguar, pagar, sacar.*)

In most *er* and *ir* verbs the following changes are made before the letter *a* or *o* in the first person singular of the present indicative and in all persons of the present subjunctive: the final *g* of the stem becomes *j; gu* becomes *g; c* becomes *z* if *cer* or *cir* in the stem is preceded by a consonant; *c* becomes *zc* if *cer* or *cir* in the stem is preceded by a vowel. (For some examples of orthographic changes see *convencer, distinguir, escoger, producir.*) Other such variations include changing an unstressed *i* between vowels to *y* in a few verbs, and adding a written accent to a final *i* or *u* of the stem of some verbs ending in *iar* and *uar* to keep the stem vowel from becoming a diphthong in certain forms of the present tenses. (For examples see *leer* and *enviar.*) Some typical verbs of this kind are given here. The infinitive, the present partici-

ple, and the past participle are shown in the left-hand column. These forms are followed by additional parts of the verb to show the changes.

18 Foreign Language

Radical-changing verbs. These verbs fall into three classes, according to the kind of phonetic change made in the stem vowel (radical vowel) that precedes the infinitive ending *ar, er,* or *ir.*

Class I (*ar* and *er* verbs): When the natural stress falls on the stem vowel *o* or *e*, the *o* becomes *ue* and the *e* becomes *ie;* these changes occur in the present indicative and the present subjunctive (in all persons except the first and second person plural) and in the singular of the affirmative imperative. (Examples are *contar* and *perder.*)

Class II (*ir* verbs): When the natural stress falls on the stem vowel *o* or *e*, the *o* becomes *ue* and the *e* becomes *ie* (as in verbs of Class I); further, when the stem vowel *o* or *e* is unstressed and is followed by an ending that contains a stressed *a, ie,* or *ió,* the *o* becomes *u* and the *e* becomes *i*. These changes occur in the present participle, in the third person singular and plural of the preterit indicative, in the first person and second person plural of the present subjunctive, and in all persons of the imperfect subjunctive. (Examples are *consentir* and *dormir.*)

Class III (*ir* verbs): When the natural stress falls on the stem vowel *e*, the *e* becomes *i;* even when unstressed, the stem vowel *e* becomes *i* if the ending that follows contains a stressed *a, ie,* or *ió.* This change from *e* to *i* occurs also in all the forms affected in verbs of Class I and Class II. (For examples of this change see *medir.*) Some typical verbs of this kind are given here.

Other irregular verbs. Because both orthographic-changing and radical-changing verbs follow definite patterns, they are less irregular than many Spanish verbs that have major irregularities in their forms. From this large group (which includes orthographic-changing and radical-changing verbs) a number of irregular verbs with the forms in which the irregularities occur are given.

—*Bernice Randall*

Other Irregular Verbs

Infinitive / Present participle / Past participle	Present	Imperfect	Future	Conditional	Preterit	Present subjunctive	Imperfect subjunctive	Imperative
dar (to give) dando dado	doy das da damos dais dan				di diste dio dimos disteis dieron	dé des dé demos deis den	diera dieras diera diéramos dierais dieran	
decir (to say) diciendo dicho	digo dices dice decimos decís dicen		diré dirás dirá diremos diréis dirán	diría dirías diría diríamos diríais dirían	dije dijiste dijo dijimos dijisteis dijeron	diga digas diga digamos digáis digan	dijera dijeras dijera dijéramos dijerais dijeran	di decid
estar (to be) estando estado	estoy estás está estamos estáis están				estuve estuviste estuvo estuvimos estuvisteis estuvieron	esté estés esté estemos estéis estén	estuviera estuvieras estuviera estuviéramos estuvierais estuvieran	está estad
haber (to have) habiendo habido	he has ha hemos habéis han	había habías había habíamos habíais habían	habré habrás habrá habremos habréis habrán	habría habrías habría habríamos habríais habrían	hube hubiste hubo hubimos hubisteis hubieron	haya hayas haya hayamos hayáis hayan	hubiera hubieras hubiera hubiéramos hubierais hubieran	
hacer (to do, make) haciendo hecho	hago haces hace hacemos hacéis hacen		haré harás hará haremos haréis harán	haría harías haría haríamos haríais harían	hice hiciste hizo hicimos hicisteis hicieron	haga hagas haga hagamos hagáis hagan	hiciera hicieras hiciera hiciéramos hicierais hicieran	haz haced
ir (to go) yendo ido	voy vas va vamos vais van	iba ibas iba íbamos ibais iban			fui fuiste fue fuimos fuisteis fueron	vaya vayas vaya vayamos vayáis vayan	fuera fueras fuera fuéramos fuerais fueran	ve id
poder (to be able) pudiendo podido	puedo puedes puede podemos podéis pueden		podré podrás podrá podremos podréis podrán	podría podrías podría podríamos podríais podrían	pude pudiste pudo pudimos pudisteis pudieron	pueda puedas pueda podamos podáis puedan	pudiera pudieras pudiera pudiéramos pudierais pudieran	
saber (to know) sabiendo sabido	sé sabes sabe sabemos sabéis saben		sabré sabrás sabrá sabremos sabréis sabrán	sabría sabrías sabría sabríamos sabríais sabrían	supe supiste supo supimos supisteis supieron	sepa sepas sepa sepamos sepáis sepan	supiera supieras supiera supiéramos supierais supieran	
ser (to be) siendo sido	soy eres es somos sois son	era eras era éramos erais eran			fui fuiste fue fuimos fuisteis fueron	sea seas sea seamos seáis sean	fuera fueras fuera fuéramos fuerais fueran	se sed
tener (to have, hold) teniendo tenido	tengo tienes tiene tenemos tenéis tienen		tendré tendrás tendrá tendremos tendréis tendrán	tendría tendrías tendría tendríamos tendríais tendrían	tuve tuviste tuvo tuvimos tuvisteis tuvieron	tenga tengas tenga tengamos tengáis tengan	tuviera tuvieras tuviera tuviéramos tuvierais tuvieran	ten tened

Machine Translations

Translation programs. Speech translation programs are at best a resource tool when used along with a basic knowledge of the languages involved—both source and end product. At worst, they are rough approximations of translations that are not usable to facilitate communications.

The source in the translated example below is an English version of a biographical essay about writer Jack London. After being translated to Spanish by a computer program, the material was then retranslated to English—with the resulting garbled verbiage.

A history. Research on machine translation began in the 1950s to produce literal translations without using linguistic rules. Programs were developed through the National Aeronautics and Space Administration (NASA) in international space projects in the 1970s that allowed the Commission of the European Communities to build on and use language conversion prototypes.

One of the resulting automatic translators, which is now accessible through the Internet, Babel Fish, asks its users to always explain to a correspondent that a machine translator is being used. This way the context is more understandable.

Input/Output. The text to be translated should be in as polished a form as is possible, containing correct grammar, spelling, punctuation, and clear concise sentences without slang. The more thorough and finished the input, the more likely the output will appear in an acceptable context as to meaning.

In the game Gossip, the original information becomes less similar with each telling; so it is with each subsequent translation by a machine translator. Likewise, idioms are seldom translated correctly. An often-quoted example of an English phrase translated to Russian, then back to English, is: Out of sight, out of mind—which ends up translated as Invisible and insane.

It's easy to understand how important context becomes when inputting material if one considers the vast number of meanings some words have. For example, consider the sentence "We will remove the lead when we return." If it's in the context of taking the dog for a walk, maybe you're removing the leash. If a news article is being edited, the speaker may be planning to delete the introductory section. If you needed to replace a too-light lead in a replaceable-lead pencil, that may be the meaning. Or maybe you plan to remove some lead-based paint from a baseboard. When there are so many potential translations, the possibilities for mistranslation are equally numerous.

Anyone looking for a literal translation from a machine will usually get only a rough approximation, its validity in large part dependent on how well the material to be translated has been communicated. Someone expecting to get foreign language homework translated by a machine language may be very disappointed with the results. On the other hand, a person with a strong grasp of the concepts of both languages being used and possessing the skills to input to maximum effectiveness will often find a translator to be a helpful resource.

Features. On the plus side, translators come with a range of features that will assist in achieving correct, clear word communication and definitions. These include:

- easy translation of a single word (while using your knowledge to further check if the definition seems out of context with the text)
- spell checking in either language with immediate feedback if you key in a word incorrectly and, if you type in a portion of a word, selections from which you can choose what the word should be
- words and phrases pronounced by native speakers, after which you record and play your own pronunciations and compare the two
- translations in all the major languages used worldwide
- translators that do not necessitate using English as a go-between language but translate directly from one language to another—such as from Spanish to Japanese
- learning games available with some programs that make the language less of a chore and more fun

Not every translator will contain all the features listed here. Each translator will need to be looked at keeping in mind what elements are needed by the user.

Perhaps the greatest features of translators are in business or social situations that involve the need for immediate communication between people. When in a pinch, people have the ability to translate languages when no other means are available.

An American business with Russian clients, for example, may need to get some basic exchange established between the business and its clients. Without a human interpreter, the translator program may be their best bet.

Another urgent language need may come with the need to learn enough of the language to say a few important words—a thank you, a phrase of explanation, a statement of position.

As with all phases of technology, improvements are always being made. Translators matching even closer the capabilities of their human counterparts may be just around the corner.

Original English Version

It had become very clear that, by the time London arrived in Alaska in the summer of 1897, he saw the Klondike gold rush as his last, best chance to break away from a life of meaningless drudgery. He had seen enough of that as a young boy working in a cannery and later as a coal-shoveler at a power station and as a worker in the school laundry.

A few of his writings had been published, and he made a valiant but unsuccessful attempt to become a professional writer. Now he sought his fortune in the frozen gold fields of the Yukon.

London settled with several other miners on Stewart Creek, about seventy miles south of the frontier town of Dawson and filed for a mining claim on nearby Henderson Creek. But, discovering that digging for gold in the rock bed was just as much hard work as anything he had ever done, he soon left the camp for Dawson.

London spent six weeks in Dawson, during which time he gathered impressions, background, and tales that he would later use in his writing.

Translated English Version

It had gotten to be very clear that, for the moment at which London arrived in Alaska in the summer of 1897, it saw that gold of Klondike undertake as the his hard one, the best occasion to break itself far from a life of the setido servitude without. It had seen enough of that like young boy who worked in cannery and more ahead like coal-shoveler in an electrical power station and worker in the laundry of the school.

Some of their writings had been published, and he did an attempt valiant but failed to make program of professional writing. Now he looked for his fortune in the congealed fields of gold of Yukon.

London placed with several other miners in Stewart Creek, near seventy miles of the south of the city of the border of Dawson and clasifió for a next demand of mining operation in Henderson Creek. But, discovering that digging for gold in the bed of the rock it was right hard work as much as any thing that he had always done, he soon to the left the field for Dawson.

London spent six weeks in Dawson, during which hour it collected printings, the bottom, and the stories that he would use more ahead in his writing.

Latin

The Latin language began as one of many dialects of a language spoken around Rome and eventually became established as the second language of educated people in the whole of the Mediterranean basin and in large portions of Europe. Though technically a "dead" language, insofar as it no longer produces native speakers, Latin lives on through many descendant languages, such as Italian, Spanish, French, and, indirectly, English. Even if Latin were not the language of rich literary, scientific, and historical traditions, it would still be worthy of close study for what it reveals about the nature and vocabulary of modern European languages.

Pronunciation.

We know two things about how ancient Latin was pronounced: (1) it could not have been pronounced like modern Italian or Church Latin, and (2) no one knows *exactly* how it was pronounced, though some reconstructions are better than others. Most consonants were pronounced much like their modern equivalents. Differences are noted in Table 1 on page 43. Long marks were not used in classical Latin, but are included as aids to students in modern elementary and intermediate texts.

Nouns.

In a sentence, a noun will have number (singular or plural), gender (masculine, feminine, or neuter), and case (explained below). Gender is a fixed quality of a noun, but number and case can change depending on how the noun is being used.

Case.

Endings attached to nouns indicate differing grammatical roles, called "cases." For the most part, Latin recognizes six such roles with discrete endings. See Table 2 on page 43.

Declensions.

A declension is a pattern of case endings. There are five declensions, and a noun may belong to only one. See Table 3 on page 43. Notes: (1) One of the characteristics of the third declension is the large variety of nominative forms. They are not infinite, but too numerous to list conveniently in a table; (2) The second and fourth declensions have a subset of neuter endings; (3) The nominative and vocative endings differ only in the singular of the second declension.

To work with a noun, you need to know its meaning, gender, and the declension to which it belongs. A dictionary gives you this information by adopting a convention for the entry. You are first given the nominative case, secondly an abbreviation for the genitive case, which is an unambiguous indicator of the declension and the true stem (if it is not apparent in the nominative), and thirdly the gender. See Table 4 on page 43.

Articles.

Latin does not have a definite article (*the*) or an indefinite article (*a, an*), but they are easily supplied in translation. **Hĕrculēs magnam partem diĕi frŭstrā cōnsŭmpsit,** *Hercules spent a great part of the day in vain.* **Iāsŏn, dux Argonautārum, năvem dēdŭxit,** *Jason, the leader of the Argonauts, launched the ship.*

Word order.

Because the case endings reveal the function a noun has in its sentence, Latin word order is much more flexible than English, where word order is critical to the syntax. Each of these sentences means, *This girl saw my friend in the road,* although with different rhetorical emphases:

Haec puella amicum meum in viā vidit; Amicum meum in viā haec puella vidit; In viā haec puella meum amicum vidit, etc.

Adjectives.

An adjective is a word that modifies a noun. In Latin, an adjective will acquire some of the characteristics of the noun it is modifying: its number, gender, and case. The modification in form of one word to match another is called "agreement." There are two classes of adjectives: those which derive their endings from the 1st and 2nd declensions, and those which use the endings of the 3rd declension.

Adjectives of the 1st and 2nd declension use 1st declension endings to modify feminine nouns, 2nd declension endings to modify masculine nouns, and 2nd declension -**um** type to modify neuter nouns. See Table 5 on page 43.

Adjectives of the third declension are slightly more complicated. There are three types. The first type has only one form for all three genders in the nominative singular. The second type has two nominative singular forms, one for the masculine and feminine, and one for the neuter. The third has different nominative forms for all three genders.

But after the nominative singular, all third declension adjectives use the standard third declension endings. Two rules that are always observed, though, are that neuter accusative forms are always the same as the neuter nominative form, and that the neuter plural nominative ending is -**ia**. Hence it follows that the accusative plural neuter ending will also be -**ia**. See Table 6 on page 43.

It is very important to note that agreement does not require endings which look alike, but endings which are equivalent in number, gender, and case. Study how the third declension adjective **brevis, -e,** *brief,* modifies the first declension noun **vita, -ae,** *f., life.* See Table 7 on page 45.

Comparative degree.

The comparative degree of adjectives is formed by adding a suffix with case endings, similar to the English method of adding -*er* or -*est* to the root of an adjective. The comparative suffix is a third declension -**ior, -ius.** Hence the adjective **certus, -a, -um,** *sure,* in the comparative degree becomes **certior, certius,** *surer,* and declines in the third declension. Singular: *Nom.* **certior / certius;** *Gen.* **certiōris;** *Dat.* **certiōri;** *Acc. m./f.* **certiōrem /** *neuter,* **certius;** *Abl.* **certiōri,** etc. Similarly, **brevis, -e,** *brief,* becomes *briefer,* **brevior, brevius; potēns, -ntis,** *powerful,* becomes **potentior, potentius,** *more powerful.*

The items being compared may be linked with the word **quam,** or the ablative of degree of difference may be used.

Vita mea brevior erat quam vitā eius or . . . **erat vitā eius,** *my life was briefer than his life.*

Superlative degree.

The superlative degree regularly adds the suffix -**issim-** plus the first and second declension case endings. Hence **certissimus, -a, -um** from **certus, -a, -um.** If the stem of the adjective ends in -**r-** or -**l-,** some variation on this rule can be expected: **ăcerrimus, -a, -um** from **ăcer, ăcris, ăcre,** *harsh,* and **facillimus, -a, -um,** from **facilis, -e,** *easy.*

As in English, some very common adjectives form their degrees irregularly by using different stems. Some Latin examples are *good, better, best:* **bonus, -a, -um; melior, melius; optimus, -a, -um;** *bad, worse, worst:* **malus, -a, -um; pĕior, pĕius; pessimus, -a, -um;** *big, bigger, biggest:* **magnus, -a, -um; măior, măius; maximus, -a, -um.**

Pompeius in sănctissimam partem templi **ingressus est,** *Pompey entered the holiest part of the temple;* **Hĕrculēs summis cum viribus collum monstri compressit,** *Hercules squeezed the neck of the monster with all his might (with greatest strength).*

Adjectives as nouns.

Consider: *the rich, the poor, the good, the bad, and the ugly.* These are simply adjectives, and an English speaker is easily able to understand the noun that each implies. As in English, Latin adjectives can be used without nouns. **Multi tē laudant,** *many people praise you;* **Omnia parăta sunt,** *all things were prepared.* **Caesar cum suis profectus est,** *Caesar set out with his own men.*

Adverbs from adjectives.

A common way of deriving adverbs is to attach indeclinable endings to the stem

Table 1

Pronunciation

Vowels	Sound	Diphthong	Sound
a / ā	dyn<u>a</u>mite / f<u>a</u>ther	ae	<u>ai</u>sle
e / ē	s<u>e</u>t / d<u>a</u>te	au	<u>ou</u>ch
i / ī	t<u>i</u>n / s<u>ee</u>n	ei	cl<u>ai</u>m
o / ō	<u>o</u>ff / r<u>o</u>de	eu	f<u>eu</u>d
u / ū	p<u>u</u>t / t<u>u</u>ne	oe	b<u>oy</u>
y	French t<u>u</u>	ui	g<u>ooey</u>

Consonants

c	always hard : <u>c</u>at	g	always hard : <u>g</u>et
i	between vowels : <u>y</u>ellow	t	always hard : <u>t</u>on
qu	As in English : <u>qu</u>ick	v	<u>w</u>here

Table 2

Case

Case	Major grammatical role
Nominative	Subject of a verb
Genitive	Possession
Dative	Indirect object
Accusative	Direct object / Object of a preposition
Ablative	Adverbial use / Object of a preposition
Vocative	Direct address

Table 3

The Five Declensions

Singular

Case	1st	2nd		3rd	4th		5th
Nominative	-a	-us (-er)	-um	—	-us	-ū	-ēs
Genitive	-ae	-ī		-is	-ūs		-ēī
Dative	-ae	-ō		-ī	-uī	-ū	-ēī
Accusative	-am	-um		-em —	-um	-ū	-em
Ablative	-ā	-ō		-e or -ī		-ū	-ē
Vocative	-a	-e	-um	—	-us	-u	-ēs

Plural

Case	1st	2nd		3rd		4th		5th
Nom. / Voc.	-ae	-ī	-a	-ēs	-(i)a	-ūs	-ua	-ēs
Genitive	-ārum	-ōrum		-(i)um		-uum		-ērum
Dative	-īs	-īs		-ibus		-ibus		-ēbus
Accusative	-ās	-ōs	-a	-ēs (-īs)	-(i)a	-ūs	-ua	-ēs
Ablative	-īs	-īs		-ibus		-ibus		-ēbus

Table 4

Nouns of Each Declension

Dictionary entry	Gender	Stem	Declension
puella, -ae, *f., girl*	feminine	puell-	1st
ager, -grī, *m., field*	masculine	agr-	2nd
alacritās, -tātis, *f., eagerness*	masculine	alacritāt-	3rd
manus, -ūs *f., hand, band*	feminine	man-	4th
diēs, diēī, *f., day*	feminine	diē-	5th

Table 5

First- and Second-Declension Adjectives

	Feminine	Masculine	Neuter
Nom.	magna	magnus	magnum
Gen.	magnae	magnī	magnī
Dat.	magnae	magnō	magnō
Acc.	magnam	magnum	magnum
Abl.	magnā	magnō	magnō
Voc.	magna	magne	magnum

Etc.

Table 6

Third-Declension Adjectives

One

	M./F./N.	
Nom.	potēns	
Gen.	potentis	
Dat.	potenti	
Acc.	potentem	potēns
Acc.	potenti	

Two

	M./F.	N.
Nom.	facilis	facile
Gen.	facilis	
Dat.	facili	
Acc.	facilem	facile
Acc.	facilī	

Three

	M.	F.	N.
Nom.	ācer	ācris	ācre
Gen.		ācris	
Dat.		ācri	
Acc.		ācrem	ācre
Acc.		ācrī	

18 Foreign Language

of an adjective: *Positive Degree:* -**ē** for first and second declension adjectives, -**(i)ter** for third declension adjectives; *Comparative Degree:* -**ius** (the neuter accusative adjectival ending); *Superlative:* -**ē** to the superlative (-**issim**-) stem.

Hence from the adjectives **longus, -a, -um,** *long,* and **ācer, ācris, ācre,** *harsh:* <u>Positive:</u> **longē,** *at length;* **ācriter,** *harshly;* <u>Comparative:</u> **longius,** *longer, at greater length;* **ācrius,** *more harshly;* <u>Superlative:</u> **longissimē,** *longest, at greatest length;* **ācerrimē,** *most harshly.*

As may be expected, irregular adjectives will exhibit some slight deviations from these rules: **bene,** *well;* **melius,** *better;* **optimē,** *best;* **magnopere,** *very much; greatly;* **magis,** *more;* **maximē,** *most.*

A very common idiom uses **quam** with the superlative degrees of adjectives and adverbs: **Perseus** <u>quam</u> <u>**ācerrimē**</u> **in mōnstrum impetum fēcit,** *Perseus attacked the monster <u>as fiercely as possible.</u>*

Questions.
Latin poses a simple question by attaching -**ne** to the end of the first word of the sentence.

Amāsne mē? *do you love me.*

Other interrogatives can anticipate the response.

Num mē amās, *you don't love me, do you?* **Nōnne mē amās,** *you love me, don't you?*

Latin has many interrogative adverbs that are used to form questions: **cūr,** *why;* **quandō,** *when;* **ubi,** *where;* **quōmodo,** *how;* **quō,** *to where;* **unde,** *from where,* etc. There are also a number of interrogative pronouns, which will be discussed below.

The ablative case.
The ablative case has a variety of special uses, which must be learned. Some of the more common are shown in Table 8 on page 45.

Other uses of cases.
Showing motion toward and away from named cities and small islands does not require prepositions such as **ad** and **ab.** The accusative case itself indicates motion toward; the ablative case alone indicates motion from. The locative case, which indicates position, is identical in form to the genitive case in first and second declension nouns, and to the ablative case in third declension nouns.

<u>**Rōmae**</u> **multī mīlitēs erant,** *there were many soldiers at Rome;* **Mīlitēs** <u>**Rōmam**</u> **venient,** *the soldiers will come to Rome,* **Mīlitēs Rōmā profectī sunt,** *the soldiers set out from Rome.*

The dative case can show possession:

<u>**Mihi**</u> **nōmen est Brūtus,** *my name is Brutus.*

The accusative case can be used to show the duration of time during which an event occurred:

Pugnātum est <u>**multās hōrās,**</u> *there was fighting for many hours.*

A common use of the genitive is description:

Scipiō <u>**magnae virtūtis**</u> **erat,** *Scipio was a man of great courage.*

The genitive case is often used after neuter pronouns:

Quid <u>**novī?**</u> *What's new* (literally, *what of new?*); **Satis** <u>**pecūniae**</u> **nēmō umquam habēbit,** *no one will ever have enough money.*

Prepositions.
Prepositions are words that show literal or figurative spatial relations between words: *in, from, to, with,* etc. In Latin, the objects of prepositions are mostly in the accusative or ablative case. A few prepositions can take either the accusative or ablative case, with a slight change in meaning. In such instances, the accusative will signify motion and the ablative will indicate position. The dictionary lists which case the preposition governs. <u>Accusative Only:</u> **ad,** *to, toward, near;* **circum,** *around;* **iuxtā,** *next to;* <u>Ablative Only:</u> **ab,** *from;* **dē,** *down from;* **ex,** *out of;* <u>Accusative or Ablative:</u> **in,** *into* or *in;* **sub,** *under;* **super,** *over* or *on top of.*

<u>**Rōmulus lēgātōs**</u> **in vicīnās** <u>**urbēs**</u> **misit,** *Romulus sent representatives into the neighboring cities;* **Castra sub montibus celeriter mūniērunt,** *they quickly fortified a camp beneath the mountains;* **Gladiātōrēs in arēnā relictī erant,** *the gladiators had been left in the sand.*

Numbers.
Latin has cardinal numbers, *one, two, three,* etc., ordinal numbers, *first, second, third,* etc., and its own symbolic system known as Roman numerals, I, II, III, etc. A few cardinal numbers act as adjectives and change their termination to agree with nouns: **ūnus, duo,** and **trēs,** for example. You can tell which are adjectives if the dictionary entry lists more than one form in the nominative. All cardinal numbers are adjectives. See Table 9 on page 45.

<u>**Novem annīs**</u> **Caesar Galliam in prōvinciae formam redēgit,** *In nine years, Caesar reduced Gaul to a province.* **Ad** <u>**tertiam**</u> <u>**vigiliam**</u> **crepitus immānis audītus est in silvā,** *towards the <u>third watch,</u> a dreadful noise was heard in the forest.* **Oppidum ā castrīs circiter MCC passuum distābat,** *the fort lay about 1,200 paces from the camp.*

Verbs.
Like nouns, verbs consist of a stem that contains the core meaning of the verb, and endings that indicate variations in the way the action is enacted. Latin verbs can indicate the following syntactical features with endings and infixes: **Person,** 1st, 2nd, 3rd; **Number,** singular, plural; **Voice,** active, passive; **Tense,** present, future, imperfect, perfect, pluperfect, future perfect; **Mood,** indicative, imperative, subjunctive, participial, infinitive.

One of the great challenges to beginning students is to memorize the seemingly limitless number of interchangeable endings and infixes that verbs can use. But with a little effort, patterns and rules can be discerned, which make the challenge, while still formidable, a little less daunting.

Verbs: present system.
Like English verbs, Latin verbs have more than one stem. Each stem is used as the root of a different tense system. For example, the complete dictionary entry for the verb *to love* is **amō, amāre, amāvī, amātus.** These are called the principal parts of the verb. The first two principal parts of all verbs—in this case **amō, amāre**—give you the information you need to form the present system of tenses: the present, future, and imperfect. We will start by examining this system and the first two principal parts.

Latin verbs are divided into four classes, called conjugations, depending on what vowel appears at the end of the present stem. The third conjugation is further divided into i-stem and non i-stem verbs, but this is not related to its stem vowel, which for both is -**e**-. The final -**re** is dropped from the second principal part to reveal the stem and the stem vowel. See Table 10 on page 45.

To the stem are added tense signs and personal endings. The personal endings for the present system are: <u>Active:</u> -**ō** (-**m**) -**s**, -**t**, -**mus**, -**tis**, -**nt**; <u>Passive:</u> -**or**, -**ris** (-**re**), -**tur**, -**mur**, -**minī**, -**ntur.**

There is no tense sign for the present tense, so the personal endings are added directly to the stem. The short **e** of the third conjugation changes with the addition of the personal endings. But the long stem vowel of the other three conjugations is nearly always visible.

amō, *I love;* **dēbētis,** *you (pl.) owe;* **dūcuntur,** *they are led;* **capiunt,** *they take;* **audīris,** *you are heard.*

The tense sign for the future of first and second conjugation verbs is -**be**-. (The short -**e**- changes as personal endings are added.) <u>Active:</u> -**bō**, -**bis**, -**bit**, -**bimus**, -**bitis**, -**bunt**; <u>Passive:</u> -**bor**, **beris**, -**bitur**, -**bimur**, -**binimī**, -**buntur.** In the future of third and fourth conjugation verbs, the tense sign is -**ē**-, with the one exception of the first person singular, where it is -**a**-: <u>Active:</u> -**am**, -**ēs**, -**et**, -**ēmus**, -**ētis**, -**ent**; <u>Passive:</u> -**ar**, -**ēris**, -**ētur**, -**ēmur**, -**ēminī**, -**entur.**

Table 8

The Ablative Case

Means	Eum baculō percussit, *he hit him with a cane*.
Manner	Magnā cum celeritāte vēnit, *he came with great speed*.
Personal Agent	Ab Caesare servātī sumus, *we were saved by Caesar*.
Cause	Stultitiā ducis urbs dēlēta est, *the city was destroyed because of the stupidity of the leader*.
Degree of difference	Puella celerius puerō cucurrit, *the girl ran faster than the boy*.
Separation	Augustus nōs metū liberāvit, *Augustus freed us from fear*.
Time	Illō tempore Rōmae paucī erant, *at that time there were few people in Rome*.
Description	Erat mōnstrum speciē horribilī, *there was a horrible looking monster*.
Specification	Perseus statūrā prōcērus erat, *Perseus was a tall man in height*.

Table 7

Adjectives

Nom.	vīta brevis
Gen.	vītae brevis
Dat.	vītae brevī
Acc.	vītam brevem
Abl.	vītā brevī
	Etc.

Table 9

Cardinal Numbers	Ordinal Numbers	Roman Numerals
1. ūnus, ūna, ūnum	1. prīmus, -a, -um	1. I
2. duo, duae, duo	2. secundus	2. II
3. trēs, tria	3. tertius	3. III
4. quattuor	4. quārtus	4. IIII or IX
5. quīnque	5. quintus	5. V
6. sex	6. sextus	6. VI
7. septem	7. septimus	7. VII
8. octō	8. octāvus	8. VIII
9. novem	9. nōnus	9. VIIII or VIX
10. decem	10. decimus	10. X
11. ūndecim	11. ūndecimus	11. XI
12. duodecim	12. duodecimus	12. XII
13. tredecim	13. tertius decimus	13. XIII
14. quattuordecim	14. quārtus decimus	14. XIIII or XIV
15. quindecim	15. quintus decimus	15. XV
16. sēdecim	16. sextus decimus	16. XVI
17. septendecim	17. septimus decimus	17. XVII
18. duodēvigintī	18. duodēvīcēnsimus	18. XVIII
19. ūndēvīginti	19. ūndēvīcēnsimus	19. XVIIII or XIX
20. vīginti	20. vīcēnsimus	20. XX

Table 10

Verbs: Present System

Principal Parts	Stem	Stem Vowel	Conjugation
amō, amāre, amāvī, amātus, *love*	amā-	-ā	1st
dēbeō, -ēre, dēbuī, dēbitus, *owe*	dēbē-	-ē	2nd
dūcō, -ere, dūxī, ductus, *lead*	dūce-	-e	3rd
capiō, -ere, cēpī, captus, *take*	cape-	-ĕ	3rd i-stem
audiō, -īre, audivi, auditus, *hear*	audi-	-i	4th

Table 11

The Verb "to be" in the Present System

Person	Present	Future	Imperfect
1st	sum	erō	eram
2nd	es	eris	erās
3rd	est	erit	erat
1st	sumus	erimus	erāmus
2nd	estis	eritis	erātis
3rd	sunt	erunt	erant

Table 12

Demonstratives

	Masc.	Fem.	Neuter
Nom.	hic	haec	hoc
Gen.	huius	huius	huius
Dat.	huic	huic	huic
Acc.	hunc	hanc	hoc
Abl.	hōc	hāc	hōc
Nom.	hae	hī	haec
	Etc.		

18 Foreign Language

amābō, *I will love;* **dēbēbitis,** *you (pl.) will owe;* **dūcentur,** *they will be led;* **capient,** *they will take;* **audiēris,** *you will be heard.*

The tense sign for the imperfect is **-bă-** for all four conjugations. It is completely regular. The addition of the personal endings never alters the final vowel.

amābam, *I used to love;* **dēbē-bātis,** *you were owing;* **dūcēbantur,** *they were being led;* **capiēbant,** *they were taking;* **audiēbāris,** *you were being heard.*

The verb "to be" in the present system.
Aside from its inherent importance, the forms of the irregular verb "to be" in the present system must be thoroughly mastered because they are used to build the perfect tense system. The dictionary entry is **sum, esse, fui, futūrus.** See Table 11 on page 45.

Perfect system active.
The tenses of the perfect system are the perfect, pluperfect, future perfect. In the active voice, these tenses are formed from the third principal part of the verb.

amō, amāre, <u>amāvi</u>, amātus
dēbeō, dēbēre, <u>dēbui</u>, dēbitus
etc.

The passive voice of the perfect system, discussed later, uses the fourth.

The perfect system active has its own set personal endings, which, unlike in the personal endings of the present system, also indicate tense. Hence there is no tense sign inserted between the stem and the personal endings in the perfect system.

The <u>perfect personal endings</u> are: **-i, -isti, -it, -imus, -istis, -ērunt;** The <u>pluperfect endings</u> are the forms of the imperfect tense of the verb **sum.** The <u>future perfect endings</u> are the forms of the future of the verb **sum** with the exception of the third person plural, which is **-erint** instead of **-erunt.**

amāvi, *I loved*
amāveram, *I had loved*
amāverō, *I will have loved*
dēbuerătis, *you (pl.) had owed*
dūxerint, *they will have led*
cēpērunt, *they took*
audivisti, *you heard*

Participial mood.
A participle is a verbal adjective. As such, it will have features of the verb it comes from—tense and voice—and features that are necessary for its role as an adjective—number, gender, and case. Therefore, a participle will have both a verbal root and adjectival endings that can be altered to agree with its object. Latin has present, future, and perfect participles, though only the future tense has both active and passive participles.

The formulae for the participles are:

<u>Present Active:</u> present stem + the third declension adjectival endings, **-ns, -ntis;**
<u>Perfect Passive:</u> fourth principal part with **-ūs, -a, -um** adjectival endings;
<u>Future Active:</u> fourth principal part + **ur** + adjectival endings **-us, -a, -um;**
<u>Future Passive:</u> first principal part + **nd** + **-us, -a, -um.**

The complete set of participles from one of our paradigm verbs should illustrate these rules. See Table 13 on page 47.

Translating a participle requires attention to the context: **Trōiāni equum in urbem <u>tractum</u> vidēbant,** *the Trojans were looking at the horse,* <u>*which had been brought into the city*</u> (literally, <u>*having been brought into the city*</u>); **Cīvēs ōrātōri <u>discessūrō</u> dōnum dedērunt,** *the citizens gave the speaker a gift* <u>*as he was about to depart*</u> (literally, <u>*going to depart*</u>).

The future passive participle is generally used to express a sense of duty or necessity, not simply something that is going to be done. This commonly used construction is called the "passive periphrastic," and the participle is called the "gerundive." The agent in this construction is expressed in the dative case: **Haec verba ōrātōri <u>dicenda erant</u>,** *these words* <u>*had to be said*</u> *by the orator.*

Perfect system passive.
The voice of the perfect system of tenses—the perfect, pluperfect, and future perfect—is formed by using the fourth principal part of the verb (also called the perfect passive participle) linked to the subject with a form of the verb **sum.** The present tense of **sum** is used for the perfect tense, the imperfect is used for the pluperfect, and the future is used for the future perfect.

Note that the case ending of the participle must agree with the subject. **Haec mulier laudāta est (erat, erit),** *this woman was (had been, will have been) praised.*

Infinitive mood.
Verbs have three tenses and two voices of the infinitive.

<u>Present Active:</u> present stem + **re;**
<u>Present Passive:</u> present stem + **ri** for 1st, 2nd, and 4th conjugation verbs, or **-i** for the 3rd;
<u>Future Active:</u> future active participle and **esse;**
<u>Future Passive (very rare):</u> supine in **-um** and **iri;**
<u>Perfect Active:</u> 3rd principal part + **isse;**
<u>Perfect Passive:</u> perfect passive participle and **esse.**

Study the infinitives of **amō.** The verb **capiō** is given in the present passive form to show how the third

conjugation differs from the other three conjugations. See Table 14 on page 47.

Imperative mood.
To give a direct command, Latin uses the present stem of the verb without an ending for the singular, and the stem + **te** for the plural: **adiuvā mē,** *help me;* **adiuvăte mē,** *help me;* **hoc age,** *do this;* **audi mē,** *hear me.*

Gerund.
The nominative verbal noun in Latin is the infinitive; e.g. **esse quam vidēri,** *being rather than seeming* (literally, *to be rather than to seem*). For the other cases, the form is identical to the future passive participle: *Nom.* **gerere,** *to conduct or conducting; Gen.* **gerendi,** *of conducting; Dat.* **gerendō,** *to or for conducting; Acc.* **gerendum,** *conducting; Abl.* **gerendō,** *by conducting.*

Personal pronouns.
The personal pronouns decline through the full case system. Table 16 on page 47 shows **ego,** *I;* **tū,** *you;* **nōs,** *we;* **vōs,** *you (pl.).*

Latin uses the demonstrative **is, ea, id** (*he, she, it*) for its third person pronoun. Its stem is simply **e-,** to which 1st and 2nd declension case endings are added. There are some exceptions, though, in the singular as shown in Table 15 below.

Since the personal ending of the verb already implies the subject, the nominative case of the personal pronouns is used only for extra emphasis.

Ego sapientiam amō, at tū amās pecūniam, *I love wisdom, but* <u>*you*</u> *love money.*

The genitive case of the 1st and 2nd person pronouns is not used to show possession. Latin prefers the possessive adjectives **meus, -a, -um,** *my;* **noster, -tra, -trum,** *our;* **tuus, -a, -um,** *your,* **vester, -tra, -trum,** *your (pl.)*

Equus <u>meus</u> in agrō visus est, *my horse was seen in the field.*

The genitive case of the pronoun is used as the object of certain verbs that require the genitive case, and in the partitive genitive construction.

<u>**Tui**</u> **semper meminerō,** *I will always remember you;* **Pars <u>mei</u> vōbiscum** (= *cum vōbis*) **post mortem meam nōn remanēbit,** *part of me will not remain with you after my death.*

Table 15

Personal Pronouns

	Masc.	Fem.	Neuter
Nom.	is	ea	id
Gen.	eius	eius	eius
Dat.	ei	ei	ei
Acc.	eum	eam	id
Abl.	eō	eā	eō

Table 13

Participial Mood

	Active	Passive
Present	amāns, amantis, *loving*	—
Future	amātūrus, *going to love*	amandus, *going to be loved*
Perfect	—	amātus, *having been loved*

Table 14

Infinitive Mood

	Active	Passive
Present	amāre, *to love*	amārī, *to be loved* capi, *to be taken*
Future	amātūrum esse, *to be going to love*	amātum irī, *to be going to be loved*
Perfect	amāvisse, *to have loved*	amātum esse, *to have been loved*

Table 16

Personal Pronouns

	Singular		Plural	
	1st	**2nd**	**1st**	**2nd**
Nom.	egō	tū	nōs	vōs
Gen.	mei	tui	nostrum nostrī	vestrum vestrī
Dat.	mihi	tibi	nōbīs	vōbīs
Acc.	mē	tē	nōs	vōs
Abl.	mē	tē	nōbīs	vōbīs

Table 17

Main Uses of the Subjunctive

Jussive:	Nunc incipiant, *let them begin now.*
Purpose clause:	Pontem rescindi iussit nē hostibus usui esset, *he ordered the bridge to be broken down so it would be useless to the enemy.*
Result clause:	Tantum erat fulgur, ut tōtum caelum vidērētur ūrī, *the lightning was so great that the whole sky seemed to burn.*
Indirect question:	Volō scire ubi hoc plaustrum invēneris, *I want to know where you found this cart.*
Some conditional sentences:	Sī modo prius hās litterās accēpissem, iam vīveret, *if only I had received this letter beforehand, he would still be alive.*
Relative clause of characteristic:	Est nēmō quī tāle crīmen mōliātur, *there is no one who would engineer such a crime.*
Relative clause of purpose:	Nuntium mīsit quī victoriam renuntiāret, *he sent a messenger to report the victory.*
Factitive clause:	Nōn forte accidit ut Caesar tam grātus esset plēbī, *it did not happen by chance that Caesar was so beloved by the plebeians.*
Indirect command:	Eum adhortātus est ut Medūsam expeteret, *he urged him to seek out Medusa.*
After verbs of fearing:	Timeō nē correptus sit febrī, *I am afraid he is taken with fever.*
Cum clause:	Cum nihil esset relictum, omnēs Rōman rediērunt, *since nothing was left, they returned to Rome.*
Quīn clause:	Haud dubium erat quīn brevī advenīret cum auxiliō, *It was hardly doubtful that he would soon arrive with aid.*

A reflexive pronoun signifies that the subject both performs and receives the action of the verb; the pronoun points back to the subject: *She helped herself*, *They saw themselves*. Latin uses the forms of the 1st and 2nd pronouns for reflexive pronouns. The third person reflexive pronoun is: *Gen.* **suī**; *Dat.* **sibi**; *Acc.* **sē**; *Abl.* **sē**. There is no distinct plural form. There is also a third person reflexive possessive adjective **suus, -a, -um,** *he/her/its/their own*.

Eius amīcus **nōs** vidit, *his/her friend saw us*; date id **eī**, *give it to him/her*. In speculō **sē** vidit, *he/she saw himself/herself in the mirror*. Pompeius **suōs** amīcōs adiūvit, *Pompey helped his (own) friends*.

Demonstratives. Two very common demonstratives are **hic, haec, hoc,** *this,* and **ille, illa, illud,** *that*. They have the same alternative genitive and dative endings in the singular: *Gen.* **-ius**; *Dat.* **-ī**. Hic, haec, hoc, is further complicated by the **-c** suffix attached to most of the case endings in the singular and in the nominative and accusative neuter plural. The **-c** causes the final **-m** of the case endings to change to **-n**. Lastly the normal stem **h-** lengthens to **hu-** in the genitive and dative singular. In the singular it declines as shown in Table 12 on page 45.

The demonstratives can be used to modify nouns, in which case they would be properly called demonstrative adjectives, or without nouns, in which case they would be properly called demonstrative pronouns.

Illae fēminae **haec** verba ad **vōs** mittent, *those women will send these words to you*; amici **illīus** in hāc urbe pācem nōn invenient, *friends of that (man or woman) will not find peace in this city*; date **illa** **huic**, *give those (things) to this (man)*.

Subjunctive mood. In the present tense, the subjunctive mood in the 2nd, 3rd, and 4th conjugations is formed by inserting an **-ā-** between the stem vowel and the personal endings. In the 1st conjugation, where the stem vowel is already **-ā-**, the stem vowel is in effect replaced with **-ē-**. Also, in non-i stem third conjugation, the stem vowel **-e-** is lost entirely with the addition of the **-ā-**.

First Conjugation: **amem, amēs, amet, amēmus, amētis, ament;**
Second Conjugation: **dēbeam, dēbeās, dēbeat, dēbeāmus, dēbeātis, dēbeant;**
Third Conjugation: **dūcam, dūcās, dūcat, dūcāmus, dūcātis, dūcant;**
Third i-stem Conjugation: **capiam, capiās, capiat, capiāmus, capiātis, capiant;**

Fourth Conjugation: **veniam, veniās, veniat, veniāmus, veniātis, veniant.**

The subjunctive of the verb **sum** is:

Present: **sĭm, sis, sit, sĭmus, sitis, sint;**
Imperfect: **essem, essēs, esset, essēmus, essētis, essent.**

The remaining three tenses of the subjunctive (the future and future perfect do not have the subjunctive mood) are quite simple. The imperfect subjunctive is, in effect, the present active infinitive plus personal endings, either active or passive. The perfect subjunctive active is the third principal part + **eri** + personal endings of the present system. The perfect subjunctive passive is the perfect passive participle with the present subjunctive of **sum.** The pluperfect subjunctive active is the perfect infinitive + personal endings of the present system. The pluperfect subjunctive passive is the perfect passive participle with the imperfect subjunctive of **sum.** Study the synopsis of the verb **capiō** in the third person singular, shown in Table 18 below.

Table 18

Subjunctive Mood

Tense	Active	Passive
Imperfect	caperet	caperētur
Perfect	cēperit	captus sit
Pluperfect	cēpisset	captus esset

The main uses of the subjunctive are shown in Table 17 on page 47.

Common irregular verbs. Like the English verb, *go, went, gone,* some Latin verbs have irregular principal parts: **ferō, ferre, tulī, lātus,** *to carry.* Such verbs are called *suppletive* because one or more of their principal parts is being *supplied* from another verb.

Another kind of irregular verb will lack one or two of the principal parts altogether: ——, ——, **coepi, coeptus,** *began;* **bibō, bibere, bibi,** ——, *to drink.* Some others will lack some forms which are found in the conjugations of other verbs. The verb **aiō,** *to say,* for example, has no infinitive, nor does it ever appear in the 1st and 2nd persons plural. Such verbs are called *defective.*

Suppletive and defective verbs will nevertheless follow the regular rules of conjugations. The most irregular verbs are those which deviate from the normal rules of conjugation. But in these verbs the irregularities are nearly always limited to the present system of tenses, and even then the exceptions are few. A quick glance at Table 19 below will reveal most of the normal rules at work.

Three common constructions.
Indirect statement—reported speech—is formed by changing the original subject nominative of the direct statement to the accusative and the original conjugated form of the verb to the infinitive. If there is a subordinate clause in the original statement, it becomes subjunctive. Direct statement: **Amicus meus trans agrum currit,** *my friend is running through the field.* As Indirect Statement: **Putō amicum meum trans argrum currere,** *I think that my friend is running across the field.* Direct statement: **Rōma ab Gallis oppugnāta est,** *Rome was attacked by the Gauls.* As indirect statement: **Dixit Rōmam ab Gallis oppugnātam esse,** *he said that Rome had been attacked by the Gauls.*

The ablative absolute construction allows Latin to state generally an attendant circumstance of the main action of the sentence with specifying the exact nature of the relationship. It is similar to the English nominative absolute: *All things being equal . . . , That said. . . .*

The ablative absolute consists of a noun or pronoun in the ablative case and a participle agreeing with it. **His verbis iūcundis ab ōrātōre dictis,**

omnēs civēs ridēre coepērunt, *when these pleasant words had been said by the orator, all the citizens began to laugh.* **Civibus ridentibus, ōrātōr alia verba iūcunda dixit,** *while the citizens were laughing, the orator said other pleasant words.* Although the verb **sum** has no present participle, Latin can imply one in the ablative absolute as follows: **Per iocum Iuliō et Caesare consulibus actum scriberent,** *as a joke, they would write that it had been done when Julius and Caesar were consuls.*

One way of showing purpose is **ad** plus the gerund or **ad** plus the gerundive agreeing with a noun. **Ad nāvigandum (ad gerendum bellum) omnia parāta sunt,** *everything for sailing (for conducting the war) was made ready.*

Deponent verbs. Many verbs lack nearly all of their active forms, and their passive forms are translated as if they were active. It is tempting to think that deponent verbs are entirely exempt from the standard rules of conjugation, but this is not so. They follow all the rules that normal verbs do inasmuch as they are able. It is easy to tell from the dictionary entry that a verb is deponent, for it will have no active forms listed. The entry will also lack a principal part for the perfect system active. See Table 20 on page 49.

A regular deponent verb will have present and future active participles, and the future passive participle is translated passively.

Other pronouns. The relative pronoun is used as the root of several other pronouns. Accordingly, becoming thoroughly acquainted with its inflection is extremely useful. For the most part, it uses 1st and 2nd declension case endings. See Table 21 on page 49.

The most common pronouns that use the forms of the relative pronoun are listed here.

Dixit ea quae dicenda erant, *he said the things which had to be said.* **Ubi est liber quem legēbās?** *where is the book which you were reading?*

Common Irregular Verbs

Two Irregular Verbs in the Present System

Principal parts	Present					Imperfect				Future	
	Indicative		Subjunctive		Indicative		Subjunctive		Indicative	
eō, īre, iī	eō	īmus	eam	eāmus	ībam	ībāmus	īrem	īrēmus	ībō	ībimus
itus	īs	ītis	eās	eātis	ībās	ībātis	īrēs	īrētis	ībis	ībitis
to go	it	eunt	eat	eant	ībat	ībant	īret	īrent	ībit	ībunt
volō,	volō	volumus	velim	velīmus	volēbam	volēbāmus	vellem	vellēmus	volam	volēmus
velle,	vīs	vultis	velīs	velītis	volēbās	volēbātis	vellēs	vellētis	volēs	volētis
voluī,	vult	volunt	velit	velint	volēbat	volēbant	vellet	vellent	volet	volent
to wish										

Table 19

Table 20

Deponent Verbs

1st conjugation	hortor, -ārī, hortātus sum, *to encourage*
2nd conjugation	vereor, -ērī, veritus sum, *to fear*
3rd conjugation	proficiscor, -ī, profectus sum, *to set out*
3rd i-stem conjugation	morior, -ī, mortuus sum, *to die*
4th conjugation	exorior, -īrī, exortus sum, *to come forth*

Table 21

Other Pronouns

Case	Masc.	Fem.	Neuter
Singular			
Nom.	quī	quae	quod
Gen.	cuius	cuius	cuius
Dat.	cui	cui	cui
Acc.	quem	quam	quod
Abl.	quō	quā	quō
Plural			
Nom.	quī	quae	quae
Gen.	quōrum	quārum	quōrum
Dat.	quibus	quibus	quibus
Acc.	quōs	quās	quae
Abl.	quibus	quibus	quibus

Some Everyday Latin

A.D.	in annō dominī, *in the year of the Lord*
A.M.	ante merīdiem, *before midday*
etc.	et cētera, *and the other things*
et al.	et āliī, *and other people*
ad infinitum	*and on without limit*
Bona fide(s)	(with the -s-) *good faith;* (without the -s-) *in good faith*
c.	circā, *about, approximately*
E pluribus unum	*one from many*
e.g.	exemplī grātiā, *for the sake of example*
Ergo	*therefore*
gravitas	*seriousness, dignity*
i.e.	id est, *that is, namely*
ipso facto	*by that very fact*
NB	Nōtā bene, *take careful note*
non sequitur	*it doesn't follow*
quid pro quo	aliquid prō aliquō, *something for something*
passim	*throughout*
per se	*through* or *in and of itself*
post mortem	*after death*
P.M.	post merīdiem, *after midday*
pro tem	prō tempore, *for the time being*
PS	post scriptum, *after (it was) written*
rigor mortis	*the stiffness of death*
Semper Fi	semper fidēlēs, *always loyal*
sic	*thus* (indicates that an error in a quotation was in the original source)

The interrogative pronoun is identical in form, with the certain exceptions in the singular. (1) The neuter nominative and accusative is **quid.** (2) The masculine and feminine are identical in form throughout all the cases of the singular, and use **quis** instead of **qui** or **quae** for the nominative.

> **Quis** est tuus pater? *who is your father?* **Quid** loquēbāris? *what were you saying?*

The interrogative adjective is the same as the relative pronoun.

> **Cui** puerō librum tuum dedit? *to which boy did he give your book?* Ē **quā** urbe ēgressus est? *from which city did he depart?*

The pronoun meaning "somebody, something" is **ali** + the forms of the interrogative pronoun. After the words **sī, nisī, num** and **nē,** the **ali-** prefix is dropped.

> Dabunt pecūniam **alicui,** *they will give money to someone;* **Sī quem** in viā videās, dic mihi, *if you should see someone on the road, tell me.*

The pronoun meaning "anybody, anything" is the interrogative pronoun plus the indeclinable suffix **quam: quisquam, quidquam** or **quicquam.**

> **Quisquam** poterat frūmentum metere, *anyone could harvest the grain;* Nec pānem **cuiquam** dedit? *and he didn't give bread to anyone?*

The pronoun meaning "some" or "a certain" is the relative pronoun plus the indeclinable suffix **-dam: quīdam, quaedam, quoddam,** or **quiddam.** A final **-m** of a case ending becomes **-n.** Hence, for example, **quendam** instead of **quemdam.** It can also be used as an adjective in a way that approaches our indefinite article.

> In nāve erat **fīlius quīdam** rēgis Aeētae, *there was in the ship a (certain) son of the king Aeetes;* Herculēs dēlēgit **quōsdam** ex suīs, *Hercules picked out some of his (men).*

The pronoun meaning "the same" is the third person demonstrative **is, ea, id** + the indeclinable suffix **-dem: īdem, eadem, idem.** As with the suffix **-dam** above, a final **-m** of a case ending becomes **-n: eandem** instead of **eamdem.** As with **quīdam** above, it can be used as an adjective.

> Quīdam ex Argonautīs **ad eandem īnsulam** pervēnērunt, *some of the Argonauts arrived at the same island;* Ōrātōr **eadem** dīxit, *the orator said the same (things).*

18 Foreign Language

The intensive adjective/pronoun, **ipse, ipsa, ipsum**, is declined like **is, ea, id**, with the irregular genitive and dative endings.

> **In illā viā vīdimus rēgem ipsum**, *we saw <u>the king himself</u> on that road;* **Vīdistī ipsa,** *you saw these very (things).*

Reading Latin. There is no secret key to learning to read Latin comfortably. It takes some talent, but mostly just lots of patience and practice. As you begin, you should make sure you understand every letter of every word—what the source and meaning of all the forms are, what the syntax of each subjunctive is, etc. If you do, you will progress smoothly from the elementary and intermediate school texts into real Latin.

The preceding digest represents probably 90 percent of the grammar you will need to know for controlled, beginning Latin texts, and 80 percent for real Latin. Read slowly through the following passage from Caesar's *Gallic Wars* (1.41), and try to see how the translation, which is deliberately left very literal, comes out of the grammar of each word.

> **Hāc ōrātiōne habitā, mīrum in modum conversae sunt omnium mentēs summaque alacritās et cupiditās bellī gerendī innāta est, princepsque decima legiō per tribūnōs militum Caesarī grātiās ēgit, quod dē sē optimum iūdicium fēcisset, sēque esse ad bellum gerendum parātissimam cōnfirmāvit.**

> *When this speech was made, in a wondrous way the minds of all were changed around, and a very great eagerness and desire of waging the war was engendered, and the tenth legion first sent greetings to Caesar through the tribunes of the soldiers, because he had the highest opinion of it, and it assured him that it was entirely ready for waging war.*

> —*Dale Grote*
> —*John Dillon*

THE HELP DESK

➤ **Help** a younger sibling or friend by reading to her and letting her read to you. Take her to the library to select books that interest her–and be prepared to read the same book several times.

➤ **Play** word games with a child–a set of magnetic letters can be used to spell words, emphasize letter sounds, and show similar words such as hat, cat, bat, fat, sat. Use magazines and newspapers for the child to find assigned words or letters–for example, circle words that start with "s" or ask the child for words that start with a particular sound.

➤ **Help** a child think about the order and possibilities of stories–ask what happens first? then what happened? but what if?, etc. Cut out comic strips, separate the pictures, have the child arrange the pictures as he chooses, and let him tell you the story.

➤ **Help** a child keep a journal of her daily activities. Sentences are good, but even isolated words and pictures are fine. Spelling correctly is good but not as important as ideas. Start with five to ten minutes a day and increase the time as the child ages and has more to report.

➤ **Use** a magazine article to mark words using prefixes or suffixes or cut out the words and paste on a sheet of paper (suffix on one, prefix on the other). Check to see if the words are legitimate or just look-alikes.

➤ **Select** a motley group of objects and guesstimate the weight, length, etc., then check with a scale or ruler.

➤ **Write** a short story about solving a problem.

➤ **Plurals** are a challenge. Make and keep running lists of words that change more than simply adding an "s"–for example, mouse/mice, etc. Make a list of special words that are the same whether singular or plural–for example, fish, shrimp, etc.

➤ **Think** of something about which you feel strongly but have a different opinion on than your parents or friends. Write a persuasive paragraph to help them understand your point of view. Now try to change their minds to your point of view.

➤ **What** are contractions? Make lists of them as you read, listen, and speak. When are most of them used? What is the difference between common and poetic contractions?

➤ **Keep** running lists of words that have multiple meanings. Illustrate each meaning with a sentence and explain if necessary. For example, "Draw the drapes" could become "close the drapes". Or sketch a picture of the drapes.

➤ **Practice** writing descriptive paragraphs of happenings, visual pictures, effects of happenings, for example, tornado, flood, snowstorm.

➤ **Pay** attention to unfamiliar words you read or hear. Learn everything you can about the word by writing it down (as it sounds if you can't spell it). Divide it into syllables (guess if you must and mark accented syllables), and then look in the dictionary for meaning, origin, and other information.

➤ **Ask** your teacher for a list of the 137 "demon words."

➤ **Make** lists of figures of speech you read or hear. Some of the easiest to identify are similes (quiet as a mouse, smooth as silk) and metaphors (fog comes in on little cat feet).

➤ **Sit** in a room, look around, and make a list of every noun you see. Start a column beside your noun list and add adjectives that describe each noun. Make another list that arranges the nouns in alphabetical order.

➤ **Write** a paragraph or more about how and why something happens; this is called expository writing and is a good way to summarize something you are learning in other classes. Why do leaves change color in the fall? How did Columbus discover America?

➤ **Read** a newspaper editorial. Do you agree or disagree? Why? If you cannot take a stand, what more do you need to know to make a decision?

➤ **Search** for newspaper and magazine articles that contain quotes. See if you can tell which are direct quotes and which are indirect quotes. Is there a difference? Are they primary or secondary quotes? How can you tell? What punctuation marks are necessary? Where do they go? Make up your own examples.

➤ **A** special part of speech that shows excitement or emotion is an interjection. Search for examples in your reading. Make up sentences of your own. How many different ones can you provide? How do you know one when you see or hear one?

➤ **Read** a newspaper daily. Select a number of columns at random and see if you can label the entire column or each paragraph as being factual, opinion, speculation, etc.

➤ **Collect** a number of letters–personal, business, even bulk mail, ads, etc. Label the parts–salutation, closing, date, any others. Is there a difference between the types of letters? Why do you think that is? Detail the differences.

➤ **Before** looking up an unfamiliar word in the dictionary, try to solve the mystery on your own. For pronunciation and spelling, say the word several times to see if it sounds like something you've heard; write it the way it sounds and divide it into syllables. Are parts of the word identifiable–root, prefix, suffix? How is it used in the sentence–noun, verb, adjective? Can you identify the meaning? Now look it up–how close was your estimate?

➤ **Can** you identify incomplete sentences? Run-on sentences? Can a sentence be both?

➤ **Practice** your research skills. Select a topic for an assignment or just for fun. Use the library card catalogue (either cards or on a computer) to make a list of possible sources. Find those sources and check the indexes. Determine the quality of your sources. Will your first finds lead to others? How?

➤ **Practice** your note-taking skills from both written and spoken information. Develop your ability to record key words, ideas, etc., so you can retrieve the thoughts after a period of time. Do you need complete sentences? Quotes? Definitions? Or simple reminders?

➤ **For** a list of helpful references, go to the *customers* section of www.southwestern.com.

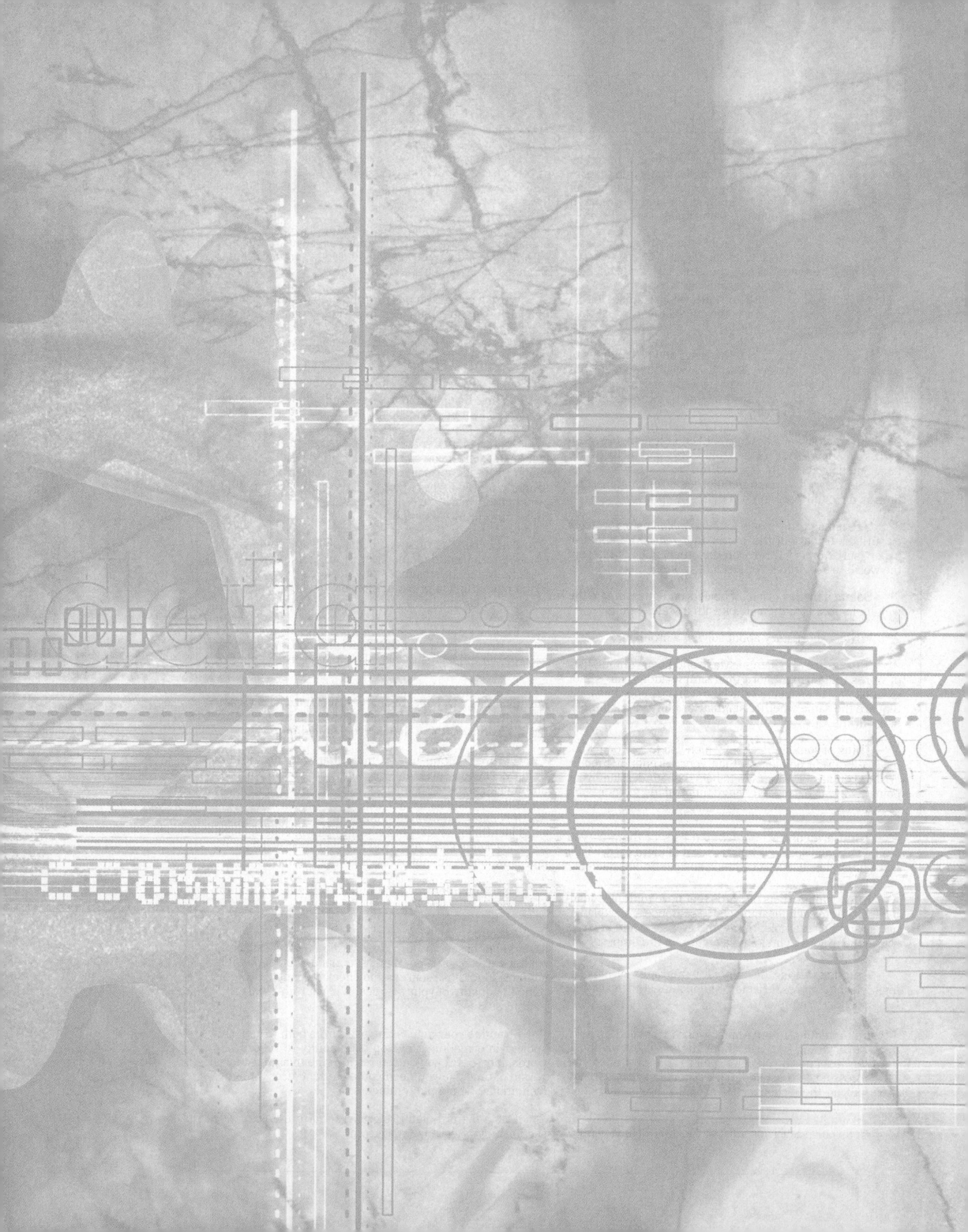

History

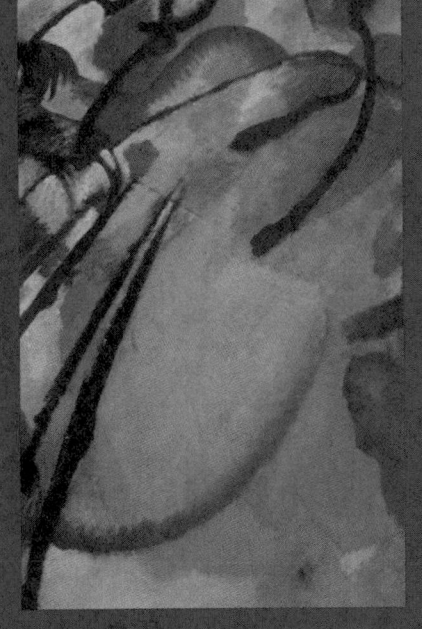

**History
of Art**

**History of
Literature**

**History of
the World**

History

Action, adventure, romance, wars, plagues, festivities, and more: All that has happened to humans over the millenia can be found in the pages of history. Many accounts of things that happened even prior to the written word have been preserved in works of art, and the oral tradition has passed through successive generations to be eventually recorded for posterity in writing.

While we normally think of history as stories, it is more than that. The history of any given period of time will contain stories of heroism and catastrophe, victory and defeat. It will tell us about the people—how they lived, who they were, what was important to them, why they did things, and what they wished they had done.

people like ourselves whose location and circumstances may have been similar to or drastically different from ours. The actions of those people may prompt feelings in us of interest, indifference, admiration, or revulsion. We can feel wonder at their accomplishments or simply their ability to survive. We can imagine ourselves living in any time and

History is a chain that connects us with those who have gone before. It allows us to feel a kinship with

any place we choose. The current popularity of historical novels bears witness to the interest in times past.

Is the appeal a yearning for a simpler time, a different location, more interesting people than those we associate with daily, or is it a need to feel the connection in whatever fashion to those who preceded us?

Our inclination to question our origin, our reason for being, what has made us what we are—as well as where we are going—can all be, if not satisfied, at least studied. After all, history is meant to be studied as well as enjoyed. A dozen historians

exemplify the time in which they lived. Simply thinking of Julius Caesar will conjure up a picture of the glory of Rome—marble buildings, togas, chariots, and gladiators.

can write about a particular time period and location and only minimally cover the same ground. Seen through the eyes of a politically astute observer or a student of human nature, the same events may not even seem to be related. Times change what we may want to know now. The Middle Ages may be best remembered for the centuries-long string of Crusades to the Middle

will attempt to unearth maps that help pinpoint the routes to the Holy Land, locations of battles, and territorial boundaries.

George Washington will summon thoughts of the Revolutionary War, knee breeches, powdered wigs, and muskets.

History is endlessly fascinating because it is about ourselves. As a wise man once said, "It balances our frustrations of how far we have to go with the satisfaction of how far we have come."

East, but a student of technology will seek out details of ship design and formulae for Damascus steel; an anthropologist may try to understand the effect on the women of the period when their men were gone for years at a time; a cartographer

The evolution of lifestyles—the architecture of buildings, the clothing, the perception and creation of beauty as expressed in art and music—is all a part of history. The contemporary language of the time period is the vehicle by which the history itself is recorded. Would the *Canterbury Tales* be as informative and fascinating when translated into late twentieth century English?

History can be traced through the accomplishments of heros and scoundrels, statesmen and traitors. If the bulk of history as embodied in the countries that rise and fall is not to your taste, find individuals who

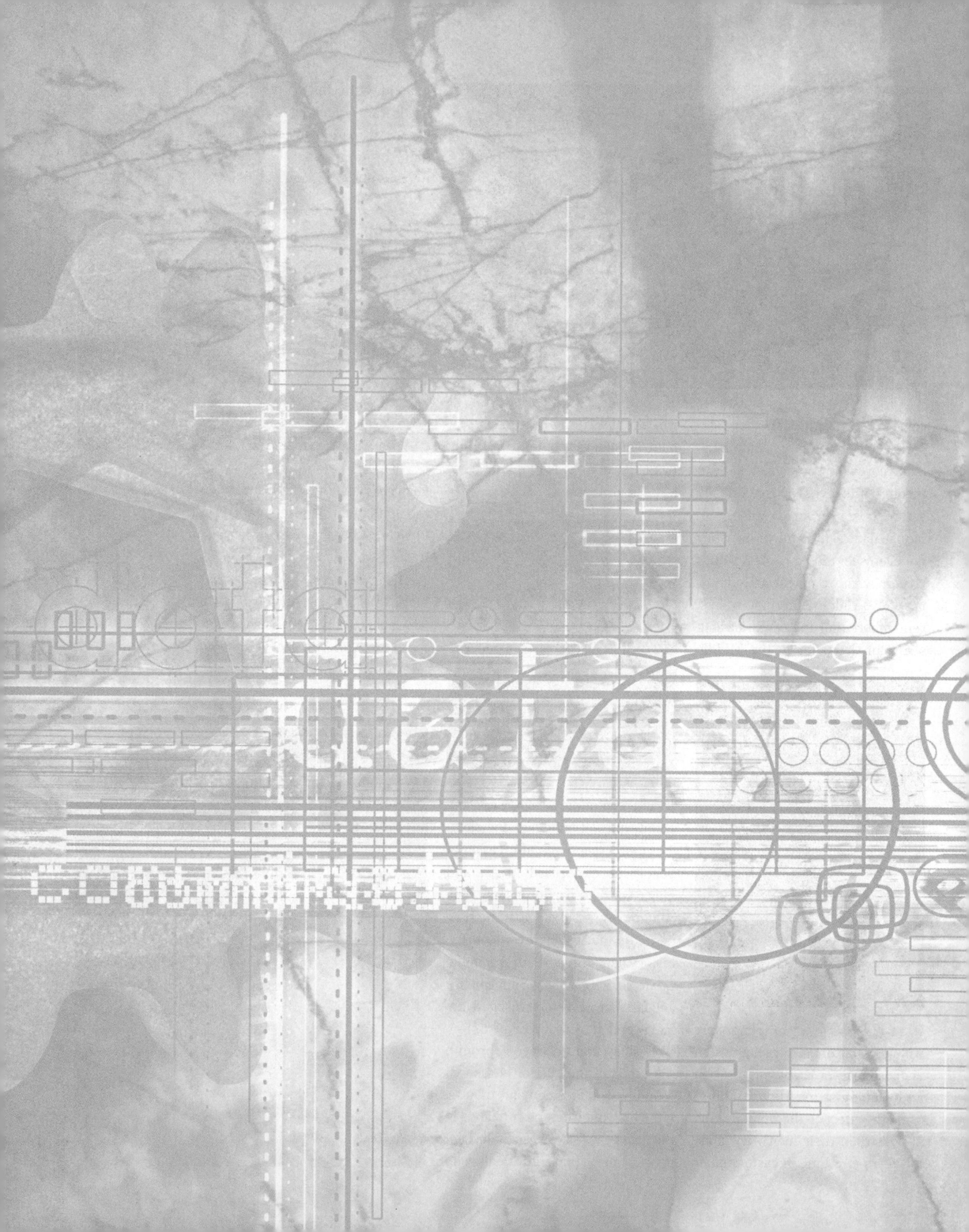

History
of Art

19

History of Art

Contents

Overleaf: *Improvisation 26
by Wassily Kandinsky*

Western Art

Western art is the name we give to the long, continuous tradition that began with ancient civilizations around the Mediterranean Sea. In the 5,000 years since the birth of civilization in Egypt and Sumeria, many nations and peoples have produced works of art that still influence our ideas today.

The spirit of innovation passed from the Egyptians and Sumerians to the ancient Greeks and later to the powerful Romans. From them, the disciplines of painting, sculpture, and architecture passed to the new countries of Europe and eventually to the New World as well. At every step, new tribes and peoples made their own contribution. The art of the West is wonderfully various, yet at the same time it is the product of a single long and distinguished tradition.

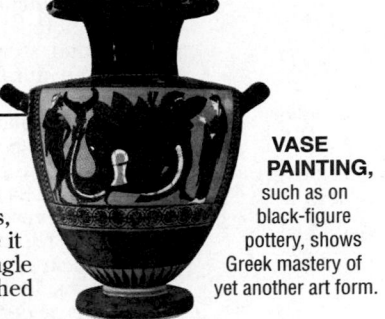

VASE PAINTING, such as on black-figure pottery, shows Greek mastery of yet another art form.

Ancient Art

Egypt

"Egypt is the gift of the Nile." That is how Herodotus, the ancient Greek historian, described the land of the pharaohs. The Nile is the longest river in the world, and it was Egypt's major means of transportation and communication. More important, it left rich deposits of alluvial soil along its banks each spring, giving the Egyptians fertile land to plant.

Egypt, protected from her enemies by thousands of miles of desert, developed in secure isolation. There was a sense of permanence and order in this land of blazing sun, and this sense is clearly reflected in the art of the ancient Egyptians.

The history of the Egyptian nation begins about 5,000 years ago when King Menes (also called Narmer) began the first of Egypt's 31 dynasties (ruling families). He did this by uniting its many small kingdoms under his own powerful rule. This important event is recorded on his palette, a ceremonial plate used for mixing eye makeup (the Egyptians painted their eyes to protect them from the glare of the sun).

The back of the palette (shown here) represents the victorious king wearing the tall crown of Upper Egypt. He prepares to kill his fallen enemy, while two other captives sprawl at his feet. To the right of the king, a hawk (who represents the god Horus) perches on a clump of papyrus (symbolizing Lower Egypt), and holds an enemy's head by a rope. This pictogram is another symbol of Menes's conquest over Lower Egypt. At the top of the palette, the king's name is written in hieroglyphics between two images of Hathor, the cow goddess.

On the opposite side of the palette, the situation is reversed and Menes, now wearing the crown of Lower Egypt, conquers the Upper Kingdom. The Narmer palette thus symbolizes the union of the country, and from this time forward, all pharaohs wore double crowns and called themselves "kings of Upper and Lower Egypt."

The palette is important both as a historical document and as a work of art. It set a standard for all future paintings and relief sculptures of important Egyptian people. The king's eye and shoulders are seen from the front, but his head, waist, and legs are viewed from the side. The artist adopted this formula so that he could show the most important parts of the body as he *knew* them to be, not just as he *saw* them in a fleeting glance. As a result, the figure has a peculiar, but permanent, look about him.

This concern with permanence can be traced to the Egyptians' view of eternal life. They believed that when a person died, the soul would continue to live as long as the body was preserved.

THE PALETTE OF NARMER, Egypt, created c 3000 B.C., portrays the ancient king about to kill an enemy. Showing human faces in profile is characteristic of early Egyptian art.

This explains why the Egyptians made mummies. Life in the next world was to be a happier existence. To insure this, the Egyptians filled their tombs with all manner of goods, including furniture, clothing, games, and even food. They also painted the tomb walls with beautiful and realistic pictures of the dead person's land, family, and slaves so that the spirit would never be in want. Of course, the most lavishly appointed tombs were those of the pharaohs, or kings.

The Egyptians believed that their pharaoh was a god. They also believed that everything, from the rising of the sun to the flooding of the Nile, depended on divine favor, so they took great measures to assure that the pharaoh's spirit would be content.

The Egyptians poured their nation's wealth into the construction of tombs for their kings. These great royal tombs went through a long period of evolution. They probably began as great mounds of earth and gradually grew into the standard form of *mastaba* (the Arabic word for "bench"). A *mastaba* is a rectangular flat-topped monument with sloping sides and a deep shaft leading to the subterranean burial chamber.

The next step was a giant one, and it came circa 2750 B.C. when King Zoser planned his eternal dwelling at Saqqara. King Zoser's resting place was built by Imhotep, the first known architect in history. By stacking six mastabas on top of one another, with the largest on the bottom and the smallest at the top, Imhotep created a "stepped pyramid": a staircase to heaven 195 feet high.

Amazing as this was, the pyramid was still only one part of the most imposing architectural complex the world had ever seen. Imhotep surrounded the pyramid with duplicates of the temples, chambers, and courtyards that King Zoser had used in his lifetime, but now their purpose was purely magical. Most of the buildings were stone dummies and were completely filled with earth and debris. The huge wall that encloses the complex, for

center
US

centre
Brit.

laborers
US

labourers
Brit.

example, has 14 massive gates, but only one of them is real. The others serve the spirit by magic.

In this brilliant architectural complex, Imhotep created the first monumental stone buildings in the world. The durability of stone was ideally suited to the eternal preservation of Zoser's body, and it became the standard building material for all future tombs. Stone was never used for houses of the living. At Saqqara, Imhotep united the past, the present, and the future for all eternity. His accomplishment was considered so great that the Egyptians came to consider him as a god.

Roughly a century after Saqqara, geometric purity was achieved during the Fourth Dynasty by smoothing out the sides of a stepped pyramid.

The result was the Great Pyramid of Cheops, the first and largest of the three pyramids of Giza near present-day Cairo. Unlike Zoser, who built his stepped tomb in the center of his magical palace, Cheops set great gateways and temples in front of the pyramid where he was to purify his soul before its journey to the next world.

The sheer size and perfection of the pyramid give us some idea of the incomparable Egyptian genius for design and engineering. More than 2,300,000 limestone blocks were cut from nearby quarries, floated across the Nile at high tide, and then dragged by slaves to the building site. Most of the stones weigh about two and a half tons, but there are some that reach the staggering weight of almost 50 tons!

Because the wheel had not yet been invented, huge gangs of laborers were forced to drag these heavy stones up temporary ramps and to lay them one on top of the other, course by course. When all the blocks were in place, the entire pyramid was faced with gleaming white limestone, so finely finished that one can barely detect the joints between the stones.

After many long years of work by untold thousands of slaves, the pyramid was completed. It was a manmade mountain measuring 755 feet on a side, and so perfectly oriented that each of its corners was exactly aligned with one of the four cardinal points (north, south, east, and west). The towering mass of the pyramid, so simple and so pure, soared almost 500 feet into the sky and totally dominated the surrounding desert. It was a symbol to all the world of the ultimate power of the pharaoh who lay buried in the center of the gigantic tomb.

Cheops's building activities were continued and even surpassed by his successor Chephren, who built the second pyramid at Giza. Chephren also created the famous 240-foot-long sphinx. This monumental stone figure, with the body of a lion and the head of a king (probably Chephren himself), was carved from a rocky bluff near the tomb. But what is the significance of this great monster? The answer is probably to be found in an ancient Egyptian myth that tells of a ferocious lion who guarded the gates of the underworld. Chephren adopted the body of the king of beasts in order to keep an eternal guard at his own tomb.

Despite all of their precautions, the Egyptians were not always successful in protecting the pharaoh's body, and in many cases the pyramids were broken into almost immediately after they were sealed. This, of course, destroyed the entire purpose of the pyramids. Their massive size was supposed to protect the pharaoh's body. In practice, they told thieves exactly where the royal treasures were buried. By the end of the Fourth Dynasty, fewer pyramids were being built, and these were generally smaller and much less conspicuous than those at Giza.

The third and last of the pyramids at Giza was built by Mycerinus, seen on the next page with his wife Khamerernebty. The king and queen take a step forward, but they are held captive in the stone block from which they were carved. Stone even fills in the spaces that we might normally expect to be open (like those between the pharaoh's arm and body). This "extra" stone strengthened the statue and protected it against breakage. Today we can appreciate how effective this measure was because the statue is still intact after more than 4,000 years.

The stiff and immobile formality of the king and queen expresses the Egyptian ideal of royal majesty. All imperfections like scars or wrinkles

PYRAMIDS: top, the plan for Zoser's pyramid with its surrounding temples and courtyards, c 2750 B.C. Below, a 19th-century view of the Sphinx and the great pyramids at Giza, c 2615–2500 B.C. The men on the foot of the Sphinx give an idea of its enormous size. The largest of the pyramids covers an area equal to 19 football fields and is nearly 50 stories high.

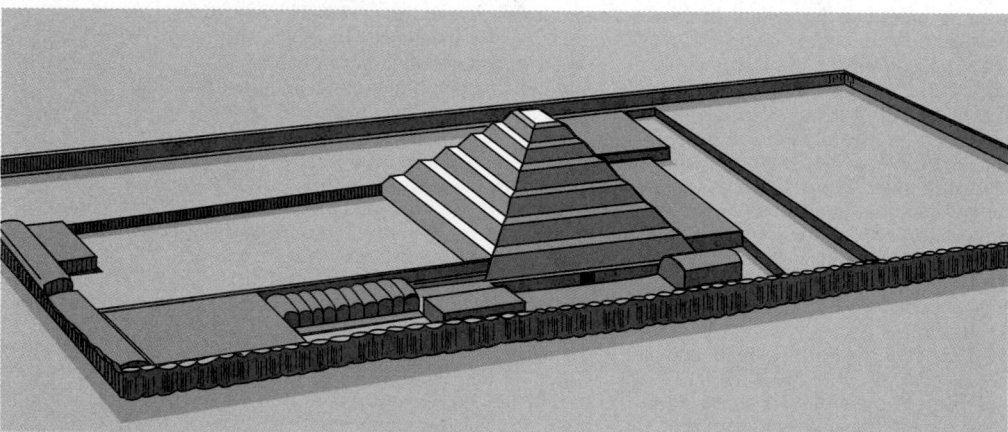

have been eliminated in order to portray the couple as perfect. This was only appropriate for an Egyptian pharaoh, who was a god and was thus perfect by definition.

About 2300 B.C. the pharaohs lost their claim to absolute authority. Many powerful officials fought for control of the government and Egypt was plunged into a dark age. During these dark years the Hyksos, an Asiatic people, attacked and subdued the country. They introduced horses, chariots, and new weapons.

In about 1570 B.C. the Egyptians cast out the invaders and ushered in the New Kingdom, characterized by great geographic expansion for Egypt and unparalleled brilliance in the arts. At first, painting, sculpture, and architecture in the New Kingdom generally adhered to the rigid standards set up some 2,000 years earlier.

Then, circa 1370 B.C., Amenhotep IV became pharaoh. In an absolutely revolutionary gesture, he forbade worship of the hundreds of Egyptian gods except for one. This was Aten, the sun god. The pharaoh closed all of the old temples and built an entirely new city (near the present Tel el-Amarna) for the exclusive worship of the sun god.

One of the effects of this religious revolution was a new interest in life in this world. And there was a consequent change in art. We can see this immediately when we compare the portrait of Amenhotep with the earlier one of Mycerinus and his queen. Previously, the pharaoh was seen as a divine king, with a strong and perfect body. But Amenhotep was depicted as he really looked: strangely shaped, with full hips, flabby belly, and a dreamy expression on his egg-shaped face. He was an impersonal and ideal king no longer. The flail and scepter, symbols of royalty, were now possessed by a man with imperfections. The pharaoh was portrayed with real emotions and his own individual personality. Realism had taken the place of idealism.

After the death of Amenhotep, this naturalistic phase in Egyptian art gradually came to a close, and artists returned to the traditional styles of stiff and monumental depiction.

After 1100 B.C., the kingdom fell into decline, and Egypt became a group of competing states. For the next 2,000 years, the country was often controlled by foreign powers. It was conquered in its turn by the Assyrians, the Persians, the armies of Alexander the Great, and the Romans. After the fall of Rome, Egypt became a part of the Byzantine Empire. Finally, in A.D. 642, it fell to the Arabs and gradually became a part of the Islamic world.

Few of the conquerors of Egypt were left untouched by its heritage of art. In all the centuries of foreign domination, the beauty of Egypt's art was prized throughout the Western world, and its ideals influenced the art of many other nations.

19 History of Art

civilization *US*

civilisation *Brit.*

The Middle East

Even as the civilization of Egypt grew and prospered, another center of civilization was developing some 500 miles to the north and east. It was the first of a succession of Middle Eastern civilizations that would deeply influence the future of art.

Mesopotamia. Where was the birthplace of civilization? Egypt is one possible place, but an equally strong case can be made for Mesopotamia, the plain between the Tigris and Euphrates rivers in present-day Iraq. Both of these early civilizations relied on agriculture made possible by fertile river valleys. By 3000 B.C., both had produced wealthy and highly sophisticated cultures. But this is where the similarities end.

Egypt was well protected by its desert boundaries, but Mesopotamia had no natural defenses. Its luxuriant plain was open to attack from all sides. Over the centuries, one nomadic tribe after another swept down on Mesopotamia and conquered it. The history of the region is a seemingly endless story of upheavals, invasions, and wars.

The "Mesopotamians" were not a distinct people. They were a mix of conquering and conquered tribes who settled in this rich land. The earliest of these tribes was the Sumerians. The Sumerians settled in the northern part of Mesopotamia before 3000 B.C.

They were a fascinating and inquisitive race: they invented the potter's wheel and one of the earliest forms of writing known to exist. This is cuneiform, a language written by making small wedge-shaped marks on a soft clay tablet. Clay, in fact, was the only material available to the Sumerians in any quantity. Unlike Egypt, Mesopotamia had no stone or timber, so its inhabitants had to build their homes and temples with sun-dried mud bricks.

Great temple complexes that were dominated by ziggurats, enormous brick "stairways to heaven," were most characteristic of Sumerian architecture. Rising several stories, and reached by steep flights of steps, these gigantic manmade mountains were crowned by religious shrines. They were the

A SUMERIAN STELA, an illustrated legal document with cuneiform writing.

Mesopotamian counterpart of the Egyptian pyramids. But the only remains of these once glorious structures are crumbling piles of earth. Unfortunately, mud bricks are far less durable than stone.

If we are lacking in Sumerian architectural remains, we are not lacking in their precious musical instruments, finely crafted goldwork, and small statuettes of gods and worshippers. The Sumerians were a deeply religious people, and the success of their civilization required them to spend great amounts of time praying to their gods. But they were also businessmen whose schedules would not permit their constant attendance at temple. The solution to this rather sticky problem was "worship by proxy." That is, the Sumerians deposited small statues in the temples to substitute for the absent person. The effect was the same as if the businessman were there himself. These little figures were often inscribed with short prayers, and they communicated with the gods through their enormous staring eyes.

By about 2360 B.C., the Sumerians had united with the Akkadians to establish an illustrious and powerful empire. But within a few hundred years, it was destroyed by the Amorite Semites who, in turn, were overcome by new waves of invaders. After centuries of turmoil, the great city of Babylon came into being. It introduced a magnificence previously unknown to Mesopotamia. Babylon was founded by Hammurabi, author of the world's first written code of laws, circa 1780 B.C. Civilized, powerful, and spectacular, Babylon became the cultural center of Mesopotamia.

Within a few short centuries, however, this brilliant civilization was devastated by the ruthless Hittites. Subsequent invasions brought the ferocious Kassites and later, the most terrifying of all, the dreaded Assyrians. The war-

like Assyrians also built enormous fortresses in order to consolidate their widespread conquests. Strangely, the Assyrians produced some very great artists who brought the art of carving in low relief to unprecedented heights.

The favorite themes of the Assyrians were military campaigns and animal hunts, which show noble beasts collapsing under Assyrian attack. Exquisitely carved wild horses attempt escape and caged lions are mercilessly slaughtered. The Assyrians delighted in showing pain, and they used their unparalleled skills of observation to portray agonized animals, bleeding and weak, their energies exhausted from the chase. Assyrian art was cruel, but it was more realistic and more vividly rendered than any other in the ancient world; it introduced emotion into art.

This is seen most compellingly in the sculptural relief on this page. The *Dying Lioness,* pierced by arrows and bleeding heavily, attempts to stand. But her back legs are paralyzed and they drag heavily behind her. Powerful forepaws bulge with exertion. She lets out a final roar; in a moment she will die.

After roughly three centuries of unthinkable atrocities, the Assyrians were defeated in the sixth century B.C. by the combined forces of their abused subjects and neighbors. Babylon rose again, more fabulous than ever. Under the rule of King Nebuchadnezzar, the city enjoyed great prosperity as an international trade center, and it became the greatest metropolis of the East. The king created the famous Hanging Gardens of Babylon, one of the Seven Wonders of the World. This spectacular structure was built of mud bricks, and like all Mesopotamian architecture, almost nothing of it remains.

One of the very few extant structures is the Ishtar Gate, the major entrance to Babylon. It, too, was made of mud bricks, but it was protected by a cover-

ing of brightly colored glazed bricks, boldly ornamented with lions, bulls, and dragons.

In the sixth century B.C., the Persians became the dominant Eastern power, and essentially ended the complicated, but brilliant, history of ancient Mesopotamia.

The Persians had been a seminomadic tribe with no great interest in art. But when their leader was proclaimed the new "king of Babylon" he sought an art worthy of the distinction. Gradually, an authentic imperial art evolved, combining Mesopotamian traditions, the native Persian love of ornament, and inspiration from Greek artists. The effects of this marriage can be best appreciated at Persepolis, the site of the most ambitious Persian palace.

The palace is an enormous structure, more than a quarter-mile long and nearly 1,000 feet wide. It is approached by a broad staircase, the walls of which are carved with an endless procession of figures paying tribute to the king. Inside, the palace's gold and silver ceilings rest on gigantic animal figures that are carved atop lofty columns.

Persian power and wealth were world renowned. In less than 50 years, the Persians were transformed from a nomadic tribe into the most powerful people on Earth. In 525 B.C. they conquered Egypt; they might have taken possession of Europe as well had it not been for the heroic resistance of the Greeks. The Persians were finally humbled in the fourth century B.C. by Alexander the Great.

The Minoans.
According to a Greek myth, the island of Crete was once ruled by a powerful king named Minos. (It is from him that the Minoans take their name.) The king's wife had given birth to a Minotaur, a terrible monster that was half man and half bull. The king was so embarrassed that he imprisoned the beast in a large maze, or labyrinth. Every seven years, the Minotaur required the sacrifice of 14 young men and women. Finally, according to the myth, the Greek hero Theseus killed the Minotaur and ended his tyranny over the island.

This was virtually all that the later Greeks knew about the Minoans. Until about 100 years ago, there was not much that could be added to this. Then, in one of the most spectacular discoveries ever made, the British archaeologist Sir Arthur Evans uncovered the vast Minoan labyrinth!

It did not contain a Minotaur, but it did contain a wealth of information about this ancient culture. As the excavation proceeded, it became clear that the legendary maze was, in fact, the sprawling palace of King Minos in the capital city of Knossos. The palace covered over four acres and included a marketplace and even a town, all arranged in a helter-skelter pattern. It's no wonder that the Greeks called it a labyrinth.

The palace was unfortified. It seems

DYING LIONESS, an Assyrian relief sculpture, c 650 B.C., shows the wounded animal with both realism and a sense of admiration.

that the Minoans, unlike almost every other ancient peoples, were not warriors. Instead, they were sailors and merchants. They lived prosperous and happy lives, and enjoyed singing, dancing, and games. Their standard of living far surpassed that of any contemporary civilization. The palace had flush toilets, running water, and a sophisticated system of ventilation. It was decorated with colorful paintings which, in their gaily flowing lines, expressed the Minoan joy of life. These paintings are strikingly different from those of the brooding Egyptians who painted the walls of tombs for the sake of the dead.

The so-called *Toreador Fresco* on this page gives some idea of the Minoans' life-loving attitude. Surrounded by a highly decorative border, two girls stand behind and before a charging bull as a boy somersaults over its back. This dangerous display was part of a religious ceremony (perhaps related to the Minotaur). But rather than stressing the hazards involved, the artist has concentrated on the playful and ornamental vitality of the scene. The same feeling characterizes virtually all Minoan art, including its beautiful pottery.

By about 2000 B.C., the Minoan civilization was already highly sophisticated. In the following centuries, it suffered several serious earthquakes, but the people were resilient and the Minoans continued to thrive—that is, until circa 1400 B.C., when the Minoans mysteriously disappeared.

The Mycenaeans.   Minoan traders often travelled to the shores of mainland Greece. Their art and civilization influenced its inhabitants, the people we call the Mycenaeans.

The Greek mainland did not have rich deposits of gold, yet the Mycenaeans amassed such vast treasures of this precious metal that 700 years later, the Greek poet Homer would describe it as "Mycenae, rich in gold." But where did the gold come from? All indications point to Egypt. It seems that the Mycenaeans were good fighters and had been paid in gold to fight as mercenaries for Egyptian warlords. The Mycenaeans' fame as warriors was later celebrated by Homer in his great epics, the *Iliad* and the *Odyssey*.

Much of our knowledge about the Mycenaeans comes from their tombs, which were filled with sumptuous treasures. These included beautiful gold cups imported from Crete, daggers inlaid with gold and silver, and death masks attached to the heads of mummified princes. These masks of finely beaten gold are powerful portrait studies of the deceased. The Mycenaeans' elaborate concern for their dead suggests that they were strongly influenced by the Egyptians.

Unlike Minoan sovereigns who lived in free-flowing unprotected palaces, Mycenaean kings lived in massive fortresses. In fact, one Mycenaean city was known as "Tiryns of the Great Walls," and was revered by the ancients as the birthplace of the legendary hero of strength, Hercules. These walls, built with huge boulders, were often 20 feet thick! This caused later Greeks to assume that they were built by the Cyclops, a mythical race of one-eyed giants.

Anyone approaching Mycenae, the capital of the Mycenaean world, is confronted by the monumental Lion Gate.

Colossal stones, some weighing as much as 18 tons, were used to construct this grand entrance. On top of the doorway is a triangular panel sculpted with mighty lions on either side of a column. This is the first example of large stone sculpture in Greek art.

Guardian lions were a common feature in both Egyptian and Mesopotamian sculpture, but combining these lions with massive defensive walls probably finds its origins with the Hittites, one of the ferocious tribes that invaded Mesopotamia. In the hands of the Mycenaeans, this motif becomes a coat of arms appropriate to conquering soldiers. It shows an alliance of the great: the kings of beasts protecting the kings of men.

Passing through the Lion Gate, a visitor would follow a path to the king's palace, or megaron. This great rectangular hall was the basic form from which the Greek temple evolved.

Mycenaean civilization flourished until the twelfth century B.C., when, during the Dorian invasion, barbarian tribes swept across Europe. Even the invincible Mycenaeans crumbled under the force of this onslaught.

The Dorian invasion signaled the end of Mycenaean power and introduced the Dark Age of Greece. People fled frantically from the invaders: some sailed to Asia Minor, others escaped to the Greek mountains, while still others simply met their deaths. Civilization all but came to an end. No buildings were constructed, almost no painting or sculpture was produced, and even the art of writing was lost. But in these bleak centuries, some important developments were taking place behind the scenes.

MINOAN AND MYCENAEAN: the *Toreador Fresco* (left) was painted by the Minoans c 1500 B.C., but was only rediscovered in the present century. *The Lion Gate* (right) was the entrance to the Mycenaean capital in Greece, c 1300 B.C.

The Greeks

From the 12th to the 8th century B.C., the inhabitants of present-day Greece settled into small communities for their common protection. Gradually, these scattered settlements developed into city-states. Each city-state was a separate entity, with its own government, its own code of laws, and its own distinct personality. There was no great king to unite them, so throughout their long history the city-states intermittently fought each other on the most bitter terms. But they had formed a sense of national identity based on a common language and some common values. In 776 B.C., these Greek-speaking city-states held their first Olympic games. From then on, all wars and rivalries were suspended temporarily every 4 years so they could once again compete in the sacred games.

Greece is a rugged country with mountains that touch the sky and ravines that seem to plunge to the center of the earth. It is of little surprise, then, that the earliest Greeks worshiped these natural wonders. But during the Dark Age a very important change took place: the gods were given human forms and personalities. In fact, they were frequently only distinguishable from humans by their immortality.

In the past, man had lived in a world dominated by wild beasts. He fought them, ate them, was fearful of them, and worshiped them. But in Greece, man was elevated above the entire animal kingdom because of his intelligence.

center
US

centre
Brit.

This recognition of man's innate worth changed the course of history, and laid the foundations for democracy, philosophy, poetry, medicine, law, and a totally humanistic style of art.

Man the rational being became the primary focus of Greek art. The Hellenes (as the Greeks called themselves) attempted to create the perfect mind and body, and thus paved the way for the concept of beauty held by the Western world. We still hold these same values, 2,500 years later.

The creation of an ideal human form did not take place overnight. It evolved slowly over the course of centuries. We might expect to trace this development in painting styles, but unfortunately almost all Greek paintings have been lost to time. Instead, we must look to pottery.

The Greeks used clay vessels for many different purposes. Some were used to carry water, others contained oil, and still others were used to store wine, honey, or grain. Each of these vases had its own name and characteristic shape. For example, the vase on this page is called a "krater." It was designed with a large opening at the top to facilitate the blending of wine and water (the Greeks never drank their wine undiluted).

This krater is one of the earliest Greek vases to come down to us. Almost the entire surface is covered with geometric ornament, horse-drawn chariots, and people with triangular torsos. It shows an ancient funeral, with the deceased person lying on a bed, surrounded by mourners who tear at their hair in despair. At this early date, the artist is still treating human form as an element of geometric decoration, but more important is the fact that he is attempting to show human emotion. From the beginning, Greek artists were interested in the way man feels.

In the following centuries vase paintings were constantly refined, and more and more attention was paid to the realistic portrayal of people. Ultimately, convincing scenes of men and gods constituted the entire decorative scheme, and abstract ornamentation was used only sparingly for borders. By the fifth century B.C., painted Greek ceramics had reached their peak of popularity and were collected throughout the ancient world.

Architecture. Like vase painting, Greek architecture went through an evolutionary process that began in the Dark Age. Once the gods were given human form, they had to be sheltered in human houses. But the homes of ordinary mortals were entirely too humble. So the Greeks looked to their ancient ancestors, the Mycenaeans, and took the form of the king's megaron from them. It was a very simple structure with upright tree trunks topped by horizontal beams. This is a basic post and lintel system of construction. It was the standard for future Greek architecture.

The crudeness of early Greek temples was gradually refined. Under Egyptian influence, stone was substituted for wood, and an elaborate system of proportions was established. The Greeks believed that "all things were in the measure of man." This applied to their gods, paintings, sculpture, and also to their architecture.

Man's body is proportional. That is, the size of his arms, legs, head, etc., are all related so that none is too big or too small. The Greeks planned their temples in much the same way, with every part related to all the others, and all parts related to man. For example, the base of a column is equivalent to man's foot, the column itself is equal to his body, and the uppermost portion relates to his head. These relationships gave Greek buildings life and the hope of perfection. The concept of proportion was as important to the Greeks as "eternity" was to the Egyptians.

Greek temples are based on the Doric, Ionic, and Corinthian orders. The very fact that they are called "orders" tells us that they are sets of rules that control the entire arrangement or order of a temple.

Each order has its own characteristics, which determine not only the size and shape of the columns and capitals (the uppermost portions of the pillars), but also the spacing of the columns, and even the type of ornaments applied to the building. The orders are based on complex systems of geometrical proportion, but they also have human correspondences. For example, the Doric order, which is austere and generally undecorated, was considered to be the masculine warrior. The delicate Ionic, with its gently spiraling capital, was the matron, and the slender and ornate Corinthian was the young maiden.

The Greeks used the orders to regulate and give life to their temples. They were considered so important that Greek architects rarely deviated from them. Indeed, the orders still continue to exert their influence after 2,500 years. Even the most casual glance will find their influence on our government buildings, banks, courthouses, and churches.

The most brilliant use of the orders is seen in the Parthenon, an enormous temple built in the fifth century B.C., the Golden Age of Greece. In plan and construction, it is as perfect a building

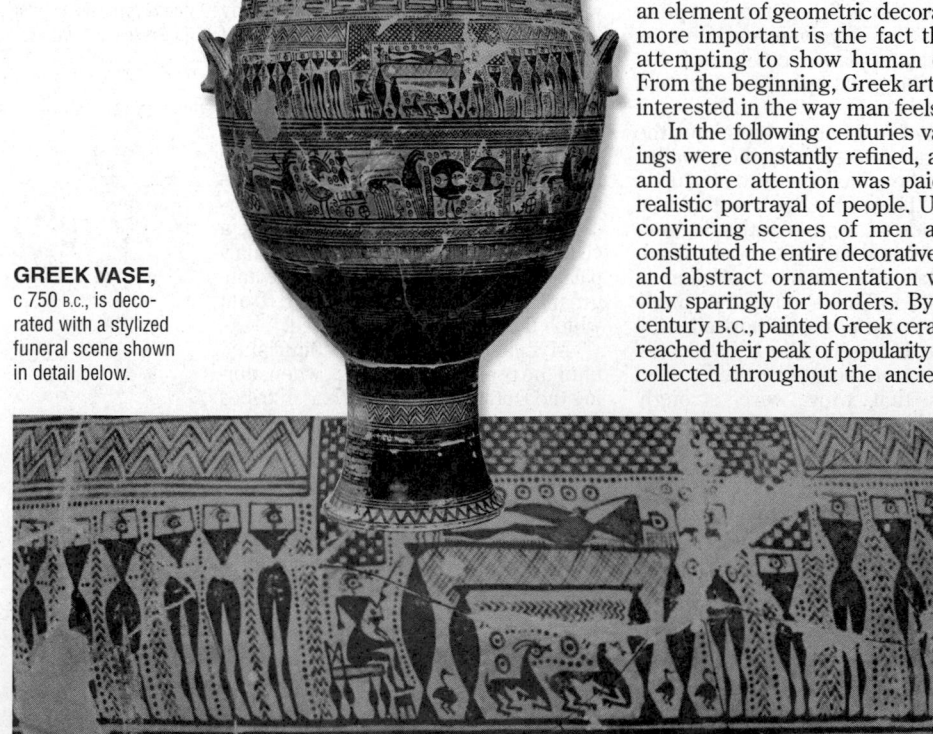

GREEK VASE, c 750 B.C., is decorated with a stylized funeral scene shown in detail below.

as is humanly possible to create. It stands on the acropolis ("high city") above modern Athens.

The original Parthenon was destroyed by the Persians in 480 B.C., but it was rebuilt by the Greek tyrant Pericles upon their defeat. No expense was spared. Built entirely of pure white marble, the temple cost more than 18 tons of gold. But it is not just the materials or cost that make the Parthenon so famous.

The architects, Ictinus and Callicrates, created a building where all elements are in perfect harmony. They did this by using curved lines. Had they used straight lines, the temple, high on the hill, would appear distorted when approached from below. So they "adjusted" every part. For instance, the columns slant back even though they look straight, and the roof and floor are not really level, but actually convex. There are dozens of similar adjustments in the Parthenon, all of which give it the appearance of perfect equilibrium. The architects created the near-perfect humanistic building by combining the best materials, the most careful planning, and the sacred orders with a profound understanding of the way man sees.

Sculpture. The humanistic qualities of Greek art are most clearly seen in sculpture. As early as the seventh century B.C., Greek artists, under the influence of Egypt, were producing large standing statues of people, one of their favorites being the kouros, a standing male youth. These figures were not quite gods, but neither were they mere men. They were heroes, semidivine figures who, like the gods, possessed perfect bodies.

The kouros on the following page is from an early stage of Greek sculpture. Like Egyptian sculpted figures, this figure has broad shoulders, a pinched waist, an extended left foot, and a general anatomical rigidity. Instead of gently modeling the youth's muscles, the sculptor has outlined them with stiff, almost geometric boundaries. This

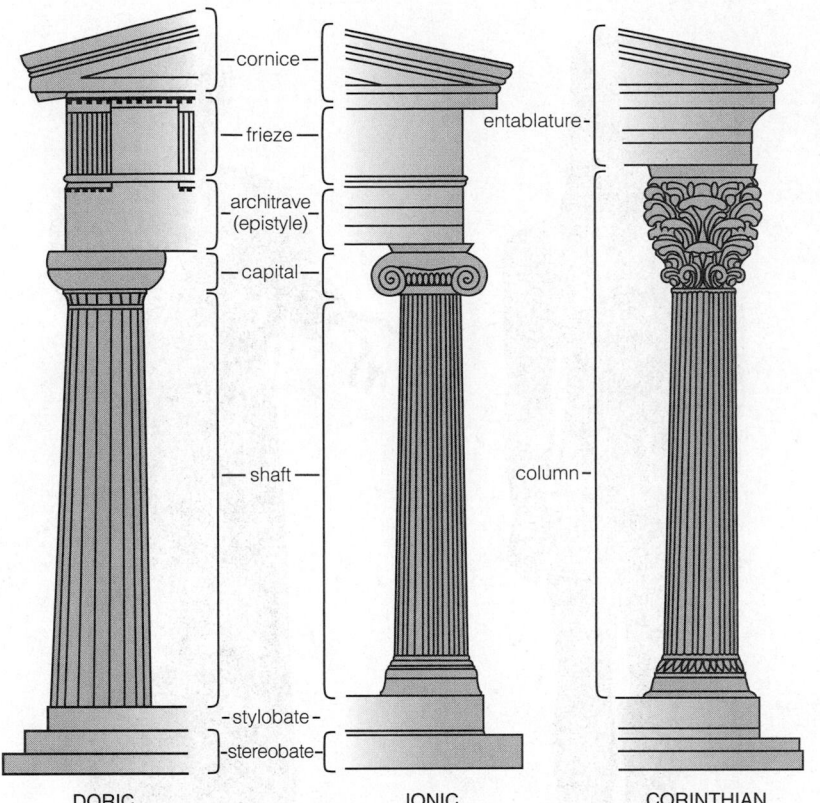

cornice

frieze

architrave (epistyle)

capital

shaft

stylobate

stereobate

entablature

column

DORIC   IONIC   CORINTHIAN

is particularly visible in the way the stomach and kneecaps are treated. The position of the arms, held close to the body, adds to the figure's stiffness. But if this kouros shares strong similarities with earlier sculpture, it also looks forward to a totally new style.

One of the most obvious differences is the figure's nakedness (Egyptian statues were always clothed). Even at this early stage, Greek sculptors were interested in the beauty of the human form. But even more important is the fact that all the "extra" stone has been cut away from the figure, leaving it to stand free. Unlike Egyptian statues, it has no reinforcing stone slab behind it,

and no stone fill between the arms and body and between the legs. This archaic kouros has taken a giant step toward "modern" free-standing forms of sculpture.

We can follow the growth of this humanizing tendency in the early classical image of the *Charioteer.* Originally, the *Charioteer* was part of a group statue with horses and a chariot. The

19 History of Art

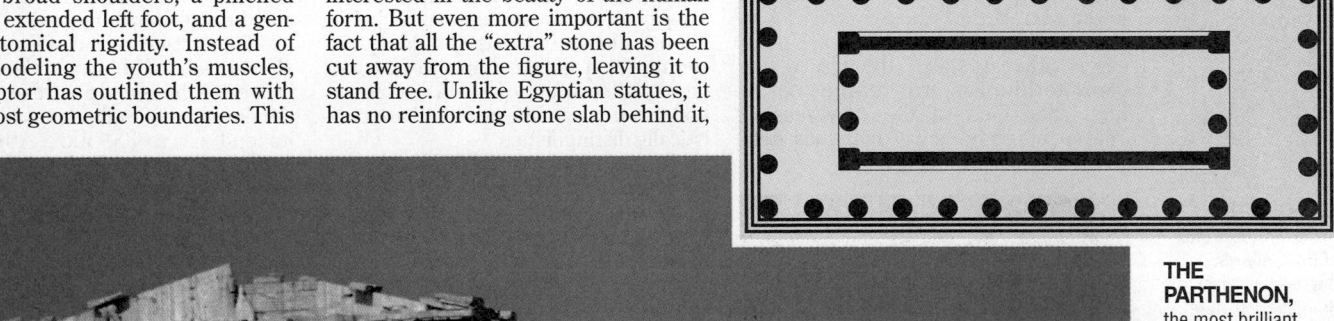

THE PARTHENON, the most brilliant surviving example of Greek architecture, was completed in 433 B.C. It is shown here in a photograph from the early 1900s. The floor plan, showing columns and interior walls, is in right top inset.

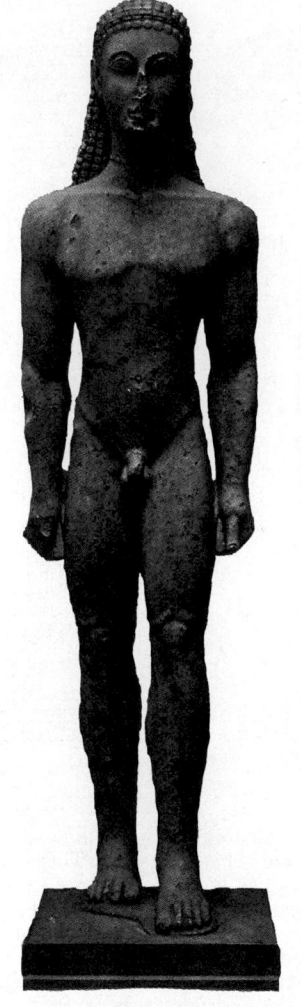

civilized
US

civilised
Brit.

LAOCOÖN,
made in Greece after 100 B.C., shows the Hellenic talent for dramatic sculpture.

statue was probably made to celebrate a victorious horse race. Admittedly, there is still a certain stiffness here, and the lower part of the athlete's skirt looks almost like a Greek column. But in every other respect, the figure has come to life. His arm reaches out to hold the reins of the now-missing chariot while his curly hair falls delicately to the sides of his face. His dark eyes are made of glass paste, and they warm his serious expression. Even the top part of his dress suggests a certain natural movement. His shoulders are slightly tilted and the drapery of the garment falls into soft folds. Natural textures of hair, skin, and cloth are realistically distinguished.

By the middle of the fifth century B.C., Greek sculpture had reached its Golden Age. The ever-threatening Persian troops were finally defeated, and Athens started to rebuild her temples on the acropolis. It was an era of wealth and optimism, a period when democracy flourished and art matured. By now sculptors had solved their early problems of naturalistic depiction. In place of former stiffness, muscular bodies gracefully bend. Sculptures are noble and quiet. A period of classical calm has set in.

The statue of Doryphorus by Polyclitos exemplifies this peak in Greek sculpture. Because Doryphorus rests his weight on only one leg, his hips and shoulders tilt slightly and a long fluid S-shaped curve runs from his head down to his extended toes. He is a great athlete, perfectly formed and impressively powerful. There is no awkwardness or clumsiness here, just

grace and beauty. Doryphorus was considered so perfect by the ancients that they established him as their standard of harmony and proportion.

The classical period of Greek art was short-lived. Old city-state rivalries between Athens and Sparta erupted into the devastating Peloponnesian War. By its end circa 400 B.C., Athens was exhausted, the prosperity of Greece was on the decline, and art took a turn toward self-conscious grace and delicacy. The most famous sculptor of this time was Praxiteles, who created works of unparalleled charm and intimacy. But there were other artists of the fourth century B.C. who worked in a very different manner: they stressed explosive action and excitement.

The fourth century B.C. was a time of tremendous change for the Greek world. Philip of Macedon, and his son Alexander the Great, changed Greece from an uneasy collection of city-states into a state under the control of one powerful leader. In the 13 years of Alexander's reign (336 B.C.–323 B.C.) Greek, or Hellenic, culture was spread throughout the civilized world. Contact with foreign cultures brought new energy to art and sometimes, as in *Laocoön,* this energy could barely be contained. A father and his two sons writhe in pain as they are attacked by serpents. They can barely maintain their balance in their desperate attempts to free themselves.

The sculptor's skill is extraordinary here, but he uses it emotionally to produce a work of violent contrasts and extravagant gestures. Unlike earlier Greek sculpture, where faces were idealized and expressionless, those of Laocoön and his sons are distorted by anguish and fright. Every part of the sculpture is electrified, even the clumps of hair that stand on end. Gone is the classical calm, gone is the ideal of man's control over nature. The height of Greek art and culture had passed. New forces were at work, and the world turned its eyes to Rome.

The Romans

Both Greece and Rome had their starts at roughly the same time. But Greek culture peaked with a brilliant climax in the fifth century B.C., while Rome was still a slowly developing hill town. In the following centuries, however, Roman military power grew and Rome began a systematic conquest of its neighbors. By the first century B.C., Rome was the leader of the world.

Early Roman life was dominated by the powerful Etruscans, who were fearsome warriors and inspired engineers. They were also gifted teachers who found receptive students in the Romans. In 509 B.C., the Romans defeated the Etruscans, using Etruscan weapons and military tactics.

One military victory followed another, until in 30 B.C. Rome became the unchallenged power of the entire Hellenistic world. The Greeks were totally subjected to Roman rule, but their culture exerted such a pervasive influence on Rome that one might well ask "who conquered whom?"

Architecture. The extent of Greek influence can be measured in the crowning glory of Roman architecture: the Pantheon in Rome. At first glance, the Pantheon looks exactly like a Greek temple, with eight huge columns crowned by a triangular pediment. But a closer look reveals that behind this classical facade are a large square block and an enormous domed cylinder. In typical fashion, the Romans took what they liked from Greek art and adapted it to their own needs. Greek and non-Greek forms are married here to produce something totally Roman and totally new: a vast interior space.

Previously, architects were only concerned with the exteriors of their buildings. Even the great temples of Greece were used like expensive stage sets. They were to be appreciated from the outside only. The interior was reserved for the gods. Today we are so accustomed to usable interiors that it is often difficult for us to imagine a time when this was not the case. With the development of interior space, the Romans turned architectural interest inside out, thus revolutionizing the course of building. Hereafter, architects would lavish considerable attention on how their buildings "worked."

When one passes through the great "Greek" porch of the Pantheon, one enters a different, totally unexpected world. The interior is a vast enclosed space, 140 feet high and just as wide. The ceiling is formed by a gigantic dome made from more than 5,000 tons of poured concrete, pierced in the center by an oculus (round window), which is the only source of illumination. The entire composition is based on a complex relationship of circles and squares masterfully integrated through color and design.

The oldest roofed building in the world, the Pantheon is an eloquent expression of Roman culture: it reflects the passion for organization, the incom-

parable engineering and architectural genius, and the authoritarian pretensions of the empire. Technically, the Pantheon was dedicated to all the gods, with its concrete dome as the dome of heaven. But it also symbolized expansive imperial extension.

Unlike the Egyptians and Greeks, who almost exclusively used stone in a post and lintel construction system, the Romans developed arches and vaults. Lacking natural stone, the Romans used brick and concrete. These materials were cheap and readily accessible, and the arches allowed great distances to be spanned safely. These were critical concerns for an empire that had to service the needs of millions of people. Roads, bridges, and sewers had to be built, and an elaborate system of aqueducts was built to insure sufficient water supplies.

Whereas Greece had lavished its architectural attentions almost solely on temples, and Egypt on tombs, the Romans used their new construction methods to erect a great variety of buildings. The empire is filled with palaces, apartment buildings, warehouses, and courts of law, not to mention great entertainment centers like the public baths and theaters. One of the most famous of these is the Colosseum, where architecture and engineering combine to create a vast structure with a seating capacity of more than 50,000. The walls of the Colosseum are composed of an endless series of brick and concrete arches, faced with a veneer of stone. In this instance, the structure has been exposed, but in many others, such as the Pantheon, thin layers of stone were used to hide the arched honeycomb wall structures.

The Romans were a practical, military people. They united a diversified world through systematic conquest, and through the imposition of a unified body of laws and culture. They were less concerned with Greek theoretical ideals than with day-to-day functionalism. This

| center
US |
| centre
Brit. |
| color
US |
| colour
Brit. |
| theaters
US |
| theatres
Brit. |

19 History of Art

THE PANTHEON at Rome (right), completed in A.D. 125, resembles a Greek temple from the outside. But its vast interior space (left) was both a major feat of engineering and a revolutionary step in architecture.

ROMAN SCULPTURE:
The Emperor Augustus (left), c 20 B.C., shows the continuing appeal of idealized forms. The portrait of a Roman (right), c 80 B.C., shows the Roman love of realism.

civilization
US

civilisation
Brit.

armor
US

armour
Brit.

watercolors
US

watercolours
Brit.

is apparent not only in their usable architecture, but in their sculpture as well.

Sculpture. The portrait of a Roman admirably demonstrates Roman practicality. Unlike idealized Egyptian or Greek sculpture, which erased all traces of age and imperfection, early Roman portraits depended on exacting realism for their impact. The sculptor here includes every wrinkle and every sagging muscle in his aged sitter's face. No attempt has been made to improve him. It is a portrait of a specific hardworking man, austere and iron-willed.

The realism of early Roman portraiture is related to religious practices. When the leader of a Roman family died, a wax mask was made of his face. It was carried in the funeral procession and then stored in a domestic shrine for ancestor worship. A full collection of these images formed the ancient Roman's family tree. Gradually, stone portraits were substituted for the more perishable wax masks.

Even while the Romans created works of such compelling realism, they were still intrigued by idealized Greek sculpture. Their houses and public buildings were flooded with Greek imports or with Roman copies of them. (In fact, it is frequently only through Roman copies that we know of lost Greek originals.)

Rome had long felt culturally inferior to the brilliant Greek civilization. This

explains why it borrowed Hellenic forms so extensively. Throughout the second century B.C., the Roman love of Greek things blossomed, reaching its peak during the next hundred years or so, particularly under Augustus, the first Roman emperor. We can see the results in *Augustus of Prima Porta,* in which Augustus is portrayed as a barefoot Greek god.

Egyptian and Mesopotamian ideas of divine kingship had reached Rome by the first century B.C. It was easy, especially in the distant parts of the empire, to conceive of the great ruler, surrounded in glory, as a divine or superhuman being. As a result, emperors were worshiped as gods in their own lifetimes. Augustus, for example, claimed descent from Venus. Reference is made to this by the small cupid (Venus's child) next to his right leg.

Augustus's semidivine nature is further suggested by his idealized form. His heroic pose is a direct imitation of the famous Greek Doryphorus, and his face, while clearly a portrait, is beautified and ageless. It is a far cry from the ruthless realism of earlier Roman images.

Augustus of Prima Porta set the standard for the representation of the ideal Roman emperor. He is a god, a hero, and a great warrior whose military victories are recorded on his armor. These qualities, together with Augustus's confident and authoritative pose, made this statue an important piece of political propaganda.

If Greek influence can be found in Roman architecture and sculpture, then we might also expect to find it in painting. We should not be surprised to learn that the Romans copied Greek subjects and techniques, and perhaps even used Greek pattern books as their guides.

Painting. The most popular method of painting in early Rome was fresco, in which the artist applied watercolors to walls covered with wet plaster. A large number of frescoes have survived in the buried cities of Pompeii and Herculaneum.

When Mt. Vesuvius erupted in A.D. 79, these two cities were buried under volcanic ash. Silently they lay below the surface of the earth for more than 1,700 years before they were uncovered. Then, within the course of a few short years, the secrets of Roman life were revealed. We discovered Roman forms of work, play, and worship, as well as how Romans dressed and what they ate. But perhaps most significant was the new insight provided into the Roman house. Undisturbed for hundreds of years, these homes still had their walls covered with brilliantly painted frescoes.

These paintings covered a wide variety of subjects. There were mythological and religious scenes, convincing architectural compositions, and delightfully naturalistic landscapes with trees, flowers, and fluttering birds. There were also vivid still-life compositions where everyday objects were isolated for their decorative effects.

One example of a Roman still life is the *Peaches and Glass Jar* fresco from Herculaneum. Unlike Egyptian tomb paintings that show flat, almost abstract objects stacked on top of each other, Roman frescoes are illusionistic. That is, the painter used perspective, light, and shade to make the objects appear three-dimensional. Using delicate greens and warm browns, the artist captured the natural beauty of fresh fruit. By the careful handling of shadows and highlights, he was able to represent a transparent glass jar partially filled with water. The painting is a casual record of the contents of a Roman cupboard, but its mastery of shape, modeling, and light marks the highest point of Roman representational skills.

Throughout the second century, the Romans continued to make advances in the arts, and the boundaries of the empire stretched farther across the globe. But even at its height of power, the great Roman state was already showing signs of strain. The empire had grown fabulously and could no longer be governed effectively. Thousands of troops were needed to guard its far-flung borders, now under constant attack by northern barbarians. The cost of maintaining such a large army brought about currency devaluation and rampant inflation.

To make matters worse, there were constant civil wars. At one point, there were 18 different claimants to the imperial throne! In such turmoil, the Romans could have little faith in a "divine and unerring" emperor.

The situation was further compounded by the incredible growth of Christianity. The new religion promised hope and salvation when the empire could only offer suffering. It told of truth and justice, and a merciful and loving God. It offered life instead of death. The resultant response to Christianity was overwhelming, culminating in mass conversions.

The existence of a new religion usually posed no particular problem for the

PEACHES AND GLASS JAR: a Roman still life buried for 1,800 years by a volcano. The fresco appears three-dimensional due to the artist's use of perspective, light, and shade.

empire. There had always been dozens of different cults peacefully coexisting. Christianity, however, was the only one to offer a direct threat to the government, not only by its sheer numbers but by its denial of the emperor's divinity. The government was undermined by this religion's insistence on exclusive devotion to the one true God. Despite its ruthless persecution by the Romans, Christianity continued to thrive. Ultimately, it succeeded the crumbling empire as the guardian of civilization.

The Early Christians

After a war-torn century, the fragmented Roman Empire was reunited by Constantine in A.D. 312. This emperor made two decisions that changed the course of world history. In 313 he made Christianity the official religion of the Roman state, and in 330 he moved the capital of the empire from Rome to Constantinople (present-day Istanbul, Turkey).

Christians at Rome. During the periods of persecution before 313, Christians did not, and could not, have public buildings for worship. Their art was hidden, and was designed only for other Christians. Yet it showed a remarkable resemblance to other Roman art. Christians and pagans differed in their beliefs, but in other ways they were much the same. They spoke the same language, performed the same jobs, and lived next door to one another. Christians, like pagans, were Roman. The result of this common tradition can be seen in Early Christian art.

A Christian painter or sculptor naturally drew on the artistic conventions with which he had grown up. Inevitably, these were pagan. So the artists simply "Christianized" their themes while maintaining many of their older motifs. Thus, the sun-god Apollo was transformed into Christ, the light of the world. The grapes and vines of Bacchus, the pagan god of wine, were baptized for Christian use and made to represent the connectedness of the Christian community.

Notable examples of Christian transformations can be found in the catacombs. These caverns under the streets of Rome were primarily used as Christian cemeteries, but they also served as hiding places during periods of persecution. Their walls were carved out to receive the bodies of the faithful, many of whom had been martyred. It has been estimated that the catacombs of Rome alone accommodated more than 4 million dead.

Frequently, small chambers were included in the catacombs for use in the celebration of Christian rites. These were decorated with religious paintings. The Early Christian artist had a difficult task because he had to represent invisible things. He solved this problem by using symbols to portray intangibles like hope, faith, and the goodness of God. His paintings became a kind of coded message, representing the most profound beliefs of the Christian faith.

In comparison with Roman frescoes, Early Christian painting is perhaps a poor affair. Its figures are frequently flat and poorly drawn, and they seem stiff and lifeless. But the Early Christian artist was not concerned with things of this world. Here the simple and clear expression of Christian belief is more

important than the Roman ideal of realism. The Early Christian artist wanted to depict the permanence of life in the next world, and the triumph of the soul over the body. These same nonnaturalistic qualities can be found in all facets of Early Christian art, including mosaics, manuscript illumination, and sculpture.

Byzantine art. When Constantine moved the capital of the Roman Empire to Constantinople, Christian art was injected with a new burst of energy. Influences from the East now entered the Christian repertoire and gave rise to a new sumptuousness. Unhappily, most of the works from the early years of Christian Constantinople have perished, and we have to look to the sixth century, under the reign of Justinian, to gain some idea of its splendor. The new style came to be known as Byzantine, after Byzantium, the ancient name of Constantinople.

By far, the most important enterprise was the construction of Hagia Sophia, the Church of Divine Wisdom. Constantine had built the first church by this name, but it was destroyed by fire. It was replaced by Justinian in the sixth century by the biggest and most structurally complex building in the world. Nonetheless, it was built in the span of only five years. The still extant church covers an area larger than three football fields and it could easily accommodate a 15-story skyscraper under its lofty dome. But it was not size alone that distinguished Hagia Sophia.

Early Christian churches in the West (that is, Rome) were based on Roman assembly halls, or basilicas. (Architects consciously avoided modeling them on the Roman temples dedicated to pagan gods.) These were low, horizontal buildings with open timber roofs that had plain brick exteriors, but they had beautifully decorated interiors. This was an architectural reflection of the inner worth of man (that is, his soul) and the lesser importance of his body.

When the imperial court moved to Constantinople, the Eastern tradition of domical buildings fused with the Western form of these elongated basilicas, thus creating the domed basilica of Hagia Sophia. By a series of daring engineering feats, the architects Anthemius of Tralles and Ictinus of Miletus managed to flood the church with light. The effect was so dazzling that people in the sixth century described the dome as being suspended from heaven by a golden chain.

The question of how to decorate the new churches posed a serious problem because large sculpture was now all but taboo: the statues in a Christian church could too easily be confused with pagan idols by the newly converted communicants. A similar, but more slowly developing, controversy was to surround painting, although it really became manifest only during the great iconoclastic battle of the eighth century.

center
US

centre
Brit.

The West favored images as "books for the illiterate," while the East forbade their use as graven images. So great was the dispute that a schism developed between the two parts of the empire—a break that has never been totally repaired.

In the sixth century, however, the controversy had not yet fully developed and fabulous mosaic programs illuminated Byzantine church interiors. Tiny glass or stone cubes, set at angles in plaster-coated walls, picked up the reflections of light and bathed the churches in a heavenly glow.

Some of the finest mosaics of this period are found in Ravenna, Italy, which had been used at times by later emperors as the seat of the empire. The mosaic program at the church of San Vitale is a beautiful example. The small segment seen here portrays the emperor Justinian and his court. There is no question that a very skilled artist executed this panel; it was, after all, an imperial commission of the greatest significance. Yet we see none of the Greek mastery of human form; nor is the Roman concern with realism apparent. Instead, we find figures with wide-staring eyes whose stiffness and rigidity remind us of Egyptian art. In contrast to that ancient style, however, these figures are hidden by flat, but sumptuously patterned robes. There is no sense of bodily weight here, and the figures seem to float above the ground on their pointed toes.

All sense of movement is denied in favor of total clarity. All incidentals are omitted in favor of the clear expression of a solemn message: Justinian in the exact center is the only figure who is wearing a halo. He is a Christ symbol and is surrounded by twelve soldiers and clerics (counterparts to the twelve apostles).

This mosaic panel has a companion piece that shows the empress Theodora with her ladies in waiting. Her dress embroidered with an image of the Three Magi, Theodora is cast in the role of the Blessed Mother. Both Justinian's and Theodora's panels are located in the choir of San Vitale, in the most sacred part of the church. The message is clear: the emperor and empress symbolize Christ and his mother; they are the vicars of God on Earth. Art has fused in the double service of the church and state, blending political and spiritual authority.

The Middle Ages

While Byzantine art flourished in the East, the Western empire collapsed under successive barbarian invasions. Vandals, Goths, and Huns, as well as Saxons, Danes, and Vikings, swarmed down from the east and the north, destroying Roman law and order, and thereby initiating the so-called Dark Ages.

For centuries this unflattering term was used to describe the period from about A.D. 500 through A.D. 900 (although sometimes it was used to describe a full 1,000 years from 400 to 1400). This period was thought to be a bleak time, a void between the brilliant cultural achievements of the Roman Empire and the revival of learning and art in Europe. Most often, the period from about 900 to 1300 is called the Middle Ages, or the medieval period, the time that separates modern Europeans from the barbarian tribes from which they originated.

More recently, we have come to understand that the Dark Ages seem dark partly because of our own ignorance. The barbarian tribes were illiterate, but they were hardly lacking in skill or creative power. We have also come to see that there is no clear division between the "Dark" and "Middle" ages. For convenience, we will consider the period from about 400 to 1300 the Middle Ages.

Early Medieval Art

Because the early invaders of Europe were wandering peoples, their art concentrated on small, easily portable objects such as weapons, harnesses, belt buckles, and jewelry. Skilled metalworkers ornamented these pieces with complicated patterns of interwoven lines and twisted animal bodies. One of their favorite techniques was cloisonné, in which strips of gold were soldered to a metal background. The spaces in between the upraised strips were filled with precious gems or enamel to produce highly colored and densely ornamented abstract designs.

Another early medieval style is called interlace. It may have come from Asia, or it may have arisen naturally from barbarian experience with woven leather thongs. Whatever its source, interlace resembles the animal style of ancient Mesopotamia and the art of the nomads of central Asia during the Early Christian era. Interlace was used to produce highly charged decorative pieces, such as snarling animal heads covered with vigorous patterns of interwoven lines. The ultimate significance of these fierce beasts leaves us puzzled; but there is some suggestion that they were used to frighten demons away. Thus, art was employed in the service of magic, just as it had been by hungry cave dwellers and

Egyptians seeking eternal life.

The interlaced animal style was put to new use in Ireland. As early as the sixth century, Christian monks had settled this land and established monasteries throughout the British Isles. These became vibrant centers of learning. When the rest of Europe was ravaged by wandering tribes, these monasteries were left as the sole guardians of civilization. Ireland escaped attack because of its isolation from the continent.

Under the combined influence of Saxon England and Celtic Ireland, barbarian interlace was Christianized for the decoration of Bibles and church manuscripts. The *Lindisfarne Gospel* is one of the most sumptuous of these early books.

The page shown here fully illustrates the pulsating new use of interlace. Dense coils in red, blue, green, and gold are compressed within a rigid geometric frame, and are overlaid by the symbol of the cross. These formal borders contrast markedly with the throbbing lacelike maze and emphasize its rhythmic motion. Fantastic beasts curl back on themselves and devour neighboring serpents, changing size and color like elastic chameleons. The intricacy of the pattern almost defies us to follow a line from beginning to end as it tirelessly threads its way through the woven net. But complexity is not confusion. The patterns are strictly controlled by symmetry, each part corresponding to the others, and all combining to form a harmonious balance of line, shape, and color.

This intricate style was also used to portray men in other contemporary manuscripts. The results were curiously knotted bodies, stiff and abstract, with all sense of human form hidden under a riot of interwoven ribbons. The barbarian craftsman, so accustomed to nonrepresentational jewelry designs, had little practice in the depiction of people. His life and art were in every way different from Roman order and realism.

colored
US

coloured
Brit.

civilization
US

civilisation
Brit.

emphasize
US

emphasise
Brit.

19 History of Art

THE LINDIS-FARNE GOSPEL is decorated with elaborate abstract patterns, revealing the artistic talent of the "uncivilized" Celts and Saxons, c 700.

Carolingian Art

centers
US

centres
Brit.

The Dark Ages seemed to come to an end on Christmas Day, A.D. 800, when Pope Leo III placed a crown on the head of Charlemagne (Charles the Great) and proclaimed him emperor of the Holy Roman Empire. Charlemagne had been King of the Franks since 768, and had created the empire through war and diplomacy. It united modern France, Germany, the Netherlands, much of central Europe, and parts of Spain and Italy. Under a dual allegiance to the secular power of the emperor and the spiritual leadership of the Pope, it revived and Christianized the concept of the Roman Empire. The empire survived, at least in name, for just over 1,000 years. During much of that time it was "neither holy, nor Roman, nor an empire," and it soon became just one of many competing European powers. But during the life of Charlemagne, it brought a great change to Europe.

Charlemagne was a lover of learning, and during his reign he tried to revive the splendors of ancient Rome. His biographer said that he transformed a dark and barbarous kingdom into one radiant with the blaze of knowledge. Charlemagne saw himself as the successor to the ancient Caesars and he invited all the best minds and finest artists to join his court in the German city of Aachen (near the modern border between West Germany, Belgium, and the Netherlands).

Charlemagne himself could not write, but he could speak Latin and understand Greek, and he enjoyed learned discussions with the scholars he summoned to court. He instituted great monastic schools and encouraged the production of church manuscripts and books of psalms, all beautifully illustrated. Some of these were painted in realistic classical style while others showed the vibrant influence of Irish ornament. To protect these expensive parchment books, craftsmen created sumptuous gold and ivory covers, frequently adorning them with precious gems.

Of all his projects, the emperor was perhaps most interested in correcting the text of the Bible. For centuries it had been copied by ignorant scribes whose mistakes had corrupted the original text. The project was directed by the brilliant monk from England, Alcuin of York. Alcuin reformed the shape of the letters of the alphabet, and the results of his work can be seen on this page. Our own clear and readable script is a direct descendant of his improvements.

In architecture as in sculpture, Charlemagne looked to the imperial past. He wanted to combine the solidity and monumentality of ancient Roman buildings with the splendor of Byzantium. The masterpiece of the period is his palace chapel, Aix-la-Chapelle. Its debt to the Byzantine style of Ravenna is unmistakable. Charlemagne imported iron railings and marble from Ravenna, and he borrowed the plan of its church of San Vitale. The end result, however, could never be confused with its Byzantine model.

Densely forested Germany had always built with timber; therefore, Charlemagne's craftsmen were not totally prepared to construct a great stone building. This is clearly seen in Aix-la-Chapelle, where the fine spatial qualities of Eastern architecture were lost to a heavy-handed manipulation of stone. Gone are the delicacy and intricacy of fluid interiors, omitted are the walls of glittering mosaics. The entire composition has been simplified and restated in stiff geometric terms. But if the sophistication of Byzantine architecture was absent, Charlemagne's chapel was still a dignified monument. It established a strong tradition of stone construction in northern Europe that was carried on for a thousand years.

Ottonian Art

When Charlemagne died in 814, his dream of a unified imperial culture died with him. His successors divided the kingdom among themselves only to have it crumble under the invasions of the Vikings, Magyars, and Saracens. Once again Europe was plunged into a dark age, perhaps more so than ever before. A glimmer of light came only in the tenth century, with the emergence of the kings of Saxony, the most extraordinary of whom was Otto I (ruled 936–973).

Determined to restore imperial traditions, Otto began a new Golden Age. Great stone churches were built on Early Christian and Carolingian models, and illuminated manuscripts were painted with new confidence and expressive power.

Shortly before the year 1000, Bishop Bernward, a distinguished patron of the arts, supported the building of a church at Hildesheim in northern Germany. In 1001 he went to Rome and gained firsthand knowledge both of classical and Christian antiquities. He may well have seen and studied the great doors of the Pantheon and of the church of Santa Sabina. Upon his return to Germany, he commissioned two bronze doors for his church.

Each of these 15-foot doors was cast in a single plate, the first of their kind since ancient Rome. Fearing confusion with pagan idols, Christian sculpture had previously been restricted to small works in metal or ivory. The bold monumentality of the bishop's doors broke with this tradition and looked forward to a time when large-scale sculpture would be reintroduced.

The bronze panel shown here is one of 16 Biblical scenes included on the doors. Having eaten of the forbidden fruit, Adam and Eve are reproached by the angry Lord. With the force of his entire body, God jabs His accusing finger at Adam, who, crouching and hiding his nakedness, points to Eve. She in turn passes the blame to the lowly serpent that snarls back at her as it cowers under the fateful tree. The drama of guilt and the origin of evil is staged theatrically against a blank ground. Gestures are exaggerated, giving the scene an air of intense pantomime. The aim of the artist was to depict the episode as clearly and as forcefully as possible. Nothing is included to distract the viewer. So strong is the emotional impact that one tends to overlook the fact that the figures are crudely ill-proportioned. The sculptor was more concerned with the portrayal of faith

AIX-LA-CHAPELLE, the palace chapel of Charlemagne, was built in 810 near the modern city of Aachen, Germany.

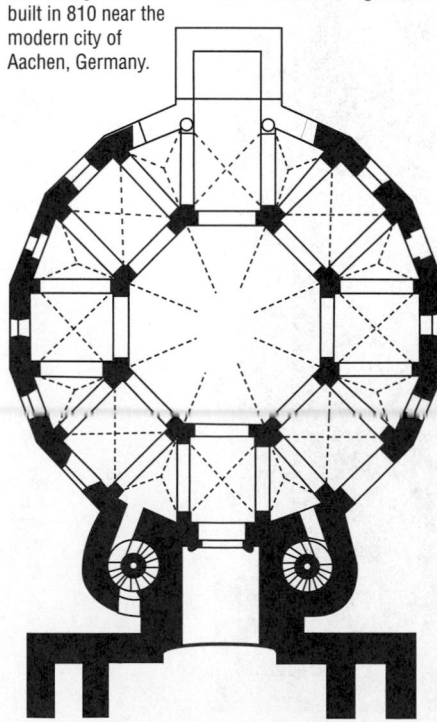

and divine justice than he was with convincing likenesses. In this, the medieval artist was distinct from most who had gone before. The Egyptians had portrayed things as they *knew* them to be, the Greeks as they *wished* them, and the Romans as they *saw* them. The medieval artist, on the contrary, depicted things as he *felt* them.

By about 1050, the rule of the Holy Roman Emperor had been limited to Germany alone. No monarch could claim universal control of the rapidly changing continent. Cities were growing, commerce was booming, and a new merchant class had arisen. Lands beyond the German borders were therefore governed by feudal lords who could deal with local requirements more effectively. It was a time when Europe as we know it began to take shape.

Romanesque Art

Feudalism was a set of complex relationships among the lord, his vassals, and peasants. In its simplest form, the lord offered protection and land in return for loyalty and agricultural and military service. Each of the many feudal kingdoms had its own problems and interests, and, as a result, each developed independently. The only true unifying force was the church. Feudal lords pledged allegiance to the church hierarchy (the bishops and the pope), and a vast international network of monasteries further unified the various regions and kingdoms. These religious communities were centers of agriculture, industry, and learning. In fact, they offered virtually the only means available for receiving an education.

Cluny. The grandest of all monasteries was the Benedictine Abbey of Cluny, from which important church reforms were initiated in the 900s. Its magnificence was such that a twelfth-century chronicler described it as "shining on earth like a second sun." Founded in the sixth century, the Benedictine Order prospered and reached its peak around 1157, when it could count over 1,200 houses from Scotland in the north and Portugal in the south to Jerusalem in the east.

Cluny's tremendous growth was directly related to the medieval preoccupation—even obsession—with eternal salvation. Crusades and pilgrimages were seen as the most effective means of insuring it. People travelled hundreds and sometimes thousands of difficult miles to visit the most sacred shrines in Christendom. With this they satisfied their desire for personal sacrifice. They believed they would be absolved of their sins as a result.

Pilgrimage churches. The most popular pilgrimage centers were Christ's tomb in Jerusalem, that of St. Peter in Rome, and Santiago da Compostela (the church of St. James the Apostle), located in the westernmost part of Spain (called "Finistera" or land's end).

Four major overland routes to Santiago da Compostela sprawled across France, merging near the Spanish border. These roads were dotted with scores of lesser churches, each possessing its own venerable relics. Roughly every 20 miles (the length of an average day's journey), there was a hospice or priory that offered food, lodging, and medical and spiritual attention to the weary pilgrim. In a sense, these way stations were the medieval Howard Johnsons along the highway.

The religious structures that developed along these routes are appropriately called "pilgrimage churches." Despite local differences in building materials, towers, and ultimate size, they share a remarkable uniformity. Their design was a calculated response to the need to accomodate large numbers of pilgrims. Their crisp logic is apparent in the plan of St. Sernin, which, like all pilgrimage churches, is characterized by extreme regularity.

The basic shape is a bold cross with a long nave (central vessel) intersected by transepts or arms. The round head or apse is the most sacred part of the church. For symbolic reasons, it almost always faces east (Christ was born in the East, the sun rises in the East, and Christ is the light of the world). Attached to the apse and the eastern sides of the transepts are a series of small chapels that hold additional relics,

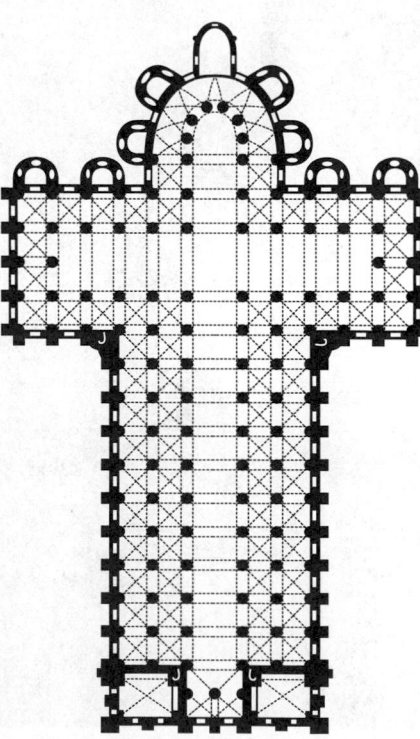

THE EXPULSION OF ADAM AND EVE, cast in bronze for the church doors of St. Michael's, Hildesheim, Germany, c 1000, tells the Biblical story with great emotional force.

ST. SERNIN, a pilgrimage church at Toulouse, France, c 1100, is built in the shape of a cross.

emphasize
US

emphasise
Brit.

colored
US

coloured
Brit.

THE LAST JUDGMENT
was created by the sculptor Giselbertus, c 1130, over the doors of the cathedral at Autun, France. The creation is dominated by the stylized Christ at center.

the central or axial one being elongated to emphasize its greater importance. The whole is surrounded by side aisles (distinguished by dotted Xs on the plan) through which pilgrims could walk without disturbing the services being held at the high altar in the apse.

The logic of the plan is carried even further in the modular use of square bays. Every portion of the church is based on a square of set size. For example, each side aisle (there are two on either side of the nave) is made up of square bays or units. One nave bay equals two of these squares, and four of them would make up the crossing (the place where the arms of the cross intersect). The result is that the entire church is interrelated. Not only did this lead to harmony and balance in design, but it offered a very practical method of construction at a time when there were no standardized yardsticks.

The length of a foot might be twelve inches in Paris, but only ten inches in another part of France. We can well imagine what disastrous consequences this could have for architecture! If, for instance, two different masons were told to build a wall 30 feet long, one would be 360 inches while the other was only 300 inches. By using a modular bay system, the medieval master mason (architect) avoided the whole problem. After determining the size of his square, he could simply tell each of two masons to build a wall ten modules long. Working from the same basic square, the two masons would produce the exact same wall.

This practical means of modular construction was to have a long and rich history. In fact, we still use a similar method in erecting modern skyscrapers with prefabricated materials cut to standard or modular lengths.

Two major problems confronted church architects in the eleventh century: how to fireproof structures whose open timber roofs were often set aflame by candles, and how to give them a dignity suitable to a house of God. Both solutions were found in the rediscovery of stone vaulting, the secrets of which had been lost during the Dark Ages. Lofty barrel vaults were now built above tremendously thick walls. The sheer weight of these supports insured vault stability but reduced the size of windows, making the churches very dark. The answer to the lighting problem was only found later in technological developments accompanying the Gothic style.

The interior of a pilgrimage church is as regular as its plan, with vertical bays marching down the length of the building in orderly fashion. The result is so compelling and so unified that it clearly distinguishes the type from earlier, more helter-skelter structures. St. Sernin and other pilgrimage churches of the eleventh century are worthy successors of Roman architecture. For this reason, this massive style is called Romanesque.

Sculpture. The development of architecture went hand in hand with the revival of sculpture. It was only natural

to want to beautify the new churches. On the one hand there were movable objects and church furniture; on the other there were large-scale stone sculptures. The purpose of these pieces, however, was not merely ornamental. In each case, decoration had the specific function of expressing Christian beliefs. It was used as a teaching tool by the church. Bronze baptismal fonts, for example, showed scenes of Christ's baptism; gold and ivory book covers depicted the authors of the four Gospels or Christ enthroned. But it was with architectural sculpture that the Romanesque had its greatest development.

Initially, architectural sculpture was confined to column capitals. Among their leaves were carved monsters, demons, and other fantastic creatures. The profound and unquestioning faith of medieval men led them to believe in the existence of such unlikely beasts and to fear them as agents of the devil. Biblical scenes were carved on other capitals to remind worshipers of miracles and other hopeful events in Christian history.

By the late eleventh century, architectural sculpture was concentrating on church portals, particularly on the tympanum (the semicircular panel above the door). No one who entered could miss the dramatic religious scenes carved above his head.

Of all themes, the Last Judgment was the most popular. Its visionary qualities gave full license to the fertile imaginations of Romanesque sculptors, as can be seen in the church of Autun. Surrounded by an almond-shaped mandorla (body halo), a flat and elongated Christ presides over the awesome process. In the lintel below, terror-stricken souls answer the summons of trumpet-blowing angels and rise from their graves to hear their final judgement. On Christ's right, calm angels lead the saved to Heaven, but on his left, hideous demons tilt the fateful scales of the damned. Insect-like devils force weeping souls into the mouth of Hell, while one unhappy figure is actually plucked from Earth by giant hands. The sculptor's skillful organization and balance of forms increase the impact of this frightful scene. Autun's tympanum was created and signed by Giselbertus, one of the earliest known medieval sculptors.

Gothic Art

The decoration of church tympanums and capitals is only one example of the growing integration of medieval architecture and sculpture. This was to reach its greatest height in the Gothic cathedrals of the twelfth and thirteenth centuries.

These were times of great change for the Middle Ages. Pilgrimages and crusades had introduced new ideas into the West and fostered the growth of a large merchant class. Interest in education became more pronounced, universities were established, and cities

(as opposed to monasteries) became the focus of medieval life. Amid this bustling activity Gothic cathedrals emerged.

Compared with Romanesque architecture, the Gothic style differs in almost every respect. Where Romanesque churches force us to our knees by their tremendous weight, Gothic buildings encourage our spirits to soar upward by their light and airy frameworks.

The Gothic style was the result both of technical developments and of a new religious and artistic vision. They first came together in Abbot Suger's Parisian church of Saint Denis (1144), and thereafter quickly spread throughout France, into England, Germany, Spain, and even reluctant Italy.

Chartres. One of the purest early Gothic buildings in France is the Cathedral of Notre Dame at Chartres. It has an enormous vertical interior, planned from the inside out. Its walls have been reduced to thin curtains pierced by tall arcades and frighteningly large windows.

Unlike Romanesque churches, Gothic cathedrals are characterized by their pointed arches. These can be seen at Chartres in the ground floor, second-story arcade, high (clerestory) windows, and even in the vaults. Pointed arches are more versatile than round arches because their height can be adjusted and they can span variable distances. (The principle is somewhat similar to opening a pair of scissors and extending its blades to any desirable distance.) Round arches, on the other hand, are inflexible: they are always half as high as they are wide. If, for example, an architect tried to vault a rectangular bay with round arches, the differing length and width of the bay would result in arches of conflicting heights. However, by using pointed arches and the "scissors principle," the architect would be able to bring all arches up to the same level and vault the nave uniformly.

Chartres' vaults tower 118 feet above the ground, pressing down and out with incredible force. But the cathedral's walls are little more than stone lattices opened by vast window expanses. How could they possibly withstand such fabulous lateral pressure? The answer lies in flying buttresses, huge piers surmounted by arches that brace the wall from the outside and channel the vault thrusts safely to the ground. Gothic interiors were thus transformed into glorious "religious greenhouses," ablaze with the mysterious colored glow of huge stained glass windows.

Ste. Chapelle. This achievement is seen most dramatically in Ste. Chapelle, the small two-story chapel that St. Louis built to house Christ's Crown of Thorns. The supporting structure has been reduced to 14 extremely slender piers between vast windows, measuring roughly 49 feet by 15 feet each.

These glazed panels (which were then the largest ever made) form a veritable illustrated Bible with thousands of

CHARTRES, built c 1150, used the flying buttress (right) to eliminate heavy wall supports and allow great windows, giving its interior a new kind of light and grace.

STE. CHAPELLE in Paris, c 1250, shows the inspired combination of graceful Gothic architecture and the perfection of stained glass for the giant windows.

**GOTHIC
SCULPTURE:**
early figures on the
exterior of the
Chartres cathedral
(1150) are stiff and
stylized compared
with those on the
cathedral at Reims
(c 1230), which show
two scenes from
the life of Mary, the
annunciation by the
angel, at left, and her
visit with Elizabeth.

figures in 1,134 different scenes from the Old and New Testaments. The jewel-like interior sparkles as the sun radiates through its multicolored stained glass.

So completely were the weight-bearing walls of Ste. Chapelle's dissolved that the architect took an unusual precaution: he stretched two iron link chains around the church, binding it against the collapse of its walls.

Gothic ideals of light and linearity were totally realized in Ste. Chapelle. Later 13th century architects strove for similar achievements, extending the skeletal principle to its very limits in their quest for skyscraping buildings. Boldly they challenged the force of gravity with vaults of ever-increasing height: 80 feet at Laon, 118 feet at Chartres, 123 feet at Reims, and 144 feet at Amiens. In 1272 they delivered the terrifying final statement of Gothic height in the awesome 156-foot vaults of Beauvais. Twelve years later, the vaults collapsed.

The disaster of Beauvais was the end of Gothic development. New churches were fewer and more modestly sized. The Gothic building boom ended.

Sculpture. The beauty of Gothic architecture depends on the harmonious balance of parts. This includes sculpture, for in the 12th and 13th centuries it was not applied to a wall, it was integrally related to the surrounding masonry.

As in Romanesque churches, sculpture was still concentrated around the portals. But now the field was extended to include complex iconographic programs that stretched over much of the exterior of the cathedral. Chartres, for example, has over 2,000 carved figures distributed among its major entrances in the west and its transept portals in the south and north.

Initially, sculpture had been subservient to its bold architectural setting. Elongated early Gothic figures, like the jamb statues around Chartres's western doors, were shaped by the tall colonettes to which they were attached. The figures are stiff and cylindrical. At first glance, they may even seem to belong more to the building than to sculpture proper. But even while these Old Testament kings and queens are encased in their architectural straitjackets, they have a life of their own. Unlike Romanesque sculpture, which was cut back into the wall, these early Gothic figures stand out in front of it. They are treated three-dimensionally, with a spatial depth new to medieval sculpture. Draperies are still handled as inscribed lines, but now they have a direct correspondence to the bodies underneath. For example, the folds fall from waists and shoulders. This, too, is a development over the purely linear patterns of earlier medieval art. Perhaps most significant, however, is the incipient naturalism of the faces at Chartres. The abstract features of Romanesque masks have been softened by a faint human quality.

This naturalistic tendency is fully matured in the jamb statues of Reims, created 75 years later. These statues reveal the astonishing influence of classical sculpture. Inspired by antiquity, the artist replaced the rigid verticality of columnar figures with convincing life-sized statues. He used the heavy folds of realistic drapery to reveal the bodies underneath. The figures turn easily toward one another, almost freed from architectural restraints. Now, after hundreds of years, people were once again thought worthy of critical artistic attention. In *The Visitation,* shown here, the two women are clearly distinguished by their ages and personalities. Mary is the youthful virgin, the ideal of feminine beauty. Pregnant with Christ, she is visited by her aged and careworn cousin, Elizabeth, soon to be the mother of John the Baptist.

Nature had been reinstated in Christian art. In the following centuries, portraits of recognizable individuals would emerge. Sculpture would break its last ties with architecture to become fully freestanding for the first time since the Roman Empire.

The Renaissance

Late Gothic naturalism began a process that, in the following centuries, was to culminate in a new kind of art. While artists in Northern Europe redirected their talents to stained glass windows (almost the only broad surfaces left in the Gothic cathedral), important changes were taking place in Italy.

As heirs to the Roman Empire and Early Christian basilicas, the states of the Italian peninsula were less devoted to the Gothic cathedral, and so had not turned their attention to stained glass. The naturalism of late Gothic times was a great influence, but it showed itself in a lively tradition of mosaic and fresco wall decoration inherited from the Byzantine culture to the east. In the 1200s, a new wave of Eastern influence washed over Italy, merging with late Gothic naturalism. This marriage of East and West set off the first artistic revolution of the new era. We have come to know this revolution as the Renaissance.

The Early Years

The leader of the revolution was a painter named Giotto.

Giotto. Shortly after 1305 Giotto began work on the small Arena Chapel in Padua. Several years later, its walls were covered with frescoes depicting the life of Christ. The *Lamentation* on this page is part of Giotto's work.

The actual dimensions of the painted figures are little more than half life size, yet they seem monumental. Giotto used large and simple forms to give his boulderlike humans a tremendous sense of weight. Like the creator of Bishop Bernward's bronze doors, Giotto avoided distracting incidentals; he focuses all attention on the tragedy of Christ's death. But unlike the Ottonian craftsman who confined his sticklike figures to an airless foreground, Giotto orchestrated his scene like a virtuoso stage director. He cast his characters so that they actually *occupy* space. Two seated figures dominate the foreground. Behind them Mary embraces her dead son. Behind Mary and her son cluster grieving mourners. A background of rocky hills and expansive sky acts as a great theater curtain and limits spatial depth to the middle- and foreground. For the first time since antiquity, the two-dimensional painted surface was treated like an open window through which we can look at the world. Instead of flat patterns on a flat plane, we are encouraged to see the drama as it might actually occur in space. And what drama it is!

When Giotto planned the frescoes, he considered some fundamental questions about man. How does he move? How does he relate to other people? How would he react to the death of his Savior? With these and similar questions, Giotto breathed a new naturalism into painting and created what are perhaps the first "modern" works of art.

Giotto made his native city of Florence a center of artistic activity. But the city of Siena made important contributions too. Its favorite son, Duccio, introduced a new refinement and elegance into painting, while his compatriot, Simone Martini, developed linear expression. Also from Siena were the Lorenzetti Brothers, who brought spatial illusion to a level previously thought to be impossible.

The International Style. For the better part of the 1300s, the papacy was divided. One line of popes lived at Avignon in southern France. At Avignon Italian and French styles of art met and blended, creating the so-called International Style. This type of painting concentrated on the glamour of courtly life, with its use of brightly colored costumes and richly decorated surfaces to convey the splendors of chivalry.

One of its finest productions was the *Très Riches Heures* of the Duke of Berry, a sumptuous prayer book illustrated by the Limbourg Brothers with the labors of the twelve months. Some of these miniatures depicted the genteel life of the aristocracy, while others were dedicated to the less fortunate lot of the peasants.

Although calendar paintings had been popular throughout the Middle Ages, the Limbourgs now used their incomparable powers of observation to produce paintings of startling reality. In fact, they studied nature so closely that they even painted shadows. This had not been done since antiquity. Their naturalistic view of the world is apparent in their *February* scene.

The top of the page (not shown here) holds the astrological chart of the month and its zodiac signs (Aquarius and Pisces).

theater
US

theatre
Brit.

center
US

centre
Brit.

colored
US

coloured
Brit.

labors
US

labours
Brit.

19 History of Art

EARLY RENAISSANCE: the *Lamentation* by Giotto, c 1305, and the *February* scene by the Limbourg Brothers, c 1415, show two important Renaissance characteristics: a new interest in drama and a new interest in portraying everyday happenings.

ST. FRANCIS BREAKS WITH HIS FATHER by Giotto has the artist's distinguishing larger-than-life-figures.

In the center is the chariot of the sun making its rounds. Below, a delightful winter scene presents one of Europe's earliest snowscapes. Its freezing temperatures are warmed by a wealth of narrative detail. Inside a small house (one wall of which has been omitted for our convenience) chilled peasants cluster around a fire. Their companion in the barnyard breathes on her frostbitten hands while sheep

THE PAZZI CHAPEL, designed by Brunelleschi, c 1440, reflects a break with earlier church design.

huddle in the fold and hungry birds scratch for food. Beyond the wicker fence one man chops trees for firewood as another drives a mule to the distant town.

The scene seems to provide an almost encyclopedic record of winter: snowy fields, leafless trees, smoke spiraling from the chimney, and even the steam of human breath lingering in crisp February air. With their calendar paintings the Limbourgs made a brilliant advance toward the artistic conquest of atmosphere. From now on artists would abandon the medieval practice of copying pattern books; they would study nature firsthand.

By extending traditional subject matter to include everyday events, the Limbourgs also broke philosophically with medieval paintings. Instead of telling sacred stories, they were concentrating on the realistic depiction of ordinary events. The very fact that paintings of this genre were included in a prayer book signals a new time. During the next century, religious and secular themes would blend inseparably. The Middle Ages had ended and the Renaissance had begun.

The new spirit. By 1400, the Renaissance was fully launched in Italy and Southern France. It was a complex phenomenon, and it affected virtually every aspect of human activity. The ineffective feudal system of the Middle Ages gave way to the modern state and to a cash economy. It was an age of discovery. During the new century, navigators would greatly expand the concept of Earth's size and complexity. For the first time since the pre-Christian era, science was uncovering new secrets. Copernicus advanced his revolutionary theory that Earth revolved around the sun. Advances in optics led to new explorations of the stars through the telescope. It was a time of almost limitless possibility, encouraged by technological advances in navigation, transportation, metallurgy, and warfare. But even more important, the Renaissance was a time of profound change in human attitudes.

Medieval man was in search of supernatural truths. He lived a fretful life constantly threatened by the Devil and plagued by worldly temptations. In the 1200s, however, St. Francis preached the goodness of God and the beauty of His earthly creations. Such teachings invited man to enjoy life in this world. It was not a rejection of Christian devotion, but a reinterpretation of it. Relieved from guilt and freed from church domination, Renaissance man began to think for himself. He looked to antiquity as the model of a more human existence. And he came to see the arts and literature as celebrations of man's intellect, achievement, and physical beauty.

In one way the Renaissance was an attempt to revive the classical age in all its glory. But in another way, the men of the Renaissance sought to produce a new

and original classical age. Men sought not just a restoration of old ways, but a rebirth—a renaissance. It was during the 1400s that the preceding centuries came to be called the Middle Ages.

The School of Florence

The spirit of the new classical age was nowhere more intense than in Florence, the illustrious home of Giotto. In the late 1200s this city had begun an enormous Gothic cathedral that was to have a great dome over its 140-foot crossing. But for a century it had remained incomplete because no one knew how to build a dome of such fabulous proportions.

Brunelleschi. Then Brunelleschi appeared on the scene. This genius was originally a goldsmith. He turned to architecture after losing a design competition in 1401 for the doors of the cathedral's baptistry. Shortly afterward, he visited Rome and was awestruck by the beauty and power of ancient ruins. He studied them closely and made hundreds of accurately measured drawings. The result of Brunelleschi's Roman visit was a new understanding of ancient architecture. When he returned to Florence, he began plans for the cathedral's dome. Within 20 years, the immense project was complete. Brunelleschi had transformed a white elephant into Florence's most celebrated landmark.

The cathedral's dome is known throughout the world as a brilliant example of Brunelleschi's engineering abilities. His powers as an architect are best seen in the chapel he built for the Pazzi family. Its small size and relatively simple structure freed Brunelleschi from complex building problems and allowed him to concentrate on the design.

His break with the Gothic is now complete. A simple stone box has replaced the soaring verticals and huge windows of the Gothic church. Great round arches, medallions, and stone pilasters (thin flat columns attached to the wall) show classical influence, but these elements are used in a new way to achieve a grace and lightness foreign to antiquity. Brunelleschi carefully broke the cool white walls into precisely defined segments, and then crowned the central space with a dome. He was the first great Renaissance architect, favoring crisp geometric clarity over Gothic complexity, and transforming the heavy classical style.

Brunelleschi's interest in geometry also led him to a momentous discovery: perspective, a system of mathematical laws that determine the diminishing size of objects as they recede farther back into space. This discovery radically altered the entire future of painting.

Masaccio. The discovery of perspective was quickly appreciated by Masaccio, the second (and the youngest) of the three great geniuses of the Early Renaissance. Masaccio grew up in the International Style. But rather than conform to its sumptuously detailed surfaces and brightly colored costumes, Masaccio brought about a revolution. He died prematurely, but in the six short years of his working life, Masaccio contributed more to art than most painters do in 40.

His last painting was the *Holy Trinity* in the church of Santa Maria Novella. By using perspective, Masaccio made the flat wall appear as if it opened into a square chapel of the kind that Brunelleschi might have built. He placed the viewpoint at the level of the viewer's eye as he stands before the fresco (about five feet from the floor) so that the viewer looks up and into the great coffered vault. The illusion is so convincing that modern scholars have been able to calculate the dimensions of the room as if it actually existed. When the painting was unveiled, it created a tremendous stir in Florence. Nothing like it had ever been created before, not even by the ancients.

The Florentines must have also been surprised by the massive figures that inhabit the chapel. Masaccio's people are not the graceful and elegant forms of the still popular International Style; they have a solidity and weight that recall the monumental work of Giotto. Masaccio uses light and shadow to model his figures, especially Christ's powerful body. Each of the figures seems to be a three-dimensional statue that could actually be touched; this adds to the illusion of spatial depth. The whole composition is based on a human pyramid, with God the Father at the top and the kneeling patrons at the bottom. All is quiet and solemn; Mary makes the only movement as she stares at the viewer and points to her crucified son.

Masaccio's *Holy Trinity* was a total statement of Early Renaissance ideals. It used perspective, light, and shadow, and a great architectural framework to portray essential Christian beliefs with a new and compelling realism.

When Masaccio died, he left no students behind. His older contemporaries developed painting in slightly different directions. Uccello and Piero della Francesca were intrigued with perspective and used it as an end in itself, creating works of austere geometric clarity. Fra Angelico, however, remained conservative. He stayed closer to the International Style and produced religious paintings of unparalleled charm and decorative effect.

Another important painter was Fra Filippo Lippi. Like Fra Angelico, he was a Dominican monk, but he shared none of Fra Angelico's piety. He was quite unsuited to religious life and was constantly in trouble, for everything from forgery to the abduction of an attractive nun (who later bore him a son). Despite his troubled life, Fra Filippo Lippi was still able to make major contributions to painting. He combined a heightened color sense with a brilliant use of line in his intensely sensuous religious paintings. Other artists, like Domenico Veneziano and Andrea Castagno, further explored the wonders of color, light, and sculptural modeling.

Donatello. The 1400s were a period of experiment in all the arts. In sculpture, the greatest personality was Donatello, who, with Brunelleschi and Masaccio, completes the Early Renaissance trio of outstanding geniuses. As a youth, Donatello was apprenticed to a stonecutter. By the age of 20 he was revered as the finest sculptor in Florence and one of the best in all of Italy. What gave Donatello this distinction? The answer is found in the authority, flexibility, and profound understanding of human nature that characterize his work.

Most sculptors of the time specialized in particular types of commissions. Some concentrated on portraits, others on relief panels, and still others on large freestanding statues. Donatello did them all. He worked in bronze, marble, and wood in both large and small scale, and he was equally at ease portraying the real, the ideal, and the spiritual. He carved moving Biblical scenes, innocent children, austere soldiers, saints, sinners, and despots. Never before had the variety of human experience been so fully treated by a single artist.

A solitary example will illustrate Donatello's brilliance. In the early 1430s he visited Rome and fell under the spell of antique sculpture. When he returned to Florence, he created the bronze statue *David* for the powerful Medici family. The sinuous David differed markedly from Donatello's earlier, more powerful work. It shows the influence of Hellenistic sculptors like Praxiteles (whom Donatello could have known through Roman copies). With this one work the classical ideal was reborn. It was the first time that this Biblical hero had been portrayed nude. Even more important, it was the first free-standing nude since antiquity. For a thousand years nakedness had been considered indecent. Only rarely was it permitted, and even then it was only as a necessary illustration to a Biblical or moral theme, as in the story of Adam and Eve. Donatello revolted, and thus began the impassioned Renaissance quest for physical beauty.

Holding a sword in his right hand and a stone in his left, David pokes at Goliath's severed head with his foot. His graceful adolescent body rests in a classical contrapposto stance that recalls the calm of Greek gods and athletes. But Donatello has replaced classical calm with a penetrating psychological drama. The brim of David's hat shadows his moody face as he casts his eyes downward. In the moments after victory he has realized his strength, ability, and personal beauty. It is a moment of self-awareness after a millennium of sleep.

The last phase of Donatello's career saw a turning away from the beautiful to

NEW REALISM was brought to painting by Masaccio's use of perspective in the *Holy Trinity* (1425) and to sculpture by Donatello's natural yet beautiful *David* (1432).

19 History of Art

colored
US

coloured
Brit.

realized
US

realised
Brit.

THE PALAZZO RUCELLAI
in Florence (1457) shows Alberti's use of classic decoration: arches and pilasters inscribed on a flat wall.

center
US

centre
Brit.

emphasize
US

emphasise
Brit.

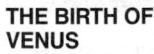

honor
US

honour
Brit.

THE BIRTH OF VENUS
by Botticelli, c 1485, introduces a classical subject to painting.

intentional distortion. In statues like his *Mary Magdalene* the sculptor extended his psychological repertoire to include the corrupting effects of sin and the power of spiritual remorse.

The length and brilliance of Donatello's career deserve the limelight, but other sculptors were also hard at work. One of the most notable was Ghiberti (whose victory in the baptistry door competition led to Brunelleschi's abandonment of sculpture for architecture). His personal grace and gift for spatial illusion made Ghiberti's studio the major training ground for the next generation of sculptors, the most outstanding of whom was Verrocchio. Other contemporaries of Donatello,

including Nanni di Banco and Luca della Robbia, developed the expressive power of sculpture via their studies of antique drapery. By the late 1400s, the quest for sculptural truth had so evolved that Pollaiuolo was supplementing the authority of antiquity with his own studies of human anatomy. He even dissected corpses to gain a better understanding of bone and musculature.

Alberti. The scientific interests of Pollaiuolo were typical of Renaissance art. Everywhere men were trying to develop valid theories on which to base their actions. Piero della Francesca's treatise on the theory of perspective was an early effort at such theory-making. With the invention of the printing press, Renaissance theory spread throughout all Italy and gradually through all of Europe through books and pamphlets.

By far the most influential spirit was Leon Battista Alberti, who wrote three treatises, *"On Painting," "On the Statue,"* and *"The Ten Books of Architecture."* As no man before him, Alberti codified Renaissance thought and established the theoretical basis of beauty. He defined it as "the harmony and concord of parts, achieved in such a manner that nothing could be added, taken away, or altered." Alberti was the first person to seriously study the first-century architectural treatise of Vitruvius, and he used it to develop his ideal system of proportions. For Alberti, contact with antiquity was not just a mental exercise. It was a way of life. We can see its results in the palace that he designed for the powerful merchant family Rucellai.

As far as the Italians knew, there were no antique houses extant. Even if there had been, their value would have been minimal as a model. Times had changed, and Renaissance homes had to accommodate modern needs. Alberti solved the problem with a compromise: he built a traditional three-story house with windows, doors, and overhanging cornice, and then he decorated it with the classical elements that Brunelleschi had reintroduced. Alberti chose the Colosseum as his model. He copied its blend of arches and vertical pilasters. But the Colosseum's numerous openings were inappropriate for a private house, so Alberti simply indicated them by inscribed lines without changing the structure of his building. In fact, the facade is just a flat wall on top of which a linear net of classical details has been overlaid. In the Palazzo Rucellai, Alberti adapted antiquity to modern needs. It was a theme to which he dedicated his entire career, reviving Roman barrel vaults, triumphal arches, and especially the orders as living parts of the new architectural vocabulary.

Alberti was a stellar intellect, but his situation was not unlike that of most artists of the later 1400s. They were confronted with the problems of how to infuse the new art with ancient spirit, how to make the teachings of antiquity their own, and in short, how to bring about a Renaissance of the classical past. Their interest led them to study classical philosophy, literature, and poetry. They were convinced of the ancients' superior wisdom, and they scoured their texts for profound universal truths.

Botticelli. The most fertile center of humanistic thought was the circle of Lorenzo de Medici, the great Florentine prince, poet, and patron of the arts. He surrounded himself with the most enlightened scholars and artists of the day, including Sandro Botticelli. Of all the painters of the age, it was he who most effectively sought to reconcile pagan and Christian philosophies. In the 1480s he painted the famous *Birth of Venus*.

Born of the sea, the goddess of love is driven to shore upon a cockle shell. She is propelled by embracing wind gods who fly behind her in a perfumed shower of roses. On land, a nymph extends a floral robe to the naked Venus. The painting has been variously interpreted. Some see it as an allegory for the birth of beauty, while others feel it represents the innocence of the human soul about to be draped in the robe of reason.

Such allegories were common in Renaissance thought. Botticelli, however, used them in a way that rejected the illusionistic breakthroughs of his predecessors. Instead of painting a convincing expanse of sea, he provided a flat plane with little V-shapes for waves. The heavy figures of Giotto and Masaccio were abandoned by him for weightless beings who delicately float on their toes. Strength and emotion are

sacrificed to linear patterns of fluttering hair and draperies, radiating shell segments, and isolating contours. Venus is like a cut-out doll pasted on top of the painting. Even attempts at perfect human proportion have given way to graceful exaggeration. But if Venus's long neck, sloping shoulders, and drooping left arm are unnatural, they emphasize the ethereal refinement of the beautiful naked goddess (the first nude Venus since antiquity). Unlike earlier Renaissance artists who strove to portray the natural world, Botticelli's mystical approach was based on the humanistic belief that man could reach God by the contemplation of beauty.

Such ideas were denounced by the fanatical monk Savonarola, who railed against the pagan attitudes of the Medici court. His puritanical attacks dampened humanistic fires and deprived Florence of its cultural leadership. Already the focus was shifting.

In Umbria, Signorelli was following up the work of Pollaiuolo and Verrocchio with violent paintings of muscular bodies; and his compatriot Perugino was laying the essential groundwork for High Renaissance spatial compositions. In Northern Italy, the literary and archaeological artist Mantagne exploited perspective in overwhelmingly realistic paintings. His influence would be felt in the later Venetian school. It crossed the Alps where it was enthusiastically received by Albrecht Dürer, the father of the Northern Renaissance.

The High Renaissance

The true successor to Florentine preeminence was Rome. The papacy was on the rise once again, and the promise of papal patronage attracted Italy's greatest talents. Architects, painters, and sculptors flocked to the Vatican to glorify the church and to satisfy the increasingly sumptuous tastes of the popes. Thus began the High Renaissance, the most illustrious period of Italian creative genius.

The new era was ushered in by men of such extraordinary genius that nothing seemed impossible. Their broad intellectual and creative horizons elevated them from lowly craftsmen to respected celebrities, reversing traditional patron-artist relationships in the process. In the past, the artist was flattered by a commission from a great prince. But now *he* bestowed the honor by agreeing to do such work. His new status gave respectability to the artistic profession and secured its place among the "fine" arts.

Leonardo. The prophet of the new age was Leonardo da Vinci, a man of such intellect that we can scarcely comprehend the breadth of his achievements. His voluminous notebooks show

that he was interested in everything: the effects of atmosphere, the growth of babies in the womb, the nature of sound, and the motion of waves and currents. His insatiable curiosity led him to explore botany, zoology, anatomy, geology, hydraulics, psychology, physiology, and optics. He also studied the flight of birds and designed a flying machine. Moreover, Leonardo was a skilled military engineer, stage designer, architect, musician, and poet. He was the universal man.

The aim of Leonardo's unbounded pursuits was the discovery of nature's eternal laws. When he was confronted by a problem, he never turned to the ancients, but used his own mind and eyes to come up with a solution. All of his scientific experiments were con-

ducted as a means of gaining more information about the visible world. To Leonardo, man's eyes were the "windows of his soul." It was only through them that he could find truth.

The significance of Leonardo's vision is apparent in his paintings. His *Last Supper* goes far beyond the mere recounting of a Biblical story. It combines perfect harmony, balance, and spatial illusion with a profound knowledge of human nature. It is a model of psychological drama revealed by artistic genius.

Leonardo's celebrity soared even moreso with his *Mona Lisa,* perhaps the most famous portrait in the world. Seated quietly, she stares at the viewer with a smile that has both captivated and confused her admirers for nearly 500 years.

PRIMAVERA
(detail) by Botticelli characteristically focuses on beauty, as evidenced in the linear patterns depicting delicate floating beings with flowing tresses and garments.

MONA LISA,
c 1508, by Leonardo
da Vinci, is perhaps
the most famous
portrait in the world.

to have been crucified. Its parts are so finely proportioned and so perfectly integrated that it stands in its courtyard like an inspired piece of monumental sculpture. Its austere Doric colonnade (appropriate to the masculine St. Peter) contrasts with the balustrade above, while its walls and niches play off each other with great three-dimensional complexity. The contrasting rhythms of solid and void, large and small, and projection and recession are orchestrated with such skill that the *Tempietto* can be likened to a beautiful symphony in stone.

It is little wonder that the creator of this architectural gem was selected by the pope to design the new church of St. Peter. The church was destined to become the most important undertaking of the 16th century, employing the greatest talents in Italy. Bramante began the process with a centralized plan, but he died before his plans were carried out. He was succeeded by a host of architects (including Raphael and Michelangelo), only some of whom recognized the importance of his scheme. Ultimately, Bramante's centralized plan was rejected as too pagan and the more traditional form of an elongated basilica was adopted.

Raphael. If Bramante achieved ideal architectural form in the High Renaissance, then it was Raphael who attained it in painting. As a child he was apprenticed to Perugino, but he quickly surpassed his master, transforming his rigid spatial compositions into works of effortless grace. Raphael's genius was already far advanced at age 21 when he painted *The Marriage of the Virgin.*

In general format, the painting owes a great deal to Perugino. But Raphael softened his master's formality, creating the delicacy and grace of a visual ballet. Sweetly the Virgin extends her hand to receive a wedding ring from St. Peter. There is no excitement, just the flow of true classical calm. The quiet is not even disturbed by the rejected suitor who breaks his rod over his knee. On the contrary, his delicate balance only adds to this scene of ideal harmony. Raphael's figures epitomize High Renaissance goals of human conduct in a logically ordered world.

The theme is continued in the piazza and dominating temple (which recalls Bramante's centralized architecture). Space curves around its circular walls and penetrates its central door to an infinite vista behind. The whole composition transcends worldly limitations. So effective is its poise, so uncluttered its space, that it exists in the spiritual realm of supernatural ideals.

The effortless grace of Raphael's paintings makes it easy for us to forget that they were the result of countless hours of unrelenting work. He learned from everyone, but adapted borrowed ideas to his own style, which stressed simplicity, dignity, and charm.

In his short life, Raphael painted some of the world's most sensitive

Her mysterious expression, sometimes seeming happy, other times sad or even jeering, is the result of *sfumato.* Leonardo invented this technique of blurred contours to obscure the transition from one plane to another. Unlike his exacting psychological studies in the *Last Supper,* he intentionally disguises Mona Lisa's true character in fuzzy shadow. The absence of precise boundaries makes her face seem to merge with the hazy landscape behind. How different she is from the cold linear figures of Botticelli.

Leonardo's superb handling of light and shade gave *Mona Lisa* the warm fleshiness of a living person. She is at once eternal and immobile, yet fleeting. Leonardo himself must have been enchanted with this dreamlike painting because he could never part with it. He carried it with him to France and kept it in his possession until his death in 1519.

Bramante. While Leonardo was in Milan he met Donato Bramante, the greatest architect of the generation. Like Brunelleschi and Alberti, Bramante was dedicated to the revival of antiquity. But he was no slavish imitator. He distilled the essence of classical architecture (symmetry, clarity, geometry, proportion, and the orders) and used it to develop the centralized church plan. Its significance can hardly be overstated. A circle is appropriate to the eternal God because it has no beginning or end. As pure geometry, it was sanctioned in antiquity as the ideal symbol of perfection, beauty, and truth. Leonardo had made sketches of centralized churches; his influence is undoubtedly at work in the *Tempietto,* or little temple, by Bramante.

Bramante erected this small shrine on the site where St. Peter was believed

Madonnas. He also created frescoes of such power that they are without equal in the history of art. The finest of these are in the Vatican and were executed for Pope Julius II. *School of Athens* is a complete artistic and spiritual statement of the High Renaissance. Unified by a complex iconography, it shows a meeting of the greatest ancient philosophers and scientists. It is an eloquent celebration of classical and Renaissance ideals, the ultimate union between pagan and Christian thought.

Michelangelo. Raphael's grace, Leonardo's science, and Bramante's geometric perfection were offset by the brooding figure of Michelangelo Buonarroti. He was a wily recluse, intolerant, jealous, and short-tempered. But he had a deep understanding of man, and his explosive genius claimed for man an almost godlike strength.

The extent of Michelangelo's skill was so great that he refused to be restricted by laws. Indeed, he even abandoned mathematical rules for perfect proportion. As far as he was concerned, beauty was in the "idea," and it was the task of the sculptor to release such slumbering concepts from their stone prisons. Removing excess stone freed the image locked inside.

Michelangelo's extraordinary talents were early recognized by Lorenzo de Medici, whose famous court introduced the youth to the most elevated humanist scholars and artists. However, Medici power collapsed in 1494 and Michelangelo fled to Bologna, and then to Rome, where he created the *Pietà*. It was his earliest masterpiece. Never before had cold white marble been transformed into such a warm and poignant vision. The Virgin Mother, beautiful and ageless, extends her left hand as she contemplates her dead son. Only the crumpled drapery across her breast reflects her grief. The wrinkled cloth simultaneously acts as a foil to the smooth refinement of Christ's body. His anatomical accuracy is the result of Michelangelo's dissection of human corpses. The crucified body shows no sign of pain. In fact, Christ's wounds are barely visible, and his dreamy face bespeaks the achievement of final peace.

When the sculpture was first exhibited in St. Peter's, no one in the awestricken crowd could believe that it was created by the 23-year-old Michelangelo. When they left, he stole back into the church and proudly carved his name on the strap across Mary's bosom. It is the only genuine signature on any of Michelangelo's sculptures.

After a 6-year absence Michelangelo returned to Florence, where he tackled the "Giant," an enormous marble block that no one else had been able to carve. Out of this impossible challenge emerged the statue of *David,* the vibrant and battle-prepared youth who became the city's symbol. A quick look at *David* deceives us. We get an initial impression of relaxation. He is the Biblical hero standing at ease, slingshot over his shoulder. But closer study reveals pulsating muscles and bulging veins that suggest tremendous pent-up energy.

With the tension of a spring about to uncoil, *David* acutely watches his approaching enemy. His penetrating stare and flaring nostrils give him a ferociousness that the Italians call *terribilita.* How different he is from Donatello's sweet young *David.* Michelangelo's statue is more closely related to those of Greek athletes like *Doryphorus.* Both celebrate the heroic physique, but next to the explosive *David,* the classical work seems feeble. This quality of pent-up passion characterized Michelangelo's life and work. It separated him totally from Raphael and other artists who were dedicated to the portrayal of calm and ideal beauty.

Michelangelo was next summoned to Rome to work on the colossal tomb of Julius II. But after six months the pope lost interest in the scheme, partly because of his construction of St. Peter's. Frustrated and sorely disappointed, Michelangelo returned to Florence. He was persuaded to come back to Rome only by the most skillful diplomacy. (The Florentines were actually afraid that the pope would blame them for harboring the artist and therefore encouraged his return.) When he finally submitted, an unhappy commission awaited. The pope wanted Michelangelo to paint the ceiling of the Sistine Chapel. The walls of the chapel already had been decorated by great painters like Botticelli, Ghirlandaio, and Perugino. Michelangelo refused. He was a sculptor, he insisted, not a painter. The pope finally had his way, and Michelangelo began work, still hoping he would soon be allowed to resume his work on the tomb.

Julius II envisioned paintings of the twelve apostles. But again, Michelangelo refused. In the end, the pope let him paint what he wanted, although Michelangelo must have had a theological advisor to guide him through complex Biblical iconography. After arranging for a crew of assistants, the artist locked himself in the chapel and allowed no one else to enter.

The ceiling was huge, covering 5,800 square feet (the equivalent of a canvas 100 feet long and 58 feet—nearly six stories—high). During the next four years, this lonely genius painted the ceiling, lying on his back on a massive platform, aided only by one mason and one apprentice.

In 1512 the doors were opened to an astonished world. Over 300 figures in every imaginable posture dramatically stretch across the vault in a narration of man's creation, fall, and redemption. The achievement was nothing less than superhuman!

IDEAL AND NATURAL blend in these High Renaissance masterpieces: Michelangelo's *David* and Raphael's *The Marriage of the Virgin,* both completed c 1504.

center
US

centre
Brit.

color
US

colour
Brit.

emphasize
US

emphasise
Brit.

THE CREATION OF ADAM, one panel of Michaelangelo's giant Sistine Chapel ceiling, is surrounded by many other figures seeming to point the viewer in other directions.

Seated in massive thrones on either side of the ceiling are the Old Testament prophets and sibyls who predicted the coming of the Messiah. Between them are triangular scenes of Christ's ancestors. In the center of the ceiling large and small panels alternate as the story of Genesis unfolds. Hosts of lesser figures appear: tiny putti (cherubs), standing sculptural figures, and muscular youths seated at the corners of the central scenes of the Creation. There is no decoration other than the human body in encyclopedic postures. The human form is the source of expressive power and the beautiful creation of God, but it is also the prison of souls yearning to be free.

One of the most famous scenes from the Sistine ceiling is the *Creation of Adam.* Beautiful and potentially strong, the first man is still one with the unformed earth. He limply extends his hand to receive the vibrant spark of life from God the Father, who approaches in a billowing robe amid an angelic escort. All attention is focused on the outstretched fingers of the two heroic figures. The Creation of Adam had been painted many times before, but never with such a profound understanding.

Upon the completion of the Sistine ceiling, Michelangelo eagerly resumed work on Julius's tomb, only to be interrupted once again. The remaining 50 years of his long life were filled with the most important painting, sculpture, and architectural commissions of the century, including the construction of St. Peter's. By the time Michelangelo died

at age 89, he had become the prototype of artistic genius: the supreme intellect who transcended law and tradition, the paramount talent who invested man with grand dignity. This artist was known by his contemporaries as the "divine" Michelangelo.

Mannerism

The extraordinary achievements of Leonardo, Raphael, and Michelangelo tend to obscure the accomplishments of other 16th century artists; for example, the lustrous color schemes of Andrea del Sarto and the unsurpassed sensuality of Correggio's religious and mythological scenes. But change was in the air.

By about 1520 High Renaissance art had reached its peak. All problems of space, color, composition, and human form seemed to have been solved. The towering geniuses of the era had succeeded in reviving antiquity and, indeed, they were confident that they had even surpassed it.

This presented the new generation of artists with an irksome question. If all artistic problems had already been solved, what was left for them to do? They decided to improve on the High Renaissance, especially the work of Michelangelo, which had taught them the benefits of artistic freedom. They rejected nature as their model and chose instead the art of their forebears. They hoped to recreate this art in a

new and interesting manner. If the High Renaissance had achieved calm, harmony, balance, and naturalism, the new "Mannerists" sought restless discord, instability, and bizarre fantasy.

Clarity and simplicity were replaced by ambiguous complexity, and paintings assumed the form of deliberately intricate puzzles. With a bold disregard of artistic conventions, the Mannerists concentrated on artificiality, distortion, and exaggeration. Pontormo, Bronzino, and Il Rosso Fiorentino ("the red head") produced strange works with clashing colors, nervous movement, and enamel-skinned people in disturbing spatial vacuums. Many of the same qualities are apparent in Parmigianino's *Madonna with the Long Neck.*

Seated with the ungainly Christ sprawled on her lap, the Madonna has been unnaturally elongated. To emphasize her elegance, Parmigianino gave the giantess a tiny oval head atop a swanlike neck, and delicate fingers that stretch like pulled taffy. She is worlds apart from Raphael's graceful Madonnas. To the Virgin's right a cluster of angels is compacted into an uncomfortably small space, only to be cut off abruptly by the picture frame. Unlike Renaissance paintings, where the figures are evenly distributed across the surface, Parmigianino's paintings intentionally contrast the two sides of his work. Our eyes pass without transition from the congested foreground to the deep background, where a haggard prophet reads an outstretched scroll. An ominous colonnade that supports nothing adds a surreal note to the painting.

The artificial and extreme sophistication of Italian Mannerism spread to France when Il Rosso, Primaticcio, and Cellini were invited to Fontainebleau by King Francis I. With them came the full repertoire of Mannerist ornament. Cellini, sculptor and goldsmith, became a court favorite with his exquisite works in precious metals. The other two artists redecorated the interior of the king's chateau. The supreme example of their achievement is the bedchamber of the duchess of Etampes, where paintings of Alexander the Great are framed by slender female stuccoes. The origin of such human supports can be traced to antiquity, but in the hands of the Mannerists classical purity was replaced by a complicated network of garlands, cherubs, grotesques, and interlocking strapwork.

As work continued at Fontainebleau, more artists were enlisted from Italy and France. So powerful was Mannerist impact that it spread beyond the royal court. Its influence is best seen in the turbulent work of Jean de Boulogne, the French sculptor who travelled to Italy to receive further training. He Italianized his name to Giovanni de Bologna and settled down in Florence to become one of the most important sculptors of the latter 1500s.

As the Mannerist vogue spread, eventually influencing even architecture, it reached the highest peak of

sophistication. Architects like Zuccari exploited its caprice with windows that look like human faces. Giulio Romano, on the other hand, worked in a more traditional idiom. His brand of Mannerism consisted of classical elements used in a most nonclassical manner to produce great architectural parodies of ancient and High Renaissance styles. His most famous work is the Palazzo del Te in Mantua, where deliberate irregularities violate the fundamental principles of humanistic architecture. A similar passion for distortion was indulged by Ammanati in the courtyard of the Pitti Palace in Florence.

The School of Venice

Throughout the 1400s, the powerful republic of Venice remained somewhat aloof from the other Italian states. It was distinguished as a separate country, culturally as well as politically, and one of its distinctions was its continued contact with the Byzantine Empire to the east.

The appeal of the great movements in art and architecture finally made their impact after 1530, and the result was a brilliant new flowering of Renaissance thought and sensibility.

Palladio. Classical architecture was introduced to Venice in the 1530s by Jacopo Samsovino. Within two decades, the new style had been perfected by Andrea de Pietro, known as Palladio (after Pallas Athena, the ancient goddess of wisdom). In Palladio, northern Italy could claim the world's greatest architectural classicist.

Palladio began as a stonemason and sculptor, but at age 30 he turned to architecture. During several trips to Rome he digested the lessons of antiquity and the theoretical writings of Vitruvius and Alberti. In 1570 he published the *Quattro Libri (The Four Books on Architecture)*, a treatise whose significance can hardly be overstated. It was eagerly seized upon by architects throughout Europe, and it later formed the basis of a classical revival in England and North America during the 1700s. Few persons in history have had such wide-ranging effects as Palladio.

Palladio is best known for his villas and churches, most of which center around his hometown of Vicenza. The most famous is the Villa Capra, known by its nickname, Villa Rotunda.

In adapting antique forms to modern residences, Palladio erroneously assumed that ancient houses were fronted by great temple porticoes, and so he incorporated one on each face of the Villa Rotunda. He used the Roman Pantheon as a model for both the porticoes and the central dome.

Centuries later, the elegance of Palladio's "classical" design, and its practical advantages (protection from the sun and ventilation), appealed to

MADONNA WITH THE LONG NECK
by Parmigianino (1535) uses crowding and the lack of visual balance for dramatic effect.

ELABORATE DECORATION
of a room at Fontainebleau, c 1540, reflects Mannerist tastes.

plantation owners in the southern United States. Thus Palladian designs became popular for the great plantations.

The austerity of Palladio's rational architecture is considerably relieved by the soft northern light of Venice. His church of San Giorgio Maggiore, for instance, might appear rigid and formal somewhere else. But here, against the brilliant blue sky, and lit by the flickering play of reflections from the water, it seems relaxed and "at home."

Painting. Palladio's interest in light was typical of Venetian artists. In fact, the Venetian school of painting was dedicated to understanding and using light and color. A distinctly Venetian style emerged with Giovanni Bellini, whose long career spanned the three generations from International Style through to the High Renaissance. He is most famous for his paintings of Madonnas, which seem to radiate with supernatural light.

To Bellini and his followers light and color were not merely something *added* to a drawn image; they were the major ingredients of painting. By contrast, the earlier Florentines and the High Renaissance masters were more concerned

RAPE OF EUROPA, c 1560, illustrates Titian's use of new effects of light and color and a new sensuousness in portraying mythological stories.

| color
US |
| colour
Brit. |
| emphasize
US |
| emphasise
Brit. |
| centered
US |
| centred
Brit. |

with draftsmanship and with depicting space, especially through perspective.

Bellini's interest in color was extended even further by his student Giorgione. Although only five paintings can be absolutely attributed to Giorgione, he ranks among the great painters of the Renaissance. His idyllic scenes of tranquil love were bathed in mysterious soft shadows.

Titian. The advances made by Bellini and Giorgione peaked in the art of Titian, the supreme colorist. A brilliant draftsman, he challenged Michelangelo as the most popular Renaissance artist.

Titian was the first painter to totally free his brush stroke from the literal description of tactile surfaces. He was not concerned with making an exact replica of how things look. He was more interested in capturing the subjects' energy and emotion as they were transformed by light. To achieve this effect, Titian used oil paints on rough-textured canvas (in place of earlier wooden panels). He began by painting the entire surface red. On top of this warm ground he added brilliantly colored figures. (A contemporary of Titian described his painted highlights as "drops of blood.") Next the painter applied layers of glaze—30 or even 40 of them—to unify his composition and to modulate the jarring effects of his exuberant colors.

The results of this technique are apparent in the *Rape of Europa,* which Titian painted in his old age. The *Rape* shows a final stage in Titian's ever-loosening use of the brush stroke. The mythological scene depicts the god Zeus (in the guise of a white bull) abducting the lovely maiden Europa. Surging forward, her red mantle waves dramatically against the sky as her friends cry out from the distant shore. Two flying cherubs and one astride a fish emphasize the compelling diagonal thrust of the painting. Titian's loosely applied paint melts the background into an indistinct multicolored haze.

During the course of his six-decade career, Titian dominated Venetian art with his portraits and his mythological and religious paintings. His achievements served as both a source and a foil to his competitors. The impetuous Tintoretto, for example, tried to emulate his color but opposed his slow and careful method of working. He was impatient with the many months that Titian lavished on his works. Tintoretto tried to combine the best of Titian with the power of Michelangelo.

The other great Venetian painter was Veronese, creator of enormous canvases that often used grand architectural settings from antiquity. Veronese's intoxicating colors and extreme illusionism bring Venetian Renaissance painting to a close. His works look

forward to the theatrical productions of the upcoming Baroque period.

The Northern Renaissance

In Italy the period from 1300 to 1600 was zealously dedicated to the revival of antiquity. Ever since Giotto, architects, painters, and sculptors had worked to reinstate classical ideals. By about 1520 total victory was theirs. In just over 200 years Italian artists had established the rules for a scientific approach to the representation of nature. Treatises on science and art abounded, and theoretical standards of perfection were thoroughly explored. Unleashed from church domination and encouraged by classical philosophy, Renaissance man came into direct contact with his physical world. He became an achiever and an independent thinker. He established the basis of modern individualism.

A simultaneous revolution was taking place north of the Alps, but its character was quite different. Whereas Italy was filled with ancient ruins, ready inspiration for the modern imitators, the North had no such ties to antiquity. Consequently, this area (consisting of modern France, Belgium, Luxembourg, most of Holland, and part of Germany) remained under Gothic influence well into the 1400s.

This is most readily apparent in Northern architecture, where the pointed Gothic look became even more elaborate. It culminated in the flamboyant style of fantastic ornament and effusive overlays.

Painting. Northern painting had a parallel development. In Italy the International Style was quickly dispelled by the new classicism. In the North, by contrast, it became a rich point of departure for several generations of painters. The movement was led by the Master of Flamalle (most probably Robert Campin). Working in the tradition of the Limbourg Brothers, Campin and his followers maintained a style of two-dimensional decoration. But they addressed a more bourgeoise audience. Northern wealth was now in the hands of successful merchants and bankers, so art had a more popular appeal. Instead of preparing illuminated manuscripts for wealthy patrons, the Northern artist came to produce large painted panels to be set above church altars. There they appealed to a broad public, rich and poor, educated and simple.

This more democratic approach also changed the artists' subject matter. In place of splendid court scenes, early Northern painters depicted middle-class domestic interiors, complete with an encyclopedic record of everything inside. This could be a serious problem for the painter of religious scenes. How could he portray supernatural events in an everyday setting? His solution was "disguised symbolism," in which almost every detail, regardless of how casual or insignificant, was imbued with a symbolic message. For example, Campin's *Merode Altarpiece* depicts the Annunciation.

An angel appears in a common Flemish home to announce to Mary her selection as the mother of Christ. Virtually all the ordinary domestic accessories are analogies for some aspect of this sacred event. Particular flowers in the painting refer to Mary's humility, chastity, and love, while a water basin denotes her purity. Towels, candles, books and other objects all play similar symbolic roles.

With his humanization of divine events, the Northern painter deprived the holy characters of their supernatural distance from man. The characters appear just like ordinary people; even their halos have been omitted. By showing an extraordinary event in an ordinary environment, the artist could indulge his delight in tiny details. The Northern painter was totally committed to the accurate *appearance* of objects (in this he opposed his Italian counterparts who used perspective, mathematics, and proportion to discover the structure behind appearances). Thus the bases of the two artistic revolutions were different. In Italy, it was centered around the revival of antiquity. In the North, it concentrated on the discovery of man in his visible world.

Jan van Eyck. The conquest of appearances was achieved by Jan and Hubert van Eyck. Their greatest combined effort was the *Ghent Altarpiece,* composed of 20 separate panels hinged together to form an enormous double-register altarpiece. It was signed by both artists and dated 1432. It is not clear what each brother contributed, but there is no doubt about the consummate skill of Jan van Eyck. So exacting was his microscopic record of the world, that even a contemporary Italian humanist called him the "prince of painters in our age." He is universally acknowledged as one of the greatest painters of all time.

Jan's acclaim stems from the almost photographic quality of his paintings, a revolutionary effect achieved through his invention of oil paints. Before the modern age, artists had to mix their own colors. They used stone to grind solid pigments into a fine powder and then they added a binding agent. Egg was the most popular. Its only drawback was that it dried quickly and so limited the artist's flexibility. Jan van Eyck substituted oil for egg. This allowed him to work much more slowly and to add many details with razor sharp accuracy.

Northern artists applied thin layers of transparent glaze on top of their pictures. This solution of oil and turpentine was mixed with color to unify the painting with a resonant glow. (We have already seen the effect of glazes on the works of Titian.) These enamel-hard layers made it seem as if one were look-

ing at the painted image through tinted panes of glass. The effect it produced was revolutionary. Glazes tend to capture light, and thus Northern paintings seem to be lit from within. Their sparkling highlights, transparent shadows, intense tonalities, and minute accuracy distinguish them from contemporary Italian work. Executed in tempera, Southern paintings appear heavy and opaque.

Jan van Eyck used his new invention to catalog reality with scrupulous honesty. His achievements are apparent in the *Arnolfini Wedding*. It shows the Italian silk merchant Giovanni Arnolfini holding his young wife's hand. He takes the vow of matrimony and raises his right hand in an oath of fidelity. The quiet ceremony takes place in his Netherlands-like bedchamber. (It was common for Italian merchants to keep a business residence in the Northern centers of international banking and trade.)

At first glance it may seem a little strange for a wedding to take place outside a church. After all, marriage is a sacrament. But if Jan has omitted conspicuous religious imagery, he has charged every household item with a symbolism that participates in the sanctity of the occasion. The dog in the foreground represents fidelity (the origi-

nal meaning of Fido). The nearby shoes identify the area as sacred. Fruit near the window symbolizes fertility, as does the small sculpted figure on the bedpost. It is St. Margaret, patron of childbirth. The small whisk brush on the back wall denotes domestic care, and the single candle burning in the chandelier (shining in broad daylight) signifies the all-seeing eye of God. Thus, while Jan has not included images of saints or angels, the spiritual exists in his symbols.

Another curious aspect of the *Arnolfini* portrait is the seeming privacy of the ceremony. Who and where are the witnesses? They are Jan van Eyck and his assistant! They are reflected in the mirror on the back wall and verified by the florid script above: "Johannes de Eyck fuit hic. 1434" (Jan van Eyck was here. 1434). The artist presented an exact depiction of what he saw; thus, the painting assumes the role of a visual marriage certificate, signed, dated, and witnessed.

Jan's techniques were irreproachable. Indeed, they were so perfect that very few painters attempted to improve on—or even imitate—his style. Instead, they sought new approaches to replace his exhaustive symbolic details. They aspired to human drama, action, and a relief from overbearing disguised symbolism. The great leader of this

ARNOLFINI WEDDING by Jan van Eyck (1434) shows the realism of Northern painters. Van Eyck's signature is shown to the right.

emphasizes
US

emphasises
Brit.

labors
US

labours
Brit.

expressive movement was Rogier van der Weyden, whose large emotional paintings became even more monumental through his contact with Italy.

After van der Weyden's death in 1464, the leadership of the Northern school of painting fell to the introspective Hugo van der Goes. His paintings, sometimes melancholy and other times passionate, infused Flemish art with an unprecedented internal drama. His greatest work, the *Portinari Altarpiece,* was installed in a Florentine church. It created a great stir among Southern artists who were mesmerized by its tremendous realism. Van der Goes' contemporary, Hans Memlinc, was also held in high regard, but his genial nature led this follower of Rogier van der Weyden to concentrate on pretty religious paintings.

The 1400s came to a disruptive close with the fantastic work of Hieronymus Bosch, one of the most intriguing and puzzling artists the world has known. Are his strange dreamlike paintings, filled with frightening beasts, hideous hybrids, and erotic plant forms, stern moral "lessons"? Or are they merely the pornographic creations of a perverse mind? Might they be the satirical work of a brazen heretic? Bosch's images are so complex that modern scholars still cannot answer these questions.

Bosch's grim view of life led him

ADAM AND EVE by Dürer (1504) puts classic figures in a Northern European setting.

back to the old pagan animal style. Yet, at the same time, he looked forward to modern art with what are perhaps the first surreal paintings.

During the 1400s Flemish art had great impact in Germany. Scores of minor masters responded to the achievements of van Eyck, van der Weyden, and their followers. But the number of truly great talents was limited. Among the distinguished roster must be included Stephan Lochner and his charming religious paintings, Conrad Witz and his realistic landscapes, and Michael Pacher and his monumental compositions emphasizing perspective. The latter was the first to establish important contacts with Italy, and thus prepare the way for what would be a veritable flood of Southern influence in the 1500s.

Graphic arts. While national isolation was beginning to dissolve, a monumental event took place in Germany: the invention of the printing press by Gutenberg. Because it permitted the inexpensive publication of books, it provided the perfect avenue for the diffusion of foreign ideas, binding the various European countries ever more closely together.

The printing press also encouraged significant changes in the graphic arts. Previously, pictures were reproduced by means of woodblocks. Designs were first drawn of the face of a block; then the background was carved away. The lines left projecting were inked and pressed onto paper. The process could be repeated as many times as desired. The technique was simple enough and Northern artists developed its expressive potential. But by 1450, even the most refined woodblocks could not accommodate the new interests in microscopic detail. Consequently, they were replaced by engravings.

The engraving process was the opposite of the woodblock process. It called for the artist to trace lines on a copper plate with a special tool called a *burin.* When the design was completely drawn, the whole plate was covered with ink. The next step was to wipe the untooled areas clean, leaving ink only in the deep linear impressions made by the burin. From this point on, it was merely a process of pressing the plate against a sheet of paper.

It took great skill to handle a burin. Lines had to be of uniform depth and thickness, and mistakes were almost impossible to correct. But in the hands of skilled craftsmen, engravings provided much more subtlety and much finer detail than even the most developed woodcut. The greatest 15th century engraver was Martin Schongauer, whose mastery of the burin let him distinguish a tremendous variety of tones and textures, ranging from furry monsters and scaly beasts to wispy feathers, human hair, and coarse crumpled cloth. Moreover, his expressive and spatial powers gave him the title "the Rogier van der Weyden of engraving."

Italian influence. As notable as Schongauer's advances may have been, they hardly prepared one for the revolutionary achievements that came about in the early 1500s. After years of only minor contact with Italy, Northern artists were seized by a sudden awareness of developments occurring beyond the Alps. They were overcome by a desire to assimilate the Italian style as thoroughly and as quickly as possible. Many went to Italy to experience the Italian Renaissance at first hand. Scores of others learned of its wonders through engravings like those of Marcantonio Raimondi, who graphically reproduced Raphael's works. The ensuing creative explosion brought the Northern Renaissance to a peak. It developed simultaneously with the Italian High Renaissance, and it ended about 1530, ten years after the decline in Italy. The greatest Northern talents were contemporaries of Bramante, Raphael, Michelangelo, Giorgione, and Titian.

Outstanding among German artists was Matthias Grünewald. He painted scenes of horrifying intensity, such as the flesh-torn Christ in the *Isenheim Altarpiece.* However, his talent lies less in his ability to portray repulsive carnage than in his ability to transform events to the level of high human drama. Grünewald's contemporary, Albrecht Altdorfer, chose a totally different vehicle for his powerful expression. He concentrated on sweeping, passionate landscapes. A third German, Lucas Cranach, developed in yet another direction. He imitated Italian sensuality, but totally rejected its classical trappings. He remained steadfast in his provincial, oddly proportioned figures, oblivious to the scientific laws of Italian art.

Dürer. Of all German personalities, there is none who could compare with Albrecht Dürer, the "da Vinci of the North" (unlike Leonardo, Dürer devoted his research almost exclusively to artistic problems). Dürer was the first Northerner to travel to Italy for the sole purpose of studying art (1495), the first Northerner to establish an international reputation, and the first to fully comprehend the aims of the Italian Renaissance. He dedicated his life to their diffusion in the North.

Dürer wrote treatises on such diverse topics as military engineering, perspective, and proportion. He was also a great painter. But it is through the graphic arts that Dürer revealed his genius. His woodcuts and engravings are unsurpassed in their beauty and excellence.

A suggestion of his extraordinary talents is provided by his engraving *Adam and Eve,* the final result of a series of preparatory drawings in which Dürer experimented with ideal proportions. Both figures are based on classical models, although Eve retains the ungainliness of an overly fleshy German matron. Adam and Eve are still somewhat awkward foreigners in the

North, Southern nudes shivering in the cold Northern forest that outlines them so dramatically. Nevertheless, they represent the first serious attempt to transplant Italian ideals beyond the Alps.

If the religious theme seems merely an excuse to show heroic nudes, it is balanced by Dürer's intellectual brand of symbolism, in which he emphasizes the conflicts of original sin. The branch that Adam holds signifies the tree of life, but the fig tree around which the serpent coils represents damnation. The elk symbolizes greed, the ox gluttony and sloth, the cat pride, and the rabbit lechery. On another level, these animals are an analogy for the diseases that man inherited as a result of Adam's and Eve's sin. In short, the engraving is a sophisticated combination of Northern and Southern, spiritual and secular motifs.

Dürer spent most of his life struggling to reconcile the Italian ideal of simple classical forms with the Northern penchant for exacting detail. The result Dürer sought was almost effortlessly achieved by Hans Holbein, whose compellingly realistic portraits assumed the monumentality of the Italian High Renaissance.

Around 1530 the tide of the Northern Renaissance was abruptly stemmed. Constant wars had drained the economy and the crisis of the Protestant revolt had challenged the very existence of art. The only area in which art developed unhampered was the Protestant Netherlands.

Breughel. Jan Gossaert, Joachim Patinir, and hosts of other minor artists came to light, but it was Pieter Breughel who led the way. Like many of his contemporaries, Breughel travelled to Italy, where he spent almost two years exploring the Mediterranean countryside. But unlike his contemporaries, he was little affected by Italy's mania for antiques. In fact, the only specific reference to his trip is the occasional appearance of a bit of Southern landscape in otherwise Northern settings. Breughel avoided the classical nude. Instead, he assimilated a sense of monumental Italian harmony into his purely Netherlands-like subject matter. He is best known for his sprawling landscapes, which might be called genre pieces.

Hunters in the Snow is one of his most popular works. In the grand tradition of the *Très Riches Heures of the Duke of Berry,* Breughel painted the labors of the twelve months (only five of which are still extant). This winter scene (January or February) shows weary hunters trudging through the snow as they return home with their dogs. To their left, women tend an outdoor fire; beyond them stretches a vast Alpine landscape enlivened by skaters and a lonely flying crow.

Breughel captured the chill of winter air with a palette of grey-greens. His simple portrayal of peasants bound to the will of nature is no more than an

objective record. The peasants are as much a part of the landscape as the barren trees or snow-covered fields. With his detached observation, Breughel was able to depict the awesome power of nature. Universal peace is disturbed only slightly by the muffled crunch of snow beneath the hunters' feet. Painted during his last period of work,

The Beggars is not dominated by nature but by humans and their suffering. Only in the background, through a gate, is a small wooded area seen. Never again did the Netherlands produce a painter so totally in communion with nature. Never again was the peasants' simple humanity portrayed with such profound dignity.

HUNTERS IN THE SNOW
by Pieter Breughel (1560) is a vast panorama of winter activities in Breughel's Netherlands. The painting reasserts the importance of the everyday life of simple people as a subject for art.

THE BEGGARS by Pieter Breughel (1568) is one of the Flemish painter's later works.

The Baroque Era

center
US

centre
Brit.

THE PIAZZA AND COLONADE OF ST. PETER'S in Rome, designed by Gianlorenzo Bernini in the 1650s, set the great church in a heroic surrounding, directing all attention toward the church itself and toward the great dome designed earlier by Michelangelo.

The 16th century was a period of artistic genius, but it was also a time of contradiction and conflict, an epoch of tremendous upheaval in virtually every sphere of human activity. The church itself was convulsed by internal abuses. The papal throne was held by a succession of despotic and unscrupulous men, including Leo X, who squandered church funds on lavish pageants and gambling. Surrounded by Renaissance splendor, and battling for secular power, the popes were as much the successors of the Roman Caesars as they were the vicars of Christ.

The relaxation of moral and religious standards provoked a reaction in Northern Europe. Martin Luther, then Zwingli and John Calvin, protested the abuses of Rome and called for reforms. The great movement that these three began is called the Protestant Reformation. It resulted in a great schism in the Western church. From this time on the one Catholic (universal) Church became the Roman Catholic Church, to distinguish it from the Lutheran, Reformed, Calvinist, and other churches of the Reformers.

The Roman church responded to this movement with its own Counter Reformation. Under the pontificates of Pius IV, Situs V, and their successors,

Christian zeal was rekindled. New religious orders were established, and there was a determined effort to directly involve the individual in the dynamism of religious experience.

The early Protestants, whose faith spread rapidly through the Northern half of the European Continent, were suspicious of the arts. In fact, some reformers made it a point to destroy statues, stained glass, and other religious works of art. The Counter Reformation saw the arts as an important part of its plan, however. So for much of the next century, the great work in the visual arts was in the Catholic South. Only gradually did art reassert itself under the Protestants.

The period, however, was more than just a time of religious turmoil. Royal families in France, Spain, and the North were well on their way to establishing absolute power. At the same time, the early Renaissance view that man was at the center of creation was being undermined by the very scientific research the reawakening had encouraged. Copernicus, Galileo, Kepler, and Newton demonstrated that man was a tiny creature on a small planet, in a corner of the universe. Exploration of the Americas, of Africa, and of Asia further

undermined men's sense of certainty and security.

Amid such religious, social, political, and scientific turmoil, it is no wonder that the character of art changed profoundly. The style that developed is known as Baroque. The origin of the name is not clear, but it may derive from the Portuguese *barocco* meaning "irregular" or "rough." It was first used unflatteringly by critics in the 1800s who condemned the style as debased classicism. Their attacks against its over-ornamented theatricality have since been moderated, and we now use Baroque to simply designate the period from 1600 to 1750.

Architecture

The seeds of Baroque theatricality first appeared on Giacomo della Porta's facade for the church of Il Gesu in Rome. As the home of the Jesuits, it exerted considerable influence, and in succeeding centuries the facade was copied around the world. But it was at Saint Peter's, the greatest project of the 16th and 17th centuries, that a truly Baroque character matured.

Pope Paul V directed Carlo Maderna

to extend Bramante's and Michelangelo's centralized plan by adding three bays to the nave. (The centralized format was now considered entirely too pagan for the seat of the Catholic Church.) Maderna was also commissioned to complete the facade, but his plans were never thoroughly executed. His work, as it stands today, is somewhat less than satisfactory. The front of the church is uncomfortably squat. It is too long, and its entrance is woefully understated. Worse yet, its horizontal sprawl tends to dwarf Michelangelo's magnificent dome.

Bernini. These unpleasant effects were alleviated by Gianlorenzo Bernini, who built the piazza (courtyard) in front of St. Peter's. The undisputed genius of the Baroque age, he was an inspired sculptor, architect, dramatist, painter, and composer. Bernini combined his many skills at the Vatican, where he created the glorious *Throne of St. Peter* and carved much of the statuary for the interior of the church. He also constructed the dramatic exterior colonnade, which reaches out like gigantic arms, embracing the entire Christian world. The colonnade transformed St. Peter's from an isolated block into one vibrantly integrated with the surrounding neighborhood. More important, Bernini's great arms (each composed of four rows of colossal Doric columns) make the facade seem taller. He accomplished this by pinching in the colonnades' straight flanks so that they mask the ends of the facade. With the terminal bays thus hidden, the facade seems more lofty and elegant as one approaches it through the sweeping piazza.

Bernini's solution was based on dramatic spatial manipulation. He used classical columns in a most theatrical way, producing a swirling tension and compelling illusion, the very hallmarks of the Baroque style. He brought these qualities to absolute refinement in his *Scala Regia* (stairway leading to the papal apartments) and in his church of Sant' Andrea in Rome.

The same spatial elements were exaggerated by Francesco Borromini, Bernini's rival and the most daring architect of the 17th century. In his little church of San Carlo alle Quattro Fontane, Borromini twisted and turned his facade as if it were rubber. Its walls project and recede like rising ocean swells, dramatically confronting the unsuspecting viewer. He replaced Renaissance static balance with pulsating energy, and Renaissance logic with unbridled emotion. Similar sensations (though considerably modified) were sought by contemporary Baroque architects like Guarino Guarini and Carlo Rainaldi.

Bernini epitomized the goals of contemporary sculptors. His *St. Theresa in Ecstacy* is the most sensuous and sublime statue ever created for the church. Wafted off her feet on a bed of clouds amid golden rays of sun, Theresa

BERNINI'S DAVID is in motion, contrasting with earlier Davids by Donatello and Michelangelo.

swoons as an angel thrusts an arrow of divine love into her bosom. The intimate scene is so constructed that painting, sculpture, and even the surrounding architecture command the viewer's full participation. Like most 17th century religious sculpture, it exists in the realm of mystical theater.

Bernini's artistic genius was already apparent in his marble *David,* which he carved at age 25. A supreme example of Baroque drama, it emphasized the essential break with Renaissance ideals. Unlike Donatello's sweet adolescent *David* or Michelangelo's brooding giant, Bernini's explosive figure springs into action. Balancing on his toes, David lunges back to hurl his stone at Goliath. His entire body strains with the thrust of physical exertion. So determined is the youth that he even bites his lip. This level of psychological tension had never been achieved before, not even in passionate Hellenistic works like Laocöon. Whereas Renaissance sculpture reveled in eternal stasis, Bernini's *David* is caught in split-second action. In another second the slingshot will be released; moments later, David will stand to watch his opponent fall. The viewer is thus irresistibly involved in completing the heroic sequence. With torpedolike force, *David* dominates his surrounding space, defying the containment of a stone block. Calm perfection, the classical ideal, has been abandoned for the fiery passion of the Counter Reformation.

Painting

A different situation is apparent in Baroque painting. Tired of Mannerist extremes, the 17th-century painters returned to nature and classical ideals. They reacted against pictorial distortion and turned to Michelangelo, Raphael, Titian, and to a lesser extent Correggio, for their essential artistic truth. Interestingly, their quest only emphasized the gap that separated them from Renaissance models, for Baroque painters were equally committed to visual truth—even when it conflicted with standards of ideal beauty. Moreover, the Counter Reformation encouraged the expression of impassioned Christianity and demanded viewer involvement.

These multiple influences gave rise to as many painting styles, all of them heroic and all of them Baroque. The Carracci Brothers, for example, combined Raphael's grace, Michelangelo's drama, and Titian's color in their animated mythological paintings in the Farnese Palace. Instead of exaggerating or distorting their High Renaissance models, they tried to recapture some of their simplicity and grandeur. Guido Reni had similar aims, although concentrating more on Raphael's fluid grace in paintings on ceilings where figures seem to dance across the clouds.

Strides toward the depiction of unlimited space gained tremendous momentum with Guercino, Pietro da Cortona, and especially Andrea dal Pozzo. In the latter's *Allegory of the Missionary Work of the Jesuits,* painted on the vaults above San Ignazio in Rome, exuberant figures thrust into the heavens with such force that they appear to surge beyond the limits of the roof. With sweeping action they thunder into the clouds, theatrically denying the distinction between real and painted space.

Baroque painters took the High Renaissance models and gave them a kind of frenzied life. Heroic ease became Herculean effort, sweet love restless passion. The power of painted movement overcame human reason and established itself as the ultimate goal of art. The viewer is drawn irresistibly into a sense of violent, but often sensuous, movement.

Caravaggio. Baroque painters believed that the Renaissance and the ancient masters had captured the essence of art. It merely remained for them to reinterpret and electrify it. This applied to all Italian painters except one: Michelangelo de Merisi, called Caravaggio, who openly denounced High Renaissance achievements. He was a rebel, an antisocial rowdy who had to flee Rome to escape charges of murder. Caravaggio spent his tragic career among the lower elements of Rome. He knew the ugly, the seamy, the dark side of human experience. And he drew on it to explore uncharted

theater
US

theatre
Brit.

emphasized
US

emphasised
Brit.

color
US

colour
Brit.

19 History of Art

territories in art. It is not surprising to learn that he was feared and hated by more than one of his contemporaries.

After an early period of mythological and genre painting, Caravaggio turned almost exclusively to religious works. His *Calling of St. Matthew* provides a compelling example of his unconventional style. The subject matter had been represented countless times before, but never with such profound psychological impact. The scene is a dingy Roman tavern. Seated among common people and young dandies, the bearded Matthew points to himself in disbelief. Why would he be chosen as an apostle? Christ's outstretched hand is a direct descendant of Michelangelo's figure of God in the Creation of Adam from the Sistine ceiling.

Caravaggio explored the power of coarse men in an unrefined environment. He abandoned decorum for cold truth. Consequently, he was charged with irreverence and disrespect. His paintings were regularly refused by the clergy who commissioned them. Still, Caravaggio refused to yield in his portrayal of grim reality. Within ten years of his death, Caravaggio's soul-searching paintings had become the major source of inspiration for Baroque painters in Italy, Spain, France, and the Netherlands. Chief among these were Velasquez, Rubens, and Rembrandt van Rijn.

During the late 1500s and early 1600s, Spain devoted herself to Counter Reformation in the form of the Inquisition, a determined effort to stamp out heresy by punishing (and often killing) the heretics. Isolated and even mysterious by nature, Spanish artists translated Italian Mannerism into a fiery brand of mysticism that agreed with the aims of the Iberian church. El Greco's flickering paintings, ablaze with Byzantine color, were the greatest expression of such religious ecstacy. But by the 17th century, Mannerist distortion was abandoned for the new Baroque style. Caravaggio's imitators, the *Tenebrisi* (the shadowy ones), carried his influence across the Pyrenees where painters like Zurbaran and Diego de Ribera enthusiastically adopted his technique of contrasting intense light and shadow. They used it to paint gruesome religious paintings wherein Christian devotion soared to unprecedented peaks.

Velasquez. The greatest painter of the day responded to Caravaggio in a totally different way. Instead of exploiting darks and lights in sacred dramas, Diego Rodriguez de Silva y Velasquez applied them to his own brand of portraiture.

In 1623 Velasquez was appointed court painter to King Philip IV, and for the next 37 years he was devoted to painting portraits of the royal family. In this time before photography, portraits provided the most important record of the royal family. Moreover, they were used to help arrange marriages and thus came to affect international relations. Needless to say, royal portraits were supposed to be flattering. But for Velasquez this was no small task. With few exceptions, Philip's family was not blessed with an attractive appearance. The situation was only compounded by the stiff and awkward costumes they wore at court. Velasquez rose to the challenge, transforming mere painted likenesses into penetrating character studies. He was one of the most gifted portraitists the world has ever known.

In two lengthy trips to Rome, Velasquez studied Italian achievements. He held no esteem for Raphael, little for the Renaissance as a whole, and perhaps even less for his Baroque contemporaries. He seems to have been influenced only by Titian's brush stroke and Caravaggio's liberating realism. But Velasquez never surrendered his Spanish individuality.

His acclaimed masterpiece is *Las Meninas* (the ladies in waiting). It is an enormous painting, the largest Velasquez ever produced. The painter represents himself inside his studio working on a large canvas (perhaps *Las Meninas* itself). To his left is the Infanta Margarita, whose kneeling maid offers a glass of water. Another maid stands between the royal child and her favorite dwarfs. Velasquez shared none of the court's perverse delight in these "human toys" and painted the dwarfs with dignity and compassion. Two more servants stand in middle ground, while a court official pauses in the door to observe the activities. To his left is a mirror that reflects the king and queen. Indeed, it might also reflect our own images because the royal couple views the scene from our own position outside the room. Brush and palette in hand, the painter stares at them (and us).

Las Meninas is one of the most complex illusionistic paintings ever created. By distributing his figures within and beyond the artist's studio, Velasquez establishes different layers of space and reality. He does this with such finesse that the studied group portrait appears to be no more than an informal gathering. The whole is transformed by diffuse shadows that dissolve distinct edges and by orchestrated highlights that dance from satin dresses to the reflected mirror image. Unlike van Eyck, who painted every tiny detail with exacting precision, Velasquez used quick brush strokes to suggest different textures. He used splashes of light, color, and shadow to create the illusion of form.

Quite aside from being a brilliant

CARAVAGGIO'S CALLING OF ST. MATTHEW drew controversy from critics who disliked the harsh reality of his works.

exploration of optical mysteries, *Las Meninas* is a testament to the artist's new professional status. Velasquez sought recognition as a noble in the illustrious Order of Santiago. At first, he was denied entry because painting was considered manual labor and below the dignity of nobility. But two years before he died, Velasquez's dream came true, and at the hand of King Philip he was inducted into the prestigious society. This honor is recorded by the red cross on the painter's doublet, which, according to tradition, was painted by the king himself. At last the respectability of the artistic profession had been realized.

Rubens. Velasquez's patronage by the Spanish court was typical of the 1600s. It was an age when royal monarchs glorified their reigns with sumptuous palaces and magnificent works of art. Foremost in royal esteem was Peter Paul Rubens, whose bouyant energy, brilliant color sense, and vibrant love of life made him the perfect instru-ment of royal pomp and ceremony.

Like Velasquez, Rubens studied in Italy. But unlike his Spanish friend, he fully adopted Italian art as the basis of his personal style. He studied antiquity, the Renaissance, and the works of his Baroque colleagues, drawing on Michelangelo's explosive power, Titian's color, Carracci's classicism, and Caravaggio's drama. He combined these influences with his native Flemish dedication to appearances. So successful was his synthesis that Rubens established a virtual monopoly over Baroque royal painting. Commissions flooded in from all over Europe.

In many cases Rubens only prepared quick color sketches for his students, who actually executed the paintings in his bustling studio. The master supervised their work and periodically stepped in to correct certain flaws or to provide glowing finishing touches.

Some idea of Rubens' universal appeal can be gained from his *Rape of the Daughters of Leucippus,* which

JUAN, A SERVANT by Velasquez helped establish the portraitist as one of the world's most renowned.

labor
US

labour
Brit.

honor
US

honour
Brit.

realized
US

realised
Brit.

recounts the abduction of two female mortals by the gods Castor and Pollux. Amid rearing horses and fluttering drapery the divine sons of Jupiter satisfy their love. The theme recalls Titian's *Rape of Europa,* as do the overly fleshy maidens. But Titian's work seems subdued in comparison with this dynamic sensuality. Rubens' work is violent. It is not the violence of struggle that activates the painting, for the gods hardly strain, and the maidens do not really resist. Instead, it is the motion of voluptuous passion rendered in sensuous tones of pearly flesh and glittering satins. Rising from a low horizon the interwoven figures sweep upward to a thundering climax. The splashing sea of female flesh reveals Rubens' primary interest: the human body in all of its healthy exuberance. More than any other painter, Rubens summed up the radiant pleasures of love.

SPACE AND ACTION, major Baroque concerns, are studied in *Las Meninas* by Velasquez (1656) and *Rape of the Daughters of Leucippus* by Rubens (1617).

19 History of Art

The Baroque art scene in Flanders was totally dominated by Rubens. The only other major painter was Anthony van Dyck, who concentrated on refined aristocratic portraits. But in neighboring Holland the situation was completely different. Constrained by sober Protestant reforms, Dutch painters shrank from any form of religious art. Nor was there a strong monarch interested in glorifying his court. When painters were thus deprived of their primary stimuli, they turned to the open market. They relied on the new class of merchants who wanted paintings as symbols of their wealth.

the middle classes with landscapes, shipping scenes, views of domestic interiors, and great numbers of still lifes. Jacob van Ruisdael, Pieter de Hooch, and Jan Steen are among the most famous of these painters, but many others produced works of extremely high quality. In a class by themselves are Frans Hals' engaging portraits and the studied interiors of Vermeer, which imbued Dutch life with an eternally quiet dignity.

Rembrandt.

The supreme talent, however, was Rembrandt van Rijn. Rembrandt's early life was a wonderful success story. His arresting powers of observation, his mysterious sense of light, and his incomparable graphic skills flooded him with more commissions than he could possibly hope to execute. But by the time he was 50, Rembrandt's luck had soured. He fell into disastrous financial difficulties and the two women he loved most had died. He abandoned his earlier robust style, in which he combined the influence of Rubens and Caravaggio. He withdrew to quiet visions bathed in silent light. He turned increasingly to contemplative religious scenes and sympathetic studies of human affliction. The same spirituality is apparent in the series of self-portraits that Rembrandt executed in the last decade of his life.

One of the most moving appears on this page. In form it derives from Raphael's portrait of *Baldassare Castiglione,* but how different this is from its aristocratic beauty. Old, tired, and plagued by bankruptcy, the artist peers into the depths of his own character. The paint of his careworn face was laid on thickly with a knife, its rough texture adding to the sense of wrinkled old age. Rembrandt used light to reveal his innermost concerns, allowing it to merge with the gloomy ground behind. There are no stiff outlines, just patches of light and shadow. With profound understanding, Rembrandt completes the Renaissance conquest of illumination. It was begun by Masaccio, developed in Leonardo's *sfumato,* and dramatized by Caravaggio. To Rembrandt light was the painter's most important tool.

In the second half of the 1600s, Rembrandt's Holland and Velasquez's Spain fell to the power of France. Under the absolute monarchy of Louis XIV, the Sun King, France replaced Rome as the artistic center of the world. It established itself as the leader in the visual arts, a position unchallenged for nearly 300 years.

Italian influences were initially strong. Bernini was invited to France and carved a swirling marble portrait of the Sun King. He also submitted a design for the royal Louvre palace. But Italian exuberance found no home in the elegant and refined French court. Bernini was dismissed and under Louis and his chief minister, Colbert, French art was systematically organized for the

**LATE
SELF-PORTRAIT**
by Rembrandt (1669)
contrasts with the
earlier portrait below.

With the new market came a change in attitude and subject matter. There were no paintings of sacred visions or royal portraits, no saints in ecstacy or rapturous nudes. Instead there were small studies of everyday life. Over 40 "little masters" supplied the demand of

aggrandizement of the king. The palace at Versailles was the crowning triumph of his absolute kingship. Never before or since has the impact of one man had such a pervasive influence over every aspect of human life.

There were, of course, outside influences, but in each case they were translated into something categorically French. For example, Dutch interpretations of Caravaggio filtered into the art of Georges de la Tour. But he simplified and abstracted them to a point of classical symmetry. So too with Louis LeNain's paintings of French peasants. But it was Nicolas Poussin who really established the classical character of French Baroque painting.

Poussin. Interestingly, Poussin spent most of his life in Rome. He had little patience with court intrigues and

tale objectively with the distance of classical logic. The lone corpse and its bearers do not evoke poignant response from the viewer; they are almost incidental to the rolling landscape dotted with classical buildings stretching back in time and place. Unlike his contemporaries, Poussin had no interest in merely recreating nature; he harbored no desire to update antiquity. He tried instead to reverse the process, and attempted to bring the 17th century back to ancient Rome.

He longed for the time when men painted only the most elevated themes. Battles, heroic actions, and religious scenes provided the stage for his classically balanced works. Poussin's style totally opposed Caravaggio's vulgar, or Rubens' vibrating, works. He strove not for emotional, but intellectual response. Accordingly, Poussin distilled his paint-

King. Pulsating shapes and restless colors were harnessed for his supreme glory. Jarring contrasts were replaced by Louis' passion for rigid symmetry. Louis used art as an international expression of his absolute power over France, a good deal of Europe, and even nature itself. Through the brilliant work of Louis Le Notre, the gardens at Versailles were made to obey the will of the king. To his great delight, natural irregularities were "corrected." Trees, bushes, lawns, and flowers were transformed into green geometry.

The binding regulations of French Baroque art were loosened in Louis' old age. By the time he died in 1715, the pendulum had swung and France joyously embraced the playful Rococo style.

But if French classicism was fated to die with Louis, it would thrive on British shores. Under the influence of Sir

BURIAL OF PHOCIAN
by Poussin (1660) brings a new kind of balance and repose to Baroque art, reflecting the stately court of King Louis XIV of France in its attempt to bring back the calm of classical art.

preferred to accept private commissions from sophisticated Frenchmen. He entertained no interest in the Renaissance (except for Raphael, whom he admired), and none at all in Italian Baroque. Instead, he skipped back to antiquity directly. His *Burial of Phocian* shows the results of Poussin's classical nostalgia. After reading the ancient writings of Plutarch, Poussin illustrated the story of Phocian, an Athenian hero who was unjustly executed by his countrymen. Denied burial in his mother country, the outcast was carried past its boundaries to a site of eternal isolation. Poussin chose to represent this painful

ing technique to a formula for classical calm. He omitted all distracting incidentals and concentrated on the almost mathematical balance of his composition. Even color was reduced to a position of secondary importance.

Poussin's concerns with austere regularity so strongly opposed the mainstream of 17th-century art that it may seem illogical to classify him as a Baroque artist. But his classicism provided a true view of France under Louis XIV. He was not so much deflating Baroque energies as redirecting their expression and purpose.

Now all things centered on the Sun

Christopher Wren and John Vanbrugh, classical logic replaced the last vestiges of the Middle Ages. In the early 1700s, under Vanbrugh, English landscape gardening achieved its first definitive shape. Wren's St. Paul's Cathedral in London combined Italian Renaissance and French Baroque classicism into something thoroughly English. Still somewhat concerned with nonclassical spatial problems, St. Paul's nevertheless anchored English interest in the past. The splendor of antiquity would be the absolute preoccupation of the following century.

—Janet Adams

Rococo and Neoclassic Art

The prevailing style of the early 1700s is called Rococo. The word derives from the French *rocaille,* or pebble, referring to the decoration of grottoes that were encrusted with pebbles and shells. Some of the most fanciful decoration in Italy had been done in the late Renaissance in the artificial grottoes of such palaces as the Pitti in Florence. It is this unrestrained decoration that is the essence of the Rococo style. The Rococo is a development of the earlier Baroque style in France, and the two share the same exuberance and energy, in contrast to the weight and stability of classic art.

Painting and Decoration

In France, the Rococo remained an interior style. It was developed and used extensively in the great *hotels,* or private houses, of the French aristocracy; these houses were built in Paris in the first part of the century. When Louis XIV died in 1715, the nobles who had been constrained to live at the court were free to build houses in Paris. These houses, or *hotels,* are found today in the section of Paris called the Marais. The exteriors of the houses are often of simple, even sober, design. The plots of land available at the time were both irregular and limited in size.

The interiors of the *hotels,* however, were lavishly decorated, reflecting the gaiety of a new age. The Regency in France (the early years of Louis XV when France was ruled by his regent) repudiated the austerity and formality of Louis XIV, both in manners and in artistic taste. Louis XV lived until 1774,

and in France the Rococo style is called Louis XV.

Paris was a major center of intellectual and artistic life of Europe in the 1700s. Much of its activity centered on the salons of the great *hotels.* The Rococo style was carried out in the furniture, in the woodwork and plastering, in the ornaments, and in the painting and sculpture.

One of the most beautiful of these Rococo rooms is the Salon de la Princesse in the Hotel de Soubise. It was decorated by Germain Boffrand between 1737 and 1740. The overwhelming impression is of lightness and movement. The cornices of the room have disappeared, lost amid the gilded woodwork, mirrors, and painting. The entire room seems to rise to the richness of the ceiling, and the whole is unified by a repetition of forms—foliage, tendrils, scrolls, and shells—that are found in the furniture as well. This decorative, flowing style is very feminine, perhaps because the salons of Paris, as well as many of the courts of Europe, were dominated by women. Maria Theresa ruled in Austria; Elizabeth and then Catherine were the first empresses of Russia; and Madame de Pompadour, Louis XV's mistress, was a major power in France. The development of taste for the Rococo, however, has as much to do with the pale women had begun to assume in the 1600s when, long before the death of Louis XIV, they began to pursue their own interests.

The French school. Painting in France in the early 1700s is dominated by Jean Watteau (1684–1721). Watteau's student Boucher, and his successor Fragonard, carried on the

Rococo tradition in painting until the French Revolution in 1789.

Watteau helped invent the Rococo style, but his paintings tower above it. He died at the age of 37, yet painted some of the most beautiful and mysterious canvases ever to be produced in France. *The Voyage to Cythera,* completed in 1717, won his admission to the French Academy, but the academy had to create a new category for it. From then on, such paintings were called *fetes galantes,* which means courtly or romantic entertainments.

This spirit characterizes most thoroughly French Rococo painting; as a literary form, it had flourished in the preceding century. In *The Voyage to Cythera,* eight couples form a cortege across the canvas. They are departing from the island of Cythera, which was holy to Venus. A statue of the goddess of love is seen on the right, adorned with garlands. The painting seems an anthology of the rite of love. Its mood is of lingering tenderness, clearly evoked by the woman at the center of the picture who is looking back over her shoulder. The couples are variations on a single theme, expressing the most graceful attitudes of love. Their movement away from the statue of Venus describes a long horizontal, gently curving line that is continued by the boat and the cupids. The whole seems to lead to an apotheosis in the figures of the cupids in the sky. This sensuous line illustrates the essential Rococo sense of movement. The setting is the most ideal of landscapes, luminescent, ephemeral, and vast. Nature is at its most benign and seems to shelter the shrine and the last couple, who have not yet gotten up.

Watteau's particular poetic powers would not be equaled again in his century. He was unique in being willing to confront delicate feelings of sadness and uncertainty, and his pictures suggest deep, but undefinable, emotion. His other well known works—a portrait called *L'Indifferent* and a portrait of the clown Gilles—also reflect this emotional depth.

Watteau's successors, François Boucher and Jean Honoré Fragonard, perpetuate the painter's genre, the *fetes galantes,* but it becomes a kind of Rococo decoration, and Watteau's psychological questioning is lost. Boucher (1703–1770) was commissioned as a young man to engrave Watteau's paintings. He helped transform Watteau's style into the full-blown Rococo. Boucher was the favorite painter of Madame de Pompadour, and later the "first painter of the king." Consequently, his influence was enormous.

Boucher's royal style can be seen in his portrait of Madame de Pompadour. The king's favorite is seen as both languorous and dignified. Her surroundings are of soft luxury and exquisite, refined taste.

THE VOYAGE TO CYTHERA by Jean Watteau shows the new warmth and emotion Rococo painters introduced into their "entertainments."

More important, Boucher perpetuated the *fetes galantes,* developing the convention of amorous idylls in a protective, rich natural world. A typical painting is the *Shepherd Piping to a Shepherdess.* It is one of Watteau's couples caught in a graceful and ideal moment of love in a setting that mirrors in its flowers and luxuriant growth the love of the human couple.

Boucher's figures, however, have little to do with Watteau. They have rather the fleshy opulence of Rubens. This is even more evident in the *Cupid a Captive* (1754) where nudes of distinct, Rubenesque proportions intertwine with the natural elements to create an atmosphere of sensuality from which any hint of human care is banished. The title of one of his allegorical pictures, *The Triumph of Venus,* indicates Boucher's philosophy: the goddess of love commands and dominates the natural world. To later viewers, this idealized state has little to do with real life.

Fragonard (1732–1806) was Boucher's pupil, and like his teacher, he was patronized by the French court. He was the last and most appreciated painter of the Rococo style in France, but his prosperity vanished with the style. After the French Revolution, the Rococo was identified with the overthrown monarchy. Fragonard died a poor man in Naples, forgotten in his native country.

The great exuberance of the Rococo style survives in Fragonard's paintings, however. They are, if possible, more sensual than Boucher's. Fragonard was a great colorist, and owes more to Rubens even than Boucher. In the *Bathers* (1765), the viewer is transported into a world that is constructed of round, sensual, human forms, foliage, and water. But Fragonard has dispensed with even a semblance of a rational, natural ordering of his elements. The foliage, the water, and the women's bodies interweave in a vision of ecstatic and unrestrained joy of the flesh. At the center of the picture is a piece of brilliant pink drapery that seems to be a kind of flag that floats like the clouds and echoes the shapes of the sheltering foliage. The play of the brilliant pink and the bright greens against the blues of the sky is intense. The enthusiasm of the bathers creates an atmosphere of excitement that is an aesthetic counterpart of pornography.

Fragonard's painting is always unashamedly sensual. In another of his well known paintings, *The Swing* (1766), the erotic element is the crux of the picture. The scene is no longer of bathing nymphs, but of a woman whose position in a swing is an unexpected, or perhaps planned, good fortune for her lover hidden in the foliage beneath her. There is an element of humor since the young woman is pushed in her swing by an elderly bishop who cannot see the young man. The woman's dress is the same brilliant floating drapery that one sees in the *Bathers.* Orange-pink, it

stands out against the dark but brilliant greens of the background. The picture is an intense dramatization of woman as an object of desire. She floats in her swing as a vision that is both idealized and humorously honest.

Realism. The style of Boucher and Fragonard was not the only possibility for painters in 18th-century France. In at least one case, great painting had nothing to do with the Rococo. Jean Baptiste Siméon Chardin (1699–1779) produced paintings of the solid bourgeoisie: interior scenes with women and children, even servants, portraying the intimacy of family life. His subject matter recalls the earlier Dutch painters such as Vermeer. The rapid, curving line of Fragonard and Boucher is absent in Chardin. He composes his pictures around large geometrical shapes, and there are many rectangles and circles in his pictures. The flat surface of the canvas, the picture plane, is divided by these shapes into distinct areas that give the illusion of stability—the moral and artistic value that the pictures extol. Chardin bathes his subjects in a gentle light that further emphasizes the calm of the pictures and makes them objects suitable for contemplation.

The picture reproduced here, *Back from the Market,* shows a servant still holding what she has brought from her shopping. She seems uncertain what to do next, and Chardin has arrested our attention on a moment without drama or grandeur. In a picture only 18 by 14 inches, Chardin renders the solidity of the walls and furniture, a fully developed space, a particular atmosphere, and the woman's passing mood. Chardin's art seems to reflect one aspect of the Enlightenment in its particularly reasonable and sane search for truth and value. It is noteworthy that Chardin was admired by Diderot, a great figure of the Age of Enlightenment.

Much less subtle than Chardin and much more patently moralistic is Jean Baptiste Greuze (1725–1805). He is best known for his scenes of moral rearmament, as in *The Return of the Prodigal Son.* Greuze does not hesitate to improve on the Christian parable—his prodigal son returns to his father's deathbed. The dramatic grief of the painting seems melodramatic and overdone. Another typical painting by Greuze is *The Village Bride,* which is a scene from the life of the lower classes. Again the sentiment of the painting is without subtlety. Greuze's paintings of this kind are perhaps most interesting as documents of a France that both exalted the common people and condemned the frivolous immorality of the upper classes. These are the views that triumph in the French Revolution.

Italy. Outside of France the greatest Rococo painter was Giovanni Battista Tiepolo (1696–1770). He was a Venetian but he worked mostly in Austria, Germany, and Spain. Unlike French Rococo pictures, the paintings of Tiepolo are enormous; often he painted frescoes as part of architectural schemes for churches and villas. His style was well adapted to its architectural function, and perhaps no one has ever painted such airy and limitless skies. They seemed to open the ceilings of the buildings themselves. His painting is distinguished by his economical and sure draftsmanship. Tiepolo needed only minimal line and shadow to create illusions of great space animated by moving figures and brilliant light.

Two other Italians of the 18th century were also adept at capturing great

MRS. ELLIOT, by Gainsborough, is one of his great portraits of English ladies.

center
US

centre
Brit.

colors
US

colours
Brit.

spaces. They were Antonio Canaletto (1697–1768) and Francesco Guardi (1712–1793). Like Tiepolo, they were Venetians, but they continued to paint easel pictures. Their main subject was their native city, of which their paintings make up an illustrated history. The festivals, lively citizens, canals, and splendid squares of Venice were recorded by both painters with care and with feeling.

England. English painting of 18th century is dominated by the portraits of English lords and ladies, as its architecture is dominated by their great houses. The first major painter of the century, William Hogarth (1697–1764), is, however, best known for his dramatic, satirical paintings. In intent, these paintings are as apt to moralize as those of Greuze, with the fundamental difference that Hogarth's are immensely humorous and entertaining. They read like scenes from novels. Engravings were made from the paintings and widely sold, the most famous series being the *Rake's Progress* (1735). The individual scenes are characterized by great detail and incident and reveal a fully developed story that the viewer can spend much time in deciphering. A typical scene is *The Orgy,* where overindulgence in wine and pleasure cost the rake his purse, which one of his lady friends deftly steals.

As are many of Hogarth's heroes, the rake is from the English upper classes. Hogarth's eloquence in exposing the weaknesses of the upper classes is overshadowed, however, by the accomplishments of other English painters in showing their strengths. Never before or since has painting so effectively and so extensively created an image of a class. The immensely rich upper classes could afford to commission the painters' work, of course, but the quality of the resulting work is a tribute to the artists' talents.

Before the 1700s, the English had imported painters from Europe. Holbein and Van Dyck, for example, made famous portraits of English kings. But the great portraitists of the 1700s were native-born.

Sir Joshua Reynolds (1723–1792) was the more conservative of two great painters, and served as president of the Royal Academy. His theory of art was deliberately classical, and he ennobled his portraits with classical motives. Thomas Gainsborough (1727–1788) began his career as a landscape painter. In one of his early pictures, the double portrait of Robert Andrews and his wife, the figures are placed in a broad expanse of English countryside that is painted with great skill and love.

Gainsborough, however, became the most sought after of portrait painters, and in the portrait of Mrs. Elliot reproduced here, it is easy to see what attracted his clients. It is hard to imagine a portrait of more elegance. At the time the portrait was made, Mrs. Elliot was the mistress of a great English lord who paid for the painting. Like most of the portraits of the time, it is life size and was meant to adorn the hall of a very large house as a guarantee of the elegance of its owners. Gainsborough gave himself wholeheartedly to the depiction of this elegance. Mrs. Elliot's tall and graceful figure is emphasized by the column behind her, and one sees the painter's delight in the shimmering splendor of her clothes and shoes. In contrast to the light concentrated in her figure and hair, all tones of silver, grey, and gold, is the dark landscape that forms the left of the picture. Mrs. Elliot seems to come in from that landscape, and her presence is a kind of rich, brilliant light that dominates both the architecture and the natural world.

Gainsborough's subjects are not always rendered with icy brilliance. In his portrait of Mrs. Richard Sheridan he treats his subject differently. Mrs. Sheridan is placed in a luxuriant and soft natural setting, and her hair, dress, and sash are of the same hues as the landscape. The woman's mood seems also a reflection of the landscape, almost melancholy. Gainsborough at his best seems to anticipate English romantic poetry. He was also brilliant in revealing great psychological insight in purely visual terms.

New directions. Gainsborough reached the highest technical level of any English painter, but his subject matter remained conservative. At the same time in England, one of the earliest manifestations of the new Romantic feeling appeared. One of the great themes of Romantic painting and literature would be the violence and passion of nature, and one of the ways of portraying that violence would be through the depiction of animals. George Stubbs (1724–1806) was a portrait painter who often painted racehorses. In 1770 he painted a picture that prefigured the new Romanticism. His *Lion Attacking a Horse* was the result of his having seen a horse killed by a lion in North Africa. His painting is much more than a recording of the event; it is its re-creation in terms that allow the expression of the greatest emotion and psychological violence.

Earlier painters of the 1700s portrayed nature as a haven for man. In Stubbs's picture, nature is a threat. The lion, the rocks, the clouds, and even the trees are dark manifestations of forces that destroy, lit peculiarly red by a storm. The horse, in its movement and in the violent contrast of its whiteness, is not so much a victim as an opposing, and also potentially frightening, force. Its mane is fire, and its teeth and head are the focus of the violence of the picture. The indulgence of this kind of violent feeling is one of the distinguishing features of Romanticism.

The painting has the same force as does the poetry of William Blake (1757–1827), another Englishman of the same period whose work was also part of the early development of Romanticism. Blake's lines recall Stubbs in their concentration of an image, in their reliance on strong contrasts of dark and light, and in their awe of violence:

> Tyger! tyger! burning bright
> In the forests of the night,
> What immortal hand or eye
> Dare frame thy fearful symmetry?

Blake was also an artist of some accomplishment. His drawings are outside the technical mainstream of art and were meant to illustrate his poems in a way reminiscent of medieval illuminations. Yet Blake and his friend Henry Fuseli (1741–1825) were proponents of the cult of the imagination that deeply influenced the Romantics in their desire to explore the world of feeling.

At the end of the 1700s, human emotion was seeking a direct outlet in art. Strangely, it was in France, where the old style had been most securely rooted, that the new art broke forth with the most violence.

Architecture

The architecture of the 1700s in Europe saw the growth of a new classicism. The Baroque style ended with a great flourish of Rococo in southern Germany and Austria in the early part of the century. But in England and France, a very pure classic style developed that quickly overcame rival styles.

Rococo. The Rococo style in France remained always decorative and was seen particularly in the interiors of the *hotels* of Paris. In southern Germany and Austria, however, the Rococo was used for a great number of churches and palaces that are Rococo in architecture as well as decoration. The Rococo architectural style owed much to earlier

Italian styles, in particular the work of Francesco Borromini and Giovanni Guarini. The classic clarity of function and space is abandoned, and the decoration of the German and Austrian churches of this period is the most exuberant development of the Rococo line.

Fine examples of the style are found all over Germany and Austria, and one of the very best is the Vierzehnheiligen (Fourteen Saints) Pilgrimage Church by Balthasar Neumann (1687–1753). The surface of the facade of the church undulates and its corners are rounded, recalling the work of Borromini. The interior of the church is perhaps the highest point ever reached by the Rococo style. The altar is placed in the center of the church, allowing the various spaces to intersect; the decoration almost completely avoids horizontal and straight lines. The effect is one of continuous flow and movement with an opulence and lightness rarely achieved in architecture. The colors of the decoration are white, gold, pale yellow, coral, blue, and pink, with the whole bathed in light. The painted ceiling completes the effect, as the upper reaches seem lost in the clouds.

Neoclassicism. In the rest of Europe the 1700s brought a style of architecture that is the antithesis of the Baroque and Rococo. Versailles, built in the second part of the 1600s, was a monument of French classicism, and the taste that determined its construction never waned in France. If anything, this taste become purified of any extraneous elements.

The architecture of Jacques Ange Gabriel (1698–1782) is a simplified, more rudimentary version of the classicism of the preceding century. Gabriel built the École Militaire and the Hotel Crillon in Paris and the Petit Trianon at Versailles, which is illustrated here. The small palace, built in the park, shows the values of weight and solidity and the clear organization of elements that are the basis of any classic art. One also sees the paring down of ornamentation,

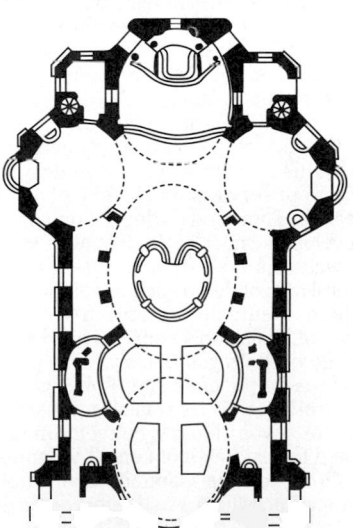

19 History of Art

ROCOCO AND NEOCLASSIC: the differences between the two competing styles are most clearly seen in architecture, where the irregular and ornate Vierzehnheiligen Church (left and below left) contrasts sharply with the Petit Trianon in France (below).

compared even with the main palace at Versailles. The Petit Trianon was built only a few years after the Vierzehn-heiligen Church, and the contrast illustrates the wide variations in taste during this period.

Another of the great neoclassic monuments of Paris is the Pantheon by Jacques Germain Soufflot (1713–1780). The Pantheon is a huge cross-shaped church on the Mont Saint Genevieve surmounted by a dome that overlooks Paris. Scholarly archaeology grew up in the 1700s, bringing a renewed interest in the buildings of Greece and Rome. The immense portico of the Pantheon is modeled on that of a Roman temple. The dome, however, is modeled on St. Paul's in London, and its proportions are those of Baroque Italy. Despite these varied elements, the effect is a classic sense of order and simplicity.

Town planning was one of the most noteworthy feats of French neoclassicism. In Nancy, the capital of the province of Lorraine, the center of the town was rebuilt along a new north-south street, with a series of beautiful squares and a palace, all in proportion to one another and unified by classical details. In Russia, too, the sense of order of classicism prevailed, and St. Petersburg (now Leningrad) became an ordered classical city.

England had had a great classic architect in the person of Inigo Jones in the 1600s, but the first great monument of 1700s England is Blenheim Place by Sir John Vanbrugh (1664–1726). Blenheim is a mixture of Baroque and classical styles on a mammoth scale. Many of the other great country houses show a search for a new, but not necessarily classical, style. Strawberry Hill, built by Horace Walpole, is in eclectic Gothic style, following a fashion of imitating Gothic ruins. In urban planning, the classic triumph on a grand scale is the architecture of John Wood and his son, who rebuilt the city of Bath, designing squares, streets, and crescents in vast classical orders.

America makes its first contribution to art history in architecture. Particularly in Virginia, the classically based Georgian style predominated. Thomas Jefferson's designs for Monticello (1769) and later for the University of Virginia modified the plain and very clear style that had already developed along Palladian lines in large houses such as Carter's Grove.

Sculpture

The 18th century was not a great age for sculpture. There were few commissions for monumental works, and the Baroque style of the preceding century was transformed into the much less serious Rococo. Rococo sculpture is small, intended to be viewed inside and close at hand. It is not without quality, but it does not rival the earlier schools. An excellent example of its charm is the *Satyr and Bacchante* of Clodion (c 1775). The statue is in terra cotta, and the movement and complicated relations of the figures are faithful to Baroque ideals despite the smaller scale.

Romantic Art

It is common among historians to think of the 18th century as ending in 1789 with the French Revolution. This date is fitting in the history of art as well; soon after the revolution, France became the center of the artistic world. Paris in the 1700s was an intellectual center, but not necessarily the city where the most important artistic creation took place. Beginning after the revolution and well into the 1900s, Paris was unquestionably the most important center in the world for painting and sculpture. With few exceptions, the history of art became the history of French art. In many ways a movement as vigorous as the Italian Renaissance took place in France in the 125 years after the revolution, and that movement led to our modern conception of art.

Painting

Goya. The greatest painter to bridge the 18th and 19th centuries, however, is not French but Spanish. Francisco Goya (1746–1828) is an isolated figure, generally considered outside the various schools of painting. He acknowledged his indebtedness to Velasquez and Rembrandt, but his painting is unlike anyone else's, and younger artists did not follow his lead. He arrived in Madrid in 1766, when Tiepolo was working there, and Goya's early painting has something of the lightness of the Rococo.

As his career developed, however, his style became increasingly his own. He was the court painter to Charles IV of Spain. He did many fine portraits, one of which is that of the king's entire family, painted in 1800. The picture recalls Velasquez's *Las Meninas* because Goya places himself in the picture in the act of painting. Indeed, the most fitting comparison for Goya is with Velasquez. The two handled paint and the use of highlights in similar fashion. There are also certain similarities of attitude in the two pictures cited. Goya's picture is famous, however, for the completely unflattering manner in which the members of the royal family are portrayed. Splendidly dressed, the adult members are at best plain and their attitudes undistinguished. The children are treated from a more hopeful point of view, and the young prince in the center of the picture has some of the mixture of fear and pride that one sees in the portrait of Don Manuel Osorio reproduced here.

Goya's themes become increasingly morbid and fantastic as he grows older. In response to the invasion of Spain by Napoleon, Goya used his painting to recall political events, as in the famous war picture *The Third of May, 1808,* a violent and emotion-filled depiction of the execution of the citizens of Madrid by a firing squad of French soldiers. Goya depicted the same kind of atrocities in a series of etchings called *Horrors of War,* and another series called *Disasters.* At the end of his life, he painted horrible fantasies, such as *Saturn Devouring His Children;* one of his etchings is called *The Dream of Reason Produces Nightmares.*

Even in his early portrait of Don Manuel Osorio, one can see Goya's profound sensitivity to the human situation and the fragility of feeling that would result in a morbid and consuming preoccupation with evil. The young child, like the prince in the portrait of the family of Charles IV, is both intently aware of the world around him and ready, it seems, to withdraw from it. He is an easy prey, like the magpie on its string. The picture has a symbolic function; the caged birds are traditional symbols of innocence, yet the child and the birds are surrounded by shadow. In the child's gaze and in his surroundings there is a brooding presence of something that is neither childlike nor beautiful. The picture seems to anticipate the disasters that Goya (and the child) would see in his own life.

David. Goya's contemporary in France was Jacques-Louis David (1748–1825), who also painted political pictures. David, too, was an official painter of a government, but his masters were republican revolutionaries rather than royalty. David saw his share of disasters, but his art remained public and even optimistic.

David is the most important painter of the French Revolution, yet paradoxically, his style has become synonymous with conservatism. David spent six years in Rome and during his time there developed a neoclassic style of painting. It was this style that he used as the moral arm of the French Revolution and which eventually became the official style of Napoleon's empire. David was a friend of the revolutionary Robespierre and was imprisoned after Robespierre's fall from power. He was also a member of the revolutionary convention that voted for the death of Louis XVI, and an authority on the Committee on Public Education, which was in charge of the art of the new republic.

In *The Death of Marat* David's style and message are clear. One sees first the absolute clarity of form: the perfectly modeled torso and drapery, which have the precision of sculpture, and the clear description of shallow illuminated space. But the picture is more than an exercise in form; it is a dramatic and impressive vehicle for a message. David's picture pays homage to the revolutionary hero and martyr Marat, who had been assassinated in his bath by the young Charlotte Corday, who was opposed to his politics. David's portrayal of the dead hero (who was his friend) is clearly a political message, stark and simple as his signing of the picture, "To Marat." Marat's fate is illuminated in this picture as if a spotlight were brought to bear upon it. David saw his painting as a clear means of communication derived from the mastery of form. His style is a return to the classical rules of Poussin, but he puts his art to the service of his political convictions. His classicism becomes a means of teaching and communication, even propaganda, in the real world of historical events.

Ingres. David's classicism was the official style of the French Academy until late in the 1800s. It was propagated most effectively by his greatest pupil, Jean Auguste Dominique Ingres (1780–1867), who himself became head of the academy. Ingres's actual study with David was not a success, and in his early years he was considered a rebel and his style a deformation of classic art. With time, however, it was seen that

he, more than anyone else, was faithful to David's principles. Chief among those principles was the preeminent importance of drawing in painting.

Classic art—architecture, painting, and sculpture—relies on the clear rendering of form, mass, and weight. In painting, the only way to convey these values is through drawing. Ingres as a draftsman was second to none, and whereas the actual forms he chose to paint differed considerably from those of David, he relied on the same careful modeling and the emphasis on contour that characterized David's style. Drawing is taught by academic discipline. Ingres more than any painter in the 1800s was the master of that discipline. Yet the classicism of Ingres was very different from that of David. Ingres used his mastery of technical means not to convey a message, but to create art that is an end in itself. Besides his portraits and a number of mythological paintings, Ingres is known for his pictures of the "odalisques," or Turkish harem slaves. These pictures are unique in the history of art for their splendor and precision. Human shapes, jewels, cloth—all contribute to help give the completely convincing illusion of reality. It is a reality that has little to do with the day to day. In this sense Ingres is closer to Boucher and Fragonard than to David.

In his portrait of Joseph Antoine Moltedo, the great gifts of Ingres are visible despite a seemingly necessary contradiction. The subject of the portrait is in no way handsome, and Ingres renders the man's plainness with scrupulous and masterful drawing. The

man's clothes, of a rich brown velvet and the whitest linen, are painted with the same care. In contrast to the man's person are objects of great, almost miraculous, beauty. The setting against which the man is painted, a distant cityscape of Rome, is of the same intense beauty. This portrait documents Ingres's particular genius: the mastery of perfect illusion. Ingres used this mastery to record the intense visual beauty he saw and obviously enjoyed, creating one of the most refined styles that ever existed in painting.

The early 1800s are commonly referred to as the Romantic era, and critics traditionally spoke of neoclassicism and Romanticism as opposites. In a sense, however, the neoclassicism of Ingres is but one school of Romanticism. His painting of the odalisques, his love of the opulent, and his treatment of landscape are all manifestations of the Romantic view of the world. The Romanticism of David and Ingres seems calm and reasonable, but it shares with the more turbulent Romanticism a desire to make visible a world that is exotic and far beyond the banality of ordinary existence.

One of the painters whose work helps shape what is commonly called Romantic painting is another of David's pupils, Baron Antoine Jean Gros (1771–1835). His best known painting, *The Pest House at Jaffa,* shows Napoleon visiting his plague-stricken troops. The painting pays homage to the emperor and, like some of David's works, carries a political message. The picture is also an attempt to describe the harrowing

19 History of Art

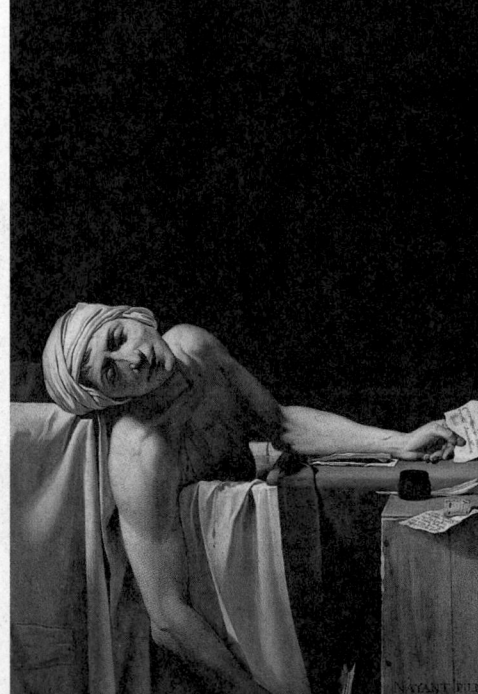

GOYA AND DAVID: The two great painters of the late 1700s produced the portrait of Don Manuel Osorio (Goya) and *The Death of Marat* (David).

experience of the pest house. It is filled with dying and agonizing nudes in an exotic setting of Moorish arches, dramatic light, and a battle-ridden city. Emotionally, the picture's intention is similar to that of Stubbs's *Lion Attacking a Horse*. This emotional violence will characterize much of the work of the later thoroughly Romantic painters Géricault and Delacroix.

Géricault.
Jean Louis Géricault (1791–1824) is the prototypical Romantic artist. He died at the age of 33 as the result of a riding accident, and horses were one of the obsessive subjects of his paintings. At 21 he had painted the *Mounted Officer of the Imperial Guard* which is a glorification of the violence of war and horses. Superhuman power concentrated in a human figure is portrayed in the movement of the horse and the rider; the rider seems to reach for a new definition of human aspiration. Géricault successfully combines a classic mastery of form and an intensely dramatic sense of color and light. The mounted officer and his rearing, turning horse are silhouetted against a fiery battlefield, and the reds of the fire in the background are reflected in the jacket, sash, and plumes of the mounted officer.

The mounted officer was painted in 1812. By 1818, when Géricault created his masterpiece, *The Raft of the Medusa*, his assumptions about life seem to have changed. The mounted officer showed power within human reach. The raft and the survivors of the sunken ship *Medusa* are a depiction of human catastrophe, where man is helpless in a natural world that can engulf him. In the exaggerated and turbulent movement of the picture, one sees the same great technical skill that characterized the earlier painting, but the sense of color has changed. *The Raft of the Medusa* is a very dark picture, and the brilliantly lit nudes of the foreground, which recall Gros's figures in the pest house, play against the dark-

ness of the sea, which is all the more somber and frightening because of the dramatically lit sky. The picture is enormous, 23 feet 6 inches by 16 feet 1 inch, almost exactly the same size as Gros's monumental picture of the pest house. Romantic painting used size as well as form and subject to create a world of violent emotion.

After *The Raft of the Medusa,* Géricault studied the heads of the victims of the guillotine and painted many portraits of madmen, seeking to understand something beyond ordinary human reason (as did Goya in the same years). Romanticism in its violent manifestations eventually led to the birth of an important new discipline, the study of human psychology. Both Géricault and Goya recognized that the human mind is a place of violence.

Delacroix.
Géricault's successor in the Romantic tradition was Eugene Delacroix (1798–1863). Delacroix inherited his subjects and his outlook from Géricault. The career of the younger painter was a continuation of Géricault's concern with the possibilities of portraying violence and drama. Delacroix's *Massacre at Chios* first won him notoriety. Depicting the disaster and violence of a real event, the massacre of Greeks by Turks on the island of Chios, it expressed the deep sympathies of the Romantics for the Greeks in their war for independence.

Delacroix is especially remembered as the proponent of a new kind of painting that saw as its prime concern the development of color. His technique is profoundly different from that of Géricault and Ingres, who was his artistic enemy for a quarter century. Géricault and Ingres were master draftsmen, but for Delacroix drawing was not as important as color. He composed his pictures with color, and his later career was a long experimentation with the possibilities of color and its application. He never

gave up his preferred Romantic subjects of violence, combat, and animals, but these subjects were painted with an increasing scientific interest in the way color functions. Delacroix kept a journal of his observations that is considered to be the most important artistic research in the art of color painting up to his time. Delacroix was immensely admired by the younger painters, who would become known as Impressionists, and by the young Van Gogh, because of his concentration on the problems of color.

Painting in England.
While the French were creating their heroic and violent versions of Romantic painting, another school of painting was developing in England; it was to have a profound effect on later painting. Joseph Turner (1775–1851) sought in many ways the same effects as French Romantic painting, but his pictures never portrayed the same intense human and animal violence. Rather, he made use of color and the grandiosity of nature to produce exalted and fantastic pictures that present a kind of expressive and emotional landscape painting. Like Delacroix, he experimented with color, but it is atmospheric, light-filled color that interests him, and his pictures lose almost all relation to reality, becoming exercises in color harmonics.

The painting of Turner's contemporary John Constable (1776–1837) was also of landscapes, but of landscapes as faithful as possible to reality. He painted recognizable views of the English countryside in great calm panoramas. Emotionally, his pictures are the opposite of those of the younger Delacroix, although an exposition of Constable's paintings in Paris in 1824 influenced both Delacroix and later French Romantics.

Constable did many oil sketches of the sites he painted, and these sketches were done out-of-doors. His painting is a study of nature, particularly as it undergoes the changes of weather and light. As his career progressed, he placed increasing confidence in the sketches; his finished pictures, even if painted indoors, preserve the quality of outdoor impressions. Painting directly from nature with scientific scrutiny was Constable's great contribution, along with his great poetic gifts.

Courbet.
Gustave Courbet (1819–1877) began a movement that is also characterized by a faithful rendering of reality. But his concern was more with the subjects of painting than with the style. His style incorporated deliberate carelessness and simplicity of surface to achieve dramatic effects of light and shade, using a palette knife as well as a brush in applying paint. His approach appealed to the later Impressionists, but his freedom in choosing his subjects was a major inspiration for younger painters. His picture *The Stone Breakers* caused a scandal when it was first shown in 1854 because the subject was considered not "artistic," even dangerously subversive.

color
US

colour
Brit.

somber
US

sombre
Brit.

THE RAFT OF THE MEDUSA
by Géricault shows the intense sense of visual drama shared by the early Romantic painters.

Manet. Painters before the time of Impressionism had been interested in the technical and stylistic problems of painting. But painters of the late 1800s changed the rules. The illusion a painter created of some real object or view had always been an important part of judging that painting. Edouard Manet (1832–1883) was perhaps the first to free painting from complete devotion to representing objective reality. This break invigorated the world of painting in Paris with an energy of creation that has rarely been equaled in the history of art. Many young painters of great talent, dedication, and intelligence made the second half of the 1800s and the early years of the 1900s a period that for painting may equal the Renaissance in Italy or 17th-century Dutch painting.

The major subjects of Manet and of the later Impressionists were the unadorned scenes of the life they found around them. Manet's first great painting, *Le Déjeuner sur l'Herbe* (Luncheon on the Grass) exploited the new freedom to paint the subject of his choice, no matter its seeming inappropriateness. Two ordinarily dressed men sit on the grass in the company of a nude woman. The picture caused a scandal. Manet's style only heightened the shock. The light is so brilliant as to minimize any modeling of the figures. They seem at the same time to be as flat as the canvas itself and to have exaggerated depth.

This is also true of the painting *Woman with a Parrot* (1866). The woman is brilliantly lit; her dressing gown reads illusionistically against the dark background, yet any particular part of it examined separately is an abstract—simply paint on canvas. Manet is less concerned with creating an illusion of a three-dimensional object than with the visual beauty of his paint, its color, the shapes it creates, and finally the brilliant light it seems to suggest. *Woman with a Parrot* is far from an abstract picture. The picture works in two ways: as a brilliantly illuminated picture of a beautifully dressed woman and as a study of the application of paint to a surface. The lemon at the bottom of the picture gives the illusion of a lemon, but also draws attention to the paint itself and to the inherent beauty of the painted surface. Other earlier painters had done similar things, particularly Velasquez, whom Manet admired. But Manet carries this double approach further than earlier artists. He is not considered an Impressionist, but in his treatment of objects like the lemon and the woman's sleeves, his breaking down of an object into highlights and patches of pure color approaches the Impressionistic style.

Degas. Manet's friend and contemporary, Edgar Degas (1834–1917), was also only on the edge of the Impressionist movement. His artistic concerns were quite different from those of the Impressionists, yet he also contributed to the movement.

Degas was in many ways the most conservative of his contemporaries, and in his work the values of the classic tradition remain intact. He was a student of Ingres and he never ceased to admire the older man's teachings. Degas was the greatest draftsman of his age. His pictures are remarkable because they preserve classical ideas of space and figure, yet experiment at the same time with flat, two-dimensional composition.

In the painting *The Tub,* reproduced here in color, one sees the value of form and Degas' skillful manipulation of three-dimensional volumes within an illusion of space. At the same time, one sees a desire for abstraction and two-dimensional design in the way the surface of the picture divides easily into flat areas of color.

Degas, for all his insistence on drawing, was also an important colorist. His painting, like that of Monet and Cézanne, is responsible for the development of a new kind of space that is dependent on color. The blues of *The Tub* create an illusion of great space that is independent of the laws of perspective, having more to do with the fullness and density of color. Gauguin, Matisse, and later painters exploited this particular quality of uniform color surfaces.

The Impressionists. The Impressionist movement was the work of Manet and Degas' slightly younger contemporaries, Monet, Pissarro, Renoir, and Sisley. The movement was

WOMAN WITH A PARROT
by Manet pointed to new developments in art.

THE TUB
by Degas uses color to effect the illusion of space.

19 History of Art

MONET'S *Morning on the Seine Near Giverny* is a typical work reflecting his mastery of light and color.

color *US*

colour *Brit.*

CÉZANNE painted a series of views of the Gulf of Marseilles from L'Estaque, studying the relationship between form and color in landscape.

moments. He painted many series employing these techniques: of snow and breaking ice in winter, of London in the fog, of the facade of Rouen cathedral, of rows of poplar trees, of haystacks. His painting gradually evolved to the state where color and its dynamics were the determining agents of the form of his pictures, yet they maintain a delicate equilibrium between observation of the real world and the purely aesthetic need of two-dimensional composition. The atmospheric space of these pictures was new in painting, and Monet's last works were enormous pictures of water and water lilies, where any constraint of composition or form had disappeared in favor of an overall color space.

Cézanne. Paul Cézanne (1839–1906) was less successful as an Impressionist, but his use of the Impressionists' methods contributed to a new synthesis of color and structure that is one of the highest points ever reached in painting. Cézanne is as great a colorist as Monet; at the same time, his pictures are the most highly and deliberately structured of all the work of the Impressionists. Cézanne developed a style of painting in which neither form nor color was sacrificed, and in which each intensified the other. Traditional three-dimensional form was relatively unimportant to the Impressionists—even two-dimensional design was absent in Monet's last pictures. But Cézanne wanted not only strong two-dimensional composition but also the classical solidity of three-dimensional form. Like Monet and the other Impressionists, Cézanne studied nature and painted series of views, such as the one shown from L'Estaque. His landscape paintings, like his still lifes, present an intense experience both of

the culmination of many ideas and practices begun by other individual artists. The Impressionists made these ideas and practices into a major school in painting. Courbet's realism and its dedication to the real, observable world; Constable's studies of sky, atmosphere, light, and landscape; and Delacroix's studies of color all came to fruition in the Impressionists' work. Their ideas were also influenced by scientific thought. A French chemist, Eugène Chevreul, had published *The Principles of Harmony and Contrast of Colors, and Their Application to the Arts* in 1839. Many of the laws discovered by Chevreul helped form the methods of Impressionism. Light was seen in its component hues; shadows were painted with their aureoles of complementary

colors; contrast or fusing was used to evoke particular optical impressions. These optical effects were achieved with unmixed pigments painted on a white ground with visible brush strokes. The hope was to recreate the effects of light and its instantaneous changes.

Claude Monet (1840–1926) went the furthest with Impressionism. *Morning on the Seine Near Giverny* is a late painting, at a time when his particular form of Impressionism had advanced well beyond naturalistic landscape painting. But even during this period Monet was pursuing the natural phenomena of light and color. He arose before dawn to station himself in his boat in different parts of his water garden at Giverny or along the Seine, choosing carefully his viewpoint and recording the light at different

GAUGUIN'S large shapes in bold colors, as in *Maternity,* was a break with the style of the Impressionists.

VAN GOGH'S self-portrait conveys intensity through brushwork, color, and pattern.

form and of light and color.

Cézanne's pictures suggest the depth and solidity of the world through a clear division between the planes and surfaces that compose it. Through his use of color, which is the most vibrant of 19th-century painting, he transforms the solidity into the movement and brilliance of light. These apparently conflicting approaches create an intense optical tension between the reading of a flat surface design and the experience of depth. This tension was taken up and developed further by the later school called cubism.

Gauguin and Van Gogh.
Manet, Degas, and the Impressionists were all working toward realism and away from it at the same time. Yet the Impressionists were still concerned with the depiction of visual reality. Two of the painters who followed were more concerned with another kind of reality. Like Blake or Géricault, they sought a deeper psychological level of meaning. Paul Gauguin and Vincent Van Gogh used the Impressionist techniques to explore more than visual perception. They made their own inner needs and desires the subject of their paintings and left the objective world behind.

Paul Gauguin (1848–1903) lived as a child in Peru. Later he was a sailor and travelled again to South America. He was also a stockbroker, who at the age of 35 devoted himself full-time to painting for the first time. He exhibited with the Impressionists and learned from Pissarro and Degas. His *Vision After the Sermon* (1888) is a depiction of Jacob wrestling with the angel as imagined by the peasant women whose backs and headdresses form the front of the picture. The emotion of the picture is heightened by the colors, which are completely freed from any necessity to be true to life. The angel is a kind of refutation of realism (Courbet had said that he could not paint an angel because he had never seen one).

He eventually abandoned France for the South Seas island of Tahiti. The emotional or spiritual values that Gauguin sought are expressed in the figures of the exotic island women. They are a far cry from the "scientific" observation of the Impressionists. The large decorative shapes and lines of the pictures and the opaque and flat, yet hot, colors show a complete repudiation of the naturalistic goals of Impressionism. Gauguin's work returns painting to the world of human expression.

Vincent Van Gogh (1853–1890), like Gauguin, painted to express his own experience. He came to France from Holland in 1886 and learned to adapt Impressionist techniques to his own purposes. The prominent use of his brush, often in small separate strokes, is his most significant technical trait. Though he was a friend of Gauguin's, both his style and his experience of reality were quite different. Van Gogh was hospitalized for mental illness, and he eventually committed suicide. In his paintings of the most unassuming objects, there is an eerie kind of intensity that one sees in his self-portraits as shown here. The intensity is conveyed by the brushwork and the creation of an intense atmosphere of color and pattern. His intensity served strictly human goals, and is a projection of his interior, turbulent world. His last painting is a picture of the field where he killed himself, a vision of yellow wheat and vivid dark blue sky. The field and the sky are empty except for the small black wings of several crows.

Seurat. Gauguin and Van Gogh are commonly called Post-Impressionists, as is another slightly younger painter,

SEURAT painted this large canvas, *Sunday Afternoon on the Island of La Grande Jatte,* using only tiny dots of color (see close-up). The technique came to be called pointillism.

Georges Seurat (1859–1891). After the 1880s, even the painters most closely associated with Impressionism, including Monet, Renoir, and Pissarro, changed their styles in some way to seek new goals. But the techniques and works of Seurat are the most conspicuous.

Like Cézanne, Seurat wanted to create an art that was solid and durable. Of all the painters of his age, he worked in the most carefully controlled fashion, trying to make a science of his technique for the analysis of form in terms of color. He worked for as long as a year on a single picture, and there are 34 known oil studies for his largest picture, *Sunday Afternoon on the Island of La Grande Jatte.*

Early in his career he learned to compose a whole picture from the smallest of brush strokes. Later he used dots of pure color. He was seeking to create volumes and space like those of Renaissance pictures while remaining faithful to Impressionists' understanding of

light and color. But his technique, sometimes called *pointillism,* had side effects. The immobility of the figures and the patterns of *La Grande Jatte* and its almost bizarre color make the painting an emotional experience more akin to a Gauguin or a Van Gogh painting than to those of the early Impressionists. The life in *La Grande Jatte* seems arrested, as if all motion and emotion were ordered stopped by the painter's will. The figures are both volume and silhouette. The painting itself reads both as a three-dimensional composition and as a flat, designed surface. This ambiguity makes it both arresting and mysterious.

Artist Henri de Toulouse-Lautrec

(1864–1901) also painted to express his emotions. He was an aristocrat and a dwarf, and he chose to live in and paint the world of Parisian nightlife. He exaggerated Degas' flat-colored planes and Manet's silhouetted figures to depict a world of extravagantly illuminated cafe and theater interiors. His color and his bold composition are instruments of strong yet tightly controlled emotion.

The 19th century in France began with the Romantic depiction of violence and grand public emotion, passed through the serene adoration of nature and light in Impressionism, and ended with the more subjective violence of the Post-Impressionists. This new subjectivity and search for a new meaning in art continued into the 20th century.

Architecture

The neoclassic style that had developed in Europe in the 1700s continued well into the 1800s. Both Europe and America saw some of their finest public buildings built in the Greek and Roman orders. The Gothic revival style that grew alongside neoclassicism was an acceptable alternative for public and private buildings by the early 1800s. When Benjamin Latrobe (1764–1820) submitted plans for the Catholic Cathedral in Baltimore he offered designs in both a neoclassic and a Gothic style. The neoclassic plan was accepted and America owes one of its most beautiful interior spaces to Latrobe's plan. Latrobe had emigrated from England, but the cathedral in Baltimore owes something to the Pantheon in Paris, and in its proportions to the original Pantheon in Rome.

Jefferson's plan for the University of Virginia complex, which was executed by Latrobe, derived again from the Roman Pantheon. The Capitol of the United States in Washington is also a

neoclassic building of impressive scale; it was designed by William Thornton at the end of the 1700s.

The flourishing of the neoclassic style in these still young American cities is an indication of its strength. In Europe, such buildings were built on a grand scale. Parts of Paris were rebuilt in the classical orders with monumental buildings dominating the vistas for which the city is famous. The Arc de Triomphe is a major monument of neoclassic Paris. Parts of London, too, were rebuilt in the neoclassic style by the architect John Nash (1752–1835).

The British Museum, which was finished in 1847 by Sir Robert Smirke, was the culmination of the neoclassic style. Its Ionic colonnade makes one of the largest expanses of classical architecture in the world. In Berlin the architect Karl Friedrich Shinkel built the Altes Museum between 1824 and 1828 on the same principle of an enormous Ionic colonnade. Even in small cities, such as Edinburgh, extensive classical facades changed the look of the city. Each city, and each architect, created different and sometimes eccentric versions of the style, but the architecture of Greece and Rome never failed as a source of inspiration.

By the time of the construction of the Paris Opera in 1861, the style was no longer truly neoclassical, but eclectic. Jean Louis Charles Garnier's architecture is a mixture of classical, Baroque, and Renaissance styles, combined to suggest great opulence. This old and overelaborated form is in stark contrast to the Impressionism that was sweeping the world of painting at the same time, illustrating the great gulf between official taste (the Paris Opera) and that of the avant-garde (the Impressionist painting).

In England, the greatest public building of the early 1800s is also eclectic in style, but it leans toward the Gothic. The old house of Parliament had burned in 1834. The architect of the new Parliament building, Sir Charles Barry, was famous for his neoclassic architecture, and it is to his assistant Augustus W. Pugin that the Gothic overlay of the building is due.

The form of the building—the clear and careful delineation of the elements and its symmetry—owes much to the classic despite its Gothic ornamentation. The building reflects the prosperity of the most powerful country in the world.

Parallel to the grand public architecture, there developed a much more simple and functional architecture, one that relied on a new building material—iron. Libraries, railroad stations, and commercial buildings were built using cast iron (later steel) frames. This engineering revolution made possible a whole new architecture. The strong but light metal frame allowed the extensive use of glass. And the standardization of structural elements made it possible to build large buildings far more quickly and cheaply. In London, the exposition building called the Crystal Palace was built in 1850 almost completely out of

THE CRYSTAL PALACE in London made use of new construction techniques that permitted the lavish use of glass.

iron and glass in only six months. In Paris, in 1889, the Galerie des Machines and the Eiffel Tower showed the possibilities of a metal superstructure using a whole new concept of style. These innovative ideas and methods would culminate in a completely new aesthetic for public buildings in the 1900s.

Sculpture

Early 1800s sculpture was dominated by neoclassicism and by its most successful proponent, Antonio Canova (1757–1822). Canova repeated and sometimes reworked the forms and attitudes of Roman sculpture, but he was capable of a refined sensuality that resembled that of Ingres.

Much more dynamic sculpture was done in France by François Rude (1784–1855), who is responsible for the gigantic figures on the Arc de Triomphe. The group, *La Marseillaise,* is approximately 42 feet by 26 feet; it shows a group of warriors being led to the defense of France by a winged figure, the goddess of liberty.

The work of Antoine Louis Barye (1795–1875) shows another Romantic preoccupation, that with animals. His *Jaguar Devouring a Hare* has the same ferocity as Stubbs's lion and horse or one of Delacroix's similar subjects.

The taste of mid-century France that produced the Paris Opera found a sculptor of exuberant vitality in Jean Baptiste Carpeaux (1827–1875). His group, *The Dance,* which was designed for the facade of the Paris Opera, is a monumental version of the taste of 100 years earlier, resembling the Rococo sculpture of Clodion. The forms, however, are more attenuated and less controlled by classic norms than are Clodion's. Carpeaux's figures suggest exploding energy unrestrained by classic norms of balance and stability.

Rodin. The great sculptor of the 19th century was Auguste Rodin (1840–1917). He worked briefly with Barye, and like the older sculptor, he preferred working in bronze. Rodin's use of the malleability of his wax and clay models also shows Barye's influence. Both men's bronzes show the same broken and irregular surfaces that come from the modeling of the soft materials of the casts.

Rodin said, however, that the great influence on his art was Michelangelo. He admired the unfinished and fragmentary state of Michelangelo's marble groups—an aspect not admired by earlier artists. Rodin used this admiration to justify his own work, which shows a tension between realism and abstract form that recalls the Impressionist painters. Rodin felt less obliged than earlier sculptors to create a facsimile of reality. He studied the reality of form and movement, as one can see in the *Walking Man.* But he used his observations to focus on the abstract problems of sculptural expression. *Walking Man* is more a study of movement and weight than it is the sculptural portrayal of a man.

At the same time, Rodin desired his work to equal the great sculptured figures of the past. He worked for many years on figures for the monumental *Gates of Hell,* which he never finished. *The Kiss* was to form one of the groups that made up the gates, and it is the clearest, most unpretentious, and most effective sculptural depiction of human love from the 1800s. Others of his sculptural groups were in a much more tragic vein, and the dominating figure of the *Gates of Hell* was to be *The Thinker.* The man, lost in brooding and merciless thought, may be the last direct expression of human emotion on the scale of Michelangelo. Like Michelangelo's sculpture, *The Thinker* makes of the human situation a philosophical and even tragic question.

Modern Art

Painting

To the end of the 1800s painting remained representational, despite tendencies of major painters toward more abstract or nonrepresentational painting. Between 1901 and 1906 there were several large exhibitions in Paris of the works of Gauguin, Van Gogh, and Cézanne, the three painters who would most strongly influence the painting of the new century.

One sees in the late work of Cézanne in particular a concern with form and color for their own sake, even though he still refers directly to the real, perceived world. It was the nonconcrete, nonrepresentational aspects of his painting that impressed younger artists, however, and helped set the direction in which painting would move.

Modern art is a movement toward nonrepresentational and abstract values; painters after 1900 divorced themselves from ties to the real world in favor of creating their own space, forms, and experience. In a sense, artists have always done this. Greek sculpture portrayed ideal rather than real human form. Renaissance paintings idealized space, exaggerating perspective in the interests of illusion. The liberties 20th-century painters took with the appearance of their subjects were only more extreme than those of earlier times. They left the idea of representation behind and sought to create visual art from the abstract elements of form, color, and design.

Matisse. The first great liberation for 20th-century painting was in the area of color, and its liberator was Henri

Matisse (1869–1954). Matisse had been trained as an academic painter, but he entered the history of art with a group of painters whose exhibition in Paris in 1905 so shocked the public and the critics that they were given the name "Fauves," or wild beasts. What caused the scandal was the paintings' extreme simplicity of form and extreme brilliance of color. Impressionist painting had made freer use of color and had maintained both harmony and subtlety. Gauguin, Van Gogh, and Lautrec had been the first to use much brighter greens, reds, and oranges. For the Fauve painters, violent use of color became the meaning of the picture itself.

Matisse's *The Red Studio* is from 1911, after the Fauve group had disbanded and individual painters were seeking their individual styles. Matisse remained faithful to the original stance of the Fauves, however. The color of *The Red Studio,* although more sober than that of some of Matisse's earlier paintings, is obviously the most expressive element of the picture. The larger part of the surface of the canvas is painted a rich brick red. Only very minimal drawing indicates the perspective of the room, yet it seems spacious partly because of the density of the color. The colors in the pictures on the walls are predominantly other reds and pinks, and the bits of blue in the pictures and the green of the plant on the table in the foreground heighten the intensity of the overall color red.

Two years earlier, Matisse had titled another painting *The Red Room (Harmony in Red)*. Harmony of color was the basis of Matisse's painting. Color was both a means of expressing

feeling and the basis of his pictures' design. He learned his use of color from Cézanne and Van Gogh, but he preferred a flatness and uniformity of hue untouched by Van Gogh's brushwork or Cézanne's description of planes. Matisse's color appeared in large calm segments, often animated, as in *The Red Studio,* by smaller bits of complementary colors. After the early Fauvist years, his use of color was never frenetic or disturbing, even when he depicted great movement, as in the large paintings of his dance series.

Matisse's drawing always remained minimal, but effective. He was able to indicate the human form in motion with the most economical lines. At the end of his long life, when he was no longer able to paint, he cut and pasted bits of colored paper to form pictures that were the most advanced of his time. Matisse more than anyone else of his era combined the classical values of painting with consistent innovation in the expressive uses of color.

Georges Rouault (1871–1958) was another painter of the original Fauve group, and he used his color and his training as a worker in stained glass to produce emotional, often religious, painting. It is a descendant of Van Gogh's early work in its portrayal of human pathos.

German expressionism.

Rouault's sensibility is entirely different from Matisse's, but it found reflection in a school of painting that developed after the Fauve period in Dresden and Munich and that is called German expressionism. Emil Nolde (1867–1956) along with Max Beckmann

color
US

colour
Brit.

THE RED STUDIO by Henri Matisse makes color the dominant element of expression, while draftsmanship is simplified and de-emphasized.

THE HOLY FACE by Rouault reflects the artist's interest in portraying emotion.

(1884–1950), Ernst Ludwig Kirchner (1880–1938), and many other German and Eastern European painters were liberated from more traditional painting by the Fauves' use of color and preference for rapid, "crude" brushwork. German painting more than any other was the inheritor of Van Gogh's subjective approach. The painters working in Germany just before 1914 made Germany's one great contribution to the history of painting. German expressionism is intensely social art and it is filled with psychological and philosophical or religious meaning. Its techniques were developed from the abstract French tradition, but it was committed in a new way to the painful psychological realities of existence. In a sense, it is a generalization and broadening of Van Gogh's subjective psychological style.

It was from the German expressionist movement that the first completely nonrepresentational painting emerged. Wassily Kandinsky (1866–1944) came to Munich from his native Russia in 1896. He brought with him the clear desire to create a new kind of painting without subject matter. He had seen one of Monet's haystack paintings in Moscow, and the painting, which to him seemed to have no subject, was a revelation of his own desires. At first his painting was mostly of landscapes in Fauve colors applied in a strong and distinct fashion, a kind of modeling of the picture surface. By 1909, his painting called *Mountain* retained only the bare suggestion of a hill-like shape. By 1912, Kandinsky was painting pictures that he called "improvisations" or "compositions" and to which he gave numbers rather than titles. He sought to let his work emerge from his unconscious mind without conscious creation.

There is no recognizable subject in Kandinsky's later painting, only a maze of lines, planes, and bright colors. Yet they still read as a kind of landscape. In a sense, they are the depiction of the fantastic landscape of Kandinsky's imagination, where color and line replace the visible objects of nature. The pictures exist primarily as color, but Kandinsky also sought a sense of movement and incident. In contrast, Matisse's world is calm and ordered.

Cubism. In France in the years immediately following the Fauve exhibition another kind of painting developed that pointed in a second important direction. Pablo Picasso was born in 1881 and settled permanently in Paris in 1904. Between 1907 and 1914 he and George Braque (1882–1963) developed the style that was called cubism. At times they worked together so closely that it is difficult to tell the pictures of one from those of the other. Cubism grows out of Cézanne's interest in the picture surfaces. Picasso was deeply impressed by the retrospective show of Cézanne's paintings in 1907, the year after Cézanne's death. The beginning of cubism can be seen in Picasso's

Les Demoiselles d'Avignon of 1907. Cézanne had talked of treating nature in terms of geometrical shapes—the cylinder, sphere, and cone. Now in the paintings of Picasso and Braque the critics could see only geometrical shapes and so they called the paintings "cubist." The crux of cubism, however, is not its geometrical shapes but the tension between the illusion of depth and the actual flatness of the canvas. That tension had already existed in major paintings of the late 1800s, but the cubists developed it as an independent value. They adopted Cézanne's methods to fracture the flat space of their pictures.

Les Demoiselles d'Avignon, along with its violence of feeling (Avignon was the red-light district of Barcelona), is equally violent in fracturing space and volume. The women's bodies are broken sharply into planes and contours that have no relation to reality, yet that indicate volume and space. The space itself remains extremely shallow, the energy of the picture seemingly concentrated on the flat surface. Certain parts of the picture, such as the masklike faces of the women on the right, are drawn. Other planes are shaded to suggest depth, but the illusion is always denied.

This crowding of the picture surface with contradictory readings of depth and flatness are the basis of cubism. From its beginning through its later development in the works of Picasso, Braque, Leger, and Duchamp, the movement was a formal study of picture space, of the function of planes, and of two-dimensional depictions of volume. In a sense, it was a return to classical concerns about form, line, and contour. The influence of the cubists was immense, and its marks can be seen in the later works of Matisse, Kandinsky, and the German expressionists. As late as the 1940s and 1950s, American abstract expressionism was using the same shallow, almost two-dimensional space.

The great disadvantage of cubism was its lack of interest in color. In *Les Demoiselles d'Avignon* the colors are earthen brown and shades of blue. In cubism's most intense phase, almost all color was banished. Later, color was used again, but it always remained of secondary importance. For years, painting seemed polarized between the apostles of form (the cubists) and the apostles of color (Matisse and his followers), the very division that Cézanne had worked so hard to deny.

Mondrian. Cubism always referred, at least indirectly, to the perceptible world, and even Kandinsky's compositions and improvisations retain the feeling of landscapes. Piet Mondrian (1872–1944) believed that cubism had not gone far enough toward formalism. After an initial cubist period, he created pictures that used a simple geometry to produce complete abstraction.

Mondrian, a Dutchman, was influenced by Van Gogh and later by cubism. During World War I, he meditated on

the theory and meaning of painting. The paintings that developed from this meditation were constructed from rectangles and squares on an asymmetrical gridlike structure. Mondrian's use of color was similarly austere and restricted to the primary colors, which, painted in uniform flat surfaces, filled some of the rectangular spaces. His colors read on the same plane with the white surfaces and the black bands of the grid, causing his paintings to seem flat, solid, and infinite. Mondrian was seeking what he called "true reality," and his paintings are a contemplation of that reality. They are, in a sense, a philosophical quest, a variation of the spirit that animated Van Gogh, Gauguin, and Seurat.

Mondrian's was one of many attempts to make of painting a means of exploring realities that were not immediately perceptible in ordinary experience. Out of Italy had come futurism and its belief in movement as the universal principle. From Russia came suprematism, which,

LES DEMOISELLES D'AVIGNON, an early painting of Picasso, is a step toward cubism, rendering the women as geometrical shapes.

PORTRAIT OF MADAME Z is another of Picasso's cubist paintings.

ABSTRACTION AND SURREALISM:
The Harlequin's Carnival (above) by Miró is amusing yet ominous, a dreamlike composition whose style is called surreal. Mondrian achieved complete abstraction in *Red, Black and White* (right), calling attention to the design above all.

center
US

centre
Brit.

like Mondrian, saw painting as a means of perceiving a reality beyond natural forms. From Zurich came Dadaism, with its contempt for society and conventional art. Dadaism was one of the symptoms of deep disillusionment caused by the horrors of World War I. In revolt against established values, Dadaism created nonart, works that were a denial of art. The movement, contradictory as it was, helped liberate artists from old assumptions and encouraged them to explore in new directions. This new freedom resulted in still another school, which was called surrealism.

FISH MAGIC by Paul Klee uses the energy of color and geometric elements.

Surrealism.

The French poet André Breton wrote the manifesto of surrealism. The movement owed much to the thought of Sigmund Freud, the psychologist who first studied subconscious thoughts and desires. Surrealism sought to discover the inner truths of the subconscious and to promote the communion of people and the natural world. The poets of surrealism practiced automatic writing, and the painters tried to give form to the images of their subconscious minds.

Joan Miró (1893–1983) was a leading surrealist painter from Spain, creating a unique personal world in his pictures. Other surrealist painters, including Salvador Dali and Max Ernst, used traditional realist painting to describe personal dream images and fantasies. Miró's world was inhabited by flat floating creatures in a timeless undetermined space. In *The Harlequin's Carnival,* a room is filled in all dimensions by creatures that seem to be both animals and toys. A certain gaiety in Miró's paintings, as in much surrealist art, lets the meanings and superstitions of the artist's childhood find life in his work. Another painter associated with the surrealists, the Swiss-German Paul Klee (1879–1940), painted and drew small pictures in delicate and diverse styles, depicting a rich life of fantasy.

Surrealist painting was anticipated by the work of Henri Rousseau (1844–1910), a man who had no training as a painter but who created exotic and mysterious landscapes inhabited by magical figures who seemed to proclaim a new age of innocence or a return to the Garden of Eden. Less optimistic but equally mysterious were the cityscapes of the Greek-Italian Giorgio de Chirico (1888–1978), who had been one of the first artists to devote his painting to the depiction of a world of his own making. His scenes of empty streets and squares of an imagined classical city seem full of prophecy and esoteric meaning. De Chirico and Rousseau have in common with the surrealists who followed them the belief that truth must proceed from the depth of a person's interior world.

Surrealism was the last major artistic movement in Europe. In the late 1930s, World War II began, and when it was over, the center of the art world had shifted. Young American artists had made New York City the center of a new movement in painting, and for the first time in history American painting became the most advanced in the world.

Abstract expressionism.

The first important painting in postwar America is called abstract expressionism, although individual artists differed considerably in style and approach. Many of them were influenced in their formative years by Arshile Gorky and by Hans Hofmann. Gorky (1904–1948) developed a style that was related to Miró's and that showed the influence of Kandinsky and the cubists. Hofmann (1880–1966) was a great colorist, but his painting also

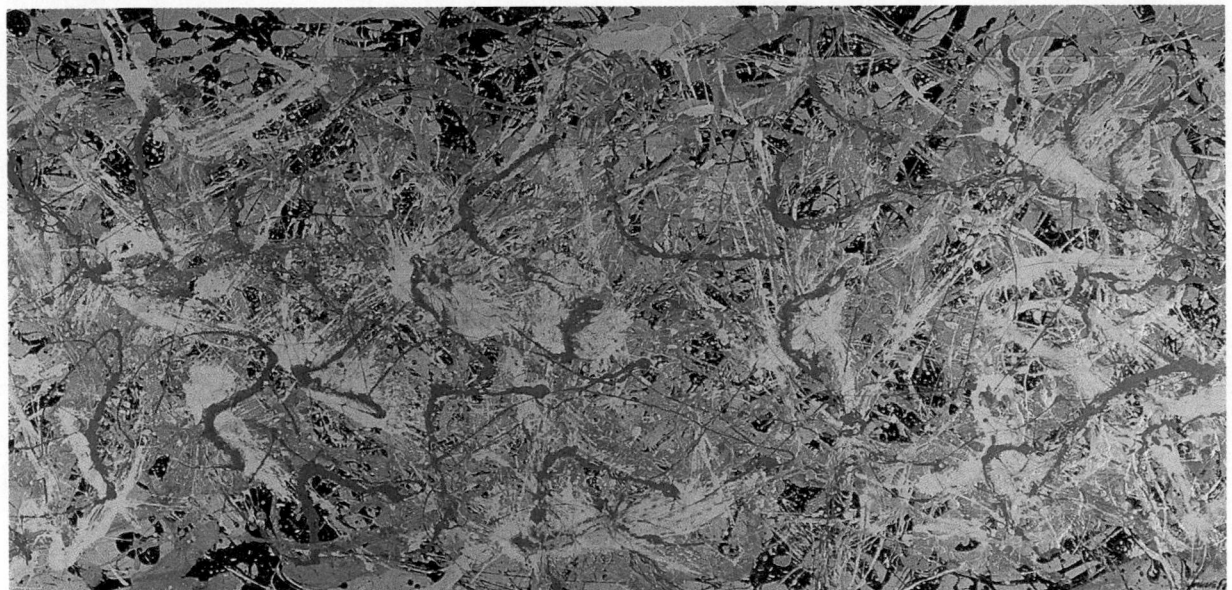

NUMBER 27, 1950
by Jackson Pollock is a masterpiece of abstract expression-ism, which flourished in New York in the 1940s and '50s. It lets one perceive an infinite space.

remained within the cubist style.

Jackson Pollock (1912–1956), the most innovative of the abstract expressionists, is best known for what is called action painting. The term describes Pollock's method, which was to pour, throw, and splatter paint onto a canvas tacked to the floor. The result, as one can see above, is not completely left to chance. The line Pollock created is no longer a drawn line; it is closer to a kind of figuration without any notion of plane or volume. The entire surface of the picture is animated by a dense, yet airy, chaos of line and color through which one can see into a kind of infinite space. Pollock's painting is the first that can be called post-cubist, since it is the first to go beyond the cubist dilemma of flatness versus depth. One sees also in Pollock's painting new possibilities for color. His dribbled lines and splotches, though always of relatively sober hues, present color in a new, different way. Pollock used raw canvas, housepaint, and metallic paints that saturated the canvas and stained it. The paint becomes a kind of dye, and the viewer sees the paint as part of the canvas rather than on top of it. Pollock did not exploit his innovation, but the genera-tion that followed made of it a new kind of painting, which, like Matisse's, had color as its prime value.

Part of the importance of American painting after World War II was its concentration on the problems that had been developed in painting in the previous hundred years in France. American painting is the continuation of a tradition that began with Delacroix and Manet. Pollock fits squarely in that tradition. The composition of his drip technique pictures, where he refuses to favor any part of the surface of the picture or to design the surface, is related in intent to Manet's enormous late pictures of water lilies.

Impressionism was a great liberating movement for color, taken up by

Matisse, and brought to America by Hans Hofmann. The American painters who followed Pollock are characterized by their attempts to make pictures that develop the fullest possibilities of color. Morris Louis (1912–1962) was one of the first painters to realize the possibilities of Pollock's stained canvases, and Louis made entire pictures of veils and stripes of pure color stained into unprimed can-vas. The optical effect of these pictures had never been seen before; the color is intense and luminescent, a pure experi-ence free of any reference to the world as it is observed. Louis was followed by other painters, notably Kenneth Noland (1924–) and Jules Olitski (1922–), both of whom continued this intense color painting.

Frank Stella (1936–) also shares Louis's concern with color, but like Cézanne he is equally interested in the structure of his picture. Stella's first pictures denied color in favor of form. In his concern for form he changed the traditional rectangular shape of the canvas, using its shape to reflect the

internal structure of the picture. In the picture reproduced here, *Bonne Bay I,* color emerges as one of Stella's con-cerns, but it is painted in a strict geometry that recalls Mondrian. Like Mondrian's, Stella's painting is a kind of two-dimensional sculpture, and like Cézanne's it is an attempt to endow color with structural strength and to make of it a kind of form. The great virtue of American painting has been its attempt to expand the traditional values of painting; its greatest achievement has been in the intelligence and the brilliance of its use of color.

Architecture

Modern architecture is all around us. It has determined the look of our cities and our towns, particularly in America, where the old is more quickly replaced by the new.

Modern architecture begins with the work of Louis Sullivan (1856–1924), a Chicago architect who began to use new

realize
US

realise
Brit.

BONNE BAY I
by Frank Stella combines geometric structure and brilliant color to produce a kind of flat sculpture.

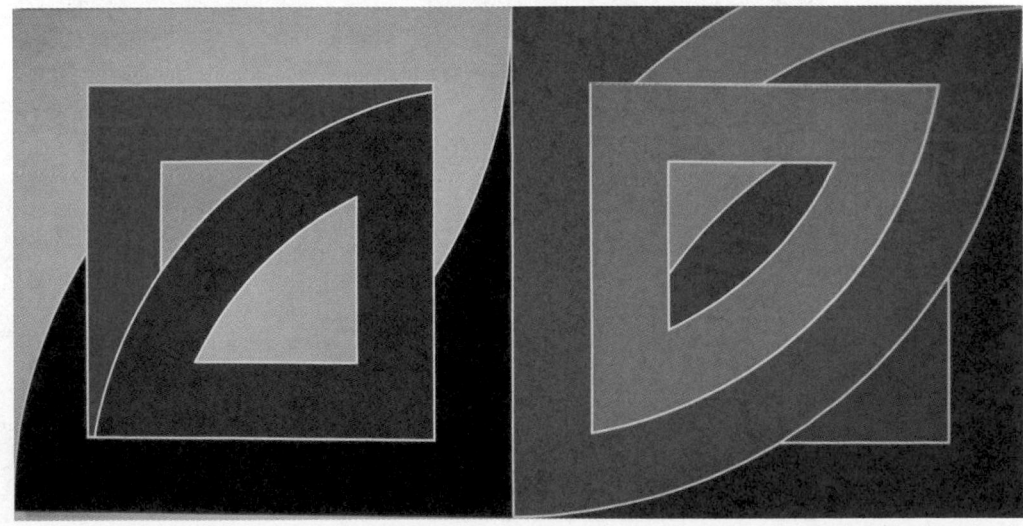

"FALLINGWATER" in Pennsylvania is a famous example of Frank Lloyd Wright's pioneering style in the design of homes.

emphasized
US

emphasised
Brit.

MODERN DIRECTIONS: the Seagram's Building in New York, designed by Miës van der Rohe, demonstrates the cool, simple lines of the international style. The Church of Notre Dame du Haut in France, designed by Le Corbusier, is a reaction using irregular lines.

structural elements—cast iron and steel—in the late 1800s. Sullivan's department store for Carson, Pirie & Scott in Chicago (1904) revealed a new functional approach to architecture. The steel frame of the building became a part of the design itself, and Sullivan came to be recognized as the father of the modern skyscraper.

At the turn of the century, there was a flourish of style called Art Nouveau. It emphasized surface decoration that was composed of curved lines in long continuous patterns and that had no precise historical model. The new methods of construction with iron and glass aided its development, making possible the curvilinear facades still visible in Brussels and Paris. Some of the best examples on a small scale were the metro (subway) stations in Paris. On a larger scale, Victor Horta (1861–1947) constructed the Maison du Peuple in Brussels. The facade is one long asymmetrical curve of steel and glass. A similar concern with curves and organic forms characterized the work of the most individual of 20th-century architects, Antonio Gaudi (1852–1926). He worked primarily in Barcelona, Spain, and designed both an Art Nouveau version of a Gothic cathedral and apartment buildings of undulating facades and stonework that simulated natural forms. Art Nouveau was short-lived, however, and its influence superficial. It quickly was supplanted by an international style of architecture from which the curve is absent.

Frank Lloyd Wright. An American and a pupil of Sullivan, Frank Lloyd Wright (1869–1959) was an important influence in 20th-century architecture. Wright's buildings are characterized by a concentration on clean, sharply accented lines and interior spaces that flow into one another. He often stripped architecture of all unnecessary surface detail, and made the blocks of the structure itself the elements of design. In domestic architecture, he sought to integrate a building and its site. One fine example is seen in the Kaufman House, which is called "Fallingwater." The house is built out over a waterfall, and the broad, horizontal planes of the decks and roofs make the building a kind of suspended sculpture in a natural setting of trees and of water. It is noteworthy that in Wright's last building, the Guggenheim Museum in New York, he placed amid the city's exclusively right-angled buildings a series of

bulbous curves, as if trying to relieve the standardized shapes of contemporary architecture.

The International Style. It is, however, the strictly rectilinear, hard-edged elements and the functionalism of Wright's style that were continued in Europe. The look of his buildings coincided exactly with the taste that is seen in Mondrian's painting and the design work of the school that grew up around it. In Germany the desire for pure forms is seen best in the work of Walter Gropius (1883–1969), who founded and designed the Bauhaus, a school of design in the town of Desau. Gropius's designs for the school itself, the most advanced of their time, established the principles of Sullivan and Wright—that a building's form should follow its function and that the structure itself should show through its style. The materials used were glass, steel, and concrete. The major facade of the studio building formed a kind of cage of glass that extended out from the steel supports and allowed a maximum of natural illumination for studios within. The clarity, precision, and symmetry of the Bauhaus and its regular volumes make it a triumph for classical principles, even in a modern style.

With the advent of Nazism in Germany, Gropius came to America as head of the Harvard Architecture School. At the same time, Miës van der Rohe (1886–1969), who was Gropius's associate at the Bauhaus, also came to America. He was responsible for applying Bauhaus principles to the American skyscraper, which he had always admired. The Seagram's Building in New York City, completed in 1956, is the realization of a plan he made 30 years previously. This elegant skyscraper is faithful in every detail to the concept of pure form and line of the Bauhaus style. The building's facade is bronze and glass, and it is raised on piers in an open space. It has had countless imitators, and is perhaps a symbol of modern American technology and commercial wealth.

In Europe, two other architects were working on equally impressive and different buildings. Le Corbusier (1887–1965) designed the Church of Notre Dame du Haut at Ronchamp in France between 1950 and 1955. The great curves, the lack of right angles and symmetry, and the closed surfaces of the walls are the opposite of Bauhaus art and the purist International Style that Le Corbusier had earlier helped to develop. Notre Dame du Haut reflects a desire for something more than the rectilinear.

In Italy, another kind of architecture was developed by Pier Luigi Nervi (1891–1979), who as an engineer used the strength of prestressed concrete to create the great dome of the Palazzetto dello Sport in Rome. His style had developed in the 1930s when he designed similar buildings for use as hangars and stadiums. In America Eero

Saarinen (1910–1961) used similar forms and the same precast concrete in the TWA terminal at New York's Kennedy airport.

The achievements of modern architecture in scale and technology are almost wondrous, and modern cities look from a distance like fabulous dreams of the imagination. However, the actual pleasure that architecture can give is often lacking, since the delights of decoration and intimacy have largely disappeared from modern construction. Architecture manifests the impersonality that is one of the by-products of the technological society.

Sculpture

Twentieth-century sculpture follows the same course as painting—toward abstraction and purity of nonrepresentational form. The development in sculpture was rapid and took place largely in the lifetime of the great Rumanian sculptor Constantin Brancusi (1876–1957). Brancusi worked in Paris most of his life. His early work owes something to Rodin, but Brancusi quickly developed his own ideas of a sculpture that would be nonrepresentational. Brancusi created and reworked a limited number of sculptures, such as the head of Mademoiselle Pogany, which in the succeeding versions became more and more simplified. By the time of *Bird in Space* (1919), Brancusi had left any detail of representation behind in favor of a sculpted shape that was an image of flight. In the idea of sculpting movement, *Bird in Space* follows Rodin's line of thinking in his *Walking Man*. Rodin's sculpture, though representational, was a step toward Brancusi's abstract rendering of flight, from which any representation of the bird had disappeared.

Most of Brancusi's sculptures were fairly small, and only in the works called *Endless Columns* did he approach the monumentality that had always been one of the aspects of major sculpture. The cubist sculpture of Picasso and Jacques Lipchitz, and almost all European sculpture before World War II, remained on a small scale. Even the futurist sculptor Umberto Boccioni (1882–1916) worked in a scale that was less than life-size.

Larger sculpture was made by Henry Moore (1898–1986) of groups of human forms that were meant to be seen out-of-doors. Moore's sculpture also moved toward a more abstract rendering of the body but remained always representational.

Abstract sculpture on a monumental scale was the achievement of the American sculptor David Smith, who just before his death in 1965 initiated his Cubi series of blocks of polished stainless steel. Perhaps of all the geometric art of the 20th century, his is the most successful. Because of the beauty of their light-reflecting surfaces,

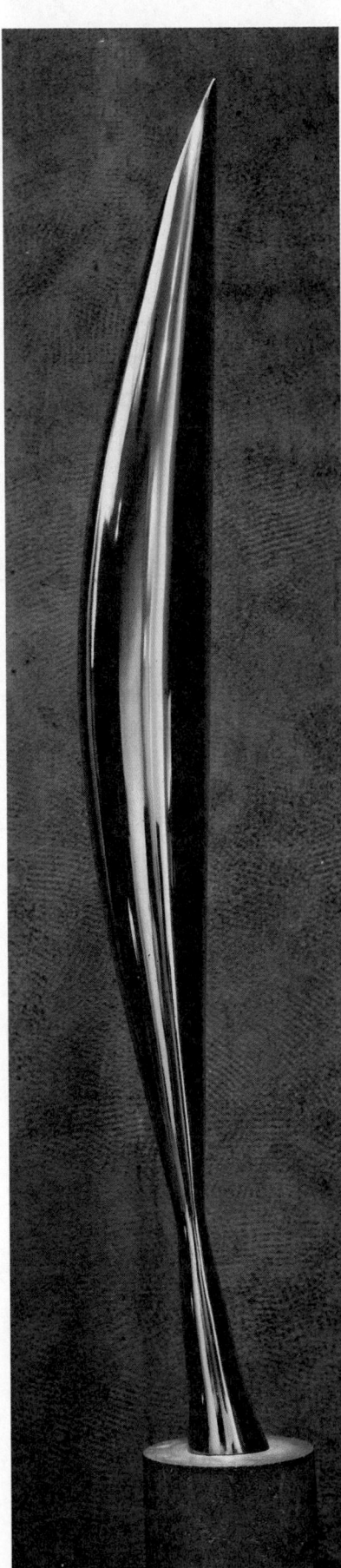

MODERN SCULPTURE approaches pure abstraction in Brancusi's *Bird in Space*, created in 1919.

19 History of Art

Smith's Cubis are visually almost sensual. They are close to an experience of painting in three dimensions, just as Stella's painting was a kind of sculpture in two dimensions. The addition of color to sculpture, begun by Picasso early in his career, added a new dimension to a traditionally monochromatic medium.

Modern sculpture, in the diversity of its styles and forms—from attenuated, eroded figures by Giacometti to minimal constructions by Richard Serra—brought new life to a medium that had lacked serious development and is impersonal, one of the by-products of the technological society.

New Directions

Even as American abstract expressionism gained international recognition in the 1950s, younger American artists went further. They questioned the conventional distinction between art and everyday life, seeking to bring art into the world of everyday experience.

One of the results of the new questioning came to be known as pop art. Robert Rauschenberg began to use everyday objects as part of his paintings. Jasper Johns shocked the art world with his straightforward painting of an American flag that filled his canvas. Was it a flag or a picture of a flag? Was it an everyday object or an art object? Johns seemed to be saying that the answer made no difference.

Pop art flourished for a dozen years, and succeeded in raising questions about art among artists and art viewers. Claes Oldenburg made giant "soft" sculptures of everyday objects. *Hamburger with Pickle* measured nearly eight feet across and was made of stuffed canvas painted in realistic colors. Andy Warhol painted a lovingly exact copy of a well known commercial soup can. George Segal peopled whole rooms with life-size plaster people doing everyday things. Roy Lichtenstein made enlarged, vividly colored frames from comic books. Many artists of the pop era sought to create new environments for audiences to experience. Some went even further and scheduled "happenings." In one famous happening, the Swiss artist Jean Tinguely gathered a group of viewers to watch one of his objects destroy itself. On schedule, it blew up, leaving only a powder mark on the floor of the museum to commemorate the event.

Many came to see art as a process rather than a product. Some who considered themselves artists wrote long plans for the construction of their work, complete with diagrams, and considered the documents themselves the product of their work. Others carried out their grand plans, sometimes modifying the very landscape to do so. Robert Smithson (1938–1973) built a long spiral-shaped jetty out into the Great Salt Lake in Utah. It has often been photographed and has a pleasing shape from the air. But what Smithson was really pointing to was the experience of walking out along the jetty, and perceiving the steady turning of the mountainous horizon as the viewer circles inward toward the center of the spiral.

How recent art movements will affect the future is difficult to predict. Every generation uses art for its own purposes and needs. The only certainty is that art most surely will continue—as an expression of the artist's being, a reflection of an audience's desires, or as pure and uncomplicated decoration.

—Richard Dickinson

American Art

Until the 1940s the work of most American artists was outside the mainstream of European art. A few American painters in the 1700s and 1800s left their homeland and established important reputations in England or France; but by leaving, they gave up the American experience.

In colonial times, an American artist was likely never to have seen the classic paintings and sculptures of Europe, and the social climate was indifferent or even hostile to the visual arts. As an anonymous writer in Boston wrote, "The Plowman that raiseth Grain is more serviceable to Mankind, than the Painter who draws only to please the eye."

MRS. RICHARD YATES, a portrait by colonial portraitist Gilbert Stuart whose likenesses of America's founding fathers brought him acclaim.

The art that existed in the early years of white settlement was of two kinds. The first was portraiture designed to keep alive the memory of a great or wealthy person. The second was folk art practiced by a wide variety of craftspersons making items such as weathervanes, furniture, quilting, and other useful items. A handful of untrained folk painters were also at work, producing flat two-dimensional portraits, often of women or children. These paintings are often called "primitives." Folk art underwent a great renaissance in the 1800s, and it survives even to the present day.

The federal period. The first American to gain wide recognition at home was John Singleton Copley (1738–1815). He was a painter of great technical gifts, yet he followed the prevailing aesthetic of New England portraiture—that a good likeness was the first measure of a portraitist. In 1774, on the eve of the American Revolution, Copley visited Europe. When war broke out, he decided to stay, settling in England.

In London, Copley met two other American expatriates, Benjamin West (1738–1820), and Gilbert Stuart (1755–1828). West pursued his career in England. Stuart returned home and established a studio in New York City. One of his 1793–94 New York portraits of Mrs. Richard Yates is shown here. It demonstrates the realistic, yet formal quality of Stuart's best work. He became

most famous, however, for his portraits of the Founding Fathers. He painted the most famous likenesses of George Washington.

Discovering the landscape. During the years of national expansion, in the early 1800s, Americans began to appreciate the artistic possibilities of the landscape all around them. In 1825, a painter named Thomas Cole (1801–1848) first displayed his large romantic paintings of the Hudson River valley, less than 100 miles from New York City. Later, he travelled through New England, making drawings and oil sketches that he would finish in his studio. Cole succeeded in capturing the hazy light and the sense of timelessness that hangs over a great river. Soon there was an enthusiastic band of other painters working along the Hudson; they came to be known as the Hudson River School.

The rugged terrain and inspiring vistas of America appealed to the romantic taste of viewers both in America and Europe. Albert Bierstadt (1830–1902) travelled extensively through the western United States after mid-century, gathering material for canvases that would dwarf those of the Hudson River painters even as the Rocky Mountains dwarfed the Catskills. Another American, Frederick Church (1826–1900), went even further afield, seeking out the wilderness of South America, Labrador, Europe, and the Middle East.

Realism. Contemporary with Bierstadt and Church, other painters sought to portray everyday life with a new kind of realism. Among the leading painters of this group were William Sidney Mount (1807–1868) and George Bingham (1811–1879). Bingham's works depicting life along the great rivers of the Midwest became especially popular through reproductions and imitations. Even as they were working, an older artist, George Catlin (1796–1872), was pursuing a similar style, portraying the American West, especially the Indians, whose way of life was rapidly disappearing.

The power of realism was most thoroughly realized, however, by two great American painters of the last half of the 1800s. Winslow Homer (1836–1910) was essentially a solitary man, and as he grew older, he became deeply fascinated with the sea and with men who relied on it for their livings. One of his late and most pessimistic paintings is *The Gulf Stream.* Homer leaves little hope for the black sailor here. The mast of his little boat has broken, the rudder is gone; a waterspout can be seen in the distance, and closer at hand, sharks circle the boat. In this battle of man against the elements, the man seems sure to lose.

Homer's contemporary, Thomas Eakins (1844–1916), was a less isolated man. His paintings often featured his family and friends. He was an insatiable student; in his eagerness to master the human anatomy, he studied at a medical school in Philadelphia. His most famous painting, *The Gross Clinic,* vividly portrays a surgical operation in progress. Eakins sought to display the painting at the Centennial Exposition in 1876, but its subject matter shocked the judges and they refused it.

Many other approaches to art were developing in the same period. Albert Pinkham Ryder (1847–1917) rejected the realism of both Homer and Eakins for a deeply individual style that anticipated later expressionistic painting. George Harnett and others developed a style of almost photographic exactness, concentrating on still-life subjects. In the far West, Frederic Remington (1861–1909), preserved the images of Indians and cowboys of the vast plains in paintings that were both realistic and filled with action.

The major contrast to the works of Homer and Eakins, however, was to be found in the art of three American expatriates in Europe. The first of these was James McNeill Whistler (1834–1903). His famous painting of his mother, called *Arrangement in Gray and Black No. 1,* reveals his intense concern with design—a concern that sometimes overcame his interest in the subjects of his portraits.

John Singer Sargent (1856–1925) was born in Italy of American parents. Although he lived in Paris most of his life, he became increasingly involved with American artists. He is most famous for his elegant portraits, many of which are engaging both as character

studies and as studies in composition and color.

The third expatriate master was Mary Cassatt (1844–1926). She began to exhibit with the French Impressionists in the 1870s and became closely associated with them. Among her special interests were portraits of mothers with children.

The Ashcan School. Up to the 1890s, the subjects of most American paintings were either genteel (influential people, "noble" landscapes) or exotic (Indians, fur traders, cowboys). A group of younger painters from Philadelphia in the 1890s was determined to break into new subject areas. They wanted to show life as it was really lived in the city as well as in the countryside and wilderness.

Led by Robert Henri, whose book *The Art Spirit* came to serve as a kind of manifesto, this group, which called itself "The Eight," extended the subject matter of painting to the lives of the middle and lower classes. The painters came to be known as "The Ashcan School." The individual artists had quite different styles and interests, but they did share a new openness to extending the subject matter of art and an antipathy to the "art for art's sake" approach championed by Whistler.

The Armory Show. Members of The Eight were eager to gain a broader audience for their work. They finally arranged to sponsor a large art show in New York City and to bring over a wide representation of modern European art, including works of Gauguin, Van Gogh, Cézanne, Matisse, Picasso, and others. The Armory Show marked the beginning of modern art in America. Critics were shocked at the abstract art from Europe, but young artists were deeply influenced. Ironically, The Eight, the sponsors of the event, were largely ignored.

America against modernism. From 1913 on, American artists were increasingly forced to choose between abstraction and the older homegrown realism. Regional painters of the 1920s and 1930s adopted a modified kind of realism, using some new techniques but holding to American values. Thomas Hart Benton, John Stewart Curry, and Grant Wood were among the more successful.

Edward Hopper (1882–1967) was a loner who took something from each school. He began by painting seascapes and landscapes in the old tradition, yet his interest in composition and especially in showing light made his work both less engaged and more

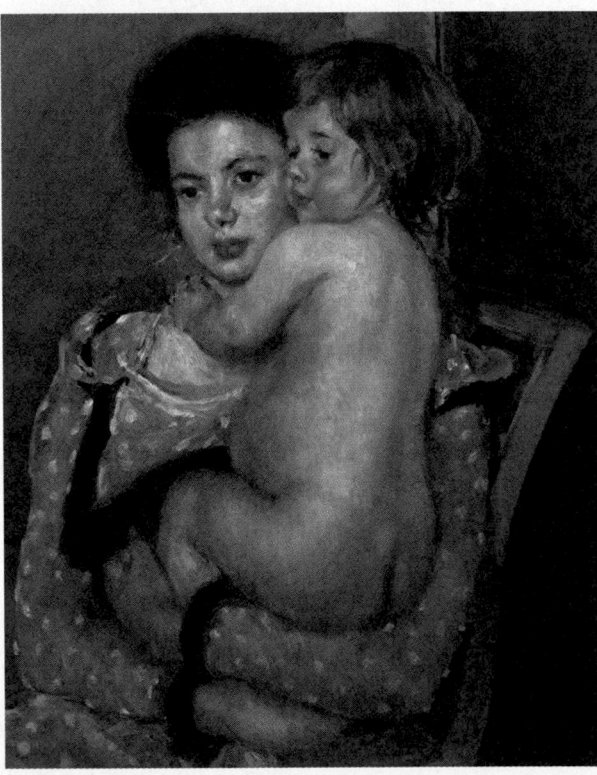

THE GULF STREAM, by Winslow Homer, shows the American devotion to realism, yet also suggests a symbolic interpretation.

REINE LEFEBVRE HOLDING A NUDE BABY by expatriate Mary Cassatt (1902).

19 History of Art

SECOND STORY SUNLIGHT by Edward Hopper portrays a warmly American scene, yet suggests a sense of isolation.

center
US

centre
Brit.

SPRING ON THE MISSOURI by Thomas Hart Benton (1945), who used a modified realism while holding on to American values.

formal. He produced haunting city scenes and seemed to revel in clearly American settings. His *Second Story Sunlight* demonstrates his deep interest in light and shade but also illustrates the separation and loneliness of his people. The scene is beautiful and yet somehow bleak—both characteristics that appear again and again in Hopper's work.

During the Great Depression of the 1930s, artists came to use their canvases as a medium for social comment and criticism. The most significant event of the decade was the establishment of the Works Progress Administration (WPA), which gave government-supported employment to visual artists, musicians, and writers. In its years of operation (1935–1943), the

While Pollock and the abstract expressionists gained a secure place in the modernist tradition, the older American tradition of realism

SEATED WOMAN by Willem de Kooning (1940). De Kooning developed a personal type of abstract expressionism.

WINTER by Andrew Wyeth (1946). Wyeth's artistic interpretation of the American experience was one of isolation and wistfulness.

WPA employed more than 3,500 artists; among them were Jackson Pollock, Willem de Kooning, and others whose works would make New York the art center of the world by 1950. By giving artists the chance to paint full time, the WPA allowed them to develop their skills and to form a sense of professionalism they had never felt before.

stubbornly survived. The paintings of Georgia O'Keeffe (herself trained in the international school) and the work of such painters as Andrew Wyeth attracted wide attention and admiration. The battle between abstraction and realism never really ended, and new skirmishes may arise in the future.

—*Lawrence Lorimer, Donald Lorimer*

Eastern Art

Although the impulse to create may have sprung from the same roots in the East and the West, the development of art took very different paths over the centuries. Only in recent times have Western students taken a deep interest in the artistic traditions of Asia. They have discovered Asian arts to be profoundly impressive, while difficult to fully understand.

Just as a Chinese observer would have to understand much about Christianity to fully appreciate the art of medieval Europe, so a Western observer must come to Eastern art with some knowledge of and sympathy for the religious and cultural past of Asia. The effort to cross cultural barriers serves as a reminder that artistic expression is closely tied to cultural values and aspirations.

The following pages offer a brief summary of artistic development in the three great centers of Asian civilization: the Indian subcontinent, China, and Japan. The arts of other Asian countries were deeply influenced by the arts of India and China.

The art of Islam has been included here even though it is not confined to Asia. Rising from the peoples of North Africa and the Arabian Peninsula, it was influenced by many older traditions as Islam itself spread. Yet it developed its own traditions, separate from those of Europe and of Asia.

India

The art of India is primarily religious. Its temples are among the world's most impressive sacred monuments in stone. Its sculpture depicts a vast array of gods and goddesses, many of which decorate the temple walls; many others are ritually worshipped in shrines and monasteries. Its paintings illustrate the mystical and mythical texts that, through the centuries, have colored the Indian imagination. Despite its religious inspiration, however, Indian art is vigorous, exuberant, and often ravishingly sensual.

The beginnings of Indian civilization reach back to the highly developed, urban Indus Valley culture that flourished in northwest India between about 3000 and 1500 B.C. The earliest known examples of Indian sculpture date from this period. Around 1500 B.C., however, the native inhabitants of the Indus Valley (Dravidians) were forced by Aryan invaders to move southward. The Aryans brought with them new forms of ritual worship, concepts of caste, and a priestly class. They also adopted elements of Dravidian worship, and from these foundations, the religious system known as Hinduism later evolved.

Buddhism. Almost no artifacts exist from the period of the Aryan invasion to the rise of Buddhist monuments after 400 B.C. Buddhism was a powerful force in India from the 300s B.C. until about A.D. 900, when it largely disappeared from India. But its impact on all the arts of Asia was and continues to be enormous. After its decline in India, it survived in many different forms throughout the rest of the Asian continent.

Buddhism was the teaching of Gautama Siddhartha, a prince, probably from Nepal, who lived between 563 and 483 B.C. According to legend, the prince as a young man was so moved by the miseries of the human condition that he renounced his worldly life and possessions to become a simple monk. He meditated under the Bodhi Tree for 49 days, until he received understanding and became the Buddha, "he who is enlightened." The historic sermon of the Buddha in the Deer Park of Benares (now Varanasi in north central India) formulated an eightfold path of conduct as a means of release from the agonizing cycle of birth and rebirth *(samsara)*. The path led to the attainment of nirvana, the extinction of all worldly desires.

The earliest Buddhist art in India dates from the Maurya period (322–185 B.C.), particularly from the reign of the Emperor Asoka, a devout Buddhist who dedicated his rule to the propagation of the Buddhist law. The characteristic monument of Buddhist art is the *stupa,* a large, solid, hemispherical relic mound that was built over the ashes of the Buddha, and later over the ashes of his disciples as well. The *stupa* was meant to be circumambulated, or walked around. The railings that enclosed the sacred area were elaborately decorated with narrative stories of previous lives of the Buddha *(Jatakas)*.

During the dynasty of the Kushans (A.D. 50–320), Buddhist iconography was codified and the story of the Buddha's life and the miracles he performed were repeated in countless numbers of reliefs decorating vast numbers of *stupas* and monasteries in the ancient province of Gandhara, in northwestern India. Here, in the wake of the invasions of Alexander the Great around 330 B.C., there flourished a hybrid art that combined Greek (and later, Roman) and oriental elements. Greco-Roman styles brought by craftsmen from the West mingled with traditional Indian subjects. Many of the images of the Buddha and other deities recall the classic Apollo or a toga-draped citizen of Rome. The standing Bodhisattva image is an early example of this mixed style. A Bodhisattva is a compassionate, semidivine being who chooses not to enter nirvana in order to assist the faithful on Earth in finding salvation. As befits his fortunate station in life, he is always shown in elaborate dress and heavily jeweled. The emphasis on the volume and folds of the

centers
US

centres
Brit.

civilization
US

civilisation
Brit.

colored
US

coloured
Brit.

A BODHISATTVA from Gandhara (C A.D. 100) shows a blend of Indian and Greco-Roman styles.

Bodhisattva's garment, his hair arrangement, and the necklace with animal head finials are typical of Hellenistic and Roman sculpture. At the same time, much of the symbolism is purely Indian. Note especially the pedestal where devotees worship the pillar of Buddhist law, rather than the Buddha figure itself.

But the principal image of Buddhist art is, of course, the Buddha himself. Anthropomorphic representations of the Buddha appeared in the early centuries of the Christian era, and can probably be linked to the rise of new Buddhist sects that emphasized *bhakti,* or devotion; these sects required the Buddha's representation in more accessible human form. The creation of the Buddha image occurred in two roughly parallel lines of development: one in Gandhara, where an Apollo type evolved; and the other in the southern Kushan capital of Mathura, near Delhi, where a more native style of Indian sculpture flourished.

The Mathura workshops produced some of ancient India's finest sculpture in the characteristic red sandstone of the region. This area was less susceptible to foreign influences than the outlying provinces of Gandhara, and its style derived from earlier, purely Indian traditions. The fertility goddesses *(yakshi)* were a popular subject for the decoration of railings and pillars in early Buddhist art. These images were a survival of the mother-goddess cult of pre-Aryan India, and in their robust and self-assured female form, with its suggestion of sensuous repose, we have the flowing grace and plastic ease char-

acteristic of the native tradition of Indian sculpture. In contrast to the naturalism of Gandharan Buddha images, the Mathura Buddha and Bodhisattva types display idealized abstract proportions combined with deep spiritual qualities.

During the reign of the imperial Guptas (A.D. 325–647), a classic Buddha image was developed, an image of idealized perfection in proportion and form. Combining and harmonizing the styles of Gandhara and Mathura, Gupta sculptors developed an image that suggested both spiritual power and physical sensuousness; that image became the classic Buddha figure of southern Asia, exported throughout Southeast Asia and Indonesia.

The Gupta Buddha type was produced at Sarnath, the site of the Buddha's first sermon. As shown here, the Buddha is always represented as a transcendental being. Marks of his divine status are usually the elongated earlobes; the *urna* between the eyebrows, like a "third eye," to suggest wisdom; and the *ushnisha* crowning the head, to symbolize his high degree of spiritual enlightenment. He is clad in a monastic robe devoid of any ornament to represent his renunciation of all earthly wealth and desires, and his right hand is raised in *abhaya mudra,* a formal gesture denoting reassurance and protection; the lowered left hand, in *varada mudra,* confers blessings and favors.

In the Sarnath images, the heavy folds of Gandharan drapery are dispensed with and a youthful human frame seems to shine with a soft

smoothness and an almost transparent luminosity of texture. The lotus-shaped eyes and the full compassionate lips recall the distinctly Indian ideal of the Mathura Buddhas.

The Gupta period was India's golden age, and its achievements in art, literature, and learning became a touchstone for the artists and literati of succeeding generations. The famous Buddhist frescoes in the cave temples of Ajanta perhaps best exemplify the luxurious, aristocratic brilliance of Gupta court and secular life. The first images of Shiva and Vishnu, the great gods of Hinduism, also date from this period.

Medieval India. Despite the brilliance of Buddhist art during this period, Buddhism began to decline after 700, and it eventually disappeared from India. Only in the northeast provinces of Bihar and Bengal did a hybrid form of Buddhism—mixed with many Hindu practices—survive. This form, with its worship of the Tantra (Manual of Ritual), magical formulas, and mystic diagrams, was transmitted to Nepal and Tibet, Southeast Asia, and eventually to China and Japan.

Hinduism, revived and reformed, became—and remained—the dominant way of life and worship in India. Even during its highest period of ascendancy, Buddhism had never completely eliminated popular Hindu beliefs. It was the ability of Hinduism to absorb diverse approaches and philosophies that accounted for its resurgence and triumph.

NINE CENTURIES OF ART:
The yakshi (left) was made in the second century A.D. at Mathura. The classic Buddha (center) is a product of the Gupta dynasty (325–647) at Sarnath. The Kandariya Mahaveda temple (right, c 1000) illustrates the resurgence of Hindu religious art.

The so-called medieval period in India dates roughly from 600 to 1200. As was the case in medieval Europe, the period was characterized by tremendous architectural activity. The collapse of Gupta power resulted in the emergence of many regional semi-feudal political dynasties, and a correspondingly varied number of art styles.

The Hindu temple, as it evolved during this period, was considered to be a replica of the cosmic world mountain, a microcosm of the universe. Its great soaring spires were decorated with a profuse array of all the divine, demonic, and mortal beings who were supposed to inhabit the universe. Gods, goddesses, musicians, dancers, ascetics, nymphs, animals, fabulous creatures, and plants were all part of the richly adorned temple walls.

The Kandariya Mahaveda temple at Khajuraho is one of the most famous of all Hindu temples. It was built sometime between 950 and 1050, and the effect of its height—more than 116 feet—is greatly increased by its deep platform base and by the vertical lines of the re-creations of the tower upon itself. A path of circumambulation is included in the whole mass of the structure. The intent was to lead the devotee through a celebration of life in all its abundant forms, to the innermost sanctum, the *garbhagrha,* where he worships his god alone. This symbolic union with the divine was expressed on the outside walls by the *mithuna* motif of eternally embracing figures representing earthly and divine love. At its best, medieval sculpture represented a natural and lively style, recalling the early Mathura emphasis on vigorous, fleshy forms. But by the beginning of the 1200s, over-refinement and a more rigid, angular style became increasingly evident; it marked the beginning of the long, slow decline of the medieval tradition.

In south India, at centers like Tanjore and Trichinopoly, the powerful Chola dynasty (850–1150) embarked on an impressive program of architectural activity; it became the creator of a new classic style. The Cholas were exceptional bronze casters. Their bronzes were not intended for decoration; they were cult images to be placed in the innermost recesses of shrines as aids for contemplation of the divine form. These images, like the earlier Buddha figures and images of all Indian gods, were composed according to certain fixed proportions that were prescribed in numerous texts *(sastras)* compiled for the technical guidance of sculptors and painters.

The Hindu pantheon is bewildering in its diversity, but it is given structure by an underlying faith in one divine being whose energy is manifested in varied forms—contemplative *(sattvic),* active *(ragasic),* and fearsome and destructive *(tamasic).* The basic Hindu trinity comprises Brahma, the Creator; Vishnu, the Preserver; and Shiva, the Destroyer.

Of these three, Vishnu and Shiva are by far the most important. Vishnu is a

solar deity and is intimately associated with kingship. Shiva's most famous representation is perhaps as Nataraja, Lord of the Dance. This is one of the great creations of Indian art, perfected by the Chola masters. Shiva reveals his divinity in dance; he is Creator, Preserver, and Destroyer at once, in perpetual motion and eternal stasis.

His upper right hand holds the drum, symbolizing sound, one of the five elements that announce creation. The corresponding left hand carries the flame, symbol of the created world. The other right hand is raised in the gesture granting freedom from fear, while the other left arm stretches across his body and points to the raised left foot, a symbol of release. The right foot holds firmly beneath it a dwarflike figure, the demon of ignorance. A flaming arch rises out of the lotus-based pedestal that supports the god, and from his high

crown a fanlike arrangement of hair and leaves emerges and flows outward toward the nearly circular arch. The head, slightly tilted back, maintains an aloof serenity within the total rhythm of the dance.

The modern era. Many local schools of Indian miniature painting flourished in north India between the 16th and 19th centuries, growing out of the earlier illustrated manuscript tradition of western India. The great patrons of Indian painting were the local Rajput rulers who dominated most of northwestern India and the hill states in the western Himalayas. Rajput themes were largely drawn from the mythology of the Hindu epics.

The Mughals (1526–1857) were the Muslim conquerors of India, and during the reigns of the three great Mughals, Akbar, Jahangir, and Shah

SHIVA, a major Hindu god shown as Lord of the Dance, from the Chola period (c 1000).

centers
US

centres
Brit.

THE TAJ MAHAL, a tomb built by the Muslim ruler Shah Jahan for his favorite wife at Agra, shows the influence of Islam on the arts in northern India. It was completed in 1652.

civilization
US

civilisation
Brit.

honoring
US

honouring
Brit.

centers
US

centres
Brit.

vigor
US

vigour
Brit.

SHANG VASE (before 1000 B.C.) was buried in the tomb of a prominent person.

Jahan, between 1556 and 1658, Persian and Hindu artists worked together to create new styles in painting, architecture, and the decorative arts. In painting, they introduced realistic portraiture. Their achievements in architecture are crowned by the most sublime of all funerary monuments, the Taj Mahal, and decorate much of the present-day city of Delhi. The Mughal interlude was brilliant, but even at the peak of their power, the Mughals never ruled a unified India. The Rajput chieftains of the north and local Hindu rajahs in the south waged intermittent war against the Muslim invaders, so that native Hindu cultural and artistic traditions, though in decline, were never completely obliterated. India remains Hindu to this day. Predominantly Islamic Pakistan and Bangladesh are independent countries.

China

The origins of Chinese culture reach back more than 4,000 years. Large numbers of ceramic burial jars, apparently produced between 2500 and 1700 B.C., have been unearthed in Kansu Province in western China; they are the earliest records we possess of Chinese civilization. These painted jars were made without the aid of a potter's wheel, and their refined forms and fluid calligraphic patterns in red, white, and black suggest the interests that were to shape much of the course of later Chinese art.

Early dynasties. In the course of the second millennium B.C., at roughly the same time as the Aryan invasion of India, the Shang dynasty (1523–1027 B.C.) emerged; it is the first recorded dynasty of China. Elaborate underground burial chambers excavated in the Shang capital of Anyang in northern Honan contained large quantities of bronze, jade, and other sacrificial objects.

Ancestor worship has always been of great importance in Chinese life, as elaborate Chinese burial practices and tomb artifacts attest. Ancestors had special powers to mediate between this world and the world beyond.

Most of the archaic Chinese bronzes, like the one shown here, were buried in the tombs of an obviously wealthy ruling elite. The ritual bronze vessels of the Shang, and of the succeeding Chou dynasty (1027–256 B.C.), served both religious and social functions. They were used to pour libations, to store food in sacrifice to an ancestor, and as gifts.

By about the tenth century A.D., vessels were classified according to their form and use into about 17 basic types, of which this Shang *Hu* is one. The *Hu* is decorated with a favorite Shang motif, a mythical monster mask, the *t'ao-t'ieh,* whose distorted features and large protruding eyes were perhaps meant to ward off evil. Its precise iconographic significance is not known. Other animal images, such as the water buffalo and ram appearing in high relief on the handles and neck of this vessel, and the winged and beaked striding dragon along its base, probably enhanced its magical properties.

In the late Chou period, sweeping curvilinear designs began to appear, and patterned motifs, often set in flat ribbon bands, decorated the surfaces not only of sacred vessels but also of items of everyday use such as mirrors, chariot fittings, and belt hooks. Long inscriptions honoring the patrons who had commissioned the objects were frequently included. Eventually, vessels approximating the ancient ritual shapes were absorbed into the traditional ceremonial ritual of Confucian temples and ancestral shrines. Under the Sung and other later dynasties, they were copied in jade, porcelain, and marble and served a wholly decorative function.

The late Chou (771–256 B.C.) period was also the great age of Chinese philosophy. Under Taoist influence, it developed the ideals for a harmonious world order. Tao means "way"; it signifies the invisible law that governs all of creation. The great ethical teacher and reformer in ancient China was Confucius (K'ung Fu-tse, 551–479 B.C.), who stressed such ethical values as moderation, piety, and familial respect. His teachings reinforced the ancient belief in ancestor worship, which, in the succeeding Han period (206 B.C.–A.D. 220), raised tomb art to new heights.

During the long period of Han rule, both Confucian ancestor worship and Taoist myths found expression in art. All the stone sculpture that survives from this period belongs to funerary monuments. The tombs of high-ranking dignitaries were guarded by large lions, rams, and other beasts, and bold and animated scenic compositions embellished the tomb walls. All the implements that the dead person had used in this life and might have need of in the next accompanied him into the tomb.

Buddhism. It was also under the Hans that Indian missionaries first brought Buddhism to China, but it was not until the fourth century, during the rule of the Six Dynasties (220–589), that the Buddhist faith became the official state religion.

KUAN-YIN, a Bodhisattva made during the classic T'ang dynasty (A.D. 618–906).

In the centuries following the death of the Buddha in India in the fifth century B.C., two major schools of Buddhist doctrine emerged. The more orthodox of these was the Hinayana tradition, which spread to the countries of Southeast Asia. The other tradition, Mahayana, spread from India and Nepal, through central Asia, to Korea, China, and Japan. Central to Mahayana philosophy is the ideal of the compassionate *Bodhisattva* ("enlightened being"), who, with a number of other legendary Buddhas and lesser deities, assists both monks and laymen in the search for eternal truth.

The earliest Buddhist monastic centers sprang up in China during the Wei dynasty (386–554). They centered around cave temples, of which the most famous are the Yun-kang caves in Shansi; the Lung-men caves in Honan; and the caves of the Thousand Buddhas at Tunhuang in the far interior of northwest China, just inside the Great Wall. Votive stelae and wall paintings found in these caves show that the Buddhas were modeled on Gandharan images. These images probably travelled to China with missionary monks and traders in the form of small portable icons in gilt bronze.

In the course of the Sui dynasty (581–618), Buddha images from Gupta India seem to have inspired a movement away from the austerely draped Wei Buddhas to more sinuous and fleshy forms. This new interest in exploring and revealing body contours culminated in the work of the great T'ang sculptors (618–906), who, like the master craftsmen of Gupta India, endowed their creations with both spiritual grace and human warmth. In this beautiful image of the Bodhisattva Kuan-Yin, a deity of mercy and compassion, we see the characteristic Chinese taste for linear and conventionalized form.

In the vital and cultured urbanity of the classic T'ang period, all the arts and sciences flourished in China. The T'ang capital, Ch'ang-an, was a large cosmopolitan city that attracted large communities of Jews, Muslims, and Christians, as well as traders and merchants from the Near East, the Caucasus, and central Asia. Large workshops existed for the manufacture of tomb figurines whose subjects reflected the diversity and vigor of the times. Musicians, merchants, dancers, implements, animals, and mythical creatures were produced in marble, jade, lacquer, and clay painted in the typical T'ang yellow, green, and white glazes.

Painting. The vibrant expansiveness of the T'ang spirit gave way in the 900s to the more conservative and isolationist Sung dynasty (960–1279), which revived much of the old Confucian ethic. The introspective mood of the new age found its richest expression in painting.

Painting was always an important art form in China, but unfortunately little

has survived from the early periods. Although painters drew their subjects from a rich variety of themes and traditions, it was in landscape painting that the Chinese particularly excelled. This genre provided the painter with a special insight into the *tao,* the unity of all things. The Chinese word for landscape painting is "mountain-water picture," and the basic motif is comprised of soaring vertical mountain peaks (yang, the male principle) and water (yin, the female principle), running down to the fertile earth. Within this lofty scale, human figures and dwelling places are of no more importance than trees and rocks.

In the *Buddhist Temple Amid Clearing Mountain Peaks,* among the most famous of all landscape paintings, the eye is first drawn to the foreground detail of trees, rocks, a bridge, water, and a monastic complex. Then the viewer's eye is slowly guided upward by the pinnacled top of the temple itself. Behind loom massive mountain heights that dominate and dwarf the entire composition yet seem to recede into the infinite distance.

Chinese paintings were typically done on scrolls, which were treasured objects to be studied and contemplated at leisure. Scrolls in the vertical format were intended for hanging on walls, while horizontal scrolls, which varied in length from two or three to as much as 40 feet, were meant to be slowly unrolled, starting at the right and moving gradually to the painting's conclusion at the left.

SUNG PAINTING (960–1279): *Buddhist Temple Amid Clearing Mountain Peaks.*

19 History of Art

PORCELAIN
(c 1400) shows
exquisite design
sense in blue
and white.

Not surprisingly, the arts of calligraphy ("beautiful writing") and ink painting are closely related in China, for they both demand the same decisive strokes and sensitivity to nuances of line. Conventions existed for rendering trees, figures, and mountain formations, and these conventions formed part of the basic training of any artist. Under the Mongol rule of the Yuan dynasty (1280–1368), a new type of painting, known as the *wen jen,* or literati, style combined the arts of painting, poetry, and calligraphy. This continued to be popular well into the 18th and 19th centuries.

Ceramics.   Native rule was restored by the Ming emperors (1368–1644), who initiated a new interest in China's past, and especially in the achievements of the old T'ang dynasty. The capital was moved to Peking, and artisan workshops were actively patronized by the imperial court. The decorative arts flourished. New techniques, such as cloisonné, were

**THE AMIDA
BUDDHA,**
(after A.D. 1000),
object of a single
salvationist faith, is
shown in deep,
peaceful meditation.

developed, and pottery and porcelain were produced in unprecedented quantities. The latter are so important in the history of ceramics that even today we continue to refer to fine dishes as "china."

In the early period, celadons (ceramic wares with grey-green or blue-green glazes) and monochromes predominated. But by the early 1400s, porcelain, a much harder and more refined ware, had become the most favored type of ceramic in China. Particularly prized were blue-and-white wares decorated with underglaze designs painted in cobalt blue, such as the decorated porcelain shown here. A powerful, multi-clawed dragon strides across a delicate floral background in a composition that is an extraordinary combination of calligraphic brushwork, virile line, and brilliant color. Such masterpieces, as well as vast quantities of commercial ware, were made at Ching-te Chen, the center of porcelain manufacture from the 1300s on. As early as the 1400s, blue-and-white porcelains had a wide market as far afield as Europe, where the art of making porcelain was not mastered for another 300 years.

The Manchu conquerors who succeeded the Ming dynasty tried to continue the high traditions they inherited in painting, ceramics, and other decorative arts. The Ch'ing dynasty (1644–1912) brings us well into the modern period. Under the Ch'ings, old designs were revived and the imperial factories produced porcelains of superb quality and of exceptional brilliance. Another ancient Chinese art, jade carving, was also revived. Perhaps it was in the demands of this exacting art that the characteristics of the Ch'ing style—impersonality, technical virtuosity, and delight in the ornate—found their most perfect expression.

Japan

As in China, Japan's prehistoric age is known to us through rich finds of ceramics. The greater part of this age is called the Jomon period (4500–200 B.C.), and derives its name from the twisted-cord type of relief decoration of its pottery. The Jomon people had migrated to the island chain from Siberia.

The next migration of peoples, the Yayoi culture (200 B.C.– A.D. 250), came to Japan from the south. The use of the potter's wheel was known to these peoples, as was the art of bronze and iron casting, most notably seen in the large ceremonial bells they designed called *dotaku.*

From the Kofun, or Tumulus, period (250–552), mound tombs survive. These tombs were surrounded by simple clay figures of humans or animals known as *haniwa.* The *haniwa* were placed in the soil around the tombs, perhaps as a means of preventing erosion. Objects found in the tombs included, among other items, three that were to assume a

special importance in Japanese culture. These were the mirror; a special type of curved jewel called *magatama;* and the sword. All three later became sacred symbols of imperial authority. Many of the tombs of this period are associated with historical emperors who were considered the direct descendants of the sun goddess Amaterasu. This belief was reinforced by the native Shinto (meaning the way or teaching of the gods) religion. Combining animistic beliefs in the beneficent spirits of nature with ancestor worship, the Shinto reverence for the pure and simple beauty of nature has survived through the centuries alongside Buddhism. It permeates Japanese culture even today.

Buddhism.   The official date of the introduction of Buddhism into Japan is traditionally given as 552 A.D., when the ruler of the Korean kingdom of Paekche sent a bronze image of the Buddha and scriptures to the Japanese court. Adoption of the new religion encouraged official missions to China, especially during the long and splendid rule of the T'ang dynasty, which was established in 618. This exposure to China at the full height of her creative power was the backdrop against which early Buddhist art in Japan developed.

The popular divinities of China's Mahayana Buddhism were enthusiastically adopted by the Japanese, as were the artistic styles and conventions of the T'angs. The Japanese dependence on mainland traditions can be seen in the famous bronze Shaka Triad (that is, Shakyamuni, the historical Buddha), one of the treasures of early Japanese art, in the Horyu-ji monastery at Nara.

The Nara period (645–794) was an age of vast temple and monastery building, modeled after Ch'ang-an, the T'ang capital of China. This ambitious building program culminated in the magnificent temple of Todai-ji, where a colossal bronze image of Vairocana, the supreme Buddha of the universe, 53 feet high, was housed in a massive wooden temple 284 feet long, 166 feet wide, and 152 feet high. Innumerable icons, paintings, precious ritual objects, and votive gifts, all executed in the classic T'ang style, are still preserved in Nara today.

From the Mahayana ideals that shaped the early history of Buddhism and Buddhist art in Japan, there emerged three major strands of doctrine to dominate Japanese religious life in subsequent centuries.

The first, esoteric Buddhism, emphasized that Buddhahood could be attained in this world by penetrating the mysteries of body, speech, and mind through incantations, spells, and magic symbols. The esoteric pantheon is vast, and its most characteristic visual representation is the *mandala,* an abstract and geometric diagram of the universe that shows the relationships between the various heavens and their countless deities. Esotericism introduced to Japan many terrifying deities who subdued

 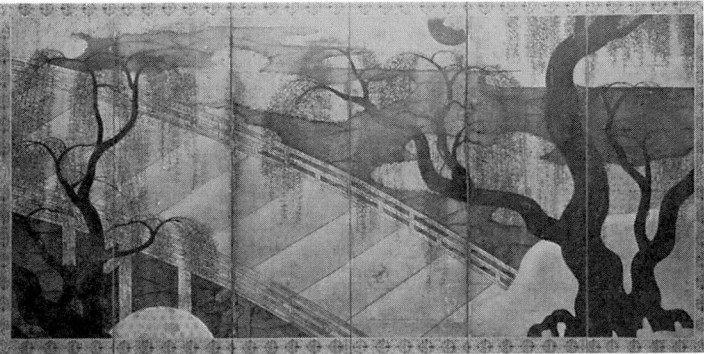

the physical obstacles to enlightenment.

Pure Land Buddhism came to Japan from China in the twelfth century, offering a single salvationist faith based on worship of the Amida Buddha—the Buddha of the Western Paradise. Pure Land mandalas evoked the paradise dwellings of Amida by showing well known shrines and landscapes. Paintings began to take on a more narrative character in an effort to provide pictorial aids in the instruction by monks of the common people. As new temples sprang up, the demand for sculptures to furnish them rapidly increased, and the assembled woodblock (*yosegi*) system of manufacture was devised and perfected by the twelfth century.

The Amida Buddha shown here is an example of this technique; it has a hollow interior. The image is over nine feet high. It is calmly and impassively seated in the cross-legged position, with its hands in the *mudra* position, denoting profound meditation. The rows of small shell-like curls that form the Buddha's *ushnisha* (one of his transcendental properties) recall the Buddha images of Gupta India, while the formal folds of the robe clearly have a Chinese prototype.

It was during the long Heian period (794–1185) that both esoteric and Pure Land Buddhism dominated Japanese culture. At the capital of Heiankyo, modern Kyoto, the powerful Fujiwara family ruled as state ministers, controlling the emperor and court politics for more than 250 years.

Heian court painters developed a specifically Japanese mode of painting and calligraphy known as *Yamato-e,* literally, "Japanese pictures." This style of painting on horizontal scrolls often had subject matter drawn from Japanese literary narrative.

In the succeeding Kamakura period (1185–1392), Japanese society took on a clearly feudal, hierarchical structure, based on the personal loyalty of vassal to master. The Kamakura *shogun* or guardians of the throne and nation dominated this hierarchy. Sculpture in the Kamakura period is distinguished by a sturdy naturalism, in contrast to the ideal beauty of the Nara period. Large portrait statues in the round emphasize true-to-life physical features, their heroic proportions reflecting the martial spirit of the Kamakura warriors.

The art form known as *e-makimono* or "painted scrolls" was one of the great achievements of this period. These are long hand scrolls, Chinese in origin, on which the Japanese painted genre subjects in continuous narrative, often ingeniously shifting perspective, tempo, and mood to suit the action of the story. Unlike the Chinese, who mainly used their scrolls for landscapes, the Japanese revealed a flair for the dramatic.

During the subsequent Muromachi (1392–1568) and Momoyama (1568–1614) periods, new warrior classes arose, creating a military rather than a feudal society. The arts came under the influence of yet another Buddhist doctrinal tradition called Zen. Zen insisted on personal self-discipline and introspection as aids to meditation, ideas that appealed to the newly emerging military clans and that found rapid acceptance.

Ink painting was favored by the Zen artists because it enabled them to illustrate in brush and ink the moment of spontaneous creativity in which spiritual enlightenment may also be achieved. This accounts for the explosive, highly dramatic flavor of many Zen paintings.

By the time Kano Masanobu founded his school in the late 15th century, the tradition had become wholly secular and decorative. The Kano were commissioned to carry out large-scale decorations of rooms in new palaces and monasteries. The pair of sixfold screens, each more than five and a half feet high and eleven feet across, entitled *The River Bridge at Uji,* is an example of such decorations. The designs are bold and sweeping, against a gleaming gold ground, and the result is one of grand but unruffled magnificence.

The modern era. The Edo period (1615–1868), which ushered Japan into the modern age, takes its name from the remote village of Edo, modern Tokyo, to which the militant Tokugawa shoguns moved their capital at the start of their long rule. A rising merchant and middle class became the real wielder of power and arbiter of taste. Edo became a city where fortunes could be quickly made and spent, and the decorative arts—textiles, lacquer ware, ceramics—of this period are famous for their brilliance of design and perfection of technique.

LANDSCAPE was a particular interest of the Japanese. *The River Bridge at Uji* (c 1500) is 11 feet long (top). *The Poem Scroll with Bamboo,* below, completed 100 years later, combines pictorial and calligraphic elements.

color
US

colour
Brit.

emphasized
US

emphasised
Brit.

flavor
US

flavour
Brit.

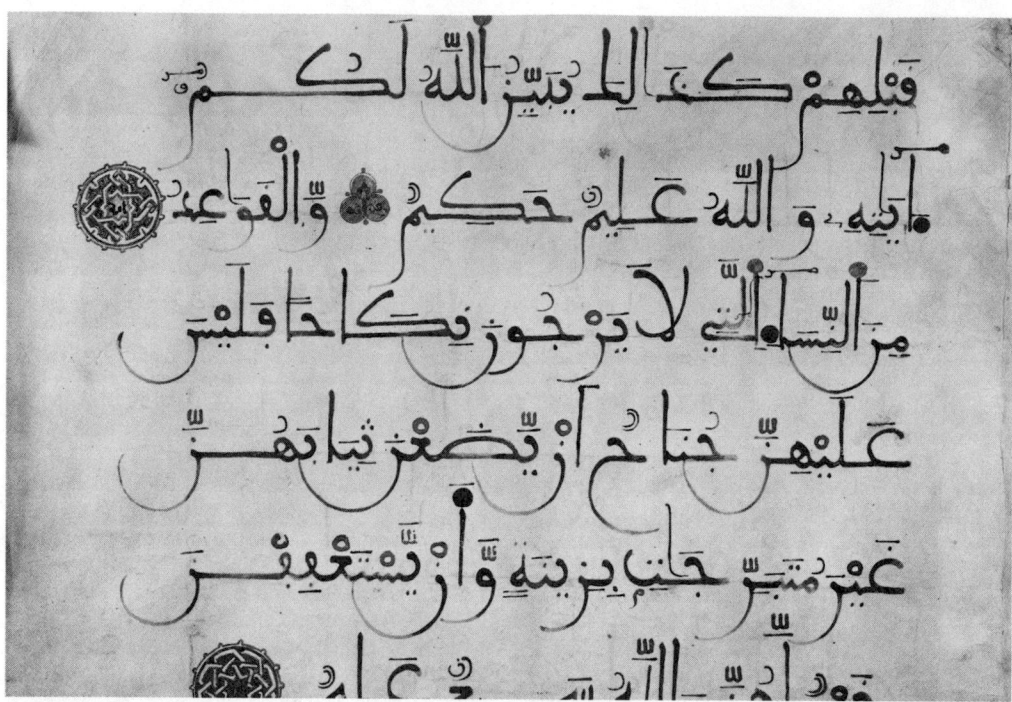

CALLIGRAPHY,
often the text of the sacred Koran, is a characteristic Muslim art form, showing a deft sense of line and form. See also the Taj Mahal in this section.

colorful
US

colourful
Brit.

center
US

centre
Brit.

TWO ACTORS
in the Ukiyo-e style is a caricature of the two stage heroes.

A distinctive style of decorative painting called *Rimpa,* a term applied to a school of painters and calligraphers, originated in the early Edo period. Its founders were the painter Sotatsu, active from about 1596 to 1623, and the distinguished calligrapher Honami Koetsu. The vigorous and sensitive *Poem Scroll with Bamboo* is a superb example of the collaborative work of these two masters. This long hand scroll is one of the rare examples of Rimpa work on silk rather than on paper. The calligraphy, at once dynamic and delicate, recalls the elegant scripts of the Heian scrolls, and appears interspersed in a carefully balanced composition of bamboo stalks and leaves. Energetic line and unerringly effective spacing are the essence of Sotatsu's style, which here boldly projects the bamboo stalks beyond the borders of the silk.

At first glance, the popular art known as *Ukiyo-e,* "paintings of the Floating World," appears to express a completely different aspect of the Japanese temperament, one that we have encountered with neither the Kano nor the Rimpa traditions. But the origins of this style, which drew its subject matter from the bravura and colorful vitality of the theatrical life of Edo, reach as far back as the lively genre scenes of the early Kamakura scrolls. Courtesans and actors were the main theme; they were depicted with humor, irony, outrageous flattery, and even undertones of sadness. This mirror of their own world had a natural appeal for the prosperous middle classes. As the market for these paintings expanded, a cheap method of reproduction by means of mass-produced polychrome woodblock prints was developed. It was through this peculiar art form of the color print that the world of Japanese art was first opened to the West in the late 1800s.

Islam

In the history of religions, Islam is relatively young. It was a monotheistic faith, founded by the Prophet Muhammad, who was born in Mecca about 570, and upon whose death in 632 an immense empire began to grow with extraordinary speed. The Arab tribesmen who were the followers of Muhammad embarked on extensive conquests, overcoming Palestine and Syria in 636, and North Africa and Persia a few years later. Eventually, the empire was to include virtually all the territory between Spain and Morocco in the west and India and Samarkand in the east. These lands were otherwise dissimilar in origin,

ethnic character, and artistic tradition.

Islamic art is too vast and varied a subject to be easily condensed. Its origins lie in the Near East, roughly in the area of the Nile, Tigris, and Euphrates rivers. The influences it absorbed were thus Sumerian, Assyrian, Babylonian, and Hellenistic, to say nothing of the Christian arts of the East—Greek, Coptic, and Syrian. From this center, as the empire spread, Muslim art extended toward Iran and central Asia in one direction, and toward the Maghreb and Spain in the other.

Unifying these extremely diverse components and traditions, however, was the revealed message of the Koran, the book of God, dictated in its entirety by Muhammad. The Koran and the other sacred text, the Hadith (the "sayings" of the Prophet), formed the basis of the holy law that regulated all aspects, social and spiritual, of the life of every Muslim. The Koran was written in the Arabic script that may be considered the most typical and widespread art form in Islam. As the conveyor of the divine message, it is invested with a nobility and an excellence that surpasses every other art. Written from right to left, along a horizontal line, the script consists of 28 letters, punctuated by diacritical marks and vowel accents. The art of Islamic calligraphy had an almost endless range of possibilities. It inevitably merged with new decorative schemes, such as floral motifs and scrolls. The exquisite *maghribi* style seen here evolved in North Africa, parts of Spain, and Islamic Africa. Gradually, calligraphic designs covered the surfaces of monuments, textiles, ceramics, paintings, and jewels, thus transferring to the objects they decorated some of the sanctity of the script itself.

In the early centuries of Islam, human forms were excluded from manuscript illuminations, wall decorations, murals, and mosaics. But the strong pictorial traditions of Hellenistic, Byzantine, and Sasanian art eventually asserted themselves, so that later Islamic art was characterized by skillful depictions of human and animal figures in a dense landscape of vegetal, geometric, or epigraphic patterns. Many Persian, Turkish, and Indian (Mughal) carpets, for example, reflect this technique.

No mention of Islamic art is complete without a reference to its architectural achievements. The Muslim place of worship is the mosque, derived from the Arabic *masjid,* "a place where one prostrates oneself [before God]." Here again, the early Muslims borrowed elements from cultures they had conquered—Christian churches, Roman basilicas, Hellenistic columns—fusing them ultimately into uniquely successful and wholly Islamic creations. The great flowering of mosque architecture between 1500 and 1700 in Ottoman Turkey, Safavid Iran, and Mughal India was the result of a long process of experimentation with existing forms.

—*Marukh Tarapor*

Photography and Cinematography

For almost two hundred years, photographers—and then cinematographers—have transferred images to film or to its counterparts. At each step of the inventive process, supplements and embellishments were added that allow the image to come across intact but enhanced in creative ways that open new fields of artistic endeavor. Images arrive today on movie and television screens, computer monitors, and the print media through the handling and direction of many skilled professionals.

Almost as soon as photography became possible, the search was on to discover ways to add motion, to insert sound, to duplicate color, to create a story line. From information to entertainment, pictures are a part of people's lives, and many of those pictures have achieved the status of art. Whether in black-and-white photos or virtual reality, the photographic arts are always in motion and offer new challenges for change to each successive generation.

Because they depended on technology for both their beginnings and evolvement, photography and cinematography were a late genre in the arts. As with most art forms, they were challenged to prove themselves as an art form worthy of recognition as such. If every amateur photographer who owned an inexpensive Brownie claimed art status for a photo, the world would be saturated with claimants. So guidelines were established. From the beginning, images were manipulated by the photographic eye on the other side of the camera.

Subject matter for a daguerreotype of the early 1800s with its carefully arranged bottle and plaster casts staked photography's claim as art. Progressively, photographers controlled the lighting, background, focus, mood, subject, color or lack of color, and processing of the finished product. And with the advent of photo shoots and moving pictures, entire crews of people worked together on projects to produce a seamless whole.

Then came digital imaging and the ability to create and re-create images outside the restraints of time and actualities. Technology combined the storytelling power of the written word with visual images to preserve the past, present, and concepts of the future in enhanced cinematography.

A DAGUERREOTYPE photo of the mid-1800s. Images were now accessible to people of all economic classes.

Photography

The visual arts preserve a record of humankind, even of preliterate cultures. Early people recorded their activities in drawings on cave walls. With time, along with more advanced methods of preserving drawings and writings, books and paintings became a means of presenting visual imagery of ideas and objects people wanted to keep. The scarcity of the means of producing and distributing these items, along with the great expense, meant that relatively few people had access to them. But as writing became a more widely distributed commodity, the procedure that would enhance and complement the text—transferring images to paper—began.

Preserving Images

In the 1800s, scientists and artists were looking for a more precise way to preserve visual images. They looked back to the Renaissance invention of the camera obscura, a method which projected an image onto a blank piece of paper, allowing an artist to sketch the image more exactly than was possible with the naked eye. If the same image were to be projected onto a chemically treated surface, they reasoned, it might be captured permanently on paper.

In 1839, William H. Fox Talbot, an Englishman, and Louis Daguerre, a Frenchman, discovered separate ways of fixing an image to a flat surface. The daguerreotype, suited to portraiture, soon replaced painted miniature portraits. Each plate was unique and no copies could be made, but soon rich and poor could afford portraits of their families and themselves. Talbot's Calotype process, which involved light-sensitive paper, was soon improved and became the basis of modern photography.

Within fifty years of Talbot's and Daguerre's inventions, thousands of photographs of the world—the Holy Land, architectural treasures of Western civilization, the newly discovered wonders of the American West—were produced and sold in albums or as stereo cards. The camera was teaching people what the far reaches of the world looked like.

In the 1880s there were two important discoveries in the field of photography: the halftone method of printing, which allowed photographs to be printed easily and cheaply, and the Kodak, a camera designed by George Eastman in 1888, which allowed anyone to pick up a camera and take photographs ("you press the button and we'll do the rest"). In 1889, one year after the introduction of the Kodak, George Eastman made another important discovery: film rolls, a transparent, flexible film base that would later make moving pictures possible.

History on Film

Color was introduced in the early 1930s. It negated the last argument made by those who had said that, based on the lack of color, photographs could not be considered art.

Throughout the twentieth century the names of photographers were becoming as familiar as those of other artists. This was especially true in Paris and in America, which were centers of photography.

Americans knew the works of nature photographer Ansel Adams, who helped create an awareness of our fragile ecological heritage and the importance of

MIGRANT MOTHER, CALIFORNIA, Dorothea Lange's 1936 photograph of an impoverished migrant mother with her children, became a remembered face of America's Great Depression.

As with all the arts, overlapping and multiple interpretations occur. Just as the subject David was presented in very different ways in the interpretations of sculptors Michelangelo, Donatelli, and Bernini, so other subjects are portrayed through the perspective of the photographer, the author, the painter.

The scope of the artist's vision in whatever medium was unlimited and often converged and/or built upon the works of other artists. Sometimes the resulting work was entirely unique, sometimes the influences on the artist were evident in the finished work.

A National Identity

Photographs have defined times and eras as no other medium could do. Cliché though the saying has become, a photograph has indeed proved to be worth a thousand words.

Photographs have stamped on our memories national endeavors—an astronaut planting a flag on the moon; tragedies—a young woman screaming in anguish at the Kent State shootings, young John John saluting the hearse bearing his slain father, the families of slain civil rights leaders; social injustices—photographer Dorothea Lange's face of poverty in the 1936 *Migrant Mother, California,* black schoolchildren

pitted against segregation in the South; wars—from Matthew Brady's Civil War photos to Viet Nam to a protester facing a tank in China's Tienemen Square. The identities of both families and of nations have been recorded and preserved in archival photographs.

Paralleling the subject matter of the Lange photograph in novel form was author John Steinbeck's *The Grapes of Wrath*. The book, about an impoverished but courageous family's migration to California, was awarded the Pulitzer Prize in 1940.

Photos such as the moon shot went on to be incorporated in books, documentaries, and movies, combining the usage of various art forms to develop a single theme.

Practical Uses

In addition to the photograph as art or photography for photography's sake, the worlds of commercial photography, news-related photography, and scientific photography now are a part of our everyday lives.

From the utilitarian uses of X-ray films that identify problems and thereby help us maintain healthful lives to catalog images that let us see the products we plan to purchase, we depend daily on the world of imagery.

preserving it. They carried from their mailboxes into their living rooms the *Time-Life* photographic works of Margaret Bourke-White.

They were moved to social action, in addition to achieving a sense of national identity, after seeing the 1955 "Family of Man" exhibition. And they marveled at the more contemporary photographic collages produced by David Hockney, and noted the messages Cindy Sherman, who included herself in her photographs, sent about stereotypical roles of women.

ASTRONAUT JAMES IRWIN salutes the American flag while standing on the moon.

A 1963 PHOTO of 3-year-old John F. Kennedy Jr. saluting as the casket of his father, slain president John F. Kennedy, is carried from the cathedral in Washington, D.C.

Cinematography

In 1887, Eadweard Muybridge, interested in giving motion to photographs, published a series of sequential photographs that analyzed the gaits of different animals. He had lined up many cameras along a stretch of track, synchronized their shutters to open at regular intervals, and then assembled the individual prints of galloping horses to obtain a split-second-by-split-second record. Muybridge proved what the naked eye could not see: that at one point none of the horses' hooves were in contact with the track.

Thomas Edison invented the kinetoscope, a machine that could show early "movies" to an individual who cranked the film loop by hand. By the early 1890s, these kinetoscopes were available to the public at penny arcades, offering a few seconds of racy or slapstick motion for a penny.

In 1896, the Lumiere brothers in Paris and Edison in New York held the first public showings of larger-than-life moving pictures on a screen for a large audience. By 1910, the movies had become a major form of popular entertainment, pulling in more money in admissions than vaudeville and Broadway together. People flocked to thousands of theaters across the country called nickelodeons.

Story Lines

The early silent movies were little more than photographed vaudeville attractions. Then Edwin S. Porter introduced narrative into film in his movie, *The Life of an American Fireman,* by crosscutting from one scene to another and creating a story. In effect, this method of editing film to include story lines created a new theater.

Other film directors soon learned the new narrative language and helped improve it. One of the earliest story types was the chase. A camera mounted on a moving car or train could wheel around, looking over its shoulder at the pursuers. The scene might actually be shot with the cars moving slowly and safely, and then shown traveling at breakneck speed.

It was a time of wild invention. By superimposing one shot over another, the filmmaker could also make it appear that a hero was hanging from a window hundreds of feet above the street, floating in the air, or even flying. By reversing the direction in which the film was run, a man who had just fallen off a building could be shown leaping back to the roof.

Film director D. W. Griffith understood that the basic unit of film was not the scene or the actor but the shot. By the careful arrangement of the long shot, medium shot, and close-up, he learned how to manipulate audience response, helping make film capable of stirring the strongest human emotions. Griffith's epics, *Birth of a Nation* and *Intolerance,* helped open up the nickelodeon to feature-length films.

Sound Recording

The first sound recordings in the early 1900s were very crude. Voices were barely understandable, and the sound of music was flat and distorted. But the appeal of a device that could capture the voice of a great singer or the exact words of a great orator encouraged continued research.

In 1927, a then little-known company, Warner Brothers, brought out *The Jazz Singer,* a sentimental story about a performer played by Al Jolson. It began silently, but in a scene with Jolson seated at a piano, he says a few words and then begins to sing.

The effect on early audiences was terrific. Within weeks, it became clear to all movie studios that they must begin to produce sound films. Over the next five years, they did. The recording arts—photography, moving pictures, and sound—had been merged to create a new art and entertainment form.

Golden Age of Film

The movies provided diversion for people during the seemingly hopeless times in the 1930s and '40s during the Great Depression and a second world war. In the movies people were powerful, rich, happy, and funny. Where private life was tedious or hopeless, the movies provided easy satisfaction.

All America went to the movies. In 1929, 90 million people a week paid admission. The figure dropped during the deepest days of the Depression, but it rose again in the late 1930s and reached a peak in 1948.

Movie palaces were built from coast to coast. They were the brightest and most striking pieces of architecture on the main streets of America, often decorated in the style of an Egyptian temple or an Italian opera house. The marquees held the brightest lights in almost any town.

One technical advance in the movies helped to produce the most popular film of the golden age of motion pictures—color. Although the movies had added sound in 1927, through the 1930s they lacked color. Technicians wrestled with the problem of color film until late in the decade, when a color process developed by Technicolor finally worked.

One of the first major films to use Technicolor was a blockbuster, a saga of the Civil War called *Gone With the Wind*

TIME EXPOSURE photography by Eadweard Muybridge was an early form of motion pictures. In a series of camera shots, he proved that all four legs of a galloping horse came off the ground at the same time.

THE KINETOSCOPE ARCADE in San Francisco in the 1890s had Kinetophones that produced music and other sounds.

(1939). It used color to great dramatic effect, notably in such scenes as the burning of Atlanta.

Decline and change.

With the availability of television, the huge popularity of the movies began to decline rapidly in the early 1950s. People stayed home in droves; movie theaters closed by the thousands, and the major studios began to lose money. There were other reasons as well, such as government regulations that resulted in studios cutting back on production.

At the same time, the new booking system opened the doors to the films of foreign directors and producers for the first time. By the 1960s, there was a significant underground of film fans entranced with the productions of Sweden's Ingmar Bergman, Italy's Federico Fellini, and many others.

These same serious fans also studied the earlier productions of Hollywood and Europe searching for artistic merit rather than box-office appeal. Gradually film was being seen not only as entertainment but also as art, and the great moviemakers, both past and present, were being honored for their contributions to a new art form.

The wide availability of family entertainment on television also influenced the kinds of movies produced for group viewing in theaters. Movie producers began to specialize, doing "adult" films for adult audiences, "teenage" films that featured contemporary music and young romance for teenagers, and occasional special children's films.

From the end of the golden age to

theaters
US

theatres
Brit.

FILM DIRECTORS
Akira Kurosawa and George Lucas discuss a model of the AT-AT walker used in *The Empire Strikes Back* from the Star Wars series, which began in the late 20th century and is continuing into the 21st.

ACTOR AL JOLSON'S voice heard in a movie of the late 1920s led to the addition of sound in most subsequent films.

the present and our multiplex theaters, the Hollywood film never regained its sense of innovation and excitement. Instead, it continued to rework older material. Westerns, which began in the early days of film, were developed into a serious form in the 1940s and '50s by directors such as John Ford and Howard Hawks. Variations on the Western theme continue to appear up to the present, particularly the space "Westerns" such as *Star Wars* and *The Empire Strikes Back,* but with few significant additions. The gangster films of the 1930s reappeared in such sensational films as *Bonnie and Clyde,* which does not have a happy ending, and three installments of *The Godfather.* Similar variations appeared in comedies and in musicals. The disaster movie came into its own as a predictable movie formula.

The growing edge of the medium was somewhere else. During the 1950s and early '60s, the producers of art films were the experimenters. But perhaps the most innovative of later cinematic work was in the neglected field of the documentary.

A younger generation of directors, often producing films for television presentation, rejected scripts and sets and artificiality in favor of portraying something real. Frederick Wiseman's defiantly noncommercial films *Titicut Follies* (1967, about a mental institution), *Hospital* (1970), and others are perhaps the best representatives of the documentary school of those years. But Wiseman also owed much to the television documentary as developed by the news bureaus of the major networks.

Toward the future.

The development of the film genre in the future is difficult to predict. Commercial film and television are hard to separate in any meaningful way. Avant-garde experiments in film and video have failed to gain wide public recognition. At the same time, filmmaking courses in schools remain extremely popular, and improved equipment makes it possible for an amateur of small means to make a movie even of feature length.

Every aspect of cinematography is in a state of change. Less than a hundred years span the introduction of sound in a film and the spectacular sound effects in contemporary epics such as the *Star Wars* sagas.

With the innovation of digital imagery toward the end of the last century, a twenty-first century of possibilities continues to evolve as a spin-off of the technique. It is a process that incorporates and is a part of many art forms.

In the 1998 movie *What Dreams May Come,* actor Robin Williams runs through the image of a canvas painting into a field of virtual flowers provided by imaging editors. Cinematographers are no longer constrained by producing what is in front of them; they use what is in their imagination, editing it in after the initial filming. As they edit, they use techniques such as Gourard shading to provide lighting that makes an unreal object appear real, causing the actual and virtual to seem to blend.

Many of the real tools required ten years ago to edit images have been replaced by the virtual tools of today. A bad photo or an uninteresting piece of film can be digitally edited and inproved or even made into a work of art. Computer-produced and -enhanced crowds, characters, and dragons need only be imagined, then inserted on an existing screen or photograph.

Timeless Art

Art flows through time, ever alive and transforming, with both past accomplishments and future possibilities providing inspiration. The need to create and to experience art spans the centuries and the continents. It is as deep a need to communicate as is speech, and as the patterns of language are universal, so are the themes and appeal of art. The stories surrounding works of art are often as intriguing as the art itself. Rock sculptings and drawings suggest that tribal societies supported artists through a division of labor that acknowledged the importance of creative talents. Off the walls of rocks, figures swim and dance through time itself, as alive with the joy of splashing through water and leaping through air as the day they were created.

Creations inspire creativity. Nowhere is this more apparent than in the symbiotic relationship of the David

sculptors—Donatello, Michelangelo, and Bernini—who drew from art of the past but interpreted the same subject in fresh and exciting new ways. These sculptings show that no work of art is totally definitive. It is always open to reinvention, reinterpretation. The Davids are products of a society that encouraged religious themes, in the process opening doors for sculptors to glorify the human form.

Society's expectations of the artist are sometimes chilling demands for conformity, as in Nazi Germany.

The artist's photographic eye, as important in the works of pre-camera portraitists as in the mood-evocative works of the expressionists, sees and reveals truth, not just pretty pictures. This clashed with Germany's political criteria that art must romanticize and glorify a happy country. Even though Otto Dix in *Randegg in the Snow, with Ravens* was able to trick the Nazis by combining the acceptable—a cozy winter landscape—with the unacceptable—skeletal trees and ravens symbolic of despair—he earlier was forced to give up his teaching post and flee his home because of his works critical of

Germany. And the works of expressionist Franz Marc, a decorated hero and casualty of World War I, were slated for destruction until an outraged public intervened. His *A Red Bull* is shown below.

In our technological society, good art remains timeless in its appeal, whether it is in a gallery or is a magnetic afterimage off a server's piece of spinning metal, broken into thousands of pieces of information and transmitted through telephone wires as sound, then translated through software into art images on a screen. Time has transported us from paints and pigments to pointers and pixels.

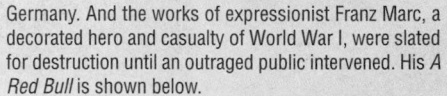

19 History of Art

THE HELP DESK

➤ **Select** something in your life—fabric, furniture, cars, etc.—and think about the influence art has made in terms of color, shape, pattern, proportion, etc. Who makes decisions about shape, color, etc., and who decides what is pleasing to the eye?

➤ **Find** a piece of art that shows movement. How is it shown? What was moving? Is it convincing?

➤ **Find** or make examples of purely imaginative art.

➤ **Find** or make examples of realistic art.

➤ **Draw** a self-portrait and portraits of each member of your family. What are the characteristics of each person that you are trying to illustrate (long hair, big nose, etc.)?

➤ **Try** to define the differences between fine art and commercial art. Add examples.

➤ **Visit** museums and commercial art galleries. Many are always free or have free days.

➤ **Visit** churches to look at stained glass windows. What do you observe most—scenes, geometric designs, brilliant colors, subdued colors, patterns, etc?

➤ **Look** at buildings—identify architectural features such as arches, columns, etc. Can you tell by looking what features are structural and what are cosmetic?

➤ **Create** a time line of development of the art you like. Note what was happening in history at the same time. Can you draw any correlation of history affecting art or vice versa?

➤ **How** does the perception of the viewer influence that person's response to art?

➤ **For** a list of helpful references, go to the *customers* section of www.southwestern.com.

Time Line of Art History

The Palette of Narmer
Egyptian
c 3000 B.C.

Statue of Mycerinus and his wife
Egyptian
c 2575 B.C.

The Lion Gate
Mycenaean
c 1300 B.C.

Dying Lioness
Assyrian relief sculpture
c 650 B.C.

Kouros
Greek
c 600 B.C.

Charioteer
Greek
c 474 B.C.

Doryphorus
Polyclitos
c 440 B.C.

Laocoön
Greek
after 100 B.C.

3000 B.C.   2500 B.C.   1500 B.C.   1000 B.C.   500 B.C.   400 B.C.   100 B.C.

Sphinx and Great Pyramids
Egyptian
c 2500–2600 B.C.

Toreador Fresco
Minoan
c 1500 B.C.

Shang Vase
Eastern/Chinese
before 1000 B.C.

Greek Vase
c 750 B.C.

The Parthenon
Greek
433 B.C.

Sculpture of a Roman
Roman
c 80 B.C.

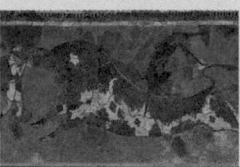

**Gothic Sculpture
at Reims**
c 1230

Ste. Chapelle
French Gothic
c 1250

February Scene
Limbourg Brothers
c 1415

Sculpture of David
Donatello
1432

Arnolfini Wedding
Jan van Eyck
1434

Mona Lisa
Leonardo da Vinci
c 1508

Madonna with the Long Neck
Parmigianino
1535

1100   1300   1500

The Last Judgment
Romanesque
c 1130

Lamentation
Giotto
c 1305

The Birth of Venus
Botticelli
c 1485

David
Michelangelo
c 1504

The Creation of Adam, Sistine Chapel
Michelangelo
1512

Hunters in the Snow
Pieter Breughel
1560

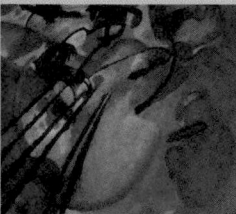

**Morning on the Seine
Near Giverny**
Monet
c 1868

**Sunday Afternoon on the Island
of La Grande Jatte**
Seurat
1886

The Gulf Stream
Winslow Homer
1899

Les Demoiselles d'Avignon
Picasso
1907

Improvisation 26
Wassily Kandinsky
1912

Bird in Space
Brancusi
1919

1800   1900

The Emperor Augustus
Roman
c 20 B.C.

The Pantheon
Roman
A.D. 125

Kuan-Yin
Eastern/T'ang dynasty
A.D. 618-906

The Lindisfarne Gospel
Celts and Saxons
c A.D. 700

Shiva
Eastern/Indian Chola period
c A.D. 1000

The Amida Buddha
Eastern/Japanese
after A.D. 1000

St.Sernin
Romanesque
c 1100

50 B.C.   **A.D. 100**   **A.D. 500**   **A.D. 1000**   **A.D. 1100**

Peaches and Glass Jar
Roman
c 79 B.C.

Bodhisattva
Eastern
c A.D. 100

Gupta Dynasty Buddha
Eastern/Indian
A.D. 325-647

Hagia Sophia
Temple, Istanbul
Byzantine
A.D. 537

Aix-La-Chapelle
Carolingian
A.D. 810

The Expulsion of Adam and Eve
Ottonian
c A.D. 1000

Rape of the Daughters of Leucippus
Rubens
1617

The Taj Mahal
Eastern/Indian
1652

Late Self-Portrait
Rembrandt
1669

Don Manuel Osorio
Goya
1700s

Mrs. Richard Yates
American/Gilbert Stuart
1793–94

The Tub
Degas
1886

1600   **1700**   **1800**

19 History of Art

Calligraphy
Islamic
1600s

Las Meninas
Velasquez
1656

Vierzehnheiligen Church
Rococo
Balthasar Neumann
1700s

The Swing
Jean Honoré Fragonard
1766

Woman with a Parrot
Manet
1866

View of the Gulf of Marseilles
Cézanne
c 1883

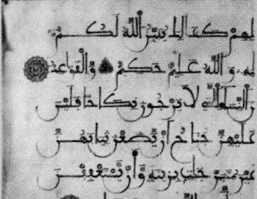

The Harlequin's Carnival
Miró
1925

"Fallingwater" in Pennsylvania
Frank Lloyd Wright
1936

Seated Woman
Willem de Kooning
1940

Spring on the Missouri
American/Thomas Hart Benton
1945

**Seagram's Building
in New York**
Miës van der Rohe
1956

Second Story Sunlight
American/Edward Hopper
1960

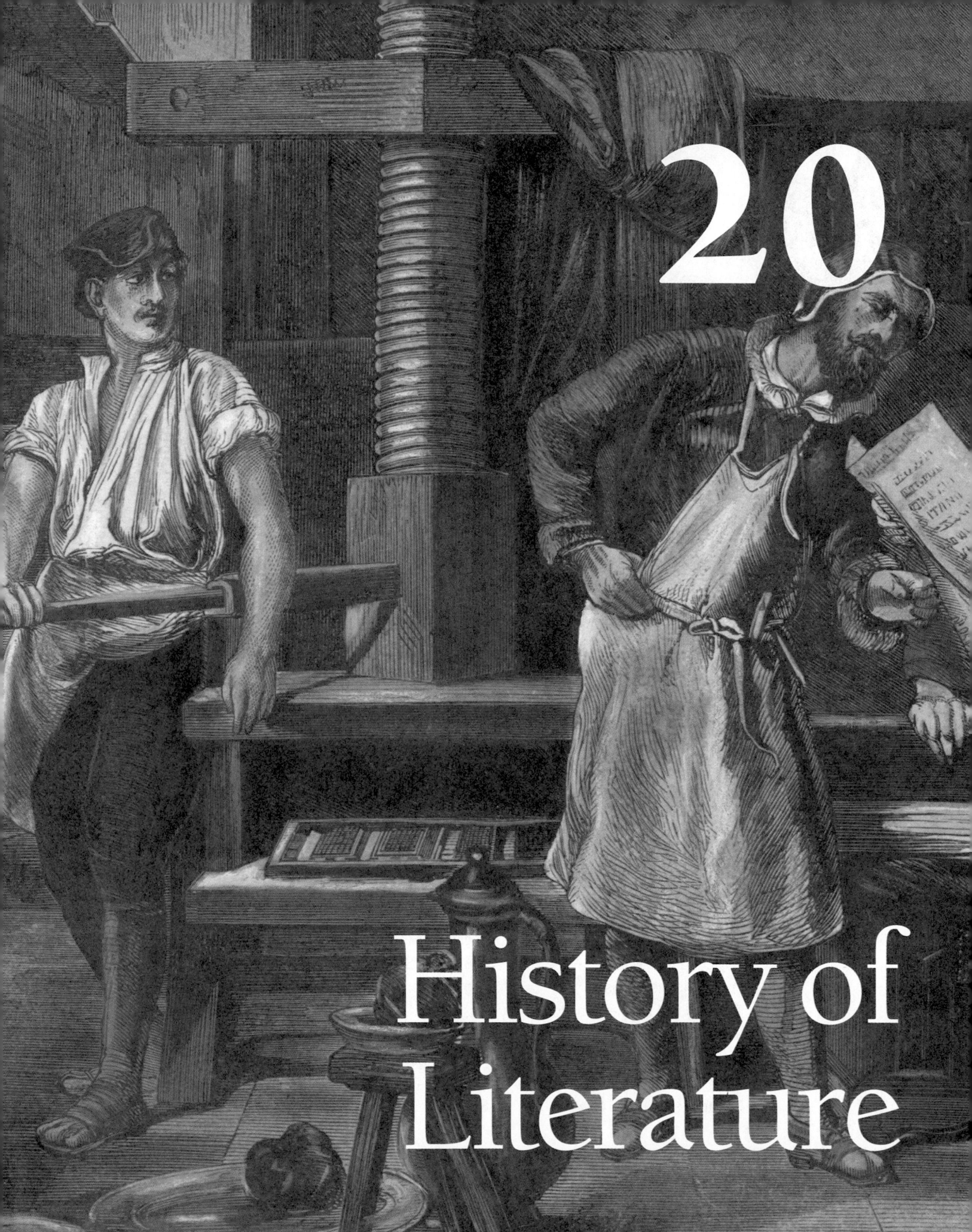

History of Literature

20

History of Literature

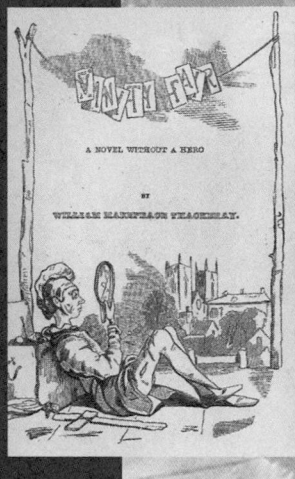

Contents

Overleaf: *Johannes Gutenberg at his printing press*

History of Literature

Ancient Literature

By the year 2000 B.C., a high level of culture and prosperity was to be found in most of the settled areas of the world. Egypt and the Minoan culture of Crete produced arts of extremely high sophistication and creativity. But beginning circa 1500, a series of catastrophes shattered this civilized world, destroying the basis of every one of the older cultures but the Egyptian. An almost universal feudal age ensued. Only after 500 years of "darkness" did the true written literatures of the world begin to emerge.

The East

China. China's first surviving documents date to about 1400 B.C. The high level of skill involved suggests written Chinese already had a long history at the time. In the Chou dynasty (1027–256 B.C.), the works ascribed to Confucianism were composed. The legendary Confucius (c 551–479 B.C.) was himself said to be a compiler of the works of earlier days. The Confucian writings we know today are later compilations done during the Han dynasty (202 B.C.–A.D. 220), at the same time as Rome's greatest age. The Five Classics (*Wu Ching*) of Confucius's canon comprise a chronicle of his home state *(Ch'un Chiu);* a system of divination based on numerology and chance *(I Ching);* a book of rituals and government *(Li Chi);* a book of historical documents *(Shu Ching);* and the great classic of Chinese lyric, the *Book of Odes (Shi Ching).* The *Book of Odes,* many of them simple folk songs, others concerning private experiences in a violent, feudal time, remains one of the world's most beautiful collections. As Confucius meant it to do, it gives human form to an ethical philosophy far in advance of its time.

The Confucian system was developed further by the teacher Mencius 372?–289? B.C.), whose *Book of Mencius* is the sole surviving collection. The *Tao Te Ching,* ascribed to Lao-tze (604–531 B.C.), and the book of essays, *Chuang-tse,* named after its author (c 369–c 286 B.C.), are works representing a philosophy of oneness with the natural opposites of the universe; the philosophy is called Taoism. It is the basis of a major Chinese religion, and its influence has been felt in many Western literatures and religions. During the Han dynasty, the philosophy was codified and explicated by scholars, and it became the basis for much of the future Chinese civilization.

India. The Indus Valley civilization was set back by the catastrophes around 1500 B.C. as well. In the centuries that followed, the region was conquered by the Aryans, an Indo-European people thought to have originated in southern Russia. They assimilated the older civilization and glorified their triumphant history in the masterpieces of Indian religion, the *Vedas.* These massive documents in verse and prose, grouped in four main categories *(Samhita, Brahmana, Aranyaka,* and the prime source of Indian mysticism, *Upanishad),* gave rise in turn to an even more massive body of commentary and explanation. A fifth category, dealing with magic and superstition *(Atharva-Veda),* extended the range even further.

A second major area of Indian literature, that dealing with the life and teachings of the Buddha (c 563–483 B.C.), stemmed from a reaction to the excessive stratification of society imposed by the Vedic priest-rulers. The canon was written down in the Pali and several other dialects in the last two centuries before Christ. The *Jatakas,* or beast-tales, of the Buddha's early lives, set the teachings deep in the tradition of popular narrative.

In the last stage of the Vedic period (c 500–200 B.C.), the *Sutras* were composed. They dealt with every aspect of ritual and of everyday life. At the same time, the Vedic form of Sanskrit, the Indian literary language, was changing to the so-called classical form. Two great heroic epics were written in the classical dialect and they became the centerpieces of Indian secular literature. The *Ramayana* is a vast poetic "family history" of the warring gods. The *Mahabharata,* vaster still, is based on old stories of the lives of royal heroes. The major set-piece of *Mahabharata* is the *Bhagavad-Gita,* which asks Hamlet-like questions about human action and suffering in conflicting circumstances. Its themes have been echoed in the literary productions of many other lands.

The rigid class system of Indian society encouraged a formal, rigidly classical court style in literature. This stifled creativity; and India, for all the richness of its religious genius, never produced the humanist classics that emerged in other areas of the world.

Persia. The period from about 650 to 450 B.C. produced the great teacher of Persian belief, Zoroaster (c 628–c 551 B.C.), in addition to Confucius, Lao-tze, the Buddha, the major Hebrew prophets,

and the early Greek philosophers. This period has been called the Age of the Great Teachers.

Zoroastrianism, whose books of law, the *Avesta,* comprise Persia's early literature and contain songs possibly written by the teacher himself, stands out especially. Its stark dualism—darkness against light, good against evil—has reappeared in religion and philosophy ever since. Such a world view is uniquely associated with the production of lyric verse. In Persia, the dualism—and the lyric poetry—survived into the next age, when the ancient civilization assimilated the tenets of Islam.

Greece

The beginnings of Western literature are concerned with religious definition, ethics, and military history. The Western classics differ from those of the East in their focus on man—for his own sake rather than for his divine significance, ethical code, or political identity. The difference appears most clearly in the classical civilizations of the Hellenes, the ancient residents of Greece whose inventions and ideas about the literary arts have carried through the succeeding 3,000 years.

LAO-TZE helped form Chinese conceptions of religion, philosophy, and literature.

Homer and the Hellenes.

The great productions of the early Hellenes were two closely related epics, the *Iliad* and the *Odyssey*. They grew out of oral materials and were first written sometime before 700 B.C. They are attributed to a man named Homer, about whom very little is known. As in many such early epics, the beauty of the *Iliad* is not in the invention of the story. That was already fixed by legend. The story concerns the war between the Hellenic states and Troy; historically, such a war may have taken place some centuries earlier, between 1500 and 1000 B.C. The fates of individual characters (Odysseus, Achilles, Hector, Agamemnon, Helen) were fixed in legend as well, and structural devices of oral composition were common to a whole class of singer- or reciter-poets. The early epics used similar descriptive epithets ("rosy-fingered dawn"), told of similar characters and situations, and sought explanations of national destiny in the legends of the past.

ODYSSEUS, warned that the tempting Sirens are irresistible, has himself tied to the mast of his ship in an episode from the *Odyssey* of Homer.

Homer represents the single inspiration in the composition of each of the poems (even though two or more poets may have had a hand in the two great works). His genius lay in using traditional materials and devices for new and surprising purposes. Rather than glorifying the Hellenic heroes, he seems to sympathize more with the family of the defeated Trojan hero. Achilles, the petulant hero of the Greek forces, is flawed at best. And Odysseus, the hero of the *Odyssey,* is more fallible than not, surviving only by his resourcefulness and capacity to endure defeat. Odysseus, whose return from the Trojan War took ten adventurous but often painful years, also represents the disaster that the war had been for Greeks and Trojans alike.

The ability to tolerate such contradictions—hero and fallible man, glorious battle and disastrous war—is a mark of the humanist tradition of Western civilization from this time forward. It appears in no civilization contemporary with Homer, and there is no sign of it before these poems in pre-Hellenic civilizations.

No works, barring the Old and New Testaments, are more essential to the later development of the West: the stories of the separate heroes, events, and gods remain nearly as current in the literature of today as they were in their own time.

The works of Homer, once set, were enacted all over the Hellenic world by travelling performers called the Homeridae. A type of poem called Homeric hymns, composed from Homer's time to the fourth century, tried to imitate the grandeur of the epic in simple, sometimes beautiful celebrations of the gods.

A rival tradition to that of Homer and the Homeridae is that of the didactic poet Hesiod. It begins perhaps 50 or 75 years later than Homer's own time. Hesiod's *Theogony* tells most of what is known about the early Greek gods. His later *Works and Days* goes further. In associating myth with a day-to-day, useful almanac of advice for farmers and merchants, Hesiod bridges the gap between the lives of the gods and the rhythms of everyday life. Hesiod was also the first poet to offer something of his own biography along the way, and to consider the poet's reactions to be an integral part of the making of the poem.

Homer's epics provided the Hellenes with a central identity for the first time, a "school" to which all conformed. Hesiod's more homely works reinforced this sense of identity. But after 650 B.C., the world began to change. Individual city-states, particularly on the Greek islands, were building prosperous commercial cultures of their own. This was Greece's age of great teachers: the philosophers Thales, Anaximander, and Anaximenes in the 500s; then Heraclitus, Pythagoras, Parmenides, and others. These thinkers considered not only ethics, but ultimately the nature of reality, and of meaning itself.

The 600s and 500s saw the development of several interrelated schools of lyric poetry. They survive today only in broken fragments, but these first "serious" lyricists set the forms, and to some extent the subject matter, for the whole classical period—nearly 1,000 years. Some of these forms and subjects are still familiar today.

The elegiac couplet, in which the second line slightly syncopates the rhythm of the first, began in the 600s as an exhortation to virtue or military valor. It became the ancients' prime vehicle for expressions of love, hate, sensuality, or grief. As used by Solon, the poet and lawgiver of Athens (c 600), it could express the injustices suffered by the poor or Solon's awareness of the privileges of the rich. Strung together in long chains, the elegiac couplet became the pastoral elegy, a lament for a dead friend portrayed as a shepherd or other innocent victim. Its form, if not its meter, carries all the way to modern times—to the *Lycidas* of Milton or *The Waste Land* of T. S. Eliot.

Other major Hellenic forms were the rushed passionate iambic, invented in the 600s; the Melic, complicated "private" stanzas employed by Sappho of Lesbos and Alcaeus of Mytilene in the 500s; and the choral ode, first performed at Sparta by Alcman.

The iambic led to the great dramatic poets of the 400s and, less directly, to the lyric poets of Latin, Catullus and Horace. Sappho and Archilochus, the two great lyric poets of Greece, also contributed greatly to later lyric poetry.

The Spartan choral ode grew more complicated over a period of perhaps 75 years. It emerged in Simonides of Ceos (556–468 B.C.) and Pindar (522?–443 B.C.) as one of the major vehicles of Greek poetry. Pindar's wildly complicated odes, largely in praise of himself, were in great demand at games and other festivals. Simonides, more conservative, was the poet of a new patriotism—it was he who wrote the elegiac epitaph for the Spartans who fell defending Thermopylae: *Stranger, go and tell the Spartans—We're still here, as they told us to be.*

Athens and tragedy.

According to tradition, tragedy began with an Attic poet named Thespis, who added an actor to the traditional chorus that chanted or spoke choral lyrics. The new poetry of theater took root in an Athens that had become the most prosperous and most politically advanced of Greek cities. Each of the successive tragic playwrights added new complexities to the form, as if to match the complications in Athens' own increasing maturity.

Much of this great period of drama coincided with the lifetime of the self-willed political leader Pericles (495–429 B.C.). During these years, Athens claimed the leadership of a coalition of cities that defeated giant Persia; then, Pericles himself began a catastrophic war with the rival city of Sparta.

ACTORS IN GREEK DRAMAS wore masks, which intensified the solemn mood.

The first of the great tragedians, Aeschylus (525–456 B.C.), had himself fought the Persians at Marathon and Salamis. His plays, frequent victors at the drama contests that were in Athens, are full of the confidence of a great time; among them are *The Persians* (472?); *Seven Against Thebes* (467); *Prometheus Bound* (date uncertain); and *Oresteia,* a trilogy (458).

By contrast, Sophocles (496?– 406 B.C.) drew away from plays of civic greatness. He was critical of the state and sought greatness in individuals. The Athens of his long life destroyed much of its own freedom and eventually lost its political independence through a prolonged state of military emergency. The treachery of the self-interested politician is a running theme in Sophocles' work, though his principal interest is the tragic victim, as in *Antigone* (c 331); *Oedipus Rex* (c 429); *Philoctetes* (409); and *Oedipus at Colonus* (401).

Euripides, the youngest of the three (480?–406 B.C.), seems to have given up on conventional patriotism altogether. He cares about the truth of characters and about the lyric power of his often complex verse. He does not believe in any grander morality than the injustice of human suffering. His plays include *Medea* (431); *Trojan Women* (415); *Electra* (413); and *Bacchae* (405). Nothing like the power of these three playwrights was to be seen again till the time of Shakespeare.

Alongside tragedy, a kind of drama now called Old Comedy was also popular. Aristophanes (448?–380 B.C.) stands out with *The Archanians* (425); *The Clouds* (423); *The Birds* (414); and *Lysistrata* (411). The writers of comedy used a mixture of bawdy humor and pointed topical reference. They mocked social pretension and shabby politics. Their form lasted only as long as Athens' original liberty. It was succeeded by the New Comedy, of which Menander (343?–291? B.C.) is the great exponent. His successful descendants may be seen in the domestic situation comedies of today.

Philosophy and history.

Athens contributed other major writers over this period. The *History,* principally of the Persian wars, by Herodotus (484?–426? B.C.), is a first attempt, rich in background information, at comprehensive history. The later *History of the Peloponnesian War* by Thucydides (471?–400? B.C.) is regarded as the first modern history, going far deeper than Herodotus. Thucydides was telling of a tragedy that happened in his own time, yet he remained committed to a dispassionate complicated view of human nature. The *Anabasis,* a memoir of military adventure, and a collection of anecdotes by the considerably younger Xenophon (434?–355? B.C.), provide

color and add to our understanding of the time.

In philosophy, Athens culminated its history of academic humanism with the *Dialogues* of Plato (427–347 B.C.), a literary masterpiece and the central canon for 2,000 years of continuity of speculative thought. Three dialogues center on the trial, defense, and death of Plato's teacher, Socrates *(Apology, Crito,* and *Phaedo).* They stand as an indictment of intolerance and as a major expression of agnostic faith. The works of Plato's pupil, Aristotle (384–322 B.C.), date from a time well past Athens' own collapse. They survive almost entirely from a later compilation of pupils' notes. Aristotle's pronouncements on literary theory were to have immense influence during the European Renaissance, almost 2,000 years after his death.

The last contribution of Hellenism lay in the rhetoric of its lawyers, including Lysias, Isocrates, and Demosthenes. They tried and failed to rally the Athenians against the Macedon of Philip and Alexander the Great.

Alexandria and Rome

Hellenism proved unable to sustain itself in its homeland, but the classical civilization passed, almost intact, first to Alexandria, the Egyptian capital built by Alexander the Great, and then to a new people, the Romans, and another language, Latin.

The Hellenistic civilization of Alexandria bubbled with fresh ideas but bore most of its fruit elsewhere. In the period when it had political as well as academic preeminence, it produced only one great poet, but he is as moving today as he was in his own time. Callimachus (c 265 B.C.) wrote with a strange blend of down-to-earth irony, philological correctness, and formal originality. He resembled a combination of Robert Frost and T. S. Eliot.

Also notable among Callimachus' prolific contemporaries were the slightly older Syracusan, Theocritus, and the somewhat younger Apollonius of Rhodes. The former began the tradition of the pastoral, based on the poet's beloved and rustic Sicily. Apollonius was an Homeric imitator, retelling the story of Jason and the Golden Fleece *(Argonautica)* and updating the heroic epic with a sentimental love story. Both were to have numerous imitators.

The greatest value of Hellenistic culture, however, was that it served the new and powerful Roman state as a window to the past. In fact, during the Roman period, the last major works in classical Greek, all prose, appeared. Among the writers were the Jewish humanist philosopher Philo (20 B.C.–A.D. 50), who anticipated Christianity's later reconciliation of classical philosophy and Old Testament faith, and the historians Josephus (A.D. 37?–100) and Dio Cassius (A.D. 155?–230?). The great biographer, Plutarch (A.D. 46–120), produced *Parallel Lives,* which served Shakespeare and many others as the best anecdotal introduction to the Greek and Roman worlds.

THEATRE OF DODON'S, where the works of the Greek dramatists were produced. Action took place on the stage and in the semicircle in front of it, surrounded on three sides by the audience.

color
US

colour
Brit.

center
US

centre
Brit.

20 History of Literature

MOLIÈRE'S COMEDIES are usually played in the elaborate costumes of the France of Louis XIV. The clothes contrast with the flawed characters Molière delighted in ridiculing.

Latest of all, the literary parodist, Lucian (second century), wrote *True History,* a deliberately absurd romantic novel that is a predecessor to the satires of Rabelais and Jonathan Swift.

The Roman republic.

Rome's serious literary works date from the time of Livius Andronicus (c 240 B.C.), who eased his life as a slave by producing plays adapted from the New Comedy into Latin. He also translated the *Odyssey* and generally made the Romans aware of the attractions of the older Greek culture during the time of Rome's great wars against Carthage. The leading military family, the Scipios, led in sponsoring Greek studies and original Latin works.

The comic playwright Plautus (254?–184 B.C.) stands as the major original talent of this time. His New Comedy farces, modeled on the Greek plays (for example, *Amphitryon; Menaechmi; Miles Gloriosus; Pseudolus*), have since served as models themselves for Shakespeare, Molière, and others. The technical innovator Quintus Ennius undertook at the turn of the second century to introduce into Latin verse the elaborate Greek rules of scansion and the hexameter. Called by Vergil the "father of Latin verse," he survives today only in fragments, as does the slightly later Lucilius, originator of Latin satire.

Many Romans, led by the conservative Cato the Elder (234–149 B.C.), fought the new style, considered weakening to the Roman character. Cato himself wrote in as rude and plainspoken a manner as he could manage. But Rome's triumphs brought the wealth and the slaves that made the weakening inevitable. Some of the slaves, from vastly more cultured backgrounds, provided important reservoirs of "native" talent.

Terence, the second-century writer of more sophisticated, if less zesty,

comedies (for example, *Phormio*), was a freed slave, born in Carthage. Polybius, (205?–125 B.C.), whose *History,* today surviving in extensive fragments, was a cross-cultural survey of the world, had been a Greek statesman and was brought to Rome as a hostage.

A century later, the slave Parthenius of Bithynia opened the techniques of the Hellenistic lyric poets to Latin poets. One of these, Gaius Valerius Catullus, wrote some of the world's most lasting lyrics, serious, scurrilous, and beautiful at once, before a premature death in 54 B.C. A second original master was the didactic poet Lucretius (96?–55 B.C.), whose *De Rerum Natura* included unique anticipations of modern scientific thought. Lucretius also displayed a frenzy for truth-telling, akin to that of the later English visionary Blake.

In the last stages of the Roman republic, dominated politically by Julius Caesar, the greatest prose came from Caesar himself, clear, interested, and alive, describing the military campaigns that opened Western Europe. Other notable prose appeared in the philosophy, orations, and especially the letters of the statesman Cicero. These later served as a model for a particularly dry style among Renaissance academics.

The biased but informative histories of Sallust (86–34 B.C.) also stand out, as does the encyclopedic curiosity of the learned Publius Varro (first century B.C.), whose study of contemporary farming practice was essential for researchers of a later age.

The Augustan age and after.

The Roman republic ended with the rise of Caesar's successor, Augustus. A certain kind of spontaneity disappeared from Latin literature. Yet the poets of the empire, beginning with those of Augustus's time, were those that carried to Europe's Middle Ages and became models for writers of the Renaissance.

The greatest of the poets of the Roman Empire was Vergil (Publius Vergilius Maro, 70–19 B.C.), who found his medium early in his *Eclogues* and *Georgics,* modeled on the pastorals of Theocritus and on Hesiod's *Works and Days.* With a young man's fire and a certain gift for mystery and prophecy, Vergil seemed to later Christian readers almost a prophet outside the faith. In his masterpiece, the *Aeneid,* he lifted his target to the model of Homer himself and sought to create an artificial myth of Rome's greatness. The *Aeneid* has been one of the world's great enduring works. It has nobility and strength of character, despite its sycophantic praise of authority throughout.

But within Vergil's own time, the old Roman temperament he celebrated had begun to disappear. For the lyric master Horace (Quintus Horatius Flaccus, 65–8 B.C.), writing in Augustus's Rome meant adopting a rigidly virtuous stance in his patriotic odes. Fortunately, he exercised more independence in private lyrics praising friendship, wine, and love. The

works of the lesser but important Tibullus (54?–18? B.C.), and Propertius (50?–15? B.C.) indicate something of the pressures of the new Roman way of life in their general dissatisfaction, even in sophisticated elegies of love.

Seemingly the most "lightweight" poet of all, Ovid (Publius Ovidius Naso, 43 B.C.–A.D. 18) was the one who caught the spirit of the age. At first a poet of love *(Amores),* he later wrote the *Metamorphoses,* the Latin work most thoroughly mined for ideas, images, and quotes by later cultures. The *Metamorphoses,* a synthesis of myths of the imagination, reflected the creative energy of an age of religious excitement, resonating in Roman mystery cults that sensed an even deeper tumult in the Eastern empire.

After the death of Ovid, exiled for a never-explained violation of the imperial morality, poetic attainment diminished. Several poets important to later generations came from Spain: Seneca the Younger, a philosopher and tragedian whose work influenced Renaissance playwrights and classicists; Seneca's nephew, the young and very talented Lucan, who lost his life in the same year as his uncle (A.D. 65) in a republican conspiracy; and the epigrammatist, Martial (A.D. 40–104).

First-century poets of great influence in the Middle Ages included the moral satirist Persius and a follower of Vergilian epic, Statius.

The last great Latin poet was Juvenal (A.D. 60?–140?), a man from the country who wrote bitter satires about the city's wickedness. Juvenal's poems won a following from many later classicists, reaching down to Dr. Johnson, whose love-hate for London in the 1700s was much like Juvenal's for Rome.

In prose, the later period boasts several important works. Histories of Livy (59 B.C.–A.D. 17) and the great Tacitus (A.D. 55–117); the technical writings of Frontinus (first century A.D.); the inaccurate but pioneering natural science of Pliny the Elder (A.D. 23–79); the letters of Pliny the Younger (A.D. 62–113); and the criticism of rhetoric and literature of Quintilian (c A.D. 35–95) all stand out.

The Two Bibles

The Hebrew-Christian Bibles represent a tradition of moral and psychological humanism as old as that of the classical world but centered on man's relation with God. They played the major inspirational role in the history of the West after the collapse of the classical civilization of Greece and Rome after A.D. 300

The Jewish Scriptures.

The early Jews spent more time in slavery than out of it. Their religion concentrated on man's self-respect as it stems from his own conscience. Escape from Egyptian bondage occurred early in the "time of troubles" (after 1500 B.C.). The oldest material in the Bible dates from this time.

From the time of David (c 1012– c 972 B.C.) to a period shortly after the fall of the Northern Kingdom (722 B.C.), at least three major hands may be seen reshaping the material of the ancient legends. Further revisions date from the period of *Deuteronomy* (600s), *Leviticus* (500s), and the century after the return from Babylonian exile (that is, after 537), when a new orthodoxy was established. The text of the *Pentateuch* (the first five books of the Jewish canon—and of the Christian Bible), which with *Joshua* represents the central witness, includes ancient material sometimes left intact, sometimes cut, reorganized, and reshaped, and sometimes amplified with new material that stemmed from rival traditions. Large bodies of interpolation, explanation, and religious, moral, or legal codes, all stemming from the needs and prevailing wisdom of the times, are included as well.

A second body of biblical wisdom grew up over the same ages. The older exemplars (for example, Joshua) were often practical as well as religious leaders. The later prophets (for example, Isaiah and Jeremiah) were Judaism's great teachers of righteousness, as often railing against a Jewish king as against foreign domination. After the writings of the prophets in importance come the works called Holy Writings (Psalms, Proverbs, Job), and Scrolls (Daniel, Song of Solomon, Lamentations). In these works, individual witness, parable, and lyric counted for very nearly as much as the Law but stood always apart from it.

The New Testament. The Gospels and the associated writings that make up the New Testament occupy a single extended generation of perhaps 150 years.

By the time of the Gospels, the greatest period of creativity in Judaism had long since ended. Aramaic and Greek

THE TORAH is used in Jewish religious services. The Hebrew text is written on parchment and kept in the ancient form of a scroll.

had replaced Hebrew both as a spoken language and as a literary tongue. Fresh thinking in Judaism continued, however. The Apocrypha (valuable works, but not with full religious authority) and such recent discoveries as the Dead Sea Scrolls give some idea of the kinds of originality involved.

The Christians knew that their teachings promised more, and demanded more, than either classicism or ritual observance had to offer. At a time when the breakdown of civilization made something like Old Testament slavery the universal condition of the Mediterranean peoples, Christianity restored a relationship with a living God irrespective of the government or culture of the day. It did so with an historic Savior of common birth but of transcending vision, the more believable for the tragic reality of his suffering.

The Gospels told their story artlessly, in simple, everyday Greek. No one has ever translated classical Greek or Latin masterpieces with full satisfac-

tion into the vernacular modern languages. The Bible, on the other hand, translates beautifully and has essentially created the modern form of several languages. The poetry of ancient Hebrew and the prose of Greek Gospels were written in languages of participation, not exclusion; they were vernacular, not highly structured, literary languages. Christianity demanded the lives of its believers and offered eternal life in return, promising in the interim the self-respect to live decently and in good conscience. The acceptance of this revelation transformed society. Nothing that kings or priests or warriors did would ever matter again in quite the same way. This vision, both Jewish and Christian, became, with classical humanism, the second great thread in the new civilization of the West. From the Middle Ages to modern times, the story of literature is woven of these two strands; in all the centuries, they have rarely been far apart, yet they have never lost their own separate identities.

The Middle Ages

Time-lapse photography can present a quickened "movie" of the otherwise imperceptible growth of a galaxy, a weather front, or a tree. The same technique, applied to the first 1,500 years after Christ, would show a whirlwind of destruction, all over the world, and then the emergence (particularly in the eighth and ninth centuries, and again in the eleventh through the thirteenth centuries) of thin veneers of culture—in Japan, China, and Islamic nations, and in isolated locations in Europe. The destruction and the gradual rebuilding remade the racial and linguistic map of the human race. The West, hardest hit of all in the early years, emerged at the end of the period with the civilization of the future, based not on the dominance of one group or language but on diversity itself. Its varied literatures made no firm

distinctions between the spoken and the written word. These literatures shared, in varying measures, the classical past, Christianity, and a new stock of Germanic and Celtic history and myth. From these new combinations grew new literatures and a new family of ideas.

The East

China. Po Chü-i (A.D. 772–846) was one of the greatest of the poets of China's classical literary age, during the T'ang dynasty. One of his famous poems tells of the unjust death of a particularly beautiful concubine. A second poem, written after Po Chü-i himself had been banished, tells of hearing a reference to the story in the song of a woman who similarly had once been famous at court.

The garments of all who heard, says Po Chü-i, were soiled with tears; not least, the coat of the junior civil servant that he himself had now become.

The poems demonstrate the range of the Chinese style. Their technique of allusion can evoke a history of current catastrophe in a few sentimental references. The poems also demonstrate the range of the Chinese reality. A highly developed and literate civil service existed at the top, with a vast continent of poverty, isolation, and "hillbilly music," as Po Chü-i called it, below.

Many Chinese, like Po Chü-i, knew the miseries of the loss of preferment at court, or of overwork and under-reward while there. Among them are three other famous Chinese poets, Li Po (perhaps 75 years Po Chü-i's senior) and Li Po's contemporaries, Tu Fu and Wang

Haiku

Basho felt that "a good poem is one in which the form of the verse, and the joining of its two parts, seem light as a shallow river flowing over its sandy bed." This is one of his most famous haiku.

Furuike ya kawazu tobikomu mizu no oto	An ancient pond— Then the sound of water Where a frog plops in

Wei. These poets left the rhymed song forms of the Confucian odes behind, writing by extremely complex rules in a concentrated style. Their immense popularity, despite the lack of any official status for much of their lives, testifies to the number of similar "minor civil servants" far-flung throughout the land.

Other important Chinese poets include the very early Ts'ao Chih and T'ao Ch'ien; and Han Yü, Li Ho, and Li Yü of the T'ang dynasty.

In the rather more academic Sung dynasty (960–1279), the most famous poet was Su Tung-p'o (1036–1101), who escaped from the growing conservatism of the time with stanza forms very nearly approaching free verse and used a sharp political tongue that frequently got him into trouble.

As the high world of the serious poet declined, however, the rather lower one of the popular storyteller proliferated. The traditional stories began as folk tales or myths. Each new teller added his own innovations, and as tellers of genius emerged (sometimes classically trained literati, writing anonymously to save face), the tradition spawned popular novels of gaiety, depth, and complexity. *The Romance of the Three Kingdoms,* probably first unraveled in the 14th century, took 200 years to attain its present set form. *All Men Are Brothers,* a realistic treatment of a Robin Hood–like adventure, and the allegory, *Monkey,* date from the same period.

Later still, truly modern novels appeared. The most famous are the *Golden Lotus* (1600s?), the *Dream of the Red Chamber* (1700s), and the *Travels of Lao Ts'an,* by a businessman. Other forms of Chinese literature included the occasional fiction written in the classical form (for example, *Strange Stories from the Liao-chai Studio,* by P'u Sungling); the popular opera and theater, based on the same tales as the early novels; and a continuous production of chronicles, encyclopedias, and philosophical and similar texts that continued at a high level almost to the modern period.

The Chinese mind in these works remains swift, keen in analysis and characterization, and tuned to the individual nuance, as it had been from the eighth century. Nevertheless, nothing resembling a modern truly representative literature appeared until Western influence, beginning in the 1800s, began a national renaissance.

Japan. Japan relates to China as the United States does to Europe— younger, bolder, but very reliant, particularly in its earliest stages, on the older race. Early Japanese literature consists of chronicles, often with mythical elements, relating to Japan's most ancient times. None of these can be traced reliably beyond the fifth century A.D. In early centuries, most literate Japanese wrote in Chinese. Inventing a Japanese written language meant a tortuous reconstruction of Chinese characters for the language.

In the eighth century, *Manyóshú,* a collection of some 4,500 beautiful poems, forms were set that Japanese poets continued to use until modern times. A roughly contemporary volume contains poems by Japanese poets in Chinese. For the 400 years of the Heian period (794–1192), the precise always extremely sensitive style of a court aristocracy filled volume after volume of anthology with the perceptions and sentiments of a highly refined people.

In prose, a similar sensitivity was applied, often in writings by women, to the intimate doings and court life of the day. *The Tale of Genji* by Murasaki Shikibu, the *Pillow Book* of Sei Shonagon, and the *Tale of Flowering Fortunes* (author unknown) are the titles of modern translations of fictional and nonfictional works of the period.

After the 1100s, civil and foreign strife paralyzed Japanese literary efforts. Nevertheless this period saw the beginning of several major forms of theater: the Nō tragedy and its accompanying farce, the kyogen. Then, reaching somewhat beyond the immediate period, came the more popular kabuki and the puppet-drama, or ningyo-shibai.

The first of these is a slow-moving, highly ritualized, intellectually demanding performance. Like the Shinto tradition of contemplative worship, it seems to want to show the essence of life by letting contradiction, and time itself, flow of its own nature. Nō has had great influence abroad. The more action-filled easier-to-understand kabuki has been, however, since its invention, the favorite of the modern Japanese.

The great figure of puppet theater and kabuki, Chikamatsu Monzaemon (1653–1724), wrote with sometimes terrifying conviction. Well ahead of westerners, he cleared the stage of nobility and made low-key beautiful poetry of the tragedy of contemporary life (as in *The Deaths at Sonezak*).

The 1600s also saw the light haiku form converted to classical purpose by the great innovator Basho and his followers. This was also the era when the Tokugawa shogunate (1603–1867) resolutely set Japan against further contact with outsiders, maintaining the nation at a deliberately feudal level, but at peace with itself, for the next 200 years.

Islam. While great events in the Far East concerned the West only at a distance, the emergence of Islam in the 600s A.D. confronted the West for many years with a rival, a threat, and, ultimately, an educator. Within the basically Arabic Islamic culture, the special mysticism of the Persian people, writing in their own language and in Arabic as well, provided a unique and lasting influence. So, too, did the confluence of Islamic, Christian, and Jewish influences in Moorish Spain.

Arabic Islam. Prior to Muhammad, Arab peoples had composed aristocratic lyrics in extremely complex verse forms extolling the virtues of the Bedouin warrior caste.

The advent of Muhammad (A.D. 570–632) and the Koran put a temporary stop to such nonreligious verse. By the mid-700s, however, Islam embraced a rich and still growing part of the world. It produced several great centers of culture, most notably at Baghdad, and in the "rebel" caliphate that ruled most of the peninsula that became Spain and Portugal.

The reborn literature remained academic until ibn al-Muqaffa, a Persian, brought Arab prose to life with a translation of the Indian beast tales, the *Panchatantra* (mid-700s). A generation later the poets abu-Nuwas and abu-al-Atahiyah wrote for the first time of contemporary Arab experience. Prose style flourished in the 800s with the writer of rationalist parables, al-Jahiz. Histories of Muhammad's life and commentary on the Koran produced works, such as those by ibn-Ishaq, al-Bukhari, and at-Tabari, that became foundations of Islamic justice. Works that influenced the West profoundly were those of the Persian physician and Aristotelian philosopher Avicenna (ibn-Sina, 980–1037), and of the Sufi theologian al-Ghazzali (1058–1111). Among historians, ibn-Khaldun (1332–1406) has a worldwide reputation. The introduction to his world history carefully analyzed historical behavior on principles akin to those of modern sociology.

Throughout this period, poetry and its related forms attained a level from which the West was to learn for many centuries. The greatest activity was focused in Baghdad. Some of the most singular talents were those of al-Mutanabbi (915–965), who wrote, he boasted, with an easy force as natural as a lark's; al-Hariri (1054–1122), who almost seems to anticipate James Joyce with his mixture of folktale simplicity and linguistic invention; and al-Maarri (d. 1057), blind and, like al-Mutanabbi, a Syrian.

To Baghdad, too, belongs much of the provenance of *The Thousand and One Nights,* a work many Muslims consider slight, but which gathers up stories from Arab sources, old Persia, and Muslim Egypt, and so serves as a 12th- to 14th-century catchall for Islamic magic and romance.

Islam in Spain. Moorish Spain was a world of extraordinary intellectual tolerance, where Arabs, Christians, and Jews taught and learned from each other. Arabic poets, such as ibn-Zaydun, ibn-Quzman, and al-Tutili, wrote to be sung, not recited, and laid the basis for what became the West's troubadour and Renaissance lyric.

The glory of Moorish Spain, however, was the originality of its scholarship. In two works he considered incidental to his monumental comparative history of religions, the philosopher and statesman ibn-Hazm (994–1064), himself a significant poet, laid down a psychology of romantic love and the nature of stress and anxiety in the human personality. Nearly contemporary with ibn-Hazm, a philosopher of the East, al-Farabi (870?–950), culminated a long tradition of Muslim scholarship in Platonism and the works of Aristotle with an extensive reconciliation between philosophy and Islam. Avempace (ibn-Bajjah, d. 1138) in Spain carried the argument further and the great philosopher Averroës (ibn Rushd, 1126–1198) carried it to the point of near heresy. Thus the Islamic philosophers (aided by Jews such as Moses Maimonides) brought Aristotle and their own long tradition of learning to the West. In St. Thomas Aquinas, their contributions would become the central philosophic issues of Europe and of the Christian church.

Such influences, in a sense, never ceased. A novel of philosophical self-reliance *(Hayy ibn-Yaqzān)* by ibn-Tufail, Averroës' friend and mentor, emerged later as a mainspring under Daniel Defoe's *Robinson Crusoe.* The poem of a visionary journey to the mountain of Heaven and Hell by the twelfth-century Spanish Sufi poet, ib-nu'l-Arabi, provided part of the inspiration and much of the detail for the greatest Christian poem of the next age, Dante's *Divine Comedy.*

Persian Islam. Persia's first literature was the work centered on its great religious teacher, Zoroaster (c 660–c 583 B.C.). Under the dominance of Islam (from the 600s A.D.), Persians gradually recovered the use of their own language and found a major role as the professional administrators of Arab, then Turkic, then Mongol Islamic empires.

The early masterpieces of prose by Islamic Persians in their own tongue are the *Siyāsatnāmeh* of Nizam-al-Mulk and the *Quābūsnāmeh* of Kai Kaus, both written in the 1000s. The first is concerned with the art of the government,

and the second with the art of self-cultivation. The *Chahār Maqālah* of Samarquandi (c 1156) is a set of gorgeously written anecdotal biographies of poets. As with the Arabs, historical writing maintained a high level in the works of writers such as Gardizi (1000s), Rashid al-Din (1250?–1318), and Ali Yazdi (d. 1524).

Poets were Persia's chief glory, however, the greatest of them adherents of Sufi mysticism. Firdausi (940?–1020) wrote a national epic, the *Shah Namah,* which is still alive in the word-for-word memory of today's Iranians. Farid ud-din Attar ("Language of Birds," early 1200s), was an allegorist concerned with man's progress toward God; Jami (1414–1492) is revered as a saint. Omar Khayyam (d. c 1123) was a mathematician whose *Rubaiyat* is famous in the West through an extraordinarily free translation by the Victorian Edward Fitzgerald.

The two great Sufi masters of love lyric were Jalal-ud-din Rumi (1207–1273) and Hafiz (1300s), who was famed for sensuality, though many of his most beautiful poems are of family, death, and the everyday world. These poets of love have had particular influence in the West and are often considered Islam's greatest poets.

India. The epics derived from the two great chains of Sanskrit legend were discussed in an earlier section. The period to A.D. 1100 was also one of enormous production in Sanskrit court epic and lyric verse. The language itself had become purely literary, not spoken, and the enormous skill and verbal ingenuity of its writers seems cold and academic today.

The Indian drama, in which aristocratic characters spoke Sanskrit and the lower classes spoke the Prakrit dialect, held more interest. The plays of Kaladasa, India's greatest poet (400s?), are still performed. Bhavabhuti (700s), another known playwright, is also among the court poets of greatest force.

The true Indian genius expressed itself most fully in the religions of transcendence and, occasionally, of reform. These religions sought an alternative to the hopelessness of the rigid caste system. For example, the literature of Jainism, written in the Prakrit dialect and in the Pali dialect of the Buddhist scholar Buddhaghosa (400s), has been of enormous influence in both the Eastern and Western worlds.

Indian mysticism includes an identification of religious knowledge with orgiastic release. The twelfth-century epic, *The Song of the Cowherd,* represents this erotic ideal.

The folk literature of India boasts what may be the world's largest storehouse of fables, beast tales, and legends. Much of this remains in the oral tradition, but in written collections, the best known of which is the *Panchatantra,* they have become part of Western folklore as well.

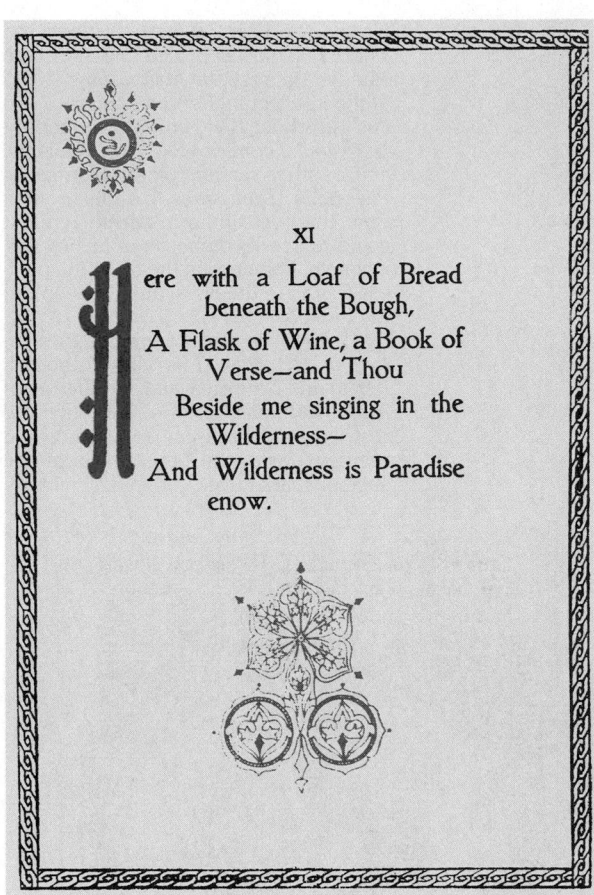

XI

Here with a Loaf of Bread
beneath the Bough,
A Flask of Wine, a Book of
Verse—and Thou
Beside me singing in the
Wilderness—
And Wilderness is Paradise
enow.

From the time of Islamic conquest, Indian classical literature declined. In recent years, the novel, play, and other literary forms of the West have provided a secular beginning on a different and much wider social scale.

THE RUBAIYAT, freely translated by Edward Fitzgerald, became a favorite with Victorians for its lyrical celebration of love and its world-weariness.

The West

The end of the classical period is often dated from the fall of Rome in the time of the barbarian invaders in the 400s. The succeeding centuries are often known as the Dark Ages, yet in these years, the new civilization of Northern Europe was slowly establishing itself.

The new culture had many roots. The classical values were obscured but never quite forgotten. Latin (in a colloquial form) was the language of the church, the one center of learning and memory that persisted through the period. At the same time, the languages and folklores of the earlier European cultures established themselves with new force as the power of Roman civilization diminished greatly.

The last classics. The inspiration of the classical world ran out in the last years of the Roman Empire, yet interest in maintaining the past continued. Athens was a museum of glories long past. Constantinople (now Istanbul, Turkey) became the capital city of the Christian Roman Empire in the 300s. Both encouraged an academic

civilization
US

civilisation
Brit.

center
US

centre
Brit.

Greek for literary use. Among the works that most appealed to those of the Middle Ages are the *Meditations* (100s) of the intellectual Roman emperor Marcus Aurelius; the genuinely touching *Hero and Leander* (400s) of Musaeus; and a rather seamy epic by Nonnus of Panopolis (*Dionysiaca,* c 450). In addition, the occasional inspired hymnist could touch deep chords of feeling; for example, Romanos in the 500s, the poetess Cassia in the 800s, and Symeon the Mystic (949–1026).

Histories in Greek included the *History of His Own Time* by Procopius (500s) and centuries later the *Alexiad* of Anna Comnena (1083?–1148). For the rest, only a continuing tradition of that resilient form, the epigram, kept the ancient spark alive.

A MEDIEVAL MONK illuminates a manuscript with miniature paintings.

Latin. Latin went on to rather a different history as the backbone, in its late vernacular form (the Vulgate), of the developing West. In its ancient literary form, however, it showed only a few gleams of talent. A "modern" novel of adventure and magical transformations, the so-called *Golden Ass* of Lucius Apuleius, intrigued later readers. So did the Latin letters of Marcus Aurelius, the emperor, and of his former tutor, Fronto. As the Roman Empire reached its end, the principal literary works included the realistic verse paragraphs of Ausonius and the decorative epics of Claudian. The Christian emphasis is evident in the hymns of Venantius Fortunatus and the anonymous, spectacularly pagan hymn *Pervigilium Veneris.*

The last significant classical writer was Boethius (480?–524), whose *The Consolation of Philosophy* served the Middle Ages as an intellectual sourcebook. Later efforts to bring back the classical style would also rely on compilers of texts on grammar, criticism,

and philology such as Ambrosius Macrobius and Priscian.

As these few sought to hold on to the ancient forms, the Latin language was developing in new directions. On one hand, it became a basis for a whole family of languages, the ancestor of modern Italian, French, Spanish, and Portuguese. At the same time, Latin itself remained the principal language of the church and of learning throughout Europe.

Although it was far from being a dead language, Latin had changed since the days of the classical authors. Most of its speakers had other mother tongues, whether Romance, Germanic, or Celtic. They were not seeking a highly refined and ornate language, but a practical one, and so the Latin Vulgate reflected the different needs of its speakers, evolving a more natural and less highly inflected grammar and a more flexible vocabulary.

The great writers in the Vulgate were more theologians and philosophers than literary men, yet the lines between disciplines were not clearly drawn.

The translation of the Bible into the Vulgate by St. Jerome (340?–420) became the important model of the simpler more immediate form. The new spirit of personal experience and confession, heralded by St. Paul, reappears in the *Confessions* of St. Augustine (354–430), whose spirit is echoed by such modern confessors as Jean Jacques Rousseau and James Joyce.

Profound debates on the nature of authority, philosophical freedom, and the role of secular knowledge accompanied the confessional tradition. From Tertullian and St. Cyprian in the 200s to the great scholastic philosophers of the high Middle Ages (1000–1400), Latin was the language of serious intellectual argument.

As the Middle Ages awoke, its secular tradition awoke too. For a time, the Vulgate competed with the new languages of Europe, and the beginnings of European literature were still in trusty old Latin: the first miracle plays; academic comedies and epics; collections of fables and bestiaries; and an increasing production from usually anonymous lyric poets. These poets—especially the Goliards of the eleventh and twelfth centuries—felt free to use Latin for their own purposes, even cheerfully defying church doctrine.

Much of the documentation of the period, too, is in Latin. In England, for example, in such great historical works as the *Ecclesiastical History of the English Nation,* by the greatest scholar of his day, St. Bede (700s), and in the half-fabulous *History of the Kings of Britain* (c 1135), by Geoffrey of Monmouth, the identity of a new nation was first expressed in the old tongue.

The first modern tongues.

Against the framework of Latin culture and church education, the several Germanic, Romance, and Celtic peoples went through the slow process of learning a "European" identity they had

never had before. Four small societies, each of brief duration, were the prophets of modern European society. They were the Anglo-Saxon, the Celtic, the Old Norse, and the Provençal.

Anglo-Saxon. Germans and Celts shared the British Isles from the time that Angles, Saxons, and Jutes began arriving from the European mainland in the 500s. Although often enemies, the peoples seem to have borrowed from each other's folklore and ideas. This seems apparent in the West's first great vernacular poem, the Anglo-Saxon epic *Beowulf* (700s), the elegiac history of the last hero of a dying Germanic people.

A hundred years later, *The Dream of the Rood* brought Christianity to a new Northern vision. In it the poet relates the history of Christ's passion through the narrative of the tree that became the cross. This device borrows from early Celtic or Germanic; yet it also seems to prefigure the spiritual personification of nature that became, in Wordsworth and others, a major English theme.

These poems stand at the head of a small but very important body of work that occupied the first of Europe's two early literary periods. Other works include *Widsith* (seventh century, the oldest Anglo-Saxon fragment), *Deor,* the *Wanderer,* the *Seafarer,* and epics of the historic battles of Maldon, and Brunaburgh. The few lines that survive from a biblically inspired *Hymn* by Caedmon almost alone suggest a new world view. Sermons and other biblical narratives exist, and the *Anglo-Saxon Chronicle,* begun at the time of King Alfred of Wessex in the ninth century, continued till 1154. The Anglo-Saxon society was strained by repeated attacks of Vikings and Danes and was finally destroyed by the arrival of the Norman French armies in 1066. Only some 250 years later did it emerge in a changed form as modern England.

The Celtic languages. The Celtic people, ancestors of today's Irish and Welsh (among others), once controlled a significant part of Europe. They were driven by succeeding invasions to the edges of the continent (the Breton region of France), to the wilderness regions of Britain (Wales, Cornwall, northern Scotland), and across the water to Ireland.

Celtic literature reaches at least back to the 500s. Among the traditional bards are the Irish Dallán Forgaill and the Welsh Aneurin, Taliesin, Myrddin ("Merlin?"), and Llywarch Hen. The Celtic languages did not produce a major European tongue, although healthy local literatures survive to this day. Their larger impact lay in their treasury of myth and legend, which has enriched the various literatures of Europe in many languages.

The principal legends are related in two major cycles of stories, the Ulster (800s) and the Fenian (1100s); and in the Welsh *Mabinogion* (1000s). The stories gradually center on the mythical court of an actual patriotic hero who brought brief peace in Britain before the Anglo-Saxon invasions. The great leader is identified as King Arthur, and his history grows and develops through successive retellings to become one of the great traditions of European civilization.

In Europe's second period of medieval creativity (eleventh to thirteenth centuries), later versions of the story evolved. These versions became the secular ideal of the new Europe, itself a "table round" of conflicting identities, but of a single pagan and Christian history. New versions of the story continue to flourish to modern times, but they have left their Celtic origins far behind.

Old Norse. As the new European societies first got their cultural legs under them in the eighth and ninth centuries, a new wave of raids and invasions, this time from the Vikings (or Norsemen) of Scandinavia, briefly stopped the awakening.

One small group of Vikings who heavily intermarried with Celts from Scotland and the Hebrides avoided the tyrannizing impact of new Norse kings by settling the small northerly island of Iceland (c 867). It became the first Western constitutional republic (930). In 300 years of independence, this tiny nation produced an astonishing literature. Icelanders preserved nearly all there is of pre-Christian Viking and Germanic religion and legend from authentic sources. The *Edda,* by Saemund the Wise, was composed before 1100. The *Prose Edda,* by Snorri Sturluson (1178–1241) is a prose adaptation, together with a discussion of the principles of Norse skaldic verse. The Icelanders also preserved Viking history in an account of Norway by Sturluson (the *Heimskringla*) and the authentic story of the first exploration of America.

But their contribution, like that of the Celts, runs deeper than their surviving texts suggest. The Icelanders represent Europe's first literary expression of the modern frontier temperament. The saga form, an extended chronicle, usually based on historical events, developed a clear narrative prose and an understated feeling for character. Its assumptions (for example, the importance of family and place) far outreach the medieval understanding of human nature.

Provençal. Of all the early creative societies, that of Provence had the greatest immediate influence. A virtually independent region, encompassing the south of modern France, Provence fell under the spell of the inquisitive and opulent culture of Islam. At the same time, its own cultural history dated from the first colonies planted by the Hellenes (from 600 B.C.). Between about 1050 and 1250, while the rest of Europe pursued war and crusades to the Holy Land, Provence was discovering a unique combination of Islamic sensuality and Western puritanism.

The developers of this new sensibility were the *troubadours,* singers of noble birth, more than 400 of whom are known by name. In lyrics of great beauty and freshness, they sang of sex-

RICHARD WAGNER based his final opera, *Parsifal,* on the epic poem *Parzival,* considered to be the climax of medieval Arthurian legend.

ual love of the purest kind and created an ideal of fervent but hopeless longing for a virtuous and unattainable woman. The nobility of the troubadours added to their appeal; their numbers included not only noblemen but more than one king.

Assisting the troubadours, there were jongleurs, of lower birth, who may have "ghosted" much of the work, but they did not receive the credit. Among them are Bernard de Ventadorn, Bertrand de Born, Peire Vidal, and Arnaut Daniel.

In the north of France, the only slightly less inspired *trouvères* spread the movement in a different dialect. They wrote less true lyric and more extended narrative. They produced one true classic, the epic *Song of Roland,* a romance of Carolingian valor that almost attains the quality of heroic myth. The character of Roland himself would be used over and over again in other European epics, perpetuating the memory of the splendor of Charlemagne's court.

The flowering of Provence ended with the disapproval of the church. Detecting heresy in the region's Christian sects, the church instituted the first Inquisition in 1233. A century of torture and persecution stamped out the heretics—and literary and musical innovation as well.

Other European peoples.

The same centuries that saw the peak of Old Norse and Provençal, and a second peak for Gaelic and Welsh, provided a similar but less concentrated brilliance in other areas of Europe. In nearly all cases, these little flowerings used Celtic myth, Germanic heroic legend, and the new lyricism of the troubadours of Provençal.

Germanic. Early in medieval times, the Swiss Abbey of St. Gall developed a tradition of scholarship, religious writing, and extended chronicle. These bore a long string of progeny in the development of the academic German mind.

Creativity started with the minnesingers, who began by imitating the troubadours, and then developed their own, somewhat more realistic style. The greatest of the minnesingers, Walther von der Vogelweide, preferred requited love to the idealized kind. He wrote with a sense of absolute pitch for the truth of experience and of his characters.

The masterpiece of the period, however, was the *Parzival* of Wolfram von Eschenbach (1170?–1220?). It belongs to the Arthurian tradition, and surpasses every other rendering of the story of the search for the Holy Grail. Wolfram writes from experience of combat as a wandering knight, of the centrality of marriage in human life, and of the connection between pleasure and the ideal in physical love. For all its elements of magical romance, his is among the first works to understand the importance of everyday life to moral experience. This concept was to become one of the West's most important themes.

Among other German works imitative of the French Arthurians, the *Tristan und Isolde* (c 1210) of Gottfried von Strassburg has special importance to later writers. Similarly, the epics from the rather different tradition of Germany's own mythic past, the *Nibelungenlied* and the *Gudrun,* have resonated down through the centuries, appearing in modern dress in the operas of Richard Wagner.

The most original of the late works, however, was the *Meier Helmbrecht,* of Wernher der Gartenaere (c 1250). It tells of a Robin Hood–type character gone wrong—blinded, maimed, rejected by his family, and hanged. This terrifying Middle Ages portrait has been largely verified by later research. Its negative power anticipates the realism that distinguishes much of later German literature.

French. French literature generally served as the model for other European vernaculars. Richest of the old Roman provinces, France had the longest continuing tradition of culture. Its Celtic heritage added a valuable component.

Chrétien de Troyes was the first, most imitated, and most prolific of the Arthurian innovators in the 1100s. In the 1200s, Guillaume de Lorris and Jean de Meung, separated by an over 40-year span, successively composed the two parts of the *Roman de la Rose,* the most celebrated allegory of love in the medieval world. In prose, Geoffroi de Villehardouin, Jean de Joinville, Jean Froissart, and Philippe de Comines, in a succession of histories and personal

ANIMAL FABLES,
such as *Reynard the Fox*,
have long been a literary staple.

memoirs over a 300-year period, laid the groundwork for the long history of French clarity and elevation of style. Standard forms of the period, common to most cultures, were the animal fables (as collected in the mock-epic *Reynard the Fox*), the short rhymed pieces sometimes taken from Greek or Latin anecdotes, the religious examples, and the rhymed epics of the *chansons de geste.*

Only one talent reached a surpassing level, however: that of the bedeviled poet François Villon (1431–1463). Villon's combining of his high literary genius with the half-criminal life he led on the Paris streets overshadows everything else of its period. Other significant poets included Rutebeuf, also a writer of miracle plays; Christine de Pisan, an early exponent of women's special viewpoint; and the graceful Charles d'Orleans.

Iberian. The major early work of Spain, the severe, powerful epic, *The*

Song of the Cid (twelfth century), deals with El Cid, the great national hero of Spain. Jewish and Moorish lyric constitute Spain's earliest poetry. Later, a body of Provençal-influenced work appeared in Portuguese; later still, both lyric and medieval heroic legend appeared.

As Spain gathered force, important writers emerged late in medieval times: Juan Rutz (*Libro de Buen Amor,* c 1330); the historian Pedro López de Ayala; and the 15th-century poets Inigo López de Mendoza and Juan de Mena. At the very end of the period, past and future crossed paths. The first printed version of *Amadis of Gaul* appeared in 1508; it was a prose romance of great medieval popularity, read until then only in manuscript form. Already in 1499 the novel *La Celestina* by Fernando de Rojas had introduced the exuberant new manner of the Italian Renaissance.

The Renaissance

Flowering in Italy

center
US

centre
Brit.

Between 1250 and 1300 in Italy, the basis of Western thought and literature began to shift in a new direction. This new movement is called the Renaissance (rebirth). Gradually, over the next two centuries, it spread through all of Europe.

In many ways, however, the early Renaissance masters in Italy were the end result—and the most impressive representatives—of the originality of the Middle Ages. Christianity had put the spiritual journey to a new life in God at the center of human existence. The new poets made that journey, too—they were believers rather than skeptics or

THE INFERNO of Dante, as illustrated in an early manuscript, shows the tortures of the damned, beset by vicious devils. Dante's hell is divided into various circles, each reserved for those guilty of a particular offense against God. Sins of the spirit, such as pride, are more severely punished than physical sins such as gluttony or sloth.

scoffers. But they saw it in a new and more personal light—not as representatives of Everyman or as mythological knights in search of the Holy Grail, but as individuals.

This spirit of moral individualism paralleled that of the independent Italian cities, which first understood the possibilities of commerce in the new age, and which were often ruled, at least nominally, on a basis of consent of the governed.

Dolce stil nuovo. Frederick II of Sicily (1194–1250) was at once Holy Roman Emperor, German king, and king of Jerusalem. The Islamic, Germanic, and Provençal influences at his court gave birth to a new school of Italian lyric poetry. Cielo dal Camo and Jacopo da Lentini (sometimes credited as inventor of the sonnet) were among the many poets of this style.

One of Frederick's older contemporaries—far from the courtly conventions—was St. Francis of Assisi (1182–1226). The beloved religious mystic enunciated the other major Italian concern of the time, that of personal religious vision. His Il Cantico della Creature expressed a faith centered on the humble, not excluding dumb animals. In his follower, Jacopone da Todi, this conscious dedication to simplicity took on a metaphysical exaltation. A similar exaltation entered the lyric of love. Guido Guinnicelli (c 1230–1276) wrote little, but with a special sincerity

that other poets promptly labeled the *dolce stil nuovo*—the sweet new style.

Guido's *canzone,* beginning *Al cor gentil ripara sempre Amore/Come a la selva augello in la verdura* (Love rests always in the gentle heart/As a bird in the protecting shade of a wood) would be echoed in the lines of Shakespeare, Milton, and Keats; more immediately, its sweetness transformed the sensibilities of Guido's younger contemporaries. Guido Cavalcanti and Guido Orlandi, among many others, writing in the Tuscan dialect, followed Guido in divorcing the spiritual ideal from the forms of knightly service or religious faith. They saw the ideal in the soul of the poet, through the intercession of human love.

Dante. One of the younger poets of this generation was Dante Alighieri (1265–1321). In 1292, he wrote *La Vita Nuova,* a great poem filled with the new sensibility. But this was only a beginning. Through the first two decades of the 1300s, Dante wrote the *Commedia* (known to later generations as *The Divine Comedy*), which was to become one of the cornerstones of Western literature.

The *Commedia* is a visionary journey through Hell, Purgatory, and Heaven. While seeking to attain to knowledge of God's creation, the poem also points in other directions. The traveller on the journey is clearly Dante himself, experiencing the trip as he tells of it. There are two guides. Through Hell and Purgatory, the great classic poet Vergil leads Dante on his way—a symbol of a new reverence for the ancient classical world. In Paradise, the guide is Dante's beloved, the beautiful Beatrice. She is an ideal symbolizing both divine and human love, a synthesis of religious and secular aspirations.

Dante also uses the *Commedia* to judge every aspect of the life of his home city, Florence, meting out the rewards or punishments deserved by its citizens after death. His concerns are strikingly modern: human psychology, individual responsibility, and love. Dante's God is not quite the God of the church. Rather God is manifest in the perfect geometry of the universe and in the essence of natural beauty (symbolized by a white rose). Dante thus essentially puts humanist principle, rather than church doctrine, at the center of the universe.

Petrarch and Boccaccio. The generation that followed Dante extended the new approach into other areas of life. The vernacular *I Trionfi* and *Canzoniere* of the poet Petrarch (1304–1374), and the collection of earthy and brilliantly perceptive stories by Giovanni Boccaccio, the *Decameron* (1348–1353), provided examples of the new man-centered stance that would influence every literature of Europe. Petrarch and Boccaccio were also among the many brilliant classicists of the day. They searched for manuscripts from the ancient past as if for new revelations from the Bible. This emphasis on recovering the classical past led men to hope for a new classical age— a new synthesis of religious and secular, Christian and pagan.

With intellectual discoveries came new critical ideas. As early as 1324 Marsilius of Padua asserted the sovereignty of the governed, not in temporal matters alone, but in religious ones, too. A hundred years later, the brilliant scholar Lorenzo Valla brought to light many inaccuracies in the Vulgate Bible by comparing it with the Hebrew and Greek originals. This implicitly challenged the view of the Latin Bible as a document fixed, changeless, and beyond criticism.

Perhaps the greatest challenge was in the matter of language itself. The Tuscan dialect of Dante, Petrarch, and Boccaccio—thanks to their brilliance—was established as Italy's literary language for the future. This achievement—the establishment of a vernacular language for literary purposes—was to be repeated over and over in coming centuries in every corner of Europe. Latin was not abandoned; English poets wrote passable Latin verse well into the 1700s. But it never again would serve as the major literary language.

The new classical age—which we know as the Renaissance—would mine the ancient classics for ideas half forgotten. But finding them, it would put them to new modern uses. The movement extended far beyond literature. In art, architecture, music, philosophy, and the physical sciences, Renaissance men would confidently bend the works of ancient Greece and Rome to their own purposes.

There was a party of reaction to this new thought and new aesthetic. Renaissance artists and scientists would be banished from their home cities (as was Dante) and even executed for heresy (as

was the scientist Giordano Bruno). But by the year 1500, the new trends were irreversible. In the great religious disputes of the 1500s, both sides—the church of Rome and the Northern reformers—were arguing as Renaissance men. The Middle Ages had ended once and for all.

England in the 1300s

England's experience was quite different from Italy's. Conquered by the Norman French in 1066, its literature became a province of the French for generations. By 1300, English writers were just beginning to rediscover their own language as the influence of the Normans diminished. This language was a far cry from the Anglo-Saxon tongue spoken before 1066. It was greatly expanded and strengthened by the addition of thousands of new words from the Norman French—especially abstract words for intellectual uses. And yet it was not French at all; its grammar and its homely everyday words were Germanic. This combination language, owing so much both to the Germanic and the Latin-based French, we call Middle English, but it is recognizable as the basis for the language we speak today.

The earliest works in Middle English date from the 1200s and their concerns are clearly those of the Middle Ages. *The Owl and the Nightingale,* for example, is a debate among the birds on the virtues of sobriety and gaiety. The *Ancren Riwle* is a day-to-day guide for young women about to take up religious meditation. And *Brut* is England's first taste of King Arthur in its own tongue, translated by Layamon from the

French. The 1300s were an eventful and often grim age in England. With the rest of Europe, England suffered a disastrous onslaught of the black plague (1348–1349). The Peasants' Revolt (1381) reflected deep social unrest, and the debate over the monarchy, which resulted in the accession of Henry IV in 1399, caused antagonisms that would result in a century of war.

In the last quarter of the century, however, there was a great flowering of literature in the almost-new language. The religious reformer John Wycliffe was instrumental in the preparation of the first (and illegal) English Bible. The second and more authoritative version (1395) was prepared principally by Wycliffe's follower, John Purvey. Defying the courtly French tradition, an

THE STORY OF KING ARTHUR and his Knights of the Round Table has been the basis for stories, books, movies, and operas.

THE DECAMERON was planned as a cycle of 100 stories told by a group of youths who had fled to the country to escape the Black Death.

otherwise unknown William Langland (1332?–1400) wrote *The Vision of Piers Plowman,* a common man's moral vision in a rough approximation of the old Anglo-Saxon alliterative line. The same line, used more subtly, and set into stanza form, appeared in *The Pearl* and *Sir Gawaine and the Green Knight,* both masterpieces and probably by the same unknown author (c 1390).

Other poets sought to adapt the European line to native purposes. John Gower's *Confessio Amantis* (c 1390) was a moral allegory of impressive power. But the greatest poet of the age, and the first great poet of the language was Geoffrey Chaucer (1340?–1400).

Chaucer.
Chaucer was a strange combination of the medieval and the Renaissance. He wrote of an England still in the Middle Ages with affection and understanding. Unlike Dante, he did not put himself at the center of his greatest works, preferring to portray a vast panoply of characters from the England of his time. At the same time, however, Chaucer was an avid disciple of the new Italian writers, particularly Petrarch and Boccaccio.

In his greatest work, *The Canterbury Tales,* he created an English version of Boccaccio's *Decameron*—a series of stories linked together by their tellers. Chaucer's work is in verse rather than prose, however, and his storytellers are filled with life and particularity; they are still recognizable to readers nearly 600 years later. The most famous of the storytellers include the lusty Wife of Bath and the courtly Knight. Each person tells a story appropriate to his character, and the narratives range from the bawdy to the solemn.

Whether considered as the culmination of the Middle Ages or as a premature Renaissance man, Chaucer is the father of English poetry and one of the most winning personalities in world literature.

The larger fortunes of England took another unpredictable turn in the years after Chaucer's death, a turn that isolated Chaucer and cut him off from later English writers. On the one hand, the social chaos of the Wars of the Roses left little time or energy for literature in the 1400s. At the same time, the language itself was undergoing changes that would make Chaucer's poetry seem strange and crude to later readers. When interest in literature revived in the 1500s, the works of Chaucer seemed out of date and out of style. He was admired but rarely imitated, a great master with few direct heirs.

Germany and the Reformation

The period from 1480 to 1530 is one of the great watersheds of history. Exploration opened Africa, India, and America to Europe. Great discoveries were made in the physical sciences. And the world population began an incredible increase that continues into the present century. The spirit of the Italian Renaissance spread through Europe, with each nationality using it in a different way. The values of society and of individuals were transformed as radically as in the early centuries of Christianity.

The secular literary response of Germanic writers to the Italian Renaissance was small. Around 1500, prosperous townfolk produced popular ballads by the thousands; they favored humorous "bits" of narrative, *Schwänke,* in verse or prose. Among the most popular collections were *Narrenschiff* or "ship of fools" (1494) by Sebastian Brant, *Till Eulenspiegel,* and the still popular beast fable tradition, *Reinke de Vos* (Reynard the Fox).

The high art and deep personal feelings of minnesingers had shifted, through the imposition of ever more complicated rules and religious content, to the new tradition of *meistersingers,* guild members of accredited skill but rarely of genius. Of the thousands of songs, fables, tales, and plays written by the most illustrious meistersinger, Hans Sachs (1494–1576, subject of the opera by Richard Wagner), only the melodies of some early Lutheran hymns still thrive.

German and Swiss drama, often on religious lines, came to life in the 1500s, but reached no high creative point. Only in 1624 did the poet and critic Martin Opitz help break German verse from imitative Latin styles (*Buch von der Deutschen Poeterey,* 1624).

CHAUCER

Near the end of his long narrative poem *Troilus and Criseyde,* Chaucer sends his "litel book" into the world. He hopes he will live long enough to write something less sad—a "comedye"—and mentions some of the classical writers he admires. In the second verse, he complains that there are too many ways of writing English and hopes that his poem will not be miscopied, but be understood wherever it is read or sung.

Go, litel book, go, litel myn tragedye,
Ther God thi makere yet, er that he dye.
So sende mygt to make in som comedye!
But litel book, no makyng thow n'envie,
But subgit be to alle poesye;
And kisse the steppes, where as thow seest pace
Virgile, Ovide, Omer, Lucan, Stace.

And for ther is so gret diversite
In Englissh and in wryting of oure tonge,
So prey I God that none myswrite the,
Ne the mysmetre for defaute of tonge.
And red wherso thow be, or elles songe,
Be thou understonde, God I biseche!
But yet to purpose of my rather speche . . . .

LE CÉLÈBRE GARGANTUA.

GARGANTUA, the celebrated giant of the works of François Rabelais, was renowned for his prodigious appetites.

The Reformation.   On another level, however, the Germanic response to the Italian awakening was revolutionary and shattering. The makers of the Protestant Reformation were learned men who used the tools of early Renaissance scholarship to new ends. As far back as 1415, a Bohemian, Jan Hus, had been burned at the stake for asserting the primacy of Scripture over ecclesiastical authority. Late in the 1400s, the great Dutch humanist and scholar, Desiderius Erasmus, writing in Latin and communicating with a wide circle of friends, composed a passionate indictment of corrupt church practices and obscurantism. His editions of Greek and Latin classics set new standards, while his Latin translation of the New Testament, working directly from the Greek text, thoroughly undermined those who rigidly interpreted faith based on the imperfect Vulgate Bible.

In the same era, the German lawyer and scholar Johann Reuchlin touched off a pre-Lutheran challenge to authority when he defended the worth of Hebrew classics. Like Erasmus and the English humanist Sir Thomas More, Reuchlin himself remained Catholic, but many of those touched by the controversy were later to join Luther in a reformed church. The Swiss Zwingli and the French John Calvin both came to Protestant stands from a critical practice learned in humanist scholarship. Philipp Melanchthon, Luther's "right hand," learned at the same time.

Martin Luther himself, while no professed humanist, was a literary genius of idiomatic German who had shaped his intellect on biblical scholarship of the first order. His translation of the Bible (1521–1531), carefully composed in a German that all could read, established a German literary language much as Dante and his contemporaries had created the literary dialect of the Italians. The Luther Bible helped give the many separate German peoples a common identity for the first time. Luther also wrote the first of the great Protestant hymns that were to create a literature of their own.

The same phenomena—translated Bible, inspired hymnody, and the beginnings of a modern literature in their image—occurred in the same period in Denmark and Sweden. Henceforth the Christian literatures of Europe would speak in conflicting voices, with consequences no one has ever quite dispelled.

Renaissance in France

As the Germanic languages spoke for the new, so the Romance languages clung to the old. The impulse to find a rule for literary correctness, even for perfection, stemmed in part from the older societies' dread of rapid change. The threat of religious reform confirmed conservative instincts.

France had as many men of secular talent as Germany had of religious. Yet it often seemed to want to clip the wings of genius before they had fully taken flight. The Huguenot poet, contributor of translated psalms to Calvin's Genevan Psalter, Clément Marot, spent time in prison for his Protestant associations, but he wrote his epigrams, rondeaux, and epistles with a seemingly unaffected lightness and grace. Till his death in 1544, he was the focus of a host of talented disciples and sometime competitors. Among them were Margaret of Navarre, his own and Rabelais' sometime patron. From a related but later school came the author of unusually direct love lyrics, Louise Labé.

The greatest name of 16th-century French lyric, however, is that of Pierre de Ronsard (1524?–1585). With his humanist master, Jean Daurat, and five others, Ronsard formed the Pléiade, named after a group of poets in Hellenist Alexandria. The Pléiade aimed to create classic poetry in the vernacular by deliberately introducing every conceivable technique and form from older examples. The famous sonnet beginning, *Quand vous serez bien vielle, au soir a la chandelle,* shows Ronsard at his best. The image was drawn from ancient authors; yet it kept its freshness into the modern era when Yeats imitated it: *When you are old and grey and full of sleep.* Such imitations (or "thefts") are one of the great wellsprings of literary renewal and may indeed create new masterpieces each time.

Ronsard's collaborators included a much admired lyric poet, Joachim du Bellay, and a playwright, Étienne Jodelle. With their contemporary Robert Garnier, they laid the foundations of serious French theater. Major rivals in Ronsard's own manner included Guillaume du Bartas.

Then came the reaction. The critic Francois de Malherbe demanded a "purer" French and a more logical sentence structure.

In the writing of prose, less inhibited by its shorter tradition, France attained its highest levels. The generation before Ronsard had already produced one of the great individual voices, that of François Rabelais (1494?–1553). His *Pantagruel* (1533) and *Gargantua* (1535), and their sequels, novels about a son and father team of giants (inspired by a popular legend), combine an explosive humor with the Renaissance learning of a born genius. A physician, humanist, and random thinker of the widest range, Rabelais lets his narrative wander to speculations of real depth on education, philosophy, or morality one moment, and on the prodigious appetites of his heroes the next.

As with an earlier titan, Lucretius, Rabelais' own vision sometimes seems to overpower him. But the depth and vitality of his first two novels especially have made his special genius a source of delight through the centuries for both intellectual and more popular audiences.

After Rabelais, two other impressive prose pieces made their appearance in the 1500s. *Institutes of the Christian Religion,* a central Protestant text written by a 27-year-old John Calvin (first in Latin, then translated to French), became a model for the closely reasoned, clearly argued advocacy that the French have made their national trademark. At least as brilliant, but of a warmer nature, were the *Essais* of Michel Eyquem de Montaigne (1533–1592). They discover a prose style of tolerance rather than argument. The pleasure of Montaigne is that of time well spent with a wise infinitely interesting friend, whose only deep commitment is to the virtues of friendship, skepticism, and self-knowledge. Montaigne is among the most influential of world writers.

The century produced great activity in a variety of other fields, including scholarship and translation. The translations of classical authors by Jacques Amyot, best known for his Plutarch's *Lives,* deserve special attention. Montaigne was one of many who credited Amyot with being the great initiator of a beautiful French style.

Italy's Decline

France, whatever its growing principles of orthodoxy, still had its best days ahead of it. The Italy of the period reached its peak and began a long decline. The middle of the 1400s saw a period of great literary promise in the Florence of the Medicis, signaled by the founding (1439) of the academy, with Marsilio Ficino at its head. Among its members were Pico della Mirandola and Leon Battista Alberti, the leading scholars of the time. Later came Lorenzo de Medici himself, a well-read man and a talented poet; and Politian (Angelo Poliziano), scholar, author of the first masque, *Orfeo,* and a poet of uncommon sweetness. But before the end of the century, the religious fanatic Savonarola had called down a severe reaction

(1481–1498) against the "pagan" learning. The 50 years that followed were to see Italy invaded and impoverished, while the church, terrified of Luther, asserted fierce intellectual discipline. Coincidentally, the recovery of Aristotle's *Poetics* in the mid-1500s seemed to offer "rules of art" by which any new form could be rejected.

A unique history demonstrates this progression. From 1480 the lively Luigi Pulci produced variants (for example, *Il Morgante Maggiore,* 1483) on the old theme of Roland (called Orlando in his Italian incarnation). They anticipated Rabelais with their mixture of brilliance and burlesque. The highly talented Matteo Boiardo spent the years till his death (1494) on another, never finished version, *Orlando Innamorato.* He introduced Arthurian material and made the story, though still lively, an allegory of love. Ludovico Ariosto eventually produced, and rewrote continuously till his death (1533), the version that won fame all over Europe, *Orlando Furioso,* as improbable as a Hollywood spectacular but as fast-moving too.

This in turn inspired Torquato Tasso, the one "deep" voice of the four, to attempt a Christian epic of the Crusades, *Jerusalem Delivered* (1575), using Ariosto's stanza, the *ottava rima.* Tasso deliberately used the Aristotelian unities (which muffled rather than freed his talent), but his work was harshly criticized as insufficiently heroic and too profane for the time. A series of subsequent personal tragedies that foreshortened Tasso's career date from this point.

The work of Tasso was to greatly influence such English poets as Spenser, Milton, and Byron in the production of their allegories. Nevertheless, all of the epics of these four Italian writers, unlike their predecessors of Dante's age, are nearly unreadable today. Tasso himself is far more moving in his shorter works than in his masterpiece.

The return to outdated medieval romance betrayed from the beginning the new uncertainty felt by a people that had suddenly grown afraid of its own voice. Within a few years, the work of Giambattista Marino set a pattern for the gilded, essentially vacant decorativeness that ended the great generations of Italian verse.

In the interval between Pulci and Tasso, other good work appeared: the *Arcadia* of Jacopo Sannazaro, the criticism of Pietro Bembo, and the professional lyricism of Giovanni Battista Guarini. But only the sonnets of the artist Michelangelo reached the old intellectual and spiritual heights.

As in France, originality fared better in prose. The most unique work, the notebooks of Leonardo da Vinci, is more document than creation. With the so-called "Madrid Codices," only recovered late in the 20th century, they offer a close portrait of an irreplaceable mind.

The writing of history produced two great exemplars. Niccolò Machiavelli (1469–1527), famous for *The Prince,* a

realistic guide to cutthroat politics, is much more himself in his *Discourses on Livy* and his *History of Florence.* He is republican in sympathy and well ahead of his time both in methods and perspective. Francesco Guicciardini (1483–1540), author of a classic account of Italian history during his own time—the disastrous first three decades of the century—outdoes even his model, Machiavelli, in his sober analysis of the process of national growth and decline. Both men had seen their flourishing careers as statesmen taken from them by events and understood the changes Italy now was to undergo.

Lesser but significant works were *The Courtier* of Baldassare Castiglione (1528), which set standards for aristocratic behavior throughout the literate West, and the *Lives of the Artists* of Giorgio Vasari, the major anecdotal and biographical source on the makers of one of the world's greatest creative periods of art. Within the same field, the *Treatise on Painting,* a practical and theoretical work by Leonardo, and the *Autobiography* of Benvenuto Cellini, an extraordinary adventure piece as well as a self-portrait of the artist-egotist, are memorable.

Fiction achieved high color, if not a high level, in the short stories of such as Matteo Bandello, Antonio Grazzini, and Agnolo Firenzuola. Probably more important were the modest fairy tales in Neapolitan dialect of the folklorist Giambattista Basile (1575–1632). Late in the period the best prose came from a new quarter entirely: the scientific writing of the physicist and astronomer Galileo, who kept away from the classical Tuscan dialect and became a fresh model for clarity and cogency for a later age.

The tyranny of the national will, however, showed plainly in the fates assigned to Italy's scientist philosophers: Giordano Bruno, whose understanding of relative location clearly anticipated today's cosmology, was burned at the stake in 1600; Tommaso Campanella, an early advocate of the primacy of experimental method, was imprisoned from 1599 to 1626; and Galileo was forced to recant in 1633 and was consigned to house arrest or rural isolation until his death.

Spain's Golden Age

Spain and England, the nations at the southern and western extremes of Europe, are connected by many historical ties over the centuries. The greatest of these is also the simplest: the gold of the New World. Imported by Spain, it fueled a boom-and-bust period of religious and political crusades that effectively stunted that country's development until modern times. The same gold, essentially stolen from the Spanish by British piracy and commerce, became in England an investment stock for many centuries of expansion and economic growth. For Spain, the period began with the discoveries of Columbus and, simultaneously, with the final recovery of a unified Spain from Islam. The only warning of decline to come lay in the age of intolerance (the Spanish Inquisition, 1478–1810) begun at the same time.

Extensive contacts with Italy (where Naples was from the mid-1400s under effective Spanish control) brought the full influence of Renaissance learning and creativity. From the beginning, the Spanish made the Renaissance an original force, with experiences from New World explorations adding a powerful element. The greatest area of Spanish work was in the theater, where other countries (except Protestant Britain) had made only the most timid of starts.

The first strides date from the late 1400s. Juan del Encina, his follower, the Portuguese Gil Vicente, and the later Bartolomé de Torres Naharro of Naples, broke from the tradition of modest religious drama and staged performances of appropriate courtly material for their noble audiences. In the late 1500s, the touring Lope de Rueda found that a marketplace audience would respond to half-improvised comic interludes. The later Juan de Cueva extended his audiences and his material even further with stories from the national epics, the old ballads of romance.

At the turn into the 1600s, a veteran of the ill-fated Spanish Armada, Lope de Vega (1562–1635) created a new form, the play of social circumstance, loosely termed *comedia* but encompassing every area of myth, legend, and contemporary material. In such works as *The King, the Greatest Alcade, El Castigo sin Venganza,* and *Peribáñez,* Lope deliberately flouted the Aristotelian rules to win popular success and opened the door to a great theatrical age.

Tirso de Molina (*The Love Rogue,* 1630, the first formal appearance of the legend of Don Juan) and Juan Ruiz de Alarcon introduced new elements in characterization and depth of conflict. The latter, born in Mexico, was among the first of the Americans who would one day return the Spanish language to greatness.

Reaching slightly beyond the limits of the period, the work of Calderón de la Barca (1600–1681) ended the great creative age. His philosophical plays (*Life Is a Dream* is the most famous) or almost any of the one-act religious plays that occupied his last years, bring up issues of belief and intellectual conviction that still occupy the Spanish mind today.

Within this 150-year span of theatrical vitality, many other literary forms saw high achievement. In poetry, Garcilaso de la Vega (1503–1536) adapted the Renaissance forms to Spanish use, especially with the invention of the rhythmically freer form called the *silva.* Publication of his verse in 1543 set a standard of serious accomplishment for

color
US

colour
Brit.

theater
US

theatre
Brit.

center
US

centre
Brit.

CERVANTES,
creator of the classic character and parable *Don Quixote.*

years to come. The Portuguese poet Luiz de Camões wrote the *Os Lusíadas,* a remarkable modern historic epic combining the age of global discovery with Portuguese antiquity. His lyric poems, too, rank him as Portugal's finest poet.

In religious writings, a mixture of intellectual seriousness and lyrical intensity reappeared with the mystic St. John of the Cross (1542–1591), whose poems were influenced by the brilliant Catholic visionary leader and author of a noted spiritual autobiography St. Theresa of Avila.

Something of the Spanish temperament may be found, too, in the "last" poet of the age, Luis de Góngora (1561–1627). But his taste sought an academically approved immortality, and the end of fresh genius dates from Góngora's success.

In prose, the strongest historical writing sprang from an utterly new source, the reports of veterans of the great explorations and American conquests. Columbus, Cortés, and others enlarged literature by simply introducing it to a new reality. The great monuments of these firsthand accounts by Bernal Díaz and Bartolomé de las Casas command new readers still. Both their works date from the later 1500s.

In fiction, the vogue of the pastoral, imitated from an earlier Portuguese model, was perfected in *Diana Enamorada* by Jorge de Montemayor. The picaresque, commencing with *Lazarillo*

de Tormes (author unknown), provided "realistic" escapism to a colorful if not always believable underworld.

The enduring genius of Spanish literature, however, undoubtedly was Miguel de Cervantes Saavedra (1547–1616), whose *Don Quixote* appeared before 1620. Cervantes belonged, like Rabelais, to no school other than that of his own bitterly ironic but always hopeful mind. Designed as a parody of chivalric literature, *Don Quixote* matured in the writing and became a parable of the whole of human existence. As with the works of Dante and Shakespeare, modern man has built it into the center of his spirit.

Finally, Spain produced in Francisco de Quevedo an exponent of that brilliant satire in which Catholic humanism was to find much of its best expression in the succeeding ages. His *Los Sueños* (1607) is a prose piece of savage force. A poet and novelist as well, Quevedo used the language with a natural power that contrasted sharply with Gongorism, the triumphant school of academic style, which he hated.

Quevedo's younger associate in the war of "ideas" against "mere words," Baltasar (Lorenzo) Gracián, won only exile and disgrace for his satiric allegory, *El Criticón.* Nevertheless, its near-existentialist view of death had great impact on the thinking of rationalist and metaphysical writers of the 18th and 19th centuries.

England Reawakens

English literature, in deep hibernation from the time of Chaucer, emerged with startling suddenness at the beginning of the 1500s. The preceding century had seen the culmination of the long religious tradition of the miracle play, preserved in several separate but related collections, and the introduction of the vice-and-virtue homilies of the morality play (as in *Everyman*).

In 1485, the year of the accession of the first Tudor king, the pioneering printer William Caxton published *Morte d'Arthur* by Sir Thomas Malory. Though little is known of the author, he set the chivalry, violence, and adulterous loves of the Arthurian legend in the realistic light of a man who has known similar experiences firsthand. The swift prose rendering has great grace and delicacy, and yet remains plainspoken throughout. It was on the person of the next king, however, that the English Renaissance was centered. Henry VIII fought the battles of political liberty and religious conscience cognizant only of his need for heirs. Eventually, Henry would establish an English church dependent on the state rather than on Rome and set a new course for English freedom.

John Skelton, Henry's boyhood tutor, was England's first lyric poet in an age. He took a strong stand on the issue of personal and sexual integrity, both in his verse and his life. From Skelton's time on, that issue cost lives.

The great poet of Henry's maturity, Sir Thomas Wyatt, had been a lover of Anne Boleyn, the woman for whom Henry abandoned the Roman Catholic Church. Boleyn, Wyatt's own son, and Wyatt's friend, the Earl of Surrey, all were to die under separate circumstances connected with the violent politics of the time. Surrey collaborated with the elder Wyatt on the first English sonnets and himself introduced the blank verse (unrhymed pentameter) that would come to full flower in the plays of Marlowe and Shakespeare.

A greater writer still was William Tyndale. His translations of the Bible, made under a ban, greatly influenced the later King James Version (1611). Yet Tyndale was to die at the stake in Europe, apparently betrayed for expressing his displeasure at the king's divorce.

The statesman who most wanted Tyndale silenced and yet the leading humanist of his age, Sir Thomas More, found himself, like his friend Erasmus, unable to break with the Catholicism of his childhood. He in turn paid for his conscience with his life.

The education of the English and their creative growth proceeded almost simultaneously. Sir Thomas More's circle, which included John Colet, Thomas Linacre, Desiderius Erasmus, and Sir Thomas Elyot, was responsible for important translations from Greek, Latin, and Italian, as well as for the estab-

lishment of new principles of education. In mid-century, Castiglione's *Courtier* and Plutarch's *Lives* appeared in English translation, the latter in the version by Sir Thomas North echoed so often by Shakespeare. The *Metamorphoses* of Ovid, translated by Arthur Golding (1567), had a similar seminal effect.

Later in the century, the accounts of explorers, firsthand or summarized, had an even more rousing effect on the free-thinking English than on the Spanish. News of the lands westward had their impact as early as More's speculative *Utopia*. Full accounts of voyages by Drake, Hawkins, Raleigh, the Cabots, and others took on the character of national epics in the making, collected most notably by Richard Hakluyt in *Principall Navigations, Voiages, and Discoveries of the English Nation* (1598–1600), a work later extended by Samuel Purchas.

Similarly, the English sense of national identity was fed by historical chronicles. Raphael Holinshed's *The Chronicles of England, Scotland and Ireland* (1577) became an important source for Shakespeare's plays.

Religious writing culminated in the sermons of Lancelot Andrewes—chief among translators of the King James Bible (1611). In a different vein, a masterpiece of the English rational but believing temperament was Richard Hooker's *Laws of Ecclesiastical Polity* (published in part, 1594).

THE TYNDALE BIBLE was published in 1525. The first page of the New Testament is shown above as it appeared in the first edition.

The *Essays* of Francis Bacon (1597 and later) expressed an early literary excitement about the possibilities of science. Thomas Harriot combined exploration, mathematical skill, and association with the "atheist" idealist poets Marlowe and Chapman, in a single lucid personality.

All of these strands—scholarly, adventurous, religious, and controversial—contributed to the astonishing fullness of this first English maturity. But the finest flower of the age was its lyric and dramatic poetry. Of the many who took part, the amateur Sir Philip Sidney (1554–1586) wrote from a life that sought to fulfill every aristocratic ideal; and the professional Edmund Spenser (1552–1599) saw poetry as a way to preferment. Others fell somewhere between these two extremes.

Sidney's pastoral *Arcadia* (1590) and sonnet sequence, *Astrophel and Stella* (1591), reveal a personality of major dimension, perhaps more important to later literature than the Italian models Sidney followed. Spenser, perhaps most himself in the amazing youthful work *The Shepheardes Calendar* (1579), created in an unfinished allegorical epic, *Faerie Queene,* whose first three books (1590) established his career, a gorgeous monstrosity that other poets (Shakespeare,

Milton, and Keats among them) have imitated and admired ever since.

Among the gentleman poets of lasting brilliance were Sir Walter Raleigh, Sir Fulke Greville, and Sir John Davies. Those who depended on patronage included George Chapman (first translator of Homer), Samuel Daniel, and Michael Drayton. Somewhere between were Thomas Campion, and the Catholic skeptic turned Protestant cleric, John Donne.

These writers generally occupied the "high," or aristocratic side of literary activity. The playwrights had the great luck of a theater that almost accidentally made its life from a wider more heterogeneous audience, leaving court performances for special occasions. Even during its greatest period (1590–1614), the theater never won the academic respectability of poetry, but it could earn a living for a playwright and afford him the scope and response necessary for greatness.

The middle 1500s had seen the first native English comedies and tragedies. In 1586, the year of Sir Philip Sidney's death, Thomas Kyd's *The Spanish Tragedy* appeared. Based on the Roman Seneca's work, its themes of revenge, betrayal, and madness struck something deep in the Elizabethan experience. Christopher Marlowe's *Tamburlaine the Great,* the next year, introduced a marvelous melodic lilt to the iambic pentameter line, together with a theme of heroism based on personal ambition rather than on public service. *Doctor Faustus,* probably written in the year of his death by murder (1593), places Marlowe with Shakespeare among those who have given the West its most basic prototypes of character and conscience.

Shakespeare. William Shakespeare, born in 1564 (the year of Michelangelo's death), died in 1616, the same year as Cervantes. He stands alone among English writers, and indeed among writers of the world. His masterpieces are not single plays but, whether by intention or not, cycles—the magical comedies of the 1590s, notably *Midsummer Night's Dream;* the historical plays later in the same decade, most fully realized in *Henry IV, Part I;* the great tragedies of the early 1600s, *Hamlet, King Lear, Othello,* and *Macbeth;* and finally the romances of the last years, especially *The Tempest.*

Throughout, Shakespeare worked with the simplest of principles, writing at the mind's own speed, using everything he read, but reworking it first, and depending for character upon the defining trait or flaw. A favorite character illustrates his range. Falstaff, the fictional drinking companion of the young Prince Hal, was based on an actual early friend, the valiant principled Sir John Fastolfe, whom the mature Henry later had executed. Shakespeare made him a drunk, a lecher, a glutton, something of a coward, and the wittiest man in England; he eventually had to change Fastolfe's name

and leave out the religious issues that brought his execution. When Prince Hal (now Henry V) rejects (rather than executes) him, Falstaff, by this time the most popular character on the English stage, dies of a broken heart. His death scene curiously echoes that of Socrates' in the *Dialogues.* Shakespeare, unable to speak openly of the religious wars that were still driving friend from friend, brother from brother, found a way to show the treachery of a king, and yet continue to glorify that king's necessary mark upon the English patriotic scene. This is myth-making on an Homeric level, yet with a realism that is thoroughly familiar to the modern temperament. The last plays grow steadily richer poetically but lose something of their dramatic fire, showing instead a moving spirit of acceptance and reconciliation.

Aside from the plays, many of which were published only after his death, Shakespeare wrote two long poems early in his career: a beautiful mysterious lyric, *The Phoenix and the Turtle,* and a collection of sonnets of highly concentrated power that rank among the great private poems of the world.

In addition to Shakespeare and Marlowe, the English theater boasted a number of other dramatists capable of moments of great force: Thomas Dekker and Philip Massinger in comedy; the collaborators Francis Beaumont and John Fletcher in comedy and tragedy; and the accomplished but nightmarishly bloodthirsty Cyril Tourneur, Thomas Middleton, John Ford, and John Webster in tragedy. Webster's *The Duchess of Malfi* (1616) stands as the masterpiece among the later plays.

The other unique figure of the age was Ben Jonson (1572–1637). Unlike Shakespeare, he was a classicist at heart, preferring emotional reserve and a controlled allusive wit derived from the structure of the Latin epigram. He led drama out of the open air and back into the schoolroom with courage and imagination. His plays, notably *Volpone* (1606) and *Bartholomew Fair* (1614) are still performed, and his use of rhymed couplets greatly influenced the neoclassicists of the late 1600s.

SHAKESPEARE

The greatest poet in the language used blank verse—unrhymed lines of ten syllables. Here, in the late play *The Tempest*, the speech of Prospero seems to be the poet's farewell and may even allude to the Globe Theater shown above.

> You do look, my son, in a movéd sort,
> As if you were dismayed. Be cheerful, sir.
> Our revels now are ended. These our actors,
> As I foretold you, were all spirits, and
> Are melted into air, into thin air.
> And, like the baseless fabric of this vision,
> The cloud-capped towers, the gorgeous palaces,
> The solemn temples, the great globe itself—
> Yea, all which it inherit—shall dissolve
> And, like this insubstantial pageant faded,
> Leave not a rack behind. We are such stuff
> As dreams are made on, and our little life
> Is rounded with a sleep. Sir, I am vexed.
> Bear with my weakness, my old brain is troubled.
> Be not disturbed with my infirmity . . . .

The Age of Reason and Conscience 1600–1789

After 1600, society was looking for a less spontaneous, more ordered universe. It sought to deny parts of Renaissance thought and to freeze the rest into a new classicism. But the revolution had already taken place. The conservative impulse—which sought to preserve not only old forms and ideas but old hereditary privilege—still had to deal with the rising new class that was gaining economic and social influence in spite of all opposition. The class of businessmen, professionals, and civil servants would seek to emulate the old nobility in some respects, but it would also seek to re-create the literary world in its own lively but determinedly middle-class image. The literature of the age, though outwardly sober and conservative, mirrors these changes throughout.

Italy and Spain

The countries of the Catholic Mediterranean, Italy, Spain, and Portugal, suffered through the 17th and 18th centuries. They were victims of economic decline and dynastic warfare, as well as the continuing conservatism of a threatened church. In the three countries, over a span of 150 years, only the tradition of humanist scholarly inquiry produced consistently solid work.

The research of the Italian archival historian Ludovico Muratori spilled over into literary history, eventually leading to a form of literary criticism that could challenge the prevailing orthodoxy. Muratori, the dramatist Francesco Maffei, the literary historian Girolamo Tiraboschi, and the historical philosopher Giovanni Battista Vico played varying roles in this. Vico's *Scienza Nuova* (1725) was a "rational" study of history concentrating on the lifespan of an entire culture, its "personality," and the circumstances of its life and death. Modern historians have learned to use this approach, making mythic sense of many otherwise intractable bits of information.

In Spain, where scholarship had just recovered its earliest literary heritage, a Benedictine monk, Benito Fijóo y Montenegro, introduced the cool, clear rationalist side of the Enlightenment, setting a point of view that would deeply influence Spanish literature through a century or more.

Beyond these few, other writers of the age were more important to their own time than to the future of literature. Italy appreciated satire (Alessandro Tassoni, Giuseppe Parini), journalism (Gasparo Gozzi, Giuseppe Baretti, and Pietro Verri), and the theater (Metastasio, Carlo Goldoni, Vittorio Alfieri, and Lorenzo da Ponte, the librettist of Mozart's *Don Giovanni* [1787]). The

Spanish Enlightenment extended into the time but not the spirit of the 1800s. In Portugal, the national taste for writing in Spanish reduced the literary output in Portuguese. Only the poet Francisco Rodrigues Lobo and the wide-ranging prose stylist, Francisco Manuel de Melo, achieved lasting reputations, both in the 1600s. After that, a strain of sincere religious writing produced the love letters of a nun, Marianna Alcoforado (first published in French in 1669), which the Portuguese have identified as a unique example of the national consciousness ever since.

France

The state of orthodoxy in the Mediterranean area did not hold in France. For nearly 100 years, beginning in the late 1500s, France enjoyed at least nominal religious toleration. During this period, the active contention of several beliefs, including that of the strongly reformist Catholic Jansenists, contributed to the keenest intellectual atmosphere to be found in Europe.

René Descartes, born before the turn of the century, announced the brilliance of the age. His *Discourse on Method,* a collection of essays (1637), opened up the question of belief, and of meaning

itself, to the logical processes implicit in mathematical thought. Blaise Pascal, a generation younger, widened the area of discussion when he seemed to suggest in his incomplete and posthumously published *Pensées* (1670) that nothing could be certainly known. His deep sense of the limits of human understanding contrasted with Descartes' greater optimism. Ironically, both men also sought to justify the Catholic faith. Pascal was persecuted for his Jansenist sympathies.

A key to the swift appreciation of these very complicated men lies in the beauty, clarity, and cogency of their very different but highly polished styles. France was a society in the making. The rights of the landed aristocracy contended with the new power of men in business, the professions, and the civil service. Style was the delicate link that held these antagonistic groups together.

Drama. The emphasis on a pure, elevated style found its most famous expression in the rhetorical verse of the French theater. In 1637 this theater produced *Le Cid* by Pierre Corneille. *Le Cid* announced a new high style and standard of action that conformed with the aspirations of the nation about to become the most powerful in Europe. Corneille's later plays and those of Jean Racine

JEAN RACINE was a great French dramatist during the age of Louis XIV.

(*Andromaque,* 1667; *Britannicus,* 1669; *Phèdre,* 1677, among others) spoke the language of Senecan classicism and conformed strictly to the unities of Aristotle, in which the action of each play took place on a single day in a single place and was of a serious nature. Yet the authentic vitality of the new French national consciousness gave these works a depth their Senecan models had lacked. Their style has typified expression of the highest French aspirations ever since.

Between Corneille and Racine in age, the great comic playwright Molière wrote on the delicate line between belief and fraud in masterpieces such as *Le Tartuffe* (1664), *Le Misanthrope* (1666), and *Le Bourgeois Gentilhomme* (1670). His mockery of society usually finds a better reception with English-speaking audiences than the tragedies of Corneille and Racine.

In a different vein, the extraordinary *Fables* of Jean de la Fontaine (1668–1694) achieved an immediacy of impact. They were simple enough to be read by children, yet they were sophisticated satire to the adults who understood the contemporary references and context.

Criticism. The 1600s were also a great period for literary criticism. The establishment of the French Academy in the 1630s gave France the first "official" court of usage and literary taste. The academy fixed both the language and literary forms, insisting on the virtue of "correctness." The better critics, such as Nicolas Boileau-Despréaux (1636–1711), recognized, however, that the genius of each great work was its power to define correctness anew.

Outside of official literary creation, several works of the late 1600s became literary models. *La Princesse de Cleves,* by Marie de la Vergne, Comtesse de la Fayette, was the first intimate piece of fiction in modern Europe. The posthumously published letters of the comtesse's friend, Madame de Sévigné, popularized epistolary collections. The worldly, often cynical epigrams of Francois de la Rochefoucauld became a model for succeeding generations.

On another level, the sermons and religious controversy of a gifted set of divines, notably Jacques Bénigne Bossuet and Francois de la Mothe Fénelon, pointed to the sharp yet civilized argument that would dominate controversial writing in the 1700s.

Thus, by 1700, the academician's emphasis on purity of speech and clarity of expression had been turned, through the pressures of a thriving society, into a search for the truth that lay under the expression, and for a logic of reform.

The Enlightenment. Before his 35th year, Voltaire (Francois Marie Arouet, 1694–1778), a self-made millionaire, had been imprisoned, brutally beaten, and imprisoned again, all unjustly and all in the name of preserving the prerogatives of the aristocratic estate. Yet he became one of the principal heroes of the movement called the Enlightenment—a sort of common man's codification of the Renaissance. Together with his associates, Voltaire came to be known as a *philosophe,* a humble teacher of wisdom, but one whose teachings led toward revolutionary self-assertion.

Voltaire's endless curiosity and irreverence was to undermine the system with its own weapons: irony and information. In *Letters Concerning the English Nation* (1733), *Éléments de la Philosophie de Newton* (1736), and *Dictionnaire Philosophique* (1764) Voltaire showed his great enthusiasm for engaging the minds of his readers.

He was a contributor to the great collective project of the age as well. The *Encyclopédie* was brought into being principally by Denis Diderot; it used not only Voltaire but a host of other talented thinkers and writers, including Montesquieu and Rousseau. This first great rationalist collection of earthly knowledge was soon perceived by the monarchy to be subversive. The first installment was published openly in 1751, but the last, in 1772, had to be secretly printed and distributed. The *Encyclopédie* was a declaration of intellectual independence for men of every class throughout Europe, allowing the curious to learn without relying on either nobleman or priest.

This strong nonfiction informational interest left its mark on other works as well. Charles de Secondat Montesquieu towers above all historians of his day with a comparative study of governments and the circumstances that mold them, *L'Esprit des Lois* (1748). His doctrines of the separation of powers and the importance of individual liberty influenced the framers of the American Constitution. The reformist political economist Anne Robert Turgot and the mathematician Marie Jean Condorcet first considered human behavior as the result of needs, rather than as blind destiny or heroic example. Voltaire's *Charles XII* headed a copious production of narrative and biographical histories, as the Duc de Saint-Simon's *Mémoires* did of personal reminiscences.

The philosophes and encyclopedists were not dry-as-dust scholars, however, as their fiction proved. Diderot's stories were perhaps his most ingratiating work. Voltaire's *Candide,* the story of an innocent who trustingly believes the philosopher's maxim that this is the best of all possible worlds, is a masterpiece, a work that is both comic and oddly tragic at the same time.

The outstanding novelist, however, was Jean Jacques Rousseau (1712–1778). He was both the least characteristic thinker of his age and its purest product. The *Nouvelle Héloïse* and *Émile,* together with the late *Confessions,* make a new connection, that between the writer's inward state (his psychology) and his contribution to the public good. For Rousseau, the spiritual journey of Christian literature remained, but he interpreted the journey in wholly personal and wholly secular terms. Man was to make his own salvation.

For Rousseau, and for most of the writers in the succeeding two centuries, a man was valuable or good not because of his station at birth or his title or his education; rather, value was to be sought inside—in the man's emotional core. This led Rousseau to speculate on the inequalities of his own society and to reconsider the very basis of society itself. Though he was no political activist, his thoughts were deeply subversive to the old French regime, suggesting the psychological basis for the revolution that would come only after Rousseau's death. He was also a prophet of an artistic and literary revolution, the great movement called Romanticism that was about to sweep Europe.

VOLTAIRE enjoyed engaging the minds of his readers, as can be seen in this excerpt from *Candide.*

STORM, SHIPWRECK, EARTHQUAKE, AND WHAT HAPPENED TO DR. PANGLOSS, TO CANDIDE AND THE ANABAPTIST JACQUES

CHAPTER V

HALF the enfeebled passengers, suffering from that inconceivable anguish which the rolling of a ship causes in the nerves and in all the humours of bodies shaken in contrary directions, did not retain strength enough even to trouble about the danger. The other half screamed and prayed; the sails were torn, the masts broken, the vessel leaking. Those worked who could, no one co-operated, no one commanded. The Anabaptist tried to help the crew a little; he was on the main-deck; a furious sailor struck him violently and stretched him on the deck; but the blow he delivered gave him so violent a shock that he fell head-first out of the ship. He remained hanging and clinging to part of the broken mast. The good Jacques ran to his aid, helped him to climb back, and from the effort he

England

The religious and philosophical issues of the 1600s led to spirited discussion and uneasy tolerance in France. In England, they led to a civil war, the violent overthrow of the monarchy (Charles I was beheaded in 1649), and an austere interregnum, a time when the throne was empty, during which literature concerned itself with controversy or (as with the theater) was outlawed. Only after the restoration of the monarchy in 1660 did the political situation become more stable and the social climate more permissive.

1600–1660. The poetry of the early 1600s was restrained and often intentionally crabbed. The exuberance of the age of Elizabeth had soured, leaving a polished but often cynical kind of "cavalier" poetry and an inward religious poetry we know as "metaphysical." Some poets worked in both styles or in some amalgam of the two. Two poets produced great poems, though small in scale: the uncommon religious poet, George Herbert (1593–1633), and Robert Herrick (1591–1674), whose work unexpectedly swims out of repetitively worked conceits to an occasional freshness and sincerity. The great favorite of the 20th century has been the eccentric Andrew Marvell (1621–1678), whose private combination of the cavalier and the metaphysical helped him reflect on the losses and achievements of his violent times.

In prose, the *Anatomy of Melancholy* (1621) of Robert Burton set out to be a psychological and physiological treatise. *Religio Medici* (1635) and *Hydriotaphia: Urne-Buriall* (1658) by the physician Sir Thomas Browne sought to reconcile science, personal faith, and the certainty of mortality. In effect, however, those books became portraits of the authors' minds, and mirrors for the speculations of their readers. With the works of Thomas Hobbes, particularly the *Leviathan* (1651), another sort of philosophical literature was born. Hobbes questioned the organization of society itself and gave little quarter to mankind, reflecting that most human lives are "nasty, brutish and short."

Hobbes's reduction of philosophy to simple and observable principles pointed forward to the great philosophical treatises of John Locke (1632–1704) and his successors, George Berkeley (1685–1753) and David Hume (1711–1776). Though not intended as pure literature, these works helped develop a precise yet idiomatic prose for practical use. It would gradually be reflected in more literary works through the 1700s.

History had a special appeal to those who were witnessing it and were often its victims. The Earl of Clarendon (Edward Hyde), an adviser to kings and an opponent of the Puritan forces of Oliver Cromwell, wrote a *History of the Rebellion* (posthumously published, 1702–1704), an important source for modern historians, but also a distinguished example of the literary polemics of the age. Thus, summing up the rebellion leader Oliver Cromwell, Clarendon writes:

> In a word, as he had all the wickednesses against which damnation is denounced and for which hellfire is prepared, so he had some virtues which have caused the memory of some men in all ages to be celebrated; and he will be looked upon by posterity as a brave, bad man.

Perhaps more important to contemporaries were the sermons and meditations of the famous preachers. The warfare of the century centered around issues of religious belief and practice, challenging the conscience of every man and woman. The meditations of John Donne stirred his listeners in the early 1600s, still echoing the exuberance of the previous age. Jeremy Taylor, a Church of England minister imprisoned and later reduced to teaching school during Cromwell's reign, published *Holy Living* (1650) and *Holy Dying* (1651), devotional books of great warmth and conviction. One of Taylor's early works, *Liberty of Prophesying*, dealt somewhat ahead of its time with the hope of religious toleration, a hope realized only after the death of thousands on both sides of the war between Episcopalian and Puritan parties.

Milton. The greatest English writer of the century was identified with the Puritan cause. John Milton (1608–1674) produced a few brilliant early poems (such as "Lycidas") before the civil war. He made vigorous efforts for the cause that eventually became Cromwell's, contributing his ability as a writer and his learning, and advising the government on both domestic and foreign affairs.

Milton had enormous talents, but he had an equally passionate sense of personal responsibility for his ideas and beliefs. His prose pamphlets in favor of divorce, and against prior censorship of the press *(Areopagitica)*, dared the prevailing ideas even of his own party.

The restoration of the monarchy (1660) ended Milton's government service. He had become blind and without property or financial resources. During the next few years he wrote the one great epic in modern English, *Paradise Lost* (1667). It retells the story of Adam and Eve and of their temptation by Satan and fall from God's favor.

The story of Satan's rebellion can be read in the light of the actual rebellion in which Milton had taken part. In fact, generations of readers have found Satan the most attractive and sympathetic character in the great poem.

In many ways *Paradise Lost* is the culmination of the Renaissance tradition of producing new classics by imitating the old. It relies heavily on Homer, Vergil, Dante, Spenser, and, of course, the Bible; but most especially it relies on the blank verse paragraphs invented by Milton's secular predecessor, Shakespeare.

In other respects, however, the great poem is strikingly modern. Milton's descriptions borrow not only from the classical languages but from the new science of his own time. His emphasis on the importance of individual conscience and choice rings true—perhaps more true to modern readers than to Milton's contemporaries.

Paradise Lost is nowhere more forward-looking than in its treatment of the relationship between Adam and Eve. For the first time in our literature, we encounter husband and wife as a unit, neither more important than the other,

---

MILTON

In the Middle Ages, romantic love had been a passion that occurred outside of marriage. John Milton's description of the devotion of Adam and Eve in *Paradise Lost* brings love and marriage together, preparing the way for scores of modern explorations of the ideal of love within marriage. In the opening lines, Adam and Eve are addressing God.

> "But Thou has promised from us two a race
> To fill the Earth, who shall with us extol
> Thy goodness infinite, both when we wake,
> And when we seek, as now, thy gift of sleep."
>   This said unanimous, and other rites
> Observing none, but adoration pure
> Which God likes best, into their inmost bower
> Handed they went; and eased the putting off
> These troublesome disguises which we wear,
> Straight side by side were laid, nor turned, I ween,
> Adam from his fair spouse, nor Eve the rites
> Mysterious of connubial love refused . . . .
> These, lulled by nightingales, embracing slept,
> And on their naked limbs the flowery roof
> Showered roses, which the morn repaired.
>   Sleep on,
> Blest pair; and O yet happiest if ye seek
> No happier state, and know to know no more.

---

theater
US

theatre
Brit.

centered
US

centred
Brit.

realized
US

realised
Brit.

sharing both joys and sorrows. Eve has none of the idealized qualities of Dante's Beatrice; nor is Adam the solitary seeker, yearning both for God and for his earthly love. This new equality of the sexes—and the new marriage relationship it allows—will be a major subject for serious writers from Milton's time to the present (see box on previous page).

The only achievement of the 1600s comparable to *Paradise Lost* was of a different order, though not dissimilar. *The Pilgrim's Progress,* by John Bunyan (in two parts, 1678 and 1684), told in spare, everyday prose of Christian's travels toward salvation. His trials and temptations and his final success offered comfort and hope to readers who felt themselves to be on the same journey. The places in the imaginary landscape— the Slough of Despond, for example, and Vanity Fair—became part of the English language. *The Pilgrim's Progress* was the most popular book in the American colonies (after the Bible) through the 1700s and well into the 1800s, rivaled only by *Robinson Crusoe* (see below).

1660–1700.   Meanwhile, at the court of the restored king, Charles II, literature of quite a different character was in fashion, particularly in the theater. The playwrights Sir George Etherege, William Wycherly, and William Congreve wrote dialogue unmatched for quickness till the present day; but their cynicism—sometimes appearing to be a rejection of all conventional moral values—makes them seem brittle and "unserious" to modern tastes.

The great literary figure in the generation after Milton's was John Dryden (1631–1700). In many ways he bridged the gap between the high seriousness of the Puritan cause and the frivolousness of the court. He first came to attention as a dramatist, specializing not in brittle comedy but in the type of bombastic tragedy popular at the time. He admired Milton and even (with Milton's permission) put *Paradise Lost* into rhyming couplets for theatrical presentation.

Dryden was a man of public affairs, and in the 1680s he assisted the government by writing political propaganda. Among these pieces, the mock epics *Absalom and Achitophel* (1681–1682) and *MacFlecknoe* (1682) rank with the greatest satires in the language. Yet, like Milton, Dryden was a man of "tender conscience." His own religious odyssey led him to the Roman Catholic Church. This choice eventually disqualified him from government service or favor.

In his later years, Dryden did much of the work that he is remembered for today. He translated Vergil's *Aeneid* into mellow and beautiful English verse, and he became the first great English literary critic. His *Essay of Dramatic Poesy* (1668) defines the English dramatic tradition in a way that is still persuasive even today. Not until Samuel Johnson nearly a hundred years later would English have a critic of such broad and generous tastes.

In an extraordinarily beautiful fragment, *The Secular Masque,* Dryden, near the end of his life, marked the century's turning with what might have been the age's epitaph:

All, all, of a piece throughout;
Thy Chase had a Beast in view;
Thy Wars brought nothing about;
Thy Lovers were all untrue.
'Tis well an Old Age is out,
And time to begin a New.

The novel.   As if in direct response, a bankrupt businessman, Daniel Defoe (1659?–1731), made the first literary stir with a brace of poems that won him, alternately, royal favor and jail. He followed with an intense career in journalism in which nearly everything in his *Review* was written by himself. Finally, in *Robinson Crusoe* (1719), *Moll Flanders* (1721), and *The Journal of the Plague Year* (1721) he turned, as many a journalist has before and since, to simulated fact without bothering to inform the public of his technique. Defoe's racy and essentially nonliterary efforts stand as one of the major building blocks of the English novel.

This new form, seemingly lightyears away from Milton's epic or Dryden's criticism, signaled the growth of an important, if less cultivated reading public. *Robinson Crusoe,* the story of a man stranded on a desert island and forced to self-reliance, struck a deep chord in the new readers. It was perhaps the most read and most durable book written in the 1700s. The novel's other building blocks included Samuel Richardson's *Pamela* (1740), a story composed of letters from an attractive young woman beset by suitors with questionable motives. Richardson's "sentimental psychology" became a major element of later fiction. In answer to Pamela came Henry Fielding's *Joseph Andrews* (1742), which brought an element of satire to the novel. Fielding parodied not only the sentimental style of Richardson, but also the classical epic, making both seem

THE
Pilgrims Progrefs:
In the fimilitude of a
DREAM.

AS I walk'd through the wildernefs of this world, I lighted on a certain place, where was a Denn; And I laid me down in that place to fleep: And as I flept I dreamed a Dream. I dreamed, and behold *I faw a Man * cloathed with Raggs, ftanding in a certain place, with his face from his own Houfe, a Book in his hand, and a great burden upon his back. I looked, and faw him open the Book, and Read therein; and as he Read, he wept and trembled: and not being able longer to contain,

* Ifa. 64. 6.
Lu. 14.33
Pf. 38. 4.
Hab. 2. 2.
A&. 16: 31.

faintly ridiculous by mixing them. Finally, Tobias Smollett's *The Adventures of Roderick Random* (1748) established the picaresque, which featured a lovable but inept hero whose misfortunes made him a kind of negative everyman. Eventually the novel would become a solid literary form in its own right. But these early efforts flew in the face of established literary standards. Their authors were conscious of being a kind of literary underground.

Beginning about mid-century with the publication of Fielding's *Tom Jones,* a sophisticated mock epic, the novel began to gain some status in the literary world. *Tom Jones* was followed by *Tristram Shandy* (1759–1767) by Laurence Sterne, a comic masterpiece in which the intended story never gets told, being constantly interrupted by the narrator's free associations. The hero is not even born until a third of the way through the book. Sterne's methods— and his "sentiment"—made him a kind of celebrity. His books were admired and laughed at in France and Germany as well as in England. With Rousseau, he was a prophet of the new sensibility that would be called Romanticism.

Among other important novels are Oliver Goldsmith's *The Vicar of Wakefield* (1766), a gentle and less revolutionary novel of sentiment, and Horace Walpole's *The Castle of Otranto* (1764), the first of the "gothic" novels, relying on an exotic or mysterious setting and on the demonic or evil possibilities of the characters. Before the turn of the century, a new master, Jane Austen, had written her first three novels, though they were not published for many years.

The Augustans.

Novelists were not the only writers to turn in new directions. Early in the century there developed a new and gentlemanly kind of literary journalism—weekly papers with informal essays on literature, politics, and other topical concerns of the day. Joseph Addison and Richard Steele produced the most famous of these papers, the *Tatler* and the *Spectator* (1709–1712), whose issues make engaging reading even today. The *Spectator* had many imitators in succeeding years. Only the *Rambler* by Samuel Johnson and, later, Goldsmith's *The Citizen of the World* are much remembered, however.

Both novelists and journalists were members of a new class: writers who could make their living with their pen alone. John Dryden was perhaps the first to succeed at this, offering the public his translations by subscription and sharing the proceeds with his printer. Other poets and men of letters followed his lead. Alexander Pope made a small fortune selling his translations of Homer, and later in the century, Samuel Johnson made both his reputation and income from the sale of his great dictionary.

Alexander Pope (1688–1744) was without doubt the most admired poet of the 1700s. He took the heroic couplet of Dryden and refined it to a fine witty point. Later poets despaired of imitating him—perhaps no English poet has had so sure and exact a sense of the language. Yet Pope's verses are cold, appealing more to the head than to the heart. Later generations have questioned his subject matter but have never been able to deny his immense talent.

Perhaps the most sympathetic strain in Pope in his capacity for moral outrage. He parodies the inconsequential concerns of the coquette by placing her in a mock epic in *The Rape of the Lock* (1712). Later, he takes apart the venal and greedy literary underworld of his time in the *Dunciad* (1728, 1742). In a more relaxed vein, his *Imitations of Horace* (1733–1739) suggest something of the feeling of Horace's Rome, akin to Pope's London. In fact, the early 1700s have come to be known as England's "Augustan Age."

For a few short years, Pope was closely associated with the other literary giant of the day, Jonathan Swift (1667–1745). Swift was no poet; rather he was a man driven by a fierce sense of moral outrage. Cruelty and false principle enraged him, and he gained his "revenge" in writing the most pointed and scathing satire ever produced in English. Swift served with Pope in the government of Queen Anne from 1710 to 1714. But when the queen died, Swift fled in disgrace to Ireland (where he had been born to Anglo-Irish parents). He served the rest of his life as the dean of the Anglican cathedral in Dublin.

Ironically, the one work of Swift's that remains a classic is *Gulliver's Travels* (1726). Swift wrote it as a parody of travel books and an indictment of mankind; it is revered as a charming children's story. The style of the book, a parody of low journalistic style, has been praised as a model for modern English. Meanwhile, the ironies Swift intended to be recognized—the small-mindedness of the tiny Lilliputians, the physical and moral monstrosity of the giant Brobdingnagians, and the perfect debasement of the filthy manlike Yahoos (far inferior to the placid horses they work for)—are often ignored or dismissed.

Three years after *Gulliver's Travels,* Swift published "A Modest Proposal," a brief and devastating suggestion in "scientific" language that the Irish, having no other means of earning a living, be encouraged to raise their own children as food for gentlemen's tables. The horrifying detail of the proposal suggests indirectly the deep sympathy Swift had for the Irish and the contempt he had for their English overlords.

Among others who associated with Pope and Swift was John Gay, a minor poet whose one great success was a "ballad opera." *The Beggar's Opera* (1728) used old English tunes to help tell the story of MacHeath, an amorous highwayman. It has never been off the stage long since it opened, and in an adaptation by German Bertolt Brecht it became *The Threepenny Opera,* a 20th-century classic with music by Kurt Weill. Even MacHeath survives in the modern adaptation as Mack the Knife in the song of that title.

The Johnson circle.

A long generation further on, another distinguished circle centered around Dr. Samuel Johnson (1709–1784). Johnson

---

centered
US

centred
Brit.

theater
US

theatre
Brit.

POPE

The heroic couplet—lines of the same length as blank verse, but rhymed one to the next—was mastered by Alexander Pope. Here, in "Epistle to Dr. Arbuthnot," he uses it to heap scorn on an evil man.

Let *Sporus* tremble—"What? that Thing of silk?
Sporus, that mere white Curd of Ass's milk?
Satire or Sense alas! can *Sporus* feel?
Who breaks a Butterfly upon a Wheel?"
Yet let me flap this Bug with gilded wings,
This painted Child of Dirt that stinks and stings;
Whose Buzz the Witty and the Fair annoys,
Yet Wit ne'er tastes, and Beauty ne'er enjoys.
So well-bred Spaniels civilly delight
In mumbling of the Game they dare not bite.
Eternal Smiles his Emptiness betray,
As shallow streams run dimpling all the way.
Whether in florid Impotence he speaks,
And, as the Prompter breathes, the Puppet squeaks;
Or, at the Ear of Eve, familiar Toad,
Half Froth, half Venom, spits himself abroad,
In Puns, of Politicks, of Tales, or Lyes,
Or Spite, or Smut, or Rymes, or Blasphemies.
His wit all see-saw between *that* and *this*,
Now high, now low, now Master up, now Miss,
And he himself one vile Antithesis . . . .

THE RAKE'S PROGRESS, a series of pointed engravings by William Hogarth, resembles Pope's pointed poetic satire. Hogarth was a friend of novelist Henry Fielding.

20 History of Literature

was a literary journalist and informal scholar who made his reputation by compiling the first great dictionary of English (1755). He accomplished (with a handful of Scottish assistants) what the French Academy took 30 years to do. The dictionary, boasting hundreds of examples of usage from English poetry, was the standard for over a century and also served as the basis for Noah Webster's American dictionaries.

Johnson's other works include a few poems, a moral fable, the essays in his weekly *Rambler,* and an edition of Shakespeare whose preface is justly famous. His great importance, however, was as a critic, and his *Lives of the Poets* (1781) redefines English poetry. Although his judgements often differed from those of later critics, Johnson's sympathies were extremely broad and generous.

Johnson's interest in biography came to its fruition in the monumental story of his own life by the younger James Boswell. Boswell's *Life of Samuel Johnson,* filled as no previous biography had been with anecdotes, conversations, and everyday details, made a larger-than-life celebrity of Johnson, nearly eclipsing his own works altogether. Boswell had more in common with Rousseau or Sterne than with Johnson, and his own psyche—at once hero-worshipping and rebellious—is an essential ingredient of his great biography.

The rest of Johnson's circle was equally remarkable. Oliver Goldsmith, shy, self-deprecating, and clumsy, managed to produce classics in three different genres: the comic play *She Stoops to Conquer* (1773), the poem "The Deserted Village" (1770), and the sentimental novel *The Vicar of Wakefield.*

Edmund Burke (1729–1797) was a member of Parliament and the most distinguished political orator of his day. He opposed the war with the American colonies and fought corruption in colonial India for decades. Ironically, he is best remembered not for these "liberal" campaigns but for his *Reflections on the French Revolution* (1790). In it, he defended England's slow evolutionary process of political reform against the radical reformers who sought to bring the French Revolution to England. Burke's early essay "On the Sublime" was an important contribution to the changing ideas of art and beauty.

Among others in the Johnsonian circle were Sir Joshua Reynolds, one of the great painters of the age; David Garrick, the great actor and theatrical entrepreneur (a boyhood friend of Johnson's); and the economist Adam Smith.

At the edges of the circle were still other distinguished men, among them David Hume, whose skeptical writings set philosophy on a new course, and whose *History of England* (1754–1762) set a new standard for historiography. The magisterial history of Edward Gibbon, *The Decline and Fall of the Roman Empire,* argues sardonically that Chris-

tianity played a central role in Rome's collapse. Finally, Richard Brinsley Sheridan warmed the Restoration style in *The Rivals* (1775) and *The School for Scandal* (1777), two enduring classics of the English theater.

New directions. Meanwhile, poetry seemed to have come to a dead end. The mild Thomas Gray and milder but lovelier William Collins tried to put new poetic substance in outworn neoclassic forms. But the true poetic impetus lay elsewhere. A group of amateur antiquarians was busy digging out England's ancient poetic past. They collected ancient ballads, studied Old English, and hunted for old manuscripts. The most influential of these "finds" proved to be forgeries: the works of Ossian translated by James Macpherson, and the "Rowley" poems of Thomas Chatterton. Authenticity aside, both seemed somehow to find a new root or starting place for future poetry. They caused great excitement in Germany as well as England. Another new sign lay in the genius of the "mad" Christopher Smart, author of the unforgettable "Song to David" (1763). It seemed that true lyric was so removed from the neoclassic tradition that one had to be fraudulent or insane to dare to write it.

As the century came near its end, this new sensibility was to transform poetry and literature, but that story properly belongs to the next age.

Romanticism and Nationalism

civilization
US

civilisation
Brit.

theater
US

theatre
Brit.

Some of the changes were external. In 1776 Britain's American colonies declared their independence, proclaiming a new set of political principles. Thirteen years later, the French rose up, first against their monarchy, then against their revolutionary leaders, finally in support of a crusade for world conquest. Other nations—the Germans, the Poles, the Scots, and the Irish— were rediscovering their national inheritances, seeking intellectual if not political independence.

At the same time, many of the changes were psychological. The late 1700s produced men that made no distinction between their public and private lives. In contrast to the decorous poets and critics of an earlier age, Rousseau, Sterne, Boswell, and others were self-involved, alert first to their own feelings and emotions and only afterward to the demands of the public. None of these new writers would be likely to serve in government or accomplish great works of scholarship. They saw their role as custodians of their own and their readers' imaginations or souls, not of their bodies or minds.

This new sensibility, with its emphasis on the individual and his identity, we know as the Romantic movement. It did not begin in a particular day or in a particular place, and many of those deeply involved in it did not consider themselves part of a movement at all. In retrospect, however, we can pick a year—1774—for convenience. And to characterize the great change, we turn to a new country and a new voice: the Germany of Johann Wolfgang von Goethe.

Germany

The great age of earlier German creativity was the Reformation of the 1500s. During the 1600s, the whole region was decimated by the Thirty Years War. Animosities between the many German states persisted for decades, and only in the 1700s did the German-speaking peoples begin a vigorous secular literature.

Perhaps the first sign of awakening was the career of Gottfried Wilhelm von Leibniz (1646–1716), a man of genius whose contributions to mathematics and philosophy were immense. Leibniz's talent for speculation and abstract thought revealed a particular trait in the German character—one seldom shared by the Germans' cousins in England.

The literary life of Germany was still simmering at a low boil at the time of Leibniz's death, but a young organist named Johann Sebastian Bach (1685–1742) had already begun composing works that would be a summation of 300 years of European music and would represent an anthology of ideas for the centuries to come.

Lessing. By mid-century, Germany was bursting with life, economic, political, and literary. The philosopher Gotthold Ephraim Lessing was constructing a theory of literature based on the model of the ancient Greeks rather than that of the Bourbon French. Lessing's classicism sought more than the ancient forms. He wanted a return to the spirit of the Athenian period. His admiration for Greek civilization has carried on in Germany to the present day. Lessing's landmark play, *Nathan the Wise* (1779), introduced a German blank verse modeled after another of his favorites, Shakespeare. His critical classic, *Laokoon* (1766), explored the differences between the visual and verbal imaginations, drawing on the discoveries of the great art historian J. J. Winckelmann. Shakespeare was brought to the national attention not only by the passionate advocacy of Lessing, but also by the translations of the talented Christoph Martin Wieland.

The philosopher Immanuel Kant (1724–1804) built on the works of Leibniz as well as on those of the Englishman David Hume. Kant, whose work was of incalculable importance to later philosophers and writers, concentrated on human powers of reason and intuition. Kant's interest in natural rather than "artificial" intellect inspired the critic Johann Gottfried von Herder (1744–1803) to suggest that artistic intuition had little to do with education or intellectual refinement. Like the language itself, Herder said, poetry rises from the collective consciousness of a people. Herder collected and edited German folk songs and encouraged others to examine the "popular" arts of the past as the English were doing at the same time.

Goethe. Herder also collaborated with Goethe and others in a pamphlet, *Von deutscher Art und Kunst,* that became the handbook of a movement termed *Sturm und Drang* (storm and stress). The movement's emphasis on the personal crises of an individual was inspired in part by Rousseau and by the new cult of "sentiment" in England. Its major result was the early work of Goethe himself. *The Sorrows of Young Werther* (1774) set Germany and all of Europe to writing novels about suicide. If German literature had ended at this point it would already have contributed a new note to the Romantic movement. But Goethe, Friedrich von Schiller, and Friedrich Hölderlin extended beyond the *Sturm und Drang* philosophy to a new lyric and drama that established the golden age of German literature.

Goethe towered over his associates. His *Faust* (in two parts, 1808 and 1832) is the greatest of all German works; a giant dramatic poem that seemed the epitome of its age. The novel of character growth, *Wilhelm Meister's Apprenticeship* (1795–1796), extended Goethe's influence on fiction. He also contributed to science, studying the morphology of living things.

But Goethe's greatest gifts remained always with the lyric: he could achieve a scene, an insight, or a passion with both perfect form and unparalleled emotional intimacy. The anthology of love lyrics *Westöstlicher Diwan* (1819) contains some of the world's most beautiful lyrics.

FAUST, the archetype of the Romantic hero, is tempted by Mephistopheles in an illustration for the play of Wolfgang von Goethe.

Schiller.

Schiller. Friedrich von Schiller stands second to his friend in the German pantheon. He was an extraordinary dramatist, often taking aim at political injustice, as in the passionately liberal *Die Räuber* (1781). Among his later plays are *Wallenstein* (a trilogy, 1798–1799), *Mary Stuart* (1800), and *William Tell* (1804).

Schiller also wrote an extensive history of the Thirty Years War and a considerable body of lyric. His "Ode to Joy" is set in the last movement of Beethoven's Choral Symphony.

After these two giants, the single novel, fragment of a play, and body of Hellenic verse produced by Friedrich Hölderlin seem a small accomplishment. Yet Hölderlin strikes true to the ears of German speakers especially, and has a kind of abstract perfection that is very much his own.

Between 1800 and Goethe's death in 1832, Romanticism swept Europe. In Germany, the emphasis shifted to prose. Jean Paul Friedrich Richter wrote sentimental, charming novels of everyday life that gained wide popularity. Friedrich von Hardenberg, who called himself Novalis, left an unfinished novel, *Heinrich von Ofterdingen* (1802), at the time of his early death, as well as a group of religious elegies, the only major lyric of his generation. At the same time, Ludwig Tieck opened the vein of the macabre and supernatural, perhaps most successfully in the later *Phantasus* (1812–1816). In the hands of the musician and novelist, E. T. A. Hoffmann, this became the gothic tale. One of the remarkable scholarly accomplishments of the age was the collection of household tales *(hausmärchen)* by the brothers Jakob and Wilhelm Grimm. The Grimms travelled the German countryside listening to old storytellers and taking the tales down word for word, thus preserving an oral tradition that may be centuries old. The Grimms were also the founders of modern philology, the study of the development of language. Their discoveries helped explain not only archaic German but also Old and Middle English.

Germany after Goethe.

Germany after Goethe. After the defeat of Napoleon, the impulse for German unification was enormous. The region was fast becoming the most advanced industrial society of Europe. At the same time, however, the mid-1800s marked the beginning of substantial emigration to the United States—people who had grown dissatisfied with religious, political, or economic disadvantage left their homeland in hopes of securing a better or freer life.

The great poet of the new age, Heinrich Heine (*Book of Songs,* 1827), left Germany in 1831 to avoid political repression and lived out his life in Paris as an advocate of liberal and radical ideas. Heine's fellow leader of the outlawed movement, Young Germany, the journalist Ludwig Börne, set both a new German prose style and a rallying point for liberals in his *Briefe aus Paris* (1830–1833). A poet of substantial talent, Georg Herwegh (*Gedichte eines Lebendigen,* 1841), retreated to exile after 1848; so, too, did the talented Ferdinand Freiligrath (*Ein Glaubensbekenntnis,* 1844).

Many novels through the late 1800s found enthusiastic readers in Germany, but none achieved the international appeal of Balzac or Dickens. In the theater, however, the developments were more significant. Early in the century, the work of Heinrich von Kleist (*The Prince of Homburg,* 1821) pointed the way toward the emotional violence of the later period. Franz Grillparzer (*A Dream Is Life,* 1817–1834; *The Jewess of Toledo,* 1855), Georg Büchner (*Danton's Death,* 1835; *Woyzek,* a fragment, published posthumously, 1850), and Friedrich Hebbel (*Judith,* 1840; *Die Nibelungen,* 1862), were all writers of significant influence. The mix of personal emotion, naturalism, and something between daydream and nightmare vision culminated in such later dramatists as Hermann Sudermann (*Die Ehre,* 1889; *Morituri,* 1897) and Gerhart Hauptmann (*The Weavers,* 1892). This theater of alienation juxtaposed outraged decency and triumphant vice in an atmosphere of social or psychological corruption.

The parallel development in music lay in the career of Richard Wagner, whose works (for example, *Der Ring des Nibelungen,* 1853–1874; *Tristan und Isolde,* 1857–1859) mirrored in myth the social agony of the times. Wagner, who wrote his own librettos, had nearly as much influence among writers as among later musicians. His marriage of structural complexity and a half-cranky, half-brilliant sexual egotism served as one of the great building blocks of 20th-century consciousness. Other writers outside the literary fold whose influence was great include Georg Hegel, who set out a philosophical system explaining cultural and national development; Karl Marx, whose reverse Hegelianism gave birth to a radical new social philosophy; Friedrich Nietzsche, whose philosophy of the *Übermensch* (superman) was the ultimate result of Romantic individualism; and psychologist Sigmund Freud, whose studies of the subconscious mind turned later writers inward in still another way.

The societies of Germany and Austria rode a rising economic tide but a declining social one. The generation of writers that would endure the period of world wars (1914–1945) seem often to have abandoned all hope. Frank Wedekind anticipated the tone of elevated self-loathing, usually with a negative sexual component that a certain kind of modernism frequently displays. His plays *Earth Spirit* (1895) and *Pandora's Box* (1903) were later used by the composer Alban Berg for his opera, *Lulu* (1934).

The work of Germany's two major modern lyricists, Stefan George (1868–1933) and Rainer Maria Rilke (*Neue Gedichte* [new poems], 1907–1908;

Duinese Elegies, 1911–1922), shared a similar background in German, French, and classical learning. Rilke seemed to achieve a directness of expression denied anyone else of his time.

As World War I drew near, the tense emotions of its age gave birth to the violent new style called expressionism. By the first year of fighting, three avant-garde expressionists, the poets Ernst Stadler, Georg Trakl, and Georg Heym, had already lost their lives, two in the trenches.

THE WRITINGS OF JAKOB AND WILHELM GRIMM have helped to preserve German stories that may be centuries old.

KARL MARX: An understanding of the writings of Karl Marx is necessary even today in fields such as economics and sociology.

England

The early German Romantics learned from the English. In the late years of the 1700s they repaid the debt. The works of Lessing, Goethe, and Schiller struck a sympathetic chord in England, helping to free aspiring poets from the restrictions of the still-admired rules of neoclassicism.

At the same time, much of the impetus for the English Romantic movement came from within the British Isles.

center
US

centre
Brit.

civilization
US

civilisation
Brit.

Poetry. The first near Romantic, the poet Robert Burns (1759–1796), spoke as a voice of reviving nationalism (*Poems, Chiefly in the Scottish Dialect,* 1786). Burns drew from the Scots' traditions and folklore and proved that a Scot need no longer be Anglicized to write great poetry in English.

Blake. The works of William Blake (1757–1827), whose *Songs of Innocence* appeared in 1789, contained a special kind of visionary independence. Its roots were partly in a tradition of religious mysticism of a deeply individual kind. Blake's later *Prophetic Books* (1793–1804) anticipated the mixture of politics, religion, and individualism that make up much of modern literature. His "high" lyric style had not been heard in England since the age of Milton. But Blake remained all but unheard in his lifetime.

Wordsworth and Coleridge. The real beginning of English Romanticism was the publication of the *Lyrical Ballads* (1798) by William Wordsworth (1770–1850) and Samuel Taylor Coleridge (1772–1834). Wordsworth, the greatest poet of the age, combined a Miltonic dignity with the plain speech and direct feeling of the English countryfolk among whom he had grown up. Coleridge's more polite and more inhibited poems often provided the trigger to Wordsworth's deeper, but slower response.

Byron. George Gordon (Lord) Byron (1788–1824), whose popularity, political involvement, and frequent lapses of taste made him the chief literary celebrity of his day, is perhaps best known for his *Don Juan* (1819–1824), a brilliant comic assertion of wit, sexuality, and physical self-confidence. Byron showed in *The Vision of Judgment* (1822) and a half-dozen lyrics even more concentrated instances of a prodigious and prodigal talent.

Keats and Shelley. John Keats (1795–1821) is probably the best loved lyric poet in the language. The great poems of the end of his life (among them, "Ode to a Nightingale," "Ode on a Grecian Urn," "To Autumn," and "La Belle Dame sans Merci") show a faith in the imagination far in advance of the symbolists. His best poems, along with those of Wordsworth, Byron, and Blake, are with Chaucer, Shakespeare, Milton, and Pope the center of English literary achievement.

Percy Bysshe Shelley (1792–1822) is a possible addition to the other four Romantic masters. Other writers continue to rediscover him, admiring his heroic intellectual conceptions and his mastery of propulsive rhythmic force.

THE NOVEL was the major form of the Victorian era. English novelist Charles Dickens wrote about members of the lower middle class, like Bob Cratchit and Tiny Tim in *A Christmas Carol.*

Almost as swiftly as the Romantic movement began, it ended. With the death of Keats, the high lyric style disappeared. Lesser writers were not of the same inspiration, and the succeeding generation seemed to hear other voices, abandoning the lyric or writing it without conviction.

The novel. Meanwhile, a new age of novelists was approaching. Jane Austen wrote three of her novels in the 1790s but published only after 1810 (*Pride and Prejudice,* 1813; *Mansfield Park,* 1814; *Emma,* 1816). She went to Keats's imaginative church of the open heart but sat at the pew of keen observation and careful structure.

Sir Walter Scott, a Scotsman, became a model for intelligent commercial success all over Europe (*Waverley,* 1814; *Ivanhoe,* 1820). Mary Shelley (*Frankenstein,* 1818) and Maria Edgeworth (*Castle Rackrent,* 1800) extended the daring of women in literature to the portrayal of psychological and social nightmares. In mid-century, an extraordinary trio, Charlotte and Emily Bronte and Elizabeth Gaskell, widened this range still further. George Eliot (Mary Ann Evans) also became a major English novelist (*The Mill on the Floss,* 1860; *Middlemarch,* 1871–1872).

There were to be no English moral giants on the scale of the great French and Russian novelists. Charles Dickens, however (*The Posthumous Papers of the Pickwick Club,* 1836–1837; *David Copperfield,* 1850; *Bleak House,* 1853; *Our Mutual Friend,* 1865; among many others), attained to something at least as

---

WORDSWORTH

These lines from Wordsworth's long poem *The Prelude* show the broad spacious quality of his verse, so new to readers accustomed to the couplets and worldly criticism of the preceding generations.

There was a Boy: ye knew him well, ye cliffs
And islands of Winander!—many a time
At evening, when the earliest stars began
To move along the edges of the hills,
Rising or setting, would he stand alone
Beneath the trees or by the glittering lake.
And there, with fingers interwoven, both hands
Pressed closely palm to palm, and to his mouth
Uplifted, he, as through an instrument,
Blew mimic hootings to the silent owls.
That they might answer him; and they would shout
Across the watery vale, and shout again,
Responsive to his call, with quivering peals,
And long haloos and screams, and echoes loud,
Redoubled and redoubled, concourse wild
Of jocund din; and, when a lengthened pause
Of silence came and baffled his best skill,
Then sometimes, in that silence while he hung
Listening, a gentle shock of mild surprise
Has carried far into his heart the voice
Of mountain torrents; or the visible scene
Would enter unawares into his mind,
With all its solemn imagery, its rocks,
Its woods, and that uncertain heaven, received
Into the bosom of the steady lake.
This Boy was taken from his mates, and died
In childhood, ere he was full twelve years old . . . .

great. He wrote, like the early Wordsworth, with the courage of the decent lower middle class, though of city rather than country folk. Every writer in Europe learned from his broad sympathies, skillful characterizations, and shrewd sense of pace. If he lacked philosophic vision, he made up for it with a stage nearly as broad and all-encompassing as Shakespeare's.

William Makepeace Thackeray, Dickens' contemporary, continued the tradition of 18th-century social satire with a new vitality and a deft hand at well turned and swift moving prose (*Vanity Fair,* 1848; *Henry Esmond,* 1852).

As the century progressed, English writers of fiction who worked at a very high level include George Meredith (*The Ordeal of Richard Feverel,* 1859), Anthony Trollope (the "Barsetshire" novels, 1855–1867), Samuel Butler (*The Way of All Flesh,* 1903), and the remarkable Thomas Hardy (*Tess of the D'Urbervilles,* 1891; *Jude the Obscure,* 1896), also recognized as among the most enduring of English poets.

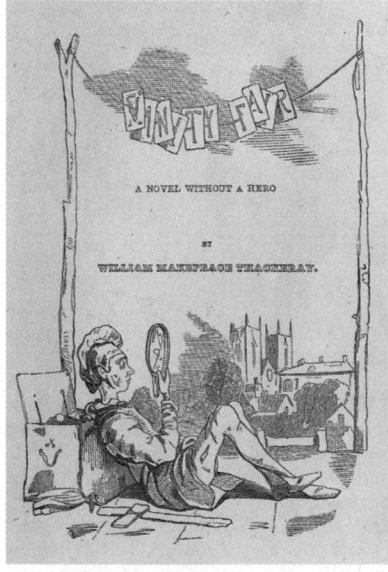

WILLIAM THACKERAY'S *Vanity Fair* featured a drawing by the author on the title page.

Victorian poetry.

Poetry underwent a difficult time after the death of Keats. The large voices among the Victorians belonged to Alfred Tennyson (*Poems,* 1832; *In Memoriam,* 1851; *Idylls of the King,* 1859–1885) and Robert Browning (*Men and Women,* 1855; *The Ring and the Book,* 1868). Both were so preoccupied with the responsibilities of national greatness that their considerable gifts were ultimately betrayed. Tennyson's saving grace is his occasional flight of sober lyric; Browning's is his delight in the sheer variety of life's ironies.

Other interesting, intelligent poets seemed unable to find a sense of identity. They include Matthew Arnold and the gifted friend whose premature elegy he was to write, Arthur Hugh Clough; and the "pre-Raphaelites," a group seeking a supposed medieval spiritual unity; the group included Dante Gabriel Rossetti, William Morris, and Coventry Patmore. Even a few of great promise seemed somehow blocked from fully realizing their gifts. These include Elizabeth Barrett Browning (*Sonnets from the Portuguese,* 1850) and Christina Rossetti (*Goblin Market,* 1862; *A Pageant,* 1881), and the novelist George Meredith (*Modern Love,* 1862).

A. C. Swinburne stands apart from the rest (*Poems and Ballads,* 1866; *Tristram of Lyonesse,* 1882). With him stands Nobel laureate (1907) Rudyard Kipling. Both are too talented to ignore, but impossible, in this age, to take altogether seriously.

Three very private lyricists, however, wrote poems that deeply impressed later generations: the novelist Thomas Hardy (*Wessex Poems,* 1898; and three other collections, to 1928); A. E. Housman (*A Shropshire Lad,* 1896); and the astonishing, and endlessly moving Gerard Manley Hopkins, whose *Poems* was not published until 1918. These three would be adopted by other literary outsiders—Irishmen, Americans, and others—after 1914.

Nonfiction. Developments in poetry and fiction were paralleled in the prose of ideas. The critics and essayists of Wordsworth's age—Coleridge (*Biographia Literaria,* 1817), William Hazlitt (*Table Talk,* 1821–1822), Charles Lamb (*Essays of Elia,* 1823–1833), Thomas De Quincey (*Confessions of an English Opium Eater,* 1821)—introduced a new Rousseauesque point of view and a corresponding psychology of literature.

Class consciousness, and the fears of its consequences, played a part in the prose of the later works of Thomas Carlyle (*Sartor Resartus,* 1833–1834), John Ruskin (*The Stones of Venice,* 1851–1853), and Walter Pater (*Studies in the History of the Renaissance,* 1873; *Marius the Epicurean,* a novel, 1885). These writers did much to advance the historical awareness of the age, but they wrote with such preciosity as to be all but unbearable to many modern readers.

Two other writers, however, the economist and philosopher John Stuart Mill (*On Liberty,* 1859; *Autobiography,* 1873), and the churchman John Henry Newman (*Apologia Pro Vita Sua,* 1864), discovered a remarkable new directness. It is as if each writer had assimilated the Romantic experience to his own purposes. Each, in fact, underwent a substantial crisis of the soul and wrote of it (see box).

The problem of doubt lay very much at the center of the age, and spiritual journeys led to uncertainty rather than to knowledge. Nowhere was this more evident than in the theory of evolution, developed independently by Alfred Russel Wallace and Charles Darwin (*Origin of Species,* 1859). Even Darwin himself might rather have clung to the old certainties rather than accept man's relationship to the animal kingdom.

Matthew Arnold shared the age's sense of uncertainty. In fact, his vision of

the sea of faith ebbing while on the shore "ignorant armies clash by night" ("Dover Beach") exemplifies the pessimism of a civilization past its prime. Yet Arnold did succeed in grasping several conditional articles of faith; even as he doubted, he expressed many of the age's certainties as well. Arnold was also the most perceptive literary critic of the age. His essays provide a summing up for the 1800s, much as Johnson's writings did for his age and Dryden's for his.

Autobiography

A newly popular form in the 1800s was the introspective account of one's own life. Two prominent Englishmen—the priest John Henry Newman and the philosopher John Stuart Mill—wrote extensively about themselves. These short excerpts are descriptions of life crises.

NEWMAN

If I looked in the mirror and did not see my face, I should have the sort of feeling which actually comes upon me, when I look into this living busy world, and see no reflexion of its Creator . . . What shall be said to this heart-piercing, bewildering fact? I can only answer, that either there is no Creator, or this living society of men is in a true sense discarded from His presence.

MILL

It occurred to me to put the question directly to myself. 'Suppose that all your objects in life were realized, that all the changes in institutions and opinions which you are looking forward to, could be completely effected at this very instant: would this be a great joy and happiness to you?' And an irrepressible self-consciousness distinctly answered, 'No!' At this my heart sank within me: the whole foundation on which my life was constructed fell down.

AMERICAN FICTION
in the early 1800s produced memorable characters, from the shy Ichabod Crane in Irving's *The Legend of Sleepy Hollow* to the heroic Natty Bumppo in Cooper's *Deerslayer* novels.

The United States

From the middle of the 1800s on, English literature found itself unexpectedly "twinned"—impressed with, yet confounded by, works from its former colonies in America. The colonies had always had writers, and after 1850, even the "mother country" could not afford to ignore them any more.

As early as 1662, the American poet Michael Wigglesworth was writing that God made man of great potential but that the stubborn creature refused to live up to it. This theme of mixed self-assertion and inadequacy would sound again and again in American letters. James Russell Lowell characterized it in 1848 as "a moral and physical stoop in the shoulders."

Religion, its ordering and its rewards, were the subject of early writings: Anne Bradstreet (c 1612–1672) and Edward Taylor (1642–1729) wrote religious verse in which a certain homeliness of conceit announced the native strain. Roger Williams (*The Bloudy Tenent of Persecution for Cause of Conscience,* 1644) stood out amid the quarrels and chronicles of the first settlers for his wholesale dedication to tolerance and his outrage at its violation.

Substantial writing began with the activities of the Founding Fathers. The works of Thomas Jefferson, Benjamin Franklin, John Adams, and Alexander Hamilton were worthy of note. The universal republican (born an Englishman) Thomas Paine (*Common Sense,* 1776; *The Rights of Man,* 1791–1792; *The Age of Reason,* 1794–1795) was prosecuted in England, imprisoned in France, and abhorred in America for his radical hatred of tyranny. Like Blake, he has always stood for an eloquent but sometimes incoherent individualism.

The Federalist Papers (1786–1788), mainly by Hamilton and James Madison, brilliantly worked out a more conservative but still rugged vision of constitutional, republican government. Thomas Jefferson, whose *A Summary View of the Rights of British America* (1774) established the intellectual grounds for American freedom of political choice, is primarily responsible for the language of the Declaration of Independence. Benjamin Franklin's famous journal, *Poor Richard's Almanack* (1732–1757), like his later *Autobiography,* demonstrates the wide range of interests and penetrating good sense that made Franklin the first of the Americans to win substantial attention abroad. The correspondence of the first years of independence is also fundamental. *The Adams-Jefferson Letters,* for example, include personal letters by Abigail Adams, a testimony to the independent women the brilliant

French critic de Tocqueville would soon call America's chief asset.

1800–1860. Formal literature first reached a high level with the generation of Washington Irving (*Rip Van Winkle* and *The Legend of Sleepy Hollow* in *The Sketch Book of Geoffrey Crayon, Gent.,* 1802–1803) and James Fenimore Cooper *(Leatherstocking Tales,* 1823–1841, which includes *The Last of the Mohicans* and *The Deerslayer).* Irving told fanciful versions of legends that originated with the Dutch and English settlers in New York City and the Hudson River valley. Cooper's stories, which were greatly admired in Europe, were early tales of frontiersmen and the mysterious American Indian. The Massachusetts writers espoused a kind of decency resembling England's Victorian values. Among those associated with this "native" school of poetry were William Cullen Bryant, Henry Wadsworth Longfellow, James Russell Lowell, and John Greenleaf Whittier. All had genuine talent, but their work seems diminished by their choice of bland subjects and decorous styles.

A renegade from this school was Ralph Waldo Emerson, the transcendentalist philosopher who led a group of moral and social reformers. They included Henry David Thoreau, the feminist Margaret Fuller, and the educational theorist Bronson Alcott.

Emerson's *Essays* of 1831 and 1844 earned him popularity and authority. But his greatness lies in his poems ("Ode," "Hamatreya," "The Apology," "Threnody," "Concord Hymn"). Clumsy, over- and under-written at the same time, both agnostic and neck-deep in nonconformist religion, and choked full of beauty, they uncannily prefigure the elements that have distinguished nearly every major American poet since.

Thoreau's *Walden* (1854) is an account of his "retirement" to the wilderness to test his self-reliance and to meditate. It, too, prefigures a whole school of modern writing in support of simple and natural living. Thoreau's earlier essay, "Civil Disobedience," became important to generations of American dissenters.

The 1850s also saw a flowering of genius in fiction. Edgar Allan Poe's eerie stories of crime and the supernatural were perhaps the first American works to have serious influence on European literature. The novelists Nathaniel Hawthorne (*The Scarlet Letter*, 1850) and Herman Melville (*Moby-Dick*, 1851) produced works of great strangeness and considerable imaginative scope.

In poetry one man has come to stand above all others of his generation. In 1855 Walt Whitman published the first edition of *Leaves of Grass*. This collection, considered strange at the time for its free verse forms and most undecorous sexual exuberance, was reissued with additions during the rest of the poet's life. The depth and power of its greatest poems has only grown with time. Among the most famous are "Song of Myself," "Crossing Brooklyn Ferry," "When Lilacs Last in the Dooryard Bloom'd" (an elegy for Abraham Lincoln), and "I Saw in Louisiana a Live-Oak Growing."

In these same years Emily Dickinson (1830–1886) was writing poems of great insight and beauty that would not be published until after her death. Her gifts of metaphor and feeling place her near the very top rank of the world's lyric poets.

1860–1914. The Civil War (1861–1865) demonstrated one more high talent in the deepest speeches of Abraham Lincoln. But the violent conflict also seemed to silence this first great wave of literary inspiration. Not even the inexhaustible Whitman attained his former level afterward.

Certain continuities, however, remained. Americans had always seen themselves first through humor. Early humorous writers often worked by overstatement and broad parody, as seemed to fit the expansive new country. They portrayed sharp New Englanders and drawling frontiersmen for an army of readers who had known few of either at firsthand. During and after the war, this tradition was taken a step further: "Artemus Ward" (Charles F. Browne) and "Petroleum V. Nasby" (David R. Locke) were slick but not unpointed comics.

Another school of writers provided more authentic local color, beginning to characterize the regional differences of the American continent. Bret Harte and Jack London portrayed California and the West; Joel Chandler Harris retold the fables and legends of the black people of the South. Later, Edgar Lee Masters and Sherwood Anderson colored in the Midwest and Willa Cather the Great Plains states.

Still another strain was that of moral outrage and reform. It began before the war in the crusade for the abolition of slavery led by William Lloyd Garrison, Wendell Phillips, John Greenleaf Whittier, Harriet Beecher Stowe (*Uncle Tom's Cabin,* 1852), and Julia Ward Howe ("Battle Hymn of the Republic," 1862).

In the so-called Gilded Age (the 1870s and '80s), as corrupt an era as America has ever known, this movement began as polite dismay, then grew to almost violent reformism as depicted in the work of Ida Tarbell, Lincoln Steffens, Upton Sinclair, and others, to whom President Teddy Roosevelt gave the name "muckrakers."

Mark Twain. All of these elements combined in the work of Mark Twain (Samuel Langhorne Clemens, 1835–1910). His comic sense was sure, his ear for American speech (especially that of his native Missouri) was nearly perfect, and his eye for fraud and moral posturing was uncanny. Twain was an adventurer, and he wrote eloquent accounts of his work on a steamboat (*Life on the Mississippi,* 1883), and as a traveller to the still-desolate West (*Roughing It,* 1872). His first great success in fiction was *The Adventures of Tom Sawyer* (1876), still a classic account of growing up mischievous in a small town. The sequel to *Sawyer,* however, became a more universal classic. *Huckleberry Finn,* the barefoot independent son of the town drunk, is one of the great characters in any literature. He runs away down the Mississippi River in the company of Jim, a runaway slave, the two completely interdependent, and the panorama of a fast-changing America unfolds before them. Huck Finn's emotional self-reliance and his special blend of knowing and innocence appear in American fiction down to the present day.

William Dean Howells became something of a teacher to Twain's generation. His own novels showed a genuine but polite realism. But perhaps his influence was greatest through the effects of his personal friendship and conversation. Among those in his circle were Hamlin Garland; Stephen Crane (*Maggie: A Girl of the Streets,* 1893; *The Red Badge of Courage,* 1895); the economist and social theorist, Thorstein Veblen (*The Theory of the Leisure Class,* 1899); and Twain himself.

Howells' realism was taken to a new level by Theodore Dreiser (*Sister Carrie,* 1900; *An American Tragedy,* 1925), who seemed barely able to write English, yet modulated it beautifully. Dreiser was among the first to write of the underside

MARK TWAIN was the greatest of America's comic writers in the late 1800s.

color *US*
colour *Brit.*

of the American experience: of the price paid for success and the costs of failure. For all his commitment to a sociological view, however, he wrote from the heart and with astonishing perceptiveness.

At the top of the social order, Henry Adams (descendant of Presidents John and John Quincy Adams) looked with shock and disappointment at the politics of the Gilded Age and looked back with longing at the supposed ideal of the Middle Ages. His emotional shellshock and perceptive insight anticipated a mood often expressed by later American intellectuals.

Whitman

Walt Whitman's poetry breaks out of rhyme and metric pattern to become a vehicle for free—yet oddly disciplined—expression.

I saw in Louisiana a live-oak growing,
All alone stood it and the moss hung down from the branches,
Without any companion it grew there uttering joyous leaves
    of dark green,
And its look, rude, unbending, lusty, made me think of myself,
But I wondered how it could utter joyous leaves standing alone
    there without its friend near, for I knew I could not.
And I broke off a twig with a certain number of leaves upon it
    and twined it around a little moss,
And brought it away, and I have placed it in sight in my room,
It is not needed to remind me of my own dear friends,
(For I believe lately I think of little else than of them,)
Yet it remains to me a curious token, it makes me think of
    manly love;
For all that, and though the live-oak glistens there in Louisiana
    solitary in a wide flat space,
Uttering joyous leaves all its life without a friend a lover near,
I know very well I could not.

20 History of Literature

English Internationalism

Swift, Goldsmith, Sheridan, and Burke were Irishmen who had made their mark in English literature. Yet to make such a mark, they had, by necessity, to Anglicize themselves, making England their cultural (if not emotional) home.

In the last quarter of the 1800s, however, Irish nationalism brought the development of a new Irish literature in English. One of the foundations of the new literary movement was the Abbey Theatre, founded by the talented Lady Augusta Gregory. Among the dramatists encouraged by the Abbey were John Millington Synge, whose *Riders to the Sea* (1904) may be the finest one-act play in the language; and Sean O'Casey, whose *Juno and the Paycock* (1924) is a classic study of the greatness and tragedy of the Irish character. Also associated with the Abbey group were the poet A. E. (George Russell) and William Butler Yeats (1865–1939), who was to become the greatest English poet of the century.

Meanwhile, in London a reawakening theater bore two thoroughly Anglicized but basically Irish playwrights: Oscar Wilde (*Lady Windermere's Fan*, 1892; *The Importance of Being Earnest*, 1895) and George Bernard Shaw (*Candida*, 1893; *Major Barbara*, 1905; *Pygmalion*, 1913; *Saint Joan*, 1923). Both Wilde and Shaw were literary sensations in London, in part because of their Irish irreverence in an otherwise decorous literary world. Shaw was undoubtedly the driest wit and one of the great geniuses in the language. He was an important figure, too, for his music and literary

theater
US

theatre
Brit.

criticism and for his successful advocacy of political and social causes in his plays and essays.

Gradually, the literature of the Irish, Americans, and English, began to blend into a new international English tradition. This had begun as early as 1876, when the American-born novelist Henry James (*The Portrait of a Lady*, 1881; *The Bostonians*, 1886; *What Maisie Knew*, 1897; *The Ambassadors*, 1903) settled permanently in London and wrote of a "Eur-America" that was a single interacting society. Polish-born novelist Joseph Conrad (*Heart of Darkness*, 1902; *Nostromo*, 1904; *The Secret Agent*, 1907) became an early example of the writer who excels in a language other than his own mother tongue.

Among the writers of this new internationalism were the American Ezra Pound, whose first book of lyrics, *Personae*, was published in 1909, and who would spend a large part of his life in Europe; T. S. Eliot, born in St. Louis and educated at Harvard, but choosing to live the rest of his life in England (*Prufrock and Other Observations*, poems, 1917); and the English novelist D. H. Lawrence (*Sons and Lovers*, 1913), who would live for years in America. These and later internationalists (W. H. Auden, Vladimir Nabokov) properly belong to the modern period, yet the trend toward one English-speaking tradition was well under way before the modern era began in 1914–1918.

Russia

If American literature was one major new force in the 1800s, Russian literature was the other. The Russians, half European and half Asian, had always stood at the outer edge of the European tradition. Their established church was orthodox, related to the Byzantine and Greek rather than to the Roman Catholic. But two great rulers of the 1700s, Peter and Catherine, had brought the Russian state closer to the European powers. The French language and taste were especially influential—and yet there remained something unique and powerful about the Russian character, a freshness that would be widely recognized and admired by the end of the 1800s.

Early Russian literature lay in the oral tradition of *byliny:* poetic legends mixing heroic figures of the Middle Ages with elements of magic and exotic trappings from Islamic and Mongol sources. Early writings in church Slavonic dealt primarily with religious matters, but included some translations of Western works.

Over the next centuries, westernizers sought to bring Russia into the European mainstream, but some of the best work came from the anti-Europeans. In the autobiography of an outstanding dissenter, the *Life of the Archpriest Avvakum* (1672–1673), the first use of colloquial Russian prose appears. "God

pays no attention to fine speech, but keeps his eye on His business," wrote this old believer, who was burned at the stake for his frankness.

The beginnings of a Russian theater and a poetry modeled on the French appeared in the 1600s. Later, as Enlightenment ideas spread at the court of the czars, the more natural verse of Mikhail V. Lomonosov (1711–1765), a scientist, historian, and humanist, and the realistic satire of the plays of Denis I. Fonvizin (*The Minor*, 1782) brought work of high achievement.

The poet Gavriil R. Derzhavin (1743–1816) wrote elaborately on a classical model. Nikolai M. Karamzin (1766–1826), author of a classic history of Russia, also had great influence through stories and travel letters written in the then-current English "sentimental" form. More prophetically, the same model in the hands of Aleksandr Radishchev (*Journey from St. Petersburg to Moscow*, 1790) earned its author a term in Siberia for its outspoken advocacy of emancipation of the serfs. Ivan A. Krylov (*Fables*, 1809) was a Russian La Fontaine who found in peasant wisdom an escape from the moral and practical restraints imposed by the czarist government.

Pushkin. The event that brought Russia into the European fold once and for all was the invasion and ultimate defeat of Napoleon's armies in 1811–1812. Within a few years, Aleksandr Pushkin (1799–1837) wrote and published works that would become the basis of a modern Russian literature. His major works include the Shakespearean-type tragedy, *Boris Godunov;* the novel *The Captain's Daughter;* a history of a peasant rebellion; and short stories such as the famous "Queen of Spades." Towering above the rest, however, is the verse novel *Eugene Onegin* (1825–1831), the great poetic masterpiece of Russian literature. Pushkin's combination of deep seriousness and lively vitality have been the envy of Russian writers ever since.

The other poets of Pushkin's generation—notably Mikhail Lermontov, Evgeny Baratynsky, Nikolai Yazykov, and Fёdor Tyutchev—also exerted great influence.

A slightly later group of writers explored the possibilities of realism, drawing especially on the experiences of the peasants. This group included Aleksei Tolstoy, Nikolai Nekrasov, and Ivan Nitkin.

In prose, the time was one of intense critical squabbling between westernizers, who favored European forms and attitudes, and "Slavophiles," who stuck to the forms and values of old Russia. The vigorous and original criticism, both social and literary, of Vissarion Grigoryevich Belinsky and Aleksandr Herzen helped turn Russian thought toward the material and moral welfare of all human beings, a social awareness that would deeply influence the 20th century.

OSCAR WILDE'S play *The Importance of Being Earnest* is a satiric look at the British clergy and nobility.

THE INSPECTOR-GENERAL in Gogol's play of that name shouts at the peasants, accusing them of dishonesty, even though he is the dishonest one.

The novel. The Russian novel reflected these social concerns. Nikolai Vasilyevich Gogol (1809–1852) began with affectionate and romantic pieces about peasant and Cossack life. But with the play *The Inspector-General* (1836) and a series of stories including "The Overcoat," he turned his attention to an almost scientific approach to social hypocrisy and poverty. Gogol never accepted easy answers. In *Dead Souls* (1842), his most unforgettable work, the behavior of the sharp operator, Chicherin—who buys lists of dead serfs from unscrupulous landowners, then uses this "property" to gain mortgages from banks—is symbolic at once of greed and of the indomitable human ability to scavenge life from death itself. Gogol was a part of a great movement to reform Russia, particularly to abolish serfdom. The medieval institution of serfdom was finally ended by the czar in 1860, the year before the beginning of America's Civil War.

Among other reformist works, *Oblomov* (1858), by Ivan Goncharov, portrayed the emptiness of the outdated but change-resistant aristocracy. *A Sportsman's Sketches* (1852), by Ivan Turgenev, had great effect in dramatizing the issue of serfdom.

Turgenev of all Russians worked most in the contemporary European manner and spent much of his time abroad. His novel *Fathers and Sons* (1861) is a prototype of the novel of the cultivated but socially alienated man that would dominate European fiction to the present day.

Tolstoy and Dostoevski. The next 20 years saw the publication of works of supreme genius by Fëdor Dostoevski *(Crime and Punishment; The Idiot; The Possessed;* and *The Brothers Karamazov);* and by Leo Tolstoy *(War and Peace; Anna Karenina).* They stand with the efforts of Dickens, Balzac, and a very few others as the major works of modern literature. Each writer developed an extensive moral philosophy. Tolstoy's matured into the nonviolence later preached by Gandhi. Dostoevski's views contributed to 20th-century existentialist thought.

These novels even surpass the writers' abilities to understand themselves. In *War and Peace,* Tolstoy set out with a deeply conservative idea, but wrote of the lives of extraordinary individuals, almost universally in conflict with the spirit of their times. In *The Brothers Karamazov,* Dostoevski intended to write about loss of faith and to follow it with a second novel about its recovery. The sequel never appeared; yet *The Brothers Karamazov* suggests its own kind of faith, even when confronted with every betrayal the world is capable of. The only affirmation is a touching of hands and an impulsive burst of tears at the conclusion. No one who has read this scene has ever forgotten it.

The succeeding generation included the poets of that strange self-criticizing lyric that is called symbolism. Vladimir Soloviev seems to herald the new movement; its most significant members included Andrei Bely and Aleksandr Blok.

Short fiction and drama. In short fiction and the drama, the new generation included Maxim Gorky and Mikhail Artzybashev. The one true inheritor of the vision of Tolstoy and Dostoevski, however, was named Anton Chekhov.

Chekhov. Chekhov was a writer of restrained yet immensely suggestive and evocative short stories and "small" plays. A doctor, he seemed almost scientific in his dissection of the Russian malaise, yet laughter and a kind of joy in human nature keep breaking in. Among his greatest works for the stage are *Uncle Vanya* (1899) and *The Cherry Orchard* (1904).

Chekhov lived at the edge of a new era in Russia. In 1905, the reformers staged an unsuccessful revolt against the czar. In 1917 and 1918, a revolution succeeded, hastened by the stresses of World War I. The next generation, including Anna Akhmatova, Osip Mandelstam, and Boris Pasternak, would carry on the tradition of literary greatness through the years of trial and repression. But their history belongs properly to the age of the moderns.

Eastern Europe

A world of languages and peoples exists between Russia and the West. The literary growth that took place in Czechoslovakia, Poland, and Hungary typifies that of the whole area.

Both Poland and the states that would become Czechoslovakia played major roles in medieval and Renaissance times. Poland's early literature, however, relied on Latin, while Czechoslovakia (then the states of Bohemia and Moravia) developed a vernacular tradition by the 1300s. By the mid-1500s, a vernacular tradition in Polish had at last taken hold.

These early years had been prosperous and powerful for Eastern Europe. But the Thirty Years War in the 1600s decimated the Protestant Czechs, and power politics steadily gnawed at Poland's boundaries and independence. Bohemia substantially lost its identity and its literature. But the Czech language began to revive in the 1700s. Hungarian began to emerge from the shadow of Latin at the same time. Only in the 1900s did the Slovak leader L'udovít Stúr finally provide his people with its own unified literary tongue.

Poland. Of the three nations, Poland had by far the strongest sense of identity. The early 19th century, with its romanticism and nationalism, produced a fervent response from young Polish writers. Four of them, writing chiefly from exile in France, were later to be thought of as fathers of a new Polish literature: the poets Adam Mickiewicz, Juliusz Slowacki, Zygmunt Krasínski, and, though hardly known till after his death, the gifted Cyprian Norwid.

As the century wore on, the first fire waned. A practical, "positivist" approach took over in Warsaw, and Poland produced fine, if less emotional works, from the novelists Boleslaw Prus and Henryk Sienkiewicz (Nobel Prize in Literature, 1905), and the playwright Gabryela Zapolska. Finally, as World War I approached, violent emotion returned, but now in the name of modernism. The dramatist Stanislaw Wyspiánski, the poets Kasimierz Tetmajer and Jan Kasprowicz, and the novelist Wladyslaw Reymont (Nobel Prize for Literature, 1924) all spoke for a free, original, and deeply patriotic literary tradition.

Czechoslovakia. The same years had seen similar advances in the Czech and Slovak tongues. The early 1800s produced the Czech poets Karel Hyneck Mácha and Jan Kollar. Mácha wrote in an international, high literary style of deep melancholy, but Kollar sought something else. A passionate spokesman for pan-Slavism, he became the spiritual father of poetry in the Slovak tongue. Each had followers in the next generation.

The years before World War I saw both a thoroughly modern and a thoroughly heroic literature in the two cousin languages, soon to be combined in one nation by the results of war.

Hungary. In Hungary, stimulated by the remarkable cultural and economic growth of Budapest, the 1800s saw an even more rapid development. Three poets successively dominated the 19th century: Mihahaaly Vörösmarty, Sándor Petöfi, and János Arany. There were several novelists, including the talented Mór Jókai. As World War I approached, a vigorous popular theater produced the internationally successful writers of sophisticated comedy, Ferenc Molnar and Ferenc Herczeg. On another level was the deeply modernist, often intellectual poetry of the literary journals, one of whose representatives, Endre Ady, won a wide European following.

The very fragmentation and competition among the peoples of East Europe seemed in the 1800s to encourage a kind of provincialism. But in the 1900s, under the pressures of war and political repression, the Eastern Europeans would help define their countries' cultural identity and yet produce works of international appeal and influence.

theater
US

theatre
Brit.

Scandinavia

The tradition of the Scandinavian tongues looked back to such medieval figures as the Danish historian Saxo Grammaticus (c 1150–c 1220) and the Swedish religious visionary, St. Bridget (c 1300–1373). Only in the 1700s did true national literatures begin to emerge. Among the pioneers were Norway's Ludvig Holberg (1684–1754), Sweden's Olof von Dalin (1708–1763) and Carl Michael Bellman (1740–1795), and Denmark's Johannes Ewald (1743–1781) and Adam Oehlenschlager (1779–1850). The task that these men had was nothing less than to establish a literary tradition despite the indifference of the cultivated intelligentsia, who looked for literature in French—and later, in the German—language.

The development of a tradition was assisted by two important nonliterary writers. Swedish scientist Emanuel Swedenborg (1688–1772) wrote on subjects ranging from engineering to physiology and psychology. Later he became a philosophical mystic whose speculations have had wide appeal. Carolus Linnaeus (1707–1778) was a botanist

and founder of the modern system of taxonomy; he wrote in a vivid, translucent style.

With the Romantic movement, a new spirit of nationalism encouraged writers in the vernacular. In Norway, newly freed from Danish domination, folk literature studies built the national consciousness (notably in great collections by Jørgen Moe and Peter Christian Asbjørnsen). In Sweden, similar research produced the work of Arvid Afzelius. Denmark produced the most significant figure of all, the educator and writer Nikolai Grundtvig (1783–1872), whose *Northern Mythology* (1808) echoed through all three of these countries.

A fourth Scandinavian literature, that of Finland, was also awakening. Important works appeared both in the Swedish language and in native Finnish. The most notable were the legend-based epic, *King Fjalar* (1844), written in Swedish by Johan Ludvig Runeberg; and the *Kalevala,* written in Finnish, a folk epic dating from the Middle Ages, but only assembled and given formal structure in the mid-1800s, written by two physicians.

From these beginnings, writers of the later 1800s entered the mainstream of European literature. In Denmark, early Romanticism gave way to a sober, reflective period, typified in the verse of Paul Møller and S. S. Blicher. The dominant author and critic of the day, Johan Heiberg (1791–1860), was perhaps most important as the inspiration for new talent. Two of his protégés attained world importance. The philosopher Søren Kierkegaard (1813–1855) defined the passionate relationship of the soul to its belief, influencing what later came to be called existentialism. Hans Christian

Andersen (1805–1875), famous as a writer of fairy tales ("The Fir-Tree," "The Ugly Duckling," "The Emperor's Nightingale"), was one of the first to understand the potential of the imagination as a subtle, independent force.

As the turn of the century approached, in common with the rest of Europe, Denmark found itself moving toward a new aesthetic of realism, led by the famous critic Georg Brandes (*Main Currents in Nineteenth-Century Literature,* 1872–1890). In the new atmosphere, major novelists included Jens Jacobsen and Henrik Pontoppidan (*The Promised Land,* 1891–1895; *Kingdom of the Dead,* 1912–1916), the poet Holger Drachmann, the later proletarian novelist Martin Andersen Nexø, and the productive and imaginative Johannes Jensen.

In Norway, an equivalent tradition of realistic self-analysis was anticipated in *The Governor's Daughters* (1854–1855), by Camilla Collett, whose publication shocked the Norwegian public. This tradition culminated in the work of Nobel Prize winners Knut Hamsun (1859–1952) and Sigrid Undset (1882–1949).

Ibsen and Strindberg. Of greatest world impact, however, were the dramas of Björnstjerne Björnson and Henrik Ibsen. A fine novelist and poet, Björnson began with epic drama but reached his peak in works that dealt with the problems of a slowly modernizing Norway (*Beyond Our Power,* a drama in two parts, 1883–1895). He was a Nobel Prize winner in 1903.

Henrik Ibsen (1828–1906) stands, with Chekhov and Shaw, among the greatest of modern playwrights. From romantic drama (*Brand,* 1866; *Peer Gynt,* 1867), through the most innova-

IBSEN AND STRINDBERG, Scandinavian giants of the modern theater, agreed only on their dark, pessimistic view of life.

tive realism (*A Doll's House,* 1879; *The Wild Duck,* 1884; *Hedda Gabler,* 1890), to a deep symbolism (*When We Dead Awaken,* 1900), he showed a rare gift for the expression of universal concerns. Ibsen had a special feeling, too, for the problems of women. At the same time, he felt little identity with his countrymen and spent most of his time abroad.

In Sweden, after a first fine burst of Romantic poets (such as Erik Geijer and Esaias Tegnér), writing turned to issues and problems. Women's rights were covered in the work of novelist and journalist Frederika Bremer. A surprising backlash of misogyny appeared in the work of talented Carl Almquist. And an iconoclastic attack on Christian orthodoxy was apparent in the writings of Abraham Rydberg.

With the coming of Johan August Strindberg (1849–1912), however, Sweden found something rather more urgent. This unpleasant but unmistakable genius was master of the entire sequence of styles from realism to expressionism. The novel *The Red Room* (1879), and such plays as *The Father* (1887), *Miss Julie* (1888), *The Dream Play* (1902), and *The Ghost Sonata* (1907), have a sweep and force that is utterly convincing.

After Strindberg, Sweden saw a literature of individuals, not movements. The poets Verner von Heidenstam (Nobel Prize, 1916), Gustaf Fröding, and Erik A. Karlfeldt (Nobel Prize, 1931), and the novelists Selma Lagerlöf (the first woman to receive the Nobel Prize, 1909) and Hjalmar Söderberg, especially stand out.

Something of the vigor of this period was communicated, too, to the former possession, Finland. Writing in Swedish, the popular novelist Zachris Topelius, the politically radical Arvid Mörne, and the poet Jarl Hemmer especially distinguished the century since Finnish independence. The free-verse poet Edith Södergran and the prose writer Runar Schildt lent a special modernity to the decade after World War I. In Finnish, the 19th century's leading writers were the novelist Alexis Kivi (Stenvall) (*The Seven Brothers,* 1870) and the feminist playwright Minna Canth. In modern times Finland produced Nobel Prize winner F. E. Sillanpää (*Fallen Asleep While Young,* 1931), the poet Eino Leino, and the mid-20th-century novelists Mika Waltari and Väinö Linna.

France

The development of French literature after the French Revolution followed a singular path. The early Romanticism of Germany and England were not picked up by the French, who were caught in the turmoil of revolution (1789), the Reign of Terror (1793–1794), and the imperial exertions of Napoleon (ending in 1815). A literary reawakening was delayed, but when it came, after 1815, it was to have great impact.

The novel. The post-Napoleonic age was one of titans in French fiction. By mid-century France had produced four of the world's great novelists—Victor Hugo (1802–1885), Honoré de Balzac (1799–1850), Stendhal (1783–1842), and Gustave Flaubert (1821–1880).

Hugo began with poetry and drama. His genius for heroic and sentimental verse is difficult to appreciate today, though Americans hear a similar note in the poetry of Walt Whitman. His play *Hernani* (1830) was one of the great landmarks of the century—and a scandal to its first audience, announcing as it did the end of the classic restraints on French drama. His great novel, *Les Misérables* (1862), was written in the romantic mode of Sir Walter Scott and of Alexandre Dumas *pere* (*The Three Musketeers,* 1844), but extends and broadens it.

Balzac's great interlinked series of novels and short stories, under the overall title *La Comedie Humaine,* "jumpcuts" characters and events. Balzac catches the moral dilemma of his materialistic society by exposing its double standards mercilessly. The occasional roughness of his technique becomes a part of the overall surface, like the graininess of a very high speed photograph.

Stendhal (*The Red and the Black,* 1831), and Flaubert (*Madame Bovary,* 1856), use a slower film, but with extremely daring subjects—adultery, female sexuality, frustrated ambitions, murder—with a seriousness that anticipates the fiction of the present century.

Drama. After Hugo's *Hernani,* the theater held much of the early excitement of Romanticism, but poetry claimed the larger talents. Hugo's own lyrics stand alone. But a host of others, including Alfred de Musset, Auguste Barbier, Alfred de Vigny, Gerard de Nerval, and Théophile Gautier brought lyricism in French poetry back to exuberant life.

By mid-century, the theater turned from serious subjects to farce, situation plays, and sentimental romance. These remain models for popular theater and films to the present day. The plays of the younger Dumas (*La Dame aux Camélias,* 1852) and Edmond Rostand (*Cyrano de Bergerac,* 1897) reveal the sentimental at its most popular.

Poetry. Poetry alone refused to give up its deep emotion and high seriousness. Charles Baudelaire (*Les Fleurs du Mal,* 1857) introduced a new ethic for the poet, working for the sake of ultimate truth—or beauty—alone, without reference to social concerns or conventions. Many others followed his example, attracted by the moral freedom his stand seemed to offer. The poems are often beautiful, but the cost of producing them was high. Arthur Rimbaud, the most prodigiously gifted of his generation (*Le Bateau Ivre, Les Illuminations),* found the emotional strains unbearable and lapsed into silence. Others who felt

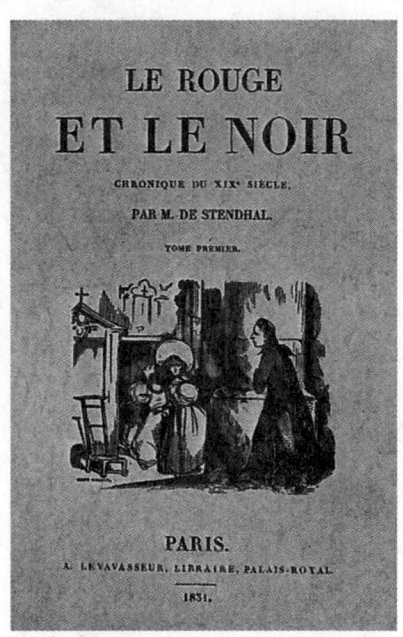

the strains were Paul Verlaine, Rimbaud's destroying and self-destructive friend; Stéphane Mallarmé, whose verbal ingenuity points the way to the Joyce of *Finnegans Wake;* Jules Laforgue, self-effacing in his best work nearly to the point of invisibility; and Charles Péguy, as stubborn in virtue as the others in diffidence or vice. To these men, the contrary roles of sinner and saint were somehow at one in the poet, who became a hero of sorts in the battle for men's souls.

Later novels. Novels, too, changed their style and path over the years, though to a greater extent than poetry, they kept their central role as public entertainment first, public statement second. George Sand (1804–1876), a woman of great influence on her age, progressed to a fiercely feminist concern with social problems of every description (*The Haunted Pool,* 1846; *Les Maitres Sonneurs,* 1853). Alphonse Daudet, the brothers Edmond and Jules Goncourt, and the extremely influential Émile Zola (whose major work was a 20-novel study of a family's dissolution) together developed what Zola called a "scientific" naturalism. Successors included the very successful Guy de Maupassant.

The lifting of naturalism to the level of high art, however, was left to Marcel Proust (1871–1922). At the beginning of *À la Recherche du Temps Perdu* (literally, "in search of lost time," but translated as *Remembrance of Things Past*), written largely before World War I, a vast flow of feelings and reminiscences begins with the remembered taste of a *madeleine,* a kind of polite macaroon, in childhood. The book ends with an elaborate but joyless party, symbolic of a society that has left its best days behind. Between beginning and end, Proust creates a world of simple sense experience that somehow comes to exemplify nearly all knowledge and feeling, including the reader's own.

Criticism. Among the many major critics of the century, Charles Sainte-Beuve (1804–1869), and the later Hippolyte Taine (1828–1893), exhibited, though in different ways, a characteristically French mode of thinking. Both sought explanations for events—and literary works—in the conditioning that produced the man or the nation. One of the early studies of a national personality was that of Alexis de Tocqueville (1805–1859), whose observations on America and Americans in *Democracy in America* (1835) seem still valid almost 170 years later.

Spain and Spanish-America

Spanish literature began to stir soon after 1833, when a turn toward political liberalism made possible the return of exiles who knew European Romanticism at first hand. Early expressions included sharp sketches by Mariano José de Larra and the poetry of José de Espronceda.

A wakening in the theater began with *Don Álvaro* (1835) by Ángel de Saavedra, and continued for about a decade. A generation later, major poets

ALEXIS DE TOCQUEVILLE'S *Democracy in America* analyzed American political and social institutions.

appeared, including Gustavo Bécquer and the remarkable Rosalía de Castro.

Beginning in the last quarter of the 1800s, Spanish novelists slowly developed a kind of realism. Notable examples include Pedro Antonio de Alarcón's *The Three-Cornered Hat* (1874), Armando Palacio Valdés's *The Joy of Captain Ribot* (1889) and *La aldea perdida* (*The Lost Village,* 1911), and Vicente Blasco Ibáñez's uncharacteristic, but world-famous war novel, *The Four Horsemen of the Apocalypse* (1916). The period produced a Nobel Prize winner in the occasionally inspired playwright José Echegaray. The energetic novelist Benito Pérez Galdós (1843–1920) wrote vast sequences of popular history, attempting to wake his people to some sense of their own past.

Like England, Spain also faced the pleasures and pains of dealing with its younger literary "twin"—Spanish America. Hispanic Americans had been writing since the gifted lyrics of the Mexican nun and feminist intellectual, Juana Inés de la Cruz (1651–1695). But true Latin American literary identity did not begin until the revolutionary ferment of the 1800s.

The experience of Andrés Bello, tutor to the great liberator of South America, Simón Bolívar, was in many ways typical of the life of Latin-American writers to this day. He spent years travelling back and forth between Europe and his native Venezuela, and eventually made a career as an educator in Chile. His poetry was based on European models, but its life stemmed from the new continent it described (*Silva a la Agricultura de la Zona Torrida,* 1826). Writers of the next generation often travelled as exiles, avoiding unstable (and often dangerous) political upheavals. The exiled Cuban poet José María Heredia, for example, published in New York and lived out his years in Mexico. The poet Esteban Echeverría and the novelist José Mármol (*Amalia,* 1851–1855), were both exiles to Uruguay from Argentina. Still later, the poet and novelist Jorge Isaacs (*María,* 1867) was driven from his Colombian plantation by civil war.

From the beginning, politics, personality, and regionalism were inextricably mixed. At mid-century, Domingo Sarmiento, in exile from Argentina (but later to become its president), wrote a classic study of tyranny by charisma, *Facundo* (1845). Others who made major careers out of the politics of reform were Ecuador's Juan Montalvo, Puerto Rico's Eugenio María de Hostos, and Peru's Manuel González Prada. Regional writing explored the worlds of the Argentine gaucho (notably, the epic *Martin Fierro,* 1872–1879, by José Hernández), and of the Peruvian past in the half-fictional historical "anecdotes" of Ricardo Palma. A rising sense of class consciousness began what would become a great literary exploration of the differences between native and European, rich and poor. Representative

works are a bitter novel about Chile's ruling class, *Martin Rivas* (1832), by Alberto Blest Gana, and *Cumandá* (1871), by Juan León Mera, about the Ecuadorian Indians.

Modernismo. Late in the 1800s, a new lyric voice was heard in the Americas. The hero of the cause of Cuban independence, José Martí, whose exile took him not only to Spain, but to New York City as well, wrote a substantial body of lyric (*Ismaelillo,* 1882). Once and for all, Martí broke completely with the stilted Spanish "classical" style, proving as much a literary as a political revolutionary. At the same time, many others were making the break, including Julian del Casal (Cuba), Salvador Díaz Mirón (Mexico), the remarkable José Asunción Silva (Colombia), and Manuel Nájera Gutiérrez (Mexico). The revolution was completed with the first book by a precocious poetic genius, the Nicaraguan Rubén Darío (*Azul,* 1888). Darío drew from the French of Baudelaire and Verlaine, but also owed much to the North Americans Whitman and Poe. The new style was called *modernismo,* and the word would echo through the first half of the 1900s.

The new writers' self-assertion ended forever Latin America's inferiority complex before the older European work. Darío excited the writers in Spain as deeply as he did those located in the Americas.

A decade later, the United States humiliatingly defeated Spain in the Spanish-American War. This provided a sharper break between the mother country and her former colonies. The Latin Americans continued to follow *modernismo.* Spain claimed Darío too, but as the source of quite a different movement. Later called "The Generation of '98," it included Spain's most celebrated minds of the time—the social thinker Ángel Ganivet; critic and moral philosopher Miguel de Unamuno (*The Tragic Sense of Life in Men and Nations,* 1913); novelist and playwright Ramon del Valle Inclán; outspoken novelist of poverty and political action, Pío Baroja (*La Lucha por la Vida,* a trilogy, 1904); essayist José Martinez Ruiz (known as "Azorin"); and playwright and Nobel Prize winner Jacinto Benavente y Martínez (*Bonds of Interest,* 1907; *The Passion Flower,* 1913). Darío himself, whether in European or American persona, continued to grow in achievement until his death in 1916.

In Latin America after Darío's death, the next movement, called *Criollismo,* sought Latin American solidarity in its unique racial mix: native Indian, European, and African.

The American Spain, with its growing population, vigor, and potential wealth, now had uniquely original literary quality. The European parent drew from this discovery a sense of new life. In the 1900s, the revival would produce, in both Spains, work in the forefront of world literature.

Modern World Literature

The literature of the modern era was deeply influenced not only by literary fashion but by world events. Among these, two were of incalculable importance. One was the awakening of the East. The European world order that had been established in 1815 at the end of the Napoleonic wars had remained in place through the 1800s. But in the early years of the 1900s, it was made obsolete by the growing power and influence of countries outside its plan. The most important of these in the beginning was Japan, though as the century progressed, the shadow of China, a state composed of nearly a quarter of mankind, loomed larger and larger.

The second world development that deeply influenced literature was the establishment of modern totalitarian states. The growth of Hitler's Nazi Party in Germany and its eventual attempt to obliterate whole segments of the population—Slavs, gypsies, Jews—reminded all men of goodwill of the thin line between civilization and savagery. In the very same years, the Stalinist terror in the Soviet Union, often aimed at writers and intellectuals, duplicated the Nazi evil under a different creed. The apparatus of modern tyranny—secret police, torture, concentration camps, forced labor—was later adopted in many parts of the developing world, particularly in South America, parts of Africa, and Southeast Asia.

Writers responded to the physical and emotional violence of the century with a new voice. The Victorian age had replaced religious faith with scientific certainty. Now that prop—and faith in man's ability to act reasonably—had also failed. Twentieth-century writers were often grim and disillusioned. At the same time, their works became symbols of the human impulse to resist, to subvert, and to survive even the most unspeakable evils.

In countries less touched by violent change, the winds of modernism continued to blow strong. With its emphasis on the interior life of the individual—and the potential there for violence as well as pleasure—modernism seemed to reflect many of the same attitudes expressed by the dissenting writers under totalitarianism. For many, modernism offered a necessary sanctuary from the horrors of world affairs—an interior, personal space where life could go on even in the midst of violence and repression.

Asia

The beginning of a new relationship between East and West begins with the victory of Japan in the Russo-Japanese War (1905) and with the establishment of the first Chinese republic in 1912. The roots of these developments lie in the late 1800s, however.

Japan. After a long period of isolation, Japan was opened once again to the outside world by an American naval officer, Matthew C. Perry, in 1854; in 1868 the Meiji restoration signaled Japan's reawakening. In literature, this meant an acceleration of translations and imitations of Western dramatic and fictional forms. The ancient literary form of the language was replaced by the vernacular at the urging of critic Shoyo Tsubouchi. The first major novel to follow this innovation was *Ukigumo* (1887–1889) by Shimei Futabatei.

Traditional Japanese fiction had had erotic (even pornographic) elements and portrayed the picaresque adventures of underworld characters. The Western works most admired by the Japanese encouraged the continuation of these elements. But the Western models also introduced a new sense of individualism and encouraged a questioning of social and political establishments.

Important writers prior to World War II included the poet Toson Shimazaki and the novelists Sosecki Natsume and Junichiro Tanizaki. Perhaps the best-known work in the West was *Rashomon,* a story told from several points of view, by novelist Ryunosuke Akutagawa.

After the defeat of the Japanese in World War II, a new generation of writers came to world attention. They included the Nobel Prize–winning novelist Yasunari Kawabata (1899–1972), his close friend Yukio Mishima (1925–1970), and Kobo Abe (*Woman in the Dunes,* 1964). All three attempted to deal with Japan's sudden emergence into the modern world and the destruction of its older traditions. They seemed disillusioned with modern Japan and reflected the tensions of the earth-shaking changes that the Japanese nation was experiencing. Both Kawabata and Mishima committed suicide.

The same sense of disillusionment was reflected in more recent novels. *Nights of a Fool* (1979) by So Aono, for example, is a tale of failed youthful rebellion involving both drugs and sex. It is familiar to Western readers, yet has particular poignance in its Japanese setting, where old traditions die hard.

China. There are fewer works known to the West from Chinese writers in this century, yet China's literature, too, is entering the international mainstream. The adoption of a vernacular and revitalization of intellectual life was begun with the May Fourth Movement in 1919. The philosopher Hu Shih, who was educated in the United States, played a major role in the movement.

Among the writers of stature in the first half of the century were Lu Hsün (1881–1936) and Ch'ien Chung-shu, author of the complex and appealing novel *Fortress Besieged* (1946).

Throughout Chinese history, literature had been enlisted in the working of political and social ends. With the victory of Chinese Communism, it retained this role, focusing much of the controversy during the Cultural Revolution of the 1970s.

Even in propagandist works, however, the marks of modern sensibilities have begun to appear. The technique, the acceptance of internal psychological development, and the emphasis on the development of character all owe something to Western influence (as does the Marxism of China's political leaders). Among the works reflecting these modern preoccupations are *Mountain Swallow* (1977) by Yang Tach'un and *A Place for Love* (1979) by Liu Hsin-Wu.

The interchange between China and the rest of the world seems destined to increase in the coming years, and will likely have great influence both on the East and the West.

civilization
US

civilisation
Brit.

labor
US

labour
Brit.

AMERICAN NAVAL OFFICER
Matthew Perry facilitated Japan's reopening to the outside world.

20 **History of Literature**

Islam. At the other geographic end of Asia (and extending through the Arabian Peninsula and North Africa), the Islamic nations seem to be nearing a period of renewed flowering and international influence. Dominated in the early century by Western nations searching for oil and other commodities, the Muslims reacted with an intense cultural conservatism. Yet they have been deeply influenced by world events, experiencing both the violence of war and the displacement, and a sudden prosperity and feeling of cultural identity.

Important writers of the early 1900s included Persia's poet of emancipation, Iradj, who contributed to the establishment of the modern nation of Iran and even advocated the emancipation of women; the novelist Sadegh Hedayet, also Iranian; the Egyptians Ahmad Shawqi and Hafiz Ibrahim; and the Turkish short story writer Mahmud Tymur.

In the second half of the century, one of the major events in the Islamic consciousness was the permanent establishment of the state of Israel, which displaced the Muslim Palestinians. The modern Palestinian poet 'Aqi expressed his wistful sense of loss in "On One Single Night." In this poem he personified his own and his people's experiences in the memory of a woman's face and the voices of children far away. Other Palestinians gave voice to more militant sentiments. Mahmud Darwish, for example, wrote that hammers in the hands of workers and guns in the hands of fighters are the only roses he wants to see.

Other important Muslim writers, reflecting in varying degrees the old traditions of Islam and the new sensibilities of this century, are the novelist of Egypt's national aspirations, Najib Mafuz; and the Algerian novelist Khateb Yassin, who brings to Arabic the influence of modern French symbolism.

The Islamic literatures have made little impression on the modern West, but the increasing importance of Islamic countries to the world economy seems certain to bring them greater influence in the years to come.

Literature of Judaism

The story of the Jews has a peculiar place in the history of the 20th century. It is a story filled with contradictions and tragedy.

From the destruction of the Temple at Jerusalem by the Romans in A.D. 70, the Jews were dispersed to many parts of the world. In the Middle Ages, communities could be found in Christian Europe, in Islamic North Africa and Spain, and as far away as India.

The Jews stubbornly retained their separate identity wherever they settled, thanks in part to the preservation of Hebrew, the language of their Scriptures. At the same time, however, they

JEWISH LIFE has been portrayed onstage in such plays as *Fiddler on the Roof*, which was based on Aleichem's novel *Tevye's Daughters*.

made major contributions to the learning and literatures of other peoples. In Islamic Spain, for example, Jewish intellectuals wrote poetry in Hebrew and Spanish and philosophy in Arabic. The philosopher Maimonides (*Guide for the Perplexed,* 1190) served as a spokesman for his entire age.

At the end of the Middle Ages, a period of persecution dispersed the Jews once again, and they turned inward. Where they found tolerance, they continued to contribute to the secular tradition. But where persecution continued, as in Eastern Europe, religious orthodoxy and a new Jewish mysticism absorbed the energy of writers and philosophers. One of the mystical reactions to orthodoxy resulted in the birth of Hasidism, an emotional and joyful but intensely separatist movement that survives to the present day.

A new secularism among the Jews in Germany is of more interest in a literary sense. The German humanist Moses Mendelssohn (1729–1786) had an important influence on early German Romanticism. At the same time, he was a major figure in the Haskalah, the Jewish Enlightenment that produced both the religious tradition of Reform Judaism, which is more open to developments in the secular and non-Jewish worlds, and the beginning of a secular literature both in Hebrew and in Yiddish, the vernacular of Eastern European Jews. Although linguistically related to German, Yiddish was written in traditional Hebrew characters. Israel Axenfeld, I. M. Dick, and I. B. Levinson were among those who began traditions of fiction and drama in Yiddish during the early 1800s.

Major writers in Hebrew during the century included the Italian "Jewish supremacist" S. D. Luzzatto, and a host of poets and novelists in Russia, including Judah Leon Gordon, famous for the purity and beauty of his language, and the novelist Mendele mocher sforim (S. Y. Abramovich). Like many Jewish writers, Mendele wrote both in Hebrew and Yiddish and often translated his stories from one language to the other.

Later in the century, in Poland, the Polish poet and novelist Isaac Loeb Peretz developed a major Yiddish tradition of stories about small local Jewish communities (*Stories and Pictures,* 1900–1901). His contemporary, Sholom Aleichem, eventually emigrated to the United States, and gradually won audiences in every major language. His novel *Tevye's Daughters* (translated 1949) became the basis of the Broadway musical *Fiddler on the Roof.*

The 1900s brought immense changes to the world community of Jews. Early in the century, an unprecedented wave of immigration made New York City a capital of world Judaism, thanks in part to the persecution of Jews in Eastern Europe. With the birth of Nazism in Germany in the 1920s and 1930s, the persecutions of earlier decades seemed pale by comparison. One of every three Jews alive at the time died at the hands of the Nazis between 1938 and 1945. Millions of others were driven from Europe, settling in North America, South America, and eventually in the newly established state of Israel.

Long before Israel was established, Jews had begun to return to their historic homeland. The social philosopher Asher Ginzberg (1856–1927) and the poet Hayyim Nahman Bialik (1873–1934) established themselves in Palestine and helped create a modern Hebrew language and style.

Among other early writers in the new Israel were Saul Tchernihovsky, a poet of great gifts, and Rachel (Rachel Blovstein), a lyric poet whose work shows an uncommon simplicity and grace. The next younger generation included Abraham Shlonsky, Leah Goldberg, and others. Shmuel Y. Agnon won the Nobel Prize for Literature in 1966. Israeli writers of the 1960s and '70s included Moshe Shamir, Amos Oz, A. Appelfeld, and S. Yizhar.

In Yiddish, important works were produced both in Israel and in the United States. The 1978 Nobel laureate was Isaac Bashevis Singer, an American whose stories first appeared in a Yiddish newspaper in New York; they were eventually translated into English and other languages. The stories were mainly about Singer's early life in the ghetto communities of Poland, but others took place in New York, Florida, Argentina, and Israel, reflecting the new dispersion—and internationalism—of the Jewish community. Other novelists, short story writers, and poets continued to write in Yiddish, although most were less prominent outside their own language.

One vital tradition of modern Jewish literature has been in the accumulation of personal histories from the Holocaust—the attempted eradication of the Jews by the Nazis. Thousands of personal accounts and analyses have appeared, yet the documentation continues to grow—a record unique in world literature in its attempt to comprehend catastrophic events through the most minute details of individual experience.

Literature of Dissent

The Soviet Union. The revolution struck at a moment of great literary ferment. Among writers, many welcomed the change, but some would soon recoil in horror as the new system hardened into tyranny; others fled Russia and lived out their lives in obscurity, cut off from their mother tongue and countrymen.

Among the émigrés were poets Konstantin Balmont, V. I. Ivanov, and Ivan A. Bunin, a master of Russian prose who won the Nobel Prize in 1933. (Another in this group was Vladimir Nabokov, who would one day win fame as a writer in English.)

THE LOWER DEPTHS, by Maxim Gorky, starred the great actor and theorist Constantin Stanislavsky at its first performance in Moscow.

Those who stayed faced years of great uncertainty. Novelist and dramatist Maxim Gorky (1868–1936) prospered during the excitement of the early 1920s; but as the party line on literary style hardened, he was forced into the narrow mold of "socialist realism" and squandered his great talent.

The poets Sergei Yesenin and Vladimir Mayakovsky both won great fame as supporters of the new regime of Lenin. But within a few years, they rejected the terrifying excesses of the new system. Marina Tsvetayeva, an astonishingly pure lyric talent, emigrated at the beginning of the revolution, but returned, unable to bear the loneliness of exile. The life of Stalinist Russia proved to be no more tolerable. She—and both Yesenin and Mayakovsky—were suicides.

Perhaps the greatest poet of the period was Osip Mandelstam, an intellectual whose lyrics look back to Pushkin and forward to the modern poets of Europe. Along with Isaac Babel, who celebrated the early revolutionary times with a mixture of Jewish humor and Cossack adventure, Mandelstam died in a labor camp. Both were victims of one of Stalin's many purges, which especially singled out writers of Jewish descent.

This tragic list of defections, suicides, and labor camp deaths is also a list of some of the century's greatest literary talents. The two finest writers who survived did so by remaining officially silent. The poet and novelist Boris Pasternak devoted most of his official time to translation. He and his gifted friend, Anna Akhmatova, continued to write privately, however, and to share their work with a small circle of trusted friends. Pasternak's novel *Doctor Zhivago* was smuggled out of the Soviet Union and published in Paris in 1957. He was awarded the Nobel Prize, but his government would not allow him to accept it.

IVAN DENISOVICH, the labor camp prisoner of Solzhenitsyn's novel, was played by Tom Courtenay in the film version.

Other writers survived after a fashion by choosing noncontroversial subjects for their novels and poetry. Stories of war (*Armored Train 14–69,* V. V. Ivanov, 1923) or revolution (*The Silent Don,* Mikhail Sholokhov, 1928–1940) were especially popular.

During the 1930s, the period of Stalin's mass purges, writers were subjected to particularly stringent controls, and it seemed that the vitality of Russian literature might be snuffed out once and for all by death and intimidation. After World War II, however, a new period of creativity began.

Memories of the heroic Soviet effort during the recent war served some writers with material for a lifetime (for example, *Days and Nights* by Konstantin Simonov, 1945, an epic of the defense of Stalingrad). Then the death of Stalin in 1953 brought a relaxation of the state's standards for writers, and a tenuous alliance was formed between established literary personalities (Ilya Ehrenburg and Aleksandr Tvardovsky, editor of an official literary magazine), young writers ambitious to extend the role of literature (Yevgeny Yevtushenko, Andrei Voznesensky, and others), and older critics of the Soviet system who had not dared speak in Stalinist times.

The most notable among this last group was Aleksandr Solzhenitsyn. After serving as an officer in World War II, Solzhenitsyn was arrested by the secret police. He served a term in the Soviet labor camps, and survived a bout with an often fatal type of cancer. The major achievement of "the thaw" in Soviet literary censorship was the publication of Solzhenitsyn's *One Day in the Life of Ivan Denisovich* (1962), thanks in part to the support of Tvardovsky. The book is a factual yet ironic account of a prisoner's day in a labor camp, and it brought the subject to the attention of Russian readers for the first time.

labor
US

labour
Brit.

20 History of Literature

The thaw was short-lived, however. None of Solzhenitsyn's other major works was ever published officially in the Soviet Union. The novels *The First Circle* (1964) and *Cancer Ward* (1966), and the long nonfiction documentary of the labor camp system, *The Gulag Archipelago* (1973–1976), were circulated secretly in typescript and finally smuggled to the West, where they were published both in Russian and in translation. Publication of the first volumes of *Gulag* earned Solzhenitsyn both a Nobel Prize and exile from his native land. He settled in the United States, living there until his return to Russia in 1994.

Solzhenitsyn's daring was followed by an extraordinary group of dissenters who risked imprisonment or exile to publish according to their own lights, most often in *samizdat* (literally "self-publishing," meaning that the works were read only secretly in typescript). Among those whose works found their way to publication in the West were the remarkable poet Joseph Brodsky, critic Andrei Sinyavsky, satirist Aleksandr Zinoviev (*The Yawning Heights,* 1979), and the recorder of prison camp life (and inspiration of Solzhenitsyn's *Gulag*) Varlam Shalamov (*Kolyma Tales,* 1978).

Eastern Europe.
The experience of writers in the countries of Eastern Europe came to resemble that of the Soviets after World War II, but their earlier histories depend on their own national fortunes.

Poland.
Poland regained its independence in the treaty ending World War I, and its writers embarked on a vigorous literary revival that owed much to the modernist ideas of Western Europe. Outstanding among the new Polish writers were members of the Skamander group, led by poets Kasimierz Wierzyński and Julian Tuwim. Wierzyński's career followed the fortunes of the nation well into modern times. During the Great Depression of the 1930s, he turned to social criticism. In 1944, he wrote a moving narrative of his wartime experience (the Poles were invaded by Germany in 1939 and were occupied throughout the war). After the takeover of Poland by a Communist government controlled by the Soviet Union, Wierzyński emigrated, but continued to write with conviction from abroad.

In the years after the war, Polish writers faced many of the moral challenges and physical dangers shared by writers in the Soviet Union. Among the works of particular distinction were the short stories of Tadeusz Borowski, who had survived a stay at the concentration camp at Auschwitz, and the novel *Ashes and Diamonds* (1948) by Jerzy Andrzejewski, which marked the beginning of a distinguished and morally independent career.

After the Soviet repression of neighboring Czechoslovakia in 1968, many Polish writers chose to emigrate. Others stayed, preferring to press for the relaxation of literary control or to wait for a change in political conditions. Among

those who stayed and those who left, a remarkably high standard was maintained, and hope persisted that one day the groups would be reunited. During the political crises of 1981, in which the Poles again reached for more independence, the great exiled poet Czeslaw Milosz (Nobel Prize, 1981) returned for the first time since 1953. He found that unofficial publication of his work made it familiar to Polish readers, just as he was familiar by similar means with the younger poets working in Poland.

Czechoslovakia and Hungary.
In a sense, these countries were formed by the Treaty of Versailles after World War I. In a brief period of independence between the wars, both established literatures of international stature.

In Czechoslovakia, the plays and novels of Karel Capek (*R.U.R.,* 1920, a futuristic play in which he coined the word "robot") were performed; they soon received international attention through translation. The novel *The Good Soldier Schweik* (1920–1923) by Jaroslav Haahasek was a wry portrait of the new nation's character.

Most remarkable of all was the work of Franz Kafka. Born in Prague of German Jewish parents, Kafka wrote in German about the frightening moral deracination of his time (*The Trial,* 1925; *The Castle,* 1926). His nightmarelike stories exerted wide influence on European letters, catching the mood of frustration and helplessness that gripped much of the war-torn Continent.

In Hungary, major figures included the poets Attila József, Miklós Radnóti (who died in a Nazi concentration camp), and Gyula Illyés; the novelists Pál Szabó and Lajos Zihaly; and the dramatist László Németh.

In the period of postwar Communist rule in Eastern Europe, neither Czechoslovakia nor Hungary was as successful as Poland in maintaining an atmosphere conducive to literature. Revolts were put down violently by Soviet forces in Hungary in 1956 and in Czechoslovakia in

MANY OF FRANZ KAFKA'S works explore religious, political, and familial authority.

ONCE IMPRISONED for his political activity, dramatist and poet Vaclav Havel became president of the Czech and Slovak Republic in 1989.

1968. Freedom of speech was energetically repressed, through intimidation, economic punishment, and imprisonment. Despite this, or perhaps because of it, writers were in the vanguard of the so-called Charter 77 human rights movement and in the democratic uprisings that toppled the Communists from power.

Among the leading writers of recent years are the Czech novelists Milan Kundera and Ivan Klima; the dramatist and novelist Pavel Kohout; and Vaclav Havel, who became president of the Czech Republic. Among the Hungarians are novelists George Konrad and Miklos Meszoly, and the poet Sandor Weöres.

Modernism

If the literature of dissent in the Soviet Union and Eastern Europe concentrated on the outward oppression of tyranny, the literatures of Western Europe concentrated on the inward—often on the oppressiveness of the writer's own mind and being.

This approach, which came to be known as "modernism," began in the late 1800s with the French poets Baudelaire, Rimbaud, and Mallarmé. The very title of Baudelaire's great work, *Les Fleurs du Mal* (The Flowers of Evil), suggests the mood that was beginning to settle on poetry even before the turn of the century. Baudelaire's poem "Le Voyage" ends with setting sail for something, but what it is is completely in doubt: "Heaven or Hell, what's the difference?"

In one of Rimbaud's poems, "Le Bateau Ivre," the journey is purely imaginary, taking place in the mind of a child while he is lying in the bottom of a rowboat tied up at the river's edge. And in a late, lonely sonnet of Mallarmé, the journey is stillborn: a swan is stuck in the ice, unable to muster the will or energy to break the ice with its wing before it utterly freezes over.

Uncertainty had arrived in many other disciplines as well. The new study of psychology, tied as it was to the subconscious, was ambiguous and dark by definition. Philosophers limited their scope of inquiry to small questions dealing with the meanings of words, having abandoned metaphysical speculations and questions of man's behavior to man. The new physics and non-Euclidean geometry called even mathematical truth into question. Perhaps worst of all, studies of society were suggesting that all governments were inherently irrational and unjust, yet they seemed ever more firmly in control, even as the prospect of war came closer with each passing day.

Yet literature during this time experienced one of its greatest rebirths. In the West, writers built on the inheritance of the French symbolists, returning to childhood, and to a simpler, if intellectually demanding, mythic way of explaining the real world. They searched the past myths from Greece and Rome, and from the Celtic and Germanic stories of the Middle Ages for parallels and patterns in which to set their own words. This new myth differed from the old in that it sought to explain not the fate of nations and peoples, but of individuals—it was subjective, rather than objective. But writers from many different backgrounds came to agree on the value of common mythological references as a way of bridging the huge gap between one human mind and another.

By its very nature, this new style of writing in the purest form appealed first to a cultured few. James Joyce's *Ulysses* (and even more, his later *Finnegans Wake*) required more previous knowledge in the reader than any influential piece of writing since the Renaissance. Yet gradually the use of symbol and myth filtered down into more popular works, until even unsophisticated readers came to understand and expect it. Gradually, a new "modern" sensibility was developed that today influences the beginning poet or short story writer as well as the scholarly professional. It is in this sense that the following pages take the word "modernism."

France

World War I sounded the death knell for French dreams of international glory. The shock of this experience can be seen in the career of the novelist Romain Rolland, whose *Jean Christophe* (1904–1912) is a confident masterpiece, but whose work over the next 40 years never dared so much again.

Among those whose careers spanned the pre- and postwar eras, the works of Colette (*The Innocent Wife,* 1903; *Cheri,* 1920; *Gigi,* 1945) seem more likely to last than those of Rolland. Confined to the intimate world of feelings and personal relations, her works reveal a talent that the world has valued more highly with each succeeding decade.

One group of French writers continued to seek for great meaning. Among them were Jules Romains and Roger Martin Du Gard (Nobel Prize, 1937), both authors of extraordinary epic cycles. Others sought significance in a revived Catholicism. Nobel laureate (1952) Francois Mauriac and Georges Bernanos were the most prominent.

France's reputation as a leader of the European avant-garde, however, was advanced by another group of writers. These included the novelist André Gide (Nobel Prize, 1947), who specialized in explorations of his characters' psychological states; Jean Cocteau (1889–1963), a writer (and filmmaker) of genuine grace, though he tended often to the bizarre; and Louis-Ferdinand Céline, who extended the tradition of self-loathing to new heights.

In the theater, Jean Giraudoux brought both innovations of style and a quixotic humanism. After 1945, the French developed the new theater of the absurd. The leading figure in this was Samuel Beckett, a transplanted Irishman whose *Waiting for Godot* (1952) became a classic of modern drama. Beckett received the Nobel Prize in 1969. Among other figures in the absurdist movement were Jean Anouilh, Jean Genet, and Eugène Ionesco.

Another strand in French writing was the cult of action. It is prefigured in the works of André Malraux (*La Condition Humaine,* 1933), but the experience of writers who served in the French Resistance during the German occupation in World War II made something more of it. Jean-Paul Sartre built a philosophy on the importance of action to defining one's existence in a meaningless world. In addition to philosophical works, his philosophical novels (*Nausea,* 1938) and plays were greatly admired. Sartre's associate Albert Camus gave further expression to the existentialist philosophy, notably in his novels *The Stranger* (1942) and *The Plague* (1947).

French poetry produced no master after World War I to match the great symbolists. Paul Valéry dominated the period between the wars, writing in the symbolist tradition. Alexis Saint-Léger Léger, writing as St. John Perse, wrote outside the main tradition, yet the quality of his verse won him the Nobel Prize in 1960. Other poets—including Paul Éluard, René Char, Louis Aragon, and André Breton—concerned themselves with the movements called surrealism and dada.

After 1950, the French popular novel retained great vitality, producing among others the polished detective stories of Georges Simenon. At the same time, serious literature seemed to languish. As always, the French excelled in criticism, however. The works of Roland Barthes, Michel Foucault, and others developed new approaches to the study of both literature and society.

The new criticism did bring one new movement to literature—an extraordinarily circumstantial style pioneered by Alain Robbe-Grillet and Marguerite Duras, and mastered by Egyptian-born Edmond Jabès in *The Book of Questions* (1963–1965).

Throughout the latter part of the century, some of the liveliest writing in French has come from outside the mother country. In parts of Africa and the Americas formerly controlled by France, a movement stressing native sources

  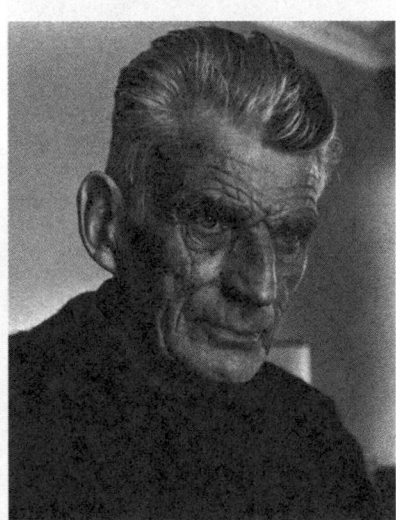

MODERNISM signaled a dramatic rebirth in literature and has influenced writers such as James Joyce (left), André Gide (center), and Samuel Beckett (right).

grew up, providing such poets as Léopold Senghor (Senegal), Léon Damas (French Guiana), and Aimé Césaire (Martinique), who may be the best French-language poet of the age.

At the same time, there was an explosion of talent among the writers of French-speaking Canada. These include poets Alain Grandbois, Claude Gauvreau, Anne Hébert, and many others; and such novelists as Gabrielle Roy, André Langevin, Marie-Claire Blais, and Madeleine Gagnon.

Italy

Through the 1800s, the Italian writers of international appeal could have been fit into a single room—a terrible fate for the people who introduced the West to civilization. Among the few were the great novelist Alessandro Manzoni (*The Betrothed,* 1827) and the remarkable poet Giacomo Leopardi (*Canti,* written 1816–1836). Later in the century, the novels of Giovanni Verga became models for realist writers of the 1900s.

Much of the literary activity of the 1800s was involved with the struggle for Italian unification. The great creative efforts of the new nation went into the grand opera, which helped to form a sense of national identity. In Verdi's *Otello* (1887) and *Falstaff* (1893), the

SIX CHARACTERS find the author and tell him what to write in Pirandello's absurdist play.

authentic Italian voice may be heard as it had not rung out in centuries (though ironically, both stories came from Shakespeare).

In the first decades of the 1900s, the rhetorical poet Gabriele D'Annunzio won great international celebrity. But it was the dramatist Luigi Pirandello who brought a genuine modernism to Italy. His *Six Characters in Search of an Author* (1921) and *Henry IV* (1922) became classics of the European theater and had great influence on later dramatists.

The period of Fascism and Italy's eventual defeat in World War II read like a play even more bitter than Pirandello dared to write. Yet literary production continued. Under Fascism, the poets Giuseppe Ungaretti, Eugenio Montale, and Salvatore Quasimodo (the last two Nobel Prize winners) developed a deliberately obscure style in order to write honestly without being silenced by the Fascist state. After World War II, their style became more accessible, but their deep human concerns remained.

Novelists included the early modernist Italo Svevo and Alberto Moravia, whose long career seemed to mirror the history and moods of the country itself. In the 1940s, novelists awakened to a new realism, and for nearly 20 years, Italian fiction was filled with a passionate and reformist spirit. Among the writers of this era were Cesare Pavese, Elio Vittorini, Carlo Levi (*Christ Stopped at Eboli,* 1945), Ignazio Silone, and Italo Calvino.

New writers have continued to appear, many from outside traditional literary circles, and writers like Calvino continued to prosper. The contemporary style most admired, however, concerns itself most often with European intellectualism rather than with the realities of Italian life.

Spain and Portugal

World War I did not have the same earth-shaking effects in Spain and Portugal as in France. The Spanish had already lost their hopes for world importance. At the same time, they were approaching a cataclysm of their own—the Spanish Civil War (1936–1939), in which the authoritarian forces of Francisco Franco overcame the socialist and reformist Republicans.

Before the Civil War, such earlier prodigies as Unamuno, Pío Baroja, and Valle Inclán were still active. Among the younger generation were novelists Ramón Pérez de Ayala and Gabriel Miró Ferrer. The brilliant critic and cultural commentator José Ortega y Gasset came to acceptance as Unamuno's successor.

But it was in lyric poetry that this generation stood out. Using the style of *modernismo* learned from South America, Juan Ramón Jiménez earned a Nobel Prize (1956), and the brothers Manuel and Antonio Machado gained international recognition.

Some 20 years younger, a new generation was even more remarkable. It included Jorge Guillén, Vicente Aleixandre (Nobel Prize, 1977), Luis Cernuda, and the great dramatist and lyric poet Federico García Lorca (*Blood Wedding,* 1933; *The House of Bernarda Alba,* 1936). Together, these poets brought Spain to the forefront of European literature, but their success was short-lived.

The Civil War sent most of the leading writers into exile, and Antonio Machado and García Lorca were killed during the fighting. The long rule of Francisco Franco was not friendly to experiment or to political comment, and many poets stayed away for the rest of their lives.

It was not until the death of Franco in the 1970s that the Spanish poets were welcomed back to their own land. By this time some major new writers had appeared. It seemed that the latter decades of the century might bring still another flowering of Spanish literary genius.

Meanwhile, in neighboring Portugal, an authoritarian regime also encouraged conservative literary styles. Only the poems of Fernando Pessoa (*Mensagem,* 1934) and the powerful realistic novel about Brazil, *A Selva* (1930) by J. M. Ferreira de Castro, stand out in the period between the wars. In the 1950s, the psychological novel *Sibila* by Agustina Bessa Luís attracted widespread admiring attention.

Only in the 1970s, during a period of political reform, did Portugal's literature reawaken. The musings of three Portuguese women published in 1974, and modeled on the *Letters of a Portuguese Nun* written centuries earlier, shocked the reading public and became one of the symbols of the movement that restored democracy to the country that same year. The voice of feminism and of frankly sexual material from a woman's point of view seemed to bring centuries of male-centered literature into question.

Since the revolution of 1974, many other new and serious works have appeared, including the frank love poems of Vitorino Nemésio, and the novel *Sinais de Fogo* by Jorge de Sena.

Latin America. The great excitement of 20th-century literature in Spanish and Portuguese continued to be in South America, however. That continent (and the Spanish-speaking countries of Central America and the Caribbean) boasted a booming economy untouched by the great wars of the century and a continuing spirit of optimism despite grave social and political problems.

In the generation born near the turn of the century, many gained international fame. Among these were poets César Vallejo of Peru, Pablo Neruda of Chile (Nobel Prize, 1971), and Octavio Paz of Mexico; and the great fiction writers Jorge Luis Borges of Argentina (*The Aleph,* 1949) and Miguel Angel Asturias of Guatemala (Nobel Prize, 1967). Others who achieved a high level on a smaller scale were the poets Gabriela

Mistral of Chile and Juana de Ibarbourou of Uruguay.

After mid-century, the older writers continued to produce, while a younger generation often equaled or surpassed them. Among the younger generation, Gabriel García Márquez of Colombia (*One Hundred Years of Solitude,* 1967) brought a truly mythical scope to the novel, and was read both in Spanish and in translation throughout the world. Other major world novelists included Carlos Fuentes of Mexico (*The Death of Artemio Cruz,* 1964) and Mario Vargas Llosa of Peru. These and other important writers (Cuba's Alejo Carpentier, Chile's José Donoso) often lived and wrote in exile as repressive regimes—both of the right and the left—came and went in their home countries. In the 1970s, many lived in or frequently visited Spain.

In Brazil, where Portuguese rather than Spanish is spoken, awakening to the new modernism arrived late through the efforts of the black poet Mario de Andrade and others. In the 1930s, the important scholarly work of sociologist Gilberto Freyre pointed toward the development of the realistic novel. Yet Brazilian writers, like their brothers in Latin America, developed a unique mix of realism and free fantasy. This mixture is exemplified in the work of Brazil's major novelist, Jorge Amado (*The Violent Land,* 1942; *Gabriela, Clove and Cinnamon,* 1958; *Tieta do Agreste,* 1977).

Among other Brazilian writers, José Lins do Rêgo was the first to write about the impoverished wilderness of the northeast. Younger writers with international followings include the poet Jorge de Lima and the novelist Clarice Lispector.

Germany

Germany stood at the center of the terrible whirlwind that consumed large parts of Europe between 1914 and 1945. Her defeat in World War I and the terms of the Versailles Treaty brought nothing but despair and foreboding. To the great cultural historian Oswald Spengler, the war itself was but one symptom of *The Decline of the West* (1918–1922). In a sense, he took the suicide of Goethe's hero Werther and applied its example to all of Europe. The bleakness of his vision matched the bleakness of the time.

The same myth of decay is evident in the novels of the great Thomas Mann (Nobel Prize, 1929), but Mann finds some solace in myth. His book *The Magic Mountain* (1924) is one of the monuments of modern literature, and Mann's output continued through still another world war.

Austria was demoted by the Versailles settlement from a superpower (with control over much of Hungary and Czechoslovakia) to a mini-state. The modernist and often bitterly ironic works of Austria's authors—including Robert Musil, Karl Kraus, and Hermann Broch—reflect the sudden change in the country's status.

The 1920s were a period of intense experimentation in Germany itself. The ruin of war and Germany's dire financial crisis hung over the era and gave it an element of cynicism, yet there was also an attitude of heedless gaiety.

The mixture of lyricism, fantasy, and nightmare that had characterized the later works of Strindberg and Wedekind dominated the theater under the name expressionism. Perhaps the most enduring production of the period was the work of a young dramatist named Bertolt Brecht. His *The Threepenny Opera* (performed in 1928), an adaptation of John Gay's *Beggar's Opera* (performed in England in 1728), with music by Kurt Weill, seemed to catch the mood of the age; it has often been produced in the years since. Its mordant songs ("Mack the Knife") are familiar in several languages. Brecht himself became a major figure in later drama as an exile in New York in the 1930s and 1940s and later as a resident of East Germany. But none of his influential "epic theater" pieces (*Mother Courage and Her Children,* 1941) was successful with American audiences.

World War I itself was the subject of perhaps the most famous novel in German written during the 1920s. *All Quiet on the Western Front* (1929) by Erich Maria Remarque is a classic of realistic war narrative and antiwar feeling. In a different vein, the novels of Hermann Hesse, turning to mysticism rather than realism or nightmare, have received constant attention in the years since their publication. His best known works include *Steppenwolf* (1927) and *Death and the Lover* (1933). He won the Nobel Prize in 1946.

With the rise of Adolf Hitler to power in the 1930s, many German writers went into exile and German literature went into eclipse. Among those who recorded the terrible time of persecution and war was the German-Jewish poet Nelly Sachs (*O, The Chimneys,* 1967). She won the Nobel Prize in 1966.

After the defeat of the Nazi forces, Germany was in ruins. Yet within a few years Germany rediscovered its literary voice. In the theater, fierce dramatists of justice called the nation to account for the terrors of its past, following in the stylistic footsteps of Brecht. Rolf Hochhuth (*The Deputy,* 1963) and Peter Weiss (*The Persecution and Assassination of Jean Paul Marat as Performed by the Inmates of the Asylum of Charenton under the Direction of the Marquis de Sade,* 1964) demonstrated the ability of the theater to question and shock. Among other dramatists of worldwide influence were the Swiss writers Max Frisch and Friedrich Dürrenmatt.

Among novelists, the major voices included Günter Grass, whose *The Tin Drum* (1959) was a sardonic review of German attitudes during the Nazi period; and Heinrich Böll, recipient of the Nobel Prize in 1972.

Germany after the war was a divided nation. While West Germany received all the benefits and hazards of rapid economic growth and contact with other Western nations, East Germany, under the control of the Soviet Union, languished. Writers there were required, as in the rest of Eastern Europe, to select topics and attitudes sympathetic to the state. Yet beginning in the late 1960s, the Eastern writers became more daring and the regime somewhat more yielding. As individuals, German writers, both East and West, continued to contribute to the larger world of literature.

MARAT/SADE: The crazed asylum inmates shocked audiences of Peter Weiss's play.

ISAK DINESEN based her novel *Out of Africa* at least partly on her experiences managing a coffee plantation in Kenya.

Scandinavia

The Scandinavian countries offered no writers of the stature of Ibsen or Strindberg in the years after 1914, yet their separate literary traditions, influenced by the international style of modernism, continued.

In Sweden, which remained neutral through both world wars and gradually erected a prosperous democratic socialist state, the major writer of the early 1900s was Pär Lagerkvist, who combined a true modernist sensibility with the characteristic reserve of his native land. Among his most important works are *The Dwarf* (1944) and *Barabbas* (1950). He was awarded a Nobel Prize in 1951.

Among other significant writers are Vilhelm Moberg, who spent considerable time in the United States and chronicled the story of Swedish immigrants to the United States in *The Emigrants* (1949), *Unto a Good Land* (1952), and *The Settlers* (1956). Novelist Harry Martinson and poet Eyvind Johnson were self-educated men who spoke for the workingman at home and who were awarded Nobel Prizes in 1974 for their advocacy.

In Norway, the modern period began with the novels of Johan Bojer (1872–1959), which sometimes approached the mythic in their sense of Norse identity. A generation younger, Sigrid Undset wrote a long trilogy about medieval Norway under the collective title *Kristin Lavransdatter* (1920–1922); it combined historical sensitivity with a very modern understanding of psychology. Undset received a Nobel Prize in 1928.

The most famous writer from Denmark in the 1900s was Baroness Karen Blixen, who wrote under the pen name Isak Dinesen both in Danish and in English. Many of her stories are set in East Africa, where she lived from 1914 to 1931. Her *Seven Gothic Tales* (1934), mysterious and understated, brought her world fame.

Two talented and original dramatists flourished in Denmark in the years between the world wars—Kaj Munk and Kjeld Abell. Munk's satirical plays showed a deep moral concern, and during the German occupation of Denmark in World War II he was put to death. Ironically, German dramatists after the war learned from him.

In recent years, leading Scandinavian writers have included the Swedish novelist Ivar Lo-Johansson, Norwegians Odd Bang-Hansen and Halldis Vesaas, and Danes Tage Skou-Hansen and Aage Dons. Although they write in languages read by only a few million, their concerns and their methods are those of the rest of Europe and of the world.

Greece

Greece only regained its political independence from the Muslim Turks after a prolonged war in the 1820s. Its literature had been held back until then by the insistence of academics on using the ancient (and by then, unspoken) form. Through the inspiration of the great poet Dionysios Solomos (1798–1857) and the crusading of later literary reformers, the poems and stories of the modern Greeks began to appear in the modern vernacular or demotic Greek, rather than in the classic language.

It was not until the 1890s, however, that writers appeared who would fully realize the promise of the new literary freedom. These men, contemporaries of France's Paul Valéry and Ireland's W.B. Yeats, produced a poetry that rivaled that of any language in the world. The most influential in this early group was Kostes Palamas. A generation later, Angelos Sikilianos began to explore the rich possibilities in Greece's mingled heritage of Christian and pagan symbols. Konstantin Kafavis has gained an international following since his death in 1933 because the lonely and pessimistic tone of his verse seemed to echo feelings in the rest of the world. In a characteristic poem, he writes, "No use to seek escape to another city. You will be a ruined man there as you are here. The city you live in follows you wherever you go."

Some poets of the next generation shared the same pessimism in the wake of Greece's involvement in both world wars. Yet an epic strain seemed still to grow even amid the pessimism. Nikos Kazantzakis wrote *The Odyssey: A Modern Sequel* (1938), a giant poem of some 33,000 lines, and later won a huge following with his novel *Zorba the Greek* (1946).

The poet George Seferis worked in another direction. His compelling mixture of intense symbolism and inventiveness made him the most influential poet from Greece in centuries. Odysseus Elytis combined modernist abstraction and characteristic Greek themes. Both Seferis and Elytis have received the Nobel Prize for Literature.

Greece has developed other forms of modern literature, from the psychological novel and play to works of Marxist advocacy. But the extraordinary success of its poets suggests wider implications for modern literature. Even as these poets become more and more Greek in their expression, they become more recognizable to the world literary scene. Like writers in Eastern Europe and Scandinavia, they contribute at once to the vitality of numerically small languages and to the creation of an international literary community.

Modern Literature in English

English was the dominant language of the 1900s, both in number of speakers and in literary achievement. The greater part of this mastery was attained in the first half of the century. The Irish supplied two masters of great importance; the Americans experienced a wave of fresh creativity as their literature came to worldwide attention; and the rest of the English-speaking world—from Great Britain, Australia, Canada, and both white and black Africa—supplied a wide range of talent.

Britain and Ireland

The first of the great world wars left Britain not defeated or destroyed, but bled white. Although it seemed the strongest nation on Earth in 1918, the rest of the century would be one long retreat from world power.

At home, the very meaning of the term British became vague. London was filling up with the residents of colonies and former colonies, acting more as a world capital for the English-speaking than as a capital for England. In fact, much of the most interesting literary activity, while centered on London, was carried on by non-Englishmen. James Joyce wrote in Switzerland and published in Paris (for largely English readers). W. B. Yeats belonged to Dublin. Ezra Pound and T. S. Eliot were Americans, one of whom circled around England, the other of whom made it his permanent home.

James Joyce. The great innovator in English in the 1900s was without doubt James Joyce. An Irishman in exile, Joyce redefined modernism for the English speakers' peculiar sensibilities. For Joyce (and for many who followed him) the story itself became a "symbol." By using the substructure of an older (and usually familiar) story, Joyce found a way of giving mythic significance to the most prosaic stuff of daily life. In *Ulysses* (1922), he used the story of Homer's *Odyssey,* yet not in the logical way that would suggest a retelling. He does not say "this is what Ulysses (Odysseus) would be like if he returned." He suggests rather that the elements of the story have quite literally repeated themselves in the lives of contemporary characters. Other tales of the past also reappear: the life of the great central character, Leopold Bloom, is a partial echo of the life of William Shakespeare.

In one sense, little about *Ulysses* is logical. First-time readers have a hard time following the story, and Joyce's reliance on a stream-of-consciousness narrative seems to put things frequently out of order. Yet in another sense, the narrative is relentlessly logical. The parts are all carefully related not only to other parts but to their "originals" in the *Odyssey* or in other sources alluded to.

The technique of *Ulysses* has immense disadvantages. It could not, for example, tell a story with a complex plot. But for relating a simple action or emotion and giving it a global significance, the technique is unrivaled. In an important way, it is a new approach to writing, and the resulting work is a new form, neither exactly a novel, a play, nor a poem, but a kind of amalgam of the three.

Yeats, Pound, and Eliot. Other strains of modernism in English were developed by the Irish William Butler Yeats and by the transplanted Americans Ezra Pound and T. S. Eliot. Yeats began as a leader of the Irish renaissance and a founder of Dublin's Abbey Theatre. Yet in the second half of his life he exerted a different influence—more on the modernist poets of English than on his own Irish countrymen. Among his collections of poetry are *The Wild Swans at Coole* (1917), *The Tower* (1928), and *Last Poems* (1940).

Ezra Pound, some 20 years younger than Yeats, brought a characteristically ornery American style to a broad range of modern poetry. He was a great literary propagandist, an early student both of oriental and of Italian Renaissance poetry, and a founder of the imagist school of poetry. His later years were darkened by his support of the Italian Fascist government during World War II. Ironically, his greatest poetry was written after the war, when he was captured by American troops, tried, imprisoned, and finally confined to a mental hospital in the United States. Readers of Pound's *Pisan Cantos* and his free translation of the Confucian *Book of Odes* will find a man slowly awakening to the enormity of his own self-betrayal and will also find some of the most beautiful American writing since Emerson.

T. S. Eliot, a protégé of Pound's, was born in St. Louis and studied at Harvard. Shortly after leaving Harvard, he went to England and lived there the rest of his life. His long poem *The Waste Land* (1922) was perhaps the most important poem in English during the 1920s. A somber work incorporating medieval myth, yet remaining resolutely in common—even prosaic—language, it set the tone for a whole generation of poets. Eliot later became a convert to Anglo-Catholicism and expressed conservative political beliefs when many other writers were liberal. Yet his poetry and his measured criticism seem sure to keep him in the top rank of poets in English.

Others who were associated with this modern school centered on London were the American poet Robert Frost, and to a lesser extent D. H. Lawrence

Robert Frost

Among American poets in the 20th century, Robert Frost was one who appealed both to serious students of poetry and to a wider audience. He brought the modernist spirit to the New England countryside, creating poems that were at once sophisticated and homespun. Below is "The Need of Being Versed in Country Things," about a house destroyed by fire.

> The house had gone to bring again
> To the midnight sky a sunset glow.
> Now the chimney was all of the house that stood,
> Like a pistil after the petals go.
>
> The barn opposed across the way,
> That would have joined the house in flame
> Had it been the will of the wind, was left
> To bear forsaken the place's name.
>
> No more it opened with all one end
> For teams that came by the stony road
> To drum on the floor with scurrying hoofs
> And brush the mow with the summer load.
>
> The birds that came to it through the air
> At broken windows flew out and in,
> Their murmur more like the sigh we sigh
> From too much dwelling on what has been.
>
> Yet for them the lilac renewed its leaf,
> And the aged elm, though touched with fire;
> And the dry pump flung up an awkward arm;
> And the fence post carried a strand of wire.
>
> For them there was really nothing sad.
> But though they rejoiced in the nest they kept,
> One had to be versed in country things
> Not to believe the phoebes wept.

(whose novels overshadowed his work as a poet), W. H. Auden, and the American William Carlos Williams.

The end of this creative ferment can be placed at the year 1939. Yeats died in that year, an old man; the second great war broke out in Europe; and James Joyce published his last work, *Finnegans Wake.* This book carried the logic of modernism to its extreme, invading even the sanctity of word meanings and coherence of phrase, creating multiple layers of meaning, and reinterpreting history as a self-centered dream. Many critics have been unable or unwilling to grant its success, yet its sales have continued to grow year after year, perhaps because, meaning or no meaning, it is one of the funniest books in the world and one of the most touching.

The Bloomsbury group. Meanwhile, a group of British writers had founded a circle nicknamed for its neighborhood, Bloomsbury. Virginia Woolf, a novelist of great gifts (*Mrs. Dalloway,* 1925; *To the Lighthouse,* 1927), was at its center. She had been influenced by the school of Yeats, Pound, and Joyce, yet her use of modernist effects had a distinctly English flavor. Others in the Bloomsbury group included the biographer Lytton Strachey (*Eminent Victorians,* 1918), the novelist E. M. Forster (*Howard's End,* 1910; *A Passage to India,* 1924), and the

realize
US

realise
Brit.

centered
US

centred
Brit.

somber
US

sombre
Brit.

flavor
US

flavour
Brit.

  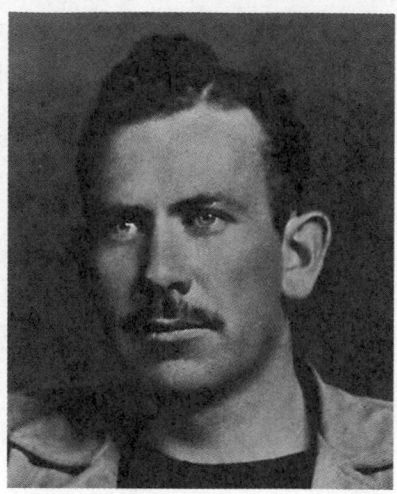

MODERN MASTERS of American literature include F. Scott Fitzgerald (left), Ernest Hemingway (center), and John Steinbeck (right). Despite their many differences, these writers shared typically American values and beliefs.

economist John Maynard Keynes. The breadth of the group's membership and interest reminds one of the earlier circle that gathered around Samuel Johnson in the late 1700s.

The English accomplished important things in the field of analysis and criticism, beginning with Keynes's *Economic Consequences of the Peace* (1919). Among other monumental works of this kind must be numbered the thoroughly individual history of World War II by former Prime Minister Winston Churchill, whose wartime speeches enriched the language as had none since the previous century. Another critic of note was the essayist and novelist George Orwell, whose *Animal Farm* (1945), an angry fable of Stalinism, has become a standard description of totalitarian government.

After the 1920s, however, the excitement in English letters diminished, and the field was left to more conservative writers, including novelists W. Somerset Maugham and Graham Greene, playwright Noel Coward, and poet Robert Graves. Young writers in the 1930s—W. H. Auden, Stephen Spender, and Christopher Isherwood—looked optimistically to socialism for new hope, but the disaster of the Spanish Civil War and the treaty signed between the Communist Soviet Union and Nazi Germany withered their enthusiasm within a few years.

After 1945. World War II shattered the power of Britain as World War I had shattered France's. Postwar literature has a kind of elegiac quality, looking backward nostalgically and forward uncertainly. A trilogy of novels by Anglo-Irish writer Joyce Cary *(Herself Surprised, To Be a Pilgrim, The Horse's Mouth)* follows a housekeeper, the old man she works for, and the visionary artist whose model and mistress she had been from 1900 to the end of World War II. The decline of the characters' fortunes is redeemed only by their stubbornness and faith. The parallel decline of Britain itself is not difficult to draw.

In a different vein, *Under the Volcano* (1947), a novel by expatriate Englishman Malcolm Lowry, tells in vivid modernist style of a talented man's alcoholic dissolution in Mexico. The protagonist considers himself an honorary British consul in the small resort community where he lives. Even as he hopes for some world-restoring success, he drags down everyone and everything important to him. The novel was unsuccessfully published in New York and only gained a wide audience after the author's death in 1958.

New life and energy came to the British theater in the 1950s from the so-called "angry young men," writers from the working classes in England angry at the disabilities imposed on them by England's rigid class structure. The group took its name from John Osborne's play *Look Back in Anger* (1956). The plays and novels of these writers introduced a new vocabulary and new concerns to the English literary scene.

A younger generation of dramatists used the advances of the earlier group to somewhat different purposes. By mixing anger, lower- and middle-class settings, and the techniques of the theater of the absurd, such writers as Tom Stoppard and Harold Pinter created a whole new type of play. Pinter especially manages to communicate in some fashion through plays in which nothing—including the air itself—seems to move (*The Birthday Party*, 1958; *Old Times*, 1970).

Among the British writers of fiction, the older ones produced extended cycles concerning the nature of upper-class life in the 1900s (C. P. Snow, Anthony Powell, Richard Hughes). A younger contingent, including Alan Sillitoe, Kingsley Amis, and D. M. Thomas, had something in common with the theater's angry young men. Finally, there was a remarkable group of women writers following in the footsteps of Ivy Compton-Burnett (1892–1969). They included Iris Murdoch, Doris Lessing (*The Golden Notebook*, 1962), and Muriel

Spark (*The Prime of Miss Jean Brodie*, 1961; *Loitering with Intent*, 1981).

The British Commonwealth

By the second half of the century, important writers in English were appearing in every corner of the globe. Although Britain had long since given up its colonial holdings, most of these outland writers were from Commonwealth countries and continued to feel some cultural ties with Britain itself.

Most notable among this group are Nobel laureate (1973) Patrick White of Australia (*The Eye of the Storm*, 1974); short story writer of the 1920s Katherine Mansfield, and the later novelist Janet Frame, of New Zealand; and novelists Hugh MacLennan (*Two Solitudes*, 1945), Brian Moore, Margaret Laurence, and Margaret Atwood of Canada.

The racial and social agonies of South Africa were movingly portrayed by Alan Paton (*Cry, the Beloved Country*, 1948) and Nadine Gordimer (*July's People*, 1981), and by dramatist Athol Fugard.

The strongest new voices, however, belonged to the writers of the black experience in Nigeria, South Africa, and the Caribbean. Among the best known are South Africa's Ezekial Mphahlele (*Down Second Avenue*, 1959) and Nigeria's Wole Soyinka (*Kongi's Harvest*, 1966). They have spearheaded a movement that now includes a wide range of distinct talents: among others, the Caribbean poet Derek Walcott and the novelist Samuel Selvon; the Nigerians Amos Tutuola, Chinua Achebe, and Gabriel Okara; the South Africans Alex La Guma, Lewis Nkosi, and Peter Abrahams; and Gambia's Lenrie Peters. The experience of the so-called Third World is also evoked by the East Indian V. S. Naipaul, who sees both the old and new worlds sympathetically, but always, through force of circumstance, from the outside.

theater
US

theatre
Brit.

The United States

1910–1940. In the decade beginning in 1910, the American literary scene was suddenly crowded with new life and energy. In London, the American T. S. Eliot published "The Love Song of J. Alfred Prufrock," his first substantial poem. Robert Frost published *A Boy's Will* and *North of Boston,* his first collections. Vachel Lindsay published three collections. A very young F. Scott Fitzgerald was hailed for his first novel, *This Side of Paradise.* And in the Middle West, there were major books of poetry (*Chicago Poems* by Carl Sandburg) and fiction (*Winesburg, Ohio* by Sherwood Anderson and *Main Street* by Sinclair Lewis). At the same time, a new dramatist named Eugene O'Neill was establishing himself as America's first great writer for the stage, and the older Theodore Dreiser was at the height of his considerable powers.

During the 1920s and 1930s, these young men came to maturity and were joined by still others: novelists Ernest Hemingway (*The Sun Also Rises,* 1926), William Faulkner (*The Sound and the Fury,* 1929), John Dos Passos (*U.S.A.,* 1930–1936), Thomas Wolfe (*Look Homeward, Angel,* 1929), and John Steinbeck (*Tortilla Flat,* 1935). Major new voices in poetry included Wallace Stevens, William Carlos Williams, the extraordinarily gifted e e cummings, and Hart Crane.

Of these writers, no fewer than six would receive the Nobel Prize: Lewis (1930), O'Neill (1936), Eliot (1948), Faulkner (1949), Hemingway (1954), and Steinbeck (1962). The awards suggest not only the quality of the work these writers produced, but also (and perhaps more accurately) how international their influence was.

To round out the picture of a 30-year period of remarkable creativity, it remains only to mention a few writers whose influence was not as immediately felt. These include Ezra Pound, whose personal influence and poetic example outlasted both long exile and suspicion of treason; Henry Miller, an American

ARTHUR MILLER'S plays depicted social awareness while showing the common man as heroic.

novelist working chiefly in Paris, who found a new excitement in portraying sex and whose books were consequently banned; the Russian émigré Vladimir Nabokov, whose modernist sensibility went somewhat against the American grain but whose influence on other writers was great; and finally, Edmund Wilson, with T. S. Eliot among the first great American literary critics, who did much to inform American readers about the currents of modern literature and culture.

American characteristics.

Taken together, these writers—of such widely varying backgrounds, tastes, and appeals—made American literature from 1910 to 1940 the most serious and influential in the world. Despite their great differences, some generalizations will help explain what they brought to world literature.

They maintained a deceptive air of natural speech in their writing, whether taking it from the American backwoods, small towns, or big cities. Even the most sophisticated, Eliot and Pound, reached their greatest heights with ordinary diction that deliberately avoided poeticisms.

Beneath this natural surface, however, something more complex was usually at work. *The Great Gatsby* by Fitzgerald, *The Sun Also Rises* by Hemingway, and *The Grapes of Wrath* by Steinbeck are all social novels on the surface—the first the story of a bootlegger's lost ideals, the second of a generation wasted by World War I, the third of the disaster of the Great Depression. Yet all three are consciously crafted to recall classical myth. Gatsby and Hemingway's heroes are all ruined "knights" resembling those in the stories of the search for the Holy Grail. *Grapes of Wrath* is a retelling of the book of Exodus—one family's odyssey across a continent in search of a promised land. (Steinbeck's later *East of Eden* uses the biblical story of the loss of paradise and the murder of Abel by Cain.)

The American writers used their mythic material with an interesting twist, however. The traditional stories usually assume that the hero has done something wrong and deserves the tragedy he lives through. But American writers tend to identify with the lawbreaker and the unfortunate and to blame society for tragedy. Fitzgerald's Nick Carraway says to Jay Gatsby, "You're worth more than the lot of them"—the seemingly upstanding and law-abiding citizens. Steinbeck clearly feels something similar for the victimized Joad family. And Hemingway spent the rest of his life trying to find heroes as worthwhile as the doomed Lady Brett Ashley and the accursed Robert Cohn.

This identification with the loser seemed even to carry over into the writers' lives. Where writers of the Soviet Union, Eastern Europe, and Third World countries often risked destruction at the hands of the state, the

American writers seemed to seek to destroy themselves.

The years of the 1930s, though darkened by the Great Depression, were still years of hope and excitement in American literature. In addition to Thomas Wolfe and Steinbeck, new writers included William Saroyan (*The Daring Young Man on the Flying Trapeze,* 1934); and a great new popular theater was evident. The increased concern with social and economic issues was shown by dramatists like Clifford Odets (*Waiting for Lefty,* 1935), but their earnestness was balanced by the wit and lightheartedness of such comic writers as George S. Kaufman and Moss Hart, collaborators on *You Can't Take It With You* (1936) and *The Man Who Came to Dinner* (1939). The period also saw the heyday of sophisticated musical comedies and film comedies, a new form that attracted many writers to Hollywood. During World War II (1941–1945), many writers worked for the U.S. government writing propaganda for the war effort.

AMERICAN PLAYWRIGHTS Clifford Odets (left) and Tennessee Williams (below) both wrote frequently of tragic families.

The 1940s. In a sense, the 1930s ended with the two great plays of the 1940s. In *The Glass Menagerie* (1944), the young Tennessee Williams deepened the domestic play, bringing to it a Chekhovian humor and an ear for the poetry of Southern speech. In *Death of a Salesman* (1949) Arthur Miller had an equal impact, enriching the play of social concern with a feeling for the complexities of family life. In the same decade, Eugene O'Neill, long out of fashion, returned to the theater with *The*

Iceman Cometh (1946). *Long Day's Journey into Night,* his last and perhaps his best play, was not produced until 1956, three years after O'Neill's death.

The new generation of writers looked to a new kind of realism. Building on the precedent of James T. Farrell, whose trilogy *Studs Lonigan* (1932–1935) had shocked the previous decade, Norman Mailer (*The Naked and the Dead,* 1948), Nelson Algren (*The Man With the Golden Arm,* 1949), and James Jones (*From Here to Eternity,* 1951) used language and explicit descriptions centering around the violence of war and sex that would have been unthinkable 20 years earlier. The first and third of these books are the two principal war novels to come from the American experience in World War II; the other is about near-wartime conditions in the big city drug trade. The latter two reached millions who might otherwise not have known about them through popular (and considerably laundered) movie versions.

At the same time, the courts of the land were reducing censorship. One of the principal battles had been fought in the 1930s over allowing the distribution of James Joyce's *Ulysses.* Later, favorable decisions allowed the sale of D. H. Lawrence's *Lady Chatterley's Lover* (1928), and finally the works of Henry Miller (*Tropic of Cancer* and *Tropic of Capricorn*).

Humor and satire. In a thoroughly different vein, the traditions of American humor continued to find literary expression. Not long after the turn of the century, newspaperman Don Marquis created archy the cockroach, who wrote a daily column in supposed blank verse, providing an insect's jaundiced views on the human race. Sportswriter Ring Lardner turned to ironic stories about baseball players and other small-town characters. Lardner's ear for flat mid-western speech—and his sense for the moral foibles of his characters—was unmatched.

In the late 1920s, a younger group of writers centered around a new magazine, *The New Yorker.* On its early staff were James Thurber and E. B. White. Beginning with reminiscences of his boyhood in Ohio, Thurber became a skilled and appealing writer in his chosen area. The surface simplicity and humor of his stories and sketches often hid a complex and sometimes bitter moralist. E. B. White often used his humor for more serious purposes. In addition to parodies, brief sketches, and light verse, he wrote polished yet informal essays on a wide variety of topics, and his children's book *Charlotte's Web* became a classic.

Among other writers in a humorous vein whom *The New Yorker* has published are Wolcott Gibbs, Dorothy Parker, S. J. Perelman, and Woody Allen.

Alone among large circulation magazines, *The New Yorker* also continued to publish serious fiction. It printed many stories by writers who also wrote

POETRY from outside the establishment came from Langston Hughes (left), a leader of the Harlem renaissance of the 1930s, and from Allen Ginsberg of the 1950s beat generation.

novels: John O'Hara (*Appointment in Samarra,* 1934), J. D. Salinger (*The Catcher in the Rye,* 1951), and Truman Capote (*Breakfast at Tiffany's,* 1958). In the 1950s and 1960s, the stories of John Cheever (*The Wapshot Chronicle,* 1957), an anatomist of suburban life and types, and of John Updike (*Rabbit, Run,* 1961) were particularly prominent. Most of these writers straddled the vague line between commercial and quality fiction; they were not highly experimental, and their range was somewhat limited, but they were among the most prolific and interesting writers of the period.

After 1950. The only strong literary movement after mid-century was that of the "beat generation." The poet Allen Ginsberg, together with novelists Jack Kerouac (*On the Road,* 1957) and the somewhat older William Burroughs (*Junkie,* 1953; *Naked Lunch,* 1959), wrote graphically of a freer way of life that conceded nothing to the politics and social mores of the day. Their acceptance of a place outside of established society and their almost obsessive search for new experience set the stage for the great youth rebellion of the 1960s.

POET SYLVIA PLATH, whose work featured themes of alienation and death, committed suicide in 1963.

Until the 1960s, American poetry was dominated by the aging generation born before 1914: cummings and Stevens, Frost and Eliot, William Carlos Williams, and the still green memory of Hart Crane.

The outspoken emotionalism and equally aggressive intelligence of Allen Ginsberg's "Howl" (1956) and "Kaddish" (1961) seemed to stir something in poets who until then had remained merely academic. Among the major works were Robert Lowell's *Life Studies* (1959) and *Notebook* (1969), and John Berryman's *77 Dream Songs* (1964) and *His Toy, His Dream, His Rest* (1968). Among other important poets of the 1950s and 1960s were Theodore Roethke, Robert Creeley, Richard Wilbur, and Sylvia Plath.

Although poetry seemed about to fall asleep again in the 1970s, poets including Denise Levertov, Gary Snyder, John Hollander, Charles Olson, and A. R. Ammons gave hope for continuing achievement.

Literary minorities. America's two literary minorities—blacks and women—seemed to look forward to different futures. American women writers from the time of Edith Wharton and Willa Cather have written freely and with passion. Many of the major figures in the Southern reawakening of the 1940s were women: Flannery O'Connor, Eudora Welty, Carson McCullers. Again in the so-called cosmopolitan style of the 1950s, Jean Stafford, Mary McCarthy, and Hortense Calisher had important places. In addition, women traditionally made up a fair proportion of the writers of popular and mass market fiction—books that make up in readership what they lack in "serious" literary value.

Gradually, however, women writers were coming to view themselves specifically as women. Many of those listed above showed the way for a fuller appreciation of women's joys and sorrows, but younger women, including novelists Anne Beattie and Mary Gordon (*Final Payments,* 1979), promised to go even further in their exploration of the subject. Women were also gaining new footholds

centering
US

centring
Brit.

in literary and cultural criticism (Susan Sontag, Gloria Steinem).

The story of black writers in America goes back into the 1800s, when Frederick Douglass won admiration as an orator and Booker T. Washington (*Up From Slavery,* 1901) used his influence to improve economic and educational conditions among blacks.

The first black poets of serious note were Countee Cullen (1903–1946) and Langston Hughes (1902–1967). Together they helped set off the Harlem renaissance of the 1920s and '30s.

In the 1940s and 1950s, black writing took a more serious and prosaic turn. Richard Wright's *Native Son* (1940) was an early attempt to tell both white and black readers what it felt like to be a black man in America. Other books in a similar vein were Ralph Ellison's *Invisible Man* (1952) and *Go Tell It on the Mountain* (1953) by James Baldwin, who wrote several novels in the next decades (*Another Country,* 1962).

In the 1960s the heartlessness of racism was exposed in *The Autobiography of Malcolm X* (1965), written with Alex Haley, *Manchild in the Promised Land* (1965) by Claude Brown, and *Soul on Ice* (1967) by Eldridge Cleaver.

The 1970s and 1980s saw a widening readership for the works of many African-American writers, including those of Maya Angelou, David Bradley, Ernest J. Gaines, Alex Haley, Toni Morrison, Ishmael Reed, Alice Walker, and John Edgar Wideman. This interest was propelled in part by the phenomenal success of Alex Haley's fact-based novel *Roots* (1976), which was adapted for an enormously successful television miniseries and sold in the millions.

In 1993 two African-American writers achieved singular recognition. In January Maya Angelou read her poem "On the Pulse of Morning" at the Presidential inauguration in Washington, D.C., and in October Toni Morrison became the twelfth American writer, second American woman, and first African American to win the Nobel Prize in Literature.

In a sense, every literary production in America can be viewed as the product of some minority: it is Irish-Catholic or big-city ethnic, western, midwestern, or southern, etc. Even the old Protestant

writer functions today as a member of a literary minority.

Among the most prominent of these groups in the 1960s and 1970s were the writers of Jewish heritage who were dealing with Jewish concerns. Their novels were often quintessentially American, yet this very fact seemed often to trouble them, to take attention away from their Jewishness. Perhaps the best known of the products of these writers was the enormously successful novel *Portnoy's Complaint* (1969) by Philip Roth, a bawdy, funny account of a Jewish boyhood and young adulthood in New Jersey and New York City.

Chaim Potok explored the Jewish-American experience, the clash of cultural values, and the nature of art and creativity in such novels as *The Chosen* (1967), *My Name Is Asher Lev* (1972), *The Book of Light* (1981), and *The Gift of Asher Lev* (1990).

A special contribution of the Jewish-American writers to American literature is their unique and affecting sense of humor. *Catch-22* (1961), a novel about the insanity of the war-time armed services, by Joseph Heller, was perhaps the most successful comedy novel of the era. Among other important writers to whom their Jewishness is a significant concern are Bernard Malamud (*The Fixer,* 1966) and the Canadian Mordecai Richler. In addition, Isaac Bashevis Singer, a Nobel laureate whose stories were written originally in Yiddish, has gained a wide audience in translation.

Perhaps foremost among serious American novelists—and incidentally among novelists of Jewish descent—is Saul Bellow, winner of the Nobel Prize in 1976. From his early *Henderson the Rain King* (1959) to *Humboldt's Gift* (1976), *The Dean's December* (1981), *More Die of Heartbreak* (1987), and *A Theft* (1989), Bellow has explored the fundamental questions of the human experience with the insight and compassion of a true master.

The future. James Joyce believed that literature is a way of obliterating the gap between past, present, and future. Remembering, recording, and prophesying are not so different from each other, because everyone's personal odyssey continues to be repeated somewhere in some form each day. Literature introduces us to the swing of life: from perplexity to reassurance and back to perplexity again. No question is ever answered but another riddle of equal magnitude takes its place.

Yet writers and readers do find a kind of solace in literature, if only in its reminder to seek the permanent and the good. *Choose something like a star,* writes Robert Frost, speaking not only of literature but of vision itself, *To stay our minds on and be stayed.*

—*Robert LaGuardia and Lawrence Lorimer*

Glossary of Literature

A

Abdiel: in Milton's *Paradise Lost,* the only one of Satan's angels who would not join the revolt against heaven.

Absurd, Literature of the: modern type of literature in which the author flouts the conventions of his chosen literary form (usually drama or novel) and uses character and situation to emphasize the meaninglessness and absurdity of his characters' lives. The ancestor of the movement is considered to be Alfred Jarry's play *Ubu Roi* (1896), and its ideas were carried forward in Franz Kafka's novels. The major absurdist writers—Albert Camus, Jean-Paul Sartre, Jean Genet, Eugène Ionesco, and Samuel Beckett—emerged during or after World War II. Later writers in the tradition include Edward Albee and Harold Pinter.

Academy: school of philosophy near Athens in ancient Greece, started by Plato about 387 B.C. It was named for Academia (Akademeia), the area in which it was located. The Academy continued to exist until 529 A.D., when it was closed by Emperor Justinian. Subsequently, the term "academy" was applied to a school of higher or special education, or to an organization made up of learned persons. Among the latter are the Royal Academy, a select British society of artists; the French Academy, a select French society of literary persons whose duties include maintaining and revising the prime dictionary of the French language; and the Swedish Academy, which serves much the same function as the French Academy and in addition awards the annual Nobel Prize in Literature.

Achates: in Vergil's *Aeneid,* a Trojan, faithful friend of Aeneas. After the fall of Troy he followed Aeneas through all his wanderings and hardships with such fidelity that his name has been used as the synonym for a loyal friend.

Acheron, GM: River of Woe, one of the four rivers of Hades. In the *Odyssey* it was the principal or boundary river of Hades over which Charon ferried the souls of the dead on their journey from the upper to the lower world. It also is used to mean the region of Hades itself.

Achilles, GM: hero of the *Iliad* and the bravest of the Greeks in the Trojan War. He was the son of Peleus, king of Thessaly, and Thetis, a sea nymph. When he was born, Thetis plunged him in the river Styx to make his body invulnerable, but neglected to protect the heel by which she held him. To save him from death in the Trojan War, she sent him to the court of King Lycomedes, where he was dressed as a girl and played with the princesses. But Troy could not be taken, and Odysseus, in the guise of a merchant, went to find him. Odysseus offered to sell jewels and weapons to the girls, and the one who chose arms he knew was Achilles; the youth gladly went off with him to war, where he was killed by Paris, who shot him with an arrow in his only vulnerable spot—the heel. *See also* Iliad.

Acrostic: any piece of writing, usually verse, in which sets of letters taken in a certain order spell a word or words. Sometimes a series, composed of the first letter in each line, spells the word or words; sometimes the final letter of each line is used; occasionally letters from the middle of the lines are chosen. If only one set of letters spells a word, the verse is a simple acrostic. If the verse contains more than one hidden series, it is called a double acrostic. The 119th Psalm is a famous acrostic (in Hebrew), and the entire book of Lamentations is a series of acrostics. However, acrostics in Hebrew in the Bible lose their distinctive form when translated. Acrostics have also been used in the making of literary puzzles.

Actaeon, GM: famous hunter who offended Artemis. One story is that he came upon her bathing, another that he boasted of being a better hunter than she. For punishment she changed him into a stag, and he was killed by his own dogs.

Adam Bede: novel by English writer George Eliot, published in 1859. It tells of the love of Adam Bede, a carpenter, for Hetty Sorrel, a pretty dairymaid, who does not love him. She is seduced and abandoned by Arthur Donnithorne, the local squire. Bede marries Dinah Morris, a Methodist preacher, who befriends Hetty.

Adonais: elegy on the death of John Keats by English poet Percy Bysshe Shelley, published in 1821. It mourns the death of Keats, condemns the critics whose reviews were thought to have hastened his death, and ends on a joyous note, hailing Keats into the company of the immortals.

Adonis, GM: beautiful youth beloved by Aphrodite. When he was killed by a wild boar, Aphrodite put him in the care of Persephone, queen of Hades, who wanted to keep him herself; Zeus then decreed that Adonis should spend six months of the year on Earth and six in the underworld. His death and return symbolize winter and summer, and his worship embodied a midsummer festival. Shakespeare's poem, "Venus and Adonis," tells the love story of the youth and the goddess.

Aegisthus: *See* House of Atreus.

Aeneas, GRM: son of Anchises and Aphrodite, and one of the heroes of the Trojan War described in Homer's *Iliad.* He married Creusa, daughter of Priam, king of Troy. When Troy was taken and in flames, Aeneas departed, bearing his old father on his shoulders and leading his little son Ascanius by the hand. The wanderings of Aeneas from this point on are celebrated in Vergil's great Latin epic, the *Aeneid. See also* Aeneid.

Aeneid: Latin epic poem by the Roman poet Vergil, left incomplete at his death in 19 B.C.; it is a classic work telling of the founding of Rome by the Trojan hero Aeneas. It narrates Aeneas's wanderings before he reaches the seven hills of Rome. Seeking a new home, he sails from Troy with a fleet of 20 ships. He is shipwrecked on the coast of Africa, where Dido, queen of Carthage, begs him to remain. She falls deeply in love with him and takes her own life in grief when the gods command him to take up his travels again. Aeneas meets her ghost when he descends into Hell to speak to his father's spirit. After seven

---

More than 1,500 titles, characters, and literary terms are listed in this glossary. Information on authors can be found in the preceding section and/or the People chapter. Symbols used here are:

G-Greek
R-Roman
N-Norse
M-myth
L-legend

An Acrostic

The first letters of each line in this poem (by a father for his children's birthdays) spell the names of the children.

Pulled by the years, he grows away from us
And upward toward manhood's might.
Under it all, we know the boy he is,
Light and worryless, the world still
all aright.

Joining her brother, she too grows away.
Undaunted by the future's wild embrace,
Day by day she strives toward womanhood.
Yet we hold still the girl, her light and
careless grace.

years of adventure and hardship, Aeneas comes to the river Tiber. Here he kills his rival, Turnus, marries Lavinia, daughter of Latinus, king of Latium, and founds the city of Lavinium. Aeneas is the legendary ancestor of the city of Rome, for his son founded Alba Longa where Romulus and Remus were born and which was superseded by Rome itself. John Dryden's famous translation of the collected writings of Vergil, including the *Aeneid,* appeared in 1697.

Aeolus, GRM: god of the winds who lived on an island where he kept the winds in a cave. One day Odysseus in his wanderings came to this place, and the kindly Aeolus gave him the four winds tied up in a leather bag with a command to the fair winds to blow the wanderers home. But one night while Odysseus slept, his sailors decided they too must share the treasure in the mysterious leather bag. They untied the string; the fierce winds rushed out and drove the ships back to Aeolus. He was so disgusted at this stupidity that he would not help them further.

Aesir, NM: race of gods that included most of the major deities: Odin, Tyr, Thor, Frigga, Balder, and Loki. The Aesir warred with the other race of gods, the Vanir (of whom the chief deities were Frey and Freya), but eventually made peace with them. Their home was Asgard.

Aesop's Fables: collection of very short stories in which animal characters behave and speak like human beings, showing the weaknesses and foibles of human nature. Each fable ends with a moral. They are attributed to Aesop, a deformed Phrygian slave who lived about 620–560 B.C. He was freed by his master and is said to have won fame for his wisdom at the court of Croesus, king of Lydia. There is a legend that Aesop saved the throne for Peisistratus, the king of Athens, by telling his fable of "King Log and King Stork" to the discontented mob that was threatening to dethrone him.

Some of the stories themselves are centuries older than Aesop and are of

Oriental origin. Babrius in the first century B.C. put them into Greek verse, and Phaedrus in the first century A.D. translated them into Latin. In the 14th century, Maximus Planudes, a monk, collected 144 fables, and from these all the later collections known as Aesop's have been taken. La Fontaine translated them into French verse during the 17th century.

Agamemnon: *See* House of Atreus.

Ahab: *See* Moby-Dick.

Ajax (the Greater), GM: one of the Greek heroes of the Trojan War. On the death of Achilles, Ajax and Odysseus were rivals for the arms of the dead hero. They fell to Odysseus, and Ajax, maddened by jealousy, killed himself. Another account of the story is found in Sophocles' tragedy *Ajax,* which tells how Ajax, blinded with insane disappointment, mistook a flock of sheep for the sons of Atreus and slew them all. When his reason returned, he was so ashamed of his deed that he killed himself with his sword.

Ajax (the Lesser), GM: one of the Greek heroes in the siege of Troy. Except for Achilles, none was swifter than he. He was skilled with the spear, but he was a great boaster. On his way home he was shipwrecked, but Poseidon cast him on a great rock. Instead of giving thanks, he bragged that he had saved himself. So Poseidon split the rock, and Ajax was drowned.

Aladdin: in *The Arabian Nights' Entertainments,* the son of a poor tailor, who finds a magic lamp and ring. Two jinn, servants of the lamp and ring, come to do the bidding of the new owner. Aladdin gains great wealth, marries the sultan's daughter, and builds a marvelous palace.

Albion: ancient poetic name for the island of Britain.

Alcestis, GM: wife of Admetus. Apollo had secured the promise of the gods that Admetus need never die, but on

condition that when his death day came, another should offer to die in his place. Alcestis willingly gave her life for her husband. But the grief of Admetus was so great that Hercules brought her back from the lower world. Her story is the subject of Euripides' play *Alcestis,* and Chaucer included her in his *Legend of Good Women.*

Alchemist, The: comedy of humours by English playwright Ben Jonson, performed in 1616. Face, a butler, invites Subtle, posing as an alchemist, and the strumpet Doll Common to use his master's house to trick numerous hypocritical townsmen out of their money. The play is an example of Jonson's use of characters dominated by "humours" (*see also* Humours). It also uses typenames, such as Tribulation Wholesome for an unctuous Puritan minister. Jonson treats the rogues Face and Subtle more sympathetically than their victims.

Alexandrian Age: period of learning and literary activity in Egypt from about 300 B.C. to 30 B.C., when Alexandria was the cultural center of the world. The great Alexandrian Library, containing the largest collection of manuscripts (400,000, it is said) of ancient times, was founded during the reign of Ptolemy Soter of Egypt (323–283 B.C.) and enlarged by his successors.

The Alexandrian period was distinguished by great scientists and mathematicians, such as Euclid, Archimedes, and Diophantus, and the last of the Greek poets, Callimachus, Theocritus, and Apollonius Rhodius.

Alexandria Quartet, The: four novels—*Justine* (1957), *Balthazar* (1958), *Mountolive* (1958), and *Clea* (1961)—by Anglo-Irish writer Lawrence Durrell. Together they tell a story of love as it exists in the atmosphere of relativity that dominates 20th-century life. Each book portrays the same characters from a different point of view, raising questions as to the nature of truth. The background is the exotic Middle Eastern city, Alexandria.

Alexandrine: *See* Stanza.

Ali Baba: in *The Arabian Nights' Entertainments* story of "Ali Baba and the Forty Thieves," a poor woodcutter who one day overhears the magic words by which the Forty Thieves enter their treasure cave. "Open Sesame," says Ali Baba when the thieves are gone; and he enters, loads his donkey with gold, and goes home. His brother also goes to the cave. But he forgets the words and cannot get out of the cave. When the thieves find him, they kill him. At last the robber captain discovers who it is that knows their secret. He hides his men in jars that he brings to Ali Baba's house, intending to jump out and kill him while he sleeps. But Morgana, the little servant girl, kills them all with boiling oil.

AESOP: A 19th-century illustration of the fable "The Sick Lion and the Fox."

emphasize
US

emphasise
Brit.

center
US

centre
Brit.

Alice's Adventures in Wonderland: classic fantasy by British mathematician Charles Lutwidge Dodgson (who wrote under the pseudonym Lewis Carroll), published in 1865. Alice falls into a rabbit hole but preserves her indestructible common sense in spite of the topsy-turvy world she discovers underground. The story has levels of satire that are appreciated by adults. However, attempts to identify Alice's queer companions, such as the March Hare, the Mad Hatter, or the Mock Turtle, with public figures in Victorian England have not been verified. As far as anyone knows, they are simply delightful nonsense creatures, originally invented by Carroll to amuse a young friend, Alice Liddell, while on a boat trip up the Thames. *Through the Looking-Glass,* a sequel, appeared in 1872; the two books, with the classic illustrations by John Tenniel, are usually published as one.

ALICE: John Tenniel's illustration of the popular heroine meeting the Dodo bird.

labors
US

labours
Brit.

Allegory: story with a literal meaning that suggests a deeper, figurative meaning. The characters often personify ideas or qualities, a type of person, or even a nation. The actions symbolize other more significant actions. An allegory is far more than a metaphor; it calls for greater length of figurative expression and a more sustained imagination on the part of both author and reader. Fables and parables are simple allegories with but one idea or moral to be put over. The long allegory can be narration or description, poetry, or drama. John Bunyan's *Pilgrim's Progress* is the most famous allegory in English—the story of Christian's trials and troubles as he seeks the Celestial City.

Alliteration: beginning two or more consecutive words, or words near together, with the same letter or sound. "Now or never," "time and tide," "spick and span" are instances of alliteration in everyday phrases.

Alliteration was the base of ancient German and Old English versification. Each line broke into two halves, with most of the accented syllables beginning with the same sound. Although no longer used as a structural base, alliteration is a common and effective device in poetry.

All Quiet on the Western Front: anti-war novel by the German writer Erich Maria Remarque, published in 1929. It shocked the world because it dealt with the everyday horrors in the trenches in a cool, matter-of-fact, realistic style known in Germany as "the new objectivity." Without heroism, patriotism, or high-sounding words, its hero, a 19-year-old conscript, endures the attrition of the war and is killed just before the armistice.

All's Well That Ends Well: one of Shakespeare's "dark comedies," first performed in 1602. Helena, daughter of a physician, claims the hand of Bertram, count of Rousillon, as her reward for having cured the king of France. He reluctantly marries her, then leaves for a war in Florence, declaring that he will have nothing to do with her until she can show him both his ring and her child by him. She follows him, disguises herself, and tricks him into giving her both; he at last accepts her.

All the King's Men: Pulitzer Prize-winning novel by U.S. author Robert Penn Warren, first published in 1946. Based on the career of Louisiana politician Huey Long, the novel relates the rise of a demagogue named Willie Stark and its effect on the narrator, his press agent, Jack Burden.

Almanach de Gotha: social register of royal and noble European families.

Amazons, GM: race of warlike women who lived in Pontus near the Euxine Sea. No men were allowed to live among them, and all the boys who were born were either killed or sent to a neighboring country to live with their fathers. In Vergil's *Aeneid,* the Amazons fought against the Greeks in the Trojan War, and their queen was killed by Achilles. One of the Twelve Labors of Hercules was to steal the girdle of their queen, Hippolyte.

Ambassadors, The: late novel by Anglo-American writer Henry James, published in 1903, in which he returns to his favorite "international theme" of contrasting European and American values. Middle-aged Lambert Strether is sent to Paris by his wealthy fiancée, the widowed Mrs. Newsome, to bring home her son Chad, who is involved with a French woman. But Strether discovers that under the tutelage of his French mistress, Chad has grown in refinement and depth. Awakened to possibilities of life that are unknown in his Massachusetts hometown, Strether betrays his trust to Mrs. Newsome, knowing he will never be forgiven, and advises Chad to stay in Paris.

Ambrosia: food of the Greek gods. Together with their drink, nectar, it made them immortal.

American Language, The: scholarly work, first published in 1919, by U.S. journalist H. L. Mencken. In it he discusses the development of the American as opposed to the English language, studying in particular the unique expressions and idioms of American English. Substantial supplements were added in 1945 and 1948.

American Tragedy, An: novel by U.S. writer Theodore Dreiser, published in 1925. Its central character, Clyde Griffiths, has a secret affair with Roberta, a fellow factory worker. Clyde is obsessed with his chances for future advancement with the company. When he meets the wealthy local belle Sondra, she becomes the symbol of his aspirations. Roberta becomes pregnant and Clyde takes her to a secluded lake, planning to drown her. Although he loses his nerve, the boat overturns, and Roberta is drowned. Clyde is executed for murder. The story was based on an actual murder case; the motive—the insidiousness of the American dream of success—was supplied by Dreiser.

Anabasis, The: history by the Greek general Xenophon, first transcribed in the fourth century B.C. It deals with an unsuccessful expedition of 10,000 Greeks to aid the Persian king Cyrus. The Greeks are cut off and make a forced retreat, a "march upcountry," through hostile territory. Xenophon, one of the leaders of the Greeks, gives a lively account of the deprivations and narrow escapes they endure before they at last reach the sea.

Anapest: *See* Foot.

Anatomy of Melancholy, The: medical treatise by the English scholar Robert Burton, first published in 1621. Burton writes about "melancholy," which for him includes all states of mind from pessimism to insanity, and gives many quotes from both ancient and contemporary authors. Thanks to Burton's wit, learning, and interest in curious facts, the book has long outlived its medical usefulness.

And Quiet Flows the Don: *See* Silent Don, The.

Androclus or **Androcles,** RL: runaway slave who hid in a lion's cave in Africa. Without fear he pulled a painful thorn from the lion's paw. In later years, Androclus was captured and thrown to the lions in the arena. But instead of attacking Androclus, one old lion fawned upon him and caressed him. Androclus and his lion were set free. G. B. Shaw based his play, *Androcles and the Lion,* on this story.

Andromache, GM: wife of the Trojan hero Hector. After the capture of Troy and the death of Hector, the Greeks threw her little son Astyanax from the walls of the city, and she was taken captive by Neoptolemus, son of Achilles. Later Andromache became the wife of

Helenus, brother of Hector. She is the subject of a tragedy by Racine, based on the *Andromache* by Euripides.

Andromeda, GM: princess of Ethiopia. Her mother, Cassiopeia, boasted that she was more beautiful than the daughters of Poseidon. In wrath Poseidon sent a sea monster to lay waste the land. Andromeda was chained to a rock in the sea as a sacrifice to be devoured by the creature. Perseus, flying home from his victory over the Gorgon Medusa, saw the beautiful maiden and saved her life. He had with him the head of Medusa; one look at it turned the monster into stone. Andromeda then married Perseus. The story is the basis of Corneille's classical drama *Andromède.*

Anglo-Saxon Chronicle: history of England up to A.D. 1154, the first prose work in Old English. The chronicle of England to the year 892 was collected from different local sources by order of Alfred the Great, who himself may have dictated the parts relating to his own time. The work was subsequently continued in various manuscripts, seven of which are still in existence.

Angry young men: group of British writers of the 1950s and 1960s, largely of working-class origin, who attacked contemporary social values in their novels and plays. The prime example is John Osborne, whose play *Look Back in Anger* (1956) made the movement famous on both sides of the Atlantic. Other writers associated with the movement are Kingsley Amis and Alan Sillitoe.

Animal Farm: anti-Utopian novel, written in the form of a beast fable, by British author George Orwell, published in 1945. A group of farm animals overthrow their human masters and set up a communal society. But the pigs gradually take over, and the commune becomes a dictatorship. While universally applicable, the fable has a particular similarity to Orwell's view of events in the Soviet Union after the Bolshevik Revolution.

Anna Karenina: major novel by Russian writer Leo Tolstoy, published in 1873–1876. Anna, a warm and beautiful woman, leaves her husband, a cold bureaucrat, for her lover, Count Vronsky. Deprived of seeing her son and snubbed by her former friends, she is reduced to abject dependency on Vronsky. At last, having persuaded herself that Vronsky loves another, she throws herself in front of a moving train. The novel is a brilliant picture of aristocratic Russian society and contains the autobiographical character Levin, whose life is based on truer values than those of society.

Antaeus, GM: one of the giant sons of Poseidon and Gaea (earth). He could not be beaten as long as he touched the earth, for he received new strength from his mother. Hercules discovered the secret of his strength, lifted the giant into the air, and strangled him.

Anthology: literally, a collection of flowers; used metaphorically for a collection of beautiful or representative passages from literature. The most famous one was *The Greek Anthology,* a collection of 4,500 short Greek elegiac poems and epigrams begun by Meleager about 60 B.C.; continued by Philippus of Thessalonica, who was first to apply the word *anthologia* to the collection; and enlarged until about A.D. 1320.

The numerous anthologies available today include anthologies of many authors' writings on a single subject, like love; of many authors' writings of a certain type, like the narrative essay; of several different works by one author; of children's literature; and of golden thoughts and sage sayings.

Antigone: tragedy by Greek dramatist Sophocles, performed in 440 B.C.; the final play of the *Oedipus* trilogy. It concerns the conflict between individual conscience and the authority of the state. Antigone, the daughter of Oedipus, piously buries the body of her brother Polynices in defiance of King Creon's decree that his body remain unburied because of his treachery. Creon orders Antigone to be buried alive. She and her intended husband Haemon, Creon's son, commit suicide, as does Creon's wife when she learns of Haemon's death.

Antony and Cleopatra: tragedy by William Shakespeare, first presented about 1607; taken from Plutarch's *Lives.* Antony, who has been living with Cleopatra in Egypt, returns to Rome and renews his ties with Octavius, marrying his sister Octavia. When Antony then returns to Cleopatra, Octavius uses this insult to his sister as an excuse for invading Egypt. He defeats Antony at sea and pursues him to Egypt. Antony, defeated and believing that Cleopatra has killed herself, runs on his sword. He finds too

ANTIGONE: Greek actress Irene Papas seeks to bury her brother in the film version.

late that the rumor is false, but lives long enough to kiss her goodnight. Cleopatra, learning that Octavius will exhibit her in Rome as a captive, kills herself by allowing herself to be bitten by an asp.

Aphorism: short sentence stating a truth or principle. An aphorism is formulated by one author, and differs from a maxim, or saying, which is folk wisdom. The term was first used by the Greek physician Hippocrates for his collection of medical principles.

Aphrodite, GM: goddess of love, beauty, and fertility. Hesiod says she was born of the foam of the sea; but in the *Iliad* she is the daughter of Zeus and Dione. In the *Odyssey* Hephaestus is her husband, and Ares her lover. She was the mother of Eros and of Aeneas by Anchises. She is identified with the Semitic fertility goddess Ishtar, called Ashtaroth in the Bible, and with the Roman goddess Venus.

ANIMAL FARM: The dominant pigs work at their office in the 1955 animated cartoon of the novel-length fable by George Orwell.

Apollo, GM: god of youth and manly beauty, son of Zeus and Leto; also called Phoebus. He was the god of poetry and music; the grasshopper was sacred to him as the symbol of song. Orpheus was his son. Apollo was also the god of healing and could avert sickness or evil; Asclepius, god of medicine, was another son. In Homer, Apollo is the god of prophecy; his oracles were unerring and were honored everywhere. The one at Delphi was the most famous. Apollo was later identified with Helios, the sun god; Artemis, his twin, was goddess of the moon. The Romans took over the worship of Apollo from the Greeks.

Apollonian: *See* Birth of Tragedy...

Apology (or *apologia*): in literature, a term borrowed from the law courts of ancient Athens, where an apology was a speech for the defense in a trial. Socrates' speeches in his defense at his trial, published by Plato, are known as *The Apology of Socrates.* Other authors have used the term as a title; at first it denoted an autobiography, but later "apology" was used for books that present the author's justification of his life.

Arabian Nights' Entertainments, The (or *The Thousand and One Nights*): famous collection of Indian, Persian, and Arabic folk tales and romances. Originally in the oral tradition, they were gathered in their present form in the 15th century and unified by the frame-story of Princess Scheherazade. Having married an embittered king who has the habit of killing his wives after his wedding night, the clever princess saves her life by starting to tell a tale each night but leaving it unfinished until the next day. After a thousand such tales, the king decides to spare her. The work became known in Europe in the 18th century. Among its best-known tales are "Ali Baba and the Forty Thieves" and "Aladdin, or the Wonderful Lamp."

Arachne, GM: Lydian maiden of great skill as a weaver. So beautiful was her work that she challenged Athena to a contest. Arachne wove a tapestry showing stories of the loves of the gods—Leda and the swan, Europa and the bull, Danae in her tower. The work was beautiful, but Athena ripped it into shreds to punish the maiden for her impiety and for daring to challenge her. Arachne then hanged herself, and Athena changed her into a spider, hanging by a thread from her own web and forever spinning. The biological name for spiders, *arachnids,* is derived from her name.

Arcadia: inland plateau of central Greece, shut in by mountains. The ancient inhabitants were shepherds and simple mountain folk. Arcadia is celebrated in the literature of many languages as a place of pastoral pleasure, contentment, and rest, and has come to symbolize the ideal country of lost or unattainable happiness.

The symbols used in this glossary are as follows:

G-Greek
R-Roman
N-Norse
M-myth
L-legend

Ares, GM: god of war; son of Zeus and Hera. In Homer's *Odyssey,* Ares is the lover of Aphrodite, whose husband Hephaestus catches them together in a net and holds them up to be laughed at by the gods. The story is typical of the low esteem in which Ares is held in Greek legend. The Romans identified Ares with their war-god Mars, for whom the month March is named.

AROUND THE WORLD: Passepartout and Phileas Fogg in the popular film.

Argonauts, GM: band of adventurers who sailed with Jason in the ship *Argo* to find the Golden Fleece. Jason, son of Aeson, king of Iolcus in Thessaly, demanded his kingdom back from his uncle Pelias, the usurper; Pelias agreed to give it up if Jason would bring back the Golden Fleece. Jason gathered a company of heroes, including Hercules, Castor and Pollux, and Theseus, and sailed to Colchis, where the fleece was guarded by a never-sleeping dragon.

Jason and the Argonauts arrived in Colchis after many adventures, but Aeetes, king of Colchis, would not give up the fleece until Jason performed several impossible tasks. Aeetes' daughter Medea, the enchantress, fell in love with Jason and helped him perform his tasks. Jason took the fleece and sailed home again on the *Argo,* taking Medea with him as his wife.

Argus, GM: monster with a hundred eyes; Hera set it to watch Io, one of Zeus's lovers. Zeus ordered Hermes to kill Argus; so Hermes played upon the lyre until all the hundred eyes were closed, then cut off the monster's head. Hera put the eyes of Argus in the tail of the peacock, her sacred bird.

Argus was also the name of the Greek shipwright who built the *Argo* (*see* Argonauts) and of Odysseus's faithful dog, the first to recognize Odysseus when he returned home ten years after the end of the Trojan War.

Ariadne, GM: daughter of Minos, king of Crete. She fell in love with Theseus, who had arranged to be sent from Athens as a sacrifice to be devoured by the Minotaur, intending to slay the monster instead. Before he entered the labyrinth, Ariadne gave him a spool of thread to unwind so he could find his way out. Theseus slew the Minotaur and returned to her, following the thread. She fled with him away from Crete, but he either abandoned her on the island of Naxos or was unwillingly blown away from the port. One story says Ariadne died of grief, another that Dionysus found her sleeping there and made her his wife.

Ariel: *See* Tempest, The.

Around the World in 80 Days: novel by French writer Jules Verne, published serially in *Le Temps,* 1871–1872. Phileas Fogg, a precise, dignified English gentleman, wagers that he can travel around the world in 80 days (then an unthinkable feat); as he sets out with his intrepid French valet Passepartout on a fabulous journey by ship, balloon, camel, elephant, and train, he is mistaken for a bank robber by Detective Fix, who pursues the two through the resulting series of adventures. Fogg wins his bet by a hair's breadth.

Artemis, GM: goddess of the hunt, of nature, and of chastity. The oldest conception of Artemis was probably as a harvest goddess. When Oenus of Calydon did not present her with a harvest offering, she sent the terrible Calydonian boar to ravage his fields. She was the goddess of nature, especially the wilderness, and her festivals were celebrated with all kinds of animals and fruits. The bear especially was associated with her, and the hind was also sacred to her. She was the protector of women and children and goddess of childbirth.

To the ancient Greeks, Artemis was daughter of Zeus and Leto and the twin of Apollo. As Apollo became known as the sun god, Artemis became goddess of the moon. The Romans identified her with their own goddess Diana.

Art for art's sake: poetic principle stating that a work of art should exist for its own sake rather than for a certain purpose, such as educating or morally uplifting the reader. The term was popularized by the French symbolist poets. Edgar Allan Poe in *The Poetic Principle* (1850) writes of "the poem written solely for the poem's sake."

Arthurian legend: cycle of verse and prose tales concerning the mythical King Arthur of Britain and his knights of the Round Table. The legend provided one of the principal themes of medieval romance throughout Europe. The Arthur of romance was of marvelous birth, conceived by Queen Igraine while his father Uther Pendragon was magically disguised as Igraine's husband. Arthur was marked for kingship as a young boy when he proved to be the only one who could remove the sword Excalibur from the stone in which it was imbedded. This feat was interpreted as a sign of the true king. (In a common variant, Arthur received Excalibur from the mysterious Lady of the Lake, also called Vivian or Nimue, who handed it up to him through the water.) Arthur married Guinevere and established his court at Camelot, where he was advised by the wizard Merlin, and where he gathered at his Round Table the flower of knighthood. It is the adventures and love affairs of the various knights that constitute the bulk of the legend. The adulterous love of Arthur's favorite knight, Lancelot, and his queen, Guinevere, led to the disintegration of the fellowship of the Round Table and Arthur's treacherous nephew Mordred attempted to usurp his throne. Though Arthur killed Mordred in battle, he was himself severely wounded. In some versions of the legend he died and was buried at Glastonbury, England. In others, Sir Bedivere threw Excalibur into the lake. The Lady's hand reached out to receive it. A barge appeared and carried Arthur to the isle of Avalon, from which he was expected to return some day, healed of his wounds.

There is some evidence that Arthur was an actual historical figure, a Celtic chieftain of the sixth century. The earliest stories about Arthur are Welsh. The chronicler Geoffrey of Monmouth describes Arthur's deeds in his largely fictitious *History of the Kings of Britain,* written in Latin in the twelfth century. The Norman-French poet Wace translated Geoffrey's history into a verse epic, *Brut,* adding the story of the Round Table. The first Arthurian poem in English was a translation of Wace's *Brut* by Layamon. The legend received its first sophisticated treatment in the romances of the French poet Chrétien de Troyes. In the 15th century the English prose *Morte d'Arthur* by Sir Thomas Malory fixed the legend in its traditional form. Modern versions include Wagner's operas *Tristan und Isolde* and *Parsifal,* Alfred Tennyson's poems *Idylls of the King* (1859–1885), and T. H. White's novel *The Once and Future King* (1958). *See also* Holy Grail; Knights of the Round Table; Gawain; Lancelot; Percival; Morgan le Fay; Merlin; *and* Morte d'Arthur.

Art of Love, The: poem by Roman poet Ovid (Publius Ovidius Naso), written in 1 B.C. It mocks the prevailing Roman tradition of didactic poetry by providing a handbook on the art of seduction down to the minutest details.

Art of Poetry, The: treatise on the art of writing poetry by the Roman poet Horace. The title was borrowed by Boileau for his book *L'Art Poetique* (1674), which set forth literary principles that were carefully followed by authors of the French classical period.

ARTHUR: The legendary king and his knights are portrayed in this 19th-century engraving as they discuss the founding of the "table round."

Asclepius: *See* Apollo.

Asgard, NM: abode of the gods, reachable only over the rainbow bridge Bifrost.

Assonance: repetition of similar, closely juxtaposed vowel sounds in a poetic passage, often used as an alternative to rhyme. For example, consider the italicized vowels in a line by W. B. Yeats: 'They will not h*u*sh, the leaves afl*u*tter round me, the b*ee*ch l*ea*ves old."

As You Like It: comedy by Shakespeare, first produced about 1599. The principal characters are the exiled Duke; his usurper brother Frederick; Frederick's daughter Celia; the Duke's daughter Rosalind; her lover Orlando; his cruel older brother Oliver; and the comic characters Audrey, Touchstone the jester, and the melancholy Jacques. The complicated plot is set in the Forest of Arden, where the exiled Duke is living and whither the other characters either flee or pursue each other. Being a good comedy, *As You Like It* ends with not one but four marriages, as well as the restoration of the Duke.

Atalanta, GM: beautiful girl who challenged all her suitors to a foot race. If she lost, she would marry the winner; if she won, the loser would be put to death. A man whose name is given in legend as either Hippomenes or Milanion eventually won her because Aphrodite had given him three of the Golden Apples of the Hesperides; he threw them in front of Atalanta as they ran, and she stopped to pick them up, thus losing the race.

Athena, GM: goddess of wisdom, industry, and war; often called Pallas Athena. She was the daughter of Zeus and Metis, and was born full grown and fully armed from the brain of Zeus. Depicted on the west pediment of her temple in Athens, the Parthenon, was the contest between her and Poseidon for the position of patron of the city. Poseidon's gift to the city was a spring (or, in some versions, the horse); Athena's was the olive tree. The people selected her, and the city was named Athens in her honor. She was also the patroness of arts and crafts and the helper and protector of the Greeks in war. The Romans identified her with Minerva.

Atlantis: fabled island in the Atlantic Ocean, west of the Pillars of Hercules. Plato and Pliny both mention it. Plato in "Timaeus" says that Atlantis was larger than Asia Minor and Libya, and was a once-ideal state that became corrupt and militaristic and used its great power to attempt to conquer the world. It was destroyed by earthquakes and sank into the sea. That such an island ever existed is doubtful, yet the question was still debated in the 1600s and 1700s by such notable writers as Montaigne and Voltaire. The idea of an advanced civilization where learning and scientific research were encouraged appealed to Western rationalists who tried to identify the lost land with America and the Canary Islands. Sir Francis Bacon entitled his essay on such a utopia of learning *The New Atlantis* (1626). Atlantis's rediscovery occurs in Jules Verne's *20,000 Leagues Under the Sea* (1870), where science, in the shape of a submarine, fulfills its promise of answers to questions such as the one regarding Atlantis's existence. In contemporary science fiction, the corrupt or ruined aspect of Atlantis is emphasized, corresponding to the modern pessimistic outlook on scientific progress.

20 History of Literature

honor
US

honour
Brit.

civilization
US

civilisation
Brit.

emphasized
US

emphasised
Brit.

Atlas, GM: one of the Titans, who rebelled against the gods and lost. Atlas's punishment was to stand forever, holding up the heavens. His one respite came when Hercules shouldered the sky so that Atlas could fetch him some of the Golden Apples of the Hesperides. Atlas returned with the apples but refused to resume his burden; Hercules tricked him by asking him to take it for a moment while Hercules made a pad

ATLAS: a Greek Titan whose rebellion brought the punishment of holding up the heavens.

for his shoulders. Later Perseus turned Atlas to stone by showing him the Gorgon's head, and Atlas became the Atlas Mountains in North Africa. Atlas was the father of the Pleiades.

The Flemish cartographer Mercator in the 1500s used a picture of Atlas holding up the world on the title page of his books of maps, and such books have since been called atlases.

Atreus: *See* House of Atreus.

Augean Stables: *See* Hercules.

Augustan Age: reign of Augustus Caesar (27 B.C.–A.D. 14), a time when Latin literature reached its highest development under the patronage of Augustus and his minister Maecenas. The great writers of the period were Vergil, Horace, Ovid, and Livy.

The reign of Queen Anne (1702–1714) is called the Augustan Age of English literature, a period notable for the writings of Steele, Swift, Pope, and Addison.

In France the term is applied to the reign of Louis XIV (1643–1715), when Corneille, Racine, and Molière wrote their brilliant plays.

Aurora: *See* Eos.

Autobiography: self-written life history. *The Confessions of St. Augustine* (late fourth and early fifth centuries) is considered the earliest autobiography in Western literature. Cellini's *Autobiography of Benvenuto Cellini* is a vivid picture of the Italian Renaissance and some of its outstanding personages, as well as of the artist himself. Rousseau's *Confessions,* published in 1782, was the first great introspective autobiography. Novels can masquerade as autobiographies, like Defoe's *Moll Flanders,* or autobiographies as novels, like Joyce's *Portrait of the Artist as a Young Man.* Among the most famous modern autobiographies are: Benjamin Franklin's *Autobiography* (first published in full, 1868); Booker T. Washington's *Up from Slavery* (1901); *The Education of Henry Adams* (1906); André Gide's *If It Die* (1926); *The Autobiography of Lincoln Steffens* (1931); Charles Lindbergh's *The Spirit of St. Louis* (1954); and Claude Brown's *Manchild in the Promised Land* (1965).

Autobiography of Alice B. Toklas, The: written by U.S. expatriate Gertrude Stein as if her secretary and companion Alice Toklas wrote it about herself. The experimental work, published in 1933, relates the story of Stein's life. In addition to describing her intellectual development and her attempt to develop a literary cubism to match her friend Picasso's visual style, she has Ms. Toklas's persona say that she knew three geniuses in her life—Pablo Picasso, Alfred North Whitehead, and Gertrude Stein.

Autocrat of the Breakfast Table: familiar essays by U.S. physician and writer Oliver Wendell Holmes, published in the first twelve issues of the *Atlantic Monthly,* 1857–1858, and soon after as a book. The setting is a boardinghouse breakfast table. The table talk—usually a monologue delivered by the Autocrat (Holmes)—rambles informally over a variety of subjects.

Avalon: *See* Arthurian legend.

B

Babbitt: novel by U.S. writer Sinclair Lewis, published in 1922. Its hero George Babbitt, a small-town businessman and town booster whose horizons are limited to Zenith (the "greatest little city in the world"), gave his name to an emergent social type. Although Babbitt eventually comes to the vague realization that Zenith and his own ideas are narrow-minded and provincial, he lacks the strength to leave or change.

Babi Yar: prison camp for Jews in Russia during World War II; the subject of two works by Soviet authors: a poem by Yevgeny Yevtushenko (1961) and a novel by Anatoly P. Kuznetsov (1966–1967).

Yevtushenko's poem decries anti-Semitism and inhumanity both in the Soviet Union and in the rest of the world. Kuznetsov recounts his eyewitness impressions of the Nazi extermination of Kiev's entire Jewish population and censures Soviet authorities for their tacit approval and attempts to cover up the incident.

Bacchus: *See* Dionysus.

Balder, NM: god of light, son of Odin and Frigga. Frigga exacted a vow from all creation never to harm Balder, but she neglected to ask the insignificant mistletoe. Arrows, stones, spears, or battle-axes could not injure him. But Loki, the mischief-maker, cut off a twig of the mistletoe and made a dart of it. He gave it to the blind Hoder and directed his aim. Balder was pierced by the dart and fell dead. Hel (death) agreed to let Balder return to life if all things in the world would weep for him. All things on Earth wept except Loki; Balder never returned, but Loki was later punished.

Ballad: traditionally, a narrative poem in simple stanza form and of unknown folk authorship. Ballads deal with folk legends, heroes, supernatural stories, unhappy love, murders, and disasters. The grim and tragic stories bear testimony to their primitive origin, for the true ballads were handed down orally from generation to generation. There were almost no written ballads before the 15th century, but the ballads themselves are centuries older.

The typical ballad stanza is the simplest of verse forms. It has four lines, of which the first and third are unrhymed and have four accents each; the second and fourth are rhymed and contain three accents each.

In the 1700s, literary scholars began to take an interest in ballads. Ballads had an enormous influence on the English and German Romantic movements. The "Rime of the Ancient Mariner" by Coleridge is an "art ballad," a literary adaptation of the folk ballad.

American ballads are of two kinds: those descended from the old Scottish or English ballads, which immigrated with the early settlers; and those that have sprung up spontaneously among mountaineers, cowboys, lumberjacks, and miners. Many of these, like the Scottish border ballads, deal with outlaws and violent death. Some, like "The Streets of Laredo," are native variants of older ballads.

Ballad of the Sad Cafe, The: novella by U.S. writer Carson McCullers, published in 1951, later dramatized by playwright Edward Albee (1963). Set in a dreary Southern small town, the action concerns the strange relationship, beginning in love and ending in violence, of three loners: a six-foot woman, her ex-convict former husband, and a tiny hunchback. Through them, the story explores the mystery and pain of loving and being loved.

Banquo: in Shakespeare's *Macbeth,* a thane (lord) who was murdered by Macbeth. Banquo's ghost returned to torment Macbeth.

Barabbas: novel by Swedish author Pär Lagerkvist, published in 1950. It describes the fate, after the Crucifixion, of the prisoner chosen to be saved instead of Jesus.

Barbara Frietchie: poem by U.S. poet John Greenleaf Whittier, published in 1864. It recounts an incident supposed to have occurred at Frederick, Maryland, during the Civil War. Barbara was a patriotic old woman who refused to lower the Union flag from her home when the Confederates under General Jackson entered the town; challenged by her courage, he did not permit his troops to molest her.

Barchester Towers: entertaining satire by English author Anthony Trollope, published in 1857. It relates the gossip about, and the ambitions of, the characters in an English diocese. The wife of the new bishop, Dr. Proudie, maneuvers to change church services, dictates who should marry whom, and assigns additional duties to disliked clergy. She and Obadiah Slope, the bishop's chaplain, are rivals for control of Barchester Towers. When Slope's hypocrisy and plotting are exposed, his hopes of a promotion are dashed, and he is banished from the town.

Battle Hymn of the Republic: poem by U.S. writer Julia Ward Howe, published in the *Atlantic Monthly* in 1862. Sung to the tune of "John Brown's Body," it became a favorite with Union soldiers in the Civil War and has remained one of the most popular of patriotic songs.

BEAT POETS rejected established values but brought back live poetry reading.

Baucis and Philemon, GM: very poor aged couple who lived in Phrygia. Zeus and Hermes, travelling in disguise, were welcomed and fed in their cottage. Not until the pitcher returned to the table miraculously filled did Baucis and Philemon realize they were entertaining gods. The old couple's prayer to die together was granted; their cottage was changed into a temple, and they were changed into trees that grew at the gate of the temple.

Bay Psalm Book: book of psalms translated from the Bible by Thomas Welde, John Eliot, Richard Mather, and other ministers of the Massachusetts Bay Colony; published in Cambridge, Massachusetts, in 1640. It is one of the first two books printed in English in the American colonies.

Beat generation: term applied to a group of cultural nonconformists in the late 1950s in the United States. "Beatniks," as they were known, were particularly associated with poetry, jazz, and the rejection of U.S. cultural values. They constituted a major Bohemian artistic movement. Chief among Beat writers were Allen Ginsberg, Jack Kerouac, Gregory Corso, and Lawrence Ferlinghetti.

Beauty and the Beast: fairy tale, first published in French (*"La Belle et la Bête"*) in 1757 but in actuality probably much older. Beauty's father, having picked a rose in the Beast's garden, is forced to send her to the Beast. She goes to live in the Beast's enchanted palace, and each day she refuses his offer of marriage. But when she finds the kind Beast wounded, she embraces and kisses him, and he turns into a handsome prince.

Becket, or the Honor of God: drama by French playwright Jean Anouilh, presented in 1959. It concerns the friendship and estrangement of King Henry II of England and Thomas à Becket, his archbishop of Canterbury, who finds his honor in the honor of God. Becket is killed by Henry's barons because he has angered the king. T. S. Eliot's *Murder in the Cathedral* deals with the same story.

Becky Sharp: *See* Vanity Fair.

Bedivere: *See* Arthurian legend.

BEGGAR'S OPERA: Captain MacHeath is visited in jail by Polly Peacham (right). In Brecht's Threepenny Opera, MacHeath became Mack the Knife.

Beggar's Opera: ballad opera by British writer John Gay, performed in 1728. It was recognized by his contemporaries as a threefold satire: (1) of the corrupt Walpole administration; (2) of contemporary Italian opera; (3) of conventional English romantic comedy, since it drew its characters from the underworld. The leading figures are the Peacham family, dealers in stolen goods; the love interest is between their daughter Polly and the gallant Captain MacHeath, a highwayman, bigamist, and murderer. German dramatist Bertolt Brecht adapted Gay's play for his satire on capitalism *The Threepenny Opera,* performed in 1928, with music by Kurt Weill.

Bellerophon, GM: son of Glaucus, king of Corinth. He committed murder and fled to Proetus, king of Argos, for protection. Antaea, Proetus's wife, fell in love with Bellerophon, and when he rejected her advances, she accused him to the king. Proetus sent him to Iobates, king of Lycia, with a secret message asking that he be put to death. Iobates sent him to kill the terrible monster Chimera, sure he would meet his death. But Bellerophon had tamed the winged horse Pegasus, and on his back he was able to approach the Chimera and kill it. After other trials, in which he was successful, Iobates saw his worth and gave him his daughter in marriage. As Euripides tells it, Bellerophon's pride led him to try flying to Mount Olympus, but Pegasus threw him and he was killed.

Belles-lettres (French term meaning "beautiful literature"): artistic, aesthetic, or imaginative literature as art, contrasted with practical, informational, or scientific writings. The term now refers especially to light essays of appreciation, prose poems, or impressionistic sketches that do not fall into any definite category.

realize
US

realise
Brit.

honor
US

honour
Brit.

20 History of Literature

Beowulf: Old English (Anglo-Saxon) epic poem in alliterative verse, written perhaps in the 700s A.D., based on a mixture of legendary and historical events that took place in sixth-century Scandinavia. It is the oldest epic in a European vernacular.

BEOWULF: The aged hero wrestles with a fire-breathing monster.

centers
US

centres
Brit.

realize
US

realise
Brit.

emphasize
US

emphasise
Brit.

somber
US

sombre
Brit.

For twelve years the monster Grendel has walked into the Danish King Hrothgar's great mead hall Heorot and devoured as many as 30 warriors in one night. The young hero Beowulf, a prince of the Geats of southern Sweden, arrives to aid Hrothgar, wrestles with Grendel, and tears off his arm. Grendel flees to his den to die. The next night his mother, the water-hag, comes to avenge her son and devours another warrior. Beowulf follows her to the bottom of the sea and, after a terrible underwater fight, kills her and cuts off the head of Grendel's corpse. The Danes celebrate their delivery with great rejoicing in the mead hall and with speeches recalling heroic deeds of the past. Beowulf returns to his own people, laden with rich gifts.

Years later Beowulf becomes king of the Geats and rules for 50 years until a fearful dragon comes to lay waste his land. Beowulf and eleven companions set out to destroy it. At sight of the fire-breathing monster, his companions, except for the loyal Wiglaf, flee. With Wiglaf's aid, the aged Beowulf kills the dragon, but he receives his own death wound in the combat. His grieving people place his body on a great funeral pyre and bury the dragon's treasure with his ashes.

Bestiary: form of medieval literature in which the supposed natural habits of animals were used as examples for teaching Christian doctrine. A well known example used was the pelican, which was said to feed her young with her own blood; her action was said to reflect Christ's redemption of man. The writers of bestiaries gleaned their information from ancient authors, from legends, and from imagination, but their books were accepted as natural histories, perpetrating belief in fabulous beasts like the unicorn, the phoenix, and the hippogriff.

Betrothed, The: novel by Italian author Alessandro Manzoni, first published in 1827; often called the greatest of modern Italian novels. The plot centers on the trials endured in 17th-century Italy by two separated lovers, Renzo and Lucia, before their eventual reunion; their adventures bring them into contact with members of almost every class in Italian society. Manzoni's characters and descriptions are famous, and the book is comparable to *Don Quixote* in its evocation of national character.

Bhagavad-Gita: *See* Mahabharata.

Biblical influence on literature: with its striking imagery, poetic wisdom, religious concepts and terms, the Bible has exerted a profound influence over many languages and cultures. In cases where no written language existed, its translation became the occasion for developing an alphabet (for example, the Cyrillic alphabet, developed c 863, is still used by Eastern Church Slavs). World literature and art have been inspired by its stories and themes. Its proverbs and turns of phrase have become such integral parts of the European languages that speakers often do not realize the origin of derivative figures of speech (as in "grapes of wrath," "handwriting on the wall," "balm of Gilead," "thorn in the flesh").

Parts of the Bible were translated into the European languages in the 1300s and 1400s. These were, for the most part, word-for-word renderings, but even these clumsy translations were a major influence on the developing languages.

During the 1500s, the Reformation encouraged more ambitious translation projects. Martin Luther in Germany and the early English translators followed Humanist principles: that is, to translate for sense rather than literally, and to translate from the original languages, Hebrew and Greek, rather than from the Vulgate Bible, itself a Latin translation.

Luther's work, completed in 1534, was a major landmark in the establishment of German as a literary language; it is still used by German Protestants today. It influenced all translations, biblical and secular, that followed.

Among the early English translators, the most influential was William Tyndale. His incomplete translation (about 1525) formed a basis for the "Great Bible" (1539) and influenced the Authorized (or King James) Bible (1611). This translation remained the standard English version for 300 years, and is still admired for its literary power. Its style influenced many generations of poets and prose writers.

The new translations and the spread of printing made the Bible available to the common people. In many homes it would be the only book. It was read privately and in groups, for inspiration, education, and entertainment. Its poetic images and syntax so influenced the imagination, phraseology, and literary taste of European writers that it is impossible to fully appreciate European and American literature without familiarity with it.

Bibliography: list of books and articles on a special subject or a certain author. For instance, a complete bibliography of Sir Walter Scott includes the titles of everything that Scott wrote, with dates of publication, all editions and formats, and every book about Scott or any of his works, as well as all magazine articles and monographs about him.

In a more general sense, bibliography is the serious study or descriptive history of all manuscripts, books, and their making, including references to authors and editions, the materials used in their makeup, and the dates and styles of their printing.

Billy Budd: late short novel by U.S. writer Herman Melville, completed in 1891–1892 and published in 1925; a parable of the eternal conflict between good and evil and the limits of human justice. Unjustly accused of mutiny by his evil superior officer Claggart, the sailor Billy Budd, a model of natural innocence, kills Claggart and accepts his punishment—death. The story was the basis for an opera by Benjamin Britten.

Biography: written history of the life of a person. In early times biography was often written for political or moral purposes. In the first century A.D. Plutarch wrote his *Parallel Lives,* comparing the careers of a score of Romans with the same number of Greeks, pair by pair; countless later writers (Shakespeare among them) drew on this work for facts and characterization. Tacitus, the Roman historian, wrote a life of his father-in-law Agricola that is a classic; and Suetonius's

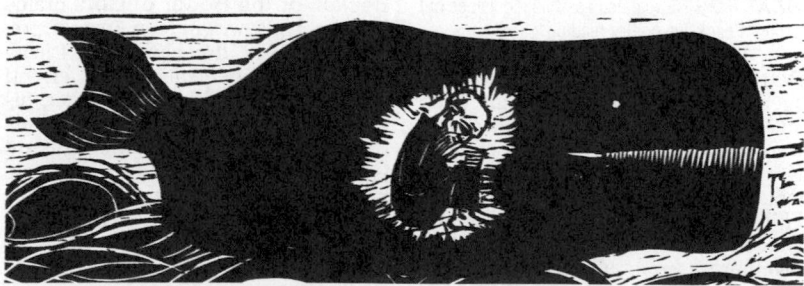

BIBLE: Jonah and the Whale, shown here in a 20th-century woodcut, is one of the many biblical stories that are familiar to all Western societies.

Lives of the Caesars (written about A.D. 120) is gossipy and full of scandal. These are samples of what is called "antique biography," written to emphasize certain moral qualities or to teach a political lesson.

Biography in English begins in the 1500s with William Roper's *Life of Sir Thomas More* and George Cavendish's *Life of Cardinal Wolsey.* In the 1600s Izaak Walton wrote *Lives* of Donne, Hooker, Herbert, and others that are the forerunners of modern personal biography. James Boswell's *Life of Samuel Johnson* (1791), considered one of the great biographies of all time, was based on Boswell's firsthand records of Johnson's sayings, habits, and most inconsequential everyday activities. Johnson himself wrote a critically important series of *Lives of the English Poets* (see entry).

In modern biography, the English writer Lytton Strachey initiated the "debunking" tradition of taking public figures down from their pedestals. In *Eminent Victorians* (1918) and *Queen Victoria* (1921), he portrayed the real person behind the popular public image, although many critics think he went out of his way to emphasize negative traits.

Although biography is an important literary form, not all biographies are or claim to be literature. Biographies may be written by historians as part of their historical studies, by family members to preserve the memory of an ancestor, or by journalists to inform readers about current personalities.

Birds, The: comedy by Greek playwright Aristophanes, first performed in 414 B.C.; generally considered the best of all ancient Greek comedies. Two Athenians, escaping from their city's courts and taxes, persuade all the birds to build a city in the air, called Cloud-Cuckooland. There they gain control of the food supplies of both men and gods, becoming rulers of the world and creating a utopia.

Birth of Tragedy from the Spirit of Music, The: essay by German philosopher Friedrich Nietzsche, published in 1872, in which the author defines two opposing dynamic cultural forces in ancient Greece. These two forces, which Nietzsche terms Dionysiac and Apollonian, are the dark, ecstatic side and the bright, rational side of man's nature; Nietzsche states that Greek tragedy was originally Dionysiac but eventually became too Apollonian, and he foresees a rebirth of "true" (that is, more Dionysiac) tragedy stemming from the work of German composer Richard Wagner.

Blank verse: unrhymed iambic penta, the most common metrical form in English dramatic and epic poetry. Shakespeare's plays, for example, are written in blank verse. It was first used by Henry Howard, Earl of Surrey, in his translations from the *Aeneid* in the 16th century. The first English drama written in blank verse was Sackville and Norton's tragedy *Gorboduc* in 1562. Christopher Marlowe made masterly use of it in his tragedy *Tamburlaine,* written in 1587. Shakespeare adopted and perfected it.

Bleak House: novel by English writer Charles Dickens, published serially, 1852–1853. It satirizes the injustice of delay in court proceedings.

Blood Wedding: drama by Spanish poet and playwright Federico García Lorca, first produced in 1933, a somber "rural tragedy" of violent passions. A timid bride runs away from her wedding feast with a former suitor, but she soon changes her mind again and wants to return. The bridegroom, who has caught up with the two, fights with the former suitor, and the two men kill each other.

Bloom, Leopold: *See* Ulysses.

Bloomsbury group: coterie of talented, elitist English intellectuals who began meeting in 1906, in the Bloomsbury district of London, to discuss philosophy and the arts and to gossip. Among others they included novelist Virginia Woolf; Fabian writer Leonard Woolf; economist John Maynard Keynes; biographer Lytton Strachey; artist Vanessa Bell; art critic Clive Bell; novelist E. M. Forster; painter Duncan Grant; and art critic/painter Roger Fry.

Bluebeard: fairy tale villain who murders his wives, one after the other, and hides them in a locked room. The story is built around the forbidden door (or forbidden chest) motif, one of the worldwide motifs of folklore. As a story,

BLUEBEARD: The monstrous husband gives Fatima the key to the forbidden door.

"Bluebeard" was first published as one of French author Charles Perrault's fairy tales. The original character is sometimes identified as the medieval French blackguard Gilles de Retz.

Bloomsbury Group's Representative Works

VIRGINIA WOOLF
Mrs. Dalloway (1925)
To the Lighthouse (1927)
A Room of One's Own (1929)
The Waves (1931)
LYTTON STRACHEY
Eminent Victorians (1918)
Queen Victoria (1921)
JOHN MAYNARD KEYNES
The Economic Consequences of the Peace (1919)
The General Theory of Employment, Interest and Money (1936)
CLIVE BELL
Civilization (1928)
Proust (1929)
E. M. FORSTER
Where Angels Fear to Tread (1905)
A Room with a View (1908)
A Passage to India (1924)
ROGER FRY
Vision and Design (1920)
Transformations (1926)
Cezanne (1927)

After murdering six wives, Bluebeard marries a seventh, named Fatima. Soon after the wedding Bluebeard goes off on a journey, leaving her all the keys of the castle but forbidding her to unlock one mysterious door. She unlocks the door and discovers the bodies of Bluebeard's dead wives. Overcome with terror, she drops the key, which becomes stained with blood and betrays her disobedience to Bluebeard on his return. She is rescued by her brothers, who kill Bluebeard. The Bluebeard story was the basis for Béla Bartók's opera *Bluebeard's Castle.*

Bohemian: originally, a native of Bohemia, a former kingdom in the area that became Czechoslovakia. The word eventually came to mean a gypsy, then any person—especially an artist or writer—who lives outside the rules of bourgeois society. The term gained currency after the publication of French author Henri Murger's *Scenes de la vie de Bohème* (1848; *Scenes from Bohemian Life*) about life in the artists' quarter in Paris; the book formed the basis for Puccini's opera *La Bohème* (1896) and established a romanticized picture of the Bohemian artist's life. *See also* Beat generation.

Boreas, GM: north wind; called Aquilo in Roman mythology.

Boris Godunov: history play by Russian poet Aleksandr Pushkin, published in 1831. It is the story of the rise of Boris, his usurpation of the throne by murdering the true Tsarevich, the rise of the pretender Dmitri, Boris's death, and the overthrow of his son by the same kind of political treachery that brought Boris to the throne. An opera of that name by Modest Mussorgsky, derived from the play, was first performed in 1874.

Bors, Sir: *See* Holy Grail.

Bottom, Nick: weaver in Shakespeare's *A Midsummer Night's Dream.* During a rehearsal for *Pyramus and Thisbe,* Puck puts an ass's head on Bottom; the fairy queen Titania falls in love with him because Oberon has put love drops on her eyes.

Bourgeois Gentilhomme, Le: *See* Would-Be Gentleman, The.

Brave New World: novel by British writer Aldous Huxley, published in 1932. Taking place in the year A.F. 632 ("after Ford" or "anno Fordi"), the novel satirizes 20th-century scientism and technocracy by portraying a society in which all social problems have been solved and life has become virtually painless but meaningless. Human beings are born from test tubes and classified for life according to intelligence—from Alphas, who are brilliant and creative, to Epsilons, whose stupidity fits them for the lowest menial jobs. People constantly pacify themselves with a tranquilizer drug called *soma.* The story is concerned with two misfits—John Savage, an Indian who has retained some of his own culture, and Bernard Marx, an Alpha who thinks too much—and their failure to adjust to the society.

Breakfast at Tiffany's: short novel by U.S. writer Truman Capote, published in 1958; a seriocomic story about the transient life of Holly Golightly, a New York playgirl.

Bridge, The: long poem by U.S. author Hart Crane, published in 1930. This mystical work explores modern American consciousness through images of the subway, the airplane, and, most importantly, the Brooklyn Bridge. Historical and legendary characters, such as Rip Van Winkle, Emily Dickinson, and Walt Whitman, are united in this effort to understand and express a national, democratic spirit.

Brobdingnag: *See* Gulliver's Travels.

Bronze Age: *See* Golden Age.

Brook Farm Institute of Agriculture and Education: community of 160 acres, organized in West Roxbury (now in Boston), Mass., in 1841 and abandoned in 1847. It was one of numerous experiments in communal living that took place in the decades before the Civil War in the United States. Because of the distinguished names that are associated with it—including Nathaniel Hawthorne, Charles A. Dana, Ralph Waldo Emerson, and Amos Bronson Alcott—it has a secure place in the nation's social history.

The principal organizer and director of the community was George Ripley, who had been a Unitarian minister and an editor of *The Dial,* a literary magazine. He was also a leader of the transcendentalists. The aim of the community was to combine the roles of worker and intellectual, to contribute to intellectual freedom, and to foster a society of cultivated people.

Among residents of Brook Farm were teachers, shoemakers, printers, and carpenters. One dollar per day was paid for work. Housing, fuel, food, and clothing were provided nearly at cost. The community thrived for a while, but eventually interest waned.

Blithedale Romance (1852), a novel by Nathaniel Hawthorne, is a fictionalized account of Brook Farm life. Hawthorne spent about six months at the farm but found the atmosphere not conducive to writing.

CALL OF THE WILD: Author Jack London, famous for his tales of adventure.

Brothers Karamazov, The: major work, often considered the masterpiece, of the Russian novelist Feodor Dostoevski, published in 1879–1880. It deals with the murder of a dissolute landowner, Feodor Karamazov, and the consequent reactions of his three sons. The eldest, Dmitri, a wild, impulsive, hard-drinking ex-soldier, a rival of his father for the favors of the fair Grushenka, is unjustly accused of the crime. The second son, Ivan, a proud, cold, and tortured intellectual incapable of love, feels guilty of the intellectual crime of despising his father and wishing him dead. The youngest son, Alyosha, is a figure of saintlike innocence, capable of undivided love. In addition to being a suspenseful story of crime and mystery, the novel is Dostoevski's vehicle for exploring his religious and social ideas. The atheism and despair of Ivan are weighed against the faith of Alyosha, but there is no easy choice between them.

Dostoevski's original aim was to write a sequel to *The Brothers Karamazov* in which faith would be restored, but he never produced such a work. Instead, *The Brothers Karamazov* introduces a multitude of characters who between them express the deep divisions in Dostoevski's mind. At the same time, they demonstrate his remarkable ability to sense their psychological heights and depths.

Brunhild: *See* Nibelungenlied.

Buddenbrooks: novel by German author Thomas Mann, first published in 1901. It is a so-called dynastic novel, recounting the decline of a North German merchant family through four generations, from bourgeois respectability to artistic frailty.

C

Caesura (Latin for "cutting"): pause or break in the middle of a line of verse, indicated by double verticals, ‖. In English verse, both old and modern, the caesura comes about the middle of a line, usually where the sense causes a natural rhetorical pause. Examples of the caesura are as follows:

I will speak out aloude ‖ I care not
  who heare it.
(From Udall's *Ralph Roister Doister.*)

Hanging so light ‖ and hanging
  so high
On the topmost twig ‖ that looks up
  at the sky.
(From Coleridge's "Christabel.")

Caliban: *See* Tempest, The.

Call of the Wild, The: story of the Alaska goldfields by U.S. writer Jack London, published in 1903. A dog named Buck is stolen as a pup from his home, shipped to Alaska, and trained as a sled dog. When his master is murdered, Buck runs away into the forest to live with the wolves and adapts to his new environment successfully. The story celebrates London's belief in the strength of primitive instincts and in the survival of the fittest.

Calydonian boar, GM: terrible boar sent by Artemis to ravage the fields of Calydon as a punishment to Oenus, king of Calydon, for failing to honor her with a harvest offering. A band of heroes hunted the boar, which was at last slain by Meleager.

Calypso: *See* Odyssey.

Camelot: *See* Arthurian legend.

Camille: work by the French writer Alexandre Dumas *fils;* first written as a novel (1848), then as a play (1852). The story centers on Marguerite Gauthier ("Camille"), a Parisian courtesan, who takes a young lover, Armand Duval, but is persuaded by his family to give him up. In the end, just before Marguerite's death from consumption, the two are reunited. The play provided a basis for Verdi's opera *La Traviata* (1853).

Candide: satirical novel by the French author Voltaire, published in 1759, directed against the notion that "everything happens for the best in this best of all possible worlds." The plot, thick with farcical misadventures (most of the incidents, however, having some precedent in history), is concerned with the sometimes divided fortunes of Candide, his beloved Cunegonde, and his tutor Dr. Pangloss, the very embodiment of optimism (a satire on the German philosopher Leibniz). In the end, somewhat reluctantly married to Cunegonde, Candide finally settles down to cultivate his garden.

Canterbury Tales, The: collection of tales, mostly in verse, by Geoffrey Chaucer; it is his masterpiece and one of the great works in English literature. The tales were written between about 1387 and 1400, the year of Chaucer's death. They tell of the poet joining a company of pilgrims on their way to Canterbury to visit the shrine of St. Thomas à Becket. To while away the journey, their host suggests that each pilgrim tell two stories going, two coming back: the pilgrim judged to have told the best tale is to get a free dinner. Chaucer only completed 24 of the tales, but these range from chivalric romance to folk tale to sermon to bawdy fable. The pilgrims, who come from all walks of life, are vividly described by Chaucer and, within the framework of the pilgrimage, he brilliantly develops their personalities. The work was influential in establishing the East Midlands dialect of English as the basis for Modern English.

Cantos: incomplete epic poem by U.S.-born poet Ezra Pound, the first parts of which were published in 1917 and the last in 1969. For the part published in 1948 *(The Pisan Cantos),* which were written while Pound was held for treason in an American military prison in Italy, the author was awarded the Bollingen Prize in Poetry for 1949. The entire work displays Pound's wide knowledge of world literature, Western and Oriental. One of the most important themes reflects the author's conviction that a capitalist system of economics is basically corrupt.

Carbonek: *See* Holy Grail.

Caretaker, The: play by British playwright Harold Pinter, first performed in 1960, about the barriers to communication between human beings in contemporary society. The plot explores a relationship between three characters: Davies, an opportunistic old tramp, is baited by a younger man, Mick, into revealing his antipathy for Aston, a former mental patient. The play uses techniques associated with the theater of the absurd.

Cassandra, GM: daughter of Priam, king of Troy, and Hecuba. Apollo gave her the gift of prophecy, but when she refused his love, he ordained that no one should believe her prophecies. Cassandra warned the Trojans to send Helen home to Greece; she warned them against the Wooden Horse; but nobody would heed her warnings. Upon the capture of Troy she fell to the lot of Agamemnon, returned to Greece with him, predicted his death and her own, and was killed by Clytemnestra. The name Cassandra has come to mean a prophet of doom.

Cassiopeia: *See* Andromeda.

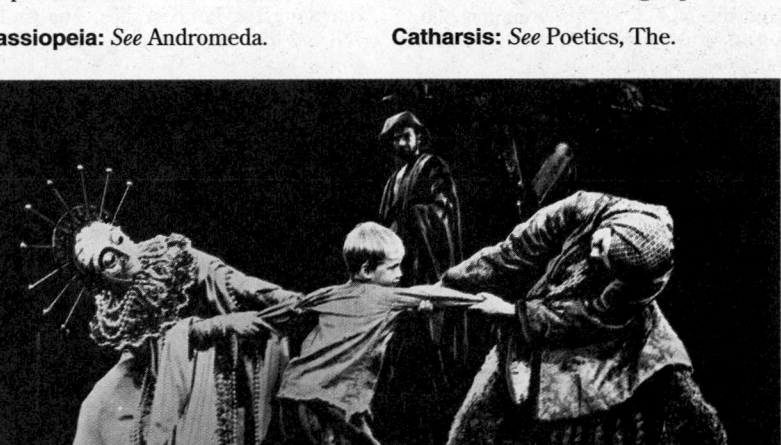

Castle, The: novel by the Czech-born, German-Jewish writer Franz Kafka, left unfinished at his death and published posthumously in 1926. A man known only as K. tries to gain entrance to a mysterious castle, but his efforts are always blocked by bureaucrats. As an allegory, the novel has been interpreted in various ways, including man's search for God.

Castor and Pollux, GM: twin brothers, also called the Dioscuri, that is, sons of Zeus. (Pollux is the Roman form; the original Greek name was Polydeuces.) The brothers took part in the voyage of the Argonauts and thus became the patrons of sailors and navigation. Castor was famous for his skill in managing horses and Pollux for his boxing. The gods rewarded their fidelity to each other by placing them together in the heavens. Their constellation is called Gemini, the Twins.

Catch-22: black comedic novel about World War II, written by U.S. author Joseph Heller, published in 1961. Yossarian, a bombardier, thinks everyone, friend or foe, is out to kill him. All he wants is to go home, but the number of missions he has to fly keeps going up. He can get out of flying more missions if he is crazy, but there's a catch: he has to tell the doctor he is crazy in order to be sent home; as soon as he does, he demonstrates the rational mind of someone who doesn't want to die; therefore he cannot be crazy. The book satirizes the military and the ideals of war and is remarkable for its vivid comic characters and situations.

Catcher in the Rye, The: novel by U.S. author J. D. Salinger, published in 1951, about youth's disenchantment with a hostile adult world. It is cast as a long, colloquial monologue spoken by Holden Caulfield, who has run away from his prep school just before Christmas vacation, preferring to head for New York rather than go home. In spite of his external sophistication, Holden maintains an incorruptible innocence during a weekend of disillusioning experiences.

Catharsis: *See* Poetics, The.

Caucasian Chalk Circle, The: play by German dramatist Bertolt Brecht, presented in 1948. In it two women contest their right to a baby they both profess to love. Brecht took his story from a classical Chinese play, "The Chalk Circle"; a similar tale is the biblical story of the judgment of Solomon (I Kings 3).

Cavalier poets: group of English courtiers who were leading Cavaliers (supporters of King Charles I of England in his struggle with Parliament). Their poems are polished and elegant and often about the trials of romantic love. Those of note are Richard Lovelace, Sir John Suckling, and Thomas Carew; Robert Herrick is usually numbered among them, though he was a clergyman rather than a courtier.

Centaurs, GM: race of half-horse, half-man beings. They lived in the mountains of Thessaly. The famous battle of the Centaurs with the Lapithae arose from a quarrel at the marriage feast of Hippodamia and Pirithous, king of the Lapithae. The Centaurs were driven out of the country. *See also* Chiron.

Cerberus, GM: three-headed dog that guarded the entrance to Hades. He prevented the living from entering and the dead from leaving. The few mortals who got by him either lulled him to sleep with music, like Orpheus, or pacified him with a drugged cake, like the Sibyl who led Aeneas to Hades. Hercules overpowered Cerberus and carried him out of Hades, one of his twelve labors; he later brought him back. *See also* Hercules.

CAUCASIAN CHALK CIRCLE: Two women struggle for a child, a common theme in world legend and literature.

centers
US

centres
Brit.

theater
US

theatre
Brit.

labors
US

labours
Brit.

20 History of Literature

Ceres: *See* Demeter; Persephone.

Changeling: in British folklore, a child of the fairies or elves left in place of a stolen human baby. This superstition was especially prevalent in the Scottish Highlands, where a newborn child was carefully watched till the day of its baptism. After that it could not be stolen by the fairies. A deformed, sickly, or idiot child was often thought to be a changeling and was cruelly treated so that the fairies would come and take it back, returning the human child they supposedly stole.

Chanson de geste (French for "song of great deeds"): any epic poem in Old French, written in the eleventh to the 15th centuries. Most of them are of unknown authorship. They deal with the emperor Charlemagne and his twelve noble peers, or paladins. They emphasize the heroic deeds of the paladins as defenders of Christianity in legendary battles against the Saracens. Others deal with the wars of the barons among themselves or against the strong, just Charlemagne. The later *chansons* graded into romance, and love or marvelous, magical adventures replaced heroism as their principal theme. The oldest, most famous, and finest is the *Chanson de Roland.* Others are *Ogier the Dane, The Pilgrimage to Jerusalem, Bertha Greatfoot,* and *Huon de Bordeaux. See also* Ganelon; Ogier the Dane; Roland.

Chanson de Roland *(The Song of Roland):* Old French *chanson de geste.* It recounts the fight of Roland, the most famous of Charlemagne's paladins, against the Saracens in 778. *See also* Roland.

Chanticleer (meaning "sing clear"): name of the cock in *Reynard the Fox* and other medieval beast fables. Chanticleer figures in Chaucer's "Nun's Priest's Tale." He is the hero of Edmond Rostand's drama *Chanticleer. See also* Reynard the Fox.

Chaos, GM: primeval formless void that existed before the creation of the world. According to Hesiod, from Chaos sprang Gaea (earth), Erebus (darkness), and Night.

Charge of the Light Brigade, The: poem by English poet Alfred Tennyson, immortalizing an incident of the Battle of Balaclava in the Crimean War. Because of an error in transmitting orders, a brigade of English cavalrymen was sent on a charge against Russian guns that could result only in their slaughter. All obeyed, evoking the poet's famous line, "Theirs not to reason why, theirs but to do or die. . . ."

Charis: in Homer's *Iliad,* the wife of Hephaestus, the god of the forge. Later the name was applied to any one of the three Graces, or Charites.

---

center
US

centre
Brit.

emphasizes
US

emphasises
Brit.

Charlemagne: king of the Franks (768–814) and emperor of the West (800–814). Charlemagne, his splendid court, and his twelve peers, or paladins, are the center of a vast cycle of romance and legend. The various *chansons de geste* celebrate the wars against the Saxons, wars in Italy and in Spain, wars with Charlemagne's own vassals and against the Saracens, his pilgrimage to Jerusalem, the false accusation against his innocent wife Blanchefleur, and the defeat of his rear guard at Roncesvalles, August 15, 778. *See also* Chanson de geste.

Charlotte's Web: children's story by U.S. writer E. B. White, published in 1952; a touching and sensitive story expressing appreciation for all forms of life. Charlotte, a spider, saves her friend Wilbur, a pig, from slaughter by weaving a web with the words "Some pig" on it, an event which, along with Charlotte's later variations, causes Wilbur's owners to think that a supernatural agent is protecting him.

HARPER & ROW

CHARLOTTE'S WEB: The spider makes a second special web for her friend Wilbur.

Charon, GM: boatman who ferried the souls of the dead across the river Styx or the river Acheron. The fare was a small coin called an obol; it was the custom to place one in the mouth of a dead person to pay his way to Hades.

Charterhouse of Parma, The: novel by French author Stendhal, published in 1839. Set in the post-Napoleonic era, the story chronicles the adventures of the profligate Fabrizio del Dongo, which culminate in the death of his mistress and their child and his own retirement to a monastery. The work is notable for its sociopolitical examination of the times, and for its analysis of the Romantic movement.

Charybdis, GM: greedy and thieving woman who stole the oxen of Hercules and, as punishment, was turned into a terrible gulf and whirlpool by Zeus. She was placed opposite the monster Scylla in the strait between Italy and Sicily. There she remained a menace to mariners and sucked down several of the ships of Odysseus. *See also* Scylla.

Cherry Orchard, The: play in four acts by Russian playwright Anton Chekhov, presented in 1904. The play mirrors Russian society at the end of the 19th century, when a long-established feudal system was giving way to social and economic changes. The cherry orchard on the estates of the once wealthy Ranevskis, representing all that was idyllic in the past, must now be sold. The Ranevskis are too inert to do much to help themselves, and in this they are contrasted with the practical Lopakhin, son of a former serf on the estate, who buys the cherry orchard, planning to cut down the trees and build houses.

Cheshire cat: appears in an old English phrase, "grin like a Cheshire cat," a simile for a broad, toothy smile. Nobody knows the origin of the comparison. In Lewis Carroll's *Alice's Adventures in Wonderland,* the Cheshire Cat vanishes by degrees until there is no cat left—just the grin.

Children's Hour, The: poem by U.S. author Henry Wadsworth Longfellow, first published in 1860. The poem is a reflection on the poet's love for his three little daughters, Alice, Allegra, and Edith. The title was used by U.S. playwright Lillian Hellman for her first staged play (1934), in which a neurotic girl wrecks a school and the lives of the two women who run it by falsely accusing them of lesbianism.

Child's Christmas in Wales, A: brief reminiscence by the Welsh poet Dylan Thomas of his boyhood Christmastime adventures, published in 1954.

Child's Garden of Verses, A: collection of poems by British author Robert Louis Stevenson, published in 1885. Among the poems, which all reflect the sense of wonder with which children explore their world, are such favorites as "My Shadow" and "The Lamplighter."

Chimera, GM: female monster with a lion's head, a goat's body, and a dragon's tail, who perpetually breathed fire. It was killed by Bellerophon riding the winged horse Pegasus. The term has come to be used for any fantastic notion or idea.

Chiron, GM: wise Centaur, skilled in medicine, who taught Asclepius the art of herbal healing. Many of the heroes of Greece were his pupils. Chiron was accidentally wounded by Hercules and placed in the heavens by Zeus as the constellation Sagittarius.

Christmas Carol, A: story by English writer Charles Dickens, published in 1843. Old Ebenezer Scrooge, a "clutching, covetous old sinner," and Tiny Tim, the crippled child of Bob Cratchit, Scrooge's downtrodden clerk, are two of the main characters. It is the story of Scrooge's regeneration: fantastic visitations by three spirits of Christmas—the ghosts of Christmas Past, Christmas Present, and Christmas Yet to Come—change him from an unfeeling money-lover to a benevolent human being who, along with other good deeds, sends a turkey to the Cratchit family to make their Christmas merry.

Chronicles of Narnia, The: collection of seven books by the literary scholar and medievalist C. S. Lewis. On one level, they are children's novels, but they can also be read as religious allegory concerning the war between good and evil. The titles are *The Lion, the Witch and the Wardrobe* (1950); *Prince Caspian: the Return to Narnia* (1951); *The Voyage of the "Dawn Treader"* (1952); *The Silver Chair* (1953); *The Horse and His Boy* (1954); *The Magician's Nephew* (1955); and *The Last Battle* (1956).

Cid, Song of the: twelfth-century heroic poem considered the first masterpiece of Spanish literature. It celebrates El Cid, Ruy (or Rodrigo) Díaz de Vivar, the great national hero of Spain of the eleventh century; he was a historical figure to whom the poem and later ballads gave almost legendary stature. *Le Cid* (1637), by French classical playwright Pierre Corneille, is the first great tragedy in modern French.

Cinderella: in world folklore, a little household drudge, cruelly treated, who attains wealth and marries a prince with the aid of a supernatural guardian. The story exists in more than 500 variants from Alaska to South Africa. The most familiar version is from the French of Charles Perrault, first translated into English about 1729.

Circe: in the *Odyssey,* a sorceress who lured travellers to her island of Aiaie and turned them into beasts by magic. When Odysseus landed there, his comrades were changed into swine. Circe could not harm Odysseus, for he was protected by the herb moly, which Hermes had given him. He compelled her to restore his companions to human form and dwelt with her for a year.

Classicism: principles and qualities ascribed to Greek and Roman literature and art, especially when used as a standard for later works. These qualities are simplicity, economy, balance, harmony, restraint, and objectivity. Classical art emphasizes overall form rather than detail, and represents general rather than particular types. Literary classicism adheres to established literary forms and fits expression to the form, rather than the form to the expression. It aims for pure, correct language, simple but elegant style, and orderliness of thought. During the late 1600s and early 1700s, classicism (or neoclassicism, as it was also called) was the dominant movement in French and English literature, as seen in the work of writers like Racine and Corneille, Dryden, and Pope. Since the beginning of the 19th

CINDERELLA: The heroine's fairy godmother prepares to make a coach-and-four out of a pumpkin and a group of small household animals.

century, Romanticism has opposed classicism by emphasizing individuality, irrationality, and self-expression—all things that classicism excluded.

Classics: in literature, productions of surpassing excellence. They represent the highest standards in literature. In a narrower sense, the classics are the works of the ancient Greek and Roman writers. In general, the classics are those works that are read and enjoyed by successive generations.

Clytemnestra: *See* House of Atreus.

Come Back, Little Sheba: play by the U.S. dramatist William Inge, presented in 1950, exploring a theme of the dependent nature of love. It depicts a crisis in the life of Doc Delaney, an alcoholic struggling to overcome his illness, and Lola, his slovenly, once-pretty wife, who still dreams about the past, her baby who died, and her lost dog, Sheba.

Comedy: play written in an entertaining manner and having a happy ending. The form originated in ancient Greece and originally signified a bawdy masque, probably a representation of the older Dionysian orgiastic rites, since plays were presented as a part of the festival of Dionysus. There are several different types of comedy: comedy of situation, like Shakespeare's *Comedy of Errors;* comedy of manners (or "high comedy"), in which the comedy is based on the mores of high society, as in the plays of William Congreve, Richard Brinsley Sheridan, Oscar Wilde, and Noel Coward; low comedy, a forthright exhibition of man's cruder instincts; farce, in which the situation and plot complications border on the preposterous; satire, as in the plays of Aristophanes and Molière; and slapstick, or pie-in-the-face. In Shakespeare's so-called dark comedies, such as *Measure for Measure,* tragic situations are resolved by means that traditionally belong to comedy. In modern plays, comical treatment of horrible or frightening situations is referred to as "black humor."

Especially during the Middle Ages, the term *comedy* was applied to nondramatic literary works that treat life seriously but do not leave the reader with a sense of

tragedy, such as Dante's *Divine Comedy. See also* Commedia dell'arte.

Commedia dell'arte: improvised comedy originating in Italy in the 1500s, based on a sketchily outlined stock plot called a scenario, embellished by farce, clowning, mime, music, and rapid patter. The *commedia* actors, often a group of professional strolling players, achieved a high degree of artistry and created a classic repertory of stock characters—Harlequin, Punchinello, Pantaloon, Pierrot, Columbine—with distinctive costumes and mannerisms. Although the names of the characters changed over the years, some of them, such as the braggart soldier Scaramuccia (or Il Capitano), go back as far as the Miles Gloriosus of Roman comedy. Others extend into the future; Beaumarchais' Figaro and Mozart's Leporello in *Don Giovanni* are descendants of the *zanni* (impudent servants), indispensable to *commedia* plays.

The *commedia* was superseded in the later 1600s in the cities by comedies with more individual characters, such as those by Molière; but the *commedia* remained popular in the small towns until the 1800s, thanks in part to the outstanding innovations of Carlo Gozzi.

Common Sense: political pamphlet by the English-born American writer and revolutionist Thomas Paine, published in 1776, calling for the immediate separation from England of the American colonies. In attacking British rule Paine wrote: "government even in its best state is but a necessary evil in its worst state, an intolerable one." The pamphlet, which was an immediate success, was widely read throughout the colonies and helped bring public opinion to support the Declaration of Independence.

Compleat Angler, The: dialogue on the superiority of the contemplative sport of fishing as against the active sport of hunting, by English author Izaak Walton, published in 1653, with additions by Charles Cotton in 1676. Although its practical importance has passed, its descriptions of natural beauty and its message of brotherly love have made it an enduring work.

Conceit: an elaborate metaphor in poetry. When a poet compares his lover's eyes to jewels, her hair to gold, he is using Petrarchan conceits. Shakespeare satirized such decorative conventions in his famous 130th sonnet, which begins, "My mistress' eyes are nothing like the sun." A metaphysical conceit is more complicated, working on several levels as it compares two images that seem to have nothing in common.

JOHN DONNE used the image of compass legs in "A Valediction: Forbidding Mourning" to represent the souls of two lovers who, though separated, are still joined. This exemplifies metaphysical conceit.

> *If they be two, they are two so*
> *As stiffe twin compasses are two,*
> *Thy soule the fixt foot, makes no show*
> *To move, but doth, if th'other doe.*
> *And though it in the center sit,*
> *Yet when the other far doth rome.*
> *It leaves, and hearkens after it,*
> *And growes erect, as that comes home.*

Confessions: autobiography, posthumously published 1781–1788, by the Swiss-born French philosopher Jean-Jacques Rousseau. Romantic and self-justifying in tone, it gives a frank account of his life, loves, and intellectual voyagings, setting a fashion for such literature, especially in France.

Confessions of a Mask: autobiographical novel by the Japanese writer Yukio Mishima, published in 1960. It deals with the sexual awakening of the author and the extreme unhappiness his homosexuality causes him.

The symbols used in this glossary are as follows:

G-Greek
R-Roman
N-Norse
M-myth
L-legend

Confessions of an English Opium Eater: English writer Thomas De Quincey's account of his own experience, published as a book in 1822. It tells how much opium he could take in a day, what the effects were, how various trivial events of his life—glorified and distorted by the influence of the drug—became the material of his dreams, and how in fear of death he gradually reduced his dosage and almost overcame the habit. This book, first published without his name, brought De Quincey a market for his writings and assured his future literary career.

Confessions of Nat Turner, The: novel by U.S. author William Styron, published in 1967; it involved Styron in controversy even as it brought him fame because of his attempt, as a white man, to represent the consciousness of Nat Turner, the black leader of the slave insurrection that took place in 1831 in Virginia. Little is known about the historical preacher; Styron in effect created his personality from his own views on slavery, racism, and the need for violence in achieving freedom.

Connecticut Yankee in King Arthur's Court, A: satirical novel by U.S. author and humorist Mark Twain, published in 1889. Hank Morgan, a brash, hard-headed, ingenious Yankee is hit on the head in a fight and is transported back to the Middle Ages—to Camelot in the year 528. Twain used the device to air his contempt for and prejudices toward Europe, the church, and monarchy.

Consolation of Philosophy, The: dialogue by the Roman statesman Boethius, written while he was in prison awaiting execution (A.D. 522–524). Boethius and his philosophic muse discuss his troubles and expound a Neoplatonic philosophy of good and evil, happiness and free will. The work was very popular for over a thousand years; it was translated into English by King Alfred, Chaucer, and Queen Elizabeth I, among others.

Consonance: repetition of identical consonant sounds in a poetic passage, with changes in the intervening vowels. Example: *bake, book, bike, back.* It is similar to alliteration, in which identical consonant sounds are also used. But, while the initial sounds of alliterative words are more important than the intervening consonants, for words in consonance it is the final consonant sound that is most significant. *Block* and *cake* are in consonance; *lamp* and *light* are alliterative.

Count of Monte Cristo, The: romantic novel by the French author Alexandre Dumas *père,* published in 1845, telling a tale of intrigue and encompassing love, hate, greed, courage, and revenge. Falsely accused of a political crime, the hero, Edmond Dantès, who is shortly to be married, is imprisoned in the Chateau d'If in the harbor of Marseilles. Managing to escape to the island of Monte Cristo, he there becomes a man of mystery, rich and powerful, before returning to take his revenge on his enemies.

Couplet: two consecutive rhyming lines of verse. The last two lines of a Shakespearean sonnet are a couplet. The most usual type is the heroic couplet, ten syllables to a line, in iambic pentameter; it was used first by Chaucer and brilliantly perfected by Pope and Dryden.

> *A perfect judge will read each work of wit*
> *With the same spirit that its author writ.*

(From Alexander Pope's "Essay on Criticism.")

Courtier, The: book by Italian Renaissance author Baldassare Castiglione, of a type called a *courtesy book:* that is, a book in which the proper attributes and behavior of a courtier and gentleman are defined. These precepts are presented in the form of a dialogue among a group of Italian gentlemen and ladies. *The Courtier* was published in Italy in 1528 and soon was translated into other languages of Europe, where it had great influence.

Courtly love: conception of love that arose from the medieval code of chivalry and from the attitude toward high-born women that was fostered by the cult of the Blessed Virgin Mary. A knight or courtier was expected to court a wise, lovely, virtuous woman who remained aloof. For her he was to write songs and poems and to do great deeds; the suffering his unrequited love inspired supposedly ennobled him. Needless to say, courtly love and marriage were incompatible. The notion was developed by the French troubadours, popularized by the court of Eleanor of Aquitaine in the 1100s, and persisted into the Elizabethan era. Its conventions are important in medieval romances, especially the Arthurian legends.

Coverley, Sir Roger de: fictional old gentleman of Worcestershire, presented by both Joseph Addison and Sir Richard Steele in many of their *Spectator* papers. Addison described him as "a gentleman that is very singular in his behavior, but his singularities proceed from his good sense."

Crane, Ichabod: *See* Legend of Sleepy Hollow, The.

Creusa: *See* Medea.

Crime and Punishment: masterly novel by the Russian writer Feodor Dostoevski, published in 1866, on the theme of redemption through suffering. The penniless student Raskolnikov believes that his natural superiority places him above the moral law of common men. He finds good reasons for committing two brutal murders, and the novel furnishes an examination of these reasons, which, one by one, are proved to be insupportable. Conscience will not permit Raskolnikov to use the money obtained through his crime, and his anguish slowly leads him to confess and embrace the consequent punishment—hard labor in Siberia—which is the gateway to his redemption.

Crisis, The: series of revolutionary pamphlets written for the American colonists by Thomas Paine from 1776 to 1783. The first, beginning "These are the times that try men's souls," was written to rally Revolutionary troops.

Criticism: the art of judging and pointing out the perfections and imperfections of works of art. Appreciation is as much a part of criticism as is detection of flaws. A good critic must have knowledge, taste, sympathy, and facility of expression. The chief objects of literary criticism are to judge, to interpret, and to give personal impressions of books.

Crito: dialogue by the Greek philosopher Plato. Socrates' friend Crito comes to the prison where Socrates is awaiting execution and outlines a plan of escape; Socrates considers whether he should escape and decides that it would be unjust, since he has lived under the laws of Athens and has no right to flout them even though he has been unjustly accused.

Croesus: sixth-century king of Lydia, who was reputed throughout the ancient world to be the richest man on Earth. He is the subject of various tales and legends told by the Greeks, most of them moral lessons concerning the fate of those who are excessively proud and prosperous.

Cronus, GM: son of Uranus (heaven) and Gaea (earth). His wife was Rhea. He was warned that a child of his would overthrow him, so he swallowed his children as soon as they were born, first Hestia, then Demeter, Hera, Hades, and Poseidon. But Rhea saved the infant Zeus by giving Cronus a swaddled stone to swallow instead. When Zeus grew up, he made Cronus vomit forth his brothers and sisters, then dethroned him.

Cry, the Beloved Country: moving novel by the South African writer Alan Paton, published in 1948, about the tragedies, both personal and national, that flow from racial persecution. The central character, Stephen Kumalo, a Zulu clergyman, finds that in Johannesburg his sister has been forced to become a prostitute and his son has become a murderer.

Cuchulain: hero of the Ulster (or Ulaid) cycle of old Irish legend. He was the son of Lug, the sun god, nephew of Conchobor, king of Ulster, and the foremost hero among the Knights of the Red Branch. He is believed to have lived in the first century A.D. At the age of twelve he guarded the possessions of Culain, the smith of Ulster, to make up to him for having killed his hound; he thereby received his name: Cu (hound) + Culain (of Culain). He married Emer, the daughter of a druid. In *The Cattle Raid of Cooley,* the most ambitious saga of the Ulster cycle, Cuchulain defends Ulster single-handedly against the forces of Connaught.

Cupid, RM: god of love; son of Venus. He is pictured as a winged, naked boy with bow and arrows. A dart from his bow would create love in the breast of whatever god or mortal it wounded. The story of Cupid and Psyche begins with his wounding himself with one of his own arrows. In this story Cupid is a youth, as was his Greek original, Eros (*see also* Psyche). But usually he is personified as a little child. The chubby little cupids commonly seen in classical and Renaissance art are called *putti* ("little boys").

Cybele: *See* Great Mother.

Cycle: all the poems, romances, and narratives dealing with a certain hero, his followers, and deeds. There are extensive cycles concerning the exploits of King Arthur and his knights, and Charlemagne and his paladins. The tales of Siegfried make up another cycle, as do those about the Ulster cycle hero Cuchulain. *See also* Arthurian legend; Chanson de geste; Nibelungenlied; Ulster cycle.

Cyclopes, GM: race of one-eyed giants who dwelt in Sicily. The word is Greek for round-eyed; Cyclops is the singular form. In the *Odyssey,* they were huge man-eating shepherds. Traditionally, they labored for Hephaestus inside Mount Etna, helping to forge the thunderbolts of Zeus. *See also* Polyphemus.

Cyrano de Bergerac: romantic drama by French playwright Edmond Rostand, first performed in 1897. Loosely based on a historical Cyrano, the hero is a poet, lover, and swordsman who is disfigured by a long nose. Though he secretly loves the same woman as his best friend, he supplies his friend with the romantic speeches to woo her. As Cyrano dies at the end, she realizes that it was his words that won her heart.

D

Dactyl: *See* Foot.

Daedalus, GM: skilled Athenian architect and sculptor. The Greek word means "cunning craftsman." Daedalus's nephew was his apprentice and bid fair to outshine his master; in jealousy Daedalus killed his nephew and fled with his son Icarus to Crete. There he built the labyrinth for King Minos (*see* Minotaur); later he and his son were shut up in the labyrinth for an offense to

CUPID: The god of love removes his blindfold in the painting by Lucas Cranach the elder.

Minos. Daedalus made wings of feathers and wax for them both, and they escaped. But Icarus flew too near the sun; the wax melted, and he fell into the sea, thereafter named the Icarian Sea. Daedalus reached Sicily in safety.

Daisy Miller: short novel by U.S. expatriate writer Henry James, published in 1878. An American girl from Schenectady is travelling in Europe with her mother. Without realizing the difference between European and small-town American conventions, the mother allows her daughter the same freedom she had at home, but Daisy's ways are misjudged in the light of a more ancient, artificial code.

Danae, GM: daughter of Acrisius, king of Argos. To prevent the fulfillment of an old prophecy that he would die at the hand of Danae's son, Acrisius shut her up in a brazen tower. But Zeus fell in love with her and visited her there concealed in a shower of gold; their son was Perseus. Acrisius set the mother and child adrift in the sea in a large chest, but they were carried safely to an island. Perseus later did kill Acrisius accidentally, fulfilling the prophecy.

Dance of Death, The: medieval allegory of the mortality of earthly things, a popular theme for mortality plays and for pictures in which a figure of death leads a line dance, as in woodcuts by Holbein and in the final scene of Ingmar Bergman's movie *The Seventh Seal. Dance of Death* has been used by a number of authors as a title; best known is a play by Swedish playwright August Strindberg, first presented in 1901, in which an aging married couple torment each other.

D'Artagnan: *See* Three Musketeers, The.

David Copperfield: semi-autobiographical novel by Charles Dickens, published 1849–1850; a sentimental story of an orphan's struggles. It deals with the sufferings of young David after his mother's death, through the cruel treatment of his stepfather, schoolmasters, and employers. Uriah Heep, a deliberately "humble" person whose hypocrisy is exceeded only by his treachery, is one of the book's many memorable characters. David finds friends, too—his aunt Betsy Trotwood, the penniless but always optimistic Mr. Micawber, and the kite-flying Mr. Dick—and matures through their kindness to become a successful writer.

Dead Souls: novel by Russian author Nikolai Gogol, first published in 1842. Pavel I. Chichikov, a swindler, works out a scheme to buy up serfs who have died but who have not yet been taken off the census rolls, then mortgage these "dead souls" to buy land. Gogol wrote a second part, in which Chichikov reforms, but he destroyed most of the manuscript just before he died.

20 History of Literature

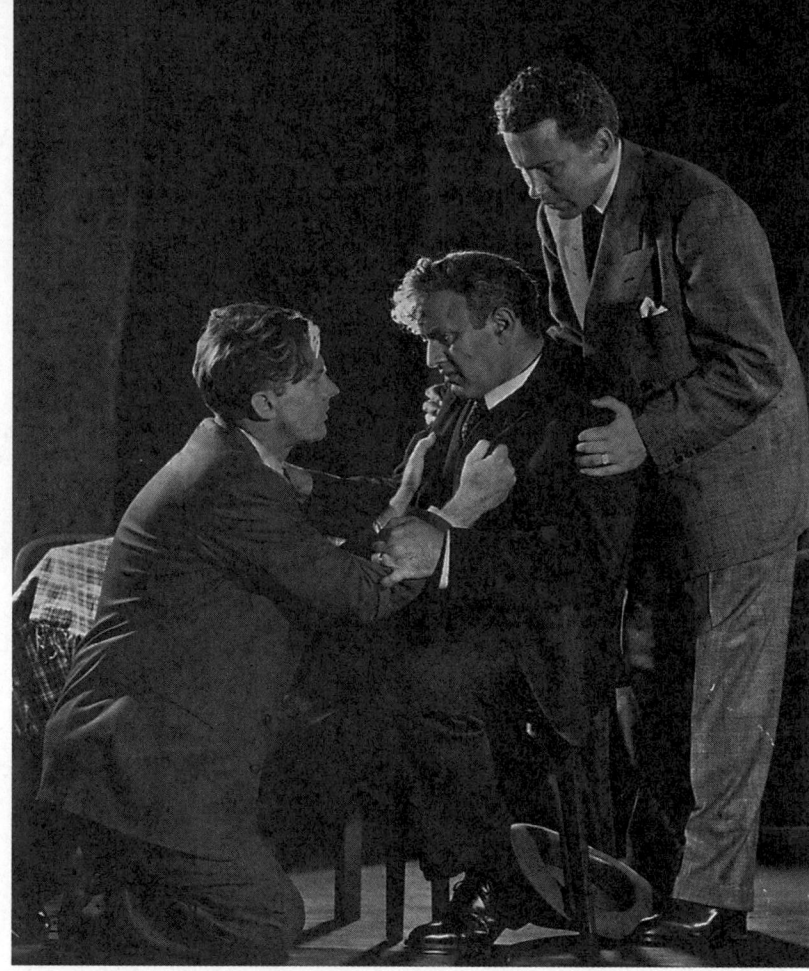

DEATH OF A SALESMAN: The defeated Willy Loman, played in the original production by Lee J. Cobb, is quizzed by his troubled sons.

Death in the Family, A: novel by U.S. writer and critic James Agee, published posthumously in 1957 and winner of a Pulitzer Prize. Partly autobiographical, the novel is a sensitive description of the effects of his father's death on a young Southern boy. The stage adaptation, *All the Way Home* (1960), by Tad Mosel, also won a Pulitzer Prize and other awards.

Death in Venice: novella by German writer Thomas Mann, published in 1912; a symbolic tale of youth and age, art and life, love and suffering. An ailing middle-aged artist, Gustav von Aschenbach, visiting Venice to regain his strength, conceives a hopeless passion for Tadzio, a young Polish boy. Though he never speaks to the boy, Aschenbach's fascination with his beauty is so great that he is unable to tear himself away from cholera-infested Venice and willingly pays the price of his life.

Death of Artemio Cruz, The: novel by Mexican author Carlos Fuentes, published in 1962. It relates the reflections of Artemio Cruz as he lies on his deathbed. His history parallels that of modern Mexico, which, in Fuentes' eyes, grows corrupt as it becomes more powerful. Starting out as the illegitimate son of a peasant and a landowner, Cruz changes from a revolutionary soldier to a rich, powerful industrialist by betraying his idealism. There is an effective change of narrative voice, from first to second to third person, a form of experimentation prevalent in much modern Latin American literature.

Death of a Salesman: play by U.S. writer Arthur Miller, first performed in 1949; a modern tragedy of an ordinary man, Willie Loman, who is an aging travelling salesman. Faced with the loss of his livelihood and the failure of his sons, whom he has inculcated with his values of achieving success through being "well-liked," Willie is bewildered by his fate. Unable to understand why this familiar American dream worked for others but not for himself, Willie commits suicide in a final, pathetic effort to rescue his family through his insurance money.

Decameron, The: collection of 100 short tales by Italian writer Giovanni Boccaccio, written about 1350, containing stories ranging from tragedy and romance to popular farce. The stories are placed in a frame in which ten Florentines, fleeing the plague of 1348, take refuge in a country villa for ten days; each tells a daily story. Boccaccio took his tales from many sources and told them in a language and a form that influenced European prose writers for centuries.

Decline and Fall of the Roman Empire, The History of the: by English historian Edward Gibbon, published 1776–1788. This classic work in six volumes considers the fall of Rome and traces the dissolution of the empire over more than a thousand years. Gibbon attributes the decline of Rome primarily to the corruption of classical Greco-Roman rational ideals by the emotional appeal of Christianity and other Eastern religions.

Deianira: *See* Hercules.

Delphic oracle: shrine of Apollo at Delphi in Greece. In ancient times it was believed that Apollo communicated with mortals at Delphi through his priestess, the Sibyl, or Pythia, who was reputed to possess special prophetic powers. Her sayings were usually uttered in obscure terms, and were subject to different interpretations.

Demeter, GM: goddess of agriculture, fertility, and marriage. She was the mother of Persephone, whom Pluto carried off to the underworld. The Romans identified Demeter with Ceres. *See also* Persephone.

Democracy in America: political analysis by French historian and political philosopher Alexis de Tocqueville, published in four volumes (two in 1835 and two in 1840); one of the early observations of the effects of democratic principles on society. Using the United States as his laboratory, Tocqueville was impressed by the disappearance of class distinctions, but expressed the fear that the danger of democracies lay in the tyranny of majority opinions over minority views.

Desdemona: *See* Othello.

Devil: personification of evil in religion, treated at times scornfully, humorously, or sympathetically in literature. Medieval morality plays tend to make the Devil an object of derision, a satyrlike buffoon. But in Dante's *Divine Comedy,* Lucifer is a gigantic brooding outcast at the center of the funnel-like Hell created by his fall. Milton's Satan, whose name before his fall was Lucifer, earns our begrudging admiration in *Paradise Lost* when he declares that he would rather "reign in Hell than serve in Heaven" (Book I:263).

In addition to being the prince of evil, the Devil is the tempter of humanity. Mephistopheles, the Devil of the Faust legend, is the elegant, horned-and-tailed gentleman whom we have come to associate with the character. He barters with Faust for his soul and they make an infernal pact. Marlowe's Mephistopheles is himself a tragic figure, a proud, fallen angel whose despair gains our reluctant sympathy even as he plots Faust's damnation. Goethe's Mephistopheles, however, is cold, cynical, and witty. When Faust slips through his hands, we rejoice in his return to being an object of scorn such as he was in morality plays (*see also* Faust). The defeated and therefore ridiculous Devil also appears in Stephen Vincent Benét's *The Devil and Daniel Webster* (see next entry).

Devil and Daniel Webster, The: short story by U.S. writer Stephen Vincent Benét, written in 1936; a humorous combination of history and folklore told in a colloquial style. Through his legendary oratorical skill, Daniel Webster wins an acquittal in the Devil's own court for

Jabez Stone, a Yankee farmer who traded his soul to the Devil for wealth and power. It later became the basis for a play and an opera.

Devil's Dictionary, The (originally titled *The Cynic's Word Book*): collection of witty definitions, written in 1906, by U.S. writer Ambrose Bierce. The entries, which originally appeared in periodicals for which Bierce wrote from 1881 to 1906, demonstrate his flair for concision and irony as well as his cynical outlook.

Dialogue: literary form in which the author uses two or more characters discussing a subject. The most famous writer of the form was the philosopher Plato, in whose dialogues his mentor Socrates discusses philosophical problems with friends. *See also* Crito; Phaedo; Republic, The; Symposium.

Diana: *See* Artemis.

Diary: daily record, usually a description of personal informal activities. The diaries of historical figures are helpful to historians in reconstructing past events and often provide intimate details of motives and manners that are not found in official records. Some are also good reading, such as the most famous diary in the English language, that of Samuel Pepys (1633–1703).

Perhaps the most famous diary of modern times is that of Anne Frank (1929–1945), a Dutch-Jewish girl who spent many months in hiding from the Nazis occupying Amsterdam.

Diary of Samuel Pepys: journal of daily events kept for the years 1660–1669 by Samuel Pepys, a British public official who was administrative head of the British navy and a friend of King Charles II. Pepys wrote in his own shorthand, which was first decoded in 1825. His accounts of the Stuart Restoration, the Great Fire of London, and many public figures and scholars of the period make it an invaluable historical document. In addition, his lively style and winning personality make the work a classic.

Dictionary: book consisting of word lists, usually arranged alphabetically. Dictionaries are of many different types, but customarily they provide information about the meaning, pronunciation, inflection, and etymology of each word listed. A dictionary may serve the needs of persons of a particular age group or educational level or include only words or proper names within a special discipline (for example, medicine, law, or biography). Dictionaries are often prescriptive; that is, they indicate that certain forms (such as spelling or pronunciation) are preferable to others.

The first distinguished and influential dictionary of English was Samuel Johnson's *A Dictionary of the English Language* (1755). The first great American lexicographer was Noah Webster, who published his *Compendious Dictionary of the English Language* (1806) and *An American Dictionary of the English Language* (1828).

The great modern historical dictionary of the English language is the *Oxford English Dictionary* (1933), a work that is made up of twelve volumes and a supplement.

Dido or **Elissa:** princess of Tyre and the legendary founder of Carthage. Her husband was murdered by her brother for his wealth, but Dido fled from Tyre with the treasure. She landed in Africa and bargained for as much land as the hide of a bull would cover. She had the hide cut into thin strips and with them enclosed enough ground to erect her citadel. A neighboring king named Iarbas coveted the city, demanded her hand in marriage, and threatened war should she refuse. Rather than marry him, she built her funeral pyre and killed herself.

In the *Aeneid,* the legendary history of the Roman people, the author, Vergil, defies accepted chronology and makes Dido a contemporary of the wandering Aeneas; she kills herself in sorrow at Aeneas's leaving her.

Dime novel: novel with a sensational adventurous story line that was originated by Edward Zane Carroll Judson under the pseudonym Ned Buntline. The first such work appeared about 1850 and originally sold for ten cents. Themes of the very popular novels often dealt with the American Revolution, the Civil War, or the Western frontier. Their popularity declined in the 1890s, when comic strips and pulp magazines gradually replaced them.

Dionysiac: *See* Birth of Tragedy...

Dionysus, GM: god of an ecstatic religion, whose cult had, by classical times, been considerably tamed. His orgiastic rites were reduced to drunken revelry, and from being a god of fruits and fertility, he became primarily the god of grapes and wine. He was called Bacchus by the Romans. According to later mythology, he was the son of Zeus and Semele, who was burned to death when she foolishly persisted in her demand to see Zeus in his full glory. Dionysus was brought up in secret by the nymphs to save him from the jealous malice of Hera, Zeus's wife. When he grew up, he travelled through the world teaching men the arts of civilization, especially the cultivation of the grape. The wild, orgiastic aspects of his cult were strongly resisted in many places. Many stories depict the sad fate of those who opposed him; those who favored him received the gift of the vine; that is, the making and use of wine. He often took on the form of a panther, tiger, goat, bull, snake, ass, or lion.

Dioscurl: *See* Castor and Pollux.

Divine Comedy, The: long allegorical poem by the Italian poet Dante Alighieri, written about 1307–1321. It expresses the poet's vision of the divine plan for justice in this world and the next. Dante originally called it *The Comedy* because it begins in sorrow and ends happily, and also because it was written in the Italian vernacular at a time when serious works were written in Latin. "Divine" was added to the title in the 16th century.

In the first book, *Inferno,* the Roman poet Vergil (the highest representative of human reason and pagan ethics)

center
US

centre
Brit.

civilization
US

civilisation
Brit.

DIVINE COMEDY: Dante took great pleasure in finding suitable punishment for evil men in *The Inferno*, but imagining the agonies, he also felt pity for the damned.

20 History of Literature

guides Dante out of a dark wood by a roundabout journey through the Afterlife. On Good Friday in the year 1300, they enter Hell, descending through nine circles, each reserved for a certain type of sin, in which the sinners become increasingly more infamous and their torments more hideous. There Dante sees well known historical figures, princes, popes, and personal enemies, all vividly characterized. The lowest circle is reserved for traitors such as Judas Iscariot, Cassius, and Brutus.

In the second book, *Purgatorio,* Vergil leads Dante through Purgatory, where he sees those who are undergoing purification and is himself purged of his sins. The gates of Paradise are as far as human reason can go, so Vergil leaves. Dante's idealized beloved, Beatrice, guides him through the nine ascending circles of Paradise, which is described in the third book, *Paradiso.* In the tenth circle, St. Bernard becomes his guide and Dante briefly experiences a vision of the Eternal Light, Divine Wisdom, or God.

The number three, symbolizing the Trinity, is used throughout as a structural principle. Thus, the work is divided into three books, each having 33 cantos. The cantos are written in *terza rima,* a three-line verse form with the rhyme scheme a-b-a b-c-b c-d-c.

Doctor Faustus: *See* Faust.

Doctor Zhivago: novel by the Russian poet Boris Pasternak, which describes life in Russia from 1900 to the late 1920s, concentrating on the conflict between the forces of pure principle and the forces of humanity and individualism. The hero, a doctor and a poet, is a passive victim of his times. Banned in Russia, the book appeared first in Italian translation in 1957 and in English in 1958. Pasternak, whose work had not been published for many years, became the symbol of the courageous, uncompromising artist. He was awarded the Nobel Prize in 1958, but did not accept it because of official Soviet disapproval.

Doll's House, A: play by Norwegian dramatist Henrik Ibsen, performed in 1879. The central figure is Nora Helmer, a pampered, spoiled housewife, who babies her children and wheedles and coaxes her husband Torvald for whatever she wants. Suddenly something ugly enters this idyllic world: Nora is blackmailed by the discredited Krogstad, from whom she had borrowed money for a trip to save Torvald's health, thoughtlessly forging her father's signature on the note. Using her usual kittenish tactics, she begs Torvald not to fire Krogstad from his bank. The attempt fails; Torvald learns the truth, characteristically vents his sanctimonious moral outrage at her deception, and vows to separate her from the children. A repentant note from Krogstad softens him up, but Nora suddenly sees Torvald clearly and realizes she can no longer tolerate a marriage that casts her

as a "doll" rather than as a responsible person. She walks out and, as the play ends, closes the door behind her.

Don Carlos: historical tragedy by German poet Friedrich Schiller, presented in 1787; a romanticized account of the Spanish king Philip II's ill-fated son Don Carlos, who died mysteriously in prison after his father had him confined for conspiracy. In this play, Don Carlos and the elder statesman, the Marquis de Posa, are portrayed as champions of liberty, opposed to Philip's cruel rule in the Spanish Netherlands. Their plotting is discovered and Philip has them both executed. The play was the basis for Verdi's opera *Don Carlos.*

DON QUIXOTE: The wayward hero and his companion set out on their adventures.

Don Juan: character originally from medieval Spanish ballad tradition, who has come to symbolize the attractive and reckless seducer. His literary history begins with *The Rake of Seville,* a tragedy by Spanish writer Tirso de Molina, first performed in 1630, which established the basic core of the legend. Don Juan seduces several honorable women and kills the father of one of them in a duel. At a later date, while planning a dinner party and a fresh seduction in the presence of a memorial statue of the man he has murdered, he arrogantly invites the statue to dinner. The "stone guest" arrives at the banquet and Don Juan is swallowed into Hell.

Other versions include *The Stone Banquet* (1665) by the French dramatist Molière, a satire rather than a tragedy, and *Don Juan Tenorio* (1844), a play by Spanish writer José Zorilla y Moral that depicts a repentant rogue who, after 30 years of knavery, is saved from Hell at

the last moment by a virtuous woman. The work that is most likely to ensure Don Juan's immortality is Mozart's opera *Don Giovanni,* written to a libretto by Lorenzo da Ponte and first performed in 1787. This superb work combines the reckless gaiety of the incorrigible Don and the comic arias of his valet Leporello, with an ominous musical undertone of impending doom.

Don Juan (pronounced Ju' an in this work), an incomplete epic by the English poet Lord Byron, published intermittently from 1819 to 1824, contains the requisite sexual escapades, but little else of the original legend. The Byronic hero is an iconoclast, leveling satiric tirades on hypocrisy in general and England in particular. George Bernard Shaw's play *Man and Superman* (1903) contains a dream interlude, *Don Juan in Hell,* that is often performed as an independent work.

Don Quixote de la Mancha: picaresque in prose, published in two parts in 1605 and 1615, by the Spanish writer Miguel de Cervantes. It began as a satire of the romances of chivalry popular in Cervantes's day.

An impoverished old gentleman, Alonzo Quixano, infatuated with knighterrantry, changes his name to Don Quixote de la Mancha, and with an uncouth peasant, Sancho Panza, as his squire, embarks on a series of misadventures. His valorous deeds, such as tilting at windmills that he believes to be giants, are inspired by a peasant girl whom he reveres as the Lady Dulcinea. Ironically, he dies thinking he has been a failure, although in his pursuit of his illusory ideals he has shown far greater nobility than his sane materialistic contemporaries have.

Don Quixote has had a lasting influence on Western literature, and Sancho Panza ranks with the great comic characters of all time; Quixote and Sancho, the visionary idealist and the practical realist, are said to represent the two facets of the Spanish character. The greatest prose work of Spanish literature, its episodic structure influenced the form of the novel in the 18th and 19th centuries.

Dover Beach: prophetic poem by the English writer Matthew Arnold, published in 1851. It reflects the negative side of Victorian self-confidence and belief in progress. It begins serenely: "The sea is calm to-night." But as the poet watches the ebbing tide, he has a vision of the "Sea of Faith" withdrawing from the world and exposing its naked reality of tragedy and pain. The poem ends with the image of the world as a "darkling plain . . . Where ignorant armies clash by night."

Dracula: novel by British writer Bram Stoker, published in 1897. This Gothic horror story became the model for innumerable stories on "the matter of Transylvania." Based on Slavic folk

realizes
US

realises
Brit.

honorable
US

honourable
Brit.

theaters
US

theatres
Brit.

legends, they deal with vampires and werewolves. Stoker's *Dracula* was a charming and cultured Transylvanian count who assumed the form of a bat at night and sucked the blood of sleeping maidens.

Dragon: fabulous monster, pictured usually as a winged, fire-breathing serpent. Its literary function is to symbolize the forces of evil a hero must overcome. Often guardian of a rich hoard, as are Beowulf's Grendel and Sigurd's Fafnir, the dragon may in fact be a mythic representation of the conquering people's enemy—an opposing tribe perhaps in possession of desirable woods or precious metals. The dragon is often associated with water (as is the Hydra slain by Hercules and the biblical Leviathan) or with fire (as is the Chimera killed by Bellerophon); it therefore can symbolize the destructive forces in nature as well.

Because of its fearsome quality, the dragon was used as an emblem in war. It appears on the shields of Agamemnon, Norse and Roman soldiers, and on royal Anglo-Saxon banners. Medieval romances recount numerous tales of dragon-slayers, such as Arthur, Tristan, and Lancelot. Other dragon-killing heroes are Hercules, Apollo, Perseus, Bellerophon, Sigurd, and Beowulf. In Christian legend, the dragon, symbolizing Satan, was overcome by the archangel Michael. Many saints, the most famous being St. George, are pictured standing upon a dragon, a symbol of their having conquered evil.

Drama: literary composition in prose or verse, representing life and character through action and dialogue; it is usually intended for performance on a stage. Many great poets were dramatists, but not all drama is literature. Because of the presence of an audience, a successful drama must entertain. But the financial success of a play is not in itself a just criterion for rating its literary merits. Many Broadway hits have become dated or have faded into oblivion, having nothing more to recommend them than fashionable ideas and, perhaps, witty dialogue.

Certain plays never become outdated, however, and these may be considered literature. Shakespeare's plays, in particular *Hamlet, Macbeth, A Midsummer Night's Dream,* and *Julius Caesar,* never cease to excite audiences; they are often performed. Molière's plays, too, are frequently revived. *Tartuffe, the Misanthrope, The Would-Be Gentleman,* and others are considered masterpieces of comic literature. People often mistakenly believe that only serious dramas, not comedy, can gain literary value. But since Aristophanes there have been comedies that rate that distinction. There are also many popular tragedies that are remembered, if at all, with embarrassment.

Of all drama, the classic Greek tragedies are perhaps the most durable, having endured for thousands of years without becoming stale. Society and religion have changed greatly since the time of Sophocles, Aeschylus, and Euripides, but their themes and poetry still have the power to move us.

In addition to plays that are meant to be performed, poets sometimes write "closet" dramas. Although the poet's ideas are expressed in dialogue, the play is intended to be read, not viewed. Milton's *Samson Agonistes* is an example. Shelley and Tennyson also wrote closet dramas.

Dramatic monologue: form of dramatic poetry in which the story is told through the voice of a single person to an imaginary audience. The writer does not intrude to offer his comments, but instead allows the reader to decide what value to place on the speaker's words. Robert Browning was the master of the form in "My Last Duchess" and "Fra Lippo Lippi."

Dramatic Poetry, Essay of: critical work by English writer John Dryden, published in 1668, during the Restoration, when the theaters were reopened. In the form of a dialogue between four friends, Dryden discusses the comparative merits of ancient, French, and English drama. Dryden sought to prove the greatness of English drama, both old and new. Through the voice of one of his characters, he shows a deep appreciation of Shakespeare and other English playwrights. He also makes a case for simplicity in writing to replace the learned and complicated metaphors that bogged down metaphysical poetry.

Dream Play, A: play by Swedish author August Strindberg, first presented in 1907. *A Dream Play* is a seminal work in avant-garde theater. Strindberg reproduced the jumpy continuity of a dream, in which characters appear, disappear, and reappear without apparent reason, and symbol is more important than substance. Indra's Daughter descends to Earth to experience human life and finds it painful. At the end of the play, having taken part in the disjointed lives and dreams of the other characters as well as her own, she promises to bring their lamentations to the throne of God.

Dr. Jekyll and Mr. Hyde: dual central character in English author Robert Louis Stevenson's *The Strange Case of Dr. Jekyll and Mr. Hyde* (1886). The doctor, a gentle, well-trusted physician engaging in chemical research, concocts a potion with which he changes himself into a mad criminal, Mr. Hyde. Jekyll finds himself helpless against the potion's effects, which eventually destroy him.

Drury Lane: street and district in London. It was named for Sir William Drury, who built a residence there during the early 1500s. It is the site of the Drury Lane Theatre, built in 1663 and rebuilt (most recently in 1812) several times after fires. The oldest English theater still in use, Drury Lane was the home of some of the greatest triumphs in the history of the English theater, most notably those of the actor David Garrick, its manager from 1747 to 1775.

Dryads, GM: wood nymphs, also called hamadryads. Unlike other nymphs, who were immortal, they lived and died with the trees in which they dwelt.

Dubliners: collection of short stories by James Joyce, published in 1914, in which Joyce portrays the middle-class world he knew in Dublin; several characters reappear in his *Ulysses.*

Duncan: *See* Macbeth.

Dunciad, The: satire in heroic couplets by English poet Alexander Pope, first published anonymously in 1728 and reissued several times in revised and extended versions. Pope directs his venom against various contemporary literary figures, chiefly ignorant critics and, in the later versions, Colley Cibber, an English actor who was appointed poet laureate in 1730.

DR. JEKYLL AND MR. HYDE: The gentle doctor and his grotesque second self were played in the film of the 1930s by Fredric March.

20 History of Literature

Dutchman: short play by U.S. writer Imamu Amiri Baraka (LeRoi Jones). It brought him recognition as an important writer and spokesman for the black nationalist movement. The two characters—a 30-year-old white woman, Lula, and a 20-year-old black man, Clay—meet on a train. Their conversation alternates between flirtation and confrontation as Clay realizes his identity as a black man in a white world.

Dwarf: in folklore, a small supernatural man living in the mountains or in the depths of the earth. Dwarfs are often represented as old men with long white beards. Sometimes helpful, sometimes malicious, they were believed to possess great knowledge; they were guardians of the earth's wealth and were skilled miners and metalworkers. The armor and swords they forged often had magical properties in legends.

DWARF: An evil dwarf in a wild natural setting.

In the households of kings and noblemen, real dwarfs were often kept as entertainers or court fools. In literature, they appear in such roles to comment on the action of normal society, from which they were excluded. Oskar, the narrator of Günter Grass's novel *The Tin Drum* (see entry), uses his willfully stunted growth to distance himself from the wartime Germany around him. This lets him observe with the mind of a man and the viewpoint of a child.

Dwarfs are often used in literature to symbolize evil human urges. The dwarf Quilp in Dickens' *The Old Curiosity Shop* represents lechery; Swift transfers the pettiness of society to the diminutive world of the Lilliputians in order to satirize his contemporaries. Benevolent dwarfs appear in Tolkien's *Lord of the Rings* as Hobbits and in Frank Baum's *Wizard of Oz* as Munchkins. In fairy tales, the dual literary function of dwarfs comes across in the character of Rumpelstiltskin, the little man who saves the heroine only to become, in his demands for an odious payment, the villain from whom the heroine must in turn be saved. The dwarfs who trick Rip Van Winkle in Washington Irving's

story are not good or evil beings, but merely mischievous.

Dybbuk: in Jewish folklore, an evil demon or soul of a dead man that takes over the body of a living person. *The Dybbuk* is a well-known play by Russian-Yiddish author S. Ansky (pen name of Solomon Rapoport), first presented in 1920. Paddy Chayefsky rewrote it as *The Tenth Man* (1960).

E

East of Eden: novel by U.S. author John Steinbeck, published in 1952. The story is based on the biblical conflict between Cain and Abel and is set in the Salinas valley of central California about the time of World War I. Violent fraternal conflict occurs first in the lives of Adam Trask and his brother Charles and then becomes evident again as Adam's twin sons, Cal and Aron, grow up. Their mother, Cathy, who deserts the twins to become a prostitute, is a key figure in the drama, as is the philosophical Chinese servant Lee.

Echo, GM: nymph who kept Hera occupied with her chatter while Zeus chased the other nymphs. Discovering the ruse, Hera in fury changed her voice to an echo. Echo fell in love with Narcissus but, being able only to repeat the last word of what he said, could never tell him of her love.

Eclogue: short pastoral poem. The word originally meant "selection," but Vergil's pastorals *(Bucolia),* imitating those of the Greek poet Theocritus, were published as *Eclogae,* and the word acquired a special meaning.

Edda: two ancient works in Old Norse or Icelandic. The first, the Poetic or Elder Edda, is a collection of Old Norse poems explaining the creation of the world and celebrating gods and heroes. It is the main source of our knowledge of Norse mythology. Most of the poems were probably composed between the tenth and 13th centuries, though some are versions of tales hundreds of years older, such as the tales of Sigurd. The Younger or Prose Edda was written by Snorri Sturluson, an Icelandic historian and statesman of the early 13th century. It is a book of Norse poetics and poetic mythology, containing many examples of the poetry of the skalds (minstrels), along with commentary by Snorri.

Eden: paradise where all living things exist in harmony. An Eden differs from a utopia in being a "natural" state rather than a perfect society. In Wells's *The Time Machine,* the Eloi may be said to be living in an Eden until the truth about their destiny becomes clear.

The notion of man's original, "natural" state, free from sin and want, had a powerful effect on Western civilization. During the 18th and 19th centuries, it

was popular in Europe to view American Indians as having lived in this state before the coming of the white man, a view fostered by Rousseau's doctrine of the "noble savage."

Elaine: *See* Lancelot.

El Dorado (Spanish for "the golden one"): originally, the name given to a mythical South American Indian chief; later the name of a legendary treasure-filled city. The chief was said to cover himself with gold dust at religious festivals. Spanish explorers searched but did not find him. The name came to mean a region where treasure and riches are to be had for the taking.

Electra: *See* House of Atreus.

Elegy: serious, meditative poem, usually containing the poet's reflections on death. A modern example of this type of poetry is Gray's "Elegy Written in a Country Churchyard." Elegy in the modern sense is usually a lament for the dead, most often a dead friend of the poet. Among the greatest elegies of this type in the English language are Milton's "Lycidas," Shelley's "Adonais" (on the death of Keats), Tennyson's "In Memoriam," Matthew Arnold's "Thyrsis," and Walt Whitman's "O Captain! My Captain!" (on the death of Lincoln).

Elegy Written in a Country Churchyard: reflective poem by English poet Thomas Gray, published in 1751. The churchyard mentioned is Stoke Poges in Buckinghamshire, England. The poem reflects upon fleeting fame and inevitable death: "The paths of glory lead but to the grave." The poem is sometimes considered an early work of the English Romantic movement.

Elizabethan Age: period roughly covered by the reign of Queen Elizabeth I in England (1558–1603) and the years directly following. A time of exploration and discovery for England, it was marked by great literary output and brilliant achievement, especially in poetry and drama. Shakespeare is the brightest name of the age. Francis Bacon, a philosopher and a lawyer for the queen, wrote brilliant essays. *The Faerie Queene,* one of the great poems in English, was written in her honor by Edmund Spenser. Sir Philip Sidney, Michael Drayton, Christopher Marlowe, Ben Jonson, John Donne, and many others helped to make the Elizabethan Age a brilliant period in English literature.

Elmer Gantry: satirical novel by U.S. writer Sinclair Lewis, published in 1927. Lewis paints a devastating portrait of the hard-drinking, woman-chasing Gantry, who turns his gift for oratory into a successful career as an evangelistic preacher, a "Professional Good Man." Lewis used the character to satirize hypocrisy and sham in U.S. religion, particularly in revivalism.

---

armor
US

armour
Brit.

civilization
US

civilisation
Brit.

honor
US

honour
Brit.

realize
US

realise
Brit.

Elysium, GM: also called the Islands of the Blest and the Elysian Fields; the abode of the good after death. Homer locates the islands somewhere in the Western ocean. Men favored by the gods went to Elysium, a land ruled by Rhadamanthus, where the sun always shines. In Vergil's *Aeneid,* the abode of the blessed is a part of the underworld, but it is a pleasant place.

Emperor's New Clothes, The: children's story by Danish writer Hans Christian Andersen. The emperor's new clothes, woven by a pair of swindlers, are supposedly made of a cloth invisible to anyone who is stupid or incompetent. When he wears them in procession, no one but a child will point out that he has no clothes on. Only then do the emperor and his people realize they have been duped. The story has been called "the truest allegory of politics."

Encyclopedia: reference work that gives information either in all general fields of knowledge or in a specific field, such as technology, sports, or music. The earliest known writer to compile information in an encyclopedic manner was a Roman, Marcus Terentius Varro; the oldest extant encyclopedia is the *Natural History* of Pliny the Elder, a work consisting of 37 books, published in A.D. 77. Pliny's work was a principal authority until after the Renaissance.

In the early 1700s, several encyclopedia-like works were published in England. But the first great encyclopedia in the modern sense was the French *Encyclopédie* of Denis Diderot, published in 28 volumes, 1751–1772. Contributors included Voltaire, Montesquieu, Rousseau, d'Alembert, and other leading thinkers of the day, known as the Encyclopedists, or *philosophes.* The encyclopedia contributed both to the spread of learning and to the consequent social discontent that helped bring on the French Revolution.

Perhaps the greatest encyclopedia published in English was the 11th edition of the *Encyclopaedia Britannica,* published in 1912, a voluminous summary of progress in all scholarly fields. Scores of encyclopedic works have since been published for many different audiences and in many special fields.

Endgame: one-act play by Irish-born French dramatist Samuel Beckett, presented in 1957. *Endgame* is a symbolic, plotless drama in the absurdist tradition; little happens, and the four characters spend the play in exchanging cryptic, allusive, and wounding remarks. The main character, Hamm, is a blind invalid; the others are his servant Clov and his aged parents, who spend the entire play in two ashcans.

Enlightenment, The: intellectual movement that swept through Europe during the 1700s. Its ideas were taken from the scientists and philosophers of the 1600s, notably Isaac Newton, René Descartes,

VOLTAIRE was a leading light in the French enlightenment of the 1700s.

and John Locke, and its perceived intent was to enlighten, or educate, society about man's reason and perfectibility, thus ridding man of prejudice and irrationality. The chief figures of the Enlightenment in France, known as the *philosophes,* included Voltaire, Rousseau, Montesquieu, and Diderot. Many of them collaborated on Diderot's *Encyclopédie.* The Enlightenment had a profound effect on politics, particularly the American and French revolutions. *See also* Encyclopedia; Philosophes.

Eos, GM: goddess of the dawn, daughter of Hyperion and Thea; known to the Romans as Aurora. Every morning she drove her chariot into the sky to announce the rising sun. Homer usually calls her "rosy-fingered Dawn." She had a penchant for carrying off good-looking young mortal men.

Epic: long narrative poem celebrating the deeds of historical or legendary heroes. The ancient Greek *Iliad* and *Odyssey* of Homer typify the ancient epic. Vergil's *Aeneid* is called the first full-length literary epic by a single author, since Homer (if there was a Homer) composed in the oral tradition. The Old English *Beowulf* stands out as the most important epic in Germanic literature, although the German *Nibelungenlied* is as well known. Like the Homeric epics, these two were composed in the oral tradition and written down later, as were the French epic *The Song of Roland* and the Spanish *Song of The Cid.* The two great literary epics of European literature are Dante's *Divine Comedy* and Milton's *Paradise Lost.* None written since then has been adjudged equal to these, but epics are still being written; Nikos Kazantzakis's *The Odyssey, A Modern Sequel* (1938) is an outstanding 20th-century example.

Epigram: in ancient Greece, an inscription (usually in verse) on a monument; hence, a short poem expressing one pointed thought. From Roman times on, the epigram was often satirical and usually ended with a witticism or a surprise. The epigrams of Martial (c A.D. 40–104), a Roman poet, became a model for later writers. An epigram is also any thought tersely and pointedly expressed in prose or verse, usually in one sentence, that sometimes seems contradictory: "Where ignorance is bliss, 'tis folly to be wise."

Epithalamium: among the ancient Greeks, a wedding poem, originally sung in chorus at the door of the bridal chamber. The Greek poet Theocritus wrote a marriage song honoring Helen and Menelaus, and the Roman poet Catullus composed a well known epithalamium. Edmund Spenser's *Epithalamion* (1595), honoring his own marriage, is the most famous in English literature; John Donne also wrote several.

Erewhon: satirical Utopian novel by English writer Samuel Butler, published in 1872. The title is an anagram of Nowhere, the literal translation of "Utopia." The book is a satire on hypocrisy, the church, parental tyranny, and society's unintelligence.

Eri-king: in Teutonic folklore, the king of the elves, who steals away human children. In later German legend, his home is the Black Forest. Goethe wrote his famous ballad "Erlkönig" on this subject; it was set to music by Franz Schubert (1816) and translated into English by Sir Walter Scott.

Erin: ancient name of Ireland.

Erinyes: *See* Furies.

Eris, GM: goddess of discord, sister of Ares. She was not invited to the wedding of Peleus and Thetis, and out of spite threw a golden apple among the guests, marked "To the fairest." Hera, Athena, and Aphrodite each claimed it and appealed to Zeus to decide. He sent them to young Paris, a shepherd on Mt. Ida. Each one made a great promise to win his favor, but when Aphrodite promised him the fairest of all women for his wife, Paris gave the prize to her. Thus Eris with her apple caused even greater strife, for when Paris saw Helen, the wife of Menelaus, he fell in love with her and carried her off to Troy; this elopement was the cause of the Trojan War.

Eros: *See* Cupid.

Essay: short literary composition, usually in prose, telling the writer's thoughts and reflections on a subject. There are three kinds of essay: the formal, polished essay on a specific subject; the technical or scientific exposition; and the personal essay.

The term "essay" was first used by the French writer Michel de Montaigne in 1571; he chose the word *essais* to designate his writings as attempts, trials, or experiments. The first of Montaigne's *Essays* came out in 1580. They were a new kind of writing, dealing with any subject or idea that came to the author's mind. They were brief or rambling, full of interruptions, personal moods, and opinions, formless and yet unified by the personality of the author.

Francis Bacon was the first of the English essayists; he put out a volume of ten essays in 1597. The *Tatler* and the *Spectator* papers (1709–1714) of Addison and Steele are witty informal essays. The *Essays of Elia* (1820–1833) by Charles Lamb are leisurely and personal; Macaulay's essays, in contrast, are impersonal and informative. Later important English essayists include Matthew Arnold, John Ruskin, Thomas Carlyle, Virginia Woolf, Alice Meynell, G. K. Chesterton, and George Orwell.

The essay is uniquely suited to expressing the writer's personal view of life, as shown in the writings of Emerson and Thoreau. Other U.S. essayists have written gently humorous or satirical pieces, like those of James Thurber or E. B. White, or have written about science and nature from a personal viewpoint, like Rachel Carson, Joseph Wood Krutch, and Loren Eiseley.

Essay on Man, An: essay in rhymed couplets by English poet Alexander Pope, published in 1733–1734. It attempts to explain the nature of man, his place in the universe, and his relation to mankind and to God. The style is epigrammatic, and many of its lines have become familiar quotations.

Eteocles: *See* Seven Against Thebes.

Ethan Frome: short novel by U.S. writer Edith Wharton, published in 1911. Ethan and his wife's cousin Mattie are driven together by the jealousy of his invalid wife Zenobia and by the long, dark Vermont winter. They attempt suicide but fail. At the end, they are all left together but miserable.

Eugene Onegin: verse novel by Russian poet Aleksandr Pushkin, published in 1831. Eugene, a shallow society gentleman, arouses the love of the innocent young Tatiana while visiting the country, but he scorns her. Later, when she is married to a prince and has become a leading society figure, he falls in love with her, but she is too honorable to countenance adultery. The book was made into an opera by Tchaikovsky (1879).

Eumaeus: *See* Odyssey.

Eumenides: *See* Furies.

Euphemism: *See* Figures of speech.

Europa, GM: daughter of Agenor, king of Phoenicia. Zeus fell in love with her, took on the shape of a beautiful bull, and mingled with the cattle of Agenor. Europa

noticed and caressed him. When she climbed upon his back, he plunged into the sea and swam off with her to Crete. She became the mother of Minos, Sarpedon, and Rhadamanthus. Subsequently, she married the king of Crete. The continent of Europe was named for her.

Eurydice: *See* Orpheus.

Eurystheus: *See* Hercules.

Everyman: English morality play, first presented about A.D. 1500. As in other morality plays, the characters are personified abstractions and the play, didactic in purpose, is intended to encourage virtue. Death has summoned Everyman, who seeks company on his journey; but his friends Beauty, Worldly Goods, and others will not come. Only Good Deeds will accompany him, though weak from neglect until Confession and Knowledge revive him. Austrian playwright Hugo von Hofmannsthal adapted *Everyman* to the problems of modern man in his *Jedermann* (1911). *See also* Morality plays.

Excalibur: *See* Arthurian legend.

F

Fable: short tale told to illustrate a truth or moral. The most common type is the beast fable, in which animals take on human characteristics. The moral is often stated at the end of the fable, but it may not be stated at all, being implicit. A fable may be made up to illustrate a proverb, or the fable may itself be reduced to a proverbial phrase ("sour grapes"; "cry wolf"). In ancient times, fables were routinely ascribed to Aesop (see also *Aesop's Fables*). After Aesop, the foremost fabulists were the 17th-century French author Jean de La Fontaine, much admired for his literary style, and the 18th–19th-century Russian author Ivan Krylov, many of whose fables are original rather than retold. More recently, James Thurber wrote a series of *Fables for Our Times* (1940), and George Orwell's *Animal Farm* (1945) is an extended beast fable. *See also* Reynard the Fox.

Faerie Queene, The: long allegorical poem by English poet Edmund Spenser. Books I to III of the projected twelve books were published in 1589; books IV to VI in 1596; and the fragmentary seventh book, the "Mutability Cantos," in 1609. *The Faerie Queene* is an epic allegory, in conscious imitation of the language of Chaucer, telling of Arthur's search for Gloriana, the Faerie Queene. Each book tells of an adventure of one of Arthur's knights, each of whom embodies a personal virtue. A moral and spiritual allegory, the poem is also an allegory of Elizabethan politics, in which Gloriana represents Queen Elizabeth. Spenser invented a unique stanza form for the work. *See also* Stanza.

POE WROTE stories of suspense and terror, like *The Fall of the House of Usher*.

Fafnir: *See* Nibelungenlied; Völsunga Saga.

Fagin: *See* Oliver Twist.

Fairies: in world folklore, a race of supernatural beings with magical powers. They are usually pictured as resembling humans, though many have the power to assume strange animal shapes. In modern children's stories fairies are usually beautiful and good, but in ancient folk belief they were dreaded, and encounters with them were dangerous. Shakespeare used mischievous spirits in *A Midsummer Night's Dream*. They are also a common device in romances.

Fairy tales: popular term for short fictional stories like "Cinderella," "Hansel and Gretel," or "Rumpelstiltskin" that are the traditional heritage of people all over the world. Although they often contain supernatural beings or elements such as witches, talking animals, or magic wands, they are not necessarily about fairies. The heroes and heroines are often children mistreated by adults, or ordinary people subject to the whims of lords and kings. A number of universal motifs borrowed from mythology recur in fairy stories, chiefly the magic aid (whether it be a ring of power or a fairy godmother) and the transformation, in which a person is changed into someone or something else. Some scholars define fairy tales, in fact, as the result of ordinary people dreaming the fulfillment of their wishes through some means remembered from myth.

The German word for fairy stories is *Märchen*, and it is used universally by folklorists. Among the many who have collected and written down or retold fairy tales, the foremost are, in France, Charles Perrault; in Germany, the Brothers Grimm; and in England, Andrew Lang. Among authors famous for their original fairy tales, the foremost is Hans Christian Andersen.

The symbols used in this glossary are as follows:

G-Greek
R-Roman
N-Norse
M-myth
L-legend

---

honorable
US

honourable
Brit.

Fall of the House of Usher, The: Gothic horror story by U.S. writer Edgar Allan Poe, published in 1839, notable for its ominous atmosphere and mounting tension. Roderick Usher, the main character, is consumed by a sense of doom that is based on a mysterious hereditary trait. The collapse of his ancestral home symbolizes the collapse of his mind.

Falstaff, Sir John: *See* Henry IV; Merry Wives of Windsor, The.

Farce: *See* Comedy.

Farewell to Arms, A: novel by U.S. writer Ernest Hemingway, published in 1929. Against the background of World War I on the Italian front, Frederick Henry, an American lieutenant and ambulance driver, and Catherine Barkley, an English nurse, fall in love. The horror and senselessness of war is one of the themes in this work, which put Hemingway's reputation as a novelist on firm ground.

Far from the Madding Crowd: novel by British writer Thomas Hardy, published in 1874. The title of the book is taken from a line of Gray's "Elegy." The central character is Bathsheba Everdene, a haughty and capricious young woman whose romantic adventures end in disillusionment.

Fata Morgana: *See* Morgan le Fay.

Fates, GRM: female spirits that presided over the destinies of both gods and men. The Greeks called them Moirai; the Romans, Parcae. They were sisters, the daughters of Zeus: Clotho, who spun out the thread of human life; Lachesis, who measured its length; and Atropos, who cut it. Aeschylus attributed to the Fates power over men and gods alike. In Norse mythology, they were the Norns, whose names were Urd, Verdandi, and Skuld; the three Weird Sisters in Shakespeare's *Macbeth* are an echo of this myth.

Fathers and Sons: novel by Russian author Ivan Turgenev, published in 1862, noted for the character Bazarov, who became the representative type of the new generation of "nihilists" (cultural and political anarchists). It depicts Russian society on the eve of the emancipation of the serfs and focuses on the contrasting values of Nikolai Petrovich Kirsanov, an aristocratic landowner, his son Arkady, a liberal freethinker, and Arkady's radical friend Bazarov.

Faun, RM: creatures of nature, half man, half goat. Faunus, identified with the Greek god Pan, was the Roman rural god of the fields. *See also* Pan; Satyrs.

Faust: figure in many legends and literary works, loosely based on a 16th-century German magician, Georg Faust. Generally, Faust is archetypical of the overreacher, one with an insatiable desire for power and knowledge.

The Tragical History of Doctor Faustus, a play by English dramatist Christopher Marlowe, first presented in 1588, is one of the two most famous dramatizations of the legend. The play is in the morality tradition and antipapist. Faustus, a good and learned man, sells his soul to Mephistopheles, the Devil, practices necromancy, and plays tricks on the pope. When payment is due, he despairs and is taken to Hell.

Faust, a poetic drama by German author Johann Wolfgang von Goethe (published in two parts, 1808 and 1832), is the other famous version of the legend. Faust is tempted by the Devil and, although he sins seriously, he remains aware of truth and goodness; he is saved by divine intervention. Faust also comes to love, but later abandons, Gretchen.

Other works based on the Faust legend include Thomas Mann's novel *Doktor Faustus* and several operas, notably Gounod's *Faust,* Boito's *Mefistofele,* and Berlioz's *The Damnation of Faust.*

Fenris Wolf or **Fenir,** NM: monster son of Loki. The gods kept him bound with the magic chain Gleipnir. In order to lure him into allowing himself to be chained, Thor placed his hand in the Wolf's mouth as a pledge; finding himself trapped, the Wolf bit Thor's hand off. It was told that the Wolf would escape at Ragnarök, swallow Odin, and be killed by Odin's son Vitharr. *See also* Ragnarök.

FATES: the three goddesses engraved after a drawing by Michelangelo.

Ficciones (Fictions): Pulitzer Prize-winning collection of short pieces, published in 1944, by the Argentine writer Jorge Luis Borges. The term *ficción,* coined by the author, represents a new genre—the story disguised as essay (including footnotes). Historical and imaginary characters, their works, and events are discussed in such a way that the reader no longer knows what is historically verifiable. Each enigmatic *ficción* serves not only as a vehicle for Borges's philosophical ideas, but also as a metaphor for a universe in which we never know what is real and what we have imagined.

Fiction: all imaginative literature in narrative or dramatic form, including drama, short stories, novels, and romances (see separate entries); it is often used as a synonym for novel. Even in historical novels the plot is imaginative. Many narrative and dramatic poems are fiction, but the term usually refers to prose.

Figures of speech: words, phrases, or statements used for expressive purposes and not meant to be taken literally. They are a part of everyday speech and are basic to slang, literature, and poetry. Common figures are:

Simile, an explicit comparison of two unrelated objects indicated by the words *like* or *as:* "The road curved like a snake."

Metaphor, a more subtle figure in which the resemblance or comparison is implied rather than actually spelled out: "You are an angel." "The road snaked around curves."

Personification, the attribution of human qualities to a nonhuman being or object: "The sun smiled down." Many myths represent ancient personifications of natural forces or objects.

Metonymy, in which one word is exchanged for another with which it is closely associated: "You can't fight City Hall" (that is, the powers that be). *Synecdoche* is a related figure in which a part is substituted for the whole, as in the use of the expression "to count noses" for counting people.

Hyperbole, an intentionally extravagant statement: "I looked in a hundred stores to find this." Its opposite is *understatement,* which represents something as less than it actually is. One form of understatement is *litotes,* in which an idea is expressed as the negative of its opposite: "He's not a bad writer." "That's not a bad idea."

Euphemism, the substitution of a more acceptable or more tactful expression for an unpleasant reality: "senior citizens" for old people; "police action" for war.

Oxymoron, the use of two or more words that are seemingly in contradiction to each other but are harmonious in some deeper sense. Milton's description of Hell, "No light, but rather darkness visible" (Paradise Lost I:63), is a famous example.

Finnegans Wake: novel by Irish-born writer James Joyce, published in 1939. It is a stream-of-consciousness experiment in form and meaning. Drawing on 17 languages, it attempts to give coherence to all human experience and, through the dreams of Humphrey Chimpden Earwicker, to find the universal myth.

Fixer, The: novel by U.S. author Bernard Malamud, published in 1966, based on a true case in czarist Russia during a period of anti-Semitism. Yakov Bok, an insignificant Jewish handyman, finds himself accused of the ritual murder of a Christian boy in Kiev; in defying this injustice and enduring his imprisonment, he attains heroic status.

Fleurs du Mal, Les *(The Flowers of Evil):* collection of poems by French poet Charles Baudelaire that embraces his entire poetic output. First published in 1857 with little success, it became one of the most influential works of modern poetry. The poems are so arranged as to constitute a symbolic, spiritual autobiography that, in theme and form, is one of the first instances of modernism. Baudelaire substitutes the terms *idéal* and *spleen* for the traditional dichotomies of good and evil. Spleen is inertia, self-involvement, pettiness, debasement. The conflict between the poet's efforts to free himself for a better life and his constant relapse into the closed, hellish world of the self provide the poems' dynamics.

Folklore: collectively, the myths, legends, folk tales, proverbs, riddles, and verse that are orally transmitted within a culture. Superstitions, children's games, and customs associated with festivals or rites of passage are also regarded as folklore; sometimes the term includes more highly developed popular arts, crafts, songs, and dances. The term "folklore" was coined in 1846 by William J. Thomas of England to describe literary and artistic survivals of an earlier age. Such relics were once called "popular antiquities."

Fool: in literature, two types of character: God's Fool, and the jester. God's Fool is the man of absolute purity of heart, knowing nothing of the ways of the world, who succeeds because of his purity; the prime example is Sir Perceval in the Arthurian legends. Dostoevski's Prince Myshkin in *The Idiot* is a more modern rendition of the type. The jester was a man retained by a ruler or noble to entertain him; the jester often had far more latitude in what he could say than any other person around a ruler, and he thus had the opportunity to serve as the ruler's conscience. A well known literary example is the fool in Shakespeare's *King Lear.*

Foot: in versification, the basic unit of meter. A foot consists of a group of two or three syllables, of which at least one is accented. The principal feet used in English poetry are:
iambus, unaccented plus accented, as in the word agree′.
trochee, accented plus unaccented, as in the word dai′ ly.
dactyl, accented plus two unaccented, as in the word des′ perate.
anapest, two unaccented plus one accented, as in the word insincere′.
spondee, two accented syllables, as in the word thir′ teen′.
See also Meter.

Forsyte Saga, The: series of novels by English writer John Galsworthy, including *The Man of Property* (1906), *In Chancery* (1920), and *To Let* (1921), published together as *The Forsyte Saga* in 1922. The history of the Forsyte family was continued in *The White Monkey* (1924), *The Silver Spoon* (1926), and *Swan Song* (1928), which were collected in *A Modern Comedy* (1929).

This social chronicle depicts the changes in manners and morals from Victorian England to the post–World War I period. According to the author, the underlying theme is the conflict beauty creates in men's lives.

For Whom the Bell Tolls: novel by U.S. writer Ernest Hemingway, published in 1940. Its hero, Robert Jordan, is an American volunteer in the Spanish Civil War who joins a band of Spanish guerrillas in the mountains and organizes their sortie to blow up a strategic bridge. He falls in love with one of the partisans, a young girl named Maria, and in the course of the book develops an awareness of the larger purpose of the war and a compassion for all oppressed people.

FRANKENSTEIN: the monster as played by Boris Karloff in the 1931 film.

Frankenstein: novel by English writer Mary Wollstonecraft Shelley, wife of the English Romantic poet. Published in 1818, before the author was 20, the novel is a sympathetic portrayal of a creature that a scientist named Frankenstein assembles from parts of corpses and then brings to life—but her creature, unlike his malevolent counterparts in later horror films, is gentle and kind, a victim of society. Only the fact that people shun him for his monstrous appearance turns him at last against humanity; he flees to Arctic regions to escape this rejection and ultimately destroys his creator. The creature in the novel was given no name, but the name of his creator, Frankenstein, eventually was applied to him also.

Free verse: verse that is rhythmical without formal meter, stanza, or rhyme. The term *vers libre* ("free verse"), coined by the 19th-century French symbolists, was adopted by a modern school of poets in Europe and the U.S. who sought to liberate poetry from conventional metrical rules. Among the early exponents of the school were Amy Lowell, Carl Sandburg, Ezra Pound, and T. S. Eliot, but it has since become the characteristic poetic idiom of the 20th century.

Free verse is not exactly new or free. The Psalms of the King James Bible and Walt Whitman's *Leaves of Grass* are early and influential examples of free verse in English. Modern poets prefer free verse because it allows them to use the natural rhythms of speech.

Frey or **Freyr,** NM: god of fertility, crops and peace. He was one of the gods called Vanir and was the brother of Freya. His marriage with Gerth (or Gerda), the frozen earth, symbolized the coming of spring.

Freya, NM: beautiful goddess of love, music, and spring; often called the Venus of the North. She was one of the Vanir and sister of Frey. In the stories of the gods and giants, Freya was forever being promised to one giant or another in exchange for some favor. In Wagner's opera *Das Rheingold,* Alberich's cursed magic ring was offered to the giants as a substitute for Freya.

Friar Tuck: in English legend, a fat short-frocked friar or priest who travelled with Robin Hood. In his first meeting with the famous outlaw, the friar displayed both his strength and his shrewdness, besting the hero in a contest of wills and proving his equal with swords. The friar later joins Robin Hood's band and becomes his confessor.

Frigga, NM: queen of the heavens, goddess of marriage, and wife of Odin; sometimes confused with Freya. With Odin she ruled heaven and earth. She was the mother of Balder. Friday was named for Frigga.

Frogs, The: play by Greek comic dramatist Aristophanes, presented in 405 B.C. Dionysus goes to Hades to fetch back a tragedian for Athens, which had none worthy of the name since the recent death of Sophocles, the last surviving of the three great writers of tragedy. He arrives in time to witness and judge a contest in tragedies between Aeschylus and Euripides. The two authors criticize each other (and Aristophanes parodies them both); in the end, Aeschylus wins. The Frogs of the title are a chorus, whose famous croaking refrain is: *Brekekekex ko-ax ko-ax.*

Furies or **Erinyes,** GM: avenging spirits who tormented wrongdoers. They were often personified as three ruthless women, daughters of earth and darkness; they are sometimes interpreted as representations of a guilty conscience. In Aeschylus's play *Eumenides,* they mercilessly pursue Orestes for his murder of his mother. The term "Eumenides" (meaning "well disposed") is a euphemism for these dreaded haunters; Aeschylus explains the name by having them renounce their lust for the blood of the guilty at the end of the play.

---

meter
US

metre
Brit.

centers
US

centres
Brit.

theater
US

theatre
Brit.

G

Gabriela, Clove and Cinnamon: novel by Brazilian author Jorge Amado, published in 1958. It masterfully explores the mysteries of love through the story of Gabriela, an extremely desirable and sensual mulatto.

Gaea or **Ge**, GM: earth goddess, both mother and wife of Uranus, and mother of the Titans: Cyclopes, Furies, Giants, and Cronus.

Galahad: chaste and perfect knight who, in later versions of Arthurian legend, achieved the quest of the Holy Grail. *See also* Holy Grail; Lancelot.

Galatea: *See* Pygmalion.

Gallic Wars, Commentaries on the: military history by Roman general and politician Julius Caesar, first published in 51 B.C. It is a terse account of his military campaigns in Gaul and Britain; it is important as a historical document for its account of the culture of the conquered people, and often used as a Latin textbook because of its direct, simple style.

Ganelon: in the Charlemagne romances, the count of Mayence, a sly and treacherous knight who was responsible for the death of Roland. *See also* Roland.

Gareth: *See* Gawain.

Gargantua and Pantagruel: comic masterpiece by the French humanist author, François Rabelais. It appeared in 1532–1564, and tells the story of the giant Gargantua, his son Pantagruel, and their companions, especially the rascally Panurge. Their adventures, recounted in five books (the fifth being of doubtful authenticity), ridicule contemporary follies and superstitions and satirize religion, politics, the law, and 16th-century French society.

Gawain: in Arthurian legend, one of the knights of the Round Table, nephew of King Arthur. Known as "the Courteous," he is the chief hero of the earlier legends and the model for young knights, though his importance declines in later legends. He was the older brother of Gareth, who was accidentally killed by Lancelot at the rescue of Guinevere from the stake. Gareth's death resulted in the breakup of the Round Table. Gawain battled Lancelot in revenge and received a fatal wound from him.

The 14th-century English poem *Sir Gawain and the Green Knight,* an anonymous epic in alliterative verse, is the most famous single Arthurian tale in English. *See also* Sir Gawain and the Green Knight.

Gemini: *See* Castor and Pollux.

Genie: *See* Jinni.

George, Saint: originally a Christian saint and martyr of the Eastern Church, who became famous for having slain a dragon and rescued a princess from it. The English soldiers of the First Crusade gave him credit for helping them to take Antioch in 1098; he became a popular saint in England and was declared the country's patron saint by Edward III in the 1300s. His flag, a red cross on a white background, was incorporated in the British flag. In medieval legend and art St. George was primarily depicted as the dragonslayer, and his victory was a common allegory for the victory of good over evil.

Geryon: *See* Hercules (Twelve Labors).

Ghost: in folk belief, an apparition, usually the disembodied spirit of a dead person not at rest. In literature, ghosts are used to create an eerie mood, to inform the other characters that all is not well, and/or to haunt a guilty conscience. Hamlet's father's ghost appears to verify Hamlet's suspicions about his mother and uncle and to demand revenge. Shakespeare uses Banquo's ghost in *Macbeth* to harass the guilt-ridden murderers. Ghosts may appear to request proper burial, as in Matthew Gregory Lewis's *The Monk,* or to forecast doom, as the demonic apparition of a raven in Edgar Allen Poe's poem seems to with his cry of "Nevermore." Poe's masterly use of ghosts in his poems and stories centers on the psychology of the haunted flesh-and-blood narrator. In many of his stories, and in Emily Bronte's *Wuthering Heights,* the ghost acts as a symbol of love's endurance beyond the grave. That mourning disturbs the sleep of the dead is a theme that occurs in folk ballads and ghost tales, and the ghost's return may be met with horror or delight by the mourner. In Dickens' *A Christmas Carol,* the ghost comes to convey a warning to Scrooge of what lies in store for him if he doesn't mend his ways.

Ghost Sonata, The: play by Swedish author August Strindberg, first presented in 1908. The best known of Strindberg's so-called chamber plays, it had considerable influence on European theater during the early part of the 20th century, chiefly on account of its masterful blending of the dreamlike and the naturalistic in this eerie tale of the tragic love of the Student and the Hyacinth Girl, Adèle.

Ghoul: in Eastern folklore, an evil spirit that opens graves and eats corpses.

Giants: in mythology and folklore, monstrous, manlike beings of superhuman strength and powers, but with ungodlike characteristics. The Greek mythological giants, the Titans, warred against the Olympian gods and were conquered and confined under Tartarus (see also *Titans*). The giants of Norse mythology were the Jotunns who are supposed to fight against the gods at Ragnarök. In Celtic mythology, the gods vanquished the Fomors, or sea giants. Giants appear in many other legends. Famous giants in literature include Rabelais' Gargantua in *Gargantua and Pantagruel* and Swift's race of Brobdingnag in *Gulliver's Travels.*

SAINT GEORGE'S rescue of a maiden from a dragon is a frequent theme in various art forms.

Gift of the Magi, The: story by U.S. writer O. Henry, who published his most famous New York stories from 1902 to 1910. O. Henry was master of the surprise-twist ending that relies on coincidence, and this story displays his talent. It tells of newlyweds who cannot afford to buy each other Christmas presents. She sells her prize possession, her beautiful long hair, to buy him a chain for his gold watch; he sells his watch in order to buy her a comb set for her hair.

Gilgamesh, The Epic of: epic poem that recounts the adventures of Gilgamesh, the great hero of Sumerian legend. The tale exists in various fragmentary versions, dating from different times between 2000 B.C. and the 600s B.C. The epic tells of the adventures and deeds of Gilgamesh and his friend Enkidu; it contains legends that have parallels in a number of other cultures and religions, such as a great flood, the killing of a sacred bull, and a number of deeds reminiscent of those of Hercules, culminating with Gilgamesh's journey in search of Enkidu after his friend's death.

GLASS MENAGERIE: the fragile Laura Wingfield and her "gentleman caller" in the wistful play by Tennessee Williams.

center
US

centre
Brit.

realizes
US

realises
Brit.

labor
US

labour
Brit.

GONE WITH THE WIND: Clark Gable (Rhett Butler) and Vivien Leigh (Scarlett O'Hara) starred in the 1939 film version.

Glass Menagerie, The: drama by U.S. playwright Tennessee Williams, presented in 1944. Invited to dinner at the home of a friend from work, Jim O'Connor unwittingly becomes the center of the family's hopes—a possible escape from home for his friend Tom Wingfield, a chance for love for Tom's withdrawn sister Laura, and the "gentleman caller" of their mother Amanda's romantic dreams. Jim gently encourages Laura and admires her beloved collection of fragile glass animals, but reveals that he is engaged, shattering their hopes. Tom, seeing his last chance vanish, at last breaks away.

Golden Age, GRM: first era of the world, when Saturn reigned and truth, innocence, and ideal happiness prevailed. There was no law, nor need for any; there were no weapons, no wars. The Romans commemorated this era every year in the festival of the Saturnalia. The Golden Age was followed by the Silver Age and Bronze Age; in every age, men and their conditions were a little worse than before. The Heroic Age followed, during which the Trojan War was fought. The classical Greeks and Romans called their own period the Iron Age and thought that things were getting worse all the time.

Golden Ass, The: Latin romance in eleven books by Roman author Apuleius, written in the second century A.D. It is written in the form of an autobiography by one Lucius, who by mistaken enchantment is changed into an ass. He recounts his travels in search of a charm to restore him to human shape, during the course of which he sees and hears many strange things. His stories are a remarkable blend of humor and realism, everyday events and fantasy; best known is the tale of Cupid and Psyche.

Golden Bough, The: classic study, by English scholar Sir James Frazer, of comparative religion and mythology, published in twelve volumes, 1890–1915. It has been an important source for writers, including T. S. Eliot, who acknowledged his indebtedness to Frazer for certain parts of *The Waste Land*. Many of the author's inferences and conclusions have been proved wrong, but the book remains important in its field. The "Golden Bough" was a tree branch that Aeneas broke off and took to the underworld as a protective charm.

Golden Bowl, The: novel by U.S. author Henry James, published in 1904, in which James examines a delicate and complicated marital tangle. Maggie Verver, a young American girl, marries an Italian prince, with whom her friend Charlotte had an affair; Charlotte marries Maggie's millionaire father but resumes her liaison with the prince. James was particularly concerned with the characters' illusions and deceptions, since everyone knows what is going on but no one chooses to admit it.

Golden Fleece: *See* Argonauts.

Gone with the Wind: phenomenally successful novel by U.S. writer Margaret Mitchell, published in 1936; an epic of the South during and after the Civil War. Scarlett O'Hara, a vivacious, spoiled Southern belle, grows and changes as the South of her girlhood is defeated and forced to change.

Good Earth, The: Pulitzer Prize–winning novel by U.S. writer Pearl Buck, published in 1931. Based on the author's observations during nearly 40 years in China, this story of a Chinese peasant family's struggles for survival became the most famous of the author's many works on that country.

Gordian knot, GL: knot tied by Gordias, king of Phrygia, so intricate and complicated that no one could untie it. An oracle prophesied that whoever should master it would rule all Asia. Alexander the Great cut it with one stroke of his sword. To "cut the Gordian knot" means to solve any problem with bold, unconventional action.

Gorgons: *See* Medusa.

Gothic novel: type of melodramatic novel, so named because the setting is often a decayed Gothic castle. Other characteristics are a terrified heroine, a lonely landscape, secret passageways, and old family secrets (which are usually dreadful). The first example of the genre was the novel *The Castle of Otranto* (1764), by the noted 18th-century English gossip Horace Walpole, in which the wicked Manfred, who rules unlawfully in Otranto, schemes to keep his throne but is at last destroyed by the ghost of the murdered rightful ruler. Among Walpole's many successors were the English writers Ann Radcliffe, whose *Mysteries of Udolpho* (1794) made her the most popular writer of the day, and "Monk" M.G. Lewis, nicknamed for his novel *The Monk* (1795), a catalogue of horrors about an abbot who is led astray by the Devil and commits numerous crimes. Perhaps the foremost writer of Gothic tales was Edgar Allan Poe; there are also elements of Gothic atmosphere in the Brontës, Hawthorne, and other Romantic writers. Later writers in the genre include Isak Dinesen.

The term Gothic has also come to be used for contemporary "formula" novels that include some of the traditional elements.

Graces, GRM: three beautiful daughters of Zeus, called Charites in Greek and Gratiae in Latin. They were Aglaia (Brilliance), Euphrosyne (Joy), and Thalia (Bloom). They accompanied the Muses and often Aphrodite, Eros, or Dionysus.

Grapes of Wrath, The: novel by U.S. author John Steinbeck, published in 1939. The book relates the moving story of a family of farmers, the Joads, forced to leave their homestead in the Oklahoma dustbowl region and head for California in search of work on the fruit farms. Beset by problems on the journey and harassed on their arrival in California, they are utterly defeated by the end of the book, though still courageous. The novel's fierce criticism of migrant workers' social and economic plight aroused the nation's conscience on its first publication.

Great Expectations: novel by English author Charles Dickens, published in 1861. Pip, a village boy brought up by the kind blacksmith Joe Gargery, meets the half-demented, jilted spinster Miss Havisham, falls in love with her ward Estella, then longs to become a gentleman. He suddenly receives wealth from an anonymous source, goes to London, and, thanks to a series of misfortunes, finally realizes that Joe Gargery's life of honest labor makes more sense than his own empty "great expectations."

Great Gatsby, The: novel by U.S. author F. Scott Fitzgerald, published in 1925, generally regarded as his greatest work. Set in New York, it is an exposure of the boredom and spiritual bankruptcy of the "jazz age," and of the thoughtless cruelty of great wealth. Its plot is concerned with the efforts of Jay Gatsby, a wealthy racketeer who poses as a playboy, to win his idealized love, the spoiled and wealthy Daisy, who is a cousin of Nick Carraway, the story's narrator. Not only does Gatsby fail, but he dies alone and deserted even by the hangers-on who had flocked to his lavish parties.

Great Mother: important deity of prehistoric origin. The Mother was originally the deity of agricultural societies; she was the earth, great and fruitful. The year was her lover, strong in the summer but dying in the autumn, only to be reborn at the winter solstice. This cycle was personified in the society's queen, who was also chief priestess; each year a new king was chosen and the old one sacrificed. The Mother was the chief deity of ancient Near Eastern and Mediterranean matriarchal societies. When these were supplanted by male-oriented societies, the Mother goddess was reduced to the position of mother of the gods.

Ancient writers identified practically every pre-Olympian goddess with the Great Mother, who for them represented an idea rather than a specific deity. Thus Rhea, Gaea, and Ops were all vaguely linked with the Mother and with each other. In the classical period, when piety for the Olympian gods had weakened, the cult of the Mother revived; she became known as Cybele. Her suitor was Attis, whom she drove mad so that he castrated or killed himself—an echo of the old rites. A corrupted form of the legend is the story of Venus and Adonis.

Grendel: in the Old English epic poem *Beowulf,* the night-stalking, man-eating monster from whom Beowulf delivered the Danes (*see also* Beowulf). An interesting modern novel, *Grendel,* written by John Gardner and published in 1971, retells the Beowulf story from the monster's point of view.

Griffin: also spelled griffon and gryphon; a fabulous monster with a lion's body and wings and the head of an eagle. It was believed by the Greeks to guard the gold of Scythia. The Greeks may have taken their notion from the statues of winged lions in Assyrian palaces and temples.

Grimm's Fairy Tales: popular name for a collection of folk tales (collected 1812–1815) by the brothers Jakob and Wilhelm Grimm of Germany, distinguished scholars and philologists. They were originally published as *Kinder und Hausmärchen (Children's and Household Tales)*. The stories were transcribed from oral recitations of peasants and other members of the vanishing class of illiterate storytellers. The work is the first example of modern folk tale scholarship. The collection contains the familiar stories of "Hansel and Gretel," "The Goose Girl," "Rumpelstiltskin," "The Frog Prince," "Snow White," and many others.

Gudrun: *See* Völsunga Saga.

Guinevere: *See* Arthurian legend.

Gulag Archipelago, The: work by Nobel Prize–winning Russian novelist Aleksandr Solzhenitsyn, published outside of Russia between 1973 and 1976. This work caused an international furor on its publication, partly because of its content—a description of conditions in Soviet labor camps between 1918 and 1956, based on the author's and other prisoners' experiences—and partly because the Soviet government stepped up its harassment of Solzhenitsyn and his family, finally exiling him to the West in February 1974.

"Gulag" is a Russian acronym for Chief Administration of Corrective Labor Camps. The work is written in a colloquial but highly emotional style and is filled with Solzhenitsyn's sense of outrage at the inhumanity of the labor camp system.

Gulliver's Travels: satire by Irish writer Jonathan Swift, published in 1726. In four parts it tells of Lemuel Gulliver's voyages to imaginary lands: Book I, to the island of Lilliput, where he finds himself a giant prisoner of a race of people six inches tall but every bit as vain and pompous as the people of his homeland; Book II, to Brobdingnag, the land of the giants, where he suffers the indignities of being swallowed and burped up by a squalling infant and being carried away by a puppy; Book III, to various countries, chief of which is the floating island of Laputa, the Cloud Cuckooland of eccentric scholars; and Book IV, to the country of the Houyhnhnms, a land where horses with an intelligence superior to that of mankind carry on an ideal government, despite the fact that they share their island with the Yahoos, a filthy and stupid race of creatures resembling humans.

GRIFFIN: The mythological monster is half eagle and half lion.

GULLIVER'S TRAVELS: Gulliver is tied to a primitive wagon and transported to the capital of Lilliput by his captors.

Gunnar: *See* Völsunga Saga.

Gunther: *See* Nibelungenlied.

Gutenberg Bible: edition of the Vulgate Bible; the first book to be printed with movable type, published in 1456. The inventor of the type and the printing press was Johann Gutenberg, a German printer.

H

Hades, GM: god of the lower world; in later myth called Pluto and other names, it being dangerous to speak his true name. The same name was applied to the dim and gloomy underworld, abode of the dead. It was surrounded by several rivers: the Styx, over which Charon ferried the shades of those duly buried; the Acheron, or the river of woe; Phlegethon, the river of fire; Cocytus, the stream of lamentation; and, in later myth, Lethe, the waters of forgetfulness. Cerberus, the three-headed dog, guarded the entrance to Hades. Tartarus was the section in which the wicked suffered torment; below Tartarus the Titans were chained. The land of the blessed, where Aeneas meets the dead heroes of Troy in the sixth book of the *Aeneid,* is a part of the underworld, but this is a later myth; for earlier authors such as Homer, all of the underworld was gloomy.

Hagen: *See* Nibelungenlied.

Hamlet: tragedy by William Shakespeare, first published in 1603. Hamlet, prince of Denmark, comes home to discover that his father is dead and his uncle, Claudius, now married to his mother, has become king. The ghost of his father reveals that Claudius murdered him, and the dead king demands vengeance. Hamlet defers action and indulges in melancholy indecision. He confronts Claudius with the truth by having the murder reenacted in a court play, breaks his relationship with the fair Ophelia, kills her father by mistake instead of Claudius, and is sent to England by the king to be put to death. But he is captured by pirates and returned to Denmark. There he finds that Ophelia, mad with grief, has drowned herself. Hamlet is killed by a poisoned sword in a fencing match with Ophelia's brother, Laertes, but stabs the king before he dies and thus finally avenges his father.

Though the plot of *Hamlet* is similar to other Elizabethan revenge tragedies, it differs in focusing its interest on Hamlet's indecision. The problem of the irresolute hero has fascinated critics and made this one of Shakespeare's most studied and analyzed plays.

Hansel and Gretel: popular folk tale first published by the Brothers Grimm in 1812. Hansel and Gretel are abandoned children who rescue themselves from a wicked witch by pushing her into the red-hot oven she has prepared to

HARLEQUIN: a French version of the clown in the Italian *commedia dell'arte.*

cook them. The story is an example of the common folk-tale motif of a stupid ogre who is tricked by his intended victim. It was adapted by the German composer Engelbert Humperdinck as a children's opera in 1893.

Harlequin: character in the *commedia dell'arte,* called Arlecchino in the Italian, often the lover of Columbine. Harlequin has a bald head and pointed cap, a mask, and a wooden sword. His typical costume is of a multicolored diamond pattern.

Harpies, GRM: ugly, foul, winged monsters with the faces of women and bodies of vultures. The word "harpy" comes from a Greek word which means to snatch; the Harpies were believed to snatch away missing persons, plunder travellers of their goods, and carry off or defile the food of offenders against the gods.

Heart Is a Lonely Hunter, The: first novel by U.S. writer Carson McCullers, published in 1940. Set in a small Georgia town, it is a poignant study of loneliness and the delusion of communication. The central image is Mr. Singer, a deaf-mute. To him the principal characters—Mick, a tomboyish adolescent girl; Biff, the owner of a seamy cafe; Jake, an alcoholic drifter; and Copeland, a black doctor—pour out their dreams, longings, and anger.

Heart of Darkness: long short story by Polish-born English author Joseph Conrad, published in 1902. The narrator, Marlow, travels to the "heart of darkness"—the jungle of cruelly exploited colonial Africa—to find in the dying Kurtz another sort of darkness and evil.

Heathcliff: *See* Wuthering Heights.

Hecate, GM: obscure goddess with great power but no clearly defined province. She later became associated with magic and sorcery, and was known as the protector of witches.

Hector: son of King Priam of Troy and his wife Hecuba; husband of Andromache and father of Astyanax. *See also* Iliad.

Hecuba, GM: principal wife of King Priam of Troy and the mother of Hector, Paris, Polyxena, Cassandra, and many other children. The Trojan War made her into a tragic figure: her sons Hector and Paris were killed; Priam was murdered after Troy fell; Polyxena was sacrificed on the tomb of Achilles; and Cassandra, who fell to the lot of Agamemnon, was murdered by Clytemnestra. Hecuba herself became the property of Odysseus. She appears in Euripides' *Trojan Women;* in his *Hecuba,* she avenges the death of her youngest son, Polydorus, in Thrace.

Hedda Gabler: late play by the Norwegian dramatist Henrik Ibsen, written in 1890. Hedda, disgusted with her didactic husband Tesman, seizes an opportunity to manipulate her former lover Løvborg, who is now involved with her schoolmate Thea; she destroys the brilliant manuscript on which his future depends and brings about his accidental death. When this crime brings her under the control of the manipulative Judge Brack, Hedda falls into deeper despair and shoots herself. One of Ibsen's most complicated heroines, Hedda has been variously interpreted as a wicked and neurotic woman or as the heroic victim of social constraints.

Heep, Uriah: *See* David Copperfield.

Heidi: children's book by Swiss writer Joanna Spyri, published in 1880. The orphaned Heidi is sent to live with her stern grandfather high in the Alps; she lives for a time in Frankfurt, where she becomes a friend of the invalid Klara, and finally returns to her beloved Alps.

Hel or **Hela,** NM: goddess of the underworld or death. She was the daughter of Loki. In her kingdom of death, Niflheim, she ruled over nine worlds, to which she allotted the dead. All those who died of sickness or old age were sent to her, but those who died in battle were sent to Valhalla.

Helen of Troy, GM: most beautiful of all women; the cause of the Trojan War. She was the daughter of Zeus and Leda, the sister of Castro and Pollux. *See also* Eris; Trojan War.

Helios, GM: sun god, later identified with Apollo. He was the father of Phaethon. Each day Helios drove his flaming chariot (the sun) drawn by four horses across the sky.

Hell: in worldwide belief, the abode of the dead, usually seen as a place of torment for the wicked. It has intrigued Western imagination at least since the time of the Greeks, who believed tortures were devised in Tartarus for the eternal torment of those who offended the gods (*see also* Sisyphus; House of Atreus). Hell is described in Vergil's *Aeneid,* Book IV, as a place of mourning rather than a place of torment. Those whose bones lie unburied beg the ferryman Charon to carry them across the river Styx, but a century must pass before he will oblige; suicides wander in this gloomy place, eternally longing for the above world sorrows they killed themselves in order to escape.

Two of the greatest evocations of Hell in Western literature are found in Dante's *Divine Comedy (Inferno)* and Milton's *Paradise Lost.* In Dante's Hell, punishments suit the sins of the damned and show the justice of the divine plan. Despite biblical references to the contrary, Dante depicts Hell as a region of cold, symbolizing the plight of the soul cut off from God: the lowest depth of Hell is a great frozen lake, over which a great winged Satan broods.

In Milton's epic, Hell is described as "A dungeon horrible, on all sides round,/ As one great furnace flamed; yet from those flames/ No light, but rather darkness visible/ Served only to discover sights of woe, . . ." (Book I: 60–64). It is an ironic tribute to these poets that readers much prefer their powerful visions of damnation to Dante's evocation of blessedness in *Paradiso* and to Milton's descriptions of Heaven and God in *Paradise Lost.*

Hellen: legendary founder of Greece. The story of Hellen is believed to have originated about the eighth century B.C. as part of a nationalist movement. According to the legend, his three sons, Dorus, Xuthus, and Aeolus, were the forefathers of the Dorian, Ionian, and Achaean Greeks (the latter two through their sons Ion and Achaeus). The Greeks in general are called Hellenes, and their culture Hellenic.

Henry IV: two-part history play by William Shakespeare, based on historical accounts of Henry's defense of the throne he had usurped from Richard II. Part I was presented in 1596, Part II in 1597.

A rebellion against Henry is led by the young Welsh rebel Hotspur, who is contrasted with Henry's own son Prince Hal, a wayward, idle youth who is less interested in affairs of state than in his drinking companions. Among them is Falstaff, one of the great comic characters of all literature—a fat old knight with enough shrewd wit to get out of all scrapes, derived ultimately from the braggart soldier of *commedia dell'arte.* At the end of Part I, Prince Hal reforms and kills Hotspur in battle. In Part II, King Henry dies and Hal rejects his disreputable cronies to assume the serious burden of kingship as Henry V.

Henry V: history play by William Shakespeare, first performed in 1599. It is a stirring representation of Henry V's victory over the French at Agincourt in 1415, portraying him as a vital young warrior king. At the close, Henry seeks to unite the two kingdoms by marrying the French princess Katharine.

Hephaestus, GM: god of fire and the forge, master smith of the gods, and patron of mortal metalworkers. He was the son of Zeus and Hera. For taking his mother's part in a quarrel Zeus hurled him down from Mt. Olympus, and after that he limped, having hurt his leg in the fall. In the *Iliad,* his wife is Charis; in the *Odyssey,* Aphrodite. His forges were believed to be under the world's volcanoes, particularly Mt. Etna. Hephaestus created Pandora, the first woman, and made the armor of Achilles. He was identified with the Roman Vulcan.

Hera, GM: sister and wife of Zeus and queen of the gods. She was the mother of Ares, Hebe, and Hephaestus and the goddess of women and marriage. Story after story pictures her as a jealous wife, taking out her resentment on the other loves of Zeus and on their children. She became identified with the Roman Juno, for whom the month June is named.

Hercules or **Heracles,** GM: celebrated and popular Greek hero, who had miraculous strength and prowess. Some stories make him the son of Zeus and Alcmene, and trace many of his troubles to Hera's jealousy: she sent two huge serpents to kill him when he was a baby but he crushed them in his cradle; she also sent a fit of madness, which caused him to kill his sons. For this misdeed, the Delphic Oracle commanded him to do penance in obedience to Eurystheus, king of Argos, who imposed on him a series of almost impossible tasks, his famous Twelve Labors (see table on next page).

There are many stories of Hercules's other feats. He freed Prometheus; killed a sea monster for Laomedon, the treacherous king of Troy who afterward refused to pay; and accompanied the Argonauts. He killed his friend Iphitus in a fit of insanity and was punished for it by being enslaved to Omphale, who set him to women's work. He died from the poison of Nessus's cloak, given him by his wife Deianira, who believed it a love charm. But he was made immortal and was married in heaven to Hebe. Hercules is usually pictured with a lion's skin cloak, a club, and a marvelous bow, which he was supposed to have willed to Philoctetes.

armor
US

armour
Brit.

Labors
US

Labours
Brit.

HENRY IV:
The old soldier Falstaff steals the limelight from the young hero-king in Shakespeare's play. Falstaff is one of the great comic characters in English literature.

20 History of Literature

labors
US

labours
Brit.

Hermaphroditus, GM: son of Hermes and Aphrodite, a beautiful man with whom the nymph Salmacis fell in love. When she prayed that she might be united with him forever, the gods merged the two into one body. In biology the term *hermaphrodite* applies to plants or animals (such as the earthworm) in which one individual is both male and female.

Hermes, GM: son of Zeus and Maia, messenger and herald of the gods. He conducted the dead to Hades. He was the god of science and invention, and invented the lyre by fastening strings across a tortoise shell. He was the guardian of travellers, roads, and commerce, was gifted with trickery, and was the protector of thieves. He stole the cattle of Admetus from under the nose of Apollo and tricked away Aphrodite's girdle. He is represented wearing a winged cap and winged sandals, and carrying the winged caduceus. The Romans identified him with Mercury.

Hero, GM: beautiful priestess of Aphrodite in the temple at Sestos on the European side of the Hellespont. She was dearly beloved by Leander, a youth on the opposite shore, who used to swim across to her every night. One night in a storm he was drowned, and Hero in despair threw herself into the waters and perished also. Christopher Marlowe's poem, "Hero and Leander," is based on this story.

Herzog: novel by U.S. writer Saul Bellow, published in 1961; a seriocomic story of alienation in modern life. Moses Herzog, an absent-minded history professor, achieves a temporary truce in the ongoing conflict between the worlds of the isolated imagination, the cultural heritage of the past, and the brutal private and public experiences of his generation by writing imaginary letters arguing his views with personal friends and public figures, both living and dead.

Hesperides, GM: daughters of Atlas and Hesperis. They were beautiful nymphs appointed to guard the Golden Apples given by Gaea to Hera on her wedding day. The wonderful garden of the Hesperides beyond the sea was guarded by a dragon that never slept. To secure some of the Golden Apples was one of the Twelve Labors of Hercules. He succeeded with the help of Atlas, according to one story; by killing the dragon, according to another.

Hestia: *See* Vesta.

Hexameter: *See* Meter.

Hiawatha: poem by U.S. poet Henry Wadsworth Longfellow, published in 1855, written in an eight-syllabled trochaic verse imitating the Finnish epic *Kalevala.* It embodies many legends and much of the culture of the North American Indians in the life of Hiawatha, son of Wenonah. He is reared by his grandmother, "daughter of the moon, Nokomis," marries Minnehaha, and becomes a hero of his people.

Hippolyte, GM: queen of the Amazons (also called Antiope). To steal her girdle was one of the Twelve Labors of Hercules. Hippolyte married the hero Theseus; their son was Hippolytus.

Hippolytus, GM: son of Theseus and Hippolyte. His stepmother, Phaedra, fell in love with him and hanged herself in shame and despair when he repulsed her. She left a note for Theseus accusing Hippolytus of trying to seduce her; Theseus cursed his son. Hippolytus fled from his father's wrath to the shore, where his horses took fright at the sea monster sent by Poseidon to destroy him. Hippolytus was dashed to death among the rocks. Euripides' *Hippolytus* (428 B.C.) is based on this version of the story, as is Jean Racine's masterpiece *Phèdre* (1677).

History of Plymouth Plantation, A: journal account of Pilgrim life from 1620 to 1647, written by William Bradford, the English-born governor of the Plymouth colony in colonial America. It was published posthumously in 1856, and provides information about the day-to-day lives of the Pilgrims.

History of Rome: massive work written by Roman historian Titus Livius (c 59 B.C.–A.D. 17), better known as Livy, from around 26 B.C. to the time of his death. Of the 142 books covering Roman history from the legendary arrival of Aeneas in Italy to the death of the emperor Tiberius's brother in 9 B.C., only 35 volumes survive. The work describes the rise of the Roman state and foreshadows its fall.

Hobbit, The: fantasy by English philologist J. R. R. Tolkien, published in 1937. The author was a scholar specializing in Old English and Old Norse, and many of the monsters, dwarfs, and trolls that appear in his stories are drawn from old legends. The Hobbits are a good-natured, peaceable race of small people who dwell in Middle-earth in the uncertain past. One of the Hobbits, Bilbo Baggins, goes off on an adventure with a wizard and several dwarfs to slay a bothersome dragon. In the course of many adventures, Bilbo finds a ring that makes its wearer invisible. This ring is the subject of a subsequent trilogy, *The Lord of the Rings. See also* Lord of the Rings.

Holinshed's Chronicles: properly titled *The Chronicles of England, Scotland, and Ireland,* a history by English author Raphael Holinshed, published in 1578; used by Shakespeare as the chief historical source for his history plays.

Holy Grail: also called the Sangreal, the platter or cup used by Christ at the Last Supper, in which Joseph of Arimathea

The symbols used in this glossary are as follows:

G-Greek
R-Roman
N-Norse
M-myth
L-legend

The Twelve Labors of Hercules

THE NEMEAN LION. Hercules strangled this monstrous man-eating lion, then skinned it.

THE HYDRA OF LERNA. Destruction of this nine-headed water snake was difficult. Since two heads grew back for each severed one, and one head was immortal, Hercules, helped by Iolaus, seared the stumps as he cut the heads off, then buried the immortal head under a great rock.

THE ERYMANTHIAN BOAR. In order to bring the boar in alive, Hercules chased it into a snowfield and tired it out.

THE ARCADIAN STAG. To capture this golden-antlered stag, Hercules chased it on foot for a year, then wounded it with an arrow.

THE STYMPHALIAN BIRDS. Hercules destroyed these man-eating birds by flushing them out with a bronze rattle and shooting them with arrows.

THE AUGEAN STABLES. Ordered to clean in one day the filthy stables of King Augeus, who had thousands of cattle, Hercules diverted the rivers Alpheus and Peneus.

THE CRETAN BULL. Hercules captured this monstrous bull, a gift of Poseidon to King Minos, then brought it to Greece and turned it loose.

THE HORSES OF DIOMEDES. Diomedes, king of Thrace, fed his mares on human flesh; Hercules tamed them by killing Diomedes and feeding him to them.

THE GIRDLE OF HIPPOLYTE. Hercules fought the Amazons, then either killed their queen Hippolyte to obtain her girdle or made it the price of her ransom.

THE CATTLE OF GERYON. Hercules journeyed to an island in the western ocean, killed the three-headed, three-trunked monster Geryon, and either brought back his cattle in a magical golden vessel given him by Helios or drove them through all of Europe to Greece.

CERBERUS. Hercules went down to Hades, seized its three-headed watchdog Cerberus, brought him up to the mortal world, then returned him to Hades.

THE GOLDEN APPLES OF THE HESPERIDES. Hercules secured the apples, Gaea's wedding present to Hera, by persuading Atlas to fetch them while he shouldered Atlas's task of holding up the sky; he then tricked Atlas into taking the burden back.

miraculously preserved the blood from the wounds of Christ. According to legend, Joseph brought the blood to Britain where it was guarded for generations. It fed or healed those who saw it, but vanished at the approach of an impure person. It disappeared when its keepers became sinful, and thereafter became the quest of many a knight. It could be found only by the chaste and perfect knight. Only Perceval, Bors, and Galahad were worthy to achieve the quest, discovering it in Carbonek Castle. In late Arthurian legend, Galahad became the one perfect and successful quester. In the older Grail cycle, however, two romances name Gawain as the quester and winner; seven name Perceval; and only one Galahad.

Hopscotch: antinovel by Argentine writer Julio Cortázar, who lived in Paris after 1951. This deliberately difficult work made him an international literary figure when it was published in 1963 because of its experimental style. In disjointed scenes and in voices that switch from first person to third, it tells the story of Horatio Oliveira, an Argentine expatriate living in Paris, and his mistress Maga, with whom he has an agreement to meet only by chance. The chapters are interchangeable, and Cortázar suggests at least two orders in which the book can be read; he invites the reader to devise others.

Horatian ode: *See* Ode.

Hornblower, Horatio: brilliant, sensitive British naval officer, hero of a series of novels by English author C. S. Forester, of which the first and perhaps best known is *Captain Horatio Hornblower* (three volumes, 1937–1939). Forester's tales eventually take Hornblower through his entire naval career, from midshipman to admiral, during and after the Napoleonic Wars. The Hornblower stories are noted for their historical accuracy and their rousing adventures; the central theme of all the tales is the loneliness of command.

Hostage, The: play by Irish author Brendan Behan, first presented in 1958. *The Hostage* is a farce; the plot is not taken seriously, and the action is often interrupted for a comic song. The hostage of the title is a British soldier, being held by members of the Irish Republican Army (IRA), in a Dublin lodging house as a hostage for the life of an IRA man captured and condemned to death by the British. Leslie, the hostage, and the maid Teresa fall in love amidst the antics of the lodgers.

House of Atreus: royal house of Greece whose descendants were doomed because of ancestral crimes of murder, incest, and cannibalism. The founder of the line was Tantalus, father of Pelops and Niobe. He was punished for serving the flesh of Pelops to the gods. Tantalus's punishment after death

was to be surrounded forever by food and water that he could not reach.

Pelops's two sons were Atreus, king of Mycenae, and Thyestes. After Thyestes seduced Atreus's wife, Atreus killed his brother's children and served their flesh to him at a royal banquet. Atreus's sons were Agamemnon, who became king of Mycenae, and Menelaus, king of Sparta, both Greek leaders of the Trojan War, which was fought over the abduction of Menelaus's wife Helen. Thyestes' son was Aegisthus. Perhaps the most famous version of the legend is the *Oresteia,* a trilogy of dramas by the Greek tragic poet Aeschylus, performed in 458 B.C.

The first play, *Agamemnon,* deals with the triumphant return of the king from the Trojan War, only to meet his death at the hands of Clytemnestra, his wife, and Aegisthus, who had become her lover. Clytemnestra, who was Helen's sister, murders her husband in revenge for his past murder of their daughter, Iphigenia, whom he had sacrificed to Artemis in order to pacify the goddess and to attain good weather for the trip to Troy. In other versions of Iphigenia's story, most notably Euripides' play *Iphigenia in Tauris,* Artemis saves her; the father, unknown to anyone but Iphigenia and the goddess, offers a deer in her place. She becomes a priestess of Artemis and later saves her brother Orestes from sacrifice.

In the second play, *Libation-Bearers* (Greek: *Choephoroe*), Agamemnon's children Orestes and Electra revenge their father's murder by killing their mother and Aegisthus. In the third play, *The Eumenides,* Orestes, who actually committed the matricide, is pursued by the Furies. The play takes place in the

realm of divine beings, where Orestes is brought to trial. He is acquitted by the persuasive arguments of Apollo.

Electra, by the Greek playwright Euripides, is another well known tragedy based on this legend, performed in 423 B.C. It is a psychological study of Orestes' accomplice, his sister, in which she plays a much more forceful role in the murder of her mother than she does in Aeschylus's play. Sophocles also used her as the central character of his tragedy, *Electra,* written between 430 and 415 B.C. Eugene O'Neill's *Mourning Becomes Electra* is a modern reworking of the same theme.

House of the Seven Gables, The: romance by U.S. author Nathaniel Hawthorne, published in 1851. The story is set in Salem, Massachusetts, and deals with a family descended from a witch-burning ancestor. The aging Hepzibah Pyncheon, who lives in the house of seven gables, has had to open a shop because of her poverty. Her old brother Clifford arrives home, his mind weakened by 30 years of unjust imprisonment. Judge Pyncheon, his cousin, who had engineered Clifford's arrest, continues to persecute the old man. But the malicious judge, the last family representative of Puritan hypocrisy, dies of apoplexy in time for old Hepzibah and Clifford to have a few years of peace; the witches' curse that has doomed the family is lifted.

Howl and Other Poems: collection of poems, published in 1956, that brought recognition to "Beat" poet Allen Ginsberg; it made him a spokesman for the generation of dropouts in the 1950s and 1960s who found themselves alienated from American society.

HOUSE OF SEVEN GABLES: This house in Salem, Massachusetts, is the setting for Hawthorne's novel. It is still standing.

**HUNCHBACK OF
NOTRE DAME:**
the gentle monster as
played by Lon Chaney
in the film.

Huckleberry Finn, The Adventures of: novel by U.S. writer Mark Twain, published in 1884; generally considered his masterpiece and one of the masterpieces of American literature. The story, told in the vivid vernacular of Huck, a true child of nature, deals with his daring act of helping Jim, a runaway slave, to escape. In an epic voyage, Huck and Jim, floating down the Mississippi on a raft, enjoy a peace, freedom, and mutual respect that is a sharp contrast to the meanness of society in the river towns where they stop. Twain uses the irony of Huck's innocent view of life to criticize the barbarity of "sivilization." The novel contains many famous comic scenes, notably those with the Duke and the Dauphin, two travelling confidence men.

Human Comedy, The: collective name given to the body of novels by French writer Honoré de Balzac. He intended to portray the private dramas of all aspects of French life—Paris and the provinces; the worlds of peasants, soldiers, businessmen, and fashionable society. The first of the series, *Les Chouans,* a historical novel, appeared in 1830. The last two works, *Cousin Bette* and *Cousin Pons,* appeared in 1847–1848 and are numbered among his masterpieces. Though Balzac did not live to complete his ambitious project, he covered an enormous range of subjects and environments. His description and psychology were realistic. He was fascinated by money, success, and failure and their effects on character.

One of the best-known works is *Eugénie Grandet* (1833), the story of a miser's daughter, who lives the life of a household drudge until her father's death makes her an heiress and she gives her money to the poor. Perhaps the most famous is *Père Goriot* (1835), the story of a bourgeois father who sacrifices his fortune and his life for the pretensions of his two snobbish daughters.

Humours: four fluids found in the human body, the proportions of which were believed by medieval and Renaissance philosophers to determine temperament. An excess of yellow bile produced a hot temper. Too much black bile gave one a melancholy outlook. Blood produced a genial disposition, and phlegm, a slow and passive one. Ben Jonson used the theory of humours in creating characters for his comedies (*see also* Alchemist, The), and Robert Burton, in *Anatomy of Melancholy,* discussed the concept from the 17th-century medical point of view.

Hunchback of Notre Dame, The: melodramatic romance by French writer Victor Hugo, published in 1831, set in the Middle Ages. Quasimodo, a mis-treated hunchback who is bell-ringer at the cathedral of Notre Dame, secretly adores the dancer Esmeralda. When a hypocritical clergyman, Frollo, falsely condemns Esmeralda as a witch, Quasimodo hides her in the belfry. Esmeralda is discovered and put to death, but the hunchback has his revenge by hurling Frollo to his death from the bell tower.

Hydra: *See* Hercules.

Hyperbole: *See* Figures of speech.

I

Iago: *See* Othello.

Iamb or **Iambus:** *See* Foot.

Icarus: *See* Daedalus.

Iceman Cometh, The: tragedy by U.S. playwright Eugene O'Neill, presented in 1946 and often considered his greatest work. Hickey, the charismatic and previously well liked travelling salesman, disrupts the lives of the inmates of the back room of Harry Hope's saloon by trying to make them give up their pipe dreams, presenting his own reformation as an example. In the end he admits that he killed his wife because he could not bear her love and forgiveness; and all but two of his cronies return to their own illusions, convinced that they saw through Hickey all the time.

Idiot, The: novel by Russian author Feodor Dostoevski, first published in 1868. In its hero, Prince Myshkin, the author intended to portray a truly good man and his effect on society; Myshkin, who is trusting, passionless, and rather simple-minded, unwittingly wrecks the lives of several persons with whom he becomes involved.

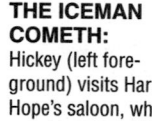

**THE ICEMAN
COMETH:**
Hickey (left foreground) visits Harry Hope's saloon, where he will challenge the illusions of the other patrons.

Idyll: short poetic description of pastoral or rustic life. Idylls take their name especially from the *Idylls* of the Greek poet Theocritus of the third century B.C. *Idyll* is sometimes used in the titles of longer narrative poems—for example, Tennyson's *Idylls of the King.*

Idylls of the King, The: long series of poems by English poet Alfred Lord Tennyson, published in twelve parts from 1859 to 1885. An allegory of the passing of an old order, based on the Arthurian legends, the work traces the life of King Arthur from his rise to the kingship with Merlin's help, through his conflict with Lancelot and Guinevere, to his death.

Igraine: *See* Arthurian legend.

Iliad: Greek epic poem by Homer. A recitative poem in the ancient bardic tradition, it was composed orally in about the ninth century B.C. and first transcribed in the sixth century B.C. It is a tale of the Trojan War, but it does not tell the whole story, only the tale known as "The Wrath of Achilles," with flashbacks to previous events of the war. The Greek hero Achilles, deprived of a slave girl by the Greeks' leader Agamemnon, sulks in his tent. When the war goes against the Greeks, he is persuaded to let his friend Patroclus fight in his armor. The Trojan hero Hector kills Patroclus, and Achilles in wrath goes out to battle, kills Hector, and drags his body in the dirt around the walls of Troy. Late at night Hector's father Priam, king of Troy, comes to Achilles and moves him to return Hector's body for burial.

Generally considered among the greatest literary works of Western civilization, the *Iliad* is the starting point for the *Odyssey* and the *Aeneid,* and, with them, has served as a model for every later epic in the classical tradition. *See also* Trojan War.

Ilium: Greek name for the city of Troy. *See also* Troy.

Imaginary Invalid, The: play by the French dramatist Molière, performed in 1673. Argan, a hypochondriac, wants a doctor for a son-in-law and tries to force his daughter to marry the preposterous Dr. Diafoirus. But Angélique loves another, and Argan finally contents himself with becoming his own doctor in a ceremonial ballet that pokes fun at the scientific jargon and pretensions of the medical profession. This play was Molière's last work; he died while playing the role of Argan.

Imagism: 20th-century American and English poetry movement that stressed direct sensory impressions and realistic images rather than abstract language and conceits. It is related to French symbolism.

The movement dates from about 1910 to 1918. Its principles were formulated by Ezra Pound in 1913. Other imagists include H. D. (Hilda Doolittle),

Richard Aldington, and F. S. Flint. Forerunners of the movement were T. E. Hulme and Ford Madox Ford. When the name was adopted by Amy Lowell and her colleagues, Pound referred to his poetry as "vorticism."

Importance of Being Earnest, The: comedy by Irish-born playwright and poet Oscar Wilde, presented in 1895. This witty and farcical masterpiece of satire pokes fun at the Victorian manners and attitudes of the upper class and clergy. The madcap plot hinges on the efforts of Jack Worthing (who has a second life in town as "Ernest") to produce a background more respectable than his real one—being found in a handbag in the cloakroom of Victoria Station—and thus satisfy Lady Bracknell, mother of the girl he loves.

Inferno: *See* Divine Comedy, The.

In Memoriam (Latin for "in memory [of]"): series of poems by English poet Alfred Tennyson, published in 1850 but written at intervals from 1833 on. They were inspired by grief for his intimate friend Arthur Hallam, who had died in 1833. The poems are one of the major elegies in English; they record the poet's sense of loss and the meditations it evokes as he works through his grief.

In Praise of Folly: satire on human nature by Dutch scholar and humanist Desiderius Erasmus, published in 1509. Though he wrote it in a week, it has always been his most popular work. The book is dedicated to Sir Thomas More, and the Latin title is a pun on his name.

Inspector General, The: comedy by Russian author Nikolai Gogol, first presented in 1836. The citizens of a small provincial town, hearing that the inspector general is coming from the capital, mistake Chlestakov, a minor civil servant, for the inspector. He takes advantage of the situation, exposes their shams and corruption, and skips town just as the real inspector general arrives.

Intimations of Immortality (in full, "Ode: Intimations of Immortality from Recollections of Early Childhood"): poem by English Romantic author William Wordsworth, published in 1807. Its argument for immortality rests on the poet's belief that our childhood is filled with memories of pre-existence that fade as we grow old: "Our birth is but a sleep and a forgetting." Yet these memories persist as intuitions or "intimations" and do not vanish altogether, even in "the light of common day."

Invictus (Latin for "unconquered"): well known poem by English writer and editor William Ernest Henley, written in 1875 while he was in a tuberculosis hospital. The much-quoted poem ends with the famous lines:

I am the master of my fate.
I am the captain of my soul.

Invisible Man, The: title of two novels. In English author H. G. Wells's novel, published in 1897, a scientist discovers a formula that makes him invisible but also turns him into a megalomaniac. U.S. author Ralph Ellison's classic novel, published in 1952, is a chronicle of the destruction of a young black man's faith in people and society, as he gradually realizes that his individuality is invisible to everyone, black and white, with whom he deals.

Iphigenia, GL: subject of the plays *Iphigenia in Aulis,* by Euripides and by Racine; and *Iphigenia in Tauris,* by Euripides and by Goethe; and of two operas by Gluck. *See also* House of Atreus.

I Promessi Sposi: *See* Betrothed, The.

Irish renaissance: literary movement in Ireland around the turn of the 20th century that was closely linked to strong political nationalism. It sought to establish an Irish national consciousness based on their culture, literature, and folklore. The movement gained its greatest strength after the Irish failed to secure home rule from England. Associated with the movement were the authors William Butler Yeats, John Millington Synge, Sean O'Faolain, Liam O'Flaherty, Frank O'Connor, Sean O'Casey, and James Joyce, though he refused to consider himself a part of it. Also associated with the movement is the Abbey Theatre in Dublin, organized by Yeats and Lady Gregory, where the plays of Yeats, Synge, O'Casey, and other Irish renaissance dramatists were given their first performances.

Iseult: *See* Tristan and Iseult.

Ishmael: narrator of Melville's *Moby-Dick,* who emphasizes his separateness from the events of the book by introducing himself in the very first line with "Call me Ishmael," the name of the biblical outcast. *See also* Moby-Dick.

Isis: chief female goddess of Egyptian mythology; the sister and wife of Osiris and the mother of Horus. She was credited with magical powers to bring the dead back to life, which she used to resurrect Osiris after Set murdered him. The worship of Isis became popular in Greece about the fourth century B.C. and was later adopted by the Romans; it lasted in Europe until the sixth century A.D. *See also* Osiris.

Ithaca: one of the Ionian islands off the west coast of Greece, it was ruled in ancient times by the Greek epic hero Odysseus.

Ivanhoe: novel by English writer Sir Walter Scott, published in 1819; a romantic, action-filled tale of chivalry set in medieval England during the reign of Richard the Lion-Hearted and focusing on the rivalry between Norman and Saxon.

armor
US

armour
Brit.

civilization
US

civilisation
Brit.

realizes
US

realises
Brit.

emphasizes
US

emphasises
Brit.

20 History of Literature

J

Jabberwock: imaginary monster in Lewis Carroll's *Through the Looking-Glass;* the creature is the subject of the famous poem "Jabberwocky" found by Alice in a Looking-Glass book. The poem contains many imaginative coined words, and the first four lines (explained by Humpty Dumpty in the Sixth Square) are famous:

> 'Twas brillig, and the slithy toves
> Did gyre and gimble in the wabe:
> All mimsy were the borogoves,
> And the mome raths outgrabe.

Jack and the Beanstalk: title of a nursery tale based on a world myth. Jack and his widowed mother are so poor that she sends him to sell their cow for food. Instead, he trades the cow for a handful of beans. His mother, angry at the foolish trade, tosses the beans out the window, where they sprout into a great stalk. The lad climbs the stalk to a giant's house where there is great wealth, outwits the giant, and returns to his mother with riches so they may both live happily ever after. This story is known among the North American Indians and South African natives.

Jack the Giant-killer: title of an old English nursery tale based on a British story first translated by Geoffrey of Monmouth. Jack, a farmer boy of Arthurian times, kills the giant of Cornwall by tricking him into a deep pit. With the help of a cloak that makes him invisible, seven-league boots of marvelous speed, and a magic sword, he kills all the giants in the land.

Jane Eyre: novel by British writer Charlotte Brontë, published in 1847. It is the strange love story of a modest and plain but intelligent governess and her ill-tempered, discourteous employer, Rochester. The impediment to their love and the cause of Rochester's moodiness is an insane wife whom he has kept hidden in the house. When Jane learns of her existence, she leaves. Later when the wife is killed and Rochester is blinded in a fire, the lovers are reunited.

Janus, RM: god of doorways, gates, and entrances; the patron of all beginnings. Janus is represented with two heads facing in opposite directions.

Jason: *See* Argonauts.

Jekyll and Hyde: *See* Dr. Jekyll and Mr. Hyde.

Jerusalem Delivered: epic poem on events of the First Crusade, written by Italian poet Torquato Tasso, published about 1580. The poem relates in 20 cantos the capture of Jerusalem by Godfrey of Bouillon and his Crusaders at the end of the eleventh century.

Jester: *See* Fool.

The symbols used in this glossary are as follows:

G-Greek
R-Roman
N-Norse
M-myth
L-legend

Jinni or **genie:** in Arabian folklore, a demon inhabiting wild and desolate places, representing the hostile elements. In Muslim literature, jinn are supernatural beings, both good and evil, constituted of fire and able to assume all manner of shapes. They are obliged to serve those who possess a magic ring, lamp, or other object.

Jocasta: *See* Oedipus.

John Brown's Body: modern epic poem for which the U.S. writer Stephen Vincent Benét won a Pulitzer Prize in 1929. This book-length narrative of Civil War days tells not only the historical events but also the moods and emotions of the war.

John Henry: in American folklore, the famous black steel driver, buried in Big Bend Tunnel, West Virginia, with his twelve-pound hammer in his hand. John Henry was the strongest and fastest of the gang at work on the Allegheny tunnel. So fast did he work that a boy had to stand by with a pail of cold water to keep his hammer cool. His boss bragged to a steam drill salesman that he needed no such modern contraption, because one of his workmen could beat a steam drill any day. A bet was laid and John Henry rose to the boast. He burst a blood vessel beating the steam drill through the rock.

Johnny Appleseed: in American folklore, a kindly, eccentric figure who travelled through the frontier territories planting apple trees. The legend is based on the activities of John Chapman, who was known as Johnny Appleseed during his lifetime (1774–1845).

Joseph and His Brothers: tetralogy of novels by German author Thomas Mann; a retelling of the Old Testament story of Joseph. The four novels are *The Stories of Jacob* (1933), *Young Joseph* 1934), *Joseph in Egypt* (1936), and *Joseph the Provider* (1943).

Joseph Andrews: novel by English novelist Henry Fielding, published in 1742. It tells the story of a virtuous servingman, Joseph Andrews. The book was begun as a parody of Richardson's *Pamela* (the story of a virtuous, long-suffering maidservant); Fielding makes his hero Pamela's brother.

Jove: *See* Zeus.

Julius Caesar: history play by Shakespeare, presented around 1599; it is about the betrayal and death of Caesar. Though warned by a soothsayer, Caesar goes to the Senate, where he is stabbed to death by Brutus, Cassius, and their fellow conspirators. Mark Antony rouses the people against the conspirators in his famous funeral oration ("Friends, Romans, countrymen . . ."), they flee Rome, and civil war ensues. The armies of Brutus and Cassius are defeated at Philippi, and both men commit suicide.

Jungle, The: muckraking novel by U.S. author Upton Sinclair, published in 1960; it was instrumental in bringing about the pure-food laws as a result of its exposé of the conditions of Chicago's meat-packing industry. It relates the experiences of a man named Jurgis Rudkis, a Lithuanian immigrant who comes to the United States in hopes of making a better life. He finds work in the stockyards, where he is cheated and exploited. He and his family descend into poverty, sickness, death, and crime. Disillusioned and alone, Rudkis hears a socialist speech and realizes that the only way workers can achieve their goal is through socialism. *See also* Muckrakers.

Jungle Books, The: two volumes of short stories published in 1894 and 1895 by Indian-born English writer Rudyard Kipling. Their hero is Mowgli, a boy brought up by a wolf pack, who learns from the wolves and other animals—Bagheera, the black panther; Kaa, the python; Baloo, the bear—the wisdom of survival in the jungle. Mowgli later joins the world of men.

Juno: *See* Hera.

Juno and the Paycock: play by Irish author Sean O'Casey, first presented in 1924. It portrays Juno Boyle, an Irish mother, who struggles through war, poverty, and the drunkenness of her comic husband Jack, the "Paycock," to maintain her family. Eventually Jack's legacy, on which the family's fortunes depended, comes to naught; Juno's son is killed by the Irish Republican Army, her pregnant daughter is abandoned, and Juno and her daughter leave the pixilated Paycock.

Jupiter: *See* Zeus.

K

Kabuki: type of Japanese drama, developed from the formal, classical Nō drama in the 1600s. It is still very popular with modern-day audiences. Kabuki is played only by male actors, who wear stylistically exaggerated makeup and act with extravagant manner. Japanese artists of the late 1800s portrayed many noted kabuki actors with characteristically ferocious expressions.

Kaievala (literally, "land of heroes"): Finnish national epic. It comprises the mythological ballads, chants, and poems of Finland handed down by the bards; it was collected by Zacharias Topelius in 1822 and again by Elias Lönnrot in 1835. Lönnrot enlarged his collection for the second book in 1849.

The poems tell myths and hero tales; they date back to very ancient times. The collection is named for the three sons of Kaleva, a Finnish giant: Vainamoinen, a seer, god of music and inventor of the harp; Ilmarinen, the smith; and the hero Lemminkainen.

KINGS: From legend (King Arthur) to nursery rhyme (King Cole) to tragedy (King Lear), royalty plays a large part in traditional literature.

Kidnapped: novel by English author Robert Louis Stevenson, published in 1886. The hero of the book, young David Balfour, is sent to sea by a treacherous and cruel uncle; while he is at sea he meets Alan Breck, a spirited and hard-fighting Jacobite. After landing in Scotland, the two of them make their way through the Highlands, avoiding the English soldiers, until David returns to his home and receives his rightful inheritance.

King Arthur: *See* Arthurian legend.

King Cole: legendary king of Britain of the third century. He is mentioned, as King Coel, in Geoffrey of Monmouth's *History of the Kings of Britain;* he is also the subject of John Masefield's poem "King Cole" and is the "merry old soul" of the nursery rhyme.

King Lear: tragedy by William Shakespeare, presented in 1606, based on folklore (retold in Holinshed) about a semilegendary King Leir of Britain. Lear demands that his three daughters declare their love for him. Hurt when Cordelia, the only honest one, doubts that she can feelingly respond to such a command, he banishes her and bestows his kingdom on his two wicked daughters, Goneril and Regan, who soon humiliate him and turn him out. Lear goes mad at the realization of his daughters' cruelty and the loss of his kingdom, and wanders through a violent storm accompanied by his Fool. All those who are loyal to Lear suffer. Cordelia returns with her husband, the king of France, and is reunited with her father, but the villainous Edmund, victorious over the French, orders her execution, and Lear dies of grief.

Knickerbocker, Diedrich: name under which Washington Irving wrote his farcical history of New York (1809). The surname Knickerbocker, an old Dutch name, was at first applied to the original Dutch colonists of New York; later the term came to mean simply any resident of New York.

Knighthood: in medieval times, soldiers pledged to the service of a liege lord. Knights were pledged also to certain codes of honor and chivalry.

In the Middle Ages, boys chosen for knighthood began their training early. At seven or eight a candidate left home and went into the service of a nobleman, where he served as a page. At 14 the boy was promoted to the office of squire. Under the tutelage of a knight, he became proficient in the use of medieval weapons—the sword, shield, mace, lance, and battle-ax. At 21 the young man was received into knighthood in an elaborate ceremony—partly religious and partly a celebration. The night before the ceremony his armor was placed before an altar where he kept an all-night prayer vigil. After a religious service and solemn vows in the morning, he was dubbed a knight.

When English longbows proved their ability to pierce French armor at the battle of Agincourt in 1415, knights became obsolete as troops. The rising central power of European kings tended to curb the feudal power of barons and orders of knighthood. The feudal system died out, and the designation of "knight" became an honorary title. Today in England, knighthood, with the title of "Sir," is conferred by the ruling sovereign upon outstanding men in various fields—science, civil service, scholarship, and many others. The equivalent title for women is "Dame."

Knights of the Round Table: in Arthurian legend, the select body of knights who sat with King Arthur at a huge round table. The traditional number of knights was 150. *See also* Arthurian legend; Gawain; Holy Grail; Lancelot; Perceval; and Siege Perilous.

Koran or **Quran:** sacred book of Islam, written in Arabic. Islamic peoples consider it the Word of God, revealed to Muhammad.

The Koran was the first book to be written in Arabic, and as such it had an enormous influence on Arabic writing and thought. An authoritative version was compiled under the Caliph Othman in the 650s A.D.; today the Cairo edition of 1919 is the standard.

Kriemhild: *See* Nibelungenlied.

Kristin Lavransdatter: trilogy of historical novels by Norwegian author Sigrid Undset, depicting a woman's life in medieval Norway. The three novels are *The Bridal Wreath* (1920), *The Mistress of Husaby* (1921), and *The Cross* (1922).

Kubla Khan: poem fragment by English Romantic poet Samuel Taylor Coleridge, published in 1816 and subtitled "A Vision in a Dream." Coleridge wrote it in 1797 under the influence of laudanum (a form of opium to which he eventually became addicted). He fell asleep over a book describing Kubla Khan. When he awoke three hours later, he realized he had composed a poem in his sleep, and managed to write down 55 lines of it before he was interrupted. The result is a haunting poem that begins:

In Xanadu did Kubla Khan
A stately pleasure-dome decree:
Where Alph, the sacred river, ran
Through caverns measureless to man
Down to a sunless sea.

| realizes *US* |
| realises *Brit.* |
| honor *US* |
| honour *Brit.* |
| armor *US* |
| armour *Brit.* |

Some Knights of the Round Table

Lancelot Gawain Tristram	known for chivalry
Bedivere Kay	the older stalwarts
Gareth Galahad Perceval	the younger knights
Mordred	the traitor

20 History of Literature

L

La Belle Dame sans Merci: ballad written in an archaic medieval style by English poet John Keats, published in 1820. It tells the story of a noble knight, destroyed by his love for a supernatural being who is beautiful but merciless. The symptoms she causes in the poet resemble those of tuberculosis, from which Keats was dying.

Labyrinth, GM: great mazelike building in Crete, built by Daedalus for King Minos to confine the Minotaur (see also entries). The word is now used for any complex and puzzling system of passageways or alleys. *Labyrinths* is also the title of an anthology of short *ficciones* selected from two story collections by Jorge Luis Borges, published in 1962. *See also* Ficciones.

Lady Chatterley's Lover: novel by the English writer D. H. Lawrence, published in 1928. Lady Chatterley's husband, Sir Clifford, is impotent. She finds fulfillment as a woman in an affair with her gamekeeper, Mellors, a man who knows no sexual restraints. This was Lawrence's last novel and the one that focuses most directly on the author's mystique of the regenerative powers of freely expressed sexuality. The work was banned in the U.S. until 1959 and in England until 1960.

Lady of the Lake or **Vivian** or **Nimue:** *See* Arthurian legend.

Laertes: *See* Hamlet; Odysseus.

Laius: *See* Oedipus.

Lake poets: three English Romantic poets—Coleridge, Wordsworth, and Southey—who are so called because they lived in England's Lake District, a region of hills and lakes in Cumberland, Westmoreland, and Lancashire. The term *Lake school* was first applied to them in ridicule in the *Edinburgh Review* in 1817.

L'allegro (Italian for "the cheerful one"): short, joyous poem by English poet John Milton, written in 1632. The poem is an idyll in praise of the delights of life in country and town and is a companion piece to the melancholy "Il Penseroso." Some well-known expressions, such as "to trip the light fantastic," derive from this poem.

Lancelot: favorite knight of King Arthur, and the lover of Queen Guinevere. His adulterous love finally led to a break with his king and divided the loyalties of the Knights of the Round Table. Lancelot fled to Brittany. When Arthur was battling Mordred for his kingdom, Lancelot returned to help him, but Arthur had died. He spent his remaining years as a penitent hermit and Guinevere entered a nunnery.

Lancelot was the father of Galahad by the Princess Elaine. Another Elaine, "the lily maid of Astolat," died for love of him. This legend is treated in Tennyson's poems "Lancelot and Elaine" and "The Lady of Shalott."

The earliest Lancelot legends portray him as the kidnapped son of King Ban de Benoic. He is educated for knighthood by the mysterious Lady of the Lake.

Laocoön, GM: Trojan priest who, with his two sons, was strangled by sea serpents. According to some sources, this punishment was visited on him for warning the Trojans not to accept the Wooden Horse of the Greeks. The agony of Laocoön and his sons, told in Vergil's *Aeneid,* is the subject of a famous classical sculptural group. This sculpture inspired "Laokoon" (1766), a classic essay on art by the German critic G. E. Lessing.

Last of the Mohicans, The: *See* Leatherstocking Tales.

Latinus: legendary king of ancient Latium, ancestor of the Latins. In Vergil's *Aeneid,* he was the king who welcomed Aeneas at the mouth of the river Tiber; Aeneas married his daughter Lavinia.

Laura: idealized beloved of the 14th-century Italian Renaissance poet Petrarch, to whom he addressed over 300 sonnets and many other lyrics. Dates of their first meeting and of Laura's death, as well as the many poems written after her death, suggest that she was a real woman rather than a poetic creation, but she has never been satisfactorily identified. These love poems constitute the poet's spiritual autobiography and were a formative influence on the development of lyric poetry, particularly in England.

Lazarillo de Tormes, The Life of: the original picaresque novel, published in 1554 by an unknown Spanish author. It inaugurated the vogue throughout Europe for the novel of the road in which the rogue hero encounters a cast of villains and thieves not only in the underworld but also in the palace, the manor, and the church.

Leander: *See* Hero.

Leatherstocking Tales: novels of early frontier life by U.S. author James Fenimore Cooper. Their hero is the white scout Natty Bumppo, known under various nicknames in the novels; he combines the Indians' knowledge of the woods with Yankee ingenuity. The series contains: *The Pioneers* (1823), *The Last of the Mohicans* (1826), *The Prairie* (1827), *The Pathfinder* (1840), and *The Deerslayer* (1841). These books were widely translated and remained popular throughout Europe long after their reputation declined in the United States.

Leaves of Grass: only collection of poems by U.S. writer Walt Whitman. First published in 1855, it was expanded and revised throughout Whitman's life. Its present form was established in 1892. In this work Whitman assumes the stance of a national bard. He celebrates himself ("Song of Myself") and his country. He celebrates democracy, fellowship, the love of men, and the love of men and women. He celebrates the eternal cycle of birth and death ("Out of the Cradle Endlessly Rocking"). When he mourns personal loss through death ("When Lilacs Last in the Dooryard Bloom'd"), all nature mourns with him. Readers were originally shocked by the poet's conceit, his prophetic tone, and his egalitarian acceptance of all aspects of life. His irregular verse form, the forerunner of free verse, was also considered unpoetic. Today this work is considered the embodiment of American Romantic nationalism.

LEAVES OF GRASS: Walt Whitman revised this collection throughout his lifetime.

Leda, GM: wife of Tyndareus. Zeus saw her bathing in a river and went to her in the shape of a swan in order to make love to her. The story inspired several works of art, notably the poem "Leda and the Swan" by W. B. Yeats. Although sources vary, Leda's children, Helen of Troy, Castor, and sometimes Pollux, are assumed to have been fathered by Zeus. Clytemnestra was her daughter by Tyndareus.

Legend: popular story that, though rooted in historical fact, cannot be verified in all its details. Many outstanding historical figures—for example, the Frankish king Charlemagne, the Celtic chieftain Arthur, the English outlaw Robin Hood, and the Spanish soldier El Cid—have, with their followers, been subjects of many legends in which the embellishments of imagination obviously outweigh historical accuracy. On the other hand, some heroes of legend, such as the Swiss William Tell, may not have existed at all, although some circumstances or persons in the tales built around them have a historical basis.

Legend of Sleepy Hollow, The: tale by U.S. writer Washington Irving, published in *The Sketch Book* in 1820. While returning late from paying court to Katrina Van Tassel, Ichabod Crane—an ungainly and timorous schoolmaster—encounters a spectral headless horseman. After a wild race with the fearful apparition, Ichabod disappears from the community. Katrina marries the daredevil horseman Brom Bones, who looks "exceedingly knowing" whenever Ichabod and his disappearance is mentioned.

Lethe, GM: one of the rivers of Hades. To drink of its waters brought forgetfulness of the past to the souls of the dead. The word means oblivion.

Let Us Now Praise Famous Men: landmark in literary journalism, published in 1941 by the U.S. poet and novelist James Agee, accompanied by photographs by Walker Evans. The work grew out of a routine magazine assignment that required Agee to live for a time among the white sharecroppers of Alabama during the Depression years. His involvement with their personal histories and their hopeless economic cycle resulted in an angry book of protest that was also a highly subjective revelation of the author's own feelings of guilt as an observer—one of the privileged living among the wretched of the earth.

Leviathan: highly influential political treatise by British philosopher Thomas Hobbes, published in 1651. A defense of secular monarchy, its pessimistic realism is surpassed only by the political doctrines of Machiavelli. Unlike many philosophers who thought man's natural goodness was corrupted by society, Hobbes believed that the life of man in the state of nature was "solitary, poor, nasty, brutish, and short." He advocated a strong authoritarian government as the only means of controlling the "war of everyone against everyone."

Life Is a Dream: play by the Spanish dramatist Pedro Calderón de la Barca, performed in 1635. Segismundo, the son of King Basilio of Poland, is thought to have died in infancy but actually has been imprisoned in a tower by his father. His father has a change of heart and has the young man drugged, dressed like a prince, and brought to the palace. Segismundo awakes, but believes he is dreaming. His father, alarmed at the prince's uncouth behavior, sends him back to prison. The people revolt and thrust kingship on the prince, who has realized that since life is as transient as a dream, only noble behavior gives it meaning.

Life of Samuel Johnson: biography of English man of letters Samuel Johnson, by James Boswell, published in 1791; perhaps the most famous biography in the English language. Boswell began to make notes and collect mater-

ial for the *Life* when he first met Dr. Johnson in 1763, continuing until Johnson's death in 1784. Boswell's own fame rests almost entirely on this biography of his friend; Johnson's fame is also dependent on this book, since his witty conversations are of as much interest as his writings.

Life on the Mississippi: autobiographical account by U.S. author Mark Twain, published in full in 1883, giving a vivid picture of his days as a Mississippi River steamboat pilot before the Civil War. The rugged apprenticeship of the river pilot, the excitement on the river levees, the steamboat races, the gambling on board the ships, and a wealth of human incident make this a classic account of river life.

Lilith: in Jewish folklore, a female demon of the night who was believed to prey on children. In medieval rabbinical literature, Lilith was Adam's first wife and was displaced by Eve, on whom she worked vengeance by threatening her children. In Goethe's *Faust,* Lilith figures as a witch in the Walpurgis Night scene.

Lilliput: *See* Gulliver's Travels.

Limerick: five-line jingle, usually nonsensical. The meter is anapestic. The first, second, and fifth lines each contain three feet and rhyme with one another. Lines three and four each contain two feet and rhyme with each other. The name is thought to come from an old custom of singing extempore nonsense verses at parties to which the chorus was always the same: "Will you come up to Limerick?" Edward Lear's *Book of Nonsense* (1846) contains many limericks. Often the limerick has a place name in the first line. Example:

There was a young lady from Niger
Who smiled as she rode on a tiger;
They came back from the ride
With the lady inside,
And the smile on the face of the tiger.

Little Foxes, The: family melodrama by U.S. playwright Lillian Hellman, presented in 1939. The play is a study of greed and evil, personified in the various members of a ruthless Southern family, the Hubbards, who viciously and eagerly set out to exploit each other and the working people of their town in order to make their enterprises rich and profitable.

Little John: devoted companion of Robin Hood. Little John was a skilled bowman whom Robin defeated in a joust; he then became second in command of the merry band. He was nicknamed Little John because of his great height.

Little Mermaid, The: fairy tale by the 19th-century Danish author Hans Christian Andersen about a mermaid who falls in love with a mortal prince. She sacrifices her voice and her mermaid's tail, enduring agonizing pain in her efforts to win his love—and an immortal soul—but fails and dies. Her suffering earns her a place with the daughters of the air, who can gain a soul through their good deeds.

Little Prince, The: children's story and parable for adults by the French aviator Antoine de Saint-Exupéry, published in 1943. The prince comes from a tiny planet where he takes care of one lovely rose. On Earth he discovers many beautiful roses. A fox teaches him that all men, foxes, and roses look alike, until love invested in one makes it different from the others.

20 **History of Literature**

realized
US

realised
Brit.

meter
US

metre
Brit.

Little Red Riding Hood: in European folklore, a little girl who goes to visit her grandmother and is eaten by a wolf who has disguised himself as her grandmother. In the version best known today, the child is rescued at the crucial moment by a passing woodcutter, and her grandmother, whom the wolf had previously eaten, is restored from the wolf's stomach. The story is known in English translations from the French of Charles Perrault and the German of the Grimm brothers.

Little Women: story by the U.S. author Louisa May Alcott, published in 1868. It is about four New England sisters, Jo, Meg, Beth, and Amy March, and was based largely on the author's own family life. Two sequels, *Little Men* (1871) and *Jo's Boys* (1886), continue the family story after the sisters are grown up and married.

LORD OF THE FLIES: This story of the return of a group of schoolboys to primitive savagery was filmed by director Peter Brook.

Lives of the English Poets: collection of biographical and critical essays by Samuel Johnson, published in two parts in 1779 and 1781. Among the 52 writers discussed are Abraham Cowley, John Milton, Alexander Pope, John Dryden, and Joseph Addison.

Lohengrin: in Germanic legend, the swan knight, a son of Parsifal, who appeared mysteriously in Antwerp in a boat drawn by swans. He rescued Princess Elsa of Brabant and married her on condition that she never ask his name. When she broke the pact, the swanboat returned on the Rhine and carried him away. The name taboo is a common motif in folk tales. This legend was the basis of Wagner's opera *Lohengrin* (composed 1847).

Loki, NM: god of evil and fire, the trickster, mischief-maker, and companion to the gods. Hel, Jormungandr the Midgard serpent, and the Fenris Wolf were his offspring. He tricked the blind god Hoder into killing Balder and refused to weep to ensure Balder's release from Hel, god-

dess of death. For this, he and his offspring were put in chains, but at the end of the world (Ragnarök) they will break loose, and they and the good gods will destroy each other.

Lolita: novel by Russian-born author Vladimir Nabokov, published in 1955; a subtle, absurdist history of the infatuation of a sophisticated middle-aged professor, Humbert Humbert, for a bubble-gum-chewing, 12-year-old American girl. It was the first of Nabokov's works in English to reach a wide popular audience.

Loneliness of the Long-Distance Runner, The: short story by the English writer Alan Sillitoe, published in 1959, in which a Borstal (reform school) boy evens his score with the system by intentionally losing a race against another school.

Long Day's Journey into Night: domestic tragedy by the U.S. dramatist Eugene O'Neill, the most personal and intimate of all his works. Written about 1941, it was not performed until 1956, three years after the author's death. The play embodies all the bitterness and ambivalence of the author's feelings toward his family. It is set in a country house in the year 1912. The characters—the four members of the Tyrone family—are patterned on O'Neill's family. The father is a matinee actor who regrets prostituting his talent; the mother is a drug addict who lives on memories of her innocent Catholic girlhood. The elder son is an alcoholic, and the younger son (O'Neill), while struggling to break away to a new life, learns he is stricken with tuberculosis, then an incurable disease.

Look Back in Anger: play by English writer John Osborne, performed in 1956, and considered the representative work of Britain's "angry young men." Jimmy Porter, an educated young man of working-class background, finds him-

self between two worlds and unable to fit into either. He vents his frustration on his middle-class wife.

Look Homeward, Angel: first novel by U.S. writer Thomas Wolfe, published in 1929. It is of the type called in Germany's *Kunstlerroman,* a novel of an artist's development. Its autobiographical hero Eugene Gant, a physical giant and precocious genius, loves and hates his hometown of Altamont (Asheville, N.C.), struggles against the limited horizons of his family, receives vague intimations of immortality from a few sympathetic people, and finally sets out on a quest for fame and fortune as a writer.

Lord Jim: major novel by Polish-born writer Joseph Conrad, written in 1900, dealing with a young English seaman who impulsively abandons his sinking ship carrying Islamic pilgrims. Unable to understand or to reconcile this ignoble act with his own self-image, Jim cannot face returning home. He lives out his life among the South Sea island natives, whose love and admiration for him are expressed in their nickname *Tuan* (Lord) Jim. But luck is against Jim. Unwittingly he betrays his native friends and meets death at their hands, a fate that finally resolves his guilt.

Lord of the Flies: novel by the English writer William Golding, published in 1954, in which a group of English schoolboys, stranded on an island, seem to reenact the Fall of Man. Their attempts to establish order, parliamentary rule, and rational priorities are defeated by mysterious forces that they all sense but cannot understand. The author suggests that these forces of evil are within man.

Lord of the Rings: trilogy of fantasy novels with allegorical overtones, written by the English scholar J. R. R. Tolkien. It consists of *The Fellowship of the Ring* (1954), *The Two Towers* (1954), and *The Return of the King* (1955). It deals with the long, often grim and terrible quest of the Hobbits to destroy the magic ring they possess in order to keep it from falling into the hands of evil powers. *See also* Hobbit, The.

Lorelei: beautiful siren whose song lures boatmen to their death. She is said to haunt a certain rock in the Rhine, which today bears her name. Her story, often considered a folk legend, was invented by the German Romantic poet Clemens Brentano in 1800. A well known German poet by Heinrich Heine, "Die Lorelei," recounts the legend.

Lost Generation: generation whose coming of age coincided with World War I, a traumatic experience that led to an abrupt break with the traditions of the past. Works of the U.S. writers of this period constitute the second great flowering of American literature. (The first was the New England renaissance.) Representative writers of the lost

The symbols used in this glossary are as follows:

G-Greek
R-Roman
N-Norse
M-myth
L-legend

generation include Ernest Hemingway, F. Scott Fitzgerald, William Faulkner, John Dos Passos, James T. Farrell, Archibald MacLeish, e e cummings, and Hart Crane, among others.

Lottery, The: haunting short story by the U.S. writer Shirley Jackson, published in 1949, in which some ordinary townspeople carry out, in an everyday fashion, a primitive magical rite of human sacrifice.

Lotus-Eaters or **Lotophagi:** in the *Odyssey,* a race of people visited by Odysseus in his wanderings. They ate only the fruit of the lotus, which caused a state of forgetfulness, languor, and contentment. Those of Odysseus's crew who tasted the lotus while they were ashore had to be bound and dragged home. Tennyson's poem, "The Lotus-Eaters," is one description of the experience.

Love Song of J. Alfred Prufrock, The: poem by the Anglo-American poet T. S. Eliot, published in *Poetry* magazine in 1915. The poem is a dramatic monologue that records the thoughts and perceptions of its narrator, Prufrock, a thoughtful, sensitive, middle-aged man who longs to express his real thoughts and emotions to his sophisticated companions but is paralyzed by insecurity. The poem is an ironic commentary on the crippling power of social convention and the unheroic quality of modern man.

Lower Depths, The: play by Russian writer Maxim Gorki, performed in 1902. It deals with some derelicts—a thief, a prostitute, an impoverished baron, an alcoholic actor—who inhabit a brutal slumlord's sleazy lodgings. A gentle hobo-philosopher, Luka, joins them and stirs their hopes for a better life. Luka leaves and they revert to their misery.

Lucifer: *See* Devil.

Lusiads, The: epic poem by Luis Vaz de Camões, published in 1572, and considered the outstanding epic of the Portuguese people. The principal concern of the poem is an account of Vasco da Gama's discovery of the sea route to India, but the action is interlaced with many accounts of the glorious history and achievements of the Portuguese. Venus, protectress of Portugal, and other mythological figures play important parts.

Lyrical Ballads: collection of poems by the English poets William Wordsworth and Samuel Taylor Coleridge, published in 1798. It is now regarded as the official opening of the English Romantic movement. It included, among many well known poems, Coleridge's "Rime of the Ancient Mariner" and Wordsworth's "Tintern Abbey." Wordsworth's preface to the second edition (1800) is the classic statement of Romantic poetic principles.

Lyric poetry: the most emotional and musical of the three divisions of poetry, the others being dramatic and epic (or narrative) poetry. A lyric expresses subjective feeling, the personal hopes, joys, sorrows, and fantasies of the author. It is usually intense and comparatively short. Sonnets, odes, hymns, and elegies are lyrics.

The word *lyric* comes from the Greek *lyra,* an ancient musical instrument of the harp type; lyrics were originally intended to be sung to the accompaniment of the lyre. The word *lyrics* still is used to mean the words of a song.

Lysistrata: comedy by the Greek poet Aristophanes, performed 411 B.C. During the war between Athens and Sparta, the women of all the Greek states, led by Lysistrata, decide to refuse to make love with their men unless they conclude the war. In spite of lapses on both sides, their bargaining is finally successful.

M

Macbeth: tragedy by Shakespeare, performed c 1606. When the Scottish noble Macbeth, thane of Cawdor, meets three witches who hail him as king of Scotland, his latent ambitions are triggered. Spurred on by his strong-willed wife, he murders King Duncan and usurps the throne. But the couple are haunted by their bloody deed. Lady Macbeth goes mad and dies. Macbeth, tormented by ghosts, is slain by the noble Macduff, and the throne is restored to Duncan's son Malcolm. The play was based on Holinshed's *Chronicles.* Macbeth was an actual historical figure.

Madame Bovary: novel by French writer Gustave Flaubert, published in 1857. It ruthlessly censures Romanticism in its portrayal of a provincial wife, Emma Bovary, who finds life married to a dull country doctor a great disappointment. Emma magnifies routine flirtations with neighboring men into grand passions, neglects her home, and spends money recklessly on affairs. Rejected by her young lover, she commits suicide. Her unsuspecting husband dies of grief, and their only child goes to the workhouse.

Madrigal: in poetry, usually a brief love lyric or pastoral poem. In music, a madrigal is also a song for several voice parts (polyphonic). It evolved during the Renaissance and was especially popular in Italy and England.

Magician of Lublin, The: novel by the Yiddish writer Isaac Bashevis Singer, published in 1960. This story of 19th-century Poland has a picaresque quality. The hero Yasha Mazur is a charismatic actor-magician who, in his travels through Poland, is loved by many women and is faithless to all. Seeing the hand of God in a series of misfortunes that befall him, the feckless Yasha becomes a penitent and retires to a solitary cell, attracting many pilgrims by his saintliness.

Magic Mountain, The: novel by German writer Thomas Mann, published in 1924. It was set in a tuberculosis sanatorium in Davos, Switzerland, on the eve of World War I, where patients from all over Europe are gathered. Young Hans Castorp comes there to visit a relative. He is beguiled by the mountain's rarefied atmosphere and dreamlike sense of timelessness, and after a small lung defect is discovered, he stays on as if spellbound, for seven years.

Mahabharata: long heroic epic of ancient India, written in Sanskrit between 350 and 600 B.C. The heroes are the Pandava brothers, who struggle to win a kingdom, then abandon it to go on a spiritual quest. The work is a compendium of Indian lore. It contains the celebrated *Bhagavad-gita* ("Song of God"), a dialogue between one of the Pandavas and the god Krishna, expressing the essence of Hindu philosophy.

Maid Marian: May Queen of English folk May Day games and morris dances in which Robin Hood also figures. In the late Robin Hood ballads and legends, she is his companion and sweetheart in Sherwood Forest.

Main Street: novel published in 1920; it established the literary reputation of U.S. author Sinclair Lewis. It satirizes life in a typical small midwestern town, Gopher Prairie, seen through the eyes of sophisticated, college-educated Carol Kennicott, who comes there as the wife of a doctor.

MACBETH: Lady Macbeth is tortured by guilt after helping to murder the king.

MRS. MALAPROP'S name in *The Rivals* comes from the French *mal à propos* ("out of place").

realizes
US

realises
Brit.

emphasized
US

emphasised
Brit.

Major Barbara: comedy by the Irish playwright George Bernard Shaw, performed in 1907. Barbara Undershaft, in rebellion against her wealthy father, a munitions maker, becomes a major in the Salvation Army and devotes her life to saving the souls of the poor. In time she discovers that the poor are more interested in soup than salvation, and realizes that her father helped them more by creating jobs and wealth than she has by joining them. Shaw's argument is that the servants of God and Mammon should unite for the benefit of all.

Malade Imaginaire, La: *See* Imaginary Invalid, The.

Malaprop, Mrs.: character in English author Richard Brinsley Sheridan's comedy *The Rivals;* she constantly misuses similar-sounding words (that is, *progeny* for *prodigy; illiterate* for *obliterate*). Such mistakes are now termed "malapropisms."

Maltese Falcon, The: classic detective novel by the U.S. writer Dashiell Hammett, published in 1930. The work was influential in removing the mystery story from the genteel country house to a realistic underworld setting; Hammett's detective, Sam Spade, is the prototype of the hard-boiled private eye. The story concerns a mysterious black statue that is so desired by the large cast of mysterious characters that they are willing to commit murder to get possession of it.

Man and Superman: philosophical comedy by Irish playwright George Bernard Shaw, published in 1903. John Tanner is a social revolutionist, utterly opposed to society's conventions and, above all, determined not to be enmeshed in love and marriage. But Ann Whitefield changes all that. The play contains a dream sequence, *Don Juan in Hell,* that is often performed separately. In it the principal characters appear as Don Juan, Doña Ana, The Statue (Stone Guest), and the Devil. As Don Juan in his dream, Tanner is a superman, but as John Tanner, he is merely a man.

Manchild in the Promised Land: autobiographical novel by U.S. author Claude Brown, published in 1965; a vivid story of a black boy growing up in New York's Harlem—the "Promised Land" its residents, Southern sharecroppers, dreamed of before migrating north. Sonny, the hero, is an accomplished thief and truant at eight; a veteran of juvenile court and reform schools; shot in the stomach while stealing at 13. He eventually escapes street life, but most of his friends end in prison or die by violence or drug overdoses.

Mandragola, La *(The Mandrake):* play by Niccolò Machiavelli, written in 1520; considered the first modern Italian comedy. Callimaco steals Lucrezia from her aged husband through a clever stratagem.

Manfred: dramatic poem by the English Romantic poet George Gordon, Lord Byron, published in 1817. Set in a lonely Gothic castle in the Alps, the poem describes the last days of the proud, tormented Manfred, who has transcended human limitations by his own study and diligence, but who is haunted by the memory of an incestuous love.

Mansfield Park: novel by English author Jane Austen, published in 1814. Fanny Price, a poor girl, is sent to live at Mansfield Park with her wealthy relatives, the Bertrams. Her spoiled cousins prove themselves ill-equipped for adult responsibilities, but Fanny falls in love with and helps redeem one of them.

Man Without a Country, The: short story by U.S. clergyman and author Edward Everett Hale, published in 1863. A naval officer, Philip Nolan, blurts out at his court-martial that he wishes never to hear of the United States again. For punishment he is compelled to live out his life on shipboard, never touching port. He dies brokenhearted, a fervent patriot.

Marco Polo, Book of: autobiographical account, written between 1300 and 1324, of the adventures of Marco Polo, a Venetian merchant travelling through Asia who became an official in China under Kubla Khan. His book greatly influenced European ideas about the world. Its concrete facts regarding the geography, history, and customs of a largely unknown continent were read with a mixture of disbelief and wonder. Maps were drawn that relied on the information in his book, making the age of exploration possible. Western eyes had been opened and a certain wanderlust took hold of Europe. Nearly two centuries later, Columbus made notes in the margins of his Latin copy of Marco Polo's adventures as he undertook his own journey to what he hoped would be Asia.

Mark: *See* Tristan and Iseult.

Marriage of Figaro, The: popular comedy by the French writer Pierre Augustine Caron de Beaumarchais, presented in 1784. It reflects the climate of opinion that paved the way for the French Revolution. Its hero is the clever and resourceful Figaro, who, in the author's earlier play, *The Barber of Seville,* helped his master Count Almaviva win the lovely Rosine for a wife. In this play Figaro is the count's rival, for Almaviva is tired of his wife and has become enamored of her maid Suzanne, Figaro's fiancée. Figaro outwits the count's attempts to seduce Suzanne. The play was not allowed on the public stage for three years because of its candid criticism of the nobility. When it was at last released, Figaro's change from friendly accomplice to bitter rival was not lost on French audiences, who were to overthrow their own masters five years afterward. The play was the basis of Mozart's opera *Le nozze di Figaro* (1786).

Mars: *See* Ares.

Mary Poppins: modern children's classic, written in 1934 by British actress and writer Pamela L. Travers. Mary Poppins is a whimsical and magical nanny of the Edwardian era in London, who uses her magical powers to entertain the children and often to solve their problems.

Masque or **mask:** early form of drama in which the actors wore enlarged figures of heads to identify the characters and magnify the voices. Dance, dumb show, and costume were emphasized over plot or character portrayal. The characters were usually mythological or allegorical. Masques were extremely popular in England in the early 1600s and found their greatest exponent in Ben Johnson.

Measure for Measure: late comedy by Shakespeare, presented in 1603. The Duke of Vienna appoints Angelo to reform the loose conduct of his subjects. Angelo institutes a harsh, puritanical rule, sentencing a young gentleman, Claudio, to death because his fiancée is pregnant. Claudio's sister, Isabella, pleads for him and Angelo agrees to release Claudio in return for Isabella's favors. The duke discovers this and arranges the exposure of his reformer's hypocrisy. He restores justice and a normal amount of sinfulness to his city.

Medea, GM: enchantress who was daughter of the king of Colchis. She fell in love with Jason when he came seeking the Golden Fleece and used her magic to help him secure it. She married and returned home with Jason. When he left her to marry Creusa, she murdered her children by him and killed her rival with a poisoned robe. Her story is told in Euripides' tragedy, *Medea,* and has been the subject of subsequent dramas and operas.

Medusa, GM: the most famous of the Gorgons, who were three dreadful sisters who had serpents for hair. The sight of her turned men into stone. Medusa was beheaded by Perseus, who escaped this fate by looking only at her mirror image in a shield given him by Athena.

Meistersinger: *See* Minnesinger.

MEDUSA: The sight of her turned men to stone. She was killed by Perseus.

"I NEVER WANT TO SEE ANY OF YOU AGAIN!"

MELODRAMA: The poster for this 1890s play suggests the exaggerated situations and emotions in melodrama, a form that survives in television soap operas.

Melodrama: originally a play with some music and singing and a highly sensational plot. Now a melodrama is any play with striking, exaggerated incidents and violent emotion; in effect, an operatic plot without music. The 19th century was the heyday of melodrama.

Menelaus: *See* House of Atreus.

Mentor: in the *Odyssey,* the faithful friend and counselor to whom Odysseus entrusted his household and the education of his son Telemachus when he left for Troy. The term is now applied to anyone who guides or influences another person's ideas.

Mephistopheles: in medieval European demonology, one of the seven lords of Hell. He was the Devil to whom Faust sold his soul in exchange for knowledge and power. *See also* Devil.

Merchant of Venice, The: comedy by Shakespeare, completed c 1597. Antonio, the merchant of Venice, borrows money from Shylock, a Jewish moneylender, so that his friend Bassanio may marry Portia. As security he offers a pound of flesh, which Shylock demands when he defaults in payment. Portia, disguised as a lawyer, saves Antonio through a legal quibble: Shylock may have the flesh but may shed no blood in taking it. The expression "a pound of flesh" has come to be used for reprisal of any kind.

Mercury: *See* Hermes.

Merlin, L: in Arthurian legend, the magician and seer who aided King Arthur in many marvelous ways. At one time when Arthur was opposed by eleven kings and one duke, Merlin caused all the tents of the enemies to fall down, and in the panic that followed, Arthur conquered his foes. By his help, too, Arthur won Guinevere for wife. Merlin made the Round Table and led Arthur to the sword (Excalibur) that he took from the marvelous hand and arm that rose out of the lake.

Mermaid or **merman:** in world folklore, a being of the sea or lakes with the upper body of a woman or man and a fish's tail. Mermaids and mermen are believed to have the power of prophecy; seeing or sometimes just hearing them can mean disaster for the observer. Similar to the birdlike sirens in this way, mermaids often lure sailors to shipwreck with their singing (see also *Sirens*). A mermaid can acquire a soul if she is loved by a human. Marriages resulting from such love often occur in fairy tales, but are usually short-lived. In Jean d'Arras's story "Chronique de la Princesse" (c 1387), the mermaid Mélusine leaves her human husband after he breaks his promise not to spy on her. The attempt of the little mermaid in Hans Christian Andersen's tale to live on land in order to be loved by a human prince results in her death. *See also* Little Mermaid, The.

Merry Wives of Windsor, The: one of Shakespeare's happiest comedies, performed in 1597, featuring his great comic character, Falstaff. Falstaff writes love letters to two married women, who compare notes and decide to teach him a lesson. Mistress Ford invites him to a rendezvous, but her husband comes home unexpectedly, and Falstaff is hidden in a clothes hamper, then dumped into the Thames. After the wives set other traps for the unwitting Falstaff, they expose his duplicity to all in a final scene. *See also* Henry IV.

Metamorphoses: collection of Greek and Roman myths retold in 15 volumes of verse by the Roman poet Ovid in the first century A.D. Among the well known stories are those of Daedalus, Jason and Medea, and Orpheus and Eurydice. Many later writers, including Chaucer and Shakespeare, drew on the *Metamorphoses.* This title was also used by the Roman satirist Apuleius for a romance that is now better known as *The Golden Ass.*

Metamorphosis, The: story by Czech-born, German Jewish writer Franz Kafka, published in 1916; his best-known short work. The story's central character, Gregor, is forced to realize his unimportance when he awakes one morning to find he has turned into a large insect.

Metaphor: *See* Figures of speech.

Metaphysical poets: label first applied derogatorily by John Dryden to a group of 17th-century English poets whose work was characterized by intellectual complexity often expressed in *conceits* (see also entry). John Donne is perhaps the most famous; others are Andrew Marvell, Abraham Cowley, Richard Crashaw, George Herbert, and Henry Vaughan. A renewed appreciation of the metaphysicals occurred in the early 1900s, and many modern poets reflect their influence.

Meter: systematic rhythm in poetry; the arrangement of syllables in a poem so that each line contains a certain number of accented syllables or metrical feet (*see also* Foot). The various meters, named for

the number of feet in a line, are: monometer (one foot), dimeter (two), trimeter (three), tetrameter (four), pentameter (five), hexameter (six), heptameter (seven), and octameter (eight).

Metonymy: *See* Figures of speech.

Micawber, Mr. Wilkins: *See* David Copperfield.

Midas, GM: king of Phrygia to whom Dionysus granted that all he touched would turn to gold. Midas soon tired of the gift when he discovered that even food and drink were transformed when he touched them. To remove the gift Dionysus bade him wash in the river Pactolus. He did so and was cured, but the sands of the river were turned to gold. The expression "the Midas touch" has come to refer to one who has a knack for moneymaking.

Middlemarch: novel by the English writer George Eliot, published in 1871–1872, considered by many her finest work. It captures the total social milieu of the provincial English town of Middlemarch. One of its principal characters is Dorothea Brooke, an idealistic young woman. She marries Edward Casaubon, a middle-aged scholar who has dedicated his life to producing a monumental work, but eventually she learns that he is a mere pedant, as empty of ideas as he is of feelings, and that his book will never be finished. After Casaubon's death, Dorothea marries his cousin, Will Ladislaw, a man more like herself.

In a parallel subplot, the ambitious young Dr. Lydgate marries the shallow Rosamond Vincy, whose materialistic values keep him constantly in debt so that he is unable to realize his plans for a new hospital.

Midgard: NM: middle earth, halfway between Heaven and Hell, the abode of humanity. It was surrounded by the great ocean, in which lived Jormungandr, the Midgard serpent, who encircled the world.

Midnight Ride of Paul Revere, The (or "Paul Revere's Ride"): much-quoted ballad by U.S. poet Henry Wadsworth Longfellow, which appeared in his *Tales of a Wayside Inn* (1863–1874).

Midsummer Night's Dream, A: comedy by Shakespeare, printed in 1600, in which courtiers mingle incongruously with the fairy king Oberon, his queen Titania, his helper Puck, and a group of clownish artisans. The plot is concerned with two pairs of lovers whose tangled affairs are first worsened but finally straightened out by fairy intervention. The clumsy attempts of the artisans to present a play, the pranks of Puck, and the songs and dances of the fairies combine to make a novel and delightful play.

Miles Gloriosus (*The Braggart Warrior*): comedy by the Roman playwright Plautus, written about 200 B.C. Its chief character, a stupid, swaggering soldier, became one of the stock comic characters of subsequent European theatrical history. In the Italian *commedia dell'arte* he was known as Il Capitano and later as Scaramouche.

Mill on the Floss, The: novel by English novelist George Eliot, published in 1860; it powerfully portrays the characters of Maggie and Tom Tulliver, children of a miller. Dark-haired, generous, impulsive Maggie is often an embarrassment to her manly, almost too-perfect brother Tom, who blocks her chance for happiness with a neighbor, Philip Wakem. Tom becomes the mainstay of the family after his father's death, then evicts Maggie because of her indiscreet adventure with Stephen Guest. The book ends with the flood of the Floss, Maggie's attempt to rescue Tom, and their reconciliation as they drown together.

Mimir, NM: giant who lived beside the root of the world tree, Yggdrasil. Here he drank from the spring that flowed from the root of the tree; its waters gave him wisdom and all knowledge of the past and the future. Odin traded one of his eyes for a drink from Mimir's spring.

Minerva: *See* Athena.

Miniver Cheevy: poem by U.S. poet Edwin Arlington Robinson, published in 1917; a brief biography of a man "born too late," who scorns the dreary, humdrum world he lives in. Drinking helps Miniver maintain his belief that if he had lived in a more heroic age, he would have been equal to it.

Minnesinger: one of the lyric poets, singers, and musicians of Germany who flourished 1150–1350. The word literally means a singer of love songs (from *minne:* "love"). The minnesinger was usually of noble birth, and his songs had to do with courtly love, the worship by a knight of some woman, often far above him in rank. The minnesingers wrote

realize US

realise Brit.

meters US

metres Brit.

Metaphysical Poets' Representative Works

JOHN DONNE (1571–1631)
 "Hymn to God the Father"
 "Death, Be Not Proud"
 "A Valediction: Forbidding Mourning"
 "Good Friday, 1613"

GEORGE HERBERT (1593–1633)
 "The Pearl"
 "The Collar"

RICHARD CRASHAW (c 1613–1649)
 "The Flaming Heart"
 "I Am the Door"

HENRY VAUGHAN (1621–1695)
 "The Retreat"
 "The World"

THOMAS TRAHERNE (1637–1674)
 "Wonder"

ANDREW MARVELL (1621–1678)
 "To His Coy Mistress"

ABRAHAM COWLEY (1618–1667)
 "The Wish"

both words and music to their songs, which were sung in the courts before knights and ladies. Contests were frequently held. As the minnesong developed, the subject matter was expanded to include political and religious themes. The greatest of all the minnesingers was Walther von der Vogelweide in the early 1200s.

The *meistersingers* of 14th- to 16th-century Germany considered themselves to be the heirs of the minnesingers, though both their music and their poetry were inferior to those of their predecessors. The most famous of the meistersingers was the shoemaker Hans Sachs, who plays an important role in Wagner's opera *Die Meistersinger* (1868).

Minos, GM: king of Crete, the son of Zeus and Europa. He was the founder of the Cretan laws and, according to the *Odyssey,* was made a judge in Hades after he died. In other legends he was the tyrant who exacted a yearly tribute from the Athenians of seven youths and seven maidens to feed the monster Minotaur. *See also* Minotaur.

Minotaur, GM: monster of Crete, half human, half bull. Its father was a beautiful white bull presented by Poseidon to King Minos, who spared its life instead of sacrificing it to the god. Minos's wife, Pasiphae, fell in love with the bull and conceived Asterius, the Minotaur, after a tryst encouraged by Poseidon. To imprison the monster, Minos ordered Daedalus to build a labyrinth. The Minotaur was killed by Theseus. *See also* Ariadne; Labyrinth; Minos.

Miracle plays: medieval dramas dealing with events from the lives of saints. Like the mystery plays, they were originally part of church services associated with particular feasts. Only a few fragmentary English miracle plays survived the Reformation, but many European examples exist. *See also* Mystery plays.

Misanthrope, Le: comedy of manners by French dramatist Molière, performed in 1666. It portrays a frivolous, fashionable world in which flattery and flirtation are the chief social graces. The hero, Alceste, is a misfit. He detests insincerity and offends everyone by speaking the truth. His only tie to society is his love for the flirt Célimène. When she refuses his offer to go off and live in seclusion with him, Alceste goes off alone.

Misérables, Les: novel by French author Victor Hugo, published in 1862. The hero, Jean Valjean, is an ex-convict who was sentenced to the galleys for stealing a loaf of bread. He becomes a successful businessman and mayor of his town, but he is hounded by Javert, a fanatical detective. When his convict past threatens the happiness of his adopted daughter Cosette, Valjean disappears. Cosette and her husband Marius, learning of his self-sacrifice, find him as he is dying.

Miss Julie: one-act tragedy by the Swedish dramatist August Strindberg, performed in 1888. On Midsummer's Eve, Miss Julie, the daughter of a count, takes part in the servants' merrymaking. Frustrated by a broken engagement, Julie flirts boldly with the handsome valet Jean and finally provokes him to seduce her. When the count comes home and rings the bell for his valet, Jean's inbred servility comes to the fore. Unable to accept the comedown from being mistress of the house to being mistress of the valet, Julie commits suicide.

Miss Lonelyhearts: novel by the U.S. writer Nathanael West, published in 1933. Miss Lonelyhearts is a newspaperman who gives advice to the lovelorn. His daily mail from "Desperate," "Anxious," "Broken-hearted," or "Sick-of-it-all" drives him to self-destructive, drunken behavior. Written with a black humor far in advance of its time, the book conveys an overwhelming mood of hopelessness.

Mnemosyne, GM: Titaness who was the goddess of memory and the mother, by Zeus, of the nine Muses.

Moby-Dick; or, The Whale: novel by U.S. author Herman Melville (1851), considered by many the finest American novel ever written. This tale of Captain Ahab's voyage in search of the great white whale that has crippled him is rich in symbolism and philosophical overtones. At the same time, it is an exciting narrative and a precise description of the New England whaling industry of the time. The narrator, Ishmael, is the only survivor of Ahab's mad quest.

Modest Proposal, A: short title of a satire by Irish-born writer Jonathan Swift, published in 1729, proposing a remedy for Ireland's poverty that will benefit all. With a series of carefully reasoned arguments, he suggests that the children of the poor, properly cooked and seasoned, would make tasty dishes at a gentleman's table and at the same time be a source of profit rather than burden to their parents.

Moirai: *See* Fates.

Moll Flanders: picaresque tale by English author Daniel Defoe, published in 1722, in which the rogue is a woman. Moll, born in prison, is left to fend for herself in England when her mother is transported to America. After she is seduced at fourteen, Moll has a series of lovers and five husbands. She later prospers as a thief, until arrested and sentenced to death. The sentence is commuted to transportation to America where, joined by one of her former husbands, a highwayman, Moll gives up her wicked ways and establishes a successful plantation.

Morality plays: medieval dramatic poems of the 15th and 16th centuries, which developed from the miracle and mystery plays. They differ from these plays, which dramatize events from Bible history or saints' lives, in that the characters are abstractions, personifications of Sin, Hate, Pride, Folly, Lust, and the like. The best-known, most imaginative, and poetic is *Everyman,* which has had successful modern production. *See also* Everyman.

Mordred: *See* Arthurian legend.

Morgan le Fay: fairy (*fay* in Middle English) who appears in Arthurian and Carolingian legend. In some Arthurian tales, she is the sister of King Arthur and one of the three queens who accompany him to Avalon to cure his wounds. Malory's *Morte d'Arthur* describes her as a malicious crone who plots to kill Arthur and her own husband, King Uriens. In some Carolingian legends, such as that of Ogier the Dane, she is celebrated for her curative powers; in others she is the Fata Morgana who gave her name to mirages in the Straits of Messina.

Morte d'Arthur: long prose narrative version of the whole Arthurian legend, written by Sir Thomas Malory, printed by William Caxton in 1485. It is through this version, rather than the numerous medieval romances, that the modern image of Arthurian legend was formed. Its emphasis is on the fellowship of the Round Table rather than courtly love. *See also* Arthurian legend; Knights of the Round Table.

The symbols used in this glossary are as follows:

G-Greek
R-Roman
N-Norse
M-myth
L-legend

20 History of Literature

Mother Courage and Her Children: play by the German playwright Bertolt Brecht, performed in 1941. It is set in the period of the Thirty Years' War. Mother Courage and her children follow the armies and sell supplies to the soldiers. But the war that brings her a living also brings death; her children Eilif, Swiss Cheese, and Kattrin are all killed. Despite her losses, Mother Courage moves on, left in the ambiguous position of being both war profiteer and victim.

MOTHER COURAGE, the heroine of Brecht's play, earned her living but lost her children as a result of the Thirty Years' War.

Mother Goose's Melody or Sonnets for the Cradle: collection of nursery rhymes and stories published in England in about 1765 by John Newbery, the first publisher of children's books. It includes the familiar "Baa, Baa, Black Sheep"; "Little Boy Blue"; "Patty Cake, Patty Cake"; and countless others. Mother Goose herself is a mysterious, untraceable figure who probably comes out of French folklore. The title, but not the rhymes, was taken from Charles Perrault's *Tales of My Mother Goose,* a fairy-tale collection first translated into English in 1729.

Mrs. Dalloway: novel by the English writer Virginia Woolf, published in 1925. The action takes place one beautiful day when Clarissa Dalloway plans and gives a party for her privileged, sophisticated circle of friends. The interactions of the guests make it quite apparent that some of them have experienced heights of passion and depths of suffering that Mrs. Dalloway herself has never experienced; being a gracious and charming hostess will be the pinnacle of her achievement.

Much Ado About Nothing: one of Shakespeare's darker comedies about love and intrigue, produced c 1598–1599. The clever woman-hater Benedick and the twice-as-clever man-hater Beatrice are finally united in a double-wedding ceremony along with the more conventional pair of lovers, Claudio and Hero.

Muckrakers: journalists and novelists of the early 20th century who devoted their energies to exposing social evils and unfair or dishonest practices in big business or government, both in fiction and in reportage. A representative work was Ida M. Tarbell's *History of the Standard Oil Company* (1904). Other works include Thomas W. Lawson's *Frenzied Finance* (1904–1905); Upton Sinclair's novel *The Jungle* (1906), dealing with the meat-packing industry; and Brand Whitlock's *The Turn of the Balance* (1907), on capital punishment. Though these writers were contemptuously dubbed "muckrakers" by President Theodore Roosevelt, some of their works stimulated reform legislation.

Murder in the Cathedral: verse drama by the Anglo-American poet T. S. Eliot, performed in 1935. It deals with the last days of St. Thomas à Becket, Archbishop of Canterbury, whose defiance of his former friend, King Henry II, results in his murder at the hands of the king's knights. The play, first performed at Canterbury Cathedral, is often staged in churches.

Murders in the Rue Morgue: short story by U.S. author Edgar Allan Poe, published in 1841 and considered the first modern detective story. It introduced the mastermind detective C. Auguste Dupin, a brilliant amateur who uncovers clues and solves the crime by his deductive skill, setting a pattern for most later detective story writers. Dupin also appeared in Poe's later stories of crime and detection.

Muse, GM: any one of the nine daughters of Zeus and Mnemosyne who were patrons and goddesses of the arts and sciences. They were: Clio (history), Euterpe (music), Thalia (comedy and pastoral poetry), Melpomene (tragedy), Terpsichore (dancing and choruses), Erato (lyric and love poetry), Polyhymnia (sacred song), Urania (astronomy), and Calliope (epic poetry).

My Antonia: novel by U.S. writer Willa Cather, published in 1918. The narrator, Jim Burden, meets Antonia Shimerda, a Bohemian immigrant, when they are both growing up in Nebraska. She works hard—first out in the fields, then later as a maid—but never loses her humor and integrity. Jim leaves to go to college. He returns 20 years later and finds that Antonia has become a middle-aged farm wife with many children who still retains the strength of character that makes her representative of the American pioneer spirit.

Mycenae, GM: ancient city, supposedly founded by Perseus and ruled by Agamemnon, the leader of the Greeks during the Trojan War (c 1250 B.C.). Following Homer's description of its site, excavations were begun in 1840 by Heinrich Schliemann in a ravine in Argos; they have yielded rich finds that include palace ruins, city walls, graves, gold cups and ornaments, bronze weapons, painted vases, and sculpture. These artifacts, along with tablets inscribed in the Linear B script (earlier found in Crete), indicate that the distinctive civilization of the Greek mainland derived from Crete.

Myshkin, Prince: *See* Idiot, The.

Mystery plays: short medieval dramatic works representing events from the Old or New Testament, especially those dealing with the birth, death, or resurrection of Christ. These plays were an elaboration of the church liturgy. They were associated with particular feasts and were originally given as part of the service. Later, as robust humor and comic byplay were introduced into the religious stories, they were forbidden in church and moved out to the courtyard or were given at markets and fairs. Famous examples are *Abraham and Isaac* and *The Harrowing of Hell.* The actors were members of local guilds or trade unions.

The surviving English mystery plays are known by the towns in which they were produced: York, Wakefield, and Chester. A fourth group of plays, formerly erroneously assigned to Coventry, are now called N-town plays.

Mystery story: popular genre of fiction in which a crime is solved, involving the elements of suspense, fear, and mystifi-

MYSTERY: Classic detective Sherlock Holmes helps the victim of a crime.

cation. Stories of detection have been known since seventh-century China; the modern detective story—the "whodunit"—is considered to have begun with Edgar Allan Poe's "Murders in the Rue Morgue" (1841), which introduced the clever amateur detective Dupin. The most famous detective of all time is Sir Arthur Conan Doyle's Sherlock Holmes, whose adventures were published between 1891 and 1927.

Among the best-known fictional detectives are Rex Stout's Nero Wolfe; Erle Stanley Gardner's lawyer-detective Perry Mason; Agatha Christie's Belgian detective Hercule Poirot and her elderly English sleuth Miss Marple; and Dorothy Sayers' aristocratic Lord Peter Wimsey. The "hard-boiled" detective, born in the United States in the 1930s, is typified by Raymond Chandler's Philip Marlowe and Dashiell Hammett's Sam Spade. Police detectives who solve crimes as part of everyday routine include Georges Simenon's Inspector Jules Maigret.

Myth: traditional story that embodies elemental and deeply felt beliefs of a people, explaining the mysteries of existence by attributing them to the actions of supernatural beings. The actors in myths are deities, or semidivine beings; if they are not, the story is a folk tale.

Certain types of myth are universal; *creation myths,* which explain how the Earth and its people came to be; *nature myths,* which personify the elements, peopling the woods, fields, mountains, and sea with gods, nymphs, and other resident spirits and giving human attributes to natural forces like the sun, moon, stars, and winds; *culture myths,* which supply reasons for tribal customs and taboos and tell how a people acquired basic elements of their culture—corn or medicine or music.

civilization
US

civilisation
Brit.

In Western culture the most familiar mythologies are those of the Greeks, the Romans, and the Norse. The Romans took much of their rich mythology from the earlier Greeks, and we know the stories more often in their Roman versions. For the equivalent names of Greek and Roman deities, see chart below.

N

Naiads, GM: Greek nymphs who presided over springs and fountains, rivers, streams, and lakes.

Naked and the Dead, The: first novel by U.S. author Norman Mailer, published in 1948; considered one of the best American novels to come out of World War II. It deals with a representative group of U.S. officers and enlisted men invading a Japanese island. The author uses a device called the "Time Machine" to switch back into the past of each of the characters engaged in the action.

Nana: novel by the French writer Émile Zola, published in 1880. It is one of a long series of naturalistic novels that traces the tainted heredity of the Rougon-Macquart family. Nana, the daughter of alcoholic parents, becomes a prostitute, but because of her unusual beauty, she rises to become an "actress" and the mistress of important men. Zola does not glamorize Nana's role as the mistress of Paris. Her stupidity, fickleness, and improvidence bring ruin to her lovers and at last to herself.

Greek and Roman Deities

GREEK	ROMAN
Aphrodite	Venus
Apollon	Apollo
Athena	Minerva
Ares	Mars
Artemis	Diana
Cronus	Saturn
Demeter	Ceres
Dionysus	Bacchus
Eros	Cupid
Hades (Pluton)	Pluto
Hephaestus	Vulcan
Hera	Juno
Heracles	Hercules
Hermes	Mercury
Hestia	Vesta
Persephone	Proserpine
Poseidon	Neptune
Zeus	Jupiter

NARCISSUS: The young man fell in love with his own image. His lover Echo could never tell him that she loved him, being able only to repeat his words back to him.

Narcissus, GM: beautiful youth for whose love Echo died. He fell in love with his own reflection in a pool, pined away with longing for the unattainable image, and was changed into the flower that bears his name. Narcissism is excessive self-love. *See also* Echo.

Narrative poetry: poems that tell stories. There are three main classifications: epic, romance, and ballad. See also separate entries.

Nathan the Wise: verse drama by the German playwright Gotthold Ephraim Lessing, published in 1779. The setting is twelfth-century Jerusalem at the time of the Crusades. The story concerns a complicated web of obligation involving a Christian Knight Templar, the Muslim Sultan Saladin, and the respected Jewish merchant Nathan. It advances a concept of religious tolerance unusual for its time. The character of Nathan was based on Lessing's friend, the Jewish philosopher Moses Mendelssohn.

Native Son: novel by Richard Wright, published in 1940; the first work by an American black to deal frankly and boldly with black-white relations. It tells the story of Bigger Thomas, a young black man who is employed as a chauffeur by the Daltons. Bigger is uneasy when Mary Dalton, a radical university student, befriends him. He helps Mary to her room when she is drunk and, to prevent her from disturbing the family, accidentally smothers her with a pillow. He then disposes of the body and engages in a series of bizarre acts to cover his deed. He is caught, tried, and sentenced to death. The mutual distrust of most black and white characters toward one another determines their behavior throughout the book.

Naturalism: movement of the late 19th century that adapted the theories of science and the objectivity of scientific method to literature and art. In France, Stendhal, Balzac, and Flaubert laid the groundwork for naturalism's leading exponents, Maupassant, Daudet, and especially Zola. The naturalistic novel was often a case history in which the character's heredity and environment, rather than his own will, determined his fate. The movement was important in late 19th-century German and English literature and had considerable effect on the work of 20th-century Italian neo-realists such as Silone, Levi, and Moravia. Some examples in American fiction are Theodore Dreiser's *American Tragedy* (1925) and James T. Farrell's

NATIVE SON by Richard Wright spoke frankly about black-white relations.

Studs Lonigan trilogy (1932–1935). In exploring the effects of environment on personality, the naturalists often chose extreme environments, such as slums or the underworld, and thus introduced new areas of subject matter to fiction.

Nausea: first novel of the French existentialist philosopher Jean-Paul Sartre, published in 1938. The hero, Antoine Roquentin, who lives the lonely life of a historical researcher, begins to have strange perceptions. He feels the chaos and unpredictability of the world around him and concludes that living is senseless in a world that so lacks meaning. He calls his feeling of malaise and self-disgust "nausea," and in the end decides that he can escape from the oppressiveness of life only in the realm of art.

Nausicaa: *See* Odyssey.

Nectar, GM: drink of the gods.

Nemesis, GM: goddess of vengeance and retribution who punished especially the proud and arrogant.

Neoclassicism: term applied to several post-Renaissance movements in art and literature (and, in modern times, music) when the classical forms and styles of Greece and Rome became the standard models. In literature its highest expression was perhaps in France during the late 1600s, in the dramas of Corneille and Racine, which adhered to classical principles with excessive rigidity. French neoclassicism influenced English literature from 1660 to the mid-1700s.

Neptune: *See* Poseidon.

Nestor: in the *Iliad,* an aged counselor of the Greeks at the time of the Trojan War, noted for wisdom and eloquence.

Newbery Medal: U.S. literary prize awarded annually since 1921 for the best juvenile book. Its name commemorates John Newbery (1713–1767), the first English publisher of children's books.

New Criticism: school of literary criticism developed in the 20th century. Its chief tenet is that a literary work stands on its intrinsic merit, regardless of its social, moral, historical, or political purpose. Its principal method is close reading—a painstaking word-for-word analysis of the text. By this method the "new critics" have revealed many subtleties and levels of meaning that were formerly overlooked in literary works. The term derives from the title of a work published in 1941 by the U.S. poet and critic John Crowe Ransom, but the method was advocated earlier by such critics as T. S. Eliot, William Empson, and I. A. Richards.

New England Renaissance or **American Renaissance:** the first flowering of a distinctive American literature that occurred between 1830 and 1870 and

The symbols used in this glossary are as follows:

G-Greek
R-Roman
N-Norse
M-myth
L-legend

NŌ MASKS show the highly stylized characters that are portrayed in the ancient Japanese form of drama.

drew its inspiration from the European Romantic movement. One center of the burgeoning culture was Boston, where the aristocratic Harvard professors Henry Wadsworth Longfellow, Oliver Wendell Holmes, and James Russell Lowell were the literary elite. Another center was the small town of Concord, Massachusetts, where Ralph Waldo Emerson and Henry David Thoreau attracted an original and eccentric circle of transcendentalist thinkers and literary friends, among whom were two of America's greatest writers, Nathaniel Hawthorne and Herman Melville. A study of this period is Van Wyck Brooks's *The Flowering of New England. See also* Transcendentalism.

New Life, The: *See* Vita Nuova, La.

Nibelungenlied, also called *The Song of the Nibelungs:* Middle German epic, written about 1200 by an unknown author. It combines the earlier Germanic legends about the hero Siegfried, who slays the dragon Fafnir to get possession of a treasure, with legends about the destruction of the rival Burgundians. The stories are unified by focusing the tale on the Burgundian princess Kriemhild, sister of Gunther, one of three brother-kings of Burgundy.

After stealing the Nibelung treasure guarded by Alberich, Siegfried goes to woo Kriemhild. In order to marry her, he must help Gunther win the northern princess Brunhild, who will only marry a man who can surpass her in feats of strength. Gunther passes the test and wins Brunhild, although his acts are actually performed by Siegfried in a cloak of invisibility. Siegfried and Kriemhild marry, but one day in a quarrel, Kriemhild reveals the deception to Brunhild. Brunhild revenges herself on Siegfried by having him slain by Gunther's loyal vassal Hagen. Hagen robs Kriemhild of Siegfried's treasure and sinks it in the Rhine. The second part of the story deals with the change in Kriemhild from a sweet-natured maiden to a tragic woman bent on revenge. After long brooding she marries Etzel (the Hunnish king Attila). Years later she invites her brothers and Hagen to visit

her and has them slain to the last man. She personally kills Hagen and is slain herself by Hildebrand, a visiting warrior at Etzel's court.

Richard Wagner's four music dramas, *The Ring of the Nibelungs* (1853–1874; comprising *The Rhinegold, The Valkyrie, Siegfried,* and *The Twilight of the Gods*), are based on the legend, but rely more heavily on earlier, more highly supernatural Norse versions (particularly the *Völsunga Saga*). *See also* Völsunga Saga.

Nimue: *See* Arthurian legend.

Nineteen Eighty-Four: novel published in 1949 by the English satirist George Orwell; a prophetic forecast of the future under totalitarian rule. It is a terrifying projection of life in the superstate watched over by Big Brother, where the book's hero, Winston Smith, has a brief escape from absolute controls on his life through a love affair, is captured by the Thought Police, and, after brainwashing, renounces all independent thought and "learns to love Big Brother."

Niobe, GM: proud mother, according to the *Iliad,* of seven sons and seven daughters. She bragged of her many children to Leto, the mother of two, Apollo and Artemis. To punish her, Apollo killed all her sons and Artemis killed all the girls. Niobe's grief was so great that in pity the gods changed her into a rock on Mt. Sipylus, from which her tears still flow when the snow above it melts.

Njal's Saga (also called *The Story of Burnt Njal*): one of the greatest of the 13th-century Icelandic sagas; it demonstrates the ethics and manners of a society whose code of justice is the blood feud. Njal is a mature man and a respected judge, the head of a large family. He is a friend and father figure to the young hero Gunnar. But the quarrels and jealousies of their wives lead to a series of aggressive acts and retaliation between the two families. Njal's attempts to settle all scores justly are defeated by the rash reprisals of his sons. The feud culminates in Gunnar's death and the burning alive of Njal and his entire family.

Nō: highly stylized form of Japanese drama involving poetry, music, and dancing, developed in the 14th century by Kan-ami and his son Zeami Motokiyo. Most of the Nō plays still performed today were written by Zeami. They have two principal characters, the Shite and the Waki. The Shite sings and dances to the accompaniment of drums and flute (or a chorus sings his part while he dances), and the Waki explains the theme. Most plays deal with supernatural beings. Often the Shite plays the dual part of a character as he was in real life and as his ghost. The gestures, costumes, and masks are in themselves a meaningful language of refinement.

Nobel Prize for Literature: most prestigious of all literary prizes, awarded annually since 1921 by the Swedish Academy in Stockholm from a fund established by Alfred Nobel, the inventor of dynamite. The winners are chosen from throughout the world on the basis of the complete body of their work. U.S. writers who have won the award include Sinclair Lewis, Eugene O'Neill, T. S. Eliot, William Faulkner, Ernest Hemingway, John Steinbeck, Saul Bellow, Isaac Bashevis Singer, and Toni Morrison.

Noble savage: term used in reference to the supposed innate goodness or moral superiority of the natural man, who is unspoiled by civilization. The concept became part of the back-to-nature philosophy of the Romantic movement and was popularized by the French writers Jean Jacques Rousseau and Chateaubriand. Some of the Indian characters in James Fenimore Cooper's *Leatherstocking Tales,* such as the wise Chingachgook and his brave son Uncas, are portrayed as noble savages having inborn virtue, grace, and delicacy of feeling.

No Exit: one-act play by the French writer Jean-Paul Sartre, produced in 1944. It deals with three characters, a man and two women, in Hell. Hell is portrayed as a windowless drawing room with ugly furnishings. They soon learn that their punishment is suited to their crimes. Having sacrificed their true natures during life for the sake of their images in other people's eyes, they are doomed to live forever only in one another's eyes.

Notes from the Underground: novel by the Russian writer Feodor Dostoevski, published in 1864. The narrator is a petty clerk who has grandiose dreams of someday humiliating all his enemies for what he has perceived as their fancied insults. In actuality his intended victims are scarcely aware of his existence, and in their presence he succeeds only in humiliating himself. He ends by taking out his bitterness on a helpless prostitute.

Novel: sustained, fictional prose narrative of considerable length, traditionally containing a realistic potrayal of life, fully developed characters, and a point of view. The novel as we know it began in the 18th century with the publication of Samuel Richardson's *Pamela.* Unlike earlier prose fiction works, *Pamela* concentrated in minute detail on the psychological development of its characters.

Among the world's most admired novelists are the English authors Henry Fielding, Jane Austen, Charles Dickens, and George Eliot; the French Honoré de Balzac and Gustave Flaubert; the Russians Feodor Dostoevski and Leo Tolstoy; the Irish James Joyce; the U.S. expatriate Henry James and writer Herman Melville. In the 20th century, the novel form has been greatly experimented with and expanded, and the merits of Latin American novelists such as Gabriel García Márquez and Jorge Amado have come to be recognized.

Nursery rhymes: verses, jingles, and poems of childhood passed on from generation to generation. Originally, some of these rhymes were adult comments on political leaders or social situations, disguised in catchy verse. Others were parts of courting songs or folk ballads. Riddles and counting-out rhymes also figure prominently in childhood poetry. Like fairy tales, nursery rhymes are often found in parallel versions in different countries. For example, "Billy Boy, Billy Boy," with slight variations, is common throughout Eastern European countries.

Nymphs, GRM: spirits of mountains, forests, trees, streams, the ocean, and springs. They were beautiful goddesses who often married human beings. Nymphs of the ocean were oceanids; nymphs of the sea, especially the Mediterranean, were nereids; nymphs of rivers, lakes, and springs were naiads; mountain nymphs were oreads; the nymphs of forests, groves, and trees were dryads.

O

Oberon: in medieval folklore, the king of the fairies or elves. He is the Alberich of German and French medieval romance, or his son. Unlike the sinister Alberich, the Oberon of Shakespeare's *Midsummer Night's Dream* is an imperious mercurial being who masterminds the evening's madness.

Octopus, The: novel by the U.S. writer Frank Norris, published in 1901; intended as the first work in a trilogy dealing with the story of wheat. The octopus is the railroad whose encroachment spells impending doom for the California wheat farmers. A second volume, *The Pit* (1903), carries the story of wheat to the Chicago stock exchange and deals with the efforts of a broker to corner the market. A third volume was incomplete at the author's death.

Ode: in classical usage, a lyric poem designed to be chanted or sung. The most famous ancient odes are those written by the Greek poet Pindar (518–438 B.C.) in celebration of heroes of the Olympic Games. The form used by Pindar is virtually inimitable. The Latin poet Horace (65–8 B.C.) wrote odes that had little resemblance to Pindaric odes; the Horatian odes are graceful and polished but informal and conversational. They were imitated by Alexander Pope and many other poets of the early 1700s. In modern usage, an ode is a sustained lyric having a dignified subject and written in an elevated tone. Wordsworth's "Intimations of Immortality" is an example (see entry).

Ode on a Grecian Urn: poem by the English poet John Keats, written in 1819. In describing a pastoral scene of love pursuit on a Greek vase, the poet expresses wonder at the enduring freshness of art.

Odin, NM: supreme god; husband of Frigga and father of Balder, Thor, Bragi, Hoder, Tyr, Vali, Vidar, Hermod, and others of the Aesir. He was the god of war, but also the god of wisdom. To become so, he paid Mimir one eye for a drink from the spring of knowledge (Mimir's well) at the foot of the world tree Yggdrasil. Two ravens attended him, Hugin and Munin (thought and memory).

Odin learned the secret of the magic runes by hanging upside down from Yggdrasil, self-wounded by a spear. By this strange rite he acquired the powers of a wizard and a poet. He is the Woden of Germanic mythology; Wednesday is Woden's day.

Odysseus: son of Laertes; called Ulysseus by the Romans; in Homer's *Iliad* and *Odyssey,* a king of Ithaca and one of the foremost of the Greek chiefs in the Trojan War. He was a suitor of Helen of Troy but married Penelope; he was so unwilling to leave her when called to rescue Helen from the Trojans that he feigned madness by plowing the sands of his native shore to avoid going to war. His ruse was discovered when his infant son Telemachus was placed in his path and he veered out of the way; he was forced to go to Troy where he distinguished himself in valor and wisdom during the years of the siege. On the death of Achilles the arms of that hero were awarded to Odysseus. The Trojan Horse was Odysseus's idea. *See also* Odyssey.

Odyssey: epic by Homer; it describes the 10 years of wandering and the hardships and adventures Odysseus encounters on his voyage home from the war. After dragging his crew away from the temptations of the Lotus-Eaters in Africa, he next escapes death from the one-eyed Cyclops, Polyphemus. He remains one year with Circe, the enchantress, and seven years with the

center
US

centre
Brit.

civilization
US

civilisation
Brit.

20 History of Literature

ocean nymph Calypso on her island Ogygia, refusing the promise of immortality in order to return home. He braves the dangers of Scylla and Charybdis, and has himself bound to the mast to escape the lure of the sirens' singing. Shipwrecked on the shores of Phaeacia, he is cared for by Nausicaa and her father, who gives him ships to continue his voyage home.

At last Odysseus reaches Ithaca, disguised as a beggar, and finds his wife Penelope surrounded by a host of insolent suitors, each coveting the kingdom. With the aid of his son Telemachus and his faithful herdsman Eumaeus, he slays them all, reigning another good 16 years. Though the *Odyssey* lacks some of the dramatic freshness and heroic poignance of the *Iliad,* and contains many episodes from folklore and oriental romance, its superbly organized structure marks it as the work of Homer. *See also* Charybdis; Circe; Lotus-Eaters; Penelope; Polyphemus; Scylla.

Oedipus, GL: son of Laius and Jocasta, king and queen of Thebes. Having been warned that he would die by the hand of his son, Laius decided to destroy the newborn child and hung him by his heels on a tree in the forest. From this incident, probably, he was named Oedipus, meaning "swell foot." A passing herdsman found the infant and saved his life, and Oedipus was adopted and reared by the king of Corinth. In his young manhood he was told by the oracle at Delphi that he was destined to kill his father and wed his own mother. Horrified, he fled from Corinth, met Laius at a crossroad, and killed him in a quarrel over the right of way.

Finally Oedipus came to Thebes where the sphinx, a winged, woman-headed monster, was daily devouring the hapless people who could not answer her riddle. Oedipus answered instantly the famous question put to him, and the monster killed herself (*see also* Sphinx).

Creon, the king of Thebes, had promised the kingdom and his sister Jocasta as wife to whomever should free the city of this peril. Thus Oedipus unknowingly married his own mother and by her had two sons, Eteocles and Polynices, and two daughters, Antigone and Ismene. When the truth of their relationship was revealed, Jocasta hanged herself and Oedipus put out his own eyes, going into exile to Colonus in Attica, followed by his faithful daughter Antigone. This story is the basis of Sophocles' famous tragedy *Oedipus Rex.*

Of Human Bondage: semi-autobiographical novel by British writer W. Somerset Maugham, published in 1915; considered his finest work. It is the story of a sensitive young man's character development and growth to maturity. Philip Carey, a crippled orphan, raised by loveless relatives, becomes enslaved by a jealous passion for a Cockney waitress, Millie, who cruelly taunts him

The symbols used in this glossary are as follows:

G-Greek
R-Roman
N-Norse
M-myth
L-legend

THE ODYSSEY: Odysseus and his crew are menaced by the one-eyed giant, the Cyclops, who is throwing huge boulders at their ship.

for his weaknesses. At last Philip frees himself from this emotional bondage, becomes a doctor, and marries an understanding woman.

Of Mice and Men: novel by U.S. writer John Steinbeck, published in 1937; a melodrama of the Depression years depicting the marginal existence of some outcasts of society. George Milton, a migrant worker, loves and protects his only friend, Lennie Small, a simple-minded giant who does not know his own strength. When Lennie unwittingly kills a flirtatious girl, George is forced to kill him to protect him from being lynched by a mob.

Ogier the Dane: one of Charlemagne's knights, also called Olger or, as a Danish national hero, Holger Danske. In early Charlemagne legends, he was a rebel who declared his intention to kill Charlemagne's son Charlot in a vendetta. Charlemagne had him imprisoned, but Archbishop Turpin protected him while

pretending to starve him. The Saracens attacked and Turpin offered Charlemagne the aid of Ogier on condition that the knight might have his revenge on Charlot. Ogier satisfied himself by slapping Charlot in the face. He and Charlemagne were reconciled, and he became one of the twelve noble peers.

Ogre: in European fairy tales, a flesh-eating giant. The word was first used by the French writer Charles Perrault in his fairy tales and may have been invented by him.

Old Man and the Sea, The: late novel by U.S. author Ernest Hemingway, published in 1952. It deals with the struggles of an old Cuban fisherman to protect a huge fish, his first catch in 84 days, from sharks. The old man fights gallantly for two days but the sharks win in the end. The book's theme of the dignity and irony of primal struggles was a return of Hemingway's original, simple heroic code.

OLIVER TWIST: In an illustration by the great 19th-century illustrator George Cruikshank, young Oliver asks the master of the workhouse for more food as his frightened friends watch.

Oliver Twist: melodramatic novel of poverty and the London underworld by British writer Charles Dickens, published serially from 1837 to 1839. Oliver, an unknown waif, escapes from a workhouse only to fall into the hands of Fagin, the master of a den of young London thieves. Fagin forces Oliver to break into a house, where the boy is caught by his intended victims, who recognize at once that he is no common criminal. Through their kindly interest, Oliver discovers his true parentage; Fagin and his crew are brought before the law, and Oliver is adopted by a wealthy gentleman.

Olympus, Mount: highest mountain in the Olympus range and in Greece; considered by the ancient Greeks to be the abode of the gods.

One Day in the Life of Ivan Denisovich: novel by Russian writer Aleksandr Solzhenitsyn, published in 1962. It describes a typical "good" day in the life of Ivan, who is a prisoner in a Soviet concentration camp in Siberia. Ivan considers the day to be good because he manages to conceal a little extra food for himself, because he incurs no unusual punishment for misconduct, and because he avoids the dreaded sentence to solitary confinement in a freezing cell that befalls one of his fellow prisoners. This was Solzhenitsyn's first novel, and the only one permitted publication in the U.S.S.R.

One Hundred Years of Solitude: novel by the Colombian writer Gabriel Garcia Márquez, published in 1967. It brought worldwide attention not only to its author but to the neglected literature of Latin America. The book chronicles the history of an imaginary isolated Colombian town, Maconda, through the stories of the members of its founding family, the Buendias, in a superb blend of myth and reality.

On Liberty: political-philosophical essay by British philosopher John Stuart Mill, published in 1859; a classic study of the problems of modern democracies. Mill argues that it is in the self-interest of the state to give its citizens the greatest amount of freedom. The state that enforces docility and discourages originality will eventually become the victim of its burdensome population of unproductive members.

Onomatopoeia: use of words to imitate natural sounds (for example, *achoo* tries to sound like a sneeze; *hahaha*, a laugh). In poetry, certain sounds or rhythms may be used to produce aural effects: a series of dactyls has the rhythm of a horse's gallop; the use of *z*-sounds has a buzzing quality. "Your life a sluice of sensation along your sides," writes D. H. Lawrence in a poem entitled "Fish," thus not only describing the fish but also creating the effect of it passing through water.

On the Road: novel by U.S. writer Jack Kerouac, published in 1957, regarded as the classic work of the Beat movement (*see also* Beat generation). A loosely structured book, written spontaneously in a few weeks, it deals with the cross-country jaunts of a group of young "Beats" in search of adventure, love, diversion, sex, enlightenment, and heightened experience. The Beat lifestyle and values—indifference to poverty, acceptance of all experience, and hunger for religious meaning—are reflected in the book.

Oracle, GRM: place where men might go to consult the gods in regard to the future and the conduct of human affairs. The answer was usually given through the voice of a priestess, after appropriate rituals had been performed and the priestess went into a trance. The message was couched in ambiguous, symbolic terms and could often be misinterpreted. The oracle of Apollo at Delphi was the most famous among the Greeks. *See also* Delphic oracle.

Oresteia: *See* House of Atreus.

Orestes: *See* House of Atreus.

Orion, GM: young and beautiful hunter, beloved by Eos and slain in jealousy by Artemis. Another story says that Artemis herself loved him and was tricked into shooting him by Apollo. After his death Orion became a major constellation in the heavens, where he appears wearing a belt studded with bright stars and carrying a club and sword.

Orlando Furioso: epic by Italian poet Ludovico Ariosto, published in 1516, enlarged in 1532. Its hero is the Roland of the Charlemagne legends, but in this version, romance takes precedence over heroic deeds. The poem's main story tells of Orlando's hopeless love for Angelica, the princess of Cathay, and his ensuing madness when Angelica elopes with a Moorish youth. Orlando's friend Astolfo makes a trip to the moon to find Orlando's wits and returns them to him.

Orpheus, GM: poet and musician of Thrace, son of Apollo and the muse Calliope. He received from Apollo the lyre, which he played so marvelously that he charmed the wild beasts and could make the trees and rocks move and the rivers stand still. When Eurydice, his wife, died from a serpent bite, Orpheus followed her to Hades and begged to be allowed to bring her back. Pluto was so moved by his music that he consented, but on condition that Eurydice follow behind and Orpheus never look back.

Orpheus promised; but just as they were leaving the world of gloom, he gave one backward look to see if she was really there. Eurydice vanished again to the realm of the dead, and Orpheus, inconsolable, returned home and vowed never more to associate with women. In revenge, the Maenads, women who cel-ebrated the rites of Dionysus, wildly tore him to pieces, throwing his head and the lyre into the river Hebrus.

Several operas have been based on this theme, of which the most famous is the German composer Christoph Gluck's *Orfeo ed Euridice* (1762).

Osiris: ancient Egyptian god and judge of the dead. He was the brother and husband of Isis and the father of Horus. As ruler of Egypt he taught civilization to his subjects. He was killed by his brother Set (Typhon) but was resurrected by Isis and Horus, who defeated Set, establishing the worship of Osiris throughout Egypt.

Othello: tragedy by Shakespeare, produced in 1604. Othello, a Moor who has become a military hero in the service of Venice, is deceived by the lies and insinuations of the villain Iago, who bears Othello a grudge for promoting Cassio instead of him. He becomes enraged at his innocent wife Desdemona, the daughter of a Venetian senator, and strangles her. When he discovers he has wronged her, he commits suicide. Operas by Rossini (1816) and by Verdi (1887) were based on the play.

Ottava rima: *See* Stanza.

Our Town: Pulitzer Prize–winning play by U.S. writer Thornton Wilder, first performed in 1938, dealing with the cycle of life in a New England town called Grovers Corners, but meant to represent Everytown. A narrator comments on the town's activities and leading citizens; the action includes the courtship and marriage of a young couple, the death in childbirth of the young wife, and her burial. More important than the plot, perhaps, was the play's imaginative structure and manner of presentation.

Overcoat, The: short story by the Russian writer Nikolai Gogol, published in 1842. Akaki Akakyevich is a poor clerk whose great deed is to purchase a new overcoat, which makes him the center of attention at the office. When thieves steal his new coat, Akaki dies of grief and becomes a ghost who haunts St. Petersburg's citizens, particularly bureaucrats, to steal their coats. Akaki became a symbol to the Russians of the insulted and injured little man.

Oxymoron: *See* Figures of speech.

P

Paladins: twelve peers of Charlemagne, inmates of his palace, and his companions at arms. The word *paladin* at first meant palace dweller and then warrior. The names of the twelve differ in the *chansons de geste* that celebrate their heroic deeds, but the most famous of the twelve were Roland and Oliver, Ganelon the traitor, Ferumbras, and Ogier the Dane.

civilization
US

civilisation
Brit.

center
US

centre
Brit.

Palladium, GM: famous statue of Pallas Athena possessed by the Trojans. No harm could befall the city so long as the statue remained within it, but Odysseus and Diomedes stole it for the Greeks, and Troy lost its protection.

Pamela, or Virtue Rewarded: first work of fiction by the pioneer English novelist Samuel Richardson, published in two parts, 1740–1741. It is also the first novel in letter form and, because this technique permits a direct and intimate revelation of the characters' thoughts and feelings, *Pamela* is regarded as the forerunner of the modern psychological novel. Pamela Andrews is a young servant girl whose letters to her anxious parents are vivid accounts of her efforts to ward off the dishonorable advances of her master, Mr. B. Even. When she is kidnapped and held incommunicado by Mr. B., she manages to sneak out letters on her progress. Mr. B. at last proposes marriage, and Pamela becomes the very model of a virtuous wife, attempting to shame Mr. B. into fidelity.

Pan, GM: god of nature, forests, fields, and wildlife; the patron of flocks and shepherds; associated especially with the pastures of Arcadia. He is represented in human shape with the legs and horns of a goat. He invented the panpipe, or shepherd's pipe, a musical instrument made of reeds. He was fond of chasing nymphs and is a symbol of eroticism. He also frightened lonely travellers. Mysterious fear that comes from no obvious cause is called "panic" after him.

Pandarus: *See* Troilus.

Pandora, GM: first woman; Zeus gave her a closed box, which he told her to give to her husband but never to open. In time Pandora became curious and opened the forbidden box. All the evils of humanity came crowding out and were let loose in the world; hope alone remained in the box, to comfort man in his afflictions.

Pantheon: temple for all the gods of a people or for their honored dead; also used to refer to all the gods. The Pantheon in Rome, built about 27 B.C. and rebuilt in the second century A.D., and the Panthéon in Paris, built between 1764 and 1781, are both marked by a great dome on top and contain the graves of many famous men.

Panza, Sancho: in Cervantes's novel *Don Quixote,* Quixote's squire, an earthbound, realistic peasant whose practical comments serve as a foil for Quixote's airy fantasies.

Paolo and Francesca: in Dante's *Inferno,* adulterous lovers who are among the most pitiable of all the sinners that Dante meets in Hell. They tell the poet how, as they were reading of Lancelot and Guinevere, their love was aroused and "That day we read no

further." In real life Francesca was the young wife of one of the counts of Rimini. She fell in love with her brother-in-law, Paolo Malatesta. When her husband discovered them together, he had them put to death (1284).

Parable: short narrative in which everyday experiences are used to illustrate a moral theme. The teachings of Christ are often couched in parables in which he likens God or himself to a king, a shepherd, a sower, a father, or an employer.

Paradise Lost: epic poem in blank verse by English poet John Milton, published in 1667. Its purpose is "to justify the ways of God to man." It relates how some of the angels revolted against God and were cast out of Heaven into Hell. They decide to revenge themselves upon the Almighty by invading Earth and leading man to sin. Satan, chief of the fallen angels, corrupts Adam and Eve and brings about their expulsion from Paradise. *Paradise Lost* is regarded as the greatest epic in the English language. Milton wrote a sequel, *Paradise Regained* (1671), which deals with the theme of redemption.

PANDORA: a watercolor by English artist and poet Dante Gabriel Rossetti.

Paradox: self-contradictory statement that nevertheless makes sense. An example is Oscar Wilde's remark, "There is only one thing in the world worse than being talked about, and that is not being talked about." Paradoxical situations, treated seriously or humorously, are often the basis for a plot.

Parallel Lives: *See* Biography.

Paris, GM: son of Priam, king of Troy. He was sought out to judge which of the three goddesses—Aphrodite, Hera, and Athena—was the fairest. Paris awarded the prize to Aphrodite, who promised him the most beautiful woman in the world for his wife. She helped him win and carry off Helen, who was the wife of Menelaus of Sparta. Thus Paris caused the Trojan War and the destruction of Troy. He was killed by an arrow shot by Philoctetes the day the city was taken. *See also* Eris.

Parody: literary form in which a serious composition, or the general manner of a serious author, is imitated in phraseology and style in order to point up the absurdities of the original. It is a particularly devastating form of criticism. Some parodies endure when their originals are forgotten.

Parzival: 13th-century German epic, written by Wolfram von Eschenbach, considered one of the greatest works of the Middle Ages. Its hero Parzival is the Arthurian knight Perceval, whose outstanding traits are innocence and simplicity. He stops at the castle of the Fisher King (Amfortas), the keeper of the Holy Grail. The Grail knights are under an enchantment and the Fisher King is dying of a wound that only a "stainless fool" can heal by proffering sympathy. Although Parzival is puzzled by the strange and wonderful things he sees there, such as the *graal,* a marvelous dish carried in a procession, and a bleeding spear, he is ashamed of calling attention to his ignorance and asks no questions. After a long spiritual quest, Parzival finds the Fisher King again and asks the question that heals the wound; he succeeds Amfortas as Grail Keeper. This story is the subject of Richard Wagner's last opera *Parsifal* (1882). *See also* Holy Grail; Perceval.

Passage to India, A: novel by British writer E. M. Forster, published in 1924. Set in colonial India, it explores the enormous gulf of misunderstanding that exists between the Indians and their British rulers. Mrs. Moore comes to India to visit her son, accompanied by his fiancée, Adela Quested. Both Englishwomen are eager to know "the real India." Mrs. Moore, who has an intuitive sympathy for Oriental thought, is able to bridge the gap between East and West in her delicate friendship with the young Indian, Dr. Aziz. But Adela is unable to rise above stereotyped reactions; while alone with Dr. Aziz in the Marabar caves, she imagines that he has assaulted her. Her accusations lead to a trial of Dr. Aziz that unleashes the repressed antagonisms of both races.

Pastoral: tradition in literature and art, invented by the Greek poet Theocritus in the third century B.C. It portrays idealized shepherds, milkmaids, or other rustics who live far from the bustle of civilized life in an idyllic never-never land (usually called Arcadia), where they engage in innocent pleasures and amorous dalliance. Pastoral poetry developed strict conventions. Its tradition was revived in the Renaissance and was extremely popular in England. Edmund Spenser's *Shepheardes Calender,* Philip Sidney's *Arcadia,* and Christopher Marlowe's "The Passionate Shepherd to His Love" are examples. Pastoral painting was important in France before the Revolution; Beethoven's sixth symphony, describing country life, is called the "Pastoral."

Paterson: long poem by U.S. doctor/poet William Carlos Williams, published in four volumes from 1946 to 1951, with a postscript entitled "Book Five" added in 1958. Writing in a vernacular, structureless style about the town of Paterson, New Jersey, Williams is really, through the depiction of a semiautobiographical character, exploring the role of man in modern America.

Patroclus: *See* Iliad.

Paul Bunyan: hero of lumber-camp folklore of the American timber country—from Michigan, Wisconsin, and Minnesota to the Pacific Northwest. The huge lumberjack became a symbol of American expansiveness and inventiveness; the tales of his incredible feats have been retold in different versions by many authors. Most say that Paul was born in Maine and rocked to sleep in a 20-foot boat off the coast. He later turned up in the midwestern forests and finally walked to Oregon because the trains were so slow. Some standard characters turn up in most of the Paul Bunyan tales: Johnny Inkslinger, his "businessman" partner; Hot Biscuit Slim, the fabulous lumber-camp cook; and of course, Babe, the Blue Ox, his most prized possession and companion. Babe was found in the Winter of the Blue Snow; he measured 42 axe handles and a plug of Star tobacco between the horns. Whenever Paul decided to move, he hitched the whole camp to Babe, and the huge ox would drag the bunkhouse, the kitchen, and all the other buildings to the new spot.

Paul himself was the greatest logger of them all. Two cuts were all he ever made for one tree. Often he made one cut with the forward swing and cut the tree behind him on the back swing. One of the most famous of the tall tales relates how Paul and Babe straightened the narrow, crooked roads in upper Michigan. Some were so crooked that they doubled back, and the men would meet themselves coming from work. So Paul hitched Babe to one end of a road, yelled "Pull," and the ox pulled the whole thing straight. Paul found he had 14 miles of extra road left, so he rolled them up and sold them to Chicago for a street—Michigan Avenue, named for the state it came from.

Pecos Bill: hero of cowboy folklore of the American West. When his parents moved to west Texas, Bill fell out of the wagon when it was crossing the Pecos River. He grew up with the coyotes and thought he was a coyote himself. One day a cowboy came along and asked him why he was "running around naked with the varmints," and that was the first inkling he had that he was human.

Deciding to take up human ways, Pecos Bill became the greatest cowhand in the West. He raised his horse, Widow-Maker, on dynamite and nitroglycerin, and no one else could ride him. Bill, though, could ride anything; he once rode a cyclone across three states until, unable to throw him, it rained out from under him and made the Grand Canyon. He invented the lariat and cattle-roping, the six-shooter, and all the best "cuss" words; and he taught the bronco how to buck. Once he saved the cattle country from a Pacific tidal wave: when he heard it was coming, he quickly threw up a levee—which was later called the Rocky Mountains.

Bill married a famous rider named Slue-Foot Sue. After she died—and there are many different legends about her fate—he was so lonely that he took to drinking nitroglycerin, but it soon lost its kick and he started adding fish hooks and barbed wire. One night, they struck together, and that little spark was the end of Pecos Bill.

Peer Gynt: poetic drama by Norwegian author Henrik Ibsen, presented in 1867. Peer is a farm boy whose egotistical appetite for life and self-gratification is at once the pride and despair of his mother Ase and the gentle girl Solveig who loves him. Peer disgraces his family by abducting a girl on her wedding night and later deserting her. He flees to the mountain trolls and marries an elf-king's daughter. He then deserts her to travel the world, where he makes and loses fortunes, trafficking in slaves or Bibles. In middle age he realizes his life is worthless and returns to Norway where he is redeemed by Solveig's abiding love for him. The *Peer Gynt Suites* by the composer Edvard Grieg were originally written as incidental music for the play.

Pegasus, GM: swift and marvelous winged horse, born from the blood of Medusa at the moment Perseus cut off her head. Hippocrene, the fountain of poetic inspiration, gushed forth when his hoof struck a rock on the Muses' mountain; hence the winged horse is a symbol of poetry. Athena gave a golden bridle to the young hero Bellerophon, who tamed Pegasus with it and went on to wonderful adventures.

Pelias: *See* Argonauts.

Peloponnesian War, The: history written by Thucydides, an Athenian general who was an eyewitness to the disastrous war between Athens and Sparta (431–404 B.C.) that brought about the demise of the Greek city-states. Believing this to have been the largest-scale war in history, the author records it in minute and objective detail. He assesses its true cause to have been the threat of the ascendancy of Athens, a democratic and mercantile naval power, to the conservative agrarian-military power, Sparta.

Pelops: *See* House of Atreus.

Penelope: wife of Odysseus. During her husband's long absence she put off her horde of suitors with the excuse that she must finish the winding sheet she was weaving for her father-in-law. Each night she unraveled the work she had done that day. Penelope's Web is still an epithet that is given to any never-finished task.

Penseroso, Il: *See* L'allegro.

Pentameter: *See* Meter.

Perceval: knight of the Round Table and the original seeker of the Holy Grail. The earliest stories about Perceval deal with the education of a simpleton and have their roots in folklore. At King Arthur's court, his many naive blunders are redeemed by his innocent charm. In later versions, Perceval became a hero in the long quest after the Holy Grail. *See also* Holy Grail; Parzival.

Père Goriot, Le: *See* Human Comedy, The.

Persephone, also called *Kore* (maiden), GM: daughter of Zeus and Demeter. She was carried off by Pluto to be his wife and queen of Hades. The prayers of Demeter moved Zeus to let Persephone return, but only if she had eaten nothing in the lower world. It was discovered that she had eaten seven pomegranate seeds and was therefore in bondage to Hades. She was allowed to spend part of the year with her mother but was compelled to return to Pluto for the other part. Her return to life symbolizes the growth of crops; her sojourn in the lower world, the planting of seed. In Roman versions, she is called Proserpina or Proserpine, daughter of Ceres.

dishonorable
US

dishonourable
Brit.

civilized
US

civilised
Brit.

realizes
US

realises
Brit.

Legendary Figures from American Folklore

Johnny Appleseed	"Snake" Magee	Rip Van Winkle
Paul Bunyan	Pecos Bill	Robinson Crusoe
John Henry		Alfred Bulltop Stormalong

Perseus, GM: son of Zeus and Danae. He founded the city of Mycenae, killed the dreadful Gorgon Medusa, and rescued Andromeda from the rock where she was chained as a sacrifice to a sea monster.

Personification: *See* Figures of speech.

Peter Pan: play for children by English author Sir James Barrie, performed in 1904. Peter is an elflike little personage who refuses to "grow up." He lures the Darling children to his home in Never-Never land where they meet the jealous fairy Tinker Bell and the terrible pirate Captain Hook.

Phaedo: dialogue by the Greek philosopher Plato, written in the fourth century B.C. It deals with the last day in the life of Socrates. In prison and condemned to death, the old philosopher discusses with his friends the immortality of the soul. At the appointed time, Socrates drinks the hemlock cheerfully, reproves his friends for their tears, and lies down to die; he dies reminding Crito that he owes a cock to Asclepius and asking him to pay the debt.

Phaedra: *See* Hippolytus.

Phaethon, GM: son of Helios, the sun god. He begged to be allowed to drive his father's great four-horse chariot across the sky. The boy soon lost control of the fiery horses; the chariot dipped too near the earth and scorched it, forming the Sahara desert, and the whole world would have been burned had not Zeus killed Phaethon with a thunderbolt.

Philemon: *See* Baucis and Philemon.

Philistines: Biblical enemy of the Israelites. In the 19th century the English critic Matthew Arnold took the term "philistine" from German student slang to refer to the prosperous members of the middle class who were indifferent to cultural and moral values.

Philoctetes, GM: hero who inherited the miraculous bow of Hercules. Because of an evil-smelling wound that would not heal, the Greeks on their way to Troy abandoned Philoctetes on the isle of Lemnos. When they learned that they needed Hercules's bow to win the war, Odysseus and Neoptolemus (or sometimes Diomedes) went to Lemnos to obtain it by treachery. Sophocles' play *Philoctetes* (409 B.C.) deals with young Neoptolemus's refusal to deceive or abandon the bitter, suffering hero. Philoctetes is brought back to Troy where his wound is healed and he slays Paris in battle. The 20th-century U.S. critic Edmund Wilson made Philoctetes the symbol of the artist in *The Wound and the Bow* (1941).

Philosophes: name applied to the French intellectual leaders of the 18th-century Enlightenment. Among them

PICTURE OF DORIAN GRAY: The portrait reflects the degeneracy of its youthful subject.

were scientists, philosophers, social critics, and writers, of whom the best-known were Denis Diderot, Voltaire, Baron de Montesquieu, Marquis de Condorcet, and Jean Jacques Rousseau, as well as the Scottish-born philosopher David Hume. Their great joint work was the compilation of a monumental *Encyclopédie* (1751–1772). Their skeptical attitudes toward religion, government, and social traditions are thought to have helped pave the way for the French Revolution. *See also* Enlightenment, The.

Phoebe, GM: name for Artemis as moon goddess.

Phoebus, GM: name for Apollo as sun god, meaning "shining."

Phoenix: fabulous bird connected with Egyptian sun worship. It was large, very beautiful, and always male; there were never two in the world at once. It was believed to live for hundreds or thousands of years. At the end of that time it built a nest in which it burned itself alive. From the ashes rose the new, young phoenix.

PHOENIX: The mythical bird rises from the ashes of an old bird in a 1602 woodcut.

Picaresque: fictional recounting of the life of a charming rogue; his or her adventures afford the writer the opportunity to satirize society as the hero encounters bigger knaves than himself

in the high courts and in church positions. The picaresque originated in 16th-century Spain, with the anonymous *Lazarillo de Tormes* as its earliest example. In English, an early picaresque is Defoe's *Moll Flanders*.

Picaresques are often considered forerunners of the novel. Later works with picaresque qualities include Voltaire's *Candide* and the novel *Roderick Random* by Tobias Smollett.

Pickwick Papers, The (more correctly, *The Posthumous Papers of the Pickwick Club*): story by English author Charles Dickens, issued in parts in 1836–1837. It is made up of a series of adventures of Samuel Pickwick, Esq., founder and president of the Pickwick Club, his valet Sam Weller, and other companions. The work made Dickens famous at the age of 24.

Picture of Dorian Gray, The: novel by the Irish-born author Oscar Wilde, written in 1891. A strikingly beautiful youth, Dorian Gray, embarks on a vicious and depraved life. His deeds do not show in his appearance but only in a portrait of himself that hangs in an upper room. The portrait reflects each new act of degeneracy and so mirrors his soul. In desperation Dorian murders the artist of the portrait, then stabs the picture. He is found dead, his body grotesquely revealing his state of corruption, his portrait once more that of a handsome, innocent youth.

Pied Piper of Hamelin, The: narrative poem by the English poet Robert Browning, published in 1842, telling a moral tale from German folklore about a magician who offered—for a fee—to rid the town of Hamelin, on the River Weser, of a plague of rats. Taking his pipe, he played the rats a tune that had them swarming after him and into the river, where they drowned. The town corporation, however, refused to pay the piper, who once more took his pipe but this time lured the town children away and into a hillside, from which they never returned.

Pierrot ("little Peter"): gentle, lovesick clown, a stock character in early French and English pantomime who replaced the earlier Italian Arlecchino (Harlequin) as the lover of Columbine.

Piers Plowman (full title, *The Vision of William Concerning Piers the Plowman*): Middle English satirical and allegorical poem of the 14th century, ascribed to William Langland. It was first printed in 1550. The form is the familiar medieval dream allegory. The poet on a May morning falls asleep upon the Malvern hills and in his dream encounters representative types of the society of his day. Piers, a simple farmer (an allegorical figure for Christ), offers to guide them to the Tower of Truth if they will first help him cultivate his field. But only a few of them are willing to help, that is, work for salvation.

Pilgrim's Progress, The: allegory by the English preacher John Bunyan, written during his imprisonment for Nonconformist views and issued in two parts, 1678 and 1684. It describes the adventures of its hero, Christian, on his way from the City of Destruction to the Celestial City. He passes through the Slough of Despond, fights with the evil Apollyon, looks on Vanity Fair, passes the castle of the Giant Despair and, after these and many other trials, arrives at the Delectable Mountains and crosses the Black River to the Shining Gate. The book's plain, direct Anglo-Saxon style made it a great popular favorite, and for many years it occupied a place second only to the Bible in English homes.

Pillars of Hercules: two headlands opposite each other at the Strait of Gibraltar, supposed to have been raised up by Hercules in his travels to find the cattle of Geryon. They were Calpe (Gibraltar in Europe) and Abila (Sierra Bullones in Africa).

Pinocchio, The Adventures of: enduring children's story by the Italian writer Carlo Lorenzini, who published it in 1883 under the pseudonym "Collodi." Pinocchio, a puppet who comes to life, has several adventures whose outcome is designed to teach young readers the difference between right and wrong: for example, whenever Pinocchio tells a lie his nose grows long; when he tells the truth, it reduces to its normal size again.

Pit and the Pendulum, The: short story by U.S. author Edgar Allan Poe, published in 1842, in which a prisoner of the Inquisition describes the harrowing tortures to which he was subjected in the dungeons of Toledo.

Pixie or **pixy:** in English folklore, a fairy or sprite who mischievously leads people astray, rattles pans, knocks over buckets, and kisses girls in the dark.

Plague, The: novel by the French existentialist philosopher Albert Camus, published in 1947. On his daily rounds in the Algerian city of Oran, the novel's doctor-hero, Bernard Rieux, notices a dead rat. More and more dead rats appear in the city, then the first human cases come, and Oran is in the grip of an epidemic of bubonic plague. Although Rieux sees the ultimate futility of his efforts, he does all he can to relieve the suffering of those around him. On the surface, the book is a vivid chronicle of a calamity, but it also may be seen as an allegory for the Nazi occupation of France and for the human condition itself; Rieux's humanistic response to a hopeless situation represents Camus' solution to man's dilemma in an absurd world.

Platonic love: generally understood as a nonsexual attachment between a man and a woman based on intellectual affinities and mutual admiration. It is not derived directly from the philosopher Plato, who believed that sexual attraction for a beautiful youth led to a love of beauty itself, which, in turn, led to a love of the Good. The modern idea of platonic love stems from the Neoplatonists of the Italian Renaissance, who popularized the concept. The poems of the sculptor Michelangelo addressed to the virtuous widow Vittoria Colonna are an expression of platonic love.

Playboy of the Western World, The: play by the Irish dramatist John Millington Synge, performed in 1907, about a young country lad, Christie Mahon, who thinks he has killed his father and, horrified, flees his home. But he is received in a nearby town (where men are scarce) as though he were a hero, bold and brave, and the flattering attentions bring about a complete change in his naturally timid personality. Christie's moment of glory is over when his father turns up alive. The play opened at Dublin's Abbey Theatre and is considered one of the masterpieces of the Irish literary renaissance. But it originally offended Irish sensitivities, and its early performances caused riots in Dublin, New York, and Philadelphia.

PINOCCHIO: an early illustration of the puppet come to life.

Pleiades, GM: seven daughters of Atlas. They were raised to a constellation in the heavens after their deaths.

Plough and the Stars, The: four-act tragicomedy by the Irish playwright Sean O'Casey, performed in 1926. It portrays some quarrelsome, gossiping, heavy-drinking occupants of a Dublin tenement during the week of the Easter Rising against the British in 1916. When the shooting starts, these brawling slum-dwellers are magically transformed. The gallantry of this rebellion against odds seems to rub off even on those who are opposed to the Irish resistance. Without denying his characters their sordid or comic moments, O'Casey conveys a picture of what the poet Yeats called the "terrible beauty" born of this event.

Plutarch's Lives: *See* Biography.

Pluto or **Pluton,** GM: most commonly used name for Hades, the god of the lower world, associating him with the god Plutus.

Plutus, GM: god of the earth's abundance and of wealth. He was the son of Demeter and was blinded by Zeus, according to some accounts, so he would bestow wealth impartially to all. Aristophanes' comedy *Plutus* (388 B.C.) deals with the restoration of his sight.

Poems, Chiefly in the Scottish Dialect: first book of poems by Scottish poet Robert Burns, published in 1786, in Kilmarnock, Scotland. (It is also known as the Kilmarnock volume.) It includes such Scottish favorites as "To a Mouse" and "To a Louse," as well as poems written in standard English, such as "The Cotter's Saturday Night." At the time that they were written, the English poems were more highly appreciated than those in the Scottish dialect, and they brought the young poet immediate fame. Later critics have favored the dialect poems.

Poetics, The: influential treatise on literary criticism, written by the Greek thinker Aristotle c 335–322 B.C. In this work, Aristotle urges the superiority of tragedy over other literary forms. He arrives at his critical principles empirically through close analysis of the tragedies that he finds most successful. Tragedy is defined by him as an "imitation of an action," in which a man of noble stature, through some "tragic flaw" *(hamartia),* rather than vice, falls from a high estate to catastrophe. Pride *(hubris),* which causes heroes to disregard laws or warnings, is a common tragic flaw. The purpose of tragedy, Aristotle believes, is to evoke terror and pity, and effect in the spectators a purgation *(catharsis)* of these emotions. Some of his observations on the limits of action and time in drama gave rise to rigid formulations—the "unities" of action, place, and time—which governed neoclassical drama in the 1600s.

Poet laureate: lifetime salaried appointment held by the official poet of the British court. The official laureateship began with the appointment of John Dryden in 1668. At one time it was considered proper for the poet laureate to commemorate national events and royal birthdays with a poem, but since 1843, no duties have been attached to the office.

Poetry: earliest and most characteristic type of literature. It seeks to express action, feeling, or thought in a concentrated imaginative way through the use

PRIDE AND PREJUDICE: The main characters, Elizabeth Bennett and Mr. Darcy, each overcome a vice to bring their romance to a happy conclusion.

of condensed, arresting, and emotive language that follows a metrical or rhythmic pattern. From the most primitive to the most sophisticated societies, poetry is regarded as having an almost magical value. Poetry is often divided into three types: lyric, narrative, and dramatic.

Point Counter Point: novel by the English writer Aldous Huxley, published in 1928; his most complex work. It deals with a set of sophisticated intellectuals who are unable to realize their expectations or to find wholeness and satisfaction in either love or work. The novel is a *roman à clef;* that is, some of the characters are thought to be based on actual literary figures such as Katherine Mansfield and D. H. Lawrence.

Polynices: *See* Seven Against Thebes.

Polyphemus: in the *Odyssey,* a Cyclops. When Odysseus and twelve of his men trespassed in his cave, Polyphemus kept them prisoner and began devouring them. Odysseus and his remaining men escaped by getting the giant drunk, putting out his eye with a burning stake, and then concealing themselves beneath the sheep as the flocks left the cave to graze. Polyphemus prayed to his father, the sea god Poseidon, that Odysseus would reach home "late . . . in evil case, with the loss of all his company, in the ship of strangers. . . ." The further misfortunes that befell Odysseus were arranged by Poseidon in answer to the Cyclops's prayer. *See also* Cyclopes.

Poor Richard's Almanack: series of almanacs by American statesman and author Benjamin Franklin, published regularly from 1732 to 1757, supposedly the work of a fictitious Richard Saunders. Many of the best-known American proverbs, such as "Early to bed and early to rise, makes a man healthy, wealthy, and wise," are from this source. Some of Poor Richard's sayings are actually of ancient origin, but Franklin often gave them an American slant. Richard's maxims on thrift were collected into a single issue, "The Way to Wealth," which enjoyed international popularity.

Porgy: novel by U.S. author DuBose Heyward, published in 1925. The story concerns Porgy, a lonely black cripple, and his love for Bess. Porgy kills Bess's former lover, Crown. While he is being questioned, Bess deserts him. The story is the basis for the folk opera *Porgy and Bess* (1935), composed in blues and jazz style by George Gershwin.

Portrait of a Lady, The: novel by U.S. expatriate author Henry James, published in 1881. It is the story of an idealistic and independent American girl, Isabel Archer, whose naiveté make her a prey of sophisticated Europeans. Isabel comes to realize her failure but proudly accepts it.

Portrait of the Artist as a Young Man, A: largely autobiographical novel by the Irish author James Joyce, published in 1916. Set in Dublin, it depicts Stephen Dedalus, its central character, through childhood, youth, and early manhood. It is about Stephen's awakening sense of

BENJAMIN FRANKLIN as a young man published *Poor Richard's Almanack.*

himself as an artist and as an individual. The book uses "stream-of-consciousness," which presents a character's thoughts and feelings without authorial comment. Stephen breaks with his social, national, family, and religious inheritance. Stephen Dedalus is also a leading character in *Ulysses* (1922).

Poseidon, GM: god of the sea and all waters. He was a son of Cronus and Rhea, and brother to Zeus and Pluto. He created the first horse and was worshiped as a god of horses. He was also the "earth-shaker," the god of earthquakes, and of bulls. He was often pictured with a trident and holding a dolphin or fish. The Romans identified him with their Neptune.

Power and the Glory, The: novel by the English writer Graham Greene, published in 1940. It is set in a certain Mexican state during a time of revolution, when religion is suppressed. The hero, Father Montez, although an alcoholic and a sinner, refuses to renounce his calling; he lives as a fugitive performing his priestly services wherever needed. When he is at last captured and shot, another priest secretly arrives to replace him.

Pre-Raphaelite Brotherhood: group of English artists and writers formed under the leadership of the poet and painter Dante Gabriel Rossetti in 1848. They chose their name to show their opposition to conventional academic painting, which they believed stemmed from the style of the Italian Renaissance painter Raphael. The Pre-Raphaelites intended to use their art as an uplifting moral device, drawing on nature for subjects; Rossetti in particular was influenced by medieval subjects and style. Although the movement was specifically directed toward painting, it attracted writers and critics, including Rossetti's brother William and sister Christina, as well as John Ruskin. Rossetti also brought together a group of younger artists, including Edward Burne-Jones and William Morris, the nucleus of the aesthetic movement of the later 1800s.

Priam: in the *Iliad,* the last of the Trojan kings. He had 50 sons, including Hector and Paris, and twelve daughters, among them Cassandra and Polyxena. He was killed by Neoptolemus, the son of Achilles, when Troy was taken. *See also* Hecuba.

Pride and Prejudice: novel by English author Jane Austen, written under the title *First Impressions* in 1796 (when she was 21) and published after considerable revision in 1813. The scene is laid in the English countryside and the plot concerns the Bennett family's attempts to find suitable husbands for their three daughters. The intimate drawing of the book's middle-class characters is done with humor and charm. Prejudice is represented by Elizabeth Bennett;

pride, by Mr. Darcy, her wealthy suitor. As Darcy overcomes his pride, Elizabeth overcomes her prejudice, and the two are happily married at last.

Prince, The: political treatise by the Italian statesman-philosopher Niccolò Machiavelli, written in 1513 and dedicated to a younger member of the Medici family. Concerned with statecraft, it drew on the past for lessons as to how a prince ought to behave, pointing to Cesare Borgia—who combined personal charisma, brute force, and political cunning in upholding his authority—as the ideal prince. *The Prince* was influential throughout Renaissance Europe, where it earned Machiavelli a reputation for diabolical cunning, and was used as a practical manual of tyranny.

Procrustes, GM: brigand who shortened or stretched out his victims until they fit his bed. He was killed in the same manner by the hero Theseus. The term "Procrustean bed" has come to mean something that one must conform to against one's nature.

Prometheus, GM: son of the Titan Iapetus; brother of Atlas and Epimetheus. His name is thought to mean "the forethinker." Prometheus has come to symbolize the struggle of human intellect and aspiration against an indifferent or hostile cosmos. In some stories, he was the creator of mankind; in all stories, he was the great hero of culture, the founder of civilization. Defying Zeus, he stole fire from heaven in a hollow fennel stalk and gave it to man, teaching him its many uses. To punish him for this act—and possibly also for his refusal to divulge the secret of Zeus's final overthrow—Zeus had him chained to a rock, where an eagle fed perpetually on his liver, which was regenerated each night only to be devoured again each day. Though this punishment was to be eternal, Prometheus was at last freed by Hercules.

Prometheus's torture and defiance are celebrated by Aeschylus in the tragedy *Prometheus Bound* (written c 478 B.C.), the only extant play of a Prometheus trilogy; the story of his triumph and liberation is told in Shelley's four-act poetic drama *Prometheus Unbound* (1820).

Prose: speech or writing that is distinguished from poetry chiefly by its lack of regular metrical pattern. Prose literature developed much later than poetry. Although prose is today generally considered more suitable for practical, expository, or narrative purposes, in ancient times, even histories and scientific or philosophical treatises were written in verse. In post-classical Europe, the Icelandic sagas (c 12th century) are the earliest examples of a highly developed prose literature. In English literature, although prose was written earlier, it was not until the emergence of the great 18th-century prose stylists—Addison, Swift, Johnson, and Burke—

that prose acquired full prestige. Later, as the novel developed as an art form, differences between prose and poetry became less distinct. Free verse is often rhythmic prose, and novelists use imagery, symbols, rhythm, and emotive language in much the same ways as they are used by poets.

Proserpina: *See* Persephone.

Proteus, GM: lesser sea god, herder of the flocks of Poseidon. He had great wisdom and could foretell the future, but would not answer questions unless compelled to. If seized, he would rapidly change from one terrifying shape to another, but if the questioner held him fast, he would finally resume his own shape and give the true answers. The word *protean,* meaning changeable, comes from his name.

Proverb: brief saying that presents in epigrammatic form a bit of traditional wisdom. Proverbs form part of the heritage of peoples throughout the world, and there is a version of most of the well known proverbs in almost all languages. "Curiosity killed the cat" and "A rolling stone gathers no moss" are typical.

Pseudonym or **nom de plume** ("pen name"): fictitious name used by a writer either to conceal his identity or simply because he prefers it. Women writers have often used masculine pen names because they did not think their work would be judged seriously if their sex were known. Some famous writers who used pseudonyms are listed below.

Psyche: heroine of a tale that is probably of Greek origin, but is known through the Latin classic *The Golden Ass* by Apuleius. Psyche is so beautiful that she incites the jealousy of the goddess Venus, who sends her son Cupid to misguide Psyche in love. But Cupid falls in

love with her himself. He visits her only at night on the condition that she does not try to behold him. One night Psyche tries to observe him with a lamp while he sleeps. Trembling at his beauty, she spills a drop of oil on him, and Cupid wakes and flees. Psyche, after performing many impossible tasks imposed on her by Venus, is at last granted immortality and reunited with Cupid.

Puck: in English folklore, a hobgoblin, usually of evil intent. In medieval times he became merely a mischievous fairy, often called Robin Goodfellow. The Puck of Shakespeare's *Midsummer Night's Dream* is a mischievous servant of Oberon.

Pun: play on words involving similar- or identical-sounding words with different meanings (one: won). Although the poet Oliver Wendell Holmes called it "the lowest form of wit" and Joseph Addison termed it "false wit," puns have a long tradition.

In early Greek and Hebrew literature, puns on names were believed to have magical properties. Since names determined fate, one could curse the enemy by finding an ominous pun in his name. Shakespeare was fond of puns, both serious and humorous, using them frequently in his plays. A famous pun appears in *Romeo and Juliet,* when Mercutio says, as he is dying, "Ask for me tomorrow and you shall find me a grave man."

The metaphysical poets also made serious use of puns. John Donne, addressing God in "Hymn to God the Father," uses the refrain, "When Thou has done, Thou hast not done . . . ." The phrase can mean either, "When you are finished (forgiving sins), you have not finished," or "When you think you have me (Donne), you still don't have me."

In the 20th century, James Joyce and his followers have continued to make extensive use of puns and other types of wordplay.

The symbols used in this glossary are as follows:

G-Greek
R-Roman
N-Norse
M-myth
L-legend

Pseudonym	Real Name
Sholom Aleichem	Solomon Rabinowitz
Guillaume Apollinaire	Wilhelm Apollinaris de Kostrowitzky
Nicholas Blake	C. Day Lewis
Lewis Carroll	Charles Lutwidge Dodgson
Joseph Conrad	Józef Teodor Konrad Korzeniowski
Isak Dinesen	Karen Blixen
George Eliot	Mary Ann Evans
Anatole France	Jacques Anatole François Thibault
Maxim Gorky	Aleksei Maksimovich Peshkov
O. Henry	William Sydney Porter
John LeCarré	Davis J. M. Carnwell
Katherine Mansfield	Kathleen Mansfield Beauchamp
André Maurois	Émile Herzog
Molière	Jean-Baptiste Poquelin
Frank O'Connor	Michael O'Conovan
George Orwell	Eric Arthur Blair
Ellery Queen	Frederic Dannay and Manfred B. Lee
George Sand	Amandine A.L. Dupin Dudevant
Stendhal	Marie-Henri Beyle
Mark Twain	Samuel L. Clemens
Voltaire	François Marie Arouet

20 History of Literature

Punch and Judy: puppet show in which the leading characters are Punch, a humpbacked, hook-nosed fellow who does outrageous and tragic things with the utmost nonchalance; his wife Judy, whom he beats to death; and his baby, whom he throws out the window. The origin of Punch is to be found in the clown Punchinello of the old *commedia dell'arte.*

PUNCH AND JUDY: a 19th-century view of the traditional puppet show characters who turn family violence into laughter.

Puss in Boots: folk tale about an animal helper that is known in a number of versions throughout the world. The best-known version is Charles Perrault's "Le Chat booté" (1697), in which a resourceful cat brings his poor master great wealth and a king's daughter for a wife.

Pygmalion, GM: sculptor who fell in love with a statue of his own creation. Venus intervened, and the statue, Galatea, came to life. The story inspired several literary works, notably George Bernard Shaw's play *Pygmalion* (1913). Shaw's Pygmalion is Henry Higgins, an English speech expert who bets that he can pass off the vulgar Cockney flower girl Eliza Doolittle as an aristocrat by teaching her to speak proper English. He succeeds brilliantly, but is astonished to find that Eliza has acquired her own power over him. This play was the basis for the musical *My Fair Lady* (1956).

Pyramus and Thisbe: story told in Ovid's *Metamorphoses* of two lovers in Babylonia who can only meet and speak through the wall between their houses. On the night they agree to run away together, Thisbe is frightened by a lion and runs away from the meeting place. Pyramus, arriving late, finds her scarf bloodied by the lion. He believes that she has been killed and falls upon his sword. Finding him dead, Thisbe also kills herself.

A riotous parody of the story is played by Bottom and his companions in Shakespeare's comedy *A Midsummer Night's Dream.*

Q

Quatrain: *See* Stanza.

R

Ragnarök, NM: the "doom of the gods" and the end of the world. It is described in the visionary poem "Völuspá" (Sibyl's Prophecy) in the Icelandic Poetic Edda. The poem foretells a great battle between the Aesir (a race of good gods) and the forces of evil, led by Hel and Loki. The Fenris Wolf kills Odin and is in turn slain by Vitharr, Odin's son. Thor and the Midgard serpent fight to the death, as do Tyr and Garm (Hel's watchdog), Loki and Heimdall (rainbow bridge watchman). The sun and the earth fall into the sea and the sky is consumed by fire. Later the slain god Balder returns from the dead, and a new and happier cycle of life begins.

Ramayana: 24,000-stanza epic poem of India, probably dating from about the beginning of the Christian Era, and attributed to a poet called Valmiki. It relates the deeds of Rama, a mythological hero, particularly his winning of the beautiful Sita for a wife, the abduction of Sita by a demon king, and his rescue of her.

Rape of the Lock, The: mock-heroic epic by English poet Alexander Pope, published in two cantos in 1712, and in five in 1714. The poem uses all the conventions of the heroic epic—an invocation to the muse; supernatural intervention; and a descent to the underworld—to embellish the story of Lord Petre's theft of a lock of hair from the fashionable belle Belinda.

Raskolnikov, Rodion: *See* Crime and Punishment.

Rasselas: romance by the English man of letters Samuel Johnson, published in 1759. In describing Prince Rasselas's fruitless wanderings in search of happiness, Johnson was leveling an attack against the optimism and simplistic formulas for achieving satisfaction that were prevalent in the 18th century. The work has often been likened to Voltaire's *Candide,* which appeared about the same time.

Raven, The: poem by U.S. author Edgar Allan Poe, published in 1845. At midnight in his chamber, the poet is visited by an ominous black bird who answers all his questions with a remorseless, "Nevermore."

Realism: in literature, the accurate representation of actual life. A reaction to the excesses of Romanticism, realism appeared, particularly in the novel, in the later part of the 19th century. Realists tended to emphasize character and its effect on motive and action, to write natural-sounding dialogue, and to dwell on details of everyday life. They abandoned such devices as unlikely coincidences, dramatic recognitions, and surprise endings, thus creating novels that were richer in texture, slower in development. Among the early masters of

realism are the French writers Balzac and Flaubert; the English writers George Eliot, Samuel Butler, and Arnold Bennett; the Russian writers Gogol, Goncharov, Tolstoy, and Chekhov; the U.S. writers William Dean Howells and Mark Twain; and the U.S. expatriate writer Henry James.

Red and the Black, The: novel by the French writer Stendhal, published in 1830. It is a powerful psychological portrait of a social outsider, Julien Sorel, who chooses to rise from his humble origins through a career in the church (the "black" as opposed to the army "red"). Ambitious, romantic, and sensitive, Julien heralded a new type of fictional hero. He ends as a condemned murderer.

Red Badge of Courage, The: novel by U.S. author Stephen Crane, published in 1895 when the author was in his mid-20s. Henry Fleming, a raw country boy, enlists at the outset of the Civil War; the book describes his mental states as he waits for action, his panic under fire, and his final conquest of cowardice through identification with his comrades. It is one of the first books to treat battle realistically rather than as a theater for displays of gallantry; Crane, however, had never been in a war.

Reliques of Ancient English Poetry: collection of traditional ballads, sonnets, songs, and romances, published in 1765 by the English bishop Thomas Percy. It was issued at a time when folk ballads were regarded as crude doggerel. The *Reliques* (or relics) drew the attention of the literary world to their power and artistry. The revival of interest in such folk materials was one of the mainsprings of the 19th-century Romantic movement.

Remembrance of Things Past: series of seven novels by the French writer Marcel Proust, published between 1913 and 1927. The novels are an autobiographical attempt to recapture the past in all its sensory reality. The narrator, beginning with his earliest memory (in *Swann's Way*), moves through free association to the re-creation of the sights, scenes, smells, and the vivid personalities that dominated his childhood. He recaptures the novelty of his first love affairs, first ventures into society, social errors, and social successes. In doing so, he creates a portrait of the snobbish, fashionable world of his day and its less elegant underside. The work is a monumental achievement both as an inner portrait of an individual's growth and change, and as an outer portrait of a society in flux. The English titles of the individual novels are *Swann's Way, Within a Budding Grove, The Guermantes Way, Cities of the Plain, The Captive, The Sweet Cheat Gone,* and *The Past Recaptured.*

Remus: *See* Romulus and Remus.

---

emphasize
US

emphasise
Brit.

theater
US

theatre
Brit.

Renascence: poem by U.S. poet Edna St. Vincent Millay, written when she was about 17, and published in 1912 in *The Lyric Year,* a collection of prize-winning poems. The poet begins with a lyrical description of her home on the Maine coast, where she is suddenly over-whelmed by an intense, painful knowledge of the suffering in the world; in death, she remembers the beauty of the living world and is reborn with a deeper love and understanding of life.

Republic, The: major dialogue by the Greek philosopher and writer Plato; an inquiry into the nature of justice. Seeking to define justice, Socrates proposes the analogy of a perfect society in which justice prevails, thus providing the first literary description of utopia (a term coined later by Sir Thomas More). He describes in detail the education of the guardians (or ruling class), and proposes, among other things, equality of the sexes, eugenic breeding, and children held in common. The dialogue contains the famous parable of the cave, in which chained prisoners attempt to interpret passing shadows. The image is a metaphor for the phenomenal world we inhabit, a mere shadow of the real world.

Restoration: period of English history beginning in 1660 when Charles II was reestablished on the throne. After the 20-year Puritan revolution, literature and drama came back into favor, and the light spirit of comedy replaced the solemnity preferred by the Puritan rulers. Among the comic dramatists of the age were William Congreve and William Wycherly, whose polished, somewhat cynical comedies of manners have remained in the English theatrical repertoire for 300 years.

The greatest literary name of the era was John Dryden. He, too, was an active dramatist, but he is best remembered for his literary criticism ("Essay on Dramatic Poetry") and his accomplished verse translations (the works of Vergil). Dryden's broad and generous appreciation of the literature of the past set the stage for the neoclassical age of Pope and Swift.

Return of the Native, The: sixth novel of English author Thomas Hardy, published in 1878. Clym Yeobright, who has been in Paris, returns to the Wessex village in which he was born, planning to open a school and improve local conditions. His decision disappoints his mother's hopes, and she is alarmed when he falls in love with Eustacia Vye,

RIME OF THE ANCIENT MARINER: Gustave Doré's 19th-century view of the cursed ship in Coleridge's great Romantic poem.

an exotic, restless, and dissatisfied girl. An aura of fateful tragedy broods over their relationship. Clym's mother meets an accidental death, Eustacia drowns herself, and Clym, his sight impaired, finds his vocation as an itinerant preacher and lecturer.

Reynard the Fox: hero of a series of fables about beasts, widely told in France, Germany, Holland, and England during the Middle Ages. The animals behave like men and are often intended as satirical portraits of knights, clergy, or nobles. The characters include Reynard the Fox, Bruin the Bear, Noble the Lion, Baldwin the Ass, Tibert the Cat, Isengrim the Wolf, Grimbert the Badger, Chanticleer the Cock, Partlet the Hen, and various others. In all the versions, though, Reynard is a trickster, representing the triumph of brains over brawn.

Rhinegold or **Rheingold:** in Germanic legend, the cursed treasure of the Nibelungs. *See also* Nibelungenlied.

Rhinoceros: play by the Rumanian-born French dramatist, Eugène Ionesco. Performed in 1960, it is a work in the tradition of the theater of the absurd. At first it seems strange when some characters in the play turn into rhinoceroses, but in time it becomes the thing to do. The main character, Bèranger, becomes an outcast because he does not conform.

Rhyme: correspondence in sound between two accented syllables, as in the words *believe/ deceive.* In poetry, the usual rhyme is end-rhyme, a correspon-dence between the final feet of two or more lines, but internal rhyme (rhyme within the line) is also common, as in the Tennyson line, "The splendor falls on castle walls."

Rhyme royal: *See* Stanza.

Rhythm: in prosody, the cadence of verse, dependent upon a succession of long and short syllables. *See also* Foot; Meter.

Richard II: historical tragedy by Shakespeare, dated 1595. The drama centers on the conflict between the young, spoiled, irresponsible King Richard and his forceful, ambitious cousin Henry Bolingbroke. After the death of Bolingbroke's father, John of Gaunt, Richard confiscates the family lands; Bolingbroke invades England while Richard is away, imprisons him on his return, and assumes possession of the throne as Henry IV. Richard is then murdered by one of Henry's followers. Shakespeare's source for the play was Holinshed's *Chronicles.*

Richard III: historical tragedy by Shakespeare, written about 1594. It deals with the hunchbacked Richard of York, who ensures his succession to the throne by murder, marriage, and political intrigue. After the death of Edward IV, Richard imprisons and later orders the murders of Edward's two young sons (the "little princes in the Tower"), whose guardian he is supposed to be. Meanwhile the rival House of Lancaster has gathered adherents, and the earl of Richmond (Henry Tudor) leads the invading army. Richard, vainly seeking a horse, is killed at the battle of Bosworth Field by Richmond (the future Henry VII, first Tudor king of England).

Shakespeare's portrayal of Richard as a villian whose character is as twisted as his back was immensely popular in Tudor England; it gave Richard a reputation for evil that cannot be wholly sustained by historical fact.

meter	*US*
metre	*Brit.*
centers	*US*
centres	*Brit.*

20 History of Literature

Some Restoration Comedies

The Old Bachelor	William Congreve	Love in a Wood,	William Wycherly
The Double Dealer		or St. James' Park	
Love for Love		The Country Wife	
The Way of the World		The Plain Dealer	

Riders to the Sea: one-act play by John Millington Synge, first performed in Dublin in 1904; one of the finest achievements of the Irish literary renaissance. A starkly tragic play, it pictures a day in an Aran Island fishing village. The old woman Maurya, who has lost four sons at sea, sees her youngest son Bartley brought home drowned.

Right You Are If You Think You Are: play by Italian dramatist Luigi Pirandello, performed in 1917. Signor Ponza and his mother-in-law Signora Frola give their accounts of the marriage of Ponza to Signora Frola's daughter. The audience is teased by conflicting stories throughout the play and left bewildered at the end.

Rime of the Ancient Mariner, The: ballad in archaic style by English Romantic poet Samuel Taylor Coleridge, published in his and Wordsworth's *Lyrical Ballads* (1798). A hoary-headed mariner detains a wedding guest with his grisly tale of a ship blown off course to the South Pole, then saved by an albatross that brings good luck and a south wind. But the mariner shoots the albatross, dooming the ship, and the bird is hung around his neck as a punishment. The ship drifts into a blazing sea around the equator; all die but the ancient mariner, who belongs to Life-in-Death. The mariner's torture finally ends, and the albatross falls into the sea, when he inadvertently blesses the water creatures. He is finally rescued, but his experience compels him to wander and tell his tale.

Ring and the Book, The: dramatic poem by English poet Robert Browning; the longest of his works, it was published in twelve books in 1868–1869. It deals with an actual murder trial in 17th-century Rome. The events of the tragedy are explained in the poem from many different points of view. The condemned man has his last words, but the reader does not know which of the many versions is the truth.

Ring of the Nibelungs, The: *See* Nibelungenlied.

Rip Van Winkle: short story by U.S. author Washington Irving, published in seven parts in his *Sketch Book of Geoffrey Crayon,* 1819–1820. Rip, a good-natured likable ne'er-do-well, goes hunting one day and meets a strange, dwarfish man who leads him into the Catskills, where a group of little men are playing ninepins. Rip drinks the liquor they offer him and falls asleep; he wakes 20 years later to find himself an old man with a long white beard. Back in his village, he discovers that his wife is dead, his daughter has married, and a republic has been established.

Rise of Silas Lapham, The: novel by the U.S. realist William Dean Howells, published in 1885. Silas Lapham, a wealthy paint manufacturer, is a self-made man who attempts to provide advantages for his daughters by building a new house in Boston's exclusive Back Bay area. But the family meets with a cold reception from proper Bostonians, and their discomfort is increased by Lapham's social errors. Though the book ends with the loss of his fortune, Lapham has risen in the sense that he has learned to maintain complete integrity in business.

ROBINSON CRUSOE: an early illustration from a Dutch edition of this world classic.

Rivals, The: lively comedy by English dramatist Richard Brinsley Sheridan, produced in 1775, when its author was 24. In order to satisfy the romantic expectations of Lydia Languish, Captain Jack Absolute woos her while claiming to be penniless Ensign Beverley. When Lydia learns that Beverley is actually the wealthy suitor that her aunt, Mrs. Malaprop, has chosen for her, she spurns him. Meanwhile, Bob Acres, also in love with Lydia, has challenged Ensign Beverley to a duel. When he reaches the field of honor and discovers the ensign to be his friend Jack Absolute, he renounces all claims to Lydia. Absolute's willingness to fight a duel over Lydia satisfies her romantic notions and she agrees to marry him. The brisk action and clever dialogue of this play have brought it continued popularity.

Robbers, The: tragedy by the German poet Friedrich Schiller, performed in 1782. It is a product of the *Sturm und Drang* period and considered the greatest success of the German Romantic theater. It deals with two brothers: Franz von Moor, who usurps his brother's inheritance and fiancée, and Karl von Moor, who becomes the outlaw leader of a robber band. In the end, Franz commits suicide and Karl surrenders to the authorities.

Robin Hood: romantic outlaw of English ballad and legend who lived with his merry companions—Little John, Friar Tuck, Will Scarlet, Allan-a-Dale, Will Stutly, and Maid Marian—in the greenery of Sherwood Forest in Nottinghamshire. Robin and his men were robbers with a difference: They waylaid rich travellers and distributed the bounty among the poor; they particularly delighted in outwitting their chief adversary, the sheriff of Nottingham. Robin himself was renowned for courage, generosity, chivalry, and marvelous skill in archery. There was probably a historical Robin Hood, perhaps in the 12th century, but attempts to identify him with various individuals are not conclusive.

Robinson Crusoe: fictional narrative by the English journalist Daniel Defoe, published in 1719; one of the most famous adventure stories ever written. Robinson Crusoe, sole survivor of a shipwreck, is cast away upon a deserted island, with only his native wits and the gifts of fortune to save him from starvation. He first rescues from the wrecked vessel tools and provisions; next he organizes his time and energy, builds a home, plants crops, and tames wild creatures. At last Crusoe sees the print of a human foot on the sand. The footprint is that of a savage whom Crusoe names Friday and adopts as a servant. The island is invaded by savages and later by European sailors; all of Crusoe's resourcefulness is needed to save his life, but he eventually masters the situation and sails back to England a prosperous man.

Rochester, Edward Fairfax: *See* Jane Eyre.

Roderick Random, The Adventures of: picaresque by English author Tobias Smollett, published in 1748; important for its descriptions of 18th-century British navy life as it relates to the adventures of the penniless Roderick Random, who makes his fortune, aided and thwarted by surprising coincidences common to the genre. *See also* Picaresque.

Roland: nephew of Charlemagne and the most famous of his paladins. The *Chanson de Roland* is the greatest of French heroic epics. It celebrates Roland's friendship with Oliver, whom he first meets as an adversary in battle. The two are so equal in arms that neither can defeat the other, and in mutual admiration they become brothers and companions. In Charlemagne's expedition into Spain against the Saracens (778), Roland distinguishes himself as a champion of Christianity. When the army is returning through the Pyrenees, Ganelon, the traitor, has Roland put in charge of the rear guard. In the pass at Roncesvalles they are outnumbered by a horde of Saracens. The main army is already far in advance, but not beyond the sound of Roland's magic horn, called Oliphant. Oliver begs him three times to sound the horn for help, but Roland is too proud; when he at last consents to call for help, it is too late to save anyone. Charlemagne hears the horn and hastens back to find his favorite warriors dead. He falls with wrath upon the Saracen army and destroys it to a man. Ganelon is examined and, discovered in his treacherous scheme, he is put to death.

Roman à clef (literally, "novel with a key"): work that portrays actual, well known people in the disguise of fictional characters. It may be read simply as a story by those who do not have the "key," but it has an additional dimension of interest for those who do. For an example, see entry on *Point Counter Point*. Many best-selling popular novels, especially those about the worlds of show business and politics are considered *romans à clef*.

Romance: form of vernacular story, originally in verse but later in prose, that developed first in France in the 12th century and spread through Europe. (The word *romance* originally meant vernacular.) Medieval romances dealt with knights, deeds of chivalry, and courtly love; they differed from earlier epics in their lack of moral grandeur and seriousness, their episodic, digressive structure, and their subjectivity. Romances are often replete with magical events, fairies, dragons, wizards, and enchantment. The three main subjects or "matters" *(matières)* of romance are the "matter of France" (tales of Charlemagne and his twelve noble peers); the "matter of Britain" (King Arthur and his knights); and the "matter of Rome" (all ancient tales, whether Greek or Roman).

In modern fiction, novels that freely idealize and are little concerned with realism are called romances.

Romanticism: in the arts, a movement that swept Europe in the late 18th and early 19th centuries, in revolt against the rational ideals of the Enlightenment. The characteristics of the Romantic movement were many and often contradictory; no one artist or work of art embodies all of them. In general, Romanticism celebrated the intuitive, the irrational, the spontaneous, and the free. Romantic poets abandoned the formal rules demanded by the classical genres to express themselves in simple lyricism. They sought inspiration in nature and in native folk songs, but most of all in themselves. Thus, the cult of the artist and the individual was born.

The movement had its origins in Germany and England, where the hold of rigidly classical French culture was less tenacious. As its influence spread, its emphasis on freedom and individuality was extended to social and political causes. Nations, like individuals, discovered and developed their distinctive personalities. The literatures of many emergent nations, including Russia and the United States, were first developed under the impact of Romanticism.

The chief writers associated with early Romantic literature are Goethe and Schiller (Germany); Wordsworth, Coleridge, Shelley, Byron, Keats, and Scott (England); Chateaubriand and Hugo (France); and Poe, Emerson, Hawthorne, Melville, Whittier, and Whitman (U.S.).

Romeo and Juliet: tragedy by Shakespeare, dated 1595–1596. Set in medieval Verona, it deals with a pair of "star-crossed lovers" who become the victims of an ancient and deadly feud between their families, the Montagues and the Capulets. Their secret marriage and plans to run away end in tragic misunderstanding, and both commit suicide. The shock causes their grief-stricken families to make a tardy peace.

Romulus and Remus: legendary founders of Rome; Romulus was supposed to have been its first king. They were twin sons of Mars and Rhea Silvia (Ilia). As infants, they were cast into the river Tiber by Amulius, Rhea's uncle, who had usurped her father's throne. The twins were found suckled by a she-wolf, then fostered by hill shepherds. In later years, they found their grandfather and restored him to his throne after killing Amulius. They decided to found a new city on the spot where the she-wolf had found them; Romulus, whom prophecies named as first king, began building a wall on the site. Remus, ridiculing him, leaped over the first stones, and Romulus killed him.

Rosinante: in *Don Quixote,* the tired, old, swaybacked, raw-boned horse on which the hero rode out to seek adventure and right wrongs.

Rubáiyát, The ("the quatrains"): verses by Omar Khayyám, a Persian philosopher and poet of the late 11th and early 12th centuries A.D. The verses record melancholy reflections upon life in vivid and simple figures, likening existence to a day's rest in a journey, or man to a clay pot. The prevailing reflection is that since life is brief and the future uncertain, one should enjoy the present with feast and song. The quatrains are known in the West through a very free translation (1859) by the English poet Edward FitzGerald.

Rumpelstiltskin: dwarf in a folk tale known in many European stories under a variety of names. For helping the heroine spin flax into gold, he demands her firstborn child, but he agrees to let her keep it if she can guess his name within three days. When the heroine manages to discover his name, he destroys himself in a temper tantrum. The version best known is from *Grimm's Fairy Tales.*

Runes: alphabet used to write Germanic languages before the Latin alphabet was adapted for that purpose.

ROMEO AND JULIET: Juliet prepares to kill herself in the 1968 film version of the play. She has awakened to discover that Romeo, having mistaken her unconscious body for dead, has killed himself in grief.

Gothic tribes in Germany used runes for writing as early as A.D. 300, but they were most widely used during Viking times in Scandinavia, where many stones for monuments with runic inscriptions are still standing. In England, a modified runic alphabet was used by the Anglo-Saxons before the Norman conquest.

S

Sabines: early Italian tribe chiefly remembered for an event in Roman legendary history known as "the rape of the Sabines." In order to provide wives for his followers, Romulus, the legendary founder of Rome, invited his Sabine neighbors to a festival, during which his men kidnapped their women. The Sabines were, in fact, conquered and assimilated by the Romans in the early third century B.C.

Saga: strictly speaking, saga refers to an Icelandic prose narrative written between the 12th and 15th centuries. Some sagas deal with the histories of Norwegian kings or the adventures of legendary heroes, but the most distinctive kind are the Family or Icelanders' sagas, which trace the histories of the early settlers of Iceland in the tenth and eleventh centuries. These artistically structured narratives are remarkable for their realism and vivid characterization. The word *saga* is now loosely applied to other long prose works, but particularly to family chronicles, such as Galsworthy's *Forsyte Saga.*

Saint Joan: play by the Anglo-Irish writer George Bernard Shaw, presented in 1923. Shaw portrays the 18-year-old Maid of Orleans as an early nationalist, a military genius on the order of Napoleon, and a feminist who demands the right to play a man's role. He views her execution as the inevitable fate of the truly superior person who, except in critical times, cannot be assimilated into society.

THE SCARLET LETTER: Hester Prynne is subjected to public exposure for her adultery.

Samson Agonistes: play by the English poet John Milton, published in 1671. It is closely modeled on the Greek tragedies and intended for reading rather than performance. It focuses on the spiritual agony that Samson endures on finding himself "Eyeless in Gaza at the mill with slaves." Its climax is the return of Samson's physical and spiritual strength, and his destruction of the Philistines as they are mocking him in their temple.

Satan: *See* Devil.

Satire: in literature, any composition—whether verse, prose, or drama—that uses irony and wit in a sustained and systematic manner to criticize human and social weaknesses. Satire ranges from urbane and polite mockery to extremely bitter indictments of human morality, such as those for which the Roman poet Juvenal (c 60–130 A.D.) is famous. Jonathan Swift's *Gulliver's Travels* and George Orwell's *Animal Farm* are other powerful social satires.

Saturn, RM: Roman god of the planting season and agriculture for whom Saturday is named. He became identified with the Greek Cronus as father of the gods, and was supposed to have reigned benevolently in Italy during the Golden Age. His festival, the Saturnalia, celebrated in December, was a feast of liberation from business, social obligation, and moral restraints. Its spirit lingers on in the celebrations of pre-Lenten carnivals and New Year's Eve.

Satyrs, GM: minor woodland gods, having human forms but the horns and legs of goats or, sometimes, the tails and ears of horses. Renowed for lechery, satyrs were descendants of Silenus and companions of Dionysus. At the great dramatic festival celebrated in Athens in honor of Dionysus, a satyr play, apparently a coarse farce, was presented by a

tragic poet after a trilogy of tragedies. Only one of these plays, Euripides' *Cyclops,* survives in its entirety. *See also* Faun; Pan.

Scarlet Letter, The: novel by U.S. author Nathaniel Hawthorne, published in 1850, considered the first great American novel. Set in the Puritan era of 17th-century Boston, it deals with the scarlet *A* that the heroine, Hester Prynne, is forced to wear as a mark of her adultery. Though she and her illegitimate daughter Pearl live as outcasts, Hester refuses to name the child's father. Hester's husband suspects the earnest minister Arthur Dimmesdale and, through a game of cat and mouse, finally breaks him down; Dimmesdale publicly confesses his guilt and bares his chest to reveal a scarlet *A* imprinted on it.

Scarlett O'Hara: *See* Gone with the Wind.

School for Scandal, The: play by the Anglo-Irish dramatist Richard Brinsley Sheridan, performed in 1777. Its satire is essentially moral, directed against hypocrisy and pretense. Its complicated plot, played out against a background of gossip and fashionable tittle-tattle, exposes Joseph Surface's duplicity in trying to win the considerable fortune of Maria, ward to Sir Peter Teazle, by making advances to Sir Peter's much younger inexperienced wife. In the end, Joseph is found out; his generous cousin Charles is rewarded with Maria's hand; and Lady Teazle, having learned a lesson about life's real values, is reconciled with her husband. The play, one of the most popular in the English language, is often revived.

Scrooge: a greedy character by Charles Dickens. *See* Christmas Carol, A.

Scylla, GM: monster who lived in a rock in the strait between Italy and Sicily, opposite the dreaded whirlpool Charybdis. Scylla originally was a nymph loved by the sea god Glaucus, who begged the enchantress Circe for a charm to melt her indifference. But Circe, herself in love with Glaucus, poisoned Scylla's bath with herbs, transforming her into a monster with six heads (each with triple rows of teeth) and twelve feet. In despair, Scylla hurled herself into the sea and settled opposite Charybdis. The strait between them became a deadly passage for mariners such as Odysseus, one of the few who managed a safe passage through it. Choosing "between Scylla and Charybdis," therefore, means choosing between two equally dangerous hazards.

Seagull, The: play by the Russian writer Anton Chekhov, presented in 1896. It introduced a new style of understated, undramatic realism to the theater. Its theme is the mystery of art.

Arkadina, a celebrated actress, needs, above everything else, to keep her beauty and the center of the stage.

Her lover, the novelist Trigorin, lives his life in order to write about it. Her young son Konstantin, struggling to become a writer, is bombarded with foolish advice; and Nina, the girl he loves, longs to experience life in order to become a great actress. Nina falls in love with Trigorin and becomes his mistress, providing him some new material. When he abandons her, she perseveres in her art, acting with a shoddy touring company, but Konstantin, despite his success as a writer, kills himself in grief over Nina's fate.

Season in Hell, A: prose poem by the French poet Arthur Rimbaud, published in 1873. In this tortured, allegorical autobiography, the 19-year-old poet celebrates himself as an outcast and one of the damned. After writing it, he burned the rest of his manuscripts and abandoned poetry.

Self-Reliance: essay by U.S. transcendentalist philosopher Ralph Waldo Emerson, published in 1841; his most popular and representative work. Its theme is the Romantic credo of individuality: "Trust thyself." Its message is that each person must trust his own instincts, even (perhaps especially) when they do not conform to the common opinion of society, "Else tomorrow a stranger will say with masterly good sense precisely what we have thought. . . ." The work contains many of Emerson's most quoted aphorisms, such as ". . . consistency is the hobgoblin of little minds. . . ."

Semele: *See* Dionysus.

Sense and Sensibility: novel by English author Jane Austen, published in 1811. Here, as in her other books, Austen paints with incomparable fidelity the middle-class English life she knew. The story reveals the nice distinction between sense and sensibility (or sentimentality) in the characters of the sisters Elinor and Marianne Dashwood. Although both are disappointed in love, Elinor keeps her balance while Marianne's impetuous emotionalism lands her in an embarrassing position. Both eventually find happiness, but Elinor manages it without even losing her dignity temporarily.

Sentimental Education, A: novel by French realist Gustave Flaubert, published in 1869. A young man from the provinces, Frédéric Moreau, supported by a wealthy and adoring mother, comes to Paris to prepare for a distinguished career. He falls in love with Mme. Arnoux, the virtuous wife of an unscrupulous art dealer. While waiting for something to come of this, Frédéric fails his examinations, drifts into casual affairs, and starts projects that he forgets to finish. Great events occur; a revolution takes place and the monarchy topples; but Frédéric's mind is elsewhere. When Mme. Arnoux finally turns to him, he is repelled by the realization that she is by then a woman of 50. Like

Flaubert's *Madame Bovary,* this novel depicts the painful contrast between subjective life and objective reality.

Sentimental Journey Through France and Italy, A: fanciful sketches of continental wanderings by the pioneer English novelist Laurence Sterne, published in 1768, just before his death. The hero of the work is the whimsical Parson Yorick, who appeared in *Tristram Shandy,* Sterne's earlier novel. *Sentimental Journey* was influential in establishing the fashion for the sentimental novel and the cult of sensibility throughout Europe.

Separate Peace, A: novel by the U.S. writer John Knowles, published in 1959; it deals with the competitive friendship of two adolescent boys in a prep school. The narrator, Gene, though intelligent and able, envies the natural grace and reckless courage of his friend, Finny. As his envy deepens into suspicion that Finny's inspired zaniness is actually calculated to bring about his downfall, their relationship assumes the aspect of a deadly contest that only one of them can survive.

Seven Against Thebes: tragedy by the Greek dramatist Aeschylus, dating from 467 B.C. It is about the fratricidal struggle of Polynices and Eteocles, the sons of Oedipus, for possession of their father's throne at Thebes. Eteocles is ruling Thebes, after having usurped the throne that he and his brother were to have shared. Argive supporters of Polynices lead an attack against each of the gates of Thebes, one after another and, one by one, they are repulsed. But at the seventh gate the attacker is Polynices, whom Eteocles meets in a combat that is fatal to both but that preserves the city.

Sherlock Holmes: most famous detective in literature, created by English physician and writer Sir Arthur Conan Doyle, whose stories about Holmes appeared from 1887 to 1927. To his admirers, Holmes in his lodgings at 221-B Baker Street, London, was as real as any contemporary celebrity—with his dressing gown, his deerstalker cap, his moody violin playing and cocaine habit, and his admiring companion Dr. Watson, who recorded his exploits. Some of the best known of his adventures, are "A Study in Scarlet" (1887), "A Scandal in Bohemia," and "The Hound of the Baskervilles" (1902).

Sherwood Forest: ancient forest in Nottinghamshire, England, famous as the hideout of the legendary robber Robin Hood and his merry men. It was once a royal forest, but much of the area is now heathland.

She Stoops to Conquer: comedy by English dramatist Oliver Goldsmith, presented in 1773. Marlow, a bashful young man, is on his way to the estate of Mr. Hardcastle to examine Hardcastle's daughter as a potential wife. In jest, Tony Lumpkin, the squire's son, tells him that the estate is an inn, and he therefore proceeds to treat Hardcastle as an innkeeper and his daughter Kate as a barmaid. Kate, sensing that Marlow likes her that way, allows the deception to continue; thus "she stoops to conquer" and gains a husband.

Short story: brief, fictional prose composition, usually involving a limited number of characters in a single illuminating incident, or creating a single intense effect or mood through the accumulation of impressions. The Romantic movement brought early examples of the form with the stories of E. T. A. Hoffmann and J. L. Tieck in Germany, and Poe and Hawthorne in the United States. The modern realistic short story, dealing with representative characters and incidents from everyday life, was per-

SHORT STORY: O. Henry was one of the most successful short story writers.

fected by the French writer Guy de Maupassant. Russian writer Anton Chekhov freed the story from self-containment and plot. In deceptively formless sketches, he was able to create stories that suggested a great deal more than they said, and whose characters seemed to have a continuing life beyond the confines of the pages.

In the United States at the turn of the century, short stories by Mark Twain, Bret Harte, and Jack London were still reminiscent of the plot-centered tale. The surprise-ending stories of O. Henry depended exclusively on plot. The stories of Hamlin Garland, Stephen Crane, Henry James, and Sherwood Anderson aimed for different kinds of realism. Since then, many major U.S. writers, including Hemingway, Faulkner, and Fitzgerald, have written distinguished short stories. U.S. writers who have made the short story a major form of expression include J. D. Salinger, John Updike, Katherine Anne Porter, Flannery O'Connor, Eudora Welty, John Cheever, and John O'Hara.

Shropshire Lad, A: first book of poems by the English poet A. E. Housman, published in 1896. These lyrics, in their simplicity of form and spareness of phrasing, introduced a new speech to English poetry. Their tone is overwhelmingly nostalgic and elegiac; they deal with the passing of youth, and the transience of love and glory.

Shylock: *See* Merchant of Venice, The.

Sibyls, GRM: inspired prophetesses. Often sibyls, the Cumaean, the Delphian, and the Erythraean were the most famous. The Sibylline Books, containing prophetic sayings written by the sibyls, were kept in the temple of Jupiter at Rome and consulted in times of national danger. They were lost when the capital burned in 82 B.C.

Siege Perilous: seat at Arthur's Round Table in which it was perilous for any knight to sit except the one destined to achieve the quest of the Holy Grail. When Galahad arrived at Arthur's court, he was able to take his place unharmed in the Siege Perilous.

Siegfried: *See* Nibelungenlied.

Sigurd: *See* Völsunga Saga.

Silas Marner: novel by English author George Eliot, published in 1861. Silas is a lonely weaver, an outcast of society, whose only pleasure is counting his money until one day, after it has been stolen, he finds an infant girl in the snow. He raises Eppie as his daughter and his benumbed natural feelings come alive. Many years later, the mystery of the theft and the secret of Eppie's parentage are revealed. Though she is the daughter of the village squire, she refuses to leave Silas to join her natural father.

Silent Don, The: historical chronicle by Soviet writer Mikhail Sholokhov, in which the Don River follows its natural course, but the people who live on its banks are caught in the upheaval of sweeping events. It tells of the Don Cossacks, and of one in particular, Gregor Melekhov, during World War I, the Russian Revolution, and the ensuing civil war. *The Silent Don* (also translated as *The Quiet Don*) was originally published in four volumes between 1928 and 1940, and was translated into English as two volumes, *And Quiet Flows the Don* (1934) and *The Don Flows Home to the Sea* (1940).

Silver Age: *See* Golden Age.

Simile: *See* Figures of speech.

Sindbad (or Sinbad) the Sailor: merchant of Baghdad whose adventures are related in *The Arabian Nights' Entertainments.* Sindbad embarks on seven voyages and, like Odysseus, encounters many marvels, including the Roc, a gigantic bird; the furry Old Man of the Sea; and a valley where huge black snakes guard rocks of diamond. In each voyage he risks a grave danger for a great reward and returns home triumphantly with his riches.

Sirens, GM: group of sea nymphs whose singing was so sweet that sailors, hearing it, leapt into the sea and were drowned. Homer says there were two sirens; later writers mention three and sometimes describe them as women with the bodies of birds. Odysseus, warned against them by Circe, plugged the ears of his sailors with wax and had himself lashed to the mast with orders to his men not to free him, no matter how desperate his signals. Thus Odysseus and his companions sailed safely by. The Argonauts escaped the sirens only because Orpheus was on board and played sweeter and more magical music than theirs. After these failures, the sirens drowned themselves.

SONGS OF INNOCENCE: a page with Blake's own illustration.

Sir Gawain and the Green Knight: Middle English verse romance known from a 14th-century manuscript that is ascribed to "The Pearl poet." It is regarded as the gem of romance literature. The mysterious Green Knight offers to let Gawain behead him on condition that he be allowed to behead Gawain in return. Gawain accepts this challenge, and cuts off the Green Knight's head. But the Green Knight picks up his head and puts it back on, making an appointment to meet Gawain the following year. Gawain keeps his bargain and, for having passed this test of courage, his life is spared.

Sirius, GM: dog of the hunter Orion, set in the sky as the constellation Canis Major. Sirius, also called the Dog Star, is the brightest star in the heavens. The period during July and August when Sirius rises at the same time as the sun was called the "dog days" by the ancients, who reckoned this period to be the hottest and unhealthiest of the year.

Sister Carrie: novel by U.S. author Theodore Dreiser, published in 1900; a naturalistic story of Carrie Meeber, who comes to Chicago from a Wisconsin farm. After a short stint as a wage slave, she is easily persuaded to become the mistress of a salesman, Drouet, and enjoys the modest comfort and finery he provides. Drouet is soon replaced by Hurstwood, a respectable man who deserts his wife and family to take Carrie to New York. Hurstwood's attempt to reestablish himself in business does not succeed and, while Carrie finds a career on stage, he steadily deteriorates and commits suicide. Because Dreiser presented the story without moral condemnation of its characters, the novel caused such an outcry that it was withdrawn by its original publisher.

Sisyphus, GM: wily king of Corinth. For his general wickedness and, according to some sources, an offense against Zeus, his punishment in Hades was to roll a huge rock to the top of a hill; just before he reached the top, the rock would roll down again, and he would have to begin anew.

In *The Myth of Sisyphus* (1942) by French existentialist philosopher Albert Camus, this legend becomes a metaphor for modern man, whose tasks are equally futile or absurd. The essay examines suicide as a logical way out of a hopeless and meaningless existence, but finds a justification for living in the struggle itself.

Six Characters in Search of an Author: experimental play by the Italian dramatist Luigi Pirandello, presented in 1921. It becomes a dramatization of the act of creating a play. While rehearsing in a theater, a director is interrupted by six characters who have never been put into a story. They demand to act out their life histories. Their complicated affairs and inconsistent actions prove too unwieldy for the director to manage, and he dismisses them, but not with complete success.

Sketch Book of Geoffrey Crayon, Gent., The: collection of sketches and tales by the U.S. writer Washington Irving, published in 1819–1820. For its best-known stories, see *Rip Van Winkle* and *Legend of Sleepy Hollow, The.*

Slaughterhouse-Five, subtitled "The Children's Crusade": novel by the U.S. writer Kurt Vonnegut, Jr., published in 1969. Billy Pilgrim, a prisoner of war in Dresden and witness to the city's destruction by firebombing in World War II, tells a story that is both a war novel and a work of science fiction. Pilgrim describes the destruction and moves back and forth in time, connecting it to his life before and after.

Sleeping Beauty: folktale that involves a slighted fairy who condemns a newborn princess to a long sleep that will begin with a prick of her finger. She can be awakened only by the kiss of a prince. The best-known versions are the Brothers Grimm's "Little Briar Rose" and Charles Perrault's *La Belle au bois dormant."* It is the subject of a popular ballet by Tchaikovsky.

Snow Country: best-known novel of the Nobel Prize–winning Japanese author Kawabata Yasunari, published in 1947. It is a slight story about the relationship of a rather cold, intellectual city gentleman with a naive geisha girl he meets at a remote hot springs resort. In a series of indelible scenes that have the quality of Japanese brush strokes, their meeting and parting is portrayed against a background world of snow and hot springs.

Socialist realism: officially approved style for art and literature in the Soviet Union and its satellites from around 1932 until the breakup of the Soviet Union in the early 1990s (except for a brief period of relaxation following the death of Stalin that became known as the Thaw). This doctrine held that any work of art or literature must reflect socialist ideals and convince the people to become better Communists. Some excellent writers—such as Maxim Gorky, Mikhail Sholokhov, Yevgeny Yevtushenko, and the East German Bertolt Brecht—were considered socialist realists, but even their work, in some respects, falls outside its bounds. Most officially approved writers were mediocre, and the government battled frequently with gifted writers unable or unwilling to adhere to the doctrine.

Songs of Innocence and of Experience: two companion series of poems by English writer, artist, and mystic William Blake, notable for their imagery, symbolism, and lyrical beauty. They first appeared together in 1794, with illuminated engravings by Blake and the subtitle "Shewing the Two Contrary States of the Human Soul"; the poems in the two series contrast the joyful, innocent view of a child with a mature view of the realities of human experience and pain.

Sonnet: poem of 14 lines (customarily in iambic pentameter), arranged in accordance with a prescribed rhyming scheme. There are two standard forms, the Italian (or Petrarchan) and the

Shakespearean (or English). They differ chiefly in that the Italian sonnet uses the first eight lines (the octet) to expose the theme, and the six remaining lines (the sestet) to resolve it, while the Shakespearean sonnet is often divided into three quatrains and ends with a summary rhymed couplet.

Sonnets from the Portuguese: sonnet sequences by English poet Elizabeth Barrett Browning, published in 1850; the artistic expression of her love for Robert Browning prior to their marriage. It contains the famous lines from the 43rd sonnet, "How do I love thee? Let me count the ways."

Sons and Lovers: autobiographical novel by English writer D. H. Lawrence, published in 1913, and considered by many his finest work. The hero, Paul Morel, is the son of a coal miner and a remarkable woman who, disappointed in her marriage, transfers her affections to her son and encourages his artistic gifts. Paul grows up and becomes involved with two women, but neither of them satisfies the expectations from love that have been created by his mother. When his mother suffers agony from cancer, Paul gives her an overdose of morphine. After her death he contemplates suicide, but eventually discovers the will to live without her.

Sorrows of Young Werther, The: novel by the German author Johann Wolfgang von Goethe, first published in 1774. The work represents Goethe's initial Romantic phase, which he later repudiated; it expressed the yearnings of young German Romantics and inspired numerous similar works and even some imitative suicides. Werther, an artistic youth, falls in love with Charlotte (Lotte), a rather conventional girl who is engaged to Albert, a decent but complacent young man. Werther's attempts to renounce Lotte, even after her marriage to Albert, prove futile. Their settled, bourgeois marriage enrages him, and his melancholy moods make the newlyweds so uncomfortable that they suggest that he cease his visits. After borrowing a pistol from Albert on the pretext of a journey, Werther shoots himself.

Sound and the Fury, The: novel by U.S. author William Faulkner, published in 1929. It recounts the last stages in the decline of a once-proud Southern family, the Compsons. It is told in an involved fashion that skips back and forth in time through the complex interior monologues of the three Compson brothers: Benjy, an idiot, protected by his brother Quentin and sister Caddy; Quentin, over-bred and oversensitive, who loves his sister too well and commits suicide; and the practical Jason, free from the family's self-destructive notions of honor and gallantry, who survives disaster to lead a respectable money-grubbing life. Caddy, the sister, is central in the thoughts of her brothers; she has left

Petrarchan Sonnet	Shakespearean Sonnet
To one who has been long in city pent 'Tis very sweet to look into the fair And open face of heaven—to breathe a prayer Full in the smile of the blue firmament. Who is more happy, when, with heart's content, Fatigued he sinks into some pleasant lair Of wavy grass, and reads a debonair And gentle tale of love and languishment? Returning home at evening, with an ear Catching the notes of Philomel—an eye Watching the sailing cloudlet's bright career, He mourns that day so soon has glided by: E'en like the passage of an angel's tear That falls through the ether silently. *John Keats*	When to the sessions of sweet silent thought I summon up remembrance of things past, I sigh the lack of many a thing I sought, And with old woes new wail my dear time's waste. Then can I drown an eye, unused to flow, For precious friends hid in death's dateless night, And weep afresh love's long since canceled woe, And moan the expense of many a vanished sight. Then can I grieve at grievances foregone, And heavily from woe to woe tell o'er The sad account of fore-bemoanèd moan, Which I new pay as if not paid before. But if the while I think on thee, dear friend, All losses are restored and sorrows end. *William Shakespeare*

town in disgrace, leaving her illegitimate daughter, also named Quentin, behind. Another central figure in the monologues and in the final narrative section of the book is the black cook Dilsey.

Spectator: 18th-century London journal, written chiefly by Joseph Addison and Richard Steele, with a few other contributors. The *Spectator* appeared from 1711 to 1712 and in 1714, following in the wake of the *Tatler,* which had a successful run from 1709 to 1711, and which was also chiefly written by Addison and Steele. The *Spectator* offered witty commentary on daily life through such fictional characters as Sir Roger de Coverley, who represented the best values of the country gentleman. He and the other characters claimed to be members of "Mr. Spectator's Club." From this stance, they commented on literature and morality. These sketches of contemporary life and problems enjoyed great popularity and were imitated all over Europe. The *Spectator* and the *Tatler* were influential in establishing the 18th-century periodical essay, which, with its informal prose style, greatly affected English journalism.

Spenserian stanza: *See* Stanza.

Sphinx, GM: winged, woman-headed monster who preyed on the citizens of Thebes with the riddle "What creature walks on four legs in the morning, two at noon, and three in the evening?" If they could not answer it, she devoured them. When Oedipus answered the riddle "Man," explaining that a baby creeps, a grown man walks upright, and an old man uses a cane, the Sphinx dashed her head against a stone and died, and Oedipus became king of Thebes. The sphinx was originally a Near Eastern art motif, with a human head and a lion's body.

Spondee: *See* Foot.

Spoon River Anthology: book of verse by U.S. poet Edgar Lee Masters, issued in book form in 1915. Inspired by the Greek Anthology, it is a series of epitaphs in the form of dramatic monologues. A succession of the departed inhabitants of an Illinois small town speak from the quiet in which "all, all are sleeping on the hill"; thus they draw vignettes of themselves and their former neighbors. The work was part of a movement to debunk the myth of idyllic life in rural and small-town America.

Sportsman's Sketches, A: collection of short stories by the Russian writer Ivan Turgenev, published in 1852. The narrator, a country gentleman, describes his casual encounters with neighbors and peasants while he roams the countryside. The common theme of these stories, though often understated, is the endless and cruel injustices that are the inevitable byproduct of serfdom. The book was a powerful influence in arousing public support for emancipation.

Stanza: unit of a poem, usually consisting of a recurring number of lines. The *quatrain* is the most common, consisting of four lines in which the rhyme pattern can be a-b-a-b or a-b-c-b. Ballad stanzas are quatrains.

Rhyme royal is a seven-line stanza in iambic pentameter in which the rhyme scheme is a-b-a-b-b-c-c. It is also called the Chaucerian stanza because of Chaucer's early use of it. *Ottava rima* is a similar stanza form, having eight lines instead of seven, and rhyming a-b-a-b-a-b-c-c. Sir Thomas Wyatt introduced it into English verse from the Italian. Byron made use of it in *Don Juan.*

The Spenserian stanza, invented by Edmund Spenser for use in *The Faerie Queen,* consists of nine iambic lines, rhyming a-b-a-b-b-c-b-c-c. The first eight lines are pentameter but the last, called an alexandrine, is hexameter.

The sonnet was originally a stanza, but is now an independent lyric. *See also* Ballad; Couplet; Sonnet.

Steppenwolf: novel by the German author Hermann Hesse, published in 1927. The story is told mainly through the bizarre journals left by mysterious protagonist Harry Haller before his disappearance. The journals tell of his conviction that he has a dual nature—that is, part domesticated human, part

The symbols used in this glossary are as follows:

G-Greek
R-Roman
N-Norse
M-myth
L-legend

20 History of Literature

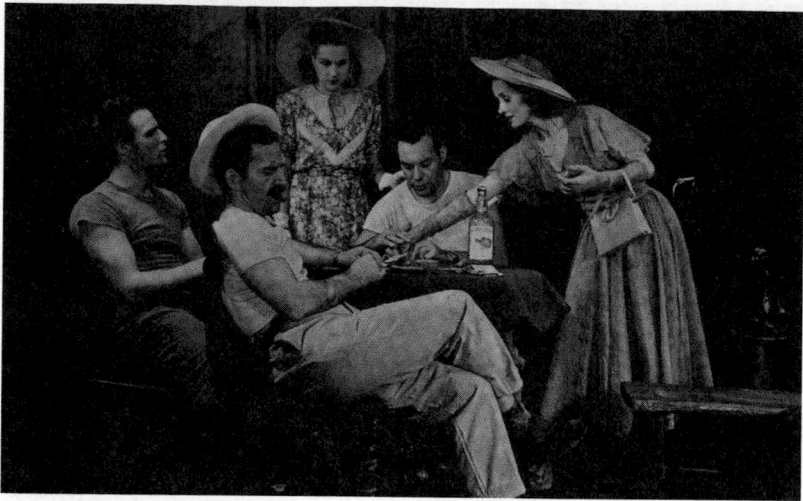

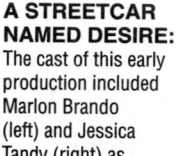

A STREETCAR NAMED DESIRE: The cast of this early production included Marlon Brando (left) and Jessica Tandy (right) as Tennessee Williams's bittersweet New Orleans characters.

honor
US

honour
Brit.

"wolf of the Steppes" *(Steppenwolf)*— and is a wild outsider who despises human life, activities, and values. The fantastic ending finds Harry in the Magic Theater "for madmen only," where he glimpses the meaning of life and decides to bear it.

Stopping by Woods on a Snowy Evening: deceptively simple, short lyric poem, written by Robert Frost in 1923, one of his best-known works. The poet, on a journey home, stops impulsively in the woods for a moment's contemplation. The seductive mystery of the deep snow, dark night, and solitude exert a powerful fascination over him that he reluctantly resists because he has "promises to keep,/ And miles to go before I sleep."

Stranger, The: novel by the French existentialist philosopher Albert Camus, published in 1942 and set in Algiers. From its opening sentences "Mother died today. Or, maybe yesterday; I can't be sure"—the reader is shocked into recognition that the narrator, Meursault (he has no first name), represents a new breed of modern man who is estranged from the deepest realities of life, even the instinct for self-preservation. Meursault adapts uncomplainingly to his absurd existence—a routine job, casual acquaintances, and aimless recreation. Nothing upsets him very much. Faced with death, however, he discovers a reason for living.

Stratford-on-Avon: English borough northwest of London on the Avon River, known for its associations with William Shakespeare, who was born there and lived there in retirement.

Stream of consciousness: phrase first applied by U.S. psychologist William James to the sum of external and internal stimuli that invade the periphery of consciousness at a given moment. Attempts to mirror this stream of images, thoughts, and impressions in literature have been made by 20th-century novelists, notably James Joyce and Virginia Woolf.

Streetcar Named Desire, A: play by U.S. author Tennessee Williams, presented in 1947 and awarded a Pulitzer Prize. Blanche Dubois, an aging Southern belle, comes to stay with her sister, Stella. Her refined behavior and coquettish manner provoke conflict with her earthy brother-in-law, Stanley Kowalski.

Studs Lonigan: trilogy of naturalistic novels by U.S. writer James T. Farrell, published between 1932 and 1935. The novels faithfully record a lower middle-class Irish environment in Chicago in the 1920s and 1930s. In boyhood, the hero, Studs, is the admired leader of the neighborhood gang. This proves to be the peak achievement of his life. As he grows older the social and cultural limitations of his milieu, the repetition of often sordid and brutal pleasures, and the dull routine of menial occupations deaden whatever spark of natural superiority he had long before his death at an early age. Although the book documents the meanness of his life in great detail, it makes Studs a figure of lyrical poignancy.

Sturm und Drang ("Storm and Stress"): period in German literature in the late 1700s that sowed the seeds of the German Romantic movement. This short-lived revolt against the Enlightenment was strongly influenced by the poetry of the Gaelic bard Ossian and the discovery of Shakespeare. Its most notable productions were dramas, characteristically tragic, turbulent, and unrestrained. Among them were the youthful Goethe's *Götz von Berlichingen* and Schiller's *Die Räuber (The Robbers)*.

Styx, GM: principal river of Hades, believed to encircle the lower world seven times. Over this river Charon ferried the souls of the dead. It was held in such terror and reverence that even the gods swore their irrevocable oaths by its name.

Sun Also Rises, The: novel by U.S. writer Ernest Hemingway, published in 1926. It deals with a group of young expatriates in Paris who drink too much and make love indiscriminately, but who seek and sometimes find purification in ritual acts—fishing in a trout stream or attending a bullfight—that suggest that they are searching for a dimly remembered innocence and honor. The work expressed the feelings of the "lost generation" of the 1920s.

Superman: concept of German philosopher Friedrich Nietzsche of the superior being: the man who overcomes and transcends himself and the limitations of his times. The idea, although variously understood, has fascinated many writers, and literary versions of the superman (usually seen negatively) were portrayed even before he was described by Nietzsche. Raskolnikov in Dostoevski's *Crime and Punishment* and Wolf Larsen in Jack London's *Sea Wolf* are both criminal supermen; those seen from a more admiring point of view include Bazarov in Turgenev's *Fathers and Sons* and architect Howard Roark in Ayn Rand's *Fountainhead*.

The Nazis in Germany derived their philosophy of the superman from Nietzsche, but it is clear in *Thus Spake Zarathustra* that Nietzsche is talking about a super-individual, not a super-state or a "master race." As Zarathustra says, there is no "way" to become a superman; the way is different for each person.

Surrealism: movement in literature and art that began in 1924, in Paris, with the poet André Breton's first surrealist manifesto. Surrealists seek to explore and express the subconscious. Dreams and hallucinations are often a source of ideas, giving surreal works their characteristic quality of fantasy. Among the most famous surrealist writers are Eugène Ionesco, Jean Genet, and Samuel Beckett.

Symbolism: widespread revolt, occurring in the late 19th century, against realism and naturalism in the arts. In essence, artists and writers turned away

Representative Works Using Stream-of-Consciousness Technique			
Principles of Psychology	William James	The Sound and the Fury	William Faulkner
Pilgrimage	Dorothy Richardson	To the Lighthouse	Virginia Woolf
Ulysses Finnegans Wake	James Joyce	Mrs. Dalloway The Waves	

from representations of objective reality to symbolic representations of their inner lives. As the Norwegian painter Edvard Munch put it: "I paint not what I see, but what I saw."

In a restricted sense, the term is associated with a group of French writers, followers of Charles Baudelaire, Stéphane Mallarmé, and Paul Verlaine, who, in a manifesto written by Jean Moréas in 1886, gave the movement its name.

Symposium (Greek for "banquet"): one of the dialogues by the ancient Greek philosopher Plato, in which his mentor Socrates and his friends, including Aristophanes, Phaedrus, Agathon (the host), and Pausanias, meet at dinner and discuss the nature of love; a latecomer, Alcibiades, makes a speech honoring Socrates. Another dialogue of the same name was written by Xenophon; it also features Socrates.

Synecdoche: *See* Figures of speech.

T

Tale of Genji, The: greatest classic of Japanese literature, written around the year 1005 by Murasaki Shikibu, a court lady. Often considered the oldest novel in the world, it portrays aristocratic life in the Heian period, an age of exquisite refinement in which an elegant society occupied itself with writing poems, painting, and viewing nature. The story is long and episodic and deals with the romantic adventures of Prince Genji, whose mistresses are sensitively and sympathetically portrayed.

Tale of Two Cities, A: novel by English writer Charles Dickens, published in 1859, set in Paris and London at the time of the French Revolution. The symbol of the revolution is Mme. DeFarge, who sits before her wine shop, knitting a scroll that records the names and crimes of the nobility.

The chief characters are Dr. Manette, whose 18-year imprisonment in the Bastille has broken his health; Lucie Manette, his daughter, who rescues him and takes him to London; Charles Darnay, a French nobleman who disavows his aristocratic family, changes his name, and goes to London; and Sydney Carton, an unconventional, alcoholic barrister. Carton and Darnay both fall in love with Lucie, but she chooses Darnay. During the terror, Darnay returns to Paris to rescue a family servant, but he is arrested and sentenced to death; for Lucie's sake, Carton takes his place and dies in his stead.

Taming of the Shrew, The: comedy by Shakespeare dated 1593–1594. The plot, given in a play, concerns Katharina, a beautiful but harsh-tongued and obstinate girl whom no one wishes to marry. Petruchio of Verona marries and tames her, mostly by inhuman treatment. Katharina becomes a wife who appears to be so loving and meek that Petruchio wins a wager he has made with his friends when she behaves docilely toward him in public.

Tam O'Shanter: narrative poem by Scottish poet Robert Burns, published in 1791, based on a local legend. It is a story about Tam, who gets drunk on market day and, with his mare Maggie, makes a spooky midnight journey home, encountering a party of dancing witches and warlocks. Unlike any other poem in Burns's repertory, this is a virtuoso's showpiece, in which the poet exhibits his bag of dazzling magic tricks and demonstrates the full range of his gifts for humor, satire, tragic insight, and elegant parody.

Tannhäuser: in German legend, a knight and minnesinger (lyrical poet) of the 13th century who entered a cave in a mountain (Venusberg) where he was to live with Venus in her court of pleasure for seven years. At length he repented and made a pilgrimage to Rome to seek forgiveness for his sins. But Pope Urban told him that he could no more be forgiven than the staff in his hand could sprout leaves. In despair, Tannhäuser turned away, discarded his staff, and returned to Venus. In a few days the dry staff miraculously bloomed, and the pope sent messengers far and wide seeking Tannhäuser, but he was never found. The story is the basis for the opera *Tannhäuser* by Richard Wagner, first performed in 1845.

Tantalus: *See* House of Atreus.

TALE OF TWO CITIES: Sydney Carton is led to the guillotine in the 1930s film version.

Tartuffe: satiric comedy by the French dramatist Molière, first presented in three acts in 1664, then expanded to five acts in 1669. The public was outraged by what it viewed as a mockery of piety. Tartuffe is a religious hypocrite who insinuates himself into the good graces of the wealthy Orgon. He convinces Orgon to disinherit his son, give Tartuffe his daughter's hand in marriage, and turn over his large estate to him. Elmire, Orgon's wife, arranges for him to overhear Tartuffe making love to her, but even then Orgon believes Tartuffe's defense. Orgon is finally turned out of his house and recognizes Tartuffe's treachery. At the last minute, the king intervenes and restores daughter and property to Orgon.

Telemachus: *See* Odysseus; Odyssey.

Tempest, The: late comedy by Shakespeare, usually dated 1612–1613. It tells the story of Prospero, an exiled magician, once duke of Milan, who causes a ship to founder on the enchanted isle where he and his daughter Miranda live. Aboard the ship are his enemies: his brother Antonio, usurper of the dukedom; the king of Naples; and his son, Ferdinand. With the help of his magic sprite Ariel, Prospero teases, beguiles, and frightens, but finally forgives his enemies, teaching them a lesson in magnanimity. Miranda and Ferdinand fall in love, and the old magician renounces his magic to return to the sober responsibilities of his dukedom. A striking minor character is Caliban, the deformed bestial slave of Prospero.

Tender Is the Night: novel by U.S. author F. Scott Fitzgerald, published in 1934, which tells of the marriage of a young psychiatrist, Dick Diver, to one of his mental patients, Nicole. Supported by Nicole's money, they are popular members of a restless fashionable international set. But Dick's loss of meaningful work and the burden of being caretaker to Nicole make him seek refuge in drink. As Nicole gains emotional strength, their marriage dissolves, and Dick drifts into obscurity and alcoholism.

Tess of the D'Urbervilles: novel by English author Thomas Hardy, published in 1891. Tess Durbeyfield, a beautiful English village girl, is a lineal descendant of the aristocratic d'Urbervilles. Alec, a son of that family, pursues and seduces Tess, then abandons her. A child is born, whom she names Sorrow, but he soon dies. Some years later the idealistic Angel Clare marries Tess, but he leaves her when, on the wedding day, she tells him of her past. He experiences a change of heart and tries again to win her love, but Alec seeks to claim her and prevent any reconciliation. Tess kills Alec, and she and Clare flee, hoping to escape from the country. They are overtaken at Stonehenge and Tess is imprisoned and sentenced to death.

Tevye the Dairyman: collection of tragicomic stories written by the Yiddish author Sholom Aleichem between 1894 and 1916. Taking place during the last years of czarist Russia, the stories purport to be monologues told to the author by Tevye as, over the years, they accidentally meet. *Tevye's Daughters,* a collection of later stories that deal with the fates of the dairyman's seven children, was published in English translation in 1949. Three of the stories became the basis of the 1960s hit musical *Fiddler on the Roof.* In the face of the unhappy destinies of his family, his people, and himself, Tevye never loses his faith in God, which is, in fact, made stronger by his trials.

Thanatopsis (Greek for "a vision of death"): reflective poem by the U.S. poet William Cullen Bryant, begun when he was only 16 and published in 1817. The poem belongs to the tradition of the English "graveyard school" of poetry, and conveys a majestic image of the immortality of the soul.

Theseus, GM: principal hero of the Athenians; he was a son of Aegeus, king of Athens, and Aethra. When he was a child, his father left a sword and sandals under a heavy rock, instructing Aethra to allow Theseus to come to him in Athens when he was big enough to move the rock. This Theseus did, taking the dangerous overland route because of his ambition to equal the fame of Hercules. He killed all the highwaymen along the way (*see also* Procrustes) and arrived in Athens already famous. He made himself known to Aegeus and vol-

Thisbe: *See* Pyramus and Thisbe.

This Side of Paradise: first novel by the U.S. writer F. Scott Fitzgerald, published in 1920. It brought him sensational fame and made him the spokesman for the jazz age generation. It deals with the boyhood and young manhood of Amory Blaine. From a midwestern background, Amory sets out to capture wealth, fame, and beautiful women, but he fails to make the grade at Princeton, achieves only a mediocre success in advertising, and loses, for lack of money, the girl he loves.

Thor, NM: god of thunder, a son of Odin. He was the god of strength and a defender in time of war, a friend of humanity. The sound of thunder was supposed to be from the rolling wheels of his chariot; the thunderbolt was his hammer, which always returned to his hand after being hurled. Thursday is named for Thor.

Thrace: name the ancient Greeks gave to the territory lying between Macedonia and the Black Sea, extending north to the Danube and south beyond the Hellespont. The ancient Greeks thought of the Thracians as savages. The chief city of Thrace was Byzantium. The territory today is divided among Turkey, Bulgaria, and Greece.

Threepenny Opera, The: *See* Beggar's Opera.

Three Sisters, The: play by the Russian dramatist Anton Chekhov, presented in 1901. It deals with three young women who live on dreams of escaping their dull provincial town and going to Moscow. They pin their hopes for escape on their brother Andrei, but he marries a stupid girl who moves into their home and tyrannizes both him and his sisters. The sisters' lives are briefly enlivened by romances with officers of the local military garrison, but these, too, end in disappointment when the regiment leaves.

Thule: name given by the Greeks and Romans to the northernmost inhabited place in the world, possibly Iceland or Norway. Described as a cold and eerie place by the Greek explorer Pytheas, who visited there around 300 B.C. after a 6-day voyage north from Britain, the region captured the literary imagination. Writers often use Vergil's phrase "ultima Thule" to describe the farthest regions. An actual Thule was founded in Greenland in 1910 by Danish explorer Knud Rasmussen.

Thus Spake Zarathustra: philosophic essay by the German philosopher Friedrich Nietzsche, written from 1883 to 1885. The work is in the form of a narrative in which the ancient Persian prophet Zoroaster (Zarathustra) is the spokesman for the author. The prophet's message is that if man is to survive he must surpass his present limitations and become a superman; his will is his most important asset. Zarathustra reviles Christianity as a religion for the protection of weaklings and a crippling hindrance to the strong individual's will to power. He celebrates a life of independence, boldness, courage, danger, and action. *See also* Superman.

Time Machine, The: science fiction fantasy by the British novelist H. G. Wells, published in 1895. The hero invents a time machine that permits him to journey into the future, where he meets a future race, the Eloi. They are charming, gentle, and dainty creatures who do no work, read no books, and eat only vegetables since animals are extinct. He then discovers, to his horror, that they share the planet with a race of underground workers, the apelike Morlocks, carnivorous creatures who exist by feeding on the Eloi.

Tin Drum, The: first novel by the German writer Günter Grass, published in 1959. The book's hero, Oskar Matzerath, is determined to thwart his father's plan to make him a grocer; he stops growing at the age of three and remains an obnoxious child, beating a tin drum throughout the rise and fall of Nazi Germany. After the war, when the survivors of the family move to West Germany, he decides to become an

THE THREE MUSKETEERS: Early film star Douglas Fairbanks plays D'Artagnan battling a host of enemies in a tavern.

unteered to free Athens from the yearly tribute of youths and maidens that had to be sent to feed the Minotaur in Crete. With the help of Ariadne, daughter of the Cretan king, Minos, he found his way in and out of the labyrinth, where he killed the Minotaur; he then carried Ariadne away with him. He later was either separated from her or deserted her (*see also* Ariadne).

After Theseus became king of Athens, he married the Amazon queen Hippolyte, by whom he had a son, Hippolytus. After her death he married Ariadne's sister Phaedra.

Three Musketeers, The: cloak-and-sword romance by the French writer Alexandre Dumas *père,* published in 1844. It deals with events in the 17th century; its hero, D'Artagnan, a dashing and reckless guardsman in the service of Louis XIII, is based on an actual historical character. His three loyal friends— the musketeers—are the bravest and most resourceful soldiers of the age. Each has a distinctive personality: the gigantic, comic Porthos is a tower of strength and dependability; Athos is reflective and clever; Aramis is dour and pessimistic.

adult and participates, as a cabaret drummer, in the postwar life. But he conceives the delusion that he is Jesus and is confined in a mental hospital from which he tells his story.

Tintern Abbey: short title for an early masterpiece of the English poet William Wordsworth, included in his and Coleridge's first collection, *Lyrical Ballads* (1798). This work deals with his characteristic theme, the mystery of the recurrence and withdrawal of grace and inspiration. The poet revisits a scene of his youth, where he had once experienced an almost mystical identification with nature, to draw spiritual sustenance from it again.

Tiresias, GM: blind prophet of Thebes whose life span several generations. He appears in Sophocles' *Oedipus Rex* and *Antigone,* in the *Odyssey,* and in many Greek legends. At one time he found two snakes copulating and killed the female. As a punishment, Tiresias was turned into a woman; somewhat later he was turned back into a man, but thereafter he possessed the knowledge and insight of both men and women.

Titans, GM: children of Uranus (heaven) and Gaea (earth). The sons were Oceanus, Coeus, Creus, Hyperion, Iapetus, and Cronus. The daughters were Theia, Rhea, Themis, Mnemosyne, Phoebe, and Tethys. The children of Cronus and Rhea were Zeus and the Olympian gods. Cronus dethroned Uranus, and Zeus in turn dethroned Cronus. In this struggle the Titans fought against the gods, were defeated, and confined under Tartarus, the deepest part of Hades.

Tom Jones (full title: *The History of Tom Jones, a Foundling*): comic novel by the pioneer English novelist Henry Fielding, published in 1749. It relates the adventures of high-spirited, impulsive, and generous Tom, who, despite many discreditable escapades, at last wins the confidence of his foster father, Squire Allworthy, and the love of beautiful Sophia Western. The novel is remarkable for its vitality and its sweeping picture of 18th-century London and country life.

Tom Sawyer, The Adventures of: classic novel of small-town American boyhood, written by U.S. author Mark Twain in 1876. It was based on his memories of growing up in Hannibal, Missouri. Tom, an imaginative boy who is fond of adventure stories, finds himself involved in a real life adventure when he and his friend Huck Finn witness a murder committed by Injun Joe. The terrified boys run away, but return in time to prevent an innocent man from being condemned for the crime. The book is a perennial favorite among children. Its sequel, *Huckleberry Finn,* is an American classic.

Tom Thumb: in English legend, the inch-high son of a plowman in the time of King Arthur. His adventures range from being swallowed by mistake to a climactic fall into the sea, where he is eaten by a fish that is then caught and taken to King Arthur's cook. The cook saves Tom's life. Tom is then presented to the king and knighted. He ends up being killed by a spider.

To the Lighthouse: novel by English writer Virginia Woolf, published in 1927. Stream-of-consciousness techniques and symbolism create the emotional atmosphere for a seaside house party. The book is dominated by the symbol of the lighthouse offshore. The people at the house party, directed by the cold, rational Mr. Ramsay, an eminent scholar troubled by self-doubt, are seen primarily through the eyes of two women: Mrs. Ramsay, a warm beautiful woman, mother of many children, who gives of herself and her concern to the point of exhaustion; and Lily Briscoe, an artist who is troubled by conflicts between other people's expectations of her as a woman and her own view of herself as an artist. The novel covers a period of about ten years, and not unil the final scene do any of the characters reach the lighthouse.

Tragedy: form of drama in which a solemn theme is set forth in action, usually proceeding to a fatal outcome. The language, whether verse or prose, is of an elevated quality. The term is now applied to novels, other literary works, and to real events that are terrible or fatal. *See also* Poetics, The.

Tragic flaw: *See* Poetics, The.

TOM JONES, title character in Richardson's 18th-century classic, was played by Albert Finney.

Transcendentalism or **New England transcendentalism:** philosophical and literary movement centered in Concord, Massachusetts, in the early 19th century; an influential part of the general

THE LEGENDARY TOM THUMB, a diminutive figure, originated in King Arthur's time.

intellectual ferment now called the American renaissance or the "flowering of New England." New England transcendentalism was an aspect of the general Romantic revolt against the rationalism of the Enlightenment and against the narrowness of organized religion.

The Concord group investigated Eastern and mystical philosophies but, above all, they sought inspiration in nature and placed their faith in intuition. Their chief spokesman was Ralph Waldo Emerson. In essays such as "Self-Reliance," he repeatedly advocated trust in hunches, instincts, feelings, and other subjective touchstones. Thus, his friend Henry David Thoreau took to the woods so that he could learn what life was about by living, a gesture that has had a powerful impact on the American imagination.

Other prominent transcendentalists were Bronson Alcott, Margaret Fuller, George Ripley, and Orestes Brownson. Although they were all fiercely individualistic, their ideas led them to champion social reforms and to found the idealistic, experimental communes of Brook Farm and Fruitlands. *See also* Brook Farm.

Treasure Island: adventure story by English writer Robert Louis Stevenson, published in 1883. Its boy hero, Jim Hawkins, gets possession of a map of an island where pirate treasure is buried. Some friends outfit a vessel to set out to search for it. But the crew of the *Hispaniola* is made up of pirates and desperadoes who are seeking the treasure themselves. The chief villain is the fascinating one-legged pirate, Long John Silver. Jim and his friends overcome the pirates and finally find the treasure.

Trial, The: novel written in German, in 1915, by the Jewish Czech writer Franz Kafka, published posthumously in 1925. A bank clerk, Joseph K., is suddenly accused of a crime by a bureaucratic official. He can never discover the exact nature of the crime, and though he devotes his life up to his execution to seeking clarification and demanding justice, all his efforts are futile. The book conveys an overwhelmingly fatalistic feeling that no man is innocent, and that there is no cure or acquittal for inner guilt. Like all Kafka's allegorical tales, it has many interpretations.

TROJAN HORSE: This "gift" was filled with Greek warriors who destroyed the city.

Tristan and Iseult: in Celtic legend, a pair of tragic lovers. Tristan, a nephew of King Mark of Cornwall, was escorting the beautiful Iseult to her wedding with the king. On the way, they accidentally drank a love potion intended for Mark and Iseult. Thereafter, they were committed to love each other forever. They made a death pact and died in each other's arms. Wagner's music drama *Tristan und Isolde* is a powerful expression of this love story. Tristan also appears in Malory's *Morte d'Arthur* as a knight of King Arthur's Round Table.

Tristram Shandy, Gentleman, The Life and Opinions of: novel by the English clergyman Laurence Sterne, published in nine volumes between 1760 and 1767. Though one of the earliest English novels, it is remarkable for its technique of free association. Tristram begins the story of his life from his conception, but as one digression leads to another, he does not actually get around to being born until Volume IV. The digressions range from bawdy anecdotes and sentimental portraits of his father and his Uncle Toby to discussions of topical problems of the day. The work was enormously popular and helped to establish the literary vogue known as the "cult of sensibility" (or sentimentality) in Europe.

Trochee: *See* Foot.

Troilus: young son of Priam, king of Troy, and Hecuba. He was killed in the Trojan War by Achilles. The legend of his love for the faithless Cresida is not a classical myth but a romance developed in the Middle Ages. Its finest expression is the poem *Troilus and Criseyde,* written in 1385 by Geoffrey Chaucer; it is also the subject of a rather cynical tragedy by Shakespeare, dated 1602–1603. The usual story is that Troilus falls in love with Cressida, the daughter of the pro-Greek Trojan priest Calchas. Pandarus arranges their meetings, and they become lovers. During a truce, Cressida is sent to the Greek camp in exchange for prisoners. Though the lovers vow fidelity, Cressida almost immediately becomes the mistress of Diomedes, plunging bewildered Troilus into jealous torments.

Trojan horse: hollow wooden horse, used during the Trojan War as a strategy by the Greeks to gain entrance to the city of Troy. Pretending to abandon the siege, the Greeks sailed away, leaving before the city gates the gigantic wooden horse with a number of men hidden inside it. Though they were warned by both Cassandra and Laocoön ("Whatever it is, I fear Greeks even when they bring gifts"), the Trojans were deceived into believing that the horse was an offering to Athena and would protect the city; they brought it inside the city walls. During the night, the Greek warriors crept out and opened the gates for their fellow Greeks, who sacked and burned the city. The story is told in the *Odyssey* and in the *Aeneid.*

Trojan War: struggle between the kingdom of Troy and an alliance of Greek kingdoms. According to legend, the war began when Paris, son of the Trojan king, Priam, carried off the beautiful Helen, wife of Menelaus, king of Sparta. Menelaus called on all the other Greek chieftains, who were bound by oath to avenge any injury done to the Spartan royal family. Under the leadership of his brother, Agamemnon, king of Mycenae, the Greek heroes Achilles, Patroclus, Odysseus, Diomedes, Nestor, and the two Ajaxes sailed across the Aegean Sea to besiege Troy.

The Trojans, led by one of Priam's sons, Hector, struggled many years to overcome their Greek foes. Victory was capricious, going from one side to the other. The gods of Olympus took sides and often interfered on behalf of their favorites.

Homer's great epic, the *Iliad,* opens in the 10th year of the war. It deals with Achilles' bitter quarrels with his leader Agamemnon, and his refusal to fight, which brings disaster to the Greeks. Some of the highlights of the *Iliad* are the death of Achilles' friend Patroclus and the funeral games held in his honor; Achilles' return to battle; his slaying of Hector and defiling of Hector's body; and the scene in which Achilles undergoes a change of heart and returns Hector's body to Priam for burial.

Tropic of Cancer: novel written by the U.S. Bohemian writer Henry Miller, describing the highs and lows of his years of poverty in Paris during the Depression. It ranges from lyrical affirmations of the joy of life to scatological descriptions of the most sordid experiences. The book was first published in Paris in 1934, but its sexual frankness caused it to be banned in the United States until 1961. Its sequel, *Tropic of Capricorn,* dealing with Miller's earlier New York years, appeared in 1962.

Troubadours: poet-musicians who flourished in Europe between the late 1000s and 1200s. They composed their poetry in the language of Provence in southern France. They invented many forms of the lyric, and were instrumental in developing the concept of courtly love and chivalry and in making the courts of Europe centers of culture. King Richard I (Richard the Lion-Hearted) of England was a troubadour himself. Others were William, duke of Aquitaine and count of Poitiers, the founder of the school; and Bertrand de Born and Arnaut Daniel, both mentioned in Dante's *Divine Comedy. See also* Courtly love; Minnesinger; Trouvères.

Trouvères: poet-musicians who wrote in the language of northern France during a period extending from the 11th century to the 14th. They flourished after the decline of the southern troubadours, whose influence is paramount in their work. Among the best known are Grace Brûlé, Thibaut IV, king of Navarre, Adam de la Halle, Colin Muset, and Rutebeuf. *See also* Minnesinger; Troubadours.

Troy: prehistoric city, background of Homer's great epic, the *Iliad.* Said to be located in northwestern Asia Minor on the southern shore of the Hellespont, Troy was a strategic port as well as the center of a prosperous farming area. On the basis of Homer's description of the region, German archaeologist Heinrich Schliemann began excavations in the Turkish mound Hisarlik from 1870 to 1890. The nine settlements that he unearthed on the site strongly indicate that the storied city really did exist. Homer's Troy is believed to be the seventh of these cities and to have flourished about 1200 B.C. *See also* Iliad; Trojan War.

Turn of the Screw, The: novel-length ghost story by U.S. expatriate writer Henry James, published in 1898. A young governess goes to an isolated country house to take care of two charming children, Miles and Flora. She sometimes sees a strange man and woman on the grounds whose descriptions match those of the former valet and governess, who are both dead. She gradually realizes that the children, though outwardly angelic, are possessed by these evil ghosts. Her attempts to free them end in tragedy.

Twelfth Night, or What You Will: comedy by Shakespeare, presented c 1600. Viola and her twin brother, Sebastian, are shipwrecked. Viola is rescued and arrives in Illyria where, disguised as a boy, she becomes a page of Duke Orsino and soon falls in love with him. The duke sends his clever page to woo Countess Olivia on his behalf; Olivia becomes enamored of the page. The situation is resolved when Sebastian, Viola's twin, arrives. He marries Olivia and Viola marries Orsino. The play is enlivened by the comic character Sir Toby Belch.

Twenty Thousand Leagues under the Sea: one of French science fiction writer Jules Verne's extraordinary voyages, published in 1870. In this tale a group of scientists become the prisoners of the fascinating Captain Nemo, who carries them off in the *Nautilus,* a strange craft of his own invention that travels underwater. The work anticipates the invention of the submarine.

Tyr or **Tiu,** NM: war god; a son of Odin. Tuesday is named for him.

U

Ubu Roi *(King Ubu):* play by the French writer Alfred Jarry, presented in 1896. Ubu, who makes himself king of Poland, is greedy, brutal, coy, and vulgar; he was first intended as a caricature of a hated schoolmaster of Jarry's youth. The play is dominated by Ubu and by other characters who look and behave like outsize puppets. Their actions embody stupidity-on-the-rampage so powerfully that the play does not have to make any sense. *Ubu Roi* shocked audiences and closed after two performances, but it is now considered the ancestor of the theater of the absurd.

Ugly Duckling, The: fairytale by the 19th-century Danish writer Hans Christian Andersen. The story deals with the loneliness of a little "duck" who is rejected by the flock because he is different. As he grows up into a beautiful swan, he realizes that being different may mean being superior. Andersen was himself a homely and ungainly youth, and this story, like many of his others, has a strongly autobiographical theme.

Ulster (or Ulaid) cycle: body of ancient Irish prose tales, written in the eighth century, dealing with King Conchobar and his knights of the Red Branch, of whom the chief hero is Cuchulain. The stories concerning these boastful, jealous, quarrelsome, chariot-riding warriors are often comic and grim, and sometimes, as in the legend of the beloved Irish heroine Deirdre, sorrowful and beautiful. The most important story is "The Cattle Raid of Cooley," in which Cuchulain, all alone, battles the forces of Connaught. *See also* Cuchulain.

20,000 LEAGUES UNDER THE SEA: Men in the *Nautilus* view a giant octopus.

Ulysses: Latin form of Odysseus. Also, a novel by the Irish writer James Joyce, published in 1922, a landmark of 20th-century fiction. The story takes place in Dublin in one day, June 16, 1904. The ordinary events of that day, as experienced by the leading characters—the autobiographical Stephen Dedalus; Leopold Bloom, a Jewish advertising salesman; his wife Molly Bloom, the eternal daughter of Eve—are carefully recorded. Intermingled are all the stimuli that touch their consciousnesses, all their bodily functions, and all their subjective mental processes, which, in the course of a day's wanderings, take them back and forth in their own lives and in the history of the human race. Joyce uses free association, interior monologue, and sometimes interpolates brilliant literary parodies. The book was banned in the United States until 1933.

Uncle Remus: chief character in several collections of tales by the U.S. writer Joel Chandler Harris, published between 1880 and 1906. The tales, told in dialect by a kindly old black man, Uncle Remus, to a little white boy on a plantation, are actually reworkings of authentic African folktales. They offer evidence of the extensive African culture brought to the New World by slaves. Most of them deal with the animal tricksters Br'er Rabbit and Br'er Fox. The best-known story is "Tar-Baby," in which a tar doll is placed in Br'er Fox's path. Angered when the doll does not move or speak to him, Br'er Fox hits it and sticks to the doll. "Sticky figure" stories are common in both African and American Indian folklore.

Uncle Tom's Cabin or, **Life Among the Lowly:** novel written in 1852 by the New England abolitionist Harriet Beecher Stowe. It had tremendous influence in arousing antislavery sentiment and is considered one of the most effective propaganda novels of all time. Miss Stowe tried to be fair to both sides. The Southern plantation owners, the St. Clares, are presented as gentle and cultured people, and their old black slave Uncle Tom is devoted to them. The villain, Simon Legree, is an overseer who whips the slaves to get more work out of them. His brutality causes Tom's death. Other major characters are the St. Clares' daughter Little Eva and her black playmate Topsy, and the young black couple Eliza and George. Eliza's escape with her baby across the ice is the book's most suspenseful event.

UNCLE TOM'S CABIN: The slave Eliza (scarcely seeming black in this 19th-century picture) escapes across thin ice from the wicked overseer Simon Legree.

Uncle Vanya: play by the Russian dramatist Anton Chekhov, presented in 1897. Vanya, an intelligent and sensitive man, manages the estate of his dead sister to provide for her scholarly husband Serebryakov and her daughter Sonya. When Serebryakov visits the estate with his new young wife Yelena, Vanya falls in love with her. He also realizes that his

UNCLE VANYA: Vanya and Yelena do not notice Yelena's hypocritical husband.

colored
US

coloured
Brit.

honor
US

honour
Brit.

brother-in-law is spoiled, selfish, and ungrateful, and his scholarly work is bogus. The final outrage occurs when Serebryakov announces his intention to sell the estate. The enraged Vanya attempts to shoot him but misses. The visitors depart, leaving Vanya and Sonya to their life of humdrum work and the realization that their goodness, patience, and sincerity will never be rewarded.

Under Milk Wood: radio play for voices by Welsh poet Dylan Thomas. It was published in 1954. In this outpouring of soaring song and verse, Thomas depicts the inhabitants of a Welsh village on a spring day. Whether they are unhappy, exotic, or a bit mad, he portrays them in lyrical terms.

Under the Volcano: novel by English writer Malcolm Lowry, published in 1947. Through effective experimental techniques, Lowry describes the despair, alcoholism, and final disintegration of Geoffrey Firmin, a former British consul living in Mexico.

Unicorn: fabulous beast resembling a horse, with a long slender horn projecting from its forehead. Unicorns were described by Aristotle and Pliny. Their horns were traditionally a sure antidote to poison, and medieval rulers valued a cup made from a unicorn's horn or a potion made from ground horn. Supposedly, the unicorn could be tamed and caught only by a virgin, in whose lap he would at once gently lay his head.

Unities: term used in drama criticism for the unities of action, time, and place that were to be observed in a play. According to these rules, a play was to deal with a single, logically connected action, performed in a single place within a single day. Aristotle mentioned the unities of action and time in the *Poetics;* his later interpreters added unity of place and insisted on the rigid application of all three. The unities were taken most seriously by the classical French dramatists of the 17th century, such as Racine and Corneille.

Up from Slavery: autobiography by U.S. educator Booker T. Washington (1856–1915), published in 1901. The son of a slave and a white man, Washington managed, through considerable effort, to get an education and, at age 25, he became president of Alabama's Tuskegee Normal and Industrial Institute for Negroes. In his book Washington stressed the importance of better education and better jobs for blacks.

Uranus, GM: personification of the sky or heaven wedded to his mother Gaea (earth). Uranus was the father of the Cyclopes, Furies, and Titans. He was dethroned by his son Cronus.

U.S.A.: trilogy of novels by the U.S. writer John Dos Passos, whose three volumes—*The 42nd Parallel* (1930); *1919* (1932); and *The Big Money* (1936)—cover American life from the eve of World War I to the early Depression years. Using a variety of expressionist techniques, the author presents episodic narratives of fictional characters from a range of regional and social milieus. Interspersed throughout are the devices of the Newsreel (snatches of actual news stories, headlines, popular songs), the Biography (lives of celebrities of the period), and the Camera Eye (subjective reminiscences). The overall effect is a portrait of a nation, colored by the author's pessimistic belief that the times are out of joint. Nobody wins in this work, neither the apparent darlings of society—film stars, public relations men, advertisers—nor the lonely outsiders.

Uther Pendragon: father of Arthur. *See* Arthurian legend.

Utopia: humanistic treatise in two parts, written in Latin by English statesman Sir Thomas More and published in 1516. It presents a critique of contemporary social and political ills, and offers a solution to them by the description of Utopia, an ideal island society where reason governs and no one grasps for power. The island has given its name (literally meaning "no place") to all such ideal societies.

V

Valhalla, NM: great hall of Odin in Asgard, where the souls of heroes slain in battle were received with rejoicing and honor (the word means "hall of the slain"). There they feasted and fought each other for sport.

Valkyries, NM: beautiful war maidens, messengers of Odin. They rode through the air above the scene of battle, selecting the warriors worthy to be slain, and carrying them to Valhalla. The name probably meant "choosers of the slain." Brunhild appears as a Valkyrie in the *Völsunga Saga* and in Wagner's opera cycle *Der Ring des Nibelungen.*

Vampire: in folklore, an "undead" person who sleeps in his grave or a coffin filled with his native earth by day but who preys on human victims to drink their blood at night. Usually the victim of a curse himself, the vampire is a sympathetic monster in literature, like the werewolf. The erotic undertones of his lust for blood and subsequent possession of virgins make him a romantic character as well. Belief in vampires is worldwide, but the most familiar vampire lore is of Slavic origin. It became popularly known through Bram Stoker's horror novel *Dracula* (1897).

Vanity Fair: novel by English writer William Makepeace Thackeray, published in 1847–1848, subtitled "A Novel Without a Hero." It satirizes social customs in early 19th-century England (the period of the Napoleonic Wars) through the contrasting histories of the fortunes of two young women—Becky Sharp, an unprincipled opportunistic charmer, and Amelia Sedley, a passive modest softhearted girl, whom life soon crushes under its weight. A well-known description of Napoleon—"He is as great as a man can be without virtue"—could well be applied to Becky Sharp. Though she may not engage the reader's sympathy, her vitality and spirit command one's fascinated attention.

Venus: *See* Aphrodite.

Verse: in general, metrical composition as differentiated from prose; specifically, one metrical line composed of a number of feet. The word "verse" is also often used to mean "stanza." The term usually refers to compositions of a superficial nature (as in "light verse") that make no pretense at being poetry.

Vesta or **Hestia,** RM: virgin goddess of the fire and hearth, not only for the home but for the state. The sacred fire in her temple was never allowed to go out and was tended by the six Vestal Virgins, chosen for their beauty and lineage. They were sworn to 30 years of chastity and were buried alive if they broke their vows.

Vicar of Wakefield, The: novel by English author Oliver Goldsmith, set in 18th-century rural England. First published in 1766, it describes a generous, kindly English vicar's noble reaction to the loss of his fortune and to succeeding mishaps that affect his five growing children.

Victorian era: in English literature, the period defined by the reign of Queen Victoria (1837–1901), an era of progress, reform, and national expansion, in which pragmatic philosophies, utilitarianism, and laissez-faire economics became dominant. The age is notable for literary productivity of all kinds, but its most typical product is the leisurely, realistic middle-class novel, such as was written in mid-century by Dickens,

Thackeray, George Eliot, and Anthony Trollope; and later on by Thomas Hardy and Joseph Conrad. Representative Victorian poets are Tennyson, Browning, and Matthew Arnold. In a narrow sense, the term *Victorian* connotes prudishness and complacency, but the great Victorian writers were all quite critical of their age. Dickens wrote more about poverty than about prosperity; Arnold called his contemporaries "philistines" and saw the "naked shingles of the world" beneath the calm facade of Dover Beach; and the historian Thomas Carlyle tried to tell his generation that man's destiny was not happiness but work.

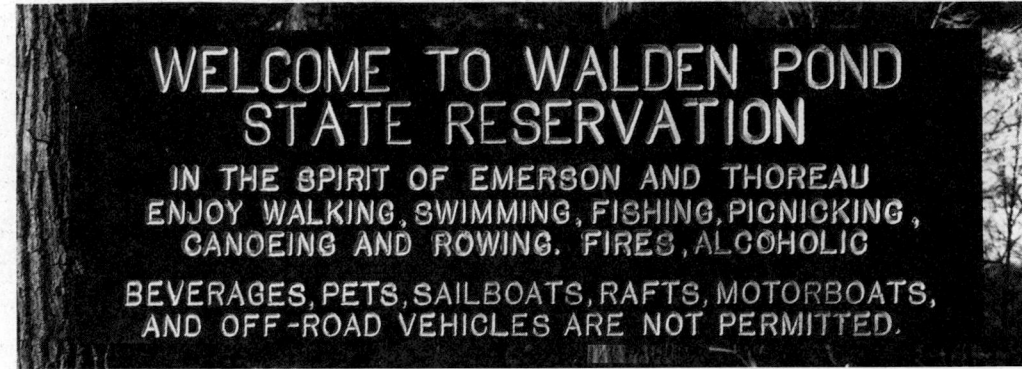

Vita Nuova, La *(The New Life):* collection of sonnets and other poems, completed in 1292, addressed by the Italian Renaissance poet Dante to his beloved Beatrice, whom he first saw at the age of nine. The poems are interspersed throughout a prose commentary that follows the development of his love for Beatrice up to and after her death.

Vivian: *See* Arthurian legend.

Völsunga Saga: 13th-century Icelandic saga, a prose narrative that draws on heroic tales that were recounted in the eddas. A slightly different version is given in the *Nibelungenlied;* the German names of the characters appear in parentheses here.

Sigurd (Siegfried) is the last of the Völsungs, who were named after Sigurd's grandfather, Völsung, the grandson of the god Odin. Sigurd kills the dragon and acquires its cursed treasure. He awakens the Valkyrie maiden Brunhild from her sleep and marries her, but soon goes on a journey to the land of the Nibelungs. There a potion makes him forget Brunhild, and he marries Gudrun (Kriemhild), sister of King Gunnar (Gunther). In disguise, he woos and wins Brunhild for Gunnar. She learns of the deception, has Sigurd killed, and kills herself. Gunnar and his brothers sink the treasure in the Rhine. Gudrun marries Atli (Etzel: based on the historical Attila the Hun), who kills her brothers in an effort to get the treasure; Gudrun then kills Atli and her two sons by him. Richard Wagner's four music dramas comprising *The Ring of the Nibelungs* are largely based on these legends. *See also* Nibelungenlied.

Vulcan: *See* Hephaestus.

W

Waiting for Godot: play by the Irish-born French writer Samuel Beckett, published in 1952 and performed in 1953, a classic of the theater of the absurd. The characters Vladimir (Didi) and Estragon (Gogo) are two tramps who are waiting in a static landscape for a Mr. Godot. Other characters come and go, senseless (but unquestioned) beat-

ings occur, farcical attempts at suicide fail. At times a messenger appears to tell them that Mr. Godot is not coming, will be delayed, or will come tomorrow. It is not clear, or not meant to be clear, who or what Godot is—God? Salvation? Grace? Death? It is only clear that waiting (the condition of life) is boring, intolerable, and absurd.

Waiting for Lefty: one-act proletarian play by the U.S. dramatist Clifford Odets, presented in 1935. The scene is a meeting of desperate taxicab drivers in the Depression era. Their cynical union boss, Fatt, has advised them not to strike; without their leader, Lefty, they are confused. While they argue, the scene switches rapidly to vignettes showing their home life and the fate of other workers facing the same dilemma. When news comes to the hall that Lefty has been killed, one of the men asks what they are to do. Actors planted in the audience, and members of the aroused audience as well, give them the answer: "Strike! Strike! Strike!"

Walden: book of essays published in 1854 by the U.S. philosopher-writer Henry David Thoreau. It describes the

WAITING FOR GODOT: The odd characters wait for the mysterious Godot but never meet him.

author's experiment in living alone in the woods for 2 years (1845–1847) in a house he built on the shores of Walden Pond. In describing the natural life and seasonal changes at the pond, Thoreau provides a reflective critical commentary on the false "playing at life" that most civilized societies mistake for living. In addition to its literary value, *Walden* has a symbolic value: It is a paean to independence and a warning to the reader to test his own values, lest he die without ever having lived.

Walpurgis Night: in German folklore, the eve of May 1st (May Day), when the Devil and the witches were believed to hold a riotous festival on the Brocken, a peak in the Harz Mountains. Goethe's *Faust* contains a scene describing Walpurgis Night.

War and Peace: epic novel by the Russian writer Leo Tolstoy, published in 1864–1869, one of the great novels of all time. It presents a panoramic view of Russian aristocratic society in the early 19th century before, during, and after Napoleon's invasion of Russia. Its numerous characters are all vividly realized, from the old aristocrat Count Bolkonsky through the young and idealistic Petya Rostov. Soldiers, peasants, princesses, simple workmen, and even Napoleon himself are portrayed. Perhaps the most memorable characters are the hero Pierre Bezukhov, a fat awkward impractical idealist, whose eccentric reflections provide a commentary of his age, and the high-spirited beauty Natasha Rostov, whom he has loved since her childhood and eventually marries.

War of the Worlds: science fiction novel by English writer H. G. Wells, published in 1898. It simulates the horror of a Martian invasion that fails only because the invaders cannot tolerate Earth's bacteria. A radio version in 1938 by Orson Welles and the Mercury Theatre players caused a great panic among listeners who thought the play was an actual news broadcast.

Waste Land, The: poem by the Anglo-American poet T. S. Eliot, published in 1922. Both stylistically and thematically it is one of the major works in modern English poetry. Its theme is that of a culture in distress, presented in a series of

WALDEN POND: The secluded refuge of Henry David Thoreau has become a state park, a turn of events Thoreau would doubtless have deplored.

theater *US*	
theatre *Brit.*	
civilized *US*	
civilised *Brit.*	
realized *US*	
realised *Brit.*	

20 History of Literature

WHO'S AFRAID OF VIRGINIA WOOLF?: Martha challenges her husband, George, an older professor, in the film version of Edward Albee's vitriolic yet moving play.

disjointed images and scenes drawn from commonplace upper- and lower-class daily life as well as from ancient, obscure fertility rituals. Its title and controlling imagery are taken from the Grail legend. The progress of the poem suggests the sick Fisher King's search through the wasteland of modern life—the Unreal City—for a cure for his illness. The poem integrates words, phrases, and images from other literary works so that the traditions of the past form a contrapuntal echo to the modern dilemma. The poem was published with several pages of notes explaining its allusions.

Waverley Novels: collective title given to the historical romances of English author Sir Walter Scott. *Waverley,* published anonymously in 1814, was the first of the series. The others, until 1827, were signed "by the author of *Waverley."* *Waverley* has the distinction of being the first historical novel. In it and in other works dealing with Scotland's heroic and colorful past, Scott touched off the springs of Romantic nationalism and became the most popular, most widely imitated novelist in Europe. His historical novels include *Guy Mannering, The Antiquary, Old Mortality, The Heart of Midlothian, Rob Roy, The Bride of Lammermoor, Ivanhoe, Quentin Durward, and Kenilworth.*

Way of All Flesh, The: novel by the English writer Samuel Butler, published posthumously in 1903. It cruelly dissects the relationships of three generations of a Victorian family. In his bitter rejection of the hypocritical piety of his clergyman father, Butler's autobiographical hero Ernest Pontifex also rejects the religion and bourgeois values that his parents represent.

Way of the World, The: play by the English dramatist William Congreve, presented in 1700, considered the outstanding comedy of the Restoration period. Like most plays of the period, its plot is fantastically complicated. Its high point is the famous bargaining scene between the lovers Mirabell and Mrs. Millamant, in which they each state their conditions for marriage. This is not the expected witty duel of the sexes; it is, instead, a frank expression of deeper values by two people who are each too intelligent to be satisfied with the "way of the world."

Werewolf: in worldwide folklore, a human being who turns into a wolf and preys on other humans. Lycanthropy, or the temporary transformation of a human being into animal form, was long assumed to be the power of witches. But in fairytales the transformation is often caused by a curse rather than an act of will, as in "Beauty and the Beast" and "The Frog Prince." Ovid relates the tale of Lycaon, a Greek king who was transformed into a wolf by Jupiter as a punishment for serving the god human flesh. However, in R. L. Stevenson's *The Strange Case of Dr. Jekyll and Mr. Hyde,* the metamorphosis is caused by the doctor's experiments and, as such, is a result of his will. When Jekyll loses control over the transformation, he fits the pattern of the victims of the curse, who are romantic, sympathetic figures. The werewolf as benevolent savior occurs in *William of Palerne,* a 14th-century English romance in which the beast aids the hero and is at last returned to human form.

Who's Afraid of Virginia Woolf?: play by the U.S. dramatist Edward Albee, first performed in 1962. A young married couple, Nick and Honey, new in the academic community, visit George and Martha, a middle-aged professor and his wife, for a drink and an evening of "fun and games." But the games played by George and Martha are deadly. They lacerate each other's egos, seduce and humiliate Nick, and attempt to destroy Honey. The games are designed to strip away illusions until all four are drunken wrecks. One suspects, however, that George and Martha will pull themselves together and play games the next night.

Wild Duck, The: symbolic drama by Norwegian playwright Henrik Ibsen, first performed in 1885. The play is a study of the illusions that sustain people in everyday life. As one character says, "Take away the life-lie from the average man and straight away you take away his happiness."

Wilhelm Meister's Apprenticeship: symbolic novel by German author Johann Wolfgang von Goethe, published in 1795–1796. It is considered the model for the apprenticeship-to-life novel, called in German *Bildungsroman,* in which a youthful hero matures. Wilhelm, the son of a merchant, is an artistic, stagestruck youth who joins a troupe of traveling players. He is disciplined into manhood by art. A sequel published in 1829, *Wilhelm Meister's Travels,* shows Wilhelm and his young son Felix setting out on a new voyage of experience and self-discovery. It apparently indicates that the apprenticeship to life is never over; that there is always more to learn. In this second novel, science and philosophy play a greater role than art.

William Tell: legendary Swiss patriot of the early 1300s, when Switzerland was ruled by Austria. Tell refused to acknowledge the Austrian governor, Gessler, by bowing to Gessler's hat, which had been set on a pole in the town square of Altdorf. As punishment, Gessler ordered Tell to show his skill with the crossbow by shooting an apple off his son's head. Tell succeeded, then warned the governor that, had he missed, he would have shot Gessler too. Tell was seized but he escaped, and later did shoot Gessler, inciting the Swiss to revolt against Austrian rule.

Tell is the subject of a famous drama by Schiller (1804), from which Rossini derived his opera *William Tell* (1829).

Wind in the Willows, The: classic children's book by English writer Kenneth Grahame, published in 1908. It is about a group of river animals—Mole, a fussy bachelor; Rat, a romantic poet; and Badger, a crabbed philosopher—and the troubles they incur because of their incorrigible young friend Toad, "the king of the Road," who has a passion for cars and reckless driving. After the conceited Toad has been imprisoned for stealing a car, and the stoats and the weasels have taken over Toad Hall, his friends help him recover his mansion, and finally succeed in reforming him.

Winesburg, Ohio: collection of poetic short stories, the masterpiece of U.S. writer Sherwood Anderson, published in 1919. The stories are linked in theme and by the central figure of the narrator, George Willard, a dreamy adolescent who aspires to be a writer. As the people of the town reveal to George their loneliness, frustration, delusions, and dreams, the inarticulate soul of Winesburg comes to life. In the final story, "Departure," George is on the train that will carry him to the city, looking back on the village of Winesburg until it disappears.

Wings of the Dove: novel by U.S. expatriate author Henry James, published in 1902. It is a novel of grand manners, for all the characters are playing a delicate game for very high stakes. Milly Theale (the dove), an American heiress in Europe, gallantly ignores the fact that she has a fatal disease. Her friend Kate Croy, who cannot marry Merton Densher for lack of money, proposes that Densher marry Milly to inherit her wealth; he shrinks from the deception, until Kate seals the bargain by becoming his mistress. Milly responds to Densher's courtship, but when she learns of his relationship with Kate, she gives up her fight for life. After her death, a letter comes to Densher; both he and Kate know it is from Milly, offering money so they can marry. But they can no longer accept the money or one another and throw the letter unopened into the fire.

Winnie-the-Pooh: children's book written by English author A. A. Milne, first published in 1926. It relates the adventures of Christopher Robin, patterned on Milne's son; his stuffed bear, named Winnie-*Ther*-Pooh; and their friends Piglet, Owl, Rabbit, Eeyore, Kanga, and Roo in a whimsical landscape where there are heffalumps but no adults. In a

THE WIZARD OF OZ: Dorothy, played by Judy Garland, comforts the Cowardly Lion (Bert Lahr) in the musical film version of the children's classic.

WINNIE-THE-POOH, a stuffed toy bear, confers with his friend Christopher Robin.

later book, *The House at Pooh Corner* (1928), a new friend, Tigger, was introduced. Milne's books were illustrated by Ernest H. Shepard.

Wisdom literature: name applied to some ancient Oriental texts and to several books of the Bible that contain philosophical speculation and ethical maxims. Sometimes the philosophy is in brief proverbs, as in the Book of Proverbs; sometimes it is in essays; and sometimes it is in parables and dialogues, as in the Book of Job.

Witch: in worldwide belief, a person with supernatural knowledge and powers, usually acquired from the Devil in exchange for his or her soul. Witches are believed to be able to change shape, transform others, cause illness and death, concoct charms, and tell the future. In literature, their prophecies never lie, but they do mislead. Shakespeare's Three Weird Sisters in *Macbeth* are the most famous witches in literature. They serve to set the ominous mood in the first scene as well as to deceive Macbeth into a false security. The convention of three cackling crones originates with the sister Fates (*see also* Fates).

In literature, witches tend to be female. Although fairytale witches are commonly conceived of as hags, in poetic usage the witch is often seductive. In the *Odyssey*, Circe is an amorous witch who transforms Odysseus's men into swine (*see also* Circe). In Coleridge's "Christabel," an evil spirit assumes the form of a beautiful girl. Keats's "La Belle Dame Sans Merci" is also a lovely enchantress who saps a young man's vitality.

Witches often play the temptress in order to acquire a soul for the Devil. The Witches' Sabbaths in Goethe's *Faust* and Hawthorne's "Young Goodman Brown" both employ beautiful witches to seduce the hero. Marlowe's Helen of Troy in *Doctor Faustus* is another instance of the Devil using sexuality to steal a soul. In M. G. Lewis's *The Monk,* a Gothic novel, the villainous lecher, at one time a respected monk, is seduced into evil by a sorceress who looks like the Madonna. Shelley, in his poem "The Witch of Atlas," expands the convention to include a witch who is both beautiful and kind.

Witches are vengeful and tend to hold grudges against following generations, as in Hawthorne's *The House of Seven Gables.* Many Gothic tales are built around undying curses falling on the heads of innocent descendants.

Wizard of Oz, The: children's story by U.S. author L. Frank Baum, first published in 1900 and titled *The Wonderful Wizard of Oz.* Baum's tale of the adventures of Dorothy and Toto, the Scarecrow, the Tin Woodman, and the Cowardly Lion was so well received that Baum continued to write books about the land of Oz until his death. The first Oz book was illustrated by W. W. Denslow; the succeeding ones by John R. Neill.

Woden: *See* Odin.

Would-Be Gentleman, The: play by the French dramatist Molière, first performed in 1670, a satire on hypocrisy. M. Jourdain, a tradesman, aspires to be a gentleman by taking strenuous training in superficial courtesies. Fortunately, his inherent but more genuinely appealing vulgarity makes him impervious to the transformation.

Woyzeck: play by the German writer Georg Büchner, published in 1879, far in advance of its time in its modern style and psychological realism. Woyzeck is a poor conscript who supports his mistress Marie and their little boy by performing services for a captain and a doctor. The doctor uses him for medical experiments—literally as a guinea pig—but he is equally a guinea pig for the captain, who delights in taxing Woyzeck's simple mind with difficult questions. They also find amusement in teasing Woyzeck with stories of Marie's

realizes
US

realises
Brit.

infidelities that Woyzeck at last realizes are true. He begins to behave strangely and to have violent dreams. One night he stabs Marie to death at a lonely pond, then dances madly at the inn, frightening everyone by his bloodstained hands and wild talk. Returning to the woods to retrieve his knife, Woyzeck drowns in the pond. The story is the basis of a modern opera, *Wozzeck,* by the German composer Alban Berg.

Wuthering Heights: novel by English writer Emily Bronte, published in 1847. Wuthering Heights is the Earnshaw estate set in the moors of northern England. Here the kindly Mr. Earnshaw brings a dark, ragged slum boy, Heathcliff, to be raised with his children Catherine and Hindley. Hindley hates the intruder and, on his father's death, reduces him to a servant. But Cathy and Heathcliff, both rebels, have already formed the intense relationship that is the core of the novel. Cathy makes a conventional marriage to genteel Edgar Linton, but cannot forget the wild Heathcliff, and he cannot forgive her betrayal. After Cathy's death, he takes revenge by marrying and mistreating Linton's weak-willed sister, acquiring the family properties, and ruining Hindley. He finds peace only by joining Cathy in death.

##

Xanadu: *See* Kubla Khan.

##

Yahoo: *See* Gulliver's Travels.

Yale school: a group of literary critics, specifically several professors of English at Yale University. The Yale school expanded on the work of French philosopher Jacques Derrida and helped popularize the deconstructionist movement in the 1970s and 1980s. The most prominent members of the group were Paul de Man and J. Hillis Miller.

Yearling, The: novel by U.S. writer Marjorie Kinnan Rawlings, published in 1938. Its subject is the turning point from boyhood to manhood in the life of 12-year-old Jody Baxter, a child of the impoverished Florida scrub country. During a period when his father is ill and the family resources are depleted, Jody finds a fawn that he raises and shares his food with. When the fawn grows up and regularly devours the family crops, his mother shoots it. Jody runs away from home, but returns to face his family with forgiveness and understanding.

Yggdrasil, NM: great world tree, an ash tree, binding together heaven, earth, and the underworld. Rooted in the underworld, where a dragon was believed to forever gnaw at the roots, its trunk supported the world, and its top reached beyond heaven. Yggdrasil was the tree of life, and also the tree of knowledge, for Mimir's well of wisdom had its source beneath its roots. It was the tree of fate as well, for beneath it sat the Norns who presided over human destiny. An eagle sat in the top, and the squirrel Ratatook ran up and down it, carrying strife.

You Know Me, Al: novel in letter form by the U.S. writer Ring Lardner, published in 1916. The letters are written by Jack Keefe, a rookie pitcher with the Chicago White Sox, to his old bush-league pal, Al. They tell Al how Keefe is the sole mainstay of his ball club, how he is pursued by beautiful women, and admired by his teammates and coaches. Subsequent letters reveal gradually that Keefe is really a second-stringer whose conceit is undamaged by reality.

Yseult: *See* Tristan and Iseult.

TRAVELERS can still visit the ruins of the home that is said to have provided the inspiration for Bronte's *Wuthering Heights.*

Z

Zephyrus, GM: god personifying the gentle west wind (the "zephyr"); called Favonius by the Romans.

Zeus, GM: supreme god identified with the Roman Jupiter. Zeus was the youngest son of Cronus and Rhea. When he was grown, Zeus overthrew his father, establishing the Olympian gods who were his brothers and sisters (*see also* Cronus). He married his sister Hera and also loved many mortal women.

Zeus was primarily king of the gods and heaven, the sky god and, especially, the thunder god. The thunderbolt was his weapon, and he was worshiped on mountain tops. His worship later took on moral and social aspects, and eventually embodied legal and political ideas as well. Zeus also was god and protector of the state and the god of personal and public oaths; murder was abhorrent to him. He was regarded in many stories as father of the world.

Zorba the Greek: novel by the Greek writer Nikos Kazantzakis, first published as *Alexis Zorba* in 1946, translated into English in 1952. It presents a rascally old Greek workman, capable of great feats of physical strength. Zorba is shown handling a mine on Crete for a bookish Briton—singing, dancing, relating amorous adventures, and even mishandling the Briton's funds. But under the impact of Zorba's uninhibited zest for life, his strait-laced employer is reeducated and becomes a freer person.

ZEUS was thought to be the sender of thunder and lightning, rain and winds. His traditional weapon was the thunderbolt.

THE HELP DESK

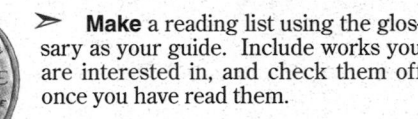

➤ **Make** a reading list using the glossary as your guide. Include works you are interested in, and check them off once you have read them.

➤ **Make** an index card for each great author discussed in HISTORY OF LITERATURE. Learn the names of the important works supplied for each author, and use them as guides for your personal reading program.

➤ **Make** index cards for the literary terms unfamiliar to you. Use the cards to study the terms and to quiz yourself.

➤ **What** are the differences/functions of author, editor, illustrator, researcher, and others?

➤ **Can** several books be related in some fashion? Why? How?

➤ **When** you finish reading a book, short story, or poem, explain why you think the title was selected. Think of an alternative title.

➤ **How** does folklore relate to literature?

➤ **What** is the difference between reality and fantasy? Fantasy and fiction? Fact and opinion?

➤ **Read** a chapter or passage and analyze what you have read— identify the motives of the characters, identify the author's viewpoint, draw your own conclusions, and identify any relationships with their cause and effect.

➤ **Review** a book or passage and identify the author's viewpoint, tone, mood, and reason for writing.

➤ **Pause** at several points while reading a book, especially fiction. Can you predict the final outcome? Do you change your mind as your reading progresses? Why or why not?

➤ **After** reading a book or story, write a summary of it. Is there a difference between a summary and a report?

➤ **Have** you found authors whose books you especially like? What is it that you like about their writing— interesting/exciting plots, characterizations, word pictures? Use examples to illustrate your points.

➤ **What** is persuasive writing? Give examples.

➤ **If** plot, style, character, and structure are the primary components of storytelling, which is most important? Is it always equally important? Can importance vary? If so, what dictates importance? Give examples.

➤ **What** constitutes a "hero" in modern fiction? Is it the same as in writings as far back as the Middle Ages? Give examples and explain.

➤ **Develop** a series of questions/criteria to govern your analysis if you were hired to review and select manuscripts for publication.

➤ **Can** you justify the continued existence of libraries in our modern society?

➤ **Discuss** feminism in fiction as a reflection of the social climate through the past 200-300 years.

➤ **Modern** fiction is frequently a product of category and formula. Draw up a list of categories, for example, detective, mystery, science fiction, spy, etc. Then select one of your favorite genres. From your own observations, develop the basic formula, then the outline of a potential book.

➤ **It** has been said that there are only a few basic plot lines in all of literature. Can you list six? Give examples of each.

➤ **Select** several biographies of the same person. Look for the differences as well as similarities. Can you tell if the author liked or disliked the subject? How complete, accurate, etc., is each?

➤ **For** a list of helpful references, go to the *customers* section of www.southwestern.com.

Pulitzer Prizes

The scope, focus, and quality of American writing in the 20th century are easily discernable by a review of the Pulitzer Prizes. Joseph Pulitzer, publisher of the St. Louis *Post-Dispatch,* New York *Herald,* and New York *Evening Herald,* endowed the School of Journalism at Columbia University and established the Pulitzer Prizes for outstanding American accomplishments in writing of various types. Although eligible writings are assessed annually, the awards are not mandatory if nothing in a field is deemed worthy.

Biography/Autobiography

AUTHORS	WORKS
Henry Adams and Douglas S. Freeman (1919)	The Education of Henry Adams
Mary W. Ashworth and John A. Carroll (1958)	George Washington Vol. III
Leonard Baker (1979)	Days of Sorrow and Pain: Leo Baeck and the Berlin Jews
Ray S. Baker (1940)	Woodrow Wilson, Life and Letters
Russell Baker (1983)	Growing Up
W. Jackson Bate (1964)	John Keats
(1978)	Samuel Johnson
Samuel F. Bemis (1950)	John Quincy Adams and the Foundations of American Foreign Policy
A. Scott Berg (1999)	Lindbergh
Albert J. Beveridge (1920)	The Life of John Marshall
Edward Bok (1921)	The Americanization of Edward Bok
William C. Bruce (1918)	Benjamin Franklin, Self-Revealed
Robert A. Caro (1975)	The Power Broker: Robert Moses and the Fall of New York
(2003)	Master of the Senate
Margaret Clapp (1948)	Forgotten First Citizen: John Bigelow
Margaret L. Coit (1951)	John C. Calhoun: American Portrait
Harvey Cushing (1926)	Life of Sir William Osler
Tyler Dennett (1934)	John Hay
David Donald (1961)	Charles Sumner and The Coming of the Civil War
David Herbert Donald (1988)	Look Homeward: A Life of Thomas Wolfe
Leon Edel (1963)	Henry James: Vol. II: The Conquest of London, 1870–1881
(1963)	Henry James: Vol. III: The Middle Years, 1881–1895
Richard Ellman (1989)	Oscar Wilde
Elizabeth Frank (1986)	Louise Bogan: A Portrait
Douglas S. Freeman (1958)	George Washington, Vols. I–VI
(1935)	R. E. Lee
Hamlin Garland (1922)	A Daughter of the Middle Border
David J. Garrow (1987)	Bearing the Cross: Martin Luther King, Jr. and the Southern Christian Leadership Conference
Katharine Graham (1998)	Personal History
Sebastian de Grazia (1990)	Machiavelli in Hell
Talbot F. Hamlin (1956)	Benjamin Henry Latrobe
Louis R. Harlan (1984)	Booker T. Washington
Joan D. Hedrick (1995)	Harriet Beecher Stowe: A Life
Burton J. Hendrick (1923)	Life and Letters of Walter H. Page
(1929)	The Training of an American: The Earlier Life and Letters of Walter H. Page
Emory Holloway (1927)	Whitman: An Interpretation in Narrative
DeWolfe Howe (1925)	Barrett Wendell and His Letters
Henry James (1931)	Charles W. Eliot
Marquis James (1938)	Andrew Jackson
(1930)	The Raven (Sam Houston)
Justin Kaplan (1967)	Mr. Clemens and Mark Twain
George F. Kennan (1968)	Memoirs (1925–1950)
John F. Kennedy (1957)	Profiles in Courage
Joseph P. Lash (1972)	Eleanor and Franklin
David Levering Lewis (1994)	W. E. B. Du Bois: Biography of a Race, 1868–1919
(2001)	W. E. B. Du Bois: The Fight for Equality and the American Century, 1919–1963
R. W. B. Lewis (1976)	Edith Wharton: A Biography
Charles A. Lindbergh (1954)	The Spirit of St. Louis

Biography/Autobiography

AUTHORS	WORKS
Carleton Mabee (1944)	The American Leonardo: The Life of Samuel F. B. Morse
John E. Mack (1977)	A Prince of Our Disorder: The Life of T. E. Lawrence
Robert K. Massie (1981)	Peter the Great: His Life and World
David J. Mays (1953)	Edmund Pendleton, 1721–1803
Frank McCourt (1997)	Angela's Ashes: A Memoir
David McCullough (1993)	Truman
(2002)	John Adams
William S. McFeely (1982)	Grant: A Biography
Jack Miles (1996)	god: a Biography
Samuel E. Morison (1943)	Admiral of the Ocean Sea
(1960)	John Paul Jones
Edmund Morris (1980)	The Rise of Theodore Roosevelt
Stephen Naifeh and Gregory White Smith (1991)	Jackson Pollock: An American Saga
Allan Nevins (1933)	Grover Cleveland
(1937)	Hamilton Fish: The Inner History of the Grant Administration
Russell B. Nye (1945)	George Bancroft: Brahmin Rebel
Ralph B. Perry (1936)	The Thought and Character of William James
Henry F. Pringle (1932)	Theodore Roosevelt
Lewis B. Puller, Jr. (1992)	Fortunate Son: The Healing of a Vietnam Vet
Michael Pupin (1924)	From Immigrant to Inventor
Merlo J. Pusey (1952)	Charles Evans Hughes
B. L. Reid (1969)	The Man from New York: John Quinn and His Friends
Laura E. Richards and Maude Howe Elliot, assisted by Florence Howe Hall (1917)	Julia Ward Howe
Charles E. Russell (1928)	The American Orchestra and Theodore Thomas
Ernest Samuels (1965)	Henry Adams
Stacy Schiff (2000)	Vera (Mrs. Vladimir Nabokov)
Arthur M. Schlesinger, Jr. (1966)	A Thousand Days
Louis Sheaffer (1974)	O'Neill, Son and Artist
Odell Shepard (1938)	Pedlar's Progress
Robert E. Sherwood (1949)	Roosevelt and Hopkins
Kenneth Silverman (1985)	The Life and Times of Cotton Mather
W. A. Swanberg (1973)	Luce and His Empire
Lawrence Thompson (1971)	Robert Frost: The Years of Triumph, 1915–1938
Carl Van Doren (1939)	Benjamin Franklin
Arthur Walworth (1959)	Woodrow Wilson: American Prophet
William Allen White (1947)	Autobiography of William Allen White
William S. White (1955)	The Taft Story
T. Harry Williams (1970)	Huey Long
Forest Wilson (1942)	Crusader in Crinoline
Ola E. Winslow (1941)	Jonathan Edwards
Linnie M. Wolfe (1946)	Son of the Wilderness

Fiction

AUTHORS	WORKS
James Agee (1958)	A Death in the Family
Margaret Ayer Barnes (1931)	Years of Grace
Saul Bellow (1976)	Humboldt's Gift
Louis Bromfield (1927)	Early Autumn
Pearl S. Buck (1932)	The Good Earth
Robert Olen Butler (1993)	A Good Scent from a Strange Mountain
Willa Cather (1923)	One of Ours
Michael Chabon (2001)	The Amazing Adventures of Kavalier & Clay

Pulitzer Prizes

Fiction

AUTHORS	WORKS
John Cheever (1979)	The Stories of John Cheever
James Gould Cozzens (1949)	Guard of Honor
Michael Cunningham (1999)	The Hours
Harold L. Davis (1936)	Honey in the Horn
Allen Drury (1960)	Advise and Consent
Jeffrey Eugenides (2003)	Middlesex
William Faulkner (1955)	The Fable
(1963)	The Reivers
Edna Ferber (1925)	So Big
Martin Flavin (1944)	Journey in the Dark
Richard Ford (1996)	Independence Day
Ellen Glasgow (1942)	In This Our Life
Shirley Ann Grau (1965)	The Keepers of the House
A. B. Guthrie, Jr. (1950)	The Way West
Ernest Hemingway (1953)	The Old Man and the Sea
John Hersey (1945)	A Bell for Adano
Oscar Hijuelos (1990)	The Mambo Kings Play Songs of Love
Josephine W. Johnson (1935)	Now in November
MacKinlay Kantor (1956)	Andersonville
William Kennedy (1984)	Ironweed
Oliver La Farge (1930)	Laughing Boy
Jhumpa Lahiri (2000)	Interpreter of Maladies
Harper Lee (1961)	To Kill a Mockingbird
Sinclair Lewis (1926)	Arrowsmith
Alison Lurie (1985)	Foreign Affairs
Norman Mailer (1980)	The Executioner's Song
Bernard Malamud (1967)	The Fixer
John P. Marquand (1938)	The Late George Apley
Larry McMurtry (1986)	Lonesome Dove
James Alan McPherson (1978)	Elbow Room
James A. Michener (1948)	Tales of the South Pacific
Caroline Miller (1934)	Lamb in His Bosom
Steven Millhauser (1997)	Martin Dressler: The Tale of an American Dreamer
Margaret Mitchell (1937)	Gone With the Wind
N. Scott Momaday (1969)	House Made of Dawn
Toni Morrison (1988)	Beloved
Edwin O'Connor (1962)	The Edge of Sadness
Julia Peterkin (1929)	Scarlet Sister Mary
Ernest Poole (1918)	His Family
Katherine Anne Porter (1966)	Collected Stories of Katherine Anne Porter
E. Annie Proulx (1994)	The Shipping News
Marjorie Kinnan Rawlings (1939)	The Yearling
Conrad Richter (1951)	The Town
Philip Roth (1998)	American Pastoral
Richard Russo (2002)	Empire Falls
Michael Shaara (1975)	The Killer Angels
Carol Shields (1995)	The Stone Diaries
Upton Sinclair (1943)	Dragon's Teeth
Jane Smiley (1992)	A Thousand Acres
Jean Stafford (1970)	Collected Stories
Wallace Stegner (1972)	Angle of Repose
John Steinbeck (1940)	The Grapes of Wrath
T. S. Stribling (1933)	The Store
William Styron (1968)	Confessions of Nat Turner
Booth Tarkington (1922)	Alice Adams
(1919)	The Magnificent Ambersons
Peter Taylor (1987)	A Summons to Memphis
Robert Lewis Taylor (1959)	The Travels of Jaimie McPheeters
John Kennedy Toole (1981)	A Confederacy of Dunces
Anne Tyler (1989)	Breathing Lessons
John Updike (1991)	Rabbit at Rest
(1982)	Rabbit is Rich
Alice Walker (1983)	The Color Purple
Robert Penn Warren (1947)	All the King's Men
Eudora Welty (1973)	The Optimist's Daughter
Edith Wharton (1921)	The Age of Innocence
Thornton Wilder (1928)	the Bridge of San Luis Rey
Margaret Wilson (1924)	The Able McLaughlins
Herman Wouk (1952)	The Caine Mutiny

Nonfiction

AUTHORS	WORKS
Ernest Becker (1974)	The Denial of Death
Herbert P. Bix (2001)	Hirohito and the Making of Modern Japan
Robert N. Butler (1976)	Why Survive? Being Old in America
Robert Coles (1973)	Children of Crisis, Vols. II & III
David Brian Davis (1967)	The Problem of Slavery in Western Culture
Jared Diamond (1998)	Guns, Germs, and Steel: The Fates of Human Societies
Annie Dillard (1975)	Pilgrim at Tinker Creek
John W. Dower (2000)	Embracing Defeat: Japan in the Wake of World War II
Rene Jules Dubos (1969)	So Human and Animal: How We are Shaped by Surroundings and Events
Will and Ariel Durant (1968)	Rousseau and Revolution
Eric H. Ericson (1970)	Gandhi's Truth
Frances Fitzgerald (1973)	Fire in the Lake: The Vietnamese and the Americans in Vietnam
Douglas R. Hofstadter (1980)	Gödel, Escher, Bach: An Eternal Golden Braid
Richard Hofstadter (1964)	Anti-intellectualism in American Life
Bert Holldobler and Edward O. Wilson (1991)	The Ants
Howard Mumford Jones (1965)	O Strange New World
Tracy Kidder (1982)	The Soul of a New Machine
Richard Kluger (1997)	Ashes to Ashes: America's Hundred Year Cigarette War, the Public Health and the Unabashed Triumph of Philip Morris
Joseph Lelyveld (1986)	Move Your Shadow
J. Anthony Lukas (1986)	Common Ground
Dale Maharidge and Michael Williamson (1990)	And Their Children After Them
Norman Mailer (1969)	The Armies of the Night
John McFee (1999)	Annals of the Former World
Diane McWhorter (2002)	Carry Me Home: Birmingham, Alabama, the Climactic Battle of the Civil Rights Revolution
Samantha Power (2003)	A Problem From Hell: America and the Age of Genocide
David Remick (1994)	Lenin's Tomb: The Last Days of the Soviet Empire
Richard Rhodes (1988)	The Making of the Atomic Bomb
Tina Rosenberg (1996)	The Haunted Land: Facing Europe's Ghosts After Communism
Carl Sagan (1978)	The Dragons of Eden
Carl E. Schorske (1981)	Fin-de-Siecle Vienna: Politics and Culture
Neil Sheehan (1989)	A Bright Shining Lie: John Paul Vann and America in Vietnam
Susan Sheehan (1983)	Is There No Place on Earth for Me?
David K. Shipler (1987)	Arab and Jew
Paul Starr (1984)	Social Transformation of American Medicine
Edwin Way Teal (1966)	Wandering Through Winter
Studs Terkel (1985)	The Good War
John Toland (1971)	The Rising Sun
Barbara W. Tuchman (1963)	The Guns of August
(1972)	Stilwell and the American Experience in China 1911–1945
William W. Warner (1977)	Beautiful Swimmers
Jonathan Weiner (1995)	The Beak of the Finch: A Story of Evolution in Our Time
Theodore White (1962)	The Making of the President 1960
Gary Wills (1993)	Lincoln at Gettysburg: The Words That Remade America
Edward O. Wilson (1979)	On Human Nature
Daniel Yergin (1992)	The Prize: The Epic Quest for Oil, Money, and Power

20 History of Literature

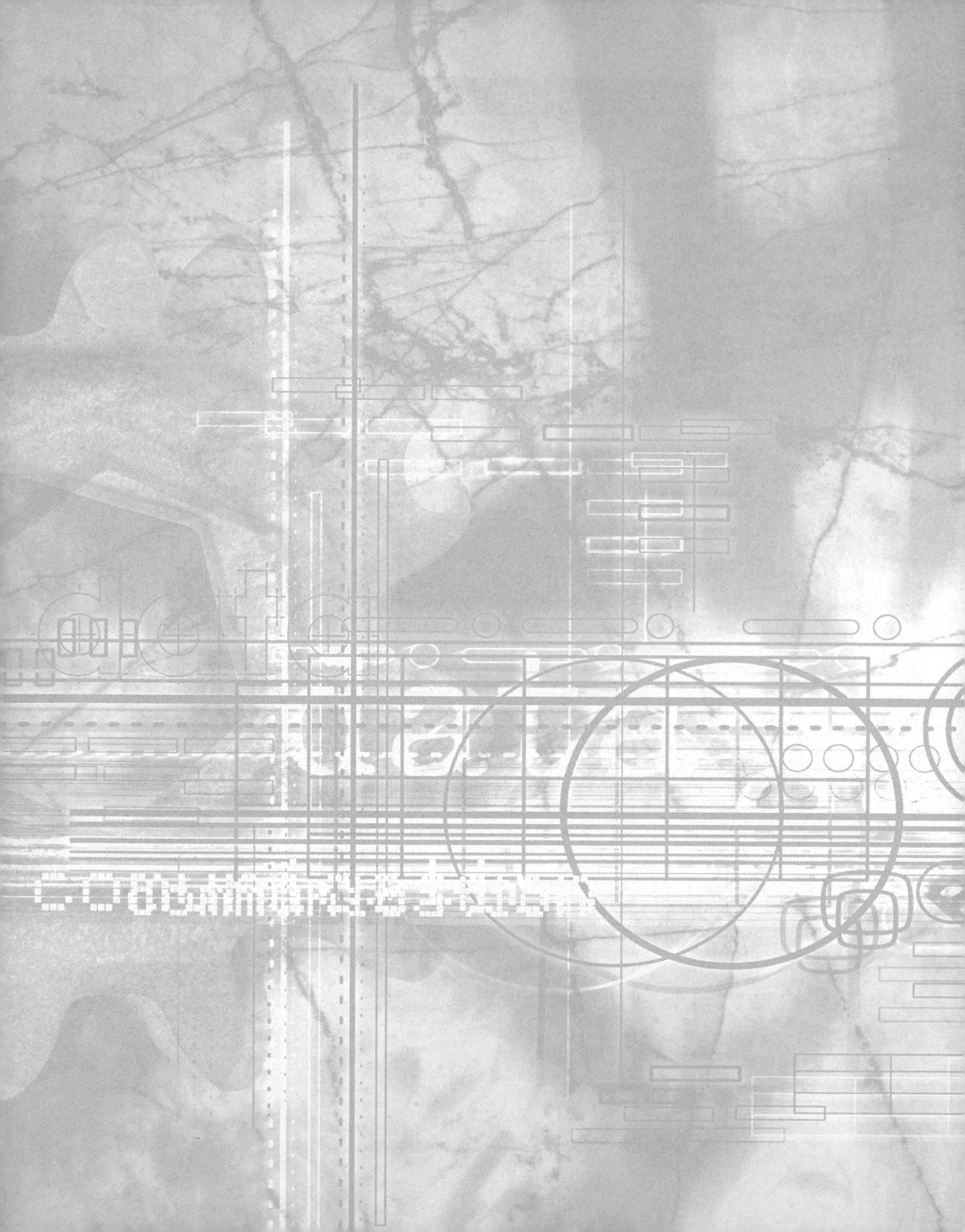

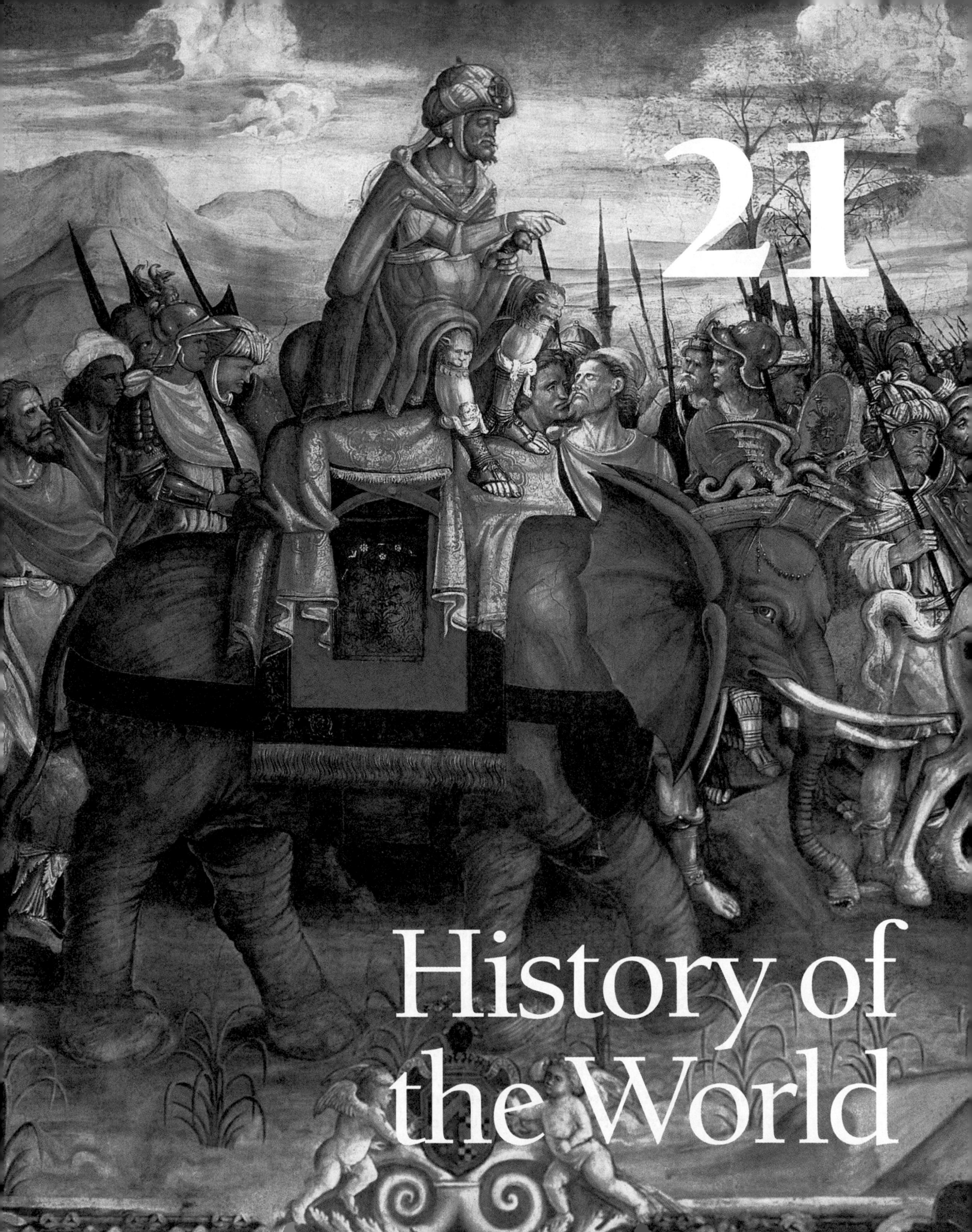

History of the World

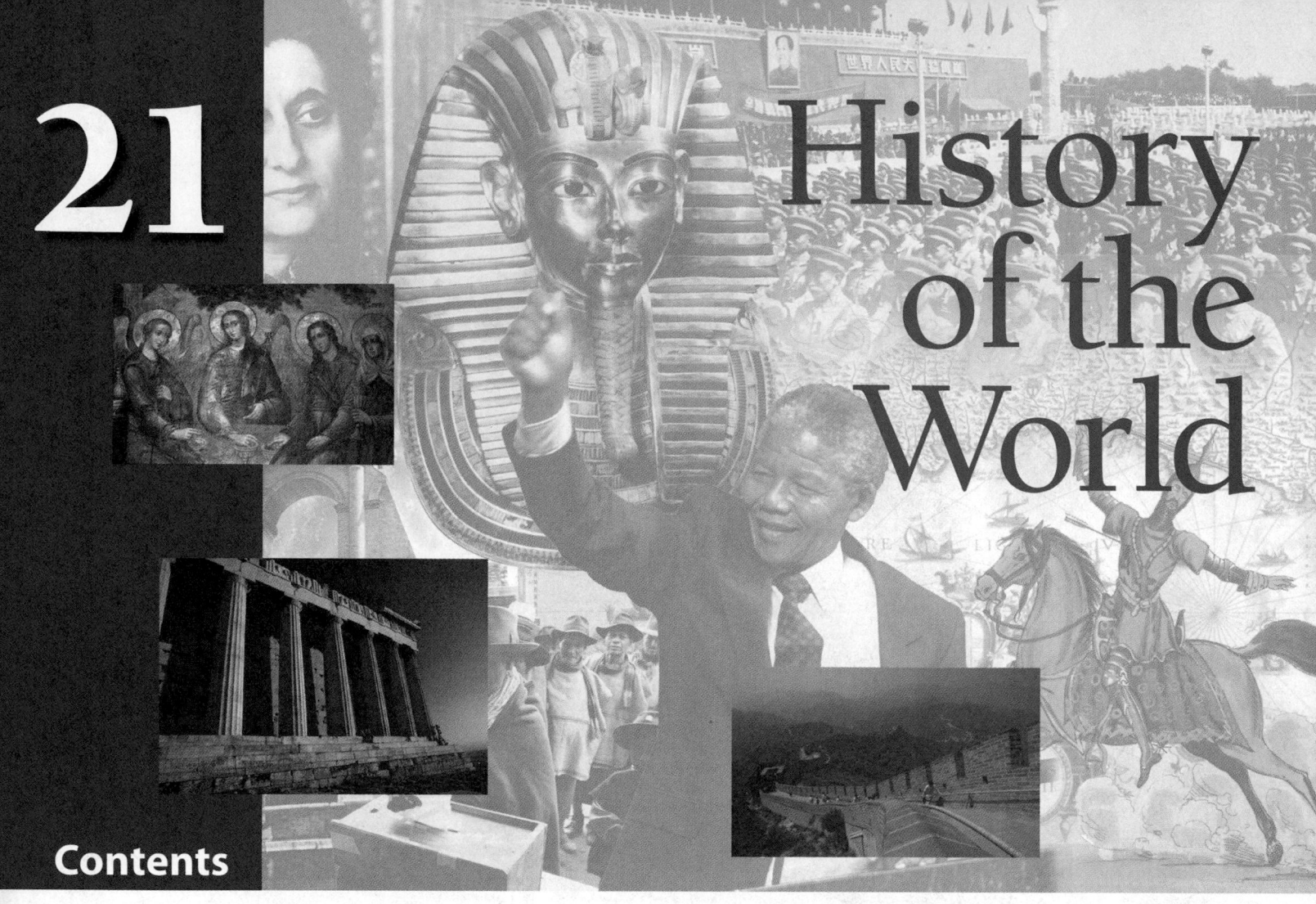

21 History of the World

Contents

Overleaf: *Hannibal crossing the mountains in Italy*

Ancient Peoples

c 3500 B.C.–A.D. 500

Historians refer to this period in history as "ancient times" or "antiquity." Its earliest date, 3500 B.C., marks the beginning of civilization on Earth. The term *civilization* describes a culture that has reached a fairly high degree of social, economic, and political development, one that has a system of writing, highly organized religion and government, advanced technology, and a high level of art. Civilization also presumes the development of urban life, as the word derived from the Latin *civil,* meaning "city dweller," implies.

Over this 4,000-year period, people across the world progressed at different speeds through various stages of development. In different places at different times, many groups moved out of the Stone Age, so-called because tools and weapons of the time were made of stone, into the Bronze Age, in which people developed metalworking and replaced stone implements with ones made of copper and then bronze. Later people progressed into the Iron Age, in which they learned to smelt and work this strong metal. Other people never left the Stone Age.

Great civilizations gathered energy and strengthened in both East and West, culminating in the crowning achievements of ancient Greece, Rome, India, and China. Historians close ancient times with the fall of the most powerful of these civilizations, Rome. The year A.D. 500 marks the end of antiquity.

Perhaps the best place to begin the journey through world history is to drop back in time to the end of the last Ice Age, about 12,000 years ago. During the Ice Age, Earth's climate was much colder than it is today. Giant glaciers, ice sheets sometimes several miles thick, spread out from the North and South poles and covered large areas of northern Europe, Asia, and North America, fully one-third of Earth's surface. The Ice Age killed off many species of plants and animals and forced humans and surviving animals to migrate to ice-free areas closer to the equator.

Gradually, though, Earth began to warm once again. The glaciers began melting and the ice receded toward the polar areas until it covered only one-twelfth of Earth. Forests grew on the newly thawed land and animals multiplied, while other plant life—fruits, grains, and vegetables—flourished once again. People began to migrate back to the newly productive lands, following the food that was again available there.

People of the Stone Age.
As the last Ice Age was ending, so was another long period in human development, the Paleolithic Age or Old Stone Age. Paleolithic people survived by hunting animals for meat and by gathering wild berries and grains. This hunting and gathering way of life kept people on the move, making nomads of them. To find the animals they hunted, they had to follow wandering herds and move on when they had picked an area clean of its edible plants.

This nomadic lifestyle caused Paleolithic people to live in small groups, often extended families of 20 to 30 people. Such groups provided enough hands to do the work without presenting too many mouths to feed. These ancient people lived in caves when they could find them, or in tents made of animal skins when they could not.

The Agricultural Revolution.
As Earth entered the postglacial period, the Neolithic Age, or New Stone Age, began. Beginning about 11,000 years ago, many people across Earth discovered that they could domesticate animals such as cattle and sheep and keep herds of them, providing a steady supply of meat and milk. They also learned that they could cultivate edible plants like grains, fruits, and vegetables in sufficient quantity to feed themselves. They therefore did not have to travel continuously to find food.

These changes marked the first great revolution in human history, the Agricultural Revolution. Now people could cease their endless wandering if they chose. They could settle in agricultural communities, build permanent homes, and put down roots. Soon villages were appearing along river banks and in mountain valleys. Villagers began to develop new skills, like making pottery and weaving baskets and cloth. They discovered the wheel and learned that they could use animals to pull plows and wheeled carts. By the time the Neolithic Age was ending in some parts of the world, about 5,500 years ago, human history was poised to begin a new and exciting era.

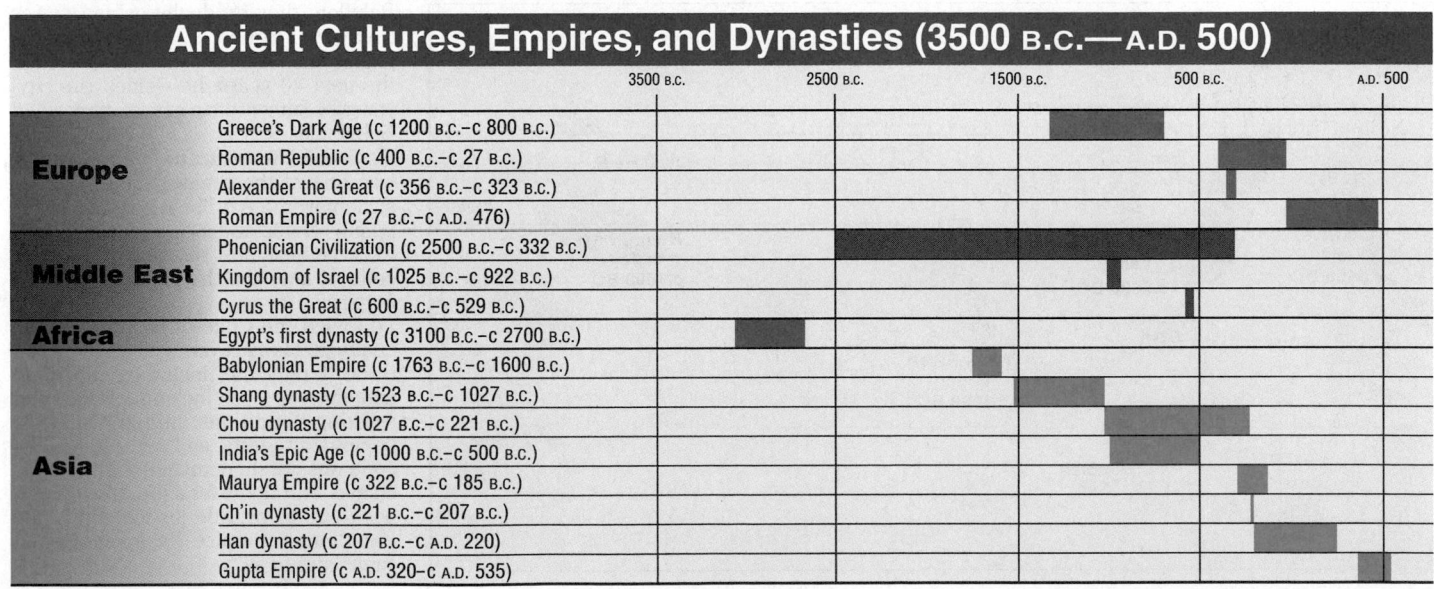

	Ancient Cultures, Empires, and Dynasties (3500 B.C.— A.D. 500)						
		3500 B.C.	2500 B.C.	1500 B.C.	500 B.C.	A.D. 500	
Europe	Greece's Dark Age (c 1200 B.C.–c 800 B.C.)				▮		
	Roman Republic (c 400 B.C.–c 27 B.C.)					▮	
	Alexander the Great (c 356 B.C.–c 323 B.C.)					▮	
	Roman Empire (c 27 B.C.–c A.D. 476)					▮▮	
Middle East	Phoenician Civilization (c 2500 B.C.–c 332 B.C.)		▮▮▮▮▮▮▮▮▮				
	Kingdom of Israel (c 1025 B.C.–c 922 B.C.)			▮			
	Cyrus the Great (c 600 B.C.–c 529 B.C.)				▮		
Africa	Egypt's first dynasty (c 3100 B.C.–c 2700 B.C.)	▮					
Asia	Babylonian Empire (c 1763 B.C.–c 1600 B.C.)			▮			
	Shang dynasty (c 1523 B.C.–c 1027 B.C.)			▮▮			
	Chou dynasty (c 1027 B.C.–c 221 B.C.)			▮▮▮			
	India's Epic Age (c 1000 B.C.–c 500 B.C.)			▮▮			
	Maurya Empire (c 322 B.C.–c 185 B.C.)				▮		
	Ch'in dynasty (c 221 B.C.–c 207 B.C.)				▮		
	Han dynasty (c 207 B.C.–c A.D. 220)				▮▮		
	Gupta Empire (c A.D. 320–c A.D. 535)					▮	

Four Great River Valley Cultures

Agriculture developed first in Southwest Asia, in the Fertile Crescent, an arc-shaped region stretching from the eastern Mediterranean to the Persian Gulf. It then spread west to North Africa and east to South and East Asia. It flourished especially in four great river valleys: the Tigris-Euphrates in Southwest Asia, the Nile in North Africa, the Indus in South Asia, and the Huang He in East Asia.

In these places, the settlement and stability that agriculture produced freed many people from the daily toil of finding the food they needed to survive. Now farmers and herdsmen could produce the necessary food while others could specialize as, for example, weavers, potters, boat makers, or woodworkers. In these fertile river valleys, civilizations began to develop for the first time.

Mesopotamia

Mesopotamia, which in Greek means "the land between two rivers," is sometimes called the "Cradle of Civilization" because the region was home to the earliest known civilization. The Tigris and Euphrates rivers run for more than 1,000 miles southward through the Fertile Crescent, in modern-day Iraq, into the Persian Gulf, carrying fertile silt with them. Each year, the rivers overflow their banks, flooding the land of Mesopotamia and renewing its soil with their silt.

By 5000 B.C., numerous farming villages dotted Mesopotamia, and by 4500 B.C., artisans there had discovered how to extract metal from copper ore by heating it with charcoal. With this discovery, the Neolithic Age ended in Mesopotamia as metal tools and weapons replaced primitive stone ones. About 3000 B.C., Mesopotamian metalworkers made another technological breakthrough. They found that copper could be made harder and could hold a sharper edge by the addition of tin, thus producing bronze. With this discovery, the Bronze Age began in Mesopotamia.

Sumer's civilization. By 3500 B.C., southern Mesopotamia, known as Sumer, was thriving. Irrigation canals transported water from the Tigris and Euphrates rivers to nourish the fields and produce crop surpluses. Agricultural plenty triggered rapid population growth and the transformation of villages into cities. There were at least a dozen cities, with names like Kish and Erech and Ur. With the appearance of cities, the world's first civilization developed.

Government. One of the major signs of civilization is an organized government. Sumer was organized into a number of powerful city-states, each ruled by a king. Each government directed the building of monuments and irrigation canals, oversaw the distribution of food, and provided for the city-state's defense.

Religion. A second sign of early civilization is the development of a set of commonly held religious beliefs. The Sumerians believed in numerous gods and goddesses, each of whom represented a different aspect of nature, for example, An, the god of heaven; Ki, the god of earth; Enlil, the god of air; and Enki, the god of water. They also believed that each city-state had its own god or goddess who protected it. As shrines to their deities, the Sumerians constructed temples, six or seven stories high, with broad stairways climbing to the top. In these temple-towers, called ziggurats, priests presided over worship of the gods and goddesses.

Cuneiform. Yet another sign of civilization is written language, and the Sumerians developed theirs about 3000 B.C. Called cuneiform, it began as pictures of objects drawn with a sharp stylus into tablets of soft clay. When the clay tablets hardened, they became permanent records of business transactions, laws, and religious teachings. In time, the pictures gave way to wedge-shaped symbols, more like the letters we know, that were easier to write. The name *cuneiform* comes from the Latin for "wedge-shaped."

The arts. The arts, a major civilizing influence, also thrived in Sumer. Brightly colored friezes covered the ziggurats and beautifully sculpted statues of the deities filled them. Music composed and played on instruments like harps and lyres was a major part of festivals and religious ceremonies. Literature in the form of epics, fables, and poems has survived on clay tablets. The longest and most famous example is the *Epic of Gilgamesh,* the tale of a heroic ruler in search of everlasting life.

Sargon of Akkad. Bitter rivalries among Sumer's city-states frequently sent them to war against one another. Such war and disunity opened them to conquest from the outside, and about 2350 B.C., the forces of Akkad, a city to the north, swept down upon them. King Sargon of Akkad conquered Sumer, making it part of his empire for a time, but later and weaker Akkadian kings allowed wars among Sumer's city-states to break out again.

The rise of Babylonia. In about 2000 B.C., waves of nomadic invaders called Amorites swarmed into Mesopotamia from west of the Euphrates. Settling in a village called Babylon, they gradually gained power over their neighbors. Then, in 1792 B.C., Hammurabi came to the throne. Over the next 40 years, he welded the city-states of Sumer into a new empire called Babylonia.

Code of Hammurabi. Hammurabi was one of the greatest rulers of the ancient world. A brilliant general, a wise administrator, and a generous patron of the arts, he is best remembered for the code of laws that he legislated for his empire.

Called the Code of Hammurabi, its nearly 300 laws covered all areas of life: trade; family life, including marriage and divorce; labor, including wages and working conditions; military service; personal property; and real estate. The code was harsh, demanding "an eye for an eye" and "a life for a life," but its purpose was to provide justice within the Babylonian Empire by applying the same laws to all.

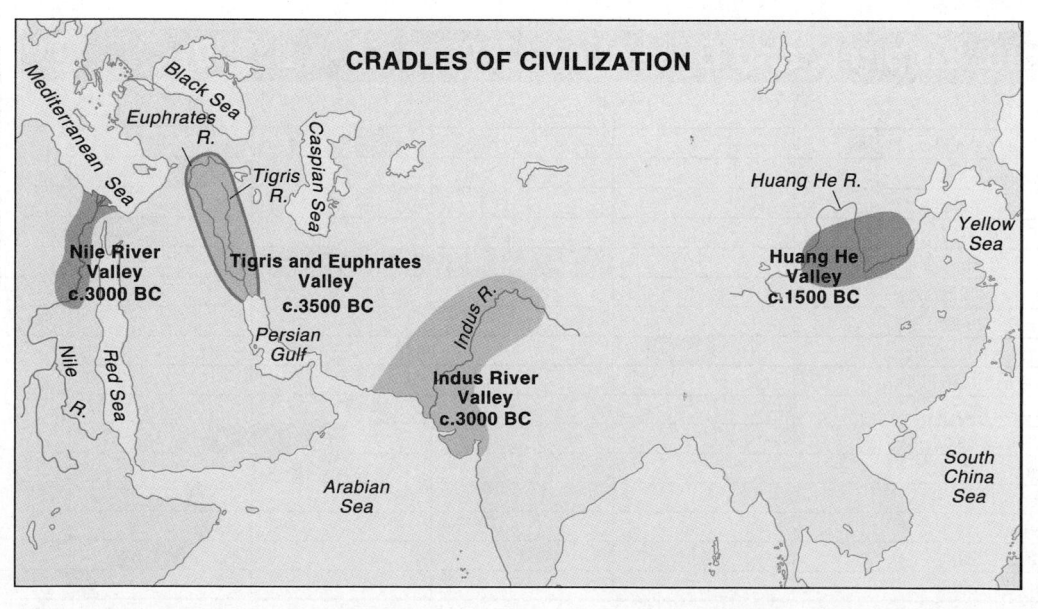

CRADLES OF CIVILIZATION

Mediterranean Sea
Black Sea
Euphrates R.
Tigris R.
Caspian Sea
Huang He R.
Yellow Sea
Nile River Valley c.3000 BC
Tigris and Euphrates Valley c.3500 BC
Persian Gulf
Indus R.
Huang He Valley c.1500 BC
Nile R.
Red Sea
Indus River Valley c.3000 BC
Arabian Sea
South China Sea

The Hittites. Hammurabi's weaker successors were not able to maintain Babylonian rule in the face of the militarily superior Hittites, warriors who conquered Mesopotamia from Asia Minor about 1550 B.C. The Hittites were the first people in history known to smelt iron. With the Hittite conquest, the Bronze Age gave way to the Iron Age in Babylonia.

Assyrian conquest. By 700 B.C., Babylonia had fallen prey to yet another invader, the mighty and fierce Assyrians. From their capital city at Nineveh on the upper Tigris River, they created an empire that stretched from the Persian Gulf to the eastern Mediterranean Sea to Egypt.

The Assyrian political administration ruled with an iron hand and demanded tribute from its conquered provinces. In 626 B.C., the Babylonians rebelled against their Assyrian masters and in 612 B.C. joined an alliance with

Egypt

At the same time that the Sumerian civilization was developing in the Tigris-Euphrates valley, another powerful civilization was emerging 600 miles to the west. Ancient Egypt, one of the longest-lived civilizations in human history, rose along the banks of the Nile River of North Africa. The Greek historian Herodotus called Egypt "the gift of the Nile," for it could not have developed without that river's life-giving waters.

Like the Tigris and Euphrates, each year the Nile flooded, overrunning its banks and inundating the land with silt, creating a ribbon of fertile soil 5 to 15 miles wide through a sun-baked desert. At its mouth, the Nile empties into the Mediterranean Sea, creating a rich delta 100 miles long and 200 miles across. During the Paleolithic Age, hunters and gatherers flocked to the generous food

Major Events — Ancient Milestones

c 4500 B.C. Copper replaces stone for tools and weapons in Mesopotamia and China.

c 3500 B.C. The wheel and the plow are invented in Mesopotamia; the sail is invented in Egypt.

c 3100 B.C. Menes unites Upper and Lower Egypt, establishing Egypt's first dynasty.

c 3000 B.C. Mesopotamian metalworkers discover bronze; major cities develop in Sumer; Sumerians invent cuneiform, a method of writing.

c 2590 B.C. The Great Pyramid of Cheops in Egypt is constructed.

c 2300 B.C. The cities of Harappa and Mohenjo-Daro emerge in the Indus Valley.

c 1792 B.C. Hammurabi comes to the throne of Babylon.

c 1770 B.C. The Code of Hammurabi is developed.

c 1550 B.C. The Hittites begin smelting iron and fashioning it into tools and weapons; a written language develops in China; the earliest form of steel is made by the Chalybes, subjects of the Hittites.

c 1490 B.C. Hatshepsut, the first woman ruler known to history, leads Egypt.

c 700 B.C. The Aryans conquer Indus valley cities.

c 605 B.C. The Hanging Gardens of Babylon are created.

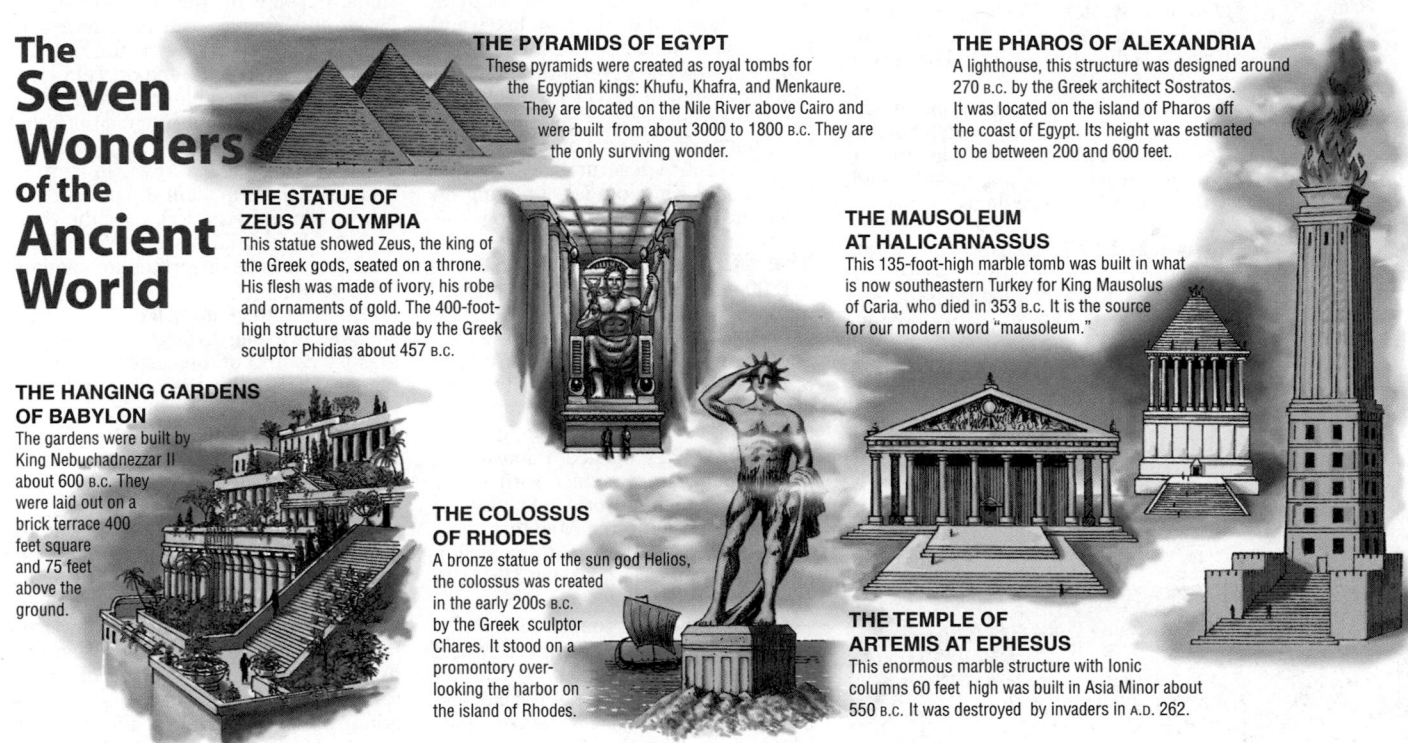

The Seven Wonders of the Ancient World

THE PYRAMIDS OF EGYPT
These pyramids were created as royal tombs for the Egyptian kings: Khufu, Khafra, and Menkaure. They are located on the Nile River above Cairo and were built from about 3000 to 1800 B.C. They are the only surviving wonder.

THE PHAROS OF ALEXANDRIA
A lighthouse, this structure was designed around 270 B.C. by the Greek architect Sostratos. It was located on the island of Pharos off the coast of Egypt. Its height was estimated to be between 200 and 600 feet.

THE STATUE OF ZEUS AT OLYMPIA
This statue showed Zeus, the king of the Greek gods, seated on a throne. His flesh was made of ivory, his robe and ornaments of gold. The 400-foot-high structure was made by the Greek sculptor Phidias about 457 B.C.

THE MAUSOLEUM AT HALICARNASSUS
This 135-foot-high marble tomb was built in what is now southeastern Turkey for King Mausolus of Caria, who died in 353 B.C. It is the source for our modern word "mausoleum."

THE HANGING GARDENS OF BABYLON
The gardens were built by King Nebuchadnezzar II about 600 B.C. They were laid out on a brick terrace 400 feet square and 75 feet above the ground.

THE COLOSSUS OF RHODES
A bronze statue of the sun god Helios, the colossus was created in the early 200s B.C. by the Greek sculptor Chares. It stood on a promontory overlooking the harbor on the island of Rhodes.

THE TEMPLE OF ARTEMIS AT EPHESUS
This enormous marble structure with Ionic columns 60 feet high was built in Asia Minor about 550 B.C. It was destroyed by invaders in A.D. 262.

other conquered states to overthrow them. The alliance won, and the New Babylonian Empire arose after Nebuchadnezzar came to the Babylonian throne in 605 B.C. and quickly subjugated all of the Fertile Crescent.

Nebuchadnezzar brought Babylon to glory as he made the city the most impressive urban center of its day. It is best remembered for the Hanging Gardens he had built there, one of the Seven Wonders of the Ancient World. But for all its glory, the New Empire barely outlived Nebuchadnezzar, crumbling in 539 B.C., less than 25 years after his death.

resources of the ancient Nile. During the Neolithic Age, they began to farm the fertile banks of the river and by 4000 B.C., farming villages lined them.

Unification of Egypt.
By 3500 B.C., the Nile region had progressed economically and politically to the point that two kingdoms developed there. Upper Egypt lay to the south (because the Nile flows north, this is the upstream area), and Lower Egypt lay to the north, bordering the Mediterranean Sea. About 3100 B.C., Menes, the king of Upper Egypt, united the two kingdoms and built his capital at Memphis, near the border between the two.

Hieroglyphics. At the same time that Egyptians were establishing their new central government, they were inventing their written language, hieroglyphics. Like the early Sumerian cuneiform, hieroglyphics used pictures to convey information and ideas; however, it was often written on scrolls of papyrus, a kind of paper made from reeds, rather than on clay tablets.

Religious beliefs. Like the Sumerians, the Egyptians believed that gods and goddesses controlled the forces of nature. The most important god in this sun-baked land was the god of the sun, Amon-Ra. Osiris was also honored as god of the Nile, and his wife Isis was

goddess of the moon. The resurrection of Osiris, symbolized each year by the flooding of the Nile, convinced the Egyptians that they too would be reborn in a life after death.

During the 2,000 years that ancient Egyptian civilization survived, 30 dynasties would rule its land, leading it through three major stages—the Old, Middle, and New Kingdoms.

The Old Kingdom

(c 2700–c 2000 B.C.). During this period, the kings of Egypt consolidated and strengthened their power over their people. Claiming descent from the god Amon-Ra, they ruled as gods themselves. They owned all the land of Egypt, and their word was law. Egyptian citizens were forced to pay taxes and rent to use the land; many of them were also forced to contribute their labor to large building projects.

The belief that the Egyptian kings

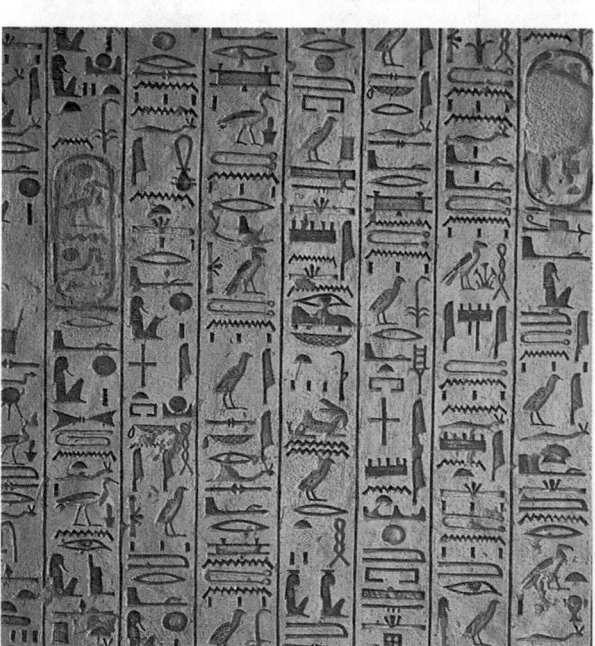

were gods led to one of the Old Kingdom's greatest achievements, construction of the pyramids. To live their lives after death in proper style, the ancient Egyptians believed they needed to be buried in magnificent tombs with lavish possessions. Consequently, construction began on monumental pyramids to house the dead rulers.

The first was the Step Pyramid, designed for Djoser about 2650 B.C. by the royal architect Imhotep. It stands over 200 feet tall. The largest of the monuments was the Great Pyramid of Khufu, a king also known as Cheops. From a base that covered 13 acres, it rose to a point that reached 48 stories above the ground. It took 100,000 workers over 20 years to bring it to completion, around 2600 B.C., making it the oldest of the Seven Wonders of the World. Such monuments gave this period yet another name, the Age of Pyramids.

By about 2300 B.C., Egyptians were being crushed by the burdens of pyramid building and by the high taxes and forced labor demanded of them. They rebelled. Now the governors who ruled the provinces of Egypt in the king's name began to demand more power for themselves. In the face of such opposition, the central government weakened and the Old Kingdom fell, bringing on 150 years of disorder and disunion.

The Middle Kingdom

(c 2050–c 1800 B.C.). About 2050 B.C., Mentuhotep II reunited Egypt and established a new capital at Thebes. Succeeding kings led Egypt into a time of unprecedented prosperity and growth. They ordered the swamps of the Nile delta to be drained to increase agriculture. They opened a flourishing Egypt to greater contact with other parts of the ancient world, encouraging trade with ports on the Mediterranean and with Mesopotamia, and capturing new lands, such as gold-rich Nubia to the south.

The Middle Kingdom also marked a golden age in Egyptian architecture and arts. Magnificent temples, which can still be visited today, rose at Karnak and Luxor, near Thebes. Literature flourished, including the *Tale of Sinuhe,* which gave rise to the familiar Sinbad the Sailor stories.

Once again, though, the central government disintegrated and civil wars raged. About 1720 B.C., Asian invaders called the Hyksos overran Egypt with superior weapons of war—horsedrawn chariots, strong bronze swords, metal armor—and for the first time, Egypt underwent the humiliation of foreign rule.

In an early example of one culture borrowing from another, the Egyptians studied the weapons and ways of warfare of their rulers. They proved such astute students that they were able to turn these new military means against the Hyksos, to expel them and establish the New Kingdom.

The New Kingdom

(c 1570–c 1090 B.C.). During this period, the Egyptian rulers began to be called *pharaohs,* from the Egyptian meaning "great house." From the start of the New Kingdom, the pharaohs again consolidated their power and devoted their time to empire building. Amenhotep I, Thutmose I, and Thutmose III proved themselves great conquerors. They extended the Egyptian Empire far to the south in Africa and into Asia along the eastern Mediterranean and across to the Euphrates River.

The mother of Thutmose III, Hatshepsut, reigned as pharaoh while Thutmose was a child. She was the first major woman ruler known to history. From 1490 to 1469 B.C., she led Egypt through a period of burgeoning foreign trade and monument building.

The Egyptian Empire reached its pinnacle of power under Amenhotep III in the early 14th century B.C. With riches that poured in from conquered lands, he built magnificent temples at Luxor and Karnak. But his successor, Amenhotep IV, weakened the empire when he attempted major religious reforms, creating a bitter struggle with wealthy and powerful Egyptian priests. His successor was nine-year-old Tutankhamen, the "boy king" who became just a puppet of the priests. He is best remembered today for the treasures of his burial place—"King Tut's tomb"—not to be unearthed for another 2,500 years.

By the 13th century B.C., Egypt was engaged in a long struggle with the Hittites for control of the eastern Mediterranean. During this time, ancient Egypt was to know its last great period, under the rule of Ramses II, another great monument builder.

Inevitably, the pharaohs' rule weakened, and again Egypt fell prey to invaders. By 1090 B.C., the power of ancient Egypt had collapsed. Over the succeeding centuries, it would be fought over and conquered by new empire builders. But the greatness of its civilization ensured that even under foreign dynasties, it was capable of high achievement. One example is the creation of Alexandria as the ancient world's foremost cultural center, especially its Great Library, the best in all antiquity.

Indus Valley

Over 2,000 miles to the east of Egypt, 1,500 miles beyond Mesopotamia, lies the Indus River, coursing south 1,000 miles from the Himalayas to the Arabian Sea, an arm of the Indian Ocean. Its lower valley, located in what is now Pakistan, is one of the most fertile plains in the world. Here, about 2500 B.C., roughly the time that the Old Kingdom was thriving in Egypt and Sumer was about to be made part of the Akkadian Empire, a civilization was emerging.

Harappa and Mohenjo-Daro.

Settlement had begun in the Indus Valley, as it had elsewhere, when hunters and gatherers evolved into Neolithic farmers living in villages along the Indus and its tributaries. By about 2300 B.C., two of these villages had grown into the cities of Harappa and Mohenjo-Daro, with close to 40,000 people in each city.

Both were marvels of city planning. At the center of each was a fortress, five stories high; from it, streets ran out in a grid, making it easy to get around. Strict government regulations decreed neat and well-constructed houses, shops, and public buildings, including public baths. Beneath the streets, brick-lined sewers carried off waste, a sanitation measure unknown in other cities of the time.

Because of its bountiful agriculture, the Indus Valley developed a thriving economy. Here cotton was cultivated for the first time. Cotton cloth, as well as fine pottery and gold jewelry, was traded as far away as Mesopotamia.

Archaeologists have unearthed thousands of small clay figures and stone seals that carry pictures and a form of writing. The pictures indicate that the Indus people probably worshipped certain animals, like sacred bulls, and gods of nature. Unfortunately, scholars have not been able to decipher the writing and perhaps never will.

About 1800 B.C., Indus Valley civilization began to decline for reasons that are unknown—possibly because of natural disasters like floods. Its death blow came about 1500 B.C. as warlike nomads from central Asia began streaming into the Indus Valley through mountain passes.

Aryan conquest. The invaders called themselves Aryans, their term for "noble ones." They quickly overran and looted the Indus towns and cities, soon conquering the entire northern plain of what is today India and Pakistan. By 700 B.C., they had established a number of Aryan kingdoms across the Indian subcontinent, each kingdom ruled by a rajah.

The Vedas. By this time, the Aryans had also developed a written language, Sanskrit. In it, they wrote the Vedas, books of sacred knowledge describing Aryan religious beliefs, known as Hinduism. The Vedas celebrated numerous gods and goddesses who personified natural phenomena, for example, the sky, fire, or lightning.

The caste system. The Aryans had been loosely divided into three social classes, from top to bottom, warriors, priests, and common people. But as their kingdoms emerged and developed, the social structure became more rigid and four major classes emerged—the Brahmans, or priests; the Kshatriyas, or warriors; the Vaisyas, or merchants; and the Sudras, or peasants and servants.

In time, these four classes hardened into castes. Once born into one caste, a person could never move into another. Eventually, the castes subdivided into some 3,000 subcastes, each with its own occupation and religious character.

At the very bottom of the social ladder were people not permitted in any caste. They were given the most degrading jobs, like carrying away human and animal waste and tanning the hides of animal carcasses. Called outcastes, these people were considered unclean and therefore "untouchable" to all caste members. This caste system was to spread and survive for centuries, with grave effects on the development of India.

Huang He Valley

At the same time the Aryans were overrunning the Indus Valley, a fourth river valley civilization was emerging 2,000 miles to the northeast, along the banks of the Huang He, in today's northern China. This river rises in the mountains of central China and flows for 3,000 miles to the sea. As it does, it passes through the Loess Plateau, where it picks up tons of fertile silt, known as loess. The color of this rich silt gives the river the name by which it has been more commonly known, the Yellow River.

About 4500 B.C., Neolithic farming villages began to appear in the Huang He valley. Archaeologists have found shards of red pottery decorated with geometric designs left by this earliest Chinese culture, the Yang Shao. A second Neolithic culture, the Lung Shan, identified by shards of wheel-made black pottery, followed the Yang Shao.

Legend tells that kings of the Hsia dynasty ruled these Neolithic peoples and that these kings taught them astronomy, chariot and boat construction, and silk manufacture. But it was not until about 1500 B.C., with the advent of the Shang dynasty, that the Chinese developed a written language and its recorded history could begin.

The Shang dynasty. The kings who founded the Shang dynasty believed that they were the "Sons of Heaven," that the god of the sky had given them the right to rule. They called this right a "Mandate from Heaven," and all succeeding dynasties would also claim it. The civilization that the Shang kings helped to found would become the longest continuous civilization the world has ever known.

Shang government was not strongly centralized. The Shang kings ruled by granting land to supporters and making them a noble class. These nobles then governed their chiefdoms under the kings' direction.

Shang kings acted as chief priests, offering sacrifices to the many gods who were believed to reside in nature and to govern natural phenomena as

well as to their ancestors, since the Chinese believed that the spirits of their ancestors could intercede with the gods for help and protection.

Written language. Under the Shangs, the Chinese developed their complex written language. Like other early writing, it relied originally on pictures of objects to convey ideas. In time, these drawings changed into symbols, growing into a total of tens of thousands of characters, some representing whole words and phrases and some representing sounds. Gradually, this number was reduced to about 10,000 characters; in recent times it has been reduced further still.

Shang scribes often wrote by using sharp sticks or brushes to draw the characters on narrow strips of bamboo, which were then bound together. That is why Chinese is written in vertical columns to this day.

Writing from the Shang period has been found on fragments of bones. Scholars have determined that such bones were used to foretell the future. If a Shang king or indeed anyone wanted to know the answer to a question— "When is a good time to plant crops?" or "Will this business deal be successful?"—he would have the question written on a piece of bone from a cow or pig. The bone was then thrown into a fire, which caused cracks to appear on it. A priest who could read such signs—an oracle—then interpreted the cracks, telling the future as the "oracle bones" presented it.

Shang achievements. The beginning of the Shang period also marked the start of the Bronze Age in China. Among the greatest of the works of the Shang period are bronze statues and vessels considered among the finest ever produced. They were widely used to offer sacrifices to ancestral spirits and to beautify the homes of the wealthy.

Shang artisans also developed white porcelain, the forerunner of modern "china" ware, and were master carvers in jade and ivory.

ABU SIMBEL, this magnificent temple for Rameses II, was nearly lost due to the construction of the Aswan Dam. A multi-nation effort to cut the temple from the rock and reassemble it safely above the rising water has preserved it for future generations.

center
US

centre
Brit.

color
US

colour
Brit.

21 **History of the World**

Cultures of the Middle East

civilizations
US

civilisations
Brit.

colonizers
US

colonisers
Brit.

centers
US

centres
Brit.

colored
US

coloured
Brit.

As the four great river civilizations were reaching their heights, other civilizations were emerging, especially in what we now call the Middle East: Southwest Asia, including Asia Minor, the eastern Mediterranean lands, and North Africa. Southwest Asia was already populated by Semitic peoples, for example, the Babylonians and the Assyrians, among many others. Now it also became a magnet for people from around the Black Sea, in what is today Ukraine, Russia, and Georgia.

About 2000 B.C., these people, called Indo-Europeans, began leaving their homelands in one of the major human migrations in history. The Aryans who invaded the Indus Valley were one Indo-European people. The Hittites who invaded Babylonia, and the Medes and Persians who moved into what is modern Iran, were also Indo-Europeans. When the Indo-Europeans streamed into the Middle East, they brought major changes with them.

The Persian Empire

The Medes and Persians began settling on the Iranian plateau about 1500 B.C. By the seventh century B.C., united under Mede leadership, they were powerful enough to become part of an alliance with Babylon that overthrew the Assyrian Empire in 612 B.C. Now, as they spread into northern Mesopotamia, they began building their own empire.

In the fifth century B.C., a Persian prince overthrew the Medes and founded the Persian Empire. As one of the finest military commanders and ablest organizers of the ancient world, Cyrus

Major Events — Middle East

c 2500 B.C. The Phoenicians establish themselves along the Mediterranean's eastern shore.

c 2000 B.C. The Indo-Europeans begin leaving the area around the Black Sea for the Middle East; this constitutes one of the major migrations in human history.

c 1280 B.C. The Hebrews return to Canaan from Egypt; the Ten Commandments are received; the Hebrews introduce the concept of monotheism, a belief in a single all-powerful god.

c 1100 B.C. The Phoenicians develop an alphabet that will become the basis for all modern European alphabets.

c 1025 B.C. Hebrew tribes unite into the kingdom of Israel.

c 600 B.C. The Persian Empire is founded by Cyrus the Great; Zoroaster rises as a religious prophet in Persia.

c 586 B.C. Judah falls to Nebuchadnezzar, the king of Babylon; the Babylonian captivity of the Hebrews begins.

c 550 B.C. The Achaemenids build the city of Persepolis in Persia.

c 536 B.C. Cyrus the Great of Persia conquers Babylonia and frees the Hebrews.

c 521 B.C. The Persians build an advanced system of roads, providing a route to China and central Asia.

c 508 B.C. Cleisthenes reorganizes the Athenian government and lays the basis for democracy.

DARIUS I, Darius Hystaspes, was one of the greatest rulers of the Persian Empire. The name Darius, common for Medo-Persian rulers, is referenced in numerous cuneiform tablets.

the Great (ruled 550–529 B.C.) succeeded in bringing Babylonia as well as all the Fertile Crescent and Asia Minor under his control. His successors would add Egypt and parts of southeastern Europe in the west, and territory as far east as the Indus River, making the Persian Empire the largest the world had yet known.

The Persians were excellent organizers and wise rulers. Darius (ruled 521–486 B.C.) divided the empire into 20 provinces, called satrapies. Governing each was a satrap who collected taxes and enforced the laws. In an effort to discourage rebellion against Persian rule, the Persians allowed the different peoples of their empire to live under their own local laws, religions, and customs.

To bind the empire together, the Persian government built an advanced system of roads. These roads facilitated contact between the emperor and the satraps and served as arteries of trade throughout the empire. The roads also provided a route to central Asia and China over which silk and other valuable goods were traded.

Zoroastrianism. The earliest Persians believed in many gods of nature. However, about 600 B.C., a religious prophet arose among them and gave them a new set of beliefs. Zoroaster preached that life is a battle between good and evil and that people must choose whether to join this struggle on the side of Ahura Mazda, the god of good, or on the side of Ahriman, the god of evil. Zoroaster predicted that the side

of good would win and that those who led moral lives would be rewarded with eternal life in paradise, while those who led evil lives would suffer eternity in hell.

Zoroastrianism set a high standard of honesty and other ethical behavior for the Persians. Its ideas of good versus evil, and of heaven and hell, would later be reflected in three major world religions, Judaism, Christianity, and Islam.

The Phoenicians

About 2500 B.C., a thousand years before the Medes and Persians began moving down onto the Iranian plateau, a Semitic people known as the Phoenicians were establishing themselves along the Mediterranean's eastern shore, in the area that is roughly present-day Lebanon. Hemmed in by mountains, the Phoenicians turned to the sea, becoming the greatest traders and colonizers of the ancient Mediterranean world. By 1000 B.C., their trading centers at Tyre, Beirut, Byblos, and Sidon dominated the commercial life of the Mediterranean.

With Egypt located to the south, Mesopotamia to the east, and Asia Minor to the north, Phoenicia became a crossroads of the ancient Middle East. Cultural influences poured into Phoenicia from all these areas, and Phoenicia's manufactured goods flowed out in a wealth-creating stream.

Among the Phoenician goods in demand was a fine woolen cloth colored with a purple dye made from local shellfish and highly prized as the royal garb for the kings of the ancient world. Other Phoenician trade goods included furniture that was made from the famous cedars of Lebanon, wine, salt, and dried fish, as well as glassware, metalware, and jewelry.

Colonization. Phoenicia's daring sailors took their ships to the edges of the known world. They sailed across the Mediterranean, through the Strait of Gibraltar, and up the Atlantic coast as far as today's England. They may also have sailed down the west coast of Africa, possibly becoming the first to round Africa at the Cape of Good Hope and to sail north through the Indian Ocean.

As the Phoenicians travelled, they carried the civilization of the Middle East with them. They founded colonies throughout the Mediterranean world, in particular on the islands of Cyprus, Malta, Sicily, and Sardinia, on the southern coast of Spain, and on the northern coast of Africa. The greatest of all the colonies was Carthage, in North Africa, which grew into a major Mediterranean power, and which would later clash with Rome for control of the sea.

The alphabet. The Phoenicians' most memorable achievement as carriers of civilization was their improvement in written language. Having become familiar in their travels with both Mesopotamian cuneiform and Egyptian hieroglyphics, they developed a simpler form of writing, creating signs that stood for single speech sounds. Though the Phoenician alphabet was not the first, the 22 symbols for consonants that the Phoenicians created became the forerunner of the Greek, Latin, and later alphabets.

The Hebrews

To the south of Phoenicia lay the land of Canaan, later known as Palestine. About 1200 B.C., the Hebrews, a Semitic people, began returning to Canaan from a long exile. With them they brought a belief in a single, all-powerful god, and a clearly delineated code of ethics. These beliefs would profoundly affect later civilizations and give rise eventually to three great world religions, Judaism, Christianity, and Islam.

Biblical beginnings. According to the Bible, the Hebrews (also called Jews and Israelites) descended from nomads who lived in Sumer. About 1800 B.C., during a time of famine, their patriarch Abraham led them away from the city of Ur in Sumer northwestward to the land of Canaan. Famine there 100 years later drove the Hebrews south into Egypt, where they were enslaved.

About 1300 B.C., their leader Moses led them in a great exodus, bringing them out of Egyptian bondage and back to Canaan. There the Hebrews, loosely organized into twelve tribes, fought the Canaanites for control of the land and

SOLOMON, known as a wise king, is shown determining which of two women is a child's true mother.

THE TEN COMMANDMENTS, or the Code of Ten Words, were given, according to the Bible, to Moses on Mount Sinai by Jehovah in the mid 15th century B.C. The commandments were part of the Mosaic law, which is parallel to parts of the earlier Code of Hammurabi.

succeeded in subjugating them. But then a new and more powerful enemy appeared, the Philistines, a non-Semitic people who had been driven out of Asia Minor and settled in southwest Palestine. (The name *Palestine* derives from the Philistines.)

The Kingdom of Israel. To overcome the Philistines, the Hebrew tribes united into the Kingdom of Israel, about 1025 B.C., under the great warrior Saul. King Saul died in battle against the Philistines in 1000 B.C., but his successor, King David, fought on and finally succeeded in restricting this enemy to one small coastal area.

Under David and later under his son Solomon, the Kingdom of Israel grew rich and powerful. Solomon inaugurated massive building projects, including a vast palace complex and the magnificent Temple of Jerusalem. But following his death in 922 B.C., his kingdom split in two, Israel in the north and Judah in the south.

Weakened by the split, Israel was crushed by the Assyrian Empire in 722 B.C. Judah managed to retain its independence until 586 B.C., when it fell to Nebuchadnezzar, king of Babylonia. He destroyed Solomon's Temple in Jerusalem and transported thousands of Hebrews back to the region of Mesopotamia. This was the so-called Babylonian Captivity. Fifty years later,

when Cyrus the Great conquered Babylonia, the Persians freed the Hebrews, but both Israel and Judah came under Persian rule.

Judaism. The Hebrews introduced the concept of monotheism, holding that there are not many gods and goddesses of nature but one God—Yahweh, or Jehovah—who created and rules the universe. The Hebrews believed that during the exodus, Yahweh revealed Himself and His Ten Commandments to Moses, who in turn revealed them to the Hebrews.

Yahweh demanded that the Hebrews live moral and ethical lives, following the laws revealed to the prophets who followed Moses and written down in the Torah, the first five books of the Old Testament. The Hebrews were to bring these laws to the rest of the world and encourage everyone to work toward respect for the individual and toward justice and peace for all. This ethical world view was a major contribution to civilization and greatly influenced the later world religions.

Judaism also holds that God acts through history to change events on earth. Both Christianity and Islam inherited this sense of history from the Jews. In fact, both of these later religions consider early Jewish history to be a record of God's actions and in a sense share a common tradition.

A VIEW FROM THE MOUNT SINAI REGION, or Horeb, shows the rocky terrain and rugged slopes in the Sinai Peninsula of Egypt. Debate continues over its exact location. Traditionally, Mount Sinai is believed to be located at Jabel Musa.

Western Cultural Development

Greece

Civilization derived from the Middle East, especially from Egypt, came to the island of Crete in the Mediterranean Sea as early as 2500 B.C. From Crete it gradually spread north to the Aegean Islands and the mainland of Greece.

Archaeology has revealed a typical Bronze Age culture still imperfectly known because of a scarcity of written records. Thus, the detailed historical information that is available from Mesopotamia, Egypt, and the Middle East in general is lacking in Crete and Greece, and the nature of Aegean culture can be learned only indirectly from its material remains.

Aegean development.
Early civilization in the Aegean is known as the Minoan period, named for the legendary King Minos of Crete. Enormous palace complexes, particularly at Knossos in Crete, show that the skills of Aegean artisans were the equal of those in the Middle East. Painted pottery and wall paintings were produced in a lively and elegant style. Marine motifs occurred frequently, an indication of the importance of the sea to these island people.

The economy of Aegean civilization rested mainly on agriculture, small manufacture, and extensive trade. Aegean trading ships ranged north to Asia Minor and south to Egypt, east to Syria, and west to Sicily. They are even thought to have gone as far as Spain to trade for tin for bronze making. Agricultural goods offered were wine, honey, and olive oil, while those sought included grain, which could be grown only in limited supplies in Aegean lands. Also imported were gold and linen thread. Famed for their craftsmanship, Aegean weavers and metalworkers produced textiles and bronze and gold metalworks that were much in demand.

The only written records of Aegean civilization are a number of inscribed tablets. A few hundred of these tablets, written in a script called Linear A, are found only on Crete and date from about 1500 B.C. Another 3,000, brief and mostly fragmentary, written in a somewhat different script called Linear B, have been found at sites on both Crete and the Greek mainland. They date from about 100 years after the Linear A tablets. Linear A is still a puzzle, but Linear B was deciphered in 1953; its language proved to be an early, primitive form of Greek.

The tablets contain records that testify to the high degree of organization in the economies of the Cretan and Greek cities.

The Linear B tablets, being in Greek, confirm both the archaeological finds and the later Greek tradition that mainland Greece came to dominate Crete, at least culturally and perhaps politically as well, shortly after 1500 B.C. By this time the first Indo-European Greek tribes, the Achaeans, had entered Greece and founded their own civilization. Evidence of considerable destruction of the Cretan palaces about that time is variously interpreted as having been caused by an earthquake or by war.

The final 300 years of the Bronze Age in the Aegean are known as the Mycenaean period, named for wealthy "golden" Mycenae, the leading Greek city of the time, where modern archaeology has uncovered the finest examples of the crafts of the late Bronze Age, especially jewelry and decorative articles of solid gold buried in the royal tombs.

The Dark Age.
The Bronze Age in Greece and Crete came to an end with barbarian invasions by a new wave of Indo-Europeans about 1200 B.C. The invaders were the Dorian Greeks from northwest Greece. The destruction they wrought was total, and for 400 years afterward the material level of culture was so low that the period is called Greece's Dark Age. Along with the splendor of the Mycenaean palaces, the art of writing was also lost, and the memory of the past remained only in oral poetry.

Contacts with the Phoenicians gradually stimulated a revival of civilized life. When the Greeks borrowed an alphabet from the Phoenicians about 800 B.C., they were already on the road to the brilliant achievements that laid the foundations of Western culture. The earliest written literature, the *Iliad* and the *Odyssey* of Homer, which recount the great deeds of Bronze Age heroes, was produced at that time.

The Greek city-state. It was also at the end of the Dark Age that the city-state, or polis, which was to become the characteristic political unit of Greece, began to appear. Greece at its height consisted of more than a thousand of these autonomous units, most of them no more than towns, each with its small area of fertile farmland and separated from its neighbors by the rugged mountains that typify the Greek landscape.

The loyalty of the citizen to his polis was fierce, and ancient Greece was never voluntarily unified. The polis dominated every aspect of life, both public and private. The city-state was so essential a part of the Greek way of life that it was thought to be part of the natural world. Aristotle's famous axiom that man is by nature "a political animal" is more correctly rendered as man is by nature "an animal who lives in a polis."

An era of growth.
The political and economic development of Greece in the 600s and 500s B.C. was very rapid. Stimulated by population growth as well as trade, the Greek cities sent boatloads of colonists throughout the Mediterranean, where they established scores of new city-states.

The main areas settled by the Greeks were the shores of the Black Sea, the Ionian coast of Asia Minor, Sicily, and southern Italy. Sicily and southern Italy, so heavily colonized, became known as Magna Graecia, or Greater Greece.

Overseas expansion was accompanied by the evolution of most Greek city-states from simple agrarian societies, ruled by a small, hereditary, landowning nobility, to violent dictatorships, to aggressive trading and manufacturing communities, with armies and navies, usually ruled under written constitutions by a fairly large class of prosperous people.

A remarkable cultural growth also took place during this period. Lyric poetry was written that, in the variety of its meters, subject matter, and imagery, was far more original than any produced in the Middle East. It was this poetry that was to form the poetic tradition of the West.

Two of the three classic architectural orders—the Doric and the Ionic —were developed. Sculpture and vase painting advanced rapidly and soon broke away from their Eastern models and developed characteristically Greek styles.

civilization *US*

civilisation *Brit.*

colonized *US*

colonised *Brit.*

meters *US*

metres *Brit.*

THE LEGENDARY TROJAN HORSE, filled with Greek soldiers hiding inside, was taken within the formerly impregnable walls of the city of Troy. When the soldiers emerged that night, the fall of Troy was accomplished.

Birth of philosophy. Perhaps the most important achievement of the period, however, was the birth of philosophy (literally, "love of wisdom"). It first appeared during the early 500s in the cities along the Ionian (Turkish) coast of the Aegean, where it was stimulated by close contact with the older cultures of Asia.

It was at Miletus, the most prominent of the Ionian cities, that Thales (whom tradition calls the first philosopher), along with a group of other pioneers, initiated the process of systematic thought. Their teachings led to the later political and moral philosophy of Plato and Aristotle, as well as to the philosophical and scientific explorations that would flower in a still later epoch of Greek history, the Hellenistic period.

The attempt of the philosophers to find a rational explanation for all phenomena, without reference to the supernatural, has been called "the discovery of the mind." It is one of the momentous achievements in the history of civilization.

The Classical period.

Ancient Greece reached its height during the 400s and 300s B.C., a time often called the Classical period. Although "the glory that was Greece," or "the Greek miracle," as succeeding ages have called this epoch, was primarily intellectual and cultural, it can be understood only within its political setting. The independent Greek city-state, the polis, provided the dynamic element.

The polis permitted a wide variety of governmental forms, customs, institutions, and attitudes, and it thereby nourished freedom and a spirit of adventurous experiment. At the same time, its very smallness inspired an intense devotion in its citizens.

In the Greek polis, public and private life were tightly interwoven. Religion, recreation, as well as entertainment, which today are considered private concerns, were usually public activities for all.

The Persian wars. The Greek cities, each immersed in its own relatively isolated development, became aware of themselves as powers in a larger world as the result of a series of invasions in the early 400s B.C., when the Persian king Darius I, and later his son Xerxes, sought to add mainland Greece to the Persian Empire. Though greatly outnumbered, the Greeks inflicted crushing defeats on the Persians at the famous battles of Marathon, Salamis, and Plataea.

Sparta and Athens. Two cities, Sparta and Athens, emerged from the wars as the leading powers in Greece. Both were much larger and more powerful than any of the other Greek cities. But Sparta and Athens were diametrically opposed in their economic and political institutions, as well as in their cultural lives and in their goals. The history of Classical Greece is generally viewed as the story of the struggle between them.

Sparta had long been recognized as the most powerful military state in Greece. Spartan life was rigid and austere, as the term "spartan" signifies. It was entirely dedicated to military strength as the means of maintaining an authoritarian society.

Spartan society was supported by the agricultural labor of the surrounding peoples, called Helots, who were completely enslaved. Spartan cultural life was narrow, as indicated by the term "laconic" (Laconia was the region in which Sparta was situated) to describe terse or succinct speech.

Athens, on the other hand, had developed into a culturally brilliant society. Trade was encouraged, opening the city to the arts and crafts of a wide region. At the close of the 500s B.C., Athens had begun one of the most venturesome political experiments in history with the creation of a direct democracy. All adult male citizens, it mattered not whether aristocrats or peasants, rich or poor, ignorant or learned, had an equal share in guiding the affairs of state, and all public matters were decided by a majority vote of citizens in the assembly, which met every ninth day.

Both the vigorous character and expansionist tendencies of Athens were expressed in the navy built a few years before the final Persian attack. This navy proved to be the deciding factor in the repulse of Persia; after the war it became the most powerful fleet in the Mediterranean.

Major Events—Western Cultures

c 2500 B.C.	A seagoing Minoan civilization develops on the island of Crete.
c 800 B.C.	*The Iliad* and *The Odyssey* are created by Homer; the city-state, or polis, begins to appear in Greece.
c 776 B.C.	The first Olympic games are held in Greece.
c 530 B.C.	Pythagoras, a mathematician and mystic, is active in Greece.
c 458 B.C.	Aeschylus produces *The Oresteia*.
c 456 B.C.	The Temple of Zeus at Olympia is completed.
c 450 B.C.	The Parthenon is built on the Acropolis in Athens.
c 433 B.C.	The first census of citizens and property is taken in Rome.
c 400 B.C.	Socrates introduces the cross-questioning (dialogue) method of teaching.
c 280 B.C.	The Colossus of Rhodes, a huge statue of the god Helios, and one of the seven wonders of the ancient world, is built overlooking the harbor on the Greek island of Rhodes.
c 55 B.C.	The first permanent stone theater is built in Rome.
c A.D. 64	A great fire destroys large sections of Rome.
c A.D. 161	During the reign of Marcus Aurelius, Stoicism becomes the dominant philosophy of the Roman Empire.
c A.D. 313	In the Edict of Milan, Christianity is granted toleration in the Roman Empire.
c A.D. 476	The western half of the Roman Empire collapses.

labor
US

labour
Brit.

vigorous
US

vigourous
Brit.

21 History of the World

ONE OF THE CULTURES of the ancient world best known today from archaeological discoveries on the island of Crete is that of the Minoans. Much of what is known about them is mysterious due to the incompletely understood written language. Highly developed architecture and art, such as the dolphin fresco shown here, as well as the decline of the civilization possibly due to earthquake and tidal wave resulting from the catastrophic eruption of Thera, may have contributed to tales of lost Atlantis. Though the culture appears to have been well known and powerful until about 1500 B.C., more complete evidence of the Minoan way of life was rediscovered only about a hundred years ago.

The Peloponnesian War. As Sparta retired to its traditional defensive isolation, after the Persian wars, Athens grasped the opportunity to grow, and in the guise of a maritime alliance, it rapidly built an empire over the Greek cities and islands of the Aegean. Athenian ambition seemed insatiable, and Sparta resented it. Allying itself with Corinth and other polises of the Peloponnesus, the southern region of mainland Greece, Sparta went to war against Athens.

The Peloponnesian War was fought for 27 years, on land and sea, from the Aegean to Sicily. It engaged the entire Greek world. Neither side was able to prevail, and the balance was finally tipped by the intervention of Persia, which provided Sparta with the funds to build a fleet. In 404 B.C., the Athenian fleet was destroyed and Athens unconditionally surrendered.

Decline of Greece. For the next 70 years, Greece was engaged in useless and destructive warfare as each of several major Greek cities in turn attempted to gain leadership, only to be met by a coalition that it could not defeat. The principle of the independent polis would not permit a voluntary national unity, nor could any single polis accomplish it by force.

The inevitable conclusion—conquest by an outside power—occurred in 338 B.C., when Philip II, king of Macedonia, a country bordering Greece to the north, defeated the Greeks at the Battle of Chaeronea. Greece's "Golden Age" came to an end, and all its cities eventually came to be subjected to Macedonian rule.

Culture of Classical Greece. In the 150 years from the Persian wars to the Battle of Chaeronea, Greece produced some of Western civilization's most precious intellectual, artistic, and literary heritage.

The Acropolis, the flat-topped hill in the center of Athens where the temples to the gods were located, had been destroyed by the Persians in 480 B.C. The rebuilding of the Acropolis represented not only the height of Athenian ambition, but of classic Greek artistic expression in sculpture and architecture.

The Parthenon, superbly designed and executed, with its elegant proportions and magnificent sculptural decoration, is the finest example of the architecture of the 400s. The other buildings, although never completed because of the Peloponnesian War, demonstrate the range and variety, as well as the quality, of classical art.

Athenian vase painting was raised to the level of a fine art, and Athenian pottery, numerous examples of which can be seen in the museums of Europe and America, was prized throughout the Mediterranean world.

Greek literary and intellectual accomplishments during this period were equally dazzling. The drama originated in Athens, where it developed not as commercial entertainment but as part of the civic and religious festival of the god Dionysus.

The tragedies written in the 400s by Aeschylus, Sophocles, and Euripides, with the grandeur of their language and subject matter, created a standard for serious literature that remains unshaken. The comedies of Aristophanes, in addition to gusto and bawdy humor, introduced the great tradition of political satire. To understand what freedom of speech and opinion meant in democratic Athens, one has only to read one of Aristophanes' antiwar plays, with its ferocious lampooning of Athens's leading politicians, and to realize that it was originally produced as part of a state festival.

The writing of history also originated in Athens in the 400s B.C. The accounts of Herodotus, the "father of history," especially his descriptions of his travels in ancient Egypt and his *Persian Wars,* are still widely read. They were followed by Thucydides' *History of the Peloponnesian War,* one of the most celebrated historical works ever written.

In philosophy, the early accomplishments of the Ionian thinkers came to maturity in the writings of Plato and Aristotle in the 300s. They raised and systematically examined the questions that human beings have probed ever since: the nature of the universe, of man, of God; the meaning of life; the relation of the individual to the state; and the whole range of scientific, metaphysical, aesthetic, and ethical inquiry.

The Hellenistic Age. In the centuries that followed, Greek culture continued, but with a difference. Greece's conqueror, Philip, king of Macedonia, planned to unite the Greeks with the Macedonians and together conquer the Persian Empire. But on the eve of his invasion, he was assassinated, leaving his 20-year-old son Alexander to carry out his plans.

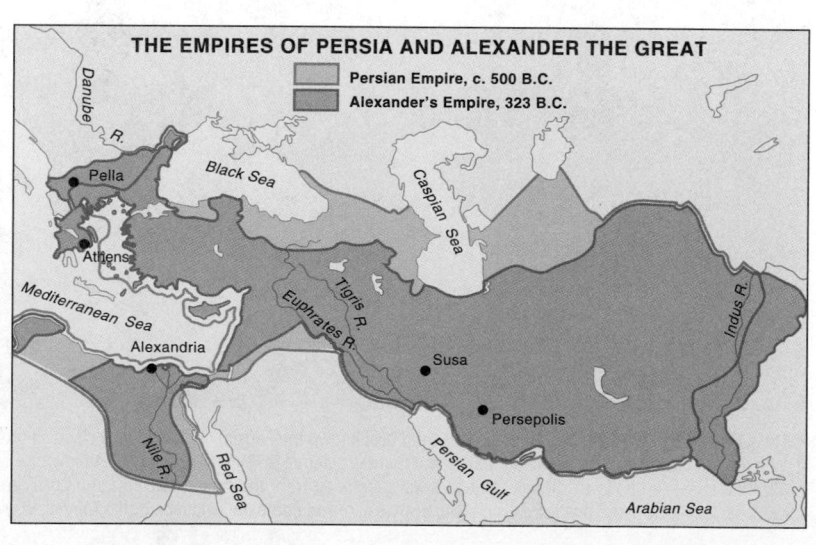

THE EMPIRES OF PERSIA AND ALEXANDER THE GREAT

- Persian Empire, c. 500 B.C.
- Alexander's Empire, 323 B.C.

Danube R. · Pella · Black Sea · Caspian Sea · Athens · Mediterranean Sea · Euphrates R. · Tigris R. · Indus R. · Alexandria · Susa · Persepolis · Nile R. · Red Sea · Persian Gulf · Arabian Sea

ANCIENT PEOPLES

Alexander the Great. Alexander soon drastically altered the Greek world, earning himself the title "the Great." In the mere 13 years between his accession to the Macedonian throne and his death at age 33 in 323 B.C., Alexander led the combined Macedonian and Greek armies in conquering all of the Persian Empire, thereby giving the Greeks mastery of the civilized world and bringing about the reciprocal influence of Greek and Middle Eastern culture throughout the immense territory that stretched from the central Mediterranean to India. The 300-year epoch that ensued is called the Hellenistic Age.

The Hellenistic world. After Alexander's death, his huge empire was fought over by his generals, called the Diadochi, who ultimately divided the empire among themselves and set up three major Hellenistic monarchies. The general Ptolemy named himself king of Egypt and founded the Ptolemaic dynasty there. A second general, Seleucus, founded a dynasty that ruled most of the Asian portions of Alexander's empire, the Seleucid Empire. Macedonia and Greece became the province of the Antigonids, descended from the general Antigonus.

To match these powerful territorial states, the old Greek city-states, recognizing the ineffectiveness of the polis in the international sphere, united in leagues. Two important political developments occurred during this period. The first was the universal acceptance of the claim of divinity, similar to that of the Egyptian pharaohs, made by the Hellenistic monarchs.

The second development came about within the Greek leagues. It involved the first significant experiments in representative government, where people chose officials to represent them, as distinct from the direct democracy of classical Athens, where each citizen voted on each issue.

Hellenistic culture. The most important contributions of the Hellenistic era were made in cultural life. Literature produced no giants to match the earlier writers, but with the spread of education and literacy, new forms of literature arose: the comedy of manners and situation, of which the major poet was Menander; pastoral poetry; didactic poetry; and the prose romance or adventure, which was the ancestor of the modern novel.

Historical writing became more professional, and histories, most of which have been lost, were written to cover all the countries newly opened to Greek curiosity. The only major historian of the period whose work has come down to us is Polybius.

In art, there was a tendency toward a more ornate and decorative style. In architecture, temples were built on a larger and more lavish scale than ever before, but the characteristic buildings were nonreligious and were typified by great tombs and by another of

PLATO'S SCHOOL OF PHILOSOPHY, shown here in an Italian mosaic, developed into what is believed to have been the first university.

the Seven Wonders of the Ancient World, the Pharos, the huge lighthouse that stood in the harbor of Alexandria in Egypt.

Science made the most spectacular progress of any period of history until modern times. The scientific inquiry begun by Aristotle was continued. In Alexandria the kings of the Ptolemaic dynasty founded the Museum, which was the first scientific institute in history. At the Museum, scholars were maintained at the expense of the state. A huge library was collected, laboratories and dissecting rooms were provided, and zoological and botanical collections were organized. Literary scholarship,

DISCOBOLOS, the Discus Thrower, represents not only the Greeks' ideal of man but also their development and passion for sport.

textual criticism, and library science were developed.

Enormous strides were made in mathematics, physics, astronomy, geography, botany, biology, and medicine. The properties of air were demonstrated; the heliocentric theory of Earth's relation to the sun was advanced; the circumference of Earth and the degrees of latitude were calculated; the motor and sensory nervous systems were discovered; the properties of cubes, cylinders, cones, and spheres were analyzed; and the techniques necessary for the measurement of curved surfaces were developed.

In philosophy, the formal schools focused their attention on ethics and their teachings began to emphasize a divine sanction for moral behavior. The most influential philosophy of the period was Stoicism, which eventually became as much a religion as a rational philosophy. The Stoics taught the immortality of the soul, the importance of doing one's assigned duty on Earth, and the brotherhood of man.

There were numerous movements in religion that created a receptive environment for the growth of Christianity. Syncretism, a belief in the fusion of the gods of one people with those of another, became prevalent and resulted in the almost universal concept of a single deity.

Most important, the Greek world absorbed the "mystery" cults of the Middle East, and thereby shifted drastically from their worship of local patron gods. These mystery religions focused on the individual and his direct, emotional communion with the divine. They taught belief in a god who had suffered, died, and been reborn. The communicant, through sacramental union with the deity, could himself achieve rebirth and salvation in the life after death.

analyzed *US*

analysed *Brit.*

emphasize *US*

emphasise *Brit.*

21 History of the World

Rome

The Hellenistic world's power was ultimately broken by conquest. The conqueror was Rome, the last and greatest organizer of the ancient world.

The early history of Rome was "invented" by the romantic propaganda of a world-state in the first century B.C.

THE PONT DU GARD, part of an aqueduct near Nîmes, France, is a striking example of the engineering ability of the ancient Romans.

emphasized
US

emphasised
Brit.

and the first century A.D. out of a combination of legend, tradition, and the desire to provide a suitable pedigree for the new rulers of the world.

Modern analysis of this "history," based on extensive archaeological research, indicates that the Romans were a local group of the Latins, one of the many Indo-European tribes who entered Italy shortly after 1000 B.C. These tribes are known collectively as the Italic peoples. The Romans were the inhabitants of a town that had a potentially advantageous location on the Tiber River, which was the last point upstream navigable by seagoing vessels.

The Romans were first ruled by a monarchy, which soon gave way to an oligarchy composed of hereditary aristocrats (patricians). The patricians, like their counterparts in the early Greek polis, ruled by means of a permanent council of elders (the Senate) and a monopoly of the state's judicial, executive, and religious offices. The mass of citizens (plebeians) met in assemblies (Comitia), whose principal function was the ratification of acts promulgated by the patricians.

Early development. Until the late 300s B.C., Rome was an insignificant state, largely agricultural and almost entirely illiterate. For a long period the Romans were culturally influenced and even ruled by the Etruscans, their neighbors across the Tiber River.

The Etruscan language is only partially understood, and thus detailed knowledge of the Etruscans is lacking today. Nevertheless, it is certain that at their height in the 600s and 500s B.C., they were far more advanced politically and culturally than the Romans.

At that time there were three powers in the western Mediterranean: the Etruscans, the Greeks of southern Italy and Sicily, and the Phoenicians, whose major commercial city was Carthage, in North Africa. In the three-way struggle for land, trade, and power, the Etruscans were the losers, and Rome's independence (traditionally dated at 509 B.C.) was a consequence of the decline of Etruscan power.

The most lasting mark made by the Etruscans was in the sphere of religion. Etruscan heritage can be seen in the complex structure and ritualism of Roman religious institutions.

Roman expansion. Following its independence from the Etruscans, Rome's development was at first inconsequential. As late as 390 B.C., a tribe of barbaric Gauls from northern Italy sacked the city. Probably as a direct result of this event, Rome began to cultivate the military prowess that was responsible for its remarkable growth. By 338 B.C., the Romans controlled the surrounding region of Latium, whose inhabitants had long been organized for military purposes in the Latin League, which Rome took over.

By the end of the 300s, they ruled the entire peninsula south of the Po River. In the following 150 years of uninterrupted military advance, Rome rose from a local power in Italy to the unchallenged ruler of most of the Mediterranean world and arbiter of the rest, over which it continued to extend its direct control.

A series of wars with Carthage, called the Punic wars, began in 264 B.C. With the destruction of Carthage in 146 B.C., Rome's rule over the western Mediterranean was absolute. In the same year, the sack and destruction of Corinth, the outcome of another series of wars that had begun in 215 B.C., completed the Roman conquest of the Greek mainland.

The rest of the Hellenistic East was subjugated piecemeal. For practical purposes, the task was completed when Rome added the last Hellenistic monarchy, Egypt, to its dominions in 30 B.C.

The republic. The nearly five centuries following Rome's independence from the Etruscans until its total control of the Mediterranean mark the period of the Roman Republic. In theory, the structure of the republic emphasized the joint power of all classes in a unified citizenry. But the gaining by the plebeians, or common people, of equal rights to those of the patricians, or aristocrats, the subject of much of the legendary early history of Rome, is illusory.

In actuality, the political and judicial equality gained by the plebeians resulted in the formation of a joint patrician-plebeian aristocracy. It was composed of a few score of the wealthiest families in Rome, who intermarried among themselves and rigorously excluded outsiders. This aristocracy maintained a monopoly over the higher offices of state, and the holders of these offices filled vacancies in the Senate.

The tightly knit oligarchy that presided over and directed the triumphant territorial expansion of Rome was motivated by a combination of patriotism and greed. Without any ideals or guiding philosophy, it treated conquest merely as an opportunity to gain unlimited wealth and power.

No better was its treatment of the citizen-farmers, whose endless military service had won the empire. Long years in the army caused neglect of small landholdings, which were taken over

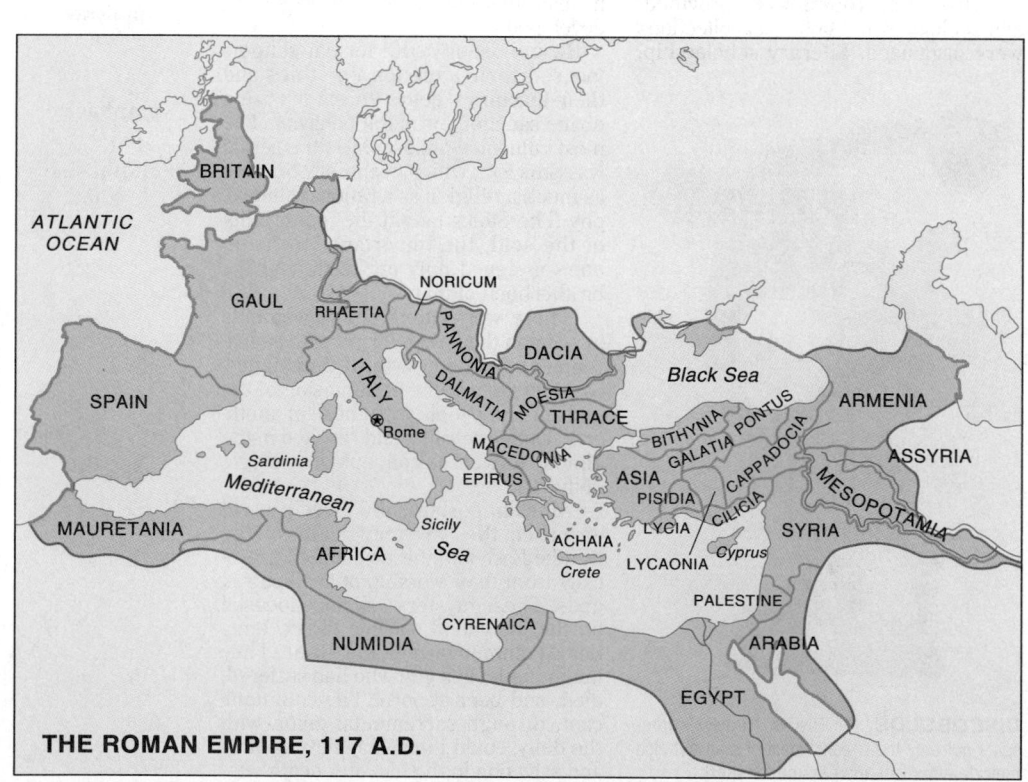

ATLANTIC OCEAN

BRITAIN

GAUL

RHAETIA

NORICUM

PANNONIA

DACIA

ITALY

DALMATIA

MOESIA

Rome

Black Sea

SPAIN

THRACE

MACEDONIA

BITHYNIA

GALATIA

PONTUS

ARMENIA

Sardinia

Mediterranean

EPIRUS

ASIA

PISIDIA

CAPPADOCIA

ASSYRIA

MESOPOTAMIA

MAURETANIA

Sicily

Sea

ACHAIA

LYCIA

CILICIA

Cyprus

SYRIA

Crete

LYCAONIA

AFRICA

PALESTINE

CYRENAICA

ARABIA

NUMIDIA

EGYPT

THE ROMAN EMPIRE, 117 A.D.

and consolidated into large estates by the senatorial aristocracy. These profitable enterprises were worked by gangs of slaves, available in whatever number was desired from the unfortunate populations defeated by Rome in war.

Popular unrest. By the end of the 100s B.C., the dispossessed small farmers, formerly the backbone of Rome's citizenry, had become a landless, rootless, unemployed mob in the city of Rome. Permanently discontented, the farmers became a chief source of the political violence that was to bring the republic to its end in the first century B.C.

Equally alienated were the wealthy businessmen, the equestrians, whose fortunes had been made by Rome's military victories but who were denied entry into the closed circle of the senatorial rulers of the state.

Ambitious demagogues exploited the general discontent to circumvent the Senate, gain control of an army, and exercise personal power. Roman territorial expansion continued, however, and even increased as reckless politicians realized the surest way to power was the command of a victorious army with which they could coerce the Senate.

Julius Caesar. After 100 years of intermittent civil strife, military coups, assassinations, and violent rioting, it is merely convention to call only the final episode in the destruction of the republic a civil war. The victor, Julius Caesar, took the office of permanent dictator, but in reality, in the few months between elimination of organized resistance and his assassination in 44 B.C., he wielded the absolute power of a Hellenistic monarch.

Of all the remarkable political figures of the first century B.C.—Tiberius and Gaius Gracchus, Marius and Sulla, Pompey, Crassus, Cicero, and the rest—Caesar appears to have been the first to

realize that however pleasurable power might be, its pursuit was not self-justifying, and that the issue at stake was how Rome's vast domain was to be governed.

The arrangements Caesar completed or launched before his sudden death made it clear that he had decided on monarchic rule aided by a Hellenistic-style centralized, permanent officialdom. The aim of empire he enunciated—eternal peace and stability, fair and equal treatment of conquered peoples, and only such taxation as proved necessary for the maintenance of a government and army to guarantee and extend these goals—goes back to the great tradition of the Persian Empire and Alexander the Great.

Caesar's death brought about a brief resumption of civil war. The victor was Caesar's nephew and heir, Octavian, who, under the title of Augustus (the Revered), realized Caesar's aims and established the governmental structure of the Roman Empire.

Roman culture. The dramatic rise of the Roman Republic and its equally dramatic self-destruction and transformation into the Roman Empire are important in world history because of the cultural developments that accompanied those transformations.

The Rome that embarked on world conquest after 300 B.C. was extremely primitive. It was a nation of simple and illiterate farmer-soldiers. There was no Latin literature at all until 250 B.C., when the first written work was produced—significantly, it was a translation into Latin of Homer's *Odyssey* by Livius Andronicus, a Greek from southern Italy.

The key to Rome's cultural achievements lay in its ability to absorb, adapt, preserve, and transmit the mighty cultural achievements of Greece. In the famous line of the Roman poet Horace, "Captive Greece captured her barbarian captor."

As Rome moved relentlessly forward on its course of conquest, its simple rustic culture was lost in that of Hellenistic Greece. Rome quickly absorbed Hel-

lenistic religious cults and ideas, philosophies, art, literature, and political institutions—all the tastes and habits of a highly sophisticated people.

In vain did conservative statesmen like Cato in the 100s B.C. inveigh against the corrupting influence of Greece. For centuries thereafter Romans continued to exhort their fellow Romans to return to the straightforward, homely virtues of their ancestors. They succeeded in shaping a Roman ideal based on the way of life of those legendary ancestors: grave, austere, simple, courageous, honest; loyal and obedient to family, religion, and state. The ideal was conspicuously lacking in subtlety, cleverness, frivolity, and intellectuality.

While giving way to the persuasive influence of Greece, the Romans, to the end of ancient times, continued to try to hold themselves to this ideal. At his best the cultivated Roman of the late republic and early empire combined the urbane, sophisticated, flexible way of the Greek with the serious, dedicated simplicity of the Roman.

Roman literature reached maturity only in the first century B.C., with the poetry of Catullus and Lucretius and the prose of Cicero. The two poets succeeded in transforming the Latin language into a subtle vehicle capable of expressing in its entirety the variety of mood, emotion, thought, and color of 500 years of Greek poetic achievement.

The immense literary productivity of Cicero performed a similar service for prose. He gave Rome a language capable of expressing the complexity of Greek philosophy and Western civilization, a prose style that remained an educational model until our day.

Under the Roman Empire, the assimilation of Greek culture was accelerated and its Roman adaptation was carried into the newly conquered barbarian lands of central and western Europe as well as to the island of Britain. With Romanization, these lands received the heritage that was to become the foundation of their own cultural tradition.

JULIUS CAESAR was one of Rome's greatest military and political leaders. He was betrayed and murdered by rebels led by Brutus, a man he had believed was his friend.

THE ROMAN COLISEUM lies in ruins. The magnificent amphitheater was the site of spectacular entertainment, such as chariot races, ship battles on an artificial lake, and wild animal shows, as well as notorious and inhumane gladiatorial combat and executions of Christians.

realized
US

realised
Brit.

color
US

colour
Brit.

civilization
US

civilisation
Brit.

21 History of the World

HADRIAN'S WALL, built by Roman soldiers, separated the north and the south of England.

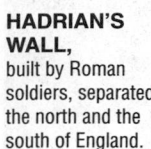

civilized
US

civilised
Brit.

emphasized
US

emphasised
Brit.

EARLY CHRISTIAN ART frequently was painted directly on wet plastered walls of churches and much has failed to survive the centuries, although some from the Byzantine period has been preserved.

The empire. The Roman Empire placed the civilized world under a single monarchic rule, although it used the political terminology of the Roman Republic and preserved such obsolete institutions as the Senate. The empire tended toward authoritarianism and military despotism, It was centuries before its autocratic nature became absolute, and by then it had begun its decline.

Its unmatched accomplishment created a system of government that enabled a vast territory and a population of about 100 million people of different races, languages, cultures, and traditions to enjoy centuries of security, stability, peace, rational and disinterested administration, and almost impartial law.

Although the early emperors of the first century A.D. led scandalous private lives, the empire they ruled actually prospered, and the centralized bureaucracy that made Rome a synonym for the art of government evolved during their reigns. By the middle of the first century A.D., that government consisted of a permanent, highly organized civil service leading from the lowest levels to the emperor, who considered himself the servant of his demanding office.

The "good emperors" of the first century created the Pax Romana, or Roman Peace, an epoch that Edward Gibbon, the great English historian of the 1700s, described as the period in which "the condition of the human race was the most happy and prosperous."

Civilization spread throughout the vast realm of the Roman Empire as scores of cities were built where formerly there had been only barbarism. A Greek lecturer who came to Rome in the 150s A.D. praised Rome's accomplishment. He stated that the new unwalled cities were meant for a world at peace—for the first time in history cities needed no local defense.

Decline and fall of the empire. The empire at its height already contained the seeds of its decay and its eventual fall. The decline and fall of the Roman Empire is one of the classic issues of history. Interpretation of the fall has ranged over the whole spectrum of causes that historians have put forth to explain historical events.

The moral explanation emphasized such matters as the private wickedness of individual emperors, the decadent luxury in which the wealthy lived, indifference to the misery of the masses, and the general malaise of a civilization that had somehow lost its dynamism and its capacity to innovate.

The social-political explanation has emphasized the divisions and conflicts of interest that developed—rich and poor, urban and rural, governmental bureaucracy and citizenry, military and civilian.

The control of the armed forces remained a problem for centuries. Army commanders always presented the threat of coups, and at various critical times made war upon each other with control of the empire as the prize.

The need for large military forces was always present because of the pressure of outside powers upon the imperial borders—in the East a revived Persian Empire, in Europe a succession of partly civilized Germanic tribes. The threat in Europe was met in the 200s by admitting whole tribes into the empire, settling them along the frontiers, and using them as defensive troops against waves of attack by other tribes still on the outside.

The problems in the 200s, and the decreasing power to deal with them, brought about an administrative revision around 300 that divided the empire into an eastern Greek-speaking half and

a western Latin-speaking half.

In spite of the efforts of individual emperors to restore unity, the two halves tended to grow further apart. By about 400 they were not only separate, but, beneath a surface of brotherhood, hostile.

Modern study of decline and fall has tended to emphasize economic factors: The failure to develop an expanding economy and an improved technology, the drain on the empire's money supply as luxury items continued to be imported from as far away as China, to be paid for in cash, and the consequent devaluation of currency, as well as the increasing burden of an ever-growing bureaucracy and an armed service paid for by a growing burden of taxation.

The development of Christianity. Coinciding with the spread of the Roman Empire in the first century A.D. was the appearance of a new religion in Palestine. There, Jesus of Nazareth, well versed in the teachings of Judaism, preached that he was the son of God, sent to redeem mankind of its sins. He told of a loving God, whom the people should love above all else. If they followed His laws set forth in the Ten Commandments of the Old Testament, and were just and forgiving with one another, after death they would join Him in the kingdom of God. Fearing that Jesus might lead other Jews in a revolt against their rule in Palestine, the Romans had Jesus crucified, but his followers, the Apostles, remained to carry on his teachings, which developed into Christianity.

Whether Christianity is to be seen as a cause of imperial decline or a symptom, or merely an accompaniment, it is true that Christianity's rise coincided with Rome's decline.

The Christian Church found a receptive world for its doctrines, a world in which the spread of mystery cults and the almost universal knowledge of the Greek language readied millions of people to receive its teachings. The early church fathers borrowed freely from Greek philosophy.

Perhaps even more important, they constructed their church along the administrative lines of the Roman Empire itself. In the 300s A.D., Christianity triumphed to become the official religion of the empire, and the church was prepared to take over the reins of authority from the failing hands of the civil and military rulers.

In the 400s the western half of the Roman Empire collapsed as invasions by the Huns of Mongolia and barbarian German tribes swept through. Through the centuries that followed, the Christian Church survived.

With its hierarchical, international structure, the church preserved in its administration the traditions of the Roman Empire. In its educational system and its monasteries, it kept alive the cultural tradition and the literary and philosophical achievements of ancient civilization.

The Flowering of Eastern Cultures

Ancient India

As Greece was going through its Dark Age and the Latins were beginning to settle Rome, the Aryans were extending their kingdoms on the South Asian subcontinent, eastward along the Ganges River and southward across the Deccan Plateau, subjugating the native populations and drawing them into the caste system. It was a period of political disunity as rival kingdoms warred frequently.

India was entering its Epic Age (c 1000–500 B.C.), so named for the magnificent pieces of religious literature it produced. Among them is the *Mahabharata*, the longest epic poem in world literature. It tells the story of war among rivals for an Aryan throne and ennobles the Aryan warrior. Its final 18 chapters, the *Bhagavad-Gita*, is a philosophical dialogue that stresses the concept of dharma, the idea that performing one's moral duty is the fulfillment of life. Another great epic is the *Ramayana*, whose leading characters personify the characteristics of the perfect man and perfect woman. From such writings, along with the earlier Vedas, sprang Hinduism, one of the two principal religions that have shaped Indian civilization.

Hinduism. Hinduism is a blend of many beliefs, those of the Aryans and of the peoples they conquered. The Brahmans, the priestly caste, preserved the sacred writings of the Epic Age and also interpreted them for the people.

In Hinduism, there are many gods, but they are all manifestations of one supreme spirit, Brahman, the World Soul. United in the spirit are a trinity of main Hindu gods—Brahma, the Creator; Vishnu, the Preserver; and Shiva, the Destroyer.

Hindus believe that everyone has a soul that is part of the World Soul. The soul longs to become reunited with the World Soul, but to do this, it must go through many reincarnations, becoming less worldly and more spiritual in each to earn salvation. Hinduism encourages living a virtuous life to achieve greater spirituality.

Solidifying the caste system. The caste system begun by the Aryans became a pillar of Hinduism. Each caste had its own strict social and religious rules, and living virtuously demanded complete acceptance of, and obedience to, these laws. According to the Hindu law of karma, if a person lived obediently as a member of his caste, he would be reincarnated into a higher caste. If he did not, he would fall back into a lower caste in his next life, or even be reincarnated as a form of animal life.

Under the caste system, the Brahmans, as the highest caste, were closest to salvation. As priests, they strengthened their position. Only they could prescribe rituals that members of other castes must observe to guide their souls to salvation. But some Hindus resented Brahman power and sought a new way toward salvation; thus Buddhism, the second of the Indian civilization's great religions, was born.

Buddhism. The founder of Buddhism, Siddhartha Gautama, wanted to break the hold the Brahmans had over Hindu life and help people find their own way to salvation, without priestly assistance. He was born in 563 B.C. in the foothills of the Himalayas, the son of a wealthy rajah. According to legend, he had never known in his luxurious life about the suffering of people until he discovered it at the age of 29. Shocked by what he saw, he renounced his life of ease to go into the outside world to learn why there was such suffering and how it might be alleviated.

After years of wandering and finding no answers, he sat down beneath a sacred fig tree to meditate. While there, he achieved "enlightenment," finding the knowledge he sought. From that experience, he became known as the Buddha, the "Enlightened One," and developed the religious philosophy that became Buddhism.

Buddha did not intend to replace Hinduism, only to reform its teachings; for example, by denying that achieving salvation required priestly rituals, or that only Brahmans were worthy of being released from the cycle of reincarnation. He said that members of any caste could reach Nirvana by living virtuously. Buddha also repudiated the Hindu gods. Although Buddha may not have intended it, Buddhism did become a movement separate from Hinduism after his death about 483 B.C.

The spread of Buddhism. Missionaries spread the teachings of Buddha throughout India and beyond in Asia. In time, Buddhism divided into two major branches. One, the Hinayana, maintained the traditional Buddhist beliefs and honored Buddha as a great teacher. This sect spread mainly to Southeast Asia, today's Myanmar (formerly Burma), Thailand, and Cambodia. Another, the Mahayana, proclaimed Buddha a god and made Buddhism a religion of priests and temples. This sect spread through central and eastern Asia, to China, Korea, and Japan.

Buddhism is sometimes described as atheistic—believing in no god at all. The followers of Buddhism would dispute this. However, the Buddhist concept of God does not have the "personhood" concept found in other religions.

The Maurya Empire. During Buddha's lifetime, the Persian Empire under Darius I annexed the Indus Valley

in northwestern India, but an alliance of Aryan kingdoms under the leadership of the kingdom of Magadha in northeastern India progressively reclaimed land from Persian control. A Magadha dynasty, called the Nine Nandas, ruled northern India from 413 B.C. until 322 B.C. A Nanda ruler and his armies confronted Alexander the Great when he invaded the Indus Valley in 326. Though defeated, the Nandas maintained their power because Alexander's troops mutinied, forcing him to withdraw.

Chandragupta Maurya. In 322 B.C., an adventurous upstart named Chandragupta Maurya seized Magadha, overthrew the Nandas, and began to build India's first great empire under the Maurya dynasty. Over the next 24 years, he brought all of northern India under his control. In 305 B.C., in one of the first major battles between East and West, Chandragupta defeated Seleucus, founder of the Seleucid Empire, and added parts of today's Afghanistan to his own empire. At its height, during the rule of Asoka, the Maurya Empire stretched from the Hindu Kush mountains to the Bay of Bengal and covered nearly all of the Indian subcontinent.

BUDDHA'S teachings came to have their greatest influence outside his homeland of India. This 72-foot-high bronze statue, the Daibutsu Buddha at Kamakura, was cast in 1252.

| civilization |
| US |
| civilisation |
| Brit. |

| honored |
| US |
| honoured |
| Brit. |

21 History of the World

Asoka. The most famous of all emperors of ancient India was Asoka, a grandson of Chandragupta; he ruled from 273 to 232 B.C. Early in his rule, he led a campaign to add the east-central Indian kingdom of Kalinga to his empire. The bloodiness of the battle so horrified him—over 100,000 were butchered—that he vowed this military campaign would be his last. He turned to the teachings of Buddhism, which he then propagated all over India. It was Asoka who sent missionaries into other parts of Asia with the civilizing tenets of Buddhism.

Asoka was a humane ruler who is still revered for his religious toleration. A Buddhist himself, he did not persecute those who remained Hindu. He is also remembered for the 84,000 hemisphere-shaped temples, called *stupas,* he built to honor Buddha.

Following Asoka's death, the Mauryan dynasty began to disintegrate. Interior factionalism, local rebellions, and outside invasions culminated with the assassination of the last Mauryan emperor in 185 B.C.

India between empires. At the start of this period, just two years after the last Mauryan emperor died, a new group of invaders, Greeks from neighboring Bactria, crossed the Hindu Kush mountains and entered India from the northwest, taking control of the northern Punjab. But by the first century B.C., their power had waned and they were overrun by nomadic Indo-European tribes—Scythians, Parthians, Afghans, and Kushans—from central Asia.

These newcomers established small states that rose and disappeared in quick succession. The most successful were the Kushans, who expanded as far east as the middle Ganges valley and as far south as the Deccan Plateau. Their rule gave northern India two centuries of peace, until their collapse in A.D. 200.

| civilizing |
| *US* |
| civilising |
| *Brit.* |
| honor |
| *US* |
| honour |
| *Brit.* |
| centers |
| *US* |
| centres |
| *Brit.* |

Major Events—Eastern Cultures

- c 1450 B.C. Earliest Indian literature, *The Vedas*, begins.
- c 563 B.C. Siddhartha Gautama, the Buddha, is born.
- c 551 B.C. K'ung Fu-tzu, Confucius, is born.
- c 500 B.C. The caste system develops in India.
- c 400 B.C. Cast iron is developed in China.
- c 300 B.C. Yin-Yang school of philosophy is introduced by Tsou Yen.
- c 206 B.C. The Great Wall of China is completed.
- 141 B.C. Wu Ti heads the Chinese Han Empire; Pax Sinica begins.

- A.D. 1 Kushans rule India for almost two centuries of peace.
- 105 Paper is invented in China.
- c 200 The great Indian epic poems, the *Mahabharata*, the *Ramayam*, and the *Bhagavad Gita*, are completed.
- c 265 The Wei, Wu, and Shu dynasties are united in China.
- 271 The magnetic compass is in use in China.
- 320 The Gupta Empire begins to reunite India; major advances in mathematics and astronomy occur; use of the decimal system begins; solar year is calculated to be 365.3586 days.
- 330 Samudragupta takes the throne in India.
- 375 Chandragupta II subdues all of northern India from the Himalayas to the Deccan Plateau.

For southern India, the period following the Mauryan collapse was more prosperous than for northern India, though its division into numerous rival states made warfare incessant. Two of its kingdoms, Pandya and Chola, engaged in thriving trade with the Roman Empire. Colonists from southern India moved eastward to the East Indies, making India the intermediary of trade between the Indies and the Hellenistic world.

The Gupta Empire. In A.D. 320, at about the time the Roman Empire started going into its decline, India was about to enter its "Classical Age." Chandragupta I (ruled 320–c 330) began to reunite much of India once again from his base in Magadha. Through conquest, his son, Samudragupta (ruled c 330–c 375), and grandson, Chandragupta II (ruled c 375–413), subdued all of northern India from the Himalayas to the Deccan Plateau. The Gupta dynasty brought peace and stability. The trade they encouraged with the Roman Empire and with Southeast Asia brought great prosperity to India.

Art and literature. Painting and sculpture reached their heights during India's Classical Age. The Gupta emperors acted as generous patrons of the arts, and brilliant artists repaid them with magnificent works.

Gupta art is probably best exemplified by the 28 monasteries and temples carved out of solid rock cliffs at Ajanta in the Deccan Plateau. There murals depict scenes from the life of Buddha as well as glorifications of the human form and human love. (To the Gupta artist, the divine was not separate from the human; the spirit was not separate from the body.)

Sanskrit literature flourished, too, with the *Panchatantra,* a collection of fables, fairy tales, and adventure stories, among them the original versions of the Western stories of "Jack the Giant Killer" and the "Seven League Boots." Indian drama moved to the forefront with works by India's greatest poet and dramatist, Kalidasa, often called "the Shakespeare of India." His best known play is *Sakuntala,* a highly romantic story of lovers separated by a curse but later happily reunited by chance.

Science and technology. The Gupta era was also a golden age for learning in India, as universities attracted scholars from all over Asia. Mathematics became an area of special expertise. Indian mathematicians developed the 0 to 9 number system as well as the decimal system. (The West later adopted these numbers as an improvement over Roman numerals.)

In medicine, too, the Indians excelled. Among other innovations, they devised means of sterilizing and keeping wounds clean, invented the scalpel, performed Caesarean sections, and even did plastic surgery.

Indian metalworkers became adept at making the best iron and finest tempered steel in the world. The Iron Pillar of Delhi, a 23-foot-high column made of solid iron, has not rusted in nearly 1,500 years and still stands as a symbol of their skill during the Gupta era.

Collapse. However, the Guptas soon went into decline. Their rule ended in A.D. 535, when Hun invaders swept into India from the northwest. They destroyed the great urban centers of the Gupta dynasty and India's Classical Age came to an end.

Ancient China

As India was entering its Epic Age in 1000 B.C., China was also entering a period of growth and creativity. In 1027 B.C., the Shang dynasty fell to the Chou, a warrior tribe of north-central China. The Chou claimed the "Mandate of Heaven" from the Shang, accusing the former rulers of having mismanaged it. The Chou established their own dynasty, which would last longer than any other, 800 years, until 221 B.C.

The Chou dynasty. With most of northern China in their domain, the Chou kings organized it into feudal states. They delegated rule of the states to relatives or local nobles, who, in turn, recognized the overlordship of the Chou kings and promised them military support.

Under the Chou, Chinese civilization made strides in its material and cultural development unrivaled by later dynasties. During the sixth century B.C., iron production developed, with more efficient weapons and tools for waging war and expanding agriculture. With the iron plow, more land was put into farming. Canal-building projects irrigated the land and provided arteries for transporting farm produce and trade goods. The population grew and China became the most densely inhabited place on Earth.

Pleased with their progress as a civilization, they considered themselves high above peoples of other parts of the world—all of whom the Chinese considered "barbarians." They proclaimed China the "Middle Kingdom," holding an exalted position between heaven and Earth.

Three philosophies. Later Chou rulers began to lose control of their empire as rivalry sent the feudal states into almost constant warfare. But within this political instability there developed a flourishing intellectual life as philosophers studied how to bring order back into Chinese life. Several schools of philosophy emerged, each with a different way to achieve societal order and each profoundly influencing Chinese civilization.

Confucianism. The first and most influential of China's great philosophers was K'ung Fu-tzu, born in 551 B.C., at about the time of Buddha in India,

Zoroaster in Persia, and the early Greek philosophers. Christian missionaries to China, two millennia later, would call him Confucius.

Confucius, as a secular rather than a religious thinker, taught that an orderly society is based on everyone having a clearly defined place, with clearly stated responsibilities. If everyone accepts those responsibilities and acts with loyalty, kindness, and hard work, society will be harmonious.

Confucianism stressed the importance of the family as the basic unit of society and therefore encouraged filial piety and ancestor worship. Confucius also taught that rulers must have high moral character in order for their governments to be virtuous. Government officials, he believed, must be both highly moral and well educated.

Taoism. While Confucius promulgated a highly rational philosophy that called for people to take an active role in the working of society's institutions, the semilegendary philosopher Lao-tze urged just the opposite. He taught that people should withdraw from such activity and instead contemplate the tao, which he defined as the universal force of nature. Only by living quietly, in harmony with nature, could people find happiness and end turmoil.

Confucianism and Taoism were assuredly rival schools of thought, yet the Chinese adopted elements of both because the philosophies complemented each other. Confucian teachings had a strong influence on public life, while Taoism provided a comforting release in private life.

Legalism. During the late Chou period, yet another school of thought emerged, Legalism. Legalists shunned both Confucian ethics and Taoist meditation, because both assumed that human nature is basically good. The Legalists believed only a strong and efficient government that strictly enforces an elaborate code of laws and harsh punishments could maintain order. A strong central government ruling a unified China was needed, and the Chinese were about to get just that.

Empire. In 221 B.C., the Ch'in dynasty came to power under the leadership of Shih Huang Ti, who was able to subjugate the warring feudal states of China and unify them. He declared himself "the first universal emperor" of China. It was from the Ch'in dynasty that China took its name.

Ch'in rule. With the help of his ruthless and efficient chief minister, Li Ssu, Shih Huang Ti reorganized China along strict Legalist lines. He divided it into 36 provinces, after effectively breaking the power of the feudal states, by taking land from the aristocrats for private ownership by the peasants who worked it. The peasants thus provided a broad tax base for the empire.

Under the Ch'in, provinces were governed by bureaucrats controlled by the empire's autocratic central government. A single, harsh empire-wide legal code replaced local laws.

To protect the empire from invading nomads from Mongolia (the Chinese knew them as the Hsiung-nu; the West would know them as the Huns), and to improve transportation and communication, Shih Huang Ti began spectacular building projects using forced labor. The first was the Great Wall of China, unifying stone and earth walls that the northern feudal states had built earlier into a single wall extending 1,400 miles from central Asia to the Yellow Sea. It was completed about 206 B.C., after the emperor's death. He also constructed roads and canals that rivaled those of Rome.

The Ch'in dynasty had unified China, but its harsh laws, forced labor, and heavy taxation brought its downfall three years after Shih Huang Ti's death in 210 B.C.

Consolidation under the Han dynasty. The Ch'in's successor, the Han dynasty, ruled China for the next 400 years, to A.D. 220, one of its most glorious periods, a time that corresponded with the late Roman Republic and the rise of the Roman Empire.

Early in their reign, the Han appeased the citizenry by lightening the burden of taxation and repealing repressive Ch'in laws. Gradually, they tempered the harsher aspects of Legalism with Confucian teachings.

The Pax Sinica. The Han Empire reached its height under the "Martial Emperor," Wu Ti, who ruled from 141 to 87 B.C. His conquering armies expanded China north to Manchuria and Korea and south to Indochina. He drove far into central Asia, annexing a long corridor to the west.

Having secured Chinese boundaries, Wu Ti ushered in the Pax Sinica, or Chinese Peace, at about the same time the Roman Empire was establishing the foundations for its Pax Romana. During this period, China and the West discovered each other and Wu Ti was quick to open trade relations between them. Soon caravans were travelling the Great Silk Route leading from China across Central Asia to the Mediterranean. Romans and Greeks treasured fine Chinese silks and works in jade and bronze, just as China treasured Western horses and Roman glass.

The civil service. Han emperors followed the Confucian stricture that government officials should be highly educated. To that end they encouraged rigorous education in Confucian ethical standards. The Han developed a system of choosing government officials based on a civil service examination that tested would-be bureaucrats on the teachings of Confucius. The civil service that resulted from this examination process lent a degree of social and political stability to Chinese life and became a model for governments elsewhere in Asia.

CONFUCIUS, a wise Chinese teacher and philosopher, is known for his sayings relating to an ethical philosophy. Confucianism stresses proper conduct, self-improvement, and the need for rulers to be righteous.

Chinese inventiveness. Under the Han dynasty, China experienced a burst of inventiveness that made the Chinese technologically superior to any people in the world. Paper made from cloth rags replaced bamboo strips for writing. The compass was developed. Iron smelting was improved by the use of the piston bellows, and steel manufacture began. Other notable inventions included the wheelbarrow and the seismograph, an instrument that could measure earthquakes several hundred miles away.

Arrival of Buddhism. Buddhism reached China during the first century A.D., but did not affect Chinese life until the Han dynasty weakened and fell, bringing 350 years of disunion and civil war. The Buddhist promise of relief from pain and suffering attracted many converts.

Prolonged disunity. Following the collapse of the Han dynasty, China broke up into three states—Wei in the north, Wu in the southeast, and Shu in the southwest. They were briefly united from 265 to 316, but a clash with Huns divided them once again.

For the next 270 years, southern China was ruled by a succession of five dynasties, none of them strong enough to retain firm control of the territories they nominally ruled. In northern China, dynasties rose and fell, most founded by conquerors from the north and Tibet. Foreign rule was a bitter pill for the Chinese to swallow, but as the conquerors came and went, the Chinese survived with their own civilization intact.

labor
US

labour
Brit.

21 History of the World

THE COMPASS is one of many important inventions dating from the Han dynasty.

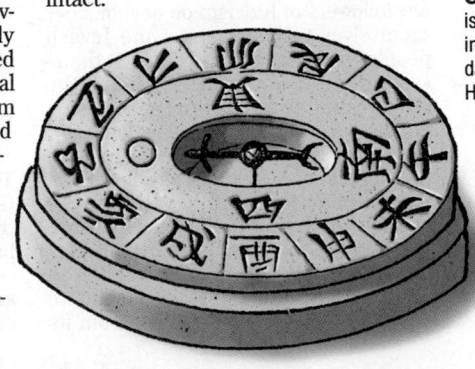

Religion and Culture

What can produce feelings of serenity or antipathy; benevolence or belligerence; surrender or resoluteness; hope or despair? Make a list of the wonders of the ancient and modern worlds and eliminate the natural wonders. What does most of the remainder have in common? Think of the most magnificent buildings in the world. Is there a common thread? Survey masterpieces of art and music. Does a recurring theme appear?

If you had even a glimmer that "religion" was the answer to the above questions, you recognize a driving force in the lives of human beings and therefore the story of those lives: what we call "history."

Religion is not a concrete formula, a one-size-fits-all answer for everyone, everywhere, every time. Religion is not confined to "civilized" people nor to "modern" humans. It is integral to the story of humankind, even though it can be manifested in myriad ways. While the recounting of historical events provides the facts of what, when, and who, much of the why requires knowledge of religion.

History crosses all religions and frequently records clashes between them. The variety of clashes cannot be numbered, any more than differences among religions can be numbered. Some focus on but a single thought and others on a multitude of ideas and rules. Some revere one god, others a host of gods. Some contemplate on an afterlife (either good or bad), others on return to life, and still others on nothing after death. Some focus on goodness and redemption, others on punishment and retribution. Some seek new members; some shun outsiders. Some are short-lived and others flourish for millennia. How can we even begin to understand history without at least a cursory knowledge and understanding of religions and their times?

Long before the development of writing, and therefore recorded history, ancient burials evidence a belief in an afterlife. The Egyptians built pyramids and practiced mummification. They dabbled in one-god/many-god religions. The Greeks ranged from total-reason-no-god beliefs to multiple-god, highly structured deities, as did the Romans, Aztecs, Incas, and Hindus at one time or another.

It is interesting to compare religions. It is said that the three largest one-god religions, Judaism, Islam, and Christianity, have more similarities than differences, and that each of them shows more inconsistencies and divisions among its sects and denominations than with each other. Witness Christianity with its wide-ranging versions from Roman and orthodox Catholicism to its array of Protestant denominations large and small, relying on differing doctrines and preaching in a multitude of languages to meet the participants' needs.

The Eastern religions boast millions of people. Though not as familiar to Europeans and Americans in their beliefs, the evidence of temples, both active and ruined, and the pageantry of religious festivals underline the longevity and importance of Hinduism, Buddhism, Shintoism, and others.

How, then, can we appreciate the why, the significance, and the aftermath of such moments in history as the Reformation, the Inquisition, the Crusades, and the Age of Exploration, which expanded the known world with the watchwords of "glory, god, and gold," unless we can study history with a knowledge and understanding of key human nature and interactions of religion?

There are a number of other religions that we have not discussed, some claiming millions or hundreds of thousands of followers. A partial listing of these other faiths includes Buddhism, Confucianism, Shintoism, Taoism, Sikhism, Jainism, Zoroastrianism, Bon, Bahai, Theosophy, Cao Dai, and Rastafarianism. In addition, many local groups in isolated places in the world continue to practice traditional religions whose origins are unknown. However, the information in this section should give you some insight into the role of religion in culture.

Here, then, is a nutshell review of some of the major, influential religions of our time.

Judaism

Although smaller than the other major religions, Judaism is nonetheless considered a major world religion. Its followers are spread over much of the world. There are only about 15 million followers of Judaism, but they have had an influence far beyond their numbers.

Judaism is the religion of a people called the Jews. The Jews are a people or national group as well as a religion. A few followers of Judaism do not consider themselves to be a part of the Jewish people, and many who consider themselves Jews do not follow or practice the religion of Judaism. For the sake of simplicity, we will generally use the word Jew to mean a follower of Judaism.

Judaism was probably the first truly *monotheistic* religion, devoted to the worship of a single all-powerful God. The Jewish faith holds that God acts through history to change events on Earth. Thus, history is important to Jews in a way that is different from its importance to people of other religions. One might imagine Buddhism without Buddha ever having lived but not Judaism without Abraham and Moses.

Both Christianity and Islam inherited this sense of history from the Jews. In fact, both of these later religions consider the history of the early Jewish nation to be part of the record of God's actions. Much of the Jewish Bible, which is the same as the Christian Old Testament, is devoted to reporting the acts of God in the history of the Jews.

Early History

The history of the Hebrews opens with God's creation of the universe. Before the universe was created, God existed, but His form then is unknowable. Then, God brought man and woman into being and gave them responsibility for the care of Earth. But they were tempted into sin and lost their direct relationship with God. In time, people began to believe in many local gods, forgetting the one God who had created the universe.

The Jews trace their history to a man named Abram, a semi-nomadic shepherd who lived about 4,000 years ago. God told Abram to take his family and followers (called the Hebrews) to Canaan, a land that today we identify with Israel. God promised Abram that he would have many descendants, who would live in Canaan. Later, as Abram and his family traveled from place to place, God reinforced this promise by making it a *covenant,* a solemn agreement, binding on both parties. The covenant bound Abram (whom God renamed Abraham) and his descendants to faithfulness to God in return for His everlasting care, so long as they abided by His precepts.

With this covenant, the Hebrews (later known as Israelites and then as

Jews) became God's chosen people, chosen to represent God to the rest of the world. The Bible shows repeatedly that God does not make it easy for his chosen ones. The history of the Jewish people is one of many difficulties.

Indeed, after the Hebrews had lived in Canaan for several hundred years, a famine arose there. They moved their families to Egypt, where food was plentiful. Although Egypt welcomed the Hebrews initially, after a time the rulers who had welcomed them were overthrown. The new rulers, known as the Pharaohs, enslaved the Israelites. The Pharaoh ordered that all male babies born to the Israelites be killed. However, God aided the Israelite mothers in helping many of their sons escape death.

One who escaped death was Moses, often considered the founder of the Jewish religion. Moses forced the Egyptians to let the Israelites go. He led them from Egypt into the desert. His goal was Canaan, the land God had promised Abraham. During the escape, God destroyed the Pharaoh's army, which was pursuing the fleeing Israelites. While in the desert, Moses received a new covenant from God in the form of the Law. Its centerpiece was the Ten Commandments, rules written by God himself on two stone tablets. These tablets, which were the center of Jewish religious life for nearly a thousand years, were kept in a wooden chest called the Ark of the Covenant. At first the Ark was housed in a tent that was carried wherever the Israelites wandered. When they occupied Canaan, the tablets were kept in a tent at Shiloh for over 200 years. The ark itself was sometimes carried by Israelite armies into battle and was hidden from enemies in moments of danger.

Eventually, the Israelites formed a kingdom called Israel. The second king, David, moved the capital to Jerusalem and planned a temple for the Ark of the Covenant. His son Solomon built the Temple and moved the Ark to it.

After Solomon's death, Israel broke into two nations, Israel in the north and Judah, whose capital was Jerusalem, in the south. In 722 B.C., Assyria conquered the northern kingdom and carried off people, many as slaves. The northern kingdom of Israel was never reestablished.

In 586 B.C., the Babylonians conquered Judah, the southern kingdom, and destroyed the temple in Jerusalem. They transported most of the Jews in Judah to Babylon. This period, known as "the Babylonian Captivity," did not last long, however, for the Persian Cyrus defeated Babylon in 539 B.C. and began to allow Jews to return home. By 515 B.C., the returning Jews had built a second Temple in Jerusalem, which lasted over 500 years. The Ark of the Covenant, however, was perhaps destroyed with the first Temple.

The Babylonian Captivity marked a turning point in the development of Jewish thought. Jews began to look for a person to restore the glories of the kingdom of Israel as it had been at its height, under David. This person would be sent by God and would make Israel and Jerusalem central among all nations. The Jewish term for the restoring king is the Messiah. Jews today still believe that a Messiah will come to usher in a period of peace and brotherhood throughout the world.

The Jewish Scriptures

The first five books of the Old Testament, known to Jews as the *Torah,* summarize what Moses reported on how God wanted the Jews to behave and record the early history of the Jewish people. Although Moses is considered the author of the Torah, the Torah is also the basic word of God. Over the years, a long series of commentaries has been written on the Torah. These commentaries were first organized into one document in the third century A.D. Over the next 300 years, treatises were written on that first organized group of commentaries. All of these were assembled in the sixth century A.D., and the whole set of commentaries on the Torah and commentaries on the commentaries is known as the *Talmud.*

Besides the Torah, Jews also consider many other historical writings, books of prophecy, songs, and sayings a part of their sacred literature. Taken with the Torah, these writings make up the Jewish *Bible,* which corresponds to the Christians' *Old Testament.*

From the Bible and Talmud, Jews learn how to conduct themselves in ways that please God. A Jew who holds to a strict monotheistic understanding of God and conducts himself according to the laws of God is fulfilling the requirements of the religion. This leaves great latitude with regard to beliefs. In other words, if you act like a Jew and believe in God, you can freely form your own opinions about other questions of religion. Thus, some Jews believe in eternal life after death much as Christians or Muslims do. Others, however, believe that the soul becomes a part of God after death but the body and the individual person cannot be recovered after death.

Late History

After the Jews returned from the Babylonian Captivity, they were usually dominated by whichever state was most powerful in the Middle East. The Jews repeatedly tried to revolt, but only the Hasmoneans (also known as the Maccabees) succeeded, and their success was short-lived. In Jesus' time, the Roman Empire dominated the Jews through a puppet kingdom. A revolt against the Romans in A.D. 70 led to the destruction of all but one wall of the sec-

PAINTINGS suggest the dress of the people of Israel in biblical times.

ond Temple. This wall is known today as the Wailing Wall. Once again the Jews were taken from their promised land and dispersed.

After the destruction of the second Temple, most Jews no longer lived in Israel. Jewish communities spread throughout the world; together they are known as the Diaspora. Since the Temple no longer existed as a focus for worship, an entirely new centerpiece had to be found. While synagogues had existed before the destruction of the second Temple, the synagogue now became a focal point for Judaism. Any group of ten Jewish males could form a body of worship, and any member of the congregation could read to the rest from the Torah.

Many of the main observances of faith, however, were centered in the home. Observances at home include Passover, celebrating the escape from Egypt and the destruction of the Pharaoh's army, and Hanukkah, celebrating the rededication of the Temple after the defeat of the Syrians in 165 B.C. These private, familial forms of worship were particularly needed by people who were dispersed into small communities.

By the 1800s there were Jewish communities in many parts of Europe, in North Africa, the Middle East, and, in lesser numbers, Australia and North and South America. Many of these communities had been persecuted (especially by Christians in Europe), and some had been driven from place to place in fear for their lives.

The greatest trial for the Jewish people came in the 1930s and '40s. Germany's Nazi government based part of its ideology on hatred of the Jews. First in Germany, later in countries the Germans occupied in World War II, the Nazis systematically killed every Jew they could locate. Millions fled Europe (many to the United States), but about one-third of all Jews alive at that time were killed. This systematic destruction of the Jewish people is known as the Holocaust.

After World War II, in 1948, the Unit-

THE WAILING WALL IN JERUSALEM is a holy place for Jews from around the world who make pilgrimages to offer prayers and to remember the survival of the Jewish people.

ed Nations set up the modern state of Israel. Many Jews from around the world moved to Israel, but others decided to stay where they were. Although the state of Israel has had to engage in several wars against neighboring Arab states to maintain its independence, the Jews are once again in control of the land that was promised to them.

Judaism Today

Today the majority of Jews live in the United States and Canada. The second largest number is in Israel. Other large groups of Jews live in Russia, France, the United Kingdom, Latin America, and South Africa. Although there has long been a population of Jews in India, its numbers have never been great.

Jewish religious practice developed somewhat differently in different parts of the world. But each community maintained the study of Hebrew (the language of the Jewish Scriptures), and there were no clear breaks into "denominations" until the 1800s. Today Jews in the U.S. are divided into four groups: Orthodox, Conservative, Reform, and Hasidic. The first three of these are separated largely by the freedom with which they interpret the Torah. The Hasidic Jews, or Hasidim, form a tradition all their own.

Orthodoxy. Before the 1800s it could be said that all Jews were Orthodox, although there have always been different schools of Jewish thought. (For example, in Jesus' time, there were the Pharisees, the Sadducees, and the Essenes.) Beginning in 1810 in Germany, however, some Jews decided that the strict interpretation of the Law found in the Talmud no longer applied. Jews who continued to follow a strict interpretation came be called Orthodox.

Orthodox Jews today continue to apply all the ancient rules of worship, including services in Hebrew, the separation of men and women during the service, and various rituals at home,

including the strict observance of dietary laws. Men wear head coverings at all times, not just during worship services. However, even among Orthodox Jews there are some disagreements, and the Orthodox congregations in the U.S. are formed into several different national organizations. About a million or a million and a half of the Jews in the United States are members of Orthodox congregations.

Reform. Abraham Geiger and Samuel Holdheim were among the early leaders of the Reform movement. The first Reform service was held in 1810.

Reform Judaism does not accept the traditional interpretations of the Law. Thus, Reform Jews do not wear head coverings during services, and services may be conducted in a language other than Hebrew. Dietary laws may not be observed at all, or some laws may be observed and others ignored. Cremation, prohibited to Orthodox Jews, is allowed. Reform Jews call their places of worship temples, not synagogues. There are about a million Reform Jews in the United States.

Conservatism. The conservative movement started in 1845 as a dispute among Reform Jews on the use of Hebrew in the worship service. Those who wanted to maintain Hebrew left the Reform movement to start the first Conservative group. Conservative Jews try to maintain a balance between the traditional ways of Judaism and the modernist spirit of Reform. For example, men and women are not separated at services, but men must wear a head covering during the service. There are about $1\frac{1}{4}$ million Conservative Jews in the United States.

If you add up the number of Orthodox, Reform, and Conservative Jews in the U.S., the sum will be more than a million short of the more than $5\frac{1}{2}$ million American Jews. While a small number of these other Jews are Hasidim, many are not affiliated with any one denomination, although they may worship at home and sometimes visit synagogues or temples.

Hasidism. In observance of Jewish law, the Hasidim are Orthodox Jews, but their movement maintains separate congregations and often separate communities from other Jews. The Hasidic movement was founded in Poland in the 1700s by Israel Ball Shem Tov. He taught that religion should be joyous and that the senses obscure the spark of the Divine inherent in every object. His followers spend much less time studying the Talmud and Torah than do Orthodox Jews. They devote themselves instead to dancing, singing, and love of nature as ways of worship. There are small communities of Hasidim in the United States, mainly in New York City, but there are also communities in Europe and Israel.

Christianity

Today the Christian religion has the most followers worldwide, about 2 billion. About one person in three throughout the world is a Christian. Christianity is the dominant religion of Europe, both Americas, and Australia, with significant numbers of followers in Asia and Africa as well.

Beliefs

Like Judaism, from which it grew, Christianity is monotheistic—its followers believe there is one and only one God. Christians also believe that God acts in history and that He is the God of the early Jewish people—the God of Abraham. The Scriptures of Judaism are part of the Christian Bible.

The earliest Christians were Jews who came to believe that Jesus of Nazareth was the Messiah the Jews had been awaiting. Jesus was born in a village called Bethlehem.

While on Earth, Jesus taught in the synagogues and outdoors, healing the sick and welcoming particularly the poor and the outcast. He said he had come to establish a new kingdom, in which people's wrongdoings would be forgiven, allowing them to achieve a new relationship with God.

When Jesus was about 33, he was arrested by the official Jewish court and turned over to the Romans, who controlled the country as part of the Roman Empire. The Romans crucified Jesus on a wooden cross. Three days after he died, according to the Gospels, he rose from the dead and visited many of his followers. Then he went to be with God the Father until the time for his return.

The night before his arrest, Jesus ate and drank with his closest followers. In this Last Supper, he told his followers to observe a similar meal to remember him. He suggested that his suffering, death, and resurrection would make a new covenant with God, replacing the covenant made between God and Abraham and Moses. In this new covenant, God forgives the sins of those who follow Jesus and offers them eternal life with God. The two parts of the Christian Bible are the Old Testament (the Jewish Scriptures), which describes God's agreement with the Jewish people, and the New Testament, which describes His new agreement.

Early Christians came to believe that Jesus, whom they called the *Christ* or the Messiah, was the Son of God, both man and God at the same time. They eventually formulated their belief in the doctrine of the Trinity. The one God expresses Himself through Three different natures: God the Father, God the Son (Christ), and God the Holy Spirit. The Trinity, one God in three different Persons, is a central mystery of the Christian faith.

After Christ went to be with God, the Holy Spirit became the principal means of continuing God's messages to people on Earth. Inspired by the Holy Spirit, Jesus' followers started the Christian Church, the formal, organized expression of their religion. The church and its members spread the *gospel,* or good news, about Christ. The church also performs the few rites that are basic to Christianity, including *baptism* (ritual purification with water) and *communion,* a rite commemorating the Last Supper. Prayer to God is a part of the faith.

The main symbol of the Christian religion is the cross, which signifies to Christians that Christ died for their sins. A schematic fish is also sometimes used.

The Early Church

Christianity began when Peter, one of Jesus' disciples, accepted Jesus as the Christ, or Messiah. Then, on the seventh Sunday after the resurrection, the Holy Spirit came to the disciples. This event, known as Pentecost ("the 50th day"), is considered by many Christians to be the birth of the Christian Church. Peter's sermon that day converted 3,000 people to the church, after which the converts lived communally and worshiped together. At this point, however, the early Christians thought of themselves as Jews who had recognized Jesus as the Messiah.

Some Jews who did not recognize Jesus as the Messiah persecuted the early Christians. However, one of the persecutors, Saul of Tarsus, had a vision of Jesus and was converted to Christianity. Under the name of Paul, he became the main missionary of the early church to non-Jews (Gentiles). As Paul converted Gentiles in Syria, Greece, and Rome, the church grew to be separate from its Jewish beginning. Paul's preaching and letters, known as "the epistles," described a church that welcomed both Jews and Gentiles.

Starting in A.D. 64, while Nero was Roman emperor, the Romans began to persecute the Christians. This continued with varying degrees of severity for about 250 years. It ended in A.D. 313, when the emperor Constantine made Christianity the state religion of the empire.

Despite the persecutions, the church grew. The letters of Paul and other followers, which were copied and read aloud at various churches, became the first part of a scripture for the new church. A few years later, the gospels (summaries of Jesus' ministry) were written. Together with a history of the early church (*The Acts of the Apostles*) and the difficult book of *Revelations,* these letters and gospels became the New Testament, the second part of Christian Scripture. It is believed that all 27 of the books of the New Testament were written between A.D. 50 and A.D. 100.

By A.D. 95, there were bishops and deacons working for the church. The bishop of Rome claimed from early on to have received authority over the rest of the church, and he can be found exercising such authority by A.D. 190. In A.D. 325 the Council of Nicaea affirmed the basic beliefs and organization of the church, with the bishop of Rome, or pope, at its head. The summary of beliefs, or *creed,* formulated at Nicaea is still used in many Christian churches.

The Roman Catholic Church

The church that took shape at the Council of Nicaea is still the largest Christian denomination. In fact, there are almost as many Roman Catholics as there are Muslims, who form the second largest religion after Christianity. More than half the world's Christians are Roman Catholic.

From the outset, Christians disagreed on many points of doctrine and belief. These disagreements were discussed at many councils, such as the one at Nicaea. Once a council decided on an issue, people who disagreed with its decision were termed *heretics* by the church. Some of the heretics had large followings and set up rival Christian churches, some lasting for hundreds of years. But the majority of Christians remained in a single church, calling it Catholic, meaning "universal."

The Roman Catholic Church traces its existence back through this majority church. The bishops of Rome traced their office back to St. Peter and gained authority over and respect from the rest of the church. Today the bishop of Rome is called the pope or "the Holy Father" and is the supreme authority in matters of faith and discipline. The senate of the Roman Catholic Church is the College of Cardinals, a group of bishops and priests who help the pope run the church. Many of the cardinals live in Rome, but others are scattered around the world, in charge of large bodies of Catholics. Most of the cardinals who do not live in Rome are also archbishops. When a pope dies, all the cardinals go to Rome to elect a new pope.

The bishops are viewed as the bearers of the apostolic succession, an unbroken line of authority going back to Christ's earliest followers. Therefore, only a bishop can ordain another bishop or a priest or confirm a person as a member of the church.

There are one or more priests in every Roman Catholic Church. The priesthood is open to men only, and

organizations
US

organisations
Brit.

recognized
US

recognised
Brit.

priests are required to take an oath of celibacy. Priests can perform all *sacraments,* except ordination and confirmation. Roman Catholics believe God's grace is transmitted to individuals through the sacraments. All seven sacraments of the Roman Catholic faith must ordinarily be performed by either a priest or a bishop.

Besides priests and bishops, the Roman Catholic Church has many different kinds of monks and nuns, men and women who take vows of poverty, chastity, and obedience. They may be teachers, medical workers, or workers in other helping professions. After the fall of the Roman Empire, monasteries preserved the learning of the classical and Early Christian worlds. Most monks are not priests.

The Roman Catholic Church is distinguished from most other Christian churches by various beliefs, most notably that the pope is supreme on Earth in matters of faith and discipline. While most Protestant churches rely solely on the Bible as their authority, Roman Catholics accept the traditions of the church as authority for many of their beliefs and practices. This has led Roman Catholics to accept seven sacraments instead of the two most Protestants accept. In addition to Communion (called the Mass or Holy Eucharist by Roman Catholics) and baptism—the two sacraments of the Protestants—Roman Catholics believe that ordination (holy orders), confirmation, penance (confession and absolution by a priest), anointing the sick (formerly known as extreme unction or the last rites), and marriage are also sacraments.

THE CHURCHES of the Eastern Orthodox religion bear testimony to the influence of the Byzantine Empire.

Roman Catholics believe that most people after death enter a place or condition called *purgatory,* staying there until they have been punished for their sins. People on Earth can reduce the length of a person's time in purgatory by prayer and other means. Roman Catholics also believe that certain holy men and women, called *saints,* can intercede with Christ for people on Earth.

Mary, Jesus' mother, occupies an important place in the Roman Catholic Church, and she is frequently asked through prayer to intercede with Christ. While most Christians believe that Mary was a virgin at Jesus' birth, Roman Catholicism says Mary herself was free from sin and that, after death, Mary's body entered heaven.

All Christian churches celebrate some form of Communion, or the Lord's Supper, but there is disagreement about the interpretation of this sacrament. Since the 1200s, however, Roman Catholics have believed that the bread and wine used in the Mass change into the true substance of the flesh and blood of Christ (although their appearance stays the same). This belief is called *transubstantiation.* Roman Catholics also believe that the sacrament of Communion represents the sacrifice of Christ on the cross.

Roman Catholicism is the predominant faith in much of southern Europe, Ireland, and South and Central America. In addition, it represents a sizable minority in the United States, Canada, Great Britain, Germany, and many parts of Africa.

Other Early Churches

A few of the churches that separated from the Roman Catholic Church in the first thousand years of Christianity have survived independently. Most prominent among these is the *Coptic Church,* which left the Roman Catholics in 451. Coptic Christians are the largest minority religious group in Egypt today. Like several other early churches that survived, the Coptic Christians are *monophysites.* Monophysites believe that Jesus Christ was divine but did not partake of a human nature. Other surviving monophysite churches include the *Armenian Church* and the *Christian Church of Ethiopia.*

The Nestorians, another early church group, became the leading Christian churches of Persia. Nestorians held that Jesus was two distinct persons, the Word and the man. They opposed calling Mary the Mother of God. They sent out many missionaries. After the conquest of Persia by the forces of Islam, the Nestorians, although tolerated by the Muslims, gradually reduced in number. Today only a small Nestorian Church survives in the mountains along the Iran-Turkey border.

Eastern Orthodox Churches

To some degree, the church in the eastern part of the Roman Empire went on a different course from the Western church for centuries. In A.D. 1054, after a dispute over whether the Holy Spirit emanated from God the Father alone or from both God the Father and Jesus Christ, the church split in two. The part that reaffirmed the older tradition (the Holy Spirit emanating from God the Father alone) became the Eastern Church. The Eastern Church rejected the pope's authority but was similar in many respects to the Roman Catholic Church. However, the Eastern Church maintained traditions that had been part of the Eastern pattern of worship even before the "great schism" with Rome.

Originally the Eastern Church was the church of the Byzantine Empire, while the Roman Catholic Church was becoming the religion of the Frankish Holy Roman Empire. Although the Eastern Church was centered in Constantinople (modern-day Istanbul), Muslim domination of Constantinople after 1453 led to a period when the Eastern Church was centered in Russia. Today the Eastern Church has separate branches in Russia, Rumania, Bulgaria, Serbia and Montenegro, Greece, Cyprus, the Czech Republic, Poland, and Finland. It also includes the Christians supervised by the patriarchs of Constantinople, Antioch, Alexandria, and Jerusalem, among the earliest bishoprics in the Christian religion.

The Eastern Church accepts as valid the first eight councils of the church. Because it holds to many early traditions of the church, the Eastern Church is called Orthodox. The state church of Greece, for example, is usually known as the Greek Orthodox Church, although officially it is the Church of Greece. In the U.S., the largest group following the Eastern rite is probably the Russian Orthodox Greek Catholic Church of America, commonly called the Russian Orthodox Church.

Although the various Eastern Orthodox churches have no central authority, their beliefs and practices are similar from church to church. The Eastern churches believe in the same seven sacraments as do the Roman Catholics, but the administration of them is different. More recent traditions in the Catholic Church, such as belief in purgatory or in the immaculate conception of Mary, are rejected by Orthodox churches. Orthodox priests are not required to be celibate, but all bishops are celibate.

The Orthodox churches have long venerated religious paintings called *icons.* Considered to be more than just paintings on wood, these icons are thought to have a power of their own. While three-dimensional statues are not acceptable to the Eastern churches, each church building includes a place for icons in front of the altar.

The Protestant Churches

In 1517 Martin Luther, a German monk, started a dispute with the Roman Catholic Church over several of its doctrines, especially the sale of *indulgences,* certificates that were said to shorten one's time in purgatory. Luther found no scriptural authority for this practice. On October 31, Luther posted 95 objections to prevailing church practices. Although no one knew it, the Protestant Reformation had begun.

Luther's confrontations with the defenders of Roman Catholic practices quickly led him to state the basic principles that varied from those of both the Roman and Orthodox churches of the time. Luther, using the Bible as his single guide, said that Christians do not need priests or the church to intervene between them and God, that God's grace is the only thing that saves sinful believers, and that only the sacraments of Communion and baptism carry with them the promise of God's grace.

Within three years of Luther's posting the 95 theses, the pope ordered that Luther recant or be excommunicated (formally deprived of the sacraments and the prayers of the church). Luther burned the order and was excommunicated. When given one more chance to recant, he refused.

Luther tried at first to avoid becoming the leader of a separate church, but his many reforms and innovations became the basis of the Protestant Reformation. These included his reform of the liturgy (the rites of worship), his stupendous translation of the Bible into German (still the Bible of German Lutherans), his introduction of hymns sung by the congregation, and his composition of the Small Catechism. Luther also changed the development of Protestantism by marrying.

Lutherans. Soon the church based on Luther's ideas was known as the Lutheran Church. It spread across Germany and Scandinavia, although parts of Germany remained Roman Catholic. By 1638 Lutheran Swedes were worshiping in what is now Delaware in the United States. In the great migrations of 1840–1910 from Europe to the United States, most of the Protestant immigrants were Lutherans from northern Europe.

Each group brought the liturgy of its own nation. By 1900 there were German, Swedish, Norwegian, Danish, and Finnish Lutherans, each with separate organizations, each worshiping in different languages. Since then, a series of mergers has reduced the number of Lutheran bodies to three large and a few small ones. Two of the large bodies, the American Lutheran Church and the Lutheran Church in America, emphasize the importance of social action. They are fairly liberal in interpreting the Bible and Luther's teachings. The other group, the Lutheran Church-Missouri Synod, is quite conservative.

Lutheran worship is formal and follows the general pattern of the ancient Catholic forms. Lutherans believe that Christ is actually present in the bread and wine of Communion, but that the bread and wine are not transubstantiated. A characteristic Lutheran practice requires that all children go through one to four years of study of the Small Catechism before they are confirmed as full members of the church.

Reformed Churches. Besides the Lutheran churches of northern Europe, other churches were started in the 1500s in reaction to the Roman Catholicism of that time. Collectively, these are known as the Reformed Churches. They were very strong in Switzerland, the Netherlands, Scotland, and Hungary. There were also widespread, but often officially suppressed, Reformed Church movements in England and France.

The Reformed Churches can be traced to a 1529 disagreement between Martin Luther and Ulrich Zwingli about Christ's actual presence during Communion. Zwingli's interpretation that only the spirit of Christ was present became the doctrine of the Reformed Churches.

But the principal architect of Reformed thought was Frenchman John Calvin. In 1533, to escape persecution in France, Calvin fled to Switzerland, which was already Protestant. There he promoted his views with a systematic exposition of Protestant thought. While Calvin relied on many of the same ideas as Luther, Calvin's logical mind led him from Luther's ideas to conclusions that Luther did not share. Most members of today's successor churches to the early Reformed Churches no longer believe in the strict Calvinist doctrine, but historically Calvin's ideas dominated the Reformed Churches.

While Calvin differed with Luther on the nature of baptism and Communion, the most influential part of his doctrine concerned sin, heaven, and hell. Calvin's approach to these subjects is known as "the five points":

1. Total depravity (people cannot do anything that God sees as good until they are among God's elect);

2. Predestination (God has elected some people to go to heaven and others to go to hell);

3. Limited atonement (Christ's death on the cross benefits only the elect);

4. Irresistibility of grace (God's decision that a person is to be among the elect cannot be resisted by the person); and

5. Perseverance of the saints (the elect cannot fall from grace).

Calvin eventually became the ruler of Geneva in Switzerland, which he tried to govern by strict Christian rules. From Switzerland, Calvin's ideas spread to start the Reformed Church in other lands. In Scotland, the church became known as the Presbyterian Church (to avoid confusion with the Church of England, which was also sometimes called "Reformed"). In France, Calvin's followers, called Huguenots, were suppressed by the state most of the time. In England, Calvin's ideas influenced the Puritans, who tried to reform the Church of England along Calvinistic lines. After failing in this, the Puritans won control of the nation under Oliver Cromwell, but England rejected the Puritan faith after Cromwell's death in 1658.

Suppression of Calvin's European followers in the 1600s led many of them to go to North America. Both the Pilgrims of Plymouth, Massachusetts, and the Puritans of the Massachusetts Bay Colony were Calvinists. The church they brought to the U.S. became the Congregationalist Church and, later, the United Church of Christ. Another migration of followers of the Reformed Churches sent Scottish Presbyterians to the U.S. in great numbers, along with Huguenots and members of the Dutch and German Reformed Churches.

Most followers of the Presbyterian Church or of the United Church of Christ are no longer strict Calvinists. Only a few members of the United Church of Christ believe in predestination. Many Presbyterians no longer believe that people are unable to cooperate with God in obtaining salvation.

Anglicans. While the Roman Church was losing members to the Lutheran and Reformed Churches, it was also losing all of England. King Henry VIII questioned the pope's authority and declared himself head of the English church in 1534.

Under Henry's successors, Edward VI and Elizabeth, the church grew increasingly like the Lutheran and Reformed Churches of the Continent. Elizabeth tried to keep the church halfway between Protestantism and Roman Catholicism.

Most Englishmen who came to settle the American colonies did not want to conform to the Church of England, but Church of England followers came as well. Individual colonies were often organized by religion, and in the 1600s only Virginia was particularly hospitable to Anglicans. In the 1700s, however, all colonies allowed diverse Christian churches, and Anglican churches were established in all of them. In the South and in New York City, the Church of England was supported with tax money (as it still is in England).

The American Revolution nearly ended Anglicanism in the colonies, since Church of England members were also often Loyalists. Many Anglicans moved to Canada or back to England. The church survived, however, changing its name to the Protestant Episcopal Church.

The Anglican churches remain both Catholic and Protestant. As in the Catholic and Orthodox churches, the Anglican Church preserves the apostolic succession of bishops and priests.

emphasize
US

emphasise
Brit.

Thus, only properly ordained bishops and priests can administer Communion or preach sermons.

Yet many Anglican beliefs are Protestant. Wide latitude of practice in the church ranges from churches with simple services focusing on the sermon to churches with elaborate liturgical rites. All seven traditional sacraments are maintained, but only Communion and baptism are viewed as necessary. Like other Protestant churches, the Anglican churches' sole authority is the Bible.

The churches that grew out of the Church of England form the Anglican communion. The Anglican communion is a group of separate churches around the world that have a line of ordination going back to the Church of England. They also share a liturgy based on the *Book of Common Prayer,* the liturgy originally prepared for the Church of England in the 1500s. There are major groups of Anglicans in England, North America, Australia, and Africa.

Baptists and Mennonites.

Baptists form the largest Protestant group in the United States. Baptist-like believers can be found throughout the history of Christianity, but it is unclear from which of these earlier groups modern Baptists come.

Around the time of the Reformation, there were scattered groups called Anabaptists in Europe. Anabaptists believed that baptism is valid only for persons who have reached faith on their own, a belief shared by Baptists today. Anabaptists in Switzerland also argued for separation of church and state, another Baptist tenet. Soon afterward, Menno Simons, a former priest, organized Anabaptists into a church known as the Mennonite Church. The earliest Baptist churches in England were founded on Mennonite ideas.

It is not clear what influence either Mennonites or English Baptists had on the American Baptist Church. In the U.S. the Baptists began to organize in the 1600s. The first Baptist churches in the New World were begun independently in Rhode Island.

Several of the basic beliefs of the Baptists enabled their churches to spread rapidly in the late 1700s and early 1800s. Baptists believe in the independence of each congregation, a belief that is helpful to a church spread out through a wilderness. The Baptist belief in religious liberty and the independence of church and state was in tune with the principles of the new nation. The Baptists made a serious effort to reach the settlers of the frontier. They ordained many part-time ministers who supported themselves by farming but who also organized congregations.

Baptists practice baptism by immersion (submerging a person completely in water) and restrict baptism to people who have come to faith in Christ; infants are not baptized. Only people so baptized can be members of the church. Baptists view Communion as a memorial

to Jesus Christ, believing that neither the body nor the spirit of Christ is present in the bread and wine.

Mennonites, although their ideas influenced the early Baptists, are not considered Baptists themselves. For one thing, Mennonites do not baptize by immersion. While the Baptists are the largest Protestant denomination in the United States, the Mennonites are one of the smallest.

Methodists.

Although the Baptists, when taken all together, are the largest Protestant denomination in the United States, the largest single Protestant organization is the United Methodist Church. Methodism grew out of 18th-century reform efforts in the Church of England. Starting in 1738, Anglican priest John Wesley and his brother Charles set up "societies," or clubs, for prayer and Bible reading. Members were expected to attend worship services in an Anglican church. By the 1760s similar Methodist societies were started in the United States.

After the American Revolution, Methodists in the U.S. started to break with the Church of England. In 1784 John Wesley sent Thomas Coke and Francis Asbury from England to help organize a Methodist Church. (In England, the Methodist Church was not fully separated from the Church of England until 1791, after John Wesley's death.)

The Methodist Church grew rapidly in the United States throughout the 1800s. One important tool was the use of circuit preachers, who traveled a circuit of hundreds of miles, preaching to a different group every day, returning to the same group every one, two, or four weeks, depending on the length of the circuit. Another factor in the Methodists' growth was their sponsorship of popular outdoor gatherings for preaching and singing called "camp meetings." Most who were converted at camp meetings became Methodists.

Methodists' beliefs are similar to those of the Anglican communion, although Methodist worship focuses more on the sermon and on hymn singing. John Wesley taught that people could become free of sin in this life, and, in general, opposed Calvin's ideas of total depravity and of an elect. Methodists today tend to avoid theological complexities, focusing more on Christ as a guide to living.

Christian churches.

In the early 1800s several different reform churches started in the U.S. These churches believed worship should be modeled more closely on the practices of the early church of the apostles. While these reform groups had much in common with the Baptists, especially their belief in each congregation's independence, there were enough differences so that the reform groups never allied themselves with the Baptists.

One aim of this reform movement was the elimination of denominations.

Therefore, the churches that are part of the movement call themselves simply Christian churches or churches of Christ. (The United Church of Christ, which has a Calvinist heritage, includes some churches that were part of this reform movement.) Some member churches of the Christian church prefer the name Disciples of Christ.

The first Christian churches were formed in 1803 under the leadership of Barton W. Stone. The Disciples of Christ grew out of efforts by Thomas Campbell and his son Alexander, which first took organized form in 1809. In 1832, Stone and Alexander Campbell urged their followers to unify, and many of the reform churches began to work together. Although the cooperating churches could not agree on a single name for themselves, their group grew rapidly. In 1906, the conservative wing of the church left to form the Churches of Christ. The Churches of Christ opposes the use of instrumental music during services and the formation of missionary societies. The present name for the part of the church that did not form the Churches of Christ is the International Convention of Christian Churches (Disciples of Christ.)

Pentecostal churches.

The fastest growing group of churches in the United States today is the group identified with the Holiness movement, or the Pentecostal movement, that began in 1906. Among the members of this group of young churches, the church called the Assemblies of God is the largest, but other large churches in the group are the Church of God in Christ, International; the Church of God in Christ; and the Church of God (Cleveland, Tennessee). The characteristic emphases of the Pentecostal bodies are on fundamentalist principles, revivalism, and a post-conversion experience called baptism in the Holy Spirit, accompanied by the sign of speaking in tongues, as experienced by followers of Jesus at Pentecost.

The Church of the Nazarene, once classed with this group, dropped "Pentecostal" from its name in 1919 to disassociate itself from the others. Positioned to the right of the Pentecostals in terms of emotionalism, Nazarenes oppose the practice of speaking in tongues; otherwise, their doctrines are similar.

Other Denominations

Other denominations include the Society of Friends (commonly known as Quakers); Unitarians; the Church of Latter-Day Saints and the Reorganized Church of Jesus Christ of Latter-Day Saints (generally known as Mormons); the Watch Tower Bible and Tract Society (known as Jehovah's Witnesses); First Church of Christ, Scientist (known as Christian Scientists); Unification Church; and Seventh Day Adventists.

Islam

The second largest religion is Islam, whose followers are called Muslims. Worldwide, there are between 600 million and 1 billion followers of Islam. The largest numbers are in Asia and Africa.

Islam is also a monotheistic faith. Its main creed is simple: "There is no God but God, and Muhammad is his prophet." A *prophet* is a human chosen by God to relate God's message on Earth. Muslims believe Muhammad was the last major prophet, but earlier prophets included those who founded Judaism and Jesus Christ. Thus, Muslims believe many of the same things that Jews and Christians do, although not always in exactly the same way.

Muhammad

Muhammad lived in Arabia about 1,400 years ago (570–632). When he was about 40, God began to speak to him. Muhammad often spent nights alone in the hills, where he received his first messages from God. Soon God's messages came to him wherever he was. God told Muhammad to transmit His message to the people of Arabia. God dictated a book to Muhammad, which was later written down and is known today as the *Koran.*

In A.D. 622 the people of Mecca, where Muhammad and his wife and daughters lived, were so upset by Muhammad's teachings that he and his followers had to flee. His escape to Medina is known as the Hegira; its date is usually considered the beginning of Islam.

Eight years after the Hegira, Muhammad returned to Mecca. By then he had so many followers that he took over the city without a struggle. From then on, the followers of Islam built a mighty empire that stretched at its height from Spain to India.

Muhammad used many Arab elements to describe Islam. The name he used for God was Allah, a name used by some Arabs for their principal god. When Muhammad returned to Mecca, he declared it a holy city. He also declared that the Kaaba, where Arabs had worshiped for many years, was to be a shrine for Allah.

The Koran retells many stories that are familiar to Jews and Christians from the Bible. It tells that the Arabs descended from the same Abraham as the Jews. Abraham had two sons, Isaac and Ishmael. Isaac became the ancestor of the Jews, and Ishmael became the ancestor of the Arabs. The Koran, however, also tells the stories of Isaac's descendants: Jacob, Joseph, Moses, David, Solomon, and Jesus Christ.

Islam is not a complicated faith. It is based on five principles:

1. Faith that there is no God but God (Allah), and Muhammad is His prophet;

2. Prayer to God five times daily;

3. Charity, shown by helping the poor and providing upkeep for places of prayer;

4. Fasting in two ways—by never drinking alcohol or eating pork and certain other foods; and by not eating, drinking, or smoking at all during daylight for one month each year (the Muslim month of Ramadan); and

5. Pilgrimage to Mecca at least once in each Muslim's life.

Muslims believe in a life after death in a paradise that is described in detail in the Koran. Paradise is for all who keep the faith. People who are evil will spend eternity in a fiery hell.

Muhammad was effectively the ruler of Arabia, as well as its religious leader, when he died. Because the state and the religion were one, a separate church was not needed. The leaders of Islam are those that people recognize as learned and holy. Unlike the Christian church, there is no central organization.

After Muhammad

When Muhammad died, his followers were in control of Arabia. He had made it clear that the state and worship of God were to be unified but had left no instructions on how to achieve this. He also did not leave detailed guidelines for worship or for living.

Muslims tried to develop specific policies from what Muhammad had done or said in various situations. The reports of Muhammad's actions and sayings, or Muhammad's Sunna, were gathered into written collections called *hadith.* From these collections and from the Koran, scholars in the seventh and eighth centuries developed a set of specific rules for worship and for life. These rules are called the *Sharia,* or Islamic law. The Sharia's relation to the Koran and to Muhammad's Sunna is similar to that of the Talmud to the Torah.

After Muhammad's death, the problems of government also had to be resolved. A small group in Medina elected Abu Bakr as *caliph* ("successor") in charge of both state and religion. Abu Bakr selected the second caliph, Umar I, who expanded the Muslim state beyond Arabia and appointed a group of elders to elect the next caliph. This resulted in the election of Muhammad's son-in-law, Ali, as the fourth caliph, but Ali made several blunders that led to his assassination. The fifth caliph then started a dynasty by naming his own son as his successor.

The *Sunnite* Muslims accept the first three caliphs as genuine. But a minority, called *Shiites,* believe Muhammad wanted Ali to be the first caliph.

Within the Sunnite and Shiite factions, there are several denominations or sects with somewhat differing beliefs. (Some small denominations are neither Sunnite nor Shiite.) Because of the identification of church with state in Islam, many of the differences between Sunnites and Shiites concern political power.

Most of the denominations or sects of Islam are centered in particular regions. For example, Saudi Arabia's state religion is Wahhabism, a Sunni denomination based on 18th-century reforms of Muslim practices. Most Iranians are Imamis. Imami is a Shiite denomination awaiting the second coming of the "hidden imam," a caliph who disappeared in A.D. 873. Many Muslim denominations expect the hidden imam to appear near the end of the world. This person, called the Mahdi, will rule the Earth along with Jesus, who will also return then. In Syria, the Druses are Shiites who regard Caliph al-Hakim as a manifestation of God, who will return as the Mahdi. The Shiite Ismalis are scattered throughout Asia and Africa. They are held together mainly by their hereditary religious leader, the Aga Khan.

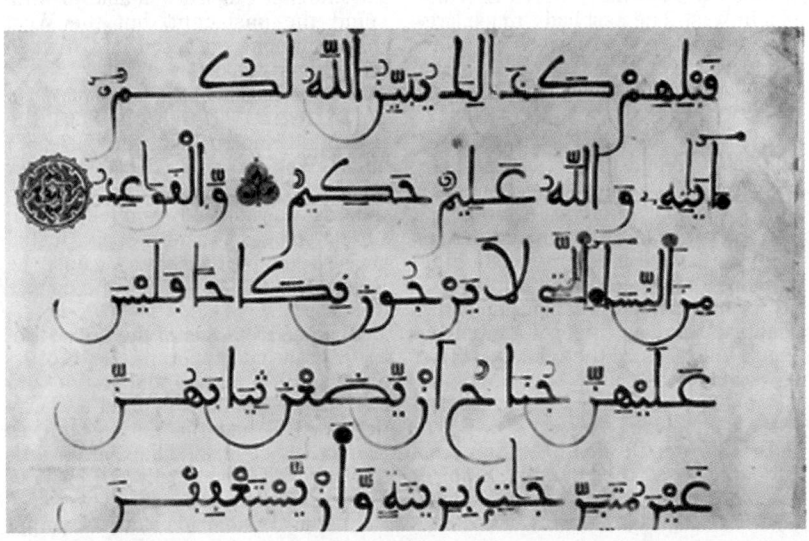

CALLIGRAPHY, often the text of the sacred Koran, is a characteristic Muslim art form, showing a deft sense of line and form. See also the Taj Mahal in the History of Art chapter.

Cultures Across The World

C A.D. 500–1500

The Middle Ages—that is what historians call the millennium of European history extending roughly from A.D. 500 to 1500. Its opening date is one of history's major dividing lines because it marks the fragmentation of the formerly glorious and widespread Roman Empire. Much of Europe was overrun by barbarian hordes, causing the collapse of the western half of the empire. The eastern half of the old empire was better able to carry on Roman civilization. This it did as the Byzantine Empire from its capital at Constantinople, the "New Rome."

For the rest of the world, this period marked a time when existing civilizations waxed and waned and new civilizations emerged. Some, like the Islamic civilization, developed in close contact with other, older civilizations; others, like those of sub-Saharan Africa and of the Americas, developed largely in isolation.

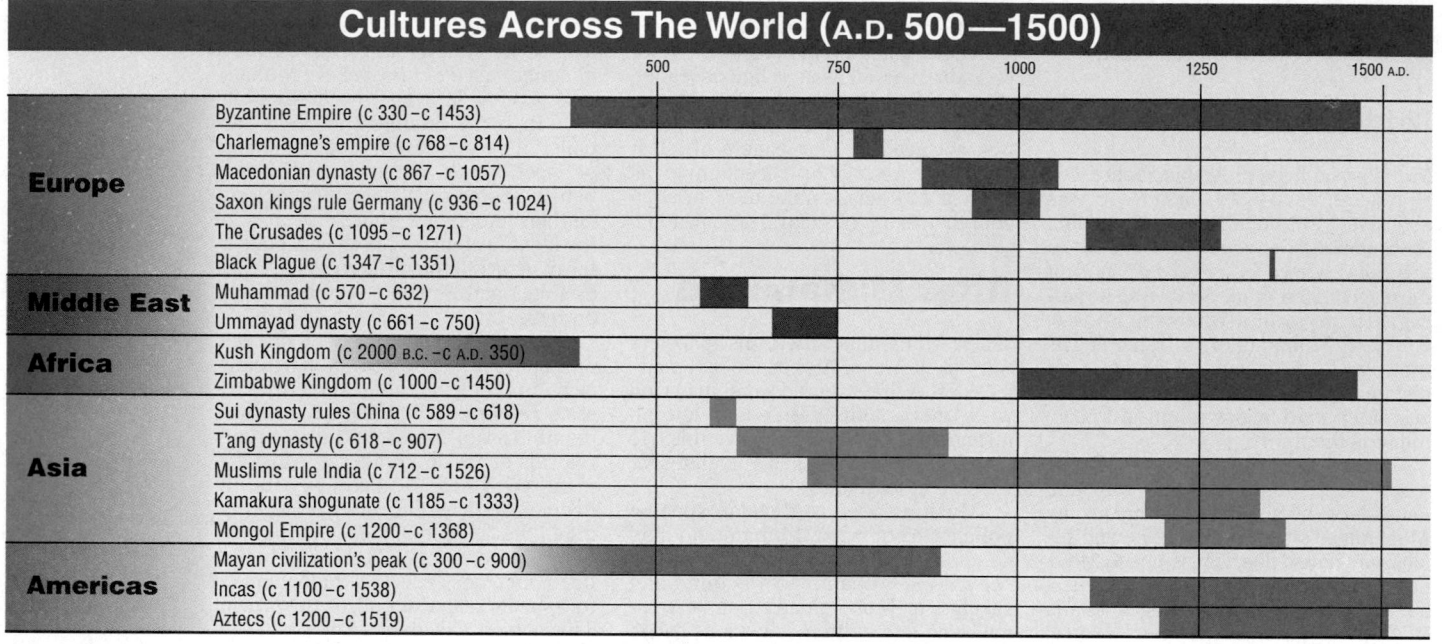

Cultures Across The World (A.D. 500—1500)

		500	750	1000	1250	1500 A.D.
Europe	Byzantine Empire (c 330 – c 1453)					
	Charlemagne's empire (c 768 – c 814)					
	Macedonian dynasty (c 867 – c 1057)					
	Saxon kings rule Germany (c 936 – c 1024)					
	The Crusades (c 1095 – c 1271)					
	Black Plague (c 1347 – c 1351)					
Middle East	Muhammad (c 570 – c 632)					
	Ummayad dynasty (c 661 – c 750)					
Africa	Kush Kingdom (c 2000 B.C. – c A.D. 350)					
	Zimbabwe Kingdom (c 1000 – c 1450)					
Asia	Sui dynasty rules China (c 589 – c 618)					
	T'ang dynasty (c 618 – c 907)					
	Muslims rule India (c 712 – c 1526)					
	Kamakura shogunate (c 1185 – c 1333)					
	Mongol Empire (c 1200 – c 1368)					
Americas	Mayan civilization's peak (c 300 – c 900)					
	Incas (c 1100 – c 1538)					
	Aztecs (c 1200 – c 1519)					

The Byzantine Empire

civilization
US

civilisation
Brit.

honor
US

honour
Brit.

center
US

centre
Brit.

Long before the Middle Ages in Europe began, the Roman Empire had been divided culturally into a Greek East and a Latin West. The East had a much larger population, many more cities, more commerce, industry, and wealth; and a richer heritage of art, literature, and philosophy.

In 286 the Roman Empire had been divided for administrative purposes into eastern and western halves by the emperor Diocletian, who established the eastern capital at Nicomedia, in Asia Minor. In 330 Emperor Constantine moved the capital to Byzantium, a small city located on the European side of the Bosporus that had been founded by Greek colonists in the 600s B.C. The new capital was called Constantinople in honor of the emperor. Today, the city is called Istanbul.

In 395, on the death of Emperor Theodosius I, the Roman Empire became divided and was ruled by two separate emperors. During the 400s, barbarians increased their pressure along the frontiers of both empires. The East Roman Empire was able to withstand the onslaught, but the West Roman Empire collapsed in 476 when its emperor was deposed.

Justinian. During the 500s, the Byzantine emperor Justinian (527–565) attempted to reconquer the West. Under the able generals Belisarius and Narses, the East was able to regain Italy, North Africa, and southeastern Spain. Justinian also fought a long war against the Persians, who had invaded the empire from the east.

Justinian was one of the greatest of the Byzantine emperors. He reorganized government administration and fortified the frontiers. In order to clarify the law, he had the entire body of Roman law codified. The Code of Justinian became eventually the basis of French, German, and Italian law.

Justinian also made a major attempt to ensure the unity of the eastern and western Christian churches, which had been steadily growing apart. He suppressed heresy and paganism and sent out numerous missionaries. This action temporarily healed the breach, but the two churches quarreled continually, and the split between western Christianity, or Roman Catholicism, and eastern Christianity, or Eastern Orthodox Christianity, became irrevocable in what is known as the Schism of 1054.

A project of more permanent value was Justinian's enormous public building program. Two of the most famous Byzantine structures still standing, the churches of Hagia Sophia in Constantinople and San Vitale in Ravenna, Italy, date from his reign.

Invasion and expansion. Justinian was succeeded by a series of weak and ineffective emperors whose reigns were marked by internal unrest and renewed barbarian and Persian invasions. Between 568 and 571, the Lombards, a barbarian tribe from Germany, conquered all of Italy except areas around the cities of Rome, Naples, and Ravenna.

In 616 Spain was lost to the Visigoths. Between 606 and 622 the Persians overran Syria, Asia Minor, Palestine, Mesopotamia, and Egypt. Slavs moved into the Balkans, and the Avars raided almost as far south as Constantinople.

In 610 Heraclius I, the son of the provincial governor of North Africa, seized the imperial throne and became the founder of a new dynasty. Heraclius reorganized the army and launched three brilliant campaigns against the Persians. By 628 the Persians were decisively defeated and the territory they had taken was regained.

The Byzantine Empire, however, had been weakened by the war. When the Arabs, who had recently been converted to Islam, embarked on a program of conquest in 634, the Byzantines were unable to stand against them. The Arabs, banded together in a formidable force, conquered the lands that Heraclius had won from the Persians, and between 673 and 678, and in 717 and 718, they besieged the city of Constantinople itself. In 698 the Arabs seized Carthage, and Byzantine rule in North Africa ended.

In 717 Leo III, the first emperor of the Isaurian dynasty (717–802), came to the throne. The first Isaurians were able leaders who managed to defeat the Muslim Arabs in Asia Minor. They were successful in several campaigns against the Bulgars, a Turkic people that threatened from the northeast.

In 802 the Isaurian dynasty ended, to be followed in 820 by the Amorian, or Phrygian, dynasty, which ruled until

THE MINARETS of Hagia Sophia from which the faithful are called to prayer in Istanbul, formerly Constantinople.

867. The last of the Amorian emperors, Michael III, was murdered by the grand chamberlain Basil, who subsequently founded the Macedonian dynasty (867–1057).

Under the Macedonians, the Byzantine Empire experienced its golden age. The Macedonian emperors were intelligent and responsible rulers who had both administrative and military ability. Byzantine culture reached its peak and Constantinople became the artistic center as well as the marketplace of the Mediterranean.

Basil II, the ablest of the Macedonian emperors, extended the empire to its greatest territorial limits. A cruel and capable general, he waged highly successful campaigns against the Arabs and Bulgars, Syria, parts of Palestine, Crete, and Cyprus, adding them to the empire. Bulgaria was conquered and divided into provinces.

Decline of the Byzantine Empire.
With the end of the Macedonian dynasty in 1057, the Byzantine Empire entered a period of decline that lasted until 1080. The empire was ruled by a succession of weak and inept emperors, and its territory was whittled away by Turkic raiders in the north, Normans in Italy, and Seljuk Turks in Syria, Palestine, and Asia Minor. The Seljuks won most of Asia Minor at the Battle of Manzikert in 1071. Internally, the Byzantine Empire was weakened by a conflict between administrative nobility in Constantinople and feudal nobility outside the capital and in the provinces.

The Crusades.
In 1081 this decline was partially checked by the advent of the Comnenian dynasty, which ruled until 1185. In 1095 the Comnenian emperor asked the Roman Catholic pope in Rome, Urban II, to send military help to recapture Byzantine lands taken by the Seljuk Turks, pleading that they included the Holy Land of Palestine, sacred to Christians as the birthplace of Jesus Christ and a place of pilgrimage. So began the Crusades, a series of military expeditions from Europe to the Middle East.

The first Crusades succeeded in winning back lands for the Byzantine Empire; but soon Crusaders grew envious of the empire's wealth. The decline of the empire was accelerated under the weak Angelus dynasty (1185–1195; 1203–1204). The Angeli lacked the power to stand against foreign enemies. The envious Europeans saw their chance.

The Latin Empire.
In 1204, during the fourth Crusade, Venetian and French leaders attacked Constantinople on the pretext of intervening on behalf of Emperor Isaac II, who was deposed by his brother Alexius III. After a siege of one month, the city fell to the Crusaders and was sacked.

The Crusaders set up a feudal state under Baldwin of Flanders that was known as the Latin Empire. The French controlled most of the former Byzantine

mainland possessions and the Venetians held most of the islands and coastal regions. Byzantine princes managed to retain control of Epirus in northwest Greece and of Nicaea and Trebizond in Asia Minor.

A Byzantine restoration.
These Byzantine princes continued to struggle against the Crusaders. Finally, in 1261, Michael VIII Palaeologus of Nicaea recaptured Constantinople and overthrew the Latin Empire. He founded the Palaeologian dynasty, which ruled for almost 200 years over a substantially reduced Byzantine Empire, consisting mainly of the area around Constantinople and parts of Greece.

Under the Palaeologi the Byzantine Empire enjoyed a cultural renaissance, but diminished physically and grew weaker politically. During the 1300s inroads into Byzantine domains were made by the Serbs in the north and Ottoman Turks in the east, while the empire was divided internally by civil war and religious controversy.

Final collapse.
In May 1453, Constantinople fell to the Ottoman sultan Muhammad II, and the last of the Byzantine emperors, Constantine XI, was killed in the battle. Athens and the Peloponnesus continued to hold out against the Turks, but within a few years they were defeated. Trebizond fell in 1461. Constantinople, for more than 1,100 years the capital of the Byzantine Empire, became the Ottoman capital.

BYZANTINE ARCHITECTURE, featuring skillfully adorned ornate tile work, still remains despite the Byzantine Empire's end in the 15th century.

Major Events — Byzantine Empire

c A.D.	286	Diocletian divides the Roman Empire into eastern and western halves.
c	330	The capital of the Roman Empire moves to Constantinople.
c	395	After the death of Theodosius I, the Roman Empire becomes completely divided and is ruled by two separate emperors.
	404	The Latin version of the Bible is completed.
	426	St. Augustine of Hippo completes *City of God*.
	455	The Vandals sack Rome.
c	867	Byzantine culture reaches a peak during the Macedonian dynasty; Constantinople becomes the artistic center and the marketplace of the Mediterranean.
	1054	The Schism of 1054 splits the church between western Christianity (Roman Catholicism) and eastern Christianity (Eastern Orthodox Christianity).
	1095	Pope Urban II, Peter the Hermit, and Walter the Penniless mount the first Crusade to take Jerusalem from the Arabs; it is the only successful crusade.
	1100	The Italians learn to distill wine to make brandy.
	1250	The goose feather (quill) is used for writing.
	1453	Constantinople falls to the Ottoman Turks.

Medieval Europe

For Europe, the western half of the old Roman Empire, the Middle Ages began with disintegration and isolation as Germanic tribes—including Franks, Burgundians, Vandals, Visigoths, and Ostrogoths—overran western Europe and set up a series of states to replace Roman rule. Now western Europe had little contact with the Mediterranean world. It would remain isolated for a long time from both the Byzantine and the Islamic civilizations.

The German tribes may have destroyed the western Roman Empire as a political entity, but they did not destroy its civilization. They took over the administrative system, the taxes, the law, and the language of the culture they conquered. They had very little immediate effect upon its agricultural base, large landed estates worked by a servile peasantry, or upon its rather limited commerce.

Frankish rule.   The Franks were one of many tribes inhabiting northern Germany. As the Roman defenses on the Rhine gradually collapsed, Frankish war bands, each under an individual king, moved into northern Gaul.

The Franks first became politically significant under the Merovingians, the family of Clovis, who became the king of all Franks about A.D. 481.

Charlemagne.   By the mid-700s, the Merovingians had declined and were replaced by the Carolingians, who inaugurated the most significant period in Frankish history. The greatest of the Carolingian kings was Charlemagne, meaning Charles the Great (ruled 768 to 814). He was the grandson of Charles Martel, who had driven the Muslims back from southern France in 732, and the son of Pepin, who had overthrown the last of the Merovingians in 751.

Charlemagne unified a vast empire and the Roman Catholic Church under his leadership. In 800 he was crowned in Rome "Emperor of the Romans," thus reviving the Roman Empire and establishing a special relationship between its "holy" emperor and the papacy. Charlemagne's rule inspired a revival of learning and literacy, and the copying of Latin texts to preserve the knowledge of classical antiquity.

By the mid-800s, the empire consisted mostly of a landed society united by a loose and decentralized political system. Upon Charlemagne's death, internal struggles for power and land ensued, and in 843 the empire was partitioned into three portions by the Treaty of Verdun. Thus weakened, it was attacked by various barbarian groups: the Vikings from Scandinavia and the Magyars from Asia. By the early 900s, Charlemagne's empire had been shattered into more than 50 political units.

The feudal system.   Feudalism emerged in Europe from the failure of the Frankish monarchy in the west to protect the kingdom from barbarian invaders. It was initially an improvisation for satisfying on a local basis the need for military protection that the larger political units were unable to provide. It was the result of a weak central government, a time of military necessity that brought about a professional fighting class, and a predominantly rural society.

Feudalism had several distinct features in Europe. The principal one was vassalage, a relationship in which one man placed himself at the service of another in return for maintenance and protection. The vassal was originally maintained by his lord's household. Later, as the position of the vassal rose in the social scale, he was supported by a grant of property, or a fief.

Feudalism was established by the mid-900s, at least in northern France. In the 1000s it spread from France to England and 100 years later to Germany. Spain and Italy, however, remained largely untouched.

Manorialism.   The institution of feudalism was inseparable from its economic base, manorialism. The fief consisted of a large landed estate or estates called villas or manors that were cultivated by a peasantry in varying degrees of economic and legal servitude. It was from the manor that the vassal derived his income and over which he exercised his political jurisdiction.

In its simplest definition, the manor was a village community of peasants tilling the soil by means of the open field system. In the open field system, arable land and meadows are divided into strips, each peasant possessing several strips in the various fields.

The High Middle Ages.   Historians often divide the Middle Ages in Europe into two periods. The early half, from the collapse of the western Roman Empire to the 1000s, a period when there was much barbarism and little education, has been called the Dark Ages. But following 1000, Europe experienced a revival in many areas, causing this period to be called the High Middle Ages.

The revival of commerce.   One of the first signs of revival in medieval Europe was the development of towns and commerce. Although trade had never quite died out along the coast of the North Sea in Europe, the source of commercial revival was Italy.

The revival of Italian commerce was given impetus by the Crusades. Beginning at the end of the 1000s, western Europeans spent 200 years vainly attempting to wrest the Holy Land from its Muslim conquerors. The Italians were in a splendid position to profit from the Crusades. They transported armies of Crusaders and pilgrims to the Holy Land and provided for them while they were there.

The Italians also imported exotic goods from Africa and the East that were in great demand in medieval Europe: spices, cloth, precious stones, and perfumes. In return, they exported what was woven in towns like Bruges, Ypres, and Ghent in the Low Countries. The wool itself came from England, and the fine finished products were traded at the famous fairs of Champagne in France. Later the Italians began to eliminate the middlemen in this prosperous trade by manufacturing their own woolen cloth.

The growth of towns.   The revival of commerce stimulated the development of towns. In the initial stages, merchants were itinerant, often travelling in caravans for mutual protection. Naturally, they sought out fortified centers as places of refuge and as markets for their goods.

At a later stage, merchants began to settle down in the most strategically located places. In due course they were surrounded by people who catered to their needs, such as blacksmiths, bakers, and cobblers. As the population expanded, houses were built outside the original fortified center, and it became necessary to protect them with another wall. Simultaneously, independent municipal governments were formed.

Thus, along with the rise of towns and commerce came the origins of a merchant class. The medieval merchant class and the social forms it produced were alien to the economic and social ethic of early medieval society. The feudal class resented its wealth and independence, and the church took a long time to recognize the activities of the

---

civilizations
US
civilisations
Brit.
centers
US
centres
Brit.
labor
US
labour
Brit.

Major Events—Medieval Europe

c 1100	The first universities in Europe are founded in Salerno (medicine), Bologna (law), and Paris (theology and philosophy).
1109	Henry I, of England, introduces a measure of length equal to the length of his arm—the yard.
c 1154	Gothic architecture spreads through Europe.
1170	Thomas à Becket, the archbishop of Canterbury in England, is assassinated.
1189	The first paper mill in Europe is established in Herault, France.
c 1202	The number zero is introduced in Europe.
1210	The teaching of Aristotle's works is forbidden at the University of Paris.
1253	The decimal system is introduced in England.
1271	Marco Polo begins his great journey to the Far East.
1290	Spectacles are invented in Italy.
c 1347	Italian ships bring rats carrying fleas infected with the Black Plague to Europe, killing 25 million people.
1380	Forged iron guns, each weighing 600 pounds, are used by Richard II to defend the Tower of London.
c 1387	Geoffrey Chaucer writes *The Canterbury Tales.*
1431	Joan of Arc is burned at the stake in France.

marketplace and the countinghouse as Christian.

The medieval church.
Another aspect of revival was the change that began to take place within the medieval church. The first manifestation of change was the emergence of religious reform.

During the 900s the increasing stability of medieval life made it possible for ordinary Christians to live lives somewhat closer to the Christian ideal than had been previously possible. In turn, they demanded that the clergy live a life superior to their own.

One of the fundamental convictions of medieval popular Christianity was that the clergy ensured the salvation of the laity by leading moral lives and by administering the sacraments.

The Cluniac reform movement, which began at the French monastery of Cluny in the early 900s, was an attempt to purify the church by restoring monastic discipline as exemplary of Christian life and by eliminating prevailing abuses in the church.

The Gregorian reform movement of the 1000s restored papal and church influence, and expanded the authority of the pope while calling for state subordination to the church.

Later, popular sects arose that challenged the assumptions of the church. These sects believed these assumptions to be based on worldliness and wealth rather than spiritual salvation. These "heresies" not only rejected the authority of the papacy, but also the intermediary position of the priesthood in administering the sacraments. They believed, instead, that the true church was a priesthood of believers who were saved through their individual religious experiences.

The Franciscan and Dominican mendicant orders also developed outside of the formal church. The Franciscans preached renunciation of the world and the value of manual labor. The Dominicans constructed an intellectual defense of church dogma, and in the 1200s developed probably the greatest

A CRUSADER is shot by a Muslim warrior using a deadly bow and arrow. It is believed that the bow was an Eastern development that was carried to Europe by returning Crusaders.

intellectual force in Europe.

The revival of learning.
During the 1000s there was also a revival of learning. The intellectual reawakening of Europe began in the monasteries, but in time it was taken over by cathedral, and then secular, schools.

The new learning was not only intellectually stimulating, it was also immensely practical. The expanding bureaucracies of the church and government demanded men who could reason as well as read and write.

In the 1200s, there was a renewed interest in the philosophy of Aristotle insofar as it revealed religious truth as compatible with human reason. St. Thomas Aquinas became a leading scholastic thinker of this age, arguing that Christian faith is a kind of supernatural knowledge.

Feudal monarchies.
Although the political prospect everywhere in Europe looked bleak at the beginning of the 900s, by the end of the century a revival began to take place. By the end of the 1200s France and England had become similar to modern nation-states,

and Germany only narrowly missed. Paradoxically, it was Germany that originally seemed to be the most likely to become a unified state.

Germany. Beginning with Otto the Great, who ruled from 936 to 973, Saxon kings ruled Germany until they were replaced by the Salian dynasty (1024–1125). The Saxons delegated great authority and power to the church, thus gaining the support of this prestigious and wealthy institution while limiting the power of the nobles. In 962 Otto was crowned Holy Roman Emperor, a title held by German kings for the next 300 years.

But the power of the church soon overshadowed that of the German state. The last two Salian kings, Henry IV and Henry V, fought bitterly with the church over the issue of lay investiture, or who had the right to name powerful church officials—the church itself or the secular rulers. It was a struggle between emperors and popes over spiritual and political authority. An uneasy compromise was reached in 1122, at the Concordat of Worms, in which the church was given the right to elect church officials but the secular rulers kept the privilege of granting them secular powers.

During the Hohenstaufen dynasty (1152–1250), the German kings tried to unify Germany under a strong monarchy, but they met unmovable resistance from northern Italy, which was then part of the Holy Roman Empire, and from the church. Germany thus remained politically fragmented and weak.

France. France did not have Germany's dynastic problems. The Capetian kings ruled France from 987 to 1328. A powerful, unified national state arose during this period.

The Capetians maintained good relations with the church, preserving their just rights while enriching the church with buildings and lands. They increased their own kingdom through marital and hereditary arrangements.

Philip II (ruled 1180–1223) wrested

EUROPE IN 1000

NORWAY
IRISH KINGDOMS
SCOTLAND
SWEDEN
DENMARK
WALES
ENGLAND
RUSSIA
ATLANTIC OCEAN
POLAND
ASTURIAS AND LEON
HOLY ROMAN EMPIRE
NAVARRE
FRANCE
BURGUNDY
CROATIA
HUNGARY
BARCELONA
CALIPHATE OF CORDOVA
Sardinia (Zeirids)
PAPAL STATE
NAPLES
BENEVENTO
SALERNO
SERBIA
BULGARIA
Black Sea
Mediterranean
BYZANTINE EMPIRE
IDRISIDS
ZEIRIDS
Sicily (Zeirids)
Sea
Crete
Cyprus

JOAN OF ARC, the Maid of Orléans, was a French peasant girl who led the French army to defeat the English at Orléans in 1429, a turning point in the Hundred Years' War.

hundred years earlier, Anglo-Saxon England had been the intellectual leader of western Europe.

By the 1000s, however, England had fallen behind. It had not kept up with the intellectual revival, economic progress, and religious reforms that were sweeping the European continent at the time.

In 1066 William of Normandy invaded England from France and captured the throne at the Battle of Hastings. The Norman Conquest of England resulted in the establishment of a feudal system far more systematic and effective than any existing in Europe. The feudal aristocracy resented the power of the monarchy, but all benefited from the establishment of unified codes of law and general order. English medieval history thereafter became a record of attempts by the nobility to limit arbitrary monarchical power while preserving the benefits of strong central government.

Henry I (ruled 1100–1135) consolidated an English system of justice and provided the foundations of English Common Law. Henry II (ruled 1154–1189), who inherited large French possessions, held his great empire together by greatly strengthening the royal power and the machinery of central government in England. The increased legal power of the monarchy brought him into open conflict with the English church, which not only had its own ecclesiastical law but often permitted its clergy to violate English civil law. When the archbishop of Canterbury, Thomas à Becket, was assassinated in 1170, during the church-state struggle, Henry performed public penance for it. Nevertheless, the royal courts continued to diminish the jurisdiction of the ecclesiastical courts.

King John (ruled 1199–1216) not only lost English possessions in France,

but was forced to yield to the papacy, and finally, in 1215, was impelled to sign the Magna Carta. This document, limiting the king's power over the aristocrats, led eventually to the emergence of Parliament, a baronial body of political representatives that first rose to power briefly during the reign of Henry III (1216–1272).

End of the Middle Ages. In 1270 the saintly Louis IX of France died while participating in the last Crusade. His successor, Philip IV, was a different kind of monarch. As we have seen, Philip fought Pope Boniface VIII and established the supremacy of the French crown over the French church.

In 1272 the pious Henry III of England was succeeded by Edward I, who similarly effected the dominance of secular over spiritual power in England. The last three decades of the 1200s thus mark the triumph of secularism in politics and the beginning of a weakening of papal authority.

In theology and philosophy, there was a similar breakdown after 1270. The major intellectual achievement of the 1200s had been the integration of Christian theology with the natural philosophy of Aristotle. In the late 1200s there was general retreat from this attempt at synthesis. In the 1300s the choice was either faith or reason, rather than a harmony of the two.

Finally, expanding population and economic growth that began in the 1000s came to a halt in the 1300s. Although the fundamental cause of this economic decline is unknown, one cause was the Black Death (1347–1351), a plague that halved the population of Europe. The 1300s saw the end of a major period of European history and the beginning of a new one; it formed a bridge between the Middle Ages and the Renaissance.

former English holdings in France from the English under King John; Louis IX (ruled 1226–1270) centralized the administration of the kingdom in Paris; and Philip IV (ruled 1285–1314) began a bitter struggle with Pope Boniface VIII over the royal right to tax the clergy. Boniface believed adamantly in papal supremacy over the state. In 1303 Philip made an unsuccessful attempt to seize the pope, who died soon after. Two years later a Frenchman was elected Pope Clement V, and in 1309 the papal seat was moved to Avignon. These events played a key role in the subsequent split within the church that came to be called the Great (or Western) Schism (1378–1417).

England. By the early 900s England had achieved both a territorial unity and an administrative sophistication unmatched in western Europe. One

---

The Middle East and Africa

The Islamic civilization that exploded onto the scene in the Middle East during the seventh century was greatly influenced by its Greek and Roman predecessors. However, several of the civilizations that emerged in Africa south of the Sahara present examples of more isolated development.

The Islamic World

The civilization that would eventually produce an empire to rival the size of Rome at its height had its beginnings in a desert wasteland that Roman legions never even tried to enter, the sandy reaches of the Arabian peninsula. It began with the founding of the third great monotheistic world religion, Islam, meaning "surrender to God," and its followers, the Muslims.

Muhammad. About 570, the founder of Islam, Muhammad, was born in the Arabian city of Mecca, 50 miles inland from Jiddha, a busy port on the Red Sea. Mecca's location made it a center of caravan trade between southern Arabia and the Red Sea. As an Arabian merchant himself, Muhammad came into contact with Jewish and Christian traders and with the teachings of their religions.

A highly contemplative man, Muhammad often walked the foothills near Mecca to meditate. There, at age 40, he had a religious experience that convinced him that there is only one God, the God of the Jews and Christians, whom Muhammad called Allah. In his revelation, Allah called upon Muhammad to perfect the religion revealed to prophets like Abraham, Moses, and Jesus, and to

preach it to the world.

Muhammad had little success at first among the Arabs, who worshiped many gods and spirits of nature. Indeed, Meccans threatened to kill Muhammad for his preaching, and he and his few followers fled to the coastal city of Medina, where he did succeed in making converts to his teachings. His flight there, called the *Hegira,* became revered by Muslims as the turning point in the development of their faith; the Hegira's date, 622, became the first year of the Muslim calendar.

By 630 Muhammad had attracted an army of followers and was able to march back to Mecca and force it to surrender to him. By the time of his death in 632, he had united all the nomadic tribes of Arabia, the Bedouins, under Islam.

CULTURES ACROSS THE WORLD

The spread of Islam. Wars of expansion followed closely upon Muhammad's death. His successors, the caliphs, made Islam into a system of government as well as a religion. They sent out their well-trained and well-equipped armies to spread both the faith and Muslim control over areas in the Middle East. By 636 Syria and Northern Palestine had fallen to Muslim forces, and by 641 all of Palestine, Mesopotamia, and Persia had also surrendered.

Conquest of Egypt followed in 642. From naval bases there, the Muslims captured the islands of Rhodes and Cyprus in the Mediterranean. They then swept west along the North African coast, capturing Carthage in 698 and making converts and allies of the Berber peoples of North Africa.

In 711 Muslim armies crossed from western North Africa over the Strait of Gibraltar to Spain, and within a decade the armies had captured nearly the entire Iberian peninsula. They got as far north as southern France, but were at last turned back there by forces under Charles Martel in 732. Muslim forces were also on the move eastward, reaching the Indus River by 724. By 750 the Islamic Empire had surpassed the size of the Roman Empire.

Division within Islam. Most of Islam's expansion took place under the rule of the Ummayad dynasty, which came to power in 661 after the Arabic Ummayad tribe fomented a civil war against the fourth caliph, Ali, a son-in-law of Muhammad. Ali was assassinated and an Ummayad became caliph, establishing his capital at Damascus in Syria.

This dispute between Ali and the Ummayads created a schism in Islam. On one side were the Sunni Muslims, or Sunnites, who accepted the Ummayad succession; on the other were the Shiites, mainly non-Arabs, who believed only a relative of Muhammad could be caliph. The schism survives today—these two sects continue to be Islam's major groups, with the Sunnites more numerous by far.

In 750 Shiite revolts in Iraq and Persia resulted in the overthrow of the Ummayad dynasty. The Abbasids, an Arabic family, tracing their descent from Muhammad's uncle, had joined the Shiites in their opposition to the Ummayads. They played upon non-Arabic, especially Persian, discontent with Arab domination of Islamic government. The Abbasids and the Persians overran the Ummayad armies and an Abbasid was named caliph. Under the Abbasids, Islamic civilization became more Persian than Arabic.

Islamic achievements. Under the Abbasids, the Muslim economy achieved unprecedented prosperity. The Arabic language and commercial ties with the continents of Asia, Africa, and Europe gave the Muslim world tremendous cohesion.

The civilization that developed under these conditions was adept at borrowing the best from the diverse peoples whom it embraced; philosophy and science were borrowed from the Greeks, and mathematics from the Indians, for example. It kept classical learn-

THE MOSQUE serves religious, military, and educational functions in Muslim life.

ing alive and synthesized scholarship from wherever it was to be found, in turn making its own original contributions to scholarship and art.

The years from 900 to 1100 were a golden age for Islamic civilization. Muhammad al-Razi, known as Rhazes to Europeans, the greatest of Muslim physicians, produced over 100 treatises on disease. The Arab scholar, Avicenna, later organized all of al-Razi's learning, as well as all the contemporary knowledge about the symptoms and treatment of diseases, into the *Canon of Medicine,* which was the world's most widely used medical book for centuries.

From the Indians, Muslim mathematicians adopted a numbering system (now called Arabic numbers) that included 0, which makes large numbers possible. They perfected algebra (from the Arabic *al-jabr,* meaning "reunion of broken parts").

Among the most famous literary works of Islamic civilization are Omar Khayyam's long romantic poem, *The Rubáiyát,* and the collected stories that make up *A Thousand and One Nights.*

The epitome of Muslim architecture is the mosque, with its domes borrowed from the Byzantines. Because Islamic law had strictures prohibiting depictions of the human form, calligraphy and geometric forms became mainstays of Muslim art.

The coming of the Ottoman Turks. The Abbasid dynasty, unable to maintain political unity, and the Islamic Empire began to break up into smaller Muslim states. In 1055 the Seljuk Turks, nomads from central Asia, who had become Muslims, gained control of Baghdad and conquered Syria, Palestine, and Asia Minor. In the 13th century, Genghis Khan, and his hordes, swept out of Mongolia and began their conquest of central and eastern Asia. In 1258 his grandson captured Baghdad and ended the rule of the Abbasids. The Mongols ruled for only a short time. In the early 14th century another Turkish force, the Ottomans, moved in.

The Ottomans had been vassals of the Seljuks in northwestern Asia Minor, and like them had converted to Islam. As Seljuk power declined, the Ottomans took over their territories and initiated more wars of expansion. By 1453 they had captured Constan-

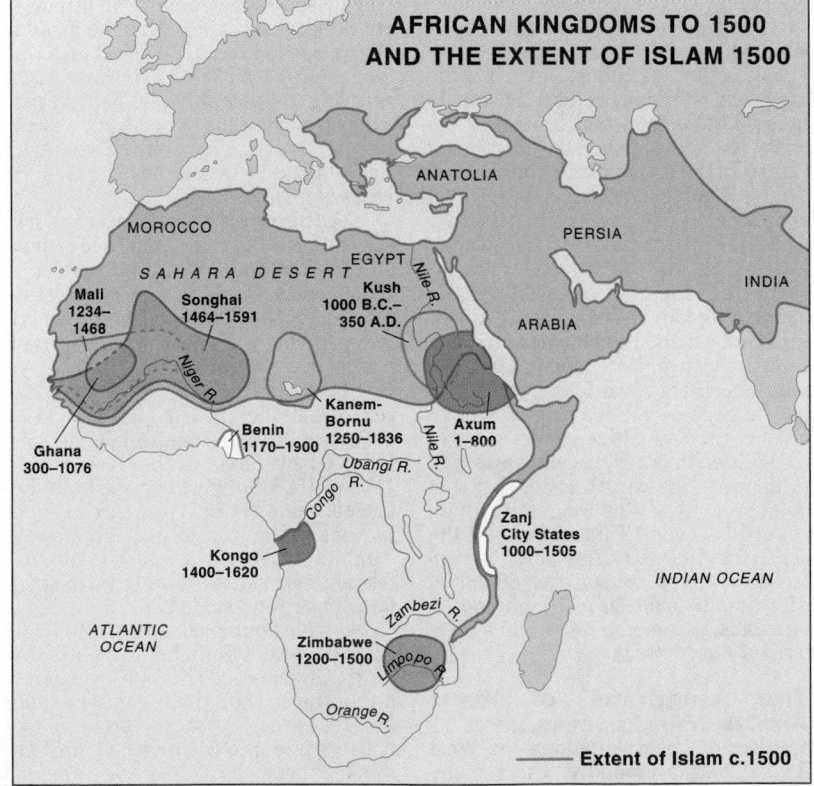

AFRICAN KINGDOMS TO 1500 AND THE EXTENT OF ISLAM 1500

ANATOLIA

MOROCCO

PERSIA

EGYPT

SAHARA DESERT

Mali 1234–1468

Songhai 1464–1591

Kush 1000 B.C.–350 A.D.

Niger R.

Nile R.

INDIA

ARABIA

Kanem-Bornu 1250–1836

Benin 1170–1900

Axum 1–800

Ghana 300–1076

Ubangi R.

Nile R.

Congo

Zanj City States 1000–1505

Kongo 1400–1620

INDIAN OCEAN

ATLANTIC OCEAN

Zambezi R.

Zimbabwe 1200–1500

Limpopo R.

Orange R.

—— Extent of Islam c.1500

tinople, and controlled much of Asia Minor and part of the Balkans. From 1453 to 1520, they made all of the Balkans, Asia Minor, territory north of the Black Sea, Syria, Palestine, northwestern Arabia, and Egypt part of the Empire. Between 1520 and 1566 they added North Africa, more of Arabia, Iraq, and parts of modern Austria and Hungary, making the Ottoman Empire the world's largest at the time.

Sub-Saharan Africa

civilization
US

civilisation
Brit.

center
US

centre
Brit.

Civilization began in Africa's Sahara and in areas south as it had elsewhere in the world. Stone Age hunters and gatherers roamed the Sahara, then a verdant area covered with grass, trees, rivers, and lakes, leaving records of themselves in cave drawings. About 5000 B.C., climatic changes began to dry the Sahara; by 1500 B.C. the Sahara had turned into the vast desert it is today. Its Stone Age inhabitants migrated, some toward the Nile valley and some into the river valleys of Africa's south and west. When they became agriculturalists, the first civilizations began to emerge, some developing in isolation, in part because of the barrier created by the Sahara Desert.

Kush and Axum. About 2000 B.C., the kingdom of Kush emerged in the Upper Nile, south of ancient Egypt in today's Sudan. Influenced by Egyptian civilization and at one time a dependency of Egypt, it developed as a major commercial center, using the Nile River and the Red Sea to trade goods with Egypt, Arabia, and Mesopotamia.

About 750 B.C., the Kush were strong enough to conquer Egypt and a Kush dynasty ruled there until 671 B.C., when the Assyrians invaded Egypt and drove them out. But Kush civilization quickly regrouped. Having learned how to make iron from the Assyrians, it became a center for iron making in Africa in its capital at Meroë. About

A.D. 200, Kush began to decline while its neighbor to the south, Axum, in what is now Ethiopia, grew stronger. Axum destroyed Kush about 350, and took over control of the area's thriving trade.

Twenty-five years earlier, King Ezana of Axum had converted to Christianity along with many of his people. The scene was thus set for the development of Christian Ethiopia. Invasion by Muslims in the seventh century did not wipe out Christianity there, though it did cut off contact with the rest of the Christian world.

East African trade. From ancient times, settlements along Africa's east coast had been involved in trade on the Indian Ocean. By 1200 numerous city-states lined the coast, combining the native Swahili-speaking culture with that of Muslim merchants, thus producing a synthesis of African and Middle Eastern civilization. Indian traders added elements of Hindu civilization.

The Swahili city-states reached their peak in the period from 1200 to 1500. Foremost among them were Malindi, Mombasa, and Kilwa. Rulers built elaborate stone mosques and enormous palaces lavishly decorated with gold and ivory. Swahili writers produced great literature; poems and ballads written in Arabic script abounded.

Central Africa and Zimbabwe. Central Africa was populated mainly by Bantu-speaking peoples who had begun a mass migration east and south from west-central Africa about 1000 B.C. Over the next 2,000 years, they founded several states along the Atlantic coast and in the Bantu interior.

One, founded near the Bantu homeland at the mouth of the Niger River by people of the Nok culture, grew into the kingdom of Benin, celebrated for its incomparable iron and bronze sculptures. Farther south was the kingdom of Kongo, at the mouth of the Congo River. There, a bureaucratic monarchy ruled six provinces that engaged in a thriving trade between the interior and Africa's west coast.

Perhaps the most powerful was the inland kingdom of Zimbabwe, between the Zambezi and the Limpopo rivers in southern Africa. Here, about A.D. 1000, migrating Bantu had found gold; Zimbabwe became the major producer of gold for the East African trade.

Ruins in the valley of Zimbabwe give evidence of the wealth and power that gold brought to this kingdom, which peaked between 1250 and 1450. At the center lies the Great Zimbabwe, a spectacular fortress spread over 60 acres, with granite walls 20 feet high and 10 feet thick, a domed temple, and a mysterious stone tower.

The kingdoms of West Africa. As in East Africa, the development of great kingdoms in West Africa was profoundly affected by

gold and trade. Trade began there in the third century, when camel caravans began crossing the Sahara, north to south, exchanging salt that West Africa did not have for gold that it did have.

Ghana. The first of West Africa's great kingdoms was Ghana, which began its development as a group of villages along the upper Niger River during the fourth century A.D. According to legend, its first rulers were Berbers from North Africa who were overthrown about A.D. 700 by the indigenous people under Kaya Maghau, who founded a new dynasty and expanded the desert trade.

During the eleventh century, Ghana reached its peak. An Arabian visitor named al-Makri recorded that the gold-rich kingdom had a 200,000-man army and an all-powerful king, thought to be divine. Two centuries later, Ghana declined for unknown reasons, and by 1203, a new leader, Sundiata, overthrew the king and founded a new kingdom called Mali.

Mali. Sundiata took over Ghana's gold trade and founded a new dynasty, which, in the mid-13th century, converted to Islam, the religion of its North African trading partners. Mali continued to expand its empire. At its height in the 14th century, Mali's kings ruled 40 million people in West Africa from their capital at Timbuktu on the Niber River.

Mansa Musa, Mali's greatest ruler, held power from 1307 to 1332 and enlarged Mali's holdings. As a devoted Muslim, he invited Muslim scholars and architects to come to Timbuktu to promote learning and to build mosques for Muslim worship.

Mansa Musa gained fame throughout the civilized world when he made a pilgrimage to Mecca in 1324. With a retinue of 60,000 and with 500 slaves each carrying a 4-pound bar of gold to pay expenses along the way, he cut a spectacular figure. The gold he spent in Egypt alone is said to have caused 20 years of inflation there.

Successors of Mansa Musa were not able to keep the Mali Empire together, as states within it went into rebellion. By the end of the 14th century, the eastern province of Songhai had won its independence; a century later, it had conquered most of Mali.

Songhai. The Empire of Songhai reached its height from 1464 to 1492 under the rule of Sonni Ali II. He was followed by Askia Muhammad, from 1493 to 1528. Songhai became both the largest empire in West Africa and the best organized to maintain power. Timbuktu became a major center of Islamic learning, its university a magnet for scholars and students.

Songhai flourished until nearly 1600, when its wealth brought the envy of the king of Morocco. With weapons unknown to Songhai—cannons and muskets—the Moroccans broke Songhai's empire into a number of smaller, weaker states.

Major Events — Middle East and Africa	
c 600	Windmills used to grind grain are built in Persia.
622	The Hegira, Muhammad's flight from Mecca to Medina, marks the first year of the Muslim calendar.
632	Muhammad unites all the nomadic tribes of Arabia under Islam.
661	A schism divides Islam into the Sunnites and the Shiites; the schism survives today.
c 750	The Islamic Empire grows larger than the Roman Empire ever was.
c 900	The golden age for Islamic civilization begins; Muhammad al-Razi produces over a hundred treatises on disease; Muslim mathematicians perfect algebra; scientists develop the astrolabe, which measures the altitude of a star and helps sailors determine their position at sea.
c 1050	Ghana, on the west coast of Africa, becomes the preeminent gold-rich kingdom in Africa; its army numbers 200,000.
c 1100	Omar Khayyam writes *The Rubáiyát*; calligraphy and geometric forms become mainstays of Muslim art.
1203	The kingdom of Mali is formed in western Africa.
1600	Moroccans destroy the Songhai Empire using cannons and muskets.

Developing Cultures of the Americas

Cultures of the Americas developed independently of those in Europe, Africa and Asia, without either side of the world being aware of the other.

The Olmecs. One of the earliest of the American civilizations were the Olmecs, located along the Gulf Coast in southern Mexico. By about 1000 B.C., their productive agrarian economy had acquired the essential features of civilization: occupational specialization; religious organization; effective government, in this case, run by a priestly ruling class; written language, in the form of hieroglyphics; and high artistic achievement, especially in architecture.

The Olmecs constructed a series of planned cities as religious centers, with stone pyramids nine and ten stories high as altars to the gods. They were marvels of masonic skill and of decorative carving. Ruins of these pyramids can still be found, along with massive stone sculptures of grim-faced heads, some weighing 20 tons.

Olmec influence spread across all of Mesoamerica, perhaps reaching its height in the city of Teotihuacan, in the northeastern Valley of Mexico. There a pyramid over 15 stories high honored the god Quetzalcoatl, pictured as a feathered serpent. By A.D. 500, this city had a population of somewhere between 100,000 and 200,000, making it the sixth largest city in the world at that time.

The Mayas. South of Teotihuacan, in the Yucatan peninsula and today's Guatemala, the Mayan civilization arose in the first millennium B.C. By A.D. 300 it had become the most splendid yet seen in the Americas.

Like the Olmecs, the Mayas built magnificent religious centers that grew into major cities such as Tikal, Palenque, and Uxmal. The cities had royal palaces occupied by a hereditary priest-king, considered the descendant of the sun god, and the priests and warrior nobles, the ruling class. Each city also had pyramid temples, some 20 stories high, built to honor the many deities the Mayas worshipped. Decoration included magnificent stone sculptures made with stone tools (the native cultures of the Americas never developed iron making). The art of mural painting reached great heights under the Mayas.

Because Mayan scholars were avid students of astronomy, observatories were another feature of their cities. The Mayas made astronomical discoveries that helped them to perfect a calendar they adopted from the earlier Olmecs but using an ingenious notational system of their own design.

In the 800s Mayan civilization collapsed. The reasons are unknown, but overpopulation, rebellion, and attack from barbarian tribes were possible causes. By 900 their great cities were abandoned and new peoples, like the Toltecs, rose to power. These peoples absorbed Mayan influences as they gained control of Mesoamerican trade, and built spectacular urban centers at Tula, in the Valley of Mexico, and Chichen Itza on the Yucatan peninsula.

The Aztecs. By the 13th century A.D., a new group of invaders, the warlike Aztecs, had migrated south from central Mexico. As they moved south, the Aztecs conquered other tribes, demanding tribute and enslaving some of the conquered people.

About 1325 the Aztecs founded their capital at Tenochtitlán, where Mexico City is located today. At that time, it was an island located in the center of a lake reachable only by causeways, making it highly defensible. Led by Montezuma I, who ruled from 1440 to 1468, the Aztecs fought for 20 years, until they had extended their empire into Guatemala, and along both the Gulf of Mexico and the Pacific coasts.

The hereditary Aztec ruler, whose people believed he was an incarnation of the sun god, governed as a despot, assisted by 38 provincial governors. A powerful military force held the system together, putting down any revolts by conquered peoples.

Aztec religion was based on the worship of gods and goddesses of natural forces. Perhaps most important was the god of the sun, Huitzilopochtli. The Aztecs believed that this god demanded human sacrifice and so they built altars atop tall pyramids on which they tore out the living hearts of the hapless victims that they abducted from conquered tribes. Then they held the still-beating organs up to the sun.

Historians sometimes draw a parallel between the Mayas and Aztecs and the Greeks and Romans. Just as the Romans borrowed much of their culture from the Greeks, so the Aztecs built their culture by borrowing from earlier Mayan and Toltec models. Also like the Romans, the Aztecs honored military discipline, direct action, and efficient imperial organization.

The Incas. Both Mayan and Aztec civilizations were outshone by the Incas of western South America. Village life had begun in the Andes Mountains about 1500 B.C. By A.D. 600 villages began to grow into cities.

Over the succeeding centuries, rival kingdoms battled one another incessantly, but in the 1100s, the Incas, of the Valley of Cuzco in modern Peru, "the children of the sun" according to their legends, began to conquer and unite the area. Under the brilliant leadership of Pachacuti, who reigned from 1438 to 1471, they brought all of the territory from northern Ecuador to central Chile, a length of 2,700 miles, and from the Pacific coast to the Amazon rain forests, into their empire.

The huge Incan Empire was a marvel of organization, with a strong central government under the authority of the hereditary emperor, considered to be the son of the Incas' most important god, Inti, god of the sun. The empire was divided into four provinces, each governed by a viceroy and each divided into 40 subsections under subgovernors. Each of these was further divided into units of ten families under the authority of a local official. A strict law code regulated all aspects of life, not unlike Hammurabi's Code in ancient Babylonia.

The Incas' engineering skill rivaled, if not surpassed, the Romans. They built a system of roads and bridges that successfully linked the highly mountainous empire, enhancing its efficient rule. Even without the wheel, which Native American cultures failed to develop, they moved massive stones to build temples and fortresses, fitting the stones so closely together that they required no mortar.

By A.D. 1500 the Incan Empire had reached its zenith under the rule of Huanyna Capac. However, a dispute over the succession to the throne, and interference by Europeans, helped to set the stage for its rapid decline in the century that followed.

THE AZTEC CALENDAR STONE, which weighs 20 tons, depicts the Aztec sun god.

honored
US

honoured
Brit.

21 **History of the World**

Major Events — The Americas

c 1000 B.C.		The Olmecs founded one of the earliest American civilizations along the Gulf Coast in southern Mexico.
c A.D. 300		The Mayan civilization in Central America creates magnificent stone sculptures with stone tools.
c	600	Incan villages begin to grow into cities in the highlands of Peru.
c	1000	The Vikings, led by Leif Ericson, reach North America, perhaps at Newfoundland; the lack of archaeological evidence leaves doubt as to the exact location.
	1300	The Aztecs dominate the central valley of Mexico.
	1454	Italian navigator Amerigo Vespucci is one of the first Europeans to recognize that North and South America are undiscovered continents.
	1492	Columbus reaches America.
	1525	Smallpox reaches the Incan Empire, killing Huayna Capac, the Incan king.
	1607	The colony of Jamestown is established in Virginia.
	1620	The Pilgrims land at Plymouth Rock, Massachusetts.
	1636	Harvard College is founded in Cambridge, Massachusetts; it is the first university in North America.

The Far East

civilizations
US

civilisations
Brit.

centered
US

centred
Brit.

While the Middle Ages in Europe saw a period of confusion, the Far East witnessed the consolidation, strengthening, and spread of the civilizations already established in India and China. Asian populations were growing and people were on the move, diffusing Indian and Chinese cultures to Japan and Southeast Asia and providing these areas with a shortcut to civilization by giving them basic institutions that they could adapt and build upon.

India Under the Muslims

India's Classical Age had come to an end when invading Huns shattered the Gupta Empire in A.D. 535. But the fabric of Indian civilization was able to withstand even this stunning blow, and a Hindu confederation succeeded in stopping the Huns.

Muslim expansion. In the early 600s, the Hindu king Harsha united much of what had been the Gupta Empire under his rule. For several decades, he governed northern India efficiently and humanely. But in later years, he grew cruel and oppressive, and he was overthrown. Northern India then broke into Rajput kingdoms, named for the people who ruled them, the descendants of earlier central Asian invaders who had intermarried with Hindus.

The resulting disunity invited Muslim invasion of India. Beginning in 712, Muslim peoples, most importantly Muslim Turks, began streaming into India through the northwest mountain passes, zealously trying to convert Hindus

to Islam and marauding through the Rajput states. By 1236 Muslims had gained control of northern India. Within another hundred years, their conquests had taken them south of the Deccan Plateau.

Establishing their capital at Delhi, along the Ganges River, they reunited India under the rule of a series of sultans in a regime called the Delhi Sultanate. Capricious and harsh, the sultans persecuted Hindu citizens, demanding taxes from them that Indians who had become Muslims did not have to pay. Many Indians did convert to Islam, especially those who preferred the Muslim principle of social equality to the rigid Hindu caste system. India divided into two separate religious streams, Hindu and Muslim, a division that threatens Indian peace and justice even today.

In 1398 Mongols, led by the brilliant general Tamerlane, overran northern India, interrupting Delhi Sultanate rule for 50 years. But in 1450 the Mongols left India, intent on new conquest elsewhere, and the sultans again took power, holding it until 1526.

China—Two Golden Ages

Unlike India, China was able to fend off foreign invasions during much of, at least, the first seven centuries of the period of the Middle Ages in Europe. Though there were occasional disruptions, it was able to enjoy a prolonged period of relative political stability.

In A.D. 580 Yang Chien, a northern Chinese general, began reunifying China after the 350 years of disorder ushered in by the collapse of the Han dynasty. In 589 he founded the Sui dynasty, which ruled China until 618. During that time, Sui kings created a centralized administration, reviving the civil service examinations begun by the Han to supply it with government officials. This reorganization provided a solid base on which two succeeding dynasties, the T'ang and Sung, could build. These dynasties brought China into two new golden ages, rivaling and surpassing that of the Han era.

The T'ang dynasty. During the T'ang period, 618 to 907, the Chinese Empire reached its greatest size yet. It subjugated two Turkic states in central Asia, made Tibet a dependency, became the overlord of Korea, and conquered Annam (modern northern Vietnam) in Indochina. The Chinese capital at Changan (modern Xian) grew to more than 2 million people, making it the world's largest city.

Government under the T'ang was highly centralized and run by a complex

bureaucracy made up mainly of scholars. These people had graduated from government universities that had trained them in Confucian learning, Chinese history, and current affairs, and they had passed civil service exams. T'ang emperors strongly supported the dissemination of Confucian philosophy, which taught loyalty and obedience to government authority.

T'ang government closely regulated the economy and encouraged its prosperity by building roads and canals to facilitate trade. The most sweeping of its building projects was the Grand Canal, which stretched 650 miles from Hangzhou (Hangchow) to Tianjin (Tientsin), linking the rich rice-growing area along the Yangtze River with fast-growing population areas along the Huang He (Yellow River). Under the T'ang, foreign trade was also encouraged, as the Silk Road used during Roman times was reopened and the port of Canton along the southern coast welcomed 100,000 foreign merchants, from Persia, Arabia, India, and the East Indies.

The T'ang era was especially brilliant in the art and technology it produced. Poetry flourished, most notably that of Li Po (c 700–762), who wrote movingly of nature, human emotions, and life's mysteries. Interest in the possibilities of learning from history encouraged an outpouring of historical writing, leading to the improvement of papermaking and the invention of block printing, which had originated in China in about 600. Gunpowder was another Chinese technological development under the T'ang, though it was used only for fireworks. The Chinese began to use gunpowder for military purposes in the tenth century, after which they developed explosive grenades and land mines.

After two centuries, the T'ang dynasty went into decline, the result of weakened emperors and ill-conceived decisions, like overtaxing peasants and persecuting Buddhists. In 907 the last T'ang emperor was deposed. Fifty years of division and disorder ensued.

The Sung dynasty. In 960 Chao K'uang-yin, a northern Chinese leader, founded China's next dynasty, which would rule until 1279. Militarily weaker than its predecessor, the Sung kept out restless Mongol invaders like the Khitan by paying them tribute in the form of silk and silver. But in 1127, another invading group, the Jurchin, came down from Manchuria and captured northern China, driving the Sung out of their capital at Kaifeng and forcing them to flee south. Now China was divided in two—the Jurchin's Chin Empire in the north and the Sung Empire in the south, with its capital at Hangzhou.

Even with this turmoil, Sung civiliza-

Major Events—Far East	
c 400	Chinese influence in language, Confucian government, and art predominates in Vietnam; the Japanese adopt Chinese writing.
c 522	Buddhism reaches Japan.
618	The T'ang dynasty in China is especially brilliant at producing art and technology.
645	Japanese art and architecture imitate Chinese styles; Japan adopts China's system of weights and measures.
712	Muslim Turks begin streaming into India through northwest mountain passes.
794	The Heian period begins in Japan; the Japanese concentrate on developing a distinctive culture and form a phonetic alphabet.
960	The Sung dynasty increases the manufacture of silk, lacquerware, and porcelain, enabling China to prosper; paper money is in use for the first time.
c 1050	Some Chinese books are printed with movable type.
1107	The Chinese invent multicolor printing, mainly to make paper money harder to counterfeit.
c 1150	The Hindu temple of Angkor Wat is created.
1275	Marco Polo arrives in China.
c 1470	Highly stylized theater emerges in Japan in the form of Nō and kabuki; haiku poetry also emerges.

tion bloomed, thanks largely to continuing commercial success. By establishing commercial colonies throughout East Asia, the Chinese took over the rich trade of their southern ports, previously controlled by foreign merchants. Trade was conducted as far away as India, Persia, and the Middle East. Increased manufacture of such goods as silk, lacquerware, and porcelain enabled the Chinese to prosper as never before. In their extensive dealings, they introduced the use of paper money for the first time in history. Sea trade also encouraged Chinese development of water clocks and paddleboats, as well as a 24-point mariner's compass. Science and cartography also were enriched, as was medicine—the Chinese developed smallpox inoculation, another first.

Chinese art and learning continued to advance under the Sung. Landscape painting reached its height as artists plumbed the depths of their Taoist love of nature to capture the rugged beauties of China with delicate brush strokes on silk. During the twelfth century, philosopher Chu Hsi (1130–1200) developed Neo-Confucianism, which synthesized the teachings of Confucianism, Buddhism, and Taoism into a single school of thought. This philosophy characterized the universe as a self-regulating order to which human beings must learn to adjust rationally.

The Mongol Empire.
By the 13th century, Chinese civilization was no longer able to hold back the Mongols, with either military might or with tribute. The Mongols then began a series of conquests that created the Mongol Empire.

Genghis Khan. The leader of the Mongols was born the son of a Mongol chief about 1167. Carrying the name Temujin, or "man of iron," he soon proved himself a great warrior, cunning, courageous, and brutal. By 1206 he earned the name Genghis Khan, or "very mighty ruler." In 1215 he and his fierce and powerful cavalries conquered northern China, occupying most of the Chin Empire and capturing Beijing, its capital.

For the next decade, he continued his empire building, taking his armies west and conquering parts of northern India as well as of Persia, Iraq, and southern Russia. After his death in 1227, his descendants continued to expand the Mongol Empire until it stretched from the Black Sea in the west to Korea in the east. It was Genghis Khan's grandson Kublai Khan who completed the conquest of China and the overthrow of the Sung dynasty in 1279. He also brought the Southeast Asian states of Burma, Annam, and Cambodia under Mongol control but failed in his attacks on Japan.

The Yuan dynasty. Kublai Khan chose the Chinese name Yuan for the dynasty he founded in 1279, and which lasted until 1368. It was the first foreign

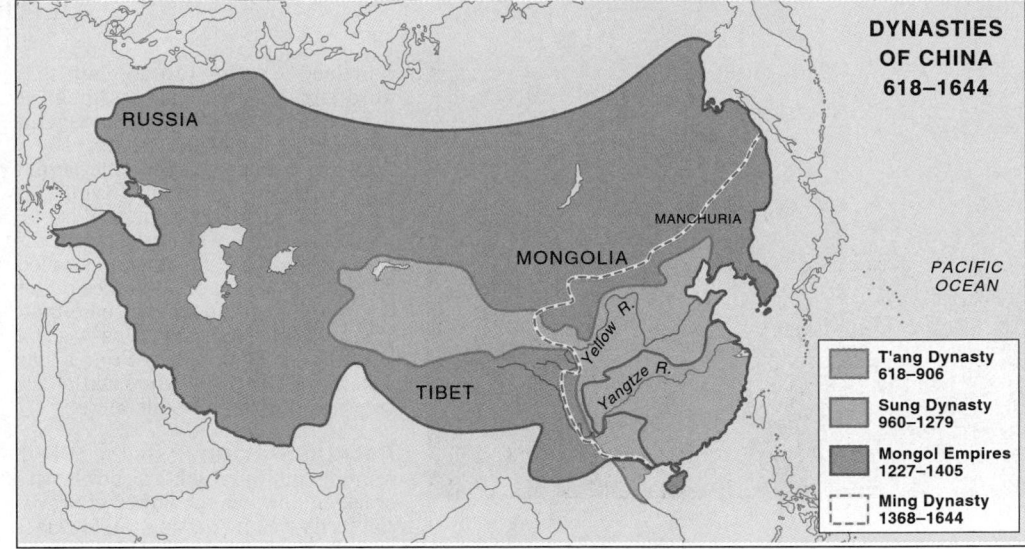

DYNASTIES OF CHINA 618–1644

RUSSIA

MANCHURIA

MONGOLIA

PACIFIC OCEAN

Yellow R.

Yangtze R.

TIBET

T'ang Dynasty 618–906

Sung Dynasty 960–1279

Mongol Empires 1227–1405

Ming Dynasty 1368–1644

dynasty to rule China. He made his capital at Beijing. High Chinese officials were replaced with Mongols, who held themselves to one set of laws while holding the Chinese to another, harsher set. Suffering reached mammoth proportions—the Chinese population dropped from 100 million to 70 million under the Mongols.

Commercial and cultural contacts with the outer world increased under the Mongols. The Italian Marco Polo was only the most famous of many Europeans who traveled to China and brought tales of its wealth, inventions, and learning back to Europe in the 13th and 14th centuries. Traders from the Middle East did the same.

Restoration under the Ming.
Under Kublai Khan's successors, Mongol rule weakened and Chu Yuanchang, a former Buddhist monk, led a successful rebellion. It culminated in 1368 with his establishment of the Ming dynasty, which ruled until 1644. Eager to remove all traces of Mongol subjugation, the Ming rulers moved quickly to restore Confucian government and bureaucracy.

THE VENETIAN TRAVELER Marco Polo returned from the East with tales Europeans could hardly believe were true.

Early in their rule, the Ming were determined to expand China's foreign interests. They encouraged foreign trade and sent out voyages of exploration to Southeast Asia, India, the Persian Gulf, and East Africa. But in the mid-1400s, for unknown reasons, the voyages were ended and China cut off its foreign contacts and withdrew into itself. At this time, it was probably the most technologically advanced civilization on Earth, but with its turn inward, it began to concentrate more on the past than the future and so gradually lost its technological edge.

The Emergence of Japan

Developing in the shadow of China, and deeply influenced by it, was the civilization of Japan, just across the Sea of Japan from Korea and Manchuria. In ancient times, migrations of Asian peoples had come to Japan by way of Korea, gradually displacing the indigenous Stone Age Ainu population. By the first century A.D., Japan's mountainous topography had encouraged these peoples to organize themselves into farming clans in numerous self-contained tribal states.

Early Japan. According to legend, the first emperor of Japan was Jimmu, a descendant of Amaterasu, the sun goddess. He is thought to have been a member of the Yamato clan, which in the early centuries A.D. extended their power over neighboring clans in central Japan. Traditionally called the "Sons of Heaven," the Yamato line of emperors of Japan is unbroken to the present.

Japan's religious beliefs were centered on the simple worship of gods and goddesses, known as *kami,* who controlled the forces of nature. Called Shinto, or "Way of the Gods," this religion advocated neither a system of ethics nor an organized priesthood.

ANGKOR WAT, Cambodia's fantastic temple city, was built in the 1100s, lost, reclaimed by the jungle, and rediscovered late in the 20th century.

civilization
US

civilisation
Brit.

centered
US

centred
Brit.

honored
US

honoured
Brit.

theater
US

theatre
Brit.

colonized
US

colonised
Brit.

Chinese influences. Just as Korea had served as a land bridge for migrations to Japan, so it served as a cultural bridge from China. Strong Chinese cultural influences began to reach Japan during the Chinese Han dynasty, in the third century A.D. Soon the Japanese became avid cultural borrowers. Having no written language of their own, they adopted Chinese writing about 400. In 522 Buddhism reached Japan. The Yamato rulers embraced it and encouraged its spread among the Japanese, eventually declaring it Japan's official religion. Confucian ideas about family loyalty and obedience to political authority were also embraced.

In 607 scholars were sent to China to study its arts and institutions. Their reports eventually convinced the Yamato that they should remodel Japanese society along Chinese lines. The so-called Taika (meaning great change) reforms, which were instituted in 645 and 646, included patterning the government after centralized T'ang rule, with its absolute monarch and its bureaucracy chosen by civil service examinations. However, this method of naming government officials never quite took hold in Japan because the emperor was forced to give many government posts to hereditary nobles. Japanese art and architecture, especially in Buddhist temples, also imitated Chinese styles. Japan adopted China's use of paper money and its system of weights and measures.

The Heian period. In 794 Japan entered a new era: the Heian period, a name taken from the Japanese term for "peace and tranquility." During this period, which lasted until 1185, Japan ended its pattern of imitating Chinese civilization and concentrated on evolving a distinctive Japanese culture. During the tenth century, a phonetic alphabet developed, freeing the Japanese from an unwieldy system of ideograms borrowed from the Chinese.

The period was marked by a change in the role of the emperor. Imperial power failed and a new clan, the Fujiwara, took control of the central government, mainly by marrying into the Yamato clan. Yamato emperors remained on the throne, but they were largely ceremonial and political figureheads as Fujiwara regents wielded the real political power.

Heian culture was centered largely in the new city of Heian (Kyoto), to which the imperial court moved in 794. Japanese poetry was enriched by the publication of the *Manyoshu,* a collection of over 4,000 poems that celebrate love of nature and human emotions. The study of human emotions was also at the heart of *The Tale of Genji,* a long novel in which Lady Murasaki of the imperial court depicted life there.

Feudal Japan. By the twelfth century, Fujiwara political power was breaking down as the power of provincial lords was increasing. Following a period of warfare among clans over who was to replace the Fujiwara, the Minamoto clan emerged victorious. In 1185 Yoritomo Minamoto established a new capital at Kakamura on Tokyo Bay. He later declared himself *shogun,* or "great general," in effect, military dictator. The emperor's court remained at Kyoto, but political power now lay in the hands of the hereditary shogunate in its headquarters at Kamakura. Military dictators held power in Japan until 1867.

Under the Kamakura shogunate, Japan was organized into a highly militaristic feudal society. Below the shogun were the *daimyo,* local lords and great warriors who had carved out huge estates that they protected with the help of *samurai,* or warrior knights. The samurai swore their loyalty to their daimyo and followed a strict code of conduct called *bushido,* meaning "the way of the warrior." Violation of this code of chivalry brought great disgrace and demanded *harakiri,* or ritual suicide. Below the samurai were the peasants who worked the daimyo's land and the artisans. Below these were the merchants, who were not honored in Japanese society, but whose influence grew as their wealth did, a result of growing foreign trade with China, Korea, and Southeast Asia.

By the early 14th century, the Kamakura shogunate was losing its control over the increasingly independent daimyo. In 1333 an alliance of daimyo overthrew the Kamakura. Five years later, in 1338, the Ashikaga family claimed the shogunate and held onto it until 1573. But the Ashikaga never gained firm control over the daimyo, and they were not helped by a schism that erupted between rival houses of their family in 1467. This schism brought on civil war that continued on and off for the next century.

Even under these circumstances, agricultural production rose and prosperity brought population and urban growth. Buddhism, especially a new sect called Zen Buddhism, exerted a major influence on life and the arts. Highly stylized theater in the form of Nō and Kabuki plays emerged, as did the *haiku* form of poetry.

Southeast Asia: World Crossroads

Southeast Asia is a tropical area of peninsulas and archipelagos whose earliest peoples probably migrated from India, Tibet, and China. The peoples of the mainland, the Indochinese and Malay peninsulas, developed mainly as agrarian peasants. Those on Pacific islands such as Sumatra, Java, Borneo, and the Philippines gravitated more toward livelihoods made from the sea, in occupations such as fishing and trade.

Foreign influences. Southeast Asia was subjected to the strong cultural, political, and religious influences of its powerful neighbors, India and China. India exerted the earliest and most powerful influence, as Hindu traders and Buddhist missionaries colonized the area. Between the fourth and fifteenth centuries A.D., Hindu-Buddhist culture—its religious beliefs, Sanskrit writing, and styles of art—came to dominate both the mainland and the islands.

Chinese influences—language, Confucian government, and art—became predominant only in Vietnam, which it conquered during the Han dynasty and ruled until the Vietnamese won their independence in the 900s.

The Khmer Empire. During the eighth and ninth centuries, several successful Hindu and Buddhist kingdoms emerged in Southeast Asia, often fighting one another for dominance. Perhaps the greatest was the Khmer Empire, which reached its height in 1200, when its rule included all of central Indochina, down to the Malay peninsula.

Prosperous and powerful, the Khmer emperors are said to have ruled in unimaginable magnificence. Their most unforgettable legacy is the temple of Angkor Wat, which one archaeologist has described as "greater than anything left us by Greece and Rome." The largest religious complex in the world, it contains 72 major monuments and is surrounded by stone walls that stretch for miles. With the fall of the Khmer Empire in the 1400s, various states in Burma, Thailand, and Vietnam struggled for mainland dominance.

The coming of the Muslims. As early as the 13th century, Muslim traders had been putting in at ports in the Malayan, Indonesian, and even Philippine archipelagos. They were eager for the spices, tin, gold, and precious woods produced there. Proselytizing Islam was as successful there as it had been elsewhere in the world, and by the 1400s most of the Malay peninsula and Indonesian archipelago had become Muslim.

Cultures In Transition

c 1500–1900

During the last centuries of the Middle Ages, the foundations for great change in the relations of the world's civilizations were laid. Until that time, Asian civilizations, such as those of India and China, had often surpassed those of Europe in power, wealth, and cultural achievements. Indeed, at the same time India was enjoying the golden age of the Guptas and China the golden age of the T'ang, Europe was struggling through its Dark Ages.

In the period following the Middle Ages, though, world power shifted. Asian civilizations declined as European civilizations grew more dynamic, soon outpacing Asia in learning, technology, and drive for empire. Largely because of European expansion, the isolation of much of the world from Europe and Asia was about to end.

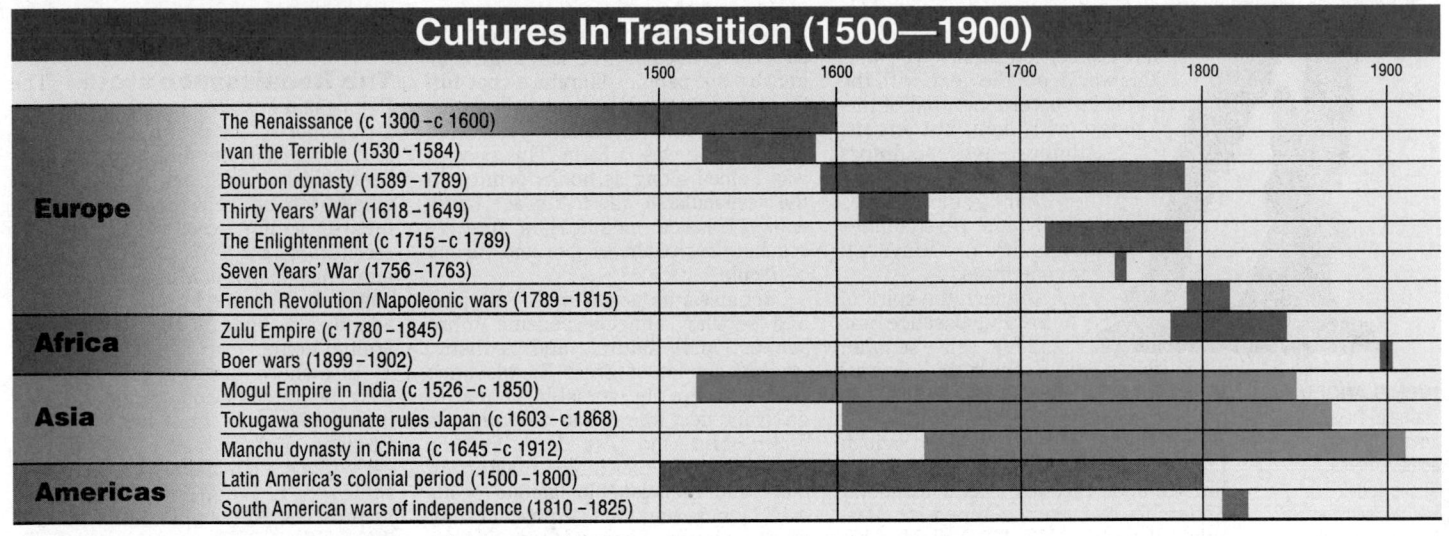

Cultures In Transition (1500—1900)							
		1500	1600	1700	1800	1900	
Europe	The Renaissance (c 1300 – c 1600)						
	Ivan the Terrible (1530 – 1584)						
	Bourbon dynasty (1589 – 1789)						
	Thirty Years' War (1618 – 1649)						
	The Enlightenment (c 1715 – c 1789)						
	Seven Years' War (1756 – 1763)						
	French Revolution / Napoleonic wars (1789 – 1815)						
Africa	Zulu Empire (c 1780 – 1845)						
	Boer wars (1899 – 1902)						
Asia	Mogul Empire in India (c 1526 – c 1850)						
	Tokugawa shogunate rules Japan (c 1603 – c 1868)						
	Manchu dynasty in China (c 1645 – c 1912)						
Americas	Latin America's colonial period (1500 – 1800)						
	South American wars of independence (1810 – 1825)						

Emerging Western Dominance

European dynamism following the Middle Ages grew largely out of a burst of individualism. During the medieval period, Europeans had been expected to subjugate themselves to the needs of the church and of the feudal manor. But as that period waned, many rebelled against medieval authority and began to seek more independence in religious thought, increased economic and political freedom, and greater general knowledge. Historians trace this ascendancy of individualism to the Renaissance.

The Renaissance

In the traditional sense, the term "Renaissance," which literally means rebirth, denotes the revival of classical learning and culture in Italy, mainly in the 1300s and 1400s, and its spread to other parts of Europe (the Northern Renaissance), mainly during the 1400s and 1500s.

The Renaissance was the first period in which men really considered themselves to be "modern"—that is, they believed their own age to be not only different from the preceding one but superior to it. The "Renaissance man" rejected the "barbarisms" and "corruptions" of the centuries since the decline of ancient Greece and Rome. He considered the medieval period decadent, thinking it a dismal, uncultured time separating the classical age from his own.

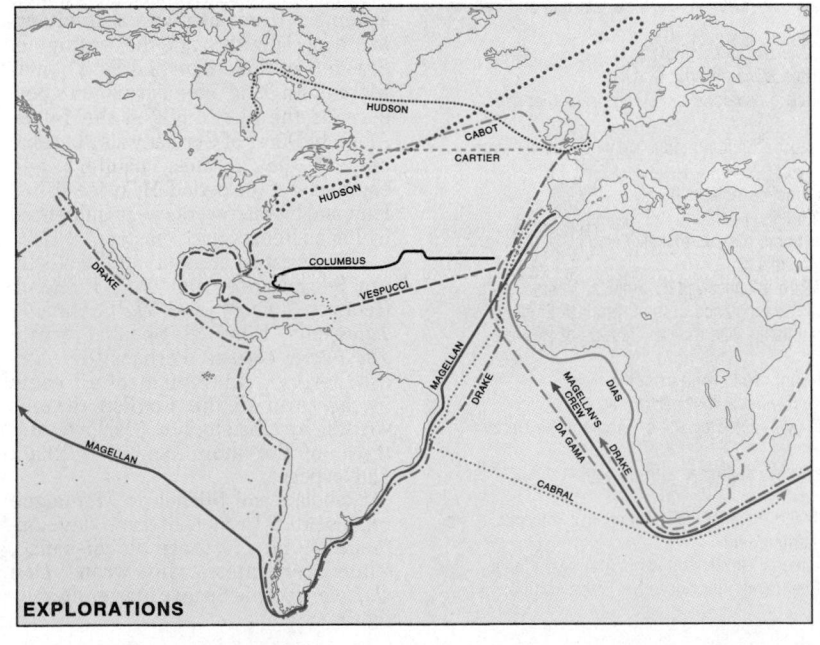

EXPLORATIONS

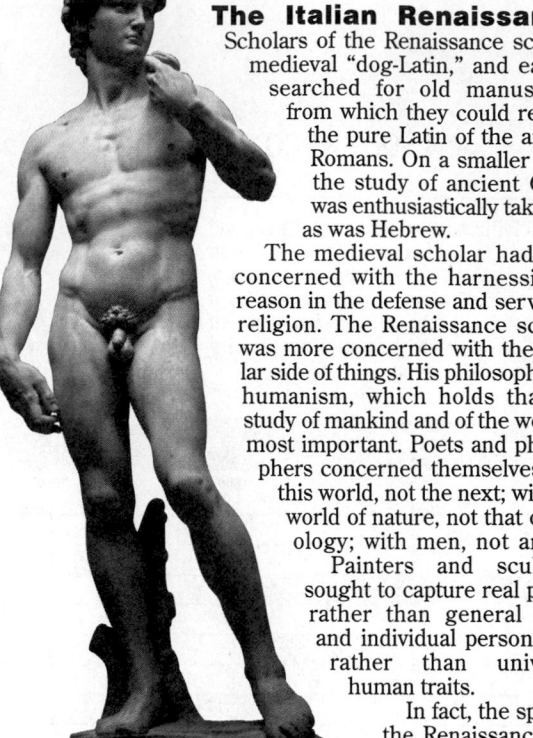

MICHELANGELO'S statue of David was among his greatest achievements. Michelangelo, as well as fellow artist Leonardo da Vinci, represented the ideal Renaissance man with his mastery of painting, sculpture, architecture, and inventiveness.

The Italian Renaissance.

Scholars of the Renaissance scorned medieval "dog-Latin," and eagerly searched for old manuscripts from which they could recover the pure Latin of the ancient Romans. On a smaller scale, the study of ancient Greek was enthusiastically taken up, as was Hebrew.

The medieval scholar had been concerned with the harnessing of reason in the defense and service of religion. The Renaissance scholar was more concerned with the secular side of things. His philosophy was humanism, which holds that the study of mankind and of the world is most important. Poets and philosophers concerned themselves with this world, not the next; with the world of nature, not that of theology; with men, not angels.

Painters and sculptors sought to capture real people rather than general types and individual personalities rather than universal human traits.

In fact, the spirit of the Renaissance was above all secular. Even the papal throne was usually occupied in this period by "Renaissance popes." Nicholas V (ruled 1447–1455) created the Vatican Library. Pius II (ruled 1458–1464) had himself been a leading classical scholar under his own name, Aeneas Silvius. Julius II (ruled 1503–1513) divided his time between making war (as ruler of the Papal States) and sponsoring enormous art projects by Michelangelo and other masters. Leo X (ruled 1513–1521) launched the ambitious rebuilding of St. Peter's Basilica in Rome.

The universities were also more secular. As centers of the "new learning," they not only concentrated heavily on secular subjects but also produced large numbers of educated laymen, not just clergy. Even the "universal man" (one who is adept at a variety of pursuits, from scholarship and poetry to the art of war), who was the Renaissance ideal, was concerned mainly with secular activities.

The Renaissance period in literature includes some of the greatest literary figures in history: Dante, who wrote *Divine Comedy;* Petrarch, famous for his sonnets and poems; and Boccaccio, author of *Decameron.*

One of the greatest Renaissance achievements was the development of a superb vernacular (the language spoken by the people) literature that furthered the development of native languages such as Italian. Until then most writing was in Latin. This change was helped along as books printed in the vernacular began to replace hand-copied classical manuscripts, thereby reaching a greater number and variety of people.

Renaissance art of both religious and secular subjects became more proportional, natural, and realistic. Among a host of great Renaissance painters were the versatile Leonardo da Vinci, best known for his paintings *Mona Lisa* and *The Last Supper;* Raphael, a remarkable master of color; and Michelangelo, famous for his fresco covering the entire ceiling of the Sistine Chapel in St. Peter's Basilica.

The Northern Renaissance.

The Northern Renaissance in Europe was conspicuous during the 1300s for its growing religious mysticism, which favored direct worship of God without an intervening priesthood. This was fostered early in Germany by the writings of Meister Eckhart and Thomas à Kempis. Humanism was also influential, especially through the writings of Erasmus of Rotterdam and Sir Thomas More of England. Flemish painters popularized the use of oils in the 1400s; Albrecht Dürer of Germany also became one of the greatest painters and engravers of the period. He twice visited Italy, and his later works were influenced by Italian Renaissance masters.

The greatest literature of the Northern Renaissance came from England. Geoffrey Chaucer wrote *The Canterbury Tales* and Edmund Spenser wrote *The Faerie Queene.* Perhaps the highest literary achievement of all came in the form of the English dramas written by Christopher Marlowe and those of the more famous William Shakespeare.

Rabelais and Michel de Montaigne represented French literary development in the Northern Renaissance, while Cervantes, who wrote *Don Quixote,* became Spain's master literary figure.

The introduction of printing.

The dissemination of this explosion of writing was amplified by the introduction of printing with movable type in Europe. In the mid-1400s, Johan Gutenberg, a goldsmith, began casting individual letters of the alphabet in metal so they could be fitted together to print one page and then easily rearranged to print another. It is estimated that before Gutenberg there were no more than 100,000 books, all laboriously hand copied, in Europe. By 1500, there were perhaps 9 million.

Although the vast majority of early printed books were theological works, including the Bible, Europe became a more literate society. The demand for knowledge increased greatly.

The Renaissance state.

The Renaissance state, in many ways a forerunner of the centralized, omnipotent modern state, developed rapidly, particularly in northern Italy's cities. Medieval republican city governments, which also ruled outlying territories, gave way to rule by an individual despot in Milan, by a wealthy oligarchy in Venice, by both in Florence, and by the pope in the Papal States around Rome.

Elsewhere, larger territorial states were being consolidated under strong monarchical rule, most importantly in England, France, and Spain. By the early 1500s, each of these countries had achieved, in rough form, its modern boundaries. Although each developed differently, royal power was markedly increased, and the centralized institutions characteristic of modern governments swiftly developed.

In England, strong government was established by the Tudor dynasty, especially by Elizabeth I (ruled 1558–1603). In France, centralization was slowed by almost constant foreign wars in the first half of the 1500s, and by civil wars in the second half. The Valois dynasty ended in 1589, and Henry IV (ruled 1589–1610) ushered in the Bourbon dynasty, which would rule France for the next 200 years.

In 1469 Spain was united under the strong rule of Ferdinand and Isabella. Maximilian I (ruled 1493–1519), the Holy Roman Emperor of the Hapsburg dynasty, inherited the Netherlands and Austria, and married his son into Spanish royalty. The resulting empire, greatest in Europe, split in 1556 between Austrian lands under Ferdinand I (ruled 1556–1564) and Spanish lands under Philip II (ruled 1556–1598). Philip brought the power of the Spanish crown to its highest peak.

The rivalry between the French crown and the Hapsburgs—especially the Spanish branch—continued until the Treaty of Pyrenees was signed in 1659, by which time French predominance in Europe had replaced Spanish. Meanwhile the Protestant Reformation had added religion to the issues states fought over.

Major Events — Renaissance

c 1300	The Renaissance, a revival of classical learning and culture in Italy, begins.
1321	Dante writes *The Divine Comedy.*
1353	Boccaccio writes *Decameron.*
1450	Johann Gutenberg develops a printing press that uses movable type.
1453	The Turks capture Constantinople; many Greek scholars escape to the west.
1506	Leonardo da Vinci completes the *Mona Lisa.*
1512	Michelangelo finishes painting the Sistine Chapel.
1517	Martin Luther posts the "95 theses," which sparks the Protestant Reformation.
1535	Sir Thomas More is beheaded by order of Henry VIII for refusing to swear allegiance to the Church of England.
1543	Copernicus publishes "On the Revolutions of Heavenly Bodies."
c 1559	Tobacco is brought to Europe from America.
1600	Shakespeare's *Hamlet* is first performed.
1609	The telescope is invented by Hans Lippershey, a Dutch scientist.
1620	The first weekly newspaper in Europe begins publication in Amsterdam.
1759	Voltaire publishes *Candide;* he is considered a leader of the European Enlightenment.
1765	Wolfgang Amadeus Mozart writes his first symphonies.
1808	Ludwig van Beethoven introduces his Fifth Symphony.

LUTHER'S posting of his "95 theses," or grievances, sparked the Reformation.

The Reformation

By the early 1500s the Catholic Church was facing serious problems, including a growing secularism in its hierarchy, ignorance among the lower clergy, and widespread abuses, such as simony (sale of church offices), pluralism (holding of more than one church office), and violation of vows of celibacy. Papal authority had been undermined, and many heresies since the 1200s, although suppressed, had left dangerous traditions.

Mysticism, especially popular in northern Europe, undermined the doctrine of "works," according to which sacraments, administered by a priest, were necessary to salvation.

Humanists pointed to errors of translation in the official Vulgate Bible. These errors destroyed the scriptural basis for some doctrines and opened the way for attack on others. In earlier periods of decline, the church had found the inner resources to reform itself; under the Renaissance papacy it did not.

Martin Luther. The matter was brought to a head by Martin Luther, a German monk and professor of theology. In 1517 Luther posted a list of grievances against the church, the "95 theses," on the cathedral door in Wittemberg, Germany. Ordered by Pope Leo X to rescind this challenge to church authority, Luther refused, saying, "On this I take my stand. I can do no other. God help me. Amen."

Luther's stand sparked the Protestant Reformation, giving rise to a number of Protestant denominations that split off from Roman Catholicism. The first of them was Lutheranism, which quickly gained followers in Germany. In Zurich, Switzerland, Ulrich Zwingli, a priest, led one splinter movement. In Geneva, French-born scholar John Calvin led another, preaching against church dogma, ritual, and pomp.

The Counter Reformation.

The Roman Catholic Church struggled to mount a Counter Reformation aimed at making internal reforms and stopping the spread of Protestantism, but initially it faltered. Many German princes adopted Protestantism, and they effectively prevented the Holy Roman Emperor Charles V (ruled 1519–1558) when he attempted to stamp it out. Lutheranism was recognized in the Holy Roman Empire by the Peace of Augsburg (1555) under the principle *cuius regio, eius religio* ("whose region, his religion"). The ruler's religion was to be the legal religion of each German state. As migration to another state was allowed, subjects were permitted to move to a state where the official religion was their own. Germany had two generations of religious peace; France and the Netherlands were torn with strife.

Bloody civil wars raged in France and the Netherlands, where Calvinism was particularly popular. In France, thousands of Calvinists, called Huguenots, were butchered in the St. Bartholomew's Day Massacre in 1572. Noble families were forced to choose between the Catholic League, part of the Catholic Counter Reformation effort, and the Huguenot armies. The matter was temporarily settled, with tolerance for the Protestant position, by the Edict of Nantes in 1598.

In the Netherlands, unpopular Spanish rule created a Protestant reformation that became as political as it was religious. The Protestant rebels, led by William of Orange, were eventually joined by the Catholics of the Low Countries in opposing Spanish rule. In 1581 the northern provinces, aided by the British, who were already at odds with Spain, separated from the southern provinces to form the Dutch United Provinces.

In 1588 Philip II of Spain, incensed at British intervention, sent the great Spanish fleet—the Invincible Armada—to conquer England and depose Queen Elizabeth I. His costly undertaking was a dismal failure, and when Henry IV took the throne in France, Catholic Spain lost its last ally in its attempt to reconquer the rebel Dutch United Provinces. To forestall defeat, Spain agreed to the Truce of Antwerp (1609–1621) and granted full independence of the Netherlands in the Peace of Westphalia (1648).

Thirty Years' War. In Germany the Catholic Counter Reformation had gained strength, and from 1608 to 1609 German princes formed rival military alliances, grouping themselves in the Protestant Union and the Catholic League. Religious and political hostility erupted into three decades of war (1618–1648), widely considered to be Europe's most destructive conflict. The four main phases of the Thirty Years' War began with revolt in Bohemia in 1618 and successive intervention by Denmark (1625–1629), Sweden (1630–1635), and France (1635–1648).

In 1635, five years after Sweden's king Gustavus Adolphus had joined the Protestant cause in the war, peace was reached. But Cardinal Richelieu of France, wishing to destroy Austrian and Spanish Hapsburg power, plotted to prolong the war. He allied France with Sweden, the Dutch princes, Savoy, and numerous German princes and was successful in weakening Hapsburg strength.

The war ended in Germany and the Netherlands in 1648 with the Peace of Westphalia, which gave France important territories on its German frontier and made the German states practically independent of the empire, and most vulnerable to French influence. Secularized church lands in Germany were returned to their 1624 holders, while Calvinists were tolerated. Spain recognized the independence of the United Provinces. The war between France and Spain, however, dragged on until 1659.

The Age of Discovery and Colonization

Europe's drive to explore and colonize overseas was as important as any other development given impetus by the Renaissance. By the end of the Middle Ages, Europeans had considerable knowledge of Asia, received from ancient writers, Crusaders in the Middle East, travellers to the Far East (of whom Marco Polo was only the most famous), and merchants involved in commerce that Venice and other cities had developed with Muslim ports in the eastern Mediterranean and the Black Sea. But they knew little of sub-Saharan Africa and were totally unaware of the existence of the Americas, Australia, and Antarctica.

centers	*US*
centres	*Brit.*
color	*US*
colour	*Brit.*
colonize	*US*
colonise	*Brit.*

TRADE FUELED THE FIRES of curiosity and courage that drove early explorers into unknown waters and lands. Many did not return.

The Great Explorers

c 1000	**Leif Ericson** of Norway reaches North America and calls the area Vinland.
1405-1434	**Cheng Ho** of China explores the coast of Vietnam, the Persian Gulf, the Red Sea, and East Africa.
1487-1488	**Bartholomeu Dias** of Portugal is the first European to round the Cape of Good Hope; he was originally part of the expedition that discovered Brazil.
1492	**Christopher Columbus**, an Italian sailing for Spain, lands in the Bahamas.
1497-1504	**Vasco da Gama** of Portugal is the first European to reach India by sea; **John Cabot** of Italy explores Newfoundland, Greenland, and the Chesapeake Bay for England; **Amerigo Vespucci** of Italy explores the eastern coasts of Central and South America.
1504-1520	**Hernán Cortés** explores the Yucatán and Mexican coasts and leads the Spanish conquest of Mexico.
1513	**Ponce de León** explores Florida and **Vasco Núñez de Balboa** crosses the Isthmus of Panama to the Pacific Ocean, both for Spain.
1519-1522	**Ferdinand Magellan's** ship *Victoria*, sponsored by Spain, is the first to circumnavigate the globe.
1531-1541	**Francisco Pizarro** of Spain explores the west coast of South America and conquers the Incas.
1534-1536	**Jacques Cartier** of France travels south on the St. Lawrence River as far as present-day Montreal.
1579	**Francis Drake** claims California for England.
1609-1611	**Henry Hudson** of England, sailing for the Dutch East India Company, explores the Chesapeake, Delaware, and New York bays.
1642	**Abel Tasman** of The Netherlands discovers Tasmania and New Zealand.
1768-1779	**James Cook** of England charts the coasts of New Zealand and the east coast of Australia; he also discovers the Hawaiian Islands.
1849-1873	**David Livingstone** of Scotland explores Africa's interior and discovers the Zambezi River and Victoria Falls.
1858	**John Hanning Speke** and **Richard Burton** of Britain are the first Europeans to visit Lake Tanganyika in Africa. Speke went on to find Lake Victoria as well.

Over the 200-year period from 1450 to 1650, all this would change. The desire of Europeans for trade goods available only from the Orient (such as spices for meat preservation, precious teak, and sandalwood from Southeast Asia, and silks, satins, and porcelain from the Far East) sent merchants in search of new and better trade routes. This search would lead to undreamed of consequences for both the Europeans and the peoples they encountered—the Aztecs and Incas of the Americas.

Portuguese leadership. Portugal, with its long Atlantic coastline on the Iberian peninsula, took the lead in searching for an all-water route to the Orient. The Portuguese hoped to reach the Indian Ocean by sailing south along the west coast of Africa, rounding its southern tip, and sailing north into the Indian Ocean. Prince Henry the Navigator sponsored a long series of voyages during the first half of the 15th century that advanced this route until first Bartholomeu Dias and then Vasco da Gama rounded Africa's southern cape. In 1498 da Gama reached Calicut in India and opened up Portuguese trade there.

A trading empire. Portugal began building a worldwide maritime trade empire that would monopolize African and Asian trade for the entire 16th century. The Portuguese had already set up trade with kingdoms of West Africa, such as Benin and Kongo, dealing largely in slaves. In East Africa, they conquered the Swahili city-states and established trading posts in Mozambique and Zanzibar. In 1510 they took control of Goa on India's west coast, and the next year captured Malacca, a center of trade on the Malay peninsula that had been held by the Muslims. From there they moved on to dominate the Moluccas, or Spice Islands, in the Indonesian archipelago, and to trade

with Ming China out of Macau and with feudal Japan.

By this time, Portugal had also gained a stake in the Americas. In 1500 a Portuguese fleet under the command of Pedro Cabral had been blown so far off course as it sailed down Africa's west coast that it crossed the Atlantic and reached Brazil. At first the Portuguese used Brazil only as a penal colony, but soon the Portuguese king was granting tracts of lands to colonists who turned them into thriving sugar plantations, using slave labor.

Spanish exploration and conquest. Spain, Portugal's neighbor, was not far behind in its explorations. Four years after Dias had first rounded the African cape, Christopher Columbus, an Italian sailing for Spain, set out to reach the East by sailing west across the Atlantic. In October of 1492 he reached the Americas, though he thought it was Asia.

The Spaniards concentrated on building their empire in the Americas, settling first in the West Indies. Hearing of kingdoms in Mexico, Central America, and South America that were rich in gold, *conquistadores* set out to conquer the native peoples and capture their wealth, which was then shared with the crown.

In 1519 Hernán Cortés launched his attack on the Aztec kingdom of Mexico. Within two years, he had destroyed the capital at Tenochtitlán, robbed the Aztecs of their gold and silver, and brought most of central Mexico under Spanish rule. Ten years later, Francisco Pizarro attacked the Inca Empire in South America. Taking advantage of the weakness caused by the division of the empire between two kings, by 1535 he had overrun the empire. In a period of only about 15 years, the two most powerful civilizations of the Americas had fallen to superior weapons and

Spanish domination.

Spain's American empire. Spain divided the vast American lands into five provinces and organized them under a central government ruled by the Council of the Indies from the Spanish capital at Madrid and by five viceroys, representatives of the king who each governed a province.

Spanish settlers arrived in America to exploit the rich silver mines of Mexico and Peru and to turn the Indian lands into giant plantations and ranches. For the Indians, life under foreign domination was a disaster. Diseases brought from Europe decimated their populations. Enslavement in Spanish mines and on Spanish plantations and ranches killed still more.

In the face of such a death toll and of Indian resistance to working for the Spanish, there was a severe labor shortage. Importation of slaves from Africa began in earnest, about 1510, and by 1650, nearly 200,000 Africans had been brought to Spanish colonies, particularly the Caribbean islands.

Dividing up the world. In 1494 Spain and Portugal signed the Treaty of Tordesillas, by which they agreed to a north-south line of demarcation running through the Azore Islands in the Atlantic Ocean. Newly discovered lands to the east of the line were put under the control of Portugal and to the west under Spain.

England, France, and the Netherlands quickly joined in the exploration and colonization of the world. As early as 1497, England sent the Italian sea captain John Cabot in search of a Northwest Passage to the Orient through North America. England laid claim to much of North America and colonized small islands in the West Indies. France and the Netherlands soon joined England in claiming land and colonizing in both places.

Across the seas in Asia, English commercial interests, which Queen Elizabeth I had chartered in 1600 as the British East India Company, struggled to establish trade with the Spice Islands. The company battled the Portuguese to win trading rights there and in India. India was also the scene of a lengthy rivalry between England and the French East India Company, established in 1664. With the British acquisition of the major ports of Bombay and Calcutta, England positioned itself for colonial predominance. The Dutch made gains in the Indonesian islands of Southeast Asia when they drove the Portuguese and the English out of the Spice Islands and won a monopoly over East Indian trade.

The commercial revolution. The revival of trade that began in medieval Europe was the first of the economic developments that constituted a full-scale revolution in the European economy. Urban commercial centers grew in size and number

center
US

centre
Brit.

labor
US

labour
Brit.

civilizations
US

civilisations
Brit.

colonized
US

colonised
Brit.

throughout Europe. Local and regional self-sufficiency was increasingly replaced by a geographical division of labor, in which regions concentrated on what they did best or what they seemed best suited for.

Long-distance commerce was stimulated by western Europe's penetration of overseas areas, which expanded the source of goods in demand and provided new markets, although both did not necessarily occur in the same area. The East, for example, had little desire for Europe's primitive exports, and demanded coined money in exchange for its spices, fine cloths, and other products.

Overseas shipping, banking, and commerce to handle increased trade volumes, stock companies to finance commercial ventures, and government protection of business and industry all increased dramatically. By 1750 small-scale medieval trading had developed into capitalism.

Absolutism in Europe

While the development of strong monarchical government progressed during the 1500s in Spain and England, and in states such as Sweden, it was interrupted in France by civil war. Yet France is the classic example of the development of absolute monarchy in the 1600s. The power of the Spanish crown declined with the power of Spain itself, and in England royal power lost ground to Parliament.

In France Cardinal Richelieu served as chief minister to Louis XIII (ruled 1610–1643) with zealous dedication. Strongly supported by Louis, he gave firm and effective rule to France, strengthening Louis' absolute royal control over a centralized government, which Richelieu helped to make dominant in Europe. Richelieu ruthlessly

SIR FRANCIS DRAKE, English explorer, court favorite, and privateer, claimed California for England.

checked the political power of the nobles and destroyed the military power of the Huguenots, though he allowed them religious tolerance to regain their loyalty. His aim was to weaken the Hapsburgs and thus make France the supreme power in Europe.

Spain's strength was exhausted by long wars. Hapsburg rule ended in 1700 and was replaced by Bourbon rule after the War of the Spanish Succession (1701–1714), which further weakened the empire.

France continued to be ruled by strong ministers after Richelieu. Cardinal Mazarin continued Richelieu's basic policies while putting down nobles' unrest caused by the curbs he imposed on the independence of the *parlements,* French courts that had the right to object to royal acts.

Louis XIV (ruled 1643–1715) established an imposing and powerful royal scene at his lavish palace at Versailles. Colbert, his minister of finance, tried to establish French economic self-sufficiency through a policy known as "mercantilism." According to this scheme, France was to export more than it imported, thus maintaining a favorable balance of trade. The surplus, paid for in gold, would enrich the national treasury. This program was only partly successful since other nations responded with anti-French mercantilist policies of their own.

The French economy was dangerously exhausted by Louis' constant wars. Louis spent many years trying to conquer the Dutch United Provinces, but he was always met by strong resistance from the European powers. The Netherlands, Sweden, and England formed a Triple Alliance against him in the 1660s, and the Austrian Hapsburgs, the German state of Brandenburg, Spain, and Denmark joined the alliance in the next decade.

Louis conquered the Rhine Palatinate in 1687, precipitating the War of the League of Augsburg (1688–1697). In 1700 he attempted to extend Bourbon control over Spain, precipitating the War of the Spanish Succession. These wars also failed because of staunch opposition from other European countries, which were determined never to allow the French and Spanish crowns to be united.

Eighteenth-Century Europe

By the end of the "Age of Louis XIV," Europe had changed. Bourbon Spain retained its American lands and was busy in foreign affairs, but remained a minor power. The Dutch United Provinces gave way to England as the dominant commercial state. Denmark's importance was past; Sweden's would soon fade. Poland would be divided among its neighbors.

The Holy Roman Empire continued

to exist as a political entity, but it had lost all importance. The Hapsburgs drew on their patrimonial lands for power and prestige, while a powerful rival, Brandenburg-Prussia, rose in northern Germany. Meanwhile, a strong Russian state was emerging. The major roles in European affairs were to be shared by France, England, Austria, Prussia, and Russia.

Rise of Prussia. The nucleus of the future kingdom of Prussia was the electorate of Brandenburg, ruled by the Hohenzollern family. Its strength grew steadily in the 1600s through inheritance and the acquisition of new territories during the long and successful reign of Frederick William, the "Great Elector" (ruled 1640–1688). This military state became even more powerful and better organized under the able Frederick William I (ruled 1713–1740).

Emergence of Russia. From the 800s, the political center of a loose grouping of Russian states was Kiev, on the Dnieper River. The Kievan state was destroyed by Mongol invaders in the 1200s, and the center of political development shifted to new settlements in the northern forests. These grew into feudal principalities, of which Muscovy, or Moscow, was the most important by the 1400s.

In this period Prince Ivan III (the "Great"; ruled 1462–1505) increased the territory and position of Moscow, reduced the threat of the Mongols to the south, and laid the foundations of modern Russia. Ivan considered himself the heir of the Byzantine Empire, now lost to the Ottoman Turks, and successor to the Byzantine and Roman emperors. He assumed the title of czar, or Caesar.

THE AGE OF ABSOLUTISM, during which the monarchs of Europe held virtually unrestricted power, was typified by the reign of Louis XIV of France. For his magnificent court and lavish support of the arts, Louis has been known as the Sun King.

THE INDUSTRIAL REVOLUTION caused profound changes in the workplace. Used to working on farms or in small shops, people increasingly were employed in large factories.

Successive czars strengthened their power within the increasingly centralized state, while extending its territory. Ivan IV ("the Terrible"; ruled 1533–1584) ruthlessly subdued the nobles, or boyars, created a centralized state administration, and expanded the empire east and west.

Following a century of relative stagnation and political turbulence, the westward advance was renewed by Peter I ("the Great"; ruled 1682–1725), who westernized many Russian institutions and cultural ideas.

His modernized, strong, centralized administration enabled Peter to seek "windows to the west." After two decades of war, Russia absorbed Sweden's Baltic lands, from Karelia to the Polish frontier, by the terms of the Treaty of Nystadt in 1721. In 1715

St. Petersburg became the new capital and Peter made advances into Turkish territories in search of a Black Sea outlet. Westernization continued during the reign of Elizabeth (1741–1762).

National rivalries. During the half century of 1733 to 1783, there occurred a series of wars fought neither in the name of religion nor against a predominant power. They were, rather, the result of colonial rivalries, territorial ambitions, and a desire to preserve a balance of power.

In the War of the Polish Succession (1733–1735), France, Spain, Italy, and Sardinia fought Poland and Russia over the election of a successor to Augustus II, king of Poland.

In the War of Austrian Succession (1740–1748), France, Spain, Saxony, and Bavaria attacked Prussia under Frederick the Great (ruled 1740–1786) to force the succession of Maria Theresa, the rightful heir to the Austrian Hapsburg throne. Britain, already at odds with Spain and France over their respective colonies in the New World, fought Spain in the War of Jenkins' Ear (1739–1748), then joined Prussia in the Seven Years' War (1756–1763), continuing the power struggle to prevent France from upsetting the European balance of power.

Britain took over most of France's colonial empire in Canada and India, and then withdrew from the continental conflict. Prussia's remarkable military machine continued to roll up victories as Frederick won Silesia. In 1772 he engineered the first of three partitions of Poland, whereby Austria, Prussia, and Russia acquired substantial Polish territory. In 1793 and 1795 Poland was split again among these powers and disappeared entirely. The Prussian Empire emerged massive and dominant on the continent. Both France and

Spain were weakened by their colonial struggles with Britain.

Prussia, newly consolidated and reformed by Frederick the Great, drew strength from the efficiency of its army and civil service. The Hapsburg domains, in east-central Europe, combined the agricultural riches of the great Hungarian Plain with the urbanity of Vienna and Prague. Even Russia, which was the most backward and the least developed of the great powers, grew stronger under its territorially ambitious sovereign, Catherine the Great (ruled 1762–1796).

The Enlightenment. The period of 1715 to 1789 in France was one of social and political decay and intellectual ferment. Absolutism had given France an effective government, but the system developed by Louis XIV required a vigorous and able monarch. Under his less capable successors, Louis XV (ruled 1715–1774) and Louis XVI (ruled 1774–1792), France lacked a dominant central force to unify the activities of ministers and councils. Government at all levels became a labyrinth of delay and resistance to change that stifled occasional attempts at reform.

Peasant resentment of aristocratic privilege and feudal dues, including enforced service, was perhaps exceeded by that of the bourgeoisie—merchants, bankers, and professional men—who by education and wealth had a claim to the political voice denied them. From this class came the *philosophes,* vigorous dissenters and critics of the Old Regime, as the prerevolution monarchy came to be called. Their ideas called for social and political revolution in France. Voltaire and Diderot were among the most influential of the *philosophes,* while the great Romanticist, Rousseau, supported many of their claims.

Revolution and National Unification in Europe

centralized
US

centralised
Brit.

The American Revolution, which ended in 1783, had a tremendous impact on Europe. The example of a people who had revolted against a monarchy, and had instituted a republican form of government, provided a boost for the political change already under way in Europe.

As the 18th century entered its final decades, Europe stood on the brink of a series of revolutions—political, social, and economic—that would shake it and much of the rest of the world. In the century to come, the changes wrought by these revolutions would forever alter the way Europe would be governed, how it would produce goods, and how the map of its political

boundaries would be drawn.

The French Revolution

In 1789 French peasant and bourgeois (middle class) resentment of aristocratic privilege finally boiled over into a revolution that tore down the Old Regime. With the defeat of the French aristocracy, the Third Estate, comprising the middle class of French society, rose to power. Other Europeans watched in horror as the ruling mobs, acting with confused and savage displays, seemed to confirm a belief in

the inability of the lower classes to exercise mature judgement in government.

The deputies of the Third Estate had formed a National Assembly and swept away the old order. But the deputies split into factions, eventually contributing to making the French Revolution a European problem.

The Girondists, the party of moderate, well-to-do burghers, in an attempt to rally the country to them and to gain ascendancy over their more radical colleagues, the Jacobins, decided on war against the European powers they believed to have been conspiring against the revolution.

Revolutionary wars and Napoleonic wars.

On April 20, 1792, the French Revolution was internationalized when France declared war on Austria. By summer, the war had expanded to include Prussia and Sardinia. By 1793 Britain, the Dutch republic, and Spain were involved. It was a war that, with only brief interludes of peace, was to last until 1815—the year of the final defeat of Napoleon Bonaparte at Waterloo.

Napoleon rose to power in France in 1799 as a champion of the revolution, but by 1804 he had proclaimed himself emperor and proceeded to expand his empire by military might. Napoleon's mighty attempt to unify all of Europe under his rule was stalled by the arousal in Germany, Russia, and elsewhere of a national consciousness that refused incorporation into a foreign-ruled empire. Napoleon's dream finally fell apart when he failed to conquer Russia. His army returned home, crippled and disoriented.

Congress of Vienna.

It is incredible that those who had witnessed the power of unleashed nationalism and the struggle between conservative aristocracy and liberal democracy could, once the fighting with France was over, feel that nothing had changed. Nevertheless, at the Congress of Vienna (1814–1815), which ended the period of the revolutionary and Napoleonic wars, this was the prevalent feeling.

The participants, led by the representatives of the Big Five—Austria, Britain, France, Prussia, and Russia—

that would supposedly permit freedom, security, and prosperity for all. France was "buffered" by the creation of the Kingdom of the Netherlands. Austria, which lost territory to the Netherlands, gained Lombardy and Venetia in Italy and was permitted to preside over a newly organized loose confederation of 39 German states. This last concession had been insisted on by Austria's genius statesman, Metternich, who feared a strong, united Germany.

The balance of power was maintained by shuffling territories and alliances so that no one state could dominate the others. The success of the Congress of Vienna is evidenced by the fact that no major European war was fought from 1815 to 1854, a record period of peace for the time.

Industrial Revolution

The Industrial Revolution grew from very humble beginnings in Britain, where its first impact was felt in the area of cotton textile manufacture.

During the 1770s and 1780s a burst of inventive genius revolutionized the textile industry. From hand operations on simple machines, such as spinning a single thread or weaving only one bolt of cloth at a time, the industry progressed to multiple spindles and complicated looms.

As the machines grew larger and more complicated, they could no longer

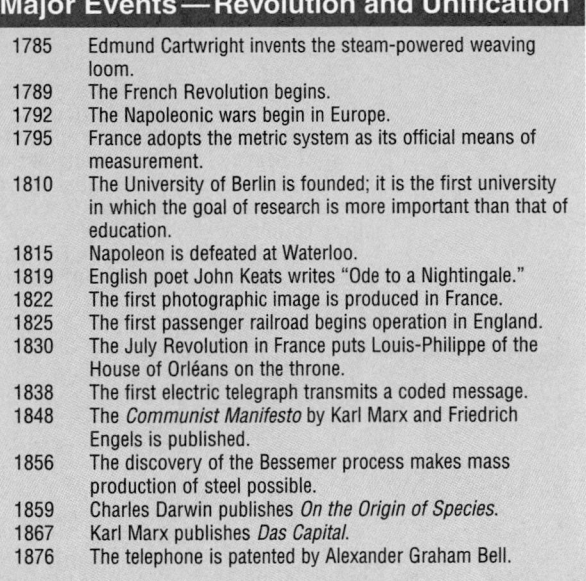

Major Events—Revolution and Unification

1785	Edmund Cartwright invents the steam-powered weaving loom.
1789	The French Revolution begins.
1792	The Napoleonic wars begin in Europe.
1795	France adopts the metric system as its official means of measurement.
1810	The University of Berlin is founded; it is the first university in which the goal of research is more important than that of education.
1815	Napoleon is defeated at Waterloo.
1819	English poet John Keats writes "Ode to a Nightingale."
1822	The first photographic image is produced in France.
1825	The first passenger railroad begins operation in England.
1830	The July Revolution in France puts Louis-Philippe of the House of Orléans on the throne.
1838	The first electric telegraph transmits a coded message.
1848	The *Communist Manifesto* by Karl Marx and Friedrich Engels is published.
1856	The discovery of the Bessemer process makes mass production of steel possible.
1859	Charles Darwin publishes *On the Origin of Species*.
1867	Karl Marx publishes *Das Capital*.
1876	The telephone is patented by Alexander Graham Bell.

portation, the only economical method of transport before the railroad, gained new importance. When rail transportation was brought to those areas, they became centers of industrial activity and prosperity.

Social effects.

The many social effects of the Industrial Revolution were as important as the material effects. It was through industrialization that western Europe was transformed from a rural to an urban civilization. Factories drew formerly rural peoples together to one spot for the purpose of production of manufactured goods. Men, women, and children worked long hours for a salary, and labor abuses became prevalent. These abuses, including child labor, unsafe conditions, overwork, and underpayment, led to the growth of socialism.

Cities sprang up everywhere and grew in size by leaps and bounds. Urbanization increased political awareness and activity among the masses, who, as rural peasants, had been traditionally isolated and disunited. The new industrial classes in Britain and France began gradually to undermine the power of the landed aristocracy. This was particularly true in Great Britain, the supreme industrial power of the world, where human labor became an important and valuable resource.

France industrialized much more slowly, and in Prussia, Austria, Russia, and most of the other nations of Europe, the time for industrialization had not yet come. Most nations feared the emergence of a proletarian, or working, class that might clamor for equal rights, and of subversive democracies resembling those of the tumultuous French Revolution. Moreover, the world economy was not ready for industrialization until the latter part of the 18th century.

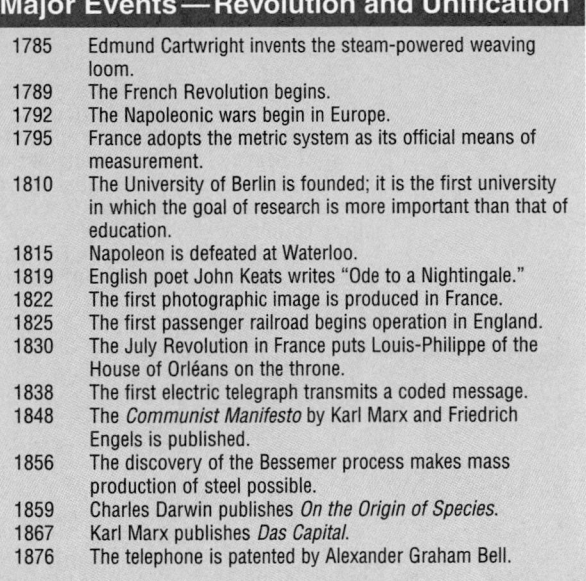

EUROPE IN 1815

— Border of the Germanic Confederation

GERMAN STATES
1. Prussia
2. Mecklenburg
3. Holstein
4. Hanover
5. Oldenburg
6. Hesse
7. Luxemburg
8. Palatinate
9. Saxony
10. Bavaria
11. Wurtemberg
12. Baden

ITALIAN STATES
13. Lombardy–Venetia
14. Sardinia
15. Parma
16. Modena
17. Tuscany
18. Papal States
19. The Two Sicilies

centers
US

centres
Brit.

civilization
US

civilisation
Brit.

labor
US

labour
Brit.

21 History of the World

all remembered the days of the Old Regime and were determined to return to them.

Except for the genius of the French diplomat Talleyrand, who argued convincingly for a return to the previous balance of power in Europe, France would have been destroyed by partitioning among the victors.

The congress finally recreated a Europe with a proper balance of power

be run by human power. Instead they were run by waterpower. Ultimately, even waterpower became insufficient. The development of the steam engine by the end of the 1700s had provided a solution to the power problem by the 1800s. Its application in the steam locomotive was to revolutionize transportation.

Areas rich in natural resources but without easy access to water trans-

Liberalism and Nationalism

With the defeat of Napoleon and the conclusion of the Vienna settlement in 1815, Europe settled down to enjoy the calm of peace. Although each nation reacted differently to the absence of war, the essential dynamic forces in every country were the same.

Despite its relative success, the Congress of Vienna totally ignored the vital

QUEEN VICTORIA'S assumption of the title of empress of India in 1876, depicted here being proclaimed in Delhi, expressed the importance of India to the British Empire.

vigor
US

vigour
Brit.

issues of nationalism and liberalism. It was this shortsightedness that eventually destroyed the peace effected for some years by the settlement.

The liberal aspirations that had been created during the revolutionary era could not be eradicated by a stroke of the pen. As the groups to which liberalism appealed grew stronger, their challenge to the constituted governments became sharper, until they later exploded into revolution.

Similarly, the nationalism that had been aroused by French occupation could not be turned off with the departure of the French. This was particularly true in Italy and Poland, where the withdrawal of the French was followed by occupation by the Austrians and the Russians.

In the period 1815 to 1848, it was the challenge of liberalism that tended to provide the greatest impetus to change. After 1848 the situation became more complicated. In some countries, notably Great Britain and Italy, liberalism retained its vigor. In other countries, such as France, its suppression led to the rise of socialism. In Austria and Germany, liberalism was submerged in a wave of nationalism.

Great Britain. In Great Britain the new class of industrial workers demanded representation in Parliament. The

situation came to a crisis following passage of the Corn Laws, which worked to the advantage of the landed aristocracy and led to more misery for the industrial class. In 1819 riots broke out and several people were killed by government troops in the Peterloo Massacre.

In the following years, though, Parliament was finally brought around to reform. The Reform Bill of 1832 gave the industrial class much greater representation in Parliament, and by 1884 the urban workers had finally been enfranchised.

France. In France, the industrial class was small and weak, but tension grew when the Bourbons were restored to the monarchy by the Congress of Vienna in 1815. Both peasants and bourgeoisie were angered by the return to power of the monarch and the aristocrats. When Charles X (ruled 1824–1830) sought to restore the prerevolutionary power of church and state by revoking the liberal rights granted by France's 1814 constitution, revolution broke out again. The July Revolution of 1830 only succeeded in turning the monarchy over to Louis Philippe of the House of Orléans; however, yet another revolution, in 1848, led to the establishment of the Second Republic.

The benefits of the new government of 1848 went to the bourgeoisie rather than to the industrial workers, who still lacked unity and influence. The working class, whose demands derived from the socialist Louis Blanc, was put down with brutal force during the June Days slaughter. This marked the origin of socialism as an active and potent force in French politics.

In 1852 Louis Napoleon, the nephew of Napoleon Bonaparte, who had been elected president in 1848, led a coup d'état and declared himself Emperor Napoleon III of the Second Empire. The empire worked hard to establish an industrial base, but it suffered diplomatic catastrophes, was decisively defeated in the 1870 Franco-Prussian War, and was generally unpopular and weak.

Austria. The rise of nationalism in Germany posed a constant threat to Metternich of Austria, who was trying to maintain Austrian rule over a weak and loosely organized German Confederation. The Hungarians, Italians, and Poles ruled by the Austrian Empire also seethed with discontent as nationalistic fervor rose to oppose foreign rule, especially that of Metternich's oppressive brand.

Metternich responded with determination. To keep the empire intact, he created a virtual police state and held back the growth of industrialism for fear that it would breed revolutionary discontent among the urban factory workers.

1848 uprisings. News of the French revolt of 1848 electrified all of Europe, and revolutions broke out everywhere.

The Hungarians seized the opportunity to break away from Vienna; the Romans overthrew papal power; the Italians in northern Italy felt their day of liberation had come; revolution even broke out in Vienna.

The Metternich system appeared to be in ruins. Yet it survived because the Austrian government called for aid from the Russian czar. The Hungarian revolution was crushed by him, the Vienna revolutionaries were successfully intimidated, and the Austrian army was left free to punish insurgents in other parts of the empire.

The Austrian Empire remained in a state of precarious equilibrium for the rest of its existence. Although it made concessions to national spirit, it never made enough to prevent nationalistic opposition.

In Prussia, a state without a middle or industrial class, the powerful military machine was operated by king and nobles working together. Following the French Revolution, the state embarked on a liberal course, allowing the abolition of serfdom and granting various concessions to the free peasantry. The result was a liberal Prussian state that elicited fierce patriotism, national pride, and loyalty from all classes of people.

National unification. A major aspect of European development in the mid-1800s was the forging of two new national states in major geographical-cultural regions—modern Germany and Italy.

An industrial middle class began to emerge in Germany in the 1840s, and it was powerfully affected by the French revolution of 1848. At the Frankfurt Assembly, representatives from the numerous German states called for popular representation in a unified Germany—but Prussian assistance, which was needed to break Austria's control, was not forthcoming.

Otto von Bismarck became the prime minister of Prussia in 1862. He began to build a liberalized state to enlist the support of the growing working and industrial classes. A constitution and progressive social legislation followed. In 1866 he forced Austria out of German affairs, and in 1870 he rallied the southern German states in the Franco-Prussian War against the French, who were beaten. Germany was at last united under Prussian influence.

In Italy, Count Cavour, prime minister of Sardinia, forged the unification of much of Italy, using liberalism as a tool for popular support in much the same way that Bismarck had done. In inciting Austria, which controlled large portions of Italy, to war in 1859, Cavour was aided by Napoleon III of France. Austria was soundly defeated, and the national patriot Giuseppe Garibaldi then succeeded in forcing Sicily and southern Italy into the new union. The new nation of Italy was proclaimed in 1861, with Victor Emmanuel of Sardinia its new king.

European Imperialism

The exploration and colonization begun by Europeans around 1500, followed by industrialization in the late 1700s, brought the far-flung parts of the world into contact as never before. The fate of the peoples of all continents would grow ever more intertwined.

Transition in Asia

Their earliest forays into Asia had left Europeans in awe of the wealth and power they found in the courts and cities of Asia's oldest civilizations. Asians were not similarly impressed with the restless and upstart Europeans they encountered, and Asian rulers, convinced of their own civilizations' superiority, did not recognize and were therefore not prepared for the global revolution under way.

India—from Moguls to the Raj.
Of Asia's major civilizations, India was the first to be profoundly affected by contact with European culture. At the beginning of the 16th century, the Muslim Delhi Sultanate was crumbling and the Hindu Rajput princes were fighting among themselves to gain control.

The Mogul Empire. This upheaval invited the Mongol attack, led by Tamerlane's descendant Babur the Tiger. Leading a small force, he succeeded in capturing Delhi in 1526 and subjugating the Rajput princes. His victory marked the beginning of India's glittering Mogul Empire. (*Mogul* is the Persian word for "Mongol.") Within 200 years, the empire covered nearly the entire Indian subcontinent.

The Mogul Empire flowered under the rule of Akbar, from 1542 to 1605. Though a Muslim himself, he worked to end Muslim discrimination against Hindus, repealing a hated Hindu-only tax and marrying a Hindu princess to try to ensure that his successors would blend Muslim and Hindu culture. Unfortunately, they did not; instead, they reinstated oppressive measures against the Hindus.

The Moguls encouraged India's artists, both Hindu and Muslim, to surpass themselves in creativity. Perhaps the greatest fruit of their artistic success is the Taj Mahal in Agra, a magnificent pink marble structure built by Mogul emperor Shah Jahan (ruled 1628–1658) as a tomb for his young wife.

The Mogul Empire reached its height of power under the rule of Aurangzeb (ruled 1658–1707), the son of Shah Jahan. Over a 50-year period, however, his ceaseless wars to bring all of the Indian subcontinent under Muslim rule weakened the Moguls and encouraged other Indian states to challenge their reign.

Among these challengers were the Marathas of the western Deccan Plateau. They saw themselves as the defenders of Hinduism against the anti-Hindu rule of the Muslim Moguls. Other challengers were the Sikhs of northern India, a sect with a strong military tradition, and the former governors of the Mogul Empire, who had carved out their own independent states.

Into this political disorder came marauding Persians, who sacked the Mogul capital at Delhi in 1739, then followed 18 years later by raiders from Afghanistan. Mogul monarchs retained the title of emperor for another century, but their realm shrank to the area surrounding Delhi, and their former empire disintegrated into hundreds of small states.

British inroads. The British East India Company, which had prospered under the Moguls, took advantage of this political unrest to strengthen its position in India. In 1757, at the Battle of Plassey, British military forces under Robert Clive defeated the ruler of Bengal, an important center of trade in northeastern India. In 1765 the East India Company forced the weak Mogul emperor to give it the right to collect all taxes in Bengal; within 20 years, the company ruled Bengal.

In 1784, the British government passed the India Act, which gave the British Parliament the right to share the power over East India Company policy in India and to name high company officials. For the next half century, the British continued to expand their control in India, incorporating large parts of it into British India, administered from London, and other parts into Indian India, ruled by local princes under British supervision.

Many Hindu and Muslim princes objected to British domination, so when in 1857 the Sepoys, Indian soldiers serving under the British, rebelled, the Indian princes supported them, in what is known as the Sepoy, or Indian, Mutiny. British troops put down the bloody revolt, but the uprising convinced Parliament to revoke the British East India Company's charter and take control of India itself. In 1858 the British Raj (from the Hindu for rule) was inaugurated as Parliament exiled the last Mogul emperor and put India under full colonial rule. In 1877 Queen Victoria of Great Britain was crowned empress of India.

Under the Crown-appointed viceroy, Great Britain continued the economic exploitation begun under the East India Company. Indian farmers were encouraged to grow cotton rather than food to supply cotton mills in England. Indian manufacture was discouraged to create a market for British manufactures in India.

To facilitate trade, Great Britain directed the construction of a vast railroad system to link the sprawling subcontinent, as well as a telegraph network. British schools were set up to educate the sons of the higher castes in English, which had become the administrative language of India. Additional courses, studied by British students, were taught to foster an Indian professional class to assist the British in carrying out colonial rule.

Ironically, British education for young Indians helped launch a movement to rid India of British rule. Learning about the struggles of the English for democracy stirred educated Indians' desire for political freedom for themselves. In 1885 Hindu nationalists founded the Indian National Congress. At first, it worked only for reforms in British rule (for example, more political power for Indians on the local level), but by the early 1900s it became a force for advocating the total expulsion of the British from India.

China—from Ming to Manchu.
By the mid-1500s, China's Ming dynasty was in decline. The population doubled between 1400 and 1600, from 75 million to 150 million. Slowing levels of production could not supply it. But, China was strong enough to resist European domination. The Mings had expelled the Portuguese, first European traders to reach China; by 1557 the Portuguese were restricted to the trading center of Macao. In the 1600s, other European traders were limited to the port city of Canton, where they were forced to comply with severe trade restrictions passed by the Chinese.

civilizations
US

civilisations
Brit.

center
US

centre
Brit.

History of the World

21

Major Events—European Imperialism	
1498	Portuguese explorer Vasco da Gama reaches India by travelling around the Cape of Good Hope.
1637	The Japanese government closes off contact with the Western world.
1644	Nurhachi, a Manchu emperor, begins to rule China.
1656	The Taj Mahal is created in Agra, India.
c 1780	The British East India Company takes over Bengal.
1784	The British government passes the India Act, giving Parliament the right to share the power of East India Company policy in India.
1796	The White Lotus Rebellion breaks out in China.
1839	The Opium War between the British and the Chinese begins.
1854	The Treaty of Kanagawa opens two Japanese ports to U.S. ships.
1858	British Parliament places India under full colonial rule.
1868	The Meiji Restoration returns power to the Japanese emperors, ushering in an era of widespread changes in Japanese foreign policy and government.
1871	Feudalism is abolished in Japan.
1885	Hindu nationalists create the Indian National Congress.
1899	The open-door policy begins in China.
1905	The Treaty of Portsmouth ends the Russo-Japanese War and establishes Japan as the dominant Far Eastern power.

The Mings' internal troubles were compounded in the 1590s by war with Japan over Korea, which weakened the empire. In the early 1600s, new enemies appeared to endanger Ming rule—people from Manchuria who called themselves Manchus. In April 1644, as Manchu armies threatened the Ming capital at Beijing (Peking), the last Ming emperor hanged himself. The following October, the Manchus declared that the Mandate of Heaven had passed to them, and a Manchu emperor took the Chinese throne. Once again the Chinese underwent foreign rule as the Manchus proclaimed themselves the Ch'ing dynasty and made Beijing their capital.

Manchu rule.   The Manchus comprised only about 2 percent of the population of China, so to rule in China, they had to have Chinese cooperation. To get it, the Ch'ing dynasty retained the Ming form of government, including the civil service examinations to select government officials. The Chinese held an overwhelming number of the 40,000 high-level government positions. The Manchus held onto key posts in the central government and in the military.

The Manchu dynasty produced two great emperors whose long rules would span about half of the dynasty's nearly 300-year rule. The first was K'ang-hsi, a brilliant military strategist and able administrator who ruled from 1661 to 1722. Under him, the Manchus not only completed the conquest of China, but also brought Mongolia under Chinese control. An avid sponsor of scholarly projects, he encouraged the teaching of Western mathematics and astronomy and supported the writing of the *History of the Ming* and the compilation of the *Complete Poems of the T'ang Dynasty.* Because he filled the role of the ideal Confucian monarch so well, he succeeded in winning over the majority of the Chinese population to Manchu rule.

In 1736, 14 years after K'ang-hsi's death, his grandson, Ch'ien-lung, began his 60-year rule and Chinese expansion continued, as Tibet and Burma were brought under Chinese control. By 1800

China covered the largest area in its long history and had a population estimated at 300 million, double its population only 200 years before.

This population explosion placed great pressure on the peasantry, whose need for land grew with their numbers. In 1796 unhappy peasants supported a revolution against Manchu domination mounted by the Buddhist White Lotus Sect. For the rest of the century, the Manchus fought to put down the White Lotus Rebellion. They finally succeeded but grew weaker in the process, setting the stage for more uprisings and for threats from trade-hungry Westerners.

Western imperialism.   Western traders were growing ever more restive and resentful of trade restrictions the Chinese had placed on them. In 1793 a British request to open more Chinese ports had been flatly rebuffed.

In the last half of the 18th century, British traders had begun to use opium produced in India to pay for the tons of Chinese tea to which their countrymen had become accustomed. The Manchu rulers became concerned about the serious addiction to opium that had infiltrated all strata of Chinese society. In 1800 the imperial government forbade the foreign traders to bring any more opium into China.

For years traders ignored the ban on opium importation, so in 1838, the Ch'ing dynasty prescribed the death penalty for opium dealing, and in 1839 it captured and burned all the chests of British-owned opium it found in Guangzhou (Canton). Britain retaliated by sending its warships to fire on Guangzhou. The Opium War had begun. For the next three years, superior British forces humiliated the Chinese. In 1842 the Ch'ing rulers were forced to pay the British an indemnity, to cede Hong Kong to British control, and to open several ports to British trade.

But when the Chinese resisted implementing this first of a series of "unequal agreements," the Opium War roared to life again as France joined

Britain in attacking China in 1856. A second Chinese defeat led to the Treaty of Tientsin in 1858. The treaty forced China to open many new ports to Westerners, including Americans and Russians, and allowed these foreigners to live and travel in China while gaining political and economic power. Eastern and Western cultures had come into conflict, militarily and economically, and Western culture had won.

National disintegration.   During this same period, internal dissension was wracking China. From 1850 to 1864, the Taiping Rebellion, a major uprising mainly of peasants, spread throughout China and took the lives of 20 to 40 million people. It so weakened the Ch'ing dynasty that it fell prey to still more foreign inroads—from both West and East.

Western powers forced China to cede pieces of territory and spheres of influence: the area north of the Amur River along the northern border of Manchuria; ports on the Pacific; rights in Manchuria to Russia; Burma to Britain; Indochina to France; Macao to Portugal; and mining rights in Shandong Province to Germany. From 1894 to 1895, during the Sino-Japanese War, Japan, China's neighbor across the East China Sea and erstwhile cultural student, fought China for control of Korea. Japan forced the crumbling Ch'ing dynasty to pay a large indemnity and to cede it vast areas, including the island of Taiwan.

In 1899 the United States, having no sphere of influence of its own in China, convinced other powers to accept the Open Door Policy, which granted equal trading privileges to all powers in China.

Angered at all these incursions, Chinese secret societies united. The Righteous Harmony Fists sought to drive all "foreign devils" out of China. In 1900 it staged the Boxer Rebellion and attacked the foreign quarter of Beijing. An army of 18,000 foreign soldiers defeated the Boxers, and once again China had to pay reparations and grant concessions.

The Ch'ing dynasty, under the old Empress Dowager Tzu-hsi, who would

ISOLATIONIST JAPAN successfully maintained its distance from the West from soon after the first Portuguese contact (below) until the arrival of Commodore Perry's gunboat (right).

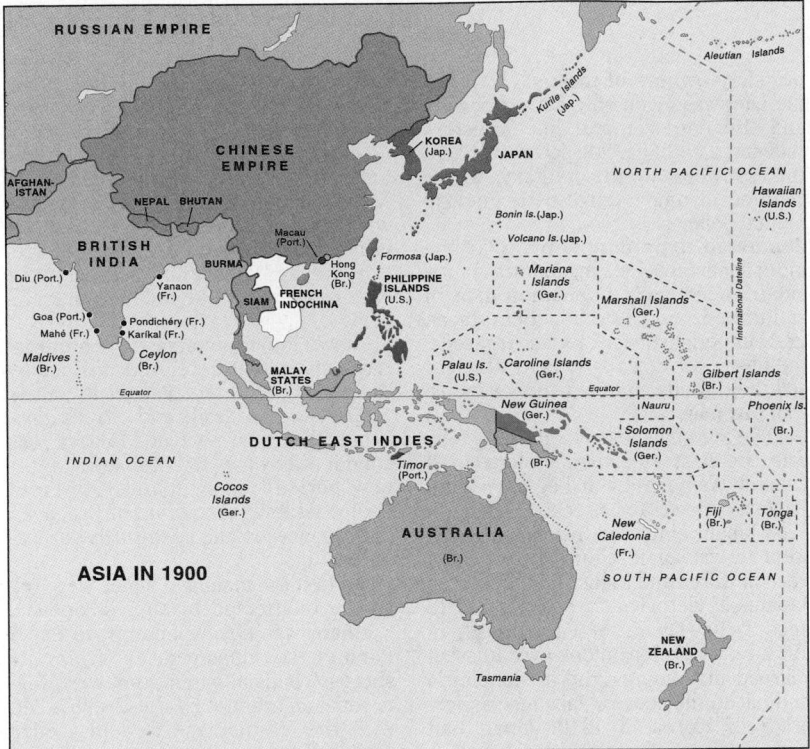

ASIA IN 1900

die in 1908, was nearing its end. An uprising in 1912 would sweep the last Manchu emperor from the Chinese throne.

Japan—feudalism to imperialism.

During the late 16th and early 17th centuries, Japan underwent its "warring states period." The shogunate's power had shrunk to nothing at the imperial capital at Kyoto. The power to govern lay in the hands of the provincial daimyo, whose wars against one another fragmented Japan as never before.

Reunification. Beginning in 1568, three military leaders, who would reunite Japan, emerged. The first was Oda Nobunaga, the son of a daimyo and a warrior of the Taira clan. After expanding his father's holdings and becoming master of three provinces, he was able to make the shogun his puppet and become dictator of central Japan.

On his death in 1582, his lieutenant Toyotomi Hideyoshi, a peasant soldier who had risen to the rank of general, continued the drive to unify Japan when he succeeded as dictator. By 1590 military conquest had made him ruler of a united Japan. It was he who led Japan to war against China in 1592 over Korea, weakening the Ming dynasty there and supplying a foretaste of later Japanese expansionism.

In 1600, two years after Hideyoshi's death, his ally Tokugawa Ieyusu completed the work of Japanese unification by taking command of the new national government and having himself declared shogun.

The Tokugawa shogunate. From its founding in 1603, the Tokugawa shogunate would rule Japan for 250 years, a period sometimes called the Pax Tokugawa. The emperor continued

to act as a figurehead, a national symbol, from his imperial court at Kyoto. The Tokugawa shoguns governed from their capital at Edo, today's Tokyo.

The Tokugawa governed in two ways. They ruled directly the one-quarter of Japan they owned, and they ruled the rest through the nearly 300 daimyo who held individual feudal estates. The shoguns' extensive military power and ingenious checks on power kept the daimyo in line and ensured the peace. One check involved "alternate attendance," a system that demanded each daimyo to spend every other year at Edo. This regulation had the dual effect of keeping the daimyo under the shogun's close observation and of causing the daimyo to spend his money to support two residences rather than to build up military power.

Once peace was established among the daimyo, their samurai evolved from rugged warriors into an educated elite who administered their daimyo's estates and acted as local government officials. The samurai became Japan's learned professional class.

Western impact. Japan had its first experience with Europeans when Portuguese merchant ships arrived there in 1542. Christian missionaries and more traders from Portugal and Spain arrived soon after. At first the Japanese were tolerant of them, allowing the missionaries to preach and make conversions, an estimated 150,000 of them by 1600. The Japanese also learned about and traded for European firearms, such as muskets, which they used in their battles for reunification. In 1600 Dutch and English merchants began to arrive in Japan, introducing intrigues to help them beat their European competitors.

The Tokugawa soon grew wary of the influence the foreigners were hav-

ing on Japan, and, following an uprising of Christian daimyo in 1637, the government closed off all contact with the Western world. It expelled all foreigners—missionaries and traders—and allowed only one Dutch trading post to remain, at Nagasaki. The government forbade all Japanese to leave the country. Christianity was bloodily stamped out wherever it had taken root.

For the next 200 years, Japan enjoyed peace and prosperity as internal trade thrived, the merchant class grew, and commercial centers evolved into great cities. But then the West, once again, began to threaten in the same imperialist fever that had propelled it into India and China.

In 1853 the United States sent a naval mission, under Commodore Matthew C. Perry, to Japan to demand that the Japanese open their country to trade. As United States Navy guns pointed at them from Edo (now Tokyo) Bay, the Japanese were well aware of the fate the Chinese had suffered at the point of British guns in the Opium War. In 1854 they reluctantly signed the Treaty of Kanagawa agreeing to American demands. Within a period of two years, Japan had signed similar treaties with Great Britain, France, Russia, and the Netherlands.

The Tokugawa shogunate's capitulation to the West stirred up fierce opposition to its continued rule in Japan. Opponents rallied around the emperor and the court at Kyoto, demanding that the emperor be returned to power and that Tokugawa military rule be overthrown. In 1866 civil war broke out between the imperial and shogunate factions, and in 1868 the imperial side won. The last Tokugawa shogun turned over his extensive estates to the 15-year-old emperor Meiji, who moved his court from Kyoto to Edo, which was renamed Tokyo. The emperor's long reign lasted until his death in 1912, a reign that was called the Meiji ("enlightened rule") Restoration.

Meiji Restoration. The Japanese leaders who emerged during the restoration's early days were young and energetic men from the samurai class. They believed that Japan's only defense against domination by Western powers was to modernize, adapting Western industrial technology and institutions to Japanese needs.

Just as the Japanese had sent representatives to China 1,200 years earlier to borrow what they could from its culture, they now sent another phalanx of borrowers to Europe and the United States. These commissions studied Western railroad and telegraph systems, factories, munitions manufacturing sites, and shipyards, and invited Western advisers to come to Japan to help build these facilities there. They studied Western military forces and chose to model a new Japanese army along German lines and a new Japanese navy along British lines, inviting both German and British officers to come to Japan and train its

centers
US

centres
Brit.

21 History of the World

officers. With their new and efficient military machine, the Japanese easily defeated China in the Sino-Japanese War of 1894–1895.

Japan's rapid militarization and industrialization was really part of a complete social, political, and economic revolution on the scale of the revolutions Western nations had undergone during the previous century. During this time, Japan's rigid social structure was loosened and occupational opportunities were broadened, thanks largely to the new compulsory education program that made Japan one of the only nations in the world with virtually no illiteracy. The universal draft calling all Japanese men to military service removed the monopoly by the samurai of that occupation and instilled in the draftees loyalty, obedience to the emperor, and the glory of death on the battlefield. The merchant class emerged with new power and prestige as the *zaibatsu,* family-owned industries, came to dominate the Japanese economy, Mitsubishi and Mitsui among them.

In 1871 feudalism was officially abolished in Japan and the central government under the emperor reorganized the old feudal estates into provinces that it could tax, legislate for, and administer uniformly. The abolition of feudalism was not without its opponents, mainly samurai bands who staged several uprisings. The most serious uprising was the Satsuma Rebellion of 1877, which the central government put down decisively, strengthening itself further.

The emperor and his cabinet formed an oligarchy that dominated the central government. Dissidents intent on even more westernization agitated to break oligarchic control and introduce more democratic government. Once again, Japan sent out a commission, this time to study Western governments. The model they adopted was the German one, and in 1889 Japan got a constitution that established a bicameral legislature, the Imperial Diet, with an upper house of peers and a lower house elected by

THE KING OF SIAM ruled over the only country in Southeast Asia that never became a European colony. The country, now called Thailand, became a prosperous center of trade.

property owners of means. However, the Diet was given only limited powers and the emperor and his ministers retained their oligarchic powers. Behind their powers lay the military, which wielded strong control over governmental policies.

Japanese expansionism. Like the industrialized Western nations, Japan experienced rapid population growth and urbanization. And like them, Japan grew imperialistic for the same reasons: the desire for new markets in which to sell their goods and the need for industrial raw materials.

The Sino-Japanese War of 1894–1895 was the first step, and victory in it caused Westerners to begin viewing Japan as a power to be reckoned with. In 1903 Japan reinforced this view when it went to war against Russia over influence in Korea and Manchuria. Repeated Japanese victories forced Russia to accept the Treaty of Portsmouth in 1905, by which Japan took over Russian railroad and mining rights in Manchuria and paved the way for Japanese annexation of Korea in 1910. Japan had become a first-class world power.

Southeast Asia—contending cultures.

In 1500 Southeast Asia was a complex mix of contending cultures. On the mainland, the influence of the formerly great Khmer Empire was limited to what is today southern Cambodia. This empire came under increasing pressure from its expansionist neighbors. To the west was the Thai kingdom of Ayutthaya, unified by Rama Thibodi in 1350 and ruled by the dynasty he founded until 1767. To the east was Vietnam. Under the Tranh dynasty (1225–1400), it had achieved some degree of political stability. Under the Le dynasty (1428–1788), it had absorbed Champa, its neighbor to the south, and had made its neighbor Laos a vassal state.

Burma was the third state vying for preeminence on mainland Southeast Asia. There, two brilliant kings, Tabinshweti (ruled 1531–1550) and Bayinnaung (ruled 1550–1581), unified the Burmese kingdoms under the Toungoo dynasty (1486–1752). Toungoo expansionism produced a series of wars against the Thais that went on from 1531 to 1605. In 1569 the Burmese captured Ayutthaya, but their triumph was short-lived. Following the death of Bayinnaung, the Thais under Nareseun expelled the Burmese from Ayutthaya.

During the 17th century there was peace between Burma and Ayutthaya: both recognized a standoff in military might. In 1767 the Burmese, under the Korbaung dynasty (1752–1885), invaded the Thais once again, but they were repelled. In 1782 a new Thai dynasty, the Chakkri (which rules Thailand to this day), came to power. It made its capital at Bangkok and then expanded to the east, occupying parts of Cambodia and Laos.

Prior to 1500, much of the Indian

archipelago had been under the domain of the Hindu Majapahet Empire, based in Java. But the coming of Islam effected its demise in 1520. A number of maritime commercial states emerged under Muslim rule, notably Malacca on the west coast of the Malay peninsula, Aceh in northern Sumatra, Demek in northern Java, and Tidore and Ternate in the eastern islands of the Indonesian archipelago.

It was into this complex of Southeast Asian states that the Europeans, led by the Portuguese, entered in the early 1500s, eager for trade and colonization. When the busy port of Malacca was conquered by the Portuguese in 1511, a new period began in the history of Southeast Asia, the period of European trade expansion and later European conquest.

At first the mainland states were relatively unaffected by the Europeans. Vietnam was strong enough to expel Portuguese missionaries from its shores. Thailand and Burma were able to repel an attempt by the Dutch allied with the Vietnamese to monopolize their trade.

Europeans were somewhat more successful in the archipelagos. By the late 1500s, Spain had gained control of the Philippines, first reached in 1521 by a Spanish expedition to circumnavigate the globe under the command of Ferdinand Magellan. Spanish missionaries succeeded in converting the majority of Filipinos to Christianity, and Hispanic culture became firmly entrenched.

In the Indonesian archipelago, the well-financed Dutch East India Company was able to force the Portuguese out in 1641. After waging war against the local sultans, the company expanded its influence over the area for the next century and a half. Dutch plantation agriculture soon displaced the traditional Indonesian economy.

The expansion of the Dutch, British, and French into Southeast Asia had begun as a commercial venture, but the effort to control trade often propelled the Europeans into political intervention, as in the case of the Dutch in Indonesia.

European governments themselves began taking over rule of the colonies from the trading interests. In 1799 the Dutch government revoked the Dutch East India Company's charter and declared the Dutch East Indies a royal colony. When Britain revoked the British East India Company's charter in 1858, taking control of the government of India, it also took responsibility for governing that company's interests in Southeast Asia. At the same time, the French government began to step up its efforts to gain imperial holdings in Southeast Asia.

By the early 1900s, all of Southeast Asia was under Western domination. Great Britain controlled Burma, Malaya, Singapore, northern Borneo, and eastern New Guinea; the Dutch held Indonesia; the French held Indochina;

and the United States controlled the Philippine Islands, having won them in its war with Spain in 1898. Only Thailand retained its sovereignty.

Australia, New Zealand, and Oceania.

The last places in the world to be settled lay, not surprisingly, far from Earth's major land masses. They included Australia, New Zealand, and the numerous islands of Oceania in the South Pacific that make up Micronesia, Melanesia, and Polynesia. Perhaps as long as 30,000 years ago, people from Southeast Asia began fanning out toward the northern coast of Australia and the western islands of Micronesia and Melanesia. Over the centuries, they continued their movement until by the 700s and 800s A.D. they reached far enough south to people Australia and Tasmania. They also reached far enough east and south to inhabit Polynesia from the Hawaiian Islands and the area from Easter Island to New Zealand. In their far-flung domains, these migrants developed in isolation from outside cultural influences.

Early history.

Australia's first settlers, the Aborigines, were a nomadic hunting and gathering people. One of the most culturally advanced of these island peoples were the Polynesian Maoris, who settled in New Zealand about 1,500 years ago. (See the AUSTRALIA AND OCEANIA volume.)

Exploration by Europeans.

Through the centuries prior to 1500, Malay fishermen and other Southeast Asian seafarers sometimes stopped briefly along Australia's uninviting northern and western shores. But they did not stay long, and Australia's existence remained unknown to the rest of the world. European scholars had long suspected the presence of a great continent in the Southern Hemisphere, believing that one was necessary to balance Europe and Asia in the Northern Hemisphere. *Terra Australis Incognita* they called it—meaning "unknown southern land."

Spanish and Portuguese sailors came close to Australia several times during the 1500s, but it was a Dutch ship, blown off its course to the Spice Islands, that made the first European contact in 1616. From then on, Dutch navigators mapped the north and northwest coasts of New Holland, as they called the island continent. In the early 1640s, Abel Janszoon Tasman sailed along Australia's south coast. He found and claimed possession of Tasmania for the Dutch East India Company, sailing along the west coast of New Zealand and so establishing Tasmania's separation from Australia.

Throughout this period, the islands of Oceania were gradually being reached by Europeans, beginning with Ferdinand Magellan's sighting in 1521 of the Mariana Islands of Micronesia. Spanish, Portuguese, Dutch, British, and French navigators continued to map Oceania's islands, filling in the world's knowledge of these "last places on Earth." Foremost among these explorers was Britain's Captain James Cook. His expeditions, in the 1760s and 1770s, charted New Zealand and Australia's east coast. He also discovered New Caledonia in Melanesia and the Cook Islands in Polynesia, and visited Tonga and the Hawaiian Islands, where he was killed in a conflict with the islanders.

European colonization.

Cook's charting of eastern Australia led to its colonization by the British. The first colonists were convicts, sentenced by British courts to settle in Australia. The agriculturally minded British quickly took over the most productive land to grow crops and to graze sheep, driving the Aborigines back into the deserts of the interior.

Australia's British colonies grew slowly at first, with free settlers replacing the convicts. By 1850 the colonial population reached 400,000. The next year, gold was discovered, setting off a rush that doubled that number in a decade. By 1900 the population had grown to 4 million.

In New Zealand, the colonization path was similar, although the British government did not designate it as a destination for convicts. Its early settlers were sealers and whalers, sailors who had jumped ship, and convicts who had escaped the penal settlements of Australia. By 1820 the British had founded several settlements in New Zealand. Like the Aborigines, the Maori natives suffered at the hands of colonists. Diseases brought by the Europeans decimated their population. In addition, the Maoris adopted European muskets, using them in intertribal wars that wiped out still more of their number. By the 1850s, the estimated pre-European population of 100,000 had been cut nearly in half.

Like the Australians, New Zealand colonists made sheep central to their economy, and their ceaseless need for new land drove them to claim ever more Maori grazing space. To try and stop further encroachment, the Maori tribes tried to unify under one king; this led to a long series of Anglo-Maori wars. The diminishing numbers of Maoris presented formidable resistance, but by 1872 they were finally beaten and the colonists continued to take their land, almost at will.

Europeans were also having an impact on the islands of Oceania during the 1800s. At first the settlers were mainly sealers and whalers or collectors of the precious woods tropical islands produced. But among these settlers were also the reprehensible "blackbirders," men who captured Melanesians and sold them into slavery to work the Australian cane fields. They also transported Polynesians to Chile and Peru to work the guano deposits. By 1850 more solid Europeans began to settle in the islands, creating a plantation agriculture that raised and exported cocoa, coconuts, coffee, and sugar.

Americans too joined in colonization, especially in the Hawaiian Islands, ruled by a Hawaiian monarchy. By 1893 the American planters there were powerful enough to depose the last Hawaiian queen, Liliuokalani, and five years later the United States annexed her former kingdom.

National development.

Following the founding of Australia's first colony in New South Wales, the British divided the continent up into additional colonies—Tasmania, Western Australia, South Australia, and Victoria. In 1850 these independent colonies won the right to self-government from the British; two years later, New Zealand won the same right. In 1901 the Australian colonies federated under the Commonwealth of Australia Constitution Act and became a dominion of the British Commonwealth. In 1907 New Zealand achieved this same status.

By 1900 Australia and New Zealand had become world leaders in the export of agricultural products such as wool and meat. Australia's rich mineral deposits made it a world leader in gold, coal, and iron ore production. At the turn of the century, New Zealanders could boast of having the highest standard of living in the world.

A MAORI CHIEF and his family sit outside their home, a carved wooden structure built on stilts. This photo was taken in 1875, three years after the Anglo-Maori wars.

colonization
US

colonisation
Brit.

JAMES COOK explored much of the Pacific before his violent death on Hawaii.

Africa

Like Asia, Africa became a magnet for European trade and territorial ambitions around 1500. For the next three and a half centuries, though, disease and African resistance helped to discourage Europeans from penetrating the interior of "the dark continent." However, some Europeans did establish trading posts and forts in certain coastal areas. From these bases they influenced African life to an extent far beyond what their small numbers would indicate. In 1870 the Europeans began coming in greater numbers. Their military and technical sophistication helped them to eventually overwhelm the Africans.

COLONIAL RULE.
After taking the city of Kumasi in Ashanti, (in present-day Ghana), Governor Maxwell compelled King Prempeh and the Queen Mother to make an act of submission to him in accordance with Ashanti custom—they accordingly bend down in front of him and Sir Francis Scott and Colonel Kempster and clasp their legs.

The Portuguese impact.
Songhai, Benin, and other well-organized kingdoms of West Africa were among the first African states that Prince Henry the Navigator's Portuguese sailors encountered on their explorations south toward the Cape of Good Hope.

The slave trade started on a small scale in the mid 1400s, but as plantation agriculture grew in the Americas, it became West Africa's major commercial activity. Between 1451 and the 1800s, it is estimated that anywhere from 10 to 15 million slaves were shipped across the Atlantic.

At first the slave trade increased the wealth and power of several African kingdoms. Ashanti (modern Ghana) and Dahomey (modern Benin) emerged as major kingdoms because of government-sanctioned slave raids. But by 1650 this trade had led to the downfall of the kingdoms when the people rebelled.

The impact of the Portuguese on East Africa was similarly devastating. They plundered Swahili city-states from Kilwa to Mombasa. In 1561 the Portuguese began a 15-year war with the Vakaranga Empire, which controlled 700 miles along the upper Zambezi River. However, soldiers of the nearby Changamire Empire objected to both the Portuguese plantations and the slave trade in Vakarangan lands. The Changamire attacked both sides, driving the Portuguese out of the interior. The Portuguese remained in Mozambique, however.

North Africa. In the 15th and 16th centuries, the Ottoman Empire expanded into North Africa, an area that earlier had been shaped, politically and socially, by the teachings of Islam. By the 18th century, Ottoman control had weakened as the strength of the empire itself waned. Four quasi-independent states emerged—Algiers (now Algeria), Tunis (now Tunisia), Tripoli (now Libya), and Egypt. The fifth state in the North African tier, Morocco, never came under Ottoman control.

European interest in Egypt began in earnest with Napoleon's invasion in 1798, as part of his effort to weaken Great Britain by cutting off its trade with the Middle East. The leader of Egyptian resistance to the French was Mehemet Ali, who later expanded his power when, in 1805, he became viceroy of Egypt. Ali began a program of costly economic reforms to improve agriculture and to build schools, railroads, and factories. To finance these improvements, he and his successors borrowed heavily from the British and the French.

With the building of the Suez Canal from 1859 to 1869, an Egyptian-French venture, Egypt's financial dependence on Europe burgeoned. The political and economic influence of Europe, and especially Great Britain, over Egyptian policies grew dramatically. In 1875 extreme financial difficulties forced Egypt's ruler, the Khedive Ismail, to sell his country's block of Suez shares to Great Britain. Britain sent military forces to occupy Egypt in 1882, declaring it a British protectorate in order to guard British financial interests. Britain then expanded its control south into the Sudan, which it ruled jointly with Egypt from 1899 as the Anglo-Egyptian Sudan.

To the west, France and Italy were staking out their claims in the impoverished and politically weak North African tier. In 1830 France sent its troops into Algiers and for the next 17 years fought the Berber tribes. With the final Berber submission, France made Algiers a colonial state. During the same time period, France was also dominating Morocco, and in 1881 it made Tunis a French protectorate. Italy set its sights on Tripoli. After declaring war on the Ottoman Empire in 1911, it took the region as its colony, renaming it Libya.

West and Central Africa. As 1500 dawned on the vast savanna lands around Lake Chad, the Islamic kingdom of Kanem-Bornu was reaching its height. Located along important trade routes to Tunis and Tripoli to the north, Egypt to the east, and the Niger River to the west, it prospered as a commercial, political, and religious center during the 16th and 17th centuries, especially under its greatest king, Indris Alooma (ruled 1580–1617).

To the west, spread across what is today northern Nigeria, were the merchant Hausa states, principally Daura, Gobir, Katsina, Kano, and Zaria. Kano became the most prosperous of these states, even surpassing Timbuktu in commercial success during the 16th century.

Still farther to the west, the Fulani people had established states in what are now Guinea and Senegal and had spread to Nigeria and Cameroon. The Fulani converted to Islam in the early 18th century. In 1804 their religious leader, Uthman dan Folio, began a holy war against several Hausa states, conquering them and creating the Fulani-Hausa Empire.

To the southeast, near Lake Victoria, several Bantu states emerged, among them Bunyoro, Buganda, Ankole, Rwanda, and Burundi. Until the mid 17th century, Bunyoro was the most powerful, but by the 19th century, Buganda had gained preeminence under a king and a well-organized form of government, with control over the region's major trade routes.

Prior to 1870, areas such as Kanem-Bornu, much of the Fulani-Hausa Empire, the Bantu states, and the interior of sub-Saharan Africa were not heavily penetrated by Europeans, who limited themselves mainly to coastal areas. But then medical advances, such as treatments for malaria and yellow fever, and improved European weapons, such as rifles, cannon, and early machine guns, neutralized the former barriers of tropical disease and African resistance. European explorers were at last able to map Africa's interior. European governments pressed in, trying to carve out vast territories to add to their empires while attempting to stifle their rivals' expansion.

Exploration had uncovered rich mineral resources in the interior as well as vast lands that could be turned into plantations for growing cash crops such as cocoa and cotton. These resources increased in importance after European countries abolished their trade in slaves during the first part of the 19th century.

To exploit these resources the French and British pushed inland from their West African coastal ports. The French captured Timbuktu and by 1874 claimed all of French West Africa, south of Algiers. In 1893 the French conquered the kingdom of Dahomey and annexed it. In 1910 France would claim still more land to the east: French Equatorial Africa.

The British annexed what is today Ghana after defeating the Ashanti kingdom in 1874; they also made Nigeria a protectorate, in 1884. By this time, Germany had joined the scramble for

African land, claiming Togo and Cameroon in West Africa, as well as German Southwest Africa (modern Namibia). The Portuguese hung onto Angola, while a new player, Belgium, gained control of the Belgian Congo, today's Democratic Republic of the Congo.

East Africa. Like West Africa, East Africa had also been disrupted by slave trade, mainly out of Portuguese-held Mozambique. This disruption weakened African political organization, facilitating European penetration of the interior from the east. In 1885 Germany proclaimed a protectorate over what it called German East Africa (modern Tanzania), arousing the consternation of Britain and France, which also harbored territorial designs on East Africa. In total disregard of the claims of African rulers, the contesting nations negotiated a settlement among themselves: Germany could retain its protectorate as long as France could claim Madagascar and Britain could press inland to create the protectorate of British East Africa (modern Kenya) and claim Uganda and the island of Zanzibar.

To the north, both France and Italy wanted control of the horn of Africa—Ethiopia and coastal Somaliland. In 1896 Italy attacked Ethiopia, but its emperor Menelik II and his well-armed and well-trained army defeated the Italians and Ethiopia maintained its independence. The French, Italians, and British agreed to divide up Somaliland among them, and Italy took control of Eritrea, to the north of Ethiopia.

Southern Africa. By 1500 the Bantu migrations had finally reached southern Africa, already inhabited by the hunting San people (also called Bushmen) and by the pastoral Khoikhoi people (commonly called Hottentots), who herded their animals as far south as the tip of the continent. The largest Bantu-speaking group to occupy southern Africa was the Nguni, subdivided into the Swazi, Zulu, and Xhosa peoples. The Sotho peoples were the next largest group, further divided into the Tswana and the Sotho. They were farmers and cattle raisers.

The Bantu did not find it necessary to form strong centralized kingdoms, but in the 17th and 18th centuries this changed because of the encroachment of European settlers. In the late 18th and early 19th centuries, the Zulu Empire emerged with the help of the brilliant military leader Shaka.

One of the earliest European settlements in southern Africa was Cape Town, founded by the Netherlands in 1652 to supply Dutch ships as they rounded the Cape of Good Hope. It grew into the thriving Cape Colony, a part of the Dutch Empire. As Dutch settlers pushed into the interior, they faced heavy resistance by indigenous Africans, many of whom they enslaved. During the Napoleonic

wars, Great Britain seized control of Cape Colony, creating conflict between the descendants of the original Dutch settlers, the Boers, and incoming British settlers. Having abolished slavery themselves, the British wanted it abolished among the Boers. They also declared English the colony's official language.

Considering this an assault on their way of life, about 100,000 Boers left Cape Colony in 1836 and began their Great Trek, a journey to the northeast to establish new colonies where they hoped to live without British interference. They founded the Orange Free State, the Transvaal inland, and Natal along the southeast coast.

The Boers' expansion brought them into conflict with the Zulu Empire, a conflict neither was able to win decisively. Having annexed Natal in 1845, the British entered the fighting, sending troops to battle the formidable Zulu warriors. Once again superior European weapons won the day, and the Zulu Empire was destroyed.

In 1852 Great Britain had recognized the sovereignty of the Boer republics of Transvaal and Orange Free State, but in 1885 gold was discovered, whetting the British appetite for this land too. A guiding force behind Britain's drive for dominion over southern Africa was Cecil Rhodes, who had made a fortune in diamonds after coming to South Africa in 1870. He had pushed British expansion northward into Bechuanaland (modern Botswana), which Britain made a protectorate in 1885, and into the area named for him, Rhodesia (mod-

ern Zambia and Zimbabwe). In 1890 he became prime minister, virtually the dictator, of Cape Colony and began to plot the seizure of the Transvaal and Orange Free State for Britain as well.

Rhodes's attempts to topple the Boer governments failed, but they created more conflict between the Boers and the British, and in 1899 the adversaries went to war. The Boer War was bitterly fought until 1902, when the Boers were

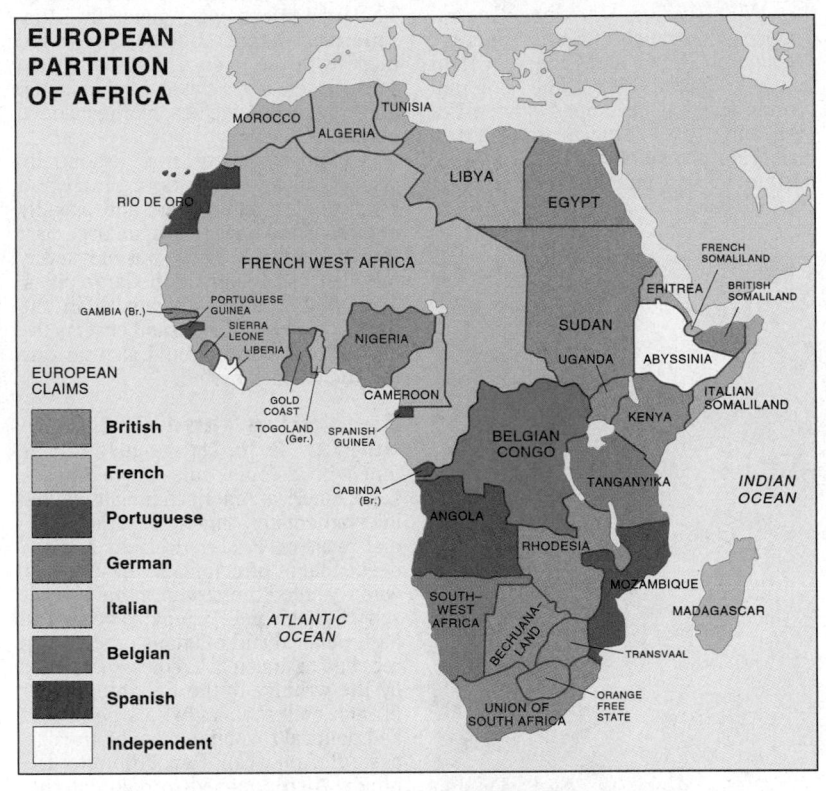

EUROPEAN PARTITION OF AFRICA

EUROPEAN CLAIMS

- British
- French
- Portuguese
- German
- Italian
- Belgian
- Spanish
- Independent

forced to surrender. In 1909 the British Cape Colony and the Boer states were united into the self-governing British dominion of the Union of South Africa.

Colonial rule. By the early 1900s, all of Africa had been carved up and placed under European rule, with the exception of Ethiopia and Liberia, an independent West African state founded in 1821 by former slaves returned from the United States. For Africans, the adjustments were daunting. Large tribes were split up among different European colonies, and small tribes, often antagonistic to one another, were combined into one colony.

Tribal law was superseded by laws handed down from the colonial powers, and tribal rulers were replaced by European officials. Land was often taken from the Africans and given to European settlers to turn into plantations or mines. In some areas, Africans were restricted to "native reserves," similar to American Indian reservations. For the Africans, it was a bewildering time as their traditional cultures were assaulted by the very different developed and industrialized European culture.

Latin America

Latin America denotes a vast area that includes Mexico, Central America, the West Indies, and South America. The name itself reflects the impact that Europeans speaking languages derived from Latin—Spanish, Portuguese, and French—had on the Americas beginning about 1500. Latin America had been carved into colonial empires by the European powers: Spain in the West Indies, Mexico, Central America, and much of South America; Portugal in Brazil; and France in Haiti in the West Indies. The colonial economies that developed during the 16th and 17th centuries were based mainly on plantation agriculture, herding, and mining, and they relied heavily on slave labor.

labor
US

labour
Brit.

honored
US

honoured
Brit.

SIMÓN BOLÍVAR
has been called the "George Washington of South America" because his victories over the Spaniards led to independence for Bolivia, Colombia, Ecuador, Peru, and Venezuela. Bolivia, once part of Peru, was named in his honor.

Colonial times. Latin America's colonial period lasted for about 300 years, through the 16th, 17th, and 18th centuries. Spain and Portugal remained the major colonial rulers in Latin America, but during the 17th century, France, England, and the Netherlands also founded colonies, mainly in the Caribbean.

Government in Latin America was highly authoritarian. Under the Spanish viceroys, individual government officials exercised great powers—legislative, executive, and judicial all at the same time. Such personal government rooted Latin America in a form of autocracy that facilitated the rise of dictators.

The Roman Catholic Church was a second major power in colonial Latin America. The church influenced every aspect of life there; in addition to its religious role, it had an important voice in government and education. It also became a major landowner. Indeed, the church came to own half of all the property in Spanish America. High church officials were generally from Spain, and they identified with the wealthy land- and mine-owning classes. The local priests were generally Latin-American native, and they identified more with the poor. Church and state were closely interrelated, a relationship that would continue beyond the colonial period.

Colonial society was essentially divided into two parts, a small and wealthy elite and a large and broadly impoverished lower class, in large part Indian and black. There was only a tiny middle class, mainly in the large cities. This dichotomy, with wealth in the hands of a few at the top and poverty the lot of the majority, would also far outlive the colonial period.

Revolution and independence. By the 18th century, discontent with colonial rule began to rack Latin America. American Indians staged intermittent uprisings against their colonial masters. Enslaved blacks and the descendants of colonists, the Creoles, who resented the power of the officials sent by Spain and Portugal to occupy all high political and religious offices, also rebelled. Educated Creoles were fired by the writings of the Enlightenment's French philosophers, who urged social and political revolution, and by the successful American Revolution to the north. Also opposed to colonial rule were the mestizos, people of mixed European and Indian blood. They objected to what they saw as their treatment as third-class citizens.

The French Revolution of 1789 and the actions of Napoleon following it sparked widespread revolutionary action in Latin America and led to its independence from direct European rule.

Haiti. The first major revolution in Latin America occurred in the French colony of Haiti, the western half of the island of Hispaniola. Following the French Revolution, the slave population of the colony demanded that the "liberty, fraternity, and equality" that the revolution promised be extended to them. When it was not, they rebelled in 1791. They found a great leader in Pierre Toussaint l'Ouverture, a Haitian black who had been in the French army. By 1801 the slaves had gained control of all of Hispaniola. Napoleon sent troops to try to recapture the island, but they ultimately failed and Haiti became Latin America's first independent nation.

South America. In 1808 Napoleon invaded Spain, threw the Spanish king Ferdinand VII off the throne, and made his own brother, Joseph Bonaparte, monarch. Spanish colonies in Latin America refused to accept this new king and took the opportunity to set up autonomous governments in what are now the countries of Argentina, Chile, Colombia, and Venezuela. When Ferdinand VII was returned to the Spanish throne in 1815, independence forces in Latin America resisted return to Spanish rule.

Simón Bolívar, a wealthy Venezuelan Creole, led the fight against Spanish government forces in northern South America. In 1819 this "Great Liberator" led a Venezuelan army across the Andes Mountains to attack and defeat the Spanish at Boyacá in Colombia. This successful campaign led to the creation of the independent nation of Gran Colombia, made up of today's Ecuador, Venezuela, Colombia, and Panama.

At the same time, two other liberators, José de San Martin and Bernardo O'Higgins, led Argentina and Chile to independence by forcing Spanish withdrawal. In 1820 San Martin moved his troops north to Peru to drive the Spanish out of their last stronghold there. In 1825 the Spanish viceroy of Peru surrendered, ending Spanish rule in South America.

Mexico and Central America. Mesoamerica followed a somewhat different path toward independence. In 1810 Miguel Hidalgo, a Mexican priest, led an army of Indian peasants against both Spanish officials and the Creoles of Mexico. Though this uprising and a subsequent peasant rebellion for land reform and the abolition of slavery failed, the rebellions convinced the wealthier classes that they should retain Spanish rule, and thus their privileged position, rather than risk social revolution.

However, in 1820, a liberal army rebellion against the king in Spain caused the conservative upper classes to change their minds and they mounted an independence movement, led by General Agustin Iturbide, that succeeded. At first organized as a constitutional monarchy, Mexico was declared a republic in 1824. In 1823 the states to the south had declared themselves the United Provinces of Central America, with their own constitution and president.

Brazil. Napoleon invaded Portugal in 1808, causing its king, John VI, to escape to Brazil and set up court in Rio de Janeiro. During his stay he encouraged the colony's economic development. In 1821 he returned to Portugal to reclaim his throne, leaving his son Pedro to rule Brazil. In 1822 Pedro proclaimed Brazil's independence from Portugal, overcame the resistance of Portuguese troops, and was crowned emperor of Brazil. A parliamentary form of government was instituted.

Monroe Doctrine. By 1825 nearly all of Latin America had become independent. Only a few, relatively small areas retained colonial rule—British Honduras in Central America; Cuba and Puerto Rico under Spain; Jamaica and the Bahamas under Britain; and the Guianas of northern South America under Britain, the Netherlands, and France.

The United States favored Latin American independence from Europe and wanted to discourage any attempts by Spain to reestablish power in the Western Hemisphere. In 1823 U.S. President James Monroe proclaimed that "the American continents are henceforth not to be considered for future colonization by any European powers." Eager to increase its trade with the newly independent states of Latin America, Great Britain helped enforce the Monroe Doctrine by using its formidable navy to discourage any European moves in that area.

Internal strife.

Simón Bolívar had hoped to unite the newly independent states into a league of constitutional republics, but clashing interests, bitter power struggles, and territorial disputes dashed this hope, and many separate nations emerged in Latin America. Though many adopted constitutions based on the United States model, true representative government would prove elusive.

Latin America's colonial background had not prepared it for democratic government. Land and wealth were concentrated in the hands of the few, mainly Creoles and the Roman Catholic Church. A great deal of political power lay in the hands of *caudillos*—tyrannical military leaders whose armies could make them dictators of the new republics. Power of any kind—political, social, or economic—totally eluded Indians, blacks, and poor mestizos, who made up the great majority of the population.

Economically, the new nations also faced formidable problems. The wars for independence had disrupted agricultural and mining production, on which the Latin American economies had been built. Foreign trade had withered, and roads and harbor facilities had fallen into disrepair. Industrialization, spreading rapidly through Europe and the United States, did not reach Latin America.

National development.

In large part, it was this foreign industrialization that would help the nations of Latin America to strengthen themselves. Industrialized nations needed raw materials that Latin America could produce in abundance and needed food products for growing populations.

As a result, both foreign investment and waves of immigrants flowed into Latin America. Roads, bridges, railroads, telegraphs, and ports were built; mining methods were improved; and new agricultural areas were developed. The countries concentrated on exporting natural resources; they supplied industrialized economies without becoming industrialized themselves.

This economic development contributed to and grew out of the young nations' improved political stability. Argentina, Brazil, Chile, Uruguay, and Costa Rica were especially successful in achieving orderly governments, though they were more oligarchic than representative.

Mexico had a more difficult struggle toward stability. For much of the period from 1833 to 1855, it was led by a corrupt *caudillo,* General Antonio López de Santa Anna. During his rule, Mexico suffered the humiliation of losing Texas, California, and the rest of the Southwest to the United States. These losses resulted from the Texas war for independence in 1836 and the Mexican War of 1846–1848. A bitter civil war (1861–1867) eventually brought on the dictatorship of Porfirio Diaz, who ruled Mexico for nearly the whole period from 1877 to 1915.

Foreign relations.

By and large, the nations of Europe honored the principles of the Monroe Doctrine. As the 1800s drew to a close, however, many Latin Americans began feeling that the United States was using the Monroe Doctrine to further its own dominance of the Western Hemisphere.

The Spanish-American War of 1898 fueled their fears. Cuban rebels had been fighting for independence from Spain. The United States declared war on Spain, ostensibly to help the rebels. Cuba won its independence from Spain, but the United States forced the Cubans to accept the Platt Amendment, under which they had to acknowledge the American right to intervene in Cuban affairs if the United States deemed it necessary. In addition to making Cuba a virtual protectorate, the United States also took control of Puerto Rico.

As the 20th century began, Latin Americans became preoccupied with the further encroachments that the "Colossus of the North," as they called the United States, might make on them.

MAXIMILIAN, whom Napoleon set up as emperor of Mexico, was executed by a firing squad after French troops were withdrawn and he was captured. He was the brother of Austrian Emperor Franz Josef.

A CARICATURE depicts England and Germany responding to the Venezuelan Blockade.

The World in the 20th Century

c 1900 to the Present

In 1900 Europe dominated the world politically, economically, and culturally. Through its imperialism, it had carved up much of Asia and Africa into colonial preserves. Through its industrialism, it had developed prospering economies, unrivaled financial power, and formidable military might.

Yet within a short time, all this would change. In 1914 Europe engulfed itself in a world war that ultimately destroyed its world primacy. Over the decades that followed, world power shifted into new hands—those of the United States and the Soviet Union. European colonies in Asia and Africa overthrew imperialism to win their independence once more.

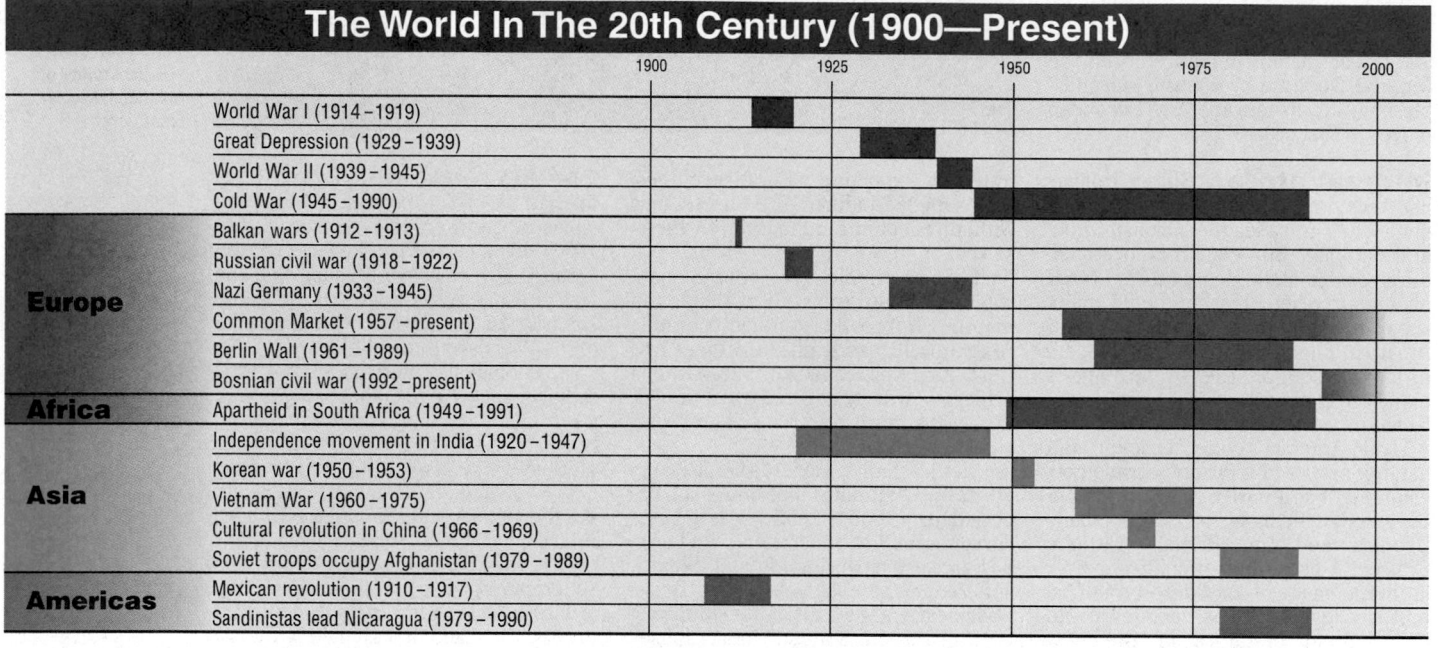

The World In The 20th Century (1900—Present)

		1900	1925	1950	1975	2000
Europe	World War I (1914–1919)					
	Great Depression (1929–1939)					
	World War II (1939–1945)					
	Cold War (1945–1990)					
	Balkan wars (1912–1913)					
	Russian civil war (1918–1922)					
	Nazi Germany (1933–1945)					
	Common Market (1957–present)					
	Berlin Wall (1961–1989)					
	Bosnian civil war (1992–present)					
Africa	Apartheid in South Africa (1949–1991)					
Asia	Independence movement in India (1920–1947)					
	Korean war (1950–1953)					
	Vietnam War (1960–1975)					
	Cultural revolution in China (1966–1969)					
	Soviet troops occupy Afghanistan (1979–1989)					
Americas	Mexican revolution (1910–1917)					
	Sandinistas lead Nicaragua (1979–1990)					

Toward World War I

Conflicting interests among the nations of Europe created dangerous rivalries for colonies, greater national glory, and superior military might. Another matter was the "Eastern question" of who would control Eastern Europe, including the Balkan peninsula north of Greece.

A System of Alliances

To understand how World War I came about, it is necessary to understand the European balance of power as the 20th century began.

Germany and Austria. Following the Franco-Prussian War (1870–1871), Germany under Otto von Bismarck realized that it needed more protection against a resurgent France, intent on recovering Alsace-Lorraine, lost in that war. The Germans feared a two-front war, with Germany caught between Russia and France.

To ensure his southern flank, Bismarck made a defensive treaty with Austria, formally known as the Austro-Hungarian Empire. This treaty, made in secret, guaranteed Austria-Hungary German support if attacked by Russia. It gave Germany a similar assurance.

Russia was Bismarck's major diplomatic concern and the most difficult country to keep within the circle of German friendship. The loss of Austria's Italian territories had turned Austrian ambitions toward the Balkans, where they conflicted with Russian interests. Russia therefore found it against its interests to become friendly with any ally of Austria.

All that Bismarck could gain was the Reinsurance Treaty, in 1887, under which Russia agreed not to support France if Germany would support Russia in the Balkans. Bismarck was dismissed in 1890, and the Reinsurance Treaty was allowed to lapse.

France and Russia. France had learned the necessity of allies with its defeat by Prussia in 1870, and it set out to remedy the lack. France's natural ally was Russia, for the two had no areas of real conflict.

Great Britain was the enemy of both. The new power of a united Germany loomed ominously. Russia was desperately seeking capital to invest; France was as eagerly looking for good investments for its wealth.

As long as Bismarck was on the scene, he was able to prevent a Franco-Russian alliance. But when he was dismissed in 1890, the two rushed to negotiate. In 1894 the Dual Alliance, aligning France and Russia, became a reality.

Britain and Italy. The two major states on the periphery of Europe—Great Britain and Italy—proved to be the most difficult to deal with diplomatically. The British felt secure behind their powerful navy and desired no permanent entanglements on the Continent. Only when its colonial empire was threatened did Britain begin to cast about for allies. This resulted from Germany's rapid buildup of its navy in the

realized
US

realised
Brit.

1890s and from its continued attempts to win colonial footholds in Africa.

By the end of the 1800s, the imperialist race had just about run its course, with France and Britain emerging the winners. Germany, demanding its place in the sun, was a threat to both colonial empires; it was natural for Britain and France to turn to each other. In 1904 the Entente Cordiale between Britain and France came into being, reversing a diplomatic pattern existing since the 1300s.

Italy proved to be a special problem. Unification had brought it more frustrations than achievements. The Italians turned outward and entered the contest for colonies. The Italians were willing to sign treaties with everyone as long as they were permitted to create a colonial empire of their own.

This was the golden age of secret diplomacy, and it was not hard to become enmeshed in conflicting alliances. Italy finally allied itself with Germany and Austria-Hungary in the Triple Alliance in 1882. But a few years later, Italy's other obligations were practically to nullify its promise to support Germany and Austria.

Military plans. The new system of alliances forced certain changes in military strategy. Germany realized that it might face a two-front war. To counter this, the Germans adopted the Schlieffen Plan.

The plan was based on two basic assumptions. The first was that the Germans could muster their armies some six weeks faster than the Russians. This would give the Germans a short but essential period in which they could fight on one front only. The second was that France would fall rapidly if a massive assault were directed down the Atlantic coast.

World War I

By the early 1900s two great power blocs, Germany and Austria-Hungary in central Europe, and a French-Russian alliance, supported by Great Britain, faced the center of Europe.

The Austrians were experiencing difficulties in the Balkans, a hotbed of nationalism. A number of small groups pledged to national liberation saw their mission in an almost messianic light.

One in Austrian-held Bosnia, headed by a Serbian patriot and secretly backed by Serbia, assassinated the Austrian archduke, Francis Ferdinand, on June 28, 1914, in Sarajevo.

The Austrians interpreted this as the first move in a new nationalist attack on the Austro-Hungarian Empire. Austria felt it had no alternative, if its empire was to survive, but to declare war on Serbia.

Outbreak. In spite of a conciliatory Serbian reply to a stiff Austrian note, the Austrians declared war on Serbia on July 28. Russia, tied by treaty to Serbia, ordered a general mobilization of its armed forces. Germany felt it then had no choice, if the Schlieffen Plan was to be effective, but to throw its military machine into gear.

Germany declared war on Russia on August 1, 1914, and on France on August 3. According to the Schlieffen Plan, the Germans had to march through Belgium. Belgium, a neutral country, refused permission for German armies to cross its territory. The Germans denounced the treaties guaranteeing Belgian neutrality and marched in. This brought Great Britain into the war on August 4.

Stalemate. During the first few weeks of the war, the Germans seemed about to prove the brilliance of the Schlieffen Plan. But French armies held at the Marne River, and the war on the western front settled down to static slaughter. An advance of 100 yards was hailed as a great victory and was purchased at a cost of thousands of dead and wounded. Machine guns, trenches, and barbed wire proved a match for the infantry and

Major Events — Toward World War I	
1901	Pablo Picasso begins his Blue period in Paris.
1903	The first successful airplane is launched by Wilbur and Orville Wright on December 17 at Kitty Hawk, North Carolina; the best flight of the day lasts 59 seconds.
1905	The first German U-boat submarine is launched; Sigmund Freud's "Jokes and Their Relation to the Unconscious" and "Three Essays on the Theory of Sexuality" are published.
1906	Canadian-American physicist Reginald Aubrey Fessenden invents the AM radio and transmits music and voice via radio waves.
1907	Louis Lumière develops color photography.
1912	The *Titanic* sinks on its maiden voyage; 1,500 people perish.
1913	French novelist Marcel Proust publishes the first volume of *Remembrance of Things Past*; Henry Ford develops conveyer belt assembly for production of the Model T automobile.
1915	The Panama Canal opens.
1916	James Joyce publishes *A Portrait of the Artist as a Young Man*.
1919	Ernest Rutherford is the first to split an atom; the first crossing of the Atlantic by air is completed by British aviators John William Alcock and Arthur Whitten Brown.

artillery. All that could be done was to wait and see which side bled to death first.

In the east the situation was more fluid. The Russian military machine began to collapse; the unpreparedness of the Russian imperial regime exposed shortages of supplies and a lack of organization.

Catastrophe was staved off for three years only because the main German force was busy in the west, and the Russian peasants were willing to die for their country. Finally, the peasants could take no more. The Russian armies dissolved at the front and revolution broke out in the Russian cities.

The deepest desire of most Russians was for peace. Vladimir Lenin, leader of the Bolshevik wing of the Russian Social Democratic Party, promised it.

With brilliant tactical insights, Lenin outmaneuvered rivals for power to bring the Bolsheviks to control of the Russian state. The net effect of the Russian Revolution in 1917 on the European conflict was to remove Russia from the war and permit the Germans one more year of battle.

War's end. In early April 1917, the United States, angered by Germany's unrestricted submarine warfare (under which it sank ships of belligerents and nonbelligerents alike), entered the conflict on the side of the Allies. This revitalization of Allied manpower, together with the cumulative effects of a British blockade of shipping in and out of German ports, brought Germany to its knees.

On November 11, 1918, the war ended and the German Empire ended with it. It remained for the victors to pick up the pieces and to try to put Europe together again. A peace conference was convened in the great Palace of Versailles, outside of Paris.

center
US

centre
Brit.

21 History of the World

WORLD WAR I

Allied Powers and Offensives
Central Powers and Offensives
Neutral Countries
Occupied by Central Powers

58

DELEGATES LEAVE THE PALACE of Versailles after the signing of the treaty that ended World War I. Among the delegates shown are President Woodrow Wilson of the United States, Georges Clemenceau of France, and Prime Minister David Lloyd George of Great Britain.

World War I

1914
June 28   Archduke Franz Ferdinand is assassinated.
July 28   Austria declares war on Serbia.
Aug. 1   Germany declares war on Russia.
Aug. 3   Germany declares war on France.
Aug. 4   Germany invades Belgium.
Aug. 10   Austria-Hungary invades Russia, opening fighting on the Eastern Front.

1915
Apr. 22   Poison gas is used for the first time by Germany.
Apr. 25   Seventy-five thousand Australian, New Zealand, British, and French troops try to open a new front at Gallipoli at the mouth of the Bosporus.
May 7   A German submarine sinks the S.S. *Lusitania*, a British liner, off the coast of Ireland; on the Eastern Front, the German and Austrian "great offensive" conquers all of Poland and Lithuania.
Aug. 20   At the Battle of Tannenburg, a vast Russian army is crushingly defeated by the Germans.

1916
Feb. 21   A strong German offensive begins at the Verdun fortress in France; the Battle of Verdun becomes the longest and bloodiest battle of World War I; over 1 million are killed.
July 1   Heavy fighting between British and German forces begins at the Battle of Somme in northern France.
Sep.   The Brusilov offensive costs the Russians over 1 million men.
Dec.   The Romanian capital of Bucharest is captured by German troops.

1917
Feb. 1   Germany begins unrestricted submarine warfare.
Apr. 6   The United States declares war on Germany.
Oct. 24   Italians are forced to retreat in the Battle of Caporetto; 600,000 Italian soldiers are lost as prisoners, deserters, or casualties.
Nov. 20   Tanks are used en masse at Cambrai, France, by the British army.
Dec. 7   The United States declares war on Austria-Hungary.

1918
Jan. 8   Woodrow Wilson introduces the Fourteen Points peace program.
Mar. 3   With the Treaty of Brest-Litovsk, Russia's new Bolshevik government withdraws from the war.
Mar. 21   Germany launches its last offensive on the Western Front.
June 20   American troops face their first important battle at Chateau-Thierry; they join with the French to stop the German advance.
Nov. 11   The armistice is signed by Germany and the Allies.

1919
June 28   The Treaty of Versailles is signed by the Allies and Germany but is never ratified by the U.S. Senate; the treaty redraws the map of Europe and forces Germany to assume responsibility for the war.

TOTAL WAR DEATHS: 15,640,000

Major Participants (total military and civilian deaths)

Allied Powers
Belgium (88,000)
Canada (55,000)
France (1,630,000)
Great Britain (1,016,000)
Italy (950,000)

Romania (375,000)
Russia (5,950,000)
United States (126,000)
Yugoslavia (128,000)

Central Powers
Austria-Hungary (2,300,000)
Bulgaria (28,000)
Germany (2,400,000)
Turkey (450,000)

Versailles settlement. When the representatives of the Allied powers met at the Palace of Versailles on January 18, 1919, they shared, with few exceptions, a grim spirit of revenge. This reflected the changes both in governments and in warfare since the Congress of Vienna had met a century before. The wars had been made by governments, not by whole peoples, and had been considered instruments of national policy. Defeat merely closed off one avenue until the game could be played again.

World War I, in contrast, was waged on a mass basis by governments dependent on the support of their people. To gain this support, governments had to arouse mass emotions. No people could be expected to sacrifice its most vigorous generation just for some diplomatic goal or dynastic gain.

War on such a scale had to have a high moral justification, such as "to make the world safe for democracy," and it had to be directed against the forces of "evil." Only in such an atmosphere of intense and unreasoning emotion could so many millions be persuaded to believe that they were not to die in vain.

Such emotions cannot be turned on and off at will, and no statesman at Versailles could have survived if he had suggested that the past be forgotten and forgiven. The greatest bloodletting in the history of Europe had just ended, and someone had to be found guilty and punished.

The obvious candidate at Versailles was Germany, and the Treaty of Versailles contained a "guilt clause," under which the Germans were to assume ultimate responsibility for the war. All else followed from this. Germany was loaded with a reparations debt that it could not possibly pay and was stripped of its colonies. Territory in Europe was taken from Germany and given to the newly created states of Czechoslovakia and Poland.

The Treaty of Versailles was a bitter pill for the Germans to swallow, but they had no choice. The British refused to lift their blockade until Germany accepted the terms of the treaty. In June 1919, the German representatives signed.

The recognition of the principle of nationalism was the one pure principle embodied in the treaty, but this too proved to be a failure. Instead of removing the pressures caused by intense nationalism that had served so long to disturb the equilibrium of Europe, the terms of the treaty merely served to aggravate the pressures in such nations as Germany and Italy. Both saw their nationalist ambitions thwarted by the peace settlement. The League of Nations, an international peacekeeping body set up under the Treaty of Versailles, would later prove powerless to stop the aggression that grew out of these ambitions.

Toward World War II

The world that emerged after World War I was a far cry from "a world made safe for democracy." In Europe, victorious nations such as Britain and France were racked with disillusionment because much of their faith in reason and in the democratic process founded on reason had been destroyed. Deprived by the war of the generation that should have provided fresh leadership in the 1920s and 1930s, these two countries pursued listless and cynical courses.

In Russia, Italy, and Germany, also exhausted and embittered by war, totalitarianism found fertile ground as ruthless leaders offered new ideologies that promised a glowing future. When a worldwide and crushing depression struck in the 1930s, totalitarian regimes became even more despotic.

During these years, the non-European world was also in tumult. Strong feelings of nationalism were driving anticolonial movements in Asia, Africa, and the Middle East. China was caught in a struggle to regain both its former autonomy and strength, while Japan grew more militaristic and expansionist. Even Latin America, though ostensibly made up of independent nations, had its problems with foreign domination.

All this turmoil would propel the world into a second world war just 20 years after the first one had ended.

Totalitarianism on the Ascent

Propelling the world toward that war was a new kind of tyranny that took hold in parts of Europe. Authoritarian regimes exercised total control over their citizens' lives. This new type of authoritarian government began with Lenin's Communist regime in Russia and climaxed with the fascist regimes of Italy and Germany.

Communist Russia. The Russian Revolution of 1917 swept the czars from the throne, but it also created a devastating four-year civil war. The Bolsheviks, now renamed the Communists, won the war and Lenin proceeded to convert Russia into the Union of Soviet Socialist Republics. Under his rule, land and industries were nationalized and the Communist Party was made the sole authorized political party.

After Lenin's death in 1924, Joseph Stalin gained control of the Communist Party and began his dictatorial rule of the Soviet Union, which would last until his death in 1953. "The very essence and foundation of our policy," Stalin said, "is to transform our land from an agricultural to an industrial country." To

do this, Stalin inaugurated a series of "five-year plans" under which the government set rigorous production quotas for farms and factories. Peasants or workers who objected were ruthlessly punished, often with exile or death. Other "enemies of the state," real or imagined political opponents, were likewise "purged." Under Stalinism, the Soviet Union did industrialize, but at a great cost.

Fascist Italy. Italy emerged from the war in frustration. In 1915 the country had finally decided to throw in its lot with Great Britain and France. The Italian soldier had fought bravely, but poor leadership and inadequate supplies had made the Italian front more of a liability than an asset to the Allies.

At the Versailles conference, Italy's demands were submerged in the demands of others. The Italians left Versailles convinced that they had been cheated of their just due only because they were not as powerful as Britain, France, or the United States.

This feeling of national humiliation, combined with the failure of unification to achieve any significant national or international goals, led to the rise in 1922 of Benito Mussolini, a young former socialist leading a national fascist movement.

At the heart of fascist political theory was a belief in the inability of the individual to run his own life satisfactorily. The leader, *il duce* in Italian, must assume the heavy burden of responsibility for the individual. Only thus would the sickness of society be cured.

Nazi Germany. The road back to a semblance of normal life seemed incredibly long and difficult in Germany. After a series of short but violent revolutions, the country settled down under the ill-fated Weimar Republic.

The experiment in democratic republican government suffered from a dire lack of the most essential ingredient—believers in the democratic process. The upper classes sneered, and the lower classes looked to socialism for salvation.

Small splinter parties appeared like mayflies in the intense heat of opposition to the Weimar Republic. Among these small splinter groups was the National Socialist German Workers Party, the Nazis. Its only real resource was the oratorical talent of its leader, or *führer,* Adolf Hitler, who was an Austrian by birth.

During the 1920s the German people attempted to dig out of the ruins of defeat. Fortunes had been wiped out, the savings of the solid middle class had disappeared in inflation, and the threat of socialism seemed ever present. In a class-conscious society such as that of

Major Events — Toward World War II	
1921	John Larson invents the polygraph (lie detector) in Nova Scotia.
1922	Benito Mussolini comes to power in Italy.
1924	Joseph Stalin gains control of the Communist Party after Lenin's death.
1925	Nellie Taylor Ross of Wyoming becomes the first woman governor.
1926	The movie *The Jazz Singer,* starring Al Jolson, introduces the era of talking motion pictures.
1927	Charles Lindbergh makes the first nonstop solo flight across the Atlantic Ocean in 33.5 hours.
1928	The quartz crystal clock is invented.
1929	Economic depression engulfs countries worldwide; FM radio is introduced; Salvador Dali, a leading artist of the surrealist movement, paints *Illuminated Pleasures.*
1930	Planet Pluto discovered by Clyde Tombaugh at Lowell University.
1933	Adolf Hitler is made chancellor in Germany.
1936	Regular public television transmission begins in Great Britain.
1939	Alexander Fleming discovers penicillin; it is considered by many to be the greatest discovery of 20th-century medical science.

Germany, loss of social status was the ultimate evil and to be avoided at all cost.

The great achievement of the Weimar Republic was that it staved off a revolution for a decade. But the drain of reparations payments on Germany's financial resources prevented the revitalization of German business and, therefore, economic stability. As a result, the financial collapse in 1929 that marked the beginning of the world economic depression of the 1930s effectively sealed the doom of the Weimar Republic.

Hitler drew broad support from the desperate middle class that was rapidly being absorbed into the lower echelons of society. But in spite of inflation, chaos, the weakness of the Weimar Republic, and the fear of the dissolution of society itself, Hitler and the Nazis did not win a majority of votes in the elections held in November 1932. In fact, the Nazis actually lost seats in the German parliament, the *Reichstag.*

Hitler was brought to power by a right-wing cabal of men high in government who persuaded the president of Germany, the aged Paul von Hindenburg, to appoint Hitler chancellor. Once in power, Hitler lost no time in bringing his Nazi underlings into positions of power.

Nationalism Around the World

Just as political change was in the air in Europe, so it was in the world outside. While European imperialism brought colonialism to much of the world, it transmitted ideas of Western democracy and nationalism as well. As the 20th century unfolded, such ideas created nationalist movements around the globe. People who wanted to break the shackles of colonialism, gain their independence, and establish their own political systems mounted rebellions in numerous nations.

The Middle East. World War I had been the death blow for the feeble Ottoman Empire, which had joined the war on the German side. As the war began, the Ottoman Empire had lost nearly all its European territory. But it still controlled Turkey and the predominantly Arab territories of Iraq, Syria, Lebanon, Palestine, Trans-Jordan, and the western coast of the Arabian peninsula. The war would change the status of all these areas.

THOMAS EDWARD LAWRENCE (1888–1935), British soldier, administrator, and author, known as Lawrence of Arabia. In World War I he helped the Arabs revolt against the Turks and was instrumental in the conquest of Palestine (1918).

labor
US

labour
Brit.

Arab revolts. Even before the war, the Arabs of the Ottoman Empire had begun to demand home rule from the Ottoman Turks. During the war, the British encouraged Arab revolts against the Ottoman Empire, now considered the enemy. They sent Colonel T. E. Lawrence (later known as Lawrence of Arabia) to assist the Arabs in their fight against Ottoman Turkish forces. British and other Allied troops occupied lands along the eastern Mediterranean.

Once the war ended, though, the Arabs found they had traded Ottoman rule for European rule. The Treaty of Versailles dismembered much of the Ottoman Empire and pieces of it were granted as mandates, areas to be administered by victorious nations. Great Britain's mandates were Iraq, Trans-Jordan, and Palestine, while France got Syria and Lebanon.

Arab nationalism simmered and often boiled up under these mandates, but Britain and France were able to

maintain their rule. Only Iraq succeeded in satisfying its nationalist yearnings by becoming an independent kingdom in 1930, though Britain remained a powerful presence there because of its interests in Iraq's newly discovered oil fields.

Conflict in Palestine. From the beginning of British rule, Palestine was a hotbed of trouble. During the war, Britain had made promises to two different groups, agreements that were certain to put the two into conflict with each another. To keep Arab support against the Ottoman Empire, Great Britain had promised that Palestine could become part of an independent Arab state. But in 1917, Britain also issued the Balfour Declaration, promising that "His Majesty's government views with favour the establishment in Palestine of a national home for the Jewish people." This Jewish movement for a homeland, called Zionism, sent thousands of Jews emigrating to predominantly Arab Palestine.

At first, Jewish immigration was small. In 1919 the Arabs outnumbered the Jews by a hundred to one. But in 1929 violence broke out between the two groups, and the situation was exacerbated by the increase in Jewish immigration as anti-Semitism in Nazi Germany sent refugees streaming toward Palestine.

Saudi Arabia. On the Arabian peninsula, two rival families contested for power—the Sauds, led by Ibn Saud, and the Huseins, led by Husein ibn Ali. In 1924–1925, the two factions went to war. The Sauds won, and in 1932 the kingdom of Saudi Arabia was established. Four years later, its economic success was assured when oil was discovered under its endless sands.

Turkey. As far back as 1902, opposition to the enfeebled Ottoman government had been growing among Turks. At that time, the Young Turks, mainly reformers who had been educated in Western universities, and young military officers began demanding constitutional government and greater political freedom.

Following World War I, there was a resurgence of nationalist feeling as the Allies, by the 1920 Treaty of Sèvres, forced the Ottoman Empire to renounce all non-Turkish possessions. The nationalists were further incensed when the Greeks invaded and occupied a part of their remaining land. The Turkish nationalists soon rallied around a military hero, Mustafa Kemal Pasha, who had earlier been active in the Young Turk movement.

Kemal proved an able and energetic leader. By 1922 his armies had driven the Greeks out of Turkish territory. The next year the Ottoman Empire was officially abolished and the Republic of Turkey was proclaimed, with the popular Kemal as its first president.

Kemal's goal was to remodel Turkey into a progressive, westernized, industrialized nation. The form of government adopted was a Western-style

parliamentary democracy, though it became one that Kemal ruled with an iron hand. He decreed that political matters were to be separated from the Islamic religion, a connection that had formerly been absolute.

To westernize his nation further, he commanded that Turks wear Western-style clothes; he even banned the wearing of the fez, the traditional brimless Turkish hat. Kemal ordered Turks to take on surnames, like the Europeans. For himself he adopted the name Ataturk, meaning "father of the Turks."

Persia. Turkey's neighbor to the east, Persia, also sought to modernize after the war. For years Britain and Russia had squabbled over control of the weak Kajar dynasty that ruled in Persia. In 1925 an army officer named Reza Khan overthrew the last Kajar shah, or king, and took power as Reza Shah Pahlevi. He followed a path similar to that of Kemal Ataturk: to industrialize and otherwise westernize his country.

India against British rule. As the 1900s dawned in India, stirrings against British rule grew violent. In 1907 and 1908 Britain changed its policies somewhat to grant Indians more participation in their local governments. But the central Indian government remained firmly under British control, and those who wanted Great Britain out of India completely found little to satisfy them.

To retain the support of India during World War I, the British promised that India would gradually be granted self-government within the British Empire. After the war, Britain passed the Government of India Act of 1919, once again granting Indians more control over provincial matters, but also once again retaining control over such national matters as taxation, foreign policy, and justice. To India's leading political party, the militantly nationalist Indian National Congress, this fell far short of expectations.

In 1920 Mohandas K. Gandhi became the leader of the Indian National Congress. Gandhi advocated civil disobedience against the British—hunger strikes, labor strikes, mass demonstrations, boycotts of British goods, and nonpayment of taxes.

Gandhi advocated other programs for India as well. These included ending the stigmatization of the caste system and freeing the untouchables, improving the status of women, and replacing the centuries-old conflict between Hindus and Muslims with a spirit of tolerance and cooperation.

Hindu-Muslim conflict. Both Hindus and Muslims wanted Great Britain out of India, but antagonism between the two groups increased as they jockeyed for position in the Indian nation that would emerge after the fight for independence was won. Disputing the claim of the predominantly Hindu Indian National Congress to leadership of the independence movement, the Muslim

League emerged in the 1930s under the leadership of Muhammad Ali Jinnah. The league wanted no part of an independent India dominated by Hindus, and the specter of a divided India, part Hindu and part Muslim, was raised.

In 1937 a new Government of India Act went into effect, providing another step toward self-government. Under it, a British viceroy remained India's chief executive, but Indians gained autonomy in provincial government and control over all central government matters except foreign affairs and defense.

China. In China, the Boxer Rebellion of 1900 signaled that the Chinese were now intent on driving out the foreign influences that so dominated their land. This intent was voiced most strongly by young Chinese who had been sent to study in Western universities. They returned to China with ideas about nationalism, liberalism, and the democratic process.

Sun Yat-sen. Their leader was Sun Yat-sen, who had studied in the United States and Hawaii and had taken a medical degree in British-held Hong Kong. Sun Yat-sen founded the Kuomintang, or Nationalist People's Party, whose first order of business was to overthrow the dying Ch'ing dynasty. This was accomplished in 1912, following a rebellion in southern China. The Kuomintang proclaimed China a republic, with Sun Yen-sen as its first president and Guangzhou its capital.

Sun Yat-sen laid out his aims in the "Three Principles of the People": political unity for a China freed of imperialist domination; democratic government; and an economy that could provide a basic living for all Chinese people.

Meeting these ambitious aims soon proved impossible. The Kuomintang republic actually controlled only a small area of China. Powerful warlords—generals with their own armies—controlled much of the rest.

In 1917 a rival government proclaimed itself in Beijing. Kuomintang leaders asked for Western help to overcome the Beijing government, but only the Soviet Union responded. The Russians sent advisers to reorganize the government and to build up strong Nationalist armies to support it. When Sun Yat-sen died in 1925, his dream of a unified China was still unfulfilled.

Chlang Kal-shek. Sun Yat-sen's successor was Chiang Kai-shek, a young general who had served as military aide to the older leader. Under Chiang, the Nationalist armies began their drive north in 1926; within two years they occupied Beijing.

But by now, dissension had broken out between two wings of the Kuomintang. On one side were the conservatives under Chiang. They rejected radical reforms, such as taking property from big landowners and giving it to peasants. On the other side were members of the Chinese Communist Party,

which had been organized in 1921.

In 1927 Chiang took advantage of a Communist-inspired workers' uprising in Guangzhou to crush the left wing. Communist advisers from the Soviet Union were expelled and many radicals were exiled. Communists scattered to the hills and mountains of southeastern China, where they set up their own administration, calling it the Chinese Soviet Republic.

By 1928 Chiang headed a Nationalist government whose capital was Nanjing. He claimed that the Nationalists governed a united Chinese republic, but the unity was illusory. Many warlords had allied themselves with Chiang and agreed on paper that they were subordinate to him. Actually, though, they maintained their power over their territories and ruled them as they had in the past.

Foreign domination. By this time, China had made some strides in freeing itself from foreign domination. In 1922 Western nations and Japan signed the Nine-Power Treaty, in which they promised not to take advantage of China or to do harm to its citizens. In 1929 ten imperialist powers gave up their claims to special rights in China.

Mao Zedong. The Chinese Communists were led by Mao Zedong, who had been a student at Beijing University when he became a founding member of the Chinese Communist Party. Mao became convinced that the way to create a Communist China was to win the support of the peasant population. To do this, the Communists made major reforms in the territories they controlled, seizing large landowners' estates, dividing them up, and distributing them to the peasants. They also

reduced the peasants' onerous tax burdens. Mao's reforms succeeded in winning over many peasants.

Japanese aggression. Civil war was disastrous for China, retarding its industrialization and making life still more miserable for the peasants. China also had to contend with aggression from Japan. In 1931 Japanese troops marched into Manchuria. In 1937 Japanese forces attacked China in great strength, beginning the second Sino-Japanese War, which lasted until 1945. The Japanese captured Shanghai and Beijing and drove Chinese forces westward in retreat. In the face of such aggression, the Nationalists and Communists agreed to a truce and united under Chiang against the Japanese. For the Chinese, the situation was desperate; by 1939 Japan had control of one-quarter of their country.

THE CHINESE COMMUNIST PARTY celebrated the 30th anniversary of its foundation with a massive display of force in Peking. Here, units of the "Army of Liberation" march past the reviewing stand, which is marked by a large portrait of Mao Zedong.

CHIANG KAI-SHEK led the Nationalist Chinese from 1925 to 1949 but fled to Taiwan, still as leader of Nationalist China, when the Communist Chinese came to power.

21 History of the World

HO CHI MINH devoted his life to ridding Vietnam of foreign domination, but did not live long enough to see the end of the Vietnam War. The city formerly known as Saigon bears his name.

center
US

centre
Brit.

Japan. Japan's designs on China began with the Sino-Japanese War of 1894–1895. In 1915 Japan presented China with the Twenty-One Demands. If China had been forced to comply, Japan would have obtained virtual control of the country. Fortunately for China, the United States was able to convince Japan to back down.

Both Japan and China entered World War I on the side of the Allies, but Japan profited from this war at China's expense. The victorious Allies agreed that Japan could take control of China's iron-rich Shantung Province from defeated Germany rather than return it to China itself. Japan also retained the rights it had won in coal- and iron-rich Manchuria as a result of the Russo-Japanese War.

Evolution in government. In the decade following World War I, Japan seemed to be moving away from oligarchic government and toward the parliamentary democracy that its constitution set forth. In 1918 Hara Takashi became prime minister, the first commoner to reach such high office. In 1925 the Universal Suffrage Bill extended the vote to all males over age 25. But the Japanese military was scornful of democracy and eager for continued military expansion.

In 1929 Hamaguchi Yoko took office as Japan's most liberal prime minister to date. He tried to reduce the military's power by cutting expenditures for it and by becoming more conciliatory toward China. He also supported agreements made at the Washington Naval Conference of 1921 and the London Conference of 1930, which limited the size of the navies that the world powers could maintain. Powerful Japanese military officials opposed the agreements.

Industrialization had paid big dividends for Japan. By the 1920s its manufactures made Japan a world leader in trade, especially in textiles. Trade had become vital to the Japanese economy.

The worldwide depression that struck in the 1930s shattered Japanese trade. Markets for Japanese exports dried up, and, with that, Japan's ability to buy food and raw materials was severely curtailed.

Amid these national troubles, the military saw its chance. In 1932 it had the new prime minister, Tsuyoshi Inukai, assassinated, ending civilian control of government. A military clique overwhelmed parliamentary democracy and set out to take the raw materials Japan needed from China. Japan's invasion of China in 1937 was part of its plan which called for Chiang to be overthrown, all Western interests to be driven out of China, and Japan, China, and Manchuria to become one economic unit under Japanese leadership.

Southeast Asia. As the 1900s began in Southeast Asia, the area remained firmly in control of Great Britain, France, and the Netherlands. But in several areas there was anticolonial agitation. One of the first nationalist movements arose in the Philippines. In 1896 Filipinos staged an uprising against the Spanish. Following the outbreak of the Spanish-American War in 1898, Filipino nationalists proclaimed the Republic of the Philippines; independence was short-lived. American rule replaced Spanish rule following a three-year war of Filipinos and Americans. However, the United States promised to train the Filipinos in self-government and grant independence in 1945.

Nationalists in Burma took their cue from their neighbors, the Indians, in agitating for independence from Great Britain, working through the General Council of Burmese Associations. In 1937 Burma gained a parliamentary system of government and chose a Burmese prime minister, but a British governor controlled foreign relations and defense.

British Malaya, leading the world in the production of tin and rubber, did not yet feel strong nationalist stirrings. It had experienced a major influx of Chinese and Indians, who had come to work on the plantations and in the commercial ventures of Malaya.

In Indochina, France maintained an oppressive political and economic hold. The French did nothing to encourage education, so the Indochinese people remained almost entirely illiterate and bound to their traditional culture. This paved the way for anticolonial agitation, especially of the anti-imperialist Communist variety.

Vietnam led the way in organizing nationalist movements. One of the earliest was founded in the 1920s by Vietnamese who had returned from France, where they had worked during World War I and had become acquainted with liberal ideas. This movement was overtaken by the Indochina Communist Party, founded in 1930 by Nguyen That Than, later known as Ho Chi Minh. The party attempted an uprising against colonial rule that year, but the French crushed it. Despite the defeat, communism would remain at the center of the Vietnamese nationalist movement.

Anticolonialism followed a similar pattern in Dutch Indonesia. The first major nationalist movement there was mounted by the Islamic Union, founded in 1912. It had little success against powerful Dutch domination. Communist anticolonialism took the form of the Indonesian Communist Party, founded in 1920, but the uprising it staged in 1926–1927 was crushed just as the one in Vietnam had been.

Southeast Asian nationalist ambitions would now have to wait for World War II before achieving success.

Africa. World War I marked the beginning of the end for colonialism in Africa. African soldiers had fought for both Great Britain and France in that war. When the soldiers returned home, they brought European ideas of nationalism with them. Then, too, some Africans were being educated in Europe, and they too returned with Western ideas of independence and self-government.

The European imperial powers were not going to give up their colonial possessions easily. Following the war, rule over colonies was simply shifted around. The Treaty of Versailles gave former German colonies in Africa as mandates to the British, French, and Belgians. German Southwest Africa (later Namibia) was given as a mandate to the Union of South Africa.

North Africa. In 1919 Egyptian nationalists, chafing under their country's status as a British protectorate, staged a revolt that was put down by British troops stationed in the country. But in 1922 Great Britain did grant Egypt independence, though the British military presence remained strong. During the 1920s and 1930s, Algeria and Morocco staged unsuccessful revolts against their French rulers.

Sub-Saharan Africa. Following the end of World War I, a black nationalist movement called Pan-Africanism emerged. Led by the black American leader Dr. W.E.B. Du Bois, it sought to end both colonialism and supremacy of

W.E.B. DU BOIS, U.S. writer, scholar, and civil rights leader

whites in Africa, and to unite Africa under black rule. The movement did not call for immediate independence, however, but for a gradual shift toward self-government and equality of the races. Pan-Africanism's most valuable contribution to African nationalism was probably the scholarship it encouraged in African studies, which generated pride in African history and culture. Pan-Africanism also produced the future leaders of African independence—Jomo Kenyatta of Kenya and Kwame Nkrumah of Ghana among them.

Independence, however, was still far in the future. In the meantime, black Africans lived under a variety of colonial structures. Africans in British colonies were governed by "indirect rule," that is, the British governed through the tribal chiefs. This worked for a time in West Africa, where the population was overwhelmingly black. In places like Kenya and Rhodesia, however, white rule was much more evident because great numbers of British had come to settle permanently.

In the British dominion of the Union of South Africa, life under white rule became the hardest for blacks. Though tensions between the British and the Boers remained high, the two white groups were united by uneasiness over the numerical superiority of the black population—three blacks to each white.

To hold onto their power, South African whites created a policy of strict segregation. They relegated many blacks to tribal reservations; limited their movements and their permits to work; gave them only the lowest paying jobs; and barred them from all political participation.

In none of the African colonies were blacks really being prepared for self-government. Both the French and the Portuguese thought of their African colonies as overseas provinces, to be ruled by their countries' laws. They saw no reason to establish political institutions that were uniquely African. Neither did the Belgians, who ruled in a highly paternalistic way, improving medical services and elementary education but giving no encouragement to African political organization.

In the years preceding World War II, feelings of nationalism gradually gathered strength in black Africa, mainly among the small educated elite. Following World War II, this group would lead a drive to end imperialism.

Latin America. As the 20th century dawned in Latin America, people warily eyed the United States and Europe, both of which had invested heavily in Latin American nations. Revolutions, border disputes, and capricious dictators kept dissension within Latin America at a boil, inviting foreign interference.

Interventionism. Such interference became apparent in the early 1900s when both Venezuela and the Dominican Republic defaulted on European loans. British, German, and Italian ships blockaded Venezuela, a first step in getting Venezuela to pay its debt. President Theodore Roosevelt of the United States stepped in to bring the matter to arbitration. In 1904 he announced the Roosevelt Corollary to the Monroe Doctrine. From now on, it stated, the United States would exercise "international police power" in Latin America. If Europeans had a dispute with a Latin American nation, the American government would do what it deemed necessary to correct the problem, including sending American troops into Latin American countries and taking over tax collection in those countries.

To Latin Americans, this was another blatant example of "Yankee imperialism" on the part of the "Colossus of the North." They were still smarting over Roosevelt's intervention in the national affairs of Colombia. There, in 1903, the Colombian government had refused to sell the United States the right to build a canal across Colombia's northern province of Panama. Roosevelt encouraged Panama to rebel against Colombia and to declare its independence. The United States then promptly recognized Panama as a sovereign nation and bought permission to build the canal from it.

Latin American-U.S. relations continued to deteriorate as the United States intervened several times in the affairs of Latin American nations. American Marines occupied and set up military governments in Nicaragua (1912–1925 and 1927–1933), Haiti (1915–1934), and the Dominican Republic (1916–1924). American troops were also sent into Mexico twice, in 1914 and 1916, as that country was torn by a highly destructive civil war. In addition, American presidents invoked the Platt Amendment to intervene in Cuba on four occasions between 1906 and 1922.

In 1933 President Franklin D. Roosevelt sought to improve relations with Latin America by proclaiming the Good Neighbor Policy. Under this policy, the Platt Amendment and the Roosevelt Corollary were revoked and American troops were withdrawn. The United States committed itself to the principle of nonintervention, and a new era in hemisphere relations began. As World War II loomed, the United States agreed to consult with the South and Central American countries on hemisphere defense, thereby modifying a policy of unilateralism that dated from the Monroe Doctrine (1823). The goodwill thus engendered provided a base for wartime solidarity. Only one Western Hemisphere country, Argentina, remains neutral.

Economic developments. In the Latin American nations the norm became economic dependency on producing one or two primary products for export. For example, Brazil depended on coffee, Venezuela on oil, Cuba on sugar, Chile on nitrates, Argentina on wheat and meat, Central American

HAILE SELASSIE was emperor of Ethiopia from 1930 to 1974, when he was deposed by an army rebellion.

countries on bananas, and Bolivia on tin.

World War I created a boom for such products that lasted well into the 1920s. But as European agricultural production recovered, prices for Latin American foodstuffs fell. When the worldwide depression struck, between 1929 and 1932, the value of Latin American exports dropped 65 percent.

During this time, Latin American governments tried to encourage the development of industries to produce consumer goods to make their countries less dependent on imports and on the necessity to sell exports. The United States and Great Britain flooded Latin America with cheap imports to discourage the competition that Latin American industry might create. However, Germany under Hitler encouraged Latin American industrialization, bartering German factory machinery for commodities.

Authoritarian regimes. The effects of the Great Depression on Latin America were similar to those elsewhere—severe unemployment, inability to pay debts, and political unrest. During the 1930s, nearly every government in Latin America was overthrown as political power shifted from landed gentry and exporters, ruined by the depression, to the emerging middle class and the military.

Since the wars for independence from Spain in the early 19th century, the military establishments of Latin America had believed that their interests were inseparable from those of their nations. In the 20th century, the military continued to exert a strong influence on government in Latin America by intervening in civil affairs. During the 1930s, several military officers emerged as dictators: Fulgencio Batista in Cuba, Rafael Trujillo in the Dominican Republic, and Anastasio Somoza in Nicaragua.

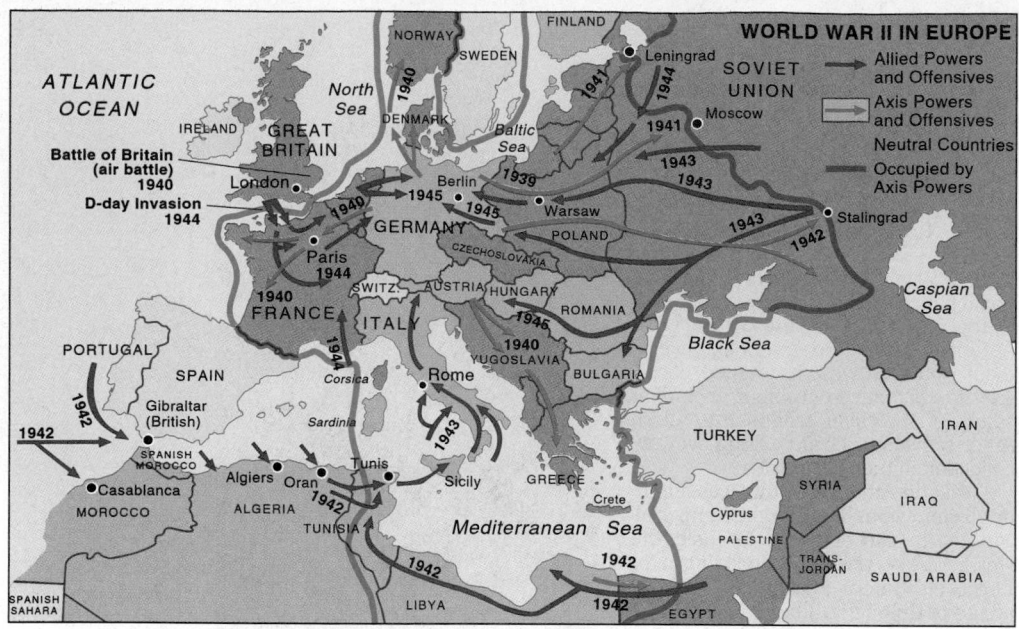

WORLD WAR II IN EUROPE

→ Allied Powers and Offensives
→ Axis Powers and Offensives
Neutral Countries
→ Occupied by Axis Powers

Social reform. The revolution in Mexico in 1910 spearheaded a drive for social reform in Latin America. Mexico led the way in appropriating land from the large landowners and redistributing it among the peasants. It also encouraged the organization of trade unions as it sought to break the hold of foreign investors over national resources and workers.

Other Latin American nations also tried to improve life for both peasants and urban workers. But rapidly growing populations helped to ensure that widespread poverty would persist.

World War II

During the 1930s, events in Europe, Asia, and Africa were leading the world inexorably toward another world war. Although few people realized it at the time, Hitler's advent to power

was the decisive moment in the first half of the 1900s. He had spelled out his program in the 1920s in his book *Mein Kampf (My Struggle),* which underlined the necessity of a resounding German military victory in Europe to restore the honor and integrity of Germany.

National expansion was a constant theme of Nazi ideology. It promoted the dogma that the Nordic, or Germanic, peoples were a superior race, and that it was the destiny of this race to rule mankind. The Jews, according to this racist doctrine, were at the opposite end of the racial ladder, an inferior race and an obstruction to the conquering path of Nazism. As a result, Jews were excluded from social and political activities, forbidden from holding religious observances, and, eventually, taken to specially constructed extermination centers where over 6 million of them were murdered.

The road to war. Hitler began his expansion in 1936 by sending German troops into a section of western Germany called the Rhineland, in direct violation of the Treaty of Versailles. In that same year, Germany signed a pact with Italy, forming a military alliance called the Rome-Berlin Axis. The year 1936 also marked Italy's conquest of Ethiopia in Africa. In 1938 German troops marched into Austria and annexed it to Germany, another violation of the Versailles treaty. None of these actions met opposition from the Allied powers.

During this same period, German and Italian fighting men and weapons were being tested in support of the rebels led by Francisco Franco in the Spanish Civil War of 1936–1939.

Next, Hitler demanded that the Sudetenland, part of Czechoslovakia, be returned to Germany. Great Britain and France, unprepared for war, agreed, with the understanding that this would be the last German expansion move. In the meantime, Japan, soon to become part of the Axis, was waging war in China.

War in Europe. In 1939 the Nazis occupied the rest of Czechoslovakia. It became clear that a line had to be drawn somewhere or Hitler would swallow all of Europe. Great Britain and France finally took a stand on the issue of Poland's territorial integrity.

Stalin recognized that Russia was unprepared for a Nazi assault should Hitler turn farther to the east and so signed a nonaggression pact with Germany that profoundly shocked Communist parties throughout the world. That pact sealed Poland's fate. On September 1, 1939, German forces began the dismemberment of Poland; and then on September 3, France and England declared war on Germany.

It took Hitler only a short time to defeat Poland. Then, in May 1940, he turned against the West. The *Wehrmacht* swept past defensive positions in France, defeated the French and British armies, and forced France to surrender on June 22, 1940. British forces managed to escape in a massive boat lift at Dunkirk, but watched helplessly as the Nazi tide, helped by Italy, spread over Greece, Crete, Norway, and North Africa. The Royal Air Force fought the gallant Battle of Britain in the skies over Great Britain during September and October of 1940. Hitler had hoped the German air attack would force the British to sue for peace. The attack failed.

In 1941 Hitler invaded Russia and committed the better part of his armies to this new conquest. In the same year, the Japanese attacked the United States naval base at Pearl Harbor and thereby brought America into the war. As American industrial might and productivity began to make itself felt, the tide began to turn against the Axis powers. The armies of the Soviet Union, aided

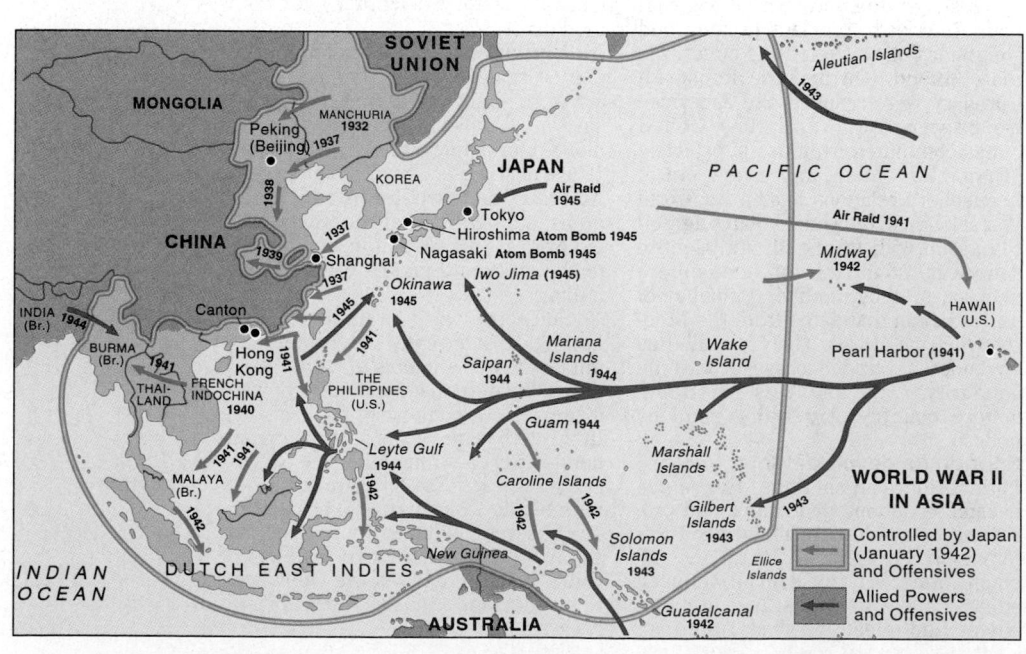

WORLD WAR II IN ASIA

→ Controlled by Japan (January 1942) and Offensives
→ Allied Powers and Offensives

by winter, halted the German advance and began to push the *Wehrmacht* back. In 1944 the British and Americans invaded France. On May 7, 1945, Germany surrendered and the war in Europe ended.

War in Asia and the Pacific.

After war began in Europe in 1939, Japan stepped up its attempt to create a new order in Asia. In 1940, with Germany's defeat of France, Japanese forces seized French Indochina; during 1941 they set out to conquer the rest of Southeast Asia, including the U.S.-held Philippines. Within six months after Pearl Harbor, the Japanese controlled nearly all of Southeast Asia as well as Pacific Islands nearly as far east as Midway and the Hawaiian Islands.

On the mainland of Asia, the Allies supported Chiang Kai-shek with supplies in China's fight against Japan. In Burma, British and Australian troops battled Japanese forces to keep supply routes open from India to China. Resistance forces such as those led by Ho Chi Minh worked against the Japanese in Indochina. Meanwhile, the United States was following an island-hopping strategy across the Pacific, capturing Japanese-held islands and turning them into bases from which an assault on Japan itself could finally be mounted.

By April 1945, Japan was being heavily bombarded. Then, on August 6, the United States dropped its newly developed atomic bomb on Hiroshima, followed by another on Nagasaki three days later. Devastated by nuclear warfare, Japan surrendered on August 14 and World War II finally ended.

Aftermath of war.

Peace came in 1945 to a Europe that had suffered more than at any time since the barbarian invasions of Rome. A new word, *genocide,* was coined to describe the Nazi attempts to wipe out the Jews and other "inferior" races of Europe. The discovery that 6 million Jews, 6 million Slavs, and others had actually been killed in special extermination camps shocked a world that thought it had seen every imaginable kind of cruelty. The moral foundations of Europe had been severely battered by this display of barbarism.

The physical state of Europe was no better. Strategic bombing had leveled cities, destroyed industries, and disrupted communications. Everything would have to be rebuilt, including the structure of governments.

Large parts of Asia also were devastated by war, especially China, which had been fighting for eight years. Little pleasure could be taken in Japan's defeat there; it meant only that civil war between Nationalists and Communists could resume. Japan had suffered massive damage, and it also had been humiliated, its military ruling regime disgraced.

World War II

1939
Sep. 1	Germany invades Poland.
Sep. 3	Britain and France declare war on Germany.
Oct.	Germany employs Sitzkrieg ("false war") tactic on the Western Front.

1940
Apr. 9	Germany invades, and quickly conquers, Denmark and Norway.
May 10	Germany invades Belgium and the Netherlands.
May 12	Germans cross the French frontier using Blitzkrieg (air, tank, and infantry "lightning strike") tactics.
May 28	German victories force the British evacuation of Dunkirk.
June 10	Italy declares war on France and Great Britain.
June 14	Germans enter Paris. The city is undefended.
June 22	France signs an armistice with Germany.
July 10	The Battle of Britain begins with German saturation bombings of British military installations, factories, and land and sea transportation sites; the British respond by destroying over 1,500 German Luftwaffe bombers.

1941
Apr. 6	Germany invades Yugoslavia and Greece.
June 22	Germany invades the Soviet Union.
Aug. 14	The Atlantic Charter, a joint declaration of war policy, is signed by Roosevelt and Churchill.
Sep. 8	German troops begin the siege of Leningrad, which lasts until January 1944.
Dec. 7	Japanese attack Pearl Harbor.
Dec. 11	The United States and Britain declare war on Japan; Germany and Italy declare war on the United States.

1942
Feb. 15	The British surrender Singapore to the Japanese.
Apr. 9	U.S. forces on Bataan in the Philippines surrender.
May 6	Americans and Filipinos on Corregidor Island in Manila Bay surrender to the Japanese.
June 6	U.S. planes destroy the Japanese fleet at the Battle of Midway.
July 10	Allied forces invade Sicily.
Aug. 7	U.S. Marines land at Guadalcanal in the first amphibious assault that allows U.S. naval forces to push back the Japanese.
Aug. 25	Hitler orders his forces to capture Stalingrad.
Oct. 23	British forces attack the Axis powers at El Alamein in Egypt.
Nov. 8	Allied troops land in Algeria and Morocco.

1943
Feb. 1	The German 6th Army surrenders at Stalingrad, a major turning point in the war in Russia.
May 13	Axis forces in northern Africa surrender.
July 25	Mussolini is deposed; Badoglio is named premier.
Sep. 3	Allied troops land at Salerno, Italy.
Sep. 8	Italy surrenders.
Sep. 10	German troops seize Rome.

1944
June 4	U.S. and British troops enter Rome.
June 6	Allied troops land in Normandy for D-day invasion.
July 20	Plot to assassinate Hitler fails.
Aug. 25	Paris is liberated.
Oct. 13	Athens is freed by the Allies.
Dec. 16	Germans strike back at U.S. troops in the Battle of the Bulge—the last major German counteroffensive.

1945
Apr. 20	Benito Mussolini is executed at Lake Como by Italian Partisans.
Apr. 30	Hitler takes his life in Berlin.
May 7	Germany surrenders unconditionally to the Allies in Reims, France, ending World War II in Europe (V-E Day).
Aug. 6	The United States drops the first atomic bomb on Hiroshima, Japan; more than 78,000 people are killed in a single minute.
Aug. 9	A second atomic bomb is dropped, on Nagasaki, Japan.
Sep. 2	Japanese sign surrender terms aboard the battleship *Missouri* (V-J Day).

TOTAL WAR DEATHS: 35,695,000

Major Participants (total military and civilian deaths)

Allied Powers		Axis Powers
Belgium (150,000)	Poland (6,445,000)	Bulgaria (24,000)
Canada (39,000)	Soviet Union (15,000,000)	Germany (4,000,000)
France (675,000)	United States (408,000)	Hungary (836,000)
Great Britain (450,000)	Yugoslavia (1,400,000)	Italy (220,000)
Netherlands (206,000)		Japan (2,000,000)
		Romania (626,000)

21 History of the World

The World Since 1945

In the half century following World War II, the world was transformed more completely and dramatically than ever before in history. Established nations changed politically and economically; new nations emerged. Rapid technological advances in warfare, transportation, and communications altered people's general view of the world. In an age of potential universal annihilation, a new perception arose that all nations must work toward a common destiny, that humanity is, in fact, a sort of "global village."

Even before the war had ended, a new international organization was founded. It was pledged to establish and maintain a just peace in the post-war world. In April 1945, representatives of 50 nations met in San Francisco to draft a charter for the United Nations (UN). Their hope was that the UN could succeed where the earlier League of Nations had failed.

For the UN, as for the League before it, world peace proved difficult to maintain. The United States and the Soviet Union emerged as powerful rivals, polarizing much of the world into a capitalist, and largely democratic, Western bloc, led by the United States, and a Communist Eastern bloc, led by the Soviet Union. This division plunged the world into a bitter ideological struggle that came to be called the Cold War. The history of the fifty years following World War II is largely the history of that struggle. From 1945 to 1950, the Cold War

centered
US
centred
Brit.

labor
US
labour
Brit.

was centered in Europe, but in the following years, it moved out to include the emerging nations of Asia, the Middle East, Africa, and Latin America.

In the late 1980s, however, the world was remade. New leadership in the Soviet Union and in Eastern Europe led to political, social, and economic changes that were inconceivable only a short time earlier.

Europe

As Allied victory became assured in the closing months of World War II, there was no coherent plan for postwar Europe. During the war the Allies had held top-level meetings at Teheran in Iran and at Yalta in the Soviet Union. At these meetings the "Big Three"—Franklin D. Roosevelt of the United States, Winston Churchill of Great Britain, and Joseph Stalin of the Soviet Union—discussed the reconstruction of postwar Europe. The question of what to do with Germany was left open. All that was decided was that there would be occupation zones—the Russians to occupy eastern Germany; Britain, United States, and France would share the western part.

The occupation zones hardened into two new countries. In 1949 the German Democratic Republic, East Germany, was established under Russian aegis. The Federal Republic of Germany, West Germany, was guarded by the British, French, and Americans. The creation of the two Germanies marked a larger phenomenon, the consolidation of Soviet rule in Eastern Europe, which, in effect, became a Soviet dependency. As Winston Churchill remarked, an iron curtain had fallen across Europe, dividing it into a Communist East and a democratic West and restricting communication and travel between the two.

The political reorganization of Europe took place at the same time that attempts were being made to revive the European economy. In 1947 George C. Marshall, the American secretary of state, proposed a plan for the economic recovery of Europe that involved heavy American subsidies. The Marshall Plan was offered to all the nations that had suffered from World War II, including the Soviet Union and the countries of Eastern Europe. The Soviet Union declined and also forced its satellites to forgo the benefits of the plan. The rest of Europe eagerly accepted the helping hand. The results were dramatic. Western Europe made a rapid economic recovery, although at a different pace in different countries, and by the 1950s, normality had been regained.

Things were different on the other side of the iron curtain. The Soviet Union determined to follow a socialist course in recovering from its terrible

losses in the war, and could do it only by political and economic domination of the lands that had fallen under its control. Countries behind the iron curtain were drawn into a close economic embrace, and their economies subordinated to Russian needs. The standard of living in the Communist countries rose with glacial slowness, in contrast to the incredible rapidity with which the standard of living in the West shot up.

Cold War in Europe. The firm hold that the Soviet Union maintained on the countries of Eastern Europe convinced the West that the Soviets intended to expand Communist influence throughout the world. In 1947 President Harry Truman of the United States instituted a policy of containment of the Soviet Union, promising American military and economic assistance to any country that felt itself threatened by Soviet domination.

In 1949 the United States initiated the North Atlantic Treaty Organization (NATO), an alliance of the United States, Canada, and ten Western European nations committed to mutual defense in the event of a Soviet attack. In May 1955, West Germany was granted membership in NATO. The Soviet Union countered by organizing the Warsaw Treaty Organization, or Warsaw Pact, a mutual defense alliance including the Soviet Union and the seven Eastern European nations it dominated. Europe was clearly split into two opposing camps, both armed but maintaining an uneasy peace.

Western European integration. The economic miracle achieved in postwar Western Europe owed much of its success to a growing spirit of unity among its nations. In 1949 the Council of Europe formed to link them socially, culturally, and economically. In 1951 Belgium, France, Italy, Luxembourg, the Netherlands, and West Germany forged the European Economic Coal and Steel Community, which served to unify these countries' coal, iron, and steel industries.

In 1957 these same nations signed the Treaty of Rome, which established the European Economic Community, or Common Market. Its aims were to eliminate barriers to free trade among its members and to facilitate the movement of labor and capital among them. The old economic walls that had served to separate the countries of Europe began to tumble down. There was not, however, universal agreement on the nature and scope of economic reforms. France, under Charles de Gaulle's leadership, played a leading role in the organization, and was able, at first, to exclude Great Britain from the Common Market. It was only in 1973 that Britain finally joined the European Community.

Major Events — The World Since 1945

1945	The Charter of the United Nations is signed by 50 countries in San Francisco on June 16.
1947	British rule ends in India.
1948	The first long-playing record is developed.
1949	NATO is established.
1950	Commercial color television begins in the United States.
1957	The Common Market is established in Europe; the first artificial satellite, *Sputnik 1*, is launched by the Soviet Union.
1960	Theodore Maimen develops the first laser using a ruby cylinder.
1961	Alan Shepard is the first U.S. astronaut in space; Soviet cosmonaut Yuri Gagarin becomes the first man to orbit Earth.
1963	U.S. President John F. Kennedy is assassinated.
1969	Neil Armstrong, an American astronaut, becomes the first man to walk on the moon, on July 21.
1974	OPEC quadruples the price of oil, causing worldwide inflation.
1975	The first personal computer is introduced; it has 256 bytes of memory.
1981	The *Columbia*, the first reusable space shuttle, completes its first orbital flight.
1985	Mikhail Gorbachev begins an era of glasnost and perestroika in the Soviet Union.
1989	Major democratic reforms sweep across Eastern Europe; Hungary declares itself a republic; Czechoslovakia forms a coalition government; democratic elections are held in Poland; the Berlin Wall is dismantled.

AT THE YALTA CONFERENCE (left to right), Winston Churchill, Franklin D. Roosevelt, and Joseph Stalin planned the post-World War II reorganization of Europe.

The existence of the Common Market cast into sharp relief those countries that were not members. Spain and Portugal had been excluded because their fascist regimes were repugnant to the founding members. In 1968 Antonio de Oliveira Salazar, the dictator of Portugal for 30 years, suffered a stroke from which he did not recover. In 1974 a full-fledged revolution overthrew the authoritarian Portuguese regime and, within a year, a democratic republic emerged. Events were not so dramatic in Spain. Francisco Franco died in 1975. Spain is now a constitutional monarchy. Elections in 1977 were the first free ones since the Spanish Civil War of 1936.

In 1986 the nations of the Common Market, now numbering twelve, took a further step toward Western European unity with the Single European Act. Under its provisions, all barriers to trade among the nations were to be removed as of 1992, when the twelve would be united in a single economic market, the largest and richest consumer and business market in the world. The act was ratified in July 1987.

The Soviet bloc. The Soviet Union had suffered during World War II more than any other nation, with an estimated loss of 20 million Russian lives. Eager to create a security zone of satellite states as a buffer between Western Europe and the Soviet Union, Stalin consolidated the Soviet hold over the Eastern European nations it had occupied during the war—Estonia, Latvia, Lithuania, Poland, East Germany, Czechoslovakia, Hungary, Romania, and Bulgaria. (Two others, Yugoslavia and Albania, succeeded in breaking away from Soviet domination, though they retained Communist governments.)

Stalin died in 1953, and after a power struggle in the Communist Party, Nikita Khrushchev became the Soviet premier. In 1956, in a secret speech that stunned the party bureaucracy, Khrushchev denounced Stalinist tyranny. He then initiated a series of reforms that aimed at "de-Stalinizing" the Soviet Union. But Khrushchev had no intention of easing Soviet domination of the Eastern bloc. In 1956 Hungary made an effort to break away, but Soviet tanks rolled in to crush the revolt. Meanwhile, discontented East Germans were fleeing to West Germany by the thousands, many through Berlin, which was still under the joint occupation of the Allies. In 1961 the Berlin Wall was built through the city by the East German government to stop the flow of refugees. In 1968 Czechoslovakia tried to liberalize its Communist rule, only to be invaded and subdued by Warsaw Pact troops ordered there by Leonid Brezhnev, Khrushchev's successor.

In 1949, in response to the Marshall Plan that revived Western Europe, the Soviet Union had set up the Council for Mutual Economic Assistance (Comecon) to promote economic unity and growth in the Soviet bloc. The Soviet Union had hoped that Comecon would make it the economic equal of the United States by the year 2000. But Comecon did not work, and unrest in the Eastern bloc grew. By the 1980s severe economic problems were weakening the Soviet Union's ability to maintain its dominance.

Poland provided a striking example of growing popular discontent within the socialist countries. The unavailability of consumer goods, high food prices, low wages, and repressive government contributed to the general unrest. In the fall of 1981, a nationwide labor movement called Solidarity emerged. Through strikes and demonstrations, it gained power and popularity until Polish Prime Minister General Wojciech Jaruzelski, under pressure from the Soviet Union, declared martial law, banned Solidarity, and imprisoned its leaders. But by the end of the decade, Poland's economic problems finally forced its Communist Party to alter its stance. Solidarity was legalized, and, after elections in 1989, Solidarity and the Communist Party fashioned a fusion government.

Much of the impetus for change in Poland and other Eastern European countries came from a change in leadership in the Soviet Union. In 1985 Mikhail Gorbachev came to power and called for a new era of *glasnost,* or "openness," across Eastern Europe.

Gorbachev permitted the countries of Eastern Europe to follow their own courses of development free of the threat of Soviet military intervention. The result was widespread repudiation of communism by these countries.

In the fall of 1989 East Germany, one of the last hard-line Communist countries, saw the virtual disintegration of its Communist Party in the face of economic chaos and revelations of party corruption. The new East German government began dismantling the Berlin Wall, the very symbol of the Cold War, and less than a year later the two Germanies were finally reunited. By the end of 1989, not only Germany had seen a revolution, but Czechoslovakia, Hungary, Romania, and Bulgaria had also disposed of their Communist governments.

In the Soviet Union, Gorbachev inaugurated freer elections, loosened government control of the media, and instituted a reorganization of the economy, including the right to run a private business, and reduction of bureaucratic Communist Party control of industrial management. Calling his economic changes *perestroika,* or "restructuring," he hoped to improve the increasingly strained condition of the Soviet economy.

In 1990 the Soviet government ended the Communist Party's monopoly of political power. However, Gorbachev's efforts to revitalize the Soviet economy and political system were not successful. The Baltic republics of Lithuania and Estonia declared independence and the Soviet Union began to fragment. Gorbachev's attempt to secure a new Union treaty among the Soviet republics ended in August 1991, when a government coup attempted but failed to remove him from power. Several more republics declared independence, and in December the Soviet Union was dissolved.

TRYGVE HALVDAN LIE (1896–1968), the lawyer, diplomat, and first secretary-general of the United Nations, is broadcasting from Luxembourg palace to all nations taking part in the Paris Conference.

Attempts at détente. At the heart of Cold War tensions was the threat of nuclear warfare. Both sides had built up their nuclear arsenals until each was capable of destroying the world many times over. The standoff created by the fear of nuclear attack came to be called the "balance of terror."

In the early 1970s, the United States and the Soviet Union began looking for ways to ease international tensions, a process that took the name *détente.* Early efforts centered on arms reduction, especially the Strategic Arms Limitations Talks (SALT), by which the superpowers agreed to limit the number of nuclear missiles and warheads each could stockpile.

Disarmament agreements grew still more important to the Soviet Union in the 1980s as economic troubles made cutting the Soviet military budget a necessity. In December 1988, Gorbachev announced a major military cutback and ordered the removal of thousands of tanks, artillery pieces, and missiles, as well as half a million Soviet troops, from Eastern Europe. For their part, the countries of Western Europe exhibited strong interest in reducing armaments on their territory as well as in increasing trade with the Soviet Union and Eastern Europe.

The collapse of the Soviet Union in 1991 marked the end of the Cold War. Key international concerns became the restructuring of the economies of the former Soviet republics and the dismantling of their holdings of the vast Soviet nuclear arsenal.

Asia

Following World War II, the nations of Asia were at last able to break the colonial grip in which they had been held. Between 1947 and 1962, independence movements fought the colonial powers

centered
US

centred
Brit.

and succeeded in instituting new national governments. These newly independent nations, along with China and Japan, struggled to develop modern economies and to achieve political stability.

The Indian subcontinent. In 1945 the British government promised that the Indian subcontinent and the British colony of Ceylon, off India's southern coast, would be granted independence no later than 1948. But as the Indians tried to draw up a constitution, the centuries-old Hindu-Muslim conflict flared again. The Muslim League demanded that India be partitioned into two states: India for the Hindus and Pakistan for the Muslims. The British government acceded, and in August 1947 British rule ended in India. In 1948 Ceylon became independent. It later renamed itself Sri Lanka.

The partition of India led to the displacement of millions and countless acts of violence, as Hindus fled Muslim Pakistan and Muslims fled Hindu India. In the exchange of more than 10 million people, about 500,000 were killed. Mohandas K. Gandhi, an opponent of partition, was another casualty, killed by an anti-Muslim Hindu fanatic in 1948.

Conditions did not improve between India and Pakistan in the decades that followed. Border disputes broke out regularly and violently, especially over the rich province of Kashmir, peopled mainly by Muslims but governed mainly by India.

Internal strife. Acrimonious disputes between groups within the newly independent states emerged as well. In 1971 civil war erupted in Pakistan, whose eastern and western sections were separated by a thousand miles on opposite sides of northern India. East Pakistan, angered at West Pakistan's dominance in government, gained India's support and fought off West Pakistani troops to become the independent state of Bangladesh in 1972.

In India, controversy over language and religion created internal dissension. When Hindi was declared the official language of India in 1965, speakers of India's 13 other major languages objected, especially the Tamil speakers of the south. The protesters saw it as an attack by the central government on provincial rights and traditions. In the 1980s, the Sikhs, a militant religious sect based in the Punjab, stepped up their demands for independence from India. The violence peaked in 1984, with the bloody suppression in June of a Sikh uprising. This action led to Prime Minister Indira Gandhi's assassination in October 1984, by two Sikh members of her bodyguard. Bloody reprisals against Sikhs followed.

During the 1980s, Sri Lanka was torn by the rebellion of its Tamil people, who resented the control that the majority people, the Sinhalese, held over Sri Lanka's government. Thousands were killed in the resulting conflict between Tamil guerrillas and the Sinhalese

government troops.

A civil war also erupted in Afghanistan, Pakistan's northern neighbor. In 1978 a coup put a pro-Soviet Communist government in power, leading to a revolt by anti-Communist Afghan rebels. The following year, the Soviet Union sent in an estimated 100,000 troops to bolster the Communist regime and help suppress the rebellion. During the nine years of war that followed, some million Afghans were killed and hundreds of thousands of Afghan refugees crossed the border into Pakistan, severely straining that country's resources. In early 1989, the last Soviet troops in Afghanistan were withdrawn. At first it was believed that the Communist regime in Kabul would soon collapse without Soviet military aid, but Afghan guerrillas were unable to score a decisive military victory. The civil war continued unabated.

Economic challenges. The rapidly growing population of South Asia puts a severe strain on the food production capabilities of the area. India's population alone, which grew from 350 million in 1947 to over 600 million in 1975, and over 1 billion in 2000, has been repeatedly threatened by famine. Only "Green Revolution" gains in food production have held it at bay. In Bangladesh, an extremely high population density and frequent devastating floods have repeatedly produced famine and homelessness. Other nations of South Asia are at risk as well.

China. At the close of World War II, after the unifying effect of the Japanese invasion had dissipated, civil war between Chiang Kai-shek's Nationalist forces and Mao Zedong's Communist "People's Liberation Army" resumed. Mao had gained the broad support of the peasants he had sought, and by 1948 the Nationalists were in full retreat and the Communists were gaining control of China. On October 1, 1949, Mao proclaimed the establishment of the People's Republic of China, with its capital at Beijing. Chiang and his remaining forces fled to the island of Formosa, or Taiwan, 100 miles off China's southeastern coast. There he proclaimed the Nationalist government of the Republic of China, with its capital at Taipei. Both claimed to be the sole legal government of all of China.

Communist economics. The government Mao established was a dictatorship of the Chinese Communist Party. Members of its People's Central Committee held all of the major civil and military positions; they were directed by Mao, who was chairman of the republic.

In 1958 Mao announced the Great Leap Forward, to speed up both agricultural and industrial production. The Great Leap Forward did not produce the dramatic results expected. Bad weather conditions, poor central planning, and oppressive working conditions impeded production.

INDIRA GANDHI, daughter of Jawaharlal Nehru, served India as prime minister from 1966 to 1977 and again from 1980 to 1984. She was assassinated in 1984 by a member of her own security guard.

THE KOREAN WAR was considered a mere police exercise when it began. Some American troops are still stationed in South Korea as monitors.

The Cultural Revolution.
By the mid-1960s, Communist leadership in China was divided between the pragmatists, who favored gradual economic development and social change, and Mao and his followers, who felt radical means had to be used to keep the process of revolution going.

In 1966 Mao launched the Great Proletarian Cultural Revolution. Paramilitary groups of students, called the Red Guards, attacked the "elite"—government officials, managers, and intellectuals—declaring them enemies of the people. Chaos ensued all over China as violence disrupted government, industrial production, and education. Not until 1969 was the army able to restore order and bring the Red Guards under control.

The Korean War.
China emerged early as a major player in the Cold War. Japan's defeat in World War II had freed Korea from 35 years of Japanese domination. At the end of the war, Soviet troops occupied the northern part of Korea and American troops the southern part. In 1948 the foreign troops pulled out, but they left a country divided into a Communist North Korea and a non-Communist South Korea.

In June 1950 North Korea invaded South Korea, in an attempt to reunite Korea under Communist rule. The United States asked the United Nations to send in troops to defend South Korea. By November, UN forces, mainly comprised of U.S. troops, had driven North Korean forces to the Chinese border. Before the North Korean army could be completely defeated, however, some 200,000 Chinese troops swept across the border to join the conflict. The fighting continued until an armistice was signed in July 1953. It returned North and South Korea to their prewar borders and statuses.

Changing foreign relations.
In the late 1950s, ideological differences began to cause strains between China and the Soviet Union. In 1959 the Soviet Union halted all aid to China and in the 1960s the two countries clashed in border skirmishes. However, as Chinese relations with the Soviet Union deteriorated, those with the United States warmed. In 1972, U.S. President Richard M. Nixon visited China, ending more than 20 years of hostility and opening diplomatic relations.

Modernizing China.
Both Mao Zedong and Prime Minister Jou En-lai, the central figures in the Chinese Communist Party for decades, died in 1976. Soon, a more pragmatic wing of the Communist Party gained control of the government. China declared its dedication to four modernizations that were to be achieved by the year 2000—in agriculture, industry, the military, and science and technology.

To achieve these aims, China moved away from Communist ideological purity and toward greater economic incentives for peasants and workers; less central planning and more entrepreneurial activity; and more contact with the West, encouraging Western investment in China and increased Western trade.

Political reforms did not keep pace with economic reforms in China, though. In June 1989 student demonstrations for greater political freedoms were brutally crushed by units of the People's Liberation Army, evoking worldwide protest.

Japan.
Unlike Germany, Japan was not divided into zones of foreign occupation after World War II. Only American forces occupied Japan.

The Allies had arrived at two major postwar aims for Japan: to eliminate any possibility of renewed Japanese militarism, and to turn Japan into a democratic state. To accomplish the first, Japan was totally demilitarized; the United States promised to provide defense for Japan should it be threatened militarily. Also, an emphasis was placed on the education of Japanese children away from militarism. For instance, textbooks were rewritten to eliminate any glorification of Japan's military tradition.

To accomplish the second goal, democratization, the Japanese emperor was required to renounce his claim to divinity; however, he was permitted to remain as a figurehead monarch. More importantly, in 1947 the Japanese adopted a new constitution that established a parliamentary form of government. It also granted women full equality, including the right to vote.

Japan's economic miracle.
By the time the American occupation ended in 1952, Japan was well on its way to not merely full economic recovery, but to creating the second highest gross national product in the world.

At first Japan concentrated its resources on the development of heavy industry and textiles. By 1957 Japan had the most modern steel mills in the world and surpassed France and West Germany in industrial production. Japan then turned to light industry, specifically high-technology products such as electronic equipment and components. By the 1970s, it had surpassed the former world leader in high technology, the United States, in many areas.

WEST MEETS EAST as the cultures of nations on opposite sides of the globe are brought together.

21 History of the World

A JAPANESE WOMAN shops at an American-style supermarket in Tokyo, Japan.

Japan's economic success resulted from three major sources: a stable, conservative government, mainly under the leadership of the Liberal Democratic Party, that has fostered pro-business policies; a well-educated work force; and a high personal savings rate, which helped to provide the capital needed for long-range business development.

However, Japan's economic miracle was achieved at high cost. Industrialization has taken its toll on the environment and has concentrated more than half of Japan's population in a heavily overcrowded 350-mile industrial corridor on the island of Honshu. Economic success has also strained relations between Japan and other industrial powers, especially the United States. Japan has developed a huge trade surplus, annually exporting goods valued at billions of dollars more than the goods it imports.

Industrial competitors accused Japan of maintaining trade policies that made it difficult or impossible for them to sell their products in the country. Since the late 1970s, the United States and other industrial nations have held negotiations with Japan to find ways to reduce its massive trade surplus. For example, the United States placed limits on the number of Japanese automobiles it would import. Japan has also been called upon to donate part of its trade surplus to less developed nations of the world.

Southeast Asia. During World War II, the Japanese occupation of Southeast Asia marked the end of Western colonialism in the region. When the Japanese withdrew, independence movements had sufficient strength to resist a return to prewar colonialism. But the end of colonialism did not occur immediately. Nor was independence accompanied by the rapid development of the political and economic stability that the nationalists had hoped for. Southeast Asia faced decades of turmoil and torment.

Independence. The first new nation to arise in Southeast Asia was the Philippines; in 1946 the United States granted Philippine independence, as provided for by a 1934 congressional act. Two years later, Britain granted independence to Burma. In 1957 British Malaya and Singapore joined with Sabah and Sarawak, on the island of Borneo, to become the independent nation of Malaysia. In 1965 Singapore withdrew and became the Republic of Singapore.

Independence for the Dutch East Indies came only after a prolonged armed struggle. Indonesian nationalists under Sukarno fought Dutch troops for four years. The Netherlands finally granted independence to the Republic of Indonesia in 1949.

France was not willing to give up its colonial possessions in Indochina.

In 1946 it granted some autonomy to Cambodia and Laos but did not grant them independence until 1953 and 1954, respectively, and only after becoming mired in a guerrilla war in another Southeast Asian colony, Vietnam. The Communist leader Ho Chi Minh, who had led the Vet Minh guerrilla resistance against the Japanese, had proclaimed Vietnam a republic in 1945, with himself as president. French military attempts to restore colonial rule ended with a major Viet Minh victory at Dien Bien Phu in 1954. The peace agreement that ended the struggle, the Geneva Accords, temporarily divided the country into a Communist North Vietnam and a non-Communist South Vietnam—pending elections leading to a reunified country. However, the regime in South Vietnam declined to hold elections, and the temporary division of Vietnam became permanent with the formation of two Vietnamese states. This division was a direct outgrowth of the Cold War.

The Vietnam War. Soon Communist guerrilla and regular forces from the north joined the southern guerrillas, called the Vietcong, and resumed the war. By 1960 open warfare against the South Vietnamese government began.

With Chinese and Soviet support, the North Vietnamese were able to keep the Vietcong supplied and fighting. The United States provided support for the South Vietnamese troops, at first sending financial aid, military equipment, and several hundred military advisers. In 1964, however, the United States decided to greatly expand military assistance to South Vietnam, adding great numbers of combat troops. By 1968, half a million American troops were fighting in Vietnam, saving South Vietnam from collapse but not defeating the Vietcong.

In 1968 American and Vietnamese diplomats began peace negotiations in Paris, but not until 1973 was a peace treaty signed. American forces withdrew from Vietnam. Shortly after, the fragile cease-fire was ignored by the North Vietnamese, who initiated a major offensive. In April 1975 Communist forces overwhelmed South Vietnamese units and took control of the south. In 1976 Vietnam was united under Communist rule and Saigon was renamed Ho Chi Minh City.

Political ferment. Vietnam's neighbors in Indochina, Laos and Cambodia, were also wrenched by war, as the Vietnamese conflict escalated during the 1960s. Civil war raged in both countries as Communist forces fought pro-Western factions.

Simultaneously with the Communist triumph in Vietnam, Communist forces fighting in Laos and Cambodia found themselves in much stronger strategic positions. In Cambodia, the Khmer Rouge routed government forces and captured Phnom Penh, the capital, in April 1975. Under Pol Pot, the Khmer Rouge forcibly removed Cambodia's

VIETCONG PRISONERS OF WAR are escorted by a U.S. soldier through rice fields during the Vietnam War.

urban population to the countryside and began a monstrous reign of terror that claimed some million Cambodian lives. Border clashes with Vietnam led to a Vietnamese invasion of Cambodia in 1977. A new, pro-Vietnamese Communist regime was installed in Phnom Penh. However, Vietnamese forces remained in Cambodia until 1989.

In Laos, the Communist Pathet Lao forces, backed by North Vietnam, scored major military gains in 1975, taking control of the country in December.

During and after these upheavals, hundreds of thousands of refugees fled from Vietnam, Cambodia, and Laos. Many unfortunate people fleeing their homes found their way to overcrowded refugee camps in Thailand, Malaysia, Indonesia, and Hong Kong. International organizations took up the complicated task of relocating the dispossessed to other countries, helping to reunite families, and aiding refugees in adjusting to life in unfamiliar surroundings and cultures.

Political turmoil and violent conflict were by no means limited to what had previously been French Indochina. Nearly all the countries of Southeast Asia faced problems of political stability. Burma, for example, had to deal both with separatist movements launched by ethnic minorities and with Communist insurgents.

Malaysia faced conflict between its major ethnic groups—the Malays, Malaysia's largest ethnic group, and the Chinese and Indians, who dominated Malaysian business and commerce. In the Philippines, Communist guerrilla forces have been active for decades, and Muslim secessionists in the south have been fighting to establish an autonomous state in Mindanao.

Economic development. Political ferment severely impeded economic development in Southeast Asia, as did rapid population growth. As rural population outstripped the land that could support it, millions crowded into the cities in search of work. These economic refugees exacerbated urban poverty, creating sprawling and squalid slums around Southeast Asian cities, notably Jakarta in Indonesia and Manila in the Philippines.

Malaysia, Singapore, and Thailand, perhaps the most stable nations in Southeast Asia, fared the best economically. They were able to produce valuable exports for the world market, thus inviting capital investment on a large scale and setting the stage for further economic expansion. Burma and Laos were the least successful in their economic development.

In 1967 Thailand, the Philippines, Malaysia, Singapore, and Indonesia formed a cooperative regional organization, the Association of Southeast Asian Nations (ASEAN). Brunei, Vietnam, Laos, Myanmar, and Cambodia have since joined. The ASEAN member countries have maintained close political and economic ties with the West.

TEL AVIV-JAFFA HARBOR provides water access for Israel's thriving manufacturing and export business.

The Middle East and North Africa

As in Asia following World War II, Western colonialism was soon to end in the Middle East and North Africa. Yet the fortunes of Western industrialized nations remained closely tied to those of the oil-rich nations of the region. In the postwar era, conflicts in the region seemed always at the flash point and a repeated threat to world peace.

Independence. By 1946 Great Britain and France were relinquishing their control of the mandates they had held in the Middle East since World War I. Syria, Lebanon, and Jordan became independent nations. In 1947 Britain turned the question of establishing a Jewish state in Palestine over to the United Nations, which proposed that Palestine be divided into a Jewish state and a Palestinian one. This plan was rejected by the Arab nations of the Middle East. Nevertheless, in 1948 the independent state of Israel was proclaimed and quickly recognized by many nations. Neighboring Arab nations, however, immediately declared war on Israel, vowing to destroy it.

In North Africa, Libya, an Italian possession since 1912, was placed under United Nations administration; in 1951 it became independent. France granted independence to Morocco and Tunisia in 1956, but was reluctant to give up oil-rich Algeria. Algerian nationalists fought a brutal eight-year guerrilla war to expel the French, who finally withdrew in 1962.

As these largely Arab nations became independent, they joined the Arab League, formed in 1945. Original members included Egypt, Syria, Lebanon, Jordan, Saudi Arabia, Iraq, and Yemen. The Arab League spearheaded opposition to the formation and existence of Israel.

The Arab-Israeli conflict.

Since its founding in 1948, Israel has fought four wars with its Arab neighbors. In the first war, armies from Egypt, Jordan, Lebanon, Syria, and Iraq invaded Israel on behalf of the Palestinians who rejected Israel's creation. Though outnumbered, the Israelis repelled the invasion and took control of a large part of Arab Palestine. Over 700,000 Arabs fled or were forced from their Palestinian homes, moving into refugee camps in surrounding Arab nations. Many of these camps still exist.

The second war began in 1956, when Egypt seized control of the Suez Canal from Great Britain. British, French, and Israeli forces attacked Egypt in response. UN intervention ended this war. In 1967, fearful of an imminent Arab attack, Israel mounted a preemptive strike against Egyptian, Syrian, and Jordanian forces. In six days, Israel destroyed the Egyptian and Syrian air forces and captured extensive territory, including the Golan Heights from Syria, the West Bank from Jordan, and the Gaza Strip and Sinai peninsula from Egypt. The fourth war was launched by Egypt and Syria in October 1973, on the Jewish holy day of Yom Kippur. After initial success, Egyptian and Syrian forces were driven back.

New hopes to end the Arab-Israeli conflict blossomed in 1993 when Israel and the Palestine Liberation Organization (PLO), led by Yasir Arafat, reached an agreement to establish Palestinian civil autonomy in Gaza and the West Bank town of Jericho. In 1994 Israel extended Palestinian self-rule in the West Bank, and Jordan and Israel ended their official state of war. In 1996, however, delays in implementing parts of the Israeli-Palestinian accord led to a new wave of violence, which continues to disrupt peace talks that thwart Arabs' and Israelis' desires to live peacefully without fear of terrorist attacks.

21   History of the World

EGYPTIAN PRESIDENT ANWAR EL-SADAT (left) and Israeli prime minister Menachem Begin shake hands at Camp David, Maryland, in 1978, watched by Jimmy Carter, 39th president of the United States.

AN AYATOLLAH visits the front during the Iran-Iraq War.

Egyptian-Israeli détente.

Originally, Egypt acted as the leader of Arab opposition to Israel. In 1952 Gamal Abdel Nasser, an Egyptian army officer, led a military coup that overthrew the Egyptian monarchy. Nasser became president of the new Republic of Egypt. Nasser, determined to eliminate all British influence from Egypt, ordered the seizure of the Suez Canal in 1956. Nasser also ordered the construction of the Aswan High Dam to control the floodwater of the Nile River.

When Nasser died suddenly in 1970, another army officer, Anwar el-Sadat, succeeded him as president. Under Sadat's leadership, Egypt fought the 1973 Yom Kippur War against Israel. In 1977 Sadat surprised the world by visiting Israel to address the Israeli parliament, the Knesset, and advance a new peace initiative. That effort foundered, but the following year, U.S. President Jimmy Carter invited Sadat and Israeli Prime Minister Menachem Begin to Camp David in Maryland to renew negotiations. In September 1978 the parties signed the Camp David accords, which established the foundations for a peace treaty between Egypt and Israel. The treaty was signed in Washington, D.C., in March 1979.

Other Arab nations condemned Egypt for establishing relations with Israel, and Egypt was expelled from the Arab League. In 1981 Sadat was assassinated by Muslim extremists in the Egyptian military. His successor, Hosni Mubarak, reaffirmed Egypt's commitment to peace with Israel, even though this policy continued to isolate Egypt from the rest of the Arab world.

Oil and OPEC.

In the years before World War II, Western companies, mainly British and American, controlled oil production in the Middle East. But after the war, the oil-producing nations of the Middle East, as well as the North African nations of Libya and Algeria, demanded more of the oil profits and greater control of production. In 1960 these countries joined with other oil-producing nations to form a cartel, the Organization of Petroleum Exporting Countries (OPEC), to regulate production and prices. Oil production has added immeasurably to the wealth of Middle Eastern and North African nations and has given them a powerful political tool—the potential to raise oil prices or cut off oil supplies as punitive measures against Western policies in the region. Such an action occurred after the Yom Kippur War of 1973, when Arab oil producers placed an embargo on oil shipments to nations supporting Israel. After lifting the embargo in 1974, OPEC again showed its power by quadrupling the price of oil. Worldwide inflation and a crippling of Western industrial growth was the result.

Flash points. Several nations in the region continue to be focal points of political instability. Long-standing religious and ethnic conflicts have contributed to this state of affairs, as have the major political and social forces that transformed the world during the 20th century.

Lebanon. Once the home of the ancient Phoenicians, Lebanon has been wracked by civil war since 1975. When the nation became independent in 1944, positions in the national government were divided among the country's religious groups, with the majority Maronite Christians predominating. By the 1970s, Muslims were in the majority in Lebanon, but the Maronites were reluctant to give up their dominant position; the result was a devastating civil conflict. Lebanese Christians are supported by Israel; the Muslims are supported by Syria and the PLO. Both Syrian and Israeli troops have made major incursions into Lebanon. UN peacekeeping forces tried without success to end the fighting.

Iran and Iraq. In 1941 Mohammed Riza Pahlavi replaced his father as shah of Iran. For the next 38 years, Iran was closely allied with the West. The shah worked to modernize Iran and turn it into a leading force in both regional and global affairs. But the shah's support of Western-style modernization enraged Muslim fundamentalists, who held that many of the reforms introduced during the shah's reign were repugnant to Muslim teachings. In 1978 Muslim fundamentalists sparked riots in Teheran. In September, martial law was imposed, but the government and military were unable to control the rising revolutionary tide.

In January 1979 the shah and his family left Iran. The Ayatollah Ruhollah Khomeini, a fundamentalist leader who had been living in exile in France, returned to Iran the following month. He established the Islamic Republic of Iran and proclaimed a worldwide Islamic revolution. In the years that followed, the kind of militant Islamic fundamentalism preached by Khomeini and his followers spread through the Muslim world, becoming a political force in the region.

In September 1980 long-standing conflicts between Iran and Iraq, particularly over control of the Shatt al-Arab waterway, exploded into full-scale war when Iraqi forces advanced into Iranian territory. In 1982 Iranian forces drove the Iraqis back across the border. The war turned into a bloody stalemate, killing a million people, interrupting oil production, and exhausting both nations. In 1988 the two nations accepted a UN cease-fire plan.

Libya. After coming to power in Libya in 1970 in a military coup, Colonel Muammar al-Qaddafi adopted a militant and provocative foreign policy that encouraged acts of terrorism, assassination, and rebellion against American, Israeli, European, and other targets. He also instigated wars with Libya's neighbors, Egypt and Chad. In spite of American economic sanctions and an American air attack on terrorist-related targets in Libya in 1986, Qaddafi remains a controversial and unpredictable figure in Middle Eastern and world politics.

Sub-Saharan Africa

In the decades following World War II, nearly 40 newly independent nations emerged in sub-Saharan Africa, free from colonial rule but facing major political, economic, and social challenges. Many were very poor, making setting up the institutions of a modern nation—efficient executive, legislative, and judicial bodies as well as educational and health systems—exceedingly difficult. Achieving national unity was another challenge. Molding a variety of tribes, many with traditions of deep enmity toward each other, into a single, homogeneous state presented further serious problems. Establishing democratic government, an ideal of most African nationalists, proved elusive; either military dictatorships or one-party rules proliferated.

Independence. British colonies led the way in winning independence. In West Africa, the Gold Coast was the first to gain independence when it became the new nation of Ghana in 1957. Nigeria became independent in 1960, and Sierra Leone gained independence in 1961. In East Africa, independence came for Tanganyika in 1961. It joined with the island of Zanzibar to become Tanzania in 1964. Uganda, Rwanda, and Burundi became independent in 1962, and Kenya in 1963. In southern Africa, Northern Rhodesia became the Republic of Zambia in 1964. Southern Rhodesia remained a British colony until 1980, when it became the independent nation of Zimbabwe.

In 1958 Guinea became the first of several independent nations to be carved out of French West Africa and French Equatorial Africa. More new nations, including Senegal, the Ivory Coast, Mauritania, Mali, Niger, Chad, Cameroon, and Gabon, were formed in 1960. In the same year, the Belgian Congo became an independent nation, eventually called the Republic of Zaire.

Portugal, however, remained unwilling to give up its colonies, the oldest in Africa. Independence for these colonies came only after bitter guerrilla wars, begun in the early 1960s, and the overthrow of the government of Portugal in a military coup in 1974. The former colonies gained independence as the nations of Angola, Mozambique, and Guinea Bissau.

Struggles for political stability. The euphoria that followed independence was soon dulled by the difficult problems facing the new countries. Often, the first problem was the task of drawing ethnically diverse groups together and establishing a sense of national unity. Leaders urged their peoples to think of themselves as more than tribal members and to accept their responsibilities as citizens of a new nation. But ethnicity was not to be denied and civil wars broke out.

In Nigeria, bitter tribal rivalry between the Hausa peoples of the north and the Ibo peoples of the east erupted in civil war, with the Ibo seceding from Nigeria and proclaiming the independent state of Biafra in 1967. After three years of war and famine, the starving Ibo surrendered and the work of reconciliation began.

Inexperience in independent national government also plagued African states. Most had little or no background in parliamentary democracy or in party politics, which encouraged the rise of dictators, often by military coup. In Uganda, Idi Amin, an illiterate noncommissioned officer, ousted the elected president and became military dictator in 1971. In eight years of brutal rule, some 300,000 Ugandans lost their lives. Amin further weakened his country by expelling all Asian citizens, who possessed the bulk of the nation's business expertise, and nationalizing all business. By the time Amin was deposed in 1979, Uganda was in deep economic trouble and mired in political and social instability.

The Cold War also contributed to political instability among the emerging nations of Africa. Through the granting or withholding of technical and financial assistance to supportive or potentially supportive nations, the United States and the Soviet Union competed for influence and strategic advantage in the region. Zaire (present-day Democratic Republic of the Congo) and Angola were among the Cold War's battlegrounds, with each superpower supporting opposing sides in civil wars.

Cold War competition was strong in the Horn of Africa, particularly in Ethiopia and Somalia in the northeast, which are strategically located near the sea lanes of the Red Sea and the Indian Ocean and the oil shipping traffic from the Persian Gulf.

Cold War alignments in the region were modified or even reversed in response to regional events as opposed to changes in the client nations' ideological positions. For example, by 1974, both Ethiopia and Somalia had forged close ties with the Soviet Union, accepting Soviet military aid and advisers and granting the Soviets permission to establish military bases in their territories. In 1977 Ethiopia and Somalia went to war over disputed land. The Soviet Union sided with Ethiopia, leading Somalia to expel the Soviets and welcome American military advisers and economic assistance. Clearly, ideology was secondary in importance to immediate political and economic conditions.

Economic challenges. Just as the newly independent African nations often lacked experience in government, they also lacked broad experience in establishing and running national economies. To overcome this obstacle, some of the new nations opted to retain close ties with the former colonial powers. Most of the former French colonies remained within the French community, and former British colonies joined the British Commonwealth.

However, there were enormous problems associated with attracting capital investment for the modernization and development of business and industry. The economies of many African nations remained primarily agricultural and extractive and therefore dependent on foreign trade. This, in turn, made them especially vulnerable to fluctuations in commodity prices and to protective measures against imports of their commodities.

OIL REFINERIES, such as this one in Saudi Arabia, process a sizeable percentage of the oil needed to fuel the industrialized nations of the world.

21 History of the World

FAMINE IN AFRICA, such as that experienced by these children in Malange, Angola, is a continuing problem and the focus of humanitarian assistance.

Nigeria's experience illustrates the way price fluctuations can affect African economies. An oil-rich nation, Nigeria benefited from the Arab oil embargo of 1974–1975, during which it became the major shipper of crude oil to the United States and other Western nations. It used some of its newfound oil wealth to finance the construction and modernization of factories, improve education, and better transportation. In the 1980s, when crude oil prices plummeted, Nigerian economic development suffered a major setback. Even Nigeria's vast oil reserves could not keep it from the fate of other African nations: a rapidly growing population fast outstripping the country's economic resources.

The constant struggle to promote economic growth has forced many African states to go heavily into foreign debt, a condition that encourages inflation, discourages investment, and contributes to political instability. Natural disasters, such as the drought and resultant famine in northeastern Africa during the 1980s, has only added to the difficulties.

NELSON MANDELA, president of the Republic of South Africa, addresses the special committee against apartheid, acknowledging the tumultuous applause following his speech in the General Assembly Hall at the United Nations.

In 1980 African heads of state met to discuss ways to deal with their economic problems. They concentrated mainly on improving economic policies, curbing corruption in the use of government funds, and promoting more careful fiscal planning. The heads of state signed the Lagos Plan of Action, which provided a blueprint for an Economic Community of Africa.

Racial strife. African independence did not automatically bring the peaceful end to white domination that the Pan-African movement had sought for decades, especially in southern Africa. In Southern Rhodesia and in the Union of South Africa, whites struggled to maintain their position of dominance.

In Southern Rhodesia, the struggle of the white minority to maintain its dominant position began even while the region was still a British colony. In 1963 the colonial government tightened restrictions on black Rhodesians, an action that provoked censure by the British government. In retaliation, the colonial government declared Rhodesian independence. In 1970 Rhodesia proclaimed itself a republic and instituted a program of complete segregation of whites and blacks. This triggered a wave of political and economic sanctions that left Rhodesia virtually isolated by the international community. This, coupled with the rise of an armed struggle by black nationalists, led ultimately to free elections, the formation of a black majority government, and Rhodesia's change of name to Zimbabwe.

The Union of South Africa continued to hold steadfastly to white rule, though whites made up only about 15 percent of the total population. In 1948 South Africa hardened its practices of racial segregation into the official policy of *apartheid,* or total separation of the races and denial of basic civil rights to blacks. Earning the scorn of the world for this action, South Africa withdrew from the British Commonwealth, declaring itself the Republic of South Africa in

1961. It also withdrew from the United Nations in 1962, after the UN imposed economic sanctions.

The struggle over apartheid gained momentum in the 1970s and 1980s. As in Rhodesia, the white-controlled government of South Africa showed great reluctance to change its policies, even in the face of growing resistance at home—by white as well as black South Africans—and the institution of political, cultural, and economic sanctions by other countries. The situation in South Africa began to change in 1990, when the new president, F.W. De Klerk, took significant steps toward the dismantling of apartheid.

Latin America

The nations of Latin America had supported the Allies during World War II (although Argentina did not declare war on Germany until 1945), and they benefited economically from Allied demand for their food exports and natural resources. But their basic problems remained—political instability; authoritarian governments; social unrest caused by the great disparity between the rich few and the many poor; and rapidly growing populations that increased by an average of 3 percent annually. Added to these woes were heavy foreign debts and high inflation. Though the nations of Latin America had been independent for over a century, they had more in common with the emerging nations of Asia and Africa than with the industrialized nations of the West.

Like Asia and Africa, Latin America felt the effects of the Cold War as the opposing American and Soviet ideologies competed for influence in the region. In 1948 the United States, hoping to strengthen the hemispheric solidarity achieved during World War II, encouraged the formation of the Organization of American States (OAS), an association of 21 Latin American nations and the United States. Its aim was to promote military, economic, and cultural cooperation in the hemisphere and to discourage the rise of Communist revolutionary movements.

Economic nationalism.
Following World War II, Latin American nations sought to free themselves from the difficulties associated with maintaining primarily extractive economies. Through industrialization and diversification, these countries sought to serve their own needs for manufactured goods as well as to create new exports for foreign trade. Industrialization became a major national priority for many nations.

Argentina, Brazil, and Mexico were most successful in industrializing; by the 1960s, they were producing steel, heavy machinery, and pharmaceuticals, which accounted for about one-fifth of their gross national products. Venezuela, Chile, Colombia, Peru, and

Uruguay also made significant industrial gains.

Rapid industrialization exacted a heavy price, however. Much of the modernization was financed by highly inflationary foreign borrowing, often with crippling effects. For example, by the mid-1980s, Brazil had run up a foreign debt in excess of $120 billion, with a monthly interest payment of $1 billion. Brazil's rate of inflation went out of control—1,000 percent in 1988 and 2,000 percent the following year. Mexico faced similar economic woes. Its vast oil reserves, discovered in the 1970s, had brought heavy foreign investment, which had grown to $105 billion by the 1980s. But after international oil prices fell in 1981, Mexico neared economic collapse, finding itself unable to pay its debts. Mexico's economic troubles highlighted the vulnerability of a national economy that relies too heavily on one commodity, especially one whose price on the international market is subject to great fluctuations.

Economic growth was also hampered by Latin America's rapidly expanding population. In Mexico, for example, between 1970 and 1990 the population nearly doubled, from 48 million to more than 85 million. The population of all of Latin America, which stood at about 283 million in 1970, was expected to double by the year 2000.

Throughout Latin America, the growing rural population outstripped the number that could be supported by available farmland. Millions of people streamed into the cities looking for employment, swelling the populations of the cities and straining their resources to the breaking point. Cities such as Rio de Janeiro and Mexico City saw the rise of sprawling slums, typified by makeshift shelters with neither running water nor sanitary facilities. Unemployment was rampant among the slum residents, and even those with jobs received wages too low to improve their standard of living. Rural poverty worsened as well.

Population growth also affected what had been a major source of Latin American exports—agricultural products. Much commercial agriculture had to give way to the production of food for home consumption, and more food had to be imported, upsetting many nations' balance of trade even further.

Authoritarianism and repression.

In the postwar period, a large number of authoritarian central governments were established, strengthened, or toppled in Latin America, often through the prominent role of the military in political affairs. In Argentina, Juan Perón came to power through a military coup in 1946, but was ousted by another coup in 1955. In the succeeding 25 years, Argentina underwent 14 changes of government, nearly all of them accomplished through violence. Bolivia, Brazil, Chile, the Dominican Republic, Ecuador, Guatemala, and Honduras also suffered coups.

Repressive dictatorships were established in both Argentina and Chile by military coups, in response to the perceived threat of political gains by left-leaning or reform movements. The military governments of these nations were ruthless in their suppression of dissent. Tens of thousands of citizens were seized by the secret police or the military and disappeared during the 1970s. After civilian control was restored, investigations revealed the magnitude of the crimes committed by the military governments against their own people.

In Panama, a new kind of dictator arose, in the person of General Manuel Noriega. Charged with aiding international drug operations and harboring fugitive drug kingpins, Noriega maintained a stranglehold on Panama largely through power derived from drug money and a large, heavily armed and personally controlled paramilitary force. Noriega's regime was toppled only with the aid of American military intervention.

Cold War effects.

Liberal and conservative political philosophies have long been at odds in Latin America, making the region a natural battleground for the Cold War struggle between the United States and the Soviet Union. Central America and Cuba were the focal points of this struggle. In 1945 Guatemala began electing a series of leftist presidents, much to the consternation of the American government. In 1954 the United States secretly supported a military coup that overthrew President Jacobo Arbenz Guzmán, a champion of major economic and social reform. In the three decades following, Guatemala suffered numerous political upheavals, as well as assassination and terrorism from both left and right.

Communism gained its strongest hold in Latin America in 1959 when a guerrilla force led by Fidel Castro overthrew the long-time Cuban dictator Fulgencio Batista. Castro soon brought Cuba squarely into the Soviet camp, receiving massive amounts of military and economic aid and actively supporting leftist or Communist-led guerrilla movements in other countries. A failed invasion of Cuba by anti-Communist Cuban exiles in 1961 was followed in 1962 with a superpower showdown over the presence in Cuba of Soviet nuclear missiles. The Soviet Union withdrew the missiles on the American assurance that it would not invade Cuba.

Cuba invested heavily in guerrilla movements in El Salvador and Nicaragua. In the 1980s, leftist guerrillas supplied by Cuba gained control of a quarter of El Salvador. In Nicaragua, Cuba supported the Sandinista guerrillas during the 1979 popular uprising against the rightist dictatorship of Anastasio Somoza Debayle. The Sandinistas gained control of the Nicaraguan revo-

MILLIONS OF INDIANS living in comparative isolation at high altitudes are now being encouraged to assume their places as participating citizens. Here, the Indians of La Campana, Colombia, cast their first votes.

lution and established a Marxist government, again with Cuban support. Soon an anti-Sandinista guerrilla movement was formed. The *contras,* or counterrevolutionaries, receiving U.S. aid, locked the Sandinistas in a fruitless and devastating civil war. As economic and social conditions deteriorated, so did the Sandinistas' standing with the people, and in 1990 they were voted out of power in an upset election.

Emerging trends.

As we begin the 21st century, certain trends have emerged and continue to emerge in Latin America. While political power has generally remained concentrated in the executive of strong central governments, there are signs that the citizenry is coming to play a larger role in the electoral process in many countries. New political parties have developed to further the interests of major groups of constituents, such as the growing middle class and the urban working class. Sentiments toward a greater degree of democracy have become increasingly pronounced, especially in Costa Rica, Venezuela, the Dominican Republic, Colombia, and Peru. Argentina, Brazil, and Mexico are making strides toward greater democracy.

In the face of widespread urban and rural poverty, the Roman Catholic Church has emerged as a strong advocate of action to improve the welfare and safeguard the human rights of the poor. Claiming 90 percent of Latin Americans as members, the church had long been considered a force of conservatism and support for the ruling elite. In recent years, however, church leaders in several Latin American countries have come to be viewed as champions of political, economic, and social reform.

Into the 21st Century

Iraq

emphasized
US

emphasised
Brit.

organization
US

organisation
Brit.

nationalized
US

nationalised
Brit.

recognizing
US

recognising
Brit.

The modern history of Iraq could just as easily be referred to as the rise and fall of the Baath Party, which ruled from 1968 until 2003. In large part, it is also the story of Saddam Hussein, since he basically *was* the Baath Party after becoming president of Iraq, chairman of the Revolutionary Command Council, prime minister and commander-in-chief in 1979. The eventual conflation of the dictator and his party is emphasized by the different goals of the Gulf Wars. During the first war, overthrowing Saddam was never a stated objective; the main goal of the second war, by sharp contrast, was to oust Saddam.

Sadly, much of modern Iraq's history takes the form of conflict and violence. To understand this troubled country is to learn about its frequent wars and the tremendous suffering of its people.

The Baath Party. The Arab Baath Socialist Resurrection Party, usually referred to simply as the Baath Party, came into power in Iraq after a quick succession of tenuous governments. As its name suggests, the party's roots are in socialism and pan-Arabism. Originating in Syria, the party was founded by a pair of students in 1947. The movement quickly spread to other Arab countries and had established a significant presence in Iraq by the early 1950s.

As the Baath Party gained momentum in Iraq, conditions were ripening for its ascendancy. Since Iraq had become an independent country in 1932, its government had been extremely unstable. From 1939 to 1958, the country was ruled by a monarch, King Faisal, who was very sympathetic to British interests. Political factions were gaining power in Iraq, but they still had no input into government decisions. These factions, broadly speaking, were composed of dedicated nationalists who resented the West in general and Great Britain in particular.

The most powerful of these factions, a group of Iraqi military officers, staged a coup d'état on July 14, 1958, killing King Faisal and his top officials. General Abdul Karim Kassem became the new head of state. Although he was well liked by the general population, especially the poor, the Baath Party did not think that he was an effective leader. The Baathists made an unsuccessful attempt on Kassem's life in 1959; Saddam Hussein himself was the would-be assassin.

A few years later, in 1963, the Baath Party tried again to kill Kassem. This time, they were successful. The party did not, however, successfully hold onto their newfound power. The first period of Baathist rule was short-lived and terribly violent: thousands of people died under their regime. About nine months after they gained power, the Baathists were pushed out by another coup.

This initial failure did not discourage the party, who spent the next years regrouping and watching their membership grow. Although Saddam was in and out of prison throughout this time, he had numerous responsibilities within the party. One of his most important jobs was as head of the secret police, an organization he spent many years developing. Much of his work was designed to ensure that the Baathist network would be more extensive and secure in the future.

In 1968, five years after their initial short-lived takeover of the government, the Baath Party seized power again. A separate group, the Arab Revolutionary Movement, had recently staged a successful coup. Much like the Baathists in 1963, this group was not strong enough to hold onto power. After a nonviolent takeover, the Baath Party controlled the Iraqi government once again.

This time, thanks in large part to the networking Saddam had performed in the interim years, the party had a tight grip on power. The new regime was headed by General Ahmed Hassan al-Bakr. Although this government was supposedly a republic, it was, in fact, a dictatorship. Eventually, the Baath Party became the only legal political party in Iraq.

Al-Bakr spent a large part of the 1970s furthering the party's socialist agenda. As a result, the oil industry became nationalized and funded many government operations, including the secret police. Throughout these years, Saddam remained a driving force within the party, but for the most part, he carefully avoided the spotlight.

Saddam assumes power. In 1979, al-Bakr officially resigned, owing to poor health. It is not entirely certain that his resignation was voluntary. In any case, Saddam placed him under house arrest immediately following his retirement. On July 16, 1979, Saddam officially assumed power. He was 42 years old. His new titles were basically a formality, since he had held most of the country's leadership responsibilities for some time.

As the new leader of a volatile government, Saddam's first priority was to protect his own political longevity. In other words, he wanted to make sure that his hold on the presidency was secure. With this goal in mind, Saddam took measures to preempt his opposition, systematically eliminating people he identified as potential threats to his position. His first step was to purge the Baath Party's inner circle.

The purge took place during a government "meeting" that would be more accurately described as a dramatically

DEPUTY PREMIER and Defense Minister Lieutenant General Hardan Tikriti, President Ahmed Hassan al-Bakr, and Chief of Staff Lieutenant General Hammad Chehab take the salute on the reviewing stand during a 1969 military parade. The parade, the first of its kind in the Arab world since the Six Day War of June 1967, celebrated the first anniversary of Baathist Party rule in Iraq.

pan-Arabism: a belief in the underlying unity of Arab nations. Stressing their similar political goals, supporters advocate an alliance of Arab countries.

staged media event. Saddam called the unsuspecting members of the Revolutionary Command Council (RCC) and other top government officials to assemble in Baghdad on July 18, 1979. There, before the gathered officials and several video cameras, Saddam tearfully revealed a secret plot designed to overthrow the Iraqi government and deliver it to Syrian rule.

The so-called Syrian Plot, according to Saddam, involved about 60 of the people in the audience. Each of the conspirators was named aloud before literally being dragged away by armed escorts. Shortly thereafter, these officials were secretly tried and executed.

There is very little doubt that Saddam invented the Syrian Plot to suit his own purposes; it is unlikely that such a conspiracy ever existed. In any case, the way in which it was revealed was designed to inspire terror in the people of Iraq. It is difficult to imagine the atmosphere of fear and paranoia that resulted from the public circulation of the Syrian Plot videotapes. It was this atmosphere that allowed Saddam's purge to expand beyond his immediate reach and into the public realm: after hundreds of high-ranking political figures were executed, fired, and/or demoted, many ordinary citizens were arrested as well.

Saddam, in effect, preempted his opposition under the guise of promoting national unity and patriotism. Anyone who openly challenged his authority was looked upon as a traitor to Iraq. The people of Iraq, government officials and citizens alike, learned that it was no longer safe to express dissent. The grim fates met by the Syrian Plot "conspirators" scared people into submission, thus securing Saddam's position as dictator.

Iran-Iraq War, 1980–1988.

After he had established his authority within Iraq, Saddam's thoughts turned to ways of extending his command beyond his own country's borders. He was keen to establish Iraq as the most powerful country in the Arab world, and he knew that assuming a position of dominance would require an impressive show of force. With these goals in mind, Saddam decided to start a conflict with Iran, an ideal target because he perceived it as both threatening and vulnerable.

The threat that Saddam perceived was mainly related to the religious orientation of the Iranian government. Around the time that Saddam came into power, Iran went through a major political upheaval: revolutionaries changed Iran's government from a monarchy to an Islamic republic in 1979. The new government was composed of Shiite Muslims who were highly antagonistic toward Iraq's Sunni-led government.

In fact, Iran's new leader, Ayatollah Khomeini, had a personal grudge against Saddam Hussein. In 1978, the shah (or king) of Iran, recognizing Khomeini's threat to his own position, asked that Khomeini be exiled from southern Iraq, where he was living. Saddam, perceiving Khomeini (a prominent figure among the Shiite population of Iraq) as a threat to his own position, happily complied with the shah's request. Thus, Saddam banished the ayatollah from Iraq only about a year before he came into power—a major mistake.

After taking control of Iran, the ayatollah made no secret of his disdain for Saddam and the Iraqi government in general. He openly expressed his interest in eventually removing the Sunnis from power. As a result, Saddam became concerned that Iran posed both short- and long-term threats to his own position. He worried that Iran would immediately support Shiite and Kurdish rebellions in Iraq and that they would possibly stage a large-scale offensive assault against Iraq in the future.

At the same time, Saddam felt that Iran would be particularly vulnerable to attack. Iran's new government was both internally unstable and internationally disliked. The regime was not widely supported by the Iranian people, and the military was disorganized. Additionally, the Iranian hostage crisis had spoiled Iran's international relations, particularly

Saddam Before the Baath

In 1937, Saddam Hussein was born into the al-Khattab clan in al-Owja, a rural village in the Tikrit region, north of Baghdad. He grew up without a father, spending the first ten years of his life with his mother and stepfather. He was poor and reportedly unhappy. In 1947, Saddam's fortune changed when he was sent to live with his uncle, Adnan Khairullah Tulfah, a wealthy member of the Sunni elite. His uncle introduced him to many politically active people and raised him to be a firm believer in pan-Arabic and anti-Zionist principles.

Saddam joined the Baath Party at the age of 20. From the beginning, he showed no compunction against killing or torture, going so far as to murder his own brother-in-law in the hopes of political advancement. Such cruelty was a precursor to his career as president, when he regularly ordered mass executions of Shiite and Kurdish Iraqis.

PRESIDENT SADDAM HUSSEIN (right) receives well-wishers on July 17, 2002, the 34th anniversary of the coup that brought the Baathists to power.

21   History of the World

CONTROL of the Shatt al-Arab waterway, on the border between Iran and Iraq, was the central issue in the Iran-Iraq War.

with the United States. Since Iran had such a bad image and had effectively alienated itself from all of the major world powers, Saddam thought it likely that the world would support his aggression, if reluctantly.

Saddam's Regime

Government Structure: The main executive and legislative power in Saddam's Iraq was the Revolutionary Command Council (RCC). This group, composed of high-ranking Baath Party officials, determined the bulk of government policy. Although the RCC contained between eight and ten members, Saddam (who served as chairman) usually made major decisions by himself.

The other major government body was the National Assembly, which was made up of 250 members who served four-year terms. There was a major discrepancy between how the National Assembly was supposed to operate and how it actually operated. Members were supposedly "elected" by the Iraqi people, but the Baath Party actually controlled elections. Furthermore, the group had no real power; while it was designed to review RCC legislation, it was never more than a formality.

Political Opposition: For a long time, the Baath Party was the only legal political party in Iraq. Even after other parties were legalized, the laws were constructed so that significant opposition was impossible. Opposing parties included the Iraqi Communist Party, the Kurdish Democratic Party, the Patriotic Union of Kurdistan, and the Da'wa Islamic Party.

War. These considerations firmly in mind, Saddam made the Shatt al-Arab waterway the vehicle for launching a war with Iran. The waterway, located where the Euphrates and Tigris Rivers meet, was a major shipping channel used by both countries. Although they had argued over it in the past, they had shared its control since the signing of a 1975 treaty. On September 17, 1980, Saddam abruptly announced that Iraq had exclusive control over the Shatt al-Arab, claiming that the treaty had not been permanently binding. The Iranian government, incredulous and incensed, denied Saddam's claim.

And so a bloody eight-year conflict began. Before examining the stages of the war in more detail, it is worth noting that Saddam initially believed the conflict would be brief (that is, resolved within a matter of months instead of years). His reasoning, although ultimately faulty, was plausible. First of all, he had recently invested massive amounts of money into Iraq's military. He felt confident that his large and well-equipped army would easily defeat Iran's, which had not yet fully recovered from the 1979 revolution. Furthermore, he assumed that the Iranian people would side with Iraq, since the new Iranian regime was widely disliked.

This was not, in fact, the case. Although they were not immediately apparent, Saddam made a number of costly miscalculations going into the war. First of all, he wrongly estimated both the might of his army and that of the Iranian army. In the early days of the war, the Iraqi army proved itself to

be less than competent. The Iranian army, although crippled by the revolution, was experienced and capable.

Sunni and Shiite Muslims

Sunni and Shiite Muslims form the two major divisions of Islam, a religion founded by Muhammad in the 600s. While both sects believe in Allah (God) and the Koran (Allah's words as recorded by Muhammad), they differ in their views regarding religious leadership and the interpretation of the Koran.

Sunnis, who account for about 85 to 90 percent of the world's Muslim population, are considered highly traditional interpreters of Islam. For this reason, Sunnis are often called Orthodox Muslims. After Muhammad's death, they named Abu Bakr his successor, or caliph. Some Muslims did not agree with this decision, saying that Ali ibn Talib was rightfully caliph. These dissenters formed the Shiite branch, which now accounts for about 10 to 15 percent of Muslims worldwide.

While the division of the Sunnis and Shiites originated with this seventh-century dispute, the two groups hold significantly different beliefs regarding the nature of religious leadership. Sunni Muslims emphasize the secular, or earthly, role of the caliph, whereas Shiites emphasize the caliph's responsibility as a spiritual leader. Furthermore, Sunnis are quite strict regarding the interpretation of doctrine, whereas Shiites believe that doctrine is both expandable and subject to reinterpretation.

Sunni and Shiite Muslims are traditionally antagonistic toward each other. Their relationship was especially strained in Saddam's Iraq. The religious makeup of Iraq's population is peculiar in that most people are Shiite Muslims. (All other Arab countries, excluding Iran, have a Sunni majority.) Saddam's regime, however, was exclusively controlled by Sunnis. In other words, the religious minority held absolute power in Iraq. This imbalance caused much suffering for the Shiite population in southern Iraq, who were continually persecuted by Saddam's government.

Additionally, the Iranian government became more stable as a direct result of the war. Under attack, the people of Iran united under their government instead of toppling it, as Saddam had expected. The new regime, seeking to establish Iran as the preeminent Arab nation, exploited feelings of national identity in much the same way that Saddam had in the early days of his presidency. In other words, fighting Iraq became an integral part of being an Iranian citizen.

The war lasted for almost a decade and was therefore both complex and eventful, but it can be broadly sketched in four stages: the Iraqi offensive, the Iranian counter-offensive, the war of attrition, and international intervention. The Iraqi offensive lasted from about 1980 to 1981. Although it became immediately obvious that the war was not going to be resolved as quickly as

Shiites During the Iran-Iraq War

During the Iran-Iraq War, Saddam was faced with a major problem: how could he keep his Shiite population loyal? How could he prevent them from supporting Iran, a country led by a prominent Shiite who used to live in Iraq? The Shiites, who made up the majority of the population in Iraq, were the only insurgency group that posed a real threat to Saddam's regime. Iran's leadership, recognizing this, stressed its Shiite identity in hopes of enlisting their support.

In an effort to prevent Iraqi Shiites from falling under the sway of the Iranians, Saddam stressed the differences between the two nations during the war. In this paradigm, religious differences were not important; the distinction that mattered was between nations. To emphasize this, Saddam went so far as to deport thousands of Shiites with Iranian origins in the early years of the war. Additionally, the Iraqi government sponsored a propaganda campaign throughout the war that stressed the unity of all Iraqi people.

As a result, many Shiites served in the lower ranks of the Iraqi army, fighting against their religious, if not national, brethren. This was ironic, considering the atrocities that Saddam would commit against the Shiites in later years. While he never staged an organized extermination campaign against them as he had the Kurds with al-Anfal, many Shiites were murdered and persecuted under the Baathist regime.

Saddam had planned, Iraq was relatively successful in these first years of the conflict. This period was marked by Iraqi aggression; at one point, Iraq occupied the Shatt al-Arab and a sizable area of Iranian borderland.

Despite these early gains, these occupations were short-lived. Iran began a series of counter-attacks (via air strikes) in 1981. They were not immediately successful, but they eventually prevented Iraq from taking more Iranian land. In late 1981, Iran unleashed a particularly grisly force: the Basij Army. This army, several hundred thousand "soldiers" strong, consisted of ordinary citizens, many of them children, most of whom were not armed. Basij soldiers employed only one tactic, which was literally to run at Iraqi soldiers. These attacks, referred to as "human waves," effectively forced Iraqi soldiers out of Iran by 1982. These gains came at a great human cost to Iran, which ultimately lost about one million lives by the war's end.

Having regained its land, Iran moved the fighting inside Iraqi borders. This shift in location marked the second stage of the war, the Iranian counter-offensive, which continued until 1984. Iraq, appalled by its turn of fortune, offered a cease-fire in 1982. (Iraq would later make similar offers at several points during the war, but this was the first.) Emboldened by their recent suc-

cess, the Iranians refused. As a result, Iraq was forced to dramatically change its military strategy; it was now fighting a defensive, rather than an offensive, war. In other words, Iraq was forced to concentrate on protecting itself rather than attacking Iran.

Nineteen eighty-four marked the beginning of the so-called war of attrition, wherein Iran hoped to eventually wear down Iraq to the point of surrender. By this point, both sides had endured heavy casualties. (Notably, Iraqi casualties dropped off sharply soon thereafter, whereas Iran went on to lose over half a million more people.) Apart from the Iranian capture of al-Faw in 1986, no major gains were made by either side during this period.

Eventually, Iran began attacking neutral foreign ships that were doing business with Iraq. Considering these attacks as a threat to the world's oil supply, the United States and other prominent Western powers felt obliged to become involved. Since Iran remained isolated from the Western world, having strained and, in some cases, terrible relationships with most countries, these powers sided predominantly with Iraq. Most of them believed that an Iranian victory would make the already volatile Middle East even more unstable. Seeking stability, the United States, France, and Great Britain decided to assist Iraq. This decision marked the final stage of the war.

United States naval units soon entered the fray, and they all but obliterated Iran's naval forces by 1988. Also, France and the Soviet Union supplied

Iraq's ground forces with advanced equipment, using technology that far surpassed the Iranian arsenal. The international powers that aligned themselves with Iraq contributed greatly to Iran's decision to accept a cease-fire in August 1988. The terms were specified in Resolution 598 of the United Nations Security Council, which had come about the year before.

Aftermath. Although the outcome of the Iran-Iraq War was actually a stalemate, Saddam celebrated it as a victory for Iraq. While it is true that Iraq successfully defended itself against the threat of an Iranian takeover, it utterly failed in terms of Saddam's original objectives for the war. He originally envisioned the war as an offensive assault on Iran that would end quickly and profitably, but ultimately, Saddam was wrong on all of these counts.

Indeed, the war was a smashing failure in terms of Iraq's well-being as a country. Before the war, the economy was in reasonably good shape. Eight years of fighting, however, had resulted in high costs of both human life and money. Iraq's economy was all but ruined, and there was little prospect of improvement. Over a quarter of a million Iraqis were dead, and the government was heavily in debt. Iraq had borrowed more than $80 billion to finance the war, and its creditors were anxious to recover their money now that the war was over.

Iraq was in no position to repay this money. Oil revenues (the country's only real source of income) had dropped by

THE MARTYRS' CEMETERY in Iran is dedicated to Iranian soliders who died in the Iran-Iraq War.

al-Anfal

Kurds, a non-Arab people of Indo-European descent, are a significant minority in Iraq, accounting for about 20 percent of the population. Since Iraq gained independence in 1932, Iraqi Kurds have fought for some level of independence or autonomy. They had very little success under Saddam's regime for two reasons: they were violently oppressed by the Iraqi government, and there was a great deal of fighting between the two major Kurdish political parties, the Kurdistan Democratic Party (KDP) and the Patriotic Union of Kurdistan (PUK).

During the Iran-Iraq War, many Kurds assisted Iranian troops in fighting against Iraq and in gathering intelligence. In 1983, the KDP helped Iran capture an Iraqi town. In retaliation, Iraqi troops abducted between 5,000 and 8,000 Kurdish males aged 12 and older from the Barzani tribe. These people were almost certainly murdered; in any case, the abductees were never heard from again.

Toward the end of the war, Saddam organized his aggression against the Kurds into a violent campaign that came to be known as al-Anfal. These atrocities, which were carried out by the military, lasted from February 1988 until September of the same year. The assault was led by Saddam's cousin, Ali Hassan al-Majid, who served as the viceroy of northern Iraq.

Al-Anfal was officially described as a counter-insurgency campaign; in other words, Iraqi troops supposedly punished the Kurds for having helped Iran during the war. It would be more accurately described as genocide, which is the mass murder of a particular ethnic group. Most of the people killed or assaulted during al-Anfal were non-combatants; more often than not, victims were innocent people (often women or children) who had taken no part in the war.

Most of the violence was leveled at areas under PUK control, although at least one assault was made against the KDP-controlled area. Most of the attacks followed a similar pattern. They usually began from the air, with soldiers dropping nerve gas or mustard gas on entire villages. (Saddam began to use chemical warfare against the Kurds as early as April 1987, but usage intensified during al-Anfal.) Shortly thereafter, ground troops were sent in to thoroughly destroy everything in sight, killing indiscriminately and demolishing entire settlements. Mass killings were a matter of course, and villages were regularly looted and burned.

Ultimately, about 80 percent of Kurdish villages were destroyed. Between 50,000 and 100,000 Kurdish people were killed. Those who survived had been, in many cases, forcibly displaced from their homes. Hundreds of thousands of Kurds were relocated. Some were placed in poorly constructed resettlement camps, while others were left with no form of compensation or assistance. Many of these "survivors" died within the first year of their displacement.

Far from being hidden from the public eye, al-Anfal was widely publicized and even celebrated by the Iraqi government. The Iranians, who had so eagerly accepted Kurdish assistance earlier in the war, did very little to assist their former allies in any way. By 1988, both the PUK and KDP headquarters had been overtaken. The Kurds, no longer having any form of organized resistance, were forced to relinquish control to the Iraqi armed forces.

authorized
US

authorised
Brit.

organized
US

organised
Brit.

more than half due to production facility damage and a large drop in oil prices worldwide. (Russia, unregulated by OPEC, flooded the world market in 1988.) Because Iraq was already so deeply in debt, no foreign aid was forthcoming. The bottom line: Saddam had no means to rebuild his ravaged country or repay his demanding creditors.

As a result, many people became increasingly unhappy with Saddam's leadership. The people of Iraq were made frustrated and miserable by the substandard living conditions that war had created. Lenders were irritated by Saddam's inability to make loan payments. Eager to appease all parties, Saddam frequently pestered OPEC to allow Iraq to sell extra oil. OPEC, however, was unresponsive to his requests.

As these pressures built, Saddam became more and more angry with his Arab neighbors, whom he felt should be more supportive of Iraq's reconstruction. He was especially enraged by two of his largest creditors, Kuwait and

The Organization of Petroleum Exporting Countries (OPEC) was established in 1960 as a way for oil exporting countries to have a measure of control over oil prices.

PHOTOS from space showed major damage to Kuwait's oil fields.

Saudi Arabia. As the self-proclaimed leader of the Arab world, Saddam felt that these countries should waive his debt as a form of tribute. When they refused to comply, Saddam became antagonistic.

Eventually, Saddam focused his anger on Kuwait. He leveled a number of (probably false) claims against his small neighbor, saying it had exceeded its OPEC quota and had stolen Iraqi oil from a shared field located beneath both countries. These assertions led to Saddam's making territorial claims on Kuwaiti land. The claims quickly evolved into threats.

Saddam's threats were especially sinister considering that he commanded the most powerful army in the Arab world. (Its might in the Middle East was second only to that of Israel.) Despite casualties from the Iran-Iraq War, the Iraqi army was one million strong. These men were experienced fighters who were incredibly poor but heavily armed. Kuwait, by contrast, was a wealthy country with a tiny army. The match was hardly even.

Saddam began openly making preparations for war with Kuwait. He gave Iran equal control over the Shatt al-Arab waterway to discourage them from arming Iraqi dissidents. (An ironic gesture, considering the same waterway had been the cause of the Iran-Iraq War.) Iraqi troops were poised at the Kuwaiti border. The international community, the United States included, did not, at this point, object vocally.

The Persian Gulf War. Assuming that the world would turn the other cheek, Saddam ordered the Iraqi army to enter Kuwait on August 2, 1990. Kuwait's 20,000-man army did not stand a chance against the swarming Iraqi troops. One week after the invasion, Saddam declared that Kuwait was the nineteenth province of Iraq. Shortly thereafter, a large number of Iraqi troops were positioned near the border between Kuwait and Saudi Arabia.

In one fell swoop, Saddam thought that he had erased two problems that had plagued him since the end of the Iran-Iraq War: he no longer owed billions of dollars to his largest creditor, and he gained more power within OPEC, thus increasing Iraq's oil quota. It seemed likely that he would stage a hostile takeover of Saudi Arabia, another country to which he was heavily indebted.

Saddam employed a number of progressively ludicrous excuses in a half-hearted attempt to disguise his blatant assault. First, he claimed that the Iraqi army was only supporting a Kuwaiti rebellion against the royal family. (This was an outlandish lie.) He also claimed that Kuwait was actually part of Iraq. In this paradigm, he was not annexing Kuwait so much as restoring its rightful homeland. Neither excuse was considered valid by the international community.

A few days after the invasion, President George H. Bush formally voiced his disapproval of Saddam's actions. His position was unequivocal: the United States would not tolerate Iraq's aggression against Kuwait. The United Nations was similarly appalled. On August 6, it imposed an embargo on Iraq, effectively blocking its ability to receive imports or make exports.

Around the same time, President Bush began building a coalition against Iraq. The international response was both supportive and swift; most of the major powers in the east and west joined immediately. Ultimately, over thirty countries became part of this group, which was alternately referred to as the anti-Iraq Coalition, the East-West Coalition, or the International Coalition.

The coalition had a single purpose: to stop Kuwait's occupation, forcing Iraq to leave immediately and unconditionally. Its narrow focus represented the common ground of all coalition countries; in other words, it was the only objective that the entire coalition could agree upon.

Many of the western coalition countries were interested in overthrowing Saddam's regime, but it is unlikely that the Arab countries would have agreed to such an agenda. In any case, Saddam's removal would have almost certainly extended the duration of the war—an unattractive possibility in the eyes of most coalition members. For these reasons, removing Saddam from power was never an official objective of the first Gulf War.

Saddam's Attempts to Disband the Coalition

As the Persian Gulf War began, Saddam was probably surprised that so many Arab countries joined the anti-Iraq coalition. He did not anticipate that his neighbors would cooperate with western powers at all, much less that they would cooperate as quickly as they did. After recovering from his shock, Saddam made several attempts to disband the coalition.

By far, his most concerted effort was his failed attempt to bring Israel into the conflict. Saddam knew that the United States was one of Israel's major allies, whereas Arab coalition members were anti-Israel. Exploiting this divide, Saddam threatened to attack Israel if the U.S. attacked Iraq.

These threats were not empty. Soon after Operation Desert Storm began, Iraq began bombing Israel with SCUD missiles. While these attacks did not result in high casualties, they successfully terrorized the Israelis.

Saddam hoped that his attacks would provoke Israel into striking back at Iraq. He believed that if it did, the Arab nations would abandon the coalition. Israel, however, did not rise to the bait; it remained out of the conflict, thwarting Saddam's plan.

Operation Desert Shield.

The King of Saudi Arabia, alarmed by the proximity of Saddam's troops, granted President Bush permission to base U.S. troops in his country. Two hundred thirty thousand American troops were sent there on August 7, signaling the beginning of Operation Desert Shield.

In response, Saddam made the first of several offers to withdraw his troops from Kuwait. It was rejected by the coalition because it was not immediate or unconditional. Bush sent an additional 200,000 American troops to Saudi Arabia, while coalition partners donated troops, equipment, and money.

Despite the imminent threat from the coalition, Saddam refused to comply with its demand. This situation continued for about six months: between August 1990 and January 1991, pressure on Iraq to leave Kuwait steadily built. Throughout this period, Saddam remained unresponsive.

The United Nations passed a resolution in November 1991 that authorized the coalition to use force against Iraq if it did not remove its troops from Kuwait prior to a January 15 deadline. This gesture, the UN mandate of the Persian Gulf War, was extremely significant. Roughly speaking, this means that the international community thought that war was the only viable alternative.

> Operation Desert Shield lasted from August 7, 1990, until January 16, 1991. The anti-Iraq coalition, led by the United States, sent hundreds of thousands of troops to protect Saudi Arabia.

Operation Desert Storm.

On January 17, 1991, Operation Desert Shield became Operation Desert Storm. Coalition forces attacked via air, beginning a treacherous bombing campaign that targeted military-related sites in Iraq and Kuwait. This air strike, which lasted about six weeks, had severe, long-term detrimental effects on the Iraqi economy. The bombing was not, at this point, limited to military sites; some targets were chosen to cause economic disruption.

As a direct result, the people of Iraq suffered terribly. Saddam was quick to exploit their distress. He repeatedly tried to mar the image of the coalition by releasing news footage that emphasized civilian suffering. In response, the coalition limited bombing targets to those that would directly affect the military; no more industrial targets were bombed. While this prevented further damage to Iraq's infrastructure, it did little to relieve the people who were already without water and electricity.

Despite the heavy bombing, Saddam did not acquiesce. Instead, he offered another conditional withdrawal on February 15, 1991. The coalition was still unwilling to compromise. The air strike

The Anti-Iraq Coalition, 1990–1991

Afghanistan	Argentina	Australia
Bangladesh	Bahrain*	Belgium
Canada	Czechoslovakia	Denmark
Egypt*	France	Germany
Greece	Honduras	Hungary
Italy	Kuwait*	Morocco*
Netherlands	New Zealand	Niger
Norway	Oman*	Pakistan
Poland	Portugal	Qatar*
Saudi Arabia*	Senegal	Sierra Leone
Singapore	South Korea	Spain
Sweden	Syria*	Turkey
United Arab Emirates*	United Kingdom	United States

(* denotes Arab countries)

ended and ground fighting began on February 24. Troops were organized under a joint command structure, with General Norman Schwarzkopf leading the non-Arab countries and Saudi Lieutenant General Khalid ibn Sultan ibn Abd al Azizl al Saud commanding Arab troops.

The ground attack did not last long. Iraqi troops surrendered or fled within a few days, prompting President Bush to declare a cease-fire on February 27. The swift defeat was attributable to several factors, namely the coalition's superior military technology and tactics. Coalition equipment and weapons were far more advanced than the Iraqi arsenal. Further, Iraqi troops were accustomed to fighting against Iran, which shared a similar fighting style. The coalition, on the other hand, used different (generally more effective) strategies.

Theses inequities led to the utter defeat of the Iraqi army, which was quickly forced out of Kuwait. The objective of the coalition was thus met: Kuwait was no longer occupied and had regained its independence. Military operations were officially over by February 28. Coalition casualties were less

AIR STRIKES and smart bombs inflicted heavy damage during the Persian Gulf War.

than 400, while tens of thousands of Iraqis had died.

In one last ghastly act of defiance, Iraqi troops dumped large amounts of Kuwaiti oil in the Persian Gulf and set fire to hundreds of oil wells as they left the country. While the fires were quelled relatively quickly (within months instead of years), the destruction was still significant. On top of the damage that Kuwait had already sustained during the war, its oil production facilities and the natural environment were further compromised.

Aftermath.

Iraq accepted the terms of a cease-fire agreement a few months after its surrender. This agreement marked the beginning of the weapons inspection fiascos that would be the bane of the western world for years to come. It also continued economic sanctions that would evolve into an utter humanitarian disaster for Iraqi citizens. These developments will be examined shortly.

Meanwhile, in the immediate wake of the war, Saddam faced several uprisings within Iraq. The Shiites and the Kurds, who had long been dissatisfied with Saddam's regime, perceived that the government had been weakened by the recent conflict. Both groups erupted into spontaneous (in effect, highly unorganized) rebellions.

The Shiites of southern Iraq rose up in March 1991. Due to a lack of strong leadership, these rebellions were swiftly stomped out by the Iraqi military. Tens of thousands of Shiites were killed, and an even larger number fled to Iran.

Almost simultaneously, the Kurds of northern Iraq rebelled. Although these rebellions were initially more successful than their southern counterparts, they were put down in less than two weeks. Between one and two million Kurds sought refuge in Turkey and Iran.

In response to the continuing atrocities of the Iraqi government against its own people, the United States, Great Britain, and France worked together to establish safe havens for the Shiites and the Kurds. These areas were called "no-fly zones" because they did not allow the Iraqi air force in designated air spaces.

A no-fly zone was established to protect the Kurds in northern Iraq in April 1991, and another was formed to safeguard the Shiites in southern Iraq in 1992. The creation of the no-fly zones was the first time that an external force attempted to regulate the atrocities committed by Saddam within Iraq.

The UN attempted to regulate Saddam in another, more powerful way: the terms of the cease-fire agreement, which Iraq formally accepted on April 6, 1991. The agreement was designed to prevent Saddam from future shows of aggression. It included severe restrictions that fall under two major categories: economic sanctions and weapons inspections. Over time, both issues evolved into unmitigated debacles.

Economic sanctions.

The UN first imposed economic sanctions on Iraq at the beginning of the Persian Gulf War. After it was over, the sanctions were viewed as a way of preventing Saddam from rebuilding his army. While the sanctions initially received worldwide backing, that support waned over the years. Eventually, most of the world viewed the sanctions as controversial at best, cruel at worst. Throughout these debates, the United States maintained that sanctions were absolutely necessary.

The sanctions became controversial for myriad reasons. Many countries had a powerful interest in seeing Iraq resume its place as one of the world's leading providers of oil. This interest was related to the money that Iraq still owed them from loans made during the Iran-Iraq War. France, for example, wanted to lift the sanctions so that Iraq could sell oil to repay its debt.

Moreover, the international community was horrified by the effects the sanctions had on Iraqi civilians. Iraq's economy was weak going into the war, but it was utterly shattered by the time it was over. The six-week bombing campaign alone had wreaked more havoc than had eight years of war with Iran. People were wounded, starving, and living in areas without basic necessities such as power and clean water. Iraq had no money to address these issues.

Furthermore, because of the economic sanctions, Iraq had no income and thus no means of buying anything for its people. After the war, thousands of Iraqis died as a direct result of not having food or medicine. Ironically, the sanctions seemed to have no ill effect on Saddam or his regime, the very people the sanctions were designed to cripple. The army was still effectively oppressing the Iraqi people, and government officials continued to lead luxurious lifestyles.

While the suffering of the Iraqi people has been widely condemned, blame has never been definitively allocated. Saddam has consistently faulted the west, claiming that the Persian Gulf War bombing campaign and sanctions had thoroughly decimated his country. The U.S., in turn, blames Saddam, saying that it was his transgressions that caused the bombing in the first place. It is difficult to assess where the Iraqi people themselves place blame.

In direct response to the concerns surrounding the effects of the economic sanctions on innocent Iraqi people, the UN Security Council passed the "oil-for-food" resolution in April 1995. (It was not accepted by Iraq until December of the following year.) The resolution was designed to maintain sanctions while alleviating civilian suffering.

The oil-for-food program allowed Iraq to sell a limited amount of oil in order to obtain food and medicine for its people. Although the quota was initially quite limited, the sanctions steadily became more lenient from that point

OIL-WELL FIRE-FIGHTERS from around the world worked together to put out Kuwait's burning oil wells. The fires were set by retreating Iraqi troops.

forward. Additionally, Saddam found ways to circumvent the restrictions. He found illegal outlets for Iraqi oil, which gave him additional income. He did not use this money to help his people.

Weapons inspections.   The second category of restrictions created by the cease-fire agreement dealt with weapons of mass destruction. Iraq agreed to dispose of its entire arsenal of these weapons and to destroy its capacity to produce them. It also agreed to allow the UN to supervise this process.

The inspections system devised by the UN was inherently flawed. The inspections depended upon Iraq, a country known to be both secretive and belligerent, for cooperation and assistance. While it is true that Saddam did not uphold his agreement to work with weapons inspectors, it is somewhat ludicrous that anyone expected him to in the first place.

While the history of weapons inspections in Iraq is long and complex, it can be summarized in a few words: Saddam was uncooperative at every possible turn. As a result, UN weapons inspectors (a group called the United Nations Special Commission, or UNSCOM) had a very hard time doing their job, which was to oversee disarmament. Inspectors needed to make sure that all weapons and weapons production facilities were destroyed but found themselves struggling to do so.

From the beginning, UNSCOM suspected that Saddam was concealing weapons of mass destruction. During the first few years of inspections, they uncovered evidence of secret stashes of biological and chemical weapons. Meanwhile, Saddam did his best to thwart, obstruct, and otherwise interfere with the inspections. The result: an aura of mystery surrounded whether these weapons existed, causing a great deal of fear and paranoia all over the world.

In an attempt to curb Saddam's violations, the UN Security Council frequently passed additional resolutions regarding weapons inspections. These efforts were essentially useless, since Saddam violated them openly. The tension heightened when Saddam expelled American weapons inspectors in November 1997. A few months later, he banished all UN weapons inspectors from Iraq. He said that inspections would be suspended until all economic sanctions had been lifted.

In response, the United States and Great Britain began a four-day bombing campaign known as Operation Desert Fox. This air strike, which began on December 16, 1998, targeted weapons stores. Public disapproval (domestically and internationally) of the bombing was extremely high.

Despite the negative media surrounding Operation Desert Fox, the U.S. and Great Britain continued to bomb Iraq regularly from January 1999 until the beginning of Operation Iraqi

AN IRAQI MAN carries a sack of flour obtained as part of the UN's oil-for-food program.

Freedom in March 2003. These bombings did not receive significant press coverage. Predictably, Saddam continued to defy inspection efforts.

Operation Iraqi Freedom.   The uncertainty surrounding Iraq's stores of weapons of mass destruction and Saddam's continued belligerence regarding inspections were the main factors that precipitated the war on Iraq in 2003. The second Gulf War, often referred to as Operation Iraqi Freedom, was extremely controversial both within the United States and abroad.

Before examining the reasons that led the United States and Great Britain to declare war upon Iraq, it is important to understand that there was a significant change in United States defense policy just after the terrorist attacks on the World Trade Center.

Its guiding principle as articulated by the Bush administration can be summarized as follows: The United States faced unprecedented danger after the September 11 attacks. This new atmosphere of terrorism required new defensive strategies, namely preemptive tactics. In other words, the United

U.S. NAVAL AND MARINE OFFICERS on the USS *Belleau-Wood* remained on high alerts even as Operation Desert Fox was ending.

States must anticipate danger and deal with it before attacks are made.

The focus on anticipatory defense marked a dramatic shift in U.S. defense policy, which was previously reactive. The new policy was much more aggressive, and many people were troubled by the implications of this shift in philosophy. They were concerned by its emphasis on potential threats, instead of actual ones. Potential danger, they reasoned, should not be treated in the same manner as actual danger.

In any case, Iraq certainly had been considered a threat by the United States for a long time. President George W. Bush considered Saddam armed and dangerous, and he felt that a preemptive war was the only way to ensure the safety of the U.S. and, to a lesser extent, the rest of the world. His justifications for this war, first and foremost, were related to the threat of Iraq's presumed weapons stores. He also cited Saddam's behavior with regard to weapons inspections and human rights abuses.

President Bush announced his intentions to the UN Security Council in March 2003, making it clear that America would attack with or without UN approval or support. Most members of the Security Council had serious reservations regarding the looming war. They felt as though President Bush was being rash and that his plan to proceed without UN backing indicated a lack of regard for international opinion.

Some people doubted the very existence of weapons of mass destruction in Iraq. (This caution proved to be well founded; after the fighting, it became apparent that there were indeed no such weapons in Iraq.) This faction argued for continuing weapons inspections in Iraq before taking any drastic action.

Suffice it to say that doubts proliferated, and the UN did not mandate the second Gulf War. This is an extremely important distinction: the UN heartily supported the Persian Gulf War but did not back the 2003 war. While the United States had deferred to the UN in the past, it did not do so in this instance.

The United States did, however, manage to assemble a coalition of countries that supported the war effort.

(Unlike the previous coalition, it did not work in collaboration with the UN.) This group is usually referred to as the "Coalition of the Willing." Ostensibly, it was larger than the one assembled during the first Gulf War. Most of the members of the Coalition of the Willing, however, provided political support, whereas most members of the first anti-Iraq coalition contributed a great deal of material support.

As a result, the 2003 coalition was not a collaborative effort in the same sense as it had been during the first Gulf War. Only three other countries—Great Britain, Australia, and Poland—contributed troops, and the United States footed the better part of the bill.

The primary objective of Operation Iraqi Freedom was to topple the Baathist regime. The war proper was launched March 20, 2003, beginning with a "decapitation attack" designed to kill Saddam. (It was unsuccessful.) Significantly, the explicit agenda for this war was to remove Saddam from power, a very different formulation than the stated goal of the Persian Gulf War.

This objective was quickly met when U.S. forces seized control of Baghdad on April 9, 2003, only a few weeks after the start of the war. The first stage of Operation Iraqi Freedom was complete: Saddam had been removed from power. By May 1, the major fighting was over.

Aftermath. Although the first stage of the war was over, substantial work had yet to be done. To begin, there was the task of bringing war criminals to justice, namely Saddam and his top officials. In the months after the fall of Saddam's regime, many high-ranking Baathists (including Saddam's sons, Qusay and Uday) were killed or arrested. After a long search, Saddam himself was finally captured in December 2003.

THE UNITED NATIONS Security Council meeting about the Iraqi situation took place just days before Operation Iraqi Freedom commenced.

The Coalition of the Willing

Afghanistan	Albania
Angola	Australia
Azerbaijan	Bulgaria
Colombia	Costa Rica
Czech Republic	Denmark
Dominican Republic	El Salvador
Eritrea	Estonia
Ethiopia	Georgia
Honduras	Hungary
Iceland	Italy
Japan	Kuwait
Latvia	Lithuania
Macedonia	Marshall Islands
Micronesia	Mongolia
Netherlands	Nicaragua
Palau	Panama
Philippines	Poland
Portugal	Romania
Rwanda	Singapore
Slovakia	Solomon Islands
South Korea	Spain
Tonga	Turkey
Uganda	Ukraine
United Kingdom	United States
Uzbekistan	

Saddam's Capture

After the Baathist regime fell in April of 2003, Saddam Hussein vanished. He went deep into hiding, disappearing so thoroughly that rumors of his death proliferated. Coalition forces began combing Iraq for a trace of his whereabouts, offering $25 million for his capture.

After an intense nine-month manhunt, Saddam was captured by United States troops on December 13, 2003. He was discovered cowering in a camouflaged hole in the ground located on a decrepit farm outside of Tikrit, near where he was born. He surrendered immediately and without struggle.

Many people were shocked by the images of a wildly disheveled Saddam hiding in a grimy hole. Theories surrounding Saddam's possible hideouts had reached near-mythical proportions, with some people proposing that he had an elaborate, luxurious underground tunnel and bunker system. While his appearance suggested that Saddam was no longer a potent political force, his capture was of high symbolic significance to Americans and Iraqis alike.

SADDAM was dirty, disheveled, and graying when captured by U.S. forces near his hometown of Tikrit.

SADDAM, discovered hiding in a hole in the ground, surrendered immediately.

MOST OF SADDAM'S presidential complex in Tikrit was built during the embargo. This palace staircase was made of white marble and coated with mother-of-pearl.

21   History of the World

AMBASSADOR PAUL BREMER holds a press conference in Baghdad.

To cope with these issues, the Coalition Provisional Authority (CPA) was established. Its essential function is to administer the reconstruction; in other words, it was designed to oversee the rebuilding of Iraq governmentally and economically. The CPA's priorities are to strengthen the Iraqi economy and foster stability in Iraq's volatile political climate. U.S. diplomat Paul Bremer serves as the organization head.

DOZENS of Iraqis helped to topple this statue of Saddam Hussein.

There was also the messy business of setting up another (this time democratic) government. Given Iraq's long history of unstable governments, this was no easy task. Furthermore, there was a pressing need to sort out the terrible problems that had resulted from Iraq's decades under a dictator with a fetish for war. Civilians were still suffering from lack of food, medicine, and basic necessities. In short, Iraq required a heavy-duty reconstruction.

Transition to Democracy

Coalition Provisional Authority (CPA): administers the reconstruction of Iraq, including political and economical development. Headed by Paul Bremer, an American diplomat.

Iraqi Governing Council (IGC): handles the day-to-day business of government. Composed of 25 Iraqis chosen by Bremer to represent the Iraq's diverse population.

Local Governance Program (LGP): provides the connection between Iraqi citizens and the CPA.

JUBILANT Iraqi policemen throw their hats in the air after graduating from an eight-week training course in Jordan. Under an agreement with the Coalition Provisional Authority, Jordan will train more than 36,000 Iraqi police officers.

Bremer appointed the Iraqi Governing Council (IGC) in July 2003. The council, an interim organization, handles the day-to-day business of running Iraq. The Council appointed interim Iraqi cabinet ministers on September 1, 2003. It will also help to lay the foundation for Iraq's new constitution.

The 25 members, who are all Iraqis, were chosen to represent all of the country's people. While Saddam's regime was composed exclusively of Arabs that were also Sunni Muslims, the Governing Council includes Shiites, Kurds, and women. IGC members come from diverse religious and ethnic backgrounds, representing the birth of representative government in Iraq.

Finally, on the local level, there is the Local Governance Program (LGP), which was designed to encourage citizens to participate in government. It acts as a liaison between the Iraqi people and the CPA. It also works to restore services like power and water.

All of these programs are designed to ease Iraq's transition into a democracy. As temporary organizations, they will disband when Iraq's government is fully rebuilt. Some people worry that this day will never come. Particular concern surrounds the Bush administration's plan to occupy Iraq for as long as necessary; the idea of the United States remaining indefinitely makes many people uncomfortable.

Furthermore, some people, including many scholars, believe that a democratic government will not be successful in Iraq. Attempting to install such a government, they contend, will prove extremely difficult and ultimately futile. Such beliefs are based on the political history of Iraq, as well as the political orientation of the region. Democracy, they argue, is an inappropriate form of government for an oil-based economy. While this point is debatable, it is true that there is no precedent for such a structure.

USAID helped set up this facility for a local town council as part of its efforts to promote local governance in Iraq.

In any case, the United States has announced goals of turning over sovereignty to the Iraqi people by mid-2004, at which point a transitional government (elected through caucuses) will assume power. The interim government will draft a constitution and ready the country for direct national elections that will establish a permanent government.

Meanwhile, there are enormous difficulties to overcome. While the task of reconstructing a broken and traumatized Iraq is hard work in itself, interim government agencies and coalition forces have faced violent resistance. Since the end of the major fighting, guerilla-style bombings and attacks have been frequent and debilitating. While U.S. forces remain optimistic, whether Iraq can be put back together under these circumstances remains to be seen.

MEMBERS of the Iraqi Governing Council meet with UN Secretary-General Kofi Annan (third from right). Pictured from left to right are Ahmed Chalabi, Governing Council member; Adel Abdul Mehdi, Governing Council deputy; Hachem Al Hassan, Governing Council deputy; Annan; Adnan Pachachi, President of the Governing Council for January 2004; and Hoshyar Zebari, Iraqi Foreign Minister.

21 History of the World

Understanding a New Global Crisis

organizations
US

organisations
Brit.

emphasized
US

emphasised
Brit.

centralized
US

centralised
Brit.

theater
US

theatre
Brit.

sympathize
US

sympathise
Brit.

During the last three decades of the 20th century, a religious revival began to sweep through much of the Muslim world. One aspect of this Islamic resurgence has been the growth of an ideology known as Islamism. Islamists are those Muslims who believe that the social and political order should be based solely on the sharia (traditional Islamic law). A return to a fully Islamic society, they argue, would bring an end to government corruption, moral decay, and social injustice and would eventually restore the Muslim world to the pre-eminent position it once held centuries ago, before the rise of the West.

By the 1970s, Islamist organizations had arisen in most Muslim countries, but the outside world paid little attention to this until 1979, when a revolution in Iran toppled the shah and led to the creation of the first modern Islamist state under the leadership of Ayatollah Khomeini. Encouraged by the events in Iran, Islamists all over the Muslim world became more assertive and saw their popularity surge during the 1980s. By 1989, Islamists had taken control of the government of Sudan. Two years later, an Islamist party won a free election in Algeria but was prevented from coming to power by the army. This led to a revolt by radical Islamists, which was finally suppressed by the government, but only after six years of civil war. Egypt experienced similar strife, marked by attacks on foreign tourists and the assassination of President Anwar Sadat in 1981.

Islamist groups also played increasingly important roles in the struggles Muslims were waging against the Soviets in Afghanistan and the Israelis in Lebanon and the occupied territories of Gaza and the West Bank. The resistance to the Soviet occupation of Afghanistan (which began in 1979) was viewed as a jihad (holy war) not only by most Afghans but by many Muslims all over the world. Similarly, the attempt to drive the Israeli army out of southern Lebanon was led by the Islamist group Hezbollah ("Party of God"). After 1987, the Israelis also found themselves facing a new Palestinian resistance group, Hamas, which was created as an explicitly Islamist alternative to Yasser Arafat's more secular Palestine Liberation Organization.

Although in the past the American government has sometimes worked with Islamist groups, particularly in Afghanistan, many Islamists view the United States as their ultimate enemy. They condemn the United States for its strong support of Israel and for its massive aid to certain Middle Eastern governments such as Egypt's, which Islamists believe are corrupt, oppressive, ungodly, and illegitimate. Moreover, American society, in their view, is materialistic and morally lax, the epito-me of everything that is wrong with secular Western culture and a dangerous source of temptation to Muslim believers everywhere. By the 1990s, a worldwide campaign of terror began to be waged against the United States by militant Islamic extremists, the most notorious being Osama bin Laden. Born to a wealthy family in Saudi Arabia, bin Laden created an international network in the 1980s to raise funds and recruit volunteers for the war against the Soviets in Afghanistan. After the Soviet withdrawal in 1989, he began to use this network, now known as Al Qaeda ("The Base"), to conduct a series of terrorist attacks on American targets at home and abroad, including a barracks in Saudi Arabia, the U.S. embassies in Kenya and Tanzania, and the U.S.S. *Cole* anchored in Aden, Yemen. By 1996, bin Laden, now an international outlaw, was living in Afghanistan under the protection of the Taliban, an Islamist militia that had taken control of most of that country in the civil war that occurred after the Soviet departure. Finally, on September 11, 2001, 19 Al Qaeda operatives simultaneously hijacked four American airliners and succeeded in crashing one into the Pentagon (below) and two into the World Trade Center towers in New York (on next page), killing more than 3,000 people, the largest loss of American lives in a single day since the Civil War. The loss of life would have almost certainly been much greater but for the courage of a group of passengers on the fourth airliner, who, in attempting to overpower their hijackers, forced the plane to crash in a field in rural Pennsylvania, far from any intended target.

The events of September 11, which came to be known simply as "9/11," sent shock waves through American society. Concerns over the vulnerability of the United States to further terrorist attacks led to increased security measures at airports, nuclear power plants, government buildings, and large public gatherings. The crisis eventually brought about the largest reorganization of the federal government in half a century, when a new Homeland Security Department officially opened its doors in January 2003. Government efforts to identify and arrest suspected terrorists living inside the United States set off debates over questions of civil liberties, immigration control, and ethnic profiling. At the same time, a groundswell of patriotic emotion created a climate of national unity not seen in America since the days of World War II, and President Bush's approval ratings soared to near record heights. The people of New York City rallied around their outgoing mayor Rudolph Giuliani, whose strong leadership during the crisis eventually earned him *Time's* Person of the Year award.

On the international front, the United States enlisted the aid of much of the world community in a concerted effort to destroy the Al Qaeda network. For the first time in its 52-year history, NATO invoked Article 5 of its mutual defense treaty, declaring the attack on America to be an attack on all its members. The British, in particular, gave unequivocal support to the United States, providing both vital intelligence information and military forces, and their prime minister, Tony Blair, became perhaps the most articulate spokesman for the campaign against terror. The ultimate goal of this campaign was to eliminate the threat posed by Al Qaeda and similar groups by making it clear that the world would no longer tolerate nations or organizations that provided aid or sanctuary to terrorists. When the Taliban refused to give up bin Laden, it was quickly overthrown by Afghan opposition forces, who received massive military support from the United States and its allies. A moderate pro-Western government under Hamid Karzai was set up in Afghanistan, but Al Qaeda cells continued to operate there and in more than 40 other countries. The truly international scope of this problem became apparent in the months after 9/11, as Al Qaeda and allied groups carried out terrorist attacks in Asia, Africa, and the Middle East. Their targets were rarely of a military nature. Instead, the attacks were usually against so-called soft targets—a discotheque on the resort island of Bali, an Israeli-owned hotel in Kenya, and a historic synagogue in Tunisia. Early in 2002, American journalist Daniel Pearl was kidnapped and

murdered in Pakistan; soon after, there were attacks on Europeans working in that country and on Pakistani Christians.

As the war on terrorism continued, President Bush increasingly emphasized the need to deal with the threat posed by Iraq's Saddam Hussein. From its first days in power, the Bush administration had argued that until Saddam was deposed or at least effectively disarmed, there could be no stability in the Middle East, and after 9/11, the United States feared that Iraq might provide terrorists with weapons of mass destruction (biological, chemical, and nuclear). President Bush pointed to Saddam's history of aggression against his neighbors (he invaded Iran in 1980 and Kuwait in 1990), his past support of terrorist groups, and his refusal to cooperate with UN weapons inspectors, whom he expelled from Iraq in 1998. In November 2002, the UN passed Resolution 1441, which demanded that Iraq account for and terminate all biological, chemical, and nuclear weapons programs or face "serious consequences," which the Bush administration interpreted to mean the removal of Saddam by military force. This threat of war provoked widespread criticism at home and abroad and caused deep divisions in NATO, the EU, and the UN Security Council. Opponents of Bush's policy argued that an attack on Iraq would further destabilize the Middle East and weaken the war on terrorism by intensifying anti-American feelings throughout the Muslim world. Bush's critics urged that the UN inspectors, whom Saddam allowed back into Iraq in November 2002, be allowed more time to do their work. Nevertheless, in March 2003, American and British forces entered Iraq.

After initially encountering unexpectedly heavy resistance, the coalition forces took control of Baghdad by mid-April, bringing to an end the Baathist regime of Saddam Hussein after only 23 days of major combat operations. A Coalition Provisional Authority began to govern the country in conjunction with an American-appointed Governing Council, composed of 25 representatives drawn from all the major religious and ethnic communities of Iraq, until full sovereignty could be restored to the Iraqi people. The difficult tasks of establishing a stable democratic government in Iraq and rebuilding its shattered economy were severely hampered by a campaign of violent resistance waged by various groups, including Baathist loyalists and militant Islamists. Coalition military personnel, foreign civilians, and Iraqis cooperating with the new government were all targeted. Most of the attacks occurred within the so-called "Sunni Triangle," the area north of Baghdad inhabited by Sunni Arabs, who had enjoyed a privileged position under Saddam's regime. Saddam himself, who had been in hiding since April, was captured by American forces near his hometown of Tikrit on December 13,

but the attacks continued into 2004. Coalition forces faced little opposition from the Kurds in northern Iraq and the Shiite Arabs in the south, the two groups that had suffered the most at the hands of Saddam, but problems did arise concerning the role these two communities would play in the new Iraqi government. The Kurds, hoping to preserve the autonomy they had gained after the 1991 Gulf War, called for a loose federal system in which each region of Iraq would be given a large measure of local self-government. The Shiites, who make up roughly 60 percent of the population, preferred a more centralized system, with direct elections for a national government. The most prominent Shiite leaders tended to be religious figures such as the Grand Ayatollah Ali Sistani, which prompted fears that Iraq might ultimately become an Islamic theocracy similar to Iran.

Before the war, President Bush and Prime Minister Blair had argued that the overthrow of Saddam Hussein was vital to the success of the worldwide campaign against terrorism, but the failure to find weapons of mass destruction in Iraq after the war and the absence of substantial evidence linking the Baathist regime to Al Qaeda and the events of 9/11 cast doubts on this argument. Critics of the war maintained that the occupation of Iraq had actually weakened the war on terror by diverting manpower and resources from the pursuit of bin Laden and by further alienating much of the Muslim world against the United States and its allies. In any event, it became clear that postwar Iraq had now become a new theater of operations for Islamists intent on waging jihad against the West. As Baathist influence within the resistance gradually faded after the capture of Saddam, Islamic extremists assumed an increasingly active role. A number of terrorist attacks, often involving suicide bombers, appeared to be the work of foreign militants linked to Al Qaeda. The attacks were aimed not only at driving out the United States and its allies but at sowing chaos and discord among the Iraqi people so that it would be impossible for a pro-Western government to rule the country after the departure of coalition forces.

Iraq was by no means the only "field of jihad" for Al Qaeda and its associates in the months after Saddam's overthrow. In response to bin Laden's call for the destruction of Muslim governments that cooperate with the United States, terrorist bombings occurred in Morocco, Saudi Arabia, Turkey, and Indonesia. In Pakistan, President Pervez Musharraf twice narrowly escaped assassination attempts by Islamic militants. The incidents in Saudi Arabia and Pakistan called attention to the complex and ambiguous relationship those two countries have long had with Islamic militancy. Since its creation in 1932, Saudi Arabia has had a close relationship with the United States, but many

Saudis admire Osama bin Laden and sympathize with the aims of Al Qaeda. Critics of the Saudi government charge that it has often appeased religious extremists within its own society and turned a blind eye to the funding of terrorist groups around the world under the guise of international Islamic charity organizations. After the bombings of 2003, however, the Saudi government began to take stronger measures against terrorist activities within its borders. In Pakistan, Musharraf's government had maintained close ties with the Taliban in Afghanistan until 2001 and had actively supported Islamic militants in their struggle against India's control of Kashmir. After 9/11, Musharraf sided with the United States in the war on terror and tried to reach a peaceful settlement with India in the dispute over Kashmir. Fiercely opposed by many Islamists in Pakistan, who now viewed him as a traitor, Musharraf became a marked man.

By the start of 2004, most of the original leadership circle of Al Qaeda had been killed or captured, including Khalid Shaikh Mohammed, believed to be the mastermind of the 9/11 attacks, but bin Laden and his chief lieutenant, Ayman Al-Zawahiri, remained at large, and their organization still posed a serious threat to world stability. Concerns over future terrorist attacks intensified in February, when Abdel Qadeer Khan, the father of the Pakistani nuclear weapons program, admitted that he had sold nuclear secrets and technology to Iran, Libya, and North Korea. President Bush and Prime Minister Blair had come under severe criticism at home when weapons of mass destruction were not found in Iraq, and official inquiries were held to investigate possible intelligence failures, but Khan's revelations revived fears that nuclear proliferation might some day provide terrorists with weapons vastly more destructive than any previously employed.

Glossary of World History

Abbasids. The second and most renowned Islamic dynasty (750–1258 A.D.). Islamic civilization reached its zenith during the first 300 years of Abbasid rule, when there was a cultural and scientific renaissance.

Agincourt, Battle of. A key battle of the Hundred Years' War between England and France was fought on October 25, 1415, at Agincourt, in northern France. An invading English army commanded by King Henry V defeated a French force more than twice its size. The victory demonstrated the superiority of the English longbow over the cumbersome armor worn by French knights on horseback.

Alsace-Lorraine. A region in northeastern France whose ownership was long contested by French and German rulers. French possessions from the 1600's, Alsace and Lorraine were acquired by Germany in 1871 after the Franco-Prussian War, then restored to France in 1919 after World War II. In World War II France was defeated by Germany in 1940 and again relinquished the region. In 1945 it was restored to France.

Atlantic Charter. A World War II joint declaration of policy and war aims agreed upon by U.S. President Franklin D. Roosevelt and British Prime Minister Winston Churchill on August 14, 1941, after a meeting held at sea off the coast of Newfoundland. The signatories disavowed any interest in territorial gain and reaffirmed their support for self-determination and self-government for all peoples.

Austro-Hungarian Empire. An empire formed in 1867 by the division of the Austrian Empire. The new entities, the empire of Austria and the kingdom of Hungary, were united in the person of a joint monarch, Franz Josef of Austria.

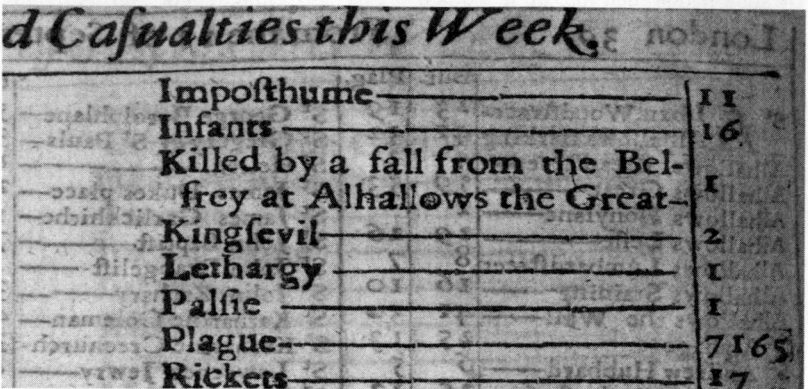

THIS EXCERPT from a September 1665 London death register shows 7,165 victims of the Great Plague in just one week.

The union, also known as the Dual Monarchy, lasted until the end of World War I in 1918.

Axis. An alliance formed by Germany, Italy, Japan, and other countries during World War II. Its foundation was the 1936 pact establishing the Rome-Berlin Axis. Germany, Italy, and Japan concluded a military and economic pact in 1940, forming what came to be known as the Rome-Berlin-Tokyo Axis.

Babylonian Captivity. Also called the Avignon papacy (1309–1376). The period during which the popes resided in Avignon, in France, rather than in Rome. Clement V (1305–1314), a Frenchman, was the first pope to take up residence in Avignon. The Avignonese popes, however, were regarded as tools of France. As a result, the prestige of the Holy See declined.

Balfour Declaration. A British foreign policy statement issued in 1917 by Foreign Secretary Arthur James Balfour. It expressed sympathy for the founding of a Jewish national home in Palestine and was an important step toward the establishment of Israel.

Barbary States. Four North African countries known today as Morocco, Algeria, Tunisia, and Libya. From the 1600's to the 1800's, the region was a stronghold for pirates and adventurers who raided shipping on the Mediterranean Sea.

Black Death. An epidemic of bubonic plague that occurred in the first half of the 14th century. It killed an estimated one-third to one-half of the population of Europe and Asia.

Boer War. A conflict fought from 1899 to 1902 in southern Africa by the Boers of the Orange Free State and the Transvaal against Great Britain. The war was sparked by conflicts between the Dutch-descended Boers and British miners, settlers, and speculators in the diamond- and gold-rich Boer states. The British defeated the Boers, annexed the Orange Free State and the Transvaal, and ultimately incorporated them into the Union of South Africa.

Brest-Litovsk, Treaty of. A World War I peace treaty signed at Brest-Litovsk in the Soviet Union on March 3, 1918, by the newly established Bolshevik government of Russia and the Central Powers. The treaty marked the withdrawal of the Soviet Union from the conflict, relieving the Central Powers of the burden of fighting a war on two fronts.

Caliph. Literally, "he who follows behind" or "successor." The title was assumed by the religious and political leaders of the Muslim community who were recognized as the successors of Muhammad (570–632).

Camp David accords. A framework for peace between Egypt and Israel worked out at Camp David, Maryland, in September, 1978. With these accords, Egypt became the first Arab state to establish diplomatic relations with Israel.

Crimean War. A war fought from 1854 to 1856 against Russia by Britain, France, Sardinia (Piedmont), and the Ottoman Empire (Turkey). The main fighting was in the Crimean peninsula, in the present-day Soviet Union. Russia sought unsuccessfully to gain territory in the eastern Mediterranean at the expense of the declining Ottoman Empire. Russia lost the war and was forced to cede the territories it had gained in the Balkans.

civilization
US

civilisation
Brit.

armor
US

armour
Brit.

OVERVIEW of a cavalry camp in the Crimean War.

WOODCUT of Muslim military leader Saladin.

Crusades. A series of wars fought from the late 11th century through the mid-13th century by Christians of western Europe to gain control of the Holy Land, which had fallen under Muslim domination. The wars are divided into four major and four minor Crusades, plus the Albigensian Crusade and the Children's Crusade.

The First Crusade (1096–1099) consisted of several mass migrations to the Holy Land. In the spring of 1096, a nonmilitary "People's Crusade." Jerusalem. It was virtually annihilated on the way. In 1097 a military force of French and Norman barons and knights succeeded in establishing the states of Antioch, Edessa, and Tripoli, and capturing Jerusalem in 1099.

The fall of Edessa to the Muslims in 1144 led to the Second Crusade (1147–1149), which achieved little.

In 1187 the Muslim leader Saladin retook Jerusalem, prompting the Third Crusade (1189–1192). The Christians regained a small coastal strip of land between Jaffa (present-day Tel Aviv-Jaffa, Israel) and Saint-Jean-d'Acre (present-day Acre, Israel).

The Fourth Crusade (1202–1204) ended with the capture and sacking of Constantinople by the Crusaders and the establishment of the Latin Empire of the East in place of the Greek Empire at Constantinople.

In 1208 Pope Innocent III proclaimed the Albigensian Crusade against the heretic Albigenses of southern France.

In the Children's Crusade of 1212, thousands of French children travelled to Marseilles, where they embarked for Alexandria, Egypt. Many were sold into slavery. A second children's contingent set out from Germany, but thousands died along the way.

The Fifth Crusade (1218–1221) was inconclusive. The Sixth Crusade (1228–1229) resulted in the regaining of Jerusalem. However, the Muslims recaptured Jerusalem in 1244.

The Seventh Crusade (1248–1254) and Eighth Crusade (1270) accomplished little. In 1291 the last Christian stronghold in the Holy Land, Acre, fell to the Muslims.

Cuban missile crisis. A confrontation between the United States and the Soviet Union in October, 1962, over the installation of Soviet missiles in Cuba. The United States secured removal of the missiles in return for dismantling missile bases in Turkey and a pledge not to invade Cuba.

Early American Civilizations. (See map this page.) Developed in the same time periods as civilizations on the other side of the world without being aware of each other.

Fascism. A political movement toward totalitarianism. Inaugurated in Italy in 1919 by Benito Mussolini, it spread to Germany, Spain, and elsewhere. It is characterized by subservience of the individual to the state and by extreme nationalism, militarism, and imperialism.

Feudalism. A social system based on land ownership in Europe and elsewhere in the world during the Middle Ages and later. It was based on reciprocal loyalty between a lord and his vassals. The vassals served the lord in return for his protection.

Franco-Prussian War. A conflict in 1870–1871 between France and the German states led by Prussia. The Prussian victory completed the unification of Germany and ended the second Napoleonic dynasty in France.

Golden Horde. A Mongol khanate that dominated Russia during the 13th and 14th centuries. In 1237 a group of Mongols led by Batu Khan, the grandson of Genghis Khan, swept westward, conquering Kiev in 1240 and advancing into Poland, Silesia, and Hungary. The Mongols ruled from Sarai, on the Volga River, extracting tribute from Russian princes. In 1391 the Golden Horde was defeated by Tamerlane and disintegrated into smaller khanates.

Good Neighbor Policy. The U.S. policy of nonintervention in the internal affairs of South and Central American republics. Announced by U.S. President Franklin D. Roosevelt in 1933, the policy departed from prior U.S. policies, which often allowed unilateral intervention in the affairs of the American republics "for their own good."

Great Depression. The worldwide economic collapse that began in 1929 and lasted through the 1930's. Marked by business failures and widespread unemployment, it helped strengthen fascism in Germany and Italy.

Hague Peace Conference. Two international meetings held at The Hague, The Netherlands, to discuss the prevention of war. The first conference,

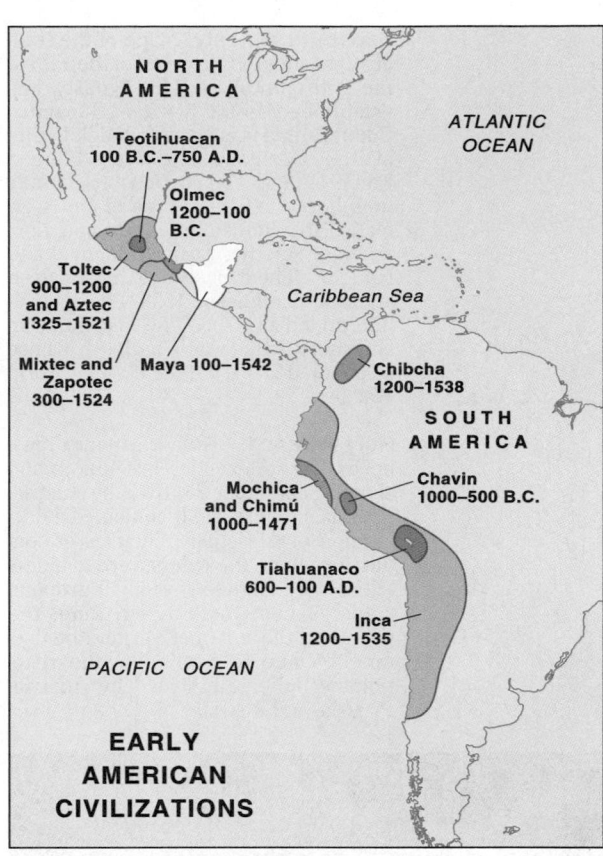

EARLY AMERICAN CIVILIZATIONS

in 1899, led to conventions for the peaceful settlement of international disputes and the definition of the rules of warfare. The second, in 1907, secured agreements on the rights and obligations of neutrals and on the collection of international debts.

Hanseatic League. A commercial confederation of cities in northern Germany formed in the 13th century to protect merchants and their goods from robbers and pirates and to secure trading privileges abroad. At the height of its power, it controlled almost all northern European trade.

DELEGATES from 26 countries meet during the first peace conference at The Hague.

Hapsburg dynasty. One of the leading dynasties of Europe from the 13th to the 20th centuries. The dynasty was established in 1273 when Hapsburg Count Rudolf was elected Rudolf I, king of the Germans and Holy Roman Emperor. Subsequent Hapsburg family members ruled as kings of the Germans, Holy Roman Emperors, and monarchs of Austria, Spain, Bohemia, and Hungary. The dynasty split into Spanish and Austrian lines in 1558. The Spanish line ended in 1700. The last Austrian Hapsburg ruler was Charles I, whose rule ended in 1918 at the close of World War I.

Holy Alliance. An agreement drawn up by Czar Alexander I of Russia and signed September 26, 1815, by Austria, Prussia, and Russia. It contained a declaration of Christian principles of conduct by which the rulers were to abide. Ultimately signed by all European rulers except the English king, the pope, and the sultan of Turkey, the document came to symbolize the reactionary policies followed by Austria, Prussia, and Russia.

PACKING CRATES containing American hams are being placed on board ship for transport to Britain under the Lend-Lease Act.

THIS IMPERIAL CROWN of the Holy Roman Empire was created circa 962.

Holy Roman Empire. A political entity founded in 962 as the restored empire of Charlemagne, which had been divided in 843. Charlemagne's empire had been considered a restoration of the Western Roman Empire, which had collapsed in 476. The Holy Roman Empire was therefore also considered a continuation of the Western Roman Empire. Primarily a loose union of Germanic states, the empire maintained a long but often strained relationship with the papacy. Its limited power was further weakened by the Protestant Reformation and the rise of Napoleon. It was dissolved in 1806.

Hundred Days. The period of March 20 to June 29, 1815, during which former emperor Napoleon I of France attempted to reestablish his rule following his escape from exile on the island of Elba. Napoleon's defeat at Waterloo, Belgium, on June 18, 1815, led to his second exile.

Hundred Years' War. A series of related wars fought between England and France from 1337 to 1453. It arose from England's claim to the French throne, based on royal descent from William I, the Norman conqueror of England. The war, fought mainly in France, brought about an end to English power on the Continent. By 1453 England controlled only the French port of Calais, which it held until 1558.

Inquisition. A medieval Roman Catholic tribunal first established by Pope Gregory IX (1227–1241) to investigate the Albigensian heresy in southern France. The inquisitors, usually Dominicans, later sought out heretics of all kinds in France, Italy, Germany, Burgundy, and Spain. The Inquisition was established in Spain in the late 15th century. The Spanish monarchs Ferdinand and Isabella used it to consolidate the power of the Spanish state and link it closely with the authority of the Roman Catholic Church.

Justinian Code. A legal code issued by Byzantine emperor Justinian I during the period from 529 to 535. It provided a comprehensive code of Roman law that became the basis for the legal codes of later European states.

Kellogg-Briand Pact. Also called the Pact of Paris. An international declaration in 1928 renouncing war as an instrument of national policy and advocating the peaceful settlement of international disputes. Eventually endorsed by more than 60 nations, it proved ineffectual because it included no provisions for enforcement.

AMONG THE RUINS of a cathedral near the Marne, French troops in 1918 used their machine guns to drive back the Germans.

League of Nations. An international organization dedicated to the preservation of world peace and the promotion of international cooperation. Inaugurated in 1920, it was dissolved in 1946. The league was weakened from the outset by the refusal of the United States to join and by its lack of real power to enforce international law.

Lend-Lease Act. An act passed in the United States in March, 1941, to provide war materials and supplies to Great Britain during World War II. After the United States's entry into the war the following December, the lend-lease program was extended to China, the Soviet Union, and 35 other Allied nations.

Lepanto, Battle of. A naval battle fought off the coast of Greece on October 7, 1571, by allied Spanish, Venetian, and papal fleets against the Ottoman Turkish fleet. The Turkish fleet was virtually destroyed, temporarily shattering the naval power of the Ottoman Empire.

Locarno Conference. A meeting in 1925 of representatives of Belgium, Great Britain, Czechoslovakia, France, Germany, and Poland in Locarno, Switzerland. The conference sought to bring peace and security to Western Europe and resulted in the Locarno Pact, a series of international treaties that restricted, for the first time in history, the right to make war.

Marathon, Battle of. A battle fought in 490 B.C. on the Plain of Marathon, near Athens, Greece, in which a greatly outnumbered army of Athenians and their allies, led by the Athenian general Miltiades, defeated a Persian army led by Darius I.

Marne, Battle of the. Two major battles of World War I fought along the Marne River in northern France. The first, from September 6 to 9, 1914, halted the initial German advance, ending German plans for the rapid defeat of France. In the second battle, July 15 to August 6, 1918, German forces were again turned back with heavy losses.

Marshall Plan. The unofficial name of the European Recovery Program (ERP), a project in which the United States gave economic assistance to war-devastated European countries after World War II.

Middle Passage. The transport of African slaves across the Atlantic Ocean to the Americas, often under brutal conditions. During the two-month voyage, the slaves were chained together and crowded below decks.

Monroe Doctrine. A foreign policy enunciated in 1823 by U.S. President James Monroe. It stated that the United States would oppose further European colonization or interference

TOP NAZI OFFICIALS were tried for war crimes in Nuremberg.

in the affairs of the nations of the western hemisphere.

Nerchinsk, Treaty of. Signed in 1689, it was the first treaty between China and Russia and the first Chinese treaty with a European power. It settled conflicts over possession of the Amur River region and was the basis for Chinese-Russian relations until the mid-19th century.

Ninety-Five Theses. The document posted by Martin Luther on the door of the cathedral in Wittenberg, Germany, on October 31, 1517, launching the Protestant Reformation. In the theses, Luther invited Catholic churchmen to debate what he considered unacceptable religious doctrines and practices.

Nuremberg trials. Trials held in Nuremberg, Germany, in 1945–1946 during which key Nazi leaders were convicted of war crimes and crimes against humanity.

Open-door policy. A term applied to the policy of allowing equal commercial opportunity to all nations in a foreign region, particularly in China in the late 19th and early 20th centuries. It was designed to counter the development of spheres of influence.

Opium War. A conflict between China and Great Britain from 1839 to 1842. It was sparked by the Chinese destruction of British consignments of the banned drug opium. Britain used the war as a pretext to force Chinese agreement to major trade concessions and to the cession of Hong Kong.

Pan-African congresses. A series of international conferences held between 1900 and 1945 by people of African descent to protest European colonialism and oppression in Africa.

symbolize
US

symbolise
Brit.

organization
US

organisation
Brit.

colonization
US

colonisation
Brit.

SHIPS at battle in Anson's Bay during the Anglo-Chinese Opium War.

21 History of the World

Papal States. A former territory of Italy over which the pope had direct rule. It existed from the time of the Donation of Pepin in 756 to the completion of the unification of Italy in 1870. The lands controlled by the pope reached their greatest extent in the 16th century, when they included much of central Italy.

Plassey, Battle of. A battle fought June 22, 1757, between a small British force and the army of Suraja Dowla, Muslim ruler of Bengal. The British victory marked the beginning of the British Empire in India.

Platea, Battle of. Battle in which the Persians were decisively defeated by the Greeks in 479 B.C. at Platea, in south-central Greece. It effectively brought the Persian wars to an end.

BRITISH GENERAL James Wolfe, who fought and died in Canada during the Seven Years' War, is depicted here leading the capture of Fort Louisbourg.

Potsdam Conference. A meeting held in July, 1945, in the German city of Potsdam by the leaders of Great Britain, the Soviet Union, and the United States to determine Allied postwar policy in Germany. The conference called for the unconditional surrender of Japan and the trial of Axis leaders for war crimes.

Russo-Japanese War. A war fought from 1904 to 1905 between Russia and Japan. It was sparked by rival interests in Korea and Manchuria. The Russian defeat established Japan as a world power.

THE DEATH of English naval commander Horatio Nelson occurred during the Battle of Trafalgar.

FRENCH PREMIER Georges Clemenceau rises to speak at the signing of the Treaty of Versailles in 1919. U.S. President Woodrow Wilson is seated to Clemenceau's right.

Seven Years' War. A war fought from 1756 to 1763 by Great Britain, the German principality of Hanover, Portugal, and Prussia against Austria, France, Russia, Sweden, Spain, and a number of German principalities. In America the struggle between Britain and France began in 1755 and was known as the French and Indian War. The war established Prussia as a major European power and Britain as the predominant colonial power.

Silk Road. The trade route that stretched from the Roman Empire to ancient China. It is the route that Marco Polo eventually followed.

Sino-Japanese War. A war fought from 1894 to 1895 between China and Japan for control of Korea. Japan's modern forces easily defeated the Chinese, who were forced to acknowledge Korean independence, pay a large indemnity, and cede territories, including Taiwan, to Japan.

Spice Islands. A former name for the Moluccas, the group of islands in eastern Indonesia between Celebes and New Guinea. The islands were the source of nutmeg, cloves, and other spices.

Tordesillas, Treaty of. A treaty between Spain and Portugal signed in 1494. It established a line of demarcation for control of colonies in the New World. The line was set at 370 leagues (about 1110 miles) west of the Cape Verde Islands. All new lands east of the line were to go to Portugal, all lands west of the line to Spain. The agreement gave Portugal the right to claim lands in Brazil. Portugal's Brazilian territories were increased by the Treaty of Madrid (1750).

Tours, Battle of. A battle fought in 732 at Tours, France. Invading Muslims from Spain were decisively defeated by the Franks led by Charles Martel, effectively ending the threat of Muslim domination in Europe north of the Pyrenees.

Trafalgar, Battle of. A British naval victory on October 21, 1805, over combined French and Spanish fleets during the Napoleonic wars. The British fleet, led by Lord Horatio Nelson, destroyed the opposing main fleet off Cape Trafalgar on the Spanish coast near the Strait of Gibraltar. Not a single British ship was destroyed, but Nelson was killed. The victory ensured British naval supremacy for the next century.

Universal Declaration of Human Rights. A declaration adopted by the United Nations General Assembly in 1948. It set forth the fundamental social, political, and economic rights of all peoples of the world.

Versailles, Treaty of. The most important of the treaties ending World

War I. The treaty was framed by Great Britain, France, Japan, and the United States, although the United States did not ratify it. It assigned responsibility for the war to Germany, required Germany to make heavy reparations payments, stripped Germany of its overseas possessions, and placed strict limits on German armed forces. The treaty also provided for establishment of the League of Nations.

Washington Conference. An international conference, also known as the Washington Naval Conference, convened by the United States from November, 1921, to February, 1922, to discuss naval disarmament and Far Eastern political affairs. The conference produced a number of treaties, including two Nine Power treaties, guaranteeing China's sovereignty and power to set tariffs; and a naval armaments treaty, creating a ten-year moratorium on the building of capital ships (ships of more than 10,000 tons displacement) and establishing ratios for the total tonnage of capital ships possessed by the United States, Great Britain, Japan, France, and Italy.

Weimar Republic. The republic established in Germany after World War I. Plagued almost continuously by political instability and severe economic problems, it was ended with the rise of Adolf Hitler to power in 1933.

Westphalia, Peace of. The group of treaties that ended the Thirty Years' War in 1648. It reduced the central authority of the Holy Roman Empire and ended the religious wars accompanying the Protestant Reformation.

Worms, Diet of. A meeting convened in 1521 by Holy Roman Emperor Charles V in Worms, Germany, to consider steps to take against Martin Luther. When Luther refused to repudiate his teachings, the diet issued the Edict of Worms, which declared Luther a heretic.

THIS 19TH CENTURY engaving depicts Martin Luther's defense of his writings before Charles V at the 1521 Diet of Worms.

THE HELP DESK

➤ **Associate** people with places and time. What country did Napoleon rule? Was that during the Crusades? What was Martin Luther's claim to fame? What did Captain Cook, Sir Francis Drake, and Magellan have in common?

➤ **Use** geography to help you understand history. What is the difference between the Old and New World? Why did Europe want to control Asia and Africa? Why did important cultures develop around the Mediterranean Sea?

➤ **Use** time lines to develop a sense of the chronology of history, that is, the order in which events happened. At first, a general awareness that Egyptian and Greek cultures came before the birth of Christ and that the Crusades preceded the discovery of America will be a help. A few specific dates will help the details fall into place.

➤ **How** can we know where we are going if we don't know where we have been? Could we have reached the current level of our existence if we had not built on the experience of the people who lived centuries ago?

➤ **What** events/inventions, etc., can you think of that have had influences on the entire world or on selected places prior to 1900? How do they relate to our modern world?

➤ **Use** your own family background to trace what locations and events in history might have been familiar to your forefathers. Take a course in genealogy to help start your search.

➤ **Make** a list of discoveries in the New World that improved or enriched life in the Old World.

➤ **The** population of the world has increased many times over in the past 200 years. To what factors can this be attributed?

➤ **Compare** and contrast the ancient Olympic games with the modern. Consider a number of elements, such as scope, events, rules, etc.

➤ **Hypothesize** a scenario for the development of written language—why, where, when, etc.

➤ **How** did the development of printing in the Middle Ages affect the course of history?

➤ **Why** has it taken so long for women to attain their current status when historically such strong leaders as Nefertiti, Elizabeth I, Catherine the Great, and Isabella made such an impact?

➤ **For** a list of helpful references, go to the *customers* section of www.southwestern.com.

World

Africa

Asia

Middle East

Australia and Oceania

Europe and Russia

North America

South America

World

When we are children we might describe something of enormous size as being "as big as the whole world." As we grow up, the world may diminish to manageable size, but "the whole world" still conjures up a picture of something huge, intriguing, colorful, and frequently exotic. It is. Though our world is small in comparison with the universe where other planets may or may not support life, it is our planet and a source of never-ending wonder, speculation, and possibilities.

While each of us is a tenant of the world, in easier-to-understand terms, we are also occupants of a continent, a country, a state or equivalent division, a city or town, a neighborhood, and perhaps even of smaller increments down to our house and our room. Our own small

place is important to us, but we also need to understand our position as a citizen of the world. How you came to be where you are is a mystery, but the importance of you in that place takes on added meaning as you learn more about the world and your place in it.

Geography may seem like a dull subject if the only thing that it means to you is maps. Ah, but what if there were no maps? Can you

imagine trying to visit your grandmother if you did not know what direction to go or how far it was or whether you needed a boat or a plane to get there? What if she lived in another town, or country, or even another continent? If you lived in the middle of the Sahara desert, would you think the world was made of sand? Or on Oahu, that the entire world was made up of tiny chunks of land surrounded by water? In a way, the land and water picture is correct

on a global scale, except that the chunks of land are huge chunks surrounded by water and are not called islands but continents.

will be developed and support large populations. On the other hand, millions of people may congregate in big cities. That may present some challenges to supporting the population with sources of food and other necessities transported from great

apparent. An old study trick is to "compare and contrast," meaning to itemize the similarities and differences. Usually the list grows longer and longer without much effort as more and more intriguing things come to your attention.

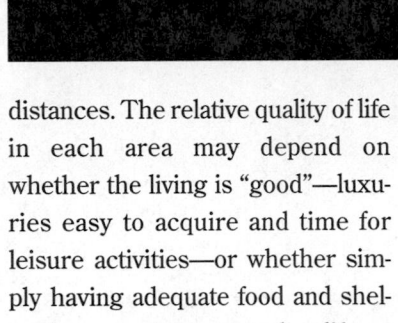

Each continent has certain characteristics, depending on the land formations, the nearness to the equator or the poles, the people who live there, and the types of plants and animals. Another very important item in characterizing the continents is the lack or abundance of mineral resources as well as the ability to produce power for industrial and domestic use. If the land has expanses of territory that are not suitable for human habitation, only the most easily accessible areas

distances. The relative quality of life in each area may depend on whether the living is "good"—luxuries easy to acquire and time for leisure activities—or whether simply having adequate food and shelter is a constant struggle—life or death, peace or war.

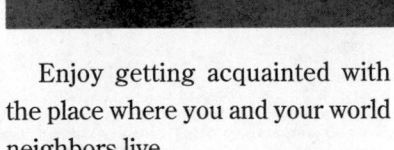

The people of each continent and country have shaped the land, the customs, and the way of life to meet their needs and desires. From the construction and design of houses to the native dress to the festivities, government, and types of jobs, each area has its differences as well as some similarities that may not be

Enjoy getting acquainted with the place where you and your world neighbors live.

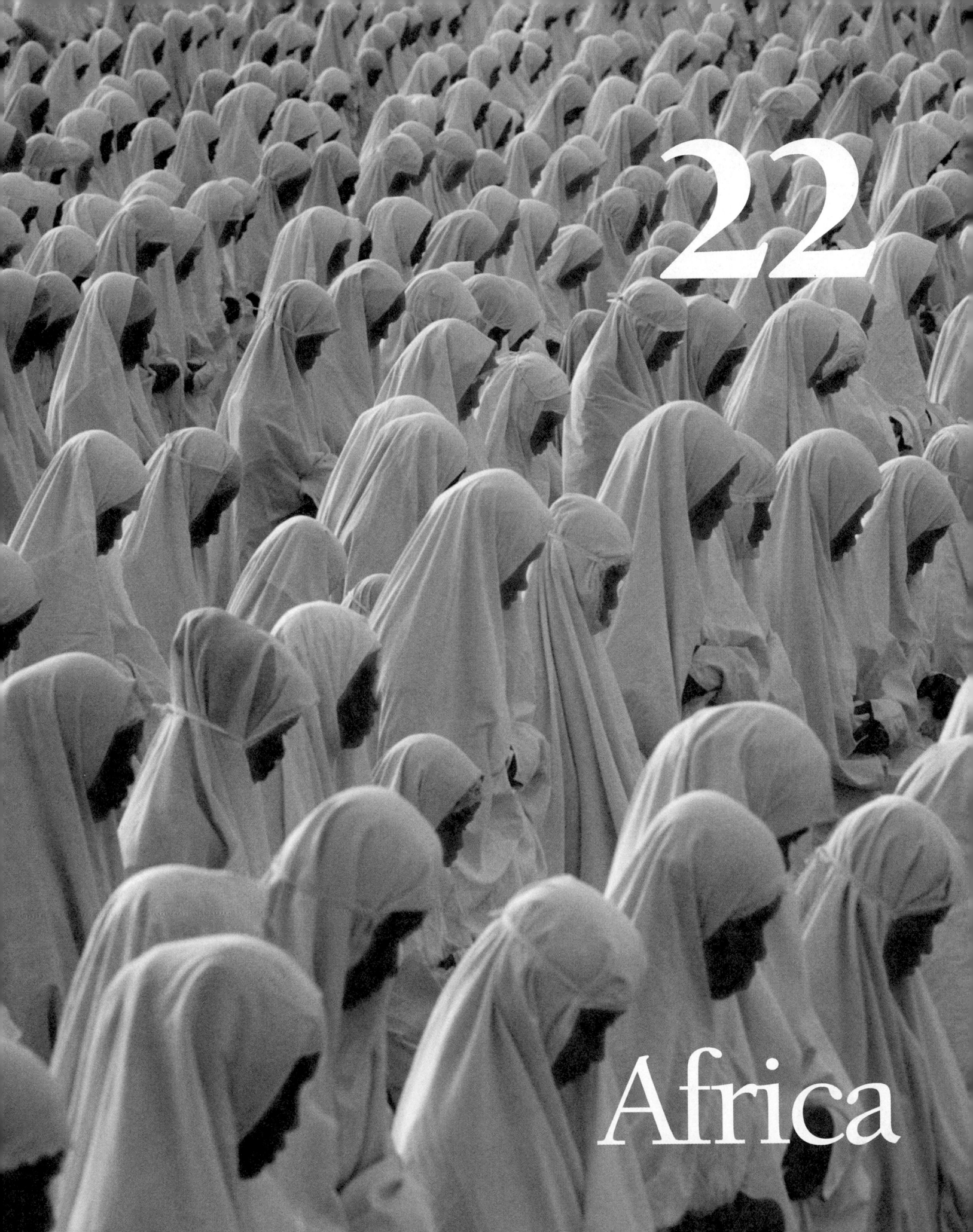

22

Africa

22 Africa

Overleaf: *Muslim Women*

Contents

Africa

kilometers
US

kilometres
Brit.

Africa, with an area of about 11.6 million square miles (30 million square kilometers) is the world's second largest continent. Its population, more than 800 million in 2000, represents over 10 percent of the world's total.

Africa south of the Sahara (also called sub-Saharan Africa) can be roughly defined as that part of the continent south of latitude 20° N. Included in this definition are the islands off the coast of West Africa, such as Bioko in the Gulf of Guinea, and the islands near the coast of East Africa, including Madagascar and Zanzibar.

The land. Africa is almost topographically homogeneous. The vast majority of the continent is occupied by an enormous plateau. On this plateau, two major divisions order the continent into distinct areas: Low and High Africa.

Low Africa refers to the area north of the Congo River and west of the Nile River. The average altitude of Low Africa is between 500 and 2,000 feet (152 and 610 meters) and is interrupted only by mountains in the northwest and by narrow coastal plains. Low Africa extends through dramatically different climatic and vegetative zones—desert, grassland, and rain forest—and includes about one-third of the continent's total area.

High Africa includes the rest of the continent—the area south and east of the Nile and Congo rivers. The average altitude is more than 3,000 feet (915 meters) above sea level. The plateau is interrupted by mountains in eastern Africa, by the coastal plains, and by the Great Rift Valley. The Great Rift Valley is an immense fissure that cuts through the plateau from the Red Sea in the north to the Shire River in South Africa; the deep valley lies below sea level in many places. High Africa also extends through the contrasting regions of savanna and desert.

There are few natural harbors along the smooth Atlantic and Indian Ocean coasts of Africa. Cliffs or steep slopes separate narrow coastal plains from the interior plateaus.

Mountains. Compared with the great mountain ranges of Europe, Asia, and the Americas, Africa does not have a great linear mountain range to speak of; the ranges occur in shorter bunches across the continent. In the north, the Atlas Mountains extend across Morocco, Algeria, and Tunisia, running roughly parallel to the Mediterranean coast. The western Atlas Mountains, or the High Atlas, contain Mount Toubkal, which reaches 13,666 feet (4,166 meters), the highest peak in the chain. There are several other snowcapped peaks in the High Atlas.

The highest peaks on the continent lie in eastern Africa and are of volcanic origin; Mount Kilimanjaro reaches 19,331 feet (5,892 meters) above sea level and is a semiactive volcano. Mount Kenya, 17,085 feet (5,208 meters), and Mount Elgon, 14,178 feet (4,322 meters), are dormant volcanoes. The Cameroon Mountains are the highest mountains in western Africa. The Tibesti, Ahaggar, and Aïr mountains rise out of the Sahara Desert. Other African ranges include the Ethiopian Massif and the central African Ruwenzori and Zambian Muchinga ranges.

Rivers. There are four major river systems in Africa. The Nile, the world's longest river, stretches 4,145 miles (6,671 kilometers) from Lake Victoria to the Mediterranean Sea. It is an important waterway and source of irrigation that supports an estimated 50 million people. The Congo is the continent's second longest river and includes the Ubangi, Kasai, and Kwango rivers as tributaries. The Zambezi River in the southeast features Victoria Falls, one of the world's most powerful waterfalls. Although 75 percent of the Niger is navigable year-round, the four major rivers are generally navigable only on the interior plateaus. Rapids and waterfalls that occur where the plateaus drop quickly to the coastal plains restrict access to the interior by boat. Other important rivers include the Senegal, Gambia, Volta, and Orange, which flow into the Atlantic Ocean; the Limpopo, which

flows to the Indian Ocean; and the Shari and Logone, which feed into Lake Chad.

Climate. The equator divides Africa climatically into roughly balanced halves. Each half can be further divided into three climatic regions.

Tropical rain forests stretch across equatorial Africa to the lakes region of eastern Africa in a belt that extends about 400 miles (645 kilometers) north and 400 miles south of the equator. Nearly half of Africa's forest area lies in the central equatorial zone. Heavy rainfall caused by converging trade winds help sustain the rain forests in the west. The high elevations in the east have inhibited further spread of the rain forests. Temperatures in the rain forest rarely reach 100°F (38°C) or drop below 70°F (27°C). The humidity is often greater than 80 percent, and 50 to 70 inches (128 to 180 centimeters) of rain falls each year.

North and south of the rain forests are two parallel belts of grassland, or savanna. The grassland is known as the Sudan in the north and the veld, or bush, in the south. Both grassland belts are between 500 and 700 miles (806 and 1,129 kilometers) wide. The belts stretch from the Atlantic Ocean to the East African lake region, where they meet, east of the rain forests. Rain is abundant close to the forest regions, about 40 inches (103 centimeters) annually. It decreases toward the desert to about 10 inches (26 centimeters). Temperatures are high, reaching over 100°F (38°C) in the summer. The transition areas between the savannas and desert regions are called steppes. They are notable for light rainfall, which varies greatly from year to year, making the areas prone to drought. The steppes of northwestern Africa are known as the Sahel.

The steppes extend to the Sahara in the north and the Kalahari and the Namib deserts in the south. The Sahara, the world's largest desert, covers 3.5 million square miles (9.1 million square kilometers), stretching from the Atlantic Ocean to the Red Sea. Summer temperatures in the Sahara average above 100°F (38°C), although the nights are much cooler. Less than 10 inches (26 centimeters) of rain falls annually. The Namib Desert is not quite as hot as the Sahara due to its smaller size and close proximity to the cool ocean. The Kalahari is almost a steppe area; many sections of the desert receive more than 15 inches (38 centimeters) of rain a year. The land remains arid because of the sandy soil and lack of water for irrigation.

The mountains receive more precipitation than the other regions. Some of the higher mountains in eastern Africa

SEVERAL million people in Egypt and Ethiopia belong to the Coptic Orthodox Church. This Coptic monastery is located in Egypt.

centimeters
US

centimetres
Brit.

receive 200 inches (513 centimeters) of precipitation a year and have milder temperatures. Sea breezes in the coastal regions help provide milder climates. Some of the coastal regions have Mediterranean climates—dry summers and wet winters.

Vegetation. The tropical forests of equatorial Africa are dense with hundreds of different species of plants. Bamboo, oil palms, and a wide variety of fruit trees are the most prevalent; mahogany, teak, ebony, and other hardwoods are the most valuable. Rubber, coffee, and cola nuts are also cultivated in the rain forests. The savannas have large numbers of acacia and baobab trees, thorny euphorbia bushes, and desert grasses. The deserts have shrubs, grasses, and weeds that can support small herds of animals. Date palms, which grow in oases in the Sahara, provide timber and palm fronds for housing. Groups of pine, cork, olive, oak, and cedar are prevalent on the coasts of the Mediterranean Sea.

Many grasslands and forests have been destroyed by agricultural and industrial development. Overgrazing of the Sudan, an area notorious for its periods of catastrophic drought, has further exacerbated food shortages throughout the region and led to the starvation of thousands of people and herds of animals. Some steppe regions have been turned almost entirely into deserts.

The people. About 70 percent of all Africans live in rural towns and villages, although the percentage of people living in cities more than doubled between 1960 and 1985. Population growth is close to 3 percent and has been at that level for 30 years. Areas of high population density exist in western Africa along the Niger; along the coast between Gambia and Cameroon; along the eastern coast from Kenya to South Africa; along the northern shores in Tunisia, Morocco, and the lower Nile; and on the East African Plateau in Ethiopia. Africa, however, is generally not overpopulated compared with other continents, but the limited amount of arable land and erratic rainfall have combined to discourage growth. Low population densities occur in the deserts, mountains, and forests.

Africa is a continent of great human diversity. It is divided among over 3,000 ethnic groups, and very few nations are ethnically homogenous. The boundaries between groups usually are not clearly defined, and the size of the ethnic groups varies widely. Almost 20 tribal groups have more than 1 million members, but most have fewer than 100,000 people.

Seventy percent of all Africans are black Africans, who predominate in the area south of the Sahara. The Hausa, Fulani, and Wolof are the largest groups in the Sahel. There are large populations of Pygmy people in the tropical forests of central and southwestern Africa. Slightly smaller populations of Bushmen, mostly San and Hottentots, live in the Kalahari Desert and in southern Africa.

Bantu-speaking people make up well over 300 different ethnic groups. Bantu is merely a linguistic classification used to distinguish people with similar backgrounds from the enormous variety of itinerant tribes; it does not denote a race or cultural group. The Mende are the largest group in the western savannas, and the Bamileke are the largest group in the northern savannas. In the eastern great lake area, the Luganda, Nyasa, and Rundi are the dominant Bantu tribes. The Zulu, Swazi, Tswana, Shona, Ndebele, and Sotho people are Bantu-speaking tribes in southern Africa.

Ethiopia and Somalia are populated mostly by Amhara and Somali people, both Kushitic tribes. Eastern Africa includes the Masai and the Dinka.

In the Sahara, Arabs and Berbers predominate, while Tuaregs and Bedouins live on the fringes of the Sahara in western and Eastern Africa respectively. The majority of the Berbers live in the deserts and mountains of Algeria, Morocco, and Tunisia.

Many Europeans and south Asians live in southern and eastern Africa. Europeans also populate many of the larger cities.

Languages. Africa is reported to have anywhere from 500 to over 1500 languages. Throughout history this hindered communication between states and within states, but they have also helped maintain cultural and ethnic ties across boundaries throughout the tumultuous years of colonialism. Four distinct stock language groups are usually cited to organize the variety.

Afroasiatic languages are mainly the languages spoken in northern Africa; they include the Berber, Kushitic, Coptic, and Arabic languages. The Afroasiatic group is the second largest, with over 100 million people speaking Arabic and another 70 million speaking Berber.

The Sudanic languages, the smallest group, are used by over 35 million people. They include Songhai and Masai and are spoken mostly in equatorial Africa.

The Niger-Congo language group is the largest. These languages are prevalent across western Africa south of the Sahara and include Hausa, Peul, and Wolof. This group also includes the 300 Bantu languages, which are spoken by peoples throughout equatorial, east, and southern Africa. The different Bantu languages are distinct and often completely unintelligible from one group to the next. Swahili is the most widely used Bantu language.

The Khoisian, or so-called click, languages are noted for their characteristic clicking sounds. Over 100,000 people in southern Africa speak Khoisian languages, with the largest group being the San in southwestern Africa.

European languages provide some inter-ethnic unity and prove invaluable in international business and politics. English and French remain the official languages spoken in most of their respective former colonies. Italian, Portuguese, and German are spoken in many different areas.

Religion. About 40 percent of the entire population of Africa follows traditional religions and animism. Animists are usually characterized by their worship of spirits believed to exist in the hills, trees, and other natural areas. The relationships between people and nature, and young and old, are strictly defined in most traditional and animist religions. The spirits of deceased ancestors are invoked for leadership and guidance. There are hundreds of local religions, with most tribal groups maintaining their own beliefs and practices.

About 300 million Africans are Muslim. A majority of the people in western Africa, including the Hausa, Kanuri, Songhai, and Malinke, have converted to Islam. Islam is the state religion in most of the countries north of the Sahara, where the Sunni Muslims dominate.

Christianity has about 350 million followers in Africa, about one-third of whom are Protestants. There are small sects of Coptic Christians in Egypt and Ethiopia, but most Christians live in sub-Saharan Africa.

Economy. Despite Africa's mineral wealth and energy resources, the continent remains relatively poor. African countries, with the exception of South Africa, have been slow to develop modern industries and farming techniques.

Agriculture. Agriculture employs three-quarters of the African work force. A majority of farmers are engaged in subsistence agriculture, using many of the same crude techniques as in the Middle East. These farmers usually produce small amounts of corn, millet, rice, sweet potatoes, peanuts, and other staple foods. Progress in agriculture has been limited by poor soil, too much or too little water, overgrazing, and overfarming. On the other hand, many thousands of African farmers are being trained in soil conservation and crop rotation, and the formation of farm cooperatives has been continually encouraged.

In many countries, modern commercial farms are the principal sources of food and export revenue. Most countries concentrate their efforts on one or two cash crops. The main African cash crops are coffee, cocoa, cotton, sugar, and bananas. Even with continuing development of commercial farming, agricultural production has not kept pace with population growth. Widespread dependence on a small number of cash crops makes many African economies prey to weather conditions, diseases, and low market prices. Large surpluses of commodities like coffee and cocoa are often as debilitating for an economy as extremely low yields brought on by drought. Many of the nations of Africa receive agricultural aid

from various countries and organizations, including the United States and the United Nations.

Between 1968 and 1985, two of the worst droughts of the century hit African economies hard. Many Africans died of starvation despite immense international aid. Mauritania, Senegal, Mali, and Niger, all on the edge of the Sahara, were particularly affected, as were Kenya and Ethiopia in the east and Mozambique and Angola in the south.

Cattle, goats, and sheep are raised in many of the savanna regions. Although coastal fishing resources are extensive, almost all of the commercial fishing is undertaken only by European countries. Most of the continental areas lack the processing and storage facilities to provide a surplus for the inland areas or for export.

KOFI ANNAN of Ghana became secretary-general of the United Nations in 1997, with a focus on reforming UN staff and operations.

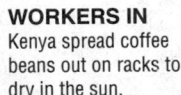

WORKERS IN Kenya spread coffee beans out on racks to dry in the sun.

MODERN FARM machinery is used on some larger farms that produce many export crops, but a large percentage of farmers in Africa continue to use simple hand tools.

The tropical forests offer ebony, mahogany, rosewood, and other cabinet woods. At one time the bulk of the world's rubber came from the tropical forests, but this production was rendered less valuable by the development of plantation rubber in Southeast Asia and by the production of synthetic rubber. To date, the economic importance of Africa's forests has come largely from by-products, such as palm oil, cork, gums, and dyes. Western Africa has begun to suffer from depletion of its forests, which occurred during the years of rapid development in the 1970s and 1980s. Nigeria, for example, had 9 million hectares of forests in the early 1960s. This was reduced to 2 million hectares by the mid-1980s.

Africa possesses 40 percent of the world's waterpower potential, but contributes only a small percentage of hydroelectric energy.

Industry. The initial economic readjustment programs of the newly independent African countries in the 1960s emphasized industrial development and sparked a short boom period for manufacturing throughout Africa. Production stagnated quickly, however, as debts accumulated. Capital was in short supply, and foreign investors were only willing to contribute toward the exploitation of raw materials. Lack of

Natural resources. The most significant contribution to the economic importance of Africa comes from the sizable oil and natural gas reserves of the Sahara. Next to fossil fuels, northern Africa's chief mineral is phosphate. Large amounts of copper are mined in the Republic of Congo, Zimbabwe, and South Africa. South Africa and several West African countries in the Congo Basin are world-leading producers of dia-

At the end of the 1980s, industry in Africa, not counting highly industrialized South Africa, represented only 1 percent of the world total. Most of that amount was concentrated in a few countries in northern and western Africa. Most industry involved the processing of food, beverages, and tobacco, and the manufacture of textiles and clothing. Heavy industry was limited to a few countries and consisted mostly of oil refining, mineral processing, and the manufacture of chemicals and building materials. The iron and steel industries in South Africa and Zimbabwe are especially important to industrial development in many African nations.

Transportation and trade. Internal trade and communication have always been difficult in Africa because one-third of the countries have no outlet to the sea. The rivers, although navigable for long distances, are treacherous near the coast because of rapids and waterfalls.

Africa has poorly developed systems for road, rail, and air travel. More than ten countries have no railroad system. Most of the continent's railroads are in South Africa, and the remaining track links inland mining and commercial agricultural regions with ports on the coasts, but there are few interior connections. Roads are generally poor, easily washed out during rainy season, and unsuited to the economical operation of vehicles. Although many countries opened national airports with regular international traffic in the 1980s, air transport remained too expensive for large-scale continental use. Radio, television, and telephone systems usually serve only the larger metropolitan areas.

Economic trends. Since the beginning of the 1980s, almost half of the sub-Saharan African countries have also instituted economic adjustment programs, mostly emphasizing agriculture while continuing small-scale industrial development and import substitution. The gains were negligible at best as corruption and mismanagement continued to reign. In fact, over the 30 years since the initial wave of independence in the 1960s, only a few countries (Botswana, Cameroon, Gabon, and others) have made improvements in the standard of living. Some countries (Equatorial Guinea, Liberia, São Tomé and Príncipe, and Zambia, among others) have watched their standard of living drop into the Third World bracket.

In 1989—roughly coinciding with the widespread changes in Eastern Europe—many of the centrally controlled economies bowed to the pressure of the continued failure of their state systems and pressure from the World Bank and International Monetary Fund and rejected socialism in favor of economic liberalization. Plans to build market economies were introduced across the continent.

At the beginning of the 1990s, however, most Africans still lived in villages and made their living from the soil. For

OVERHUNTING and environmental destruction are endangering animals like this lioness and her cub in Kenya.

monds. Manganese, chromium ore, and bauxite, the source of aluminum, are mined in large quantities in West Africa. High-quality iron ore is also an important export earner. Africa depends heavily on world demand for its raw materials and consequently is often left at the mercy of market prices.

capital, skilled labor, and adequate transportation facilities made it very difficult for African countries to compete in the world market and severely inhibited further development. Government corruption and poor management stigmatized the economies and made investors even more wary.

the most part, African countries were faced with widespread unemployment, enormous debt, and further problems with restructuring their economies.

Almost all African countries are associated with the European Union to some degree.

Government and politics.
Exposure to Western influences during World War II intensified the desire of Africans for freedom and progress. Beginning in the mid-1950s, France, Britain, and Belgium bowed to pressure from African nationalists and relinquished control of their colonies. Portuguese colonies gained independence after bloody revolutions.

African independence. The newly independent nations were confronted by many difficult problems, primarily associated with internal disunion and economic underdevelopment. Initial efforts to establish multiparty democratic systems gave way to domination by single-party military regimes. Most governments considered themselves African socialists although they owed little to European socialism. They were characterized by centralized economic planning.

For the majority of the last three decades, all but a few African countries have been run as single-party states

with authoritarian leaders. Although Africa's most renowned despots—Macias Nguema of Equatorial Guinea, Jean Bedel Bokassa of the Central African Republic, and Idi Amin of Uganda—were all deposed in 1978, and other military regimes gave way to civilian rule, dictatorships and single-party states were still the dominant political form as over half of the nations in Africa remained under military rule in the mid-1980s.

Since independence, almost all African nations have followed a foreign policy of nonalignment, accepting aid from both the Western and Eastern blocs. By the 1970s many African nations were also accepting aid from China and Japan.

Pan-Africanism. The young nations of Africa readily joined regional and international organizations in an attempt to speed development. The ideal of pan-Africanism, or the unity of all African peoples, found expression in the Organization of African Unity (OAU), which was founded in May of 1963 by 30 African nations at a conference in Addis Ababa, Ethiopia. The OAU has continued to contribute to solidarity throughout Africa, establishing regional development and cooperation.

African states have come to wield considerable voting power in the United Nations (UN) General Assembly, where

they make up nearly one-third of the membership. Most of the new nations of Africa view the UN as the key to continued advance in such areas as health and education.

Through the UN and the OAU, Africa has become a force in international relations.

Africa today. The trend toward single-party states changed rapidly in the early 1990s as Africa became a part of the global movement toward pluralism. Many experts saw it as a reaction to the fall of communism in Eastern Europe and the demise of apartheid—two seemingly impregnable institutions. Campaigns challenging long-established single-party rulers have been initiated in over a dozen countries, including the Republic of Congo, Ghana, Togo, Guinea, Kenya, Zambia, and the Democratic Republic of the Congo. In 1991 Benin's president, Mathiew Kerekou, who had ruled for 18 years, became the first African leader to be voted out of office. Cape Verde and São Tomé and Príncipe held multiparty elections. In the Republic of Congo, President Denis Sassou-Nguesso and his Marxist Party were deposed and a multiparty democracy was established. The decade's most dramatic change, however, occurred in South Africa, which ended apartheid, adopted a democratic constitution, and held free elections.

THESE WOMEN are participating in an Islamic ceremony. Islam is one of the leading religions in Africa, with nearly 300 million adherents.

22 Africa

aluminum
US

aluminium
Brit.

emphasized
US

emphasised
Brit.

labor
US

labour
Brit.

Countries of Africa

Algeria

Official name: *People's Democratic Republic of Algeria*
Area: *919,352 sq. mi., 2,381,740 sq. km.*
Type of government: *Republic*
Population: *32,278,000*
Capital and largest city: *Algiers (Pop., metro. area, 1,904,000)*
Languages: *Arabic (official), Berber dialects, French*
Literacy: *62%;* **Currency:** *Dinar*
Per capita GDP: *$5,600 (Rank: 81st)*

kilometers
US
kilometres
Brit.

labor
US
labour
Brit.

The land. Most of Algeria is part of the vast desert waste of the Sahara. A narrow northern zone, where the bulk of the people live, is dominated by two parallel east-west mountain chains—the Tell Atlas and the Saharan Atlas. Both are part of the massive Atlas Mountains, which stretch across northern Africa. The Tell Atlas is a series of coastal mountains and valleys parallel to the Mediterranean Sea. The Saharan Atlas lies about 200 miles (323 kilometers) inland. Between the two ranges is a plateau area where Algeria's most fertile soils are found.

Most of the desert surface of southern Algeria is composed of rock and gravel, but there are some large sand areas. In the southeast are the Ahaggar Mountains, a volcanic rock mass whose highest peak, Mount Tahat, reaches above 9,800 feet (3,000 meters). The barren Sahara region is sparsely populated.

In Algeria's coastal region, the winters are mild and rainy and the summers are hot and dry. The plateau region receives little rain, about 12 inches (31 centimeters) annually. The Sahara is hot and dry and receives less than 4 inches (10 centimeters) of rain a year.

The people. Most of Algeria's rapidly growing population is Muslim of Arab, Berber, or mixed Arab-Berber stock. More than 1 million people of European origin left Algeria after independence was won in 1962, leaving the country with only about 75,000 European residents.

Algeria has a high literacy rate compared with other African nations. Education is free and compulsory to age 16. The population is almost 50 percent urban. Ninety-one percent of the population live along the Mediterranean coast on 12 percent of the land. The largest cities are Algiers, the capital; Oran (population, 745,000); Constantine (564,000); and Annaba (271,000).

Economy. Algeria has traditionally been an agricultural country. Although only 3 percent of the entire country's land is arable, one-third of the labor force is employed in agriculture. The bulk of its produce, which consists of wheat and barley and a variety of vegetables and fruits, comes from the region between the Tell Atlas and the Mediterranean. For many years the most valuable export was wine.

Industry and mining account for over half of the gross national product,

SAND DUNES cover much of Algeria.

compared with under 10 percent from agricultural products. Rich oil and gas fields were discovered in the Sahara in the 1950s. Petroleum and natural gas now account for almost 98 percent of Algeria's total exports. Iron ore and phosphate are also important exports.

Algerian industry is dominated by state-owned factories manufacturing steel, petrochemicals, fertilizers, and cement. Algeria's main trading partners are France, Italy, the United States, the Netherlands, and Canada.

Government. The head of state is a president who is popularly elected to a 5-year term. The president appoints a prime minister and the members of a Cabinet of Ministers. Legislative power is exercised by a bicameral parliament, which includes the 389-member National People's Assembly whose members are popularly elected for 5-year terms. The constitution allows for a multiparty system.

History. The territory of present-day Algeria was invaded many times and dominated by many peoples before the country won its independence in 1962. Until the modern era, Algeria was often a part of larger units that included parts of present-day Morocco and Tunisia.

The earliest known settlers were Berber-speaking peoples. The Phoenicians, who arrived in about 1200 B.C., established control over part of North Africa. Their rule ended in 146 B.C. with the fall of Carthage to Rome.

Roman domination ended with invasions by the Vandals in the A.D. 400s. In the sixth century the region came under Byzantine rule. In the seventh century the Arabs began to sweep through North Africa, and Algeria became part of the Arab-dominated Muslim world, which stretched from Spain to Arabia.

Ottoman era. In the early 1500s the Spanish, crusading against the Muslims

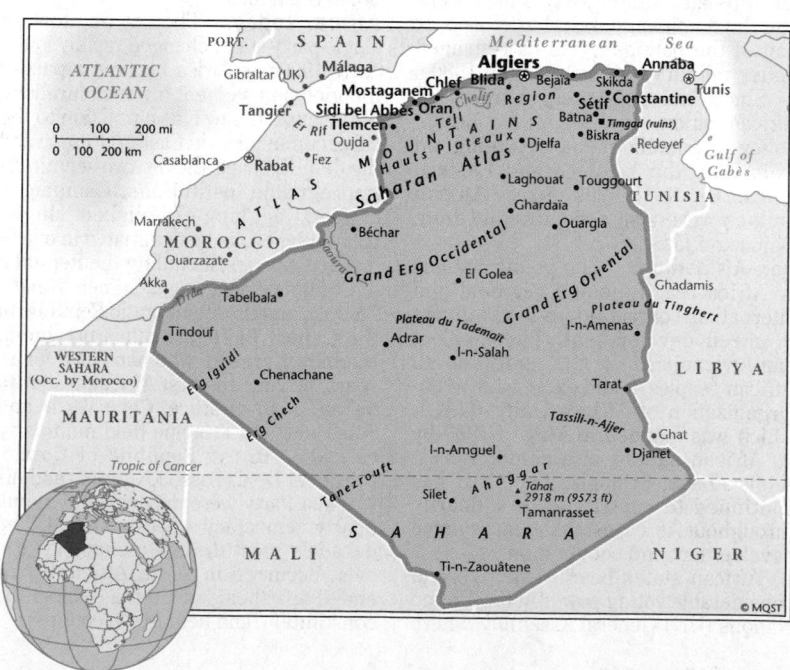

who had withdrawn from Spain to North Africa, captured several Algerian cities. The inhabitants of Algeria appealed for help to a Muslim commander, Khayr ad-Din, who drove the Spanish from Algiers in 1519. He offered allegiance to the Ottoman Empire in return for men and supplies. With Turkish aid, the Spanish were driven out of Algeria.

Algeria remained formally part of the Ottoman Empire until 1830. As an Ottoman province, its boundaries came to be roughly those of the modern Algerian state. Because of its great distance from Istanbul, Algeria became a Turkish regency in name only, and a Turkish *dey,* or governor, ruled the country almost as an independent state. The Turks held control of the coastal region, but the interior remained largely under traditional tribal rule.

French rule. The French occupation of Algeria began in 1830 with the capture of Algiers. The Turkish dey quickly capitulated, but native Algeria, led by Abd-el-Kadir (Abd-al-Qadir), resisted. Not until 1847, when Abd-el-Kadir was captured, did France secure control over most of the country.

Large numbers of French and other Europeans settled in Algeria soon after the defeat of Abd-el-Kadir, and by 1900 Europeans made up 14 percent of Algeria's total population. The new settlers built up the Algerian economy, developing commercial agriculture for the French market. But the development served the needs of only the French Algerians, who gradually gained control of most of the best land.

By the early 1900s, the lack of economic opportunities and political inequalities created growing unrest within the Muslim majority. Algerian desire for self-determination grew following World War II. In 1954 an armed rebellion against the French was begun by the National Liberation Front (FLN). The FLN slowly won the allegiance of most of the non-European population during a bitter struggle in the years that followed.

Finally, in 1960, after a military effort that brought 500,000 French troops to Algeria and resulted in a series of French domestic political crises, French President de Gaulle agreed to negotiate with the FLN.

The two countries reached agreement only after months of bargaining. During that period part of the French army based in Algeria attempted a military coup against de Gaulle. In addition, a last-ditch terrorist campaign against French withdrawal was waged by the Secret Army Organization (OAS) in Europe. On July 3, 1962, after 132 years of French rule, Algeria became independent.

Independence. The fruits of victory were almost lost in a near civil war that erupted immediately after independence was granted. Ahmed Ben Bella, a leader of the FLN who had been imprisoned in France since 1956, made a successful bid for power with the support of the FLN army.

By the end of 1962 Ben Bella had been elected premier by a newly formed national assembly, and he appeared to be securely in power. In June 1965, however, Ben Bella was deposed in a bloodless coup led by the army, and Houari Boumédienne, a military leader of the independence struggle, emerged as head of the new regime. Boumédienne's military regime declared war on Israel in 1967, subsequently breaking off relations with the United States and allying itself more closely with the Soviet Union. Relations with the United States were reestablished in 1974.

A semidemocratic constitution was granted in 1976, and in the elections of 1977 Boumédienne was elected president. He died the following year and Chadli Benjedid was elected president.

In response to severe rioting and protesting in 1988, Algeria revised its constitution to permit political parties and guarantee freedom of expression and the right to strike.

In the first round of multiparty national elections in December 1991, the fundamentalist Islamic Salvation Front (FIS) was the clear winner, causing alarm that Algeria might become a fundamentalist Islamic state. In January 1992 President Benjedid dissolved the assembly and resigned, turning power over to a five-member Council of State, which canceled the second round of elections and declared a state of emergency. Armed conflict between government forces and Islamic guerrillas escalated in 1992 and 1993, in part because of the unwieldy nature of the Council of State. FIS's armed wing disbanded in 2000, and many militants surrendered. However, residual fighting continues.

Angola

Official name: *Republic of Angola*
Area: *481,226 sq. mi.,*
    1,246,700 sq. km.
Type of government: *Transition*
Population: *10,554,000*
Capital and largest city: *Luanda*
    (Pop., metro. area, 1,822,000)
Languages: *Portuguese (official),*
    African dialects
Literacy: *42%;* **Currency:** *Kwanza*
Per capita GDP: *$1,330*
    (Rank: 157th)

The land. Most of Angola lies on the deeply dissected Bihé Plateau, which has an average elevation of 4,000 feet (1,220 meters). A narrow coastal plain skirts the plateau on the west, and in the east a higher plateau rises to 7,000 feet (2,134 meters).

A portion of Angola, the small Cabinda region, about 2,800 square miles (7,252 square kilometers) in area, is an enclave separated from Angola proper by the Democratic Republic of the Congo. Low-lying Cabinda is covered by dense tropical jungle.

Much of the interior of Angola is heavily forested. Some portions of the east are swampy; the Moçâmedes Desert lies in the southwest. Many rivers, the Zambezi and tributaries of the Congo River among them, rush down from the plateau toward the borders.

Angola's climate is varied. Cabinda and the coastal and northern regions are tropical, with high heat and humidity. The south and southeast are generally drier. The lower areas are hot, and the higher regions cool. The greatest amount of rainfall—about 70 inches (180 centimeters) annually—is in the Mayombe Forest in Cabinda, while the smallest amount—less than 2 inches (5 centimeters)—falls on the coast.

The people. The overwhelming majority of the people are Bantu of many tribal groups, including the Kongo, Kimbundu, Ovimbundu, and Chokwe. About 1 percent of the population is European, and there is a small group of mixed African and European origin.

BAZAARS in Africa carry brightly colored handwoven rugs and other handicrafts.

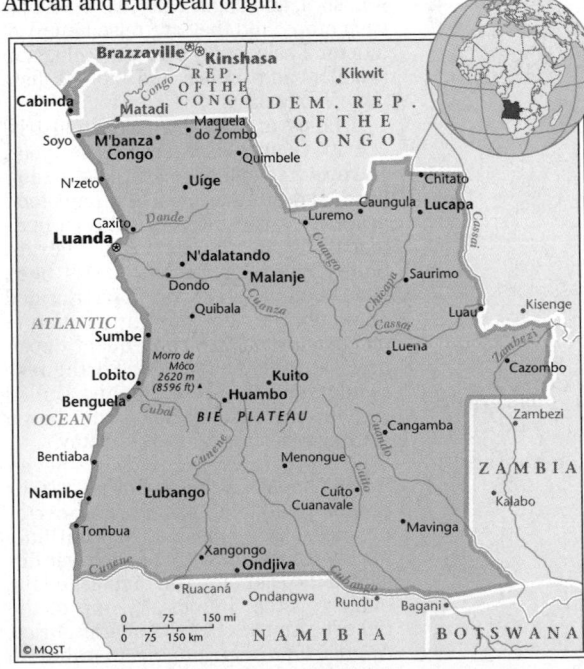

COFFEE, raised on large plantations, is one of Angola's leading exports.

The diverse ethnic backgrounds of the population contribute a wide variety of spoken languages to the country. No single African language reaches beyond its ethnic area, however, Portuguese is used throughout the country. Because of government emphasis on education, literacy has improved greatly since independence.

More than 70 percent of the people are concentrated in the west, the central highlands, and the north. The population is only 25 percent urban. Major cities include Luanda, the capital, and Huambo (population, metro. area, 400,000).

Economy. Angola is a rich land. There are diamonds, oil, copper, manganese, iron, gold, and other minerals, and the hydroelectric potential is considerable. Farming is the chief economic activity of most of the people, however.

The basic food crops are manioc, corn, rice, and vegetables. Coffee, cotton, sisal, and sugar cane are the major cash crops, and they are raised on plantations. The country's forests yield palm products and timber, and there is fishing off the coasts.

Mining is Angola's major industrial activity. Oil was discovered in the 1960s, and over 22.5 million metric tons are now produced annually. Oil refining, food processing, and building material manufacturing are the leading industries. Some hydroelectric power has been developed. The economy deteriorated markedly after the abrupt transition to independence. The subsequent departure of about 350,000 Portuguese residents, who were mostly skilled laborers and civil servants, caused even greater problems for the economy.

Under the guidance of the Soviet Union, Angola nationalized most of its economy, although some private-sector business was allowed to continue, mostly in agriculture. The civil war disrupted the economy and diminished the quality of life. Potentially one of the richest countries in sub-Saharan Africa, Angola has been unable to rebound from these periods of strife.

laborers
US

laborers
Brit.

Oil, natural gas, coffee, gold, iron ore, fish products, corn, and sisal are the country's chief exports. Machinery and vehicles, textiles, drugs, and manufactured goods are imported. Angola's main trading partners are the United States, Germany, France, Cuba, Portugal, and Brazil.

Government. The head of the Angolan government is its president, who is assisted by a council of ministers. The legislature consists of a unicameral National People's Assembly. Angola has, since 1991, moved toward multiparty democracy. The two main political parties are the Popular Front for the Liberation of Angola (MPLA) and the National Union for the Total Independence of Angola (UNITA).

History. Large-scale migrations of Bantu-speaking Africans originating in what is now the Nigeria-Cameroon border region began populating Angola about A.D. 500. The area's first inhabitants, hunter-gatherers related to today's Khoisan people of southwestern Africa, were eventually driven out by the more advanced Bantu. The Bantu introduced iron technology, agriculture, and sophisticated social systems to the region.

Angola was part of the large, advanced Bantu-speaking kingdom of Kongo when it was visited in 1482 by the Portuguese explorer Diego Cão. Friendly relations were established, and Portugal sent missionaries, traders, and settlers to the territory in the 1500s. Portions of the territory later came under direct Portuguese administration, but when Kongo began to disintegrate, Portugal did little to develop or exploit the region's resources.

During the 1600s the Portuguese defeated Dutch attempts to win control of Angola, and in the 1700s and 1800s Angola was a major source of slaves for Portugal's colony of Brazil. In 1878 slaving was prohibited and replaced by a system of contract labor. Under the contract system, men over 18 who were employed fewer than 6 months a year could be forced to work. Women and young children were frequently drafted

to meet labor needs as well.

Portugal's title to Angola was affirmed and the colony's boundaries set in 1885 and 1886. Colonial development was largely in private hands until the 1930s, when the government encouraged the Portuguese to settle there.

The government initiated full exploitation of the area's resources and imposed centralized control by breaking the power of local chiefs. Portugal's official policy was to incorporate Angola into the culture, society, and economy of European Portugal.

Nationalism. Although some political participation was permitted Angolans after 1951, when Angola was declared an overseas province, the government failed to meet the educational, health, and welfare needs of the majority of the people. This neglect spurred the growth of a nationalist movement, and in 1961 an insurrection broke out in Cabinda and northern Angola.

Portugal moved to suppress the revolt by military force, but guerrilla warfare continued in the north and nationalist leaders established a government in exile that demanded independence.

The United Nations urged Portugal to liberate its prized and profitable colony, but instead Portugal attempted to improve Angola's economic, social, and educational conditions. It initiated programs of industrialization and oil production to modernize the economy. But guerrilla warfare continued up to 1974, as the United States, South Africa, the Soviet Union, and Zaire competed for influence in the colony.

After years of bloody warfare and economic decline caused by massive Portuguese emigration, the guerrillas, helped by Soviet-aided Cuban troops, established an independent Marxist regime in 1975. South African troops staged an unsuccessful attack on the new regime in 1978.

The Marxist regime, led by the Popular Movement for the Liberation of Angola (MPLA), controlled most of Angola for the next 13 years. The National Union for the Total Independence of Angola (UNITA), an avowed anti-Communist group backed by the United States and South Africa, continued to engage the MPLA forces throughout the 1980s. The National Front for the Liberation of Angola (FNLA), an anti-Communist group assisted mostly by Zaire, continued low-level guerrilla warfare in the north.

In December 1988, Cuba signed an accord agreeing to the removal of all its troops by July 1991. In 1989 South Africa stopped supporting UNITA.

A cease-fire between government forces and antigovernment forces was declared on May 31, 1991. National elections were held in September 1992. However, UNITA failed to defeat the ruling MPLA. Serious fighting resumed in late 1998 and continued until a cease-fire in 2002 after rebel leader Jonas Savimbi was killed. Up to 1.5 million lives may have been lost during the 30 years of civil war.

Benin

Official name: *Republic of Benin*
Area: *43,471 sq. mi.,*
112,620 sq. km.
Type of government: *Multiparty*
democracy
Population: *6,835,000*
Capital: *Porto-Novo*
(Pop., 233,000)
Largest city: *Cotonou*
(Pop., 651,000)
Languages: *French (official), Fon,*
Yoruba, tribal dialects
Literacy: *38%*
Currency: *CFA franc*
Per capita GDP: *$1,040*
(Rank: 166th)

The land. Most of Benin, formerly called Dahomey, lies at an elevation of less than 1,000 feet (305 meters) above sea level. Benin has a narrow, sandy coastline. Behind this coastal area are marshes and lagoons. The mainland begins in a low-lying clay plain that is intensively cultivated. There are grasslands in the north.

A low dividing ridge crosses the country at its greatest width. Rivers south of the ridge drain into the sea. To the north are tributaries of the Volta and Niger rivers.

The climate in the coastal region is hot and humid. Between 30 and 50 inches (77 and 128 centimeters) of rain fall annually. In the north it is dry from November to June and rainy from June to November.
The people. The population of Benin includes many ethnic groups. The Fons live in the southern part of the country. The Nagots live in western Benin and in the areas near the cities of Porto-Novo and Abomey. The Baribas live in the north. Other ethnic groups are the Peuls, the Sanbas, the Aïzo, the Yoruba, and the Adjas. There is a small European population.

More than two-thirds of the people live in the south. The northern half of the country is sparsely populated. Most people live in rural areas. Animism is

practiced by the majority of the people; however, there are significant minorities of Christians and Muslims.

The port of Cotonou is Benin's largest city and economic center. Porto-Novo, the capital, is the second largest city. Other important cities include Parakou (population, 145,000); Abomey (67,000); and Kandi (73,000).
Economy. Almost 80 percent of Benin's population is engaged in subsistence agriculture, while livestock and fishing contribute additional income. Cotton, corn, coffee, peanuts, and millet are the main cash crops.

Mineral deposits of iron, gold, and chromite are largely unexploited. Industry is mostly small-scale, centered on the processing of palm oil, sugar, and cotton and the manufacture of consumer goods. Industry employs about 16 percent of the workforce.

Trade consists of importing food and manufactured goods and exporting cotton, crude oil, and palm oil products. Benin's main trading partners are France, the Netherlands, Japan, Italy, and the United States.
Government. In 1989 Benin began a move toward multiparty democracy from its previous Marxist ideology, adopting a constitution in December 1990. Transition was complete by April 1991.

The executive branch consists of a president, who is both chief of state and head of the government, and the Council of Ministers. The president is elected by popular vote to a 5-year term. The Council of Ministers is appointed by the president.

The legislature is the unicameral National Assembly. The 83 members are elected by popular vote to 4-year terms.
History. Many rich and highly organized kingdoms existed in the area of present-day Benin. The most famous was the Fon kingdom of Abomey, established in 1625, whose ruler had conquered other coastal states by the early 1700s.

Portuguese traders came to what is now Porto-Novo in the 1600s. With the rise of the slave trade the English, Dutch, Spanish, and French also came to the area. European slave companies dealt largely with the foreign minister of the kingdom of Abomey.
French rule. In 1851 the French established themselves at Cotonou, and in 1890 hostilities broke out between France and Abomey. France established a protectorate over the area and exiled the king while continuing to use tribal chiefs in administering the region. The boundaries of Benin, then called Dahomey, were defined by 1898, and in 1904 Dahomey became part of the Federation of French West Africa.

Local conflicts dominated Dahomey's politics after World War II. In 1947 France introduced a territorial assembly, and Sourou-Migan Apithy, a southern leader, and Hubert Maga, a northerner, were elected to the French

National Assembly. But regional movements did not solidify into a single national organization.

France granted Dahomey internal autonomy in 1957, and Apithy was elected prime minister. In 1958 Dahomey voted to become a member of the French Community.
Independence. France granted Dahomey its independence in August 1960. Several parties merged, and Maga was elected president. Party unity did not last, however, and a military coup overthrew Maga in October 1963.

This was the first of five coups to unsettle the country since independence. In the fifth one, in October of 1972, Major Mathieu Kerekou took over the government. He began formulating a "new society" based on Marxist-Leninist principles. In November of 1975 he announced that the country's name was being changed from Dahomey to the People's Republic of Benin.

A new constitution was granted in 1977, but allegations of government corruption and attempted coups persisted. Benin's economy continued to be dependent on French aid and attempts to modernize it have met with little success so far.

In 1989 thousands of people demonstrated against President Kerekou's authoritarian government. Kerekou responded by announcing that Marxism-Leninism would no longer be the state ideology. Still, a series of crippling strikes and antigovernment demonstrations were launched, and finally Kerekou agreed to step down. In 1991 the first free presidential election in nearly three decades was held.

meters
US

metres
Brit.

centers
US

centres
Brit.

Botswana

Official name: *Republic of*
Botswana
Area: *231,804 sq. mi.,*
600,370 sq. km.
Type of government:
Parliamentary republic
Population: *1,579,000*
Capital and largest city: *Gaborone*
(Pop., 186,000)
Languages: *English (official),*
Setswana
Literacy: *70%;* **Currency:** *Pula*
Per capita GDP: *$7,800*
(Rank: 65th)

The land. The Kalahari Desert occupies most of central and western Botswana. This dry region, covered with sand, grass, and thorn bush, has no rivers. The land in eastern Botswana is well watered and fertile. The Okavango River flows into northern Botswana and forms an area of swamps and marshes. The Molopo and Limpopo rivers run along the southern border.

Northern Botswana has a tropical climate. Farther south, the climate is

22 Africa

THE APPEAL of the natural beauty of the Kalahari Desert is seen here in a sunset.

hot and dry. The north receives an average of 27 inches (69 centimeters) of rain a year, but the south receives less than 9 inches (23 centimeters).

The people. Most of Botswana's people speak a Bantu language. There are eight principal tribes in Botswana, each with its own traditional tribal area. The Bamangwato is the largest tribal group. Eighty percent of the people live in villages in the eastern part of the country. An estimated 40,000 Batswana work in neighboring African countries, mainly in the Republic of South Africa. The major cities in Botswana are Gaborone, the capital; Mahalapye (population, 40,000); and Serowe (42,000).

Economy. Historically, Botswana's economy has been based on cattle raising and farming. Eighty percent of the workforce is engaged in agriculture, although only about 50 percent of the nation's food is produced domestically. The basic food crops of Botswana include corn, sorghum, peanuts, and fruits and vegetables.

The mining of diamonds, copper, and nickel has been the most significant factor in the country's vast economic improvement since 1966. Botswana's strong financial position is due mostly to the sale of diamonds, which accounts for over 75 percent of the country's export receipts. Botswana's major trading partners are Switzerland, South Africa, and the United States.

Government. The head of state and chief executive of Botswana is the president, elected along with the legislature, the National Assembly. Assembly candidates must indicate their choice for president; the presidential candidate with the greatest number of supporters elected to the assembly becomes president. A House of Chiefs, composed of members of the eight dominant tribes, serves as an advisory body to the National Assembly. General elections are held at least every 5 years.

centimeters
US

centimetres
Brit.

center
US

centre
Brit.

History. The region's earliest inhabitants are believed to have been the San. Sotho people began populating Botswana about 1600 from the southwest. In the early 1800s, Tswana-speaking people were driven into Botswana from the Transvaal, in present-day South Africa, by invading Zulus. In the years following, there were tribal wars and conflicts with Boers from the Transvaal.

British rule. In 1885 the British placed present-day Botswana under their protection. They viewed the area, which they called Bechuanaland, as economically useless, but strategically important because it served as an access route to the north, which was then unoccupied by whites. The land served also as a wedge between the Germans, then in South-West Africa (Namibia), and their Boer allies, in the Transvaal. In 1895 the British government incorporated the land south of the Molopo River into the Cape Colony, later a part of South Africa.

The British instituted indirect rule in the protectorate, allowing the Botswana chiefs to retain their authority under the protection of the British Crown. The protectorate soon became economically dependent upon South Africa, into which the British had long assumed all of Bechuanaland would eventually be incorporated.

The protectorate progressed slowly until after World War II, when political change became rapid, spurred by the development of nationalism in other parts of Africa. In 1950 a Joint Advisory Council was established; it gave the Botswana people more influence in the national government. The Joint Advisory Council created a legislative council that further established a popular presence in the government and that led the campaign for independence.

Independence. Botswana achieved self-rule in 1960 and Seretse Khama became the country's elected president. A moderate, he founded the Bechuanaland Democratic Party. Great Britain granted the country its independence on September 30, 1966.

Khama ruled a democratic, nonracial government that clashed with the racist regimes in South Africa and Rhodesia (now Zimbabwe). Violence erupted in 1978 over the issue of Rhodesian workers in Botswana; many civil servants were angry about the continued foreign presence in government positions. The government restored order by establishing a policy that would, in time, replace all government personnel from foreign countries with citizens of Botswana. Khama died in 1980 and was succeeded by Dr. Quett K. J. Masire. Masire retired in 1998 and was succeeded by Vice President Festus Mogae. Mogae won the 1999 election.

Today Botswana is one of the few flourishing democracies in Africa. Botswana opposed South Africa's policy of apartheid, even though their economies are closely linked.

Burkina Faso

Official name: *Burkina Faso*
Area: *105,841 sq. mi.,*
274,200 sq. km.
Type of government:
Parliamentary
Population: *12,887,000*
Capital and largest city:
Ouagadougou
(Pop., 634,000)
Languages: *French (official), tribal dialects*
Literacy: *36%*
Currency: *CFA franc*
Per capita GDP: *$1,040*
(Rank: 167th)

The land. Most of Burkina Faso, formerly called Upper Volta, is occupied by sandy plains. In the east, along the border with Niger, is a region of swamps. The Volta Noire, or Black Volta, the Volta Rouge, or Red Volta, and the Volta Blanche, or White Volta, flow through the country.

The climate in most of Burkina Faso is hot and dry. Annual rainfall varies from about 40 inches (103 centimeters) in the south to less than 10 inches (26 centimeters) in the extreme north and northeast.

The people. There are many different tribal groups in Burkina Faso. Almost half of the population is of the Mossi tribe. Other large tribal groups include the Bobo, the Gurunsi, the Samo, and the Marka. There is a small French population.

The largest cities are Ouagadougou, the capital, and Bobo-Dioulasso (population, 269,000).

The majority of the people are animists, although there are significant minorities of Muslims and Christians. Over 90 percent of the people live in rural areas and most of the population is concentrated in the south and center of the country. A high population density, by African standards, causes migrations of thousands of people for seasonal agricultural work in neighboring Côte d'Ivoire and Ghana.

Economy. Burkina Faso, hindered by a lack of water resources, by poor soil, and by its landlocked location, is a poor country. Only 17 percent of its gross national product is derived from industry, while over two-fifths of it comes from agriculture.

The basic food crops are millet and sorghum. Peanuts and cotton are also grown. Cattle, sheep, and goats are raised in most parts of the country.

Industry is poorly developed. There are deposits of manganese, bauxite, and gold, but mining is undeveloped. Many people work outside the country, mostly in Ghana and Côte d'Ivoire. A railroad connects Ouagadougou with the Ivorian port of Abidjan.

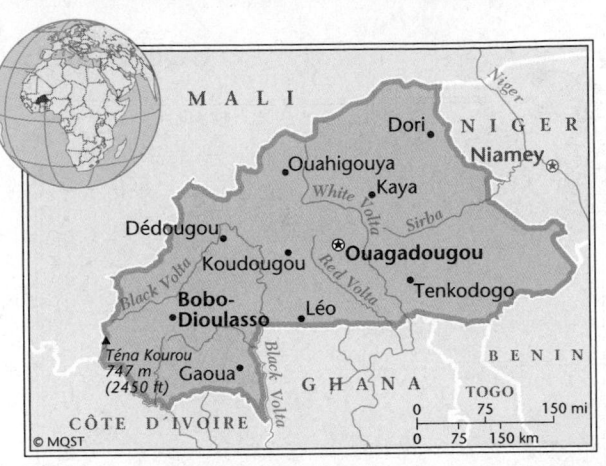

STAMP
of the Upper Volta,
now known as
Burkina Faso

Burkina Faso's main imports are foodstuffs, textiles, and machinery. The major exports are oilseeds, cotton, live animals, and hides and skins. Most trade is conducted with Ghana, Côte d'Ivoire, and France. Burkina Faso is a member of an economic union with Benin, Côte d'Ivoire, Niger, and Togo.

Government. By a new constitution adopted in 1991, the head of state is a president who appoints a prime minister. The president is elected by popular vote to a 5-year term. Legislative power rests with a 111-member assembly whose members are elected to 5-year terms.

History. In about A.D. 1000 the Mossi people migrated into Burkina Faso and established there two principal kingdoms—Ouagadougou and Yatenga. The kingdoms competed with the Dagomba and Mamprussi peoples to the south for primacy in the area. In about 1300 the Mossi came into conflict with the warriors of the ancient empires of Mali and Songhai.

In the 1400s and 1500s Mossi armies raided areas beyond Tombouctou, in present-day Mali. They later raided areas in what is now Benin and Nigeria. The Mossi successfully guarded the northern approach routes to Burkina Faso until the 1800s, when the French began to conquer the area.

French rule. France gained control over most of the region in 1896, and in 1904 the area became part of the colony of Upper Senegal and Niger. In 1919 a separate colony of Upper Volta was created. In 1932 Upper Volta was divided among Niger, Côte d'Ivoire, and French Sudan (present-day Mali), but the territory was reestablished as a single unit in 1947.

During the 1950s politics in Upper Volta largely reflected African, rather than exclusively national, considerations. At that time a local branch of the African Democratic Rally (RDA), an African regional organization with headquarters in Côte d'Ivoire, had many followers in Upper Volta. In the late 1950s, however, the Upper Volta branch of the RDA began to take up national issues and joined with a smaller reform group to form the Voltaic Democratic Union (VDU).

Independence. In August 1960 Upper Volta became independent. In 1966 Lieutenant Colonel Sangoulé Lamizana led a successful military coup, suspended the constitution, and established a provisional government. Civilian rule was restored in 1978, but it lasted only 2 years. Coups in 1980 and 1983 both installed military governments. In 1984 Upper Volta changed its name to Burkina Faso. During the coup of 1987, President Thomas Sankara was killed and a new military council was subsequently formed. In 1991 a new constitution was adopted and Blaise Compaoré was elected president; he ran unopposed. Legislative elections were held in 1992.

Despite cyclical drought and chronic political unrest—four coups in the 1980s alone—new data indicate that the country is making economic headway. Burkina Faso can boast of being one of the few African countries that enjoyed growth in per capita gross national product during the 1980s.

Burundi

Official name: *Republic of Burundi*
Area: *10,742 sq. mi., 27,830 sq. km.*
Type of government: *Republic*
Population: *5,965,000*
Capital and largest city:
    Bujumbura
    (Pop., 235,000)
Languages: *Kirundi and French (both official), Swahili*
Literacy: *35%;* **Currency:** *Franc*
Per capita GDP: *$600*
    (Rank: 188th)

The land. Plateaus, lying at elevations of between 2,500 and 3,500 feet (762 and 1,067 kilometers), cover most of Burundi. The Great Rift Valley, which stretches along Burundi's western boundary, is bordered by peaks above 7,000 feet (2,134 kilometers). Lake Tanganyika acts as the northwestern border for about 80 miles (129 kilometers). The country's land surface is badly eroded, and soil erosion is a serious problem. Burundi has a tropical climate that is moderated by the country's high elevation. Rainfall ranges from more than 55 inches (141 centimeters) in the mountains to less than 40 inches (102 centimeters) along the shores of Lake Tanganyika.

The people. Two tribal groups are dominant in Burundi, the Hutu and the Tutsi, or Watusi. The Hutu, constituting about 85 percent of the population, are mostly farmers. The Tutsi, who make up about 15 percent of the total, are traditionally herdsmen and warriors. The Tutsi long dominated the Hutu and provided the ruling class.

Burundi is one of the most densely populated areas in sub-Saharan Africa, although the only urban areas are in Bujumbura, the capital, and Gitega. Most of the people live on family farms throughout the highlands.

Economy. More than 90 percent of the population of Burundi is engaged in subsistence farming. Famine remains a threat whenever the weather is bad during the growing season.

Coffee, grown almost exclusively by individual farmers on privately owned plots, provides up to 90 percent of Burundi's export revenue. The government has encouraged tea and cotton production to reduce dependence on coffee.

Burundi's main trading partners are Germany, Belgium, France, and Iran.

Government. A 1992 constitution was supplanted in 1998 following a 1996 coup in which the president was overthrown. In 2001 a president was sworn in to hold office temporarily as the first step toward national elections in 3 years.

History. The Twa were probably Burundi's first inhabitants. The Twa are a Pygmy people known mostly as hunters and pottery makers. The Hutu, the largest ethnic group in Burundi, began a migration into the area that spanned hundreds of years and was not completed until the eleventh century. The Tutsi, who probably came south from the area of Ethiopia, overran Burundi and Rwanda in the 1500s and a Tutsi aristocracy headed by a *mwami,* or king, established its rule.

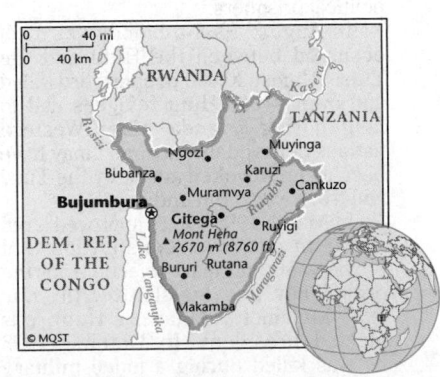

MOST CHILDREN in Burundi grow up on farms.

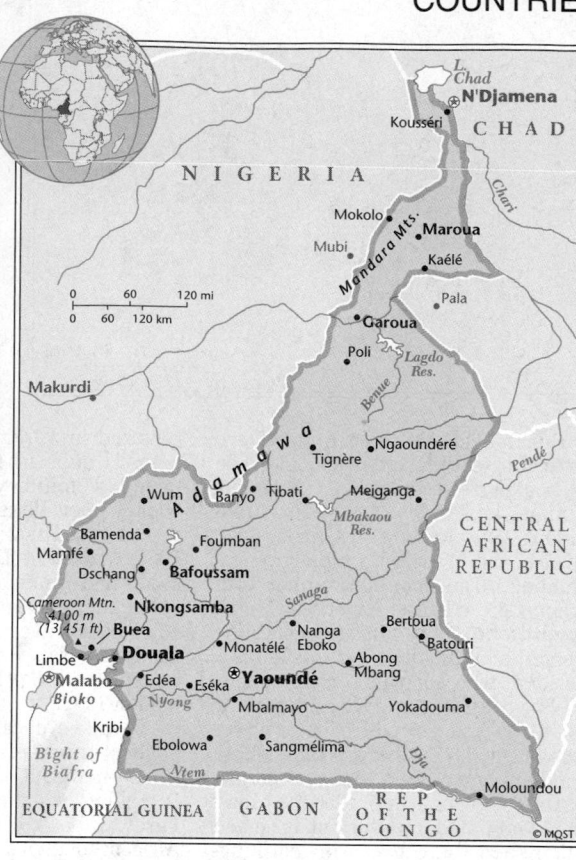

center
US

centre
Brit.

meters
US

metres
Brit.

aluminum
US

aluminium
Brit.

In 1890 Germany seized the area of present-day Burundi and Rwanda, which became known as Ruanda-Urundi. Belgium occupied the region in 1916 during World War I. After the war Ruanda-Urundi became a Belgian mandate under the League of Nations. Ruanda-Urundi became a UN trust territory in 1946.

Burundi became independent on July 1, 1962. Moderate Tutsi and Hutu formed the National Union and Progress Party, which became the majority party in Burundi. Mwami Mwambutsa IV, who had come to the throne in 1915, became chief of state.

In 1966 the monarchy was overthrown and a republic established. Rivalry between the elite Tutsi and the discontented Hutu erupted into civil war in 1972–1973. Mass executions followed. The Supreme Military Council under Jean-Baptiste Bagaza came to power in 1976 but was overthrown in 1987 by Pierre Buyoya. Buyoya and the Military Committee for National Salvation restored religious freedom and freed political prisoners.

In August 1988 a bloody skirmish occurred between the Hutu and the Tutsi. Almost 20,000 people were killed and over 60,000 Hutu refugees fled to neighboring Rwanda. Many Western nations believed the skirmish may have been an unprovoked attack by the Tutsi and froze aid to Burundi.

In March 1992 voters approved a referendum on a new constitution that provides for multiparty elections for the presidency and legislature. In June 1993 Melchior Ndadaye, a Hutu, was elected president. In October 1993 he was killed during a foiled military coup. Years of ethnic violence followed. A 2001 peace agreement between the Tutsi-dominated army and Hutu rebels put a transitional government in place, but fighting continued. In November 2003 both sides signed a power-sharing plan toward ending the 10-year civil war.

Cameroon

Official name: *Republic of Cameroon*

Area: *184,946 sq. mi., 475,440 sq. km.*

Type of government: *Unitary republic*

Population: *15,428,000*

Capital: *Yaoundé (Pop., 649,000)*

Largest city: *Douala (Pop., 810,000)*

Languages: *English, French (both official)*

Literacy: *63%*

Currency: *CFA franc*

Per capita GDP: *$1,700 (Rank: 143rd)*

The land. Cameroon has a varied landscape. In the north are broad grasslands. In the center of the country is the Adamawa Plateau, with elevations of between 2,600 and 5,000 feet (793 and 1,524 meters) above sea level. In the south is a densely forested plateau averaging 2,000 feet (610 meters) in elevation. The volcanic Mt. Cameroon, which rises over 13,300 feet (4,055 meters), is near the coast. The coastal region and the southeastern plateau are covered by thick tropical rain forests.

The climate throughout the country is hot and humid. Some regions in the south receive as much as 180 inches (462 centimeters) of rain each year.

The people. More than a hundred different tribes live in Cameroon. Bamileke, Kirdi, and Fulani peoples live in central and northern Cameroon. Bantu-speaking peoples inhabit parts of southern Cameroon. Some Pygmies live in the forests of the south. Cameroon's largest cities include Yaoundé, the capital, and Douala, the major port on Cameroon's Atlantic coast.

Economy. The oil industry in Cameroon accounts for 60 percent of the country's export earnings. Since offshore oil production began in 1978, it has played a major role in Cameroon's economic growth. Crude oil exports go mainly to the United States.

Seventy percent of the work force is engaged in agriculture, allowing Cameroon to be self-sufficient in staple foods. The major export crops are coffee, cocoa, and timber. Other agricultural products include bananas, rubber, cotton, peanuts, and palm oil. Most crops are grown on large plantations, although cocoa, the traditional cash crop, is still produced on small family farms.

Cameroon's industry is dominated by the processing of agricultural products and the refining of oil. The aluminum smelting, steel producing, and leather tanning industries are growing in importance. The government plays a large role in the industrial sector.

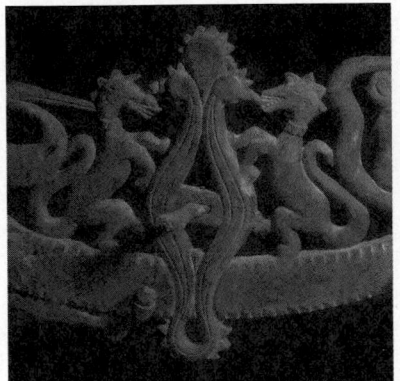

A STONE carving from Cameroon

Cameroon's imports include manufactured goods, machinery, transportation equipment, and chemicals. Major trading partners are France, the Netherlands, Japan, and the United States.

Government. The government of Cameroon is headed by a president who has strong executive powers and is popularly elected to a 7-year term. Legislative powers rest with the National Assembly. The assembly has 180 members elected to 5-year terms by universal suffrage.

History. Cameroon was the original home of an agricultural Bantu people who swept westward across central Africa in prehistoric times. Between the 1600s and 1800s, the Portuguese and British established trading posts in the area. In 1884 Germany established the Kamerun protectorate, which covered about the same area as the present-day republic.

After World War I the German protectorate was divided into separate French and British mandates under the League of Nations. The two mandates later became UN trust territories. France acquired the larger share of the former German territory. Great Britain acquired two disconnected land areas. The territory in the north was inhabited by Muslim Fulani, who had a feudal system closely allied with that of northern Nigeria. The territory in the southwest was a humid forest area with Bantu inhabitants.

France administered its territory as part of the Federation of French Equatorial Africa. East Cameroon received internal autonomy from France in 1958, and full independence in 1960 under Ahmadou Ahidjo. Great Britain administered its territory with Nigeria, using local chiefs and permitting some representation in Nigerian assemblies.

In 1961 the northern region expressed the desire to remain with Nigeria, but the southern region voted to join the Republic of Cameroon. A federal republic was formed on October 1.

In 1972 East and West Cameroon were joined into a united republic by popular referendum and the federal system was abandoned. Ahidjo was president of Cameroon from 1961 until his resignation in 1982. He was replaced by Paul Biya, his prime minister, who was reelected in 1988.

In 1986 a toxic volcanic gas eruption from Lake Nios killed over 1,500 people. International aid and scientific teams helped deal with the situation. In the late 1980s, Cameroon faced a depression in the world market for its three main exports—oil, cocoa, and coffee. The government responded with renewed efforts to restructure the economy, securing financing from the International Monetary Fund and a loan from the World Bank.

Cape Verde

Official name: *Republic of Cape Verde*

Area: *1,568 sq. mi., 4,030 sq. km.*

Type of government: *Republic*

Population: *409,000*

Capital and largest city: *Praia (Pop., 103,000)*

Languages: *Portuguese (official), Crioulo (national)*

Literacy: *72%*

Currency: *Escudo*

Per capita GDP: *$1,500 (Rank: 151st)*

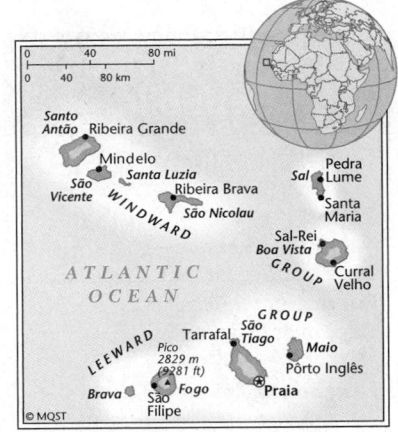

The land. Cape Verde consists of ten islands and several islets. The islands are volcanic in origin and are mountainous. The only active volcano is Mt. Cano on Fogo Island. Mt. Cano reaches 9,282 feet (2,835 meters).

The islands are divided into two groups. The Barlovento (windward) group consists of Santo Antão, São Vicente, Santa Luzia, São Nicolau, Sal Rei, and Boa Vista. The Sotavento (leeward) group includes Maio, São Tiago, Fogo, and Brava.

The climate varies from island to island, but is generally hot and dry. In Praia, the capital, the average annual rainfall is only 9.5 inches (24 centimeters) and the average annual temperature is about 75°F (24°C).

The people. The majority of the population is of mixed African and Portuguese descent. About one-third is African, and a very small proportion is European. Portuguese is the official language, but a Creole dialect of Portuguese and other languages is widely spoken. Seventy percent of the people live in rural areas and 50 percent of the people live on the island of São Tiago.

Drought and famine have compelled many of the people to emigrate; of the estimated 1 million people of Cape Verdean ancestry in the world, only about one-third actually live on the islands. The largest towns are Praia, the capital, on São Tiago, and Mindelo (population, 68,000) on São Vicente.

Economy. The islands have no exploitable mineral resources, and their soil is generally too dry and poor to support vegetation. Bananas, coffee, nuts, oilseeds, and corn are raised, and some salt is produced. Fish are abundant off the coasts and some livestock is grazed. The islands have several good ports, and the refueling of ships is the main economic activity.

Trade is limited. Coffee, bananas, and nuts are exported, and foodstuffs, textiles, and building materials are imported. Most trade is with Portugal, the Netherlands, and Angola.

Government. The executive branch is comprised of a president elected by popular vote to a 5-year term and an appointed prime minister and council of ministers. The legislature is the 72-member unicameral National Assembly whose members are elected by popular vote to 5-year terms.

History. The Cape Verde Islands were uninhabited when they were discovered in 1456 by the Portuguese. The Portuguese began to settle the islands in the late 1400s and early 1500s, and African slaves began to be imported. In 1587 a governor was appointed for the colony, and in the 1600s and 1700s settlers from Spain, Italy, and Great Britain joined the Portuguese on the islands. The colony thrived on plantation agriculture and trading.

In 1951 the colony was made an overseas province of Portugal, and in 1961 the islanders received full Portuguese citizenship.

In 1956, however, the African Party for the Independence of Guinea-Bissau and Cape Verde (PAIGC) formed and began demanding economic and political reform in both countries. PAIGC began an armed rebellion in Guinea-Bissau (Portuguese Guinea) in 1961. The rebellion grew into a war and the Soviet Union sent 10,000 troops to support PAIGC forces. After gaining control of most of the land in Guinea-Bissau, PAIGC began an aggressive political movement in Cape Verde, eventually pressuring the government into forming a coalition government with both Portuguese and Cape Verdean members in 1974. Cape Verde became independent of Portugal on July 5, 1975.

In the first 10 years of independence, Cape Verde was severely plagued with devastating droughts and famines.

In 1990 PAIGC gave up the political monopoly it had enjoyed ever since independence. Pedro Pires became president in 2001.

Central African Republic

Official name: *Central African Republic*
Area: *240,470 sq. mi., 622,980 sq. km.*
Type of government: *Republic*
Population: *3,623,000*
Capital and largest city: *Bangui (Pop., 452,000)*
Languages: *French (official), Sangho (national)*
Literacy: *60%*
Currency: *CFA franc*
Per capita GDP: *$1,300 (Rank: 158th)*

The land. The Central African Republic lies on a plateau with an average elevation of 2,000 feet (610 meters) above sea level. In the east are mountains with heights ranging up to almost 4,600 feet (1,402 meters). There are forests in the south, but savanna woodlands and grasslands cover most of the country. Tributaries of the Shari River in the north, and of the Ubangi River to the south, flow through the country.

Because of the altitude, the climate is mild. In the north, annual rainfall averages 50 inches (128 centimeters), while rainfall in the south often exceeds 75 inches (192 centimeters).

The people. The Central African Republic is a sparsely populated country inhabited by peoples of the Mandjia-Baya, Banda, M'Baka, and Zande tribes. A few thousand Europeans live in Bangui, the capital, and in other smaller towns. More than 70 percent of the population live in rural areas.

Economy. The main impediment to economic development in the Central African Republic is the country's landlocked position and poor transportation infrastructure. Agriculture employs 70 percent of the population and accounts for 60 percent of total export receipts. The principal agricultural exports are coffee, cotton, timber, and tobacco. The chief agricultural areas are in and around the cities of Bossangoa and Bambari. Livestock raising is a growing industry and the government hoped for production to double by the year 2000.

The diamond industry accounts for 30 percent of export receipts. Small amounts of gold are exported, and uranium, limestone, and iron ore are also mined. Diamonds and gold are mined mostly by individual prospectors.

The country's industrial sector is limited mostly to the processing of agricultural and forestry products. Many industries directed toward import substitution—such as assembling motorcycles and bicycles, and manufacturing textiles, cigarettes, and beverages—have started production in recent years.

Chief among the Central African Republic's trading partners are France, Belgium, Italy, Japan, and the United States.

Government. A new constitution was adopted in 1995. The executive branch consists of a president, a prime minister, and a Council of Ministers. The president is elected for a term of 6 years. The legislative branch consists of a 109-member National Assembly.

History. Archaeological findings—great stone foundations near Bouar and stone tools in the east—seem to indicate that people lived in the region thousands of years ago. However, any other records are virtually nonexistent before the 19th century.

The French entered the region in the mid-1800s and gave it the name Ubangi-Shari. They met with little opposition from the tribesmen who lived there.

In 1899 France permitted private companies to develop the region. Company abuses resulted in loss of life from forced labor and disease, and loss of capital because of inefficient management practices. In 1910 France united Ubangi-Shari with present-day Chad, the Congo (Brazzaville), and Gabon in the Federation of French Equatorial Africa.

meters
US

metres
Brit.

labor
US

labour
Brit.

TRADITIONAL practices for work such as laundry still prevail in much of Africa.

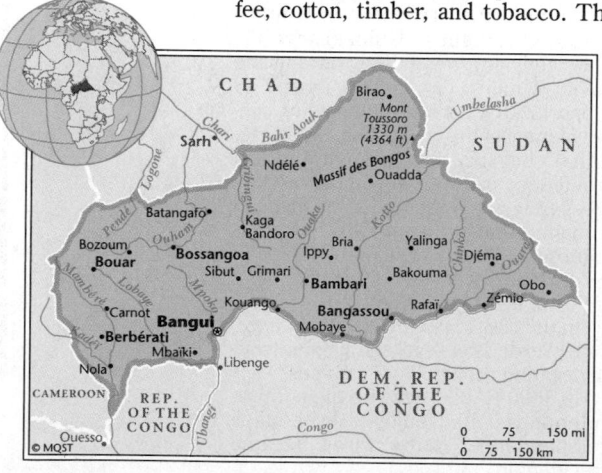

In 1946 France reorganized the administration and introduced territorial assemblies. Barthélémy Boganda, a political leader in Ubangi-Shari, created the Movement for the Social Evolution of Black Africa (MESAN). Boganda was elected to the territorial assembly in 1952, and by 1956 MESAN had won all the seats in the assembly.

Ubangi-Shari voted to join the French Community in 1958 as an individual member, thus ending the Federation of Equatorial Africa. Boganda became the nation's first premier. Ubangi-Shari changed its name to the Central African Republic. Boganda was killed in an airplane crash in 1959, and the assembly elected Boganda's cousin and political associate, David Dacko, president of the republic. Complete independence came on August 13, 1960. Dacko dissolved all opposition parties in 1962.

In 1965 Colonel Jean Bedel Bokassa deposed Dacko and assumed the position of chief of state. In 1976 he proclaimed the country to be a monarchy, the Central African Empire, with himself as emperor.

Bokassa ruled the country harshly and tyrannically from 1976 to 1979. A French-aided coup in 1979 restored the republic with Dacko as president. Another coup in 1981 removed Dacko and instituted a military government led by General André Kolingba. In 1985 the military government was dissolved and a new government was formed with increased civilian participation. In 1986 a new constitution ushered in a popularly elected government. The following years, however, saw dissidence, violence, and coup attempts. In a 2003 coup, General Francois Bozize seized power, promising future elections.

Chad

Official name: *Republic of Chad*
Area: *499,476 sq. mi.,*
    1,284,000 sq. km.
Type of government: *Republic*
Population: *8,971,000*
Capital and largest city:
    N'Djamena (Pop., 547,000)
Languages: *French, Arabic (both*
    official), Sara
Literacy: *40%*
Currency: *CFA franc*
Per capita GDP: *$1,030*
    (Rank: 168th)

The land. Most of Chad is a vast plain. The northern region of the country forms part of the Sahara. Grasslands cover central and southern Chad. The country's lowest point is the dry Bodele Depression, in north-central Chad. In the extreme north is the Tibasti Massif, with elevations of about 11,000 feet (3,354 meters). The country's most important rivers are the Shari and the Logone. Lake Chad, in the west, fluctuates in size from 4,000 to 10,000 square

miles (10,360 to 25,900 square kilometers) due to extremely flat land and the varying flow of the rivers that feed it.

Northern Chad is hot and dry and receives less than 10 inches (25.6 centimeters) of rain a year. The climate in the south is more tropical, and rainfall averages about 40 inches (103 centimeters) a year.

The people. Chad is sparsely populated. Arabs and Hamitic people live in the north and are mostly Muslim. The Sara, the largest tribal group in Chad, live in the south and are divided between Christianity and animism. Chad's major cities are N'Djamena, the capital; Moundou (population, 103,000); and Sarh (80,000).

Economy. Subsistence farming and fishing engage over 80 percent of Chad's workforce. Chadian farmers produce millet, sorghum, rice, sweet potatoes, and peanuts for domestic consumption. Chad's economy is heavily dependent on cotton, which accounts for 43 percent of the nation's exports.

Industry is centered on the processing of agricultural products. The few industries that do exist are hampered by a lack of transportation facilities.

Chad imports petroleum, textiles, machinery, and transportation equipment. The trade deficit is made up by French aid. Most trade is with France, Nigeria, Cameroon, and the United States.

Government. Chad's government is in transition. The president is head of state and governs with a prime minister and Council of State, and a legislative body, the National Assembly.

History. The area that is now Chad was for many centuries an important crossroads. From about 200 B.C. to A.D. 1000 its inhabitants maintained close contact with the people of the Nile valley, with whom they shared a similar culture.

Christianity flourished in central Chad in about A.D. 300. Later, nomadic peoples from Darfur, in modern western Sudan, overran Chad, dispersed the indigenous inhabitants, and created an empire known as Kanem in the region near Lake Chad. In the 11th century, Islam penetrated the area. From that time on the peoples of Chad strengthened their commercial ties with the peoples of the Mediterranean coast.

In the period from about 1000 to 1600 many internal and foreign wars were fought. As a result, the Kanem Empire moved its center to Bornu, on the southwestern side of Lake Chad in what is now northern Nigeria.

Both the sultanate of Baguirmi, in southwestern Chad, and the Ouadaï Empire, in the east, became powerful. They maintained their control until the late 1800s. At that time Rabih az-Zubayr, a warlord and slave trader from Sudan, gained control of Chad.

The French, who had established themselves in Chad in the 1890s, defeated Rabih in 1900 and proceeded to conquer all of Chad. The present boundaries of Chad were established in 1913. In 1920 Chad became a member of the Federation of French Equatorial Africa.

During World War II Chad supported Free France and contained important Allied bases. Postwar politics were at first largely controlled by the French. After 1958, however, African leaders rapidly gained prominence. France gave Chad its independence in August 1960, and François Tombalbaye became the country's first president. Tombalbaye was assassinated in a coup in 1975.

Libyan-backed Muslims from the northern part of the country have waged guerrilla warfare against the Bantu-dominated governments of Chad since 1966. They staged an ill-fated major offensive in 1979.

A coup in 1979, backed by Nigeria, ousted the military government. The country became the scene of a bloody civil war from 1979 to 1982, as opposing factions fought for government control.

Libyan-backed supporters of former President Goukouni Oueddei, who had been forced out in 1982, invaded Chad in 1983 and were able to occupy the northern third of the country. President Hissen Habré was supported by France and the United States and succeeded in removing most of the Libyan influence in 1987. Libya's Muammar Qaddafi declared an end to the 20-year war with Chad in 1988, formally recognizing the Habré government. Idriss Deby took charge of the government after a bloodless coup forced Habré to flee in December 1990. Despite some movement toward democratic reform, power remained in the hands of a northern ethnic oligarchy.

Deby won multiparty elections in 1996 and 2001. A democratic movement against the government, which began in 1998, and clashes between the government and rebels persist; however, a cease-fire was signed in 2003.

centered
US

centred
Brit.

22 Africa

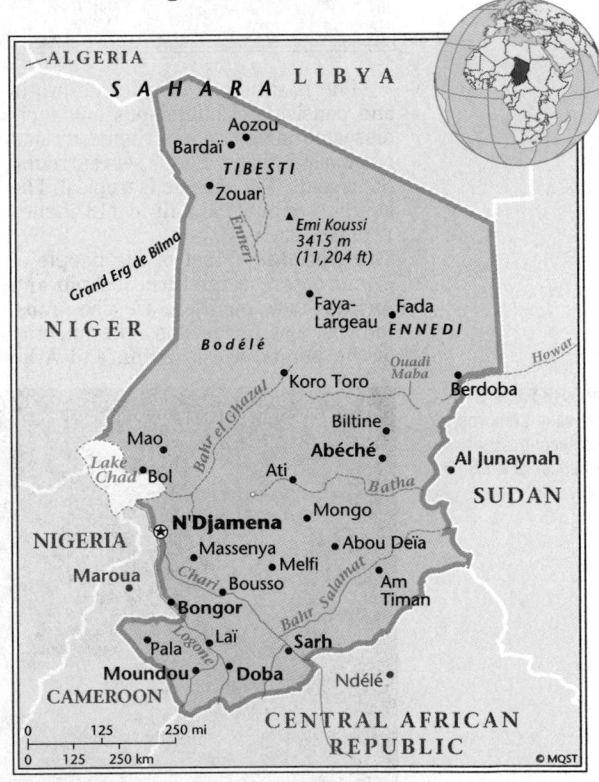

Comoros

Official name: *Federal Islamic Republic of the Comoros*
Area: *838 sq. mi., 2,170 sq. km.*
Type of government: *Independent republic*
Population: *614,000*
Capital and largest city: *Moroni (Pop., 30,000)*
Languages: *French and Arabic (both official), Comoran*
Literacy: *57%*
Currency: *Franc*
Per capita GDP: *$710 (Rank: 184th)*

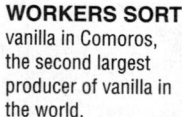

kilometers
US

kilometres
Brit.

The land. Comoros consists of three main islands. Nzwani, formerly Anjouan, is 164 square miles (425 square kilometers); Mwali, formerly Moheli, is 112 square miles (290 square kilometers); and Njazidja, formerly Grand Comore, is 443 square miles (1,147 square kilometers). Moroni, the capital, is located on Njazidja.

The islands are of volcanic origin and consist of mountainous or deeply dissected plateau cores ringed by narrow coastal plains. Coral reefs surround the islands. The climate is tropical. The average annual rainfall is 113 inches (289 centimeters).

The people. Most of the people of Comoros are a mixture of Arab and African stock, but there are also Arabs, Indians, and Europeans. The majority of the people are Muslim, and Arab culture predominates. The largest towns are Moroni, the capital, and Mutsamudu (population, 17,000).

Economy. Agriculture is the mainstay of the comorian economy and employs about 87 percent of the population. Rice, corn, vegetables, and fruits are raised for local consumption. The chief commercial crops are vanilla, of which Comoros is the world's second largest producer, spices, coffee, sisal, and coconuts. The islands have almost no mineral resources.

Comoros's main trading partners are France, the United States, Germany, Kenya, and Kuwait.

Government. A 2001 constitution resulted in the reunification of the three islands. It provides for each island to have its own president, with a federal presidency having overall authority and rotating between the islands every 4 years.

History. The Comoro Islands have been known since ancient times. They were conquered by Arabs in the 600s. In the 1500s they were visited by the Portuguese, French, and Dutch, and the French established a settlement. In the 1800s the Arab kingdoms on the islands were attacked by Malagasy armies from Madagascar, and years of warfare followed. France took control of the islands between 1866 and 1909.

The French expanded agricultural production by opening plantations. In 1912 the islands were joined with Madagascar into a single French colony. In 1946 they were granted internal autonomy.

On July 6, 1976, the islands declared their final independence from French rule. The island of Mayotte opposed independence and chose to maintain its ties with France.

A constitution was ratified in 1978 and Ahmed Abdallah was elected to a 6-year term as president. Abdallah was reelected unopposed in 1984 and given the authority to appoint governors to each of the main islands. He was assassinated in 1989 during an attempted coup. Said Mohamed Djohar was elected president in 1990. Colonel Azali Assoumani seized power in 1999.

Upon ratification of a new constitution in 2001, Assoumani resigned his position and ran for president in the 2002 elections, winning with 75 percent of the vote.

Congo, Democratic Republic of the

Official name: *Democratic Republic of the Congo*
Area: *905,328 sq. mi., 2,345,410 sq. km.*
Type of government: *Republic*
Population: *55,042,000*
Capital and largest city: *Kinshasa (Pop., 4,657,000)*
Languages: *French (official), Lingala, Swahili*
Literacy: *77%*
Currency: *Zaire*
Per capita GDP: *$590 (Rank: 189th)*

Much of the country now known as the Democratic Republic of the Congo was originally a native nation known as the Luba in the 16th century. It later became a colony of Belgium, and was known as the Belgian Congo. After independence in 1960, it was known as the Congo. In 1971 the name was changed to Zaire and in 1997, it became the Democratic Republic of the Congo.

The land. Tropical grasslands and forests are typical of most of the country's landscape. The interior is a vast plain with swamps in some places. The Mitumba Mountains lie along most of the eastern border and include Mt. Ruwenzori, which has an elevation of about 16,800 feet (5,122 meters). There are also highlands in the south.

There are many lakes along the eastern border, including lakes Albert, Edward, Kivu, Tanganyika, and Mweru. The Zaire River, formerly called the Congo River, flows through part of the northeast and along the western border. The Ubangi and Kasai rivers are the main tributaries flowing into the middle Congo River.

The climate throughout the country is tropical. About 71 inches (182 centimeters) of rain fall annually. Areas in the north and in the south receive less rainfall.

The people. Most of the indigenous population is Bantu, although over 200 ethnic groups are represented, including the Tutsis, Hutus, Kongo, Lulua, Bashi, Mongo, Hamite, and Pygmies. Over 100,000 Europeans live in the country, more than half of whom are Belgian. About two-thirds of the people are Christian, a small number are Muslim, and most of the remainder follow traditional tribal religions.

The main cities include Kinshasa, the capital; Lubumbashi (population, 565,000); Mbuji-Mayi (486,000); and Kisangani (318,000). About 70 percent of the population live in rural areas. Over 700 languages and dialects are spoken.

Economy. Since 1960, the economy has been seriously disrupted by political instability and civil wars. When it held

WORKERS SORT vanilla in Comoros, the second largest producer of vanilla in the world.

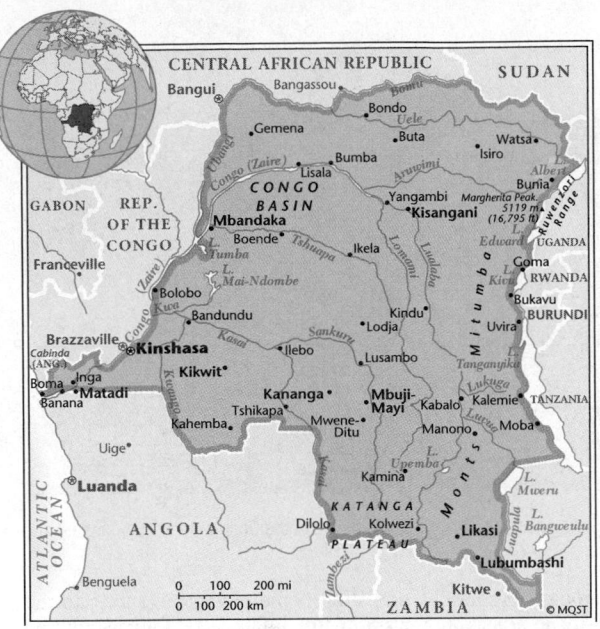

A YOUTH opens cacao pods to gather the beans.

the Congo as a colony, Belgium developed the country's rich mineral resources and built railroads to complement river navigation.

The mineral riches include copper, which accounts for half of the country's export revenues, cobalt, of which the Democratic Republic of the Congo is the world's biggest producer, and industrial diamonds, of which it is the world's second largest producer.

Industry is based mostly in Kinshasa, where the best electricity and transportation facilities exist. Production is directed almost exclusively toward the domestic market. Food processing, textiles, construction, and transport equipment are the largest industries.

The country possesses great reserves of water and oil, including 140 million barrels of oil reserves and 13 percent of the world's hydroelectric potential. Although both resources are relatively unexploited, significant strides have been made in development in the 1980s. Petroleum from the offshore oil fields has become one of the largest sources of export revenue.

Seventy percent of the population is engaged in agriculture, which has traditionally been considered the base of the economy. The main crops are cassava, plantain, sugar cane, corn, rice, and fruit.

The United States and many European Union countries are the chief trading partners. The country's main exports include copper, cobalt, diamonds, oil, tin, palm oil, coffee, cacao, rubber, tea, and cotton. The main imports are foodstuffs, petroleum products, transportation equipment, and textiles.

Government. The country is currently ruled as a dictatorship, but is in transition to a possible representative government. A self-appointed president resides over a cabinet and a 300-member legislature he appoints. A new constitution is to result from ongoing meetings between Congolese factions.

History. The earliest inhabitants were the Pygmies. The Kongo, Kuba, Luba,

and Lunda were Bantu-speaking tribes that moved in from the southeast of what is now Nigeria. The first kingdom to emerge was the Luba, which was created in the 16th century.

Portuguese sailors reached the region in 1482, but the area remained largely unknown until the late 1800s. Between 1874 and 1877 the British explorer Henry Stanley explored the area. In 1884 Belgium's King Leopold II obtained European recognition of a Congo Free State at the Berlin Conference on African Affairs.

Colonial Rule. Between 1885 and 1908 Leopold's agents used unscrupulous methods to secure labor to exploit the Congo's rubber and ivory resources. Mistreatment of the people created an international scandal, and in 1908 Leopold turned over control of the area to the Belgian Parliament.

Under Belgian rule there was economic advancement, and a high literacy rate was achieved. But there was little secondary education and no higher education until the founding of Lovanium University in 1954. The administration encouraged vocational training and the breaking of tribal ties, but would not allow the inhabitants opportunities to gain political experience.

In 1954 the Kongo people, led by Joseph Kasavubu, demanded political rights and autonomy from the rest of the country. From then on the tempo of political change greatly accelerated. In 1955 Belgium discussed a plan for citizenship, but in response to growing African pressure, Belgium announced in January 1960, that independence would be granted on June 30.

Independence. The country held elections in the midst of turmoil. Patrice Lumumba, leader of the National Congolese Movement, became the prime minister, and Kasavubu won the next highest position of president.

Lumumba's government faced both a mutiny in the army and the flight of most of the country's European technicians and administrators. The Congo's

richest province, Katanga, under the leadership of Moise Tshombe, seceded from the new republic in July 1960.

Lumumba was overthrown in September 1960, and by 1963 UN forces had ended Katanga's secession. In 1964 Tshombe, a friend of the United States and Europe, became prime minister despite the objections of many African states, which saw him as a tool of European mining interests.

Joseph Mobutu (now Marshall Mobutu Sésé Seko) became president and head of state following a 1965 military coup. Political stability and some economic progress were finally achieved under his long rule. His attempt in 1974 to "Africanize" the economy left the country with a scarcity of capital and skilled labor. In 1971, the name of the country was changed to Zaire.

In the mid-1970s Zaire tried to help Angolan forces prevent a Soviet-backed leftist takeover of that government. However, leftist forces finally won, and since 1977 the new Angolan government has aided Katanga (now called Shaba) Province rebels in their renewed secessionist movement.

Between 1978 and 1986, Zaire enjoyed a relatively calm period, but in the late 1980s opposition to Mobutu's rule grew. In 1991 Mobutu convened a transitional High Council to draft a new constitution and prepare for multiparty elections. In 1992 the council declared itself sovereign and named Etienne Tshisekedi, Mobutu's leading opponent, prime minister. In March 1993, Mobutu sanctioned a second government headed by Faustin Birindwa. Ethnic violence and economic collapse accelerated through 1993.

Much of the unrest has been related to the fact that the boundaries of the country as drawn by European powers in 1885 failed to take into account tribal, ethnic, or economic implications. Fighting among the Tutsis and Hutus in Burundi and Rwanda in the 1990s spilled over into Zaire, where many refugees fled. Civil war broke out in 1996 between forces of President Mobutu and rebel forces under Laurent Desire Kabila, and on May 18, 1997, Kabila's rebel troops captured the capitol of Kinshasa. Kabila took over as the country's self-declared president the following day.

Following the takeover, the country was renamed the Democratic Republic of the Congo, with pledges by Kabila to institute democratic rule. His regime was challenged by a rebellion in 1998. A cease-fire was signed in July 1999, but sporadic fighting continued. Kabila was assassinated in January 2001. His son, Joseph Kabila, succeeded him and quickly began overtures to end the war. In 2002 a power-sharing agreement was reached with the rebels and peace accords were signed with both Rwanda and Uganda. Despite these efforts fighting continued into 2003. In April 2003 a new constitution was signed and in July a new government which included former rebels was put in place.

kilometer *US*

kilometre *Brit.*

centered *US*

centred *Brit.*

Congo, Republic of

Official name: *Republic of the Congo*
Area: *132,012 sq. mi., 342,000 sq. km.*
Type of government: *Republic*
Population: *2,908,000*
Capital and largest city: *Brazzaville (Pop., 596,000)*
Languages: *French (official), Lingala, Kikongo*
Literacy: *75%*
Currency: *CFA franc*
Per capita GDP: *$900 (Rank: 172nd)*

The land. The Republic of Congo has a varied geography. Along the coast is a relatively cool and practically treeless plain. Farther inland is the wet and forested Mayombé Escarpment, which is cut by the Kouilou River. The Niari Basin, a 200-mile- (320-kilometer-) wide region of woodlands and grassy plains, lies east of the escarpment; north of it are the grassy Batéké plateaus. The Congo and Ubangi rivers form the eastern border.

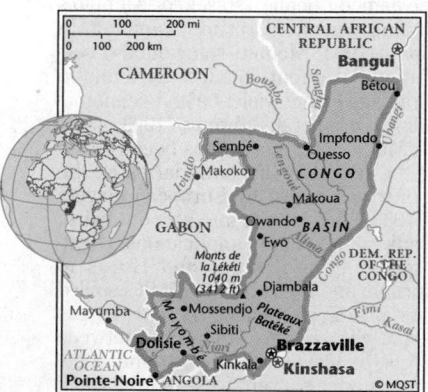

THE ENSLAVEMENT of Africans by European traders began in the Congo in the 16th century and continued until the 19th century.

The country has a tropical climate. Annual rainfall is usually at least 50 inches (128 centimeters).
The people. There are many different ethnic groups in the Republic of Congo. The Kongo, Sanga, Teke, and Ubangi are the largest groups. Almost 60 percent of the population live in urban areas. Although 90 percent of the children attend free, compulsory schools, only 50 percent of the population is literate.

The country's major cities include Brazzaville, the capital and major river port, and Pointe Noire (population, 298,000), a port city on the Atlantic Ocean.
Economy. About 27 percent of the population is engaged in subsistence farming. Bananas, manioc, peanuts, rice, tropical fruits, and corn are grown for local consumption. Forestry is very important to the economy.

The country has a well-developed transportation system. The Congo-Ocean railroad links Brazzaville and Pointe Noire, and the Congo and Ubangi rivers provide excellent water routes for the Congo and neighboring countries.

The largest source of income is from mining. Rich potash deposits were depleted by 1977, but offshore oil was discovered in 1973 and its production and refining have prospered since then. Copper, gold, lead, and zinc are mined, and there are rich unexploited deposits of iron ore. Some industrial development has occurred, including the building of factories that process timber, textiles, chemicals, and cement. In 1977 most industry was nationalized.

The Republic of Congo depends heavily on imported goods. Ninety percent of the meat consumed is imported. The country also imports machinery and consumer goods. Its exports include timber, diamonds, and petroleum. The main trading partners are France, the United States, Italy, Germany, Spain, Japan, and Brazil.
Government. A new constitution adopted in 2002 provides for a popularly elected president who appoints a prime minister and a council of ministers. Legislative power rests with an elected bicameral legislature.
History. The area was believed to be largely uninhabited when the Mboshi

and Vili people began migrating to the area in the 1400s. The Lali people, an offshoot of the Kongo kingdom centered in nearby Angola, overran the Mboshi and Vili people. Portuguese explorers had already begun trading with these people at that time. The original trade in gold and ivory was replaced by the slave trade. British, Dutch, and French companies joined the trade until slaving was abolished in the 1800s.
French rule. The French explorer Pierre Savorgnan de Brazza reached the area in 1873, and signed an agreement with the Teke king. The French obtained European recognition of their influence over the region of the present-day Republic of Congo at the Berlin Conference on African Affairs in 1884.

The French called the area Middle Congo. In 1910 France joined the Middle Congo with present-day Gabon, Chad, and the Central African Republic to form the Federation of French Equatorial Africa.

France gave private companies control over developing the country, but company rule was harsh. Africans were deprived of legal rights, and in the 1920s African political dissatisfaction could be seen in the rise of various local religious sects. The most important sect was the Matswa among the Kongo.

The Middle Congo supported Free France during World War II. In 1944, in gratitude for its support, France held a conference to discuss colonial reforms

DAVID LIVINGSTONE was the first European to explore much of sub-Saharan Africa.

in Brazzaville. Shortly after, the Middle Congo became an overseas territory within the French Union, and many political parties developed, largely along tribal lines.

Independence. In the mid-1950s Fulbert Youlou became the dominant political figure in the country. Youlou, a Kongo and a Roman Catholic priest, had gained the support of the Matswa. In 1958 the Middle Congo agreed to join the French Community. In 1959 Youlou became the first president; the Republic of Congo became independent on August 15, 1960.

Following a military coup in 1963, the Congo came increasingly under the influence of the Communist nations, especially China and the Soviet Union. Another successful coup in 1968 proclaimed the Congo Africa's first "people's republic." A succession of presidents from the Congolese Labor Party headed the government during the 1970s and 1980s. In 1979 a single-list election was held for national and regional assemblies and Denis Sassou-Nguesso was elected president.

In 1986 the Congolese government signed a loan agreement with the International Monetary Fund in an attempt to balance the budget and boost productivity outside of the oil industry.

In 1991 a national conference was convened to institute wide-ranging reforms. President Sassou-Nguesso was forced to appoint a new prime minister and to accept free elections. A new constitution was approved in 1992 and Pascal Lissouba was elected president in a free election. A brief civil war restored Sassou-Nguesso to the office. A new constitution was approved in 2002.

Côte d'Ivoire

Official name: *Republic of Côte d'Ivoire*

Area: *124,470 sq. mi., 322,460 sq. km.*

Type of government: *Republic*

Population: *16,598,000*

Capital: *Yamoussoukro (Pop., 107,000)*

Largest city: *Abidjan (Pop., 1,929,000)*

Languages: *French (official), native dialects*

Literacy: *49%*

Currency: *CFA franc*

Per capita GDP: *$1,550 (Rank: 149th)*

The land. Côte d'Ivoire was called the Ivory Coast until 1985. The surface of Côte d'Ivoire is relatively flat. There are plantations along the eastern coast, beyond which are tropical rain forests. Forests stand along the western coast as well. North of the forests is savanna. There are mountains in the west and

northwest with elevations above 5,000 feet (1,524 meters).

Three rivers flow from north to south—the Sassandra in the west, the Bandama, and the Comoé in the east. The Cavally River flows along part of Côte d'Ivoire's western border.

Côte d'Ivoire has a hot, tropical climate. The coastal region receives an average of about 80 inches (205 centimeters) of rain each year, and the northern part of the country receives an average of about 50 inches (128 centimeters) yearly.

The people. There are many ethnic groups in Côte d'Ivoire. The most important are the Baule, Senufo, Agni, and Kru. Côte d'Ivoire's largest city and major port is Abidjan. Bouaké (population, 330,000) is the second largest city.

Economy. Côte d'Ivoire's economic life depends heavily on agriculture. The country's most important crops are coffee, cacao, pineapples, and bananas. Although most of Côte d'Ivoire's land is undeveloped, it is one of the world's leading producers of both coffee and cacao. Once grown on large European-owned plantations, both are now raised mainly on small African-owned farms. The basic food crops are yams, manioc, and rice. Fishing is also important to the economy. Côte d'Ivoire's industries include food processing, textiles, and oil refining. Lumbering is very prosperous, as is the mining of diamonds and manganese. Oil has been extracted since 1980, although in the initial ten years of production, reserves of oil were found to be small and very difficult to exploit.

Côte d'Ivoire's major imports are machinery, petroleum products, and consumer goods. Exports include coffee, cocoa, bananas, timber, and pineapples. France is the country's most significant trading partner, along with Germany and other European Union members.

Government. Côte d'Ivoire has a presidential system of government. Executive powers are vested in a president, who is popularly elected to a 5-year term. Legislative power is held by a 225-member National Assembly. Assembly members are elected by universal suffrage to 5-year terms.

History. The important Muslim city of Kong in the north of present-day Côte d'Ivoire dates from the eleventh century as a caravan trade center. African kingdoms in the southeast of the country date from the time of the expansion of the Ashanti people from present-day Ghana in the 1700s and 1800s.

French rule. France had contacts with Côte d'Ivoire in the 1600s and 1700s. In 1893 France established a colony, and in 1904 the colony was made a part of the Federation of French West Africa. But the total conquest of the area was not completed until the end of World War I.

There was little freedom of political expression for Africans until after World War II. At that time Felix Houphouët-Boigny founded the Democratic Party of Côte d'Ivoire (PDCI), a local section of the African Democratic Rally. The

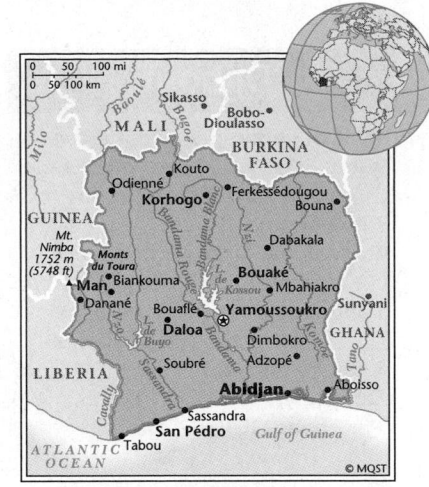

PDCI grew rapidly and became the dominant political force in the country.

In 1946 the colony became a territory within the French Union. With support from French Communists and the French administration, Houphouët-Boigny was elected to the French National Assembly.

He gained fame in the assembly for his law abolishing forced labor. France then attempted to suppress the PDCI, and as a result many regional parties sprang up. In 1950 Houphouët-Boigny broke with the Communists and adopted a pro-French policy. He rebuilt his party, benefiting from prosperity created by a coffee boom.

Independence. From 1956 to 1959 Houphouët-Boigny was a member of successive French administrations. In 1958 his country voted overwhelmingly to become an autonomous member of the French Community.

Côte d'Ivoire became independent on August 7, 1960, and Houphouët-Boigny was unanimously elected president of the republic. All opposition parties were silenced, and the PDCI became the country's sole legal political party, a status it still enjoys.

Côte d'Ivoire became a leader of African pro-Western sentiments under the long, peaceful, and prosperous rule of Houphouët-Boigny. Its economy developed rapidly, with growth of about 7 percent each year from 1960 to 1980. The country made a successful transition from a European-operated to an African-operated economy.

However, in the late 1980s, depressed prices for cacao and coffee and rising discontent with the government led to protests by workers and students in 1989. Multiparty elections were held in 1990, ending 30 years of single-party rule.

In December 1993 President Houphouet-Boigny, revered as the father of his country, died. He was succeeded by the speaker of the parliament, Henri Konan-Bedie, who was ousted by a coup in 1999. In October 2000 Laurent Gbagbo became president. Civil war erupted after a 2002 coup attempt, but peace was declared 9 months later with a power-sharing agreement. French and West African peacekeepers enforce a tenuous cease-fire amid distrust on both sides.

labor
US

labour
Brit.

Djibouti

Official name: *Republic of Djibouti*
Area: *8,558 sq. mi., 22,000 sq. km.*
Type of government: *Republic*
Population: *447,000*
Capital and largest city: *Djibouti
(Pop., metro. area, 62,000)*
Languages: *French and Arabic
(both official), Somali, Afar*
Literacy: *46%*
Currency: *Franc*
Per capita GDP: *$1,400
(Rank: 154th)*

The land. Most of the country is desert. The interior is a low, rolling desert basin. North of the Gulf of Tadjoura, the Mabla and Gouda mountains rise to a peak of just under 6,000 feet (1,829 meters). Their slopes hold the territory's only forests. The coastline is low and flat except along the southern shore of the Gulf of Tadjoura, which is steep. The climate is hot and dry. The average annual rainfall is only about 5 inches (13 centimeters).

The people. The original inhabitants of the region are the Issa Somalis and the Hamitic Afars. There are now large minorities of Arabs and Europeans. Almost all the people are Muslim, and they speak French, Afar, Arabic, and Somali. Most of the Issas and Afars are seminomadic. The principal cities are Djibouti, Tadjoura, Obock, Dikhil, and Ali Sabieh.

Economy. The country's strategic location at the mouth of the Red Sea and its status as a free-trade zone ensures its economic importance. Its only known mineral resource is salt, which is largely unexploited. Herding, especially of goats, is the chief activity of the people. Some farming is possible with irrigation near the coast. Vegetables, melons, and dates are the main crops. Shipbuilding and construction are the only industries. About fifty percent of the population is unemployed.

Trade is the mainstay of the economy. A modern port at Djibouti, the capital, is an important refueling, storage, and distribution point for Red Sea and Indian Ocean commerce. Djibouti exports hides, skins, and coffee, mostly to Middle Eastern and African countries. Food, transportation equipment, and petroleum products are imported from foreign nations.

Government. The republic is headed by a president aided by a prime minister and a cabinet. There is a unicameral legislative Parliament with 65 elected members. Since 1981 a single party, People's Progress Assembly (RPP), has ruled, despite the institution of a multiparty constitution in 1992.

History. Ablé immigrants came to the area from Arabia in the third century B.C. and settled mostly in the north. The Afars, descendants of the Ablé, were herders who settled mainly in the south. Eventually, the Somali Issas pushed the Afars out of the south and settled on the coasts. Missionaries brought Islam to the area in A.D. 825.

In 1837 Rochet d'Hericourt explored Djibouti for France. Further expeditions established ties between the French and local kingdoms. In 1862 Afar chiefs ceded power to the French government; by 1869 French trading settlements and ports were prospering.

Treaties signed in the 1880s with the Afars and the Issas extended French authority, and in 1896 the territory became known as the colony of French Somaliland. The city of Djibouti rapidly became an important port and refueling station; in the early 1900s a railroad was built between it and the capital of Ethiopia.

In 1946 the colony was made an overseas territory of France, and in 1956 it was granted internal self-government. In the 1950s and 1960s France initiated programs to improve education and welfare in the territory and to broaden its economy. In 1967, acting on a request by the territorial assembly, the French National Assembly changed the name French Somaliland to the more accurate French Territory of Afars and Issas. In a 1967 referendum the people voted to remain under French control.

Ethiopia, whose people are ethnically related to the Afars, and Somalia, whose people are ethnically related to the Issas, clashed over territorial disputes as well as over the fairness of the vote that deprived both of the possibility of absorbing the colony. In 1977, after 115 years of French rule, Afars and Issas became the independent nation of Djibouti. In 1978 there were hostilities, with Ethiopia and Somalia charging each other with interference in Djibouti's internal affairs. Djibouti accepted large numbers of refugees and immigrants fleeing the confrontation. It welcomed French and U.S. military protection. A peace accord in 1994 ended a 3-year uprising by Afars rebels.

Four thousand French troops are currently stationed in Djibouti and are the mainstay of the country's economy. France also gives extensive financial aid to ensure the stability of the country.

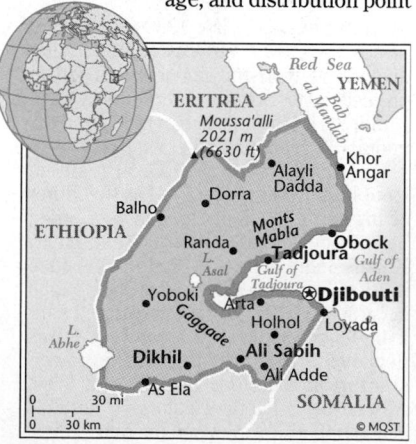

Egypt

Official name: *Arab Republic of
Egypt*
Area: *389,564 sq. mi.,
1,001,450 sq. km.*
Type of government: *Republic*
Population: *73,313,000*
Capital and largest city: *Cairo
(Pop., 6,801,000)*
Languages: *Arabic (official),
English, French*
Literacy: *51%*
Currency: *Pound*
Per capital GDP: *$3,700
(Rank: 102nd)*

The land. Egypt consists of two principal regions that are divided by the Suez Canal. East of the canal is the Sinai peninsula, rugged desert country with only a few oases. In the south, the Sinai peninsula is dominated by Jabal Katerina, the highest mountain in Egypt, which reaches 8,668 feet (2,643 meters). The region west of the canal is mainly desert.

The Nile River flows northward through the western region. The fertile valley formed by the river is between 2 and 10 miles (3 and 16 kilometers) wide and about 950 miles (1,532 kilometers) long. In the north the valley widens into a delta through which the Nile reaches the Mediterranean Sea. The desert begins at the edge of the valley. A large valley called the Faiyum Depression lies to the southwest of Cairo, near the town of Al-Faiyum; it is what remains of ancient Lake Moeris. The depression is extremely fertile, with many gardens and orchards. The flow of the Nile is regulated by several large dams that provide maximum water for irrigation.

The Arabian Desert (known in Egypt

STATUE OF PHARAOH Mycerinus and his wife, c2575 B.C.

Map labels (Djibouti): Red Sea, YEMEN, Bab al Mandab, ERITREA, Moussa'alli 2021 m (6630 ft), Khor Angar, Alayli Dadda, Dorra, Balho, ETHIOPIA, Monts Mabla, Randa, L. Asal, Obock, Tadjoura, Gulf of Tadjoura, Gulf of Aden, Yoboki, Arta, Djibouti, L. Abhe, Gaggade, Holhol, Loyada, Dikhil, Ali Sabih, Ali Adde, As Ela, SOMALIA, 30 mi, 30 km, © MQST

Margin box: meters *US* / metres *Brit.*

as the Eastern Desert) lies between the Nile and the Red Sea. The desert is bordered in the east by mountains reaching as high as 7,175 feet (2,188 meters). There are few oases and the region is very sparsely populated.

The Libyan Desert (known in Egypt as the Western Desert), part of the eastern Sahara, is a large, arid plain. Enormous sand dunes provide a significant barrier at the Egyptian-Libyan border. There are no settlements at all in the southern portion of the Libyan Desert.

Summers in Egypt are very hot and dry—with temperatures often reaching 107°F (42°C) in the shade—and winters are warm and dry. A little winter rain, about 1.1 inches (2.8 centimeters), falls in the area of Alexandria, in the north.

The people. The population of Egypt is concentrated in the Nile valley and its delta. The country has a high rate of population growth and the government employs an active birth control program. Egypt is the second most populous country on the African continent. Almost 99 percent of the people live in less than 4 percent of the total area.

Most Egyptians are descended from Hamitic peoples who inhabited the Nile valley in ancient times. There is some mixture of Arab stock from the time of the Muslim conquest in the 600s. Over 90 percent of the people are Muslim and Arabic-speaking. Most of the remaining people are Copts (Egyptian Christians). Nomadic herdsmen, or Bedouins, roam the desert regions in search of food and water for their livestock.

The major cities are Cairo, the capital, near the junction of the Nile valley and the delta; Alexandria (population, 3,339,000), the main Mediterranean seaport; Giza (2,222,000); Shubrâ al-Khayma (871,000); and Port Said (472,000).

Economy. Egypt's economy, traditionally based on agriculture, is industrializing rapidly to counter high unemployment created partly by rapid increases in population growth. Nonetheless, agriculture still employs more than one-third of the labor force.

Cotton is the major crop, followed by sugar, rice, and corn. The Nile River and its Aswan Dam provide abundant irrigation as well as hydroelectric power.

The main industries process the cotton grown in the country. Modern textile and chemical plants have been established in many towns, especially in and near Tanta, near the Mediterranean Sea. Armament industries have also been founded. Tourism provides additional income.

Egypt's revenues from the operation of the Suez Canal were halted in 1967 when the Arab-Israeli war broke out. The canal did not regain its former significance again until the late 1970s, when it became a major oil-shipment route.

Most Egyptian energy needs are supplied by its own oil. In 1987, 45 million metric tons of crude oil were produced. Coal was discovered in the late 1960s, as

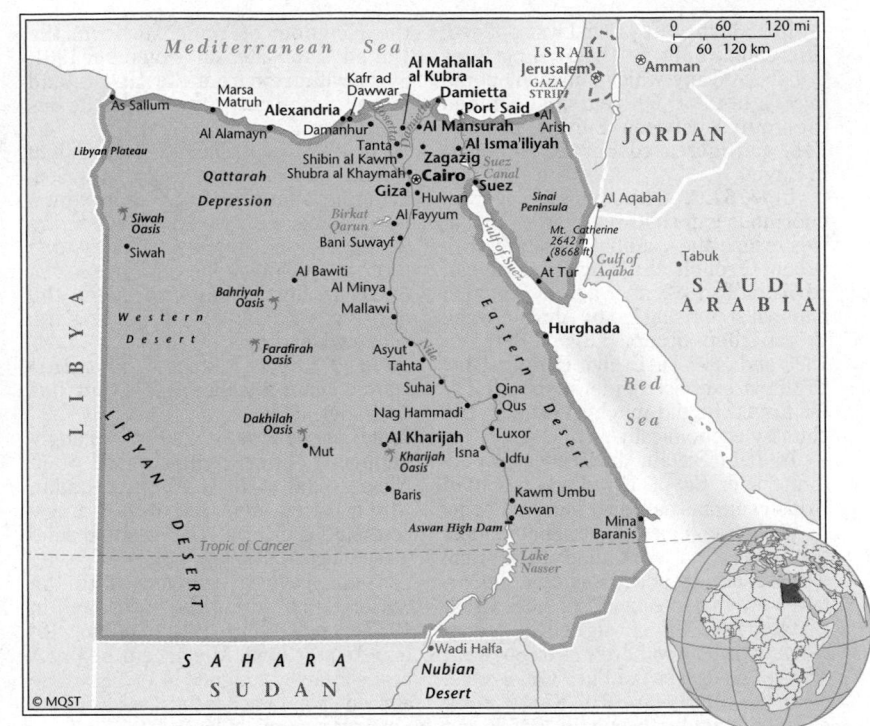

was uranium in the late 1970s. Iron ore is mined and converted into steel. Although the private sector is expanding, almost all heavy and large industries are still controlled by the state.

Imports include cereals, machinery, and raw materials. The main exports are cotton, petroleum, and textiles. Most trade is conducted with the United States, European Union countries, and Japan. Egypt receives extensive economic aid from many of these same nations.

Government. The Arab Republic of Egypt has a presidential system of government. The president is nominated by the legislature and approved by popular vote. He is elected to a 6-year term. The president appoints a cabinet, headed by a prime minister, which is responsible to the legislature.

Legislative power is vested in the 454-member People's Assembly. The Advisory Council is a 264-member consultative body.

History. Civilization has existed in Egypt for over 5,000 years. Successive Egyptian dynasties ruled until foreign invaders overran the country. The first of these invasions occurred in 945 B.C., when a Libyan prince, Sheshonk, seized control of Egypt. Libyans ruled Egypt until the late 700s B.C., when an Ethiopian dynasty took power. In about 670 B.C. Assyrians took over the country, only to be conquered by Persians in 525 B.C. For more information about Egyptian history, see the HISTORY OF THE WORLD volume.

In 332 B.C. Alexander the Great of Macedonia conquered Egypt and brought the country into his empire. At Alexander's death in 323 B.C., one of his generals, Ptolemy, took control of Egypt and founded the Ptolemaic dynasty. Egyptian culture and politics became infused with the Greek tradition. Egypt

prospered—academies were built and trade was encouraged.

In 30 B.C. Egypt, weakened by internal conflicts, fell to the powerful forces of Rome. During the Roman occupation, probably in about the A.D. 300s, Christianity spread to Egypt, and the Coptic Church, the church of Christian Egyptians, was established.

Islam. Egypt remained under Roman authority until A.D. 639. In that year, Muslim Arabs conquered Egypt. Since that time, Egypt has been closely identified with the Islamic world. The Muslims converted most of the Egyptian people, and Egypt became a major part of the early Muslim empires.

In 969 a Muslim dynasty, the Fatimid, established its control over Egypt and made Cairo its capital. In the 1100s Christian Crusaders threatened the Muslim empire. Saladin, a Syrian officer, came to the aid of the Muslim rulers, repulsed the Christian troops, and in 1169 founded the Ayyubid dynasty, which lasted for a century.

In 1250 the slave guards of the Ayyubids, the Mamluks, seized control of the country and ruled it until 1517. In that year the Ottoman Turks defeated the Mamluks and absorbed Egypt into the Ottoman Empire. But the Ottoman Turks maintained only loose control over Egypt, and they left the Mamluks most of their former political power.

European influence. In 1798 Napoleon I of France invaded Egypt, but French rule was short-lived. In 1801 British and Ottoman forces expelled the French. In 1805 an Albanian Muslim soldier, Muhammad Ali, seized power and established a dynasty that lasted until 1952. Although Muhammad Ali and his successors did much to westernize Egypt, their attempts were only partially successful.

civilization
US

civilisation
Brit.

22 Africa

In 1869 the Suez Canal was opened. The canal, built by the French Suez Canal Company, which obtained operating rights for 99 years, shortened the routes between Europe and the East and increased Europe's interest in Egypt.

In 1876 Egypt, near bankruptcy from enormous expenditures from efforts to westernize the country, was forced to accept French and English financial advisers. In 1882, after a brief Egyptian nationalist uprising led by Ahmad Arabi, British troops occupied Egypt. Between 1883 and 1907 Sir Evelyn Baring (Lord Cromer) exercised chief responsibility for Egypt; he did much to develop the country economically.

In 1914 Britain declared a protectorate over Egypt. Egyptians resented British rule and called for independence. In 1922 Britain gave Egypt limited independence, but continued to control defense, foreign policy, and other important matters. On August 26, 1936, Great Britain and Egypt signed a treaty whereby Britain withdrew its troops from all regions except the Suez Canal zone.

In the same year, 1936, King Farouk succeeded to the throne. In 1945 Egypt and six other Arab nations formed the Arab League to promote unity among member nations. In 1948 Egypt and the other Arab nations fought an unsuccessful war against the newly created state of Israel. Israel drove the invaders out, and the United Nations negotiated separate armistice agreements between the Arab states and Israel, but no final peace treaty was signed. Egypt obtained control of the Gaza Strip, a small area on the Mediterranean Sea that had once been part of Palestine.

Republic. After the 1948 Arab-Israeli clash, Egypt, troubled by failure in the war, a corrupt regime, and social unrest, fell into political turmoil. In 1952 an army group called the Free Officers seized control of the government and forced the king to abdicate.

General Muhammad Najib (Naguib) became prime minister. In June 1953 Egypt became a republic, and Najib became president. In 1954 Lieutenant Colonel Gamal Abdel Nasser, a leader of the military revolt, ousted Najib and assumed the position of president.

In 1956 the United States withdrew offers of a loan for the building of a high dam at Aswan. Because of the withdrawal of the loan offer, Nasser nationalized the Suez Canal and announced his intention to use canal revenues to build the dam. Nasser also accepted large-scale Soviet aid for the project. A dispute over free access to the canal arose after nationalization, and a new conflict erupted. British, French, and Israeli forces attacked in October 1956, and after a brief but intensive struggle, both sides accepted a UN cease-fire.

United Arab Republic. On February 1, 1958, Egypt, in an effort to build Arab unity, joined with Syria to form the United Arab Republic (U.A.R.). The following month, the U.A.R. joined with the Kingdom of Yemen to form the United Arab States. In September 1961, Syria withdrew from the U.A.R., and three months later Egypt ended its ties with Yemen.

In 1967 Egypt blockaded the Gulf of Aqaba, Israel's outlet to the Red Sea, bringing about a brief war in which Israeli forces were victorious and during which they occupied some Egyptian territory, including the Sinai peninsula. A UN-arranged cease-fire ended the fighting, with Israel still holding the occupied territory.

In 1973 Egypt, allied with other Arab states, again attacked Israel, but was again defeated.

Contemporary Egypt. The increasingly unpopular Nasser regime ended when Nasser died in 1970. Anwar el-Sadat, who replaced him, promulgated a new constitution in 1971 and permitted political parties to develop.

Sadat severed relations with the Soviet Union during the 1970s, and in 1977 entered into peace talks with Israel's president, Menachem Begin. A peace treaty was signed in 1979, and the agreed-upon Israeli withdrawal from the Sinai was completed in 1982.

Sadat was assassinated in 1981 by Muslim extremists. He was succeeded by his vice president, Hosni Mubarak. Mubarak improved relations with the Arab world and played a more active role in the United Nations. Egypt sent troops to Saudi Arabia in 1990 as part of the allied response to Iraq's invasion of Kuwait.

In the early 1990s Egypt's move toward democratization was hampered by rapid population growth, economic difficulties, and the rise of a violent Islamic fundamentalist movement that sought to topple the Mubarak government and establish an Islamic state in Egypt.

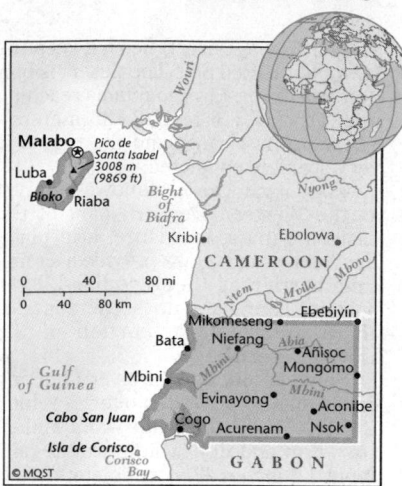

Equatorial Guinea

Official name: *Republic of Equatorial Guinea*

Area: *10,827 sq. mi., 28,050 sq. km.*

Type of government: *Transition*

Population: *498,000*

Capital and largest city: *Malabo (Pop., 30,000)*

Languages: *Spanish (official), Fang, Bubi, English, Pidgin*

Literacy: *79%*

Currency: *CFA franc*

Per capita GDP: *$2,100 (Rank: 132nd)*

The land. Equatorial Guinea, formerly known as Spanish Guinea, consists of two provinces—Río Muni and Bioko. In Río Muni, a coastal plain gives way some 12 miles (20 kilometers) inland to a higher, rolling plateau, which rises in the east to a hilly region. Bioko Province occupies two islands and several islets. Bioko Island consists of two volcanoes separated by a narrow valley. Its coastline is steep, except in the southwest, where there is an excellent harbor at San Carlos. Annobón, the smaller island, is also volcanic in origin, and has a rugged terrain.

The climate of Equatorial Guinea is tropical, with very high heat and humidity throughout the year. The average annual rainfall is about 75 inches (192 centimeters).

The people. Most of the people of Bioko are descended from the islands' native people, the Bubes. There are also Europeans and other Africans. Most of Río Muni's population are descendants of the Fang people. There are also people of other African tribal groups and a small number of Europeans. Río Muni's population is nearly triple that of Bioko.

Equatorial Guinea is sparsely populated, with only 15 percent of the population living in urban areas. The largest towns are the capital, Malabo, and Bata.

Catholicism is the predominant religion, although there are some Protestants, Muslims, and people who have held to traditional religions. Spanish is the official language, but a number of African languages are spoken.

Economy. Equatorial Guinea's economy is chiefly agricultural, and its mineral resources—titanium, iron ore, manganese, uranium, and alluvial gold—remain largely unexplored and unexploited. The main products are cacao, grown on Bioko plantations, and coffee, timber, and forest products from Río Muni. The country has very little manufacturing.

Most of Equatorial Guinea's trade is conducted with France, Spain, Italy, and Germany.

Government. A new constitution came into effect in November of 1991. Under the constitution, the president appoints a prime minister and a Council of Ministers. The legislature is an 80-member House of People's Representatives.

History. The first inhabitants of Equatorial Guinea are believed to have been Pygmies. Between the 17th and 19th

kilometers
US

kilometres
Brit.

centuries, Bantu migrations populated the coasts. The Fang arrived later and the Bubes emigrated to Bioko from Cameroon in several waves.

Fernâo do Pó, a Portuguese explorer, reached Bioko and the nearby mainland in the 1470s. The Portuguese claimed the islands and retained control until 1778, when they were ceded to Spain. Possession of the mainland was disputed until 1900, when the Treaty of Paris granted Río Muni to Spain. Settlers established plantations using African laborers.

In the 1950s and 1960s Spain's goal was the improvement of the welfare of the people, the expansion of the economy, and the incorporation of the territory into the Spanish nation.

Equatorial Guinea was granted internal self-government in 1963 and in 1968 was granted independence.

Having assumed dictatorial power by 1969, president Francisco Macias Nguema led a bloody reign of terror for 11 years. In attempting to establish Río Muni's predominance, he reestablished slavery and deprived the people of Equatorial Guinea of their human and civil rights.

Macias was executed following a coup in 1979 that established a military regime. A new constitution, approved in 1982, prepared the way for a return to civilian government.

In 1984 France became Equatorial Guinea's leading trade partner. France's role has continued to increase since Equatorial Guinea's entry into the CFA franc zone in 1985.

The first presidential elections since independence were held in 1989. Obiang Nguema Mbasogo was the sole candidate. He is still in office, although subsequent elections were widely seen as flawed. Elections have been marred by violence, allegations of fraud, and arrests of opposition leaders.

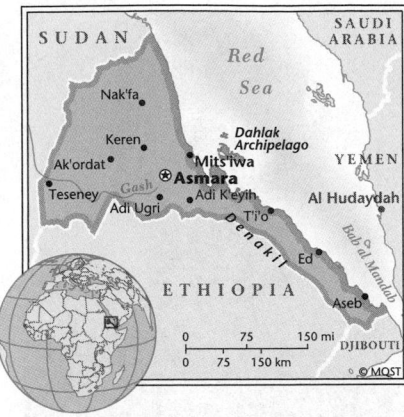

Eritrea

Official name: *State of Eritrea*
Area: *47,194 sq. mi.,*
121,320 sq. km.
Type of government: *Transition*
Population: *4,306,000*
Capital and largest city: *Asmara*
(Pop., 358,000)
Languages: *Tigre, Kunama, Arabic,*
Nora Bana, Cushitic dialects
Literacy: *25%*
Currency: *Ethiopian birr*
Per capita GDP: *$740*
(Rank: 183rd)

The land. Eritrea's varied terrain is dominated by its interior highlands, which are an extension of the Ethiopian Highlands and which rise to about 7,000 feet (2,134 meters) in elevation. These highlands are cut by numerous rivers and streams. The northern coastal region of Eritrea, along the Red Sea, has a semiarid climate in the northwest and an arid climate in the southeast, which is part of the Danakil Desert. The coastal lowlands receive an average of about 8 inches (21 centimeters) of rainfall annually. Rainfall in the interior highlands is significantly higher, increasing with altitude to approximately 40 inches (103 centimeters) annually.

The people. There are a number of ethnic groups living in Eritrea, the most numerous being the Tigre, which make up about half the population. Other important groups include the Kunama, Afar, and Bilen.

Eritrea's major urban center is its capital, Asmara. Other important cities include the ports of Aseb and Massawa. About 80 percent of Eritrea's people live in rural areas.

Economy. Eritrea's main economic activity is agriculture, which employs about 80 percent of the population. However, Eritrea's long war with Ethiopia, drought, and deforestation have limited its agricultural production.

Most of Eritrea's numerous light industries were shut down or removed during the war with Ethiopia. Fishing and salt production are important economic activities.

Eritrea has a number of potentially profitable natural resources, including gold, copper, potash, and iron ore.

Government. Eritrea's government is in transition, pending implementation of a democratic constitution and election of a permanent government. Executive power is held by the president, who presides over a cabinet and legislature. Legislative authority is exercised by a 150-member National Assembly, whose members are to be popularly elected.

History. Eritrea was the site of the powerful kingdom of Axum, which flourished from the first to the ninth centuries A.D. Over the centuries, parts of Eritrea came under the control of others, including the Ottoman Empire and Egypt.

Beginning in 1869, Eritrea gradually came under the control of Italy, which declared Eritrea a colony in 1890. In 1941, during World War II, Eritrea became a British protectorate and a center of Allied operations against Axis forces in the region.

In 1952 Eritrea was federated with Ethiopia, but it retained considerable domestic autonomy. However, the Ethiopian central government's encroachments on Eritrean autonomy fueled sentiments for independence, which by 1961 turned into armed conflict. The 1970s and 1980s saw the rise of the Eritrean People's Liberation Front (EPLF) as the leading force in the war against Ethiopia. The overthrow in April 1991 of Ethiopia's Marxist government was followed one month later by the EPLF's capture of Asmara and establishment of the Provisional Government of Eritrea.

In April of 1993 Eritreans voted in a UN-sponsored referendum to establish an independent Eritrea. The Ethiopian government acknowledged Eritrea's independence in May.

In February 1994 the EPLF changed its name to the People's Front for Democracy and Justice (PFDJ). The 75 members of its central committee were appointed to, and constitute half the membership of, the transitional government's National Assembly.

In March 1994 the provisional government of Eritrea established a Constitutional Commission, charged it with the task of drafting a democratic constitution, and called for multiparty national elections within four years. It has since focused its efforts on rebuilding the country, which had been completely devastated by three decades of war and repeated droughts.

laborers
US

labourers
Brit.

center
US

centre
Brit.

FAMINE
and civil wars between Ethiopia and Eritrea for several decades have caused hardship for refugees such as these.

22 Africa

Ethiopia

Official name: *Federal Democratic Republic of Ethiopia*

Area: *438,452 sq. mi., 1,127,127 sq. km.*

Type of government: *Federal republic*

Population: *65,254,000*

Capital and largest city: *Addis Ababa (Pop., 2,424,000)*

Languages: *Amharic (official), Tigrinya, Orominga, Arabic, English, Somali, Guaraginga*

Literacy: *36%*

Currency: *Birr*

Per capita GDP: *$700 (Rank: 185th)*

HAILE SELASSIE, emperor of Ethiopia until his deposition in 1974

meters
US

metres
Brit.

meager
US

meagre
Brit.

The land. Most of Ethiopia is occupied by the Ethiopian Highlands, a region formed of a tremendous thickness of volcanic lava split by deep gorges and canyons. The Great Rift Valley divides the highlands along a line running southwest from the east-central part of the country.

A large mountain mass northwest of the Great Rift Valley rises more than 15,000 feet (4,573 meters). There is a plateau in the southeast with elevations above 10,000 feet (3,049 meters). In the northern part of the country, close to the Red Sea, is a low-lying desert region, the Danakil Depression.

There are many rivers and lakes in Ethiopia. At the western end of the Rift Valley is the Omo River, which drains into Lake Rudolf along the border with Kenya. Lake Tana, near the center of the Ethiopian Highlands, is the source of the Blue Nile. The Tekeze River, another Nile tributary, originates near the eastern slope of the highlands. The Awash River in the eastern end of the Rift Valley flows northeast through a dry plain to its final destination in Lake Abbé.

The climate is influenced by altitude. In the Ethiopian Highlands average rainfall varies from 40 inches (103 centimeters) in the north to 80 inches (205 centimeters) in the southwest. The lowlands receive less than 8 inches (21 centimeters) of rain.

The people. There are many ethnic groups in Ethiopia. Among the most important are the Oromo, Amhara, Tigré, and Sidamo peoples. The Amhara people live in the central highlands, the Tigré in the northern part of the country. The Oromo are the dominant tribe in southern Ethiopia.

Both the Amhara and Tigré peoples are Coptic Christians. Some Oromo are Muslim, some are Christian, and some are pagan. The Oromo live in the south and also in parts of central Ethiopia.

Ethiopia's major cities include Addis Ababa, the capital; Dire Dawa (population, 208,000); Gonder (142,000); and Nazret (164,000).

Economy. Ethiopia's meager economy depends on agriculture; the most important crop is coffee. Eighty percent of the people are involved in agriculture, which accounts for 90 percent of export earnings. Most farmers, however, are engaged only in producing basic food crops, and about half the farmland is planted with grains. Severe drought and the ongoing civil war caused a tremendous drop in agricultural production, which led to famine during the 1980s. Hundreds of thousands of Ethiopians and most of Ethiopia's livestock died of starvation. Western countries and international relief agencies contributed enormous amounts of food and assistance; the United States alone contributed $456 million for various relief projects.

Although Ethiopia has deposits of gold, platinum, and other minerals, mining is poorly developed, partly due to the costs of overland transportation. Industrial production greatly increased in the 1960s, giving the country textile and food processing plants. Ethiopia's many rivers provide a potential source for hydroelectric power, a shortage of which, along with a shortage of advanced technology, limits further industrialization.

Coffee is the main export item, while petroleum products, machinery, and consumer goods are the chief imports. Ethiopia's main trading partners include the United States, Saudi Arabia, Germany, Japan, Italy, and France.

Government. A new constitution was adopted in 1994. By its terms, legislative power resides with a bicameral legislature, consisting of a lower chamber, whose 548 members are popularly elected, and an upper chamber, whose 108 members are elected by the country's nine state assemblies. The head of state is a president who is elected by the lower chamber of the legislature, the House of People's Representatives.

History. Ethiopia is one of the world's oldest kingdoms, and the historical and archaeological records of Ethiopian culture go back to about 500 B.C. The present-day rulers claim descent from the Queen of Sheba, whose descendents ruled over the ancient Semitic-speaking Sabean people, whose origins are in southern Arabia.

Ethiopia was under Semitic influence until A.D. 324, when the emperor Azana was converted to Christianity. Muslims invaded Ethiopia in the 600s. The Muslims converted the Oromo and pushed the Amhara to the highlands, where they remained cut off from the rest of the world until the early 1500s.

In the 1400s Portugal sent an expedition to Ethiopia. In 1527 Muslims overran Ethiopia, but with the aid of Portugal, Ethiopia expelled the Muslim sultan in 1541. Portuguese Jesuits came to Ethiopia and tried to bring the Ethiopian Christians into the Roman Catholic Church. In 1632 the emperor, Fasilides, expelled the Jesuits.

Political unrest, poor relations with Great Britain, and religious wars marked the period until 1887. At that time Italy attempted to gain territory in Ethiopia. Italy proclaimed Ethiopia a protectorate in 1889, and in 1895 the Italian army invaded Ethiopia. Italy was defeated at the Battle of Aduwa in 1896 but retained the coastal region.

Contemporary Ethiopia. In 1916 Ras Tafari became the regent for the empress Zauditu. He succeeded to the throne at her death in 1930 and took the name Haile Selassie. In 1935 Italy, then under the rule of Benito Mussolini, renewed its claims on Ethiopia and invaded the country. The emperor unsuccessfully appealed to the League of Nations for help. In 1936 Italy united Ethiopia, Eritrea, and Italian Somaliland to form Italian East Africa.

In 1941 English and Ethiopian troops defeated the Italian occupation forces and Haile Selassie returned to

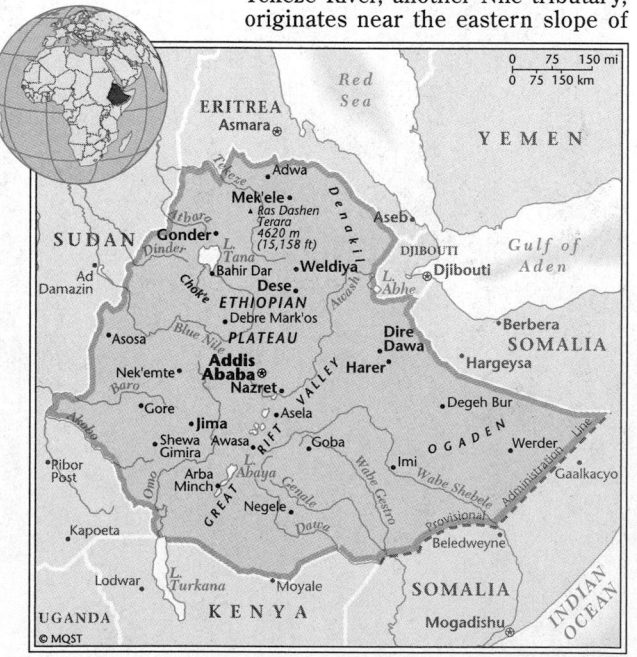

the throne. In 1962 Eritrea was federated with Ethiopia, but the Eritrean Liberation Front led repeated attempts after 1970 to effect secession. Fighting also recurred in sporadic border disputes with Somalia over control of the Ogaden region. Somalia also lent support to the Eritrean rebels.

Strikes, student protests, and army rebellion led to the deposition of Haile Selassie in 1974; he died a year later.

The new military government began a socialist restructuring of the society and economy. Several bloody coups ensued until 1977, when Mariam Haile Mengistu, a ruthless dictator, assumed leadership of the nation and its socialist revolution.

Several years of severe drought in Ethiopia and neighboring countries resulted in the mid-1980s in widespread famine. Between 1984 and 1985, it was estimated that 300,000 lives were lost to famine. The drought abated in 1987 but resumed in 1988, causing widespread famine once again.

After decades of dispute, Eritrean rebel forces seized control of the entire Province of Eritrea in June 1991. The rebel government hoped to establish independence from Ethiopia even though an independent Eritrea would leave Ethiopia landlocked and without the use of its two major ports.

At the same time, rebels from the northern Tigré Province forced Ethiopia's president to flee. A transitional government was established in Addis Ababa and plans were made for multiparty national elections to be held by early 1994.

In April of 1993 Eritreans voted in a UN-sponsored referendum to establish an independent Eritrea. The Ethiopian government acknowledged Eritrea's independence in May. A 2-year border war ended in December 2000.

Gabon

Official name: *Gabonese Republic*
Area: *103,321 sq. mi., 267,670 sq. km.*
Type of government: *Republic*
Population: *1,288,000*
Capital and largest city: *Libreville (Pop., 420,000)*
Languages: *French (official), Fang, Myene, Bateke*
Literacy: *63%*
Currency: *CFA franc*
Per capita GDP: *$5,500 (Rank: 82nd)*

The land. Most of Gabon is covered by wet tropical forests. Inland from a coastal plain is the edge of the African Plateau, called the Crystal Mountains in the north and the Mayombé Mountains in the south. In the southeast are the Batéké plateaus, comprised of grasslands.

Gabon lies on the equator and the climate throughout the country is hot and humid. Annual rainfall varies from 59 inches (151 centimeters) in the south to 157 inches (403 centimeters) in the north. There is a long dry season from May to September. The average annual temperature is about 80°F (27°C).

The people. There are many different tribal groups in Gabon, most of which are Bantu-speaking. The Fang, who migrated from the north in the 1800s, form the largest group. There are also peoples of the Myene, Bapounou, and Eshira tribes, as well as over 40 other tribal groups with separate languages and cultures.

Gabon is thinly populated. Most of the people live in rural areas. The major city is the capital, Libreville. Port-Gentil (population, 79,000) is Gabon's major port. Other cities include Franceville (31,000), Oyem (22,000), and Lambaréné (15,000).

Economy. The economy of Gabon is based largely on mining and forestry, although most of the people are engaged in subsistence farming. Manioc, corn, and bananas are the country's main crops.

Gabon is one of the richest of the black African nations because of its mining, which accounts for about one-third of the gross national product, and its lumbering. Both enterprises are largely foreign-owned. Gabon has some of the world's largest deposits of manganese, iron ore, and uranium. Offshore oil deposits have been exploited, and about 10 million metric tons, accounting for over 60 percent of the nation's export revenues, are produced annually. Gabon exports petroleum, wood, manganese, and uranium; it imports foodstuffs and manufactured goods. Most of its trade is with France and the United States.

Government. Gabon has a presidential system of government. Executive power is vested in a president popularly elected to a 7-year term. Legislative power rests with a bicameral legislature consisting of the 120-member National Assembly, elected by direct popular vote, and the 91-member Senate, whose members are elected by municipal councils and department assemblies. In 1990 opposition parties were legalized for the first time since 1968.

History. Little is known of the early history of the Gabon area. Bantu tribal groups came into the area beginning about 1200. They remained isolated in the dense forests and retained their separate cultures. One group, the Fang, fought their way to the coast after hearing about the arrival of European traders. In the 1400s Portuguese explorers established trade relations with the Loango kingdom. The original trade in gold dust, ivory, palm oil, and wood soon gave way to slaving.

French rule. Slave trading was abolished in the early 1800s, and in 1849 France established a center for freed slaves at Libreville. In 1899 France began granting concessions to private companies to develop the region. Company abuses led to depopulation, depletion of resources, and loss of capital. In 1910 Gabon became part of French Equatorial Africa.

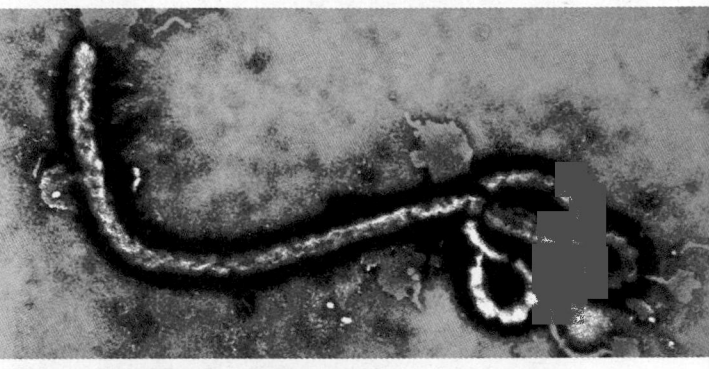

THE DEADLY Ebola virus was first identified in the Congo area of western Africa.

Political activities before World War II were confined mainly to groups in Libreville, religious cults, and Fang tribal societies. After the war, France liberalized its colonial system, and in 1946 it created the French Union. Gabon was permitted to establish territorial assemblies and to elect deputies to the French National Assembly. Jean-Hilaire Aubame, representing the northern Fang people, was elected to the French assembly.

Self-rule. France granted Gabon internal self-government in 1957. Leon M'Ba, representing the southern Fang and other groups in his party, the Gabonese Democratic Bloc (BDG), became prime minister of a coalition government that included Aubame's party.

Gabon became a member of the French Community in 1958 but broke its ties with French Equatorial Africa, from which it had long desired to secede because of its own wealth.

Gabon became independent on August 17, 1960, and M'Ba was elected president. Early in 1964 a military coup threatened the regime, but the French intervened in support of M'Ba. In 1964 M'Ba's party won a majority of seats in the National Assembly, and M'Ba continued as president until his death in 1967. He was succeeded by Albert Bongo (now Omar Bongo). In 1968 the BDG became the Gabon Democratic Party. Bongo was elected in 1973 and in every subsequent election. Constitutional reform led to a multiparty system in the 1990s; however, a 2003 constitutional change

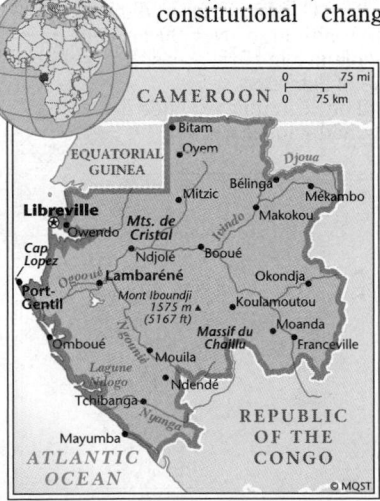

center *US*

centre *Brit.*

makes it possible for Bongo to remain in power indefinitely

France still has great influence on Gabon's economy and French troops are stationed in the country. Bongo has sought to establish closer ties with other European Union nations. New oil funds in the late 1980s, and the opening of the Rabi-Kounga oil field in 1989, brought international oil companies into Gabon and helped buoy the slumping economy.

The Gambia

Official name: *Republic of The Gambia*
Area: *4,396 sq. mi., 11,300 sq. km.*
Type of government: *Republic*
Population: *1,456,000*
Capital: *Banjul*
        (Pop., 42,000)
Largest city: *Serrekunda*
        (Pop., 151,000)
Languages: *English (official), Mandinka, Wolof, Fula*
Literacy: *48%*
Currency: *Dalasi*
Per capita GDP: *$1,770*
        (Rank: 140th)

The land. The Gambia is dominated by the Gambia River, which flows through the narrow country from east to west for over 200 miles (323 kilometers). Mangrove swamps line the river for about 150 miles (241 kilometers) inland from the ocean. Beyond the swamps the land is grassy with patches of sandy soil. The Gambia is low lying with a maximum altitude of 239 feet (73 meters). Sandstone plateaus cover the region farthest from the river.

The climate is tropical. The Gambia receives about 40 inches (103 centimeters) of rain a year. The rainy season lasts from June to October.

The people. A number of peoples live in The Gambia. Among the larger groups are the Malinke, Wolof, and Fulani, most of whom are Muslims.

The Gambia is fairly densely populated, although over 90 percent of its people live in rural areas. It has a high rate of illiteracy.

The Gambia's major city and capital, Banjul,

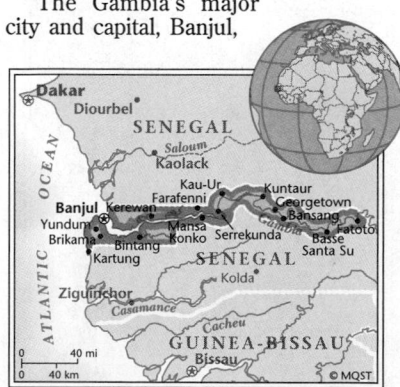

is on St. Mary's Island at the mouth of the Gambia River. The Gambia's largest city, Serrekunda (population, 151,000), lies in the middle of the country.

Economy. The Gambia's economy depends on agriculture. The main crop is peanuts. Sorghum and rice are also grown. Agriculture accounts for nearly 60 percent of the gross national product and employs 80 percent of the nation's labor force. Tourism and fishing are increasing in importance. There are few mineral deposits and little industry in the country.

Peanuts accounted for over 75 percent of the value of exports. The Gambia imports rice, wheat, sugar, petroleum products, motor vehicles, and manufactured goods. The Gambia's main trading partners are Ghana, European Union countries, Japan, and the United States.

Government. Legislative power rests with the National Assembly, which has 53 members, 48 of whom are elected. The head of state is the president, who is elected by popular vote to a 5-year term; number of terms is unrestricted.

History. A Carthaginian, Hanno, may have sailed up the Gambia River in the 500s B.C. During the A.D. 900s, the Gambia region was a distant outpost of the empires of Ghana and Mali.

In the 1400s the Portuguese explored the Gambia region and traded with the people there, mostly the Wolof and Malinke, as did Dutch, English, and French merchants in the following years. Between the 1500s and 1700s, there was a large slave trade with America.

By the 1700s the British and French had established trading posts and forts at the mouth of the Gambia River. British and French merchants competed vigorously throughout the 1700s for control of trade with The Gambia, but in 1783 The Gambia was awarded to Great Britain by treaty.

British rule. Throughout the 1800s British merchants trading on the Gambia River resisted proposals that The Gambia should become part of French-controlled Senegal.

After World War II Britain faced the problem of Senegalese demands for The Gambia. Gambians had mixed feelings about union with Senegal. They realized that their country could not be economically successful, but there were significant differences in language and culture between the two countries.

Self-rule. In 1963 The Gambia became self-governing with Dawda Jawara as prime minister. Independence came in February 1965. The Gambia became a republic in 1970, and Jawara was elected president.

In 1994 Jawara was overthrown in a bloodless coup. A military government, headed by Yahya Jammeh, suspended the constitution and banned political parties. A new constitution and subsequent elections returned the country to civilian rule.

Ghana

Official name: *Republic of Ghana*
Area: *92,076 sq. mi., 238,540 sq. km.*
Type of government: *Constitutional democracy*
Population: *20,163,000*
Capital and largest city: *Accra (Pop., 860,000)*
Languages: *English (official), African dialects*
Literacy: *65%*
Currency: *Cedi*
Per capita GDP: *$1,980 (Rank: 136th)*

The land. Grasslands and forests occupy much of Ghana's land. Half the country has an elevation of less than 500 feet (152 meters). The Volta River and its principal tributaries, the Black Volta, White Volta, and Oti, drain all of northern Ghana and about half of the south. Extensive grassy plains and isolated hills are typical of the Volta basin landscape. The south and west of Ghana are hilly and forested.

In the southeast the Volta River flows between the Akwapim Hills and the Togo Mountains. At that point there is a large dam and power plant, at Akosombo. The damming of the Volta River created a large lake, 3,300 square miles (8,542 square kilometers) in area, called Lake Volta. The climate throughout the country is tropical. Rainfall varies from more than 80 inches (205 centimeters) in the southwest to less than 40 inches (103 centimeters) in the north.

The people. Many Ghanaians are Akan-speaking people, mainly Fanti along the coast and Ashanti farther inland. The Ga people, who are related by culture and language to the Ashanti, live around the city of Accra. In the north are people who speak languages of the Gur family.

About one-third of Ghana's population is literate and over two-thirds live in rural areas.

Ghana's major cities include the capital, Accra; Kumasi (population, 349,000); and Tamale (137,000).

Economy. Ghana's economy progressed rapidly after the 1950s, but its growth has now leveled off. Nearly half of the gross national product comes from agricultural products, and about 15 percent from manufacturing and mining. Fifty-five percent of the work force is engaged in farming.

Ghana is the world's top cacao producer, and yams, rice, corn, and grains are basic food crops. Lumbering is a significant economic activity.

Ghana is rich in mineral deposits, especially diamonds, manganese, gold, and bauxite. Ghana's industrial base is relatively advanced compared with that

kilometers
US

kilometres
Brit.

labor
US

labour
Brit.

realized
US

realised
Brit.

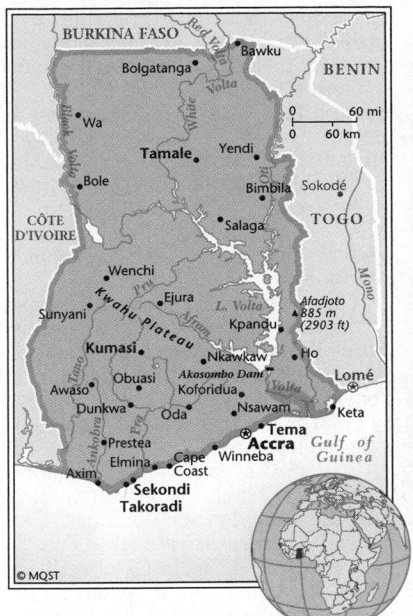

AFRICAN women display examples of their art of weaving.

of many other African countries. Tema's aluminum production and hydroelectric power from the Volta River Project helped stimulate industrial growth. The industrial sector suffered in the 1980s due to a shortage of imported raw material. Ghana is in the process of liberalizing its economy, allowing many industries to become private to stimulate growth.

The major exports are cocoa, gold, diamonds, manganese, timber, and aluminum. Ghana imports manufactured goods, machinery, food, and chemicals. The country's major trading partners are Great Britain, the United States, Germany, Japan, and the Netherlands.

Government. A new constitution was approved by referendum in April 1992. By its terms, the head of state is a president who is popularly elected to a 4-year term and who may serve two terms. Legislative power is exercised by a 200-member parliament whose members are popularly elected and serve 4-year terms. The members of a Council of Ministers are appointed by the president and approved by the parliament.

History. Ghana is named after a medieval empire in western Africa, although medieval Ghana was located in present-day Mali. The name *Ghana* was chosen because it was believed that people from the ancient empire had migrated to the coastal region.

In 1471 Portuguese explorers encountered the Fanti people, who were then migrating southward. In the years that followed, several European countries engaged in trade for gold, ivory, and slaves supplied by the Ashanti through Fanti middlemen.

British rule. The British and the Ashanti waged wars throughout the 1800s. In 1874 the British finally achieved victory and formed the coastal area of Ghana into the Gold Coast colony. In 1896 Britain exiled the Ashanti king, Prempeh I, and in 1901 the British established the colony of Ashanti, which included the interior north of the Gold Coast colony.

In the same year, 1901, the Northern Territories, the region to the north of Ashanti, became a British protectorate. The German colony of Western Togoland became a British mandate under the League of Nations after World War I, and was administered together with the Gold Coast.

In the 1920s railroads were built and cacao became an important export. A new class of educated Africans formed trade unions, professional associations, and cultural groups, and began to contest the power of traditional chiefs, through whom Britain administered the country.

After World War II, Ashanti representatives were given seats in the colony's legislative council, which had been established at the beginning of colonial rule, and in 1946 the council acquired an African majority.

In 1947 Joseph Danquah organized a nationalist movement, the United Gold Coast Convention (UGCC). Kwame Nkrumah broke away from UGCC in 1949 and founded the Convention People's Party (CPP). Riots broke out in 1950 in support of Ghanaian independence, and Nkrumah was arrested by the British for his conspicuous role in the disturbances.

Nkrumah's party won elections held in 1951, and he was released to become a member of the government. In 1952 he became prime minister. Although the CPP won elections held in 1954 and 1956, newly formed regional parties challenged its power. Several of these parties merged into the National Liberation Movement, which called for a federation of regions rather than a unified state.

Independence. In March 1957, the Gold Coast, Ashanti, the Northern Territories, and British Togoland became indpendent as the nation of Ghana. Ghana became a republic in July 1960, and Nkrumah was elected president.

Nkrumah became a leader in Pan-African affairs.

The CPP remained dominant, but strong political opposition developed. The regime became increasingly authoritarian, and its opponents resorted to plotting and an attempted assassination of the president.

In 1964 Nkrumah acquired dictatorial powers. He ran the country into debt, and his regime was accused of corruption. Nkrumah was deposed following a 1966 military coup. There was another bloodless military coup in 1972. In 1979 Lieutenant Jerry Rawlings led a group of noncommissioned officers in a violent coup. However, Rawlings and his Armed Forces Revolutionary Council (AFRC) soon restored civil constitutional rule.

Charges of ineffectiveness led to another coup in 1981 organized by Rawlings and the AFRC. Rawlings suspended the constitution and created a seven-member governing body committed to the decentralization of government.

In 1988 local district elections were held throughout the country—the first elections in 8 years. The success of these elections encouraged the government to continue liberalized reforms.

Rawlings was constitutionally prevented from seeking a third term and was succeeded by John Kufuor.

THE ASHANTI of Ghana were at war with the British for most of the 19th century, until their defeat in 1874.

AFRICAN CLOTH displays unique patterns and many rich colors.

Guinea

Official name: *Republic of Guinea*
Area: *95,640 sq. mi.,*
245,860 sq. km.
Type of government: *Republic*
Population: *8,816,000*
Capital and largest city: *Conakry*
(Pop., 705,000)
Languages: *French*
Literacy: *36%*
Currency: *Franc*
Per capita GDP: *$1,970*
(Rank: 137th)

meters
US
metres
Brit.

The land. The countryside of Guinea is quite varied. There is a wide, rainy coastal plain, but farther inland the land is drier and has elevations of more than 3,000 feet (914 meters) above sea level. In the central part of the country is the mountain region of Fouta Djallon. From the mountains the land descends to the east into the drainage basins of the Senegal and Niger rivers. There are grasslands and forests in the east.

The climate is tropical. Rainfall varies from 59 inches (151 centimeters) in Upper Guinea to 170 inches (436 centimeters) on the coast.

The people. There are many different ethnic groups in Guinea. The larger groups are the Fulani, Malinke, and Susu. The Fulani live in the mountainous Fouta Djallon. The Malinke live in the savanna regions of Upper Guinea. The Susu live on the coast and the inland plain. Seven different national languages are used widely.

Most of the people live in rural areas, although many migrated to urban areas in the 1980s. Guinea's largest city is the capital, Conakry, situated on Tombo Island off the mainland of Guinea. Conakry is also Guinea's major port. Other important cities include Labé (population, 65,000) and Kankan (89,000).

Economy. Two-fifths of the gross national product is derived from agriculture, one-fifth from mining, and about 14 percent from manufacturing. More than 80 percent of the work force is engaged in agriculture. Cash crops include bananas, coffee, palm products, peanuts, and pineapples. Manioc, fruits, millet, and rice are basic food crops.

Guinea has the richest bauxite deposits in the world. Iron ore, diamonds, and gold are also mined. The country has abundant hydroelectric power.

Alumina and bauxite account for more than 80 percent of export earnings. Guinea trades mainly with the United States and Western Europe. Its main imports are petroleum products, machinery, and foodstuffs.

Government. A new constitution, promulgated in 1991, and a law enacted in 1992, established Guinea as a multiparty democracy. Legislative power resides with the National Assembly, whose 114 members are popularly elected. The head of state is a president, who is also directly elected. The first presidential election was held in 1993, the first legislative elections in 1995.

History. During the 11th century, the kingdom of Ghana occupied most of present-day Guinea. The Mali, or Malinke, Empire, based in Mali, ruled the region in the 13th century. Islam took root during the Mali reign, gaining large numbers of followers among the nobility and townspeople.

During the 15th century, the Malinke people of Guinea were in regular contact with European sailors and merchants. They also traded across the Sahara. The Malinke ruled until the 16th century, when the Songhai Empire of Gao took control of eastern Guinea and the Fulani asserted dominance in the west and north. Many of the Fulani of Upper Guinea became Muslims.

In the early 1700s Muslims in the Fouta Djallon region revolted against their pagan rulers and created a state of their own.

The French began to acquire portions of Guinea in the 1800s. The indigenous peoples fought against these acquisitions, but they were largely unsuccessful. Samory Touré, a warrior who assembled his own army and ruled much of Upper Guinea, fought a frequently victorious guerrilla war against the French in the 1880s and 1890s. By 1898, however, French armies had forced Samory into exile.

French rule. In 1895 Guinea became a part of French West Africa, and was subject to direct rule from France. In the Muslim area of Fouta Djallon, however, France initiated a system of indirect rule. Schools and hospitals were provided in both the coastal and interior areas.

The peoples of the coastal region, particularly those of Conakry, became thoroughly acquainted with French culture. A railroad was built that linked Conakry to Kankan, in upper Guinea, by 1925, thus making the export of tropical products possible.

In 1946 Guinea became a territory within the French Union, but Guinea was the only French territory that refused to join the newly formed French Community in 1958. In October 1958, under the leadership of Sékou Touré, Guinea became independent.

Independence. At the time of independence, France withdrew financial and administrative help, causing a serious crisis in Guinea. France resumed ties in 1963.

From 1958 to 1984 Guinea experienced economic difficulties and the loss of civil and human rights under the dictatorial and communistic rule of President Touré.

After Touré's death in 1984, the Guinean military staged a bloodless coup. President Lansana Conté, one of the coup's leaders, instituted an economic reform program in 1985 designed to completely restructure and revitalize the economy. Continued government corruption and dissatisfaction with the initial reforms led to riots in 1987 and 1988.

Unrest in Sierra Leone and Liberia has spilled over into Guinea, threatening its fragile stability.

Guinea-Bissau

Official name: *Republic of*
Guinea-Bissau
Area: *14,051 sq. mi.,*
36,120 sq. km.
Type of government: *Republic*
Population: *1,333,000*
Capital and largest city: *Bissau*
(Pop., 109,000)
Languages: *Portuguese (official),*
Criolo, African dialects
Literacy: *34%*
Currency: *Peso*
Per capita GDP: *$900*
(Rank: 173rd)

The land. Guinea-Bissau consists of a mainland with a deeply indented coast, and a number of offshore islands, including those of the Bijagós archipelago. Most of the country consists of low coastal plain, much of which is swampy. In the east is a higher, drier savanna region. The highest point in the country, in the southeast, rises only 800 feet (243 meters) above sea level.

There are many rivers and streams, and the Cacheu, Mansôa, Gêba, and Crubal rivers have large deltas. The tropical climate is characterized by high temperatures and extreme humidity. Annual rainfall is more than 40 inches (103 centimeters). When the rivers are flooded and the tide is high, almost a third of the country's land can disappear under water.

The people. The population is made up of many diverse tribal groups. The Fulani and Malinke live in the north and the northeast, the Balante and Pepel in the southern coastal regions, and the Mandyako and Mancanha in the central and northern coastal areas.

Many languages are spoken, including Portuguese and African languages, but a Creole patois is the most commonly understood tongue. The majority of the people are animists, although a significant minority are Muslim, and a small percentage are Christian.

Eighty-seven percent of the people in the sparsely settled country live in rural areas. Bissau is the capital and largest city (population, 109,000); the rest of the country is divided into regions, the largest of which are Ohio, Cacheu, and Bafatá.

Economy. Guinea-Bissau has little mining, but potentially large bauxite deposits may someday help to diversify its economy. Meanwhile, Guinea-Bissau remains basically an agricultural land, and its standard of living is very low. Ninety percent of the workforce is engaged in agriculture, although only 8 percent of the total area of the country is cultivated. The country's forests are exploited for their timber. The main commercial crops are palm kernels and peanuts raised on European-owned plantations. Basic food crops include rice, millet, coconuts, manioc, beans, and bananas. There is little industry, although the government is trying to develop industries around the abundant fish and shellfish resources.

Almost all of the country's limited trade is with Portugal. Cashews, peanuts, and palm kernels are the chief exports, and machinery and consumer goods are imported.

Government. In 1994 the first multiparty legislative and presidential elec-

GUINEA'S CASH CROPS include dates and other palm products, peanuts, bananas, pineapples, and coffee.

tions were held. The president is elected by popular vote to a 5-year term. The 100 members of the National People's Assembly are popularly elected to 4-year terms.

History. Little is known of the early history of Guinea-Bissau. The first inhabitants were hunters and fishermen. The Fulani eventually moved to the inland regions, while the coast was settled by small communities of farmers. In the 13th century, the Mali Empire moved into the region and built the Gabu kingdom.

Portuguese sailors were the first Europeans to visit present-day Guinea-Bissau, in 1446. Portugal established trading posts and ports at the mouth of the rivers and on the Bijagós islands. In the late 1400s the region was made a dependency of the nearby Portuguese colony of the Cape Verde Islands. From the late 1500s through the mid-1800s, the colony, like the whole of West Africa, prospered from the slave trade.

Portugal occupied only coastal portions of the territory, and sent very few permanent settlers. In the 1800s Portuguese claims to the region were disputed by Great Britain and France.

In the middle 1800s, the slave trade was effectively stopped after years of pressure by British, French, and African leaders. The Portuguese were forced to travel inland in search of new profits. In the late 1800s agreement was reached on the division of west-central Africa among the European powers, and Portuguese control of the area was formally recognized.

Portuguese attempts to control the interior led to rebellions among the Africans, who were particularly angered by Portugal's participation in the slave trade. The rebellions were put down by 1915, and Portuguese settlers expanded their plantations in the colony. In the 1930s colonial administration was centralized.

In 1951 the colony was made an overseas province. Portugal did little to develop the economy and virtually ignored the education, health, and general welfare needs of the African population. Forced labor, under the "contract labor" system, remained the rule. The contract labor system involved the subjugation of an individual or a group of individuals to an employer for a length of time prescribed in a "contract" or agreement. The terms of the contracts were often harsh, reflecting the severity of slavery. However, in 1961 Portugal formally granted full Portuguese citizenship to African Guineans.

With encouragement from neighboring African states, a national liberation movement developed in the early 1960s. In 1961 a rebellion for independence began. The Portuguese armed forces proved unable to quell the uprising and by 1970 the rebel forces controlled two-thirds of the country. A constitution was granted in 1973, and on September 10, 1974, Guinea-Bissau became the first Portuguese territory in Africa to win independence. Portugal, having been the first of the European nations to colonize Africa, was among the last to relinquish its colonies.

Dissatisfaction with a proposed merger of Guinea-Bissau with Cape Verde brought about the overthrow of the government in a coup on November 14, 1980. A new constitution approved in 1984 reinstated the National Assembly. The first multiparty elections were held in 1994. An interim government installed after a 1998 civil war turned power over to President Kumba Yala in February 2000. He was deposed in a military coup in September 2003 and an interim president installed.

Ivory Coast

See Côte d'Ivoire

labor
US

labour
Brit.

colonize
US

colonise
Brit.

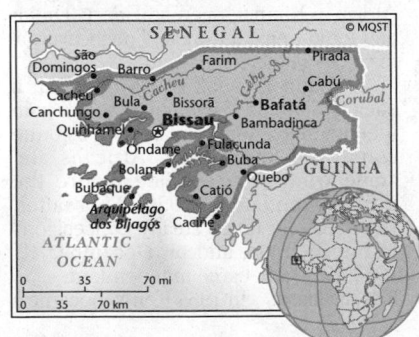

Kenya

Official name: *Republic of Kenya*
Area: *226,651 sq. mi.,*
   582,650 sq. km.
Type of government: *Republic*
Population: 31,223,000
Capital and largest city: *Nairobi*
   (Pop., 2,143,000)
Languages: *English, Swahili*
Literacy: 78%
Currency: *Shilling*
Per capita GDP: *$1,000*
   (Rank: 169th)

HERDERS tend their livestock on the African plain.

meters
US
metres
Brit.

The land. Kenya has a varied landscape. The land is low in both northern Kenya and eastern Kenya behind the coast. Except for the area around Mombasa, the eastern and northern regions are too dry for intensive settlement. Lake Turkana extends into the Great Rift Valley in northern Kenya. In the southeastern part of the country the land is flat and dry. There is a highland region in the west and southwest.

The highland terrain is extremely varied. The Rift Valley cuts through this area and there are also lakes and volcanic peaks, including Mt. Kenya, which has an elevation of over 17,000 feet (5,183 meters). Huge Lake Victoria borders Kenya's southwestern corner. Three-fourths of Kenya is semiarid and receives less than 20 inches (51 centimeters) of rain annually. In the highlands precipitation is more abundant, varying between 35 and 60 inches (77 and 158 centimeters) annually.

The people. Kenya's peoples belong to many different tribes. The largest tribes are the Kikuyu, Luo, Luhya, Masai, and Kamba. The Kikuyu have played an important role in Kenya's political history. There are also small minorities of Europeans, Asians, and Arabs.

Kenya's largest city is its capital city, Nairobi. Mombasa (population, 465,000),

on the Indian Ocean, is the country's major port. Other large cities include Kisumu (185,000) and Nakuru (163,000). Kenya's population is 90 percent rural.

Economy. Kenya's economy is based on private enterprise supported by the government. Agriculture is the foundation of the economy, with the highlands as the most productive region. Many crops are grown on European-owned plantations, including coffee, tea, and sisal. While coffee and tea are its most important crops, Kenya is the world's largest producer of pyrethrum, a vegetable ingredient used in certain insecticides. The staples of the country, produced by Africans and Europeans, include corn, wheat, vegetables, dairy products, and meat. Almost 80 percent of the work force is engaged in agriculture. Undependable weather conditions and a shortage of arable land—only 20 percent of the land is cultivable—hamper the agricultural industry. The high population growth rate further inhibits growth and stability.

Although Kenya is not well endowed with mineral resources, the country is a major producer of soda ash. The Kenyan government has made efforts to develop the country's industry and has encouraged tourism, largely safaris from Nairobi to see the country's varied wildlife. The country's principal industries include food and tobacco processing and textile, glass, and chemical manufacturing.

Kenya's main imports are petroleum, machinery, chemicals, food, and fabrics. Exports include coffee, tea, sisal, sugar, cotton, pyrethrum, and petroleum products. The tourist industry is the largest foreign exchange earner. The country's main trading partners are Great Britain, the United States, Germany, the Netherlands, and Japan.

Government. Kenya has a presidential system of government. Executive power is held by a president, who is popularly elected from among the members of the legislature. The legislature is the unicameral National Assembly. Assembly members are popularly elected to 5-year terms. In 1991 the National Assembly amended the constitution, making Kenya a multiparty state.

History. Fossils found in Kenya suggest that humans lived in the area 2.6

million years ago. Evidence shows that Kushitic-speaking people, who occupied the area from 1000 B.C., began trading with the Arabs in the first century A.D. Slave trading between the Arabs and the people of Kenya existed for many centuries. By the 1600s Turks and Portuguese had joined the trade, but in the early 1800s Great Britain had outlawed the slave trade.

British rule. In 1887 the sultan of Zanzibar, who had nominal control of the region, granted the British East African Company control over all of present-day Kenya in return for a fixed sum of money. Great Britain declared the area a protectorate in 1895. In the same year Britain began building a railroad from Mombasa to Uganda with the aid of Indian laborers.

To make the railroad pay for itself by transporting agricultural products, the British government encouraged Europeans to settle and farm in Kenya by offering long-term land leases in the highlands. Britain set up reserves of land for Africans displaced by European settlers outside the highlands and established a legislative council in the region in 1907. In 1920 all but the coastal area became a Crown colony. The coastal region became the Kenya Protectorate.

Nationalism. In 1938 the highland region, which became known as the "white highlands," was officially closed for settlement to all but Europeans. The European community came to dominate political affairs. Meanwhile, the African population, especially the numerous Kikuyu people, was increasing and crowding the reserves. Many Africans were forced to seek work in the new cities. Although an African was nominated to the legislative council in 1944, power remained in the hands of the white settlers and unrest grew among the Africans. Kikuyu, such as Harry Thuku and Jomo Kenyatta, created political organizations in the 1940s.

Starting in 1952 the Mau Mau, a society of militant Kikuyu trying to gain independence for Kenya, terrorized the country. Thousands of Africans and some whites were killed before the uprising ended in 1956. Thereafter, Great Britain made steady concessions to the Africans, and on December 12, 1963, Kenya became independent.

Independence. In 1964 Kenya became a

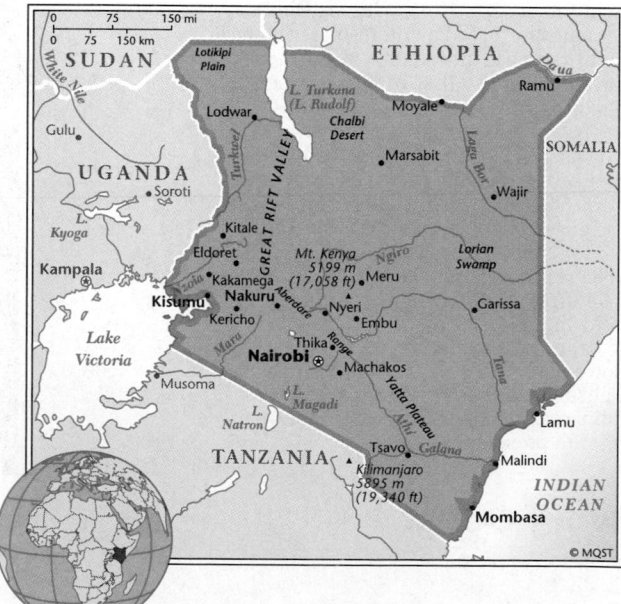

SUDAN
ETHIOPIA
Lotikipi
Plain
White Nile
Lodwar
L. Turkana
(L. Rudolf)
Moyale
Daua
Ramu
Gulu
Chalbi
Desert
UGANDA
Soroti
Marsabit
SOMALIA
L.
Kyoga
Kitale
Wajir
Kampala
Eldoret
Mt. Kenya
5199 m
(17,058 ft)
Lorian
Swamp
Kakamega
Meru
Kisumu
Nakuru
Nyeri
Garissa
Kericho
Embu
Lake
Victoria
Thika
Nairobi
Machakos
Musoma
L.
Magadi
Yatta Plateau
Lamu
TANZANIA
Tsavo
Galana
Kilimanjaro
5895 m
(19,340 ft)
Malindi
Mombasa
INDIAN
OCEAN
© MQST

republic with Jomo Kenyatta (1891–1978) as its first president. Kenyatta's regime gave Kenya a peaceful and relatively stable beginning, although charges of government corruption were made in 1974–1975. Daniel Arap Moi became president in 1978 and was reelected in 1983 and 1988. In 1980 military and economic aid was accepted from the United States, which, in return, gained access to Kenya's military bases.

During the early 1980s and early 1990s, Kenya faced the problems of drought, a high population growth rate, a weakening economy, and ethnic violence. In December 1992 and 1997 elections that were free if not completely fair, Moi was reelected president. However, in 1993 the country was plunged into bloody ethnic strife. Moi was required constitutionally to step down in 2002 and was replaced by Mwai Kibaki, ending almost 40 years of rule by Moi's party.

Lesotho

Official name: *Kingdom of Lesotho*
Area: *11,715 sq. mi., 30,350 sq. km.*
Type of government:
    Constitutional monarchy
Population: *1,858,000*
Capital and largest city: *Maseru*
    (Pop., 138,000)
Languages: *English, Sesotho, Zulu,*
    Xhosa
Literacy: *83%;* **Currency:** *Loti*
Per capita GDP: *$2,450*
    (Rank: 125th)

The land. The Drakensberg Mountains dominate most of Lesotho. The mountains reach elevations of about 11,000 feet (3,354 meters) above sea level, but they have areas of grassland and alpine pasture. Lowlands in the west occupy about one-quarter of Lesotho. The Orange River and its tributaries flow through the country.

The climate is temperate. The winter months frequently bring heavy snow; while summer temperatures reach up to 90°F (32°C). Rainfall averages about 28 inches (72 centimeters) a year.

The people. Almost the entire population is made up of Africans of the Sotho tribe. Most of the people live in the lowlands. The majority of the population is Christian. Many thousands of Sotho are employed in the Republic of South Africa because Lesotho cannot support them. Lesotho's only major city is its capital, Maseru. Almost all of Lesotho's people live in rural areas.

Economy. Lesotho is a poverty-stricken nation. Its economy is based on subsistence agriculture, livestock raising, and the earnings of workers employed in South Africa. Subsistence farming engages about 86 percent of the workforce. The chief crops are corn, beans, sorghum, peas, and wheat. Cattle, sheep, and goats are raised throughout the country, and hides, wool, and mohair are produced.

There are only a few small industries in Lesotho. Mineral deposits, except for diamonds, have not been discovered. Diamond mining is important to the economy.

Lesotho imports food, machinery, vehicles, manufactured goods, and petroleum products. Exports include wool and mohair, diamonds, and livestock. Most of Lesotho's trade is with the Republic of South Africa, with which Lesotho has a customs union. Lesotho receives financial aid from Great Britain.

Government. In 1990 the king, who held executive and legislative authority, was stripped of power. After a 1991 coup the king was returned to the throne as a figurehead and a constitution was instituted. Legislative power resides with a bicameral parliament, the Senate (principal chiefs and members of the ruling party), and the Assembly (popularly elected). The leader of the majority party of the Assembly becomes the prime minister.

History. The Sotho tribal grouping emerged in the early 1800s from the union of Bantu-speaking peoples under the leadership of a northern chief, Moshoeshoe. Moshoeshoe had successfully defended these peoples from raiding Zulu and Ndebele bands.

The newly organized nation ran into conflict with the Boers, Dutch farmers migrating northward from the Orange Free State. The conflicts led Moshoeshoe to sign a treaty of friendship with

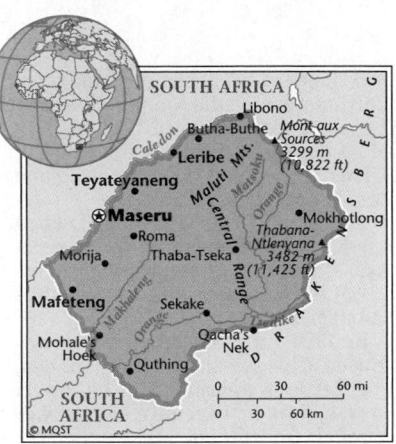

the British governor of Cape Colony. In 1868 Great Britain declared a protectorate over this territory, which they called Basutoland, to prevent seizure of the country by the neighboring Orange Free State.

British rule. In 1871, a year after the death of Moshoeshoe, the British gave control of Basutoland to Cape Colony. Between 1880 and 1882 Cape Colony troops waged the Gun Wars, a series of military campaigns, to disarm Basutoland's inhabitants, who had rebelled against Cape Colony rule. The effort failed, and Cape Colony abandoned the territory. In 1884 Basutoland became a British High Commission Territory.

The British administered the territory through a resident commissioner who rarely acted contrary to the wishes of the paramount chief. Sotho traditional law survived under British rule.

Basutoland's economic affairs were tied to those of South Africa, and until 1948 Great Britain assumed that South Africa would eventually incorporate Basutoland. Union with South Africa was unacceptable to Basutoland, however, because of South Africa's policy of apartheid, or rigid separation of the races.

Nationalism. In the 1950s the Basutoland African Congress, an African nationalist organization, campaigned for Basutoland's independence. The congress also sought support from Great Britain and the United Nations to lessen Basutoland's economic dependence on South Africa.

In 1964 Britain abolished the High Commission and appointed a representative to Basutoland. On October 4,

MANY WILD ANIMALS populate Kenya's national parks and game preserves and attract a large number of tourists each year.

1966, Basutoland became an independent member of the Commonwealth. The new nation, renamed Lesotho, was led by the Sotho chief, Moshoeshoe II. In 1967 the king accepted the role of a constitutional monarch.

In 1970 Prime Minister Leabua Jonathan seized control of the government. A military coup overthrew Jonathan in 1986 and reinstated King Moshoeshoe II as chief of state.

In 1990 King Moshoeshoe II was stripped of his power and exiled. His son, King Letsie, was installed in his place, but was given no executive authority. A National Constituent Assembly was established to create a new constitution and lead Lesotho back to democratic civilian rule. A coup in 1991 ousted Justin Lekhanya as chairman of the military council. Parliamentary elections were held in 1993.

Liberia

Official name: *Republic of Liberia*
Area: *43,323 sq. mi.,*
111,370 sq. km.
Type of government: *Republic*
Population: *3,262,000*
Capital and largest city: *Monrovia*
(Pop., 421,000)
Languages: *English (official),*
Niger-Congo
Literacy: *38%;* **Currency:** *Dollar*
Per capita GDP: *$1,100*
(Rank: 164th)

The land.   Most of Liberia is occupied by hills and low uplands. The country has a rocky coastline, beyond which are swampy plains. In the north, along the border with Guinea, are the grass-covered Nimba Mountains, with elevations of about 4,500 feet (1,372 meters). The Lofa, St. Paul, St. John, and Cestos rivers flow through the country.

Liberia has a hot and humid tropical climate and is one of the rainiest areas in Western Africa. The rainy season extends from May through October. Rainfall aver-

meters
US

metres
Brit.

colonizers
US

colonisers
Brit.

RUBBER tree plantations help support Liberia's economy.

ages more than 140 inches (359 centimeters) a year in the coastal region and over 100 inches (256 centimeters) a year in the interior of the country.

The people.   There are two distinct population groups in Liberia—the Americo-Liberians, descended from blacks brought to Liberia from the United States during the 1800s, and the tribal peoples, who form the majority of Liberia's people. Liberia's indigenous tribes include the Kpelle, Bassa, Gio, Kru, and Grebo.

The major cities of Liberia are Monrovia, the capital and largest city, and Buchanan.

Economy.   Liberia's economy is based on subsistence agriculture, mining, and rubber growing. Eighty percent of the workforce is engaged in agriculture. The people raise cassava, rice, palm fruit, and bananas for local consumption. Commercial fishing is a growing industry.

Liberia exported only palm oil products, coffee, and cassava until 1926, when the Firestone Rubber Company established rubber plantations in Liberia and lent the government capital for development. In the 1960s other private companies established rubber plantations, and in 1986 over 4.75 million cubic meters were produced, mostly by foreign companies.

Two-thirds of Liberia's national product comes from mining. The nation is a top iron ore producer. Diamonds are also important.

Liberia's main imports are food, fuel, and machinery. The main exports are iron ore and natural rubber. Coffee, cocoa, and timber are also grown for export. Most trade is conducted with the United States, Germany, Italy, the Netherlands, and Japan.

Government.   After years of civil war, free and open presidential and legisla-

tive elections were held in 1997. The president and bicameral legislature are elected by popular vote.

History.   Liberia's tribal groups migrated to the area between the 12th and the 16th centuries. A large number of people arrived as refugees from the destruction of the Songhai Empire in the 15th century.

Europeans also began establishing trading posts in Liberia in the 15th century. In 1822 the American Colonization Society began to settle freed slaves from the United States in Liberia. Malaria killed most of the original colonizers, but several new groups followed. They negotiated treaties with the native tribes until consolidation of the land was completed in 1838.

Agents of the American Colonization Society administered the region until July 26, 1847, when Liberia declared its independence. Most world powers quickly recognized the new nation's independence, but the United States withheld recognition until 1862.

In the early 1900s Liberia was faced with a financial crisis when the world market price for its coffee dropped. Liberia sought the aid of foreign countries. In 1926 the Firestone Rubber Company leased large land areas from Liberia, providing an important source of revenue. In the 1930s a League of Nations study of labor conditions uncovered widespread forced labor. This resulted in the resignation of Liberia's president, Charles D. B. King.

During World War II U.S. soldiers built the first roads into the interior, and in 1948 a modern port built with U.S. money opened at Monrovia.

William V. S. Tubman was president of Liberia from 1944 to 1971. He ended the Firestone's monopoly in the rubber industry by inaugurating an open-door policy of international investment. He also initiated the development of the country's rich resources of iron ore. Tubman died in 1971 and was succeeded by William R. Tolbert, who attempted to reform the government but met with growing discontent over the minority Americo-Liberian rule. As he turned to oppressive forms of control, riots broke out in 1979. In a military coup in 1980, Tolbert and many of his top aides were killed.

The military government, led by Samuel K. Doe, suspended the constitution but promised to return the government to civilian rule. A new constitution was drafted and elections were held in 1985. Doe was elected president and inaugurated in 1986.

Regional disputes over continued government corruption erupted into a civil war in 1989, when Libyan-backed followers of Charles Taylor, the leader of the National Patriotic Front, invaded Liberia from Côte d'Ivoire. Doe was killed in 1990 by rebel forces. Before the first cease-fire was declared in 1990, over 20,000 Liberians had been killed and 500,000 had been uprooted. Fighting continued, with periodic cease-fires, until July 1993

Three years of civil war culminated in the summer of 2003 when rebels surrounded Monrovia intent on overthrowing Taylor. After the arrival of Nigerian peacekeepers and under international pressure, Taylor stepped down on August 11, 2003 and took promised asylum in Nigeria. In October government representatives and rebel factions chose a leader for an interim government. Sporadic fighting continues and UN peacekeepers remain.

Libya

Official name: *Great Socialist People's Libyan Arab Jamahiriya*

Area: *684,461 sq. mi., 1,759,540 sq. km.*

Type of government: *Dictatorship*

Population: *5,369,000*

Capital and largest city: *Tripoli (Pop., 1,500,000)*

Language: *Arabic, Italian, English*

Literacy: *76%;* **Currency:** *Dinar*

Per capita GDP: *$7,600 (Rank: 66th)*

The land. Libya is almost entirely desert. Less than 2 percent of the land is cultivated, and less than 1 percent is forested.

The Gulf of Sidra (Sirte) divides Libya's Mediterranean coast into two major segments, northern Tripolitania in the west and northern Cyrenaica in the east. There are oases in the coastal region separated from each other by sand dunes and salt marshes. There are highlands beyond the coast, including

the Jebel Nafusah in Tripolitania and the Jebel at Akhdar in Cyrenaica.

The Sahara, the desert that covers most of North Africa, has many landscapes, three of which are important in Libya—upland bare rock surfaces, as in the Hammada al-Hamra in southern Tripolitania; gravel-covered plains, as in the Serir Tibesti in the south; and areas of extensive sand dunes, as in the Idehan Murzuk in the southwestern Fezzan region and the Calansho Sand Sea in the east.

There are few oases in southern and eastern Libya. Oases are more common in the Fezzan, where they are usually formed by springs and wells in valleys and at the foot of escarpments.

Libya does not have any year-round rivers, but there are dry water routes in many parts of the country. There are deep, salty lakes in Libya, the largest of which is Arrashia, in Cyrenaica. Rainfall averages about 14 inches (36 centimeters) a year along the Mediterranean coast. There is virtually no rainfall in the desert regions.

The people. Most of the people in Libya are Arabic-speaking Sunni Muslims of mixed Arab and Berber origin. There are also some Berber-speaking peoples in northern Libya and in the desert region. Italians form the largest European community in Libya. A large portion of the labor force is foreign.

Libya is one of Africa's least densely populated countries. Ninety percent of the people live on less than 10 percent of the land. Only at oases in the Sahara and near the borders of the Mediterranean Sea is permanent human habitation possible. Many of the people are nomads who must move about in the desert in search of grazing land for their flocks. Fifty percent of the population is under age 15. Most of the cities and towns are concentrated in the coastal region. Libya's largest cities are Tripoli, the capital; Banghazi (population, 800,000); and Misurata (360,000).

Economy. The modern economy of Libya is based on oil production. The traditional part of the economy is based on dates and other produce of the coast and oases, flocks and herds raised by the nomads, the catch of Mediterranean fishermen, and urban crafts.

Since 1959 economic life has been almost completely altered by the production of petroleum, particularly from the Zelten and Dahra fields, both of which have pipelines leading to the Gulf of Sidra. In 1989 Libya produced over 53 million metric tons of petroleum, an enormous amount that now accounts for over half of the country's gross national product and for 95 percent of export earnings.

Almost 20 percent of the population is engaged in subsistence farming, although only 5 percent of the land is arable. Barley, date palms, citrus fruits, and peanuts are grown, mostly in the coastal region, where there is sufficient rainfall for crops. Date palms are also grown in the desert oases. Sheep, camels, and goats are raised by nomads,

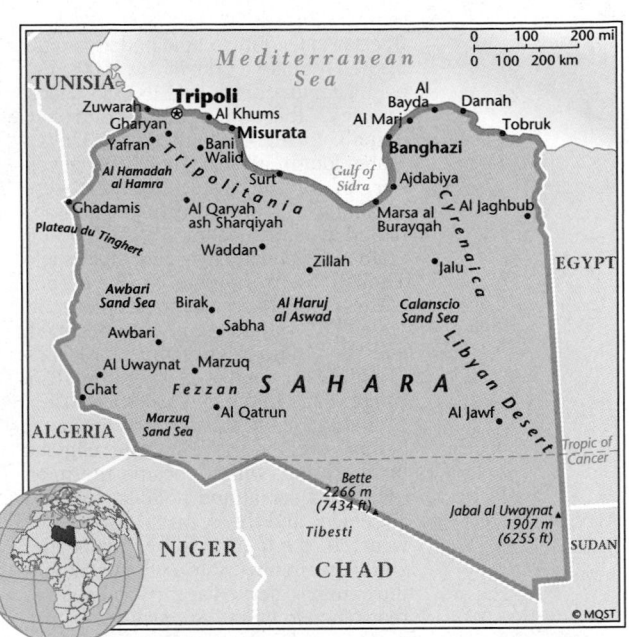

mainly in Cyrenaica. Forty percent of Libya's food is imported.

Libya's industry centers on the production and processing of its oil and its agricultural products. There are canneries in Tripolitania that process fish caught in the coastal waters. The country's main imports are food, chemicals, manufactured goods, textiles, iron and steel, and machinery. Although Libya's chief export is petroleum, hides and skins, peanuts, and fruits are also important exports. Most of Libya's trade is conducted with Italy, Germany, France, Spain, and Great Britain.

Government. The General People's Congress (GPC) is officially the highest policy-making body in Libya. The GPC is made up of officials from the provincial and municipal congresses. The GPC appoints the general secretary, effectively the prime minister, and the General People's Committee, which has executive power. A revolutionary leader, however, is the de facto chief of state.

History. Libya's three main regions have had a separate existence for most of the country's history. Even after the Arab conquest of the region in the mid-600s, Cyrenaica was administered for the most part from Egypt and Tripolitania was administered by dynasties in northwestern Africa. The Fezzan has also had its own distinctive history. Regional differences are still important in modern-day Libya.

labor
US

labour
Brit.

centers
US

centres
Brit.

MANY OF THE people of Libya are nomads who depend upon the camel for their livelihood.

Ottoman era. Libya came under the rule of the Ottoman Turks in the 1500s. For over a century, from 1711 to 1835, a local dynasty, the Qaramanli, controlled Tripoli. In the early 1800s the United States fought against the bey, or governor, of Tripoli, whose pirates were raiding U.S. ships. European nations united to eliminate piracy in the Barbary States—Tripoli in Libya plus Algiers and Tunis to the west—thus cutting off one of the major sources of government revenue. The Qaramanli regime declined, and the Ottoman government reestablished direct control of Tripoli in 1835.

Italian rule. In the mid-1800s a Muslim, Muhammad ibn Ali, known as the Great Sanusi, created the Sanusian religious brotherhood, which became the most important social and political force in Cyrenaica and the Fezzan. In 1911 Italy wrested control of Libya from the Ottoman Empire after a short war, and the Sanusiya served as the focal point of resistance to Italian colonialism.

During World War II major battles were fought in Libya. The North African campaigns virtually wiped out the Italian colonial settlements. After the war a defeated Italy was stripped of its colonies. A deadlock over which major power should assume trusteeship for Libya led to the decision to give the former colony complete independence.

Independence. Libya became a unified state in 1963, and the Sanusian chief, Idris, became king. Increased oil revenues were channeled into low-cost housing, education, and roads. This policy continues under Colonel Muammar al-Qadhafi, who took power in 1969 and was elected leader of the Revolutionary Command Council in 1977. The council advocates unity of all Arab countries and has taken steps to rid the country of foreign investors.

Qadhafi has led Libya into socialism and Muslim traditionalism. After 1975 Soviet political ties were strengthened, but Libya, while supporting communism as an international ideal, makes its own domestic and external decisions. It engaged in border clashes with Egypt and Chad in 1977 (fighting in Chad lasted until 1987), and in 1979 aided Uganda's government against a rebellion.

Libya is a virtual police state under the rule of Qadhafi, who has provided facilities, training, and support for international terrorists. In 1986 the United States imposed economic sanctions against Libya in response to its support of terrorist groups. Later that year, U.S. warplanes were sent to attack terrorist-related targets in Tripoli and Benghazi.

In March 1992 the United Nations imposed sanctions against Libya for its refusal to allow the extradition of two nationals suspected of involvement in the bombing of a Pan American Airways jetliner over Lockerbie, Scotland, in 1988. In 1999 Libya surrendered the suspects. But, only when Libya admitted liability and paid remuneration to victims' families in 2003, did the UN formally remove sanctions.

Madagascar

Official name: *Republic of Madagascar*
Area: *226,597 sq. mi., 587,040 sq. km.*
Type of government: *Republic*
Population: *16,473,000*
Capital and largest city:
Antananarivo
(Pop., 1,103,000)
Languages: *Malagasy, French (both official)*
Literacy: *80%;* **Currency:** *Franc*
Per capita GDP: *$870*
(Rank: 175th)

The land. An island nation off the east coast of Africa, Madagascar is about 1,000 miles (1,613 kilometers) long and 360 miles (581 kilometers) at its greatest width, making it the world's fourth-largest island. Most of the island is dominated by a great interior highland, which has an average elevation of about 4,000 feet (1,220 meters) above sea level.

The highland contains deep canyons and volcanic mountains, with elevations as high as about 9,400 feet (2,866 meters). Steep cliffs border the highlands, especially in the east. The major rivers are the Mangoky, Betsiboka, and Tsiribihina.

Trade winds bring heavy rains, about 146 inches (374 centimeters) annually, to eastern Madagascar, but it is dry to the west of the cliffs and in the south, where less than 14 inches (36 centimeters) of rain fall annually.

In recent years the island of Madagascar has become dangerously deforested, causing severe soil erosion.

The people. Madagascar's indigenous population is made up of 18 different ethnic groups. The largest is the Merina, who live mainly in the central highlands and are important in the political life of the country. The Betsimisaraka are the largest coastal group. The Betsileo people live in the central highlands. The country's largest city is its capital, Antananarivo, which is situated in the highlands. Other cities include Fianarantsoa (population, 109,000) and Toamasina (138,000).

The population is predominantly rural. The majority of the people are animists, although a large minority of people are Christian.

Economy. The economy of the island nation has suffered because of its isolation. Madagascar's economy is based on agriculture. Eighty-five percent of the work force is engaged in farming, which provides about 80 percent of the country's export earnings. Coffee, vanilla, rice, sugar, and cloves are the principal cash crops. Rice, corn, bananas, and sweet potatoes are the main food crops. Livestock raising is an important activity in the west and the south.

Although mineral resources are considerable, they are not well developed.

However, Madagascar is a major producer of graphite. The island also began producing bauxite, chromium, and nickel in the 1970s; most hopes for the economy's future growth rest on the developing mining industry.

Food processing is the main industry, while the oil refining, fertilizer, textile, and cement production industries are growing.

In 1986 the government initiated economic reforms directed at developing self-sufficiency in food production as well as increasing exports. Despite rigorous reforms, Madagascar remained strapped with debt and unable to increase agricultural production above the level of population growth.

Imports include manufactured goods, especially textiles, iron and steel, machinery, petroleum products, and food. Major exports include coffee, cloves, vanilla, sugar, tobacco and animal products. Most trade is conducted with France, Germany, and the United States. Madagascar receives economic assistance from France.

Government. A new constitution was approved by referendum in 1992. By its terms, the head of state is a president who is popularly elected to a 5-year term. Legislative power resides with a bicameral parliament consisting of a National Assembly, whose members are popularly elected, and a Senate, whose members are appointed by an electoral college and by the president. The National Assembly chooses a prime minister.

History. Historians believe that Madagascar was first inhabited during the first century A.D., when Indonesian explorers arrived, probably by way of southern India and eastern Africa. They are considered the distant ancestors of the Merina and Betsileo.

Arab traders established small, feudal principalities along the Madagascar coast as early as the 1000s or 1100s. In

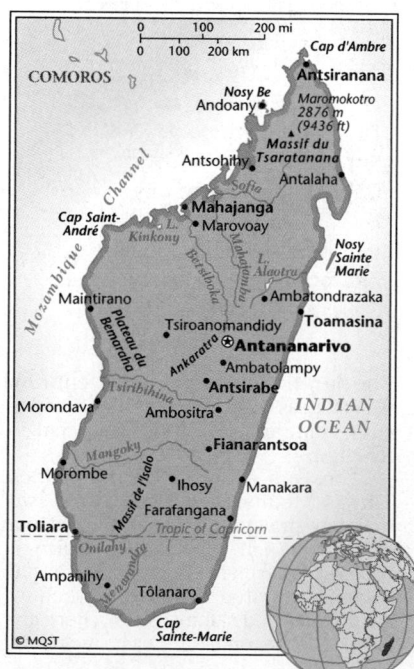

the 1500s and 1600s, Dutch, French, and British merchants established trading and supply posts on the island as part of their routes to India. Buccaneers established a short-lived republic on the island in the 1700s.

During the 1500s and 1600s the indigenous peoples were involved in civil wars. Confederations and military commands were established on the island, but most collapsed because of internal strains or the rebellion of subjugated peoples. In the central plateau, however, the Merina people slowly expanded their area.

In the early 1800s a Merina king, Radama I, brought European advisers to his court, welcomed missionaries, and instituted education in the Malagasy language. Later rulers played the British and the French off against one another. In 1890 French claims to Madagascar were recognized by Great Britain, and in 1896 Madagascar became a French colony. France abolished the Merina monarchy and exiled the queen. By 1904 the French controlled the island.

Contemporary Madagascar. Local nationalist movements emerged briefly during World War I and again in the 1920s. In 1947 discontent over land confiscation and the periodic imposition of involuntary labor led to a serious revolt. France suppressed the revolt and took steps to develop Madagascar's economy, but also prohibited political activity.

In 1956 France changed its policy toward overseas possessions and permitted political activity in all French African colonies. Of the several political parties that emerged in Madagascar, the nationalist Social Democratic Party (PSD) won power.

In October 1958, under the leadership of the PSD headed by Philibert Tsiranana, Madagascar became an autonomous republic within the French Community. In June 1960 the country became the Malagasy Republic (later reverting to Madagascar), an independent republic with a presidential system of government. Discontent over European control of the economy led to civil unrest, culminating in military coups in 1972 and 1975. Massive Chinese aid was

THE TRUE LEMUR is an arboreal primate, 20 species of which live in Madagascar.

accepted and French-owned plantations were nationalized. Political and civil disturbances have continued, however, and President Didier Ratsiraka, resorted to stern military rule to maintain order.

In the early 1980s, Ratsiraka tried to create a one-party state, but he met with fierce opposition. New political parties have formed since and a period of censorship of the press has ended.

In 1989 the first multiparty elections in 14 years were held in Madagascar. Ratsiraka was elected for a third term. Open parliamentary elections were also held in 1989. In 1991 demonstrations broke out in protest of government corruption, including the alleged rigging of election results. In February 1993 Albert Zafy defeated Ratsiraka for the presidency, but Ratsiraka was reelected in 1997. Inconclusive elections in 2001 resulted in Ratsiraka and another candidate claiming victory. After a recount and minor skirmishes, Marc Ravalomanana became president.

Malawi

Official name: *Republic of Malawi*
Area: *45,733 sq. mi., 118,480 sq. km.*
Type of government: *Multiparty democracy*
Population: *11,393,000*
Capital: *Lilongwe (Pop., 440,000)*
Largest city: *Blantyre (Pop., 502,000)*
Languages: *English, Chichewa (both official)*
Literacy: *58%*
Currency: *Kwacha*
Per capita GDP: *$660 (Rank: 186th)*

The land. Most of Malawi is occupied by mountains and plateaus. Because of its rugged terrain, Malawi has been described as "Switzerland without snow." The Great Rift Valley runs through Malawi in a north-south line. Lake Nyasa, or Malawi, which stretches along the eastern border, lies in the valley. The Shire River, the lake's outlet, flows southward into Mozambique.

West of the lake the land climbs steeply to a plateau with elevations between 4,000 and 7,000 feet (1,220 and 2,134 meters). The Shire Highlands are south of Lake Nyasa. East of the Shire River is Mt. Mlanje, which has an elevation of about 9,800 feet (2,988 meters).

The lake region of Malawi has a generally hot, humid climate. Temperatures throughout the rest of the country vary with differences in altitude. Average annual rainfall varies between 33 and 59 inches (85 and 151 centimeters).

The people. Most of Malawi's people are Bantu-speaking. The largest groups, the Nyanja and the Chewa, live mainly near Lake Nyasa. The Chewa live on the

west side of the lake in the central region. The Nyanja live to the south of the lake. The Nyanja are descendants of early inhabitants of Malawi. There are also communities of European and Asians.

Lilongwe, the country's capital, in central Malawi; Blantyre (population, 502,000) and Zomba (66,000) in the southern part of the country; and Mzuzu (87,000) in the north are Malawi's largest cities.

Most of the people live in rural areas. Malawi is a fairly densely populated country.

Economy. The economy of Malawi is based on agriculture. Ninety percent of the population is engaged in subsistence farming. Malawi's resources cannot support its population, and many workers find employment in nearby countries. Basic food crops include corn, millet, cassava, peanuts, and rice. Commercial crops include cotton, tobacco, sugar, and tea.

Industry consists mostly of processing agricultural products; consumer goods and construction materials are also manufactured. The mining of coal is helping to reduce coal imports. Industry now contributes 13 percent of the gross national product, compared with 50 percent contributed by agriculture. Tourism is also increasing in importance, but Malawi's landlocked position and its limited transportation system have slowed development.

The country's major imports are industrial materials, mostly iron and steel, machinery, consumer goods, and transportation equipment. Exports include tobacco, tea, sugar, coffee, and cotton. Most of Malawi's trade is with South Africa, Great Britain, and the United States.

Government. Malawi is headed by a president who controls a parliament of 141 elected members and an unlimited number of appointed members. In 1993 Malawians approved a referendum for multiparty democracy.

History. Malawi owes its name to the Malawi,

labor
US

labour
Brit.

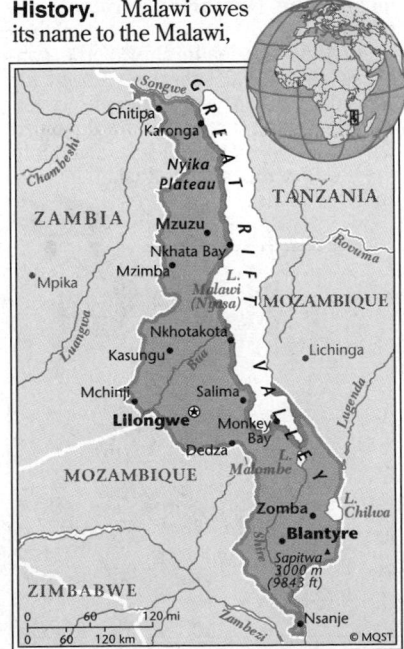

or Maravi, people who entered the area in the 15th century. The Malawi divided when they reached the northern end of Lake Nyasa. One group, ancestors of the present-day Chewa, migrated south to the west bank of the lake. The other group, ancestors of the Nyanja, travelled down the east side of the lake and settled in the area south of the lake. By A.D. 1500, the two groups combined to establish one vast empire. In the mid-1500s, Portuguese explorers were the first Europeans to encounter the Malawi Empire.

The western shore of Lake Nyasa became a popular route for Bantu-speaking immigrants entering central Africa from the north, and by the 1800s the area's dense population made it a favorite target for Arab slave raiders, who bought slaves from the Bantus.

European interest in present-day Malawi originated in the 1870s, after the explorations of David Livingstone and other Scottish missionaries who were anxious to put an end to the slave trade. In 1889 missionary pressure for governmental action against the Arab slave traders and the threat of Portuguese occupation led Great Britain to declare the area the British Central Africa Protectorate.

Cecil Rhodes's British South Africa Company financed the region's administration in the early years of the protectorate, but a dispute over political control led the British government to accept complete responsibility for the territory. In 1907 the name of the area was changed to Nyasaland.

Nationalism. African nationalist movements developed early in Nyasaland, organized by politically conscious laborers returning from work in the mines of Northern and Southern Rhodesia (now Zambia and Zimbabwe) and South Africa. Because of resentment of British colonial policies and fear of federation with both the Rhodesias, nationalists formed the Nyasaland African Congress in 1944.

In 1951 the leadership of the congress demanded self-government for Nyasaland. Two years later, however, against African sentiment, Britain joined the two Rhodesians and Nyasaland into the Federation of Rhodesia and Nyasaland.

Nationalists, under the leadership of Dr. Hastings Banda, attracted wide support in denouncing the federation. Great Britain finally agreed to an African-elected majority in the Nyasaland legislative council, and in 1961 elections. Dr. Banda's nationalist Malawi Congress Party won an impressive victory.

Independence. Great Britain formally dissolved the federation in 1963, and on July 6, 1964, the country of Malawi became independent, with Banda as its prime minister.

In 1966 Malawi became a republic, and Banda became the first president. In 1967 Malawi signed a trade agreement with South Africa, despite South Africa's policy of apartheid and the opposition of other African countries. The two countries remained at odds over the apartheid issue, but maintained close economic ties.

Dr. Banda was declared president for life in 1970, and his control has become increasingly dictatorial since then. He dismissed his cabinet in 1977.

Mozambican refugees began fleeing to Malawi in large numbers in the middle 1980s; by the end of the decade, almost 500,000 refugees were living in Malawi. The government continued to offer assistance and refuge, although the refugees put an enormous strain on the economy. Bakili Muluzi was elected president in 1994 in the first free election, and reelected in 1999.

AFRICAN SCULPTURE has influenced Western art in the 20th century.

interethnic harmony, which is relatively rare among African states.

Mali is very sparsely populated. Most of the people live in small towns and villages. The country's largest cities are Bamako, the capital; Ségou (population, 88,000); Mopti (82,000); and Sikasso (157,000). Most are near the Niger River or its tributaries.

Economy. The economy of Mali is based on agriculture. About 75 percent of the work force is engaged in agricultural activities. Millet, rice, and corn are the basic food crops. The principal commercial crops are peanuts and cotton. Fish from the Niger River are also an important export. Cattle, sheep, and goats are raised, mainly in central and northern Mali. Cotton and livestock account for almost 90 percent of Mali's annual export earnings.

The Niger River valley is the most productive region in Mali. There is a large irrigation project on the upper part of the river.

There is very little mining, although there are deposits of salt, bauxite, phosphates, manganese, zinc, copper, and gold. Industry consists mainly of agricultural processing for domestic consumption and export. Industrial development is hampered by the country's landlocked position.

Other important exports are peanuts and dried fish. Major imports include manufactured goods—especially textiles, iron and steel, and machinery—and sugar. Most trade is conducted with neighboring countries and with France, Belgium, and Germany.

Government. A new constitution adopted in 1992 provides for multiparty government. Executive power is vested in a president, who is elected to a 5-year term. The president appoints a prime minister, who in turn appoints a Council of Ministers. Legislative power rests with a 147-seat National Assembly whose members are elected to 5-year terms.

History. Evidence of human life in Mali goes back about 4,200 years. Mali

laborers *US*

labourers *Brit.*

centimeters *US*

centimetres *Brit.*

Mali

Official name: *Republic of Mali*
Area: *478,714 sq. mi., 1,240,192 sq. km.*
Type of government: *Republic*
Population: *11,300,000*
Capital and largest city: *Bamako (Pop., 1,179,000)*
Languages: *French (official), Bambara, African dialects*
Literacy: *38%*
Currency: *CFA franc*
Per capita GDP: *$840 (Rank: 178th)*

The land. Most of Mali is flat, with areas of low plateaus. The vast desert wasteland of the Sahara occupies the northern third of the country. In the northeast is the Adrar des Iforas mountain region.

The Niger River flows through southern Mali, and the Senegal River flows from southwestern Mali. The desert region is hot and dry, but the southern part of the country is cooler. The most rain is received in the south, about 35 inches (90 centimeters) annually, while almost no rain falls in the northern desert.

The people. There are many different ethnic groups in Mali. The largest are the Mande, followed by the Fulani and over 20 others. Mali has a legacy of

A MOSQUE in Mopti, Mali

became a popular area as the Sahara dried out during the same period. The medieval kingdom of Ghana prospered in Mali and portions of Mauritania and Senegal between A.D. 800 and 1050. Trade was brisk during this period because of Mali's position as an outpost for trans-Saharan trade. Ghana thrived in the trade of gold and slaves. Islam was introduced to the kingdom in the 10th century. In the early A.D. 1200s Sundiata, a powerful leader of a group of Mande people, defeated Sumanguru, ruler of the Susu kingdom of Kaniaga, and created the Mali Empire. By the 1300s this empire stretched from the Gambia River to what is now the northwestern border of Nigeria. The people of Mali traded gold from the upper Niger and Senegal River regions for the salt of the Sahara and luxury goods from northwestern Africa.

In the early 1300s, Mali's most illustrious ruler, Mansa Musa (ruled 1312–1337), extended the empire from Niger to the southern Sahara. The Mali Empire was well known to the Arab world, particularly following a lavish pilgrimage by the emperor to Mecca in 1324.

In the late 1400s the then-ruler of Mali was overthrown by the king of the new state of Songhai. The Songhai kings governed the vast area once loyal to Musa until 1591, when a Moroccan army crossed the Sahara and defeated the Songhai. The Moroccan army was not strong enough to control the entire empire, and the territory broke up into smaller city-states.

During the 1800s two Muslim reformers, Ahmadu Lobo and al-Hajj Umar, created Islamic theocracies in the region. The creation of the Islamic states was one phase of a wave of religious revivalism that swept tropical Africa south of the Sahara.

French rule. France at that time was extending its colonial rule southward from northern Africa, and al-Hajj Umar's state clashed with French forces. By 1880 France had emerged victorious, and in 1895 France formed the colony of the Soudan, which it administered as part of French West Africa. In 1946 this area became a territory, and in 1958 the territory became an autonomous member of the French Community.

In 1959 France joined the Soudan with Senegal to form the Mali Federation, and in June 1960 the federation became an autonomous member of the French Community. Two months later Senegal withdrew from the federation, and on September 22, 1960, the former Soudan withdrew from the French Community and proclaimed itself the Republic of Mali.

Independence. Modibo Keita became the first president of the new republic in 1960. He was ousted in 1968 in a bloodless coup led by army officers; Moussa Traoré took over the presidency. Traoré was elected as president in 1979 when Mali's new constitution came into effect.

Under Keita, Mali, aided by China, had turned to socialism. Traoré quickly dissolved the agricultural collectives and encouraged private enterprise, so that exports and agricultural production, especially of cotton, improved significantly. However, the economy suffered from severe droughts and famines. Mali receives economic aid from many countries, especially France.

Economic decline during the 1980s was met with outbreaks of protest in 1991, and Traoré was overthrown. A new constitution was approved and Alpha Oumar Konare became president in a free election in 1992. Free elections continue.

Mauritania

Official name: *Islamic Republic of Mauritania*

Area: *397,850 sq. mi., 1,030,700 sq. km.*

Type of government: *Republic*

Population: *2,829,000*

Capital and largest city:
Nouakchott
(Pop., metro. area, 612,000)

Languages: *Hasaniya Arabic and Wolof (both official), Pular, Soninke*

Literacy: *41%*

Currency: *Ouguiya*

Per capita GDP: *$1,800 (Rank 139th)*

The land. About three-fourths of Mauritania is desert. In the west long lines of sand dunes are separated by broad lowlands. In the north and east rocky desert surfaces are common. There is cultivated land in the southwest, near the Senegal River, which flows along the country's southwestern border. The climate of Mauritania is generally hot and dry. Rainfall varies from less than 4 inches (10 centimeters) annually in the desert to 25 inches (64 centimeters) in the extreme south.

The people. Most Mauritanians are nomadic Moors, people of mixed Berber and Arab stock. Black Africans, mostly Tukulor and Fulani, live in southern Mauritania, mainly near the Senegal River; Tuareg people live in the central part of the country. Mauritania's largest cities are Nouakchott, the capital; Nouâdhibou (population, metro. area, 76,000); and Kaédi (metro. area, 107,000).

Nearly all of the people are Muslims. Mauritania is lightly populated. Because of the endemic drought in the early 1980s, many nomads and oasis dwellers have migrated to urban areas.

Economy. Following its independence, Mauritania developed mining enterprises, but it remains a poor country with a small gross national product. Its gross national product is now about 30 percent agricultural and 25 percent industrial.

Agriculture is based on livestock breeding. Sheep, cattle, goats, and camels are raised, mainly in central and northern Mauritania. The only considerable area of cultivated land is in the Chemanna, the Mauritanian part of the Senegal River valley. About 80 percent of the population is engaged in subsistence agriculture.

The basic food crops are millet, dates, rice, and corn. Acacia trees, the source of gum arabic, are grown in the central part of the country. Fish from the Senegal River also provide an important source of income.

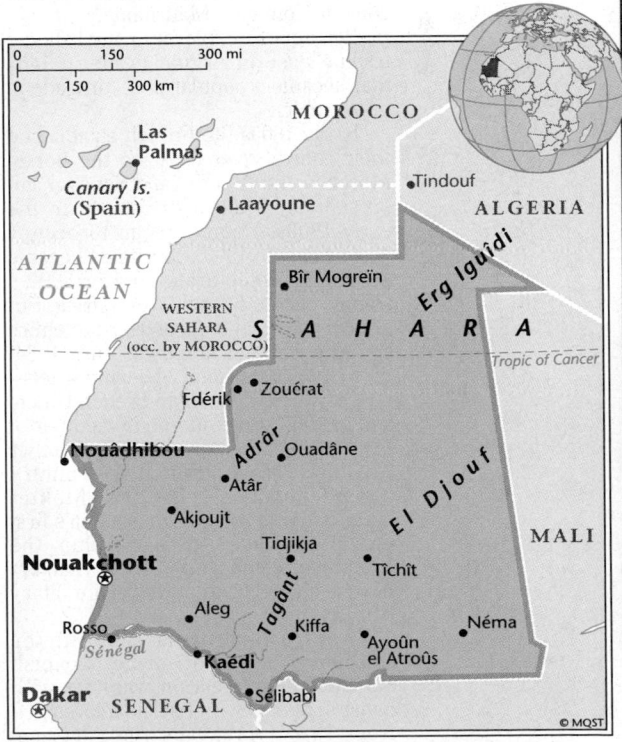

The country's mining wealth is based on its iron ore deposits, mainly at Fdérik in the north. Gypsum and copper are also important.

Iron ore, fish, and fish products are the major exports. Major imports are manufactured goods, machinery, and foodstuffs. Most trade is conducted with France, Italy, Spain, and Japan.

Government. A new constitution, implemented in 1991, established Mauritania as a multiparty democracy. The head of state is a president who is popularly elected. The president appoints a prime minister, who is head of government. Legislative power resides with a bicameral legislature, consisting of an 81-member National Assembly and a 56-member Senate.

History. In about the ninth century, a confederation of nomadic Berbers entered Mauritania from the north and forced the existing black population southward. The Berbers adopted Islam in the 900s, but retained many of their traditional beliefs. In the 11th century, they united to form the Almoravids, which quickly became a powerful religious and political force.

The Almoravids overran Morocco, western Algeria, and Muslim Spain. Their leaders founded the famous city of Marrakesh, in Morocco, and established a dynasty that lasted almost a hundred years. A branch of the Almoravids went south and conquered the empire of Ghana in 1076. Starting in the 1300s, nomadic Arabs migrated into Mauritania.

After hundreds of years of migration, the Beni Hasan, a branch of the Bedouins, asserted dominance over the Berbers in Mali and Mauritania in the 15th century. The intermarriage that occurred between Bedouins and Berbers created the Moors, who would come to dominate Mauritania.

Portuguese explorers established a trading post on Arguin Island in 1461 that became a popular post for trade in gum arabic.

In the 1800s the French established their control over areas to the north, Morocco and Algeria, and Senegal and present-day Mali to the south. In the early 1900s, France began to occupy Mauritania. In 1903 Mauritania became a French protectorate, and in 1920 a colony, part of French West Africa. But effective French control over the entire country was not achieved until 1934.

In 1946 Mauritania became a territory in the newly formed French Union, and in 1958 an autonomous member of the French Community. On November 28, 1960, France granted the country its independence. In 1961 Moktar Ould Daddah became Mauritania's first president. Under his leadership, the country was modernized somewhat, but he was ousted from power in a military coup in 1978.

In 1976 Mauritania annexed the southern portion of former Spanish Sahara, but this action was met with Saharan guerrilla reprisal attacks staged from 1976 to 1980 by the Algerian-backed Polisario Front. Mauritania's ruling military government renounced its claim to the territory in 1980 and Morocco promptly annexed it.

In 1986 and 1987, Mauritania held regional and local elections in a step toward restoring democracy.

In 1989, 40,000 black Senegalese workers were expelled from Mauritania, sparking border disputes between Mauritania and Senegal.

The first multiparty presidential election was held in 1992, but in 2002 some opposition parties were banned, ensuring the 2003 reelection of the sitting president, Maaoya Ould Sid Amed Taya, who has been in power since taking control of the government in 1984.

Mauritius

Official name: *Republic of Mauritius*
Area: *718 sq. mi., 1,860 sq. km.*
Type of government:
 Parliamentary democracy
Population: *1,200,000*
Capital and largest city:
 Port Louis (Pop., 128,000)
Languages: *English (official), French, Creole, Hindi*
Literacy: *83%;* **Currency:** *Rupee*
Per capita GDP: *$10,800*
 (Rank: 46th)

The land. Mauritius is an island nation that includes the island of Mauritius, Rodrigues Island, and the smaller islands of the Agalega and Cargados Carajos archipelagos. The islands of Mauritius are volcanic in origin, and Rodrigues Island rises sharply from the sea. On Mauritius, a 2,200-foot (671-meter) central plateau is rimmed by rocky mountains. Many rivers and streams flow down from the mountains. Rodrigues Island is mountainous and barren except for some fertile valleys. The Agalega Islands are low and fertile, and the Cargados Carajos Islands are little more than rocky reefs.

The country's climate is semitropical, with hot summers, cool winters, and high humidity. Rainfall is heavy—from 50 to 200 inches (128 to 513 centimeters) a year on all the islands. Cyclones are a frequent danger, especially between December and April.

The people. The population density of Mauritius is very high—almost 1,200 persons per square mile (1,935 per square kilometer).

The people of Mauritius are of varied origins, and the population is divided along ethnic lines. About two-thirds of the population is Indo-Mauritian, of Indian background; a very small minority is Sino-Mauritian, of Chinese descent; and about a third is of European, African, and mixed origins.

Major cities include Port Louis, the capital; Beau Bassin-Rose Hill (population, 104,000); Curepipe (79,000); and Quatre Bornes (72,000).

Economy. Mauritius depends heavily on sugar; about 90 percent of all cultivated land is devoted to the crop. Decreases in sugar prices and recurring cyclones that damage the sugar crops have hurt the economy.

Tea, tobacco, and fish add to the national income, and there are valuable, but unexploited, forest resources.

Production of textiles has become the country's largest industry. Sugar cane processing is another leading industry, with sugar and molasses the principal products. A related industry is the making of fiber bags for the sugar. Newer industries produce cigarettes, tea, soap, beverages, and construction materials. Tourism has also become important.

Clothing is the main export, although sugar still accounts for 34 percent of export revenues. Foodstuffs, fuels, fats, chemicals, and manufactured goods must be imported.

Most trade is with Great Britain, France, the United States, and Germany. Mauritius owes at least part of its relative economic strength to its history as a colony of both Britain and France. It enjoys special trade privileges with both countries.

Government. Mauritius's constitution, revised in 1991, provides for a president who is elected to a 5-year term by a National Assembly of up to 72 members, including 62 who are elected directly. Legislators also serve 5-year terms. The president appoints a prime minister and a Council of Ministers.

History. The uninhabited island of Mauritius was known for many centuries to Arab and Malay sailors, who probably first used it for shelter before 1000. Portuguese sailors landed on the island in the 1500s, but they did not establish settlements. The Dutch, who named the island Mauritius for their ruler, Prince Maurice, attempted to establish a colony but failed.

No successful settlement was made until 1715, when the French East India Company claimed the island for France and renamed it Ile de France. The French began sugar cultivation using slave labor.

In 1767 the French government took control from the company and made the island a naval base for use in France's

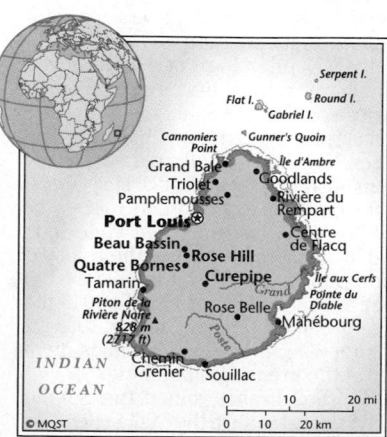

---

labor
US

labour
Brit.

meter
US

metre
Brit.

fiber
US

fibre
Brit.

struggle with Great Britain for control of India. Britain captured Ile de France in 1810, and in 1814 the Treaty of Paris awarded it the island.

British rule. Renamed Mauritius, the island was Britain's main source of sugar during the 1800s. Few Britons settled there, however, and French cultural influence remained strong. In 1833 Britain abolished slavery on Mauritius, and indentured workers, mostly from India, were brought to work the sugar plantations.

The economy grew increasingly dependent on sugar, which was subject to damage by cyclones and drought and to sharp fluctuations in world market prices.

After 1886 limited home rule was granted to Mauritius. The islands moved gradually toward fuller self-government, led mostly by the Indo-Mauritians, the dominant political force on the island.

Independence. A leader of the independence movement, Seewoosagur Ramgoolam was elected the country's first prime minister after internal self-government was granted in 1964. Mauritius moved rapidly toward independence, which was granted in March 1968. Bitter communal riots marked the months preceding and immediately following independence.

Serious labor problems in 1971 resulted in extensive strikes, and a state of emergency was proclaimed. The people of Mauritius enjoyed political freedom, but unemployment and overpopulation were still major problems.

In 1980 the government began an economic adjustment program that began to pay off as the historically troubled economy reached the end of the decade. Tourism became an important foreign exchange earner. The textile industry grew larger than the sugar industry, even though the sugar industry continued to produce at high levels. In 1989 Mauritius launched Africa's first offshore banking center, which is designed to attract international interests.

Morocco

Official name: *Kingdom of Morocco*
Area: *172,368 sq. mi.,*
        446,550 sq. km.
Type of government:
        Constitutional monarchy
Population: *31,168,000*
Capital: *Rabat*
        (Pop., metro. area, 1,220,000)
Largest city: *Casablanca*
        (Pop., metro. area, 2,943,000)
Languages: *Arabic (official),*
        French, Berber dialects
Literacy: *44%*
Currency: *Dirham*
Per capita GDP: *$3,700*
        (Rank: 105th)

The land. The western end of the Atlas Mountain system dominates Morocco. In

the north the Rif Atlas runs parallel to the Mediterranean Sea. The Middle Atlas, which has elevations of over 10,900 feet (3,323 meters), and the Grand Atlas, which has elevations of over 13,600 feet (4,146 meters), run through central Morocco. The Anti-Atlas, in the southwest, borders the desert region of the Sahara, which stretches along eastern and southern Morocco.

The Moroccan Meseta, or plateau, lies on the Atlantic side of the Grand Atlas and Middle Atlas. It is irrigated in places, as at Marrakesh, and is crossed by rivers leading into lowland plains. The Moulouya River and valley are east of the Middle Atlas.

The Grand Atlas and Middle Atlas intercept rain-bearing winds that bring moisture to the north and west and cause desert conditions in the south and near-desert conditions in the east. Rainfall is more plentiful in the north, where almost 35 inches (90 centimeters) fall annually; it decreases to the south to as low as 4 inches (10 centimeters) in the western Sahara.

Ceuta and Melilla, two Spanish enclaves in northern Morocco, are the last vestiges of European colonialism in the area.

The people. The Moroccans are descended from Berbers, possibly the original inhabitants of the area, and from Arab settlers. Most of the people are Sunni Muslim, although there is a small Jewish population. There

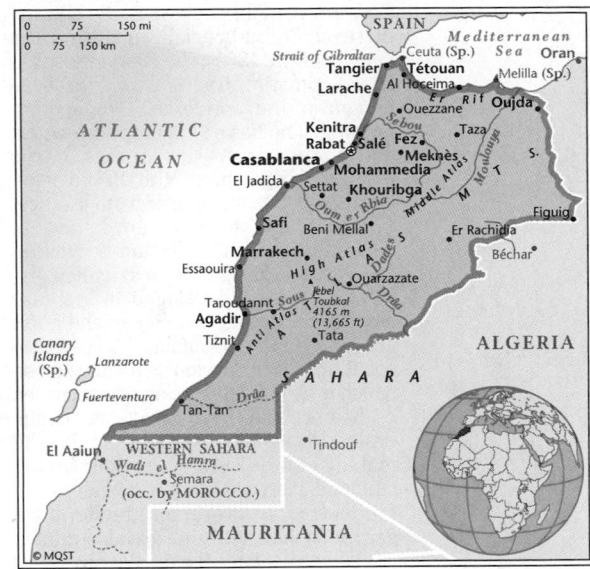

are small communities of Europeans, mainly French and Spanish.

Most people live west of the Atlas Mountains. Morocco's major cities (metro. areas) include Rabat, the capital; Casablanca (population, 2,943,000), an industrial and commercial center and port; Marrakesh (602,000); Fez (564,000); and Meknès (401,000).

The country's recent rapid rise in population—about 3 percent each year—contributes to its high rates of unemployment.

center
US

centre
Brit.

MOROCCAN SOLDIERS are skilled horsemen like their forebears, the Berbers and Arab settlers.

Economy. Although Morocco became increasingly industrialized during the decade of the 1980s, the economy still is based primarily on agriculture. Forty-two percent of the workforce is engaged in farming. The basic food crops are wheat and barley, corn, wine grapes, citrus fruits, and vegetables. With the aid of foreign capital, particularly from France, Morocco has become an important source of seasonal fruits and vegetables for Western Europe. Large irrigation projects have been developed to increase agricultural production. Sheep and goats are raised in the mountains. Morocco has spent heavily to develop its fishing sector, which is potentially a major export earner.

Morocco has deposits of several minerals. Phosphate rock, used in the making of fertilizers, is the most important, and Morocco is a world leader in its production. Iron ore, anthracite, manganese, cobalt, and zinc are also mined.

Morocco's largest industry processes phosphates into phosphoric acid and fertilizers. Oil refining is the second largest industrial activity. There are a number of small industries in the country. Cement, Moroccan leather, flour, sugar, and other products are produced. Tourism has become an important industry, and overseas Moroccan workers return a significant portion of their incomes to their native land.

The major imports are petroleum products, food, manufactured goods, especially iron and steel and textiles, and machinery. Morocco's exports include phosphates, phosphoric acid, citrus fruit, and clothing. Most trade is conducted with France and other European Union nations.

Government. Morocco is a constitutional monarchy. The king appoints a prime minister and other ministers. The prime minister has considerable authority. The legislature is bicameral. The upper house is elected indirectly by influential groups; the lower chamber is popularly elected.

History. The earliest known inhabitants of present-day Morocco were Berbers. In the 600s B.C. Phoenicians established trading posts in the region.

meters *US*
metres *Brit.*

OUTDOOR MARKETS appeal to the important tourist trade in Morocco.

In the second century A.D. Rome established a province in northwestern Morocco. Roman domination came to an end in the 400s with the invasion of the Vandals.

In the early 700s Muslim armies invaded Morocco, and the Berbers gradually adopted Islam. In the late 700s most of the country united under Idris, a member of the Alid family. His son founded the city of Fez.

In A.D. 1056 Berber tribes formed a powerful religious and political force, the Almoravids. They founded the city of Marrakesh in 1062 and established a dynasty that ruled until 1147. The Almohads, another Berber confederation, defeated the Almoravids and established a dynasty that lasted until 1269. The Marinid dynasty succeeded the Almohads.

In 1544 Morocco came under the rule of another Alid dynasty, the Sa'dis, and in 1664 yet another branch of the Alids, the Filalis, or Alawites, assumed control.

France was given an exclusive trade treaty in 1767. Border disputes erupted with the French in Algiers soon after. In 1844 Morocco was defeated by the French in the northeast. In 1860 Spain and Great Britain gained leading trade positions throughout the coastal regions. In 1884 Spain claimed a protectorate along Morocco's southern coast.

European control. In the early 1900s Great Britain, Spain, France, and Germany competed for control of Morocco. In 1912 the Moroccan sultan was forced to sign the Treaty of Fez with France, and most of Morocco became a French protectorate. In the same year Spain obtained control of a region in the north and one in the south. In 1923 the city of Tangier became an international zone.

In 1921 a leader in the Rif Mountains, Abd el-Krim, led an uprising against the Spanish and then fought a combined Spanish and French force. He was defeated in 1926. After 1925 the government of French Morocco was more centralized and the European population in Morocco began steadily to increase.

Nationalism. Nationalism in Morocco began to develop in the late 1920s. In 1927 France placed Muhammad bin Yusuf (Muhammad V) on the throne, believing he would act favorably toward France. The French assumption appeared valid when in 1930 Muhammad signed the Berber *Dahir,* which downgraded the importance of Islamic law. After that, however, Muhammad responded to the appeals of the nationalists, to France's alarm.

By the time of World War II Muhammad was cautiously cooperating with the nationalists while maintaining favorable relations with France. During World War II, Morocco supported the Vichy government in France until the Allies invaded North Africa in 1942. In 1953 France forced Muhammad to abdicate in order to end his nationalist activity. He went into exile, but as a result nationalist disturbances intensified. In 1955 France accepted the

necessity of dealing with Muhammad, and he returned to Morocco in triumph.

Independence. Negotiations quickly led to independence for French Morocco, achieved on March 2, 1956. By agreements in April 1956 and April 1958, the Spanish zones were granted independence. In October 1956 Tangier was incorporated into Morocco. In 1969 Ifni, a former Spanish enclave, was ceded to Morocco.

Morocco claimed all of Spanish Sahara, but in 1975 Mauritania was granted the region's southern portion. The Algerian-backed Polisario Front (Saharan liberation army) fought to establish an independent Western Sahara. In 1979 Mauritania renounced its claim to the southern portion and by 1980 Morocco, aided by the United States, had annexed the entire region.

King Hassan II ascended to the throne in 1961; a year later he made Morocco a constitutional monarchy. His own authority was greatly restricted by a new constitution in 1972. After 1973 Hassan, pressured by public opinion, began a broad program of "Moroccanization" of the nation's economy. Foreign-owned farms were nationalized. Morocco has its own form of socialism, which permits considerable private enterprise.

In the late 1980s and early 1990s, Morocco's economy grew steadily, despite poor harvests, a depressed world market for phosphates, and a burgeoning population. The government's steady privatization of businesses and industry and foreign investment have helped to bring political and economic stability.

Mozambique

Official name: *Republic of Mozambique*
Area: *309,413 sq. mi., 801,590 sq. km.*
Type of government: *Republic*
Population: *17,324,000*
Capital and largest city: *Maputo (Pop., 967,000)*
Languages: *Portuguese (official), indigenous dialects*
Literacy: *42%;* **Currency:** *Metical*
Per capita GDP: *$900 (Rank: 174th)*

The land. Most of the long, irregularly shaped land consists of flat or rolling plateau ranging from 800 to 2,000 feet (244 to 610 meters) in elevation. In the east a narrow lowland skirts a coast, and in the west a zone of high plateaus and mountains reaches a peak of nearly 8,000 feet (2,439 meters). The most important of the country's many rivers are the Zambezi, which crosses central Mozambique, and the Limpopo, in the south.

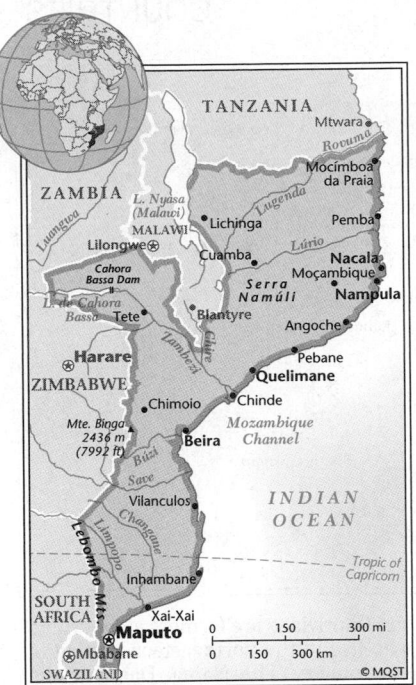

The climate is hot and humid along the coast, especially in the north, where 40 inches (103 centimeters) of rain fall annually. Temperatures are moderate in the interior, which is also drier, with only 30 inches (77 centimeters) of precipitation falling annually.

The people. The great majority of Mozambique's population is African. Europeans constitute the largest minority, and the remainder are of Asian and mixed backgrounds. Most of the Africans belong to a variety of Bantu tribes. The largest groups are the Makua and Tsonga. Most of the people follow traditional religions, but there are also Muslims and Roman Catholics.

Major cities include Maputo, Beira (population, metro. area, 413,000), and Nampula (303,000). Fifty percent of the population lived in the central provinces of Zambezia and Nampula until hundreds of thousands fled the area during uprisings between 1986 and 1988.

Economy. Mozambique is a very poor land, with a primarily agricultural economy. Agriculture accounts for over 80 percent of the labor force and for about 90 percent of export revenue. Mineral resources have not been fully exploited, although some coal, bismuth, bauxite, and copper are mined. Mining and industry are increasing gradually as hydroelectric power becomes available. Most of the country's forests stand uncut.

Farming is especially productive in the river valleys and in the north, where sugar cane, cotton, corn, copra, tea, sisal, manioc, fruits, and vegetables are raised. Most farms have been collectivized and many industries have been nationalized since 1975.

Industry is limited to the processing of agricultural products, the milling of cotton textiles, and the manufacture of such items as rope, soap, cement, tires, hand tools, and leather goods. An important contribution to the economy is made by money earned by Mozambique laborers hired to work in the mines of neighboring Zimbabwe and of South Africa; however, the number of workers has decreased sizably in the last two decades.

Nuts, cotton, sisal, sugar, and copra are among the leading exports, and food, machinery, vehicles, fuels, and industrial raw materials are among the imports. The bulk of the country's trade is with Japan, the United States, Spain, Portugal, and Germany. The economy depends heavily on foreign assistance.

Government. By the terms of its constitution of 1990, executive power is vested in a president and cabinet led by a prime minister. The legislature is the 250-member, popularly elected Assembly of the Republic. The new constitution legalized opposition parties and introduced a bill of rights.

History. Mozambique has been inhabited for many centuries by Bantu peoples. Between the 10th and 14th centuries, sophisticated city-states, such as Sofala, near present-day Beira, developed on the basis of iron and gold exports to Asia and the Arab world. When the Portuguese, the first Europeans to reach the region, arrived in the early 1500s, Arab trading colonies had been established along the coast. In the 1530s the Portuguese sacked the coastal trading cities and broke the trade network established with Africa and India. The Portuguese then established a monopoly over sea trade and began to explore the interior.

Unsuccessful in their search for gold and silver, the Portuguese turned to the slave trade for revenue. The slave trade had been carried on before the arrival of the Europeans, but the Portuguese expanded it and it soon became the colony's most profitable enterprise.

Soldier-settlers, called *prazeros,* established petty chieftainships in the interior. They seized African villages, which they converted into peasant colonies, and ruled independent of Portuguese authority. Slavery was legally abolished in 1878, but the labor situation scarcely changed. *Prazeros* kept their slaves, but referred to them as "contractual laborers." Local officials cooperated with the *prazeros* by declaring unemployed Africans vagrants and thus eligible to be forced into contracts requiring them to work for the Europeans.

In the 1930s Portugal tightened its control over its colonies. The government took over the exploitation of the colonies' resources.

In 1951 Mozambique's status was changed to that of an overseas province, and in 1961 Portugal granted its African

CHILDREN lend a hand in Mozambique.

labor
US

labour
Brit.

FARMING VILLAGES such as this are productive in the river valley and in the north in Mozambique.

SAND DUNES stretch for miles along the Atlantic coastline of the desert in Namibia.

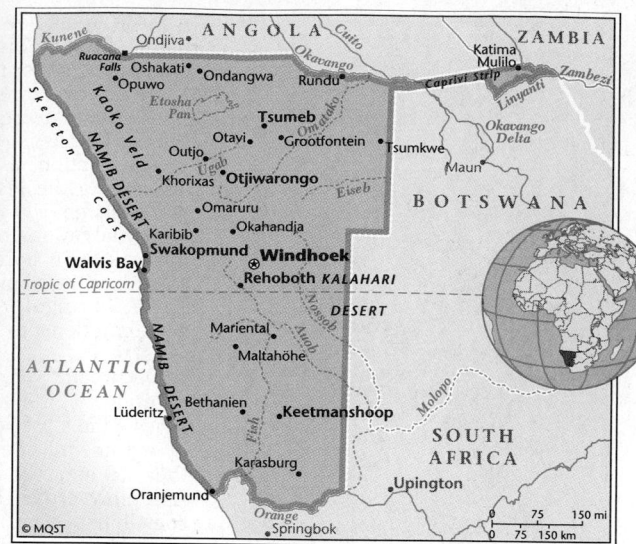

inhabitants full Portuguese citizenship. Although some reforms were initiated in 1961 to improve the welfare and education of the Africans, little progress was made. Forced labor continued in many places, and African political rights were limited.

In the 1960s the United Nations and many countries, and some groups within Mozambique, increased pressure on Portugal to improve conditions in the colony and at least to grant Mozambique self-determination. With support from other African states, a Mozambique nationalist liberation organization developed. In 1964 it began a rebellion against Portugal. Guerrilla warfare, concentrated in the north, continued throughout the 1960s despite an increase in Portuguese military strength in Mozambique to counter it.

Since its independence on June 25, 1975, Mozambique has been torn apart by a civil war between guerrillas of the Mozambique National Resistance (Renamo) and supporters of Frelimo, the party of the Marxist-socialist government. Renamo originally was supported by South Africa and Rhodesia. In 1984 South Africa and Mozambique signed a nonaggression accord.

During the 1980s Renamo closed down about a third of Mozambique's health clinics and schools. Renamo was better equipped than the government. That fact, in addition to the government's political and economic problems, led to Mozambique's complete devastation.

Starvation worsened in the late 1980s because of periods of drought and flooding. Relief efforts were only partially successful because of guerrilla interference and government inefficiency and corruption.

In 1990 the government moved to adopt a multiparty system. In October 1992 both sides signed a cease-fire. In December a UN peacekeeping force was sent in to supervise the truce and the disarming of the combatants, and prepare for elections in 1994. President Joaquim Chissano was reelected in 1999.

Namibia

Official name: *Republic of Namibia*
Area: *318,611 sq. mi.,*
825,418 sq. km
Type of government: *Republic*
Population: *1,897,000*
Capital and largest city: *Windhoek*
(Pop., 147,000)
Languages: *English (official),*
Afrikaans, German
Literacy: *38%*
Currency: *South African rand*
Per capita GDP: *$4,500*
(Rank: 94th)

The land. Most of Namibia (formerly called South-West Africa) is set on a high plateau that is an extension of the main South African plateau. The plateau averages an altitude of 3,600 feet (1,080 kilometers) above sea level. The Namib Desert stretches along the coast and is mostly uninhabited. The east is occupied by the Kalahari Desert, which has small stretches of grazing land. The northeastern border extends in a thin 186-mile (300-kilometer) strip of land that projects between the borders of Angola, Zambia, and Botswana; the region is called the Caprivi Strip. Walvis Bay is a South African enclave in Namibia that is one of the most important ports in western Africa. The future of Walvis Bay is being negotiated.

The climate is hot and dry. Rainfall averages 22 inches (56 centimeters) annu- ally in the north, 6 inches (15 centimeters) in the south, and about 2 inches (5 centimeters) on the coast. Except for a few springs, there is no surface water in the country.

The people. The population of Namibia is made up of many different ethnic groups. The largest are the Ovambo, Damara, Herero, Kavango, Caprivians, and Nama.

The Ovambo make up over half of the population. The Ovambo, Kavango,

and Caprivians are farmers and herders who live in the northeastern section of the country. The Nama, Damara, and Herero live in the central region of Namibia. A European minority lives primarily in the south. The Nama and Damara groups speak Khoisian, while most of the other ethnic groups speak Bantu-related languages.

The main cities include Windhoek, the capital; Swakopmund (population, 18,000); Rundu (19,000); and Keetmanshoop (15,000).

Economy. Mining is the backbone of Namibia's economy. It accounts for over 80 percent of export earnings while employing less than 10 percent of the population.

Agriculture engages about 60 percent of Namibia's workforce and is the second most important sector of the economy. The modern European-dominated sector consists mainly of ranching; the traditional African sector is made up of subsistence farmers growing millet, sorghum, corn, and peanuts. Industry employs about 10 percent of the population and is comprised mostly of the food processing and mining equipment industries.

Uranium oxide and diamonds are the main exports; tin, lithium, cesium, and rubidium contribute smaller shares. Namibia's main trading partners are South Africa, Germany, France, and the United States.

Government. Nambia's constitution, approved in February 1990, created a multiparty republic with a president elected to serve 5-year terms. The legislature is made up of a 72-seat, popularly elected National Assembly and the 26-seat National Council, chosen from the regional councils.

History. Bushmen are generally acknowledged to be the first inhabitants of the region. The Nama and the Damara were later inhabitants, and the Bantu-speaking Ovambo and Herero eventually migrated from the north.

The Namib Desert provided a formidable barrier to European exploration until the late 18th century. Great Britain claimed Walvis Bay in 1878 and incorporated it into the Cape of Good Hope colony in 1884. In 1883 a German trader claimed the rest of the coastal region, from the Congo River to 26° south latitude, after negotiations with a local chief. In 1884 South-West Africa, as Namibia was then called, was declared a German protectorate.

As World War I approached, the Union of South Africa occupied German South-West Africa at the request of the Allied powers. On December 17, 1920, South Africa took over South-West Africa under a mandate from the League of Nations. The mandate gave South Africa full governmental power over the territory.

The League of Nations was dissolved in 1946 and the mandate system was taken over by the United Nations' trusteeship system, but South Africa refused to place the territory under a trusteeship agreement. Instead, South Africa applied for South-West Africa's annexation into the union.

International pressure was put on South Africa to free the territory. The pressure became more intense in the 1960s when many European nations began granting independence to their colonies and trust territories in Africa. In 1966 the United Nations terminated South Africa's mandate and established a United Nations Council for South-West Africa. However, South Africa continued to administer the territory.

The South-West Africa People's Organization (SWAPO) began guerrilla attacks on South African forces. SWAPO forces were originally based in Zambia. As hostilities intensified over the years, however, guerrilla efforts were launched from newly independent Angola.

In 1968 the United Nations changed the name of the territory to Namibia. In 1971 the International Court of Justice ruled that South Africa's presence in Namibia was illegal.

Prompted by increasing international pressure, South Africa convened the Turnhalle Conference in 1975. The conference brought together leaders of Namibia's various indigenous groups to discuss the area's future. By the end of 1976, the conference agreed on a constitution incorporating continued separation of the races with a 2-year timetable for independence. South Africa proceeded with the plan, holding elections for a European-dominated National Assembly even though SWAPO and the United Nations Security Council rejected the proposal.

South Africa eventually disbanded the National Assembly and resumed direct control of Namibia.

In December 1988 South Africa finally agreed to withdraw from Namibia when an agreement was signed by Angola, Cuba, and South Africa that ended the civil war in Angola and mandated the withdrawal of all Cuban forces from Angola and Namibia. South Africa had insisted that it would not grant independence while Cuban troops were still present in Angola.

SWAPO emerged as the strongest of Namibia's 40-odd political parties in 1989 elections. The government maintained close ties with Cuba, whose troops fought alongside SWAPO guerrillas against South African forces. All Cuban troops returned to Cuba by 1991.

On March 21, 1990, Namibia achieved independence and became a member of the Commonwealth. During the transition period, all political prisoners were freed and discriminatory legislation was abolished.

Niger

Official name: *Republic of Niger*
Area: *492,863 sq. mi.,*
  1,267,000 sq. km.
Type of government: *Republic*
Population: *10,760,000*
Capital and largest city: *Niamey*
  (Pop., 397,000)
Languages: *French (official),*
  Hausa, Djerma
Literacy: *15%*
Currency: *CFA franc*
Per capita GDP: *$820*
  (Rank: 180th)

The land. Much of Niger is flat. In the north there is desert and in the east there are scrubby and grassy lowlands. In north-central Niger a great mass of volcanic mountains known as the Aïr rise to elevations of almost 6,000 feet (1,829 meters). Lake Chad lies at the southeastern corner of Niger. The Niger River flows through southwestern Niger. Niger's climate is hot and dry. Half of Niger receives less than 4 inches (10 centimeters) of rain each year. Rainfall averages about 20 inches (51 centimeters) a year near Nigeria.

The people. There are four main ethnic groups in Niger—the Hausa, Djerma, Fulani, and Tuareg. The Hausa and the Djerma are sedentary farmers living in the arable southern region. The Fulani and Tuareg are nomadic or seminomadic livestock-raising peoples. The southern part of the country is heavily populated, especially near the Niger River. Most of the people are Muslim. Niger's largest cities are Niamey, the capital; Zinder (population, 120,000); and Maradi (111,000). Over 90 percent of the people live in rural areas in this sparsely populated country.

Economy. Uranium deposits discovered in the northern desert contribute about two-thirds of the nation's exports. Tin and tungsten also are mined. Industry is poorly developed.

About 90 percent of the workforce is engaged in farming and herding. The basic food crops are millet, sorghum, rice, beans, and wheat; the main commercial crops are peanuts, cotton, cowpeas, and tobacco. Most of the cultivated land is near the border with Nigeria. Cattle, sheep, and goats are raised in most parts of the country.

The main imports are manufactured goods, machinery, and petroleum products. Uranium is the major export, and peanuts, cowpeas, livestock, and vegetables are also significant. Nigeria and European Union countries are Niger's chief trading partners.

Government. By the terms of a constitution adopted in 1992, the head of state is a president who is elected to a 5-year term and appoints a prime minister. Legislative power is held by an 83-member National Assembly whose legislators are elected to 5-year terms.

History. At times portions of Niger have been claimed by the empires of Songhai, Mali, Gao, Kanem, and Bornu. Much of what is now western Niger was part of the Songhai Empire, which flourished from the 1400s to the late 1500s, when it was conquered by a Moroccan army. During the same period, the city-states of the Hausa people in southern Niger maintained their independence from foreign domination. In the north the nomadic Tuareg roamed the arid fringe of the Sahara. All of these peoples traded with North Africa, and the city of Zinder was a center for commercial caravans.

In the early 1800s the Hausa region was engulfed in revolution. Usuman dan Fodio, a Fulani Muslim cleric, led a holy war, or *jihad,* against the Hausa ruling class of Gobia, one of the more important city-states. He voiced the long-standing religious and social complaints of the subjects of the Hausa rulers.

The war lasted from 1804 to 1810, by which time nearly all the Hausa states had come under Fulani rule. In time, all of southern Niger and northern Nigeria owed allegiance to Fulani overlords.

French rule. The power of the Fulani rulers, and of the Tuareg, was broken by the French, whose army conquered what is now Niger between 1890 and 1914. Beginning in 1895 Niger was administered as part of French West Africa. After World War II Niger became a territory within the French Union.

center
US

centre
Brit.

22 Africa

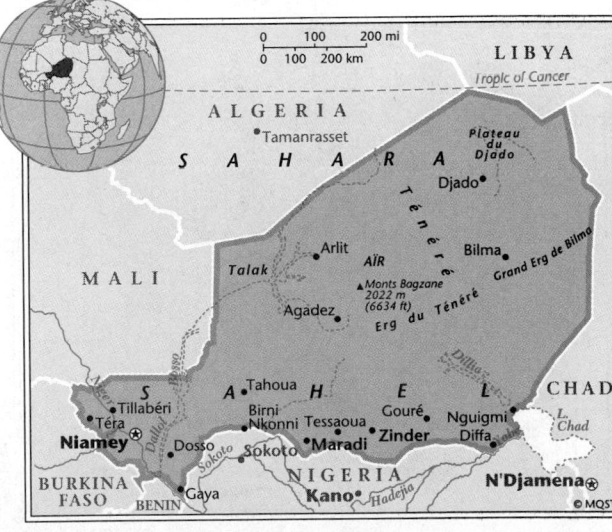

In 1958 the Niger Progressive Party, led by Hamani Diori, won an overwhelming majority of seats in the territorial assembly. In that year Niger became an autonomous member of the French Community. The assembly soon dissolved all opposition parties.

Independence. On August 3, 1960, Niger became independent and Diori became president. He was ousted in a 1974 military coup. The leader of the coup, Seyni Kountche, became president and the Supreme Military Council was created to administer the government. Niger suffered from drought and famine between 1968 and 1975. Massive UN and U.S. aid was supplied during the crisis. Drought struck again in the early 1980s.

In 1987 Kountche died of natural causes and Ali Saibou was elected president by the Supreme Military Council. A new constitution was ratified, and in 1989 presidential elections, Saibou was the only candidate allowed on the ballot.

In 1990 thousands of nomadic Tuaregs returned to Niger. Tensions led to guerrilla warfare in 1991. In 1992 a constitution established a multiparty political system. Presidential and legislative elections were held in 1993. Following, coups in 1996 and 1999, a council was created to facilitate transition to civilian rule.

meters
US

metres
Brit.

Nigeria

Official name: *Federal Republic of Nigeria*
Area: *359,346 sq. mi., 923,770 sq. km.*
Type of government: *Military*
Population: *130,500,000*
Capital: *Abuja (Pop., 107,000)*
Largest city: *Lagos (Pop., 5,195,000)*
Languages: *English (official), Hausa, Ibo, Yoruba, Fulani*
Literacy: *57%;* **Currency:** *Naira*
Per capita GDP: *$840 (Rank: 179th)*

The land. Most of Nigeria is occupied by plains or low rolling hills. There are tropical forests and mangrove swamps along the coast. The Niger River, which flows through south-central Nigeria, forms a large delta where it reaches the ocean.

There are grassy savannas in central Nigeria, north of the junction of the Niger and Benue rivers. In the north-central part of the country is the Jos Plateau, which has an elevation of almost 6,000 feet (1,829 meters) above sea level. There is grassland and desert in the far north. The Adamawa Mountains are in the southwest.

The climate of Nigeria is hot and humid. Some areas in the south receive as much as 150 inches (385 centimeters) of rain each year.

The people. Nigeria is the most populous country in Africa. There are four main ethnic groups in Nigeria—the Yoruba, Ibo, Hausa, and Fulani. The Fulani and Hausa peoples are predominantly Muslim and are concentrated in northern Nigeria. The Yoruba live mainly in the southwest, and the Ibo in the east. The Yoruba are divided almost evenly between Islam and Christianity, while the Ibo are predominantly Catholic.

The country's largest cities include Lagos; Ibadan (population, 1,835,000), in the southwest; Ogbomosho (433,000), in the southwest; and Kano (2,167,000), in the north. Although nearly 80 percent of the population still live in rural areas,

Nigeria has more than 30 cities with populations exceeding 100,000.

Economy. Nigeria is the wealthiest of all black African nations because of its rich oil deposits, mainly in the Niger delta. Oil, discovered in 1958, accounts for 95 percent of the nation's exports. Eighty-one million metric tons of oil were produced in 1989. Gas, coal, tin, and columbite are other natural resources.

Nigerian industry is supported by abundant hydroelectric power from the Niger River. Steel manufacturing and oil refining are the main industries. Textiles, cement, and automobiles are also manufactured.

Nigeria's agriculture, the mainstay of the economy before 1960, is based on the production of peanuts, oil palm products, cacao, coffee, cotton, and rubber. The country's basic food crops include yams and corn. Nigeria has rich forest resources, and timber is exported. Fish from the Niger River and poultry farming provide additional sources of food. Cattle are raised mainly in the northern part of the country. Most trade is with the United States, France, Germany, and Great Britain.

Government. A constitution adopted in May 1999 provides for a president who is elected by popular vote for no more than two 4-year terms and for a bicameral popularly elected legislature.

History. The many peoples of Nigeria have a rich heritage. In about the 12th century, the Yoruba settled in western

NIGERIA boasts the highest population in Africa. It also has the wealthiest economy of the black African countries.

NIGERIAN ceremonial mask

Nigeria, while in the north the Hausa established agricultural states. In southern Nigeria the early states of Ife and Benin produced sculpture that is now world famous. In the 1200s the Hausa in the north were converted to Islam by the Fulani from eastern Africa. In the early 1800s a Fulani leader, Usuman dan Fodio, conquered the Hausa, replacing the Hausa dynasties with Fulani emirs.

Portuguese traders came to Nigeria in 1472, and Portugal and other European countries shared in the lucrative slave trade that developed. The British penetrated the area beginning in 1807 to halt the slave trade. Lagos was occupied by Great Britain in 1861, and the United Africa Company, later known as the Royal Niger Company, opened the Niger valley to trade. In 1885 the Oil Rivers Protectorate was set up in the coastal region.

British rule. The British government took over direct administration of the protectorate in 1891, and by 1893, with the addition of a region beyond the coast, formed the Niger Coast Protectorate. In 1900 it became the Protectorate of Southern Nigeria. In the same year the territory of the Royal Niger Company became the Protectorate of Northern Nigeria. In 1903 the emirates of the north came under British control.

The protectorates were united in 1914, and after World War I the former German colony of Cameroon was added as a mandate under the League of Nations. In 1939 southern Nigeria was divided into the Eastern and Western provinces.

Nigerians had begun to seek greater freedom before World War I, but nationalist movements tended to be regional. Most prominent were the Northern Peoples' Congress (NPC) led by Sir Ahmadu Bello, the Action Group in the Western region led by Chief Obafemi Awolowo, and the National Council of Nigeria and Cameroons (NCNC) led by Dr. Nnamdi Azikiwe. After World War II regional legislatures and elections were introduced throughout the country.

In 1954 the first national elections were held, and the NPC and NCNC obtained the most votes. Eastern and Western Nigeria became self-governing in 1957; but the less-developed north did not become self-governing until 1959.

Independence. On October 1, 1960, Nigeria became an independent nation. In 1961 a UN plebiscite was held in the British Cameroons, and the Northern Cameroons voted to become part of the new Nigeria, which then consisted of three regions—Eastern, Western, and Northern Nigeria. On October 1, 1963, Nigeria became a republic. In 1966 two successive coups resulted in the establishment of a military regime. A year later, the Ibos, frustrated by the northern Muslims' apparent monopoly on political power and oil revenues, proclaimed the independent Republic of Biafra. After a bloody civil war, the Ibos were defeated, but Nigeria was badly weakened. Severe droughts and famines between 1968 and 1974 further wracked the country.

The military continued to dominate Nigerian politics. In 1985 a coup installed General Ibrahim Babangida, who delayed restoring the country to civilian rule. In 1989 a new constitution, providing for a civilian government and multiparty elections in 1993, was adopted. In June 1993 presidential elections were held, but Babangida annulled the election, stepped down as president, and appointed Ernest Shonekan as head of an interim government. After months of unrest, the military, led by General Sani Abacha, took control. Former general Olusegun Obasanjo became president in 1999 following free elections. Fighting between Muslim and Christian factions which has plagued Nigeria since 1999 threatens the country's stability.

Rwanda

Official name: *Rwandese Republic*
Area: *10,167 sq. mi., 26,340 sq. km.*
Type of government: *Republic*
Population: *7,668,000*
Capital and largest city: *Kigali (Pop., 234,000)*
Languages: *French, Kinyarwanda, Kiswahili*
Literacy: *48%;* **Currency:** *Franc*
Per capita GDP: *$1,000 (Rank: 171st)*

The land. Rwanda is composed mainly of hills and uplands. A continuous chain of mountains with elevations above 6,500 feet (1,982 meters) runs along Rwanda's western border. An eroded plateau slopes eastward from the mountains. In the north there are active volcanoes in the Virunga Mountains, which reach an elevation of over 14,700 feet (4,482 meters). The Kagera River drains Rwanda's plateau. Lake Kivu is in western Rwanda.

There are two wet and two dry seasons each year. In most places between 40 and 60 inches (103 and 154 centimeters) of rain fall during the year.

The people. There are three ethnic groups in Rwanda—the Hutu, the Tutsi,

THE MOUNTAIN GORILLA inhabits the upland regions in Rwanda.

and the Twa. Until recently the Hutu, by far the majority of the population, were dominated by the minority Tutsi under a feudal system. The Twa, Pygmy forest-dwellers, are probably descendants of Rwanda's original inhabitants.

Rwanda's population density is the highest in sub-Saharan Africa; it also has a high annual rate of population increase. Almost all the people are subsistence farmers living in rural areas. The population density results in high emigration rates.

About three-quarters of the population are Christians, mostly Roman Catholics; the majority of the other citizens are animists. Major cities include Kigali, the capital; Butare; and Ruhengeri.

Economy. About 45 percent of Rwanda's gross national product is derived from agriculture. The basic food crops are beans, corn, and sweet potatoes, and the basic cash crops are coffee and tea, which account for almost 90 percent of export earnings. Cattle are numerous and are a symbol of both wealth and social position. Soil erosion and drought are constant problems throughout the country.

Although Rwanda has deposits of cassiterite, tungsten, and other minerals, the country's resources have not been fully developed. Industry consists of brewing, food processing, cigarette production, and textile manufacturing.

Rwanda's principal exports are coffee, tea, tin, and tungsten. Imports include

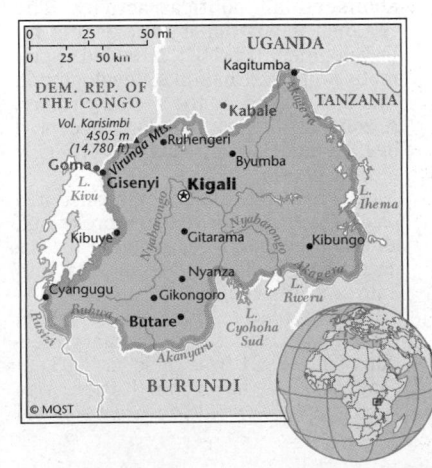

foodstuffs, textiles, machinery, chemicals, and petroleum products. Most trade is with Kenya and the European Union nations.

Government. Rwanda's president is assisted by a 17-member presidentially appointed cabinet of ministers. The 1978 constitution vests legislative power in a 70-member unicameral body. The president and legislature are elected by universal suffrage. The government is, however, currently in transition.

History. The Tutsi, who probably came from Ethiopia, invaded Rwanda in the 1500s. They established themselves as a ruling aristocracy, headed by a mwami, or king, over the agricultural Hutu.

In 1894 the first European, Graf von Goetzen, a German, reached the kingdom; in 1899 Germany established a protectorate over the region. Germany administered the area as part of German East Africa until World War I. After the war the protectorate became a mandate of Belgium under the League of Nations. Belgium was to administer the region with present-day Burundi as Ruanda-Urundi. In 1946 it became a UN trust territory.

Belgium permitted little African political activity, and until the 1950s supported traditional Tutsi rule over the Hutu majority. At that time Africans organized political parties along ethnic lines, and the tribal Party of the Hutu Emancipation Movement (PARMEHUTU), composed mainly of Hutu, opposed the Tutsi-dominated National Rwandan Union (UNAR). Tension between the Hutu and the Tutsi led to civil war in 1959. The Hutu ended Tutsi dominance, and large numbers of Tutsi fled to neighboring countries.

In elections held in 1961, PARMEHUTU won an overwhelming victory. The Belgium trusteeship was ended on June 28, 1962, and Rwanda was declared an independent republic on July 1, 1962. Grégoire Kayibanda of PARMEHUTU became president.

Kayibanda initiated a policy of reconciliation and appointed Tutsi ministers to his cabinet. But in 1963 fighting again broke out between the Tutsi and the Hutu. In July of 1973 Kayibanda was deposed in a bloodless military coup.

The military took power under the leadership of Juvenal Habyarimana and abolished all political activity. The National Revolutionary Movement for Development (MRND), intended to promote unity and national development, was established by the military rulers. A constitution was popularly accepted in 1978 and Habyarimana was officially elected president.

In 1994 Habyarimana was killed in a plane crash. Ethnic violence broke out, and some 200,000 people were massacred. Two million refugees fled into Zaire and Tanzania.

The first local elections were held in 1999, and the first parliamentary elections since 1994 were held in 2003. In May 2003 a new constitution was approved which would ensure a political

balance between the Hutu and Tutsi, a move toward ending the ethnic violence that has plagued the country.

São Tomé and Príncipe

Official name: *Democratic Republic of São Tomé and Príncipe*
Area: *371 sq. mi., 960 sq. km.*
Type of government: *Republic*
Population: *170,000*
Capital and largest city: *São Tomé (Pop., 5,700)*
Language: *Portuguese*
Literacy: *79%;* **Currency:** *Dobra*
Per capita GDP: *$1,200 (Rank: 161st)*

The land. The country consists of the islands of São Tomé and Príncipe and some small islets. The islands are volcanic in origin and consist of a hilly, forested interior ringed by a wide, flat, coastal plain. São Tomé's highest peak reaches 6,313 feet (1,925 meters) above sea level. Príncipe's elevations are generally below 3,000 feet (915 meters).

São Tomé and Príncipe's climate is extremely hot. The humidity is high and rainfall is heavy. Annual rainfall ranges from 40 inches (103 centimeters) in the town of São Tomé to 100 inches (256 centimeters) on the nearby peaks.

The people. São Tomé, the southern of the two islands, has nearly 15 times as many inhabitants as the slightly smaller Príncipe. Many laborers have been imported in recent years from the countries of Angola and Mozambique. They work on plantations run by white settlers on which local residents refuse to work. The population is composed of people with mixed heritages, descendants of African slaves, Cape Verdeans, and Portuguese settlers. The two major towns are São Tomé, the capital, and São António.

Economy. The island nation's economy has steadily declined owing to price decreases in its major crop, cacao, and nationalization of more than 50 percent of the plantations. The economy is still based primarily on the cultivation of cacao but copra, coffee, coconuts, palm oil, and cinchona are also important commercial crops. Industry is limited to the processing of agricultural products.

The country has a serious balance of trade problem. Cacao, palm, coconut products, and coffee are exported. Food, fuel, textiles, and other necessities are imported. The country's main trading partners include Portugal, Germany, the Netherlands, and China.

Government. On July 12, 1975, the islands were granted independence by Portugal. The country is headed by a president who appoints a prime minister (chosen by the legislature) to assist in

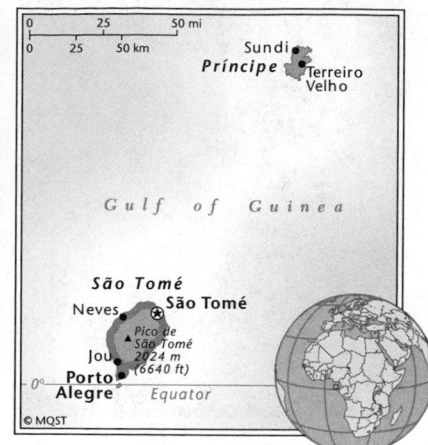

executive decision making. Legislative power is vested in a unicameral National Assembly whose members are elected by direct popular vote to 4-year terms.

History. The islands were uninhabited when discovered by the Portuguese in 1471. They were made a Portuguese colony in 1522 and an overseas province of Portugal in 1951. The colony was settled by Portuguese, many of whom were exiles, and by peoples of western Africa. Sugar plantations were established, but they were replaced by the slave trade as the chief economic activity. Cacao and coffee took over the island's economy in the 19th century.

In the mid-1960s São Tomé became a staging area for European mercenaries hired to subdue uprisings for independence in the Portuguese territories on the African mainland.

In an effort to revive the faltering economy, the government is encouraging private enterprise to stimulate foreign investment in the islands. The country's first free elections were held in 1991, but instability continues amid coup attempts, the most recent in 2003. The discovery of oil in the Gulf of Guinea, the proceeds of which will be shared with Nigeria, should have a dramatic effect on this small country.

Senegal

Official name: *Republic of Senegal*
Area: *75,318 sq.mi., 196,190 sq. km.*
Type of government: *Republic*
Population: *10,311,000*
Capital and largest city: *Dakar (Pop., 880,000)*
Languages: *French (official), Wolof, Pulaar, Diola, Mandinka*
Literacy: *39%*
Currency: *CFA franc*
Per capita GDP: *$1,580 (Rank: 148th)*

The land. Senegal is occupied mostly by lowlands with elevations below 650 feet (198 meters) and sandy plains are

LEOPOLD SENGHOR brought democracy to Senegal.

typical of most parts of the country. Senegal lies largely in Africa's Sahelian zone, a region of sparse grass and spiny trees.

There are plateaus in the southeast of the country with elevations up to about 1,640 feet (500 meters), and swamps and tropical rain forests in the southwest. The Cape Verde peninsula, Senegal's, and Africa's, westernmost point, protrudes into the Atlantic Ocean.

Four major rivers flow through the country—the Senegal in the north, the Gambia and Saloum in central Senegal, and the Casamance in the south.

Temperatures are moderate in most parts of the country. Some regions in southern Senegal receive as much as 60 inches (154 centimeters) of rain each year. The peninsula receives about 24 inches (62 centimeters) a year.

The people. There are many tribal groups in Senegal. The largest are the Wolof, the Fulani, the Serer, the Diola, and the Tukulor. The small number of non-Africans mainly are Europeans, Syrians, and Lebanese.

Dakar, the capital, is Senegal's largest city. Other large cities (metro. areas) are Thiès (population, 256,000); Kaolack (228,000); and Saint-Louis (148,000).

Two-thirds of the nation's people live in rural areas.

Economy. About 30 percent of Senegal's gross national product is derived from agriculture, and 20 percent from industry. Sixty percent of the workforce is engaged in agriculture. The basic food crops are millet, sorghum, and rice. Peanuts are the main cash crop. Fishing is also important.

Senegal has rich phosphate deposits. Industry is centered in Dakar and is well developed. The largest industries are the textile, food processing, and beverage industries. Peanuts, phosphates, and fish are processed for export. Tourism is growing rapidly.

The main Senegalese imports are textiles, machinery, and foodstuffs. The principal exports are peanuts, peanut oil, and phosphates. Most of Senegal's trade is conducted with France, Nigeria, Great Britain, and the United States.

Government. Senegal has a presidential system of government. Executive power is held by a president who is popularly elected to a 5-year term. Legislative power is held by a 120-member National Assembly. Assembly members are popularly elected to 5-year terms.

History. Between about the 400s and 200s B.C. the peoples of what is now Senegal traded by sea with the Carthaginians. During the next millennium they traded with the merchants of ancient Ghana and Mali.

Portuguese sailors visited the shores of Senegal during the 1400s, and beginning in the 1500s French, Dutch, and British merchants came to the region. In the late 1600s the French established settlements at Saint Louis and on Gorée Island, near the Cape Verde peninsula.

Under a succession of energetic colonial governors, the French tried to transform Senegal into a profitable outpost of their empire. But few Frenchmen could be induced to settle there, and wars with Great Britain over control of the area were costly. Britain conquered Senegal in the 1750s and administered the area in union with Gambia as the Crown colony of Senegambia.

French rule. By the 1800s France had gradually reestablished its control over most of the country. Only at that time did the French alter the indigenous way of life. From 1854 to 1865, under governor Louis-Léon-César Faidherbe, the French subjugated the people living between Saint Louis and Gorée Island and asserted their authority over the peoples living on both banks of the Senegal River.

The Senegalese opposed the French at every turn. Muslims along the Senegal River, many of whom had become subject to a Fulani-ruled empire in the 1700s, unsuccessfully fought the French. In the interior, al-Hajj 'Umar, a Muslim reformer who had created Islamic States in the region in the 1800s, temporarily halted the French advance.

In 1904 Dakar became the capital of French West Africa. The more important schools and hospitals of French West Africa were located there, and Senegal's coastal region became the most westernized part of French West Africa.

In 1946 Senegal became a territory within the French Union. In elections held in 1951 and 1957, Léopold Senghor, a French-educated poet, led the Senegalese Progressive Union to victory. In 1958 Senegal became an autonomous member of the French Community.

Independence. In 1959 France joined Senegal with present-day Mali to form the Mali Federation. On August 20, 1960, Senegal withdrew from the federation and proclaimed its independence. Senghor became Senegal's first president.

During Senghor's long and stable rule, Senegal normalized relations with Mali (1963) and improved its relations with the Arab states. In the mid-1970s Senghor allowed the establishment of political parties and free elections, making Senegal one of the most democratic nations in Africa.

centered
US

centred
Brit.

There have been attempts to improve the lagging economy through diversification, but Senegal remains largely dependent on French aid.

In 1982 Senegal and Gambia formed a confederation, called Senegambia, but it was dissolved in 1989.

In 1989 Senegal faced its most serious crisis since becoming independent. The 1988 presidential election results were met with rioting that led to a national state of emergency. After stability was restored, the opposition forces continued clandestine protests. A border dispute between Senegal and Mauritania erupted into ethnic violence in 1989. Abdoulaye Wade was elected president in April 2000 in the country's first multiparty elections.

Seychelles

Official name: *Republic of Seychelles*
Area: *176 sq. mi., 455 sq. km.*
Type of government: *Republic*
Population: *80,000 (2000 est.)*
Capital and largest city: *Victoria (Pop., 25,000)*
Languages: *English, French (both official), Creole*
Literacy: *58%*
Currency: *Rupee*
Per capita GDP: *$7,600 (Rank: 67th)*

meters
US

metres
Brit.

centers
US

centres
Brit.

The land. The Seychelles archipelago consists of about 90 islands and islets in the Indian Ocean with two distinct collections of islands.

The Mahé group includes about 40 granite islands within a 35-mile (56-kilometer) radius of the main island, Mahé. The islands are rocky, usually with a mountainous, forested interior, often rising 3,000 feet (914 meters) above sea level and ringed by a low, flat coastal plain. Mahé is 57 square miles (148 square kilometers) and is the site of Victoria, the capital.

The Coralline islands are coral, barren, and virtually uninhabitable. These islands rise only a few feet above sea level.

The climate is warm, with heavy rainfall averaging 92 inches (236 centimeters) annually in Victoria. Other important islands include Silhouette, Praslin, La Digue, and Curieuse.
The people. Population density is uneven, with four-fifths of the people living on Mahé, the principal island. Most of the inhabitants are descendants of early French settlers and their African slaves. The majority of the population is Roman Catholic. Creole, English, and French are all official languages, but most of the population speaks Creole.
Economy. A rapidly developing tourism industry has created virtually full employment and has helped the

economy greatly since the 1971 opening of the first commercial airport. Most of the islanders subsist by farming small plots and fishing. Projects have been undertaken to diversify agriculture and to expand fishing into a commercial activity.

Large plantations produce coconuts, palms, and spices, especially cinnamon; the country's industries process these products. Seychelles lacks natural resources and has no mining industries. Copra and cinnamon products are the main exports, but they are far outweighed by consumer imports.

The main trading partners of the Seychelles are France, Great Britain, South Africa, and Pakistan.
Government. According to the nation's 1979 constitution, the People's Progressive Party was the only party in Seychelles, but a 1991 amendment to the constitution legalized opposition parties. Executive power is vested in a president who is assisted by the unicameral, 34-member National Assembly.
History. The Seychelles were uninhabited when discovered by the Portuguese in the early 1500s. They were not settled until the mid-1700s, when the French established communities on the islands and claimed them for France.

Great Britain received the islands in 1814 by the Treaty of Paris and administered them with the Mauritius colony until 1888, when the two were separated. In 1903 Seychelles became a Crown colony.

Seychelles became an independent nation June 28, 1976, ending nearly 160 years of British colonial rule. It had a pro-Western foreign policy, but in a military coup in 1977 a socialist regime deposed the president and took control of the government. The regime leader has retained the presidency despite the successful institution of a multiparty system.

With income from thriving tourism, the government built a welfare state, offering free health care and education and a housing policy providing a home for every family.

Sierra Leone

Official name: *Republic of Sierra Leone*
Area: *27,907 sq. mi., 71,740 sq. km.*
Type of government: *Military*
Population: *5,565,000*
Capital and largest city: *Freetown (Pop., 470,000)*
Languages: *English (official), Krio, Temne, Mende*
Literacy: *31%;* **Currency:** *Leone*
Per capita GDP: *$500 (Rank: 191st)*

The land. Sierra Leone has a varied landscape. In the northwest a mountainous peninsula extends into the Atlantic. Inland from the peninsula and in other places along the coast there are swampy plains. Farther inland are plateaus.

There are forests and grasslands in the north and east. In the northeast are the Loma Mountains, with a peak elevation of over 6,390 feet (1,948 meters). Many rivers flow through the country, including the Rokel and the Moa.

Sierra Leone has a tropical climate, receiving about 145 inches (372 centimeters) of rain each year.
The people. There are some 20 tribal groups in Sierra Leone, the largest of which are the Mende and the Temne. The Mende live mainly in the south and the Temne in the north. There are also several thousand Creoles, descendants of freed slaves who came to Sierra Leone in the 1700s and 1800s. Islam and Christianity are the major religions practiced among the population.

The Creoles live mainly in and near Freetown, the country's capital and largest city. Bo, Kenema, and Makeni are also major urban centers. Freetown is the site of the third-largest harbor in the world.
Economy. The economy of Sierra Leone is based on agriculture, which engages over 70 percent of the workforce. The basic food crops are rice, cassava, corn, and sweet potatoes. Palm kernels, cacao, kola nuts, ginger, and coffee are important commercial crops. Fishing is also an important source of income for the people along the coast. Industry is confined to the manufacturing of consumer goods, such as cigarettes, alcoholic beverages, nails, and paint.

Sierra Leone has rich mineral resources, and the country is one of the world's major producers of diamonds. It also has the world's greatest deposits of rutile, a mineral, used in paint manufacture, first commercially mined here in 1979. Rutile now accounts for 50 percent of Sierra Leone's exports. Bauxite, cacao, diamonds, and coffee are also important. Imports include food, petroleum, capital goods, and consumer goods. Main trading partners are Great Britain, Nigeria, the Netherlands, and the United States.
Government. Sierra Leone is a multiparty democracy. The head of state is a president, popularly elected to a 5-year

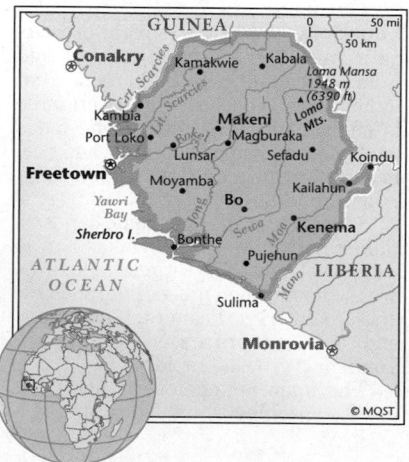

term. The legislature is a unicameral parliament of 124 members, 112 of whom are elected by popular vote, and 12 who are paramount chiefs representing the country's districts.

History. The Temne predominated in present-day Sierra Leone by the 12th century A.D. The Mende and Loko arrived shortly thereafter. Their communities were very small and there was no central government.

The Portuguese explorer Pedro da Cintra visited Sierra Leone in 1462 and gave the area its name, which means Lion Mountain. The course of Sierra Leone's modern history was affected by the proclamation in 1772 by Great Britain's Lord Chief Justice William Mansfield that slavery was never acknowledged by law; consequently, slaves held in England were set free.

In London and in other British cities, freed slaves found it difficult to obtain employment, and they constituted a source of embarrassment to the British government. The government gave its support to the plan of a private company, the Society for the Abolition of Slavery, to ship the freed slaves to Africa.

In 1788 the first shipload of freed slaves settled in present-day Sierra Leone. First by purchase and later by force, they acquired land and built villages near what later became Freetown. In 1791 the Sierra Leone Company began administering the settlement. New groups of freed slaves came to Sierra Leone from Nova Scotia and Jamaica.

British rule. In 1808 the coastal area became a British Crown colony. The colony grew in wealth and importance, new settlements were made along the coast, and the settlers began to increase their trade contacts with the tribes of the interior. The settlers also took more and more tribal land. In the early 1800s the number of settlers was increased by the addition of slaves freed at sea by a British patrol stationed in Freetown.

In 1896, in a move to prevent French territorial expansion, the British government established a protectorate over the interior. The two regions—the colony and the protectorate—were administered separately until 1924. British administrative policy during the 1930s and 1940s helped to integrate the peoples of the protectorate with those of the colony. It also worked to eliminate the antagonism between the descendants of the settlers, the Creoles, and the Africans.

At first the peoples of the coast felt superior because of their higher educational level, but the growth of indigenous political movements reversed this. In 1951 Milton Margai, a Mende physician from the protectorate, led the Sierra Leone People's Party to an important electoral victory over the combined opposition of the parties loyal to two Creoles, Dr. H. C. Bankole-Bright and I. T. A. Wallace-Johnson.

Independence. When Sierra Leone became independent on April 27, 1961, Margai became the country's first prime minister.

The All People's Congress took control of the government in 1969, and by popular referendum an official one-party state was established in 1978. Political turmoil has ensued since the nation's independence, including several military coups, disputed elections in 1967, and the attempted overthrow and assassination of President Siaka Stevens in 1971. A republic was proclaimed on April 19, 1971. Stevens was reelected in 1978.

In response to continued government corruption and a depressed economy, student and public employee protests broke out in 1984 and 1985 and led to rioting. The protestors clamored for multiparty elections. Still, Joseph Momoh was elected on October 1, 1985, in a single-party referendum.

The civil war in neighboring Liberia spilled over into Sierra Leone in 1991, triggering events that led to a military coup in 1992. Another military coup, in 1996, led to multiparty national elections in that year. UN peacekeepers remain in the country.

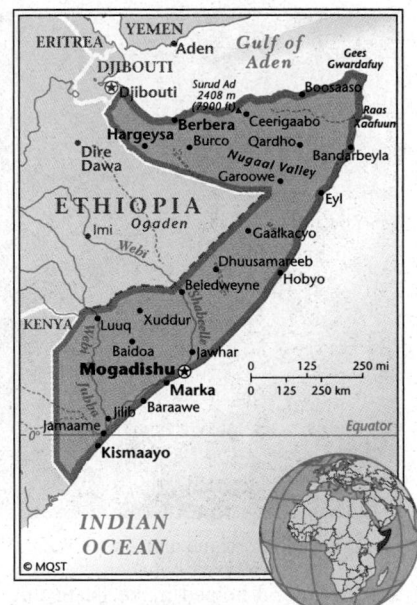

Somalia

Official name: *Somalia*
Area: *248,050 sq. mi.,*
637,660 sq. km.
Type of government: *Transition*
Population: *7,753,000*
Capital and largest city:
Mogadishu
(Pop., 230,000)
Languages: *Somali (official),*
Arabic, Italian, English
Literacy: *38%*
Currency: *Shilling*
Per capita GDP: *$550*
(Rank: 190th)

The land. Located in the easternmost part of Africa, Somalia occupies most of a peninsula that juts into the Indian Ocean. Most of Somalia is occupied by a high plain. The north is mountainous, with the plateaus rising 3,000 to 7,000 feet (915 to 2,134 meters) above sea level. The Mijertins region, also in the north, reaches elevations of 8,250 feet (2,515 kilometers). South and west of the plateau the plain reaches only 2,000 feet (610 kilometers). Near the eastern coast the plain is sandy, and gives way inland to low hills.

Although the southwestern part of the country receives about 20 inches (51 centimeters) of rain each year, semiarid and arid conditions prevail in most parts. The northern part of the country receives less than 10 inches (26 centimeters) of rain each year. The main rivers are the Juba and the Shabelle.

The people. Somalia has a relatively homogeneous population. Most of the inhabitants are Somali, a people of mixed Ethiopian, Arab, and Indian ancestry. A distinct Somali culture developed over the centuries. The majority of the population shares common Somali traditions and language, and the Islamic faith. Bantu-speaking people live in the southern part of the country.

Somalia is sparsely populated and over two-thirds of the population live in rural areas. More than half of the rural dwellers are nomadic or seminomadic herders. Mogadishu, the capital, is Somalia's largest city. Other major cities include Hargeysa, Baidoa, and Burco.

Economy. Somalia's economy is based on herding. Camels, sheep, and goats are raised in most parts of the country.

The basic food crops are corn and sorghum, and the main cash crop is bananas, which are grown mainly on irrigated plantations in the southern part of the country. Sugar cane and a variety of fruits also are grown.

Industry consists mainly of meat and fish processing, sugar refining, and leather tanning. Somalia has deposits of iron ore, gypsum, beryl, and columbite, but mineral deposits have not been fully exploited. The main imports are rice, petroleum products, textiles, and machinery. The main exports are bananas, live animals, hides and skins, cotton, and frankincense. Most trade is conducted with Italy, Kenya, Saudi Arabia, and the United States.

Government. According to its 1979 constitution, Somalia is headed by a president who is elected to a 7-year term and a 177-member unicameral People's Assembly. The government, however, is currently in transition.

History. In about the 900s the Galla people, who were originally from Ethiopia, migrated into what is now Somalia and pushed the indigenous agricultural Bantu people southward. Between the 1200s and 1300s the Somali people, who migrated from the Ethiopian highlands and northern Kenya, displaced the Galla.

South Africa

Official name: *Republic of South Africa*
Area: *470,886 sq. mi., 1,219,912 sq. km.*
Type of government: *Republic*
Population: *42,716,000*
Capital: *Pretoria (administrative) (Pop. 692,000)*
Largest city: *Cape Town (Pop., metro. area, 2,898,000)*
Languages: *11 official languages, including Afrikaans, English, Xhosa, Zulu, Sotho*
Literacy: *85%*
Currency: *Rand*
Per capita GDP: *$9,400 (Rank: 52nd)*

Arabs and Persians made settlements on the northern coast between the 800s and 1500s and helped make Islam the dominant religion. In the early 1800s the sultan of Zanzibar obtained control of the southern part of the country.

The protectorates. Egyptians occupied the area of Somalia between 1874 and 1885. The Egyptian occupation was ended when Great Britain established a protectorate over the northern part of the country. Under the terms of an agreement made with the sultan of Zanzibar, Italy established the Protectorate of Somalia in the south in 1889.

Between 1900 and 1920 both the British and the Italians fought a rebellion led by a Muslim religious leader, Sayyid Muhammad ibn 'Abd Allah Hasan, whom they called the "Mad Mullah."

In the 1920s and 1930s the fascist government of Italy maintained firm control of the south and encouraged settlement by Italian colonists. Italy used the region as a staging base to attack Ethiopia in 1934. After World War II broke out, Great Britain took over the administration of the Italian protectorate in 1941.

Postwar politics centered on reuniting the Somali people. Haja Muhammad Hussein, leader of the Somali Youth League (SYL), a nationalist movement he had founded in 1943, called for unification of the Italian and British protectorates under a single UN trusteeship.

In 1949, however, the UN General Assembly voted to return southern Somalia to Italy as a trusteeship for a 10-year period so that Italy could prepare the region for independence. In 1956 elections were held and Abdullah Issa of the SYL became the first prime minister of Somalia.

In 1954 a British-Ethiopian agreement granted the Haud area, a semi-arid, grassy plain that lies in southwest Somalia and southeast Ethiopia, to Ethiopia, but the Somali people retained the right to graze their cattle on the land. A legislative council was created in British Somaliland in 1957, and on June 26, 1960, Britain granted Somaliland its independence.

Independence. On July 1, 1960, after the Italian trusteeship ended, the Italian and British regions were united to form Somalia.

At the time of independence Ethiopia forbade the Somali to graze cattle in Ogaden. Both countries claimed the area, and fighting erupted in 1963. Fighting also broke out with Kenya over disputed land.

Members of all political parties united in the Somali National Congress to deal with the territorial claims of Somalia to land in Ethiopia, northern Kenya, and French Somaliland (present-day Djibouti). In 1977–1978 war in Ogaden broke out against Ethiopia. Somalia, which had established close ties with the Soviet Union, ordered Soviet troops out of its country because of Soviet assistance to Ethiopia. Soviet-armed Cuban troops helped Ethiopia push Somalia out of Ogaden, but tensions persisted. In 1988, Somalia and Ethiopia reached a peace agreement.

Following a 1969 military coup, Somalia's businesses were partly nationalized. After 1975 a newly formed one-party socialist state collectivized farms.

Somalia had an anti-Western foreign policy, but refugees from Ogaden after the war received extensive aid from the West and from Arab states. The massive immigration of refugees, which began in 1977, added to the problems caused by droughts and famines in the mid-1970s.

In 1991 President Mohammed Siyad Barre was forced to flee. One rebel group, the United Somali Congress, took power, naming Ali Mahdi Mohammed interim president. But a dispute between Ali Mahdi and General Mohammed Farah Aidid plunged the country into civil war and anarchy, and a 2-year drought brought on widespread famine. In 1992 U.S. forces spearheaded a United Nations operation to restore order and oversee delivery of relief supplies. In 1995, after suffering significant casualties, the UN withdrew. A Transitional National Government (TNG) was created in 2000, with a 3-year mandate to create a Somali government, but in 2004 there was yet to be a government in place.

The land. Most of South Africa is occupied by a plateau that slopes inward from its rim. The most striking feature of the landscape is the Great Escarpment, which borders the plateau in an almost unbroken line running southward from the northeastern corner of the country, rounding the southern coast and continuing northward on South Africa's western side. The upper edge of the escarpment is over 5,000 feet (1,524 meters) above sea level.

South Africa's highest point is in the east, where the Drakensberg, a mountainous region, reaches an elevation of over 11,400 feet (3,476 meters) above sea level.

Between the oceans and the foot of the Great Escarpment is a coastal zone about 100 miles (161 kilometers) wide. This region consists of greatly eroded, steplike land cut by streams and valleys, especially in the wetter, eastern side of the country. In the south these steps

YOUNG SOUTH AFRICANS wearing period military uniforms

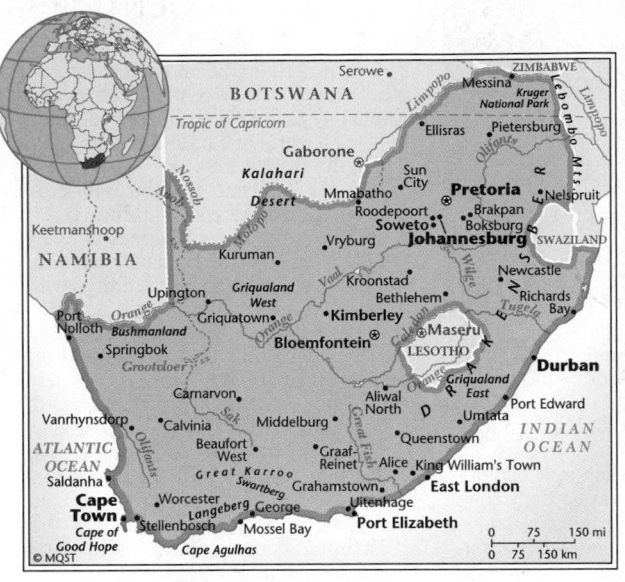

59

PREHISTORIC
drawing of a camel
in Africa

labor
US

labour
Brit.

color
US

colour
Brit.

NELSON MANDELA
was voted the first
black president of
South Africa in 1994.

22 Africa

give way to long, low mountains known as the Cape Ranges, some of which reach the sea in peninsulas.

Cape Agulhas, the southernmost point of Africa, separates the Atlantic Ocean on its west from the Indian Ocean on its east. The most famous point on the Atlantic coast is the Cape of Good Hope.

Most of the plateau is drained by the Orange River and its principal tributary, the Vaal. Both rivers flow westward from the Great Escarpment. The Aughrabies Falls are at the head of a deep canyon leading to the Atlantic Ocean at the point where the Orange River leaves the surface of the plateau. The northern half of the Transvaal is drained by the Limpopo River, which forms the border with Zimbabwe.

Climate. Rainfall in South Africa is much heavier on the east coast and on some parts of the Cape Ranges than on the plateau surface. Half of the country receives less than 20 inches (51 centimeters) of rain a year, and water-supply problems are common, particularly in the west. The climate is moderate in most parts of the country. Northern and eastern Transvaal are tropically hot, but most of South Africa has cool winters.

The people. The majority of the South African people are black Africans, about 70 percent of whom are Bantu-speaking peoples. Among the main tribal groups are the Zulu, Xhosa, and Sotho. About two-thirds of the black Africans live either on farms owned by whites or on reserves established by the government.

Europeans make up the largest minority group. A majority of them are Afrikaners—Afrikaans-speaking people descended from Dutch, German, and French Huguenot settlers. Most of the remainder of the Europeans are of British descent. There are small minorities of people of mixed origin, largely descended from the indigenous Khoikhoi, European and Malay settlers, and Asians, largely of Indian origin. Most of the people are Christians, although there are significant groups of Muslims and Hindus.

The major metropolitan areas of South Africa include the capital, Pretoria; Cape Town, in Cape Province, South Africa's legislative capital and major port; Johannesburg (population, 752,000), in the Transvaal, a major commercial center and industrial city; Durban (669,000), in Natal, the Indian Ocean outlet for the Transvaal and the center of the English-speaking and Indian business communities; and Port Elizabeth (775,000), in Cape Province, an industrial city and port.

Economy. South Africa has the most highly developed industrial economy of any African country. Economic development has been made possible largely by South Africa's rich mineral resources, especially diamonds and gold.

Black African labor plays an essential part in South Africa's growing economy. Although black Africans form the bulk of unskilled labor in industry, agriculture, and mining, they are generally barred from the skilled labor force. The whites are the most prosperous group in South Africa, with incomes, material comforts, and health and education standards equal to those of Western Europe. The black South Africans suffer from poverty akin to that of the Third World. Although Coloreds and Asians are economically better off than the black Africans, they are not as prosperous as the whites.

Agriculture. Under 10 percent of the gross national product comes from agricultural production. Most farming is done on large, white-owned farms. Agriculture employs a considerable proportion of Afrikaners and most black Africans. Crop production, however, is restricted by limited rainfall and poor soil in most parts of the country.

The basic food crops are corn, sugar, sorghum, and peanuts. Fruits, especially citrus and grapes, are the most important commercial crops. They are grown mainly in the region inland from Cape Town. Cattle and sheep are raised, and wool and hides are important exports.

Mining and manufacturing. Manufacturing developed rapidly after World War II and is now the largest contributor to the economy. The sector is dominated by the manufacture of metal products, especially steel, automobiles, and chemicals. Food and tobacco processing also are important. The government owns many industries, but it encourages private enterprise.

Mining provides the capital and supports the markets required for economic growth. South Africa has rich mineral resources, and it is one of the world's largest producers of diamonds and gold. In 1986 over 10 million metric carats of diamonds were produced. Gold accounts

SPRINGBOK herds are part of the teeming wildlife on the African plains.

for 40 percent of South Africa's export earnings. It comes from mines in the Witwatersrand, in the northern part of the country, and from Odendaalsrus, in central South Africa. Waste materials at the gold mines are reprocessed to yield uranium. South Africa also has vast resources of coal and iron ore.

Trade. Long-standing trade sanctions levied against South Africa by world leaders as an expression of opposition to apartheid were greatly intensified and combined with new sanctions in the 1980s. Trade with most of the world was hindered, although the South African government found ways to circumvent sanctions: oil, for example, was imported through third-party relations.

Iron and steel, copper, diamonds, fruit, and wool are important exports. Imports include machinery, chemical products, and consumer items.

Government. South Africa is a republic. Its government is undergoing a period of intense transition as the nation faces the stresses of eliminating apartheid in all aspects of its political and social life. In September 1993 the government voted to establish a Transition Council, consisting of members representing every major political group and government jurisdiction, to oversee preparations for the first multiparty national elections in 1994. The council drafted, and the parliament approved, an interim constitution establishing a bicameral parliament, one house to be popularly elected and the other to be elected by the provincial legislatures. A new constitution was certified and went into effect in February 1997. It is being implemented in phases.

labor
US

labour
Brit.

color
US

colour
Brit.

kilometers
US

kilometres
Brit.

CAPE TOWN is the legislative capital and a major port of South Africa.

History. Bantu peoples from northern Africa came to South Africa in the 1400s or 1500s, destroying or intermarrying with the indigenous people, the Khoikhoi.

In the 1480s a Portuguese explorer, Bartholomeu Dias, rounded the Cape of Good Hope. But permanent European settlements were not made in South Africa until 1652, when the Dutch East India Company founded Cape Town as a supply base for voyages to the East Indies. The base developed into the Cape Colony, composed of Dutch settlers who supplied food for passing ships. Because cash crops would not grow well in the poor soil, the farmers, called Boers, turned to hunting and cattle raising.

Pushing eastward, the Boers repeatedly clashed with the Bantu over grazing land, water, and cattle thefts. By the end of the 1700s, Boer pressure on the Bantu peoples' already crowded land gave rise to a powerful military organization led by Shaka (c 1787–1828), chief of a Bantu clan called the Zulu. Shaka forged Bantu tribes into a nation covering much of modern South Africa.

British-Boer conflict. The British seized control of the colony in 1795. They stimulated the economy and extended the government to the frontier. Great Britain abolished slavery in 1834, and in 1836 it returned to the Bantus territory captured from them by the Boers.

The Boers, irritated by the liberal racial policies and the new legal institutions of the British, undertook a mass migration to the east known as the Great Trek. During the migration, the Boers destroyed the Zulu forces.

To deny the Boers access to the sea, the British annexed the seaport city of Natal (now Durban) from them in 1844. The Boers then journeyed to the north and founded the republics of the Transvaal and the Orange Free State, which Great Britain recognized as independent states in the 1850s.

The discovery of diamonds in 1867 and gold in 1886 in the two republics attracted many English-speaking immigrants. British and Afrikaner businessmen cooperated in Cape Colony, but the discovery of gold only strained relations between Britain and the Transvaal. The Transvaal refused to enter into any political or economic union with Britain's colonies.

In 1895 Cape Colony's prime minister, Cecil Rhodes, supported the Jameson Raid, an attempt to overthrow the Transvaal's president, Paul Kruger, and install an English-speaking government. The

raid turned the political conflict into an ethnic conflict between Afrikaners and Englishmen. In 1899 the dispute erupted into the Boer—or South African—War, which the British won.

By 1902 Great Britain had conquered the Afrikaner republics, but it granted them self-government in 1906. On May 31, 1910, the British colonies of Cape Colony and Natal were united with the former republics to form an independent Union of South Africa. At that time reserves of land were marked off for occupation by the Bantu.

The union. During World War I South Africa fought with Britain against Germany. Led by two Afrikaners, Jan Christiaan Smuts and Louis Botha, South African forces captured the German colony of South-West Africa. In 1919 Smuts became South Africa's first prime minister.

After World War I a steady price for gold and cheap labor encouraged the country to industrialize. Taxes, drought, and overcrowding on government-created reserves had driven many young black Africans off the land in search of jobs. Racial segregation was extended into industry and labor agitation became a punishable crime.

In the 1920s the National Party, formed by conservative Afrikaners, came to power. The party extended racial segregation beyond the industrial color bar. Apartheid came to include residential segregation, prohibitions against individual ownership of land by black Africans, restriction of movement, separate and unequal educational facilities, and denial of the vote to black Africans.

In 1952 the African National Congress, an association formed in 1912 to protest racial discrimination, organized boycotts and demonstrations to protest the racial laws. The government retaliated by jailing some 10,000 participants and by enacting a severe law declaring government critics "subversive."

In 1960 South African police fired into a crowd of nonwhites demonstrating against racial policies in Sharpeville, some 30 miles (48 kilometers) south of Johannesburg, killing 69 people. World opinion rallied against South Africa, but the government turned a deaf ear. In 1961 Albert Luthuli, a Zulu chief, received the Nobel Peace Prize for advocating peaceful methods for resolving South Africa's racial problems.

The republic. On May 31, 1961, South Africa withdrew from the British Commonwealth and became a republic. In 1962 South Africa withdrew its delegation to the United Nations when the General Assembly voted economic sanctions against it because of its racial policies. But heavy British and U.S. investments in South Africa blocked the effective application of sanctions.

In 1963 South Africa created the Transkei, an all-African Bantustan, or homeland, with a government separate from, but not independent of, the republic. In 1976 Transkei was declared an independent homeland, as was

Bophuthatswana in 1977, Venda in 1979, and Ciskei in 1981.

South Africa's determined and strictly enforced policies of apartheid have led to great racial strife, often culminating in violence. In 1976, during racial rioting, about 600 people, mostly Bantus, were killed.

In the 1980s, the United States and other Western nations joined African nations in a call for black majority rule in South Africa. Many nations and international corporations imposed economic sanctions and withdrew their investments from South Africa.

South Africa continued to be ruled by a white minority until 1984, when people of mixed race and Asians were allowed limited representation. In 1986 the Pass Laws that prohibited blacks from moving to the cities were abolished; blacks were given an advisory role in government and were allowed to hold South African citizenship.

In 1990 President F. W. de Klerk removed a ban on the African National Congress (ANC) and freed Nelson Mandela, one of its leaders, who had been imprisoned for 28 years. The following year de Klerk secured the repeal of key laws supporting the system of apartheid.

In 1993 a Transition Council was established in South Africa and an interim constitution was adopted, both major steps toward fully democratic elections in April 1994. As expected, the African National Congress won over 60 percent of the vote, and Nelson Mandela became the first black president of South Africa.

For their efforts to bring about a peaceful end to apartheid in South Africa, F. W. de Klerk and Nelson Mandela were awarded jointly the 1993 Nobel Peace Prize. Thabo Mbeki became president in 1999.

Sudan

Official name: *Republic of the Sudan*

Area: *947,760 sq. mi., 2,505,810 sq. km.*

Type of government: *Military*

Population: *37,090,000*

Capital: *Khartoum (Pop., 947,000)*

Largest city: *Omdurman (Pop., 1,271,000)*

Languages: *Arabic (official), English, Nubian, Ta Bedawie*

Literacy: *46%*

Currency: *Pound*

Per capita GDP: *$1,360 (Rank: 156th)*

The land. Sudan, the largest country in extent in Africa, has a varied landscape. Most of northern Sudan is occupied by the desert region of the Sahara. The Nile River flows north through central Sudan, creating a fertile region. The river's two main branches, the Blue Nile and the White Nile, meet at Khartoum, Sudan's capital, and then the great, single river flows northward into Egypt.

In west-central Sudan the Marra Mountains reach elevations well above 10,000 feet (3,049 meters). East of the Marra Mountains is the Kordofan Plateau. In central Sudan the Nuba Mountains reach elevations of over 4,300 feet (1,311 meters). South of Khartoum, in east-central Sudan, there are tropical savanna lands.

In the south there are tropical rain forests, and in the extreme southern part of the country the White Nile overflows to create a swampy region called the Sudd. The Atbara River, a tributary of the Nile, flows through eastern Sudan.

Rainfall averages only about 4 inches (10 centimeters) a year in east-central Sudan, and the Red Sea coast is arid and hot. It is relatively rainy in the western mountain region, and the south has a humid tropical climate.

The people. There are two distinct groups of people in Sudan: Arab-Africans in the northern region of Khartoum, Kordofan, Darfur, Central, Eastern, and Northern; and black African tribes in Southern Region.

Most of the Arab-Africans, who make up the majority of Sudan's population, are Arabic-speaking. They are divided into great tribal groups, including the Jaaliin, Shaiqiyya, and Kababish. Most of these people are Muslims. The more important non-Arabic-speaking peoples in northern Sudan are the Beja, who live near the Red Sea; the Nubians, who live along the Nile from Dongola to the Egyptian border; the Negroid Nuba, in southern Kordofan; and the Negroid Fur, who live in Darfur.

The southern tribes make up about one-fifth of the population. The major tribes include the Dinka, Shilluk, and Nuer. Most of the people of the southern tribes are animists, although there is a small minority of Christians.

Economy. The economy of Sudan is based on agriculture. The main food crops

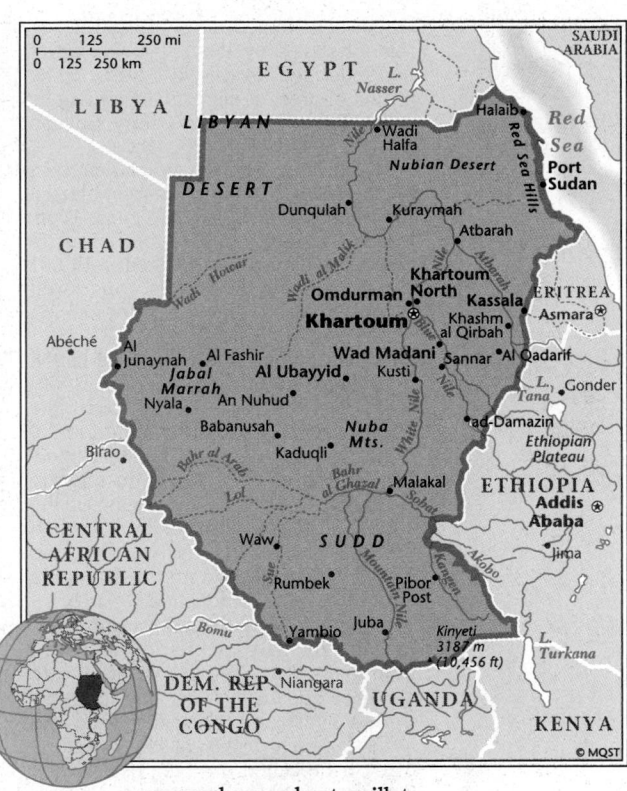

THE DATE PALM is one of the world's oldest crop plants. They have been cultivated for 5,000 years or more.

are sorghum, wheat, millet, sesame seeds, peanuts, castor beans, and dates. The major cash crop, grown primarily in the Gezira flat between the Blue and White Nile, is cotton. Sudan is, for the most part, self-sufficient in food. Almost 80 percent of its workers are farmers.

Gum arabic is produced for export, and camels and sheep are raised in many parts of the country.

Sudan's industry is concerned primarily with processing agricultural products. Although Sudan extracts iron ore, chromite, and other minerals, its mining is underdeveloped. An inadequate trans-portation infrastructure continues to hinder economic development.

Substantial petroleum reserves were discovered in the mid-1970s; these reserves could make Sudan self-sufficient in that area, but ongoing civil unrest has stopped development in the industry.

The major imports are petroleum products, textiles, machinery, and foodstuffs. The major exports are cotton, sorghum, sesame seed, and gum arabic. Most trade is conducted with Saudi Arabia, Egypt, and European Union nations.

Government. In 1983 Sudan was divided into regions, each led by a governor. In 1989 a coup suspended the regional governorships. Each region was placed under a military leader. The regions rely heavily on the central government, which is still run by the military, for economic support. Although the government is in transition and a president is now elected by popular vote, there remains skepticism that any real changes are imminent.

History. Sudan's history has always been closely linked with that of Egypt. In about 3000 B.C. the pharaohs of ancient

Egypt sent expeditions into Sudan to raid for slaves; by about 2000 B.C. Egypt had extended its rule into Sudan. The region of present-day Sudan came to be called Kush. The power of Egypt began to decline after about 2000 B.C.

A Nubian leader from Napata, in north-central Sudan, proclaimed himself king of Kush in 750 B.C. He gained control of Egypt and established a Sudanese dynasty that lasted until 661 B.C., when the Assyrians conquered Egypt. After that time, Egyptian civilization in Sudan declined.

The kingdom of Kush reestablished itself as an independent state and survived until about A.D. 350, at which time it was destroyed by the kingdom of Axum, in Ethiopia. After that, black peoples from the south began to migrate into northern Sudan. Beginning in the 500s the peoples of northern Sudan became Christians, and two Christian dynasties, the kingdoms of Maqurra and Alwa, were established.

In the late 1200s the Mamluks, a Muslim dynasty in Egypt, destroyed Maqurra. Arabs began migrating into northern Sudan, and many of the people were converted to Islam. Alwa survived until the early 1500s, at which time a black tribe called the Funj established the powerful Muslim state of Sennar. Until its decline some 300 years later, the Funj dynasty provided Sudan with unity and security.

Egyptian conquest of Sudan began in 1820, and Sennar was overrun by Egyptian armies. At the junction of the White and Blue Niles, Egypt created a military and administrative center, Khartoum, which became the capital of Egyptian Sudan. Egyptian rule lasted until 1885. In that year a Sudanese, Muhammad Ahmad, often called al-Mahdi, captured Khartoum after a 4-year religious and political struggle against Egyptian rule.
Condominium. Sudan remained under the firm control of al-Mahdi's successor until an Anglo-Egyptian military force conquered Sudan in 1898. Sudan became a condominium ruled jointly by Great Britain and Egypt in 1899, but in fact Britain controlled Sudan. The period of British rule was considered by many a model of colonial administration, achieving security and economic development.

Although nationalist movements emerged in the 1920s, they became important only during World War II. The local nationalist movement was strongly marked by rivalry between two major Muslim religious brotherhoods, the Khatmiya and the Ansar. The Khatmiya, led by Sayyid Ali al-Mirghani, favored union with Egypt. The Ansar, led by Sayyid Abd al-Rahman, a son of Muhammad Ahmad, took a more pro-British stand and favored complete independence.

In 1953 Egypt and Britain granted Sudan self-government, and soon all sides were able to agree on complete independence for Sudan. A parliament was established in January 1954, and the National Unionist Party, which represented a more secular policy than the brotherhoods, formed the first cabinet. On January 1, 1956, Sudan became an independent republic.
Independence. The Umma Party, mainly composed of Ansar supporters, and the People's Democratic Party, largely Khatmiya supporters, formed a coalition, and in July 1956 the National Unionist Party was forced from power. Political instability ensued and, following a 1969 military coup, General Gaafar al-Nimeiry took control of the newly formed socialist state.

In spite of some student unrest, considerable stability was achieved. The southern provinces had gone into rebellion against the north in 1963 and were granted regional autonomy in 1975.

Nimeiry led Sudan out of favor with the Soviet Union, a strong ally before the 1972 purges of the Communist Party.

In 1985 Nimeiry was overthrown in a military coup led by his defense minister, Abdel Rahman el-Dahab.

In 1989 the government was again overthrown in a coup led by Omar Ahmed al-Bashir. The Bashir government imposed Islamic law throughout Sudan. Factional fighting continued after the coup as it has for most of the last 30 years. Historically, the fighting was caused by southern Sudanese resentment of northern Sudanese domination of the government.

Also in 1989, the country was split between the Sudanese People's Liberation Army (SPLA), which controlled large areas of the southern provinces, and the new national government, which controlled the northern provinces and the major towns and cities in the south.

Years of civil unrest led many to flee the country and inhibited agricultural production. This and years of drought caused widespread starvation throughout the 1990s. The situation improved somewhat and an increase in oil exportation showed promise for the country. Agreements between the government and the rebels in 2002 and 2003 regarding a future power-sharing government brought hope of eventual stability.

Swaziland

Official name: *Kingdom of Swaziland*

Area: *6,701 sq. mi., 17,360 sq. km.*

Type of government: *Monarchy*

Population: *1,150,000*

Capital and largest city: *Mbabane (Pop., 38,000)*

Languages: *English, siSwati (both official)*

Literacy: *78%*

Currency: *Lilangeni*

Per capita GDP: *$4,200 (Rank: 97th)*

The land. Swaziland possesses three well-defined veld, or grassland,

regions—the highveld, middleveld, and lowveld. The highveld, in western Swaziland, is mountainous and has an average elevation of 3,500 feet (1,067 kilometers). To the east is the middleveld, with an average elevation of 2,000 feet (610 kilometers). The lowveld, in eastern Swaziland, has average elevations of 1,000 feet (305 kilometers). The Lubombo, a plateau region, is in the extreme eastern part of the country.

The highveld is humid and receives between 40 and 90 inches (103 and 231 centimeters) of rain each year. The climate in the middleveld and Lubombo plateau is subtropical and drier, receiving between 30 and 45 inches (77 and 115 centimeters) of rain each year. The lowveld receives between 20 and 30 inches (51 and 77 centimeters) of rain each year.
The people. Most of the people of Swaziland belong to the Bantu Swazi tribe. The Swazi have traditionally been a pastoral people. Eighty percent of the Swazi live in rural areas. There are also a small number of Bantu people of the Zulu group in southern Swaziland.

About 3 percent of the people are of European origin, mainly Afrikaans-speaking in southern Swaziland and English or Afrikaans-speaking in the north. There is a small community of people of mixed European and African descent that controls a great deal of the economy. Over half of the people are Christian; the remainder practice traditional, indigenous religions.

There are only two large cities in Swaziland—Mbabane, the capital, and Manzini, formerly known as Bremersdorp, the country's geographic and commercial center and a lively market town.
Economy. About 25 percent of Swaziland's gross national product is contributed by agriculture and about 25 percent by mining and industry combined. The economy is more diversified than most others in Africa, owing largely to the country's fertile soil, rich forests, abundant water supply, and gambling casino at the Royal Swazi Hotel, which contributes extensive government revenues.

THE APPEAL of a child's face is universal.

In recent years the Swazi have become successful farmers. The basic food crops are corn, beans, peanuts, and sorghum. The chief cash crops are sugar, wood pulp, fruits, cotton, and tobacco. Fifty-six percent of the land is held by the government in trust for the Swazi nation. The remaining land is privately owned.

Cattle are raised in most parts of the country. The Swazi have traditionally valued cattle as a symbol of social status; only in recent years have cattle acquired economic importance. Forestry, mainly in the highveld, is of growing importance to the economy.

Swaziland's mineral resources include large deposits of iron ore and asbestos. There are also deposits of coal, gold, tin, barytes, and pyrophyllite. Iron ore mined at Ngwenya, in western Swaziland, is carried by rail to the port of Maputo, in Mozambique, for export. However, iron ore deposits were severely depleted by 1978 and health concerns precipitated a serious decline in demand for asbestos. Sugar refining, fruit canning, and wood pulp processing are now the main manufacturing activities. In addition, the textile industry has been growing rapidly.

Swaziland's main imports are food, machinery, and petroleum products. The leading exports are sugar, wood pulp, and fruit. Most trade is conducted with South Africa, Great Britain, and Japan.

Swaziland has close economic ties with South Africa, and many Swazis find work there. Customs duties for Swaziland are collected by South Africa, and Swaziland receives a fixed percentage of South Africa's customs revenue each year. Swaziland also uses South African currency.

THE RHINOCEROS has been placed on the list of endangered species.

Government. Swaziland is a monarchy and has a parliamentary system of government. The legislature is a bicameral Parliament (Libandla) led by a prime minister. The king chooses 20 of the 30 Senate members and 10 of the 65 House of Assembly members. Parliament functions chiefly as the king's advisory council.

History. In the mid-1700s the Ngoni broke away from the main body of Bantu peoples. They came into conflict with another group of Bantu people, the Zulu, and by the early 1800s the Zulu had forced them northward into present-day Swaziland.

A Ngoni chief, Sobhuza, founded the Swazi nation by fusing several Ngoni clans with some Sotho people they had conquered. Sobhuza's son Mswati extended Swazi power and prestige among neighboring peoples.

European influence. Europeans began to settle in the area in the 1800s, and the Swazi ruler granted them many land concessions. Both the British colony of Natal, in present-day South Africa, and the Afrikaner, or Boer, Republic of the Transvaal, also in present-day South Africa, claimed Swaziland. In 1890 a compromise was reached, and a provisional government was established; it was composed of representatives of the Swazi, the British, and the Transvaal Afrikaners.

To appease the Afrikaners, the British ceded administration of Swaziland to the Transvaal in 1894, despite Swazi protests. In the Boer, or South African, War (1899–1902), the British conquered the Transvaal and assumed control of Swaziland. In 1907 the British High Commissioner for South Africa took over the administration.

The rise of nationalism in the 1940s and 1950s threatened the Swazi aristocracy and the white community, both of whom feared the loss of power and privilege. In 1960 these groups requested Great Britain to grant a constitution that would preserve the status quo. A British-sponsored constitution promulgated in 1964, which instituted popular elections for the national legislature, was the first step toward the transfer of sovereignty.

Independence. Traditionalist forces, led by the Swazi chief Sobhuza II, formed the Imbokodvo Party, which won a majority of seats in the legislative council in Swaziland's first elections in 1964. In April 1967 Britain granted Swaziland self-government; independence was gained on September 6, 1968.

In 1973 King Sobhuza II repealed the constitution; he replaced it with a new one in 1978 that makes the king the chief of state. Sobhuza II died in 1982 and was replaced by two different queen regents until Mswati III became king in 1986.

Swaziland was an important ally of South Africa during the period of tough sanctions in the 1980s, and was used as a base for a good portion of South Africa's international trade. When Mswati III came of age in April 1986,

he began to loosen his country's ties with South Africa. The Swazi government has actively pursued assistance from other countries.

Tanzania

Official name: *United Republic of Tanzania*

Area: *364,805 sq. mi., 945,090 sq. km.*

Type of government: *Republic*

Population: *35,302,000*

Capital: *Dodoma (Pop., 204,000)*

Largest city: *Dar es Salaam (Pop., 1,361,000)*

Languages: *Swahili, English*

Literacy: *68%;* **Currency:** *Shilling*

Per capita GDP: *$610 (Rank: 187th)*

The land. Tanzania was formed in 1964 by the merger of the mainland nation of Tanganyika and the offshore islands of Zanzibar and Pemba.

Tanganyika is by far the larger part of the republic, with an area of some 361,800 square miles (937,062 square kilometers). Zanzibar, which includes Zanzibar and Pemba islands, has an area of 1,020 square miles (2,642 square kilometers).

Tanganyika is occupied mainly by a high, semiarid plateau, with mountain masses in the northeast and southwest. Mt. Kilimanjaro, the highest point in Africa, reaching 19,331 feet (5,892 meters) above sea level, is near the Kenya border, and Lake Victoria is part of the northern lowland. The narrow coastal plain, with an average width of 20 miles (32 kilometers), reaches inland to the edge of the plateau. The Rufiji River flows through central Tanganyika.

MOUNT KILIMANJARO looms over the landscape in Tanzania.

Zanzibar and Pemba are low-lying coral islands with many inlets. There are mangrove swamps on the islands. The islands' temperatures are high from December to March and lower between June and October. Heavy rains fall in April and May, and there are light rains in November and December. Average annual rainfall is between 60 and 80 inches (154 and 205 centimeters).

The people. Over 96 percent of Tanzania's population live on the mainland, and the country's largest city, Dar es Salaam, is on the coast of Tanganyika. About 90 percent of the labor force is occupied by subsistence farming.

Tanganyika's people include members of some 120 tribes, most of which are Bantu. The largest tribe is the Sukuma. There are also groups of Arabs, Europeans, and people of Indian and Pakistani origin.

Zanzibar and Pemba also have many different peoples, including Shirazis, who are descendants of ancient Persians, Africans from the mainland, Arabs, Asians, and people from the Comoro Islands. Over 90 percent of the population live in rural areas. Tanzania's principal cities include Dodoma, the capital; Dar es Salaam, the former capital; Mwanza (population, 223,000); Mbeya (153,000); and Zanzibar Town (158,000).

Economy. The economy of Tanzania is based on agriculture. Agriculture employs 90 percent of the workforce and provides 85 percent of exports. The basic food crops are rice, corn, and sorghum.

In Tanganyika, cotton, coffee, and sisal, a fiber used in rope, are the most important commercial crops.

Sisal and coffee are generally grown on mountain slopes, and cotton is produced mainly in the lowlands near Lake Victoria. Cattle are currently raised in most parts of the mainland.

Large quantities of cloves are grown on plantations in Zanzibar and Pemba. Coconuts are an important commercial crop. In addition, fishing is significant in the economy.

Industry in Tanzania consists mainly of food processing. Mineral resources are considerable on the mainland, but they are widely distributed and transportation costs are high. Diamonds are mined, and there are also deposits of lead, gold, and iron ore.

Agriculture, which accounts for over half of the gross national product, is largely collectivized. Industry, which contributes less than 10 percent of the gross national product, has become increasingly nationalized since 1967. Today most of the manufacturing industry is state-controlled, although the government is slowly instituting measures to liberalize the economy.

The major imports are petroleum products, textiles, and machinery. The major exports are sisal, coffee, cotton, and cloves. Most trade is with Germany, Great Britain, and the United States.

Government. Tanzania has been ruled since 1977 by its Revolutionary Party. A president and vice president are elected on the same ballot to a 5-year term. Legislative power is held by a 274-member National Assembly. Zanzibar elects its own 50-member House of Representatives which enacts laws applying to Zanzibar. Additionally Zanzibar elects a president who presides over matters internal to Zanzibar.

History. The 1964 union of Tanganyika and Zanzibar merged the histories of two separate regions.

Zanzibar. Arabs began colonizing Zanzibar in the 700s. Portuguese arrived in the late 1500s and brought the area under Portuguese rule. About 1700, Arabs from Oman broke Portugal's control of the islands and established a sultanate. The Arabs developed a prosperous slave market and encouraged the growth of clove plantations.

In the 1800s Great Britain gained control of the islands and ended the slave trade. In 1890 Britain formally established a protectorate over Zanzibar. The sultan remained as nominal ruler, however, and until 1956 the islands were ruled primarily by Arabs under British supervision.

Two political parties were formed in the 1950s—the Zanzibar Nationalist Party (ZNP), representing the Arabs, and the Afro-Shirazi Party (ASP), representing mainly the African population and some Shirazi. In 1957 the ASP split and the Zanzibar and Pemba Peoples' Party (ZPPP) was formed.

On June 24, 1963, Zanzibar became self-governing; elections were held in July. Although the African-dominated ASP won the largest number of votes, the government was controlled by a coalition of the ZNP and ZPPP.

Zanzibar received its independence on December 9, 1963, and Sheik Muhammad Shamte became prime minister of the coalition government. The opposition, consisting largely of Africans, staged a bloody coup against Arab rule on January 12, 1964. The sultan was overthrown and a republic proclaimed. Sheik Adeid Amani Karume, leader of the ASP, became president. Karume asked Tanganyika to provide assistance to restore order. Zanzibar and Tanganyika were united at Karume's request.

Tanganyika. In the 700s Arabs also established settlements in the coastal region of Tanganyika. The Portuguese settled in the region in the late 1400s. The Arabs developed a prosperous slave trade in the interior that flourished until the 1800s, when it was checked by Christian missionaries led by David Livingstone.

Germany began colonizing the area in 1884, and in 1890 the region became part of German East Africa. After World War I Tanganyika became a British mandate under the League of Nations, and in 1946 it became a UN trust territory. Nationalism grew in the 1950s, and in 1954 Julius Nyerere formed a nationalist political party, the Tanganyika African National Union (TANU). The candidates of TANU were victorious in the first elections for a legislative council, held in 1958.

In 1959 Britain took steps to establish self-government for Tanganyika, which became fully independent on December 9, 1961. A republic was proclaimed in 1962.

United republic. Tanzania was created in 1964 by the merger of Tanganyika and Zanzibar. Nyerere, president of Tanganyika since 1961, became the president of the United Republic of Tanzania in 1964.

In the 1960s and 1970s Nyerere introduced a form of socialism in which there was communal farming, the goal of national self-reliance for workers, and the nationalization of many privately owned businesses.

The revolutionary army that was responsible for the 1964 overthrow of the sultan of Zanzibar joined with revolutionary forces in Tanzania in the successful execution of the 1977 military coup there. The Revolutionary Party that took power was repressive and socialistic.

In 1979 the Tanzanian army was welcomed as Uganda's liberator when it marched into that country on a retaliatory mission. Tanzanian forces ended up deposing Uganda's ruthless despot, Idi Amin. Tanzania is in the midst of a potentially enormous period of change. As it continues to move toward liberalizing the economy, the government is being pressed by opposing factions. Foreign aid donors want reforms to speed up greatly with a completely free market as the goal. Old guard politicians oppose abandoning socialism. President Ali Mwinyi has guided reform programs according to his own slow pace.

Discontent in Zanzibar erupted into violence in early 1988. Many residents of Zanzibar contended that secession was the only answer to their problems.

In 1992 the ruling Revolutionary Party approved a constitutional change to allow multiparty politics. In 1995 the first multiparty elections took place.

labor
US

labour
Brit.

fiber
US

fibre
Brit.

Togo

Official name: *Togolese Republic*
Area: *21,921 sq. mi., 56,790 sq. km.*
Type of government: *Transition*
Population: *5,299,000*
Capital and largest city: *Lomé*
   (Pop., 450,000)
Languages: *French (official), Ewe,*
   Mina, Kabye, Dagomba
Literacy: *52%;*
Currency: *CFA franc*
Per capita GDP: *$1,500*
   (Rank: 153rd)

The land. Grasslands occupy most of Togo. There is a sandy coast behind which are lagoons. Inland from the lagoons is the Terre de Barre, a low, clay plain that rises to a sandy plateau. The Togo Atakora Mountains cross the center of the country, whose highest elevation at Pic Baumann is 3,235 feet (986 meters). The Mono and Ogou rivers flow through Togo. The climate is hot and humid. Annual rainfall varies from 28 to 63 inches (72 to 162 centimeters) throughout the country.

The people. There are many different ethnic groups in Togo. The largest groups are the Ewe (25 percent of the population) in the south and the Kabre (15 percent of the population) in the north. Lomé is Togo's largest city, other cities include Sokodé and Kpalimé.

About half of the people are animists. Less than one-third are Christians (mostly Roman Catholic); the rest are Muslims. Togo has a rapidly growing population, with about a 3 percent annual rise in recent years. The population is unevenly distributed; most is concentrated in the south and along the major north-south highway connecting the coast to the Sahel.

Economy. Agriculture and commerce are the main economic activities in Togo. Eighty percent of the population are engaged in agriculture. Yams, rice, corn, millet, and sorghum, grown mainly in the interior, are the principal food crops. Cotton, cacao, and coffee are the leading commercial crops. Palm products, such as copra and palm oil, are important, and the peoples near the coast and the lagoons prepare copra and coconut oil. Togo is self-sufficient in basic foodstuffs when harvests are normal.

Togo has rich phosphate deposits; approximately 3 million tons are shipped annually, accounting for almost 35 percent of export earnings. Mining and industry are relatively undeveloped, though, and account for only about one-fifth of the country's gross national product, while agriculture accounts for nearly two-fifths.

Togo's main imports are machinery, foodstuffs, consumer goods, and fuels. The major exports are phosphate, cotton, coffee, and cacao. Most trade is conducted with European Union nations.

Government. In July 1991 a constitutional conference voted to suspend Togo's 1979 constitution, dissolve its National Assembly, and declare its backers sovereign. In August it stripped the president of most of his powers and appointed a prime minister as head of a transitional government. In October a commission was formed to draft a new constitution for Togo. In 1992 a new constitution was adopted.

History. Between about the 1200s and the 1800s many African tribal kingdoms established their rule over the area of present-day Togo. In the 1400s Portugal developed trade relations with the Ewe. By the mid-1890s Germany had established a protectorate over Togo. After World War I the German protectorate was divided into separate British and French mandates under the League of Nations. In 1946 the mandates became trust territories under the UN.

Great Britain administered its trust territory along with the Gold Coast colony. In 1956 British Togoland voted to join the Gold Coast, which became the independent nation of Ghana in 1957.

After World War II France established a locally elected territorial assembly in French Togoland. In 1956 French Togoland obtained internal self-government from France. Nicolas Grunitzky, of the Togolese Progressive Party, became the country's first prime minister. Grunitzky's party lost elections held in 1958 and his brother-in-law, Sylvanus Olympio, leader of the Committee for the Togolese Unity Party, succeeded him.

Independence. On April 27, 1960, Togo became independent. Lieutenant Colonel Etienne Eyadéma led a successful coup in 1967. Eyadéma has been Togo's president ever since.

In 1986, 70 Togolese dissidents attempted to overthrow the Eyadéma government but the insurrection was halted after 2 days of fighting. In 1987 Togo established a National Human Rights Commission to investigate complaints of human rights abuses.

In 1991, after several weeks of violent demonstrations, President Eyadéma agreed to set up a transitional government, to hold multiparty elections, and to rewrite the constitution. A constitution was adopted and multiparty elections instituted; however, Eyadéma remains president and validity of elections are in question.

Tunisia

Official name: *Republic of Tunisia*
Area: *63,153 sq. mi., 163,610 sq. km.*
Type of government: *Republic*
Population: *9,816,000*
Capital and largest city: *Tunis*
   (Pop., 702,000)
Languages: *Arabic (official),*
   French
Literacy: *67%*
Currency: *Dinar*
Per capita GDP: *$6,600*
   (Rank: 75th)

The land. Tunisia has four contrasting geographical regions—the Sahel, or plains, along the east coast; a steppe region inland from the coast; the Atlas mountain system in the north; and a low-lying desert region, part of the Sahara, in the south.

The Sahel is occupied by low rolling hills. Paralleling the eastern coast, but farther inland, is the flatter steppe region. The Tell Atlas in the far north is separated from the Saharan Atlas, or High Tell, by the Medjerda River valley. The Tell Atlas extends to the coast in Cape Blanc, and the Saharan Atlas extends to the coast in Cape Bon. The highest peaks are Mount Chambi, which rises to 5,066 feet (1,544 meters)

center
US

centre
Brit.

meters
US

metres
Brit.

near the Algerian border, and Mount Mrhila, which reaches 4,521 feet (1,378 meters) southwest of Tunis.

South of the mountains is the Shott el Jerid, a large salt lake close to sea level that receives some streams from the mountains. In the southwest, along the boundary with Algeria, lies part of the Grand Erg Oriental, a major sand area of the Sahara.

In the northern part of the country winters are mild and rainy and summers are hot and dry. Annual rainfall in the north averages 16 inches (41 centimeters). South of the Shott el Jerid the climate is hot and dry with less than 4 inches (10 centimeters) of rain a year.

The people. Most of Tunisia's people are descended from indigenous Berber-speaking peoples and later Arab immigrants. There are small communities of Jews and Europeans, mainly French, Italian, and Maltese, and nomadic Berber tribes in the desert.

Tunis, the capital, is the country's largest city and principal port. Other important cities are Sfax (population, 249,000); Bizerte (106,000); Gabès (105,000); and Sousse (125,000). Kairouan (110,000), southwest of Tunis, is a historic Muslim holy city.

Tunisia's population, over half urban, has grown at a rapid rate of over 2 percent a year during the last decade. Literacy has also increased over that period, owing to aggressive government educational programs.

Economy. Tunisia has been working toward a more open economy. In 1986 an aggressive reform program was instituted, encouraging growth in the private sector. The population growth and improved literacy have created a surplus of skilled labor. Thirty percent of the workforce are occupied by farming; another 30 percent are distributed among manufacturing, construction, and mining.

Industry and mining combined account for over 30 percent of Tunisia's gross national product, while commerce and banking account for just under 25 percent, and agriculture for under 20 percent.

Tunisia has rich phosphate, iron ore, and oil deposits that account for most of its mining and industry. Food processing is also significant.

Tunisia is one of the world's leading producers of olive oil; wheat, barley, and olives are the main crops. Figs, citrus fruits, and wine grapes are also grown, and livestock raising is the major occupation of the nomads.

The major imports are food, lumber, textiles, and machinery. The major exports are oil, phosphates, olive oil, and fruits. Most trade is conducted with European Union countries, particularly France, Italy, and Germany.

Government. Tunisia has a presidential system of government. Executive power is vested in a president who is popularly elected to a 5-year term. Legislative power is held by the 182-member unicameral Chamber of Deputies, which is also popularly elected every 5 years.

History. In 814 B.C. the Phoenicians founded the city of Carthage, near the site of present-day Tunis. In 146 B.C. Rome destroyed Carthage, and Tunisia came under Roman domination. Roman rule ended in the A.D. 400s with invasions by the Vandals. In the 500s the region came under Byzantine rule.

A decisive break in Tunisian history occurred with the arrival of Muslim Arabs in the mid-600s. Although the native people were the most Romanized and Christianized people of northwestern Africa, Tunisia became part of the Arab-Muslim world.

Tunisia shared the fortunes of the dynasties that arose in northern Africa and Spain. In the early 800s the Aghlabids gained control of Tunisia. The Fatimids controlled much of Tunisia in the 900s, and in the 1100s a Morocco-based dynasty, the Almohad, gained control. In 1228 the Almohads were succeeded by the Hafsids, who ruled Tunisia until the early 1500s, when the Ottoman Turks began a series of invasions.

By 1574 Tunisia had become part of the Ottoman Empire, but it was soon able to achieve a considerable measure of self-rule. In 1705 an Ottoman Turkish ruler of Tunisia, owing allegiance to the sultan, established the Husaynid dynasty, which lasted until the monarchy was abolished in 1957.

The local Tunisian government attempted internal reforms and westernization early in the 1800s, but Tunisia soon fell victim to foreign indebtedness and increasing European interference. In 1881, after a brief military campaign, France established a protectorate over Tunisia.

French administration. Although large numbers of French and other Europeans settled in the country, native institutions were left largely intact. Tunisians learned technical skills from the French and benefited from the country's economic growth without being overwhelmed in the process.

Nationalism developed rapidly after World War I, and the Tunisian struggle for independence came to be personified by Habib Bourguiba, who organized the Neo-Destour Party in 1934. The Neo-Destour grew out of an earlier, more traditional party, the Destour, or Constitution Party.

After a long period of intermittent negotiations and armed struggle, France agreed to grant Tunisia internal self-government in 1954. On March 20, 1956, France granted Tunisia complete independence, and in 1957 Tunisia become a republic with Bourguiba as president.

Independence. Tunisia, after independence, made impressive improvements in education and economic development. Diplomatically, the period from 1956 until neighboring Algeria won its independence from France in 1962 placed Tunisia in the delicate position of attempting to maintain relations with France while supporting the Algerian independence movement.

In 1961 fighting erupted in Tunisia between the French and the Tunisian supporters of the Algerians. Relations between the two worsened. In 1962 France moved out of its naval base in Bizerte. In 1964 the government nationalized French holdings in Tunisia, and France ended its technical and economic assistance.

Tunisia restored relations with France in 1968, but lost favor with the Arab states for its support of Egyptian-Israeli peace moves. Tension with Libya increased after the two nations failed to carry through with a proposed merger in 1974. In 1980 Libya attacked Gafsa in Tunisia.

Bourguiba was elected president for life in 1974. Labor riots in 1978 became widespread as many political opponents of the president denounced his autocratic rule. Bourguiba was a liberal autocrat, respecting human rights and allowing the economy to prosper. In 1983 Bourguiba legalized two opposition political parties.

In November 1987 Prime Minister Zine al-Abidine Ben Ali declared Bourguiba senile and replaced him as president. Ben Ali was elected president in April 1989.

Ben Ali opened up the political system—giving amnesty to former opponents and liberalizing laws governing the public sector. Other broad-ranging economic reforms were instituted to encourage foreign investment.

Uganda

Official name: *Republic of Uganda*
Area: *91,820 sq. m.,*
236,040 sq. km.
Type of government: *Republic*
Population: *24,889,000*
Capital and largest city: *Kampala*
(Pop., 1,209,000)
Languages: *English (official),*
Luganda, Swahili, Banto
Literacy: *63%*
Currency: *Shilling*
Per capita GDP: *$1,200*
(Rank: 162nd)

The land. Most of Uganda is occupied by a plateau with elevations between 3,000 and 6,000 feet (915 and 1,829 meters) above sea level. The Ruwenzori Mountains run along the western border, reaching an elevation of more than 16,760 feet (5,110 meters) at Mt. Margherita. In the east Mt. Elgon reaches an elevation of almost 14,180 feet (4,323 meters).

Lake Victoria is at the southeastern corner of Uganda. Lakes Edward and Albert are in western Uganda, and Lake Kyoga is in central Uganda. The Albert Nile and the Victoria Nile are among the country's many rivers.

Uganda has a tropical climate. In the northeast rainfall averages about 20 inches (51 centimeters) a year, but in the southwest and west it averages

meters
US

metres
Brit.

labor
US

labour
Brit.

COUNTRIES

Uganda has rich copper deposits, as well as deposits of iron ore and cobalt.

Most industry is engaged in the processing of Uganda's mineral and agricultural products. The Owen Falls hydroelectric plant, near Lake Victoria, supplies most of the country's electricity, and industry is concentrated in the Owen Falls region.

The major imports are textiles, petroleum products, iron and steel, and machinery. The principal exports are coffee, tea, tobacco, cotton, and copper. Most trade is conducted with Great Britain, Kenya, the United States, and Italy. Uganda has close economic ties with Kenya and Tanzania.

Government. In a 1986 coup, the National Resistance Council seized power and named Yoweri Museveni president. A new constitution in 1995 banned political parties, but nonparty legislative and presidential elections were held in 1996.

History. Between the 1400s and 1600s various peoples established kingdoms in present-day Uganda. In the 1600s the Buganda kingdom became powerful and conquered many of the existing states.

James Augustus Grant and John Hanning Speke explored the source of the Nile in 1862 and established trade relations between Great Britain and Mutesa I, the *kabaka,* or king, of Buganda. Protestant and Roman Catholic missionaries followed, as well as Muslims, who were in contact with neighboring regions. In the 1880s Mutesa's son and successor, Mwanga, attempted to stop the spread of Christianity in the area, and many Christians were killed.

British rule. In 1888 the Imperial British East Africa Company concluded a treaty with Buganda, and the kingdom came under the company's administration. The company withdrew from the area because of economic difficulties, and in 1894 Great Britain established a protectorate over the region. By 1896 the protectorate included all of present-day Uganda.

In 1900 the Buganda regent signed the Uganda Agreement with Britain; it established administrative arrangements that were to endure until Uganda achieved self-government in 1962. The kabaka, with his *lukiko,* or assembly, was recognized as the ruler of Uganda as long as he cooperated with Britain. Four regions were marked out—Eastern, Western, Northern, and Buganda. The Buganda region occupied south-central Uganda.

Britain established a legislative council following World War I, and African members were appointed to the council after World War II. In 1953 Buganda demanded independence from the rest of Uganda. It feared being forced into federation with the British protectorate of Kenya and Tanganyika, and thereby coming under the control of Kenya's white settler community. In the same year, Kabaka Edward Mutesa II was exiled after refusing to nominate Bugandan members to the legislative council.

Independence. In March of 1962, Uganda was granted self-rule. Milton Obote, prime minister, led a coalition party that was able to incorporate Buganda peacefully. On October 9, 1962, Uganda became independent, with Obote as prime minister and the king of Buganda, Edward Mutesa II, as president.

In 1966 Obote took full control of the government, suspended the constitution, and ousted President Mutesa. Obote assumed the position of president. In January of 1971 Obote was overthrown by troops led by General Idi Amin, who then named himself president.

Amin, a Muslim traditionalist, became president for life, expelled most Asians from the country in 1972, abolished the parliament, and opened virtual warfare against the Christian tribes. Amin's harsh and repressive tactics, as well as his avid attempts to Africanize the economy, led to shortages of skilled labor, a decrease in exports, excessive inflation, and hostile relations with Western Europe and the United States. Over 100,000 Ugandans were murdered

AFRICA'S MAIN cash crops are cacao, coffee, cotton, bananas, and sugar cane, seen growing here.

between 50 and 60 inches (128 and 154 centimeters) a year.

The people. There are many tribal groups in Uganda, most of which are Bantu-speaking. The largest Bantu tribe is the Ganda. Other large groups include the Teso, the Nkole, and the Soga. There are also peoples of Nilotic and Nilo-Hamitic stock, and small communities of Asians and Europeans.

Uganda's largest cities include Kampala, the capital; Jinja (population, 87,000); and Entebbe (58,000). All three are near Lake Victoria. Over 90 percent of the people live in rural areas. The population is concentrated in southern Uganda. Two-thirds of the people are Christian and the rest are animists and Muslims.

Economy. Uganda's economy is based on agriculture. About 80 percent of the workforce is engaged in agricultural endeavors. The basic food crops are corn, beans, and cassava, and the main cash crops are cotton and coffee. Coffee accounts for nearly 90 percent of the country's exports. Tobacco, sugar cane, and tea are also grown. Cattle are raised in many parts of the country, and fish from Uganda's lakes are important to the economy.

MORE THAN 90 percent of Ugandans live in rural areas, such as in this camp of round huts.

endeavors
US

endeavours
Brit.

meters
US

metres
Brit.

by members of Amin's regime. When Amin ordered an invasion of Tanzania in 1978, Tanzanian troops marched into Uganda and were welcomed as its liberators. Amin was ousted.

Political anarchy ensued until 1980, when Obote returned to rule. He restored good relations with the West, and although he promised to respect human rights and provide a liberal administration, changes were slow in coming.

Obote was overthrown in a military coup in 1985 and Yoweri Museveni organized a new government. Over the succeeding years, Museveni's government took enormous steps toward restoring stability and rebuilding the economy. Uganda experienced fast economic growth, but inflation and government corruption continue to be major obstacles to further growth.

Zambia

Official name: *Republic of Zambia*
Area: *290,507 sq. mi., 752,610 sq. km.*
Type of government: *Republic*
Population: *10,149,000*
Capital and largest city: *Lusaka (Pop., 1,270,000)*
Languages: *English (official), indigenous dialects*
Literacy: *79%;* **Currency:** *Kwacha*
Per capita GDP: *$880 (Rank: 176th)*

The land.   Most of Zambia is occupied by a high plain, with elevations between 3,000 and 4,000 feet (915 and 1,220 meters) above sea level. In the east are the Muchinga Mountains, with a peak of over 6,000 feet (1,829 meters).

The Zambezi River flows along the border with Zimbabwe, and the Luangwa and Kafue rivers, tributaries of the Zambezi, flow through Zambia. Along the Zambezi River is Victoria Falls, where the river plunges more than 300 feet (92 meters) into a deep canyon. Kariba Lake, formed by the Kariba Dam on the Zambezi River, is one of the largest man-made lakes in the world.

Zambia has a subtropical climate. The country receives between 25 and 30 inches (64 and 77 centimeters) of rain a year.

The people.   Most of the people in Zambia are Bantu. The largest ethnic groups are the Bemba, Tsonga, Chewa, and Lozi. About 1 percent of the population is European. Most Europeans live in the north-central part of the country. There are also some Asians and people of mixed origins.

About 40 percent of the people live in urban areas, with the largest concentrations being in the northern copper belt towns. The main cities include Lusaka, the capital; Ndola (population, 442,000); Kitwe (467,000); and Chingola (212,000).

Economy.   Mining accounts for half of the gross national product, while agriculture and manufacturing contribute about 20 percent each. About 90 percent of all export revenues come from copper and cobalt production. North-central Zambia is known as the Copper Belt. Over half of the country's energy demands are met by its domestic waterpower reserves. There is also an oil pipeline from Tanzania. Zinc and lead are mined along with copper and cobalt. Zambia is working desperately to diversify the economy and reduce dependence on the mining industry.

Zambia's basic food crops are corn, cassava, millet, rice, soybeans, and wheat. Tobacco, peanuts, and cotton also are grown. Many of Zambia's farms and industries were nationalized by 1975 in an effort to close the gap between the prosperity of the white minority and the destitution and poverty of the black majority.

The main imports are textiles, petroleum products, iron and steel, and machinery. The major exports are copper, zinc, and tobacco. Most trade is conducted with European Union countries, Japan, South Africa, and the United States.

Government.   Zambia has a presidential system of government. Executive power is vested in a president who is popularly elected to a 5-year term and is limited to two terms. The president appoints a vice president. Legislative power rests with the 150-member National Assembly. Assembly members are popularly elected to 5-year terms.

History.   Waves of Bantu-speaking immigrants began arriving in the 15th century, with the largest numbers arriving in the late 17th century. In the early 1800s, Mulambwa, chief of one Bantu tribe, the Lozi, built a powerful state in northwest Barotseland.

In the 1830s the Lozi state crumbled before the Kololo, a military band composed of different Bantu clans. In the 1860s, however, the Lozi reestablished their dominance in Barotseland.

In the mid-1800s Europeans began to settle in present-day Zambia, and in 1890 Cecil Rhodes's British South Africa Company obtained a monopoly over mining rights.

Control of the region by the British South Africa Company ended in 1923, and the British government took over the administration of Northern Rhodesia. Southern Rhodesia, however, became self-governing, and white settler governments came to power there. Thus, when representatives of the Southern Rhodesian government and the white settlers of Northern Rhodesia, at a meeting in Victoria Falls in 1936, decided to work for the union of the two countries, the Africans of Northern Rhodesia were outraged. Nonetheless, in 1953 Great Britain established the Federation of Rhodesia and Nyasaland.

Opposition from African nationalists in Northern Rhodesia and Nyasaland led Britain to dissolve the federation in December 1963. On October 24, 1964, Northern Rhodesia became the independent nation of Zambia. Kenneth Kaunda became the first president and maintained that position until 1991.

Kaunda led black African opposition to white minority rule and the South African apartheid policy of separate societies. He aligned Zambia, economically, with Tanzania, while accepting aid from Communist as well as democratic nations in order to reduce Zambia's economic dependence on South Africa.

Zambia under Kaunda was a one-party state. Although he made a sincere effort to improve the lives of Zambians, economic problems and political unrest led Kaunda in 1990 to approve legislation providing for multiparty elections. In August 1991 a new constitution was approved by the National Assembly, and in October, in free and fair elections, Frederick Chiluba was elected president. Free elections continue.

Zimbabwe

Official name: *Republic of Zimbabwe*
Area: *150,764 sq. mi., 390,580 sq. km.*
Type of government: *Parliamentary democracy*
Population: *12,463,000*
Capital and largest city: *Harare (Pop., 1,189,000)*
Languages: *English (official), Shona, Sindebele*
Literacy: *85%*
Currency: *Dollar*
Per capita GDP: *$2,450 (Rank: 126th)*

The land. Most of Zimbabwe is occupied by a high level plateau that has an elevation of over 3,000 feet (915 meters) above sea level. Most of the country's farms are located here. In east-central Zimbabwe are the Inyanga Mountains, with elevations of about 8,500 feet (2,592 meters).

The only extensive lowlands are in the southeast, near the Limpopo River and its principal tributary, the Shashi. The Zambezi River flows along part of the northern border, and many other rivers flow through the country.

The lowlands are hot and dry, but temperatures on the plateau above 3,500 feet (1,067 meters) are moderate. Rainfall is confined to the period from October to April, with an average between 63 and 76 inches (162 and 195 centimeters) annually.

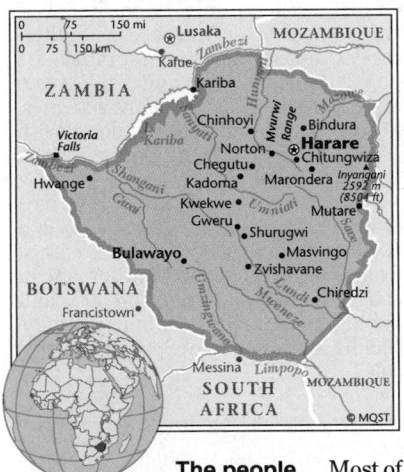

The people. Most of the population of Zimbabwe is Bantu, mainly of the Shona tribe in the east and the Ndebele in the southwest. The Ndebele are related to the Zulu people of South Africa. There is a small minority of European origin. Eighty percent of the population live in rural areas. Half the people practice syncretic religions, which are part Christian and part animist, and the rest are Christians and animists.

The major cities are Harare, the capital; Bulawayo (population, 622,000); and Chitungwiza (275,000).

Economy. Most of the people are subsistence farmers. In 1991 the government began a plan designed to move more than 110,000 families onto 15 million acres of fertile land previously owned by white farmers.

Despite serious water shortages, Zimbabwe has important agricultural production. Zimbabwe is self-sufficient in food production and agriculture accounts for almost 40 percent of the export revenues. It also employs a majority of the labor force. The basic crops are corn and grains. The major commercial crops are tobacco and sugar.

Zimbabwe has rich mineral resources, particularly gold, asbestos, and chromium ore. Nickel has become important in recent years. Oil is in short supply, but industry is more highly developed in Zimbabwe than in most African countries.

Tobacco, cotton, and gold are Zimbabwe's main exports, while machinery, electricity, chemicals, and processed goods are its main imports. Zimbabwe's main trading partners are South Africa and the U.K.

Government. Zimbabwe is headed by a president elected by popular vote. The president appoints two co-vice presidents and a cabinet which is responsible to the House of Assembly. The legislature consists of a unicameral 150-member House of Assembly. One hundred and twenty of the members of the House of Assembly are elected by universal suffrage, twelve are appointed by the president, ten are chiefs elected by the country's tribal chiefs, and eight are provincial governors.

History. Ancient cave paintings and tools found in what is now Zimbabwe provide evidence that people lived there during the Stone Age. As early as A.D. 800, the Bushmen in the region were mining minerals for trade. In about A.D. 1000 Bantu tribes from central Africa drove off the aboriginal Bushmen.

The Bantu founded the Zimbabwe civilization, which left imposing stone ruins. In the 1400s another Bantu people, the Shona, expelled or absorbed their predecessors and built the Monomotapa Empire, which was based on gold mining. By the mid-1400s, the empire reached all the way to the coast in Mozambique.

In the 1600s Portuguese from Mozambique ravaged the African states in the Zambezi valley, and the Monomotapa Empire collapsed. By the 1800s the power of the Portuguese had declined. In the early 1800s another Bantu tribe, the Ndebele, subjugated the Shona.

British control. Ndebeleland lay in the path of British expansion northward from Cape Colony in South Africa, and in 1888 the Ndebele king accepted British protection over the area. He also granted to Cecil Rhodes a monopoly over mining rights for his British South Africa Company.

In 1953 Great Britain established the Federation of Rhodesia and Nyasaland, but on December 31, 1963, the federation was dissolved. Northern Rhodesia and Nyasaland became independent as Zambia and Malawi, respectively, and Southern Rhodesia remained under British control as the self-governing colony of Rhodesia.

Independence. The Rhodesian government pressed for independence, but Britain refused, insisting on assurances of adequate representation for the country's African majority. Despite Britain's position, Prime Minister Ian Smith declared Rhodesia independent on November 11, 1965. Britain responded by leading an international economic embargo against the country. The discord led to a civil war with guerrilla activity (aided by Mozambique and Zambia) aimed at overthrowing Smith's government and establishing a multiracial one in its place.

Elections to a new government were finally held in 1979, and the radical

VICTORIA FALLS
in Zambia is a 355-foot cataract, one of the seven natural wonders of the world.

nationalist advocate, Robert Mugabe, was elected prime minister. He promised that his regime would work to mend old wounds and promote equitable political and economic representation of all races.

Britain accepted Zimbabwe's independence in 1980 and Zimbabwe began to normalize economic, international, and domestic affairs. In 1987 the constitution was amended to end the separate electoral roll for white voters and to establish an executive presidency to replace the president/prime minister executive. In 1990 Mugabe was elected president with 78 percent of the vote, although only 54 percent of the eligible voters cast their ballots.

The country has become more unsettled in the last several years. The pace of black resettlement onto previously white-owned farms was accelerated, amid reports of widespread intimidation of, lack of compensation for, and abuse of the white farmers. Experts say that such radical land reform will slash food production and further damage an economy already severely weakened by excessive government deficits and an inflation rate approaching 100 percent, both brought about partly by Zimbabwe's involvement in the war in the Democratic Republic of the Congo. Foreign aid has dwindled (in part because of concerns about human rights abuses and Mugabe's recent political actions); the lack of foreign currency has in turn led to severe shortages of vital imports. Mugabe was reelected in 2002 in a vote most regarded as rigged.

As Mugabe faced his first serious political opposition, several controversial laws were passed, among them laws making criticism of the president a crime and requiring government approval of independent journalists' writings.

Continued human rights violations led to Zimbabwe's suspension from the Commonwealth of Nations. In response the country withdrew from the group in December 2003.

civilization
US

civilisation
Brit.

Dependencies in Africa

French Dependency

Mayotte (145 sq. mi., 375 sq. km), a tiny island that was formerly part of the Comoros Islands, has a population of 171,000. Located just northwest of Madagascar, it voted to become a department of France in 1976, when the rest of the Comoros became independent. Its fertile soil produces vanilla, coffee, and copra.

Moroccan Dependency

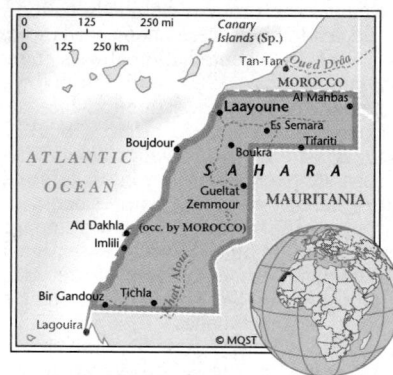

Western Sahara

(102,679 sq. mi., 266,000 sq. km), formerly called Spanish Sahara, is located in northwestern Africa adjacent to Morocco and has a population of 256,000. Until 1976 the area was an overseas province of Spain. Following the Spanish departure, the area was first divided between Morocco and Mauritania, then taken over entirely by Morocco, although the Moroccan claim to the territory is not recognized. The Polisario Front, a guerrilla movement, seeks to make it an independent nation. Phosphate mining is the most important economic activity. The principal town is the capital, El Aaiún.

Norwegian Dependency

Bouvet Island (22 sq. mi., 58 sq. km.), an uninhabited island in the South Atlantic, is covered by glaciers and lies between the southern tip of South Africa and Antarctica. An automatic meteorological station that supplies data via satellite to Norway is the only evidence of development on the island.

Portuguese Dependency

The Madeira Islands (307 sq. mi., 795 sq. km) are located 360 miles northwest of Morocco, in the Atlantic Ocean. They consist of two island groups, with a total population of 245,000. The Madeiras are, by choice, still a Portuguese dependency, though the islands have their own political and administrative organization and a Regional Assembly. The economy is largely based on agriculture. Bananas and sugar cane are the chief crops. The fishing and tourist industries also are important.

Spanish Dependencies

The Canary Islands (2,807 sq. mi., 7,270 sq. km), in the Atlantic Ocean off the west coast of Morocco, form two provinces of Spain. Tenerife is the most important of this group of islands. There are several significant commercial ports on the islands, including Las Palmas and Santa Cruz. The two provinces—Santa Cruz de Tenerife and Las Palmas de Gran Canaria—have a combined population of 1,694,000. The economy of the islands is based on agriculture, primarily sugar cane, fruits, and vegetables. Resorts and tourism on several of the islands are also important to the economy.

Ceuta (7.5 sq. mi., 19 sq. km) is a small enclave on Morocco's Mediterranean coast opposite Gibraltar. Its population is 72,000, and fishing and tourism are its main economic activities. Morocco claimed Ceuta, along with Melilla, in 1975. It is the closest African port to Europe.

Melilla (4.8 sq. mi., 12 sq. km) is a small enclave located 200 miles east of Ceuta on Morocco's Mediterranean coast. Its population is 66,000, and fishing is its main economic activity. Melilla is a remnant of Spanish colonial rule.

THE SAHARA DESERT reaches from coast to coast across northern Africa, covering an area about the same size as the United States.

Cities of Africa

Abidjan, the largest city of Côte d'Ivoire. The city is located on the Ebrie Lagoon, which is connected to the Gulf of Guinea by the Vridi Canal. Abidjan has modern port facilities and is the terminus of a highway network and railroads from landlocked west African countries. Pop., 1,929,000.

Accra, the capital of Ghana. The city lies on the Gulf of Guinea and is a seaport. Accra has an international airport and is linked by railroad to the agricultural districts of Ghana's interior. The University of Ghana is located in Accra. Pop., 860,000.

Addis Ababa, the capital and largest city of Ethiopia. It is situated in a hilly region in the central part of the country. Addis Ababa is the country's chief commercial, industrial, and educational center. Its industries produce cement, textiles, food, processed tobacco, beverages, and leather goods. Ethiopia's first university, the National University, was founded at Addis Ababa in 1961. It is also the site of the headquarters of the Organization of African Unity (OAU). Pop., 2,424,000.

Alexandria, situated west of the Rosetta mouth of the Nile River on the Mediterranean Sea, the principal seaport and second largest city of Egypt. Alexandria was founded by Alexander the Great in 332 B.C. It became an important port and intellectual center and was also famous for its lighthouse, which was one of the seven wonders of the ancient world, its library, and its school of medicine. Pop., 3,339,000.

Algiers, the capital of Algeria, the major Mediterranean port on the northwest coast of Africa. The city's port handles such exports as wool, fruits and vegetables, and wine, most of which are sent to France. Local industries produce cement, metal products, chemicals, machinery, and paper. Tourism is also important. Pop., 1,504,000.

Antananarivo, formerly Tananarive, the capital of Madagascar, situated on a basalt ridge on the east-central part of Madagascar Island. The city is an administrative, agricultural, and commercial center; its industries include food products, textiles, and cigarettes. Pop., 1,103,000.

Aswan, the capital of Aswan Governorate in Egypt, located on the east bank of the Nile River, about 550 miles (886 km) south of Cairo. The city is the site of the Aswan and Aswan High dams. Aswan's dry, mild climate makes it a popular tourist resort during the winter months. Industries include a fertilizer plant and copper and steel mills. Significant amounts of red granite are quarried here. Pop., 220,000.

Bamako, the capital of Mali, situated on the Niger River, in the southwestern part of the country. It serves as the trade center for the surrounding area and exports peanuts, cotton, and tobacco. Bamako is connected to Dakar in Senegal by rail and has an international airport. Pop., 1,179,000.

Bangui, the capital of the Central African Republic, located on the Ubangi River, near the Democratic Republic of the Congo border. The city's port handles almost all of the republic's foreign trade. Bangui is linked by road with Chad, Cameroon, and Sudan, and has an international airport. Local industry consists of food processing and the manufacture of textiles, timber, and metal products. Pop., 452,000.

Banjul, formerly Bathurst, seaport and capital of The Gambia, located on St. Mary's Island at the mouth of the Gambia River. It is the commercial center of The Gambia, and peanut processing is the chief industry. Pop., 42,000.

Bissau, on the west coast of Africa, the capital and chief port of Guinea-Bissau. The major exports are peanuts, palm products, timber, and copra. It is linked by rivers to communities in the interior and has an airport. Pop., 109,000.

Brazzaville, the capital and largest city of the Republic of Congo, on the Zaire River directly opposite Kinshasa. Brazzaville is an important river port and the country's commercial and educational center. Major industries include food processing, and the manufacture of textiles, construction materials, chemicals, and timber. Pop., 596,000.

CAIRO, the capital of Egypt, is a thriving metropolis.

Bujumbura, the capital of Burundi, in east-central Africa, located at the northern end of Lake Tanganyika. The city, which was formerly called Usumbura, is an important lake port and trade center for agricultural produce from the surrounding region. Pop., 235,000.

Cairo, the capital of Egypt and the largest city in Africa, on the Nile River, at the head of the Nile Delta. It is an important transportation, commercial, and industrial center. Manufactures include metals, plastics, food products, textiles, and chemicals. Al-Ahzar University, founded in A.D. 970, is the world's oldest and largest center of Islamic scholarship. Cairo has many museums, mosques, and universities. Pop., 6,801,000.

Cape Town, the legislative capital of the Republic of South Africa and the capital of Cape Province. Cape Town is located on the southwestern shore of Table Bay, near the southern tip of Africa. It is an important manufacturing center whose industries include textiles, clothing, chemicals, oil refining, fertilizers, food processing, and ship repair. It is a very busy port. Exports include diamonds, fruit, gold, and other minerals. Pop., metro. area, 2,898,000.

center
US

centre
Brit.

CAPE TOWN, in South Africa, is a vital center for industries such as oil refining and ship repair.

22 Africa

Casablanca, the largest city in Morocco, on the Atlantic coast of North Africa. Possessing one of the world's largest artificial ports, Casablanca handles most of Morocco's passenger traffic and foreign trade. Phosphates are the city's chief export. Industries include textiles, cement, and glass manufacture. Pop., metro. area, 2,943,000.

Conakry, the capital of Guinea, on the island of Tombo. The island is linked to the mainland by a causeway. Conakry is Guinea's largest city, chief port, and a commercial and industrial center. Exports include bauxite and iron ore. Pop., 705,000.

Dakar, the capital and chief seaport of Senegal, located on the Cape Verde peninsula on Africa's west coast. The city, which has a strategic location and an excellent harbor, is a transportation center with important air, rail, and shipping facilities.

Peanuts are the principal export. Dakar's industries produce canned fish, refined sugar, chocolate, peanut oil, and textiles. The city is the seat of the University of Dakar, the Pasteur Institute, and the Institut Français d'Afrique Noire. Pop., 880,000.

Dar es Salaam, the former capital of Tanzania, a major seaport of East Africa. The city is an administrative, transportation, and economic center. Among its exports are coffee, sisal, cotton, gold, diamonds, and tin. Dar es Salaam's industries produce textiles, cement, pharmaceuticals, and processed foods. Pop., 1,361,000.

Djibouti, the capital of Djibouti and an East African port, located on the Gulf of Tadjoura. Djibouti is the terminal of a railroad that originates in Addis Ababa, Ethiopia; the city's exports are mainly Ethiopian products. They include coffee, hides and skins, and oilseeds. Pop., metro. area, 62,000.

Freetown, the capital and chief port of Sierra Leone. It is located on the estuary of the Sierra Leone River and has an excellent harbor. Freetown is the transportation and commercial center of Sierra Leone. Exports include plastics, sugar, and cement. Pop., 470,000.

Gaborone, the capital of Botswana, primarily an administrative and cultural center. The economy is made up of light industries and textile manufacturing. Pop., 186,000.

Harare, or Salisbury, the capital of Zimbabwe, located in the northeastern part of the country. Surrounded by a rich gold-mining region, it is a transportation and commercial center for southeastern Africa. It has steel and textile mills, and tobacco processing is a major industry. Pop., 1,189,000.

Johannesburg, the largest city in the Republic of South Africa, in southern Transvaal Province, about 30 miles (48 km) southwest of Pretoria. Johannesburg is situated on a plateau 5,750 feet (1,753 m) above sea level. It is the industrial and commercial center of South Africa. Gold mining is the chief industry; important manufactures include cut diamonds, chemicals, textiles, plastics, and paper products. Pop., 752,000.

Kampala, the capital of Uganda, situated in east-central Africa, near the equator. The city is a trade and transportation center for the surrounding region, which produces coffee, tea, sugar cane, cotton, tobacco, and livestock. It is the seat of Makerere University. Pop., 1,209,000.

Khartoum, the capital of Sudan, in northern Africa, situated near the junction of the White Nile and the Blue Nile. Khartoum is the communications, commercial, financial, and educational center of Sudan. It contains modern stores and boulevards as well as a bazaar and several mosques and churches. Pop., 947,000.

Kigali, the capital of Rwanda, situated about 135 miles (218 km) south of the equator in central Africa. It lies in a poor agricultural area; iron and tin are mined, and hides and cattle are the main source of income. Pop., 234,000.

Kinshasa, formerly Léopoldville, the capital and largest city of the Democratic Republic of Congo, situated in west-central African on the Zaire (Congo) River opposite Brazzaville. Kinshasa is the cultural, administrative, financial, commercial, and transportation center of the country. Its industries manufacture chemicals, textiles, processed foods, mineral oils, and cement. It is the seat of Lovanium University. Pop., 4,657,000.

Lagos, the former capital and major port of Nigeria, located on the mainland and on islands in Lagos Lagoon, off the Gulf of Guinea. The islands are connected to the mainland by bridges. Its manufactures include textiles, chemicals, and metal products. Lagos is connected by road and rail to other Nigerian cities and is served by an international airport. Pop., 5,195,000.

Libreville, capital of Gabon, located 30 miles (48 km) north of the equator on the Atlantic Ocean. It is Gabon's largest city and a major port. Hardwoods, cement, and ceramics are exported. Pop., 420,000.

Lilongwe, capital of Malawi, situated 50 miles (80 km) west of Lake Nyasa, in southeast Africa. It lies in a fertile agricultural area and is a center for tourism and commerce. Pop., 440,000.

Lomé, the capital and major seaport of Togo, located on the Gulf of Guinea. The city is the commercial and industrial center of the country. It exports phosphate, cacao, coffee, copra, timber, and palm oil. Lomé is connected by railroad with the cities of the interior. Pop., 450,000.

Luanda, a seaport on the west-central coast of Africa, capital of Angola. The city is Angola's major industrial center. It produces soap, tobacco, and plastics. There is also a large oil refinery. Luanda's chief exports are coffee, sugar, cotton, fish, and manganese. It is linked to Malange and Casengo in the interior by rail and is served by an airport as well. Pop., metro. area, 1,822,000.

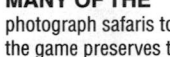

center
US

centre
Brit.

MANY OF THE photograph safaris to the game preserves to spot wildlife such as these giraffes have a starting point in Nairobi.

Lusaka, the capital of Zambia, located in the south-central part of the country. The city lies in an agricultural region and is the hub of a road and rail network that links it to the Democratic Republic of the Congo, Tanzania, and Malawi. Pop., 1,270,000.

Malabo, formerly Santa Isabel, the capital of Equatorial Guinea, located on the island of Bioko (Macias Nguema) off the west-central coast of Africa. It is a seaport that exports cacao and coffee raised on local plantations. Pop., 30,000.

Maputo, formerly Lourenço Marques, the capital and largest city of Mozambique, located on an inlet of the Indian Ocean, near the country's southern border. It is the country's administrative, communications, and commercial center. Its modern port exports coal, cotton, ores, sugar, and hardwoods. Its chief manufactures are cement, pottery, food products, textiles, pharmaceuticals, and rubber. Pop., 967,000.

Marrakesh, in west-central Morocco, on the western slopes of the Grand Atlas Mountains in North Africa. Marrakesh is one of the largest cities of Morocco and a major Muslim religious center. Manufactures include wool, flour, carpets, and leather goods. Pop., metro. area, 602,000.

Maseru, the capital of Lesotho, in southern Africa. The city is located near the western border with the Republic of South Africa. Maseru is the nation's transportation and commercial center. Pop., 138,000.

Mbabane, the capital and chief town of Swaziland, a former British protectorate in southeastern Africa. It is located about 95 miles (153 km) southwest of Maputo, capital of Mozambique, with which it is linked by rail. Mbabane is popular in southern Africa for its casinos. Exports from Mbabane include iron ore and asbestos. Pop., 38,000.

Mogadishu, the capital and chief port of Somalia, in eastern Africa. It lies on the Indian Ocean, about 700 miles (1,130 km) southeast of Addis Ababa, the capital of Ethiopia. Mogadishu exports bananas, charcoal, livestock, and animal hides. Pop., 230,000.

Mombasa, the chief port of Kenya, off the coast of eastern Africa. Mombasa is located on a small island in the Indian Ocean and is linked to the mainland by a causeway, a bridge, and ferries. The city exports coffee, cotton, tea, sugar, and animal skins. Pop., 465,000.

Monrovia, the capital and chief port of Liberia in West Africa. Monrovia is located on Cape Montserrado, near the mouth of the Saint Paul River, on the Atlantic Ocean. Exports include rubber, iron ore, gold, and coffee. The city was named for U.S. President James Monroe. Pop., 421,000.

UNITED NATIONS FORCES mounted an operation to restore order and ensure delivery of relief supplies to Mogadishu and all of Somalia when unrest plunged the country into civil war in 1992.

Moroni, the capital of the Comoro Islands, at the north entrance to the Mozambique Channel. Moroni is located on the east coast of Grande Comore Island. It is the chief port for the country's export of vanilla and spices. Pop., 30,000.

Nairobi, the capital and largest city of Kenya. It is the focus of several rail lines that carry coffee, cotton, tea, and sisal from parts of Kenya and Uganda to the Indian Ocean port of Mombasa. Its principal industries include meat packing, flour milling, and manufacture of clothing, chemicals, foodstuffs, and various paper products. Pop., 2,143,000.

N'Djamena, formerly Fort-Lamy, the capital of Chad, located about 70 miles (112 km) south of Lake Chad. It is the largest city and chief transportation, industrial, and commercial center of Chad. Pop., 547,000.

Niamey, the capital of Niger. An inland port on the Niger River, it is a market center for the agricultural products of the region. Pop., 397,000.

Nouakchott, capital of Mauritania. Lying 4 miles (6.5 km) from the Atlantic Ocean, it is a market center with a deep-water port. Pop., metro. area, 612,000.

Ouagadougou, the capital and leading city of Burkina Faso. It is connected by rail with Abidjan, a port on the Côte d'Ivoire. Ouagadougou is the trade center for the surrounding agricultural region. Its main exports are peanuts, cotton, and handicrafts. Pop., 634,000.

Port Louis, the capital and chief port of Mauritius, an island in the Indian Ocean about 500 miles (800 km) east of Madagascar. Sugar, the main crop and export of Mauritius, is shipped from Port Louis. Pop., 128,000.

ZEBRAS LIVE in the grasslands of eastern and southern Africa.

22 Africa

PRAIA
is the capital
of Cape Verde, a
cluster of islands off
the coast of Senegal.

center
US

centre
Brit.

Porto-Novo, the capital of Benin, situated on the southern coast of western Africa, on the Gulf of Guinea. Porto-Novo is a seaport that exports palm products and cotton. Pop., 233,000.

Praia, the capital of Cape Verde, a group of islands that lie in the Atlantic Ocean, about 500 miles (800 km) west of the coast of Africa. Situated on São Tiago Island, Praia is a seaport that exports citrus fruits, sugar cane, and coffee. Pop., 103,000.

Pretoria, the administrative capital of South Africa and the capital of Transvaal Province, situated on the Apies River about 34 miles (55 km) northeast of Johannesburg. Pretoria is a transportation, industrial, and political center, and the seat of two universities. Its manufactures include steel, chemicals, ceramics, glassware, processed foods, and tobacco. Pop., metro. area, 692,000.

Rabat, the capital of Morocco, situated on the south bank of the Bou Regneg River, near its mouth on the Atlantic Ocean. Local handicraft industries produce leather goods, baskets, tapestries, and embroidered cloth. The city is the site of Mohammed V University. Pop., metro. area, 1,220,000.

Salisbury. *See* Harare.

São Tomé, capital and port city of São Tomé and Príncipe. It lies on the island of São Tomé in the Gulf of Guinea. It exports cacao, coffee, and coconuts raised on the island. Pop., 5,700.

Tripoli, the capital of Libya, situated in northwestern Libya on the Mediterranean Sea. The city is a transportation and trading center. Its industries produce textiles, rugs, sponges, tobacco products, and salt. Pop., 1,500,000.

Tunis, the capital of Tunisia, situated in the northeastern part of the country on the Lake of Tunis. Tunis is connected to the Mediterranean Sea by a canal that ends at the subsidiary port, Halq al Wadi. The city is the major commercial, industrial, and transportation center of the country. Its products include processed foods, textiles, metal goods, carpets, and olive oil. Pop., 702,000.

Victoria, seaport and capital of the Seychelles, on an archipelago in the Indian Ocean. The city lies on Mahé Island and exports the island's cinnamon, fish, and coconut products. Pop., 25,000.

Windhoek, the capital of Namibia, or South-West Africa. It is located about 250 miles (400 km) east of Walvis Bay. Windhoek is Namibia's administrative, economic, and transportation center and is linked by railroad to South Africa. It ships Persian lamb skins and produces meat, clothing, and bone-meal. Namibia is also renowned for its red and white wines. Pop., 147,000.

Yaoundé, the capital of Cameroon in western Africa. It is located in the west-central part of the country, about 130 miles (210 km) east of Dauala, its port on the Atlantic Ocean. Yaoundé is

Cameroon's commercial and educational center. It is also a transportation center and market for the region's coffee, cacao, copra, sugar cane, and textiles. Pop., 649,000.

AN AFRICAN WOMAN in traditional dress

Glossary of Africa

Aden, Gulf of. An arm of the Indian Ocean, bounded on the north by Arabia and on the south by Africa's Somali coast. The gulf is 500 miles (885 km) long and connects with the Red Sea to the west through the Bab al Mandeb Strait.

African National Congress. An association formed in 1912 to protest racial discrimination in South Africa. Decades of racial strife followed, resulting in the banning of the ANC. Economic sanctions were imposed by the United Nations against South Africa, and as part of the resolution that gave citizenship and a role in government to blacks in the country, the ban on the ANC was removed in 1990.

Afrikaans. Language spoken by the majority of white and mixed race South Africans. It is derived from Dutch and has evolved over the centuries to its present form through interaction between the native South African tribes and the Dutch settlers.

Apartheid. An Afrikaans word with the meaning "separateness." It is used to describe the South African government's policy from 1948 to 1991 of rigid separation of the races and plans for their separate development.

The policy was put into effect through a series of far-reaching laws governing the social, economic, political, and educational affairs of South Africa's people. These laws recognized four groups: whites; Bantu, or black Africans; Coloreds, of mixed racial origin; and Asians, predominantly people of Indian origin.

Apartheid benefited the minority white population enormously. For example, 87 percent of the land was reserved for whites. Nonwhites were restricted in virtually every sphere of activity. The system sparked strong opposition within South Africa and was bitterly attacked throughout the world. Many countries instituted economic sanctions against South Africa. In the 1980s the government instituted minor reforms, but the essential injustice of apartheid remained unaddressed until 1990 and 1991, when the key apartheid laws were repealed.

Atlas Mountains. A 1,500-mile-long (2,415 km) mountain system of North Africa, extending from the southwest coast of Morocco westward to Cape Bon on the northeast coast of Tunisia. The Atlas system includes the Anti-Atlas in the southwest; the Grand, or High, Atlas in central Morocco; and the Saharan Atlas stretching across northern Algeria. The Grand Atlas includes Toubkal, 13,661 feet (4,167 m), the highest peak in the Atlas system.

Bantu. An agricultural tribe that originally inhabited the area known as Cameroon today, and swept westward across Africa in prehistoric times. It does not now represent a cultural group, but has become a linguistic classification for the 300 different ethnic groups that speak Bantu.

Boers. Dutch settlers who came to South Africa as a result of the founding of Cape Town by the Dutch East India Company in 1652. The Boers were originally farmers who turned to hunting and cattle raising and came into conflict with the Bantu people over rights to land and water. This gave rise to the war with the Zulu and other Bantu tribes, which united under the leadership of Shaka.

Cameroon. The name of a volcanic mountain that rises over 13,300 feet near the coast of the country with the same name.

Cape Agulhas. The southernmost point of Africa. It separates the Atlantic Ocean on its west from the Indian Ocean on its east.

Cape of Good Hope. A point of land at the southwestern tip of Africa, on the Atlantic Ocean.

Chad. A lake in north-central Africa, located at the junction of the boundaries of Chad, Niger, Cameroon, and Nigeria. Lake Chad is fed by the Chari and Logone rivers and, while it has no outlet, it remains fresh. Its area fluctuates between 4,000 and 10,000 square miles (10,360 and 25,900 sq. km).

Dahomey. The name by which Benin was known until 1904, when it became part of the Federation of French West Africa. France granted the country its independence in 1960, and after several coups, the country became the People's Republic of Benin in 1975 under Mathieu Kerekou.

Great Rift Valley. The longest depression in Earth's crust, actually a succession of rift valleys, extending 3,000 miles (4,839 km) from Syria to Mozambique and averaging 35 miles (57 km) wide. The valley sinks below sea level in some places—as at the Dead Sea—and rises as high as 9,000 feet (2,743 km) above sea level in some of the adjacent plateau regions. The valley is often an obstacle to travel from east to west.

Hutu. The name of the most numerous of the two tribes that make up the population of Burundi, constituting about 85 percent of the total. Civil war and ethnic violence has existed between this group and the ruling Tutsi tribe since 1972, resulting in many deaths and the flight of more than 60,000 Hutus to neighboring Rwanda.

Kalahari. A desert of southern Africa, with an area of more than 100,000 square miles (260,000 sq. km). It extends southward from Lake Ngami through central Botswana into northern South Africa as far as the Orange River and westward from Botswana into Namibia (South-West Africa).

APARTHEID SIGNS were a common sight in South Africa before 1991.

color
US

colour
Brit.

22 Africa

Kilimanjaro. The highest mountain in Africa, located on the border of Kenya and Tanzania. Kibo, the site of relatively recent volcanic activity, is the highest peak at 19,331 feet (5,892 m). It is covered by glaciers. Mawenzi, the other main peak, is 17,564 feet (5,354 m) and has no glaciers.

Niger. A major river in West Africa, rising in southeastern Guinea and flowing northeast into Mali and then southeast through Niger and Nigeria. The river flows for about 2,600 miles (4,200 km) and empties into the Gulf of Guinea. About 80 miles (130 km) from its mouth, the Niger forms an extensive delta.

Nile. The longest river in Africa and in the world. Its course can be traced from the Kagera River headwaters in northern Tanzania to the Mediterranean Sea, a distance of 4,145 miles (6,673 km). The Nile proper is formed by the joining of the White Nile and the Blue Nile at Khartoum, in Sudan. The White Nile flows north from Tanzania into Uganda and Sudan, where it is joined by its major tributaries, the Ghazal and the Sobat, before joining the Blue Nile. The Nile proper continues north through Egypt and forms an extensive delta north of Cairo.

Nyasa. The third largest lake in Africa, located on the borders of Tanzania, Malawi, and Mozambique. The lake has a surface area of 11,430 square miles (29,604 sq. km) and a mountainous shoreline. Its only outlet is the Shire River, a tributary of the Zambezi River.

Islam. The name given to the religion preached by the Prophet Muhammad, who was born in Mecca about A.D. 570. He claimed to be the messenger from the one God, Allah. His followers are called Muslim, an Arabic word that means "one who submits." About 300 million Africans are Muslims, and Islam is the state religion in most of the countries north of the Sahara.

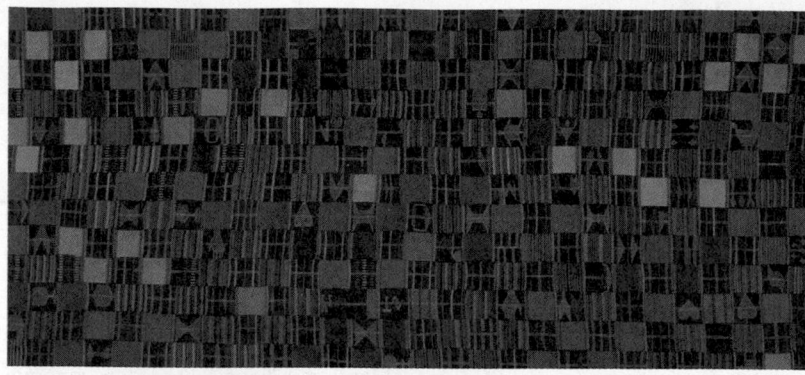

AFRICAN TEXTILES ARE noted worldwide for their interesting patterns and vivid hues.

Kush. The name by which present-day Sudan was known when it furnished slaves for Egypt as early as 3000 B.C. A Nubian leader proclaimed himself king of Kush in 750 B.C., and gained control of Egypt, where he established a dynasty that lasted until conquest by the Assyrians in 661 B.C.

Mahé. The main island of the Seychelles. The name also refers to the 40 granite islands in the Mahé group within a 35-mile radius of the main island.

Olduvai Gorge. The portion of the Great Rift Valley in northern Tanzania where remains have been found of some of the world's oldest hominids. Anthropologist Louis Leakey and other members of his family have discovered tools and other evidence of early human life as well as bones in the area.

Organization of African Unity (OAU). Established in Addis Ababa, Ethiopia, in 1963, its charter describes its purpose as promoting respect for the sovereignty and territorial integrity of its member states and the removal of all colonial influences in Africa. The political leaders of member nations meet annually to set policy and settle disputes. Although its actual authority is limited, the 50-member OAU continues to contribute to the stability of the continent.

Red Sea. An inland sea between northeastern Africa and the Arabian peninsula, part of the Great Rift Valley system. It is about 1,300 miles (2,100 km) long and between 130 to 250 miles (210 to 400 km) wide. The sea is connected to the Mediterranean by the Suez Canal and to the Gulf of Aden through the strait of Bab al Mandeb.

Safari. An African trip organized formerly to hunt wild animals. Today most wild animals are protected in animal preserves, and most safaris are for the purpose of observing and photographing the animals.

Sahara. A desert region of North Africa extending about 3,000 miles (4,800 km) from west to east and 1,000 miles (1,600 km) from north to south. It is the world's largest desert, and includes high plateaus, such as the Tibesti, Ahaggar, and Aïr; depressions such as the Qattara; and plains 600 to 1,200 feet (180 to 360 m) above sea level. The landscape includes only 20 percent sandy desert, or erg, and extensive stony desert, or reg. Rainfall averages less than 10 inches (26 cm) a year, and the only permanent rivers are the Nile and Niger. Inhabited largely by nomadic people, the desert has rich mineral deposits.

Sahel. A semiarid region that lies between the Sahara Desert and the tropical zones of western Africa. The Sahel stretches east from the coast of the Atlantic to Chad.

Shott el Jerid. A large salt lake south of the mountains in the north of Tunisia. The lake is close to sea level and receives some streams from the mountains.

Tanganyika. An African lake on the border of Tanzania and the Democratic Republic of the Congo. It is 420 miles (676 km) long and has an area of 12,700 square miles (32,893 sq. km). Its depth of 4,710 feet (1,436 m) makes it the world's second deepest lake.

Tutsi. One of the two dominant tribal groups in Burundi. Also known as Watusi, the tribe is traditionally herdsmen and warriors, and, although Tutsi

MEERKATS SEEM TO pose for the photograph safaris popular with tourists to southern Africa.

HOMINID FOSSILS, such as these 3-million-year-old fragments, have been discovered in the Olduvai Gorge and at sites in South Africa.

make up only about 15 percent of the total population, they are the traditional ruling class. Civil war and ethnic violence between this group and the Hutus has flaired in the country since 1972.

Upper Volta.   The name by which Burkina Faso was formerly known, as a territory of France. The country, known as Haute Volta in French, became independent in 1960.

Victoria.   A famous large lake in east-central Africa, the world's second largest freshwater lake. Lake Victoria lies mainly in Uganda and Tanzania, but borders on Kenya. The lake, which is about 250 miles (400 km) long and 200 miles (320 km) wide, is the major source of the Nile River.

Victoria Falls.   A waterfall in southern Africa on the Zambezi River between Zambia and Zimbabwe. The falls are 5,580 feet (1,700 m) wide and drop 355 feet (108 m).

Volta.   A river system of Ghana, about 1,000 miles (1,600 km) long. The Volta, which empties into the Gulf of Guinea, is formed by the joining of the Black Volta and the White Volta, both of which rise in Upper Volta.

Zagros Mountains.   A mountain range in southwestern Iran that forms the western and southern borders of the Iranian plateau. The range is about 600 miles (965 km) long and rises to a height of 15,000 feet (4,570 m).

Zaire.   Or Congo, a river in central Africa. With its tributaries, it is one of the world's longest river systems, draining about 1.4 million square miles (3.6 million sq. km) The Lualaba, its headstream, rises on the Katanga Plateau in Zaire and flows north to join the Luapula and Lukuga rivers. Before turning to the west at Kisangani, where it becomes the Zaire proper, the river crosses the 60-mile (96-km) stretch of the Boyoma (Stanley) Falls. About 350 miles (564 km) from its mouth, it widens to form Malebo (Stanley) Pool, where Brazzaville and Kinshasa are located, at the end of the inland navigation route. The Zaire then falls some 850 feet (260 m) over a series of waterfalls, which lead into the river's estuary.

A STONE figure typical of the work found in the Zaire, or Congo, River area

THE HELP DESK

➤   **Spend** some time each day locating countries and cities in Africa that are in the news on a map or globe.

➤   **Make** a list of great civilizations—Egyptian, Mayan, Incan. Locate the area and arrange in the order of their height of power. Then arrange them in order of length of power.

➤   **Document** your family's ethnic heritage. What country did your forefathers come from? When did they come? Why? Who? What famous people share your background? Older relatives would be a good source of information.

➤   **Study** the maps that show where the ancient civilizations developed. Note that most were around rivers. Why do you think that happened?

➤   **As** you study Africa, try to analyze the manner in which people adapted to their environment.

➤   **Study** the continental map. Pay particular attention to the locator inset map that will help you locate the portion of the globe Africa occupies. Is it in the Northern or Southern hemisphere? In the Eastern or Western hemisphere? Is it north or south of the equator? What are the major physical features—any large rivers, mountains, deserts? Make a list of the names of those features.

➤   **Review** the historical background of one of the countries. Does it date back thousands or hundreds of years, or is it much younger? Write a short report noting major events in the history in chronological order. Compare the events in the country to events in countries nearby. Is there any similarity? Are they friends or enemies? Do the people speak the same language? What are other similarities or differences that you have detected? Don't forget to use the History of the World volume for related information.

➤   **Look** at the photographs. What can you learn about the climate, geographical features, and the people? Test yourself. As you read the newspapers and listen to the news, as you hear the names of the countries, can you visualize the area so that the information is more meaningful?

➤   **For** a list of helpful references, go to the *customers* section of www.southwestern.com.

23

Asia

23

Asia

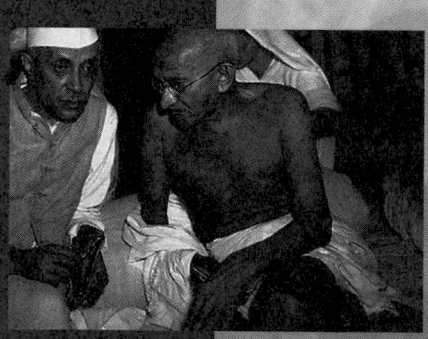

Overleaf: *Mount Fuji*

Contents

Asia

A Note about Spellings

As with any language that is written in a script other than the Roman alphabet, Arabic is, at times, difficult to transliterate into English, and there is no single universally accepted system for doing so. This difficulty also arises with words from other languages that are, or have been in the past, written in the Arabic script, such as Farsi and Turkish. When rendering Arabic words into English, this publication follows standard modern international practice, avoiding, for example, the use of diacritics, which some systems of transliteration employ.

Note on the Country Listings

Most of the information included in the following section is self-explanatory; however, some of the recurring statistical information requires a word of explanation about its importance.

Literacy

The literacy rate, that is, the percentage of people in a country who can read out of the total population, gives an important indication of the level of education in that country.

Per capita GDP

This figure represents the gross domestic product of the country divided by the total population; it provides an indication of the standard of living in each country. This figure is of necessity given as an estimate. (Each country's current world rank is also provided.)

Population

Population estimates are based on the most recent data available. Whenever possible, they are based on census or other official figures.

Asia is the largest contintent, both in land mass and in population. Although the countries of the Middle East are located on the continent of Asia, they comprise a separate region, and the information about them will be found in the MIDDLE EAST volume. The region extends from Saudi Arabia north to Turkey, and from Iran west to the Mediterranean Sea.

Asia also geographically includes the part of Russia east of the Ural Mountains, but in political, historical, and cultural terms, Russia is usually considered part of Europe. For that reason, this chapter will contain only geographical information about Asian Russia. Other information on Russia will be found in the EUROPE AND RUSSIA volume.

The populations of this large and geographically diverse area are varied. The people belong to many different ethnic groups, with differing ancestry, customs, and religions. The largest ethnic groups include the Arabs in the southwest and the Chinese in the east. The number of languages and dialects spoken serve as a barrier to cooperation, with one Indian state alone having more than 375 languages and dialects.

civilizations
US

civilisations
Brit.

These different groups often dislike and distrust each other and this can sometimes lead to violence.

Physical types vary from populations with coarse hair and a fold of skin across the inner corner of their eyes to those with fine hair and no inner eyelid fold, or those with dark skin and curly hair.

The countries of Asia and the Middle East have many different forms of political organization. India, Israel, and Japan operate under democratic principles. A few nations, such as Bhutan and Saudi Arabia, still have kings. Communist governments rule Vietnam, China, and North Korea. Iran is a theocratic republic. At times of political unrest, military leaders have taken control of Asian and Middle Eastern countries, giving rise to powerful leaders.

Asia was the birthplace of several of the world's earliest civilizations. One of the first developed in the crescent formed by the Tigris and Euphrates Rivers in the Middle East by about 3500 B.C. The rivers allowed irrigation of the alluvial plains in that area, creating agricultural surpluses necessary to support the rise of large cities. Cuneiform writing developed there around 3000 B.C.

There are evidences of trade between this Mesopotamian culture and the Indus Valley culture, which is dated to 2,500 to 2,000 years before Christ. Excavations at the great cities of Mohenjo-daro and Harappa have demonstrated that some of these people, in addition to engaging in long-distance trade, were literate, were craft specialists, and lived in cities with a complex society.

The Chinese Shang dynasty had begun developing writing around 1,400 years before the present, with its earliest form being that of glyphs inscribed on bones. The Chinese writing system later influenced the development of both Korean and Japanese writing systems.

The continent was also the birthplace of the world's major religions, including Buddhism, Hinduism, Islam, Judaism, Shinto, Taoism, and Confucianism. Although Christianity has more followers than any other world religion, it has never become a major faith in Asia. More Asians practice Hinduism than any other religion. It is the major faith in both India and Nepal. Islam is the next most popular religion, but it is the most widespread geographically. Buddhism is practiced mostly in east and southeast Asia.

Asia has been traditionally defined as those lands bounded on the east by the Pacific ocean and on the west by Europe. The most northern parts of Russian Asia lie within the frozen Arctic area and the most southern parts of the continent lie in the tropics near the equator. It contains some of the world's largest and smallest countries as well as some that contain the most dense and the least dense populations per square mile.

The land. The continent of Asia generally is divided into four subregions, each of which tends to be unified climatically, geographically, and culturally. *South Asia* comprises Pakistan, India, Sri Lanka, Bangladesh, Bhutan, and Nepal; *Southeast Asia* includes the Indochinese peninsula, Indonesia, and the Philippines; *East Asia* includes the eastern third of China, Korea, Taiwan, and Japan; and *Central Asia* includes the western two-thirds of China, Mongolia, Tibet, Afghanistan, Kazakhstan,

Kyrgyzstan, Tajikistan, Turkmenistan, and Uzbekistan.

Mountains. Asia is dominated by a large mountain mass at its center. The focus of this extensive range is the Pamir Knot, a rugged plateau region located north of the Indian subcontinent, where the borders of China, India, Tajikistan, Pakistan, and Afghanistan meet.

West of the Pamir plateau, which is sometimes referred to as the roof of the world, the mountains of the Hindu Kush extend west through Afghanistan toward the Plateau of Iran.

The Tien Shan range extends north from the Pamirs into northern China and Mongolia. To the northeast the Tien Shan merges into the Altai range, which extends from Mongolia into southern Kazakhstan.

The Karakorum range extends east of the Pamirs into the Kunlun range, which arcs into central China around the northern edge of the Tibetan Plateau. Between the Tien Shan and Altai ranges

center
US

centre
Brit.

THE ETHEREAL mist-shrouded hills near the city of Guilin are the subject for many of China's most famous paintings.

23 Asia

THE LITERACY RATE varies widely in Asian countries, but great emphasis has been placed on education in recent years, with fierce competition for the best schools in developed countries like Japan.

IRRIGATED TERRACES for rice increase the amount of arable land in many Asian countries, which depend heavily on rice as a staple.

in the north and the Kunlun Mountains lie the vast, arid Gobi and Taklamakan deserts and the great Mongolian Plains.

The Himalayas, to the south and southeast of the Pamirs, form a giant east-to-west arc running 1,500 miles (2,400 km) along the northern edge of India, from the Indus River in the northwest to the Brahmaputra River in the southeast.

Between the Himalayan and Kunlun ranges is the huge Tibetan Plateau. This region of about 471,000 square miles (1,220,207 sq. km) has an average elevation of about 16,000 feet (4,875 m).

The Himalayan range and its related plateau are considered to have been formed by the merging of the Indian subcontinent with the Asian mainland. The enormous forces produced by the convergence of the two giant landmasses caused folding of the continental crust and formation of the Himalayas. It is thought that the forces of uplift created by the sinking of the northern edge of the Indian landmass beneath the Asian landmass built up the Tibetan Plateau. In geological time, the Himalayas are considered a youthful mountain range.

The Himalayas contain the tallest mountains in the world, including Mt. Everest, at 29,035 feet (8849 m) the highest in the world. Because of their great height and steepness, the Himalayas are a formidable barrier, effectively dividing northern and southern Asia.

At the eastern end of the Himalayas are several mountain chains that spread like fingers southward into Southeast Asia. Of these, the Annam Cordillera in Vietnam and Laos, the Tanen Taungghi in Myanmar and Thailand, and the Arakan Yoma in Myanmar are the most important.

Rivers. River valleys have been extremely important to the continent's development. Population tends to be concentrated along the fertile valleys and deltas of the many rivers that rise in the central mountain core.

Central Asia is dominated by the Amu Darya and Syr Darya rivers. Both empty into the Aral Sea, another important body of water in Central Asia. Owing to excessive irrigation, however, the sea level of the Aral is dropping to perilously low levels and water from the rivers is becoming a scarce natural resource.

The Indus and Brahmaputra rivers, two of the most important rivers of South Asia, rise very near each other on the southern edge of the Tibetan Plateau and then run in opposite directions. The Indus, about 1,800 miles (2,900 km) long, flows northwest around the northern end of the Himalayas, then south to the Arabian Sea. The Brahmaputra, about 1,680 miles (2,710 km) long, flows to the eastern end of the Himalayas and then south to the Bay of Bengal. Another important South Asian river, the Ganges, rises in the Himalayas in northern India and flows about 1560 miles (2520 km) southeast to the Bay of Bengal.

The principal rivers of Southeast Asia are the Irrawaddy and the Salween of Myanmar, the Chao Phraya of Thailand, the Red of northern Vietnam, and the Mekong. The Mekong rises in eastern Tibet and flows southward 2,600 miles (4,200 km) through China and into Laos, where it forms much of the border of Laos with Thailand. It then flows across Cambodia and into southern Vietnam, where it spreads into a large, fertile delta.

In China the principal rivers are the Huang He and the Yangtze (Chang Kiang), both of which also rise in Tibet. The Huang He flows about 2,900 miles (4,700 km) into the Yellow Sea. The Yangtze flows some 3,400 miles (5,490 km) to the East China Sea.

Japan has many rivers, providing ample irrigation and some sources for hydroelectric power, but none is of particular significance.

The islands. The islands of Asia and the Pacific are generally of three types: mountainous, volcanic, and coral. Most of the islands of Southeast and East Asia are mountainous or volcanic or a combination of the two. They are arranged in several arcs that are associated with mainland ranges.

The arc formed by the Andaman and Nicobar islands in the Bay of Bengal, Sumatra, Java, and the lesser Sunda Islands is a continuation of the Arakan Yoma range in Myanmar and is volcanically active. The island of Borneo is an extension of the Malay peninsula. All these islands are situated on an extension of the Asian continent called the Sunda Shelf. The Philippines, Sulawesi, and the Moluccas are essentially the tops of mountains situated on the edge of the Sunda Shelf.

The arc of the Japanese islands follows the juncture of several mainland and oceanic ridges that extend along the Pacific coast of the Asian mainland. This complex of ridges runs from Sakhalin down through Japan and the Ryukyu Islands to Taiwan. All of these island arcs are characterized by extensive volcanic and seismic activity.

Climate. Asia's weather is dominated by the climatic pattern known as monsoon. During the winter, high-pressure areas form over the cold land, causing a flow of cold dry air toward the low-pressure areas over the warmer seas and oceans. The centers of high pressure during Asian winters are generally located in Siberia, the Asiatic part of Russia. The Himalayan barrier reduces the effects of the winter monsoon on the lands beyond, from Pakistan to southeastern China. However, in areas not protected by mountain barriers, such as Mongolia, northern and central China, and Korea, the winters are bitterly cold and severe.

During the summer, the wind pattern of the monsoon is reversed. Low-pressure areas form over the land, particularly in the Punjab region of northern India and in the Gobi Desert region of China. Hot, moisture-laden air from the oceans and seas flows across the land toward the centers of low pressure. The mountain barriers force the air to rise and cool, thus reducing its ability to carry moisture. For this reason, the rich, fertile lands on the coastal side of the mountain barriers receive abundant monsoon rainfall and the inland regions of Asia receive very little precipitation.

Vegetation. Asia has a wide range of vegetation zones. Desert conditions prevail in central and west-central Asia. Vegetation is sparse in the desert zone, but the lands to the north, east, and southeast of this region constitute a belt of low grassland called steppe. Vegetation in this zone is drought resistant and hardy and supports a larger variety and number of animals. In eastern Asia, temperate grasslands merge into forest. In west-central Asia, the vast Plateau of Tibet, classified as alpine tundra, gives way along the Himalayas to a tropical rain forest extending along the northern rim of the Indian subcontinent southeast through most of Southeast Asia. Forest and grassland prevail in India, diminishing to steppe and desert in Afghanistan.

The people. Asia's population density averages about 250 people per square mile. However, local and regional population densities vary widely. For example, the population density of Mongolia, which has 2.4 million people in an area twice the size of Texas, averages 4 people per square mile. Also, some mountainous and desert areas in central Asia have essentially zero population density. These may be contrasted with Singapore and Hong Kong, which have population densities approaching 12,000 and 14,600 people per square mile, respectively.

Throughout Asia, the population tends to be concentrated in the fertile plains, river valleys, and coastal regions. Most of Japan's population, for example, lives in cities situated along the coasts.

Asia's cultural and ethnic variety reflects its geographical features and long history of early civilization, migration, and invasion. Some of Asia's ethnic groups are quite large. The Han Chinese constitute the majority population of China, one of the centers of early Asian civilization. The Koreans of North and South Korea and the Japanese of Japan also constitute the majority groups of their respective countries.

India, the second center of early Asian civilization, has developed a large number of distinct groups with a wide variety of linguistic, religious, and cultural traditions. Generally, however, the various ethnic groups may be organized into two larger groups: the Indo-Aryans, an Indo-European subgroup concentrated primarily in the northern areas of India; and the Dravidians, concentrated generally in southern India.

Southeast Asia, located between the two great centers of ancient Asian culture, is characterized by a wide variety of ethnic groups, including the Burmese, Thais, Laos, Khmers, Vietnamese, Malays, and Filipinos. Small culturally separate groups are found in remote mountain areas as well as on the islands of the Pacific.

Certain migratory patterns that have helped shape Asia's ethnic diversity are known because they continued into relatively recent times. For example, in India the population tended to migrate from the northwest toward the south and east. Southeast Asia was repeatedly invaded by various southern Chinese tribes. The Philippine islands were settled in waves by Malay groups from Indonesia and the Malay peninsula. From central Asia the Mongols pushed west as far as Europe, south into Afghanistan and India, and east into China.

Language. Many hundreds of languages are spoken in Asia. Most have been shown to be related, although sometimes distantly, to one of a number of language groups.

The largest language group in Asia is Sino-Tibetan, which includes Chinese, Tibetan, Burman, and Thai. There are several forms of Chinese, with Mandarin Chinese being the most widely used language in China. Within each form of Chinese are separate dialects.

Two language families predominate on the Indian subcontinent. The Dravidian languages, which include Tamil, Telugu, Kannada (Kanarese), and Malayalam, are spoken in southern India and Sri Lanka. The Indo-European family predominates in northern India, Afghanistan, Pakistan, and Bangladesh, and includes Hindi, Dari, Pushtu, Urdu, Baluchi, Punjabi (Panjabi), and Bangla (Bengali). Sinhalese, the language of about three-fourths of the population of Sri Lanka, is an Indo-European language that shows heavy Dravidian influence. English is used in India, Pakistan, and Bangladesh.

Central Asia is dominated by languages of the Ural-Altaic family, which includes Mongolian and Manchu. The Austro-Asiatic family includes Khmer (Cambodian) and the languages of the Nicobar islands. French is still used in Indochina.

The languages of the Malay peninsula and most of the islands of Southeast Asia and the Pacific belong to the Malayo-Polynesian group of languages. Malay, Bahasa Indonesia, Tagalog, Samoan, and Hawaiian are among these languages.

The many languages of New Guinea do not appear to be related to any other group of languages. This is also true of the aboriginal languages of Australia as well as the Vietnamese, Korean, and Japanese languages.

Religion. Most of the world's great religions are represented in Asia and Australasia.

Hinduism, the religion with the largest number of followers in Asia, began in the Indus River valley in what is now Pakistan. Over the millennia it has developed into a complicated religious and social structure. Hinduism is now

THE KALEIDOSCOPE of activity in Tokyo is evidence of both its importance as a commercial center and the overcrowding that results from being the world's largest urban center.

THE GANGES RIVER in India is sacred to Hindu pilgrims, thousands of whom travel there each year to purify themselves by bathing in its waters.

practiced primarily in India and Nepal, but also in Bhutan and in Fiji, where many Indians have settled. Jainism and Sikhism, two religions closely related to Hinduism, are also practiced in India.

Buddhism has fewer followers but is distributed over a larger area. Originating in India, it is the major religion of Tibet, Mongolia, and of much of Southeast Asia, but it is also practiced in China, Japan, and other parts of Asia. However, it long ago ceased to be a major religion in India. There are two main branches of Buddhism: Mahayana, which is practiced in the northern parts of Asia; and Theravada, which is practiced primarily in Southeast Asia.

Islam, the third major religion of Asia, was brought from the Middle East by Muslim traders. It is the primary religion of the people of Afghanistan, Kazakhstan, Kyrgyzstan, Tajikistan, Turkmenistan, Uzbekistan, Pakistan, Bangladesh, Malaysia, and Indonesia. There are also significant communities of Muslims in western China. Islam has two main sects: The Shiites adhere to strict fundamentalist precepts, and the Sunnis follow less stringent interpretations.

Confucianism, which is more a system of ethical behavior than a religion, and Taoism developed in China. Confucianism spread to Korea, Japan, and Vietnam. Taoism also spread to other lands. Shinto, the indigenous religion of Japan, encompasses numerous major and minor sects.

Economy. In economic development, as in many other things, Asia is a continent of contrasts. Countries that are desperately poor, such as Bangladesh, Cambodia, and Vietnam, exist side by side with wealthy countries, such as Japan, South Korea, and Singapore.

During colonial times, the Asian economies were geared primarily to exploitation of raw materials for the industries of the colonizing countries. Today, despite significant progress by some governments to promote domestic processing of locally produced raw materials, a large part of the exports from the Asian mainland still are processed in Europe, North America, and Japan.

Attempting to develop financial stability, Asian countries have joined together to create various organizations to foster economic improvement. The

colonizing
US

colonising
Brit.

labor
US

labour
Brit.

aluminum
US

aluminium
Brit.

centers
US

centres
Brit.

Association of Southeast Asian Nations (ASEAN) was established in 1967 by Brunei, Indonesia, Malaysia, the Philippines, Singapore, and Thailand. The organization, created to encourage economic cooperation among member nations, has sponsored programs that encourage foreign investment. It also engages in special efforts to attract members of the European Community. ASEAN is currently considering plans to establish a common market, to be known as AFTA (ASEAN Free Trade Area), by 2008; however, many doubt the feasibility of this goal.

ASEAN has traditionally shied away from political matters. In 1992 the organization changed its stance, however, when it called for the establishment of a Zone of Peace, Freedom, and Neutrality (ZOPFAN); this zone would require military as well as economic cooperation.

Another cooperative organization, the Asian Development Bank, was created in 1966 to fund developmental projects, enable Asian countries to coordinate economic activities, and provide technical assistance. This assistance is offered through a Technical Assistance Special Fund and the Japan Special Fund. The bank created the Asian Development Fund in 1974 to aid the least developed nations in Asia. As of 1990, 34 Asian nations and 15 non-Asian countries were members of the bank.

Agriculture. The economy of Asia is dominated by agriculture, which employs more than 60 percent of the labor force. Countries that are not highly developed employ a greater percentage of their work forces in agriculture. For example, in Bhutan 95 percent of the labor force is agricultural. In Nepal 91 percent of the labor force works in agriculture. In the two largest countries, China and India, the numbers are 68 and 70 percent, respectively. This may be contrasted with such developed countries as Singapore and Japan, where the work forces are, respectively, 1 and 9 percent agricultural.

Farming methods remain traditional for the most part, with little or no mecha-

RICE is the main food throughout much of Asia and is also the most important agricultural product. Some countries still have to import rice.

nization or application of Western-style farming techniques. The development of hardy new strains of rice, wheat, and other grains that produce higher yields has helped to increase agricultural production. Partly because of this, some countries, such as India, which have long suffered shortfalls in grain production, have become net exporters.

Rice, the main food throughout much of Asia, is also the main agricultural product. India and China are the leading rice producers and also the leading producers of Asia's second most important crop, wheat.

Other important crops include barley, corn, millet, and sorghum. Important export crops include tea, rubber, cotton, jute, and sugar cane. Copra, the dried meat of the coconut, is an important export for many Pacific island nations. Hog production is important in China.

Natural resources. Asia is richly endowed with a great variety of natural resources. Forests provide a valuable export product for a number of countries, particularly Japan and the countries of South and Southeast Asia. However, overcutting of forests in Southeast Asia is leading to serious problems for the region. The denuding of the mountains slopes in Nepal has been partially blamed for the periodic flooding that occurs in Bangladesh. Ecologists are becoming increasingly concerned with the destruction of the rain forests in Southeast Asia.

Fishing is an important activity throughout much of Asia. Japan is the leading fishing nation of Asia and the world. Other major fishing nations are China, Thailand, the Philippines, and Indonesia. Asia is also quite rich in fossil fuel resources. Indonesia, China, and Malay-sia have large reserves of oil and natural gas, as do Uzbekistan, Turkmenistan, and Kazakhstan. China also has vast coal reserves. Other nations, such as India, are just beginning to exploit their oil reserves.

Asia contains important reserves of almost all the minerals required by the industrial world, including major deposits of graphite, tin, tungsten, aluminum, iron, chromium, mercury, zinc, and manganese.

Industry. Asian industrialization has been delayed to some extent by its colonial past. There was little incentive to introduce manufacturing technology during the era of European colonialism in Asia. Also, the generally inadequate development of transportation in much of Asia has complicated the delivery of raw materials to processing and manufacturing centers.

Asian industry has focused primarily on the processing of its raw materials and agricultural products. However, the postwar rise of Japan as the third largest industrial economy in the world and similar successes in Taiwan, South Korea, Singapore, and Hong Kong are encouraging signs for the future. Japan's success, for example, has given it the capital necessary to launch new industries and invest in cooperative ventures in other Asian countries. China and India also have developed substantial industrial and manufacturing capabilities, although the percentage of each country's industrial work force is still relatively low.

Major industries in modern Asia include electronics, textiles, chemicals, petrochemicals, aluminum, steel, automobile manufacturing, and arms production.

Government and politics.

Prior to the period of European colonial expansion into Asia, the region was divided largely into a number of kingdoms, principalities, and empires. In the 18th and 19th centuries, European influence and control over the region expanded in direct proportion to the rise in European control of Asian trade and commerce. With the exception of Siam (Thailand) and Japan, virtually every Asian country fell under European control.

As the European colonial system weakened in the late 19th to mid-20th centuries, strong nationalist movements gained momentum under the leadership of Western-educated Asian leaders. Much of Asia's recent political history is that of newly independent nations struggling to achieve or maintain political stability while trying to overcome economic handicaps created at least partially by colonialism.

Modern Asia has been greatly affected by the Cold War and the collapse of the Soviet Union in 1991. The Soviet Union, with its vast Asian territories, and China competed with each other for control of the region after the end of World War II; the United States sought to check the advancement of both countries. Many Asian nations thus found themselves dominated by foreign powers once again. The rivalry also fostered the growth of military strength in Asia. In 1991 six of the world's nine largest armies were to be found on the continent of Asia. They were the armies of China, North Korea, South Korea, Vietnam, India, and Pakistan.

The collapse of the Soviet Union has drastically changed politics throughout Asia, creating a continent of shifting alliances and new economic and political priorities. While both China and the United States have motives for seeking to fill the vacuum created by the disappearance of the Soviet Union, many Asian nations prefer to work toward creating governments capable of maintaining stability without relying on either of these powers.

East Asia. Modern East Asia is dominated by Japan, Asia's strongest economic power.

Japan's establishment of a Japanese-dominated economic program, called the Greater East Asia Co-Prosperity Sphere, led ultimately to Asia's involvement in World War II and Japan's defeat by the Allies. Following the war, Japan was required to adopt its current system of parliamentary democracy. The postwar constitution of Japan also placed a cap on military spending and limited military action to self-defense.

Programs of economic and technical assistance helped Japan on its postwar course of steady economic growth. This, in turn, has helped give Japan one of the most stable governments in the world. The Japanese government's commitment to scientific research and development and long-term industrial planning has greatly helped the nation's economic and political stability. With increasing economic power, Japan has also taken some tentative steps toward exercising greater political influence in the world. Its history of aggression prior to and during World War II, however, has forced the country to show great delicacy in its diplomatic relations with other Asian countries, especially Korea and China. Japan is also reluctant to follow policies requiring military intervention, both because of its constitutional restraints and because of lack of popular support for such measures. While Japan's success has greatly benefited its people and ensures stability in East Asia, it has also created tensions with some of its trading partners, particularly the United States, which has accused the government of unfair trading practices such as protectionism. Some less developed Asian countries have also accused Japan of reviving colonialism because of Japan's practice of buying materials at low cost and exporting some manufacturing jobs (along with attendant environmental problems) to poor Asian countries where wages are far lower.

Other East Asian countries, such as Taiwan and South Korea, have also experienced economic booms, and there has been much discussion of the rising importance of the "Four Tigers" (South Korea, Taiwan, Hong Kong, and the Southeast Asian nation of Singapore) and of the rise of the Pacific Rim (East Asia and the west coast of the United States) as a significant economic arena.

South Korea's phenomenal rate of growth in the 1970s and 1980s had moderated by the early 1990s, however. Consumer and worker discontent, added to long-standing opposition to repressive government policies, contributed to increased political problems in South Korea. Nonetheless, South Korea still had a far higher standard of living than that of its northern neighbor, North Korea. The dissolution of the Soviet Union, North Korea's strongest ally, has led to some speculation that the two countries, created after the end of World War II, will reunite. Although leaders of the two countries have agreed to resume communications, no steps toward reunification have yet been taken, in part because of the enormous cost of integrating the North Korean economy with that of the South. At the least, however, North Korea will be forced to seek new economic partners and South Korea might be a logical first choice.

The collapse of the Soviet Union also had an effect on China, Asia's most powerful Communist nation. There, the

FREE ENTERPRISE, such as this jade market, has long flourished in Hong Kong, but merchants are still unsure about its future under the People's Republic of China.

prospect of sweeping change seemed to work both for and against the movement for economic and political reform. China, which became an independent republic in 1912, became a Communist country in 1949 after a long struggle between non-Communist Nationalist forces and a Communist guerrilla movement. After establishing a Communist government, China became a basically totalitarian state. In the 1980s a reform movement began making steady progress. The movement was effectively halted in June 1989, however, when military force was used against Chinese demonstrators in Beijing's Tiananmen Square. One result of the violent repression was a severe weakening of the faith once held by many Chinese in the ability of communism to solve China's problems. The government began introducing limited free-market economic strategies and encouraging investment from abroad. China also began strengthening its economic ties to Taiwan and to Hong Kong. Hong Kong had been a Crown Colony of the United Kingdom, which signed an agreement stipulating that Great Britain could lease Hong Kong for 99 years. China and Great Britain signed an agreement in 1984 ensuring that Hong Kong could maintain its capitalist economy for 50 years after the expiration of the lease. Economic uncertainty after Hong Kong's return to Chinese control in 1997 caused thousands of Hong Kong's wealthy citizens to leave, although many have since returned.

Southeast Asia. Events in Southeast Asia over the past 30 years have shown that the West's fears concerning communism in Asia were unrealistic.

An ideological rift developed between the People's Republic of China and the Soviet Union in the late 1950s and early 1960s and had ripple effects throughout Southeast Asia, especially in Vietnam. There, a Communist-led guerrilla movement in French-held Indochina culminated in the establishment in 1954 of Communist North Vietnam and non-Communist South Vietnam. North

Vietnam, aligned with the Soviet Union, came into direct conflict with China and also with the Communist Khmer Rouge government of Cambodia, which it toppled in 1979. Cambodia has still not recovered political or economic stability. The war between the divided Vietnamese country also involved Laos and massive troop support from the United States in the South.

While part of Southeast Asia was occupied with the Vietnam War, the countries of Singapore, Brunei, the Philippines, Indonesia, Malaysia, and Thailand established the Association of South East Asian Nations (ASEAN) in 1967 to foster economic and social development. Of the member nations, only Thailand borders the more troubled countries of Southeast Asia. The countries, while not as economically powerful as Japan, South Korea, and Hong Kong, have created a center of relative stability in a chaotic part of the world. They have also formed a number of mutually beneficial arrangements among themselves. For instance, Singapore has a number of engineers and skilled workers, but little room for building factories, while Malaysia has land available, but little money for investment and a small skilled labor force. Singapore's foreign investment ventures in Malaysia have proved profitable for both countries.

Economic crises have impeded progress in some of these countries, however. In the Philippines, economic woes contributed to government problems with the Philippine Communist guerrilla movement as well as several attempted coups by dissident political and military leaders.

Despite such occasional obstacles, economists predict that the member nations of ASEAN will develop into industrialized nations of major economic significance in the years to come.

THIS SINGAPORE woman wears a red mark made of sandalwood paste that originally would have signified that she was married. In recent years, young women have adopted the mark as merely a decorative element.

Central Asia. The collapse of the Soviet Union has had the strongest repercussions in Central Asia, a region that is heir to various cultural legacies, including those of ancient China, Persia, India, the Ottoman Empire, and Imperial Russia. Today, although most inhabitants of Central Asia are of Mongolian descent, cultural and ethnic diversity are creating unrest in various countries.

Central Asia was the object of what Rudyard Kipling called "The Great Game" during the 19th century, when Great Britain and Russia competed for control in the area. Later, Russia, as part of the Soviet Union, won an important round of the game when the U.S.S.R. divided the region into five Soviet Republics. When the Soviet Union collapsed in 1991, the former republics declared their independence. Because of the republics' significant natural resources and their proximity to the Middle East, the region once again has become an important element in global politics. Turkey, Russia, and Iran are among the most interested players of the new game. Meanwhile, the new countries are struggling to establish politically and economically sound institutions.

Like other former republics of the Soviet Union, the Central Asian republics are experiencing high rates of inflation and much difficulty with the disappearance of subsidies and central planning from Moscow. In an effort to overcome the economic difficulties facing the new countries, the five Asian republics established an organization called the United States of Central Asia in early 1993. The organization agreed to work toward the creation of a common market and to coordinate the attempts of member nations to master the economic disorder they are facing, although no specific policies were established.

Unlike their European counterparts, most Central Asian republics chose to retain communist governments. Of the five republics, only Kyrgyzstan has established a democratic government. Many of the countries maintain that the communist system of government is best suited to controlling the ethnic unrest that is disturbing Kazakhstan, Tajikistan, and Uzbekistan. Violence in these countries has erupted as a result of hastily drawn borders that created ethnic minorities in the countries when they were first absorbed by the Soviet Union. The violence, also fueled by government opposition to Muslim fundamentalists, exacerbates the already formidable problems facing the new nations.

The future of the Asian republics and their oil reserves is of special concern to their neighbors. Russia, although wary of becoming involved in internal disputes after the Soviet Union's experiences in Afghanistan, is concerned about the fate of ethnic Russians living in predominantly Muslim republics. Iran, meanwhile, is a Muslim theocracy eager to find allies in the region. Turkey, on the other hand, is a moder-

ate Muslim country closely allied to the West; it would prefer to see its new neighbors follow a less provocative course. Much needed foreign investment in the region is limited. Onlookers wait to see the outcome of the region's metamorphosis.

Afghanistan endured bitter fighting between the communist government and rebels for ten years, with Soviet intervention causing controversy until the Soviet troops withdrew in 1989. War between the government and guerillas escalated; eventually, part of Afghanistan was controlled by a loose coalition and part by the fundamentalist Islamic Taliban. A U.S.-led military campaign, in response to the September 2001 terrorist attacks, toppled the Taliban. Afghanistan's new multiparty government remains shaky, and sporadic fighting continues.

South Asia. South Asia is also beset by ethnic discord and financial worries. In addition to the strained relations between Hindu India and Muslim Pakistan and Bangladesh, the region's tensions are increased by internal unrest related to religious or ethnic minorities in many countries. In the early 1990s Indian Muslims became the target of violent attacks by Hindus. In Sri Lanka the Tamil ethnic minority launched guerrilla attacks to fight for the establishment of an autonomous region in the northeastern portion of the country.

The economies of South Asian countries are as troubled as their people. For many years South Asia was dependent on traditional farming techniques that were unable to sustain the region's fast-growing population. When agricultural advancements created a Green Revolution in the area, it was hoped that conditions in South Asia might improve, but natural disasters continued to devastate the area (particularly in Bangladesh), overpopulation remained a serious problem, and both India and Pakistan allocated large portions of their budgets to military endeavors.

The collapse of the Soviet Union, one of India's major trading partners and sources of military technology, forced India to rethink its cumbersome economic policies, which foster state monopolies of some industries and discourage foreign investment. Steps have been taken to liberalize the economy, and many foreign investors are interested in establishing themselves in India, which could provide a foothold in South Asia, a huge potential market, and a source of labor cheaper than that of industrialized nations. The region's ability to achieve and maintain stability, a main consideration for many investors, remains to be seen.

As Asia moves into the 21st century, its leaders have become increasingly aware that its future is intertwined with that of the world. It is widely believed that only through international cooperation, especially on political and economic levels, will the nations of Asia be able to meet the challenges to come.

Countries of Asia

Afghanistan

Official name: *Islamic Republic of Afghanistan*
Area: *249,936 sq. mi., 647,500 sq. km.*
Type of government: *Republic*
Population: *27,756,000*
Capital and largest city: *Kabul (Pop. 1,527,000)*
Languages: *Pashtu, Dari*
Literacy: *36%*
Currency: *Afghani*
Per capita GNP: *$800 (Rank: 182nd)*

The land. Afghanistan is a high country, with an average elevation of about 6,000 feet above sea level. A great central mountain core dominates the landscape. In the east, the Hindu Kush ranges rise to more than 20,000 feet. The Koh-i-Baba and Paropamisus ranges, with elevations of 10,000 to 15,000 feet, fan out toward the west.

Near the western border the land drops to Seistan, a barren plateau at an elevation of 1,500 feet. East of Seistan are two deserts, the Dasht-i-Margo and the Registan.

Four large rivers flow from the central mountains through the country's major inhabited regions. The Amu Darya (Oxus) drains the hilly northeast and forms part of the border with the Soviet Union. The Hari Rud flows west from the Paropamisus. The richest regions are the valleys of the Helmand and its tributaries, in the southwest, and the valley of the Kabul, which flows east to the Indus.

Afghanistan's climate is characterized by extremes. In the lower regions average temperatures range from over 115°F in summer to -10°F in winter. Mountain temperatures may vary by as much as 50°F in one day, although south of the mountains temperatures are more moderate. Winds are high throughout the country. Average precipitation ranges from 2 inches a year in the west to 12 inches in the east.

The people. Afghanistan's central position in Asia has given it a varied population. Over half the people are Pukhtun (also called Pashtun or Pathan), a tribal group related to the Persians and Indians. Their language is Pushtu. Other major groups are the Hazara, who speak a mixed Persian-Turkish dialect, the Turkic-speaking Uzbek and Turkoman, and the Tajik, whose language is Dari, a dialect of Persian.

Most Afghans live in rural villages. The urban population is about 15 percent of the total population. The major cities are Kabul in the east, Herat in the west, and Kandahar in the south.

More than one-third of the population fled to Pakistan or Iran during and after the Soviet invasion in 1979. About half of the people later returned.

Economy. Afghanistan's economy is poor and is based on farming and herding, although no more than 25 percent of the land can be cultivated and only about 12 percent is farmed. Mineral resources include coal, oil, gas, iron, salt, copper, gold, and lapis lazuli.

Karakul sheep are Afghanistan's most valuable agricultural commodity, providing meat, milk, and fat for domestic consumption and skins for export. Goats, cattle, horses, donkeys, and camels also are raised. The leading crops are wheat, other grains, cotton, sugar beets, opium poppies, and a great variety of fruits and vegetables.

Leather processing, textile weaving, and flour milling are the only well established manufacturing industries.

Projects have been initiated to develop coal and hydroelectric resources; to expand transportation and communications facilities; and to improve education and health services.

Following the 1978 communist coup and the 1979 Soviet invasion of Afghanistan, Western financial aid virtually dried up. The Soviet Union and the Comecon countries became the primary providers of technical and financial assistance.

Due principally to sales of natural gas, Afghanistan for a time maintained a favorable balance of trade. Gas accounts for about 35 percent of total exports. Now exports include opium, fruits and nuts, carpets, karakul skins, and cotton. Imports include food, petroleum products, and manufactured items.

Principal trading partners have been the United Kingdom, West Germany, the U.S, Netherlands, Pakistan, and Iran.

Government. A 2004 constitution provides for a directly elected president, a bicameral national assembly, and an independent judiciary.

History. Afghanistan lies at the crossroads of ancient Asian migration routes, and its early history is a story of invasions and conquests. The country has been inhabited since prehistory, but the first known settlers were Aryans, who passed through Afghanistan on their way to India in about 1500 B.C.

By the 500s B.C., Aryana, as the area was known, was part of the Persian Empire. In 328 B.C. it was conquered by Alexander the Great. After Alexander's

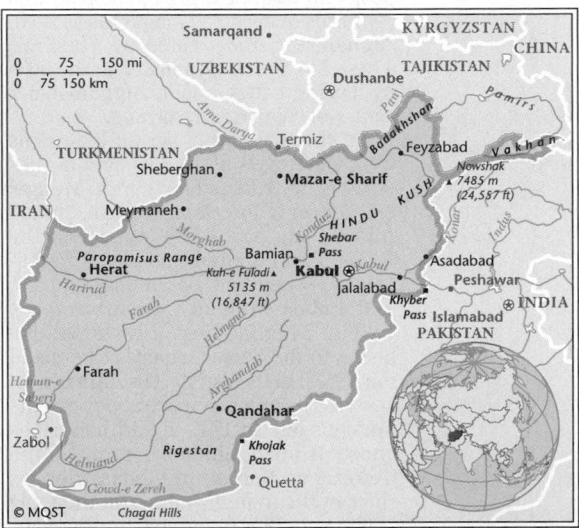

A VILLAGE in Afghanistan clings to the side of the mountain range that dominates the landscape of the rugged countryside.

death, it was divided between the Seleucid Empire of Persia and Bactria, a kingdom in the north. In the 100s B.C. these kingdoms fell before invasions from the north by nomadic tribes from central Asia.

Islam. In the late 600s and early 700s Arab armies invaded and converted the people to Islam. During the next several centuries many small kingdoms arose in Afghanistan, most ruled by Muslims. These kingdoms, dominated in the 900s by Turkic tribes, made Afghanistan a center of culture and learning.

In the 1200s the Turkic kingdoms were destroyed by the Mongol armies of Genghis Khan. The Turkic-Mongol conqueror Tamerlane (Timur) made Afghanistan part of his empire in the 1300s. Two hundred years later Tamerlane's descendant Babur founded the vast Indian Mughal (Mogul) empire.

The Mughals lost most of Afghanistan to the Safavid rulers of Persia in the 1600s. In the early 1700s Afghanistan asserted its independence and drove the Persians out. In 1747 the Afghan tribes chose Ahmad Shah Durrani, of the Sadozay section of the Abdali tribe, as ruler of the united country. In the early 1800s rebellions toppled the dynasty.

Foreign interference. Several civil wars for control of the throne left the country vulnerable to foreign invasion. By the 1800s control of Afghanistan had also become a goal of Russia and of Great Britain, whose Indian territory bordered Afghanistan. By 1839 Dost Muhammad, a Barakzay tribal leader strongly opposed to foreign control, held the throne. To protect its position in India and the Near East, Britain sought to place a more friendly ruler in power. This led to an Anglo-Afghan war between 1839 and 1842.

The British captured Dost Muhammad, but they could not put down a rebellion in the country and withdrew. For the next 36 years, Afghanistan's history was marked by civil war, Russian advances, Persian invasions, and, in 1878, by renewed war with Britain. In 1879, having won the war, Britain in effect made Afghanistan a buffer state between British and Russian imperialist ambitions.

In 1880 Abd-ar-Rahman came to the throne and cooperated with the British when it benefited Afghanistan. He pacified rebellious tribesmen; the boundaries between Afghanistan, Russia, and British India were set.

Afghanistan was neutral during World War I, but anti-British sentiment spread, nationalism developed, and in 1919 nationalists led a war against Britain. Neither side won, but the British allowed the country to conduct its own foreign affairs. Afghanistan's right to domestic self-rule had been promised in an Anglo-Russian agreement in 1907.

Modernization. After the war a new king, Amanullah, began to modernize the country. His reforms were extreme, costly, and unpopular, and in 1929 he was deposed during a tribal rebellion. Mohammed Nadir, a Pashtun leader, came to power. Afghanistan was neutral during World War II.

Under Nadir Shah and his son, Mohammed Zahir Shah, Afghanistan was gradually modernized. Democratic forms and processes were introduced, the economy developed, and some Western ideas were adopted.

In 1964 the Afghans received a written constitution that provided for democratic reforms, but the constitution was abolished when Zahir Shah was overthrown in 1973 by some army officers.

In 1978 another military coup brought the Communist People's Democratic Party of Afghanistan (PDPA) to power. Its unpopular policies led to widespread civil unrest. In September 1979 President Noor Mohammad Taraki was killed during a coup led by Hafizullah Amin, his prime minister. The Soviet Union, claiming to be bound by a 1978 Treaty of Friendship, invaded the country in December.

The Soviets deposed Amin. The new government, headed until 1986 by Babrak Karmal, and then by Najibullah, was highly unpopular. A strong guerrilla movement, supplied by Western and Middle Eastern countries, forced the Soviets to maintain a heavy military presence in Afghanistan.

The Soviets withdrew their forces in 1989, and the war between the government and guerrilla movements escalated. Najibullah resigned in April 1992.

Burhanuddin Rabbani became president in June 1992, but the coalition Northern Alliance still controlled part of the country and the fundamentalist Islamic Taliban seized control elsewhere. Osama bin Laden, a wealthy Saudi who had left Afghanistan in 1990, returned in 1996. He gave financial support to the repressive Taliban regime, and his fighters fought alongside Taliban troops. The U.S.-led military campaign against bin Laden, begun in response to the September 11, 2001, terrorist attacks in New York City and Washington, D.C., toppled the Taliban. (For more background, see "Understanding a New Global Crisis" in the HISTORY OF THE WORLD volume.) Even with a new government in place and ratification of a new constitution, the situation in Afghanistan remains precarious.

LORD FREDERICK ROBERTS is seen here with a group of Indian nobles at the end of the Afghan War in which the boundaries were set between Afghanistan, Russia, and British India.

Bangladesh

Official name: *People's Republic of Bangladesh*
Area: *55,584 sq. mi., 144,000 sq. km.*
Type of government: *Republic*
Population: *135,657,000*
Capital and largest city: *Dhaka (Pop., 4,232,000)*
Languages: *Bangla (official), English*
Literacy: *56%*
Currency: *Taka*
Per capita GDP: *$1,750 (Rank: 142nd)*

The land. The land is dominated by the Ganges, Brahmaputra, and Meghna river deltas. The rivers branch into many small tributaries that weave throughout the land. They flood frequently, leaving rich deposits of soil, but also causing great loss of life and damage to land and property.

Land elevations in northwest Bangladesh seldom exceed 300 feet above sea level. Eastern Bangladesh is dominated by the Chittagong Hill tracts, which rise sharply as high as 3,000 feet.

Bangladesh has a monsoon climate, with mild winters and hot summers. It is one of the rainiest areas in the world, with annual rainfall ranging from 50 to 200 inches.

The people. The population currently increases nearly 3 percent a year, and the country's density of 1,969 people per square mile is one of the highest in the world. Ninety-one percent of this population is rural. Most of the people are Indo-Aryan Bengalis. There are also many Biharis, who migrated from India after 1947, and native tribal peoples living in the hill areas. Seventy percent of the labor force is engaged in agriculture, mostly on a subsistence level.

Dhaka, the capital, is also the largest city in Bangladesh. Chittagong (population, 1,364,000), in the east, is the country's largest port.

Economy. Bangladesh is an extremely poor country with an unskilled labor force. Most of the population is engaged in subsistence farming. The most important crops are rice, jute, tea, and sugar.

Manufacturing contributes only about 8 percent of the gross domestic product. The manufacture of products from raw jute, such as burlap sacks and carpet backing, is important. Increasingly important is textile manufacture, both for domestic consumption and for export.

Bangladesh imports far more than it exports; the difference is made up primarily from the aid it receives from other countries. Primary exports are jute and jute products, textiles, frozen fish, leather, and tea. Imports include industrial goods, food, petroleum, and consumer goods.

Government. The head of government is a prime minister, who is usually the leader of the legislature's majority party. The legislature is a popularly elected parliament of 300 members. Office of president is normally ceremonial in nature.

History. The history of Bangladesh is closely tied to that of the rest of the Indian subcontinent. Though there were periods of independence for Bengal (the region of which Bangladesh is a part), its history is largely one of invasion and domination.

In 1193 the first of several invasions that eventually converted much of the region to Islam occurred. In 1576 Bengal was conquered by the Mughal Empire, which was centered in Delhi, India.

In 1514 the Portuguese built several trading posts in Bengal, but they were driven out in 1632. They were followed by Dutch, French, and British traders. By the end of the 19th century, the British had pushed the other European powers out of the area.

Bangladesh was administered as part of British India until 1947, when the region was partitioned into separate Hindu and Muslim nations and India and Pakistan were created. Pakistan consisted of present Pakistan plus the eastern portion of Bengal, which was known as East Pakistan.

From the beginning there were tensions between East Pakistan and the West Pakistan-dominated government.

In December 1970 the Awami League (a Bengali nationalist party), led by the enormously popular Sheik Mujibur Rahman, won a majority of the seats (167 of 313) in the Pakistan National Assembly. This unexpectedly large showing in the first national elections held in Pakistan since independence emphasized the fissure between the Bengali-speaking people of East Pakistan and their rulers.

On March 1, 1971, Pakistan's President Ayub Khan announced that the convening of the National Assembly would be postponed. Leaders of the Awami League claimed they were being cheated of the fruits of the election. Widespread rioting in the Bengali province ensued, and strikes crippled many cities.

On March 25, President Ayub Khan ordered the Pakistan national army into the Bengali province to crush dissent. Sheik Mujibur Rahman, who had in a radio broadcast declared the independence of Bangladesh, was arrested. The death toll of this phase of the civil war was estimated by some observers to be in the hundreds of thousands. In addition, several million Bengalis fled to neighboring India, which thereafter gave extensive aid to Bangladesh. In December 1971 India entered the war on the side of Bangladesh, and the Pakistani forces were quickly defeated.

Bangladesh was proclaimed an independent state with Sheik Mujibur Rahman as its prime minister.

Incensed by economic chaos and governmental corruption, a military group seized power on August 15, 1975. Mujibur Rahman and his family were killed. Parliamentary government was reinstated by the constitution of 1977 and in 1979 Ziaur Rahman was elected to the presidency.

Rahman was killed during an attempted coup in 1981. A second coup in 1982 succeeded in installing a military government, led by Hussain Mohammad Ershad. Martial law was lifted slowly and Ershad was elected president in 1986 in an election that was boycotted by the opposition parties. In 1990 a pro-democracy movement forced Ershad to resign and in 1991 free elections were held and continue.

Dangerous levels of naturally occurring arsenic have been found in ground water, causing a public-health crisis.

Bhutan

Official name: *Kingdom of Bhutan*
Area: *18,142 sq. mi., 47,000 sq. km.*
Type of government: *Monarchy*
Population: *2,094,000*
Capital and largest city: *Thimphu (Pop., 8,900)*
Languages: *Dzongkha (official), various dialects*
Literacy: *42%*
Currency: *Ngultrum*
Per capita GDP: *$1,200 (Rank: 60th)*

The land. Bhutan is no more than 190 miles long and 90 miles wide, but it has three distinct geographical zones. Within 20 miles of its northern border is a wild and snowy region, where peaks of the eastern Himalayas tower to almost 25,000 feet. A central zone, about 40 miles wide, ranges in elevation from 3,500 feet to 10,000 feet; it is forested with evergreens. The southern region, which

THE INFLUENCE of the monasteries has been very strong in Bhutan since the 1500s, when conquering Mongol tribes placed the country under the spiritual authority of the Dalai Lama of Tibet.

labor
US

labour
Brit.

centered
US

centred
Brit.

emphasized
US

emphasised
Brit.

23 Asia

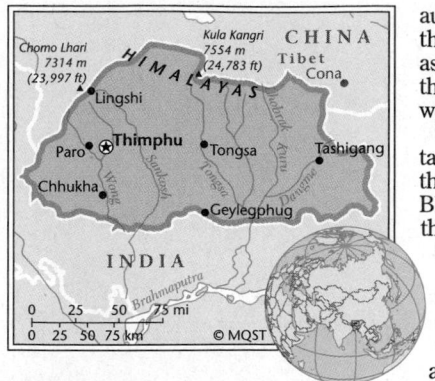

grades into the Brahmaputra River valley, is low and mostly covered with dense semitropical forest.

Several rivers flow south through Bhutan. The most important are the Amo Chu, the Sankosh, and the Dangme Chu.

Bhutan's climate varies with elevation. In the north, where alpine tundra conditions prevail, the cold is extreme, and glaciers fill the higher valleys. The central zone is temperate, and rainfall averages 40 to 60 inches a year. The southern region has a semitropical climate—heat and humidity are extreme, and up to 300 inches of rain may fall in a year.

The people. Bhutan's population is concentrated in the river valleys of the temperate central region. About two-thirds of the people are Bhotia, a Tibetan-speaking group. A Nepali minority makes up about one-quarter of the population.

Economy. Agriculture is the basis of Bhutan's economy, employing 90 percent of the population. Bhutan's forests are valuable. Deposits of dolomite, coal, gypsum, limestone, and other minerals have been unexploited.

Farms are concentrated in the rich river valleys, and they produce a surplus of food. The major crops are rice, wheat, corn, barley, and millet. Fruits and vegetables are also raised. Yaks, goats, and cattle are herded.

Bhutan is one of the world's least developed countries. Manufacturing accounts for only 1.5 percent of employment. Products include weaving, woodwork, cement, textiles, and plywood. Tourism is a big contributor to the economy.

India is Bhutan's largest trading partner and donor of aid, accounting for 90 percent of Bhutan's exports. Exports include cement, fruit, cardamom, timber, and handicrafts. Imports include food, textiles, and machinery.

Government. Bhutan is a monarchy ruled by a hereditary king. The king is advised by a Council of Ministers and a Royal Advisory Council.

Legislative functions are handled by the National Assembly. The assembly has 150 members, of which 105 are popularly elected; the remainder are monastic representatives, or appointed by the king.

History. Little is known of Bhutan's early history. In the 1500s Tibetans conquered the Mongol tribes that inhabited the land and placed it under the spiritual authority of the Dalai Lama of Tibet. In the 1700s China conquered Tibet and assumed control over Bhutan jointly with the Dalai Lama, but the country actually was governed by local tribal chieftains.

In 1774, after several raids by Bhutanese hill tribesmen on British India, the English East India Company forced Bhutan to grant it trading privileges through the important Himalayan passes that Bhutan controlled. But the raids continued, and in 1865 British troops subdued the hill tribesmen and annexed Bhutan's eastern region.

In 1885, after years of feuding among tribal chieftains, one leader, Ugyen Wangchuk, gained dominance over all the tribes. He cooperated with the British and by 1907 established himself as the maharaja of Bhutan. During the early 1900s China tried unsuccessfully to reassert control over the country, but in 1910 an Anglo-Bhutanese treaty recognized Bhutan's sovereignty. Its foreign affairs were to be managed by Britain, which also agreed to pay compensation for the territory annexed in 1865. Bhutan remained largely isolated from the rest of the world for half a century. In 1949 India agreed to assume Britain's responsibilities in Bhutan.

Bhutan began to assert its independence a bit more strongly and joined the UN in 1971. In 1991 a prodemocracy movement which the government believed to be instigated by Nepali immigrants resulted in eviction to UN refugee camps in Nepal where they have remained for over a decade. In recent years the monarchy has made concessions, including a draft constitution, toward the country becoming a parliamentary democracy.

Brunei

Official name: *Negara Brunei Darussalam*

Area: *2,227 sq. mi., 5,770 sq. km.*

Type of government: *Constitutional sultanate*

Population: *351,000*

Capital and largest city: *Bandar Seri Begawan (Pop., 50,000)*

Languages: *Malay (official), English, Chinese*

Literacy: *88%*

Currency: *Dollar*

Per capita GDP: *$18,000 (Rank: 32nd)*

The land and people. Brunei is split into two separate sections by an offshoot of the Malaysian state of Sarawak. The western and larger section consists of the districts of Belait, Tutong, and Brunei and Muara. In the east is the district of Temburong.

Much of the land is rugged and hilly. The land is drained by the Belait, Tutong, Brunei, and Temburong rivers. Much of the land in these river valleys is swampy, and little of Brunei is suitable for cultivation. Rainfall averages about 150 inches per year, with coastal areas receiving less, and inland areas receiving up to 200 inches.

About two-thirds of the people are Malays, and there is a large minority of Chinese. There are small minorities of native peoples and of Indian. Most of the people live in the coastal areas, especially around the oil centers of Seria and Kuala Belait.

Economy. Brunei's economy is overwhelmingly dominated by the exploitation of oil and natural gas resources. As a result, Brunei has the highest per capita income in east Asia, and among the highest in the world. Current government objectives emphasize the development of nonpetroleum industries in recognition of the fact that Brunei's petroleum reserves are expected to run out about the year 2015.

Government. Although Brunei has a constitution, much of it has been suspended. The head of state is the sultan, and he holds complete authority over the country. He is assisted by a Council of Ministers.

History. Very little is known of the early history of Brunei. There were early contacts with both China and India, and through the latter Brunei's rulers were converted to Islam. By the beginning of the 16th century, the Brunei sultanate controlled all of the island of Borneo as well as a part of what is now the Philippines.

In 1600 the Portuguese established a trading post at Bandar Seri Begawan, and over the next two centuries the city became a center of European trade.

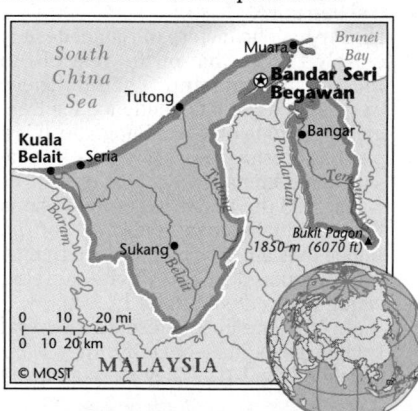

During the 18th and 19th centuries, Brunei lost more and more territory to European traders and adventurers. Finally, in 1888, the sultan appealed for aid to the British, who responded by making Brunei a protectorate.

The discovery of oil in 1929 increased the importance of Brunei. In 1959 a new constitution was promulgated; it returned full executive power to the sultan. In 1963 the sultan declined an invitation to join the new Malaysian federation.

In 1979 Brunei and Great Britain signed an agreement granting Brunei total independence. On January 1, 1984, that agreement went into effect.

Burma
See Myanmar

Cambodia (Kampuchea)

Official name: *Kingdom of Cambodia*

Area: *69,881 sq. mi., 181,040 sq. km.*

Type of government: *Constitutional monarchy*

Population: *12,890,000*

Capital and largest city: *Phnom Penh (Pop., 1,000,000)*

Languages: *Khmer (official), French*

Literacy: *35%*

Currency: *Riel*

Per capita GDP: *$1,500 (Rank: 150th)*

The land. Cambodia occupies the mountain-rimmed basin of the lower Mekong River. At the center of the basin, only a few feet above sea level, is Tonle Sap, a lake that serves as an overflow basin for the floods of the Mekong. It has an area of about 1,000 square miles and a depth of 5 feet during the dry season, but it increases to four times that area and 10 times that depth during the rainy season.

Cambodia's highest point, in the Cardamom Mountains along the southwest border of the basin, is only slightly under 6,000 feet. Separated from the Cardamoms by a narrow lowland corridor in the northwest are the Dangrek Mountains, which rim the basin on the north. East of the basin, the Moi plateau rises to between 1,500 and 4,000 feet.

Cambodia has a tropical climate, with rainy summers and dry winters. Year-round temperatures range from 70°F to 100°F, and the humidity is high. An average of 60 inches of rain a year falls in the basin, and the mountains receive about 80 inches a year.

The people. Cambodia's population is quite homogeneous. Most of the people are Khmers, or native Cambodians. They are Theravada Buddhists and speak Khmer, or Cambodian. There are minorities of Vietnamese, Chinese, and Chams, and some small tribal groups in the hills.

Population is concentrated along the Mekong River and around Tonle Sap.

Economy. The Cambodian economy has been in a shambles since the beginning of civil war in the early 1970s. Until then, Cambodia had a self-sufficient economy, producing enough rice and other agricultural products to be a net exporter of food.

Agriculture is still the backbone of the economy though at much reduced levels. The principal products are rice, rubber, cotton, tobacco, pepper, beans, and kapok. The Tonle Sap and the Gulf of Thailand yield large catches of fish.

Cambodia's principal natural resource is its rich soil, but valuable hardwood forests, high-grade iron ore deposits, and phosphate deposits are also important.

Even before the onset of war, Cambodia had little industry, though a beginning was being made. Tobacco, rubber, lumber, textile, and food processing plants were being built. Since 1975 some of the plants that were destroyed have been rebuilt.

Foreign trade has remained at a very low level. Cambodia's main exports are rubber, rice, timber, pepper, and semiprecious stones. Imports include food, medicine, machinery, and military equipment. Most trade is with Vietnam and the Comecon countries.

Government. A United Nations-supervised election in May 1993 saw the first free elections in Cambodia in two decades. Some 90 percent of eligible voters cast ballots for the members of a new 120-member National Assembly. In September 1993 the National Assembly adopted a new constitution that established the king as head of state. The constitution provided the king with limited but not completely defined powers over the legislative, executive, and judicial branches. The head of government is the prime minister. Legislative power is held by the National Assembly.

History. Cambodia's history extends back at least as far as the A.D. 100s, when the Kingdom of Funan, in southern Cambodia, was established. It gained power over territory in present-day Thailand, Malaya, Vietnam, and Laos. During the 500s, the kingdom of the Chenla, to the north, overthrew the Funan Empire.

By about 800, the Khmers, inhabitants of southern Cambodia who may have been descended from Indians, united with the Cham, an Indonesian people of the northern Malay peninsula. They conquered the Chenla and established an empire centered at Angkor, on the plain northeast of Tonle Sap. Their culture was predominantly Indian and their religion similar to Hinduism.

For the next 400 years Khmer god-kings ruled an empire that included large areas of Southeast Asia. Their rice-growing civilization was quite advanced, and evidence remains of great temples, roads, irrigation projects, and public buildings at Angkor, including the

civizilation
US

civilisation
Brit.

THE WAT,
or temple, at Angkor in Cambodia is part of the remains of the city that was the capital of the culture that thrived there from the 800s to the 1400s.

Temple of Angkor Wat. Khmer power declined during the 1300s. In 1431 the Siamese conquered Angkor, and the Khmer kings retreated to the region near Phnom Penh.

During succeeding decades, the Khmers fought several disastrous wars with their former subjects, the Cham, the Thais, and the Vietnamese, and lost much of their territory. By the mid-1800s, when French colonists began to settle in Indochina, Cambodia was a minor state plagued by dynastic disputes and in danger of being divided between the Siamese and the Vietnamese.

French control. In 1863 France made Cambodia a protectorate. Except for preventing its partition, the French generally ignored Cambodia. They fostered little social or economic change and allowed the Cambodian monarchy to continue to function. During the 1930s Cambodian nationalism began to grow, and it turned into anti-French feeling during World War II, when Vichy France allowed Japan to use bases in Cambodia and permitted Thailand to occupy some Cambodian territory.

In 1945 Japan briefly took direct control of the Cambodian government, but King Norodom Sihanouk proclaimed his country's independence. In 1953 the French, having allowed Cambodia complete internal self-government after the war, turned control of the military over to the Cambodians. In 1954 Vietnamese communist forces invaded Cambodia, joining anti-French guerrillas who had been active there since 1945. A Geneva conference held late in the year ended the fighting, and the troops were withdrawn.

Independence. In 1955 King Sihanouk abdicated in favor of his father and assumed the title of prince. He consolidated the nation's political strength and founded a political party, the People's Socialist Community. In 1960, when Sihanouk's father died, the prince was elected chief of state. He was chosen to lead a council to act as regent for his mother.

The country concentrated on economic and social development and remained at peace despite violent conflicts raging in neighboring Southeast Asian nations. In the early 1960s, however, when the Vietnam War intensified, Cambodia feared for its safety and sought international guarantees of its neutrality.

Although Cambodia did not become directly involved in the Vietnam War, for five years it was ravaged by a civil war between government forces, backed by the United States and South Vietnam, and the United National Cambodian Front, supported by North Vietnam and China.

In 1975 Sihanouk, who had been ousted by General Lon Nol in 1970, came out of exile in Beijing to lead the Khmer Rouge in a communist invasion of Phnom Penh, which fell to him on April 17.

He soon lost power to Pol Pot, the prime minister of the new government, who directed mass evacuations of cities and towns as the nation's population was set to work in the fields and clearing forests. An isolationist policy tried to hide from the world the forced labor, mass executions, and near total destruction of culture, education, and civilization that ensued.

The Vietnam-backed Kampuchean National United Front for National Salvation drove Pol Pot into exile when it captured Phnom Penh on January 7, 1979. A new government headed by Heng Samrin was formed; it maintained its power with the assistance of Vietnamese troops.

A government in exile, led by Sihanouk, Khieu Samphan, and Son Sann, leaders of the three largest guerrilla movements, supported a guerrilla army in Cambodia. In 1991 a cease-fire was accepted by all factions. A United Nations-sponsored election in 1993 saw a victory for Sihanouk, who was restored as king and who named his son, Prince Norodom Ranariddh, prime minister. A coalition government formed in 1998 brought some stability and the surrender of the remaining Khmer Rouge.

China

Republic of China

See Taiwan

The land. China is an immense country, and only the Soviet Union and Canada are larger in area. Mainland China's length from east to west is approximately the same as that of the United States, and its range from north to south is equivalent to that from Puerto Rico to Labrador.

The huge territory of mainland China is divided into 21 provinces, five autonomous regions, and two municipalities—Beijing, the capital, and Shanghai. The autonomous regions are more than administrative units. Each of the five—Guangxi-Zhuang, Tibet, Xinjiang-Uygur, Ningxia-Hui, and Inner Mongolia—contains a majority of non-Chinese people, and each has a history and culture different from China's.

Regions. Geographically, it is conventional to divide China into five regions—China Proper, Manchuria, Tibet, Xinjiang, and Mongolia. China Proper, the region south of the Great Wall and east of Tibet, occupies a third of the land. It is the geographical and historical core of the country, containing the bulk of the population and the roots of Chinese civilization in the Huang He (Yellow River) valley.

The other four regions comprise what is often called Outer China. Manchuria, northeast of China Proper, is more sparsely populated and contains rich mineral deposits. Tibet, in the southwest, lies high in the Himalayas and has a very small population. Xinjiang, in the northwest, is arid and inhabited mainly by Uygur peoples. The Mongolian region, Inner Mongolia, north of China Proper, is arid and peopled primarily by Mongols.

China's provinces serve as administrative subdivisions; some provinces include parts of two major regions. The provinces and the regions also have distinctive cultures with recognizable dialects, if not individual languages, and customs, social patterns, and traditions that exist independently within the larger framework of Chinese culture.

Highlands dominate China's terrain. High mountains thrusting eastward from the southwest include the Himalayas and their foothills.

These mountain systems and the high, barren plateau of Tibet in their center form the world's most formidable land barrier, separating the Hindu civilization of South Asia from the Chinese civilization of East Asia. The eastern edge of these mountains also contains the sources of China's two great rivers, the Yangtze and the Huang He.

Between this mountainous mass and a northern spur, the towering Tien Shan in Xinjiang, is the Taklimakan desert. Along the northern rim of China are the Ordos desert and the eastern fringe of the Gobi desert, bound on the east by the Greater Khingan range, which marks the western edge of Manchuria.

China Proper and Manchuria are crisscrossed by less formidable highlands that follow two major sets of intersecting structural areas, one trending northeast to southwest and the other intersecting it east to west.

The northeast-southwest axis is marked in the east by the Fujian Massif, the Shandong and Liaodong peninsulas, and the Manchurian highlands bordering Korea in the northeast. The central portion of this axis is formed by the Greater Khingan range in Manchuria and the Wutai and Luliang ranges in Shanxi province farther south.

This line is a major physical and cultural division of eastern Asia. To the west of it, elevations are from 3,000 to 6,000 feet higher than to its east. The west is arid, the east is humid; the western economy is based on pastoral activities, the eastern on sedentary agriculture.

The series of east-west trending chains is represented at the far north by the Lesser Khingan mountains, at the southern edge of Mongolia by the Yin Shan, and in the far south by the Nan Ling mountains, a series of hills and low mountains between the Yangtze and the Xi rivers. By far the most important mountains of the east-west axis are those of the Qin Ling, which bisect China Proper.

The Qin Ling has a physical and cultural significance similar to that of the north-south Khingan divide. South China, below these mountains, is generally warm and humid, whereas north China tends to be cold and dry.

China's few major lowlands and plateaus lie in China Proper and Manchuria, among the intersecting lines of highlands. In the northeast the Manchurian Plain's grasslands contain some of China's most fertile soils.

The flat and fertile North China Plain is essentially a giant compound delta of the Huang He, the Huai, and the Yangtze rivers. The 100,000-square-mile Yangtze Basin is rich with alluvial soils. The mountain-ringed Sichuan basin on the upper Yangtze River includes about 75,000 square miles of rolling terrain.

The most important region in south China, the Canton lowlands, the compound delta of the Xi, Bei, and Zhu (Pearl) rivers, is a key agricultural, industrial, and commercial center.

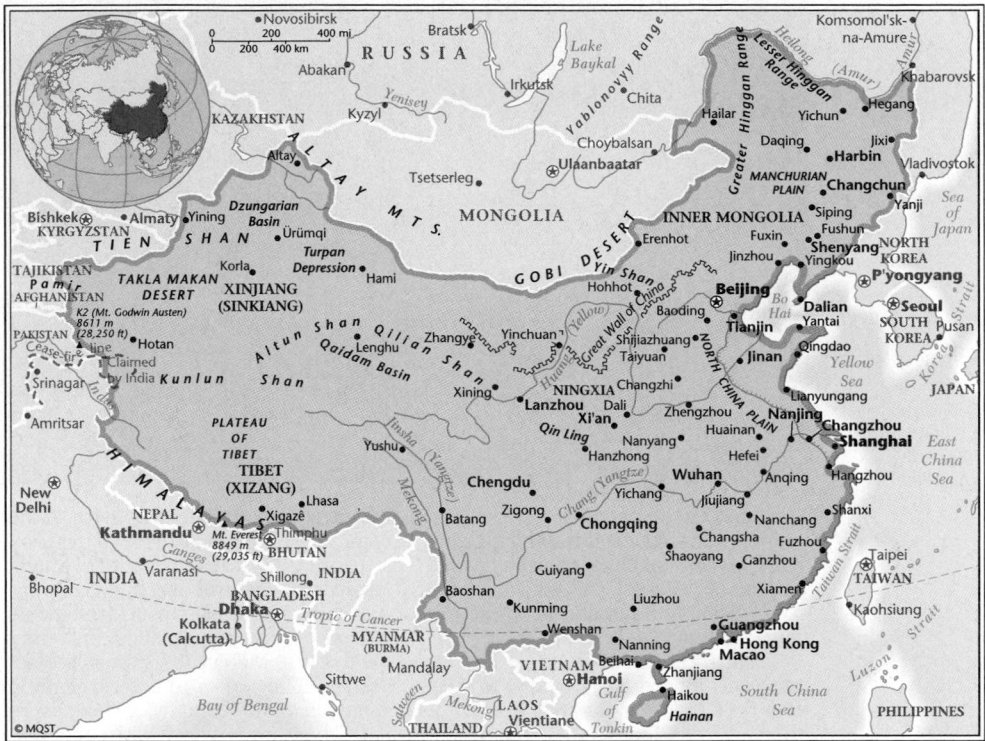

THE PHILOSOPHY founded by Confucius about 500 B.C. was a moral code of personal and public conduct rather than a religion, for it does not teach the worship of a God or a life after death.

Rivers. Almost all of China's rivers, which are concentrated in the eastern portion of the country, flow east or south toward the sea. The most important in the south is the Xi, formed by streams flowing from the eastern Tibetan foothills.

The Yangtze rises in the eastern Tibetan Plateau and twists some 3,200 miles through south-central China, passing through deeply etched gorges in Sichuan and emptying into the East China Sea at Shanghai.

The Huang He rises near the Yangtze and flows north along a winding course, making a great bend northward around the Ordos desert and on eastward between Shanxi and Henan provinces. It empties into the Bo Hai gulf, an inlet of the Yellow Sea.

Both the Huang He and the Yangtze are subject to frequent and vicious floods and sudden changes of course, but both supply the water and the soil to raise food for the huge concentration of people in their valleys.

Climate. China's climate is determined by the winter and summer monsoons. Cold dry air from Siberia moves across China in the winter, and hot moist winds from the Pacific flow inland during the summer, bringing the heavy rains.

Most of China lies in the temperate zone, but climate varies extensively from region to region. North China and Manchuria have long, severe winters. Rainfall is under 20 inches a year, and the growing season is less than 200 days. But farther south, the growing season lengthens, ultimately permitting year-round agriculture in the southernmost parts of China. Precipitation also increases greatly, averaging 40 to 80 inches annually.

The people. China contains approximately one-quarter of the world's people. About 90 percent of the people live in the eastern third of China. The overall population density of China is about 327 people per square mile, but this figure can vary greatly, from near zero in portions of the west, to over 2,000 people per square mile along the coast.

Although many ethnic groups make up China's population, more than 90 percent of the people are of the Han group, the people commonly considered "Chinese." The Han have great cultural unity and share the same written language, but they speak many regional dialects of Chinese. The Beijing dialect, or

PAINTINGS reflect the manner of dress and lifestyles in Imperial China.

RICE, a daily staple of the Chinese diet, is grown mainly in the fertile Yangtze River basin and in the south of China.

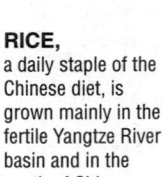

THE SECRET of making silk from the cocoons of the silkworm was carefully guarded from its discovery about 2700 B.C. until Muslim traders brought the worms to Spain and Sicily in the 800s and 900s.

Mandarin, is the national language; it is taught in the schools throughout China. The Chinese language is written in ideographs, or "characters," that carry the same meaning no matter how one pronounces the word they represent.

About 6 percent of China's people are non-Han Chinese. They belong to more than 50 ethnic groups that live in the areas surrounding China Proper. The Zhuang, a Thai-speaking people in southeastern China, are the largest minority. The Yi, also in the south, are another large group. Along the western and northwestern frontiers Tibetans, Uygurs, and Mongols are in the majority, and the Manchu people are in the northeast.

The Chinese religious tradition is an amalgam of primitive animistic beliefs linked to the agricultural nature of Chinese society and to the literate religious traditions of Confucianism, Taoism, and Buddhism. Confucianism provides the philosophic, moral, and ethical underpinnings of Chinese society and culture; however, aspects of Confucianism have religious overtones for the average Chinese.

Economy. China traditionally has been an agricultural land, and this is true today, despite considerable industrialization since the advent of the communist regime in 1949.

Until 1979 the government maintained strict control over the economy. Agriculture was collectivized and industrial output centrally planned. Following the death of Mao in 1976, the new leadership followed a more pragmatic approach to the economy, allowing more individual initiative. A long-range 20-year plan provides for a 10-year period of transition to a less centralized economy, and calls for, among other things, the development of light industry, tourism, agriculture, energy, and a rising standard of living.

Natural resources. Exploration and development of China's mineral resources was not undertaken on a large scale until the 1950s and 1960s.

China has enough large reserves of coal to last some 400 years at present usage rates. Oil is found in Manchuria, Xinjiang, and in the central Yangtze basin, as well as along the continental shelf. In 1986 China produced 911 million barrels of oil, making it the sixth largest producer of oil in the world.

Agriculture. Poor climate, rough terrain, and inadequate soil or water prohibit farming in a large part of China. With an estimated 270 million acres, or about 11 percent of China's total area, under cultivation, there is still less than half an acre of farmland per person.

Starting in 1979, some of the farms that were collectivized in the 1950s were returned to family control under the new program of economic liberalization. Households contracted with the government to produce a certain amount of a crop. Anything above that amount could be sold either to the government at a higher price or on the open market.

Agricultural production rose an average of 7.9 percent per year from 1979 to 1983, in contrast to a rise of about only 3 percent per year from the 1950s through most of the 1970s. Though much of the credit for this rise must be given to the new economic reforms, and to new pricing policies, some credit must go to earlier state investment in pesticides, fertilizer, farm equipment, and large-scale works such as irrigation projects.

China's chief crops are wheat, raised chiefly in north China and Manchuria, and rice, grown mainly in the Yangtze basin and south China. Other important crops include barley, millet, kaoliang, soybeans, cotton, tobacco, and tea. There is little livestock raising, but there is some fishing off the coasts and in the rivers.

Industry. In 1984 the government brought about sweeping changes in the industrial sector. A move was made away from centralized control of all manufacturing toward more control by local management. The government will continue, as it has in the past, to provide policy and long-range planning for some products. For many other products, however, it appears that the government intends to let the marketplace regulate production.

Trade. Foreign trade historically played a small role in the Chinese economy. Because of a desire for self-sufficiency and a shortage of export commodities, until the 1980s the Chinese adopted a conservative policy toward foreign trade, using it primarily to obtain technology.

Recently, however, trade restrictions with the West have loosened considerably. Special economic areas have been set up in which foreign investment is encouraged.

Principal exports include petroleum, light industrial goods, chemicals, and agricultural goods. Imports include grain, consumer goods, textiles, and advanced technology. Ninety percent of China's trade is with noncommunist countries, principally Hong Kong, Japan, and the United States.

Government. The government which was established by Communist China in 1949 is embodied in a 1954 constitution. The government is dominated by the Communist Party.

Supreme legislative and executive power is vested nominally in an elected National People's Congress. The congress chooses a standing committee to act for it between sessions. The congress also elects a state council, led by a prime minister, to administer the government, and a president, who acts as head of state.

The actual seat of power is the Chinese Communist Party's Political Bureau, or Politburo, of the party's Central Committee. It determines national policy, and its chairman is usually the key figure in the government. Only party-supported candidates are elected to public office, although party membership is not required for election. Most important government posts are held by party leaders.

History. China has a long continuous history. The remains of prehistoric "Peking man," found in north China, date back as far as 1 million years. The valley of the Yellow River on the North China Plain was the site of one of the earliest human societies, which developed a unique culture.

First dynasties. Heroic legends tell of a Hsia dynasty founded by an emperor Yü in 2205 B.C. There is no firm evidence of its existence, however, and the first documented Chinese dynasty is the Shang, or Yin. Exact dates of ancient Chinese events are often disputed, but the Shang dynasty was founded in 1766 or 1523 B.C. on the North China Plain.

The Chou. During the Chou dynasty (about 1027–256 B.C.) a loose confederation of feudal states was organized. Wealth was based on land ownership and the economy was based on agriculture. Warrior nobles formed the upper class, and village peasant society was communal.

Agricultural and military technology improved, canals were built, a monetary economy developed, population grew, contact was made with western Asian countries, and trade prospered. Art, music, and literature all flourished, but the Chou is known primarily for its philosophers.

Three of the most important philosophers who founded schools of thought between 600 and 300 B.C. were Lao Tzu, Confucius, and Hsüntzu. Lao Tzu, who was probably several writers, taught that there is a natural order to the universe, of which man is a part. Confucius and his student and interpreter Mencius laid the foundation for much of China's social order, moral code, and political development. Confucius taught that a perfect moral order can be realized if one follows certain norms of social behavior (li) set forth by ancient sages. His idea of a well ordered, well educated, and mutually cooperative society stood as the Chinese ideal for many centuries. Hsüntzu laid the basis for the "legalist" school of thought, which provided the philosophical foundation for an

THE GREAT WALL, the longest structure ever built, was designed to protect China's northern borders. Although sections of defensive walls existed before, most of the wall dates from the Ming Dynasty (1368–1644 A.D.).

authoritarian state led by an absolute ruler and ordered by strict laws.

The legalist doctrine found followers when the Ch'in conquered the Chou and established leadership over the Chou subject states. This semibarbarous, authoritarian state (221–206 B.C.), following its unification of the formerly warring states, contributed to agricultural prosperity through the construction of an elaborate irrigation system. Its strong central government permitted the growth of social stability and military strength. The Ch'in dynasty, which gave China its name, extended Chinese rule south to modern Canton and west across the Plateau of Yunnan, founding the first Chinese empire. The Ch'in ruler soon after began construction of the Great Wall to keep out invaders from the north, the only exposed frontier. Political chaos followed his death (210 B.C.). The eventual succession of Liu Pang marked the beginning of the long-lasting native Han dynasty (206 B.C.–220 A.D.).

The Han. The Han emperors built an empire that became one of the world's greatest states. Political order was maintained by the concession of local rule to outlying regions of the empire. Foreign invasions were thwarted, and during the expansionist reign (141–87 B.C.) of Wu Ti, the empire absorbed most of the territory that is now part of modern China.

Under the later Han emperors, who introduced state control over parts of the economy, China grew prosperous. Public works as well as cultural and educational achievements marked the period.

The dynasty was interrupted (9–23 A.D.) by the revolutionary rule of Wang Mang. Concerned about social and economic inequality, he championed land reform and the nationalization of the great landed estates.

The Han dynasty was restored, but tensions between the ruling class and the peasants increased. Peasant rebellions and fighting between rival lords were frequent in the 100s A.D. Professional armies moved into local areas to keep the peace and soon came under the control of the local lords.

Three leaders of these armies grew to such power that they divided the empire into three semi-independent kingdoms—the Wei, the Wu, and the Shu Han. Imperial power disintegrated, and the last Han emperor died in 220.

The six dynasties. For the next 370 years China was merely a collection of petty states, most of them at war with one another, and none able to dominate the others. The period was known as the era of the "six dynasties," as six houses in succession managed to gain the throne, but none actually ruled China.

In the 300s and 400s nomads conquered China's northern frontier region, although the natural mountain and desert barriers prevented them from penetrating farther. Many northern Chinese migrated southward, and during the 300s and 400s they spread their culture into Southeast Asia.

COMMUNIST LEADERS' portraits hang over the gate to the Forbidden City of the former Chinese Emperors.

While military invasion from the north disrupted China, the spread of Buddhism, the Indian religion, altered China's traditional social base. Confucianism had fallen from favor because of the failure of the Han dynasty, which had been built on it. Taoism also grew in strength and soon rivaled Confucianism in importance.

During the brief Sui dynasty (581–618) the central government was restored to its former power, the Great Wall was rebuilt, the economy was revitalized, and the northern territories were reconquered. In trying to expand Chinese territory the Sui met disastrous defeats at the hands of the Koguryo people of Korea in the north and Turkic tribes in the west. Following these defeats, a rebellion toppled the Sui.

A brief period of turmoil followed the end of the Sui. Li Yüan, a Sui bureaucrat of Chinese and "barbarian" descent, with the support of Turkic tribes from central Asia, became emperor of China in 618, founding the T'ang dynasty (618–907).

The T'ang. The 300-year T'ang era was one of China's most brilliant. In the 600s T'ang rulers consolidated their control of the government and made China's borders secure against further invasion by forming an alliance with the powerful, warlike Uygurs. T'ang government was efficient, economical, and more just to all classes.

Agriculture and trade prospered. Chinese thinkers assimilated Buddhism, Taoism, and Confucianism and developed a unified philosophical base for society. Under the T'ang, poetry, painting, sculpture, scholarship, and science flourished and attracted artists and scholars from other lands.

T'ang peace and prosperity were interrupted in the mid-700s by a revolt led by An Lu-shan, a "barbarian" who had the command of some Chinese armies. The uprising resulted in a bloody civil war. Thus weakened, the empire was left open to attack by its neighbors, and the late 700s were marked by invasions by such peoples as the Uygurs and Tibetans.

realized
US

realised
Brit.

23 Asia

The Sung. The Sung dynasty (960–1279), which finally won the competition for power in 960, led China into the modern age. Sung leaders reformed the military and reorganized the government by creating a large, well salaried, honest, and efficient civil service. They won the support of the masses by reducing taxes, abolishing the traditional forced *labor*, providing loans to farmers, and initiating public works projects.

The arts and sciences continued to advance, spurred by the widespread use of printing. The Sung empire was not a strong military state, however. By 1234 the north had fallen before the Mongols, who had begun in the 1100s to conquer an empire that eventually included all of Asia north of India.

The Yüan. In 1260 Kublai, a leader of the Mongols, was elected khan, ruler of the Mongol empire. Eleven years later he proclaimed the Yüan dynasty (1271–1368) in northern China. By 1279 the dynasty controlled the entire country, and China became a subdivision of the Mongol empire. One European adventurer, Marco Polo of Venice, visited Kublai Khan's court, and his reports excited European interest in the unknown empire.

Despite rule by non-Chinese, central China retained its traditional culture and social organization and remained remarkably unified. In the 1300s Chinese antagonism to foreigners sparked rebellions against the Mongols. These rebellions, and rivalries among the Mongols themselves, led to the disintegration of the Yüan dynasty in the mid-1300s.

The Chinese leaders of the rebellion against the Mongols competed among themselves for the throne. Chu Yüan-chang, a Buddhist from northwestern China, emerged dominant and in 1368 established himself as the first emperor of the Ming dynasty (1368–1644).

The Ming. By 1382 Ming rulers had driven the Mongols out of China Proper,

SPECTACULAR mountains rise precipitously over farmland in the narrow valleys of Guangxi Province in southeastern China.

THIS AGELESS setting is particularly appropriate for the practice of t'ai chi chuan, the ancient Chinese exercises for relaxation.

and by the 1400s they had regained control of all but the western third and the northern fringe of present-day China. In 1421 Yung-lo moved the capital from Nanking, where it had been since the founding of the dynasty, to Beijing, where a walled "forbidden city" became the center of imperial rule.

The Ming emperors proclaimed China supreme in all the world, and indeed China wielded great power throughout Asia. From its Asian neighbors China demanded tribute, *emphasizing* its preeminence; in return it offered financial aid and military protection. Ming expansion of foreign contacts improved Chinese prosperity and influenced the country's cultural growth. For the first time, large numbers of Christian missionaries and Western merchants visited China.

Largely due to paralyzing internal corruption, diverse opposition to the dynasty surfaced in the early 17th century. In the 1630s a bandit, Li Tzu-ch'eng, gained control of northern China, and his rebellion soon spread. He gained the support of many groups in society, won control of most of China, and soon conquered Beijing.

By the 1640s the Manchus, a non-Chinese people who lived in the region northeast of China Proper, had begun to penetrate China. They joined the government troops in defeating the rebels and then used their position of power to establish the Ch'ing dynasty (1644–1912).

The Ch'ing. Much of the early Ch'ing period was spent in putting down resistance by the supporters of the Ming regime and in subduing the non-Chinese neighbors of China Proper and annexing their territory.

By about 1800 the Ch'ing had expanded to the boundaries of present-day China and beyond, to Taiwan in the east, across Mongolia and coastal Siberia in the north, and to Tibet in the west.

The Manchus did not attempt to replace Chinese customs; rather, they continued the political and economic policies of their Ming predecessors, maintaining strict state control over all

areas of Chinese life. Chinese culture and scholarship continued to flourish in the traditional pattern through the 1700s.

At the same time, the Western world was beginning to take an active interest in the Far East. European states were beginning to establish trading colonies in the nations near China.

The Portuguese in the 1500s were the first to trade with China; they were followed by the Dutch and the British. The English East India Company established a trading station at Canton in the late 1600s and throughout the 1700s carried on a brisk trade in tea through Canton.

As Western influence began to challenge traditional concepts of Chinese society, Chinese leadership entered a decline. The Ch'ing rulers became mired in fruitless military activity, and their court became riddled with corruption. Prosperity began to wane as the population level began to soar and the traditional economy could not support it.

Western impact. Ch'ing policy confined foreign trade to the one port of Canton, in the south. There foreign traders were only allowed contacts with a licensed monopoly group of Chinese merchants. The British, dissatisfied with the trading conditions, tried to establish diplomatic relations in the 1790s. But the imperial authorities insisted that any country wishing to establish relations with China must accept the status of a tributary state.

By the end of the 1700s, foreign traders found a large Chinese demand for opium and local officials ready to cooperate in smuggling it into China. Efforts to suppress the trade by an able imperial official led to the Opium War in 1839. The British, with complete naval superiority and small parties of Indian troops under British officers, defeated the Chinese armies.

Under the Treaty of Nanking (1842), ending the war, China ceded Hong Kong to Britain and opened five more ports to foreign trade. Later treaties established extraterritoriality (putting foreigners under the jurisdiction of their own consuls, not Chinese laws), the most-favored-nation principle (a concession to one foreign power shared by all), and the right of missionaries to work in China.

The result was a system that survived until the 1940s, under which foreigners in China had a privileged position largely exempt from Chinese control. The treaty ports under foreign jurisdiction became the main commercial and industrial centers, and the customs service, from which developed the post office, came under foreign control.

The Manchu regime was further weakened in the mid-1800s by the Taiping rebellion (1850–1864). Led by a religious mystic with the aid of a military officer, a large force of rebels marched toward Beijing conquering the territory along their route.

The Taiping leaders overran large parts of central China and set up a totalitarian state with a distorted Christianity as a religion. The Taiping and later rebellions in northern and western China were suppressed only when local officials raised new armies that remained loyal to their organizers rather than to the central government.

The able officials who rose in this period of crisis realized that China must modernize to survive, but they had to contend with very strong conservatism. After 1860, moreover, the court was dominated by the empress dowager, skilled at intrigue but an extreme conservative and ignorant of the outside world. Thus, attempts at modernization were slow and halfhearted, and often ended when sponsoring officials moved to other positions.

Treaty system. Problems raised by the presence of foreigners worsened. Canton, where most of the Westerners were concentrated, was especially rebellious because of its resentment of the British conquest in the Opium War. Friction between the Cantonese and the foreigners grew so intense that in 1857 and 1858 French and British troops, using the need to protect their interests as an excuse, seized and occupied the city.

In settlement of this conflict, the treaties of Tientsin opened more ports to foreigners, legalized the importation of opium, permitted the establishment of European diplomatic missions at Beijing, allowed missionaries and traders to enter the interior of the country, and exacted further indemnities from the Chinese.

The Ch'ing rulers, giving the matter second thought, refused to admit foreign ambassadors to Beijing. In reprisal, British and French armies stormed Beijing in 1860 and burned the summer palace.

Having thus proved the weakness of the imperial government, the British and French saw an advantage in maintaining a weak dynasty that they could control, and they assisted the Ch'ing rulers in putting down the bloody rebellions throughout the country. The Ch'ing remained on the throne, but they and China were dependent on the Westerners who flooded the once isolated empire after 1860.

The imperial government still made no major attempts to reform its administration or modernize its economy and society, and China continued to be humiliated as it became weaker and more and more subservient to the foreign powers.

Renewed conflict. In 1874 the Ch'ing proved unable to prevent Japan from invading Taiwan. They avoided losing the island only through Western diplomatic maneuvers. In the 1880s France occupied Indochina, part of the traditional Chinese tribute system. In 1887 Portugal was granted Macao, a port near Hong Kong.

Relations with Japan, which had made a rapid transition from its traditional ways to the technological and political sophistication of the 1800s, grew tense. Korea, long a tributary of China, slipped into Japanese control in the 1860s and 1870s, when China did not protest Japan's recognition of Korea as an independent state.

In 1885 both China and Japan agreed to withdraw their troops from Korea, but continuing intrigue and growing Korean nationalism led in 1894 to war between Korea and China and to a Sino-Japanese war.

By early 1895 Japanese forces had all but destroyed China's army and navy. China was forced to recognize Korean independence, cede Taiwan, the Liaotung peninsula, and the Pescadores to Japan, pay a huge indemnity, and open more ports to foreigners.

Reform efforts. In 1894 Dr. Sun Yat-sen (Sun Wen) organized one of the earliest secret revolutionary societies whose goal was the overthrow of the Ch'ing. Students organized "study societies" to develop theories of reform. Philosophers reinterpreted Confucianism to permit modernization and reform within Chinese traditional ideology.

A new style Chinese army was organized under Yuan Shih-k'ai with German instructors, and an officers' training school was established. Its cadets later rose to dominant positions. Chiang Kai-shek went to this school and then to an officers' training course in Japan.

In 1898 the emperor started a program of drastic reforms guided by advisers who were Confucian scholars but who realized the need to modernize. The conservatives rallied around the empress dowager who, with the support of Yuan Shih-k'ai, imprisoned the emperor and reversed the reforms.

The reactionaries who came to power with the defeat of China's attempts at domestic reforms hoped to restore China to its position of isolation. Thus, in 1899, when Italy sought concession of a port, the demand was rejected violently. An antiforeign militia, called the "Righteous and Harmonious Fists," or "Boxers," was organized in eastern China.

The Boxer Rebellion. The Boxer Rebellion in 1900 was the last major uprising against foreign intervention in China. The Boxers, assisted by some imperial army units, besieged the foreign diplomatic quarter in Beijing. The empress dowager declared war on all the major foreign powers, although local officials in south and central China promptly negotiated neutrality for the areas they controlled. An international expedition captured Beijing and the powers imposed further restrictions on Chinese sovereignty.

Republican revolution. By that time a new opposition was developing under leaders educated outside the traditional system. Sun Yat-sen (1865–1925) became the leader of a revolutionary republican movement, winning support from Chinese students in Japan, overseas Chinese communities, and secret societies. He also had some powerful Japanese supporters.

After several unsuccessful attempts, the revolution succeeded in 1911. The Manchu court called on Yuan Shih-k'ai to suppress the uprising. After winning some battles, he then negotiated to join the revolution if he were first made president of the republic. As president, he made himself independent of the parliament in which Sun Yat-sen's Kuomintang Party had a majority, defeated a Kuomintang uprising against him, and finally tried to make himself emperor.

In place of the constitution, which was to have been ratified by the parliament, Yuan ruled under a "constitutional compact," which he announced in 1914 and which gave him a ten-year term as president.

The establishment of the republic did not lessen the financial and political power wielded by foreign nations, however, and Chinese political instability left China even more unprepared to cope with foreign interference. When World War I broke out in 1914, China became the diplomatic and occasionally the military battleground for Russia, Japan, and Germany.

Nor was the war the only source of violence in China. A successful rebellion broke out in 1915 in Yunnan, led by Yuan's opponents in response to his assumption of the title of emperor.

Yuan's death in 1916 left all real power in the hands of local military

centers
US

centres
Brit.

realized
US

realised
Brit.

THE BOXER REBELLION in China was precipitated in 1900 by the formation of secret societies to resist Western influences and religions.

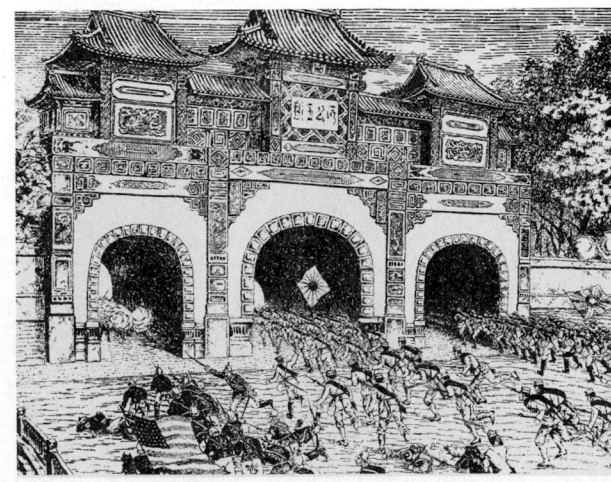

CHINA STILL produces more raw silk than any other country. These spools will be shipped to a mill to be woven.

commanders, and a period of continual civil wars began. The warlords gave first priority to their own power, but otherwise differed greatly.

With China itself divided, the end of World War I also found Manchuria in the hands of Japan and Mongolia under Russian domination. The Versailles Treaty, which ended the war, allowed Japan to retain Shantung, and China refused to sign the document.

At the Washington Conference in 1922, the Allied powers agreed to reconsider their demands for extraterritorial rights, to respect China's territorial integrity, and to assist China in the formation of a stable government. A Sino-Japanese treaty was arranged by which Japan was to withdraw from Shantung.

This official end to foreign intervention came too late, however. No one government led China, and in 1920 the country was plunged into open civil war among the warlords.

CHIANG KAI-SHEK, the Chinese general during World War II, assumed leadership of the government in 1925, but fled with his government to Taiwan in 1949, when Communists took over the mainland.

Kuomintang. By 1920 the old Confucian order was discredited and parliamentary democracy had failed. The Western democracies seemed to have betrayed their principles by helping Yuan Shih-k'ai to destroy the parliament and by backing Japanese claims on China after World War I. In this situation, Chinese intellectuals were attracted by what the Soviet Union claimed to offer. The Chinese Communist Party was founded in 1921 but, until 1924, it had only a few hundred members.

Also in 1924 a Kuomintang congress met to plan the party's future. It accepted Communists as members and employed Soviet advisers to train members in military and political tactics. Sun Yat-sen died in 1925, and leadership of the Kuomintang passed to Chiang Kai-shek.

With Soviet aid, Chiang suppressed the warlords and gained control of northern China. Soon, however, a split opened between the conservative Nationalists, led by Chiang, and the radicals and Communists. The radicals and Communists established a government at Wuhan, and the Nationalists set up a government at Nanking.

After a brief reconciliation, the two factions split widely apart. In 1927 Mao Tse-tung, a Communist Party leader, organized a peasant uprising in Hunan Province. When the uprising was suppressed, the Communists retreated into the interior and organized an anti-Kuomintang revolutionary army. In June, 1928, Chiang and a purged Kuomintang captured Beijing and proclaimed a single government for the whole of China with its capital at Nanking.

Between 1928 and 1937 the new Kuomintang National government made real though uneven progress in national reconstruction. It had full control only

in the lower Yangtze valley. Elsewhere local warlords remained powerful and often challenged the central government. The Japanese seized Manchuria in 1931, fought at Shanghai in 1932, and tried to extend their influence in north China. The national government gave a high priority to modernizing its army with the help of German advisers, but tried to postpone a showdown with Japan until it had some chance of fighting successfully. This gave the appearance of an appeasement policy, which became increasingly unpopular. In civil affairs, there was great improvement in administration and a well managed currency reform. There were fairly successful experiments in rural reconstruction in some local areas, but several innovative laws were not effectively enforced.

When, in 1936, it became apparent that Japan was preparing for total war with China, Chiang was kidnapped by Nationalists who attempted to force him to postpone internal struggles to meet the threat posed by Japan. After his release, Chiang concluded a truce with the Communists, and the Nationalists and Communists formed a united front against Japan.

War with Japan. In 1937 Japan opened a major offensive against China. Japanese troops met surprisingly strong resistance from Communist and Nationalist forces, but by 1939 they had conquered and occupied the eastern third of China, the country's heartland. From this large mainland base, Japan entered World War II.

During the war, the British, Soviet, and U.S. governments aided the Chinese by sending supplies through western China. In 1943 Britain and the United States abrogated all treaties giving them special rights in China and promised President Chiang that they would force Japanese restitution of Chinese territories after the war.

Although the Chinese Communists did not change their theoretical beliefs, their practical policies from 1937 to 1946 were reformist. They initiated sweeping agricultural reforms and effectively reorganized local government and the system of taxation.

The National government, on the other hand, failed to use the surge of patriotic enthusiasm in the early war years to put through the essential reforms that could have increased its efficiency and enabled it to compete with the Communists for popular support. Failure to reform the tax system led to accelerating inflation, with all its demoralizing effects. Late in the war, Soviet troops occupied Manchuria and stripped the industrially developed area of its machinery.

When the war ended in 1945, civil war again broke out between the Nationalists and the Communists. A U.S. mission, led by General George C. Marshall, tried without success to mediate the conflict.

Renewed struggle. At the outset, the National government had a larger and much better equipped army than the Communists, and was backed by a larger population and greater resources. It threw away these advantages by inept strategy, poor army leadership, and bad civil administration. The leaders reacted to increasing difficulties by a growing reluctance to face unpleasant realities. American advisers could never induce them to admit that drastic reforms were essential for their survival.

The Communists won most of the battles and in 1949 captured the Nationalists' restored capital, Nanking, and proclaimed the People's Republic of China from Beijing. Chiang Kai-shek and his government fled to the island of Taiwan, where they established themselves at Taipei.

Communist regime. The outbreak of the Korean War (1950–1953) aided the Communist government. It rallied popular support against the United States and United Nations forces and gained prestige by successfully repelling an invasion across the Yalu River and pushing back U.S.-UN forces led by General Douglas MacArthur.

By 1952 the Communist Party had consolidated its control of the mainland, and in 1953 it announced the first five-year economic plan to industrialize China. However, plans for enacting the program were not drawn up until 1955. With aid from the Soviet Union, China's strong central government and well disciplined party, backed by a strong army, made great strides in repairing the damage done by years of warfare. The communist government collectivized agriculture and worked for the rapid industrialization of China.

In 1956 the government called for a "Great Leap Forward," which aimed at replacing family and village life with communal life, and which hoped to have each citizen participate in all phases of the economic development program.

But the first plan and the subordination of agriculture to industrial growth proved to be disastrous mistakes. Combined with floods and poor initial organization, they caused a great decline in crop production. Moreover, industrialization did not proceed at the pace the communist planners had hoped, and it was not until the early 1960s that China's economy seemed based on a firm foundation.

In foreign affairs communist China concentrated on extending its influence throughout eastern and Southeast Asia. Communist Chinese troops had aided North Korean forces in the Korean War and supported communist guerrilla bands in Laos, Vietnam, Cambodia, and elsewhere. Also, despite its own need for food and funds, the communist government sent financial and technical aid to other nations.

China's progress was interrupted in the mid-1960s by events stemming from an ideological conflict growing between the Soviet Union and China since the mid-1950s. The dispute became an open break in the early 1960s.

The Chinese government declared itself ideologically purer than the Soviet Union, which it claimed had compromised communism with Western ideas. China felt that the Soviets' withdrawal from Cuba during the Cuban missile crisis in 1962 was just one example of the U.S.S.R.'s soft-line approach to the noncommunist nations.

Chairman Mao carried his ideological campaign further in 1966 by proclaiming a "proletarian cultural revolution" to purge China of "revisionist," or regressive, tendencies. He charged that China's party apparatus had become a privileged ruling group "taking the capitalist road," and organized the Red Guards from university and middle-school students to attack the party apparatus.

Schools were closed, agricultural and industrial production interrupted, and the government's administrative machinery disrupted. Nonetheless, China successfully continued its research and development programs in atomic weapons, and exploded its first thermonuclear device in 1964.

Beginning in the early 1970s, Mao began to lead China out of the cultural revolution. His death in 1976 led to a struggle for power between the radicals and moderates in government. The radicals, led by Mao's widow and three others, made a bid for power that failed. Labeled the "Gang of Four," they were arrested and denounced.

In July 1977 they were expelled from the Communist Party while Deng Xiaoping, an able administrator who himself had been purged, was restored to the Politburo.

The new party leadership pursued a more pragmatic approach to the country's problems. The economy was liberalized, making it more responsive to the laws of supply and demand. Some of the reforms instituted included providing long-term leases on individual farms and more realistic prices for products, and reducing the level of state ownership of industry.

In 1984 an agreement was reached with Great Britain providing for the return of Hong Kong to China in 1997.

The reforms were not without opponents. In 1987 a number of old-line Maoists were forced to resign from the Politburo. Deng Xiaoping gradually turned over leadership to his protégé, Zhao Ziyang. In late 1987 Deng became the first top Chinese Communist leader to retire voluntarily. Zhao Ziyang succeeded him as general secretary of the Communist Party. Li Peng became acting prime minister in April 1988.

In 1989 "pro-democracy" demonstrations were staged in Beijing and Shanghai. After months of open protest, the army fired on the demonstrators in Tiananmen Square, Beijing, killing hundreds and injuring thousands more.

Despite the following crackdown, China seemed to continue its move toward a more liberalized economy but political control remains tight.

India

Official name: *Republic of India*
Area: *1,269,010 sq. mi., 3,287,590 sq. km.*
Type of government: *Federal republic*
Population: *1,034,173,000*
Capital: *New Delhi (Pop., 295,000)*
Largest city: *Mumbai (Pop., 11,914,000)*
Languages: *16 official, including Hindi and English*
Literacy: *52%*
Currency: *Rupee*
Per capita GDP: *$2,540 (Rank: 122nd)*

The land. India, approximately one-third the size of the United States, stretches about 2,000 miles from north to south. The country has three major land regions: the Himalayas and associated mountain ranges in the north, the Indus-Ganges-Brahmaputra plain in north-central India, and the Deccan Plateau in the south.

Land regions. The Himalayas extend from east to west for 1,500 miles, interrupted by the Indus and Brahmaputra rivers. The mountains range from 150 to 200 miles in width, from north to south.

The vast Indus-Ganges-Brahmaputra plain, which lies between the Himalayas and the Deccan Plateau, is formed by the Indus, the Ganges, and the Brahmaputra rivers and their many tributaries, stretching from the western border with Pakistan across northern India to Bangladesh.

The Deccan Plateau, which forms the triangle-shaped peninsular portion of the Indian subcontinent, is bounded by the Vindhya and Satpura mountains in the north. Running southwest to northeast for about 800 miles, they rise from 1,500

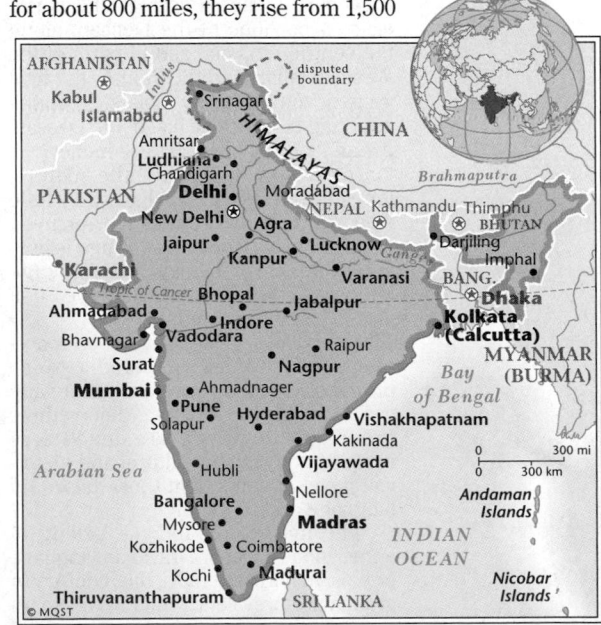

to over 4,000 feet. Unlike the great plains, where the rivers are fed by mountain snows and flow all year, the rivers of the plateaus flow seasonally and depend on the monsoon rains. Since less rain falls in the Deccan Plateau, it is much more arid and supports a less dense population.

The plateau is bounded along the Arabian Sea coast by the Western Ghats and along the Bay of Bengal by the Eastern Ghats. Near the southern tip of the peninsula, the Western Ghats have peaks of over 8,000 feet. The Eastern Ghats have an average height of 1,500 to 2,000 feet.

The northern edge of the plateau is drained by a series of rivers flowing northward to the Gangetic plain. The Narbada and Tapti rivers in the northwestern portion of the plateau drain westward into the Gulf of Cambay. The major rivers of the plateau rise on the eastern flanks of the Western Ghats, flow eastward across the plateau, and drain into the Bay of Bengal. The largest of these rivers are the Godavari, Krishna, and Cauvery.

Climate. The Himalayas shield the Indian subcontinent from the main body of the Eurasian land mass. As a result, the climate of the subcontinent is unique. In winter, high pressure systems in the Punjab region of central Pakistan and northwestern India produce winds that move down the Gangetic plain into the Bay of Bengal. Winters are generally dry in most of the subcontinent.

During March, April, and May, there is little air movement and the subcontinent begins to heat up, creating low pressure conditions in the north. By the end of May or the beginning of June, the summer monsoons arrive, bringing rain into the Ganges valley.

Rainfall varies considerably. On the Ganges-Brahmaputra delta, in the Khasi and Chittagong hills, Assam, the southern zone of the Himalayas, and along the Malabar coast, the total rainfall may exceed 80 inches a year. In the northeastern portions of the Deccan, along the southeast coast, and in parts of the Western Ghats and the Punjab, the total ranges from 40 to 80 inches. In Kathiawar and the western half of the Deccan, the annual rainfall is 20 to 40 inches.

In the southern half of the country, temperatures are tropical and vary little from month to month. In northern India, however, the annual range is considerable. In January the average temperature in the north may be 30°F lower than in the south.

The people. There have been movements of peoples into India since prehistoric times. The result is a wide variety of physical types. Major ethnic groupings, however, are much less important in tracing cultural and historical developments than those based on language and religion.

The majority of Indians belong to either Indo-Aryan or Dravidian language groups. In northern India, the Indo-Aryan groups are prevalent, while in the south

MOTHER TERESA, the Yugoslav-born Catholic nun, was awarded the Nobel Peace Prize in 1979 for her humanitarian work among the sick and poor of India.

Dravidian languages are most common. Tribal people who live in the Himalaya regions speak a number of languages.

Fourteen major languages are spoken in India, and these are broken up into hundreds of local dialects. Hindi is the official language, although English is still widely used in government and is the common means of communication among educated Indians.

The vast majority of Indians are Hindus, but India has one of the world's largest Muslim communities. In addition, there are minorities of Christians, Sikhs, Buddhists, and Jains.

India is second only to China in population, and there is great geographic variation in its distribution. Most Indians live in the Gangetic lowlands and the coastal areas. There, rural population densities approach 2,000 persons per square mile in the more crowded districts. Overall, India's population density is 644 persons per square mile.

The most recent census showed an increase in population of nearly 25 percent during the decade since the previous census, and in recent years there has been a striking decline in the death rate. This is generally attributed to better sanitation and health care, the control of epidemics, increased food production, and general economic improvement. This rapid population growth places a heavy burden on the nation's economy. The government has embarked on a family planning program in an attempt to sharply reduce the rate of population increase.

About 25 percent of India's population live in urban areas. India's most populous cities are Kolkata, Mumbai, Delhi, and Madras.

Economy. India has great economic problems. There is not enough cultivated land or industry to support the country's population, and unemploy-

ment and underemployment are high.

Natural resources. India has most of the mineral resources required for industrial expansion. It has one of the largest high-grade iron ore reserves in the world, as well as large deposits of coal. Other important deposits include bauxite, chromite, lead, manganese, and tin.

PILGRIMS BATHE in the waters of the Ganges in hope of curing illness; others come there to die, believing that those who die there will be carried to Paradise.

AGRICULTURAL PRODUCTION IN INDIA, which continues to suffer food shortages, has grown, but there are still great numbers of subsistence farmers.

Agriculture. India traditionally has had great difficulty feeding its population. Since independence, however, agricultural production has averaged a growth rate of about 3 percent per year. A yearly rise in production of at least 2 percent is necessary to keep pace with the population increase.

A large majority of India's people, about 68 percent, are employed in agriculture, though agriculture accounts for only 38 percent of India's gross domestic product. It is estimated that roughly 50 percent of India's total area is cultivated.

Despite the gains in agricultural production, there are still great numbers of subsistence farmers. The average size of a farm is 6.5 acres; at least 34 percent of rural households possesses less than half an acre.

One of the chief hazards to Indian agricultural development is lack of water. Much of the Indian government's effort to improve agriculture has been invested in increasing irrigation. India is surpassed only by China in the acreage under irrigation.

Increased use of chemical fertilizers and the sowing of high-yield and drought-resistant strains of grain also have contributed greatly to the rise in production. Principal crops include rice, wheat, coffee, sugar cane, cotton, jute, and tea.

India has one of the largest cattle herds in the world, and though religious beliefs forbid their slaughter for meat, better management of dairy farming has resulted in India's becoming self-sufficient in dairy products.

Industry. Industrial production contributes about one-fifth of the domestic product. The government is seeking ways to increase the role of manufacturing in the economy.

Manufacturing in India can be divided into two groups. The first group consists of handicraft industries organized on a household or guild basis. These industries are small, producing light consumer goods such as cotton cloth, jewelry, sugar, and soap. The second group is made up of modern factory industries that manufacture cotton and silk textiles, mill iron and steel, produce chemicals and pharmaceuticals, and refine part of the domestic production of crude oil.

An increase in electric power generating facilities has been a major target of the various 5-year plans. By 1985 there was a capacity of about 40 million kilowatts. The sources for this energy are hydroelectric, thermal, and, to a limited extent, nuclear.

Trade. India generally has suffered an unfavorable trade balance, importing more than it exports. Since independence India has moved away from a dependence on traditional exports such as tea and textiles, although they still constitute a large part of its exports, and toward the export of manufactured goods. India's exports include crude oil, engineering goods, precious stones, and handicrafts.

In the past, India has been a large importer of food, but as it has achieved self-sufficiency in food production, these imports have declined. India's principal imports are petroleum, machinery, fertilizers, and steel.

India's trade is carried on chiefly with the United States, Japan, and the European Union.

Government. India is a democratic republic and has a parliamentary system of government. The head of state is the president, who is elected to a 5-year term by the members of the national and the state legislatures. Effective executive power is exercised by a prime minister, who is almost always the leader of the majority political party in parliament at the time.

Parliament consists of two houses, the *Rajya Sabha* (Council of States) and the *Lok Sabha* (House of the People). The Council of States consists of up to 250 members, who are indirectly elected to 6-year terms. The House of the People may have up to 545 members, most of them elected by universal suffrage.

The organization of India's 28 state governments is similar to that of the federal government. Each has a legislature and an administration headed by a governor, who is appointed by the president. India also has seven Union Territories, governed indirectly by the president.

India has played a prominent role in international affairs as a leader of the nonaligned nations—those countries that seek to avoid identification with the world's great power blocks.

History. Evidence of the first permanent village settlements in India, dating from about 3000 B.C., is found in what is now Pakistan, in the hilly areas of southern Baluchistan. Some time after the appearance of these settlements, a great urban civilization developed in the Indus Valley, which lasted from about 2500 to 1500 B.C. It is probable that this civilization was related to the great river valley civilization of Sumer that had already appeared in Mesopotamia, but there is little evidence of direct borrowing.

Between 2000 and 1500 B.C., Aryans, or Indo-Europeans, spread from their homeland (probably western Russia) to Europe, Mesopotamia, and India. The Aryans gradually advanced from northwestern India through the Punjab, down into the Gangetic plain. By 900 B.C. they had probably begun to penetrate the Deccan Plateau.

The Aryans subjugated the native inhabitants, and by the 600s B.C., the tribal communities were being absorbed into various small kingdoms that had hereditary monarchs and capital cities.

Changes also took place in the Aryan religion. The simple rites of the *Rig-Veda,* the most ancient of the Aryan religious texts, gave way to elaborate rituals that exalted the role of the Brahmins, or priestly class.

The emphasis on the importance of the Brahminic priesthood and absorption of religious practices from many sources transformed the older Aryan cult into Hinduism, the religious structure that influenced the later history of India.

The first empires (600 B.C.–A.D. 300). By the 600s B.C., a number of small kingdoms had appeared in northern India, the most important of which were Kosala, between the Ganges and the Nepal mountains, and Magadha, south of the Ganges in modern Bihar. In the 500s B.C. this area of the Gangetic plain also produced Buddhism and Jainism, two great religions that denied the authority of the old Vedic scriptures and the supremacy of the Brahminic priesthood.

By the beginning of the 300s B.C., Magadha, ruled by the Nandas, had become the dominant power in the Gangetic plain. In about 322 B.C. the Nanda dynasty was overthrown by Chandragupta Maurya, who embarked on a policy of conquest that brought under his control most of northern India, including part of modern Afghanistan, and much of southern India.

The Mauryan Empire was ruled from the splendid capital of Pataliputra (modern Patna). Asoka (about 273–232 B.C.), Chandragupta's grandson, turned his back on territorial expansion and sought to make Buddhist ethics the guiding force for a kingdom of righteousness.

On rock walls and pillars all over the kingdom, he had engraved the principles of conduct that his people were to follow. In these edicts he emphasized honesty, obedience to parents and teachers, religious toleration, and service to others. The beginning of the Buddhist shrines that were to provide

civilization
US

civilisation
Brit.

emphasized
US

emphasised
Brit.

THE LITERACY rate in India has improved with government-sponsored programs such as this one in an open-air school in the countryside.

centers
US

centres
Brit.

civilization
US

civilisation
Brit.

many of the great masterpieces of Indian art date from Asoka's reign, when Buddhism became the religion of kings and merchants and made important contributions to philosophy.

The Mauryan Empire disintegrated soon after Asoka's death, when foreign invaders entered from the northwest. The invaders included the people known as Sakas, or Scythians, and the Kushan, a Central Asian people who were the most influential. They established a strong kingdom in northern India in the first century A.D. that lasted for nearly 200 years. Their greatest king, Kanishka (about 78–110 A.D.), supported Buddhism, and during his reign missionaries carried Buddhism to central Asia. From there it was eventually transmitted to China and other parts of East Asia.

In most of southern India Mauryan control had probably never been very strong, and in the extreme south three kingdoms—the Chola, the Pandya, and the Chera—had existed independently during Asoka's reign. These three kingdoms, with periods of decay and obscurity, continued to exist up to the 1100s A.D. Following the disintegration of the Mauryan Empire, the history of southern Indian tended to be quite separate from that of the north. From the first century B.C. to about 200 A.D., most of the Deccan was controlled by the Satavahanas, who ruled from Andhra Pradesh.

Guptas and Rajputs (300–1200 A.D.). After the downfall of the Kushan, no empire developed in northern India until the 300s, when the Guptas, a family from the Magadha region (modern Bihar), built up a powerful new kingdom. Under Samudragupta (about 330–375 A.D.) and his son Chandragupta II (about 375–413 A.D.), the dynasty's power spread all over northern India. The principal cities of the empire were Pataliputra and Ujjain.

The Gupta period was an age of great activity in literature, the fine arts, religion, science, and philosophy. Its intellectual and artistic accomplishments reflected a prosperity and state of material well-being perhaps never again matched in India's history. During this golden age, Buddhism and Jainism remained important, but Hinduism, which had developed its characteristic social laws and devotional rituals, had become dominant.

A central Asian people, the Huns, invaded northern India in the 400s, and although their empire was short-lived, it destroyed the power of the Guptas.

Attempts were made in the following century, notably by Harsha (606–647), to recreate a single political authority in northern India, but none of these efforts was particularly successful. By the 800s northern India was split up into many kingdoms ruled by Rajputs, members of the Hindu warrior class.

Developments in southern India. During the period of Gupta and Rajput ascendancy in northern India, southern India was controlled by various regional kingdoms. The Chalukyas, who ruled from Badami in the western Deccan, were dominant from about 600 to 750 A.D. Their major enemies were the Pallavas, whose capital was Kanchipuram. The Pallavas ruled from the 300s until the end of the 700s, when they were overthrown by the Chola kings of Tanjore.

The Cholas maintained control of all the territory south of the Tungabhadra River from about 850 to 1200, when they were usurped by the revived power of the Pandyas at Madura.

The southern kingdoms were the centers of cultural and religious movements.

AKBAR THE GREAT was one of the earliest Indian rulers to deal with European traders.

Most of the rulers were great builders, and they adorned their kingdoms with magnificent temples and palaces. The Pallavas were responsible for the series of rock-carved temples at Mamallapuram and the great temple complex at Kanchipuram. The Cholas built numerous temples, the most famous of which is at Tanjore, and decorated them with stone and bronze sculpture.

Muslim dominance (1200–1700). The first impact of Islam on India came in 712, when Arab control was established over Sind, in the lower Indus River valley. The Rajput kings of northern India prevented the Arabs' further expansion.

A dynasty of Afghan Turks from Ghor overcame the Rajputs in 1192 at Taraori. They established a sultanate at Delhi and from there gradually extended their control over all northern India. Under Ala-ad-din Khalji (1296–1316), the Turks conquered southern India. This new empire, the greatest in India since that of the Mauryas, fell apart after Ala-ad-din's death.

Weakened by Tamerlane's raids from central Asia in the late 1300s, the Delhi sultanate lost all but parts of the Punjab and the Gangetic plain by 1500. But permanent changes had been effected in the pattern of Indian civilization by the 300 years of Muslim occupation. A large Muslim minority had been created, and Islamic ideas and values had begun to influence Indian life. Orthodox Hinduism remained the most popular religion, however.

A new group of invaders entered India in 1526, led by Babur, a Mongol chieftain who had founded a kingdom at Kabul. He defeated the Delhi sultan at Panipat in 1526 and made himself master of the Gangetic plain up to Patna. He was succeeded by his son Humayun, who was driven out of India in 1540. Humayun was succeeded by his son Akbar (ruled 1556–1605), the founder of the Mughal Empire. Akbar pursued an aggressive policy of expansion that brought all of northern India under his control.

Akbar's reign is one of the most vital in Indian history, for he initiated policies that had a lasting influence. At the very beginning of the conquests, the Muslims had been faced with the problem of the proper treatment of the Hindus. Akbar enunciated a policy of universal toleration, the most obvious sign of which was the abolition of the *jizya*, the discriminatory tax. Akbar also instituted far-reaching administrative reforms, including the expansion of the revenue system, careful surveys of all cultivated land, and reforms of the taxation system.

Akbar's successors continued his policy of consolidation and expansion up to the middle of the 17th century. The Taj Mahal and the Pearl Mosque at Agra were built at this time.

Aurangzeb (1658–1707) reversed the religious policy initiated by Akbar. As a devout Muslim, he looked with disfavor on the growing power and prosperity of the Hindus, and as a statesman he probably questioned the possibility of holding the empire together without the loyalty of a Muslim ruling class. The discriminatory taxes were reimposed on the Hindus, the building of new temples was forbidden, and an attempt was made to replace Hindu government officials with Muslims.

Aurangzeb also embarked on a policy of territorial expansion and acquisition that brought all of India, except the extreme southern tip, under Mughal control.

Aurangzeb's vast empire began to crumble within a generation of his death. Rebellions broke out everywhere in the Mughal Empire, and a series of weak successors to the throne were unable to control the administration effectively. In 1739 northern India was invaded by Nadir Shah of Persia. By 1750 the empire was reduced to the territory around Delhi.

Western dominance and unification. The Marathas were the most important of the regional powers that emerged from the wreckage of the Mughal Empire. By 1760 they controlled all of central India and much of the south. Their expansion was checked in 1761 with their defeat at Panipat by a combined Mughal and Afghan army, and further halted in the 1780s by the rising power of the English East India Company.

The English had been in India since 1600 as traders, but the company became important as a political power only after the decline of Mughal power. In 1757 it interfered in a succession dispute over the throne of Bengal, and by 1765 it was in effective control of Bengal's resources, which it used to pay for the cost of expansion. By 1820 it was the paramount power in India, and soon all of India was brought under its control.

In 1857 the Great Mutiny, also called the Sepoy Mutiny, in northern India was instigated by the company's Indian soldiers, but it was abetted by other groups in the population that had special grievances against the new power.

The rebellion was crushed, and the East India Company lost its power to rule. A new administration was created, directly responsible to the British Crown. It directly ruled Bengal, Bombay, Madras, the Punjab, and the United Provinces (modern Uttar Pradesh). Indirect control was exercised over the remaining two-fifths of the territory through about 600 Indian princes. Although these rulers had internal autonomy, they had no control over their relations with other states.

The political unity achieved in the 1800s was made possible by a number of factors. The development of modern communications and transportation brought all India under the immediate control of the central government through telegraphs, railways, and steamships.

An efficient civil service was also created for the first time. A uniform legal system introduced Western ideas and methods of jurisprudence. Finally, English was the language used not only in administration but also in higher education. Colleges and universities gave Indians a common means of communication as well as a common knowledge of Western thought.

The rise of nationalism. The emergence of a nationalist movement in the late 1800s was the direct result of political unification. Educated Indians became aware simultaneously of the Western tradition of political freedom, the dependent state of their own country, and the glory of their past history. The nationalist movement had its formal beginnings in 1885 with the founding of the Indian National Congress by Allan Octavian Hume and a small group of Indian intellectuals.

The nationalist movement, with its demands for responsible government and a larger degree of independence, was complicated by Hindu-Muslim relations. Muslim leaders argued that responsible government based on direct popular representation would mean that Muslims, who constituted 25 percent of the population, would be a permanent minority ruled by Hindus. This led to the founding in 1906 of the Muslim League.

The British responded to the demands of the nationalists in 1909 through the Morley-Minto Reforms. They allowed the direct election of a number of Indians to provincial legislatures, and gave the Muslims separate electorates to ensure their adequate representation. The Indian National Congress denounced this as an attempt by the British to continue their hold over India by turning one religion against another.

The next response to nationalist demands came in 1919, when a new constitution, called the Montagu-Chelmsford Reforms, increased the power of the elected representatives in the provinces and widened the franchise. Indian political leaders were disappointed with the constitution, for they felt the British had, through the control of finance, kept all the important sources of power in their own hands.

The Indian National Congress, under the leadership of Mohandas K. (Mahatma) Gandhi, passed a resolution in 1920 condemning the new system of government; it began a campaign of nonviolent noncooperation. This became the characteristic method of the congress in its struggle against the British from that time on.

Gandhi's great achievement was to make the demand for independence a mass movement through the use of terminology and symbols drawn from traditional Indian religion and culture rather than from Western political thought. His chief lieutenant was Jawaharlal Nehru, who appealed to the intellectuals of India as well as to the country's masses.

Gandhi's success tended to alienate the Muslims, who increasingly argued that when freedom came, provision should be made for the Muslims to control their own destinies. Muhammad Ali Jinnah emerged as the leader of the Muslims.

The Government of India Act of 1935 was another unsuccessful attempt to give the Indians a sense of responsibility in government. When World War II broke out in 1939, the congress leaders resigned their government posts to protest their country's involvement in the war.

In 1945 a new Labour government in Britain entered into negotiations with the leaders of the congress and the Muslim League. Jinnah insisted that Nehru's demands for British withdrawal and the election of a constituent assembly to decide the future of the country would leave the Muslims without any protection against the Hindu majority. Following outbreaks of Hindu-Muslim violence in 1947, the congress consented to the creation of a separate Muslim state.

Independence. On August 15, 1947, British rule ended in India. A Muslim state, Pakistan, was formed from territories in the west and east, with Jinnah as governor-general and Liaqat Ali Khan

THE BEAUTIFUL TAJ MAHAL was built by Shah Jahan as the tomb of his favorite wife, Mumtaz Mahal, who died in 1629.

Labor *US*

Labour *Brit.*

INDIA'S REVERED LEADERS, Jawaharlal Nehru and Mohandas Gandhi, led a peaceful movement for independence from Great Britain, using traditional Indian values as motivation.

as prime minister. The remainder of British India became the Dominion of India, which inherited British India's organization and international obligations and rights. Nehru became prime minister and Lord Mountbatten governor-general.

With partition, violence flared along the border, particularly between West Pakistan and the Indian part of Punjab, as Hindus fled to India and Muslims to Pakistan. The two governments finally succeeded in stopping these bloody riots, but as the bitterness lingered. Gandhi was assassinated (January 30, 1948) by a Hindu extremist. Nehru then became leader of the new India.

The memory of violence on both sides, and dislike by most Indians of the fact of partition, have strained relations between the two countries. Other issues include the use of the Indus River for irrigation, payment of compensation for property left behind by refugees, and disputes over Kashmir.

On January 26, 1950, India adopted a new constitution, by which it became a sovereign republic but remained a member of the Commonwealth of Nations. In 1952 and in elections in 1957 and 1962, the Indian National Congress won a majority of seats in the national legislature. Jawaharlal Nehru, as head of the Congress Party, remained prime minister until his death in 1964.

Contemporary India. Since independence, one of India's major foreign policy concerns has been its relationship with Pakistan. Relations between the two were never good but they worsened during 1962, when Pakistan agreed to negotiate a treaty with China to define a part of the frontier west of the Karakorum Pass held by Pakistan but claimed by India.

A new quarrel broke out in April 1965 over the boundaries between the two in the Rann of Kutch, a desolate territory on the western coast. Fighting broke out, but a truce was arranged in June 1965. Two months later fighting again erupted between the two nations, this time along the border between Indian- and Pakistani-controlled parts of Kashmir.

In 1971 the civil war between East and West Pakistan, in which India supported the rebellious East (Bangladesh), resulted in some 10 million refugees crossing into India.

Indira Gandhi, the daughter of Nehru and an important figure in the Congress Party, became prime minister in 1966. She won a landslide victory in 1971, even though Gandhi had dissolved the lower house of Parliament the year before.

In 1975 political unrest led Gandhi to suspend civil liberties and arrest hundreds of political opponents. She also imposed "emergency rule" and postponed scheduled national elections. She initiated an unpopular program of forced sterilization and population control. When elections were finally held in 1977, she was defeated in her bid for reelection.

Morarji Desai and then Charan Singh served as prime ministers before

INDIRA GANDHI, daughter-in-law of Mahatma Gandhi, hoped to restore order to the fragmenting Indian society as prime minister, but she was assassinated in 1984.

January 1980, when Indira Gandhi led her Congress Party to a stunning upset. Gandhi was reinstated as prime minister amid hopes that she could curb inflation and restore order to the increasingly fragmented Indian society.

The 1980s brought an upsurge in religious violence. In 1984 militant Sikhs, agitating for more autonomy for the Punjab, were ejected from the Golden Temple by the army. It is estimated that about a thousand people died during the 2-day battle.

In October of 1984 Indira Gandhi was assassinated by two Sikh members of her bodyguard. Her death touched off a period of violence by Hindus against Sikhs. In December another terrible tragedy struck India. A leak of highly toxic gas at a Union Carbide pesticide plant in Bhopal caused the deaths of more than 2,000 people; hundreds of thousands more were injured.

Indira Gandhi's son Rajiv succeeded her as prime minister. Gandhi proved unable to live up to his promises to clamp down on government corruption and religious violence, and he was voted out of power in 1989. While campaigning for reelection in 1991, he was assassinated. Current Prime Minister Atal Behari Vajpayee was elected in 1998.

An ongoing dispute with Pakistan over Kashmir erupts into violence periodically, but 2003 saw great strides in normalizing relations between the countries.

Indonesia

Official name: *Republic of Indonesia*
Area: *740,904 sq. mi., 1,919,440 sq. km.*
Type of government: *Republic*
Population: *231,326,000*
Capital and largest city: *Jakarta (Pop., 9,374,000)*
Languages: *Bahasa Indonesian (official), Javanese, English*
Literacy: *84%*
Currency: *Rupiah*
Per capita GDP: *$3,000 (Rank: 116th)*

The land. Indonesia consists of over 13,500 islands and stretches some 3,000 miles from east to west and some 1,500 miles from north to south across the equator. The islands are divided into three main groups—the Greater Sundas in the west; the Lesser Sundas in the south; and the Moluccas in the east.

The Greater Sundas include Indonesia's largest and most important islands—Java, Sumatra, Borneo, and Sulawesi (Celebes). The western part of New Guinea, West Irian, is also part of Indonesia.

A typical Indonesian island consists of a core of high mountains and hills ringed by coastal plains. The islands are divided into three geologic regions. The largest islands, in the northwestern portion of the archipelago, are out-croppings of the Sunda Shelf, a submerged extension of the continent of Asia. The southeastern islands are part of the Sahul Shelf, the continental shelf of Australia and New Guinea.

Between these two stable geologic regions lies a third region still in formation. It is marked by a semicircular band of some 300 volcanoes, of which 60 are considered active.

Indonesia has an equatorial climate moderated by the influence of the sea. Temperatures are high, but not excessively so, and stable throughout the year, usually ranging between 75° F and 90° F. Rainfall is generally heavy, between 40 and 100 inches a year.

The people. Indonesia is ranked fourth among the nations in population. Almost two-thirds of the people live on Java, which accounts for only one-tenth of the country's area. Population is extremely dense near Jakarta, the capital.

The two next largest Indonesian cities are also on Java—Surabaja, the leading port, and Bandung, a cultural and educational center. Parts of Sumatra and Bali are also heavily populated.

Most Indonesians are Malays, but the population is divided into many ethnic and cultural groups. It is estimated that there are over 250 languages spoken in Indonesia. At independence, Bahasa Indonesian was chosen as a national

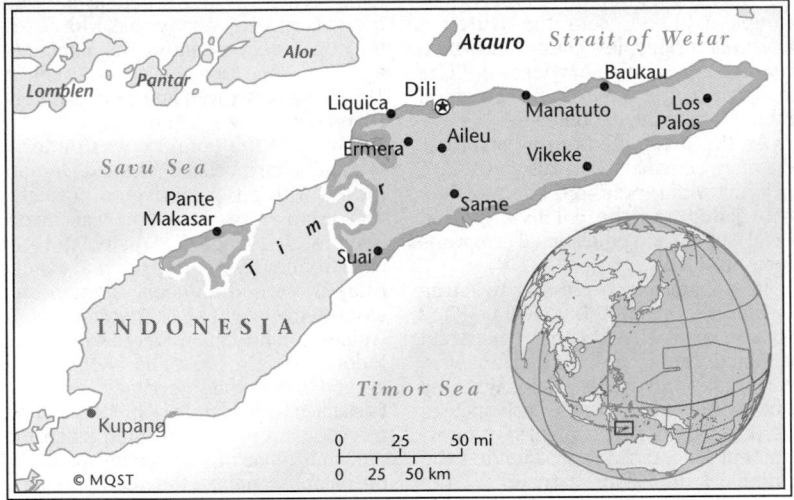

language to be used in government and taught in the schools. The language is based on a form of Malay widely used in trade. Approximately 90 percent of Indonesians are Muslims; most of the rest are Hindus, Christians, and Buddhists. There are Chinese and Arab minorities.

Eighty-two percent of the Indonesian population live in rural areas and 74 percent of the labor force is employed in agriculture.

Economy. Indonesia has made important progress since the dark years of the 1950s and 1960s, when political instability and mismanagement left the economy a shambles.

The largest reserves of petroleum in the Far East are in Sumatra, Borneo, Java, and Ceram. In 1986 Indonesia produced nearly 445 million barrels of oil and accounted for about 2 percent of the world's oil production. Indonesia's economy is dependent on oil, which accounts for almost 70 percent of export earnings and about 55 percent of government revenue.

Indonesia is also a leading world producer of tin, mining 22,000 metric tons in 1985.

There is also bauxite on Bintan, sulfur and manganese on Java, nickel on Sulawesi, and abundant iron ore and low-grade coal in Sumatra, Java, and Borneo. In addition to their rich resources, the islands are covered by valuable forests, which provide teak, sandalwood, bamboo, resins, and oils.

Most of Indonesia's resources are undeveloped, however, and agriculture is the mainstay of the economy, providing about 25 percent of gross domestic product (GDP). The equatorial climate permits year-round farming. Agricultural products raised primarily for export include cinchona (source of quinine), rubber, coffee, tea, copra, palm oil, sisal, tobacco, sugar, cocoa, indigo, and pepper and other spices. The basic food crops include rice, corn, sweet potatoes, peanuts, soybeans, bananas, manioc, and vegetables.

Manufacturing industries make up only about 13 percent of GDP. The government has encouraged the development of industries based on the exploitation of Indonesia's own natural resources. A recent ban on the export of logs has encouraged the processed lumber industry and helped make Indonesia the leading exporter of plywood. Indonesia is also the world's largest producer of liquefied natural gas.

Indonesia's imports include machinery, transport equipment, and textiles. Its largest trading partners are Japan, the United States, and Singapore.

Government. Executive power is held by a president who is both chief of state and head of government. The president is elected every five years by a People's Consultative Assembly, which meets only once and sets state policy. Legislative authority rests with the 500-member House of People's Representatives.

Although Indonesia is nominally a democracy, the army has held considerable influence since independence. This influence is felt not only in the government, where members of the military hold a number of important posts, but also in important national industries, where army personnel often hold top positions. This situation is formalized in the philosophy of "two functions," which holds that the armed forces have a social role as well as a military one.

History. Indonesia has been inhabited since prehistoric times, and remains of one of the earliest humans have been found on Java. By the 100s B.C., Malay people had developed on the islands of the archipelago simple societies based on fishing, agriculture, and seafaring. In the 100s A.D., Indian peoples began to come to the islands, first as traders and then as settlers.

Early kingdoms. By the 500s and 600s many small Indian-Malayan Buddhist and Hindu kingdoms had been established on the islands, and a variety of cultures and societies developed. These societies built up a vigorous trade with nearby island and mainland states, and with India and China.

The first of these kingdoms to achieve significance beyond its own island territory was Srivijaya, on Sumatra. It developed a high Buddhist culture and an advanced civilization, and by the 800s it controlled an empire that included part of the Malay peninsula as well as most of the Indonesian islands.

In the 1100s internal conflicts and threats of attack from the mainland weakened Srivijayan control over the islands, and a new kingdom centered at Majapahit, on Java, gained power. After leading a defense of the islands against an attack by the Mongols in the late 1200s, the Javanese kingdom became the dominant influence in the archipelago.

labor
US
labour
Brit.

civilization
US
civilisation
Brit.

AGRICULTURE is the basis for the Indonesian economy, much of it carried to market by timeless methods.

DANCE
is the most famous
art form of Indonesia.
Typical are dances
depicting life of the
old Javanese royal
courts and Balinese
folk dances.

In the 1300s and 1400s Muslim Arabs began to settle in Indonesia, and by the late 1400s Islamic influence had weakened the older Hindu and Buddhist kingdoms. By the early 1500s there was no single powerful state governing Indonesia. In the 1400s and 1500s European traders began visiting the islands, attracted by the fame of the spices, woods, and other goods of the "East Indies" and the "Spice Islands," as Indonesia was called.

European control. The Portuguese were the first Europeans to establish trading posts in the islands. By the mid-1500s they held military control over most of the islands, and they attempted to convert the islanders to Christianity. Islam spread rapidly through the islands as one weapon against the European invaders.

Portugal held a virtual monopoly of the islands' trade by 1580, when Spain acquired the Portuguese crown. Spain's European rivals, especially England and The Netherlands, then redoubled their efforts to break the monopoly. The Dutch, with the help of Muslim islanders, gained a foothold on the islands.

In 1602 the Dutch formed the Dutch East India Company. During the 1600s the company drove out the Portuguese and other European traders and subdued the islanders. The Dutch trading center of Batavia (modern Jakarta), on western Java, grew into a prosperous center for the rich trade of the islands. The Dutch were joined in the 1700s by Chinese immigrants, whose plantations first developed the islands' agricultural potential and who began investing in the colony's business.

Dutch rule. In 1798 The Netherlands took direct control of the colony from the East India Company. The company's government had grown corrupt and inefficient, and The Netherlands needed the islands as a naval base during the Napoleonic wars. Moreover, the colony had proved even richer than expected. In the early 1800s the French and the British briefly occupied The Netherlands East Indies, but the Dutch resumed control in 1816.

During the 1800s the Dutch reaped great riches from the colony through a

center
US

centre
Brit.

system of state-regulated, privately owned plantations. The Europeans' concentration on producing export crops to the exclusion of subsistence crops led to frequent famines and to the misuse and depletion of the islands' resources.

Although the Dutch encouraged and educated some islanders and did not prohibit their owning businesses or farms, the majority of Indonesians were illiterate, poor, and powerless. Colonial regulations protected native workers from mistreatment, but most of them were severely exploited.

In the early 1900s resentment of colonial inequities led to Indonesian nationalist movements. Led by Dutch-educated Indonesian intellectuals, the movements grew rapidly. In 1916 these groups obtained from the Dutch a *Volksraad,* or people's council, in which Indonesians could participate. The council had little authority, however, and did not satisfy the nationalists.

As the nationalists grew stronger and more active in the 1920s and 1930s, they met with repression. Their leaders were jailed and the colony's limited social welfare and educational programs were curtailed.

In 1942, during World War II, Japanese forces invaded Indonesia. They quickly crushed the Dutch defenses and occupied the islands. The Japanese encouraged Indonesian nationalism by allowing the Indonesians to participate in the occupation government. One government leader, Sukarno, founded the National Indonesian Party, one of the country's major nationalist organizations.

Indonesian leaders who opposed the Japanese established a government-in-exile in Australia. There they outlined a plan for a gradual postwar separation of Indonesia from control of The Netherlands.

In 1945, three days after the Japanese surrender, Sukarno and Muhammad Hatta, another nationalist leader, proclaimed the independence of the Republic of Indonesia.

Independence. Several years of political conflict and warfare followed, with Sukarno's government fighting not only the Dutch, who attempted to reestablish their control, but more conservative nationalist groups as well. In 1949 The Netherlands yielded sovereignty over the islands.

An independent federal union was established, loosely united with The Netherlands. However, dissatisfaction with this organization led in 1950 to the abolition of the federal state and the creation of the centralized Republic of Indonesia, which included all the islands.

The new country was faced from the start with the problem of unifying a large number of islands with a variety of cultures and no tradition of unity. It tried to solve this problem with a strong central government. Between 1950 and 1955, Sukarno, the nation's first president, held great power, appointing all local officials and all members of parliament.

The country held its first elections

in 1955 for both a parliament and a constituent assembly, which was to draft a permanent constitution. Of Indonesia's 29 political parties, the Communists emerged from the elections as one of the four strongest, along with two Muslim parties and Sukarno's Nationalist Party.

The army objected to the Communists' influence in the government, and in 1958 army officers on Sumatra rebelled, sparking an uprising that spread to Sulawesi and many smaller islands. The rebellions were quelled in 1961.

Between 1957 and 1959 Dutch property was seized, Dutch businesses harassed, and all Dutch citizens were ordered out of Indonesia. The resulting economic crisis compounded the problems created by the rebellion and left the government very weak. Moreover, the constituent assembly was unable to agree on plans for a new constitution. In 1959 it was dissolved and a government reorganization was begun.

By 1960 the country was under a system Sukarno called "Guided Democracy"—with an executive so powerful that popular participation was effectively stifled—but dissension did not end. Conflicts with the Dutch also continued, with Indonesia demanding sovereignty over The Netherlands' New Guinea colony, called West Irian by the Indonesians. In 1963 The Netherlands agreed to surrender territory.

Contemporary Indonesia. In 1963 a new, more violent dispute erupted when the Sukarno government moved to block the establishment of the nearby Federation of Malaysia, formed by the union of four former British colonial areas—Malaya, Singapore, Sarawak, and Sabah (North Borneo).

The Indonesian government soon began a "Crush Malaysia" campaign. Border fighting was frequent, and in 1965 Indonesia announced its withdrawal from the United Nations after Malaysia was admitted to membership.

Hostility to Malaysia was one aspect of Sukarno's general opposition to all European involvement in Southeast Asia. In 1965 Indonesia nationalized all foreign-owned businesses in the country, and although it officially remained neutral in foreign affairs, the government strengthened its ties with Communist China as its opposition to Western nations stiffened.

Indonesia's pro-Beijing Communist Party grew in power, and in October, 1965, attempted to seize the government. The coup attempt was crushed by the army, and it is estimated that more than 100,000 Indonesian Communists were killed in the aftermath. Many thousands of Indonesia's Chinese residents were murdered or driven from their homes. Some of Sukarno's top aides were convicted of complicity in the communist plot.

The army officially took control of the government in 1966 and Lieutenant General Suharto became prime minister. Sukarno retained the post of president until March 1967, when the

Peoples' Consultative Assembly dismissed him and appointed Suharto president. Elections kept Suharto in office until 1997 when he stepped down amid a severe economic crisis.

Suharto's military government concentrated on rebuilding the economy, ravaged by years of violence and political upheavals. Although oil income since the 1960s strengthened the economy, there was an uneven distribution of this new wealth, accompanied by charges of unfair economic advantages to Chinese and Japanese minorities. Student riots erupted over the issue in 1974, and even though they were readily put down, the government pursued a course of reform.

Suharto also sought closer ties with noncommunist nations. Japanese and U.S. financial aid and investments were significant outcomes of this policy.

Indonesia also took a more active role in regional affairs. In 1966 friendly relations were reestablished with Malaysia. In 1988 Indonesia hosted talks between the various warring factions in Cambodia. Indonesia broke relations with China in 1967 and remains strongly anticommunist.

In 1976 Indonesia annexed the former Portuguese colony of East Timor during a civil war on the island. Thousands of civilians were reported killed during the takeover.

On August 30, 1999, the East Timorese voted overwhelmingly to separate from Indonesia. United Nations peacekeepers arrived in September to restore order. The last Indonesian soldiers left East Timor in October, 24 years after the annexation. East Timor was under UN administration pending its formal independence, which came in May 2002.

Japan

Official name: *Japan*
Area: *145,844 sq. mi.,
377,835 sq. km.*
Type of government:
Constitutional monarchy
Population: *127,066,000*
Capital and largest city: *Tokyo
(Pop., 8,130,000)*
Language: *Japanese*
Literacy: *99%*
Currency: *Yen*
Per capita GDP: *$28,000
(Rank: 10th)*

The land. The Japanese archipelago consists of over 3,000 islands and extends 2,000 miles from northeast to southwest. But 98 percent of the area lies within the four major islands of Honshu (87,300 square miles); Hokkaido (30,300 square miles); Kyushu (16,200 square miles); and Shikoku (7,200 square miles).

Most of the country is mountainous, with only about 15 percent of the

land sufficiently level for cultivation. The country's limited plains areas are concentrated on Honshu. Japanese civilization, not surprisingly, has developed primarily in the limited space occupied by four major plains, those around Tokyo, Nagoya, Kyoto-Osaka, and Kitakyushu. Roughly half of the nation's population lives in these areas.

Many of the mountains are folded ranges upthrust from the Pacific floor. Japan is crossed by seven principal volcanic chains containing 192 major volcanoes, 58 of which are active. An average of four seismic shocks a day are recorded. Volcanoes produce the highest peaks in the country. Mount Fuji, a dormant volcano on Honshu, has an elevation of 12,389 feet.

Japan's rivers are short and swift with greatly varying water levels. The Inland Sea serves Japan as a major waterway. It is about 250 miles long and is connected with the Pacific Ocean and with the Korea Strait.

The coastline of the Sea of Japan has few indentations and consequently has few good harbors. The southern coast of Honshu contains Japan's most important harbors and ports, such as Tokyo, Yokohama, Nagoya, Osaka, and Kobe.
Climate. Japan's climate, subtropical in the south and cooler in the north, is generally mild and pleasant. The average mean January temperature is 45°F in southern Kyushu and 14°F in Hokkaido. August is usually the hottest month of the year, with a mean of 81°F in the south and 69°F in the north.

Western Hokkaido, eastern Honshu, and the Inland Sea region receive 40 to 60 inches of rain a year. In central Honshu and along the Sea of Japan 100 to 120 inches of rain is not uncommon. In most parts of the country maximum rains occur in the early summer.
The people. The Japanese are a Mongoloid people with a mixture of Malay and Caucasoid stocks. The only important minority group consists of about 600,000 Koreans. There are small groups of Chinese and Europeans, and remnants of the aboriginal people, the Ainu.

The indigenous religion of Japan is Shinto, which emphasizes ritual cleanliness and the living, moving spirit of nature. The second important religion is Buddhism, which came to Japan in the sixth century from China.

Education is very important to the Japanese. The country's level of literacy is one of the highest in the world. The school dropout rate is very low, and nearly one-third of all high school graduates attend college.

The Japanese inhabit one of the world's most heavily populated lands, with a density of about 818 people per square mile. Moreover, because the nation is so mountainous, more than 4,000 persons live in each arable square mile. Japan has eleven cities claiming more than 1 million inhabitants, the largest being Tokyo, Yokohama (3.4 million), Osaka (2.6), Nagoya (2.2), Sapporo (1.8), Kyoto (1.5), and Kobe (1.5).

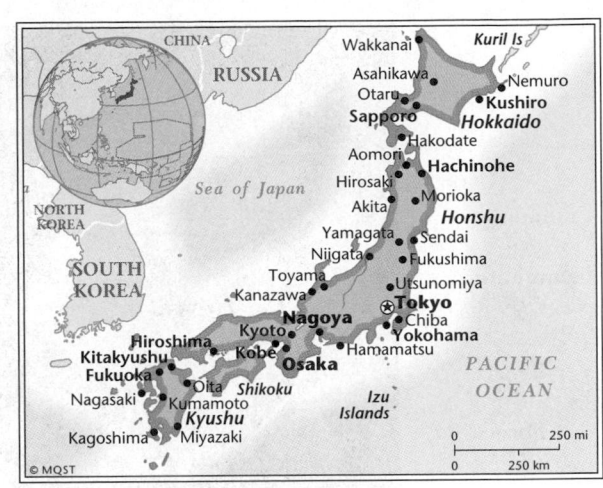

Economy. Japan's economic performance since World War II has been phenomenal. Despite a poverty of natural resources, Japan has become a leading nation in the world economy. The country's economy expanded at an annual rate of about 11 percent from 1947 to 1952, slowed during the 1950s, and then grew by 10 percent a year during the 1960s. Growth was slower during the 1970s owing to soaring oil prices, but it still remained stronger than in other major nations. By 1980 the gross national product (GNP) had passed the trillion-dollar mark, the third highest in the world, and average family income approximated that of the United States. In the early 1990s, however, Japan's economy was stalled by a worldwide recession and growing East Asian competition.
Natural resources. Japan has a large variety of mineral resources, but the deposits are small and inadequate for Japan's advanced level of industrial development. Coal is the main mineral resource, but most of it is of low grade. Most basic industrial materials must be imported.

Materials in which domestic production is sufficient are lead, zinc, arsenic, bismuth, pyrite, sulfur, limestone, gypsum, barite, silica, and dolomite. Vanadium, chromium, molybdenum, tungsten, titanium, tin, manganese, and iron ore also are produced, but large imports still are required to meet the economy's needs.

Japan's mountainous terrain and abundant rainfall help make the country

civilization
US

civilisation
Brit.

emphasizes
US

emphasises
Brit.

**EARLY
JAPANESE
PAINTINGS**
frequently depicted
Buddhist subjects and
employed techniques
and compositions
from China.

JAPAN PRODUCES more cultured pearls than any other country in the world, raising them in carefully tended oyster beds.

aluminum
US

aluminium
Brit.

fiber
US

fibre
Brit.

WORKERS
discuss quality
control at an
electronics plant
in Japan.

the fourth largest producer of hydro-electricity in the world.

Agriculture. Agriculture's position in Japan's economy has declined since World War II, even though production has increased. Agriculture contributed 21 percent to the gross domestic product in 1953, but less than 5 percent at the beginning of the 1980s. At the same time, Japanese farmers, despite a decrease in their actual numbers, are increasingly affluent; their income increased fivefold in the 20 years from 1955 to 1975.

The average Japanese farm of about $2\frac{1}{2}$ acres is intensively cultivated. Such techniques as fertilizer use, irrigation, multiple cropping, and terracing place Japan's crop yields per acre among the highest in the world.

About half the cultivated land is used for the production of paddy rice, the staple of the Japanese diet. Barley, wheat, potatoes, pulses, vegetables, and fruits also are grown.

Fishing. Fish ranks second to rice in the Japanese diet and is the principal source of protein. Japanese coastal waters contain a great variety of fish.

The sardine catch leads in both volume and value, although herring and mackerel are important in northern waters. In addition to coastal fishing, Japan has a large fleet that goes to distant fishing grounds in the north and south Pacific.

Forestry. About two-thirds of Japan is covered by productive forests, which are the source of building materials, fuel, paper, and other articles. Oak, laurel, and bamboo grow in southern Japan. A mixed forest, including maple, ash, birch, cypress, and pine, is found in central Japan. Conifers such as spruce, fir, and hemlock grow in northern Japan. However, domestic production of timber provides only about 40 percent of Japan's needs.

Industry. Despite its limited resources, Japan is an industrial giant, having

invested heavily over the last three decades in the construction of both light and heavy industrial plants.

A telling index of the magnitude of Japan's industrial success is a list of areas in which the country is a world leader: rayon and acetate fabrics, plastics, aluminum, synthetic rubber, resins, raw silk, crude steel, cotton fabrics, watches, cameras and lenses, pianos, calculators, television and radio sets, wood pulp, motorcycles, ships, automobiles, and chemicals.

Textile production has experienced a transition in recent years, as synthetic fabrics have challenged Japan's silk and cotton industries. As a consequence, Japan's synthetic fiber production increased nearly twentyfold from the war era to the late 1970s, enabling Japan to continue as the world's second leading producer of fabrics.

A major growth industry has been the manufacture of transportation vehicles. Since the war, Japan's motorcycle industry has become dominant in the world market; its shipbuilders have produced more tonnage than all other nations combined, despite recent cutbacks owed to European pressures; and in 1980 Japan passed the United States as the largest automobile producer in the world.

Another important postwar development has been Japan's rise as a producer of electronic equipment, such as television sets, videocassette recorders, and computers. Japan ranks with the United States as a leader in the futuristic "smart machine" industry that has grown from the electronics-computer revolution.

Trade. Deficient both in arable land and natural resources, Japan is heavily dependent on foreign trade. Raw materials, foodstuffs, and fuel are Japan's principal imports, especially cereals, sugar, raw cotton and wool, iron ore, bauxite, copper ore, coking coal, crude rubber, and crude petroleum. Almost all of Japan's exports are manufactured goods. Markets for these goods are found in Canada and Australia, but mostly in the United States, where Japan has concentrated its foreign investments in recent years.

Government. Japan is a constitutional monarchy with a parliamentary system of government. The emperor is the symbol of the state, and executive power is wielded by a prime minister and cabinet responsible to the legislature, the Diet. The prime minister, chosen by the Diet from among its members, appoints the cabinet ministers, at least half of whom must be members of the Diet.

The Diet is composed of the House of Representatives, whose 480 members are elected to four-year terms, and the House of Councillors, with 247 members elected to six-year terms. A portion of the councillors are elected by the nation at large, and a portion are elected from local constituencies.

History. Although the first inhabitants of Japan were ancestors of the Ainu, a Caucasoid people, archaeological evidence indicates that most of the early Japanese were Mongoloid invaders from Korea, who first appeared in Japan in the early centuries A.D. They brought with them a bronze and iron civilization and founded the Japanese state.

Early Japan was ruled by numerous clans, one of which, the Yamato, gained supremacy by the 300s or 400s. From the Yamato descended the Japanese royal family, although Japanese tradition maintained that the Sun Goddess of the Yamato chiefs was the progenitor of the imperial family.

An emigration of Chinese artisans and scholars in the first century A.D. introduced Japan to the advanced civilization of China. The introduction (mid-sixth century) of Buddhism particularly revolutionized Japanese arts and architecture.

Between 607 and the mid-800s, a series of Japanese missions went to the Chinese court. The missions included officials, scholars, artists, and Buddhist monks. They remained in China for periods of study and many became influential on their return to Japan.

A complex centralized administration in the Chinese manner was established and Chinese-style cities were built. Nara was built as the capital in 710. It was replaced by Kyoto in 794. Less successfully imitated by the Japanese were China's provincial administration and land distribution systems, which were strongly opposed by the clans.

Such cultural borrowings as Buddhism and Buddhist art were the most enduring. Attempts to adapt the Chinese writing system to the Japanese language were largely unsuccessful and made writing unnecessarily difficult. After 200 years of imitation, a native Japanese culture began to emerge, and in 838 the last Japanese embassy was sent to China.

MORE THAN 50,000 pilgrims a year climb to the top of Mount Fuji, which the Japanese consider sacred.

A brilliant Japanese court life developed, which came to be dominated by the Fujiwara family. The Fujiwara gained control over the imperial family through intermarriage, and from about 850 on its head acted either as regent or as civil dictator.

While the Fujiwara dominated the court in the 900s and 1000s, real power came to reside in the provincial knights and their families. Of all these families, the Minamoto emerged as the most powerful in 1185. Its chief, Yoritomo, settled in Kamakura and gave himself the title of shogun, or generalissimo.

Kamakura era. By appointing its men as estate managers throughout the country, the Kamakura group was able to control both peasants and court nobles, whose incomes came from the Kamakura-managed estates. The Kamakura group became the only real central government in Japan.

Upon Yoritomo's death, the Hojo family assumed power, ruling through a puppet shogun from the Fujiwara family and then from the royal family.

By the late 1200s the Kamakura system had begun to disintegrate, although Kamakura soldiers were able to repel Mongol invasions ordered by Kublai Khan in 1274 and 1281. The strain of warding off Mongol invasion attempts had weakened the Kamakura shogunate, and in 1331 a retired emperor, Daigo II, led a revolt against the Kamakura. The result was a bitter struggle. In 1338 Ashikaga Takauji had himself proclaimed shogun; his successors ended the conflict in 1392. The Ashikaga shoguns never acquired the same degree of authority as the Kamakura shoguns, but they preserved a measure of stability until 1467. During this period of political collapse, commerce and manufacturing prospered and trade with China expanded.

Political reunification came in the late 1500s when Oda Nobunaga, a feudal lord, seized Kyoto in 1568 and became ruler of central Japan. His successor, Hideyoshi, assumed power in 1582 and reunited the entire country. He attempted an invasion of Korea in 1592, but was repulsed by Chinese forces. Hideyoshi was succeeded in 1598 by Tokugawa Ieyasu, who took the title of shogun in 1603.

Tokugawa era. Tokugawa and his successors created a political system that remained unchanged for 250 years. The price of stability and peace, however, was an oppressive and reactionary government. Social stability was achieved by the creation of a strict class system. Foreign relations and Western influence, especially Christianity, had flourished in the late 16th century. Both now became the targets of bitter reactionary politics. The Spanish and Portuguese were expelled, and in 1638 the Japanese were forbidden to go abroad. In the same year, the thriving Christian community was liquidated by fierce oppression and persecution.

By the 18th century a wealthy merchant class, merged through intermarriage with the warriors, began to undermine the austere Confucianism encouraged by the Tokugawa shoguns.

JAPAN PASSED the United States as the world's largest producer of automobiles in 1980.

There was also a revival of interest in the West.

Commodore Matthew Perry conveyed (1853 to 1854) strong American insistence on establishing trade; this underscored demands to end Japan's isolation. In 1858 a full commercial treaty with the United States was signed, and similar agreements with European countries followed. Foreign businesses were set up in Yokohama, which soon became a major world port.

Meiji restoration. The Tokugawa regime lost national confidence by negotiating a treaty with a foreign power, and in 1867 the new shogun voluntarily surrendered control of the country to the emperor, a return to royal rule called the Meiji restoration.

The new Meiji government quickly set Japan on a course that would bring two generations of breathtaking transformation. Leaders went abroad to study Western institutions and invited Western advisers to Japan. From what they learned, the Japanese created new structures suited to Japan's goal of modernization. Compulsory education, a standard land tax, universal military conscription, and a constitution that made Japan a constitutional monarchy in 1889 were among the acquisitions.

The costs of modernization were borne mostly by the peasants, who paid new land taxes instead of feudal dues. Foreign investment, with its risk of foreign control, was limited, and new industries developed by the government were sold cheaply to private Japanese firms. With a strong army and navy, and a large industrial complex, Japan was ready to test itself as a world military power.

Expansionism. A quarrel with China over Korea provoked the Sino-Japanese War of 1894–1895, which was easily won by Japan. Clashes of interest with Russia over Korea and Manchuria led to the Russo-Japanese War of 1904–1905, a war won by the Japanese after a series of stunning victories on land and on sea.

Korea was annexed in 1910. Japan now had the opportunity to become the leader of a modernizing pan-Asian movement, but the movement was neglected in favor of attempts to secure dominance in Asia by military force.

In 1914 Japan, as Britain's ally, declared war on Germany in World War I. Seeking to take advantage of the situation, Japan attempted to dominate China. These plans were upset largely through diplomacy initiated by the United States. Thereafter, extreme nationalism flourished in Japan. Japan's "divine mission" to rule Asia and, ultimately, the world, was preached. Meanwhile, the world economic crisis of the 1930s increased support for nationalist extremism.

To maintain its economy and large population, Japan was desperately in need of foreign markets where it could obtain supplies and sell its exports. With the Depression, Japan became subject to the will of other nations' tariff policies.

By the 1930s many Japanese, especially the militarists, were eager to engage in a policy of colonial expansion to obtain sources of raw materials and markets. Although the emperor and many leading statesmen disliked the army extremists, they were unwilling to produce a public scandal by acting decisively against them. This culminated in the invasion of Manchuria in 1931. Full-scale war with China started in 1937.

World War II. Meanwhile, in 1936, Japan had signed with Germany the Anti-Comintern Pact. Finally, in 1940, the Rome-Berlin-Tokyo Axis was established. To break the economic blockade set up by the Western nations, especially the United States, in protest against Japanese aggression, Japan attacked Pearl Harbor on December 7, 1941, without warning.

After many important initial Japanese successes, the United States and its allies counterattacked. By 1943 Japan was in retreat. Yet Japan did not surrender until August 14, 1945, after the United States dropped the world's first atomic bombs on the Japanese cities of Hiroshima and Nagasaki.

Japan was occupied by U.S. forces under the command of General Douglas MacArthur, and attempts at a thorough democratization of the country were started. Emperor Hirohito disclaimed his divinity, and in 1946 a new constitution gave power to a parliament chosen by universal suffrage, with the emperor as a constitutional monarch. The constitution also included effective civil liberties clauses. Reforms to strengthen labor unions, break up business cartels, and end the rural landlord system also supported democracy.

Contemporary Japan. Economic recovery was slow after the destruction wrought by the war, but the rapidly changing international situation provoked sharp modifications in U.S. policy in regard to Japan. Since Japan regained its independence (September 8, 1951), Japan and the United States have maintained exceptionally close ties. A mutual security treaty (also September 8, 1951) promised American protection of Japan in return for the right to maintain U.S. bases there. Though trade competition has created strains, basic cooperation has never diminished. A symbol of this close relationship was America's return to Japan in 1972 of the Ryukyu Islands won in World War II.

The Korean War, from 1950 to 1953, sparked a startling increase in Japan's industrial output. This growth has been somewhat slowed since 1970 because of inflation caused largely by high oil prices.

One key to Japan's postwar adjustment has been a stable government dominated by the conservative Liberal Democratic Party, which held the office of prime minister until 1993 and has won almost every election since its formation in 1955. Under prime ministers like Yoshida Shigeru (1946–1947, 1948–1954) and Sato Eisaku (1964–1972), the party gave Japan both political stability and a highly business-oriented climate.

The party suffered reverses in the 1970s because of corruption scandals that beset Prime Minister Tanaka Kakuei and several years of economic slowdown, but it still retained power.

In 1982 Yasuhiro Nakasone became prime minister. During his terms in office he worked to improve Japan's status as a world power, responding to the perception that Japan was not accepting fully its responsibilities as a world economic leader. Under his administration, Japan increased development aid to Southeast Asia and the Pacific basin and improved ties with neighbors such as China.

A series of government corruption scandals shook Japan in the late 1980s and early 1990s. In 1994 Tomiichi Murayama became the first Socialist prime minister since 1948. Junichiro Koizumi became prime minister in 2001.

In January 1995 a powerful earthquake struck Kobe, leaving more than

labor
US

labour
Brit.

JAPANESE CHILDREN enjoy noodles, that delicacy for which Italy and the rest of the world have to thank Asia.

5,000 people dead and tens of thousands homeless. In March 1995 terrorists released a powerful nerve gas in Tokyo's subways. Ten people died; thousands became ill.

Kampuchea

See Cambodia

Kazakhstan

Official name: *Republic of Kazakhstan*
Area: *1,048,878 sq. mi., 2,717,300 sq. km.*
Type of government: *Republic*
Population: *16,742,000*
Capital: *Astana (Pop., 313,000)*
Largest city: *Almaty (Pop., 1,129,000)*
Languages: *Kazakh, Russian*
Literacy: *98%*
Currency: *Tenge*
Per capita GDP: *$5,900 (Rank: 78th)*

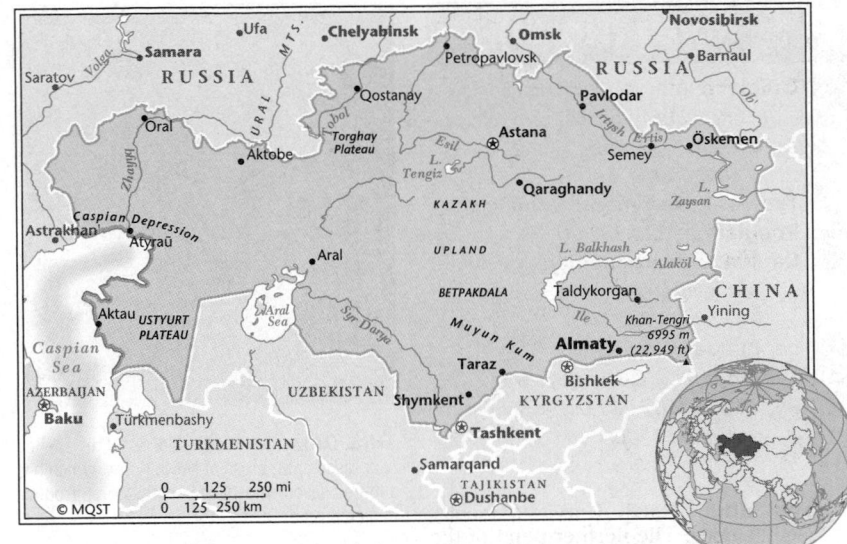

The land. Kazakhstan, the second largest of the former Soviet republics, is located in Central Asia. The northern and western parts of Kazakhstan consist of lowlands. The central part of the country is rolling plains and plateaus, with smaller mountain regions in the south and east, where the highest peak is about 5,000 feet (1,500 meters). The Turanian Depression, in the west and south, is the site of an ancient seabed. In Lake Balkhash, more than 400 miles (650 kilometers) long, brackish water dominates in the eastern part and fresh water in the western part.

Major rivers include the Ural, flowing south into the Caspian Sea, and the Syr Darya, which traverses the steppe from the Pamir-Tien Shan mountain ranges to the Aral Sea. The Irtysh, Ishim, and Tobol rivers flow north to the Ob River, whose waters empty into the Arctic Ocean. Kazakhstan has more than 1,400 miles (2,250 kilometers) of coastline on the Caspian Sea, the world's largest inland body of water. Climate is of the continental type, with temperatures ranging from 90°F (32°C) in summer to 3°F (-16°C) in winter. There are wide variations in rainfall. The central and northwestern areas are characterized by dry winds. Steppes and deserts are common in Kazakhstan, and woodlands are rare.
The people. The population of Kazakhstan contains almost equal proportions of Kazakhs and Russians, as well as many other nationalities, including Germans, Uzbeks, and Crimean Tatars. Many of these peoples were brought to Kazakhstan during periods of intense agricultural and industrial development. Kazakhs are traditionally Muslim.
Economy. Mineral resources abound in Kazakhstan, where there are large reserves of coal, tungsten, iron ore, lead, copper, zinc, manganese, and molybdenum. In the Caspian Depression are found oil and natural gas. Ranked third among the industrial republics of the former Soviet Union, Kazakhstan produces steel, rolled ferrous metals, machinery, chemicals, and textiles, as well as fuel and electric power.

Major food-processing industries include sugar, butter, preserves, and canned meat and fish production. Where once the land was devoted primarily to cattle, large areas are now under cultivation, with irrigation available on more than 2 million hectares. Important crops are wheat, cotton, potatoes, sugar beets, and fruit. Sheep, exceeding 36 million in 1990, are raised for high-quality wool. Cattle, goats, and pigs are also raised, and fishing is well developed and profitable. With its unusually varied resources, Kazakhstan is relatively self-sufficient.
Government. The head of state is a popularly elected president. The head of government is a prime minister appointed by the president. There is a bicameral legislature. Kazakhstan is a member of the Commonwealth of Independent States.
History. Kazakhs descended from Mongol and Turkic tribes that came to the area about the first century B.C. For most of their history, Kazakhs were divided into small nomadic groups of cattle breeders and herdsmen. In the early 17th century, these groups were brought together in three federations, or hordes, that later came under the protection and control of the Russian czar. A large influx of Russian and Ukrainian peasants arrived after the abolition of serfdom in Russia in 1861, and the new settlers were given Kazakh lands. Fiercely resentful, the Kazakhs revolted against Russian rule in 1916 and suffered great losses in the ensuing repressions. Civil war plagued the area after the Bolshevik revolution of 1917.

After territorial reorganizations and name changes, the region became in 1936 a full Union republic; it was officially named the Kazakh Soviet Socialist Republic. The early 1930s saw a new wave of immigration, as a massive effort was undertaken by the Soviets to industrialize some areas, collectivize farming, and settle the nomadic population. By 1953 the amount of tilled land had doubled. Between 1954 and 1959, under the Soviet leader Nikita Khrushchev, the virgin lands program was introduced, resulting in the cultivation of large areas that had lain fallow or never seen a plow. The population of ethnic Russians rose dramatically as immigrants came to work on newly tilled land, in nuclear testing sites, at the Baikonur space center, and in vast industrial plants in the north. Severe environmental problems resulted from rapid industrialization and its attendant pollution, as well as from nuclear testing, particularly near Semipalatinsk. High unemployment rates and economic hard times contributed to interethnic turbulence between Kazakhs and other, more skilled and educated groups.

State sovereignty was declared in October 1990, and the republic's independence from the U.S.S.R. was proclaimed in December 1991. Nursultan Nazarbayev, who had been named head of the republic shortly before it declared its autonomy, was elected president in 1991 in an election in which he was the only candidate. Other candidates were barred from the ballot under unusually strict nominating rules. He retained the post in 1998 after a widely criticized election.

(For more information on the history of Kazakhstan during the Soviet period, see the article on Russia in the EUROPE AND RUSSIA volume.)

meters
US

metres
Brit.

center
US

centre
Brit.

THE NOMADIC PEOPLE of Kazakhstan live in collapsible tents called yurts, the interiors of which are quite comfortable.

23 Asia

Korea (North)

Official name: *Democratic People's Republic of Korea*
Area: *46,528 sq. mi., 120,540 sq. km.*
Type of government: *Communist*
Population: *22,215,000*
Capital and largest city: *P'yŏngyang (Pop., 2,741,000)*
Language: *Korean*
Literacy: *99%;* **Currency:** *Won*
Per capita GDP: *$1,000 (Rank: 170th)*

center
US

centre
Brit.

The land. North Korea is mostly mountainous. The northern end of the Taebaek mountains, which extend down the Korean peninsula, and the Hamgyong mountains, which run southwest to northeast, dominate the country. Lowlands occupy the western part of the country, along the Yellow Sea.

North Korea's most important rivers are the Yalu and the Tumen, which form most of the border with China, and the Taedong, which flows through the capital city of P'yŏngyang.

The climate in North Korea is dominated by long cold winters and short summers, although along the western coast temperatures tend to be more moderate.

The people. North Korea's population is both ethnically and linguistically homogeneous. Nearly all the population are believed to be Korean, although there may be a small minority of Chinese.

The population of North Korea is unevenly distributed, with a much higher density along the west coast than in the interior or the east coast. P'yŏngyang is by far the largest city. Other important cities include Hamhung (710,000), Ch'ŏngjin (582,000), Sinuiju (326,000), and Wonsan (300,000).

Although the constitution permits North Koreans to practice religion, in reality the government actively discourages any religious participation.

Economy. The North Korean economy is patterned on the Soviet model. Industrial capacity is mostly owned by the state, and agriculture has been collectivized.

THIS DAMAGED MAIZE CROP spelled near-disaster for areas of North Korea, which has suffered severe shortfalls in agricultural produce in recent years.

North Korea is rich in natural resources. Mineral resources include coal, manganese, iron ore, uranium, and zinc. Because of the many swift streams and rivers, hydroelectric potential is high.

Heavy industry is well developed in North Korea. Significant manufactures include products such as steel, cement, and fertilizer. The severe climate found in most of North Korea means that the growing season is quite short. However, investments in fertilizers and mechanization have recently made the country self-sufficient in food.

Most of North Korea's trade is with other socialist countries. Principal exports include machinery, steel, metal ores, textiles, and chemicals. Imports include petroleum, food, rubber, and machinery.

Government. North Korea is nominally ruled by a Supreme People's Assembly that elects a Central Committee to act for it between its short sessions. In actuality the Communist Party dominates political life. Its central political committee determines national policy and its chairman is the key figure in government.

History. *Note: For Korean history prior to the end of the Korean War, see article on South Korea.*

Postwar. Following World War II, a government based on the Soviet pattern was established in North Korea. It was dominated by a newly formed Communist Party, and was greatly influenced by China's new communist government. Kim Il Sung became its leader. Following the Korean War, Kim established a degree of independence from both China and the Soviet Union. He carried a "cult of personality" to extreme lengths in one of the most tightly regimented and closed communist societies.

No peace treaty was ever signed between North and South Korea following the Korean War. Reunification remains one of Kim's central goals, and North Korea has pursued that goal using both diplomacy and violence.

Talks between the two Koreas on normalizing relations have been held periodically.

North Korea has periodically used violence to try to destabilize the South Korean government. Among its acts of aggression were attempts in 1968 and 1974 to assassinate South Korean president Park and a 1983 bombing of South Korean officials in Rangoon, Burma.

Kim Il Sung died in 1994; he was succeeded by his son, Kim Jong Il.

North Korea has admitted producing nuclear weapons and withdrew from the Nuclear Non-Proliferation Treaty in 2003. Negotiations regarding the dismantling of the nuclear weapons program continue.

Korea (South)

Official name: *Republic of Korea*
Area: *38,013 sq. mi., 98,480 sq. km.*
Type of government: *Republic*
Population: *47,963,000*
Capital and largest city: *Seoul (Pop., 9,854,000)*
Language: *Korean, English*
Literacy: *98%;* **Currency:** *Won*
Per capita GDP: *$19,400 (Rank: 28th)*

The land. The eastern part of South Korea is dominated by the Taebaek mountains, and the center of the country by an offshoot called the Sobaek range, which runs from northeast to southwest. The most fertile areas of the country are the lowlands along the west coast between the mountains and the Yellow Sea. The Han, the Kum, and the Naktong are South Korea's most important rivers. The south and west coasts are dotted by numerous small islands. The larger island of Cheju is located about 50 miles off the south coast.

The climate is generally temperate. Summers are hot and humid, and winters are cold and dry. Yearly rainfall averages about 60 inches along the west coast, falling mostly during the summer months.

The people. South Korea has a very ethnically homogenous population. There is, apart from Koreans, only a small minority of Chinese origin. Most South Koreans are either Confucian or Buddhist, but there are also many Christians. Ch'ondogyo, a mixture of Confucian, Taoist, and Buddhist teachings, also has numerous adherents.

South Korea is quite densely populated, with 1121 people per square mile. In 1988 about 65 percent of the population lived in urban areas. Seoul is by far the largest city, but other important cities include the ports of Inchon and Pusan and the interior cities of Taegu and Kwangju.

The economy. South Korea is one of the so-called "little dragons" of Asia. Driven by high levels of exports, the country achieved an astonishing growth rate of about 10 percent per year during the 1960s and 1970s.

The division of the Korean peninsula in 1945 left the South Korean economy in terrible shape. The south had little in the way of natural resources and most of the industrial development to that time had taken place in the north.

Light industry has grown rapidly in South Korea since the 1950s. Textiles, clothing, paper, and electronic equipment are produced. Heavy industry also has increased, including such products as steel, motor vehicles, chemicals, and ships.

Agriculture's importance to the South Korean economy has declined as the importance of industry has increased. Today agriculture and industry each employ about one-quarter of the population. Principal agricultural products include rice, barley, potatoes, and fruits and vegetables. Forestry is important, but many forests have been depleted.

Major exports include transport equipment, textiles, electrical products, and steel. Imports include oil, food, machinery, and raw materials. Japan and the United States are by far South Korea's largest trading partners.

Government. Following revision of the constitution in 1987, South Korea has as head of state a president popularly elected every five years. Legislative power rests with the National Assembly, which has 273 members elected to four-year terms.

History. Korea was settled more than 3,000 years ago, probably by peoples from Manchuria or northern China. They lived by hunting, fishing, and herding, and over many centuries developed a culture unique to the peninsula. The first known state of any significance was the kingdom of Choson, which was founded in the 190s B.C. By 108 B.C. Han Chinese had conquered Choson and established Chinese colonies in Korea, one of which, Lolang, survived until the 300s A.D.

Agriculture and iron smelting appeared in southeastern Korea by the first century A.D., but the area was not politically unified until the 300s, when three native Korean kingdoms had developed—Koguryo in the north, Paekche in the southwest, and Silla in the southeast.

Silla grew in power under the strong leadership of a political and military elite, and in the 600s, with aid from China, it conquered Paekche and Koguryo. Silla ruled a unified peninsula for almost 250 years, a period considered the golden age of Buddhism. The government was efficiently run, society was well organized and peaceful, trade prospered, the arts flourished, and Buddhist culture and learning took firm root. By the 800s, however, Silla began to collapse.

In the period of confusion that followed, some powerful merchant communities developed trade relations with China and Japan.

By the 900s, rebel leaders had revived the Koguryo state, conquered the rest of Korea, and in 918 founded the Koryo dynasty. The Koryo restored order by establishing a centralized, bureaucratic government. The new government did nothing to remedy the inequitable division of land and power that had split Korean society, however.

By the mid-1000s the court was dominated by a succession of powerful families, and by the mid-1100s the whole system was in a state of collapse as a result of factional fights and revolts. By 1258 Korea had fallen to the Mongols and the Koryo kings became Mongol vassals.

A WORKER inspects a silicon wafer in the "clean room" of a factory in South Korea.

Korea suffered greatly under the Mongols, but by the late 1300s it was independent again, under the Yi.

The era of the Yi dynasty is considered the golden age of Confucianism in Korea. Confucian emphasis on learning produced an elite of scholars and was responsible in the 1400s for the development of an alphabet, called *hangul,* for the Korean language. Confucian ethics served to widen the divisions within the traditional social and economic order, and factionalism severely weakened the country.

In the late 1500s Korea was devastated by Japanese invasions. An invasion in 1592 led to the Japanese conquest of most of Korea, but China came to the aid of its vassal state and the Japanese were driven out. A second invasion in 1597 led to further destruction, and Korea never fully recovered. In the 1620s and 1630s, it was overrun by Manchu armies and became totally dependent on China for support and protection.

New Influences. The destruction of the old social and economic orders, and the weakening of traditional values, left Korea open to new influences. Christian missionaries began to visit the country in the 1600s, and by 1800 they had won many converts and had introduced Western learning and ideals into the peninsula.

Also by the 1800s, a new middle class of craftsmen and merchants had replaced the old feudal landlords as the dominant and most prosperous group in society. Trade with Japan thrived, and the appearance of trading ships from Western nations in the 1800s promised even greater prosperity.

The Korean government tried unsuccessfully to maintain traditional society by repressing Western learning and banning foreign trade. Moreover, by the mid-1800s China had lost much of its power and was unable to serve as Korea's protector or as its agent in foreign affairs.

Foreign rivalries. Japan and China vied for political, commercial, and diplomatic control of Korea. To back its position, China invited the United States, Britain, Germany, Italy, France, and Russia to enter into trade and diplomatic relations with Korea, and in the 1800s Korea

KOREAN FISHERMEN dry lines of squid for the market.

A CHEERFUL GATHERING of children in South Korea.

became a diplomatic battleground for the world's great powers. The Korean government was sharply divided into rival factions and became extremely unstable.

An antiforeign and nationalistic religious uprising in 1894 opened the door for Japanese troops to move into Korea to protect Japanese interests. This precipitated the Sino-Japanese War that ended in 1895 in victory for Japan, forcing China to relinquish all claims to Korea.

Russia, with interests and influence in Korea second only to those of China, challenged Japanese dominance over Korean affairs. Russo-Japanese rivalry led to war between the two in 1904. The treaty ending the war in 1905 recognized Japan's dominant position in Korea, and in 1910 Japan annexed Korea, making it a colony.

THE SUMMER OLYMPICS of 1988 were held in Seoul, South Korea.

Japanese rule. Korea was ruled despotically, and Japan was concerned only with economic exploitation of the land and the people. The Japanese developed the country's industries and resources by using forced labor, gave the best land and jobs to Japanese, and tried to impose their culture on Koreans.

Japan's rule was bitterly resented, and an independence movement soon developed. Although it was able to do little against the Japanese, its leaders aligned themselves during World War II with the Allies, who were fighting Japan—China, Britain, the United States, and, at war's end, the Soviet Union.

Divided land. In 1945 Soviet and U.S. troops liberated the peninsula from the Japanese. To facilitate acceptance of the Japanese surrender and to prepare the country for independence, the two agreed to divide their authority in Korea at the 38th parallel. U.S. and Soviet representatives could not agree on the formation of a provisional government for a reunited country, or on the withdrawal of their troops. In the south, a constituent assembly was elected and a constitution adopted. Syngman Rhee, a leader of the independence movement, was elected to the presidency.

In 1949 Soviet and U.S. forces withdrew and the 38th parallel became the boundary between rival Korean states. The division of the country added to the difficulties it faced in recovering from years of war and colonial rule, and Korea became a focus of the worldwide confrontation between the United States and the Soviet Union.

In June, 1950, the North Koreans tried to unify Korea by conquering the South, and they certainly would have succeeded but for United Nations-sponsored U.S. intervention. General Douglas MacArthur came near to unifying Korea by conquering North Korea, but he was driven back by Chinese intervention. A truce negotiation in 1953 left the frontier between the two Koreas not far from the prewar one.

In the postwar years President Syngman Rhee became increasingly dictatorial. He was overthrown in 1960 in a revolt started by student demonstrators. An ineffective civilian government that was overthrown by the army in 1961 ensued.

The government became dominated by General Park Chung Hee. Although he allowed the restoration of some democratic systems, the power of the presidency, which Park assumed, was strengthened, and little dissent was permitted. He was elected president five times before being assassinated in 1979. Park's tenure emphasized the reform and modernization of the South Korean economy. As a result, South Korea has one of the strongest economies in Asia.

In 1980 the army, led by Chun Doo Hwan, again imposed martial law, sometimes brutally. The reaction by the military to a protest in Kwangju left 170 people dead and put a stain on the government that it has not yet overcome. Martial law ended in 1981, and South Korea returned to a strong indirectly elected presidential system of government.

In 1983 South Korea was rocked by two tragedies. In September the Soviet Union shot down a Korean passenger plane, killing 269 people. In October a bomb blast in Burma killed 17 South Korean officials, including four cabinet ministers and two principal advisers to Chun.

Popular antigovernment demonstrations in 1987 forced Chun's resignation. His successor, Roh Tae Woo, supported a referendum on a new constitution that provided for direct election of the president. The constitution was approved and Roh was elected over his opponents. The 1988 Summer Olympics were held in Seoul.

In 1992 Kim Young Sam, a former dissident, was elected president. Kim Dae-jung was elected president in 1998.

Talks between North and South Korea on reunification began in 1990. Kim Dae-jung won the 2000 Nobel Prize for his work toward reconciliation with North Korea. Talks have since stalled.

Kyrgyzstan

Official name: *Kyrgyz Republic*
Area: *76,621 sq. mi.,*
198,500 sq. km.
Type of government: *Republic*
Population: *4,822,000*
Capital and largest city: *Bishkek*
(formerly Frunze)
(Pop., 754,000)
Languages: *Kirghiz, Russian*
Literacy: *97%;* **Currency:** *Som*
Per capita GDP: *$2,800*
(Rank: 119th)

The land. Kyrgyzstan (formerly called Kirghizia), in the northeastern part of Central Asia, lies within the vast Tien Shan mountain complex. Its peaks reach as high as 24,406 feet (7,439 meters) on its eastern border. In the south lies the Pamir mountain system. There are many valleys and plateaus at elevations of 6,000 to 9,000 feet (1,800 to 2,750 meters). The few lowlands exist mainly in the valleys of the Chu and Fergana rivers in the southwest part of the country. In the northeast, a great basin contains Lake Issyk-Kul, also called the Kyrgyz Sea. A natural wonder with 300 miles (480 kilometers) of coastline, the lake's intensely blue waters are warmed by volcanic action. Temperatures remain moderate along the lake shore in spite of surrounding mountains.

Kyrgyzstan's largest river is the Narin, flowing into the Fergana valley, and on its banks is a series of new hydroelectric power stations. Climate is influenced by Kyrgyzstan's great altitudes and permanently snow-covered mountains, by its great distance from the oceans, and by an abrupt change in elevation from the neighboring Central Asian deserts and plains to the north, west, and southeast. Summer temperatures in the lowlands reach as high as 109°F (43°C), but average about 82°F (28°C). January temperatures average -0.5°F (-18°C). Rainfall in the valleys ranges from 4 to 20 inches a year, with 30 to 40 inches falling in the Fergana and Kyrgyz mountains.

The people. The Kyrgyz, once known as the Kara-Kyrgyz, are an ancient Turkic people with strong tribal traditions and a long history as one of Central Asia's great nomadic, pastoral groups. A noticeable Mongol strain was acquired after Genghis Khan and the Mongol hordes invaded the region in the 13th century.

The raising of sheep, horses, and cattle remains the most important Kyrgyz occupation. However, many social changes have resulted from the forced settling of nomadic peoples by the Soviet regime, and from the merging of small, individual farms into state-run collectives.

Kyrgyz cultural life is enriched by its oral tradition of folk tales and poetry, handed down from generation to generation by storytellers and bards.

Today the Kyrgyz form roughly half of the population, which also includes Russians, Uzbeks, Ukrainians, Germans, and Tatars. Most Kyrgyz are Muslim.
Economy. The old tradition of livestock breeding continues to thrive in Kyrgyzstan, with sheep and goats predominating over cattle and pigs. Yaks are raised for their meat and as dairy cattle, grazing mainly in high-altitude pastures unsuitable for other animals. The small, strong Kyrgyzian horses are bred as draft animals and for their meat.

Important crops are cotton, sugar beets, tobacco, opium poppies, and grains, together with fruit, grapes and vegetables. Other important branches of agriculture are the raising of silkworms and beekeeping. Agriculture is now largely mechanized in Kyrgyzstan, and the republic manufactures the specialized machinery needed for the rugged mountain terrain. Irrigation projects have greatly increased agricultural output, especially of cotton.

Natural resources include coal, with large reserves in the Karakichi region of the inner Tien Shan mountain complex, as well as mercury, antimony, zinc, tungsten, and uranium. More than half of Kyrgyzstan's electrical power is generated by hydroelectric stations. Industry centers on the mining and processing of raw materials, together with the manufacture of machinery and instruments.

Food processing is of considerable importance, with sugar refineries producing 415,000 metric tons in 1989. Economic reforms are under way, but the raising of prices and lowering of wages are causing great hardship.
Government. Kyrgyzstan is a republic whose latest constitution expands presidential powers. The president is elected by popular vote to a 5-year term. A prime minister and cabinet are appointed by the president. Members of the bicameral legislature are elected by popular vote to 4-year terms.

Independence from the Soviet Union was formally declared on August 31, 1991. Kyrgyzstan is a member of the Commonwealth of Independent States.
History. The nomadic Kyrgyz lived originally around the Upper Yenisey River near Mongolia, and later settled in the Tien Shan region of what is now Kyrgyzstan. The area successively came under the control of the Mongols, the Kalmyks, and Manchus, and in the 17th century the Kyrgyz became Chinese subjects. In the 19th century, they were ruled by the khanate (state) of Kokand.

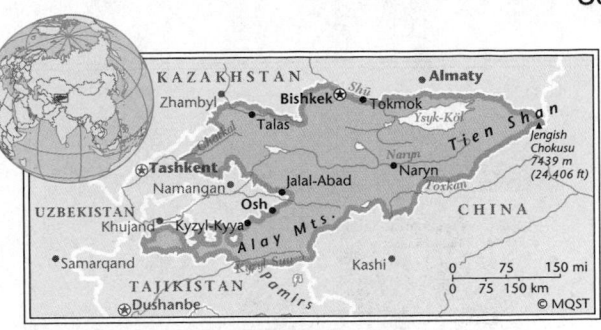

Between 1855 and 1876 the khanate was taken over by Russia and made part of the Russian empire. Still clinging to their nomadic way of life, the Kyrgyz opposed compulsory enlistment in the czarist army in 1916. They fought against Bolshevik control between 1917 and 1922, enduring a period of great violence and famine. In 1924 the region became the Kara-Kyrgyz Autonomous Province, and in 1936 was declared a Soviet Socialist Republic.

As in neighboring Kazakhstan, the 1920s and 1930s were characterized by land reform, collectivization of farms, and efforts to settle the nomadic peoples. Although Kyrgyz nationalists vigorously resisted the changes imposed by the Soviets, they were repressed and forced to submit to a government manned almost entirely by ethnic Russians. Since the establishment of nongovernment opposition parties in the 1980s, conflicts over land and housing, particularly around Osh, have led to violence between Kyrgyz and Uzbeks. These confrontations contributed to the election in October 1991 of the reform candidate Askar Akaev. He won reelection in 2000, and a 2003 referendum expanded his powers.

Kyrgyzstan became an independent country upon the dissolution of the Soviet Union in 1991.

(For more information on the history of Kyrgyzstan during the Soviet period, see the article on Russia in the EUROPE AND RUSSIA volume.)

labor
US

labour
Brit.

meters
US

metres
Brit.

centers
US

centres
Brit.

Laos

Official name: *Lao People's*
Democratic Republic
Area: *91,405 sq. mi.,*
236,800 sq. km.
Type of government: *Communist*
Population: *5,778,000*
Capital and largest city: *Vientiane*
(Pop., 331,000)
Languages: *Lao (official), French*
Literacy: *57%;* **Currency:** *Kip*
Per capita GDP: *$1,630*
(Rank: 147th)

The land. Laos is a long, narrow country, broader in the north, with a southern panhandle that narrows at one point to little more than 50 miles in width. In the northern region sandstone and limestone plateaus are deeply etched by the

labor
US

labour
Brit.

centered
US

centred
Brit.

manganese, gold, coal, and copper, but these have not been explored. Tin, gypsum, salt, and limestone are mined in small amounts.

Almost all of the country is forested with potentially valuable timber, and the soil is very rich, especially in the valleys of the Mekong River and its tributaries.

Subsistence agriculture dominates the economy. The major crop is rice, but yields are very low. Vegetables, spices, and some fruits, including bananas, mangoes, and pineapples, are grown throughout the country. Cotton is widely raised, and there is some commercial tobacco farming around Vientiane.

Many upland tribes still follow the "slash and burn" form of farming. These farmers clear the forest by cutting down the smaller trees and burning the refuse. In the fields thus cleared, they plant a variety of crops for a few seasons and then abandon the field to the forest to start over again at another clearing. When all the land within a certain radius of the village has been exploited, the people migrate to a new area.

Foreign trade is of little importance in the economy, and the balance of trade is very poor. The main exports are hydroelectric power, tin, coffee, soybeans, leather, and forest products such as wood, cardamom, benzoin, and lac. Petroleum, machinery, manufactured goods, and foodstuffs are principal imports.

Government.   Laos is a republic with a president as titular head of state. The basic power rests with the prime minister, who is also the secretary-general of the Lao People's Democratic Party (the only political party).

History.   The aboriginal Kha people of Laos were joined in the mid-1200s by the Lao, one tribe of the Thai people who fled the Mongol invasion of south-central China and settled the northern edge of the Indochinese peninsula. They established many small kingdoms that were in almost constant competition for control of the entire region.

Lan Xang.   In the mid-1300s, Fa-Ngum, ruler of a kingdom centered in Muang Swa, on the upper Mekong River, conquered most of the kingdoms of Laos and northern Siam (Thailand) and united them in the empire of Lan Xang, the "Land of a Million Elephants." The

culture and religion of India, transmitted through tribes south of Laos, heavily influenced Lao culture. Fa-Ngum adopted Buddhism and made his capital a center of Buddhist culture.

His son, Sam Sene T'ai, consolidated the kingdom and established an efficient administration. By the late 1300s Lan Xang was a powerful, peaceful kingdom that had grown prosperous as a producer of forest products and as a center of trade in Southeast Asia.

During the 1500s attacks by powerful neighbors of Laos—Annam to its east, and Siam (present Thailand) and Burma to its west—weakened Lan Xang and lowered its prestige. During this period the Lao capital was moved south, to Vientiane, and Muang Swa was made a temple city and renamed Luang Prabang.

Civil strife.   In the late 1500s Laos was torn by violent dynastic struggles that left it poverty-stricken and defenseless against tribal rebellions and attacks by its neighbors. By the early 1700s, this civil strife had split Laos into three rival states, one ruled from Luang Prabang, one from Vientiane, and the third from Champassak in southern Laos.

No state could regain the former power, prosperity, and prestige that the unified kingdom had enjoyed, and each sought the aid of Siam, Annam, and Burma in conquering the others. As a result, Laos continued to be torn by conflict throughout the 1700s. By the early 1800s Siam had conquered the kingdoms and had annexed Laos.

During the 1800s European explorers, traders, and missionaries began to visit Laos. Although Laos itself, with few riches and no access to the sea, held little attraction for the Europeans, competition was keen among the European states for control of all the territory in Southeast Asia.

French control.   By the late 1800s only Siam, which included Laos, separated British Burma from French Cambodia. The British wanted Siam to remain independent, and the French wanted to gain control of Siam. In 1893, in an effort to hold off French conquest, Siam ceded to France all its territory east of the Mekong, which included most of Laos. In 1904 most of the remainder of present-day Laos became French.

The French imposed peace on the warlike Lao tribes and kingdoms, and they allowed Lao leaders to participate in the government. They modernized the government, abolished slavery, and brought education and medical care to the Lao. The French also attempted to develop the country's natural resources and improve its economy, but the world economic Depression of the 1930s hindered any real economic progress.

Japan occupied all of Indochina during World War II, and during the Japanese occupation Lao nationalism began to grow. A "Free Laos" government was organized and it took over when the Japanese withdrew. After the war, the French made an unsuccessful attempt to reestablish their control. In 1947 the Lao

Mekong River and its tributaries. The long, almost impassable range of mountains called the Annam Cordillera forms nearly the entire eastern border of Laos. The western border is formed primarily by the Mekong River; its fertile valley supports most of the population.

Laos has a tropical climate, with high humidity and temperatures averaging between 80°F and 90°F.

The people.   Laos is an ethnically diverse country. The Lao and the Tai are related to the Thai people of Thailand, and they speak related languages. The Meo and Man in northern Laos are related to peoples in southern China. The Kha are most closely related to the Mon-Khmer peoples of Cambodia. Buddhism is the principal organized religion in Laos, but animist beliefs and practices are widespread.

Laos is sparsely populated and 85 percent of the population live in rural areas. There is no large metropolis. Vientiane, the administrative capital, is the largest city. Luang Prabang, the royal capital, ranks second, with a much smaller population.

Economy.   Laos is a poor country with an undeveloped economy and an unskilled, largely illiterate labor force. It is thought to have deposits of iron ore,

SUBSISTENCE AGRICULTURE is the mainstay of the Laotian economy, and many upland farmers still clear the forest for planting by the "slash and burn" method.

adopted a constitution establishing a monarchy and a parliament. In 1949 Laos became an independent state within the French Union.

Opposition to the French was quite violent elsewhere in Indochina. In Vietnam open war, supported by communist forces, was raging against the French, and in 1953 the communist-dominated Vietminh forces of Vietnam invaded Laos. In 1954 the French gave up the struggle in Vietnam.

Independence. A peace conference held at Geneva later in 1954 officially ended the war and recognized Laos as a sovereign state.

Political and economic chaos reigned in Laos after 1954, as the governments that came to power were too unstable to deal with the many factions within Laos or to repair the social and economic damage of years of warfare. In addition, communists from Vietnam organized a rebel army, the Lao People's Liberation Army, originally called the Pathet Lao.

Numerous conflicts between the Pathet Lao and neutralist royal forces resulted in almost constant civil war after 1960. The situation was aggravated by the war in neighboring Vietnam, as the Vietminh established invasion bases in Laos.

The United States and South Vietnam frequently bombed Vietminh bases in Laos before the Vietnam War ended in 1973. At that time a coalition communist-Royalist government was formed in Laos. In August 1975 the Vietminh-backed Pathet Lao took control of Laos. The king was forced to abdicate and a Communist government, strongly influenced by Vietnam, was instituted.

With the dissolution of the Soviet Union in 1991, Laos loosened its ties with Russia but strengthened its ties with China and Vietnam. It became more lenient toward capitalist ventures and joined ASEAN in 1997.

Malaysia

Official name: *Malaysia*
Area: *127,284 sq. mi.,*
329,750 sq. km.
Type of government:
Constitutional monarchy
Population: *22,662,000*
Capital and largest city:
Kuala Lumpur
(Pop., 1,379,000)
Languages: *Malay, Chinese*
dialects, English, Tamil
Literacy: *84%;* **Currency:** *Ringgit*
Per capita GDP: *$9,000*
(Rank: 54th)

The land. Malaysia includes West Malaysia (the former British colony of Malaya) on the southern end of the Malay peninsula, and East Malaysia, consisting of the states of Sarawak (on northwest Borneo) and Sabah (north Borneo).

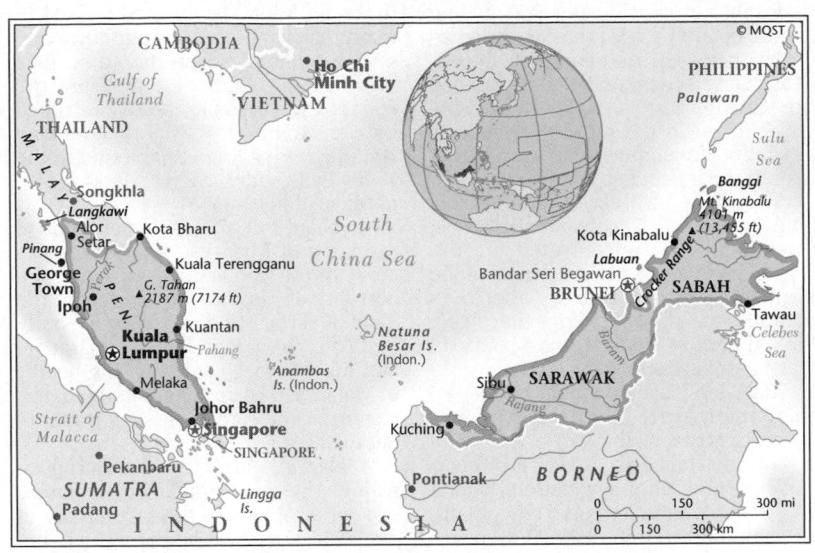

West Malaysia consists of a narrow central core of low, jungle-covered mountains rising up from swampy mineral-rich coastal plains. East Malaysia has a mountainous interior and a narrow border of swampy coastal plains. Small islands lie off the coasts of both West and East Malaysia. Of the many rivers that thread Malaysia, the most important are the Pahang, in West Malaysia, and the Rajang, in East Malaysia.

The Malaysian climate is equatorial. The year-round temperature averages 80°F, and an annual average of 100 inches of rain falls on the country as a whole.

The people. The Malaysian population is quite varied. Just under half of the people are Muslim Malays who speak Malay. Slightly more than one-third are Chinese. The Chinese are primarily urban; the Malays are predominantly rural. Indians and Pakistanis make up about 10 percent of the population; the remainder consists of a variety of native islanders, mostly in East Malaysia.

Population is concentrated in the coastal regions. It is densest in the western half of West Malaysia, where the country's largest cities are located—Kuala Lumpur, the Federation's capital; Ipoh (population, 383,000); and George Town (220,000), a port city on Penang Island in the Malacca Strait.

Malaysia's population has urbanized considerably since World War II. Today, 35 percent of the population live in urban areas, with many people living in urban centers that exist as planned agricultural settlements.

Economy. Malaysia has a prosperous and growing economy, largely because of its wealth of natural resources, especially rubber and tin. Malaysia is the world's leading producer of natural rubber, with an output of over 1.5 million metric tons in 1984. Most of the rubber comes from West Malaysia.

Malaysia's abundance of high-grade tin ore, concentrated on the west coast of the Malay peninsula, has made it the world's largest producer of tin, mining 41,000 metric tons in 1984. Forests cover more than 75 percent of Malaysian territory and are one of the most valuable resources, supplying timber, palm oil, hemp, and coconut products. Bauxite, iron ore, and petroleum also are found in Malaysia.

MALAYSIA
is the world's leading producer of natural rubber. The processing of rubber, seen here, and tin are the country's two major industries.

center
US

centre
Brit.

realized
US

realised
Brit.

labor
US

labour
Brit.

Rubber processing and tin smelting are the country's major industries. In an effort to lessen its economic dependence on two commodities—rubber and tin—that fluctuate sharply in value, the government in the mid-1960s encouraged the development of diversified manufacturing industries.

Very little of Malaysia's cultivable land is devoted to subsistence crops. Rice paddies, concentrated in the coastal lowlands, account for most of the farmland, and the country's farmers raise less than half of the rice they need. Fish, the other staple of the Malaysian diet, are abundant off the coasts.

Malaysia has a favorable balance of trade, with West Malaysia making a much larger contribution to the country's trade than East Malaysia. Important exports include petroleum and natural gas, electric and electronic equipment, rubber, and tin. Imports include transport equipment, machinery, and food products. Malaysia's major trading partners are Japan, Singapore, and the United States.

Government. Malaysia is a constitutional monarchy. The paramount ruler, or king, is elected to a five-year term by the nine hereditary rulers of the states of West Malaysia from among themselves. He serves as chief of state and as Muslim religious leader. Actual executive power is wielded by the prime minister and cabinet, who are responsible to a parliament.

The 69-member Senate, the upper house of parliament, is partly elected by the state legislatures and partly appointed by the king. The more powerful 193-member House of Representatives is popularly elected. Parliament shares legislative power with the state legislatures.

History. The territory of present-day Malaysia was inhabited in ancient

RICE PADDIES such as these are concentrated in the coastal lowlands of Malaysia and account for most of the farmland.

times by Malay peoples who lived in many small coastal kingdoms and whose economies were based on fishing, farming, and trading. From the 800s to the 1200s they were controlled by the far more powerful Sumatran Buddhist Srivijayan empire, and in the 1300s by the Javanese Hindu kingdom of Majapahit.

In about 1400 a Malay ruler founded the state of Malacca, on the western coast of the peninsula. Its capital, the port city of Malacca, soon became the most important trading center in Southeast Asia. During the 1400s Arab traders and missionaries converted the people of Malacca to Islam. The state became a center for the spread of Islam throughout the area.

Malacca's port interested European nations that were establishing colonies in southern Asia in the late 1400s. In 1511 Malacca fell to the Portuguese, but in 1641 the Portuguese were ousted by the Dutch. The Europeans did not develop the territory or attempt to bring all of Malaya under their authority. Malacca gradually declined in importance except as a port on the sea route between Asia and Europe.

British role. In 1795 Britain took Malacca from the Dutch. In 1826 it was consolidated with the British settlements at Penang, at the northern end of the Strait of Malacca, and with Singapore, at the southern end of the peninsula, to form the Colony of the Straits Settlements.

In the mid-1800s an English adventurer, James Brooke, gained control of Sarawak in northwest Borneo. In 1881 a British chartered company took over what is now Sabah in north Borneo. Thus an arc of British influence developed across the northern edge of the island world at the same time that

Dutch influence was slowly growing in what is now Indonesia. The Dutch and the British formally apportioned the area by treaties in 1824 and 1891.

After the opening of the Suez Canal in 1869, Southeast Asian trade became more profitable and important, and competition increased among European states for territory in the region. Also in the late 1800s, the wealth of Malaya's tin mines was realized and it attracted the interest of the British.

By 1914 Britain had concluded treaties making protectorates of the sultanates on the Malay peninsula. Once the British presence guaranteed their security, Chinese miners came in large numbers to Malaya. These workers formed the nucleus of the state's large Chinese minority.

Malaya soon was the world's leading producer and exporter of tin. In the early 1900s the British also developed rubber plantations on the peninsula. The rubber industry was manned largely by Indian labor, and the Malay states soon ranked as the world's leading producers of rubber.

By the 1920s, with a well-ordered government under British administration and a prosperous economy run by Chinese and Indian labor, Malaya was economically, politically, and socially unique in Southeast Asia. The great alien immigration that had left the native Malays and their sultans a bare majority in their own land inhibited the development of any nationalist movements.

Malayan nationalism grew during World War II, when the country was occupied by Japanese forces. Under Japanese direction, the Malayans were largely self-governing, and a desire for full independence followed liberation from the Japanese.

In 1948, after two years of an unsatisfactory trial union, the protected Malay states were united to form the Federation of Malaya. In June 1948, guerrilla fighting broke out, instigated by Chinese Communists with the support of part of the Malayan Chinese population. Rivalries and conflicts between the Chinese and the Malays within Malaya helped to keep the war going. With the aid of British troops, the federation government gradually defeated the guerrillas.

Independence. In 1957 Malaya became fully independent under a constitution that attempted to balance carefully the power of the Chinese and the Malay portions of the population.

In 1961 the self-governing British colony of Singapore proposed union with Malaya as a step to ensure its economic position. Malaya agreed on the condition that the British colonies on Borneo, with their Malay population, be admitted to the union to balance Singapore's Chinese population.

In 1963 the union took place, creating the Federation of Malaysia, with Tunku Abdul Rahman as leader of the new state. The inclusion of the Borneo states

aroused the opposition of two neighboring states, Indonesia and the Philippines.

The Philippines suspended diplomatic relations, and Indonesia began a "Crush Malaysia" campaign. The campaign led to open fighting between 1964 and 1966, when the fall from power of Indonesia's President Sukarno ended Indonesia's opposition to the federation.

Meanwhile, tensions mounted between Malaysia, with the majority of its population being Malays, and Singapore, ruled by its Chinese majority. In 1965 Singapore seceded.

Perhaps Malaysia's most persistent problem since independence has been the uneasy relationship among its three main ethnic groups. In 1969 riots broke out against Chinese Malaysians because of their disproportionate control of wealth. As a result, the constitution was suspended until 1971, and legislation was passed that assured ethnic Malays preferential treatment in education and employment. In the 1980s the government used the security laws enacted at that time to restrict political opposition.

In 2003 after 22 years in office, Mohamad Mahatir retired as prime minister. His tenure was marked by great economic growth as well as authoritarianism.

Maldives

Official name: *Republic of Maldives*
Area: *116 sq. mi., 300 sq. km.*
Type of government: *Republic*
Population: *320,000*
Capital and largest city: *Male*
(Pop., 74,000)
Languages: *Divehi, English*
Literacy: *93%;* **Currency:** *Rufiyaa*
Per capita GDP: *$3,870*
(Rank: 100th)

The land and people. The country is formed of some 2,000 islands in the Indian Ocean grouped into 12 atolls, or island groups. Most of the islands are small and low-lying, and only about 220 are inhabited.

The Maldivians are an amalgam of people from Sri Lanka, India, Southeast Asia, the Middle East, and Africa. They speak a language similar to Elu, or old Sinhalese, the language of ancient Sir Lanka. Almost all the people are Muslim. Population is densest near the center of the island group, on Male Atoll, which is the site of the capital and largest city, Male.

The overall population density on the crowded islands is 1,753 people per square mile, although most islands have fewer than 1,000 inhabitants.

Economy. Maldives, for such a tiny country, has a relatively diverse economy. Fishing is an important industry, employing about 45 percent of the population and supporting a canning and drying industry. The country also

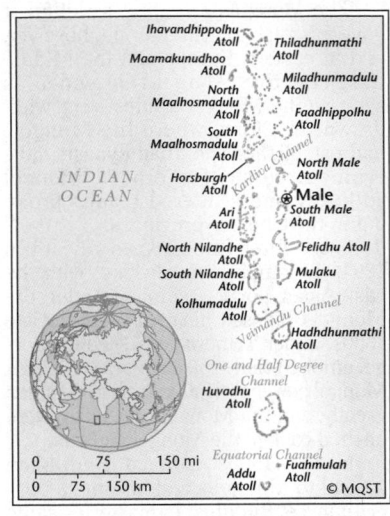

supports some garment manufacture. Tourism accounts for about one-fifth of economic activity. Maldives is known particularly for its desert-island atmosphere.

Maldives exports textiles and fish products. Imports include manufactured goods and food products. Major trading partners are Sri Lanka, Singapore, and the United States.

Government. The president is nominated by the legislature and confirmed by national referendum. The legislature has 50 members; 42 popularly elected and 8 appointed by the president.

History. The Maldive islands have been inhabited by people of the Indian Ocean region for many centuries. These people had strong ties with the island of Sri Lanka and were long required to pay tribute to the kings of Kandy in Sri Lanka. During the 1500s the islands were under the nominal control of Portugal, and during the 1600s they were under Dutch rule.

Great Britain made Sri Lanka a crown colony in 1789 and assumed indirect authority over the Maldive islands. In 1887 the islands became a British protectorate. During World War II, Britain built an important air base on Gan Island.

The 1950s were years of great unrest for the islands. In 1953 the national assembly abolished the sultanate and proclaimed a republic, but in 1954 an insurrection resulted in the restoration of the sultanate. British attempts to reactivate its air base on Gan led to clashes between those opposing and those favoring the British presence on the islands. Moreover, the government was unable to deal with the islands' severe food shortage.

Discontent in 1958 led to an insurrection in Suvadiva, south of Male. A rebel leader declared Suvadiva a republic and requested aid from Britain. Britain granted the aid, arousing strong anti-British feeling in Male. In 1959 the Suvadiva rebellion ended and the British were allowed to reopen their air base. During the early 1960s the Maldivian government and Great Britain negotiated the islands' future, and in 1965 a

treaty between Great Britain and the Maldive islands granted full sovereignty to the country. Britain was allowed to retain control of the Gan Island base, although they abandoned it in 1976, and agreed to provide aid to the new nation. In a referendum held in 1968, the Maldive islands voted to become a republic. Ibrahim Nasir, the former prime minister, became the Maldives' first president.

Maumoon Abdul Gayoom was elected president in 1978 and was reelected for a sixth term in 2003. In 1980 a coup using mercenaries was attempted and the subsequent investigation implicated former president Nasir.

Mongolia

Official name: *Mongolia*
Area: *604,090 sq. mi., 1,565,000 sq. km.*
Type of government: *Republic*
Population: *2,674,000*
Capital and largest city: *Ulaanbaatar (Pop., 760,000)*
Languages: *Khalkha Mongol, Turkic*
Literacy: *98%*
Currency: *Tughrik*
Per capita GDP: *$1,770 (Rank: 141st)*

The land. Much of Mongolia occupies the grassy, rolling Mongolian Plain, which ranges in elevation from 3,000 to 6,000 feet. Mountains in the north and west rise to between 5,000 and 11,000 feet. Along the southwestern border, the Altai range towers over 12,000 feet. In the south and southeast, the Mongolian Plain becomes the barren desert of the Gobi Depression, which extends into Inner Mongolia.

All of Mongolia's principal rivers flow northward, toward the Soviet Union. They include the Selenge and the Orkhon, which empty into Lake Baykal, and the Kerulen, an important tributary of the Amur River.

Mongolia's climate is generally dry and is characterized by long, cold winters and short, cool summers. Precipitation increases from south to north, ranging from less than 5 inches to 15 inches a year.

The people. The population is almost entirely Mongol, divided into a number of groups, of which the Khalkha is by far the largest. There are minorities of other Mongols, and some Russians and Chinese. Lamaist Buddhism is the dominant religion, but its practice has been restricted since the 1930s.

Over half the population is rural, and some is seminomadic. Population is concentrated in the northern half of the country. About 25 percent of the people live in Ulaanbaatar, the capital, in east central Mongolia.

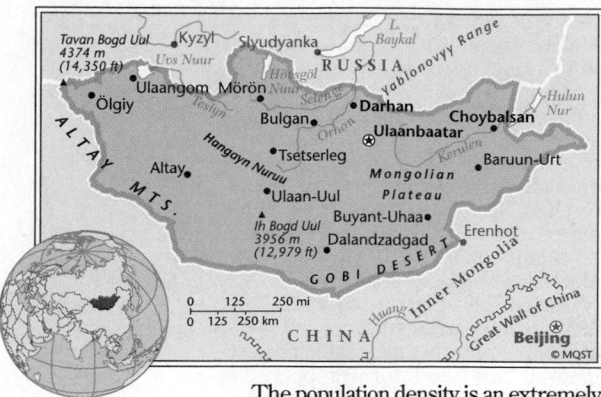

The population density is an extremely sparse three persons per square mile.

Economy. Livestock herding, the Mongol's traditional way of life, remains the mainstay of the country's economy. The country's huge herds of sheep, goats, cattle, horses, and camels provide most necessities, including food, clothing, shelter, and transport, as well as goods for export. The main crops are grain, potatoes, and some vegetables. Agriculture is collectivized on the Soviet model.

Mongolia's resources include coal, copper, gold, iron, molybdenum, and petroleum. The country's considerable hydroelectric capacity is being developed. Industrialization has been recent and relatively rapid. Manufactures include building materials, textiles, and processed foodstuffs.

Mongolia exports farm and animal products and some metal ores. Consumer goods, raw materials, and machinery are imported. Mongolian trade is primarily with communist countries. Mongolia receives large amounts of aid from the Soviet Union.

Government. Power is vested in a popularly elected assembly, the Khural. Until 1990, however, political power actually rested with the country's Communist Party, the Mongolian People's Revolutionary Party (MPRP). The party proposed all candidates for the Khural, and its political bureau set national policy.

In 1992 a new constitution was adopted; it established a 76-member parliament. In free and fair multiparty elections the MPRP was victorious, gaining a 70-seat majority.

History. The early Mongols were divided into many rival nomadic tribes. They lived by herding and raiding neighboring tribes and states. By the beginning of the 1200s, the Mongols held the territory all around the Gobi.

Expansion. The first leader to unite the Mongol tribes was Genghis Khan, the "very mighty king," in 1203. He led the Mongols in the conquest of northern China, eastern Russia, and the Islamic lands of the Near East.

After Genghis Khan's death in 1227, his son, Ogotai, led the Mongols across Hungary and Poland and as far west as Vienna. Ogotai's death in 1241 forced the Mongols to retreat to elect a new khan. Kublai Khan, their choice, conquered all of China and Korea and controlled much of Southeast Asia.

The Mongols proved less skillful at governing than at conquering, however, and in eastern Europe and the Middle East effective Mongol rule ended as soon as the Mongol armies were withdrawn. In China, where the Mongols had established the Yüan dynasty, government corruption eroded Mongol authority and scattered revolts broke out in the Chinese provinces.

Decline. After Kublai Khan's death in 1294, the empire was divided, with the east Asian portion coming under the Mongol-Chinese Chin dynasty. In the late 1300s, under Tamerlane, a second Mongol empire briefly ruled western Asia. But Mongol power and influence had declined greatly, and the Mongols gradually were pushed back to the Mongolian Plain.

In the 1500s Lamaist Buddhism spread to Mongolia and became a powerful force. Buddhist monasteries came to hold much of the land, and a large proportion of the male population became monks.

In the 1600s Inner Mongolia came under the control of the Manchus, who conquered China in 1644 and established the Ch'ing dynasty. Despite Mongol resistance, the Manchus had conquered almost all of Outer Mongolia by the 1680s, and Mongolia became a province of China. In the early 1700s, Russia began to exert a strong influence on northwestern Mongolia.

Apart from its contacts with China and Russia, during the 1700s and 1800s Mongolia remained isolated from the outside world. Mongolians came to resent their Chinese administrators, who governed the region as though it were a colony, and Chinese settlers, who appropriated grazing land for farm use.

Autonomy. Manchu power had declined by the early 1900s, and Japan and Russia agreed to share influence in Mongolia, with Japan controlling eastern Inner Mongolia and Russia dominating Outer Mongolia. In 1911 a revolution in China overthrew the Manchu dynasty, and the people of Outer Mongolia, with Russian support, toppled the Chinese provincial government and proclaimed the autonomy of Outer Mongolia. The Mongolians chose a lama, the *hutukhtu,* or "living Buddha," as nominal ruler.

People's republic. During the 1920s and 1930s, the government promoted radical and rapid economic and social change. The economic power of the Chinese in Mongolia was destroyed, and the power of the Buddhist lamas was crushed. All opposition to government programs was suppressed.

Inner Mongolia had remained a Chinese province, and in the 1930s it was occupied by Japanese forces. Japanese occupation posed a threat to the Mongolian People's Republic, and in 1939 Soviet and Mongol troops drove the Japanese from the border area.

The Mongolian People's Republic participated briefly in World War II. In 1945, as part of the war settlement, the people of Outer Mongolia confirmed in a referendum their desire to be independent of China; in 1946 China, under Chiang Kai-shek, recognized Outer Mongolia's independence. In 1950, after a communist government had been established in China, the Chinese communists and the Soviets agreed to guarantee the independence of the Mongolian People's Republic.

In the late 1950s Mongolia began to expand its contacts with the West, and in 1961 Mongolia became a member of the United Nations. In the early 1960s, when a split developed between Communist China and the Soviet Union, Mongolia sided with the Soviets. In 1990, as the Soviet Union was dissolving, Mongolia's Communist Party completely replaced its top leadership with members dedicated to political and economic reform and renounced its monopoly on political power. The parliament amended the constitution to allow for multiparty elections, in which the former communists won a majority. With the exception of the 1996 election, the communists have continued to control the government.

Myanmar (Burma)

Official name: *Union of Myanmar*
Area: *261,901 sq. mi.,*
    678,500 sq. km.
Type of government: *Military*
Population: *42,282,000*
Capital and largest city: *Yangon*
    (Pop., 2,513,000)
Language: *Burmese*
Literacy: *83%;* **Currency:** *Kyat*
Per capita GDP: *$1,500*
    (Rank: 152nd)

The land. Myanmar, formerly called Burma, is a diamond-shaped country with a long extension stretching southward into the Malay peninsula. The Tenasserim coast, in the south, and the Arakan coast, to the north, are rocky and steep. The central coast is shallow and filled with sandbars.

Along the coast the densely forested Arakan mountain range rises more than 10,000 feet and extends into a region of hills in the country's northwest corner. Central Myanmar is a low basin through which flows the Chindwin and Irrawaddy rivers and, east of a low range of hills, the Sittang River. In the east is the hilly Shan Plateau, about 3,000 feet in elevation, threaded by the Salween River and its tributaries.

The Irrawaddy River dominates Myanmar's terrain. It rises in the far north and flows southward for approximately 1,400 miles before entering the Gulf of Martaban at the head of the Andaman Sea. It is navigable for about 875 miles inland, and it leaves a deposit of rich soil in its valley and delta. The delta is 150 miles wide and extends about 180 miles inland from the sea.

Myanmar has a tropical climate. Average winter temperatures range

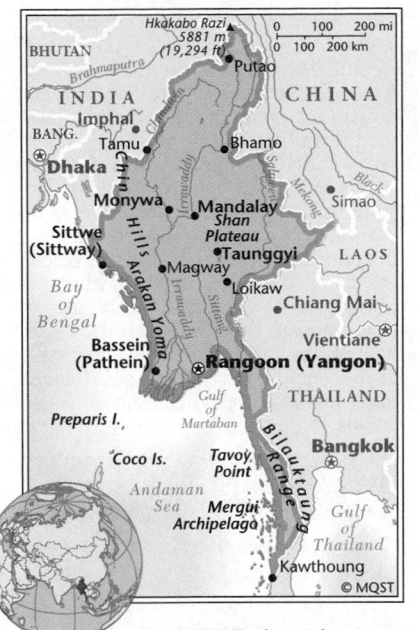

THIS PADUANG woman of Myanmar wears the traditional brass necklaces of her people.

from 70°F along the coast, where humidity is very high, to 60°F in the interior. The summer temperatures rise above 100°F. In southwestern and northeastern Myanmar, monsoons are common and rainfall is generally heavy—about 80 inches a year in the northeast and up to 200 inches in the southwest. Tropical forests cover these wet regions. Central Myanmar is a treeless, grassy plain that receives only about 25 inches of rainfall a year.

The people.   The people of Myanmar are divided into a number of traditional tribal and language groups. The dominant people are the Burmans, who speak Burmese, a Sino-Tibetan language, and use an alphabet similar to that of Sanskrit. The larger minority groups are the Chin, Shan, and Kachin peoples of the hill regions, and the Karen of lower Myanmar.

Buddhism is the major religion of Myanmar, although there is also an active Muslim minority.

Population is densest in the river valleys. Seventy-five percent of the population is rural. Yangon is the largest city in Myanmar. Other important cities include Mandalay, Pegu, Bassein, and Moulmein.

Economy.   Myanmar is a country with rich natural resources. Over half of the country is forested, and there are valuable stands of teak and ironwood. Myanmar's mineral riches include petroleum, lignite, lead, tin, tungsten, copper, iron, nickel, zinc, silver, gold, jade, amber, and rubies. All are mined to some extent but none has been fully exploited.

Myanmar's most valuable resource is its soil, which is extremely fertile in the river valleys. Agriculture employs about 70 percent of the population. The chief crop is rice, which is grown on approximately two-thirds of the cultivated land, mostly in the rich, moist delta region. Peanuts, sugar, sesame, cotton, and tobacco are also raised. Fishing is important along the coast.

Most of Myanmar's few industries are concerned with the processing of agricultural goods or the extraction of such natural resources as timber and oil. Light industry has increased recently, but Myanmar's economic planning is geared mainly toward the increased exploitation of agriculture and petroleum. Industry has been heavily nationalized since the early 1960s.

Myanmar's exports consist mainly of rice, teak, and ores and metals. Most of these exports go to Indonesia, Singapore, Sri Lanka, and Japan. Myanmar's imports consist mainly of finished goods and machinery. One-third of these imports come from Japan, while China, the United States, and Great Britain also contribute significantly. A large black market provides goods that are unavailable in official markets.

Government.   By its constitution, Myanmar is a one-party socialist state. A 485-member People's Assembly is elected to a four-year term. The assembly elects the members of the chief policy-making body, the Council of State,

as well as the Council of Ministers, which is responsible for the administration of the government. The head of state is the chairman of the Council of State, and the head of government is the head of the Council of Ministers. However, since 1988 Myanmar has been ruled by a military junta.

History.   The easy migration and invasion routes along the Sittang and Irrawaddy river valleys have helped make Myanmar's history turbulent. The earliest known settlers were the Pyu, who had moved into the region by the late 600s. In the late 700s a more powerful people, the Mon, settled in the delta region of lower Myanmar.

The Burmans.   The Burman people immigrated from northeastern Tibet during the 900s. They came in such large numbers that they were able to occupy all of central and southern Myanmar and parts of Thailand, and they soon dominated the entire region. At first the Burmans were divided into many small clans, but in the mid-1000s one clan chieftain, Anawrahta, united all the Burmans.

PAGODAS, or towerlike temples, are the best-known expression of art in Myanmar. Here a man prays before a typical Buddhist shrine.

A CHILD WEARS the colorful clothing associated with special celebrations in Myanmar.

PUPPETS are examples of the woodcarving for which the craftsmen of Myanmar are well known.

The Burmans conquered the Mon and adopted much of their culture, which focused on warfare and religion. The king was deified, and many great temples were built in their fortresslike capital, Pagan.

In 1287 Pagan fell to the Mongols, and the empire collapsed. The Mongols took over central Myanmar, the Mon reestablished their southern kingdom, and a newly powerful people, the Shan, established a group of states in the northeastern hills. The Shan led the Burmans in resistance to the Mongols and drove the Mongols out of the region in the early 1300s.

In the 1750s a powerful Burman dynasty arose under Alaungpaya, who reunited the Shan, Burman, and Mon kingdoms and conquered portions of India and Thailand. The destruction wrought by centuries of violence, and the stagnation created by an archaic system of government, weakened the country, which came to be known as Burma, and it was unable to meet a strong challenge from British merchant interests.

British rule. Between 1824 and 1826 the British drove the Burmese out of northeastern India and occupied the Arakan and Tenasserim coasts. The Burmese refused to grant trading privileges to the British, and by 1886 the British had conquered all Burma and made it a part of British India.

Burma's economy and government were modernized under British rule. Burma became the world's leading exporter of teakwood, and the Irrawaddy delta became one of the world's leading producers of rice. Missionaries, especially from the United States, began working in Burma's upland areas, and many of the hill peoples were converted to Christianity.

Many Burmese resented the British and the Indians, who had come to play a prominent role in economic affairs. After World War I a wave of nationalism led to strikes, riots, and, in 1931, to a brief but large-scale rebellion. The British introduced democratic forms of government in the 1920s and 1930s, and in 1937 granted a constitution separating Burma from India.

By the beginning of World War II, Burma had a prosperous economy and a fairly stable political system, but Japanese occupation in 1942 and British reconquest in 1944 caused great economic destruction.

Independence. After the war a group of nationalists who had organized an anti-Japanese army and a political network during the occupation led a drive for independence. As the Anti-Fascist Peoples Freedom League (AFPFL) they emerged as the dominant political party after the British granted Burma its independence in 1948.

Violent political disputes and tribal rebellions kept the nation in disorder from 1948 until 1952, when the Burmese government, under Prime Minister U Nu, succeeded in restoring its authority. Some social and economic gains were made during the 1950s, but corruption and lack of skills slowed progress. Moreover, the national government was too weak to cope with the demands of the minorities for greater autonomy or with communist-led insurrections.

In 1958, faced with dissension within the ruling AFPFL, conflict among Burma's other parties, and the imminence of rebellion and civil war, U Nu asked General Ne Win to take power. Army rule brought a measure of peace to the country, and elections in 1960 restored civilian government under U Nu.

In 1962, with a rebellion among the Shan and a threat of total civil war, Ne Win led an army coup and again took control of the government. In 1963 and 1964 most large businesses were nationalized and the repatriation of many Indians and Pakistanis was ordered. Ne Win's government led Burma on an isolationist course, steering clear of affiliations with the big powers and keeping foreign contacts to a minimum. Ne Win created a one-party state led by the Burma Socialist Program Party (BSPP).

In the 1980s, a growing number of people in Burma called for the military to restore democratic rule. In 1988 Ne Win resigned and called for political reforms. In 1989 the country was renamed Myanmar. The following year, in free elections, the opposition National League for Democracy was victorious, but the military ignored the election.

Myanmar's leading opposition figure is Daw Aung San Suu Kyi, daughter of Aung San, the nationalist leader assassinated in 1947 and revered as the father of independent Burma. Suu Kyi was placed under house arrest until 1995, when the military showed signs of trying to accommodate the opposition. However, by 1996 the army moved again to stifle all dissent. Suu Kyi was again placed under house arrest where she remained in 2004.

Nepal

Official name: *Kingdom of Nepal*
Area: *54,349 sq. mi.,*
  140,800 sq. km.
Type of government:
  Parliamentary democracy
Population: *25,874,000*
Capital and largest city:
  Kathmandu (Pop., 421,000)
Language: *Nepali*
Literacy: *28%;* **Currency:** *Rupee*
Per capita GDP: *$1,400*
  (Rank: 155th)

The land. Nepal can be divided into three distinct geographical regions, each extending east to west. The Great Himalayas dominate the northern region, an area of spectacular alpine scenery with many of the world's tallest mountains. There are eight peaks with elevations of over 26,000 feet, and Mt. Everest, on the Nepal-Tibet border, with an elevation of 29,035 feet, is the tallest mountain in the world. The lower portions of this region are forested. The climate is very cold and rather dry.

The second region, in central Nepal, is also mountainous. Elevations range from 4,500 in the valley bottoms to 10,000 feet. Most of the lower slopes and valleys are cultivated.

The most important part of the central region is the Kathmandu Valley, the heart of the country. Only 18 by 15 miles in area and surrounded by high mountains, it contains the country's main towns—Kathmandu, the capital, Patan, and Bhadgeon. The valley is well watered, receiving about 58 inches of precipitation annually, and has a moderate climate.

The third region, called the terai, is a narrow belt 10 to 20 miles wide next to the Indian border. Most of the terai is heavily wooded. Its climate is hot and humid, with rainfall averaging 60 inches a year. Winters can be quite pleasant, however.

Many rivers flow from the Himalayas through Nepal, including the Kosi, the Trisuli, the Baghmati, the Gandak, and the Karnali.

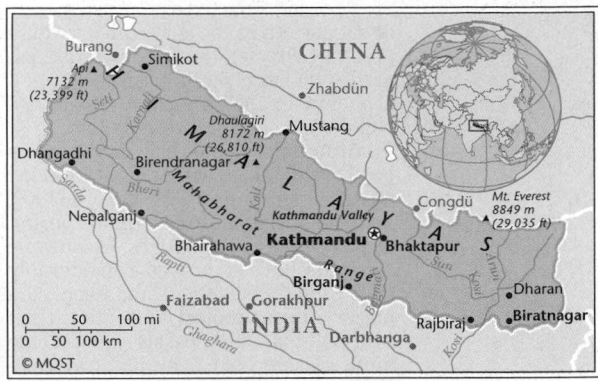

MT. EVEREST, on the border between Nepal and Tibet, is the highest mountain in the world, with an elevation of 29,035 feet.

The people.   Nepal's population is concentrated in the central region, especially the Kathmandu Valley, and in the southern region, the terai. The north is sparsely populated.

The Nepalese are descendants of Mongols and peoples of northern India. They are traditionally divided along tribal lines, with the Gurkha the dominant group. The minority Newar and Sherpa peoples are Mongol-Tibetan. The Nepalese speak Nepali and a variety of hill dialects. Nepal is officially a Hindu country, although there is a Buddhist minority. Ninety-three percent of the population is rural and 93 percent of the labor force works in agriculture.

Economy.   The Nepalese economy is based on agriculture, but the country is rich in natural resources. Nepal's mineral resources include copper, iron, sulfur, coal, hematite, and bauxite, but they remain virtually untapped because of Nepal's isolation and lack of transportation facilities.

Because of its many rapid rivers, Nepal has a large hydroelectric potential. A number of joint Indian-Nepali hydroelectric projects have been undertaken.

The country's best farmland, in the south, produces rice, jute, mustard, tobacco, wheat, linseed, sugar cane, and a surplus of cereal grains. There are also many acres of valuable forest. The majority of farmers in the central region eke out a subsistence living cultivating small, terraced plots of irrigated land.

Herding is the main activity of the Sherpa in the north, who graze sheep, goats, and yaks on the Himalayan slopes. Wheat and barley are grown in the valley bottoms of the north.

An important source of income and foreign exchange has been the service of Gurkha soldiers in the British and Indian armies. Nepal relies on financial and technical assistance from the United States, China, and India.

Nepal's international trade is limited.

The main exports are rice, jute, wool, timber, linseed, and hides. Textiles, fuels, medicines, footwear, and industrial raw materials are imported. Most trade is with India, although Japan has figured increasingly as a trading partner.

Government.   Nepal has a king, who is head of state. Under a constitution adopted in 1990, power resides in a 205-member, popularly elected House of Representatives. The majority party in the House chooses the prime minister, who is the head of government. The first parliamentary elections under this system were held in 1991.

History.   The earliest inhabitants of the Kathmandu Valley were the Newars, who lived under a tribal form of government and developed a religion and customs representing a blend of Buddhism and Hinduism. In the first centuries A.D., the valley came under the rule of Indian kings, who consolidated Indian influence in Nepal in the form of the Hindu religion and culture and monarchical government.

When the last of the dynasty of Indian kings, the Malla, began to weaken in the 1400s, the country returned to tribal government. In the 1500s a western principality, Gurkha, gained strength under the Shah dynasty, whose most famous ruler, Prithvi Narayan, conquered the Katmandu Valley in 1769 and created the modern Nepalese state.

Expansionism.   Combining military ambition with an unusual talent for administration, Prithvi Narayan extended his rule eastward to Darjeeling, now in India, and his descendants expanded Nepalese hegemony to the east as far as Kashmir and to the south into present-day India.

Two Nepalese invasions of Tibet, in 1788 and 1791, brought retaliation from China, which had gained suzerainty over Tibet. Nepal was forced to withdraw from Tibet and to pay tribute to China. The payments ceased in 1908.

Nepalese expansionism soon turned southward and confronted the British, who were extending their control of India northward in the Ganges valley. The Nepalese refused to negotiate with the British and permitted frequent raids into the Indian plains.

The British were able to subdue the Nepalese marauders and reach a settlement with Nepal in 1816, in the Treaty of Sagauli. The treaty established Nepal's boundary with India and gave Britain a deciding influence in Nepalese foreign relations. Gurkha soldiers began to be used by British armies.

Rana rule.   Struggles for power in the early 1800s weakened Nepal and in 1846 resulted in the establishment of rule by the prime ministers, the Ranas. Rana rule, supported by the army and the British in India, was marked by conspiracies and assassinations within the extended Rana family and the isolation of Nepal from modernizing influences.

In the 1900s in India, Nepalese intellectuals laid the groundwork for a movement supported by the titular ruler, King Tribhuvana, to unseat the Ranas and institute a program of reform and advancement. After India achieved independence in 1950, the Nepalese National Congress, modeled on the Indian Congress Party, led a reform drive that was backed by the new government in India.

The Ranas responded with legislative concessions in 1950, but revolts broke out and with Indian encouragement King Tribhuvana was able to end Rana power in 1951. The political and administrative turmoil accompanying the downfall of the Ranas lasted for eight years, while the country was held together by the newly found power of the king. Tribhuvana died in 1955 and was succeeded by his son, Mahendra.

Contemporary Nepal.   With Chinese power increasing in Tibet, threatening the security of both Nepal and India, King Mahendra, in 1959, promulgated a new constitution, giving himself supreme executive powers but also providing for a legislature.

In 1960 King Mahendra outlawed political parties and reinstated direct royal rule, but authorized a system of panchayats, or councils. The king's provisions for what he called "democracy from below" led to a resurgence of popular support.

labor
US

labour
Brit.

23 Asia

The king attracted a progressive body of supporters in the government with a program directed toward modernization of the still largely traditional society and economy. In 1963 the caste system and childhood marriages were abolished.

Although Nepal has traditionally been closely allied with India, it canceled an arms agreement with India in 1969, charging that nation with harboring Nepalese political fugitives. Meanwhile relations have improved considerably with China. Recently, China financed a major highway project connecting Tibet with Kathmandu. Nepal also has become more closely linked, by highways and airline service, with India and Pakistan.

King Mahendra died in 1972 and was succeeded by his son, Birendra Bir Bikram Shah Dev. In 1990 a pro-democracy movement swept Nepal, forcing King Birendra to accept political parties and a new constitution. In 1991 the moderate Nepal Congress Party won a majority in the new government.

In a bizarre episode in 2001, King Birendra was killed by his son, Dipendra. Prince Dipendra also killed his mother and several other members of the royal family before shooting himself. While in a coma, he was crowned king. Upon his death, three days later, his brother, Gyanendra, became king.

A Communist rebel movement seeking abolishment of the monarchy has been of concern since 1996. Despite periodic cease-fires and peace talks, rebel attacks continue.

labor
US

labour
Brit.

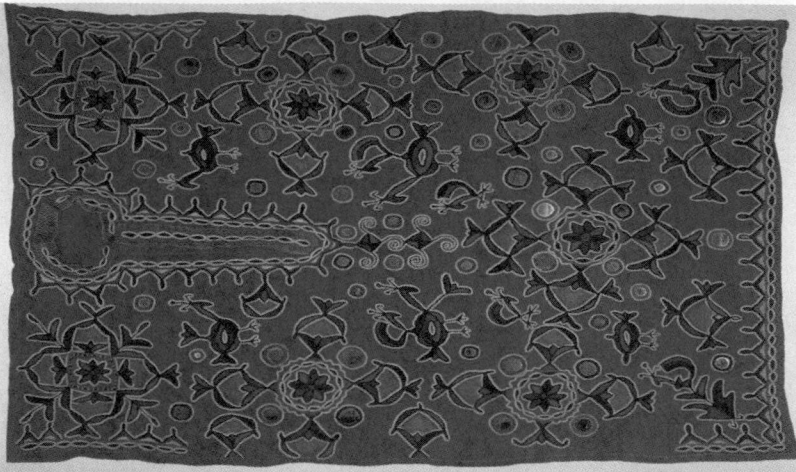

BEAUTIFUL PRAYER RUGS such as this are important possessions of Muslims, who pray toward Mecca several times daily. Ninety-five percent of Pakistanis are Muslim.

Pakistan

Official name: *Islamic Republic of Pakistan*

Area: *310,321 sq. mi., 803,940 sq. km.*

Type of government: *Republic*

Population: *147,663,000*

Capital: *Islamabad (Pop., 529,000)*

Largest city: *Karachi (Pop., 9,339,000)*

Languages: *Urdu (official), English, Punjabi*

Literacy: *43%;* **Currency:** *Rupee*

Per capita GDP: *$2,100 (Rank: 133rd)*

The land. Pakistan can be divided into five separate geographic regions. Baluchistan, in the southwest, is an arid region of mountains and valleys. The Makran Coast forms a narrow corridor connecting the Indus valley with Iran. The Northwest Frontier is a mountain and hill region whose many mountain passes, including the Khyber Pass, historically have been the gateways to the Indian subcontinent. Punjab, in the upper Indus valley, is the traditional economic, political, and cultural heart of Pakistan, a land rich in wheat and with a growing industrial capacity. Sind, a desert region, occupies the lower Indus valley.

The people. The people of Pakistan are a mixture of many groups. Two-thirds of the population is Punjabi; the rest is mostly Sindhi, Pashtun, Urdu, or Baluchi. Urdu is the national language, but English is widely used.

Over 95 percent of the people are Muslims, but there are significant Christian and Hindu minorities.

Aggressive government educational policies in recent years have raised Pakistan's literacy rate significantly, but it is still quite low.

Pakistan's natural population increase is high. Three-quarters of the population is rural. Only three cities have populations over 1 million: the major port of Karachi (9.3 million), the industrial city of Lahore (5.1 million), and Faisalabad (2 million).

Economy. About half the labor force is employed in agriculture. Pakistan has an extensive system of irrigation. The principal crops include wheat, cotton, rice, corn, and sugar cane.

At Pakistan's partition from India in 1947, the country had almost no industrial base, but after substantial investment, industry accounts for about 13 percent of employment. Manufactures include textiles, carpets, steel, fertilizer, cement, and petroleum products.

Pakistan's largest export is cotton, both raw and processed. Also exported are rice, leather, and fish products. Imports include machinery, fuels, and consumer goods. An important contribution to the economy is made by Pakistanis working abroad, especially in the Middle East, who send a portion of their wages home to their families. Japan, the United States, and Saudi Arabia are principal trade partners.

Government. Following a 1977 military coup, democratic processes were only gradually restored. A constitutional amendment in 1986 bound Pakistan to observe Islamic law.

According to the constitution, the president is head of state and is elected by an electoral college. The head of government is the prime minister, who is chosen by the president and confirmed by the popularly elected National Assembly. The National Assembly consists of 217 members elected to 5-year terms. The upper legislative house is the 87-member Senate, indirectly elected by provincial and tribal leaders for a term of 6 years.

History. Pakistan's existence as a separate Muslim state is rooted in the early history of northern India. Islam began to influence northern India in the early 600s, when Muslim sailors from Arabia visited the coast of Sind, at the mouth of the Indus. Muslim conquerors ruled Sind from the 600s and spread Islam there.

In the 1000s, Muslims from Afghanistan began extending their rule over territory in northwest India. Until the 1800s Afghans, Turks, Arabs, and finally the Mughals (or Moguls) ruled all or part of northern India, establishing many small kingdoms and princely states that at times were unified into empires. In addition to their religion, the Muslims brought Persian and Arabic art, literature, learning, and customs to produce a way of life different from that of Hindu India to the south.

Britain began extending its influence over India in the 1700s. By the early 1900s the British controlled most of the Muslim territories, and by the mid-1800s, with the addition of Punjab and Sind, the British were in firm command of all of India.

In the late 1800s, when Indian leaders began to demand a stronger voice in their country's government, Muslims made up about one-quarter of India's population. The Indian National Congress, formed in 1885 to work for self-government, spoke for all India and included prominent Muslims. Its composition, however, was predominantly Hindu.

Muslim autonomy. The positive movement toward autonomy for Indian Muslims began soon after the Indian nationalist movement was organized, and in part as a result of its organization. Sir Sayyid Ahmad Khan and other Muslim leaders argued that there was a distinct Muslim nation in India that should not be submerged in the Hindu majority. This, they contended, would happen if the British left the country and a fully representative government was introduced.

While urging Muslims to improve their relatively backward condition through education and commerce, Sir Sayyid recommended that they not participate in the activities of the Indian National Congress.

Muslim League. In 1906 Muslims founded the All India Muslim League to press for protection and advantages for Muslims. Although its goal, self-government for India, was the same as that of the National Congress, the organizations could not agree on a plan to divide power.

Violence between Hindus and Muslims in the 1920s and 1930s, as well as continued sponsorship of a Hindu revival, widened the split within the nationalist movement. The final blow to unity came in 1937, when the Indian National Congress gained control of most provincial legislatures popularly elected on a broadened franchise. The Muslim League believed that the policies of these Congress majorities discriminated against Muslims.

It was after 1937 that Muhammad Ali Jinnah, a former Indian National Congress leader and advocate of Hindu-Muslim unity, began a drive for the creation of a separate Muslim state. By 1940, under Jinnah's leadership, the Muslim League resolved that a Muslim state should be created when India gained independence.

In 1946 negotiations took place for a transfer of power to Indians, but the Congress and the League could not agree on terms for establishing an interim government, or for drafting a constitution for the new state. The British had strongly supported a unified India, but they had also encouraged Muslim ambitions.

Partition. In 1947, when the Hindu-Muslim stalemate could not be broken, Britain acquiesced to Muslim demands for a separate state. It was to consist of all contiguous areas with Muslim majorities in British India. Bengal in the east and the Punjab in the west were divided and the princely states adjacent to Pakistan were given the choice of joining one of the new states. This resulted in the creation of a country with two nonadjoining sections.

On August 15, 1947, Pakistan became an independent nation within the British Commonwealth. Muhammad Ali Jinnah became Pakistan's first governor-general.

Partition created serious problems for both India and Pakistan. Communal rioting, especially in the Punjab, killed thousands. The economies of the two countries were disrupted by large migrations of Muslims to Pakistan and Hindus to India.

The cultural difference between the eastern and western parts of the new state caused antagonism and sharpened struggles for political power. Pakistani political leadership faltered after the death in 1948 of Jinnah and the assassination in 1951 of Liaqat Ali Khan, Pakistan's first prime minister. Delays in creating a constitution extended the period of instability.

The republic. A republican constitution was adopted in 1956. But years of political turmoil had weakened the economy, and the decentralized federal system established by the constitution could do little to solve the country's economic problems.

Relations with India, bitter after decades of religious conflict, grew more hostile in the mid-1950s over the issue of Kashmir. India gained control of the bulk of Kashmir, but the region had a Muslim majority; Pakistan said Kashmir should be made part of the Muslim state. This worsened Pakistan's internal political and economic situation.

In 1958 a group of military leaders under General Muhammad Ayub Khan took over the government. The new government took firm control of economic activity and initiated modernization programs that improved the economy.

In 1962 a new constitution was adopted; martial law was gradually lifted and civil rights restored. In 1965 President Ayub Khan won reelection handily. The country's economy improved in the mid-1960s under government development programs using aid from abroad. In 1965 the Kashmir dispute again broke into open warfare.

Violent protests erupted in East Pakistan in 1969 as its population demanded political autonomy. Ayub Khan was forced to resign; General Yahya Khan declared martial law. In December 1971, East Pakistan declared itself the independent state of Bangladesh. Yahya Khan resigned and Zulfikar Ali Bhutto, leader of the Peoples' Party, became Pakistan's first civilian president.

Bhutto sought to reestablish peaceful relations with India. He initiated land reforms and government control of industry. In 1973 he permitted the formation of a parliamentary form of government. He was deposed during a military coup in 1977 and was executed in 1979. New president Muhammad Zia ul-Haw instituted absolute military rule. Martial law was lifted in 1985, and democratic processes were revived. Zia was killed in 1988 in an airplane explosion. Benazir Bhutto, daughter of Zulfikar Ali Bhutto, became prime minister in 1988 but was not reelected in 1990. In 1993 Bhutto was returned as prime minister of a coalition government.

Prime Minister Mohammad Nawaz Sharif's government fell in an October 1999 coup, and General Pervez Musharraf seized control and suspended the constitution. In a 2004 election, which most opposition parties boycotted, Musharraf retained the presidency.

An ongoing dispute with India over Kashmir erupts into violence periodically, but 2003 saw great strides in normalizing relations between the two countries.

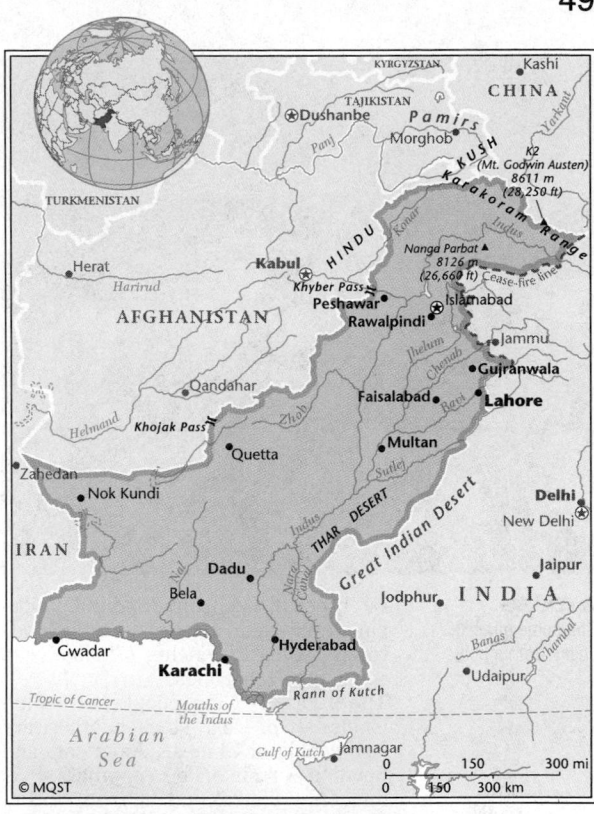

Philippines

Official name: *Republic of the Philippines*
Area: *115,800 sq. mi., 300,000 sq. km.*
Type of government: *Republic*
Population: *82,995,000*
Capital and largest city: *Manila (Pop., 1,581,000)*
Languages: *Filipino, English*
Literacy: *95%;* **Currency:** *Peso*
Per capita GDP: *$4,000 (Rank: 99th)*

The land. There are more than 7,000 islands within the Philippine archipelago, but the eleven largest islands account for 94 percent of the country's total land area. The largest islands are Luzon (40,420 square miles) and Mindanao (36,537 square miles). Each of the remaining islands is less than 6,000 square miles in area.

Most of the islands are hilly or mountainous, with only limited areas of level land. In the northern half of Luzon, the principal island, there are several mountain ranges running from north to south. The Sierra Madre range runs parallel to the northeastern coast, and the Central Cordillera forms the spine of the island. Between the two ranges is the Cagayan Plain, one of the two sizable lowlands on Luzon.

Average monthly temperatures at sea level range from 76°F to 84°F year-round. Although it is cooler at higher altitudes, temperatures below 60°F

A YOUNG
Philippine girl sells shells from a boat.

labor
US

labour
Brit.

center
US

centre
Brit.

RICE FIELDS,
like these at Banaue, occupy about half of the land devoted to farming in the Philippines.

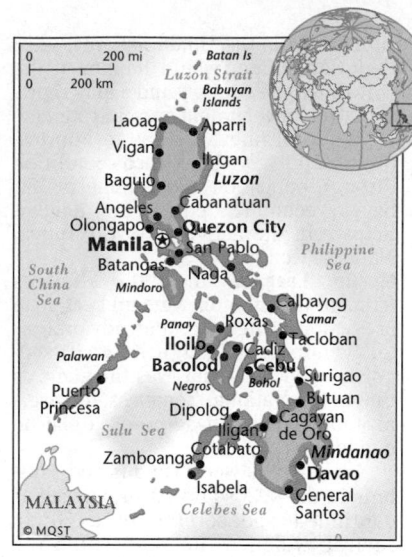

rarely occur. Typhoons strike the Philippines every year. Most of the Philippines receive at least 60 inches of rain a year, some up to 125 inches.

The people. Most people in the Philippines are of Malay stock, but there are also people of Chinese, American, and Spanish origin. The population is unevenly distributed. Luzon, Cebu, Negros, Bohul, Leyte, and Panay are the most heavily populated islands. The largest city is Manila, on Luzon.

Most Filipinos are Christian, but there are also minorities of Muslims in northern Luzon and western Mindanao. Many local languages are spoken in the Philippines. Pilipino, the official language, is derived from Tagalog, the language spoken around Manila. English is also widely spoken.

Economy. The economy of the Philippines is based on agriculture, and about 50 percent of the labor force is dependent on agriculture for its livelihood.

About one-third of the land is arable, and about three-quarters of that is devoted to domestic food crops.

While rice and fish are the two mainstays of the Filipino diet, the islands do not catch enough fish for their own population's demands. Self-sufficiency in rice production was only recently attained. Rice occupies almost one-half of the cropped land. Corn and coconuts are also important crops. Other crops of some significance include root crops, fruits, nuts, sugar cane, abaca, tobacco, ramie, kapok, and rubber.

The number of persons engaged in fishing is second only to the number in agriculture. Fishing is becoming an increasingly important industry.

Forests cover about 50 percent of the country and are among the most important resources of the Philippines.

The Philippines has considerable mineral wealth, and is a leading producer of copper and gold. Also extracted are nickel, zinc, cobalt, coal, and silver.

Before independence in 1946, industry was confined largely to processing agricultural products. Since independence, the government has promoted industrialization, and by 1986 manufactured goods contributed nearly one-quarter of the gross national product. A number of consumer goods industries have been established or expanded, and some heavy industry has been established. In the 1980s an emphasis was placed on developing export-producing industries.

The main imports are machinery, chemicals, food, iron and steel products, and petroleum. The major exports are electronic goods, clothing, coconut oil, copper, gold, and bananas. Most trade is conducted with the United States and Japan. The Philippines receives economic aid from the United States.

Government. Under the new 1987 constitution, the head of state is the president, who is popularly elected to a six-year term. Legislative authority, as in the United States, rests with a 24-member Senate and a 214-member House of Representatives.

History. The earliest arrivals to the Philippine archipelago are thought to have been a dark-skinned people who migrated across land bridges from Southeast Asia 20,000 to 30,000 years ago. The next migrants to arrive on the islands were Malay peoples from the Indonesian islands.

The Philippine islands were known to traders from China and Southeast Asia at least as early as the 14th century. During this period, Arab traders introduced Islam to the islands.

Ferdinand Magellan visited the Philippines in 1521 and claimed the islands for Spain. In 1571 Miguel López de Legazpe, a Spanish soldier, established the first Spanish settlement in the islands and extended Spanish control over Cebu, Leyte, Mindanao, Panay, and central Luzon. In 1571 he took possession of Manila and made it the capital of the territory.

Long before the Spanish conquest, the Philippines traded with China. Later, Spanish galleons brought silver to Manila from the port of Acapulco in Mexico to trade with the Chinese for luxury goods, and Manila became an important trading center.

Under Spanish rule, Christianity and Western legal concepts and customs were introduced into the Philippines, and a centralized government was established. In the 1800s resentment against Spanish rule grew, and by the end of the 1800s the Filipinos had staged a number of revolts.

In 1896 José Rizal, a leading Filipino patriot, was executed for his part in uprisings that broke out in that year. His death spurred the revolutionary movement. Spain promised to grant Filipino representation in Madrid and to permit wider autonomy for the islands, but it failed to keep these promises, and the Filipinos, led by General Francisco Makabulas, renewed the struggle against Spanish rule.

U.S. rule. In April 1898, the United States declared war on Spain, after the U.S. battleship *Maine* was destroyed in Havana harbor, in Cuba, which was also under Spanish rule. By that time the Filipinos were fighting the Spanish in the Philippines. In August 1898, U.S. forces occupied Manila. In the Treaty of Paris, signed on December 10, 1898, Spain ceded the Philippines to the United States for $20 million.

In 1899 a war of insurrection against the United States was led by Emilio Aguinaldo, head of the anti-Spanish rebellion of 1896. In 1901 Aguinaldo was captured and the uprising was ended.

Between the summer of 1900 and the summer of 1901 the islands were administered by a military governor while the Taft Commission, established by President William McKinley and headed by William Howard Taft, drew up plans for a civil government. The plan provided for a legislature with an appointed upper house and an elected assembly. In 1907 the first assembly elections were held.

Time Line of Philippine History

Early population composed of a native group of unknown origin called Negritos, who were joined by groups of Malaysians and Indonesians from Southeast Asia. Chinese and Japanese traders reached the islands sometime before 1000 A.D.

1300–1400	Muslim traders and Arab missionaries traveled to the Philippines and converted the Moros of Mindanao and the Sulu Archipeligo to Islam.
1521	Spanish explorer Ferdinand Magellan landed in the Philippines in what is now Cebu Harbor during the first around-the-world voyage. After having claimed the islands for Spain, he was killed while attempting to help one Filipino group fight another.
1542–43	An expedition by Spain was launched from Mexico. Spanish admiral Ruy Lopez de Villalobos visited the islands and named them Las Filipinos (The Philippines) in honor of the prince (who was to become King Philip II of Spain).
1565	General Miguel Lopez de Legaspi established the first permanent Spanish settlement on Cebu Island.
1571	Legaspi founded Manila.
mid 1500s– mid 1700s	Spanish rule strengthened in spite of continuing conflicts with the Filipinos, especially the Moros. Spanish friars converted most of the people to Roman Catholicism.
1762–1764	The British occupied Manila briefly.
mid 1700s– late 1800s	Spanish resumed rule of the islands and continued to put down revolts, spread Catholicism, and establish a few schools and many churches.
mid 1800s	Manila was opened to foreign trade. As the economy improved, some Filipinos became well-to-do and opted to send their children away for their education. Those who returned were to try to influence the Spanish to improve social and political conditions.
1896	José Rizal became a leader of the Philippine independence movement. He was arrested and executed by firing squad. His successor, Emilio Aguinaldo, led a revolt against the Spaniards and, in return for promises of reform, left the islands.
1898	The Spanish-American War, which was focused on ousting Spain from Cuba, involved the Philippines in both action and results.
May 1, 1898	Commodore George Dewey sailed into Manila Bay with the U.S. Pacific fleet. Destroyed the Spanish Pacific fleet at anchor with a cost of only eight wounded Americans. His order to the captain of his flagship is one of the great wartime quotes: "You may fire when ready, Gridley."
June 12, 1898	The Philippines declare independence from Spain. Aguinaldo returned and joined the American forces with his newly formed Filipino army. A group of his supporters elected him president on June 23.
Aug. 13, 1898	Manila was occupied by Filipino and American soldiers.
1898–1899	The end of the war marked a major change in both Philippine and American fortunes. The Spanish ceded the islands to the United States and U.S. paid $20 million for specific island holdings, not to be interpreted as a purchase of the islands themselves. American sentiments ranged from approval that viewed the new "global empire" as evidence of America's "manifest destiny," to being completely appalled by America's "imperialist" foreign policy. At one point Andrew Carnegie offered to buy the Philippines for $20 million and give the country its freedom.
Feb. 4, 1899	Emilio Aguinaldo led a guerilla rebellion against American rule, claiming that the islands had been promised immediate independence (there is no evidence to support this contention). The rebellion lasted until Aguinaldo's capture on March 23, 1901, by General Frederick Funston at Palawan, Luzon. The rebellion was declared officially over on April 19. Americans viewed this as the most unpopular U.S. war to date.
1900	Amnesty was granted to Filipino insurgents by a proclamation issued by General Arthur MacArthur, military governor of the Philippines (and father of Douglas MacArthur, who spent 1903, the year following his graduation from West Point, helping to map the Philippines).
1901	William Howard Taft (later to be U.S. president) became the first American governor of the Philippines. He engineered the sale and transfer of ownership of Catholic Church lands to 50,000 new Filipino landowners.
1901–1934	With the avowed intention of granting independence to the Philippines at a still-to-be-determined date, the U.S. set about preparing the island's people to become self-governing. Schools were established and health issues addressed. A raging cholera epidemic in 1905 was particularly difficult, even though President Theodore Roosevelt personally cut through red tape to provide quinine to victims. Of course the drug had no effect on cholera but the attention focused on the problem evidenced American concern. In spite of resistance to quarantine procedures and institution of sanitation standards, the epidemic was contained. Lessons learned continue to provide protection worldwide.
1902	U.S. Congress, declaring the islands an unorganized territory and inhabitants territorial citizens, authorized a governing commission appointed by the president. On July 4, Theodore Roosevelt issued the order establishing civil government and granting amnesty to political prisoners.
1909	The Payne Bill passed the U.S. Congress and introduced trade privileges to the Philippines.
1913	The Underwood Act provided free trade between the U.S. and the islands, which remained in effect until Jan. 1, 1941.
1921	The policy of gradual self-government was set back when Leonard Wood, appointed governor-general, ruled in a semi-military manner.
1933	The Howes-Cutting Act passed by the U.S. Congress provided for the complete independence of the islands in 10 years. President Herbert Hoover vetoed and was overridden by Congress, but the act was rejected by the Philippine legislature.
Mar. 24, 1934	The Tydings-McDuffie Act passes Congress. It spelled out a plan leading to complete independence for the Philippines on July 4, 1946, and was approved by the Philippine legislature on May 1.
1935	The Commonwealth of the Philippines was established, with Manuel Zuezon elected as the first president.
Dec. 7, 1941	The Philippines were attacked by Japan at the same time that the attack on Pearl Harbor, Hawaii, occurred.
Dec. 10, 1941	Japan invaded Luzon where General Douglas MacArthur commanded the defending U.S. and Philippine forces.

23 Asia

Time Line of Philippine History

Jan. 2, 1942	Manila fell to the Japanese, forcing General MacArthur and his combined U.S. and Philippine forces to withdraw to Bataan peninsula on Luzon.
Mar. 17, 1942	When defense of Bataan became hopeless, a presidential order from Franklin Roosevelt directed MacArthur to withdraw to Australia, where he was named Commander-in-Chief of the Southwest Pacific Command. His departure was marked by his promise that "I shall return."
Apr. 9, 1942	Bataan fell to the Japanese, and Gen. Jonathan Wainwright, with 3,500 soldiers and nurses, withdrew to the island of Corregidor in Manila Bay.
Apr. 10, 1942	The Bataan Death March began at dawn. American and Philippine prisoners taken at Bataan were forced to march 85 miles in six days on only one meal of rice. After atrocities and hardships, the prisoners were interred until the end of the war released them. Thousands died.
May 6, 1942	Corregidor fell, and General Wainwright with his troops surrendered the fortress to General Tomouki Yamashita.
1941–1944	The Philippines were occupied by Japanese forces.
Oct. 20, 1944	American troops landed at Leyte, fulfilling MacArthur's promise to return. During this campaign the first kamikaze suicide plane was used.
Oct 23–26, 1944	Battle of Leyte Gulf, the largest naval battle of WWII, ends with the Japanese fleet suffering heavy losses and the successful invasion of the Philippines.
Jan. 9, 1945	The U.S. Sixth Army invaded Luzon and a task force of 850 ships sailed into Lingayen Gulf, 100 miles north of Manila.
Feb. 7, 1945	MacArthur returned to Manila.
Apr. 24, 1945	The conference to form the United Nations opened in San Francisco with fifty delegates, including the Philippines. The charter signed June 26 made the Philippine Islands a charter member of the UN.
July 5, 1945	MacArthur declared the islands liberated although some fighting continued.
Aug. 15, 1945	V-J Day (Victory over Japan).
July 4, 1946	Republic of the Philippines established with Manuel Roxas as the first president of the completely independent islands. (Roxas had spent the war appearing to assist the Japanese but was actually a spy for the Philippine underground movement.)
1948	Quezon City, named for the first president of the Commonwealth, became the official capital but Manila continued as the chief governmental and business center.
late 1940s–early 1950s	A communist rebellion aimed at the government and breaking up large land holdings broke out on Luzon. The "Huks" at one point had control of five provinces but were overcome by Philippine forces and surrendered in 1954.
1954	The Philippines joined the South East Asia Treaty Organization (SEATO), a mutual defense organization modeled on NATO (North Atlantic Treaty Organization).
1957	Ramón Magsaysay, popular president of the islands, was killed in a plane crash not long before the election he was expected to win.
1959	Military bases in the islands that had been leased to the U.S. for ninety-nine years have the leases reduced to twenty-five years.
1965	Ferdinand Marcos elected president of the Philippines.
1970	Student rioting in Manila protested the corruption of the government of President Marcos. After a number of casualties occurred when the students were fired on by government forces, Marcos said he would not run for a third term.
1972	Marcos declared martial law in the face of communist guerilla activities. Marcos continues as president and assumes legislative powers.
1981	Marcos ends martial law and returns powers to the National Assembly. The constitution is amended by plebiscite to change the form of government from a parliamentary to a presidential system. Marcos elected to a new six-year term.
1983	Benigno Aquino, Jr., a leader of opposition to Marcos, returned from three years of exile in the U.S. and was assassinated at the airport. A Philippine court acquitted all 26 people accused of the murder in 1985.
1986	Corazon Aquino, widow of Benigno, wins presidential election; Marcos' dictatorial regime ends. He flees to exile first on Guam, later Hawaii.
1987	President Aquino's proposed new constitution is approved by 80 percent of the voters and a two-house legislature is established.
1988	Agreement between the Philippines and U.S. permits Clark Air Force Base and Subic Bay Naval Station to continue operating until late 1991.
1989	A rebellion of army troops threatened the government of President Aquino but was suppressed. (A factor in the victory was the order by U.S. President Bush that American fighter planes keep rebel planes on the ground.) Ferdinand Marcos died in exile after having been declared too ill to stand trial on charges related to missing Filipino funds. His body was not returned to the islands for burial until 1993.
1990	Imelda Marcos, widow of Ferdinand and considered a co-conspirator with him, was indicted and tried in U.S. Federal Court on racketeering charges related to the missing $200 million and its concealment by using it to buy art, jewelry, and real estate in the United States. She was acquitted.
1991	Mount Pinatubo erupts. Strained U.S.–Philippine relations led to ordering withdrawal of U.S. forces from Subic Bay, ending American military presence that began in 1898 with the Spanish-American War.
1992	Fidel Ramos succeeded Corazon Aquino as president. Ramos had led the movement ousting Marcos and defended Aquino against several coup attempts.
1992–1998	Muslim separatists, particularly focusing on the southern islands, including Mindanao, cause problems with the government.
1998	Joseph Estrada elected president.
2001	Joseph Estrada forced from office amid charges of wrongdoing. He fought that assertion in spite of having been replaced by his former vice-president, Gloria Macapagal-Arroyo. Mount Mayon erupts.
2002	Two hostages being held for more than a year by rebel group Abu Sayyaf were killed during a rescue attempt. A third hostage, wounded during the fighting, was rescued.

In 1934 President Franklin Roosevelt signed the Tydings-McDuffie Act, stipulating that independence was to be granted the Philippines in 1946. Under the terms of the act, the Philippines, in 1935, became a self-governing commonwealth headed by an elected president. Manuel Quezon was the first president.

On December 7, 1941, Japanese forces struck the islands, and on January 2, 1942, Manila was occupied by the Japanese. Valiant battles were fought on Bataan peninsula and Corregidor island, but the Philippines were forced to surrender in May 1942.

Japan established a puppet government in which many Filipinos served. Quezon established a government-in-exile in Washington, D.C., and Americans and Filipinos organized a large-scale guerrilla movement.

Early in the war the peasant farmers created an army, the Hukbalahap, commonly called Huk, led by Luis Taruc. The Huks rallied the rural population and killed some 25,000 Japanese and their Filipino supporters.

On October 20, 1944, U.S. troops, supported by Filipino guerrillas, landed on the island of Leyte, and on February 23, 1945, after a fierce three-week battle, the Allied forces captured Manila.

Independence. On July 4, 1946, the Philippines became independent. The new government faced rebuilding the country's economy; dealing with the rebellion of the Huk, which had become a Communist-dominated group; and handling the unpopular abuse by American businesses of what was called "parity," or equal rights with their Filipino counte parts.

Under the leadership of President Ramón Magsaysay, elected in 1953, the Huk rebellion was suppressed by a newly strengthened army, which also acted to control political corruption and abuse. Magsaysay was killed in a plane crash in 1957. His successors were beset by economic problems aggravated by sharp population increases, stress over the Americans' privileged position in the nation, and renewed political corruption.

Ferdinand Marcos became president in 1965. In the face of rising criticism and terrorism, he declared martial law in 1972. The assassination, in 1983, of Benigno S. Aquino, an opposition leader, provoked a national crisis. Allegations that the Marcos government was involved in the assassination caused widespread rioting.

In 1986, within weeks after Marcos declared himself the winner in presidential elections believed to be fraudulent, demonstrations and defection of military units forced him into exile. Opposition candidate Corazon Aquino, Benigno Aquino's widow, became president. Aquino completed her term, despite economic crises, attempted coups, and strained U.S.-Philippine relations. In 1991 the U.S. closed Clark Air Base and Subic Bay Naval Station, ending its military presence in the Philippines. U.S. advisors arrived in early 2002 to train the Philippine army in antiterrorism techniques.

Singapore

Official name: *Republic of Singapore*
Area: *244 sq. mi., 633 sq. km.*
Type of government: *Republic*
Population: *4,453,000*
Capital: *Singapore*
Languages: *English, Chinese, Malay, Tamil (all official)*
Literacy: *94%;* **Currency:** *Dollar*
Per capita GDP: *$24,700 (Rank: 22nd)*

The land. The nation of Singapore consists of the large island of Singapore and some 55 low-lying islets within 10 miles of its eastern and southern shores. On Singapore Island, a coastal plain surrounds a central plateau that has a peak of 581 feet. Once swampland and jungle, most of the island has been cleared for farming and building. The island is about 26 miles long and 14 miles wide.

Singapore's climate is hot and humid. The average year-round temperature is about 81°F, and an average of 96 inches of rain falls each year.

The people. Singapore is very densely populated, with over 11,789 persons per square mile. An extremely high rate of population growth was slowed down by a determined government program of birth control. The majority of the country's population live in the capital and largest city, Singapore, on the southern coast of Singapore Island.

About three-quarters of Singapore's people are of Chinese descent. Malays and Indonesians make up some 14 percent. About 8 percent are of Indian and Pakistani origins, and there are small groups of Europeans and people of mixed ethnic backgrounds.

Malay is the national language, and Malay, Mandarin, Chinese, English, and Tamil, an Indian language, are official languages. Many of the dominant Chinese adhere to Confucianism, Taoism, and Buddhism. Most of the Malays and Pakistanis are Muslim, the Indians are largely Hindu and Sikh, and there are many Christians.

Economy. Singapore is one of Asia's "little dragons," so called because of the strength of its economy in relation to the size of the country. Singapore's prosperity is based on its location on important sea routes between the Indian Ocean, the South China Sea, and the Pacific and on its large, industrious population. Singapore is the commercial and financial center of Southeast Asia, and a large share of the region's trade passes through its port, the second largest in the world. This activity has given Singapore the third highest per capita income in Asia.

Singapore's industry traditionally has been based on processing Southeast Asia's natural products, such as tin, rubber, spices, copra, coffee, and timber. Attempts have been made to develop heavy industry to broaden Singapore's economic base. As a result industries like petroleum refining and shipbuilding have become important. A more recent trend has been a move toward producing high value-added goods for export, such as consumer electronics.

Trade. Commerce, especially transshipment trade, remains a major factor in Singapore's economy, however. The country processes Asian goods for export and distributes imports to Asian market centers.

A large part of the value of Singapore's trade is for transshipped goods. Electronics, machinery, petroleum products, and rubber are principal exports. Imports

DETAIL OF FRIEZE
from the Kaliamman Temple, a Buddhist temple in Singapore

PRAYERS
in many forms are offered in Singapore, where the religions of the people are as varied as their origins.

include crude oil, foodstuffs, machinery, and many types of manufactured goods. The United States, Japan, and Malaysia are primary trading partners.

Government. Singapore is a republic with a parliamentary system of government. The head of state is the president, who is elected by popular vote to a 6-year term. Executive powers are exercised by a cabinet, headed by a prime minister, responsible to the parliament. The parliament has one house with 84 members elected under a system of compulsory universal suffrage. The People's Action Party is the only political party with power.

History. Singapore had become an important commercial center by the A.D. 1100s. In 1377 Singapore city was destroyed by Java, and it lost its trading importance. In 1819 Sir Thomas Stamford Raffles, a British East India Company agent, established a trading post on the island. Commerce flourished, and in 1824 the British purchased Singapore.

British rule. In 1826 Britain established the "Straits Settlements," combining Singapore with two former rival trading centers, Malacca and Penang. In 1867, as their prosperity and importance increased, the settlements were raised to the status of British crown colony.

The opening of the Suez Canal in 1869 and the development of steamships increased Europe's trade with the Far East and further bolstered Singapore's prosperity. In the late 1800s profitable tin smelting and rubber processing were added to the island's trading activities.

In the 1920s the British established a major naval base at Singapore, and in the 1930s an air base. In 1942, during World War II, Japan captured Singapore and occupied it until the British recaptured it in 1945. In 1946 Singapore was separated from Penang and Malacca and made a separate crown colony.

In the 1950s Singapore moved toward self-government, and in 1959 it was granted full internal autonomy. The major political force in the country became the largely Chinese People's Action Party.

Independence. In 1963 Singapore joined the new nation of Malaysia, formed of Malaya, Sabah (North Borneo), and Sarawak. Singapore's dominant economic position and its Chinese majority led to friction with Malaysia's federal government. As a result, in 1965 Singapore reluctantly withdrew from the federation and became a sovereign state.

Lee Kuan Yew, prime minister from 1959 to 1990, was regarded as greatly responsible for Singapore's remarkable economic growth in the 1960s and 1970s, but he was criticized for his authoritarian style. His chosen successor, Goh Chok Tong, was returned to office by election in 1991. In 1993 the first direct presidential election took place.

The nation pursues close economic and political relations with Malaysia and its other Asian neighbors, while attempting to maintain nonalignment with the world's major powers.

---

center
US

centre
Brit.

laborers
US

labourers
Brit.

civilization
US

civilisation
Brit.

Sri Lanka

Official name: *Democratic Socialist Republic of Sri Lanka*
Area: *25,326 sq. mi., 65,610 sq. km.*
Type of government: *Republic*
Population: *19,577,000*
Capital and largest city: *Colombo (Pop., 642,000)*
Languages: *Sinhala (official), Tamil, English*
Literacy: *90%;* **Currency:** *Rupee*
Per capita GDP: *$3,250 (Rank: 112th)*

The land. Sri Lanka's coastline is low and sandy except for the area around the Jaffna Peninsula, in the north, and at Trincomalee, in the east. Both have excellent natural harbors. In the interior of southern Sri Lanka, mountainous highlands rise from the coastal plain to a peak of over 8,000 feet. The north is largely a flat plain with an elevation only slightly above sea level.

Sri Lanka has a tropical climate, with average year-round temperatures ranging between 80°F and 100°F. It is cooler in the mountains. Humidity is high throughout the country, but especially in the southwest, where as much as 200 inches of rain a year may fall. About 50 inches fall yearly on the rest of the country.

The people. More than two-thirds of the people of Sri Lanka are Sinhalese, and speak Sinhala, an Indic language. Most are Buddhist. Almost one-quarter of the people are Tamils, a people of southern Indian origin who speak Tamil, a Dravidian language. Most Tamils are Hindus. The Tamils are divided between Sri Lanka Tamils, those who have been Sri Lankan for many generations, and Indian Tamils, the descendants of Indian laborers brought to the island in the 1800s.

Smaller minorities include Muslim Arabs, Burghers—descendants of Dutch colonists—Eurasians, Muslim Malays, and Veddas, descendants of the island's first settlers. Relations among the various groups have not always been good, and there have been bitter conflicts between the Sinhalese and the Tamils.

The population is concentrated in the southwestern corner of the island and in places along the coasts. It grew at a rapid rate of about 2.5 percent a year between 1963 and 1971. Since then, however, a national birth-control program has helped to reduce the annual increase. The most populous cities include the capital, Colombo; Dehiwela-Mt. Lavinia (population, 210,000); Moratuwa (177,000); Jaffna (129,000); Galle (91,000); and Kandy (110,000).

Economy. Sri Lanka's economy is based almost completely on agriculture, which employs 45 percent of the labor force. The soil is Sri Lanka's most important natural resource. The leading crops

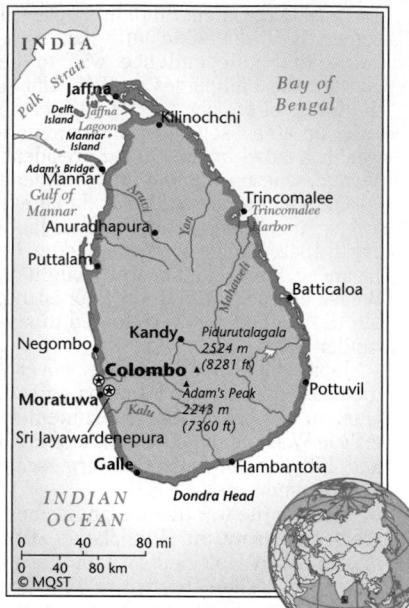

of tea, rubber, coconuts, and spices are grown on large plantations. Tea is grown in the highlands, rubber in the wet lowlands, and coconuts in drier coastal regions. Small farms produce ample supplies of rice and vegetables. Fish are abundant off the coasts.

Sri Lanka's few industries are mainly concerned with processing tea, rubber, and coconuts. There are also factories producing textiles, cement, soap, and other consumer items.

Sri Lanka relies heavily on foreign trade for many commodities. Tea, textiles and garments, rubber, and coconut products account for most of the exports, which are shipped mainly to the United States, Egypt, and West Germany. The major imports, including foodstuffs, petroleum products, textiles, fertilizers, and machinery, come mainly from Saudi Arabia, Japan, and the United States.

Government. In 1978 Sri Lanka received a new constitution that provided for a strong popularly elected president as head of state. The president appoints the prime minister and cabinet and can dismiss them.

Legislative power is held by a unicameral parliament with 225 members. The president also has the power to dismiss the parliament.

History. Sri Lanka's first known inhabitants were a primitive people, the Veddas. In the 500s B.C., they were conquered by the Sinhalese, an Aryan people from northern India. The Sinhalese established a kingdom in the north central portion of the island, and constructed irrigation works to enable them to grow rice in the dry region. By the 200s B.C. Sinhalese civilization was quite advanced, and its culture, centered on Buddhism, had produced many magnificent temples, especially in the capital at Anuradhapura.

The kingdom was subjected to attacks and invasions by people from

TEA IS ONE OF SRI LANKA'S leading crops. Most of the tea plantations, such as this one in Nuwara Eliya, are in the highlands.

Taiwan

Official name: *Republic of China*
Area: *13,888 sq. mi., 35,980 sq. km.*
Type of government: *Multiparty democracy*
Population: *22,454,000*
Capital and largest city: *Taipei (Pop., 2,720,000)*
Language: *Mandarin Chinese (official), Taiwanese, Hakka dialects*
Literacy: *94% (1998 est.)*
Currency: *Dollar*
Per capita GDP: *$17,200 (Rank: 35th)*

southern India, and it was conquered in the A.D. 900s by the Chola empire. The Chola were driven out in the 1000s, but some Chola cultural influences remained. During the 1000s Arab traders began to stop at Sri Lanka, and some settled on the island.

Between the 1200s and 1400s, the island was attacked by Malay and Chinese adventurers, as well as by Indians. In the 1300s the Hindu Tamil people of southern India invaded Sri Lanka and settled in the northern part of the island, forcing the Sinhalese to the south.

European influence. In the 1500s Portuguese traders arrived in Sri Lanka, drawn by the high quality of the cinnamon that the islanders grew. They soon destroyed the Tamil kingdom and established control over the coastal regions. The Sinhalese retreated to the highland interior, around Kandy. In 1638 traders of the Dutch East India Company arrived.

By 1658, aided by the king of Kandy, the Dutch had driven out the Portuguese and had taken over the spice trade. The Dutch exerted little control over the island's government. During the 1600s and 1700s the Sinhalese kingdom of Kandy underwent a cultural revival and grew in power, controlling some smaller islands in the Indian Ocean.

In 1796 the British replaced the Dutch in the coastal areas, and in 1802 made the island the crown colony of Ceylon. By 1815, with the aid of some of the Kandyans, the British took control of the island, including Kandy. The British expanded the area of cultivated land, planted tea and rubber, and improved irrigation facilities in the north. They established schools and introduced Western forms of government.

In 1931 Ceylon was granted limited self-government. Parliamentary elections were held in 1947, and on February 4, 1948, Ceylon was granted sovereignty as an independent member of the Commonwealth of Nations.

Independence. Independent Ceylon concentrated on developing its economy

and improving the lot of its people through social welfare programs. From the mid-1950s to the mid-1960s, Ceylonese politics was dominated by the socialist Sri Lanka Freedom Party (SLFP). S.W.R.D. Bandaranaike, leader of the SLFP, was prime minister from 1956 until his assassination in 1959. His widow became prime minister in 1960 and the country followed strongly socialist policies, with many businesses being nationalized. The government's methods were unpopular, and it fell in 1964.

Under the more moderate United National Party (UNP), elected in 1965, the socialist program continued, but encouragement was given to private business to speed economic growth. The UNP government concentrated on uniting the many factions of Ceylon's society.

Mrs. Bandaranaike was elected prime minister again in 1970. She severely suppressed left-wing rioters who wanted more rapid socialization and an end to the nation's economic problems.

In 1972 a new constitution was adopted; it declared Ceylon to be the Republic of Sri Lanka, and ended the role of the British queen as monarch. Sri Lanka remained, however, a member of the Commonwealth.

Another new constitution in 1978 provided for a presidential government after the UNP had ousted Mrs. Bandaranaike in the election of 1977. Junius Jayewardene, leader of the UNP, then became president.

A separatist movement among the minority Tamils erupted in violence in 1983, and continued for 20 years. Peacekeeping efforts by India failed. Upheaval in the country has included presidential assassination. After years of conflict, the 2001 election of Ranil Wickremesinghe as prime minister seemed to pave the way for a possible end to hostilities. Norway helped broker a peace agreement in early 2002, resulting in subsequent productive meetings, and talks began in September 2002.

The land. The island of Taiwan is mountainous. Its major range, the Chungyang, runs from north to south in the eastern third of the island. It contains many peaks over 10,000 feet high, and its highest peak, Yü Shan, is more than 13,000 feet high. To the east, across a narrow rift valley, a coastal range rises to a maximum of 7,000 feet and then drops sharply into the sea. Many rivers flow east and west from the Chungyang range.

To the west of the mountains the land slopes to a fertile coastal plain that is the heartland of the island. It is only some 25 miles at its widest, but its width is being extended by continuous sedimentation along the shallow west coast. The west coast contains the island's best harbors.

Taiwan's climate is semitropical. Annual precipitation varies from 50 inches in the mountains to 200 inches on the coasts. During winter, from October to April, north to northeast winds bring

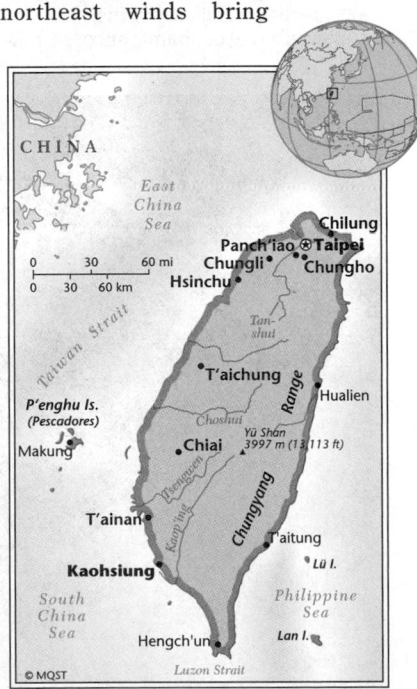

much rain to the northern areas. In summer, the winds are chiefly from the south and southwest, and it is during this period that most of the south receives its maximum rain. From May to November, the island may be struck by typhoons.

Temperatures in the lowlands rarely drop below 60°F. The higher elevations are colder, and the higher peaks have prolonged snow cover.

The people. Taiwan was settled by Chinese from Fukien and Kwantung provinces during the period from the 1600s to the 1900s. There was a large influx of people from all parts of the mainland in the late 1940s and early 1950s. There are also small numbers of aborigines who are considered to have come from Polynesian stock. Mandarin Chinese is the official language of Taiwan; however, many native Taiwanese speak the Amoy dialect of Chinese.

Taiwan is densely populated, with some 1,693 people per square mile in 1993. Sixty-seven percent of the population is urban. The most populous cities are the capital, Taipei; Kaohsiung (population, 1,387,000); T'aitung (108,000); and T'ainan (720,000).

Economy. Taiwan has one of the world's fastest growing economies, and the second highest per capita income in East Asia, after Japan.

The island's natural resources are limited to coal, natural gas, hydroelectric power, and its main resources, fertile land and abundant water.

Agriculture continues to play an important role in the economy. As only one-quarter of the island's land can be cultivated, farming is intensive and two or three crops a year are raised on the same land. Rice is the major crop, and the staple of the diet. Sugar cane, raised primarily for export, is second in importance. Sweet potatoes, soybeans, tea, peanuts, and fruits are also significant items.

Taiwan's real economic success, how-ever, has come from light manufacturing geared to the export market. Heavy industry has also been successful, including steel, shipbuilding, and oil refining.

Taiwan relies heavily on its export market for the strength of its economy. Exports include electronic equipment, plastics, footwear, toys, textiles, and other consumer goods. Imports are largely raw materials and capital goods to support industry and food. Its major trading partners are the United States, Japan, and Hong Kong.

Government. The Republic of China (also called Nationalist China) is the continuation of the nationalist government that fled mainland China under Chiang Kai-shek in 1949. It claims to be the legitimate government of all China, but its authority is confined to Taiwan. The People's Republic of China insists that Taiwan is an integral part of Chinese territory. Taiwan has a republican form of government.

The executive branch of government is quite strong. It consists of a president and vice president elected by popular vote to four-year terms, and a premier and cabinet appointed by the president.

The National Assembly, a nonstanding body, is responsible for amending the constitution, impeaching the president, and changing national borders. Primary legislative responsibility rests with the 225-member Legislative Yuan. Historically both bodies have been dominated by Nationalist Chinese leaders, but changes in recent years permitted greater Taiwanese representation. This culminated in 2000 with the first peaceful transfer of power to the Democratic Progressive Party, which now holds the majority of the seats in the Legislative Yuan, thus ending more than 50 years of Nationalist rule.

History. Most of Taiwan's history prior to 1949 is coincidental with China's, now known as the People's Republic of China.

In 1624 the island of Taiwan, inhabited by aborigines and a small number of Chinese, was seized by the Dutch. In 1661 a Ming dynasty loyalist, Cheng Cheng-kung (Koxinga), drove out the Dutch and made Taiwan a base from which he hoped to reconquer the mainland from the Manchus, but Manchu armies regained control in 1683.

In 1896, following the first Sino-Japanese war, Taiwan was ceded to Japan. For a half-century, until the end of World War II, Japan invested heavily in the Taiwanese economy, preparing the island for its later, great economic success.

In 1945, when the Nationalists took over the government of Taiwan, they were faced immediately with difficulties in governing the island. Descendants of the mainland Chinese who had settled Taiwan in the 1600s regarded themselves as native Taiwanese, different from the mainland people. Some had hoped for complete independence for Taiwan after the Japanese withdrew.

The sufferings of the Taiwanese under outside rule, their unmet demands for independence, and the ineptitude and harshness of the Nationalist government after 1945, combined to create severe friction between the Taiwanese and the mainlanders. The situation worsened, and in 1947 the Taiwanese rebelled. The revolt was crushed ruthlessly.

When the Nationalists lost to Communist forces on the mainland in 1949, they moved their government, their army, and some 3 million of their citizens to Taiwan. There, President Chiang Kai-shek proclaimed a government of all China and declared his intention to return to the mainland.

In 1950 Communist China declared Taiwan to be a part of its territory and announced its intention to reclaim it. The U.S. Navy protected the island and prevented any contemplated mainland invasion attempt.

TAIWAN'S ECONOMY relies heavily on its export market. Many of the exports are electronic equipment, such as the computers being tested in this factory.

Taiwan's history in the 1950s and 1960s was shaped by the claim of both Chinas to be the sole representative of the Chinese people. Because of the rivalry, low-level military activities continued between the two Chinas in the 1950s and 1960s, flaring up into several crises—the battle for the tiny islands of Quemoy and Matsu in the late 1950s, and the buildup of Communist and Nationalist troops on facing coasts in the early 1960s.

The division radically affected the nation's foreign affairs as well. Taiwan committed itself to maintaining its position in the noncommunist world as the sole legal government of China, and it refused to deal officially with any nation that recognized Communist China.

The United States not only protected the island with U.S. naval forces, but gave the Nationalists their main diplomatic support, trained the Nationalist army, and provided the aid that made possible Taiwan's economic growth.

The Kuomintang claim to all China affected Taiwan's domestic politics in other ways. Full-scale national elections were postponed until the return to the mainland, and the republic's affairs remained in the hands of the National Assembly, which elects the president. Twice it amended the constitution to permit President Chiang Kai-shek to be reelected.

In the early 1960s the Kuomintang moved to strengthen its control over Taiwan's politics in response to a widening of opposition activities. In 1966 the National Assembly greatly increased the powers of the presidency, at the same time promising that elections would be held for the assembly on Taiwan.

In 1971 Taiwan lost its seat in the United Nations to the People's Republic of China. In 1979 the United States recognized the People's Republic as China's legal government. In 1980 it failed to renew the mutual security and defense pact it had signed in 1954 with Taiwan, but it continues to maintain a "privileged relations" status.

Chiang, the center of the Nationalist movement for over 50 years, died in 1975. His son, Chiang Ching-kuo, the premier, was named chairman of the Central Committee of the Kuomintang Party. In 1978 he was elected president.

In 1987 Chiang Ching-kuo lifted martial law. Chiang died in 1988 and was succeeded by Lee Teng-hui, the country's first native Taiwanese president. Lee continued the process of reform, and in 1991 declared an end to Taiwan's 43-year emergency rule. In open elections later that year the Kuomintang was returned to power. Taiwan continues its move away from reunification through election of pro-independence candidates. In 2003 relations between Taiwan and China became even more strained with continued calls for a referendum on independence and the call for removal of missiles aimed at Taiwan.

Tajikistan

Official name: *Republic of Tajikistan*
Area: *55,237 sq. mi., 143,100 sq. km.*
Type of government: *Republic*
Population: *6,720,000*
Capital and largest city: *Dushanbe (Pop., 529,000)*
Languages: *Tajik (official), Russian*
Literacy: *98%,* **Currency:** *Ruble*
Per capita GDP: *$1,140 (Rank: 163rd)*

The land. The republic of Tajikistan is in the mountainous southeastern portion of Central Asia. It includes in the Pamir Mountains in the east, the Gorno-Badakhshan Autonomous Region (population, 161,000), which comprises 24,590 square miles (63,700 square kilometers) on the borders of Afghanistan and China. More than half of Tajikistan is situated above 10,000 feet (3,000 meters). Tajikistan has the highest peaks of the former Soviet Union, in the northern Pamir region: Communism Peak at 24,590 feet (7,495 meters) and Lenin Peak at 23,405 feet (7,143 meters). The southern Tien Shan Mountains occupy the central part of the republic.

The Tajik Fergana valley in the north, and the hot, dry Gissar and Vakhsh valleys to the southwest, contain most of Tajikistan's people and agriculture. From vast glaciers, including Fedchenko Galcier, some of the world's longest fast-flowing rivers and their tributaries provide irrigation for many farms. The largest river is the Amu Darya, forming the boundary between Tajikistan and Afghanistan. Severe earthquakes and landslides are common throughout the republic. Lake Kara-Kul, a salt lake in the Pamirs at almost 13,000 feet (3,900 meters) is the largest in Tajikistan.

The climate is strongly continental, hot in summer and very cold in winter, but it changes with altitude. Temperatures in Tajikistan range from 86.5°F (30.3°C) during the southern summer to -3.3°F (-19.6°C) in the highlands in winter.

The people. Tajiks, forming more than 62 percent of the population, are an Iranian people whose ancestors may have originated in Sogdiana, part of the ancient Persian Empire. Their language is similar to Persian and is written in a modified Cyrillic script. The Tajiks are closely related to the Muslim Uzbeks, who make up 23 percent of the population. Unlike many Central Asians, Tajiks have been a sedentary rather than nomadic people. Although Tajiks have been a separate ethnic group since as early as the eighth century, they were long a part of larger Uzbek regions with only semi-independent status.

Tajikistan has a high rate of population increase, especially in the region of Gorno-Badakhshan. It had one of the lowest standards of living in the former Soviet Union. However, literacy increased dramatically under the Soviet regime. Women were emancipated officially in the 1920s, and by 1977 they made up almost 40 percent of office and industrial workers.

Economy. Tajikistan has a variety of mineral resources, mainly in the north; they include brown coal, iron, lead, zinc, mercury, antimony, tin, tungsten, and gold. There are deposits of uranium and radium, as well as precious and semi-precious stones. Oil and natural gas are extracted in some areas. Besides mining, Tajikistan's industries include mineral processing, textile machinery production, cotton and silk milling, and carpetmaking.

Hydroelectric power generated by the republic's many rivers is developing fast and playing an important role in both industry and agriculture. Major power plants have been built on the Syr Darya and Vakhsh rivers, with a thermal power station installed near Dushanbe. A network of canals includes the Vakhsh and Gissar, constructed in the late 1930s. The Great Fergana and North Fergana canals and extensive irrigation systems were built after World War II.

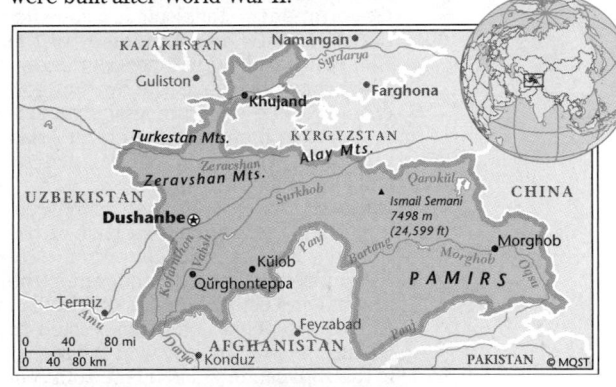

Long-staple cotton is one of the mainstays of the economy, with most of the crop grown in the valleys of the southwest and northwest. Irrigation techniques, in use since ancient times, greatly increased the yield of cotton, rice, barley, and oats. Orchard fruits such as pears, apricots, apples, cherries, figs, and pomegranates flourish on the lower mountain slopes. Mulberry trees are grown for the silk industry.

center
US

centre
Brit.

kilometers
US

kilometres
Brit.

THE COTTON so important to the Tajikistan economy is mostly grown in the valleys of the southwest and northwest.

23 Asia

COUNTRIES

DESTROYED BUILDINGS are evidence of the civil unrest in Khatlon, Tajikistan.

US

labour
Brit.

Livestock breeding is an important factor in Tajikistan's agriculture, with sheep predominating over cattle, goats, and pigs. Karakul sheep are raised for their high-quality wool.

Government.   Tajikistan is a constitutional republic and a member of the Commonwealth of Independent States. The prime minister is the head of government. The governmental structure is similar to that of other Central Asian republics, with executive, legislative, and judicial branches.

History.   As early as the second century B.C., the region was part of the Persian Empire and the empire of Alexander the Great. Conquered in the seventh and eighth centuries by Iranian Arabs, the people were converted to Islam. The Mongols invaded the region in the 13th century, and by the 16th century it had become part of the Uzbek emirate (khanate) of Bukhara. In the mid-1800s, Russia took over the northern Tajik areas, while Bukhara continued to control the south. After the Russian Revolution of 1917, Tajikistan's northern territories were included in the Turkestan Autonomous Soviet Socialist Republic, with other regions becoming part of the Uzbek Soviet Socialist Republic. In 1924 the Tajik Autonomous Soviet Socialist Republic was formed within the Uzbek Soviet Socialist Republic. Modern Tajikistan was created out of the areas of Bukhara and Turkestan already heavily populated by Tajiks; it became the Tajik Soviet Socialist Republic in 1929. Tajiks strongly resisted Soviet efforts at collectivization and land reform in the 1930s, and the ensuing repressions caused long-lasting hostility.

Since the unsuccessful coup of August 1991, in Moscow, the Communist Party has been outlawed and reinstated on several occasions. After declaring independence from the Soviet Union on September 9, 1991, Tajikistan became a member of the Commonwealth of Independent States in December 1991. A provisional Council of State governed the country following the resignation in September 1992 of President Rakhomon Nabiev. A civil war that began after independence culminated in the implementation of a peace agreement in 2000, but peace remains tenuous.

(For more information on the history of Tajikistan during the Soviet period, see the article on Russia in the EUROPE AND RUSSIA volume.)

Thailand

Official name: *Kingdom of Thailand*
Area: *198,404 sq., mi., 514,000 sq. km.*
Type of government: *Constitutional monarchy*
Population: *63,645,000*
Capital and largest city: *Bangkok (Pop., metro. area, 6,355,000)*
Language: *Thai, English*
Literacy: *94%*
Currency: *Baht*
Per capita GDP: *$6,600 (Rank: 74th)*

The land.   Thailand has several distinct land regions. The north-south trending Bilauktaung mountain range follows the border with Burma. It extends southward across the Kra Isthmus into peninsular Thailand, which forms the backbone of the great Malay peninsula.

In northwestern Thailand, a mountainous upland area, with an elevation of 600 to 3,000 feet above sea level, lies between the Salween and the Mekong river basins. It contains the major tributaries of the Chao Phraya, the principal river system of the country.

The basin of the Chao Phraya, which contains the fertile Bangkok Plain, is the core region of Thailand. The basin has an inverted U-shaped outline, with the Dawna and the Bilauktaung mountain ranges on the west, the uplands of the hilly Shan Plateau on the north, and the Phetchabun Mountains on the east.

The Phetchabun Mountains form the western margin of the Khorat Plateau, a rolling basin with elevations generally below 700 feet. Rising in the Khorat Plateau is the Mun River, the chief Thai tributary of the Mekong River. The Dang Raek scarp establishes the southern boundary of the Khorat Plateau; between this scarp and the Cardamom Mountains on the Gulf of Thailand coast, a narrow lowland connects the Tonle Sap basin of Kampuchea with the delta of the Chao Phraya.

Climate.   Thailand lies within the monsoon area of Southeast Asia, but due to the rain shadow effect of the surrounding mountains, annual precipitation is limited in the lowlands. Temperatures are generally quite high.

The people.   Almost all of Thailand's people are Thai, related to the people of Laos and eastern Myanmar. They speak Thai, and most are Buddhists. The largest minority group is Chinese.

Compared with most Southeast Asian countries, Thailand, with a population density of about 297 people per square mile, is rather thinly settled.

Population is concentrated in the river valleys, especially that of the Chao Phraya. Bangkok (Krung Thep), the capital and by far the largest city, is located near the mouth of the Chao Phraya.

Economy.   Thailand is a relatively prosperous country. Agriculture is the basis of economic life, but industry based largely on the exploitation of Thailand's rich natural resources has increased in recent years.

Forestry, mining, and related operations are the country's leading nonagricultural activities. Thailand is the world's second greatest producer of tin, although mining as a whole employs only 1 percent of the total labor force. In the early 1970s, a substantial amount of petroleum and gas was discovered in the Gulf of Thailand; the production from these fields is helping to reduce Thailand's dependency on imported oil.

One of Thailand's most valuable resources is timber. About one-quarter of the country is covered by forests. Tropical evergreen rain forests in the mountains contain a great variety of hardwoods, and dense monsoon forests contain teak, of which Thailand is one of the world's leading producers. However, overexploitation is leading to rapid depletion of the forests. There is an abundance of fish in the waters off Thailand's long coast and in its many rivers.

Agriculture.   Thailand has rich soil and agriculture employs about 60 percent of the labor force. Although farming methods tend to be rather primitive, so much

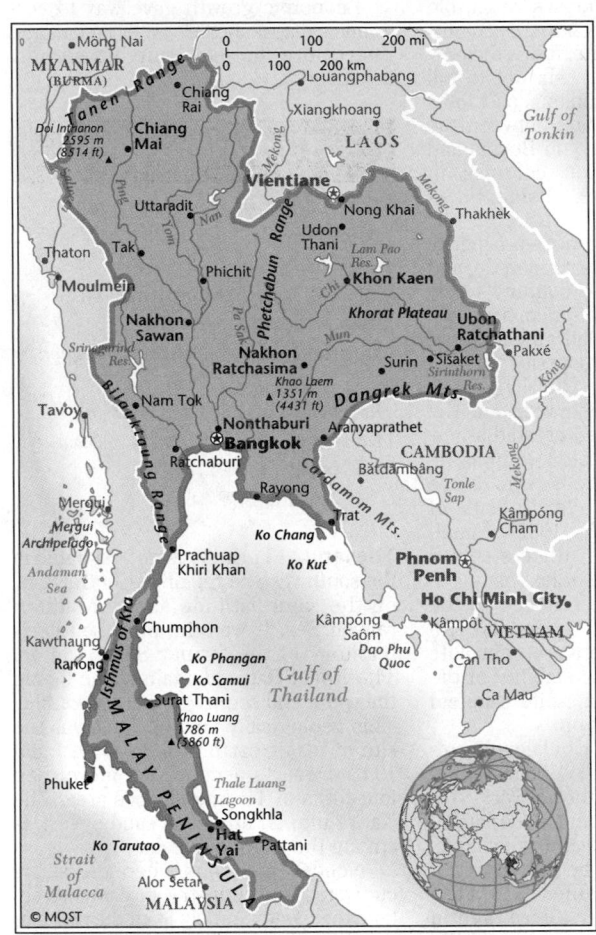

TRADITIONAL ways are still preserved by the Thai people, who are related to the people of Laos and eastern Myanmar.

MOST THAI people are Buddhists and take pride in their beautiful temples.

land is under cultivation, about 44 percent of the total area, that Thailand is a large net exporter of food and agricultural products.

Most Thai farms are small and individually owned, except for the rich Bangkok region estates, which use tenant farmers to cultivate rice. Rice is by far the largest crop.

Other agricultural activities include rubber production, both on large estates and on small holdings. Some short-staple cotton is produced on the peninsula in the northern sections of the central plain. Other crops include tobacco, sugar cane, corn, fruits, cassava, peanuts, soybeans, coconuts, sesame, castor beans, silk, and peppers.

Manufacturing is becoming an increasingly important part of the Thai economy. Although most industry is involved in the processing of Thailand's natural resources and agricultural products, the government is actively promoting export industries like electronics assembly and textile manufacture, and its heavy industries like cement production and natural gas liquefaction.

Trade. Thailand's international trade depends primarily on the country's farms, forests, and mines. Rice, rubber, tapioca, electronics, and textiles are major exports. Fuels and manufactured goods are the major imports. Japan, the United States, and the European Union are Thailand's major trading partners.

Government. Thailand is a constitutional monarchy with the king as head of state. The king approves the selection of the prime minister, who is chosen from the House of Representatives. Legislative power rests with a bicameral National Assembly, consisting of a 500-member House of Representatives and a 200-member Senate. The House and Senate members are elected by popular vote to four-year terms.

History. The Thai have a long history. People speaking closely related dialects of the Thai language have been living throughout the hilly region of southern China and northern Southeast Asia since nearly the beginning of recorded history. Modern Thailand has its origins in a state created by small warring bands of Thai-speaking people who moved down into the lowlands of the Chao Phraya valley in the A.D. 1200s.

In the late 1200s, under their first important kingdom, Sukhothai, the Thai conquered most of the area of present-day Thailand from Mon and Khmer peoples. They adopted the Theravada Buddhism of their Mon subjects and the political system of the Khmer rulers whom they displaced.

Between the 1300s and the 1700s, the Thai ruled from a capital located at Ayutthaya, about 75 miles north of modern Bangkok. The Thai state, like others in Southeast Asia at that time, had no real

boundaries. The king ruled his palace-city and its surrounding area directly.

The king exercised some control over most of the Chao Phraya plain through semiautonomous noble-officials. At times Thai kings were strong enough to exact tribute from more distant vassals in Malaya, Cambodia, Laos, and northern Thailand. Wars were common and generally were fought to enforce claims to tribute or to capture new subjects rather than to acquire territory.

Chakri dynasty. In the 1500s the Burmese overran the kingdom and sacked Ayutthaya. The Thai recovered, only to suffer another crushing defeat by Burma in 1767. A powerful Thai revival led to the founding of a strong, new dynasty, the Chakri, in 1782. The Chakri kings established their capital at the port city of Bangkok, and it was from there that Thailand—called Siam by Westerners—faced European imperialism in the 1800s.

The Chakri kings, unlike their Burmese, Vietnamese, and Chinese counterparts, were actively interested in commerce and aware of what was happening in the world outside. In 1855 King Mongkut willingly signed a treaty with the British opening Siam to international trade; he took the first step to modernize the monarchy.

Mongkut's first son, Chulalongkorn, ruled from 1868 to 1910. He steered the country toward modernization while

23 Asia

IRONICALLY, ELEPHANTS were used in the logging that reduced their habitat in Thailand. Steps are being taken now to protect both forests and elephants.

avoiding the dangers presented by European imperialists and Siamese reactionaries.

Slowly but steadily Chulalongkorn abolished slavery, replaced traditional forced labor with monetary taxes, drawn in part from rapidly rising exports of rice and teak, and reorganized the administration with the help of European advisers. He was obliged to yield control of large vassal areas to the British and French, but at the same time he greatly extended the area effectively ruled by Bangkok.

centimeters
US

centimetres
Brit.

MOST THAI farms are small and individually owned. A market like this might offer anything from corn, fruits, and coconuts to rice, cotton, and peppers.

During Chulalongkorn's reign, old Siam was transformed into a recognizably modern nation-state. It was the only country in Southeast Asia not to fall under colonial rule, thanks in part to its position as a buffer state between the British colonial territory in Burma and India and the French colonies in Indochina. The name Thailand was adopted in 1939.

In the early 1900s, Siam's prosperity grew as demands for its rubber, tin, and timber increased. The country's new progressive social, economic, and educational policies enabled all classes of Thais to share in its prosperity.

Constitutional monarchy. Chulalongkorn's successors were less able men, and the changes he inaugurated created a new class of Western-educated administrators and army officers who were increasingly restive under the rule of absolute monarchy. In 1932 a small group of civilians and officers seized power in a swift and bloodless coup.

The Chakris were reduced to the status of constitutional monarchs. The king's willingness to give up absolute rule contributed to the stability of the constitutional system despite frequent changes of administration.

In a continuation of Chulalongkorn's "survival diplomacy," the Thais joined Japan as a passive ally during World War II to avoid invasion and occupation. When Japan's defeat became inevitable, Thailand quietly let it be known that it supported the Allies. After 1945 Thailand was actively pro-Western, and in 1954 was a founding member of the Southeast Asia Treaty Organization (SEATO), although, following its well-established neutralist tradition, it also attempted to maintain informal, friendly contacts with Communist China.

Modern Thailand. King Bhumibol Adulyadej ascended the throne following the death of his older brother in 1946. In the decades after the war Thailand concentrated on industrializing and modernizing its economy and on protecting itself from the military conflicts that still raged in Southeast Asia.

Internal conflicts and persistent communist guerrilla activities have resulted in several military coups. While these takeovers often resulted in the suspension of constitutional and civil rights, they did not weaken Thailand's political stability. Although the governments were autocratic, they were not oppressive.

A bloody military takeover in 1976 was followed by another in 1977. A democratic constitution was provided in 1978, and in February 1980, the prime minister resigned in the face of rising oil prices, inflation, and unemployment; he was succeeded by Prem Tinsulanonda who remained in office until 1988. In 1991 the military again took over the government. In 1992, after violent clashes with pro-democracy demonstrators, the military agreed to national elections. Chuan Leekpai, an opponent of military rule, became prime minister.

Economic growth gave way to economic collapse in 1997. After bailout and restructure, the economy has steadily improved.

Turkmenistan

Official name: *Turkmenistan*
Area: *188,407 sq. mi., 488,100 sq. km.*
Type of government: *Republic*
Population: *4,689,000*
Capital and largest city: *Ashgabat (Pop., 407,000)*
Languages: *Turkmen, Russian*
Literacy: *98%;* **Currency:** *Manat*
Per capita GDP: *$4,700 (Rank: 89th)*

The land. Turkmenistan is situated in the southwestern region of Central Asia, on the same latitude as the Mediterranean Sea. It was the most southerly territory of the former Soviet Union. The Kopet-Dag mountain range lies in the south and southwest of the republic. This geologically young range was the site of major earthquakes in 1929 and 1948. Deserts account for more than four-fifths of Turkmenistan's area. The Kara-Kum, an immense sand desert, is among the world's largest.

Nondesert regions, where the land is cultivated and industry has prospered, take their water supply from the oases of the Kopet-Dag foothills and those of the republic's principal rivers. These include the Amu Darya (called the Oxus in ancient times), which flows toward the Aral Sea along Turkmenistan's northeastern border, the Murgab, and the Tedzhen. With a strongly continental climate, temperatures range from an average of -25°F (-4°C) in winter to 82°F (28°C) in summer. In the southeast Kara-Kum, temperatures occasionally reach 122°F (50°C).

Rainfall, occurring mostly in the spring, seldom exceeds 3 inches (8 centimeters) per year in the northwest, with mountain areas receiving about 12 inches (30 centimeters) per year.

The people. Turkmen descendants of the medieval Oghuz tribes are the principal ethnic group. The Turkmen were originally pastoral nomads divided into many tribes and clans. Eight independent tribal groups were identified in 1863. They include the larger Tekke, Ersari, and Yomut tribes, and the smaller Chaudor, Salor, Sarik, Goklan, and Alieli tribes.

Before the of Russian and later Soviet domination, many Turkmen were mercenaries in the service of various Central Asian rulers. Much of the population lives in the Kopet-Dag oasis in the south and the Amu Darya valley of the northeast. Traditional occupations such as raising livestock (including camels and horses), growing long-staple cotton, and carpet-making provide income for many people.

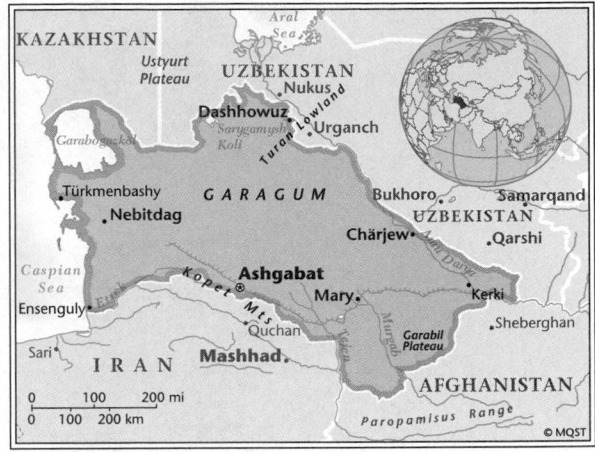

TURKMEN MARKETS display carpets, world-famous for their beautiful designs and durability. The carpets are a leading export for Turkmenistan.

Turkmen is a southern Turkic language. First written in Arabic script, it was changed to Latin script in 1929 and to Cyrillic in 1940. It has recently been replaced (1992) by a Latin-based Turkish script. The principal religion of indigenous Turkmen is Sunni Muslim, with elements of Sufi mysticism.

Economy. Oil and natural gas extraction and cotton growing are the most important elements of Turkmenistan's economy. Oil and gas resources are tapped mainly in the west and from offshore sites in the Caspian Sea. Mineral deposits include coal, sulfur, magnesium, and salt, with about 50 new salt mines in the Kara-Kum Desert.

Industrialization has been slow to develop in Turkmenistan, but the republic now has chemical plants, metal-processing works, and production of oil-refining and agricultural equipment, as well as cotton-ginning industries and silk-weaving mills.

Agriculture is concentrated on cotton, fodder and cereal crops, fruit, melons, and grapes. Karakul sheep are raised for their beautiful much prized pelts. Turkmen carpets, famous for their varied designs and durability, are an important export.

Government. The structure of government follows that of other Central Asian republics, with an executive branch consisting of the president and Council of Ministers, a legislative branch, and a judicial branch in the form of a Supreme Court. Turkmenistan is a member of the Commonwealth of Independent States.

History. Turkmenistan was ruled by Arabs in the eighth century and by Seljuk Turks in the 11th century. The country was conquered by Genghis Khan in the 13th century and by Tamerlane in the 14th century. The southern tribes were ruled by Persia from the 15th to 17th centuries, while the northern groups were controlled by the Uzbek khanates of Khiva and Bukhara.

Russian efforts to expand into Turkmen territory resulted in the disastrous Battle of Gok Tepe in 1881, when some 150,000 Turkmen were killed. By 1895 Russian domination was established.

After the Bolsheviks failed to take control in 1917, Soviet forces were sent to Ashkabad. The Turkestan Autonomous Soviet Socialist Republic was created in 1918 and it formally entered the Soviet Union. In 1924 the Turkmen Soviet Socialist Republic was organized as part of the National Delimitation of Central Asia. Soviet policies of collectivization, compulsory settlement of nomadic groups, and repression of Muslim religious practice and intellectual freedom met with strong resistance as late as the mid-1930s. Turkmenistan declared its independence in October 1991, and joined the Commonwealth of Independent States in December 1991.

Saparmurad Niyazov, head of state, was elected president in 1990, reelected in 1992 in a one-candidate contest, and voted president-for-life by a parliament of his choosing.

(For more information on the history of Turkmenistan during the Soviet period, see the article on Russia in the EUROPE AND RUSSIA volume.)

Uzbekistan

Official name: *Republic of Uzbekistan*

Area: *172,696 sq. mi., 447,400 sq. km.*

Type of government: *Republic*

Population: *25,563,000*

Capital and largest city: *Tashkent (Pop., 2,143,000)*

Languages: *Uzbek, Russian, Tajik*

Literacy: *99%;* **Currency:** *Som*

Per capita GDP: *$2,500 (Rank: 124th)*

The land. The republic of Uzbekistan, at the core of Central Asia, includes the Karakalpak Autonomous Republic in the north. Much of Uzbekistan is made up of desert, semidesert, and steppe. Almost 50 percent of the republic is permanent pastureland. In the north and northwest lie steppes that extend into Kazakhstan, with lowland desert areas in the southwest. Eastern Uzbekistan contains parts of the Tien Shan mountain ranges, interspersed with fertile valleys and rich oases that support a large number of people. The vast and productive Fergana valley is densely populated.

Major rivers are the Amu Darya on the southwestern boundary and the Syr Darya on the northeastern border. All other rivers in the republic begin in the mountains, are extensively tapped for irrigation, and eventually disappear into the desert sands. Irrigation networks that are used for agriculture total more than 93,150 miles (150,000 kilometers).

Uzbekistan's climate is strongly continental and generally very dry, with rainfall averaging about 8 inches (20 centimeters) per year. Temperatures in the

23 Asia

centrated mainly on cotton cleaning, silk weaving, and food processing.

Cotton is the republic's chief crop, thriving in the Uzbek climate and assisted by extensive irrigation. The oases of the Fergana valley, Zeravsha, Tashkent, and Khorezm produce, besides cotton, rice, fruit, and silk. In 1990 Uzbekistan produced about 62 percent of all cotton grown in the Soviet Union, as well as 50 percent of its rice and 60 percent of its alfalfa. The western desert and semidesert regions provide rich pastureland for livestock raising, particularly Karakul sheep.

Government.   Uzbekistan is a republic, but with authoritarian presidential rule, and is a member of the Commonwealth of Independent States. As in other Central Asian republics, the government is divided into an executive branch consisting of a president and a Cabinet of Ministers, a legislative branch with 250 members, and a judicial branch.

History.   There is evidence that humans lived in Uzbekistan as long as 55,000 to 70,000 years ago. The area was a part of the ancient Persian Empire, and was captured in the fourth century B.C. by Alexander the Great. Arab forces invaded in the eighth century A.D. and converted the nomadic Turkic peoples to Islam.

Controlled by the Seljuk Turks of Khorezm in the 12th century, then devastated by Genghis Khan and the Mongols in the 13th century, the region became part of the empire of Tamerlane (Timur) in the 14th century and flourished under his rule. Nomadic Uzbeks came down from the north in the early 1500s and mingled with the local population.

After the Uzbek khanates of Khiva, Bukhara, and Kokand were created, the area was annexed by Russia in the 1880s, and Russian immigrants began coming to Uzbekistan in large numbers. In 1917, despite Uzbek resistance, Soviet control was established in Tashkent, and the region became part of the Russian republic as the Turkestan Autonomous Soviet Socialist Republic in 1918.

The khanates of Khiva and Bukhara, made into people's republics in 1920, became Soviet Socialist Republics later, and eventually joined the Uzbek Soviet Socialist Republic, formed in 1924 from areas populated by Uzbeks.

Under Soviet rule, agriculture was modernized and new industries were introduced. Manned chiefly by Russians, industry expanded during World War II, when Russian factories were installed in Uzbekistan's safer territory. In 1960 irrigation was made available to the so-called southern Hungry Steppe, and in 1963 a large area was transferred from Kazakhstan to Uzbekistan to achieve better use of the land.

Uzbekistan proclaimed its independence in 1991 and joined the Commonwealth of Independent States.

(For more information on the history of Uzbekistan during the Soviet period, see the article on Russia in the EUROPE AND RUSSIA volume.)

Vietnam

Official name: *Socialist Republic of Vietnam*
Area: *127,210 sq. mi., 329,560 sq. km.*
Type of government: *Communist*
Population: *80,577,000*
Capital: *Hanoi (Pop., 2,464,000)*
Largest city: *Ho Chi Minh City (Pop., 4,990,000)*
Languages: *Vietnamese (official), French, Chinese, English*
Literacy: *94%;* **Currency:** *Dong*
Per capita GDP: *$2,100 (Rank: 134th)*

The land.   Vietnam is a narrow S-shaped strip of territory that consists of two large river deltas—the Red and Mekong—and a connecting mountain range—the Annam Cordillera.

Lying entirely within the tropics, all the lowlands of Vietnam have warm, moist, frost-free weather. The total amount of rainfall and the maximum period of rainfall depend upon exposure to the northeast and southwest monsoons. The average range of temperatures is from 60° to 90°F over most of the country.

From mid-September to March, the northeast monsoons bring cool weather to the Red River delta area, rain to the entire east coast, and sunny skies to the Mekong delta. From June to September, the southwest monsoons bring high humidity and rain to all of Vietnam. From July to November, the country is subjected to irregular and sometimes damaging typhoons.

The core of northern Vietnam is the Red River delta, in the eastern part. It is the compound delta of the Red, the Black, and other lesser rivers, most of which originate in adjacent China and Laos. Mountains and highlands dominate the landscape throughout the entire western and northern parts of the region.

South of the 17th parallel, the Annam Cordillera and its foothills form a central massif. It occupies some two-thirds of the southern area and leaves room for only a few small, enclosed coastal plains. The south's only major lowland lies in the swampy delta of the Mekong River at the southern tip of the country.

The people.   Almost all of the people are Vietnamese, descended from Mongol and Indonesian peoples.

The largest minority group is the Chinese, most of whom live in Hanoi, Haiphong, and Ho Chi Minh City.

The second largest minority consists of Montagnards, the aboriginal people of the country, who are of Malay-Indonesian or Mon stock, and who lead seminomadic lives in the mountains.

The third largest group is the Khmers, who are concentrated mostly

southern lowlands often exceed 104°F (40°C) in summer, which lasts from May to October. During the relatively short winter in the north, mean temperature is about 10°F (-12°C), occasionally reaching as low as -36°F (-38°C).

The people.   Forming more than 70 percent of the population, Uzbeks are a complex ethnic mixture. Their ancestors were the ancient peoples of Sogdiana, Shash, Fergana, and Khorezm, as well as Iranian and Turkic nomads mingled in the 15th century with Uzbek nomads from the north. Their name comes from the ruler Öz Beg Khan (died c 1340), from whom the Uzbeks claim to be descended.

In the 19th century a large number of Russian immigrants came to Uzbekistan and other lands of Central Asia and settled mostly in urban areas.

Important traditional occupations include cotton and rice farming, silkworm breeding, and the raising of livestock. With an ancient national heritage, Uzbek cultural life is rich and varied. Colorful national dress is still worn, particularly on holidays, and many customs and traditions survive in the form of folk art, song, interior decoration, rugs, special foods, and folk festivals.

The official language is Uzbek, a member of the Eastern Turkic language group, written since 1940 in Cyrillic script. Most Uzbeks are Sunni Muslim.

Economy.   Although uranium, copper, tungsten, aluminum ore, and gold are mined in Uzbekistan, natural gas, oil, and coal are the country's most valuable natural resources. Pipelines carry natural gas from Djaikak to Tashkent and from Fergana to Kokand, and there is a pipeline linking Bukhara to the Ural Mountains. Gas is used to power many local industries, which benefit as well from power generated by hydroelectric plants on the larger rivers.

The republic is a producer of machinery and heavy equipment, with emphasis on machines for cotton production and textiles, for irrigation projects, and for road-building. The chemical industry in Uzbekistan provides fertilizers for cotton growing, and cotton wastes and by-products are used in the manufacture of chemical products. Light industry is con-

colorful
US

colourful
Brit.

aluminum
US

aluminium
Brit.

HO CHI MINH was the leader of the communist government in North Vietnam. His efforts to unify the country led to the Vietnam war. Ho Chi Minh City is the largest city in Vietnam.

along the Cambodian border. There are also minorities of Cham (remnants of a 16th-century kingdom), Indian, and Malay peoples, and in the mountainous areas of the north and northwest are members of the Muong, Tai, Meo, and a number of smaller tribes.

In the northern section of the country, the population is concentrated in the Red River delta. In the southern section, the most densely settled area is in the Mekong delta region, especially around Ho Chi Minh City. The overall population density for Vietnam in 1993 was 571 persons per square mile.

Large numbers of people have fled Vietnam since 1975. A disproportionate number of these are ethnic Chinese who have claimed discrimination.

Economy. The economy of Vietnam, which has been in a state of disarray for decades, has been reorganized on the Soviet model. Part of the difficulty has been the integration of the socialist north with the south, which had been strongly capitalistic until 1975. Economic performance since the end of the Vietnam War has been very poor. However, in 1986 reforms were begun that loosened the tight controls on all aspects of the economy. It was hoped that these reforms would help make the economy more productive.

The Vietnamese economy is primarily agricultural, with rice production the leading activity. After very low production in the 1970s, the 1980s saw an increase in the amount of rice produced. The two major agricultural regions are the deltas of the Mekong and Red rivers. Agriculture in the north has been largely collectivized. An elaborate irrigation system of dams, dikes, and reservoirs put into operation in the Red River delta greatly increased the output of rice. Other agricultural products include corn, potatoes, soybeans, and coffee.

After rice, fish is the most important staple of the Vietnamese diet. The size of

the fish catch also increased during the 1980s, after a low period caused in part by loss of fishing boats used in emigration.

Manufacturing is plagued by equipment failure and unreliable sources of raw materials. Important industries include food processing, textiles, cement, fertilizers, and chemicals.

Most of Vietnam's trade is currently with Hong Kong and with Japan and its neighbors in Southeast Asia. Principal exports include raw materials, agricultural products, handicrafts, and seafood. Imports include petroleum, transportation equipment, chemicals, and fertilizers. Trade with Europe, the United States, and nations of the former Soviet Union is growing.

Government. Vietnam's government is democratic in form, but it is basically controlled by the Communist Party. The constitution vests supreme governmental authority in the popularly elected National Assembly, which chooses a standing committee to act for it between its short sessions and elects a president as head of state. The president appoints the prime minister and other cabinet members.

The Communist Party, however, nominates all candidates for the National Assembly, and government leaders are usually top officers of the party. The politburo of the party's central committee determines national policy.

History. Vietnam has been inhabited for many centuries, but little is known of its early history. It is thought to have been settled by people from elsewhere in Indochina and from neighboring islands, and by people moving southward from China.

By about 500 B.C., a kingdom had been established by these Viet peoples, as they called themselves. It extended from present-day northern Vietnam across the modern southern Chinese province of Kwangtung. In the 200s B.C., the Viet began to feel the cultural influence of China, and their kingdom was conquered by generals of the disintegrating Ch'in dynasty of China.

Chinese rule. The Ch'in ruled until 111 B.C., when armies of the Han dynasty, the successor to the Ch'in, conquered Vietnam and annexed it to China. It remained Chinese for about 1,000 years. The Vietnamese managed to retain their own culture despite the influences of Chinese economics, religion, and language.

The T'ang dynasty came to power in China in 618 and asserted strict authority over the "pacified South," or An-Nam, as Vietnam came to be called.

Independence. In 907 the T'ang dynasty collapsed, and the Vietnamese successfully rebelled. In 939 a rebel leader, Ngo Quyen, founded a Vietnamese dynasty that by 940 had regained control of all the territory from the 17th parallel to the southern Chinese province of Yünnan. China never recognized Annam's independence, and the country remained under nominal Chinese control.

The first strong dynasty was the Li (1009–1225), which launched a success-

ful drive to regain territory from the Chams of Champa. In 1471, after the Chams had been severely weakened by civil war, the Vietnamese were able to conquer the entire Champa kingdom and extend their Annamese empire across Cochin China, in the south, and into present-day Cambodia. Annam had become a great power in Southeast Asia, but its era of unity, power, prestige, and peace, was short.

Dissension. The 1500s were years of political upheaval. In 1620 civil war erupted between two powerful families—the Trinh in the north, or Tonkin, and the Nguyen in the south, or Annam. Each supported and controlled rival dynasties.

While the Vietnamese were fighting each other during the 1700s, Europeans began establishing colonies in Southeast Asia. Missionaries, explorers, and merchants arrived in Vietnam from Great Britain, France, The Netherlands, Portugal, and Spain. Despite their internal warfare, the Vietnamese successfully prevented any of the foreigners from establishing colonies. But Roman Catholic missionaries, most of whom were French, were successful in converting and influencing many people.

THE MEKONG RIVER delta is home to over half the people of southern Vietnam. It is the chief agricultural area of Vietnam.

Unification. One of the missionaries, Pigneau de Behaine, had become a close adviser of Nguyen Anh, the emperor of Annam. Through him, in 1787, the emperor first requested French aid in conquering all of Vietnam. French volunteer sailors and soldiers helped reorganize and train the Annamese army. They helped Nguyen Anh put down a rebellion in Annam and then assisted him in a successful attack upon Tonkin.

By 1802 the Annamese had conquered all of Tonkin, and in 1802 Nguyen Any proclaimed himself Emperor Gia-Long of all Vietnam, which included much of present-day Cambodia as well. Gia-Long restored peace to his newly unified country. He practiced toleration of all religions and permitted friendly Westerners to live in the country. His death in 1820, however, brought to the throne Minh-Mang, who was anti-Western and anti-Christian.

France tried to open Vietnam to trade by offering to negotiate commercial and diplomatic treaties with Minh-Mang. He rejected all offers and in 1826 broke off formal relations with France. In the 1830s he ordered the persecution of Christians.

Minh-Mang's successor, Thieu-Tri, practiced even harsher persecution of the missionaries and merchants, most of whom were French. It worsened under Thieu-Tri's successor, Tu-Doc, and when, in 1857, a Spanish bishop was executed, France joined Spain in attacking Vietnam.

French conquest. France's emperor, Napoleon III, seized the opportunity to increase French influence in the area. Following the occupation in 1859 of Saigon and French military success in 1861 in Cochin China, Tu-Doc ceded control of the southern region to France in 1862.

Tu-Doc obtained Chinese protection for his remaining kingdom (Annam and Tonkin) in the 1870s, but the French still captured Tonkin. In 1884 the Treaty of Hue placed all of Vietnam under French protection.

China protested but was not prepared to fight. France established its control over the region and in 1887 united Cambodia, Cochin China, Annam, and Tonkin into the colony of French Indochina.

Rebellions were frequent. In the 1920s France granted the Vietnamese a partially-elected council to advise the colonial government. Vietnamese representation was not effective, however, and in 1930–1931 more violent rebellions occurred. They were put down harshly. Opposition to French rule grew and Vietnamese nationalist groups were organized.

World War II. In 1940, after the outbreak of World War II, Japan invaded and occupied Vietnam, and took control of the colony from the Vichy French regime. The Japanese permitted Vietnamese leaders to participate more fully in the government than the French had, and although the Japanese exploited the country economically, they gave the people greater freedom.

During the war, the Communist Vietminh, led by Ho Chi Minh, became the first anti-Japanese guerrilla force in Vietnam. In March, 1945, near the end of the war, Japan declared Vietnam independent.

In August, 1945, Ho's forces seized Hanoi and demanded the abdication of the emperor, Bao Dai. In September Ho proclaimed the independence of the Democratic Republic of Vietnam. A struggle for power followed among the Vietminh, the non-Communist Vietnamese, and the French forces.

Division. In December, 1946, full-scale war broke out between French soldiers and Vietminh forces. The people tended to support the Vietminh. Communist countries aided the rebels, especially after 1949, when a communist regime came to power in China.

Finally, in 1954, at the Battle of Dien Bien Phu, the French suffered a shattering defeat and decided to withdraw. The 1954 Geneva Conference, which arranged for a cease-fire, provisionally divided Vietnam into northern and southern sectors at the 17th parallel. The unification of Vietnam was to be achieved by general elections to be held in July, 1956, in both sectors under international supervision. In the north, the Democratic Republic of Vietnam was led by its president, Ho Chi Minh, and was dominated by the Communist Party.

In the south, Ngo Dinh Diem, a Roman Catholic who was prime minister under Emperor Bao Dai, took over the government when Bao Dai left the country in 1954. As the result of a referendum held in 1955, a republic was established in South Vietnam, with Diem as president. Diem refused to participate in the elections mandated by the Geneva Conference.

Diem's government proved unable to solve South Vietnam's problems. Political power was concentrated in Diem's family, and his brother, Ngo Dinh Nhu, organized a secret police

force to enforce Diem's policies. Hostility toward the increasingly repressive regime aided the organization of communist-supported rebels, the Vietcong, who opened guerrilla activity in the late 1950s.

Vietnam War. The United States committed itself to supporting the Diem regime and sent military and political advisers to train the South Vietnamese army and to assist the government. Little headway was made against either the insurgents or the country's pressing social and economic problems, due in part to widespread corruption in the government.

Resentment against the government increased, especially among Buddhist leaders, who believed the government discriminated against Buddhists. Antigovernment riots, led by the Buddhists, broke out in Saigon and Hue. In November 1963, a military group seized power and killed Diem.

The war intensified as the United States expanded its role from training and advising to actual combat in the early 1960s. Also assisting the South Vietnamese army were Australian, Filipino, Korean, New Zealand, and Thai forces. Air raids began carrying the war to the north in 1965. U.S. troop strength reached its peak in April of 1969.

In January of 1973, in Paris, an agreement was signed providing for a cease-fire in place and calling for a political settlement of the conflict. The United States began withdrawing its last remaining troops, but hostilities continued between North and South Vietnam. In early 1975 the North Vietnamese opened a successful offensive, which brought about the complete defeat of the South Vietnamese forces. In June, a Provisional Revolutionary Government established an administration in Saigon.

Steps were undertaken to transform the society along the lines of the North. Vietnam was officially reunified in 1976.

Vietnam joined the United Nations without incident in 1977, and in 1978 joined the Soviet trading bloc, known as Comecon.

Vietnamese forces invaded Cambodia in 1977, and heavy fighting lasted for two years. China, already disturbed by Vietnam's domestic discrimination against Chinese residents, cut financial aid to the new communist government and invaded some of the country's northern provinces on February 17, 1979. Relations with China remained tense through the mid-1980s.

Vietnam withdrew its forces from Cambodia in 1989 under intense international pressure.

The collapse of the Soviet Union in 1991 and the consequent end of economic aid left the Vietnamese economy in severe trouble and forced badly needed economic reforms.

Vietnam and United States relations improved throughout the 1990s as U.S. trade restrictions were relaxed and Vietnam increased efforts to account for still-missing American servicemen.

SAIGON, the capital of South Vietnam, was evacuated by U.S. ground troops in 1973 and fell to the communists in 1975.

Cities of Asia

Agra, in northern India, on the Yamuna River in Uttar Pradesh State. One of the oldest cities in India, Agra is famous as the site of the Taj Mahal, the Red Fort, and other historic monuments. It is an important agricultural center and is well known for metal inlay work. Pop., 1,260,000.

Ahmadabad, one of the largest cities in India, in Gujarat (formerly Mysore) State in western India, on the Sabarmati River about 500 miles (805 km) north of Bombay. The city was founded in the 15th century, and it is known especially for its architecture, which reflects Hindu, Muslim, and Jain influences. It is also a major industrial, commercial, and transportation center noted for its cotton and textiles. Pop., 3,515,000.

Allahabad, in Uttar Pradesh State in northern India, at the confluence of the Ganges and Yamuna rivers. The city is a shipping and trade center for local agricultural produce, especially sugar cane and cotton. Allahabad is also a holy city for Hindus. It was built in 1583 by the Mughal emperor Akbar the Great on the site of ancient Prayag and has many historic monuments. Pop., 990,000.

Ashgabat, formerly Ashkhabad, then Poltoratsk, the largest city of Turkmenistan. It lies in an oasis on the edge of the Kara-Kum Desert, about 25 miles (40 km) from the Iranian border. Founded in 1881 as a Russian fort, it was an important station on the Transcaspian Railway. Ashgabat was made the capital of the Turkmen Soviet Socialist Republic in 1924. In 1948 it was devastated by an earthquake and has since been rebuilt. Pop., 407,000.

Astana, formerly Aqmola or Akmola, the capital of Kazakhstan. It lies on the banks of the Ishim (Esil) River in the north central part of the country. It was founded in 1854 as a fortress and was a small mining town until the 1950s, when it became the center of a large agricultural project. In 1994 the Kazakhstan government began transferring the national capital from Almaty to Astana. Pop., 313,000.

Bangalore, the capital and largest city of Karnataka State in southern India, and the fifth largest city in India. Founded in the 16th century, it is an industrial, transportation, educational, and communications center. Its products include aircraft, machine tools, railway coaches, electrical and electronic equipment, pharmaceuticals, textiles, and glassware. Pop. 4,292,000.

Bangkok, the largest city and capital of Thailand, located on the Chao Phraya River about 20 miles (32 km) inland from the Gulf of Siam. It is Thailand's industrial center and major port and handles most of the country's foreign trade. It is an important rail center and has one of the most modern airports in Southeast Asia. Pop., metro. area, 6,355,000.

Bassein, or Pathein, a port of Myanmar, on the Bassein River, which flows into the Bay of Bengal. It lies in a rice-growing region, and rice is its chief export. Pop., 144,000.

Beijing, or Peking, the capital of China, situated in northeastern China at the northern end of the Grand Canal. The city is an air and rail center, with links throughout China and connections with Russia and Korea. Its major industries produce steel, transportation equipment, agricultural machinery, and textiles. Beijing, the political, financial, cultural, and educational center of the country, is an ancient walled city that comprises the Inner City in the north, the Outer City in the south, and recently annexed suburban areas. Pop., 7,362,000.

Bishkek, formerly Frunze, the capital and largest city of Kyrgyzstan, located in the Chu River valley in the north central part of the country. Founded in 1878, it expanded rapidly after becoming the capital of the Kirghiz Soviet Socialist Republic in 1936, and after the installation of machine-building industries moved from Russia during World War II. The city is Kyrgyzstan's most important educational and cultural center. Pop., 753,000.

Bombay (now Mumbai), the capital of Maharashtra State, located on the west coast of India. The city is a major commercial, financial, and industrial center. As a port, Mumbai ranks second only to Calcutta. Mumbai has many educational institutions, the best-known of which is the renowned University of Bombay. Pop., 11,914,000.

Bukhara, or Bukhoro, a city in southwestern Uzbekistan, located in an important cotton-growing region of the Zeravshan River valley. Founded around the first century A.D., it was conquered by Genghis Khan and the Mongols in 1220, and by Tamerlane in 1370. It is a center of Islamic learning, intellectual activity and traditional handicrafts. Bukhara contains notable religious monuments, mosques, and madrasas (Muslim seminaries). Pop., 238,000.

Calcutta (now Kolkata), the second largest city in India, about 80 miles (130 km) north of the Bay of Bengal. It is the capital of West Bengal State. Kolkata is one of the world's busiest ports. Pop., 4,580,000.

center
US

centre
Brit.

THE MODERN CITY OF MUMBAI was founded by Portuguese traders as a trading post in the 1530s. Its present population of almost 12 million has led to serious problems of overcrowding.

Canton. See Guangzhou.

Cebu, the capital of Cebu Province, on the eastern coast of Cebu Island in the south-central Philippines. It is one of the country's largest cities, its second busiest port, after Manila, and home of several universities. Its products include textiles, ships, automobiles, chemicals, processed foods, furniture, and cosmetics. Visited by Ferdinand Magellan in 1521, Cebu became the site in 1565 of the first Spanish settlement in the Philippines. Pop., 719,000.

Ch'ŏngjin, a city in northern North Korea, the capital of North Hamyong Province. Located on the Sea of Japan, it was controlled by the Japanese from 1910 to 1945 and was a center for the Japanese invasion of China in the 1930s. It is a major industrial and rail center, producing iron and steel, ships, machinery, chemicals, and textiles. Pop., 582,000.

Chongqing, in southeastern Szechwan Province, southern China, at the junction of the Yangtze and Chia-ling rivers. The city is the major river port and industrial center of southwest China. It was the capital of China from 1937 to 1945. Pop., 3,127,000.

Colombo, the capital, largest city, and chief port of Sri Lanka. It is located on the island's southwestern coast. Colombo exports most of Sri lanka's tea, coconut products, cotton, and rubber. It is the site of several Buddhist and Hindu temples and of Colombo University. Pop., 642,000.

Da Nang, an excellent seaport in east-central Vietnam. It is Vietnam's fourth-largest city. Pop., 680,000.

Delhi, or Old Delhi, a city in north-central India close to New Delhi, the capital, in the union territory of Delhi. It has served as the capital city of various conquerors and is an important rail and trade center. It is famous for its handicrafts in metals and ivory. Pop., 9,817,000.

Dhaka, or Dacca, the capital of Bangladesh, between the Meghna and Ganges rivers. The city is a trade and processing center and is noted for the production of gold and silver jewelry, textiles, tea, paper, carved shells, and jute. It is the seat of the University of Dacca. Pop., 4,232,000.

Djakarta. See Jakarta.

Dushanbe, formerly Dyushambe, then Stalinabad, the capital of Tajikistan, on the Dushanbinka (Varsob) River in the Gissar Valley, in the southwest. A modern, planned city and a major transport junction, it is an important industrial, cultural, and educational center. Because the area is prone to earthquakes, many buildings are one-story. Pop., 529,000.

Guangzhou, formerly Canton, in southern China, on the Pearl River, about 80 miles (130 km) from the South China Sea. It is the capital of Kwangtung Province. A major river port, it manufactures chemicals, paper, textiles, cement, and machinery. Pop., 3,935,000.

Hanoi, the capital of Vietnam, situated on the Red River delta. The city is an important commercial and industrial center. Pop., 2,464,000.

Hiroshima, a Japanese seaport, the capital of Hiroshima Prefecture, lying on the Inland Sea. The city is an important industrial, commercial, and cultural center for the surrounding area. Its manufactures include textiles, machinery, tools, and canned goods. Hiroshima

was the target of a U.S. atom bomb attack at the end of World War II. The city, which was almost completely destroyed by the bomb, has been rebuilt. Pop., 1,126,000.

Ho Chi Minh City, formerly Saigon (the capital of South Vietnam from 1954 to 1976), near the southeastern coast of Vietnam. It is a commercial and transportation center, and with its suburb, Cholon, is a major port and industrial complex. Pop., 4,990,000.

Hong Kong, (413 square miles) has 6,708,000 people. A Crown Colony at the mouth of the Canton River in southern China, it is 90 miles south of Canton. The British annexed it in 1841, then added the islands of the New Territories and leased it from China in 1898 for 99 years. Hong Kong receives a heavy flow of Chinese refugees and is a commercially thriving colony. Shipping, banking, textile and electronics industries, and tourism do very well. The colony is 80 percent urban. Hong Kong has become one of the most important trading centers of Southeast Asia. Victoria is its capital. In 1984 Great Britain and the People's Republic of China signed an agreement by which Hong Kong passed into control of the People's Republic in July, 1997, as a Special Administrative Region. Under the agreement, China agreed to permit Hong Kong's social and economic system to remain unchanged for another 50 years.

Hue, a port city in central Vietnam. The city was once the capital of the Vietnamese empire in Indochina, and of the French colonial state of Annam. It was a major battleground of the Vietnam War. Pop., 292,000.

Inchon, a port and industrial city in northwestern South Korea. It is the main port for Seoul, which is about 25 miles (40 km) east northeast and is served by road and rail links. Its products include iron, steel, petroleum products, chemicals, textiles, machinery, salt, and lumber. An amphibious landing of UN forces at Inchon in September, 1950, during the Korean War, halted and ultimately routed the North Korean invasion of South Korea. Pop., 2,466,000.

Islamabad, the capital of Pakistan, just northeast of Rawalpindi in northern Pakistan. The city has light manufacturing industries. Pop., 529,000.

Jakarta, or Djakarta, seaport and capital of Indonesia, on the northwest coast of Java. It is the largest city of Indonesia. Pop., 9,374,000.

Kabul, the capital of Afghanistan, situated on the Kabul River about 50 miles (80 km) from the Pakistani border and the Khyber Pass. The city is a commercial center and the seat of Kabul

APPREHENSION ABOUT THE future of Hong Kong as a Special Administrative Region of the People's Republic of China has led to the exodus of some of its commercial interests.

University and other educational institutions. Pop., 1,527,000.

Karachi, the largest city and most important port of Pakistan, situated on the Arabian Sea near the delta of the Indus River. The city has excellent air, rail, and shipping facilities. Its industries produce textiles, chemicals, transportation equipment, steel, and ships. Pop., 9,339,000.

Kathmandu, the capital and commercial center of Nepal. The city is a marketing center for rice, fruit, vegetables, and livestock raised in the area. Kathmandu has some small industries. Pop., 421,000.

Khodzhent, or Khujand, formerly Leninabad, a city in Tajikistan, on the Syr Darya River. It is the second largest city of Tajikistan and a center of silk production and carpet making. Pop., 165,000.

Kuala Lumpur, the capital city of Malaysia, situated on the western part of the Malay peninsula, about 200 miles (320 km) northwest of Singapore. It is a transportation center with industries based on rubber and tin production. Pop., 1,379,000.

Kyoto, the former capital of Japan, situated on west-central Honshu Island. Kyoto is a cultural and artistic center known for its handicraft industries. There are many temples and shrines in the city, and parts of the old imperial palace are preserved. The city is visited by many tourists. Pop., 1,468,000.

Lhasa, capital of Tibet Autonomous Region, southwestern China, on a tributary of the Brahmaputra River. It was long known as the Forbidden City because of the hostility to foreigners of its many lamas, who have now been suppressed and dispersed by the Chinese. It is the site of magnificent palaces of the former Dalai Lama and impressive temples and monasteries. Pop., 376,000.

Macau, (6 square miles) is an enclave on the south China coast, 40 miles west of Hong Kong. It includes a province and two small islands and has 437,000 people. Broad autonomy was granted it in 1976. Macau is a thriving urban commercial center. Its free gold trade, tourism, and fishing are other major sources of income. Macau passed into control of the People's Republic of China in 1999.

Makasar. See Ujung Pandang.

Mandalay, on the left bank of the Irrawaddy River in central Myanmar, about 350 miles (565 km) north of Yangon. Mandalay is an important religious and cultural center. The leading industry is silk weaving. Pop., 533,000.

Manila, the largest city, chief port, and capital of the Philippines. It lies on Luzon Island on Manila Bay. The city is a transportation, manufacturing, cultural, and educational center. Its products include chemicals, coconut oil, textiles, tobacco, drugs, paints, and rope. Pop., 1,581,000.

Nagasaki, a seaport on the west coast of Kyushu Island, Japan. Opened to foreign trade in 1568, it has had the longest contact with the Western world of any Japanese city. A large steel rolling mill and nearby coal fields have made it an important shipbuilding and industrial center. The inner city was destroyed on August 9, 1945, by the second U.S. atomic bomb used in warfare. Pop., 423,000.

Nagoya, a city of Japan, located on the south coast of Honshu Island at the head of Ise Bay. A major port and industrial and rail center, the city produces pottery and porcelain, textiles, machine tools, automobiles, and chemicals. Pop., 2,171,000.

Nanjing, formerly Nanking, the capital of Jiangsu Province, China. It is on the Yangtze River, which seagoing vessels can navigate to the city. Rail lines connect it to Beijing and Shanghai. Traditional industries include the manufacture of silk and cotton cloth and a durable cotton fabric called Nankeen. Iron, oil, and food-processing plants also have been established. Manufactures include textiles, machinery, chemicals, trucks, and electronic equipment.

An important cultural and educational center, Nanjing is the site of scientific research institutes and several institutions of higher learning, including Nanjing University. It was the capital of Nationalist China from 1928 to 1937 and again from 1946 to 1949. Pop., 2,678,000.

Nara, a Japanese city within 50 miles (80 km) of Kyoto and Osaka. It was the first capital of Japan, from 710 to 784. Pop., 366,000.

New Delhi, the capital of India, situated in the north-central part of the country on the west bank of the Yamuna River. New Delhi lies south of Delhi. It is a transportation and trade center with some light industries, textile mills, and printing plants. New Delhi was constructed as an administrative center. The seat of government was transferred from Calcutta to Delhi in 1912 and to New Delhi in 1931. Pop., 295,000.

Osaka, a Japanese port, situated on the southwestern coast of Honshu Island. Osaka is one of the most important industrial and commercial centers of Japan. Its industries produce a wide variety of goods, including cotton textiles, automobiles, steel, and chemicals. Pop., 2,599,000.

Osh, a city in southwestern Kyrgyzstan, situated on the Akbura River near the Alai Mountain foothills. One of the oldest settlements of Central Asia, for centuries it was an important silk-processing center and a major station on the old trade routes to India and China. Silk and cotton textiles are still produced there. The city is the site of Tash-Sulayman (Takht-i-Suleyman), or Solomon's Throne, a curiously shaped rock that has been a place of pilgrimage for Muslims. Pop., 220,000.

Palembang, a river port of Indonesia, situated in southeastern Sumatra on the Musi River. It is the most important trade center and the largest city of Sumatra. Palembang has important oil refineries and exports oil and petroleum products, rubber, coffee, spices, and coal. Pop., 1,416,000.

center
US

centre
Brit.

MACAU was founded as a permanent settlement for trading by the Portuguese in 1557. It gained broad autonomy in 1976, but it passed into control of the People's Republic of China in 1999.

SINGAPORE is the capital of the small country in southeast Asia with the same name. The city is built around the harbor and the export and import activities upon which it relies.

Patna, a city on the Ganges River in northeastern India, the capital of Bihar State. It is a transportation and trade center that produces grains, oilseeds, and sugar cane. The city is considered sacred by the Sikhs and is the seat of two universities. Pop., 1,377,000.

Peking. See Beijing.

Peshawar, in Pakistan, strategically situated near the Khyber Pass. The city serves as a gateway to Afghanistan and central Asia. Peshawar, a road and rail junction, is the trade center for a region that produces grain, oilseed, cotton, and sugar cane. Pop., 983,000.

Phnom Penh, the capital and commercial center of Cambodia, situated at the junction of the Tonle Sap and Mekong rivers. Phnom Penh is a rail center and a river port. Pop., 1,000,000.

Pune, or Poona, a city in west-central India, about 80 miles (130 km) southeast of Bombay. A transportation and commercial center, Pune has a number of military facilities. Manufactures include machinery, textiles, chemicals, munitions, and paper. Pune is a major cultural and educational center. Pop., 2,540,000.

Pusan, a seaport in southeastern South Korea, about 200 miles (320 km) southeast of Seoul on the Korea Strait. Pusan is a major commercial and industrial center. It has several colleges and the National Museum and Art Gallery. Pop., 3,655,000.

P'yŏngyang, the capital of North Korea, situated on the Taedong River in the western part of the country. The city is a center of heavy industry and manufactures steel, rubber, cement, and

chemicals. Pop., 2,741,000.

Rangoon, or Yangon, the capital of Myanmar, 21 miles (34 km) from the Gulf of Martaban. It is Myanmar's largest city and chief port. The city is the seat of the University of Rangoon. The skyline is dominated by the 368-foot Shwe Dagon Pagoda, which is covered with gold leaf. Pop., 2,513,000.

Saigon. See Ho Chi Minh City.

Samarkand, or Samarqand, known to the ancient Greeks as Maracanda, in

Uzbekistan, in the Zeravshan River valley. Said to be one of the world's oldest existing cities, it was the capital of Sogdiana and fell to Alexander the Great in 329 B.C. Its position on the trade route between the Middle East and China made the city a great prize. Samarkand was the capital of Tamerlane's empire in the 14th century and became famous for its splendid palaces and gardens. Many of its magnificent monuments and mosques still stand, including the restored tomb of Tamerlane and the ancient observatory of Ulug-Bek, Tamerlane's grandson. Pop., 362,000.

Sapporo, located on Hokkaido, the northernmost island of Japan. It is the country's third largest city in area and fifth largest in population. It is known for its annual International Snow Festival and was the site of the 1972 Winter Olympics. Pop., 1,822,000.

Seoul, the capital of South Korea, situated near the Han River in the northwestern corner of the country. The cultural and economic center of South Korea, it is the site of several colleges. It is connected by a railway with its port, Inchon. Pop., 9,854,000.

Shanghai, a port city on the eastern coast of China, near the mouth of the Yangtze River. It is the largest city in China and is a major industrial and commercial center. It is an important cultural and educational center with many universities and scientific institutes. It also has several museums and theaters. Pop., 8,214,000.

Shenyang, formerly Mukden, in northeastern China, on the Hun River. It is the capital of Liaoning Province and a major

THE CITY OF SHANGHAI developed as a small Chinese trading center as early as the Song dynasty (960–1279). It was forced to open to foreign trade by the British after the Opium War in 1842.

industrial city. It is also an educational and cultural center with historic buildings and monuments. Pop., 4,670,000.

Singapore, a seaport and capital of Singapore, on Singapore Island off the southern tip of the Malay peninsula. It is a major commercial and industrial center. Pop., 4,131,000.

Surabaya, a seaport on the northeast coast of the Indonesian island of Java. It exports rubber, oil, sugar, spices, tobacco, and other local goods, and has shipyards, oil refineries, textile mills, rubber processing plants, and chemical factories. Pop., 2,801,000.

Surat, a major 17th and 18th century port and trading town renowned for its silks and brocades. It was the first European settlement in India. It remains a center for silk weaves and carpet and textile manufacture. Pop., 1,499,000

Suzhou, a port city in eastern China, on the Grand Canal in Jiangsu Province. Silk and cotton textiles are its chief manufactures, along with handcrafted items. Famous for its natural beauty and its many canals, it is called the Venice of China. Pop., 883,000.

Taipei, the capital of Taiwan, situated at the northern end of the island. The city is the commercial and industrial center of Taiwan, with good transportation facilities. Taipei is the seat of National Taiwan University. Pop., 2,720,000.

Taiyuan, a city of east-central China situated on the Fen River, about 265 miles (425 km) southwest of Beijing. Taiyuan is an industrial and rail center, lying near important iron and coal fields. Its industries produce iron and steel, agricultural equipment, and chemicals. The city also has machine shops, textile mills, and oil refineries. Pop., 2,052,000.

Tashkent, the capital of Uzbekistan, situated in the foothills of the Tien Shan Mountains, in an oasis in the Chirchik River valley. It flourished as a trade hub on the ancient caravan route from Samarkand to Peking. An important cultural and educational center, it was largely rebuilt after a major earthquake in 1966. Pop., 2,143,000.

Thimphu, or Thimbu, the capital and largest city of Bhutan. Located on the Wong Chu River in the Himalaya Mountains, it is the site of Tashi Chho Dzong, a fortified monastery dating from the 13th century and now converted and used for government offices. Bhutan's capital since 1962, it is accessible by highway and air links. Pop., 8,900.

Tianjin, a port of northeastern China, situated at the junction of the Pie River and the Grand Canal, about 80 miles (130 km) southeast of Beijing. Tianjin is a commercial and industrial center

that handles much of the import-export trade of the surrounding region. It is also the seat of several institutions of higher education, including Nankai University and Tianjin University. Pop., 5,855,000.

Tokyo, the capital of Japan and one of the largest cities in the world, situated on Honshu Island in Tokyo Bay. The city is the administrative, economic, and industrial center of Japan. Tokyo is served by an excellent port, many railroads, an international airport, an extensive highway system, and a rapid transit system. It is also Japan's cultural, educational, and religious center. It is the seat of Tokyo University and has many museums, theaters, and religious shrines. Pop., 8,130,000.

Ujung Pandang, a port in Southeast Asia, on the island of Celebes, or Sulawesi, in Indonesia. It is one of Indonesia's largest cities. Exports include coffee, copra, rice, and spices. Pop., 1,154,000.

Ulaanbaatar, capital of the Mongolian People's Republic, located on the Tuula River. It is connected by a branch of the Trans-Siberian railroad and by air with Russia and China. Pop., 760,000.

Uralsk, a city in western Kazakhstan, on the Ural River, about 170 miles (275 km) west southwest of Orenburg. Founded in the 17th century by Cossacks, it became a center of the Cossack independence movement. Its products include leather, footwear, furs, and agricultural products. Pop., 195,000.

Varanasi, formerly Benares, in north-central India, on the Ganges River in Uttar Pradesh State. One of India's oldest cities, it is the holiest city of the Hindus, who visit it as pilgrims to bathe

in the sacred waters of the Ganges. The city is also sacred to Jains, Sikhs, and Buddhists. A cultural center, the city is the seat of Benares Hindu University and Benares Sanskrit University. Pop., 1,101,000.

Vientiane, the administrative capital of Laos, on the Mekong River near the border with Thailand. The city is a commercial center, dealing in textiles and agricultural and wood products. Pop., 331,000.

Wuhan, in east-central China, at the confluence of the Han and Yangtze rivers. It was formed by the merger of three cities, Hankow, Hanyang, and Wuchang, and is the capital of Hubei Province. Wuhan is central China's industrial, administrative, and transportation center. Pop., 4,040,000.

Yogyakarta, in southern Java, Indonesia, at the foot of volcanic Mt. Merapi, 175 miles (280 km) southwest of Surabaya. The city is the cultural center of Java and is noted for its drama and dance festivals, the Islamic University of Indonesia, and its colleges. The Buddhist temple, Borobudur, and the palace of the sultans attract many tourists each year. Pop., 431,000.

Yokohama, a seaport in southeastern Honshu, Japan, in Tokyo Bay. The city is part of the urban-industrial complex around Tokyo and is the seat of four universities. It also has many churches, temples, shrines, gardens, and parks. Pop., 3,427,000.

Zhengzhou (Chengchow), the capital of Henan Province in east-central China, an important railroad junction and the center for a large textile industry. Pop., 1,797,000.

THE TOKYO Metropolitan Prefecture is the world's largest urban center, having all of the problems common to a city of that size, while still retaining a strong traditional orientation.

Glossary of Asia

Amu Darya. A river of Central Asia, known in ancient times as the Oxus. It rises in the mountains of northeastern Afghanistan and flows some 1,579 miles (2,540 km) northwest to the Aral Sea, forming part of the border between Afghanistan and Tajikistan. Much of its water has been diverted for irrigation, causing a decline in the size of the Aral Sea.

Angkor. An extensive ruin in west-central Cambodia, just north of Tonle Sap. Once the capital of the Khmer Empire, which flourished from the 9th to the 15th century, it is the site of the temples Angkor Wat, dating to the 12th century, and Angkor Thom, dating to the 13th century. Restoration, begun in the 1920s, has been badly disrupted by political turmoil in Cambodia.

Aral Sea. A large lake or inland sea in Central Asia, situated between Kazakhstan and Uzbekistan. The sea's main tributaries are the Amu Darya and the Syr Darya. Once the world's fourth-largest lake, it has been reduced in size and its salinity level has been raised because of water diversion from its tributaries for irrigation projects.

Ashikaga dynasty. The reigning Japanese dynasty from 1336 to 1568. The name is derived from the city of Ashikaga, located north of Tokyo, which was the ancestral home of the Ashikaga shoguns, or military rulers.

Asia Minor. A peninsula of southwestern Asia, lying west of a line between the Gulf of Iskenderun and the Black Sea. It is bounded on the west by the Aegean Sea and on the south by the Mediterranean. Its former name, Anatolia, is used for the Asian part of modern Turkey.

Association of Southeast Asian Nations (ASEAN). An organization formed in 1967 that seeks to promote the stability, cultural development, and

MOST OF BORNEO'S inhabitants are Dayaks, who live in villages like this along the coast and in the mountains.

economic progress of the Southeast Asian region. Its members are Brunei, Indonesia, Malaysia, the Philippines, Singapore, and Thailand.

Ava. The capital of Burma and the name given to Burmese rulers from 1364 to 1555. Ava was located on the Irrawaddy River, about six miles south of Mandalay. The Ava rulers had cultural and military relations with rulers as far away as China and Ceylon.

Bandung Conference. Also known as the Asian-African Conference, a meeting of delegates from 29 nations of Asia and Africa held in April, 1955, at Bandung, Indonesia.

The conference was an attempt by African and Asian states to increase their influence in international affairs by acting together on issues of mutual concern. They agreed on closer economic and cultural cooperation and endorsed the principles of self-determination and human rights as expressed in the UN Charter. The conference condemned colonialism, and several of the Asian leaders condemned communism as well.

No machinery was set up to implement the proposals of the conference, and the states remained divided in their attitudes toward both communism and cooperation with the West. The conference did, however, draw attention to Asian and African nations, their problems, and their potential strength as a nonaligned unit in world politics.

Borneo. An island lying between the South China Sea on the north and the west, the Java Sea on the south, and the Makasar Strait, Celebes Sea, and Sulu Sea on the east. The island, about 290,000 square miles (751,000 sq. km) in area, is the third-largest in the world. Indonesia, Malaysia, and Brunei share the island. The Indonesian part is called Kalimantan.

Bushido. The unwritten feudal code of conduct for the Japanese Samurai, or warrior class. The code, the "way of the warrior," developed during the Kamakura period (1185–1333) and was based on Zen Buddhist and Confucian tradition. It emphasized courage, physical and mental toughness, loyalty, and filial piety. With the abolition of the feudal system in the early 1870s, the code became a general ethical standard for all Japanese.

Caste. From the Portuguese word *casta,* "breed" or "race," the system of hereditary social units in Indian Hindu society. There are four major caste divisions—Brahmans, priests and scholars;

Kshatriyas, warriors and administrators; Vaisyas, shepherds, merchants, and artisans; and Sudras, laborers and servants. The four main castes are divided into numerous subcastes. Outside the caste system are the untouchables, or outcasts. They occupy the lowest social, economic, and religious position in traditional Hindu society. The importance in India of the caste system has diminished. Since the 1930s, largely as a result of the work of Mohandas K. Gandhi, the government of India has taken steps to place the untouchables on an equal footing with the rest of Hindu society.

Champa. An ancient Southeast Asian kingdom that existed in the coastal region of present-day central Vietnam from the 100s to the 1700s. It was founded by the Chams, a people related to the Indonesians who had been strongly influenced by Indian culture. Descendants of the Chams are still to be found in modern Kampuchea and Vietnam.

Chao Phraya. The principal river of Thailand, formed from the Ping, Wang, Yom, and Nan tributaries, which rise in the northern mountains and then merge at Nakhon Sawan. The river's total length is about 225 miles (362 km) from the mountains to its mouth on the Gulf of Thailand.

Ch'ondogyo. A Korean religious sect founded in the 1860s, known first as Tonghak (Eastern learning). Ch'ondogyo, which means "society of the heavenly way," incorporated many concepts of other religions and philosophical systems, including those of Buddhism, neo-Confucianism, Taoism, and Roman Catholicism. The founder of the Tonghak movement, a scholar named Ch'oe Che-u, was executed in 1864 on charges of heresy, but the movement grew after his death. Most of its followers were peasants.

Ch'ondogyo was a traditionalist and antiforeign movement that developed in opposition to Roman Catholic Christianity, known in Korea as Sohak (Western learning). The hostility between the followers of Tonghak and the followers of Sohak became the basis for a major uprising in 1894, the Tonghak Rebellion, which was crushed only after Chinese and Japanese troops intervened on opposing sides. The immediate consequence of this intervention was the struggle between China and Japan for control of Korea in the Sino-Japanese War of 1894–1895. This war led to Japanese domination of Korea after 1896. Despite continued persecution under

THE BUSHIDO code of the Samurai held the members of Japan's warrior class to requirements of self-discipline and bravery in combat.

the Japanese until 1945, Ch'ondogyo survived, and in 1979 there were 1,100,000 members.

Colombo Plan.   A plan for cooperative efforts to raise standards of living and strengthen the economies of the developing nations of South and Southeast Asia. It was published on November 28, 1950, by a committee of Commonwealth ministers; it came into effect on July 1, 1951. It has several times been extended. The member nations assist each other on a bilateral basis. The aid includes technical assistance, loans, equipment, educational programs, and food supplies.

Its members are Afghanistan, Australia, Bangladesh, Bhutan, Burma, Cambodia, Canada, Fiji, India, Indonesia, Iran, Japan, Laos, Malaysia, the Maldives, Nepal, New Zealand, Pakistan, Papua New Guinea, the Philippines, Singapore, South Korea, Sri Lanka, Thailand, the United Kingdom, and the United States.

Daimyo.   Japanese feudal chiefs, or territorial lords. The origins of the daimyo can be traced to the local lords of the 1000s, who can properly be called daimyo after the 1500s. The daimyo became especially prominent during the later portion of the Ashikaga period (1336–1568) and the early part of the Tokugawa period (1603–1867).

After 1600 most of Japan was divided into feudal domains, called *han,* of which the daimyo were rulers. Although the daimyo were allowed virtual autonomy within their own realms, the central Tokugawa government developed an intricate system of controls to prevent the daimyo from becoming a military threat to their central authority.

In 1871 an imperial decree abolished feudal domains and marked the end of the daimyo as feudal lords. The daimyo were given governmental pensions and were classified as nobles. In

1876 they were given lump-sum payments in the form of government bonds. Many became members of Japan's growing commercial class.

Euphrates.   A river in southwest Asia that rises in eastern Turkey. It flows southeast for 1,700 miles (2,737 km) through Syria and Iraq to the Persian Gulf. The river is formed by two headstreams, the Kara and the Murat. At about 120 miles (193 km) from the Persian Gulf, the Euphrates joins the Tigris River to form the Shatt al-Arab.

Syria and Iraq depend on the Euphrates for irrigation. Ancient peoples built a complex system of canals that allowed the Tigris and Euphrates plain to support the civilizations of Babylonia, Assyria, and later of Persia.

Everest.   A mountain in the Himalayas, between Nepal and Tibet. It is the highest mountain in the world, rising to 29,035 feet (8,849 m).

Examination system.   A system of nationwide examinations by which Chinese men became eligible for appointment to the Chinese civil service and thus members of the ruling group in traditional Chinese society.

By about 100 A.D., China had developed a civil-service system based on merit. Under the Sung dynasty (960–1279), the examination system became the most important means of recruiting civil servants, and during the Ming dynasty (1368–1644) methods were developed to ensure complete impartiality in the grading and selection process. The system remained virtually unchanged until the 1900s.

The examinations were held every three years. They were given at three successive levels—the local, or prefectural, level; the capital; and the royal palace. About 10 percent of the candidates passed at each stage. After passing the last stage, candidates were eligible for official positions.

Although the examinations were theoretically open to all, success depended on years of study and, often, tutoring by scholars. This limited candidates to the sons of well-to-do families. Sometimes extended families or clans sponsored students in their preparation for the examinations.

One of the weaknesses of the system was the heavy emphasis given to the Four Books, considered the most important works of Confucianism, and the Five Classics, five ancient works on songs, documents, prophecy, historical annals, and rituals. Literary style was very important and little attention was given to practical affairs.

Between 1901 and 1906 the examination system was gradually abolished and a modern school system instituted in which Western subjects were taught.

Ganges.   A river of South Asia that rises in the Himalayas and flows south and east for about 1,500 miles (2,496

km) through northern India and Bangladesh to the Bay of Bengal. It is heavily used for transportation and provides power for industries and water for irrigation. The Gangetic Plain is formed by the river in northern India. The Ganges is a sacred river for Hindus.

The major southern tributaries of the Ganges are the Son and the Jamna. Major northern tributaries are the Kosi, the Gogra, and the Gandak. As it flows through Bangladesh, the Ganges is joined by the Brahmaputra River about 100 miles (160 km) from its mouth to form the Padma and the world's largest delta.

Gaza Strip.   A narrow section of desertlike land that stretches along the western coast of the Mediterranean Sea. Israel has occupied the area since the Six-Day War of 1967, although Egypt still claims the territory. The majority of people in the Gaza Strip are Palestinians.

Ghaznavids.   An Islamic dynasty that arose in Ghazni, Afghanistan, in the late 900s. It ruled northeastern Iran, Afghanistan, and northern India.

In 977 the Turkish slave commander Sebuktigin became governor of eastern Afghanistan. He established a tradition of raiding the plains of India, but remained a subject of the Samanid empire. Sebuktigin's son Mahmud (998–1030) became fully independent and greatly enlarged Ghaznavid territory. He raided deep into India, moving down the Ganges River to sack the cities of Mathura and Kanauj, and into the Kathiawar (Saurashtra) Peninsula. Mahmud set the northern frontier at the Amu Darya and annexed an area southeast of the Aral Sea. In 1029 he seized Hamadan, in western Iran.

Under Mahmud's son the western portion of the empire fell to the Seljuk Turks. By 1059 the Ghaznavids held only eastern Afghanistan and northwestern India. Attempts to reassert Ghaznavid influence led to the sack of Ghazni by Ghurids, a dynasty based in central Afghanistan, or Ghur. In 1151 a Ghurid, Ala ad Din Husayn, destroyed the city. The Ghurids extinguished the Ghaznavid line in 1186.

Gobi.   A desert region in northern China and southeastern Mongolia. Asia's largest desert, the Gobi covers about 500,000 square miles (1,295,000 sq. km).

Hainan.   A large Chinese island, about 13,200 square miles (34,190 sq. km) in area, lying about 15 miles (24 km) south of the mainland. The island is mountainous, thickly forested, and rich in minerals.

Himalayas.   A mountain system in southeastern Asia containing the world's highest peaks. The range extends for about 1,600 miles (2,575 km) from Kashmir in the west to Assam in the east. It forms an arc separating the subcontinent of India from the rest of Asia.

The system may be divided into three sections—the Greater Himalayas

emphasized
US

emphasised
Brit.

laborers
US

labourers
Brit.

civilizations
US

civilisations
Brit.

in the north, with an average elevation of about 20,000 feet; the Lesser Himalayas in the center, averaging about 11,000 feet; and the Outer Himalayas in the south, with average elevations of about 3,500 feet. The Greater Himalayas contain Mt. Everest.

The Himalayas are primarily responsible for the extreme dryness of western China, because they block the wet monsoon winds before they can reach the interior. By contrast, the southern slopes of the mountains receive a considerable amount of rain and snowfall. The Himalayas hold the sources of several of Asia's important rivers, including the Ganges, the Brahmaputra, and the Indus.

Hindu Kush. A mountain range in northeastern Afghanistan that extends for about 600 miles (965 km) along the border with Pakistan as far as Kashmir. The mountains form a natural barrier for northern Afghanistan, Pakistan, and India. The highest peak is Tirich Mir, 26,000 feet (7,700 m) above sea level. The Hindu Kush is a watershed between the Amu and Indu river systems.

Hong or Cohong. A small group of Chinese business firms licensed to carry on trade with the West. This merchant guild enjoyed a monopoly of Chinese trade with Western nations. The Hong monopoly came to be located in Canton in the 1700s, and the Hong merchants were involved in worldwide trade, much of it with the English East India Company. By the 1830s the Canton system had become antiquated, and the Treaty of Nanking, which ended the Opium War (1839–1842) between Britain and China, abolished the Hong monopoly at Canton.

Huang He. Or Yellow River. The second longest river of China. The Huang

THE HIMALAYAS, whose name means House of Snow or the Snowy Range, provide a dramatic backdrop for this monastery tucked into a mountain fastness.

He rises in the Kunlun Mountains of northwestern China and flows in a generally easterly direction for 2,900 miles (4,670 km), emptying into the Gulf of Chihli. Its tributaries include the Fen, Huai, and Wei rivers. The river has been the cause of numerous floods.

Indochina. A general name for the peninsula of Southeast Asia occupied by Vietnam, Laos, Cambodia, Thailand, Burma, and the mainland portion of Malaysia. French Indochina was a French colony that included present-day Cambodia, Laos, and Vietnam.

Indus. One of the major rivers of South Asia. Rising on the northern slopes of the Kailas range of southwestern Tibet, it flows northwest into Kashmir, then southwest through central Pakistan to the Arabian Sea—a total of more than 1,800 miles (2,900 km). Its major tributaries include the Chenab, the Sutlej, the Jhelum, and the Ravi.

Irrawaddy. A major river of Burma that rises in the north and flows for more than 1,300 miles (2,090 km) to empty into the Gulf of Martaban of the Bay of Bengal near Rangoon. The delta of the Irrawaddy is about 150 miles (240 km) long. The river's chief tributaries are the Nmai and the Chindwin.

Irtysh. A river of Central Asia. Rising in the Altai Mountains in China, it flows west and northwest some 2,640 miles (4,248 km) through Kazakhstan and into Russia, where it joins the Ob. The Irtysh is navigable for much of its length. Two large hydroelectric stations have been constructed on its upper course.

Khyber Pass. A pass in a range of the Hindu Kush on the border between Afghanistan and Pakistan, about 33 miles (53 km) long and between 50 and 600 feet (15 and 183 m) wide. The pass has had continuing strategic and historical importance since the fifth century B.C.

Konbaung dynasty. The last Burmese dynasty, ruling from 1752 to 1885. The dynasty was founded by a north Burmese leader who took the name Alaungpaya (1752–1760), meaning "embryo Buddha." His conquests formed the basis for the modern Burmese state.

By the mid-1700s the Toungoo dynasty (1486–1752), whose court was at Ava in central Burma, had fallen into decline. The Toungoo had been defeated by the Mon, whose power was centered in the south, at Pegu, the Manipuri of the northwest, and the Shan of the northeast.

Between 1752 and 1757 Alaungpaya succeeded in reuniting Burma. In 1753 he cleared the capital city, Ava, of its Mon conquerors, and built a new capital at Shwebo. In 1757, he took Pegu, which completed his conquest of the Mon. In 1760, he invaded Siam (Thailand), but was wounded and returned to Burma, where he died.

Alaungpaya's successors, Hsinbyushin (1763–1776), Bodawpaya (1781–1819), and Bagyidaw (1819–1837), continued his policy of conquest. By 1824, the Burmese advance threatened the interests of the British East India Company in India. In 1824, the British declared war on Burma, initiating the first Burmese war (1824–1825). The Burmese were defeated, and by the Treaty of Yandabu of 1826 Britain annexed Assam, Arakan, Manipur, and the Tenasserim coast. In a second Burmese war (1852–1853) the British annexed Peg, and with the third Burmese war (1885–1886), the Konbaung dynasty came to an end. In 1885, the British took Mandalay, then the Burmese capital. On January 1, 1886, Burma was officially annexed by Great Britain.

Kopet-Dag. A mountain range of Central Asia. It extends northwest to southeast some 400 miles (644 km) along the border between Iran and Turkmenistan. With elevations up to 9,650 feet (2,941 m), it is the only important upland in Turkmenistan. The capital city of Ashkhabad is located at the base of the Kopet-Dag range.

Korean War. An undeclared war, officially termed a "conflict" by the U.S. government, fought from 1950 to 1953 by South Korea and various members of the United Nations, primarily the United States, against North Korea and Chinese communist troops aided by the Soviet Union.

Korea, which was part of the Japanese empire from 1910 to 1945, was partitioned at the end of World War II. Under the terms of the 1945 Yalta agreement between the United States and the Soviet Union, Korea was divided at the 38th parallel. Soviet forces occupied the northern part of the country, and United States forces occupied the south.

In 1948 a communist regime was established in North Korea, the Democratic People's Republic of Korea, with Kim Il Sung as prime minister. In South Korea, elections held in 1948 resulted in the establishment of the Republic of Korea, with Syngman Rhee as president. In June, 1950, a year after U.S. occupation forces had been withdrawn from South Korea, North Korean troops invaded the south.

The United States was the first to aid South Korea, but it quickly received support from the United Nations. The UN Security Council was able to pass a measure authorizing a police action in Korea partly because the Soviet delegation had boycotted the meeting and was unable to veto the resolution.

At the beginning of the war the South Korean and UN forces were driven southward, almost off the peninsula. In September, 1950, an amphibious landing by U.S. troops at Inchon forced the North Koreans into retreat. During the next 70 days North Korean forces were pushed back almost to the Yalu River, which forms the Chinese-Korean boundary.

In November, 1950, a well equipped Chinese communist army of 200,000 crossed the Yalu to counterattack. They drove the UN divisions steadily back, and by January, 1951, communist forces were 70 miles below the 38th parallel. The UN troops then began another offensive, which carried them across the 38th parallel on March 31.

On July 10, 1951, the first of many negotiating sessions began at Kaesong. The fighting continued, however. An armistice was finally signed at Panmunjom in 1953. Korea remained divided, with roughly the same boundary between north and south as that observed before the conflict. An international inspection team was established to maintain the armistice.

Krakatoa, or Krakatau. A volcanic island between Sumatra and Java whose eruption in 1883 was the most violent ever recorded. The sound of the explosion was heard as far away as Japan and Turkey. Nearly five cubic miles (21 cu. km) of fragmented material was ejected into the atmosphere by a series of explosions.

Malay Archipelago. The world's largest island group extending east from the Malay peninsula between the Pacific and Indian oceans. It includes the islands of the Philippines and Indonesia, and, sometimes, New Guinea.

Malay peninsula. A projection of mainland Southeast Asia between the Andaman Sea, on the west, and the Gulf of Thailand, which is an arm of the South China Sea, on the east. It is occupied by Burma, Thailand, and Malaysia.

Manchuria. A northeastern region of China, consisting today of the provinces of Jilin, Liaoning, and Heilongjiang. Rich in natural resources, it was coveted by both Russia and Japan. Japan seized it in 1931 and created the puppet state called Manchukuo.

Mandarins. The name given to Chinese officials by Westerners before the Chinese revolution of 1911. After passing a rigorous series of examinations, the Mandarins were made responsible for all aspects of government.

The Mandarins were prevented from accumulating power by not being allowed to serve in their native provinces, by serving only three years in any one area, and by being subject to review by a board of censors, which investigated the administration of provincial governments.

Mataram. A kingdom in central Java that rose to power in the 1600s, after the fall of the Majapahit kingdom.

The Mataram kingdom was threatened by the Dutch, who had established trading posts in Indonesia. When the Matarami leader, Sunan Agung, sought to expand his influence into northwestern Java, he met resistance from the Dutch and was eventually defeated.

In 1646 the Dutch signed a trade treaty with Agung's successor, Amangkurat I. Dutch relations with Mataram remained more or less stable until 1674, when a rebellion broke out threatening Amangkurat's reign. In this first Javanese war of succession, Amangkurat was forced to flee his capital and seek Dutch protection.

The Mataram kingdom was further weakened in the 1700s by two more wars: the second Javanese war of succession (1719–1723) and the third Javanese war of succession (1749–1757). The third war eventually turned into a rebellion against Dutch control and resulted in the partition of Mataram in 1755.

May Fourth Movement. An intellectual movement in China that was at its height from about 1917 to the early 1920s. During this period Chinese intellectuals were attracted by Western ideas; they were critical of traditional Chinese values that were based on Confucian teachings.

An important attack on the Confucian tradition was a demand by Chinese intellectuals that the traditional Chinese literary language be abandoned. Written Chinese was very different from spoken Chinese, and Chinese intellectuals considered it inadequate for scientific studies, for popular education, and for a literature expressing new ideas. A new written language based on the spoken language was created, and, soon after, textbooks in the new writing began to be used in primary schools.

The May Fourth Movement takes its name from the May fourth incident of 1919, in which university students and professors in Peking demonstrated in protest against the refusal of the Paris Peace Conference to return Shantung to China. Shantung had been seized by the Japanese during World War I.

Mekong. A major river of southeastern Asia, rising in the Tangkula Mountains in eastern Tibet. It follows a twisting, mostly southeasterly course for 2,600 miles (4,185 km) before emptying into the South China Sea through a wide delta at the southern tip of Indochina in Vietnam.

The Mekong's major tributaries include the Mun, the Hou, the Khong, the Srepok, and the Chinit. The river marks parts of the China-Myanmar, Myanmar-Laos, and Laos-Thailand borders. It is navigable to north-central Laos and has a fertile valley and delta.

Nerchinsk, Treaty of. Signed in 1689, the first treaty between China and Russia and the first Chinese treaty with a European power. It settled conflicts over possession of the Amur River region and was the basis for Chinese-Russian relations until the mid-1800s.

New democracy. A political phrase originated by the Chinese communist leader Mao Zedong in a 1940 essay entitled "On the New Democracy." The document announced that the goal of the new democracy was the creation of a "democratic" state ruled by several revolutionary classes under the control of the working class, or proletariat.

In 1941 Mao announced that a "new democratic" government should be composed of all parties in addition to representatives from nonpartisan groups. In 1945 a Chinese Communist Party conference again advocated coalition government. In 1949 Mao stated that the new government should be a "democratic coalition" under communist leadership and should also be a dictatorship directed against the "enemies of the people." The people were categorized into four classes—proletariat, peasantry, petty bourgeoisie, and national bourgeoisie.

New Guinea. The world's second largest island, lying in the southwest Pacific Ocean, north of Australia. The island, with an area of 320,000 square miles (829,000 sq. km), has a mountainous interior. New Guinea has mangrove and sandalwood forests and contains deposits of gold, oil, cobalt, and nickel. New Guinea is shared by West Irian, a province of Indonesia, and Papua New Guinea.

Open-door policy. A policy of allowing equal commercial opportunity to all nations in a particular foreign region. The policy, which came to refer particularly to China in the late 1800s and early 1900s, was designed to counter the development of spheres of influence, in which one country has exclusive trading privileges in a specific area.

The term "open door" was first used by U.S. Secretary of State John Hay in 1899. Hay joined with Britain in opposing plans by France, Germany, and Russia to establish areas of exclusive interest in China. Hay won partial agreement for an open-door policy from the powers.

In 1900 the Boxer Rebellion broke out in China, and the possibility arose that China would be partitioned among the powers. Again the United States proposed an open-door policy to the other major powers, and once again it met with limited success.

The Washington Conference of 1921 had as one of its aims the formal recognition of the open-door policy in China. Among the conference participants who agreed to the plan was Japan. The open-door policy remained more or less in effect until 1931, when Japan invaded China and took the rich northeastern region of Manchuria.

Opium War. A conflict between China and Great Britain from 1839 to 1842. Britain, wanting to force China to open up to more trade, used the pretext of a Chinese ban on the import of opium and the destruction of a British supply of the drug. Britain won the war easily. By the Treaty of Nanking, China was forced to give the British important

categorized
US

categorised
Brit.

23 Asia

trade concessions and cede them the island of Hong Kong, as well as pay a large indemnity.

Pamir.   A mountain range in Tajikistan, in central Asia, lying along the borders of Pakistan, Kashmir, and China, north of the Hindu Kush and Karakorum ranges. Peaks in the Pamirs rise to almost 25,000 feet (7,620 m) above sea level.

Plassey, Battle of.   A battle fought June 22, 1757, between a small British force and the army of Suraja Dowla (Sirajah-daulah), Muslim ruler of Bengal, which resulted in the reduction of French influence in India and the beginning of the British Indian empire.

The battle took place shortly after the outbreak of the Seven Years' War (1756–1763) between Britain and France. When the war began, Robert Clive of the British East India Company decided to oust the French from their trading stations in Bengal. The French, however, were protected by Suraja Dowla, who expelled the British from Calcutta.

After capturing the city, he ordered 146 Englishmen locked up in a small windowless room (later known as the Black Hole of Calcutta) for one night, during which most of them died of suffocation.

Soon thereafter Clive's small force defeated Suraja Dowla at Plassey, about 80 miles north of Calcutta. Clive put a puppet ruler on the Bengal throne, and the English rapidly established complete control of the Bengal region.

Samil Movement.   A peaceful national demonstration held throughout Korea on March 1, 1919. It is sometimes called the March First Movement. Korean patriots, whose country had been annexed by Japan in 1910, announced Korean independence in a proclamation read in every town. The demonstrators were harshly suppressed, however, and the movement failed.

San-Min Chu-I, or Three Principles of the People.   A political statement written by Sun Yat-sen in the early 1900s to guide a republican revolution in China. The three principles were nationalism, democracy, and socialism.

Sun's "nationalism" was anti-Manchu and anti-imperialist. Sun's "democracy" involved a constitution with five powers—executive, legislative, judicial, examination, and censorial. Sun's "socialism" meant merely the application of a single tax to put a limit on the accumulation of capital. The three principles became part of Kuomintang ideology.

Satsuma Rebellion.   An uprising in Japan in 1877 in the former province of Satsuma. The rebellion was led by conservative samurai (aristocratic warriors) who opposed the movement of Japan's new government, established by the Meiji Restoration, toward a constitutional monarchy.

The samurai, having been stripped of many of their traditional privileges and sources of income, attacked an army installation at Kagoshima. Government forces rushed to the area. Heavy fighting ensued, and the samurai were eventually defeated.

The Satsuma Rebellion, which was the last armed insurrection against the Meiji regime, marked the end of the feudal powers and prerogatives of the samurai.

Shogun.   A short form for *Seii-tai-shogun,* Japanese for "barbarian-quelling generalissimo," a title first given to outstanding generals in Japan in the 700s. By the 1100s a feudal system had developed in Japan and a hereditary clique headed by a warrior, Yoritomo, came to govern much of the country. Although the official seat of government was the court at Kyoto, Yoritomo's private government was more powerful. The title of shogun came to apply to all the hereditary military dictators who were to rule Japan for the next 600 years. The shoguns' administrations were known as shogunates.

Sinai.   A triangular peninsula that forms the easternmost portion of Egypt. It extends southward from a 150-mile-long (240-km) Mediterranean coast for over 200 miles (320 km) to the northern tip of the Red Sea. Two extensions of the Red Sea—the Gulf of Suez and the Gulf of Aqaba—form the western and the eastern boundaries of the peninsula. The extensive central plateau of Al-Tih rises to the south and culminates in Gebel Katherina, 8,652 feet (2,637 m) high. Nearby is Musa Mountain, thought by many to be the Mount Sinai referred to in the Old Testament.

South Asian Association for Regional Cooperation (SAARC).   A regional organization that attempts to promote economic cooperation among member nations.

Tet.   The popular name for the Vietnamese New Year festival, celebrated during the first seven days of the year. Because the yearly cycle is determined according to the lunar calendar, Tet can fall in January or February. The name of the holiday was attached to a major North Vietnamese and Vietcong offensive during the Vietnam War, launched on January 30, 1968, to coincide with that year's Tet festival.

Tibet.   A plateau region in southwestern China of about 471,700 square miles (1,221,700 sq. km), bordered on the south by the Himalayas and on the north by the Kunlun Mountains. Both the terrain and climate of Tibet are quite harsh, and it supports only a small population (1,970,000 in 1985). Tibet maintained its independence for much of its history; however, China several times tried to gain dominance over the area, with mixed success. The most recent invasion

came in 1950, when the new Chinese communist regime annexed Tibet. Tibet has not submitted easily to Chinese rule, and there have been several uprisings, notably in 1959 and 1987.

Timurid Empire.   An empire in central Asia and western Persia in the 15th and 16th centuries ruled by descendants of Tamerlane (Timur). Established by Tamerlane's son Shah Rukh, it turned the cities of Samarkand and Herat into centers of culture and scientific learning. Babur, a Timurid descendant, founded the Mughal dynasty in India in 1526.

Tonle Sap, or Great Lake.   In west-central Cambodia, the largest lake in Southeast Asia. It is a natural reservoir of the Mekong River, to which it is connected through the Tonle Sap River. Commercial fishing is an important activity on the lake.

Turtle ships.   Ironclad naval vessels used by the Korean admiral Yi Sun Sin to fight the Japanese, who had invaded Korea in 1592. Yi's "turtle ships" defeated the Japanese navy and the Japanese were forced to withdraw. Some consider the turtle ships the world's first armored warships.

Vietnam War.   A guerrilla war dating from the collapse of the French colonial empire in Southeast Asia in 1945, following World War II. Initially a nationalist struggle, the conflict grew and eventually involved both Asian and non-Asian nations.

The war in Vietnam began in 1945 as a struggle between Vietnamese nationalists seeking independence and French colonial forces attempting to reestablish French rule after the defeat of Japan, which had invaded and occupied the area during World War II. The Viet Minh, as the Vietnamese forces were known, were led by Ho Chi Minh, a long-time communist.

A crucial battle in the French struggle to retain control of Vietnam was fought in 1954 at Dien Bien Phu. The Viet Minh won a decisive victory and the French agreed to withdraw.

An international conference was held in Geneva, Switzerland, in 1954. The terms of the Geneva agreement provided for the division of Vietnam at the 17th parallel. The north became a communist-controlled republic led by Ho Chi Minh, and the south became a monarchy with a weak emperor, Bao Dai, and a strong prime minister, Ngo Dinh Diem. In 1955 a republic with a powerful president was established in the south. Diem served as the first president and won U.S. support.

Almost immediately after the partition of Vietnam, South Vietnam began to be infiltrated by guerrilla forces, known as the Vietcong, from the north.

The Diem government was unable to cope with domestic problems or conduct a successful campaign against the

---

centers
US

centres
Brit.

armored
US

armoured
Brit.

insurgents. Resentment against the Diem regime culminated in a bloody coup in November, 1963. Diem was killed and the government was seized by a military junta.

A change in the nature of the war came in 1965, when U.S. air attacks on North Vietnam were begun and U.S. combat troop strength in South Vietnam was sharply increased.

Late in January, 1968, the Vietcong launched the Tet offensive, a major attack that weakened morale in the United States and South Vietnam.

World pressure for settlement of the conflict brought a meeting of both sides in Paris in May, 1968, but the fighting continued until January 23, 1973, when a peace settlement was finally announced. In early 1975 North Vietnamese and Vietcong forces launched a new offensive and the South Vietnamese military effort collapsed. On April 29 U.S. President Gerald Ford ordered the complete evacuation of all remaining U.S. personnel. On April 30 the South Vieamese president surrendered unconditionally to the Vietcong.

Warlords. Chinese military leaders who controlled many large areas of China and competed with one another for increased power and territory. The period 1916 to 1928 is often called the warlord era in modern Chinese history. Warlords remained in control of some areas of China until the advent of the communist regime in 1949.

Yalu. A river that rises in northeastern Korea and forms part of the North Korea-China border. It flows for 500 miles (800 km), emptying into Korea Bay.

Yangban. A Korean term meaning "two groups" and referring specifically to the civil and military branches of the bureaucracy. The term generally designates the whole landowning official class, however. During the Yi dynasty (1392–1910), important official posts were held exclusively by the landowning class, or *yangban*. Although Korea, like China, used an examination system to recruit competent men for government service, the examinations were usually open only to members of yangban families. After Korea became a Japanese protectorate in 1905, the Japanese abolished the yangban's status.

Yangtze. One of the principal rivers of China and of the world. It rises in the Kunlun Mountains and follows a twisting course for 3,434 miles (5,530 km) before it empties into the East China Sea. The portion east of its rugged gorges—about one-sixth of its length—is navigable by ocean vessels.

THE HELP DESK

➤ **Look** at maps and globes with a younger sibling or friend. What do they represent? Make some simple maps and diagrams, such as a floor plan of your house, the block you live on, school, or playground. Help the child learn directions: Start with up, down, right, and left, and progress to directions. Help the child tell the difference between depictions of land and water on a globe and learn to identify the continents and major countries by name.

➤ **Imagine** a route you travel frequently, for example, home to school or home to the mall. Write instructions to lead someone unfamiliar with the route. Include directions, distances, landmarks, etc. Test your skill by having someone follow your instructions.

➤ **Draw** a map illustrating the above instructions. Be sure it uses standard mapping guidelines with North at the top and a rough distance indication if possible.

➤ **Make** a map of play dough or salt clay that shows mountains, lakes, rivers, plains, peninsulas, etc. Just for practice, your first map can be an imaginary place with many features. Then make one of a country in Asia.

➤ **Look** at the participation of different groups at different times in the country's history, for example, Hindus and Indian independence.

➤ **Do** you like to sample different foods? Indian, Chinese, Thai, etc? What distinguishes the cuisines? Why are they different?

➤ **Make** a list of the largest cities. How does the size of those cities compare with cities that you are familiar with? Why do you think that people began to live in that area and continued to live there?

➤ **Study** the continental map. Pay particular attention to the locator inset map that will help you locate the portion of the globe Asia occupies. Is it in the Northern or Southern hemisphere? In the Eastern or Western hemisphere? Is it north or south of the equator? What are the major physical features—any large rivers, mountains, deserts? Make a list of the names of those features.

➤ **Use** the locator inset map to pinpoint the country and then turn to the continent map to confirm the location. Look at the list of physical features you made as you studied the continental map. Do any of those features appear in the country you are studying? How do you think the presence of that feature affects the country?

➤ **Document** your family's ethnic heritage. What country did your forefathers come from? When did they come? Why did they leave their homeland? Who? What famous people share your background? Older relatives would be a good source of information.

➤ **Look** at the photographs in this section. What can you learn about the climate, geographical features, and the people? As you read newspapers and listen to the news, pay particular attention to the names of countries and regions. Visualize the area so that the information is more meaningful to you.

➤ **Study** the information box for each country. What can you determine from each set of facts? Is the country large or small? Rich or poor? Heavily or sparsely populated? Is it an industrial nation or an agricultural one? Are the people well educated?

➤ **Plan** a trip. Select a destination from the place you are to another place in Asia. Where would you stop along the way? How would you travel from one place to another? How long would each leg of the trip require? What kind of clothes should you take? Can you find out what kind of money you should have at each stop? What languages will you be likely to hear?

➤ **For** a list of helpful references, go to the *customers* section of www.southwestern.com.

Middle East

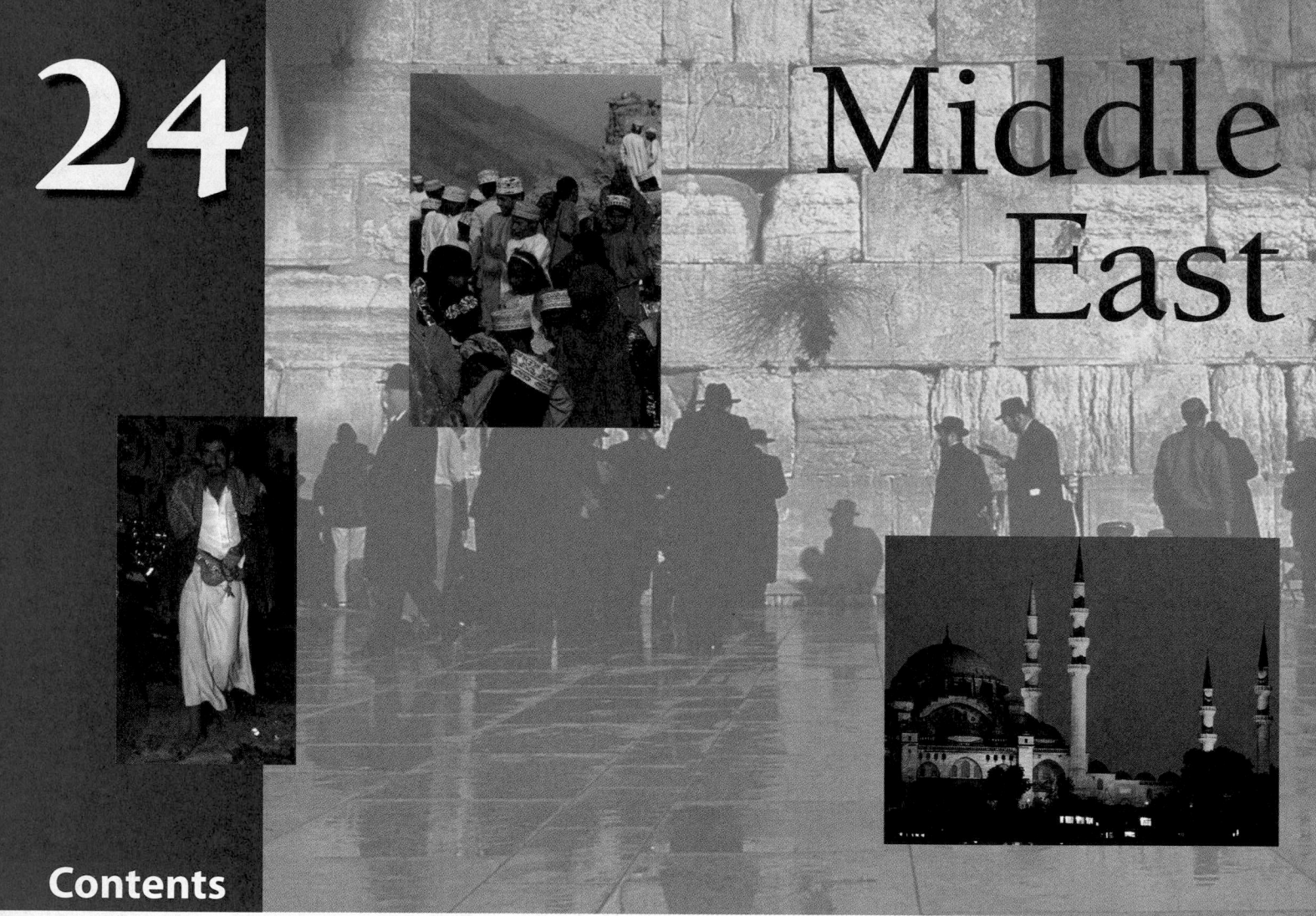

24 Middle East

Contents

A Note about Spellings

As with any language that is written in a script other than the Roman alphabet, Arabic is, at times, difficult to transliterate into English, and there is no single universally accepted system for doing so. This difficulty also arises with words from other languages that are, or have been in the past, written in the Arabic script, such as Farsi and Turkish.

When rendering Arabic words into English, this publication follows standard modern international practice, avoiding, for example, the use of diacritics, which some systems of transliteration employ.

Overleaf: *Pearl Monument, Bahrain*

Middle East

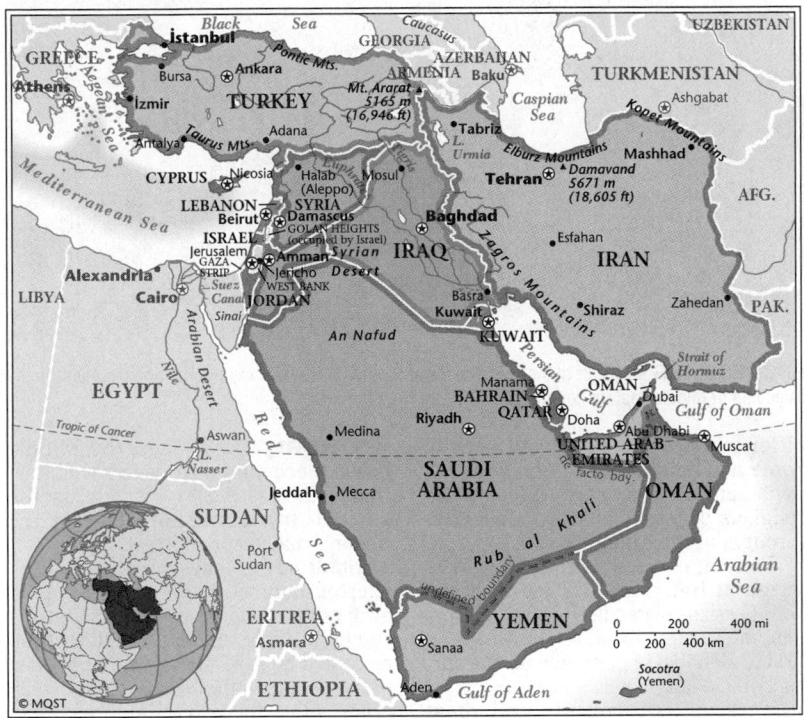

The Middle East includes all of Turkey, Cyprus, and the entire Sinai and Arabian peninsulas. It extends as far east as Iran's eastern border with Pakistan and Afghanistan; as far north as the Turkish and Iranian borders with Azerbaijan, Armenia, Georgia, Bulgaria, Greece, and the Black and Caspian seas; as far west as the easternmost waters of the Aegean and Mediterranean seas, and the border between the Sinai peninsula and Egypt; and as far south as the Red and Arabian seas. The population of this region is over 230 million.

The land. The topography of the Middle East is dominated by mountains and deserts. The region consists largely of the Arabian peninsula, which contains the vast central plateau of the Arabian Desert. The desert rises gradually from sea level along the Persian Gulf, and westward to the highland regions that dominate the Red Sea coast. The Syrian Desert lies farther north and extends across the borders of Jordan, Iraq, Saudi Arabia, and Syria.

The Bosporus and Dardanelles straits in northwestern Turkey connect the Black and Mediterranean seas. The Persian Gulf is both the source of and chief waterway for the Middle East's rich oil trade. The Red Sea has become a major international trade route since the completion of the Suez Canal in 1869, which connects the Red and Mediterranean seas. The Suez Canal provides the shortest path between ports in Europe and Asia.

Mountains. Four important mountain ranges spread out from northwestern Turkey: the Elburz Mountains stretch along the northern border of Iran; the Zagros Mountains run through southwestern Iran; the Taurus Mountains lie in southern Turkey; and the Pontic Mountains dominate northern Turkey. Characterized by jagged peaks, abject drops, and deep valleys, they are often compared with the American Rockies and the European Alps. The two highest peaks in the Middle East are Mount Damavand, which is 18,665 feet (5,691 meters) above sea level in the Elburz Mountains, and Mount Ararat, which is 16,934 feet (5,163 meters) high and lies on the northeastern border of Turkey. Mountains run parallel to the Red Sea in Saudi Arabia and along the coast of the Gulf of Aden in Yemen. A smaller range extends from Turkey into Lebanon. The mountains in Oman are part of the Iranian Zagros range.

Rivers. The one great river system in the Middle East—the Tigris and Euphrates—rises in Turkey. The Euphrates winds through Syria before reaching Iraq, where it meets the Tigris, and the two flow into the Shatt al-Arab, a river that drains into the Persian Gulf. As early as 2400 B.C., civilizations created elaborate irrigation systems connected to the Tigris and the Euphrates that supplied large productive farms.

The Jordan River and the Litani, in Lebanon, are important year-round sources of water. Many other rivers contain water only during the rainy seasons. The Sakarya, Kisil Irmak, and Yesil Irmak are three of Turkey's many large rivers.

Climate. The varying topography of the Middle East divides the region into discrete climatic zones. Only the coastal and mountain regions receive more than 10 inches (26 centimeters) of rain annually. Most areas receive rain only during the winter months.

The interior desert regions of the Middle East face some of the highest temperatures in the world during the summer months, often reaching above 135°F (57°C). The winters are much cooler. In the southern area of the interior, which includes Yemen, Oman, and southern Saudi Arabia, entire years pass without any measurable amount of rain, while at other times rainfall totals several feet in a few months. The shores of the Mediterranean, Black, and Caspian seas receive dependable precipitation and generally have a more temperate climate. In the northern mountains winter temperatures average below 32°F (0°C). The mountains of Yemen and Lebanon receive snow regularly in the winter months, but their temperatures are generally not as low as in the northern ranges.

Vegetation. The desert areas of the Middle East are severely inhibited by the sandy soil, which cannot support tree growth or most varieties of vegetation without irrigation. Some plants have adapted to the conditions and have formed small areas of vegetation. These desert plants, however, are generally not edible by domesticated animals. Overgrazing has depleted most areas of grassland that still existed at the turn of the century and has precipitated the further encroachment of the desert. Soil loss from wind and river erosion is the biggest obstacle for vegetation in Turkey, Libya, and Iran.

Oranges, bananas, apricots, and dates thrive in the river valleys as well as in many coastal areas. Nonindigenous plants have been introduced from areas around the world: rice from Asia; cotton, tobacco, potatoes, and corn from Europe and the Americas. Ancient forests in the Middle East have been severely depleted during modern times. Younger, lush forests thrive on the southern coasts of the Black and Caspian seas, and various evergreens and shrubs are found in most of the coastal regions.

meters
US

metres
Brit.

civilizations
US

civilisations
Brit.

MUSLIMS
are called to prayer five times each day and participate wherever they happen to be.

PROCESSIONS form part of the celebrations and ceremonies that are important observances in the calendars of Middle Eastern countries.

The people. The extreme aridity of the Middle East has caused the population to be distributed unevenly; towns and cities have grown mostly around coastal areas, inland oases, and river valleys. The mountain regions have also created isolated communities. Most people are farmers, nomadic herders, or city dwellers.

A high population growth rate, above 2.5 percent, has put an enormous strain on the environment and the economy. The cities have been forced to adapt rapidly to constant growth and an influx of people. The growth of urban areas has also had the effect of bringing diverse cultures into close contact.

Arabs and Jews—both Semitic peoples—are two of the largest population groups. Persians, the largest Indo-European group, dominate Iran, and the Turkish people dominate Turkey. There are also significant minorities of Kurds in Iran, Iraq, and Turkey; Greeks and Turks in Cyprus; and Copts and Armenians throughout the region.

Languages. The languages of the Middle East can be divided into three groups: Semitic, Persian (or Indo-Iranian), and Turkish.

Semitic languages originated in the Middle East and are spoken by the majority of people there. Hebrew, which had almost completely disappeared as a living language, is the official language of Israel. Arabic is the official language of Syria, Lebanon, Jordan, Iraq, and Saudi Arabia. Because it is the language of the Koran, it is used to some degree throughout the Muslim world. The different Arabic dialects differ widely from region to region. Some ancient Semitic languages, like Syriac and Aramaic, are still used for religious purposes among small sects throughout the Middle East.

Persian, or Farsi, is the official language of Iran. Kurdish and Baluchi, both Persian-related languages, are spoken in Turkey, Iraq, and Iran. The Arabic alphabet is generally used today for Persian languages.

Turkish is spoken throughout Turkey, in Turkish Cyprus, and in parts of Iran. Turkish is a Ural-Altaic language and is related to the languages of Scandinavia, Hungary, the Balkans, and central Asia.

Religion. Islam is the dominant religion in the Middle East. The majority of Muslims in the Middle East are either Sunni Muslims or Shiite Muslims. The major distinction between the two groups is that Sunnis believe in allowing community leaders to elect new leaders, or *caliphs,* while Shiites believe that only descendants of Muhammad can succeed as leaders. Shiite Islam is the official religion of Iran; it has large populations of followers in Iraq, Yemen, Syria, and Lebanon. Sunni Islam is the main religion in Jordan and Kuwait. Other smaller Islamic sects, such as the Alawis in Syria or the Ibadhi Kharijites in Oman, exist throughout the Middle East.

In spite of the dominance of Islam, many other religions continue to exist in significant numbers. Christianity has a large and diverse following. Significant numbers of Maronites live in Lebanon, and the Greek Orthodox are gathered in small numbers in many different countries. Judaism is the official religion of Israel; there are also small communities of Samaritans and Karaites. Zoroastrians still practice in Iran, the Yazidis gather in Iraq, and the Druze congregate in the mountain regions of Syria and Lebanon.

Economy. Although the Middle Eastern economy has been revolutionized by the vast wealth earned from the oil industry, agriculture is still the region's main economic activity.

Agriculture. Many governments have exerted control over traditional land ownership, building commercial farms and limiting the amount of land that can be owned by a private citizen. Still, most of the people in the Middle East live by crude subsistence farming. Less than 10 percent of the region's total land is cultivated. Extensive irrigation systems are required for most of the new commercial farms. Generally, Middle Eastern farmers use outdated techniques and get along without many of the innovations of the modern world. The cash crops are cotton and tobacco. Wheat, barley, and rye are the staple crops in the north, and corn and millet are the main crops in the south. Fruits and nuts are also produced.

Nomads herd livestock in the deserts and grasslands, as they have done for thousands of years. Fishing is important locally in most of the coastal areas, with largest production coming from Turkey, Egypt, and Yemen.

Natural resources. The extraction of mineral resources is the most prosperous activity in the Middle East. Over half of the world's known oil reserves are located here, mostly along the Persian Gulf coasts. The revenues from this trade have been used to benefit the exporting countries by improving education systems and transportation infrastructures, as well as by greatly modernizing and developing the industrial sectors of the economy.

Significant amounts of coal, iron ore, mercury, and magnesite are mined in Turkey. Israel, Jordan, and Syria are major producers of phosphates.

Industry. Oil processing is the main industry in the Middle East. Textile and construction material manufacturing,

INTRODUCTION

along with food processing, are also important industries.

Israel and Turkey have the most progressive and diverse industrial sectors. Many of the region's automobiles are manufactured in these two countries, and steel manufactured in Turkey is an important commodity for development in the entire region.

Transportation and trade. Historically, the Middle East has almost always been a major route for intercontinental travel. Today, within the individual countries, road and rail systems are generally underdeveloped. Turkey and Israel have the most extensive networks of paved roads. Turkey, Israel, Egypt, and Iran have the largest railroad networks. Donkeys and camels are still used extensively, along with automobiles, for ground transportation. International connecting airports exist in most major cities, and connecting air transportation is available in most towns.

Economic trends. In the last 20 years, the Middle East has become a major market for arms manufacturers from both the East and West. In 1987 the countries of the Middle East purchased almost $18 billion worth of military hardware, which represents almost 40 percent of the world arms market. The sale of arms has become a major political tool for countries hoping to improve ties with the oil-rich nations of the Middle East. During the Iran-Iraq War, the two countries accumulated enormous debts by purchasing arms, the largest suppliers of which were the United States, the Soviet Union, France, and China. Many countries have begun to build their own arms industries. Israel and Egypt are the most advanced.

The oil industry in the Middle East and Africa faced a crisis in the early 1980s as demand fell by about 45 percent and prices fell as a result. Demand began to grow again in 1986 and had returned to normal levels by the end of the decade.

In response to the crisis, members of the Organization of Petroleum Exporting Countries (OPEC) began purchasing oil-related assets—refineries and service stations—particularly in the United States. Gulf Oil Company, for example, has been taken over by Kuwaiti interests. OPEC hoped to exert control over more levels of the industry to avoid future crises. The realization that their economies are effectively fueled by nonrenewable petroleum resources has compelled many OPEC nations to initiate programs designed to restructure and diversify their economies.

Government and politics.

After World War II, British-mandated Palestine, claimed by both Arabs and Jews, was to be divided into an Arab state and a Jewish state according to a plan laid out by the United Nations (UN). In 1948, after the British mandate expired, the Jews established the state of Israel with their portion of the allotted territory. The Palestinians rejected the UN plan, and the ensuing arguments erupted into an Arab-Israeli war that lasted into 1949 and left the issue unresolved. War broke out again in 1967 and in 1973 as the Arab states, led by Egypt, tried to regain Israeli-occupied territories.

An active Palestinian terrorist movement, aimed at destroying the Israeli nation, has caused further violence and political disruption in the Middle East since the 1960s. The Palestine Liberation Organization (PLO), which has engineered these terrorist attacks, continues to insist on the return of Israeli-occupied areas to Palestinian rule, although the PLO did finally recognize Israel at the end of the 1980s to improve their international political standing.

The Arab-Israeli dispute has especially broad international implications. The Arab states have used their great deposits of oil as a tool to enforce anti-Israeli policies. Manipulating oil prices on several occasions demonstrated the Arabs' dangerous power over the industrialized nations of both East and West. In 1973, during the Arab-Israeli War, the oil supply to Western nations and Japan was cut off, and the resulting high oil prices caused a worldwide recession.

The majority of Middle Eastern states are unified only in their Islamic faith, which has dominated the region for centuries. The violent Iranian Islamic revolution of 1979 proved Islam to be a potent vehicle for nationalistic aspirations.

The Middle East today. The year 1991 appeared to mark a new era in the Middle East. The anti-Iraq coalition that assembled for the Persian Gulf War aligned the unlikely trio of Saudi Arabia, Egypt, and Syria. The presence of Western nations in the coalition was a striking departure from the traditional anti-Western Arab stance. The unity of the Arab League had been fractured by a variety of ideological disputes, mostly concerning OPEC and Israel, preceding the formation of the coalition, and the new alliance was portentous of a more stable future. The demise of the Eastern European power base led many Middle Eastern countries to explore new avenues for support—Syria, for example, turned to the U.S. for military and economic support—opening new lines of communication between the Middle East and the Western world. Israel and its Arab neighbors even gathered in Madrid, Spain, for negotiations to resolve their differences. Subsequent events have shown, however, that the Arab-Israeli situation has instead worsened considerably.

ANTIQUE ARABIC CERAMIC TILES are valued not only for their beauty but also for the information they provide about life in Middle East countries.

Countries of the Middle East

Bahrain

Official name: *State of Bahrain*
Area: *241 sq. mi., 620 sq. km.*
Type of government: *Monarchy*
Population: *656,000*
Capital and largest city: *Manama*
  (Pop., 140,000)
Languages: *Arabic (official),*
  English, Farsi, Urdu
Literacy: *89%*
Currency: *Dinar*
Per capita GDP: *$13,000*
  (Rank: 43rd)

The land. Bahrain occupies an archipelago of 35 islands in the Persian Gulf. The country's major islands are Bahrain, Sitra, Muharraq, Umm Al-Nassan, Jidda, and Hawar. Bahrain, the largest island, is about 30 miles (48 kilometers) long and 10 miles (16 kilometers) wide. All of the islands are barren, with extremely hot and humid climates. Only about 3 inches (8 centimeters) of rain falls on them annually, and their only water comes from underground springs. Cities developed around these springs.

The people. Bahrain is one of the most densely populated countries in the world, with over 1,300 people per square mile. The population is mostly Arab. There are also Arabs from other countries, Asians, and European oil workers in the country. Native Bahrainis are overwhelmingly Muslim.

Almost 40 percent of the population live in Manama. Other major cities include Jidhafs (population, 45,000); Rifa'a (50,000); and Isa Town (35,000).

Economy. Oil is Bahrain's principal natural resource and chief export. Reserves are being rapidly depleted, though, and annual production has dropped from nearly 4 million metric tons in the early 1970s to 2.15 million in 1989. Additional income is derived from processing Saudi Arabian crude oil. The oil business continues to dominate the economy. Petroleum production and processing account for about 85 percent of export receipts. Since 1975 Bahrain's gas industry has been nationalized, as has 60 percent of its oil industry. Ninety percent of the labor force is engaged in mining and industry. Bahrain has also become an international banking center.

Dates, grain, vegetables, and citrus fruits are raised in the islands' oases. Trade passing through Manama, one of the best ports in the Persian Gulf, is an important source of income. Aluminum smelting and international banking are Bahrain's largest non-oil industries.

Bahrain's imports are mostly machinery, chemicals, and food. Major trading partners are Great Britain, Saudi Arabia, the United States, and Japan.

Government. The nation's first Parliament was created in 1973, but it was dissolved in 1975. Bahrain is now a constitutional monarchy, but the emir has absolute authority. He is aided by a cabinet led by a prime minister, all of whom he appoints. A parliamentary election in 2002, however, is paving the way for a more democratized country.

History. As early as 3000 B.C., Bahrain, then named Dilmun, was considered a thriving commercial center known for its pearling industry. Several thousand burial mounds in the north of the main island have been dated to the Sumerian period in 3000 B.C. The islands were mentioned by Persian, Greek, and Roman explorers.

Their strategic location and rich beds of pearl oysters attracted several conquerors. In 1507 Portugal occupied the islands and held them until 1602, when the Persians conquered them.

In 1782 Arab tribes seized power and founded the Khalifa dynasty. In 1820 Bahrain entered into treaty relations with Great Britain, and in 1861 the two countries concluded a treaty for the protection of Bahrain.

The discovery of oil in 1931 brought Bahrain sudden international importance and radically changed the islanders' traditional way of life. Iran laid claim to the islands and protested the British presence there.

In the mid-1950s and mid-1960s, Bahraini pan-Arab nationalists incited anti-British riots and called for union with other Arab states. The Khalifa dynasty maintained its control, however, and Bahrain remained under British protection until independence in 1971.

Bahrain took part in the 1973–1974 Arab oil embargo against the United States and other nations, after which the government took controlling interest in the oil industry.

The Iran-Iraq War and the 1991 Gulf War severely limited business activity in the Persian Gulf. Bahrain's economy stands to benefit greatly from any rejuvenation of trade during peacetime.

A movement toward democratization that began in 1999 continues. In 2002 Bahrain held its first parliamentary election in 29 years.

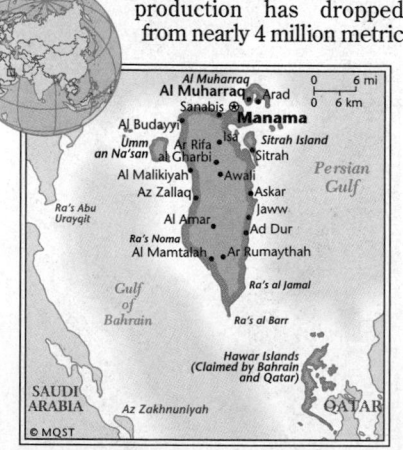

Cyprus

Official name: *Republic of Cyprus*
Area: *3,571 sq. mi., 9,250 sq. km.*
Type of government: *Republic*
Population: *767,000*
Capital and largest city: *Nicosia*
  (Pop., 273,000)
Languages: *Greek, Turkish*
  (both official), English
Literacy: *97%;* **Currency:** *Pound*
Per capita GDP: *Greek area,*
  $15,000; (Rank: 40th);
  Turkish area, $7,000
  (Rank: 69th)

The land. The island of Cyprus is mountainous. Two ranges rim the coasts—the Kyrenia Mountains in the north and the Olympus Mountains in the south. A wide, fertile plain occupies the center of the island. Summers are hot and dry, and winters are cool with occasional rain. Annual rainfall is usually less than 15 inches (38 centimeters) in the lowlands.

The people. About four-fifths of the Cypriots are Greek Christians, and one-fifth are Turkish Muslims. The island's population is concentrated in the central plains, espe-

THE CITADEL OF BAM, the well-preserved archaeological site of a 12th-century fortified town in Iran.

cially around Nicosia, and along the southern coast, in the port cities of Limassol (population, 95,000) and Larnaca (115,000).

Cyprus is densely populated, with about 175 people per square mile (282 persons per square kilometer); over half live in rural areas. Great Britain maintains two separate sovereign areas in Cyprus, where it has military bases.

Economy. Copper, asbestos, and iron mined in the Olympus Mountains are among Cyprus's principal exports. Vegetables, oranges, and wines produced for the European market are also important. Wheat, olives, and carob (a cattle fodder) are grown. The island has developed very little heavy industry, but there are many light manufacturing plants. Among the principal manufactured products are food, beverages, textiles, tobacco, leather goods, and chemicals. Tourism is also an important source of income.

Cyprus is heavily dependent on imports of fuel, raw materials, heavy machinery, and transportation equipment. Cyprus's main trading partners are Great Britain and other European Community countries, and many Middle Eastern and African nations.

Government. The Republic of Cyprus was politically separated in 1975 from the northern Turkish-controlled part of the island, seized in 1974. The Turkish Cypriot state, created by referendum, also has a republican form of government. Both are governed by separate presidents and elected legislative assemblies. The Greek Cypriots control the only internationally recognized government. The Turkish Cypriot government, called the Turkish Republic of Northern Cyprus, is recognized only by Turkey.

History. People have lived on Cyprus since before 4000 B.C. The ancient Greeks traded with Cyprus and established colonies on the island. From about 800 B.C. to modern times, Cyprus was ruled by whatever nation dominated the adjacent seas. Phoenicians, Assyrians, Persians, Romans, Byzantines, Arabs, European Crusaders, and Venetians all occupied the island at various times.

In 1571 the Ottoman Turks conquered Cyprus and held it until 1878, when Great Britain took control. During the period of Ottoman rule a Turkish-speaking Muslim minority developed alongside the original Greek-speaking Christian majority. In 1914, at the beginning of World War I,

Great Britain formally annexed Cyprus from the Ottoman Empire, which had allied itself with Britain's enemy Germany. In 1925 the island became a British Crown colony.

During the years of Venetian and Ottoman government, the island underwent an economic and cultural decline, but as a British colony it experienced a revival. With this revival came an awakening of national consciousness and a rising demand on the part of Greek Cypriots for *enosis,* union with Greece, a demand that Turkish Cypriots opposed. In 1955 Greek Cypriots began a guerrilla war against the British in order to force them to grant the island independence.

Independence. In 1959, after years of fighting, an agreement signed by Great Britain, Greece, and Turkey granted Cyprus independence with safeguards for the rights of the Turkish minority.

Archbishop Makarios, head of the Cypriot Orthodox Church and leader of the Greek community, became president, with a Turkish Cypriot leader as vice president. Friction between the Greek and Turkish communities paralyzed the new government.

In 1963, Makarios proposed constitutional changes that the Turkish minority felt would reduce their rights. This disagreement led to an armed conflict between Greek and Turkish Cypriots; Greece and Turkey intervened. A UN peacekeeping force finally mediated a cease-fire, but no solution was reached.

Makarios was temporarily deposed in a 1974 coup, and Turkey invaded the island. A Turkish Cypriot state was created in the northern part of the island in 1975. It declared itself a republic in 1983 and adopted a constitution and held elections in 1985. Since Makarios's death in 1977, there have been renewed attempts to unify the two sectors of Cyprus.

A new president of Cyprus, George Vassiliou, took office in February of 1988. Vassiliou showed a readiness to take the concerns of the Turkish Cypriots into account, and the Cypriots also began to show greater flexibility. Both sides began talks on a UN plan to establish a two-state federation. No resolution was forthcoming. UN-led talks resumed in 1999 and continued through 2002, but, again, no resolution was reached. Cyprus is to join the EU in 2004. Benefits of membership will only be extended to the Greek side until the Turkish side makes concessions toward reunification.

Iran

Official name: *Islamic Republic of Iran*

Area: *636,128 sq. mi., 1,648,000 sq. km.*

Type of government: *Theocratic republic*

Population: *67,538,000*

Capital and largest city: *Tehran (Pop., 6,759,000)*

Languages: *Persian, Turkish, Kurdish, Arabic*

Literacy: *72%*

Currency: *Rial*

Per capita GDP: *$7,000 (Rank: 70th)*

The land. Central Iran lies on a great plateau that has an average elevation of 4,000 feet (1,220 meters) above sea level. It contains two barren, salty deserts—the Dasht-e-Kavir and the Dash-e-Lut. West and south of the plateau are the

rugged Zagros Mountains; to the north the Elburz range rises to over 18,000 feet (5,488 meters) above sea level. Mount Damavand, an inactive volcano northeast of Teheran in the Elburz Mountains, is Iran's highest peak at 18,386 feet (5,604 meters). Narrow, fertile lowlands skirt the country's seacoasts.

Iran's climate varies from region to region. Rainfall averages only 12 inches (31 centimeters) a year for the country as a whole, but the plateau receives less than 5 inches (2 centimeters) and the mountains and northern coasts may receive as much as 40 inches (103 centimeters) annually. In the central deserts summer temperatures rise above 120°F (50°C), but the mountain areas are cooler both in summer and in winter.

The people. Population is concentrated on the lower mountain slopes and in the coastal regions. Ancient Iran was settled by tribes that migrated into the region from Europe. Modern Iran's population also includes Arabs, Jews, Armenians, nomadic Kurds, Baluchi, Turkomans, and Bakhtiari, all highly independent minorities.

Most of the people are Muslims, over 90 percent of whom are Shiite, the remainder being Sunni. Half the people live in rural areas, half in urban areas. The major cities include Teheran, the capital; Meshed, or Mashhad (population, 1,887,000); Isfahan, or Esfahan (1,266,000); and Tabriz (1,191,000).

Economy. The wealth of Iran is derived from oil, but farming and herding are the occupations of most Iranians. The bulk of the cultivated land is in the moist northwest, where wheat and barley are the leading crops. Corn, rice, sugar beets, tea, tobacco, and fruits also are raised. Cotton thrives on the edges of the plateau, and goats, sheep, and camels are grazed in semidesert areas. Fishing prospers on the Caspian coast. Poultry farmers have expanded production with government aid since the 1979 revolution.

Iran has 10 percent of the world's oil resources, but annual production dropped from 260 to 145 million metric tons between 1978 and 1979, at the time of the revolution; it has remained at that level. The oil industry was nationalized in 1951, but several international companies are still involved in the ownership and operation of various Iranian petroleum enterprises new 5-year plan, passed in January 1990, was directed toward transferring control of state industries to the private sector. Revenues from oil production and refining constitute the largest single portion of Iran's income.

Most of Iran's industries process agricultural products, producing cotton and wool textiles, dried fruits, cigarettes, vegetable oils, and leather. Carpet-weaving is an ancient craft that is still important. In 1988 Bandar Abbas was the only fully operational non-oil port; the others, which were damaged during the Iran-Iraq War, had not been reconstructed.

Japan, Germany, Turkey, Italy, and Great Britain are the major trading partners. Iran imports machinery, iron and

AN AYATOLLAH, or religious leader, from Ahwaz visits the front in the 1980s war between Iran and Iraq over disputed territories.

steel, electrical goods, and grain. It exports mostly crude oil, which accounts for 90 percent of the total export revenue, and petroleum products.

Government. The Iranian constitution, ratified in 1979, gives supreme authority to the "Spiritual Leader." A 12-member Council of Experts appoints the Spiritual Leader and interprets the constitution. Six of the members are religious men selected by the leader and six are elected by the assembly. The president, popularly elected for 4-year terms, has full executive authority. The position of prime minister has been abolished. The legislature is the 290-member unicameral Islamic Consultative Assembly.

History. The modern history of the Middle East began in Iran in 1908, when the region's first oil was found there. In ancient times, too, Iran—or Persia—was important as the core of the great Persian Empire, which ruled the entire Near East in the 500s and 400s B.C. Alexander the Great conquered the empire in the 300s B.C., and his successors were defeated by Parthians, who lived in modern-day northeastern Iran, in the 200s B.C. It was not until the A.D. 200s that Persians regained control of their land, under the Sasanian dynasty.

Sasanians ruled until 641, when they were overthrown by Arab armies that converted the Persians to Islam. Seljuk Turks replaced the Arabs as rulers in the eleventh century, and they in turn were overthrown by the Mongols in the 1200s. When the Mongol Empire disintegrated in the 1500s, Persians again took control and rebuilt and reunited their country.

Under Nader Shah, who ruled in the 1700s, the Persians drove out invading Afghans and went on to conquer Afghanistan and part of India. Civil war followed Nader's death in 1747 and caused the loss of all the newly conquered territory. The Qajar faction emerged dominant from the civil wars and founded a dynasty that ruled until the 1920s.

Although Persia remained sovereign during the 1800s and early 1900s, it was subject to the competing economic and political influences of Russia and Great

Britain. In 1905 a rebellion broke out among Persians who objected to the weak shah's dependence on foreign states, and in 1906 the shah yielded to the rebel's demands for a constitution and an elected assembly.

Riza Shah. Foreign interference increased after the discovery of oil in 1908, however, and in 1921 Riza Pahlavi, an army officer, led a coup that drove the pro-British shah into exile. In 1923 Pahlavi became prime minister, and in 1925 the Majlis proclaimed him shah.

Riza Shah began the modernization of Persia. During his reign, communications, education, and industry were expanded and the judiciary, military, and all of society began to be reordered on a Western pattern. Great Britain retained its influence only as the operator of the Iranian oil fields.

During World War II Iran declared itself neutral, but Great Britain and Russia occupied the country. In 1941 the Allies forced Riza Shah to yield the throne to his son, Muhammad Riza.

Contemporary Iran. After the war a strong Iranian nationalist movement developed, with the ending of foreign control as its primary goal. Mohammad Mossadegh, a leader of the nationalists, became prime minister in 1951 and ruled as a dictator.

During Mossadegh's ministry the British-owned oil fields were nationalized. Iran was unable to market the oil without foreign help, however, and the country faced financial ruin. In 1953 the shah removed Mossadegh from office and had him arrested.

Oil production began again in 1954 under the direction of British, U.S., French, and Dutch companies that shared the profits with Iran. Oil revenues were spent on programs of social and economic reform as industrialization and modernization were rapidly increased.

Shah Muhammad Riza Pahlavi, crowned in 1967, eventually established strict martial law to control his rivals, which included Islamic fundamentalists and political conservatives. Labor strikes and riots spurred further military reaction as production dropped. The shah's U.S.-aided military adventures in neighboring lands further undermined his popularity; he was finally deposed by militant revolutionaries in February 1979. Ayatollah Khomeini, an exiled leader of the Shi'a community, returned to Iran and was appointed Spiritual Leader. He appointed a provisional government and proclaimed the country the Islamic Republic of Iran.

Militants seized the U.S. embassy in Teheran on November 4, 1979, and held 53 Americans hostage until January 1981, seriously damaging U.S.-Iranian relations.

In September 1980 Iran and Iraq began a sporadic bloody war brought on by border disputes. Other Persian Gulf nations began to feel threatened by Iran's success in the war. In 1987 an increased naval presence by the United States and other countries, to protect shipping in the Gulf, created a volatile situation. In July 1988 a cease-fire was declared between Iran and Iraq.

Khomeini's death in June 1989 had a major impact on the political system. Hashemi Rafsanjani was elected president and a new constitution was implemented. The new government initiated economic reforms, reducing the state's role in the economy, and pledged to improve relations with the West.

Iran remained neutral during the Persian Gulf War, although it let Iraqi aircraft land in Iran. In the wake of the conflict, Iran has moderated somewhat its revolutionary tone and militant anti-Western stance. At the same time it has conducted a massive weapons buildup that has proved a drain on its still-struggling economy.

Overwhelming victories in recent presidential and parliamentary elections show that support has grown for a reform movement that presses for liberalization of the country. This is, however, at odds with religious conservatives of the judiciary and the supreme leader and presents a struggle for Iran's future identity.

24 Middle East

Iraq

Official name: *Republic of Iraq*
Area: *168,710 sq. mi., 437,072 sq. km.*
Type of government: *Republic*
Population: *24,002,000*
Capital and largest city: *Baghdad (Pop., 3,841,000)*
Languages: *Arabic, Kurdish, Assyrian, Armenian*
Literacy: *40%;* **Currency:** *Dinar*
Per capita GDP: *$2,400 (Rank: 127th)*

The land. The high Zagros Mountains rim Iraq on the north and east, reaching as high as 10,000 feet (3,049 meters) above sea level. The western and southwestern regions are desert.

Central Iraq consists of a "lower plain," in the southern part of the Tigris and Euphrates valley, that never rises above 300 feet (92 meters), and an "upper plain," a rolling, hilly region in the northeast of the country.

About 5 inches (13 centimeters) of rain fall yearly on the lower plain; the upper plain receives about 15 inches (39 centimeters) of rain a year. The rest of the country is quite dry. Summer temperatures in Iraq's desert areas often climb above 120°F (50°C), but averages for the country as a whole range from about 50°F (17°C) in winter to 95°F (35°C) in summer.

The people. The population is concentrated in the river valleys. Most Iraqis are Arab, but the population also includes a large Kurdish minority in the northeast. Bedouin tribes live in the southwest. Nearly three-quarters of the population is literate and two-thirds live in urban areas. The most important cities include Baghdad, the capital; Mosul (population, 664,000); Kirkuk (419,000); and Basra (406,000).

Economy. Oil, the most important part of Iraq's economy, has contributed to the country's improving standard of living. Oil accounts for half the gross national product; 101.2 million metric tons were produced in 1987. The richest fields are at Kirkuk, Mosul, and Basra. The oil industry was nationalized in 1972.

Iraq has some light industries that produce chiefly building materials, textiles, carpets, cigarettes, dried fruits, and leather goods. Iraqi industry was once state-owned; since 1987 it has become increasingly privately owned.

Agriculture is also important to the economy, employing 30 percent of the work force. Farmers in the fertile central plain grow barley, wheat, rice, tobacco, cotton, and dates. Sheep are raised on the upper plain and on the fringes of the desert. Large-scale irrigation and flood-control programs were undertaken in the 1950s and 1960s to create more farmland. The irrigation systems are in need of major repairs, although the problem has been partially alleviated by a new series of major dams.

The country's chief export is oil, which accounts for 95 percent of export earnings. Barley, dates, wool, and cotton are also exported. Imports include foodstuffs, machinery, iron, and steel. Turkey, the United States, Brazil, and Japan are Iraq's principal trading partners.

Government. According to its 1970 constitution, Iraq is ruled by the socialistic Revolutionary Command Council, which elects the president and appoints a council of ministers. The legislative body is the 250-member unicameral National Assembly. Elections to the legislature were held in 1980, for the first time since 1958. There is one political party.

History. Modern Iraq is the site of ancient Mesopotamia, "the land between the rivers," where the oldest known civilization—that of the Sumerians—flourished in about 3000 B.C. Other great empires—Babylonia, Assyria, and Persia—followed Sumer in the fertile lowlands between the Tigris and the Euphrates rivers.

In A.D. 750 Arab Muslims conquered the region and converted the people to Islam. Arab rule continued until 1258, when Mongol armies devastated the country. Iraq made little recovery under the Ottoman Turks, who took power in 1638 and ruled the area until World War I.

After the war Great Britain received a League of Nations mandate over Iraq. In 1921 Iraqis chose as king Emir Faisal of the Arabian province of Hejaz, and Iraq was proclaimed a constitutional monarchy, gaining independence.

Independence. In 1932 the League of Nations recognized Iraq's sovereignty by admitting it as a full member. Faisal died in 1933 and was succeeded by his son Ghazi, who reigned until his death in 1939. Ghazi's young son and heir, Faisal II, was a minor, and a regent ruled in his name.

civilization
US

civilisation
Brit.

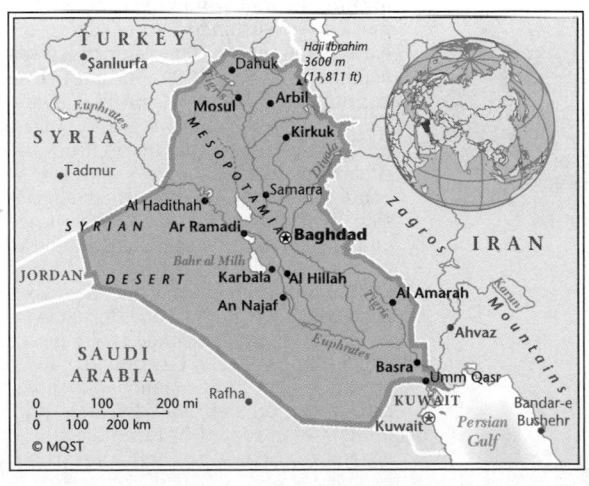

Iraq's modern history has been turbulent. During the 1930s, minority groups rebelled against the new government and nationalists fought against the presence of British personnel and troops. During 1941 a pro-Nazi group briefly controlled the government, but it was overthrown, and Iraq supported the Allies in World War II.

Faisal II came of age in 1953, but in 1958 army officers led by General Abdel Karim Qasim overthrew the government, assassinated King Faisal, and proclaimed Iraq a republic. Qasim became premier but was killed in February 1963 during another coup, in which Abdel Salaam Arif took power. **Contemporary Iraq.** After an unsuccessful attempt to form a federation with Egypt and Syria, Arif, in November 1963, split with the pan-Arab leaders in the U.A.R. and Syria. In 1964 a new constitution took effect that favored alliance, but not a merger, with the U.A.R.

Arif died in an accident in 1966, and his brother, Abdel Rahman Arif, became president. Several attempted coups in 1965 and 1966 resulted in a long series of governmental reorganizations. In 1968 Abdel Arif was ousted. A Revolutionary Command Council took power, and Ahmed Al Bakr was chosen president.

A major domestic problem began in 1961 when rebel Kurds demanded the establishment of an independent Kurdish state. Some Kurdish autonomy was granted in 1966 and again in 1974, but fighting, especially heavy in 1974, 1975, and 1979, continued. Iraqi bombings of Kurdish villages in Iran worsened relations between those two countries. In 1979 Saddam Hussein, Bakr's vice president, was installed as the new president.

As border conflicts increased and Iran fell into revolution, a major Iranian-Iraqi war broke out in 1980. The brutal war left some 300,000 Iraqis dead before a cease-fire was declared in July 1988. Peace negotiations began later that year.

Iraq also participated in the 1948–1949, 1967, and 1973 Arab wars against Israel. It led the united Arab protest against the Israeli-Egyptian peace accords of 1978–1979.

On August 2, 1990, Iraqi troops invaded Kuwait without warning. They met little resistance and easily seized Kuwait's oil fields. The Emir of Kuwait escaped to Saudi Arabia and Iraq announced its annexation of Kuwait.

The United Nations voted to impose total economic sanctions on Iraq and American and British forces were sent to Saudi Arabia to prevent further aggression. On January 16, 1991, after peace talks failed, an international coalition of forces, including those of the United States, began a campaign of air attacks designed to force Iraqi troops to withdraw from Kuwait. Iraq responded with missile attacks on Israel and on Saudi Arabia. A ground offensive was launched by coalition forces on February 24. The Iraqi military was routed in three days. Iraq agreed to a cease-fire and Iraqi troops began withdrawing on March 2, 1991.

Small-scale rioting and factional fighting ensued in Iraq after the cease-fire; thousands of Kurdish Iraqis escaped to Turkey and Iran. International organizations brought food and supplies to the fleeing Kurds, many of whom were stranded in the mountains between Iraq and Turkey without provisions. The Iraqi army quelled the rebellion, and Saddam remained president.

The cease-fire required that all Iraq's nuclear, chemical, biological, and ballistic weapons be destroyed, but UN inspection teams were alternately expelled or obstructed in their work, so UN sanctions remained in place. After the terrorist attacks on the U.S. in 2001, the Bush administration believed the Middle East would remain unstable until Saddam was deposed and feared that Iraq would provide terrorists with weapons of mass destruction. A 2002 UN resolution threatened "serious consequences," which the U.S. took to mean Saddam's removal by force.

A U.S.- and British-led coalition attacked Iraq in early 2003. The war was essentially over by mid-April, but the reconstruction that followed was marred by violence. Forces continued to meet resistance from factions loyal to Saddam, who had escaped during the fall of Baghdad. In July Saddam's sons were killed in a raid, and by September a Governing Council and cabinet were in place. Despite this progress, guerrilla attacks and suicide bombings continued; targets included UN headquarters, the Jordanian embassy, holy shrines, and police stations. In September a member of the Governing Council was ambushed and killed. In December Saddam was captured; coalition forces had hoped this would stem the continuing attacks, but there was no discernable change. Transfer of power to the interim government was to take place by July 2004, but the particulars were disputed and the UN was called on to intercede.

Israel

Official name: *State of Israel*
Area: *8,017 sq. miles, 20,770 sq. km.*
Type of government: *Republic*
Population: *6,030,000*
Capital (disputed) and largest city: *Jerusalem (Pop., 628,000)*
Languages: *Hebrew (official), Arabic, English*
Literacy: *95%*
Currency: *New Israeli shekel (NIS)*
Per capita GDP: *$19,000 (Rank: 31st)*

The land. Israel is a small irregularly shaped country with a varied landscape. A narrow, fertile plain borders the Mediterranean. In central Israel, the hilly Judaean plateau rises east of the coastal plain. In the north rise the high-

lands of Galilee, a region of rolling hills and rich valleys. Mount Meron, located in the far north near Safad, rises to 3,963 feet (1,208 meters). Near Israel's eastern border the land drops sharply into the valley of the Jordan River. The wedge-shaped, barren Negev Desert, in the south, occupies more than half of Israel's land area.

The Jordan, Israel's principal river, flows along the northeastern border into Israel's largest freshwater lake, the Sea of Galilee, and on into the Dead Sea. Smaller streams run through the northern and central portions of the country, but in the southern regions only dry riverbeds are found.

The southern desert receives almost no rain, but rainfall in the northern and central areas averages 20 inches (51 centimeters) a year, most of it falling during the winter and spring.

The people. Since 1948, when Israel became a state, nearly 2 million Jews from many parts of the world have poured into the area. Most Arabs fled Israel during the 1948–1949 Arab-Israeli war, although many Arabs still remain and many others have emigrated since.

Israel is the most literate country in the Middle East. With nearly 500 people per square mile, Israel is densely populated and overwhelmingly urban.

Population is concentrated in the more fertile and temperate northern and central regions of Israel. The two largest cities, Tel Aviv-Jaffa (population, 348,000) and Haifa (265,000), are on the coast. Jerusalem, the capital, lies in the center of the Judaean Hills.

Economy. The people of Israel have worked hard to meet the challenge of a harsh land. In an area that a few decades ago had only a subsistence agriculture, Israelis have developed manufacturing industries and have increased agricultural production to feed an expanding population and to export their products.

Israel's desert lands hold a great variety of mineral resources. Potash and salts are obtained from the Dead Sea, copper is mined in the southern Negev,

---

meters
US

metres
Brit.

center
US

centre
Brit.

(For more background on Iraq, see Into the 21st Century in the HISTORY OF THE WORLD volume.)

and stone is quarried in the center of the country. Israel has some oil and natural gas, but not enough to meet its needs. Diamonds, which are cut and polished in Israel, account for one-fourth of the total export revenues.

Nearly one-third of Israel's gross national product is derived from manufacturing, while agriculture contributes 10 percent. Israel's land is intensively cultivated. In areas that once were swamps or deserts, farmers use every available piece of land and every drop of water to raise their crops. About one-third of the cultivated land is irrigated.

Citrus fruit, grown on the coastal plain, is the most important farm product, and it is one of Israel's principal exports. Grains, tobacco, grapes, olives, and other fruits are grown in Galilee. Farmers on the fringes of the Negev raise cotton and dates. Nomadic herdsmen graze goats and sheep in the Negev, and dairy farming prospers in the north and on the plain.

Manufacturing and general technological development have drastically improved the Israelis' standard of living in the last two decades. The refining of domestic oil and of crude oil shipped to Haifa is the country's most important heavy industry. Other heavy industry includes chemical production, metal processing, and machinery manufacturing. Israelis work in many light industries, including diamond polishing, textile weaving, glass making, food processing, and wine making. Aeronautics, electronics, biotechnology, and agricultural technology are the biggest growth industries today.

Many industries and farms are operated as cooperatives or collectives. Most of Israel's factory, farm, and office workers belong to Histradrut, the leading national labor union, which provides a wide variety of social and economic services.

A RABBI reads the Torah, the religious law of the Jewish people that is found in the first five books of the Bible.

Machinery and electronics are the most important exports; diamonds, citrus fruits, and manufactured goods are also significant. Imports are mostly oil and capital goods.

Most of Israel's trade is with the United States, Great Britain, France, and Germany. Grants as well as loans from the United States, reparations payments from Germany, technical aid from the United Nations, and contributions from private groups and individuals around the world help to support the Israeli economy.

Government. Israel's form of government is a republic. The chief of state is a president, who is elected every five years by the parliament, or Knesset. With the advice of the Knesset, the president appoints a prime minister to act as chief executive. The prime minister and the cabinet he chooses are responsible to the parliament.

The 120 members of the unicameral Knesset are popularly elected to terms of four years. Participation in government is open to all Israeli citizens, including non-Jews.

History. Although the state of Israel is new, the land is ancient. In about 2000 B.C., wandering tribes of Hebrews appeared in Canaan, later called Palestine. Perhaps 500 years later, a group of Hebrews was conquered and enslaved by the Egyptians.

After 1200 B.C., Hebrews once again inhabited Palestine and developed a society based on herding and agriculture. Over the next thousand years the Hebrew culture and religion developed; produced the Hebrew Bible, the Old Testament; gave root to Christianity; and contributed its part to the foundation of Western civilization.

Despite the strength and importance of their culture, the Jews were never powerful militarily or politically. In the 900s B.C. the Hebrew kingdom split in two—the kingdom of Israel in the north and the kingdom of Judah (the source of the word Jew) in the south. By 586 B.C. both kingdoms had been conquered and most Jews were in exile in Babylonia. Fifty years later Babylon fell and the Jews were permitted to return to Palestine.

Those who returned settled in southern Palestine and rebuilt Jerusalem. They were free from foreign domination only briefly, however. Palestine became in turn a province of Persia (538–332 B.C.); of Alexander the Great's empire (332–323 B.C.); of Egypt (323–198 B.C.); and of the Syrian Seleucid dynasty (198–168 B.C.).

The Jews maintained their own society and culture, however, and it was during the period after the Babylonian captivity that the Hebrew Bible was compiled from earlier and contemporary writings.

In 168 B.C. the Jews successfully rebelled against the Seleucids, only to be subjugated in 63 B.C. by the Romans. In 70 A.D. the Jews tried to throw off Roman rule, but they were crushed and their capital city, Jerusalem, was destroyed.

The Diaspora. Many Jews left Palestine and scattered throughout the world in what was called the *Diaspora,* or the dispersion. Palestine remained in the hands of the Romans and their successors, the Byzantines, until the 600s. Then the armies of a new religion, Islam, made Palestine part of a vast Arab empire.

Four hundred years later, the Seljuk Turks conquered Palestine, but they were soon challenged by the Christian Crusaders, who penetrated the country. Finally, Egypt drove out the Crusaders and held Palestine until it became a part of the Ottoman Turkish Empire in the 1500s. Palestine remained Turkish until the end of World War I.

Many of the dispersed Jews had never been completely accepted into the societies in which they had settled. Often they were victims of prejudice and persecution, but they maintained their religion, their culture, and the hope that they would one day return to Palestine, or "Zion."

Zionism. During the 1800s a Zionist, or nationalist, movement arose, and small groups of Jews returned to Palestine as pioneers. The first Zionist Congress was held in 1897 at Basel, Switzerland, under the leadership of Theodore Herzl, an Austrian Jew.

The congress greatly strengthened the efforts of the early idealistic pioneers and formulated the Basel Program, which called for the settlement of Jews in Palestine and the creation of a homeland there for the Jewish people. Zionism as an international mass movement included both religious idealists and political nationalists, and it won the support of many non-Jews.

The Zionists tried to persuade Turkey to allow the mass settlement of Jews in Palestine, but the request was refused. In 1917, during World War I, Great Britain's foreign secretary, Arthur Balfour, publicly announced Britain's support for the Zionist program.

The Balfour Declaration pledged to facilitate "the establishment in Palestine of a national home for the Jewish people" without injuring the non-Jewish population already living there. Britain occupied Palestine during the war. In

PAINTINGS suggest the dress of the people of Israel in biblical times.

labor
US

labour
Brit.

civilization
US

civilisation
Brit.

1922 the League of Nations gave Britain a mandate over Palestine—then including both present-day Israel and Jordan—that obliged it to fulfill the Balfour pledge. **British mandate.** The Zionists were well organized. They established organizations to encourage immigration, handle finances, set up political structures, and plan extensive agricultural and industrial development. The Jewish community developed alongside the traditional Arab society, but Jewish immigration and land purchases and the pioneer spirit of the Jews encountered Arab resistance.

The British sought to appease the Arabs by restricting Jewish activity. In 1939–1940 they drastically limited Jewish immigration and land purchases to keep Jews a minority in Palestine. The Arabs were not satisfied.

During World War II the Palestinian Arab leader, the mufti of Jerusalem, cooperated with the Germans. The Jews supported the British in the war, and a Jewish brigade fought in the Middle East and in Europe.

Jews defied the British effort to close Palestine to refugees from Nazi countries, and many Jews entered Palestine despite British opposition. Opinion in the non-Arab world began to turn against Great Britain. By the end of the war the deadlock over Palestine was complete. Britain, unable to find a solution satisfactory to all sides, submitted the dilemma to the United Nations in February 1947. **Statehood.** In November 1947 the United Nations voted to terminate the British mandate and to partition Palestine into an Arab state, a Jewish state, and a multinational enclave around Jerusalem. The British left Palestine May 15, 1948, and an Israeli government recognized by most non-Arab states took power.

Sporadic fighting had broken out in Palestine immediately after the UN partition resolution. On the heels of the British withdrawal, the Arab states of the Middle East, united in the Arab League, invaded Israel. The Israelis drove the invaders out, and in 1949 the United Nations negotiated separate armistice agreements between Israel and the Arab states. But no final peace treaty was signed, and a formal state of war continued.

The Arabs refused to recognize Israel and employed tactics of encirclement, noncommunication, economic boycott, and border harassment. When Egypt began a military buildup on Israel's frontier in 1956, Israel invaded Egyptian

---

labor
US

labour
Brit.

THE WAILING WALL IN JERUSALEM is a holy place for Jews from around the world who make pilgrimages to offer prayers and to remember the survival of the Jewish people.

---

territory. The United Nations soon arranged a cease-fire.

After several years of uneasy peace, local clashes broke out along the Israeli-Syrian border in 1967. Egypt denied Israel access to the Gulf of Aqaba and massed troops on Israel's border. Israel struck out at Egypt and at Jordan, which had joined the conflict, occupying the Gaza Strip; the Sinai Peninsula; the part of Jordan west of the Jordan River, called the West Bank; and the heights east of the Sea of Galilee, called the Golan Heights. A cease-fire was established after about four months, and it remained more or less in effect until October of 1973, when Egypt launched an attack across the Suez Canal and Syrian forces struck the Golan Heights. In 18 days the United Nations worked out a cease-fire. A disengagement agreement was agreed to by Egypt and Israel in December of 1973, and by Syria and Israel in May of 1974.

Prime Minister Menachem Begin, elected in 1977, and Egypt's President Anwar el-Sadat, signed a peace treaty in 1979. The treaty arranged for Israel's withdrawal from the Egyptian territory it had annexed.

Attempts for a peaceful resolution of the conflict between Israel and the Arab states have been greatly hindered by the terrorist anti-Israeli policies of the Palestine Liberation Organization (PLO), led by Yasir Arafat. Israeli-PLO tension led to a limited war between Lebanon and Israel in 1978 and an Israeli invasion of Lebanon in 1982, which forced the temporary withdrawal of the PLO from that country. By 1984 Israel had over 30,000 citizens in the West Bank area. The old "green line" that had separated the West Bank from Israel became increasingly blurred by new Jewish settlements.

In December 1987 a Palestinian uprising, called the *intifada*, erupted on the West Bank and in the Gaza Strip to protest occupation of the territories by Israel. In July 1988 Jordan renounced claims to the West Bank in favor of the PLO. In November 1988 the PLO declared an independent Palestinian state in the occupied territories, but it was not accorded much international recognition. Later, in an attempt to gain diplomatic recognition, the PLO recognized the right of Israel to exist.

In the late 1980s and early 1990s, tens of thousands of Soviet Jews emigrated to Israel. The government, led by Yitzhak Shamir, sought U.S. loan

---

guarantees for new construction but opposed the U.S. requirement that Israel halt new construction in the West Bank. In June 1992 the Labor Party won the national elections and Yitzhak Rabin became prime minister. Rabin halted new construction and revitalized talks with Palestinian representatives. In September 1993 Israeli and PLO representatives signed, in Washington, D.C., a Declaration of Principles on the establishment of Palestinian self-rule in Gaza and the West Bank city of Jericho.

Israel and Jordan signed a peace agreement in 1994. In November 1995 Rabin was assassinated by Yigal Amir, a Jew who objected to the peace process and to handing over any territory to the Palestinians. Then, under the renewed leadership of Shimon Peres, Israel's first direct election of a prime minister was won by Benjamin Netanyahu. Netanyahu's tenure was marred by bitter internal division, and the centrist Ehud Barak defeated him decisively in 1999. Barak was unable to reach a peace accord with the Palestinians, the status of Jerusalem being the major point of contention, and, in the fall of 2000, new waves of violence erupted in the West Bank and Gaza Strip. Barak's popularity plummeted, and he called for early elections, in which he lost to the more militant former defense minister Ariel Sharon.

Despite attempts by the U.S., UN, European Union, and Russia to facilitate the Israeli-Palestinian peace process and occasional cease-fires, violence continues in the region and no resolution seems imminent.

Jordan

Official name: *Hashemite Kingdom of Jordan*
Area: *34,436 sq. mi., 89,213 sq. km.*
Type of government:
  Constitutional monarchy
Population: *5,307,000*
Capital and largest city: *Amman (Pop., 1,147,000)*
Languages: *Arabic (official), English*
Literacy: *87%;* **Currency:** *Dinar*
Per capita GDP: *$4,300 (Rank: 96th)*

The land. Most of Jordan is barren land. Almost the entire eastern half of the country is desert, partly covered by salt or lava. In the west a hilly region separates the desert from a wide, deep gorge that runs the length of the country. The Jordan River flows through the northern part of this gorge, from the Sea of Galilee into the salty Dead Sea, and provides the boundary between Jordan and Israel.

South of the Dead Sea is a dry riverbed, the Wadi al Araba, which runs to the Gulf of Aqaba. Mount Ramm, near Aqaba, is Jordan's highest peak; it

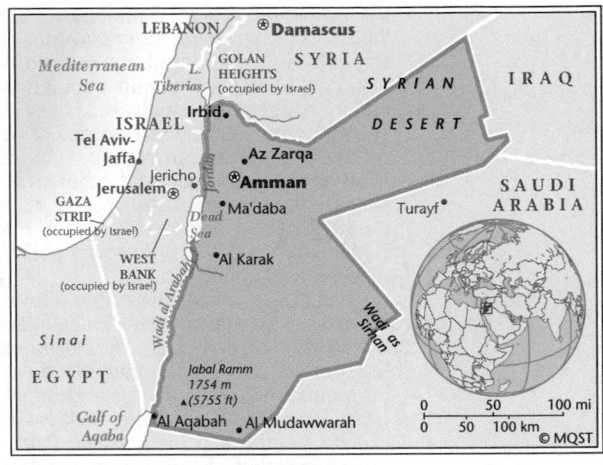

PETRA was an ancient city in what is now Jordan. The Franks occupied it during the Crusades until 1189, after which time it fell to ruin.

rises 5,755 feet (1,760 kilometers) above sea level. West of the Jordan River lies the fertile West Bank region, which was seized by Jordan from Palestine in 1948 and occupied by Israel in 1967.

In the western uplands, Jordan's climate is mild, with 15 to 25 inches (39 to 64 centimeters) of rainfall a year. Almost no rain falls in the desert, where summer temperatures rise above 120°F (50°C).

The people.　Most of the people are Arabs, many having emigrated from Palestine during the 1948–1949 Arab-Israeli war. An overwhelming majority of the people are Sunni Muslims. The Bedouins make up a small minority in eastern Jordan and small minorities of Circassians, Armenians, and Kurds also live in Jordan.

Almost 60 percent of the population is urban. Major cities include Amman, the capital; Az Zarqa (population, 429,000); and Irbid (247,000).

Economy.　Jordan is a very poor, arid country, with little surface water, infertile soil, and few exploitable resources. Potash, phosphates, and limestone, mined around the Dead Sea, are Jordan's most important minerals. Some marble, gypsum, manganese, and ceramic clays are also mined, and there are believed to be large untapped reserves of copper, iron, sulfur, and silicon.

Only about 10 percent of Jordan's land is suitable for cultivation, and only part of that is farmed. The best growing regions are in the moist northwest, but even there some irrigation is necessary. Barley and wheat are the main crops. Beans, tobacco, and citrus and other fruits grow in the Jordan valley, and grapes, dates, figs, olives, and nuts are raised in the drier areas. Goats, sheep, camels, and horses also are raised. Major industries are food processing, clothing and cement manufacture, and tourism.

Chemicals, phosphates, potash, and manufactured goods are the most important of Jordan's exports. The country imports primarily foodstuffs, petroleum, pharmaceuticals, textiles, and machinery. Most trade is with other Arab states, the United States, Great

Britain, and Germany.

Government.　Jordan is a constitutional monarchy. The hereditary head of state is a king who wields great authority over all branches of government. He appoints the prime minister and other members of the cabinet and may dismiss them at will.

The ministers are also responsible to the lower house of the National Assembly, the House of Representatives, which is elected every 4 years by universal suffrage. Members of the upper house, the Senate, are appointed by the king.

History.　Civilization in the region of Jordan probably began around 2000 B.C., when Semitic Amorities settled around the Jordan River in the area called Canaan. As a part of Syria, the region was occupied by a succession of Middle Eastern empires. The last was the Ottoman Empire, which controlled the country from the 1500s into the 1900s.

After World War I Jordan became part of a new Syrian kingdom, which came under French control. In 1922 the League of Nations gave Great Britain a mandate over Palestine and Transjordan, as the territory between the Jordan River and Saudi Arabia was called. In 1923 Transjordan gained semi-independent status within the mandate area.

Emir Abdullah ibn al-Husayn, an Arabian ruler, governed with British advice. He was the first of the Hashemite ("of Hashem," or "Husayn") dynasty. For the next 20 years the country moved toward independence with British assistance. Transjordanian troops aided the Allies in World War II, and a treaty signed in 1946 with Great Britain established Transjordan's sovereignty. Great Britain retained great influence, however.

In 1948–1949 Transjordan participated in the Arab war against the newly proclaimed state of Israel. Abdullah annexed a portion of Palestine just west of the Jordan River and changed the country's name from Transjordan, "across the Jordan," to Jordan.

Contemporary Jordan.　King Abdullah was assassinated in 1951, and his son

and heir, Talal, was judged incompetent. Talal's son, Hussein, came to the throne in 1952. Hussein sought British aid in meeting the country's pressing economic and social problems. But the presence in the country of a large number of Palestinian refugees demanding renewed war with Israel led to political instability.

Anti-Western riots in 1955 and 1956 forced the departure from the country of all British personnel and an end to British assistance. In 1957 and 1958 King Hussein himself barely avoided being deposed during a government upheaval.

The territory Jordan had annexed from Palestine in 1948, the West Bank of Jordan and Jerusalem, was regained by Israel in the 1967 war. King Hussein imposed martial law after the war.

Palestinian guerrillas based in Jordan continued to mount raids on Israel. Jordanian troops tried, unsuccessfully, to squelch these raids. Other Arab states supported the Palestinians, and, in 1974, at an Arab summit meeting, the Palestine Liberation Organization was designated as the sole representative of

KING HUSSEIN of Jordan agreed with Israeli Prime Minister Yitzhak Rabin to end the state of war that had existed since 1948.

the Arabs in the West Bank territories. The Jordanian government accepted this, although it heightened tensions between Jordan's Bedouin population and the Palestinian population. Hussein subsequently dissolved Parliament to reduce its Palestinian representation.

Hussein led Jordan and other Arab states in their condemnation of Egypt for its 1979 peace treaty with Israel. He replaced Jordan's pro-Western policy with political nonalignment.

Jordan's economy has suffered from the persistent warfare and Palestinian terrorism that has been carried on in the region for years. Its unemployment problems were seriously heightened when Israel reoccupied the West Bank in 1967, thus forcing large-scale Palestinian emigration into neighboring Jordan. Meanwhile, the fertile agricultural lands and irrigation water supplies of the West Bank were lost. Jordan's ailing economy receives aid from the Arab oil states, but the United States has continued its support as well.

In 1988 Jordan cut legal and administrative ties with the Israeli-occupied West Bank. King Hussein asserted himself as an advocate of Middle Eastern peace initiatives. In 1989 the government lifted martial law, which had been in force since 1967. This act was the first major step in Jordan's proposed move toward liberalization.

In 1991 Jordan opposed military action against Iraq in the Persian Gulf War, a position that isolated it interna-

tionally. In June 1991 Taher Masri, a Palestinian who advocated a negotiated peace in the Middle East, became prime minister. In November he was succeeded by Sharif Zaid ibn Shaker, who continued Masri's efforts to restore Jordan's ties with Egypt, Syria, and the U.S. Upon Hussein's death in 1999, his oldest son, Abdullah II, ascended to the throne.

Kuwait

Official name: *State of Kuwait*
Area: *6,932 sq. mi., 17,820 sq. km.*
Type of government:
   Constitutional monarchy
Population: *2,112,000*
Capital and largest city: *Kuwait*
   (Pop., 193,000)
Languages: *Arabic (official),*
   English
Literacy: *79%*
Currency: *Dinar*
Per capita GDP: *$15,100*
   (Rank: 39th)

The land.   Kuwait's surface is level desert broken by only a single ridge of hills and a few small oases. Nine islands are included in the national territory, but only one, Failaka, is inhabited. The climate is extremely hot, and almost no rain falls, usually only between 1 and 7

inches (3 and 18 centimeters). Less than 9 percent of the land is arable, and most of the country's water is desalinated seawater.

The people.   Native Kuwaitis are Arabs but there are large minorities of Indians, Iranians, and non-Kuwaiti Arabs as well as European and U.S. oil workers. Three-quarters of the labor force is comprised of foreign workers, largely Palestinians employed in either government work or the oil industry. The Kuwaiti government plans to trim the number of foreign workers from 1.6 million to 600,000. Almost all Kuwaitis live in urban areas. Most are Sunni Muslims. Important cities are Kuwait, the capital, and As Salimiyah, a suburb of Kuwait City.

Economy.   Oil is Kuwait's only important natural resource. An estimated one-fifth of the world's proven oil reserves lie beneath Kuwait's land and off its coasts. Fruits and vegetables are grown in oases, and large desert areas have been irrigated.

Oil accounts for 85 percent of the country's exports; 91 million metric tons were produced in 1989. The government took control of 60 percent of the industry in 1974. Many foreign companies are involved in the oil enterprise and they pay large royalties to Kuwait.

Oil processing is the main industry, although there is also food processing and chemical production. Much of the oil money is used to finance social welfare programs and economic development projects. About 600 of Kuwait's 950 oil wells were set on fire by Iraqi troops during the Gulf War. Production was not able to resume until 1992. Experts estimate that Kuwait lost $120 million a day in oil revenues because of the fires.

Kuwait's major export is oil, but processed foods, leather goods, building materials, and other manufactures are also exported. Imports include vehicles, foodstuffs, and raw materials. Kuwait's chief trading partners are Japan, the United States, Germany, Italy, and Great Britain.

Government.   Kuwait is a constitutional monarchy in which the ruler, an emir, has great power. The emir is assisted by a prime minister and a council of ministers. The legislative body is the National Assembly, made up of 50 elected members.

AN ESTIMATED one-fifth of the world's proven oil reserves lie beneath Kuwait, where oil processing is the main industry and oil is the major export.

History. Kuwait was first settled in the early 1700s by Arab people from the interior of Arabia. It grew prosperous as a trading center and a pearl fishery. Attacks from southern Arabia in the late 1700s impoverished the country, but by the end of the 1800s the economy had recovered.

In 1899, after attempts by the Ottoman Empire to annex Kuwait, the country signed a treaty of protection with Great Britain. By that treaty and a later agreement, Britain assumed responsibility for Kuwait's foreign affairs and defense.

The beginnings of full-scale oil production in 1946 radically changed the way of life of the people of Kuwait. Within 20 years the country had become a wealthy welfare state.

Kuwait gained full independence in June 1961, when the 1899 treaty with Britain was canceled and replaced by a treaty of friendship. Within the month, Iraq announced its intention of annexing Kuwait, which it claimed as Iraqi territory. British troops were sent to protect Kuwait, and later an international force of the Arab League replaced the British troops. Arab League forces remained in Kuwait until the threat from Iraq ended in 1962. The dispute was not finally settled until 1963, however, when new leaders seized power in Iraq.

Since 1962 the Kuwait Fund for Arab Economic Development has been a major source of funds for development projects in other Arab lands. In 1967, after renewed Arab-Israeli hostilities caused severe economic problems in many Arab states, Kuwait increased its aid to these Arab lands.

On August 2, 1990, Kuwait was invaded by Iraq, without provocation or warning. The emir of Kuwait, Jaber al Sabah, was able to escape, but his brother, Sheikh Fahd, was killed.

After the United Nations imposed severe economic sanctions on Iraq, and months of negotiations failed, an international coalition of forces launched a full-scale air attack. After a month of continual bombings, Iraqi military installations were decimated. Then the coalition troops, mostly American and British soldiers, engaged Iraqi troops and forced them to surrender. Iraq agreed to a cease-fire and began withdrawing its troops on March 2, 1991.

The Iraqi occupation wreaked havoc in Kuwait. An estimated $20- to $30-billion worth of damage was done during the 7-month occupation. Over 2,000 Kuwaiti citizens were reported missing. In addition, entire Kuwaiti oil fields were set on fire by retreating Iraqi troops.

After the war, the emir was pressured by the people of Kuwait to form a more democratic government and, in 1992 parliamentary elections, opposition groups won 31 of 50 assembly seats. However, later democratic reforms of the emir were defeated by the National Assembly and in 2003 traditionalists swept elections winning 47 of the 50 seats.

Lebanon

Official name: *Lebanese Republic*
Area: *4,014 sq. mi., 10,000 sq. km.*
Type of government: *Republic*
Population: *3,678,000*
Capital and largest city: *Beirut*
(Pop., 475,000)
Languages: *Arabic (official), French, English, Armenian*
Literacy: *86%*; **Currency:** *Pound*
Per capita GDP: *$5,200*
(Rank: 84th)

The land. Mountains cover more than half of Lebanon. The Lebanon Mountains run through the center of the country, and the Sharqi, or Anti-Lebanon, chain extends along the eastern border. The highest summit is Qurnet-es-Sauda, in the Lebanon Mountains, which reaches 10,131 feet (3,089 meters). A narrow, fertile plain lies between the coast and the Lebanon Mountains; the Bekáa, a fertile valley, lies between the Lebanon and the Sharqi ranges. Lebanon's major river, the Litani, flows through the Bekáa.

The climate is mild and moist. Yearly rainfall averages between 30 and 50 inches (77 and 128 centimeters).

The people. The Lebanese people are largely Arab. Approximately half the population is Christian and half is Muslim. There are many separate sects within each community. The largest are the Maronite Christians and the Sunni Muslims.

The population is concentrated in port cities along the coast, especially in Beirut, the capital; Tripoli (population, 128,000); and Zahla. Heavy emigration, primarily to North and South America, has characterized the Lebanese population since the 1860s, and there are almost as many Lebanese living abroad as in Lebanon. Many emigrants maintain economic and social ties with Lebanon and contribute to the country's economic and cultural life.

Lebanon is very densely populated, with nearly 800 people per square mile (308 people per square kilometer). Its population is 60 percent urban.

Economy. Lebanon's economy is more diversified than that of many other Middle Eastern nations. Agriculture, industry, and trade are all important. The country has no major exploitable mineral resources except for some deposits of iron ore.

Agriculture occupies almost 20 percent of the labor force and contributes 9 percent of the gross national product. The leading crops are wheat, barley, corn, tobacco, olives, and citrus and other fruits. Sheep, pastured in the mountains, and timber forests, in central Lebanon, are also of economic importance.

The availability of a well-educated and skilled labor force and the development of the country's great hydroelectric resources was instrumental in

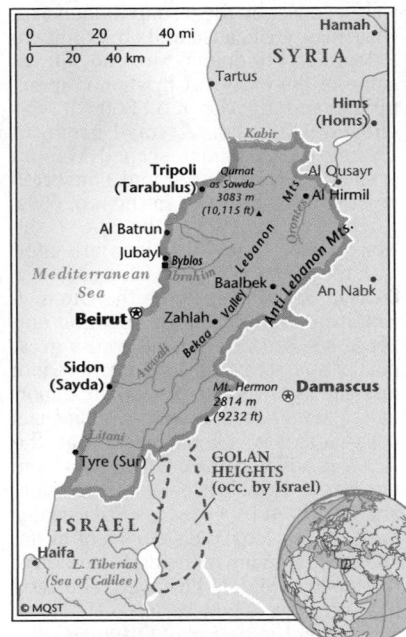

enabling Lebanon's industry to expand rapidly after 1960.

Lumber and food processing, textile weaving, oil refining, and cement production are the leading industries. Income from tourism is also important.

Serious factional infighting since 1975 has provided obstacles to the struggling economy. The destruction of property and the constant interruptions of the normal patterns of economic affairs have all but halted Lebanon's plans to establish itself as the hub of economic activity in the Middle East. Lebanon's main exports are agricultural products. The major imports include machinery, textiles, and manufactured consumer goods. Lebanon's main trading partners are Saudi Arabia, France, Switzerland, and the United States.

Government. Lebanon is a republic in which power is divided between Christians and Muslims. A Christian president, elected by a unicameral Parliament, is head of state. The president is elected for 6 years and is not eligible for immediate reelection. A prime minister, who is Muslim, and a cabinet are responsible to Parliament. A newly formed executive council acts as an intermediary between the president, the prime minister, and the speaker of Parliament. The 128 members of Parliament are popularly elected under a system by which each religious group elects a number of representatives in proportion to its membership.

History. Lebanon is an ancient land. In its forests grew the cedars of Lebanon mentioned in the Old Testament. Its excellent ports have made it a vital trading center since ancient times. Before 2000 B.C. the area was the home of the Canaanites. Later it was the home of the Phoenicians, who were the leading traders of the ancient world. In the 800s B.C. Lebanon was conquered by the Assyrians.

Lebanon's history has been closely associated with that of Syria, but Lebanon was set apart by the strong influence of Christianity. Because of its proximity to Palestine, Phoenicia was the site of some of the earliest Christian communities, and by the A.D. 300s it was entirely Christian. A small group of Lebanese Christians escaped Muslim armies that conquered and converted most of Syria-Lebanon in the A.D. 600s. Their descendants became the Maronites—Arab Christians affiliated with the Roman Catholic Church.

Ottoman era. In the 1500s the Ottoman Empire conquered both Lebanon and Syria, but Lebanon was allowed a great deal of autonomy. This relative freedom and the country's commercial importance placed Lebanon in an advantageous position that it maintained through the 1800s. In addition, the presence of a large number of British and French missionary schools and colleges made it a center for Arab intellectual development in the 1800s. Here many of the early leaders of the modern Middle East were educated in Western ways and learning.

During the period of Ottoman rule, Lebanese Christian and Muslim communities expanded, and the two occasionally came into conflict. In 1860 a revolt by Christian peasants against Muslim overlords touched off widespread religious strife, eventually leading to civil war. Great Britain and France intervened and forced Turkey to give Lebanon an autonomous government that divided power between the Christians and the Muslims.

Independence. After the defeat of the Ottoman Empire in World War I, France received a League of Nations mandate over Lebanon. In 1941, following Germany's defeat of France in World War II, a free Lebanese government proclaimed the country's independence of the German-controlled Vichy French administration.

A treaty recognizing Lebanon's sovereignty was signed in 1943 by Lebanon and the Free French government. In 1945 Lebanon was admitted to the United Nations; it also joined the Arab League. All foreign troops had left the country by 1946, and in 1947 elections were held.

During the 1950s and 1960s Lebanon strengthened its economy and expanded social welfare and development programs.

Civil war flared again in 1975, with Palestinians and leftist Muslims teamed against Christian Maronite factions of the army and Israeli-backed Christians. UN troops temporarily reestablished peace.

The use of southern Lebanon by the Palestine Liberation Organization (PLO) as a base from which to conduct terrorist attacks against Israel led, in 1982, to the invasion of Lebanon by Israel. The defeat of the Palestinian forces led to the withdrawal of the PLO from part of Lebanon.

Since the beginning of the civil war in 1975, foreign countries have tried to help restore order. In 1983 multinational peacekeeping forces were installed in Beirut to support the elected government. After attacks on the U.S. embassy, and on the headquarters of the U.S. and

French units, the forces were withdrawn. More recently, in 1986, Syrian troops moved into Beirut to oversee a cease-fire agreement, but fighting broke out between Lebanese factions anyway.

In 1989 Rene Muawed was assassinated 17 days after being elected president. Elias Hrawi was elected in his place. Hrawi established the Second Republic by signing constitutional amendments in 1990. These amendments created an executive council that would serve as an intermediary between the president, prime minister, and speaker of Parliament. The president's right to remove the prime minister and dissolve the assembly was eliminated.

In 1990 General Michel Aoun, the commander of the army, who had launched his own bloody "war of liberation" against Syria against the wishes of the Hrawi government, was ousted by Syrian troops and forced to flee. The new government slowly reasserted its authority over the country. Parliamentary elections, the first since 1972, were held in August and September of 1992. Israel withdrew its troops in May 2000.

Oman

Official name: *Sultanate of Oman*
Area: *82,647 sq. mi.,*
  212,460 sq. km.
Type of government: *Monarchy*
Population: *2,713,000*
Capital and largest city: *Muscat*
  (Pop., 41,000)
Languages: *Arabic (official),*
  English, Baluchi, Urdu
Literacy: *80%;* **Currency:** *Rial*
Per capita GDP: *$8,200*
  (Rank: 64th)

The land. A narrow plain skirts the country's 1,000-mile (1,613-kilometer) coastline. The northwestern portion of the plain, the Batina, is quite fertile. Rugged mountains rise sharply to nearly 10,000 feet (3,049 meters) above the plain. In the interior is a low, barren plateau, the eastern end of the vast Rub'al Khali, or "Empty Quarter," of the Arabian peninsula. The climate throughout the country is hot and dry. Rainfall averages between 3 and 4 inches (8 and 10 centimeters) each year.

The people. The native peoples are Arab, but there are Baluchi, Persian, Indian, and African minorities. Population is concentrated in three main regions—Muscat, in the northeast; Oman, in the mountains; and Dhofar, on the Arabian Sea coast. Oman is sparsely populated and almost all of its people live in rural areas.

Economy. Oman's major product and resource is oil, which was first produced in 1967. In 1987, 28.2 million metric tons were produced, and oil accounted for almost 95 percent of

the nation's exports. Copper has also become a significant export in recent years. In 1989 almost 15,000 tons of refined copper were produced.

Agriculture and fishing dominate the traditional way of life. Dates are the leading agricultural product, and coconuts, cereals, and citrus fruits also are grown. Large herds of camels still are raised in the interior, and there is good fishing off the coast. There is very little industry other than oil processing.

The decline in world oil prices in the mid-1980s encouraged the government to accelerate plans for the decentralization of its economy. Emphasis was placed on improving the farming and fishing industries, making both areas more open to the private sector. Change occurred slowly because shipping lanes often were obstructed during the Iran-Iraq War and the Persian Gulf War. Even greater oil reserves were discovered at the end of the 1980s. The economy remained very stable.

Trade is prosperous. Oman's nonoil exports are processed copper, dates, and fish. Imports include machinery, transportation equipment, manufactured goods, and food. Japan, the United Arab Emirates, South Korea, and Great Britain are the chief trading partners.

Government. The sultan of Oman is an absolute monarch who rules with the aid of his ministers. The sultanate has no constitution, legislature, or legal political parties. There is a two-chamber legislature which is basically advisory in nature. Upper chamber members are appointed by the monarch. Lower-chamber members are elected, but monarch can negate election results.

History. Arab peoples have inhabited Muscat and Oman for many centuries. Because of its strategic position at the mouth of the Persian Gulf, the land attracted conquerors seeking control of the gulf. In 1508 the Portuguese occupied Muscat, and during the following century they competed for control with the Ottoman Turks.

By 1650 the native Arabs had driven out both the Portuguese and the Turks. Arab control was not secure, however,

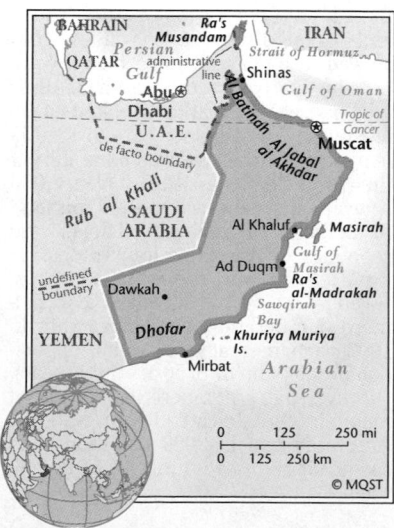

PEOPLE IN BRIGHTLY colored clothing gather at a market in Fanja, Oman.

until 1737, when Ahmad ibn Said fought off a Persian invasion.

During the 1700s and 1800s the sultanate extended its control over parts of southern Iran and eastern Africa. In the late 1800s, however, internal political disputes divided the region between coastal Muscat and interior Oman. The power of both declined, and foreign territories they had held were lost.

In 1891 Muscat granted special privileges to Great Britain in return for British protection. Close ties with Britain were reaffirmed several times in the 1900s by treaties of friendship. In the mid-1950s British-led troops helped the sultan of Muscat put down a rebellion in the interior. Following this conflict, the United Nations acknowledged the sovereignty of Muscat over Oman.

Sultan Said bin Taimur was overthrown by his liberal, British-educated son, Qaboos, in the coup of 1970. Sultan Qaboos initiated domestic development programs, promised to establish a constitutional monarchy when Oman was "ready" for it, and supported the 1979 Egyptian-Israeli peace treaty that was condemned by most other Arab nations.

Qaboos fought leftist rebels in Dhofar from 1970 to 1975; the conflict was rekindled again in the late 1970s. Military and economic treaties signed with the United States in 1980 permitted the latter's use of Oman's military facilities on the Persian Gulf.

In 1997 Qaboos gave women the right to be elected and in 2003 voting rights were extended to all citizens.

Qatar

Official name: *State of Qatar*
Area: *4,279 sq. mi., 11,000 sq. km.*
Type of government: *Monarchy*
Population: *793,000*
Capital and largest city: *Doha*
  (Pop., 264,000)
Languages: *Arabic (official),*
  English
Literacy: *79%*
Currency: *Riyal*
Per capita GDP: *$21,200*
  (Rank: 24th)

The land. The Qatar peninsula is mostly a low plain thinly covered with sand, although some small hills and higher elevations lie in the northwest. The north is partially arable but the south is completely arid. The peninsula protrudes 100 miles (160 kilometers) from the Arabian mainland into the Persian Gulf.

The climate is hot and dry, and rainfall is less than 4 inches (10 centimeters) a year. There are no rivers and only a few small oases in the east, therefore all drinking water is provided by desalination plants.

The people. The people of Qatar are of Arab stock but also include Indians, Iranians, and Pakistanis. Over 80 percent of both the popula-

tion and the labor force is comprised of foreigners. More than 70 percent of the population live in Doha, the capital.

Economy. Qatar lacks skilled native labor, but it is one of the richest nations in the world. Oil is its only natural resource, and the country has almost no cultivable land. Fishing, pearl diving, and the herding of goats and camels were the main means of livelihood before the discovery of oil; they continue to contribute to the economy.

Oil production, begun in 1949, is the country's only significant industry and it accounts for most of the gross national product. Qatar produced 20 million metric tons of oil in 1989. In 1977 all gas and oil reserves were nationalized. Foreign oil companies pay large royalty fees to Qatar's sheik.

Oil and pearls are Qatar's main exports, while food, machinery, and raw materials are its chief imports. Most trade is with Japan, European Union nations, and the United States.

Government. Qatar is under the absolute rule of a hereditary sheik, who is assisted by the Council of Ministers, the supreme executive body, and by a 35-member advisory council.

History. Qatar has been inhabited by Arab peoples for many centuries. The sheiks of Qatar were compelled to pay tribute to the sheiks of Bahrain for protection and support until 1872. In 1868 Qatar entered into the first of a series of treaties with Great Britain, which was then building a strong position in the Persian Gulf. Between 1872 and 1914, however, the Ottoman Turks maintained a fort in Qatar and controlled the country.

In a treaty signed in 1916, Qatar's sheiks granted Great Britain special diplomatic and commercial rights in return for protection. The discovery of oil in 1939 brought wealth and international importance to the sheikdom. In 1971 Britain terminated all of its treaty relationships with the Persian Gulf sheikdoms and withdrew. On September 3, 1971, Qatar declared itself to be a fully independent state. In 1972 and

labor
US

labour
Brit.

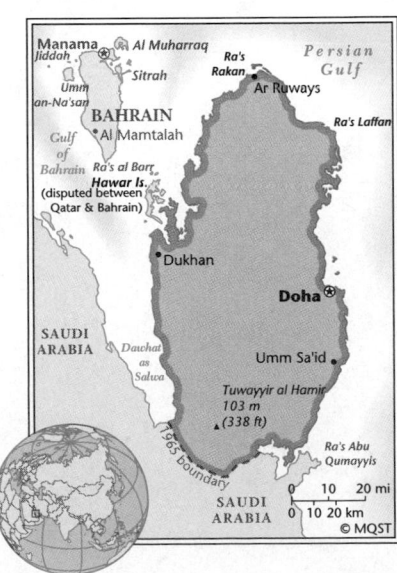

1995 bloodless palace coups were staged by sons against their reigning fathers.

Qatar, still very dependent on oil, was hit hard by falling oil prices and the decade of war and unrest in the Persian Gulf in the 1980s. The largest single gas deposits in the world were discovered in the offshore mine known as North Field. The discovery renewed optimism and spurred new foreign investment in Qatar.

In the late 1990s Qatar began implementing democratic reforms, including women's suffrage and allowing a free press.

Saudi Arabia

Official name: *Kingdom of Saudi Arabia*
Area: *762,666 sq. mi., 1,960,582 sq. km.*
Type of government: *Monarchy*
Population: *23,513,000*
Capital and largest city: *Riyadh (Pop., 2,776,000)*
Language: *Arabic*
Literacy: *78%;* **Currency:** *Riyal*
Per capita GDP: *$10,600 (Rank: 47th)*

meters
US

metres
Brit.

labor
US

labour
Brit.

center
US

centre
Brit.

The land. Most of the surface of Saudi Arabia is barren. A narrow, infertile plain, the Tihama, lies along the western coast. To its east the Hejaz Mountains, in the north, and the Asir Mountains, in the south, rise sharply to 11,000 feet (3,354 meters). These treeless, sandstone and lava mountains slope into an interior plateau, which consists of two desert regions—An Nafud, in the north, and the Rub'al Khali, in the south.

The interior plain occupies about 90 percent of the country's area and is largely uninhabited. Along the eastern border, rolling coastal plains slope into the Persian Gulf.

Saudi Arabia has no rivers—only wadis, dry riverbeds where rainfall

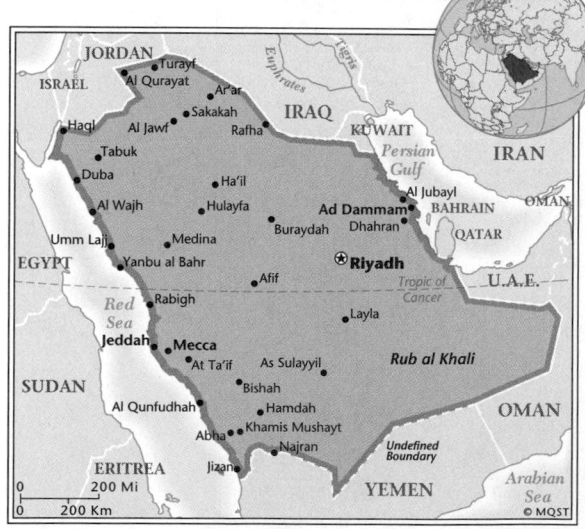

THIS PATRIOT MISSILE launcher was deployed during Operation Desert Shield.

may run off. Underground water is tapped by wells.

Saudi Arabia's climate is hot and dry. Summer daytime temperatures often climb to over 125°F (52°C) in most of the country, but nights, especially in the desert, can be quite cold. In the mountains and along the eastern coast the average year-round temperature is a more moderate 80°F (27°C). Rainfall is rare, and the deserts may go for years without any rain.

The people. Most Saudi Arabians are Arabic-speaking Muslims. The country's population is clustered around its few oases, watered by underground springs, where are located the cities of Riyadh, the capital; Jeddah (population, 2,046,000); Mecca (966,000); and Medina (608,000).

Nomadic Bedouin tribesmen have long roamed the deserts. Government programs have been settling the nomads in areas where irrigation can make sedentary life possible.

Almost 50 percent of the population is comprised of foreigners who fill the gap created by Saudi Arabia's lack of skilled labor.

Economy. Over 60 percent of Saudi Arabia's gross national product comes from mining and industry, compared with 4 percent from agriculture. The country has the world's second highest production rate of oil, with 209.5 million metric tons of crude oil produced in 1987. Saudi Arabia increased production between 1987 and 1989 to force down world oil prices and reestablish discipline among OPEC (Organization of Petroleum Exporting Countries) oil producers. Aramco (Arabian American Oil Company), the world's single most productive oil company, was nationalized by Saudi Arabia in 1979. The principal refinery is on the east coast, at Ras Tanura.

Oil revenues are used to provide free education and health care for Saudi Arabians, government funding, and domestic improvements, including industrialization and agricultural expansion and modernization. The largest industrial plants produce petrochemicals, fertilizers, and steel.

Many of the people in Saudi Arabia live as farmers or herders. The country's only major crops are grains, citrus fruits, and dates, which are grown in oases. Sheep, goats, and camels graze in Saudi Arabia's vast deserts. There is some pearl diving and fishing along the coasts. Money spent in the country by Muslim pilgrims to the holy cities of Mecca and Medina is the second most important source of income.

Saudi Arabia's prosperous international trade is based on oil. Foodstuffs, textiles, clothing, machinery, and transportation equipment are imported. Saudi Arabia's major trading partners are the United States, Japan, Great Britain, Italy, and France.

Government. Saudi Arabia is a monarchy with a king who serves as the country's political and religious leader. The king appoints a Council of Ministers. In 1992 a constitution was instituted which set forth the government's responsibilities.

History. Saudi Arabia became a nation in 1926, but the territory of Saudi Arabia originally known simply as Arabia has been inhabited since ancient times by Arab herdsmen and traders, and it was the site of several ancient kingdoms. Muhammad the prophet was born in the trading city of Mecca in A.D. 570, and the city became an important center of the Muslim religion.

During the century following Muhammad's death in 632, Muslim armies conquered North Africa and the entire Middle East and Muslim power extended into Spain. Religious disputes and competition for power soon brought disorder to Arabia, however. It was divided into two major sheikdoms—Nejd in the interior of the peninsula and the Hejaz in the west—and many petty states.

Parts of Arabia were conquered in the 1200s by the Egyptians and in the 1500s by the Ottoman Turks. The conquerors were most interested in the Hejaz because of the importance of controlling the Muslim holy city of Mecca, its capital.

Wahhabis. In Nejd in the 1700s a Muslim sect whose goal was to reform Islam was founded by Muhammad Ibn Abd al-Wahhab. His followers, the Wahhabis, allied with Muhammad ibn Saud, a ruler of part of Nejd.

Saud's successors carried Wahhabism to the Persian Gulf, and by 1806 they had wrested the Hejaz from the Sharifs, the rulers of Mecca who had controlled the Hejaz. But Saud's Wahhabis were driven back into the interior of Nejd by Turkish and Egyptian troops. In Nejd they lost power to the rival sheikdom of al-Rashid.

Nearly 100 years later, in 1902, Saud's direct descendant, Abd-al-Aziz ibn Saud, conquered Nejd's capital, Riyadh, and took control from the Rashids. By 1913 Saud had defeated the Rashids and had driven the Ottomans from most of central Arabia.

In 1916 Saud's rival for power, Sharif Husayn of Mecca, led a pan-Arab revolt against the Turks that carried his sons to the thrones of the new Arab states of Iraq and Transjordan (present-day Jordan). After World War I uneasy relations between the Husayns and the Saudis led to warfare in 1924. The Saudis captured the Hejaz and forced out the Husayns.

In 1926 Saud united Nejd and the Hejaz and two small dependencies, Asir and Hasa, into a Wahhabist state. He proclaimed himself king of the entire region, which he named Saudi Arabia in 1932.

Contemporary Saudi Arabia. Under Saud the modernization of Arabia began, and the discovery of oil in 1938 greatly speeded up the process by providing a source of income for the government. Large-scale oil production began in 1945, after World War II. Oil revenues made possible social changes that promised to affect radically Saudi Arabian life, but the country somehow maintained internal political and social stability. Abd-al-Aziz ibn Saud's son, Saud, succeeded him in 1953, but in 1964 he was replaced by his half brother, Faisal.

Saudi Arabia has supported conservative Arabian societies, and it aided both Yemen and Oman when those countries faced political revolts or invasions. It refused to help Egypt, a country leaning toward radical social change, during the 1967 Arab-Israeli war, but it did support the Arab cause during the 1948–1949 and the 1973 Arab-Israeli wars.

Saudi Arabia works hard to moderate Arab conflicts and affairs. It buys armaments from the West and redistributes them to Arab nations at its discretion. It was a leader of the Arab oil boycott of 1973–1974 designed to force the formulation of anti-Israeli policies by Western nations, and it rebuked Egypt for its role in the 1979 Egypt-Israeli peace treaty.

King Faisal was assassinated in 1975 and was succeeded by Crown Prince Khalid, who reigned until his death in 1982. Crown Prince Fahd then became king.

In response to the 1990 Iraqi invasion of Kuwait, King Fahd requested support from the United States to guard against the possible invasion of Saudi Arabia. Saudi Arabia then became a primary strategic location for the allied effort against Iraq in the Gulf War. Saudi Arabia also contributed 20,000 troops and over 200 tanks to the coalition.

The Saudi Arabian invitation to the United States military marked a significant change in Middle Eastern relations with the West; a country that historically had opposed the West turned to the largest Western power for defense against another Arab country.

On March 1, 1992, King Fahd issued three decrees that significantly altered the Saudi government. They provided for a 60-member Consultative Council whose members will be appointed by the king for 4-year terms and will review and propose laws and advise the Cabinet. The decrees also included a Saudi bill of rights.

In August 2003, following the war in Iraq, U.S. troops withdrew from Saudi Arabia, where they had been stationed since the Gulf War.

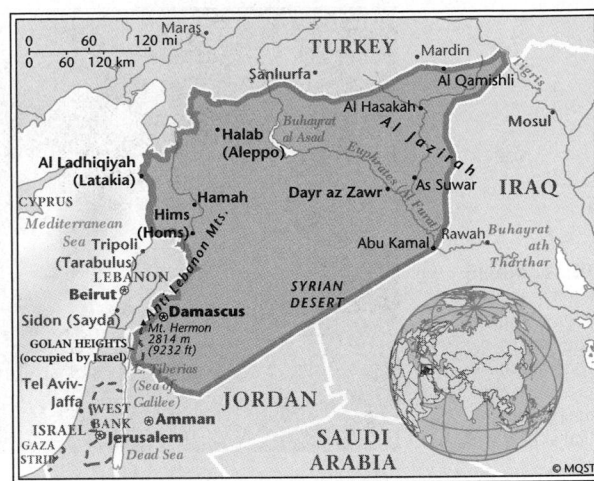

Syria

Official name: *Syrian Arab Republic*

Area: *71,480 sq. mi., 185,180 sq. km.*

Type of government: *Republic*

Population: *17,156,000*

Capital: *Damascus (Pop., 1,394,000)*

Largest city: *Aleppo (Pop., 1,583,000)*

Languages: *Arabic (official), Kurdish, Armenian, Aramaic*

Literacy: *71%;* **Currency:** *Pound*

Per capita GDP: *$3,200 (Rank: 113th)*

The land. A narrow, fertile plain follows Syria's Mediterranean coast. To its east the rugged Alawite and Anti-Lebanon mountains rise to over 9,000 feet (2,744 meters) on the northwestern border.

The Orontes River waters a fertile valley east of the mountains. In northern and northeastern Syria are the rolling plains and rich valley of the Euphrates River. In central Syria, arid, rolling hills give way to the barren Syrian Desert, which occupies the south-eastern corner of the country.

Syria's coastal climate is mild and rather moist, with about 30 inches (76 centimeters) of rain each year along the coast. Central and eastern Syria are quite dry; only about 10 inches (25 centimeters) of rain fall there annually. The area also has the hot summers and cold winters of the desert.

The people. Most Syrians are Arabs, but the population also includes Kurds and Armenians. Population is densest in the Euphrates River valley and along the fertile coastal plain in the west between the coastal mountains and the desert. Damascus, the capital and largest city, lies in the southwest near the Lebanese border. Another important city is Homs, or Hims, (population, 540,000). Half of the population live in urban areas. The Shi'a Muslim community dominates the government, although it makes up a minority of the population. Almost three-quarters of the people are Sunni Muslims; there are also significant numbers of other types of Muslims and of Christians.

Economy. About one-fifth of Syria's gross national product is derived from industry, one-fifth from commerce, and slightly less than from agriculture. The country's main natural resource is oil, 13.5 million metric tons of which was produced in 1988. Oil accounts for over half of Syria's exports. Phosphates are also mined.

Agriculture. About one-third of the country's land is cultivated and one-third is suitable for pasturage. Most

RURAL VILLAGERS on the plains of northwestern Syria build beehive-shaped houses of sun-dried mud bricks.

THE ROMANS left much evidence of their occupation in the eastern Mediterranean. The ruins of this amphitheater are found at Basra.

farmland is in the west and north, and much requires irrigation. A land redistribution program in the 1950s and 1960s created many small farms from large estates. Twenty-five percent of the work force is engaged in agriculture. Most land is privately owned.

The leading farm crops are cotton, wheat, and barley. Corn and other grains, dates, olives, sugar beets, and tobacco are also raised, and wool and silk are important commodities. Large herds of goats and sheep are grazed on the central plains. The government controls the agricultural collection, processing, and distribution industries.

Industry. Textiles account for the largest portion of Syria's manufacturing output. Sugar, leather products, dried fruits, and wines are the leading manufactures outside of the textile industry. Gypsum and asphalt are processed. Many industrial, commercial, and financial enterprises were nationalized in the 1960s.

Trade. International trade is important in the Syrian economy, and the country's chief port, Latakia, is a major Middle Eastern commercial center. Syria collects fees on oil from Iraq carried to the Mediterranean by pipeline across Syria. Oil, cotton, woven fabric, phosphates, and live animals are the chief exports, and machinery, clothing, foodstuffs, and other consumer items are imported.

Most trading activity is controlled by the government. Italy, Romania, the former Soviet Union, the United States, France, and Germany are Syria's leading trading partners. In 1988, 45 percent of the government's expenditures went to defense.

Government. According to a 1973 constitution, Syria is headed by a president who is elected to a seven-year term. The prime minister is head of the Council of Ministers, which shares executive power with the president. The legislature is the unicameral People's Council, whose 250 members are elected.

History. The modern nation of Syria has its roots in the ancient region of Syria, which was the site of some of the earliest civilizations. Syria was a center of the trade routes used by the great nations of the ancient world.

center
US

centre
Brit.

civilizations
US

civilisations
Brit.

Located between the Tigris-Euphrates valley and the Nile valley, it was often the object of rivalry between the powerful nations that grew up in both valleys. Trade and war between the civilizations to the north and south of Syria brought many different peoples and cultures to the area.

Between 2000 B.C. and 333 B.C., the Akkadians, the Sumerians, the Amorites, the Hittites, the Egyptians, the Assyrians, and the Persians successively occupied parts of the Syrian region. During that time three groups, the Hebrews, the Aramaeans, and the Canaanites, made permanent settlements.

In 333 B.C. Alexander the Great conquered Syria from the Persian Empire. After his death, Syria went to one of his generals, Seleucus, who founded the Seleucid dynasty that ruled Syria (including modern Israel, Lebanon, and Jordan) until the Roman conquest in 64 B.C. Syria was one of the first Roman provinces to have had Christianity, in the first century A.D., and Syria's language, Aramaic, was the language of most early Christians.

In the 630s Muslim Arab armies conquered the region. Islam replaced Christianity, Arabic replaced Aramaic, and Syria became an Arab country. The city of Damascus became the center of a great Arab empire and Syria's prosperity increased.

As the Arab empire weakened, however, Syria entered a decline. Ruled by outsiders, it suffered neglect. The Christian Crusades against the Muslim Middle East in the 1000s, 1100s, and 1200s did great damage to Syria and its economy, and the invasions of Mongols and Tatars from the north and east in the 1200s and 1300s left Syria weak and impoverished.

Ottoman rule. In 1516 the Ottoman Turks conquered Syria and made it part of their empire. Under the Ottoman Turks Syria remained peaceful, but neglect and poor government caused the economy and cultural life to decline further, especially in the 1700s, when the disintegration of the empire brought anarchy to Syria.

The opening of the Suez Canal in 1869 took away much of the trade between the Mediterranean and the Indian Ocean that had previously passed overland through Syria. Some economic improvements were made in the late 1800s, but the country remained largely undeveloped.

Nationalism. Also in the late 1800s, Syria began to feel the impact of the spirit of nationalism that had been growing in Europe. Syria became a center for an Arab cultural revival and for Arab nationalism, and Syrians demanded self-government.

When the Ottoman Empire entered World War I on the side of Germany, Syria cooperated with the Allies. In return, Great Britain supported Syrian Arab nationalism and aided a successful 1916 Arab uprising against the Ottoman government.

At the end of the war in 1918, French troops made an attempt to occupy the country, but Faisal ibn-Husayn, a leader

ISRAELI SOLDIERS set up a large machine gun in the Golan Heights, an area that has been under dispute with Syria since the 1967 Arab-Israeli war.

COUNTRIES

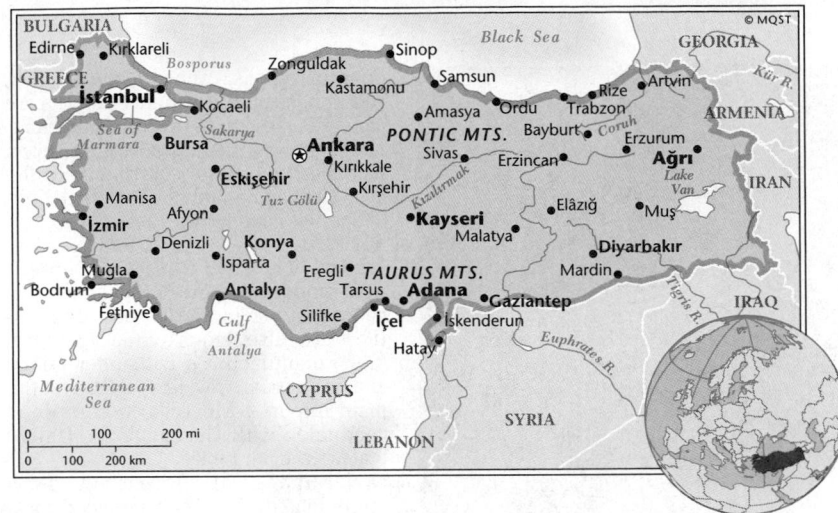

of the nationalist rebellion, proclaimed Syria's sovereignty. A Syrian National Congress was called, and in 1920 Faisal was proclaimed king. France, which had received a League of Nations mandate over Syria, deposed Faisal later in 1920 and set up its own government.

Syrian discontent with French rule led in 1925 to a two-year rebellion, which the French put down harshly. Discontent grew. In 1930 the French proposed a constitution that would have made the country a republic but would not have granted complete independence. The Syrians rejected it.

Independence. In 1941, during World War II, the Vichy French government of Syria was driven out by British and Free French forces. Syria was formally declared an independent republic, although British and French troops did not withdraw until after the war, in 1946.

In 1943 Shukri al-Kuwatly was elected the first president of the republic, and in 1945 Syria entered the United Nations and joined other Arab states in forming the Arab League.

Turmoil marked the first two decades of the republic, and the military became the dominant factor in political life. In 1949 an army officer, Husni al-Zaim, ousted the civilian government. More coups followed, and from 1949 to 1954 the government was dominated by Colonel Adib Shishakly, who ruled behind the official presidency of Hashim al-Atasi. In 1954 Shishakly was forced into exile, and the next year al-Kuwatly again became president.

In 1958 Syria merged with Egypt to create the United Arab Republic (U.A.R.), with Egypt's Gamal Abdel Nasser as president. In 1961 the Cairo government imposed an unpopular socialist program on the Syrian part of the U.A.R., and Syria withdrew from the union.

Contemporary Syria. Political instability increased. In March 1963 a military coup overthrew the government and a new cabinet was appointed. The new cabinet was dominated by Baathists, members of the Baath Party, advocating a socialist and pan-Arab program.

Following a 1970 military coup, a socialist state was established under the stabilizing presidency of Hafez al-Assad. The socialist Baath Party became Syria's only legal party. As a leader of pro-Palestine Liberation Organization (PLO) and pan-Arabian politics, Syria received massive Soviet military and economic aid. The Soviets, however, were somewhat alienated by Syria's intervention in 1976 in Lebanon's civil war involving Palestinian guerrillas and by Syria's ousting of its national Communist Party. Upon his father's death in June 2000, Bashar al-Assad was named president.

Syria's Golan Heights, on its western border, has been occupied by Israel since the 1967 Arab-Israeli war. Syria has been a leader of the Arab opposition to the 1979 Egyptian-Israeli peace treaty.

Serious internal dissension has been created since the late 1970s by increasing violence between the privileged ruling Shiite Alawite sect, to which Assad belongs, and the Sunni Muslims. Moreover, Syrian-Iraqi relations have seriously deteriorated. In 1982 Syrian and Israeli forces clashed during the Israeli invasion of Lebanon.

In the late 1980s, Syria found itself increasingly isolated in international politics. In 1986 the European Community imposed economic sanctions on Syria for its alleged support of international terrorism. Syria's relationship with the Soviet Union, its only superpower supporter, was weakened by improved Soviet-Israeli relations in the late 1980s and ended with the collapse of the Soviet Union in 1991.

Syria was instrumental in ending the civil war in Lebanon in 1989. In 1991 Syria and Lebanon signed a mutual security treaty that virtually secured Syria's hegemony over its neighbor.

Syria joined the coalition forces against Iraq during the 1991 Gulf War. Syria's role in the war helped renew relations with Egypt and other moderate Arab nations. By 1993 Syria's relations with the U.S. were also improving.

Syrian-Israeli peace talks took place sporadically during the 1990s, resuming in 1999. Talks broke down quickly over return of the Golan Heights to Syria.

Turkey

Official name: *Republic of Turkey*
Area: *301,304 sq. mi., 780,580 sq. km.*
Type of government: *Republican parliamentary democracy*
Population: *67,309,000*
Capital: *Ankara (Pop., 3,203,000)*
Largest city: *Istanbul (Pop., 8,803,000)*
Languages: *Turkish (official), Kurdish, Arabic*
Literacy: *85%;* **Currency:** *Lira*
Per capita GDP: *$7,000 (Rank: 71st)*

The land. Thrace, the small European portion of Turkey on the Balkan peninsula, consists of rolling plains bounded by uplands in the north and a mountainous coastline in the south. It is separated from Anatolia, the section of the country located in Asia Minor, by a small sea—the Sea of Marmara—and two straits—the Bosporus in the east and the Dardanelles in the west.

In Asian Turkey the Pontic Mountains, rising over 11,000 feet (3,354 meters), follow the shores of the Black Sea. The Taurus mountain range on the southern coast rises to a peak of over 11,500 feet (3,506 meters) above the Mediterranean. Narrow, fertile plains separate both ranges from the sea.

Between the mountain ranges is the Anatolian Plateau, with an average elevation of 3,000 feet (915 meters). Toward the west the plain breaks into a series of fertile river valleys separated by low ridges. In the east the plateau merges with the Pontic and Taurus mountains in the rugged highland of Armenia, where Mt. Ararat, Turkey's highest point, rises to 16,946 feet (7,973 meters). Turkey's largest lakes—Van, in the east and Tuz, in the west—are saltwater lakes.

Many rivers flow from Turkey's highlands toward the long coastline. The longest is the Kizil, which rises in the eastern highlands and flows west and north to empty into the Black Sea. Other important rivers are the Firat, or Euphrates, which rises in Turkey and flows south, the Ceyhan in central Anatolia, and the Sakarya in the northwest.

Climate. Thrace and coastal Anatolia have a mild, moist climate. Rainfall averages 20 to 40 inches (51 to 102 centimeters) annually. Most rain falls in the winter.

In the dry Anatolian Plateau only 10 to 20 inches (26 to 51 centimeters) of rain fall a year, and temperatures are hotter in summer and colder in winter than on the coasts. The inland mountains have a colder climate and are often snow-covered.

The people. Most Turks are Turkish—related to peoples of central Asia—and they speak Turkish. Almost the entire population is Muslim, though there are small minorities of Christians and Jews. The largest minority group is the Kurds, a seminomadic people who inhabit the eastern highlands. There are also small Greek and Armenian minorities.

meters
US

metres
Brit.

COSTUMES of the Byzantine Empire reflect the richness and magnificence that is also typical of the art and architecture of the period.

Fifty-five percent of the people live in urban areas. Many others live in squatter villages around the cities' edges. The densest population is in northwestern Anatolia and eastern Thrace, where Istanbul (population, 8,803,000), the country's largest city, is located. The capital, Ankara, is in central Anatolia. Other important cities include Izmir (population, 2,232,000); Adana (1,131,000); and Bursa (1,195,000).

Economy. Turkey is presently engaged in the transition from a centrally controlled economy to a free market one. Throughout its history the area that is now Turkey has been famous for its agricultural and mineral products. Turkey's economy is still heavily based on agriculture, but industry has expanded greatly since 1950.

Turkey's wide variety of known minerals include rich deposits of coal and chrome and fairly large reserves of oil, zinc, copper, iron, and lead. Turkey also has abundant waterpower and an electrical power capacity (three-quarters of which is thermal) that has helped the rapid growth of its industries. About 20 percent of the gross national product is now contributed by agriculture, although it employs about 56 percent of the work force. About 30 percent of the gross national product is provided by industry.

Agriculture. Over half of the labor force is occupied by farming and herding. Some one-third of the land area is cultivated, and over one-third is used for pasture. Sheep, goats, cattle, and other livestock are grazed on the Anatolian plain and in the eastern highlands.

Cereals, especially wheat, are the major farm crops. Cotton and sugar beets are also important, and legumes, citrus and other fruits, and nuts are raised as well. Tobacco is the most important commercial crop. Most farms are small, and agricultural methods are generally outmoded and inefficient. Evergreen forests cover some 13 percent of the country's area, and forestry is important. There is some fishing off the coasts.

Industry. Textile weaving and oil refining are the leading industries. Refined sugar, flour, paper, tobacco products,

labor
US

labour
Brit.

civilization
US

civilisation
Brit.

dried fruits, oils, canned foods, cement, and iron, steel, and chrome products are among Turkey's most important manufactured products. Automobile manufacturing has become a large contributor to the economy and many state-owned light industries have grown rapidly since the mid-1970s.

Trade. The chief exports are agricultural products, especially grain, tobacco, cotton, and sugar. Metal ores and textiles are also exported. Machinery, fuels, manufactured consumer goods and industrial raw materials are the main imports. Most Turkish trade is conducted with Germany, the United States, Iraq, and Italy.

Government. A new constitution was promulgated in 1982. It provided for a strong presidency with a term of seven years. The president is assisted by a prime minister and a cabinet. The unicameral legislative body is the 550-member Grand National Assembly.

History. Although the Turks did not appear there until the Middle Ages, the region called Turkey has been inhabited since ancient times. The history of the land extends back nearly 4000 years to the civilization of the Hittites and earlier.

After conquests by Persians, Greeks, and Romans, Turkey became, in the 200s A.D., the core of the eastern half of the Roman Empire. In 330 A.D. Constantinople (the modern Istanbul) became the capital of the Byzantine Empire, the successor to the Roman Empire.

In the 900s the first Turks, the Seljuks, migrated into Asia Minor from central Asia. In the eleventh century the Seljuks conquered territory in Anatolia, adopted Islam, and established a kingdom ruled from central Turkey. The Byzantine emperors, with the aid of Christian Crusaders, defended western Anatolia and the rest of the empire from the Seljuks, who were overrun by the Mongols in the 1200s.

Ottomans. A second group of Turks renewed the attack on the Byzantine Empire in the late 1200s. These were the Ottomans named after their leader Osman. After 200 years, the Ottomans conquered the empire, capturing the capital, Constantinople, in 1453.

From Constantinople the Ottomans ruled a mighty empire that reached its height under Suleiman the Magnificent (ruled 1520 to 1566). It stretched from Austria in the north to the Indian Ocean in the south, and from Persia (Iran) in the east to Algeria in the west.

The Ottoman Empire in the 1500s was not only the largest and the most powerful state in the world, but the most efficiently governed as well. Its society was ordered along a feudalistic pattern, and its leaders combined political power with religious influence. The Ottoman Empire had an administrative bureaucracy, a court system, and an excellent army and navy.

Decline. The 300 years following Suleiman's reign, however, witnessed an almost uninterrupted decline. A disastrous defeat by the armies of the Holy Roman Empire in 1571 ended Ottoman military supremacy. Governmental administration collapsed under weak sultans and corruption. Military discipline crumbled.

Local authorities gradually assumed power, and by the 1800s many provinces were independent in fact, if not in name. In addition, France, Great Britain, Austria, and Russia conquered parts of the empire, and the Balkan provinces rebelled, leaving Turkey only Thrace of its once considerable European possessions. The Ottoman Empire in the 1800s had become the "sick man of Europe."

THE BLUE MOSQUE or Hagia Sophia in Istanbul is the most beautiful, in a city that is known for its beautiful Islamic houses of worship.

THE EMPEROR JUSTINIAN, who built the Hagia Sophia as a Christian church, appears here as a saint.

Toward the end of the 1800s progress was made in reforming the government and restoring order. The era also saw the beginning of a cultural and literary revival. In 1876 Abdul-Hamid II took the throne and a liberal constitution was proclaimed.

The sultan soon ended the reform efforts, however. He revoked the constitution, abused his subjects, especially minority groups, and took Turkey into wars that resulted in disastrous losses.

Young Turks. In the discontent caused by his failures and abuses, a revolutionary party was formed, the Committee of Union and Progress, or the "Young Turks." The party hoped to restore Turkish power by westernizing the country and by expanding Turkish territory.

In 1908, with the support of the army, the Young Turks forced Abdul-Hamid to grant a new constitution and parliamentary government. In 1909 he was deposed and replaced by his brother.

Soon, however, the Young Turks divided into factions. Moreover, in trying to regain lost territories they gave up still more. As each of their projects failed, their government grew more despotic. By 1913 a military wing of the party assumed power by a coup d'etat.

Under this government Turkey entered World War I on the side of Germany and suffered terrible losses. During the war, the Turkish government deported Armenians en masse from Anatolia because they were believed to be supporters of the Russian forces. Over 600,000 Armenians were massacred during their journey. When the war ended in 1918, the country was occupied by troops from many Allied countries and was threatened with partition among the Allied states. All that

remained of the Ottoman Empire was Anatolia and Thrace, and the Young Turk government fled into exile.

In 1920 a nationalist party organized an unofficial Turkish government under Mustafa Kemal to drive out the Allied occupation forces. Kemal, with the support of the majority of Turks, organized an army and by 1923 had forced the Allies to leave and to recognize Turkey's sovereignty over Asia Minor and eastern Thrace in the Treaty of Lausanne.

The republic. In October, 1923, Turkey was proclaimed a republic, with an elected legislature and with Kemal as president. The political and religious authority of the old sultanate and the caliphate were abolished.

Kemal, who was later given the surname "Ataturk," or "father of the Turks," radically reformed Turkish government, economy, and society, turning its medieval Islamic social and political structure into that of a modern, Western-style nation. At Ataturk's death in 1938, his prime minister, Ismet Inonu, became the president and continued the country's westernization program.

Turkey did not participate in World War II, but it favored the Allies. After the war it pursued a pro-Western policy, joining the North Atlantic Treaty Organization. Turkey was aided in its fight against expanding Communist influence by U.S. economic aid under the Truman Doctrine and the Marshall Plan.

In 1950 the Democratic Party took power from Inonu's Republican People's Party government. The Democratic-led government faced rising discontent at home. Economic expansion and modernization had proceeded rapidly, and in 1950 severe inflation threatened the economy. The government responded

with unpopular financial restrictions. Unrest was met with repression, which the people, especially Turkey's new educated class, resented.

Contemporary Turkey. In 1960 a military group seized power. They established a second republic by 1961. Inonu became prime minister. He initiated economic development programs that were designed to develop natural resources, modernize agriculture, and expand industry at a moderate pace. Inonu was defeated in the 1965 elections. He was succeeded by Suat Urguplu, a member of the Justice Party. Later that year the Justice Party formed a new government.

During this period Turkey's foreign relations were complicated by its proximity to the Soviet Union and its friendship with Israel. Turkey invaded Cyprus in 1974, helping the minority Turkish Cypriots to occupy the northern part of the island. The invasion strained Turkish-U.S. and Turkish-Greek relations.

Prolonged political and economic unrest resulted in civil riots and subsequent changes in government in the next decade. Ethnic and religious tensions mounted in the mid-1970s, accompanied by extensive terrorist activity. As the republic was on the verge of crumbling, owing to increased violence and incipient civil war, martial law was proclaimed. The government was taken over by the military in 1980.

The Turkish economy grew steadily after reforms were launched in 1980, although inflation and interest rates remained high. Martial law was lifted in 1984.

Thousands died in clashes between Turkey's military and native Kurds during the 1980s and 1990s. The Kurds, about 20 percent of the population, at

meters
US

metres
Brit.

labor
US

labour
Brit.

aluminum
US

aluminium
Brit.

center
US

centre
Brit.

first sought independence, and still press for an autonomous state, or federation with Turkey.

In recent years Turkey's aspiration to European Union (EU) membership has led to steps in government reform. This includes a 2003 law reducing the military's political influence. EU membership is predicated on reform in the areas of human rights, minority protection, and democratic principles.

United Arab Emirates

Official name: *United Arab Emirates*
Area: *29,401 sq. mi., 75,581 sq. km.*
Type of government: *Federation*
Population: *2,446,000*
Capital: *Abu Dhabi (Pop., 399,000)*
Largest city: *Dubai (Pop., 669,000)*
Languages: *Arabic (official), Persian, English, Hindi, Urdu*
Literacy: *79%;* **Currency:** *Dirham*
Per capita GDP: *$21,100 (Rank: 25th)*

The land. The emirates lie on a mostly flat coastal plain. The majority of the land is dominated by a barren desert dotted with a few oases. At the eastern end of the country, along the coast, lie the western Hajar Mountains, which rise to 10,000 feet (3,048 meters) in some places.

In the desert regions, temperatures often reach 120°F (50°C) in the shade. Rainfall averages 3 inches (8 centimeters) a year. In the mountain region, the climate is cooler and about 15 inches (38 centimeters) of rain fall annually.
The people. The native Arabs account for only a quarter of the total population. The remainder of the people are Arabs

A CHILD CAMEL JOCKEY gets ready for a camel race in Dubai, United Arab Emirates.

SINCE 1976, oil has been the mainstay of the economy of the United Arab Emirates. Seen here is a section of an off-shore oil rig on the ship *Offshore Mercury.*

from other countries, Iranians, Pakistanis, and Indians. Foreigners, working mostly in the oil industry, account for nearly 90 percent of the labor force.

Ninety percent of the people live in urban areas. Most of the people are Sunni Muslims, and there are small minorities of Christians and Hindus. Arabic is the official language, but English is commonly used. The largest cities are Dubai, capital of Dubai State, and Abu Dhabi, the provisional federal capital. Both of these cities are strategically situated on the country's Persian Gulf coast.

Economy. Despite spending eight years on the fringes of the Iran-Iraq War and enduring a dramatic slump in the oil industry during the mid-1980s, the United Arab Emirates emerged from the decade even stronger than before. The fall in oil revenues led the United Arab Emirates to concentrate its efforts on diversifying the economy. The development of alternative domestic industries—especially the manufacture of aluminum, building materials, plastics, and other consumer goods—has helped to strengthen the union of the emirates.

Nomadic grazing of livestock, pearl diving, fishing, trading and date farming were once the only means of livelihood in the states. They became of secondary importance after 1958, when the production of oil became the main-

stay of the economy. Since 1976 the government has owned 60 percent of the country's two major oil companies. International banking has also become a significant aspect of the economy. Foreign investment, especially from France, is heavy.

The United Arab Emirates is one of the richest countries in the Persian Gulf, and the emirate of Abu Dhabi controls most of that wealth. Abu Dhabi produced 55.6 million metric tons of oil in 1988. Dubai, the chief port and commercial center, produced 17 million metric tons, the second largest amount. Sharjah oil resources are just beginning to be developed.

Oil accounts for 95 percent of the export revenues, although hides, dates, and other agricultural products are also exported. Foodstuffs, machinery, and consumer items are the main imports. Japan, the United States, South Korea, and the EU countries are the country's chief trading partners.
Government. The United Arab Emirates, a federation formed on December 2, 1971, is ruled by an elected sheik and a Federal Supreme Council (FSC) composed of the seven rulers of the seven states. The seven emirates are Abu Dhabi, Ajman, Dubai, Fujairah, Ras al-Khaimah, Sharjah, and Umm al Qaiwain. The FSC is the de facto legislative body. The unicameral National Council, with 40 members appointed by the FSC, serves as an advisory body.

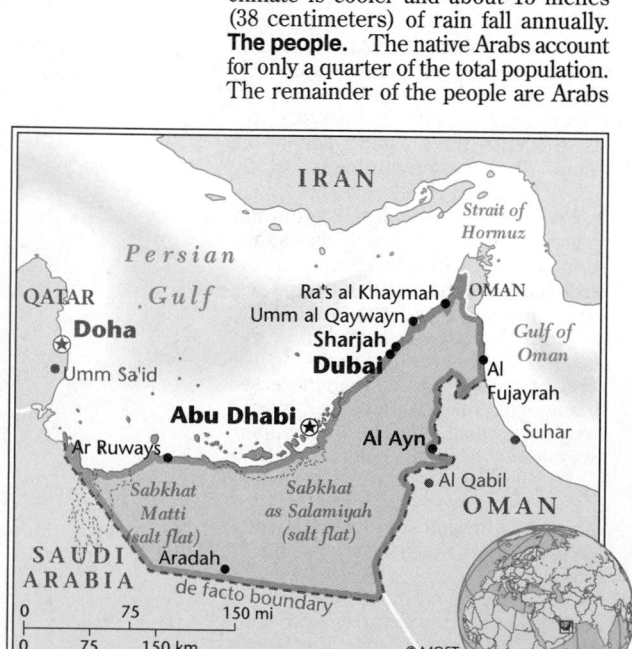

IRAN

Strait of Hormuz

Persian Gulf

QATAR
Doha
• Umm Sa'id

Ra's al Khaymah
Umm al Qaywayn
Sharjah
Dubai
OMAN

Gulf of Oman

Al Fujayrah
Suhar

Abu Dhabi
Al Ayn
• Ar Ruways
Al Qabil
Sabkhat Matti (salt flat)
Sabkhat as Salamiyah (salt flat)
OMAN
SAUDI ARABIA
Aradah
de facto boundary

0   75   150 mi
0   75   150 km

© MQST

History. For centuries the sheiks of the region known as the Trucial Oman battled for control of the territory. In the 1500s, when Portugal controlled the Persian Gulf, the sheiks turned to piracy and the slave trade. By the 1700s their ships ranged over the entire Persian Gulf and into the Arabian Sea. They waged undeclared war against the English East India Company, the principal trader in the area.

At the beginning of the 1800s the company and Great Britain suppressed the piracy, and in 1820 they signed a treaty of peace with the sheikdoms. By later agreements the sheiks promised to abandon slavery and piracy, turned control of their foreign affairs and defense over to Great Britain, and granted the British exclusive trading privileges.

Until the 1950s the sheikdoms experienced little internal or external strife. The discovery of oil in the 1950s, however, and the wealth and influx of foreigners that oil production brought to the states, disrupted the traditional society. In the 1960s programs were initiated to use oil revenues for health care, education, and technological improvements.

In the 1950s and 1960s border disputes with neighboring states were frequent. In 1971, after Britain withdrew from the area, six of the sheikdoms entered into a union and the seventh joined in 1972. Qatar and Bahrain were offered membership in the union, but both declined. In 1979 the United Arab Emirates severed diplomatic relations with Egypt to show its disapproval of the Egyptian-Israeli peace treaty signed in that year.

Yemen

Official name: *Republic of Yemen*
Area: *205,380 sq. mi., 527,970 sq. km.*
Type of government: *Republic*
Population: *18,701,000*
Capital and largest city: *Sanaa (Pop., 927,000)*
Language: *Arabic*
Literacy: *38%;* **Currency:** *Rial*
Per capita GDP: *$820 (Rank: 181st)*

The land. A low plain, 5 to 10 miles (8 to 16 kilometers) wide, extends along the coast of Yemen. The inland regions rise into highlands. In the eastern portion of the country the highlands seldom rise above 7,000 feet (2,134 meters). In the middle of the eastern region is a broad valley with many oases called the Hadramawt. In the western and central regions, many rugged mountains rise to over 12,000 feet (3,659 kilometers). To the north of the eastern highlands is the Rub'al Khali Desert. To the east of the western mountains the highland regions descend to a dry, arid plateau.

In the desert and along the coastal plains less than 10 inches (26 centimeters) of rain fall a year. In the desert, the temperatures often rise to over 130°F (54°C). A more temperate climate prevails in the mountains and the central plateau, where an average of 12 inches (32 centimeters) of rain fall a year.

The people. The Yemeni are Arab Muslims of the Sunni and Shi'a sects. Over 80 percent of the population live in rural areas. Yemenis are mostly sedentary, with the majority of the people living in small villages and towns throughout the highlands and along the coasts.

The main cities include San'a, the capital; Aden (population, 401,000), the economic capital and major port; and Ta'izz, or Taizz (290,000), a commercial center.

Economy. Yemen is one of the poorest countries in the world and it receives extensive aid from the oil-rich Arab states and from the United States and other industrialized countries.

Herding and farming are the principal occupations of the Yemeni people. Cotton, grains, fruits, and qat, a mild narcotic, are raised, and sheep and goats are grazed on the fringes of the desert. There is also some fishing on the coasts.

The port city of Aden is the principal commercial center for the lower Arabian peninsula. It has a large oil refinery and oil storage facilities, and is a major Arabian port for oil exporting and ship refueling. Minor oil discoveries in the 1980s led to investment and development by international oil companies.

Yemen imports the majority of its commodities and food. The country's main trading partners include Germany, the United States, Great Britain, Japan, France, and Italy.

Government. The newly united Yemeni Republic was created in 1990,

ABU DHABI
is both the name of the most influential state in the United Arab Emirates and the city that is the federation's capital. Its economy depends heavily on the oil that was discovered there in 1958.

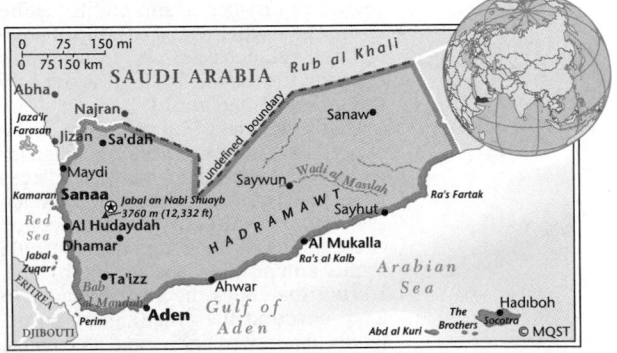

THE VILLAGE of Kawkaban is typical of those located in the rugged mountains in Yemen's western and central regions.

removing the border lines drawn during partition. A president is elected by popular vote to a seven-year term. A bicameral legislature consists of a Shura Council, appointed by the president, and a House of Representatives, elected by popular vote.

History. During the first millennium A.D., the sheikdoms that made up the territory of Yemen were controlled by Egyptians, Turks, and Yemenis before being ruled by independent sultans. The best known of these early states was Saba or, as it was called in the Bible, Sheba. A high degree of economic prosperity earned the country the name of *Arabia Felix* among the Greeks and Romans.

Yemen's prosperity was based on an elaborate system of irrigation and the export of frankincense, precious jewels, and spices. Yemen also controlled a large part of the trade between India and the Mediterranean.

In the first centuries A.D., prosperity declined as the India-Mediterranean trade moved along new routes. In the early sixth century, Christian Ethiopians crossed the Red Sea and conquered the country.

Yemen was converted to Islam in the seventh century and formed part of the Islamic empires ruled successively from Medina, Damascus, and Baghdad. A revival of prosperity and culture came under the Zaydi imams, a family of political and religious leaders. In the ninth century the Zaydi founded a dynasty that ruled Yemen until 1962.

In the 16th and 17th centuries, Portugal and the Ottoman Turks competed for control of Yemen, but their invading forces were driven off. During the next 200 years the country suffered another decline caused by its isolation from the new trade routes around the Cape of Good Hope. During the 1800s the British, eager to keep peace in the area, signed agreements to protect neighboring sheikdoms.

In 1872 the Ottoman Turks succeeded in making Yemen part of their empire, but Yemeni resistance continued in the highlands until World War I. The Ottoman Empire was forced to withdraw in 1918, at the end of World War I, leaving Yemen an independent nation under the Zaydi ruler.

The imam Yahya closed the country to outsiders, and although Yemen joined the Arab League in 1945 and the United Nations in 1947, it had almost no contact with the rest of the world. In 1948 Yahya was killed during an attempted revolution, and his son, Ahmad, succeeded him.

Ahmad gradually allowed foreign diplomats into Yemen. In 1958 Yemen and the United Arab Republic formed a federation, the United Arab States. By early 1962 the union had been abolished, however.

A republic was declared following a military coup in 1962, after which a civil war raged between the royalist forces of the deposed imam and republican army troops. The war involved the rest of the Middle East. Egypt sent arms and troops to aid the republicans, and Jordan and Saudi Arabia provided the royalists with weapons and money.

The civil war finally ended with the establishment of a leftist socialist state in South Yemen in 1969. South Yemen was proclaimed The People's Democratic Republic. Massive nationalization projects and repressive rule ensued. North Yemen remained a republic: the Yemen Arab Republic. There were continued coups and violence.

As a merger of Yemen and South Yemen was nearing implementation in 1978, the presidents of both countries were assassinated, resulting in war between the Yemens in 1979. South Yemen received massive Soviet aid and Yemen was supported by Saudi Arabia and the United States.

Intermittent border skirmishes were waged throughout the 1980s, while the possibility of unification was still being explored. Relations between the two Yemens became warmer in 1989; the border between the two countries was opened and visa restrictions were canceled.

Finally, on May 22, 1990, the two Yemens merged. President Ali Abdullah Saleh of North Yemen was elected president of the new union. Ali Salem al-Baidh, former secretary-general of the South's ruling Socialist Party, was chosen vice president. A brief civil war in 1994 was without major incident.

SEEN HERE are qat chewers in a Yemen bazaar. Qat is a shrub grown by Arabs for the leaves, which furnish a stimulant narcotic when chewed or brewed for tea.

Cities of the Middle East

Abu Dhabi, city on the Persian Gulf, temporary capital of the United Arab Emirates. Oil production is its chief industry. Pop., 399,000.

Amman, the capital of Jordan, in the northwestern part of the country, about 25 miles (40 km) northeast of the Dead Sea. Amman is Jordan's chief industrial and commercial center and the hub of a rail and highway network. The area is famous for colored marble. Industries include food processing and manufacture of textiles and leather goods. Pop., 1,147,000.

Ankara, the capital of Turkey and second largest city, located on the central Anatolian plateau on the Ankara River. The city is an important commercial, industrial, and cultural center. Ankara markets and processes agricultural products of the region and is famous for the production of Angora goat wool, or mohair. Other manufactures include cement, textiles, leather goods, and tile. Pop., 3,203,000.

Baghdad, the capital and largest city of Iraq, located on both banks of the Tigris River, in the east-central part of the country. The city is the intellectual, commercial, and industrial center of Iraq. The chief industry is oil refining, but factories manufacture a variety of products, including shoes, clothing, and cement. Damage to the city was sustained during the Iran-Iraq and Gulf Wars, and again when Baghdad became the focus of U.S. and British forces searching for Saddam Hussein during their war with Iraq. Pop., 3,841,000.

Beirut, the capital of Lebanon, located on the eastern shore of the Mediterranean Sea, at the foot of the Lebanon Mountains. Long an important center for east-west trade, Beirut is a busy port and transportation center. It lies on the Cairo-Istanbul-Baghdad railway, is the hub of a good road network, and has an international airport. Beirut is also a banking and an educational center. Many areas of the city were destroyed during Lebanon's civil war. Pop., 475,000.

Bethlehem, located about 5 miles (8 km) southwest of Jerusalem. It is part of the West Bank, which has been occupied by Israel since 1967. Bethlehem was the birthplace of Jesus. The Church of the Nativity, built by Emperor Constantine in 330 a.d., occupies the reputed site of the stable where Jesus was born. The major business in Bethlehem is the sale of souvenirs to tourists and pilgrims. Pop., 22,000.

Damascus, the capital of Syria, situated in the southwestern part of the country on the Barada River. The city is located in an oasis that has been continuously inhabited since prehistoric times. Modern Damascus is a major Middle Eastern administrative, communications, commercial, and industrial center. Its products include cement, glass, textiles, and sugar.

Damascus was a noted marketplace on caravan routes during ancient and medieval times. The city retains its ancient citadel, bazaars, Roman gates, and historic churches. The bazaars are renowned for their silks, brass, and copper ware. Pop., 1,394,000.

Doha, the capital and chief port of Qatar, located on the east side of the Qatar peninsula on the Persian Gulf. Since the discovery of oil in Qatar in the 1940s, Doha has become an important commercial center. Oil is its chief export. Pop., 264,000.

Istanbul, the largest city in Turkey, located on the western, or European, bank of the Bosporus strait, near its entrance to the Sea of Marmara. It is the only city in the world that lies on two continents. One of the Mediterranean's busiest ports, Istanbul is Turkey's principal transportation, commercial, and industrial center. Its manufactures include processed foods, tobacco, leather goods, cement, glass, and soap. The city was the capital of the Byzantine and Ottoman empires and has many historic buildings. The most famous of these is Hagia Sophia, a sixth-century church that is now a museum, whose dome dominates the city. The city was formerly called Constantinople, in ancient times, Byzantium. Pop., 8,803,000.

Jerusalem, one of the great religious centers of the world, a holy place of Jews, Christians, and Muslims, and the capital of Israel. Jerusalem is located in the Judean Hills of central Palestine, about 35 miles (56 km) from the Mediterranean Sea and about 13 miles (21 km) west of the Dead Sea. The Old City of Jerusalem contains most of the holy places, while the New City is the religious, economic, and administrative center of the state of Israel. During the brief Arab-Israeli war of June 1967, Israeli troops captured the Old City, which has been integrated with the Israeli sector. Pop., 628,000.

Kuwait, capital of Kuwait and a port at the northwestern end of the Persian Gulf. The city was severely damaged during the Iraqi occupation and subsequent Persian Gulf War. The main export is oil. Pearls and hides are also exported. Pop., 193,000.

Manama, capital and principal city of Bahrain, situated on Bahrain Island, on the Persian Gulf. Refining and exporting petroleum are the port city's main industries; there is also some shipbuilding and fishing. Pop., 140,000.

Mecca, chief holy city of the Muslim world, located in west-central Saudi Arabia, east of Jidda. Mecca is the birthplace of Muhammad. It contains the Kaaba, chief shrine of Islam, which is visited by many thousands of pilgrims each year. The city is also the capital of the province of Hejaz and a commercial center. Pop., 966,000.

Muscat, capital of Oman, a country in the southeastern part of the Arabian peninsula. This walled city is located on Muscat Bay, an arm of the Gulf of Oman, at the entrance to the Persian Gulf. Pop., 41,000.

Nicosia, capital of Cyprus, an island in the eastern Mediterranean Sea. It is divided into separate Turkish and Greek sectors. It is a commercial center of the Messaori Plain, which produces wheat, wine, olive oil, almonds, citrus fruits, and livestock. Textiles, leather, machine tools, and cigarettes are manufactured there. Pop., 273,000.

Riyadh, capital of Saudi Arabia, located in the east-central part of the country on the Nejd Plateau. Riyadh, the commercial and educational center of the kingdom, serves as a trade center for the dates, vegetables, and grain produced in the surrounding area. The city expanded rapidly when huge oil deposits were discovered. Riyadh was an important base for coalition forces during the Persian Gulf War. Pop., 2,776,000.

Sanaa, capital of Yemen, located in a high mountain valley in southwestern Arabia. It lies in the center of a rich, irrigated, agricultural region that produces fruits and coffee. This walled city is also the cultural and commercial center for the area. Pop., 927,000.

Teheran, or Tehran, capital of Iran (formerly Persia), situated in the north, about 70 miles (110 km) from the Caspian Sea. The city is the cultural, industrial, and transportation center of Iran. Manufactures include cotton, glass, metal products, construction materials, and automobile parts. Pop., 6,759,000.

colored
US

coloured
Brit.

center
US

centre
Brit.

Glossary of the Middle East

Aden, Gulf of. An arm of the Indian Ocean, bounded on the north by Arabia and on the south by Africa's Somali coast. The gulf is 500 miles (885 km) long and connects with the Red Sea to the west through the Bab al Mandeb Strait.

Aqaba, Gulf of. An extension of the Red Sea lying between the Sinai and the Arabian peninsulas. The gulf is 110 miles (177 km) long and from 5 to 17 miles (8 to 27 km) wide.

Arabia. A large peninsula in southwestern Asia, separated from the bulk of the continent in the northeast by the Persian Gulf and the Gulf of Oman. High mountains along the western and southern boundaries are separated from the Red Sea on the west and the Gulf of Aden on the south by narrow coastal plains. The central Arabian Plateau slopes gently eastward into the Persian Gulf basin. It is about 1,200 miles (1,930 km) long with a maximum breadth of 1,300 miles (2,090 km). Its area is about 1 million square miles (2.6 million sq. km) in all.

Arab League. Officially the League of Arab States. An organization of Arab nations in northern Africa and the Middle East formed March 22, 1945. Membership in 1991 included Algeria, Bahrain, Djibouti, Egypt, Iraq, Jordan, Kuwait, Lebanon, Libya, Mauritania, Morocco, Oman, the Palestine Liberation Organization, Qatar, Saudi Arabia, Somalia, Sudan, Syria, Tunisia, the United Arab Emirates, and Yemen.

THIS ARAB town in the West Bank in Israel is in an area disrupted by violence and conflict between Palestinian and Israeli settlers.

The Arab league was organized to promote the common social, economic, and cultural interests of the Arab peoples. The members attempt to work together in the fields of foreign policy, law, education, finance, and trade.

Egypt's membership was suspended in 1979 after it signed a peace treaty with Israel, and the league's headquarters were moved from Cairo to Tunis. Egypt was readmitted in 1989.

Dead Sea. A salt lake, about 400 square miles (1,036 sq. km) in area, on the Israel-Jordan border, into which the Jordan River flows. Lying 1,296 feet (395 m) below sea level, its shores and surface are at the lowest known point of land on Earth. Due to evaporation, it is saltier than seawater and contains many other minerals as well.

Jordan. A river in the Middle East that rises in four headstreams in the Anti-Lebanon Mountains of Syria. It flows south for some 200 miles (320 km) in Israel and Jordan through the Sea of Galilee and into the Dead Sea. The Yarmuk River is the principal tributary of the Jordan, whose course lies in the Great Rift Valley.

Negev. A semidesert region in southern Israel. The Negev contains copper, potash, phosphate, and oil deposits. Limited agriculture is carried on with water brought from the north.

Orontes. A 246-mile-long (396 km) river in western Syria. It rises in northeastern Lebanon and flows north to the Turkish border, where it turns and flows west to the Mediterranean Sea.

Persian Gulf. A shallow extension of the Arabian Sea, bounded by the United Arab Emirates, Qatar, Saudi Arabia, Kuwait, Iraq, and Iran. It is some 550 miles (885 km) long and is connected with the Gulf of Oman to the southeast.

Red Sea. An inland sea between northeastern Africa and the Arabian peninsula, part of the Great Rift Valley system. It is about 1,300 miles (2,100 km) long and between 130 to 250 miles (210 to 400 km) wide. The sea is connected to the Mediterranean by the Suez Canal and to the Gulf of Aden through the strait of Bab al Mandeb.

THE SALT LAKE
known as the Dead Sea is mentioned in the Bible as the Salt Sea. Its shores have yielded many ancient scrolls, which are the oldest known manuscripts of Biblical writings.

Sinai. A triangular peninsula that forms the easternmost portion of Egypt. It extends southward from a 150-mile-long (240-km.) Mediterranean coast for over 200 miles (320 km) to the northern tip of the Red Sea. Two extensions of the Red Sea—the Gulf of Suez and the Gulf of Aqaba—form the western and eastern boundaries of the peninsula. The exten- sive central plateau of Al-Tih rises to the south and culminates in Gebel Katherina, 8,652 feet (2,637 m) high. Nearby is Musa Mountain, thought by many to be the Mount Sinai of the Old Testament.

West Bank. A section of land west of the Jordan River between Israel and Jor- dan, which covers approximately 2,270 square miles (5,900 sq. km). The West Bank has been administered by Israel since 1967. The peace treaty signed by Egypt and Israel in 1979 was aimed, in part, at establishing a 5-year period of Palestinian self-rule in the area. The Palestinians have continued to push for complete autonomy, while Israelis con- tinue to build new settlements in the area.

THE HELP DESK

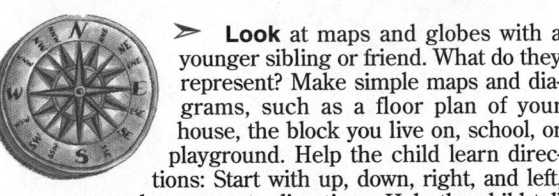

➤ **Look** at maps and globes with a younger sibling or friend. What do they represent? Make simple maps and dia- grams, such as a floor plan of your house, the block you live on, school, or playground. Help the child learn direc- tions: Start with up, down, right, and left, and progress to directions. Help the child tell the difference between land and water on a globe and iden- tify the continents and major countries by name.

➤ **Imagine** a route you travel frequently, for example, home to school or home to the mall. Write instructions to lead someone unfamiliar with the route. Include directions, distances, landmarks, etc. Test your skill by having some- one follow your instructions.

➤ **Draw** a map illustrating the above instructions. Be sure it uses standard mapping guidelines with North at the top and a rough distance indication if possible.

➤ **Make** a map of play dough or salt clay that shows mountains, lakes, rivers, plains, peninsulas, etc. Just for practice, your first map can be an imaginary place with many features. Then make one of a country in the Middle East.

➤ **Look** at the participation of different groups at differ- ent times in the country's history, for example, Islamic revolutionaries in Iran.

➤ **Do** you like to sample different foods? Jewish, Lebanese, etc? What distinguishes the cuisines? Why?

➤ **Make** a list of the largest cities. How does the size of those cities compare with cities that you are familiar with? Why do you think that people began to live in that area and continued to live there?

➤ **Study** the continental map. Pay particular attention to the locator inset map that will help you locate the portion of the globe the Middle East occupies. Is it in the Northern or Southern hemisphere? In the Eastern or Western hemi- sphere? Is it north or south of the equator? What are the major physical features—any large rivers, mountains, deserts? Make a list of the names of those features.

➤ **Use** the locator inset map to pinpoint the country and then turn to the continent map to confirm the location. Look at the list of physical features you made as you stud- ied the continental map. Do any of those features appear in the country you are studying? How do you think the pres- ence of that feature affects the country?

➤ **Spend** some time each day locating countries and cities that are in the news on a map or globe.

➤ **As** you study the Middle East, try to analyze the man- ner in which people adapted to their environment.

➤ **Document** your family's ethnic heritage. What coun- try did your forefathers come from? When did they come? Why? Who? What famous people share your background? Older relatives would be a good source of information.

➤ **Look** at the photographs in this section. What can you learn about the climate, geographical features, and the people? As you read newspapers and listen to the news, pay particular attention to the names of countries and regions. Visualize the area so that the information is more mean- ingful to you.

➤ **Study** the information box for each country. What can you determine from each set of facts? Is the country large or small? Rich or poor? Heavily or sparsely popu- lated? Is it an industrial nation or an agricultural one? Are the people well educated?

➤ **Make** a list of important people in the development of the country. As you note events in your historical report, watch for names of people associated with those events. Read the newspapers and listen to news reports to add cur- rent names to your list of people. See if you can find pictures of current rulers or other important people and try to determine why they are important to the country. See if the people on your list appear in other volumes of the Vol- ume Library by checking the Index.

➤ **Review** the historical background of the country. Is it a country that dates back thousands or hundreds of years or is it much younger? Write a short report noting major events in the history in chronological order. Now compare those events to events in countries nearby. Is there any sim- ilarity? Are they friends or enemies? Do the people speak the same language? What are other similarities or differ- ences that you have detected? Don't forget to use the History of World volume for related information.

➤ **Continue** your study of the world. If you have Book 3 of the *Volume Library*, study the more detailed maps of the countries. Use the blank map outlines to locate countries, physical features, and cities.

➤ **Plan** a trip. Select a destination from the place you are to another place in the Middle East. Where would you stop along the way? How would you travel from one place to another? How long would each leg of the trip require? What kind of clothes should you take? Can you find out what kind of money you should have at each stop? What lan- guages will you be likely to hear?

➤ **For** a list of helpful references, go to the *customers* section of www.southwestern.com.

25

Australia
and Oceania

25

Australia and Oceania

Contents

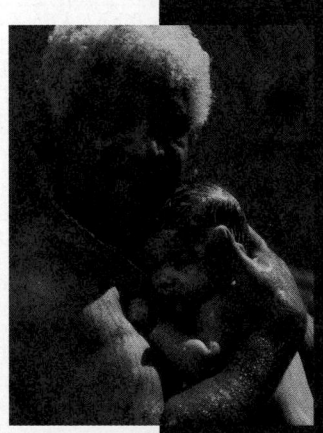

Australia and Oceania

colonization
US

colonisation
Brit.

The last places in the world to be settled lay, not surprisingly, far from Earth's major land masses. They included Australia, New Zealand, and the numerous islands of Oceania in the South Pacific that make up Micronesia, Melanesia, and Polynesia. Perhaps as long as 30,000 years ago, people from Southeast Asia began fanning out toward the northern coast of Australia and the western islands of Micronesia and Melanesia. Over the centuries, they continued their movement until by the A.D. 700s and 800s they reached far enough south to people Australia and Tasmania. They also reached far enough east and south to inhabit Polynesia from the Hawaiian Islands and the area from Easter Island to New Zealand. In their far-flung domains, these migrants developed in isolation from outside cultural influences.

Australia's first settlers were the aborigines, a nomadic hunting and gathering people who believed that the gods had created Earth during the "dreamtime" and that once the gods had finished, they instructed human beings never to change anything on Earth. The aborigines followed this admonition by making no changes in the land through agriculture or mining. They ranged over the often harsh environments of Australia taking only what they needed to survive and then moving on, never developing a written language and never changing their way of life over the millennia.

The people of the islands of Oceania did turn to agriculture. Their search for new land to farm kept them moving ever eastward across the South Pacific. Their extensive travels made them master seamen, able to navigate thousands of miles using only the sun's position, the roll of the waves, and the direction of the birds' flight.

One of the most culturally advanced of these island peoples were the Polynesian Maoris, who began settling in New Zealand about 1500 years ago. There they farmed the rich soil and lived in tribes in small villages whose focal point was the *marae*, the meeting house where they worshipped their pantheon of eight major gods. Stories of these gods were passed down in a rich oral tradition.

Through the centuries prior to 1500, Malay fishermen and other Southeast Asian seafarers sometimes stopped briefly along Australia's uninviting northern and western shores. But they did not stay long, and Australia's existence remained unknown to the rest of the world. European scholars had long suspected the presence of a great continent in the southern hemisphere, believing that one was necessary to balance Europe and Asia in the northern hemisphere. *Terra Australis Incognita* they called it—meaning "unknown southern land."

Spanish and Portuguese sailors came close to Australia several times during the 1500s, but it was a Dutch ship, blown off its course to the Spice Islands, that made the first European contact in 1616. From then on, Dutch navigators mapped the north and northwest coasts of New Holland, as they called the island continent. In the early 1640s Abel Janszoon Tasman sailed along Australia's south coast. He found and claimed possession of Tasmania for the Dutch East India Company, sailing along the west coast of New Zealand and so establishing Tasmania's separation from Australia.

Throughout this period, the islands of Oceania were gradually being reached by Europeans, beginning with Ferdinand Magellan's sighting in 1521 of the Mariana Islands of Micronesia. Spanish, Portuguese, Dutch, British, and French navigators continued to map Oceania's islands, filling in the world's knowledge of these "last places on Earth." Foremost among these explorers was Britain's Captain James Cook. His expeditions in the 1760s and 1770s charted New Zealand and Australia's east coast. He also discovered New Caledonia in Melanesia and the Cook Islands in Polynesia, and visited

Tonga and the Hawaiian Islands, where he was killed in a conflict with the islanders.

Cook's charting of eastern Australia led to its colonization by the British. The first colonists were convicts, sentenced by British courts to settle in Australia. The agriculturally minded British quickly took over the most productive land to grow crops and to graze sheep, driving the aborigines back into the deserts of the interior.

Australia's British colonies grew slowly at first, with free settlers replacing the convicts. By 1850 the colonial population reached 400,000. The next year gold was discovered, setting off a rush that doubled that number in a decade. By 1900 the population had grown to 4 million.

In New Zealand the colonization path was similar, although the British government did not designate it as a destination for convicts. Its early settlers were sealers and whalers, sailors who had jumped ship, and convicts who had escaped the penal settlements of Australia. By 1820 the British had founded several settlements in New Zealand. Like the Aborigines, the Maori natives suffered at the hands of colonists. Diseases brought by the Europeans decimated their population. In addition, the Maoris adopted European muskets, using them in intertribal wars that wiped out still more of their number. By the 1850s the estimated pre-European population of 100,000 had been cut nearly in half.

Like the Australians, New Zealand colonists made sheep central to their economy, and their ceaseless need for new land drove them to claim ever more Maori grazing space. To try and stop further encroachment, the Maori tribes tried to unify under one king; this led to a long series of Anglo-Maori wars. The diminishing numbers of Maoris presented formidable resistance, but by 1872 they were finally beaten and the colonists continued to take their land, almost at will.

Europeans were also having an impact on the islands of Oceania during the 1800s. At first the settlers were mainly sealers and whalers or collectors of the precious woods tropical islands produced. But among these settlers were also the reprehensible "blackbirders," men who captured Melanesians and sold them into slavery to work the Australian cane fields. They also transported Polynesians to Chile and Peru to work the guano deposits. By 1850 more solid Europeans began to settle in the islands, creating a plantation agriculture that raised and exported cocoa, coconuts, coffee, and sugar.

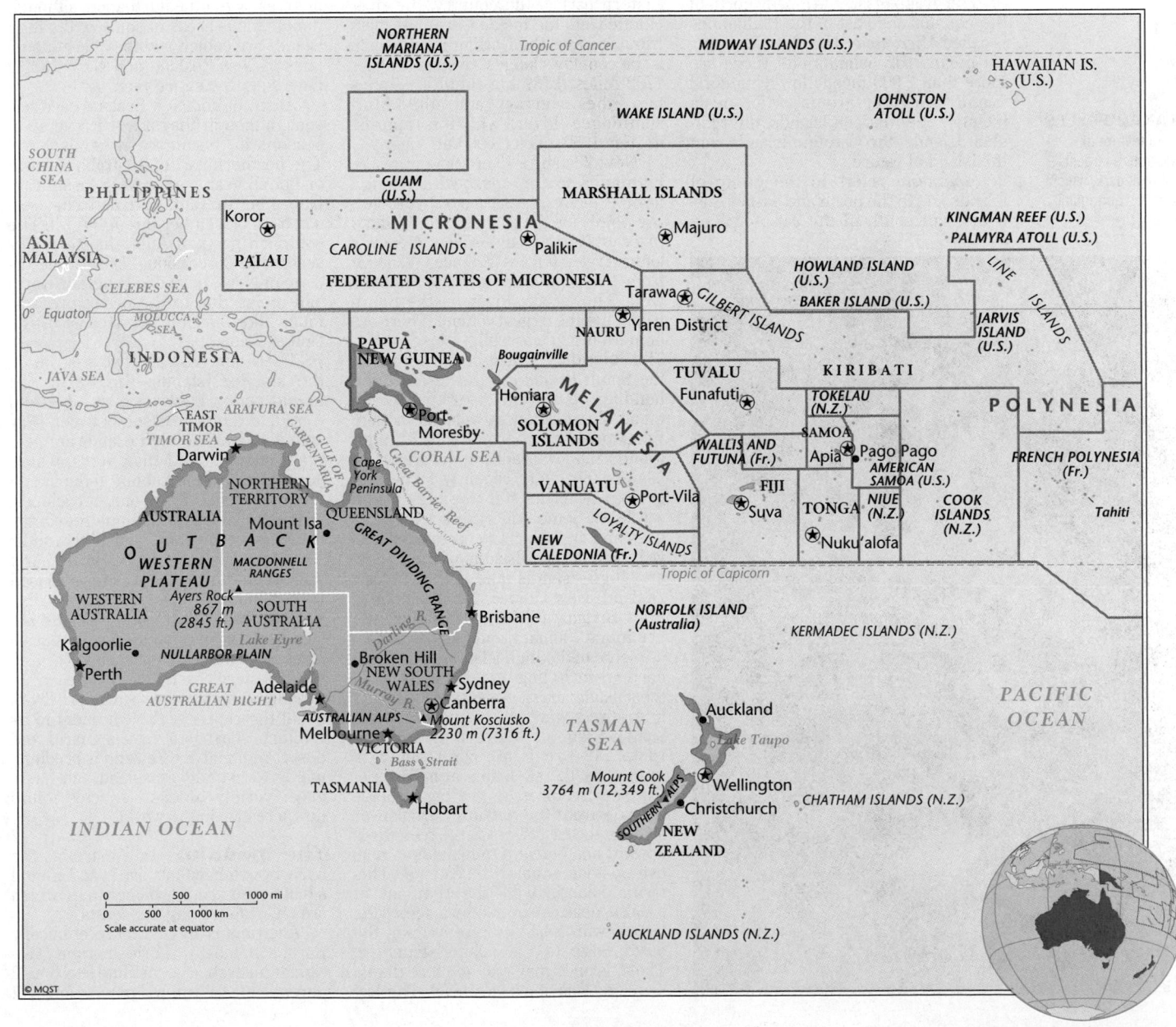

meter
US

metre
Brit.

center
US

centre
Brit.

KAKADU FALLS
are a feature of
Australia's largest
national park, which
also has aboriginal
rock art.

The land. The smaller Pacific islands are generally divided into three groups based on their geography and cultural backgrounds: *Polynesia, Micronesia,* and *Melanesia*. The biggest island, Australia, is surrounded by water, like an island, but it is classed as a continent, and is sometimes referred to as the island continent.

Polynesia is spread over the largest area of the South Pacific, stretching from Midway Island in the north to New Zealand in the south, a distance of 5,000 miles. Easter Island is the easternmost island in the group, lying about two-thirds of the way to the continent of South America. This island group also includes New Zealand, by far the largest island in the group. This group includes French Polynesia and the Cook Islands. Although Hawaii is culturally the northernmost point in the Polynesian triangle, it is now part of the United States and is discussed in the NORTH AMERICA volume.

The group of islands mostly north of the equator and east of the Philippines is called *Micronesia*. The word Micronesia means tiny islands and there are more than 2,000 mostly low-lying coral islands in the group. Micronesia includes the Mariana Islands, the Marshall Islands, the Caroline Islands, and the island of Nauru.

Melanesia refers to the group of islands just to the north and east of Australia, but south of the equator. The

word Melanesia means black islands and refers to the large amount of melanin, or dark pigment, that is found in the skin of the Melanesian people. Melanesia includes New Guinea, the Solomon Islands, New Caledonia, Fiji, and Vanuatu. Although Fiji is geographically a part of Melanesia, it is culturally more like Polynesia.

Mountains. Australia is the flattest of the seven continents, and its only significant mountain range, the Eastern Highlands, also known as the Great Dividing Range, reaches its highest point at Mount Kosciusko, which has an elevation of 7316 feet (2230 m). The Eastern Hills of New Zealand's North Island run from East Cape to Cook Strait. The Southern Alps and High Country cover most of the South Island of New Zealand, and include some of the island's most spectacular scenery.

Rivers. The major river in Australia is the Murray, which is 1609 miles (2589km) long. Located in the southeastern part of the country, the river empties into the Indian Ocean. Its main tributaries are the Darling River, which is the country's longest river, flowing for 1702 miles (2739 km) until it empties into the Murray, and the Murrumbidgee River, which is approximately 1050 miles (1690 km) long.

New Zealand's rivers flow from the highlands to the coast with enough force to serve as sources of hydroelectric power for the islands. The Waikato River on North Island is New Zealand's longest river. It flows 264 miles (425 km) from the highlands into the Hauraki Gulf. The Clutha River on the South Island has the largest volume. There are numerous lakes as well.

The islands. Most of the islands of the South Pacific are the result of the building up and the wearing down of mountains formed by volcanic action. Consequently, there are now high islands and low islands in the area. The islands that were recently formed in geological terms still rise high above sea level. Some still have active volcanoes and are subject to earthquakes as well. The largest islands of the Pacific are high islands and include New Zealand, New Guinea, New Caledonia, New Britain, Fiji, the Marianas, the Solomons, Vanuatu, and Samoa.

Some of the high islands have developed an encircling reef on the flanks of the volcanic mass, protecting the island from direct wave action and forming a shallow lagoon between it and the island. The reefs are coral, which is formed by the skeletons of millions of tiny sea creatures. As the high islands subside from the action of erosion or shifts in the earth's crust, the reef grows upward and outward to maintain a relative position equal with sea level. This forms islands with the remnant of basaltic peaks encircled by a deep wide lagoon with a barrier reef forming the outer edge of the island structure. These islands may rise no more than a meter or less above sea level. The low

islands include the Tuamotu, Tuvalu, Gilbert, Marshall, and Phoenix groups.

An atoll is formed when the barrier reef of an "almost atoll" has kept pace with the subsidence of the foundation taking the volcanic island below sea level and forming the irregular ringlet of the typical atoll. Although small in size, the atoll has the largest distribution of any island type in the Pacific basin. It is also the type of island most affected by relative changes in sea level, by tsunamis, or waves formed by earthquakes, and by wind storms.

Other types of islands include the elevated barrier reef, which show emergence and tilting in a seismically active area. Palau and Yap in the Western Carolines, Guam, and the Northern Marianas show signs of this recent emergence.

Climate. Most of the islands of the Pacific lie between the equator and the Tropic of Capricorn and are considered tropical. Most enjoy a mild climate with temperatures that average about 75 degrees, with little fluctuation, although mountainous areas in some of the high islands are cooler, and the tallest mountains in New Zealand and New Guinea have snow the entire year.

Australia and New Zealand have seasons, although they are the reverse of seasons in the northern hemisphere. The northern part of Australia is warm or hot all year, with a wet season from November through April and a dry season from November through April. The southern parts of Australia have four seasons and occasional frosts. The climate of New Zealand is generally warm and moist, due to the ocean breezes, much like the northwest coast of the United States.

There are basically two seasons in the smaller islands: the warm and humid period between November and April and the dry season between May and October. The high islands are generally more humid than atolls, where you can enjoy the cooling influence of the trade winds. Typhoons, or cyclones, strike the islands with some regularity, bringing heavy rains and high winds. These are thought to be particularly numerous during the warming caused by El Niño.

Vegetation. The Pacific islands are largely tropical. Australia has extensive forests on its northern, eastern, and southwestern coasts, changing inland to broadleaf shrub and savanna. From about the center of the continent to its western coast is a vast semiarid and desert region. New Zealand is predominantly forest and grassland and has a great variety of plant species found nowhere else in the world.

The people. In Australia, the majority of inhabitants live in and around a half dozen major urban centers, which are all located along the coasts.

Australia is by and large ethnically European, mostly of British origin. Aboriginal Australians constitute less than 2 percent of Australia's population, yet

THE PAINTINGS OF PAUL GAUGUIN celebrated the beauty of the land and the people of Tahiti.

their culture and history have had a significant impact on the development of modern Australian culture.

Most of the people in New Zealand are descendants of British settlers who came there in the 1800s. The largest minority group is the Maoris, the Polynesian people who originally settled the islands.

The inhabitants of the Pacific Islands probably came from southeast Asia many thousands of years ago. During periods of lower sea levels, they probably came by land. Later, as land masses became separated by water, they developed a tradition of travel by canoe. These various migrations developed some distinguishing physical characteristics between Melanesian, Polynesian, and Micronesian island populations, many of which exist in some part today, although the differences have become less obvious with modern travel.

Language. Most of the languages of the Pacific Islands belong to the Malayo-Polynesian group of languages. Although English is the most widely used language in the Pacific Islands, with French and Japanese the main language of some islands, there are actually more than 1,000 languages in the islands. Many of these languages are related and probably diverge the most widely in their written form, as a result of the various interpretations to the spoken word applied by the various missionaries who first made it into a written language. The languages of New Guinea and the aboriginal groups of Australia, however, do not appear to be related to any other group of languages.

Religion. Christianity is the main religion of Australia and New Zealand. Christianity has also been the main religion of the smaller islands since the 1800s, when the missionaries brought it to the islands, although it is combined with elements of earlier religions in some of the islands.

Economy. Australia and New Zealand have well developed economies, with Australia dependent largely upon agricultural and mining industries, and New Zealand dependent upon agriculture and manufacturing. The economies of the smaller islands, however, are largely at the subsistence level, with most people producing the things they consume, or with heavy subsidies from the countries upon which they depend. Tourism is becoming an important element in the economies of many of these countries, as they search for means to develop.

Agriculture. Although only about 5 percent of the workers of Australia are involved in agriculture, they produce nearly all of the food for the country, due in part to the heavy mechanization of the farming industry. The main farm products, and the primary exports, are cattle, wheat, wool, dairy products, sugar cane, and fruit. New Zealand raises and exports a great deal of dairy products, as well as meat from cattle, and meat and wool from sheep.

Agriculture is the primary industry of most of the islands of the Pacific, with the main exports being sugar from sugar cane, cocoa, and coffee. Many of the islands were engaged in the production of copra, or dried coconut from which coconut oil is extracted, but the market for that has decreased in recent years. Although there is a great abundance of fresh fruit, the distances involved and the depressed economies of these islands make it difficult to get their produce to market.

Natural resources. Australia depends heavily on its mineral resources, and it has become one of the world's leading mining countries. Deposits of gold, silver, lead, copper, zinc, and tin have been mined since the 1800s. Recently bauxite, iron ore, coal, natural gas, oil, and nickel have been discovered.

New Zealand's greatest natural resource is the hydroelectric power generated by the dammed rivers. Land suitable for farming, grazing, and foresting constitutes another primary resource.

The smaller islands have few natural resources such as minerals. The low islands tend to have soil that is scarce and too poor for serious farming. The high islands have richer soil and adequate rainfall, but may be too steep or heavily covered with vegetation to make farming practical. Fish and sea products are plentiful, but the islands lack the infrastructure to exploit them adequately, and have leased fishing rights to more developed nations. Recently, overtures have been made by some of these nations to lease the rights to "mine" the manganese nodules that lie on the ocean bottom in the territorial waters of several of these small island groups.

Industry. In addition to its mining industry, Australia produces many of the goods consumed in the country. Factories also produce goods for export, including processed foods, chemicals, and textiles, in addition to manufactured metal products. The processing of New Zealand's agricultural products for consumption and export is her major industry. There is little industry on the small islands, although French Polynesia continues to develop the culture of black pearls, which are popular on the world market.

Tourism. Industry related to tourism is becoming very important in the Pacific Islands, and this has been greatly enhanced by the availability of air service. There is a growing number of tourists who enjoy the scenery, climate, and water sports. This has encouraged the building of roads, hotels, shops, and restaurants, and the development of tourist attractions. The Cook Islands, for example, now has a hospitality training center, which trains students in the tourism trade, including classes for every position from tour guide to cook and waiter.

The distances of the Pacific Islands and the cost entailed with travelling those distances has been a factor in the continued growth of this industry. At the present, most of the tourist trade in the area involves travel between islands, or travel between the islands and Southeast Asia or Japan. The fact that the Olympics for the year 2000 were held in Australia greatly enhanced world travel to the South Pacific.

AYERS ROCK in Uluru National Park is one of Australia's most famous landmarks. Its caves are covered with aboriginal rock paintings.

WITH NO THREAT IN SIGHT, an ostrich hides its head in the sand of the desert which covers about one-third of Australia.

World war in the Pacific.

The South Pacific became a focus of World War II when Japan bombed Pearl Harbor in Hawaii on December 7, 1941, and the United States, Great Britain, and Canada declared war on Japan the following day. After the United States began bombing raids on Japan in 1942, the Japanese turned their eyes toward the islands in the south in order to provide a buffer zone for defense. The battle of the Coral Sea northeast of Australia was indecisive, but served to check Japan's threat to Australia.

The Japanese next sent their fleet against the United States fleet at Midway. Although the U.S. bombers were slow and outdated, the importance of the use of aircraft and aircraft carriers was proved in this first decisive victory against the Japanese in the Pacific. The focus next turned to the south Pacific, with engagements on New Guinea and Guadalcanal, occupied by the Japanese. The Japanese had evacuated Guadalcanal by early 1943, but fighting continued on New Guinea until 1944.

The Pacific campaign continued with engagements that carried the Allies across the Gilbert, Marshall, Caroline and Mariana islands in the central Pacific toward the Philippines. The strategy followed was to bypass the islands strongly held by the Japanese and to capture the islands that were weakly held in order to establish bases

from which to strike. The capture of Guam and other islands in the Marianas brought Admiral Nimitz and the Allied fleet within bombing distance of Japan and striking distance of the heavily held Philippines.

After the taking of the Philippines in March of 1945, Allied superiority of the seas was established. This, combined with the success of campaigns in China, Burma and India, began to turn the tide in the Allied favor against Japan. Using the islands of Iwo Jima and Okinawa, the raids against the Japanese homeland were stepped up, culminating in the dropping of two atomic bombs and the Japanese signing of surrender on September 2, 1945.

Nuclear testing.

Since 1945, at least one nuclear test has taken place in the south Pacific each year, and over 250 nuclear devices have been tested by the combined programs of the United States, Great Britain and France. Testing by the United States and Great Britain ended in 1963, but testing by the French only ended in 1996, under growing protests by the inhabitants of French Polynesia. The atolls of Moruroa and Fangataufa in French Polynesia were ceded to France, however, by the Tahitian Territorial Assembly in 1964, so even if French Polynesia should become independent, these areas would still be accessible for nuclear testing if France chose to do so.

Recent trends.

The most influential countries in this region are Australia and New Zealand, both members of the Commonwealth of Nations, formerly known as the British Commonwealth. Despite their European heritage, which is shared to varying degrees by many of the neighboring islands formerly held as European colonies, the countries of Australasia are leaning toward closer ties to Asia rather than Western nations. The main reasons for this shift in alliance are the rise of Asian economies and the demise of the Soviet Union. Asia has become the main market for exports (chiefly natural resources) as Great Britain and the United States face economic troubles.

Politically, the end of the Cold War has also changed the tenor of the region. While the Cold War remained a major factor in world politics, the United States saw its alliance with Australia and New Zealand as strategically important. Treaties among the countries (referred to as ANZUS), already weakened by New Zealand's refusal to accept any warship unwilling to declare itself free of nuclear weapons, became less vital with the elimination of the Soviet Union. While ties between Australasia and Western nations remain close, closer relations with Asia also seem inevitable.

As Asia moves toward the 21st century, its leaders have become increasingly aware that its future is intertwined with that of the world. It is widely believed that only through international cooperation, especially on political and economic levels, will the nations of Asia and Australasia be able to meet the challenges to come.

As with other Third-World peoples, the people of the south Pacific have experienced a cultural reawakening in recent decades. The exploration of traditional art, mythology, language, music, dance, and ritual has resulted in the recovery of a great sense of national pride. The fleet of canoes, which was constructed and sailed by traditional methods between the southern islands and Hawaii is part of this renaissance. Pupu Arioi, in French Polynesia, is a small but dedicated organization that focuses on teaching children about their Polynesian heritage.

A look at the list of dependencies at the end of this volume will reveal that there are more dependencies in this area than in any other part of the world. Today, there is a growing friction in the area caused by the desire of many of these island nations for independence in a setting in which that is not economic feasible and in which most of the islands are not able to survive without subsidies from developed countries. Many of the islands are beset by internal economic difficulties that make it difficult to concentrate on developing potential sources for income. These will be some of the tensions that are carried into the 21st century as the island nations strive to take their places in a world economy.

Countries of Australia and Oceania

Australia

Official name: *Commonwealth of Australia*

Area: *2,967,124 sq. mi., 7,686,850 sq. km*

Type of government: *Federal parliamentary*

Population: *19,547,000*

Capital: *Canberra (Pop., 312,000)*

Largest city: *Sydney (Pop., metro. area, 3,948,000)*

Languages: *English (official), indigenous dialects*

Literacy: *100%*

Currency: *Dollar*

Per capita GDP: *$27,000 (Rank: 13th)*

The land. The Commonwealth of Australia is composed of six states and two mainland territories. The states are New South Wales, Queensland, South Australia, Tasmania, Victoria, and Western Australia. The two internal territories are the Northern Territory and the Australian Capital Territory.

Australia's external territories and colonies are mostly former British colonies. They include Christmas Island and the Cocos (Keeling) Islands, both once incorporated in the British colony of Singapore; Norfolk Island, an old British penal colony that was inhabited in 1856 by descendants of the mutineers of the HMS *Bounty;* Heard and McDonald islands; Ashmore and Cartier islands; Coral Sea Island Territory; and the Australian Antarctic Territory.

Australia contains some of the oldest and most stable portions of Earth's surface. It may once have formed part of an ancient continent known as Gondwanaland, also consisting of Africa, parts of the Indian subcontinent, and Brazil.

Regions. Australia has three main land regions—the Western Plateau, Central Lowlands, and Eastern Highlands. The Western Plateau occupies approximately the western half of the continent. It has an average elevation of about 1,200 feet above sea level. It is mostly flat but has some isolated mountain ranges, such as the Macdonnell and Musgrave Ranges in the eastern part of the plateau, which rise to almost 5,000 feet above sea level, and the Hamersley Range in the northwest. The central portion of the plateau is mostly desert.

The Central Lowlands, lying east of the Western Plateau, has an aver-age elevation of about 500 feet, although Lake Eyre, in the southern part of the region, lies about 40 feet below sea level. Marine sediments, laid down about 50 million years ago, cover much of the region.

Sedimentary rocks in the northern part of the Central Lowlands form the Great Artesian Basin, an important source of underground water in an area that receives very little rain. The Murray-Darling-Murrumbidgee Basin, Australia's most extensive river system, occupies the southeastern portion of the lowlands.

The Eastern Highlands, sometimes known as the Great Dividing Range, is a collection of many mountain ranges and plateaus that run parallel to Australia's east coast. Among the ranges are the Australian Alps, Hunter Mountains, Blue Mountains, Liverpool Range, and Darling Downs. Mount Kosciusko, which rises more than 7,300 feet in the Australian Alps, is Australia's highest peak.

The island of Tasmania, about 130 miles from the Australian mainland, contains an extension of the Eastern Highlands. The highlands form a central plateau containing many natural lakes.

The Great Barrier Reef, a collection of islands, cays, and reefs, stretches for some 1,250 miles along the northern half of the east coast. Parts of the reef are formed from the same rocks as the mainland; others consist of the skeletons of millions of tiny coral polyps that have solidified into reefs and islands.

Climate. Australia's winter season extends from June to August, and summer from December to February. Winters are mild almost everywhere; summers are warm to hot.

The interior parts of the Central Lowlands and Western Plateau are extremely arid, and Lake Eyre is usually completely

AUSTRALIA is home to many animals, such as this koala, that are found nowhere else in the world.

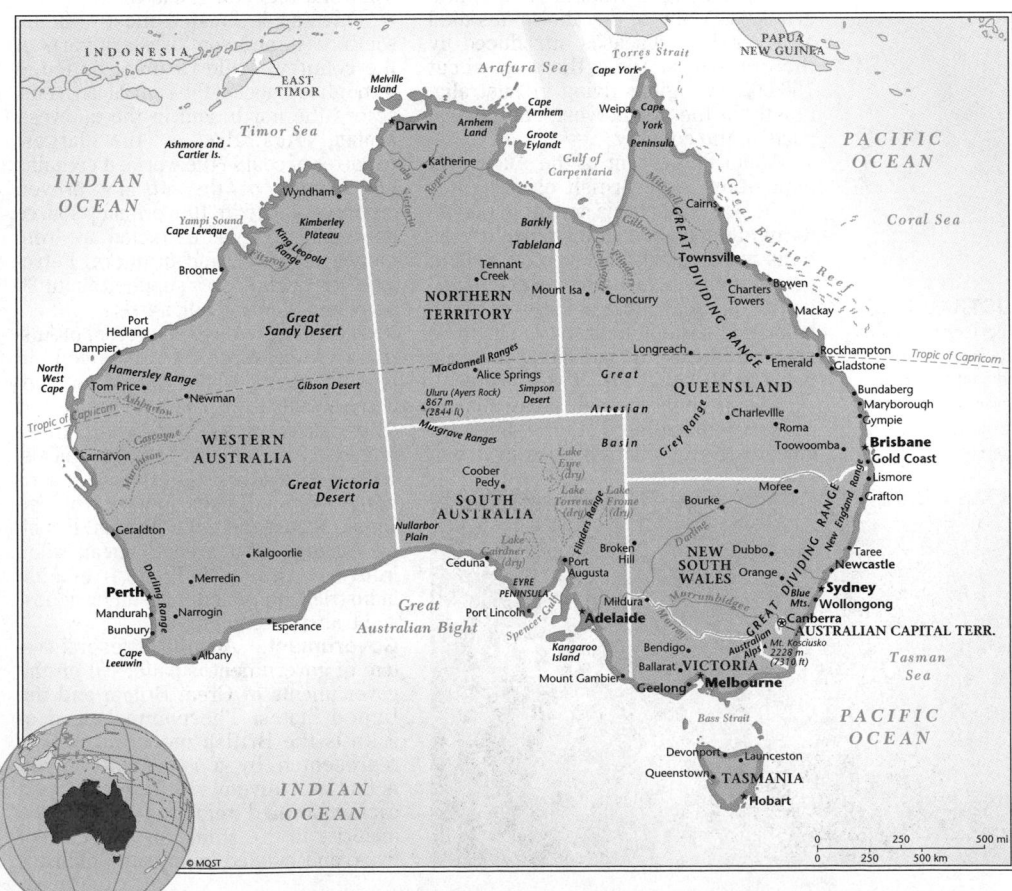

dry. The northern coastal region receives heavy seasonal rainfall. Australia's southwestern corner receives winter rain. The only area to receive year-round rain is the southeastern corner. Rainfall over most of the interior averages less than 10 inches a year, creating constant concern over drought.
Plant life. Because of Australia's dryness, forests are found only in the southwest and along the eastern and northern coasts. Almost half the continent is covered with semidesert scrub or sand dunes. Another large portion has mixed grass and tree cover.

Australia's dryness, coupled with the continent's long isolation from the rest of the world, has led to the development of many unique species of plants and animals. Typically Australian are the eucalyptus and acacia types of plants, which together account for more than a thousand different species. These plants form the dominant nongrass vegetation.
Animal life. The continent is famous for its distinctive animal life, especially the platypus, kangaroo, wallaby, and koala. Rabbits, although not native to Australia, are so numerous that they have been labeled pests.

The kookaburra, emu, Australian lyrebird, and black swan are among the more famous of some 650 species of birds found in Australia.
The people. When the first European settlers arrived in Australia in the late 1700s, they found an estimated 300,000 aborigines living there. The aborigines are related to small groups of people living in other areas of southern Asia. Many of the aborigines died as a result of diseases introduced by the Europeans. Today there are about 150,000 aborigines living in Australia, mostly in the north, west, and central parts of the country.

About 95 percent of the Australian population is of British origin. After World War II Australia sought to double its immigration rate. Immigration restrictions were eased and over 2.5 million people came to Australia between 1947 and 1975, causing the native-born population composition to drop from 90 to 80 percent. The overall population increase between 1970 and 1976 was 1.5 percent.

The population of Australia is unevenly distributed. Eighty-five percent of the population lives in urban

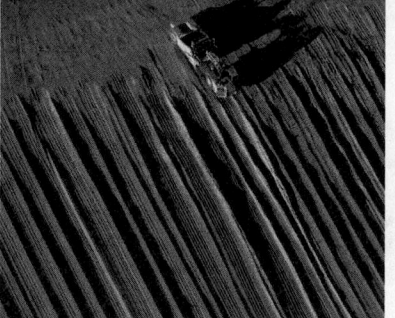

MINING is one of Australia's most important industries. Seen here is a rutile mine.

areas that are, for the most part, on or near the coast. The extremely arid interior of the continent has almost no permanent population.

Sydney, the capital of New South Wales, is the largest of Australia's cities and an important economic center. Melbourne, the capital and largest city of Victoria, is also a major economic center. Canberra, the national capital, is located in the Australian Capital Territory.
Economy. The Australian economy traditionally has been heavily dependent on agriculture and on the processing of raw materials. In recent decades, however, there has been a shift toward the manufacturing and service industries. Together they represent about 93 percent of employment.
Agriculture. Even though agriculture now employs only about 6 percent of the Australian population, and produces only about 5 percent of the nation's gross domestic product (GDP), it still accounts for over 40 percent of export earnings. The primary agricultural products are wheat and other grains, meat, wool, fruits and vegetables, and wine.

Farming is located mostly in the south, east, and southwestern parts of the country, while ranching is found throughout most of the central lowlands, across the north, and in the far west.
Mining. Australia is the largest exporter of coal in the world; it contains one-quarter of the world's proven reserves of bauxite (the primary source of aluminum). Also extracted are iron, nickel, lead, tin, and uranium. Petroleum production now supplies about 80 percent of domestic oil needs.
Manufacturing. About 20 percent of Australia's workforce is employed in manufacturing. Major industrial products include transport equipment and other machinery, food products, textiles, processed metals, and petro-chemicals.
Trade. Australia's biggest trading partner is, by far, Japan, followed by the United States and Great Britain. Principal exports include coal, wheat, wool, iron ore, and beef. Imports include industrial equipment, consumer goods, and transport equipment.
Government. Australia's federal system of government is patterned on the governments of Great Britain and the United States. The nominal head of state is the British monarch, who is represented by a governor-general. Actual executive power is wielded by a cabinet, formed from the party with the majority in the House of Representatives, and headed by a prime minister

responsible to Parliament.

Parliament has two houses—the 76-member Senate, with members elected to six-year terms, and the 150-member House of Representatives, popularly elected to three-year terms.

Each of Australia's six states has its own parliament and premier to deal with local matters. The organization of the state parliaments varies from state to state. The Northern Territory is self-governing, and the Australian Capital Territory is administered by the federal government.

Australia is a member of the Commonwealth of Nations, and close ties are maintained with Britain and other Commonwealth countries. Australia is also a member of the Colombo Plan in Asia and the Organization for Economic Cooperation and Development (OECD); it plays an active role in the United Nations. Australia works in cooperation with the European Union (EU), as, in addition to sharing many common views, the EU is Australia's largest trading partner and source of foreign investment.
History. The original settlers of Australia, the aborigines, arrived on the continent about 12,000 years ago from Southeast Asia. These people lived at an extremely primitive level, with very little in the way of material culture, but with a highly developed ability to survive in a hostile natural environment.

In the 1600s Portuguese, Spanish, and Dutch navigators explored the southern hemisphere. In 1606 a Spanish commander, Luis Vaez de Torres, sailed through the strait that now bears his name, off the northeastern tip of the mainland. In the same year Willem Jansz explored the region around the Gulf of Carpentaria.

Abel Tasman discovered the island of Tasmania in 1642. In 1770 Captain James Cook made extensive explorations of the continent's east coast, and later claimed it for England.
Settlement. Britain made the first settlement in Australia in 1788, when Arthur Phillip led 1030 people (including 726 convicts) to Port Jackson, which eventually became the great city of Sydney. Britain established a second colony in 1803–1804 in Tasmania.

The early history of the settlements was dominated by the convict system, and by the struggle of the free settlers to establish their rights as Englishmen. The colony's first economic objective was agricultural self-sufficiency, and when a convict's time expired, he was encouraged to set up a small farm.

By 1796 Merino sheep had been introduced into the colony; wool soon became an extremely important industry. The dynamic wool industry spread rapidly after the 1820s and provided an export commodity that has since been basic to the Australian economy.

Because sheep ranching requires broad fields and a small workforce, each colony tended to develop a single urban center, usually near a port. In 1829 settlers founded Perth, in Western Australia; in 1835, Melbourne, in the Port Phillip

district of what was then New South Wales; and in 1836, Adelaide, in South Australia. Except for Western Australia, these new colonies were for free men only.

The early 1800s were also marked by the further efforts of former convicts to establish their civil rights and of the colonies to achieve self-government. Many Australians and Englishmen strongly attacked the convict system on the grounds that it morally damaged Australian society, had ceased to be a punishment for English criminals, did not rehabilitate prisoners, and unfairly competed with free labor. Britain ceased sending convicts to New South Wales in 1840, to Tasmania in 1853, and to Western Australia in 1868.

Self-rule. Progress toward self-rule developed as the number of free colonists grew. In 1850 the British Parliament passed the Australian Colonies Government Act, which allowed the Australian colonies to organize legislatures. The act also formed the Port Phillip district of New South Wales into the separate colony of Victoria, and provided for the separation of Queensland from New South Wales in 1859. Western Australia waited until 1890 for responsible government, however.

In 1851 gold was discovered in eastern Australia, and the ensuing gold rush brought a rapid rise in the population, from some 400,000 in 1850 to 1,146,000 in 1860.

Also in the 1890s, in the midst of a worldwide financial depression, a serious shipping, shearing, and mining strike erupted in Australia. The effects of the strike were intensified by a severe drought, which reduced the numbers of sheep and cattle. At that time trade unions grew in importance, and the first politically-oriented labor parties emerged.

Commonwealth. In 1897–1898, a convention met to draft a federal constitution. In 1900 Britain accepted a federal framework for Australia, and the Commonwealth of Australia came into being on January 1, 1901.

A significant development between 1901 and the outbreak of World War I was the impact of the Labour Party, organized in 1891. Trade unions saw the need for political support for social welfare legislation, but the Labour Party, representing the unions, entered federal politics reluctantly. It felt the best prospects for success lay in influencing the state governments.

In 1902 the Labour Party allied itself with Alfred Deakin, who became prime minister. Labour supported a white Australia position: they wanted to keep out Asians, whom they feared as cheap labor.

At the outbreak of World War I, Australia was weak in manufacturing. After foodstuffs and raw materials, its major export for war was manpower. Of a total population of about 4 million people, Australia mobilized some 400,000 men and sent 332,000 volunteers overseas.

In 1915 William Morris Hughes, leader of the Labour Party, became prime minister. Hughes advocated conscription for overseas service, but a popular referendum twice defeated his attempts. A rift developed within the party following the defeats. Hughes broke from the Labour Party and organized a National War Government. His followers formed the Nationalist Party in opposition to the Labour Party.

Interwar era. After the war, the Commonwealth came under the rule of a coalition of the Nationalists and a new group, the Country Party. The Country Party was formed in 1918 by farmers who felt that rural areas were not adequately represented.

With war production over, the government emphasized land industries, but the markets failed. There was a postwar recession, exports declined, and tremendous imports left companies without means to finance purchases. The rural industries, except for wool, had to be supported by high, government-fixed domestic prices.

The worldwide Depression of the 1930s hit Australia hard because of the sharp drop in prices for its exports. Former Nationalist and Labour Party members formed the United Australia Party to meet the results of the Depression with sound finance.

World War II. At the onset of war in Europe in 1939, Australian troops were sent to fight Axis forces in the Middle East. However, following the Japanese attack on Pearl Harbor, Hawaii, in 1941, and then the fall of Singapore and the bombing of Darwin in 1942, troops were recalled from the Middle East to defend home territory. As military reverses forced Great Britain to reduce its role in the defense of Australia, the Australian government fostered closer ties with the United States. Australian forces were involved in the Battle of the Coral Sea and in land battles in New Guinea and Borneo.

After 1945. The war had provided a big boon to industrialization, helping to lift Australia out of the Depression of the 1930s. In 1941 Australia had elected a Labour government, and it enacted a series of important social welfare programs. It also introduced a program of aid to immigrants, prompting a huge influx from Europe.

In 1949 a coalition of the Liberal and Country parties, led by Robert Menzies, defeated the Labour Party in a national election. Menzies emphasized free enterprise and opposition to communism. One consequence of the election of Menzies was the further strengthening of ties with the United States. Australia joined with New Zealand and the United States to form the ANZUS defensive alliance, and sent troops to fight alongside United Nations forces in Korea and United States forces in Vietnam.

During the decades following the end of World War II, Australia has experienced rapid economic expansion. The discovery of important deposits of metals, coal, and petroleum boosted manufacturing growth and introduced a period of prosperity.

The Liberal-Country coalition remained in power under five successive prime ministers. In 1972, however, the Labour Party attained the majority in the House of Representatives but failed in the Senate. Prime Minister Gough Whitlam's attempts to pass legislation were often balked by the Senate. In 1975 the Senate refused to approve the budget, hoping to force an election. When Whitlam refused to call one, the governor-general, in an unprecedented move, dismissed him, and called for new elections.

The Liberal Party, led by Malcolm Fraser, won the subsequent election. The economic situation in the late 1970s and early 1980s was marked by high unemployment and inflation, low export prices, and ineffective management by Fraser.

In 1983 elections the Liberals were turned out of office by the Labour Party, led by Robert Hawke. Hawke sought consensus between business and labor, reduced expenditures, and increased exports. In 1991 he was succeeded by Paul Keating, who led Labour to a fourth straight victory in 1993 despite a continuing recession. John Winston Howard has been prime minister since 1996. A referendum to change Australia's status from a commonwealth headed by Britain's monarch to an independent republic was defeated in 1999.

labor
US

labour
Brit.

emphasized
US

emphasised
Brit.

25 Australia and Oceania

THE SYDNEY OPERA HOUSE, standing on a peninsula in Sydney Harbor, is a famous city landmark.

Fiji

Official name: *Republic of the Fiji Islands*
Area: *7,052 sq. mi., 18,270 sq. km*
Type of government: *Republic*
Population: *856,000*
Capital and largest city: *Suva (on Viti Levu) (Pop., 92,000)*
Languages: *English (official), Fijian, Hindustani*
Literacy: *93%;* **Currency:** *Dollar*
Per capita GDP: *$5,200 (Rank: 83rd)*

The land and people. Fiji consists of two large islands, Viti Levu and Vanua Levu, and many islets and atolls. The islands are coral-rimmed and consist primarily of densely forested volcanic mountains etched by rapidly flowing rivers. The climate is tropical, with high year-round temperature and humidity.

Nearly three-quarters of the people live on Viti Levu. The population is divided between Fijians, a Melanesian people, and people of Indian origin. There are also small groups of Europeans and Chinese. English is the official language.

Economy. The islands have forest resources, gold and copper deposits, and rich farmland in river deltas. Agriculture is the mainstay of the economy, with fruits, sugar cane, coconuts, cacao, and rice the chief commercial crops. Timber milling, gold mining, and the processing of sugar and copra are the chief industries. Tourism is an important source of income.

Agricultural products are the main exports, and manufactured goods, fuels, and equipment are imported. Great Britain, Australia, and Japan are the islands' major trading partners.

laborers
US

labourers
Brit.

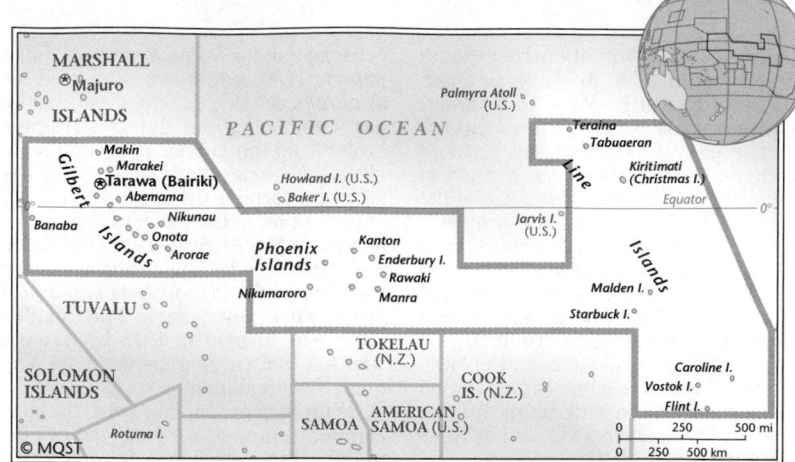

Government. Until 1987, when a coup toppled the government, Fiji was a parliamentary democracy whose head of state was the British monarch. A new constitution, adopted in 1990, provides for a bicameral parliament.

History. Little is known of the islands before they were visited in the 1600s by the Dutch. They were virtually ignored by Europeans until the 1700s, when traders came in search of sandalwood and coconut products. The traders were followed by Christian missionaries.

Tribal warfare raged in the mid-1800s, and in 1874 the tribal chiefs ceded power to Great Britain. Plantations were established in the late 1800s, and Indian laborers were imported to work them. The economy prospered on farming and forestry. The Indians soon grew to be a majority of the population, and disputes between the Indians and Melanesians continued into the 1900s. In 1966 a constitution came into effect that divided representation between the Indians and Melanesians.

In 1987, following an election that would increase the influence of the Indian majority, a coup removed the government. The coup leader, Sitiveni Rabuka, a Melanesian army officer, declared Fiji a republic and promised a new constitution that would guarantee Melanesian control of the government. Free elections in 1999 were followed by a coup in 2000.

Kiribati

Official name: *Republic of Kiribati*
Area: *277 sq. mi., 717 sq. km*
Type of government: *Republic*
Population: *96,000*
Capital: *Tarawa (Pop., metro. area, 25,000)*
Languages: *English (official), Gilbertese*
Literacy: *20%*
Currency: *Australian dollar*
Per capita GDP: *$840 (Rank: 177th)*

The land and people. Kiribati is scattered across more than 2 million square miles of the west central Pacific. It consists of four groups of atolls, including the sixteen Gilbert Islands, eight Phoenix Islands, eight Line Islands (one group of five and another group of three), and Banaba, or Ocean Island.

All of the islands are low-lying coral atolls, except Banaba, which is of volcanic origin with a rugged, mountainous terrain. The islands' climate is hot and humid, with rainfall ranging from 40 to 120 inches annually.

Most of the people of Kiribati are Micronesian, but there is also a small minority of Polynesians. Over 90 percent of the population live on the Gilbert Islands, and about one-third on the single island of Tarawa. The Phoenix Islands are not permanently inhabited.

FAMILY TIES are extremely strong among the people of Polynesia.

Economy. Banaba once had rich phosphate deposits, the mining of which was the economic mainstay of the islands until deposits were depleted in 1980. Since then Kiribati has been faced with the challenge of developing a diversified economy. Coconuts are grown, and copra is the main export. Kiribati also exports fish and fish products and receives income from the sale of the right to fish in its waters.

Government. The head of both state and government is the president. The legislature of the republic is a unicameral House of Assembly. It has 39 elected members and 3 others.

History. The first Europeans to sight the islands may have been Spanish sailors in the 1500s, but most were discovered in the late 1700s and early 1800s by British seamen.

Great Britain proclaimed the Gilbert and Ellice islands a protectorate in 1888 and added Ocean Island in 1900. At the request of the inhabitants, it annexed the islands as a colony in 1916. The other islands were added to the colony between 1916 and 1938. British settlers established copra plantations, and the British government has used the islands as cable stations, ports, and radar stations.

The Gilbert Islands were the scene of heavy fighting in World War II. After the war, efforts were made to expand the economy of the islands, to extend self-government, and to relieve population pressure on the crowded islands.

In 1975 the Ellice Islands severed ties with the territory and became a separate territory under the name Tuvalu, which is now independent.

Kiribati became an independent republic on July 12, 1979. Banaba has actively sought separation since the inception of the new republic.

Marshall Islands

Official name: *Republic of the Marshall Islands*
Area: *70 sq. mi., 181 sq. km*
Type of government: *Constitutional*
Population: *55,000*
Capital: *Majuro (Pop., 18,000)*
Languages: *English, Marshallese (both official), Japanese*
Literacy: *94%*
Currency: *U.S. dollar*
Per capita GDP: *$1,600 (Rank: 146th)*

The land and people. The Marshall Islands are a group of 34 islands in the Pacific Ocean east of the Philippines. The islands consist of two roughly parallel chains of coral atolls: the Ratak chain, with 16 atolls, and the Ralik chain, with 18 atolls. The most populous atolls are Kwajalein and Majuro.

The population is Micronesian. Most of the population is Christian, principally Protestant.

Economy. The majority of the Marshall islanders are subsistence farmers and fishermen. The principal crops are coconut, taro, yams, breadfruit, and vegetables. Most of the small amount of industry is involved in processing the coconut and fish harvests.

Fish products, copra, and coconut oil are the principal exports. Imports include food, machinery, and textiles. Rent for the U.S. missile tracking base

on Kwajalein Atoll and aid from the United States are important contributions to the economy.

Government. The head of state is the president, who is elected by the 33-member legislative Nitijela from among its members. The members of the Nitijela are elected to 4-year terms. A 12-member Council of Iroij (traditional chiefs) advises the president and cabinet.

History. The Marshall Islands were probably originally settled from islands to the west and south. They were first sighted by Europeans in the 16th century, when the Spanish explored the region. However, little value was placed on the islands, and no formal claim by a European power was established until 1886, when Spain and Britain recognized German control over the islands.

At the beginning of World War I, Japan took control of the Marshalls from Germany, and in 1920 obtained a League of Nations mandate to administer the islands. The Marshall Islands, in particular Kwajalein Atoll, saw heavy fighting during World War II.

After the war, the islands were administered by the United States under a United Nations mandate as part of the Trust Territory of the Pacific. From 1946 to 1958 the United States used the Bikini and Enewetak atolls as testing sites for nuclear weapons.

After a failed attempt to unite all of the Trust Territory into one independent nation, the Marshall Islands became the Republic of the Marshall Islands in 1979. The islands became a sovereign nation in 1986 when a Compact of Free Association took effect. The compact leaves defense and foreign policy matters in the control of the United States.

Micronesia, Federated States of

Official name: *Federated States of Micronesia*
Area: *271 sq. mi., 702 sq. km*
Type of government: *Constitutional*
Population: *136,000*
Capital: *Palikir (Pop., 7,000)*
Languages: *English, indigenous dialects*
Literacy: *89%*
Currency: *U.S. dollar*
Per capita GDP: *$2,000 (Rank: 135th)*

The land and people. The Federated States of Micronesia comprises 607 islands spread across the southern Pacific Ocean. Consisting of most of the Caroline Island chain, the Federated States is about 2,000 miles across, from Yap Island in the west to Kosrae Island in the east.

The islands are of coral and volcanic origin. The islands of Yap and Truk, and the islands Kosrae and Ponape, are the most densely settled parts of the nation.

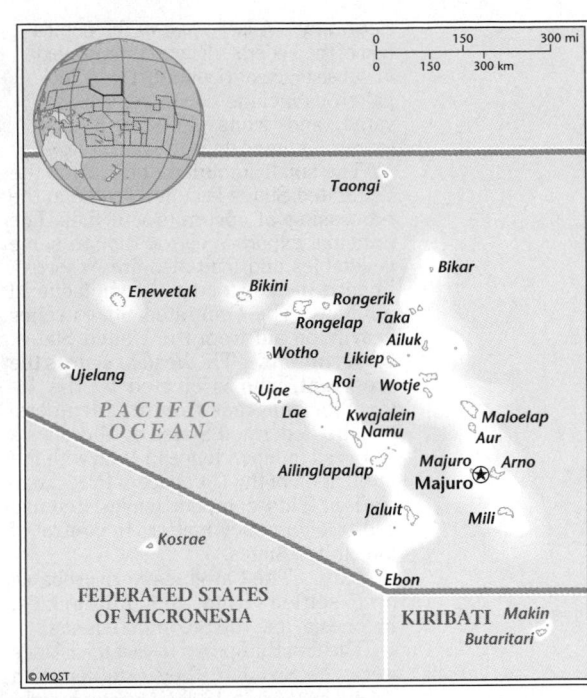

The Yap group has four large, hilly islands and seven smaller islands. The Truk island group consists of eleven islands encircled by a coral reef.

Most of the population of the Federated States is Micronesian. However, the islands are culturally and linguistically diverse. There are eight major indigenous languages spoken in the Federated States, although English is the official language.

The Federated States attained independence in 1986 under a Compact of Free Association with the U.S.

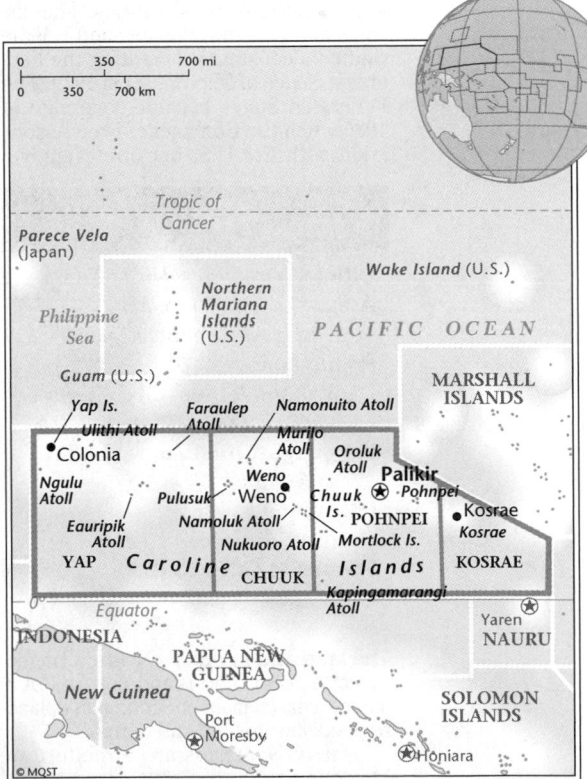

Economy. A large part of the population of the Federated States is employed in subsistence agriculture. The principal crops include coconuts, cassava, yams, and fruits. Fishing is also extremely important to the economy.

The small amount of industry in the Federated States is concentrated in the processing of coconuts and fish. The principal export is copra, though some vegetables and fruit also are exported. Imports include food and manufactured products. The Federated States relies heavily on aid from the United States.

Government. The head of state is the president, who is elected by the 14-member congress from its members.

The Federated States of Micronesia achieved independence in 1986 with the ratification of the Compact of Free Association. This compact leaves defense and foreign policy matters in control of the United States.

History. The Carolines were probably first settled from the Philippines, Indonesia, and the Solomon Islands.

The first Europeans to visit the islands were the Spanish; they established a colony in 1668. In 1899 Germany bought the Carolines from Spain and held them until World War I. Japan received a League of Nations mandate over the islands in 1920.

During World War II the islands saw heavy fighting between U.S. and Japanese forces. In 1947 the United Nations joined the Caroline, Northern Mariana, and Marshall islands as the Trust Territory of the Pacific Islands, under U.S. administration.

An attempt to create a constitution to unite the territory pointed up regional differences and led to its division into four separate political entities. The districts of Yap, Truk, Ponape, and Kosrae ratified a constitution creating the Federated States of Micronesia in 1979. The Federated States became sovereign in 1986 when the Compact of Free Association with the U.S. became effective.

Nauru

Official name: *Republic of Nauru*
Area: *8 sq. mi., 21 sq. km*
Type of government: *Republic*
Population: *12,000*
Capital and largest city: *Yaren*
    (Pop. 4,000)
Languages: *Nauruan (official),*
    English
Literacy: *99%*
Currency: *Australian dollar*
Per capita GDP: *$5,000*
    (Rank: 86th)

The land and people. Nauru is ringed by coral reefs. The island consists of a narrow coastal plain encircling an upland region. Nauru is hot and humid.

Native Nauruans are a mixture of Micronesian and Polynesian stock.

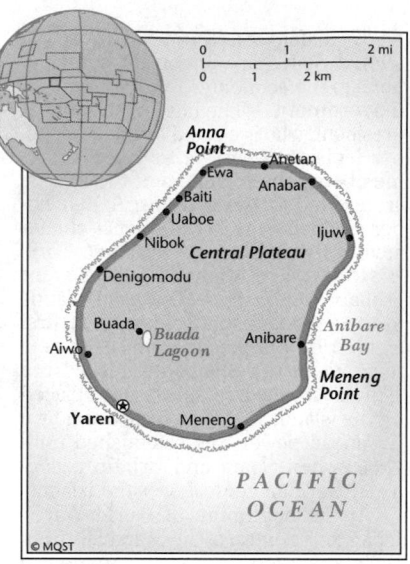

Most are Christian. Chinese and other foreign workers and European administrators and managers make up about half the population.

Economy. The island's economy is almost totally dependent on phosphate mining, although coconuts and other fruits and a few vegetables are raised on the coastal plain. The production of phosphates is Nauru's chief industry, and the island is one of the world's leading producers of phosphate rock, exporting about 2 million metric tons a year. The Nauruans took control of the phosphate industry from the British Phosphate Corporation in 1970. The Nauruan people now enjoy one of the world's highest standards of living.

Phosphates are the only exports, and food, machinery, and consumer goods are imported. Most trade is with Australia, New Zealand, Japan, and Britain. Efforts are currently under way to diversify the economy in preparation for the predicted depletion of the phosphate deposits in the 1990s.

Government. Nauru's government is headed by a president, who is chosen by a popularly elected legislature from among its members. The legislature's 18 members are elected to 3-year terms.

History. Nauru was discovered in 1798 by a British explorer, but for over a century it remained a beachcombers' refuge and a minor source of copra. In 1888 possession passed to Germany.

In 1900 Nauru was found to be rich in phosphate rock, the basis of a fertilizer then coming into extensive use in Australia and New Zealand. By agreement with the Germans, phosphate mining was undertaken by an Australian-based British company.

After World War I, in 1919, Nauru was entrusted to Great Britain, but Australia administered economic and political affairs. Phosphate production was shared by Australia, New Zealand, and Great Britain. Occupied by the Japanese in World War II, the island was reoccupied in 1945 by Australian troops.

Following the war, it became a UN trust territory under joint Australian, British, and New Zealand authority, with Australia administering the island.

In 1966 the UN General Assembly recommended that the trustee nations make the island habitable again when the phosphate is depleted by replacing all soil that had been removed with the rock. The island became an independent nation on January 31, 1968.

Much of the 1980s was marked by instability as no party was able to gain a clear majority in parliament until 1987. Nauru joined the UN in 1999.

New Zealand

Official name: *New Zealand*
Area: *103,710 sq. mi.,*
    268,680 sq. km
Type of government:
    Parliamentary democracy
Population: *3,908,000*
Capital: *Wellington*
    (Pop., 164,000)
Largest city: *Auckland*
    (Pop., 368,000)
Languages: *English, Maori*
Literacy: *99%*
Currency: *Dollar*
Per capita GDP: *$19,500*
    (Rank: 27th)

The land. New Zealand is made up of two main islands, North Island and South Island, and several smaller islands, including Stewart Island and the Chatham Islands.

New Zealand is a relatively mountainous country. The Southern Alps extend along the length of South Island, and there are 28 peaks with elevations over 10,000 feet above sea level. The highest peak, reaching an elevation of 12,349 feet, is Mt. Cook, in the west-central part of South Island. The eastern part of South Island contains several areas of level land at fairly low elevations, notably the Canterbury and Southland plains. Cook Strait separates North Island from South Island.

North Island has four volcanic peaks with elevations of over 6,000 feet, the highest of which is Ruapehu, with an elevation of 9,175 feet. Among the larger lowland regions of North Island are the Waikato-Thames Plain and the Manawatu-Horowhenua Coastal Plain.

There are many rivers on the islands, including the Waikato, Wanganui, and Rangitaiki on North Island, and the Waitaki, Oreti, and Clutha on South Island.

Climate. New Zealand has a damp, mild climate, which is strongly influenced by the small size of the islands in relation to the vastness of the surrounding ocean. The waters surrounding the country tend to moderate its temperatures, so that the winters are relatively mild and the summers comparatively cool.

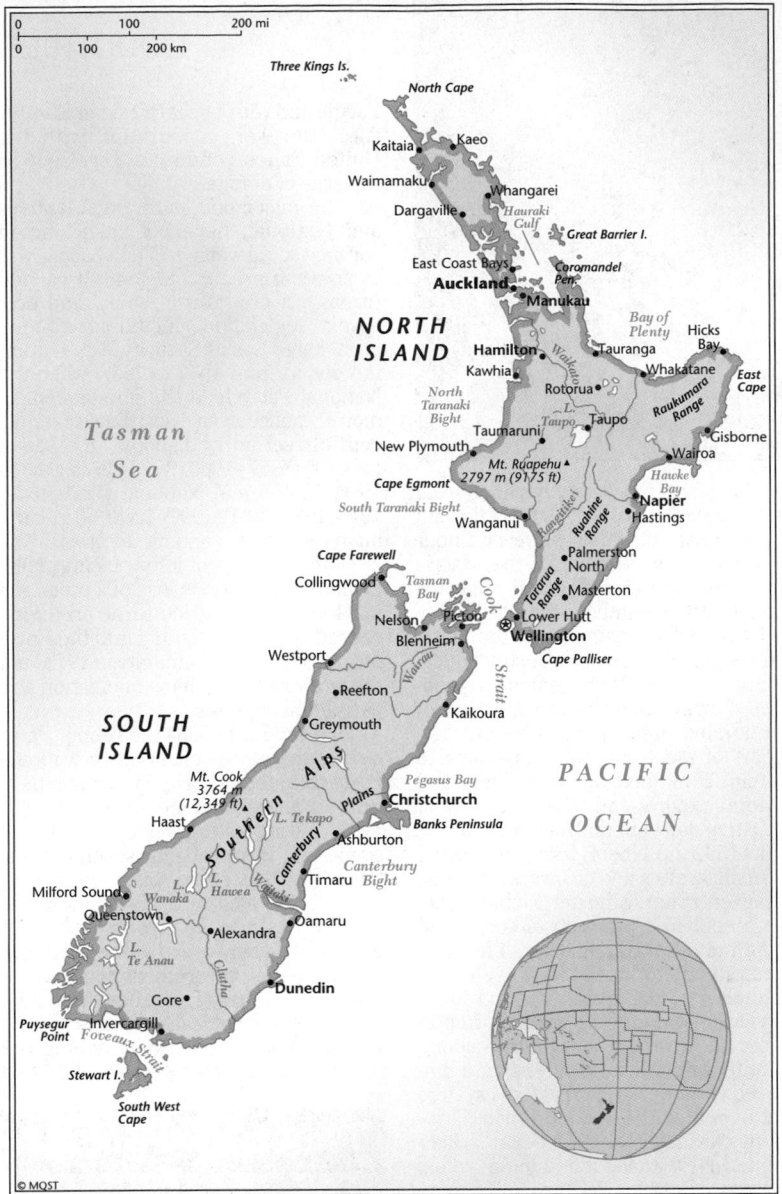

vegetables are grown mainly on North Island and in the north of South Island.
Mining and manufacturing. New Zealand is not an important mining country, but enough coal is mined to meet local needs in most years and some gold is produced. Because of a lack of major mineral resources and a limited home market, New Zealand did not develop a great number of manufacturing industries in the past. Today, however, in an attempt to diversify its economy, New Zealand is building up the manufacturing sector. Increased steel and aluminum manufacturing has been particularly significant. Most manufacturing is still concerned with the processing of dairy products, the canning and freezing of vegetables, and leather and wool preparation.

Industrialization has called for increased energy sources. The Maui offshore gas field was discovered in 1969, and recently an oil refinery was built in the country. Hydroelectric power provides almost 80 percent of the country's electricity needs.

Auckland is the principal manufacturing center, with woodworking, textile, brewing, and light engineering plants. Both Auckland and Christchurch have automobile assembly plants that use some components of New Zealand manufacture.
Trade. New Zealand's trade structure has changed drastically since the 1950s. Great Britain, which for many years accounted for approximately 60 percent of New Zealand's exports and imports, is now involved in less than 20 percent. On the other hand, trade with the United States and Australia has increased greatly, and trade with Japan has gone from practically zero to about 15 percent of the country's total.

There has also been a change in the products exported, with agricultural products dropping from 95 to 60 percent of the total and manufactured goods, including unwrought aluminum, rising to approximately 40 percent. The major exports, however, are still meat, dairy products, and wool. Principal imports are fuels, chemicals, food, machinery, and other manufactured goods.

aluminum
US
aluminium
Brit.
center
US
centre
Brit.

THE SPECTACULAR SCENERY of the New Zealand Alps

Only a small area of South Island receives less than 20 inches of rain a year, whereas many parts of both North and South islands receive over 50 inches of rain a year. The greatest rainfall occurs in the western part of South Island, where some areas receive over 200 inches a year.
Dependencies. New Zealand is responsible for several former British colonies. Tokelau has been one of New Zealand's overseas territories since 1949. Ross Dependency in Antarctica attained the same status in 1923. New Zealand is responsible for the external affairs and defense of its two self-governing territories, the Cook Islands, self-governing since 1965, and Niue Island, self governing since 1974.
The people. About 85 percent of New Zealanders are of British descent. A small percentage of New Zealanders are descended from other European settlers. The Maori, a people of Polynesian stock, migrated to New Zealand from the Pacific islands beginning in the 900s. Maoris now make up about 9 percent of the population.

About three-quarters of the people live on North Island. Eighty-four percent of New Zealanders are urban dwellers, and two cities, Auckland and Wellington, along with their suburbs, account for over one-third of the population.
Economy. New Zealand is primarily an agricultural country. At one time all of North Island and most of South Island were forested. In the 1800s European settlers cleared large areas to establish farms, and today only about 20 percent of New Zealand is forested.
Agriculture. The country's mild climate and its grasslands provide excellent conditions for pastoral industries, and agri-culture employs about 10 percent of the population. Sheep are raised in most parts of the country, and New Zealand is one of the world's largest exporters of wool. Dairying is also an important agricultural industry in New Zealand. Most of the dairying is confined to North Island. The principal products are butter and cheese.

On South Island, wheat, oats, barley, and turnips are grown. Fruits and

NEW ZEALAND is one of the world's largest exporters of wool.

Government. New Zealand has a parliamentary system of government. The head of state is the British monarch, who is represented in New Zealand by a governor-general. Actual executive power is vested in a prime minister and a cabinet responsible to the legislature. Legislative power is held by a 120-member House of Representatives. House members are popularly elected to 3-year terms.

History. The Maori migrated to New Zealand between the 900s and 1300s. In 1642 the Dutch navigator Abel Tasman sighted the islands of New Zealand, but they were not visited by Europeans again until 1769, when Captain James Cook accurately charted the coasts.

Only after European settlement in Australia in the late 1700s and early 1800s did Europeans develop an interest in New Zealand. From the 1790s to the 1840s, Europeans exploited New Zealand's timber, seals, whales, and flax and established a port of call at the Bay of Islands, on North Island.

Missionaries worked among the Maoris while Britain sought to maintain order on the islands and stimulate trade without assuming governmental responsibility. Perhaps 2,000 Europeans then lived in New Zealand.

British rule. In 1840 settlement began in earnest. In that year the British signed the Treaty of Waitangi with the Maoris. By this treaty Britain extended its sovereignty over New Zealand and promised protection of Maori land rights and equality in a biracial society. In 1841 New Zealand became a crown colony.

In quick succession, settlements were made at Wellington and Auckland, and at Nelson, Dunedin, and Christchurch on South Island. The British settlers intended to develop an economy based on crop production, but sheep grazing and wool production proved more feasible and profitable. In 1852 Britain granted a constitution providing for a loose federation of six provinces, and in 1856 a parliamentary system of government was permanently established.

Federal government. Gold was discovered in the 1860s on South Island, and gold rushes brought men and capital. In that same decade North Island was preoccupied with wars between Maori tribes and settlers over land. The Maoris were defeated in 1872; after that many Maoris refused to cooperate with the government.

labor
US

labour
Brit.

emphasized
US

emphasised
Brit.

The Maori population declined from about 100,000 in 1840 to 40,000 at the end of the 1800s. After that, however, under educated Maori leadership, the Maoris developed into an influential minority, and today they number over 290,000.

New Zealand stagnated in the 1880s and people left the island. Technological changes solved New Zealand's problems, however, as the introduction of refrigerated shipping made possible the export of meat and dairy products to Britain. This development diversified pastoral exports and triggered a rapid growth of dairying on North Island.

In 1891 the Liberal Party, supported by small farmers and city workers, came to power. Prime Minister Richard Seddon launched a program of social and economic experimentation. The government introduced land reforms, compulsory labor arbitration, and social services. Trade unions grew in importance. These progressive reforms, along with technological changes and improved export prices, provided a system that benefited the common man, farmers in particular. In 1907 Great Britain granted New Zealand dominion status.

Dominion. Between 1912 and 1935 a more conservative government, supported mainly by North Island farmers, remained in office almost without a break.

New Zealand gained new importance within the British empire as a supplier of dairy products, meat, and wool to Great Britain. New Zealand soldiers campaigned with British forces against the Central Powers in World War I.

Politically important in the years from 1916 to 1935 was the rise of the Labour Party, supported by a growing industrial working class. In 1935 Labour came to office and held power continuously for 14 years.

The world economic depression of the 1930s hit New Zealand hard. The Labor government arranged guaranteed prices for farmers, and took control of exports and imports, foreign exchange, and banking. It emphasized the redistribution of income, elaborated a social security system, and promoted factory industries to balance the economy. In effect, the government sought to socialize national income rather than the means of production.

Contemporary New Zealand. In 1939 New Zealand entered World War II, collaborating with the United States in the Pacific and with Great Britain in Europe. After the war, cooperation with the United States continued, especially in the area of defense.

The major political parties, Labour and National, have been working to advance social welfare. When Labour was in power from 1935 to 1949, it carried through a program of social and economic legislation, including a comprehensive Social Security Act. During the period from 1949 to 1957, when the National Party held the government, it moved cautiously in discarding economic controls set up by Labour. Since then, Labour (1957–1960, 1972–1975, 1984–1990, 1999–) and National (1960–1972, 1975–1984, 1990–1999) have been careful in removing economic controls.

The main problems facing New Zealand today are its loss of a protected market for its agricultural products, caused by Britain's entry into the European Economic Community in 1973, and the worldwide problems of inflation and petroleum supplies.

In elections in 1984 the Labour Party ousted the more conservative National Party from the majority in parliament. It won an unprecedented second term in 1987. During its first term, Labour was successful in privatizing several industries that had been government run, such as the electrical distribution system. It was also able to substantially deregulate many areas of the economy.

In 1986 the government began a new policy of refusing to allow visits by United States nuclear warships to New Zealand ports, thereby breaching the ANZUS defense alliance.

Papua New Guinea

Official name: *Independent State of Papua New Guinea*
Area: *178,212 sq. mi., 461,690 sq. km*
Type of government: *Parliamentary democracy*
Population: *5,172,000*
Capital and largest city: *Port Moresby (Pop., 174,000)*
Languages: *English (official), Pidgin, Motu, indigenous dialects*
Literacy: *65%;* **Currency:** *Kina*
Per capita GDP: *$2,400 (Rank: 128th)*

The land and people. The country of Papua New Guinea consists of the eastern half of the South Pacific island of New Guinea, the islands of the former territory of New Guinea, and several other island groups east of New Guinea, including the islands New Britain, New Ireland, and Bougainville. The interior and eastern tip of Papua proper are extremely mountainous, but there are

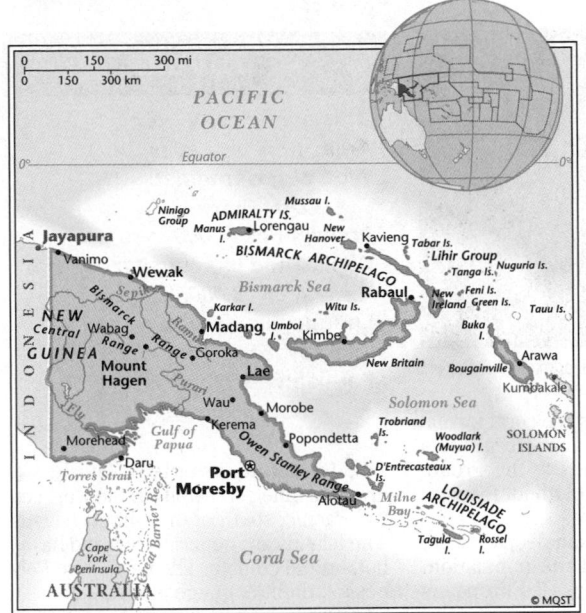

lowlands in the north, south, and west. There are many rivers. The outlying islands are mountainous, and coral reefs ring Papua and most of the islands.

Indigenous Melanesian peoples form the bulk of the population. There are also Europeans, Asians, and many extremely isolated tribal groups of the western hill regions. There are several hundred languages spoken in Papua New Guinea. Two languages, Hiri Motu and a form of pidgin English, are widely spoken. Standard English is the official language.

Economy. The economy is based on agriculture. Coconuts, cacao, coffee, and rubber are the chief commercial crops. There is also commercial forestry and fishing. Most industry is involved in the processing of the country's agricultural products, but light manufacturing is developing. Papua New Guinea has some important mineral deposits, including copper and gold, which, because of their inaccessibility, are only beginning to be exploited.

Government. Papua New Guinea is a member of the British Commonwealth, and the British monarch is head of state. Executive power is held by the prime minister, who is the leader of the majority party in the 109-member parliament.

History. Human remains found in New Guinea date back at least 10,000 years. New Guinea and the adjacent islands were inhabited by Melanesian peoples when they were first visited by the Spanish and Dutch in the 1600s. No European settlement was made until 1828, when the Dutch occupied the western half of New Guinea. In 1883, after a German company had begun trading in eastern New Guinea, Australia occupied Papua without British approval. In 1884 Britain made southeastern New Guinea a protectorate as British New Guinea. Australia was given full sovereignty over the area in 1905.

New Guinea was occupied by Japanese forces during World War II, and the area was the site of bitter fighting. After the war, economic development projects were begun. Forestry and fishing were developed and new industries were started. Popular participation in government also increased. The country became self-governing in 1973 and achieved full independence in 1975.

Bougainville, rich in copper deposits, tried to secede several times in the mid-1970s, but its attempts were crushed. A secessionist movement, often violent, took place again between 1989 and 1998. A cease-fire was declared in April of that year.

Solomon Islands

Official name: *Solomon Islands*

Area: *10,982 sq. mi., 29,450 sq. km*

Type of government:
Parliamentary democracy

Population: *495,000*

Capital and largest city: *Honiara*
(Pop., 49,000)

Languages: *English (official), Pidgin, indigenous dialects*

Literacy: *13%;* **Currency:** *Dollar*

Per capita GDP: *$1,700*
(Rank: 145th)

The land and people. The Solomon Islands consists of about a dozen large islands and many small islets. The islands are of two types, mountainous and volcanic, and low-lying coral atolls. The climate is warm and rainfall is heavy.

Melanesian, Polynesian, and Micronesian people make up the bulk of the population, and there is a small group of Europeans. English is the official language, but pidgin English is more widely spoken.

Economy. The islands' forests are a rich source of valuable hardwoods, and there are deposits of gold and other minerals that are only partially exploited.

Most people live by subsistence farming and fishing. Coconuts and cocoa are the chief commercial crops.

Coconut products, fish, cocoa, and timber are the chief exports, and manufactured goods, fuels, and food are imported. Japan and Australia are the principal trade partners.

Government. The Solomon Islands is a member of the British Commonwealth, and the British monarch is its head of state. The head of government is the prime minister, who is elected by a 50-member parliament.

History. Little is known of the islands before they were visited by the Spanish in 1567. They were soon lost to Europeans again, and were rediscovered by the French only in 1792. The islands served Europeans as a source of copra and cheap labor. In the 1880s and 1890s Great Britain assumed control of the islands and established a protectorate. British authorities took steps to halt "blackbirding," the forcible recruiting of island labor. At the same time, British settlers established plantations, Christian missions, and trading posts.

INDIGENOUS MELANESIAN PEOPLES form the bulk of the population of Papua New Guinea.

labor
US

labour
Brit.

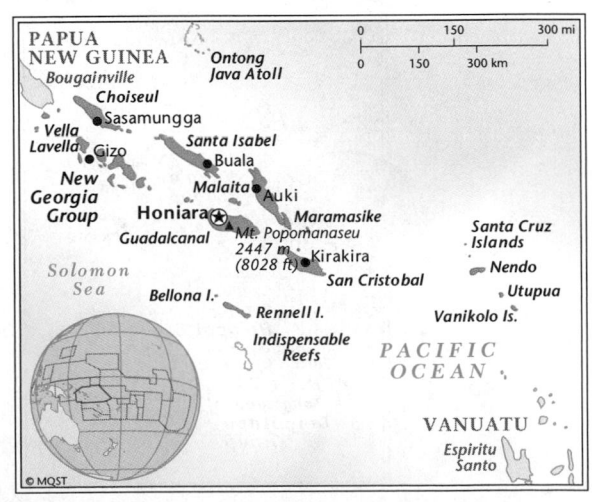

The islands, especially Guadalcanal in the southwest, were the scene of fierce fighting between Japanese and Allied troops in World War II. In the decades after the war, Great Britain concentrated on raising the islanders' standard of living and expanding the local economy by developing natural resources.

From the end of the war, the Solomon Islanders began to press Britain for self-government. Following a short period of representative councils, the islands received a constitution in 1974 and on July 7, 1978, they became an independent member of the British Commonwealth.

Five years of ethnic violence and the resulting lawlessness became so intense that the government appealed for assistance from neighboring countries. In July 2003 as international peacekeeping force led by Australia arrived to help restore order. In August warlord Harold Keke surrendered. Although some forces began leaving in October, others remain.

Tonga

Official name: *Kingdom of Tonga*
Area: *289 sq. mi., 748 sq. km*
Type of government:
Constitutional monarchy
Population: *106,000*
Capital and largest city:
Nuku'alofa (Pop., 22,000)
Languages: *Tongan (official), English*
Literacy: *99%*
Currency: *Pa'anga*
Per capita GDP: *$2,200
(Rank: 131st)*

The land and people. The Tonga, or Friendly, Islands include about 170 small islands that form three major groups—Tongatapu, the largest, in the south; Ha'a-pai; and Vava'u, in the north. Some of the islands are volcanic in origin and have a mountainous,

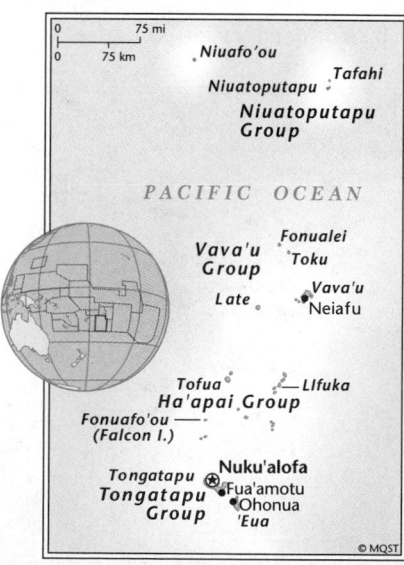

rugged terrain. Others are coral formations and are flat and low. Coral reefs ring most of the islands of the group. The climate is mild throughout the year and rainfall is moderate.

Tongans, a Polynesian people, make up a large majority of the population. There are small groups of Europeans and other islanders. English and Tongan, a Polynesian language, are spoken. Most of the people are Protestant.
Economy. The Tongan economy is based on agriculture. Coconuts, bananas, vanilla beans, and pineapples are the main commercial crops, and taros, yams, fruits, and corn are grown for local consumption. Pigs and cattle are raised, and there is some fishing.

With no mineral resources and no important fuel resources, the islands' only industry is copra production. Tonga exports copra, vanilla beans, and fruit and imports foodstuffs, fuels, and machinery. Australia, New Zealand, and Japan are Tonga's principal trading partners.
Government. Tonga is a constitutional monarchy with a hereditary king who appoints the prime minister. The legislative assembly consists of nine nobles who are elected by their peers, nine popularly elected people's representatives, and the twelve members of the cabinet.
History. Tongan history extends back to the 900s or earlier, when the first Tongan ruling dynasty is considered to have been founded. Europeans reached the islands in the 1600s, and in the late 1700s European ships began to visit Tonga. By the mid-1800s most of the Tonga islanders had been converted to Christianity.

The islands were most recently united into a single kingdom in 1845, when Taufa'ahau Tupou, the king of Ha'apai, won the thrones of Vava'u and Tongatapu as well. The king granted a democratic constitution in 1875. In 1900 Tonga and Great Britain signed a treaty and the islands became a British protectorate, retaining their autonomy while leaving defense and foreign affairs to Britain.

Tongan troops participated in World War II in the Solomon Islands, and Allied bases were established in Tonga.

Under a new treaty ratified in 1959, Tonga received greater local autonomy, and in 1965 Britain further relaxed its authority over Tonga. The islands became fully independent in 1970. Tonga gained UN membership in 1999.

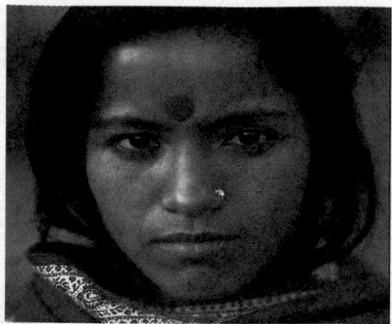

THE PEOPLE of Tonga are primarily Polynesian.

Tuvalu

Official name: *Tuvalu*
Area: *10 sq. mi., 26 sq. km*
Type of government:
Democracy
Population: *11,000*
Capital and largest city: *Funafuti
(Pop., 4,000)*
Languages: *Tuvaluan, English*
Literacy: *55%;* **Currency:** *Dollar*
Per capita GDP: *$1,100
(Rank: 165th)*

The land and people. Tuvalu is a group of nine coral atolls in the west central Pacific, south of the Gilbert Islands. The islands are generally low and have a hot, humid climate. The people are Polynesian; their language is Tuvaluan.
Economy. There are many pandanus groves and coconut groves on the islands. The natives engage in fishing, farming, and the production of copra, which is the chief export. The economy also relies on income from the sale of postage stamps and on remittances from overseas workers. A trust fund has been set up by Australia, New Zealand, and Great Britain to provide income for the future.
Government. Tuvalu is a member of the Commonwealth, and its head of state is the British monarch. The 15-member parliament elects a prime minister.
History. The islands were discovered in 1764 by Captain John Byron, grandfather of Lord Byron. They were made a British protectorate in 1892 and were included in the colony of Gilbert and Ellice Islands, which was created in 1916. Separation from the Gilbert and Ellice territory took place in 1975; at that time the name of Ellice Islands was changed to Tuvalu. Independence was obtained in 1978.

Tuvalu receives extensive British economic aid, but it remains basically dependent on its single cash crop, copra. Many of its citizens seek employment overseas in the phosphate industry in the Republic of Kiribati.

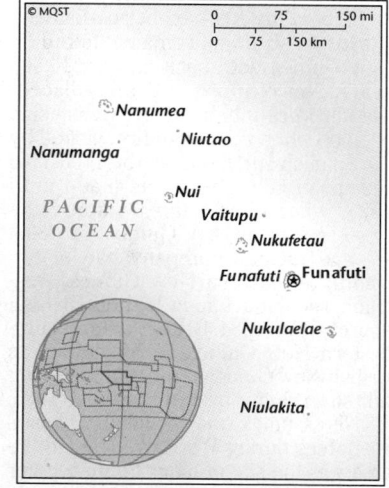

Vanuatu

Official name: *Republic of Vanuatu*
Area: *5,697 sq. mi., 14,760 sq. km*
Type of government: *Republic*
Population: *196,000*
Capital and largest city: *Port-Vila*
   (Pop., 30,000)
Languages: *Bislama, English,*
   French (all official)
Literacy: *53%;* **Currency:** *Vatu*
Per capita GDP: *$1,300*
   (Rank: 159th)

The land and people. Vanuatu consists of about 80 islands. The islands are of volcanic origin and have rugged, mountainous interiors rimmed by low coastal plains. The climate is hot and humid throughout the year.

Most of the islanders are Melanesian, and there are people of British and French origin. Vanuatu is 18 percent urban with a density of only 29 people per square mile. It is a primitive and technologically backward nation with a low literacy rate. Most of the labor force consists of peasant farmers.

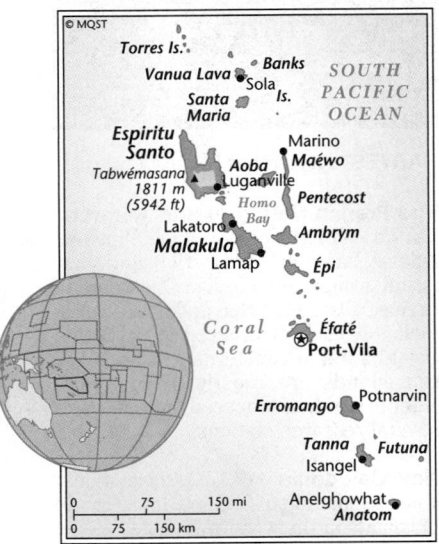

Economy. The economy is agricultural, with coconut and cacao the chief commercial crops. Yams, bananas, breadfruit, and manioc are grown for local consumption. Large herds of cattle are raised, and there is considerable fishing. Industry is limited to the processing of farm products, hides, and fish. The country exports copra, beef, fish, and cocoa. Imports include manufactured goods, food, and fuel. Principal trading partners include Australia and the Netherlands.

Government. The republic has a unicameral legislature, the Parliament. It has 52 elected members. The head of state is the president, who is indirectly elected to a four-year term. The Parliament elects a prime minister from among its own members.

History. Vanuatu has been occupied for many centuries by Melanesians. European planters and traders began visiting the islands after their discovery in 1606 by the Spanish.

By the mid-1800s, British and French settlers outnumbered other Europeans, and in 1887 the two nations formed a commission to protect their mutual interests. In 1906 joint control of the islands was established. In the mid-1900s, projects were undertaken to modernize and expand the islands' economy and to improve the health and welfare of the islanders.

The constitution, which was granted in 1979, provided for pre-independence elections. A fear of the nationalization of the plantations and the possibility of creating a tax-free haven led to a controversy over the desirability of independence.

Separatist movements on both Espiritu Santo and Tanna led to violence after elections that favored the pro-nationalist party. In May 1980 Jimmy Stevens led a revolt on Espiritu Santo, which attempted to declare independence as Vemarana.

Anglo-French forces crushed the revolt, and the nationhood of a united Vanuatu was preserved. Papua New Guinea forces have been stationed in the country since its independence, to maintain peace and control separatist violence.

In 1987 the Western powers were alarmed when the Vanuatu government signed a one-year agreement with the Soviet Union allowing Soviet fishing boats to operate in Vanuatu's territorial waters.

Samoa

Official name: *Independent State of*
   Samoa
Area: *1,104 sq. mi., 2,860 sq. km*
Type of government:
   Constitutional monarchy
Population: *179,000*
Capital and largest city: *Apia*
   (Pop., metro. area, 34,000)
Languages: *Samoan (Polynesian),*
   English
Literacy: *80%,* **Currency:** *Tala*
Per capita GDP: *$3,500*
   (Rank: 107th)

The land and people. Samoa (known as Western Samoa until 1997) is made up of two large islands, Savai'i (660 square miles) and Upolu (430 square miles), and several small islands, including Manono and Apolima. Volcanic in origin, they are almost entirely surrounded by coral reefs. Mountains form the core of the two major islands, reaching an elevation of 3,608 feet in Upolu and 6,094 feet in Savai'i.

Samoa has a tropical climate. Temperatures average about 80°F (26.7°C), and yearly rainfall is 112 inches.

Most of the people of Samoa are of Polynesian stock, and most are Christian. About 70 percent of the people live in Upolu, and about 28 percent live on Savai'i. Apia, on Upolu, is the commercial center of the islands and the only city of any size.

Most Samoans live in traditional extended family communities in small coastal villages.

Economy. The economy of Samoa is based on agriculture. Sixty-seven percent of the labor force are agricultural workers. Most of these people are engaged in crude subsistence farming. The basic food crops are taro, yams, breadfruit, and papaya. Fish are also important in the diet of the people, and poultry and pigs are raised. Cocoa, coconuts, and bananas are grown for export. The islands have few mineral resources, and there is little industry.

The major imports are food, fuel, textiles, and machinery. The major exports are bananas, coconut oil, timber, cocoa, and copra. Most trade is with New Zealand and Australia.

Government. The constitution provides for a head of state, known as *O le Ao o le Malo*. The present head of state rules for life but future heads of state will be elected by the legislature to a five-year term. Executive power is exercised by a cabinet headed by a prime minister responsible to the legislature.

Legislative powers are held by the Legislative Assembly. The assembly has 49 members, who serve for 5 years. Samoans elect 47 of the members, and non-Samoans elect 2. Only chiefs or matai (members of the titled class) may serve in the assembly.

History. Archaeological evidence suggests that the Samoan islands were first settled before 1000 B.C., perhaps from islands farther south. It is believed that much of the eastern part of Polynesia may have been settled from Samoa.

The first European to visit Samoa was a Dutch explorer, Jacob Roggeveen, in 1722. The islands were later visited by other explorers, but European penetration did not begin until 1830, initiated by British missionaries.

Foreign interests. The British were interested in the islands as a place for missionary work, trade, and the development of plantations. U.S. interest centered on trade and control of the harbor at Pago Pago, in present-day American Samoa. The Germans came first to trade and then developed the largest plantation interests on the islands. New Zealand also held an interest in the islands.

center
US

centre
Brit.

labor
US

labour
Brit.

25 Australia and Oceania

The last three decades of the 1800s saw periodic clashes arising from efforts of the three great powers to settle the Samoan question. Much of the time they assumed that Samoa would be independent, but with one of the powers exercising a dominant political influence in the islands. The United States, firmly in control of Pago Pago, was most consistently concerned with Samoan independence.

By a 1900 international agreement, the islands were divided. Germany gained control of present-day Samoa and granted Great Britain territories elsewhere in the Pacific. The United States annexed eastern Samoa. From 1900 to World War I, Western Samoa was a German colony.

New Zealanders occupied the islands of Western Samoa early in the war, and in 1920 began to administer them as a League of Nations mandate. In 1946 Western Samoa became a United Nations trust territory under New Zealand's administration, and in 1959 it became self-governing.

Independence. In 1961 a plebiscite was held under UN supervision, and the people voted overwhelmingly for independence. On January 1, 1962, Samoa became the first independent Polynesian state of modern times. Close ties were maintained with New Zealand, which continues to provide economic aid and educational assistance.

Dependencies in Australia and Oceania

Australian Dependencies

Australian Antarctic Territory (2,472,000 square miles), in Antarctica, is uninhabited except for scientific research stations.

Christmas Island (52 square miles), with 474 people, is 230 miles south of Java, in the Indian Ocean. Phosphate extraction has historically been the economic mainstay of the island. A commercial space-launch site is being developed.

The Cocos (Keeling) Islands (5.4 square miles) have 632 people. Located in the Indian Ocean, 1,700 miles northwest of Australia, they consist of two atolls with 27 small islands. Home, with three-quarters of the population, is the main island. West Island, at about 6 miles from end to end, is the largest. The Cocos were purchased by Australia in 1978.

The Coral Sea Islands Territory (8.5 square miles) is virtually uninhabited. Located east of Queensland, Australia, it is administered from Norfolk.

The Heard and McDonald Islands (113 square miles) are uninhabited islands in the Indian Ocean 2,575 miles southwest of Australia.

Norfolk Island (13.5 square miles), with 1,800 people, is located in the South Pacific, 900 miles northeast of Australia. It is inhabited largely by descendants of the *Bounty* mutineers, who went there in 1856. It received limited domestic rule in 1979. The islanders live mainly from tourism and the sale of postage stamps.

Chilean Dependencies

Easter Island (63 square miles) has 3,800 people. It is in the Pacific Ocean, 2,300 miles west of Chile. Sheep grazing is its economic mainstay.

Sala y Gomez Island (.05 square mile) is an uninhabited island in the Pacific Ocean, 250 miles east of Easter Island.

French Departments and Territories

Clipperton Island (2 square miles), formerly part of French Polynesia, was separated from it in 1979. Located 700 miles southwest of Mexico in the East Pacific, it is uninhabited.

French Polynesia (1,359 square miles) has a population of 258,000. It includes about 130 islands in the South Pacific. Its most important member is Tahiti, one of the Society Islands group, which includes the Windward and Leeward island groups. Tahiti was discovered by Captain James Cook in 1769. It is a beautiful island with a large tourist industry. Over half the population of French Polynesia lives on Tahiti. Also part of French Polynesia are the Tuamotu Archipelago, the Marquesas Islands, and the Austral or Tubuai Islands. Nuclear testing on the islands has instigated an international dispute since it began in 1966. The capital is Papeete on Tahiti.

HARVESTING seaweed in an outrigger canoe

The French Southern and Antarctic Lands (169,805 square miles) include Adelie Land on Antarctica and four island groups in the Indian Ocean, south of Australia: Kerguélen and Crozet archipelagos, each discovered in 1772, and Saint-Paul and Amsterdam islands. All the islands are mostly uninhabited. Adelie Land, discovered in 1840, has several research stations.

New Caledonia (7,172 square miles) has a population of 208,000. It is a group of islands in the western Pacific Ocean, 110 miles east of Australia. New Caledonia is the largest of the islands, which include the Isle of Pines, the Loyalty Islands, the Huon Islands, and the Chesterfield Islands. Discovered in 1774, New Caledonia was a French convict station from 1871 to 1896. It is the world's third largest producer of nickel. Its capital is Noumea.

Réunion (969 square miles) is the only French Department in this area of the world, while New Caledonia, the Wallis and Futuna Islands, French Polynesia, and French Southern and Antarctic Lands are French Territories. Réunion has a population of 744,000. It is a volcanic island in the Indian Ocean, 420 miles east of Madagascar. It has been a French possession since 1653. Its capital is St. Denis.

MANY OF THE ISLANDS of the South Pacific were involved in the Pacific theater of World War II. Some still have U.S. military bases.

The Wallis and Futuna Islands (106 square miles) have a population of 15,600. Located in the southwest Pacific between Fiji and Samoa, the islands were dependencies but elected in 1961 to become a French overseas territory. The capital is Mata-Utu.

New Zealand Dependencies

The Cook Islands (93 square miles) have a population of 21,000. They are in the South Pacific, 2,000 miles northeast of New Zealand. They include the Northern Group, with seven atolls, and the Southern Group, with eight atolls. They accepted domestic self-government in 1965.

Niue (100 square miles), with a population of 2,100, is in the South Pacific, 400 miles west of the Cook Islands. It was given internal self-rule in 1974.

Ross Dependency (160,000 square miles) in Antarctica was established in 1923. It is uninhabited but has several research stations. The principal station, Scott Base, is manned year-round.

The Tokelau Islands (4 square miles) have a population of 1,400. They are in the South Pacific, 300 miles north of Samoa. They include the atolls of Atafu, Nukunonu, and Fakaofo. The population is principally Polynesian and has close ties to Samoa.

Norwegian Dependencies

Peter I Island (69 square miles) is an uninhabited Antarctic island south of the South Shetland Islands. The island was first explored by a Norwegian expedition in 1929, and was made a dependency in 1933.

Queen Maud Land is an uninhabited region of Antarctica that had been visited only by Norwegian explorers before it was claimed by Norway in 1939.

United Kingdom Dependencies

The British Indian Ocean Territory (23 square miles), formed in 1965, has no indigenous population and includes the five atolls of the Chagos Archipelago, of which Diego Garcia is the most important member. The other atolls are Peros Banhos, Salomon, Eagle, and Egmont. The territory is 1,180 miles northeast of Mauritius. Major U.S. air and naval bases are stationed on Diego Garcia.

The Pitcairn Islands (17 square miles), located in the South Pacific Ocean about midway between Peru and New Zealand, includes Pitcairn Island and the uninhabited Henderson, Ducie, and Oeno islands. Pitcairn Island has a population of 47, most of whom are descendants of the *Bounty* mutineers. The only community is Adamstown.

United States Dependencies

American Samoa (76 square miles), 1,600 miles northeast of New Zealand, in the Pacific, has 69,000 people. It includes six small islands of the Samoan group, plus Swains Island. It has been American since 1899, except for Swains, which was added in 1925. The territory's constitution, ratified in 1966, provides for a bicameral legislature and a popularly elected governor. The capital is Fagotogo on the Island of Tutuila.

Guam (212 square miles), the largest and southernmost of the Mariana Islands, has a population of 161,000. Located in the western Pacific, it is about 1500 miles south of Japan. First colonized by the Spanish in the 17th century, it is now a manufacturing and oil-refining center. U.S. military bases are on the island, which is also a popular resort. In 1979 its U.S. citizens voted down a proposed constitution that would give the island more self-government but would deprive the citizens of U.S. citizenship rights. Agana is the capital.

Howland, Baker, and Jarvis Islands (2.7 square miles) are uninhabited South Pacific islands, 1,500 to 2,000 miles south and southwest of Hawaii.

Johnston Atoll (91 square miles) is located in the Pacific, 715 miles southwest of Hawaii. American-controlled since 1858, it is now administered by the U.S. Air Force. It has been used for nuclear tests.

Kingman Reef (0.4 square mile) is an uninhabited American dependency (since 1922) in the Pacific, 35 miles northwest of Palmyra Island. It became a U.S. naval station in 1934.

The Midway Islands (1.9 square miles), with a population of 40, are in the Northern Pacific, 1,200 miles northwest of Hawaii. They include an atoll plus the two islets called Sand and Eastern. Controlled by the U.S. Navy since 1903, Midway was the scene of several famous World War II air and sea battles.

Commonwealth of the Northern Mariana Islands (184 square miles) approved commonwealth status in 1975 and a new constitution went into effect in 1986. The islands were formerly part of the Trust Territory of the Pacific Islands. The 16 islands are located north of Guam, and there are 77,300 people. The chief island and governmental center is Saipan.

Republic of Palau (177 square miles) is located about 530 miles southeast of the Philippines. Palau was the last state remaining in the UN-mandated Trust Territory of the Pacific Islands, which was established after World War II and included some 2,100 islands in the area commonly known as Micronesia. Palau includes 26 islands and several hundred islets; it has a population of 19,000. Its capital is Koror, on the island of Babelthaup. In October 1994 Palau entered into the Compact of Free Association with the United States, by which Palau is self-governing in internal affairs but the United States retains responsibility for defense and other external affairs. Palau was admitted to the United Nations in December 1994.

Palmyra Island (4 square miles), an atoll with over 50 islets, is in the Pacific, 1,000 miles southwest of Hawaii. It is privately owned and uninhabited, but is administered by the Department of Interior. It became American in 1898 along with Hawaii, from which it was separated in 1959, when Hawaii gained statehood.

Trust Territory of the Pacific Islands. *See* Republic of Palau.

Wake Island (2.5 square miles), unincorporated territory administered by the Department of Interior, is an atoll of three small islands 2,300 miles west of Honolulu, Hawaii. Military personnel have left, but some civilian personnel remain.

For more information on the U.S. Pacific territories see the NORTH AMERICA volume.

THE WATERS OF FRENCH POLYNESIA are some of the most beautiful in the world.

colonized	*US*
colonised	*Brit.*
center	*US*
centre	*Brit.*

TOURISM is a very important part of the economy of the Pacific Islands, and one they are working to promote.

Cities of Australia and Oceania

Adelaide, the capital and largest city of South Australia State, in southern Australia, located on the Torrens River in a rich agricultural and mineral-producing region. Founded in 1836, it is one of Australia's main commercial, industrial, and transportation centers. Its products include chemicals, machinery, electronic equipment, textiles, automotive parts, and petroleum. Pop., metro. area, 1,044,000.

Apia, the capital, largest city, and chief port of Samoa (formerly Western Samoa), on the north coast of the island of Upolu. Chief exports are copra, bananas, and cocoa. Pop., metro. area, 34,000.

Auckland, the chief port of New Zealand, located on North Island between the harbors of Waitemata and Manukau. Auckland is New Zealand's largest industrial center. It is also the site of the University of Auckland and the Auckland War Memorial Museum, noted for its Maori collection. Pop., 368,000.

Brisbane, the capital and principal port of Queensland, Australia, on the Brisbane River, 14 miles (23 km.) from Moreton Bay. Brisbane is a commercial and manufacturing center and is the seat of the University of Queensland. Pop., metro. area, 1,609,000.

Canberra, the capital of Australia, in the Australian Capital Territory, in the southeastern corner of New South Wales. A model city, Canberra was founded in 1913 and became the seat of government in 1927. The Australian National University is located there. Pop., 312,000.

Melbourne, the capital, largest city, and chief port of Victoria State, Australia. It is located at the mouth of the Yarra River on Port Phillip Bay, in southeastern Australia. The city is an important railroad terminus and one of Australia's leading commercial centers. Manufactures include electrical goods, motor vehicles, textiles, and processed foods. Pop., metro. area, 3,339,000.

Perth, the capital and major city of Western Australia State, on the Swan River estuary in western Australia. Founded in 1829, it grew with the discovery of gold in the region in the 1890s, and with its connection with the transcontinental railroad in 1917. Its products include steel, aluminum, machinery, cement, petroleum proucts, and fertilizer. The port of Fremantle, at the mouth of the Swan River on the Indian Ocean, is now part of the Perth metropolitan area. Pop., metro. area, 1,307,000.

Port Moresby, the capital of Papua New Guinea, in the South Pacific Ocean. Port Moresby lies on the southern coast, on the Gulf of Papua. It is a commercial center that exports copper, rubber, and wood products. Pop., 174,000.

Suva, the capital of Fiji, situated on the southeastern coast of Viti Levu Island. It is a port of call on international shipping routes, and it processes and exports fruits, sugar, coconuts, cacao, and timber. Pop., 92,000.

Sydney, the capital of New South Wales, on the southeastern coast of Australia. It is the country's largest city and chief industrial and commercial center. It has a deep natural harbor and an excellent port. Sydney is the site of several colleges and of the national art and history museums. Pop., metro. area, 3,948,000.

Wellington, the capital of New Zealand. It is located at the southwestern tip of North Island, overlooking Cook Strait. Wellington has a large harbor and is the financial, manufacturing, commercial, and transportation center of New Zealand. Pop., 164,000.

centers
US

centres
Brit.

aluminum
US

aluminium
Brit.

SYDNEY HARBOR, overlooked by the Sydney Opera House, is almost as busy as a metropolitan freeway, hosting both commercial and pleasure crafts.

Glossary of Australia and Oceania

Colombo Plan, a plan for cooperative efforts to raise standards of living and strengthen the economies of the developing nations of South and Southeast Asia. It was published on November 28, 1950, by a committee of Commonwealth ministers; it came into effect on July 1, 1951. It has several times been extended. The member nations assist each other on a bilateral basis. The aid includes technical assistance, loans, equipment, educational programs, and food supplies.

It's members are Afghanistan, Australia, Bangladesh, Bhutan, Burma, Cambodia, Canada, Fiji, India, Indonesia, Iran, Japan, Laos, Malaysia, Maldives, Nepal, New Zealand, Pakistan, Papua New Guinea, the Philippines, Singapore, South Korea, Sri Lanka, Thailand, the United Kingdom, and the United States.

Great Barrier Reef, a coral reef that extends 1250 miles (2000 km.) off the coast of northeastern Australia and southeastern New Guinea at the edge of the continental shelf. It protects the coastline and forms a channel that contains many small coral islets, which attract students and tourists.

Murray, Australia's principal river rising near Mt. Kosciusko in southeastern Australia and flowing westward for 1609 miles (2590 km.) to Encounter Bay, off the Indian Ocean on the south Australian coast. With its tributary, the Darling River, it forms a watercourse 2310 miles (3719 km.) long.

New Guinea, the world's second largest island, lying in the southwest Pacific Ocean, north of Australia. The island, with an area of 320,000 square miles (829,000 sq. km.), has a mountainous interior. New Guinea has mangrove and sandalwood forests and contains deposits of gold, oil, cobalt, and nickel. New Guinea is shared by West Irian, a province of Indonesia, and Papua New Guinea.

South Pacific Forum, regional organization of independent and self-governing states. Representatives of the member governments meet to discuss issues of importance to the South Pacific region. In 1994 the members were Australia, the Cook Islands, Fiji, Kiribati, the Marshall Islands, the Federated States of Micronesia, Nauru, New Zealand, Niue, Papua New Guinea, the Solomon Islands, Tonga, Tuvalu, Vanuatu, and Samoa (formerly Western Samoa).

Tasmania, an island 150 miles (240 km.) off the southeastern coast of Australia, lying between the Indian Ocean and the Tasman Sea. About 180 miles by 190 miles (290 by 306 km.), Tasmania is geologically a continuation of the Australian continent. A high central plateau is surrounded by forested mountains in the west and agricultural lands in the north and southeast.

AUSTRALIA'S GREAT BARRIER REEF is one of the most spectacular in the world; it attracts students and tourists alike.

MANY TRIBAL PEOPLES in New Guinea still live in traditional villages and practice traditional ways, such as the dance seen here.

The Help Desk

➤ **When** traveling across time zones, practice thinking, "If it is _____ o'clock in Sydney, then it must be _____ o'clock in Chicago."

➤ **Use** play dough or salt clay to make a map of Australia, New Zealand, or one of the islands. Show mountains, lakes, rivers, plains, peninsulas, etc.

➤ **Select** a destination from the place you are to another place in Australia or Oceania. Where would you stop along the way? How would you travel from one place to another? How long would each leg of the trip require? What kind of clothes should you take? Can you find out what kind of money you should have at each stop?

➤ **For** a list of helpful references, go to the *customers* section of www.southwestern.com.

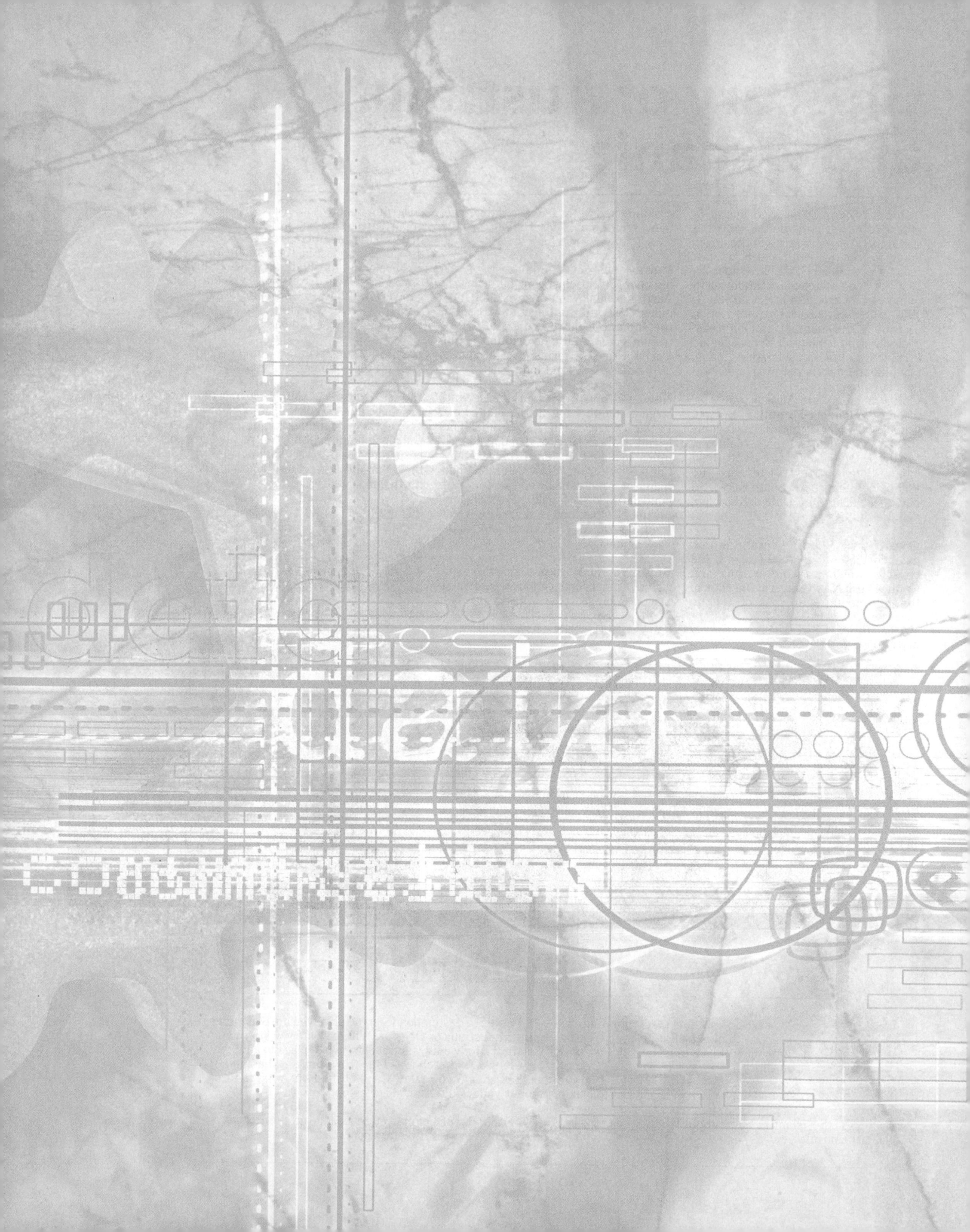

26

Europe
and Russia

26

Europe and Russia

Contents

Europe and Russia

Europe is bounded on the west by the Atlantic Ocean, on the south by the Mediterranean Sea, and on the north by the Arctic Ocean.

The eastern boundary is somewhat arbitrary. Unlike the other continents, Europe does not have a clearly delineated landmass and is considered a continent more for its cultural homogeneity than for its geography. By convention, however, the eastern boundary of Europe has come to be regarded as a line extending along the Ural Mountains to the Caspian Sea, then northeast along the Caucasus Mountains to the Black Sea.

This boundary, although following clearly defined geographical features, has the disadvantage of placing the western tip of Turkey in Europe and the rest in the Middle East. It also places the western part of Russia in Europe and the vast eastern part in Asia. Because the historical forces that helped shape Turkey are interwoven with the history of the Middle East, the country is discussed in the MIDDLE EAST volume. However, Russia, dominated by its European population, is discussed in the EUROPE AND RUSSIA volume as if it were entirely a European nation.

Also considered part of the European continent are a number of islands, including the British Isles, Iceland, the Spitsbergen Islands, and the Shetland

Islands in the North Atlantic. Although Greenland is technically part of North America, because of its cultural and political connection with Scandinavia, it, too, is treated as part of Europe. Of the islands and island groups in the Mediterranean Sea, only Cyprus is not considered part of Europe.

The land. Europe is roughly wedge-shaped, with its base along the Ural Mountains in the east and its pointed end extending west into the Atlantic Ocean. In the north, the Scandinavian peninsula extends southeast into the North and Baltic seas. West and north of Scandinavia is the Norwegian Sea, and north of Russia is the Barents Sea. Both of these seas are arms of the Arctic Ocean. In the southern part of the continent, the Balkan and Italian peninsulas extend southward into the Mediterranean Sea.

Because of its numerous peninsulas and irregular coastlines, Europe has the largest ratio of coastline to land area of the world's continents. Estimates of the length of the coastline range up to 50,000 miles (81,000 kilometers). Glaciation and other geological activity have produced many harbors and inlets. Of particular interest is the western coast of Norway, with its steep-sided *fjords*.

Europe can be divided into four basic topographical regions, running in

east-west bands. The northernmost of these bands is a region of highlands running from the northern British Isles across Scandinavia. This region has a generally harsh climate and poor soil and is sparsely populated. Of the Scandinavian countries, Norway and Sweden have the least productive land, a result of massive glaciation and scouring of previous ice ages.

The next region to the south is a band of lowland that runs through western France, southeastern England, Belgium, the Netherlands, Denmark, northern Germany, Poland, Ukraine, and large portions of Russia. The land of this region, which is known as the European Plain, is the most productive area in Europe. The land is covered with sedimentary material, much of it deposited by glaciation. The soil is fertile and the region is heavily cultivated. The European Plain is also highly industrialized. These two factors have produced one of the most densely populated regions in the world.

The next region, called the Central Uplands, is a plateau region that stretches from Spain through central France. It marks the southern boundary of the European Plain from Germany to Poland.

The fourth region of Europe is the alpine mountain region in the south, which stretches from the Sierra Nevada

kilometers
US
kilometres
Brit.

mountain system of southern Spain to the Caucasus Mountains in southeastern Europe. In terms of geological time, this region is still relatively young. Continuing volcanic and seismic activity offer clear evidence that the land of southern Europe is still undergoing changes.

Mountains. Southern Europe is dominated by mountains. Perhaps the most important and best known of its mountain ranges is the Alps, which constitutes a formidable barrier between northern and southern Europe.

The Alps are a complicated mountain system having a number of different branches. Essentially, however, it runs in an arc from southeastern France to eastern Austria. The eastern end of the system splits, with one branch, the Dinaric Alps, running south through the Balkan peninsula. The other branch, called the Carpathian Mountains, runs

east through the Czech Republic and Slovakia, then south into Romania.

The sharp peaks and steep sides of the Alps are indications that the range is still young. Its snowcapped peaks and glaciers are reminders of Europe's geological past, when much of the continent was covered with ice. The glaciers of past ages carved the deep alpine valleys of Switzerland and northern Italy.

Another important mountain range in Europe, the Pyrenees, forms the border between Spain and France; it is a natural barrier between the Iberian peninsula and the rest of Europe. The Sierra Nevada range, located in southeastern Spain, is part of a group of mountain ranges known collectively as the Sierra Nevada system. The Sierra Nevada range includes peaks that rival the Pyrenees in height and grandeur. This range also includes the southernmost glacier in Europe.

Other important ranges in southern Europe include the Apennines, which run the length of the Italian peninsula; and the Balkan Mountains, which run east and west through southern Serbia and Montenegro and Bulgaria. To the north of the Balkans, the Transylvania Alps also run in an east-west direction and join the Carpathian range at its southern tip.

In far eastern Europe, the Ural Mountains cut Russia on a north to south axis. Unlike the alpine mountain system, the Urals are relatively low in elevation and have the rounded appearance typical of older mountain systems.

Located between the Caspian and Black seas, the formidable Caucasus Mountains help complete a natural land-water barrier between Europe and the Middle East. The Caucasus is a youthful range and is on a center of seismic activity. Mt. Elbrus is the tallest peak in the

center
US

centre
Brit.

26 Europe and Russia

meters
US

metres
Brit.

Caucasus range and also the tallest mountain in Europe, rising to 18,510 feet (5,640 meters) above sea level. To the northeast, on the northern shore of the Caspian Sea, is the lowest elevation in Europe, measured at 92 feet (28 meters) below sea level.

Rivers. Europe's rivers have been extremely important to its economic development. Many of them are navigable for considerable distances inland, facilitating the transport of goods and people. Many of the navigable rivers have been connected by man-made canals to increase their utility as shipping routes. Thus, it is possible to cross from one end of the continent to the other by small boat.

Because of the peninsular arrangement of much of Europe, most of the continent's rivers rise in central mountain areas and run outward to the surrounding seas. Among the important rivers that empty into the Atlantic Ocean are the Guadalquivir, Guadiana, Tagus, and Douro rivers of Spain and Portugal; and the Garonne, Loire, and Seine rivers of France.

The most important river of northern Europe is the Rhine. It rises in eastern Switzerland and flows 820 miles (1,320 kilometers) through Germany and the Netherlands, emptying into the North Sea. Also flowing into the North Sea is the Elbe, which passes through Germany and the Czech Republic. Flowing into the Baltic Sea through Poland are the Oder and the Vistula.

One of the most important rivers in Eastern Europe is the Danube. The Danube rises in southern Germany and flows 1,750 miles (2,820 kilometers) to the Black Sea. Along the way it passes through or forms part of the borders of Austria, Slovakia, Hungary, Croatia, Serbia and Montenegro, Bulgaria, and Romania.

Europe's longest river is the Volga. It follows a roundabout route of 2,290 miles (3,690 kilometers) from its source near Moscow, east and then south to the

ACID RAIN from industrial pollution is a matter of growing concern among environmentalists, as the forests of Europe are being destroyed.

Caspian Sea. A number of tributary rivers empty into the Volga, extending its basin across much of Russian Europe. A canal and river waterway link the Volga to the Black and Baltic seas.

Other important rivers of eastern Europe include the Dnieper, Europe's third-longest river, and the Dniester, both of which flow through Ukraine and empty into the Black Sea.

In southern Europe, most Mediterranean rivers are short and their flows tend to be seasonal, with the rivers drying up during the warm summer months when there is little rain. The exceptions are the Ebro in Spain, the Rhône in France, and the Po in Italy. All three rise and receive most of their volume of water in mountain systems outside the Mediterranean basin.

Climate. Europe has four basic climatic regions. The Mediterranean region in the southern part of the continent is characterized by wet, mild winters and hot, dry summers. Most of this region's moisture is brought by prevailing westerly winds from the Atlantic Ocean, so the western end of the Mediterranean basin tends to receive more precipitation than the eastern end.

The maritime climate is influenced by the relatively warm waters of the North Atlantic Ocean. Areas that have a maritime climate include northwestern Spain, western France, Belgium, the Netherlands, Denmark, southern Sweden, Norway, the British Isles, Iceland, and northern Germany. These areas have abundant year-round rainfall, with moderate temperatures both summer and winter.

The continental climate is found primarily in eastern Europe. It is characterized somewhat by lower amounts of precipitation and harsh winters. Most of the rainfall in this region occurs during the warm summer months.

The fourth climatic region occurs where the continental climate merges into the maritime climate. This region

encompasses eastern France, southern Germany, Switzerland, Austria, and eastern Europe. The climate is characterized by cold winters, with heavy snowfall in the mountain areas. Summers tend to be warm and generally drier than in western Europe.

Vegetation. Long ago a good part of Europe was densely forested. Much of the original forest cover was removed, particularly in western Europe, as the continent's population and need for farmland increased. However, most areas of Europe still have substantial woodland. In coastal areas far north, near the Arctic, only tundra vegetation such as mosses, lichens, and small shrubs thrive. Coniferous forests cover most of Sweden, Finland, and northern Russia. Mixed broadleaf and coniferous forests are found in the middle of the continent from central Europe east to the Urals. Large areas in the Mediterranean have been dedicated to the cultivation of olive, fig, citrus, and other fruit trees.

The people. In 2002 Europe's population of 749,792,000 accounted for almost 12 percent of the world's people. Europe is a densely populated continent, although density varies widely from place to place, largely because of geographic factors. The rocky and mountainous northern interior parts of Norway and Sweden, for example, are not suitable for agricultural activities and are generally inhospitable, so these areas are relatively sparsely settled. Similarly, the extremely mountainous areas of central Italy have a much lower population density than the Plain of Lombardy in northern Italy. This large rolling plain, situated between the Apennines and the Alps, has one of the highest population densities in Europe.

The areas of highest population density generally follow a strip that begins in southern England and continues east across northern France, the Low Countries, Germany, the Czech Republic, Slovakia, southern Poland, Ukraine, and Russia. Europe's largest cities are London (population, metro. area, 7,652,000) and Moscow (8,297,000).

Two major factors account for Europe's ability to support a large population within a relatively small area. The fertility of the European Plain has remained high despite centuries of concentrated agricultural activity. Improvements in agriculture have helped to keep Europe's growing population from outstripping its food supply. Europe's industrialization and economic diversification help to support its population.

Population growth. Europe's population is growing substantially slower than the population of the world on average. Europe's rate of growth for the period 1980 to 1990 was 0.3 percent, compared with a world growth rate of 1.7 percent. This is explained by two factors. Europe's death rate is slightly below that of the world average, and its birth

THE TEMPLE OF POSEIDON in Greece stands sentinel over the Mediterranean Sea, the home of the Greek god of the sea.

rate is substantially lower than that of the world average.

Ethnic diversity. In addition to its high population density, Europe also has a remarkably large number of ethnic groups for its relatively small area. One reason for this is that Europe has been invaded many times by many different migratory peoples.

Although humans lived in Europe as far back as 35,000 years ago, the continent was sparsely populated until well after the close of the last Ice Age. Europe presented no major barriers to people migrating from the east, and over the course of time successive waves of people settled in the region. Europe has seen large influxes even in recent times. Large ethnic groups may be identified with modern nations, such as the French with France and the Swedes with Sweden, but other ethnic groups, such as the Basques of France and Spain and the Lapps of Norway, are not representative of a nation's entire population. Many of Europe's ethnic groups are identified by a variety of cultural factors, such as language, religion, and history. In many parts of Europe ethnic identity, long subordinated to the nation state, emerged in the late 1980s and early 1990s as a major political force. Yugoslavia and Czechoslovakia dissolved as a result of ethnic divisiveness, and the resultant countries, along with Ukraine and Russia, continued to face problems created by ethnic minorities.

Languages. Most of Europe's contemporary ethnic groups are defined principally by language. About 35 distinct languages are now spoken in Europe, in addition to many more dialects. Almost all these languages and dialects fall into the Indo-European language group and are thus related to each other. Most of the Indo-European languages in Europe

can be divided into three principal groups: Romance languages, Germanic languages, and Slavic languages.

The Romance languages are those that developed in provinces of the Roman Empire and that are descended from Latin, the language of the ancient Romans. The principal Romance languages include Italian, French, Spanish, Portuguese, and Romanian.

The Germanic languages were spread by migrating German tribes and evolved into the modern languages of German, English, Dutch, Danish, Norwegian, Swedish, and Icelandic.

The Slavic languages predominate in Eastern Europe. These include Polish, Czech, Slovak, Slovene, Russian, Belorussian, Ukrainian, Serbo-Croatian, Bulgarian, and Macedonian.

Other Indo-European languages not belonging to the three groups listed above include Greek, Albanian, Lithuanian, and Latvian. Remnants of Celtic, a very early Indo-European language, are found in the Breton language spoken in Brittany, in the Gaelic languages of Ireland and Scotland, and in the Welsh language.

There are some European languages that do not belong to the Indo-European group. The majority of these are found in Russia. They include the Uralic languages, such as Finnish, Karelian, Samoyedic, Lapp, Estonian, and Hungarian; the Altaic languages, including Turkish, Azerbaijani, and Kazakh; and the Caucasian languages of southern Russia and Georgia. Basque, which is spoken in the northern Pyrenees region of both France and Spain, appears to be unrelated to any other language in Europe or elsewhere.

Religion. The principal religions throughout most of Europe are Christian, a legacy of the Roman Empire. Christianity was adopted as the official religion by the Romans toward the end of the Roman Empire. As Roman power declined and barbarian assaults hastened the empire's disintegration, the early Christian Church became the conservator of ancient history and learning, thereby establishing itself as a link between the ancient and modern ages.

With the division of the Roman Empire into a western (later Holy Roman) empire and an eastern (later Byzantine) empire, the Christian Church became divided into the western Roman Catholic Church and the Eastern Orthodox Church. Both branches of Christianity helped preserve knowledge through the Middle Ages. The period of the Renaissance in Europe in the 16th century also saw the rise of Protestantism, the third major branch of Christianity.

SUNFLOWERS are an important cash crop in several European countries. Their pressed seeds produce the world's third most important vegetable oil.

Roman Catholicism is the dominant religion in Ireland, Spain, Portugal, France, Belgium, Italy, the Czech and Slovak republics, Poland, Hungary, Croatia, Slovenia, and Lithuania. Protestant faiths predominate in England, Scotland, Scandinavia, Finland, Estonia, and Latvia. Roman Catholicism and Protestantism both have adherents in Germany, Switzerland, and Northern Ireland. The Orthodox faith has a majority of followers in Romania, Bulgaria, Yugoslavia, Ukraine, and Russia. The religions of Islam and Judaism have also played important roles in the development of Europe. Islamic influence in Spain at the height of the Arab Empire contributed greatly to European culture. The Turks of the Ottoman Empire, a major European force between the 15th and early 20th centuries, were also Islamic. Today Islam is practiced by only a small minority of Europeans. It is strong in Bosnia, Macedonia, and parts of Ukraine and Russia.

The Middle Ages saw the rise of substantial Jewish communities in Europe, particularly in central and eastern Europe. These communities were almost entirely destroyed during World War II. After the war a large percentage of the surviving Jews lived in the Soviet Union, where the practice of their religion was hampered by a policy that attempted to discourage all organized religion. Present-day European Jews live mostly in France, Great Britain, Ukraine, and Russia, though many Jews are now emigrating from the former Soviet Union.

Economy. For centuries, agriculture was the foundation of the European economy. It provided the basis for the growth of Europe's large population and set the stage for Europe's rise as a center of trade and industry. Europe's large workforce and abundant natural resources ensured its industrial development. In addition, its overall high level of education, especially in central and western Europe, has helped it during the transition from heavy industry to high technology and service industries.

Agriculture. Intensive use of fertilizers and the development of advanced agricultural techniques have enabled European farmers to produce large crops even in marginal soils. The result is that Europe is one of the most productive agricultural areas in the world. Major products include potatoes, wheat, rye, barley, corn, meat, and dairy products. The region of greatest agricultural output is in western and central Europe. Vast areas of farmland stretching through Ukraine and Russia, as far as the Urals, produce large quantities of wheat, but farm production is significantly less efficient than in western Europe. This can be attributed to poorer soil, less favorable climate, and less advanced farming techniques.

Forestry thrives in northern Scandinavia, Finland, and northern Russia. In the Mediterranean, production of fruits and vegetables is important. Fishing is principally important off the coast of Norway, in the North Sea, and in the North Atlantic.

Natural resources. Many areas of Europe are rich in iron and coal, two key resources for industry. Large deposits of coal are found in Great Britain, northern France, southern Belgium, western Germany, Poland, Ukraine, and Russia. Iron ore is found in Britain, Sweden, France, Ukraine, and Russia. Large reserves of petroleum and natural gas are being developed in the North Sea. Russia also produces petroleum and has oil and gas fields in the south, southwest, and Siberia. Diamonds, emeralds, and gold are also found in Russia. A variety of other minerals are found throughout Europe.

Industry. The Industrial Revolution began in Great Britain in the mid-18th century with the development of machines to apply first waterpower and then steam power to manufacturing. The result was a rapid changeover from small cottage and village industries to centralized, more efficient, and internationally competitive industries based on factories, mills, and foundries. Mechanized industry, plus techniques for producing the advanced machinery and the raw materials needed, led to increased preeminence for British manufacturing, but only for a time.

The Industrial Revolution began to spread to the rest of Europe in the 19th century. Abundance of coal, iron, and other minerals in many parts of Europe made it possible to establish heavy industries, especially in iron and steel, chemicals, heavy equipment, and shipbuilding. Manufacture of textiles, automobiles, machinery, and a vast array of other goods also developed. Today Europe plays an increasingly important role in high-technology industries, including aerospace, electronics, and communications.

Cooperation between British and French industries led to the development of the supersonic jet Concorde. The European Space Agency, organized by several European nations to promote technological growth, is playing an important part in rocket and satellite technology and space research.

In the 1980s, European engineers applied the latest technological advances to the development of high-speed rail transportation. A German prototype using magnets to lift a moving train slightly off its tracks clocked a speed of 240 miles (387 kilometers) per hour on a test track. In France the world's fastest train began service, reaching a top speed of 186 miles (300 kilometers) per hour in its run between Paris and Le Mans.

Transportation and trade. In addition to Europe's well-developed system of river and canal transportation, it has built an extensive and efficient system of rail, highway, and air transport. In 1988 construction began on the Eurotunnel, a 31-mile (50-kilometer) rail tunnel beneath the English Channel that enables rail passengers to travel between Paris and London in about three hours. The tunnel was completed in the mid-1990s.

In recent years the volume of air traffic handled by European airports has increased significantly, prompting the airline industry to move toward an improved air traffic control system.

A number of European countries maintain large merchant fleets. The ports of Rotterdam, Marseille, London, Antwerp, Genoa, and Hamburg are among the busiest in the world.

The largest part of European trade is between the European nations themselves. The leading trading nation in Europe is Germany. Other major trading nations include Great Britain, France, Russia, Ukraine, The Netherlands, and Italy.

---

center
US

centre
Brit.

kilometers
US

kilometres
Brit.

THE CHUNNEL, or Eurotunnel, under the English Channel offers three-hour service by rail between London, England, and Paris, France.

THE CONCORDE, designed jointly by France and Great Britain, began service in the 1970s, but suspended service in 2003 for economic reasons. A supersonic plane, it had a speed of about 775 miles per hour.

Tourism, long an important industry in many countries, has become a major factor in the European economy since the end of World War II.

Economic communities. The idea of the integration of the various states of Europe into a pan-European federation dates back several centuries. However, not until the 20th century did the movement toward European integration gain momentum. The destruction of almost a generation in World War I sparked several pan-European movements, but these were unable to overcome the objections of national governments. The devastation visited upon Europe during World War II, the development of nuclear weapons, and the possibility of Europe's—and the world's—total extinction in any subsequent war were powerful new arguments for the political, social, and economic integration of Europe.

In Eastern Europe the Communist countries, led by the Soviet Union, formed the Council for Mutual Economic Assistance (COMECON). COMECON, established in 1949 to coordinate industrial development and production and promote trade, proved unable to meet its goals effectively, and in 1991, with the demise of the Soviet Union, the organization was disbanded. Former members sought to form new economic ties, not only among themselves, but also with the United States, the nations of Western Europe, and the industrial nations of Asia.

Western Europe, meanwhile, had developed its own economic organizations. During World War II, the governments in exile of Belgium, the Netherlands, and Luxembourg agreed to form a customs union to promote trade and economic growth, particularly in the coal and steel industries. In 1948 the first elements of the trade agreement, designed to eliminate tariffs between the member countries and establish a unified external tariff system, went into effect. Within a few years, production and profit in selected industries had risen dramatically. The success of Benelux, as the union came to be known, set the stage for the broader integration of European economies.

In 1951 the Benelux nations and France, West Germany, and Italy signed a treaty establishing the European Coal and Steel Community (ECSC). The signatories agreed to remove all trade barriers between the countries in the coal, steel, and iron industries and to promote the free movement of labor and materials for those industries. The success of ECSC sparked an economic boom in Western Europe, despite the limited scope of the treaty. In 1957 the movement toward a more comprehensive system of economic integration led to the Treaty of Rome, under which the ECSC nations formed the European Economic Community (EEC), also known as the Common Market. The goal of the EEC was to remove all trade barriers between member nations, encourage the free flow of labor and capital within the community, and establish a common external tariff structure.

At the same time, the member nations established a separate organization, the European Atomic Energy Community (Euratom), to promote the development and growth of nuclear industries and technology. In 1959 seven nations—Austria, Denmark, Great Britain, Norway, Portugal, Sweden, and Switzerland—established another trade community, the European Free Trade Association (EFTA) in an effort to promote economic growth without giving up individual power to control external tariffs. Finland and Ireland subsequently joined EFTA. The EFTA nations agreed to eliminate internal tariffs on industrial and manufactured goods, but not on agricultural products. Economic growth among EFTA members improved but came nowhere near the growth enjoyed by EEC members. Denmark, Great Britain, and Ireland eventually left to join the EEC.

In 1967 the EEC merged with the ECSC and Euratom to form a joint organization called the European Communities (EC). The goals of the EC were to achieve the total elimination of internal trade and economic barriers and establish a uniform external tariff structure. According to the EC's Single European Act of 1986, sometimes referred to as Project 1992, 282 measures were to have been enacted by December 31, 1992. They would enable goods, services, money, and labor to move freely among member nations. Although the goal was not met in its entirety, significant progress has been made in some areas.

labor
US

labour
Brit.

THE TREATY OF ROME established the European Community, designed to eliminate trade barriers between member countries.

As part of the EC's efforts to ease commerce among the various countries, the organization established the European Monetary System (EMS) in 1979. The EMS relied on an exchange rate mechanism designed to ensure that the values of member nations' currencies remain within reasonable range of one another. Problems with the system became apparent in 1992, when Britain and Italy withdrew temporarily from the EMS.

In 1992 the Maastricht Treaty called for the creation of a common currency and a central European bank as well as European citizenship and cooperation in foreign policy and defense. The treaty, which required each nation's approval, was rejected by Danish voters and only narrowly passed in France. Denmark and Great Britain approved the treaty, with conditions, in 1993, but Germany's approval was challenged in court.

With ratification of the treaty in November 1993, the EC became known as the European Union (EU). At the time the EU included Belgium, Denmark, France, Germany, Greece, Ireland, Italy, Luxembourg, the Netherlands, Portugal, Spain, and the United Kingdom. In 1995 Austria, Finland, and Sweden became members of the EU. The former Eastern Bloc nations of the Czech Republic, Estonia, Hungary, Latvia, Lithuania, Poland, Slovakia, and Slovenia, as well as Cyprus and Malta, became members in 2004. The EU has forged close ties with EFTA, which, as the European Economic Area, complies with EU regulations. EFTA now consists of Iceland, Liechtenstein, Norway, and Switzerland.

The political structure of the EU includes the Council of the EU, with representatives from each member government, which is the principal decision-making body; a 20-member European Commission which is politically independent and represents the interests of the EU as a whole; a Court of Justice, which rules on disputes concerning EU laws and regulations; and a 624-member (as of April 2003) European Parliament, whose representatives are directly elected by voters in the member countries. The parliament shares with the Council both the power to legislate and authority over the EU budget. It also has the power to approve/reject nominations of Commissioners.

The 2004 expansion necessitated steps be taken in order to ensure that the EU would continue to operate efficiently with 25 or more members. To that end, the Treaty of Nice, which went into effect on February 1, 2003, set new rules regarding the size and functions of the various EU institutions.

Government and politics.
Most of the countries of Europe are republics or constitutional monarchies with popularly elected representative governments. Until recently, however, the nations of central and eastern Europe were governed by authoritarian communist regimes. At present, the trend in those nations, including the countries of the former Soviet Union, is toward political pluralism and representative government. Political parties in Europe run the gamut from conservative, rightist groups to radical or revolutionary leftist constituencies. The majority parties are much closer to the political center and tend to be flexible in their approach to major issues. The existence of ultraconservative political parties, such as the National Front in France, the Italian Social Movement, and the Republican Party in Germany, has prompted a degree of alarm among observers of the European political scene. Indeed, some rightist splinter groups once more embrace the slogans and symbols of the fascist and Nazi movements.

In the years following World War II, the power and influence of Communist parties in Europe reached a peak. Despite efforts on the part of the Communist movement to redefine its principles and goals in light of the major changes in eastern Europe, it failed to maintain its hold on the region. Central and eastern Europe underwent dramatic changes during the 1980s and early 1990s, culminating in the demise of communist control.

Socialist principles are still strong in European politics, however, as evidenced by the Socialist Party of France, the Social Democratic Party of Germany, and the Labour Party of Great Britain.

The 1970s and 1980s saw the rise in Western Europe of a new political movement called the Green Party. Its major concerns were continuing tensions between the superpowers, the militarization of Europe, and the growing environmental problems facing Europe and the world.

In the 1980s the Green Party led the opposition to the deployment of new nuclear weapons in Europe as well as to the upgrading of existing weapons systems. In 1989 the party posted substantial gains in elections to the European Parliament. The Green Party remained a relatively small opposition group, however.

Recent history. Shattered by two world wars, Europe settled into a period of relative stability following the end of World War II. The most distinctive feature of post-World War II Europe was what British Prime Minister Winston S. Churchill described in 1946 as the iron curtain between Soviet bloc nations and Western Europe. Tension between the two competing systems of government resulted in the Cold War, which dominated world politics for almost 50 years. After Mikhail S. Gorbachev became general secretary of the Communist Party of the Soviet Union in 1985, he called for the political and economic restructuring of the ailing Soviet system, and renounced the use of military force to intervene in the affairs of other nations. Soon, the barrier between the communist and western blocs began to crumble.

Poland became the first communist nation to establish a non-communist national government. In 1989 strikes and mass demonstrations led to the toppling of the communist governments of Czechoslovakia and East Germany, and in Romania the communist regime was overthrown by force. Reforms were also instituted in Bulgaria, Yugoslavia, and even the Soviet Union.

The 1989 dismantling of the Berlin Wall, erected in 1961, and a symbol of the division of Europe between democratic and communist governments for almost 30 years, was followed by the reunification of Germany in 1990.

In 1991 the Baltic republics of Latvia, Lithuania, and Estonia broke away completely from the Soviet Union. The Soviet Union itself disintegrated after an attempted coup in August 1991, leaving in its wake 15 new countries. Eleven of the new republics formed the Commonwealth of Independent States (CIS), a loose organization designed to provide the new states with continuity in economic and foreign affairs.

Yugoslavia also began to disintegrate in 1991, with Bosnia and Herzegovina, Croatia, and Slovenia all declaring their independence from the federal government. Serbian troops moved into Croatia and Bosnia and Herzegovina, where they remained for 4 years. Elections in Czechoslovakia in 1992 set the stage for the dissolution of that country as well. In January 1993, the country was divided peacefully into the Czech Republic and Slovakia. In 2003 Yugoslavia was dissolved and the remaining two republics formed the loose federation of Serbia and Montenegro.

Other nations of eastern Europe are also faced with the problems of political division along ethnic lines.

---

center
US

centre
Brit.

labor
US

labour
Brit.

THE CHARM
of street cafes is
one of the pleasures
of European life
for locals and
travellers alike.

THE 1989 DISMANTLING of the Berlin Wall signaled the reunification of Germany and the end of the Cold War.

Military alliances. The North Atlantic Treaty Organization (NATO) was formed in 1949 to protect the nations of Western Europe from military attack, specifically from the Soviet bloc countries. Its original members included Belgium, Canada, Denmark, France, Great Britain, Iceland, Italy, Luxembourg, the Netherlands, Norway, Portugal, and the U.S. Greece and Turkey joined in 1951, and a newly rearmed West Germany joined in 1955. France withdrew from military participation in 1966. Spain joined the alliance in 1982. The Czech Republic, Hungary, and Poland joined in 1999. Bulgaria, Estonia, Latvia, Lithuania, Romania, Slovakia, and Slovenia joined in 2004.

In response to the NATO alliance, and particularly the rearmament of West Germany and its admission to NATO, in 1955 the Soviet Union organized the Warsaw Treaty Organization, or Warsaw Pact. Its original members were Albania, Bulgaria, Czechoslovakia, East Germany, Hungary, Poland, Romania, and the Soviet Union.

The purpose of the organization was primarily to protect member nations from external military threats, but it also legalized the presence and movement of Soviet forces within the borders of the member states, thus guaranteeing the continued dominance of the Soviet Union and communism in those nations.

Albania severed diplomatic relations with the Soviet Union in 1961 and withdrew from the Warsaw Pact in 1968.

Warsaw Pact forces were used in Czechoslovakia in 1968 to enforce what came to be known as the Brezhnev Doctrine, which sanctioned the use of Soviet military force to protect other communist governments. The doctrine was ultimately repudiated by Gorbachev and the Soviet government. The end of communist domination of eastern Europe called into question the continuing function and objectives of the Warsaw Pact, and in 1991 the Pact was disbanded. Major Soviet troop withdrawals from eastern Europe reduced the likelihood of a sudden, overwhelming strike against Western Europe. The successful negotiation of the Strategic Arms Reduction Treaties (START) between the Soviet Union (which was later replaced by Russia, Ukraine, Belarus, and Kazakhstan) and the United States in 1991 and 1993 further altered the military balance in Europe. With the threat of nuclear war lessened, NATO's role in maintaining Europe's security was reevaluated.

Today the political, social, and economic order of Europe is undergoing revolutionary change. The dynamic forces now at work on the continent will almost certainly have a profound effect, the nature of which is yet unknown, on the entire world.

THEN PRIME MINISTER of England Margaret Thatcher enters NATO headquarters in Brussels to confer with other leaders of the pact.

Countries of Europe and Russia

Albania

Official name: *Republic of Albania*
Area: *11,100 sq. mi., 28,750 sq. km.*
Type of government: *Emerging democracy*
Population: *3,545,000*
Capital and largest city: *Tirana (Pop., 244,000)*
Languages: *Albanian (official), Greek*
Literacy: *93%*
Currency: *Lek*
Per capita GDP: *$4,500 (Rank: 93rd)*

The land. Albania is a mountainous land. A southern extension of the Dinaric Alps covers more than two-thirds of the country. Level land is found only along rivers and near the coast. Albania's rivers are few and short, and they flow westward, to the Adriatic. Three large lakes lie astride Albania's borders—Scutari, in the northwest, and Ohrid and Prespa, in the east.

The climate along the coast is Mediterranean, with warm, dry summers and mild, damp winters. The vegetation there is of the *maquis* type—dry evergreen bushes and small trees. Farther east the rainfall is considerably higher, and winters can be quite severe.

The people. Almost all of the people are Albanians, but there is a small Greek minority in the south, along the Greek border. Almost 2 million Albanians live across the border in Serbia and Montenegro's Kosovo-Metohija region. The population of Albania is increasing far faster than anywhere else in Europe. Over 60 percent of the population is rural.

The Albanians are divided into two main groups, each with its own mutually intelligible dialect. The Ghegs live in the northern half of the country, and the Tosks live in the southern half. Before religious institutions were banned in 1967, most Albanians were Muslims. About 20 percent of the people were Orthodox Christians, and 10 percent were Roman Catholics.

Economy. Albania has long been the poorest country in Europe. By 1945, 90 percent of the population was still employed in agriculture. Since then, the government has sought to transform the country from an agricultural to an agricultural-industrial nation. The government has followed the Soviet model of economic development, with strong central planning, state-controlled industry, and collectivized agriculture.

Agriculture still employs about half of Albania's people, although there is little land that can be cultivated and the soil is poor. Wheat, corn, and potatoes are the principal grain crops, and cotton, tobacco, and sunflowers are the main industrial crops. Large quantities of fruit are produced. Livestock includes cattle, goats, and sheep. Sheep are the most important.

Albania has considerable mineral resources, but the rough landscape makes it difficult to exploit them. The major minerals include oil, lignite coal, chromium, copper, iron, and nickel.

Oil extraction has increased rapidly since 1960, with 3 million metric tons of crude being extracted in 1987. Albania has a large hydroelectric potential, some of which is exploited to produce about 80 percent of domestic needs. Electricity is also exported to neighboring Serbia and Montenegro.

Industrial production is mainly concerned with the processing of Albania's mineral and agricultural resources. Petroleum processing, chemical production, iron and copper smelting, and food processing are all important industries.

The major exports are minerals and metals and agricultural products, such as fruit, wine, and tobacco. Imports consist largely of machinery and transportation equipment. Albania's principal trading partners are Serbia and Montenegro, the Czech Republic, and Italy.

Government. Albania has a 140-member legislature of one house, the People's Assembly. A direct popular vote determines the election of 100 members. The remaining 40 are elected by proportional vote. Members are elected to 4-year terms. The president is elected by the People's Assembly for a 5-year term and the prime minister is appointed by the president.

History. Illyrian tribes from central Europe migrated into the area of present-day Albania in about 2000 B.C. The region was called Epirus by the ancient Greeks, who established colonies along the coast. In the 200s B.C., Pyrrhus of Epirus built a powerful state and in 280 he invaded Italy. He was defeated, and internal unrest led to the disintegration of the state.

Roman era. Rome conquered the Illyrian states by 167 B.C., and the region became fairly prosperous from its geographic position astride Rome's trade routes to the East. Many Albanians became prominent in Roman life, and the towns generally became Roman in culture. In 395 the Roman Empire was divided into eastern and western halves, and Albania became part of the Eastern Empire.

During the A.D. 400s, a number of barbarian tribes invaded the region, and during the 600s and 700s, Slavic peoples began to settle in the lowland areas. During the 800s and 900s, the region was included in a Bulgarian state, but Byzantine rule was reestablished in 1018.

In 1054, a schism in the Christian Church led to a new era of conflict. Normans and Crusaders, representatives of the Western, or Roman Catholic, Church, invaded the country and fought against adherents of the Eastern, or Orthodox, Church.

The decline of Byzantium in the 1100s was accompanied by the establishment of Albanian principalities, and in 1230 by the reimposition of Bulgarian rule. During the later 1200s, the Anjou rulers of Sicily established themselves in parts of Albania, and in the mid-1300s the region was part of a Serbian empire.

Ottoman rule. The Ottoman Turks began the conquest of Albania in the 1300s, and by 1389 most of the country was under Ottoman control. Albania remained under Turkish control until 1912. There were many risings against Ottoman rule during the 1400s, and in 1443 a major rising was led by Gjergj Kastrioti (George Castriota), popularly known by his Turkish name, Skander, plus his title, beg ("Skanderbeg").

In 1444 a general assembly of Albanian notables created an Albanian league with Skanderbeg as president. The

Albanian state collapsed after the death of Skanderbeg in 1468.

During the period of Ottoman rule, local officials, often Albanians, gained control of large areas, and they made these lands hereditary possessions. The population came to be divided into three main groups—Muslims, educated in Turkish; Orthodox Christians, educated in Greek; and Roman Catholics, educated in Italian.

In the 1800s the Ottoman Empire was near collapse, and Albania became a focal point for the ambitions of several states. Serbia, Montenegro, and Greece, staked out claims to Albanian lands.

In 1912 the first Balkan War was fought against Turkey by Bulgaria, Greece, Serbia, and Montenegro. The Greeks, Serbs, and Montenegrins planned to divide Albania among themselves. But the Albanians proclaimed their independence in the city of Vlonë in November 1912 and petitioned the great powers of Europe for recognition.

The powers agreed to the establishment of an autonomous Albanian state under the suzerainty of the Ottoman sultan, and set out the boundaries of the new state. The boundaries included only about half the area and half the people traditionally considered Albanian by the Albanians.

Independence.   In 1913 the powers recognized Albania as an independent nation with the stipulation that it be under a 10-year period of control by them. The new nation was to be a monarchy, and the powers chose a German prince, William of Wied, to head the new state. World War I broke out in 1914, and William left the country.

After the war, Italy, Serbia, Greece, and Montenegro all put forth claims to Albanian territories. But in 1920 Albania won recognition of its full independence and membership in the League of Nations.

The new Albanian government was weak. The country was poor, most of the people were illiterate, and neighboring nations interfered in the country's troubled politics. In 1928 a regional chieftain proclaimed himself King Zog I. In 1939 Italian troops invaded Albania and on April 12 incorporated the economically depressed country into the Italian Empire. Traditionally Albanian areas in Serbia (Kosovo) and in Greece (Cameria) were added to the puppet Albanian state. But Italian efforts to win Albanian support met with little success.

Communist rule.   During World War II, national resistance to Italian and German occupation was organized under communist control. By the end of the war in 1945, the Communist Party, led by Enver Hoxha, after ruthlessly eliminating all noncommunist opposition, had established firm control over the country.

The Yugoslav communist-led resistance movement had given significant aid to the Albanians during the war, and ties between the two countries remained close during the first years of the new regime. In 1948, however, when Yugoslavia and the Soviet Union split, the Albanians supported the Soviet Union.

Ties with the Soviet Union remained close until after the death of Stalin in 1953. When Albanian leaders continued to espouse pro-Stalinist views, the new Soviet regime denounced Albania in 1961. The Soviet Union withdrew its military installations from Albania and ceased all economic assistance to the country. These actions led Albania to seek assistance from the People's Republic of China. China offered financial aid and trading rights to Albania, and close ties resulted.

With the death of China's leader, Mao Zedong, in 1977, however, came a clash of ideologies. The new Chinese government sought better relations with the West and Albanians charged that this moderate line was compromising the Communist goal of international revolution. By 1978 China had cut all financial and military aid to Albania. Following this break, Albania reaffirmed its intention to pursue a policy of self-sufficient nonalignment with foreign powers.

The 1980s saw a marked lessening of the country's extreme isolation and improvement in its relations with neighboring and other countries, particularly after the death of Hoxha in 1985.

In 1991 civil unrest arose after a communist victory in open elections. In 1992 the communists were swept from power in new elections, but the economy then collapsed and thousands left to work in other countries. International observers judged the 2000 elections acceptable, but serious problems remain.

Andorra

Official name: *Principality of Andorra*

Area: *174 sq. mi., 450 sq. km.*

Type of government: *Parliamentary democracy*

Population: *68,000*

Capital and largest city: *Andorra la Vella (Pop., 21,000)*

Languages: *Catalan (official), French, Castilian*

Literacy: *100%*

Currency: *Euro*

Per capita GDP: *$19,000 (Rank: 29th)*

The land and people.   Andorra is one of Europe's smallest countries. It has a rugged landscape dominated by the Pyrenees Mountains. These mountains rise from 6,500 to over 9,000 feet (2,000 to 2,700 meters).

Andorrans are descendants of a people known to the ancient Romans. They speak Catalan, the language of Catalonia, a region that encompasses northeastern Spain and southeastern France. The population of Andorra is 60 percent Spanish, 30 percent Andorran, and includes a French minority.

Economy.   Although tiny, Andorra is prosperous. Its major natural resources are waterpower, from several lakes and

BREAD LINES in Albania reflect the fact that, although its economy is growing, the nation is still the poorest country in Europe.

meters *US*

metres *Brit.*

the Valira River; small deposits of iron and lead; and timber. Only a small part of the land can be farmed. Rye, wheat, vegetables, and tobacco are grown, but Andorra depends on Spain and France for most of its food.

Tourism and trade contribute heavily to the economy. The country's status as a duty-free area and its reputation as a center for winter and summer mountain sports attract great numbers of visitors each year. Andorra exports primarily tobacco, cigarettes, and timber products, especially to Spain and France.

Government. Since the 13th century, sovereignty over Andorra had been exercised jointly by the Roman Catholic bishop of Urgel, in Spain, and by the French president. In March of 1993, the citizens of Andorra approved a constitutional referendum that established the country as a parliamentary co-principality and authorized the formation of the first parliament in Andorra's history.

History. Andorra's history as a state traditionally extends back to Charlemagne, who is said to have driven the Muslims from the region. The country gained semi-independent status in 1278, when the bishop of Urgel and the French counts of Foix assumed joint sovereignty over the "Valleys of Andorra," with the right to collect tribute.

The arrangement endured, but the counts of Foix were replaced by the princes and kings of Navarre, the kings of France, and then the presidents of France. Nominal tribute is still paid to the cosovereigns.

Because of its small size and geographic isolation, Andorra escaped involvement in modern European wars. In the 1950s and 1960s, however, the increasing importance of the tourist trade led to fuller involvement in European affairs and to a thriving economy.

Spain's entry into the European Community in 1986, and the expected creation of a single European market in 1992, changed the economic relationship between duty-free Andorra and its neighbors. Many immigrants, legal and illegal, are drawn by its robust economy and lack of income taxes.

---

center
US

centre
Brit.

meters
US

metres
Brit.

civilizations
US

civilisations
Brit.

THIS TURKISH SETTLEMENT on the Armenian steppe is a reminder of the forced exodus of thousands of Turkish Armenians from border areas in 1915.

Armenia

Official name: *Republic of Armenia*
Area: *11,503 sq. mi.*
29,800 sq. km.
Type of government: *Republic*
Population: *3,330,000*
Capital and largest city: *Yerevan*
(Pop., 1,247,000)
Languages: *Armenian, Russian*
Literacy: *99%;* **Currency:** *Dram*
Per capita GDP: *$3,300*
(Rank: 109th)

The land. The landlocked republic of Armenia, at an average altitude of 5,900 feet (1,800 meters), lies just south of the Caucasus Mountains. It is the smallest of 15 republics of the former Soviet Union. The northwestern highlands combine mountains, lava plateaus, extinct volcanoes, and deep gorges carved by rivers. The highest peak is Mount Aragats in the northwest, with a height of 13,400 feet (4,090 meters). The Sevan Depression of eastern Armenia, at an altitude of 6,200 feet (1,900 meters), contains Lake Sevan, one of the largest mountain lakes in the world. It empties into the turbulent Razdan River and feeds an array of irrigation networks and hydroelectric stations. In the southwest, the Ararat Plain is bisected by the Araks River, which flows to the Caspian Sea.

Armenia has a variety of landscapes, from semidesert to steppe, forest, alpine pasture, and high-altitude tundra. The climate is unusually varied and changes with elevation. Summers in the lowland plains are hot and long, with temperatures as high as 108°F (42°C). Winter temperatures average about 23°F (–5°C), with much lower readings in high-altitude regions. Rainfall in the mountains reaches nearly 315 inches (800 centimeters) per year, with 80 to 160 inches (200 to 400 centimeters) in the lowland areas.

The people. Forming 93 percent of the population, Armenians are descended from the highlanders of ancient Armenia, a region and former kingdom of Asia Minor. They are ethnically homogeneous and enjoy a rich cultural heritage and strong national identity. The population of the republic tripled in the 50 years between 1920 and 1970. Agriculture remains an important occupation, but with increasing urbanization and industrialization, more than 62 percent of the people live in urban areas.

Christianity has been the dominant religion since its adoption in the early fourth century A.D. Most Armenians today belong to the Armenian Apostolic (Orthodox) Church or to the Armenian (Roman) Catholic Church.

Economy. The republic has substantial deposits of copper, molybdenum, gold, and silver. Recent industrialization has been greatly assisted by the development of hydroelectric plants on Lake Sevan and the Razdan River. Armenia's principal manufactured products are machine tools, electrical power machinery, nonferrous metals, and chemicals. Up-to-date light industry is geared to textiles, carpets, and footwear. High-quality wines and cognacs are also produced for export. Most of Armenia's industry is located in the cities of Yerevan, Kumayri, and Kirovakan. Agricultural output is primarily wine grapes, tobacco, fruit, sugar beets, potatoes, and cotton.

Government. Armenia has a one-house, 131-member legislature, the National Assembly. Members are elected by popular vote every 5 years. A prime minister is appointed by a president, who is chief of state.

History. Occupying the eastern part of ancient Armenia, one of the world's oldest civilizations, the republic has a long history dating back to the sixth century B.C. Armenia has been invaded and controlled by Alexander the Great, Romans, Persians, Byzantines, Mongols, and Ottoman Turks. In 1828 czarist Russia obtained the region of present-day Armenia from Persia. For centuries the target of persecution because of their religion, in 1915 thousands of Armenians perished during a forced exodus from Turkish border areas. After a brief period of indepen-

© MQST

dence, Soviet forces established control in 1920. Armenia joined the Soviet Union as part of the Transcaucasian Soviet Socialist Republic in 1922, and in 1936 it was declared a separate constituent republic.

Armenia has been engaged since 1983 in a territorial dispute over the Armenian Christian enclave of Nagorno-Karabakh, situated in Muslim Azerbaijan. Through multinational negotiations progress is now being made to resolve the issue. Economic stability has been seriously affected by this crisis, and by the disastrous earthquake of 1988. In 1991, following the dissolution of the Soviet Union, Armenia joined the Commonwealth of Independent States.

(For more information about the history of Armenia as part of the Soviet Union, see the article on Russia.)

Austria

Official name: *Republic of Austria*
Area: *32,375 sq. mi., 83,850 sq. km.*
Type of government: *Federal republic*
Population: *8,170,000*
Capital and largest city: *Vienna (Pop., 1,562,000)*
Language: *German*
Literacy: *98%*
Currency: *Euro*
Per capita GDP: *$27,700 (Rank: 11th)*

The land. Austria is a landlocked, mountainous country. The Austrian Alps run west to east from the Swiss border and occupy nearly all of central and southern Austria. Aside from a few prosperous valleys, the Alps are rugged and barren, with many ice-covered peaks.

North of the Alps lies a hilly area that grades into a forested plateau region between the Danube River and the Czech border. In the northeastern corner of the plateau is the fertile and heavily populated Vienna basin. The navigable Danube crosses northern Austria on its way to the Black Sea, and its many tributaries thread the country.

The Austrian climate varies greatly from region to region. For the country as a whole, the average temperature in January is 22°F (6°C), and in July 64°F (18°C). The Alps, however, are colder in winter and cooler in summer. Rainfall averages between 30 and 40 inches (76 and 102 centimeters) a year.

The people. The people of Austria are almost entirely German-speaking, but there are some who speak other languages, including Croatian, Czech, and Slovene. Most of the population is Roman Catholic.

The most densely populated areas are on the northern and southern edges of the Alps, especially along the Danube River in the north. The mountainous central part of the country is sparsely settled. Vienna, in the northeast, is Austria's largest city, with almost 20 percent of the country's total population. Other important cities include Graz (population, 227,000), Linz (186,000), Salzburg (145,000), and Innsbruck (114,000).

Economy. Austria is a prosperous country, marked since World War II by above average economic growth and relatively low unemployment. Manufacturing and services gradually replaced agriculture in economic importance.

In 1946 the Austrian government nationalized much of the country's industry. In the 1980s government-owned industry still employed almost 20 percent of the industrial workforce. In recent years, the economy has moved away from dependence on heavy industries, such as steel, toward industries such as chemicals, plastics, paper, and electronics.

Austria is the world's largest producer of magnesite, which is used in various chemical processes. It also has reserves of iron, lead, and zinc. The country's extensive forests have made lumber an important export, and extensive development of hydroelectric potential has been a boon to industrial development.

Owing to a lack of good farmland, agriculture now contributes less than 5 percent of the gross domestic product, and employs less than 10 percent of the workforce. Even so, more than 80 percent of Austria's food requirements are met by domestic production.

Most trade is with Western Europe, and a free trade pact has been negotiated with the European Union in order to protect access to that market. Major exports include chemicals, transport equipment, iron and steel, and wood products. Imports include machinery, fuels, raw materials, and food products. A persistent trade deficit is largely offset by an important tourist industry.

Government. Austria is a federal republic made up of nine states. The Federal Assembly consists of two houses. The 183-member National Council is elected every 4 years in a system of proportional representation. The Federal Council has 64 members elected by the provincial assemblies.

A president, elected to a 6-year term, is head of state. He appoints the chancellor, or prime minister, who is usually the head of the majority party, as the head of government.

ST. STEPHEN'S CATHEDRAL in Vienna is an example of the Old World landmarks for which the city is famous.

By the 1955 treaty restoring its sovereignty, Austria may possess only defensive weapons and must maintain neutrality in world affairs.

History. The Danube River basin was an important roadway for peoples migrating from the east many centuries ago. The Romans established military posts and settlements in the area, but by the 400s A.D. migrating Germanic tribes from the north, and Slavic tribes from the east had forced the Romans out of the region. By about 800 the area had become part of the vast empire of Charlemagne, who made it the eastern kingdom, the "Ostmark" or "Osterreich," of his realm.

In 955 Otto I, founder of the Holy Roman Empire, drove out the Magyar peoples who had begun invading the region from the east starting in the 880s. From 976 until 1246, when the line died out, the Babenberg dynasty extended their control over most of Austria.

In 1282 Austria became a possession of the Hapsburg family. The Hapsburgs ruled Austria for over 600 years and held a dominant position in the Holy Roman Empire. Through the strength of their dynasty the country achieved a position of leadership in Europe during the 1500s, 1600s, and 1700s. During that time Austria was the center of a Hapsburg empire that controlled territory throughout Europe.

The empire. In 1804, two years before the Holy Roman Empire was dissolved, Hapsburg emperor Francis II declared himself emperor of Austria and Austria itself became an empire. In the following 50 years, the Austrian Empire, led by its

center
US

centre
Brit.

THE CITY OF SALZBURG in Austria is known for its music and theater festivals.

foreign minister, Prince Klemens von Metternich, played a major role in the series of military and political alliances that characterized European affairs during the Napoleonic and later eras.

The Austrian Empire included parts of modern southern Poland and the western Ukraine; most of Czechoslovakia, Hungary, and northern Italy; part of the Balkan peninsula; and the many different and often restless nationalities that lived in those regions. Austria's government was highly centralized and conservative.

In the 1840s and 1850s liberal and nationalist revolutions broke out in the Austrian Empire. These rebellions weakened the government's power and led to reforms that only partly satisfied the empire's rebellious subject peoples—particularly the Croatians, Czechs, and Hungarians. Austria's loss of absolute control over its people weakened its international position.

In 1867 the many separate German states were united under Prussia, Austria's rival in German politics, in a North German Confederation. The unification of Germany forced Austria, in order to retain some internal stability and international power, to make the restive Hungarian region of the empire an equal partner with the German part. The two states were joined in the Dual Monarchy of Austria-Hungary in 1867.

Creation of the Dual Monarchy, controlled by the Germans of Austria and the Magyar people of Hungary, left the Slavic subject peoples in Bohemia and the Balkans dissatisfied. The discontent of the Slavs was an important cause of World War I, which began in 1914 when a Slav from Serbia assassinated Archduke Francis Ferdinand, the heir to the Austro-Hungarian throne. Austria-Hungary declared war on Serbia, and was joined by Germany. Serbia was supported by czarist Russia, which was in turn supported by France and Britain. (See HISTORY OF THE WORLD.)

The German allies were defeated, and at the end of the war in 1918 the Hapsburg empire lay in ruins. In 1918 the emperor abdicated and was replaced by a provisional government. The provisional assembly declared its desire to unite with Germany, but the Allied powers prohibited Austrian-German unification by the Treaty of St. Germain (1919).

The Allies divided much of Austria's old territory among Italy, an independent Hungary, a restored Poland, and the new states of Czechoslovakia and Yugoslavia.

The first republic. In 1920 a permanent government was formed, and its members drafted a constitution. Austria, now a small, overwhelmingly German-speaking nation, was made a federal republic.

Two political parties dominated the republic—the conservative Christian Socialists and the liberal Social Democrats. The Christian Socialist Party drew its principal support from the wealthy landowners and manufacturers, the clergy, and the farmers. It favored some

form of authoritarian government. The Social Democrats mainly represented the urban workers and followed a socialist program. A small, nationalistic faction favoring union with Germany grew rapidly in size during the 1920s.

The first republic faced serious difficulties from its earliest years. In 1920 the government had to use force to prevent parts of the country from seceding and joining Germany. Pressure for unification with Germany, or *Anschluss*, was to plague the republic continually. The Austrian economy avoided total collapse only by receiving financial grants from the League of Nations between 1922 and 1925.

In 1926 a serious conflict opened between the Christian Socialist national government and the Social Democrats. The Social Democrats governed the province that included the capital city, Vienna, where one-quarter of the country's population then lived.

In Vienna the Social Democrats had financed social welfare programs for the workers by heavily taxing the rich. The conservative Christian Socialists objected strongly to these programs. The conflict, centered in Vienna, frequently became violent.

A new Christian Socialist national government elected in 1929 set the restoration of order as its primary goal. It banned political parties. In 1930 it signed a treaty of friendship and protection with Benito Mussolini's fascist government of Italy.

A financial crisis in 1932 seriously weakened the national government, which proved unable to handle the continuing political conflicts. The National Socialist (Nazi) Party's growing power in Germany inspired the Austrian nationalists. The nationalists' strongest opposition came from the Social Democrats, and the conflict between the two parties grew violent.

Dictatorship. A Christian Socialist cabinet formed in 1932 by Chancellor Engelbert Dollfuss was determined to restore public order. In 1933 Dollfuss dissolved the legislature and restricted the rights of free speech, press, and assembly. He also tried to ban the Austrian Nazi party in 1933, but met with firm German opposition.

Faced with the threat of a German invasion, Dollfuss made himself dictator in 1933 to strengthen his position. On July 25, 1934, however, he was assassinated by Austrian Nazis.

Kurt von Schuschnigg continued the dictatorship, which relied on heavy economic aid and military protection from Italy, its only buffer against a German takeover. Domestic disorder soon was to cripple the nation, however, as nationalists and socialists bitterly attacked each other.

As Hitler gained the friendship of Mussolini, Nazi activity increased in Austria. In 1938 Schuschnigg was forced to recognize the Austrian Nazi party and to include members of the Nazi party in his cabinet.

Anschluss. In a last effort to save Austria, Schuschnigg tried to show the world that Austrians did not want to join Germany. Hitler then began massing troops on the Austrian border. Schuschnigg resigned, and Artur von Seyss-Inquart, the Nazi minister of the interior, replaced him as chancellor. In March 1938 Seyss-Inquart announced Austria's union with Germany and invited the German army into the country. The Anschluss had been accomplished.

The Allies hoped to avoid a second war by letting Hitler take Austria, so they made no objection to the *Anschluss.* In 1939, when World War II did begin, Austria was an integral part of Nazi Germany.

The cost of the war was high for Austria. Over 500,000 Austrian military personnel and civilians were killed, including some 60,000 Jews who died in Nazi concentration camps. (See HISTORY OF THE WORLD volume.) In addition, Austria was heavily bombed by the Allies and much of its industrial base was destroyed.

Contemporary Austria. Following the German defeat in 1945, Austria was divided into four zones, each occupied by one of the major Allied powers—the Soviet Union, Britain, France, and the United States. Austria's status after the war was complicated by Allied confusion over whether to treat the country as a victim of German aggression or as a willing participant in the war.

The constitution of 1920 was restored and a coalition government was formed. Allied forces withdrew in 1955 upon the signing of a treaty that committed Austria to neutrality, prohibited union with Germany, and required that Austria pay reparations to the Soviet Union.

After difficult initial postwar years, the Austrian economy recovered quickly. By 1955 the economy was almost back to prewar levels, and in the succeeding decades it grew strongly.

The Austrian political scene has remained stable. Except for the period from 1970 to 1983, when the Socialist Party held an absolute majority in the National Council, the country has generally been ruled by coalition governments. In 1986 the election of former UN secretary-general Kurt Waldheim to the Austrian presidency drew international criticism because of allegations that he had been involved in Nazi atrocities during World War II. Waldheim chose not to seek reelection in 1992 and Thomas Klestil, candidate of the conservative People's Party, was elected president.

In 1995 Austria became a member of the European Union, but retained its strict neutrality and refused to allow the stationing of foreign troops within its borders.

Azerbaijan

Official name: *Republic of Azerbaijan*

Area: *33,428 sq. mi., 86,600 sq. km.*

Type of government: *Republic*

Population: *7,798,000*

Capital and largest city: *Baku (Pop., 1,792,000)*

Languages: *Azeri, Russian, Armenian*

Literacy: *97%;* **Currency:** *Manat*

Per capita GDP: *$3,300 (Rank: 110th)*

The land. Occupying southeastern Transcaucasia on the Caspian Sea's western shore, Azerbaijan includes the geographically separate Nakhichevan Autonomous Republic. The northern limit of Azerbaijan is formed by the Great Caucasus Mountains, where the highest peak is Mount Bazardyuki, reaching 13,500 feet (4,145 meters). In the southwest, the Little (Lesser) Caucasus mountain system contains picturesque Gök-Göl Tarn (Lake Gyoygyol) at a height of 4,500 feet (1,372 meters). In the east is the vast Kura-Araks lowland area, named for the principal river and its tributary. This area includes the Shirvan, Milskaya, and Mugan steppes. An extensive system of canals irrigates much of the lowland area.

The climate in central and eastern Azerbaijan is dry and subtropical, with mild winters and very hot summers. The southeast is characterized by high

meters
US

metres
Brit.

humidity. Winters in the mountain regions are moderately cold.

The people. Forming 83 percent of the population, Azerbaijanis live in an area said to be settled since Paleolithic times. They are a predominantly Turkic people, combined with Iranian and other Transcaucasian strains, and are famed for their longevity. Forty-eight out of every 100,000 persons reach the age of 100 or more. Minority populations include approximately 400,000 Russians, more than 90 percent living in the cities, and about the same number of ethnic Armenians, who inhabit the contested area of Nagorno-Karabakh. Several million Azerbaijanis reside in nearby Iran and maintain their Turkic language. Intellectual and cultural life has flourished in the region for centuries, and modern Azerbaijanis are still known for their musical tradition, especially in the realm of improvised song. Illiteracy was almost completely eliminated under the Soviet regime.

The dominant religion is Islam, although the Armenian population of Nagorno-Karabakh remains Christian.

Economy. With rich reserves of oil, mainly on and in the Caspian Sea near Baku, Azerbaijan has been a major oil producer since the late 1800s. Other nat-

THE COMPOSITIONS of Austrian Franz Joseph Haydn, seen here with his family, were important in the development of musical style and taste in the 1700s.

ural resources include gas, iodobromide waters, zinc, iron, lead, copper, and the limestone and marble used in building. The republic produces equipment for the oil and natural gas industry as well as heavy machinery, chemicals, and textiles. Fisheries, especially on the Caspian Sea, are noted for their fine caviar made from sturgeon roe.

Raw cotton and tobacco are the most valuable crops, and the production of wine grapes continues to increase. Tea, wheat, fruits, and nuts are also grown. Livestock consists mostly of sheep and goats, with Karabakh riding horses raised for export.

Government. Azerbaijan is a constitutional republic. The three branches of government include the executive, which consists of the president, prime minister, and Council of Ministers; the legislature, in the form of the National Assembly with 125 members; and the judicial branch.

History. Modern Azerbaijan occupies the northern part of an historic area known as Albania in ancient times. Its history is closely mingled with that of Armenia and Persia. Azerbaijan was controlled at various times by Persians, Muslim Arabs, Mongolian Turkic tribes, Ottoman Turks, and Genghis Khan's Mongol hordes.

Russia acquired the territory from Persia in 1828 through the Treaty of Turkmenchai. The 19th century saw a period of industrial development under Russian rule, particularly after the completion of a major railway link from Baku to central Russia. An independent republic was created in 1918 and toppled in 1920 by Red Army forces. The Azerbaijan Soviet Socialist Republic, formed that same year, later joined the Transcaucasian Soviet Socialist Republic, and in 1936 it was made a separate union republic.

Since 1988 attention has been focused on the enclave of Nagorno-Karabakh, where Armenian Christian inhabitants have been agitating for secession from Muslim Azerbaijan.

meters
US

metres
Brit.

colonized
US

colonised
Brit.

CHRISTIAN KARABAKHS
and Kachins seek refuge from civil unrest in Azerbaijan.

In 1991, upon the dissolution of the Soviet Union, Azerbaijan declared its independence and became a member of the Commonwealth of Independent States.

(For more information about the history of Azerbaijan as part of the Soviet Union, see the article on Russia.)

Belarus

Official name: *Republic of Belarus*
Area: *80,155 sq. mi., 207,600 sq. km.*
Type of government: *Republic*
Population: *10,335,000*
Capital and largest city: *Minsk (Pop., 1,677,000)*
Languages: *Byelorussian, Russian*
Literacy: *98%*
Currency: *Ruble*
Per capita GDP: *$8,200 (Rank: 63rd)*

The land. The republic of Belarus, formerly Byelorussia (White Russia), is a region of hilly lowlands. Dzerzhinsky Mountain, the highest in the republic, is a mere 1,135 feet (346 meters) above sea level. Northern lowlands are marked by sloping ridges created by glacial debris. Areas of marshy land in the southwest combine in the east with the swamps of the Dnieper Lowland. Large forests, mostly of pine, fir, birch, and alder, cover about a third of Belarus, giving variety to the flat landscape.

Belarus contains more than 4,000 lakes and many rivers. The great Dnieper River, the third-longest river of Europe, flows southward to the Black Sea. Other major rivers include the Pripyat and Berezina, tributaries of the Dnieper, and the Western Dvina in the north and Neman in the west, flowing to the Baltic Sea.

Climate is affected by the proximity of the Baltic Sea

and is characterized by temperate summers and mild winters with frequent periods of thaw. Rainfall averages 22 to 28 inches (55 to 70 centimeters) per year.

The people. Belarussians, making up almost 80 percent of the population, are descended in part from East Slavic tribes that colonized the region between the fifth and eighth centuries. They are enriched by an ancient culture, including literary traditions dating from the 11th century.

Ruled by the Russian Empire in the 19th century, many Belarussians, particularly Jews, emigrated to the United States to escape difficult conditions at home. The population was further reduced during the period of collectivization in the 1930s, when many who opposed Stalin's policy were deported or killed. Thousands perished during World War II, which also saw the destruction of most of the remaining Jewish population.

Today the central part of the republic contains its most densely inhabited areas, while the swamplands of the south are thinly settled.

Economy. Once thought lacking in mineral resources, Belarus is now exploiting deposits of high-quality oil, coal, brown coal, rock salt, and potassium salt. Its peat marshes, covering more than 6 million acres (2.5 million hectares), are an important asset used for fertilizer and fuel and in the chemical industry.

Major industrial output is concentrated in engineering equipment, heavy-duty trucks and agricultural machinery, cars, and textiles. Chemical plants produce potassium fertilizer and oil by-products. Woodworking industries make plywood and pressboard for building, furniture, and matches.

The republic's chief crops are potatoes, rye, wheat, barley, oats, and sugar beets. Flax is grown in the north and hemp in the south.

Government. Belarus is a constitutional republic. A president is elected to a 5-year term by popular vote, and a prime minister is appointed by the president. The legislature consists of the Council of the Republic with 64 members and the Chamber of Representatives with 110 members.

History. Settled around the seventh century, Belarus was controlled by Kiev until the Mongol invasion of the 13th century. The dukes of Lithuania conquered the area in the 14th century, and a large number of Jews settled there.

During the partition of Poland between 1772 and 1795, Belarus became part of the Russian Empire. The country sustained great damage during conflicts between Russia and Poland, and in Napoleon's campaign of 1812. Further devastation was inflicted during World War I and in the Soviet-Polish War of 1919–1920, concluded in 1921 by the Treaty of Riga, which ceded western Belarus to Poland. The eastern area joined the Soviet Union in 1920 as the Belorussian Soviet Socialist Republic.

LATVIA

0　　　75 mi
0　　75 km

Velikiye Luki

Daugavpils

LITHUANIA

Polatsk

Pastavy

Vitsyebsk

Vilnius

Maladzyechna

Orsha

Smolensk

RUSSIA

Dzyarzhynskaya Hara
Lida
346 m
(1135 ft) ▲ **Minsk**

Smalyavichy

Mahilyow

Hrodna

Krychaw

Vawkavysk
Baranavichy

Asipovichy

Babruysk

Byelaruskaya

Zhlobin

Salihorsk

Bryansk

Rechytsa

Homyel'

Brest

Dnieper-Bug Canal　Pinsk

Pripyats

Mazyr

Pripyats Marshes

•Chernihiv

POLAND

Chornobyl'

UKRAINE

Kiev
Reservoir

© MQST

West Belarus was retaken by the Red Army in 1939 and became part of the Soviet Socialist Republic.

After surviving the purges of the 1930s under Stalin and the terrible destruction of World War II, Belarus emerged as one of the more successful and stable republics of the Soviet Union. Following the dissolution of the Soviet Union in 1991, Belarus became a member of the Commonwealth of Independent States (CIS) and its capital, Minsk, was chosen as the site of CIS meetings.

(For more information about the history of Belarus as part of the Russian Empire and Soviet Union, see the article on Russia.)

Belgium

Official name: *Kingdom of Belgium*
Area: *11,787 sq. mi., 30,536 sq. km.*
Type of government: *Federal parliamentary democracy*
Population: *10,275,000*
Capital: *Brussels (Pop., 137,000)*
Largest city: *Antwerp (Pop., 449,000)*
Languages: *Dutch, French, German (all official)*
Literacy: *98%*
Currency: *Euro*
Per capita GDP: *$29,000 (Rank: 7th)*

The land. Most of Belgium consists of low-lying plains. In the southeast, however, the country is quite hilly, and this highland wood and pasture zone—the Ardennes Forest—is rather sparsely settled. The main rivers in Belgium are the Schelde, the Sambre, and the Meuse.

Belgium has little variation in climate. Its mild winters and cool summers are characterized by light rainfall, high humidity, and partial cloudiness. In the southeast, however, the higher elevations cause somewhat cooler summers and distinctly colder winters, and the precipitation is much heavier.

The people. Belgium can be nearly evenly divided linguistically, and, to a certain extent, culturally, by an east-west line. In the north are the Flemings, who make up about 55 percent of the population. They speak Flemish, which is a language closely related to Dutch. In the south, the French-speaking Walloons are dominant. Brussels is bilingual. There is also a small minority of Germans near the eastern border. The people of Belgium are overwhelmingly Roman Catholic.

The relatively stable population is one of the densest in the Western world, with 840 people per square mile. It is 95 percent urban.

Economy. Belgium is a highly industrialized nation, although, apart from coal, the country has almost no natural mineral resources. It enjoyed, until recently, one of the highest standards of living in Western Europe. In the 1980s Belgium experienced high unemployment and high levels of government debt linked to shrinking foreign demand for traditional Belgian products such as steel. The encouragement of new high-technology industries has begun to restore the country to its previous prosperity.

Agriculture. Belgium is a very fertile country. Even though agriculture employs only about 2 percent of the population, it remains highly productive and supplies a large part of the country's needs.

Industry. With heavy investment in new, more competitive technology, Belgium has been able to rescue some of its important heavy industries. Steel production, metal fabrication, and machinery manufacture remain an important part of the economy. Belgium also produces chemicals, textiles, and glass.

New high-technology industries are becoming increasingly important as the country searches for export products.

Trade. Trade is extremely important to the Belgian economy. It is one of the largest exporters, per capita, in the world. Because Belgium has few exportable natural resources of its own, it relies heavily on adding value to imported resources, which are then reexported.

Major exports include machinery, chemicals, food, and iron and steel. Imports include machinery, fuel, and food. Belgium is joined with Luxembourg in a customs union. In addition it is a member of the European Union (EU). Most of its trade is with other members of the EU.

Government. The head of state in Belgium is the king. Executive power is exercised by the king and his ministers. No act of the king is effective, however, unless countersigned by a minister. Ministers, including a prime minister, are appointed by the king from among the members of the majority party in parliament, and they are responsible to parliament.

Legislative power is exercised by the parliament, which consists of two houses, the 71-member Senate and the 150-member Chamber of Representatives, and by the king, who sanctions and promulgates the laws. Members of the Chamber of Representatives are popularly elected on the basis of proportional representation. The Senate members are partly directly and partly indirectly elected every 4 years.

History. The Belgae, or Belgians, were one of the Gallic tribes conquered by Julius Caesar in the first century B.C., and the area that is now Belgium became part of the Roman Empire. Roman occupation was followed by invasions of Franks between the A.D. 200s and 400s. After 476 Belgium was ruled by the Merovingians, and later it became part of Charlemagne's empire (800–843).

During the Middle Ages, Belgium existed as a group of duchies, which in 1384 came under the control of the dukes

of Burgundy in eastern France. Belgium passed to the Hapsburgs through marriage in 1477 and subsequently became part of the Holy Roman Empire. On the resignation of the Holy Roman Emperor Charles V in 1556, Belgium, along with the Netherlands, passed to Philip II of Spain.

The northern provinces of the Netherlands, or Holland, formed the Union of Utrecht and declared their independence in 1581. But the provinces that constitute modern Belgium continued to be ruled by Spain and then by Austria (1713) until conquered by France in 1792.

Belgium became part of Napoleon's empire in 1801. The Congress of Vienna (1814–1815), which redrew the map of Europe after Napoleon's defeat, united Belgium with Holland in the Kingdom of the Netherlands.

The union of the two failed to take into consideration the difference in character between the two regions, however. Holland was Protestant, Germanic, agricultural, and commercial, whereas Belgium was Roman Catholic, French-oriented, and industrial. Holland favored a policy of free trade, and Belgium sought high tariffs to protect its industry.

ANTWERP, long known as one of the strongest fortresses in Europe, is famous for its beautiful architecture.

THE HEADQUARTERS of the European Union in Brussels.

color *US*

colour *Brit.*

MANY HOUSES IN BRUSSELS were built in the 1600s by wealthy merchants.

Independence. In 1830 the Belgians revolted. King William I sent Dutch troops into Brussels to suppress the revolution, but they were unsuccessful. A provisional government was established, and with the agreement of France and Britain, Prince Leopold of Saxe-Coburg-Gotha was elected king. Within a year, after several conferences, the great powers recognized the independence of Belgium and in 1839 guaranteed its neutrality.

Under Leopold I, who ruled from 1831 to 1865, Belgium's economy expanded rapidly, and under Leopold II (1865–1909) Belgium acquired a vast empire in the African Congo. By the end of the 1800s, Belgium had transformed itself from an oligarchy governed by a small middle class to a democracy based on universal suffrage with very advanced social welfare programs.

Belgian neutrality was violated by Germany during both World War I and World War II. German troops first entered Belgium on August 4, 1914, after Germany repudiated the treaty guaranteeing Belgian neutrality. The resulting destruction and death toll were enormous.

War damage in Belgium in World War I amounted to more than $7 billion. The tremendous cost of reconstruction after the war caused a rapid rise in the national debt, inflation, and other financial problems that were to plague the country for almost 20 years. Economic problems increased demands for social legislation, and popular dissatisfaction was expressed politically. As a result, the interwar period was characterized by a series of short-lived governments.

During World War II, the Germans attacked Belgium on May 10, 1940. On May 28, King Leopold III surrendered to avoid further bloodshed. It was felt, however, that his early surrender weakened Allied strategy and many patriotic Belgians were outraged. Leopold spent the remainder of the war as a German prisoner. The second German occupation was far worse than the first. Damage was more extensive and many more lives were lost.

After the war ended, criticism of Leopold's wartime record was so strong that he was unable to return to Belgium immediately. The Belgians voted on March 12, 1950, to recall King Leopold to the throne. Opposition continued to prove so bitter, however, that Leopold abdicated in 1951 in favor of his son, who became King Baudouin. He ruled until his death on July 31, 1993, when he was succeeded by his brother, who became King Albert II.

Contemporary Belgium. Early during the postwar period, Belgium recognized the pressing need for economic cooperation among the nations of Europe. In 1957 Belgium, along with five other nations, signed the treaty establishing the Common Market.

One of the main concerns of the government during the 1950s was the increasing political unrest in the mineral-rich Belgian Congo. Independence was granted to the Congo on June 30, 1960, and the loss of this important market and source of raw materials dealt a severe blow to the Belgian economy. Belgian business interests supported a separatist faction in the province of Katanga. The resulting civil war inevitably caused an international crisis.

The long-standing hostility between French- and Flemish-speaking Belgians has remained the most difficult and divisive problem of the postwar period. Three semiautonomous and politically equal regions were created by constitutional revision in 1971—French-speaking Wallonia, Flemish-speaking Flanders, and the bilingual Brussels region. However, language divisions still continue to color politics as well as decisions about education and culture.

Bosnia and Herzegovina

Official name: *Bosnia and Herzegovina*

Area: *19,781 sq. mi., 51,233 sq. km.*

Type of government: *Emerging democracy*

Population: *3,964,000*

Capital and largest city: *Sarajevo (Pop., 529,000)*

Language: *Serbo-Croatian*

Literacy: *90%;* **Currency:** *Dinar*

Per capita GDP: *$1,800 (Rank: 138th)*

The land. Located on the Balkan peninsula, Bosnia and Herzegovina is a small, triangular country bordered on the northwest by the Sava River and to the east by the Drina River. Other important rivers are the Bosna (from which Bosnia derives its name), the Una, the Vrbas, and the Neretva. No natural harbors are found on the country's 13-mile (21-kilometer) stretch of coastline on the Adriatic Sea.

Bosnia, in the north, is a mountainous area with heavy forests that features the Dinaric Alps in the east. Herzegovina, to the south, has level land more suitable for farming.

The sirocco, a wind from the southwest that brings rain to the area, and the bora, a fierce wind from the northnortheast, are important in determining the region's weather. Although these winds are factors in both Bosnia and Herzegovina, the climates of the two areas differ. Bosnia is generally mild, with cold winters, while Herzegovina is more subtropical, with dry, extremely hot summers and a rainy season lasting from October until January.

The people. Bosnia and Herzegovina is populated by a volatile mix of Slavs, Serbs, and Croats. The majority of the Slavs are Muslims belonging to the Sunni sect, while most Serbs are Eastern Orthodox. The Croatian population is predominantly Roman Catholic. The country has only one official language, Serbo-Croatian, which is written in both the Cyrillic and Roman alphabets. Major cities in Bosnia and Herzegovina are Sarajevo, the country's capital, Banja Luka (population, 196,000), and Mostar (127,000), the capital of the region of Herzegovina.

Economy. Timber, coal, iron, bauxite, and other minerals are among the country's important natural resources. Its chief agricultural products are corn, wheat, oats, barley, sugar beets, flax, cotton, and tobacco.

Although in recent years the area has relied less on agriculture and more on industry, the economy is troubled as a result of the country's political turmoil during the early 1990s. In 1991 Bosnia

and Herzegovina had an inflation rate of 1,000 percent and an unemployment rate of 25 percent.

Government. When the republic of Bosnia and Herzegovina became an internationally recognized independent country in 1992, it established a democratic republic with a bicameral parliament. Each of the country's three major ethnic groups is represented by its own political party and elected president.

History. The republic of Bosnia and Herzegovina is the site of Roman ruins that date back to the time when the area was part of the Roman provinces of Illyricum and Pannonia. When Slavic people from the north settled in the region in the sixth and seventh centuries, many of the Roman colonists retreated to what is now Albania.

The Slavs who remained became known as Serbs and Croats. An independent country for most of the period from the ninth to the eleventh centuries (the region was briefly united with two other Serbian principalities from 1081 to 1101), Bosnia came under Hungarian rule during the twelfth century. Religious differences between the Croats, linked to the Roman Catholic Hungarians, and Serbs, influenced by the Eastern Orthodox Church, caused political unrest in the region. The situation was further complicated by the emergence of the Bogomils, a heretical Christian sect whose members were drawn chiefly from the nobility.

Muslim Turks of the Ottoman Empire gained control of the area beginning in 1463, and Islam became a new major religion. Bosnia and Herzegovina remained part of the Ottoman Empire until the 19th century, when a peasant revolt in 1875 led to an all-out war involving Austria-Hungary and other European forces. The war ended in 1878, and Bosnia and Herzegovina came under the rule of the Austrian-Hungarian Empire.

As nationalism emerged as a growing force in Europe, ethnic groups in Bosnia and Herzegovina, as in other Balkan areas, became increasingly dissatisfied. The unrest finally erupted when a Serbian nationalist assassinated Archduke Francis Ferdinand, heir to the Austrian throne, during his visit to Sarajevo on June 28, 1914. The event triggered World War I. At the end of the war, both Bosnia and Herzegovina became part of the Kingdom of Serbs, Croats, and Slovenes, which became Yugoslavia in 1929. (See the article on Serbia and Montenegro for a history of the region between 1918 and 1991.)

In 1991, amid continued ethnic hostilities throughout Yugoslavia and the collapse of the Soviet Union, Bosnia and Herzegovina declared itself independent. The European Community (later the European Union) ruled that the new nation could not be recognized as such until a referendum was held. Bosnian Serbs opposed the results of the March 1992 referendum, which established the country's independence, and fighting erupted in April.

Enlisting the help of Yugoslavia's largely Serbian army, ethnic Serbs in Bosnia and Herzegovina besieged the capital city of Sarajevo. The neighboring republic of Croatia allied itself with Bosnia and Herzegovina in June, but in the next month Croatia created what it called the Croatian Community of Herceg-Bosna, leading to speculation that the region might be divided between Croatia and Serbia.

By December 1992 Serbian forces had gained control of two-thirds of the country, using violence and terror to achieve "ethnic cleansing," the forcible removal or killing of non-Serbians. In 1994 Bosnian Muslims and Croats joined to form a federation. In 1995, after NATO forces bombed Bosnian Serb targets, the presidents of Bosnia, Serbia, and Croatia signed a peace accord in Paris, France, following U.S.-sponsored negotiations held in Dayton, Ohio. A NATO-led stabilization force remains in place to deter renewed hostilities.

kilometer
US

kilometre
Brit.

26 Europe and Russia

THE FIERCE recent conflict in Bosnia and Herzegovina has caused much destruction and human suffering.

Bulgaria

Official name: *Republic of Bulgaria*
Area: *42,811 sq. mi.,*
110,910 sq. km.
Type of government: *Emerging*
democracy
Population: *7,621,000*
Capital and largest city: *Sofia*
(Pop., 1,191,000)
Language: *Bulgarian*
Literacy: *98%;* **Currency:** *Lev*
Per capita GDP: *$6,600*
(Rank: 73rd)

RILA MONASTERY, of the Bulgarian Orthodox Church in Bulgaria, survived years of communist repression.

The land. Mountains and plains alternate in Bulgaria to form four major geographical regions. In the north is the Danube basin, a low, fertile plateau crossed at the Bulgarian-Romanian boundary by the Danube River.

At the eastern end of the Danube basin is a large limestone plateau region. To the south of the basin, arching southeastward from Bulgaria's northwestern corner to the Black Sea, are the Balkan Mountains, ranging from 3,000 to over 7,000 feet (920 to 2,100 meters) in elevation. The entire southwestern corner of the country is also mountainous, with the Rhodope Range rising to over 9,000 feet (3,783 meters).

Between the two mountainous regions, in central Bulgaria, is the basin of the Maritsa River. At its eastern end, the basin widens and opens into the Black Sea. At its western end is the heartland of Bulgaria, the Sofia basin.

The Bulgarian climate varies from region to region. The Danube plateau has cold, snowy winters and hot summers. The Maritsa basin, farther south, is protected by the mountains to the north and has milder winters. The mountains throughout the country tend to have harsher weather, with seasonal variations.
The people. Nearly 90 percent of the people are Bulgarians. They speak Bulgarian, a south Slavic language, and use an alphabet similar to the Russian. The larger minority groups include Turks, Macedonians, Romanians, Armenians, and gypsies. Most of the people belong to the Bulgarian Orthodox Church, an independent Eastern Orthodox Christ-

ian body. Islam is the largest of the minority religions.

Population is densest in the Sofia basin, especially around Sofia, the capital, which is a rapidly growing industrial center as well as the administrative and intellectual heart of the country. Other large urban centers are Plovdiv (population, 340,000) in the Maritsa valley; Varna (305,000) and Burgas (212,000), the leading Black Sea ports; and Ruse (183,000), the largest Danubian port.
Economy. From 1945 to 1989, Bulgaria followed the Soviet economic model, wherein the state owns all the means of production and regulates all economic activity. Bulgaria's economy, traditionally based on agriculture, was industrialized rapidly under Communist leadership. In the 1980s, Bulgaria loosened ties with the Soviet Union.

As a result of industrialization, agriculture's significance to the Bulgarian economy dropped sharply. In 1986 it accounted for 17 percent of the national product and employed 19 percent of the labor force. However, Bulgarian agriculture remains among the most efficient in Eastern Europe. Wheat and corn are the leading cereal crops; tobacco, sugar beets, cotton, and soybeans are also important crops. Livestock husbandry, fishing, and forestry are other significant contributors to the economy.

Bulgaria has important deposits of coal, iron, copper, lead, and zinc. The country, however, has limited reserves of oil and natural gas, and must therefore import a large percentage of its energy needs.

Industry, which was nationalized in 1947, accounts for almost half of the national product, and it employs about one-third of the workforce. The nation's leading industries include metalworking, oil refining, iron and steel production, machinery manufacture, chemical production, and

electricity production. The traditionally important light industries, including textiles and weaving, leather tooling, woodworking, and tobacco processing, thrive on a smaller scale. In the 1980s emphasis was placed on developing high-technology industries such as electronics and biotechnology.

Bulgaria's international trade has increased greatly since the 1950s; it now contributes about half of the national income. Principal exports include agricultural and food products, textiles and clothing, and machinery. Imports include fuel, machinery, and timber. About 80 percent of Bulgaria's trade is with other Eastern European countries. Since Bulgaria began to privatize its industries and establish a market economy, it has been faced with loss of markets, high unemployment, and high inflation. By the mid-1990s the economy showed little growth.
Government. Free elections held in June 1990 ended the Communist Party's monopoly of Bulgarian political life. In 1991 a Grand National Assembly completed work on a new constitution, which went into effect in July. It established Bulgaria as a democratic state and provided for a popularly elected, 240-member parliament. The head of state is the president, who is directly elected for a 5-year term. The head of government is the prime minister. The first parliamentary elections were held in October 1991.
History. Bulgaria's location has made the country subject to competing Slavic, Byzantine, Ottoman Turkish, and West European influences. Bulgaria's history has been marked by frequent conquest and domination by foreign powers. Present-day Bulgaria was part of the Roman Empire by the middle of the first century A.D. By the 500s, a variety of Slavic tribes had settled in the region.

meters
US

metres
Brit.

center
US

centre
Brit.

labor
US

labour
Brit.

CITY SQUARE IN SOFIA, Bulgaria, the country's capital and largest city.

In the 600s the Bulgars, a warlike people from the northern shores of the Black Sea, conquered the Slavs and settled in the territory. By the 700s the Bulgars had organized a state, the first Bulgarian Empire, and for the next hundred years they resisted conquest by the Byzantine Empire. In 817 a Bulgarian-Byzantine treaty established peace between the two nations.

From about 853 to 927, under the emperors Boris and Simeon, the Bulgarian Empire reached its height. Boris consolidated his power by putting down rebellious nobles, and his armies conquered new territory. During that time the Bulgars were converted to Christianity. Simeon continued the expansion of the empire, and made Sofia a center of learning and culture. At his death the Bulgarian Empire controlled much of the Balkan peninsula. In the late 900s, however, Bulgarian territory began to fall to Byzantine armies, and by 1018 the entire nation had been conquered.

During the 1100s, when the Byzantine Empire had begun to disintegrate, a second Bulgarian Empire was established. During the 200 years that the second empire flourished, Bulgaria again became the dominant power in the Balkans. Continual warfare weakened it, however, and in 1393, the country was again conquered by Byzantium.

Ottoman rule. The brief period of brilliance and expansion of the second empire was followed by 500 years of rule by the Ottoman Turks. Under the Ottomans, Bulgaria was isolated from both the Western and the Slavic worlds. Ottoman control of the country was complete, and only those Bulgarians who became Muslims could achieve positions of authority. But life for the peasants—the bulk of the population—was probably no more difficult than under Bulgarian rulers.

During the second half of the 1800s, Bulgarian nationalism became an active force. The Ottoman Empire had become weak, and Bulgarians were able to assume greater control over their own affairs. They established a national school system, an active press, and a newly independent Bulgarian Church. In 1876 a revolt against the Turks was crushed with vicious ferocity. This provided Russia, an enemy of the Ottomans, with an excuse to go to war with Turkey in 1877.

Independence. Russia was victorious, and in 1878 the Treaty of Berlin granted independence to the principality of Bulgaria, the northern section of present-day Bulgaria. The southern two-thirds, known as Eastern Rumelia, received independence separately. The area remained the center of international political and territorial disputes until 1885, when the two regions were united as Bulgaria.

The new nation was governed by nationalist leaders until 1908, when Prince Ferdinand proclaimed it a kingdom. In the years between 1886 and 1912, Bulgaria made substantial economic and political progress under a democratic constitution. Domestic progress was jeopardized by territorial quarrels, however. Bulgaria claimed Macedonia from Serbia and Greece, Thrace from Greece and Turkey, and southern Dobruja from Romania.

These territorial disputes led, in 1912, to the first Balkan War, which Bulgaria and its Balkan allies won against Turkey. In the second Balkan War, in 1913, Bulgaria lost territories to its former allies, Greece and Serbia, and to Romania and Turkey. When Germany and Austria promised the return of these territories, Bulgaria sided with them in World War I. Germany and its allies lost the war, and the 1919 Treaty of Neuilly forced Bulgaria to cede still more territory—to Yugoslavia, Greece, and Romania.

The losses embittered Bulgaria's domestic politics and foreign relations during the decades between the two world wars. Relations with Greece and Yugoslavia were especially uneasy, and border disputes were frequent. Resentment within Bulgaria led to the loss of many social and economic gains. Premier Aleksandr Stamboliski, the effective political leader of the time, instituted many reforms, but his methods were unpopular and aroused further resentment.

In 1923 a militant nationalist organization, IMRO (Internal Macedonian Revolutionary Organization), helped overthrow the Stamboliski government. IMRO played a large part in precipitating a series of government crises during the next 10 years. After a decade of disorder, the military seized control in 1934.

A second coup staged by the king took place in 1935. The king suspended the constitution and made himself a dictator. Bulgaria's continuing territorial ambitions and close trade ties with Germany brought it into World War II on the German side in 1941; however, Bulgaria was careful to avoid declaring war on the Soviet Union.

Communist rule. Toward the end of the war, in September 1944, the Soviet Union declared war on Bulgaria, and within a week Soviet forces occupied the country. In 1945 elections were held, and a government that was led by a communist-dominated Fatherland Front came to power.

Bulgarians voted in 1946 to abolish the monarchy and establish a republic. By 1948 the communists had removed all independent voices from the government, and communist rule was absolute.

Bulgarian communists who had led the resistance and organized the republic gradually were replaced by those controlled from the Soviet Union.

After the war Bulgaria closely followed the Soviet lead in both internal and external policy decisions. It earned the reputation of being one of Moscow's most loyal allies. Following the Soviet lead in 1948, Bulgaria broke ties with Tito's Yugoslavia. In 1968 the country participated in the invasion of Czechoslovakia.

In 1989, amid growing demands for political and economic change, Todor I. Zhivkov, for 35 years Bulgaria's leader, resigned. The next year the Communist Party became the Bulgarian Socialist Party. In 1992 Zhelyu Zhelev won the country's first direct presidential election.

In parliamentary elections in 1991, the small Turkish Movement for Rights and Freedom gained the balance of power against the opposition Union of Democratic Forces and the Socialists. It was hoped that the new importance of Bulgaria's Muslim Turkish minority would help end decades of violent oppression. Power shifted back and forth through the 1990s. Bulgaria joined NATO in 2004.

THE CHURCHES of the Eastern Orthodox religion bear testimony to the influence of the Byzantine Empire, of which Bulgaria became a part in 1018.

Croatia

Official name: *Republic of Croatia*
Area: *21,829 sq. mi., 56,538 sq. km.*
Type of government:
  Parliamentary democracy
Population: *4,391,000*
Capital and largest city: *Zagreb*
  (Pop., 692,000)
Language: *Serbo-Croatian*
Literacy: *97%;* **Currency:** *Kuna*
Per capita GDP: *$8,800*
  (Rank: 57th)

kilometers
US

kilometres
Brit.

center
US

centre
Brit.

aluminum
US

aluminium
Brit.

civilization
US

civilisation
Brit.

A WOMAN WATCHES from the window of a decorated house in the Czech Republic.

The land. Croatia is a hook-shaped country on the Adriatic Sea. Some 600 islands off the coast are also part of the country. The coastal region, which includes the Istrian peninsula in the north, is interrupted for 13 miles (21 kilometers) by Bosnia and Herzegovina's short coastline, and then resumes again. About one-third of Croatia is forested.

Croatia has three distinct geographic regions. Mountain ranges, chief among which are the Dinaric Alps, characterize Dalmatia, which is the area parallel to the coastline south of the Velebit Mountains. Hills roll across the north, referred to as the Zagorje region. Flat, fertile land dominates the country's inland region, known as the Pannonian Plain. The coastline enjoys a mild, Mediterranean climate, while the rest of the country has a more continental climate, with cold winters and warm summers.

The country's major rivers are the Sava, flowing diagonally from the northwest to the southeast and forming part of the country's border with Bosnia and Herzegovina; the Drava, which separates Croatia from Hungary; and the Danube, which flows along part of the border with Serbia and Montenegro.

The people. Most of the people living in the country are ethnic Croats who are Roman Catholic, although a minority population of Serbs, who are Eastern Orthodox, play an important role in the nation.

After Zagreb, the country's capital, Croatia's next largest city is Split (population, 175,000), a shipbuilding center in the middle of the coastline. Other important cities are Rijeka (144,000), the country's chief port, located near the northern end of the coast; Osijek (90,000), on the Drava River; and the historic old city of Dubrovnik (30,000), at the southern end of the Croatian coast.

Economy. Copper, bauxite, coal, oil, and timber are important natural resources of Croatia. Manufacturing and mining are the largest industries in the country, producing aluminum products, paper, textiles, petroleum products, chemicals, iron, and steel.

Agriculture also contributes to the economy. Olives and wine are major agricultural products, and corn, oats, sugar beets, wheat, and potatoes are grown on the Pannonian Plain.

Government. The independent republic of Croatia was established in 1991 as a parliamentary democracy. A president and legislature are elected by popular vote. The legislature is the 151-member one-house Assembly, or Sabor. A prime minister is nominated by the president from the party holding a majority in the Sabor.

History. When Croats migrated during the sixth century from the area known today as the Ukraine to what is now Croatia, they found themselves in the Roman provinces of Pannonia and Dalmatia. Whereas the Romans had first conquered the Adriatic trading centers as early as the sixth century B.C., and then moved inland, the Croats reversed the process, taking first the inland regions and then pushing toward the sea. The Croats established a farming civilization governed by tribal chiefs. After being converted to Christianity in the seventh century, the Croats found themselves divided, with those in Pannonia claimed as part of the Frankish Empire and those in Dalmatia claimed as part of the Byzantine Empire.

In 925 the Croats established their own kingdom, recognized by Pope John X. The country's security was threatened by the Venetians, who were encroaching on the Dalmatian territories; the Bulgarians, who briefly threatened Pannonia; and the Byzantine Empire, which exerted its influence under the guise of assisting the country against the first two enemies. In the eleventh century Croatia freed itself from Byzantine power by halting relations with Byzantium and intensifying its association with the papacy.

Although Croatia's power increased, internal conflicts ultimately destroyed the country's independence. Croatia's king, Dimitrije Zvonimir, was killed in 1089 when he attempted to persuade his subjects to join Pope Gregory XII's war against Byzantium. In the chaos that followed, Byzantium took Dalmatia, and King László of Hungary claimed the Croatian crown and the Pannonian territories on the basis of his relationship to Zvonimir, his brother-in-law. When the Dalmatian Croats recognized a king other than the Hungarian sovereign, the pope, supporting his Catholic allies, suggested that Hungary wage war to enforce fealty. The war ended with the Pacta Conventa, which led to Croatia's 800-year relationship with Hungary. The status of Croatia varied throughout this period, but Hungarian influence remained firm.

During the 15th century, Dalmatia was sold to the Venetians, who ruled the area for the following 400 years. The rest of Croatia fell to the Turks when the Ottoman Empire invaded the Balkans during the 15th and 16th centuries. When Hungary proved unable to provide effective protection against the Turks, Croatian and Hungarian nobles elected the Hapsburg King Ferdinand I of Austria as sovereign. Austria then limited the powers of the Sabor, the Croatian legislative body, and ordered Hungarian, German, Austrian, and Serb troops to protect the Croatian border. Croatia thus became a buffer state

© MQST

between the Ottoman Empire and western Europe.

In 1724 Hungary, also under the control of the Hapsburgs, annexed Croatia, although Croatia continued to claim autonomy. As Hungarian claims to Croatia strengthened, Croatian nationalism also grew. Despite Croatia's active opposition to Hungarian control in 1848, Croatia was assigned to Hungary when the Hapsburgs established the Austrian-Hungarian Empire in 1867. Croatian nationalism remained a potent force in the area's politics in the years that followed.

In 1918 Croatia formally declared its independence from Austria-Hungary and then joined the new Kingdom of Serbs, Croats, and Slovenes, which became Yugoslavia in 1929. (See the article on Serbia and Montenegro for the history of Croatia from 1918 to 1991.)

Croatian nationalism led to secession from Yugoslavia in 1991, and in 1992 the European Community (later the European Union) recognized the new country. Croatia's declaration of independence led to a bloody conflict with the Yugoslavian army, a predominantly Serbian force, which claimed to be protecting the interests of ethnic Serbs. The UN became involved in peacekeeping efforts. Ethnic regions changed hands often throughout the 1990s. In 2000 Croatia welcomed back banished Serbs and entered into talks with Bosnia and Yugoslavia.

Czech Republic

Official name: *Czech Republic*
Area: *30,387 sq. mi., 78,703 sq. km.*
Type of government:
Parliamentary democracy
Population: *10,257,000*
Capital and largest city: *Prague*
(Pop. 1,179,000)
Languages: *Czech, Slovak*
Literacy: *100%;* **Currency:** *Koruna*
Per capita GDP: *$15,300*
(Rank: 38th)

The land. The Czech Republic consists of the historic regions of Bohemia, or Czecy, in the west, Moravia in the east, and a small segment of Silesia in the north. In Bohemia, the western part of the country, the rolling plateau of the Bohemian Quadrangle is rimmed with mountains. The Bohemian Forest in the southwest, the Erzgebirge Range in the northwest, and Silesia's Sudeten Range in the north all rise above 4,000 feet (1,220 meters). The hills of the Bohemian-Moravian Uplands form the eastern limit of the plateau. The Elbe (Labe) River and its tributaries drain the entire region. Flowing northwest, the Elbe provides a route to the North Sea.

Moravia, in the eastern part of the republic, is a wide passageway of river valleys and low hills drained by the Morava and Oder rivers. The Morava flows south toward the Danube River, which provides access to the Black Sea. The Oder flows north toward the Baltic. The country's climate is moderate, although considerable regional differences exist.

The people. The majority of the people living in the Czech Republic are of Czech or Moravian descent, though there are small minorities of Slovaks, Hungarians, Gypsies, and other ethnic groups.

Population is densest in central Bohemia, especially around Prague, the capital, largest city, and cultural and economic center of the country. Other important cities are Brno (population, 379,000) and Ostrava (319,000).

Economy. Approximately 60 percent of the Czech Republic's gross domestic product is derived from industries such as aircraft production, oil refining, textiles, and glass and crystal manufacturing. Agriculture and food processing also play a significant role in the country's economy. The country's few natural resources include coal, iron, and limited quantities of nonferrous metals.

Beginning in 1989 economic reforms such as privatization, liberalization of prices and foreign trade, and conversion to a Western-style market economy were introduced to Czechoslovakia, causing some economic discomfort. Much of Czechoslovakia's industry was located in its Czech Republic, and the bulk of foreign investment in the country was aimed at enterprises in that region. As a result, the republic was able to achieve a low unemployment rate, curb inflation, and attract foreign investment while moving to privatize its economy.

Government. A bicameral, popularly elected parliament elects the president. The president serves a 5-year term and is limited to two terms. The president appoints the prime minister, who is the head of the government.

History. The basins of the Elbe, Oder, and Morava rivers, protected by the surrounding mountains, had been settled by Slavic peoples by the sixth century A.D. By the seventh century some tribal and geographical distinctions had been made between Czechs, Moravians, and Slovaks.

Moravia developed most quickly, and by the end of the ninth century Moravian princes ruled an empire, called the Great Moravian Empire, that included Slovakia and parts of present-day Austria and Hungary. Moravian subjects became Christians during the ninth century. In the early 10th century, the Moravian Empire was conquered by the Magyar people of Hungary.

Bohemia. The Czech tribes of Bohemia were gradually united during the ninth and tenth centuries. By the end of the that period, one leader ruled Bohemia and the western portion of the Moravian Empire. In the 11th century the kingdom of Bohemia became part of the Holy Roman Empire, but its military power and political strength were great enough to permit the state a good deal

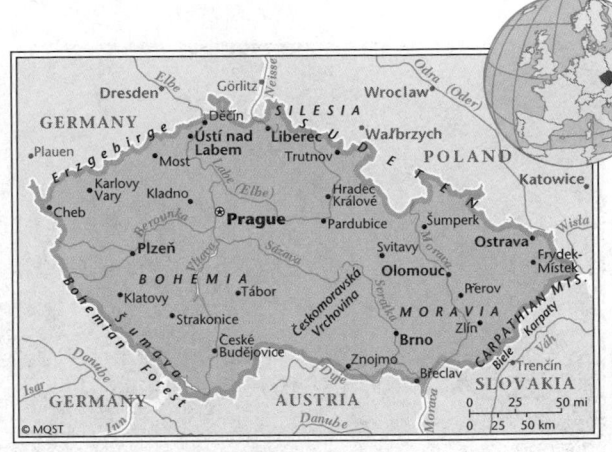

of independence. Its wealth, prestige, and cultural and political leadership reached a peak in the 14th century, when King Charles I of Bohemia became Holy Roman Emperor as Charles IV. Charles made Prague the capital of his empire. A generous supporter of the arts and education, he founded Charles University.

During the 15th century, especially after the execution in 1415 of a Bohemian religious reformer, John Hus, conflict within Bohemia and between Bohemia and the empire led to a gradual decline in the kingdom's prestige. In 1526 a Hapsburg of Austria was elected king of Bohemia. In 1547 the Bohemian crown became the hereditary possession of the Hapsburgs, who ruled Bohemia together with Austria and Hungary. Hapsburgs also ruled the Holy Roman Empire.

BOHEMIAN KINGS were crowned in the beautiful church of St. Vitus in Prague.

THE BEAUTIFUL CITY OF PRAGUE lies on both banks of the Vltava River, connected by several bridges.

centered
US

centred
Brit.

TOMBSTONES in a cemetery in the Czech Republic testify to the age of the city, which was probably founded in the 800s.

The Bohemian nobles resented the Hapsburg king, not only because he was not a Czech, but also because he was a Roman Catholic (during the late 16th century many Bohemians had become Protestants). In 1618 the Bohemian nobles rebelled. The rebellion raged until 1620, when the Bohemian rebels were defeated at the Battle of White Mountain, near Prague. Hapsburg control of Bohemia remained firm for the next two centuries.

In the early 19th century the pan-Slav movement developed in Bohemia and Slovakia, and in 1848 it contributed to a Slavic revolt against the German-speaking Austrians.

The rebellion was put down by 1849, but the movement gained strength as Austria lost power to Prussia and gradually relaxed its rule. In 1867 Austria's reception of the Magyars of Hungary into an equal partnership in a dual Austrian-Hungarian monarchy served to spur the Slavic independence movement. By the last decades of the 19th century, Austria-Hungary's encouragement of industrialization in Bohemia

had made the Czechs one of the most prosperous people of Europe.

By the time World War I began, the Czechs were economically, emotionally, and politically ready to take advantage of the turmoil the war caused in Austria-Hungary. Czech and Slovak soldiers surrendered independently to the Allied armies and fought against Austria-Hungary, thus winning support in the Allied countries for their independence movements.

During the war Tomáš Masaryk, the leader of the Czech national movement, and Slovak leaders, such as Milan Hodža, agreed to unite in a new country, and they formed a provisional government. After the war the Allies recognized the provisional government as the representative of the Czech and Slovak peoples, and in 1918 Czechoslovak independence was proclaimed.

Independence. The new state was formally recognized in 1919 in the Treaty of St. Germain. A democratic constitution was adopted, and Masaryk became the first president. He was succeeded in 1935 by his associate, Eduard Beneš.

Czechoslovakia became the most democratic and prosperous country in eastern Europe. Although equal status had been granted to Czechs and Slovaks, the new state was based largely on Czech political and economic leadership centered in Prague. The Slovaks, after a thousand years of rule by Hungary, were not as advanced as the Czechs politically or economically.

Friction between Czechs and Slovaks mounted over political, economic, religious, educational, and social issues. To these difficulties was added the dissatisfaction of a sizable German minority included in the new state. The Germans, concentrated in the strategic Sudeten region of northwestern Czechoslovakia, resented rule by Czechs and Slovaks, whom they had dominated for centuries.

Charging discrimination and claiming they had no real voice in government, Sudeten Germans served as German agents within Czechoslovakia. Their complaints and Hitler's diplomatic and military pressures created a severe international crisis that led in 1938 to the Munich Agreement.

Britain and France agreed at Munich to the division of Czechoslovakia and the transfer of one-third of its population and its vital defenses to Germany. Poland and Hungary also took areas they had long claimed. In return, Hitler promised to leave untouched the remainder of Czechoslovakia. In 1939, despite this promise, German troops occupied the rest of Czechoslovakia, declaring the Czech area a protectorate and creating a separate puppet state in Slovakia.

During World War II, a major Czechoslovakian resistance movement was organized; Czechoslovakian Communists played a prominent role. In 1944–1945 Soviet troops liberated Slovakia, Mor-avia, and most of Bohemia from the Germans. U.S. forces liberated western Bohemia in 1945, but the Soviets insisted that their troops be allowed to free the capital, Prague. This gained for the Soviet Union the bulk of the prestige associated with the country's liberation.

Communist rule. The presence of Soviet troops and the desire of President Beneš and other Czechoslovak leaders to cooperate with the Soviet Union enabled the communists to position themselves for a successful coup d'etat in 1948.

During the 1950s the communist-controlled government nationalized all large-scale business and industry and collectivized agriculture. The government concentrated on developing Slovakia and on building up heavy industry in Bohemia. Czechoslovakia became one of the most productive states in the Soviet bloc.

Later, as the economy began to slump, Czech Communist Party chairman Alexander Dubček led a movement, during what became known as the Prague Spring, to establish a humanistic-socialist democracy in which Slovakian autonomy would be recognized. As the movement reached its height in August

1968, Soviet and other Eastern bloc troops invaded the nation and placed the ultraconservatives back in power.

In the resulting shake-up, Gustav Husak became head of the Communist Party. Husak led a purge of the party that removed the reformist membership. The reforms that had been instituted were dismantled.

In November of 1989 the so-called Velvet Revolution succeeded in forcing the communist government to resign after huge demonstrations were staged in Prague. This time the Soviet Union did not intervene. In December the dissident playwright and human rights activist Vaclav Havel became president of Czechoslovakia and the country began dismantling the old socialist policies and economic system.

Three years later, in December 1992, the country agreed to dissolve into two separate nations, the Czech Republic and the Slovak Republic. This decision was ostensibly the result of the June elections, in which the two republics chose leaders with sharply differing views on the best means of establishing a Western-style economy. The Czechs favored rapid implementation of economic reforms, while the more economically troubled Slovaks sought to introduce the reforms gradually to their republic. Rather than compromise, the two leaders decided to split the country. Without a referendum, the Czechoslovakian government approved the dissolution of the 74-year-old nation and on January 1, 1993, the Czech and Slovak republics were born. The Czech Republic joined the European Union in 2004.

Denmark

Official name: *Kingdom of Denmark*

Area: *16,625 sq. mi., 43,070 sq. km.*

Type of government: *Constitutional monarchy*

Population: *5,369,000*

Capital and largest city: *Copenhagen (Pop., 501,000)*

Languages: *Danish, Faroese, Greenlandic*

Literacy: *100%*

Currency: *Krone*

Per capita GDP: *$29,000 (Rank: 8th)*

The land. Denmark consists of the Jutland peninsula, four main islands—Fyn, Sjaelland, Lolland, and Bornholm—and 478 smaller islands, 99 of which are inhabited. The self-governing Faeroe Islands, in the North Atlantic southeast of Iceland, and Greenland, an island off the coast of northeastern North America, are dependencies of Denmark.

Denmark has a long, deeply indented coastline that affords many fine harbors. Almost all of Denmark consists of low plains. The highest point, in hilly east Jutland, is less than 600 feet (180 meters) above sea level, and there are many small lakes, ponds, and streams throughout the country.

Denmark's climate is generally mild and moist. Average temperatures range from about 32°F (0°C) in January to 62°F (17°C) in July. Rainfall averages about 24 inches (61 centimeters) a year in the east and about 30 inches (76 centimeters) in the west. In the western part of the country, winters are warmer, summers cooler.

The people. The Danish population is quite homogeneous, although there is a small German minority in south Jutland. Danish is the universal language, and 97 percent of the Danes belong to the Danish Lutheran Church.

Overall population density is high, but the rate of population growth is low. The most heavily populated regions are northern Fyn, eastern Jutland, and eastern Sjaelland, especially the Copenhagen area, where almost 20 percent of the population lives. Western Jutland, which is rather barren, is sparsely settled.

Economy. Denmark has one of the highest gross national products per capita of any country in Europe. The country's prosperity is based on its very efficient farming, light industry, and commerce. There are few mineral resources other than building stone, sand, and clay, although in recent years production from North Sea petroleum wells is meeting an increasing proportion of the country's energy needs.

Over half of Denmark's land is cultivated. Agriculture employs about 3 percent of the population, and although it contributed only about 5 percent to the national product, it accounted for more than one-quarter of total exports. Farms are small and privately owned, but farmers are organized into cooperative societies for purchasing, processing, and marketing their produce, and for improving production. Dairying and the production of meat, especially pork, are the most important farm activities. Fishing is also an important activity.

Manufacturing employs about 28 percent of the labor force, and production has increased rapidly in the last two decades. Processed foods, textiles, chemicals, and light machinery are leading industrial products. Tourism and shipping are also significant sources of income.

Denmark has experienced serious trade deficits in recent years. It has joined international organizations to establish new markets for its exports.

Most of Denmark's trade is with Western Europe and the United States. Leading imports are heavy machinery, raw materials, iron and steel products, and fuel. Leading exports are meat, fish, dairy products, manufactured goods, and light machinery.

Government. Denmark is a constitutional monarchy with the queen as head of state. The queen appoints a prime minister and a cabinet who wield executive power and are responsible to the parliament, the Folketing. The parliament has one house with 179 members and is popularly elected under a system of proportional representation. Greenland and the Faeroe Islands are represented in the Folketing by two members each.

History. Archaeological evidence indicates that primitive societies may have existed in the region of present-day Denmark as early as 10,000 years ago. Beginning about 2500 B.C., a society based on agriculture developed in the area. Early Danish peoples may have included the Cimbri and Teutons, warlike tribes described in Roman histories as inhabiting the region in the first century B.C.

By the A.D. 800s, Danish Vikings had developed a society with a complex social organization. The Viking period, between about 800 and 1050, was turbulent. Scandinavian adventurers—raiders, merchants, and eventually settlers—visited the Caspian Sea, Iceland, Greenland, and possibly even North America, and raided England and Western Europe. During the 900s Christianity was introduced into the region, and by about 1035 it had become the dominant religion.

26 Europe and Russia

meters
US

metres
Brit.

labor
US

labour
Brit.

COPENHAGEN is a major port, with part of the city located on the east coast of the island of Sjaelland, and other parts on Amager.

THE LITTLE MERMAID of Hans Christian Andersen's fairy tale watches over Copenhagen's harbor.

kilometers
US

klilometres
Brit.

The inhabitants of Denmark remained divided into separate communities until about 950, when one chieftain, Harold Bluetooth, began uniting the tribal kingdoms. The consolidation continued gradually until the 1000s, when King Canute (1014–1035) ruled a single Danish kingdom. Canute also expanded his power over England and Norway, but this Anglo-Scandinavian empire did not survive his death.

By the mid-1200s a highly organized, semifeudal society had developed, with a strong central monarchy limited by a council of royal advisers firmly based on a middle class of farmers and artisans. During the 1200s and 1300s, Denmark took over territory in the Baltic area, Norway, and Sweden.

Union. In 1397 both Norway (with its possessions—the Faeroe Islands, Greenland, and Iceland) and Sweden were united under the Danish crown in what is known as the Union of Kalmar. This union survived, at least in form, for over a century. At the beginning of the Protestant Reformation in the early 1500s, Scandinavia was torn by religious disputes and social conflicts. As a result, Sweden in 1523 asserted its independence, but Norway remained under Danish rule.

Wars with Sweden were frequent well into the 1600s. A peace settlement was finally reached in 1660; under it, Denmark surrendered to Sweden the southern part of the Scandinavian peninsula. In the same year, the monarchy became absolute as the result of a rebellion among townsmen in support of the throne. Led by several strong rulers, Denmark-Norway regained lost territory from Sweden.

In the 1700s, however, the monarchy weakened and a form of parliamentary government was introduced, and industry and trade expanded. During the Napoleonic period of the early 1800s, the monarchy of Denmark-Norway allied itself with France against England and Sweden. As a result of the defeat of Napoleon, Denmark lost Norway to Sweden.

Nationalism and reform. After the Napoleonic wars a nationalist and liberal movement developed in Denmark that was directed toward rebuilding and reforming the country. A constitution was adopted that limited the monarchy, created a national assembly, and guaranteed civil liberties.

The Danish nationalist movement was partly responsible for attempts to bring under Danish rule the duchies of Schleswig and Holstein, at the southern end of the Jutland peninsula. Although the duchies had once been ruled by Danes, all but the predominantly Danish northern section of Schleswig was German in language and loyalty, and the German states disputed Danish claims to the territory. The conflict led to two Danish-German wars, one from 1848 to 1850 and another in 1864. An 1864 settlement forced Denmark to relinquish all claims to the duchies.

The latter half of the 1800s was an era of continuing reform in Denmark. The cooperative movement was organized, and broad social welfare measures were gradually introduced. The constitution underwent several revisions, and by 1914 Denmark had already achieved a fully democratic parliamentary government.

Modern Denmark. Denmark remained neutral during World War I. In 1918 Iceland was granted independence, but it remained united with Denmark under the Danish crown.

Denmark faced a series of economic crises in the years following World War I. Attempts at recovery were thwarted by the worldwide depression of the late 1920s and early 1930s. In the mid-1930s, however, Denmark made an excellent recovery, enacting advanced social legislation that remained in effect long after the depression had ended.

Denmark again proclaimed its neutrality at the beginning of World War II, but in April 1940 German forces invaded and occupied the country. King Christian X refused to go into exile or to yield to the Germans, and the Danes governed themselves until 1943, when the Germans assumed direct control. Denmark was liberated in May 1945.

Denmark's economy had been badly damaged during the German occupation, but by the early 1950s prosperity had returned. In 1953 a new constitution was adopted. It removed Greenland from colonial status and substituted a unicameral for a bicameral legislature.

Frederik IX succeeded to the throne in 1947. The 1953 constitution changed the law of succession to allow for female accession to the throne. Upon Frederik's death in 1972, his daughter, Margrethe, became queen.

Danish politics since the 1950s has been complex, though changes have taken place gradually. The existence of a large number of political parties has made compromise an essential element in Danish political life; since 1945 no single party has been able to command a majority in the Folketing.

Denmark ended its long-standing policy of isolation when it joined the North Atlantic Treaty Organization (NATO) in 1949 and the European Economic Community, or Common Market, in 1972.

Relations with NATO became strained in 1988 when the Folketing passed a resolution which, in effect, closed Danish ports to NATO warships. However, a compromise was reached.

Estonia

Official name: *Republic of Estonia*
Area: *17,413 sq. mi., 45,100 sq. km.*
Type of government: *Republic*
Population: *1,416,000*
Capital and largest city: *Tallinn (Pop., 398,000)*
Languages: *Estonian (official), Latvian, Lithuanian, Russian*
Literacy: *100%*
Currency: *Kroon*
Per capita GDP: *$10,900 (Rank: 45th)*

The land. In addition to mainland Estonia, the country also includes over 800 islands and islets in the Baltic Sea. The largest island is Saaremaa, which covers some 1,048 square miles (2,714 square kilometers).

Most of mainland Estonia is low, rolling terrain. Many lakes and rivers are seen throughout the mainland, the longest rivers being the Parnu and the Kasari. Forests of pine, fir, birch, and other varieties cover almost 30 percent of the terrain. The climate is temperate and relatively humid. Winter temperatures average about 35°F (1.7°C), and the warm summer temperatures seldom rise above 65°F (18°C). About 27 inches (69 centimeters) of precipitation fall annually.

The people. Almost 70 percent of the people are Estonian, most of them

A CASTLE IN TALLINN, the capital and largest city in Estonia.

Lutheran. About a quarter of the people are Russian. Most live in Tallinn, the capital, and other urban areas in the east. Small minorities of Ukrainians, Finns, and Belarussians also are found throughout Estonia. Estonian, a language related to Finnish and Hungarian, is used most widely. Major cities include Tallinn (population, 398,000) and Tartu (101,000).

Economy. Estonia was granted economic autonomy in 1989 and in the 1990s moved to transform its economy to a free market system. The large collective farms were placed into private hands and by 1995 privatization of industry was virtually complete. Viewing trade as key to economic growth, the government adopted business-protection laws to attract foreign investment.

Raising animals for meat and milk is the principal agricultural activity. The leading crops are potatoes and various grains. As 49 percent of the country is covered with forests, timber processing is a significant industry.

Mining is also an important source of income, producing large amounts of shale, peat, and phosphorites. A factory in Kohtla-Jarve extracts oil from the shale, which is the primary energy source for Estonian industry.

Government. By a new constitution adopted in June 1992, Estonia is a republic. Legislative power is exercised by the 101-member Riigikogu, or parliament, whose members are elected to 4-year terms. The members of the Riigikogu elect the head of state, the president, whose term of office is 5 years. The head of government is the prime minister, who is appointed by the president and presides over the Council of Ministers.

History. Evidence from civilizations of the Aesti people, ancestors of Estonians now living in the region, dates back over 2,000 years. Estonia was divided into four small regions and eight discrete provinces by the Aesti tribes. The country remained in much the same political form for many centuries, during which the Estonians developed extensive trade relationships with the Roman Empire and various Germanic tribes.

The Aesti remained independent until the ninth century, when Vikings raided the coastal regions and established strongholds throughout the area. In the 13th century, Estonia was invaded and conquered by the Knights of the Sword, a German religious-military order that organized a feudal system, subjugating the native Aesti. The order also brought Christianity to the area. Eventually, Estonia was divided between the German Knights of the Sword, who controlled the south, and their Danish counterparts in the north.

By the 16th century, the Protestant Reformation had reached Estonia, and a large percentage of the population converted to Lutheranism to defy their German feudal lords. In 1561 Swedish troops took control of southern Estonia from the Germans; they maintained control in the area until Peter I of Russia drove the Swedes out in the early 18th century. Estonia remained a province of Russia for two centuries.

After the Russian revolution in 1917, Estonia proclaimed its independence and established a democratic government that was eventually recognized by the new Soviet government.

In 1940 the Soviet army occupied Estonia, forcibly installed a communist government, and absorbed Estonia into

MANY OF TALLINN'S beautiful churches and other buildings were built from the 1200s to the 1500s.

the Soviet Union. Sixty thousand Estonians were killed or deported during the following year. Germany occupied Estonia for 3 years during World War II, beginning in 1941. After World War II, the Soviet Union set up collectivized farms and state-run industries throughout Estonia. The Soviet government also began a process of forced integration—sending Russian troops and government officials, as well as large numbers of other non-Baltic peoples, to Estonia. Urban population doubled in the first 40 years of communist rule. Many nations, including the United States, refused to recognize the incorporation of Estonia or the other Baltic states into the Soviet Union.

The communists faced opposition throughout their domination of Estonia. During the period of *perestroika* in the Soviet Union that began in the 1980s, the Estonian opposition was able to function openly and spark a new wave of nationalism.

In 1991 after the collapse of the Soviet Union, Estonia became an independent republic and was admitted to the UN. Elections have resulted in tenuous coalition governments and several resignations by prime ministers. Estonia became a member of both NATO and the EU in 2004.

(For information about the history of Estonia as part of the Soviet Union, see the article on Russia.)

Finland

Official name: *Republic of Finland*
Area: *130,128 sq. mi., 337,030 sq. km.*
Type of government: *Republic*
Population: *5,184,000*
Capital and largest city: *Helsinki (Pop., 560,000)*
Languages: *Finnish, Swedish (both official)*
Literacy: *100%*
Currency: *Euro*
Per capita GDP: *$26,200 (Rank: 17th)*

The land. The name Finland means "land of fens and marshes," and much of Finland is quite low and swampy. Ten percent of the land area is occupied by about 50,000 lakes. The southwestern third of Finland lies on a low coastal plain. Elevations rise to above 1,000 feet (305 meters) only in the northern third of the country, where densely forested uplands extend into the barren Lapland region of the far north.

About one-third of Finland lies north of the Arctic Circle, but the sea moderates the climate, especially in the south. Finland has long cold winters and short warm summers. Snow covers the ground for from four months of the year in the south to almost 8 months in parts

civilizations
US

civilisations
Brit.

centimeters
US

centimetres
Brit.

labor
US

labour
Brit.

of the north. Rainfall averages 30 inches (76 centimeters) in the southwest and decreases toward the north.

The people. Finland is sparsely populated. Population is concentrated in the southwestern third of the country, especially along the coast near Finland's largest cities, which include Helsinki, the capital; Tampere (population, 198,000); and Turku (174,000).

The majority of the people speak Finnish, a language of the Uralic family related to Estonian and Hungarian. For historical reasons, Swedish is also an official language, but it is spoken by fewer than 10 percent of the people. Most Finns are Lutheran, but there are Orthodox Christian, Jewish, Roman Catholic, and other Protestant groups.

The seminomadic Lapps of the far north make up about 0.5 percent of the population. They remain generally isolated from Finnish life.

Economy. Finland's economy is heavily dependent on the exploitation of its rich forests. Almost two-thirds of the country is forested, and forestry products account for more than one-third of exports. Finland has very limited mineral resources aside from considerable copper deposits, although small amounts of nickel, lead, zinc, and iron are mined.

Manufacturing employs about 25 percent of the workforce. Wood and paper products are the principal manufactured goods. Copper smelting and iron and steel production are also important. Shipbuilding and shipping are valuable industries.

Agriculture is of decreasing importance in Finland. Agriculture and forestry together employ under 15 percent of the labor force, compared with nearly 50 percent after World War II

PRODUCE COMES TO MARKET by boat in Finland. The country's name means "land of fens and marshes."

although agricultural production is still nearly 85 percent of domestic consumption. Less than ten percent of the land is under cultivation, and farming is confined almost entirely to the south. Dairying is a major activity, and such hardy crops as hay, fodder, and cereals are grown. Coastal fishing is prosperous.

Finland's exports include paper and wood pulp, timber and wood products, machinery, and transportation equipment. The major imports are heavy machinery and vehicles, finished consumer goods, fuels, and chemicals. Most of Finland's trade is with Sweden, Great Britain, and Germany.

Government. Finland is a republic with a president as head of state and chief executive. The head of government is a prime minister who heads a cabinet responsible to parliament. The 200 members of parliament, which has one house, are popularly elected to four-year terms under a system of proportional representation.

History. Finland contains archaeological evidence of human settlement as early as the Stone Age, over 50,000 years ago. Modern Finland was settled by people who migrated from the eastern Baltic region in about 100 A.D. For many centuries they lived in a tribal society based on hunting, trapping, and fur trading.

In the 1100s Sweden conquered the Finnish tribes and converted them to Christianity. The Finns absorbed a great deal of Western culture through Swedish influence, and with Sweden adopted Lutheranism in the 1500s. From 1362, Finland participated in the election of the Swedish monarchs, and was considered an integral part of Sweden.

For most of the 600 years that Sweden controlled Finland, the Swedes and the Russians competed for control of the Baltic region, and Finland was often their battleground. One of the results of repeated and often harsh Russian occupations was a growing lack of faith in Sweden's ability to protect Finland.

Finally, in 1808, during the Napoleonic wars, Sweden lost Finland to Russia. Emperor Alexander of Russia made Finland an autonomous grand duchy and allowed it to govern itself. The Finns enjoyed a great deal of autonomy throughout the 1800s. However, during the reign of the last czar, Nicholas II (1894–1917), Russian imperialism resulted in the loss of Finnish home rule.

Independence. Finland took advantage of the turmoil caused in Russia by the 1917 revolutions and proclaimed its independence on December 6. In January 1918, civil war broke out in Finland between the communists and socialists, called the Reds, and conservative factions, called the Whites. Aided by German troops, the Whites won and established a republic.

In the 1920s and 1930s the Finns passed legislation for advanced social and economic reforms. But the young republic was harassed by extremist organizations and some attempted coups throughout the 1930s. A socialist coalition finally restored order in 1937.

In 1939 the Soviet Union invaded Finland. After an initially strong defense, Finland was defeated. In the

REINDEER are raised by the seminomadic Lapps of the far north of Finland.

peace treaty, Finland lost territory. When Germany attacked the Soviet Union in 1941, it was aided by Finland, which hoped to regain the territory. When Germany began to suffer losses in Russia, Finland sued for peace. In the armistice more territory was lost to the Soviet Union, and reparation payments were agreed to.

After the war, Finland sought to maintain neutrality in international affairs, promoting good relations with East and West European nations. However, Finland's economy suffered as a result of the changes that swept the Soviet Union, for decades one of Finland's major trading partners, in the late 1980s and early 1990s. A full member of the European Free Trade Association since 1986, Finland also became a member of the European Union in 1995.

France

Official name: *French Republic*
Area: *211,209 sq. mi.,*
    547,030 sq. km.
Type of government: *Republic*
Population: *59,925,000*
Capital and largest city: *Paris*
    (Pop., metro. area, 9,664,507)
Language: *French*
Literacy: *99%*
Currency: *Euro*
Per capita GDP: *$25,700*
    (Rank: 18th)

The land. France has a varied terrain. High, rugged mountains dominate the southern part of the country, where the Pyrenees form the French border with Spain. In the southeast the Alps extend along the borders with Italy and most of Switzerland. Lower, more rounded mountains are the Jura and Vosges in the northeast, the Massif Central, which dominates the southeastern half of the country, and the Massif Armoricain, which forms the spine of Brittany.

Lowland plains are found along the Atlantic coast and in the valleys formed by France's principal rivers. The Seine, in the northwest, flows into the English Channel. The Loire and the Garonne flow into the Atlantic Ocean. The Rhône flows south into the Mediterranean Sea. The Rhine forms part of the French border with Germany.

Climate. Most of France has a maritime climate, with cool winters and mild summers. The southern coast has a typical Mediterranean climate, with hot, dry summers and mild, rainier winters. The greatest seasonal variations in temperature occur in the east and in the highland areas.

Overseas dependencies. France, once the master of a vast overseas empire, offered French territories the opportunity to gain their independence in 1958. Some chose to remain associ-

ated with France. French "overseas departments," as they are called, now include the following:

• French Guiana, on the northeast coast of South America.

• Guadeloupe and Martinique, both part of the Lesser Antilles of the West Indies.

• Réunion, an island in the Indian Ocean.

• Mayotte, in the Mozambique Channel off the east coast of Africa.

• St. Pierre and Miquelon, small islands off the southern coast of Newfoundland.

French "overseas territories" include the following:

• French Polynesia, in the South Pacific Ocean, includes the Society Islands group (the Windward and Leeward Islands), which includes the beautiful island of Tahiti, the Tuamotu Archipelago, the Gambier Islands, the Austral or Tubuai Islands, and the Marquesas Islands.

• New Caledonia, in the western Pacific Ocean, east of Australia.

• Wallis and Futuna Islands in the South Pacific Ocean

• Southern and Antarctic Territories, which are mostly uninhabited and include the Kerguelen Islands, Crozet Islands, Amsterdam Island, Saint-Paul Island, and Terre Adélie.

For more information on the French overseas territories and departments consult the Asia, Middle East, Australia and Oceania, North America, and South America volumes.

The people. France has one of Europe's most homogeneous populations. There is a strong feeling of cultural unity, and France has been troubled very little by minority unrest.

French is the universal language, and more than 95 percent of the people are Roman Catholic. Breton, Flemish,

German, Catalan, and Basque are spoken in the border areas by relatively few people. The most substantial linguistic minorities are the German-speaking population in Alsace and the Breton population of Brittany.

The population has grown sharply since World War II, but this increase has become more moderate in recent years. In addition to the native population, there are 3.7 million foreign residents, most of whom have come from four Mediterranean countries—Algeria, Italy, Portugal, and Spain. These countries provided workers during the economic expansion of the 1960s and 1970s, but since the late 1970s this immigration has been more and more strictly controlled because of an increase in unemployment.

France's population is fairly evenly distributed throughout the country. Only a few areas, such as the high Alps and parts of the infertile Landes district, near the Spanish border, are sparsely populated, and only a small number of industrial areas are densely settled.

Paris, the capital, has one of the densest concentrations in the world. This concentration has contributed to the predominance of the city in the administrative, economic, and cultural life of the country; however, in recent years there has been a movement to the suburbs and smaller centers. The government has also tried to encourage regional development.

Other major urban areas include the industrial city of Lyon (population, metro. area, 1,349,000); France's principal seaport, Marseille (metro area, 1,350,000); the manufacturing center of Lille (191,000); the seaport and industrial center of Bordeaux (219,000); the manufacturing and marketing center of Toulouse (398,000); and Nice (346,000).

Economy. France is the fourth largest economy in the world, after the United

centers
US

centres
Brit.

A BRIDGE
over the Lot River in
Cahors, a town in the
southwest of France

States, Japan, and Germany. It is strong in all sectors, including agriculture, manufacturing, and the service industries.

France has a mixed economy, with a larger share of the economy than is usual for a capitalist country controlled by the government. The government has long owned or held a controlling interest in a number of the most important French industries, such as automobile and aircraft manufacture and banking. In the mid-1980s this trend was reversed somewhat when a conservative administration privatized many state-held businesses.

The French economy is greatly aided by the freight and passenger-carrying capacity of a well-developed state-owned railroad system. A high-speed train between Paris and Lyons was inaugurated in 1983, and additional high-speed links are planned. A significant amount of freight is also carried by an extensive system of internal canals and navigable rivers.

Strong governmental direction of the economy under a series of formal development plans contributed greatly to France's economic growth. The plans involve close cooperation between government and private business and have been successful in channeling resources and balancing economic growth.

Natural resources. France's mineral endowment is varied and, by European standards, moderately rich. There are major deposits of iron ore, in Lorraine, and bauxite, from which aluminum is made, in the southeast. There are many coalfields scattered throughout the country, but mining them is expensive and much of the coal is of modest quality. France has no domestic production of petroleum and must therefore import a large percentage of its energy needs. The expected depletion of natural gas

aluminum
US

aluminium
Brit.

reserves by the end of the century only makes the situation worse.

The abundant waterpower of the Alps, Pyrenees, and Massif Central place France second in Europe in developed hydroelectric capacity, allowing the country to produce one-quarter of its domestic needs. Nuclear power supplies about half of total electricity needs. France remains committed to nuclear power despite growing hostility toward it in the rest of Western Europe.

Agriculture. France leads Western Europe in agricultural production; it exports more farm products than any other European country. Agriculture accounts for about one-sixth of total exports.

France has always had the advantage of large tracts of fertile soil and a varied climate, but has often been handicapped by overly small farms and outmoded techniques. However, larger units, increased mechanization, chemical fertilizers, extended irrigation, and the stimulus of the Common Market have increased production dramatically. Agriculture now employs only about 8 percent of the workforce. France ranks high in the production of grain, meat, milk, cheese, wine, and fruit.

Industry. France is one of the world's most important industrial nations, and industry employs about one-third of the working population. Important industries include steel and steel products, aluminum, chemicals, motor vehicles, aircraft, and textiles. In recent years France has also taken a strong position in new industries such as telecommunications.

France's major exports include agricultural products, armaments, steel, chemicals, transportation equipment, foodstuffs, pottery, glassware, natural and synthetic rubber, and textiles. The principal imports include petroleum products and fuels, ores, raw textiles, and machine tools.

About half of French trade is within the European Union, but France also trades extensively with Japan, Switzerland, and the United States. In addition, France has sought to build up trade with Eastern Europe, the former Soviet Union, Communist China, and the developing countries of Asia, Africa, and Latin America.

Government. France is a democratic republic. The constitution of the Fifth Republic was adopted in 1958. The head of state and chief executive is the president, who is directly elected to a 5-year term. The president appoints a prime minister and council of ministers, or cabinet, as well as all other officials.

The constitution grants the president the right to dissolve the powerful lower house of the legislature, the National Assembly, after conferring with the prime minister, and the right to call new elections. In a national emergency, the president may assume all executive and legislative powers.

Legislative authority is vested in the parliament, which consists of the National Assembly and the Senate. The stronger of the two houses is the National Assembly, whose 577 deputies are popularly elected to 5-year terms under a system of proportional representation. The 321 members of the Senate are elected by regional and city electoral colleges to 9-year terms. The National Assembly can cause the government to fall with a vote of censure; therefore, it has considerable influence on the choice of the prime minister and cabinet.

History. The territory of France, known in ancient times as Gaul, was inhabited by Celtic tribes when Julius Caesar led his Roman legions into the region in 58 B.C. By 51 B.C. Caesar had brought all of Gaul under his

WELL-TENDED VINEYARDS drink in the sunlight in the Bordeaux region of southwestern France. Workers harvest grapes in northeastern France (inset).

COUNTRIES

control. The Romans introduced the Latin language and Christianity to the Gauls.

For over 200 years the region was prosperous, but as the Roman Empire began to disintegrate, Germanic tribes, among them Visigoths, Franks, and Burgundians, established themselves in various parts of Gaul.

The Merovingians. In the late 400s the Franks, led by Clovis I, the first of the Merovingian kings (ruled 481–511), succeeded in conquering Gaul and western Germany. Clovis conquered most of what had been Roman Gaul, established the Merovingians as the ruling dynasty of the Franks, and was instrumental in converting his people to Christianity.

Clovis, however, regarded the Frankish kingdom not as a state but as his private property, and he divided it among his four surviving sons when he died. This practice, which was continued by the Frankish monarchy, was the leading cause of the chronic civil wars that plagued Frankish history.

By the middle of the 600s, continual civil strife had taken its toll on the power and prestige of the Merovingian kings. At about the same time their wealth had dwindled because of their lavish grants of land to the church and to their noble retainers in return for government service.

As the Merovingians became poorer they became weaker. On the other hand, the church and leading noble families gained enormously in wealth and political power.

In the 600s the Carolingians, who were the royal stewards of the Merovingians, assumed most of the royal authority. In 732 the Carolingian Charles Martel thwarted Muslim invaders at Tours in west central France, halting the Muslim threat to France and enhancing the prestige of his house. But Charles did not depose the Merovingians, who continued as nominal rulers of the Franks until 751, when Charles's son, Pepin the Short, seized the throne.

The Carolingians. Pepin's son, Charlemagne, or Charles the Great, who ruled from 768 to 814, won control of most of western Europe. He created a powerful empire, which he administered efficiently. Charlemagne was a patron of learning, and scholars from all of western Europe came to his capital, Aachen. Charlemagne cooperated closely with the church, and in 800 Pope Leo III crowned him emperor of the Romans, which legitimized Charlemagne's rule over the former Western Roman Empire.

The strength of the Carolingian empire was dependent on the genius of Charlemagne. His son, Louis the Pious (ruled 814–840), was incapable of maintaining a strong hold over the kingdom. The centralized administration collapsed, and Louis' three sons struggled among themselves for supremacy. In 843 they signed the Treaty of Verdun, which divided the Carolingian Empire into three parts.

The eastern region, Germany, was awarded to Louis the German; the western region, France, went to Charles the Bald; and the middle strip, which included northern Italy and Alsace-Lorraine, was given to Lothair I, who also retained the title of emperor of the Romans. The partition of 843 marked the beginnings of modern France and Germany.

Carolingian rule declined rapidly in the 800s and 900s. New barbarian invasions shook Europe, and political power fell into the hands of feudal lords. Economic life shrank and became centered on the self-sufficient manor. In northwestern France Viking invaders established themselves in the region that came to be known as Normandy; after the passage of centuries, they were assimilated into the Frankish population.

The Capetians. The Carolingian dynasty died out in 987, and the powerful nobles chose Hugh Capet as king. The Capetian kings—Hugh and his descendants—brought authority and prestige to the French crown. They used force sparingly and built up their power and possessions by the strategic marriages of their sons and daughters to the great feudal families of France, waiting patiently until they inherited their lands. They were careful to preserve their just rights over the French church but at the same time they enriched it with buildings and lands. France became the largest, richest, and most populous kingdom in medieval Europe.

The first important French king was Louis VI (ruled 1108–1137), whose principal achievement was to gain complete control of the royal patrimony itself, the Isle de France. He also married his son and heir to Eleanor of Aquitaine, the duchess of the largest feudal principality in France.

After 15 years, Louis VII (ruled 1137–1180) divorced Eleanor, ostensibly because they were too closely related, but, in fact, because she had not produced a male heir. Louis then married a daughter of the King of Castile, who died childless. Within five weeks of her death he married the Countess of Champagne, who did produce a male heir, the future Philip II.

Philip II (ruled 1180–1223) was determined to regain the territory gained through marriage by Henry II of England and unify all of France with himself as absolute monarch. Philip succeeded in wresting control of Normandy, Anjou, Maine, Poitou, and Touraine from the English between 1202 and 1204.

During the reign of Louis IX (1226–1270) the royal court began to evolve into a central bureaucracy. Louis established a high court of justice, known as the *parlement*, and reorganized the royal treasury into a more workable body of government.

The last great Capetian king was Philip IV (ruled 1285–1314), who completed the administrative organization and territorial development of the French medieval state. He also taxed the French clergy, who had been exempt from direct royal taxation. This in turn led to a conflict with Pope Boniface VIII, who held the most extreme views of any medieval pope concerning papal supremacy and clerical independence.

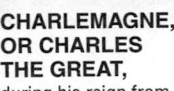

CHARLEMAGNE, OR CHARLES THE GREAT, during his reign from 768 to 814, created a powerful empire that included most of western Europe.

26 Europe and Russia

THE LOUVRE was originally built as a fortress by Phillip II in about 1200. The structure now houses one of the largest museums in the world and has a modern glass addition designed by I. M. Pei.

centered
US

centred
Brit.

AT HIGH TIDE, the waters of the bay make an island of the steep rock upon which the beautiful Abbey of Mont-St.-Michel stands.

JOAN OF ARC died as a result of English justice, but not before she strengthened the will of Charles VII to drive the English out of all of France except Calais.

In his confrontation with the papacy Philip was completely victorious. He gained the right to tax the French clergy and after the death of Boniface secured the election of a French pope. For over 70 years the popes reigned from Avignon under the supervision of the French monarchs.

For 300 years the continuity of the Capetian kings and their policies had run like a bright thread through French history. When Philip IV died in 1314, the French monarchy was at its height. Moreover, Philip left three adult sons behind him. In a little more than a decade, however, they were all dead and the medieval French monarchy died with them.

The Valois kings. The throne passed to one of Philip's nephews, Philip VI (ruled 1328–1350), who was the first of the Valois dynasty. Under the Valois, royal power continued to grow, despite some major setbacks.

In 1337 the right of Philip VI to the throne was challenged by his distant cousin, Edward III of England. This led to a long, complex dynastic conflict from 1337 to 1453 known as the Hundred Years' War. During this war the French crown also faced a revolt of French peasants, the *Jacquerie* of 1358; a Parisian insurrection; and bitter civil strife among powerful French nobles, particularly those of Armagnac and Burgundy.

In 1420 Henry V of England, who had defeated the French at Agincourt in 1415, forced the Valois king, Charles VI, to disown his own son and make Henry the heir to the French throne. However, the dauphin, as the French heir to the throne was known, fought back. With the help of Joan of Arc, who escorted him to Reims, where in 1429 he was crowned Charles VII (ruled 1422–1461), he managed to drive the English out of all of France except Calais by 1453.

During the Hundred Years' War the French kings had begun to create a more effective army by placing it under royal control, supporting it with royal funds, and selecting its officers. They also obtained a special direct tax on land, called the *taille*, which they did not give up at the end of the protracted conflict.

Louis XI (ruled 1461–1483) inherited a monarchy that had almost absolute power and that was no longer threatened by foreign intervention. Louis destroyed the power of the remaining feudal lords and brought most of present-day France under royal control. Louis continued to reinforce the strength of the monarchy and sought ways to ally the throne with the growing middle class.

Louis XI's son, Charles VIII (ruled 1483–1498), introduced a French policy of expansion abroad with campaigns in Italy. Although they were unsuccessful, they succeeded in stimulating French interest in Italian Renaissance culture. Charles's cousin, Francis I (ruled 1515–1547), continued the Italian campaigns and initiated French support of German Protestants as a means of weakening the rival Hapsburg dynasty.

Henry II (ruled 1547–1559) won a foothold in Lorraine by seizing the bishoprics of Toul, Metz, and Verdun from the Holy Roman Emperor Charles V. The French also captured Calais, the last English possession in France, and ended the Italian wars.

Religious conflict. After Henry's death, his three sons ruled France in succession—Francis II (1559–1560), Charles IX (1560–1574), and Henry III (1574–1589). During most of that period, the queen mother, Catherine de Medici, dominated political life.

Catherine and her sons were unable to maintain control in the face of Calvinism, rivalry between the powerful Catholic Guise and Protestant Bourbon families, and the intervention of Hapsburg Spain in French affairs.

The Huguenots, as the French Calvinists were called, created the greatest problems for the three Medici mon-

archs. During their reigns the royal army was intermittently engaged in a fierce civil war with Huguenot forces.

The struggle reached its bloodiest point in 1572, when Catherine incited Parisian Catholics against a large assemblage of Huguenots gathered in the capital to attend the wedding of Margaret of Valois, Catherine's daughter, and the Huguenot Henry of Bourbon, king of Navarre. The Massacre of St. Bartholomew's Day ensued, resulting in the death of many Protestants.

The leadership of the Huguenots fell to Henry of Navarre, who had successfully escaped the massacre. When the Valois line ended in 1589 amid the confusion of civil and religious strife, Henry returned to Paris to ascend the throne as the famous Henry IV (ruled 1589–1610), the first of France's Bourbon kings.

Bourbon rule. The Bourbons made France a relatively centralized state and a world power. Henry IV took several steps to bring order to divided France. He became a Roman Catholic to consolidate his position as king, but in 1598 he issued the Edict of Nantes, which gave the Huguenots religious rights and political guarantees. He defeated or bought off rebellious nobles and rebuilt the economy.

After initial difficulties, his successor, Louis XIII (ruled 1610–1643), was able to continue the expansion of royal power by delegating authority to Cardinal Richelieu. Richelieu, an important force from 1624 to 1642, crushed rebellious Huguenots while allowing them religious privileges; forced the nobles to demolish fortifications that did not protect the frontiers; developed the technique of sending out royal inspectors, or *intendants*, to supervise local administration; and ruthlessly suppressed conspiracies against the regime.

Richelieu had increased royal power and improved administration through a central bureaucracy of competent experts who owed their fortunes and loyalty to him and the king. He also placed the government of the provinces under royal officials who had arbitrary authority to take over many of the duties and powers of traditional local officials. His innovations were to greatly improve the effectiveness of the government, especially law enforcement and the administration of justice. Increased taxes and more efficient tax collection strengthened the crown both financially and politically.

Outside France, the cardinal intervened in Germany's religious conflict, the Thirty Years' War, on the side of the Protestant princes to prevent the consolidation of Hapsburg power.

After Richelieu's death in 1642, Cardinal Mazarin carried on his work, surviving a series of revolts—called the *Fronde*—by the nobility and *parlements*, who sought greater participation in government. They were put down with great difficulty, but proved to be the nobility's last rebellion in defense of medieval privileges.

NOTRE DAME CATHEDRAL is one of Europe's most famous landmarks and stands as a masterpiece of Gothic architecture.

Mazarin also brought the Thirty Years' War to an end in 1648 with the Peace of Westphalia. This settlement strengthened the French foothold in Lorraine and won France most of Alsace. Although the Austrian Hapsburgs had conceded defeat, the Spanish Hapsburgs continued to fight until 1659, when they yielded some territories in the Pyrenees and the Lowlands.

Louis XIV. With the death of Cardinal Mazarin in 1661, Louis XIV (ruled 1643–1715) began to rule France personally. By that time France was already the most unified, most populous, and wealthiest state in Europe. Louis, known as "the Sun King," further strengthened the power of the monarchy and reinforced French hegemony in Europe.

Louis excluded the great nobles from his councils in favor of reliable middle-class officials, domesticated the troublesome aristocracy in his splendid palace at Versailles, silenced opposition from the *parlements,* used *intendants* to enforce his will in the provinces, and avoided convening the Estates-General, or national assembly.

Jean Baptiste Colbert, his controller general of finance, encouraged the development of industry with favors and protection; the Marquis de Louvois, minister of war, reorganized the army; and the Marquis de Vauban, a military engineer, improved military fortifications. In North America, French explorers and soldiers built an empire extending from the St. Lawrence River and the Great Lakes to the mouth of the Mississippi River on the Gulf of Mexico.

The work of modernizing France was only half completed, however. The tax system remained riddled with exemptions and inequities; internal customs barriers still impeded commerce outside of central France; and underneath the royal superstructure lay a confusion of local administrative organs, courts, and laws inherited from the past.

Louis, moreover, weakened French economic life when he revoked the Edict of Nantes in 1685, suppressing the remaining Protestant rights. This led to the emigration of thousands of Huguenots, large numbers of whom were merchants, manufacturers, and craftsmen.

Colbert, meanwhile, was establishing an economy based on "mercantilism." This policy aims at economic self-sufficiency and a favorable balance of trade. Exports exceed imports and the surplus is paid for in gold, thus increasing national wealth and power. Colbert's mercantilist tactics—protective tariffs and prohibitions, subsidies and monopolies to stimulate native industries, shipping, and so forth—were only partially successful.

Other nations were more advanced industrially and commercially. They responded with anti-French mercantilist policies of their own, while the king's wars crippled the program by draining the economy.

Louis' wars, inspired primarily by a desire for glory, drained French resources and made his reign unpopular. As a result of the first three wars (War of Devolution, 1667–1668; Dutch War, 1672–1678; and War of the League of Augsburg, 1688–1697), France acquired bits of the Spanish Netherlands, the Franche-Comté, in east-central France, and Alsace.

After the War of the Spanish Succession (1701–1714), however, waged against a Grand Alliance of European powers, France had to recognize English claims to Newfoundland, Nova Scotia, and Hudson Bay territory in North America.

At Louis' death in 1715, France was economically exhausted—but the economy was more fully developed and sounder than it had been before Colbert.

Decline of the monarchy. In the 1700s the French monarchy began to lose its power and prestige. Louis XV (ruled 1715–1774) preferred private pleasure to the tasks of government. French intellectuals of the Enlightenment, a contemporary philosophic movement characterized by its emphasis on the idea of universal human progress, campaigned for social and political reform.

Although their ideas influenced large numbers of the bourgeoisie and many European "enlightened despots" of the period, Louis XV chose to ignore them. Ministers quarreled, necessary reforms were defeated, and the *parlements* repeatedly challenged royal authority on behalf of vested interests.

France also became involved in several new wars. The War of the Polish Succession (1733–1735) ensured that France would eventually acquire the rest of Lorraine, but the War of the Austrian Succession (1740–1748) ended in stalemate. Finally, the Seven Years' War (1756–1763), fought after a "diplomatic revolution" in which France became allied with its old rival, Hapsburg Austria, resulted in the loss of French Canada to the British.

Louis XVI (ruled 1774–1792) was a well intentioned ruler, but he, too, lacked determination. Early in his reign he was faced with the problem of the public debt, swelled by war costs and aid to the American rebels against England. The antiquated tax system could not provide enough funds to balance the budget, and the nation faced bankruptcy.

A series of reform ministers who saw the need to tax the upper classes were

THE WINGED VICTORY OF SAMOTHRACE, a statue of the Greek goddess Nike, is one of the Louvre's most famous attractions.

THE PALACE OF VERSAILLES was built by Louis XIV in the 1600s and served as the royal residence until the French Revolution.

dismissed. Finally, as the crisis mounted, a program was proposed that would force the aristocracy to assume their share of the tax burden. They rebelled, maintaining that the Estates-General—an assembly representing the three estates of French society, clergy, nobility, and commoners—alone had the authority to approve new taxes. In 1789, hopeful of consolidating their position, the aristocracy compelled the king to summon the Estates-General for the first time in 175 years.

The revolution. The three estates were to sit separately, with one vote apiece, giving the first two estates (the nobility and the clergy), which represented a tiny minority, a two-to-one advantage. But the Third Estate proclaimed itself the National Assembly, and swore that it would not be dissolved until it had written a constitution for France. With this famous "Tennis Court Oath" made on June 20, 1789, and the storming of the Bastille on July 14, the French Revolution was clearly at hand.

NAPOLEON PROCLAIMED HIMSELF emperor of France in 1804, then conquered much of Europe before his final defeat at Waterloo in 1815.

The revolutionaries then destroyed the remnants of feudalism, swept away antiquated laws and local institutions, guaranteed certain basic civil rights, and created a constitutional monarchy with a fairly democratic legislative assembly.

They antagonized many Frenchmen when they seized church property to gain revenue and proceeded to turn the church into a government department with elected priests paid by the state and virtually detached from Rome. The revolution also produced economic disorder and high prices, which kept the country unsettled. Even more serious for the new constitutional monarchy was the public distrust of Louis XVI and his queen, Marie Antoinette.

Even before the constitution went into effect in the autumn of 1791, the royal family had tried to escape the country. The leaders of the legislative assembly became convinced that reactionary European rulers were allying against them and on April 20, 1792, they declared war on Austria, inaugurating the wars of the French Revolution, which were to last until 1815. The monarchy was overthrown by a Parisian insurrection on August 10.

The First Republic. On September 21, 1792, a new revolutionary assembly, the National Convention, announced the establishment of the First Republic. The convention delegates, elected by universal suffrage, were republicans; they proceeded to draft a republican constitution. At the convention, the radical Jacobin Party, which was allied with the Parisian populace, gradually defeated the moderate Girondists.

A Reign of Terror occurred in 1793–1794, when the Jacobin leaders of the convention formed a Committee of Public Safety to conduct government affairs. Faced with foreign invasion, serious threats of counterrevolution, and grave economic problems, the committee created a "revolutionary government" designed to crush its enemies and prepare the way for the establishment of a democratic republic.

This revolutionary government, led by Maximilien de Robespierre, featured a centralized dictatorship, a single party, a police regime, a dictated economy, and mass propaganda. Thousands of Girondists and counter-revolutionaries, as well as Louis XVI and Marie Antoinette, were executed.

To win the war—which had expanded by the spring of 1793 to include Prussia, Sardinia, Britain, the Dutch Republic, and Spain—the government drafted the entire able-bodied male population. With the largest army ever organized in Europe, the French Republic turned the tide of war in its favor.

The Directory. In July, 1794, Robespierre was overthrown by the more moderate members of the convention. A reaction against the terror followed, culminating in 1795 in the establishment of a conservative republic called the Directory, because executive authority was shared by five directors.

Under the Directory (1795–1799), France experienced ineffective and unstable government at home, but enjoyed marked military success abroad. France won control over Belgium, the Rhineland, and much of Italy. In 1799 Napoleon Bonaparte, the republic's most successful general, overthrew the Directory and proclaimed himself consul. In 1802 he made himself consul for life, and in 1804, emperor. Each change was approved by the people in a plebiscite.

Napoleonic period. Within France Napoleon created a political system that was an amalgam of the old monarchy and the revolution. He made himself a hereditary, divine-right ruler and formed a new aristocracy composed of those who served the state well. He made peace with the Roman Catholic Church in 1801 in a concordat with the pope, although he did not return the clergy's confiscated lands.

Napoleon issued a new civil law code, usually known as the Napoleonic Code, which was intended to assure all citizens of equality under the law. He introduced a tax system that was more efficient and equitable than that of the old regime and he instituted administrative reforms that gave France a modern, highly organized, and fully centralized bureaucracy.

Abroad, France absorbed Belgium, Holland, the Rhineland, and part of Italy. Napoleon set up puppet states in western Germany, Switzerland, Italy, and Poland, and forced Austria, Prussia, and Russia into an alliance. However, failure to crush Britain either militarily or economically, a costly war in Spain, and a disastrous campaign in Russia led in 1814 to Napoleon's defeat by a European coalition. Napoleon's attempt to regain control—known as the Hundred Days—ended in his final defeat at Waterloo, Belgium, in 1815.

Restoration. Under the terms of the peace agreement concluded at the Congress of Vienna in 1815, France's territory was reduced to what it had been in 1792. The Bourbons had been restored to the French throne in 1814. The Bourbons could not restore the old regime, however, and in 1814 Louis XVIII (ruled 1814–1824) issued the Constitutional Charter to win the support of the bourgeoisie and the peasants. The charter limited the power of the ambitious émigré aristocrats who had

THE ROYAL PALACE of the Tuileries stood on the right bank of the Seine in Paris until much of it was destroyed in 1871. The gardens laid out in the 1600s remain.

recently returned to France from their exile, guaranteed basic liberties, and created a constitutional monarchy similar to that in Britain.

The king headed a chamber of peers whom he appointed and a chamber of deputies chosen by a small electorate.

When Charles X (ruled 1824–1830) succeeded Louis, he immediately made it clear that he wished to reestablish the prerevolutionary order.

Charles chose reactionary ministers, granted indemnities to the nobles whose lands had been confiscated during the revolution, and entrusted public education to the clergy. The chamber, dominated by the bourgeoisie, opposed the king's actions.

Charles dissolved the chamber and called for new elections, but the majority of the electorate failed to support his policies. He retaliated by promulgating the July Ordinances, which restricted the freedom of the press, reduced the size of the electorate, and again dissolved the chamber of deputies.

Fearing that the ordinances were a prelude to a coup d'état, liberal intellectuals incited the Parisians to revolt in the July Revolution of 1830. Charles abdicated, and a constitutional monarchy was established. A cousin of the deposed ruler, Louis Philippe, duke of Orléans, became the new king.

The July Monarchy. To the disappointment of the republicans, the liberal middle class, and the workers, the July Monarchy, as Louis Philippe's reign was called, proved to be as opposed to social and economic reforms as the previous regime had been.

The revolution had merely shifted the power from one small group to another: the upper middle class, or *haute bourgeoisie,* had replaced the

nobility. Like their aristocratic predecessors, the bourgeoisie refused to widen voting privileges, and they used their newly acquired power to develop industries and businesses for their own material gains, in effect simply trading one oppressive regime for another.

Many groups opposed the July Monarchy. The Legitimists wanted Charles X or his grandson, the duke of Bordeaux, restored to the throne; the republicans wanted universal suffrage and a republic; the workers demanded better working conditions and a voice in the government.

The workers joined with the republicans, both groups believing that only a radical change in the country's political structure could bring about improved social conditions. On February 22, 1848, rioting broke out in Paris, and two days later Louis Philippe abdicated.

The Second Republic. A provisional government headed by the poet Alphonse de Lamartine and the journalist Louis Blanc was established. Blanc, strongly in favor of social reform, established National Workshops to provide jobs for the unemployed. He was unable to provide enough work for everyone, however, and in the ensuing dissension dissolved the workshops. The closing of the workshops was followed by rioting, which was finally suppressed by the army.

In November 1848, an assembly completed the drafting of a new constitution, which provided for a legislature of one house and a president with strong powers to be elected by universal suffrage. In December 1848, the first presidential election under the Second Republic was held. The vote made Louis Napoleon, a nephew of Napoleon Bonaparte, president, and revealed that the country as a whole, especially the

French peasantry, was much more conservative than the vocal Paris populace.

Second Empire. In an almost bloodless coup d'état in 1851, Louis Napoleon declared the national legislature dissolved. The liberal dreams of a generation were dissipated on December 2, 1852, when Louis Napoleon became by plebiscite Emperor Napoleon III.

The Second Empire witnessed feverish attempts to create an industrial base. It was hoped that using state funds for industrial enterprises and encouraging technological innovation could accomplish a true industrial revolution.

But France still remained woefully behind both Britain and the rising state of Prussia. Just how far behind became clear in 1870, when Prussia inflicted a surprising and humiliating defeat on Napoleon III's France in the Franco-Prussian War.

The news of Napoleon III's surrender on September 4, 1870, to the Germans was the last straw for a nation that had already been embarrassed by a series of diplomatic catastrophes in the 1860s.

The Third Republic. On September 4, 1870, the Third Republic was born. A provisional government of national defense raised an army to try to prevent the Germans from occupying the city of Paris, but the Parisians were defeated after a four-month siege. Under the terms of the peace treaty negotiated between Bismarck and Adolphe Thiers, the head of the National Assembly, France was forced to cede Alsace and

MANY BEAUTIFUL CHATEAUX of the Loire valley, such as this one at Villandry, survived the destruction of the French Revolution.

part of Lorraine to Germany and to pay a huge indemnity.

Before the treaty was signed, the Third Republic was confronted by an insurrection in Paris, which evolved into a civil war. Unwilling to concede defeat to the Prussians, the Parisians drove the French government troops out of the capital in March, 1871, and formed their own municipal regime—the Paris Commune. Civil war raged for two months until the supporters of the National Assembly managed to suppress the commune.

Although the Third Republic started badly, it survived until 1940. The republic, headed by Thiers, was provisional at first since a majority of deputies in the National Assembly favored a monarchy. But the monarchists were badly divided between supporters of the Bourbon and Orleans lines, and gradually the voters turned to conservative republican candidates.

During the Third Republic there was a rapid change in cabinets—more than 50 before World War I. Since presidents did not call elections when ministries were voted out, deputies were not afraid to overthrow a cabinet. More important, France did not develop large, disciplined political parties such as those in Britain. Instead, after a century of ideological conflict, there was a multitude of small parties.

This system, which continued into the Fourth Republic, was not as unstable as it seemed, however. Changing ministries were composed of many of the same men who represented coalitions of center parties. Also, behind the shifting ministries stood the Napoleonic administrative structure, with its centralized bureaucracy.

The republic weathered a number of crises—such as a threatened coup in 1889 and the Dreyfus affair in the late 1890s. In 1894 Alfred Dreyfus, a Jewish army officer, was convicted of treason. Later evidence pointed to his innocence, but the army refused to reopen the case. Monarchists, conservatives, and militarists as well opposed reopening the case, wishing not only to stand behind the army but to disgrace the republic. The country was bitterly divided.

In 1898 the case was reopened, and the following year Dreyfus was pardoned. In 1906 he was exonerated. Thus, the Dreyfus affair ultimately discredited the monarchists and strengthened the republic.

The Third Republic proved politically radical but socially conservative. Republicans led by Jules Ferry restricted the role of the church in education, and the schools were expected to turn out loyal republicans.

In social welfare legislation, however, the republic lagged behind Germany and Britain. The Radical Socialists, who held the balance of power in the chamber before World War I, proved radical in name only.

Industry expanded, but not as rapidly as in other nations, and the population barely increased at all. Yet French trade grew considerably as a result of extensive colonial expansion in Africa and Southeast Asia (Indochina). By 1914 France's colonial empire was second only to Britain's.

To protect its colonial interests and to secure its position against Germany, France strengthened its army and navy, formed the Dual Alliance with Russia in 1894, and entered the Entente Cordiale with Britain in 1904. Rather than risk losing a vital ally, France supported Russia in the Balkan crisis that precipitated World War I.

World War I. In August, 1914, German troops drove westward through Belgium to invade France; soon most of Europe was involved in the conflict. Britain supported France, and the United States entered the conflict on their side in 1917. For four years most of the fighting on the western front was carried out in northeastern France. Over 1 million French soldiers lost their lives and untold physical damage was done.

Although the Allies did eventually defeat Germany, after the 1917 Bolshevik Revolution Russia was lost as an ally, and France still faced a powerful German state. Under the terms of the Treaty of Versailles (1919), France was granted a 15-year occupation of the Rhineland, which was to be permanently demilitarized.

Germany was disarmed, and France was given Alsace-Lorraine, large war reparations, and some former German colonies. The period from 1919 to 1925 was marked by labor unrest and serious inflation. French foreign policy was based on a tough line against Germany, and in 1921 France formed an alliance with Poland. France occupied the Ruhr in 1923 to force reparation payments from Germany.

Interwar France. From 1925 to 1932 France pursued a more conciliatory German policy, although France allied itself with the nations of the Little Entente—Czechoslovakia, Romania, and Yugoslavia. The Locarno treaties of 1925, guaranteeing the Versailles frontiers and providing for arbitration of disputes, seemed to ensure European stability. At home, prosperity obscured the need for social legislation, although a modest social security system was approved. The world economic depression of the 1930s and the rise of Adolf Hitler in Germany, ended this quiet interlude.

Unemployment, growing insecurity, and a succession of ineffective ministries gave rise to extreme right-wing groups, who were as militant, antirepublican, and antidemocratic as their prototypes in Italy and Germany. In 1934, when the government was alleged to be involved in a financial scandal, the rightists staged anti-parliamentary riots.

In response to the right-wing threat, the Socialist, the Radical Socialist, and the Communist parties formed a political bloc, known as the Popular Front; this bloc came to power in 1936. The Popular Front's prime minister, Léon Blum, promised to bring about moderate reforms that were well within a capitalistic economic system.

Blum won parliamentary approval to establish collective bargaining, a 40-hour work week, paid vacations, closer government control over national financial affairs, nationalization of the arms industry, and cultural programs for the lower classes. But in 1938 France returned to economic and social conservatism under Prime Minister Edouard Daladier.

With its finances exhausted, lacking British support, preoccupied with internal politics, and with an influential right wing sympathetic to Mussolini, France avoided taking action against the growing aggressiveness of Nazi Germany.

France failed to halt German rearmament in 1935, remilitarization of the Rhineland in 1936, or the annexation of Austria and dismemberment of Czechoslovakia in 1938. The Nazi-Soviet nonaggression pact of 1939 left France without a powerful ally on Germany's east.

World War II. In 1939 World War II began with Germany's attack on Poland. France was economically stagnant, politically badly divided, and militarily unprepared. In May 1940, France collapsed before the German *blitzkrieg*, and on June 22 an armistice was signed with the Nazis.

Northern and western France were occupied by the Germans. In the southeast the Germans set up a puppet government that was headed by Marshal Henri-Philippe Pétain. This was known as the Vichy regime after the town that was its capital. The Vichy government effectively came to an end in 1942 following the Allied invasion of North Africa, when Germany occupied the remainder of France.

center
US

centre
Brit.

labor
US

labour
Brit.

HITLER POSES before the Eiffel Tower in Paris during the German occupation of France in World War II.

General Charles de Gaulle and a handful of Frenchmen escaped to London and formed the French Committee of National Liberation (the Free French). At first the committee functioned to recruit Frenchmen to continue the fight against Germany, but eventually it took the form of a provisional government ready to take control of France after the defeat of Germany.

France was liberated in August, 1944, by Allied forces, which included contingents of the Free French under General de Gaulle. During the immediate postliberation period, de Gaulle presided over a provisional government, but he resigned in 1946 because of communist and socialist opposition to a constitution providing for a strong executive. The constitution resulted in a government similar in many ways to that of the Third Republic.

The Fourth Republic. After the resignation of de Gaulle, a coalition of communists, socialists, and members of the MRP (the Catholic Popular Republican Movement) carried through various social reforms and nationalized the country's most important power, transportation, and banking facilities.

Soon, however, the coalition broke up over ideological differences and Cold War tensions, and France once more returned to social and economic conservatism. Beset by inflation, strikes, and foreign exchange problems, the French economy was modernized and production increased with the help of U.S. aid under the Marshall Plan, which was inaugurated in 1947.

The most serious problem facing the Fourth Republic was the struggle to maintain the French colonial empire. France waged a losing war in Indochina against pro-independence forces from 1946 to 1954, when it was forced to withdraw. A few months later France was in a costly colonial war in Algeria, where there were many French settlers.

THE FAMOUS PHOTOGRAPH of a Frenchman weeping at the invasion of France by Hitler's forces expresses the grief of the entire nation.

Finally, weakened by the old pattern of rapidly changing ministries, the Fourth Republic was destroyed in 1958 by an attempted coup led by French soldiers and settlers in Algeria determined to forestall an agreement between the French government and Algerian nationalists.

The Fifth Republic. De Gaulle returned to power as head of France's Fifth Republic, which placed extensive powers in the hands of the president. In 1962 de Gaulle recognized Algerian independence. Meanwhile, France had granted independence to most of its numerous other African dependencies.

During the first decade of the Fifth Republic, France enjoyed stability and prosperity and played an ambitious role in foreign affairs. De Gaulle built France into a major power free from the constraints of other nations, particularly the United States. Under his leadership, France developed its own nuclear force. To a certain extent, his policy succeeded; France has become influential in those African countries that were formerly French colonies.

The Gaullist regime tottered in 1968 when a student rebellion touched off a national strike. De Gaulle resigned in 1969 after the defeat of a referendum for his proposals for constitutional reform, and died a year later. His successor, Georges Pompidou, initiated reforms to benefit blue-collar workers, but died in office in 1974.

A new union of the left in 1972 led to increased leftist representation in parliament. In elections to choose Pompidou's successor, the socialist François Mitterrand was narrowly defeated by moderate conservative Valéry Giscard D'Estaing.

Giscard's tenure was marked by a severe downturn of the economy that derailed many of his intended reforms. This, combined with government scandals and dissatisfaction with Giscard's personal style, led to his defeat at the polls in 1981 by François Mitterrand.

In subsequent elections to the National Assembly, socialists won an absolute majority, gaining an impressive mandate for reform. Among other changes, the socialist government nationalized many large businesses, increased the level of social benefits, and instituted judiciary reforms. However, the economy did not improve, and in 1984 legislative elections a center-right coalition gained a majority in the assembly.

In a situation hitherto unknown in the Fifth Republic, Mitterrand was forced to appoint a prime minister not of his own party: Jacques Chirac, a conservative. During this period Chirac reversed many of the changes that had been instituted by the socialists.

Mitterrand defeated Chirac in the presidential election of 1988. With the collapse of communism, he moved to improve ties with united Germany and strengthen Frances's position in European and international affairs. However, continued economic problems at home led to rising dissatisfaction with the socialist government. Chirac was elected president in 1995.

GENERAL CHARLES DE GAULLE formed a provisional French government in London during World War II. He later participated in the liberation of France, commanding contingents of the Free French.

26 Europe and Russia

Georgia

Official name: *Georgia*
Area: *26,904 sq. mi., 69,700 sq. km.*
Type of government: *Republic*
Population: *4,961,000*
Capital and largest city: *T'bilisi,*
    (Pop., 1,399,000)
Languages: *Georgian, Russian*
Literacy: *99%;* **Currency:** *Lari*
Per capita GDP: *$3,100*
    (Rank: 114th)

meters
US

metres
Brit.

The land. The republic of Georgia lies at the eastern end of the Black Sea, and includes the Abkhaz and Adzhar autonomous republics and the Yugo-Ossetian autonomous oblast (region). The Great Caucasus mountain range in the north traverses the country from east to west, with peaks such as Shkhara and Rustaveli reaching more than 16,000 feet (4,875 meters). Mount Kazbek, at 16,500 feet (5,030 meters) is an extinct volcano that towers above Daryal Pass.

In the south, running generally parallel to the northern mountains, are the ranges and plateaus of the Lesser (Little) Caucasus. Although 85 percent of the republic is rugged mountain terrain, variety is provided by a strip of lowland between the Great and Lesser Caucasus; it also crosses the country from east to west. Near the Black Sea are the Kolkhida Lowlands, once an area of stagnant swamp, which have been drained and reclaimed for the cultivation of subtropical and other crops.

Principal rivers of western Georgia are the Inguri, Rioni, and Kodoni, which descend from the Great Caucasus and flow to the Black Sea. In central Georgia, the Kura (Mtkvari) River runs along the high plateau called the Kartalinian Plain.

Climate varies from humid subtropical in the western lowlands near the Black Sea, to alpine in the northern and southern mountains, to dry in the eastern Kura steppes. Temperatures average about 41°F (5°C) in western coastal areas, where winters are mild, and rainfall there totals 40 to 80 inches (100 to 200 centimeters) per year.

The people. The name Georgia stems from Gorj, the Persian name for the region's native people. Georgians, forming about 70 percent of the population, are influenced by an ancient culture and rich traditions, some dating back to the fourth century B.C. Long known for their ability as fighters, for their generosity, and good looks, Georgians also tend to live very long lives.

A strongly nationalistic people, Georgians were controlled for centuries by foreign invaders, and they reflect the intermingling of many ethnic groups. At one time, their principal occupations were farming and the raising of livestock. Under the Soviet regime, however, the urban population more than trebled from 1913 to 1974, while the rural element increased by only one-quarter.

Georgians have been Christian since the fourth century. Their language is related to the Ibero-Caucasian family of languages and is written in Georgian script. In addition, a standard literary language has been in use since about the fifth century.

The mountain village of Gori is the birthplace of Iosip Djugashvili, who later took the name Joseph Stalin and became Georgia's most famous son.

Economy. Georgia has important deposits of coal, oil, manganese, and marble. Major industries include mining, metallurgy, machine building, chemicals, construction materials, oil, and oil products. The supply of fuel and power is well developed, with many hydroelectric stations and coal- and gas-powered plants providing a solid base for industrialization.

Agriculture is both diverse and mechanized, emphasizing grains, fruit, grapes, tea, and vegetables. Wines have been made in Georgia for centuries, with more than 500 varieties of grapes in use. The resorts on the Black Sea draw many tourists and provide an important source of income.

Government. Georgia obtained independence from the Soviet Union in 1991. The Georgian constitution, implemented in 1995, provides for a popularly elected 235-member parliament. The president is both chief of state and head of the government, and is elected by popular vote to a 5-year term.

History. The first Georgian kingdom dates back to the fourth century B.C. After a long period of domination by Persians, Armenians, and Turks, the Georgian people were united in the 12th and 13th centuries and enjoyed a brief return to independence and prosperity. Devastated in the Mongol invasions of the 13th century, and by Tamerlane in the late 14th century, Georgia later became the focus of a long struggle between Persia and Turkey. In the 16th century it was divided into principalities, some ruled by Persia and others by Turkey. Between 1783 and 1830 the territory was acquired by Russia.

Georgia declared its independence in 1918, but was forced to submit to the Soviet government in 1922. With Armenia and Azerbaijan, it became part of the Transcaucasian Soviet Socialist Republic that same year, and was made a separate Soviet republic in 1936.

In 1991 Georgia declared independence from the Soviet Union and Zviad Gamsakhurdia was elected president. In 1992 he was ousted by opposition forces who claimed he had become increasingly authoritarian. Eduard Shevardnadze was then elected president. In 1993 Georgia suffered major setbacks in fighting with secessionist forces in Abkhazia, in northwestern Georgia. After parliamentary elections in 2003 which were seen as fraudulent, demonstrators called for Shevardnadze's resignation. After an initial standoff he conceded and in early 2004 opposition leader Mikhail Saakashvili was elected president.

(For more information about the history of Georgia as part of the Soviet Union, see the article on Russia.)

Germany

Official name: *Federal Republic of*
    Germany
Area: *137,804 sq. mi.,*
    356,910 sq. km.
Type of government: *Federal*
    republic
Population: *82,351,000*
Capital and largest city: *Berlin*
    (Pop., 3,382,000)
Language: *German*
Literacy: *99%;* **Currency:** *Euro*
Per capita GDP: *$26,600*
    (Rank: 16th)

The land. The northern area of Germany is on the low-lying North German Plain. This area of flat land, broken by low hills, lakes, and swamps, is quite fertile. The central region of Germany, the Central Uplands, is covered by relatively low, heavily forested mountain ranges and plateaus cut by numerous river valleys. The southern region is upland country dominated by the Erzgebirge (Ore Mountains), the mountainous Thuringian Forest region, the Harz Mountains, and the northernmost ranges of the Alps. These mountain ranges are drained by the many tributaries of the Elbe River, the principal river of eastern Germany. The Rhine River rises in the Alps and flows through the western part of the country. It is navigable along its entire course in Germany. Important tributaries of the Rhine include the Mosel, the Main, the Neckar, and the Ruhr. Other important rivers include the Danube, which rises in southwestern Germany and flows east to the Austrian border; and the Wesser, which rises in the Central Uplands and flows north to the North Sea.

| 0 | 40 | 80 mi |
| 0 | 40 | 80 km |

Maykop
Cherkessk
RUSSIA
Sochi
Mt. Elbrus
5642 m
(18,510 ft)   Nalchik
Gagra
Shkhara
5068 m
(16,627 ft)
Sokhumi
Jvari
RUSSIA
Mqinvartsveri
5047 m
(16,558 ft)
K'ut'aisi
Black
Sea
P'ot'i
Mtkvari
Lagodekhi
Ba'tumi   LESSER
T'bilisi
Rust'avi   Tsit'eli-Tsqaro
Artvin   CAUCASUS
TURKEY   ARMENIA   AZERBAIJAN
Gyumri
Vanadzor   Mingäçevir Reservoir
© MQST
Caspian
Sea

The climate is moderated by Germany's location with respect to the Atlantic Ocean and North Sea. Temperatures tend to be lower in the central and southern regions. This means temperature is about 30°F (–1°C) in the winter and about 65°F (18°C) in the summer. Rainfall varies from as much as 50 inches (127 centimeters) annually in parts of the southern highlands to about 20 inches (51 centimeters) in some parts of the lowland regions.

The people. Germany has been from ancient times a place of migration for a large variety of ethnic types. This fact is evident in the diverse physical characteristics of the population. Eastern Germany has a very homogeneous ethnically German and German-speaking population. In the west, while most people speak standard German, regional dialects are still spoken. The vast majority of the eastern German population is at least nominally Protestant, with less than 10 percent being Roman Catholic. In the west, the population is evenly split between Roman Catholicism and Protestantism. Western Germany has a significant number of migrant workers, mostly from southern European countries.

Germany has one of the highest population densities in all of Europe. The great majority of the population live in urban areas. Eastern Germany has a slightly higher population density than most of its neighbors, though still considerably lower than that of western Germany.

The largest German city is Berlin, which was the capital of Germany until 1945 and was declared the capital of the new Germany in 1990. Other important urban centers include Hamburg (population, 1,715,000), Munich (1,210,000), Cologne (963,000), Leipzig (493,000),

Dresden (478,000), and Chemnitz, formerly Karl-Marx-Stadt (259,000).

The population figures for German cities may change significantly in the initial years of reunification. When the East German borders were originally opened it was estimated that some 2,000 people fled the country daily. However, reunification, a new democratically elected government, the establishment of free markets, and a greater sense of freedom is expected to bring many easterners back home and also draw western merchants, businessmen, and workers to the east to help offset the original population losses.

Economy. As of July 1, 1990, the deutsche mark became the common currency of Germany and East German industry was placed under the West German rules of corporate activity. The economic merger transformed East Germany's 8,000 state-owned companies into joint stock ventures, with a special government trust set up to guarantee liquidity through the early stages of economic merger. Many East German enterprises were found to be obsolete and deemed unlikely ever to become competitive in the world economy. In addition, a number of nuclear power facilities were ruled unsafe and shut down, further hindering economic renewal in the east. Raising the East German economic infrastructure up to western standards will require the investment of billions of dollars over the coming years. Inflation and high unemployment are apt to be significant obstacles in the short term, at least, and possibly for many years.

In the postwar decades, West Germany became the leading industrial nation in Europe and the fourth-largest in the world, after the United States, the

Soviet Union, and Japan.

Germany is not particularly well endowed with mineral resources. However, it does have important deposits of coal, iron, and potash. Domestic production of petroleum and natural gas account for only a small portion of the nation's requirements.

Agriculture has declined dramatically in importance since World War II. In the west in the late 1980s, there were less than half the number of farms as in 1949; in 1986 agriculture employed only about 5 percent of the workforce. Agriculture employed about 10 percent of the workforce in East Germany. The

centers
US

centres
Brit.

THE FLAT TERRAIN and rich soil along the Mosel River in the Rhineland region of western Germany support intensive agriculture and large population centers.

INDUSTRY is the most important sector of Germany's economy, and automobile production at plants like this BMW facility is one of the leading industries.

most important crops in Germany include cereal grains such as wheat and rye, potatoes, and sugar beets. Dairy farming is also important.

By far the most important sector of the economy, and the driving force behind the West German recovery, has been industry. It provides 43 percent of the gross domestic product and employs 32 percent of the population. The most important industries include electrical and mechanical engineering, vehicle production, electronics, and chemicals. West Germany is also strong in the new high-technology computer, telecommunications, and office equipment industries. Important East German industries include the manufacture of chemicals, transport equipment and vehicles, and machine tools, with recent emphasis placed on the development of the high-technology industries of electronics and biotechnology.

West German prosperity is due in large measure to its extremely high level of exports. In 1987 West Germany exported more, measured by value, than any other country in the world. The country's principal trade partners are the other members of the European Community, the United States, Austria, and Switzerland.

The East German economy was also driven by industry. Its industrial output ranked second in the European Communist bloc after the Soviet Union, its major trading partner. In the 1970s and 1980s, however, its industries were not

modernized, and production fell as skilled workers left to find employment in the West.

Government. Reunification of Germany in 1990 after 45 years of postwar division involved the merger of West Germany, a federal union of eleven Laender, or states, with East Germany. One of the early tasks of reunification was to merge the 15 East German districts into five states that could function within the German federation.

The German head of state is a president, although actual power rests with a chancellor, or prime minister, elected by the Bundestag, the lower house of the legislature. The chancellor and a cabinet are responsible to the legislature.

The deputies of the Bundestag are popularly elected to four-year terms. The members of the less powerful upper house, which is called the Bundesrat, are chosen by the governments of the individual Laender. The legislature has 598 members, approximately one-fourth of whom represent the five reconstituted Laender of eastern Germany.

History. Political division is not new to Germany. With no major natural boundaries save the Alps to the south, the territory has been open to invasion from east, north, and west. In ancient times there were many small, tribal states, all subject to easy conquest. Among the earliest settlers were the Teutons, a Germanic people.

The territory was divided among several Teutonic tribes—the Franks, the Saxons, and the Thuringians—led by elective kings. Beginning in the 200s A.D., other Germanic peoples from the east settled in the area—notably the Goths and the Burgundians. The Romans made several unsuccessful attempts to conquer the Germanic tribes, but no single ruler gained control of the entire region until the 300s, when the Huns swept across the land.

Both the Huns and the Vandals, who followed soon after, were migratory, warlike peoples whose main goal was conquest, and their rule over the settled tribes was brief. It was only the Franks, who settled in the Rhine valley in the late 300s, who eventually attempted to permanently unite the Germanic peoples.

Frankish kingdom. The Franks expanded westward from the Rhine into Gaul, driving out the Roman legions stationed there. They adopted Christianity and won the support of the popes, whose power by the 500s was greater than that of Rome. The Franks defeated the other Germanic tribes and in 732 fought off a Muslim invasion of Europe.

The Franks reached the height of their power under Charles the Great, or Charlemagne, who became king in 768. Under Charlemagne, the Franks controlled a vast territory ranging from central Italy on the south to the Baltic Sea on the north, and from the Pyrenees on the west to the Elbe River on the east. Charlemagne accepted the role of protector of the popes, and in 800 he was

crowned emperor in Rome, an act that laid the religious and political foundations for the later Holy Roman Empire.

The unity Charlemagne achieved did not long survive him. Several decades of disunity followed his death in 814, and in 843 the Treaty of Verdun divided his territories into three parts. The eastern, predominantly German, portion, between the Rhine and the Elbe rivers, went to Louis the German; it became the core of modern Germany while the west became modern France.

The Saxons. The tribal loyalties and ambitions existing before Charlemagne's time had not been forgotten. Each major tribal unit had formed a country, and the dukes and princes who led them vied for control of the German throne. By the early 900s, one German clan, the Saxons, had emerged dominant. Its first ruler, Henry the Fowler, extended German territory to the Oder River and defended it against attacks from Magyar and Slavic peoples to the south.

A Saxon king, Otto I, in 962, was given the crown of Italy and became the first Holy Roman Emperor as a reward for aiding the pope. The Holy Roman Empire revived, at least in name, the old Roman Empire and gave to Germany the empire's prestige as well as the support of the papacy.

By about 1030, the Holy Roman Empire was a prosperous feudal nation with thriving towns and vigorous trade. Henry III, who became emperor in 1039, probably held more actual power than any previous emperor.

Henry was the last emperor with such power, however. After his death in 1056 a regent ruled for his young heir, and the period of the regency was fatal for the strength of the German throne. Both the church and the nobility had become dissatisfied with their lack of power. By the 1070s the pope and the emperor were in open conflict over the distribution of political and religious power. The local princes sided with the papacy to reduce the strength of the emperor.

The conflict continued into the mid-1200s, and although both emperors and popes won victories, the final result was

THE FIRST GERMAN PRINCE to wear the magnificent crown of the Holy Roman Empire was Rudolf of the House of Hapsburg in Austria.

a great loss of power for both. The empire disintegrated into anarchy in the 1250s. For a 20-year period known as the "Great Interregnum," no one man ruled Germany, although many tried. Moreover, as each faction grew in power—the princes, the dukes, the bishops, and the towns—a tradition of disunity was firmly established and it became even harder to consolidate political power.

It was only in 1273, at the insistence of Pope Gregory X, who feared the growing power of France, that the German princes elected one of their number to be Holy Roman Emperor. Their choice was Rudolf of the House of Hapsburg in Austria, then a minor princely house. Rudolf took steps to ensure the continuance on the throne of members of his family, and later Hapsburg emperors became powerful.

The Hapsburgs. During the Middle Ages, the Hapsburg emperors added to the territory under their control, but the unification of the German states did not follow the Hapsburg rise to power. The German emperor was an elected king by tradition and by a law enacted in 1356. As he could rule only with the consent of the princes who elected him, the German emperor constantly had to make concessions to them, and he was unable to rule as firmly as a hereditary monarch could.

Because of the weakness of the central government, the German states were less an empire than a federation dominated by the stronger states. Nearly constant competition for power kept the German states in turmoil from the 1300s to the 1800s, but the Hapsburg family remained the dominant power through the 1700s.

Administrative and economic policies initiated during the 1100s had encouraged the development of towns. By the middle of the 1300s, these policies, coupled with a renewed interest in the arts and an expanding economy, had transformed many towns into "free cities"—large autonomous units free from the control of local princes. From the middle of the 1200s to the middle of the 1400s, the influence of German cities rivaled that of German princes.

Despite the fragmentation of the Holy Roman Empire, it reached the height of its power and size in the early 1500s under Emperor Charles V, who, by inheritance and marriage, ruled Spain, Portugal, Belgium, and The Netherlands as well as the German states. It was during his reign, however, that religious controversy flared, contributing to the final disintegration of the empire. In 1517 Martin Luther, an Augustinian monk, called for reforms in the Roman Catholic Church.

Reformation. The Lutheran Reformation attracted many more radical social, political, and religious reformers, and they became a threat to both the church and the empire. Charles V led a diet, or council, at Worms in 1521 to try Luther. The council banned the spread of any

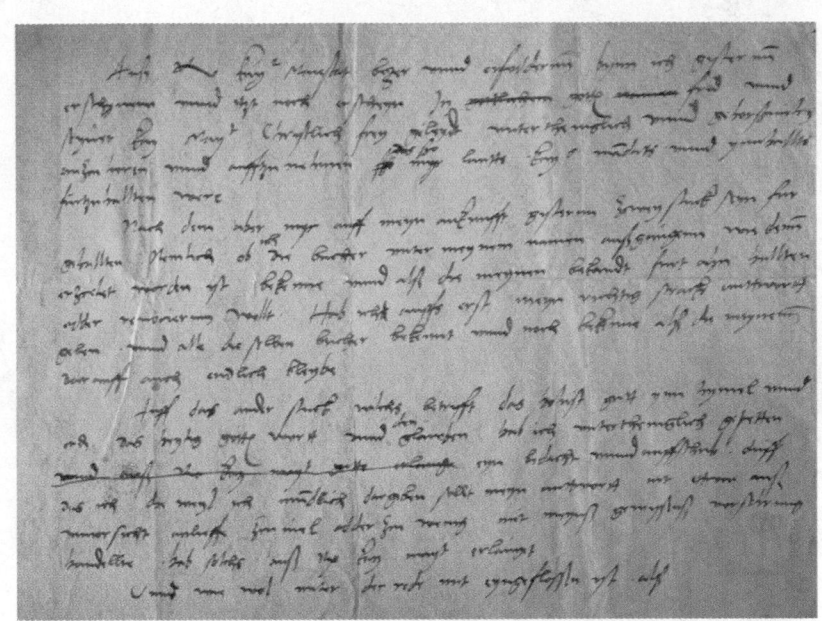

PART OF THE DOCUMENT in which Martin Luther called for reforms in the Roman Catholic Church, setting in motion the Reformation and the foundations of Protestantism

new doctrines. The reformers continued, however, encouraged by power-seeking princes, who adopted their reforms as a means of opposing the emperor.

The progress of the Reformation was speeded by Charles's involvement in a series of wars with France. In Germany, disputes among the proliferating Protestant sects and between Protestants and Roman Catholics led to a series of religious wars, which were ended in 1555 by the Peace of Augsburg.

The peace settlement marked the final collapse of the emperor's real power. It granted to each prince within the empire the right to determine the religion of his subjects. In 1556 Charles abdicated, leaving his Spanish possessions to his son Philip, and his German dominions to his brother, Ferdinand.

The Peace of Augsburg had not finally settled the religious disputes, and it had only aggravated Germany's political confusion. In 1618 fighting began again in the Thirty Years' War. At first the war was confined to the Roman Catholic-Protestant conflict, but almost immediately the old issues of prince versus emperor, and federation versus empire, were renewed.

The war spread and eventually involved most of continental Europe as well as England and Sweden. The German states, however, were the focus of the conflict, and the death and devastation visited upon the Germans was appalling. The Peace of Westphalia, which settled the war in 1648, formalized German disunity by giving the local princes more power than the emperor. Each of the 300 separate German states received the right to conduct its own diplomacy, determine the religion of its people, and vote on the emperor's right to collect taxes, raise an army, or conduct foreign policy.

Germany's enemies, notably France, gained from German fragmentation, which greatly diminished its international power.

Rise of Prussia. During the latter half of the 1600s, Prussia, known then as Brandenburg, began to grow from a small duchy into the most powerful state in Germany. Prussia's ruling Hohenzollern house increased the territory within its domain and, at the same time, established an efficient, centralized administration to control it. The army, officered by the nobility, became the central institution of the state.

Decisive in Prussia's ascendancy to power within Germany was the succession to the throne in 1740 of Frederick

PICTURESQUE FRIEBURG in the Black Forest is famous for its cuckoo clocks.

FAIRY-TALE CASTLES
still dot the German landscape. Mad King Ludwig's Schloss Neuschwanstein was the inspiration for Disney's castle.

THE GOTHIC CATHEDRAL
of Munich is one of the city's best-loved landmarks.

II, called the Great, a man of driving force and shrewd statesmanship. Immediately upon assuming the throne he invaded Silesia, a large and wealthy Austrian territory. Finally, in 1763, Prussia won the disputed Silesian territory, which doubled Prussia's population and natural resources. Germany was then polarized between northern Germany, dominated by Prussia, and southern Germany, led by Austria.

Prussia's rapid rise to power had been due in large part to Frederick the Great, and after his death in 1786, the system he had built could not function effectively. Thus in 1806, when the French armies of Napoleon were conquering Europe, Prussia offered little resistance and fell to Napoleon after the Battle of Jena.

Napoleonic era. By 1806 Napoleon controlled most of the German states, which he organized into the Confederation of the Rhine. He persuaded the Austrian emperor, Francis I, formally to dissolve the Holy Roman Empire. In 1809 Austria yielded to the French, and Napoleon's troops occupied all of Germany.

The French occupation ended in 1813, after Austria reluctantly joined forces with Prussia and Russia in a war of liberation that pushed Napoleon's armies west of the Rhine. But the fairly brief French occupation had wrought changes in Germany more significant than the formal dissolution of the Holy Roman Empire.

Germany was still a collection of states, but the Napoleonic Confederation of the Rhine had reduced their number and the Congress of Vienna, in 1815, after Napoleon's defeat, accepted the reduction by setting up the Germanic Confederation, a loose grouping of 38 independent German states.

Prussia had pressed for a more unified Germany, but the congress encouraged the autonomy of the states as sought by the Austrian foreign minister, Prince Klemens von Metternich. Metternich's shrewd leadership led to tightened monarchical control over the social, political, and economic life of Austria. This "Metternich system" also enabled the Austrian Empire to exercise

control over the south German states and avoid conflict with Prussia over dominance in a unified Germany.

In Prussia, too, the movement for reform—which before 1815 had resulted in tax and administrative reforms and the abolition of serfdom—began to lag as reactionary forces triumphed over liberalism throughout Germany.

The Napoleonic wars had awakened democratic and nationalistic movements that the German governments felt must be repressed. Under the leadership of Austria's Metternich, the German states imposed tight controls on all civil liberties, especially on the activities of the universities. These controls only spurred the liberals and nationalists to resist, and in 1848 they rebelled against Metternich's reactionary policies.

Risings of 1848. Inspired by a similar revolution in Paris, large numbers of Austrians, mostly in Vienna, organized and demanded a constitution. Metternich fled Austria, and the emperor granted a constitution and abdicated in December, 1848.

The rebellion had spread from Vienna to the Hapsburg's Hungarian and Slavic subject peoples. A new Austrian emperor, Francis Joseph I, concentrated on crushing the rebellions in Hungary and the Slavic areas, ignoring the more peaceful rebellion among the Germans.

The rebellious Germans demanded not only political and social liberties, but the political union of Germany. Most German states elected liberal local governments, which in turn elected liberal representatives to a national assembly that met in Frankfurt in May, 1848, to establish a republic. In 1849 the assembly drafted a democratic constitution for a unified German state and elected Prussia's ruler, Frederick William IV, emperor of the new nation.

Some of the states opposed the new organization, however, and Austria, which with Russia's help had quelled the Hungarian and Slavic revolutions in early 1849, refused to join the unification movement that would have forced it to give up its non-German territories in joining Germany.

Frederick William IV, unwilling to accept the throne from an elected assembly, refused the imperial crown, and by 1850 the old constitution of the Germanic Confederation had been readopted and the unification and reform efforts of the assembly had failed. Austria was once more able to impose a superficial calm on Germany after putting down the 1848 rebellions, but it could not stem the movement for German unification.

Unification. In 1844 Prussia had encouraged unification by organizing a customs union, the Zollverein, of more than half the German states, but excluding Austria. Unification efforts gathered strength after 1862 under the leadership of Otto von Bismarck, Prussia's chief minister. He followed a policy of "blood and iron" in leading Germany to European dominance.

Bismarck had soon centralized and strengthened Prussia's government and pressed the development of the army and expansion into new territory. Prussia sought to control the two predominantly German duchies of Schleswig and Holstein that Denmark claimed. In 1864 Austria aided Prussia to drive out the Danes, but Bismarck's subsequent attempt to control Holstein angered Austria, and war between the two was only narrowly averted.

War did break out between them for seven weeks in 1866. In the Seven Weeks' War Prussian forces easily defeated Austria, and as a result in 1867, a constitution was adopted for a new confederation excluding Austria and several south German states.

Constitutionally a federal state, the new North German Confederation was actually under Prussian control. Austria, having lost control of Germany, was forced to admit Hungary as an equal partner in a dual monarchy, and Austrian history diverged from the history of Germany.

German Empire. Prussia quickly became the greatest power in Europe and was able to roundly defeat France in 1870–1871 in the Franco-Prussian War, a conflict over dynastic claims to the throne of Spain. Prussia forced France to accept a harsh, cruel, and humiliating settlement—France ceded the industrially rich territories of Alsace and Lorraine, paid a large indemnity, and supported a German army of occupation.

Now the dominant figure of all Europe, Bismarck also succeeded in 1871 in bringing the south German states, again excluding Austria, into the North German Confederation. He became the first chancellor, or prime minister, of the German Empire. William I was proclaimed the emperor.

The new German state was a curious mixture of democratic and authoritarian institutions. Advanced social welfare laws existed side by side with legislation curbing the Roman Catholic Church and suppressing the socialists. Both the central government and the 25 states constituting the union had monarchical forms of government.

Each state enjoyed a large degree of autonomy, although the federal government, or *Reich,* was empowered to administer a common communications system, maintain an army, and conduct foreign affairs. In addition to the kaiser, or emperor, the federal government had a legislature with two houses—the *Bundesrat,* where the states received representation, and the *Reichstag,* where the people were represented through a system of universal suffrage.

The economic growth of the new empire was astounding. In 1860, for example, German steel production did not even equal that of France; by 1900 it exceeded that of both England and France combined. By 1900, moreover, German naval power approached that of Great Britain, the traditional "mistress of the sea."

Germany's political prestige also grew, as a result not only of its strengthened economic and military position but also of the capable leadership of the "iron chancellor." Bismarck soon consolidated the new Germany's continental position by alliances in 1882 with Austria-Hungary and Italy, in the Triple Alliance, and in 1887 with Russia.

Bismarck fell from power in 1890, when the new emperor, William II, who opposed his authoritarian measures and his diplomatic techniques, decided to conduct German diplomacy personally.

Under William II, Germany followed a policy of aggressive imperialism that divided Europe into two opposing camps—pro-German and anti-German. William antagonized Britain by enlarging the German navy, enraged his ally Russia by competing with it for territory in the Near East, and made no attempt to improve relations with France, which had been poor since the loss of Alsace-Lorraine.

German aggressiveness drew France and Britain, traditional enemies, closer together. In the Entente Cordiale of 1904, the two settled several longstanding disputes and united in opposition to Germany. In 1905 William tested the entente by openly urging independence for the French protectorate of Morocco.

The entente proved solid, and in 1906 France and Britain led the Algeciras Conference of European powers, which berated Germany for its insult to France. In 1907 Russia, Germany's former ally, entered the British-French alliance, forming the Triple Entente. In 1911 Germany precipitated a second "Moroccan Crisis" and was again rebuked.

World War I. The European powers were able to settle the incidents of 1905 and 1911 peacefully, but crisis followed crisis in the Balkan region. Bulgaria and Turkey, having lost territory in Balkan wars in 1912 and in 1913, joined Germany, Austria-Hungary, and Italy to form the alliance of Central Powers in opposition to the Triple Entente.

In 1914 a crisis caused by the assassination of Archduke Francis Ferdinand, heir to the Austrian throne, led to World War I. Bosnia, where the assassination occurred, was an Austrian territory, but as the assassin was Serbian, and as Serbia had led Pan-Slav activity in Bosnia, Austria threatened reprisals against Serbia. Germany supported Austria, while Russia backed Serbia.

Both sides misjudged the seriousness of the situation, and the war that resulted involved the allies of Germany and Russia and eventually all of Europe as well as the United States, Japan, and the Middle East. Germany had predicted that the war would be short, but the war lasted four years, and Germany was unable to maintain the strength of its forces.

In 1918, with defeat imminent, rebellions broke out in the German territories, resulting in the abdication of the emperor and the declaration of a Ger-

man republic. The peace settlements exacted huge reparations; confiscated German overseas possessions and non-German-speaking European territories; and disarmed the country.

Weimar Republic. A republic was formally established in July, 1919, when the Weimar constitution was adopted. The new German state faced difficulties from its beginning, especially in dealing with the humiliation of the dictated peace and in bearing the heavy burden of reparations, which led to inflation and a currency collapse.

The lack of a tradition of unity and of parliamentary democracy provided a shaky foundation for the new government, made more unstable by attacks from the communists on the extreme left and authoritarian nationalists on the extreme right.

In 1929, just as the government had begun to solve its economic and political problems and had begun to be reintegrated into Europe by joining the League of Nations, the worldwide economic depression struck. Unemployment increased and with it came widespread resentment against the existing German government. The heavy victories of extremist parties in elections held in 1930 reflected the growing popular discontent.

On the left, the communists scored heavily, and on the right, Adolf Hitler's National Socialist, or Nazi, Party, gained enough seats to become the second-largest party in the *Reichstag.* In 1932 elections, the Nazis became the largest single party in the *Reichstag,* and in 1933 Adolf Hitler was appointed chancellor.

Nazi era. Hitler came to power partly by heading a highly organized political party, and partly because the brand of nationalism that he preached was attractive to the Germans, who were

UNDER WILHELM, OR WILLIAM II, Germany followed a policy of aggressive imperialism that divided Europe into two opposing camps and led to World War I.

26 Europe and Russia

humiliated by defeat in the war, impoverished by the depression, and fearful for their property in the face of communism.

He promised to create a revitalized, strengthened Germany—a Germany stronger than the First Reich, the Holy Roman Empire, or the Second Reich, Bismarck's empire. He assured Germans that they were capable of greatness because they were descended from the strong, pure, "Aryan race" of Teutons, and he directed their hostility toward Jews and non-Germans, especially the Slavs.

Although the Nazi Party received only 44 percent of the vote in elections held in late 1933, Hitler proclaimed that the elections had made him the spokesman of all Germany. The *Reichstag* granted him dictatorial powers and suspended the constitution. Germany was transformed from a federal state into a highly centralized state. The office of president was abolished, and Hitler assumed all powers of state.

Economic policy was determined by the central government, and unemployment was reduced by public works projects and massive rearmament. All opposition parties were banned and strict censorship was imposed. The legal system was reorganized to place the needs of the state above accepted standards of justice, and concentration camps were opened to imprison and often kill Hitler's "convicted" political opponents.

The camps came to be used primarily for the imprisonment and murder of Jews, as anti-Semitism became an increasingly important part of the Nazi program. Jews were forbidden to teach, hold office, attend universities, or engage in many businesses; non-Jews were ordered to ostracize them and to boycott Jewish businesses. Between 1935 and 1945, Hitler's regime killed some 6 million European Jews and another 9 to 10 million Gypsies, Slavs, and political opponents.

The basis of Hitler's early foreign policy was hostility to conditions imposed on Germany by the Versailles treaty system that ended World War I. In 1933 Germany ended its membership in the League of Nations. Hitler abrogated German agreements to remain neutral, and began to rearm the country. Thereafter, Germany moved to prepare for war and for expansion to the east.

In 1936 and 1937, Germany entered into treaties with Japan and Italy. Italy, led by the fascist dictator Benito Mussolini, became an especially close ally, forming one half of the "Rome-Berlin Axis." One common feature of these treaties was their declaration of opposition to communism, but in 1939 Hitler entered into a nonaggression pact with the communist government of the Soviet Union.

Hitler also refused to obey the territorial limits set by the Versailles settlement. Using the desire to unite all German-speaking peoples as an excuse, Hitler annexed Austria in 1938 and in 1939 took part, then all, of Czechoslovakia. The World War I Allies did not strongly object to his actions, hoping to appease him and prevent a second world conflict.

World War II. Until 1939 Hitler had gained territory and allies bloodlessly, but in that summer he demanded that the Free City of Danzig, within Poland's borders, be "restored" to the Reich. When he was refused, Germany invaded Poland and occupied Danzig. Britain and France, bound by treaty to protect Poland and realizing that Hitler could not be appeased, declared war on Germany on September 3, 1939.

The major German offensive against the west began in 1940, when German troops overran the neutral states of Denmark, Norway, The Netherlands, and Belgium, and invaded France. Then in June 1941, German armies broke the nonaggression pact and invaded the Soviet Union.

In December 1941, the United States entered the war against Hitler, and in 1942 Soviet troops began a counteroffensive. Before the tide turned in favor of the Allies, Hitler controlled by conquest or alliances almost all of continental Europe as far east as the outskirts of Moscow and territories in North Africa and the Middle East.

The main Allied counteroffensive began in June 1944, when British, Canadian, and U.S. troops landed on the beaches of Normandy. By September 1944, the Allies had reached the German border. When Soviet troops reached the outskirts of Berlin from the east in May 1945, and the fall of the city seemed imminent, Hitler committed suicide. The Germans surrendered, and the war was over.

Occupation. The leaders of the four major allied nations met at Potsdam, Germany, in July 1945, and partitioned Germany into four zones of occupation. The Soviet Union occupied the portion east of the Elbe River and the United States, Britain, and France divided the territory to the west.

Portions of Germany east of the Oder and Neisse rivers were placed under the administration of Poland, which was dominated by the Soviet Union. The Allies also divided Berlin

U.S. INFANTRYMEN hold up a captured German Nazi flag during World War II.

into four occupation zones and established the Allied Control Council to coordinate the occupation.

West Germany. The Soviets did not cooperate with the other members of the council, and in 1948, after several policy disputes with the Soviet Union, France, Britain, and the United States merged their sectors and gave the new zone a large measure of self-government.

Later in the same year, elections were held in western Germany and a federal constitution was agreed upon. The Soviet Union tried to force the Allies to leave Berlin and to allow unification on Soviet terms by blockading Berlin in 1949, but a massive airlift broke the blockade.

Britain, France, and the United States maintained nominal control over West Germany until 1955, when the Federal Republic of Germany became fully sovereign.

In the early 1950s West Germany concentrated on repairing the destruction wrought by the war, and worked to develop and expand its industry. By the mid-1960s, the country had become a leading industrial nation.

In 1961 the East Germans built the Berlin Wall, which physically divided the city and became the symbol of divided Germany and the continuation of the Cold War. West Berlin had, by that time, become a model Western urban center and a sharp contrast to Communist East Berlin.

West Germany's political recovery paralleled its economic recovery. Under the leadership of Konrad Adenauer and his conservative Christian Democratic Party, West Germany became integrated into Western Europe as a staunch ally of the West. However, a resurgence of extreme right-wing nationalism in the mid-1960s disturbed the government and led in 1966 to the formation of an alliance of the Christian Democrats and their traditional opponents, the liberal Social Democrats. Willy Brandt, leader of the Social Democratic Party, became chancellor in 1969.

Brandt inaugurated a new foreign policy, *Ostpolitik,* or "eastern policy," which sought accommodation with the Soviet Union and other communist nations. Friendship treaties were signed with the Soviet Union and Poland in 1970, with East Germany in 1972, and with Czechoslovakia in 1973. For these efforts Brandt received the Nobel Peace Prize in 1971, but he resigned in 1974 following the discovery that one of his aides was an East German spy.

Helmut Schmidt, also a Social Democrat, succeeded him in time to face an economic recession induced by oil-import shortages, which resulted in high unemployment and inflation. By 1975 the crisis had passed and prosperity resumed.

In 1982 a worsening economic climate and a general trend toward conservatism led to the ousting of Schmidt by a parliamentary no-confidence vote. He was replaced by Christian Democrat Helmut Kohl. Kohl resigned in January 2000.

In the 1980s, a new player in West German politics was the environmentalist Green Party, reflecting a growing concern among West Germans about the deteriorating environment. In 1987 elections, the Greens polled over 8 percent of the vote, giving them considerable influence as a possible coalition partner.

East Germany. The post-World War II Soviet occupation of eastern Germany had a dual puopose. The primary goal was the institution of a government that would be pro-Soviet and therefore no threat. The secondary goal was the collection of reparation payments for war damages in the Soviet Union.

In furtherance of the first goal, the German Democratic Republic was proclaimed on October 7, 1949. The new government was patterned on the Soviet Union, and was firmly in the control of the German Communist party, the Socialist Unity Party.

The road back to economic health for the new state was impeded by several factors. Of great impact was the Soviet demand for reparations, which was met by the wholesale dismantling, and transport to the Soviet Union, of East German industry. In addition, large numbers of refugees, many of them skilled workers, fled East Germany for the West. By 1961, when the Berlin wall was built to halt the flow, it is estimated

that more than 3 million refugees had left East Germany.

In 1953 the raising of work quotas in some industries led to massive strikes and demands for free elections. The East German authorities lost control of the situation and called in Soviet troops to restore order.

Starting in the early 1960s, the East German economy began to grow quickly. By the 1980s it had become a major industrial nation, and the wealthiest Eastern bloc country.

For its first two decades, East Germany had great difficulty in gaining international recognition of its independent status. All moves toward such recognition were blocked by West Germany and the United States. In 1972, however, the two Germanys signed a treaty providing mutual recognition, and the following year both were admitted to the United Nations. Relations between the two countries have been steadily improving since.

In the 1980s, East Germany was recalcitrant in following the Soviet lead in reforming its economy and political system. Discontent finally erupted in 1989. In the spring, Hungary opened its border with Austria, enabling East Germans visiting that country to cross to the West. Some 30,000 East Germans eventually reached West Germany by this route, in the biggest East German exodus since 1961. Thousands more sought refuge in foreign embassies and eventually were sent to West Germany aboard sealed East German trains.

Through the summer and early fall the movement in East Germany for freedom and democracy grew. Mass demonstrations in Leipzig, Berlin, and other cities led to the resignation of the old communist leadership. On November 9, the new leadership permitted free travel through the Berlin Wall and between the two Germanys and promised free elections.

In the March 1990 elections, the Christian Democrats and other parties supporting reunification won a plurality of the vote. This strong showing, coupled with the disintegration of the East German Communist Party and the worsening economic situation, greatly accelerated reunification. Economic

WEST GERMAN PROSPERITY is due in large part to its high level of exports, many of which are shipped through the important port of Hamburg.

center
US

centre
Brit.

26 **Europe and Russia**

THE INTERNATIONAL CONFERENCE CENTER is a landmark in Berlin.

union between the two Germanys went into effect on July 1, and political union was achieved on October 3. Elections for the new all-German parliament were scheduled for December.

The enlarged Federal Republic of Germany chose to remain within the NATO alliance. East Germany, just prior to reunification, withdrew from the Warsaw Treaty Organization.

The reunification of Germany had profound immediate effects on Europe and the world and promised to have an even greater impact in years to come. With the virtual disintegration of the Warsaw Pact military alliance and subsequent bilateral agreements on conventional force limits in Europe, Germany became an important member of a new European system of collective security.

In the early 1990s, the German government undertook the enormous tasks of rebuilding the economy of eastern Germany and aiding the orderly transition of the states of Eastern Europe and the former Soviet Union to free market economies. It also faced the specter of neo-Nazi violence directed at Germany's large foreign population.

labor
US

labour
Brit.

civilization
US

civilisation
Brit.

Greece

Official name: *Hellenic Republic*
Area: *50,929 sq. mi.,*
131,940 sq. km.
Type of government: *Presidential*
parliamentary
Population: *10,645,000*
Capital and largest city: *Athens*
(Pop., 746,000)
Language: *Greek*
Literacy: *97%;* **Currency:** *Euro*
Per capita GDP: *$19,000*
(Rank: 30th)

The land. Greece is a mountainous country with many small peninsulas that jut out into the Mediterranean Sea. Almost one-fifth of the total land area of

Greece consists of islands, the largest of which are Crete, Rhodes, Lesbos, Chios, and Samos.

West of the mainland are the Ionian Islands. To the east, in the Aegean Sea, are the Cyclades, Sporades, Dodecanese, and other island groups. The Peloponnesus is joined to the mainland by the narrow Isthmus of Corinth.

The surface of Greece is mainly rough and hilly, and there is very little flat land. The rugged Pindus Mountains dominate the landscape of western mainland Greece from the northern border to the southern coast. Plains are few and lie mostly along the eastern coast. They are isolated by intervening highlands. Rivers are short and usually dry in summer.

The climate varies from region to region. In general, the south and east have hot, dry summers, and mild, moist, windy winters. In the north and west winters are rather cold, summers are hot, and rainfall is more abundant than in the south and east.

The people. Almost the entire population of the country is Greek, but there are small minorities of Bulgarians, Turks, Slavs, and Albanians in the border areas. Greek Orthodox is the predominant religion, although there is a very small minority of Muslims.

Population is densest along the eastern coast, in the Athens region, in the major towns of Macedonia in the north, and on a few of the islands. The southern Peloponnesus and the more mountainous interior are sparsely populated. Apart from Athens, the most important cities include Thessaloniki (population, 364,000), Piraeus (176,000), and Patras (163,000). Greece has traditionally had a high rate of emigration, and Greeks have settled throughout the world.

Economy. Greece is not a prosperous country by Western standards, but its economy has industrialized and generally improved significantly since World War II. Holding membership in the European Union (EU) has been of considerable benefit to Greece, as it receives a large share of EU development funds.

Agriculture employs about one-quarter of the labor force. It is a mainstay of the economy, despite the fact that less than 30 percent of the land is suitable for cultivation. Greece's generally poor soils are suitable for only a limited variety of crops, and productivity is low. Principal crops include olives, grapes, cotton, tobacco, and grains. Sheep and goats are herded in the northwest hills.

Industry accounts for about 25 percent of employment. Most businesses remain small and unproductive, and are relatively uncompetitive with rivals in Western Europe. Principal products include textiles, clothing, processed foods, chemicals, electrical equipment, and cement. Greece has generally had an unfavorable balance of trade. The expenditures of tourists in Greece, and the remittances of Greeks abroad, partially offset the large deficit.

The chief exports are tobacco, fruit, cotton, wine, olives and olive oil, and mineral ores. The main imports are machinery and vehicles, lumber, textiles, manufactured consumer goods, foodstuffs, chemicals, and petroleum. Greece's leading trading partner is Germany, followed by Japan, Italy, and France.

Government. Greece has a republican form of government. The president, who is chief of state, is elected by parliament. The head of government is a prime minister appointed by the president. The prime minister is generally the head of the majority party in parliament. The parliament is unicameral, with 300 members who are elected by direct popular vote to 4-year terms.

History. Modern Greece has roots in the classical Greek civilization that flourished on the Hellenic peninsula in ancient times. Between about 800 B.C. and 300 B.C., the Greeks developed a culture that laid the foundation for much of later Western civilization.

In B.C. 338 Greece was conquered by its northern neighbor, Macedonia. Greek culture was spread throughout Macedonia's vast Middle Eastern and Mediterranean empire, all of which, including Greece itself, eventually came under the control of Rome.

In 285 A.D. the Roman Empire was divided, and Greece became part of the eastern section, ruled from Byzantium. In 330 Byzantium, renamed Constantinople, became the capital of all that remained of the Roman Empire. As a part of what later became the Byzantine Empire, the Greeks were still the cultural and intellectual leaders of the eastern Mediterranean.

While western Europe struggled with the disorder produced by barbarian invasions, the Orthodox Christian, Greco-Roman civilization of the eastern empire maintained its stability. Greek cultural influence was dependent on Byzantine political strength, however, and the eastern empire was unable to withstand the onslaught of a new power in Asia Minor, the Ottoman Turks.

In the 1000s, the Turks began to attack the Byzantine Empire. Over a period of 400 years they conquered Byzantine territory bit by bit until, in 1453, they captured Constantinople.

Ottoman rule. The Greeks did not fare badly under the Ottomans. They had some self-government, and Greeks in Constantinople, called Phanariots, filled positions in the Ottoman administration. The Turks did not force Greek Christians to convert to Islam, although those who did enjoyed status in the Muslim society.

For the most part, the Ottoman government ignored Greeks living outside Asia Minor, and in many cases neglected them. What remained of Classical Greek culture decayed, and the people of Greece sank into poverty.

The Greeks were far from content under Turkish rule, however. In the 1700s those Greeks still living in the

THE GREEK CULTURE, exemplified by the beautiful Parthenon on the Acropolis in Athens, influenced much of the Mediterranean world.

Hellenic peninsula began to develop a feeling of national pride and a desire for independence. Moreover, in the 1700s the Ottoman government began to loosen control over its more distant territories.

The Greek economy, exhausted since Roman times, began to revive, and Greek trade, industry, and shipping expanded. At the same time self-government began to develop on the local level. The spirit of nationalism swept Europe in the early 1800s, and Greek nationalism took the form of a desire for full freedom from Turkey; it included the goal of uniting all Greek-speaking people into one nation.

Independence. The Greek struggle for independence began in 1821, when Alexander Ypsilanti, a leader of a secret revolutionary organization, Philiké Hetairia, or Society of Friends, led a revolt in the Phanariot-governed principalities of Moldavia and Walachia which are now part of Romania.

Ypsilanti had hoped for aid from neighboring Russia, but he received no support and was defeated. Uprisings also broke out in the south of Greece, however, and continued despite severe Turkish reprisals.

By 1822 the rebellion was countrywide, and the Greeks declared their independence. Over the next few years, Greek guerrilla forces won control of much of their territory from the Ottoman Turks. In 1825, however, the Ottoman Empire gained the support of Egypt, nominally a part of the empire. The untrained Greek guerrillas could not stand up against the power and organization of the Turkish-Egyptian army, and the Greeks steadily lost the land they had won.

The rebels would have met total defeat if they had not received help in 1827 from Britain, France, and Russia. All three had interests in the Balkans, and all opposed Turkish domination of the region. The European nations agreed to join in finding or forcing a solution to the war. They tried to impose an armistice and urged the Ottoman Empire to grant independence to Greece.

When the Turks refused, the European powers ordered a blockade to enforce a truce and to prevent the Turkish forces from receiving supplies. In enforcing the blockade, ships from Britain, Russia, and France destroyed most of the Egyptian fleet when it tried to bring troops and supplies into the port of Navarino in October 1827.

In 1828 Russia declared war on the Ottoman Empire, and by so doing aided the Greeks. Although the war grew out of a Russo-Turkish territorial dispute, Russia also saw an advantage in weakening the empire by driving the Turks from Greece.

Russia defeated the Ottoman Empire in August 1829, and the Treaty of Adrianople, which ended the war, contained a provision granting independence to Greece. Turkey agreed to accept the London Protocol of March, 1829, in which the three European powers decided that Greece—which then included only the Peloponnesus, the Cyclades, and central Greece—would be an autonomous state under a king to be chosen from among the royal families of Europe.

The Greeks, however, already had a government. In 1827 they had chosen an assembly and elected a president, Ioannes Kapodistrias. He was assassinated in 1831, however, and Greece then accepted the powers' choice of a Bavarian prince, Otto, as king.

A new nation. The new state faced great problems. Many Greeks wished to continue fighting to liberate territory inhabited by Greeks but not governed by Greece. The economy, severely damaged by the revolution, was weak—there was little manufacturing and

A PRIEST of the Greek Orthodox Church, the predominant religion of Greece.

The Olympics

According to legend, Hercules was commanded by the gods to clean out the huge stables of Augeas, king of the Greek City of Elis. Hercules accomplished the task in one day by diverting the direction of two rivers so that they flowed through the stables. To celebrate, Hercules began the Olympic Games, in honor of Zeus, the chief Greek god.

The cities of Pisa and Elis each claimed to have created the idea of the Olympics in the Olympia valley. In 884 B.C. a truce was declared so that the games could be held in peace. Emissaries were sent to inform others of the truce; they bore a message engraved on a metal disc with the words in five circles. The five linked circles are still the Olympic symbol, which is instantly recognizable. The rings represent the continents of Africa, Asia, Australia, Europe, and the Americas. The colors of the rings, blue, yellow, black, green, and red, on the white background, have symbolic significance. The flag of each nation competing in the Olympic games contains at least one of the colors. The Olympic motto, Citius, Altius, Fortius, translates from the Latin as Swifter, Higher, Stronger, the goals of all the Olympic competitors.

No records were kept of the earliest Olympic Games. Indeed, the whole affair lasted just one day and consisted of a race of about 200 yards (one stade). The first champion was a young cook, Coroebus of Elis, who was the victor in 776 B.C.

In time, additional events were added, including boxing, wrestling, chariot racing, jumping, discus and javelin throwing, and races for runners wearing armor. The games took on a carnival atmosphere.

Olympic winners were considered heroes. The crowning achievement was to win the pentathlon, which consisted of five events: jumping, foot racing, discus throwing, javelin throwing, and wrestling. Whoever won three of the first four events was the champion; if no one won three, wrestling was the deciding event.

A particularly vicious "sport" of the later games was called pancratium; it was a fierce combination of boxing and wrestling. There were no holds barred. During one match a boxer named Arrachion had a toehold on his opponent, who gripped Arrachion's throat and began to choke him. With one last effort Arrachion twisted his opponent's leg severely, causing him to raise one arm in defeat. At that instant Arrachion choked to death. He had won the match but lost his life. Perhaps the greatest of all pancratium champions was Theagenes of Thasos, who was reputed to have won a total of 1400 matches.

As the Olympic Games grew in popularity, contestants came from Rome, Asia, and Africa. The games became a travesty. More and more professional athletes were entered. By the time Rome conquered the Greek cities, the Olympics were more spectacle than athletic event.

At last, in A.D. 394, the games were outlawed by the Christian emperor of Rome, Theodosius I. For almost 16 centuries the Olympics were forgotten. Only legends and poems remained to tell of the ancient glory of the games, the high ideals, and the great champions.

Between 1875 and 1881 German archaeologists uncovered in Greece the area that was once the site of the temples and stadium. One visitor to the excavation was French scholar Baron Pierre de Coubertin. His suggestion that the Olympics be started again finally was implemented, and the first "new" Olympiad was held in 1896 in Athens.

A crowd of 50,000 saw the lighting of the torch, which had been carried by relays of runners from the Olympia valley

JAYNE TORVILL AND CHRISTOPHER DEAN at the 1984 Sarajevo Olympics.

to the Greek capital. Athletes from 13 nations marched into the stadium and were greeted by the cheering throng. The U.S. athletes won most of the events; however, the honor of Greece was upheld when a 25-year-old country shepherd named Spiridon Loues won the great marathon race.

After the success of the 1896 Olympics, there was considerable sentiment to hold all future games in Athens, but Baron de Coubertin believed the site should be changed for each Olympiad. Paris was chosen for 1900, then St. Louis in the United States in 1904. A special Olympics was held in 1906 in Athens and the regular Olympics in 1908 were in London.

The 1912 Olympics took place in Stockholm, Sweden. Many additional events had been added, including swimming, various racing distances, yachting, and the shot put.

Because of World War I and its effects, the 1916 games were never held. In 1924 the winter Olympics were begun at Chamonix, France, with events in hockey, skiing, and figure skating. The summer games were held in Paris. The Olympics had become a truly international event, with two sections of the games (winter and summer sports) held in different cities every four years. They were held every fourth year thereafter except for 1944, during World War II.

In 1980 the United States did not participate in the summer Olympics, held in Moscow, as a protest against Russia's invasion of Afghanistan. Many nations of the world did send teams. In 1984, at the Los Angeles games, the Chinese participated for the first time since 1952. However, the Soviet Union, along with most of its allies, did not participate, because of insufficient security. In 1992, for the first time in 20 years, every nation with a National Olympic Committee was represented. Beginning in 1994, every other year became an Olympic year, rather than every fourth year, with the summer and winter games alternating.

The Olympics

The modern Olympics have produced numerous athletes who have won everlasting fame. Among them are:

- Jim Thorpe of the United States, a Sac and Fox Indian. In 1912 Thorpe won both the pentathlon and decathlon events; however, he was deprived of his medals when it was discovered that he had played professional baseball, thus losing his amateur standing.
- Jesse Owens of the United States. Of the 66-man American track and field squad for the 1936 Olympics in Berlin, Germany, ten were blacks. These ten outscored every other national team, winning a total of eight gold, three silver, and two bronze medals. Owens won four golds. Adolf Hitler, the leader of Germany, believed blacks were an inferior race and refused to award the medals to black Americans personally.
- Sonja Henie of Norway. The first of a series of outstanding figure skaters, "the Norwegian doll" won the gold medal in her event in 1928, 1932, and 1936 before turning professional and becoming a movie star.
- Emil Zatopek of Czechoslovakia. In 1952 Zatopek broke three running records: the 10,000 meter, the 5,000 meter, and the marathon.
- Mark Spitz of the United States. In 1972 Spitz won a record seven gold medals in swimming events.
- Olga Korbut of the Soviet Union and Nadia Comaneci of Romania, two of the world's greatest gymnasts. Korbut won two gold medals in the 1972 games, and seven perfect 10s helped Comaneci win three gold, one silver, and one bronze medal in 1976.
- Eric Heiden of the United States. During the 1980 Winter Games, Heiden won gold medals in all five of the men's speedskating events.
- The 1980 United States hockey team. This squad, made up of amateurs from college teams, scored one of the great upsets in Olympic history, defeating the heavily favored national team of the Soviet Union, and going on to win a gold medal.
- Jayne Torvill and Christopher Dean of Britain. Skating to Ravel's "Bolero," ice dancers Torvill and Dean won gold in 1984, receiving a total of twelve perfect 6.0s.
- Greg Louganis of the United States. Louganis was the first diver to win the same gold medals in successive Olympics. He won gold in 1984 and 1988 in the 3-meter springboard and 10-meter platform dive.
- Katarina Witt of East Germany. Witt was the first woman since Sonja Henie to defend the women's Olympic title in figure skating. She won gold medals in 1984 and 1988.
- Florence Griffith Joyner of the United States. In 1988 Griffith Joyner became the first woman to win four Olympic running medals: three gold and one silver.
- Carl Lewis and Michael Johnson, both of the United States. In 1996 Carl Lewis became only the fourth person to win the same individual event four times when he earned gold for the long jump. During the same Olympics, Johnson set a world record in the 200 meter run and became the first man to win gold in both the 200 and 400 meters at one Olympiad.
- Jim Shea of the United States. In 2002 Shea became the third generation of his family to participate in the Olympics. He won the hearts of viewers when he carried a photo of his grandfather inside his helmet during competition. His 91-year-old grandfather, who had been a gold medalist in the 1932 games, had been killed in a traffic accident just 17 days before the opening ceremonies. Shea went on to win a gold medal in skeleton, which was making a reappearance at the games after a 54-year absence.

SITES OF MODERN OLYMPIC GAMES

Year	Summer Games	Winter Games
1896	Athens, Greece	
1900	Paris, France	
1904	St. Louis, U.S.A.	
1906	Athens, Greece	
1908	London, England	
1912	Stockholm, Sweden	
1920	Antwerp, Belgium	
1924	Paris, France	Chamonix, France
1928	Amsterdam, Netherlands	St. Moritz, Switzerland
1932	Los Angeles, U.S.A.	Lake Placid, U.S.A.
1936	Berlin, Germany	Garmisch-Partenkirchen, Germany
1948	London, England	St. Moritz, Switzerland
1952	Helsinki, Finland	Oslo, Norway
1956	Melbourne, Australia	Cortina d'Ampezzo, Italy
1960	Rome, Italy	Squaw Valley, U.S.A.
1964	Tokyo, Japan	Innsbruck, Austria
1968	Mexico City, Mexico	Grenoble, France
1972	Munich, Germany	Sapporo, Japan
1976	Montreal, Canada	Innsbruck, Austria
1980	Moscow, U.S.S.R.	Lake Placid, U.S.A.
1984	Los Angeles, U.S.A.	Sarajevo, Yugoslavia
1988	Seoul, S. Korea	Calgary, Canada
1992	Barcelona, Spain	Albertville, France
1994		Lillehammer, Norway
1996	Atlanta, U.S.A.	
1998		Nagano, Japan
2000	Sydney, Australia	
2002		Salt Lake City, U.S.A.
2004	Athens, Greece	
2006		Turin, Italy
2008	Beijing, China	
2010		Vancouver, Canada

GREG LOUGANIS at the 1984 Summer Olympics in Los Angeles.

THE WHITE BUILDINGS and blue waters of the Greek Islands make them one of the world's most popular tourist destinations.

YARN IS STILL SPUN by hand in the rural areas of Greece.

agricultural techniques were old-fashioned and inefficient. A sense of local pride hindered administration by a national government.

Otto's attempts to solve these problems led to a highly centralized, bureaucratic government that was too clumsy to be effective and too complex for the people to deal with. In addition, the European powers still had great influence in Greek politics.

In 1843 two political factions, one supported by the British and one by the Russians, rebelled against the king. The rebels demanded a constitution and an elected assembly. Otto agreed to these demands and established a constitutional monarchy. The new system worked almost as poorly as absolute rule had, and in 1862 Otto was deposed.

In the following year a Danish prince was named king as George I of Greece (ruled 1863–1913). The Greeks had selected another leader, but accepted the powers' choice of George when Britain turned over to Greece the Ionian Islands, which had been a British protectorate.

George's attempts to transform Greece into a country governed by the most advanced parliamentary institutions were only partly successful. The Greeks' lack of education and their inexperience with parliamentary government resulted in a rapid turnover of governments.

The first leader to have any success in establishing an efficient Greek government was Eleutherios Venizelos, who became prime minister in 1910. Venizelos won a strong majority in parliament in 1911 and was able to pass a revised constitution that allowed for more stable parliamentary government.

Venizelos reorganized and simplified the bureaucracy and reduced the power of the army in government affairs. During his first years in office, the educational system was broadened and large estates were divided among small farmers.

Expansion. During the reign of George I, Greece made many additions to its territory. The European powers exerted great efforts to prevent this expansion from resulting in a clash with the Ottoman Empire that could lead to a general European war. In 1881 the powers forced the empire to yield most of Epirus and Thessaly to Greece as part of the settlement of the Russo-Turkish War of 1877.

In 1896 Greece, trying to aid a rebellion in Crete against Turkish rule, did go to war against the Ottoman Empire, and was soundly defeated. But Britain, France, and Russia forced the empire to evacuate Crete, which was then occupied by the three powers and by Italy. Crete successfully rebelled in 1905, and in 1908 declared its union with Greece. The European alliance withdrew its forces the following year.

Greece entered another territorial war before World War I. In the spring of 1912 Premier Venizelos made an alliance with Bulgaria, and in the follow-

ing fall Greece and Bulgaria—with its ally, Serbia—declared war on the Ottoman Empire over conflicting territorial claims. Greece and its allies won this First Balkan War, and in 1913, by the Treaty of London, the Ottoman Empire gave up its claims to Crete and ceded Macedonia to the Balkan allies.

Another Balkan war in the summer of 1913, fought by Greece, Serbia, and Romania against Bulgaria, determined which state would receive what part of the territory. By the Treaty of Bucharest, Greece gained part of Macedonia and another section of Epirus.

In World War I, Premier Venizelos urged Greek intervention on the side of the Allies (Britain, Russia, and France). King Constantine, who had come to the throne after his father's death in 1913, preferred to remain neutral. It was not until 1917, after an Allied ultimatum forced Constantine to yield the throne to his son, Alexander, that Greece entered the war against Germany.

Greek troops fought primarily in the Balkans, and at the end of the war the Treaty of Sèvres gave Greece eastern Thrace, the Turkish islands in the Aegean, and a mandate to occupy a part of Turkey's mainland. The new Republic of Turkey opposed the treaty, however, and in 1920 a Greek army invaded Turkey, only to meet disastrous defeat in 1922. King Constantine, who had regained the throne after Alexander's death in 1920, was forced to abdicate again.

Search for stability. Constantine's son became king as George II, but his government was forced out of office in 1923 by a powerful faction that favored a republican form of government. In 1924 this faction formed a revolutionary government that proclaimed Greece a republic. The republic was a failure. The leaders of the new government could not agree on policy, and after a rapid succession of governments, George II was restored to the throne in 1935.

COBBLED STREETS in Greek villages permit only the foot traffic for which they were originally constructed.

THE SOIL OF GREECE is generally poor but proves ideal for the groves of olive trees so closely associated with the country.

Greece's extreme political instability left the nation helpless in the face of serious problems. The greatest difficulties were economic. Weak industry, unproductive agriculture, and an extremely high birthrate kept the people in poverty. The world economic depression of the 1930s was particularly severe for Greece because of its dependence on exporting such costly items as wine and olive oil.

In 1936 King George appointed General Ioannes Metaxas as premier after a parliamentary election gave no party a majority. Metaxas dissolved parliament and made himself dictator. His fascist-like regimentation of society was unpopular, but he relieved some of the country's economic problems.

World War II ended the Metaxas dictatorship, but brought enormous economic, social, and political problems. The Greeks successfully fought off an Italian invasion attempt in 1940, but in 1941 German forces conquered the country and occupied it until 1944.

Civil war. During the war George Papandreou, a leader of the Greek parliament, formed a government in exile. After the war, however, his government remained in office for only three months in 1945. Its rivals for power were two opposing political organizations formed during the war.

A Communist-led resistance group had political and economic control of the countryside, and a right-wing royalist faction dominated parliament. An election in 1946 restored the monarchy, but by the time King George returned a few weeks later, a civil war had broken out.

Greece's desperate political and economic troubles inflamed the war, which continued with support from Yugoslavia for the Communist guerrillas and with U.S. aid for the government forces. In 1947 Yugoslavia withdrew military assistance from the rebels and the United States gave large-scale financial and military aid to the country under the Truman Doctrine. By 1949 Greek government troops were able to subdue the rebels.

Contemporary Greece. The 1950s were a period of relative stability for Greece. The government of Constantine Karamanlis lasted for eight years, from 1955 to 1963, and presided over a long overdue economic recovery.

However, the stability was short-lived. Between the years 1963 and 1967, Greece endured almost continual government crises. No one party succeeded in winning a majority in parliament, and George Papandreou led a series of coalition cabinets that were bogged down in endless disputes with King Constantine II, who had inherited the throne in 1964.

In 1967 military leaders staged a coup to avert a leftist rebellion allegedly being planned by Papandreou's son, Andreas.

Conservative and reactionary policies ensued until a new but bloodless military coup in 1973 paved the way for civilian government; Constantine Karamanlis became prime minister in 1974. By popular referendum in that year, the monarchy was replaced with a republic.

Karamanlis and his New Democracy (ND) Party were again victorious in 1977, but lost some strength to the leftist Panhellenic Socialist Movement (PASOK). In 1981 elections, PASOK, led by Andreas Papandreou, attained an absolute majority in parliament.

Allegations of corruption preceding the 1989 elections contributed to the loss of the Socialist majority in the parliament. The New Democracy Party formed a short-lived coalition, then was returned to power under Constantine Mitsotakis in new elections in 1990. His severe austerity measures helped Papandreou and the Socialists to regain control of the government in 1993.

Relations with Turkey continue to be difficult. In 1974 a Greek-backed coup on the island of Cyprus led to an invasion of the island by Turkey. War between Greece and Turkey was only narrowly avoided, and Cyprus continues to be a sore spot. The two countries also have an unresolved dispute over the mineral rights to the continental shelf under the Aegean Sea.

During the 1970s and early 1980s relations with the United States were strained because of what the Greeks perceived as support for Turkey. From 1974 to 1980 Greece withdrew from the military arm of NATO and has periodically threatened to close U.S. military bases in the country.

Hungary

Official name: *Republic of Hungary*
Area: *35,919 sq. mi., 93,030 sq. km.*
Type of government: *Republic*
Population: *10,075,000*
Capital and largest city: *Budapest*
    (Pop., 1,825,000)
Language: *Hungarian*
Literacy: *99%;* **Currency:** *Forint*
Per capita GDP: *$13,300*
    (Rank: 42nd)

The land. Most of Hungary is flat land less than 600 feet (183 meters) in elevation. The lowlands fall into two main areas divided by the Central Hungarian Uplands. In the northwest lies the fertile Lesser Hungarian Plain, drained by tributaries of the Danube. The Greater Hungarian Plain occupies the southeastern half of the country and is crossed by the Danube. West of the Danube, the Greater Hungarian Plain is rolling land that rises gradually toward the south, culminating in the Mecsek uplands in the southernmost part of Hungary. East of the Danube the plain is almost completely level, drained by tributaries of the Danube and dotted with lakes.

The central uplands consist of ranges of hills and low mountains. West of the Danube, in Transdanubia, are the Bakony and Vértes ranges. East of the Danube, in the north-central part of the country, are the higher Börzsöny, Cserhát, Mátra, and Bükk ranges, which reach a height of over 3,000 feet (915 meters).

meters
US

metres
Brit.

The Danube forms part of the boundary between Hungary and the Czech Republic and cuts through the Hungarian upland. The Danube's important tributaries in Hungary are the Drava (Drau) and the Tisza. Lake Balaton, along the southwestern edge of the central uplands, is Hungary's largest lake.

Hungary's climate varies from region to region. Summer temperatures average 71°F (22°C) and winter temperatures average 31°F (–1°C). About 25 inches (64 centimeters) of rain fall each year. The greater plain tends to be hotter and drier, the uplands somewhat colder and wetter.

The people. Over 95 percent of the population is Magyar, or Hungarian. The Hungarian language is related to Estonian and Finnish and is unrelated to any of the other languages spoken in Europe. About two-thirds of the people are Roman Catholic, and most of the rest are Protestant. There are small minorities of Germans, Slovaks, Serbs and Croats, and Romanians. There are significant numbers of Hungarians living in neighboring countries, particularly Romania, the Czech Republic, Slovakia, and Serbia and Montenegro.

Almost 60 percent of the people are urban dwellers and one-third of these live in the capital, Budapest, which is the political, cultural, economic, and intellectual center of the country. Other important cities are Debrecen (population, 204,000), an eastern university town; Miskolc (173,000), an industrial center in the

---

centimeters
US

centimetres
Brit.

center
US

centre
Brit.

aluminum
US

aluminium
Brit.

THE CAFES OF THE MARKET in Hungary attract sightseers as well as shoppers.

---

northeast; Szeged (159,000), a southeastern city known for its textiles and food products and also for its strong paprika; and Pécs (158,000), near the center of an important southern mining district.

Economy. The Hungarian economy, traditionally based on agriculture and light industry, became industrialized under the communist regime that took power in 1947.

In the 1980s, as the economy stagnated and foreign debt grew alarmingly, Hungary became one of the first Eastern European countries to take advantage of the new calls from the Soviet Union for economic liberalization and reorganization. After an initial period of rapid improvement in the standard of living, after reform measures were instituted, stagnation set in. At the end of the decade, the government planned complete transition to a market economy.

Natural resources. Bauxite, the ore from which aluminum is obtained, is the most important mineral, and Hungary is one of the world's largest producers, mining over 3 million metric tons in 1986. Uranium is mined in the southwest, and there are also deposits of manganese. Coal is Hungary's prime source of energy, but the reserves are mostly of low quality. There is some natural gas and hydroelectric power. In 1986, 2 million metric tons of oil were produced in Hungary, but Soviet oil imports are still considerable.

Agriculture. Agriculture accounts for about 20 percent of Hungary's national product, and is an important source of exports. Hungary's soil is quite rich and is especially suitable for raising grains. Corn, the leading crop, and wheat, barley, and rye represent about half of the total crop acreage. Potatoes, sugar beets, sunflowers, and tobacco are the main industrial crops. Warm summers enable Hungary to produce table and wine grapes, fruit, and vegetables. Almost all agriculture has now been collectivized.

Industry. Under the communist regime, there had been a distinct shift from light to heavy industry. Nearly half of the national product now comes from industry. More recent developments have been aimed at an increased output of consumer goods.

Iron, steel, chemicals, machinery, and textiles are the major industrial products. Aluminum and computers have become significant additions to this list in recent years.

Trade. Hungary generally has an equitable balance of trade. Raw materials, farm products, processed foods, and some machinery are exported. Oil, raw materials, textiles, and machinery are imported. Much of Hungary's trade is with the European Union.

Government. Under a revised constitution, signed in 1989, a democratically elected president is given full executive authority and designated as chief of state. The president is joined by an elected prime minister, considered the head of government, and by a unicameral legislative branch made up of a 386-member National Assembly.

Democratic elections held in 1990 elected former dissident Arpad Goncz to a 5-year term as president and reduced the communist Party to a small minority in the National Assembly, which is dominated by the Democratic Forum and the Free Democrats.

History. The Hungarian plains and the Danube valley lie along a major ancient European migration route; they offered good settlement sites for early European peoples. The territory, known to the Romans as Pannonia, was inhabited by a succession of Germanic and Slavic tribes and by the Huns between about 1000 B.C. and the A.D. 800s. In the late 800s the Magyars, a people from the Ural Mountains, arrived on the Pannonian plains and conquered and mixed with the Slavic people settled there.

The Magyars were a seminomadic and warlike people. Under their leader, Prince Árpád, they expanded their territory at the expense of nearby Germanic and Slavic kingdoms. In 955 they were defeated by the Germans. The Magyars, by then a mixture of Magyar, Slavic, and Germanic peoples, retreated to territory in the Danube basin and settled into an agricultural way of life.

The Hungarian kingdom. By the end of the 900s, the Magyars had developed a stable government and a well-organized feudal society. In 997 Stephen, a descendant of Árpád, became Hungary's first king. Stephen established strong ties with western, rather than eastern, Europe and with the Roman Catholic Church.

During Stephen's reign, the Magyars became Christian. Stephen began what was to become a long struggle to weaken the great nobles and centralize Hungary's government. During Stephen's reign, Hungary's territory was considerably expanded.

Several decades of dynastic warfare followed Stephen's death in 1038, but order was restored in 1077, when Ladislas I, also of Árpád's line, became king. For the next 150 years Hungary's territory grew, its prosperity increased, and its ties with the West strengthened.

Hungary was unable to resolve conflicts between the king and the nobles, however. The nobles' feuds and rebellions against the king threatened the stability of the nation and left the country unprotected, as the nobles were responsible for its defense.

In 1241 Mongol armies swept across Hungary, meeting little opposition. The destruction they wrought was repaired, but by the end of the 1200s no solution had been found to the dispute between the king and the nobles. Their rivalries for power permitted a foreigner, Charles of Anjou, to take the throne in 1308.

Hungary's new rulers also held thrones in other countries, and as a result of the foreign involvements of Charles and his descendants during the 1300s and early 1400s, Hungary became increasingly active in the diplomatic affairs of western Europe.

Hunyadi. In the early 1400s, the Ottoman Turks posed a threat to

LITTLE GIRLS ON BICYCLES take time from an outing to pose beside the Danube in Budapest.

Europe, and Hungary assumed the role of protector of the West. Between 1437 and 1456 Hungarian armies led by a powerful nobleman, János Hunyadi, blocked attempted Turkish invasions of Europe.

Hunyadi's son, Matthias, became king of Hungary in 1458 and led the country to its peak of greatness. He broke the power of the great nobles, organized an efficient centralized administration, and introduced the art and learning of the Renaissance into Hungary.

In an attempt to become leader of a united central Europe that could crush the Ottoman Turks, Matthias conquered territory in Bohemia, where he was named king, and in Silesia, Moravia, and Austria. At his death in 1490, Hungary was the most powerful state in western Europe. Matthias's successors, however, were weak men. They lost most of his political and territorial gains and took no action against the Turks.

Ottoman era. In the early 1500s the Turks began once again to move toward Hungary, and in 1526 they overwhelmed the country. Although the Turks were the nominal overlords of all Hungary, in fact the country was divided into three parts.

Northern and western Hungary were ruled by the Hapsburgs of Austria, who succeeded to the throne of Hungary in 1526. In the northeast, the principality of Transylvania grew so powerful that it was independent in all but name. The Turks controlled central Hungary.

Throughout the country there was turmoil. The Magyars resented Austrian and Turkish rule; Hungary's Slavic peoples resented the Austrians, the Turks, and the Magyars; and the Magyar nobility was split between those who had gained power by supporting the Turks and those who had fought against the Turks.

To these frictions was added religious strife arising from the Protestant Reformation. The Hungarians were unable to resolve their differences or to throw off Turkish rule.

Austrian rule. In 1686 Austria's armies drove the Turks out of the region, and Austria assumed complete rule over the Magyar and Slavic peoples of Hungary. Austria did little to rebuild the country, which was still laboring under an outmoded feudal structure and which had been ravaged by years of warfare. Austrian rule was harsh and autocratic at first, and was unpopular with all Hungarians.

The Austrian rulers of the latter half of the 1700s were more liberal, however. They improved the economy and expanded the educational system, which in turn stimulated efforts for more radical reforms. Organizations were formed by democratic, progressive nationalists, and in the late 1700s and early 1800s, inspired by the French Revolution, they led demands for social, economic, and governmental reforms.

The Austrian emperor, with the support of the conservative Hungarian nobility, refused the demands and harshly repressed the movement. Repression only intensified the revolutionary spirit. In 1848, when liberal, democratic rebellions were breaking out all over Europe, Hungarian nationalistic reformers led an uprising against the Austrian Empire and demanded independence as a democratic state. The emperor yielded, the Hungarian nobles fled, and a republican government was established.

The new regime abolished the country's feudal, social, and economic organization, but the republic was short-lived. In 1849, under orders from a new emperor, Austrian and Russian troops crushed the republic, and Hungary once more became a subject state. The old order could not be restored by force, however, and Hungary remained the most independent of all of Austria's territories.

The Dual Monarchy. After 1848 Austria steadily lost power to Prussia, and in 1867 Prussia organized a union of German states that excluded Austria. The Hungarians took that opportunity to demand independence. In the same year, 1867, Austria and Hungary arrived at a compromise by which the Dual Monarchy of Austria-Hungary was formed.

The two states shared control of foreign policy, finance, and defense. Hungary, however, was a self-governing state that ruled Slavic subjects as well as Magyars. The Slavs resented Magyar rule, which was no better than Austrian rule had been.

Austria-Hungary had joined the alliances creating the Central Powers, and in 1914 entered World War I. In 1918 Hungary went down to defeat with its allies. When defeat was imminent, a rebellion broke out in Hungary, and in November 1918, a republic was pro-

laboring
US

labouring
Brit.

26 Europe and Russia

A FRAMED VIEW of the domed Parliament building in Budapest.

THE OLD CITY of Pest can be seen from the old city of Buda, which is on the opposite side of the Danube. A third city of Obuda joined with the two to form Budapest in 1873.

honors
US

honours
Brit.

meters
US

metres
Brit.

claimed, but in 1919 the Communist Party assumed control. Communist rule was overthrown at the end of 1919 by monarchists, who chose Admiral Miklós Horthy as regent in 1920.

The regency. In June 1920 the Hungarian government signed the Treaty of Trianon, which officially ended World War I for Hungary and which stripped Hungary of much of its territory and power. Under the treaty, Hungary ceded almost three-quarters of its land and two-thirds of its population to Austria, Romania, and the new states of Czechoslovakia and Yugoslavia. In 1921 Hungary's king, who attempted to return, was exiled.

The regency remained in power throughout the 1920s and 1930s. It was a conservative and authoritarian government, and all efforts at reform were stifled. Hungarian foreign policy was based on opposition to the Treaty of Trianon, and the government sought to recover the lands and peoples lost under the treaty.

The regency was bitterly hostile to the "Little Entente" of the new Slavic states and to their western patron, France. It was equally hostile to the Soviet Union because of the brief but violent and destructive communist dictatorship of 1919.

The government of the regency thus was attracted by the political and territorial aims of Adolf Hitler of Germany and Benito Mussolini of Italy. Despite strong opposition within Hungary from monarchists, communists, and democratic liberals, right-wing nationalists prevailed

in the government. In 1934 Hungary entered a political and economic alliance with Italy and Austria and thereafter moved closer to the National Socialist (Nazi) government of Germany.

During World War II, in 1939 and 1940, Adolf Hitler restored to Hungary parts of its former territories in Romania and Czechoslovakia. In November 1940 Hungary formally allied itself with the Axis powers, although Hungarians did not fight in the war at first.

The Germans used the country as a base to delay Soviet advances into central Europe, and in 1944 Germany took direct control of the government. In the winter of 1944–1945, Soviet troops invaded and occupied Hungary, and when the war ended they were in firm control of the country.

Communist rule. After the war a communist dictatorship with close ties to the Soviet Union was established under the leadership of Mátyás Rakosi. The communist regime did not enjoy wide support and used repression and terrorism to stay in power. Communist efforts to transform the basis of Hungary's economy from feudalistic agriculture to state-owned heavy industry were inefficient and damaged the country's economy.

Economic, political, and social grievances fanned Hungarian nationalism and desire for independence from Soviet control. After the death of Joseph Stalin in 1953, the Hungarian Communist Party split between advocates of continuing tight controls over all aspects of life and those seeking a more moderate course.

In October 1956 demonstrations against the government erupted and led to a popular uprising that had wide support, even from the Communist prime minister, Imre Nagy; but it was crushed by Soviet troops and tanks.

Janos Kadár, who had defected to the Soviets from Nagy's cabinet, became prime minister and first secretary of the Communist Party. In 1958, after a secret trial, Nagy was executed. The Hungarian Communist Party, which had disintegrated during the revolution, was completely reorganized.

The methods used by Kadár to consolidate power were repressive, but when the government's position was more secure Kadár began to relax controls and allow an increasing measure of freedom. Under Kadár's administration, economic programs were reorganized to achieve greater efficiency and a better balance between agriculture and industry.

Some free enterprise was permitted, consumers and producers were given a greater voice in the economy, and trade with non-communist countries was expanded. The standard of living rose, and by the mid-1960s Kadár's regime was among the least repressive of the governments of Eastern Europe.

During the 1980s, however, the economy slumped. By the late 1980s foreign debt per capita was the highest in Eastern Europe, and the standard of living was declining. Kadár's government was

seen as incapable of making the necessary reforms to revive the economy.

With the reforms in the Soviet Union came demands for similar economic and political changes in Hungary. During the 1988 party conference Kadár and the conservatives were turned out by reform-minded members led by Karoly Grosz. Several startling indications of change were seen soon after, including the dismantling of fences marking the border with Austria and the funeral and reburial with full honors of Imre Nagy, leader of the failed 1956 revolution. A new constitution was signed in 1989 and democratic elections were held in 1990. Hungary joined NATO in 1999 and the EU in 2004.

Iceland

Official name: *Republic of Iceland*
Area: *39,758 sq. mi.,*
103,000 sq. km.
Type of government: *Republic*
Population: *279,000*
Capital and largest city: *Reykjavik*
(Pop., 111,000)
Language: *Icelandic*
Literacy: *100%;* **Currency:** *Krona*
Per capita GDP: *$27,100*
(Rank: 12th)

The land. Iceland has a rugged, barren terrain. It is quite mountainous, with a central core of highlands rising about 5,000 feet (1,500 meters). Glaciers cover large areas of the country, and many rivers run down from the glaciers. The largest glacier on the island is Vatnajökull, which covers over 3,100 square miles (7,700 square kilometers).

Iceland is of volcanic origin, and volcanoes are still quite active. Hot springs are common in the volcanic areas. In the early 1960s a new volcanic island, Surtsey, rose in Iceland's coastal waters.

Iceland's climate is much milder than one might expect from its latitude because it is moderated by the Gulf Stream that warms the island's coasts. Average temperatures range between 30°F and 52°F (–1°C and 11°C) throughout the year. Almost 50 inches

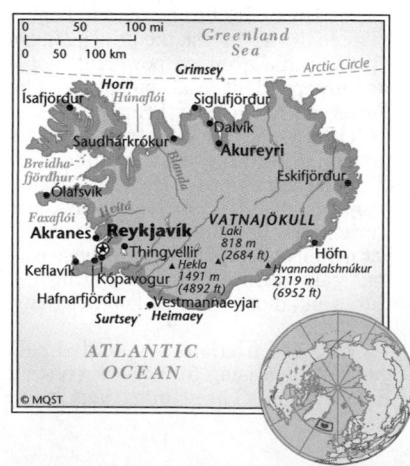

(127 centimeters) of rain fall in the southern lowlands. The far north receives an average of only 15 inches (38 centimeters).

The people. Iceland is still rather sparsely settled, with only six people per square mile. Its rapidly rising population is found mostly on the southwestern coast, with almost half of it centered around Reykjavik. Almost 90 percent of the population is urban.

Iceland's population is quite homogeneous. Almost all the people are Scandinavian in origin, and Icelandic, a Scandinavian tongue, is the universal language. Over 95 percent of the population is Lutheran.

Economy. Despite its barrenness, Iceland is a moderately prosperous country with an economy based largely on fishing and trade. The chief natural resources are its rushing rivers, which provide hydroelectric power, its thermal springs, which provide heat, and its geographic position near rich fishing banks and along a major route between Europe and North America.

Less than 1 percent of the land is cultivated, and only hay, root crops, and other hardy crops can be grown. Grazing land is available and sheep raising and dairying are of some importance. Hothouse vegetable and fruit production provide locally grown produce.

Fishing and related activities make the greatest single contribution to the Icelandic economy. Cod and herring, from coastal waters and from the Grand Banks near Canada, are the chief catches. Fishing and fish processing constitute the bulk of Iceland's industrial activity.

To diversify its economy, Iceland rapidly developed new industries in the 1950s and 1960s. Of particular importance are energy-intensive industries that can make use of Iceland's cheap hydroelectric and geothermal power. The aluminum industry is particularly prosperous, although most of the aluminum ore is imported.

HOMES IN ICELAND tend to be scattered in a sparsely settled landscape that averages only six people per square mile. However, fishing makes the country moderately prosperous.

Trade is vital to the Icelandic economy. Fresh and processed fish and fish products account for over 70 percent of the country's exports. Other exports include aluminum, ferro-silicon, and wool products. Raw materials, foodstuffs, machinery, many manufactured goods, petroleum products, and ships must be imported. Most of Iceland's trade is with Great Britain, the United States, Germany, Japan, and the Scandinavian countries.

Government. Iceland is a republic with a president, who has limited powers, as head of state. The president is elected by popular vote to a four-year term. Actual executive power rests with a prime minister and cabinet responsible to the legislature. The prime minister is appointed by the president. Members of the cabinet are appointed by the prime minister with the approval of the legislature. Members of the 63-member unicameral legislature, the Althing, are popularly elected.

History. Iceland was settled in the late 800s by Norwegian Vikings. Immigration increased through the 900s, with settlers coming from the British Isles as well as from Norway. By the end of the 900s, the descendants of those first settlers had established their own system of representative government, with a constitution, a court system, and the Althing.

The yearly Althing, the meeting of chieftains and popular representatives, soon became the social and cultural center of Icelandic life, as well as the country's legislature and supreme court. In 1000 the Althing adopted Christianity as the religion for the entire country. During the 900s and 1000s, Vikings from Iceland made many voyages of exploration. They discovered and settled Greenland and visited North America.

Dissension among the Icelanders during the early 1200s led to the breakdown of government, and in 1262 Iceland joined with Norway and submitted to the rule of the Norwegian king, although nominally remaining self-governing. In 1387 the kingdoms of Denmark and Norway were united, but Iceland remained legally Norwegian until 1814.

Between the 1300s and the 1700s the island was struck by many natural disasters, including volcanic eruptions, plagues, and floods. Denmark-Norway did little to alleviate the resulting famine. Moreover, trade monopolies and other commercial regulations of the 1600s and 1700s served to further the interests of Norway and Denmark rather than those of Iceland.

Danish rule. Norway was separated from Denmark in 1814, but Iceland remained under Danish sovereignty. In the early 1800s, Iceland began to recover from the effects of natural disasters, and a spirit of nationalism spread through the island, leading to demands for independence. The first step toward increased autonomy was the restoration of some authority to the Althing in 1843.

In 1854 Denmark relaxed its trade restrictions and Iceland's economy began to improve. In 1874 Iceland was granted a new constitution, which provided for Icelandic self-government under the supervision of a Danish minister. The island became completely self-governing in 1904.

ICELAND WAS SETTLED BY NORWEGIAN VIKINGS in the 800s, bringing their own system of representative government. Shown here is the archaeological site of the first Viking parliament.

26 Europe and Russia

centered
US
centred
Brit.

aluminum
US
aluminium
Brit.

Independence. After World War I Iceland demanded the self-determination that had been granted to other nations by the Treaty of Versailles. In 1918 a Danish-Icelandic treaty recognized Iceland's independence within a union with the Danish crown, and Denmark remained responsible for Iceland's foreign affairs and defense.

During the 1920s and 1930s Iceland was generally isolated from the rest of the world. During World War II, however, Iceland was of great strategic importance as an Allied air and naval base. After its occupation by Germany in 1940, Denmark was unable to handle Icelandic affairs. In 1944 Iceland proclaimed itself a sovereign republic.

During the 1940s and 1950s Iceland concentrated on expanding and balancing its economy. The island began to participate more fully in world affairs and it became increasingly dependent on international trade agreements and defense pacts. It was also an important link on international air routes as well as a strategically important NATO base.

In the early 1960s, at Iceland's request, the United States withdrew most of its troops from Iceland. This trend was reversed under the direction of a new conservative coalition that came to power in Iceland following the 1974 elections. There are now nearly 3,000 U.S. NATO military personnel stationed in Iceland.

In 1972 Iceland extended its fishery limit from 12 to 50 miles, and in 1975 it extended the limit to 200 miles. The government said that the extension was necessary to protect the fish stocks, vital to the nation's economy. Tensions mounted between Iceland and Great Britain over this issue, until the British finally consented to Iceland's extended fishing rights in 1976. In 1985 the Althing declared the country to be nuclear-free, thereby banning the entry of ships carrying nuclear weapons.

meters
US

metres
Brit.

labor
US

labour
Brit.

centers
US

centres
Brit.

Ireland

Official name: *Ireland*
Area: *27,128 sq. mi., 70,280 sq. km.*
Type of government: *Republic*
Population: *3,883,000*
Capital and largest city: *Dublin*
    (Pop., 495,000)
Languages: *English, Irish*
    (both official)
Literacy: *98%*
Currency: *Euro*
Per capita GDP: *$28,500*
    (Rank: 9th)

The land. The Republic of Ireland occupies the southwestern five-sixths of the island of Ireland, one of the two main British Isles. The northeastern sixth of the island makes up Northern Ireland, which is part of the United Kingdom.

Ireland is an old, low, glaciated plateau with few elevations above 2,000 feet (610 meters). There is a central plain, opening more widely on the east, fringed by higher and more rugged land, especially in the north and southwest. Drainage is a problem, and much of Ireland is covered by odd-shaped lakes, marshes, and peat bogs.

The combination of damp, acid soils, a very damp climate, and uncertain drainage has restricted forest growth and greatly limited the variety of agriculture. More than one-third of Ireland is classified as bog, although there are sizable tracts of excellent grassland suitable for raising livestock.

The climate is dominated by maritime influences. Winters are mild and summers are quite cool. The humidity is high, rain is abundant and frequent, and clouds and fog are common. Dublin has a temperature range of only 20°F (7°C), with August averaging 62°F (17°C) and January 42°F (6°C).

The people. The Irish people are culturally quite homogeneous. Irish, or Gaelic, a Celtic Indo-European language related to other Gaelic languages of the British Isles, is the official first language; it is spoken in the southern and western coastal regions of Cork, Kerry, Mayo, and Donegal. English, however, is universally spoken, and official documents are printed in English and Irish. About 94 percent of the population is Roman Catholic. Most of the remainder is Anglican or Protestant.

Ireland's population declined steadily from the late 1840s until the 1960s. In the 1840s potato diseases began to attack the country's principal crop, and famine precipitated a flood of emigrants to North America and other areas. A high rate of celibacy and a low birthrate contributed to the decline in population.

Dublin, the capital, is by far the largest city, and one-quarter of the entire population of Ireland resides in the Dublin area.

Economy. Ireland's economy has become increasingly diversified in the last two decades. Traditionally an agricultural state, Ireland now has a labor force that is composed of 28 percent manufacturing workers and only 15 percent agricultural laborers.

Agriculture is still, however, quite important to the economy, providing nearly one-quarter of total exports. Principal crops include wheat, barley, oats, potatoes, and sugar beets. Grazing land is plentiful in Ireland, and livestock-raising for meat, dairy, and wool is an important activity.

Although Ireland was once thought to be nearly devoid of mineral wealth, recent discoveries of significant deposits of lead, zinc, and copper have been made. Peat is an important energy source, and small deposits of oil and natural gas are being exploited.

The government has aggressively promoted industrial expansion over the last several decades. As a result, there has been a significant amount of foreign investment in Ireland, helping to expand such industries as electronics manufacture. However, much industry is still involved in processing agricultural products. Other important industries include chemicals, textiles, and paper production.

Ireland's principal exports are food products, live animals, chemicals, electronics, and machinery. Imports include petroleum, grains, transport equipment, and machinery. Great Britain is by far Ireland's most important trading partner, but trade with other European Community members is also important.

Government. Ireland is a republic. The head of state is the president, who is elected to a term of 7 years. Executive powers are wielded by a prime minister, who is usually the leader of the majority party in the Dail, or house of representatives. He is appointed by the president on the recommendation of the house of representatives.

Legislative power is vested in the Parliament, which includes the 166-member Dail elected on the basis of proportional representation, and the 60-member Senate, which is partly elected and partly appointed by the incumbent prime minister.

History. In the 300s B.C., the Celts crossed from Europe to Ireland and easily defeated the indigenous population there. The Celts soon divided the country into a number of small independent kingdoms.

Ireland lived in isolation until the A.D. 400s, when St. Patrick landed on the island to spread Christianity among the generally pagan populace. Christianity quickly took hold, and a brilliant scholarly tradition was begun at newly founded monasteries that became widely known centers of learning and culture.

In the 800s the island was invaded by the Northmen, or Vikings, who raided the land periodically. They were not defeated until 1014, when a great Irish king, Brian Boru, routed them at Clontarf, near Dublin.

In 1167 King Henry II of England invaded Ireland upon the invitation of a

CHRISTIANITY SPREAD among the Celtic kingdoms of Ireland when St. Patrick arrived in the 400s. The Celtic cross is unique to that branch of the church.

deposed Irish king, Dermot MacMurrough. The Irish were defeated, and in 1171 Henry established his personal rule over the country.

English rule. In time, England relaxed its control, partly because its attention was almost totally given to the Hundred Years' War (1338–1453) with France and to the internal Wars of the Roses (1455–1485). A considerable degree of autonomy had gradually been obtained by the local aristocracy, and the era is known as the period of "aristocratic home rule." Direct English control was actually reduced to an area around Dublin known as the Pale.

It was not until 1494, under Henry VII, that English power was reestablished throughout the island. During the Tudor dynasty, the major issues that were to poison relations between the two countries—religion, land ownership, and home rule—began to arise.

Henry VIII broke with the papacy in 1534 and attempted to eradicate Roman Catholicism from Ireland.

Mary I, Henry's daughter, tried to force the assimilation of the Irish by confiscating the lands of the Irish lords who refused to conform and distributing them to English settlers. Elizabeth I continued this system, which came to be known as "plantation," and excluded the Irish from any significant role in the administration.

A great rebellion—known as the "Tyrone Wars"—finally broke out in 1597, and its leaders—Hugh O'Donnell and Hugh O'Neill, earl of Tyrone—became two of the most celebrated Irish heroes. After a series of victories, they were finally defeated in 1601 by the English at Kinsale.

Under England's Stuart king, James I, Scottish settlers were given lands in Ulster. As a result, a new rebellion started in 1641, when the Ulstermen massacred many of the usurpers of their lands. Terrible revenge was taken in 1649 by England's Puritan dictator, Oliver Cromwell. The population of the town of Drogheda in eastern Ireland was slaughtered, and most of the land still remaining in Irish hands was confiscated.

Conditions were better under Charles II, and they improved greatly under James II, who was a Roman Catholic. The Glorious Revolution of 1688, however, soon removed him from the throne, and he was finally defeated on Irish soil at the Battle of the Boyne in 1690.

Eventually the Penal Laws—a series of laws first formulated under James I that sought to reduce the power of the Irish—were made more stringent, and economic measures ruinous to the Irish nation were enacted. Tension mounted.

It was only in 1798, however, that a major revolution, led by Wolfe Tone, was attempted. The effort failed, and England then deprived Ireland of its own Parliament. In 1800 Ireland was united to England and allowed representation in the English Parliament.

The period of union. A great disaster, the "potato famine," struck the island in 1845, causing about 1 million deaths in a few years. A massive emigration then began, chiefly to the United States.

Emigrants living in the United States founded the Fenian Society to continue the struggle against Britain. In 1873 the Home Rule League was formed in Ireland. Its outstanding figure was Charles Stewart Parnell, a brilliant and extremely popular leader.

Later, a more active movement, the Sinn Féin, came to the fore. On Easter Monday, 1916, in the middle of World War I, several hundred of its members rose in Dublin, but the rebellion was put down by British troops. In the following years, the IRA (Irish Republican Army), which became the military branch of Sinn Féin, beleaguered the British with bombings, raids, and street battles.

Free state and republic. After the war, the Sinn Féin triumphed in elections held in 1918, winning most of the Irish seats in the British Parliament. These candidates refused to go to England, and set up their own Parliament, declaring Ireland an independent republic.

A period of political upheaval followed, during which the British tried to maintain order by pouring troops into the country. But in 1922 Britain recognized the Irish Free State and granted it dominion status. The six northern, predominantly Protestant, counties of Ulster chose to remain part of the United Kingdom. The new situation provoked profound, violent dissension among the Irish.

Under Prime Minister (later president) Eamon de Valera, a new constitution was promulgated in 1937, whereby the sovereign country of Ireland, or Eire, was proclaimed. In 1948 the last ties with the British Commonwealth were cut and Ireland became a republic on April 18, 1949. Eamon de Valera served as prime minister and then as president until 1973.

Ireland has faced severe economic problems since the mid-1970s, partly because of the recession in Britain and partly because of the energy crisis brought on by the inflated price of imported oil. The energy crisis became especially severe in 1979.

Ireland joined the European Community (EC) in 1973 in the hopes of easing its economic situation. As one of the least developed countries in the EC, it received extensive economic aid, however the situation remained difficult. In the late 1980s unemployment ran as high as 18 percent, although inflation appeared to have been brought under control.

AN IRISH SCHOOLBOY before the ruins of a fort

BLARNEY CASTLE near Cork houses the Blarney Stone, which was set there in 1446. Legends abound about the origin, but today kissing the stone is thought to bestow the gift of sweet speech.

The status of Northern Ireland has continued to be of exceptional concern to the Irish government. Following the assassination of the British ambassador to Dublin, as well as other terrorist atrocities committed by the IRA, Ireland committed itself more fully than ever to the pursuit of reunification through democratic means. A peace settlement for Northern Ireland was approved in 1998; however, despite a transfer of power to the Northern Irish Republic and IRA assurance of disarmament, the situation remains unresolved with little progress toward a resolution.

Italy

Official name: *Italian Republic*
Area: *116,275 sq. mi.,*
301,230 sq. km.
Type of government: *Republic*
Population: *57,927,000*
Capital and largest city: *Rome*
(Pop., 2,460,000)
Languages: *Italian (official),*
German, French, Slovene
Literacy: *98%*
Currency: *Euro*
Per capita GDP: *$25,000*
(Rank: 21st)

The land. The country is a boot-shaped peninsula measuring about 750 miles (1,209 kilometers) in length and averaging about 125 miles (202 kilometers) in width. Its territory includes two large islands—Sicily, lying just off the toe of the boot, and Sardinia, lying 130 miles (210 kilometers) off the southwest coast—as well as a number of smaller islands.

ITALIAN YOUNG PEOPLE socialize in a village square in Tuscany.

Much of Italy is hilly or mountainous, and the amount of land suitable for agriculture is limited. The Alps run along the entire northern border. In the northeast they curve south to form the Apennines, which extend down through the peninsula into the toe of the boot and across to Sicily. The only sizable plain is the valley of the Po River in the north, although there are coastal plains and numerous interior basins.

Italy's major rivers are the Po, the Adige, the Arno, and the Tiber. Many shorter streams originate in the Apennines and flow toward the Adriatic or Tyrrhenian coasts.

Italy's climate is varied. The north has a continental climate, with warm summers and cold winters, which are often accompanied by heavy snowfall in the more mountainous regions. Southern Italy has a typically Mediterranean climate, with hot, dry summers and mild, rainy winters.

Rainfall varies, generally decreasing toward the southeast. The north averages over 30 inches (76 centimeters) a year, but parts of Apulia, at the heel of the boot, receive less than 15 inches (38 centimeters).

The people. The country is densely settled with nearly 500 people per square mile. Overpopulation has long plagued Italy and has led to a heavy outflow of Italians to the rest of Europe and to many other parts of the world. The currently low rate of population growth has helped make the economy more manageable.

Italian is the nearly universal language. There are a few small linguistic minority groups. More than 99 percent of the people are at least nominally Roman Catholic.

Italy is traditionally urban, and over 70 percent of the population live in cities and towns. Rome, Milan, Turin, and Naples have more than 1 million inhabitants and over 40 other Italian cities have populations of more than 100,000.

Economy. Before the mid-1950s, the Italian economy was largely dependent on agriculture and tourism. Although both are still important, their relative weight in the economy has declined in the wake of industrial expansion since then. Italy has become one of the top seven industrial countries in the world.

An important factor in the Italian economy is the tremendous difference in the standard of living between the north and south. The north is highly industrialized and has the country's more fertile farmland, which is the most intensively cultivated land in southern Europe. The south is heavily populated and suffers chronically from high unemployment. It is much poorer and far less developed, having little industry and small, inefficient farms. The government has actively sought to bring economic and industrial development in the south up to the level enjoyed in the north.

Natural resources. Italy is poor in natural resources. Sulfur bauxite, zinc, lead, and mercury are mined in quantity and large amounts of limestone and marble are quarried. Italy is essentially dependent on foreign oil to supply energy for its industries, although it does produce some natural gas and has a good supply of hydroelectric power.

Agriculture. Agriculture still employs 12 percent of the labor force and accounts for about 5 percent of the national product. In recent years, production has greatly improved through land consolidation, increased mechanization, and improved methods of agriculture.

The Po valley, which has an extensive irrigation system, raises all the nation's rice, most of its wheat, and three-fourths of its corn. Yields per acre compare favorably with those of northwestern Europe and rank among the world's highest. The region also supports many cattle and produces substantial quantities of wine.

Southern Italy grows a variety of vegetables, fruits, and nuts. Among the most important of these are olives, peas, beans, grapes, citrus fruits, and almonds. Livestock also is raised in the south, but sheep and goats are more numerous than cattle.

Industry. The government plays an important role in Italian industry. Three state-owned holding companies—the Industrial Reconstruction Institute, National Hydrocarbons Agency, and National Power Authority—control a major part of the country's industrial capital. Government holdings are heavily concentrated in iron and steel, engineering and telecommunications, shipbuilding and shipping, petroleum, gas, and electric power.

Most of Italy's industry is concentrated in the northwestern part of the Po valley, particularly in the triangle formed by the cities of Milan, Turin, and Genoa. Textiles, refined and fabricated metals, machinery, vehicles, and electrical and office equipment are the most important manufacturers.

Trade. Italy's main exports are textiles, vehicles, electrical equipment, machinery, chemicals, fruits and vegetables, and wine. Principal imports include iron and steel, petroleum, coal, chemicals, foodstuffs, timber and paper products, and raw cotton and wool.

The nation's most important trading partners are Germany, the United States, France, Britain, Switzerland, and the Netherlands.

Government. Italy is a democratic republic with a parliamentary form of government. The chief of state is the president, who is elected to a 7-year term by the legislature. The president has the power to dissolve the legislature and call for new elections. He also nominates the prime minister, who must then be approved by the legislature.

The prime minister chooses the ministers who form his cabinet from among the members of the legislature.

The legislature consists of the 630-member Chamber of Deputies and the 315-member Senate. Both chambers are directly elected on the basis of proportional representation to 5-year terms. The Senate also includes a small number of lifetime members and former presidents of the republic. Legislation may originate in either house and must be passed by a majority of both.

History. Italy has been inhabited since very early times, and traces of Paleolithic and Neolithic cultures have been found throughout the peninsula. In about 2000 B.C. a group of people closely related to the ancient Greeks entered Italy from the north and gradually established themselves throughout the peninsula.

Approximately 1,100 years later the Etruscans, who may have come from Asia Minor, settled in north-central Italy, and subjugated the local inhabitants. In the 700s and 600s B.C., the Greeks colonized parts of southern Italy and Sicily. They dominated the area to such an extent that it was known as *Magna Graecia,* or Greater Greece.

In 388 B.C. Rome, an insignificant city-state that until 100 years earlier had been dominated by the Etruscans, gained control of the surrounding area of Latium. By 270 B.C. the Romans had conquered all of Italy, and the history of Italy from the 200s B.C. to the A.D. 400s is largely the history of Rome and the Roman Empire.

In the A.D. 400s Italy was invaded by peoples from central and eastern Europe, including the Visigoths, Ostrogoths, Heruli, and Huns. In 476 the last Roman emperor in the west, Romulus

Augustulus, was deposed by Odoacer, a Heruli chieftain. Odoacer ruled until 493, when he was killed by Theodoric, king of the Ostrogoths. Theodoric established a kingdom that lasted until 553, when Italy was conquered by the emperor of the east, who ruled from Byzantium.

The Byzantines were unable to defend Italy, and in 568 it was invaded by a Germanic tribe, the Lombards. The Lombards gained control of most of the peninsula except Rome, Ravenna, and Naples. Furthermore, in 726 Pope Gregory II, who had quarreled with the Byzantine emperor over ecclesiastical matters, declared Rome and the Roman church independent.

Rome's independence was continually threatened by the Lombards, and the popes began to turn to the Carolingian kings of the Franks for help. In 756 Pepin subdued the Lombards and forced them to cede part of central Italy to Pope Stephen II, creating the nucleus of the Papal States.

Pepin's son Charlemagne deposed the last Lombard king in 774, and in 800 Charlemagne was crowned the emperor of the Romans by Pope Leo III. Italy was ruled by the Franks until 887, when the Carolingian Empire finally disintegrated.

A century of turmoil followed, during which Muslims established themselves in southern Italy and Sicily. Order was restored in 962 with the coronation by Pope John XII of Otto I of Saxony as emperor of Italy and Germany. This union of Italy and Germany marked the beginning of the Holy Roman Empire.

The German emperors, who were mainly concerned with domestic affairs, rarely visited Italy, and the northern and central parts of the country were ruled by warring feudal lords. In the south the Normans wrested control of Sicily from the Muslims and of Apulia and Calabria, at the tip of the peninsula, from the

Byzantines. The Normans then established the Kingdom of the Two Sicilies.

City-states. During the 900s cities began to develop, particularly in north-central Italy, and by the 100s and 1100s they had become independent communes. The Italian cities prospered as a result of the Crusades and increased existing trade with the Muslim world. Venice and many of the other cities in the north became Europe's thriving marketplaces and banking centers.

Strong rivalries existed between these cities and prevented even partial national unification. By the end of the 1200s Italy was divided into several hundred city-states. In the 1300s and 1400s several republics, such as Genoa and Venice, and the ruling families of a number of other cities, including the Medici of Florence, the Visconti and Sforza of Milan, and the Este of Ferrara, grew extremely rich and powerful through trade.

THE RUINS OF THE COLOSSEUM still bear silent testimony to the glory that was Rome.

colonized
US

colonised
Brit.

centers
US

centres
Brit.

ITALIAN SCULPTOR GHIBERTI'S depiction of Christ on this panel typifies his ability to lend grace and spatial illusion to works of art.

VENICE, the "Queen of the Adriatic," floats on more than 100 islands and uses canals as thoroughfares.

There was constant warfare among the city-states, and Italy became prey to its more powerful neighbors. But the era of the city-states saw the development of the Renaissance, and the intellectual and artistic works of the Italian Renaissance remain even today as a symbol of cultural greatness.

The descent of Charles VIII of France into Italy in 1494 began the Italian Wars, which arose over rival French and Spanish claims to the throne of the Kingdom of Naples. The wars did not end until 1559, when the Treaty of Cateau-Cambrésis was signed. The treaty recognized Spanish supremacy in Italy and marked the end of independence for most of the Italian states.

Foreign domination. The War of the Spanish Succession (1701–1713) and the War of the Polish Succession (1733–1735) increased foreign domination of Italy. At the end of the War of the Austrian Succession, which lasted from 1740 to 1748, the only independent states left were the declining republics of Venice, Genoa, and Lucca; the Papal States; and the Kingdom of Sardinia, established in 1720 under the House of Savoy. Most of the rest of Italy was under the control of the Hapsburgs of Austria.

Although divided and under foreign domination, Italy during the 1700s enjoyed enlightened rule. The rulers of Italy, inspired by the principles of rationalism, which emphasized the idea of universal human progress, embarked on a program of government reform.

By about 1790, however, the French Revolution had caused a reactionary spirit. Nonetheless, many Italians had become familiar with progressive ideas, and when the French emperor, Napoleon Bonaparte, won Lombardy from the Austrians in 1796, a movement for independence and unity developed and spread throughout the peninsula of Italy.

emphasized *US*
emphasised *Brit.*

realized *US*
realised *Brit.*

Under the protection of Napoleon, several new republics were created. In 1799 Napoleon was driven out of Italy by the Russian and Austrian armies of the Second Coalition, formed in the previous year by Russia, Britain, Austria, Naples, Portugal, and the Ottoman Empire. But Napoleon returned in 1801 and was crowned king of Italy in 1805.

The government of Napoleon was one of enlightened despotism. Although the Italians had little political freedom, many economic, administrative, and educational reforms were carried out.

The Napoleonic Empire collapsed in 1814, and the Congress of Vienna, which met to redraw the map of Europe, restored the old regimes in Italy. Austrian influence was dominant in the peninsula. By and large the restoration was reactionary, and most of Napoleon's reforms were repealed.

Risorgimento. Many Italians, especially those of the middle class who had benefited the most under Napoleonic government, realized how advantageous a strong central government could be. This realization, the memory of the earlier reform governments of the 1700s, the recent republican experiments, and a growing feeling of nationalism, all contributed to the development of the risorgimento, or resurgence, and the desire for a united and independent Italy.

Some of the more daring patriots joined secret societies whose aim was to overthrow the existing governments. The most important of these societies was the Carbonari. The Carbonari staged a revolution in Naples in 1820 that overthrew the monarchy there and set up a constitutional government. But Austrian troops defeated the rebels the following year.

The Carbonari also led a number of less-successful revolutions—in Piedmont in 1821 and in Modena, Parma,

and the Papal States in 1831–1832. Soon after the failure of these uprisings, the Carbonari began to decline. It was largely replaced by Giovine Italia (Young Italy), founded in 1831 by Giuseppe Mazzini, a former member of the Carbonari.

Mazzini believed that God's will was an independent Italy that would take the lead in the spiritual and political regeneration of Europe. During the 1840s and 1850s Mazzini incited numerous revolts throughout Italy, all of which were unsuccessful.

Unification. Italian unification was finally brought about by Count Camillo Benso di Cavour, prime minister of the Kingdom of Sardinia. Cavour understood that foreign aid was needed to free Italy from Austrian domination. In 1858 Cavour met secretly with Napoleon III of France at Plombières and promised him Nice and Savoy in return for military assistance against the Austrians.

War broke out in 1859 and the Austrians soon were defeated, but the Sardinians were able to gain only Lombardy. Meanwhile, however, the regions Tuscany, Modena, Parma, and Romagna had declared their independence and formed provisional governments. Under the sanction of Napoleon III, plebiscites were held in March, 1860, and the four states voted for union with Sardinia in a larger kingdom.

In May, 1860, Giuseppe Garibaldi, a nationalist leader, landed in Sicily with 1,000 volunteers. By September he had won not only Sicily, but Naples as well. Sardinian troops then marched into the Papal States, but France intervened on behalf of the pope.

Nonetheless, the Kingdom of Italy, excluding Rome, was proclaimed in 1861 under Victor Emmanuel, the king of Sardinia. In 1870 French troops were withdrawn from Rome when war broke out between France and Prussia, and the Papal States and Rome were added to the new kingdom.

THE BEAUTIFUL CATHEDRAL in Milan is one of Europe's largest churches. It has more than 3,000 statues, including the life-size figures on the marble spires.

The Kingdom of Italy was a constitutional monarchy with a parliamentary form of government. The two major political forces were the Right, which was conservative, and the Left, which was radical. From 1860 to 1876 the government was controlled mainly by the Right. A highly centralized government was formed. It set about the task of establishing national armed forces, restoring the country's finances, modernizing the transportation system, encouraging industry, and improving agriculture.

This program was continued and expanded by the Left, which held power from 1876 to 1891. The right to vote was extended, elementary education was made compulsory, administrative and legal reforms were instituted, and the army and navy were strengthened.

Expansion. In the late 1800s and early 1900s many Italians felt that the acquisition of colonies was necessary to Italy's international prestige, and Italy embarked on a program of colonial expansion in Africa. In 1885 Italy began the occupation of Eritrea, and in 1889 southern Somaliland was obtained. Territory in present-day Libya was added to Italy's African possessions in 1912. These colonies, for the most part desert, proved to be a heavy drain on Italy's economy.

In 1882 Italy, Germany, and Austria-Hungary formed the Triple Alliance against France. A year earlier France had occupied Tunisia, where there was a large Italian population. The Triple Alliance was renewed in 1887, 1891, 1902, and 1912.

World War I broke out in July 1914, and Italy proclaimed its neutrality in the conflict, which pitted the Central Powers, led by Germany and Austria-Hungary, against the Allied Powers, led by Britain, France, and Russia. Italy maintained that it was not bound by the terms of the Triple Alliance inasmuch as Austria was an aggressor.

Within Italy feelings were divided as to whether the country should remain neutral throughout the course of the conflict. Many Italians felt that they should not let the war end without trying to secure territory in the Balkans and firmly establish the border with Austria, which was open to question.

To secure these ends, Italy began negotiations with Austria. The Austrians proved evasive, and on April 26, 1915, Italy concluded the secret Treaty of London with the Allies. In the event of Allied victory, the treaty promised Italy Trentino, the south Tyrol, Istria, Gorizia, Gradisca, the city of Trieste, some of the Dalmation Islands, the Dodecanese Islands, part of Germany's African colonies, and the seaport of Adalia on the coast of Asia Minor.

Italy declared war on Austria-Hungary in May 1915 and in August 1916 declared war on Germany. Italian troops fought the Austrians and Germans along the northern frontier for four years with varying degrees of success. In 1918 they held firm against a major offensive launched in June, and in November won a decisive victory at Vittorio Veneto.

Fascism. At the 1919 Versailles Peace Conference, which ended the war, Italy won little of what it had been promised. The resulting popular discontent, together with postwar social and political unrest, contributed to development of an extreme nationalistic movement, fascism, led by Benito Mussolini. Fascism was embraced primarily by discontented members of the lower middle class.

On October 28, 1922, the fascists staged a march on Rome. King Victor Emmanuel III, rather than use the military to put down the revolt, asked Mussolini to form a government. Mussolini was named prime minister and gradually created a dictatorial regime. Parliament became his puppet, and in 1938 the lower house, the Chamber of Deputies, was replaced by the Chamber of Fasces and Corporations, whose members were appointed by the Fascist Party.

Fascist foreign policy was imperialistic. In defiance of the League of Nations, Mussolini invaded Ethiopia in October 1935, and, following the conquest of Ethiopia, Victor Emmanuel assumed the title of emperor of Ethiopia. In 1937 Italy withdrew from the League of Nations. In 1939 it conquered Albania and Victor Emmanuel was named its king.

Mussolini also supported fascist movements abroad. He aided General Francisco Franco in the Spanish Civil War of 1936–1939, and supported Adolf Hitler in Germany's annexation of Austria and Czechoslovakia. On May 22, 1939, he concluded an alliance with Germany, establishing the Rome-Berlin Axis.

World War II. Following the outbreak of World War II in September 1939, Mussolini declared Italy's neutrality. But in June 1940, when France was on the verge of defeat, he invaded southern

BENITO MUSSOLINI led Italy into the Second World War on the side of the Axis.

BREAD REPRESENTS the hearty fare of Italy, one of the world's most popular cuisines.

France, bringing Italy into the war. The Italian troops were ill-prepared and were soon demoralized by disaster after disaster. General discontent grew as the war continued, and German troops moved into Italy.

On July 25, 1943, the king dismissed Mussolini as head of the government. A new government was formed by Marshal Pietro Badoglio. The Allies invaded Sicily in July and August of 1943, and in September Italy surrendered. Mussolini proclaimed a "social republic" in the German-controlled north; this lasted until the country was completely liberated in 1945.

On May 9, 1946, Victor Emmanuel abdicated in favor of his son, who became King Humbert II. But the monarchy had lost its popularity as a result of its cooperation with Mussolini, and a referendum held in June made Italy a republic. A new constitution was adopted in 1947, and in 1948 Luigi Einaudi became president.

Republic. Italy soon developed three major political parties—the Christian Democrats, the Socialists, and the Communists. Center-right coalitions ruled Italy through most of the post-war era. The nation began to industrialize and improve its economy as it cooperated closely with the United States and the nations of Western Europe in the postwar revival.

Economic problems, which worsened after 1973, are rooted in Italy's dependence on inflated foreign oil imports. High unemployment and widespread workers' strikes have resulted.

Amid this turmoil, the Communist Party, disavowing its ties with the Soviet Union, made strong gains in the elections of 1976 and 1980. It now ranks

center
US

centre
Brit.

closely behind the Christian Democrats as the most influential party of the center-left coalition.

Since the 1970s the government has been harassed by neofascist and radical leftist terrorist activities. In 1978 former prime minister Moro was assassinated by the Red Brigade terrorists, and right-wing terrorists are alleged to have set the bomb at the Bologna train station where 84 people were killed in 1980.

The governing coalitions that result from Italy's system of proportional representation are often fragile. The unusually long tenure of the Socialist prime minister Bettino Craxi, from 1983 to 1987, at the head of a Socialist-Christian Democrat coalition, provided a time of relative stability.

From 1986 to 1987 Italy held the biggest organized crime trial ever. All told, 452 Mafia suspects were tried and 319 received prison terms.

Craxi resigned in 1987. Several short-lived governments followed, as the country was rocked by revelations of official corruption. In January 1994 Carlo Azeglio Ciampi, who had instituted important reforms, resigned as prime minister; he became prime minister again in 1999.

In 2001 Silvio Berlusconi became prime minister. Tax fraud and bribery charges plagued his term. With cases against him pending, in 2003 the parliament passed a law providing immunity to top government officials, thus suspending any actions against him while in office.

center
US

centre
Brit.

centimeters
US

centimetres
Brit.

labor
US

labour
Brit.

RIGA BECAME THE CAPITAL of an independent Latvia in 1918 and again in 1991, when the country broke away from the Soviet Union.

Latvia

Official name: *Republic of Latvia*
Area: *24,749 sq. mi., 64,100 sq. km.*
Type of government: *Republic*
Population: *2,367,000*
Capital and largest city: *Riga*
    (Pop., 793,000)
Languages: *Lettish, Lithuanian, Russian*
Literacy: *100%;* **Currency:** *Lat*
Per capita GDP: *$8,300*
    (Rank: 62nd)

The land. Latvia is dominated by a low-lying plain that is broken only by low, rolling hills. Two-thirds of the country is covered by wooded areas. The Daugava, Latvia's major river, supplies substantial hydroelectric power, but it is navigable for only a short distance from its outlet on the Baltic Sea. The Gulf of Riga and the many, mostly man-made, Latvian ports bordering it are critical for the country's prosperity.

The moderate climate is influenced by the prevailing air masses from the Baltic Sea and nearby Atlantic Ocean. Summers near the coast are warm and very wet, and winters are mild, with mean temperatures usually hovering around 32°F (0°C). Summer temperatures in the interior are cooler, and winters are much longer and colder. Between 22 and 30 inches (56 and 77 centimeters) of precipitation fall annually.

The people. Only 53 percent of the population is Latvian, also known as Lett. Almost 30 percent of the population is Russian. In contrast to the other Baltic states, an overwhelming majority of native Latvians live in urban areas. Latvian, a Baltic language related to Lithuanian, is still used widely. More than half of the citizens are Lutheran, with the remaining portion being predominantly Roman Catholic.

The principal cities of Latvia are Riga, the capital; Daugavpils (population, 115,000); and Liepāja (95,000).

Economy. Latvia is the most industrialized of the Baltic countries. A skilled labor force has enabled Latvia to create a diversified industrial base. Manufacture of machines and metals is the largest activity. Heavy industries build ships, trains, and agricultural equipment. Radios, refrigerators, and washing machines are also produced in great quantities. Light industry includes textile and clothing manufacture. The bulk of industrial activity is based in Riga, although steps have been made toward decentralizing the manufacturing base.

Agriculture is directed toward domestic consumption, with the most important products being butter, cheese, and bacon. Wheat, beets, potatoes, and vegetables are the main crops.

Before independence, a significant percentage of Soviet trade was conducted through Latvian ports. Maintaining ties to Latvia is thought to be crucial economically and strategically for Russia. Latvia may be able to use this to secure economic stability.

Government. In 1991 the Latvian government restored key portions of the nation's pre-Soviet 1922 constitution, establishing Latvia as a parliamentary republic. In June 1993 Latvian voters elected a new 100-member parliament. The head of state is the president and the head of government is the prime minister.

History. Latvia was first settled by Balts, primarily the Kur, Latgale, and Liv. Between the first and sixth centuries A.D., Latvia was recognized throughout Europe for its cultural progress. Extensive trade routes linked the region to the Roman Empire and to German states. After the demise of the Roman Empire, Latvia developed new trade relationships with Scandinavian countries. In the ninth century, however, the Vikings raided Latvian territory and gained control of the coastal regions.

The Knights of the Sword, the crusading German sect that had already captured Estonia, seized Latvia in 1230. The combined state they created was known as Livonia. German-influenced towns and churches were built and trade routes were established; Riga became known as a major trading post during this period. A feudal system was established, and the native population was reduced to serfdom.

Swedish troops defeated the Germans and the Poles in the Livonian War (1558–1583) and established control in the north, allowing Poland to maintain control in the south and effectively splitting the country between Catholicism and Lutheranism.

Russia, under Peter I (the Great), conquered both regions in 1721 and maintained control until the Russian Revolution, after which Latvia proclaimed independence.

In 1939, after 22 years of independence, Latvia was subjugated by the Soviet Union and incorporated as a republic. In 1940, the first full year of Soviet occupation, 35,000 Latvians were killed or exiled to Siberia. After a 3-year German occupation during World War II, communism was reinstalled, the economy was centralized, and the Supreme

Soviet of the Soviet Union exerted complete authority over the territory.

During the ensuing decades, the percentage of the population that was native Latvian was reduced from about three-quarters to just over half—mostly due to government-sponsored Russian immigration—while the total population grew. Russians were given many top positions in government and commerce, and hundreds of thousands of Soviet soldiers were stationed throughout the country. Religious activities were severely inhibited by strict Soviet laws.

An underground resistance movement survived the decades of Soviet domination and was given new life by the period of openness, or perestroika, instituted in the Soviet Union during the mid-1980s by Mikhail Gorbachev.

In 1990 the legislature of Latvia announced a plan for gradual independence. Months of disputes and demonstrations that included the threat of economic sanctions from the Soviet government ensued. Despite continued warnings from the Kremlin, Latvian nationalists continued to protest for independence.

After the Soviet coup in August 1991 left the central government weakened, Latvia, along with Lithuania and Estonia, seized the opportunity for action and declared full independence.

After almost every European nation and the United States recognized Latvian

THE FREEDOM MONUMENT stands as a tribute to the spirit of Latvian independence.

independence, the Soviets recognized Latvia as an autonomous state and the United Nations accepted it as a member. Latvia joined NATO and the EU in 2004.

Liechtenstein

Official name: *Principality of Liechtenstein*
Area: *62 sq. mi., 160 sq. km.*
Type of government: *Constitutional monarchy*
Population: *33,000*
Capital and largest city: *Vaduz (Pop., 5,100)*
Language: *German;* **Literacy:** *100%*
Currency: *Swiss franc*
Per capita GDP: *$23,000 (Rank: 23rd)*

The land. Liechtenstein is a very small independent principality located between Austria and Switzerland. It extends no more than 16 miles (26 kilometers) from north to south and 7 miles (11 kilometers) from east to west.

The Alps dominate the country's landscape in the east, rising to over 8,000 feet (2,400 meters). Western Liechtenstein lies in the valley of the Rhine River, which flows along the country's western border. Winters are long and cold, but summers are mild.

The people. Liechtenstein's small population is concentrated in the Rhine valley, where Vaduz, the capital and only large town, is located. The official language is German; however, most people speak Alemannic, a Germanic dialect. More than 90 percent of the population is Roman Catholic.

Since the nation began to industrialize, after 1950, it has attracted large numbers of foreign workers, who account for one-third of the population.

Economy. Liechtenstein's economy was once based almost entirely on agriculture, but by the mid-1900s industry had become the main source of income. In 1930, for instance, 70 percent of the nation's labor force was involved in agriculture. Today that figure is less than 2 percent. Cattle, dairy, corn, fruit, and potatoes are the leading farm products.

Liechtenstein's hydroelectric power resources, good transportation facilities, and skilled labor force combine to attract industry. Major manufactured products include precision instruments, small machine parts, pharmaceuticals, and false teeth. Textiles, ceramics, leather goods, and processed foods also are produced.

A large portion of the country's income consists of registration fees paid by foreign companies that incorporate in the principality because of its favorable tax policies. Banking is becoming increasingly important because of strict secrecy laws. Sales to collectors of postage stamps also contribute to the economy, as does tourism.

Liechtenstein has a favorable balance of trade, as its exports earn a great deal and it imports only a few items. It trades heavily with Western Europe, particularly Switzerland and Austria, and the United States. It has a customs union with Switzerland.

Government. Liechtenstein is a constitutional monarchy ruled by a prince of the House of Liechtenstein. A head of government, an assistant head, and three councilors, all appointed by the prince, are responsible to a 25-member, popularly elected Diet. Switzerland represents the country's interests abroad.

History. In ancient times, Liechtenstein's territory was part of the Roman province of Rhaetia. During the 1300s and 1400s, the Holy Roman Empire's county of Vaduz and barony of Schellenburg were united under a single count. By 1712 this feudal state had come into the possession of the Liechtenstein family.

In 1719 the Holy Roman Emperor granted the fief to the family as the Principality of Liechtenstein, and at the dissolution of the Holy Roman Empire in 1806, it became fully independent. Since then, to secure protection, diplomatic representation, and trade advantages, it has become associated with several states, including the Flemish Confederation, the German Confederation, and Austria-Hungary.

In 1919, after Austria-Hungary's defeat in World War I, Switzerland agreed to represent Liechtenstein abroad. In 1921 Liechtenstein established a democratic form of government, adopted Swiss currency, and entrusted postal and telecommunications services to Switzerland. In 1924 they formed a customs union.

Liechtenstein avoided involvement in World War II. The country concentrated on developing its economy, and today its people enjoy a high standard of living. Since the 1960s Liechtenstein has been seeking closer cooperation with other small European states.

In 1984 Prince Franz Josef handed over the executive authority to his son Hans Adam. In 1989 Hans Adam II became head of state.

26 Europe and Russia

meters
US

metres
Brit.

centered
US

centred
Brit.

Lithuania

Official name: *Republic of Lithuania*
Area: *25,174 sq. mi., 65,200 sq. km.*
Type of government: *Republic*
Population: *3,601,000*
Capital and largest city: *Vilnius (Pop., 578,000)*
Languages: *Lithuanian (official), Polish, Russian*
Literacy: *98%;* **Currency:** *Lita*
Per capita GDP: *$8,400 (Rank: 61st)*

The land. Lithuania is dominated by a low plain region that lies between hills in the east and west. Few of the hills reach very high; the highest point in the country is Mount Jouzapine, which is only 958 feet (292 meters) above sea level. About a quarter of the land is covered by forests. The coastal regions are separated from

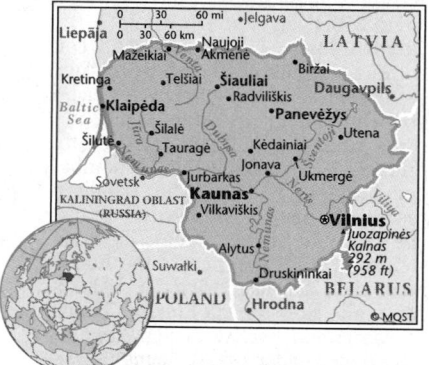

the Baltic Sea by a narrow strip of sand dunes.

The climate is moderate due mostly to Lithuania's proximity to the sea. Near the coasts the summers are warm and the winters mild. The interior of the country is generally colder than the coasts year-round. Annual precipitation is between 24 and 34 inches (62 and 87 centimeters).

The people. Eighty percent of the population is Lithuanian, although many Lithuanians left the country in mass migrations in the 19th and 20th centuries. A significant minority of Russians live in urban areas, along with smaller minorities of Belorussians and Jews. Many Poles inhabit the countryside. Most of the Lithuanians and Poles from rural villages are Roman Catholic.

Lithuanian remains a popular and vital language. The principal cities are Vilnius, the capital; Kaunas (population, 414,000); and Klaipeda (203,000).

Economy. The Lithuanian economy is based on agriculture. Livestock raising occupies the largest number of people. Pigs, horses, and cattle are raised on large collective farms. Dairy farming is also important, and sugar beets, flax, potatoes, and vegetables are the main crops.

The countryside is rich in a variety of mineral resources, including sulfates, iron ore, and limestone. Oil has recently been discovered offshore in the Baltic Sea.

Industry is centered around production of machine tools and precision instruments. Lithuania is a major manufacturer of radio and television equipment in Eastern Europe. Manufacture of clothing and furniture is also important. When Lithuania was a part of the Soviet Union, it enjoyed a higher standard of living than most other Soviet republics.

The Lithuanian economy became intricately linked with that of the Soviet Union during the 51 years of Soviet domination, so it will take many years for the economies of Lithuania and Russia to adjust.

Government. A freely elected 141-member parliament, known as the Supreme Soviet until 1990, is Lithuania's legislative body. The chief of state is a president, who serves a 5-year term and is elected by popular vote. The president, on the approval of the parliament, appoints a premier, who is the head of the government.

History. Archaeological evidence indicates that ancestors of the Lithuanian people settled in the area as early as 1500 B.C. The two main groups were the Samogitians and the Augshtaitians.

During the centuries that followed, the coastal regions of Lithuania traded across Europe and Asia and maintained a level of independence while being continually ravaged by forays of Goths, Poles, Germans, and Russians. Between the seventh and eleventh centuries, Lithuanian tribes staved off a campaign of raids from the Vikings.

In the 13th century, the Knights of the Sword, the German religious order that had already captured Estonia and Latvia, launched an invasion of the area. The Lithuanian tribes united under Mindaugas and repelled the invaders. The descendants of the Mindaugas created the Grand Duchy of Lithuania, which eventually expanded as far south as the Ukraine and established itself as a world power by the end of the 14th century.

In 1386, in response to a new German threat, the Lithuanian dukes established a union with Poland and, through marriage, the grand duke was named the king of Poland. In 1409 Polish and Lithuanian forces drove the remaining German invaders out.

In 1569 Poland and Lithuania created an official federation with a common monarch. Poles came to dominate the monarchy—increasing Polish influence in Lithuania. In the late 18th century, the Third Partition of Poland divided Poland's territory among Austria, Prussia, and Russia, causing Lithuania to be split between Prussia and Russia, with the larger share going to Russia.

BOATERS ROW
across Lake Galve to the restored 15th-century Castle of Trakai, the former capital of Lithuania.

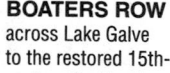

Lithuania declared independence from Russia in 1917 and remained autonomous until 1940, when it was coerced into the Soviet Union. After German occupation during World War II, major reforms were instituted to integrate agriculture and industry with the rest of the Soviet system. In the first quarter century of communist rule, economic production increased dramatically and industrial centers grew substantially. By 1980, however, the constant pressure to maintain high rates of production had taken its toll. The resulting food shortages and stagnating economy caused discontent. In the mid-1980s, Lithuanian nationalist leaders demanded greater freedom, sparking debate throughout the country.

In 1990 the Lithuanian parliament declared full independence, and the Soviet Union responded with a fuel embargo. Thirteen people were killed and a hundred were wounded by the Soviet army during the demonstrations in Vilnius that followed. The failed Soviet coup in August 1991 allowed Lithuania to press for independence when the central government was splintered and weakened.

On September 6, 1991, the government of the Soviet Union officially recognized Lithuania's independence.

On September 17, 1991, Lithuania was officially admitted into the United Nations. The Lithuanian government refused to join the newly formed Commonwealth of Independent States. The commonwealth's open economy, however, eased Lithuania's transition to an autonomous market economy. Lithuania was admitted to both NATO and the EU in 2004.

(For more information about the history of Lithuania as part of the Soviet Union, see the article on Russia.)

Luxembourg

Official name: *Grand Duchy of Luxembourg*

Area: *999 sq. mi., 2,588 sq. km.*

Type of government:
Constitutional monarchy

Population: *449,000*

Population growth rate: *0.6%*

Capital and largest city:
Luxembourg (Pop., 77,000)

Languages: *Luxembourgish, French, German*

Literacy: *100%;* **Currency:** *Euro*

Per capita GDP: *$44,000*
(Rank: 1st)

The land. The southern third of Luxembourg is part of the Lorraine Plateau; it consists of rolling plains. The northern two-thirds of the country is part of the Ardennes and is hilly and wooded. Its principal river is the Sauer.

Luxembourg has a temperate, rainy climate. Winters are mild, summers cool. Summer temperatures average 60°F (16°C). Rainfall averages about 30 inches (76 centimeters) a year.

The people. Luxembourgers are a mixture of nationalities—primarily French, Dutch, German, and Belgian. French is frequently used for official purposes, but German and Luxembourgish, a Germanic dialect, are widely spoken. More than 95 percent of the population are Roman Catholic. A large number of foreign workers are resident in the country. The only important urban center is the capital, Luxembourg.

Economy. The main support of Luxembourg's economy is the iron and steel industry. There are large iron ore deposits in southwestern Luxembourg, and there is coal nearby in Germany. This combination has made Luxembourg one of Western Europe's major iron and steel producers, with steel alone accounting for more than a third of all exports.

About 5 percent of the labor force is employed in agriculture, which is troubled by low yields. Livestock is raised, and the principal crops are potatoes, wheat, barley, and wine grapes.

Banking and financial services are a growing sector of the economy, primarily because of banking secrecy laws, a central location in Europe, and a multilingual population.

In 1922 Luxembourg and Belgium formed an economic union that abolished the customs frontier between them. The union was dissolved in 1940, but was reestablished in 1945. In 1948 a customs union, known as the Benelux Customs Union, went into effect among Luxembourg, Belgium, and the Netherlands. Full economic union of the countries has existed since 1960.

Because of its small domestic market, foreign trade is extremely important to the economy. Major imports include fuels, motor vehicles and parts, machinery, and a variety of manufactured goods. Principal exports include steel, plastics, rubber, machinery, and textiles. Luxembourg's major trading partners include Belgium, Germany, France, and the Netherlands.

Government. Luxembourg is a constitutional monarchy with a grand duke as chief of state. Executive power is exercised by the duke and the Council of Ministers. The council, or cabinet, is headed by a prime minister.

Legislative power rests with the 60-member Chamber of Deputies, which is directly elected to a term of 5 years. The Council of State, an advisory body of elder statesmen appointed by the grand duke, deliberates on proposed legislation and expresses its opinion on other matters referred to it, but its decisions can be overruled by the Chamber of Deputies.

History. The name Luxembourg is derived from the castle of Lützelburg, the seat of Count Siegfried I, under whose sway several lands were united in the 900s. The size of the country gradually increased under a series of able rulers. In 1308 Count Henry of Luxembourg became Holy Roman Emperor. In 1354 his grandson, Emperor Charles IV, expanded Luxembourg's territories and made it a duchy.

Luxembourg was conquered by Philip the Good of Burgundy in 1443. In 1477 it passed to the Hapsburgs through marriage, and in 1555 Philip II of Spain received it from Charles V as part of the Low Countries. Luxembourg was conquered by Louis XIV and ruled by France until 1697, when it was restored to Spain.

It was ruled by Austria from 1714 until 1795, when it again came under French rule. Luxembourg was annexed to the French Republic and subsequently became a part of the Napoleonic Empire. At the Congress of Vienna (1814–1815), Luxembourg was made a grand duchy, ruled by William I, who was also king of the Kingdom of the Netherlands.

Luxembourg was associated with Belgium when it seceded from the Netherlands in 1830, but in 1839 part of the country merged with Belgium and the rest remained an independent grand duchy under the personal rule of the Netherlands' king.

Lacking economic ties with the Netherlands, Luxembourg became associated with the German states, and in 1866, upon dissolution of the German Confederation, Luxembourg was made neutral. The crown then passed to Grand Duke Adolphe of Nassau in 1890, thus breaking the direct tie with the Dutch monarchy.

Modern Luxembourg. Luxembourg was invaded by the Germans in 1914, at the outbreak of World War I, and remained under German occupation throughout the war. In 1919 a referendum confirmed the desire of the country to remain a duchy.

Luxembourg's neutrality was violated again in World War II, when German troops occupied the Low Countries in 1940. Grand Duchess Charlotte, granddaughter of Adolphe, and the cabinet carried on a government in exile in London and Montreal, Canada. The country was liberated in 1944.

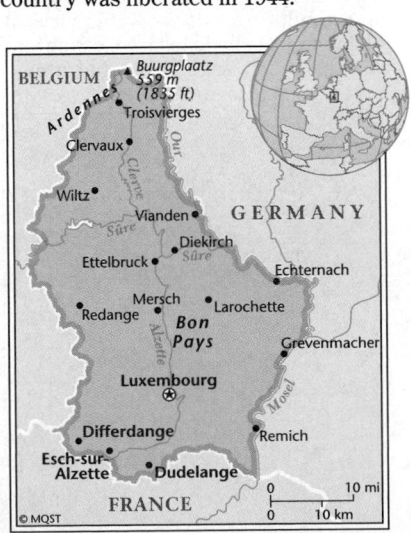

labor
US

labour
Brit.

26 Europe and Russia

In 1949 Luxembourg abandoned its neutrality and joined NATO. In 1957 it joined the European Economic Community (later the EU). It now cooperates closely with Western European countries in economic matters.

Macedonia

Official name: *The Former Yugoslav Republic of Macedonia*
Area: *9,778 sq. mi., 25,333 sq. km.*
Type of government: *Emerging democracy*
Population: *2,055,000*
Capital and largest city: *Skopje (Pop., 545,000)*
Languages: *Macedonian, Albanian*
Currency: *Denar*
Per capita GDP: *$5,000 (Rank: 85th)*

The land. Macedonia is a rugged land of mountains and forests. The country's most important mountain ranges are the Kouf and Nide, which act as a border between Macedonia and Greek Macedonia. Of the country's three major rivers, the Aliakmon, the Strymon, and the Vardar, the final one is the most important. Two large lakes, Ohrid and Prespa, straddle the southeastern border. Macedonia's climate is continental, with hot summers and cold winters made colder by the vardarac, a harsh wind that blows down from the mountains in central Macedonia.

The people. Ethnic Macedonians, who generally practice the Eastern Orthodox religion, are the largest element of Macedonia's population. Most members of the country's two important minority groups, the Albanians and Turks, are of the Islamic faith. Bitola, in southern Macedonia, is the country's second-largest city (Skopje, the capital, is the largest), with an estimated population of 108,000.

Economy. Macedonia is not a highly industrialized country and relies heavily on agriculture for its economic survival. Major crops include tobacco, cotton, and various fruits, vegetables, and grains.

ALEXANDER THE GREAT of Macedonia conquered most of what was then considered the civilized world, spreading Greek ideas and customs.

Bua cattle, known for their ability to withstand harsh conditions, are raised in Macedonia, as are sheep and water buffalo. Mineral resources include iron ore, lead, zinc, nickel, and silver. Handicrafts are also an important element of Macedonia's national economy.

Government. Macedonia is an emerging democracy with a popularly elected president and legislature.

History. Modern Macedonia is a portion of a historic region, also called Macedonia, which encompassed modern Macedonia as well as parts of southwestern Bulgaria and northern Greece.

The long, complex history of Macedonia dates back to well before the birth of Alexander the Great. Ancient Macedonia was one of the many independent governments that existed in the Hellenic world. In 338 B.C. Philip II won the Battle of Chaeronea, establishing Macedonia's preeminence. Philip's son, Alexander the Great, succeeded to the throne in 336 B.C., and Macedonia's power became legendary. Upon Alexander's death in 323 B.C., rival forces struggled to gain control of Macedonia. Stability returned about 276 B.C., when Antigonus was elected king and his descendants were recognized as heirs to the throne.

In 146 B.C. Macedonia became a Roman province. When the Roman Empire was divided in A.D. 395, Macedonia became part of the Byzantine Empire. Throughout the sixth and seventh centuries, Slavs and Bulgars began invading Macedonia, and despite Byzantine efforts to retain control, the area eventually was taken over by the First Bulgarian Empire. Between the 7th and 14th centuries, Macedonia was ruled by the Bulgars; by a Slavic Macedonian calling himself Czar Samuel; by the Byzantines, who assumed power after a brutal battle in 1014; by the Serbs; and finally, beginning in the 14th century, by the Turks of the Ottoman Empire. At approximately the same time, Muslim Albanians began settling in Macedonia.

For over 500 years, while the Turks governed Macedonia, Christian Macedonians found themselves living in an Islamic country. The *hajduk,* outlaws who attempted to resist the Ottoman government, and the Orthodox Church, although restricted, managed to foster the ethnic identity of Macedonians, but Ottoman control remained firm.

In 1878 the Treaty of San Stefano, which concluded the Russo-Turkish Wars, awarded most of Macedonia to Bulgaria, but it was returned to the Ottoman Empire in the same year in accordance with the Treaty of Berlin. (This treaty was the product of the Congress of Berlin, a meeting of the major European powers held to check Russian advances in the area.)

Macedonia became a point of dispute among several European nations. Although Bulgaria pointed to linguistic affinities between Bulgarian and Macedonian to support its claims that the two nations were closely related and should be ruled by the same government, the Serbs asserted that the Macedonians were culturally Slavs and the Greeks claimed that they were really Slavic-speaking Greeks.

The rise of European nationalism led Macedonians to seek independence, and the Vatreshna Makedonska Revolutisionna Organizatsia (VMRO, the Internal Macedonian Revolutionary Organization) was organized in 1893 to work toward this end. Unrest in Macedonia soon erupted into violence. Failed rebellions in 1902 and 1903 attracted international attention, and in the interest of maintaining stability in the volatile Balkans, Macedonia was divided into zones to be regulated by British, French, Italian, Austrian, and Russian forces. In response to the demands of the Balkan League, comprising Bulgaria, Serbia, Montenegro, and Greece, a new Turkish government (sometimes referred to as the Young Turks) agreed to reform their policies in Macedonia. The European troops withdrew in anticipation of the promised changes, but the reforms proved inadequate and another uprising took place in 1909. These internal conflicts were quickly followed by the Balkan Wars (1912 and 1913) and then by World War I. During the dismantling of the Ottoman Empire following World War I, Macedonia was divided among Greece, Bulgaria, and Yugoslavia.

(For a history of modern Macedonia from 1918 to 1992, see the article on Serbia and Montenegro.)

The Macedonian declaration of independence in January 1992 was the country's recent effort to establish its sovereignty. While Bosnia and Herzegovina, Croatia, and Slovenia successfully managed to gain recognition from the European Community, Greece strongly opposed the recognition of Macedonia, suggesting that the use of the name "Macedonia" was at best an affront to Greece and at worst proof that Macedonia would later attempt to claim the area in northern Greece that bears the same name. The European Community (later the European Union) and the United States announced in July 1992 that they would not accept the new country unless the republic's name was changed. Greece and Serbia established a trade embargo against Macedonia, which nonetheless continued to maintain its right to establish an independent country. Greece lifted its embargo in 1995, and the two countries have normalized relations.

Malta

Official name: *Republic of Malta*
Area: *124 sq. mi., 320 sq. km.*
Type of government:
    Parliamentary democracy
Population: *397,000*
Capital and largest city: *Valletta*
    (Pop., 7,600)
Languages: *Maltese, English*
    (both official)
Literacy: *89%;* **Currency:** *Lira*
Per capita GDP: *$17,000*
    (Rank: 36th)

The land. The Maltese islands include Malta, Comino, and Gozo. The islands are flat and consist of limestone rock covered with a thin layer of soil. There are very few trees and no rivers or lakes.

The climate is semitropical, with mild winters and hot summers. An average of 20 inches (51 centimeters) of rain falls on the islands, but it varies greatly from year to year.

The people. The Maltese are a Mediterranean people who speak a Semitic language. Maltese culture exhibits varying degrees of Arab, Italian, and British influence. The population is almost entirely Roman Catholic. Malta's density of population is extremely high—over 2,800 persons per square mile. Emigration, especially since the end of World War II, has been high and directed mainly to Australia, Britain, and Canada.

Economy. Malta is in the process of developing its economy. Its only resources are its people, its geographic location, and its limestone.

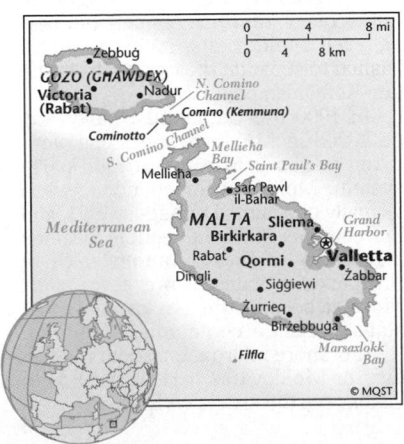

Tourism has become a leading source of income in recent years. Manufacturing began on Malta in the early 1960s and now employs about a quarter of the labor force. Significant manufactured products include textiles, rubber products, and processed foods. Shipbuilding is the main industry.

Agriculture is relatively insignificant to the economy. Potatoes, tomatoes, grapes, and wheat are the main crops. Fishing is important.

The leading exports are clothing, semiconductors, agricultural produce, processed foods, textiles, and cut flowers. The leading imports are textiles, machinery, foodstuffs, petroleum, and consumer goods.

Government. Malta became a republic within the Commonwealth in 1974. The chief of state is a president, who appoints a prime minister, usually the majority leader of the legislature. The popularly elected unicameral legislature has approximately 65 seats, but this varies, as additional seats are given to the party with the largest popular vote.

History. Malta, called Melita in ancient times, and its sister island, Gozo, were once inhabited by people whose stone monuments still exist. A refuge for ships following Mediterranean trade routes, the islands were visited by Phoenicians and Greeks, and in the 200s B.C. they passed under Carthaginian rule. Malta became a Roman possession in 216 B.C. During the first century A.D., the Maltese adopted Christianity.

After the dissolution of the Roman Empire, Malta passed successively to the Byzantine Empire, the Arabs, Sicily, the Spanish kingdom of Aragon, and then to the united kingdoms of Aragon and Castile. In the early 1500s, the Holy Roman Emperor received Malta from Spain by inheritance, and in 1530 he granted it to the Order of the Hospital of St. John of Jerusalem.

The knights, who served as protectors of religious pilgrims, regarded Malta as an outpost for the defense of Christianity. They withstood attacks by the Muslim Turks, including a long siege in 1565. The island under the knights was supported and protected by the nations of Europe, and it grew prosperous from Mediterranean trade.

The military strength and effectiveness of the order declined during the 1600s and 1700s, and in 1798 Napoleon Bonaparte of France occupied Malta. Two years later, with the aid of the Maltese, a British force drove out the French, and the Maltese requested permanent British protection. In 1814 Malta became a British crown colony and a vital British naval base.

British rule. The islanders had partial self-government during the 1800s. They were self-governing during the 1920s and 1930s, but two issues sharply divided the island—the choice of Maltese or Italian as an official language and church-state relations. The conflict grew so bitter that home rule was abolished in 1936.

During World War II, Malta had great strategic value. It withstood heavy German and Italian air bombardments and was a base for the Anglo-U.S. invasion of Sicily in 1943. In 1942 Britain awarded the George Cross to the Maltese people for their bravery during the bombardments.

Independence. After the war, the country worked to achieve sufficient unity to allow restoration of complete internal self-government, which it received in 1962. Maltese and English were made the official languages, and Roman Catholicism was declared the official religion. In 1964 the British granted the country full independence. In 1974 it became a republic.

Malta concentrated on expanding its economy to end its dependence on the British naval base, which had been its major source of income and which was being closed down. By 1979 the British had abandoned the base. Malta has since become a major financial center and a tourist destination. In 2004 Malta joined the EU.

MANY STONE MONUMENTS of Malta date to the time when the Phoenicians colonized the islands, about 1000 B.C.

centimeters
US

centimetres
Brit.

labor
US

labour
Brit.

26   **Europe and Russia**

Moldova

Official name: *Republic of Moldova*
Area: *13,008 sq. mi., 33,700 sq. km.*
Type of government: *Republic*
Population: *4,435,000*
Capital and largest city: *Chişinău*
(*Kishinyov*)
(*Pop. 658,000*)
Languages: *Moldovan, Russian*
(*both official*)*, Gagauz*
Literacy: *96%;* **Currency:** *Leu*
Per capita GDP: *$3,000*
(*Rank: 117th*)

kilometers
US

kilometres
Brit.

The land. The republic of Moldova is located just west of the Carpathian Mountains. The Prut River, a tributary of the Danube, forms the western border with Romania and meanders southward to the Black Sea. The Dniester (Dnestr) River, 877 miles (1,411 kilometers) long, rises in the southwestern Ukraine and follows a winding course to the Black Sea near Odessa. The largest river of Moldova, it skirts the western boundary of the republic. Much of Moldova lies between these two rivers.

Northern Moldova contains flat plains, or steppes, at an elevation of some 500 to 650 feet (150 to 200 meters), as well as somewhat higher forested uplands and dramatic limestone ridges along the Prut. The central uplands, where the highest point is Mount Balaneshty at 1,409 feet (430 meters), are characterized by deep valleys and steep, forested slopes. The Budzhak Plain, in the south, is cut by many gullies and ravines.

The proximity of Moldova to the Black Sea gives it a mild climate. Annual temperatures average about 45.9°F (7.7°C) in the north, with somewhat higher temperatures in the south. Average rainfall is approximately 18 to 22 inches (45 to 55 centimeters) per year, although wide variations do occur. Heavier rainfall in the summer months has resulted in severe land erosion in many areas.

Moldovian soils are fertile, with an abundance of the black soils, called chernozem, in which grains, tobacco, and sugar beet crops thrive.

The people. Moldova ranks among the most densely populated regions of the former Soviet Union, with an average of 336 persons per square mile. Moldavians, or ethnic Romanians, make up the largest part of the population. In addition, there are sizable Ukrainian, Russian, Jewish, and Bulgarian minorities, and a small Christian minority of Gagauz people.

Ethnic disturbances have occurred recently in the Trans-Dniester region largely inhabited by Slavs opposed to the possibility of Moldovian reunification with Romania.

Today the official language of Moldova is Moldovan, a member of the Romance language group, originally written in Roman script. In an effort to separate Moldavians from their Romanian neighbors, in 1940 the Soviet government ordered that the Cyrillic alphabet be used when writing. The use of Roman script was restored in 1989.

Economy. Although Moldova has few natural resources, industry is diversified and well developed. The main industrial emphasis is on food processing, but machine building, power engineering, building materials, chemicals, and textiles are also important. The food industry includes canning of fruits and vegetables, wine making (as well as production of champagne and brandies), sugar refining, and pressing of vegetable oils. Moldova recently supplied almost a third of the Soviet Union's tobacco. Specially designed tractors are produced for use in vineyards and in orchards.

Hydroelectric stations and thermoelectric plants provide ample electricity to Moldova and also supply electrical power to Bulgaria and southern Ukraine.

Agriculture continues to play a leading role in the Moldovian economy. Important crops are sugar beets, grains, wine grapes, vegetables, and fruits. Farming is largely mechanized. Specialized farming is concentrated in tobacco, in the large vineyards of the southern and central regions and the orchards of the north and southeast, and in the sunflower seeds that flourish throughout the republic. Livestock raising includes chickens, pigs, cattle, and goats. Sheep, particularly the Karakul breed, are raised mainly in the south.

Government. Moldova is a republic. The executive branch of government consists of a president, who is elected by parliament to a 4-year term, and a council of ministers, selected by a prime minister. Both are with the approval of parliament. The prime minister is appointed by the president, also upon approval of the parliament. The parliament has 101 members, who are elected through electoral blocs by popular vote to 4-year terms.

History. Moldova's history is closely linked to that of the old province of Moldavia, a region lying east of Transylvania and separated from it by the Carpathian Mountains. Modern Moldova consists of a small portion of the old province.

Moldavia was controlled by Scythia during the first millennium B.C. Later it formed part of the province of Dacia under the rule of the Roman Empire, and thereafter upheld its Latin speech through a long series of foreign rulers. It was part of the Kievan state in the ninth to eleventh centuries A.D. After the Mongol invasions, in the mid-14th century, it became a principality that included the territories of Bukovina and Bessarabia. In the 16th century, the Ottoman Turks took control of Bessarabia, the area of eastern Moldavia between the Prut and Dniester rivers, and held it until it was ceded to the Russian Empire in 1812. The remaining portion of Moldavia stayed under Turkish control.

After the formation of the Soviet Union by the Bolsheviks, the Moldavian Autonomous Soviet Socialist Republic (ASSR) was created in 1924 from districts that had once been part of the Podolsk region in western Ukraine, an area inhabited by Ukrainians but claimed nevertheless by Romania. In addition, Bessarabia became part of Greater Romania in 1918. The Nazi-Soviet Pact of 1939, however, required that Romania give up Bessarabia and northern Bukovina to the Soviet Union. As a result, most of Bessarabia was joined to the lands of the Moldavian ASSR and a new Moldavian Soviet Socialist Republic was formed in 1940. (The remaining areas of Bessarabia and northern Bukovina were joined to the Ukrainian Soviet Socialist Republic.) Romania captured the region in 1941, during World War II, and held it until 1944, when it was retaken by the Soviet Union and made a union republic.

After World War II, the Soviets went to great lengths to separate Moldova and Romania socially and politically. Use of the Cyrillic alphabet became mandatory in Moldova, and many Russians and Ukrainians were encouraged to immigrate there. These policies angered Moldovians, many of whom wished to separate their group from the non-Romanian populace.

In 1990 the Communist Party was outlawed in Moldova, and steps were taken to reorganize into a multiparty system. Moldovian independence was formally proclaimed in August 1991, and in December 1991, the republic became a member of the Commonwealth of Independent States. However, in 2001, Moldova became the first former Soviet state to elect a communist president.

(For more information about the history of Moldova as part of the Soviet Union, see the article on Russia.)

UKRAINE
Dniester
Briceni
Bălţi Rîbniţa Kotovs'k
UKRAINE
Iaşi Chişinău Bender (Tighina) Tiraspol
ROMANIA
Bacău
UKRAINE
Cahul
Galaţi Izmail Black Sea
Danube

Codrii

0 35 70 mi
0 35 70 km
© MQST

Monaco

Official name: *Principality of Monaco*

Area: *.73 sq. mi., 1.9 sq. km.*

Type of government: *Constitutional monarchy*

Population: *32,000*

Capital and largest city: *Monaco (Pop., 27,000)*

Languages: *French (official), English, Italian, Monegasque*

Literacy: *99%;* **Currency:** *Euro*

Per capita GDP: *$27,000 (Rank: 14th)*

The land and people. Monaco is the second smallest independent country in the world. It is set into steep cliffs surrounding an excellent harbor on the Mediterranean Sea. Its climate is mild and rather dry.

There are four sections in the principality—Monte Carlo, the newer, eastern part of the city; La Condamine, surrounding the harbor; Monaco-Ville, which lies atop a rocky promontory jutting into the Mediterranean; and Fontvielle, where landfill has added new area to the city.

A majority of the population is from other European countries, and only slightly more than one-tenth of the people are native Monagasques. French is the official language, however, Italian and Monégasque also are spoken. Roman Catholicism is the predominant religion.

Economy. Tourists enjoy Monaco's beaches and gambling casino, the major source of Monaco's income. The country also has light industries producing plastics, microelectronics, precision tools, and luxury consumer items.

Monaco has no income tax, and it has long served the wealthy as a refuge from taxes. Low corporate taxes also have helped attract many corporate branch offices.

Government. Monaco is governed by a prince, who is assisted by a small appointed cabinet. An elected 18-member National Council shares legislative power with the prince. France is responsible for Monaco's defense, but the principality maintains its own consulates throughout the world.

History. The ancient Phoenicians, Greeks, Carthaginians, and Romans all used Monaco's harbor. In the 600s and 700s, Monaco was occupied by the Lombards, who built a fortress on its rocky promontory. In the 800s the fortress fell to the Saracens.

Monaco became part of the Holy Roman Empire, and in the 900s it was granted to a leading family of Genoa, which later took the name Grimaldi. The Grimaldis did not exercise their rights over the territory until the late 1200s, when they were driven from Genoa as a result of political feuds.

The tiny state was in constant danger of being overwhelmed by its larger neighbors. With its fortress and its excellent harbor and port facilities, Monaco was coveted by Genoa, Savoy, Florence, France, and Spain. Monaco managed to maintain its independence, however, and in 1512 the right of the Grimaldis to rule Monaco was formally acknowledged by the king of France.

After the French Revolution, in 1793, France annexed the principality. The sovereignty of the Grimaldis was restored in 1814, and in 1815 the Treaty of Vienna made Monaco a protectorate of the Kingdom of Sardinia. In 1861 the principality once more came under the protection of France. In 1911 Monaco adopted a constitution, ending the absolute rule of the princes.

During the early 1900s, the principality developed into a fashionable resort. It is well known for its gambling casino at Monte Carlo.

The current ruler, Prince Rainier III, acceded to the throne in 1949. In 1956 he married the American film star Grace Kelly.

Monaco was admitted to the UN in 1993.

THE BEAUTIFUL HARBOR and beaches, along with the gambling casinos, make tourism the main industry in Monte Carlo.

Netherlands

Official name: *Kingdom of the Netherlands*

Area: *16,033 sq. mi., 41,536 sq. km.*

Type of government: *Constitutional monarchy*

Population: *16,068,000*

Capital and largest city: *Amsterdam (Pop., 734,000)*

Language: *Dutch*

Literacy: *99%;* **Currency:** *Euro*

Per capita GDP: *$26,900 (Rank: 15th)*

The land. The Netherlands consists mostly of low plains, although there are some hilly sections in the east. Much of the land along the coast lies below sea level. It is protected by dikes and kept dry by drainage systems. The Dutch have a much higher percentage of reclaimed land than any nation in Europe. The West Frisian Islands lie along the northern coast.

The climate is maritime, with cool summers, mild winters, and high humidity. Rainfall is ample.

The Netherlands Antilles, a fully autonomous part of the kingdom, is all that remains of a once vast overseas empire controlled by the Dutch.

The people. The Netherlands is one of the most densely settled of the world's developed nations, with some 1030 people per square mile. The population is densest in the western half of the country. The largest city is Amsterdam. Other major cities include Rotterdam (population, 606,000); The Hague (441,000); Utrecht (258,000); and Eindhoven (203,000).

The population is homogeneous and is an ancient mixture of Germanic and Celtic stock. There are no large ethnic minorities, although religious differences have been the basis of some past friction. About 40 percent of the

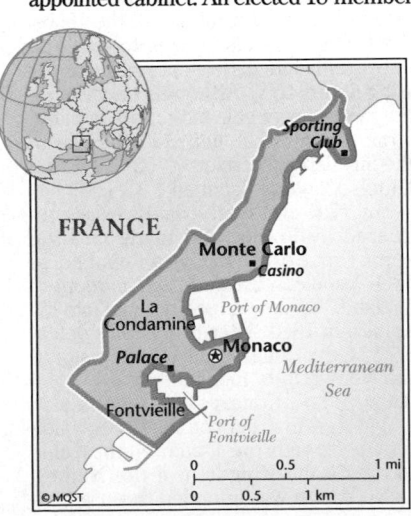

CHEESE, seen here in a cheese market, and tulips are the products most closely linked with the Netherlands.

labor
US

labour
Brit.

FRANZ HALS was a famous Dutch painter in the 1600s. He painted group portraits, some of civic groups such as the regents at right, in addition to individuals.

population is Roman Catholic, and 30 percent is Protestant.

Economy. The Netherlands is located along the heavily trafficked North Sea coast, and commerce is a mainstay of the Dutch economy. The Dutch merchant fleet is one of Europe's largest, and Rotterdam is the continent's leading port.

The Netherlands industrialized considerably after World War II, although mostly without the aid of industrial raw materials. Since 1959 great quantities of oil and natural gas have been discovered. Europe's largest natural gas field, in Groningen province, provides for almost half of the country's energy needs. About half of this gas is exported. In 1985, 3.7 million metric tons of oil were produced in the Netherlands, with most of the refining done at Pernis, near Rotterdam.

Agriculture, hindered by poor soil and climate, accounts for about 4 percent of the national product and only 5 percent of the labor force. Despite this,

Dutch agriculture uses intensive and highly efficient methods, and yields per acre and per animal are among the highest in the world. Principal agricultural products include grains, dairy products, and meat.

Twenty-eight percent of the labor force is engaged in manufacturing. Major industrial products include steel and other finished metals, transportation equipment, machinery, chemicals, refined petroleum, radios, textiles, ships, and a variety of processed foodstuffs.

In 1948 the Benelux Customs Union, linking Belgium, Luxembourg, and the Netherlands, went into effect. Full economic union of the three countries has existed since 1960. Exports include petroleum, natural gas, chemicals, refined petroleum, metal and electrical goods, textiles, and food products. Major imports are industrial raw materials, which make up about one-third of the total; foodstuffs; fuels; and a variety of consumer goods.

The Netherlands' chief trading partners are the other members of the European Union.

Government. The Netherlands is a constitutional monarchy. The sovereign is head of state, but executive power is exercised by a prime minister and cabinet. The prime minister must normally be able to command a majority of votes in the legislature, however, ministers may not simultaneously be members of parliament. The monarch also appoints a council of state that advises the cabinet.

Legislative power is held by the States-General, which consists of two houses. The upper house is called the First Chamber, and its 75 members are chosen by provincial legislatures for 4-year terms. The 150 members of the lower house, the Second Chamber, are directly elected and serve 4-year terms.

History. When Roman legions commanded by Julius Caesar first advanced into The Netherlands in 57 B.C., the area was inhabited by Celtic and Germanic tribes. The region south of the Rhine became a part of the Roman Empire, and remained so until A.D. 400, when the Netherlands came under the control of

the Franks. The Netherlands was part of Charlemagne's empire from 800 until 843. After the breakup of the empire, the Netherlands emerged as a group of duchies, most often under the control of German princes. After 1384 they were ruled by the dukes of Burgundy.

Mary of Burgundy was married to the future Holy Roman Emperor Maximilian I in 1477, and in 1493 the Netherlands became part of the Holy Roman Empire. After the resignation of Emperor Charles V in 1555, the empire was divided, and the Netherlands passed to Philip II of Spain.

During the second half of the 1600s, many of the Dutch accepted Calvinism. Philip, a devout Roman Catholic, saw the suppression of Protestantism as a paramount goal and introduced the Inquisition into the Netherlands. Religious persecution intensified the conflict between the Dutch and the Spaniards. In addition to religious freedom, the Dutch sought economic independence and self-rule, and they strongly resented foreign domination.

Independence. In 1579 the seven northern provinces formed the Union of Utrecht, and 2 years later they proclaimed their independence. A bloody civil war was fought until 1609, when a 12-year truce was signed. Under the leadership of William of Orange, the Dutch Netherlands achieved de facto independence.

At the end of the truce, Spain resumed the war, but the Dutch were more than able to hold their own, and in 1648 the Treaty of Westphalia formally recognized the independence of the United Netherlands. The southern provinces continued to be ruled by Spain, and then by Austria until the end of the 1700s.

During the 1600s the Dutch nation reached its political and cultural height. The Dutch established a colonial empire, and for a brief time the Netherlands was the leading commercial power in Europe. Dutch supremacy was broken by a series of naval wars fought with England (1652–1654; 1665–1667) that soon reduced the Netherlands to the status of a second-rate power.

During the second half of the 1600s, the Dutch were also trying to stem the expansionist tendencies of France under King Louis XIV. Although successful, they were never able to recover from the strain of the effort, and after the War of the Spanish Succession (1702–1713), the Dutch economy declined.

In 1795 the Netherlands was conquered by France and made into the puppet state of the Batavian Republic. In 1806 Napoleon created the Kingdom of Holland, which was incorporated into his empire in 1810. After Napoleon's defeat in 1814, the Congress of Vienna restored the Netherlands' independence.

Union. The Congress of Vienna also joined the Austrian and former Spanish provinces with the Dutch Netherlands to create the Kingdom of the Netherlands, which was intended to serve as a

AMSTERDAM is a city of more than 100 canals lined with handsome old houses, many of which date from the 1600s.

bulwark against future French expansion. But the union between Belgium and Holland was short-lived.

Holland was Germanic in orientation, Calvinistic in religion, and in favor of a policy of free trade; Belgium was French in orientation, predominantly Roman Catholic, and in favor of high tariffs to protect its growing industry. In 1830 a revolution broke out in Belgium that eventually resulted in the separation of the two countries.

Modern Netherlands. The Netherlands remained neutral in World War I. It was invaded by the Germans during World War II, suffering greatly during German occupation. Queen Wilhelmina escaped to London and led her country in exile. After liberation in 1944, she was restored to her throne. In 1948, after a reign of 50 years, she abdicated in favor of her daughter, Juliana, who turned the throne over to her daughter, Beatrix, in 1980.

During the postwar period, the Netherlands lost a large portion of its colonial possessions. A nationalist rebellion broke out in Indonesia in 1945, and in 1949 the Dutch granted the country its independence. In 1954 the American colonies of Dutch Guiana and the Netherlands Antilles gained internal self-government, but they remained in the kingdom as equal partners of the Netherlands. In 1962 Netherlands New Guinea (West Irian) was transferred to Indonesia and, in 1975, Dutch Guiana, or Surinam, became independent.

There were massive emigrations to the Netherlands from Indonesia after 1949, and from Surinam after 1975. Terrorist activity in the Netherlands has been carried on by a militant group supporting the independence of the South Moluccan islands from Indonesia.

The Netherlands' system of proportional representation in parliament makes it difficult for any one party to achieve an absolute majority. Since World War II the country usually has been ruled by center-right coalitions led by the Christian Democratic Party.

Norway

Official name: *Kingdom of Norway*
Area: *125,182 sq. mi., 324,220 sq. km.*
Type of government: *Constitutional monarchy*
Population: *4,525,000*
Capital and largest city: *Oslo (Pop., 513,000)*
Language: *Norwegian*
Literacy: *100%*
Currency: *Krone*
Per capita GDP: *$31,800 (Rank: 4th)*

The land. Norway is a long, narrow country described as being "all mountains and sea." It is almost totally devoid of plains. Most of the terrain is rugged and mountainous, but there is a high, hilly plateau region in the center of the country.

The Kjölen Mountains follow the border with Sweden. They rise to about 8,000 feet (2,400 meters) in the south-central region, and steep slopes plunge into the Skagerrak along the coast.

Norway's long coastline is penetrated by almost innumerable deep, sheltered, navigable inlets, or fjords, and is protected from the open sea by a fringe of islands. Many lakes lie scattered throughout Norway, and many rivers and streams rush down from the mountains. The only rivers of any length are the Glåma, Lågen, and Rauma, in southern Norway.

More than one-third of the country lies north of the Arctic Circle, and two arctic islands, Jan Mayen and Spitsbergen (Svalbard), are part of Norway.

Norway's climate is varied. The south has a temperate marine climate, with cool summers, mild winters, and much cloudiness. The warm North Atlantic drift keeps the entire coast ice-free all year. In the north and in the higher elevations, the climate is colder and more severe. Precipitation is plentiful, particularly in the mountainous areas.

The people. Norway has one of Europe's smallest populations, with about 34 persons per square mile. The interior and the northern two-thirds of the country are sparsely inhabited, and most of the people live along the southern coast, where Norway's main cities, Oslo, Bergen (population, 233,000), and Trondheim (151,000), are located.

Almost all of the people are Norwegian. Norwegian is the universal language and Evangelical Lutheranism is the established state religion, although there is complete religious freedom. In the far north there is a minority (about 0.5 percent of the population) of seminomadic Lapps, who have their own language and culture.

Economy. Norway's economy traditionally was based on merchant shipping, fishing, forestry, and agriculture. In the 1900s the country began to expand its industry by developing and utilizing its natural resources.

Although its economy operates on small volume, Norway was one of the world's richest countries per capita even before its oil and gas reserves began to be exploited in the 1970s.

Hydroelectric power was Norway's main domestic energy source before the discovery of great oil reserves and natural gas fields in the North Sea. Hydroelectric power is still important, though; over 99 percent of the country's electricity is hydroelectric. In 1987, 50 million metric tons of oil were produced in Norway, more than the country uses domestically.

Agriculture. Less than 5 percent of Norway's land is cultivable, and in 1987 agriculture contributed less than 3 percent to the domestic product. Agriculture employs about 5 percent of the labor force. The major emphasis is on livestock raising and dairying. Hardy grains, potatoes, and some fruits and vegetables also are grown.

Commercial fishing still prospers, and forestry is important too.

Manufacturing. Norwegian industry received a tremendous boost in the 1950s and 1960s from the rapid development of hydroelectric power.

In 1987 manufacturing contributed 15 percent of the national product. Among the newer industries made possible by cheap

26 Europe and Russia

VIKINGS
explored the North Atlantic and travelled as far as North America in ships like this one on display in Oslo.

> **colonized**
> *US*
>
> **colonised**
> *Brit.*

and abundant electricity are the electrometallurgical and electrochemical industries. Major manufactured products include machinery, ships, and land vehicles. Lumber and pulp and paper mills are also important, and fish processing plants produce some of Norway's major exports.

Trade. Norway's new status as a major oil supplier has improved its volume as well as its balance of trade considerably. Oil and gas account for over one-third of total exports.

Major imports are ships and boats, machinery, petroleum products, textiles, and foodstuffs. Metals and ores, pulp and paper, and fish and fish products are the leading nonoil exports. Sweden, Great Britain, Germany, the United States, and Denmark are Norway's major trading partners.

Government. Norway is a constitutional monarchy, with a king as head of state. Actual executive power is wielded by a prime minister and cabinet responsible to parliament.

MANY VILLAGES
in sparsely settled rural Norway rely heavily on fishing for their livelihood.

The parliament, called the Storting, is popularly elected every four years. It elects one-quarter of its 165 members to sit as an upper house, the Lagting. The remainder of the Storting is called the Odelsting. Most legislative actions are taken by the united Storting.

History. Archaeological evidence indicates that man lived in Norway as early as 8,000 years ago. Beginning about 7,000 years ago, a variety of wandering tribes from the north and south appeared in Scandinavia. Germanic tribes, the main forebears of the present Norwegian people, had established themselves in the land by about 500 B.C.

For the next 1,000 years, during the eras of the Roman Empire and the barbarian migrations, tribal groups in Norway shifted and resettled, competing for dominance over the region.

During the 800s A.D. the tribal communities were gradually united, and Harold Fairhair (Harald Haarfager) became Norway's first king. The united tribes began to expand their territory, and from the late 800s through the early 1000s, Norwegian Vikings explored and colonized the shores of Britain, Ireland, the Faroe Islands, Iceland, Greenland, and probably North America.

During several brief intervals in the late 900s and early 1000s, the country was under Danish rule, but Norwegian kings always regained control, and by the mid-1000s the monarchy was quite strong.

Early kingdom. Through the efforts of King Olaf Tryggvesson and King Olaf Haraldsson in the late 900s and early 1000s, Christianity was introduced into Norway. As the church gained influence, it challenged royal power and was supported by members of the landowning aristocracy, whose power was growing.

Civil wars filled the period between the mid-1100s and the mid-1200s, but the strength of the monarchy was maintained, and the 1200s marked the high point of Norwegian power and prosperity. Between 1217 and 1263, during the reign of King Haakon IV, Iceland and Greenland were added to the realm. Norwegian art and literature flourished, and King Magnus VI sponsored a codification of law for the entire country in the 1270s.

This era of greatness was short-lived, however. In the mid-1300s, the plague killed half of Norway's population and crippled the country. The merchants of the German Hanseatic League gained a firm grip on Norwegian economic life. Moreover, the Norwegian royal succession became entangled with that of Sweden and Denmark.

In 1380 King Olaf V, the last of Harold Fairhair's dynasty, became king of both Norway and Denmark. When he died in 1387, his mother, Queen Margaret of Denmark, combined the thrones of both kingdoms. In 1397 Sweden was added to form the Kalmar Union, which was completely dominated by Denmark.

Norway was the weakest member, and its territory, prestige, and autonomy declined steadily in the 1400s. The union was frequently torn by internal struggles, and in 1523 Sweden broke away.

Danish union. Norway remained linked with Denmark as part of a kingdom ruled and administered by Danes. With Denmark, Norway became Lutheran in 1536. Norway shared Danish wars, including a series of territorial and dynastic struggles with Sweden between the 1560s and the 1720s.

Between 1588 and 1648, the Norwegians did enjoy some economic benefits from Danish rule. King Christian IV reformed the administration of Norway and initiated the development of Norwegian resources. Absolutists who ruled Denmark-Norway after 1660 stimulated Norway's economy by expanding exports and founding new towns.

Modest but steady economic growth continued through the 1700s and helped to lay the basis for the development of a Norwegian national consciousness. In 1807 Denmark granted Norwegian requests for a degree of self-government. The French Revolution and the hardships endured during the Napoleonic wars stimulated Norwegian nationalism. In 1814 Sweden, which had opposed Napoleon and had won a victory over Denmark, forced Denmark to cede Norway. (Denmark had supported Napoleon.)

Swedish union. The Norwegians rose in protest and refused to recognize Swedish rule. They convened a national assembly, which adopted a liberal constitution in May 1814, and they elected the Danish prince Christian Frederick as their king.

The crown prince of Sweden invaded the country and succeeded in taking the Norwegian throne. Nevertheless, the Norwegians, by their resistance, secured a great deal of autonomy before they would accept union with Sweden. Norway was granted an elected Storting, and was proclaimed indivisible and independent; it was joined in union with the Swedish crown. The Storting ratified the union in 1815.

During the 1800s, Norway underwent a national renaissance. Scholarly and scientific activities widened, and arts and letters flourished. The economy of Norway-Sweden improved steadily during the 1800s.

MOST NORWEGIANS live in towns like Alesund along the southern and southwestern coast, where the warm North Atlantic Current of the Gulf Stream alleviates the winters.

As their strength increased, Norwegian liberal intellectuals grew restless under arbitrary kings. Sweden granted concessions, including a system of free education, complete religious freedom, and expansion of voting rights.

The reform movement accelerated, and in 1872 the first Norwegian trade union was formed. In the 1880s a parliamentary government was introduced, based on universal male suffrage. In the 1890s Norwegian demands for complete independence grew, led by Johan Sverdrup. The economies of both Norway and Sweden were booming, with Norway's merchant fleet serving as the basis of the prosperity.

Renewed independence. As Norway's international trade expanded, the Norwegian Storting requested permission to handle Norway's consular affairs under its own flag. When the Swedish king refused, the Norwegian Storting declared Norway independent in June, 1905. Norway elected the Danish prince Charles to be king as Haakon VII. Sweden accepted Norway's declaration of independence in October 1905.

Norway was well prepared for independence by its material progress, political activism, and social reforms of the late 1800s. Democratic reform continued in Norway after independence. The royal veto over the Storting was abolished, the vote was extended to women, and social welfare programs were initiated.

Norway remained neutral in World War I, but its vital merchant fleet was severely damaged. After the war, the nation suffered an economic depression that was intensified by the world economic depression of the 1930s.

Economic and social reforms initiated during the 1920s and 1930s included the formation of cooperative enterprises, the institution of national collective bargaining, and the expansion of social welfare legislation under the leadership of liberal, labor, and left-wing farmers' party governments. A Labor government elected in 1935 was successful in ending Norway's economic crisis by expanding the government's economic role.

In 1940 during World War II, Germany invaded Norway, and despite stiff Norwegian resistance, Nazi troops conquered and occupied the country. King Haakon rallied resistance to the Germans, and the Norwegian home front played a prominent part in Norway's liberation from the Germans in 1945.

Contemporary Norway. Norway participated actively in postwar international affairs. In 1945 it became a charter member of the United Nations and a Norwegian, Trygve Lie, became the first UN secretary general. Although its neighbors pressed for a Scandinavian defense union, Norway joined NATO in 1949. At the same time it encouraged the social, economic, and cultural unity of the Scandinavian nations. In 1952 Norway joined the Nordic Council, formed to encourage Scandinavian cooperation.

Having shared a common border with the Soviet Union, Norway had to be circumspect in its foreign policy during the era of the Cold War between the Soviet Union and the United States, but it remained anti-Communist in domestic politics and tended to be pro-Western in international affairs. In 1957 King Haakon died and was succeeded by his son, Olav V.

Since 1950 Norway has concentrated on expanding and modernizing its economy and developing its natural resources, particularly its waterpower. The growth of industry was not rapid enough to support Norway's broad social welfare programs, and in the early 1960s the economy began to falter. The Labor government, which is Marxist in theory but permissive toward the development of free enterprise, bore the brunt of popular dissatisfaction because of the many generous social welfare programs it had introduced.

Coalition governments have ruled since 1965, with the Labor and Conservative parties sharing most of the power.

In a national referendum in 1972, Norwegians rejected membership in the European Economic Community (EEC). Subsequently, in July 1973, a free-trade agreement for manufactured goods was negotiated with the EEC. In 1994 Norway rejected joining the EU (which superseded the EEC).

Poland

Official name: *Republic of Poland*
Area: *120,726 sq. mi., 312,680 sq. km.*
Type of government: *Democratic*
Population: *38,625,000*
Capital and largest city: *Warsaw (Pop., 1,610,000)*
Language: *Polish*
Literacy: *99%;* **Currency:** *Zloty*
Per capita GDP: *$9,500 (Rank: 51st)*

The land. The greatest part of Poland is level to rolling lowland, although there are local variations in relief.

Central Poland is a flat plain and the only noticeable relief features are deeply cut river valleys. The Vistula, Poland's largest and longest river, crosses the eastern part of this plain and flows north to the Baltic. The Oder flows north along the western border.

Southern Poland is mountainous. To the west lies the Sudeten range, to the east, the Carpathian Mountains. The two mountain systems are separated by the uppermost valley of the Oder River, which is known as the Moravian Gate.

Most of Poland has a climate characterized by wide yearly temperature variations. Winters are cold and snowy, and summers are warm and dry.

The people. Before World War II Poland was a state with substantial minorities—Byelorussians, Germans,

labor
US

labour
Brit.

Jews, and Ukrainians. After World War II and its turmoil it became largely homogeneous. The former religious and linguistic minorities were either exterminated during the wartime German occupation or forced to leave Poland after 1945. The Byelorussians and Ukrainians had been concentrated in the eastern regions annexed by the Soviet Union. The population is now nearly all Polish-speaking and Roman Catholic, though there are small Greek Orthodox and Protestant groups.

Warsaw is Poland's capital and largest city. Other major cities include Łódź (population, 787,000), which is primarily industrial, and Kraków (741,000), which was untouched by the war and is full of monuments to Poland's past. Gdańsk (Danzig) (455,000), at the mouth of the Vistula, on the Baltic, is Poland's first port for freight traffic.

Economy.   After World War II, the Polish economy grew slowly, mostly owing to poor decisions and management by the central government. In 1989, as the communist regime was being swept away, inflation rose to 640 percent and shortages of food and other consumer goods grew. The new government initiated a "shock therapy" program of austerity measures as it moved toward establishing a market economy and attempting to become competitive in the world economy.

Natural resources.   Coal is Poland's most valuable mineral resource and its major source of energy. Polish coal deposits, located largely in Upper and Lower Silesia, the middle and upper valley of the Oder River, are extensive. Poland is one of the world's largest coal producers. Poland also has substantial deposits of copper, zinc, lead, and sulfur.

Agriculture.   Agriculture is very important to the Polish economy, producing a large share of exports and employing nearly 30 percent of the work force. Polish agriculture differed fundamentally from that in most other communist-controlled countries, for little land is collectivized. Nearly nine-tenths of Poland's agricultural land is privately

center
US

centre
Brit.

A FARMER HARVESTS
a crop of potatoes on a farm near Kraków, Poland.

cultivated. Farms are generally small, averaging between 8 and 30 acres. Animal power is still widely used in farming, although agricultural machinery is beginning to be produced in increasing quantities.

The government has encouraged the raising of livestock, with an emphasis on pigs and sheep. Poland generally produces enough meat to fill domestic needs, and meat and meat products have been important exports.

Rye is the principal crop, but large quantities of wheat, barley, and oats also are grown, along with potatoes for food, fodder, and alcohol.

Industry.   Industry contributes slightly less than half of the gross domestic product. Poland's largest industrial center is located in Upper Silesia, in the southwestern part of the country, near the country's major coal deposits. Iron and steel, heavy machinery, chemicals, shipbuilding, textiles, and processed foods are the main products of Polish industry.

Trade.   Poland's exports include coal, pork products, and ships. Principal imports are petroleum, cotton, iron ore,

COAL IS POLAND'S most valuable mineral resource and its major source of energy, providing fuel for power stations.

wheat, and metalworking machinery.

Government.   According to the agreement worked out between the Communist Party and the trade union Solidarity in 1989, Poland has a bicameral legislature. The 100-member upper house, the Senate, is popularly elected from an open ballot. The 460-member lower house, the Sejm, initially had 65 percent of its seats reserved for the Communist Party.

Executive authority is held by a prime minister and cabinet responsible to the Sejm. The chief of state is a president, elected by popular vote for four years, who has the power to dissolve parliament and call new elections. Both the president and the Senate can veto legislation passed by the Sejm.

History.   The Poles were originally one of several Slavic tribes that settled between the Oder and Vistula rivers before the 700s. During the 900s they joined with neighboring peoples to fight off a series of invasions by Germanic tribes; they became unified under the Piast dynasty.

In 966 one of the early Piast rulers, Prince Mieszko, accepted Christianity. Mieszko's successors expanded Polish domains, especially to the east. In 1138, with the death of Boleslav III, Poland entered a period of political disintegration that was worsened by attacks from the Mongols.

Under Casimir the Great (ruled 1333–1370), however, Poland revived. Casimir strengthened the central government, consolidated Polish territory, developed agriculture, and constructed roads and bridges. In 1364 he founded the University of Kraków, one of the oldest institutions of higher learning in eastern Europe.

On the death of Casimir in 1370, the Piast dynasty died out and the crown passed to Louis I of Hungary, Casimir's nephew. Louis was succeeded by his daughter Jadwiga, who in 1386 married Ladislas Jagello of Lithuania. Under the Jagellons, cultural activity reached a peak and Poland greatly extended its territory, which by the mid-1500s stretched from the Baltic to the Black Sea.

The Jagellon dynasty ended in 1572 with the death of Sigismund Augustus, and for 200 years the succession to the Polish throne was contested by the various ruling houses of Europe. The succession was further complicated by the fact that the king was elected by the Polish parliament, which was composed of the nobility.

Any noble could block any measure by his one vote. This practice, known as the *liberum veto,* not only made the election of a new monarch extraordinarily difficult, but almost paralyzed the central government.

Partition. In 1764 a pro-Russian Polish nobleman, Stanislas Poniatowski, was made king through pressure exerted by Russia. This interference by Russia was resented by the Polish nobles, who rebelled in 1768. Russian troops crushed the rebellion, but Prussia and Austria feared that Russia would absorb Poland to their disadvantage. As a result, in 1772, the three countries agreed to partition Poland. The result was that Russia, Prussia, and Austria annexed territories adjoining them, and Poland lost approximately one-third of its land.

Alarmed, the Poles sought to strengthen their government and institute various reforms. Russia, however, invaded Poland again in 1793 and the country was once more partitioned, with Russia and Prussia each annexing more land. A third partition by Russia, Prussia, and Austria took place in 1795, and Poland was wiped off the map.

In 1807 Napoleon I of France created the Grand Duchy of Warsaw out of the Polish territories that had been annexed by Prussia. Although nominally independent, the Grand Duchy was really a puppet state. After Napoleon's defeat, the Congress of Vienna, held in 1814–1815, divided the Grand Duchy among Russia, Prussia, and Austria. Thousands of Polish intellectuals left the country for other nations in western Europe, where they kept the spirit of Polish nationalism alive.

Life for Poles in the three territories varied. In Russian Poland, despite some persecution, Poles took part in Russian national life. In Austrian Poland, the Poles gained important political privileges and frequently held posts in the Austrian government service. In Prussian Poland, the Poles were politically oppressed but became strong economically.

Throughout the 1800s, however, all Poles sought to rid themselves of foreign rule. Uprisings in Russian Poland took place in 1830 and 1863 but were brutally crushed.

Independence. At the turn of the century the movement for independence gained momentum. A few years before the outbreak of World War I, Jozef Pilsudski, a nationalist leader, secretly trained an army to fight for a reconstituted Polish nation. During World War I, exiled Polish leaders formed the Polish

National Committee in Paris, which was recognized by the Allies as the spokesman for Poland. When U.S. President Woodrow Wilson enunciated his Fourteen Points in 1918, he called for the establishment of an independent Polish nation.

The Central Powers were defeated in 1918, and Pilsudski established an independent Polish government in Warsaw. Under the terms of the Treaty of Versailles in 1919, Poland regained most of Polish territory from Prussia and much of Upper Silesia. The region around the Lithuanian city of Vilna, which both countries claimed, was granted to Lithuania in 1920 but seized by Poland in 1922.

Poland gained access to the sea through the Polish Corridor, a narrow strip of land that cut through Germany to the port of Danzig, which was made a free city under the supervision of the League of Nations. Poland's claim to territories in the east, however, soon resulted in a clash with the Soviet Union.

The Allies had suggested a border between Poland and the Soviet Union based on ethnic lines, with the non-Polish territories in the east going to the Soviet Union. This suggested border, known as the Curzon Line, was rejected by the Poles, and in 1920 fighting broke out between Poland and the Soviet Union. A peace treaty signed at Riga in 1921 made Poland's frontier much the same as it had been before the partition in 1795.

Interwar era. In the same year Poland adopted a democratic constitution that provided for a parliamentary form of government. The new republic, lacking a strong executive and subject to the conflicting demands of many different political parties, was unable to deal effectively with the myriad problems caused by bringing together territories that had been parts of other states for more than 100 years and with large minorities of other nationalities, including Ukrainians, Byelorussians, and Germans.

In 1926 Józef Piłsudski headed a military coup that overthrew the existing government and established himself as dictator. On his death in 1935, a group of army colonels continued the dictatorship.

World War II. The rise to power of Adolf Hitler in Germany, the disintegration of the League of Nations, and the collapse of the various efforts within Europe to establish regional security arrangements led, on September 1, 1939, to World War II. The war began with a German invasion of Poland from the west, and two weeks later the Soviet Union invaded from the east. The Poles fought bravely, but were quickly overwhelmed. A government in exile was established in London, and Polish units fought with the Allies throughout the war. During the war the large Jewish minority in Poland was virtually exterminated by the Nazis.

In April 1943, the Soviet government broke relations with the Polish government in London, and in July 1944, it created the Polish Committee of

National Liberation on conquered Polish territory. In January 1945, the Soviet Union reorganized the committee as the government of Poland.

British and U.S. efforts to ensure the active participation of democratic groups in this government and to guarantee free elections in Poland were unsuccessful, and after controlled elections in January, 1947, a communist government was firmly in power.

Communist rule. The history of Poland under communism followed that of the other states of Eastern Europe, with the destruction of rival political groups, the purge of the Communist Party itself, rapid industrialization, forced collectivization of agriculture, a mass indoctrination effort, and complete control of the army and internal security police by the Soviet Union.

This pattern was broken in the summer of 1956, when riots for "bread and freedom" in Poznań sparked a successful revolt against Soviet rule. Wladysaw Gomułka became the new first secretary of the Polish Communist Party. He led Poland into an era of distinctly Polish-style socialism.

Collectivization was reduced, industry was somewhat decentralized, and consumer production was increased. But as the people were given more free-

A MONUMENT commemorates the ghetto where 500,000 Jews were confined during the second world war. As a result of hunger, disease, and execution by the Germans, only 60,000 remained at the end of the war.

POSTWAR BUILDINGS and the underground transportation system in Warsaw are modern contrasts to the historic landmarks of the city.

dom, and as relations with the West improved, there were increased demands for a better standard of living and working conditions. Gomułka, faced with a cultural revolution, resorted to repression.

In 1970 workers' strikes forced Gomułka's resignation in favor of Edward Gierek. As the head of a large and inefficient bureaucracy, Gierek had little success in appeasing the populace. In 1976 workers led a new series of strikes in response to new price rises. Incensed by constitutional amendments that favored the Soviet position in Poland, they began a human rights and working peoples' movement.

The government made mild concessions to the strikers, but a new massive series of strikes paralyzed the national economy in 1980. Party leadership changed hands again. The workers were given the right to strike, and the promise of gradual wage increases. The independent labor organization, Solidarity, was officially recognized.

In 1981, as the economic and political situation worsened and the danger of Soviet intervention loomed, the government declared martial law and outlawed Solidarity. In 1989 Solidarity was legalized, and in parliamentary elections it became the dominant force in the government. In 1990 the Communist Party disbanded and the Solidarity leader was elected president. The new government instituted a radical economic program that stimulated growth but also raised unemployment and drastically cut social programs. In elections in 1993 a coalition of two socialist parties gained a majority of seats in parliament and Waldemar Pawlak, head of the Polish Peasants Party, became prime minister. Poland joined the EU in 2004.

labor
US

labour
Brit.

meters
US

metres
Brit.

fibers
US

fibres
Brit.

Portugal

Official name: *Portuguese Republic*
Area: *35,552 sq. mi., 92,080 sq. km.*
Type of government: *Republic*
Population: *10,084,000*
Capital and largest city: *Lisbon*
    (Pop., 565,000)
Language: *Portuguese*
Literacy: *87%*
Currency: *Euro*
Per capita GDP: *$18,000*
    (Rank: 33rd)

The land.   Portugal has three major geographic regions. In the northeast the western fringe of the high tablelands of central Spain produces a fairly rugged terrain. Narrow mountain ranges rise to elevations of more than 3,000 feet (915 meters) above sea level and extend almost to the Atlantic. In the west is a broad coastal plain that widens toward the south. The southeast is covered by low, rolling hills.

Portugal's principal rivers are the

Douro in the north; the Tagus, which divides the country almost equally into northern and southern regions; and the Guadiana in the southeast. The wide, protected mouth of the Tagus gives the city of Lisbon one of the world's finest natural harbors.

Portugal has a temperate maritime climate. Winters are generally mild, except in the highland areas where they are cold and snowy. Summers are warm in the north and hot in the south. North of the Tagus rainfall averages nearly 30 inches (76 centimeters) annually, but it is less than 20 inches (51 centimeters) along the southern coast.

The Madeira islands and the Azores, lying respectively, about 1,000 and 750 miles (1,600 and 1,200 kilometers) to the southeast in the Atlantic Ocean, are integral parts of Portugal.

The people.   Portugal has no significant minority groups. Portuguese is the universal language, and the majority of the people are Roman Catholic.

The population is concentrated in the north along the coast from the region of Setúbal to the Spanish border, and is especially dense in the lower Tagus and in the lower and middle Douro River valleys. The country is sparsely settled south of the Tagus and along the entire eastern border.

Portugal's population is nearly two-thirds rural. Lisbon and Porto (population, 263,000) are the largest cities.

Economy.   Portugal is still one of Europe's poorest countries. As industry has steadily increased, however, the gross national product and its per capita value have risen significantly.

One of Portugal's main economic problems is its lack of energy and mineral resources. Wolfram, from which tungsten is produced, is the most important mineral mined. Hydroelectric

power has increased recently, but as industry becomes more important, Portugal becomes more dependent on oil, all of which is imported.

Portugal is one-third forested, and forest products (cork, turpentine, rosin, and timber) are major export items. Fishing, particularly for tuna and sardines, is an important and prosperous economic activity.

Portugal is traditionally an agricultural country, but its labor force today is slightly more dependent on manufacturing jobs, employing 35 percent of the labor force, than agricultural ones, employing 22 percent of the labor force. Industry and agriculture are both hindered by a poor, although improving, transportation system.

Portugal's major agricultural product is wine; the country is known both for its port and its Madeira. Other important crops include wheat, corn, potatoes, and tomatoes.

Portugal's small but expanding industrial sector produces canned seafood, textiles, ceramics, electronic equipment, steel, wood pulp and paper, and petrochemical products. The expanding ship repair and shipbuilding facilities promise to add significantly to the economy.

Trade.   Portugal's major exports include clothing, textiles, wine, cork, pulpwood, and processed foods. Principal imports are manufactured goods, machinery, transportation equipment, coal, petroleum, wheat, sugar, cotton, and other raw fibers. The country's chief trading partners are the countries of Western Europe.

Government.   Portugal is a republic with a president as head of state who is directly elected to a 5-year term. Executive authority is held by a prime minister and Council of Ministers appointed by the president. These officials are responsible to the unicameral, 230-member Assembly of the Republic. Members are popularly elected to 4-year terms. There is also a Council of State, a body acting as consultant to the president.

History.   The history of Portugal is inseparable from that of Spain until the 1000s. In 1055 Ferdinand I of León and Castile began to reconquer from the Muslims, or Moors, the northern part of present-day Portugal and organize it as a country. In 1094 Ferdinand granted the country of Portugal to Henry of Burgundy, who had distinguished himself in the campaign against the Muslims.

Afonso Henriques of the Burgundian dynasty became count in 1128 and declared Portugal independent of Castile. In 1143, in the Treaty of Zamora, Castile formally recognized Portuguese independence, and Afonso Henriques was proclaimed king.

Afonso continued to push the Muslims southward, and in 1147 he captured Lisbon and established a frontier on the Tagus River. Afonso's immediate successors, Sancho I, Afonso II, and Sancho II, extended Portugal to its present boundaries, which were attained in 1249.

ROMAN RUINS at Conimbrige near present-day Coimbra in Portugal

LISBON, THE CAPITAL and largest city of Portugal, is home to about 20 percent of the country's population.

Avís dynasty. Afonso's direct descendants reigned until 1385, when John I of Avís seized the throne and successfully defended Portugal against Castilian invasion. During the 1400s the Portuguese kingdom consolidated its power and began to expand overseas.

Under the direction of Prince Henry the Navigator (1394–1460), the third son of King John I, Portugal discovered and colonized the Madeira Islands, the Azores, and the Cape Verde Islands, and explored far down the west coast of Africa.

John II (ruled 1481–1495) further advanced Portuguese exploration, and in 1488 Bartholomew Dias reached the Cape of Good Hope. During the reign of Manuel I (1495–1521), the Portuguese sailed to India, discovered Brazil, and began to establish a vast empire through the acquisition of territories in the East Indies and Southeast Asia.

During the 1500s Eastern trade brought great profits for a time, but holding such extensive territories proved difficult and eventually the empire proved a disastrous drain. Reckless spending, persecution of the Jews, who were prominent in banking and finance, and the introduction of the Inquisition further weakened the small kingdom.

Bragança dynasty. In 1580 the Portuguese throne fell vacant and was seized by Philip II of Spain. Philip and his son and grandson ruled for 60 years, during which time Portugal was little more than a conquered province. The kingdom regained its independence in 1640, when the Portuguese revolted and elected John of Bragança to the throne, but by that time most of Portugal's eastern empire had been lost to the Dutch and the English.

The 1700s brought a revived prosperity largely owed to the trade and newly discovered wealth of Brazil. In the mid-1700s the country was ruled by the Marquis of Pombal, a powerful minister of Joseph Emanuel (ruled 1750–1777).

Although he was often seen as ruthless, Pombal sought to strengthen the monarchy, develop trade and agriculture, and reorganize the nation's army and navy. He also attempted to break the power of the church and the nobility in order to weaken existing class differences. The Braganças proved unable to cope with the international problems resulting from the French Revolution of 1789, and in 1807 the country was itself conquered by Napoleon I of France.

The Braganças fled to Brazil and did not return until 1822, seven years after Napoleon's final defeat at the Battle of Waterloo. In the same year Brazil declared its independence and Portugal was beset by a series of political and constitutional struggles that lasted until the mid-1800s.

The reigns of Peter V (1853–1861) and Louis I (1861–1889) brought some measure of political calm. Portugal attempted to balance the budget and reduce poverty, but little progress was made and discontent with the monarchy grew.

The reign of Carlos I (1889–1908) brought no improvement. The king was financially extravagant and licentious. Popular discontent increased and Carlos was assassinated in 1908. His son Manuel II was also financially irresponsible, and following an insurrection in Lisbon in 1910, he was forced to flee the country. Portuguese leaders immediately proclaimed a republic but political conditions remained extremely chaotic and a total of 18 revolutions took place during the next 16 years.

Modern Portugal. During World War I Portugal fought on the side of the Allies, but the government was continually threatened by pro-German factions that attempted to seize power.

In 1926 a junta of military officers, headed by General António Oscar de Fragoso Carmona, seized power. In 1928, unable to handle economic problems, the generals appointed a professor of economics, António de Oliveira Salazar, finance minister. In 1932 Salazar became premier, or prime minister, and soon established a long-lasting dictatorship. Although he did not assume the presidency, he arranged for the successive election of figureheads while firmly holding power himself.

colonized
US

colonised
Brit.

THE MONUMENT to the Discoverers celebrates Portugal's explorations, which led to the establishment of a vast empire in parts of Africa, Asia, and South America.

Portugal remained neutral in World War II but provided Britain with raw materials from its African possessions and the right to establish a military base in the Azores.

Salazar retired in 1968. A military coup in 1974 was followed by elections in 1975, in which the Socialist Party won the most seats but failed to win a majority. Between 1974 and 1987 Portugal had 17 unstable governments. In 1987 the right-of-center Social Democrats won an absolute majority in the assembly and became the dominant party in Portugal.

Portugal joined the European Community (EC) (later the European Union) in 1986. A program of austerity and privatization of state-controlled industry and business, coupled with development funds from the EC and steady increases in foreign investment, helped to revitalize Portugal's economy.

center
US

centre
Brit.

meters
US

metres
Brit.

THE CASTLE OF VLAD TEPES, or Vlad the Impaler, stands in Romania south of Transylvania. He was the inspiration for the story of *Dracula*.

Romania

Official name: *Romania*
Area: *91,675 sq. mi.,*
237,500 sq. km.
Type of government: *Republic*
Population: *22,318,000*
Capital and largest city: *Bucharest*
(Pop., 2,009,000)
Languages: *Romanian (official),*
Hungarian, German
Literacy: *97%;* **Currency:** *Leu*
Per capita GDP: *$6,800*
(Rank: 72nd)

The land. The land surface of Romania is dominated by the great arc-shaped mountain system formed by the Carpathians and the Transylvanian Alps. The Carpathians run from the northwest to the southeast, where they meet the Transylvanian Alps. The Transylvanian Alps run across the country from the southeast to the southwest, ending at the Danube River.

West and north of these mountains lies Transylvania. This triangular plateau is drained by the Mures and Somes rivers, which flow northeast toward Hungary. The Transylvanian plateau is

separated from the Hungarian plain by the low Bihor Mountains. Beyond the Bihor, Romania controls a long, narrow strip of the Hungarian plain.

The region between the Carpathians and the Prut River, part of the border with Ukraine, is known as Moldavia. The area that lies between the Danube and the Transylvanian Alps is Walachia. Between the Danube and the Black Sea lies the Romanian portion of the Dobruja Plateau.

The Danube is Romania's largest river, but for much of its course it forms the border with Bulgaria and Serbia and Montenegro. The Olt and Siret, which cross the lowlands of Walachia and Moldavia, are the Danube's most important tributaries.

Most of Romania has a continental climate with hot, dry summers and cold, windy, snowy winters.

The people. Romanians represent the great majority of the total population. There are significant minorities of Hungarians and Germans in the country. Other small minority groups include Ukrainians, Gypsies, Russians, Serbs, and Croats. The minorities are concentrated in western Romania.

Romanians, unlike their neighbors, are descended from Romans, Greeks, and Celts. The Romanian language, which is derived from Latin, belongs to the Romance group. Its vocabulary, however, contains substantial borrowings from the Slavic languages.

The population is divided almost equally between rural and urban areas.

Bucharest, the capital, is also the political, artistic, and intellectual center. It is a sprawling metropolis that contains few relics of its long history. Other important cities include Constanța (population, 337,000) on the Black Sea; Timișoara (330,000) in the west; and Cluj-Napoca (329,000) and Brașov (310,000) in Transylvania.

Economy. Before World War II, Romania was largely an agricultural nation, but under the communist regime great emphasis has been placed on industrial development. After many years of high

growth, the economy slumped in the 1980s. Industrial and agricultural production fell, and per capita income and the living standard declined drastically. Efforts to move toward a market economy have been stalled since 1990, and the government has sought to stem rising inflation and declining productivity.

Natural resources. Oil is Romania's most important resource, with about 10.5 million metric tons produced annually. The principal oil fields are located along the southern and eastern flanks of the main mountain system, in Walachia and Moldavia.

Romania also has major deposits of natural gas near its oil fields and in Transylvania. The production of natural gas has been growing rapidly and its current annual production rate is about 27 billion cubic meters, making Romania one of the world's leading producers.

Coal is increasing rapidly in importance. It now supplies about 50 percent of the nation's energy and is expected to supply two-thirds by the 1990s.

Romania also mines iron, manganese, bauxite, gold, silver, and uranium, but is dependent on imported iron ore and coal.

Agriculture. About 28 percent of the workforce is employed in agriculture. While production has increased in recent years, it has been at a much slower rate than that of industrial production. Cereals, especially corn and wheat, are the country's major crops. Potatoes and sugar beets also are grown.

Industry. Although Romanian industrialization has been rapid, it has been directed toward the development of heavy industry rather than the production of consumer goods. In 1985 Romania produced almost 13 million metric tons of steel, almost 35 times as much as in 1948.

Substantial progress also has been made in the production of iron, machinery, and chemicals, as well as in nonferrous metallurgy. Textiles and food processing are the most important light industries.

Trade. The country's relatively small volume of trade is slowly increasing. During the 1980s, the generally favorable

balance of trade was due mainly to severe restrictions on imports. Romania's chief exports include electric motors, petroleum products, food products, factory equipment, wood products, ball bearings, and transformers. Major imports include automobiles, iron ore, finished rolled metal, coking coal and industrial coke, and industrial equipment.

Important trading partners are Egypt, Germany, the Commonwealth of Independent States, and Italy.

Government. Romania is a republic. Following the overthrow of the communist regime in 1989, a new constitution was approved by an elected Constituent Assembly in November 1991, and ratified in a national referendum the following month. The constitution provides for a bicameral legislature consisting of a 140-seat Senate and a 345-seat Chamber of Deputies, whose members are chosen by direct election on the basis of proportional representation.

Executive power is held by a president, who is directly elected and may serve a maximum of two terms. The president appoints the prime minister, who heads a Council of Ministers.

History. During the 300s B.C., what is now Romania was settled by the Dacians, a people related to the Thracians in Greece. In about 60 B.C., the Dacians were united by Burebistas. The Roman emperor Trajan conquered the Dacian kingdom in 105–106 A.D., and in 107 made it a Roman province. Roman rule last until 271, when the emperor Aurelian, who was faced with the threat of barbarian invasions and various problems within the empire, withdrew Roman troops together with a substantial part of the population.

For the following 700 years, Romania was swept by successive waves of barbarian invaders, including the Visigoths, Huns, Lombards, Avars, Slavs, and Magyars. These invasions all but obliterated the original Dacian population, even though their language survived.

During the 1200s two chief principalities, Moldavia and Walachia, emerged. The principalities were prevented from gaining power, however, by the strength of their neighbors, Poland, Hungary, and the Ottoman Empire. By the 1500s, the Moldavian and Walachian princes were reduced to paying heavy tribute to the Ottoman Turks.

For a brief period duing the late 1500s, Michael the Brave of Walachia succeeded in defeating the Turks and uniting the two principalities. But on his death in 1601 the Turks regained control of the area. Early in the 1700s, Moldavia and Walachia allied themselves with Peter the Great of Russia in his campaign against the Turks, but the joint effort failed.

Phanariot rule. The Turks appointed Phanariots, wealthy Byzantine Greeks, to the thrones of Moldavia and Walachia. The Ottoman sultan usually sold the throne to the highest bidder, and the Phanariot princes sought to extort enough money from the populace

to show a profit over their original investment. The Phanariot period was one of misery for the Romanians.

From 1802 to 1812, as the result of wars between the Russians and Turks, the principalities were occupied by the Russians. The Peace of Bucharest in 1812 restored Ottoman control, but the Moldavian province of Bessarabia remained in Russian hands.

In 1821 revolutions against the Phanariots took place in Moldavia and Walachia. Although the revolts failed, the Turks replaced the Greeks with native princes. In 1829, as a result of the Russo-Turkish War of 1828–1829, the Russians once again were able to occupy the principalities.

Autonomy. Russia withdrew in 1834, and Moldavia and Walachia were granted autonomy under Ottoman suzerainty. During the following 14 years, the principalities made progress in education, agriculture, and trade.

In 1848 Romanian intellectuals staged revolutions in Moldavia and Walachia to secure social and political reforms. The revolt in Moldavia was quickly put down, but in Walachia the rebels established a republic. The Russians and Turks both intervened to suppress the republican government, and the princes were restored under an arrangement whereby they were elected to seven-year terms of office.

As a result of the Crimean War (1854–1856), in which the Russians were soundly defeated by the British, French, Sardinians, and Turks, it was decided that a commission would determine the future status of the principalities. Elections were held in 1857, and Moldavia and Walachia voted for union under one prince. But the Convention of Paris, held in 1858, decided that the principalities were to have a central control commission but separate legislatures and separate princes. Both Moldavia and Walachia then elected the same prince, Alexander Cuza.

In 1861 the principalities succeeded in having their union recognized by the Turks and the European powers, and in 1862 they established a single legislature and cabinet. Cuza, however, proved to be unpopular and in 1866 he was forced to abdicate.

Independence. Cuza was replaced by Charles of Hohenzollern-Sigmaringen, who reigned as Carol I. After the Russo-Turkish War of 1877–1878, in which Romania sided with Russia, the Turks were forced to recognize Romanian independence, which was accepted internationally by the Treaty of Berlin in 1878. In 1881 Carol became Romania's first king.

In the years following independence, Romania was governed by a conservative and authoritarian land-owning class that allied the country and its economic and political development with Germany and Austria-Hungary. Nonetheless, the desire to gain Transylvania and Bukovina from Austria-Hungary led Romania to enter World War I on the side of the Allies in 1916.

TRADITIONAL COSTUMES are still worn in Romania for celebrations and festivals.

Romania emerged from the war having gained not only those two territories but also Bessarabia from the Soviet Union and eastern Banat from Austria-Hungary, which had a large Magyar (Hungarian) population.

In the postwar period, the government remained conservative and authoritarian. In the 1930s the world economic depression brought financial hardship to the Romanians, especially to the peasantry. Dissatisfaction was expressed politically and the Romanian Communist Party and the strongly pro-German fascist Iron Guard grew in strength.

Dictatorship. In 1938 several factors, including a mounting agricultural crisis and a need to control the power of the Iron Guard in the face of increasing pressure from Nazi Germany, led Carol II to establish a royal dictatorship. Nonetheless, in 1940 Germany and Italy forced Carol to cede Transylvania to Hungary and southern Dobruja to Bulgaria in an agreement known as the Vienna Award.

ROMANIA'S MONASTERIES, many famous for painted walls, survived the communist years by avoiding political activities.

The Romanian people were outraged and the king was forced to abdicate.

Carol was succeeded by his son Michael, and the government was taken over by General Ion Antonescu, the former prime minister under Carol, who had strong Iron Guard leanings and who maintained a complete dictatorship.

During World War II Romania was occupied by the Germans and participated in Germany's campaign against the Soviet Union. In August 1944 King Michael overthrew Antonescu's dictatorship and entered the war on the side of the Allies. Romania restored Bessarabia and Bukovina to the Soviet Union, which in turn nullified the Vienna Award.

Communist rule. Following World War II, despite the presence of an Allied Control Council in the country, the Soviet Union managed to take control of Romania. King Michael abdicated in December 1947, and Romania was proclaimed a people's republic. By 1952 nationalist communist leaders had been replaced by pro-Soviet Romanian communists, who gave the nation a Soviet-style constitution. Agricultural collectivization and forced industrialization followed.

In the mid-1960s Romania began to act independently of Soviet control in both domestic and international concerns. It formally declared its independence in 1964, and in 1965 it adopted a new constitution that made it a socialist republic. It followed a policy of neutrality between the Soviet Union and China. It maintained close economic ties with Comecon nations and also with non-communist nations.

In 1965 Nicolae Ceausescu became first secretary of the Communist Party. He strengthened his repressive rule by appointing many of his friends and family members to a number of important government posts. In the 1980s Ceausescu refused to follow the Soviet lead in economic and political reform.

Ceausescu resigned in 1989 and was executed. Democratic elections were held in May 1990 and a multiparty government was formed. In 1992 Ion Iliescu, a former communist, was elected president in a free and fair election. He was returned to power again in 2000. Romania joined NATO in 2004.

Russia

Official name: *Russian Federation*
Area: *6,591,027 sq. mi.,*
17,075,200 sq. km.
Type of government: *Federation*
Population: *144,979,000*
Capital and largest city: *Moscow*
(Pop., 8,297,000)
Language: *Russian*
Literacy: *98%;* **Currency:** *Ruble*
Per capita GDP: *$8,800*
(Rank: 58th)

The land. The Russian Federation, formerly the largest republic of the Soviet Union, is the world's largest sovereign power in territory. Russia extends over two continents, occupying much of eastern Europe and all of northern Asia. A natural boundary between the European and Asian parts of the country is formed by the Ural Mountains, the Ural River, and the Caspian Sea.

Physical regions. Russia may be divided into four major land regions. The European-West Siberian plain is the great plain that extends from the European border into Siberia, broken only by the Ural Mountains. The great majority of the Russian people live within the confines of this plain. It stretches northward all the way to the Arctic Ocean and eastward to the Yenisey River.

Beginning at the Yenisey, the Central Siberian Plateau extends to the Lena River. Covered almost entirely by forest, it is sparsely settled. Beyond the Lena, stretching eastward to the Pacific Ocean and the Bering Strait, is eastern Siberia. Vast mountain chains divide this desolate area into subregions, most of which are drained by rivers that flow into the Arctic Ocean. The far eastern region is Russia's link with China, Japan, and the Pacific Ocean.

Mountain systems. The mountain ranges of Russia vary greatly in size, elevation, and characteristics. The Ural Mountains are for the most part a low, worn-down range, highly mineralized, and one of the principal centers of Russian mining and manufacturing.

In the southwest the eastern part of the Caucasus Mountains runs some 700 miles (1,125 kilometers) from the Black Sea to the Caspian Sea. The mountains form the traditional boundary between European Russia and the countries of the Near East.

The Sayan Mountains lie in southern Siberia and overlook the deepest lake in the world, Lake Baykal. Separat-

centers
US

centres
Brit.

kilometers
US

kilometres
Brit.

ing eastern Siberia from eastern Mongolia and Manchuria are the Yablonovy and Stanovoy ranges. In the northeast is a mountainous area that is composed of the Verkhoyansk, Cherskiy, and Kolyma ranges.

Vegetation zones. The combined result of the influences of surface features, climate, and soils on the land of Russia is the existence of several different vegetation zones that extend in an east-west direction across Russian territory.

In the far north, along the shores of the Arctic Ocean, on the Arctic islands, and inland for a distance varying from 100 to 400 miles (160 to 650 kilometers), is the tundra zone. This is an arctic desert, where low year-round temperatures inhibit the growth and variety of vegetation. During the greater part of the year it is an empty, storm-swept place, covered with snow and ice.

South of the tundra and stretching across the entire width of Russia is the northern forest zone, or taiga. The taiga is composed mostly of coniferous evergreen trees—pine, fir, and larch—interspersed with clumps of birches.

South of the taiga, in the European part of Russia, is a triangle-shaped mixed forest zone with its points located near the cities of St. Petersburg in the northwest, Bryansk in the southwest, and Perm in the Urals.

Much of the original mixed forest has long since been cut, and substantial areas are under the plow. Moscow and St. Petersburg, the two largest Russian cities, are located within this zone, as are some of the leading Russian industrial areas and the majority of the Russian population.

South of the mixed forest is the grassland zone, or steppe. This area is covered with black earth, one of the most fertile soils on our planet. Virtually all of the steppe in the European part of Russia and in western Siberia is now under cultivation.

Climate. With the exception of a few coastal areas on the Black and Caspian seas, the greatest part of Russia has a continental climate, characterized by extremes of temperature and rainfall.

Winter temperatures throughout most of Russia are well below freezing, but temperatures are lowest in the northeast. Summers, on the other hand, are likely to be warm, except in the far north regions.

A large percent of the area of Russia is covered by permafrost, or permanently frozen soil that varies in depth from one foot to several hundred feet and thaws only a few inches during the summer months. Agriculture, as well as road and railroad building, can be carried out only with extreme difficulty and at great expense on this permanently frozen ground.

The people. Although Russia is a multiethnic state, the vast majority of the population is Russian. The Russian people are part of the East Slavic group of nationalities, which also includes Ukrainians and Belorussians (White

Russians). Most Russians either have no religious affiliation or belong to the Russian Orthodox Church. A small number are Roman Catholic, Protestant, Jewish, or Muslim.

Ethnic groups. Russia's Jewish minority has decreased sharply since the early part of the 20th century, primarily owing to the persecution of Jews in German-occupied parts of the Soviet Union during World War II and the looser emigration policies established in the 1980s. Today's Jewish minority includes those Jews living in the Jewish Autonomous Religion in the far eastern part of the country.

Ethnic Germans live on the Volga River, where their ancestors settled in the 18th century, while people who speak Uralic languages, such as Estonian and Finnish, are found in the northwest part of the country. Turkic-speaking peoples (including Tatars, Yakuts, and Bashkirs) also form a small segment of the population, as do the peoples of the eastern Caucasus Mountains, where groups such as the Circassians and Abkhaz live. Many Turkic and Caucasoid people are Muslims belonging to the Sunni sect. In the far east, Koreans and Buryats, related to the Mongols of neighboring Mongolia, live in southern Siberia. Buddhism is the predominant religion of these people.

Distribution. Owing to climate and geography, the distribution of population is very uneven in Russia. The majority of the people live within the European part of the country, but there has been a marked increase in the population east of the Urals and the Caspian Sea. During and immediately after World War II, there was considerable migration to Siberia and the far eastern regions.

There has also been a substantial migration from the countryside to the cities. In 1940, 67 percent of the population was rural. In 1990 only 34 percent of the people lived in nonurban areas, although this is still a considerably larger proportion than is found in most of Western Europe and North America. Moscow, St. Petersburg (formerly Leningrad, population, 4,678,000), and Nizhniy Novgorod (formerly Gorky, 1,358,000) are among the country's largest cities.

Economy. In the 50 years following the Russian Revolution, the Soviet Union made significant economic progress, changing from an agricultural to an industrial nation with a gross output second only to that of the United States. Soviet gains, however, were made by concentrating on heavy industry at the expense of consumer goods, services, and agriculture.

In the 1960s and 1970s, the rate of economic growth decreased considerably. In spite of reforms designed to decentralize industrial management and to increase productivity, the economy still remained sluggish and the basic problems continued. Soviet technology lagged behind that of the West, the cen-

tral system of planning and management was cumbersome, and agriculture was relatively unproductive.

Pursuing a policy of *perestroika* (reconstruction), Soviet leader Mikhail Gorbachev encouraged the introduction of economic reform when he assumed office in 1985, but there was little improvement in the economy. A combination of political and economic conditions ultimately led to the disintegration of the Soviet Union.

Present-day Russia. The economy that Russia inherited was the product of nearly 75 years of Soviet central planning. In an effort to jolt the economy,

THE ONION DOMES of St. Basil's Cathedral in Moscow reflect the Byzantine heritage of the Russian Orthodox Church.

THE GOVERNMENT-OWNED GUM department store on Red Square sold only domestic goods prior to the dismantling of the Soviet Union.

Russian president Boris Yeltsin introduced a series of drastic reforms designed by his chief economist, Yegor Gaidar, who also assumed the position of prime minister. The main elements of Gaidar's strategy were the privatization of state-owned factories, shops, and farm collectives; a price liberalization policy enabling sellers to set their own prices (with the exception of some necessities, on which the government imposed ceilings); and the liberalization of foreign trade policies. The plan also called for shifting many of the federal government's former responsibilities to state or local authorities, thus decreasing federal expenditures and increasing revenues by imposing a value-added tax.

Foreign governments considering granting aid to the new country, and the International Monetary Fund, a major source of economic aid, approved the measures and supported Yeltsin's positions. The state and local governments were unprepared for their new tasks, however, and Russian citizens, straining to pay the higher prices on their old salaries, found the new economic conditions overly burdensome. Businesses also found it difficult to function in the new environment.

Throughout 1991 inflation rose at dizzying rates while joblessness increased, productivity decreased, and general chaos reigned. Parliament finally forced Yeltsin to replace Yegor Gaidar with Viktor Chernomyrdin, who advocated easing the reform policies in an effort to alleviate the suffering of the general public. Many economists believed Gaidar's methods, though unpleasant, to be the most likely means of achieving economic health and feared that Chernomyrdin, in his attempts to appease opponents of the reforms, would lead Russia back to communist-style systems.

Natural resources. Russia is rich in natural resources. Most metals and minerals are produced in such quantities that imports from abroad are of minor importance.

There are large deposits of iron ore, copper, lead, zinc, nickel, chrome, manganese, bauxite, and mercury. Russia produces substantial quantities of gold and emeralds, and following the discovery of a large deposit of diamonds in Siberia, the country became one of the

labor
US

labour
Brit.

A GRAVEL PIT IN SIBERIA, which is rich in mineral deposits

CABBAGE is an important part of Russia's agricultural yield. The inefficient state-run collective farms have been reorganized, but Russia still imports food.

world's leading diamond producers. Russia also has abundant fuel resources. Coal is a major fuel used in transportation, homes, and factories. In 1992 Russia produced 338 million tons of coal.

Oil, a major export, is an important source of foreign currency for Russia. Oil is sold to other Commonwealth countries, however, at well below market prices. After World War II, the oil fields between the Ural Mountains and the middle Volga River became the leading producers. Major oil fields are also found along the northern edge of the Caucasus and in the far east. Pipelines not only connect the Volga-Ural fields with the major industrial areas in the European and Siberian parts of Russia, but with Poland, Germany, the Czech Republic, and Hungary. In 1992 Russia produced 394 million tons of oil. The refusal of Tatarstan and Chechen-Ingushetia, two regions within Russia, to join the new Russian federation is significant because these are oil-producing regions.

The most important natural gas deposits lie near the Arctic Circle, north of the west Siberian lowlands in the Urengory fields. A major pipeline from Siberia to Western Europe is under construction in order to increase exports.

Agriculture. Use of arable land in Russia is severely hampered by cold in the north, so agricultural activity is limited to the southern regions of the country. The northerly location of the country results in a short growing season. In addition, the long distances between warm seas and croplands render rainfall limited and unpredictable.

These severe handicaps are partly responsible for the low yields that have characterized agricultural production. In addition, cropland has not been extended into areas of marginal rainfall and plants that could mature quickly in areas farther north, where growing seasons are very short, have not been developed.

To these environmental adversities, the Soviet system added man-made difficulties. Virtually all available land was placed under either collective or state

farm control. This deprived farmers of incentives. The reluctance of the government to offer farm workers sufficient rewards for their labor, and the policy of directing investments into industry while ignoring the needs of agriculture, added further difficulties. An interesting characteristic of Soviet farming was the significance of the private sector in the production of certain essential foods. Although farmland was owned by collective and state farms, farm workers were entitled to small plots of land, usually about half an acre in size but never more than one acre. The produce of these plots was either consumed by the worker's family or, more frequently, sold directly to consumers, outside of the state's control.

The reforms instituted by the Russian government in 1992 expanded this feature of the agricultural sector. Requiring that the land held by collectives or state farms be made available to individual farmers and that all enterprises be privatized, the government hoped to increase production. Many farmers were unable to afford the necessary farming equipment, however, and by the spring of 1992 only 4 percent of all agricultural workers were private farmers.

Grains, the leading crop, include wheat, rye, barley, oats, and corn. Russia exports considerable amounts of flax, and produces part of the hemp its industry consumes. Sugar beets, tobacco, and oilseeds—sunflower, rapeseed, and castor beans—are among the leading crop used by industry.

Soviet livestock suffered severe losses during the drive for collectivization (1929–1933), when nearly half the cattle and two-thirds of the hogs in the country were destroyed by farmers unwilling to turn over their animals to collective ownership. The livestock levels of 1929 were not regained until 1956, and further growth, with the exception of hogs, has been very slow. The output of meat, milk, eggs, and other dairy products remains well below that of the United States and Western Europe.

Industry. From 1945 until its collapse in 1991, the Soviet Union ranked next to the United States as the world's largest producer of iron and steel. The industry continues to be of great significance to the new Russian economy.

Before the Revolution of 1917, Russian industry was concentrated in the European part of the country. St. Petersburg and Moscow were among the leading centers of light industry. However, heavy industry was concentrated in the Ukraine.

The temporary loss of much of Russia's industrial capacity during World War I and the civil war that followed led to efforts to decentralize industry and to develop new centers removed from the vulnerable western borders of the Soviet Union.

Russia's central industrial region, in the Moscow area, contains the country's most valuable industries, producing electrical equipment and automobiles as well as various consumer goods, including textiles.

The Ural industrial region owes its present large-scale development to Soviet planning. It produces iron and steel, petroleum and its byproducts, heavy machinery, and chemicals.

Also dictated by the Soviet government, the Siberian lowlands and adjacent river valleys near the Russian-Chinese border produce coal and a variety of metals.

In accordance with its policy of industrial decentralization, the Russian government has developed other, smaller industrial centers to lessen the dependence of its far-flung territories on the major industrial areas, thereby reducing the burden on its transportation system.

Some of the important smaller industrial centers are located in Transcaucasia and the far east.

Trade. Major Russian exports include petroleum, gas, textiles, chemicals, timber, iron ore, industrial equipment, and iron and steel. Principal imports are ships, wheat, sugar, clothing, raw materials, and industrial machinery.

Government. In September 1993 President Boris Yeltsin dissolved the Russian legislature, the Supreme Soviet, and called for new elections. In November Yeltsin approved a draft constitution that established a new bicameral legislature. Members of the 178-member upper house, the Federation Council, and the lower house, the Duma, are directly elected to four-year terms, as is the president, who is limited to two terms in office. The constitution, which is subject to amendment, gives the president strong powers, including the authority to dissolve the Duma under certain circumstances. Voters approved the constitution and elected a new parliament in December 1993. In March 1998 Yeltsin fired his cabinet members and reorganized the government.

Russia is a federation with a central government and regional governments, each making policies. Procedures are set forth to resolve conflicting policy issues. Russia includes 21 autonomous republics, 10 autonomous regions, and 1 autonomous province, as well as other provinces and territories.

Russia was a founding member of the Commonwealth of Independent States, an organization formed by eleven of the former republics of the Soviet Union after its collapse in 1991. Russia continues to be a leader in the organization.

History. Archaeological evidence indicates that various societies existed in European Russia before there were written records. The earliest Slavic inhabitants probably arrived from an unknown point of origin several hundred years before the birth of Christ. Their settlements tended to concentrate in the south, near the Black Sea, and along the river systems that stretch inland from the Baltic and Black seas.

The river routes made it possible for groups of Scandinavian Vikings, or Varangian warriors and traders, to move through the same regions. From this composite of Slavs, Scandinavians, and the remnants of earlier populations, the oldest Russian state emerged during the 800s A.D. Kievan Rus was a confederation of principalities. Its two most important cities, Kiev and Velikiy Novgorod, were located along the major river trade routes. The Kievan principalities contained a mixture of merchants, peasants, and warrior-politicians.

Kievan Rus. Kiev's power and wealth, and its social and political structure, were rooted in an agrarian as well as a commercial economy. This duality made for complex patterns of political administration. Kievan society was eventually undermined by strife among claimants to the princely thrones that characterized the administrative system. Kiev finally fell in 1240 to the Mongols who invaded from the east.

Three centuries earlier, Orthodox Christianity had been introduced into Kievan Russia from the Byzantine Empire. It was destined to make a lasting impression on Russia.

Rise of Moscow. The Mongol conquerors permitted religious and political

centers
US

centres
Brit.

26 Europe and Russia

TRANSPORTATION IS A PROBLEM in the vast land expanse of Russia. The country's important seaports carry most of the foreign trade.

A FAMILIAR LANDMARK in Russia is its unique wood houses.

center
US

centre
Brit.

autonomy in Russia, as Kievan Rus disintegrated into a number of tiny principalities (appanages) whose rulers owed allegiance to the Mongol khans. The Russian Orthodox Church continued to function and serve the local population.

In the 1300s a few of the appanage princes were able to increase their holdings by purchase, marriage, or conquest. Among these was Ivan I (ruled 1325–1340), who ruled the principality of Muscovy, or Moscow. By the time of Ivan's death, Moscow, which was an active trading center at the confluence of the Moscow and Uka rivers, had secured some important advantages over its neighbors.

Ivan III.   Under Prince Ivan III (ruled 1462–1505), called "the Great," Moscow succeeded in establishing its sovereign authority over important independent principalities in central European Russia as well as over more frontier territories to the east and north.

The most important challenge to Muscovite expansion was the flourishing commercial principality of Novgorod. Nevertheless, the principality fell easily under Muscovite pressure in 1478. Muscovy then incorporated other independent principalities and began to challenge Mongol control.

By 1480 the Mongols had been overthrown, although Tatar heirs of the empire continued to raid and harass Moscow. The main sources of conflict in the early 1500s were the Baltic countries of Poland, Lithuania, and Sweden.

Meanwhile, serious internal problems had developed.

To ensure continued support from their boyar warriors and administrators, the Muscovite princes had often rewarded them with special privileges and large grants of land. As a result, the power of the boyars increased and some members of this Muscovite aristocracy began to challenge the authority of the sovereign prince himself.

Muscovite Russia.   Ivan IV (ruled 1533–1584), wishing to continue the expansionist policies of his predecessors and determined to preserve and increase sovereign authority, met these problems aggressively. Sometimes called "the Terrible," he was one of the most brutal and bloody figures in Russian history. Taking for himself the title of czar (caesar), he proceeded to employ all the absolute political power of an autocrat.

During the first years of Ivan IV's reign, the young czar undertook reforms generally regarded as enlightened and necessary. Muscovy was a patchwork of formerly independent principalities and separate local units of varying independence, and the Muscovite state was badly in need of administrative reorganization and legal reform.

Among Ivan's measures were a codification of laws (*Sudebnik* of 1550) and a reorganization of local administration. In 1549 Ivan ordered the convocation of the first national assembly, or *Zemski Sobor*.

During the 1550s Ivan also became deeply involved in wars of territorial expansion. At first Muscovite military campaigns were concentrated against khanates at Kazan on the middle Volga River, at Astrakhan, and in the Crimea.

A much more serious campaign began in 1557 against the inhabitants of the eastern Baltic region, who blocked Russian access to the Baltic Sea and northern Europe. This conflict gradually expanded until Ivan IV's armies were involved in an exhausting war with the large and powerful states of Poland and Sweden.

Centralization.   At the same time the czar's policies of expansion and domestic reform ran into mounting opposition, particularly from the boyars, who felt themselves threatened by administrative reforms and who bore the burden of the military campaigns. This political struggle came to a head in the early 1560s, when Ivan IV renounced the throne and retired to a monastery. Ivan returned only after the boyars and the church agreed to meet certain of his demands.

The victorious czar then organized the central territories of Muscovy as a separate administrative unit subservient to his will. Using handpicked men, called *oprichniks,* Ivan began to punish as "evildoers" anyone who objected to his policies of expansion and creation of a centralized state.

A virtual reign of terror was unleashed against the boyars, and Muscovy was plunged into near civil war. Crushing most opposition, Ivan IV became far more powerful than any previous Muscovite prince.

Feodor I (ruled 1584–1598), Ivan IV's successor, was too weak to master the legacy of power and antagonism bequeathed him by his father, and real authority began to fall into the hands of court favorites. When Feodor died, the ancient Muscovite dynasty died with him.

The period immediately following the death of Feodor, dominated by increased domestic strife, foreign wars and, finally, Polish invasion, is known as the Time of Troubles (1598–1613). Poland was eventually defeated, and peasant uprisings and other social disorders were suppressed. The Time of Troubles ended in 1613 with the accession to the throne of the new Romanov dynasty.

Romanovs.   Physically exhausted and verging on economic ruin, Russian society only slowly regained the international independence and domestic order that had characterized it in the early days of Ivan IV. The first Romanovs were unable to claim the prestige and authority of the earlier rulers of Moscow.

Nevertheless, Czar Michael Romanov (ruled 1613–1645) and his successor, Czar Alexis (ruled 1645–1676), managed to reassert and extend centralized autocratic authority and to restore some measure of prosperity.

Serfdom.   By the 1600s the institution of serfdom had become central to the functioning of the state. Exploitation of the large areas of land granted by the czars to their royal servitors since the early days of Muscovite expansion was feasible only through the use of serf labor.

A community of interest between the warrior landowners and the czar known as the *pomiestie* system developed. The noble landowner became responsible not only for providing soldiers and military leadership during times of war, but also for administering the land under his control.

Gradually the landowner became the immediate representative of authority over the peasant who worked the land. To ensure social stability and to placate an increasingly demanding nobility, the state made it more difficult for the peasant legally to escape bondage to land and lord.

Renewed expansion. By the mid-1600s Russia had largely regained the territory it had lost during the Time of Troubles. With the decline of Poland and Sweden, the west was again open to Russian expansion. In the south the power of the Turks, who had captured Constantinople in 1453, was also waning.

Despite a major schism in the Russian Orthodox Church and the peasant rebellion of Stenka Razin, Russian society prospered in this period. Trade with Western Europe grew, and educated Russians became increasingly attracted to Western organization and technology. It was Peter the Great, however, who initiated an era of rapid modernization and reform.

Peter the Great. Peter's reign (1689–1725) inaugurated the imperial period of Russian history. One of Peter's major goals was to modernize Russia as quickly as possible. He made the church subordinate to the state, reorganized the central government and provincial administration, and introduced a new military and civil service based on merit. Peter also required the nobility to serve the state, undertook tax and financial reforms, and developed trade and industry.

Following the acquisition of the eastern Baltic coastlands from Sweden in 1703, Peter built a new capital, St. Petersburg, on the Gulf of Finland. He called the city Russia's window to the West.

Peter launched a vigorous program of reforming and westernizing Russian ideas, manners, and customs. This, like his military efforts and centralization policies, was often unpopular. By the end of his reign in 1725, it was clear that Russia had become a major power in Europe and that old Muscovy had been transformed into the Russian Empire.

Early empire. Certain of Peter's reforms remained largely intact under the czars of the 1700s. The nobility pressed for and eventually received greater and finally absolute authority over their serfs, while owing fewer and fewer obligations to the state. Finally, in 1762, the nobility was freed entirely from compulsory state service.

The emergence of the nobility from the service position it had occupied under Peter was in part due to the weakness or indifference of his successors. Lax leadership allowed groups such as the Guards' Regiments in St. Petersburg, which were composed exclusively of nobles, to gain power. During the reign of the powerful, brilliant Catherine II "the Great" (1762–1796), the nobles suffered no loss of power. Catherine, who had come to the throne through a coup d'etat, needed their political backing and administrative talents. On the other hand, public office and thus public power came to be held by a group of individuals drawn from an increasingly smaller professionalized reservoir of nobles and civil servants.

The bureaucracy continued to be dominated by the nobility, but many nobles settled into a life of apathy and indolence on their estates. As a result, in the 1800s, men of various classes, or *raznochintsi,* began to fill the lower ranks of the administration, and the direct authority and influence of the nobility was gradually reduced.

Imperial expansion. By the end of Catherine the Great's reign in 1796, Russian control of the Ukraine had been consolidated and areas north of the Black Sea that had been protectorates of the Ottoman Empire had been added to the Russian state.

All of Siberia to the Pacific Ocean and more and more of central Asia had also been incorporated into the Russian Empire, which had become by far the largest land state in the world. Most important, however, Russian expansion brought with it direct and constant contact with the great European powers—France, Britain, Austria, and Prussia.

Contact with the powers resulted in Russian involvement in major European wars of the 1700s and Russian participation between 1772 and 1795 in the partitions of Poland. Thus, the Russian Empire found it difficult to escape involvement in the wars of the French Revolution and the Napoleonic wars (1789–1815).

Alexander I. In 1812, despite efforts by Alexander I (ruled 1801–1825) to hold Russia aloof from the Napoleonic struggle in the west, Napoleon invaded Russia. After heroic resistance and desperate suffering, the Russian armies forced the French to retreat. Russia joined Austria and Prussia in a coalition that helped defeat Napoleon in 1813–1814, thus raising Russia to new heights of importance in European affairs.

During the first years of his reign, Alexander welcomed the possibility of undertaking extensive reforms, including the easing or abolition of serfdom and the drawing up of a constitution for the empire, but the projects themselves were never effectively realized.

When real reform failed to materialize, a protest movement was formed by educated Russians who had been inspired by the ideals of the French Revolution. By the mid-1800s demands for radical social and economic reform had grown into a chorus of opposition to the government.

PETER THE GREAT is portrayed at Poltava as he celebrates his victory over the Swedes under Charles XII in 1709, establishing Russia as a major European power.

Nicholas I. Unfortunately, Alexander's successor, Nicholas I (ruled 1825–1855), was naturally conservative and did not favor reform. Furthermore, his accession to the throne was immediately followed by the Decembrist Revolt, an attempted seizure of the government by a group of liberal and reform-minded officers and nobles. The uprising made Nicholas determined to dominate not only the actions but the thoughts of his subjects.

The government attempted to protect society from radical political and social influences, and it viewed most

26 Europe and Russia

DURING THE REIGN of Catherine the Great, the Russian Empire became the largest state in the world, incorporating all of Siberia and much of central Asia.

THE ALEXANDER COLUMN commemorates the Russian ruler who resisted Napoleon's armies and forced them to retreat.

realized
US

realised
Brit.

THE MAGNIFICENT WEDDING of Nicholas and Alexandra was the last wedding of a czar in Russia. In 1918 revolutionaries killed the entire royal family.

proposals for change with great suspicion. It practiced strict censorship and instituted an early form of the secret police. These policies were disastrous for Russia. They not only allowed severe problems to go unsolved, but also stifled Russia intellectually, technologically, and economically at a time when Europe was being transformed by the profound changes resulting from the Industrial and the French revolutions.

Despite the repression carried out by Nicholas, a small band of intellectuals continued to oppose the government, some from exile in Western Europe. Brilliant writers like Tolstoy and Dostoevsky and a number of fine musicians and painters rose to prominence.

Nicholas intervened several times against revolutions in Europe and tried to expand Russian influence in the Balkans. This latter policy led to a major conflict with Britain, France, and the Ottoman Empire in the Crimean War (1853–1856). The resulting defeat of Russian armies on Russian soil by countries supplying their troops by sea over many thousands of miles led many Russians to conclude that a major overhaul of their society and government was needed.

Reform. On Nicholas's death in 1855 the new czar, Alexander II (ruled 1855–1881), realized that the time for action on reforms had come. In 1861 the serfs were freed.

Additional reforms encouraged economic growth and social change, which were seen as essential to Russia's survival in the modern European world. They included reforms in state finance, in local government, in the judicial system, and in military administration. But the inertia of a tradition-bound society, combined with the conservatism of the landed nobility and the government bureaucracy, prevented rapid social improvement.

As a result, liberal critics were not stilled by Alexander's reforms and they became increasingly frustrated and isolated from society as a whole. After the 1860s their dissatisfaction was manifested by the formation of groups dedicated to overthrowing the autocracy. In 1881 one of these groups assassinated Alexander II, hoping thereby to touch off a revolution.

Alexander III. Although Alexander III (ruled 1881–1894) succeeded in crushing his father's assassins, the revolutionary movement continued to grow. It grew not only inside Russia, but also among the many Russian émigrés in Western Europe.

Alexander III determined to meet the problems of Russian society with force and more thorough bureaucratic control. But this extreme reaction could not prevent industrialization and urbanization and the social changes that accompanied them.

Consequently, in the 1880s government policy became ambivalent. The ministry of finance promoted rapid change, while the ministry of the interior remained extremely conservative. At the same time Russia's position in international affairs was delicate, and in contrast to its most powerful European neighbors, Russia became politically and militarily weaker.

Nicholas II. The situation was not improved when the weak and indecisive Nicholas II (ruled 1894–1917) succeeded Alexander III in 1894. Nicholas pursued the same domestic policies as his predecessor and continued his conservatism and repression. But a major social and political crisis was brewing. The peasantry, deprived of land and burdened by taxes, was angry and restless. Marxists and other intellectuals spread revolutionary ideas among the newly urbanized workers, who were poorly paid and badly housed. Several non-Russian ethnic groups within the empire developed a nationalist spirit and began to seek greater autonomy. Russian liberals demanded civil freedoms and a more responsible government. Before long a disaster in foreign affairs touched off Russia's first modern revolution.

The Revolution of 1905. Conflicting interests in east Asia led to war (1904–1905) between Russia and a recently strengthened and westernized Japan, and the Russians experienced a series of humiliating defeats on land and sea.

The domestic repercussions were serious. In addition to the burdensome and unimaginative rule of Nicholas II, basic changes were taking place in the social and economic structure of Russia. The disastrous war with Japan resulted in the rapid and unforeseen growth of a broadly based revolutionary movement.

In January 1905, imperial troops opened fire on a crowd of unarmed workers trying to present a petition of grievances to the czar. This incident, known as "Bloody Sunday," fanned the fires of revolution that spread widely in the cities and countryside, and even to some units of the armed forces.

The czar offered minor concessions, but they failed to stem the tide. By the autumn of 1905, peasant riots and seizures of landlords' estates, together with a general strike, virtually paralyzed the government. With the situation out of control, Nicholas II reluctantly endorsed reform. He issued the October Manifesto, which promised basic civil liberties and the convocation of a national assembly, the Duma.

The Duma did not have full parliamentary powers, and its members were chosen by indirect and unequal suffrage. Moreover, the czar retained sovereignty over the country, and when the first two Dumas elected turned out to be critical of the government, he dissolved them.

In 1906 Nicholas dismissed the somewhat liberal Count Witte as prime minister and appointed Peter A. Stolypin, who promptly revised the electoral laws to weight the franchise even more heavily in favor of the propertied classes.

As a result, Duma deputies on the right supported the czar and his policies, and liberal leaders and parties of the center tried to work within the Duma.

The liberals and moderates worked to achieve necessary reform and to extend gradually the Duma's authority and influence so that it might become a representative parliament like those of Western democracies. The few deputies of the extreme left, primarily Social Democrats (Marxists), continued to oppose the government wholeheartedly.

In 1907 the continued restlessness of the peasantry, caused by land hunger and general economic hardship, led Prime Minister Stolypin to introduce agrarian reforms. He sought to break up the traditional peasant commune, under which land was owned collectively, and to encourage individual peasant proprietors.

It was hoped that if the peasants became property owners they would have a stake in the existing social order and develop a less revolutionary attitude. The transfer of land belonging to the state and to the nobles into peasant hands also was stepped up. World War I interrupted these reforms before their full impact could be measured.

World War I. In the years after the Revolution of 1905, the Russian economy generally prospered and limited social and educational reforms were initiated, but at the same time dissatisfaction among the workers increased. Whether Russia was at that period headed for a new social crisis or for a peaceful evolution is unclear. In any case, the war cut off these developments and made a revolution much more likely.

For several decades before 1914 Russia and Austria-Hungary had been vying for influence in the Balkans. Russia aspired to serve as protector of the Slavic peoples there, and in August, 1914, when Serbia, under pressure from Austria-Hungary, turned to Russia for help, the Russians decided to back Serbia, even though many Russian leaders realized that Russia was ill-prepared for war and might not be able to withstand the strain on its resources.

Russia's leaders hoped the war would be short and victorious, and that they would receive substantial territorial gains in the Balkans. These hopes were to be bitterly shattered. The war soon proved disastrous for the Russians as superior German and Austro-Hungarian armies battered the Russian forces.

Losses in men and equipment were high, mismanagement of supplies and of the general war effort was common, and morale sagged badly, both at the front and at home. By 1916 the economy as a whole had begun to collapse and there were severe food and fuel shortages in the cities.

The situation was complicated by a general disintegration in leadership at the highest levels. Gregory Rasputin, a charlatan "holy man," had acquired considerable influence over Empress Alexandra as a result of his success on several occasions in preventing her only son, the heir to the throne, from dying of hemophilia.

In 1915 Nicholas II decided to go to the front to take personal command of the armies. Rasputin, through his hold on Alexandra, began to have a strong influence on the appointment of ministers and the formation of government policy. Although Rasputin was murdered in 1916 by a group of patriotic noblemen, the weakness, inefficiency, and political ineptitude of the government persisted.

Revolution. The situation became critical in March 1917. Quite unexpectedly, food riots, coupled with strikes, lockouts, and general labor unrest, led to a mass demonstration in the capital, St. Petersburg, against which the government proved powerless. Within one week the czar had been toppled from the throne. He and his family were later executed.

With the collapse of the government there was no legally constituted authority, but two centers of power sprang up. One was the Provisional Government, a temporary committee formed by members of the Duma to rule until elections could be held for a constituent assembly. The other was the Petrograd Soviet (Council) of Workers' and Soldiers' Deputies, an institution that had existed briefly during the Revolution of 1905.

Provisional Government and Soviet. The Soviet was more representative of the Russian people than the Provisional Government. The Soviet fell at first under the domination of doctrinaire socialists, primarily the Mensheviks

center	
US	
centre	
Brit.	
labor	
US	
labour	
Brit.	

26 Europe and Russia

THE HERMITAGE in St. Petersburg, once a residence of the czar, is now Russia's largest museum.

UNDER COMMUNIST RULE, parades were held annually to celebrate the Russian revolution.

labor
US

labour
Brit.

(moderate Marxists) and social revolutionaries (agrarian socialists). At that time the extreme wing of the Marxists in Russia, the Bolsheviks, constituted only a tiny minority of the Soviet.

A compromise between the Soviet and the Provisional Government was reached, and the Soviet agreed to let the Provisional Government run the basic governmental system provided that civil liberties and other democratic guarantees were maintained. The Soviet retained control over certain services, such as communications, and exerted a strong influence in the army. The resulting dual power system provided a rather shaky government for a society wracked by revolution and war.

Moreover, there were a number of basic social and economic issues on which the Provisional Government and the Soviet disagreed. The leaders of the Provisional Government wanted to continue the war until victory could be achieved. The leaders of the Soviet wanted a rapid end to the war and opposed any annexations of territory by the victors.

For the masses, the key issues were the ending of the war, distribution of land, and better living conditions. The general population wanted immediate peace and instant reform. V. I. Lenin, leader of the Bolshevik, or extremist, faction of the Russian Marxists, stepped into this breach.

Bolsheviks. Taking advantage of the basic desires as well as the growing radicalism of the masses, Lenin propounded the slogan, "Peace, land, and bread," and saw that the Soviet might be the means by which his Bolshevik party could seize power. As a result, after an abortive popular uprising in the summer of 1917, Lenin, with the brilliant assistance of Leon Trotsky, seized power in Petrograd (now St. Petersburg) on October 25–26,

1917, and shortly thereafter in most of Russia. This "October Revolution," which became the November Revolution after the Russian calendar was changed, easily overthrew the existing moderate regime and instituted sweeping changes in Russia.

Soviet Union. After the Bolshevik seizure of power, Lenin turned to the tasks of consolidating the authority of his government and meeting the basic demands of the people. He called for peace and nationalized all land, although he permitted the peasants to use the acreage they had seized during the revolution. Lenin also decreed the separation of church and state and nationalized major industries and banks.

Lenin promulgated a new "socialist" constitution for the newly created Russian Soviet Federated Socialist Republic (R.S.F.S.R.). He encouraged the formation of separate but closely allied socialist republics under Bolshevik control in non-Russian areas of the former czarist empire. Between 1922 and 1924 these were joined to the R.S.F.S.R. to form the Union of Soviet Socialist Republics (U.S.S.R.).

Dictatorship. Lenin suppressed opposition parties and ended freedom of expression. He also dissolved the Constituent Assembly, which he had allowed to be elected in November 1917, when it convened with the Bolsheviks. In addition, he established secret police to ferret out and punish "counterrevolutionaries."

Despite considerable opposition not only within the Bolshevik party but throughout the country, Lenin finally forced through his policy of obtaining peace for Russia. On March 3, 1918, the war with Germany and Austria-Hungary was ended by the Treaty of Brest-Litovsk.

Under the terms of the treaty, Russia suffered heavy territorial and economic

losses. The treaty outraged many patriotic Russians and contributed to the outbreak of civil war between Bolshevik supporters (Reds) and those opposed to the new Soviet government (Whites). The treaty also helped lead to intervention in Russia by U.S. and Allied troops.

The Western powers, furious at what they considered Russia's betrayal of the common cause against German militarism, and desperately eager to reestablish an eastern front against Germany, sent small forces to northern Russia and Siberia and money, supplies, and advisers to various anti-Bolshevik forces.

After the end of World War I, in November 1918, the Allies continued halfhearted intervention in hope of overthrowing the Bolshevik regime. But by the end of 1920, the Soviet government had succeeded in defeating its internal and external foes, although the country was exhausted, near starvation, and demoralized.

Ruthlessly putting down peasant protests and disorders as well as a serious popular uprising at the city and naval base of Kronstadt, Lenin made it clear that the Bolsheviks would not tolerate opposition from the people. In addition, at the tenth party congress in 1921, Lenin crushed dissent within the party itself, making it clear that the leadership would not tolerate opposition from the rank and file. Thus the foundation was laid for dictatorship over Russia by the Communist Party.

NEP. Lenin began reconstruction of the devastated country by launching the New Economic Policy, or NEP, under which some of the controls and centralization that had characterized the previous period of wartime communism were abandoned.

Considered a temporary expedient from the start, the NEP did not solve the problem of how to increase Russia's productive forces and build an economy firm enough to support the socialist society envisaged by the communist leaders. By 1927, however, the economy had been restored to its 1913 level and Soviet leaders were faced with the problem of establishing new goals.

This situation was complicated by a power struggle within the Communist Party following Lenin's death in 1924. Joseph Stalin, the general secretary of the party, emerged victorious, first defeating Leon Trotsky and his "left" supporters, and then the so-called right opposition. Stalin established one-man rule over both the party and the country.

Stalinism. After expelling Trotsky from the party's politburo, Stalin then adopted Trotsky's domestic policy, which called for rapid and extensive industrialization. To achieve this, the first five-year plan was begun in 1928 and completed ahead of schedule in 1932. To obtain the labor and capital for industrialization, Stalin found it necessary to force the peasants onto state-owned collective farms.

POSTERS OF STALIN established his position among the leaders of the revolution in Russia.

Massive peasant resistance bordered on civil war, and an estimated 5 to 10 million peasants were killed, died of starvation, or were exiled to Siberia and central Asia. But by 1933 Stalin had won.

He established complete party control over every aspect of private and public life and created a totalitarian regime known as Stalinism. At the cost not only of lives but of an almost total loss of freedom, Soviet society achieved remarkable industrial growth during the decade of the 1930s.

Fearing that critics of his program were springing up within the party, Stalin began a great purge in 1936, starting with former party colleagues and rivals. The elimination of alleged "traitors to the party" soon spread to all levels of the party and to people in all walks of Soviet life.

Many thousands were arrested, imprisoned, exiled to slave labor camps, or executed. The bloodbath finally ended in 1938, but by then terror had become a major ingredient of Soviet daily life under the Stalinist regime.

Foreign policy. During the 1920s Soviet foreign policy had been directed at gaining recognition and support for the new Soviet state and preventing the possibility of Western intervention in Russia, as had occurred during the revolution. Soviet leaders proposed disarmament and, later, the formation of alliances against Nazi Germany and fascist Italy. But Stalin finally became disillusioned with the appeasement policies of France and England and in August, 1939, ignoring communist ideology, which decried fascism, and the anguished protests of millions of communists and Soviet sympathizers around the world, Stalin signed a nonaggression pact with Hitler. In so doing he bought time and some territory in Eastern Europe, but he also allowed Hitler to conquer Poland and France, which meant that by June, 1941, Hitler was able to launch a major offensive against the Soviet Union.

World War II. After sweeping initial successes facilitated by inadequate Soviet preparations, the Nazi armies were checked before Moscow and Leningrad (formerly Petrograd) in the late fall of 1941. Britain and the United States furnished considerable aid to the Soviet Union, and all three nations subscribed to general war aims set forth in the Atlantic Charter.

Despite the considerable successes of the Germans in 1942, the heroic Soviet forces remained intact while suffering staggering losses. They inflicted a major defeat on the Nazi armies in the last months of 1942 at the hard-fought Battle of Stalingrad, in the present-day city of Volgograd.

From that time on, Soviet troops began to push the Germans back, a process assisted by the British-U.S. landing in France in June, 1944. Attacked on two fronts, the Germans

STALIN AND CHIANG KAI-SHEK were allies during World War I and until Chiang repudiated communism and retreated to Taiwan with his government.

surrendered in May, 1945. The Soviet Union attacked Japan on August 8, 1945, and easily occupied Manchuria.

Cold War. After victory the Soviet Union faced two major problems: reconstruction and its relationship with its Western allies. Despite attempts in a series of wartime conferences to work out cooperative arrangements for the postwar period, friction soon arose between the Western powers and the Soviet Union, marking the beginning of the Cold War.

The chief issues were Germany and Eastern Europe. The Soviet Union, which had agreed to joint four-power occupation of Germany, began to extract unilateral reparations to assist its own reconstruction efforts. As a result, Germany soon became divided into a pro-Allied West Germany and a Soviet-dominated East Germany.

In Eastern Europe the Soviet Union, whose armies had liberated much of the area from German domination, exerted pressure to ensure the emergence of pro-Soviet governments despite Soviet promises at the Yalta Conference (1945) that free elections would be held in those countries.

Between 1946 and 1948 one country after another in Eastern Europe came under Soviet domination over the protests of the Western nations.

It was widely believed in the West that Stalin intended not only to ensure the security of the Soviet Union, but also to aid the spread of socialist revolutions in the world. It was also believed that an opportunity for Soviet expansion in Western Europe had arisen through the disorder left by the war and the large communist parties that existed in France and Italy.

The Western powers responded with military and massive economic aid to Western Europe, hoping to contain Soviet and communist expansion.

The iron curtain. At home, Stalin launched a renewed program of industrialization and totalitarianism. The mild freedom of thought and activity that had been permitted during the war was ended, and strict adherence to anti-Western and nationalistic dogma was demanded in all areas of Soviet life.

To keep out Western influence, Stalin drew an "iron curtain" between Western and Eastern Europe, cutting off all contacts and normal interchange. At the same time he forced the Soviet people to make even greater sacrifices to rebuild the country and to further advance the process of industrialization. The Soviet Union was determined to compensate itself for its terrible losses in the war, and this it could do only by exploiting the lands that had fallen under its control. The countries behind the iron curtain were drawn into a close economic embrace and their economies were subordinated to Russian needs. The standard of living rose with glacial slowness, a pace that was emphasized by the incredible rapidity with which the standard of living in the West shot up.

emphasized
US
emphasised
Brit.

Post-Stalin era. When Stalin died in 1953, there was a change in Soviet foreign and domestic policy. At home, the new leaders were eager to eliminate the worst abuses of Stalinism without undermining their own control. After a brief struggle for power, Nikita S. Khrushchev emerged as the strongest figure.

Blaming evils in the Soviet system on Stalin personally, Khrushchev attempted to reduce substantially the use of terror and to increase material incentives to achieve higher economic performance. To do this meant encouraging initiative, providing a higher standard of living, and permitting a slightly wider range for intellectual and artistic creativity.

Khrushchev was deposed in 1964, largely because of the personal and arbitrary nature of his rule, but his successors, Leonid Brezhnev and Aleksei Kosygin, themselves followed the same policies.

RUSSIA'S SPACE station Mir was in orbit around Earth for 15 years.

kilometers
US

kilometres
Brit.

Although skilled Soviet cosmonauts achieved a number of successes in space following the launching of the first Soviet space vehicle, *Sputnik,* in 1957, and although housing and living conditions improved, Soviet society faced severe problems in the late 1960s and 1970s. The rate of industrial growth slowed and the economy was sluggish, partly because of the difficulties involved in planning centrally for such a large and complex industrialized society. The agricultural sector performed erratically, and in years of poor weather, notably in 1973 and 1974, the Soviet Union was forced to buy millions of tons of wheat abroad, primarily from the United States.

In this period a small number of intellectuals and scientists began openly to criticize the party and government in what came to be known as the "dissident movement." Although the government soon exiled some prominent dissidents, such as the writer Aleksandr Solzhenitsyn, and permitted some Jewish dissidents to emigrate, the movement

was not eliminated and remained a thorn in the side of the government. Moreover, the commitment to communism of many citizens, particularly young people, seemed more and more formalistic or nonexistent, despite the adoption of a new constitution and extensive discussions about the future communist society.

Peaceful coexistence. In foreign policy, the Soviet leaders accepted the realities of the nuclear age and espoused a policy of peaceful coexistence. Realizing that the Soviet Union and the United States had the nuclear capability to destroy each other, the two nations decided that the contest between capitalism and communism must take place on nonmilitary grounds.

Improved Soviet-American relations during this era of détente resulted in agreements between the two super-powers regarding nuclear nonproliferation (SALT I, 1972), joint space missions, trade arrangements, and cultural and educational exchanges.

These conciliatory efforts overshadowed areas of tension in U.S.-Soviet relations, such as the crisis in 1962 over Soviet attempts to place missiles in Cuba. The American government also criticized Soviet support for revolutions in Ethiopia, Angola, and other parts of Africa, and Soviet encouragement of Palestinian ambitions in the Near East. For its part, the Soviet government expressed strong displeasure over American policy in Vietnam and over warmer U.S. relations with communist China.

From the 1950s through the 1970s, the Soviet Union faced a series of challenges within the communist camp. Yugoslavia, expelled from the socialist bloc in 1948, continued to pursue an independent course throughout the period. In 1956 the Soviet government intervened by force to put down an inspired revolt in Hungary, and in 1968 it used armed intervention to oust a democratic socialist regime in Czechoslovakia. This last intervention was justified by what came to be called the Brezhnev Doctrine: that the Soviet Union has the right to use military force against a neighbor if it feels that events in that country threaten Soviet security.

More critical dissension arose between the Soviet Union and China, where a communist regime had won power in 1949 with little Soviet aid. Taking a harder line toward world capitalism, the Chinese communists sought to replace the Soviet Union as the leader of the international communist movement. While the Chinese denounced Soviet revisionism and appeasement, the Soviet leaders accused the Chinese of adventurism and war mongering.

In 1978 the Soviets began to repudiate the parts of the 1975 European security pact that called for freer movement of people and ideas. They jailed dissidents but allowed over 130,000 Jews and 40,000 Germans to emigrate.

In 1979 the Soviet Union invaded Afghanistan in order to restore a government that had been overthrown in a

RUSSIA'S INTEREST in nuclear research during the Cold War is reflected in this monument to the atom in Chelyabinsk.

coup. The invasion caused widespread condemnation of the Soviet Union and led to a souring of U.S.-Soviet relations. The SALT II arms limitation treaty, which had been signed by U.S. President Jimmy Carter and Soviet leader Brezhnev, but was not ratified by the U.S. Senate, was shelved. Economic sanctions against the Soviet Union were applied, and a partial boycott of the 1980 Moscow Olympics was organized.

Soviet forces were finally withdrawn from Afghanistan in 1989 after a long and inconclusive struggle against antigovernment guerrillas. The Soviet experience in Afghanistan has often been compared with the American experience in Vietnam, especially in some of the war's domestic consequences: considerable popular disillusionment with the military and the mistreatment of returning veterans.

Gorbachev. In 1982 Brezhnev died and power passed in quick succession to two of his contemporaries, Yuri Andropov, who died in 1984, and Konstantin Chernenko, who died in 1985. It was considered the start of a new ruling generation when Mikhail Gorbachev, a much younger man, was chosen to succeed Chernenko.

It quickly became apparent that Gorbachev was different from his predecessors. His foreign policy was marked by rapid progress in nuclear arms reductions negotiations. In 1987 Gorbachev signed the Intermediate Range Nuclear Forces Treaty (INF) which required both the Soviet Union and the United States to eliminate all land-based missiles capable of striking targets within a range of 300 to 3,400 miles (500 to 5,000 kilometers). Gorbachev also advanced the

MIKHAIL GORBACHEV'S reform policies of *glasnost* and *perestroika* led to a new openness in political debate in the Soviet Union and contributed to its disintegration.

START (Strategic Arms Reduction Treaty) talks, which had been under way since 1982. His efforts resulted in the 1991 treaty under which the Soviet Union and the United States both agreed to reduce their strategic nuclear weapons by 30 percent.

Domestically, Gorbachev initiated reforms in the Soviet political and economic systems. These reforms came to be characterized by the terms *glasnost,* meaning "openness," and *perestroika,* meaning "reconstruction."

In furtherance of glasnost, Gorbachev restructured government and political life, allowing more dissent and reducing the role of the Communist Party while promoting the democratization of government. Reforms under perestroika attempted to introduce the market forces of supply and demand to the economy and to make individual business enterprises responsible for their own profits and losses.

The economy responded slowly to the reforms and was hindered by bureaucratic intransigence. By the end of the 1980s little progress had been made.

Political reforms had led in 1989 to relatively open elections. In the newly organized Congress of People's Deputies, communist candidates were embarrassingly ignored by Soviet voters. Several of the most heavily populated Soviet republics openly sought autonomy, threatening economic independence as well. Although Gorbachev had been elected president of the Soviet Union, he faced serious challenges by Communist Party dissidents.

The new openness in political debate led to other difficult problems for Gorbachev, not the least of which was a rise in nationalist feelings among the many national minorities. Among the more vociferous of the minorities were the Baltic republics of Latvia, Lithuania, and Estonia. In 1990, after heated disputes over the pace and nature of reform, Boris Yeltsin, the president of the Russian Republic, quit the Communist Party and Eduard Shevardnadze resigned from his post as Soviet foreign minister.

With a fractured government and a severely troubled economy, Gorbachev managed to sign an agreement with the leaders of nine republics for a treaty that would shape a new union. One month after the agreement was signed, hard-line communists launched a coup d'etat, seizing control of the Soviet government and placing Gorbachev under house arrest at his vacation home in the Crimea. In response, Boris Yeltsin denounced the coup conspirators and led a resistance movement that resulted in thousands of Russians demonstrating outside the Russian Parliament building. The coup leaders' lack of organization and popular support, as well as their inability to silence the resistance movement, led to the failure of the coup after 3 days. Gorbachev was returned to office and immediately outlawed the Communist Party. Latvia, Lithuania, and Estonia declared their independence and were recognized by the central command.

With economic conditions continuing to disintegrate and the union near bankruptcy, Russia declared its independence in a drive to save the economy and precipitate widespread reform. The newly independent Russia forged an agreement with Ukraine and Belarus (formerly Byelorussia), creating the Commonwealth of Independent States. Despite objections from Gorbachev, eight other republics soon joined the Commonwealth.

On December 25, 1991, Mikhail Gorbachev resigned his post as leader of the Soviet Union, and the Russian flag was flown over the Kremlin. Russia subsequently took over the Soviet UN seat and the Soviet parliament. The new Commonwealth is not a state, but an organization through which international stability and security can be maintained. Members agreed to honor arms treaties negotiated by the Soviet Union and developed policies regarding the military of the former superpower. Of foremost importance was the agreement to continue nuclear arms reduction, as stipulated under the 1991 START treaty, and to place control of nuclear weapons under one authority.

However, rivalry between Russia and Ukraine complicated relations between the two countries. As part of an arms reduction plan, Ukraine, Belarus, and Kazakhstan agreed to destroy their nuclear weapons or transfer them to Russia. Ukraine was especially wary of this arrangement, protesting that it gave Russia undue power and placed the other republics at a disadvantage. Two other points of contention were the status of the former Soviet Union's Black Sea fleet, claimed by both countries, and the future of the Crimea, a Ukrainian-held region with a large Russian population that had declared its independence from Ukraine. Ultimately, Russia and Ukraine agreed to share the fleet and its attendant expenses, and Russia dropped its request that the 1954 Soviet decision to grant the Crimea to Ukraine be reevaluated.

Although Ukraine had still not ratified the first START treaty, in January 1993 Boris Yeltsin signed a second treaty that committed Russia and the United States to eliminating all heavy, land-based nuclear missiles, thus severely limiting first-strike capabilities on both sides.

While foreign affairs demanded close attention, internal difficulties also arose during its first year of post-Soviet independence. Yeltsin's first act as president of the independent Russian federation was to implement a dramatic program of economic reform, causing widespread hardship and controversy.

In September 1993 Yeltsin ordered the Russian parliament dissolved, sparking a violent confrontation in October. He approved a new draft constitution and called for new elections. On December 12, Russians elected a new parliament and approved the constitution. An opposition bloc of communist and nationalist legislators was elected, however, and in January 1994 Yeltsin chose a new cabinet less inclined to radical reform. Yeltsin resigned in December 1999 and appointed then-prime minister Vladimir Putin acting president. Putin was elected president in March 2000.

Putin, who came to the position having never held elected office, brought a political stability not seen during the Yeltsin era. He maintains a high approval rating, despite some observers seeing many of his actions as autocratic. Some see as evidence the arrest on Putin's orders of Russia's wealthiest man, a supporter of liberal opposition parties, on fraud and tax evasion charges. Parliamentary elections in 2003 were swept by a party loyal to the president. He saw this as a validation of the course he had set as president, while observers criticized the elections because of bias in the state-run media and official support at all levels of government for the party.

Conflict with separatist rebels continues in the republic of Chechnya, subsequent to the Chechen-Russian war of 1994–1996. Bomb attacks in the country attributed to Chechen rebels continue despite Chechens voting to approve a regional constitution and the election of a president in the republic. With international observers questioning the fairness of the election, the effectiveness of such measures remains unknown.

honor
US

honour
Brit.

26 Europe and Russia

San Marino

Official name: *Republic of San Marino*
Area: *23 sq. mi., 60 sq. km.*
Type of government: *Republic*
Population: *28,000*
Capital and largest city: *San Marino (Pop., 2,800)*
Language: *Italian*
Literacy: *96%*
Currency: *Euro*
Per capita GDP: *$34,600 (Rank: 3rd)*

The land. San Marino is the third smallest state in the world after Vatican City and Monaco. San Marino consists almost entirely of one mountain, the three-peaked Mt. Titano, which rises over 2,300 feet (700 meters). Several rivers rush down the mountain. The most important rivers are the Fumicello, Ausa, and San Marino.

San Marino's climate is mild, with rather cold winters and warm summers. Rainfall is moderate.

The people. Almost all of San Marino's population is of Italian descent, and the official language is Italian. Most Sammarinesi are Catholic. A large number of citizens live abroad.

Most of the population is concentrated in twelve towns lying around the base and on the peaks of Mt. Titano. The largest town, Borgo Maggiore, is on one peak of the mountain. The capital, San Marino, is on the highest peak.

Economy. San Marino is a moderately prosperous country. Its chief natural resources are farm and pasture land and magnificent scenery, which attracts many tourists.

Farming is an important occupation. Grapes and wheat are the leading crops, and dairying is important too. San Marino's industries, an increasingly important part of the economy, produce textiles, building materials, paper, leather goods, pottery, bricks, cement, wine, and candy. Tourism and the sale of postage stamps contribute heavily to the country's income. San Marino has a customs union with Italy and uses Italian currency.

meters
US

metres
Brit.

RACING FANS watch the Formula One cars in the Imola Grand Prix in San Marino.

Government. San Marino is a republic. Legislative power is vested in a 60-member assembly, the Great and General Council, which is popularly elected every 5 years.

Twice yearly the council appoints from among its members two captains regent who, with the Congress of State, or cabinet, wield executive power. San Marino is represented diplomatically abroad by Italy.

History. According to tradition, San Marino was founded in the A.D. 300s by Marinus, a Christian stonemason from Dalmatia who was fleeing from religious persecution. Marinus is said to have been later made a saint, San Marino. The earliest document definitely establishing San Marino's existence as an independent commune, however, is dated 885. San Marino was apparently self-governing at that time.

San Marino's rugged terrain and its political and economic insignificance protected it from destruction by medieval invaders of Italy and helped to keep it generally aloof from violent political and religious feuds that disrupted Italy during the 1200s and 1300s.

In the 1400s and 1500s, San Marino avoided incorporation into the Papal States and was able to expand its territory somewhat. In the 1500s it was controlled for a brief period by the powerful Italian Borgia family, but in 1549 Pope Paul III proclaimed its independence and sovereignty.

When Napoleon I of France conquered Italy in the late 1700s, he spared the tiny republic. When the many states of Italy were united in 1861, San Marino did not join the new nation. In 1862 it entered a customs union with Italy, and in 1879 San Marino and Italy signed a lasting treaty of friendship.

San Marino entered World War I as an ally of Italy, and in the 1930s, when Benito Mussolini led the fascist government of Italy, San Marino adopted a fascist form of government. In World War II, it proclaimed its neutrality and was a haven for refugees, but it was bombed by Allied planes and suffered damage from ground fighting.

After the war, in the late 1940s, a communist-socialist coalition government was elected. It held power until 1957, when the more conservative Christian Democratic Party took control. In 1978 the Christian Democrats finally lost control of the assembly when a communist-led coalition won a majority of seats. In 1986 the communists and the Christian Democrats formed a coalition, in what was called a "historic compromise."

Slovakia

Official name: *Slovak Republic*
Area: *18,859 sq. mi., 48,845 sq. km.*
Type of government: *Parliamentary democracy*
Population: *5,422,000*
Capital and largest city: *Bratislava (Pop., 429,000)*
Languages: *Slovak, Hungarian*
Literacy: *99%*
Currency: *Koruna*
Per capita GDP: *$12,200 (Rank: 44th)*

The land. Slovakia is a country of high mountains in the north, where the Carpathian range, represented by the High and Low Tatras mountains, reaches a peak of more than 8,000 feet (2,439 meters). There are lowlands in the southeast, where the Vah and Hron rivers flow south to the Danube. This region, known as the Hungarian Plain, supports much of the country's agricul-

SPIS CASTLE overlooks a village at the foot of the hill in Slovakia.

ture. A series of mountains, hills, and plateaus connects the two areas. Bratislava, the capital, and Kosice (population, 235,000) are major urban areas.

The people. The majority of the people living in the Slovak Republic are of Slovak descent, although a sizable Hungarian minority exists owing to the historical association of the two countries. Small Polish and Ukrainian populations also reside within the country.

Economy. Slovakia's natural resources include coal, timber, natural gas, and various metals such as antimony, mercury, copper, lead, and zinc. Major industries are armaments, shipbuilding, textiles, glass, chemicals, and oil refining. Agriculture comprises a little over 10 percent of the total gross national product, with farmers raising wheat, corn, rye, fruits, and vegetables.

The division of Czechoslovakia creates serious difficulties for Slovakia, a country already saddled with an unemployment rate of almost 12 percent and a history of dependence on subsidies from the Czech federal budget. As the new country faces the daunting task of establishing and funding its own government, military, and bureaucracy, many economists speculate that deficit spending and rampant inflation will be unavoidable.

Government. The chief of state is a president, who is elected by direct popular vote to a 5-year term. The legislature is the single-chamber 150-member National Council. The members are elected to 4-year terms based on proportional representation. The prime minister is usually the leader of the majority party in the National Council election and is appointed by the president.

History. Present-day Slovakia is believed to have been first inhabited by members of Illyrian tribes. Celts followed, and then Germanic tribes. The Slovaks, a Slavic people, first migrated to the area from Silesia in the fifth century. The Avars overran Slovakia in the sixth century, and ruled until the ninth century, when the Great Moravian Empire, encompassing Slovakia, Moravia, Bohemia, Silesia, and parts of Poland, came to power and brought Christianity to the region. Moravian control was quickly supplanted by Magyar domination, however, when the Avars requested assistance from their Magyar neighbors in what is now Hungary. The Magyars wrested Slovakia from the Moravians in 1907, and the region remained under Hungarian domination for the next thousand years, while Bohemia and Moravia became part of the Holy Roman Empire.

The conquering Magyars exerted considerable influence on Slovakia, reducing the Slovaks to serfs. Ukrainian mountain people migrated to what is now Slovakia in the 11th century, and German miners settled in the east during the 12th century. Czech Hussites fleeing religious persecution in their country contributed to the national heritage in the 15th century, but despite contact with these groups, the population remained predominantly Slovak and Hungarian.

The Protestant Reformation gained some followers in the 16th century, with Slovaks and Germans following Luther and Magyars following Calvin, but the majority of the population remained Catholic. Thus, the religious upheavals that disturbed much of Europe did not disrupt Slovakia. Contact with the Czechs and with the Protestant reformers, along with the growth of a small bourgoisie as towns and cities developed, fanned hopes for better conditions, leading to periodic attempts to improve the situation of Slovaks within the Magyar Empire. The efforts met with little success, and Slovak culture was maintained mainly through folk traditions and the clergy, who were among the few Slovaks able to obtain an education.

In 1526, when the Turks defeated the Hungarians at the Battle of Mohács, the Hungarians moved their court to Slovakia. The move improved conditions slightly for some Slovaks, but the vast majority of natives continued to suffer poverty and discrimination under Hungarian rule.

Hapsburg victories against the Ottoman Empire reestablished the old Hungarian Empire in 1711. The Hapsburgs initially established policies favoring the non-Hungarian population of the area in an effort to stem Hungarian ambitions. At the same time, the Slovak experienced a national awakening, leading Slovak intellectuals to develop various theories concerning the relationship between Slovaks and Czechs. Some believed the two nationalities to be distinct; others described them as related but different; and still others claimed they were one, supporting Pan-Slavism and the establishment of a Czechoslovak nation. Hungarians countered Hapsburg domination with their own movement of renewed pride in their national heritage. Hungarian supremacy eventually prevailed.

When the revolutions of 1848 shook Europe, the Slovaks presented their "Demands of the Slovak Nation." The manifesto called for the establishment of schools in which Slovak would be the language of instruction, the right to use Slovak in courts of law and local administrations, and the right to establish a Slovak assembly. The Hungarian government quickly dismissed the Slovak demands and employed Hungarian troops to crush any opposition. The Slovaks turned to the Austrian Empire for aid, but were rebuffed. Nonetheless, efforts to promote Slovakian autonomy within Hungary continued. In 1861 a second list of demands was presented unsuccessfully to the government, and a cultural organization known as the *Matica Slovenska* was founded.

In 1867 waning Hapsburg power resulted in the establishment of the Austro-Hungarian Empire. The new arrangement prompted the Hungarians to exercise their increased influence at the expense of the Slovaks. The *Matica Slovenska* was banned, and the Slovak language was forbidden in all but elementary schools. Political and economic discrimination persisted. The Slovaks responded by establishing the Pan-Slavic Slovak National Party and intensifying their attempts to achieve autonomy.

Tension between Hungarians and Slovaks grew steadily, and when World War I broke out the Slovaks were reluctant to support their Hungarian rulers. Slovak soldiers, like their Czech counterparts, surrendered to the Allies and fought against the Hungarians. Throughout the war Czechs, eager to free themselves of Austrian dominance, and Slovaks, long

RUSSIAN-BUILT apartment blocks provide housing in Slovenia.

kilometers
US

kilometres
Brit.

aluminum
US

aluminium
Brit.

oppressed by the Hungarians, worked together to promote the creation of a country in which Czechs and Slovaks would be independent. A provisional government was put together by Czech leaders, notably Tomáš Masaryk, and Slovak leaders, including Milan Hoda, Milan Stefánika, Vavro Srobar, and Father Andrej Hlinka. Ethnic Slovaks in the United States supported the movement and sponsored a meeting held in Pittsburgh, Pennsylvania. The resulting Pittsburgh Declaration, signed May 30, 1918, was not an official document but it signaled the coming of Slovak independence. Czechoslovakia was formally recognized in 1919 as a result of the Treaty of St. Germain. (For a history of Slovakia between 1916 and 1989, see the article on the Czech Republic.)

After the "Velvet Revolution" of 1989, as the new Czechoslovakia began its program of economic reform, Slovakia suffered more financial hardships than did the Czech half of the republic. With less foreign investment, fewer productive industries, and more economic ties to the former Eastern bloc, the economy flagged and unemployment rose. Prague subsidized the republic's economy, but improvements were negligible. Czechs, experiencing difficulties of their own, complained of having to support Slovakia, while Slovaks chafed under what they saw as Czech condescension.

In June 1992 the two republics elected leaders with opposing views on the best way of continuing economic reform. The leaders decided to disband the country rather than compromise their views. Despite the tensions between Czechs and Slovaks, citizens of both republics were wary of dividing the nation, fearing increased economic difficulties and less political prestige.

In the absence of a national referendum, however, the government proceeded to dissolve Czechoslovakia into two countries. The creation of the Slovak Republic on January 1, 1993 provided Slovaks with independence for the first time in more than a thousand years. Slovakia joined NATO and the EU in 2004.

Slovenia

Official name: *Republic of Slovenia*
Area: *7,836 sq. mi., 20,296 sq. km.*
Type of government: *Emerging democracy*
Population: *1,933,000*
Capital and largest city: *Ljubljana (Pop., 264,000)*
Languages: *Slovenian, Serbo-Croatian*
Literacy: *99%,* **Currency:** *Tolar*
Per capita GDP: *$18,000 (Rank: 34th)*

The land. The northernmost of the former Yugoslavian republics, Slovenia includes the mountains of the Julian Alps (where Slovenia's highest mountain, Mount Triglav, is found) and the Karawanken range, the Adriatic coastline, and the fertile Pannonian Plain. Almost half of Slovenia is forested. The climate depends on the region. Along the Adriatic the climate is Mediterranean; the mountainous areas have an alpine climate; the interior's climate is continental. Many rivers flow through the country, including the Soa, the Savinja, the Mura, the Drava (which has been dammed to provide hydroelectric power), and the Sava. The country is famous for its mineral springs at Cjele, and the vast Postojna Caves, which have an area of 12 square miles (19 square kilometers).

The people. Slovenia is one of the most homogeneous of the former Yugoslavian republics, with a population primarily of Slovenes. Most Slovenes are Roman Catholic, although there are a few Protestants and a very small Muslim minority. Although the main language is Slovenian, Serbo-Croatian, Hungarian, and Italian are also spoken. In addition to Ljubljana, Maribor (population, 109,000), Celje (48,000), and Kranj (51,000) are important cities. Approximately 51 percent of the population live in urban areas.

Economy. Slovenia is an industrialized country in which mining, manufacturing, steel production, and textiles are major elements of the economy. Tourism and agriculture are also important. Its agricul-

tural products include livestock (cattle and pigs), corn, wheat, sugar beets, potatoes, and grapes. Coal, iron, mercury, aluminum, and timber are among the country's most valuable natural resources. Germany is Slovenia's major trading partner. Although the prolonged civil wars disrupting other former Yugoslavian republics are not present in Slovenia, the young country's new economy is still experiencing some difficulty. By 1994 the country had reduced its inflation rate to 20 percent, however.

Government. Slovenia is a parliamentary democratic republic. The legislature is a single-chamber body, known as the National Assembly. The National Assembly has 90 members. Forty of the members are directly elected; fifty are elected by means of proportional representation. Members are elected to 4-year terms. The number of directly elected and proportionally elected members varies from election to election. A president, who is the chief of state, is elected by popular vote to a 5-year term. The president nominates a prime minister, who is usually the leader of the majority party or majority coalition in the National Assembly election.

History. A Roman province from the first century until the collapse of the Roman Empire, Slovenia was overrun in the sixth century by a Slavic people calling themselves Slovenes. The area was ruled by Bavaria from 743 until 788, when the Franks took control. When the Carolingian Empire was divided in the ninth century, Slovenia was returned to Bavarian rule, which gradually gave way to Hapsburg dominion late in the 14th century. The German rulers of the region oppressed the Slovenes and attempted to strip them of their national identity, but Slovenian pride survived, largely through the work of local Roman Catholic priests. A few peasant uprisings during the 15th and 16th centuries reflected Slovenian dissatisfaction but did not result in any real changes for the populace. Buffered by the southern regions of the Hapsburg Empire, Slovenia was never taken by the Ottoman Empire and remained a Roman Catholic nation throughout the period of Turkish supremacy in the Balkan peninsula. In the 16th century the Protestant Reformation attracted some Slovenian followers, who also saw in the Reformation the possibility of political freedom from Hapsburg Austria, but Catholic forces quickly checked the movement.

Conditions for the Slovenians improved slightly in the 18th century, when the Hapsburgs introduced some reforms to the region, but Austrian dominance was never seriously threatened. Throughout the period of Hapsburg rule, German was the official language, and Slovenian was spoken chiefly by the peasants. It was not until 1809, when Slovenia became a French province under Napoleon's authority, that Slovenian was encouraged and used in official transactions. By 1814 Napoleon had been defeated and Slovenia was returned to

Austria. The brief period of national awakening experienced under Napoleon's rule encouraged Slovenians to seek independence from the Hapsburgs. In 1848 Slovenia unsuccessfully tried to establish itself as a separate province within the Austrian Empire.

By the 1870s Slovenia was interested in joining with other South Slavs (Serbs and Croats) to form an independent country. Nothing came of this interest until 1918, when Slovenia formally joined the Kingdom of Serbs, Croats, and Slovenes. (For a history of Slovenia between 1918 and 1991, see the article on Serbia and Montenegro.)

Slovenian nationalism led to the country's declaration of independence from Yugoslavia in 1991. A brief conflict with federal troops was followed by the suspension of the declaration of independence for 3 months. During that period negotiators participated in peace talks sponsored by the European Community (EC). Independence was declared again on October 8, 1991, and Germany recognized the new country in December of the same year. The EC [later the European Union (EU)] granted recognition in January 1992, and in May Slovenia became a member of the United Nations. Slovenia joined both NATO and the EU in 2004.

Soviet Union

The Union of Soviet Socialist Republics, or Soviet Union, was dissolved in 1991. As a result, each of its republics became an independent country.

Information on Kazakhstan, Kyrgyzstan, Tajikistan, Turkmenistan, and Uzbekistan can be found in the Asia volume country listings. Armenia, Azerbaijan, Belarus, Estonia, Georgia, Latvia, Lithuania, Moldova, Russia, and Ukraine can be found in the country listings in this volume.

Spain

Official name: *Kingdom of Spain*
Area: *194,834 sq. mi.,*
504,750 sq. km.
Type of government:
Parliamentary monarchy
Population: *40,153,000*
Capital and largest city: *Madrid*
(Pop., 2,939,000)
Languages: *Spanish (official),*
Catalan, Galician, Basque
Literacy: *97%;* **Currency:** *Euro*
Per capita GDP: *$20,700*
(Rank: 26th)

The land. Most of Spain consists of a high tableland, the Meseta, which has an average elevation of more than 2,500 feet (762 meters) above sea level. Most of the Meseta is flat, but it has many hilly and mountainous areas.

The principal mountain ranges of the Meseta are the Sierra de Gata, the Sierra de Gredos, and the Sierra de Guadarrama, to the west and north of Madrid; the Sierra Morena in the south-central area; and the Cantabrian Mountains in the north. Northeastern Spain is dominated by the rugged Pyrenees, which run along the border with France, isolating the Iberian peninsula as a whole from the rest of Europe.

There is a relatively narrow coastal plain in the east, along the Mediterranean, which widens substantially only in the lower Ebro River valley. This plain is broken in many places by mountains that extend to the sea. In southwestern Andalusia, along the Atlantic shore, the coastal plain is fairly wide.

Spain's major rivers are the Ebro, the Douro, the Tagus, the Guadiana, and the Guadalquivir. The Guadalquivir is the only river navigable for any significant distance.

Climate. The climate of Spain is varied. The southern and eastern coasts have a Mediterranean climate, with long, hot, dry summers and short, cool, moderately rainy winters.

The interior has a continental climate, with very hot summers and cold winters. It is generally quite dry. Galicia and the northern coast have a maritime climate, by far the rainiest in Spain. The higher elevations experience cooler summers and much colder winters.

The Canary Islands, which lie about 800 miles (1,300 kilometers) off the southwest coast, and the Balearic Islands, in the Mediterranean off the east coast, are also part of Spain.

The people. The Spanish people reflect strong regional differences because of the country's historical development and mountainous terrain, which helps isolate one part of the country from another.

The official language is Castilian Spanish, which is generally understood throughout the country. Numerous regional dialects are spoken, however. Catalan, spoken in the northeast, Basque, spoken in the mountains of the north, and Galician, spoken in the northwest, differ greatly from Castilian.

Until 1978 the state religion was Roman Catholicism, and more than 90 percent of the population is at least nominally Roman Catholic. There are small minorities of Jews, Muslims, and Protestants.

Spain's principal city is the capital, Madrid, located almost at the geographic center of the country. Spain's second largest city is the Mediterranean port of Barcelona (population, 1,504,000). Other major cities are Valencia (738,000), Seville (685,000), Zaragoza (615,000), and Bilbao (350,000).

Economy. The Spanish economy is one of the least developed in Western Europe. Nonetheless, substantial improvement has taken place since 1960.

center
US

centre
Brit.

MOST CAVE PAINTINGS
in northern Spain are of the animals that prehistoric man hunted.

THE SPECTACLE of the bullfight, or *corrida,* is popular in Spain. It originated there as a sport in the 1700s, although some forms of bullfighting existed before then.

labor
US

labour
Brit.

civilization
US

civilisation
Brit.

Since 1960 Spain has sought to increase the national income and to improve production efficiency in order to compete in the world market. The result of this planning has been a rise in the standard of living and a rapid growth of industry, which now accounts for 31 percent of the labor force and one-third of the national product. Agriculture, which employed 41 percent of the labor force in 1960, now provides for only 14 percent of labor and about 6 percent of the national product. Foreign investment and tourism rose significantly during this period.

Natural resources. Spain's mineral resources compare favorably with those of the rest of southern Europe, but the production of some materials, such as mercury, pyrites, and potash, has decreased considerably because quality deposits of these have been nearly exhausted.

Spain's mineral industry does produce substantial quantities of coal (anthracite), lignite, iron ore, lead, manganese, tin, zinc, and wolfram.

Oil has been discovered in recent years, but most of Spain's oil is still imported. Hydroelectric capacity is small, while nuclear energy is gaining in importance.

Agriculture. In the past Spain was traditionally an agricultural nation, but low levels of technical progress, poor land distribution, and the careless depletion of national forests have decreased the importance of agriculture in the economy as compared with industry. Nevertheless, agriculture remains an important contributor to the economy.

Grains, fruits, and vegetables are the chief products. These include wheat, barley, grapes, olives, and oranges. Sheep, cattle, and poultry are raised. In addition, Spain is one of the world's leaders in cork production and has one of the world's largest fishing fleets.

Industry. Spain's industry is becoming increasingly important to the country's economy. The government actively encourages industrial growth, particularly in new high-technology fields. Much of Spain's industry is concentrated in Catalonia, centered on the port city of Barcelona. Spain's most important industries include steel, shipbuilding, textiles, food processing, and automobiles.

Trade. The country's principal exports are oranges, nuts, fish, vegetables, wine, textiles, and iron and steel. Chief imports include machinery, foodstuffs, chemicals, manufactured goods, and petroleum. Spain's major trading partners are the United States, Germany, France, and Great Britain.

Government. According to Spain's 1978 constitution, the monarch is now a figurehead, although the present king, Juan Carlos, wields great influence. Actual power under the constitution lies with the bicameral Cortes Generales, with a 350-member Congress of Deputies and a 259-member Senate. All legislature members are elected to four-year terms.

The head of government is the President of the Government named by the king and responsible to the Cortes Generales. The king also appoints, on the president's recommendation, a cabinet.

History. Spain was peopled in prehistoric times by primitive Basques and Iberians. In about 900 B.C. Celts began entering the peninsula from the north.

The Phoenicians began founding trading colonies on the southeastern coast in about 800 B.C., and the Greeks followed suit from about 500 B.C. The Phoenician city of Carthage, in North Africa, acquired control over southern Spain during the 200s B.C. In 202 B.C. Rome defeated Carthage in the Second Punic War and completed the conquest of Spain. By the beginning of the first century A.D., Roman control over the peninsula was undisputed.

Under Roman rule, classical civilization entered Spain and it soon became one of the most Romanized provinces of the empire. Spain made significant contributions to Latin literature and produced one of Rome's greatest emperors, Trajan. Spain was also one of the first parts of the empire to accept Christianity.

In 409 A.D. Spain was overrun by the Vandals, in turn driven out by the Visigoths. In 419 the Visigoths established a kingdom that included Spain and southern France. They contributed little to Spain culturally and put up little resistance when Arab and Berber Muslims invaded the country in 711. The Muslims, or Moors as they were called, ruled most of Spain from Córdoba, which became the center of a brilliant civilization.

Reconquest. A small Christian nucleus survived the Muslim invasions in the Asturian Mountains, which in 722 became the kingdom of Asturias. The establishment of this kingdom marked the beginning of the Reconquest, the 800-year struggle of the Christians in the north to retake Iberia from the Muslims.

In addition to Asturias, which evolved into the kingdom of León in the 1000s, there arose the Christian kingdoms of Aragon and Navarre, the county of Catalonia, and the county—later the kingdom—of Castile. Each of these medieval Christian states had its own body of laws and feudal customs. Each also had a *côrtes,* or representative assembly.

For 300 years these kingdoms waged unsuccessful wars with the Caliphate of Córdoba, the ruling power of Muslim Spain. In the 1000s civil war among the Muslims shattered the unity of the caliphate. Its disintegration aided the Reconquest, and by 1300 the

MANY OF THE BASQUES who live in the Pyrenees raise sheep on land that is suitable for little else.

Christians had reduced the Muslim hold to a narrow strip in southern Spain known as the kingdom of Granada.

Aragon and Catalonia had merged in the 1100s, and Castile and León had done the same in the 1200s, but Portugal separated from Castile in 1143 and became an independent kingdom. Further unification of Christian Spain was brought about by the marriage in 1469 of Ferdinand of Aragon (ruled 1479–1516) and Queen Isabella of Castile (ruled 1474–1504).

In 1478 they supported the Inquisition, whose stern ecclesiastical courts sought out the thousands of converted Jews and Muslims living in Spain whose allegiance to Roman Catholicism was doubted.

In 1492 Ferdinand and Isabella conquered Granada, the last Muslim stronghold. To unify the country completely they expelled the remaining Jews and Muslims. In the same year, Christopher Columbus discovered the New World and claimed it for Spain, thus opening up vast new territories for colonization.

The Hapsburgs.   Joanna, the daughter of Ferdinand and Isabella, married Philip of Hapsburg, the heir to the Holy Roman Empire and to much of northern Europe. Their son, Charles I of Spain (ruled 1516–1556), became the Holy Roman Emperor Charles V in 1519.

Charles encouraged Spanish colonial expansion, and during his reign Spain gained control of most of Mexico, Central America and northwestern South America. In his role as emperor, however, he embroiled Spain in a series of wars against France. A devout Roman Catholic, he made an unsuccessful attempt to defeat Lutheranism in Germany and engaged in a long struggle against the Muslims of North Africa.

Philip II.   Charles's son, Philip II (ruled 1556–1598), did not succeed to the Holy Roman Empire, but he did inherit Spain; the New World possessions; Franche-Comté in France; Milan and Naples in Italy; and the Netherlands. As staunch a Roman Catholic as his father, Philip's foreign policy was often largely the result of his religious convictions.

Philip was determined to suppress Protestantism among his subjects in the Netherlands, but his attempts failed and the Netherlands declared its independence from Spain in 1581. His greatest failure, however, was his attempt to conquer England, which was not only Protestant but also Spain's rival for control of the seas.

In 1588 Philip launched the Spanish Armada against the English. The armada was largely destroyed; its destruction marked the beginning of the end of Spanish sea power. Philip's only notable success in foreign affairs was the acquisition of Portugal in 1580.

Decline and renewal.   Spain declined rapidly in the 1600s, partially as a result of mediocre and indolent kings who left governing to inferior ministers. The country grew poorer, government revenue proved insufficient despite heavy gold imports from Spain's American colonies, and the population declined. The Dutch and English crippled Spanish trade on the seas, and Portugal regained its independence in 1640.

The nation was at its weakest when Charles II (ruled 1665–1700) died without heirs and the throne passed to Philip V (ruled 1700–1746) of the French Bourbon line. Under the Bourbons, Spain underwent a revival in the 1700s. Trade and industry grew, the population increased, colonial administration improved, and the Spanish army and navy regained some of their former strength. These gains, however, were swept away during the Napoleonic era.

Spain in the 1800s.   In 1807 Napoleon I of France seized the Spanish throne for his brother Joseph, and the Spanish monarch, Ferdinand VII, was forced to abdicate. The Spanish carried on guerrilla warfare against the French, and in 1813, aided by the British, they finally drove Napoleon's troops from the peninsula.

In 1814 Ferdinand VII was restored to the throne, but Spain had been seriously weakened. The mainland American colonies, which had proclaimed their independence during Ferdinand's reign, were completely lost by 1825. A family quarrel among Spanish Bourbons over the throne led to a fierce civil war, the Carlist struggle, that raged from 1834 to 1839.

The reign of Isabella II, who had come to the throne in 1833 as an infant, was marked by political unrest and internal disorder. In addition, she was personally unpopular and in 1868 was forced to abdicate.

After an experiment with an imported Italian monarch, Amadeo I (ruled 1871–1873), a republic was established in 1873. The following year, however, Isabella's son, Alfonso XII (ruled 1875–1885), came of age and was recalled to the throne.

Alfonso XII died in 1885 and was succeeded by Alfonso XIII (ruled 1885–1931), who was born after his father's death. In 1898 Spain fought the disastrous Spanish-American War with the United States. In the war it lost Cuba, Puerto Rico, the Philippines, and Guam, reducing Spain's colonial empire to a few minor holdings in Africa.

Instability.   Spain was neutral in World War I, but the wartime demand for goods led to an expansion of Spanish industry. In the postwar period, when the demand for goods and munitions ceased, Spain suffered labor problems and political instability. The country was also burdened with the financial and military problem of putting down uprisings in Spanish Morocco, where a Spanish zone had been established in the early 1900s.

In 1921 a military disaster in Morocco seriously threatened the monarchy. The political situation grew steadily worse, and in 1923 General Miguel Primo de Rivera seized power

VELÁSQUEZ painted this portrait of Carlos, or Charles I, under whom Spain expanded its colonial empire.

with the king's consent and established a dictatorship. Primo de Rivera resigned in 1930 and the republicans took advantage of the overwhelming majority they had won in parliamentary elections in 1931 to proclaim a republic.

The Second Spanish Republic, which attempted liberal reforms, was unpopular with the Roman Catholic Church and the aristocracy. General dissatisfaction with the republic increased as the world economic depression of the 1930s began to affect Spain.

The armed forces, the monarchists, the land-owning aristocracy, and the church were united in their opposition to the republic. The republic was

FERDINAND VII was forced to abdicate the Spanish throne when Napoleon seized it for his brother Joseph.

supported, on the other hand, by Socialists, Communists, Republicans, and various liberal groups.

Civil war. Following a Republican victory in elections held in 1936, violence broke out and the army, led by General José Sanjurjo, rose against the government. General Sanjurjo was killed in a plane crash, and General Francisco Franco assumed leadership of the rebels.

Soon after the outbreak of hostilities, foreign nations began to intervene. The Republicans, as the supporters of the government were called, were aided by sympathizers in the United States and other countries, as well as by the Soviet Union. Franco and the Nationalists received large-scale aid from Nazi Germany and fascist Italy, and by 1939 the Republicans were defeated.

Franco set up a dictatorship and governed with the title "El Caudillo," or "the leader," aided by the Falangists, the Spanish equivalent of the Italian fascists.

Contemporary Spain. Although he was openly favorable to the Axis powers in World War II, Franco remained neutral. In 1947 Franco promulgated the Law of Succession, which restored the monarchy by providing for the election of a king by a Regency Council after his death.

In 1953, during the Cold War, the United States changed its previously unfavorable attitude toward Franco's government and obtained military bases in Spain. Franco's government became somewhat less reactionary in the mid-1960s and it granted a new constitution in 1966.

Franco died in 1975 and Juan Carlos, the grandson of the last reigning king, Alfonso XIII, became king of Spain. Juan Carlos turned out to be staunchly pro-democracy and actively encouraged its development. A new constitution was ratified in 1978 making Spain a parliamentary monarchy. It also disestablished Roman Catholicism as the state religion and guaranteed civil rights.

Spain's return to democracy was not completely smooth. In 1981 a group of Civil Guards seized the Cortes, taking the deputies hostage. One military commander sent his troops into the streets in support of the coup. However, the personal intervention of Juan Carlos elicited the loyalty of the remaining army commanders and the coup collapsed. In 1982 another plot by some members of the armed forces to overthrow the government was uncovered and its leaders arrested.

The governments elected in 1977 and 1979 were run by the center-right party, the Union of the Democratic Center. However, in the 1982 elections, public reaction to the attempted coups led the Socialist Party to an absolute majority in the Cortes. Felipe González Márquez, leader of the Socialists, and therefore prime minister, proved to be a popular leader. The Socialists won a majority in 1986 and retained power with pluralities in 1990 and 1993.

One of the most difficult problems Spain has faced has been the prolonged terrorism by Basque separatists who want independence for the Basque provinces. Although the government has been unable to end the terrorism, indiscriminate violence against civilians by ETA, the terrorist group, has lost them support.

center *US*

centre *Brit.*

meters *US*

metres *Brit.*

Sweden

Official name: *Kingdom of Sweden*
Area: *173,732 sq. mi., 449,964 sq. km.*
Type of government: *Constitutional monarchy*
Population: *8,877,000*
Capital and largest city: *Stockholm (Pop., 755,000)*
Language: *Swedish*
Literacy: *99%*
Currency: *Krona*
Per capita GDP: *$25,400 (Rank: 19th)*

The land. Sweden may be divided into two geographic regions—the Norrland, the northern two-thirds of the country, and the south. Part of the Norrland lies north of the Arctic Circle. In western Norrland, the Kjölen Mountains, the mountainous backbone of the Scandinavian peninsula, rise to nearly 7,000 feet (2,134 meters). The Northern Plateau occupies the center, and in the east there is a relatively narrow coastal plain. The main rivers of the region drain eastward into the Gulf of Bothnia.

The southern third of Sweden includes the broad, level Central Lowland and Skåne, a flat plain in the extreme south. These two regions are separated by a rough upland zone, the Småland Plateau, which has many rivers and includes Sweden's largest lakes, Vänern and Vättern.

Each region has a distinct climate. The Norrland is subarctic, with long, cold winters and short, cool summers. The severity of the climate increases to the north and in the higher elevations. Southern Sweden has much milder winters and slightly warmer, although still cool, summers. The country as a whole is rather dry, receiving only about 20 inches (51 centimeters) of rainfall a year, most of it in the south.

The people. The Swedish people are ethnically and culturally homogeneous. Swedish is the universal language, and the dominant religion is Lutheranism. There are small minorities of Lapps and Finns in the north. Sweden has a large number of immigrants, mostly from other Scandinavian countries and from the Balkan countries.

Although Sweden is one of Europe's largest countries in area, its population density, about 49 people per square mile, is one of Europe's lowest. The population growth rate, only about 0.2

percent a year in the 1980s, is one of the world's lowest and life expectancy is among the world's highest.

Over 80 percent of the Swedes live in urban areas, particularly in the southern third of the country.

Sweden's major cities include Stockholm, the capital, on the southeast coast; Göteborg (population, 471,000), on the southwest coast; and Malmö (462,000), near the southern tip of Sweden.

Economy. Sweden has a highly industrialized economy based on rich natural resources. All of Norrland and much of the south are heavily forested, and the dense timber stands make Sweden's forestry output one of Europe's largest. Sweden's many swift rivers and streams are harnessed for electricity, and hydroelectricity now accounts for about 45 percent of total electrical production. Nuclear energy is also highly

A GIRL crowned in a wreath of candles celebrates St. Lucia's Day, which marks the beginning of Yuletide in Sweden.

developed; it accounts for about 50 percent of the total.

Sweden's most important mineral resource is its exceptionally large deposit of high-quality iron ore. There are also modest reserves of lead, zinc, manganese, tungsten, sulfur, copper, gold, and silver. Sweden also has large deposits of uranium, although they are not extensively exploited.

Agriculture. Owing to poor climate, poor soil, and rough topography, only about 7 percent of the land can be cultivated, most of it in the south. Agriculture employs only about 5 percent of the labor force. Nevertheless, efficient farming techniques produce high yields per acre and agricultural production accounts for about 80 percent of domestic needs.

Dairying is the main agricultural activity, and dairy products account for about half of farm revenues. Oats, wheat, rye, barley, and potatoes are the main crops. Commercial fishing prospers and provides important export products. Forests cover over half of Sweden's total land area, and forest products are an important part of the economy, accounting for over 15 percent of the total exports.

Manufacturing and shipping. Manufacturing is the most important part of the Swedish economy. It employs 23 percent of the national labor force and contributes about one-quarter of the national product, but its rapid growth since World War I has slowed considerably since the mid-1970s. Most Swedish industry is privately owned, but the government is directly involved in the operation of many enterprises, especially the waterpower industry.

Although there is some iron and steel production, metalworking, and shipbuilding, emphasis has been placed on producing electrical machinery, vehicles, furniture, scientific instruments, chemicals, pulp and paper, procelain, and glass.

Trade. The leading imports are machinery, petroleum products, iron and steel products, and foodstuffs. The major exports are machinery, lumber and wood pulp, iron and steel, paper and cardboard, sawed timber, and transportation equipment. Most Swedish trade is with Germany, Great Britain, the United States, Denmark, and Norway.

Government. Sweden is a constitutional monarchy, with a king as head of state. A new constitution was granted in 1975. Actual executive power is exercised by a prime minister and cabinet responsible to the legislature, the Riksdag.

The Riksdag became a unicameral body in 1971. Its 349 members are elected for four-year terms. Of these, 310 are elected by proportional representation and the other 39 seats are distributed to ensure that the parties are represented according to the votes they poll.

History. In about 1000 B.C., Germanic peoples related to modern-day Swedes appeared. The settlers remained divided into numerous small bands and king-

doms until about 600 A.D., when two large tribal groups became dominant—the Goths on the shores of Lake Vättern, and the Svear in the area of Lake Mälaren, near Stockholm.

As other Scandinavian Vikings, or adventurers, sailed westward between 800 and 1050, Sweden's Vikings thrust eastward along European river systems. In the 1100s they established colonies on the eastern shore of the Baltic and governed territory between the Baltic and the Black seas in Russia.

Although the kingdoms of Gothia and Svealand were united in the early 800s, competition for power continued between the Goths and the Svear. Nevertheless, by the end of the 1100s a unified Swedish state had emerged in which Svear, or Swedish, influence prevailed.

Christianity spread to Sweden in the 800s, and by 1000 the church was a powerful influence. During the 1100s Christianity was an important part of the culture the Swedes carried to the Finnish peoples of the territories they conquered.

The 1200s and early 1300s were turbulent, as a newly formed land-owning aristocracy challenged the political and economic dominance of a powerful middle class of townsmen and merchants. Contacts with the German merchants of the Hanseatic League introduced strong German influence into Sweden in the 1300s, and in 1363 a member of the German family of Mecklenburg took the Swedish throne.

Kalmar Union. When opposition to the king arose, the nobility, in 1388, called on Margaret, queen of Denmark and Norway, to intervene. She became ruler of Sweden and laid the foundation for the Kalmar Union (1397–1483), which united the three kingdoms. The union was dominated by Denmark, and throughout the 1400s Sweden remained a restless partner.

Both the peasants and the nobility rebelled against the Danish rulers in the 1400s, and Sweden gradually regained its autonomy. In 1520 Denmark, trying to reassert its supremacy, invaded Sweden and killed Swedish nationalist leaders. This sparked a nationalist revolt led by Gustavus Vasa, a young nobleman.

Vasa kings. Sweden succeeded in breaking away from the Kalmar Union, and in 1523 Gustavus became the first king of the House of Vasa. He had the strong support of the merchants and townsmen, and one of his first acts was to end the German Hanseatic League's monopoly of trade in the Baltic area. During his rule, too, the Reformation came to Sweden, and by the mid-1500s Lutheranism was the dominant religion.

Under generally able kings of the House of Vasa, Sweden developed a prosperous economy and a position of prestige and power in the world. In 1630 the intervention of King Gustavus II Adolphus on the side of Protestantism in the

labor
US

labour
Brit.

A GUARD in a sentry box is a colorful trapping of monarchy in Sweden.

STOCKHOLM IS BUILT on the mainland of Sweden and on 14 small islands connected by bridges. Riddarholmen Island (right) is one of the oldest sections of the city.

religious-political conflict of the Thirty Years' War was decisive in making Protestantism dominant in northern Europe.

Sweden spent most of the rest of the 1600s and the early 1700s in wars of conquest against Poland, Russia, and Denmark. Sweden's greatest soldier-king, Charles XII, died in 1718, and Russia soon won from Sweden most of the territory conquered from Poland and Denmark in the previous century.

The country returned briefly to constitutional government, but absolutism was restored in 1772 under Gustavus III, who feared that Sweden would come totally under the control of Prussia. At first he ruled as an "enlightened despot," introducing progressive and liberal measures, but in the 1780s his rule began to grow more repressive.

Gustavus invaded Russian Finland in an unsuccessful attempt to regain dominance in the Baltic. Aristocratic opposition and intrigue resulted in his assassination in 1792.

Turmoil followed the death of Gustavus. His successor, Gustavus IV, lost Sweden's Finnish provinces in still another war with Russia in 1808, and he was forced by the dissatisfied nobility to abdicate in 1809. Charles XIII was then chosen to succeed him. In 1809 a new constitution was adopted giving great power to the aristocracy.

Charles XIII had no heir and the nation was in need of a strong leader. In 1810 a French marshal, Jean Baptiste Bernadotte, was elected crown prince under the name Charles John.

Reforms and growth. In 1812 Sweden joined the coalition against Napoleonic France, and the end of the Napoleonic era brought major territorial changes. In 1814 Sweden acquired control of Norway from Denmark and the two states were joined in a personal union under the Swedish king. The aged Charles XIII continued to rule in name only until 1818, when Charles John came officially to power.

Charles John's tendency toward arbitrary rule stimulated liberal reform movements. Under his successor, Oscar I, the Liberals made some headway toward universal education and the limitation of royal power. Under Oscar's successor, Charles XV, they achieved economic and political liberalization and, in 1866, a two-chambered legislature was authorized.

During the later 1800s, Sweden underwent rapid industrialization, especially after 1872, when Oscar II came to the throne and initiated programs that made Sweden a commercial and industrial state. The social upheaval that accompanied rapid industrialization resulted in progressive social welfare and suffrage legislation, the growth of trade unionism, and the development of cooperatives.

Prosperity and political reform affected Norway, too, and by the 1890s Norwegian nationalism was a major force. In 1905, partly because of a dispute over consular service, Norway proclaimed its independence, which Sweden accepted late in the year.

Modern Sweden. Political and social progress continued in the 1900s. Under Gustavus V, who came to the throne in 1907, universal suffrage and a system of proportional representation were introduced. In 1914 Sweden's Socialist Party won about one-third of the seats in the lower house of the legislature, and the pace of social legislation accelerated.

Sweden managed to stay neutral in World War I and suffered little from it. During the 1920s and 1930s, under continuing Socialist direction, prosperity continued. Sweden successfully combatted the world economic depression of the 1930s by heavily involving the government in the economy and introducing unemployment insurance legislation.

When Adolf Hitler's Nazi party came to power in Germany in the 1930s, Sweden armed itself but maintained its neutrality. Its neutrality was severely

tested in 1939, when Finland was invaded by the Soviet Union, and later in 1940, during World War II, when Denmark and Norway were attacked and occupied by German forces. Sweden was forced to make some concessions to Germany, but it also gave asylum to refugees.

After the war, Sweden's economy continued to expand. Prosperity and a successful combination of socialism and individualism combined to produce a stable society. For 63 of the 72 years between 1932 and 2004, Sweden was led by the liberal Social Democratic Party.

Sweden has participated actively in the international organizations of the postwar world and used its historic position of neutrality to work for international peace. It has worked hard for tighter Scandinavian unity.

In 1986 the country was rocked when Prime Minister Olof Palme was murdered on a Stockholm street.

In 1994 voters approved Sweden's joining the European Union. Although supportive of the European monetary union, Sweden did not adopt the Euro as the monetary unit for the country.

Switzerland

Official name: *Swiss Confederation*
Area: *15,942 sq. mi., 41,290 sq. km.*
Type of government:
Federal republic
Population: *7,302,000*
Capital: *Bern
(Pop., 122,000)*
Largest city: *Zurich
(Pop., 341,000)*
Languages: *German, French, Italian, Romansch
(all official)*
Literacy: *99%*
Currency: *Franc*
Per capita GDP: *$31,700
(Rank: 5th)*

The land. Switzerland has three major physical regions: the Jura Mountains in the northwest, the central Swiss Plateau, and the Alps, which cover the southern three-fifths of the country.

Switzerland has many lakes, of which Lake Geneva is the largest. The principal rivers are the Rhine and the Rhône, which have

SNOW-COVERED SLOPES of the Swiss Alps attract thousands of skiers yearly.

their headwaters high in the Swiss Alps, only a few miles from one another.

Switzerland's climate is humid, with mild to cool summers and mostly cold winters. Winters increase in severity with altitude, and the more rugged parts of the Alps are very cold and snowy. In the south and along Lake Geneva the climate is much milder.

The people. The Swiss are descended from several different ethnic groups. Rhaetic and Celtic tribes that lived in Switzerland in Roman times were overwhelmed by the Germanic Alemanni and Burgundians in the 400s. Roman culture and the Latin language stayed strongest in the south. These ethnic differences have remained embedded in local speech.

Switzerland has four official languages—French, German, Italian, and Romansch—and most Swiss have at least a working knowledge of more than one language. About two-thirds of the population speaks German. The Swiss are evenly divided between Protestantism and Roman Catholicism.

Switzerland's natural rate of population growth is average for a European nation, but its net growth is the highest in Europe because of heavy immigration. The highest population density is found on the Swiss Plateau, in an east-west band from Zürich to Geneva, and in the Rhine corridor.

Switzerland's most heavily populated cities, in order, are Zürich (population, 341,000), Basel (165,000), Geneva (176,000), and Bern (122,000).

Economy. Switzerland has few natural resources and agriculture is limited by the rugged terrain. But the Swiss have developed a prosperous economy based on the manufacture of high-quality, low-bulk goods, such as watches and clocks, that involve a high degree of skilled workmanship. These goods have an excellent reputation and a steady market abroad.

The economy has also been aided by the country's political stability and policy of strict neutrality, which have made it a great international banking and insurance center. Switzerland also derives large revenues from international traffic, mainly between West Germany and Italy, and from tourism.

Natural resources. Switzerland has no important mineral deposits other than salt and stone. But the country's rivers provide an excellent source of hydroelectric power, which the Swiss have developed to compensate for the lack of fuels. It provides the nation with 59 percent of its electrical needs.

Agriculture. Agriculture employs only about 7 percent of the labor force. It is efficient but production does not meet domestic requirements.

The raising of livestock, particularly dairy cattle, is the most important agricultural activity. The major crops are wheat, potatoes, sugar beet, and fruit.

Industry. Swiss industry, employing 35 percent of the labor force, must import a large part of its raw materials. Most of its products are exported. The most important industries produce textiles, chemicals, pharmaceuticals, clocks and watches, and precision machinery.

Trade. The country's chief exports are watches and clocks, pharmaceuticals, chemicals, textiles, and machinery. Major imports include foodstuffs, heavy machinery, iron and steel, motor vehicles, raw fibers, and petroleum.

Switzerland conducts the bulk of its trade with Germany, France, Italy, the United States, and Great Britain.

Government. Switzerland is a federal republic of 26 cantons, which are similar to provinces or states. The executive branch consists of the Federal Council, composed of seven ministers who head various administrative departments, chosen by the Federal Assembly.

The head of state is the president, who is elected to a one-year term from among the members of the Federal Council by the legislature. The president has comparatively little power and cannot serve consecutive terms.

Legislative power is vested in a bicameral Federal Assembly consisting of the Council of States and the National Council. The Council of States has 46 members. The National Council has 200 members directly elected on the basis of proportional representation to four-year terms.

Women did not gain the right to vote in federal elections until 1971, and, until the passage in 1982 of a constitutional amendment guaranteeing equal rights, were still prohibited from participating in some local elections.

History. The earliest recorded inhabitants of present-day Switzerland were a number of Celtic tribes, among them the Helvetii, who had at an earlier time probably conquered the Rhaeti, who also lived in the area. In the first century B.C. these tribes were defeated by the Romans under Julius Caesar, and Switzerland became Roman territory.

During the 400s A.D., when Roman power began to decline, the area was conquered by the Alemanni, the

center
US

centre
Brit.

labor
US

labour
Brit.

fibers
US

fibres
Brit.

26 Europe and Russia

PICTURESQUE TOWNS
and villages of Switzerland reflect the high standard of living of the Swiss people.

HAY HARVEST
in St. Moritz

Burgundians, and the Franks. By the early 800s, Switzerland had become part of Charlemagne's empire, although it became divided under Charlemagne's successors.

Independence. During the 1200s the area around Lake Lucerne came under the rule of the Swabian Hapsburg family. In 1291 the Swiss communities, or cantons, of Schwyz, Uri, and Unterwalden entered into a defensive league, or confederation, against the Hapsburgs, whose rule was extremely oppressive. The Hapsburgs were decisively defeated in 1315 at the Battle of Morgarten, and the cantons were able to gain their independence.

By 1513 the confederation had expanded to include 13 cantons, and Switzerland became an important military power. Swiss expansionism, however, was permanently checked by Francis I of France, who won a crushing victory over the Swiss at Marignano in 1515.

In the 1500s the Reformation, led by Ulrich Zwingli in Zürich and John Calvin in Geneva, provoked a civil war between Roman Catholic and Protestant cantons and seriously weakened the league. Switzerland remained neutral throughout the Thirty Years' War, but was able to gain international recognition of its independence and neutrality in 1648 at the Peace of Westphalia, which ended the conflict.

For 100 years following the Peace of Westphalia, Switzerland was in decline. This came to an end in the mid-1700s with the growth of industry and an intellectual renaissance. In 1798, during the French revolutionary wars, the confederation was replaced by the French-sponsored Helvetic Republic, which had a strong central government and abolished the sovereignty of the cantons.

Neutrality. In 1815 the Congress of Vienna, which redrew the map of Europe after Napoleon's defeat, reaffirmed Switzerland's independence and neutrality. It also drew up a federal plan for the cantons that granted them a large degree of individual autonomy. In 1848 a new constitution strengthened the central government. It was revised in 1874 to strengthen central authority even further.

In the 1800s and 1900s Switzerland's neutrality led many international organizations to choose the country as the site of their headquarters. The country stayed neutral, although heavily armed, throughout both world wars.

Contemporary Switzerland. In 1946, in order to maintain its neutrality, Switzerland decided not to join the United Nations, but it finally joined in 2002. UN European headquarters are in Geneva.

Postwar prosperity, especially in the 1950s and 1960s, led to an influx of foreign workers into labor-short Switzerland. Today 20 percent of the national labor force is composed of foreign workers.

Reaction against the presence of so many foreign workers, strongest in the financial and industrial center of Zürich, led the Swiss government in 1967, 1970, and 1974 to announce referendums to impose constitutional limitations on the number of foreign workers admitted into the country. Each popular vote opposed the restrictions, but voting was close and tension continues to mount over the issue.

Since 1959 Switzerland has been led by a coalition of the four main parties, the Social Democrats, Radical Democrats, Christian Democrats, and the People's Party. This coalition has resulted in the maintenance of a stable political life. Parliamentary elections in 2003 threatened this balance when the right-wing Swiss People's Party received the majority vote, making the future of such a coalition uncertain.

labor
US

labour
Brit.

center
US

centre
Brit.

Ukraine

Official name: *Ukraine*
Area: *233,028 sq. mi.,*
603,700 sq. km.
Type of government: *Republic*
Population: *48,396,000*
Capital and largest city: *Kiev*
(Pop., 2,590,000)
Languages: *Ukrainian (official),*
Russian, Romanian, Polish
Literacy: *98%;* **Currency:** *Hryvnya*
Per capita GDP: *$4,200*
(Rank: 98th)

The land. Ukraine, located on the East European Plain, is a land of many rivers and few mountains. Most of Ukraine's rivers, including the Dnieper (Ukraine's longest river), flow toward the southeast and empty into the Black Sea. The country's only mountain ranges are the Carpathian Mountains in the southwest and the Crimean Mountains, situated between the Black Sea and the Sea of Azov. The climate in Ukraine is basically temperate, although it ranges from Mediterranean in parts of the Crimean peninsula to continental in the north.

The people. The majority of the people living in Ukraine are East Slavs (Ukrainians, Russians, and Belorussians), with ethnic Ukrainians constituting the largest part of the population. Many ethnic minorities, including Moldovians, Jews, Poles, Lithuanians, Khazars, Tatars, and Khazaks also live in Ukraine. Ukrainian is the most widely spoken language in the country. The main religion is Ukrainian Orthodox, a branch of the Eastern Orthodox Church. Most Ukrainians who are Catholic follow the Eastern rite. A small portion of the population is Jewish or Muslim. Almost a third of the Ukrainian population live in rural areas. Major cities in Ukraine include the capital city of Kiev; Kharkiv (population, 1,494,000), a major industrial center; Donets'k (1,050,000); and Odesa (1,002,000).

Economy. Ukraine's many natural resources include coal, lignite (brown coal), peat, iron ore, mercury, titanium, manganese, bauxite, and mercury. Historically referred to as the breadbasket of Russia, Ukraine produces grains and sugar beets. In addition to mining and agriculture, the manufacture of industrial equipment, machinery, and chemicals contributes significantly to the country's economy.

Upon declaring itself independent of the Soviet Union in 1991, Ukraine embarked on a series of modest economic reforms. While the reforms were not as far-reaching as those in Russia, the economy nonetheless suffered a sharp drop in production and spiraling inflation, estimated at a monthly rate of 30 percent. The damage was due in part to the country's dependence on imports from Russia, which was undergoing tumultuous changes, and in part to the fact that the old communist economic policies were not sustainable. In the spring of 1992, the Ukrainian parliament decided to replace the Russian ruble with the karbovanets, which was replaced in 1996 by a new currency, the hryvna. To aid the troubled economy, Prime Minister Leonid Kuchma advocated more vigorous reforms in late 1992, including a stronger privatization policy, liberalization of prices, severe cuts in subsidies, and a strict monetary policy. However, critics feared the measures Kuchma proposed would lead to the same type of economic difficulties encountered in Russia.

Government. The Ukrainian government's Supreme Council is a legislative body consisting of 225 elected members. The president nominates the prime minister, who is then approved by the legislature. Ukraine is a member of the United Nations, having held a seat since its days as a Soviet republic.

History. Ukraine was first settled about 6000 B.C. Between the eighth and first centuries B.C., the nomadic Scythians ruled the region. Successive invasions by various European tribes were followed by the arrival of the Turkic-speaking Khazars in the seventh century A.D. The Khazars ruled the area until 965, when they were defeated by a Scandinavian people called the Varangians, who had already conquered Novgorod and Kiev to establish Kievan Rus.

Kievan Rus continued to expand until it encompassed present-day Ukraine and Belarus, as well as parts of Russia and

Scandinavia. It was destroyed in the 13th century, when the Tatars invaded. The remains of the state were divided between Lithuania-Poland and Russia in the 14th century, and Ukrainians were forced to work the land as serfs. Some Ukrainians escaped to the empty regions of southwestern Ukraine and became known as Khazaks (Cossacks), the Turkic word for outlaws. As the Tatars continued to threaten Ukraine, the Cossacks were hired as soldiers by both the Poles and the Russians. The Cossacks believed their military service freed them from serfdom, but the Poles recognized only registered Cossacks as militiamen and considered the rest to be serfs or outlaws. In 1648 the Cossacks revolted against the Poles and established an independent state. The Cossack state was quickly attacked by Polish forces.

When the Cossacks applied to Moscow for aid in 1654, the Russians responded by fighting Poland and absorbing the Cossack state. One branch of the Cossacks then allied itself with the Turks of the Ottoman Empire and continued its struggle against the Poles. Meanwhile, Cossacks living under Russian rule forged an alliance with Sweden in an attempt to establish an independent Ukraine. Russia's defeat of Sweden in 1709 put an end to these Cossack ambitions. Ukraine was not only divided politically between Poland and Russia, but also by religious differences: The Poles in Ukraine were Roman Catholic; Ukrainians under Polish rule were Catholics following the Eastern rite; and Ukrainians under Russian rule were Eastern Orthodox. When Poland collapsed in the 18th century, Ukraine was once again divided, this time between Russia and Austria.

Nationalism grew in Ukraine throughout the 19th century, but little progress was made toward achieving independence. The upheaval created by World War I and the Russian Revolution of 1917 finally enabled Ukraine to gain an opportunity for independence. A Central Rada (council) was established in Kiev in 1917, but by 1920 Russia had established the Ukrainian Socialist Soviet Republic, and the western portions of Ukraine were divided among Poland, Czechoslovakia, and Romania.

When the Union of Soviet Socialist Republics was established in 1922, Ukraine was one of the constituent states. Although Soviet rule improved the literacy rate among Ukrainians and bettered their economic conditions somewhat, Ukrainian resistance continued. Ukrainian opponents to the collectivization of farms were harshly punished under the Stalinist regime, which created an artificial famine in the area. World War II brought further devastation to the region, though the Allied victory led to the reunification of Ukraine. In 1954 the Soviet Union added the Crimean to Ukraine. After the nuclear disaster at Chernobyl in 1986, a number of opposition groups increased their resistance to the Soviet regime. Intellectuals, environmentalists, religious organizations, and workers all expressed their opposition to the government throughout the 1980s. Mikhail Gorbachev's efforts to reform the government did little to appease Ukrainians, and on August 24, 1991, the Ukrainian Supreme Soviet declared Ukraine's independence. The declaration was supported in a December referendum. (For a detailed history of the period between 1922 and 1991, see the article on Russia.)

As an independent country, Ukraine helped found the Commonwealth of Independent States in December, 1991, but it was wary of Russia's possible domination of the organization. Ukraine was the first of the former Soviet republics to create an independent army and demanded a share of the Black Sea fleet, which it initially claimed in its entirety.

Although Ukraine agreed in principle to the Strategic Arms Reduction Treaty (START) negotiated between the Soviet Union and the United States in 1991, Ukraine had not ratified the treaty by the end of January 1993, thus making it impossible to enforce START II, signed by Russia and the United States earlier in the month. Ukraine objected primarily to granting Russia full control of all nuclear weapons, despite having agreed to such an arrangement in Lisbon in the spring of 1992. The delay in compliance was explained by claims that Ukraine would be endangered by relinquishing its nuclear weapons and would not receive enough financial aid from the United States and European countries once the nuclear bargaining chip was lost. Ukraine, however, relented and the last nuclear warhead was removed to Russia in June 1996.

Leonid Kuchma, who had called for closer ties with Russia, was elected president in 1994. In 2001 and 2002, amid allegations of involvement in a journalist's death and shipments of military equipment to Iraq, some called for his resignation, but he remains in power.

A TRADITIONAL VILLAGE of wooden houses has been recreated in Ukraine.

United Kingdom

Official name: *United Kingdom of Great Britain and Northern Ireland*

Area: *94,251 sq. mi., 244,174 sq. km.*

Type of government: *Constitutional monarchy*

Population: *59,912,000*

Capital and largest city: *London (Pop., metro. area, 7,652,000)*

Languages: *English (official), Welsh, Gaelic*

Literacy: *99%*

Currency: *Pound*

Per capita GDP: *$25,300 (Rank: 20th)*

meters
US

metres
Brit.

center
US

centre
Brit.

labor
US

labour
Brit.

The land. The United Kingdom of Great Britain and Northern Ireland, usually referred to as Great Britain or Britain, covers most of the British Isles, off the northwest coast of continental Europe.

The major island, Great Britain, includes England in the south and east, Wales in the west, and Scotland in the north. Northern Ireland, part of the United Kingdom, shares the island of Ireland with the independent Republic of Ireland.

Most of the islands near Great Britain, including the Hebrides, Shetland, and Orkney groups off Scotland and the Isle of Wight off England, are British. The Channel Islands in the English Channel and the Isle of Man in the Irish Sea are British dependencies.

A complex geological structure gives the British Isles a varied topography despite their limited size. On Great Britain a moderately high highland region arches northward from the Cambrian Mountains in Wales and the Cotswold Hills in Western England. It extends through the Pennine Mountains in north-central England and the Cheviot Hills, the Southern Uplands, and the Grampian Mountains of Scotland to the Scottish Highlands, where the nation's highest peak, Ben Nevis, rises to 4,406 feet (1,343 meters).

Most of England is occupied by low plains. In central England the Midlands occupy the basins of the Mersey and the Trent rivers between the Cotswolds to the south and the Pennines to the north. In the south and east the lowlands are called the Downs and Fens. The Central Lowland, in Scotland between the Southern Upland and the Highlands, is the only major lowland outside of England.

Narrow plains skirt the deeply indented coasts of Wales, northern England, and southern Scotland, but the highlands of northern Scotland drop sharply into the sea. The northern and western sections of Northern Ireland are rolling uplands, leveling off in the south and east.

The most important of Britain's rivers are the Thames and the Severn in England and the Tweed and the Clyde in Scotland. Most British lakes are in the Lake District of northwestern England and in the Scottish highlands, which are also marked by long, narrow fjordlike inlets. Britain's largest lake, Lough Neagh, lies in the center of Northern Ireland.

Climate. Britain has a temperate maritime climate. The cold temperatures usual for the islands' northerly location are moderated by the warm Gulf Stream flowing just west of the islands and by warm winds off the Atlantic Ocean. As a result, winters are generally mild and summers cool, with few temperature extremes. Average temperatures are about 40°F (4°C) in winter and 60°F (16°C) in summer.

Rainfall ranges from 20 inches (51 centimeters) a year in the southeast to 120 inches (305 centimeters) on the west coast, and averages about 40 inches (102 centimeters) for the country as a whole.

The people. Britain is one of the world's most densely settled countries, with 606 people per square mile. The bulk of the country's population live in England and Wales. Britain is also a highly urbanized nation, and 90 percent of Britons live in cities or suburbs.

Britain's population is quite homogeneous. Most Britons are descendants of Celtic, Scandinavian, French, and Germanic peoples who settled in the islands by the twelfth century.

English is the universal language, although the Celtic languages of Welsh and Gaelic are spoken in the north and west. The Church of England (Anglican Church) is the established church and the dominant religion, but other Protestant denominations and Roman Catholicism are also important.

The few ethnic minority groups of any significance are made up of immigrants from member nations of the British Commonwealth of Nations. Most prominent are people from the West Indies, India, and Pakistan.

Economy. Britain has one of the lower per capita incomes in Europe; however, the country remains a major industrial and trading nation. During the 1980s Britain finally began to move out of the economic slump that had troubled it for most of the postwar years.

Natural resources. In 1975 production from the North Sea oil fields began. By 1987 Britain was the sixth largest oil producer in the world, extracting 122 million metric tons. Britain's natural resources also include abundant fields of excellent coal and rich iron ore deposits, mostly in the Pennines, as well as quantities of limestone, gravel, chalk, and fine clays. There are also small deposits of zinc, tin, and lead, and bauxite is mined in northern Ireland.

Agriculture. The soils of Britain's lowlands and river valleys, especially in eastern England and northern Ireland, are quite fertile, but limited in quantity. The highlands are generally unsuitable for farming, but they provide excellent grazing land.

Agriculture, though highly productive, contributes only 3 percent of the gross domestic product and occupies less than 3 percent of the labor force. However, agricultural production provides about three-quarters of domestic food needs.

A great variety of crops are raised. Wheat and barley are important, and fruits, vegetables, and other grains also are raised. Dairy farming prospers, particularly in Wales, Northern Ireland, the Scottish lowlands, and western England. Large herds of sheep are grazed in the Highlands and the Midlands, and pigs, poultry, and beef cattle are important throughout the country.

Fishing contributes less than 1 percent of the GDP, but it has long provided an important item in the British diet and is vital to the economies of Scotland and the northern islands.

Industry. Britain is a highly industrialized nation, and manufacturing contributes about one-quarter of the gross domestic product, one of the highest percentages in the world. British industry, originally based on its coal, iron, and wool, was forced to shift in the mid-1900s to keep pace with modern technology and to meet the varied demands of modern markets. Heavy industry remains central to the British economy, however.

England, Great Britain, United Kingdom

These venerable state names are sometimes confused when referred to by foreign writers and speakers.

England (capital, London) is a part of Great Britain and of the United Kingdom. It is made up largely of the area south of the river Tweed, which separates England from Scotland. England emerged as a distinct political entity in the ninth century.

Great Britain, or **Britain**, considered as a unit, comprises England, Wales, and Scotland plus certain small adjacent islands. Wales was politically incorporated into England by Henry VIII in 1536. The Act of Union, in 1707, formally united Scotland with England. Ever since, England and Scotland have been ruled by one monarch, from 1603, and by a single Parliament, from 1707.

The **United Kingdom** is the kingdom of Great Britain and, since 1922, Northern Ireland. The term United Kingdom referred to Great Britain and all of Ireland from 1801, when the two countries were united by an act of Parliament, until 1920, when Ireland was partitioned. The two entities have since been known as Northern Ireland and the Republic of Ireland.

THE UNITED KINGDOM includes England, Scotland, Wales, and Northern Ireland. The constitutional monarch, Queen Elizabeth II, lives in England. Also pictured here are a pastoral scene in the hills of Scotland, fishermen of Wales, and a mural depicting the civil strife in Northern Ireland.

Iron and steelworking, metal finishing, chemical production, shipbuilding, and manufacture of machinery, machine tools, aircraft, and vehicles are the most important activities. Textiles, both wool and the newer synthetics, are an important element in British industry. Food processing is also important.

The centers of British heavy industry are in the Midlands, in southern Wales, in the Scottish lowlands, and, to a lesser extent, in coastal Northern Ireland and on the northern English coast. Greater London is the center of British light industry; it is also the commercial and financial center of the country.

The British government plays an active role in the economy, stimulating and regulating agriculture and industry and providing broad social services for the British people. The government owns and operates in whole or in part the country's rail and air transport systems, its coal and steel industries, and its radio, television, and telecommunications networks.

Trade. International trade is vital to Britain's economy, and Britain for many years was the world's first ranking trading nation. Foodstuffs constitute the largest single class of imports, and fuels, industrial raw materials, and finished and semifinished consumer goods are also imported. Machinery, petroleum, vehicles, and scientific instruments are the leading exports. Textiles, chemicals, metals, and other manufactured goods are important as well.

26 Europe and Russia

Tea

For centuries, tea has been one of the most widely distributed and popular commodities in the world's trade markets. It has a serendipitous bent—its discovery, addition of ice, and packaging in bags being the products of chance occurrences. Fortunes have been made from the sale of tea, battles have been fought over it, and highly structured rituals and ceremonies have accompanied the serving of tea.

Teas for Tea

- Breakfast teas often are chosen for their bright color and brisk flavor. They include Ceylon, Indian, African, and blends, including Assam or Chinese Keemun.

- Low tea, so called because it was served in the low part of the afternoon, traditionally was served by aristocracy and featured small gourmet delicacies. For this early-afternoon tea, choices may include flavored or scented teas such as mango or peach, as well as China and green teas—teas that are less brisk than those often associated with breakfast servings.

- High tea, originally more identified with the working class, was a substantial meal served at the end of the workday. In addition to the lighter teas, which may be served at both low and high teas, the choices are quite open for high tea. Additional offerings include stronger teas such as Assam, Earl Grey, Orange Pekoe, and Darjeeling, often preferred because of its versatility.

History of Tea. According to lore, more than five thousand years ago a Chinese ruler known for his scientific knowledge, in addition to his patronage of the arts, applied that knowledge and required that drinking water be boiled as a safety measure. While traveling one day, the emperor Shen Nung had his servants boiling the water for drinking when some leaves from a bush blew into the water. Deciding to test the infusion, or tea, the emperor drank some, found it to his liking, and the rest is history. *Ch'a Ching* **and Other Writings.** The first well-researched work on the subject of tea was a book, the *Ch'a Ching,* written in 800 A.D. Influenced by his monastic upbringing, poet and author Lu Yu wrote extensively of tea cultivation methods and preparations. His Zen Buddhist philosophy was prevalent in the writings, and it was this association that was carried along with tea seeds to Japan, where again tea was used in ceremonies to enhance religious meditation. As Irish-Greek historian and journalist Lafcadio Hearn observed of the early Japanese ritual, "The supremely important matter is that the act be performed in the most perfect, most polite, most graceful, most charming manner possible."

Arrival in Britany. Although the importation of tea from tropical and subtropical regions to Europe began in the late 1500s, Great Britain didn't begin sampling the brew until the mid-1600s. At that time its American colonists, early tea drinkers thanks to Dutch importers, consumed more than did citizens of the Mother Country.

A Tea Tax, A Revolution, and Variations. With its base in Britain, the East India Trading Company gained a trade monopoly, keeping the price of tea high. As the empire sought ways in the 1770s to pay for the French and Indian War fought in America, heavy taxation of the colonies became a means of doing so. A tea tax was one of many taxes imposed, against which the colonists rebelled, saying they had no legislative representation. Counting on the high usage of tea by the colonists as leverage, the tax was required. The colonists pledged not to drink tea, however, and had a tea party of their own in which they dumped a shipment in Boston harbor. As British troops were quartered in Boston homes, a revolution soon followed, resulting in independence for Americans.

While tea went on to become the national drink of Great Britain, many of its variations were developed in the United States. A batch of hot tea to be served as samples at a world's fair exposition in St. Louis lost its appeal because of the hot weather. So ice was added, launching another way to serve the drink. Tea in bags and instant tea were also first used in the United States.

Kinds of Tea and Packagings. Tea is categorized as either black, green, or oolong, depending on how the leaves are processed. From these three types, blends often are created and flavorings are added. Herbal teas, however, contain portions of various plants, such as berries, flowers, and roots, but they have no tea leaves.

Tea plants thrive in tropical and subtropical regions. Among countries producing the majority of the world's tea are China, India, Sri Lanka, Kenya, Japan, Indonesia, and Turkey.

Tea is a most versatile product. On the grocery shelves one finds loose tea, loose tea specially blended for automatic iced tea or drip coffee makers, iced tea brews, blends, decaffeinated tea, tea bags, tea bags specifically blended to be iced, instant tea, breakfast tea, herbal teas with flavors and spices, and still the rows of tea products continue. They come in tins, boxes, bags, quart cans, and jars.

Tea can be steeped in individual cups, in tea bells, or in teapots of porcelain, silver, metal, or earthenware. Teacups and saucers are part of tableware sets or can be purchased separately in sets. Those who have exacting standards as to what constitutes a proper cup of tea often question additions such as lemon, milk, or sugar, and have strong opinions on such things as proportion of tea to water and water temperature.

Other Uses. The leaves are sometimes studied by fortunetellers, and they are sometimes used as healing poultices. Because antioxidants, which are thought to fight cancer and heart diseases, are found at high levels in tea, many people drink tea as a health supplement.

A TRADITIONAL CREAM TEA, consisting of scones and baps (rolls) served with clotted cream and jam, is served outdoors in the garden of a tea shop in Cornwall.

Tea

Especially favored for its contributions to longevity is green tea. Studies comparing lifespans of Japanese women who drank excessive amounts of green tea, as compared to those who didn't, suggested the tea drinkers lived longer. Proponents of green tea in the diet praise its immune-bolstering properties, health-inducing agents, and aids to digestion.

What's For Tea? Depending on the occasion, what is served for tea as a dining function depends on the time of day and degree of formality involved. Breakfast foods are served at morning teas. High tea usually calls for more food, with a carefully planned atmosphere and attention to detail in serving. Finger foods, salads, and sweets—along with the traditional scones and jam—are typical accompaniments to the cups of tea.

A Fine Cup of Tea

6 cups freshly drawn cold tap water or bottled water
2 to 3 teaspoons Darjeeling blend tea
Milk or cream
Sweetener (sugar or sugar syrup)
Citrus slices and juice (lemon, lime, or orange)
Fresh mint sprigs and whole cloves

Pour a small amount of hot water into the teapot to heat the pot. Bring the cold water just to a boil in a teakettle. Discard the warming water in the teapot and immediately add the tea to the pot. Pour the boiling water in the kettle over the tea. Let steep for 5 minutes before straining into cups. Serve with milk, sweetener, citrus slices and juice, mint and cloves.

THIS WORKMAN in London in 1915 interrupts his work for a few minutes to have his "high" tea.

Although the time of day for high tea may be about the same as for afternoon tea—four or five in the afternoon—the afternoon tea is lighter and serves as a bridge between lunch and dinner. A nursery or schoolroom tea provides more filling foods than does the afternoon tea. Other sources of tea and light refreshment are commercial establishments such as tea gardens and tea shops.

Purposes of the Social Tea. A tea may serve many social functions. It can involve meditation, enlightening conversations, and mild exercise about the grounds. It may serve as a springboard for rowdy conversations and competitions or, conversely, as an information exchange that can range from educated discussions to mere gossip, depending on the direction set by the host and the propensities of the guests.

For the host who wants to provide quality food and drink but also to maintain an atmosphere conducive to exchanges with artistic and social merit, the choice of participants is just as important as the tea itself. Likewise, a tea accompanied by boisterous games and wagers would not attract the contemplative meditator nor be successful if the partakers viewed the function as an opportunity to discuss business or fashions.

However it's prepared or served, the popularity of a good cup of hot tea has remained undiminished over the years. Tea's place in the scheme of things was well described by Rudyard Kipling in *Natural Theology:* "We had a kettle; we let it leak: Our not repairing made it worse. We haven't had any tea for a week . . . The bottom is out of the Universe."

Speaking of Tea

All well-regulated families set apart an hour every morning for tea and bread and butter. —Joseph Addison

I am in no way interested in immortality, but only in the taste of tea. —Lu T'ung

There is no trouble so great or grave that cannot be much diminished by a nice cup of tea. —Bernard-Paul Heroux

A TABLE laid with cakes, a teapot, and other tea things entices tea participants to an inviting seat in front of a cozy fire.

ENIGMATIC STONEHENGE is among the ancient landmarks of Britain. The oldest parts probably date as far back as 3100 B.C.

meter
US

metre
Brit.

Since Britain's accession to the European Common Market, trade with European countries has gained in importance relative to the Commonwealth countries. Other important trading partners include the United States, Japan, and the Scandinavian countries.

Government. Britain is a constitutional monarchy with a parliamentary system of government. The British monarch is head of state. Actual executive power is wielded by a prime minister and cabinet responsible to the legislature, Parliament. Parliament has two houses—a popularly elected lower house, the 659-member House of Commons, and the less powerful, hereditary and appointive upper house, the House of Lords. The House of Lords has 693 members, although generally less than one-third of this number attend sessions.

Britain does not have a single written constitution; rather, its government is based on a series of documents, judicial decisions, and traditions that have the force of law. These define all the civil rights of British citizens and outline the powers of the departments of government.

History. (Please refer to page 114 for a list of the English kings and queens.)

The British Isles have been inhabited since prehistoric times. In about 600 B.C. Celtic peoples from the mainland of Europe began to settle on the island. They were divided into two groups: Gaels and Britons. The Gaels arrived first and settled in the north and west. The Britons occupied the south and east.

Mysteries of Stonehenge. Among the earliest and most famous monuments found in Britain is Stonehenge, a curious, circular group of huge standing stones dating from prehistoric times. For centuries people have wondered about this strange templelike structure located on Salisbury Plain in Wiltshire, England, southwest of London: Who built it and why? Even the name "Stonehenge," first recorded in the twelfth century, is something of an enigma, but it probably has some connection with the notion of stones "hanging" in the air (stone + *hengen*, in Old English, referring to something hung up).

Though questions still remain, British archaeologists have unraveled many of the mysteries surrounding Stonehenge. They think it was probably built in three separate stages, beginning about 3100 B.C. At that time, native Neolithic people dug the circular, 20-foot- (6-meter-) wide ditch that encloses the present site. Along the inside perimeter of the 320-foot- (98-meter-) wide circle, the builders also inexplicably dug and then refilled 56 holes (used later for burials). The entrance to Stonehenge was marked by a break in the circular ditch and two parallel entry stones set up on the northeast of the circle.

Neolithic builders made extensive changes in the original Stonehenge about 2100 B.C. The entrance, roughly aligned with sunrise at summer solstice, was widened into what is now called the Avenue, and two unfinished circles of bluestone pillars were set up inside the circular trench. The pillars, weighing about 4 tons each, were somehow brought to the site from Wales, over 200 miles (320 kilometers) away.

One hundred years later, the now-familiar circle of larger stone uprights topped by stone lintels replaced the bluestone pillars. Inside the linteled circle, another series of upright stones with lintels formed a horseshoe, the open end being aligned with the entrance. Weighing some 50 tons each, these larger stones were up to 30 feet (9 meters) long and had joints cut in them. We still do not know how they were transported from about 20 miles (32 kilometers) away, but one theory holds they were carried by a glacier.

Over the following centuries more work was done on Stonehenge, including setting up the bluestone pillars in a circle between the linteled circle and horseshoe. The last work on Stonehenge dates from about 1100 B.C., when the Avenue was extended almost 2 miles (3 kilometers) to the nearby Avon River. Sometime after that, Stonehenge was abandoned for reasons unknown.

We still do not know what purpose Stonehenge served, but most likely some sort of services were held there. A connection with sun worship is possible, because Stonehenge was aligned with sunrise at the summer solstice. One thing is certain: Neither the Romans nor the Druids built Stonehenge, as was once popularly believed. Archaeological work has shown that the monument was built long before either group arrived in Britain.

The Roman general Julius Caesar invaded the British Isles in 55 B.C. and found Gaels and Britons living in informal communities whose economies were based on agriculture, metalworking, and trade. But the Romans did not seriously attempt to conquer Britain until 43 A.D., when under the emperor Claudius a military expedition invaded the island and occupied part of present-day England.

The Romans established settlements, founded cities, built roads and forts, and eventually extended Roman civil and military administration up to the present-day Scottish border. There the emperor Hadrian had a wall built in the 120s to protect the Roman part of the island from the hostile Celtic and Pictish tribes that remained outside Roman control. From the 40s A.D. to the 300s, England was Roman and its history was part of that of Rome.

As England shared in Rome's greatness, it shared in its decline. In 367 the Picts and the Scots breached Hadrian's wall. Within the next 50 years Rome withdrew its troops from Britain to defend the empire in other areas. This resulted in a degeneration of culture, law, and prosperity. It left Britain vulnerable to foreign invasions. From about 450 to 600 successive waves of invaders from northern Germany—Jutes, Angles, and Saxons—conquered the Celts or forced them to retreat to the western areas of the island, into Cornwall and Wales.

The various tribes of Anglo-Saxon invaders eventually created a number of kingdoms in the various parts of the island that each had settled. The most important kingdoms were Northumbria in the northeast; Mercia in the

THE STONE WALL built by the Romans across northern England to protect the frontier and control trade was named for the emperor Hadrian.

The Commonwealth of Nations

The Commonwealth of Nations, known from 1931 to 1946 as the British Commonwealth of Nations, is a voluntary association of the United Kingdom and a number of independent nations and dependencies that once were part of the British Empire.

Commonwealth members are not bound by treaty and are not subject to a common set of laws or foreign policy. Their unity stems from their heritage as part of the former British Empire, their recognition of the British monarch as the symbolic head of the Commonwealth, and their desire to seek the benefits of cooperation and consultation.

The roots of the Commonwealth of Nations were established with the rapid growth of the British Empire in the 17th and 18th centuries. The inadequacy of the British Parliament to supervise all details of colonial government led to the rise of more or less internally independent colonial governments.

In the 19th and early 20th centuries, the confederation of British colonies into large units led to the emergence of Australia, New Zealand, Canada, and South Africa as self-governing dominions in 1907. In 1931, by the Statute of Westminster, these dominions and Newfoundland and Ireland were declared sovereign states freely associated within the British Commonwealth of Nations.

The events of World War II and international developments following the war contributed to the expansion of the Commonwealth. As former British colonies achieved independence, many chose to become members. Other members, such as Ireland, South Africa, Fiji, and Pakistan, chose to leave the association. South Africa, Figi, and Pakistan have since rejoined.

The prime ministers of the Commonwealth nations meet periodically to discuss matters of common concern. A Commonwealth secretariat was established in 1965 to coordinate consultation and exchange of information among the members.

Commonwealth Member Nations

Antiqua and Barbuda	Namibia
Australia	Nauru
Bahamas	New Zealand
Bangladesh	Nigeria
Barbados	Pakistan
Belize	Papua New Guinea
Botswana	Saint Kitts and Nevis
Brunei	Saint Lucia
Cameroon	Saint Vincent and the
Canada	Grenadines
Cyprus	Samoa
Dominica	Seychelles
Fiji	Sierra Leone
The Gambia	Singapore
Ghana	Solomon Islands
Grenada	South Africa
Guyana	Sri Lanka
India	Swaziland
Jamaica	Tanzania
Kenya	Tonga
Kiribati	Trinidad and Tobago
Lesotho	Tuvalu
Malawi	Uganda
Malaysia	United Kingdom
Maldives	Vanuatu
Malta	Zambia
Mauritius	Zimbabwe (withdrew in 2003)
Mozambique	

26 Europe and Russia

Midlands; and Wessex, stretching from London westward to the Severn River. The other kingdoms included East Anglia, Essex, Kent, and Sussex in the south and east.

In the 600s the Anglo-Saxon kingdoms began to be converted to Christianity through the influence of a missionary from Rome, Augustine. It was Augustine who baptized Ethelbert, king of Kent, and in 601 became the first archbishop of Canterbury.

Monastic life flourished in England and produced notable figures like the Venerable Bede (673–735), a monk at Jarrow who wrote a history of the English people. Through the work of the monasteries, the Germanic Anglo-Saxon tongue became a written language, English. Church structure developed early, and religious leaders exerted great influence, especially in Mercia and Wessex.

Rivalries among the kingdoms prevented any real unity for many centuries. Mercia, under Offa II (ruled 757–796), and Wessex, led by Egbert of Wessex (ruled 802–839), underwent marked political development and extended their boundaries westward. By the early 800s a unique English social and political structure had taken shape, and the once warlike Anglo-Saxons had become a settled, agricultural people enjoying peace and stability. Protected only by an army of untrained farmers, however, they were prey to more warlike peoples.

The "Danes," or Vikings, who were the inhabitants of what are now Denmark, Sweden, and Norway, began raiding the east coast of Britain in 787. In the 850s they began a systematic conquest of the island, and by 870 all of the Anglo-Saxon kingdoms except Wessex had surrendered.

Wessex, led by King Alfred the Great (ruled 871–899), successfully resisted, and in 878 Alfred made a treaty with the Danes that divided England along a line running from London northwest to the Irish Sea. The area northeast of the line remained in Danish hands and was called the "Danelaw." The area southwest of the line was an enlarged kingdom of Wessex.

Alfred created in Wessex a strong political and cultural unit, and in 955 his grandson was able to conquer the Danelaw. Alfred's descendants soon became the first kings of all England.

In about 980 the Danes renewed their raids. Ethelred the Unready (ruled 978–1016) attempted to buy off the Danes by paying tribute to them, but by 1017 England had fallen to the Scandinavians.

Ethelred and his son both died in 1016, and the Danish king, Canute, became the king of England (ruled 1017–1035) as well. He established an orderly government, but his two sons lacked his ability and one of Alfred's descendants, Edward the Confessor, became king (ruled 1042–1066).

During Edward's reign, two groups competed for power. One was led by Godwin, the earl of Wessex, and his son Harold. Their rivals were Normans, the descendants of a group of marauding Northmen who in 910 had settled opposite England's south coast on the French peninsula that came to be called Normandy.

Norman conquest. On the death of the English king Edward the Confessor in 1066, the council of the realm elected Harold, earl of Wessex, king. William of Normandy, a cousin of Edward, maintained that Edward had promised him the throne. William invaded England in October, 1066, and defeated the English at the Battle of Hastings.

The Battle of Hastings, 1066. Among the greatest battles in English history, Hastings had consequences reaching far beyond the battlefield itself. First and foremost was that the battle secured the Norman conquest of England, but the victory also put an entirely new, Norman nobility in control of Anglo-Saxon England and introduced the French language and culture there as well. The impact on English culture was enormous.

The immediate cause for the Battle of Hastings was a dynastic struggle for the English throne. William, duke of Normandy, was a cousin of England's King Edward the Confessor and probably had been promised the throne. But just before Edward died in 1066, he named as his successor England's most powerful nobleman, Harold, earl of Wessex. Duke William refused to accept the change and organized his followers from Normandy (now part of modern France) and a large contingent of mercenaries into an army. In all, he may have had somewhat more than 7000 soldiers, but estimates vary widely.

A REENACTMENT of the Battle of Hastings, which secured the Norman conquest of England by William of Normandy in 1066

William and his army crossed the English Channel in late September, landing at Pevensey on England's southern coast. Meanwhile, King Harold hurriedly gathered an army of 7,000 men, many of them peasants with no real combat experience, and rushed southward to meet William's army. By October 14 Harold had taken up a defensive position on a ridge outside Hastings, massing his best troops in the center and deploying the inexperienced militiamen to either side. William prepared to attack early that morning.

At first the attack at dawn went badly for William's Norman troops. They approached the ridge in three lines, archers first, infantry next, and horse-mounted knights in the rear. The archers waited too long to fire their opening volley, however, and when the infantry moved up the ridge, javelins and rocks rained down upon them. The Norman cavalry attacked next, faltered before a punishing English counterattack, and then retreated. The day seemed lost, but William rallied the troops, leading a successful cavalry charge against English soldiers who had unwisely pursued the Normans down the ridge.

William drew out and cut down still more English soldiers by having his own troops attack and then pretend to retreat in panic. But repeated Norman charges up the ridge failed to dislodge the main body of Harold's troops.

The battle dragged on, with William alternating his attacks between volleys of arrows and frontal assaults. By late afternoon Harold still held the ridge, but two of his brothers had been killed and his troops were growing weary. Then King Harold himself was killed by an arrow, and when darkness fell his troops scattered in the forest behind the ridge.

William, who narrowly escaped being killed himself while pursuing Harold's fleeing troops, next led his army to London and seized the government. He was crowned William I, king of England, in Westminster Abbey on Christmas Day, 1066.

As the result of William's conquest, England received a new royal dynasty, a new aristocracy, a new architecture (Norman Romanesque), a new language (Norman French), and a new institution (feudalism). But William the Conqueror preserved much that was useful from the Anglo-Saxon past—the law, the courts, the tax system, the national militia, and the administrative machinery. The conquest enabled William to establish a feudal system far more systematic and effective than any existing in Europe.

By 1085 William's rule over England was firm. His Norman followers held lands throughout the kingdom and acknowledged him as their feudal overlord; his castles were built at strategic points to protect the land from internal and external violence.

The feudal aristocracy of England was resentful of the power of the monarchy from the beginning. On the other hand, the benefits of the law and order brought about by this power were obvious to everyone. The political theme of English medieval history is thus a search for ways to prevent royal power from becoming arbitrary while preserving the very real benefits of strong central government.

In religious matters, William and his successors worked to make the church in England conform to the standards of the papacy while preventing papal influence in England from becoming superior to their own.

Most important, William's conquest of England bound the island, through Normandy, to Latin Christendom and turned it away from the ties it had had with Scandinavian lands, peoples, and customs.

Henry I. When William died in 1087 he left the kingdom of England to his second son, William Rufus (William II, ruled 1087–1100), who lacked most of his father's wisdom and ruled oppressively. Another of William the Conqueror's sons, Henry I (ruled 1100–1135), who followed William II to the throne, showed something of his father's skill and energy in government and administration.

Tower of London. The imposing fortress called the Tower of London dates back to the eleventh century and the first years of William the Conqueror's reign. Over the centuries English monarchs expanded the original, temporary fortress situated along the Thames River and used it variously as a palace, royal mint, archive for public records, prison, and place of execution. The Tower once even housed a royal collection of wild animals, including an elephant and a polar bear.

William the Conqueror built the first structure, the central White Tower of white limestone, in about 1078. Inside the 90-foot- (27-meter-) high, nearly square tower were a dungeon and living quarters for nobles, soldiers, and servants. Royal bedrooms and a council chamber occupied the top floor. Both Henry I (ruled 1101 to 1135) and Henry II (ruled 1154 to 1189) added other buildings, and during the reign of Richard I (ruled 1189 to 1199), large sums were spent fortifying the growing complex.

Thick encircling walls with smaller towers were added later, and eventually the whole complex occupied over 18 acres. The inner wall surrounding the White Tower has 13 towers, including Wakefield Tower, where Britain's crown jewels are stored. The outer wall has six towers and is surrounded by a moat (left dry since 1843). A smaller wall, built mainly by Henry VIII (ruled 1509 to 1547), surrounds the outer edge of the moat. The Tower has a land entrance as well as a river entrance, which is called Traitor's Gate because many state prisoners were brought to the Tower by way of the Thames.

King Stephen (ruled 1135 to 1154) became the first English monarch to reside in the Tower (1140). The Tower remained a royal residence for nearly five centuries and was the site of weddings, balls, and many other happy occasions, but it is generally remembered as a notorious prison and place of executions.

Bishop Ralf Flambard became the Tower's first prisoner after being arrested for selling benefices in 1101. A resourceful criminal, Flambard succeeded in getting his guards drunk and escaped through a window by sliding

THE OLDEST PORTIONS of the Tower of London date from the time of William the Conqueror in the late 1000s, and they house relics from that period.

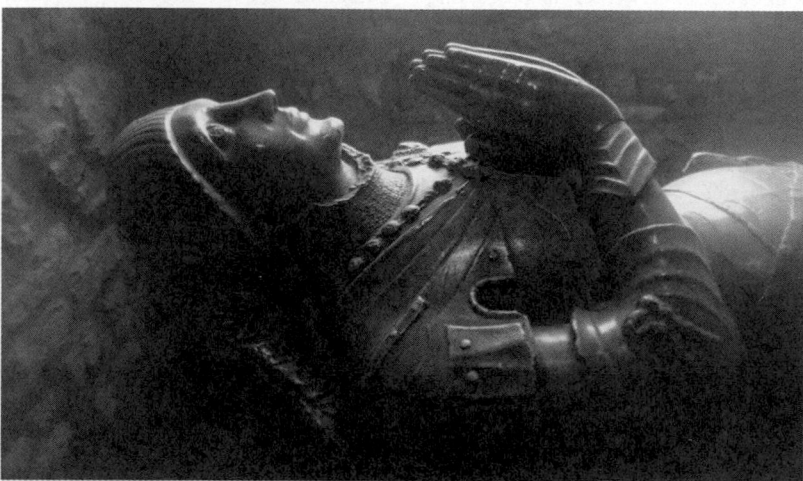

down a rope. The many Tower prisoners who followed during the next centuries were not nearly so fortunate. They suffered long periods of imprisonment, torture, and, when the sovereign pleased, execution. Among the famous prisoners executed at the Tower were Henry VI, Edward I (and his brother), Anne Boleyn and Catherine Howard (both wives of Henry VIII), Henry's minister Thomas Cromwell, Lady Jane Grey, Sir Walter Raleigh, and the Catholic Martyr Sir Thomas More.

Though the Tower has not been a royal residence since the reign of James I (1603 to 1625), and the last prisoners were long ago released, it remains in use today as an arsenal, museum, and place to store the crown jewels. A popular London landmark, it is still guarded by yeoman warders, called "Beefeaters," who wear colorful costumes and daily entertain tourists with stories about the Tower's illustrious, sometimes infamous, past.

Because some disputed his right to the throne, Henry's first acts as king were bids for popular favor. One of the most significant was his issuance of a charter promising to remedy many grievances the people had held against his predecessor. By this limiting of the king's own powers, his charter proved a precedent for later demands upon royal prerogatives.

Henry also made legal and administrative reforms. He appointed travelling justices, or judges, who brought the legal expertise of the royal court to the English shires. Their accumulated experience later resulted in the beginnings of English common law.

Henry established a central finance office, the Exchequer, for the fair receipt and adequate accounting of the royal revenue. He was also successful in foreign affairs, being able to reconquer Normandy and reunite it with the English crown.

Henry II. Many of the gains in the direction of an ordered royal government were lost when dynastic disputes followed Henry I's death in 1135. The king left no direct male heir, and the nobles' rivalry for power brought near anarchy between 1135 and 1154. In 1154 Henry I's grandson, Henry of Anjou, gained the throne as Henry II (ruled 1154–1189).

Through inheritance and marriage, Henry controlled nearly all of southwestern France and was thus lord of not only England but of continental territories far larger than those directly controlled by the actual king of France. Ireland, too, came at least nominally under the English king's authority when in 1154 Pope Adrian IV allowed Henry to extend his kingdom there.

Henry II strengthened the position of the monarchy, which had been weakened during the dynastic struggle. By defining royal rights, he strengthened the position of the king over the barons. He was able to hold together his vast and diverse possessions in France, involving immense financial commit-

A DETAIL from *A Tournament of the Knights of the Round Table Before King Arthur and Queen Geunevere* from Chretien de Troyes' *Romance of King Arthur*

colorful *US*

colourful *Brit.*

26 Europe and Russia

ments, while he also strengthened the royal power and the machinery of the central government.

Henry II also carried forward the legal reforms of Henry I. He extended the use of the sworn testimony of "jurors" to help in arresting criminals. It is largely due to Henry II that English common law, not Roman law, and trial by jury, not trial by inquisition, became the English legal tradition.

The expansion of royal judicial activity brought Henry into conflict with the church, which was also expanding its legal system, and with his own archbishop of Canterbury, Thomas à Becket. The bitter struggle that ensued culminated in the assassination of Becket at the high altar of Canterbury Cathedral in 1170.

Although Henry did not order the assassination, he did perform public penance for it. Subsequently, the principle of "benefit of clergy," or immunity from secular courts, remained a feature of English law. In practice, however, the

Origins of the King Arthur Legend

The Roman withdrawal from Britain in 410 A.D. marked the beginning of a troubled period. Celts remaining in England came under attack from the Picts in the north and from the Angles and Saxons, members of Germanic tribes that crossed the English Channel in search of new lands. By the next century the Celts, forced westward by the Angles and Saxons, had settled in what is now Wales.

Is it possible that the legendary King Arthur was based in fact on an early Celtish leader who fought against the Anglo-Saxon invaders? Some of the earliest written literature making mention of Arthur is indeed Welsh, and by the eleventh century, the Welsh had evolved romanticized stories about Arthur's heroic military exploits. Among the first recorded references to a warrior named Arthur is a Welsh poem composed about 600. A Welsh text from the ninth century, *Historia Brittonum*, mentions Arthur as a high king of the Britons and names twelve battles he won against the Saxons and Picts. Arthur's victory at Badon is mentioned in the tenth-century Welsh text *Annales Cambriae*, which also says that Arthur fell during fighting at Camlann.

Welsh sources and an unnamed historical work served as the basis for another important work in the literature of King Arthur, Geoffrey of Monmouth's twelfth-century *History of the Kings of Britain (Historia Regnum Britanniae)*. His fictionalized biography gave the first organized account of Arthur as a great conqueror and greatly influenced the later medieval literature on the Arthurian legend. But Geoffrey apparently merged the Welsh Arthur legends with a historical figure called Riothamus, King of the Britons. Riothamus, a title that means supreme king, led an army of Britons into Gaul during the last years of the Western Roman Empire (fifth century). Geoffrey's Arthur likewise leads his army on an expedition into Gaul, and like the historical Riothamus, was betrayed to the barbarians and disappeared while retreating toward Avallon, the island in Celtic legend represented as a paradise to which Arthur and other heroes were carried after death.

Evidence for the existence of a real King Arthur remains very sketchy. The Welsh Arthur and the historical Riothamus conceivably might have been one and the same. But scholars have found serious conflicts in what little literature remains, and the Welsh Arthur may have no basis in fact whatsoever. Or he may be a composite of two leaders.

Still, there is tantalizing evidence that some parts of the Arthur legend do derive from fact. For example, archaeologists have identified Cadbury Castle in southern England as one of the more likely sites for King Arthur's legendary Camelot. In fact, the castle was apparently refortified at about the right time in the fifth century, and some have speculated that Riothamus was the king who oversaw those changes.

Ruling Houses of England and of the United Kingdom

The House of Plantagenet. Eight kings from this house, now properly called Angevin, ruled medieval England for over two centuries, between 1154 and 1399. Descended from the French counts of Anjou, these kings also ruled extensive domains in France until the early 1200s. The Plantagenets' long reign witnessed the Crusades, unrest at home and attempts at curbing royal powers (notably the Magna Carta and early forms of Parliament), and the onset of the Hundred Years' War with France. The last Plantagenet kings proved especially unpopular and so helped bring about the downfall of their dynasty.

The name "Plantagenet" is believed to have originated as a nickname of Geoffrey, count of Anjou, either because he often planted broom (genus *Genista*) around his hunting blinds or because he wore a sprig of broom in his cap. At any rate, Count Geoffrey married Matilda, daughter of England's King Henry I. They produced a son who became England's King Henry II, the first in the Plantagenet line.

Henry's accession in 1154 marked the end of a ruinous civil war in England, and he proved a strong ruler. But Henry was forced to divide his attention between ruling England and ruling his extensive lands in France, which he inherited from his father, Geoffrey. The Plantagenet kings who followed were similarly distracted by holdings on the Continent, until the French kings conquered most of them.

Henry's two sons, Richard I "Coeur de Lion" (Lionheart), who ruled 1189 to 1199, and John, who ruled 1199 to 1216, succeeded him. Richard spent most of his reign leading the

King Henry VIII

Third Crusade, and John so abused his power that he was forced to sign the Magna Carta, placing the king under English law and limiting his powers (1215). Considered one of England's bad kings, John also lost nearly all the English domains in France.

A succession of sons then followed their fathers to the throne: Henry III (ruled 1216 to 1272), Edward I (ruled 1272 to 1307), Edward II (ruled 1307 to 1327), and Edward III (ruled 1327 to 1377). Edward III had five sons, but it was his grandson by his first son who succeeded him. Richard II (ruled 1377 to 1399) proved unable to control his barons. With unrest mounting, he was overthrown in favor of Henry IV, who was also a grandson of Edward III (by Edward's third son). Richard's fall from power marked the end of the direct Plantagenet line, Henry IV being a member of the related House of Lancaster.

House of Lancaster. The Lancastrian kings reigned between 1399 and 1471, a tumultuous period embracing the end of the Hundred Years' War and much of the civil war called the Wars of the Roses. Fought between the Lancastrians and the rival House of York for control of the English throne, the Wars of the Roses eventually ended Lancastrian rule and brought the Yorkists to power.

The Lancastrian line originated in 1267 when Edmund "Crouchback," the youngest son of King Henry III, was created earl of Lancaster. Edmund gained the nickname "Crouchback" (meaning crossed back) because he had been a crusader and so was privileged to wear the cross. Eventually, Edmund's granddaughter and sole surviving heir married John of Gaunt, King Edward III's third son, thereby investing John with the title of duke of Lancaster. Meanwhile, the last king of the Plantagenet line, Richard II, proved an ineffectual ruler. He came largely under John of Gaunt's control, but when John died in 1399, King Richard II exiled his oldest son, Henry Bolingbroke, and seized the Lancastrian lands.

Later in 1399, Bolingbroke invaded England and forced the unpopular Richard II to abdicate in his favor. Bolingbroke, the first Lancastrian king, based his claim to the throne on his descent from Henry III; he was crowned Henry IV and ruled from 1399 to 1413. Nevertheless, Henry faced revolts in Wales and at home, which strained the country's finances and weakened his government.

His son, Henry V (ruled 1413 to 1422), was a popular and effective king who restored order in England and who won important victories in France during the Hundred Years' War. He died from a fever in 1422, bringing his one-year-old son to the throne as Henry VI. Henry VI proved the most unfortunate of the line.

During Henry VI's early years, when the government was run by Henry's uncles, the tide of the Hundred Years' War turned against England. The situation steadily worsened and by war's end, in 1453, England had lost virtually all the territory it had won in France. Loss in the war heightened discontent with Henry's reign. Two years later, in 1455, members of the House of York challenged Henry on the battlefield and so began the Wars of the Roses. The badges worn by the combatants provided the name for the wars: The Yorkists wore a white rose and the Lancastrians a red rose.

Following a Yorkist victory at the Battle of Mortimer's Cross (1461), Edward IV was proclaimed king. Lancastrians afterward revolted against Edward and during one uprising in 1465, Henry was captured and imprisoned in the Tower of London. Five years later, a new revolt against Edward briefly restored Henry VI as king (1470 to 1471). The Yorkists regained the throne in 1471, however, and this time executed Henry. Henry's death without a male heir ended the direct line of the House of Lancaster.

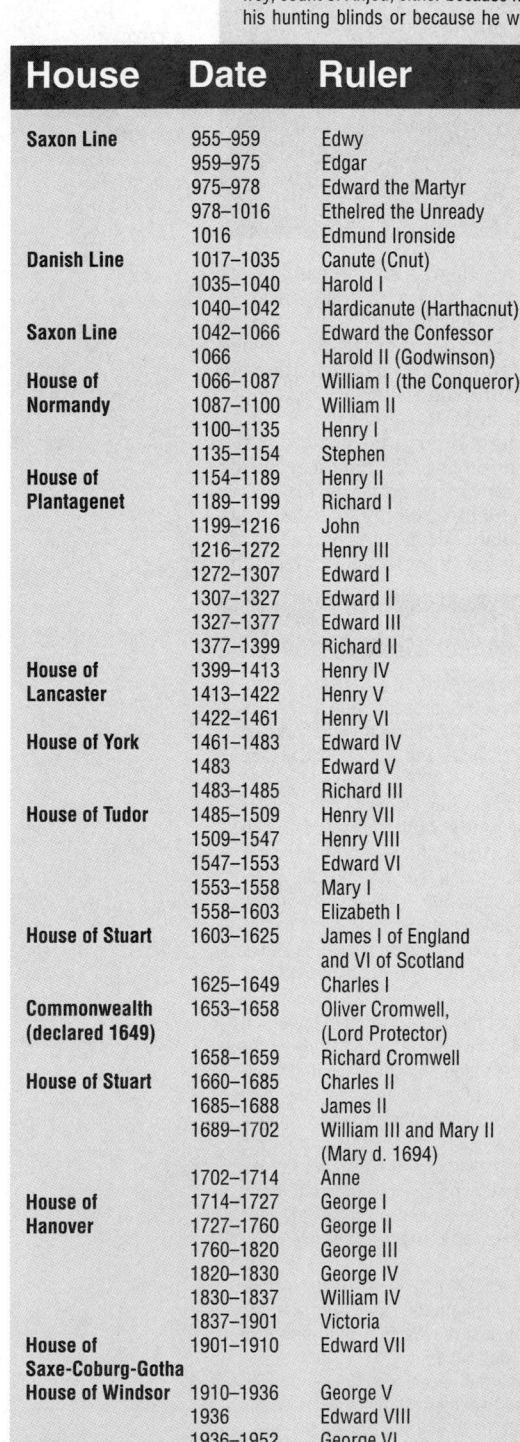

House	Date	Ruler
Saxon Line	955–959	Edwy
	959–975	Edgar
	975–978	Edward the Martyr
	978–1016	Ethelred the Unready
	1016	Edmund Ironside
Danish Line	1017–1035	Canute (Cnut)
	1035–1040	Harold I
	1040–1042	Hardicanute (Harthacnut)
Saxon Line	1042–1066	Edward the Confessor
	1066	Harold II (Godwinson)
House of Normandy	1066–1087	William I (the Conqueror)
	1087–1100	William II
	1100–1135	Henry I
	1135–1154	Stephen
House of Plantagenet	1154–1189	Henry II
	1189–1199	Richard I
	1199–1216	John
	1216–1272	Henry III
	1272–1307	Edward I
	1307–1327	Edward II
	1327–1377	Edward III
	1377–1399	Richard II
House of Lancaster	1399–1413	Henry IV
	1413–1422	Henry V
	1422–1461	Henry VI
House of York	1461–1483	Edward IV
	1483	Edward V
	1483–1485	Richard III
House of Tudor	1485–1509	Henry VII
	1509–1547	Henry VIII
	1547–1553	Edward VI
	1553–1558	Mary I
	1558–1603	Elizabeth I
House of Stuart	1603–1625	James I of England and VI of Scotland
	1625–1649	Charles I
Commonwealth (declared 1649)	1653–1658	Oliver Cromwell, (Lord Protector)
	1658–1659	Richard Cromwell
House of Stuart	1660–1685	Charles II
	1685–1688	James II
	1689–1702	William III and Mary II (Mary d. 1694)
	1702–1714	Anne
House of Hanover	1714–1727	George I
	1727–1760	George II
	1760–1820	George III
	1820–1830	George IV
	1830–1837	William IV
	1837–1901	Victoria
House of Saxe-Coburg-Gotha	1901–1910	Edward VII
House of Windsor	1910–1936	George V
	1936	Edward VIII
	1936–1952	George VI
	1952–	Elizabeth II

Ruling Houses of England and of the United Kingdom

House of York. The House of York, rivals of the Lancastrians for the English throne, supplied three kings—Edward IV, Edward, and Richard III—who ruled England only briefly, from 1461 to 1485. Yorkist claims to the throne sparked the bloody Wars of the Roses, which raged from 1455 to 1485.

The House of York originated in 1385 when Edmund of Langley, King Edward III's fifth son, was created Duke of York. The rival House of Lancaster, however, which had ruled England since 1399, traced its lineage back to Edward III's third son. By 1455 the ravages of the Hundred Years' War and the ineffective rule of Lancastrian king Henry VI provided an opportunity for Richard, duke of York, to seize the throne. Richard not only claimed descent from Edward III's fifth son, but also (on his mother's side) from Edward's third son.

Though victories on the battlefield eventually forced Henry VI to name Richard as his successor, Richard was killed at the Battle of Wakefield (1460). Richard's son Edward marched on London in the next year and was proclaimed King Edward IV.

Edward ruled from 1461 until 1470, when the Lancastrians drove him out of the country and restored Henry VI. Edward returned the following year with new allies, however, and regained the throne. Henry was executed soon after, and Edward's reign was undisturbed until his death in 1483.

Trouble began anew when Edward's son, Edward V, took the throne. Only 13 years old, he soon fell prey to his father's brother, the Duke of Gloucester. Gloucester had Edward and his ten-year-old brother Richard declared illegitimate and locked the two princes in the Tower of London. Gloucester then took power in 1483 as Richard III and apparently had young Edward and his brother murdered (their bones were finally discovered in the Tower in 1674).

Richard's actions and the widespread belief that he planned to marry Edward's daughter Elizabeth turned many Yorkists against him, bolstering support for Henry Tudor, a Lancastrian claimant to the throne. In 1485, two years after Richard had seized power, Henry Tudor defeated him at the Battle of Bosworth Field. Richard died in the battle, and Henry Tudor took the throne as Henry VII, thus ending the short reign of the Yorkist kings.

House of Tudor. Kings and queens of the Tudor house ruled England from 1485 to 1603. During their long reign, the Tudors expanded the powers of the monarchy, created the Church of England, and helped make the English navy a strong force on the high seas. Furthermore, two of their number, Henry VIII and Queen Elizabeth, rank among the most famous English monarchs of all time. While the family can be traced back to a 13th-century Welshman, it was Owen Tudor, a squire in King Henry V's court, who introduced so-called royal blood into the line. After Henry's death, Tudor married the widowed queen, Catherine of Valois, and had five children by her. One of his sons, Edmund, earl of Richmond, married Margaret Beaufort, who also had ties to the royal house of Lancaster. Their son Henry Tudor became the first Tudor king in 1485.

Henry's ascent to the throne was by no means smooth. The bloody Wars of the Roses had been raging on and off for some 30 years, with Yorkist King Edward IV finally gaining the crown. But after Edward IV's death in 1483, his brother Richard seized the throne (as Richard III). This angered Yorkists, throwing additional support to Henry Tudor, who claimed the throne based on his ties to the House of Lancaster.

Henry Tudor made good his claim by defeating and killing Richard at the Battle of Bosworth Field in 1485. He also married Edward IV's daughter Elizabeth, and so united both Yorkist and Lancastrian claims in his own newly founded Tudor dynasty. As Henry VII (ruled 1485 to 1509), he proved a wise and effective ruler, and his three children also furthered Tudor interests. His son, Henry VIII (ruled 1509 to 1547), succeeded him; his daughter Mary Tudor married French King Louis XII, and another daughter, Margaret Tudor, married Scottish King James IV.

Henry VIII's reign was marked by his creation of the Church of England in 1534 and his ruthless search for a wife who would bear him a male heir (he divorced or executed four of his six wives). Henry ultimately fathered three children, two daughters and a son, and eventually all three ruled England—Edward VI (ruled 1547 to 1553); Mary I (ruled 1553 to 1558); and Elizabeth I (ruled 1558 to 1603).

Young Edward was only nine when he succeeded to the throne; he died of tuberculosis just six years later. Mary, also not of strong constitution, was the wife of Spain's King of Phillip II and reigned in England for just five years before dying. Her attempts to restore England to Catholicism in that short time were accompanied by persecutions of Protestants

King James I

that earned her the sobriquet Bloody Queen Mary.

Henry's second daughter, Elizabeth, proved to be the most effective and enduring ruler of Henry's children. A popular queen, she streamlined the government, increased the powers of the monarchy, encouraged efforts at colonization and overseas trading ventures, and oversaw a period in which literature and the arts flourished.

Because Queen Elizabeth died without heirs, however, the Tudor line came to an end with her in 1603. That brought the Scottish House of Stuart to power in England, based on the marriage of Margaret Tudor to Scotland's King James IV a century earlier.

House of Stuart. The Stuart line of kings came to power in England after the last Tudor monarch, Queen Elizabeth I, died without an heir. The six Stuart sovereigns reigned between 1603 and 1714, a troubled period marked by arbitrary rule, revolts, and the ascendancy of parliament.

Ancestors of the Stuart family date back to eleventh-century Brittany, but the name did not emerge until after a family member was appointed steward to the king of Scotland. The French spelling of Stewart, "Stuart," was adopted during the 1500s. Well before that, however, the Stuarts had become Scotland's royal family. In the 1300s a family member named Walter married Marjory, daughter of Scotland's King Robert I. Their son, Robert II, ascended the throne as the first Stuart king of Scotland, in 1371.

Stuart kings ruled Scotland until 1625, and the last of them, James VI, also ascended the English throne, as King James I (ruled 1603 to 1625). His claim to the English throne came through his great-grandmother

Ruling Houses of England and of the United Kingdom

Margaret Tudor, who was Henry VII's daughter. James was extravagant and unpopular, and his relations with Parliament deteriorated seriously, setting the stage for the English Civil War.

Charles I (ruled 1625 to 1649) succeeded his father and engaged in struggles with Parliament, which refused to yield to arbitrary rule. Finally, the country plunged into civil war between Charles' royalist supporters and the parliamentarians. The parliamentarians ultimately won, beheaded Charles I (1649), and briefly abolished the monarchy by establishing the Commonwealth (1648–1660). The monarchy was restored under Charles' son, Charles II (ruled 1660 to 1685). During his reign London was first ravaged by the plague and then destroyed by the Great Fire in the 1660s. Charles II also had his problems with Parliament, which he dissolved in 1681. After his death four years later, Charles' brother, King James II (ruled 1685 to 1688), succeeded him.

A Catholic and an unpopular ruler, James II infuriated Parliament by his attempts to promote Catholicism. With the backing of Parliament, James II was forced to abdicate and was replaced by William and Mary in the so-called Glorious Revolution of 1688. Both William and Mary (ruled 1689 to 1702) had ties to the Stuart family and both were Protestants, which was what Parliament wanted.

By 1702, both had died without heirs, and the problem of a successor arose again. Many Stuart claimants were ruled out because the Act of Settlement, passed in 1701, now barred Catholics from succeeding to the throne. So Queen Anne (ruled 1702 to 1714), a Protestant daughter of James II, was chosen to reign.

When in 1707 the Act of Union joined England, Scotland, and Wales, Anne became the first sovereign to rule over the new kingdom of Great Britain. In that same year, she also became the last British monarch to use the royal veto power.

Queen Anne died without heirs, and by the Act of Settlement, various Catholic Stuarts were bypassed in favor of a Protestant from the House of Hanover, George I. The Stuart line thus ended with Queen Anne.

House of Hanover. Six monarchs from this family ruled Great Britain for almost 200 years, between 1714 and 1901. They successfully defended the throne against several rebellions by Stuart claimants, watched as Parliament's power steadily grew at their expense, lost the American colonies, gained India and a vast new worldwide colonial empire, presided over Britain's Industrial Revolution, and saw their nation through numerous bloody wars in the 1700s and 1800s as Britain rose to become a world power.

The Hanover family, of German origin, was named for the German electorate of Hanover, which it ruled from 1692. The family had ties to the Stuart kings of England through James I's granddaughter Sophia, but many other Stuarts preceded them in the normal line of succession. All that changed when Parliament imposed the Act of Settlement in 1701.

Enacted to bar Catholics from succeeding to the throne, the act meant that only Protestant Stuarts could take the throne. When the last Protestant Stuart, Queen Anne, died without heirs in 1714, the Hanover family suddenly jumped to the head of the line of succession. Since George III (ruled 1760 to 1820) was the first Hanoverian king born in Britain, and he proved more popular than either his father or grandfather. His tumultuous reign saw the rise of the Industrial Revolution and economic prosperity, the American Revolution, the French revolutionary wars, the Napoleonic wars, and the War of 1812. George III went insane in 1810 and died ten years later.

Two other succeeding Hanoverian kings, George IV (ruled 1820 to 1830) and his brother, William IV (ruled 1830 to 1837), had brief reigns.

William IV was succeeded by his niece Victoria, certainly one of the most famous British monarchs of all time. With her succession, the English and Hanoverian thrones were separated, however, because women could not succeed to the Hanoverian throne. Victoria's uncle became king of Hanover instead.

Nevertheless, Victoria left her mark on England. As queen from 1837 to 1901, she was the longest reigning monarch in British history and presided over a nation that by then was the world's greatest commercial and colonial power.

The line of Hanoverian monarchs came to an end with Victoria, because her son and successor, Edward VII, by tradition took his father's name, Wettin of Saxe-Coburg-Gotha. The family changed its name to Windsor in the early 1900s.

House of Windsor. Monarchs of the Windsor family have ruled Great Britain since 1901, following the death of Queen Victoria, the last sovereign from the House of Hanover. During their reign the Windsors have led Britain through two world wars and have seen the monarchy reduced to a largely ceremonial role.

The Windsors' original family name, Wettin of Saxe-Coburg-Gotha, belonged to Queen Victoria's German-born husband, Albert. Because of anti-German sentiment in Britain during World War I, King George V changed the family name to Windsor by royal proclamation in 1917. Queen Elizabeth II further strengthened the identity of the Windsor name with the monarchy by decreeing that her descendants in the male line would retain it. Traditionally, her children would have assumed their father's surname, Mountbatten, but in 1960 the queen decided that descendants with the titles of prince, princess, or royal highness would retain the Windsor name. All others would have the name Mountbatten-Windsor.

Queen Elizabeth II

Queen Victoria (ruled 1837 to 1901) was the last ruler of the House of Hanover because her son and successor, Edward VII, followed tradition and took his father's family name, Wettin of Saxe-Coburg-Gotha. During her long reign, the British empire reached its height. Edward did not become king until late in his life and so reigned only from 1901 to 1910. His son, George V (ruled 1910 to 1936), was a popular king who traveled extensively with his wife, Queen Mary, and who often appeared in public.

When King George died in 1936, his son's succession brought on a major crisis within the royal family. Price Edward had been a popular heir apparent; however, during the 1930s, he met an American socialite named Wallis Simpson, then living in London with her second husband. Edward and Mrs. Simpson fell in love, and soon after he became king as Edward VIII in 1936, she started proceedings for her second divorce. A twice-divorced American woman was deemed unacceptable as a queen, however, and King Edward faced the difficult choice between ruling Britain or marrying the woman he loved. Edward abdicated on December 10, 1936. After declaring in a famous radio broadcast that he had given up the throne for "the woman I love," Edward married Mrs. Simpson in 1937.

Edward's younger brother succeeded him as King George VI (ruled 1936 to 1952). He reigned during the difficult years of World War II, but died suddenly in 1952, bringing his daughter, Queen Elizabeth II, to the throne. She continues to reign.

The 1981 marriage of Elizabeth's eldest son and heir apparent, Prince Charles, became a public celebration televised worldwide. Controversy has plagued the royal family in recent years, including broken marriages and divorce. Prince Charles separated from his wife, Princess Diana, in 1992, a divorce was finalized in 1997, and Diana died in a car accident shortly thereafter.

royal courts steadily diminished the jurisdiction of the ecclesiastical courts.

Richard I. Henry was succeeded by his son Richard (ruled 1189–1199). Richard I, "the Lionhearted," was great in legend but of little importance in fact as far as England was concerned. Throughout almost all of his reign he was engaged in the Third Crusade, which kept him out of the country.

The absence of King Richard did not cause the degeneration of royal power, largely as a result of Henry II's reforms and the work of Hubert Walter, who was archbishop of Canterbury and his chief minister.

By the 1100s English society was well settled into its particular pattern of feudalism. Differing from continental feudalism, the English manorial system led more to internal peace than to internal conflict, for, with armed castles required to be licensed by the king and thus few in number, the noblemen of England were more gentlemen landowners than warriors. Feudal duties to higher lords, including the king, were fulfilled more often through the courts of law than through war.

John. Richard was succeeded by his brother John. During John's reign (1199–1216), England lost its continental Angevin possessions, including Normandy itself, to France. Moreover, John's attempts to control the nomination of the archbishop of Canterbury failed, and in 1213 he had to humble himself before the pope and acknowledge that England was a papal fief.

In his attempt to extend royal power at the expense of the barons, especially in the dispensing of justice and the levying of taxes, John was brought to heel by a revolt of the barons. In 1215, at Runnymede, the discontented nobles forced him to grant a long and detailed charter, which came to be known as the Great Charter, or *Magna Carta.*

The Magna Carta was not a charter of liberties for all Englishmen. It was a catalog of baronial grievances against the excessive financial exactions of English kings in general, and of John in particular.

The Magna Carta was not an attempt to destroy the real benefits of strong central government. It attempted to limit kingship rather than destroy it. As the first attempt to limit the authority of the king, the Magna Carta pointed toward the most important development in England during the 1200s, the growth of Parliament.

Henry III. The nobility increased its control over the monarchy during the reign of John's son, Henry III (ruled 1216–1272).

From the point of view of the English, Henry had four faults: his subservience to the papacy; his subservience to foreign favorites, the French relatives of his wife and mother; his defeats at the hands of the Welsh and Scots; and his inability to recover English possessions in France. In 1258 the barons revolted and set up their own government, and Henry III remained king in name only.

The baronial council of government called for a "Model Parliament" in 1265. It was to be attended by two knights elected from each shire and, for the first time, two representatives from each city and borough.

Under this threat to their power, however, the king and the more conservative barons rallied, and late in 1265 the king's forces led by his son, Prince Edward, defeated the barons in battle. The baronial rebellion and experiment with government ended. All charters granted were annulled.

Edward I. Edward (ruled 1272–1307) decided that he could utilize a Parliament that brought together the greater clergy, nobility, and town leaders. Envisioning Parliament as a broad-based advisory council, he realized that it could effectively announce royal policy and influence public opinion. Moreover, Parliament could be most useful in opening to the king new sources of revenue beyond the limited and inadequate income that the crown derived from its traditional source, fixed feudal dues.

Edward needed new sources of money and support because of his ambitious foreign and domestic policies. While he was making inroads in the power of the barons and the church in England, he was at war with France on the continent to defend one of his French territories. Even more aggressive and costly were the wars he waged in Wales and Scotland.

Wales had for centuries been a troublesome and occasionally threatening land on the western frontier of the English kingdom. In the early 1200s Wales had been united under Llewelyn the Great (ruled 1194–1240) and had begun to exploit the rifts existing among English political factions.

In the late 1200s Edward I decided that the peace of England required the conquest of Wales, and by 1284 he had conquered the kingdom. Although Welsh laws, customs, and language survived, independent Wales ceased to exist, and Edward's castles dominated the land. In 1301 Edward proclaimed his son and heir the "Prince of Wales."

Edward had less success in Scotland, the kingdom to the north. Scotland, like Wales, had had a troubled domestic history, and for centuries had been a threat to England. After the death in 1286 of its king, Alexander III, Scotland found itself without a ruler and prey to the evils arising from a disputed succession to the throne. Edward I was called in to choose a king, and in 1292 he declared John Baliol king of Scotland. Taking advantage of his position, Edward then made extensive demands on the Scots.

To resist the king's aggression, the Scots made a military alliance with the king of France. John Baliol, William Wallace, and Robert Bruce led Scotland in wars against English domination. These wars continued for over 30 years and did not end until 1328, when King Edward III recognized Bruce's title to the Scottish crown.

Edward II. Although Edward left his son, Edward II (ruled 1307–1327), the benefits of advancements in the laws and institutions of the realm, he also left a drained treasury, an exhausting war in Scotland, and a host of enemies at home and abroad. Edward II was not the man to overcome these difficulties.

In Edward II's reign, the barons sought with some success to supervise royal policy through a commission known as the Lord's Ordainers. When, in 1327, Edward, surrounded by plots and conspiracy, was deposed and murdered, it was Parliament that named his successor, proclaiming his 15-year-old son King Edward III.

Edward III. The young king came to the throne during a turbulent period in England's social and political development. During the 1200s and early 1300s English cultural and economic life had quickened, and the speed of the resulting social change was increased by a long series of wars and a major epidemic during the 1300s.

English cities and towns, which had grown into thriving centers of trade, had developed a particularly active commerce in cloth with the Low Countries—Belgium, the Netherlands, and Luxembourg.

In part to ensure the continuation of this commerce and to foil the attempts of the French king to interrupt it, Edward III (ruled 1327–1377) in 1337 began a conflict with the French that lasted so long it earned the name the Hundred Years' War.

Britain enjoyed early victories but suffered both from financial exhaustion and from the violent onset in 1348 of the plague known as the Black Death. The plague killed perhaps one-third of the English population and about half of that of Europe.

By causing a manpower shortage that broke the traditional bonds of the

26 Europe and Russia

realized
US

realised
Brit.

centers
US

centres
Brit.

THE FOUR LEADERS of the First Crusade were Godfrey of Bouillon, Raymond of Toulouse, Robert of Flanders, and Bohemond of Taranto.

A FAMOUS SIGHT in London is the Tower Bridge, the lower center portion of which can be pivoted to allow ships to pass.

serf to the land and the manor, the Black Death hastened the process of social change. Feudalism began to disintegrate and the position of the towns and of a

London Bridge

London Bridge once provided the only means of crossing the Thames River except by water, and so it became an important facet of the city's life. The Romans probably built the first bridge (of wood) sometime between 100 and 400 A.D., and wooden structures remained in use until the 13th century. At that time, the first stone bridge, the one of nursery rhyme fame, was built by a chaplain named Peter of Colechurch.

Completed by 1209, Colechurch's bridge spanned the Thames with 19 arches of varying widths and two drawbridges. But its most unusual features were the church, shops, and houses built on it—they rose anywhere from three to seven stories high. These buildings and the many shops lining the roadway added to the hubbub of commercial traffic on this key London artery, and for centuries London Bridge was regarded as a choice business and residential location.

Over the centuries the bridge became the scene of various calamities, including fires. The first blaze broke out just three years after its completion. Fires at both ends suddenly trapped sightseers and firemen, and some 3000 people were killed by fire and drowning. In 1282 five arches collapsed and in 1633 another fire burned half the bridge. This time a servant had left a tub of hot ashes under a stairway. The bridge was again severely damaged in the Great Fire of London in September of 1666.

At least one calamity had a happier ending. One day in 1536 a baby girl named Anne, the daughter of a cloth worker, fell from the bridge. In an instant a brave young apprentice named Edward Osborn dived into the murky waters, rescuing the helpless infant from certain death. Years later Anne's father became a wealthy man but never forgot his gratitude to Osborn. When Anne reached marriageable age she had many suitors, but in the end she was betrothed to none other than Osborn, who went on to enjoy high regard in London and eventually became lord mayor.

Old London Bridge lost its status as London's sole Thames crossing on completion of Westminster Bridge in 1750. And despite extensive renovations during the 1750s, the aging bridge was nearing the end of its useful life. Finally, in 1831, a new London Bridge was completed upstream, and the old bridge was demolished.

The new bridge, designed by John Rennie and built by his son, was a conventional stone structure with just five arches and no buildings on it. Opened officially by King William IV, the new London Bridge remained in use until 1972, when yet another bridge was built. This one is a six-lane, three-span, prestressed concrete structure. The stone facing of the previous bridge was dismantled and shipped to Lake Havasu City, Arizona, in the United States, where it now serves as a tourist attraction.

newly formed middle class was strengthened. Aided by the collapse of feudal loyalties and by the new spirit of nationalism inspired by the wars with France, the English monarchy in the late 1300s was able to centralize its power at the expense of the local lords and clergy.

The new social order not only increased the power of the monarchy, it also enhanced the status of the representatives of the expanding middle class in Parliament.

Between 1339 and 1349 the knights and burgesses began to be designated as the "Commons" because they had begun electing a common speaker to represent them before the king.

The continuing wars with France also strengthened Parliament, as the growth of parliamentary power depended primarily on the control of taxation, and Edward III was continually in need of funds to wage war. He asked Parliament to take on the burden of levying taxes, and Parliament consented to grant the funds in return for the king's remedying grievances or giving additional privileges sought by Commons.

By the end of Edward's reign, Parliament's power was great. Not only had the nobles succeeded in increasing their control over finance, but they had also secured an important role in formulating legislation; they had even exerted occasional pressures to control executive policy.

Richard II. In the wars with France, the English suffered many defeats. By 1375 the burdens of war and taxation had added to the discontent the lower classes felt in a time of rapid social change and economic instability. This discontent led in 1381 to a briefly successful "Peasants' Revolt."

Richard II (ruled 1377–1399) responded to foreign failures and domestic unrest with arbitrary rule. This made many enemies who rallied behind Richard's cousin, Henry of Lancaster, in

1399 and forced Richard to abdicate.

Henry IV. The proclamation of Henry of Lancaster as King Henry IV (ruled 1399–1413) by Parliament marked a great step in the growth of Parliament. Henry reigned as a frankly constitutional monarch. By putting down several rebellions and invasions, Henry was able to pass on to his son Henry V a kingdom more secure than the one he had taken. It looked as though stability had indeed returned to England.

Henry V. Henry V (ruled 1413–1422) was able to pursue the long war with France with remarkable success. By his victories and by his marriage to the daughter of the king of France, Henry became heir to the French throne in 1420. But two years later, he unexpectedly died, and left only an infant son, Henry VI. Both France and England thus were ruled by regents, and under these circumstances, not surprisingly, both kingdoms deteriorated.

Henry VI. France recovered first. It improved its military position, and between 1429 and 1431 the tide of battle began to turn against the English.

England's reverses on the Continent had repercussions at home. Unfavorable terms accepted after England's losses caused the House of Commons to raise treason charges against the king's ministers. A brief rebellion by landed gentry followed and weakened the shaky hold of Henry VI (ruled 1422–1461) on the throne. In 1455 the weakness of the monarchy caused rivalries among contenders for the throne to erupt into civil war.

Henry VI's Lancastrian followers opposed the supporters of other descendants of Edward III, who were led by Richard of York, Henry's cousin. The conflicts that arose between the two houses were known collectively as the War of the Roses because the traditional badge worn by Lancastrians was the red rose and the Yorkists' badge was the white rose.

Bloody civil war between the houses dragged on for 30 years, with the leaders of each faction claiming the right by inheritance to be king. An end seemed to be in sight in 1461. Richard of York had been killed the year before, but his son, Edward, defeated the Lancastrians in that year.

York. Edward of York was proclaimed king as Edward IV (ruled 1461–1483). His reign and that of his brother, Richard III (1483–1485), were marked by continuing warfare and violence. Many powerful groups in England, including Yorkists, turned to Henry Tudor, earl of Richmond. Henry had only a remote claim to the throne as a Lancastrian, but he had resided safely in France during the dynastic wars. Henry invaded England in 1485 and defeated Richard III's army. As a result of Richard's death in the battle, Henry gained the crown as Henry VII.

Henry VII. Henry VII (ruled 1485–1509) had come to the throne through military victory and parliamentary consent; hereditary right had played little part. He sought to make his throne secure for himself and his descendants and to bring peace and order back to England. To achieve both ends, in 1486 he united the formerly warring houses by marrying Elizabeth of York, the eldest daughter of Edward IV, and founding the Tudor dynasty.

Under the Tudors, England entered one of its greatest eras. Under Henry's guidance, the first royal navy was built and the Cabots explored the coasts of North America, preparing the way for English colonies there.

Henry VIII. Henry VII's son, Henry VIII (ruled 1509–1547), led England into participation in the diplomatic and military affairs of Europe. From 1515 to 1529, Thomas Wolsey, lord chancellor, was his brilliant adviser and agent in foreign affairs.

Henry became obsessed with a personal struggle against the Catholic Church. The papal courts at Rome, in 1529, refused to permit his divorce from Catherine of Aragon, who had failed to bear him a male heir. Moreover, Henry resented the authority of the pope, a foreign religious figure, over the political concerns of England. His predecessors had tried for centuries to limit church authority. Henry VII had come close to subordinating the nobility to the monarchy, but the church remained, with its courts, laws, taxes, and massive properties. Henry's divorce would provide the occasion for a sweeping reform of relations between the monarchy and the church.

By 1533 Henry had an English court invalidate his marriage to Catherine, and he married Anne Boleyn. In 1534 Henry passed an Act of Supremacy, making himself and his successors head of the church in England. All appeals to Rome thereafter became illegal.

Although at the time that Henry defied the church the Protestant Reformation was sweeping Europe, the

impetus for England's "reformation" was more political than religious. The Anglican Church differed little from the Roman Catholic Church, except that Henry, not the pope, was its head.

Henry's marriage to Anne Boleyn did not serve his dynastic purposes. In 1533 she bore him a daughter, Elizabeth, but no son. In 1536 he had Anne executed, and he married Jane Seymour, who died in 1537 while giving birth to a son, Edward. Two other wives preceded Henry's sixth, Catherine Parr, who survived him.

Edward VI. Henry's actions had made religion a vital issue in English politics, and its importance increased after Henry's death. Henry was succeeded by his ten-year-old son, Edward VI (ruled 1547–1553), whose policies were determined by the duke of Somerset and the duke of Northumberland, both of whom worked to make the English church far more Protestant than it was.

Mary I. After Edward VI's death, the crown passed to Mary (ruled 1553–1558), the devoutly Roman Catholic daughter of Henry VIII and Catherine of Aragon. Mary tried unsuccessfully to restore Roman Catholicism in England. She married Philip II of Spain, heir to the Holy Roman Empire, but their marriage was unpopular because of English fears of intervention and domination by Roman Catholic Spain.

Mary's persecution of Protestants earned her the name "Bloody Mary," although in her insistence on a single national religion she was in company with every other European ruler in the 1500s. Her death brought her half-sister, Elizabeth, to the throne.

Elizabeth I. Elizabeth (ruled 1558–1603) saw the importance of bringing order and peace to the realm, and with the help of talented advisers available to her she found the means and developed the policies to do so with remarkable success.

In the area of religion, Elizabeth moved cautiously, not making a decision until Parliament did. By the Acts of Supremacy (1559) and Uniformity

(1563), passed by Parliament, she achieved a broad religious settlement that was moderate enough to satisfy the great majority of her subjects.

Elizabeth increased royal power by gaining widespread popular support through ensuring the welfare of the people. Elizabeth initiated a program of national regulation of economic and social affairs unprecedented in Europe. Currency was stabilized, and industry was stimulated by grants of patents and monopolies. The "poor laws" provided relief for the disabled and the indigent, and the Statute of Apprentices regulated the hours and conditions of labor. Laws against religious dissent were enforced only when they threatened the peace of the realm.

The economic vitality of the kingdom found expression in the formation, near the end of Elizabeth's reign, of a number of trading companies—the most famous of which was the East India Company—that established commercial relations and trading outposts in many parts of the world.

Elizabeth also used the English institutions of government to her, and England's benefit. Under the Tudors, the Privy Council, consisting of the monarch's personal advisers, usually led Parliament, which passed into law many of the measures initiated by the council. The centralizing of these institutions, together with the elimination of older ones associated with feudalism or Roman Catholicism, made the English machinery of government more efficient.

Elizabeth's government brought England international prestige as well. By successfully facing a series of crises brought on by the Spanish king and other Roman Catholic leaders determined to restore Roman Catholicism in England, Elizabeth gained new respect for her country.

Moreover, in Elizabeth's reign English sailors broke the Spanish monopoly of trade with the New World and established England as a leading maritime nation. They plundered Spanish galleons,

TOURNAMENTS, a feature of the feudal system, were a form of ritualized battle and probably served as military training and testing.

26 Europe and Russia

labor *US*

labour *Brit.*

CATHERINE PARR, the sixth wife of Henry VIII, survived him when he died in 1547.

Robert "The Bruce" and the Spider's Web

Revered today as a Scottish national hero, Robert "the Bruce" was a medieval nobleman who led the rebellious Scots to independence from the English. The victory was hard fought, but persistence proved to be the key. Bruce had lost a series of battles to the English and finally was forced to flee Scotland. Instead of accepting defeat, however, he returned and by his victory at the now famous Battle of Bannockburn, secured Scotland's independence in 1314.

The Scots had revolted against their English overlords late in the 13th century, and by 1306 Robert "the Bruce," a nobleman related by marriage to Scotland's royal family, had been crowned king by his followers. The English had the upper hand, though, because they controlled much of the countryside. In 1306 they routed Bruce's forces, executed three of his brothers, and even took his wife captive. Bruce fled Scotland, going into hiding on Rathlin Island off the coast of Ireland.

All seemed lost, but legend tells how Bruce may have found his inspiration to carry on. One day, while hiding on Rathlin Island, according to the legend, Bruce watched a spider fail six times while trying to attach its web. Having failed himself six times in battle against the English, he watched all the more intently as the determined spider tried a seventh time. When it succeeded, Bruce saw that by persisting he, too, could win.

Returning to Scotland in 1307, Bruce gained new supporters and with them gradually recaptured the castles that had fallen into English hands. The fighting culminated in the decisive Battle of Bannockburn on June 23–24, 1314, when a large English force tried to come to the aid of nearby Stirling Castle, the last English stronghold in Scotland. Though outnumbered almost three to one, Bruce led his army into battle and by taking advantage of the terrain routed the English troops. With the battle already won, a wave of some 2000 angry Scottish irregulars swept onto the battlefield and put to death any of the English not fortunate enough to escape.

Bruce thus took the throne (as Robert I) and freed Scotland from the yoke of English rule. But the English steadfastly refused to recognize Scotland's independence, even though they had no chance of reconquering it. Persisting as he had before, Robert I launched repeated raids into northern England in hopes of forcing the English to terms. The final victory came in 1328, when England finally made peace with Scotland. By the Treaty of Northampton, England recognized Robert I as king of Scotland and abandoned all claims to the kingdom. Destined to be remembered as the champion of Scotland's independence, Robert I had little time to savor this final victory. He died the following year.

raided Spanish colonial outposts, and seized Spanish treasure. These exploits increased English national pride and awareness of the importance of the sea to England's world position.

England's growing maritime supremacy led Philip II of Spain to build a great armada in 1586 to destroy the English fleet and to make possible the conquest of England.

Sinking the "Invincible" Armada. Angered by England's refusal to restore Catholicism as the national religion and by its support for rebels in the Spanish Netherlands, Spanish King Philip II decided to invade England and make himself king. Philip planned to assemble a mighty fleet that would keep English warships at bay and enable him to convoy some 30,000 troops from the Spanish Netherlands across the English Channel to England. Thus, Philip gave birth to Spain's "invincible" armada, unwittingly setting the stage for a historic naval defeat in 1588.

England's Queen Elizabeth, well aware of Philip's plan, began organizing a fleet to defend England. She had Sir Francis Drake, Sir John Hawkins, and Sir Martin Frobisher at her service, and they helped develop a daring plan to ward off the invasion. Though their fleet

was smaller, the English decided to use its speed, maneuverability, and long-range cannon to attack the slower Spanish ships from a distance. This was a sharp break from the way in which previous naval battles had been fought. Traditionally, ships closed on one another for ramming and boarding by armed soldiers.

Even before the armada sailed in 1588, it seemed less than invincible. In fact, Sir Francis Drake delivered the first proof of that while the armada was still assembling at Cadiz, Spain. Drake brazenly sailed into the harbor and promptly destroyed 33 Spanish ships. Next, while the damaged Spanish fleet was being repaired, its commander suddenly died. The Marquess de Santa Cruz, Spain's most distinguished admiral, was replaced by the Duke of Medina Sidonia, who had no combat experience.

Things went no better when the armada set sail in May, 1588. Soon after leaving Cadiz, the flotilla of 130 ships (including about 40 warships), ran headlong into a storm that tossed the armada—and the 27,000 sailors and soldiers aboard the ships—around like so many corks. Damage sent the armada back to port for a month or so before it sailed again in July. This time the Spanish ships reached the English Channel without incident, but the English ships lay in wait for them.

A running battle developed in the Channel, with the English ships—numbering less than a hundred—laying off

at a distance and firing their long-range cannon at the armada. The British had a clear advantage in this type of fight. Though they had fewer cannon, they actually had more long-range cannon than all the Spanish ships combined. Over half the Spanish cannon were light antipersonnel weapons designed to repel boarding parties.

So long as the Spanish ships maintained their defensive formation though, the British proved unable to do any serious damage. But they did gain one important advantage—both sides used up ammunition for their heavy cannon in the three days of skirmishing. Being close to home, the British warships were able to take on additional gunpowder and shot. The armada put into Calais (now in France) on August 6, 1588, to refill its empty magazines and begin taking aboard additional soldiers for the invasion.

The English struck that very night, however, before the Spanish could even begin loading their ships. Hoping to scatter the Spanish fleet, the English sent eight burning ships into the harbor. Panicked Spanish captains obliged by cutting loose their anchors and sailing helter-skelter for open water rather than risk seeing their ships catch fire. With the armada now out of formation and out of ammunition, the British attacked at dawn off Gravelines, in the Channel. The furious British cannon fire sank three Spanish ships and badly damaged many others before ammunition ran low.

Order of the Garter

The oldest order of chivalry in Europe, England's Order of the Garter, was established c 1344 by King Edward III. Records about its founding have been lost, but the traditional story tells of how an incident involving King Edward led to its creation. The king was dancing at a ball one evening with Joan, Countess of Salisbury, when her garter fell to the floor. Bystanders looked with amusement at the embarrassed countess, but King Edward quickly retrieved the garter and, putting it on his own leg, said gallantly in French, *"Honi soit qui mal y pense"* (Shamed be he who thinks evil of it).

Edward, to commemorate the incident, held a great feast at Windsor Castle on April 23, St. George's Day. Knights were entertained lavishly at a 200-foot-long table, and all participated in a great jousting tournament. The Order of the Garter thus was founded, with St. George as its patron saint.

Another account has it that Edward displayed a blue garter at the Battle of Crécy (1346) during the Hundred Years' War to signal his soldiers to begin fighting. After winning a decisive victory over the larger French force, King Edward created the Order of the Garter to celebrate his success. The garter thus became part of the knights' formal attire and is to this day worn with full regalia below the left knee.

The order today is the highest order of English knighthood and the most prestigious civil and military honor in Britain. The British monarch and the Prince of Wales automatically become members, and only the monarch has the right to name new knight companions to the order. There are at present 25 companions, but other categories of membership have been added over the many centuries of the order's existence. Members of the royal family become royal knight companions, for example, and descendants of King George I and King George II are "extra knights." Foreign dignitaries may also be appointed extra knights.

By custom, each knight has a stall in St. George's Chapel at Windsor Castle, where are kept the knight's banner, helmet, and a plate bearing the knight's coat of arms. When a knight dies, the banner and helmet are removed, but the plate is left mounted in the stall, leaving a permanent record of the knight's coat of arms. The earliest plate dates from about 1394, just a few decades after the order was started.

ELIZABETH I brought prosperity to the nation and increased its prestige internationally.

Then luck turned in the Spaniards' favor, or so it seemed. A sudden squall enabled the Spanish ships to escape by sailing northward around the British Isles and back to Spain. But the escape route proved even more deadly than the British warships. Low on supplies and ill-prepared for the northerly voyage, the Spanish endured freezing cold, starvation, and brutal North Sea gales during their passage around Scotland. One after another, ships foundered at sea, ran aground, or were sunk or captured by the British. Only 60 badly damaged ships ever made it back to Spain, and some 15,000 Spaniards died in the ill-fated venture.

The Spanish, then the greatest European power, had been humiliated, and England was saved from invasion.

James I. Elizabeth never married, and upon her death in 1603, the crown passed to James VI of Scotland, son of her cousin, Mary of Scotland. James (ruled 1603–1625) became the first of the Stuart kings as James I of England. Although the crowns of England and Scotland were united in one person, the kingdoms remained separate.

Religion was one of the first issues confronting James. Dissatisfaction with the vagueness of Elizabeth's church settlement had increased in the late 1500s, and many hoped further changes could be made in the law to eliminate vestiges of Roman Catholicism in the Church of England. The term "Puritan" came to be applied to those who were dissatisfied.

These Puritans turned first to Parliament to achieve the desired church reform, but with little effect. James, himself an Anglican, was unwilling to commit himself on the issue and gave the Puritans little more than permission to make a new translation of the Bible. The king's stubbornness was one cause for the departure of numbers of Puritans to America, where they established the Massachusetts Bay Colony—it was the second English colony in the New World. Jamestown, a settlement in Virginia, had been the first.

Roman Catholics, too, were unhappy over James's refusal to revoke the Elizabethan anti-Roman Catholic laws. In 1605 Guy Fawkes and others formed what came to be known as the Gunpowder Plot. They planned to blow up Parliament on November 5. The plot was discovered the day before, and Fawkes and his fellow conspirators were executed. The plot aroused strong new anti-Roman Catholic feeling and led to further repressions.

James was unsuccessful in dealing with Parliament, and during his reign the conflicts between king and Commons over religion, foreign policy, and economic affairs grew. The central and most important dispute was over the extent of royal authority.

James held to the "divine right" theory of kingship—royal authority came from God and the king was above the law. James's ineptitude in handling the institutions of government caused the Commons to become equally rigid in asserting the rights of subjects and in fixing constitutional limits upon the arbitrary use of royal power.

Unable to deal with Parliament, James ruled without it almost continuously from 1611 to 1621. Parliament's hostility toward James impelled it to develop powerful procedures and strong leaders capable of initiating and carrying through policies. The conflicts between the king and the Commons grew still sharper during the reign of James's son, Charles I.

Charles I. The economic and governmental policies of Charles (ruled 1625–1649) hardened and enlarged opposition to his rule. After dissolving two Parliaments that opposed his arbitrary rule, Charles was forced by Parliament in 1628 to grant the Petition of Right, a document that declared illegal certain royal taxes, such as forced loans, and practices, such as arbitrary imprisonment. Charles had had to reconvene Parliament and grant its demands because he needed parliamentary approval to finance English involvement in the Thirty Years' War, a European religious and political conflict that had begun in 1618.

When Parliament continued to refuse funds, Charles ruled without it between 1628 and 1640, resorting to makeshift methods of taxation and dictatorial behavior, which alienated the populace. In 1640, when the additional expense of a war with Scotland forced Charles to reconvene Parliament, the members were ready to challenge the king.

In 1641 the House of Commons formulated a program called the "Grand Remonstrance" that would have created a limited parliamentary monarchy in England and that would have modified the episcopal organization of the church. Charles accused the parliamentary leaders of treason.

In 1642 civil war began between the royalists, called Cavaliers, who supported the king, and the parliamentarians, called Roundheads. The Cavaliers were generally Anglican nobles or gentry; the Roundheads were mostly Puritan burghers and townsmen who wanted to abolish the episcopacy. Led by Oliver Cromwell, the parliamentarians finally defeated the royalists in 1648.

Commonwealth. Charles I was tried and beheaded early in 1649. The monarchy and the House of Lords were abolished and England was declared to be a commonwealth. An executive council led by Cromwell as "protector" ran the government.

Between 1649 and 1658 Cromwell had as much difficulty with Parliament as Charles had had, and several times he found it necessary to dismiss it. His revolutionary government made little progress with the constitutional experiments it had planned. One of the few benefits of the commonwealth was the support it gave to Puritan colonists in America. In Scotland and Ireland, however, its excessive zeal only alienated the population and made future union more difficult.

Charles II. After Cromwell's death in 1658, the protectorate was too weak to survive for long, and in 1660 Charles I's son took the throne as Charles II (ruled 1660–1685). Religion continued to be the central issue, and in the 1670s Parliament passed a series of laws directed against Catholic and Protestant dissenters. Much of the parliamentary debate centered on a bill that would have excluded Charles's brother, James, from the throne because he was a Roman Catholic. During this debate the party labels "Whig" and "Tory" came into general use.

Whig designated one favoring religious toleration and the exclusion of James, that is, asserting parliamentary control over the succession. Tory designated one favoring an intolerant and exclusive Anglican Church policy and the hereditary right of kingship, even if it should involve bringing a Roman Catholic to the throne.

Great Fire of London. Among the worst fires London has ever seen, the Great Fire cut a 500-acre swath through much of the city between September 2 and September 6, 1666. The fire destroyed everything in its path, and by the time it had been brought under control, over 13,000 houses, 87 churches, dozens of public buildings, and numerous other structures lay in ruins. Over 100,000 people were left homeless, but miraculously only eight people lost their lives.

London had suffered through a drought during the summer of 1666, after having been ravaged the year before by an outbreak of bubonic plague, which killed 15 percent of the population. By September the parched city was ripe for a major fire, and its narrow streets lined with houses and shops

> **centered**
> *US*
>
> **centred**
> *Brit.*

CLAUDE MONET painted the Houses of Parliament with the Waterloo Bridge.

presented near-perfect conditions for spreading it. The spark came about 2 A.M. on September 2, when fire broke out in a bakery shop on Pudding Lane, between the Tower of London and London Bridge.

The lord mayor, Sir Thomas Bloodworth, was roused from his sleep an hour later, when the fire spread to an inn across the street from the bakery. Angry at having his sleep disturbed, Bloodworth dismissed the danger and went back to bed, leaving firefighters to handle the seemingly inconsequential blaze. A church caught fire next, then the tinder-dry Thames Street wharves, and suddenly there was no stopping the growing conflagration. When Londoners awoke that morning, some 300 houses and London Bridge were already on fire. Lord Mayor Bloodworth had reawakened and had joined the firefighters desperately trying to control the fire.

By September 4 the blaze had consumed half the city and sent Londoners fleeing ahead of it with any possessions they could carry. Nothing, it seemed, could halt the fire. Firefighters even pulled down rows of houses ahead of the flames, but the flames jumped over these ineffective firebreaks. The famous English diarist Samuel Pepys witnessed the fire and reported that at one point the flames stretched for over a mile. "How horridly the sky looks, all on fire in the night," he wrote.

Four days after starting, the Great Fire of London was finally brought under control. By then, about four-fifths of the city had been destroyed, forcing about 100,000 Londoners to camp in the fields outside the city with little or no shelter. King Charles II promised to supply them with bread, and rebuilding began soon after.

This time, however, the streets were made somewhat wider and houses were built of brick instead of wood to prevent a repetition of the disaster. By 1672 London had largely been rebuilt.

James II. The 1680s led to the firm establishment of a constitutionally limited monarchy in England.

James II (ruled 1685–1688) followed his brother to the throne in 1685, and most Englishmen were willing to be loyal to him and accept his declaration that he would defend the Anglican Church and keep his own Roman Catholic loyalties a purely private matter. By 1688, however, James's actions, such as giving Roman Catholics high positions in his council and in the army, and harshness toward Anglican opponents, had caused many to contemplate acting against him.

The birth of a son to James's wife in June, 1688, brought this discontent to a head, for in the absence of a son, the throne would have gone to James's daughter, Mary. Mary, a staunch Protestant, was married to William of Orange, head of the Dutch state and leader of the Protestant forces in Europe against Roman Catholic Louis XIV of France. Thus Mary's succession and the future of Protestantism in England seemed doubtful.

In June, 1688, a small group of both Whigs and Tories invited William of Orange to invade England; William and an army landed in England in November, 1688. Finding little support in England against this challenge, James II fled to France.

William III and Mary II. In accepting a Declaration of Rights along with the crown, William and Mary (ruled 1689–1694) accepted constitutional limitations upon their royal authority, which were written into the Bill of Rights. The absolutist theory of divine right was dead. The monarch ruled by grace of legally constituted popular representatives who could remove authority as well as grant it.

Sir Walter Raleigh, Elizabethan Adventurer

Courtier, poet, and above all adventurer, Sir Walter Raleigh was a man of his times. Queen Elizabeth's reign (1558 to 1603) was an exciting era, marked by England's rise as a naval power, early efforts at exploring and colonizing distant lands, and the flowering of the English Renaissance. It was also a time for driving passions—for learning, power, or riches—and of seemingly infinite possibilities for those adventurous enough to gamble their fortunes or their lives. Raleigh put himself and his fortune at risk.

During his early years, Raleigh fought for the Protestants in the French Wars of Religion and in the 1570s studied at Oxford University. By 1578 he had returned to military adventures, first in a pirating venture against the Spanish and then as a soldier fighting for the British Crown against rebels in Ireland (1580). After securing introductions at Queen Elizabeth's court, he quickly attracted her attention.

By 1582 Raleigh had become a favorite of the queen, and his fortunes soared. The queen granted him huge estates in Ireland and made him captain of her guard in 1587.

A bold and controversial figure, Raleigh was unpopular with other courtiers. He had an interest in skeptical philosophy and mathematics and, as an accomplished poet, demonstrated his sensitivity. His poetry no doubt helped keep him in the queen's good graces and his poem *Cynthia* was written in her honor.

But Raleigh was also an adventurous visionary who organized the first efforts at establishing the New World colony of Virginia (from 1585). Wanting him close by, the queen refused to let him accompany the colonists, however. His early ventures failed to establish permanent settlements, but they paved the way for successful colonies founded soon afterward.

Having made his fortune, Raleigh also wanted to have a family. Elizabeth's interest in him had faded by the late 1580s, but even so he dared not risk her wrath by marrying publicly. So, possibly as early as 1588, Raleigh secretly married one of the queen's ladies in waiting. He could not hide his son's birth, however, and when the jealous queen found out in 1592, she locked Raleigh and his wife away in the Tower of London. Eventually, Raleigh managed to buy their release.

No longer required to attend the queen, Raleigh returned to adventuring. In 1595 he led an expedition up Guyana's Orinoco River in search of Eldorado, the legendary city of gold. He found some gold mines, but not Eldorado, and on his return took part in military actions against the Spanish.

Raleigh's fortunes suffered a dramatic turn when James I became king in 1603. His hostility toward Spain displeased James, who wanted peace, and in that same year Raleigh was convicted on trumped up charges of plotting against the king. Imprisoned in the Tower of London from 1603 to 1616, he was finally released to search again for Eldorado. As part of the bargain, Raleigh solemnly promised King James he would not offend Spain.

Everything rode on the success of this last venture, but Raleigh failed to find the legendary city. Worse yet, one of his lieutenants burned a Spanish settlement in Guyana during the fruitless search. When Raleigh returned, he tried to explain the broken promise, but King James refused to listen. Raleigh was executed in 1618.

The events of the Glorious Revolution were confirmed in a number of statutes. By then, the monarch could not suspend acts of Parliament, and was required to convene Parliament annually. In addition, Roman Catholics were excluded from the throne, but limited toleration was granted to Protestant dissenters.

As king, William had to deal with unrest in Scotland and Ireland. Scotland, though still officially ruled by the English king, was more loyal to the deposed James II than to England, and William only barely managed to maintain his position there. Roman Catholic Ireland, still smarting from harsh treatment under Cromwell, was even more rebellious, and the Protestant king responded with severity.

When the political situation in England stabilized, William brought England into the League of Augsburg, an alliance that united both Protestant and Roman Catholic Europe against the territorial aggression of Louis XIV of France. War began in 1689 and continued with brief interludes of peace until 1713.

Anne. Despite strong allies and Parliament's support of the war, England and its allies did not begin to win until William's successor, Mary's sister Anne (ruled 1702–1714), appointed John Churchill, first duke of Marlborough, as commander of the armed forces. His brilliant victories resulted in the defeat of Louis XIV's policies and led to the Treaty of Utrecht in 1713.

By the terms of the treaty, England received Gibraltar and Minorca in the Mediterranean and the Hudson Bay Region and Newfoundland in Canada. In addition, Britain gained trading rights with Spanish colonies and a monopoly of the slave trade in Europe for the next 30 years.

At the head of this embryonic empire was the newly formed United Kingdom. Scotland and England had been formally joined in 1707 into Great Britain. All the British Isles were under control of the British monarch, although Ireland's membership in the union was in little more than name.

None of Queen Anne's children outlived her, and upon her death the parliamentary rules concerning the succession operated, thus excluding Roman Catholic Stuart rulers.

House of Hanover. Next in line was the head of the German state of Hanover, a descendant of James I. He ascended the throne of England as George I (ruled 1714–1727). Because George I and his son, George II (ruled 1727–1760), spoke poor English, had little knowledge of British politics, and were more interested in their German state, Britain's development as a nation governed by ministers advanced rapidly during their reigns.

Cabinet government had gradually developed from the monarchs' custom of using members of the Privy Council as their agents in Parliament. Because it was expedient to have a united cabinet supported by the majority in Commons, the kings found it necessary to consider the desires of Parliament when choosing a cabinet. George I and George II were often absent from cabinet meetings, thus allowing the ministers great autonomy. This custom hardened in time into a precedent.

Both Georges employed the political genius of their adviser, Sir Robert

26 Europe and Russia

THE GREAT FIRE OF LONDON in 1666 burned most of the city, leaving more than 100,000 people homeless.

Buckingham Palace

Buckingham Palace, the London residence of British monarchs since 1837, is among the world's most famous buildings. Built around an enclosed courtyard, the palace has about 600 rooms, including a great ballroom and a covered swimming pool, and is surrounded by some 45 acres of gardens. The palace today is a fittingly grand and imposing structure for the royal family, but it was not always so.

Buckingham Palace is a distant cousin of the original Buckingham House, a red brick mansion built between 1702 and 1705 for John Sheffield, first duke of Buckingham. Some years later, in 1762, King George III bought the large structure from the duke's heir and made it a family residence. George III enlarged Buckingham House, but his son, George IV, wanted a newer, even grander palace built on the site when he became king in 1820.

Parliament balked at the 500,000 pounds King George wanted to spend and instead authorized a sum "not less than" 200,000 pounds for repairs and improvements. George IV was determined to have something new, and while retaining much of the original shell, he made the new palace much larger and more costly than Parliament had authorized. Critics complained, and a parliamentary committee sharply questioned architect John Nash, but still the bills piled up and work on the palace seemed no nearer completion.

The project outlasted King George, who died in 1830, architect John Nash, who was fired in 1830, and George's brother, King William IV, who died in 1837. When Victoria became queen in 1837 and took up residence there, she confronted a nightmare of problems large and small—doors would not shut, bells would not ring, drains would not work, bathrooms were not ventilated, and many of the thousand windows were stuck shut.

Nevertheless the queen grew fond of Buckingham Palace, as did the monarchs who have succeeded her. During Victoria's reign the central courtyard was completely enclosed by adding the east front in 1847, and in 1855 work on the ballroom was finished. With the exception of the east front, which was replaced in 1913, the palace was essentially completed under Victoria's stewardship. Total cost exceeded 700,000 pounds.

centers
US

centres
Brit.

BUCKINGHAM PALACE has over 600 rooms, including private rooms and offices for the royal family and their staffs in addition to rooms for formal occasions.

Walpole (served 1721–1742), in making the machinery of government work. Walpole was the first man in British history to warrant designation as prime minister. Walpole's policies gave England political stability, and his reforms of fiscal and commercial regulations stimulated internal industry, shipping, and foreign trade. Moreover, he refused to let England become involved in European conflicts.

During the peaceful ministry of Walpole, a war party emerged eager to extend English penetration of Spanish America. Spain's attempts to check English violations of the Peace of Utrecht of 1713 led to incidents that were used to arouse support for a "patritic" war. The War of Jenkins' Ear (1739–1748) was named for a publicized atrocity in which it was alleged that Spanish soldiers had cut off the ear of an English seaman, but it was really over trade. It soon merged with the War of Austrian Succession (1740–1748), which had imperial and commercial overtones, as Europe's overseas colonies and international trading privileges were at stake.

Hostilities, ended in 1748, resumed in 1756 as the Seven Years' War, more directly between England and France, the leading European powers. The conflict stemmed mostly from rivalries in North America and India. Britain's victory in the war, directed by the war minister William Pitt, made England the foremost colonial and commercial power in the world. By the Peace of Paris of 1763, England received most French possessions in North America east of the Mississippi and increased trading power in India.

George III. The attempts of George III (ruled 1760–1820) to strengthen the ties between England and the colonies ended in 1775 with the outbreak of the American war of independence.

That war cost Britain the American Colonies—the most valuable portion of its empire. The loss of revenues from taxation was offset, however, by the properous trade that developed with the new nation.

George's policies were more successful after 1783, when he named Pitt's son, William Pitt the Younger, as prime minister. Pitt's genius for finance led to economic reforms, and he did much to eliminate governmental corruption. Above all, he organized the war effort against the French Empire under Napoleon in the early 1800s.

During the century following Napoleon's defeat in 1815, England enjoyed relative peace. Pitt's attempt to incorporate Ireland into the United Kingdom failed in 1801, however, when George forbade religious freedoms for Irish Roman Catholics.

English society had changed rapidly since the mid-1700s. As industrialization increased tremendously, so did the population, especially in the new industrial urban centers. By 1815 Britain was the world's supreme industrial nation, resulting in both national power and stability.

Birth of the Industrial Revolution. Signs of the technological, economic, and social changes wrought by the Industrial Revolution can be found throughout much of the world today. Reliance on factories and machinery for manufacturing goods, the growth of large cities, and greatly improved transportation are among the many effects of this socioeconomic revolution that began in Britain during the second half of the 18th century.

Why did the Industrial Revolution start in Britain? Historians point to important technological advances made there, but other underlying factors were present as well. For example, from the late 1600s, Britain enjoyed a long period of political stability, and with the founding of the Bank of England in 1694, the kingdom boasted a strong banking and credit system that encouraged the growth of capitalism. Britain's existing class of merchant's also provided a well spring for the newer commercial entrepreneurs who would eventually build and operate the factories, foundries, and railroads.

Prince of Wales

The title Prince of Wales is traditionally held by the English monarch's eldest son and heir apparent. It is the highest title the sovereign's oldest son may hold and it is reserved solely for him as heir apparent, though it is not inherited. Instead, each sovereign may confer the title.

The Prince of Wales holds his title only until being crowned king. The title ceases to exist on his accession, to be revived when the new sovereign grants it to his son and heir.

A Welsh nobleman originally adopted the title Prince of Wales in 1244, a few decades before the English conquered Wales. After defeating the Welsh, English King Edward I executed the last native Prince of Wales, David III, in 1283; some years later, in 1301, Edward named his own son Prince of Wales. The future Edward II thus became the first male heir apparent to hold the title, which has since been granted to nearly every one of the oldest sons of the English monarchs.

Among the best-known Princes of Wales have been the future George IV, Edward VII, and Edward VIII. The future George IV, by his own admission "too fond of women and wine," spent much of his life as the Prince of Wales before becoming king in 1820. He reigned until 1830. Likewise, the future Edward VII remained heir apparent for many years. Immensely popular, he was Queen Victoria's son and was created Prince of Wales in 1841, just a month after his birth. He finally became king in 1901, at age 59. He reigned until 1910. The future Edward VIII also proved a popular Prince of Wales, but he is usually remembered for abdicating in 1936, after serving as king for less than a year. He gave up the throne to marry a twice-divorced American woman, Mrs. Wallis Warfield Spencer Simpson, better known as the Duchess of Windsor.

The current Prince of Wales, Charles, was granted the title in 1958 by his mother, Queen Elizabeth II. He was ten years old at the time. Prince Charles has also proved a popular, if sometimes withdrawn, Prince of Wales. Charles' marriage to Diana in 1981 and subsequent divorce in 1997 have caused speculation that their son William might become Elizabeth's successor, though Charles has spent over four decades as heir apparent.

26 Europe and Russia

THE APPEAL of the great playwright and poet William Shakespeare is just as strong today as it was when he wrote in Elizabethan England.

The most immediate causes of Britain's Industrial Revolution were technological advances made during the 1700s, particularly in textile production; for example, the invention of the so-called flying shuttle for weaving in 1733, the water-powered mechanical yarn spinning machine in 1769, and Edmond Cartwright's steam-powered loom in 1785. These and other new inventions led to the building of large textile factories and transformed what was once a small cottage industry into a thriving national industry with an enormous output.

While textiles led the way, other parts of the British economy also benefited from important technological advances. For example, coke replaced charcoal for iron smelting in about 1750, making iron production much more efficient. But probably the most important innovation was James Watt's improved steam engine, which he perfected in the late 1700s. Steam engines suddenly provided a ready source of power for the big manufacturing machines of the industrial age, replacing earlier wind-power and water-power devices. In the early 1800s, steam engines also revolutionized transportation by powering locomotives and steamships.

When factory-building accelerated during the mid-1700s in Britain, fundamental social and economic changes associated with the Industrial Revolution began to occur. For example, independent craftsmen faded in importance because they could not compete with machines that produced more quickly and efficiently. Meanwhile, farmers left their lands to work in the industrial towns and cities, creating a new industrial working class benefiting from higher factory wages.

The Industrial Revolution also gave Britain important economic advantages, and the government actively sought to prevent its spread to other nations. Export of manufacturing methods, machinery, and even skilled workers was outlawed, but eventually the temptations proved too great. In about 1807, two British entrepreneurs set up the first British-style machine shops in Liege, Belgium; thus began the export of the Industrial Revolution to countries outside Britain. During the century that followed, the British-born economic and social revolution spread throughout much of the world.

THE ARMLEY MILL Industrial Museum in Leeds preserves many artifacts such as this handloom from the time of the Industrial Revolution.

The Industrial Revolution and its emerging middle class elicited reactionary policies from the conservative, aristocratic Tories who dominated Parliament. Moreover, by the time George IV (ruled 1820–1830) took the throne, parliamentary policy merely required royal approval, which had come to be taken for granted.

The basic problem remained the partition of power. The old aristocracy, armed with the lessons it felt it had learned from the French Revolution, was more adamant than ever in refusing to yield its control over the state.

Further, it was generally accepted, according to the theory of "virtual representation," that a member of Parliament represented the best interests of Britain, not the specific interests of any particular locality. Some liberal Tories, however, felt that public protests of injustice had validity and responded by passing legislation reforming labor, criminal, and religious toleration laws.

The Tories refused to reform electoral laws, however, which, written centuries before the radical population shifts and class changes forced by the Industrial Revolution, deprived many citizens of representation. The Tories lost the 1830 election on this issue of election reform, and the new Whig, or liberal, majority in the House of Commons gave priority to the issue and began a gradual reform of the electoral system.

After considerable maneuvering and difficulties, the Whigs were successful in 1832, when the Reform Bill fundamentally altered the nature and philosophy of Parliament. Henceforth, the concept of actual representation was to gain steadily on that of virtual representation.

Victoria. Reform was achieved in other areas as well. For the remainder of the 1800s, both Whig and Tory cabinets under Queen Victoria (ruled 1837–1901) passed masses of legislation that radically changed the structure of English society.

Slavery in the colonies was abolished in 1833. Factory acts limited working hours and set standards for conditions and wages, while other laws regulated trade unions. Poor laws established national relief programs. As the century drew to a close, Parliament overhauled the judiciary and the educational systems and established a public health system.

During Victoria's reign many English people felt that their constitution and society had reached a perfect balance that ensured peace at home and abroad and guaranteed continued prosperity. England seemed to be at a peak of power and progress.

Industry and trade had made Britain the most prosperous state in the world. It became the leading political power after the 1850s, when it acquired colonies all over the world. Benjamin Disraeli, who became prime minister in 1868, was the guiding light of English imperialism. In 1875 he acquired a controlling interest in the Suez Canal Company. By the end of the century, Britain had gained colonies or commercial interests in the Far East, the Middle East, and Africa, in addition to its older colonies in North America and the Caribbean.

Britain's Colonial Empire. The most successful of all the European empire builders, Great Britain ranked as the world's leading colonial power by the close of the 19th century. Backed by its supremacy as a sea power, Britain controlled a far-flung empire stretching around the world. Its possessions ranged from tiny island colonies in the West Indies and elsewhere to the vast expanses of Canada in North America, India in the Asian subcontinent, Australia in the South Pacific, and a host of colonies in southern and western Africa.

The English did not begin actively colonizing foreign lands until the reign of Queen Elizabeth I, and the Orient with its lucrative spice trade was initially of most interest. Elizabeth chartered the East India Company in 1600, and as an agent of British imperialism the company gradually expanded British control over the Indian subcontinent. But colonies founded in Canada, America, and the Caribbean in the early 1600s developed more quickly and so became the basis for Britain's first great colonial empire.

The rapid spread of colonial settlements in North America created a strong demand for British goods, making the colonies an important facet of Britain's economy. This raised the stakes in a fierce rivalry with the French, who also had colonial interests in North America. Between 1689 and 1763, a series of wars over colonial territories erupted between the British, French, and Spanish—King William's War, Queen Anne's War, King George's War, and the French and Indian War. Britain emerged the clear winner and by the Treaty of Paris (1763) gained control of French holdings in Canada, America (except lands west of the Mississippi), the Grenadines, Senegal, and Spanish Florida. With Britain also gaining the upper hand in India, it now possessed the world's leading colonial empire—not as large as Spain's but easily the wealthiest.

The loss of the American colonies two decades later shocked the British but did not deter them. Seeking a global network of maritime bases and trading posts, Britain expanded its colonial interests in the South Atlantic, Africa, the Far East, and South Pacific. By 1815 Britain had built what is often called its "second empire," composed of Canada, India, Australia, and dozens of other colonies in Africa and elsewhere. As the world's leading colonial power, Britain was able to further expand its holdings later in the century, when Africa was carved up by the European powers. It also exercised considerable influence in China and Southeast Asia.

Colonial rivalry increased toward the end of the 19th century, especially as newer colonial powers like Germany, Japan, and Italy sought to build their own empires. The rivalries contributed to the outbreak of World War I and cost some combatants their colonial possessions. Britain meanwhile gained a considerable presence in the Mideast, though most of the new territories were League of Nations mandates.

Pressure for independence in Britain's overseas territories increased steadily during the early 1900s and eventually helped break up the empire. In 1931 Britain created the British Commonwealth, and by the Statute of Westminster formally recognized the autonomy of dominions within it. World War II, however, hastened the pace of decolonization. Britain, seriously weakened by the war, was in no position to confront widespread demands for independence. Beginning in the late 1940s, the government hastened to divest itself of most of its remaining

labor
US

labour
Brit.

THE CORONATION OF VICTORIA signaled a long period of peace, prosperity, and reform for the commonwealth.

overseas possessions, including India, Mideast territories, and colonies in Africa.

But Britain's imperial role brought the country into conflict with other colonial powers. All the major European countries were establishing colonies in Africa and Asia, and Britain sought to compete. It became involved in a series of crises and conflicts over colonial territories, from the Afghan and Zulu wars of the late 1870s through the South African Boer War of 1899 to 1902.

By the end of the 1800s the optimism and confidence that had marked the mid-1800s had waned considerably in Britain. In addition to conflicts abroad, industry at home ceased to enjoy the unquestioned superiority it had once held over other nations, and agriculture began to suffer from foreign competition.

Edward VII. In the early years of the 1900s, during the reign of Queen Victoria's son Edward VII (1901–1910), two Liberal governments passed radical social welfare legislation, including old-age pensions and provisions for national unemployment and medical insurance.

In 1909 the Liberals in the House of Commons introduced a radical "people's budget" designed to put the burden of taxes on the rich. By refusing to pass the bill, the House of Lords was deprived of its dominant position in the government.

George V. In 1910, the year that George V (ruled 1910–1936) came to the throne, the House of Commons passed a law limiting the power of the Lords over the Commons on all issues.

Ireland remained a problem. In 1912 the introduction of a series of bills that would have provided home rule for Ireland led to a crisis between the government and the people of Protestant Ulster, who declared their intention to resist home rule. A showdown was prevented only by the outbreak of war in Europe in 1914.

A series of international crises involving the great powers after 1900 had encouraged Britain to make alliances with France (1904) and Russia (1907) to counteract the Triple Alliance of Germany, Austria-Hungary, and Italy. A dispute between Austria-Hungary and Serbia in the summer of 1914 led to the outbreak of World War I. Britain declared war on Germany on August 4, 1914.

The war was costly for England and resulted in a staggering loss of men before it ended in November, 1918. The war also severely damaged the British economy and drained industrial resources. As a result, Britain lost its preeminent world economic position to newly industrialized nations that had suffered less during the war, notably the United States.

British international political power declined as well as the nation's colonial empire began to disintegrate. At a conference in 1926, Britain and its domains agreed to form an association in which no member should have subordinate status—the British Commonwealth of Nations. The era of British imperial power was drawing to a close. The Commonwealth agreement was formalized in 1931 by the Statute of Westminster.

The United Kingdom itself lost one of its members when Ireland rebelled

SALISBURY IS FAMOUS for its cathedral. The "new" town, built in the 1200s, replaced Sarum, a town with evidence of occupation since prehistoric times.

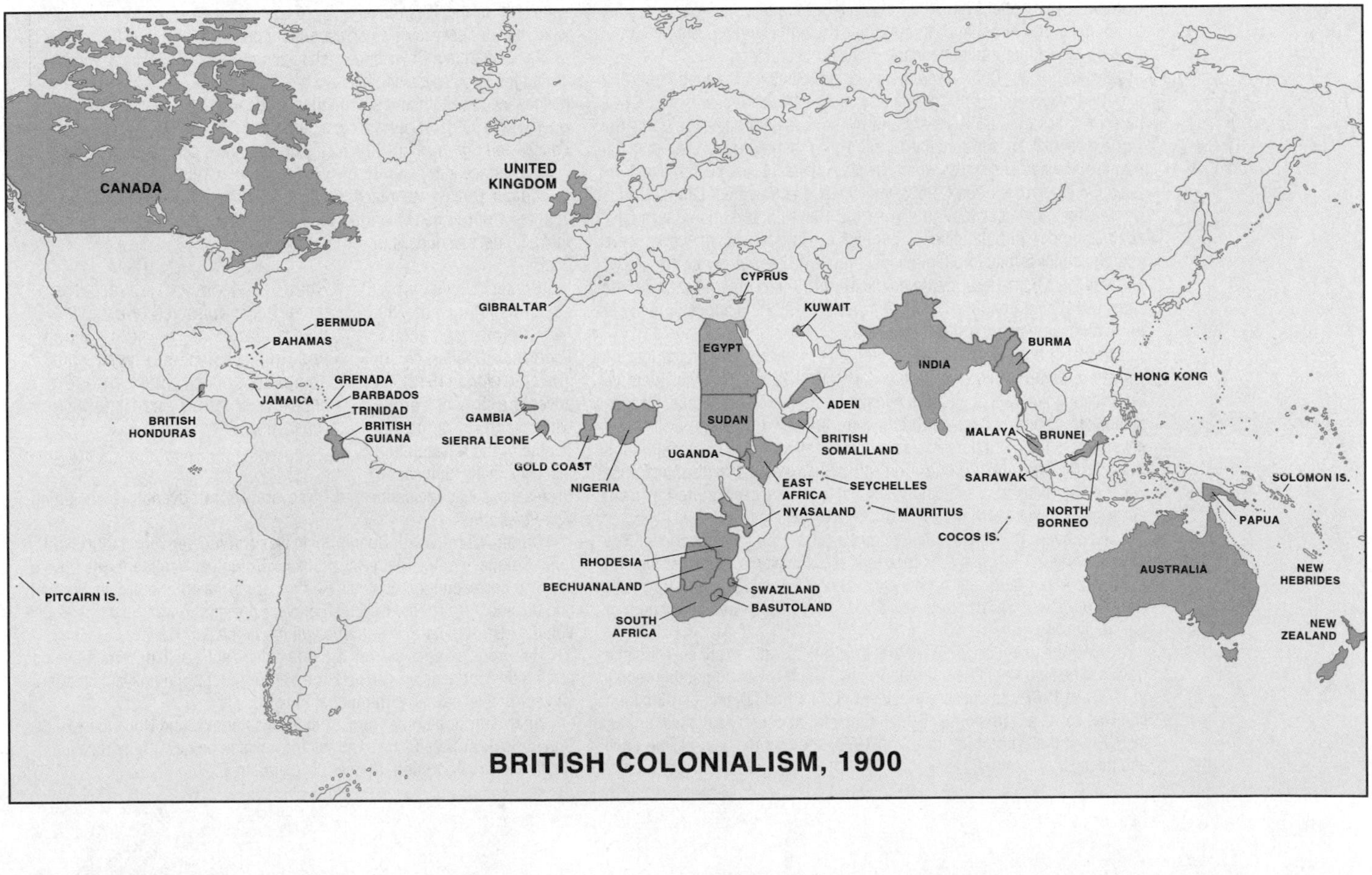

BRITISH COLONIALISM, 1900

CANADA
UNITED KINGDOM
BERMUDA
BAHAMAS
GRENADA
BARBADOS
JAMAICA
TRINIDAD
BRITISH HONDURAS
BRITISH GUIANA
PITCAIRN IS.
GIBRALTAR
CYPRUS
KUWAIT
EGYPT
INDIA
BURMA
HONG KONG
GAMBIA
SIERRA LEONE
GOLD COAST
NIGERIA
SUDAN
UGANDA
ADEN
BRITISH SOMALILAND
EAST AFRICA
SEYCHELLES
NYASALAND
MAURITIUS
COCOS IS.
MALAYA
BRUNEI
SARAWAK
NORTH BORNEO
SOLOMON IS.
PAPUA
RHODESIA
BECHUANALAND
SWAZILAND
BASUTOLAND
SOUTH AFRICA
AUSTRALIA
NEW HEBRIDES
NEW ZEALAND

Some Popular British Authors

Agatha Christie is perhaps the most successful mystery writer in the world. Her books have sold over 100 million copies and have been translated into 100 languages. Christie wrote more than 75 novels and short story collections as well as a number of theatrical plays during a writing career that spanned more than 50 years.

Agatha Mary Clarissa Miller was born in 1890 in Torquay, Devon, England. She had no formal education but was taught at home by her mother. She was sent to school in Paris when she was 16 to study singing and piano. In 1914 she married Colonel Archibald Christie, an aviator in the Royal Flying Corps, and they had one daughter, Rosiland, before divorcing in 1928. She did, however, keep using the name Christie professionally. In 1930 she married Max Mallowan, an archeologist whom she accompanied on yearly excavations to Syria and Iraq.

> Her books have sold over 100 million copies and have been translated into 100 languages. At the time of her death, in 1976, she was the best-selling English novelist of all time.

Christie wrote her first novel, in 1920 while working as a nurse in a Red Cross Hospital during World War I. The book introduced Hercule Poirot, an eccentric, egotistical Belgian detective with a funny mustache, who, through the years, would appear in over 25 novels and short stories. He will most likely be remembered for his ability to solve complicated mysteries with the help of his "little grey cells."

Christie's other principal detective, Miss Jane Marple, was a shrewd, very inquisitive elderly spinster. She lived in the English village of St. Mary Mead and seemed a very unlikely detective. First introduced in the 1930 novel *The Murder at the Vicarage*, Miss Marple was featured in twelve novels, with her final appearance in Christie's last published novel, *Sleeping Murder* (1976).

Christie first gained recognition with *The Murder of Roger Ackroyd* (1926). She went on to write 75 best-selling novels, many serialized in popular magazines in England and the United States. Much of the success of her books is due to her ability to weave an interesting web of plots, forcing the reader to think on a certain path by her misdirection through dialogue and pointless hints. Her characters were often led to murder due to financial problems, and, through her deceptive writing, Christie often fooled her readers into suspecting innocent characters.

Several of her books were adapted into plays for the stage. In 1952 she tried playwriting, and the result was *The Mousetrap,* which at 8,862 performances over 21 years at London's Ambassadors Theatre holds the world's record for the longest running play at one theater. Among the numerous plays she wrote were *The Unexpected Guest* (1958) and *Witness for the Prosecution* (1953), which was the New York Drama Critics Circle choice for best foreign play of the 1954–55 season and was later adapted into a popular film. A number of Christie's other works were adapted successfully into films, including, in 1974, *Murder on the Orient Express* (1934), in 1978, *Death on the Nile* (1937), in 1982, *Evil Under the Sun* (1941) and, in 1980, *The Mirror Crack'd* (1962). In addition, many of her works were adapted for television.

In 1926, the year her mother died, her husband announced that he wanted a divorce because he had fallen in love with another woman. What happened next seemed to be taken from one of her books. Christie disappeared, and her whereabouts were unknown until she was found several days later at a hotel registered under an assumed name. Although there has been much speculation, no details about the disappearance were ever released. Archibald said that she had been suffering from amnesia. The two were finally divorced two years later.

Her novels *Murder in Mesopotamia* (1936) and *Death on the Nile* (1937) were set in the exotic locations she traveled to with her second husband, Max Mallowan, on his excavation trips to Syria and Iraq. She also wrote *Come Tell Me How You Live* in 1947, which was an account of her many trips.

Using the pseudonym Mary Westmacott, Christie wrote six romance novels. She also wrote her autobiography, which appeared posthumously in 1977. In 1967 she became president of the British Detection Club, and she was made a Dame of the British Empire, her country's highest honor, in 1971. At the time of her death, in 1976, she was the best-selling English novelist of all time.

Sir Arthur Conan Doyle is best known for creating master sleuth, Sherlock Holmes; his sidekick, Dr. Watson; and Holmes' archenemy, Professor Moriarty. Sherlock Holmes' adventures have been followed worldwide by millions of readers, who become enthralled with his ability to solve crimes through keen observation and deductive reasoning. Fans have formed many Sherlock Holmes clubs such as the Baker Street Irregulars in New York and the Sherlock Holmes Society in London. Although Conan Doyle wrote other well-received novels and adventures, they are overshadowed by the popularity of Sherlock Holmes.

Born in 1859 in Edinburgh, Scotland, Arthur was one of ten children. His father was a civil servant, and it was a struggle for the family to make ends meet on his limited income. Conan Doyle was educated at home and at a local school until he was sent first to a Jesuit preparatory school, then a Jesuit secondary school. Conan Doyle did not care for the strict rules and discipline, but he was a better than average student. Rather than have her son dedicate his life to the Jesuits in return for his education, Conan Doyle's mother was able to meet the tuition expenses.

Conan Doyle attended the University of Edinburgh, where he studied medicine. While there, he met two professors he later patterned two of his characters after—the imposing, outspoken Professor George Edward Challenger of *The Lost World* and Sherlock Holmes. He practiced medicine from 1882 until 1891, and during the slow periods while building his practice, he began to write.

Sherlock Holmes first appeared in *A Study in Scarlet* in 1887. Next came *The Sign of the Four* in 1890. Conan Doyle also began writing short stories which featured Holmes for *Strand Magazine*. He soon tired of Holmes and wanted to concentrate on more serious work, so in *The Final Problem*, in an 1893 issue of *Strand*, he killed him off. There was such a public outcry that Conan Doyle had to bring Holmes back to life. Altogether Sherlock Holmes appeared in 56 short stories and two more novels, *The Hound of the Baskervilles* and *The Valley of Fear*.

Conan Doyle's first historical novel was *Micah Clarke* (1889). He wrote several more successful historical novels, including *The White Company* (1890), *Rodney Stone* (1896), and *Sir Nigel* (1906). While in Egypt in 1895, Conan Doyle was inspired by his surroundings to write *The Tragedy of the Korosko*. During that visit fighting broke out between the British and the Dervishes. Conan Doyle became an honorary war correspondent for the *Westminster Gazette*, an experience that proved helpful when he later served as a correspondent during World War I.

In 1899 Conan Doyle supervised a temporary hospital facility in Africa during the Boer War. Upon his return to England, he wrote about his experiences living in filth and surrounded by death and disease in *The Great Boer War* (1900). He also wrote a pamphlet, *The War In South Africa: Its Causes and Conduct,* in 1902, justifying England's participation in the war. For his service and support, he was knighted in 1902.

Conan Doyle was married twice. His first wife, Louise Hawkins, suffered from ill health during their entire marriage. She died in 1906. In 1907 he married Jean Leckie.

Conan Doyle introduced another of his better-known characters, Professor Challenger, in *The Lost World* (1912), an adventure story of a group who venture into the depths of the Amazon and discover living dinosaurs.

> Sherlock Holmes' adventures have been followed worldwide by millions of readers, who become enthralled with his ability to solve crimes through keen observation and deductive reasoning.

Professor Challenger appeared in several more adventures, including *The Poison Belt*.

During World War I, Conan Doyle was a volunteer with the Crowborough Company of the Sixth Royal Sussex Volunteer Regiment. His travels as a war correspondent took him to the battlefronts of the British, French, and Italians. As a tribute to British bravery during the war, he wrote a six-volume history, *The British Campaign in France and Flanders*.

He wrote extensively on the subject of spiritualism, and traveled around the world lecturing. His strong feelings regarding psychic matters and spirituality earned him much criticism.

After returning home from a trip to Scandinavia and Holland in 1929, Conan Doyle suffered a heart attack from which he never fully recovered. He died in Crowborough, Sussex, England, in 1930.

Some Popular British Authors

Thomas Hardy produced fifteen novels, one of which was never published, fifty-three short stories, and several volumes of poetry during a literary career that spanned nearly sixty years. Born in 1840 in Higher Bockhampton, Dorset, England, he grew up in a rural area, upon which he based the fictional county of Wessex, the setting for many of his novels and short stories.

At sixteen he began an architect apprenticeship, and in 1862 he became a draftsman for an office in London. He eventually took a position with architect G. R. Crickmay. During this time, Hardy met Emma Gifford, who in 1874 became his wife. She was supportive of his literary endeavors, and his 1873 novel was based somewhat on their courtship. They resided in both Dorset and London. She died in 1912.

In London, Hardy became involved with the city's cultural life but soon became disillusioned with society and the social structure of the classes. His religious faith also began to decline, and he gave up his earlier dream of obtaining a university education and ordination as an Anglican priest. Always studious, Hardy began reading poetry, then writing it. His first poems were rejected by the publishers; however, revised versions published in later volumes are considered to be among his finest work.

> Thomas Hardy produced fifteen novels, fifty-three short stories, and several volumes of poetry during a literary career that spanned nearly sixty years.

Hardy's first novel, *The Poor Man and the Lady* (1868), was rejected by publishers. He was advised to write a less opinionated, more artistic novel with more detail in the plot. The result, *Desperate Remedies* (1871), was published anonymously and received mixed reviews.

In his next novel, the well-received *Under the Greenwood Tree* (1872), Hardy was beginning to find his own voice. Loosely based on his father, the book is referred to as the first of the Wessex novels. After *A Pair of Blue Eyes* (1873) was published, Hardy serialized it for *Tinsley's Magazine*, then wrote a serial for the more important *Cornhill Magazine*. The serial was *Far From the Madding Crowd* (1874). This novel popularized his writings because of his use of humor, tragedy, melodrama, and the idyllic settings. He used Wessex as the setting for all his novels and stories that followed.

The next few novels Hardy wrote met with uneven reviews and reception. *The Hand of Ethelberta* (1876), a social commentary on the British class system, was not well received. However, *The Return of the Native* (1878) was well liked for the imagery Hardy used to evoke the countryside he had known as a child. Set in the Napoleonic period, *The Trumpet-Major* was published in 1880. His next two novels, *A Laodicean* (1881) and *Two on a Tower* (1882), are considered to be two of his lesser works.

The Hardys moved to Dorchester in 1883, where he lived for the rest of his life. Incorporating details of Dorchester's topography and history, he wrote *The Mayor of Casterbridge* (1886), a tragic story.

Hardy's first volume of short stories, *Wessex Tales*, was published in 1888. Instead of focusing on Victorian aristocrats, these stories told of artists and shepherds. *A Group of Noble Dames* (1891) was his next collection of short stories. The stories, as well as his next collection, *Life's Little Ironies* (1894), look at how people, especially women, react to extreme social situations and expose the inconsistencies within Victorian society. His last volume was *A Changed Man* (1913).

Hardy's final two novels, *Tess of the d'Urbervilles* (1891) and *Jude The Obscure* (1895), are considered by most critics to be his best. Both are tragedies with working class people at the center. His frank treatment of sexual attraction was a shock to people of the time, and both books were harshly criticized. At this time Hardy stopped writing novels and returned to writing poetry. Because of Hardy's reputation as a novelist, his first collection of poems, *Wessex Poems* (1898), was slow to be received. But the publication a few years later of *The Dynasts,* an epic poetic drama, helped reinforce Hardy's reputation as a great nineteenth- and twentieth-century writer.

When his wife, Emma, died, Hardy wrote a collection of poems that was later included in *Satires of Circumstance* (1914). In 1914 Hardy married Florence Emily Dugdale. He published *Moments of Vision* (1917), *Late Lyrics and Earlier* (1922), and *Human Shows* (1925), while in his seventies and eighties, and wrote for a collection called *Winter Words*, published after his death. Hardy died in 1928.

George Bernard Shaw, born in Dublin in 1856, was the youngest of three children. Shaw did not like school and, by the age of 16 he was working as a clerk in a land agent's office.

He was knowledgeable about art, music, and literature due to his mother's influence. Just prior to Shaw turning sixteen, his sisters and mother, a professional singer, moved to London. In 1876 Shaw joined them after deciding to become a writer. His first novel, *Immaturity*, written in 1879, went unpublished until 1930. His following four novels were also refused by the publishers. During the 1880s he became a Socialist and helped found the Fabian Society, a middle-class Socialist group whose goal was to transform Britain into a socialist state through reform and education rather than revolution.

In 1895 Shaw became theater critic for the *Saturday Review*, making a name for himself for his witty writing and new ideas, and began to write plays. A great admirer of Henrik Ibsen, Shaw believed Ibsen's plays showed a realism and seriousness that was lacking on the London stage, and Shaw wanted to pattern his work after Ibsen's. His first group of plays, *Plays Pleasant and Unpleasant*, included *Widowers' Houses* (1892), an attack on slum landlords, and *Mrs. Warren's Profession*, which dealt with prostitution. Because of the subject matter, the latter, written in 1893, was not produced until 1902. The pleasant *Arms and the Man* (1894) and *Candida* (1897) were more lighthearted and witty.

In 1898 Shaw married Charlotte Payne-Townshend. His next group of plays included *Caesar and Cleopatra* (1901), considered one of his best works, in which Cleopatra is a mean-spirited child of 16, while Caesar is a philosophical and lonely man.

Establishing himself as a major playwright as he used comedy and satiric wit to explore and expose the part society plays in its own evils, Shaw did not become well known in England until a series of his plays were performed at the Royal Court Theatre from 1904 through 1907. *Man and Superman* (1905) presents the idea that humanity is one level of the evolution of God. *Androcles and the Lion* (1912) has the theme that for a life to be worth living, one must have something worth dying for. Performed in 1913,

> Shaw's ability to give a voice to his beliefs and ideals through his intelligent and witty writing made him one of England's best-known playwrights. His plays are produced more than those of any other English playwright, with the exception of William Shakespeare.

Pygmalion, a comedy about class distinction, is one of Shaw's comic masterpieces. Phonetician Henry Higgins gives lessons to a Cockney flower girl so she may be presented as a proper lady to society. The experiment is a success, but their different backgrounds bring repercussions. In 1938 *Pygmalion* was turned into a film that won an Academy Award for Shaw, and in 1956 it was adapted into a musical, *My Fair Lady*, first for the stage and, in 1964, as a motion picture.

During World War I Shaw stopped writing plays. He wrote a pamphlet, "Common Sense About the War," in which he argued for negotiations for peace, charging that Great Britain and its Allies as well as Germany were equally responsible for the war. His public speeches made him an outcast and nearly ruined his reputation. He wrote one major play during this time, *Heartbreak House* (performed 1920), an outlet for his bitterness and disappointment with British politics and society.

The 1920 canonization of Joan of Arc sparked Shaw's interest. The result was his masterpiece, *Saint Joan* (1923), a depiction of her life and sainthood. Shaw received much praise for this work, and it led to his being awarded the Nobel Prize for Literature in 1925.

A feminist with continued strong political beliefs, Shaw in 1928 wrote *The Intelligent Woman's Guide to Socialism and Capitalism*. He also produced *The Apple Cart*, which dealt with his political beliefs and his uncertainty about humans' abilities to govern themselves. In 1950, after a fall from a tree, he died at the age of 94.

Shaw's ability to give a voice to his beliefs and ideals through his intelligent and witty writing made him one of England's best-known playwrights. His plays are produced more than those of any other English playwright, with the exception of William Shakespeare. His talent for combining comedy and drama in making social statements is a large part of what makes his plays so popular even today.

in 1920. In 1922 it became the Irish Free State, and only Ulster, in the north, remained British.

Britain's main problems in the 1900s were economic. Neither the coalition Liberal-Conservative governments nor the first governments of the new Labour Party, nor the Conservative governments in power between 1918 and 1931, improved England's poor economic situation.

The economy never fully recovered after World War I, and unemployment spread. As Britain lost colonies and fell behind in manufacturing, its trade also declined. The worldwide economic depression of the 1930s worsened Britain's situation.

George VI. In 1936 Edward VIII came to the throne and abdicated in less than a year to marry a divorced American woman. He was succeeded by his brother George VI (ruled 1936–1952). A national coalition government of Conservatives, Liberals, and Laborites, formed in 1931, held power throughout the 1930s.

The government's attempts to cope with the Great Depression extended Britain's broad social welfare programs and introduced great control by the government over industry and trade. Little progress was made, however, and the Depression's cure was left largely to time.

Inactivity marked the coalition's foreign policy. Britain had entered into the collective security agreements of the League of Nations and the Locarno Pact in the 1920s, but, in a policy of appeasement, it failed to stand by these agreements when confronted by the aggressive foreign policies of fascist Italy and Nazi Germany.

The policy of appeasement reached its peak in 1938 when Prime Minister Neville Chamberlain consented to Nazi occupation of the Sudeten German region of Czechoslovakia in meetings with Adolf Hitler at Munich. In March, 1939, Hitler repudiated the Munich agreements by annexing the remainder of Czechoslovakia.

World War II. Realizing the failure of Chamberlain's appeasement policy, the British and French governments reaffirmed their guarantee of the independence of Poland. By the end of the summer, however, Hitler invaded Poland, and on September 3, 1939, Britain and France declared war on Germany.

Within nine months Holland, Belgium, and France had fallen, and Britain stood virtually alone against the Germans. In May, 1940, Winston Churchill succeeded Chamberlain as prime minister. As head of a coalition government, he provided vigorous leadership in the resistance to German air attacks in 1940 and 1941.

Surviving the Blitz: Britain's "Finest Hour". Standing virtually alone against the Nazi military might early in World War II, Britain persevered and narrowly won what could have been a disastrous defeat in the Battle of Britain. Adolf Hitler had begun preparing to invade

| laborites |
| US |
| labourites |
| *Brit.* |

THE STUBBORN RESOLVE of Prime Minister Winston Churchill inspired the English people to fight on when all seemed lost in the Second World War.

Britain immediately after France fell in June, 1940, believing a massive air assault would crush the Royal Air Force (RAF) and clear the way for his invasion. But Hitler sorely underestimated the courage and determination of the RAF pilots. Nor did he anticipate the stubborn resolve of Britain's wartime leader, Prime Minister Winston Churchill, who inspired his people to fight on even when all seemed lost.

Before World War II Churchill had been a high-level government official and something of a political maverick. So on becoming prime minister in May 1940, he told the House of Commons he had "nothing to offer but blood, toil, tears and sweat." Indeed, just weeks later, British army troops narrowly escaped annihilation at Dunkirk; now they were barely able to defend their homeland.

At each crisis, Churchill, with his trademark cigar and "V" for victory sign, found the words needed to rally the British people. Speaking before the House of Commons after France fell to the Nazis in June 1940, Churchill warned that the Battle of Britain was about to begin. Should Britain fall, he said, it would plunge Europe into a new dark age. Churchill then made his famous appeal to his people: "Let us therefore brace ourselves to our duties and so bear ourselves that if the British Empire and its Commonwealth last for a thousand years men will still say, 'This was their finest hour.'"

The Battle of Britain began in July with Luftwaffe attacks on British ports and shipping. Then, in early August, the Germans shifted to massive day and night attacks, mainly directed at RAF installations. The RAF had only 650 fighters against the Luftwaffe's 1300 bombers and 900 fighters, so that it was a desperate fight from the beginning.

But thanks to Britain's newly developed radar, the RAF skillfully concentrated its fighters and shot down hundreds of German planes. The German bombers still kept coming, however, and by the last week of August 1940, the RAF was nearly beaten.

Then, a German bombing raid against London on August 23 prompted the British to retaliate by bombing Berlin. Embarrassed and enraged by the unexpected attacks, Hitler ordered the Luftwaffe to concentrate its bombing on London. September brought furious German attacks on the city. The destruction peaked on September 15, when over 1000 German bombers and 700 fighters hit London in a daylong attack. The blitz killed thousands of Londoners and demolished large parts of the city, but it proved a godsend to the beleaguered RAF.

While London took a terrible beating, the RAF repaired its badly damaged airfields and control installations. The remaining RAF fighters were also able to concentrate their strength over the relatively small area of the city. And while Hitler may have thought bombing London would break the British, it only stiffened their resolve. Londoners grimly endured the onslaught while overhead RAF Spitfire fighters continued knocking down German planes by the hundreds.

By the end of September, the staggering losses finally forced the Luftwaffe to halt its daylight bombing attacks, and two weeks later Hitler abandoned all plans to invade Britain. Bombing raids dropped off sharply during October and, by month's end, the British had clearly won the Battle of Britain. The cost was great—the British lost 915 planes and the Germans 1733—but RAF fighter pilots saved Britain by maintaining control of the skies. As Churchill said later, "Never, in the field of human conflict, was so much owed by so many to so few."

Churchill led Britain into alliances with the Soviet Union and the United States that brought about the defeat of Italy in 1943 and of Germany in 1945. After the war, Britain took on a large measure of responsibility in the making of the peace and in the subsequent formation of the United Nations. In July, 1945, a general election replaced Churchill with a Labor government led by Clement Attlee.

Postwar Britain. When the war in Europe ended, in May 1945, beleaguered Britain faced a difficult adjustment to the postwar world. Six years of war had exhausted its military, shattered the economy, and left the country nearly bankrupt. Britain had lost its leadership in world trade, banking, and shipping to the United States, and could no longer even defend its far-flung colonies, much less force them to wait any longer for independence. British cities lay in ruins, but above all the people were tired. They had lost loved ones and endured years of rationing and other privations during the war.

At the general election in mid-1945, voters turned away from Prime Minister Churchill, the wartime hero and Conservative Party leader, to hand a landslide victory to Clement Attlee and his Labour Party. Attlee used the vote as a mandate for change and instituted sweeping reforms during his first year and a half as prime minister, including the nationalization of railroads, coal mining, steel production, trucking, ports, utilities, and the Bank of England. Meanwhile, Labour also enacted sweeping social welfare reforms, creating a welfare system that nationalized hospitals and included a national health care system.

Another accomplishment of Attlee's government was to divest with relative grace much of Britain's remaining colonial empire. Britain withdrew from India and Pakistan in 1947 and Burma and Ceylon (now Sri Lanka) in the next year. Attlee also led the nation out of its Mideast holdings—Jordan (1946), Palestine (1948), and Egypt (1948, except for the Suez Canal)—and laid the groundwork for the independence of other colonies in Africa and elsewhere during the 1960s, 1970s, and 1980s. Meanwhile, he continued Britain's firm alliance with the United States during the early Cold War years and led his country into the pro-West North Atlantic Treaty Organization in 1949.

But by 1947 Britain's economic situation had become desperate. Cities remained in ruins, the economy struggled to get back on peacetime footing, and many basic necessities were in short supply. Through the Marshall Plan, the United States began providing badly needed financial aid on a massive scale from 1948, but hardships continued for some years. Attlee devalued the British pound in 1949 to stimulate exports, but rationing of food, fuel, and other consumer goods remained in force into the 1950s.

Return to prosperity. Continuing economic problems helped force a change of government in 1951, and so began a long period of Conservative Party government that lasted until 1964. During that time the economy recovered and the country prospered. Conservatives denationalized the Bank of England and certain industries, but left intact Labour's social reforms. Construction also began on a vast network of highways, until then virtually unknown in Britain, promoting growth of the trucking industry at the expense of the country's ailing railroads.

Winston Churchill, again chosen as prime minister, served from 1951 until 1955, when age and poor health forced his retirement. The two most important events during his administration were the Korean War (1950 to 1953) and the death of King George VI (1952). Queen Elizabeth II succeeded her father and was crowned amid the splendor of a formal coronation ceremony in 1953. Britain also revealed in 1952 that it had built an atomic bomb, thus joining the United States and Soviet Union as a nuclear power.

A NAVAL BATTLE during the reign of Henry VII, who was better known for his diplomatic victories than his military victories

26 Europe and Russia

Mary Rose: Lost and Found

When the medieval English ship *Mary Rose* sank accidentally on July 19, 1545, it ranked among the most advanced warships of King Henry VIII's navy. Lost with nearly all hands aboard that fateful day, the *Mary Rose* rested in its watery grave just outside England's Portsmouth Harbor for the next four centuries. But thanks to the mud and silt blanketing the wreck, *Mary Rose* was preserved in remarkably good condition. The prize of King Henry's fleet thus became a priceless time capsule of 16th-century seafaring life just waiting for the arrival of modern underwater archaeologists.

Built in 1509, the *Mary Rose* had been extensively refitted in the years before 1545 and was among the first warships to carry additional heavy cannons below the main deck. The extra cannons added 24 tons to the weight of the *Mary Rose,* however, and because the guns were mounted close to the waterline, closable gunports had to be added to prevent swamping in heavy seas. Furthermore, during battle the *Mary Rose* was burdened with even more weight. In addition to ammunition and supplies for its normal crew of 415 sailors, the *Mary Rose* also carried almost 300 soldiers, including archers armed with longbows.

When the *Mary Rose* joined an English fleet leaving Portsmouth Harbor on July 19, 1545, it was fully loaded and heading into battle against a huge French fleet attempting to invade England. The ship's gunports were open, and its captain, Vice Admiral Sir George Carew, may have been only dimly aware that his ship was dangerously top-heavy because of the overloading. Carew ordered the *Mary Rose* to turn to engage the nearby French ships. But instead of a pitched sea battle, what followed was one of the worst disasters in English naval history.

The *Mary Rose* answered the helm by turning hard to starboard, and the extra weight made the ship heel over more than normal. Water suddenly rushed into the open gunports below the main deck, and horrified sailors scrambled to escape the incoming torrent.

The swamped ship sank so quickly that few survived. Within a minute the *Mary Rose* disappeared beneath the waves, taking 630 of the 700 men aboard.

The English tried but failed to salvage the *Mary Rose* soon after turning back the French invasion. Then, in 1836, John and Charles Deane, inventors of the first practical diving helmet, stumbled on the wreck and spent four years salvaging various artifacts. Extensive salvage work did not begin until 1971, when British underwater archaeologists rediscovered the wreck.

The Mary Rose Trust was formed and for the next 11 years, archaeologists made over 30,000 dives to systematically search for and remove artifacts from the site. The wreck yielded over 17,000 artifacts, many of them in good condition. Divers retrieved 139 longbows, some still resilient enough after four centuries to be strung and shot, 2,500 arrows, compasses, cloth and leather items, and even the remains of food. Among the most prized items was a remarkably well-preserved surgeon's chest containing ointments, syringes, and a large wooden mallet used for anesthetizing patients. (The surgeon put a metal helmet, also found, over the patient's head before striking the numbing blow.)

The biggest treasure of all was the starboard half of the hull, which had been preserved virtually intact by the mud. In late 1982, 437 years after the ship went to the bottom, the remains of its hull again broke the surface, raised in one piece by a complex system of scaffolds and slings. The hull, along with some 2,500 artifacts, is now displayed in a museum established by the Mary Rose Trust in Portsmouth, England.

British Ballet

Ballet Origins. Ballet developed in Europe. It originated in France, but its roots can be traced to Renaissance Italy of the 1400s and 1500s. During this period, dancing became more elaborate and ostentatious. The Italian nobility used dance to demonstrate their wealth and refinement. They were quickly imitated by wealthy bankers and merchants in the cities.

By 1500, dance spectacles, organized and directed by dancing masters, had become very elaborate. At banquets and other formal entertainments, costumed dancers, often representing figures from classical mythology, presented series of carefully rehearsed and polished dances, somewhat like amateur floor shows.

From Italy to France. When Catherine de Médicis, the Italian-born member of the ruling family of Florence, became queen of France, she introduced into the French court the same kind of entertainment she had known in Italy. In 1581, she arranged for *Le Ballet Comique de la Reine* to be performed in honor of a royal wedding.

The glorious production lasted for almost six hours and is considered by many historians to be the first ballet. In addition to dancing, it included specially composed music, singing, and spoken verse. It was a great success, and for the next century, dance entertainments of this kind were a principal diversion of the nobility of Europe.

Professionally trained dancers began to replace members of court as ballet developed and the dancing became more lively and athletic. During this same period, the 1700s, ballet came to be seen as an art form independent of singing, one consisting solely of the dance and its musical accompaniment.

Ballet and Romanticism. In the early 1800s, Romanticism took hold in ballet. The stories that were told in romantic ballet often took place in the dreamlike world of the supernatural, offering an escape from the real world. Ballet technique expanded as women began to dance on their toes. A result of fascination with dreams and enchantment, toe dancing represented being lifted into another world. The quintessential ballet of this period is *Giselle.* It offers everything the Romantics prized: country life, madness, and the supernatural.

Dance in Britain. In the early 1900s, two remarkable women, Marie Rambert and Ninette de Valois, began the development of British ballet.

Marie Rambert, born in Warsaw, was studying medicine when she saw performances of dancers Anna Pavlova and Isadora Duncan. She was so taken with what she saw that she gave up medicine and began to study dance. She became a teacher and worked with Diaghilev and Nijinsky on the original production of *Rite of Spring.*

Arriving in London in 1917, Rambert continued her dance studies, and in 1920 she established a dance school. In 1926 she founded the Ballet Rambert. Under Rambert's direction for thirty years, the company nurtured young talent but lost them to other companies. The company was reorganized in the 1960s, emphasizing modern dance.

As a child, Ninette de Valois attended theater school and performed with a touring children's theater company. In 1918 she became principal dancer with the British National Opera; in 1923 she became a soloist with Diaghilev's Ballets Russes.

After leaving Diaghilev in 1926, she began staging performances at the Old Vic Theatre in London. De Valois was the choreographic director to the Old Vic, the Festival Theatre in Cambridge, as well as to the Abbey Theatre in Dublin from 1926 to 1931.

In 1931, de Valois and Lilian Baylis founded the Vic-Wells Ballet, so called because the company performed at both the Sadler's Wells Theatre and the Old Vic Theatre. During the 1930s, de Valois created many new works, including *The Rake's Progress, The Haunted Ballroom,* and *Don Quixote.*

The company changed its name to the Sadler's Wells Ballet in 1940 after the Sadler's Wells Theatre was bombed during the war; in 1946 the ballet company became the resident company of the Royal Opera House. De Valois then founded a second company called Sadler's Wells Theatre Ballet, which was housed at the Sadler's Wells Theatre.

The Royal Ballet. In 1956 a royal charter was granted to both companies. The Sadler's Wells Ballet became the Royal Ballet, and Sadler's Wells Theatre Ballet became the Touring Company of The Royal Ballet. Today, the touring company is housed in Birmingham and is known as the Birming-

ham Royal Ballet. Retiring in 1963, after thirty-two years as director, de Valois remained active for many years as an advisor.

De Valois encouraged many young choreographers, among them Frederick Ashton, who became the principal choreographer for her company from 1935 until his retirement in 1970 and who served as director of the Royal Ballet from 1963 to 1970. He was knighted in 1962.

Ashton created a large varied reper-

DANCE GROUP performing Frederick Ashton's ballet, *Symphonic Variations.*

toire, ranging from ballets with no story, such as *Symphonic Variations,* to the more dramatic *A Month in the Country,* and the playful *Tales of Beatrix Potter.* He, along with the radiant English ballerina Margot Fonteyn, created a British ballet style that was known for its refinement and sensitivity to musical phrasing.

Fonteyn joined the Vic-Wells Ballet School in 1934 and became a soloist a year later dancing in de Valois' *Haunted Ballroom.* Establishing her reputation as perhaps the greatest British ballerina of all time, Fonteyn was identified with Frederick Ashton in many ballets he created just for her, including *Symphonic Variations* and, most notably, *Ondine.*

In 1954 Fonteyn became president of the Royal Academy of Dancing and, in 1959, she was guest artist to the Royal Ballet. At a time when she seemed to be scaling back on the amount of dancing she was doing, Fonteyn entered into a partnership with dancer Rudolf Nureyev. This partnership, which lasted throughout the 1960s, became legendary. Their first ballet performed together was *Giselle,* and with it the most famous partnering in ballet was born.

English National Ballet. The Gala Performances of Ballet gave its first performance in 1950. Established as a showcase for Alicia Markova and Anton Dolin, two of Britain's premier dancers, the touring company is still in existence today operating under the name English National Ballet. The partnership of Markova and Dolin began when they formed Britain's first touring ballet company in 1935.

They toured throughout the country for the next two years performing such classics as *Giselle, Swan Lake Act II,* and "The Kingdom of Sweets" from *The Nutcracker.* They returned to London in 1948, after the second World War, and danced with various companies, including Sadler's Wells Ballet.

In 1950 they presented five Gala Performances with Ballet Rambert. The performances were so successful that it was proposed that they follow the season with a regional tour. The programs were made up of one- or two-act ballets, and during that first season they toured for eleven weeks.

In honor of the Festival of Britain, the company's name was changed to Festival Ballet, and when the company first toured abroad, the name was extended to that of London's Festival Ballet. In order to make billing easier, the name London Festival Ballet was adopted in 1969, and in 1989 it was renamed, becoming known at that time as the more formal English National Ballet.

In the 1960s, in response to audiences' interest in longer, more-dramatic works, full-evening works were commissioned, including *The Snow Maiden* and *Peer Gynt.* Rudolf Nureyev was among the artists who worked with the company, and two of his works, *The Sleeping Beauty* and *Romeo and Juliet,* which were created in the 1970s, became instant classics.

In the 1980s the goal of the artistic director was to make it the best touring company in the world. Today, the English National Ballet is still a touring company that remains true to Anton Dolin's vision of bringing quality ballet to the general public at affordable prices.

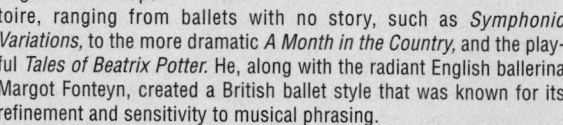

theater
US

theatre
Brit.

National Flag of Britain

The national flag of Great Britain, also known as the Union Jack, the Union Flag, or the British Union Flag, was officially adopted January 1, 1801. Its design represents the three heraldic crosses of St. George, St. Andrew, and St. Patrick, whose emblems represent England, Scotland, and Ireland, respectively. The composite of these insignia results in a visual realization of Great Britain's governmental structure of multiple countries united under a single sovereign. Notably, the dragon, which is the emblem of Wales, was omitted from the design. This is because Wales was no longer a separate principality when the flag's design was conceived.

St. George has been the patron saint of England since the 1270s. His emblem is a red cross on a white background. This symbol constituted the design of England's national flag until the first part of the seventeenth century. Similarly, Scotland had a separate national flag, which featured the symbol of their patron saint, St. Andrew. The Scottish flag featured a diagonal white cross imposed over a blue background.

A political shift occurred when James VI of Scotland (who later assumed the title of James I) inherited the English throne in 1603. Soon thereafter, he joined England and Scotland in a personal union, so called because he continued to rule each of the two countries as a separate kingdom. Since the English and Scottish governments were not integrated, each country maintained an individual flag until 1606. At that point, a debate arose regarding which country's flag would be appropriate to fly at sea. The dispute was settled when James I issued a royal proclamation declaring that the designs of the English and Scottish flags would be combined (see box).

The new flag, which was to be flown from all ships belonging to England or Scotland, integrated the symbols of the two flags by laying St. George's cross over the cross of St. Andrew. Initially, the design was not well received. The English felt slighted because the white background of St. George's cross was obscured. The Scots were similarly uncomfortable with the positioning of their emblem, as St. Andrew's cross lay under the English insignia.

The Proclamation

Whereas some difference has arisen between our Subjects of South and North Britain, Travelling by Sea, about the bearing of their flags, for avoiding of all such contentions hereafter, We have with the advice of our Council ordered That from henceforth all our subjects of the Isle and Kingdom of Great Britain and the Members thereof shall bear in their maintop the Red Cross, commonly called St George's Cross, and the White Cross, commonly called St Andrew's Cross, joined together, according to a form made by our Heralds and sent by Us to our Admiral to be published to our said Subjects. And in their foretop Our Subjects of South Britain shall wear the Red Cross only as they were wont, and our Subjects of North Britain in their Foretop the White Cross only as they were accustomed. Wherefore We will and command all our Subjects to be conformable and obedient to this Our Order, and that from henceforth they do not use to bear their flags in any other Sort, as they will answer the contrary at their Peril.

> Given at our Palace of Westminster the 12th day of April in the 4th year of our Reign of Great Britain France and Ireland Annoq. Domini 1606.

Despite its opposition, the design endured, probably because it was strictly reserved for nautical use. It was, however, discontinued for a brief period beginning in 1649 (when England became a Commonwealth), but the flag was restored in 1660. Even then, the flag was not flown on land until 1707, when England, Scotland, and Wales joined to form Great Britain, which united the kingdoms under a single government.

Throughout its evolution to this point, the flag was referred to as either the British flag or the flag of Britain; the term "Union Jack" had yet to enter the vernacular. Now, the phrase has gained so much popularity that it is used more often than any other of the flag's names. Despite its prevalence in modern vocabularies, the exact origin of "Union Jack" remains unknown, although a number of theories exist.

Some historians believe the term "Union Jack" originated from the "jackets" that were worn by English and Scottish soldiers. Others name the source as James I's name in Latin (Jacobus) or French (Jacques) translation. Most people, however, contend that it was derived from the use of "jack" to mean "small." Many proponents of this theory cite a proclamation issued by Charles II, who declared that the Union Flag should be flown by Royal Navy ships as a jack, or small flag at the bowsprit. In any case, it is widely held that the phrase came into common usage around the time of Queen Anne's reign from 1702 to 1714.

In 1800, a hugely significant political shift occurred when the Act of Union was passed. This Act ended the Irish Parliament and created the United Kingdom of Great Britain and Ireland. At the time the Act became effective in 1801, a new flag was approved. The purpose of the new design was to acknowledge Ireland's new status; therefore, the symbol of St. Patrick, the patron saint of Ireland, was incorporated with the other two crosses. The symbol, which depicted a diagonal red cross on a white background, was integrated by placing the diagonal red cross over the white cross of St. Andrew. Thus, the first official flag of Great Britain was born. The same design as that approved in 1801 is used today.

> Great Britain's new flag was originally reserved for the King's exclusive use. It was flown only from his forts and castles; its use was forbidden elsewhere. Today, the Union Jack flies from a diverse group of locations, including royal and government buildings, residential homes, businesses, and other institutions across the United Kingdom.

Great Britain's new flag was originally reserved for the King's exclusive use. It was flown only from his forts and castles; its use was forbidden elsewhere. Over time, its use has become much less restricted. Today, the Union Jack flies from a diverse group of locations, including royal and government buildings, residential homes, businesses, and other institutions across the United Kingdom. Notably, civilian ships cannot fly the Union Jack; particular designs are reserved for their use.

Many traditions surround the flight of the British Union Flag. Most famously, it flies above Buckingham Palace, Windsor Castle, and Sandringham when the Queen is not in residence. Additionally, the flag is flown at half-mast upon the occasion of a death in the royal family. The flag is displayed in front of government buildings on certain holidays, including Commonwealth Day, the Queen's official birthday, Remembrance Day, State Opening and Propagation of Parliament, St. David's Day, St. George's Day, St. Andrew's Day, and St. Patrick's Day.

Victory at Trafalgar

At war against Napoleonic France, British warships commanded by Admiral Horatio Nelson crushed a combined French and Spanish fleet at Trafalgar on October 21, 1805. This famous naval battle destroyed French naval power without loss of even a single British ship, but still this victory came at a great price. Admiral Nelson, among Britain's greatest naval heroes of all time, was killed as the battle drew to its close.

Nelson, who had gone to sea at age 12 and had become a captain before turning 21, had distinguished himself as a high-ranking British naval officer in the earlier French Revolutionary Wars (1792–1802). Blinded in the right eye during a battle in 1794, he lost his right arm in another naval action in 1797. Yet he returned to sea and won important victories at Cape St. Vincent (1797) and the Battle of the Nile (1798), which wrecked the French fleet and left Napoleon's army bottled up in Egypt.

Admiral Nelson had been pursuing the remnants of the French navy for several months in 1805 when he finally caught them off Cape Trafalgar, Spain, outside the Strait of Gibraltar. The French fleet, a combined force of 18 French and 15 Spanish warships, was commanded by Admiral Pierre Villeneuve. Villeneuve turned his ships northward to form a single, ragged line. Nelson, aboard his flagship HMS *Victory*, responded by forming his 27 ships into two parallel lines and attacking at a right angle to the Franco-Spanish column. Minutes before the battle began, Nelson signaled his now-famous message: "England expects that every man will do his duty."

The five-hour battle began at noon, with the British warships cutting the Franco-Spanish line in two and then proceeding to capture 18 enemy ships and thousands of sailors in the brutal fighting. Even Admiral Villeneuve and his ship were captured, but Nelson would not live to savor his victory. Just a half hour before the battle ended, he was mortally wounded as the *Victory* attacked the French warship *Redoutable*. A sniper perched on the *Redoutable*'s topmast felled the British hero as the two ships closed. Clearly a tragic victory for Britain, Trafalgar nevertheless established Britain's naval supremacy for the next hundred years.

IN THE BATTLE of Trafalgar, Horatio Nelson's British fleet defeated a combined French and Spanish fleet, giving England control of the sea.

Churchill's foreign secretary, Anthony Eden, succeeded him as prime minister in 1955. Soon after, however, Eden made a critical miscalculation in the 1956 Suez crisis. After the Egyptians nationalized the canal in 1956, both Britain and France used troops to retake it, but intense criticism at home and abroad forced them to turn the canal over to the United Nations. Shaken by the public outcry, Eden stepped down in early 1957.

Two other Conservative prime ministers followed, Harold Macmillan (served 1957 to 1963) and Sir Alexander Douglas-Home (1963 to 1964). While Britain was sufficiently prosperous during the late 1950s to decline membership in the newly formed European Economic Community (EEC), the situation changed in the early 1960s. A steady drop in Britain's share of world trade, increasing imports, inflation, declining productivity, and increasing trade union unrest all conspired to send the economy into a decline. However, France now blocked Britain's attempts to join the EEC.

Labour returns. The Labour Party came back into power in 1964 with Harold Wilson as prime minister. Wilson had no better luck than his predecessors at overcoming France's opposition to Britain's EEC membership, and his efforts at turning the economy around—including controls on imports and wages—proved unpopular.

Far worse for Britain was the start of violence between Protestants and Catholics in Northern Ireland during the late 1960s. Amid the fight over Catholics' civil rights, acts of terrorism became commonplace and eventually spilled over into England itself. Every government from Wilson's onward grappled with the problem, seemingly to no avail. Wilson sent in British troops, and after 1972 the British government ruled Northern Ireland directly in an effort to guarantee civil rights of the Catholic minority. In 1985 the British government even gave Ireland a role in governing Northern Ireland, but Irish Republican Army attacks continued into the 1990s.

The Conservative Party returned to power in 1970, and under Prime Minister Edward Heath governed until 1974. Probably the most important accomplishment during the Heath administration was Britain's entry into the EEC (1973), at last opening up the Common Market to British goods and furthering the process of European unification. But a series of strikes—by dockworkers, postal workers, and coal miners—crippled Britain's economy. The strike, coupled with the Arab oil embargo, forced Heath to declare a state of emergency in 1973. Meanwhile, the oil shortages gave Britain every reason to develop the promising North Sea oil fields, which began producing oil in the mid-1970s.

North Sea oil. Until discovery of North Sea oil and natural gas fields in the late 1960s, Britain relied almost completely on imported oil. Development of the rich North Sea oil fields, which are centered off Scotland's northeast coast, quickly made Britain a major player in the international petroleum market. By 1992 Britain ranked fifth in natural gas production worldwide and ninth in oil production. From then, combined oil and gas revenues accounted for 1.3 percent of Britain's gross national product.

Early discoveries of natural gas off The Netherlands coast in 1959 barely hinted at the vast oil and gas stores hidden farther north off the Scottish coast. Natural gas was discovered there first in 1965, and by 1967 an undersea pipeline brought the gas directly from offshore rigs to the mainland. Two years later drillers tapped into the huge undersea oil deposits off the Scottish coast. In 1976 the first North Sea crude was piped from what became one of the largest oil fields, the so-called Forties field.

Because of Britain's need for oil and the instability of the international oil market during the 1970s, the vast North Sea oil fields were developed rapidly. Twenty-four oil fields were producing by 1983, and the government as of 1995 licensed private companies to exploit over 50 offshore oil fields in return for a 45 percent tax on revenues. The Forties, Brent, Piper, and Ninian oil fields currently lead

THE OFFSHORE oil and gas fields in the North Sea have made Britain a major player in the international petroleum market.

centered
US

centred
Brit.

Oxford University

OXFORD UNIVERSITY, a major center of learning since the 13th century, has many fine buildings in the Gothic Revival style.

Among the oldest universities in Britain, Oxford was first organized in the early 1100s. Education was a church responsibility, and students were affiliated with the church and enjoyed the privileges of clerical life. The school had no place of its own in the early years and held classes in church buildings or in hired halls in the town of Oxford.

The school began growing in the mid-1100s, when it unexpectedly benefitted from troubles between England and France. Reacting to the international difficulties, French officials barred English students from further study at the University of Paris after about 1167. These displaced students swelled the ranks at Oxford, and by the next century Oxford was firmly established as an institution of higher learning. Teaching there focused originally on theology, liberal arts, law, and medicine.

Oxford's original colleges amounted to nothing more than boardinghouses for the poorer students, but they soon evolved into what became the model for all new Oxford colleges that followed. Each college became a community of scholars and teachers living and studying together. Each had its own entryway, usually through a gatehouse, and was built around one or more courtyards, which came to be called quadrangles. The oldest existing college at Oxford was established in 1249 as University College. Balliol College was founded in 1263, followed by Merton College a year later.

The British Crown issued charters to Oxford during the 1200s and in 1571 Parliament formally approved the incorporation of Oxford University. Meanwhile, 14 other colleges had been formed during the ensuing three centuries, among them Christ Church (1546). The university continued expanding by founding other colleges, and the curriculum was eventually expanded and modernized. Thus, over the centuries, Oxford became a leading university known throughout the world for academic excellence.

Among the many distinguished individuals who studied at Oxford were the scholars Erasmus and Sir Thomas More. Roger Bacon conducted many of his famous scientific experiments at Oxford, while astronomer Edmund Halley and physicist Robert Boyle also studied there. So, too, did Henry VIII's famous lord chancellor, Cardinal Wolsey, the Elizabethan courtier Sir Walter Raleigh, Quaker leader William Penn, and the founder of Methodism, John Wesley. Many notable British prime ministers were also students, including William Pitt the Elder, William Gladstone, and more recently, Harold Macmillan and Margaret Thatcher. Literary figures at Oxford included T. S. Eliot and Oscar Wilde. Cecil Rhodes, who studied there and later made a fortune in South Africa, endowed Oxford's famous Rhodes scholarship program.

gas leak, the sound was followed by a tremendous explosion and fire that split the rig in two. Fire instantly engulfed the wreckage, killing everyone inside the living quarters and forcing those outside on the platform to jump to the water below. Only 166 of the 229 workers on Piper Alpha survived, in the worst accident in the British sector of the North Sea fields.

Piper Alpha has proven the exception in an otherwise good overall safety record, and developing the North Sea oil fields has provided much-needed income for the British economy. Exports of surplus oil and gas improved Britain's balance of payments, while the rigs, pipelines, refineries, and other facilities created tens of thousands of jobs.

Britain's oil boom is not expected to last beyond the 20th century, and some experts believe the flow of North Sea oil has already peaked. But exploration in the North Sea continues to uncover additional reserves, guaranteeing Britain at least some oil into the next century.

Harold Wilson and the Labour Party returned to power after the 1974 elections. Prime Minister Wilson immediately gave in to the coal miners' demands in order to end the disastrous strike, but labor unrest continued, fueled by rising prices and opposition to EEC membership. Labour Party leader James Callaghan fared no better when he took over as prime minister in 1976. Indeed, by the winter of 1978–1979, government seemed unable to control the striking unions, and for the first time since 1924, Commons ousted a prime minister in a vote of no confidence.

Thatcher takes control. Dubbed the "Iron Lady," Conservative party leader Margaret Thatcher became Britain's first woman prime minister in 1979. She proved to be both a popular and effective administrator and held office for an unprecedented eleven years, making her Britain's longest-serving prime

meter
US

metre
Brit.

labor
US

labour
Brit.

"IRON LADY"
Conservative party leader Margaret Thatcher became Britain's first woman prime minister in 1979.

in North Sea crude oil production. Over 35 offshore natural gas fields also have been developed, with Ravenspurn, Indefatigable, North, and Leman ranking among the top producers.

The key to developing North Sea oil has been the massive steel offshore oil platforms. Standing like tiny islands in the harsh and stormy North Sea, they are built to withstand 100-foot (30-meter) waves and 160-mile-per-hour winds. Long steel legs anchor them to the sea floor and support the platforms

150 feet (46 meters) or more above the water, where drilling equipment and living quarters for workers are located. Hundreds of men live and work on a rig for months at a time.

Extracting oil and gas can be a dangerous business, however, and nowhere was that made clearer than on the Piper Alpha platform in July, 1988. The North Sea was unusually calm that day, when one worker suddenly heard a noise he described as something "screaming like a banshee." Probably a high-pressure

THE CHANGING OF THE GUARD in London is an enduring part of the panoply of monarchy, enjoyed by the English and visitors alike.

minister since 1827. Thatcher ended labor unrest, restored a measure of economic stability and national pride, and instituted sweeping changes designed to end socialism in Britain.

Probably her most important accomplishment was winning the power struggle with the unruly unions. This she did bit by bit, beginning with laws against boycotts and secondary strikes, and then moving up to imposing stiff fines for violations and ending such pro-union measures as the closed shop. The final showdown came in 1984, when coal miners staged a violent one-year strike to protest the closing of inefficient mines. Thatcher's resolute stand marked a signal victory for the government.

Her handling of economic matters was every bit as dramatic. While imposing tough deflationary policies to curb the economic crisis, she privatized almost every industry the Labour Party had nationalized since World War II. Unemployment rose, but ultimately profits from privatization helped boost the economy, as did the windfall from the developing North Sea oil fields. Thatcher also promoted less government interference in the economy, cut back on social welfare programs, and reduced taxes.

In foreign affairs her administration scored notable successes, beginning with resolution of the crisis in Rhodesia (now Zimbabwe) in 1980. Two years later, Prime Minister Thatcher gained wide approval for her decisive handling of the Falkland Islands crisis. Following an invasion of the British territory by Argentine troops, she ordered it retaken by force. The speedy, albeit costly, victory helped restore a measure of British national pride and contributed much to Thatcher's popularity.

Falkland Islands War. Fought for national pride and possession of a tiny island group some 300 miles (483 kilometers) off Argentina's southern coast, the Falkland Islands War was a brief conflict involving air, sea, and land forces. British Prime Minister Margaret Thatcher's resolute response to Argentina's aggression and the quick, overwhelming victory of the British forces in the war reasserted Britain's position as a military power. The action also bolstered Prime Minister Thatcher's reputation at home and abroad.

Claims to the Falklands and associated islands had been disputed since the 1600s, but Britain occupied the islands in 1833 and governed them as a colony for the next century and a half. Frustrated by years of unsuccessful negotiations aimed at getting the islands, Argentina broke off talks early in 1982 and threatened to take matters into its own hands.

The Chunnel

For the first time since a land bridge disappeared 10,000 years ago, the Channel Tunnel has linked Britain directly with mainland Europe. Nicknamed the "Chunnel," the 31-mile (50-kilometer) tunnel under the English Channel is an engineering marvel that cost billions to complete, but the big savings in time for transporting passengers and freight between England and France appeared to make the project economically viable. The high-speed rail service under the English Channel slashes a train trip between London and Paris from seven hours by rail (and ferry) to about two and three-quarters hours via the Chunnel.

For almost two centuries, engineers had dreamed about such a tunnel, but the magnitude of the project, the cost, and even international political difficulties kept it from coming to fruition. As early as 1802, planners proposed a tunnel carrying horse-drawn carriages under the channel, but hostilities between Britain and Napoleon's French Empire sank that project. Work on another tunnel project actually began in 1881, but it was abandoned two years later because the British feared subversives might use it to infiltrate their country. Another attempt, in 1974, ended after only a year because of unexpectedly high costs and worries about the environment.

Finally, in late 1987, a privately financed British-French company called Eurotunnel began digging tunnels from Folkestone on the English side of the channel and from Calais on the French side. The project was enormous, involving the boring of three tubes 31 miles (50 kilometers) long and 150 feet (46 meters) under the channel bottom. The two main tunnels were 25 feet (8 meters) wide, and the service tunnel running parallel between them was 15^1/$_2$ feet (4.7 meters) wide.

Delays and massive cost overruns plagued the project, and old fears in Britain about the dangers of being linked with continental Europe resurfaced. Nevertheless, construction companies working from both sides of the channel managed to link up the service tunnel in 1990 and the two main rail tunnels in 1991. The Chunnel was formally opened during a ceremony in 1994.

The final price tag for the Chunnel has been put at more than 9 billion pounds (about $15 billion U.S.), but that must be measured against the economic potential of the project. Eurotunnel offers standard rail service and drive-on, drive-off shuttle train service for cars and trucks. In the first five years of operation, 28 million people and 12 million tons of freight passed through the Chunnel.

Nothing happened until March 19, 1982, when some 60 scrap-metal salvagers from Argentina landed on South Georgia Island. Venting nationalistic urges, they raised the Argentine flag over the island and left a few of their number behind to enforce the claim. The move apparently sparked Argentina's military government into action, because on April 2 some 2000 Argentine troops landed on the Falkland Islands and promptly overwhelmed the 84-man British garrison at Port Stanley, the capital.

Argentina steadfastly refused Prime Minister Thatcher's demands to withdraw and eventually put some 20,000 troops on the Falklands. Thatcher meanwhile gave the go-ahead for a military operation to retake the islands, and as of April 28, Britain declared a 200-mile (322-kilometer) war zone around the islands. British air attacks on the Falklands began on May 1. British planes consistently outgunned Argentina's fighters by a wide margin. For their part, Argentinian planes sank several British warships, including two destroyers, two frigates, and other craft.

The war belonged to the British, however. Their troops made an amphibious landing north of Port Stanley on May 21 and three days later began advancing southward to surround Port Stanley. Though there was some stiff resistance, British troops took up positions around the capital in early June. One by one, strategic positions fell into British hands and during an assault on the night of June 13–14, Argentinian resistance collapsed. The military governor formally surrendered on June 14.

Britain lost 256 servicemen while retaking the Falklands. Argentina fared considerably worse, losing 750 soldiers and sailors, a cruiser sunk by a British submarine, and numerous fighter aircraft. The humiliating loss sorely embarrassed Argentina's military government and contributed to its downfall in 1983. An elected civilian government has held power in Argentina ever since.

Britain's success in the Falklands was attributed to a certain extent to logistical and material support from the United States, which found itself in a difficult position during the conflict. On the one hand, the longstanding U.S.-British ties of friendship and alliance had been strengthened by the similar political philosophies of Thatcher and U.S. President Ronald Reagan. On the other hand, critics argued that U.S. support of Great Britain in the war ran counter to the longstanding U.S. Monroe Doctrine opposing European involvement in affairs in the western hemisphere.

During her long term of office Prime Minister Thatcher also remained a staunch U.S. ally, returned Hong Kong to the Chinese (as of 1997), entered into an agreement with the French to build a railroad tunnel under the English Channel (1986), signed (with the United States and the Soviet Union) the Intermediate Nuclear Forces Treaty to eliminate intermediate range nuclear weapons (1987), and reluctantly agreed to Britain's membership in the European Monetary Union (1989). By 1990 though, inflation, rising unemployment, and her determined stand on a new and unpopular poll tax caused her popularity to slip, forcing her resignation in 1990.

Conservative government continued under Prime Minister John Major, who scrapped the poll tax (1991) and grappled with a full-blown recession (from 1991). Soon after taking office, Major sent British troops to fight in the Persian Gulf War. At home, he had little success in stopping IRA terrorist attacks and, like Thatcher, worried about Britain's monetary union with neighboring European countries. But in 1993 Major backed and won ratification of the controversial Maastricht Treaty for furthering political and economic union among European nations. In the same year his government also enacted a bill to privatize British railroads.

Despite deepening economic recession, which became Great Britain's longest since before World War II, Major and the Conservative Party won a majority in general elections in April 1992. By the fall, however, a financial crisis prompted the withdrawal of the pound sterling from the European Union's Exchange Rate Mechanism (ERM). Conservatives were weakened by bitter disagreement over the question of European union.

In 1993 Major overcame significant opposition within his own party in July when he secured a vote of confidence on the government's policy on the Maastricht Treaty. In August the treaty was ratified.

In 1993 continuing talks were initiated between members of the British government and officials of the IRA. By early December a peace initiative was announced between Major's government and the IRA, a process that continued into 1994 and 1995. An agreement was forged in 1998 and the IRA disarmed in 2001.

Britain played a prominent role in the Bosnian conflict, sending troops to distribute humanitarian supplies. Britain's troops also helped establish and maintain what peace could be found between the warring factions.

Labourite Tony Blair was elected prime minister in 1997.

Blair gave immediate and vocal support to the U.S. after the terrorist attacks in September 2001. Britain sent its elite troops to aid in the ensuing war in Afghanistan. In 2003 British troops also joined with those of the United States in a war with Iraq to end the regime of Saddam Hussein.

IRA— Irish Republican Army

In 1905 an Irish movement known as *Sinn Fein* (Irish: We Ourselves) was formed to promote the independence of Ireland and the revival of Irish culture and language. Today it is dedicated to the political unification of Northern Ireland and the Republic of Ireland. The IRA, the military arm of Sinn Fein, employs violence in its attempt to achieve union. The IRA maintained a low level of armed activity through the late 1960s, when Sinn Fein, by then a political party known as *Fianna Fáil* (Irish: Fenians of Ireland) split in two. The radical minority became known as the Provisional IRA, the remainder as the Official IRA. It is the Provisionals who stepped up violence against British security forces and the Protestant establishment in Northern Ireland.

LEADERS
of the provisional
Irish Republican Army

138

Vatican City

Official name: *State of the Vatican City*
Area: *0.17 sq. mi., 0.44 sq. km.*
Type of government: *Monarchical-sacerdotal state*
Population: *840*
Languages: *Italian, Latin (both official)*
Literacy: *100%*
Currency: *Euro*

THE SQUARE IN FRONT of St. Peter's Basilica in the Vatican is frequently filled with throngs of worshipers and sightseers.

The land. Vatican City, in Rome, Italy, is the world's smallest sovereign state. It is the seat of administration of the Roman Catholic Church and residence of the pope. The term "the Vatican" is frequently used to refer to both the central administration of the church and the government of Vatican City.

Vatican City lies on the west bank of the Tiber River. It includes St. Peter's Basilica, St. Peter's Square, the Vatican palaces, Belvedere Park, and the Vatican Gardens.

The Vatican also exercises extraterritorial sovereignty over a dozen buildings and some territory in or near Rome, including the basilicas of St. Mary Major, St. John Lateran, and St. Paul outside the Walls; the pope's summer residence at Castel Gandolfo; and the Vatican radio station at Santa Maria di Galeria.

The Vatican population consists of clergy of all nations, the Vatican guard, and a number of lay personnel.

Government. The Vatican is ruled by the pope, who has absolute power. He delegates much of the actual administration to the Pontifical Commission for the State of the Vatican City. The commission is headed by a governor.

The Vatican's diplomatic relations with foreign countries are carried out by the Secretariat of State. The Vatican maintains diplomatic ties with about 108 countries. The pope is pledged to neutrality in political disputes between governments except when his mediation is requested by both sides. There is also a permanent UN observer.

History. The traditional seat of the papacy has always been Rome. Throughout the Middle Ages the popes controlled not only the city of Rome but large territories in central Italy, the Papal States. The popes lost most of the territory that formed the Papal States during the Italian struggle for unification in the 1850s and 1860s.

In 1849 a Roman Republic was declared, and France, intervening on behalf of the pope, sent troops to Rome. The Kingdom of Italy was formed in 1861, and in 1870, when French troops were withdrawn on the outbreak of the Franco-Prussian War, Rome was added to the new kingdom.

In 1871 the Italian government passed the Law of Guarantees granting the papacy full sovereignty over Vatican City and an annual income from the Italian treasury. The pope refused the offer. The 1929 Lateran Treaties restored relations with Italy, however.

The treaties recognized the sovereignty of the papacy within Vatican City, regulated the status of the church in Italy, and arranged for an indemnity to be paid to the papacy as compensation for the loss of the Papal States. In 1947 the terms of the Lateran Treaties were incorporated into the constitution of the Italian Republic itself.

In 1976 the treaties were revised so that Roman Catholicism would no longer be recognized as Italy's official religion and religious education would no longer be required in schools.

In 1984 the United States established diplomatic ties with the Vatican.

Serbia and Montenegro
(formerly Yugoslavia)

Official name: *Serbia and Montenegro*
Area: *39,518 sq. mi., 102,350 sq. km.*
Type of government: *Republic*
Population: *10,658,000*
Capital and largest city: *Belgrade (Pop., 1,619,000)*
Language: *Serbo-Croatian, Albanian*
Literacy: *93%*
Currency: *Dinar, euro*
Per capita GDP: *$2,370 (Rank: 129th)*

The land. Within Serbia are the autonomous provinces of Kosovo in the south and Vojvodina in the north. Serbia is a mountainous country, especially in the south, with many rivers. Northern Serbia and Vojvodina form part of the fertile Panonian Plain, while mountains dominate Kosovo and southern Serbia. Important rivers in Serbia include the Danube, the Ibar, the Zapadna, the Morava, the Niava, and the Sava. The Danube forms Europe's deepest gorge, the Iron Gate Gorge, also in Serbia.

Montenegro, to the southwest of Serbia, is also a mountainous region with many rivers and an Adriatic coastline along the Gulf of Kotor. Much of the land is made up of the limestone formations known as karst. The main mountain ranges in Montenegro are the Black Mountains, which give the country its name, and the Dinaric Alps. The region's many rivers include the Zeta, whose valley provides a large part of the arable land in the area, the Moraa, the Bojana, the Piva, the Tara, and the Lim.

The climate ranges from Mediterranean along Montenegro's coast, to continental in the inland regions of Serbia, to alpine in the high mountains of both republics.

The people. Serbia, excluding the autonomous provinces of Vojvodina and Kosovo, is mainly populated by ethnic Serbs. Vojvodina is home to Serbs, Croats, and Hungarians, who constitute an estimated 20 percent of the population. Approximately 90 percent of Kosovo's population is Albanian. Montenegro is dominated by Montenegrins, who are ethnically, historically, and culturally linked to the Serbs, although there is an Albanian minority. Both Serbs and Montenegrins speak Serbo-Croatian and use the Cyrillic alphabet. In Vojvodina the Croats use the Roman alphabet, and Hungarian is also spoken. Most inhabitants of Kosovo speak Albanian, as do the ethnic Albanians in Montenegro.

The country is largely Eastern Orthodox, although the Croats and Hungarians tend to practice Roman Catholicism, and the Albanian population is largely Muslim. Major cities include Belgrade, the capital of both Serbia and the federal republic; Novi Sad (population, 291,000), the capital of Vojvodina; Podgorica (173,000), the capital of Montenegro; and Priština (47,000), the capital of Kosovo.

THE VATICAN MUSEUM holds many of the world's art treasures, such as the Laocoön.

Economy. Serbia and Vojvodina are fairly prosperous regions, while both Kosovo and Montenegro are burdened with underdeveloped economies. Minerals, including lead, zinc, gold, silver, and copper, are among the natural resources found in Serbia. Vojvodina has oil reserves and natural gas. Coal, lead, zinc, and nickel are mined in Kosovo. In addition to their industrial contributions, Vojvodina and Serbia also provide the bulk of the country's agricultural products. Sugar beets and grains are grown on their fertile plains. Livestock, especially pigs and sheep, add to the agricultural element of the economy. Montenegro's economy is largely based on tourism, sheep raising, and mining.

Government. The government has a president who is elected by direct popular vote. A legislative body, the Federal Assembly, is comprised of the Chamber of Republics and the Chamber of Citizens. The Federal Executive Council performs the government's administrative duties.

History. Present-day Serbia, once a part of the Roman Empire's provincial territories, was settled by Serbs in the seventh century. During the ninth and tenth centuries, both the Byzantine and Bulgarian empires sought to incorporate the Slavs, with the Byzantines eventually succeeding. After a series of successful battles against the Byzantines in the twelfth century, the Serbs managed to establish themselves as an independent state. Late in the century parts of Montenegro were added to the Serbian Empire, led by Stephen Nemanja.

Despite an alliance between Serbia and the Second Bulgarian Empire, the Bulgars joined other powerful empires seeking to assume control of Serbia during the 13th century. The attempts proved unsuccessful, and Serbian power increased throughout the first half of the 14th century under the leadership of Stephen Duan. When his son, Uro, came to the throne in 1355, however, Serbia's fortunes declined. Disaster struck in 1389 at the Battle of Kosovo, when the Ottoman Empire defeated the Serbs, causing many to flee to the mountains of Montenegro.

Throughout the 14th and 15th centuries, the Turks strengthened their hold on the Balkans. Montenegro fended off Turkish attempts to take the region by putting itself under Venetian rule. By 1484 the Ottoman Empire had swallowed Albania and Herzegovina. The Turks moved closer to Montenegro, but, although threatened, Montenegro was never actually conquered by the Ottoman Empire.

Serbs, meanwhile, sought refuge in Hungary until 1526, when the Turks defeated the Hungarians. The Serbs remained under Turkish control until 1683, when the Austrians defeated the Ottoman Empire at Vienna. The Austrians managed to push the Ottoman Empire back to Kosovo, and Serbs joined the attack, but in the end the Turks prevailed. Again under the rule of the Ottoman Empire, Serbs fled to Hungary once more, where they were promised a region in which they would be free to practice the Eastern Orthodox rite and elect their own military governor, known as a *vojvoda*. The promises proved illusory. The region in which the Serbs settled is present-day Vojvodina, which still has a large Hungarian population.

Throughout the 18th century, while Serbia was a battleground for Austrian, Hungarian, and Turkish ambitions, Montenegro established a firm alliance with Russia. In 1804 Serbia, under the leadership of the rebel Karageorge, revolted against the Ottoman Empire. The Serbs attempted to gain assistance from Russia and Austria, but both countries refused. Alone, Serbia shook itself free of the Ottoman Empire in December 1806. Shortly thereafter the Russians declared war on the Turks and, when both Russia and the Ottoman Empire turned to Serbia for help, the Serbians sided with Russia. The sporadic conflict between Russia and Turkey concluded in 1812 with the signing of the Treaty of Bucharest, which made provisions for the Serbs but declared that the specifics of the agreement were to be worked out by Serbia and Turkey. When Turkey demanded that Serbia formally surrender in 1813, the Serbs refused, leading to a Turkish attack that ended with a victory for the Ottoman Empire. Serb rebel forces, led by Karageorge, fled to Austria, and those left in Serbia were slaughtered or sold as slaves. Serbia was divided into three districts to be governed by Turkey.

Two years later Milo Obrenovi, one of the Serbian district heads appointed by the Turks, led the Serbs in another revolt. This time Russia supported

Serbia. In 1830 the Ottoman Empire was pressured into recognizing Serbia as an independent principality, and Milo was acknowledged as its prince. Although Milo's heirs were supposed to inherit the throne, popular opinion turned against him, and in 1842 Alexander, the exiled son of Karageorge, was elected prince, creating a dangerous rivalry between the two families. Alexander began discussing the establishment of a South Slave state in which all Christians in the area, whether Roman Catholic or Eastern Orthodox, would unite against the Muslim rulers of the Ottoman Empire. However, he lost the throne in 1858 and Milo was again named prince. Milo's son Michael successfully managed to establish a Balkan League comprising Serbia, Montenegro, Bulgaria, Greece, and Romania, but when he was assassinated in 1868 his son was unable to hold the league together.

Russia once again declared war on Turkey in 1877, and Serbia once more joined the fray. The Russo-Turkish War, won by Russia and Serbia, was concluded in 1878 by the Treaty of San Stefano, which granted Serbia independence. The treaty was superseded by the Treaty of Berlin, which also recognized Serbia as an independent country but granted it more territory. In addition, the Treaty of Berlin recognized Montenegro as an independent nation almost twice its former size.

As the century ended, Serbia and Montenegro were influenced by the growth of nationalism. Despite indepen-

PEPPERS are closely associated with central Europe and the Balkan countries. Ground pepper comes in dozens of flavors, from sweet and mild to fiery hot.

regent, Prince Paul, courted the Germans for economic reasons, despite popular sentiment. By 1939 Germany dominated Yugoslavia politically, and in 1941, despite efforts to remain neutral, Yugoslavia felt itself forced to sign the Axis Pact. King Peter II reacted by organizing a military coup, which was swiftly crushed when Germany invaded in April 1941.

Germany occupied Serbia and part of Vojvodina throughout the war, established a puppet state in Croatia that also included Bosnia-Herzegovina and parts of Slovenia, and allowed Italy to occupy southern Slovenia, Dalmatia, and Montenegro. Italy also created a puppet state of Albania and Kosovo. Hungary occupied what remained of Vojvodina, Slovenia, and Croatia, and Bulgaria occupied Macedonia and southern Serbia. Serbs formed two guerrilla groups to fight the Germans: the Chetniks, supporters of the exiled monarchy, and the Partisans, Communists led by Josip Broz Tito. Many Croats supported the Germans, who had given them their own state in which they were free of Serbian control, and Croatian forces brutally carried out oppressive policies against Serbs, Jews, and Gypsies throughout the war. The Chetniks and Partisans, temporarily working together against the Nazis, soon found them-

dence, the Balkan nations continued to be dominated by Austria-Hungary, Russia, and Turkey. Strained relations between Serbia, pledged to further the interests of Austria-Hungary, and Montenegro, which had allied itself with Russia, worsened in 1907 when Montenegro implicated Serbia in a plot to assassinate the Montenegrin sovereign, Nicholas. Nonetheless, the two countries cooperated in 1910 to fight the Turks in the Balkan Wars of 1912–1913, and in 1914 the two countries began discussing the possibility of unification.

With the assassination of Austria-Hungary's heir to the throne, Archduke Francis Ferdinand, by a Serbian national, World War I broke out. Montenegro and Serbia were allies during the war, and at its end in 1918, the two countries joined Croatia, Dalmatia, Bosnia, Herzegovina, Slovenia, and Vojvodina to form the new Kingdom of Serbs, Croats, and Slovenes, to be ruled by the Serbian king. The Pan-Slavism that had inspired the new country quickly gave way to infighting among the various nationalities and religious groups, most of whom objected to what was perceived as the undue influence of the Serbs, who dominated the army and government. Disputes arose about whether the country should have a centralized government or a looser arrangement consisting of independent states within a federation. In an effort to quiet the unrest, King Alexander made himself dictator in 1929 and changed the name of the country to Yugoslavia. He also divided the country into nine *banovina,* or administrative provinces, and divided what had been Serbia

among five of the provinces, creating Serbian minorities in those areas.

Throughout the 1930s, Yugoslavia's government, led by King Peter II's

PEOPLE CELEBRATE in Slovenia, one of the six autonomous republics created from Yugoslavia by Marshal Tito in 1945.

THE FIELDS OF YUGOSLAVIA saw tanks as well as farming equipment due to ethnic unrest in the Balkan countries during the 1990s.

selves fighting each other when the Chetniks decided that German reprisals were taking too heavy a toll on the Serbian population and began cooperating with the Germans. The Allies, who first supported the non-communist Chetniks, were eventually forced to recognize the Partisans as their partners in Yugoslavia.

When World War II ended, the Allies encouraged the formation of a coalition between the monarchists and the Communists, but Tito quickly took control of the country and had the monarchy abolished in 1945. Tito divided the country into six autonomous republics: Serbia (including Vojvodina and Kosovo), Montenegro, Slovenia, Bosnia-Herzegovina, Croatia, and Macedonia. In an effort to recover from the damage wrought by the war, he implemented a series of land reforms, industrial plans, and central economic policies. Wartime collaborators and political opponents were given harsh punishments, including execution.

Tito's first policies were closely modeled on those of Stalin's Soviet Union, but he gradually began modifying them, drawing sharp criticism from Stalin. In 1948 the Soviet Union succeeded in having Yugoslavia expelled from Cominform (Communist Information Bureau), even though the headquarters were in Belgrade. Yugoslavia then embarked on a campaign to placate the Soviets without capitulating entirely. Relations between the two countries remained strained, and in 1949 Yugoslavia was also expelled from Comecon (Council for Mutual Economic Assistance).

Although Yugoslavian relations with the West were also difficult, the West exploited the differences between the Soviet Union and Yugoslavia by offering economic assistance. In the early 1950s Yugoslavia introduced economic reforms, which in turn led to political reforms, and Tito established his foreign policy of non-alignment. Under this policy, Yugoslavia would not fall under Soviet or Western dominance, but would work with other developing nations, such as China, India, and Cuba, to voice their needs effectively. Economic and political reforms continued throughout the 1960s, with political reforms leading various ethnic groups to hope for more freedom. Croats and Macedonians expressed the desire to use their own languages, and Albanians in Kosovo struggled for political autonomy.

In 1968 relations with the Soviet Union worsened when the Soviet invasion of Czechoslovakia was denounced by Yugoslavia. Internally, Albanians staged demonstrations to protest their conditions in the underdeveloped regions of Kosovo and Macedonia. In 1971 Tito attempted to ease internal problems by establishing a collective presidency that was to be shared by representatives from all six republics and from the two autonomous provinces of Vojvodina and Kosovo. The arrangement was perceived by the Croats as an indication that real autonomy might be possible. The government reacted sharply to Croat demonstrations, however, and suspicions deepened between the republics urging central government (chiefly Serbia and Montenegro) and those seeking a federation of independent nations. In 1974 Tito pushed through a new constitution that strengthened the central government.

Upon Tito's death in 1980, the office of the presidency was rotated among the representatives from various republics. The arrangement seemed to work, despite severe ethnic tensions, until 1991, when Slovenia, Croatia, and Bosnia-Herzegovina declared themselves independent, followed by Macedonia in 1992. Serbia, citing concern for ethnic Serbs in those areas, fought the disintegration of Yugoslavia both politically and militarily, and the country quickly collapsed into chaos, with charges of military abuses and brutality on all sides. The Serbs were accused of implementing policies of ethnic cleansing in Serb-dominated areas of the breakaway republics, while Serbs claimed that they were in danger of being oppressed in the newly created countries. The European Community and the United Nations intervened with only limited success, and Yugoslavia formally conceded that the Socialist Federal Republic of Yugoslavia had ceased to exist when, in April 1992, Serbia and Montenegro established the Federal Republic of Yugoslavia.

In 1999, the Serbs' massive expulsion of ethnic Albanians in Kosovo led NATO to bomb Serbia and send in peacekeepers. Former president Slobodan Milosevic is on trial for war crimes and atrocities.

In February 2003 Yugoslavia dissolved itself, forming the new state of Serbia and Montenegro, a loose federation of the two republics. In 2006 Montenegro can hold a referendum on independence.

Dependencies in Europe

REINDEER are able to survive in the cold weather of Greenland, where they are still hunted.

Danish Dependencies

The Faroe Islands (541 sq. mi., 1400 sq. km) are a group of 17 inhabited islands, including Streymoy, Eysturoy, and Váagar, and many inlets. The islands are located in the Atlantic Ocean, 300 miles northeast of the Shetlands. The Faroes, with a population of 46,000, are self-governing, but as an integral part of the Danish kingdom they also have two representatives in the Danish parliament. The islands have been Danish since 1380. Fishing, whaling, and sheep herding are the most important economic activities.

Greenland (839,782 sq. mi., 2,175,600 sq. km), the largest island in the world, is located in the North Atlantic Ocean and the Polar Sea. It became a Danish province in 1953 and was granted internal self-rule in 1979. With 56,000 people, it has two representatives in the Danish parliament. There is some mining on the island, although most resources are unexplored. Fishing and fur hunting are the main economic activities. Nuuk, formerly called Gothab, is the capital.

Norwegian Dependencies

Jan Mayen (144 sq. mi., 373 sq. km) is an uninhabited island, 300 miles northeast of Iceland, above the Arctic Circle. Discovered by Henry Hudson in the early 1600s, it has been a Norwegian dependency since 1929. An Icelandic-Norwegian dispute concerning part of its offshore area was settled in 1980. A research station is located there.

Svalbard (23,957 sq. mi., 62,049 sq. km), a group of islands in the Arctic Ocean, has a population of 2,500. It has been a Norwegian dependency since 1925. Spitsbergen is the most important of these islands, which also include North East Land, Barents Island, and Edge Island. There are rich coal deposits here, particularly on Spitsbergen. They are exploited by Norwegian and Russian mining camps.

United Kingdom Dependencies

The Channel Islands (120 sq. mi., 311 sq. km), a group of islands off the northwest coast of France, have been direct dependencies of the English Crown since the Norman Conquest of England in 1066. The principal islands are Jersey and Guernsey, although there are seven smaller islands in the group. The economy of the islands relies heavily on tourism from England, Scotland, and Wales, as well from Europe and the United States, but dairying and truck farming are also important.

Gibraltar (2.3 sq. mi., 6.5 sq. km), a massive, rocky headland on the southern coast of Spain, at the entrance to the Mediterranean Sea, has 27,000 people. It has been a British Crown colony since 1704. Although in 1966 Spain demanded its independence, in 1967, by popular referendum, Gibraltar chose to remain British. Spain closed its border with Gibraltar in 1969, but reopened it in 1982. Gibraltar's economy revolves around its flourishing tourism industry and the needs of its British naval base.

The Isle of Man (227 sq. mi., 588 sq. km), in the Irish Sea, is not part of the U.K. The island, with a population of 74,000, is a direct dependency of the British Crown, and as such it is not subject to acts of the British Parliament but has its own legislature. The island was ruled successively by Norway, Scotland, and England and became a Crown possession in 1765. Tourism is the mainstay of the economy. Douglas, the capital, is the largest town.

THE ROCK OF GIBRALTAR, a British Crown colony since 1704, occupies a militarily strategic position at the entrance to the Mediterranean Sea.

Cities of Europe and Russia

Amsterdam, the capital of the Netherlands, located in the province of North Holland. The city lies at the junction of the Amstel and IJ rivers near the IJsselmeer (formerly the Zuider Zee). It is connected by canal with the North Sea and the Rhine River.

Amsterdam is the commercial and industrial center of the Netherlands and one of its busiest ports. Its most important manufactures include iron and steel, machinery, chemicals, paper, printed matter, and beer. Amsterdam also is a center of the international diamond-cutting industry. Pop., 734,000.

Andorra-la-Vella, capital and largest town of the principality of Andorra, located on the Valira River in the Pyrenees. Principal industries include tourism and commerce. Pop., 21,000.

Antwerp, the second largest city in Belgium and the country's chief port. It is located on the Scheldt River about 55 miles (88 km) inland from the North Sea. Antwerp has one of the world's largest harbors and is among the busiest ports in Europe.

Antwerp's industries include petroleum refining, chemicals, automobile assembly, diamond cutting, and electronics. The city has many historic buildings and art treasures. Pop., 449,000.

Athens, the capital and largest city of Greece, located on the Attic Plain, about five miles inland from its port of Piraeus on the Saronic Gulf. Named after the classical Greek goddess of wisdom, Athens was the cultural center of ancient Greece. The flat-topped hill of the Acropolis, which overlooks the city, contains the ruins of some of the most beautiful buildings of ancient Greece.

Modern Athens is the center of Greece's political, cultural, and economic life. The products of its wide variety of industries include ships, food, steel, chemicals, beverages, and textiles. Athens is one of the busiest ports on the Mediterranean Sea, and lies on major railroad and airline routes. Pop., 746,000.

Baku, the capital of Azerbaijan. The city is located on the Apsheron peninsula reaching into the Caspian Sea. A flourishing medieval trade and craft center, Baku came under Persian rule from 1509 to 1723, and again in 1735. It was annexed by Russia in 1806, and in the 1880s became a major site of oil drilling, refining, and shipbuilding. Pop., 1,792,000.

Barcelona, on the northeast Mediterranean coast of Spain, the capital of

Barcelona Province and the second largest city in the country. Barcelona is Spain's leading manufacturing center and its largest port. Its major industries produce textiles, chemicals, machinery, pharmaceuticals, and cosmetics. Pop., 1,504,000.

Basel, in northern Switzerland, situated on the Rhine River near the French and German borders. It is the second largest city in Switzerland and serves Switzerland as a major river port. Basel is also an important railroad junction and travel center. The chief local industries produce dyes, chemicals, silk textiles, and pharmaceuticals. Pop., 165,000.

Belfast, the capital of Northern Ireland, located on the east coast, at the mouth of the Lagan River. The city is Northern Ireland's leading port and manufacturing center. Belfast's industries produce linen and other textiles, ships, aircraft, processed foods, tobacco, and whiskey. Many educational institutions are in Belfast, including Queen's University. Pop., 277,000.

Belgrade, the capital of Serbia and Montenegro, located on the Danube River, about 50 miles (80 km) from the Romanian border. The city is an active port and a transportation and industrial center. Belgrade's industries produce chemicals, machine tools, farm equipment, electrical equipment, paper, textiles, and processed foods. The seat of

the University of Belgrade, it has many museums. Pop., 1,619,000.

Berlin, the capital of Germany, located on the Spree and Havel rivers. Berlin was the capital of Germany until the end of World War II, when it was divided into four zones and occupied by the United States, France, Britain, and the Soviet Union.

In 1949 the American, British, and French zones became West Berlin and the Soviet zone became East Berlin. East Berlin became the capital of East Germany and West Berlin, although it has close ties with West Germany, was not a constitutional part of the latter. Upon the reunification of Germany in 1990, Berlin again became the capital. Berlin is a financial, commercial, and manufacturing center whose chief products are textiles, porcelain and china, electrical equipment, many types of machinery, and foodstuffs. Pop., 3,382,000.

Bern, the capital of Switzerland and of Bern Canton, located in the west-central part of the country, on the Aare River. Its varied manufactures include chemicals, precision instruments, machinery, and chocolate. It is a cultural, educational, banking, and commercial center. Pop., 122,000.

Birmingham, in south-central England, located in the West Midlands. The second largest city in Great Britain,

THE HARBOR CITY of Barcelona is Spain's major industrial city and was host to the 1992 Summer Olympic Games.

center *US*

centre *Brit.*

centers
US

centres
Brit.

Birmingham is one of the world's leading industrial centers. The city specializes in the manufacture of motor vehicles, bicycles, machinery, and electrical products. The production of iron, steel, and nonferrous metals is also important. Pop., metro. area, 2,296,000.

Bologna, in north-central Italy, at the foot of the Apennines, about 50 miles (80 km) north of Florence. Bologna is the capital of the political region of Emilia-Romagna. The city is an industrial, commercial, and educational center. Manufactures include machinery, chemicals, electric motors, and shoes. Bologna is also a tourist center and an important agricultural market. Pop., 370,000.

Bonn, the former capital of West Germany, situated on the Rhine River, 15 miles (24 km) south of Cologne. Long an educational and cultural center, the city is noted for its architecture, its museums, and its university. After it became the West German capital in 1949, Bonn expanded rapidly. The city's industries produce electrical equipment, chemicals, pharmaceuticals, and precision instruments. Pop., 302,000.

THE WORKS
of great architects, artists, and writers made Florence, Italy, a center for the arts and gave rise to the Renaissance.

Bordeaux, in southwestern France, located on the Garonne River. The city is an important seaport and a leading commercial and cultural center. Its principal industries are oil refining,

EDINBURGH, Scotland's capital city, is a cultural and educational center with many noteworthy historic buildings.

furniture making, and food processing. It produces and exports red and white wines that are world famous. The history of Bordeaux dates back to Roman times, and in old sections there are Roman ruins and medieval buildings. Pop., 219,000.

Bratislava, the capital of Slovakia, located on the Danube River near the Slovakian, Hungarian, and Austrian borders. Founded by the Romans, it became an important trade center and was the capital of Hungary from 1526 until 1784. Bratislava was recognized as part of Czechoslovakia in 1918 and became the capital of Slovakia in 1993. Shipping, oil refining, food processing, textiles, metals, and chemicals are major industries. Pop., 429,000.

Brussels, the capital and largest city of Belgium, located near the center of the country, on the Senne River. Brussels is an important administrative, financial, and cultural center. The city manufactures chemicals, machinery, textiles, electrical equipment, and rubber goods. Brussels is famous for its lace and carpets. Pop., 137,000.

Bucharest, the capital and largest city of Romania, located in central Walachia, on the Dimbovita River. The city is the country's commercial, industrial, and cultural center. Its industries produce machinery, electrical equipment, textiles, clothing, chemicals, transportation equipment, and processed foods. Bucharest is known for its many cultural and educational institutions. Pop., 2,009,000.

Budapest, the capital and largest city of Hungary, on the Danube River, in the north-central part of the country. As Hungary's largest industrial center, Budapest produces iron and steel, textiles, electronic equipment, many pharmaceuticals, machinery, and processed foods. The city is also the cultural and educational center of Hungary and has several museums and libraries. It is the seat of the Academy of Sciences. Pop., 1,825,000.

Cardiff, the capital and largest city of Wales, at the mouth of the Taff River, on the Bristol Channel in western Britain. Cardiff is the cultural and educational center of Wales. Its major industries include food processing, iron and steel manufacture, and ship repairing. Pop., 305,000.

Chişinău, the capital and largest city of Moldova, situated in the republic's central region on the Byk River. An old monastery town settled in the early 15th century, it passed to the Turks in the 1700s. It was acquired by Russia in 1812 and became the center of Bessarabia. Chişinău was part of Romania from 1918 until 1940, when the Soviet Union seized it and made it the capital of the Moldavian Soviet Socialist Republic. Most of the city's large Jewish population perished during World War II. Today it is the industrial, commercial, and cultural center of Moldova. Pop., 658,000.

Cologne, or Köln, in western Germany, on the Rhine River in the state of North Rhine-Westphalia. The Rhineland's most important industrial center, Cologne manufactures iron and steel, machinery, and textiles. Its insurance and engineering industries are also important. It is a busy river port and has extensive shipyards. It is also a leading cultural and educational center. Cologne Cathedral is the city's most famous landmark. Pop., 963,000.

Copenhagen, or København, the capital and largest city of Denmark, lying on Sjaelland and Amager islands. An important industrial center, the city produces ships, machinery, and chemicals. It has an excellent natural harbor and is a major European port. The city is the seat of Copenhagen University and the cultural center of Denmark. Pop., 501,000.

Donetsk, a city in Ukraine, on the Kalmius River. It is the leading industrial center of the Donets Basin, with coal mines, foundries, metallurgical plants, chemical works, and machinery plants. It has a university and several technical colleges. Pop., 1,050,000.

Dresden, a German industrial city situated on the Elbe River. The city was almost completely destroyed by Allied bombing during World War II. Its manufactures include chemicals, machinery, optical instruments, and glass. It is also an important river port. The city's buildings include some excellent examples of Baroque architecture. Pop., 478,000.

Dublin, the capital, largest city, and chief port of the Republic of Ireland, located on Ireland's east coast near the mouth of the Liffey River. Dublin is a major transportation, commercial, and administrative center. Its industries include brewing and distilling, glassmaking, and textile-weaving. The city is Ireland's cultural and educational center, containing a large university, a cathedral, and many museums and libraries. Pop., 495,000.

Edinburgh, the capital of Scotland. It is located on the south shore of the Firth of Forth in southeastern Scotland. Edinburgh is a residential and administrative city. It is noted for its cultural and educational activities and historic buildings. The principal industries are food processing, engineering, papermaking, chemicals, and distilling. Pop., 430,000.

Florence, in central Italy, on the banks of the Arno River, in the western Apennines. It is the capital of Tuscany and a center of commerce and light industry. One of the world's foremost art centers, Florence attracts many tourists. Handicrafts include textiles, pottery, jewelry, and leather goods. A flood in 1966 damaged many art treasures and buildings. Pop., 352,000.

Frankfurt-am-Main, in west-central Germany, on the Main River, about 100 miles (160 km) southeast of Cologne. A leading industrial city, Frankfurt's manufactures include machinery, electrical equipment, and chemicals. The city is a commercial and financial center and its location makes it the transportation hub of West Germany. Frankfurt is also an educational and cultural center. Pop., 646,000.

Gdańsk, formerly Danzig, a Polish seaport situated on the Baltic Sea, on the delta of the Vistula River. The port of Gdańsk handles coal, lumber, and grain. Products of the city's varied industries include ships, processed foods, and chemicals. Pop., 455,000.

Geneva, the capital of Geneva canton in southwestern Switzerland, located on the Rhône River at the southern end of Lake Geneva. The city serves as a banking center and as the headquarters for a number of international organizations. Its industries include tourism and the manufacture of clocks, jewelry, precision tools, surgical and optical equipment, leather goods, and textiles.

Geneva is an ancient city that became important during the Reformation. It is an intellectual and cultural center with many schools, museums, and libraries. Pop., 176,000.

Glasgow, a port and industrial city of west-central Scotland, lying on the Clyde River. Glasgow is the largest city in Scotland, with extensive docks and shipyards. Its principal products are textiles, food, and chemicals. Its engineering and printing industries are also important. Pop., metro. area, 630,000.

The Hague, the seat of the Netherlands' legislature and royal residence, and the capital of the province of South Holland. The Hague lies near the country's west coast. It is the site of the headquarters of several international organizations. Banking and insurance are important industries. The Hague is mainly a residential city. Pop., 441,000.

Hamburg, the capital of the German state of Hamburg, with which it is coextensive, situated at the confluence of the Elbe, Aster, and Bille rivers, near the North Sea. Hamburg is Germany's largest seaport and an important industrial center as well. Shipping and shipbuilding are the city's major industries. Pop., 1,715,000.

Helsinki, the capital and largest city of Finland. It is situated on the southern coast, on the Gulf of Finland. Helsinki is a major seaport and the country's chief trading center. Shipbuilding is Helsinki's leading industry. The production of textiles, foodstuffs, paper and wood products, and ceramics is also important. Helsinki is an educational center with a university and several colleges. Pop., 560,000.

Kiev, the capital of Ukraine, situated on the Dnieper River about 450 miles (725 km) southwest of Moscow. Kiev is a commercial, industrial, and transportation center. Its industries produce precision instruments and tools, electric motors, agricultural machines, and electrical equipment.

Kiev was the capital of a Russian principality in the 800s, and the first seat of the Russian Orthodox Church. It is an educational and cultural center, with museums, old churches, monasteries, and a national library. Pop., 2,590,000.

Kraków, or Cracow, a city in southern Poland on the Vistula River. It is a rail and commercial center that manufactures machinery, construction materials, chemicals, paper, and clothing. The city is also a cultural and educational center, with medieval buildings, a Gothic cathedral, a castle, and a university. Pop., 741,000.

26 Europe and Russia

THE HAGUE has been the location of many international conferences seeking peaceful solutions to problems between wars. It is the site of the Peace Palace, built in the 1900s.

LISBON IS A BUSY PORT located on the estuary of the Tagus River on the Atlantic Ocean. Its varied architecture reflects both Moorish and Renaissance design.

Leeds, in north-central England, on the Aire River, about 165 miles (266 km) northwest of London. It is the center of England's wool industry. Manufactures include textiles and clothing, iron and steel, electronics, machinery, chemicals, and leather goods. The city is an important cultural and educational center. Pop., metro. area, 1,446,000.

Lisbon, the capital and largest city of Portugal, located at the mouth of the Tagus River on the Atlantic Ocean. It is Portugal's leading port, and it exports the country's fish, olive oil, and wine. Lisbon contains most of the country's industry and produces refined oil, electronics, textiles, chemicals, processed foods, and tile. The city has many beautiful churches and a number of interesting Moorish and Renaissance buildings. Pop., 565,000.

Liverpool, an important British port and the center of a large metropolitan area. It is situated on the Mersey River, near the Irish Sea. The city's economy is based on shipping and warehouse storage, especially of cotton, wool, tobacco, and grain. Liverpool is a rail and distribution center. Its industries produce flour, refined sugar, electrical equipment, chemicals, and rubber. Pop., metro. area, 838,000.

Ljubljana, the capital, largest city, and economic and cultural center of Slovenia, on the Ljubljana River in central Slovenia. Founded by the Romans as Emona in 34 B.C., it became part of the Hapsburg Empire in 1277 and of Yugoslavia in 1918. Ljubljana became the capital of the Republic of Slovenia in 1991. An important transportation and industrial center, it produces textiles, paper, chemicals, and electrical equipment. Pop., 264,000.

Lódź, the second largest city of Poland, about 75 miles (120 km) southwest of Warsaw. It is an important transportation and industrial center and produces such diverse products as textiles and machinery, electrical equipment, chemicals, and processed foods. Pop., 787,000.

London, the capital of the United Kingdom, and one of the world's largest cities, located on the Thames River about 40 miles (65 km) from the North Sea. London is Great Britain's major port and commercial center. Its industries produce mostly finished consumer goods, including clothing, metal and electrical goods, chemicals, processed goods, plastics, and cigarettes. London is also a major center for banking, insurance, publishing, andprinting.

A city since Roman times, London has many points of historical interest. Its fine educational institutions, libraries, and museums make it an important cultural and intellectual center. London is joined to other parts of Great Britain and the world by an excellent network of land, sea, and air transportation. Pop., metro. area, 7,652,000.

Luxembourg, the capital of Luxembourg, located in the south-central part of the country. The city is an industrial, commercial, and cultural center. Luxembourg's industries produce iron and steel, textiles, leather goods, machinery, and processed foods. It is also a banking center. Pop., 77,000.

Lyon, city in France, situated at the confluence of the Saône and Rhône rivers, in the southeastern part of the country. Lyon is a major commercial and industrial center.

The leading industry is the manufacture of silk textiles, but the city also produces chemicals, drugs, dyes, and electrical machinery. A stock exchange and international banks make it a financial center, and yearly international trade fairs are held in the city. Over 2,000 years old, Lyon has many sections of historical interest. Pop., metro. area, 1,348,832.

Madrid, the capital and largest city of Spain. The city is located in the region of New Castile, at the geographical center of the Iberian peninsula. Madrid is situated on a plateau at 2,100 feet above sea level, and is on the Manzanares River. It is Spain's leading administrative, financial, and cultural center. It is also among the nation's chief educational and tourist centers. Manufactures include transportation equipment, machinery, leather goods, optical and electrical equipment, plastics, and chemicals. Pop., 2,939,000.

Manchester, in northwestern England, on the Irwell River in Lancashire, about 30 miles (48 km) northeast of Liverpool. Britain's leading manufacturing center, Manchester is among the world's chief producers of cotton goods. Other products include plastics, electronic equipment, machinery, chemicals, and rubber goods. Manchester is a railroad junction and an ocean port linked to the Irish Sea by the deepwater Manchester Ship Canal. Pop., metro. area, 2,277,000.

Marseille, or Marseilles, in southeastern France, its chief port on the

MUNICH, CAPITAL OF BAVARIA, is a manufacturing center located on the Isar River, just north of the Bavarian Alps in southeastern Germany.

Mediterranean Sea, and the country's third largest city. It is located on the Gulf of Lion, about 25 miles (40 km) east of the mouth of the Rhône River. It is the capital of the department of Bouches-du-Rhône and a leading industrial center. Manufactures include petroleum products, chemicals, machinery, sugar, textiles, and olive oil. Pop., metro. area, 1,349,772.

Milan, in northern Italy, located between the foothills of the Alps and the Po River, near the border with Switzerland. Milan is the second largest city in Italy and the nation's leading industrial, financial, and commercial center. Manufactures include men's and women's clothing, aircraft, motor vehicles, heavy machinery, chemicals, and textiles. Pop., 1,183,000.

Minsk, the capital city of Belarus, located on the Svisloch River near the western border with Poland, on the main railway line between Warsaw and Moscow. It is the country's commercial, industrial, and cultural center. Settled more than 900 years ago, it was the capital of Minsk principality in 1101 and became part of Lithuania in 1326. After passing to Poland, it was reclaimed by Russia in the second partition of Poland in 1793. Minsk has been severely damaged several times, notably by Napoleon in 1812, during the German occupation of 1918, and during World War II. A center of Jewish life during the Middle Ages, the city was home to a large Jewish population until World War II. Pop. 1,677,000.

Moscow, the capital and largest city of Russia. It is located on both banks of the Moscow River, about 400 miles (640 km) southeast of Leningrad. Moscow is the Soviet Union's industrial, political, and transportation center. Manufactures include motor vehicles, machinery, electrical equipment, chemicals, textiles, and steel.

Moscow is the administrative and cultural center of the nation. Major city landmarks include the Kremlin, Red Square, St. Basil's Cathedral, and Lenin's tomb. Moscow is a center of education, with many universities and other schools. Pop., 8,297,000.

Munich, or München, capital of the state of Bavaria and the third largest city in Germany. Munich is situated on the Isar River, about 25 miles (40 km) north of the Bavarian Alps in southeastern Germany. The city is an important industrial, commercial, and transportation center.

In addition to beer, for which the city is famous, Munich manufactures vehicles, machinery, optical and precision instruments, chemicals, and textiles. The city is also a major cultural, educational, and tourist center. Pop., 1,210,000.

Naples, or Napoli, a major seaport in Italy on the Bay of Naples, off the Tyrrhenian Sea. It is 10 miles (16 km) northwest of Mount Vesuvius. It is a port and industrial center and important for the manufacture of ships, automobiles, textiles, porcelain, wine, and machinery.

Naples was founded several hundred years before the birth of Christ. Many relics from the ruins of Pompeii are in the National Museum. Naples has medieval and Renaissance buildings, as well as a university, libraries, and museums. Pop., 993,000.

Oslo, the capital of Norway, lying at the northern end of Oslo Fjord, near the Skaggerak. The largest city in Norway, Oslo is also the country's principal port and its administrative, commercial, and industrial center. Industrial activities include shipbuilding and the manufacture of textiles, paper products, and chemicals. The city has many historic sites and cultural institutions, and is the seat of the University of Oslo. Pop., 513,000.

Oxford, a city in central England, situated on the Thames River. Oxford is the seat of Oxford University, which was founded in the 1100s. Oxford's industries include the production of steel and automobiles and printing and publishing. Pop., 134,000.

Palermo, an Italian port, the capital of the province of Palermo and of Sicily. The city has shipyards and warehouses, and its industries produce wine, chemicals, textiles, and cement. Palermo, which is thought to be over 2500 years old, has many historical and architectural monuments. Pop., 653,000.

Paris, the capital of France, situated in east-central France on the Seine River. The city is the administrative and commercial hub of France, and one of the most important cultural and intellectual centers of the world. Its collections of art and architecture are outstanding, and its excellent educational facilities attract scholars and students from all over the world.

Among the best known points of interest in Paris are the Louvre art museum, Notre Dame Cathedral, the opera, and the Eiffel Tower. Paris is also a thriving industrial city that produces machinery, high-tech electronic equipment, automobiles, and airplanes. Pop., metro. area, 9,664,507.

Pisa, in north-central Italy, on the Arno River, near the Ligurian Sea. The city is a commercial and industrial center whose manufactures include textiles, glass, pharmaceuticals, machine tools, and processed foods. It has many art treasures and notable buildings, including the famous Leaning Tower whose stability is in doubt. Pop., 85,000.

Porto, or Oporto, the second largest city of Portugal, situated on the Atlantic coast at the mouth of the Douro River. Porto is known for the export of port wine. Its industries produce beverages, textiles, clothing, and pottery. Pop., 263,000

Prague, the capital of the Czech Republic, on the Vltava (Moldau) River. The city is an educational center and a transportation hub. Its manufactures include machinery, steel, automobiles, chemicals, and food and beverages. Prague has many historic monuments representing the Romanesque, Gothic, Italian late Renaissance, and Baroque styles. Pop., 1,179,000.

PRAGUE IS CALLED "City of a Hundred Spires" because of the many church spires that define the capital city's skyline.

REYKJAVIK IS ICELAND'S CAPITAL and largest metropolitan area, with more than half the country's population.

Reykjavik, the capital of Iceland, located on the southwestern coast of the country. It is the country's leading seaport and only major city. Reykjavik has a large fishing industry, busy shipyards, and a textiles industry. It is the site of a university. Pop., 111,000.

Riga, the capital of Latvia, situated on the western Dvina River near the mouth of the Gulf of Riga, an inlet of the Baltic Sea. It is the largest Baltic city and is known generally as a beach resort. Its industrial sector specializes in the manufacture of telephone, radio, and other electrical equipment, machine tools, and chemicals. Pop., 793,000.

Rome, the capital of Italy, located in the west-central part of the country, on the Tiber River, 17 miles (27 km) inland from the Tyrrhenian Sea. Rome has been a major center of civilization for over 2,000 years. It was the capital of the Roman Empire and retained its importance during the Middle Ages as the seat of the papacy. In the 1500s and 1600s Rome became the center of the Italian Renaissance, and many magnificent palaces and churches, decorated with beautiful sculptures and paintings, were built.

Modern Rome is the cultural, financial, and transportation center of Italy. Its industries include engineering, chemical production, motion pictures, food processing, printing, and publishing. Pop., 2,460,000.

Rostov, a city in southeastern Russia, on the Don River, about 30 miles (48 km) from its mouth on the Sea of Azov. It is an important port, transportation, and industrial center whose manufactures include farm machinery, barges, ball bearings, electrical equipment, chemicals, road-making machinery, clothing, and processed foods. It has a university and several institutions of higher learning. Pop., 1,004,000.

Rotterdam, city in the Netherlands, on the New Maas River, an outlet of the Rhine River, near the North Sea. With easy access to both the North Sea and

Rhine River, Rotterdam is one of the busiest ports in Europe. Shipping and shipbuilding are Rotterdam's leading industries, but chemicals, paper, furniture, refined petroleum, clothing, and processed foods are also produced. Pop., 606,000.

Ruse, on the Danube River, about 40 miles (65 km) south of Bucharest. The city is Bulgaria's largest port on the Danube and an important transportation center. Ruse's major industries produce railroad equipment, textiles, processed foods, refined petroleum, and agricultural implements. Pop., 183,000.

St. Petersburg, formerly Leningrad, the second largest city in Russia, located at the mouth of the Neva River on the Gulf of Finland, an inlet of the Baltic Sea. The city was known as Leningrad from 1924 until 1991. It was founded by Peter the Great in 1702, and from 1712 until 1918 was the capital of Russia. During World War II St. Petersburg, then called Leningrad, withstood a siege by German forces for over two years.

St. Petersburg is a major industrial center. Its industries produce electrical equipment, precision tools, machinery, chemicals, textiles, and paper. It is also an important shipbuilding center. The city has many cultural and educational institutions, including the Hermitage art museum and the University of St. Petersburg. Pop., 4,678,000.

Sarajevo, the capital and largest city of Bosnia and Herzegovina, on the Miljacka River about 125 miles (200 km) southwest of Belgrade. Captured by the Turks in the 15th century, it became a major Muslim trading and cultural center. Sarajevo was occupied by Austria-Hungary in 1878 and was the scene of the assassination of Austrian Archduke Francis Ferdinand in 1914 by a Serbian nationalist, the event that triggered World War I. Host of the 1984 Winter Olympic Games, it became capital of Bosnia and Herzegovina in 1992, but has been devastated by fighting between Muslim and Serbian factions. Pop., 529,000.

Seville, port on the Guadalquivir River, in southern Spain. Historically important as a center of Moorish Spain and of colonial trade with the Americas, the city is today an important commercial center. Manufactures include cigarettes, textiles, armaments, and porcelain. Pop., 685,000.

Sofia, the capital and largest city of Bulgaria, situated in the western foothills of the Balkan Mountains. It is the economic center of the country, with industries producing machinery, electrical equipment, textiles, and processed foods. Sofia is the home of the country's main educational institutions. Pop., 1,191,000.

Stockholm, the capital and largest city of Sweden. It is situated in the southeast, on Mälaren Lake, near the Baltic Sea. The city is an important port and its industries include food-processing plants, chemical and machinery factories, and paper and textile mills. It is an

THE GONDOLAS AND CANALS of Venice draw many tourists to this romantic center of art and architecture in northeastern Italy.

center
US

centre
Brit.

civilization
US

civilisation
Brit.

important commercial and financial center, and its schools, museums, libraries, and theaters give it great cultural importance. Pop., 755,000.

Tallinn, the capital of Estonia, located on the Gulf of Finland. The city has been an important seaport for many centuries and has become a center for manufacturing in the 20th century. Its major industries produce electrical equipment, textiles, furniture, and paper. It has large military and naval bases that are remnants from the years of Soviet control. Pop., 398,000.

Tampere, in southwestern Finland, on Lake Nasijarvi. A cultural, transportation, and industrial hub, it is a leading textile center and its industries include lumber mills, machinery, and leather-processing plants. It is notable for its modern architecture as well as for its university and technological institute. Pop., 198,000.

T'bilisi, or Tiflis, the capital of the Republic of Georgia. The city, which lies on the Kura River, is a resort known for its thermal springs. It is also an agricultural and economic center. Tbilisi's industries produce textiles and clothing, wood products, machinery, plastics, and industrial equipment. Pop., 1,399,000.

Thessaloniki, or Salonika, a seaport in northeastern Greece. It is Greece's second largest city and an important commercial and industrial center. Leading manufactures include petroleum products, chemicals, steel, textiles, and construction materials. Thessaloniki is famous for its many fine Byzantine churches. Pop., 364,000.

Tirana, the capital of Albania. Tirana is served by Durrës, an Adriatic seaport. The city is a commercial and industrial center in an agricultural region well known for the production of olives. Tirana's manufactures include building materials, metal products, food processing, and textiles. Tirana is the seat of a university, a science institute, and museums. Pop., 244,000.

Trieste, a port in northeastern Italy, situated on the Adriatic Sea, near the border with Serbia and Montenegro. Following World War II, the city was made part of a free territory, but in the 1950s it was incorporated into Italy and surrounding territory into what was then Yugoslavia. The main industries are shipbuilding and shipping; there are also steel mills and oil refineries. Pop., 210,000.

Utrecht, in central Netherlands, on the Oude Rijn River, 20 miles (32 km) southeast of Amsterdam. The city is a finance, transportation, and industrial center whose manufactures include machinery, aluminum, chemicals, cement, and processed food. Utrecht has many museums and splendid

medieval churches. The university is the largest of the Dutch state universities, with many specialized schools and a large library. Pop., 258,000.

Vaduz, capital of the European principality of Liechtenstein, situated on the banks of the Rhine River. As the country's chief city, it is primarily an administrative center. Tourism is important. Pop., 5,100.

Valletta, capital and seaport of Malta, on the northeast coast. For many years the port was an important base for the British navy, but by 1979 the base was closed. Much of the city's economic activity still centers around the port, and tourism is becoming increasingly important. Pop., 7,600.

Venice, or Venezia, the capital of the province of Venezia, in northeastern Italy. Occupying more than 100 islets in a lagoon off the Adriatic Sea, the city is built on a foundation of sunken piles and is connected with the mainland by bridges. Transportation in the city is by boat along numerous canals.

Venice is noted for its outstanding architecture in a variety of styles, and it has long been an artistic center. The city's chief source of income is tourism. Its few light industries produce glass, jewelry, textiles, furniture, and handicrafts. Pop., 266,000.

Vienna, the capital of Austria, located in the northeastern part of the country on the Danube River. Vienna is Austria's major commercial and industrial city, producing chemicals, textiles and clothing, machinery, paper, and food products. Vienna was for centuries a European cultural center. With its state university, technical schools, and music, drama, and fine arts academies, Vienna is still an important intellectual center. Pop., 1,562,000.

Vilnius, formerly Vilna, the capital of Lithuania, located on the Neris River. It is an active industrial center whose chief manufactures include agricultural machinery, electrical and electronic equipment, chemicals, and textiles. It is the cultural center of Lithuania and the seat of Lithuania University, founded in 1579. Pop., 578,000.

Vladivostok, a port on the Sea of Japan, in southeastern Siberia in Russia. It is the country's most important port on the Pacific Ocean and is kept open in the winter by icebreakers. The city is the eastern terminus of the Trans-Siberian Railroad. Fishing fleets are based in Vladivostok. The city's industries include fish canning, shipbuilding, and mineral refining. Pop., 607,000.

Warsaw, the capital and largest city of Poland. Located on the Vistula River in the east-central part of the country, Warsaw is the commercial, political, educational, and cultural center of Poland.

ST. STEPHEN'S CATHEDRAL is one of Vienna's many well-known cultural landmarks.

Manufactures include machinery, chemicals, electrical equipment, textiles, clothing, and food products. Pop., 1,610,000.

Wroclaw, in southern Poland, on both banks of the Oder River, about 190 miles (300 km) southwest of Warsaw. Wroclaw, German Breslau, is a river port and railroad junction. Manufactures include machinery, chemicals, textiles, and food products. Pop., 634,000.

Yerevan, the capital of Armenia, in the south of the republic, 14 miles (23 km) from the Turkish border, on the Razdan River. Yerevan is an important administrative, industrial, and cultural center. It was the site of the fortress of Yerbuni in 783 and developed as a crossroads on the trade route between Transcaucasia and India. Ceded to Russia in 1828, Yerevan became the capital of the Armenian Soviet Socialist Republic in 1920 and of the Republic of Armenia in 1991. Pop., 1,247,000.

Zagreb, the capital of Croatia, on the Sava River. Zagreb is the largest city and the commercial, financial, cultural, and educational center of Croatia. Manufactures include machinery, textiles, chemicals, paper and metal products. Pop., 692,000.

Zürich, in Switzerland, at the mouth of the Limmat River, at the northwest end of Lake Zürich. It is the capital of the canton of Zürich and the largest city in Switzerland. The city is the industrial, commercial, and financial center of the country, with many banks and financial institutions that are internationally renowed. Manufactures include machinery, textiles, machine tools, turbines, radios, and paper. The city is also a cultural, educational, and tourist center. Pop., 341,000.

theaters
US

theatres
Brit.

aluminum
US

aluminium
Brit.

Glossary of Europe and Russia

Adriatic Sea. An arm of the Mediterranean Sea lying between Italy on the southwest and Montenegro and Albania on the northeast. The Adriatic is about 500 miles (800 km) long and 100 miles (160 km) wide. To the south, the Strait of Otranto links it with the Ionian Sea.

Aegean Sea. An arm of the Mediterranean Sea between Greece and Turkey. The Aegean is about 400 miles (645 km) long and 200 miles (320 km) wide, and drains south into the Sea of Crete. It contains many dry, rocky islands, including those in the Cyclades, Sporades, and Dodecanese groups.

Alps. An extensive and complex mountain system in central Europe, extending about 700 miles (1,130 km) from southeastern France east through Switzerland and southwestern Austria and south into Slovenia. The highest peak is Mont Blanc, which towers 15,781 feet (4,813 m). The range is narrow in the west and wider to the east. A variety of regional names are applied to the Alps. Some of the most important sections follow:

Bernese Alps, in west central Switzerland, north of the Rhône River.

Carnic Alps, along the Italian-Austrian border.

Dinaric Alps, in Bosnia and Hertzegovina and Montenegro, running northwest to southeast parallel to their coasts.

Dolomites, in northeastern Italy.

Julian Alps, in Slovenia along the Italian border.

Lepontine Alps, along the Swiss-Italian border, east of the Pennine Alps.

Maritime Alps, in southeastern France along the Italian border.

Pennine Alps, along the Swiss-Italian border, bounded on the north by the valley of the Rhône River.

Altai. A mountain system extending about 1,300 miles (2,100 km) from southern Siberia southeast into China and Mongolia. The headwaters of the Ob and Irtysh rivers are in the Altai system. The Altai mountains are rich in minerals, particularly gold, silver, lead, copper, and zinc. The northeastern ranges are densely forested.

Apennines. A mountain range that forms the backbone of peninsular Italy. The Apennines extend in a long arc from the Ligurian Alps in northwestern Italy to Calabria in the south, about 850 miles (1,370 km). The highest peak, Monte Corno, is 9,560 feet (2,916 m). Pastures and forest cover the upper slopes, and fruits and grains are grown in the valleys.

Azov, Sea of. Northern branch of the Black Sea. The world's shallowest sea, it has an area of 14,500 square miles (37,555 sq. km). The Crimean peninsula forms its western and southern shores. The sea is connected to the Black Sea by the Kerch Strait. Kerch, Zhdanov, and Taganrog are important cities on the Sea of Azov.

Baikal. Lake in south-central Siberia, in Russia, one of the world's largest lakes. Lake Baikal covers an area of 12,200 square miles (31,600 sq. km). Its maximum depth of 5,710 feet (1,740 m) makes it the deepest lake in the world.

Balearic Islands. A group of islands in the Mediterranean Sea off the east coast of Spain that makes up the Spanish province of Baleares. There are 16 islands altogether. The largest are Majorca, Minorca, Ibiza, Formentera, and Cabrera. The islands are popular vacation spots. They produce mostly fruits and wines.

Balkan wars. Two conflicts fought in the Balkan peninsula whose outcomes

THE EUROPEAN ALPS cover a distance of about 700 miles through France, Switzerland, Austria, and Slovenia.

THE CUISINE OF THE BASQUES is widely appreciated, although the origins and language of the people are little understood.

established the conditions for the outbreak of World War I. In the First Balkan War (October, 1912–May, 1913), the allied states of Serbia, Bulgaria, Greece, and Montenegro defeated the Ottoman Turks, strengthening Serbia and Bulgaria at the expense of the Ottoman Empire. In the Second Balkan War (June–July, 1913), a coalition of Balkan states defeated Bulgaria. The ensuing peace settlement stripped Bulgaria of most of its gains from the first war and further increased the power of Serbia. Serbia's gains in these wars produced a regional rivalry with Austria-Hungary that led to war in 1914 and its expansion into the larger conflict of World War I.

Baltic Sea. An arm of the North Atlantic Ocean separating the Scandinavian peninsula and Finland from the rest of continental Europe. It flows into the North Sea to the west through the Kattegat and the Skagerrak. The Baltic is the world's largest body of brackish water. It covers an area of 160,000 square miles (415,000 sq. km). The Baltic has two large branches—the Gulf of Bothnia in the north and the Gulf of Finland in the east.

Barents Sea. A part of the Arctic Ocean lying north of Russia and Norway and bounded on the east and north by the islands of Novaya Zemlya, Franz Josef Land, and Svalbard. On the west the Barents Sea flows into the Norwegian Sea.

Basques. A people living on the Bay of Biscay at the western end of the Pyrenees in both Spain and France. The origin of the Basques is unknown, and their language appears to be unrelated to any other. A strong nationalist movement has been responsible for acts of terrorism.

Black Forest. A mountainous region in southwestern Germany. The mountains reach summits of nearly 5,000 feet (1,525 m) and are thickly forested. They contain the sources of the Danube and Neckar rivers.

Black Sea. A large inland sea between southeastern Europe and Asia, lying north of Asian Turkey, west of Russia, south of Ukraine, and east of Romania, Bulgaria, and European Turkey. About 170,000 square miles (440,000 sq. km) in area, it receives the Danube, the Dniester, the Dnieper, and other major rivers. The Sea of Azov, a small arm of the Black Sea, lies to the north. The Bosporus, the Sea of Marmara, and the Dardanelles link the Black Sea with the Aegean.

Bosporus. A strait between European and Asian Turkey. It joins the Sea of Marmara with the Black Sea, and is 19 miles (31 km) long.

Bothnia, Gulf of. The northern arm of the Baltic Sea. It lies between Sweden and Finland.

Bourbon. An important European ruling family. Members held the thrones of France (1589–1792, 1814–1848), Spain (1700–1931, 1975–), and Naples and Sicily (1735–1861).

Capetian dynasty. A ruling house of France (987–1328) whose kings, through conquest and statecraft, laid the foundations of modern France.

Carlists. Supporters of the claims to the Spanish throne of Don Carlos María Isodro de Borbón (1788–1855) and his descendants. Following the death of his brother, King Ferdinand VII, in 1833, Don Carlos claimed the throne on the basis of the Spanish Salic Law of 1713, which prohibited females from succeeding to the throne. In 1830 King Ferdinand had formally abrogated the Salic Law, and in 1833 his infant daughter became Queen Isabella II. The Carlists fought two wars (1834–1839 and 1873–1876) and staged several uprisings in support of Don Carlos's claim. The Carlists continued to influence Spanish politics into the early 1900s.

Carpathian Mountains. A mountain system of central and eastern Europe extending more than 1,000 miles (1,610 km) through the Czech Republic and Slovakia, Hungary, Poland, Romania,

and Ukraine. Although a continuation of the Alps, the Carpathians are more rounded and lower than the Alps; the highest peak, Mt. Gerlach, is 8,711 feet (2,657 m). The Carpathians contain the sources of many rivers, including the Vistula and the Dniester.

Caspian Sea. The world's largest inland sea, between Russia and Iran, at the border of Europe and Asia. It is about 750 miles (1,208 km) long and averages 200 miles (320 km) in width. There are no outlets, but the Ural, Volga, Kura, Terek, and Atrek rivers flow into the Caspian.

Caucasus Mountains. An extensive mountain range between the Black and Caspian seas, often considered as part of the boundary between Europe and Asia. The Greater Caucasus, in the north, is about 750 miles (1,208 km) long, and the highest peak, Mt. Elbrus, is 18,481 feet (5,637 m). Volcanic in origin, this chain has hot springs and occasional earthquakes. The Lesser Caucasus, in the south, is a mountain system formed in part by the northern ranges of the Armenian Highland.

Chartism. An English working-class movement that advocated parliamentary reform between 1836 and 1848. The movement originated when workers in London prepared a program known as the People's Charter. They demanded annual parliaments, universal male suffrage, vote by secret ballot, equal electoral districts, abolition of property requirements for membership in the House of Commons, and salaries for members.

The People's Charter was published in 1838, and the Chartists attempted unsuccessfully in 1839, 1842, and 1848 to have petitions incorporating the Charter accepted by Parliament. After 1848, economic conditions improved and the movement gradually lost influence. Most of the objectives of the Chartist movement were ultimately realized.

Chersky Mountains. An important range of eastern Russia. It is located to the north of the Sea of Okhotsk and runs generally southeast to northwest. Its highest elevation is 10,217 feet (3,113 m).

Comecon. *See* Council for Mutual Economic Assistance.

Comintern. The name given the Communist Third International, an organization founded in 1919 dedicated to spreading the communist revolution worldwide. It was dissolved by Joseph Stalin in 1943 in an effort to promote greater solidarity among the Allied powers during World War II. Comintern had been preceded by two socialist international organizations. The First International was formed in 1872 and dissolved in 1876. The Second International was formed in 1889 and dissolved in 1920, although it had ceased to function in 1914 at the beginning of World War I.

Commonwealth of Independent States (CIS). Organization established by the Soviet republics of Russia, Ukraine, and Belarus in 1991 as the Soviet Union faced imminent collapse. The Commonwealth promotes economic and political cooperation among

realized
US

realised
Brit.

26 Europe and Russia

GERMANY'S BLACK FOREST, so named because of its dark evergreens, is the setting for many fairy tales and folk stories.

STACKS OF SALT on the island of Corsica, known as the birthplace of Napoleon and later occupied by his forces in 1796

its eleven fully independent republics, which also include Armenia, Azerbaijan, Kazakhstan, Kyrgyzstan, Moldova, Tajikistan, Turkmenistan, and Uzbekistan.

Corsica. A French island in the Mediterranean about 100 miles (160 km) southeast of the French coast. It is 3,352 square miles (8,682 sq. km) in area and is mountainous. The highest peak is Mont Cinto, 8891 feet (2,710 m).

Cossacks. Descendants of Tartars and escaped Ukrainian serfs who settled along the Dnieper and Don rivers in Russia. Renowned for their fierceness in battle and love of freedom, the Cossacks made several attempts to establish an independent state. Cossack units were important elements of the czarist army, but were also notorious for their pogroms against Jewish communities.

Council for Mutual Economic Assistance. Also known as CMEA or Comecon. An organization of communist countries that sought to develop and coordinate the economies of its member nations. Comecon was founded in 1949 by the Soviet Union, Bulgaria, Czechoslovakia, Hungary, Poland, and Romania. Albania joined later that year but stopped participating in 1961. The former East Germany joined in 1950, Mongolia in 1962, Cuba in 1972, and Vietnam in 1978. It was disbanded in 1991.

Council of Europe. An organization of Western European nations with the purpose of promoting greater unity among its members, particularly in the areas of economic and social development, human rights, and environmental improvement. As the international organization with the widest Western European membership, the council is an important forum for the discussion of regional affairs. The membership expanded substantially in the early 1990s, following the breakup of the Soviet Union, increasing to 40 members by the end of 1996, and 45 by 2004.

Crimea. Located between the Black Sea and the Sea of Azov, the Crimean peninsula, or Crimea, is known for its pleasant climate and strategic location. It was the site of the Crimean War, fought from 1853 to 1856, in which Russia was defeated by an alliance of England, France, Turkey, and Sardinia, which sought to limit Russia's influence in the region. Crimea became part of the Soviet Union in 1921, after several years of bloody conflict. More recently, the area has been a point of contention between Russia and Ukraine.

Danube. A major river of central and southeastern Europe. It rises in the Black Forest of Germany and flows for some 1,775 miles (2,858 km) through or along the borders of eight countries before emptying into the Black Sea. Its major tributaries include the Drava, Sava, Tisza, and Prut rivers.

Dardanelles. An important strait separating parts of European and Asian Turkey. It links the Aegean Sea and the Sea of Marmara and is 38 miles (61 km) long and 0.75 to 4 miles (1.2 km to 6.4 km) wide. Its ancient name was the Hellespont.

Declaration of the Rights of Man and of the Citizen. A document adopted by the French Constituent Assembly on August 27, 1789, and later used as the preamble to the French Constitution of 1791. The declaration, defining a citizen's inalienable rights, was based on the principles of the Enlightenment and the American Declaration of Independence. It expounds the basic philosophy of the French Revolution and was a call for liberal reform throughout Europe in the 1800s.

Delphic Oracle. The shrine of Apollo at Delphi in Phocis, Greece. In ancient times it was believed that Apollo communicated with mortals at Delphi through his priestess, who was reputed to have prophetic powers. The word "oracle" refers to the site of Apollo's temple as well as to the messages transmitted by the priestess.

Dnieper. A major river of western Russia. It rises near Smolensk and flows southwest and south for over 1,400 miles (2,255 km), emptying into the Black Sea. Its tributaries include the Sozh, Desna, and Berezina rivers.

The Dnieper is navigable for most of its course, and it is an important producer of hydroelectric power. It drains an area of 195,000 square miles (505,000 sq. km).

Don. A major river of western Russia. It rises in the Central Russian Upland, southwest of Moscow. The river flows in a generally southerly direction between the Dnieper and the Volga rivers for about 1,225 miles (1,972 km) before emptying into the Gulf of Taganrog of the Sea of Azov.

Tributaries of the Don include the Donets, Medveditsa, Sal, and Manych rivers. Seagoing ships can travel as far as Rostov, and the entire course is navigable by smaller vessels.

Douro. Also known as Duero. A river that crosses northern Spain and Portugal. Rising in north-central Spain, the river flows westward for 556 miles (897 km), forming part of the border between Spain and Portugal, before emptying into the Atlantic Ocean near the Portuguese city of Porto. In Portugal the Douro has been extensively developed for hydroelectric power.

Ebro. The longest river in Spain. It rises in the Cantabrian Mountains in northern Spain and runs eastward 565 miles (911 km) to the Mediterranean Sea. The river is used extensively for

THE TEMPLE OF APOLLO at Delphi was inhabited by the oracle, who delivered messages believed to be from the god of sunlight.

irrigation and the production of hydro-electric power.

Elbe. An important river of the Czech Republic and Germany. The river originates in the Czech Republic and flows 724 miles (1,168 km) through Germany to its outlet on the North Sea below Hamburg. The Elbe is navigable throughout most of its course and canals connect it to other important European waterways. In addition to Hamburg, the Elbe flows past the important industrial cities of Dresden and Magdeburg.

English Channel. A body of water between England and France that joins the Atlantic Ocean and the North Sea. It is 21 miles (34 km) wide at its narrowest extent, the Strait of Dover, and 112 miles (180 km) at its greatest.

Etruscans. An ancient people who inhabited northern and central Italy and established a thriving civilization in the centuries before the rise of Rome. The region that they controlled, from the Po valley in the north to central Italy in the south, was known in ancient times as Etruria.

The Etruscan civilization arose around 900 B.C. The Etruscans established independent city-states that were organized into several loose confederations. The inability of the Etruscan cities to work together for the common good led to their eventual conquest by the Romans, who were ruled by Etruscan kings for a century until their overthrow about 509 B.C.

Etruscan wealth was based on the trade of wine, olives, grain, iron, copper, and other commodities throughout the Mediterranean region and north into central Europe. The power of the Etruscans began to decline in the early sixth century B.C., and all of Etruria was eventually absorbed by the Romans. Etruscans were accomplished artisans, metalworkers, and engineers, and much of their learning was passed on to the Romans.

European Communities (EC). An international European organization that was formed in 1967 by the merger of the executive bodies of the European Coal and Steel Community (ECSC), the European Atomic Energy Community (Euratom), and the European Economic Community (EEC or Common Market).

The EC had its origin in the destruction visited upon Europe by World War II. The ECSC was created in 1951 by the Treaty of Paris. This organization worked to remove all trade barriers to the movement of coal, iron, steel, and scrap metal among the signatory nations. In 1957 the Treaties of Rome created Euratom to develop the nuclear energy industry and the EEC to work toward free trade and a common economic policy.

In 1992, with the implementation of the Maastricht Treaty on European Union, the EC was merged into a new organization, the European Union (EU), to promote further European integration. EU membership includes the 12 EC nations listed below:

Member nation	Year joined
Belgium	1951
Denmark	1973
France	1951
Germany	1951
Greece	1981
Ireland	1973
Italy	1951
Luxembourg	1951
Netherlands	1951
Portugal	1986
Spain	1986
United Kingdom	1973

ETRUSCAN ARTISANS left a rich cultural heritage, the best-preserved examples of which are wall paintings on tombs.

Additionally Austria, Finland, and Sweden were admitted in 1995. In 2004 the EU expanded to include Cyprus, the Czech Republic, Estonia, Hungary, Latvia, Lithuania, Malta, Poland, Slovakia, and Slovenia.

European Free Trade Association (EFTA). An international organization formed in 1960 to promote the expansion of free trade among its members. Although similar to the European Communities in its goals, EFTA does not seek political unification among member nations. Each member state maintains separate ties with nonmember nations. The four current members of EFTA are Iceland, Liechtenstein, Norway, and Switzerland. Six former members, Austria, Denmark, Finland, Portugal, Sweden, and the United Kingdom, are now members of the European Union.

European Union (EU). *See* European Communities.

Garonne. An important river of southeastern France. The Garonne rises in the Spanish Pyrenees about 30 miles (48 km) from the French border. It flows some 357 miles (576 km) to the Atlantic Ocean, past the major cities of Toulouse and Bordeaux, and joins with the Dordogne River about 40 miles (65 km) from the ocean to form the Gironde estuary. A canal joins the Garonne at Toulouse with the Mediterranean Sea.

Geneva. A crescent-shaped lake on the border of France and Switzerland, 224 square miles (580 sq. km) in area.

Gibraltar, Strait of. A body of water at the western end of the Mediterranean Sea between Spain and Morocco. It joins the Mediterranean and the Atlantic Ocean. About 8 miles (13 km) wide at its narrowest point, the strait has enormous strategic importance.

Glasnost. A Russian word meaning "openness," used to describe the relaxing of government controls on life in the Soviet Union. The policy was begun by Mikhail Gorbachev in 1986. Glasnost had a major effect on the domestic and foreign media, allowing them unprecedented latitude in the discussion of political and social problems and criticism of the government and its leaders.

Glorious Revolution. A coup in England in 1688 in which the Roman Catholic king James II was overthrown in favor of his Protestant daughter, Mary II, and her husband, William III.

Greenland. In area, the largest island in the world, 840,000 square miles (2,176,170 sq. km). A dependency and former colony of Denmark, it lies northeast of North America and is washed by the North Atlantic and Arctic oceans and by the Greenland Sea. About three-

civilization
US

civilisation
Brit.

26 Europe and Russia

quarters of its area lies above the Arctic Circle, and almost seven-eighths of Greenland is covered by ice.

Guelphs and Ghibellines. Opposing political factions important in Italy during the late Middle Ages, when popes and emperors vied for political supremacy. The names of the papal (Guelph) and imperial (Ghibelline) parties derived from two rival factions of the German nobility in the 12th century. The conflicts involved questions of allegiance to the pope or emperor, and also economic and social differences within communities and political differences among them. The nobility tended to be Ghibelline and the communes Guelph, but individual communes were often split internally, and neighboring communes frequently fought one another.

Hebrides. A group of islands off the west coast of Scotland. They are separated into the Outer Hebrides and the Inner Hebrides by the North Minch and Little Minch straits. Altogether there are about 500 islands in the group, of which about 100 are inhabited. Principal economic activities are fishing, agriculture, tourism, and the production of woolens. Total population of the islands is about 30,000.

Hohenzollern. A German ruling family, important chiefly as the ruling House of Brandenburg (1415–1918) and its successor state Prussia. The last three kings of Prussia (1871–1918) were also the emperors of Germany.

Hussites. Followers of John Hus (1369?–1415), a Bohemian religious reformer who criticized the Roman Catholic Church for its dogmas and abuses and placed final authority in the Bible rather than the church. Opposition to the Hussites led to a series of wars in the early 15th century. Many historians view the Hussite movement as a forerunner of the Protestant Reformation.

Iberia. A peninsula in the southwestern corner of Europe, between the Mediterranean Sea and the Atlantic Ocean, occupied by Spain and Portugal. It is ringed with the Pyrenees and the Cantabrian Mountains on the north, the Sierra da Estrella on the west, and the Cordillera Penibética on the southeast.

The interior is also mountainous, with the Sierra Morena and Sierra de Guadarrama the most important chains. The major rivers crossing the peninsula are the Duero, the Tejo (Tagus), the Guadiana, the Ebro, and the Guadalquivir.

Irish Sea. A sea about 40,000 square miles (103,630 sq. km) in area, between Ireland and Great Britain. It is connected to the Atlantic Ocean by the North Channel in the north and St. George's Channel in the south. The Isle of Man is in the Irish Sea.

Irtysh. *See* Ob.

Jacobins. A political club that dominated the French Revolution in 1793 and 1794 under the leadership of Maximilien Robespierre. It was responsible for the Reign of Terror, during which thousands of French citizens were put to death by guillotine. The Jacobins were suppressed after Robespierre was executed on July 27, 1794.

Jacobites. The name given to partisans of the descendants of James II, the Stuart king of England who was forced to flee the country in the Glorious Revolution of 1688.

James II died in exile in 1701, and the Stuart claim to the British throne was taken up by his son, known as James III to the Jacobites. Historians call him "the Old Pretender," the name used for him by his opponents.

In 1714 the German elector of Hanover became king of Great Britain as George I. Shortly thereafter the Old Pretender landed in Scotland. Aided by followers from the Scottish Highlands, he tried to organize a revolt. The uprising was badly organized and it failed.

In 1745 the Pretender's son, called the "Young Pretender" or "Bonnie Prince Charlie," landed in Scotland. This new attempt at revolt was also crushed, and the British government decided to destroy Jacobitism in the Scottish Highlands once and for all by breaking up the Highland clans.

Kamchatka. A peninsula on the Pacific coast of Russia, between the Bering Sea

and the Sea of Okhotsk. It is about 750 miles (1,210 km) long and reaches a maximum of 300 miles (484 km) in width. The peninsula has many geysers, hot springs, and a number of active volcanoes, including the highest peak in Siberia, Klyuchevskaya Sopka. The climate is considered to be severe and as a result the peninsula is lightly populated.

Kattegat. A strait between Sweden on the east and the Danish Jutland peninsula on the west. It connects the Baltic Sea to the Skagerrak and the North Sea.

Kolyma. The name of both a major river and a mountain range in eastern Siberia. The Kolyma Mountains are located north of the Sea of Okhotsk and run generally southwest to northeast, parallel to the Pacific coast. The Kolyma River rises in the Kolyma Mountains and flows 1,323 miles (2,134 km) north to the Arctic Ocean.

Lapps. A people inhabiting Lapland, which includes northern Norway, Sweden, Finland, and the Kola peninsula of Russia. Although the Lapps are thought of primarily as nomadic reindeer herders and hunters, only a small percentage of the total Lapp population is nomadic. Most Lapps live a relatively settled life that includes agriculture, fishing, trapping, and reindeer herding. The Lapp language consists of three distinct, mutually unintelligible, dialects.

Lena. A river in eastern Siberia, Russia. Originating near Lake Baikal in southern Siberia, the Lena is the longest river in Russia. It flows north 2,653 miles (4,279 km) to the Laptev Sea, part of the Arctic Ocean. The Lena and its associated tributary rivers, including the Aldan, Vilyuy, Vitim, and Olekma, drain an area of about 1 million square miles (2,591,000 sq. km). The principal city on the Lena is Yakutsk.

Loire. The longest river of France. It rises in the Cevennes Mountains in the southeast, flows northwest and west for 634 miles (1,020 km), and empties into the Bay of Biscay through a wide estuary at St. Nazaire.

Lombard League. A military coalition formed by the towns of Lombardy, in northern Italy, against the German emperor, Frederick I (Barbarossa, 1152–1190). The league was formed after Frederick's fourth expedition to Italy (1166–1168) and was composed of the Lombard towns joined by Venice and the Normans of Sicily.

Frederick invaded northern Italy again in 1174. In 1176 he was defeated by the league at Legnano. This was the first time since the fall of Rome that professional cavalry was defeated by an army of nonprofessional foot soldiers. By the Peace of Constance, drawn up in 1183, the independence of the Lombard towns was recognized.

DETAIL OF A COLOR PRINT depicting the 1794 execution of Robespierre, leader of the Jacobins during the French Revolution

GLOSSARY

A second Lombard League was formed about 1230, when the German emperor Frederick II renewed German claims on Italy.

Long Parliament. A British Parliament that theoretically sat for 20 years, from November 1640, to March 1660, without holding new elections.

The Stuart king Charles I had decided to rule without Parliament in 1629. In 1640, however, he was forced to convoke Parliament to raise funds to crush a revolt in Scotland. The Parliament was a revolutionary body. One of its leaders was the Puritan Oliver Cromwell. It insisted on the execution of the king's chief advisers.

In 1642 war broke out between Parliament and the king. In return for Scottish army support, Parliament passed the Solemn League and Covenant in September 1643, establishing Presbyterianism as the official religion of England, Ireland, and Scotland.

The parliamentary forces defeated the royalists, and Cromwell wanted Charles I executed. But about a hundred members of Parliament protested, and Cromwell used the army to exclude them from Parliament. Parliament then consisted of about 50 members; it was known as the Rump Parliament. The Rump did have Charles I executed in January 1649.

Lucerne. A lake in central Switzerland. It is roughly cross-shaped, 44 square miles (114 sq. km) in area, and bounded by the cantons of Lucerne, Unterwalden, Uri, and Schwyz.

Marne. A river that rises in eastern France and flows north and west for about 325 miles (525 km) into the Seine at Charenton.

Mediterranean Sea. The largest inland sea in the world, 2,400 miles (3,865 km) long and up to 1,000 miles

THE COLORFUL WOOLEN CLOTHING worn by Lapp men for ceremonial occasions is also practical for the cold climate they inhabit.

(1,600 km) wide. It separates the continents of Europe to the north, Asia to the east, and Africa to the south. The Mediterranean is linked with the Atlantic Ocean by the Strait of Gibraltar and with the Red Sea by the man-made Suez Canal.

The irregularly shaped sea is divided into two deep basins by the Italian peninsula, the island of Sicily, and a submarine ridge joining Sicily and Tunisia. There are islands in each basin. The eastern basin, connected to the Black Sea by the Bosporus and the Dardanelles, has two northern extensions, the Adriatic and Aegean seas.

The Mediterranean basin has hot, dry summers and warm, wet winters.

Meuse. A river that rises in northeastern France and flows through Belgium and the Netherlands for 580 miles (935 km) into the North Sea. In the Netherlands, the Meuse becomes the Maas.

NATO. *See* North Atlantic Treaty Organization.

North Atlantic Treaty Organization (NATO). A defensive alliance of many Western European, North Atlantic, and Mediterranean nations. NATO came into existence in 1949 in response to the Soviet military presence in Europe. It is an arrangement by which member nations agree that an attack on any member nation will be considered an attack on all. The members of NATO are Belgium, Bulgaria, Canada, the Czech Republic, Denmark, Estonia, France, Germany, Greece, Hungary, Iceland, Italy, Latvia, Lithuania, Luxem-

bourg, the Netherlands, Norway, Poland, Portugal, Romania, Slovakia, Slovenia, Spain, Turkey, the United Kingdom, and the United States.

North Sea. An arm of the North Atlantic Ocean separating Britain from the northwestern European mainland.

Norwegian Sea. A part of the Arctic Ocean lying off the coast of Norway. It is bounded on the south by the Faroe and Shetland islands, on the west by Iceland and Greenland, and on the north by Spitsbergen.

Nuremberg laws. Decrees promulgated in 1935 by Adolf Hitler's Third Reich depriving all Jewish Germans of the rights of citizenship. The laws also forbade intermarriage between Jews and non-Jews. The same laws became applicable in Austria in 1938, when Germany annexed that country.

Ob. A river in western Siberia, one of the great rivers of Russia. It begins in southern Siberia at the confluence of the Biya and Katun rivers, whose headwaters are located in the Altai Mountains. The Ob flows about 2,290 miles (3,694 km) to the Gulf of Ob, which extends about 600 miles (968 km) inland from the Arctic Ocean. Southwest of the Gulf of Ob, the river is joined by the Irtysh River, which also rises in the Altai group and is longer than the Ob. Together the Ob-Irtysh river system drains an area larger than the Mississippi drainage basin. The rivers and associated tributaries make up some 17,500 miles (28,225 km) of navigable waterway.

CHAMBORD is a well-known example of the fortresses/chateaus that line the valley of the Loire River in France.

Oder. A river in central Europe, about 560 miles (900 km) long. It rises in the Czech Republic, flows north through western Poland, is joined by the Neisse River, and continues north to the Baltic Sea. The Oder forms part of the border between Germany and Poland.

Old Regime. In French, *ancien régime*, the term used to describe French society and government in the period before the French Revolution of 1789. The phrase refers to a society in which many characteristics of medieval life persisted.

French society before the revolution was divided into three "estates," or classes. The first and second estates, the clergy and nobility, had many privileges, rights, and immunities denied to the third, the common people.

The tax structure under the Old Regime was complex and inequitable, and the system of weights and measures was irregular. Society was regulated by conflicting legal codes and government was headed by an absolute monarch.

Olympus. A mountain range in Greece, near the coast of Thessaly. Mt. Olympus, 9,570 feet (2,917 km), the highest point in the range and in Greece, was thought in ancient times to be the home of the gods.

Orkney Islands. A group of about 70 small islands lying off the northern tip of Scotland. The Orkney Islands were a Danish possession until the 15th century, when they were acquired by Scotland. About 19,000 people live on the islands.

Peloponnesus. A large peninsula and province of southern Greece, connected with the mainland by the narrow Isthmus of Corinth. The Peloponnesus is the site of ancient Corinth and Sparta.

Perestroika. A Russian word meaning "restructuring." Mikhail Gorbachev used the word in 1987 in his call for reform in the Soviet Union. The term quickly came into general use to signify the reorganization of the Soviet economy to make it more responsive to consumer demand, and the reorganization of the Soviet political system to make it more democratic.

Pyrenees. A major European mountain range extending some 270 miles (435 km) along the entire Spanish-French border, from the Bay of Biscay to the south coast of the Gulf of Lions. The highest peak is Pico de Aneto, 11,168 feet (3,404 m).

Rhine. A West European river that rises in the Swiss Alps and flows north and west, forming parts of the boundaries of the countries of Liechtenstein, Switzerland, France, and Germany. In Germany it crosses a rich, densely populated, and highly industrialized region before turning west into The Netherlands, where it divides into two branches, the Nederrijn and the Waal, which empty into the North Sea.

The Rhine is 820 miles (1,320 km) long, and its major tributaries include the Neckar, Main, Ruhr, Lippe, and Moselle rivers. It is navigable for most of its course, and is connected by many canals with other major European river systems.

Rhône. A west European river that flows some 500 miles (800 km) through Switzerland and France. It rises in the Swiss Alps, passes through Lake Geneva, and crosses into France. Joined at Lyon by the Saône River, it turns south and empties into the Mediterranean Sea west of Marseille.

Riviera. A Mediterranean seacoast in southern France and northwestern Italy. Its blue water and white beaches have made it one of the world's most popular resort areas.

Romanov dynasty. The line of czars who ruled Russia from 1613 until the Russian Revolution in 1917. They traced their lineage to Anastasia Romanova, first wife of the czar Ivan the Terrible (ruled 1547–1584). The line ended with the assassination of the last czar, Nicholas II, and his son Alexis in 1917.

Sardinia. The second largest island in the Mediterranean Sea, lying to the west of and belonging to Italy. Sardinia, which has a long and violent history, has been occupied successively by

STANDING STONES on the Orkney Islands may date from the same period as Stonehenge; there is archaeological evidence of occupation of the islands from about 3000 B.C.

ROMANTIC CASTLES overlook the Rhine, an important shipping link in the highly industrialized area.

Carthaginians, Romans, Vandals, Byzantines, Saracens, and Spaniards. The island is generally poor, although it has some important natural resources and a growing tourist industry.

Scandinavia. A large, mountainous peninsula of northwestern Europe washed by the Arctic Ocean on the north, the Norwegian Sea on the west, the North Sea, Skagerrak and Kattegat straits on the south, and the Baltic Sea and Gulf of Bothnia on the southeast. It is shared by the nations of Norway and Sweden.

Seine. A river of northern France that rises in the highlands northwest of Dijon. It flows through Paris and empties into the English Channel at Le Havre after a course of 482 miles (776 km).

Shetland Islands. An island group lying about 130 miles (210 km) off the north coast of Scotland. The islands are sparsely populated, with people living on some 20 of the 100 islands. Like the Orkney Islands, the Shetland Islands were acquired by Scotland from Denmark in the 15th century.

Siberia. The region of Russia extending east from the Ural Mountains to the Pacific Ocean, bordered on the north by the Arctic Ocean and bordered on the south by Kazakhstan, China, and Mongolia. Siberia encompasses an area of over 5 million square miles (12,953,000 sq. km), but has a population density of only about seven people per square mile. The region has a great wealth of natural resources; however, its severe

climate hampers exploitation of those resources. Siberia was the traditional place of exile for criminals, political dissenters, and citizens caught up in the Russian prison system. It is also an area of great natural resources.

Sicily. The largest island of the Mediterranean. Politically a part of Italy, Sicily is separated from the southwestern tip of the Italian mainland by the

narrow Strait of Messina. Most of Sicily is mountainous and rugged, and the climate is dry and mild.

Skagerrak. A strait between Norway and Denmark, about 150 miles (240 km) long and 80 miles (130 km) wide. It leads into the North Sea in the southwest and the Kattegat in the northeast, and forms an important link in the North Sea-Baltic waterway.

THE INVITING HARBORS of the Riviera in France and Italy make this resort area one of the most popular in the Mediterranean.

Ural Mountains. A mountain system in Russia that extends for about 1300 miles (2,100 km) from the Kara Sea to the Ural River, forming the traditional geographic boundary between Europe and Asia. The Urals can be divided into three sections—the Northern Urals, which contain the highest peaks; the Central Urals, which are gently rounded; and the Southern Urals, which are formed by three parallel ranges.

Vesuvius. An active volcano in Italy, lying on the eastern shore of the Bay of Naples. Vesuvius is about 4,000 feet (1,220 m) above sea level, but its exact height varies with each eruption. In 79 A.D. it buried Roman Pompeii.

Vistula. The longest river in Poland. The Vistula rises on the north slopes of the Carpathian Mountains in southeastern Poland and flows 675 miles (1089 km) to the Baltic Sea. A number of important cities are located on the banks of the Vistula, including Kraków, Warsaw, and Gdansk. The river is navigable to above Kraków, and canals link it to other important waterways in Eastern Europe.

THE TOWER BRIDGE, located at the Tower of London, is one of several bridges that cross the Thames River.

Stuart. The dynastic name of rulers of Scotland (1371–1714) and England (1603–1714). The last Tudor ruler, Elizabeth I, died childless in 1603. Her cousin, James VI of Scotland, took the English throne as James I, effectively uniting the two countries. The Stuart rulers of England were James I, Charles I, Charles II, James II, William III and Mary II (joint rulers), and Anne.

Tagus. The longest river of the Iberian peninsula. It rises in Spain's eastern mountains, flows west across Spain, and forms a small section of the border with Portugal before turning southwest to enter the Atlantic Ocean at Lisbon after a course of 626 miles (1,008 km).

Tatars. Also called Tartars. Turkic-speaking Muslim peoples who live in Russia near the Volga River region. The name once referred to Mongol and other Asiatic peoples who invaded Europe and became powerful in Russia.

Thames. A river 210 miles (338 km) long in southern Britain. It rises in Gloucestershire, flows east into the densely settled fertile English Lowlands, through London, and empties into the North Sea.

Transylvania. A plateau region in central Romania bounded on the north, east, and south by the Carpathian Mountains and the Transylvania Alps. The region had a long history as an independent principality. It is the scene of considerable ethnic tension between a large Hungarian minority and the Romanian majority.

Tudor. The dynastic name of the English royal family that ruled from 1485 to 1603. Tudor rulers of England included Henry VII, Henry VIII, Edward VI, Mary I, and Elizabeth I. The Tudor line was succeeded by the Scottish Stuart line.

Tyrrhenian Sea. An arm of the Mediterranean Sea. It lies between Italy on the east, Corsica and Sardinia on the west, and Sicily on the south.

Ural. A river in the west-central Russia. It rises in the southern Ural Mountains and flows southwest, and south again, emptying into the Caspian Sea. The river is about 1,500 miles (2,415 km) long.

Volga. The longest river of Russia and of Europe, 2,293 miles (3,692 km) long. It rises in the Valdai Hills northwest of Moscow and follows a winding course to the Caspian Sea. The Volga flows first east and southeast to Kazan, and then generally south to Astrakhan, where it forms an extensive delta. Canals join the Volga to the Baltic and Black Sea river systems.

Warsaw Pact. A defensive alliance formed in 1955 by the Soviet Union and its Eastern European allies. The alliance was organized in response to the admission of West Germany to the North Atlantic Treaty Organization (NATO).

THE ARCHAEOLOGICAL SITE of Pompeii has been partially excavated from the layers of ash deposited on it by the eruption of Vesuvius in 79 A.D.

Its members were the Soviet Union, Bulgaria, Czechoslovakia, Hungary, Poland, and Romania. Albania and East Germany withdrew in 1968 and 1990 respectively. It was completely disbanded in 1991.

Wars of the Roses. A series of dynastic wars fought from 1455 to 1485 between rival branches of the English royal family. The wars are so named because of the roses that were the symbol of each faction: red for the House of Lancaster and white for the House of York. The civil wars ended when the factions were united by the marriage of Henry VII to Elizabeth of York.

Yenisey. A major river of Asia, located in Siberia. It is formed from the Greater Yenisey, rising in the Sayan Mountains of Mongolia, and the Lesser Yenisey, rising in the Siberian highlands. They meet at Kyzyl to form the Yenisey proper. It is over 2,500 miles (4,000 km) long. Major tributaries of the Yenisey include the Lower Tunguska, Stony Tunguska, Angara, and Abakan rivers. The Yenisey empties into the Yenisey Gulf of the Kara Sea.

THE VOLGA RIVER is dear to the hearts of Russians. This scene of barge handlers by Repin (c. 1870 or 1871) hangs in the State Museum in St. Petersburg.

26 Europe and Russia

THE HELP DESK

➤ **Spend** some time each day locating countries and cities that are in the news on a map or globe.

➤ **Do** you like to sample different foods? French, Italian, German, etc? What distinguishes each of the above cuisines? Why?

➤ **As** you read about different historical places, use current maps to find modern locations with the same names, for example, Rome, GA; Troy, NY; etc.

➤ **Study** the maps that show where the ancient civilizations developed. Note that most were around rivers. Why do you think that happened?

➤ **Document** your family's ethnic heritage. What country did your forefathers come from? When did they come? Why? Who? What famous people share your background? Older relatives would be a particularly good source for this type of information.

➤ **Help** plan the next family vacation. Where would you like to go or what would you like to do? Write to tourist bureaus and chambers of commerce (the library can help find addresses and give you other ideas). Use the information to plot routes, fun places, etc. Keep a journal of the trip. What would you do again; what do you wish you hadn't done?

➤ **Study** the continental map. Pay particular attention to the locator inset map that will help you locate the portion of the globe that Europe and Russia occupy. Are they in the Northern or Southern Hemisphere? In the Eastern or Western hemisphere? Are they north or south of the equator? What are the major physical features— any large rivers, mountains, deserts? Make a list of the names of those features.

➤ **Study** the individual country maps. Use the locator inset map to pinpoint the country and then turn to the continent map to confirm the location. Look at the list of physical features you made as you studied the continental map. Do any of those features appear in the country you are studying? How do you think the presence of that feature affects the country?

➤ **Make** a list of the largest cities. How does the size of those cities compare with cities that you are familiar with? Why do you think that people began to live in that area and continued to live there?

➤ **Plan** a trip. Select a destination from the place you are to a place in Europe or Russia. Where would you stop along the way? How would you travel from one place to another? How long would each leg of the trip require? What kind of clothes should you take? Can you find out what kind of money you should have at each stop?

➤ **Review** the historical background of the country. Is it a country that dates back thousands or hundreds of years, or is it much younger? Write a short report noting major events in the history in chronological order. Now compare those events to events in countries nearby. Is there any similarity? Are they friends or enemies? Do the people speak the same language? What are other similarities or differences that you have detected? Don't forget to use the History of the World volume for related information.

➤ **Make** a list of people important in the development of one of the countries. As you note events in your historical report, watch for names of people associated with those events. Read newspapers and listen to the news to add current names to your list. See if you can find pictures of current rulers or other important people, and try to determine why they are important to the country. Check the Index to see if any of them are discussed elsewhere in The Volume Library.

➤ **When** traveling across time zones, practice thinking, "If it is ____ o'clock in London, then it must be ____ o'clock in Moscow."

➤ **Look** at maps and globes with a younger sibling or friend. What do they represent? Make simple maps and diagrams such as a floor plan of your house, the block you live on, school, and playground. Help the child learn directions—start with up, down, right, and left, and progress to north, south, east and west. Help the child tell the difference between land and water on a globe and identify the continents and major countries by name.

➤ **Imagine** a route you travel frequently, for example, home to school or home to mall. Write instructions to lead someone unfamiliar with the route. Include directions, distances, landmarks, etc. Test your skill by having someone follow your instructions.

➤ **Draw** a map illustrating the above instructions. Be sure it uses standard mapping guidelines with North at the top and a rough distance indication if possible.

➤ **For** a list of helpful references, go to the *customers* section of www.southwestern.com.

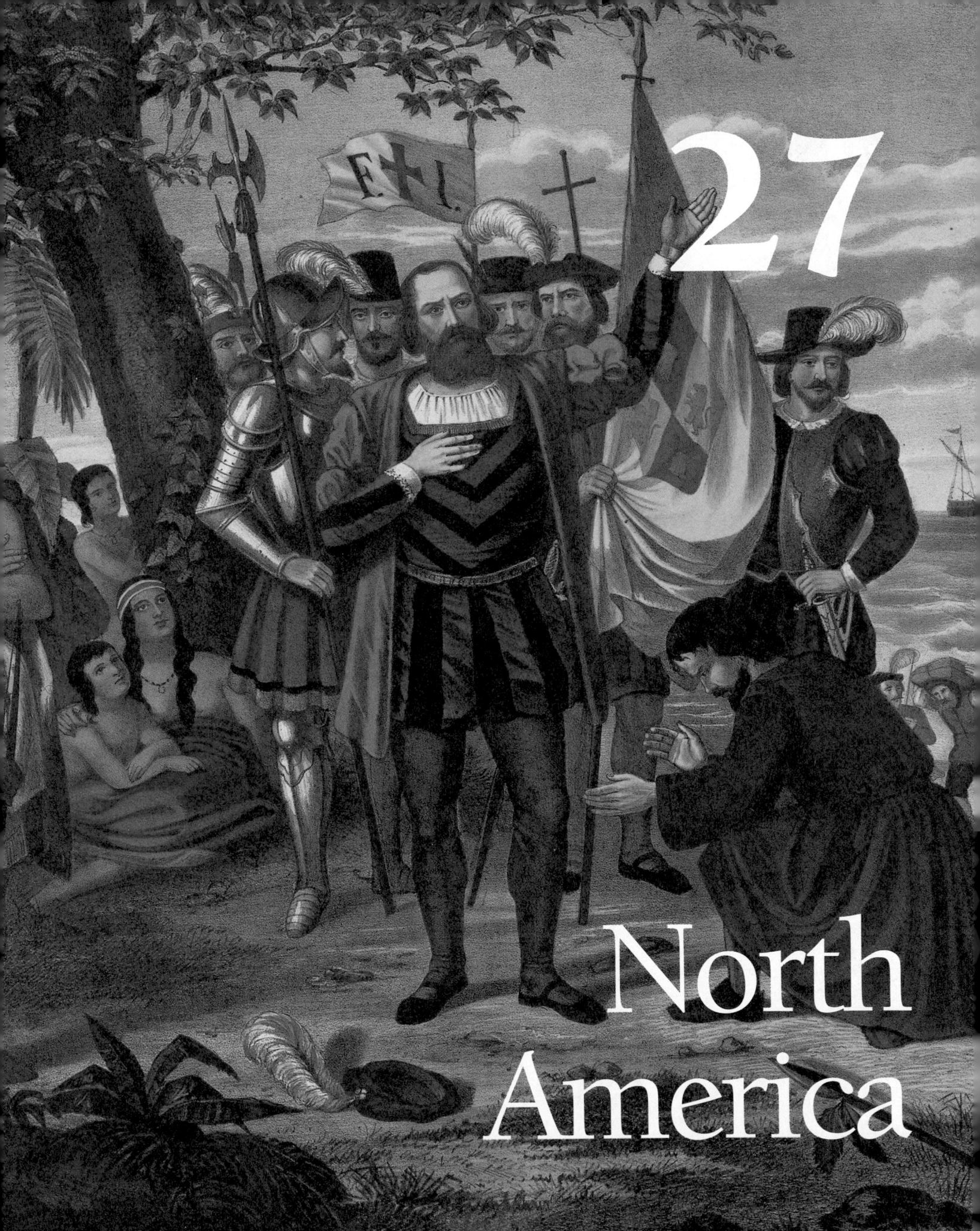

27

North
America

27 North America

Overleaf: *Columbus landing in America*

Contents

North America

The North American continent includes Canada, Greenland, the United States, Mexico, the countries of Central America, and the islands of the West Indies in the Caribbean Sea. It is the third largest continent in landmass, covering about 9,360,000 square miles, and has the fourth largest population, with about 499 million people.

The major part of North America is made up of Canada and the United States. The two countries together are sometimes referred to as Anglo-America because many of their settlers came from England, and English is the major language spoken.

Mexico and Central America have historical and cultural ties with South America, and Spanish is the main language. They are discussed as a unit in this volume. The Caribbean islands make up the third unit in the volume. The large icy island of Greenland is a dependency of Denmark and is discussed in the EUROPE AND RUSSIA volume because of its cultural, political, and economic ties with Europe.

North America has many extremes of climate and environment. In the far north, the arctic reaches of Alaska and northern Canada remain perpetually frozen, but the southwestern United States has produced one of the highest temperatures recorded on Earth, in Death Valley, California. The American southwest is characteristically hot and dry, yet the Pacific northwest, including the states of Oregon and Washington and the Canadian Province of British Columbia, annually records an abundance of rainfall. Mexico and Central America offer contrasts from cool and dry highlands to

tropical coastal areas, and from cloud forests to rain forests. The West Indies have consistently balmy weather and tropical conditions.

The North American people are as diverse as the land in which they dwell. Across the continent are hundreds of groups of Native Americans, whose ancestors came across the landmass that originally connected the continent with Asia, where the Bering Sea is today. They were probably following the herds of the mammals upon which they depended.

Archaeological finds continue to push the date of that first migration further and further back, and some believe that they may have come as early as 35,000 years ago. From these hunters developed the many groups of Native Americans that inhabited the continent when it was discovered by Europeans.

Canada and the United States were settled primarily by the English, although the French were also heavily involved in the settlement of Canada and have left their imprint on the Province of Quebec. Today their population is a melting pot of the nationalities that have found refuge in both countries. The Spanish were the primary colonizers of Mexico and Central America, and many European countries claimed colonies in the West Indies, where the population also demonstrates the influence of black Africans brought in as slaves to work in agriculture.

Anglo-America is rich in natural resources, with many underground resources such as oil, coal, and natural gas. It also has rich agricultural lands and forests. It produces about a third of

THE STARS AND STRIPES are an integral part of a Fourth of July celebration for children all over the United States.

the world's manufactured goods and grows more agricultural products than any other country, much of which it exports.

The countries of Canada, Mexico, and the United States are united in a trade agreement called the North American Free Trade Agreement (NAFTA), creating one of the world's largest free-trade zones. The agreement took effect in 1994, replacing a similar agreement between Canada and the United States signed in 1989. In a world that is recognizing the realities of a global economy, but is faced with growing nationalism and ethnic identification, it is hoped that this agreement will serve as a model for future agreements.

YOUNG GIRLS participate in a traditional celebration in Mexico.

SCHOOLCHILDREN absorbed in their school activities in Canada reflect the importance placed on education in that country.

The United States and Canada

Canada and the United States together have an area of 7.5 million square miles (19.3 million square kilometers). They extend from the Gulf of Mexico on the south to the Arctic Ocean on the north, and from the Atlantic Ocean on the east to the Pacific Ocean on the west, where they are separated from Asia by the Bering Strait. The two countries are among the world's leading industrial nations and rank high in economic development and in per capita wealth.

Although independent of each other, Canada and the United States share a complex web of cultural, social, and economic ties. English is a predominant language in both countries, although French is the predominant language in the Province of Quebec in Canada. Both Canada and the United States were shaped in part by British political and cultural ideas during their formative years. Today these two countries have a combined population almost five times that of Great Britain. They have also developed a social and cultural life that has been profoundly enriched by immigrants from many other nations.

The land. Canada and the United States can be divided into seven physiographic regions: the Western Highlands; the Coastal Range; the Basin and Range; the Eastern Highlands, including the Canadian Shield; the Eastern Coastal Plain; the Inland, or Interior, Plain; and the Ozark-Ouachita Highlands.

In the western part of the continent, the Western Highlands run roughly northwest to southeast from Alaska through western Canada into Mexico. The core of the Western Highlands is a chain of seismically active mountain

ranges known collectively as the Rocky Mountains. These ranges extend from British Columbia in western Canada to central New Mexico in the United States. North of the Rocky Mountains are the Mackenzie Mountains in the Yukon, the Alaska Range in southern Alaska, and the Brooks Range in northern Alaska. South of the Rockies extend two major mountain ranges, the Sierra Madre Occidental and the Sierra Madre Oriental ranges of Mexico. The highest point in North America is the peak of Mt. McKinley, in the Alaska Range, which rises to 20,320 feet (6,194 meters) above sea level.

West of the Rocky Mountains and running parallel to the Pacific are the Coast Mountains, which extend from Alaska to southern British Columbia. South of the Coast Mountains rises the Coastal Range, which includes the Cascade Mountains in Washington and Oregon and the Sierra Nevada in California. Between the Coastal Range and the Rocky Mountains is the Basin and Range region, a huge arid-to-semiarid complex of plateaus broken by short mountain ranges and deeply carved canyons. To the southwest the plateau declines to the lowest elevation on the North American continent, 282 feet (86 meters) below sea level at Death Valley, California.

The Eastern Highlands, although significantly less imposing than the Western Highlands, is the oldest geologic formation in North America. Consequently, weathering and geological forces have had a much longer time to work on the topography, and a great variety of terrains can be found in this vast region. In the northeastern corner of the continent, the Canadian Shield, the oldest part of the Eastern Highlands, extends from the coast of Labrador to the west around Hudson Bay and then northwest to the Arctic. This enormous plateau extends south into parts of Minnesota, Wisconsin, Michigan, and New York in the United States.

To the east of the Canadian Shield, the Eastern Highlands continues as a cordillera of related uplands and mountain ranges that extends from northern Labrador into the Laurentian Highlands of Quebec and then south into the Appalachian Mountain system, which roughly parallels the Atlantic coast from Newfoundland in Canada to Georgia and Alabama in the United States.

To the east of the Appalachians is the Eastern Coastal Plain, a lowland area that is relatively narrow in the north but broadens considerably in the south, extending south across a large part of Florida and west, past the southern limit of the Appalachians, along the Gulf of Mexico.

Between the Western and Eastern highlands, extending from central Canada to southwestern Texas, lies a great, fertile lowland called the Inland, or Interior, Plain, or more commonly, Great Plains. This region, which over geologic time was repeatedly submerged under inland seas and then uplifted,

centered
US

centred
Brit.

centimeters
US

centimetres
Brit.

THE ROCKY MOUNTAINS are a seismically active mountain range that extends from British Columbia in western Canada to central New Mexico in the United States.

consists of layers of sedimentary rock upon which have been built rich, deep soils. The Inland Plain extends north through the continent from the Gulf of Mexico, rising slightly in elevation to the edge of the Canadian Shield, and continuing northwest along the Mackenzie River basin to the Arctic Ocean. In the United States, the eastern portion of this region rises in elevation to meet the western hills of the Appalachians. The western portion rises steadily to the eastern base of the Rocky Mountains.

The Ozark-Ouachita Highlands is an isolated region centered in Arkansas and southern Missouri. It includes the Ouachita Mountains, situated in west-central Arkansas south of the Arkansas River, and the Ozark Plateau, north of the Arkansas River at the northwest corner of Arkansas and southwest corner of Missouri.

Rivers and lakes. The largest river system in North America is that formed by the Mississippi River and its numerous tributaries, which provide drainage for the southern part of the Inland Plain.

Many other rivers not a part of the Mississippi system empty into the Gulf of Mexico. First among these is the Rio Grande, which rises in southwestern Colorado and flows generally southeastward some 1,885 miles (3,033 kilometers), forming part of the U.S. border with Mexico, where the river is known as the Río Bravo.

The Great Lakes-St. Lawrence River system, shared by the United States and Canada, drains the surrounding lands, carrying its waters northeastward into the Atlantic Ocean. The five Great Lakes—Superior, Michigan, Huron, Erie, and Ontario—constitute one of the most notable physiographic features of the continent and the largest freshwater system on Earth.

The northern part of the Inland Plain is drained largely by the Mackenzie River system, which flows into the Beaufort Sea. The Mackenzie River system ranks as one of the major river systems of the world.

Hudson Bay drains a large portion of Canada. Among the numerous rivers that flow into the bay are the Churchill, Nelson, and Severn.

Several major rivers flow westward from the Great Divide, including the Yukon, which rises in Yukon Territory and flows southwestward through Alaska to the Bering Sea; the Columbia, which rises in British Columbia and flows to the Pacific Ocean; and the Colorado, which rises in northwestern Colorado and flows west and south to the Gulf of California, an arm of the Pacific Ocean.

Climate. The northern part of North America, including most of Alaska and interior northern Canada, is arctic or subarctic. The subsoil stays frozen year-round and is known as permafrost (see the discussion of permafrost on page 41 in the EARTH volume). Winter temperatures average approximately -10° to -30°F (-23° to -34°C), and summer temperatures average about 40° to 60°F (4° to 16°C). Precipitation ranges from less than 10 inches (25 centimeters) to about 20 inches (50 centimeters) annually, almost entirely in the form of snow.

The Pacific coastal region, from southern Alaska to northern California, has a much milder climate, with temperatures averaging from about 20° to 50°F (-7° to 10°C) in the winter and 50° to 70°F (10° to 21°C) in the summer. Rainfall is abundant, ranging from 40 to 80 inches (102 to 204 centimeters) annually.

Western Canada east of the coastal ranges has a milder climate than that of the northern interior, with winter temperatures ranging from about -10° to 20°F (-23° to -7°C) in winter to about 60° to 70°F (16° to 21°C) in the summer. Annual precipitation ranges from about 10 to 40 inches (25 to 102 centimeters), with lower precipitation occurring inland.

The eastern two-thirds of the continent, exclusive of interior and northern Canada, have a generally moderate and moist climate, with average temperatures and precipitation levels increasing from north to south and from west to east. Average winter temperatures range from about 10° to 30°F (-12° to -1°C) across the Great Lakes and into eastern Canada and the northeastern United States to 50° to 70°F (10° to 21°C) in the southeast from Georgia and Florida along the Gulf Coast to eastern Texas. Summer temperatures average about 60° to 75°F (16° to 24°C) across the Great Lakes and St. Lawrence River valley and into New England and the Maritime Provinces. In the south, summer temperatures average about 90°F (32°C). Annual precipitation ranges from about 20 to 40 inches (51 to 102 centimeters) in the north, and about 40 to 60 inches (102 to 152 centimeters) from the Maritime Provinces and coastal New England through the southeastern United States and the Ohio and Mississippi river valleys. Parts of the Gulf Coast and the southern tip of Florida receive 80 inches (203 centimeters) or more of rainfall annually.

The southwestern United States and the Basin and Range region have the warmest and driest climates in North America. Winter temperatures average from below 40°F (4°C) in the north to about 60°F (16°C) in the south. However, summer temperatures average from 80° to more than 90°F (27° to 32°C) and summer temperatures in the southern part of the region frequently exceed 100°F (38°C). Annual precipitation ranges from less than 10 inches (25 centimeters) to about 25 inches (64 centimeters).

Vegetation. North America has a broad variety of vegetation, the most prominent feature being a vast coniferous forest extending from Newfoundland and around the southern shore of Hudson Bay, then stretching northwest, extending arms westward into interior Alaska and southward across the coastal mountain ranges and the Rocky Mountains. Southeastern Canada, from Newfoundland through the St. Lawrence River valley and the Great Lakes region, has mixed coniferous and broadleaf forests.

The eastern half of the United States has mixed coniferous and broadleaf forests in the northeast, broadleaf forests from the Mid-Atlantic states to the upper Mississippi River valley, and mixed coniferous and broadleaf forests in the southeast and along the lower Mississippi valley and the eastern Gulf Coast.

The eastern half of the Inland Plain, from the western Gulf Coast and south-

LIGHTHOUSE ROCK is a prominent feature of the rugged landscape in Palo Duro Canyon State Park. With more than 16,000 acres, the park is the largest in Texas.

eastern Texas into west-central Canada, is primarily temperate, tall grass prairie. To the west the tall grasses thin out to short grass prairie, or steppe, and in the southwest to desert scrub. The Basin and Range region has a sparse covering of desert vegetation.

The northern rim of the continent, from the Aleutian Islands along coastal Alaska and through far northern Canada, is tundra.

The people. The population of the United States is 281,422,000 (2000 Census) and that of Canada is 31,902,000 (2002 estimate). The population density for the United States was 80 persons per square mile (31 persons per square kilometer), less than three-quarters of the world average, and for Canada 9 persons per square mile (3 persons per square kilometer).

The bulk of Canada's population live in a small corridor extending over southeastern Quebec and Ontario and in a pocket of the Pacific Northwest

centered on the city of Vancouver. Both areas have moderate climates, are rich in natural resources, and are well situated for growth.

The population of the United States is clustered in a small number of zones. The oldest is an urban corridor along the East Coast from north of Boston, Massachusetts, to Washington, D.C.

A second zone is located along the southern shores of the Great Lakes, extending from western New York to eastern Wisconsin.

The third zone in the United States is located on the Pacific coast of California. A fourth center of population is in Texas, and a fifth is on the Florida peninsula. These last two are the most rapidly growing of the five urban corridors of the United States.

The rugged terrain of the Western Highlands limits the growth of population, as do the terrain and arid climate of the Basin and Range region. Similarly, the frozen expanses of northern Canada and interior Alaska have extremely sparse populations.

North America is a continent of ethnic diversity, less in Canada than in the United States. Most Canadians are descended from immigrants from the British Isles or from France.

THE BEAUTIFUL FOLIAGE in New England and the Atlantic Provinces in Canada is a major tourist attraction in the fall.

Note on the Country Listings

Most of the information included in the following section is self-explanatory; however, some of the recurring statistical information requires a word of explanation about its importance.

Literacy. The literacy rate, that is, the percentage of people who can read out of the total population, gives an important indication of the level of education in a country.

Per capita GDP. This is the gross domestic product divided by the total population; it provides an indication of the standard of living in each country. (Each country's current world rank is also provided.)

The ethnic diversity of the United States is almost legendary. The leading countries of origin include Germany, England, Ireland, Italy, Mexico, France, Poland, The Netherlands, Scotland, Sweden, Norway, and Russia. About 12 percent of the U.S. population is of African descent. About 9.5 percent is of Hispanic origin, and about 3 percent is of Asian origin. Native Americans number almost 2 million.

Languages. The great majority of the population of the United States speak English, but a growing segment, about 14 percent of the population, speak a language other than English. Spanish has become an important language, particularly in the southwestern United States. In Canada the predominant languages are English and French. French is the predominant language in use in the Province of Quebec, and many Canadians are fluent in both French and English.

Religion. Christianity is the predominant faith in the United States. The 1990 Census recorded more than 86 million members of Protestant churches and more than 58 million members of the Roman Catholic Church. Among the Protestant churches there are a number of Baptist denominations, including the Southern Baptist Convention, with some 15 million members, and the National Baptist Convention (U.S.A.), with about 8 million members. Other Protestant denominations include the United Methodist Church, the Church of God in Christ, the Evangelical Lutheran Church, the Church of Jesus Christ of Latter-Day Saints (the Mormons), the Presbyterian Church (U.S.A.), the African Methodist Episcopal Church, and the Episcopal Church. Almost 6 million persons are members of the Jewish faith. Islam is a small but growing religion in the United States. In Canada Roman Catholicism has the largest number of adherents, followed by Protestantism, Judaism,

and Buddhism. The leading Protestant denomination is the Anglican Church of Canada.

Economy. The United States and Canada have a combined gross national product of over $6 trillion, almost double that of Japan and almost four times that of Germany. Per capita incomes of both countries are among the highest in the world. Worker productivity is the highest in the world. North America possesses an abundance of natural resources, especially those needed to support a modern industrial economy. The North American transportation system is large, diversified, and highly efficient, and its communications systems are broad-ranging and sophisticated. North America has an abundance of institutions of higher learning and industrial research and development centers; they provide the knowledge and innovations that keep the continent's high-technology economy growing.

Manufacturing is an important activity in eastern Canada, and the development of natural resources, including timber, minerals, and petroleum, in eastern and western Canada is a key component of the country's economy.

Agriculture. The Inland Plain of North America has been called the world's breadbasket. The United States and Canada are the leading wheat exporters in the world, with combined sales in excess of $6.5 billion annually. Together the two countries produced 96,791,000 metric tons of wheat in 1992, about 17 percent of the world total. The United States is the world's leading producer of corn; Canada ranks twelfth. In 1992 the United States and Canada together produced 245,657,000 metric tons of corn, about 46 percent of the world total.

The two countries produce many other crops, including rye, oats, barley, soybeans, and potatoes. Cotton is important in the southern United States.

The United States and Canada harvest about 7 million metric tons of fish annually, about 7 percent of the world total. The United States is the world's leading meat producer, processing more than 31 million tons of meat, almost 17 percent of the world total, in 1993. Livestock include dairy and beef cattle, sheep, hogs, chickens, and turkeys.

Only about 4 percent of North America's workforce is engaged in agriculture, including farming, animal husbandry, fishing, and forestry. The percentage rises when agriculture-related employment, as in transportation, storage, manufacture and repair of machinery, and food processing, is included. Nonetheless, the figure indicates a remarkable efficiency in North American agriculture.

Natural resources. Timber industries are located in the Pacific Northwest, centered in British Columbia and the states of Washington, Oregon, and northern California. Southeastern Ontario and Quebec and northern New England are heavily forested and are centers of timber-related industries, as is the southeastern United States.

North America has important petroleum and natural gas reserves. The most important oil fields are in Texas, Oklahoma, Arkansas, Louisiana, and Alaska. Oil fields have also been developed in western Canada, mostly in Alberta and Saskatchewan.

North America is rich in coal, with fields in Nova Scotia and western Canada, the Appalachian region of the eastern United States, Texas, and Michigan. Nearly all the continent's supply of anthracite is located in Pennsylvania.

High-grade iron ore is found in Labrador and around Lake Superior, including southwestern Ontario and northern Minnesota and Wisconsin. Southeastern Ontario is rich in platinum, nickel, and copper. Northern Manitoba contains large reserves of zinc ore, as well as copper and nickel. The United States and Canada have reserves of uranium ore, and both are major producers of aluminum and sulfur. Canada is a major producer of potash, zinc, and nickel, and the United States is a major producer of iron, copper, lead, and salt.

Industry. The North American industrial heartland stretches from New England and southern Quebec through southern Ontario and the Great Lakes region. It produces almost every conceivable product, from iron and steel to processed foods, automobiles, plastics, paper products, jewelry, machine tools, textiles, and high-technology electronic equipment. However, recent decades have seen the expansion of industry in other regions. The center of the automobile industry is in Michigan and southern Ontario, but factories have been built in Tennessee and Ohio. Textiles and furniture are important in the southeastern United States. Washington State is the home of a great aerospace and high-technology corporation, and California is the home of numerous computer hardware and software developers

centers
US
centres
Brit.

aluminum
US
aluminium
Brit.

THE VAST WHEAT FIELDS of the Inland Plain of North America have been called the world's breadbasket, producing about 17 percent of the world's total wheat yearly.

THE TIMBER INDUSTRIES are important to the economies of the Pacific Northwest, northern New England, and southeastern Ontario and Quebec.

and manufacturers. Refining of petroleum and petroleum products is centered in Texas and Louisiana, and Texas has become an important manufacturing center for electrical and electronic equipment, machinery, and transportation equipment. The Southwest has become an important manufacturing center.

Transportation and trade. The growth of transportation and trade in North America has paralleled the growth of its population and its economic activities. In the 17th and 18th centuries, there were few roads, and even the best, which connected the main population centers, were difficult to traverse. The 19th century saw improvement and expansion of the road system and a boom in canal construction in the United States. Railroad mileage and use reached a peak in North America in the 1920s and 1930s, then began to decline as automobiles, buses, trucks, and airplanes became important, then dominant, forms of transportation. The 1940s and 1950s saw a boom in road and highway construction in the United States and Canada. Today North America's road, rail, air, and waterborne systems provide transportation to and from most parts of the continent.

The United States and Canada are each other's most important trading partners. The United States receives about three-quarters of Canada's exports and supplies about two-thirds of its imports. Canada's second most important trading partner is Japan, followed by the United Kingdom.

Economic trends. The North American Free Trade Agreement (NAFTA), which was signed in 1992 by the United States, Canada, and Mexico, and went into effect in 1994, gradually eliminates virtually all tariffs and other impediments to trade and investment among the three countries, creating a single, integrated economic bloc. An important part of the accord was the restructuring of Mexico's trade relationship with the United States. The elimination of Mexico's steep tariffs and prohibitive regulations on U.S. goods will increase U.S. exports to Mexico, and it is expected that investment in Mexico will also increase, providing that country with the capital to build new industries and sell more products to the United States and Canada.

Government and politics. The United States and Canada have adopted representative forms of government. Each system is an outgrowth of British government and law, yet the two systems have marked differences as well as distinct similarities. The difference in form is due at least in part to the fact that the U.S. system of government was established after a rupture in relations between Great Britain and its 13 American colonies, whereas the Canadian system of government was established over a long period of political connection between Canada and Great Britain.

Like the British system, the Canadian federal government has a bicameral Parliament. The lower house, the popularly elected House of Commons, is similar to its British counterpart, and its upper house, the appointed Senate, is similar to the British House of Lords. The head of government is the prime minister, leader of the majority party (or majority coalition) in Parliament. The head of state is the British monarch, who is represented by an appointed governor-general.

The United States federal government also has a bicameral legislature, known collectively as the Congress. The upper house, or Senate, includes two members from each of the 50 states. Originally, members of the Senate were chosen by the state legislatures, but in 1913 the U.S. Constitution was amended to enable direct election of U.S. senators. The lower house of Congress, the House of Representatives, consists of 435 members. The number of House members apportioned to each state is determined by population, according to the census taken every ten years. The head of state is the president, popularly elected.

As the 21st century gets under way, the United States and Canada face important political and economic challenges at home and abroad. Into this period of rapid change they bring the ideals of representative democracy and international cooperation and the determination to work peacefully toward a better future for all.

NAFTA, the North American Free Trade Agreement between the United States, Canada, and Mexico, has aroused strong sentiments on both sides of the issue.

United States

The United States Today

The United States of America is one of the largest countries in the world, both in area and in population. In area, it ranks fourth behind Russia, Canada, and China. In population, it ranks third, behind China and India. Economically, it is the most powerful nation in the world. Its standard of living is by far the highest of all large countries, but in terms of per capita income it ranks behind several smaller countries in the oil-rich Middle East and in northern Europe.

Two great forces have formed the United States—immigration and development. Many Americans can trace their ancestry to people who arrived in America during its first 200 years.

The earliest immigrants brought with them a determination to conquer the vast and nearly empty continent. They invented new means of transportation to cross it, new communications to keep in touch across its great distances, and new implements to farm its lands, recover its natural resources, and encourage trade. They developed a new kind of government as well.

The story of immigration and development is to a large degree the story of

kilometers
US

kilometres
Brit.

American history. But to understand it fully, one must know about the land itself and about the people of the United States today.

United States

Official name: *United States of America*
Area: *3,655,318 sq. mi., 9,372,610 sq. km.*
Type of government: *Republic*
Population: *281,421,906*
Capital: *Washington, D.C. (Pop., 572,000)*
Largest city: *New York City, New York (Pop., 8,008,000)*
Languages: *English, Spanish*
Literacy: *97%;* **Currency:** *Dollar*
Per capita GDP: *$36,300 (Rank: 2nd)*

The land. The main landmass of the United States, accommodating 48 of its

50 states, occupies the central part of the North American continent, bordering Canada to the north and Mexico to the south. U.S. lands stretch from a long Atlantic coastline in the east to the Pacific in the west.

The state of Alaska is a vast frigid region in the northwest corner of North America, separated from the 48 contiguous states by the Canadian Province of British Columbia. Hawaii is an island chain in the Pacific, some 2,000 miles (3,218 kilometers) southwest of California.

The landmass of the 48 contiguous states is defined by four regions of mountains and highlands. The first of these is the Coastal range, running parallel to the Pacific shoreline. The second range is the Rocky Mountains, which runs from northern Idaho and Montana south and east as far as north-central New Mexico.

A third mountain chain, the Appalachians, runs roughly parallel to the Atlantic coast from Maine in the north to Alabama in the south.

The fourth mountain region is the Ozark-Ouachita Highlands, in Arkansas and southern Missouri.

The other main landforms of the United States can be defined in relation to these mountain ranges. In the West, between the Coastal and Rocky Mountain ranges, is the Basin and Range region. In the East and South, along the Atlantic and Gulf of Mexico coasts, are the coastal plains. Finally, in the great midland region between the Rockies and the Appalachians is the Inland Plain, one of the most productive agricultural regions in the world.

Alaska has extensive ranges of coastal mountains, including the highest point in North America (Mt. McKinley, 20,320 feet [6,194 meters] above sea level); these mountains separate a narrow coastal area from the state's vast arctic interior. The Hawaiian Islands are of volcanic origin.

Climate. In general, the climate of the United States is temperate. Temperatures are generally higher in the south and lower in the north. Precipitation is, for the most part, higher in the east and lower in the west.

The Northeastern states are generally cool and damp. Winter low temperatures range from 0° to 30°F (-18° to -1°C) and summer highs range from 70° to 90°F (21° to 32°C). Precipitation is moderate, ranging from 30 to 45 inches (76 to 114 centimeters). The Southeast is warm and humid. Summer highs average near 90°F (32°C) and winter lows range from 30° to 60°F (-18° to 16°C). In southern Florida and along the Gulf coast of Alabama and Mississippi, precipitation is over 60 inches (152 centimeters) a year; in the rest of the region it ranges from 45 to 60 inches (114 to 152 centimeters).

The Southwestern region is warm and very dry. Except in high mountain regions, summer high temperatures average above 90°F (32°C), and precipitation averages between 10 and 25 inches (25 and 64 centimeters). The deserts of Arizona and California receive less than 10 inches (25 centimeters) of rain a year and routinely record high temperatures over 100°F (38°C).

In general, the Northwestern region is cold and dry. Winter lows average from 0° to 20°F (-18° to -7°C), and summer highs approach 90°F (32°C). The inland regions show the greatest temperature extremes in the country: readings over 100°F (38°C) in summer and well below zero in winter are common. Precipitation ranges from 15 to 30 inches (38 to 76 centimeters). A narrow strip between the Pacific and the Coastal mountains in Washington, Oregon, and northern California has a much damper and more temperate climate.

The Pacific shore of Alaska has a damp, temperate climate. Inland regions east and north of the Coastal mountains are bitter cold. Temperatures in Hawaii vary from 60° to 80°F (16° to 27°C) year-round. Precipitation varies from moderate at low altitudes and along southwest shores to over 100 inches (254 centimeters) per year at high altitudes and along northeast shores.

The people. The population of the world has increased rapidly in the last 200 years, but the rate of increase in the United States during that period is even greater than that of the world average. From a base of fewer than 4 million in 1790, the U.S. population increased to 200 million in 1970. In recent years, the rate of population growth has increased, after a short period of decrease. In absolute numbers, the country gained some 32 million people between 1990 and 2000 to record a total population of 281,421,906.

The regions. Population is not distributed evenly throughout the country, and population growth and other characteristics differ from one section to another. In order to make these differences clear, the United States has been divided into eleven regions.

The regions, as shown in the map on page 73, are defined as follows:

Southwest states: California, Arizona, Nevada, Hawaii

Northwest states: Oregon, Idaho, Washington, Alaska

Mountain states: Montana, Wyoming, Utah, Colorado, New Mexico

Oil states: Texas, Louisiana, Oklahoma, Arkansas

Grain states: Missouri, Kansas, Nebraska, Iowa, South Dakota, North Dakota, Minnesota

Great Lakes states: Wisconsin, Illinois, Indiana, Michigan, Ohio

South-Central states: Kentucky, Tennessee, Mississippi, Alabama

South Atlantic states: Florida, Georgia, South Carolina, North Carolina

Tidewater states: Virginia, West Virginia, Maryland, Delaware (and the District of Columbia)

Mid-Atlantic states: Pennsylvania, New Jersey, New York

New England states: Connecticut, Rhode Island, Massachusetts, Vermont, New Hampshire, Maine

In area, the Western regions are much larger than those in the East. The five regions west of the Mississippi River occupy three-quarters of the U.S. land area.

Population, on the other hand, is heavily concentrated in the regions east of the Mississippi, which contain over 60 percent of the population on only 25 percent of the land.

Population growth. The population increase between 1990 and 2000 was unevenly distributed among the regions. Over 50 percent of the increase occurred in only three regions. The Southwest and the South Atlantic gained more than 13 million, and the Oil states gained 4 million. All regions in the West grew at rates well above the national average.

Minorities and ethnic groups. During the 1800s Americans of foreign birth or parentage constituted a large part of the total population. Today the foreign-born make up less than 9 percent of the total population. There are, however, several important minority groups in the United States.

Of the total population of 281.4 million recorded in the 2000 Census,

DISABLED VETERANS watch a Veterans Day service in Springfield, Massachusetts.

- 36.4 million, or 12.9 percent, of all Americans identified themselves as African Americans;
- 35.0 million, or about 12 percent, were of Hispanic descent;
- 15 million, or about 5.3 percent, were designated "Other" by the Census; these included those who did not identify themselves as belonging to one of the categories provided, such as White, Black, American Indian, Asian or Pacific Islander;
- 12.7 million, or about 4.2 percent, were designated under the category Asian or Pacific Islander.

African Americans. Most African Americans have ancestral roots in the Southern states, and about half of them still live in the South. They account for 20 percent of the total population in the South Atlantic, Tidewater, and South-Central regions.

Between 1920 and 1970, millions of African Americans moved to cities in Northeastern states, where there were more employment opportunities and

27 North America

U.S. Population 1800–2000

YEAR	POPULATION	INCREASE	% INCREASE
1800	5,308,483		
1810	7,239,881	1,931,398	36.3
1820	9,638,453	2,398,572	33.1
1830	12,866,020	3,227,567	33.5
1840	17,069,453	4,203,433	32.7
1850	23,191,876	6,122,423	35.9
1860	31,443,321	8,251,445	35.6
1870	38,558,371	7,115,050	22.6
1880	50.155,783	11,597.410	30.1
1890	62,947,714	12,791,931	25.5
1900	75,994,575	13,046,861	20.7
1910	91,972,266	15,977,691	21.0
1920	105,710,620	13,738,354	14.9
1930	122,775,046	17,064,426	16.1
1940	131,669,275	8,894,229	6.8
1950	150,697,361	19,028,086	14.5
1960	179,323,175	28,625,814	19.0
1970	203,302,031	23,978,856	13.3
1980	226,515,349	23,202,794	11.4
1990	248,709,873	22,194,524	9.8
2000	281,421,906	32,712,033	13.2

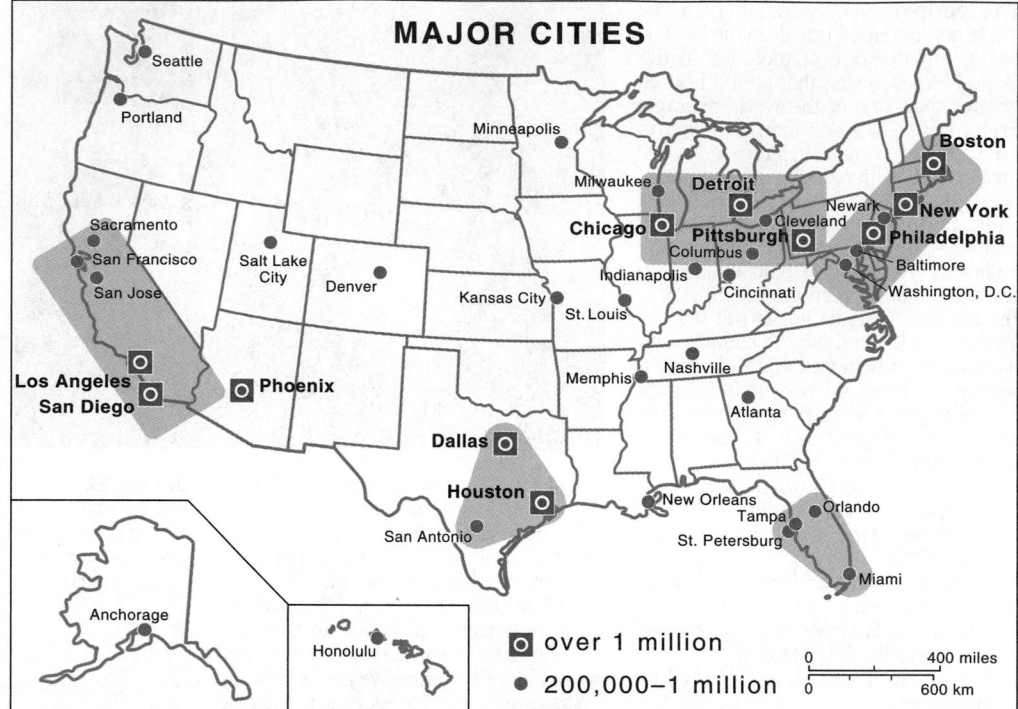

MAJOR CITIES

over 1 million
200,000–1 million

0   400 miles
0   600 km

MAJOR CITIES form large corridors of high population density and business activity. These metropolitan areas may each contain many smaller cities.

center
US

centre
Brit.

kilometers
US

kilometres
Brit.

where racial segregation was not established by law. More than 10.7 million, almost a third of the national total, live in the Great Lakes and Mid-Atlantic regions.

Hispanics. Americans of Hispanic origin include a large group of Mexican descent; many from Puerto Rico and other Caribbean islands; and smaller numbers who trace their heritage to South America, Central America, or Spain.

Americans of Hispanic descent are heavily concentrated in the Southwest, Mountain, and Oil regions. Altogether, nearly two-thirds of all Hispanics live in these three regions.

There are also considerable concentrations of Hispanic Americans in the Mid-Atlantic states (principally in and around New York City), and in the Great Lakes and South Atlantic regions. Miami, Florida, has the largest population of Cuban-Americans in the country.

Asians and others. By far the largest concentrations of those who designated themselves in the 2000 Census under the categories "Asian" or "Native Hawaiian and other Pacific Islander" are in the Southwest, Northwest, and Mountain regions. In the 2000 Census, around 5 million persons in these three regions designated themselves as such. They represent almost 48 percent of the national total in this category.

Religion. About 60 percent of Americans report affiliation with a religious group. The great majority, some 144 million persons, are members of a Christian church. Nearly 6 million are Jewish; about 4 million are members of the Church of Jesus Christ of Latter-Day Saints, or Mormons. Finally, 3 to 4 million adhere to a variety of other religions, including Islam and Buddhism. In the last decade Islam has grown significantly in the United States.

Members of particular religious groups are often predominant in one geographical region and sparsely represented in another. Half the Jewish population lives in or near New York City, while many others live in Florida and California.

Roman Catholics are heavily represented in the large cities of the Northeast and the Midwest. In addition, many Hispanic Americans, who are heavily concentrated in the Southwest, are Roman Catholics.

Protestant denominations are not too heavily represented in Northeastern cities, but they make up the overwhelming majority in most of the South and Midwest. Baptist churches are predominant in the South, while Methodist churches predominate in the Midwest outside of large cities.

The economy. Because of its size, both in area and population, the United States has a remarkably large and diversified economy. Its major industries include manufacturing, agriculture, and the extraction and refining of a wide variety of mineral products. In recent years, services—from data processing to the provision of lodging for tourists—have played an ever larger role in the economy, providing more jobs than all production of goods combined.

Income. Personal income in the United States is among the highest in the world, ranking behind a handful of small countries in northern Europe and the oil-rich Middle East. Measured on a per capita (per person) basis, income has increased rapidly, from less than $600 in 1940 to $25,379 in 2000. Although the cost of living has also increased rapidly during the same period, average Americans have far greater purchasing power currently

than their predecessors in the 1940s and '50s.

Manufacturing. Production of manufactured goods has traditionally been the basis of an advanced economy. In 1997 value added by manufacturing in the United States came to more than $1.8 trillion.

Almost half the value added was produced by the Great Lakes, Mid-Atlantic, and South Atlantic regions. Another quarter came from the Southwest and Oil regions.

The decline of heavy industry in the Northeast regions because of foreign competition, sluggish economic conditions, and other factors, seems likely to reduce that area's importance in manufacturing, at least in the short term, as the region develops new high-technology industries. The Sun Belt regions are attracting many new industries, and, as population trends indicate, workers from the Northeast are moving to the South and West to compete for the new jobs there. Industrial growth is especially rapid in the Oil and South Atlantic regions.

Agriculture. In 1997 farm marketings in the United States exceeded $197 billion. More than a quarter of this total, $51 billion, was produced by the Grain states. Combined with the output of the Oil and Great Lakes states, the total for the central regions is more than half the national output. The Southwest, which includes California, the largest and most productive agricultural state, contributed more than 13 percent of the national total, with a range of crops from citrus to cotton to wine grapes.

Minerals. The most important mineral product economically is oil. In mineral production, the Oil states contributed more than 45 percent of the national total of $134 billion in 1997.

The Oil and Mountain regions together account for over half of the total production. Oil production in Alaska is significant as well.

Other regions produce valuable products as well—iron ore in the Great Lakes area; coal in the Appalachian fields (spread through several regions), and in other widely separated regions; and a variety of valuable metals and minerals in the West.

Trade and services. The contribution of trade and services to the total economy is somewhat difficult to assess. Altogether, wholesale, retail trade, and service establishments paid more than $1.4 trillion in wages and salaries in 1997. The heaviest activity was in the densely populated urban areas in the Mid-Atlantic, Great Lakes, and Southwest regions. These three areas accounted for almost 50 percent of the total payrolls in those fields.

Retail and wholesale trade are especially strong in California, New York, and Texas. The service economy is most active in California, Texas, and Florida; the Great Lakes region; and along the East Coast, from Washington, D.C., to Boston, Massachusetts.

Major cities. For political purposes, cities are still defined by city limits. But for most other purposes, they are better defined as metropolitan areas—clumps of cities, towns, and suburban areas that most often center around the largest city in the area. All populations in this section are given for standard metropolitan areas as defined by the U.S. Census Bureau.

In all, 50 cities had metropolitan populations of more than 1 million in 2000. The 6 largest have between 6 and 21 million; 17 have between 2 and 6 million; and the remaining 27 have between 1 and 2 million. Together these metropolitan areas had almost 164 million people.

All of the U.S. regions have at least one metropolitan area of a million or more. These large cities are not evenly distributed. They tend to develop in long corridors or in clusters. Six of these major metropolitan areas are part of a corridor that runs from Boston, Massachusetts, to Washington, D.C., along the Atlantic seaboard. The corridor is the home of more than 37 million people.

A second corridor stretches along the southern shores of the Great Lakes, from Pittsburgh, Pennsylvania, and Rochester, New York, in the east, to Chicago, Illinois, and Milwaukee, Wisconsin, in the west. This corridor has traditionally been the industrial heartland of the United States.

A third urban corridor is growing along the Pacific coast from San Francisco to San Diego, California. The largest center along this corridor is the Los Angeles area, a vast region that contains over 15 million people.

Two other clusters of large cities have grown more recently in Texas and Florida.

There are about 40 additional metropolitan areas in the United States with between 500,000 and 1 million people.

Transportation. The development and prosperity of the United States has always depended on efficient transportation capable of operating over the country's vast distances. The economic development of the Northeastern states depended on good ocean ports, and later on rivers, canals, and roads leading to the interior. The railroad made the rapid development of the Midwest and Far West possible. More recently, the use of air transportation has been essential to the statehood and economic well-being of Alaska and Hawaii.

The principal means of transportation currently, however, is the automobile. A vast system of paved roads was developed by the states in the 1930s and 1940s. In 1957 the federal government established a new system of limited access roads, called interstate highways. During the next 20 years, much of the system was completed, and it constitutes one of the largest civil construction efforts in the world. It consists of some 42,500 miles (68,400 kilometers) of multilane highway built to exacting standards.

Long-distance travel, both for business and pleasure, has shifted more and more to the air. The United States

has the largest domestic airline industry in the world. Airports in important regional centers such as Atlanta and Chicago are among the busiest in the world. International travel is especially important to airports in New York, Los Angeles, and Seattle.

Communications. Rapid communication has played an important role in the country's economic and social development.

Today, about half of all the telephones in the world are in use in the United States. Electronic switching equipment and advanced satellite technology have enabled direct dialing and automatic billing of almost all calls within the country and of many international calls. The telephone system is also used as a connection between computers, typesetting equipment, and many other electronic devices.

The United States was a pioneer in the development of radio and television. Today, television and radio stations provide local programming and bring both entertainment and news from distant parts of the country and the world.

Education. A large majority of Americans receive both elementary and secondary education in public schools. Half the adult population has completed more than twelve years of schooling, and more than half of recent high-school graduates enroll for college.

Over 13 million Americans are enrolled in some 3,600 institutions of higher education. Nearly 80 percent are enrolled at publicly supported institutions.

The arts. Aspiring writers, painters, and musicians have traditionally flocked to the large cities of the Eastern seaboard. In the 1800s, Boston and Philadelphia were the major cultural and art centers. In the early 1900s, New York was the major center of the arts, rivaled only by Chicago. As recently as the 1960s, the "Big Five" symphony orchestras were those in Boston, New York, Philadelphia, Cleveland, and Chicago. To these can be added many other fine orchestras, including the Cincinnati, Houston, Pittsburgh, St. Louis, and San Francisco symphony orchestras, the Los Angeles Philharmonic, and the National Symphony Orchestra in Washington, D.C.

Although the Eastern cities remain important in the arts, many Southern and Western cities have become important as well.

Museums play a significant part in the nation's cultural life, and despite severe financial constraints in recent years, American museums have seen a steady rise in annual attendance. The United States has more than 6,000 museums of all types, including art, general, natural history, and scientific.

World prospects. The 1900s have been called "the American Century," and through the first half of the century, the United States gradually took on a role of world leadership. Since 1960, however, the country has faced serious challenges, both from within and with-

out. Perhaps the most serious of these have been the economic challenges of increasing dependence on costly foreign oil, and increasing international competition in the manufacture of basic industrial goods.

The demise of the Soviet Union and the end of the Cold War marked the beginning of a new era in world politics. Potentially, the global map of power and influence is likely to be redrawn in the next decade. Although many threats to peace appear to have been eliminated, terrorism is on the upswing and world leadership will be an infinitely more difficult task.

At home, the country continues to wrestle with racial issues that have haunted it since the Constitution was drawn up more than 200 years ago. Poverty and unemployment, the depletion of natural resources, and air and water pollution are among the nation's major problems.

Nonetheless, the country remains prosperous and more peaceful than any country of its size in the history of the world.

THE INTERSTATE system in the United States is one of the world's largest civil construction efforts, consisting of 42,500 miles of multilane highways.

27 North America

ABOUT HALF the population of the United States receives more than 12 years of schooling.

United States History

Exploring and Settling North America

The first Americans. The history of the exploration and settlement of the United States properly begins with the arrival of small groups of people who crossed a land bridge, commonly called the Bering land bridge, that once stretched from Asia to North America. Sometime between 50,000 and 20,000 years ago, these hunters and, new evidence suggests, fishermen began tracking game and seeking fish across this land bridge, travelling from Siberia to what is now Alaska. It is possible that these groups arrived in two or even three separate waves of migration. Genetic differences between the Inuit of Canada and Alaska and North American Indians suggest at least two separate groups crossed the Bering land bridge. As the bands' numbers grew, they moved deeper into North America and down into Central and South America. Then,

about 10,000 years ago, the world climate warmed, causing massive melting of the polar ice sheet that covered much of the continent. The ocean rose up and covered the land bridge, creating what we know as the Bering Strait.

These first Americans, who came to be called Indians, were grouped in a variety of tribes. It is estimated that at their most numerous, there were 2,000 tribes in North America alone. They spoke at least 200 different languages and followed different ways of life. Perhaps a million Indians lived in the area that has since become the United States and Canada. Modern researchers suggest that 3 million lived in what is now Mexico and Central America, and another 20 million lived in South America.

Indian land regions. Geography was the main factor in determining the way of life of these first Americans. Different tribes developed different cultures, largely influenced by the characteristics of the land regions in which they made their homes. In the area that would become the contiguous United

States, there were five land regions that were home to five major cultural groups of Indians.

The Eastern Woodlands. This area, stretching all the way from Canada to the Gulf of Mexico and from the Atlantic coast to west of the Mississippi River, was the largest land region. The Eastern Woodlands were characterized by abundant inland waterways and coastal waters, forests filled with game, and good soil. In this environment, the tribes of the area became hunters and farmers. In the colder north, hunting was a more important activity than farming. Moose, beaver, deer, bear, wild ducks, and geese were main sources of food, as were fish, and along the Atlantic coast, clams. Wild rice was, and still is, gathered in the area that is now Wisconsin. Farther to the south, corn and other crops were important.

The many tribes that occupied the Eastern Woodlands fell into three language groups. The largest group, the Algonquian, was scattered from Canada to Virginia and included the Algonquin, Ottawa, and Ojibwa tribes centered

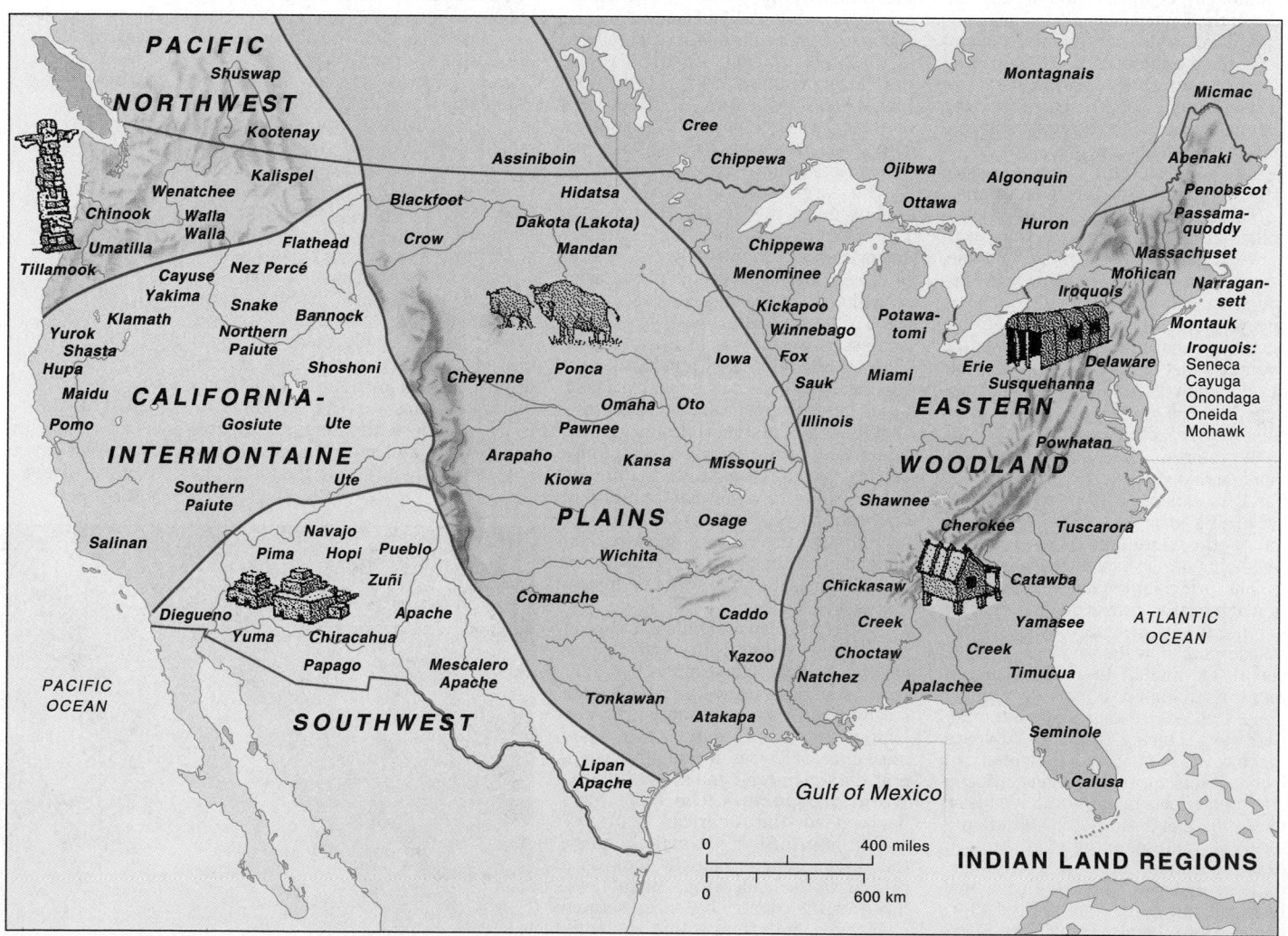

INDIAN LAND REGIONS

around and north of the Great Lakes; the Abenaki of Maine; the Delaware; the Powhatans of Virginia; and the Miami and Illinois to the west. The second group, the Iroquoian, was centered in present-day New York State and included the five original member tribes of the Iroquois Confederacy, the Mohawk, Oneida, Onondaga, Cayuga, and Seneca, and, after 1722, the Tuscaroras, who migrated to New York from the southeast. The third group, the Muskogean, extended south from Virginia to Florida and west to the Mississippi and included the Creek, Choctaw, and Chickasaw.

The Plains. Stretching from the Mississippi River westward to the Rocky Mountains and from Canada southward to Mexico, the Plains were flatlands covered by tough grass. The Plains Indians lived for the most part in villages along streams and rivers. The men were hunters and the women were farmers, raising mainly corn, squash, and beans. Among the tribes that made the Plains their home were the Pawnee, Mandan, Hidatsa, Cheyenne, Dakota (Sioux), Blackfoot, Arapaho, and Comanche.

The buffalo was central to the life of the Plains Indians. It is estimated that at one time from 45 to 50 million buffalo roamed North America, grazing mainly in this region. The Plains Indians hunted the huge beasts and used buffalo meat for food; buffalo skins for tepees, blankets, and shields; and even dried buffalo manure for heating fuel. In the 18th century, Plains Indians acquired large numbers of horses, which gave them much greater mobility and proved enormously valuable in hunting. Plains Indians became outstanding horse breeders and arguably the best horsemen in the world.

Winters on the Plains were often harsh, as cold arctic weather swept down from the north. During winter, the Plains Indians stayed close to home, in their villages. But with the coming of summer, they packed up to go on long buffalo hunts, during which they lived as nomads.

The Pacific Northwest. This area extended along the Pacific coast from southern Alaska through present-day Oregon and Washington. It was an area of great abundance. In the mild, wet climate, wild berries and other foods grew easily and plentifully. The many rivers were rich in salmon, and the coastal waters teemed with sea mammals that could be captured for their meat and warm furs. Thick forests of cedar and fir trees reached all the way down to the beaches, so wood was plentiful for building houses and hollowed-out canoes. Within the forests, game abounded. Farming was largely unnecessary because there was enough food that could be gathered or hunted. All in all, the Indians of the Pacific Northwest were well provided with food and the materials needed for shelter. Among the tribes in this region were the Tillamook, Chinook, Nootka, and Kwakiutl, and Tlingit of the northwest coast, and the inland

tribes of the Klamath, Modoc, Umatilla, Spokan, Flathead, and Nez Percé.

The California-Intermountain. Resources were not quite so abundant in much of this region, which included what is now California and the Great Basin that lies between the Rocky Mountains and the Cascade and Sierra Nevada ranges. The mild climate of California made it suitable for farming and for gathering foods that grew wild, like berries, acorns, and roots. Clothing and housing could be quite simple, requiring a minimum of raw materials. California was the home of a large number of American Indians from many tribes, including the Chumash, Pomo, Hupa, and Mohave.

Life was much harder for the Indians of the Intermountain area. Here the climate was dry and ill-suited to farming. Winters amid the mountains were harsh, and finding food was nearly impossible. People travelled in small hunting bands, finding what food they could and storing it in caves to carry them through the winter storms. Tribes inhabiting the Great Basin region included the Ute, Paiute, Shoshone, and Bannock.

The Southwest. This huge, dry land region covers present-day Arizona, New Mexico, and southern Colorado and Utah. It is marked by steep-walled canyons, few rivers, and stretches of flat desert land. Yet the Indians who settled here, including the Hopi, Zuni, Navajo, and Apache, were able not only to survive, but also to develop highly organized and comfortable societies. Some of the groups built their villages, or pueblos, against the canyon walls, making them resemble today's apartment buildings. They reached their lodgings by climbing ladders, and these ladders could be pulled up in case of attack.

The dry land and climate of the Southwest did not provide much food naturally, but some of the Indians devised methods of irrigation that enabled them to grow much of the food they needed, mainly corn, beans, and squash. They supplemented this with foods they could hunt or gather.

The Age of Discovery. Far to the east of the North American continent, events were taking shape that would one day bring profound changes to the lives of American Indians. In western Europe, new and powerful nations were emerging from the feudal Middle Ages. By the end of the 1400s, nations like England, France, Spain, Portugal, and the Netherlands had been organized and strengthened by strong monarchs. A new merchant class had become increasingly important, and it was eager to extend its buying and selling powers to new markets and products. Europeans began to take an interest in the world outside their own boundaries. They sought new learning and discoveries.

Travels of the Vikings. The first Europeans to explore the Americas probably did so centuries before the 1400s. The Vikings were daring seafarers who sailed from Norway, Sweden,

and Denmark westward into the Atlantic Ocean from the 800s on. Having explored and settled Iceland and then Greenland, they went on to the North American coastline around A.D. 1000. Their travels took them to present-day Newfoundland and Labrador, where they attempted to establish settlements. But repeated attacks by the Indians, or *skrellings,* as the Vikings called them, drove the would-be settlers away and back to Greenland.

Voyages of the Portuguese. As the Vikings were looking to the West, the people of several other European nations were looking to the East. The Crusades of the 1100s and 1200s had acquainted Europeans with the useful and beautiful goods of the Middle East and Asia— spices, silks, polished steel, perfumes, and fine pottery. The overland routes to these regions were slow, expensive, and often dangerous. Merchants and sailors were looking for faster and more economical sea routes. (For more information about European exploration, see Cultures in Transition, in the HISTORY OF THE WORLD volume.)

The Portuguese were the first to succeed in this search. In 1487–1488, Bartholomeu Dias sailed down the western coast of Africa into the then-mysterious and forbidding waters near the southern tip of the continent. A few years later, in 1497–1498, Vasco da Gama followed Dias's route and continued on up along Africa's east coast, through the Indian Ocean, and on to India. Soon the sailors and traders of other Atlantic nations were following the same route to successful trade.

Columbus and the Spaniards. In the meantime, an Italian seaman from Genoa, Christopher Columbus, believed he could find a sea route to the East that was even shorter. Like most knowledgeable people of his time, Columbus believed that Earth is round rather than flat. Thus, he determined, it was possible to reach the East by sailing west.

27 North America

TRIBES OF THE IROQUOIS CONFEDERACY constituted one of the three language groups that occupied the Eastern Woodlands when the European explorers arrived.

He judged the distance to Asia to be only about 3,500 miles (5,600 kilometers). In 1484 he tried to get the Portuguese to finance an expedition across the Atlantic, but he was not successful. He moved to Spain and spent several more years trying to obtain backing for his plan. Finally, in 1492, he convinced Queen Isabella of Spain to finance his voyage.

In August 1492, Columbus set sail with three ships, the *Niña,* the *Pinta,* and the *Santa Maria,* and a crew of about 90, from Palos, Spain. Two months and about 3,500 miles (5,600 kilometers) later, he landed on a tiny island that he named San Salvador, today one of the islands of the Bahamas. Thinking he had reached the Indies—the islands of present-day Indonesia—he called the people of the island Indians. He sailed on and reached what he thought was China. Actually, it was the island of Cuba. In December Columbus discovered the island of Hispaniola, where he established La Navidad, the first Spanish settlement in the New World. In later years, he made three more voyages. He never found the riches of the East that he sought, and he died thinking that he had indeed reached Asia.

Later Spanish explorers found the golden treasures of the great Indian civilizations of the Aztecs of Mexico, the Mayans of Central America, and the Incas of Peru. These finds encouraged more Spanish exploration, some of it farther to the north. In 1513 Juan Ponce de León, who had already found gold on the island of Puerto Rico, travelled farther west in search of a legendary "Fountain of Youth." His explorations took him up and down the coasts of Florida. In 1539 Hernando De Soto began a search for gold. His travels took him from Florida through what are now the Carolinas and as far west as present-day Oklahoma. During the same period, Francisco Coronado led an expedition in search of another legend, "the Seven Cities of Gold."

In 1528 a Spanish expedition led by Pánfilo de Narváez had landed in Florida but met with great hardship and set sail for Mexico, only to be shipwrecked on the coast of Texas. Most of the party died, but a small group, including Alvar Núñez Cabeza de Vaca, survived and began an eight-year journey through the interior, part of the time as prisoners of the Indians. In 1536 Cabeza de Vaca made his way to Mexico with three other survivors. His account of his travels included the legend of seven fabulously wealthy cities located somewhere to the north.

This story prompted Coronado to make his journey into the Southwest in 1540. Coronado's quest for wealth was as fruitless as Ponce de León's had been, but he did explore the U.S. Southwest, including the Grand Canyon.

The French, English, and Dutch. The wealth that Spain was finding in the newly found lands aroused the interest of other European nations. They wanted riches from the new lands, and they also

kilometers
US

kilometres
Brit.

civilizations
US

civilisations
Brit.

colonize
US

colonise
Brit.

THE DUTCH established their first major settlement in the New World on the island of Manhattan in 1626 and called it New Amsterdam.

wanted a way through North America to Asia, a "Northwest Passage."

In 1524 the king of France sent Giovanni da Verrazano to explore the North American coast and find a likely waterway west. He reached the coast of North America, probably in the Carolinas, then worked his way north to New York Harbor and on to Nova Scotia. Verrazano did not find a westward passage to the Orient, but on the basis of his explorations, France laid claim to North America. Later explorers for France, like Jacques Cartier in 1535 and 1536, began penetrating the continent by way of the St. Lawrence River in Canada. Following this route in 1673, Louis Joliet and Père Jacques Marquette, and then in 1682 Robert de La Salle, penetrated as far as the Mississippi River and down to the Gulf of Mexico.

England had begun sending its explorers to North America as early as 1497. In that year, John Cabot reached the continent's shores and claimed the "new-found-land" for England. About 80 years later, another English explorer, Martin Frobisher, tried to find a Northwest Passage. His voyage took him as far as Frobisher Bay in Canada. About 35 years later, Henry Hudson, an English seaman sailing for the Dutch, penetrated still deeper into Canada in search of a passage to China. He reached Hudson Bay. The previous year, he had made another attempt, exploring Delaware Bay and then following the Hudson River in what is now New York as far as the present-day city of Albany. On the basis of this expedition, the Dutch laid claim to an area extending up the Hudson River and down the Delaware River south of Delaware Bay.

Colonizing America. The Western European nations may have begun by seeking treasure in the New World, but gradually they decided to colonize the lands to which they laid claim. A colony could supply raw materials to a mother country and provide markets for goods that the mother country produced. In that way the mother country could become self-sufficient and eliminate the need to buy from other nations.

Spanish, French, and Dutch settlement. The Spanish were the first to actually establish colonies in the New World. They had claimed part of South America as well as the islands of the Caribbean, Central America, Mexico, Florida, and the region west of the Mississippi River through to California. They called the North American portion of their claim New Spain.

In 1565 the Spanish founded the first permanent European settlement in what would one day be the United States. They established the fort and village of St. Augustine along the Atlantic coast of Florida. In years to come, the Spanish would found many more settlements along the Pacific coast in California.

Cartier and the French explorers who followed him informed France of the vast riches in fish to be found along the coast of North America, especially on the Grand Banks of Newfoundland. Their explorations along inland waterways called the attention of France to a potential fortune in furs in the New World from a seemingly endless supply of fur-bearing animals.

These attractions brought French settlers to New France, as the French called the territory they claimed. The territory included the St. Lawrence

River valley, the Great Lakes, and the Mississippi River valley. The French established most of their larger settlements, such as Quebec and Montreal, in Canada, but they also founded smaller communities around their trading posts, especially along the Mississippi River.

The Dutch also acted on their claims to North American territory. Dutch settlers left their own land-poor nation to establish farms along the rich river valleys of New Netherland. Their major settlement was New Amsterdam, established in 1626 on the island of Manhattan, which the Dutch governor Peter Minuit had bought from the Manhattan Indians for about 60 guilders worth of goods. (A guilder was about one day's pay for a Dutch laborer.) New Amsterdam soon became an important trading center for shipping farm products and furs back to The Netherlands and elsewhere.

Early English settlements. Nearly a century passed after John Cabot's explorations before England finally began its first attempts at settlement of North America. In 1585 Sir Walter Raleigh, an English adventurer, writer, and favorite of Queen Elizabeth I, sent an expedition to colonize the vast new land of Virginia, the coast of which had been explored by a Raleigh expedition the year before. The colonists landed at Roanoke Island, off the coast of what is now North Carolina. The settlers fared poorly and, before a relief ship arrived in 1586, returned to England aboard the fleet of Sir Francis Drake, who had been harassing the Spanish in the West Indies. Raleigh sent another expedition to Roanoke in 1587. Again, the ship that brought the settlers had to return to England for supplies, and it was unable to return to Roanoke Island until 1591. When it did, it found no sign of the settlers, only the word CROATOAN carved on a tree. This was the name of an Indian tribe that lived in the area. The fate of the settlers of the "Lost Colony" remains a mystery, but Roanoke Colony was the birthplace, on August 18, 1587, of Virginia Dare, the first English child born in America.

Jamestown. The next attempt at settlement was made in 1607. A group of about 120 settlers arrived in present-day Virginia and founded a community they called Jamestown. These settlers were just as unprepared as the earlier ones to cope with the hardships of their new surroundings. The land they had chosen for their settlement was low and swampy and not good for farming. When winter came, it proved to be very harsh, and fully two-thirds of the settlers died.

For the next three years, the settlers were often on the verge of starvation, and Indian attacks were common. More settlers died. Yet somehow, thanks in part to the strong leadership of Captain John Smith, who was made president of the colony's governing council in the fall of 1608, the colonists held on, and Jamestown survived. It became England's first permanent settlement in the

ABOUT 120 ENGLISH SETTLERS came across the Atlantic and established a community they called Jamestown in 1607 in present-day Virginia.

New World, and the Virginia Colony was established.

Plymouth. The Pilgrims, who were persecuted for their religious beliefs in England, founded the next permanent settlement. They came to America in search of a place where they might worship as they pleased. In September of 1620, a group of 102 Pilgrims crowded aboard a tiny ship called the *Mayflower* and set sail from England to America. They headed for Virginia, but storms drove them off course and sent them northward toward Cape Cod Bay, in what is now Massachusetts.

In November they anchored in the bay and drew up a plan of government in which they promised to make "just and equal laws . . . for the general good." In their "Mayflower Compact," they agreed to abide by the will of the majority in governing themselves. In December they sighted and chose the place where they would make their new home, and moved ashore. They named their settlement Plymouth after the port in England from which they had sailed.

Like the settlers at Jamestown, the Pilgrims faced great hardships in that first winter. Half of them died, yet the remainder stayed on and, with the help of Indians who were friendly to them, they learned how to farm, fish, and hunt in their strange new home. In autumn they harvested their first crops and with the Indians celebrated the first Thanksgiving in the New World.

Massachusetts Bay Colony. Eight years after the Pilgrims arrived in Massachusetts, a larger group of people in search of religious freedom came to settle there. They were called the Puritans because they thought that the established Church of England, of which they disapproved, was in need of purification.

The Puritans came to the New World to escape persecution.

They established their first community at Salem in September of 1628 and soon founded other settlements in Massachusetts, among them Boston. Massachusetts Bay Colony thrived. In 1632 Boston became its capital, and in 1691, Plymouth joined the Massachusetts Bay Colony.

The Thirteen Colonies. The English government colonized the New World by granting charters to lands it claimed to corporations and individuals. The recipients of land grants then recruited settlers and financed the establishment of their colonies. In return, they hoped the colonies would become profitable.

Between 1607 and 1730, 13 English colonies were established along the Atlantic coast, stretching from Maine (then a part of Massachusetts) in the north to Georgia in the south. The colonies can be divided into three

27 North America

THE ENGLISH PILGRIMS came ashore at a place they called Plymouth in 1620 and drew up the Mayflower Compact, agreeing to abide by the will of the majority in governing themselves.

kilometers
US

kilometres
Brit.

honor
US

honour
Brit.

groups—New England, the Middle Colonies, and the Southern Colonies. **New England.** In addition to Massachusetts, the colonies of New England included Rhode Island, Connecticut, and New Hampshire. The founding of these latter colonies stemmed in large part from trouble in Massachusetts. The Puritan leaders there were very serious about their religion and demanded that people living in Massachusetts follow Puritan beliefs and practices. But not all Puritans agreed. Roger Williams, a brilliant young Puritan minister, came to Massachusetts from England in 1631. He disagreed strongly with many practices of both the Puritan church and the government it ran. As a result, he was banished and forced to leave the colony. In 1636 he and a few followers founded a new settlement, which they called Providence. This was the beginning of the colony of Rhode Island. Williams established a government independent of religious belief, and he encouraged toleration for the members of most religious faiths. Williams was able to get a charter from the English king for his new colony, which soon grew and prospered.

WILLIAM PENN, a Quaker, founded Pennsylvania as a place of religious freedom and fair representation. He agreed to pay the Indians for most of the land he claimed in the territory.

Other Puritans also left Massachusetts in disagreement with the government there. Thomas Hooker, also a Puritan minister, sought greater religious and governmental freedom. He and his followers moved to a trading post on the Connecticut River and established a town they called Hartford. It joined with the settlements of Windsor and Wethersfield and in 1639 drew up a democratic form of government called the Fundamental Orders, which became the basis for the colony of Connecticut. New Hampshire was also settled in part by those who dissented from the religious tenets that held sway in Massachusetts.
The Middle Colonies. New York, Delaware, New Jersey, and Pennsylvania constituted the Middle Colonies. The first settlers in this area had been Dutch, and much of the region was claimed by The Netherlands. The Dutch had founded settlements in Connecticut and claimed the land in Delaware that had been settled in 1838 by the New Sweden

Company. In 1655 the Dutch finally succeeded in gaining control of New Sweden. This ended the Swedish threat to New Netherland, but in the next few years Dutch and English interests in the region led to numerous difficulties. Finally, in 1664, the English sent four warships into the harbor of New Amsterdam and demanded that New Netherland come under English rule. The governor of New Netherland, Peter Stuyvesant, was highly unpopular with the Dutch settlers. The settlers put up no resistance to the English, and thus New Amsterdam became New York, named for the Duke of York, whom the English king had appointed proprietor of the settlement.

The Duke of York then gave the territory south of New York to two of his friends, Lord John Berkeley and Sir George Carteret. They divided the land into East Jersey and West Jersey and became proprietors of the two areas, which would eventually become New Jersey. The colony of Delaware also went from Dutch to English control at this time.

In 1682 another colonial proprietor arrived to create a colony where his religious sect could find religious freedom. William Penn, the son of a wealthy English admiral, had joined the Society of Friends, or Quakers, in England. Like the Pilgrims and the Puritans, the Quakers suffered from religious persecution in England.

When Penn's father died, it was discovered that the king of England had owed him a large sum of money. William Penn asked that the debt be paid in the form of a charter that would give him the right to establish a colony. In 1681 the king granted Penn an area of some 48,000 square miles (124,272 square kilometers).

When Penn came to visit this heavily wooded territory in the following year, he named it Pennsylvania ("Penn's woods"). There he set out a plan of government for his colony, the Great Charter and Frame of Government. In it he stated that all colonists in Pennsylvania would have freedom of religion and that all men who owned land or paid taxes could elect representatives to make the colony's laws. Pamphlets advertising Penn's new colony were distributed throughout the countries of Western Europe. Soon settlers from the British Isles, Germany, Scandinavia, and France were pouring into Pennsylvania.
The Southern Colonies. Of the Southern Colonies—Virginia, Maryland, North Carolina, South Carolina, and Georgia—Virginia is the oldest, going back to the founding of Jamestown in 1607. Maryland is next. About 25 years after Jamestown, the English nobleman George Calvert (first Lord Baltimore) sought to establish a colony that offered religious freedom to Roman Catholics. Like the Quakers, Catholics were denied freedom of religion in England.

King Charles I decided to grant Lord Baltimore 12,000 acres (4,860 hectares)

KING GEORGE II of England, who ruled between 1727 and 1760, granted the charters that resulted in the settlement of many of the American colonies. His son inherited the conflict that followed.

just north of the Virginia Colony. But Baltimore died before the charter was issued, and his son Cecilius Calvert, second Lord Baltimore, became proprietor. In 1634 about 200 settlers came to the colony, which Calvert, who never travelled to it, called Maryland, in honor of the queen consort, Henrietta Maria.

North Carolina and South Carolina were the next Southern Colonies to be settled, although at first they were one big colony called Carolina. Carolina is the Latin form of Charles, named in honor of Charles II, England's king from 1660 to 1685. Charles in 1663 had given the land grant for Carolina to eight noblemen who became proprietors of the colony. In 1669 the proprietors issued the Fundamental Constitutions, written in part by John Locke, which established a feudal form of government for Carolina that later brought the proprietors into conflict with the colonists. Difficulties with the Spanish and the Indians, and economic conflicts between the northern and southern parts of the colony, weakened the proprietors' control and ultimately brought them into conflict with the Crown, which in 1729 reestablished direct control of Carolina and made North and South Carolina royal colonies.

Georgia was the last of the colonies to be established. In 1732 an English nobleman, James Oglethorpe, wanted to found a place where people who had fallen into debt could start again. The usual procedure for dealing with such unfortunates in England was to send them to debtors' prison.

The king, George II, granted Oglethorpe and 19 other men a 21-year charter making them trustees of a generous tract of land south and west of the Savannah River. Oglethorpe and 30 families set out for Georgia, named for their benefactor, and there they began the difficult work of carving a settlement out of the wilderness. Savannah was settled in 1733 and the colony grew slowly. Economic growth was hampered in part by

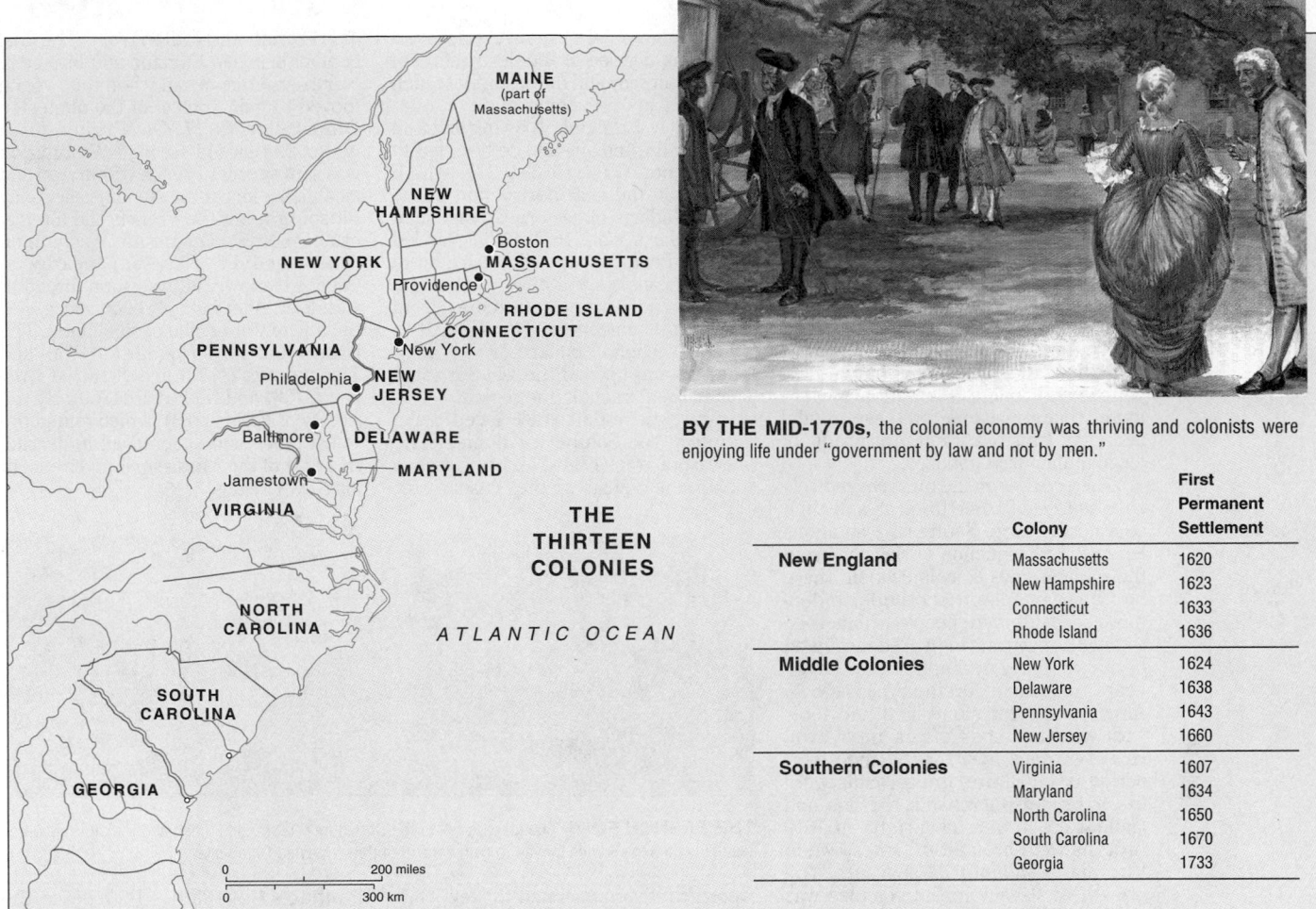

BY THE MID-1770s, the colonial economy was thriving and colonists were enjoying life under "government by law and not by men."

THE THIRTEEN COLONIES

ATLANTIC OCEAN

MAINE (part of Massachusetts)

NEW HAMPSHIRE

Boston
MASSACHUSETTS

NEW YORK
Providence
RHODE ISLAND
New York
CONNECTICUT

PENNSYLVANIA

Philadelphia
NEW JERSEY

Baltimore
DELAWARE

MARYLAND

Jamestown

VIRGINIA

NORTH CAROLINA

SOUTH CAROLINA

GEORGIA

0   200 miles
0   300 km

	Colony	First Permanent Settlement
New England	Massachusetts	1620
	New Hampshire	1623
	Connecticut	1633
	Rhode Island	1636
Middle Colonies	New York	1624
	Delaware	1638
	Pennsylvania	1643
	New Jersey	1660
Southern Colonies	Virginia	1607
	Maryland	1634
	North Carolina	1650
	South Carolina	1670
	Georgia	1733

land restrictions and, until 1749, by the prohibition of slavery. In 1752 Georgia became a royal colony.

Colonial life. By the 1750s, the population of the 13 colonies stood at about a million and a half people, spread fairly thinly along the Atlantic coast. Most people lived on farms. A few important cities had developed: Philadelphia, Boston, New York, and Charleston, South Carolina. But even the largest of them, Philadelphia, still had fewer than 20,000 people. The colonists were overwhelmingly from the British Isles.

Representative government. The desire for representative government ran deep and strong in the colonies. The Mayflower Compact had established a pattern 130 years earlier of developing a set of written laws, of "government by law and not by men." Even before the Mayflower Compact, in 1619, the House of Burgesses had been formed in Virginia. The burgesses were the elected representatives of the Virginia colonists, and they met to determine what laws they would live under and what taxes they would pay.

The Fundamental Orders of Connecticut, which had been drawn up in 1639, was based on an earlier plan of government in the Massachusetts Bay Colony. It provided for the election of a governor and representatives to an upper house and lower house of legislature by the eligible voters of the colony. The earlier Massachusetts plan had made membership in the Puritan church a prerequisite for voting, but the Connecticut plan did not. However, the Fundamental Orders still contained quite a few restrictions. For example, the governor had to be "always a member of some approved congregation" and "formerly of the magistracy." The voters were limited to "freemen" who had been "admitted Inhabitants" by the town in which they lived and who had taken an "oath of fidelity."

The government of each colony was also determined by the kind of colony it was. Royal colonies (New Hampshire, Massachusetts, New York, New Jersey, Virginia, North Carolina, South Carolina, and Georgia) were under the direct authority of the king; proprietary colonies (Maryland, Delaware, and Pennsylvania) were under the authority of one or more proprietors; and the self-governing colonies (Rhode Island and Connecticut) had no direct supervision.

All of the colonies had a governor, a council to advise the governor, and an assembly (like the House of Burgesses). In royal colonies, the king selected the governor and the governor chose his council. The voters elected the members of the assembly. In proprietary colonies, the proprietor selected the governor, who then selected his council. In self-governing colonies, the voters elected the governor, his council, and the assembly.

For laws to be enacted by colonial governments, they had to be approved by the governors and the assemblies. They then had to be approved by the English government. This need for mutual approval sometimes led to disagreements between assemblies and governors or proprietors and between colonial governments and England.

The colonial economy. The economy created by the colonists was based largely on agriculture. The type of farming and other economic pursuits differed from section to section.

In New England, farms were generally not more than about ten acres (four hectares) of frequently rocky soil. Corn was the basic crop, and the colonists made it a staple of their diet, as cornmeal bread or mush. They fed the stalks to their livestock and used the husks to make mattresses.

The sea was also important to the New England economy. Many fishing villages sprang up along the coast, and when weather permitted, hundreds of fishing boats went out to gather cod and haddock from the rich waters. Shipbuilding flourished as the colonists used their forests for this new industry. New England merchants soon developed a busy trade with Europe, Africa, and even China.

The Middle Colonies were blessed with richer soil than that of New England, and soon they had developed into the breadbasket of American colonies. Wheat was the main crop, and it soon became a major export. Port cities like New York and Philadelphia attracted artisans who produced a wide variety of useful and fine goods, like hats, furniture, wigs, and carriages.

In the Southern Colonies, rich soil, flat land, and a warm climate combined to promote the development of large plantations that produced tobacco, rice, cotton, and indigo. Plantation owners found ready markets for these goods, and they traded agricultural products for manufactured goods.

The need for an inexpensive and reliable source of labor to clear and then operate the large Southern plantations led to the introduction of slavery. From the earliest days of colonization, there had been people in servitude. Indentured servants were people who agreed to work as servants for a predetermined period of time, perhaps five or seven years, in return for their passage to America and for some land and tools with which to start off on their own. However, once they had finished their period of indenture, the servants were free to become merchants, artisans, and landowners in their own right. In 1619 Africans were brought to Jamestown in Virginia as indentured servants. The growth of slavery in the colonies was slow at first, but by the late 1600s Africans were being brought to American shores in great numbers as slaves, to work for masters for their entire lives. All of the colonies were involved in this: The bulk of African slaves went to the Southern Colonies, but many were brought to America by New England slave traders.

> **labor**
> *US*
>
> **labour**
> *Brit.*

Creating the American Republic

War and disagreement. The rapid expansion of the English colonies in the 1600s led to conflict, first with the American Indian tribes whose lands were being absorbed by English settlements, then with the French, whose claims in North America conflicted with the claims of the British.

Indian wars. Conflict between English settlers and Indians became inevitable as the number of colonists increased and as the colonies began to build on and cultivate ever greater tracts of land.

The settlements of Virginia and Maryland, which had had friendly relations with the tribes of the Powhatan Confederacy until the death of Powhatan in 1618, were attacked in 1622 by Powhatan's successor. The colonists launched a swift and bloody reprisal, but in 1644 the confederacy launched another, more devastating attack. This time the colonial response was overwhelming and led to the destruction of the confederacy and the seizure of much of the Indians' remaining lands.

In New England, growing friction between the Indians and settlers led to the Pequot War (1636–1637), which resulted in the near destruction of the Pequot Indians of eastern Connecticut. King Philip's War (1675–1676) was led by King Philip, or Metacomet, leader of the Wampanoags and head of a confederacy of Indian tribes stretching from Maine to Connecticut. The war led to the destruction of Indian power in New England and opened the way for rapid colonial settlement in the region.

American Indians also faced dislocation in the Southern colonies. The Tuscarora War (1711–1712) in Carolina led to the defeat of the Tuscaroras, whose survivors migrated to New York and became the sixth tribe of the Iroquois Confederacy. In 1715 the Yamassee Indians of lower Carolina launched an initially successful war against English settlers, but they were ultimately defeated and driven into Florida.

King William's War. By the end of the 1600s, French and English rivalry in the Hudson Bay and St. Lawrence River regions had reached the breaking point. In 1689 war broke out between England and France. The American phase of the war was called King William's War, after the English king, William III. Fighting in North America was inconclusive, and the Treaty of Ryswick (1697) restored all conquered lands to their original owners. After the war ended, France stepped up settlement in the Ohio and Mississippi river valleys.

Queen Anne's War. In 1702 Britain went to war against France in the War of the Spanish Succession to prevent France from gaining control of the Spanish throne. The American phase of the war, named after Queen Anne of England, went in favor of the English colonists, who attacked and burned Spanish-held St. Augustine (1702), captured all but one of the 14 missions in northwestern Florida (1704), and captured Port Royal, Nova Scotia (1710), but failed to take Quebec (1711). By the Treaty of Utrecht (1713), Britain gained Hudson Bay, Newfoundland, and Nova Scotia. France became more determined than ever to develop its western holdings.

The French and Indian War. The final conflict between England and France in North America began when the French moved to gain control of the contested Ohio Valley. In 1754 a Virginia force under 22-year-old George Washington was sent to order French withdrawal and establish a fort at the site of present-day Pittsburgh, but the French had already established Ft. Duquesne. Washington established Ft. Necessity nearby at Great Meadows but was soon forced to withdraw. After initial French successes, the tide of war turned against them. The British took forts Duquesne (1758) and Ticonderoga (1759) and captured Quebec (1759) and Montreal (1760). By the Treaty of Paris (1763), which ended the war, France surrendered all its territories east of the Mississippi River except for New Orleans.

THE FRENCH FORT Ticonderoga fell to the British in 1759 in the French and Indian War, which resulted when the French moved to gain control of the contested Ohio Valley.

Pontiac's Rebellion. With peace, the colonists looked forward to settling the new lands to the west, but the Indian tribes living in the upper Ohio Valley opposed British expansion. In 1763 an uprising led by the Ottawa chief Pontiac was launched against English outposts in the region. Although initially successful, the rebellion was unable to counter British force, and Pontiac signed a peace treaty in 1766.

Meanwhile, in October of 1763, the British government had issued a proclamation prohibiting colonial expansion to the west of the Appalachian Mountains. The following year the British began to pass laws raising taxes on the colonies to help pay off the large debt incurred in fighting the French. The colonists objected to these actions by Parliament, and resentment of the British government began to grow.

Actions and reactions. For 150 years, the people of the American colonies had lived in relative freedom. British rule over them had been lax, partly because the British government did not have any centralized authority to oversee colonial affairs.

Following the French and Indian War, however, British rule began to tighten. The mother country had always placed some trade restrictions on the colonies. For example, the Navigation Acts passed during the 1600s included provisions stating that all goods shipped into and out of the colonies had to be transported

PONTIAC, an Ottawa chief, led a rebellion against English expansion in the upper Ohio Valley in 1763. He was forced to sign a treaty of peace with the British in 1766.

on British-owned or colonial-owned ships; that goods going from the colonies to other nations of Europe had to pass first through British ports, where the British could collect taxes on them; and that some colonial goods—like sugar, tobacco, cotton, molasses, indigo, and rice—could be shipped only to Britain.

There were also some restrictions on the goods the colonists were allowed to manufacture (so they would not be competitive with British manufactures). Enforcement of these restrictions was never very firm, and colonists engaged in massive smuggling to get around them. As the British government sought new revenues, it attempted to enforce these trade laws and impose new ones.

The Grenville Acts. In 1764 Lord George Grenville, Britain's prime minister and Chancellor of the Exchequer, began a campaign to strengthen British authority over the colonies. The Sugar Act (1764) imposed new duties on many goods shipped to the colonists from Britain. The Quartering Act (1765) required colonial governments to provide housing and supplies for British troops stationed in the colonies. The Stamp Act (1765) required the purchase of a tax stamp for every legal document, newspaper, pamphlet, or broadside issued in the colonies. Even playing cards and dice required a tax stamp.

American protest against these measures was immediate and loud. Colonial merchants complained that the Sugar Act duties were more than they could afford. Colonial governments refused to obey the Quartering Act. But the Stamp Act drew the greatest fire. In Virginia's House of Burgesses, Patrick Henry condemned it and the English king, saying of his defiance, "If this be treason, make the most of it!"

Groups of angry colonists organized the Sons of Liberty, who openly defied the act by attacking stamp tax collectors. In October of 1765, representatives from nine colonies formed a Stamp Act Congress, which sent a formal protest to King George III asserting that only colonial assemblies had the right to tax the colonists. "Taxation without representation is tyranny," they cried. In response to this protest and to a growing refusal by colonists to buy or use the stamps, as well as a petition by London merchants who had been hurt by a growing colonial boycott of British goods, the hated Stamp Act was repealed in 1766. But Parliament also passed a law declaring

the colonies to be subordinate to the British government, which had "full power and authority" to make laws concerning them.

The Townshend Acts. Lord Grenville was forced to resign, but his ideas still had support in Charles Townshend, the new Chancellor of the Exchequer. In 1767 Townshend persuaded the British Parliament to place a new set of revenue-producing duties on glass, lead, paper, paints, and tea brought into the colonies. The colonists saw these duties as thinly disguised taxes.

Some Americans determined to avoid paying the new duties by smuggling goods, others by refusing to buy them. Imports of the listed goods went down by 50 percent. The Virginia House of Burgesses passed the Virginia Resolves, stating that only the colonial government had the authority to tax its citizens. In the North, Boston became a hotbed of resistance. Britain stationed troops there to keep the peace and enforce the duties.

The citizens of Boston, forced to provide for the quartering of British troops, grew more and more angry. On March 5, 1770, their anger exploded into violence. As a crowd of Bostonians taunted red-coated soldiers standing guard near the Customs House, a shot rang out, and the soldiers opened fire on the crowd. When the smoke cleared, five of the colonists lay dead or dying in the snow. Word of this "Boston Massacre" spread quickly through the colonies.

In the next month, the British government repealed all the Townshend duties except the one on tea. It left that as an indication of its right to tax the colonists.

Organized resistance. Following the Boston Massacre, Samuel Adams, a Boston lawyer, began organizing a large number of Committees of Correspondence, intended to keep tabs on British actions in the colonies and to pass

THE BOSTON MASSACRE occurred in 1770, when British troops fired on citizens angered by the duties passed by British Parliament on glass, lead, paper, paints, and tea brought into the colonies.

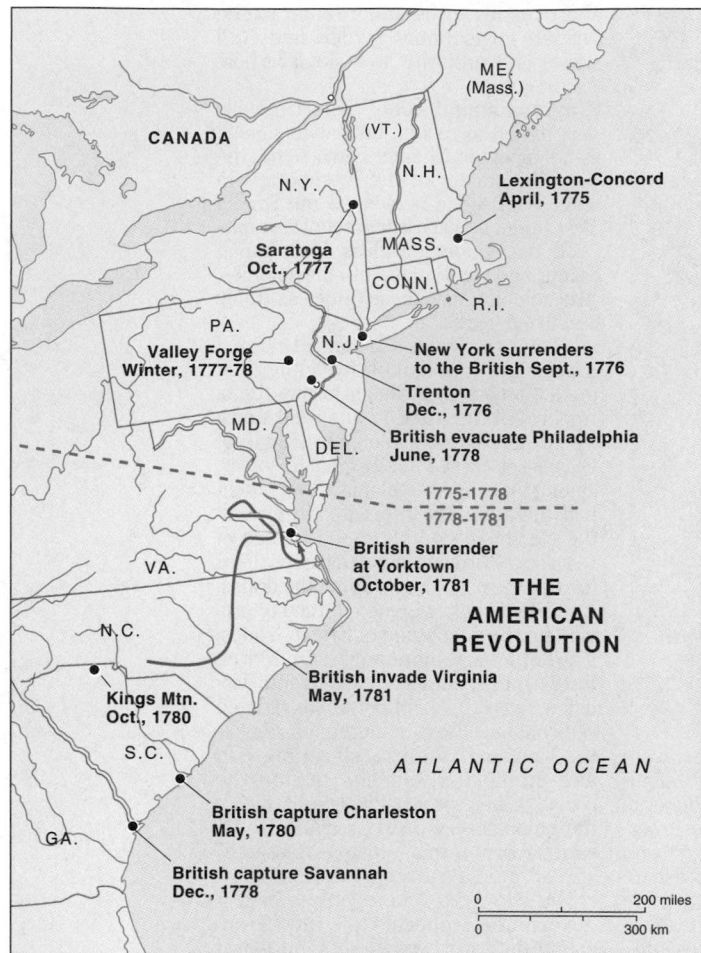

THE AMERICAN REVOLUTION

ME. (Mass.)

CANADA

(VT.)

N.Y.

N.H.

Lexington-Concord
April, 1775

Saratoga
Oct., 1777

MASS.

CONN.

R.I.

PA.

N.J.

Valley Forge
Winter, 1777-78

New York surrenders
to the British Sept., 1776

Trenton
Dec., 1776

MD.

DEL.

British evacuate Philadelphia
June, 1778

1775-1778
1778-1781

British surrender
at Yorktown
October, 1781

VA.

N.C.

British invade Virginia
May, 1781

Kings Mtn.
Oct., 1780

S.C.

ATLANTIC OCEAN

British capture Charleston
May, 1780

GA.

British capture Savannah
Dec., 1778

0   200 miles
0   300 km

COLONISTS dressed as Indians stole aboard ships in Boston Harbor in 1773 and threw overboard the tea from the hated East India Company that threatened to put colonial tea merchants out of business.

THE DECLARATION OF INDEPENDENCE from Great Britain was adopted by the Continental Congress on July 4, 1776.

information along to other colonists. The committees encouraged opposition to British actions. Soon there were Committees of Correspondence in nearly every colony. In addition to Sam Adams, the members included John Hancock and James Otis of Massachusetts, and Patrick Henry and Thomas Jefferson of Virginia.

In 1773 the British passed the Tea Act, which favored the East India Company, a British tea-selling company, and threatened to put colonial tea merchants out of business. In the dark of night on December 16, 1773, some 50 Sons of Liberty disguised as Indians stole aboard three ships anchored in Boston Harbor that were loaded with tea from the hated British tea company. They threw all of the tea overboard. This "Boston Tea Party" enraged the British government.

The Intolerable Acts. The British were quick to retaliate. Early in 1774, Parliament began passing a series of Coercive Acts, called "Intolerable Acts" in America. The first act, the Boston Port Bill, closed Boston Harbor to all shipping. This threatened the people of Boston with shortages of food and with business failures. Another act took the Massachusetts government out of colonial hands and placed it effectively under British rule. It also forced the colonists to get written permission from

the governor to hold any town meeting other than the annual meeting held to elect selectmen or other local officials.

Toward independence. The British government intended that the Coercive Acts would punish and isolate Massachusetts. Instead, the acts served to rally the other colonies to the defense of Massachusetts. At the first news of Boston's fate, the Virginia House of Burgesses called for a meeting of representatives from all the colonies to draw up a united protest.

The First Continental Congress. In September of 1774, 56 delegates from twelve colonies (only Georgia was absent) met in Philadelphia, where they took the following steps:

1. Declared the Coercive Acts null and void.
2. Pledged that their colonies would not buy goods from Britain.
3. Urged the colonists of Massachusetts not to pay any taxes to their military government.
4. Encouraged Massachusetts to organize a militia.
5. Sent a formal protest to King George III.
6. Planned to meet again the following May.

Parliament and the king replied to the protest by sending more troops to the colonies to put down any unrest.

Lexington and Concord. The military governor of Massachusetts, General Thomas Gage, soon learned that the colonists were training a militia of "Minutemen," so-called because they could mobilize at a minute's notice. The Minutemen had a supply of guns and ammunition at Concord, a few miles outside Boston. Gage ordered some 700 British soldiers to march from Boston to Concord and capture or destroy the supplies in a surprise raid. But the colonists set up a system to warn the people when the British troops made their move.

On the night of April 18, 1775, a light flashed from the tower of Boston's Old North Church. It alerted Paul Revere and William Dawson to race along the roads to Concord on horseback, warning that "the British are coming."

When the British got to Lexington, they were met by Captain Thomas Parker's company of 70 Minutemen. "If they mean to have war," said Parker, "let it begin here." Gunfire exploded and eight Minutemen fell dead. The British continued on to Concord, where they destroyed the militia's supplies and confronted a force of some 400 Minutemen at Concord's Old North Bridge before beginning a retreat to Boston. By that time, some 30 towns in eastern Massachusetts had been roused, and their 3700 Minutemen sniped at the retreating British troops from behind walls and trees. British casualties were almost 300 dead, wounded, or missing.

The Second Continental Congress. Less than a month later, on May 10, 1775, the Second Continental Congress assembled in Philadelphia. This time all the colonies sent delegates, among them George Washington, John Adams, Benjamin Franklin, Thomas Jefferson, and John Hancock.

The Congress petitioned the English king to repeal the Intolerable Acts and to refrain from making any more "unprovoked attacks," such as those that occurred at Lexington and Concord. The Congress also asked the colonies to send soldiers to help the Minutemen, who were still fighting around Boston. It named George Washington as the commander of the forces, which formed the core of the Continental Army, also authorized by Congress.

Before Washington could reach Boston, however, a major conflict flared between Americans and British there. The Americans had dug in at Breed's Hill and Bunker Hill north of Boston. On June 17, 1775, General Gage sent 2,400 British troops to dislodge them. The Americans initially stuck to their guns, but after three charges, the British troops drove them out. This victory in the Battle of Bunker Hill cost the British about 1000 casualties.

Still, the Continental Congress did not call for total revolution against Britain. Many Americans were still loyal to the British Crown; they simply wanted to end what they saw as Britain's unfair and wrongful actions toward them. In July Congress adopted a conciliatory petition, known as the Olive Branch Petition, to be sent to the king in hopes of restoring peace. But in September the colonists learned that the king had refused the petition and also declared that the colonies were in revolt and that Britain would take military action against them.

In May of 1776, the Second Continental Congress met once more and declared, "It appears absolutely irreconcilable to reason and good conscience for the people . . . to support any government under the Crown of Great Britain."

The Declaration of Independence. In June 1776, Richard Henry Lee of Virginia brought a motion before the Continental Congress: *"Resolved,* that these United Colonies are, and of right ought to be, free and independent States." Five delegates—Thomas Jefferson, Benjamin Franklin, John Adams, Robert R. Livingston, and Roger Sherman—began preparing a declaration to embody this motion. Thomas Jefferson did most of the writing, and in July, the Declaration of Independence was presented to the Continental Congress.

This historic document was composed of two parts: a preamble that justified the colonists' rights as God-given, and a list of grievances against the tyrannical King George III. On July 4, 1776, the Congress adopted the declaration. The new United States now was on the way to full revolution.

The Declaration of Independence

Adopted by the Continental Congress, July 4, 1776

When in the Course of Human Events, it becomes necessary for one People to dissolve the Political Bands which have connected them with another, and to assume among the Powers of the Earth, the separate and equal Station to which the Laws of Nature and of Nature's God entitle them, a decent Respect to the Opinions of Mankind requires that they should declare the causes which impel them to the Separation.

We hold these Truths to be self-evident, that all Men are created equal, that they are endowed by their Creator with certain unalienable Rights, that among these are Life, Liberty, and the Pursuit of Happiness—That to secure these Rights, Governments are instituted among Men, deriving their just Powers from the Consent of the Governed, that whenever any Form of Government becomes destructive of these Ends, it is the Right of the People to alter or to abolish it, and to institute new Government, laying its Foundation on such Principles, and organizing its Powers in such Form, as to them shall seem most likely to effect their Safety and Happiness. Prudence, indeed, will dictate that Governments long established should not be changed for light and transient Causes; and accordingly all Experience hath shewn, that Mankind are more disposed to suffer, while Evils are sufferable, than to right themselves by abolishing the Forms to which they are accustomed. But when a long Train of Abuses and Usurpations, pursuing invariably the same Object, evinces a Design to reduce them under absolute Despotism, it is their Right, it is their Duty, to throw off such Government, and to provide new Guards for their future Security. Such has been the patient Sufferance of these Colonies; and such is now the Necessity which constrains them to alter their former Systems of Government.

(Here follows a list of specific complaints against the King and the British government.)

We, therefore, the Representatives of the UNITED STATES OF AMERICA, in GENERAL CONGRESS, Assembled, appealing to the Supreme Judge of the World for the Rectitude of our Intentions, do, in the Name, and by Authority of the good People of these Colonies, solemnly Publish and Declare, That these United Colonies are, and of Right ought to be, FREE AND INDEPENDENT STATES; that they are absolved from all Allegiance to the British Crown, and that all political Connection between them and the State of Great-Britain, is and ought to be totally dissolved; and that as FREE AND INDEPENDENT STATES, they have full Power to levy War, conclude Peace, contract Alliances, establish Commerce, and to do all other Acts and Things which INDEPENDENT STATES may of right do. And for the support of this Declaration, with a firm Reliance on the Protection of divine Providence, we mutally pledge to each other our Lives, our Fortunes, and our sacred Honor.

The American Revolution.

By July 4, 1776, the Revolution was more than a year old. Following Lexington and Concord, Boston lay under siege for nearly a year as the Americans continued to fight to drive the British out. On March 4, 1776, Washington's forces occupied Dorchester Heights and began to move up artillery that had been captured at Ft. Ticonderoga on May 10, 1775, by a force under Ethan Allen. From the Heights Washington's guns commanded Boston. On March 7 the British commander, General William Howe, decided to evacuate Boston, and on March 26 the British forces sailed to a friendlier base in Canada.

War in the Middle Colonies. In the summer of 1776, General Howe landed 30,000 British troops in New York City. Washington had moved his troops there from Boston, but they were no match for the British force. Howe easily defeated the Americans on Long Island on August 27 and occupied New York City on September 15.

Trenton and Princeton. Washington retreated north, crossed the Hudson, then moved through New Jersey and into Pennsylvania in the autumn. As winter set in, the British believed that the war would wind down, but Washington surprised them. On Christmas night, Washington and 6,000 troops crossed the icy Delaware River to attack the British garrison at Trenton, New Jersey. The force there, made up of Hessian (German) mercenaries hired by the British, quickly surrendered. Washington moved on to Princeton, where his men captured two British regiments with their guns and supplies.

GENERAL WASHINGTON captured two British regiments with their guns and supplies in his famous charge at Princeton.

THE BITTER WINTER shared by General Washington and his troops at Valley Forge in 1777–1778 was a time of starvation, disease, and suffering.

colors
US

colours
Brit.

Saratoga. In 1777 British General John Burgoyne presented a plan he thought would crush all effective American resistance. He believed that the Hudson River valley was the key. If the British could win command there, they could gain full control of New York and cut off New England from the other colonies.

Burgoyne's plan called for him to lead an army south from Montreal in Canada to the Hudson River. A second army, under the command of Colonel Barry St. Leger, was to enter western New York from Canada over Lake Ontario and sweep in from the west. A third army, under General Howe, was to move up the Hudson River from New York City toward Albany.

The plan did not work. St. Leger's force was stopped by an American force under General Nicholas Herkimer and retreated to Canada. General Howe, instead of moving north up the Hudson, moved south, capturing Philadelphia on September 26 after defeating Washington at Brandywine two weeks earlier. On October 4 he again defeated Washington's troops, at Germantown. Burgoyne's troops marched south as far as Saratoga, north of Albany, where the Continental Army surrounded them and forced their surrender on October 17, 1777.

The Battle of Saratoga proved to be the turning point of the American Revolution. It weakened the British and strengthened American morale, and it also helped to convince France that the Americans could win the war. The French decided to support the Americans with troops and supplies, and they signed a treaty of alliance on February 6, 1778.

Valley Forge. Following the loss of Philadelphia, Washington moved his troops to Valley Forge in Pennsylvania for winter encampment. The winter of 1777–1778 was a terrible period of starvation, disease, and suffering for the American troops. Yet they endured, and thanks to military drill and training, they came out a stronger army than before.

War at sea. The powerful British navy had little to fear from the rebellious Americans. The Continental Congress had authorized an American navy in 1775, but there was little money to build ships and the British easily destroyed most of the ships that were built. Some owners of fishing boats or merchant ships equipped their vessels with guns and went to sea as privateers, harassing British shipping and sometimes capturing trading ships.

The most famous naval battle of the American Revolution was fought off the coast of England on September 23, 1779, between the American ship *Bonhomme Richard,* an old French warship under the command of Captain John Paul Jones, and the larger British ship *Serapis.* After several hours of battle, the *Bonhomme Richard* was close to sinking when Jones brought it near to the *Serapis.* Thinking that the American ship wanted to surrender, the British captain asked, "Have you struck your colors?"

Jones shouted his famous reply, "I have not yet begun to fight!"

With that, Jones's men raked the British with musket fire and hand grenades and each crew tried to board the other ship, without success. More than half the Americans were killed or wounded, but Jones captured the *Serapis.* He transferred his crew from the badly damaged *Bonhomme Richard,* which sank two days later.

CAPTAIN JOHN PAUL JONES captured the larger British ship, *Serapis,* in the famous battle in which he declared, "I have not yet begun to fight!"

The American Revolution 1766–1783

In the following listing of battles and events in the American Revolution, (A) indicates an American force and (B) a British force. The winning commanders appear in italics.

1766–1774
Mar. 8, 1766 Repeal of the Stamp Act.
Mar. 5, 1770 Boston Massacre.
June 9, 1772 Burning of the customs schooner *Gaspé*.
Dec. 16, 1773 Boston Tea Party.
Sept. 5 to Oct. 6, 1774 First Continental Congress.

1775
Apr. 18 Paul Revere's ride.
Apr. 19 Fight at Lexington and Concord: *Capt. John Parker (A)*; Maj. John Pitcairn (B).
May 10 Capture of Ticonderoga: *Ethan Allen (A)*; Capt. Delaplace (B).
May 10 to Mar. 3, 1789 Second Continental Congress.
May 12 Capture of Crown Point: *Seth Warner (A)*.
June 17 Battle of Bunker Hill: *William Prescott (A)*; Gov. Thomas Gage (B).
July 3 Washington assumes command of the Continental Army at Boston.
July to Mar. 1776 Siege of Boston: *George Washington (A)*; Sir William Howe (B).
Sept. to Dec. American invasion of Canada: Gen. Richard Montgomery (A); Sir Guy Carleton (B).
Nov. 12 Capture of Montreal: *Gen. Richard Montgomery (A)*; Sir Guy Carleton (B).

1776
Mar. 7–26 British evacuate Boston.
July 4 Declaration of Independence adopted by Continental Congress in Philadelphia.
Aug. 27 Battle of Long Island, N.Y.: George Washington (A); *Sir William Howe (B)*.
Sept. 15 Occupation of New York City by British.
Sept. 16 Battle of Harlem Heights: George Washington (A); *Sir William Howe (B)*.
Sept. 22 Nathan Hale executed as a spy.
Oct. 11–13 Naval battle on Lake Champlain: Benedict Arnold (A); *Sir Guy Carleton (B)*.
Oct. 28 Battle of White Plains: George Washington (A); *Sir William Howe (B)*.
Nov. 16 Loss of Fort Washington, N.Y.: Col. Robert Magaw (A); *Sir William Howe (B)*.
Nov. to Dec. Washington's retreat through New Jersey.
Dec. 25 Washington crosses the Delaware River.
Dec. 26 Battle of Trenton, N.J.: *George Washington (A)*; Johann G. Rall (B).

1777
Jan. 3 Battle of Princeton, N.J.: *George Washington (A)*; Lt. Col. Mawhood (B).
Apr. 25–26 British raid and burn Danbury: *Benedict Arnold and David Wooster (A)*; Col. William Tryon (B).
July 5 Americans evacuate Ticonderoga: Arthur St. Clair (A).

Aug. 3–22 Siege of Ft. Stanwix (Schuyler—now Rome), N.Y.: *Peter Gansevoort (A)*; Barry St. Leger (B).
Sept. 11 Battle of Brandywine, Pa.: George Washington (A); *Sir William Howe (B)*.
Sept. 19 Continental Congress flees Philadelphia to York, Pa.
Sept. 21 The Paoli "Massacre," Pa.: Anthony Wayne (A); *Gen. Grey (B)*.
Sept. 26 British occupy Philadelphia.
Oct. 4 Battle of Germantown, Pa.: George Washington (A); *Sir William Howe (B)*.
Oct. 6 British capture forts Montgomery and Clinton, N.Y., on the Hudson: James Clinton (A); *Henry Clinton (B)*.
Oct. 17 Surrender of the British Army at Saratoga, N.Y., by Sir John Burgoyne.
Nov. 15 Articles of Confederation submitted to the states for ratification.
Dec. 19 to June 17, 1778 Washington's army encamped at Valley Forge, Pa.

1778
Jan. Conway Cabel seeking removal of Washington from command of American army exposed.
Feb. 6 Franco-American treaty of alliance signed in Paris.
June 18 British evacuate Philadelphia.
June 28 Battle of Monmouth, N.J.: *George Washington (A)*; Sir Henry Clinton (B).
July 4 Wyoming (Pa.) Massacre: Col. Zebulon Butler (A); *Col. John Butler (B)*.
July 4 to Aug. 12 Gen Charles Lee court-martialed for conduct at Battle of Monmouth.
July 11 Arrival of French fleet under Comte d'Estaing off Sandy Hook, N.Y.
Aug. 8–11 Siege of Newport, R.I.: George Washington (A); *Sir Henry Clinton (B)*.
Nov. 11 Cherry Valley (Pa.) Massacre by Indians led by Chief Joseph Brant (B).
Dec. 29 Capture of Savannah, Ga., by British Gen. Robert Howe (A); *Lt. Col. Archibald Campbell (B)*.

1779
Jan. 29 British conquest of Georgia completed: Gen. Robert Howe (A); *Lt. Col. Archibald Campbell (B)*.
Feb. 25 Capture of Vincennes, Ind.: *George Rogers Clark (A)*; Henry Hamilton (B).
Mar. 3 Battle of Briar Creek, Ga.: Col. John Ashe (A); *Lt. Col. Prevost (B)*.
July 5 Plundering and burning of New Haven, Conn., by British led by Gov. William Tryon.
July 15 Storming of Stony Point, N.Y.: *Anthony Wayne (A)*; Lt. Col. Henry Johnson (B).
Sept. 23 Naval action, *Bonhomme Richard* and *Serapis: John Paul Jones (A)*; Richard Pearson (B).
Sept. 29 to Oct. 9 American siege of Savannah, Ga.: Benjamin Lincoln (A); *Sir James Wright (B)*.

Oct. 9 American assault at Savannah and death of Pulaski: Benjamin Lincoln (A); *Sir James Wright (B)*.

1780
Apr. 10 to May 12 British siege of Charleston, S.C.: Benjamin Lincoln (A); *Sir Henry Clinton (B)*.
May 12 American surrender of Charleston, S.C.: Benjamin Lincoln (A); *Sir Henry Clinton (B)*.
July 10 Arrival of French troops under Rochambeau at Newport, R.I.
July 25 Gen. Horatio Gates assumes command of American army in the South.
Aug. 6 Battle of Hanging Rock, S.C.: *Thomas Sumter (A)*; Banastre Tarleton (B).
Aug. 16 Battle of Camden, S.C.: Horatio Gates (A); *Lord Cornwallis (B)*.
Sept. 21 Benedict Arnold's treason uncovered.
Oct. 2 John André executed at Tappan, N.Y., as a spy.
Dec. 4 Gen. Nathanael Greene assumes command of the American army in the South.

1781
Jan. 1 Mutiny of Pennsylvania line in Washington's army at Morristown, N.J.
Jan. 17 Battle of Cowpens, S.C.: *Col. Daniel Morgan (A)*; Banastre Tarleton (B).
Jan. 20 Mutiny of the New Jersey line in Washington's army at Morristown, N.J.
Mar. 1 Articles of Confederation become effective.
Mar. 15 Battle of Guilford Courthouse, N.C.: Nathanael Greene (A); *Lord Cornwallis (B)*.
Sept. 8 Battle of Eutaw Springs, S.C.: *Nathanael Greene (A)*; Lt. Col. Alexander Stewart (B).
Sept. 28 to Oct. 19 Siege of Yorktown, Va.: *George Washington (A)*; Lord Cornwallis (B).
Oct. 19 Surrender of Yorktown, Va.: *George Washington (A)*; Lord Cornwallis (B).

1782
July 11 British evacuate Savannah, Ga.
Nov. 30 Preliminary Treaty of Peace between the United States and Great Britain in Paris.
Dec. 14 British evacuate Charleston, S.C.

1783
Sept. 3 Definitive Treaty of Peace between the United States and Great Britain signed in Paris.
Nov. 25 British evacuate New York City.
Dec. 4 Washington delivers his Farewell Address to his officers in Fraunces Tavern, New York City.
Dec. 23 Washington resigns as commander in chief of the American army.

War in the South. In 1778 the British developed a new military plan. They attacked the Southern Colonies, intending to march northward. In December British forces attacked Savannah, the major port of Georgia. The attack succeeded and the British soon took control of most of the colony. In 1780 British forces under the command of General Charles Cornwallis sailed into the South Carolina port of Charleston and captured it. British troops soon began the march north to capture the Carolinas.

However, when Cornwallis's men reached Kings Mountain in North Carolina on October 7, a few hundred Kentucky and Tennessee riflemen wiped out half of Cornwallis's army. In the next few months, the British lost additional battles in the Carolinas to Americans under the command of generals Nathanael Greene and Daniel Morgan. In the end, the British were able to hold onto Savannah and Charleston but nothing else.

Yorktown. In the spring of 1781 Cornwallis moved north from Wilmington, North Carolina, to invade Virginia. Opposing the British advance was a small American force under the command of the Marquis de Lafayette, a young French nobleman who had offered his military services to the Continental Congress. Cornwallis and Lafayette fought to a stalemate. Cornwallis made camp at Yorktown, Virginia, on the Chesapeake Bay, where he waited for a British fleet that was to resupply him with fresh troops, ammunition, and provisions.

Before Cornwallis could receive help, however, Washington and his army, along with French troops commanded by Marshal Rochambeau, moved south to Virginia to attack by land. The French fleet arrived to blockade Chesapeake Bay, cutting off any possibility of resupply or escape by sea for the British. Surrounded and cut off, Cornwallis was forced to surrender. He

GENERAL CHARLES CORNWALLIS surrendered to the Americans at Yorktown on October 18, 1781, although sporadic fighting continued in the colonies for another year.

THE CONSTITUTION OF THE UNITED STATES established a form of government predicated on the idea that government was of the people, by the people, and for the people.

and his force of over 7,000 men laid down their arms on October 18, 1781. Sporadic fighting continued in the colonies for the next year, but essentially the American Revolution was over and an independent nation had been born.

Establishing a new government.

Now that the war had ended, it was time to draw up the terms of peace. The Continental Congress sent Benjamin Franklin, John Jay, and John Adams to Paris to meet with the commissioners of the British government. Thomas Jefferson and Henry Laurens were also appointed but did not go to Paris. The British wanted to grant little more than independence to their former colonies, but through sheer tenacity, the American commissioners gained further concessions: fishing rights in Canadian waters and ownership of the entire Ohio River valley. By the Treaty of Paris, signed in 1783, the United States stretched from Canada to Spanish Florida and from the Atlantic coast to the Mississippi River. Now the nation had to set about the task of governing itself in peacetime.

Articles of Confederation. Shortly after the Declaration of Independence had been adopted in 1776, the Second Continental Congress drew up a plan of government called the Articles of Confederation. The Articles were adopted by Congress on November 15, 1777, and were ratified on March 1, 1781. They provided for the continuation of Congress, with state delegates appointed and paid by each state, and they gave Congress the right to declare and carry on war, build a navy, manage all foreign and Indian affairs, settle interstate disputes, coin money, and create post offices.

Weaknesses within the Articles quickly became obvious. Congress could neither levy nor collect taxes; it could only name the amount needed and wait for the states to supply it. It could pass laws, but it had no way of enforcing them. Also, no change or improvement could be made in the Articles without the unanimous vote of all the states, which meant that one state could thwart the will of the remaining twelve.

Under the Articles of Confederation, Congress was able to shape one far-reaching measure—the Ordinance of 1787, also called the Northwest Ordinance—which determined the future of the Northwest Territory, the area west of the colonies and north of the Ohio River. The ordinance provided for the formation of no less than three or more than five states in the territory, and stated that each new state could be admitted into the union when its population reached 60,000. Slavery was forbidden in the area, but this provision did not affect fugitive slaves from other states, or slaves already in the territory. Five states grew out of the old Northwest Territory—Ohio (1803), Indiana (1816), Illinois (1818), Michigan (1837), and Wisconsin (1848). The nation now had a working method by which future states could enter the union.

But the Articles were unable to alleviate the growing rivalries and disputes among the states or to deal with the nation's inability to deal adequately with foreign affairs. In 1787 Congress called a convention to draw up a plan that

would correct the weaknesses of the Articles of Confederation.

Writing the Constitution. In May, 1787, 55 delegates from eleven states (Rhode Island was absent, and New Hampshire's delegates arrived later) met in Philadelphia. Among them were the nation's most prominent leaders. George Washington was chosen president of the convention. James Madison, Alexander Hamilton, Benjamin Franklin, and Gouverneur Morris were among the delegates. The delegates soon decided not to revise the existing Articles, but instead to prepare an entirely new constitution.

Problems became obvious immediately. States with large populations clashed with smaller states over the matter of representation in Congress. Small states feared that lesser representation would put them at the mercy of larger states. Connecticut proposed a solution: The lower house of Congress, the House of Representatives, would represent the people of the states on the basis of population. Large states would have more representatives than small states. The upper house, the Senate, would have equal representation from each state, large or small.

Another problem arose between states that had large slave populations and states that did not. The slave states wanted the slaves counted as part of their populations in determining how many representatives they would have in the House. But they did not want slaves counted as part of their populations when it came to determining what taxes each state should pay. The non-slave states could not agree. Once again, a compromise was found. Only three-fifths of the slaves would be counted, for both representation and tax purposes.

The convention also separated the national government into three branches—legislative (Congress), to make laws; executive (president), to carry out laws; and judicial (Supreme Court and other national courts), to interpret laws. The convention also agreed that the United States should have a federal system of government in which the national, or federal, government would share power with the state governments.

On September 17, 1787, the delegates adopted the Constitution. Now they had to go back to their states to convince the state governments to vote for its adoption too. Only when two-thirds of the states ratified the Constitution would it become the law of the land.

Ratification. The Constitution met with a great deal of opposition in the various states. Numerous groups opposed it, as did some prominent patriots. Men like Patrick Henry and Samuel Adams fought ratification because they believed that the Constitution created too strong a central government; they feared tyranny. Other Americans argued that the Constitution created a government that would favor the rich over the poor and middle classes. Men like Thomas Jefferson thought that the Constitution must include a "bill of rights" that would protect citizens' personal liberties—for example, freedom of speech, press, and religion—against the powers of the new government.

The Federalist Papers, a series of essays written by Alexander Hamilton, James Madison, and John Jay, defended the Constitution and helped win support for it. Gradually, the states began ratifying the Constitution. Ratification was secured in Massachusetts only on condition that a bill of proposed amendments be added to it. (They were incorporated into the first ten amendments, or Bill of Rights.) On June 21, 1788, the vote of the ninth ratifying state (New Hampshire) made the Constitution "the supreme law of the land." (See also GOVERNMENT AND LAW volume, the Constitution section.)

Founding a new nation. The first step in implementing the Constitution was to elect a president and the members of Congress. The Constitution provided for an electoral college, composed of elected representatives from each state, to cast votes for the president and vice president. On February 4 (the first Wednesday in February), 1789, the electoral college chose George Washington as president and John Adams as vice president. On April 30 Washington took the oath of office in New York City, the nation's temporary capital. (In 1790 it would be moved to Philadelphia and in 1800 to Washington, D.C.)

Congress met and quickly established a cabinet system to aid the president. Executive departments of state, treasury, and war as well as an office of attorney general and postmaster general were included. By passing the Judiciary Act of 1789, Congress set up the Supreme Court and 16 lower federal courts.

Domestic problems. The Revolutionary War had left the United States government deeply in debt, both to American citizens and to foreign governments. The nation was also in need of many costly internal improvements—roads, for example. Secretary of the Treasury Alexander Hamilton, a leader of the Federalists, felt that the central government should take strong action to solve these financial problems. He proposed that tariffs be raised and that new taxes be levied on certain American goods, like liquor. He further proposed that a national bank, the Bank of the United States, be established by private investors to handle tax revenues and to print money. (Previously, each state printed its own money.)

Secretary of State Thomas Jefferson opposed Hamilton's plan, feeling that it favored the wealthy, landed class at the expense of the farmers. He also objected to the national bank because the Constitution had not specifically provided for such a bank, and because "all powers not delegated to the United States, by the Constitution, nor prohibited by it to the states, are reserved to the states, or to the people."

Hamilton argued that in addition to the express powers enumerated in the Constitution, there were also implied powers that could be "employed as an instrument or means of carrying into execution any of the specified powers."

Hamilton's plan was put in place, but it pointed up a deep division in beliefs about how the nation should be governed. Hamilton and the Federalists favored a strong and active federal government and opposed the limitation of its powers strictly to those specifically granted to it in the Constitution. The Democratic-Republicans, led by Jefferson, did not want to see a strong central government. They felt that strong state powers were the surest way to protect the individual rights of the people. In the following years, the two factions

THE NEW CONSTITUTION was adopted in Philadelphia on September 17, 1787.

hardened into rival political parties, forming the basis of a two-party system.

In 1791 Hamilton sponsored and secured passage of a bill raising an excise tax on the manufacture of liquor. Hamilton's new tax soon led to rebellion. Farmers in Pennsylvania, who made whiskey from the grain they grew, banded together in 1794. They refused to pay the tax and drove the tax collectors away. President Washington used troops to crush this "Whiskey Rebellion" and end defiance of federal authority.

Foreign affairs. In 1789 the United States's old ally, France, had a revolution of its own, overthrowing the monarchy. In 1793 the new republican government went to war with Britain and Spain. France expected American support, but President Washington proclaimed that the nation would remain strictly neutral.

Remaining neutral proved very difficult. Both French and British ships harassed American shipping, and the British even began taking American sailors off their ships and impressing them into the British navy. In addition, the French minister to the United States, Edmond Genêt, known as Citizen Genêt, compromised American neutrality by commissioning French privateers and organizing expeditions against British territories.

These and other problems prompted President Washington to open negotiations with the warring nations. In 1794 he sent John Jay to Britain as his representative. The result was the Jay Treaty, which was signed on November 19, 1794; it did not succeed in ending British impressment, but it did extract a promise that British troops would be removed from the Northwest Territory, reducing the threat of war in North America.

The next year, Washington sent Charles C. Pinckney to Spain. The result was the Pinckney Treaty, signed on October 27, 1795. The treaty gave Americans free use of the Mississippi River

and let them establish warehouses in New Orleans.

The XYZ Affair. In 1797 John Adams, a Federalist, became president, and he continued negotiations with foreign governments. The French had broken off diplomatic relations with the United States because of the Jay Treaty and the perception that the United States was favoring Great Britain in its foreign policy. President Adams sent diplomats to France to try to reestablish peaceful relations, but the French minister of foreign affairs, Talleyrand, not only refused to see the Americans but also sent three French agents to them to demand huge bribes as payment for a peaceful settlement. When the American people learned in 1798 of this XYZ Affair (the French agents were never named and were referred to simply as X, Y, and Z), they were outraged. Federalists demanded that the United States declare war on France. The Democratic-Republicans resisted, and tensions grew.

An undeclared naval war followed the establishment of a Navy Department in May of 1798 and the repeal in July of the 1778 treaties of alliance with France, which were superseded by a new treaty, the Convention of 1800.

Alien and Sedition Acts. Popular feeling at the height of the French crisis led the Federalists to push Congress to pass four laws known collectively as the Alien and Sedition Acts in 1798. The Alien Act, passed on June 25, gave the president the power to deport any foreigner who seemed a menace to the nation; the Sedition Act, passed on July 24, imposed fines and imprisonment upon anyone who opposed government measures or published "false, scandalous and malicious" attacks on Congress or the president. The Naturalization Act, passed on June 18, required a 14-year residency in the United States before any alien could gain citizenship. The Alien Enemies Act, passed on July 6, gave the president the authority to apprehend, imprison, or deport any

alien subjects of an enemy nation in time of war.

The Democratic-Republican group accused the Federalists of launching a "reign of terror." Kentucky and Virginia passed resolutions in 1798 that denied the federal government any powers not explicitly given by the Constitution, and declared that the states had the right to nullify what they believed to be unconstitutional acts of Congress.

Jeffersonian democracy. In 1800, John Adams was defeated for another term as president by Thomas Jefferson, and the Democratic-Republicans took over. Jefferson, who was a firm believer in limited government, promised to preside over "a wise and frugal government which shall restrain men from injuring one another, and shall leave them otherwise free to regulate their own pursuits in industry and improvement."

Tripolitan War. In 1801 the United States came into conflict with Tripoli, one of the Barbary States on the Mediterranean coast of north Africa, when Tripoli's pasha demanded an increased tribute to prevent American ships in the Mediterranean Sea from being seized or attacked. Jefferson refused to pay the increased tribute and sent a fleet to the Mediterranean to blockade the port of Tripoli. In 1803 the U.S. frigate *Philadelphia* was captured, but it was destroyed in Tripoli Harbor by an American force led by Stephen Decatur. In 1805 an American force captured the Tripolitan city of Derna. Soon after a peace settlement, ending the tribute but requiring U.S. ransom for American prisoners held in Tripoli, ended the conflict. The United States, however, continued to pay tribute to other Barbary States until 1815.

The Louisiana Purchase. In 1803 President Jefferson was offered an opportunity to double the size of the United States. France under Napoleon had been embroiled in European wars for several years and was in terrible need of money. Napoleon, after being asked under what conditions he would consider selling

THE FOUNDERS of a new nation included some remarkable men. Left to right: Benjamin Franklin, already 70 years old at the time of independence, but still young enough to serve as a diplomat and to help frame the Constitution when past 80; George Washington, war hero and the first president of the young country; John Adams, first framer of American foreign policy; Alexander Hamilton, influential member of the Constitutional Convention and contributor to *The Federalist;* and Thomas Jefferson, scholar, architect, author of the Declaration of Independence, and defender of the rights of the common man.

BENJAMIN FRANKLIN **GEORGE WASHINGTON** **JOHN ADAMS** **ALEXANDER HAMILTON** **THOMAS JEFFERSON**

New Orleans and West Florida, offered to sell the Louisiana Territory, a vast area between the Mississippi River and the Rocky Mountains, for only $15 million, or a few cents an acre. Afraid that Napoleon would change his mind, Jefferson's negotiators, Robert R. Livingston and James Monroe, snapped up the offer. Congress voted to ratify the Louisiana Purchase, and the United States redrew its boundaries. In 1810 West Florida, which Jefferson viewed as part of Louisiana but which was considered by Spain to be part of Spanish Florida, was annexed.

Embargo Act of 1807. Britain and France continued to interfere with American freedom on the seas. Both sought to keep the other from benefiting from American trade. Finally, Jefferson persuaded Congress to pass an Embargo Act, a law forbidding American ships to call on foreign ports. He hoped this loss of American goods would make Britain and France stop their interference, but it only hurt American traders. In 1809 trade was resumed with all nations but Britain and France.

The War of 1812. In March, 1809, James Madison, another Democratic-Republican from Virginia, succeeded Jefferson as president. British offenses against American shipping continued. In addition, the British were encouraging Indians along the western frontier to attack American settlers. Members of Congress, called "war hawks," demanded a declaration of war on Britain. In June of 1812, President Madison delivered a war message to Congress, which passed a declaration of war on June 18.

The young nation was too weak to fight a war against a major power, but the British were fighting the French at the time, so they could spare few troops or ships to fight the Americans. However, they did launch a successful blockade of American ports and, after Napoleon's fall in 1814, were able to bring new forces to bear against the United States. They were even able to capture Washington, D.C., in August of 1814, and set it afire in retaliation for the American burning of York (Toronto) the year before. But they did not press their advantage, and soon the Americans began winning battles. The most stunning American victory took place at New Orleans, at the mouth of the Mississippi River. American troops led by General Andrew Jackson defeated the British at New Orleans on January 8, 1815. The British suffered some 2,000 casualties, but American losses were only 8 dead and 13 wounded.

Actually, this final battle never had to be fought. Representatives of Britain and the United States had been meeting in Belgium to discuss peace. On December 24, 1814, they signed a peace treaty, but news of it had not reached the United States.

The 1814 peace treaty, the Treaty of Ghent, marked the beginning of better relations between the United States and Britain. The European wars had finally ended, so interference with American shipping ended too. The treaty provided the basis for the peaceful settlement of a number of disagreements between the two countries. This allowed the United States to enter a long period of uninterrupted westward expansion and development.

National Growth and Expansion

The Era of Good Feelings.
Following the War of 1812, America took its place as a full-fledged nation in the world. At home, there was a growing sense of unity and nationalism. Even political partisanship seemed to fade as the Federalist Party lost support and the Democratic-Republican Party gained more strength. In 1816 the Democratic-Republican candidate, James Monroe of Virginia, easily won the presidency, to which he was reelected in 1820. The years of his presidency are often referred to as "the Era of Good Feelings."

Economic growth. The Federalist Party had been steadily weakening for a number of years, but many of its principles had not. The Democratic-Republicans had gradually adopted many of Hamilton's ideas for strong federal government and federal participation in the nation's economic life. Therefore, they passed the Tariff of 1816, which placed high tariffs on British-made goods coming into the country to protect budding American manufactures.

In that same year, Congress chartered the Second Bank of the United States (the first one had been chartered for only 20 years and Congress had failed to renew its charter when the matter came up for a vote in 1811). Like its predecessor, it was owned by private investors and it handled government revenues and issued bank notes, the national currency. It also regulated the policies of state banks and extended loans to encourage the growth of industry.

Recognizing that if industry were to grow it would require a good transportation system to tie the nation together, Congress passed in early 1817 a bill establishing a fund to help finance the construction of "a perfect system of roads and canals." However, outgoing President Madison vetoed the bill, halting temporarily the federal program for internal improvements. Congress later made successful appropriations to help finance the Cumberland Road, or National Road, running westward from Baltimore, Maryland, to Vandalia, Illinois. However, Congress refused to finance construction of the Erie Canal, which was ultimately approved by the New York legislature. The canal, which when completed in 1825 ran from Albany to Buffalo, on Lake Erie, opened a shipping passage from the Atlantic Ocean to the Great Lakes. This transportation system not only aided the

BETSY ROSS is reputed to have made the first official flag of the United States in 1776. A replica flies outside her restored home in Philadelphia.

growth of industry, but also the movement of hundreds of thousands of settlers westward. Its success sparked similar ventures throughout the nation.

Expanding boundaries. President Monroe's secretary of state, John Quincy Adams, the son of the former president, felt very strongly that the United States must expand its "natural boundaries" (take over all of North America). In 1818 a military force under the command of General Andrew Jackson advanced into Florida to pursue hostile Seminole Indians using Spanish territory as a refuge. This action helped convince Spain that Adams's intention to secure Florida for the United States was not to be ignored.

In 1819 Adams was able to receive Florida from Spain, for the sum of $5 million, under the terms of the Adams Onis Treaty.

The previous year, under the provisions of the Convention of 1818, the United States and Great Britain settled the border between the United States and Canada at the 49th parallel from Lake of the Woods, Minnesota, to the Rocky Mountains. By this, the United States gained some land from Canada, in what are now North Dakota, South Dakota, and Minnesota. However, no agreement was reached on the Oregon Territory west of the Rockies, which both countries claimed, so the treaty provided for joint occupation of the territory for ten years.

The Monroe Doctrine. Secretary of State Adams believed there was a threat to the United States from Europe far to the south of the nation's borders as well. Many of the Spanish colonies in Latin America were rebelling against their European masters and declaring themselves independent nations. Several of Spain's European allies expressed interest in helping Spain to regain the lost colonies. The idea of European nations coming to conquer areas in the western hemisphere greatly alarmed Adams, who feared they might also come into conflict with the United States.

On the advice of Adams, President Monroe enunciated a new doctrine in his State of the Union message to Congress in 1823. He warned Europe that any attempt at conquest or colonization with the western hemisphere would be looked on as an "unfriendly disposition to the United States." The new nation had little power to back up this "Monroe Doctrine," and it had no force in terms of United States or international law, but fortunately the British agreed to it, and the powerful British navy was able to prevent European intervention in the western hemisphere. The Monroe Doctrine became firmly established as part of the nation's political practice.

Development of economic sections.
By the end of Monroe's second term, the Era of Good Feelings was drawing to a close. In the election of 1824, the candidates—John Quincy Adams of Massachusetts, William Crawford of Georgia, Henry Clay of Kentucky, and Andrew Jackson of Tennessee—were called Republicans, but they were divided along sectional lines.

The nation was developing distinct economic sections—the North, the South, and the West. Each section favored a particular candidate. Jackson won the most popular votes, but he did not have a majority in the electoral college. The election was, therefore, thrown into the

House of Representatives, where Clay gave his support to Adams, who was then chosen president. When Adams subsequently made Clay his secretary of state, Jackson supporters charged that Clay had thrown the election in return for the appointment. It was an unfair charge, but for the rest of his career Clay was haunted by it. Jackson became Clay's enemy, and many in the West felt betrayed.

The industrial North. As early as the late 1700s, the Industrial Revolution, which was already well established in Britain, was coming to life in the United States, most particularly in the North, which included the New England and Mid-Atlantic states. The many rushing waterways of the North supplied a ready source of available energy to power factory machines. In 1790 Samuel Slater built a cotton thread spinning mill in Pawtucket, Rhode Island. Within the next 25 years, textile mills sprang up all over New England, and the American factory system was born.

At about the same time, the young and inventive Eli Whitney developed a new method of manufacture by creating interchangeable parts. In 1798 Whitney secured a contract to provide 10,000 muskets to the United States government. He opened a factory near New Haven, Connecticut, and developed machines to produce uniform, interchangeable parts for the firearms. This meant that relatively unskilled workers could produce an enormous number of muskets, which could all be easily assembled and just as easily repaired. This was a vast departure from the old way, in which a gunsmith turned out one gun at a time by hand. Soon other products were being manufactured using the principles advanced by Whitney.

The emerging factory production system gave impetus to many other industries. Iron and steel were needed for factory and farm machines. Coal was necessary to help make the iron and steel and to power factory machines.

New growing industry demanded improved transportation, and during the period from the 1820s to the 1850s, new canals and roads were being built throughout the North. At the same time, new forms of transportation were also appearing. In 1802 John Stevens demonstrated a propeller-driven steam ferry on the Hudson River, and a practical steamboat was developed by Robert Fulton in 1807. In 1809 Stevens demonstrated the first ocean-going steamboat, which sailed—or steamed—from New York to Philadelphia. By 1820 steam navigation was common on the rivers and lakes of the North. In 1826 Stevens installed a steam locomotive on a circular track at his New Jersey home; four years later a number of railroads were operating or under construction in the United States. In 1830 there were about 28 miles (45 kilometers) of railroad track in the United States, some of it for horse-drawn traffic on short runs. In 1840 the mileage increased to 2,800 (4,500 kilometers), and by 1860 to more than 30,000 (48,270 kilometers). Two-thirds of the mileage was in the North, and Chicago was the undisputed rail center of the nation.

The need for labor to run the North's growing industries brought on rapid population growth. Immigrant workers came by the thousands, and the at-home birthrate rose as well. Between the 1820s and the 1850s, the population of the North more than doubled. Philadelphia tripled and New York City and Boston quadrupled.

The agricultural South. As the North became more industrialized and urbanized, the South maintained a very different character, remaining agricultural and rural. It also developed an economic system and a social structure that differed from that of the North.

The economic system of the South was dominated by the production of cotton. Prior to 1793, cotton had been a very expensive crop to produce. Before it could be sold, sticky seeds had to be cleaned out of it by hand, a process that produced only one pound of cotton per day per worker. But in 1793, Eli Whitney, travelling in the South, recognized the solution to the problem and invented a cotton gin (short for *engine*) that made it possible for one worker to clean 50 pounds of cotton a day. Whitney's cotton gin was so simple to duplicate that soon there were cotton gins throughout the South, and most of the profits Whitney realized from his invention went into lawsuits for patent infringement.

Now cotton became highly profitable. Planters in search of cheap land left the seaboard states and established large plantations in western Georgia, Alabama, Mississippi, and even farther west. Labor was needed to work the plantations, and the planters relied on slaves. Slavery, an institution that had been diminishing somewhat in the South, experienced a burst of growth. In 1790 the number of slaves in the United States was almost 700,000. By 1820 the number was more

THE EMERGING FACTORY production system generated by the Industrial Revolution gave rise to many industries in the North. This sloss furnace was associated with the iron and steel industry.

THE SOUTH maintained an economic system and a social structure largely rural in nature and based on agriculture and the labor provided by slaves.

than 1.5 million, and by 1860 more than 3.9 million. Gradually, the South became the producer of two-thirds of the world's supply of cotton.

The South benefited from its plantation economy, but it had to share the benefits with the North. Northern shippers handled most of the cotton, and Northern manufacturers sold many goods to the South, which had not built up manufactures of its own.

The frontier West. For most of the colonial years, the Mid-Atlantic region had been the breadbasket of the nation. But as droves of settlers crossed the Appalachian Mountains following the War of 1812, the rich lands of the West became the new breadbasket. Many of the settlers headed for the Old Northwest, which grew in population more than tenfold between the 1820s and the 1850s. Others headed for the area south of the Ohio River and settled in Kentucky and Tennessee. Still others moved farther on, across the Mississippi River into Iowa, Missouri, and beyond.

The fertile prairie lands fell quickly to the plow, especially to the all-cast-iron one introduced to the region in the 1820s, then to the steel one developed by John Deere in 1837.

Another boost to American agriculture came in 1831 when Cyrus Hall McCormick developed the first successful reaper. McCormick patented his reaper in 1834 and in 1847 moved from his native Virginia to Chicago, where he began large-scale production. McCormick's reaper greatly increased American wheat production. Other farm machines were developed, including seeders, cultivators, and threshers, revolutionizing American agricultural production.

Bumper crops of corn and wheat soon provided not only enough grain to feed the United States, but also enough for export. Beef, pork, and poultry joined grain as important Western farm products.

The federal government favored this Western settlement. Its first service to the settlers was removing the Indians from the land by driving them farther west. The Land Act of 1800, passed by Congress to amend and augment the Land Act of 1796, reduced the minimum purchase size from 640 to 320 acres (259 to 130 hectares) and extended the time to complete the purchase from one to four years. The Land Act of 1820 provided land to be sold in 80-acre (32-hectare) tracts at only $1.25 an acre. Such prices were irresistible to farmers from small farms in New England, as well as to immigrant farmers from Ireland, Germany, and Scandinavia.

Improvements in transportation also helped fuel the great growth of the West. Steamboat shipping on the Mississippi brought farm products down to the busy seaport of New Orleans and returned with manufactured products for the region's farms, towns, and plantations. Agricultural products could also be shipped along the Great Lakes, then placed on canal barges and sent to the East Coast through the canal systems. These same shipping arteries also made it easy to get manufactured goods to markets in the West. The extension of railroads made shipment even faster and cheaper and aided the growth of cities such as St. Louis, Cincinnati, and Chicago.

The development of the agricultural West made greater industrialization of the nation possible. The West provided the food the North needed to feed its ever-growing numbers of industrial workers.

The growth of democracy. The election of 1824 had pointed up the differing interests of the developing economic sections. For example, the industrial North wanted high tariffs on manufactured goods entering the United States to reduce competition from imported goods and to aid the growth of its domestic industries. The agricultural South believed that high tariffs raised the prices of manufactured goods it had to buy, and so favored low tariffs. The West, the newest and least developed section, favored federal spending on roads and other improvements, but other sections resisted the higher taxes that would be required to pay for Western growth and development.

Then, too, there was the issue of slavery. The South believed its economy was thoroughly dependent on slavery and therefore defended it strongly. Elements in the North, however, objected to it just as strongly.

The Missouri Compromise. The issue of slavery, which had been growing for two decades, became a major national problem for the first time when Missouri applied to become a state in 1818. Missouri had been settled by people from the South who expected it to become a slave state. But in early 1819, when the bill for Missouri statehood came before the House of Representatives, an amendment was added that prohibited the further introduction of slaves and provided for the eventual elimination of slavery in Missouri. The bill passed the House but was voted down in the Senate. In December of 1819, Congress passed legislation admit-

ting Alabama as a slave state, thus equalizing slave and nonslave state representation in the Senate at eleven apiece. When Congress began considering the admission of Maine, the struggle between proslavery and antislavery forces in Congress became deadlocked. Speaker of the House Henry Clay of Kentucky fashioned a complicated agreement that came to be known as the Missouri Compromise. Missouri would be admitted as a slave state, but slavery would be prohibited in the remaining lands of the Louisiana Purchase north of the parallel 36° 30′. Maine would be admitted as a free state, restoring the balance of slave and free states at twelve

THE OREGON TRAIL was the longest of the overland routes carrying settlers across the continent from Independence, Missouri, to the Pacific Northwest.

THE MISSOURI COMPROMISE stated Missouri would be admitted as a slave state, but slavery would be prohibited in the remaining lands of the Louisiana Purchase north of the parallel 36/30.

civilized
US

civilised
Brit.

each. The compromise settled the immediate problem, but the issue of slavery would continue to plague the nation.

The party system. Andrew Jackson, a Westerner, had been the popular vote winner but the ultimate loser in the presidential election of 1824. Jackson began campaigning for the election of 1828 as soon as the 1824 decision was reached. By this time, the Republican Party was splitting along ideological lines. Adams and his supporters were calling themselves the National Republicans, reflecting their belief in strong and active national government. Jackson and his supporters characterized the National Republicans as the "aristocratic" party of the wealthy and the powerful. The Jacksonians called themselves Democrats to stress their concern for the common man.

Jackson's triumph. Several factors favored Jackson's election over Adams in 1828. Since the revolution, the right to vote had been gradually extended to "the common man" to whom Jackson appealed. Property qualifications and payment of land taxes generally ceased to curtail suffrage. The right to vote continued to be limited to white adult males (excluding women and blacks), but between 1824 and 1828 alone, the number of voters doubled.

Another factor favoring Jackson was his attack on the Tariff of 1828, which had been engineered by the Jacksonians in Congress. The bill authorized such high tariffs that even the Northern interests, which supported protectionism, were expected to vote against it, causing it to fail and embarrassing the Adams administration. To the surprise of its authors, the bill passed and became law. The "Tariff of Abominations," as it came to be known, enraged the agricultural South and caused many Southerners to support Jackson (as did many Westerners, who were voting for one of their own).

Jackson won by a landslide in the electoral college, tallying up 178 votes to 83 for Adams. However, the popular vote was closer, 647,231 for Jackson against

509,097 for Adams. Adams took only New England, Delaware, and New Jersey. Jackson easily took the South and the West, as well as states with many wage earners, such as New York and Pennsylvania. John C. Calhoun, who had been vice president under Adams, was reelected. Jackson's election ushered in a period that came to be known as "the Era of the Common Man." During this time Jackson attacked government policies that he thought protected privileged groups, and suffrage was extended still further.

The spoils system. Jackson believed that people should not remain in government service for a long time. If they did, he contended, they would lose their concern for the public welfare and instead concentrate on holding their own jobs. He therefore advocated a policy of rotation in public office. He also believed that "to the victor belong the spoils," a saying that would be used by William L. Marcy, senator from New York, in a speech in the Senate in 1832. Jackson began replacing people who opposed him with people who had supported his candidacy and were faithful to him.

Although Jackson set a precedent for this so-called "spoils system" in filling government jobs, he did not invent it. The spoils system had long been a part of state politics, and other presidents had removed people from office in order to reward friends and supporters. Jackson actually replaced only about one-fifth of federal officeholders for political reasons. Later presidents would extend the system, thus causing a massive turnover of officeholders with each new administration.

Removal of the Indians. Jackson often spoke out for retaining the rights of the states in the face of attempts by the federal government to exercise its power. He argued for those rights when he supported Georgia's attempt to take over the land of the Cherokee Indians, one of the five major tribes remaining in the Southeast, known collectively as the Five Civilized Tribes, and relocate them

west of the Mississippi River. The Cherokees brought their case against removal to the Supreme Court in 1832 by challenging the authority of Georgia over Cherokee lands. The court, under Chief Justice John Marshall, declared that "the Cherokee Nation . . . is a distinct community, occupying its own territory, with boundaries accurately described, in which the laws of Georgia can have no force."

Jackson agreed with Georgia. He thus refused to enforce the High Court's decision. "John Marshall has made his decision," Jackson remarked, "now let him enforce it." As a result, the entire Cherokee nation was marched westward, under U.S. Army guard. Fully one-fourth of them died along the way.

Nullification. Another issue concerning states' rights arose in response to the so-called Tariff of Abominations. The South from the beginning had opposed, for economic and philosophical reasons, any form of protectionist tariff, and John C. Calhoun of South Carolina, Jackson's vice president, was a vociferous opponent of the tariff. In 1828 he had written a tract (published anonymously) stating that if Congress passed legislation that did undue injury to any state, that legislation was unconstitutional and the state had a right to declare it null and void. (In this, Calhoun echoed the contentions of the Virginia and Kentucky resolutions of 1798.)

In January of 1830, on the floor of Congress, Daniel Webster, senator from Massachusetts, and Robert Hayne, senator from South Carolina, debated the matter of federal versus states' rights. Webster argued that the federal government had final authority because it was the agent of all the people, not merely the people of one state. Only the Supreme Court, not the states, had the right to decide whether laws were constitutional. He warned that if this proposition were not accepted by all states, the states would one day go to war against each other. "Liberty *and* Union, now and forever, one and inseparable!" was his final plea.

In July of 1832, however, a new tariff was passed by Congress. Although it was not as excessive as the Tariff of 1828, it still was a protectionist measure and Southern opposition sprang up again. In October, the South Carolina legislature called for a state convention. On November 24, it adopted the Ordinance of Nullification, which declared the tariff null within the state; the legislature prepared to defend this stand by force of arms if necessary. Furthermore, any attempt by the federal government to enforce the tariff would dissolve all political connection between South Carolina and the United States. In other words, South Carolina would secede from the Union.

Jackson was personally opposed to the tariff, but he would not tolerate a possible disruption to the Union. He sent South Carolina a sharp warning emphasizing that "the laws of the United

States must be executed." He also asked Congress to pass the Force Bill, giving him authority to enforce the tariff. "The Great Compromiser," Henry Clay, pushed a compromise bill through Congress; it provided for a ten-year decrease in tariffs so that all tariffs would be lowered by at least half. This satisfied South Carolina for the time. It rescinded the Ordinance of Nullification, and talk of nullification ceased.

Meanwhile, the growing rift between Jackson and Vice President Calhoun had become a complete break. Senator Hayne (of the Webster-Hayne debate) had been elected governor of South Carolina and had resigned from the Senate. Calhoun was elected to Hayne's seat in the Senate and resigned from the Vice presidency.

The bank fight. A prime Jackson target as a bastion of special privilege was the privately controlled Second Bank of the United States. From the beginning Jackson had challenged the constitutionality of the bank. He saw it as a tool of the rich to oppress the poor and to prevent state banks and small businesses from expanding their commercial activities. He also saw that the bank's private stockholders could grow rich on government funds.

In 1832, Nicholas Biddle, the president of the bank, was encouraged by Henry Clay to seek renewal of the bank's charter, even though the existing charter would not run out until 1836. Biddle applied to Congress for renewal. Congress voted to renew the bank's charter, and Jackson vetoed the bill. Renewal of the charter became a campaign issue later that year as Jackson's National Republican opponent, Clay, campaigned against Jackson's veto and for the bank. After Jackson won the election easily, he set out to destroy the bank. He did so by withdrawing government funds and by making no more deposits. Instead, the

government deposits were given to state banks owned by Democrats—"pet banks" they soon came to be called. The effect was to cripple the U.S. bank. In 1836 Biddle secured a charter from the state of Pennsylvania, but the bank failed a few years later in the depression that followed the Panic of 1837.

National political parties. The approach of the 1832 presidential election brought an important change in the way Americans chose their candidates. Prior to 1832, presidential candidates had been chosen by congressional caucuses, state legislatures, or other bodies of limited scope and representation. The rise of sectional candidates caused further problems, as evidenced by the 1824 election, which had to be decided in the

House of Representatives. It became clear that the political parties needed to become formal national organizations and that a new mechanism was required to pick party candidates.

In September of 1831 a new party, the Anti-Masonic Party, had nominated William Wirt for the presidency. The party began in New York State after a man who had been investigating the mysteries of Freemasonry suddenly disappeared and subsequent investigations revealed the extensive involvement of Masons in state politics. The party expanded its interest to national issues and in 1831 introduced the first national convention and the first party platform. In December of 1831 the National Republicans held their first national convention and nominated Henry Clay for president. In May of 1832 the Democratic Party, at its first national convention, nominated Andrew Jackson.

In the 1832 election Jackson won 219 electoral votes to Clay's 49. Wirt, head of the nation's first "third party," won 7 votes. Jackson won 687,502 popular votes to Clay's 530,189. Because Clay had made the Bank of the United States an issue in the election, Jackson considered his victory a vindication of his policy by the American people.

Panic and depression. Jackson's crippling of the U.S. bank following the 1832 election had severe financial repercussions. In 1837, shortly after the election of Jackson's vice president and hand-picked successor, Martin Van Buren, the nation neared financial collapse. Without the restraining influence of the Second Bank of the United States on issuing money, a great deal of currency was printed that had little backing in gold or silver. Credit was easy and borrowing reached record heights. Inflation and speculation were rampant. Jackson had attempted to cool the heated economy by returning, in part at least, to the use of gold or silver—hard currency—in place of paper money with the Treasury Department's issuance of

the Specie Circular on July 11, 1836. In an attempt to curb land speculation, it required payments for public lands to be made in gold or silver or, in limited cases, in Virginia land scrip. An extension allowed any "actual settler or bona fide resident" to use paper money. This dealt a severe blow to the boom. Soon mortgages were going unpaid, banks were failing, and factories were closing. This Panic of 1837 led to the worst depression in the nation's history to date.

The financial gloom helped to defeat President Van Buren's bid for reelection in 1840. By that time, Henry Clay and the National Republicans had joined together with many of Jackson's enemies, including John C. Calhoun, to form the Whig Party. The party's candidate in 1840 was William Henry Harrison, who in 1811 had led an attack on the Shawnee Indians in Indiana that came to be called the Battle of Tippecanoe. Harrison was portrayed as an Indian-fighting hero, a man of the people. In the election Harrison won a landslide of 234 electoral votes to Van Buren's 60. But the Whig victory was soon muted. Just one month after taking office, Harrison died of pneumonia. His vice president, John Tyler, a compromise candidate who did not support many Whig policies, succeeded him.

DANIEL WEBSTER, the senator from Massachusetts, championed the side of the federal government in the debate over states' rights.

ANDREW JACKSON had won national acclaim in a stunning American victory over the British in New Orleans in the War of 1812.

Manifest destiny. As Americans filled up the Ohio and Mississippi valleys, the nation looked farther west. Said writer John Louis Sullivan in 1845, "Our manifest destiny is to overspread the continent allotted by Providence for the free development of our yearly multiplying millions." But the area was not simply the Americans' for the taking. Not only were there hundreds of thousands of American Indians there, many of them driven westward by earlier American settlement, but other nations were laying claim to the West. The Oregon Territory had been claimed by Britain. Mexico, which in 1821 had thrown off the yoke of Spanish rule, included the area west of the Louisiana Purchase, from the Gulf Coast through Texas and California to the southern boundary of Oregon.

The Oregon Territory. In 1818 the United States and Britain had agreed to share the rights to the Oregon Territory, which included what are now Oregon, Washington, Idaho, and part of Canada. This ten-year agreement had been renewed in 1827 with no term limitation but with the provision that either country could end the agreement by giving one year's notice.

The first non-Indians to come to the Oregon Territory were the rugged so-called "mountain men," hunters and trappers of the valuable fur-bearing animals there, especially beaver. Although these were wandering men, permanent settlements were founded on the sites of fur-trading posts. One was Astoria, on the Pacific coast, named for John Jacob Astor, founder and owner of the American Fur Company.

BLACK HAWK, seen here with his son, was the Sauk Indian chief who led the struggle against the westward movement of settlers. He was defeated in the Black Hawk War in 1830.

By the 1830s, the mountain men had destroyed most of the beavers, but there was now a new job they could take on, leading wagon trains of American settlers to the fertile land west of the Rockies. The route they followed was the Oregon Trail, beginning in Independence, Missouri, and stretching as far as Astoria and later Portland, Oregon.

Soon American settlers vastly outnumbered the British in the Oregon Territory, and expansionist-minded Americans were calling for the United States to take sole ownership of the entire Pacific Northwest, up to the parallel 54°40′. "Fifty-four forty or fight"

became their rallying cry. For a while, war with Britain threatened, but neither nation wanted war. The Oregon Treaty of 1846 divided the Oregon Territory at the 49th parallel, a continuation of the boundary between Canada and the United States from Minnesota west to the Rocky Mountains.

Texas. From the 1720s, the Spanish had claimed all of what is now Texas, but only about 4,000 Spanish settlers lived there by the 1820s. In 1821, Mexico gained its independence from Spain and wanted to make Texas, which had been claimed by Spain as part of New Spain, its northern province. Eager to attract settlers there, the Mexican government granted permission to Moses Austin and 300 other American settlers to start a colony in Texas. Under Moses's son Stephen, the colony was founded in 1821, and thus began a mass movement of American settlers into Texas. By the end of the 1820s, there were about 20,000 Americans living there, versus 4,000 Mexicans.

It was not long before there was severe friction between the Texans and the Mexican government. The Mexicans were Roman Catholics, and the Americans predominantly Protestants. Misunderstandings were also caused by the language difference between the Spanish and the English. In addition, the Americans were mainly Southerners who had brought slaves with them. Mexico tried various measures to maintain its weakening control over the region, but most of them only made the problem worse. Finally, the central government prohibited further immigration and outlawed slavery in Texas. In 1833, Antonio López de Santa Anna established himself as dictator of Mexico and sent troops to restore the central government's control of Texas. Armed clashes followed in 1835. In February of 1836, Santa Anna advanced into Texas commanding an army some 6,000 strong. On February 23 he began a siege of the Alamo, at San Antonio, garrisoned by some 187 Texan volunteers. On March 2 at Washington, Texas, the independent Republic of Texas was declared, and Sam Houston was named commander of the army. On March 6, the Alamo fell and Santa Anna had all of its defenders killed. On March 27, some 300 Texan fighters captured at Goliad were killed by Santa Anna's order. But on April 21, Santa Anna was defeated and captured by a smaller force led by Houston, and he was forced to agree to Texan independence, a promise he later broke. In October Houston became president of independent Texas.

In 1837, Houston applied for permission for Texas to enter the United States. President Jackson favored annexing Texas, but he saw two problems: probable war with Mexico and the admission of a slave state that would tip the delicate balance between North and South. Jackson refused to support annexation.

In 1843 Houston again approached the United States government on

annexation. President Tyler, eager for American expansion, was finally able, in February, 1845, to put a joint resolution through Congress authorizing annexation. On December 29 Texas became the Union's 28th state. Mexico broke off diplomatic relations with the United States.

California. During the same period, the area west of Texas, through California, was also in ferment. Like Texas, this area had been part of New Spain and it became Mexican in 1821. The Spanish had sparsely settled the area, mainly with a chain of missions founded by Franciscan friars along the California coast.

By 1845 there were about 700 Americans living in California. In previous years, both Jackson and Tyler had tried unsuccessfully to buy California from Mexico. Then, in the election of 1844, Democrat James K. Polk, a true expansionist, ran on a platform favoring both the annexation of Texas and the acquisition of California. His main opponent, Whig candidate Henry Clay, was less interested in making Texas an issue.

The election was extremely close, particularly in the popular vote, but Polk gained 170 electoral votes to Clay's 105. After Polk took office, he encouraged Americans in California to rebel against the Mexican government. They did, and on June 14, 1846, after the Mexican War had begun, American rebels proclaimed the California Republic and raised their flag, showing a grizzly bear and a lone star. On July 7, U.S. naval forces landed at Monterey and declared California a part of the United States. U.S. Army Captain John C. Frémont took command of the Californian forces and drove all Mexican troops out of northern California.

War with Mexico. The immediate cause of the war with Mexico was the claim of Texas that the Rio Grande was its southwestern boundary. Mexico claimed the region as far north and east as the Nueces River. In May 1845, President Polk sent General Zachary Taylor and his troops to the disputed border, and in July the American forces advanced to the Rio Grande. On April 25, 1846, Mexican forces crossed the Rio Grande and attacked the American troops, killing 16. On May 13, 1846, Congress declared war on Mexico, and Mexico's formal declaration followed.

The dispute over the Texas border may have sparked the war, but the underlying cause was the American government's desire to gain, once and for all, the Mexican territory between the current United States and the Pacific. Western and Southern states responded enthusiastically, but many in the Northern states were critical of the government's actions, fearing a Southern conspiracy to secure more territory for the extension of slavery.

The American military strategy called for four moves. General Taylor was to hold the Rio Grande; General Winfield Scott was to land at the Mexican port of Veracruz and advance on Mexico City, the capital; Colonel Stephen Kearny was

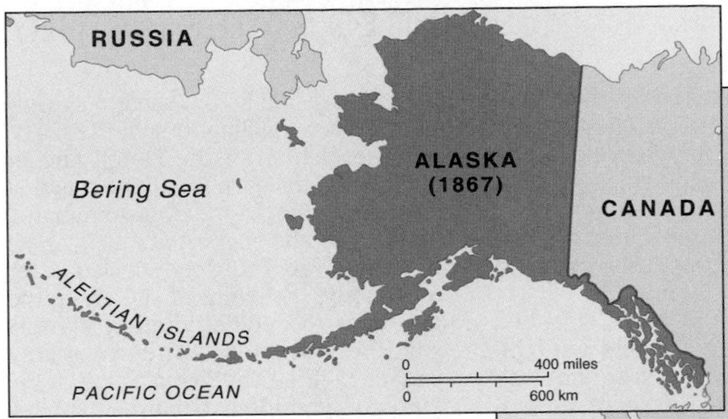

Map: TERRITORIAL EXPANSION OF THE UNITED STATES

RUSSIA

Bering Sea

ALASKA
(1867)

CANADA

ALEUTIAN ISLANDS

PACIFIC OCEAN

0   400 miles
0   600 km

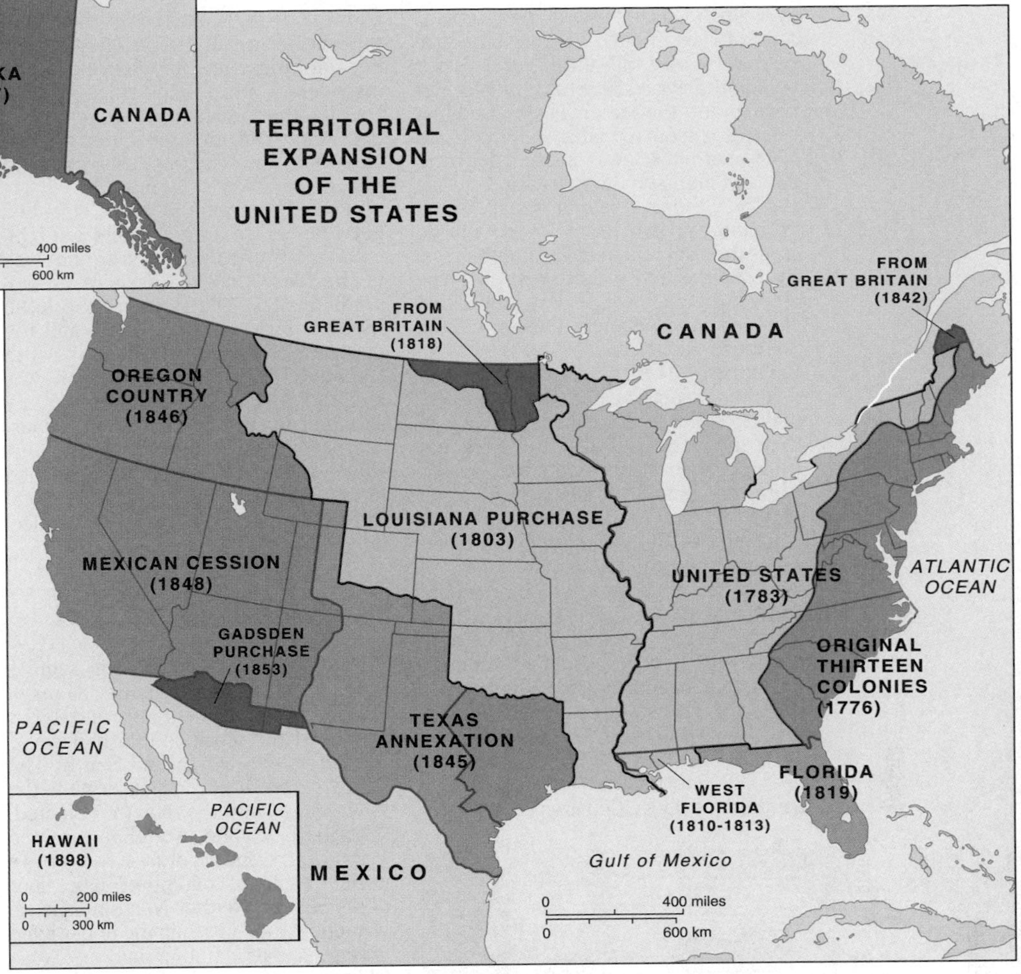

TERRITORIAL
EXPANSION
OF THE
UNITED STATES

CANADA

FROM
GREAT BRITAIN
(1842)

FROM
GREAT BRITAIN
(1818)

OREGON
COUNTRY
(1846)

LOUISIANA PURCHASE
(1803)

MEXICAN CESSION
(1848)

UNITED STATES
(1783)

ATLANTIC
OCEAN

GADSDEN
PURCHASE
(1853)

ORIGINAL
THIRTEEN
COLONIES
(1776)

PACIFIC
OCEAN

TEXAS
ANNEXATION
(1845)

FLORIDA
(1819)

WEST
FLORIDA
(1810-1813)

PACIFIC
OCEAN

HAWAII
(1898)

MEXICO

Gulf of Mexico

0   200 miles
0   300 km

0   400 miles
0   600 km

---

to take and hold New Mexico, then push on to California to join the forces there under Captain Frémont; and Commodore Robert F. Stockton was to position a fleet in the Pacific off the California shore.

All four campaigns were marked with success. Taylor followed up his early victories by taking Matamoros and Monterey. He then took some 10,000 men south to reinforce Scott's march from the coast to Mexico City. Mexican General Santa Anna, with an army of 20,000, attacked a force of about 4,000 Americans at Buena Vista on February 22, 1847. The American force held, and after a desperate two-day battle, routed the Mexicans. This battle made Taylor the hero of the war and put him in the White House in 1849.

In March 1847 Scott landed at Veracruz, took the city, and began his march on the Mexican capital. He drove Santa Anna from the pass at Cerro Gordo and continued his advance, taking city after city. On September 14, Santa Anna retreated from Mexico City. Scott's army entered and kept possession until a peace treaty was signed.

On February 2, 1848, Mexico and the United States signed the Treaty of Guadalupe Hidalgo. By its terms, Mexico conceded the border question: The Rio Grande henceforth would be the southwest boundary of Texas. It also ceded to the United States, for $15 million, the territories now known as California, Utah, Arizona, and New Mexico. The United States now stretched "from sea to shining sea." As if this great land acquisition were not enough of a bonanza, news that gold had been discovered on the property of John Augustus Sutter in the Sacramento Valley on January 24, 1848, set off a gold rush to California. Some 80,000 "Forty-Niners" arrived in California in one year.

Settling the Last West.
In the drive for American conquest of the continent from coast to coast, settlers largely bypassed the "Last West," the area running roughly from the 98th to the 120th meridian. This area, made up of the Great Plains and the basins, plateaus, and mountains of the Rocky Mountain region, seemed forbidding to settlers. Lack of rainfall and sparse vegetation caused its early explorers to call it the Great American Desert. Settlers were put off by the plow-breaking tough grass that covered the plains, as well as by the flatness, dryness, and treelessness of the area. The Great American Desert offered

little promise for agriculture, so settlers moved through it as quickly as they could and on to the more inviting lands of California and the Pacific Northwest.

Mining and cattle.
During the 1850s, though, settlers began coming in large numbers. Some were drawn by mining strikes, as prospectors discovered that the Rocky Mountain region was rich in precious ores. A gold strike near Denver, Colorado, caused the Pike's Peak rush of 1859, which brought 50,000 prospectors in just a few months. In the same year, the greatest deposits of gold and silver ever found were discovered in the Comstock Lode, near Virginia City, Nevada, drawing 20,000 prospectors. Two years later, a gold strike at Last Chance Gulch in Montana brought thousands more. In 1875 gold was discovered in the Black Hills of the Dakotas, creating the Homestake Mine near Deadwood.

A growing cattle industry was also bringing in settlers. Millions of longhorns, descendants of cattle brought by the Spanish settlers, roamed lower Texas. As the demand for meat grew in the increasingly populous East, cowboys rounded up the cattle and moved them northward on "the long drive" to such railroad towns as Abilene and Dodge City in Kansas. From these towns the cattle could be shipped to meat-packing houses in Chicago.

Western railroads.
By the 1850s the American government was eager to link the nation with a transcontinental railroad, but disagreements over the route such a railroad should take combined with other, more pressing problems, such as the fight over slavery and the threat of Southern secession, to stall any serious consideration of the venture. But when the Civil War began, a new incentive to build a transcontinental railroad was introduced. The railroad would bring the West closer to the North, thereby helping the Union cause. On July 1, 1862, President Abraham Lincoln signed the Pacific Railway Act, which provided low-cost loans and granted huge tracts of government-owned land to private railroad companies with the provision that they use the money made

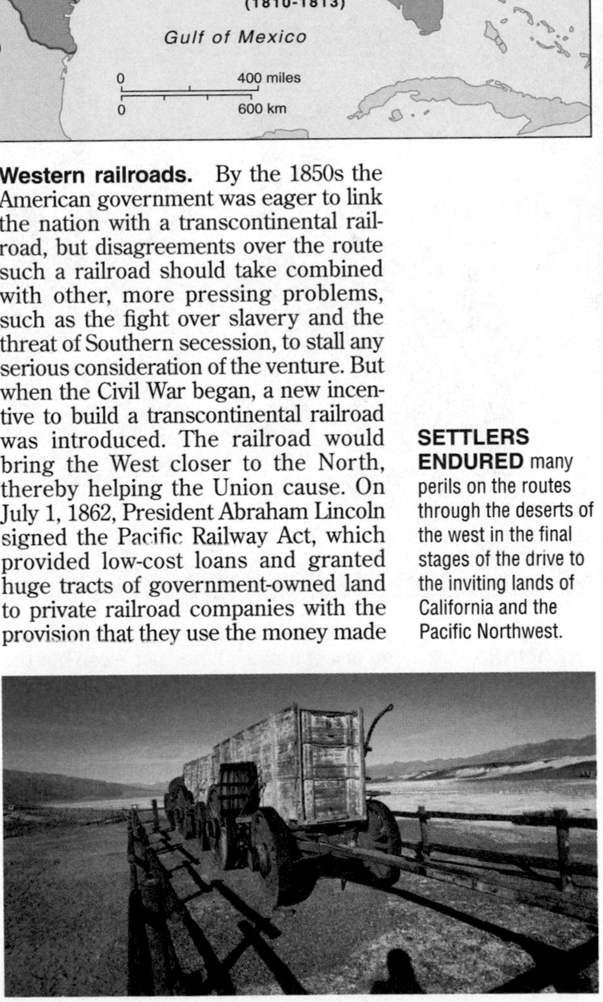

SETTLERS ENDURED many perils on the routes through the deserts of the west in the final stages of the drive to the inviting lands of California and the Pacific Northwest.

by selling the land to build new railroads. A great race to build a transcontinental railroad began, with the Central Pacific building eastward from Sacramento, California, and the Union Pacific building westward from Omaha, Nebraska. In 1864 another act was passed doubling the land grants to the railroads. On May 10, 1869, the two sets of tracks met at Promontory, Utah. It was now possible to cross the nation in only a matter of days. By 1890 the entire Last West could be crossed by such railroads as the Great Northern, the Northern Pacific, and the Southern Pacific.

Farming. The railroads did a great deal to attract farmers to the Great Plains. Railroad companies advertised their land sales all over the East and Europe. The Homestead Act, which Abraham Lincoln signed into law on May 20, 1862, was another attraction. Through it, the government offered settlers 160-acre (65-hectare) plots of land at no cost if they lived on the land and developed it for 5 years. Farmers could also buy plots for $1.25 an acre after living on them for only 6 months. Improvements in farm machinery made the Great Plains more suited to agriculture than it had been. As a result, by the 1880s, Kansas and Nebraska were covered with wheat fields. Farm production from the newly settled area soared.

BUILDING THE TRANSCONTINENTAL RAILROAD led inevitably to the loss of lands claimed by the Indians and led to the government policy of restricted Indian lands, or reservations.

The Indians. American settlers had at last conquered the Last West, but the losers were the Indians. To them the Last West was their last home. Many of the Indians had been forced there by white settlements in other parts of the country. Some Plains Indian tribes had lived there for centuries or longer, but others such as the Dakotas (or Sioux) had been driven onto the Plains by white settlement or by other tribes.

In 1851 the American government launched a reservation policy under which it tried to restrict the Indians to designated areas (very often the poorest ones, which the settlers did not want),

allowing settlers to take over the rest of the land. However, if a designated area became attractive, as when gold was discovered in the Black Hills of South Dakota, the Indians were driven off so that American fortune hunters could exploit the new riches that the land offered.

For the next 25 years, clashes between protesting Indians and the U.S. Army were all too frequent—as in the Sand Creek Massacre in Colorado in 1864, the Battle of the Little Bighorn in Montana in 1876, and the massacre at Wounded Knee in South Dakota in 1890. But the outcome was inevitable. The Indians were finally subdued and restricted to reservations. The Dawes Severalty Act of 1887 dissolved Indian tribes by law and divided the reservation land among individual Indians, weakening the tribes' collective power.

A House Divided

Toward disunion. The acquisition and settlement of the new lands of the West during the 1840s and 1850s worsened the tensions that had developed between North and South. The South wanted to extend slavery into the new areas, but the North objected. Whether new states would be admitted to the Union as slave or free states was a frequent point of contention on the floor of the Senate. Neither North nor South wanted the other to gain the upper hand in representation in that body.

Wilmot Proviso. In 1846, during the Mexican War, President Polk sent a bill to Congress requesting $2 million to be used, if needed, to compensate Mexico for territory annexed by the United States. Congressman David Wilmot of Pennsylvania introduced an amendment establishing "as an express and fundamental condition to the acquisition of any territory from the Republic of Mexico" the prohibition of slavery "in any part of said territory." The question of the extension of slavery, which had been simmering since the Missouri Compromise in 1820, was suddenly brought to a full boil. A furious debate ensued in both houses of Congress. On August 8, the amended bill passed in the House of Representatives, but it was killed when the Senate refused to consider it. Another appropriation bill came up in 1847, and Wilmot sponsored another amendment excluding slavery in the territories. The bill passed in the House, but the Senate again refused to consider it, passing another bill without the amendment. The House then approved the Senate bill. The Wilmot Proviso failed in Congress, but its principle became the key plank in both the Free-Soil and the Republican Party platforms.

Election of 1848. Slavery in the territories became the key issue in the national election of 1848. In May the Democratic convention was boycotted by the New York faction called Barn-

burners, a group so opposed to slavery that they were willing to split the party, after the fashion of the Dutch farmer who burned his barn to kill the rats that were in it. The Democrats nominated Lewis Cass, who supported the principle of "popular sovereignty" or "squatter sovereignty," the right of settlers in the territories to decide whether slavery would be permitted in the states they formed. In June the Whig Party nominated for president General Zachary Taylor, the hero of the Mexican War and a slaveholder. Soon after, the Barnburners nominated Martin Van Buren, who in August was also endorsed by the Free-Soil Party, made up of a coalition of anti-slavery forces. Taylor won the election with 163 electoral votes to 127 for Cass. Van Buren won no electoral votes, but his candidacy cost Cass the election.

Compromise of 1850. By 1849 the number of free and slave states stood at 15 each. But now California was applying to enter the Union as a free state, a prospect the South did not favor since it would tip the balance in favor of the North.

Added to the California question were a number of other issues, but all revolved around the central issue, slavery. Northerners objected to the trading of slaves in Washington, D.C., virtually in the shadow of the Capitol Building. Southerners complained that there were no effective laws to help them reclaim fugitive slaves who were escaping to the North. Southerners were also concerned about attempts to prohibit the extension of slavery in new states.

Henry Clay, now a senator from Kentucky, proposed a compromise, as he had 30 years earlier with the Missouri Compromise. In the North's favor, he proposed that California be admitted as a free state and that slave trade be abolished within Washington, D.C. In the South's favor, he proposed that New Mexico be divided into two territories— New Mexico and Utah—and that each have the right to popular sovereignty. He also proposed that a strict new Fugitive Slave Law be adopted.

Clay introduced his resolutions in the Senate on January 29, 1850, in the midst of the most dangerous crisis the nation had seen to date. Calls had been made for secession and for the dissolution of the Union and had been met by President Taylor's firm commitment to preserve the Union.

The compromise Clay proposed brought to the Senate floor the most important and impressive debate in the country's history. Clay urged compromise and was supported eloquently by Daniel Webster of Massachusetts and by Stephen A. Douglas of Illinois. John C. Calhoun, longtime champion of the South and of states' rights, opposed the compromise, as did Jefferson Davis of Mississippi, William H. Seward of New York, and Salmon P. Chase of Ohio.

In March Calhoun died. The measures lingered in the Senate. Then on July 9, President Taylor died and was succeeded by Vice President Millard

The Movement for Abolition of Slavery

Black slavery was established in the American colonies shortly after the first Africans were brought to America in 1619. In the next two centuries, slavery became an economic necessity in the minds of many Southern planters, especially after the invention of the cotton gin. By 1820, more than 2 million black slaves labored in the United States, and by 1860, the number had grown to nearly 4 million.

There had always been some moral qualms about slavery in the nation—Thomas Jefferson, a Southern slaveholder himself, had voiced some of them before 1800. But in the 1800s, antislavery feeling grew, especially in the Northern and Western states. In 1816, the American Colonization Society was founded; its aim was to buy slaves, free them, and return them to Africa, to a newly founded country called Liberia. The society met with very limited success—by 1831, only about 1400 former slaves had been relocated to Liberia.

In the meantime, other attempts were being made to abolish slavery in the United States. In 1829, David Walker, a free black, published the *Appeal*, in which he urged black Americans to strike for their freedom. In 1831, William Lloyd Garrison began publishing a newspaper called the *Liberator*, in which he demanded freedom for slaves, claiming that slavery was forbidden by the Declaration of Independence.

In 1833, Garrison helped organize the American Anti-Slavery Society, and served as its president for two decades. Other prominent abolitionists were the poets John Greenleaf Whittier and James Russell Lowell; reformers Wendell Phillips and Theodore Weld; Lucretia Mott; and the Grimke sisters, Angelina and Sarah, Southerners who had left South Carolina in protest against slavery.

One of the most effective speakers of the 1,000-chapter Anti-Slavery Society was Frederick Douglass, a former slave who had educated himself and who had proved to be a formidable fighter against unwilling servitude. Sojourner Truth, another freed slave, sought, like Douglass, to influence public opinion.

In 1840, abolitionists formed the Liberty Party and ran a presidential candidate who favored abolition. With the formation of the Republican Party in 1854, abolitionists found their political home.

While advocating that the nation end slavery through law, many abolitionists acted to free slaves by helping them to escape along the "underground railroad." Slaves seeking freedom would follow the North Star, to make their way up to Canada. Abolitionists along the way hid the fleeing slaves in their homes and farms by day.

The Civil War, The Emancipation Proclamation, and the 13th Amendment brought the abolitionist movement to a successful conclusion.

HARRIET TUBMAN, who was born a slave, escaped and became an abolitionist, operating successful underground railroad escape routes for other slaves.

a border disagreement left over from the Treaty of Guadalupe Hidalgo, which had ended the Mexican War. Mexico agreed to sell almost 30,000 square miles (77,700 square kilometers) of territory, south of the Gila River and between the Rio Grande and the Colorado River, for $15 million. The treaty, signed on December 30, 1853, was ratified in June of 1854, but the sale price was reduced to $10 million.

Perry expedition. Meanwhile, a naval expedition to Japan, commissioned by President Fillmore and headed by Commodore Matthew C. Perry, arrived there in July of 1853. Japan had been closed to Western nations for about two centuries. On March 31, 1854, on his second visit to Japan, Perry secured a treaty that opened two Japanese ports to American trade, gained protection for shipwrecked sailors and other Americans in Japan, and led to subsequent agreements between the two nations.

Kansas-Nebraska Act. In 1854 came another direct confrontation over slavery. Senator Stephen A. Douglas proposed a bill that would start the vast, unorganized territory west of Minnesota, Iowa, and Missouri on the way to statehood. The Kansas-Nebraska Act, passed in May 1854, divided the territory into Kansas and Nebraska. The provisions of the Missouri Compromise were repealed, and the doctrine of popular sovereignty was applied in both territories.

Immediately, proslavery and antislavery interests began sending armed settlers to the new territories, especially to Kansas, neighbor of the slave state of Missouri. When it came time to vote for representatives to the Kansas legislature, proslavery settlers outnumbered antislavery forces. But to make sure of victory, proslavery Missourians crossed the border, voted illegally, and gave the proslavery party an overwhelming victory. Antislavery settlers, calling it a stolen election, set up their own legislature. For the next 4 years, a state of civil war existed in "Bleeding Kansas."

Sectionalism and politics. Both the Whig Party and the Democratic Party had supporters in the North and South, and since Tyler's time, they had more or less alternated in winning the White House. But the divisions within the Whig Party had grown as sectional strains had worsened, and the Kansas-Nebraska Act tore the party apart.

In July of 1854, antislavery forces from both the Whig and the Democratic parties met in Jackson, Michigan, and formed the Republican Party. By 1856 the Republicans had become strong enough to run John C. Frémont for president. His Democratic opponent, James Buchanan, won by 174 electoral votes to 114. Millard Fillmore, who had gained the nomination of the virtually dead Whig Party and also the American, or "Know-Nothing," Party, won eight electoral votes. The Know-Nothing Party was anti-foreigner, anti-Catholic, and short-lived.

Fillmore who, unlike Taylor, favored compromise.

In September of 1850, Congress passed the five measures that made up the Compromise of 1850, but once again, compromise did not settle the slavery question. Newspapers in the North were soon protesting the new Fugitive Slave Law, calling it "a hateful statute of kidnappers." Protest and outrage grew with the publication in 1852 of abolitionist Harriet Beecher Stowe's *Uncle Tom's Cabin*, which movingly described the cruelties of slave life and the desperation of the slaves who fled from it and

stirred antislavery feelings to a fever pitch in the North.

Fillmore's support of the compromise, particularly the Fugitive Slave Law, made him powerful enemies in the Whig Party, which in June of 1852 nominated General Winfield Scott for the presidency. Scott was defeated in the election by the Democratic candidate, Franklin Pierce, who polled 254 electoral votes to Scott's 42, in a landslide that marked the Whig Party's last hurrah in national politics.

Gadsden Purchase. In 1853 Pierce sent James Gadsden to Mexico to settle

On March 6, 1857, two days after Buchanan's inauguration, the Supreme Court handed down a momentous decision brought on by the suit of Dred Scott, a black man who insisted he was a free man rather than a slave by virtue of having lived in a free state. The High Court declared that no slave and no individual of slave ancestry could be a citizen of the United States or appeal to a federal court. It further decided that slaves were "property" to be transported from state to state, and that Congress could not prohibit slavery in the territories and was bound by the Constitution to protect it.

This decision delighted the South because it implied that slavery was protected throughout the nation by constitutional guarantees. Northerners were outraged at the ruling, and the Republican Party called for congressional legislation against the extension of slavery into the territories.

John Brown. In the midst of the sectional ferment, an antislavery veteran of the "Bleeding Kansas" fights named John Brown attempted to launch a popular uprising against slavery. In 1855 Brown had moved from Ohio to Kansas to join five of his sons in the fight against proslavery elements from Missouri. After a bloody attack at Lawrence, Kansas, on May 21 by proslavery men, Brown and six others attacked a proslavery encampment on the Pottawatomie Creek and

armory
US

armoury
Brit.

kilometers
US

kilometres
Brit.

Robert E. Lee to retake the armory and capture Brown. After a two-day siege, the Marines succeeded. Brown was tried for treason and then hanged on December 2, 1859.

The episode horrified and terrified the South, raising the specter of slave uprisings. Such violent revolts were not unknown. In 1831 a slave named Nat Turner led an uprising in Virginia that claimed more than 50 white people's lives before it was crushed. An unknown number of blacks were killed in reprisal. Turner and a number of his followers were hanged. With this in mind, many in the South now felt its existence as a slaveholding territory might well depend on separation from the Union.

The election of 1860. The entire nation anxiously awaited the next election. When the Democratic convention met, Democrats from the North had a majority. They favored Senator Stephen A. Douglas of Illinois, an advocate of popular sovereignty. This so upset the Democrats from the South, who thought that the slavery issue had been solved by the Dred Scott case, that the convention adjourned without having nominated a candidate. When it reconvened two months later, delegates from the Deep South were absent. Douglas was chosen the candidate of the Northern Democrats. The Southern Democrats split off and nominated John C. Breckinridge of Kentucky.

brought him national prominence. In the 1860 presidential race, Lincoln ran on a platform that did not push abolition of slavery but did restrict its extension into territories. The platform also favored a tariff and a homestead act for Western lands, thus strengthening its appeal to the North and the West.

Lincoln won only 40 percent of the popular vote, but he captured 180 electoral votes, well over Breckinridge's 72 votes and Douglas's 12 votes. Even John Bell, candidate of the splinter Constitutional Union Party, beat Douglas, winning 39 electoral votes.

Secession. The election of Lincoln, the representative of a party that had support only in the North, galvanized the South into action. Fearful of being unable to maintain its power in the federal government and to protect itself against the power of the industrial North, the South began to seriously entertain ideas of secession. "Fire-eaters" preached the need for secession and maintained that it could be accomplished without civil war because the North, threatened with the loss of cotton and the Southern market, would not dare to oppose secession forcibly.

South Carolina, long a place where a belief in the doctrine of nullification had thrived, led the movement for secession. On December 20, 1860, it declared itself a free and independent state. By February 1861 all the other states of the lower South—Mississippi, Florida, Alabama, Georgia, Louisiana, and Texas—had taken similar action. On February 4 delegates from these seven states met in Montgomery, Alabama, to form the Confederate States of America. Five days later they elected Jefferson Davis of Mississippi as president and Alexander H. Stevens of Georgia, who, like Davis, had been against secession, as vice president. The Confederate constitution stressed state sovereignty, prohibited high protective tariffs, and recognized "the institution of Negro slavery as it now exists in the Confederate States."

The young Confederacy took over many federal forts and arsenals in the South. In April 1861 Fort Sumter, in the harbor of Charleston, South Carolina, was under siege. Lincoln, hoping to keep the states of the upper South—Virginia, Arkansas, Tennessee, and North Carolina—from seceding, and hoping to avoid war, had thus far not acted to oppose the Confederate takeovers. But he did order Fort Sumter to be resupplied with food and notified the South Carolina authorities of the nature of the resupply effort. On April 11 the Confederates ordered the commander of the garrison, Major Robert Anderson, to surrender the fort. Anderson refused to comply but let it be known that in a few days he would be forced, due to lack of supplies, to evacuate the fort anyway. This the Confederates could not, or would not, wait for, and on April 12, Confederate batteries began bombarding the fort. The next day, after 33 hours of bombardment, Anderson surrendered; the next day, the

THE ANTISLAVERY uprising led by John Brown at Harper's Ferry resulted in his hanging, but reinforced the South's fears of slave revolts.

killed five people. In August he and a small band of antislavery fighters battled against a much larger force of proslavery men, gaining Brown even more notoriety and convincing him that only by bloodshed could slavery be ended.

On the night of October 15, 1859, Brown and a small band of followers attacked and took the federal armory at Harpers Ferry, Virginia. President Buchanan ordered a force of U.S. Marines under the command of Colonel

The Republicans nominated Abraham Lincoln of Illinois. Lincoln had served one term in Congress, but had turned away from politics to practice law in Illinois. However, his opposition to the Kansas-Nebraska Act brought him back into politics. He supported the Republican Party in 1856, and in 1858 ran against Douglas for the Senate. He lost the election, but the series of debates he had with Douglas, which came to be known as the Lincoln-Douglas debates,

Union			Confederacy	
California	Maryland	New York	Alabama	North Carolina
Connecticut	Massachusetts	Ohio	Arkansas	South Carolina
Delaware	Michigan	Oregon	Florida	Tennessee
Illinois	Minnesota	Pennsylvania	Georgia	Texas
Indiana	Missouri	Rhode Island	Louisiana	Virginia
Iowa	Nevada	Vermont	Mississippi	
Kansas	New Hampshire	West Virginia		
Kentucky	New Jersey	Wisconsin		

garrison evacuated the fort. The first shots of the Civil War had been fired.

The Civil War. The day after the surrender of Fort Sumter, President Lincoln issued a proclamation calling for 75,000 troops to suppress the insurrection facing the Union. By December 1861, 600,000 men were in the Union army. In the South the call for volunteers met with an equally ardent response, and many brilliant officers resigned from the U.S. Army to go home and serve their states. Among them was the unparalleled Robert E. Lee, who declined Lincoln's offer of the command of the Union forces. After Virginia seceded, Lee agonized over what to do, and finally decided to serve his state as commander of the Army of Virginia.

Within a month, four more states had gone over to the Confederacy. First went Virginia, but its western section remained loyal to the Union and was admitted to the Union as the state of West Virginia. Arkansas, Tennessee, and North Carolina followed. In June the capital of the Confederacy was moved from Montgomery, Alabama, to Richmond, Virginia. President Davis licensed Southern privateers to seize U.S. vessels. In April, Lincoln had proclaimed a blockade of Southern ports, although at the outset he did not have the means to enforce it.

Unequal sides. At the beginning of the war, the North and South each hoped to gain victory in a short war—90 days perhaps. But the war would be a prolonged one—four years in all.

The South had the advantage in military talent. In addition to Lee, it boasted the West Point–trained generals Pierre G. T. Beauregard, Thomas J. (later "Stonewall") Jackson, J. E. B. Stuart, and Joseph E. Johnston. Among the South's disadvantages was the weakening effect of a states' rights ideology on the execution of the war.

Among the North's advantages were its much larger population (23 million versus fewer than 9 million in the South); its factories (110,000 versus 18,000), capable of being converted to the production of war supplies; and its railroad mileage (27,000 miles, 43,000 kilometers, versus 8,400 miles, 13,500 kilometers), for moving troops and supplies.

Strategy. As war began, the South had no intention of invading the North. It hoped, and many believed, that the North would not go to war to preserve the Union. Failing that, the Southern strategists planned to wage a defensive war against Northern attacks, with the hope that reported defeats would cause the North to wear down and finally leave the South alone. They also hoped that Great Britain and France, needing Southern cotton, would soon recognize the Confederacy. The Northern strategy was quite different. Union forces would have to invade the South and isolate it in order to defeat the Southern armies and preserve the Union.

The North's broad strategy was proposed by General Winfield Scott, a veteran of the war with Mexico. Named the Anaconda Plan (for the python that crushes its victims to death), it aimed to split the South into three parts, first by capturing the Mississippi River valley and thus isolating the states west of the Mississippi River; second by splitting the sections east and west of the Appalachians. Once the areas were isolated from one another, a naval blockade, extending from Virginia to Texas, would strangle the South.

Early battles. Implementing this broad strategy would take time, but some Northern tacticians had a more immediate plan—to capture the Confederate capital of Richmond and so demoralize the South that its surrender would follow.

First Bull Run. To that end, in July 1861, Lincoln sent the Army of the Potomac, though poorly trained and inexperienced, to attack a Confederate force camped at Manassas Junction in northern Virginia, not far south of Washington, D.C. The two sides joined in battle at Bull Run. At first, the Union forces under General Irvin McDowell seemed to be winning against the Confederate forces under General P. G. T. Beauregard. But their advance was stopped by General Thomas Jonathan Jackson, who earned his nickname "Stonewall" in this battle by standing (it was later claimed) calmly in the midst of the fighting, like a stone wall. Jackson's Confederate reinforcements put the Union troops to rout. The North could now see that a long war was probably ahead.

Peninsular campaign. Lincoln decided to name General George B. McClellan general in chief of the Union forces. After eight long months of retrenchment and training, during which the Army of the Potomac swelled to some 160,000 strong, McClellan refused to advance against the Confederates. Meanwhile, commanders in other fields were scoring victories, notably Grant in Tennessee. Finally, in March, McClellan began to move the army by sea to the Yorktown peninsula. McClellan planned to outflank the Army of Northern Virginia under General Joseph E. Johnston, capture Richmond, and end the war quickly. In April, McClellan, who had been removed as general in chief, began moving his Army of the Potomac up the peninsula, but too slowly to outmaneuver Johnston. Nonetheless, McClellan's advance forces came within five miles (eight kilometers) of Richmond.

The Confederates struck fiercely at Seven Pines but were driven off. Johnston was wounded and General Robert E. Lee took command. Lee saw a golden opportunity to destroy the Army of the Potomac and end the war quickly. He struck McClellan's army at the end of June in the Seven Days battles, but was unable to coordinate all the forces in his

PRESIDENT ABRAHAM LINCOLN, seen here with his cabinet, took office under threats by the South to secede from the Union.

27 North America

THE CIVIL WAR
was fought primarily
by foot soldiers, most
of them untrained,
and the deaths due to
battle, privation, and
disease were the
highest ever suffered
in an American war.

command effectively. McClellan was
able to withdraw to a better position
south of Richmond. Lee withdrew his
forces closer to Richmond and waited,
but McClellan did not renew the attack.
The Peninsular campaign ground to a
halt. On July 11 President Lincoln
named General Henry E. Halleck general in chief, and soon Halleck ordered
McClellan to move back north.

Monitor **and** *Merrimack.*   The Peninsular
campaign was almost canceled by the
appearance on March 8, off Hampton
Roads, Virginia, of the 20-gun Confederate ironclad ram *Virginia.* It had been
built on the raised hull of the Union ship
Merrimack, which had been deliberately
destroyed in the evacuation of Norfolk
Navy Yard early in the war. The *Virginia,*
still commonly known by its earlier
name, destroyed two Union ships, ran a
third aground, and returned for the kill
on March 9, when it met the federal ironclad *Monitor.* The *Monitor* had only two
guns mounted in a single turret, but it
fought the *Virginia* to a draw and forced
it to retire. This was the first battle in history between ironclad warships. On May
10, when the Confederates evacuated

ROBERT E. LEE
surrendered his
Virginia landholdings
to lead the
Confederate Army.
He was successful
in early campaigns
against the Armies
of the Potomac
and Virginia.

Norfolk, they destroyed the *Virginia* to
keep it from being captured.

Second Bull Run.   Lincoln and Halleck
created a new army, the Army of Virginia, under the command of General
John Pope. This army joined with
McClellan's and marched on Richmond
in the summer of 1862. But like the
Union army of 1861, it too was stopped
at Bull Run in a battle waged there on
August 29 and 30; it sustained 16,000
casualties. The Army of Virginia, as
unsuccessful as that of the Potomac,
was disbanded.

Antietam.   The defeat of the Union in its
attempts on Richmond freed Lee and his
troops. To the amazement of the North,
Lee set out to invade the border state of
Maryland in an effort to cut roads, rail
lines, and communications, take prisoners, capture supplies, wreak havoc,
isolate and threaten Washington, D.C.,
impress England and France, and, last
but not least, demoralize the North. In
late summer, McClellan moved his
troops to stop Lee. On September 17,
1862, Union and Confederate forces
met in the bloodiest battle of the war, at
Antietam Creek in Maryland. McClellan, with nearly twice the forces available
to Lee, fought the Confederate army to a
draw, but allowed Lee's army to retreat
when he failed to press his advantage
and destroy the scattering troops. Upset
by McClellan's lack of aggressiveness,
Lincoln in November relieved him of
command. There were no victors at
Antietam, where almost 5,000 died and
more than 18,000 were wounded. The
Union lost another chance to end the
war, and the Confederacy lost a victory
that could have earned it diplomatic
recognition.

Fredericksburg and Chancellorsville.   Union
troops, now under the new general
in chief Ambrose E. Burnside, made
another attempt on Richmond in mid-
December 1862. Once again, Lee's
smaller army stopped the Army of the
Potomac, this time at Fredericksburg,
and sent them reeling back to Washington. Lincoln next tried General Joseph
"Fighting Joe" Hooker, who again
marched on Richmond, in late April of
1863. This time Union troops reached
only as far as Chancellorsville, where
once again they met defeat at Lee's hand,
suffering a loss of 17,000 dead, wounded,
or missing. When hearing the news of
yet another defeat, Lincoln cried, "My
God! My God! What will the country say?
What will the country say?"

U.S.-British relations.   At the beginning of the war, both France and Great
Britain declared neutrality, but events
were to bring Britain and the United
States close to war. On November 8,
1861, the U.S. naval vessel *San Jacinto*
stopped the British steamer *Trent* and
seized the Confederate commissioners
to Britain and France, James M. Mason
and John Slidell. The British were outraged and war was averted only when, on
December 26, Mason and Slidell were
ordered released. Relations between the
two countries were also strained in 1862
when the Confederate raider *Alabama,*

outfitted in Liverpool, was allowed to sail
from England and begin preying on
Union shipping. The *Alabama* and other
raiders fitted out in England caused enormous losses and aroused much anger
against Britain. The damage claims
against Britain for allowing the raiders to
sail out of its ports, known collectively as
the *Alabama* claims, were not settled
until 1872, when an international commission awarded $15.5 million in
damages to the United States.

The Emancipation Proclamation.
Lincoln's aim from the beginning had
been the preservation of the Union. He
had opposed the extension of slavery in
the territories and had stated that
sooner or later the country would be all
slave or all free, but that it could not
remain forever divided on the issue. In a
speech in Springfield, Illinois, on June
17, 1858, he had quoted the Bible in reference to slavery: "A house divided
against itself cannot stand." But in his
inaugural address, he had tried to reas-
sure the South: "The government will
not assail you." He had had no intention
of attacking slavery in the South.

Toward the end of 1862, Lincoln
sensed, however, that the long, discouraging war could be won only with the
impetus provided by a new emotional
lift. He decided that now was the time to
take a moral stand and raise the banner
for the slave.

On January 1, 1863, the Emancipation Proclamation was issued. It
proclaimed that all slaves in areas still in
a state of rebellion were henceforward
free. It did not state that slaves in Union-
held territories or in border states loyal
to the Union were free. Since the Union
was not in control of the areas the
proclamation covered, the Emancipation Proclamation did not actually free
any slaves. But it did change the nature
of the war, from one of national patriotism to one of a crusade for the
oppressed. And in so doing, the proclamation also made it more difficult for
Great Britain, which opposed slavery, to
recognize the Confederacy now that
slavery was a main issue in contention.

Draft riots.   In March, 1863, faced with
the need to raise more troops, Congress
instituted the first national military draft.
The draft act provided that any draftee
could fulfill his obligation by paying $300
or hiring a substitute. Because only the
wealthy could escape conscription, the
act became known as the poor man's
draft. It triggered four days of bloody
riots in New York City, beginning on July
13, in which mobs of white workers beat
and murdered hundreds of people, particularly blacks, attacked police and
firemen, and destroyed many buildings.
By the time the riots were ended by
National Guard troops on July 16, about
1,000 people had been killed or wounded.
Congress authorized three more drafts
during the war, none of which provoked
anything like the New York riots. In all
four drafts, relatively few men were
actually drafted. Most of the conscription quotas were met by volunteer
enlistments.

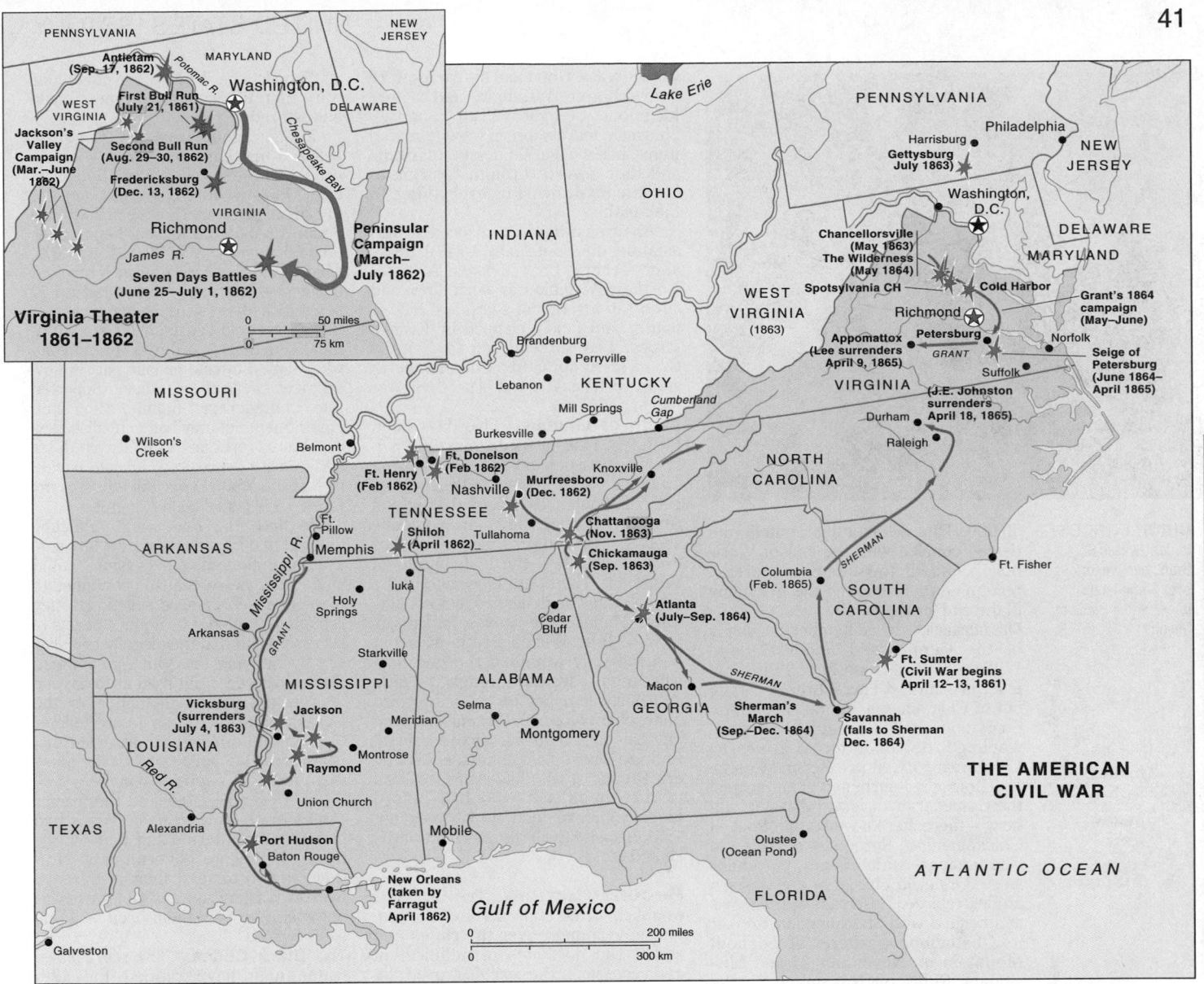

Virginia Theater 1861–1862 (inset map)

- Antietam (Sep. 17, 1862)
- First Bull Run (July 21, 1861)
- Jackson's Valley Campaign (Mar.–June 1862)
- Second Bull Run (Aug. 29–30, 1862)
- Fredericksburg (Dec. 13, 1862)
- Richmond
- Washington, D.C.
- Peninsular Campaign (March–July 1862)
- Seven Days Battles (June 25–July 1, 1862)
- *James R.*
- *Potomac R.*
- *Chesapeake Bay*

PENNSYLVANIA — MARYLAND — NEW JERSEY — DELAWARE — WEST VIRGINIA — VIRGINIA

0 — 50 miles / 0 — 75 km

THE AMERICAN CIVIL WAR

Main map labels:
- Lake Erie
- PENNSYLVANIA — Harrisburg, Philadelphia, Gettysburg July 1863
- NEW JERSEY — DELAWARE — MARYLAND
- Washington, D.C.
- Chancellorsville (May 1863)
- The Wilderness (May 1864)
- Spotsylvania CH
- Cold Harbor
- Grant's 1864 campaign (May–June)
- Richmond
- Petersburg — GRANT
- Norfolk — Suffolk
- Appomattox (Lee surrenders April 9, 1865)
- Seige of Petersburg (June 1864–April 1865)
- J.E. Johnston surrenders April 18, 1865
- WEST VIRGINIA (1863)
- VIRGINIA
- Durham — Raleigh
- NORTH CAROLINA
- OHIO — INDIANA
- Brandenburg — Perryville — Lebanon — Mill Springs
- KENTUCKY — Cumberland Gap
- Burkesville — Knoxville
- MISSOURI — Wilson's Creek — Belmont
- Ft. Henry (Feb 1862) — Ft. Donelson (Feb 1862)
- Nashville — Murfreesboro (Dec. 1862)
- Chattanooga (Nov. 1863)
- Chickamauga (Sep. 1863)
- SHERMAN
- Columbia (Feb. 1865)
- SOUTH CAROLINA
- Ft. Fisher
- ARKANSAS — Ft. Pillow — Memphis — Shiloh (April 1862) — Tullahoma
- *Mississippi R.* — GRANT
- Iuka — Holy Springs — Starkville
- Arkansas
- Atlanta (July–Sep. 1864)
- Cedar Bluff
- Ft. Sumter (Civil War begins April 12–13, 1861)
- MISSISSIPPI — Vicksburg (surrenders July 4, 1863) — Jackson — Raymond — Union Church — Montrose — Meridian
- ALABAMA — Selma — Montgomery
- GEORGIA — Macon
- Sherman's March (Sep.–Dec. 1864)
- Savannah (falls to Sherman Dec. 1864)
- LOUISIANA — *Red R.* — Alexandria
- Port Hudson — Baton Rouge
- Mobile
- New Orleans (taken by Farragut April 1862)
- TEXAS — Galveston
- *Gulf of Mexico*
- Olustee (Ocean Pond)
- FLORIDA
- ATLANTIC OCEAN

0 — 200 miles / 0 — 300 km

Turning points. While war raged in the East, it was also being fought in the West, as Union troops tried to capture control of the entire Mississippi River valley. Combined Army and Navy operations, under the command of General Ulysses S. Grant and Commodore Andrew H. Foote, were bringing the Union a number of stunning victories. From February to June 1862, through victories at Fort Donelson and Fort Henry and at Shiloh and Memphis, Union forces had recaptured western Tennessee. On April 26 Union admiral David S. Farragut's naval squadron had captured New Orleans, the Confederacy's most important port, at the mouth of the Mississippi River. Now only Confederate control of Vicksburg, Mississippi, kept the Union from succeeding in taking the entire Mississippi valley and cutting off the Confederate states west of the Mississippi.

Vicksburg. Situated on high bluffs overlooking the Mississippi River, surrounded by many swamps and rivers, strongly fortified and well garrisoned, the Confederate fortress at Vicksburg was very difficult to attack. After several failures, Grant decided to attack from the south. In April 1863, he moved 20,000 men down the Mississippi to a point south of Vicksburg. Using every sort of draft animal to be found on the surrounding plantations and farms to carry their supplies, Grant's troops marched north toward Vicksburg. Then they suddenly turned right—away from Vicksburg. First they captured and destroyed Jackson, Mississippi, an important Southern railroad and munitions center. The next day they turned west, and on May 16 they defeated a considerable part of the Vicksburg garrison. Two days later, Grant had completely surrounded Vicksburg. After a 47-day siege, the city finally surrendered, on July 4. The Mississippi valley portion of the Anaconda Plan had been achieved.

Gettysburg. At exactly the same time, another momentous battle was raging in the East. President Davis and General Lee had decided that Lee should bring the war up into Pennsylvania, to try and draw Grant away from Vicksburg and, with luck, strike a death blow after the North's failures at Fredericksburg and Chancellorsville. The Southern plan was to march up to Harrisburg, capture it, and advance on Philadelphia and New York if the North did not sue for peace. A victorious campaign on Northern soil might bring British recognition, which would swing the war in favor of the South. Lincoln sent Union troops under General George C. Meade to stop Lee. The two forces met unexpectedly near Gettysburg. The bloody struggle continued from July 1 through July 3, 1863. The Confederates pressed the superior Union forces hard the first two days but were unable to gain the advantage. On July 3 Lee, believing that an all-out charge on the Union center would put Meade's army to rout, ordered a frontal assault on the Union lines along the aptly named Cemetery Ridge. Here the South met defeat, and General George C. Pickett's division, which led the charge, was almost annihilated. It is estimated that the total number of losses of Union and Confederate dead, wounded, and missing was between 40,000 and

THE UNION strategy called for a three-pronged attack intended to split the Confederacy into three sections.

center
US

centre
Brit.

UNION FORCES under Ulysses S. Grant were victorious over Confederate forces at the Battle of Shiloh.

theater
US

theatre
Brit.

GEORGE PICKETT led the Confederate charge at Gettysburg, which resulted in a stunning Southern loss. The count of dead, wounded, and missing on both sides was between 40,000 and 50,000.

50,000. This devastating Confederate defeat, coupled with the loss of Vicksburg, ended the hope of foreign recognition and marked the beginning of the end for the South.

Chickamauga. In September the Army of the Cumberland under General William S. Rosecrans forced the Confederates under General Braxton Bragg out of Chattanooga, Tennessee, but on September 19–20, Bragg's army overwhelmed the Union forces at nearby Chickamauga, Georgia. General George H. Thomas's determined stand against the Confederates averted disaster, and he was thereafter known as the "Rock of Chickamauga." Rosecrans retreated to Chattanooga, which Bragg put under siege. Grant, in charge of the western armies, replaced Rosecrans with Thomas and rushed with Sherman and Hooker to Chattanooga, where, at Lookout Mountain on November 24 and Missionary Ridge on November 25, the combined Union forces routed Bragg's army and secured eastern Tennessee. Now the stage was set for Sherman's march to Atlanta and the sea.

Union victory. General Grant, who on March 9, 1864, became general in chief of all Union armies, devised a three-point plan to end the war. Union forces under General Philip Sheridan were to invade the rich Shenandoah valley and destroy everything of value to the

Confederacy. Grant and his troops were to march from Washington and capture Richmond. General William Tecumseh Sherman and his forces were to march from Chattanooga, Tennessee, to Atlanta and then sweep through Georgia to Savannah, destroying everything in their path.

All three campaigns succeeded, devastating the South. On April 9, 1865, after General Lee's beloved Army of Northern Virginia was worn down and cut off in a series of sharp and bloody battles and finally trapped by Grant's forces, Lee surrendered to General Grant at Appomattox Courthouse in southwestern Virginia. The Civil War had ended.

Death of Lincoln. Five days later, President Lincoln was attending a performance of a play entitled *Our American Cousin* at Ford's Theater in Washington, D.C. At about 10 o'clock on the night of April 14, a shot rang out. Someone shouted, "Sic semper tyrannis!" ("Thus ever to tyrants"—the state motto of Virginia.) "The South is avenged!" the man shouted as he leaped to the stage, ran off behind the scenes, and disappeared. John Wilkes Booth, an actor, had mortally wounded the one man who might have put through the difficult postwar policy of "malice toward none; charity for all." The war was over, but Lincoln was dead. Vice President Andrew Johnson of Tennessee, a southern Democrat who had remained loyal to the Union and who had helped Lincoln gain reelection in November, 1864, became the 17th president of the United States.

Reconstruction. The Civil War established the supremacy of the federal government over the states and ended the doctrines of nullification and secession. The war destroyed the influence of the Southern planters in national government, giving dominance to the Northern industrialists. This so enhanced the prestige of the Republican Party that it controlled the federal government until well into the 20th century. As a result, businessmen carried the nation into a new period of industrialization and Western expansion.

Lincoln's plan. Lincoln's desire had been to restore civil government throughout the broken South as quickly as possible. "Let us bind up the nation's wounds. Let us do all we can to achieve and cherish a just and lasting peace," he had urged. In 1863, he proclaimed that each formerly rebellious state could reestablish its own government when it met two conditions. First, 10 percent of its citizens who had voted in 1860 had to swear an oath to "faithfully support and defend the Constitution of the United States" in order to be pardoned. Lincoln withheld pardons from high-ranking Confederate leaders, former U.S. congressmen and judges who supported the rebellion, and military officers, effectively cutting them off from political power. Second, the state had to

abolish slavery. When these conditions were met, the state government could be restored.

Many Republicans in Congress believed that Lincoln's plan was far too lenient. These so-called "Radical Republicans" insisted that Congress, not the President, determine how to deal with the South. In 1864 the Radical Republicans pushed through the Wade-Davis Bill, which set forth a harsher plan. It required that a majority of white males (not just 10 percent) had to swear allegiance before the state could reestablish its government. Further, it ordered that anyone who wanted to vote or take part in government swear never to have supported the Confederacy. Finally, the state government not only had to abolish slavery, but to repudiate Confederate debts and its act of secession. Lincoln pocket vetoed the Wade-Davis Bill, but support for its ideas persisted in Congress.

At first, the Radical Republicans thought that President Andrew Johnson, a bitter opponent of secession, would share their views. Johnson continued to demand of reorganized states that they repudiate Confederate debts and acts of secession and that they legally end slavery by ratifying the 13th Amendment. But he offered a full pardon to anyone who would swear allegiance to the Constitution, including many former Confederate officials. He asserted that Reconstruction policy was for the president, and not Congress, to make.

By December, 1865, all the former Confederate states except Texas had met Johnson's terms and had reorganized their state governments. Now they wanted to send their representatives to Washington, but Congress was not willing to take them back on Johnson's terms.

The Black Codes. The reorganized states may have ratified the 13th Amendment, but that did not mean that they wanted to give equal rights to the newly freed blacks, called *freedmen*. In March 1865, Congress had established the Freedmen's Bureau, to help impoverished freedmen to make new lives.

A CANNON stands on Lookout Mountain, relic of the battle at Chattanooga which secured eastern Tennessee for the Union.

The American Civil War 1861–1865

In the following listing of battles and events in the Civil War, (U) represents the Union (Northern) army, while (C) represents the Confederate (Southern) army. Italics denote winning generals; (k) signifies killed.

1860
Nov. 6 Election of Abraham Lincoln.
Dec. 20 Secession of South Carolina.

1861
Feb. 9 Jefferson Davis elected president of the Confederate States of America (C.S. of A.).
Feb. 18 Davis inaugurated at Montgomery, Ala.
Mar. 4 Lincoln inaugurated at Washington, D.C.
Apr. 12-13 Bombardment and surrender of Ft. Sumter, Charleston Harbor, S.C.
Apr. 19 Blockade of Southern ports declared by President Lincoln.
May 6 Confederate Congress passes act recognizing state of war between the U.S. and the C.S. of A.
May 26 Richmond, Va., becomes capital of the C.S. of A.
July 21 First Battle of Bull Run (Manassas, Va.): Irvin McDowell (U); *J.E. Johnston and P.G.T. Beauregard (C)*.
Aug. 10 Battle of Wilson's Creek, Mo.: Nathaniel Lyon (U); *Ben McCulloch (C)*.
Oct. 21 Battle of Ball's Bluff, Va.: C.P. Stone (U); *N.G. Evans (C)*.
Nov. 7 Battle of Belmont, Mo.: Ulysses S. Grant (U): *L. Polk (C)*.
Nov. 8 Removal of James Mason and John Slidell from the British steamer *Trent*.
Nov. 20 Creation of Committee on the Conduct of the War by Union Congress.

1862
Jan. 19 Battle of Mill Springs (or Logan's Cross Roads), Ky.: *G.H. Thomas (U)*; G. B. Crittenden (C).
Feb. 6 Fall of Fort Henry, Tenn.: *Ulysses S. Grant (U)*; L. Tilghman (C).
Feb. 14-16 Siege and surrender of Ft. Donelson, Tenn.: *Ulysses S. Grant (U)*; S.B. Buckner (C).
Feb. 21 Battle of Valverde, N.M.: *E.R.S. Canby (U)*; H.H.Sibley (C).
Mar. to June 9 Jackson's Valley campaign (Va.): N.P. Banks (U); *T.J. Jackson (C)*.
Mar. 9 Battle of *Monitor* and *Merrimack* in Hampton Roads, Va.: *J. L. Worden (U)*; C.R. Jones (C).
Apr. 5 to May 4 Siege of Yorktown, Va.: *G.B. McClellan (U)*; J.B. Magruder (C).
Apr. 6-7 Battle of Shiloh (or Pittsburgh Landing), Tenn.: *Ulysses S. Grant (U)*; A.S. Johnston (k) and P.G.T. Beauregard (C).
Apr. 16 First Confederate Conscription Act.
Apr. 26 Surrender of New Orleans, La.: *B.F. Butler (U)*; Mansfield Lovell (C).
May 31 to June 1 Battle of Seven Pines (or Fair Oaks), Va.: *G.B. McClellan (U)*; J.E. Johnston and G.W. Smith (C).
June 1 Robert E. Lee (C) appointed to command Army of Northern Virginia.
June 26 to July 1 Seven Days battles, Va.: G.B. McClellan (U); *Robert E. Lee (C)*.
July 17 Second Union Confiscation Act passed.
Aug. 29-30 Second Battle of Bull Run (or Groveton), Va.: John Pope (U); *Robert E. Lee (C)*.
Sept. 17 Battle of Antietam (or Sharpsburg), Md.: G.B. McClellan (U); R.E. Lee (C). *Draw*.
Sept. 19 Battle of Iuka, Miss.: *W.S. Rosecrans (U)*; Sterling Price (C).
Sept. 24 Union Presidential suspension of writ of *habeas corpus*.
Oct. 3-4 Battle of Iuka, Miss.: *W.S. Rosecrans (U)*; E. Van Dorn (C).

Oct. 8 Battle of Perryville, Ky.: D.C. Buell (U); *Braxton Bragg (C)*.
Nov. 16 to July 4, 1863 Vicksburg, Miss., campaign: *Ulysses S. Grant (U)*; J.C. Pemberton (C).
Dec. 13 Battle of Fredericksburg, Va.: A.E. Burnside (U); *Robert E. Lee (C)*.
Dec. 20 Holly Springs, Miss., depot captured and burned; R.C. Murphy (U); *E. Van Dorn (C)*.
Dec. 31 to Jan. 3, 1863 Battle of Stones River (or Murfreesboro), Tenn.: W.S. Rosecrans (U); Braxton Bragg (C). *Draw*.

1863
Jan. 1 Emancipation Proclamation.
Jan. 1 Galveston, Tex., recaptured: I.S. Burrell (U); *J.B. Magruder (C)*.
Feb. 25 Union National Bank Act effective.
Mar. 3 Union Federal Draft Act.
Apr. 11 to May 4 Siege of Suffolk, Va.: *John J. Peck (U)*; James Longstreet (C).
Apr. 27 to May 5 Campaign and Battle of Chancellorsville, Va.: Joseph Hooker (U); *Robert E. Lee (C)*.
May 19 to July 4 Siege and surrender of Vicksburg, Miss.: *Ulysses S. Grant (U)*; J.C. Pemberton (C).
May 27 to July 8 Siege and surrender of Port Hudson, La.: *N.P. Banks (U)*; Franklin Gardner (C).
June 9 Cavalry battle of Brandy Station, Va.: Alfred Pleasanton (U); *Jeb Stuart (C)*.
June 20 West Virginia admitted to Union.
June 23-30 Tullahoma, Tenn., campaign: *W.S. Rosecrans (U)*; Braxton Bragg (C).
July 1-3 Battle of Gettysburg, Pa.: *G.G. Meade (U)*; Robert E. Lee (C).
July 4 Surrender of Vicksburg, Miss.: *Ulysses S. Grant (U)*; J.C. Pemberton (C).
July 8 Surrender of Port Hudson, La.: *N.P. Banks (U)*; Franklin Gardner (C).
July 13-16 New York City draft riots.
Sept. 19-20 Battle of Chickamauga, Ga.: W.S. Rosecrans (U); *B. Bragg (C)*.
Sept. 21 to Nov. 25 Siege and Battle of Chattanooga, Tenn.: *W.S. Rosecrans, G.H. Thomas, U.S. Grant (U)*; B. Bragg (C).
Nov. 17 to Dec. 5 Siege of Knoxville, Tenn.: *A.E. Burnside (U)*; J. Longstreet (C).

1864
Feb. 3 to Mar. 5 Meridian, Miss., campaign: W. T. Sherman (U); L. Polk (C). No decision.
Feb. 20 Battle of Olustee (or Ocean Pond), Fla.: Truman Seymour (U); *Jos. Finegan (C)*.
Mar. 9 U.S. Grant appointed general in chief of Union armies.
Mar. 10 to May 22 Red River, La., campaign: N.P. Banks (U); *Richard Taylor (C)*.
Apr. 12 Capture of Fort Pillow, Tenn.: L.F. Booth (k); *N.B. Forest (C)*.
May 5-6 Battle of the Wilderness, Va.: *Ulysses S. Grant (U)*; Robert E. Lee (C).
May 5 to Sept. 2 Atlanta, Ga., campaign: *W.T. Sherman (U)*; J.E. Johnston and J.B. Hood (C).
May 8-12 Operations about Spotsylvania Court House, Va.: Ulysses S. Grant (U); Robert E. Lee (C). No decision.
May 11 Cavalry battle at Yellow Tavern, Va.: *P.H. Sheridan (U)*; Jeb Stuart (k) (C).
May 15 Battle of New Market, Va.: Franz Sigel (U); *J.C. Breckinridge (C)*.
May 25-27 Battle of New Hope Church, Ga.: J. Hooker (U); *J.E. Johnston (C)*.

June 3 Battle of Cold Harbor, Va.: Ulysses S. Grant (U); *Robert E. Lee (C)*.
June 10 Battle of Brice's Cross Roads, Miss.: S.D. Sturgis (U); *N.B. Forrest (C)*.
June 18 to Apr. 1, 1865 Siege of Petersburg, Va.: *Ulysses S. Grant (U)*; Robert E. Lee (C).
June 19 Naval battle. *Alabama* and *Kearsarge*, off French coast; *John A. Winslow (U)*; Raphael Semmes(C).
July 6-12 Early's raid on Washington, D.C.: *Ulysses S. Grant (U)*; J. E. Early (C).
July 9 Battle of Monocacy, Md.: Lew Wallace (U); *J.E. Early (C)*.
Aug. 5 Naval battle in Mobile Bay, Ala.: *D.G. Farragut (U)*; Percival Drayton (C).
Aug. 7 to Oct. 25 Shenandoah Valley, Va., campaign: *P.H. Sheridan (U)*; J.E. Early (C).
Sept. 1 Evacuation of Atlanta, Ga.: *W.T. Sherman (U)*; J.B. Hood (C).
Oct. 19 Battle of Cedar Creek, Va.: *P.H. Sheridan (U)*; J.E. Early (C).
Oct. 23 Battle of Westport, Mo.: *S.R. Curtis (U)*; Sterling Price (C).
Nov. 8 Lincoln reelected president.
Nov. 15 to Dec. 21 Raid through Georgia from Atlanta to coast: *W.T. Sherman (U)*; G.W. Smith and W.J. Hardee (C).
Nov. 21 to Dec. 16 Hood's Tennessee campaign: *G.H. Thomas (U)*; J.B. Hood (C).
Nov. 30 Battle of Franklin, Tenn.: *J. Scofield (U)*; J.B. Hood (C).
Dec. 15-16 Battle of Nashville, Tenn.: *G.H. Thomas (U)*; J.B. Hood (C).
Dec. 21 Capture of Savannah, Ga.: *W.T. Sherman (U)*; W.J. Hardee (C).

1865
Jan. 13-15 Battle of Ft. Fisher, N.C.: *A.H. Terry (U)*; W.H. Whiting (k) (C).
Feb. 3 Hampton Roads, Va., peace conference.
Feb. 6 Robert E. Lee appointed general in chief of all Confederate forces.
Feb. 17 Columbia, S.C., captured and destroyed by fire: *W.T. Sherman (U)*.
Feb. 18 Charleston, S.C., evacuated by Confederate troops.
Mar. 4 Abraham Lincoln inaugurated for second term.
Apr. 1 Battle of Five Forks, Va.: *P.H. Sheridan (U)*; G.E. Pickett (C).
Apr. 2 Capture of Selma, Ala.: *J.H. Wilson (U)*; N.B. Forrest (C).
Apr. 2 Confederate evacuation of Richmond, Va.
Apr. 9 Confederate surrender at Appomattox Court House, Va. *Ulysses S. Grant (U)*; Robert E. Lee (C).
Apr. 12 Capture of Mobile, Ala.: *E.R.S. Canby (U)*; D.H. Maury (C).
Apr. 15 Death of President Lincoln. Andrew Johnson inaugurated as president.
Apr. 26 Confederate surrender at Durham, N.C.: *W.T. Sherman (U)*; J.E. Johnston (C).
May 4 Surrender of Confederate forces in Louisiana: *E.R.S. Canby (U)*; R. Taylor (C).
May 10 Jefferson Davis captured at Irwinsville, Ga.
May 26 Surrender of Trans-Mississippi Dept.: *E.R.S. Canby (U)*; Kirby Smith (C).
June 2 Surrender of Galveston, Tex.: *H.K. Thatcher (U)*; Kirby Smith (C).
Nov. 6 Final Confederate surrender—*Shenandoah*, Capt. James Waddell, to British authorities at Liverpool, England.

labor
US

labour
Brit.

color
US

colour
Brit.

The bureau offered funds for food and education and protection in labor contracts and local troubles. But life remained desperate for the former slaves, as it did for all the South's poor. As the reorganized state governments drew up their laws in 1865 and 1866, they incorporated a number of acts called Black Codes. The Black Codes denied the freedmen many rights of citizenship. They forbade blacks from carrying arms, required that they serve an apprenticeship while underage, governed their employment, and instituted curfews. Thus blacks were once again relegated to social, economic, and political inferiority in America.

Johnson and Congress. Many members of Congress were outraged by the Black Codes. In February 1866, they voted to renew the Freedmen's Bureau and extend its powers to protect blacks. Johnson vetoed the bill. (In July a new version of the bill was passed and Johnson's veto was overridden.) In April Congress passed the Civil Rights Act, which declared that freedmen were U.S. citizens entitled "to full and equal benefit of the laws." Johnson vetoed this act, too, stating that it was unconstitutional and granted the federal government power at the expense of the states. This time, an angry Congress overrode Johnson's veto, but fearing that the Supreme Court might agree with the president, it proposed the 14th Amendment, which guaranteed citizenship to blacks.

CARPETBAGGERS were Northerners who went South to profit from its defeat in the Civil War.

Johnson objected to the 14th Amendment, too, as an invasion of states' rights, and advised Southern states not to ratify it. In the congressional elections of 1866, Johnson sought to gather strength for his policies in Congress by campaigning for candidates that would support them. The effect was disastrous. Republicans who opposed him won overwhelmingly.

Control of Reconstruction was now firmly in the hands of Congress.

Congress was quick to pass the Reconstruction Act of 1867 over Johnson's veto. The act made new demands on the reorganizing Southern states and divided the South into five military districts, each under the control of a military commander. The commander was to register the voters, exclude prominent Confederate leaders, and include all other male citizens "of whatever race, color, or previous condition of servitude." These voters were to elect a state convention to frame a state constitution. If this constitution satisfied Congress, and if the state legislature ratified the 14th Amendment, the state would be readmitted to the Union.

Impeachment of Johnson. Congress backed up its Reconstruction Act with other laws that limited Johnson's role in Reconstruction. One was the Tenure of Office Act, which denied the president the right to dismiss civilian government officials who had been "appointed by and with the advice and consent of the Senate" without Senate approval. Through this act, Congress would be able to keep in office those officials who were friendly to Congress, in spite of Johnson's wishes.

In 1867, Johnson came into conflict with Secretary of War Edwin M. Stanton over the appointment of commanders of the military districts in the South; on February 21, 1868, Johnson removed Stanton from office. Radical Republicans saw this as an opportunity to get rid of Johnson, so the House voted to bring articles of impeachment against him on February 24, 1868, and on March 2 and 3, passed eleven articles of impeachment outlining what it saw as the president's "high misdemeanors" in office.

From March 30 to May 26, Johnson stood trial on the charges, with the Senate as jury and Chief Justice Salmon P. Chase as judge. In two votes, on May 16 and May 26, 35 senators voted Johnson guilty, one short of the necessary two-thirds majority. Johnson could remain in office, but his power was greatly diminished. That fall, he did not attempt to run again. General Grant, now a popular war hero, was elected president.

The South reacts. By 1871, all the former Confederate states had reorganized their governments, under generally Republican domination, and had been readmitted to the Union. Thanks to the newly passed 15th Amendment, blacks now had the right to vote, which they did, generally for Republicans. Several black representatives were elected to state and federal office. Much to the chagrin of many white Southerners, carpetbaggers—Northerners who had moved to the South following the war—were exerting some power in Southern state governments. So were scalawags, Southerners who had stayed loyal to the Union during the war and supported Reconstruction under the Republicans.

Economic conditions were desperate. Planters and farmers faced ruin,

with much of their land destroyed and their labor supply now freed. Landless former slaves turned to sharecropping to survive, often working a plot of their former masters' land and living no better than they had before, and in some cases worse. Little by little, though, the South began rebuilding itself. A "New South" was beginning to emerge.

It soon became obvious that some white Southerners wanted to maintain strict control over blacks and to end black participation in voting and government. Secret groups like the Ku Klux Klan and the Knights of the White Camellia were formed to keep both blacks and white Republicans intimidated and away from elections. To try to combat such actions, Congress passed the Force Act in 1870 and the Ku Klux Klan Act in 1871.

Reconstruction ends. As time wore on, the North began losing interest in Reconstruction. Radical Republicans, notably the fiery congressman Thaddeus Stevens of Pennsylvania, who died in 1868, were rapidly passing from the scene. Government corruption, which seemed to flourish during Grant's administration, became the new focus of attention. Union troops that had long occupied the South were being pulled out. The last of them left in April 1877, one month after the inauguration of Rutherford B. Hayes as president. Southern governments moved out of Republican hands and into Democratic ones. Reconstruction had come to an end.

Coming of Age

An industrial giant. Though the beginnings of industrial growth in the United States are usually traced to the 1830s and 1840s, the greatest surge of growth began after the Civil War. In the next 50 years, industrial expansion completely changed the United States— from agricultural to industrial, from rural to urban, from inward-looking to outward-looking. The United States soon evolved into a major world power.

Growth of industry. The nation's phenomenal industrial growth was spurred by four fortuitous circumstances. First, the United States was blessed with a seemingly endless supply of natural resources—vast reserves of coal, iron ore, oil, copper, zinc, gold, and silver. It also had generous supplies of lumber and excellent conditions for agriculture. Second, markets for American industrial output were growing. From 1870 to 1920, some 25 million immigrants came to the United States, and the birthrate of the native-born population increased, causing the population to grow from 38 million to 106 million.

This provided a vast industrial and agricultural workforce and an enormous number of customers for American goods. Home markets alone were able to absorb nearly 95 percent of American output.

Third, favorable government attitudes toward industry also encouraged growth. Business enjoyed the benefits of high tariffs, a general reluctance to curb the excesses of industry, and many other incentives. Finally, innovative industrial leaders appeared: clever, talented inventors; resourceful business organizers; and ingenious investment bankers who could assemble necessary capital.

All of these forces combined to cause American industrial production to grow fivefold by 1900, and to continue this phenomenal growth into the 20th century. The United States was on its way to becoming the greatest industrial producer in the world.

Rise of big business. Before 1865, most businesses had been owned by a single proprietor or by a few partners. As businesses grew, it became apparent that many small, competing businesses were not necessarily the most efficient way to turn a profit. Instead, financiers formed large corporations by buying and merging small firms.

One example was Andrew Carnegie, the son of Scottish immigrants, who between 1868 and 1899 assembled all of the elements that go into steel production—coal and ore mining, water and rail shipping to steel plants, steel-making, shipping to customers—into one vast enterprise, the Carnegie Steel Company. Another example was John D. Rockefeller, who brought together many small, independent oil refineries and combined them into the giant Standard Oil Company, which controlled virtually all oil production in the United States by 1880.

Such businesses as these contributed to economic growth, but they also created monopolies that destroyed competition. Soon the cry went up that the government must intervene and control the monopolies. Said one advocate of control, Henry Demarest Lloyd, "If the tendency of combination is inevitable, control of it is imperative."

The federal government responded with legislation. The Interstate Commerce Act of 1887 established the Interstate Commerce Commission to keep railroads from giving lower prices through rebates to some large businesses. The Sherman Antitrust Act of 1890 was passed "to protect trade and commerce against unlawful restraints and monopolies." Both laws were ineffective, however, since those in high government office had little interest in placing limits on large industrial combinations.

Communication and transportation. It is impossible to imagine America's dramatic industrial growth without advances in communication and transportation. Telegraphy, which had been developed by Samuel F. B. Morse and first demonstrated on an experimental line between Baltimore and Washington, D.C., in 1844, introduced rapid communication before the Civil War. In 1866, Cyrus Field, after several unsuccessful attempts, laid the first transatlantic cable, linking Europe and the United States. In the 1870s, Thomas Edison introduced numerous improvements in telegraphy. In 1876,

Immigration and the United States

The United States has taken in more immigrants than any other nation in the world. During colonial times, about 1 million immigrants arrived, mostly from the British Isles. In the decades following American independence, immigrants kept arriving at the rate of about 10,000 a year. Then, in the 1830s alone, more than 600,000 arrived, an average of 60,000 per year.

In the 1840s, the surge of immigrants nearly tripled. Famine in Ireland and political unrest in Germany drove citizens to scrape together the steerage fare, crowd into sailing ships, and suffer the uncomfortable and treacherous transatlantic journey. In that decade, 1,700,000 immigrants arrived in the United States, to be followed in the 1850s by 2,600,000 more. Over the next three decades, another 10 million arrived, mainly from Great Britain, Ireland, and Germany, joined by farmers from soil-poor Scandinavia.

The migration preceding 1885 is often referred to as the "old migration"; it consisted mostly of people from Northern and Western Europe. The migration after 1885 is known as the "new migration"; it consisted of many more immigrants from Southern and Eastern Europe. Poverty, political unrest, and religious persecution in Austria-Hungary, Italy, Russia, Greece, Rumania, and Turkey impelled more than 8 million people to leave for the United States between 1890 and 1910. In the two decades following, another 16 million followed them.

It was not until the United States was more than a hundred years old that it placed any restrictions on immigration. In 1882, Congress passed the Chinese Exclusion Act, which barred any further immigration from China. In 1907, the United States concluded a "gentlemen's agreement" with Japan to exclude any further immigration from that country.

Legislation during the 1920s cut back severely on the number of immigrants admitted and set up quotas that discriminated against immigrants not from Northern and Western Europe.

More recent waves of immigration have included refugees from Europe made homeless before and after World War II. In 1965, a new Immigration and Nationality Act abolished the old quotas and opened up immigration to Hispanics from Latin America and to Asians. Each year, more than 300,000 of these people are taken in legally, but this number cannot keep pace with the number who want to enter. As a result, illegal immigration is today at an all-time high.

Alexander Graham Bell marked the nation's centennial by showing his "speaking machine," or telephone, which would one day form the basis of American Telephone & Telegraph. At about the same time, Edison developed the carbon button microphone, which turned Bell's telephone into a practical device. In 1877, Edison developed the phonograph, and in 1878 the first practical incandescent lamp; he was also on the way to developing the means to produce and distribute electricity, to power everything from doorbells to streetlights.

Transportation was totally transformed with the massive expansion of the railroads. Electric trolley cars, elevated trains, and subways enabled cities

to expand beyond all previous dreams. Finally, there came the automobile. In 1900 there were about 3,500 cars in the United States. By 1920, there were 9 million, thanks in large part to the enterprise of Henry Ford. He made the automobile an ordinary possession of the average family through the economy of assembly line mass production. Between 1910 and 1917, his company sold more than a million and a half Model T's, and each year the price went *down*—beginning at $950 and ending at $360.

During this period, another form of transportation was literally spreading its wings. Two bicycle mechanics, Orville and Wilbur Wright, developed an airplane, which they first flew successfully

OVER 200 MILLION PEOPLE such as this family (above left) passed through this processing center for immigrants on Ellis Island in New York Harbor between 1892 and 1954.

on the beach at Kitty Hawk, North Carolina, on December 17, 1903. The original Wright plane was a frail machine, but over the years the brothers improved their craft and in 1909 a Wright machine was purchased by the U.S. Army Signal Corps, a clear sign that the airplane was more than just an interesting toy. Other aviation pioneers, such as Glenn Curtiss, advanced the fledgling aviation industry, but air transportation did not affect the economy until after 1920. Nonetheless, the early success of powered flight at the turn of the century gave hopes that one day no mountain, jungle, or ocean would stand between one person or country and another.

Struggles of labor. The Carnegies, the Rockefellers, and the Fords were growing rich, and a comfortable middle class, made up largely of business managers and clerical workers, was growing as well. But a large mass of people were not benefiting from the rapid industrialization. Industrial laborers worked 70-

Pennsylvania, by Uriah Stephens. Its first national assembly was held in 1878. The organization championed many reforms, including the 8-hour workday and strict laws against child labor. By 1886, its membership, made up of skilled and unskilled laborers in many industries, had risen to 700,000. But on May 4 of that year, a riot in Haymarket Square in Chicago, which had been preceded on May 1 by an unsuccessful general strike of workers demanding an 8-hour workday, led to bloodshed and death. Police tried to break up a meeting of anarchist workers, and a bomb exploded, killing seven policemen. Although it was never learned who had thrown the bomb, eight anarchists were tried and convicted on charges relating to the riot. Seven were sentenced to death and 1 to 15 years in prison. The riot turned many Americans against the idea of labor unions. Union supporters were accused of being socialists or communists and were widely thought to be un-American.

to unionize and better wages and conditions would be a continuing struggle for many decades.

Growth of cities. Cities were where the large workforces were, and so industrialists built their plants in or near cities. Once the plants were there, many more workers moved to the cities, causing them to double or triple in size in as short a time as 20 years. In 1880, less than a quarter of the American population lived in cities; by 1900, well over half of Americans did.

The cities were exciting places, with such attractions as giant department stores like Marshall Field's in Chicago, Wanamaker's in Philadelphia, and Macy's in New York. They were also centers of theater, music, the arts, and sports. New trolley cars and elevated trains could carry the wealthy and the middle class to comfortable homes at the outskirts of the cities.

But cities had their seamier sides, too. Housing for the poor was dark and overcrowded. The mortality rate among the occupants of tenements, especially among children, was shockingly high. City governments paid little attention. Powerful political machines were too busy stealing money from city treasuries or taking bribes from builders and other special interests.

The drive for reform. Corruption in city government paralleled corruption at state and federal levels. During the Grant administration (1869 to 1877), members of Grant's administration were convicted of taking bribes and of stealing from tax revenues. The weaknesses of the "spoils system" became all too obvious, as corruption by federal appointees reached a new high.

Crédit Mobilier scandal. In 1872, it was revealed that the owners of the Union Pacific Railroad had diverted millions of dollars of construction funds by establishing their own construction company, Crédit Mobilier of America, to build the transcontinental railroad. In order to preclude a congressional investigation, one of the owners, Congressman Oakes Ames of Massachusetts, had distributed shares of Crédit Mobilier stock "where they will do us the most good," to fellow congressmen. Among those who had received stock were Vice President Schuyler Colfax, Speaker of the House James G. Blaine, and Congressman James A. Garfield of Ohio. The scandal fueled demands for political reform.

Tilden-Hayes dispute. President Grant was reelected in 1872, defeating Democratic candidate Horace Greeley of New York, but his administration was weakened by an economic recession and by revelations of political corruption. In 1876, the Republicans nominated Rutherford B. Hayes for the presidency, and the Democrats chose Samuel J. Tilden. In the election Tilden won a majority in the popular vote, but the Republicans challenged the electoral votes in four crucial states. An electoral commission, voting along party lines,

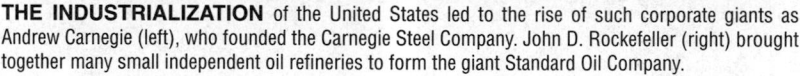

THE INDUSTRIALIZATION of the United States led to the rise of such corporate giants as Andrew Carnegie (left), who founded the Carnegie Steel Company. John D. Rockefeller (right) brought together many small independent oil refineries to form the giant Standard Oil Company.

and 80-hour weeks for less than 20 cents an hour, often in dirty and unsafe conditions. Immigrants made up a large percentage of these workers, and the children of the poor were well represented—as many as 2 million children were working in factories in 1900.

Life for the working class was very uncertain. An injury could throw a person out of work, and when it did, there was no pay. Depressions, too, were common, causing unemployment and hardship every 10 years or so. There was no unemployment compensation or other public assistance to replace wages.

Following the idea that "In union there is strength," workers made several attempts to unionize themselves, to try to get management to agree to higher wages, shorter hours, better working conditions, and an end to child labor. An early attempt was made by the Knights of Labor, formed in 1869 in Philadelphia,

The American Federation of Labor, founded in 1886 under the leadership of cigar-maker Samuel Gompers, weathered this storm. It soon gained strength from the Knights of Labor, which began to weaken after 1886. By 1904, the federation's membership had grown to over a million mostly skilled workers.

Business owners and managers were generally hostile to labor unions. The government, too, had little use for unions, declaring that they defied antitrust laws when they went on strike because they were "in restraint of trade." Nevertheless, strikes were frequent and often bloody. In 1892 a strike at the Carnegie Steel Works at Homestead, near Pittsburgh, resulted in nine strikers and three company guards dead. In 1894, a strike at Pullman's Palace Car Company near Chicago caused federal troops to be brought in on the side of management. Labor agitation for both freedom

awarded all the disputed electoral votes to Hayes, giving him a one-vote majority and the election.

Civil service. Agitation to end the spoils system became particularly strong after the assassination of President James A. Garfield, in 1881. Garfield, a "dark horse" compromise candidate at the Republican convention, had beaten the Democratic nominee, Winfield Scott Hancock, by only 7,000 popular votes. On July 2, 1881, Garfield was shot by Charles J. Guiteau, a man who had wanted an appointment to a government job but had not gotten it. Garfield died on July 19. His successor was Chester A. Arthur, who fought tenaciously against the spoils system. In 1883, the Pendleton Act was passed; it set up a Civil Service Commission and decreed that many government jobs were to be awarded on the basis of competitive examinations rather than political favor.

Populism. Although industry may have been booming, helping industrialists and bankers in the East to grow rich, agriculture was suffering during the late 1800s. Farm production was up, but farm prices were steadily declining, and farmers in the South and Midwest were sinking deeper into debt. The farmers saw the railroads as their enemies. They believed the railroads charged them too much to ship their farm products. They also did not trust the bankers, who they believed hoarded gold and did not allow enough money to circulate to help the farmers pay their debts. The farmers favored the "free coinage of silver," which would allow the government to print paper money backed by the nation's plentiful silver supply to give the farmers the dollars they needed to become solvent again.

In 1891, agrarian interests formed the Populist Party, which favored the free coinage of silver, government ownership of the railroads, a graduated income tax, an eight-hour workday, and popular election of senators (at the time, senators were elected by the state legislatures). The Populist Party ran candidates in the presidential elections of both 1892 and 1896, but the party never really gained much power. Farm prices began to rise, diminishing farmer discontent, and populism faded away.

Progressivism. Populism may have lost strength, but many of its reform ideas had not. They were picked up and expanded by a new movement—Progressivism. The Progressives, who came from both the Republican and Democratic parties, believed that continuous progress was possible, that life in the United States could improve for everyone. They believed that the nation's rapid industrialization and urbanization had harmed the working poor, and that big business had become too powerful and was crushing small business. They further believed that individual citizens did not have enough power in determining how their government was run and that government corruption at all levels had therefore flourished.

Many Progressives concentrated on eliminating the awful living conditions that existed in all too many of the nation's cities. They made more comfortable citizens aware of the poverty and lack of sanitation in city tenements. As a result, cities began passing laws that set modern building standards to alleviate some unhealthful conditions. Cities also began setting up public boards of health.

In the early 1900s, state legislatures, with the urging of Progressives, began passing laws to reduce the length of workdays, to force employers to make machinery safer, and to outlaw or limit child labor. Public systems of industrial accident insurance were also set up to help compensate workers who were injured on the job.

State and city government. The Progressives used two methods to reclaim state and city government from corruption and inefficiency. One struck at the power of party bosses. "Give the government back to the people!" was the cry. The second method was to hire experts to run government, rather than trust party professionals.

Wisconsin, under Robert Marion ("Fighting Bob") La Follette, its Progressive Republican governor, took the lead in reforming state government. As part of the "Wisconsin Idea," the state legislature adopted the direct primary, giving citizens, not party bosses, the right to choose candidates for office. Soon other states were adopting other

measures for "direct democracy." In 1913, the states ratified the 17th Amendment, which provided for the election of senators by popular vote.

Some other Progressive measures included the secret ballot; initiative, which gave voters the right to suggest laws to their legislators; referendum, which gave voters the right to vote directly on certain bills; and recall, which gave voters the right to remove officials.

Many city governments at this time also adopted a city manager type of government. The city manager was a professional administrator who was expected to run municipal government along the most efficient, rather than the most politically rewarding, lines.

Roosevelt's Square Deal. The Progressives achieved real national power when one of their own, Republican Theodore Roosevelt, became president in 1901. An energetic reformer as governor of New York, Roosevelt had made powerful enemies in the Republican Party. They decided to sidetrack his political career by making him William McKinley's vice presidential running mate in the 1900 election. McKinley was elected, but Roosevelt unexpectedly came to office at age 42, when McKinley died on September 14, eight days after being shot at the Pan-American Exposition in Buffalo, New York.

Roosevelt firmly believed that all Americans should get what he called "a square deal," that government should

ORVILLE AND WILBUR WRIGHT developed the first airplane, which they flew successfully at Kitty Hawk, North Carolina, in December of 1903.

Three American Crusades

The Progressive movement, like its predecessor, the Populist movement, was made up of crusaders and activists. Three of the movement's causes helped change American institutions in the years before 1920—the graduated income tax, Prohibition, and women's voting rights.

Why would anyone crusade for an income tax? Farmers especially favored it as a way to get nonlandowning city dwellers to share the tax burden. The farmers opposed high tariffs, a common way to raise revenues at the time. Income taxes had been levied previously, but in 1894 the Supreme Court declared them unconstitutional. Agitation for them continued, though, and in 1913, the 16th Amendment was ratified, giving Congress "the power to lay and collect taxes on income." Today, income taxes are the government's single largest source of revenue.

The drive for Prohibition began in the early 1800s, led by concerned women and churchmen who deplored the effect of hard drinking on the family. They began a crusade for *temperance*, by which they meant the avoidance of all use of alcohol. In 1874, the Women's Christian Temperance Union (WCTU) was formed, and its members went into saloons where they prayed and sang hymns to discourage drinking. Carry Nation, one of the most vociferous crusaders, took a hatchet into saloons and smashed the liquor kegs.

By 1917, the crusade against alcohol had succeeded in getting Congress to approve the 18th Amendment, and in 1919 the amendment was ratified by three-quarters of the states. However, Americans found that they did not like living "dry," and in 1933, the 21st Amendment was passed; it repealed Prohibition.

The WCTU was helpful in working for another constitutional amendment, one that would not be repealed: extension of voting rights to women. The suffrage movement began in 1848 in Seneca Falls, New York. There, under the leadership of Lucretia Mott and Elizabeth Cady Stanton, a women's rights convention met; it demanded equal rights for women, including the right to vote. In 1869, Stanton and Susan B. Anthony formed the National Woman Suffrage Association; its aim was to get Congress to pass an amendment giving women the vote. The struggle was a long one. It was not until 50 years later, in 1920, that women got what they wanted—the 19th Amendment guaranteeing women's suffrage.

SUFFRAGETTES under the leadership of Susan B. Anthony and Elizabeth Stanton campaigned for the right to vote.

protect all segments of the population, not just a few chosen ones. This belief was put to the test in May 1902, when 150,000 coal miners went on strike in Pennsylvania's anthracite mines, which were owned by a combination of coal-carrying railroads. In previous strikes, the federal government had sided with management rather than labor. But under Roosevelt, the government came to the aid of the striking workers, forcing the reluctant owners to accept the arbitration of a commission, which awarded a shorter workday and a 10 percent pay increase to the miners but did not grant their key demand, recognition of their union, the United Mine Workers of America.

Trust busting. Roosevelt quickly made known his distaste for what he called "bad trusts," business combinations that used their great financial power to kill competition and thus increase their profits. The government brought many prosecutions against trusts; 44 of the cases were decided in the government's favor. Many railroads and shippers were convicted of illicit rebating. Among the most famous trust exposures of this period was the suit against the Standard Oil Company, which was convicted of receiving and giving such rebates and was ordered to dissolve in 1907.

Conservation. In the month of May 1908, Roosevelt called the Conservation Congress to take up the question of saving the nation's rapidly dwindling natural resources. The Reclamation Act of 1902 had already provided for the irrigation of arid Western areas. The renewal of forests, the protection of wildlife, and the development of water-power were provided for as a result of the Conservation Congress.

Consumer protection. Reporters referred to as muckrakers heightened awareness of public needs. After reading a novel by Upton Sinclair entitled *The Jungle,* which described the unsanitary conditions of the meat-packing industry in Chicago, Theodore Roosevelt became an avid supporter of legislation to protect consumers from unsanitary or otherwise harmful products. The year 1906 saw passage of the Meat Inspection Act, giving government inspectors the right to check sanitary conditions in meat-packing plants, and the Pure Food and Drug Act, which prohibited the use of harmful ingredients in food and medicinal products.

After Roosevelt. In 1908 Roosevelt decided not to run again and helped his friend William Howard Taft win the Republican nomination and ultimately the election. Taft followed many of Roosevelt's Progressive reform policies, including prosecuting trusts and improving the lot of labor. A separate Department of Labor was established, and government workers were given an eight-hour workday.

Even so, Taft fell into disfavor with Roosevelt, beginning with Taft's support of the highly protectionist Payne-Aldrich Tariff of 1909. This issue divided the Republican Party and strengthened the Republican Insurgent movement against Taft. In 1912 Roosevelt decided to try for the Republican nomination. But the Republicans controlling the party and the national convention stuck with Taft, and Roosevelt bolted to become the candidate of the newly established Progressive Party. This split among the Republicans ensured the landslide election of the Progressive Democratic candidate, Woodrow Wilson.

Wilson, too, had reformist aims. He lowered tariffs, which had remained high during so many Republican administrations; reformed the banking system and established the Federal Reserve System, giving the government more control over finance; and continued the work of controlling the trusts.

The Clayton Antitrust Act of 1914 listed in detail all the practices condemned by the courts, particularly rebates, secret agreements, price privileges, and interlocking directorates between banks, railroads, and coal companies. It asserted that the labor of a human being is not a commodity, and it exempted from antitrust laws all nonprofit-making labor and farm groups. This provision gave labor unions new freedom to organize and operate.

The Federal Trade Commission Act of 1914 established the Federal Trade Commission to prevent unfair competition in interstate commerce.

THE ENTERPRISE OF HENRY FORD made the automobile available to the average family through the economy of assembly-line mass production.

Becoming a world power.
Prior to the Civil War, the United States took little part in world affairs. But its burgeoning industrialization following the war led to a demand for foreign markets and raw materials. The United States began to play an ever-increasing role in world affairs. By the turn of the century, it had become a leading world power, with possessions scattered all over the globe, especially in Latin America and Asia.

Imperialism. The first American stirrings toward empire occurred in 1867 when Secretary of State William H. Seward prevailed on Congress to buy Alaska from Russia for $7.2 million. The purchase was derisively called "Seward's folly" until great reserves of gold were found there 30 years later, setting off a mad gold rush. In 1867, Seward also arranged for the United States to buy the Midway Islands in the Pacific. In 1889 the United States joined Germany and Britain in a joint protectorate of the Samoan Islands in the South Pacific.

Nearer at hand, some 2,000 miles (3,200 kilometers) off the California coast, lay the Hawaiian Islands, where American missionaries had gone to convert the islanders, and where sugar growers and traders had become rich and powerful. By the 1890s, these business interests were eager to take total control of the islands by removing the Hawaiian monarch, Queen Liliuokalani, from the throne. In January 1893, with the help of U.S. Marines, they achieved their goal, but President Grover Cleveland secured the restoration of Queen Liliuokalani as head of the new government and opposed annexation. In 1898, during the Spanish-American War, Congress annexed the Hawaiian Islands to the United States.

War clouds. Cuba, lying just a few miles off the Florida shore, had long been trying to get out from under Spanish rule, through guerrilla warfare and uprisings. Following an insurrection in Cuba in 1895, Spain sent General Valeriano Weyler to crush the rebellion. Reports of his pitiless treatment of the Cuban people earned American sympathy for the Cuban cause. This sympathy was not lessened by the $50 million in American capital invested in Cuba. Many influential Americans wished to oust Spain from the western hemisphere for economic and strategic reasons and to acquire Spain's possessions in both the Caribbean and the Pacific.

In 1898 riots in Havana prompted Cleveland's successor, President William McKinley, to send the U.S. battleship *Maine* to the Havana harbor to protect American citizens and property. On the night of February 15, the *Maine* blew up in the harbor, killing 266 American sailors. It was never proven that Spain was responsible for the disaster, but newspapers played up the incident until the American public was eager for war. In March, the U.S. government demanded that Spain cease hostilities in Cuba. By April 10, Spain had agreed, but the next day McKinley delivered a war message to Congress anyway. On April 19, Congress demanded that Spain relinquish its claims in Cuba, recognized Cuban independence, and authorized military intervention. On April 24, Spain declared war, and on April 25, the United States resolved that a state of war had existed since April 21.

The Spanish-American War. Naval actions began at once. The U.S. North Atlantic Squadron was ordered to blockade Cuba and head off the Spanish fleet assumed to be heading there. Commodore George Dewey, in command of the Pacific squadron, in February had been directed by Assistant Secretary of the Navy Theodore Roosevelt to prepare for action and, in the event of war, to advance on Manila Bay in the Philippine Islands to destroy the Spanish fleet stationed there. Dewey began his bombardment about 5 A.M. on May 1 and had destroyed the Spanish fleet by 12:30 with no losses. The elusive Spanish Atlantic fleet sailed into Santiago Harbor in Cuba in May, and Commodore Winfield S. Schley effectively blockaded the harbor by May 28.

General William R. Shafter and 17,000 troops (including the famous volunteer cavalry regiment, the Rough Riders, led by Colonel Leonard Wood and Lieutenant Colonel Theodore Roosevelt) landed at Daiquiri near Santiago in June. El Caney was taken by General Henry Lawton on July 1. The same day, the Rough Riders helped storm and capture San Juan Hill. Fearing the destruction of Admiral Pascual Cervera's fleet, which was caught between land and sea, General Ramón Blanco in Santiago ordered the fleet to make a run for the open sea. On July 3 Cervera sailed out of the harbor to dare the blockade, and the battle that followed left not one Spanish vessel afloat. The U.S. Navy then bombarded Santiago unhindered, and the city surrendered on July 17.

An armistice was signed on August 12; on December 10, 1898, a peace treaty was signed in Paris. Spain gave up all claims to Cuba, Puerto Rico, and Guam, and sold the Philippine Islands to the United States for $20 million.

Aftermath. Now that the United States had expanded its territory and influence in the Caribbean and Pacific, it had to work out ways to deal with its new responsibilities.

labor
US

labour
Brit.

kilometers
US

kilometres
Brit.

27 North America

ROUGH RIDERS, led by Theodore Roosevelt, captured San Juan Hill in Cuba in the Spanish-American War.

50

Cuba. Cuba received a provisional government under General Leonard Wood, who had been promoted from the rank of colonel for his actions during the war. Wood's military rule greatly improved education and sanitation on the island. Yellow fever was wiped out in Havana through the efforts of an Army commission headed by Major Walter Reed, a U.S. Army surgeon, and Major William C. Gorgas, in charge of the Army sanitation program.

In February 1901, Cuba framed a constitution patterned after the U.S. Constitution. As a condition of American withdrawal from the island, the Cubans added an amendment guaranteeing that Cuba would permit no foreign interference or control by treaty of any kind, and reserving to the United States the right to intervene, at its own will, in behalf of Cuba's peace or independence.

Puerto Rico. Puerto Rico remained under U.S. military control until the Foraker Act of 1900 established a civil government with an American governor and executive council appointed by the American president, and a house of representatives elected by the inhabitants. This was far from satisfactory to the Puerto Ricans, because control of their government actually rested with the American executive council, and because

the temporary American regime established in Manila.

The United States countered with a force of 50,000 troops that engaged in a three-year guerrilla war, killing thousands of Filipinos before putting down the revolt and restoring order.

Anti-imperialists denounced U.S. occupation of the Philippines, but the imperialists carried the day. They argued that the United States would now increase its national prestige, promote new business enterprises, tap the expanding trade with the Orient, frustrate the designs of other expanding powers in the Pacific, particularly Germany, and "uplift and civilize" the people of the islands.

In July 1901, William Howard Taft, who had previously headed a commission to organize a civil government for the Philippines, became the islands' first civil governor. In the Jones Act of 1916, the Filipinos were promised independence as soon as a stable civil government had been established, but independence did not arrive until 1946.

The troubled hemisphere.
Now that the United States had overseas possessions and global responsibilities, it took an even more militant stand in the western hemisphere.

Colombia. The treaty provided that the United States would buy a strip of land across the isthmus. The Senate ratified this treaty, but Colombia rejected it. With the tacit assistance of President Roosevelt, the inhabitants of Panama rebelled against Colombia and established an independent republic.

U.S. naval forces prevented Colombian troops from using military force in Panama to quell the rebellion. The new government was recognized within three days by the United States, and its independence was immediately guaranteed. In February 1904, the Hay-Bunau-Varilla Treaty between the United States and the new Panamanian government was ratified. Panama by the treaty permanently leased a zone 10 miles (16 kilometers) wide across the isthmus for $10 million and a perpetual annual payment of $250,000.

Digging began at once, but no great progress was made until an Army sanitation program under William C. Gorgas, now a colonel, brought rampant yellow fever and malaria under control, and engineers decided to build a lock-type instead of a sea-level canal. In 1907, the project was transferred to the Army engineers under Colonel George W. Goethals. At a cost of $400 million and thousands of lives, the "big ditch" was completed in 1914.

The Roosevelt Corollary. Several European nations had made large loans to Latin American countries and were now demanding repayment. In fact, they were threatening to use force. This threat prompted Roosevelt to promulgate a new policy. According to the Monroe Doctrine, the United States became the guardian of the western hemisphere; now it must on occasion take the responsibility to police all of the international difficulties in the area. If any nation of the hemisphere were unable to meet its financial obligations or protect the lives and property of foreigners, the United States would intervene. Roosevelt and his successors, Taft and Wilson, made frequent use of this declared right to intervene in Latin America's affairs—in Nicaragua, the Dominican Republic, and Haiti, for example—to the lasting resentment of the Latin Americans.

Trouble with Mexico. During the early 1900s, Mexico underwent a series of revolutions. In 1913 General Victoriano Huerta seized control of the government. President Taft and his successor, Woodrow Wilson, adopted a strong moral tone. Both presidents refused to recognize Huerta's new regime, and Wilson indicated that the regime did not represent the will of the Mexican people and that it rested only on force. Wilson's stand was a departure from traditional American policy. Indeed, Wilson went so far as to engage in efforts to bring down the Huerta regime.

Huerta retaliated against American citizens and their property, arresting American naval personnel in 1914. The United States promptly seized the

THE PANAMA CANAL was completed by United States Army engineers in 1914, at a total cost of $400 million.

U.S. citizenship was denied them. Finally, an act passed in 1917 gave them their own legislature and U.S. citizenship.

The Philippines. American overseas expansion came to a head in regard to the Philippines. Living on approximately 80 islands more than 6,000 miles (9,654 kilometers) from America's west coast were some 7 million Filipinos from over 80 tribes. A common desire to be free of foreign control united them. Under the leadership of Emilio Aguinaldo, the Filipinos tried, in February 1899, to oust

The Panama Canal. With navies and political interests in the Atlantic and Pacific, U.S. politicians and businessmen wanted to be capable of moving ships more quickly between the oceans. President Roosevelt eagerly supported a project to dig a canal across the Isthmus of Panama, in what was part of Colombia. A French company had tried to dig a canal across the isthmus in the 1880s but had failed. In 1903 Secretary John Hay concluded the Hay-Herrán Treaty between the United States and

kilometers *US*
kilometres *Brit.*

civilize *US*
civilise *Brit.*

PRESIDENT THEODORE ROOSEVELT'S foreign policy of "talking softly and carrying a big stick" was codified as the Roosevelt Corollary to the Monroe Doctrine.

Mexican port of Veracruz. War between the two neighbors seemed imminent. Wilson accepted mediation of the dispute by the so-called ABC Powers—Argentina, Brazil, and Chile—who recommended Huerta's resignation and establishment of a provisional government. Huerta fled Mexico, and a reform leader, Venustiano Carranza, seized power. Wilson immediately recognized his government.

But the trouble was not over. Pancho Villa, an anti-Carranza revolutionary, showed his displeasure with the American recognition of Carranza by raiding Columbus, New Mexico, in March of 1916 and killing 17 Americans. With Carranza's permission, Wilson sent a punitive military expedition under General John J. Pershing into Mexico to capture Villa. Pershing failed, and the Americans withdrew in January 1917. Other foreign problems were demanding American attention.

America in World War I.
The drive for empire among European nations had created bitter rivalries. Fearful and jealous of one another, the European countries had formed alliances for their mutual protection. In 1907 two major alliances faced each other—the Triple Entente, or simply the Allies, including Britain, France, and Russia; and the Triple Alliance, or Central Powers, including Germany, Austria-Hungary, and, until 1914, also including Italy. The situation grew increasingly volatile.

On June 28, 1914, the heir to the Austro-Hungarian throne, Archduke Franz Ferdinand, was riding in an open limousine through the streets of Sarajevo, Bosnia, a part of the Austro-Hungarian Empire. In the crowd stood a young student from Serbia, Gavril Princip, who believed that Bosnia should be freed from Austria-Hungary and become a part of Serbia. As the limousine paused near Princip, he raised a gun and fired twice, killing both the archduke and his wife.

This single act propelled all of Europe into war, as Austria-Hungary declared war on Serbia on July 28, Russia (considering itself Serbia's protector) prepared to fight Austria-Hungary, and Germany declared war on Russia on August 1, and on France two days later. Britain declared war on Germany on August 4. World war had begun between the two alliances.

Neutrality. In August 1914, President Wilson urged Americans to stay neutral: "Be impartial in thought as well as in action, neutral in fact as well as in name." At first, Americans seemed willing to follow this course.

The warring nations were eager for the food and munitions that the United States could provide, and orders for guns and food flooded the United States from both sides. Britain, however, was using its navy to set up a blockade of Germany in an effort to starve that nation out. Americans were angered when British ships harassed American shipping headed for Germany, but in an effort to stay neutral, the United States took no action. To break the blockade, Germany resorted to its submarines, or U-boats, which could strike British ships and ships heading for Britain. The United States protested U-boat warfare, since it sometimes cost American lives and property.

On May 1, the first American ship to be sunk, the tanker *Gulflight,* was torpedoed off the British Isles. Then on May 7, 1915, a German U-boat sank the British passenger liner *Lusitania* off the coast of Ireland, with the loss of nearly 1,200 lives, including 128 Americans. Americans feared that they were losing their freedom of the seas. The sinking of the *Lusitania* aroused great anger in the United States, and as a result Germany in September promised to stop sinking passenger ships without warning.

Closer to war. In 1916, Wilson won a close election over his Republican opponent, Charles Evans Hughes, using the slogan "He Kept Us Out of War." But three events combined to end American neutrality. The first was Germany's return to "unlimited submarine warfare" on February 1, 1917, causing Wilson to break off diplomatic relations with Germany. The second was the discovery in early March of the so-called Zimmerman telegram. Written by German Foreign Minister Arthur Zimmerman to the German minister in Mexico, the message instructed him to urge Mexico to join the Central Powers against the United States should the United States declare war on the Central Powers. In return, Germany offered Mexico the return of Texas, New Mexico, and Arizona after the defeat of the United States. The third decisive event was the opening phase of the Russian Revolution in March. This phase saw the abdication of the czar and the establishment of a pro-Allied provisional government that declared its intention to continue the war against the Central Powers but that was by no means in full control of the country.

On April 2, 1917, President Wilson asked Congress for a declaration of war against Germany. "The world must be made safe for democracy," he stated. On April 6 Congress declared war, and the United States joined the Allies.

Into battle. By this time, the Allies were in a desperate situation. They had been fighting for nearly three years, and the war was in stalemate. On the western front, troops on both sides faced each other from trenches stretching down a long front through France. The British had lost one-third of their troops, the French over half. And both countries were fast running out of food and military supplies. In July the Russians launched a major offensive that turned into a disaster, and in November the Bolsheviks seized power and moved quickly to take Russia out of the war. Now the Central Powers could concentrate their forces on the western front.

The first task for the United States was to raise an army. Within three months, over a million men had volunteered, but many more would be needed. So on May 18, 1917, the Selective Service Act was passed, providing for the draft of what eventually turned out to be nearly 3 million men.

The next task was to mobilize American agriculture and industry to provide for both the American forces and those

POSTERS STIRRED patriotic fervor during World War I, the "war to end all wars."

ALLIED FORCES repulsed German offenses in savage battles on French soil, such as this one at Verdun.

honoring
US

honouring
Brit.

kilometers
US

kilometres
Brit.

labor
US

labour
Brit.

of the hard-pressed Allies. The government tripled the amount of food sent to the Allies, through both greater farm production and conservation of food on the home front. (Citizens were encouraged to save food by honoring "wheatless Mondays" and "meatless Tuesdays.") Federal agencies also took control of the American economy, telling manufacturers what to produce for the war effort.

On the home front, women rushed in to fill the jobs left by departing volunteers and draftees. For the first time, women became auto mechanics, mail carriers, and trolley conductors. Also for the first time, women lawyers and doctors were allowed to work for government agencies. Morale was kept up by the Committee on Public Information, which sent out 75,000 speakers to rally enthusiasm for the war. Movie stars and other entertainers appeared before large groups to encourage them to buy "Liberty Bonds" to help the government finance the war. To aid in that financing, income tax rates were raised.

War in France. It took time for the U.S. Army to mobilize, and relatively few American troops reached France until March of 1918. President Wilson had chosen General John J. Pershing, veteran of the Battle of San Juan Hill during the Spanish-American War and commander of the Pancho Villa expedition, to head the American Expeditionary Force (AEF). Pershing insisted that the AEF fight as a separate force, not as a part of British or French forces. By spring of 1918, the AEF was in the thick of the war.

In March 1918, the Germans began a series of offensives that pushed the Allied lines back, creating two bulges, or salients, that threatened Paris. The Germans hoped to strike a devastating blow and end the war before the growing American forces could turn the tide against them. The first important American action was on May 28 at Cantigny, north of Paris, where the 1st Division overran the German defenses and held them against several fierce counterattacks. On June 4 the United States 2nd Division halted the German advance at Chateau-Thierry, on the Marne River northeast of Paris, and from June 6 to 24 American troops fought a bloody but victorious battle for Belleau Wood, to the northwest.

On July 15, the Germans launched their last offensive, across the Marne. When it ground to a halt, the Allies, including about 250,000 Americans, counterattacked on July 18 in the Aisne-Marne offensive. On September 12 and 13, Americans attacked and destroyed a German salient around St. Mihiel, about 150 miles (241 kilometers) east of Paris. Then, on September 26, U.S. troops attacked the Germans in the Argonne Forest, opening the Meuse-Argonne offensive, between the Argonne Forest and the Meuse River. Over a million Americans fought there; in November, they triumphed. On November 11, 1918, Germany signed the terms of surrender. Wilson's "war to end war" was over. (For more information about World War I, see The World in the 20th Century in the HISTORY OF THE WORLD volume.)

A search for a just peace. Before the war had ended, Wilson had proposed "Fourteen Points" on which he thought the peace should be built. Among these was the proposition that all peoples should have the right to self-determination. Former colonies, for example, and national groups within the Austro-Hungarian Empire should be able to choose for themselves how they wanted to be ruled. Another point proposed a League of Nations, where all nations might settle their differences peaceably.

For a while, Wilson thought he might make his Fourteen Points a reality; he was enthusiastically welcomed by European crowds as he made his way to Versailles to work out the peace treaty. But the other Allied leaders were more interested in punishing Germany than in implementing Wilson's ideals. The Treaty of Versailles did provide for a League of Nations, but it demanded huge reparations from a war-impoverished Germany. Germany was stripped of its colonies and forced to accept full responsibility for the war; this unfortunate action helped to ensure that European war would soon come again.

Wilson fared little better at home, where he found bitter opposition to the League of Nations. Fearing that such a league would have too much power over American foreign affairs, Congress voted against approving the Treaty of Versailles. Wilson, whose health was broken during a cross-country campaign for the league, found his hopes for a "just peace" irreparably shattered.

The American Age

Feast and famine. As American troops began arriving home, the nation was in a mood to forget war and foreign entanglement and the rapid social changes brought on by war. Americans welcomed the message of Warren G. Harding, Republican senator from Ohio: "America's present need is not heroics but healing, not nostrums but normalcy . . . not surgery but serenity. . . ." In 1920, the American people turned away from the Democrats and the controversy over the League of Nations and elected Harding president, under whose administration they hoped the nation would enjoy "a return to normalcy."

Unrest. The 1920s are often looked back on as a crazy, fun-loving era—the Roaring Twenties, the Era of Wonderful Nonsense, the Jazz Age. But the '20s had its deeply serious side. The decade began with a recession, marked by rising prices and unemployment. Labor unrest followed, and with it frequent strikes.

The Red scare. Many Americans were quick to blame the strikes on communist influences within labor unions. A wave of bombings, blamed on "foreign anarchists," fueled American fears that the "Reds" were plotting to overthrow the American government.

In January of 1920, Attorney General A. Mitchell Palmer ordered a series of raids on groups suspected of "un-American" ties. Some 6,000 suspects were arrested in 33 cities, and over 500 were deported. Yet no overthrow plots were ever uncovered, and many Americans began to feel that the raids were trampling on the Bill of Rights. By the end of the year, the Red scare had died down.

The Palmer raids of 1920 were not the beginning of political repression in the United States. A number of raids had been conducted in 1919. A special target of the crackdown during this period was a Marxist-oriented labor organization called the Industrial Workers of the World (IWW). Formed in Chicago in 1905, its leaders included

Eugene V. Debs and William D. ("Big Bill") Haywood. It sought the organization of all workers into large national industrial unions, and its promotion of the theory of class struggle appealed especially to unskilled and migrant workers, particularly Western miners and lumberjacks and Eastern textile workers. It opposed American entry into World War I. Many of its leaders were jailed, and its membership dwindled in the '20s. Some joined the Workers (or Communist) Party, or the Communist Labor Party, both of which were founded in 1919.

Immigration restricted. American distrust and dislike for the large numbers of immigrants arriving from southern and eastern Europe did not die down, however. In May of 1921, Congress passed the Emergency Quota Act, which severely limited, by nationality, the number of immigrants who could enter the United States to 3 percent of the number of persons of that nationality living in the United States as of the census of 1910. As the law was due to expire in June of 1924, Congress, in May, passed the Immigration Act of 1924. It decreed that only a small number of immigrants from southern and eastern European countries could enter the United States; immigrants from northern and western Europe were favored. Congress did this by choosing the census of 1890 to determine population by nationality and by lowering the number admitted annually to 2 percent. In 1929 the total number of immigrants allowed in annually was lowered to 150,000.

The Ku Klux Klan. Fear of the new and the strange was especially strong in the small towns of the South and Midwest. There, prejudice against blacks had long been strong, but now it was joined by hatred of Catholics and Jews, groups that included many of the new immigrants. These prejudices and hatreds led to a revival of the Ku Klux Klan, reestablished in Georgia in 1915. By 1923 the Klan's membership had grown to 4 million people bent on preserving America for white, "native-born" Protestants. The Klan's methods were to terrorize those who did not fit their definition of an American.

Political scandal. It has been said that the only qualification Warren G. Harding had to be president was that he looked like one. Harding was an affable man, given to playing poker with his pals. His cronyism was the basis for his selection of many cabinet and executive officers, and their greed resulted in massive political corruption. His attorney general, Harry Daugherty, made a fortune by selling government favors. Harding's friend Charles Forbes, whom he named head of the new Veterans' Bureau, helped himself and his friends to $200 million of the bureau's funds. Harding's secretary of the interior, Albert B. Fall, took more than $400,000 in bribes in return for issuing leases to government oil land reserved strictly for U.S. Navy use, at Teapot Dome in

Wyoming and Elk Hills in California, to private oil developers. The scandals were the most serious since those of the Grant era 50 years earlier.

Word of all this corruption was just starting to come out when, on August 2, 1923, Harding died suddenly in San Francisco while on a trip to the West Coast. He was succeeded by his vice president, a dour and laconic former governor of Massachusetts, Calvin Coolidge.

Prosperity. The advent of "Silent Cal" began a period that came to be called "Coolidge prosperity." During this time tariffs went up and income tax rates went down. Antitrust legislation was not enforced. Coolidge's attitude toward business could not have been more encouraging: "The business of America is business," he declared. During the 1920s, industrial production nearly doubled.

Not everyone was sharing in Coolidge prosperity. Agricultural production had grown impressively during World War I as American food entered world markets. Farmers had taken mortgages on new land and put it under cultivation. Now, as Europe got back on its feet and could meet much of its own agricultural need, prices for American farm products fell. As a result, it was becoming increasingly difficult for American farmers to meet their mortgage payments, and banks began repossessing their farms.

Organized labor also suffered during the 1920s. Hostility toward labor unions ran high, and the unions lost several of the safeguards that they had won during the Progressive Era, as the Supreme Court found unions in violation of antitrust legislation.

FLAPPERS were the prototype for the uninhibited period of prosperity that followed World War I.

PRESIDENT WILSON'S vision of a "just peace" was not realized to his satisfaction after World War I, but the treaty did provide for a League of Nations.

UNITED STATES POSTAGE
$1 WOODROW WILSON 1913-1921 $1

27 North America

GEORGE SEGAL'S statues of men in a bread line recall Franklin D. Roosevelt's economic programs during the Great Depression.

labor
US

labour
Brit.

Technological advances. The 1920s were years of rapid technological growth. In 1920 the first regular radio broadcasting station, KDKA in Pittsburgh, Pennsylvania, went on the air. It was joined by other stations, and the radio industry began to boom. In 1926, the National Broadcasting Company (NBC) became the first radio network, followed in 1927 by the Columbia Broadcasting System (CBS). Later, NBC was divided, and one part became the American Broadcasting Company (ABC).

Aviation advanced rapidly as well. The first coast-to-coast airmail service was introduced in 1920. The Air Commerce Act of 1926 provided federal aid for the development of airports and air transportation. Also in 1926 Robert H. Goddard opened the age of modern rocketry when he launched the first successful liquid-fuel rocket.

On May 22, 1927, Charles A. Lindbergh, Jr., made the first nonstop flight from New York to Paris, France. A year later, Amelia Earhart, a member of a three-person crew, became the first woman to fly across the Atlantic. In 1932 she became the first woman to fly solo across the Atlantic.

In 1921 Colonel William ("Billy") Mitchell demonstrated the military value of aviation when he directed the aerial bombing and sinking of a captured German battleship. Mitchell openly challenged, and questioned the patriotism of, military leaders and politicians who refused to recognize the importance of air power to the national defense. In 1925 he was courtmartialed. Mitchell resigned from the Army in 1926, but the events of World War II were to prove him right.

Boom to bust. In 1924, despite a continuing agricultural slump and the growing discontent of organized labor over government policies and recent court rulings that favored owners over

workers, Coolidge won the presidential election handily. But in 1928 Coolidge announced, "I do not choose to run," and the Republicans nominated Herbert Hoover as their candidate. To run against him, the Democrats named Alfred E. Smith, governor of New York, the first Roman Catholic to run for the presidency for a major party. Satisfied with the prosperity under the two previous Republicans, the voters overwhelmingly elected Hoover. Smith was also hurt in part by prejudice against Catholics, which was especially strong in the South, as well as by his support of repeal of the 18th Amendment and the end of Prohibition.

Problems. Farm problems continued to plague the country. President Coolidge had vetoed several measures authorizing federal aid to help support agricultural prices and find foreign markets for American produce, stating that such measures constituted price-fixing, favored special interests, and invited retaliation by foreign markets. In June 1929 Congress passed the Agricultural Marketing Act, which established a Federal Farm Board to help farmers set up privately owned cooperatives and corporations to buy and hold farm surpluses and help stabilize prices. The program did little to remedy the problem.

A better remedy might have been to lower the tariff barriers and thus facilitate world buying and selling. Instead, in 1930, Congress passed the highest protective tariff in its history, the Hawley-Smoot Tariff. Within two years, the United States lost over $5 billion in world trade.

With its world trade down, the nation had an excessive supply of manufactured goods. High productivity had, by the end of the 1920s, produced a great overstock. Factories soon began cutting back on production, thus cutting back on manufacturing jobs.

The crash. One of the causes of the seeming prosperity of the 1920s was the busy stock market. Speculation in stocks had become nothing short of a national mania. Stock prices kept going up and up until they were dangerously overpriced. Speculators kept borrowing more money to buy more stocks. By 1929 a total of $9 billion was owed to banks as a result of stock speculation. Then, on October 29, 1929, the bubble finally burst. Prices had been going down steadily, and nervous speculators were trying to sell their stocks as quickly as they could. On that "Black Tuesday," they dumped 16 million shares on the market and there was no one who wanted to buy. The stock market had crashed. Soon the nation's other economic ills would become apparent to all, and the worst depression in the nation's history was under way.

The Great Depression. In the three years following the crash, the national situation became desperate and human suffering grew. Between 1929 and 1932, farm income shrank by 50 percent. Industry was operating at half its former rate. In 1932 alone, 32,000 businesses failed, and so did nearly 1,500 banks, wiping out the life savings of millions of Americans. The number of unemployed Americans reached over 12 million—fully one-quarter of the workforce. One million Americans took to the road, trying to find work, and local and state charities could not deal with the widespread destitution.

Hoover opposed measures for direct federal relief on various political and moral grounds, but he launched a huge program of public works in 1930 to try to stem unemployment. In 1932 he secured passage of the bill for the Reconstruction Finance Corporation, which lent $2 billion to banks, railroads, and other industries. But, because the Great Depression was worldwide, nothing short of world recovery could stem the economic disaster.

Election of 1932. Amid growing domestic economic crises, the Republicans renominated Hoover. The Democrats chose New York Governor Franklin D. Roosevelt, a distant cousin of former President Theodore Roosevelt. As governor, Roosevelt had set up a relief program for New York, and he promised to set up relief programs on a national scale if elected.

Despite having suffered a crippling attack of polio in 1921, Roosevelt was one of the most active and appealing of young Democrats. Like his presidential cousin, he had served as assistant secretary of the Navy, in the Wilson administration, and he had been the Democrats' vice presidential candidate in 1920. He had made a dramatic appearance on crutches at the hotly contested 1924 convention to nominate the governor of New York, Al Smith, and, at Smith's urging, had run successfully for governor in 1928. Roosevelt toured the country promising people a "New Deal." He won a landslide victory as voters rejected Hoover's administration, which many blamed for their economic problems. Roosevelt won 472 electoral votes to Hoover's 59. More importantly, the Democrats gained firm control of both houses of Congress.

The New Deal. As soon as he was elected, Roosevelt and his advisers, called his "brain trust," began shaping a series of domestic social and economic programs—the New Deal. The New Deal had three main objectives: *relief* for those hit hardest by the Depression; *recovery* for the nation's economy; and *reform* to prevent another depression.

Roosevelt took office on March 4, 1933, saying: "The nation asks for action and action now. We must act and act quickly." He sought to assure Americans that the country's problems could be solved. "This great nation will endure," he told them, and stated that it was his "firm belief that the only thing we have to fear is fear itself." It was exactly what the American people wanted to hear. In the now-famous first hundred days, Congress responded to the president's programs by passing a raft of emergency recovery measures in banking, industry, and agriculture. (See chart below.)

The first thing Roosevelt did was declare a "bank holiday," closing all the banks to give inspectors sufficient time to determine which were sound enough to continue doing business. Then Congress passed the Emergency Banking Law, giving the president the power to reorganize insolvent national banks. To help revive industry, Congress passed the National Industrial Recovery Act (NIRA) to establish codes for industries to eliminate unfair competition, abolish child labor and sweat shops, establish minimum wages and maximum hours, create additional jobs for the unemployed, and enable labor to organize freely and bargain collectively. To aid agriculture, Congress passed the Agricultural Adjustment Act (AAA) to control production of farm goods through subsidies aimed at lowering production and to lend money to farmers.

Congress also passed a number of relief acts, some offering direct aid to the needy and some offering jobs in public works. The Civilian Conservation Corps (CCC) and Public Works Administration employed millions. Other measures created the Tennessee Valley Authority (TVA) to develop a depressed area covering parts of seven states; the Securities and Exchange Commission (SEC) to regulate the stock market; Social Security legislation to provide old-age insurance; and the National Labor Relations Board (NLRB) to monitor labor disputes.

Constitutional amendments. In January, as President-elect Roosevelt waited to take office, the 20th Amendment to the Constitution was ratified. It moved the date of the presidential and vice presidential inauguration from March 4 to January 20 and also required sessions of Congress to open on January 3 of each year. These provisions, which reduced the time between a president's election and inauguration, eliminated the "lame duck" session of Congress following each national election, which included members who had not gained reelection.

On February 20 Congress passed the 21st Amendment, repealing the 18th Amendment. Roosevelt had supported repeal of Prohibition, which had been ineffectively enforced, had promoted the growth of organized crime, and had lost favor among many Americans. The amendment called for ratification within seven years by state conventions organized for the purpose. It was ratified on December 5, 1933.

Social Security Act. One of the most far-reaching laws enacted during the New Deal was the Social Security Act, which was passed by Congress on August 14, 1935, and provided the foundation for the nation's Social Security system. It authorized funds for old-age

The First Hundred Days

Franklin D. Roosevelt took office on March 4, 1933. In the first months of his term, aided by a sense of crisis in the country and a Democratic majority in the Congress, he passed bills designed to help the needy and shore up the economic structure of the nation. The major acts were:

Emergency Banking Relief Act, March 9	Imposed federal regulation on the banking business
Civilian Conservation Reforestation Relief Act, March 31	Provided jobs for young men on federal conservation projects
Federal Emergency Relief Act, May 12	Granted funds to states for relief of the poor; provided 4 million civil works jobs
Agricultural Adjustment Act, May 12	Paid farmers subsidies for reducing production and made federal loans available
Tennessee Valley Authority Act, May 18	Created Tennessee Valley Authority to provide jobs, electrical power, and flood control
Federal Securities Act, May 27	Tightened regulation of securities markets; required fuller disclosure about securities in order to protect investors
Home Owners' Refinancing Act, June 13	Provided federal mortgages to those in danger of losing their homes because of unemployment
Glass-Steagall Banking Act, June 16	Created the Federal Deposit Insurance Corporation to insure bank deposits up to $5,000
National Industrial Recovery Act, June 16	Suspended antitrust laws; granted new rights to labor; created the National Labor Board

Some of these acts were temporary and some provisions were later ruled unconstitutional; but many provisions endured and some agencies are still active and important.

benefits, unemployment compensation, aid to dependent children, and other services, and established equal taxes on employees and their employers based on the employees' wages to pay for the programs.

Roosevelt and the Supreme Court. Many of the New Deal measures represented incredible departures from previous governmental practices, and their constitutionality was called into question. The Supreme Court found both the AAA and the NIRA unconstitutional. An angry President Roosevelt blamed this defeat of his policies on the fact that the Supreme Court was made up of "nine old men," six of them over 70 years old and seven of them appointees of Republican presidents. In February, 1937, Roosevelt proposed that Congress reorganize the High Court, giving the president the right to name a new justice for each one who did not retire by age 70. This was intended to enable Roosevelt to install his own appointees, who would be more likely to be sympathetic to the laws he proposed. Congress angrily accused him of trying to "pack the court," and denied his proposal, leaving the membership of the court as it had been.

WORLD WAR II called millions of American women into the workforce and changed forever the structure of American society.

Effects of the New Deal. The New Deal did not return the nation to prosperity at once. In fact, its radical features and broad scope raised bitter and vocal opposition: It had significantly altered the government but had failed to reach the objectives it had set. The 1936 presidential election became a referendum on the New Deal. When the votes were counted, Roosevelt had beaten his Republican opponent, Alfred M. Landon, by 11 million popular votes, winning 523 electoral votes to Landon's 8.

When Roosevelt began his second term in 1937, he had to state that he still saw "one-third of the nation ill-housed, ill-clad, ill-nourished." But the New Deal, which by 1938 was running out of steam, had made the most profound, dramatic, and lasting changes in government in American history. Government had grown larger than ever before and it had moved into many new phases of American life. Direct government intervention and regulation—in business, social welfare, and human security—reached heights undreamed of a few years earlier. Even after the Depression ended, government's right to intervene and regulate was widely accepted.

War and responsibility. The worldwide Depression had paved the way for the rise of rightist military dictators in Europe. Adolf Hitler and the Nazi Party took control of Germany; Francisco Franco and the Falangists had seized power in Spain after a bloody three-year civil war; and Benito Mussolini and the fascists ruled Italy. Half a world away, in Japan, another government dominated by the military came to power. The German, Italian, and Japanese dictatorships were bent on expansion, and soon each was on the move—Japan into China in 1931, Italy into Africa in 1935, and Germany into Austria and Czechoslovakia in 1938. In the mid-1930s, the three signed a series of mutual assistance pacts and became known as the Axis powers.

War in Europe. At first, the Allies, Britain and France, had regarded fascism with forbearance, as a political aberration that would pass away in time, then accepted it reluctantly because it offered a defense against encroachments into Western Europe by Soviet communism under the iron rule of Stalin. To appease Hitler, the Allies agreed to sacrifice Czechoslovakia to German expansionism by the terms of the 1938 Munich Pact. But on September 1, 1939, Hitler's tanks rolled into Poland, an ally of Britain and France, and the Allied nations had no choice but to declare war on Germany.

The Germans were prepared for war and the Allies were not. In the spring of 1940, in a repeat of the *blitzkrieg* (lightning war) that had overwhelmed Poland, Hitler rapidly conquered Denmark, Norway, The Netherlands, Belgium, and France, leaving Britain to fight alone. In 1941 Hitler tore up a mutual nonaggression pact he had signed with Stalin on the eve of the war and attacked the Soviet Union, which immediately joined Britain as an ally.

From neutrality to aid. Once again, popular sentiment in the United States favored staying out of foreign troubles. In 1935 and 1937, Congress passed a series of laws known as the Neutrality Acts to ensure that the United States would isolate itself from war. But as in 1917, the United States would find neutrality impossible to maintain. On September 5, 1939, the United States declared its neutrality, but in November it passed a new Neutrality Act that repealed an arms embargo imposed by the 1937 act. The new act legalized the sale of arms and munitions to belligerents on a "cash and carry" basis; the belligerents had to pay for their purchases and transport them on their own ships.

In the fall of 1940, Roosevelt had won an unprecedented third term as president, all the while maintaining that the United States would not involve itself in any foreign war. But by that time, it had become clear that the nation could no longer remain uninvolved. On June 10, Italy had declared war on France and Great Britain and Roosevelt had declared, "We will extend to the opponents of force the material resources of this nation." In September, the United States gave Britain 50 destroyers in return for leases for military bases in Newfoundland, Bermuda, and other sites in the western hemisphere. On December 29, in a radio "fireside chat," Roosevelt told Americans that their nation must become the "arsenal of democracy," providing money and military equipment to those nations resisting German forces. In his January, 1941, message to Congress, Roosevelt asked for a lend-lease plan to assist the Allies. He also set forth the "four freedoms" that he believed were the birthright of all human beings: freedom of speech and of worship, freedom from want and from fear.

In March, Congress approved the Lend-Lease Act, which supplied beleaguered Britain with guns, tanks, ships, and planes. In August, President Roosevelt and British Prime Minister Winston Churchill issued the joint statement known as the Atlantic Charter; it contained eight principles of national policy, including a renunciation of territorial gain, support of political determination of all peoples, and abandonment of the use of force by all nations. Then, in November, Congress repealed the Neutrality Acts, as American shipping was already fighting an undeclared naval war with Germany in the North Atlantic.

Pearl Harbor. As the European colonial powers were weakened by the war in Europe, Japanese militarists saw an opportunity to step up their plan to drive all colonial powers, including the United States, from East Asia. They wanted to establish their own "New Order" in Asia, but President Roosevelt and Secretary of State Cordell Hull resisted these efforts. When the Japanese occupied French Indochina (Vietnam and Cambodia) in July of 1941, the president froze Japanese assets in the United States and embargoed shipments of the oil and scrap iron that were desperately needed in Japan. Britain followed suit. In November 1941, negotiations over trade, the status of China, and territorial expansion in Asia began between the United States and Japan. Japan demanded an end to all U.S. and British influence in Asia. While the talks were going on, a Japanese fleet set out across the Pacific toward Hawaii.

On the morning of Sunday, December 7, 1941, Japanese fighters, bombers, and submarines attacked the American naval base at Pearl Harbor in Hawaii. Nineteen U.S. ships were sunk or badly damaged; more than 2,300 Americans were killed. The following day, President Roosevelt spoke to Congress, referring to the "day which will live in infamy" and asking for a declaration acknowledging that a state of war existed between the United States and Japan. Within a few hours, war was declared. Three days later, the other Axis powers, Germany and Italy, also declared war on the United States.

The United States now found itself facing war on two fronts—in Europe and in the Pacific. Roosevelt determined that the situation in Europe was the more desperate—if Britain and the Soviet Union fell, the United States would be totally on its own.

Americans in wartime. Industry and agriculture mobilized to create a giant wartime production apparatus, shifting as quickly as possible from consumer goods to military supplies and equipment. The wartime economy provided millions of new jobs, higher wages and overtime pay, factory jobs for women, and profitable war contracts for manufacturers.

Many government agencies were set up to regulate prices, wages, and rents; allocate materials; and coordinate production. Rationing systems were set up for scarce goods such as gasoline, sugar, coffee, and rubber.

Fearful of further Japanese attacks and of enemy spies and sabotage, many Americans, particularly on the West Coast, became suspicious of all people

AIR POWER played a significant role in war for the first time.

of Japanese ancestry, even those born in the United States, the Nisei. President Roosevelt, in a move that would later be condemned by many Americans, authorized inland "relocation camps" and the forced removal of 100,000 Japanese-Americans from their homes and property.

As early as September 1940, Congress passed the Selective Service Act, the first U.S. peacetime draft. In December 1941, the limits were broadened to include men 20 to 44 years of age. In May 1942, Congress authorized the formation of women's noncombat branches in the Navy (WAVES), Army (WACS), Air Force (WAFS), Coast Guard (SPARS), and Marines. In all, more than 16 million Americans served in military units during the war.

Allied cooperation. Throughout the war, the leaders of the "Big Three"—Roosevelt for the United States, Churchill for Britain, and Stalin for the Soviet Union—as well as other Allied civilian and military leaders, met regularly to work out wartime strategy and to plan for postwar peace. The major disagreement among the three was the timing of the Allied invasion of Western Europe. The Soviet Union was suffering enormous losses on the eastern front; it insisted that Britain and the United States invade France without delay. But in August of 1942, at a meeting in Moscow, Churchill told Stalin that Allied forces were not yet strong enough to invade Europe. As if to prove the point, an Allied raid on the Channel city of Dieppe shortly after the conference suffered extremely heavy losses, but it gained important information about amphibious operations that would later save many lives.

AMERICA joined the war after the Japanese bombing of Pearl Harbor, and American naval power eventually turned the tide of the war in the Pacific.

Major Events of World War II

1939–1941

German armies attack Poland on September 1, 1939. The Allied powers, led by Britain and France, declare war on the Axis (Germany and Italy). By July 1940, the Axis powers overrun Denmark, Norway, Belgium, Holland, and France, and threaten Britain. In June 1941, they invade the Soviet Union.

Meanwhile, the Japanese, allied with the Axis, take control of South Asia and the Pacific. On December 7, 1941, they attack Pearl Harbor, a U.S. Navy base in Hawaii. Within days, the United States declares war on all Axis nations.

Events in Europe/*Events in the Pacific

1942

* Jan.-May. Japanese capture the Philippines and Burma.
* May. U.S. forces drive off Japanese fleet in Coral Sea.
* June. U.S. defends Midway Island, defeats Japanese fleet.
* Aug. U.S. forces land on Guadalcanal, face bitter fight.

  Nov. U.S. and Allied forces land in North Africa.

1943

  Feb. Soviets begin long offensive to retake Stalingrad and drive Germans from U.S.S.R. in bloodiest campaign of war.
* Feb. U.S. completes conquest of Guadalcanal.

  May. Allied forces drive all Axis troops from North Africa.

  July-Aug. Allies invade and occupy Sicily.
* July. U.S. begins drive on Solomon Islands.

  Sept. Allies invade the mainland of Italy.

1944

* Jan.-May. Allied air forces begin heavy bombardment of Germany.
* U.S. defeats Japanese in New Guinea.

  June-Aug. Rome liberated June 4; Allies invade France at Normandy beaches June 6; Paris liberated August 25.
* June. U.S. forces capture Saipan, Guam.
* Oct. U.S. fleet crushes Japanese fleet at Leyte Gulf, gains foothold in Philippines.

  Dec. Battle of the Bulge; German counteroffensive drives Allies back in Belgium. Allies hold at Bastogne.

1945

* Feb. Manila, capital of the Philippines, is liberated.
* Apr.-June. U.S. approaches Japan, captures Okinawa.

  Apr.-May. Fall of Germany: British, U.S., and Soviet forces meet; Berlin falls May 2; Germany surrenders May 8.

  May-June. U.S. bombards Japan, prepared for invasion.
* Aug. 6 and 9. U.S. drops atom bombs on Hiroshima and Nagasaki.
* Japan surrenders August 14.

INFANTRYMEN hold up a captured German Nazi flag during World War II.

On November 8, British and American troops landed in North Africa, where the British had been fighting German forces under General Erwin Rommel for a year. After bitter fighting, the Germans were defeated by May of 1943. This paved the way for the invasion of Sicily in July and of Italy in September.

War in the Pacific. Meanwhile, the United States began to take the initiative against the Japanese. On April 18, 1942, Colonel James H. Doolittle led a squadron of carrier-based B-25 bombers in a raid on Tokyo, an event that shocked the Japanese and greatly helped to restore American confidence. In the next month, in the Battle of the Coral Sea, the United States Navy stopped a Japanese invasion of southern New Guinea as preparation for an invasion of Australia. This was the first naval battle in which all the fighting was done by carrier-based aircraft. The Battle of Midway in June halted a Japanese invasion of Midway Island. The Japanese lost four aircraft carriers, and the tide began to turn against Japan. In August United States Marines landed at Guadalcanal, beginning a long and bloody struggle for the Solomon Islands.

Allied conferences. In January of 1943, Roosevelt and Churchill met at Casablanca, Morocco, and agreed that the Allies would continue to prosecute the war until total and unconditional surrender by the Axis was achieved. At the Trident Conference in Washington, D.C., in May of that year, they worked out plans for the invasion of Italy and scheduled the long-awaited invasion of France for May of 1944. At the Teheran Conference in Iran in November of 1943, Roosevelt, Churchill, and Stalin met to coordinate plans for the invasion of Europe and to discuss postwar political issues.

The fall of the Axis. In July of 1943, after Allied forces invaded Sicily, Mussolini and the fascist government in Italy were overthrown. The new Italian government surrendered soon after the

Allied invasion of Italy, but Mussolini escaped to northern Italy and proclaimed a new fascist republic. Fierce fighting continued into 1944. On June 4, U.S. troops entered Rome, the first European capital to be liberated by the Allies.

The long-awaited invasion of Western Europe came on June 6, 1944, with the invasion of Normandy. With massive air support, American, British, Canadian, and other Allied troops moved across France; French forces led by Charles de Gaulle entered Paris in August. The Soviet army moved on Germany from the east. But the Nazis were not yet beaten. In September they launched the first V-2 rocket attack against London. This weapon caused even more damage than the V-1 "flying bombs," which had first been launched against London in June. In December, Hitler launched an all-out offensive in the Ardennes, which caused a large bulge in the Allied lines. This Battle of the Bulge, as it soon was called, proved to be a disaster for the Germans, and sped up the invasion of Germany on both fronts. At the end of April 1945, Hitler and many top Nazis committed suicide; others fled. Germany surrendered unconditionally, and the war in Europe ended on May 8, 1945.

War in Asia raged on with no sign of abating as American forces moved on Japan from the east, "island hopping" in bloody campaigns that forced an ever-tightening ring around Japan. In October of 1944, the Battle of Leyte Gulf marked the end of Japanese naval power and cleared the way for the liberation of the Philippines. In November large-scale bombing of Japan began.

In February of 1945, at the Yalta Conference in the Crimea, Roosevelt, Churchill, and Stalin met to plan for the postwar occupation of Germany, the reorganization of Europe, the entry of Russia into the war against Japan, and a conference to draw up a charter for the United Nations. In July the United States, Britain, and the Soviet Union met in Potsdam, near Berlin, to decide on how Germany would be occupied. On August 6, 1945, the newly developed atomic bomb was dropped on the Japanese industrial city of Hiroshima, killing 100,000 people. On August 9 a second bomb was dropped on Nagasaki. The next day Japan surrendered, and Allied victory was declared on August 15. Japanese officials signed the document of surrender on September 2. World War II was over, after the loss of over 405,000 American lives among millions of casualties worldwide. In addition, the atomic age had begun and the stage was set for a new kind of conflict. (For more information about World War II, see The World in the 20th Century in the HISTORY OF THE WORLD volume.)

Roosevelt to Truman. President Roosevelt did not live to see either the German surrender or the use of the atom bomb and the Japanese surrender. In 1944, although aging and ill, the President had run for a fourth term and had easily beaten the Republican candidate, New York State governor Thomas E. Dewey. Less than three months after his fourth inauguration, Roosevelt died, on April 12, 1945, after suffering a stroke at his winter home in Warm Springs, Georgia. He was succeeded by his vice president, Harry S. Truman, a blunt, plainspoken former senator from Missouri.

During the war, Roosevelt had urged the formation of a new international organization to replace the League of Nations as a stronger, more effective force for peace. On April 25, 1945, as

GENERAL DOUGLAS MACARTHUR accepted the surrender of the Japanese on September 2, 1945.

provided by the agreement at the Yalta Conference, 50 nations met in San Francisco to draft a charter for the new United Nations.

A serious disagreement between the United States and the Soviet Union on use of the veto in the Security Council delayed the signing of the UN Charter until June 26, 1945.

Prosperity and suspicion.

When the war ended, the United States found itself the world's leading industrial and military power. Its wartime Allies and the Axis nations were severely war-damaged and they faced the monu-

mental task of rebuilding their industries and cities. The United States, on the other hand, was relatively untouched. Its most pressing problems were to convert from a wartime to a peacetime economy and to absorb the returning military veterans into civilian life.

Readjustment. America was able to convert to peace with surprising ease. The armed forces were demobilized rapidly, and returning service personnel were aided by the so-called G.I. Bill of Rights, which had been passed by Congress in 1944. The bill offered money for tuition and living expenses to those who wanted to go to college or to training schools; low-cost loans to those who wanted to buy homes or start up businesses; and unemployment benefits to those who were seeking jobs. Millions of veterans took advantage of these opportunities, at once raising the educational level of the nation and sending the building industry into a period of unprecedented boom.

Inflation. The period of readjustment, however, was not without its problems. Americans had built up savings of over $135 billion during the war, and now they were eager to spend it. Consumer demand for goods that were scarce during the war kept the factories busy. But the supply of consumer goods could not keep pace with the demand, and prices soared as soon as wartime price controls were lifted. Within a single year, the cost of living rose by 50 percent.

The Taft-Hartley Act. Inflation brought on a rash of strikes as workers demanded pay increases that would allow them to keep up with rising prices. A wave of antiunion feeling resulted, and in 1947, a Republican Congress passed the Taft-Hartley Act, which took away some of the power that labor had gained in the New Deal era. Among other provisions, it banned the closed shop, required an 80-day cooling-off period before a strike could begin in a vital industry, and forbade unions from contributing to political campaigns. Denounced by labor and rejected by Truman, the bill was passed over his veto.

labor
US

labour
Brit.

27 North America

CHURCHILL, ROOSEVELT, AND STALIN met at Yalta in the Crimea in 1945 to plan the strategy of the war and the ensuing peace.

Cold War. The Soviet Union insisted on keeping a tight hold on the nations of Eastern Europe, and by 1947 it became evident that it also wanted to expand communist influence into Greece and Turkey, a move that the Western Allies vehemently opposed.

The Truman Doctrine. Civil war in Greece, in which communists were trying to gain control of the government, and Soviet demands for territorial concessions by Turkey, caused Truman to take important steps to stop further communist expansion in Europe. In March 1947, he announced what came to be called the Truman Doctrine, stating that it "must be the policy of the United States to support free people who are resisting attempted subjugation." Truman asked Congress to authorize millions of dollars in economic and military aid for Greece, Turkey, and any other nation that wanted to fight communist takeover. In May Congress appropriated funds for Greek-Turkish aid.

The Marshall Plan. Truman's policy of containment of communism was carried even further by his secretary of state, George C. Marshall. Seeing that the economically dislocated countries of Europe were all subject to communist influence, Marshall announced on June 5, 1947, that the American government was willing to provide economic aid to any country that agreed to work for its own recovery. This was the basis of the European Recovery Plan (ERP), also called the Marshall Plan, for the reconstruction and rehabilitation of Europe.

Through this plan, Congress appropriated what was then an enormous sum, $12.5 billion, in aid to countries in Western Europe (the countries of Eastern Europe were offered the same aid, but the Soviet Union did not allow them to accept), beginning in 1948. This aid

JOSEPH STALIN'S role shifted from ally to foe as disagreements arose over the reorganization of Germany and the proliferation of nuclear weapons.

helped Western Europe to become independent and self-supporting once again.

The Berlin blockade. In June of 1948, a direct confrontation between the Western nations and the Soviet Union arose in Berlin. All of eastern Germany had been occupied solely by the Russians, with the exception of the German capital of Berlin. Here Americans, French, British, and Russians controlled different zones within the city. Wanting to drive the Western nations out of this eastern area, Soviet troops blocked the routes of access—highways and railroads—that the Western powers had to the city in an effort to cut off the city's supplies.

But the Western powers would not be driven out. They mounted a massive airlift into Berlin, flying in enough cargo each day to keep Berlin's 2 million residents, as well as their own troops, supplied. In May of 1949, after 321 days, the Russians lifted the blockade. Yet there remained basic disagreements between the Soviet Union and the Western powers over the reorganization of Germany. In September the parliament of the Federal Republic of Germany met in Bonn, and in the following month the German Democratic Republic was established in Russian-controlled eastern Germany.

NATO. Recognizing that an "iron curtain"—Winston Churchill's phrase—separated Europe into two parts, the Western powers established the North Atlantic Treaty Organization (NATO), a regional mutual security alliance, in April 1949. The original members were the United States, Canada, eight Western European nations, Turkey, and Greece.

The election of 1948. Inflation, the spread of communism, and accusations of corruption in his administration had made Truman look like an easy candidate to beat in 1948. The platform he

offered, which he called the Fair Deal, promised to extend many New Deal programs—higher minimum wage and Social Security benefits; more support for housing, agriculture, and education; and a system of government insurance for medical expenses. But left-leaning Democrats, wanting more, broke away to form the Progressive Party, with former Vice President Henry A. Wallace as their candidate. Truman's insistence on equal rights for blacks and other minorities alienated many Southern Democrats, so they too broke away to form the States' Rights Party with South Carolina Governor J. Strom Thurmond as their candidate.

Jubilant Republicans chose Thomas E. Dewey again and awaited a landslide victory. But Truman began an extensive "whistle-stop campaign," travelling by train through communities across the nation and stopping to address the voters at stations along the way. He polled about 2 million more votes than Dewey and won 303 electoral votes to Dewey's 189, marking one of the great political comebacks in American politics.

The Korean War. At the end of World War II, Korea had been divided into zones of occupation, with the United States controlling the country up to the 38th parallel and the Soviet Union controlling territory above the 38th parallel. As had been the case in Germany, the Soviets and the Western powers could not agree on reunification, and two separate states were established. The Cold War turned hot on June 25, 1950, when communist North Korean troops crossed the 38th parallel and attacked non-communist South Korea. During the previous year, a long civil war in China had ended with the triumph of the communists. The People's Republic of China was now the ally of the Soviet Union and of North Korea. Fearful that if one Asian nation were conquered, others would soon fall to the communists, the United States sent its troops as part of a UN force to aid South Korea.

By November, the UN troops had driven the North Koreans back behind their border and were continuing north, almost to the Chinese border. At that point, the Chinese intervened, sending the UN troops retreating southward. For the next two and a half years, the fighting continued, until finally a cease-fire was signed on July 27, 1953, essentially restoring the old border between North and South Korea. The war cost 157,530 U.S. casualties, including 54,246 dead.

The Korean War demonstrated the strong determination of the United States to resist communist aggression around the world, but it also revealed the dangers and the tremendous cost of American involvement in a land war in Asia.

Disagreement on the conduct of the war between General Douglas MacArthur, commander of UN forces in Korea, and President Truman led to MacArthur's removal from command. MacArthur had publicly advocated air

Major Events of the Korean War

1950

June 25	North Korean forces invade South Korea.
June 27	UN authorizes the use of UN forces to repel the North Koreans. President Truman orders U.S. forces to South Korea.
June 28	Seoul falls to North Koreans.
July 8	General Douglas MacArthur is named UN commander in Korea.
Aug. 6	North Koreans open a major drive to destroy UN forces.
Sept. 15	UN forces land at Inchon, near Seoul and the 38th parallel, and drive the North Korean army north toward Manchuria.
Nov. 24	General MacArthur launches an end-the-war offensive in northern Korea.
Nov. 26	Chinese launch a massive counterattack. UN forces begin retreat, then stabilize front near 38th parallel.

1951

Apr. 11	General MacArthur is relieved of command. General Matthew Ridgway is named UN commander in Korea.
July 10	Armistice talks begin.

1953

July 27	Armistice is signed and goes into effect.

and naval strikes against targets in China in order to secure the defeat of Chinese and North Korean forces. Truman, seeking to prevent the conflict from expanding into a full-fledged world war, opposed such measures.

This tactical disagreement highlighted the flaw inherent in so-called limited warfare: Military objectives and political objectives do not necessarily coincide.

In Korea, UN forces halted North Korean aggression, but the 1953 armistice produced little more than a fragile armed truce.

Assassination attempt. On November 1, 1950, two members of a Puerto Rican nationalist group tried to assassinate President Truman at Blair House in Washington, D.C. Truman was unharmed, but one assassin and a guard were killed in the attack. The surviving assassin was tried and convicted of murder in 1951.

Presidential term limit. The strain of the presidency had clearly worn down President Roosevelt and may possibly have led to his death. Some felt that the presidency had become such a powerful and demanding office that no person should be allowed to serve more than two terms. On February 27, 1951, the 22nd Amendment was ratified. It stated that no person could serve more than two presidential terms, and that anyone who served more than two years of another president's term could serve only one more term.

McCarthyism. A fear of communist activity both abroad and at home dominated much American thinking during the late 1940s and early 1950s. Senator Joseph McCarthy of Wisconsin charged that there were communists in American government in 1950, claiming he had a list of 205 communists or pro-communists working in the State Department. In that same year, former State Department official Alger Hiss, accused of spying for

the Soviet Union 20 years earlier, was convicted of perjury. In 1953 Ethel and Julius Rosenberg, convicted of treason for stealing sketches of the atomic bomb, were executed.

Other private and public investigations went on throughout the country; they involved former members of the Communist Party, their associates, and others simply suspected of radical tendencies. Many people were unfairly dismissed from their jobs, and many organizations and institutions required loyalty oaths of their employees. Though few charges were ever proved, many people were labeled "security risks."

Then, in early 1954, McCarthy accused the U.S. Army of harboring known communists. The televised Army-McCarthy hearings showed the American public McCarthy's unfair tactics, and public opinion began turning against him. In December McCarthy's colleagues in the Senate censured him for "conduct unbecoming a member," and "McCarthyism" faded away.

Eisenhower years. In 1952, the Republicans chose General Dwight D. Eisenhower as their candidate for president. Eisenhower had resigned as the

commander of SHAPE (Supreme Command Allied Powers in Europe) to run for the presidency, vowing that if he were elected, he would go to Korea. At this time the war had become a brutal stalemate. Adlai E. Stevenson, governor of Illinois, was the Democratic candidate. A respected liberal, Stevenson failed to overcome the popular sentiment for "Ike," and Eisenhower won by a large margin.

Domestic affairs. The Eisenhower years saw the development of unprecedented prosperity in the United States. Population growth, brought on largely by a "baby boom" after the war, encouraged tremendous building activity in many sectors: houses (mostly in new suburbs), highways on which to reach them, schools, and shopping centers. In addition, science and technology, pushed ahead by wartime research, helped industries such as plastics, electronics, and television to grow.

Foreign affairs. Eisenhower appointed John Foster Dulles as his secretary of state. Dulles committed the United States to the theory of "massive retaliation"—which relied on the use of the U.S. nuclear arsenal against communist aggression.

The United States and the Soviet Union began competing furiously in an arms race, constructing new and more potent nuclear weapons. In November of 1952 the United States had tested a new type of atomic weapon, the hydrogen bomb, which had many times the destructive power of the first atomic bombs. In 1953, the Soviet Union exploded its first hydrogen bomb. Rockets carrying nuclear warheads and atomic submarines equipped with missiles were stockpiled in huge numbers.

In the mid-1950s, following the death of Stalin, there was a thaw in Soviet-American relations as the two powers attempted to move closer to peaceful coexistence. The two nations planned a summit conference in 1960. Shortly before the meeting, however, an American U-2 reconnaissance plane was brought down inside the Soviet Union. The pilot, Francis Gary Powers, confessed to his spy mission but President Eisenhower refused to apologize, so the Soviet Union angrily withdrew from the planned summit.

centers
US

centres
Brit.

apologize
US

apologise
Brit.

27 North America

THE 1950s were a decade of unprecedented prosperity in the United States, with tremendous building activity and mobility.

New Challenges

Crises and crusades. The decade of the 1960s began on a note of hope. In November 1960, Democrat John F. Kennedy, at age 43, became the youngest man ever elected to the American presidency, as well as the first Roman Catholic. After defeating Senator Hubert H. Humphrey of Minnesota in a well-planned and well-financed primary campaign, Kennedy chose Senator Lyndon B. Johnson of Texas, his main opponent at the Democratic convention, as his running mate. In the election in November, Kennedy narrowly defeated Republican Richard M. Nixon, Eisenhower's vice president, winning the popular vote by a majority of less than 120,000.

THE ELECTION of John F. Kennedy, shown above with astronaut John Glenn, ushered in a decade of hope and innovation—a hope cut short by his assassination in 1963.

Kennedy's victory was secured in part by his performance in four televised debates with Nixon, during which Nixon appeared to be less comfortable and less prepared than Kennedy. Interestingly, TV audiences that watched the Kennedy-Nixon debates tended to say that Kennedy had won the debates, but audiences that had listened to the debates on radio said that Nixon had won. Nixon's lack of preparedness was surprising in light of the fact that in the 1952 election campaign, Nixon, after being accused of benefiting from a "secret" campaign fund, went on television and defended himself and his candidacy brilliantly in an address that came to be known as the "Checkers speech." (Nixon had ended the speech with a reference to his children's dog Checkers.)

During the 1960 campaign, Kennedy had promised the voters that he would name a "ministry of talent" as cabinet advisers. Fulfilling that promise, he gathered around him people distinguished by their youthfulness, academic background, and vigor. Kennedy's inaugural address was an inspiring appeal to his fellow citizens to join him in pushing toward a "New Frontier," both at home and abroad.

Kennedy offered several innovative programs. He pressed for new and better relations with Latin America through a $10 billion Alliance for Progress, a cooperative program that went into effect in September of 1961 and was joined by all the nations of Latin America except for Cuba. To strengthen the image of the United States abroad, and at the same time help underdeveloped nations, he suggested and implemented the unique and successful Peace Corps. The corps was established by executive order in March 1961, and enacted into law in September of that year. It was comprised mainly of youthful volunteers who served overseas at subsistence wages as teachers, agricultural advisers, public health workers, engineers, and community advisers.

At home Kennedy offered new programs in housing, education, urban renewal, and medical care for the aged, but nearly all his proposals were blocked by Congress. One important legislative victory was the passage in 1962 of the Trade Expansion Act, designed to stimulate American foreign trade by giving the president new powers to negotiate tariff reductions.

The Cuban crisis. In 1959 Fidel Castro, a young lawyer, had successfully led a revolution in Cuba against the government of dictator Fulgencio Batista. As premier, Castro turned increasingly to communist nations for aid. Cuban-American relations were strained in May 1959, when a law was passed in Cuba authorizing the expropriation of large landholdings, forbidding foreigners to buy or inherit land, and barring foreigners from owning stock in sugarcane ventures. In 1960, Castro issued decrees authorizing the seizure of property and businesses owned by Americans in Cuba. In 1960, Cuba established full diplomatic relations with the Soviet Union and recognized the People's Republic of China and North Korea, and U.S.-Cuban relations further deteriorated. In January 1961, President Eisenhower ordered the severing of diplomatic relations with Cuba.

The Eisenhower administration also had been helping to organize an invasion of Cuba. Shortly after taking office, Kennedy decided to allow the plan to proceed, and on April 17, 1961, an American-equipped army of about 1,500 anti-Castro Cuban exiles landed at the Bay of Pigs. American officials had believed that the Cuban people and Castro's own troops would support the invaders, but there was no popular uprising. Kennedy refused to give the foundering invasion force, which had become stranded on the beach, open American air support. As a result, the attack was decisively repulsed and most of the invaders captured or killed. The Bay of Pigs fiasco aroused anti-American sentiment throughout Latin America and the world, and the United States was regarded as an aggressor.

In October 1962, the U.S. Central Intelligence Agency (CIA), which had hopelessly bungled the Bay of Pigs operation, informed Kennedy that the Soviet Union was establishing nuclear missile launch sites in Cuba. This time the CIA was right. On October 22, in a bold, dramatic television speech, Kennedy explained the situation to the American people, and warned the Soviets that the United States would consider any missile "launched from Cuba against any nation in the western hemisphere as an attack by the Soviet Union on the United States, requiring a full retaliatory response upon the Soviet Union." Kennedy also announced that in response to this threat to the western hemisphere, he had ordered a naval "quarantine" of Cuba. Any ships carrying offensive weapons to Cuba would be turned back by the U.S. Navy. He also demanded that the Soviet Union dismantle the newly constructed missile bases in Cuba. Five tense days followed, but almost at the last moment, Soviet Premier Nikita Khrushchev backed down, and on October 26 he offered to withdraw the missiles in return for a promise that the United States would not invade Cuba. Kennedy, ignoring Khrushchev's demand that U.S. missiles in Turkey be dismantled, agreed on the next day to the earlier conditions, and on October 28 the crisis was over.

Following the Cuban missile crisis, Kennedy took steps to ease the threat of nuclear destruction. In the spring of 1963, the missiles in Turkey were withdrawn. Also, a "hot line" teletype connection was set up between Washington and Moscow; it afforded direct communication between the two heads of state in times of crisis. After further efforts, the United States, the Soviet Union, and Great Britain signed a nuclear test ban treaty in 1963, banning testing of nuclear weapons in the atmosphere and underwater.

Race for space. In 1957, as the United States was beginning to develop a satellite to send into orbit around Earth, Americans were stunned when they learned that on October 4 the Soviet Union had succeeded in placing its satellite *Sputnik* into orbit. Fearing that the United States was falling behind in rocket technology, the Eisenhower administration stepped up its space program, and on January 31, 1958, it launched *Explorer 1*. The United States and the Soviet Union vied with each other to see who could build more powerful (and potentially weapons-carrying) rockets.

In an address to Congress on May 25, 1961, Kennedy announced a new goal for the space program: to land a man on the moon and return him safely to Earth. The Mercury program had just launched the first American in space, Alan Shepard, on May 5, 1961. On February 20, 1962, astronaut John Glenn made the first U.S. orbital flight around Earth. In the mid-1960s, the Gemini program followed, sending a series of two-man spacecraft into orbit.

With the Apollo program that followed, Kennedy's goal was achieved. In July of 1969, astronauts Neil Armstrong, Edwin Aldrin, and Michael Collins accomplished the first manned landing on the moon. As Armstrong set foot on the moon on July 20, he said, "That's one small step for a man, one giant leap for mankind."

But despite the success of the space program, the growing signs of "peaceful coexistence" between the Soviet Union and the United States, and a prosperity unequaled in American history, major problems loomed on the horizon. The increasing involvement of the United States in the conflict in Vietnam was becoming a difficult issue. Kennedy's support for the domestic civil rights movement had caused trouble in the Democratic Party, particularly in the South. In November Kennedy decided to go to Texas to try to heal a party rift that threatened to tip the state to the Republicans in the next election.

On November 22, 1963, while riding in a motorcade in Dallas, Texas, Kennedy was shot by a gunman hiding in a nearby building. He died shortly afterward of a rifle bullet wound in his brain. Police soon arrested 24-year-old Lee Harvey Oswald, a former Marine who had once defected to the Soviet Union. Two days later, the accused assassin was himself killed by Jack Ruby, a Dallas nightclub owner, as police were moving Oswald from one jail to another. Millions of television watchers saw the shooting. A commission chaired by Chief Justice Earl Warren concluded that the assassination had been Oswald's doing alone, but many Americans remained unconvinced.

Lyndon Baines Johnson, who had accompanied Kennedy to Texas, was sworn in as president aboard the presidential jet, *Air Force One.* Johnson had had a long and successful career as a congressional leader.

The Great Society.   President Johnson pledged himself to carry out Kennedy's domestic program and to build a new momentum for social change in the United States. In February of 1964, Congress passed a tax cut that had originally been introduced by the Kennedy administration. The act, which was approved by overwhelming majorities in both houses of Congress, decreased individual and corporate income tax

rates. In August 1964, Congress passed the Economic Opportunity Act, which began a federal "war on poverty." The Office of Economic Opportunity (OEO) was created to operate a federal Job Corps, VISTA (Volunteers in Service to America), community action programs, a program for migrant workers, and the Head Start program for disadvantaged preschool children.

As Johnson pressed forward his ambitious program of domestic legislation, foreign events began to take center stage. American involvement in the war in Vietnam grew in 1964 and became one of the key issues of the presidential campaign. In October Nikita Khrushchev was removed from power in the Soviet Union, prompting questions among Americans about the future.

In August, Johnson won the Democratic nomination easily and chose Senator Hubert H. Humphrey of Minnesota as his running mate. The month before, the Republican Party had nominated Senator Barry M. Goldwater of Arizona, a staunch conservative who opposed big government and liberal politics with such vigor that many began to think of him as an extremist who was too reckless to be entrusted with the power of the presidency in the Nuclear Age.

In the November election Johnson beat Goldwater by almost 26 million popular votes, winning 486 electoral votes to Goldwater's 52 in one of the great landslides in American political history.

Johnson considered the election to be a mandate for his domestic programs, which he believed would turn the nation into the "Great Society." He got Congress to pass many more programs to assist public schools, the aged, and the poor. Other measures increased Social Security benefits and the minimum wage.

Perhaps the most ambitious program passed by Congress was the Medicare Bill, which Johnson signed into law on July 30, 1965. The program was designed to make medical and hospital care affordable for all Americans aged 65 and older. The campaign for national health care had been begun in 1945 by Harry S. Truman, so it was fitting that Johnson signed the bill in Truman's presence, at the Truman Library in Independence, Missouri.

AMERICAN DISTRUST of the growing American involvement in Vietnam was a key issue in the presidential campaign in 1964.

center
US

centre
Brit.

27 North America

THE UNITED STATES lost the race with Russia to launch the first satellite to orbit the earth, but successfully landed the first man on the moon in 1969.

MARTIN LUTHER KING, JR., was the leader of the civil rights movement, which sought to extend full civil rights to the nation's blacks.

Struggle for civil rights. The Great Society also sought to extend full civil rights to the nation's blacks. The perceived need for civil rights had arisen many years before, in the days of slavery, and had made rapid strides in the years just after the Civil War, only to be nearly crushed in 1896 by the Supreme Court ruling in the case of *Plessy* v. *Ferguson.* In that case the High Court ruled that separation of the races was legal provided that blacks had access to separate but equal accommodations. But the movement gained new impetus in the 1940s and 1950s. An early target was desegregation of American public schools. On May 17, 1954, the Supreme Court handed down a momentous decision forbidding school segregation. The unanimous ruling in *Brown* v. *Board of Education of Topeka* held that "separate but equal" schools were "inherently unequal," thereby overturning the ruling upon which racial segregation had relief for almost six decades. The High Court ruled that school desegregation should begin at once. Widespread resistance in the South slowed implementation, and federal troops and marshals were sometimes called in to enforce school desegregation.

In an effort to desegregate public transportation, 26-year-old Reverend Martin Luther King, Jr., led a year-long boycott of the buses of Montgomery, Alabama, beginning in December 1955, after Rosa Parks had been arrested for refusing to give up her seat to a white passenger on a bus. In November 1956, the Supreme Court affirmed a lower court ruling that the buses be desegregated. In 1961 "Freedom Riders," interracial groups, travelled together on interstate buses through the South in an effort to get the federal government to enforce a 1946 Supreme Court ruling that had ordered desegregation of long-distance buses. The Freedom Rides sparked numerous violent confrontations, but they were ultimately successful, as were many "sit-ins" for the purpose of desegregating eating and entertainment establishments in the South.

By 1963 King was recognized as the major leader of the civil rights movement. On August 28, 1963, more than 200,000 civil rights supporters joined in a march on Washington to show Congress their desire for civil rights legislation. King addressed the vast crowd, describing his dream of full equality and respect between blacks and whites.

Congress responded with the Civil Rights Act of 1964, which President Kennedy asked for in June 1963, and President Johnson signed on July 2, 1964. The act outlawed racial discrimination in employment and public accommodations. The Voting Rights Act of 1965, which President Johnson submitted to Congress in March 1965, and which was signed into law on August 6, provided for federal supervision to allow blacks to register where they had been previously denied the right to vote. The Civil Rights Act of 1968, signed by Johnson on April 11, 1968, attempted to guarantee blacks the right to open housing.

With all this legislative action, though, blacks were still struggling for the opportunities that full civil rights were intended to afford them. In 1967 the Kerner Commission, a government group that had studied riots in black neighborhoods of Los Angeles and other cities, concluded that "Our nation is moving toward two societies, one black, one white, separate and unequal."

Vietnam. After World War II, France had tried to reestablish control over its colony of Indochina (Vietnam), only to be defeated by Vietnamese forces led by the Communist Ho Chi Minh in 1954. France left Indochina, which was divided into a Communist-controlled northern state and a non-Communist southern state led by Ngo Dinh Diem, who had been put into power with U.S. help. The arrangement was to be temporary, pending countrywide elections, but Diem refused to allow the elections to take place. Beginning in the late 1950s, North Vietnam backed Vietnamese guerrillas who were fighting to overthrow the regime of South Vietnam. The Northerners wanted to reunite Vietnam under a Communist government. Presidents Eisenhower and Kennedy had sent military advisers and supplies to help South Vietnam.

As the situation grew more and more desperate for South Vietnam, President Johnson began increasing American involvement in the fighting. In August of 1964, after an American destroyer, on an intelligence mission off the coast of North Vietnam in the Gulf of Tonkin, was attacked by North Vietnamese patrol boats, Congress passed the Gulf of Tonkin Resolution, which authorized the president "to take all necessary measures to repel any armed attack against the forces of the United States and to prevent further aggression."

Soon American planes were bombing targets in North Vietnam, and in March 1965, the first American combat troops were sent to South Vietnam. In the next three years, great numbers of American troops were fighting in South Vietnam, half a million by the end of 1967 and 540,000 in 1968. Johnson's hope was to hold off the North Vietnamese and guerrilla forces long enough to give the South Vietnamese a chance to build up their army and their government. But as time passed, it became obvious that this strategy was not working. Corruption, incompetence, and factionalism gravely weakened the South Vietnamese government and led to numerous coups and uprisings.

Antiwar movement. Organized protest against the seemingly endless war began when college students staged "teach-ins" to portray the conflict as a civil war in which the United States should not be involved. Their disillusion spread to other citizens, until the antiwar movement claimed millions of supporters.

Fight for women's rights. The activism of the 1960s spawned a new crusade for women's rights. One spark for the movement was the publication in 1963 of Betty Friedan's book *The Feminine Mystique.* The book identified many of the inequalities women suffered in American life—social, political, and economic. Three years later, Friedan founded NOW, the National Organization for Women, which demanded, among other things, equal educational opportunities for women; equal pay for equal work; wider job opportunities; publicly funded day-care centers; and the repeal of laws banning abortion.

The Equal Pay Act of 1963 had guaranteed equal pay for equal work, and the Civil Rights Act of 1964 prohibited job discrimination on the basis of sex as well as race, but the passage of legislation did

HO CHI MINH led the forces of the North Vietnamese in their attempt to overthrow the regime of South Vietnam.

centers
US

centres
Brit.

honor
US

honour
Brit.

Major Events of the Vietnam War

1945 Ho Chi Minh declares independence of Vietnam September 2, but French soon move to reassert authority in Indochina.

1954 French are defeated at Dien Bien Phu May 7.
Truce agreement at Geneva in July divides Vietnam pending nationwide elections.
Ho establishes Decmocratic Republic of Vietnam in north; former emperor Bao Dai sets up rival government in south with Ngo Dinh Diem as prime minister.

1955 Diem refuses to participate in nationwide elections.

1960 National Liberation Front, or Vietcong, founded; organizes guerrilla operations in south.

1964 North Vietnamese gunboats attack U.S. destroyer *Maddox* August 2. Gulf of Tonkin Resolution passed August 7. U.S. warplanes bomb North Vietnam.

1965 First sustained bombing of North Vietnam begins February 24.
First U.S. combat troops land at Da Nang March 8.

1968 Tet offensive launched January 31. My Lai massacre committed in March. Paris peace talks begin in May. U.S. troop strength rises to 540,000.

1969 President Nixon announces withdrawal of 25,000 troops June 8. Troop level down to 480,000 by year's end.

1970 U.S. and South Vietnamese troops invade Cambodia April 30.

1971 U.S. and South Vietnamese forces invade Laos February 8.

1972 President Nixon orders mining of Haiphong harbor in May, bombing of Hanoi and Haiphong in December.

1973 Cease-fire agreement signed in Paris January 27.
Last U.S. forces withdrawn from Vietnam March 29.

1975 North Vietnamese launch new offensive in January, capture Saigon April 30.

27 North America

THE AMBIGUITIES of the intense guerrilla warfare in the jungles of Vietnam increased the growing discomfort of the American people with the conflict.

not guarantee compliance. The crusade for legalizing abortion was advanced by a Supreme Court ruling in January 1973, striking down state antiabortion laws in Texas, in the case of *Roe* v. *Wade,* and in Georgia, in the case of *Doe* v. *Bolton.* The Court ruled that state laws could not prohibit a woman from having an abortion in the first three months of a pregnancy, that the constitutional right to privacy left such a decision in the hands of the woman and her physician. But strong opposition on religious and moral grounds continued.

In 1972 Congress passed the Equal Rights Amendment (ERA), which stated, "Equality of rights under the law shall not be denied or abridged by the United States or any state on account of sex." But the amendment failed to be ratified by the necessary 38 states, and it did not take effect.

The end of optimism. In January of 1968, trouble in Asia expanded beyond the borders of Vietnam when North Korean gunboats seized in international waters the intelligence ship U.S.S. *Pueblo.* The crew was imprisoned and tortured and was not released until December. One month after the *Pueblo* seizure, the North Vietnamese staged an ambitious offensive during the most important Vietnamese festival, Tet, the lunar New Year celebration. North Vietnamese and Vietcong forces assaulted scores of towns and cities, from Hue in the northern part of South Vietnam to Saigon in the south. Although it turned into a military defeat of major proportions for the Communists, the Tet offensive also showed the American public how little control non-Communist forces had in South Vietnam. On April 4 Martin Luther King, Jr., was shot dead in Memphis, Tennessee, by James Earl Ray. Rage swept the nation and riots broke out in over 170 cities.

In March President Johnson, undermined by lack of success in Vietnam and by antiwar protests at home, announced that he would not seek reelection. Senator Eugene McCarthy of Minnesota, who opposed the war, had run a very strong second to Johnson in the New Hampshire primary, and soon after, Robert Kennedy, brother of the slain president, announced that he, too, was a candidate for the Democratic nomination. Just after midnight on June 5, following his victory in the California presidential primary, Kennedy was shot by gunman Sirhan Sirhan. Robert Kennedy died on June 6.

In August a deeply divided Democratic Party met in Chicago for a turbulent convention marked by violent clashes between police and antiwar protestors. Vice President Hubert Humphrey won the nomination over Eugene McCarthy, who had campaigned as the peace candidate. The Republicans chose former Vice President Richard M. Nixon. A major third-party contender was Governor George C. Wallace of Alabama. Nixon won the election by one of the narrowest popular vote margins in U.S. history, receiving 43.4 percent of the popular vote to Humphrey's 42.7 percent.

Nixon came to office with the promise of ending the Vietnam War. "The greatest honor history can bestow is the title peacemaker," he said in his inaugural address. On the domestic scene, the economy was slowing down, resulting in increased unemployment and inflation.

Ending the Vietnam War. Nixon's original plan was to "Vietnamize" the war—to withdraw U.S. troops gradually and turn the war over to the South Vietnamese. In 1969 U.S. troop strength in South Vietnam began to drop, and President Nixon announced plans to reduce troop levels by 110,000. Antiwar

THE MEMORIAL TO THE VIETNAM WAR DEAD has been beneficial in healing the scars to the American psyche caused by the Vietnam conflict.

gasoline *US*

petrol *Brit.*

bills were introduced to curb the president's power to commit the United States to war without the consent of Congress; and proposals were made for a fixed deadline for the withdrawal of all American forces.

Peace negotiations had begun in Paris in May 1968, but progress had been slow and frustrating. By the end of 1971, U.S. troop strength had dropped below 200,000 and South Vietnamese troops were doing more and more of the fighting. By the end of 1972, progress had been made on a comprehensive peace plan, but it stalled over the deadline for withdrawal. Finally, on January 27, 1973, an agreement was signed. Terms included a cease-fire, withdrawal of American troops, and return of all American prisoners of war.

In 1974 the South Vietnamese military continued to hold its own against Communist forces, after fighting was renewed following U.S. withdrawal. But reductions in U.S. aid limited its ability to fight.

In January 1975, the communists opened their final offensive in northern South Vietnam and within two months the South Vietnamese forces were in full retreat. In April the last Americans were evacuated, and within days, South Vietnam was entirely in communist hands. U.S. involvement in the conflict had cost 58,000 American lives, many billions of dollars, and a crisis of confidence in government.

The Soviet Union and China. In November 1969, the United States and the Soviet Union ratified a nuclear non-proliferation treaty. Then, in February of 1972, President Nixon became the first U.S. president to visit the People's

protestors, however, continued to demonstrate for an immediate end to American involvement; a nationwide "moratorium" was held in October, and in November details of an American massacre of Vietnamese civilians at a place called My Lai were revealed.

Despite Nixon's policy of troop withdrawal, in April 1970, he sent American and South Vietnamese troops into Cambodia to clear out border sanctuaries used as supply bases by North Vietnamese and Vietcong guerrilla forces. The public's reaction to the move was intense. Antiwar demonstrations were held across the nation. Four students at Kent State University, in Ohio, were killed by National Guard troops during a demonstration on May 4, 1970, and 448 colleges closed down in protest. On May 14 two students were killed at Jackson State College, in Mississippi, in a violent confrontation with police.

In February of the next year, South Vietnamese forces, with U.S. air and artillery support, invaded neighboring Laos to cut off the "Ho Chi Minh Trail," a well-worn Communist supply line through dense vegetation. Again there was intense reaction against American involvement. Congress repealed the Gulf of Tonkin Resolution, the original mandate for massive U.S. involvement;

Republic of China, ending nearly 25 years of diplomatic separation. Nixon and the Chinese leaders agreed to increase trade between the two nations and to allow journalistic, scientific, and cultural exchanges. In May Nixon visited the Soviet Union and signed a treaty limiting antiballistic missiles, a result of the Strategic Arms Limitation Talks (SALT).

The faltering economy. As American participation in the Vietnam War wound down, the U.S. economy became the major political issue. The unemployment rate climbed steadily until 5 million were out of work in 1971. At the same time, inflation reduced the value of the dollar, industry produced below capacity, and many American goods were uncompetitive on the world market. The nation was entering a period of "stagflation," economic stagnation combined with inflation.

Nixon announced a program in August 1971 that included a wage-price freeze, tax cuts, a surcharge on certain imports, and devaluation of the dollar. For a while, it seemed that stagflation might be beaten, but when the wage-price controls were lifted in early 1973, prices leapt once again.

Oil crisis. A major contributor to continuing high inflation in the United States was the high price of oil. As a longtime ally of Israel, the United States incurred the wrath of the Arab nations, which provided 25 percent of all American oil, by supporting Israel after it was attacked by Egypt and Syria in October 1973. The Arabs punished the United States by refusing to export oil to the country, and prices for petroleum and gasoline soared, raising inflation rates. However, when the oil embargo was

ARAB OIL-PRODUCING COUNTRIES punished the United States for supporting Israel in 1973 by refusing to export oil to the U.S.

ended in March 1974, American oil problems did not end. The Organization of Petroleum Exporting Countries (OPEC), which had instituted steep price increases in 1973, continued to raise oil prices.

1972 election and Watergate. In 1972, President Nixon announced his candidacy for reelection, and in August he and Vice President Spiro Agnew were renominated at the Republican National Convention.

Nixon's Committee to Reelect the President used political tactics that were referred to as "dirty tricks." Such tactics helped to scuttle the candidacy of the Democratic front-runner, Senator Edmund Muskie of Maine, as the Nixon camp tried to ensure the nomination of the weakest Democratic candidate, whom they judged to be Senator George S. McGovern of South Dakota, a liberal Democrat who favored a quick end to the continuing U.S. involvement in Vietnam.

In May George Wallace of Alabama, who had chosen to seek the Democratic nomination rather than mount another third-party campaign, was shot by a mentally unbalanced would-be assassin at a campaign rally. Wallace was permanently paralyzed, and his campaign wound down rapidly.

At the Democratic convention in July, McGovern was nominated on the first ballot. His chosen running mate, Senator Thomas F. Eagleton of Missouri, withdrew from the ticket after it was revealed that he had received psychiatric treatment for depression. He was replaced by R. Sargent Shriver.

In the November election, Nixon defeated McGovern in a landslide, winning by almost 18 million popular votes and gaining 520 electoral votes to McGovern's 17. But the sweetness of the victory was to be short-lived for Nixon.

Prior to the national party conventions and the election, during the night of June 16–17, there had been a puzzling break-in at Democratic National Headquarters in the Watergate apartment complex in Washington, D.C. Five men employed by the Committee to Reelect the President were arrested after breaking in to plant electronic surveillance equipment in the offices.

When the five defendants went on trial in early 1973, it became apparent that the break-in was instigated, and then covered up, by high White House officials. Nixon denied any role in planning the break-in or the subsequent cover-up, but in February of 1973, the Senate convened a seven-member select committee to investigate the Watergate affair. In April Nixon announced that two of his top aides, H. R. Haldeman and John Ehrlichman, were resigning, and that he had also asked for the resignation of White House counsel John W. Dean. Later disclosures connected these aides to the scandal.

In May the Justice Department appointed Archibald Cox to act as special prosecutor in the Watergate investigation, and the Senate select committee

THE RESIGNATION OF RICHARD NIXON (far right) in 1974 paved the way for Vice President Gerald Ford (second from left). Democrat Jimmy Carter (second from right) won the election in 1976 but lost to Republican Ronald Reagan (far left) in 1980.

began its investigation of the Watergate affair. John Dean testified that Nixon was involved in the cover-up. Testimony from Attorney General John Mitchell and others uncovered various other illegal activities directed by officials within or working on instructions from the White House. Another revelation disclosed that Nixon's office contained recorders on which all conversations had been taped. Nixon refused to surrender the tape recordings on grounds of executive privilege and national security. Nixon offered written summaries of the recordings requested by the investigating bodies, and ordered Cox to halt his demands for the tapes. Cox refused. On Saturday, October 20, 1973, in what came to be called the Saturday Night Massacre, Nixon ordered Attorney General Elliot Richardson to fire Cox. Richardson resigned, as did his deputy William D. Ruckelshaus. Finally, Robert H. Bork, solicitor general, fired Cox.

News of the affair enraged Congress, the courts, and the public. Nixon finally gave up some tapes, one with a crucial erasure, to the federal court demanding them. In July 1974, under Supreme Court direction, he surrendered other complete tapes that were later used to convict his former aides and Attorney General Mitchell of conspiracy to obstruct justice.

Agnew resigns. In the midst of the Watergate investigations, Vice President Agnew was undergoing an investigation on a totally unrelated matter—the alleged acceptance of bribes from construction companies while he was governor of Maryland. On October 10, 1973, Agnew resigned as vice president,

shortly after entering a no-contest plea on a single charge of income tax evasion.

Under the provisions of the 25th Amendment, which provided for presidential and vice presidential succession and was ratified on February 10, 1967, Nixon selected a successor to Agnew. His choice was Representative Gerald R. Ford of Michigan, a 25-year veteran of Congress.

Nixon falls. In early 1974, the House Judiciary Committee began studying the possibility that Nixon had committed impeachable offenses. On July 30 the committee approved three articles of impeachment.

A few days later, Nixon released a statement and a transcript showing that he had authorized an attempt to use the CIA to block the FBI investigation of the Watergate break-in six days after the burglary had occurred. This revelation eroded most of Nixon's remaining support. On August 8, 1974, Nixon announced his resignation.

The next day, Gerald R. Ford was sworn in as president. One month later, on September 8, he issued a pardon to Nixon for all federal crimes he "committed or may have committed or taken part in" while president.

Ford's presidency. In accordance with the 25th Amendment, Ford nominated a vice president to replace himself. He chose former governor Nelson A. Rockefeller of New York. For the first time since the Constitution was adopted, both the president and vice president were appointed rather than elected.

Ford acted to carry out both the domestic and foreign policies set forth by Nixon and Secretary of State Henry

THE IRAN-IRAQ WAR threatened to slow the much-needed flow of oil to the United States.

THE SPACE RACE continued under President Reagan.

Meanwhile, Cambodia fell to the Communist Khmer Rouge in April, and South Vietnam was defeated by the Communists from the north. On May 12, Cambodian gunboats seized the American freighter *Mayaguez*, and Ford ordered U.S. forces to recover the ship and its 39-man crew.

In September 1975, Ford escaped two assassination attempts, the first in Sacramento, California, on September 5, and the second in San Francisco on September 22.

Carter is elected. In 1976 Ford chose to seek a full elected term as president. After fighting off a strong challenge by Ronald Reagan for the nomination, Ford, who had major differences with Rockefeller, chose Senator Robert Dole of Kansas as his running mate. The Democratic nominee was former governor Jimmy Carter of Georgia. Ford's pardon of Nixon, in effect putting the former president above the law, hurt him in the election. Carter defeated Ford, winning 51 percent of the popular vote in a very close race.

Carter undertook many domestic programs, including civil service reform, deregulation of the airline industry, promotion of energy conservation, and development of new, renewable sources of energy. During his administration the Department of Energy and the Department of Education were established.

Relinquishing the Panama Canal. After 13 years of negotiation, in September 1977, the United States and Panama reached agreement on the terms of a new Panama Canal treaty. The treaty would place the canal and the Canal Zone under complete Panamanian control by the end of the century. Debate over the treaty was heated. Opponents contended that "giving away the Panama Canal" threatened national security. Finally, Congress ratified the treaty by a close vote in April 1978.

Camp David. Carter's greatest triumph came in April 1979, when he called together Israeli leader Menachem Begin and Egyptian leader Anwar el-Sadat at the Presidential retreat at Camp David, Maryland. There, for 13 days, the leaders worked out a treaty to end 30 years of war between Egypt and Israel. The treaty provided a framework for the Israeli return of captured land to Egypt, a process that was eventually completed in 1982.

Hostage to Iran. One of the staunchest allies of the United States in the Middle East was the Shah of Iran, Mohammed Riza Pahlevi, who had sought to modernize his oil-rich country. In 1979 he was overthrown by political and religious opponents who believed modernization undermined the religious beliefs and practices of Islam.

After the exiled Shah, dying of cancer, came to the United States for medical treatment, Iranian militants seized the American embassy in the capital at Teheran on November 4, 1979, and took 52 Americans hostage. Despite all American efforts, both diplomatic

Kissinger. Domestically, the dual problem of the 1974–1975 recession and high inflation placed the country's economy in serious condition. In October Ford introduced an economic plan whose slogan was "Whip Inflation Now," or WIN. However, by early 1975, nationwide unemployment had passed 8 percent while prices continued to rise. Ford vetoed a number of bills in an attempt to control government spending.

and military, the hostages were not freed until January 1981, after spending 444 days in captivity.

The Carter Doctrine. In December 1979, the Soviet Union invaded Afghanistan, on Iran's border. Carter tried to punish the Russians by cutting off the sale to them of such American products as grain. He also withdrew the United States team from the 1980 Olympics, held in Moscow. Then, in an effort to keep the Soviet Union from moving any farther into the Middle East, he declared the "Carter Doctrine"—that any Soviet moves on the Persian Gulf would be met by American military response.

Changing direction. By the time the election of 1980 approached, President Carter's popularity was at a very low ebb—a poll showed that he had the approval of only 21 percent of the American people. Energy shortages and high fuel costs, unemployment and inflation, and seemingly worsening international relations had sadly disillusioned the American electorate.

Reagan elected. At the Democratic National Convention in August, Carter halted a bid for the nomination by Senator Edward M. Kennedy of Massachusetts that left the party weakened. In July Ronald Reagan won the Republican nomination and chose George Bush, one of his closest opponents, as his running mate. In November Reagan defeated Carter in a landslide. Reagan's election brought the first basic change in federal government policy in nearly half a century. Reagan said he would cut government spending, balance the budget, reduce taxes, and rebuild defense forces.

Reagan had no chance to put his policies into effect before he was seriously wounded on March 30 by John W. Hinckley in an assassination attempt. He made a rapid recovery.

The economy was sluggish, however, and inflation and unemployment were high. Reagan's economic policy came to be known as "Reaganomics" or "supply-side economics." It called for tax cuts that would spur savings and presumably increase capital investment and create jobs. This policy was designed to reduce inflation, lower interest rates, and increase government revenues.

On August 4 Congress approved a Reagan tax reduction bill that cut income tax rates by 25 percent in three stages, ending July 1, 1983. The economy began to improve, but the budget deficit began to rise, partly because of large increases in military expenses. The Reagan administration attempted to cut domestic programs in such fields as social welfare and education, but largely failed because the Democrats controlled the House of Representatives throughout Reagan's presidency.

In 1980, the last year of the Carter administration, the federal deficit was almost $74 billion. In 1983 it rose to almost $208 billion, and in 1986 to more than $221 billion.

RUSSIA'S MIKHAIL GORBACHEV and President Ronald Reagan signed in 1987 the first treaty in history to provide for nuclear arms reductions.

Foreign affairs. The Reagan presidency faced numerous problems, including war in the Middle East, terrorism, civil war in Nicaragua, and negotiations with the Soviet Union.

On August 20, 1982, some 800 U.S. Marines landed in Beirut, Lebanon, as part of a multinational peacekeeping force. On October 23, 1983, an explosive-laden truck leveled the Marines' headquarters, killing 241 Marine and Navy troops. Earlier, on April 18, another bomb had nearly destroyed the U.S. embassy in Beirut, killing 63 persons, including 17 Americans.

With Iran and Iraq at war, there was danger to the heavy traffic of oil tankers in the Persian Gulf. A large percentage of the oil imported by the United States came from the Middle East, and by 1984, after several years of declining demand, oil imports began to increase again. Accordingly, U.S. Navy ships were sent to the Persian Gulf in February, 1984; they later began to convoy neutral shipping. On May 17, 1987, an Iraqi warplane mistakenly fired a missile at the U.S. frigate *Stark,* killing 37 crewmen. An even greater tragedy came on July 3, 1988, when the U.S. cruiser *Vincennes* mistakenly shot down an Iranian passenger jet, killing all 290 persons aboard.

The Reagan administration had earlier identified Libya as an abettor of worldwide terrorism. On April 14, 1986, Reagan ordered an air strike against Libya, following a bombing of a discotheque in West Berlin on April 5, in which one American serviceman was instantly killed and one fatally injured. U.S. Air Force and Navy planes blasted five military bases and terrorist training centers near Tripoli and Benghazi.

The administration exhibited a particular dislike for the Marxist-oriented Sandinista regime in Nicaragua. Opposed to it were the Contras, representing both democratic forces and the remnants of the brutal regime the Sandinistas had overthrown. Reagan sought throughout his presidency to secure financial aid for the Contras, whom he called "freedom fighters." At first Congress obliged, but later it resisted appropriations for any but humanitarian aid.

More successful was the invasion of the tiny Caribbean nation of Grenada on October 25, 1983, undertaken to oust a pro-Cuban Marxist group that had seized power in a bloody coup. The invasion succeeded, although a discouraging lack of preparation and coordination was revealed.

Also a success was U.S. participation in negotiations for the withdrawal of Soviet troops from Afghanistan. On April 14, 1988, the U.S.S.R. agreed to begin a phased withdrawal; it was completed in February 1989.

During his presidency, Reagan held four summit meetings (in Geneva, Reykjavik, Moscow, and Washington) with General Secretary Mikhail Gorbachev of the Soviet Union. The meetings led to the first treaty in history to provide for nuclear arms reductions. Signed on December 8, 1987, and ratified by the U.S. Senate on May 27, 1988, the treaty called for the destruction of 2,611 U.S. and Soviet medium- and short-range missiles in Europe.

In November 1984, Reagan defeated Walter Mondale, who had been vice president under Jimmy Carter, and gained reelection in a landslide, carrying 49 of the 50 states and winning 525 electoral votes to Mondale's 13. Reagan's second term was marred by scandal. It was revealed on November 3, 1986, that the United States had been secretly selling arms to Iran in the hope

of securing the release of Americans held hostage in Lebanon by Islamic terrorists. Some funds from the sales had been secretly diverted to the Nicaraguan Contras. John M. Poindexter, the national security adviser, resigned and his assistant, Marine Colonel Oliver L. North, was dismissed. Both were convicted in 1990 on federal charges, but in 1991 the convictions were overturned on appeal. On December 24, 1992, President Bush pardoned six other officials involved in the scandal, including Caspar W. Weinberger, former secretary of defense, who was to have gone on trial in January 1993.

Domestic matters. In the area of domestic legislation, several significant laws were enacted during the Reagan presidency. On October 22, 1986, Reagan signed a bill providing the most sweeping tax reform in 40 years. It lowered taxes for individuals and increased taxes by about the same amount for businesses and corporations. The law also eliminated various deductions. A major reform of the immigration laws was signed on November 6, 1986. It prohibited employers from hiring illegal aliens, but it also provided the means for many aliens to secure legal status in the United States.

In November 1988, Vice President George Bush was elected president, easily defeating his Democratic opponent, Governor Michael S. Dukakis of Massachusetts.

On January 2, 1989, the United States and Canada signed a free trade agreement intended to eliminate tariffs and reduce other trade barriers by the end of the century.

On August 9, 1989, President Bush signed a law to bail out the nation's savings and loan associations. Having been freed of certain regulatory restrictions,

centers
US

centres
Brit.

many savings and loan institutions failed because of ill-considered loans, poor management, and criminal activity. It was estimated that it would cost at least $300 billion to bail them out.

Supreme Court changes. When President Reagan took office in January of 1981, Republicans looked forward to the opportunity of influencing the course of government in the long term through the appointment of more conservative justices to the Supreme Court. In 1981 Justice Potter Stewart resigned and Reagan nominated Sandra Day O'Connor, who was confirmed by Congress on September 21. She became the first woman justice to serve on the Supreme Court.

In July 1986, Warren E. Burger retired as chief justice. Reagan nominated Supreme Court justice William H. Rehnquist to succeed him, and Antonin Scalia to fill Rehnquist's vacated seat. On September 17 the Senate confirmed both appointments. Scalia was confirmed unanimously, but Rehnquist met with considerable Senate opposition.

In 1987 Lewis F. Powell, Jr., retired from the Court. Reagan's first nominee, Robert H. Bork, was not confirmed by the Senate, and his second, Douglas Ginsburg, withdrew after admitting he had used marijuana as a college student and teacher. The third nominee, Anthony Kennedy, was confirmed unanimously on February 8, 1988.

In 1990 William J. Brennan, Jr., retired from the Court, and President Bush nominated David H. Souter, who was confirmed on October 2.

In 1991 Thurgood Marshall retired and Bush nominated Clarence Thomas. After charges of sexual harassment

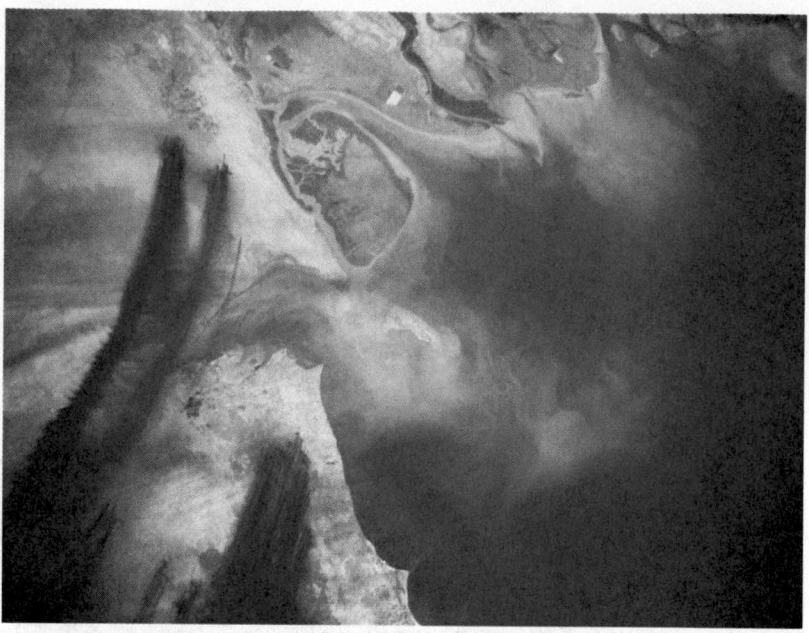

PHOTOGRAPHS FROM SPACE indicate the extent of the damage to oil fields in Kuwait during the Gulf War.

were suddenly leveled against Thomas by Anita Hill, a law professor and Thomas's former employee, Thomas categorically denied the accusations and angrily charged the televised Senate confirmation hearing with perpetrating a "high-tech lynching." On October 15 Thomas was confirmed by the Senate in a 52 to 48 vote.

The nation enters the 1990s. In mid-1990 a recession began to grip the country. It was marked by a high unemployment rate that did not go down until late 1992. Meanwhile, the annual federal deficit was about $300 billion, and the national debt by the end of 1992 was approaching $4 trillion.

Domestic legislation enacted during the Bush Presidency included a landmark law to protect disabled persons against discrimination (July 26, 1990); the Clean Air Act of 1990, tightening pollution standards (November 15); the Immigration Act of 1990, which set new quotas for persons to be admitted to the United States (November 29); the Civil Rights Act of 1991, which made it easier for employees to sue employers on grounds of discrimination (November 21); and as an aid to inner cities, a law that would provide grants and loans for housing and business (June 22, 1992). This last act was the result of one of the worst urban riots in U.S. history. On April 29 a jury in California acquitted four white Los Angeles policemen of charges of having beaten a black man, even though a video camera had recorded the incident. The ensuing riot in a predominantly African-American area of the city resulted in 52 deaths, the destruction of some 600 buildings, and much looting.

In December of 1989, President Bush ordered U.S. military forces into Panama to depose its dictator, Manuel

Noriega, who had been indicted by two U.S. grand juries in February 1988 on charges of drug trafficking and racketeering. U.S. troops engaged in a brief conflict with vastly outnumbered Panamanian troops. Noriega surrendered and was convicted in a U.S. federal court July 10, 1992. He was sentenced to 40 years' confinement.

On July 31, 1991, Bush and Mikhail Gorbachev, president of the Soviet Union, signed the Strategic Arms Reduction Treaty (START), an agreement calling for large cuts in nuclear weapons. The United States would reduce its arsenal from about 12,000 to about 9,500 missiles, and the Soviets from about 11,300 to about 6,900. A further reduction in nuclear arms was agreed to on December 29, 1992. By 2003, U.S. warheads would be cut to 3,500 and those of Russia to 3,000.

The signing of this second Strategic Arms Reduction Treaty (START II) in Moscow on January 3, 1993, highlighted the enormous changes that had occurred in international politics during President Bush's term of office. An unsuccessful coup in the Soviet Union in August 1991 had accelerated its dissolution, which was formalized that December. President Boris N. Yeltsin of Russia, who had played a central role in defeating the coup and in replacing the Soviet Union with the less-centralized Commonwealth of Independent States, signed START II with President Bush.

However, it was clear that new difficulties had arisen, for Russia was not the only former Soviet republic to possess nuclear weapons. Ukraine and Kazakhstan also held significant portions of the Soviet nuclear stockpile, and further agreements would be required to establish procedures to provide for their elimination.

SANDRA DAY O'CONNOR was nominated to the Supreme Court by President Reagan and became the first woman to hold that position.

In response to the August 1990 Iraqi invasion of Kuwait, an international coalition of forces, including the U.S. military, was sent to the Arabian peninsula to defend against further aggression in the region. On January 16, 1991, coalition forces launched a military campaign to liberate Kuwait. After a six-week air battle and a five-day ground war, Iraqi troops and resources were decimated and remaining Iraqi forces were driven out of Kuwait. Iraq accepted on March 3 the terms of a United Nations resolution that called for, among other points, the inspection of all chemical and nuclear weapons and facilities.

The U.S. force of 532,000 in the Persian Gulf was the most significant U.S. military deployment since the Vietnam War. The war in the Gulf, in contrast with the war in Vietnam, received unusually high levels of approval in the United States, in part because of the speed and decisiveness of the victory and the low number of casualties (less than 200 dead and less than 500 wounded for U.S. forces), and in part because of an almost flawless public relations campaign by the Defense Department.

Under the auspices of the United Nations, U.S. armed forces landed in Somalia on December 9, 1992, inaugurating Operation Restore Hope. This mission was intended to expedite the distribution of food to a nation where civil war and drought had already cost some 300,000 lives, with another million in danger of starvation. The relief mission was a great success, but administration hopes to have all U.S. military forces leave Somalia rapidly were frustrated by continuing conflicts between rival warlords and the inability to restore functioning political and police authority in Somalia.

On December 17, 1992, Canada, Mexico, and the United States signed the North American Free Trade Agreement (NAFTA), which would eliminate import taxes and other barriers to trade in all of North America.

The NAFTA agreement and the economic recession became central issues in the 1992 presidential campaign. In early 1992, Texas billionaire businessman H. Ross Perot entered the campaign as an independent candidate. He attacked both parties for their inability to control deficit spending and reduce the national debt and pledged, if elected, to reform government and end deficit spending.

In July the Democratic National Convention nominated Governor Bill Clinton of Arkansas for the presidency and Senator Al Gore of Tennessee for the vice presidency. Clinton called for greater emphasis on training for high-technology jobs, education, and technology, and for a program of national health insurance.

In August the Republican National Convention renominated President Bush and Vice President Dan Quayle.

The economic indicators did little to support Bush's argument that the recession was over, and he and Quayle failed in their attempts to portray Clinton as simply another "tax and spend liberal." In November Clinton defeated Bush, winning 370 electoral votes to Bush's 168. Perot won no electoral votes, but he received more than 19 million popular votes, the most for a third-party candidate since Theodore Roosevelt in 1912.

A feature of the 1992 balloting was the election of four women to Senate seats, bringing the total to six, the most ever, including the first black female elected to that office. In the balloting for the House of Representatives, the number of women elected to Congress rose to 47; African Americans to 38; and Hispanic Americans to 17, more than double the existing number.

Clinton took office January 20, 1993, with the presidency and both houses of Congress controlled by the same political party for the first time in twelve years.

Early in his administration Clinton seemed to become sidetracked by issues that had not been central to his campaign, such as ending the ban on homosexuals serving in the military. He was also hurt by several ill-advised and ultimately unsuccessful nominations for high-level government positions. However, his administration soon focused its efforts on passage of a budget bill incorporating tax increases and spending cuts to reduce the federal deficit by $500 billion over five years. The bill was passed by Congress on August 7, 1993, and signed by Clinton on August 10. After passage of the budget bill, the Clinton administration focused on ratification of the NAFTA agreement and introduction of a national health insurance program, whose formulation had been overseen by Hillary Rodham Clinton, President Clinton's wife. The NAFTA bill passed by a narrow vote in November 1993, but the health insurance bill was killed before it reached the Senate or House floors. In September 1994, Senate majority leader George Mitchell announced that he would not introduce health care reform legislation during the current session of Congress. Congressional leaders from both parties declared that they would renew their efforts for health care reform in 1995, after the midterm elections.

In 1993 Justice Byron R. White retired from the Supreme Court. Clinton nominated Ruth Bader Ginsburg, who was confirmed by Congress on August 3 and sworn in on August 10, becoming the second woman justice of the Supreme Court. In April of 1994, Supreme Court justice Harry A. Blackmun announced that he would retire at the end of the Court's term, on June 30, after 24 years of service. President Clinton nominated Judge Stephen G. Breyer of the First Circuit Court of Appeals. After relatively smooth confirmation hearings, Breyer was approved unanimously by the Senate Judiciary Committee on July 19 and confirmed by the full Senate on July 29.

In other matters, Clinton moved to extend foreign assistance to Russia and Eastern Europe and to help the UN establish peace and stability in Somalia and in war-torn Bosnia. At home, Clinton signed a $6.2 billion relief bill to aid Americans in the flood-ravaged Midwest. **Midterm elections.** In 1994 the Clinton administration achieved some notable successes but seemed unable to convince the American electorate of their significance. The administration received a boost in popularity for its role in securing the historic accord on Palestinian autonomy signed by Israel and the Palestine Liberation Organization in May 1994. President Clinton's use of American military force to restore

THE SPEED AND DECISIVENESS of the air strikes and smart missiles played a significant role in the Gulf War.

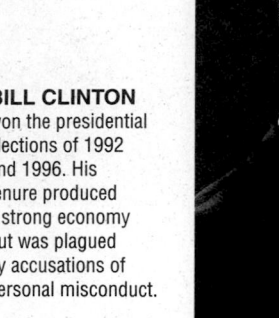

BILL CLINTON won the presidential elections of 1992 and 1996. His tenure produced a strong economy but was plagued by accusations of personal misconduct.

center
US

centre
Brit.

Haitian president Jean-Bertrand Aristide to power in September received only mild approval.

The U.S. signing, shortly before the national elections, of the General Agreement on Tariffs and Trade (GATT), by which some 124 signatory nations agreed to reduce tariffs and trade restrictions over a period of 20 years, was hobbled by a delay in ratification in Congress. Some members voiced concern that the extremely complex treaty had not been examined carefully enough. Others claimed that some of its provisions, notably the establishment of a World Trade Organization to regulate treaty provisions and arbitrate disputes among signatory nations, would impinge on U.S. sovereignty. However, after the election President Clinton was able to secure majorities among both parties in both houses of Congress in support of the treaty. On November 29, 1994, the House approved the accord 288 to 146, and on December 1 the Senate approved it 76 to 24. Passage of GATT was viewed as a major achievement.

In domestic affairs, the administration pointed with pride to numerous signs of a strong economy. However, both Congress and the administration were hurt by their inability to deal successfully with such issues as health care and campaign finance reform.

In September of 1994 some 300 Republican candidates for Congress signed a so-called "Contract with America," pledging that within the first 100 days of a new Republican-controlled Congress, they would introduce legislation to cut taxes, increase defense spending, overhaul the welfare system, and secure constitutional amendments to balance the budget and establish congressional term limits.

In the elections on November 8, the Republicans gained control of both houses of Congress, for the first time since 1952, taking a 227 to 199 (with one

independent) majority in the House of Representatives and a 53 to 46 majority in the Senate.

Clinton redefined. In the aftermath of the 1994 midterm elections, President Clinton moved toward the political center, focusing on a few important issues and defending the issues and programs he felt were threatened by the Republican-controlled Congress.

The Republicans in the House of Representatives had made it clear that they sought to dismantle whole agencies, departments, and programs of the federal government and to force Clinton to accept plans for balancing the federal budget in seven years. In late 1995 President Clinton vetoed the budget passed by Congress, vowing to prevent overzealous Republican cuts in funding for Medicare, the environment, education, and health. The result of the standoff was that funding authorization for the government ran out and much of the federal government ground to a halt. A second shutdown occurred in December. Polls showed that increasing numbers of citizens blamed not the Clinton administration but the Republicans for the shutdown and the legislative deadlock. The popularity of House majority leader Newt Gingrich plummeted, and the president's standing began to recover.

President Clinton's moves to partially accommodate the Republican opposition cost him the support of some members of his party. He accepted the Republican plan to balance the federal budget by the year 2002 after failing to gain any support for a less draconian ten-year plan. In August 1996, President Clinton signed into law a sweeping reform of the welfare system that limited benefits, instituted work requirements, and assigned greater responsibility for financing and administering welfare programs to the states.

In other legislation, the Senate ratified the START II strategic arms reduction treaty in January 1996. In August, President Clinton signed legislation raising the minimum wage to $5.15 an hour, effective July 1, 1997.

In international affairs, the Clinton administration scored a major breakthrough when it brokered a Bosnian peace accord. In November 1995, the leaders of Bosnia, Croatia, and Serbia met near Dayton, Ohio, and agreed to a peace plan that called for a UN peacekeeping force of 60,000. President Clinton announced that some 20,000 U.S. troops would take part in the peace mission, but stipulated that all American forces would be withdrawn within a year. The plan received the support of Clinton's eventual opponent in the 1996 presidential election, Senate majority leader Robert Dole.

After securing the Republican nomination for the presidency, Dole retired from the Senate to campaign full time. The keystone of the Republican campaign was a 15 percent tax cut to stimulate economic growth. Voters greeted the proposal with little support, and the energetic attacks on President Clinton

by H. Ross Perot, candidate of the fledgling Reform Party, did not help Dole either. On November 5, 1996, Clinton was reelected with a 49 percent plurality, becoming the first Democratic president since Franklin D. Roosevelt to be elected to a second term. The Republicans failed to win the presidency but kept their majority in the House of Representatives and increased the Senate majority to 55 seats to the Democrats' 45.

Much of Clinton's second term in office was marred by his legal difficulties. During the course of a sexual harassment lawsuit brought against Clinton by Paula Jones, a former Arkansas state employee, Independent Counsel Kenneth Starr accused Clinton of lying to a federal grand jury about his relationship with Monica Lewinsky, a former White House intern. After months of denials and sordid revelations, Clinton finally admitted the affair with Lewinsky. On December 19, 1998, he became only the second president to be impeached (accused), on charges of perjury and obstruction of justice. He was acquitted on February 12, 1999.

In 2000, former vice president Al Gore ran against Texas governor George W. Bush for the presidency. On election night, November 7, after winning Florida's 25 electoral votes, Bush was declared the winner by news networks, and Gore called Bush to concede. Hours later, the Florida vote looked too close to call and Gore rescinded his concession. After weeks of complicated legal wrangling, the United States Supreme Court ruled 5-4 to stop the recounts in Florida, which in effect accorded the state to Bush by a margin of some 537 votes. The next day, December 13, Gore conceded again. Bush was inaugurated on January 20, 2001.

GEORGE W. BUSH and his father, George H. Bush, are the second father and son to be elected U.S. president. The others were John Adams and John Quincy Adams.

The States and Territories

The states that make up the United States each have considerable independence in pursuing their own affairs, and they are given important powers in the Constitution itself. In recent years, the federal government has grown to be more powerful than the individual states. But in spite of this, the states have maintained a strong sense of diversity, owing to a combination of geographical, historical, social, political, and economic differences.

Regional differences have played an important part in the development of the United States. They have encouraged rapid development of new land and new resources and promoted a sense of cultural diversity and tolerance. On the other hand, these same regional differences also led to the nation's greatest tragedy—the Civil War, in which social, political, and economic differences were resolved by force.

In this section, you will find first the flags of the states and territories, then information on the U.S. flag. Next you will find a general overview of the states, divided into 11 regions. A general overview of the regions is presented first, with regional maps showing how member states fit together. Then information on each state is presented separately. The regions are arranged geographically in order of appearance; the states follow in alphabetical order.

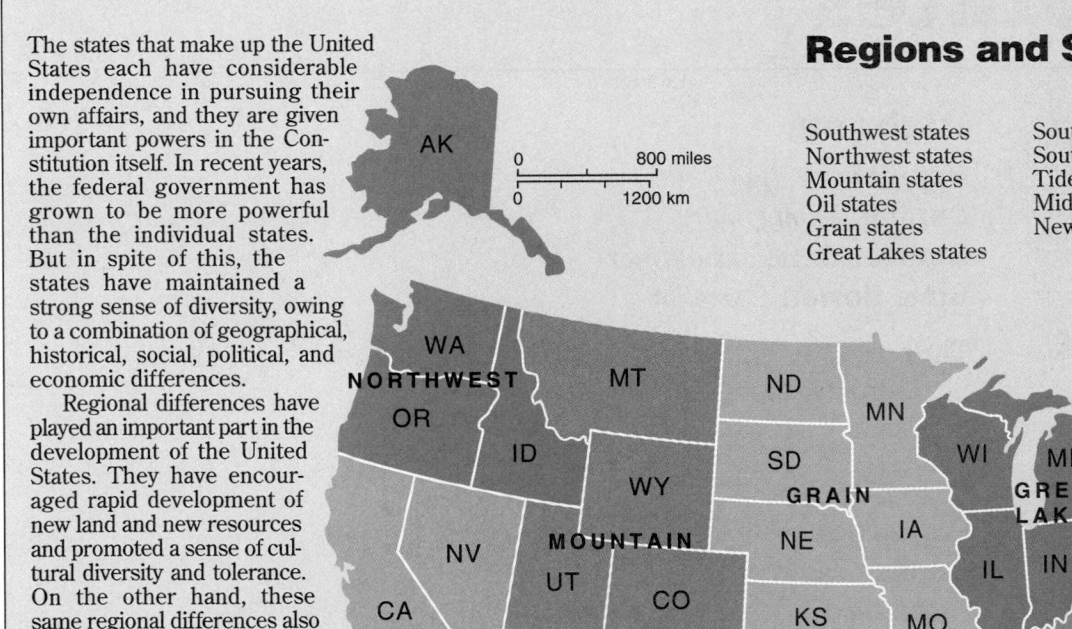

Regions and States

Southwest states
Northwest states
Mountain states
Oil states
Grain states
Great Lakes states

South-Central states
South Atlantic states
Tidewater states
Mid-Atlantic states
New England states

Where To Find Each State

Flags of the United States

Alabama

Population: *4,447,100*
Capital: *Montgomery*
State bird: *Yellowhammer*
State flower: *Camellia*

The red "X" resembles the Civil War Southern battle flag feature, St. Andrew's cross.

Alaska

Population: *626,932*
Capital: *Juneau*
State bird: *Willow ptarmigan*
State flower: *Forget-me-not*

The North Star indicates Alaska's status as the northernmost state. The Big Dipper, or Great Bear, is a symbol of strength.

Arizona

Population: *5,130,632*
Capital: *Phoenix*
State bird: *Cactus wren*
State flower: *Saguaro cactus blossom*

A copper-colored star denotes Arizona's status as the largest copper producer in the U.S. Thirteen rays represent a setting sun and original colonies. Colors refer to the state's heritages: blue and yellow are state colors; blue and red are U.S. colors; and red and yellow are colors of Spanish Conquistadors.

Arkansas

Population: *2,673,400*
Capital: *Little Rock*
State bird: *Mockingbird*
State flower: *Apple blossom*

The diamond represents diamond mining. The 25 white stars represent the state's position as the 25th state. The three lower blue stars refer to three things: France, Spain, and the U.S., the countries that owned the state prior to its admittance to the Union; the date of the Louisiana Purchase, 1803; the state's being the third formed from the Louisiana Purchase. The remaining blue star stands for the Confederacy.

California

Population: *33,871,648*
Capital: *Sacramento*
State bird: *California quail*
State flower: *California poppy*

The flag's grizzly bear, the official state animal, symbolizes courage.

Colorado

Population: *4,301,261*
Capital: *Denver*
State bird: *Lark bunting*
State flower: *White and lavender columbine*

The colors symbolize features of the state's landscape—blue for clear skies, white for snow-capped mountains, red for the color of the earth, and gold for the sun.

Connecticut

Population: *3,405,565*
Capital: *Hartford*
State bird: *American robin*
State flower: *Mountain laurel*

Grape vines refer to the wild grape vines that grow throughout the state and also to the colony that was transplanted from Europe to the New World.

Delaware

Population: *783,600*
Capital: *Dover*
State bird: *Blue hen chicken*
State flower: *Peach blossom*

The wheat, corn, and ox represent agricultural prosperity. The date, December 7, 1787, is when Delaware became the first state to ratify the Constitution. A ship represents the ship-building industry and coastal commerce. A farmer represents contributions of the farming industry and a soldier stands for the state's commitment to the fight for freedom.

Florida

Population: *15,982,378*
Capital: *Tallahassee*
State bird: *Mockingbird*
State flower: *Orange blossom*

The state's great seal and motto are combined. The great seal depicts a Native American woman surrounded by a beautiful Florida landscape of water, beach, palms, and sun.

Georgia

Population: *8,186,453*
Capital: *Atlanta*
State bird: *Brown thrasher*
State flower: *Cherokee rose*

The current design incorporates bands of red and white and a blue canton with the Georgia coat of arms and 13 stars which represent the original states. Debate continues over the design. It was changed in 2001 and again in 2003. A referendum will be held to decide which of these will be the final design.

Hawaii

Population: *1,211,537*
Capital: *Honolulu*
State bird: *Hawaiian goose*
State flower: *Yellow hibiscus*

Commissioned when Hawaii was an independent kingdom, this flag has represented Hawaii throughout its history as a kingdom, territory, republic, and state. The eight stripes represent the islands that make up the state.

Idaho

Population: *1,293,953*
Capital: *Boise*
State bird: *Mountain bluebird*
State flower: *Syringa*

The state seal includes a robed woman who represents liberty and justice. A man holds a pickaxe and shovel, representing mining. The Shoshone River winds through woods that represent the timber industry, and a plowman represents the agriculture industry.

Illinois

Population: *12,419,293*
Capital: *Springfield*
State bird: *Cardinal*
State flower: *Purple violet*

The state seal includes an American eagle holding a shield reminiscent of the national flag. The 13 stars on the shield represent the original colonies. The dates 1868 and 1818 are the years the state seal was adopted and Illinois became the 21st state, respectively.

Indiana

Population: *6,080,485*
Capital: *Indianapolis*
State bird: *Cardinal*
State flower: *Peony*

A flaming torch symbolizes liberty. Nineteen stars signify Indiana's status as the 19th state. Thirteen outer stars signify original states. Five inner stars represent the next five states. The largest star represents Indiana.

Iowa

Population: *2,926,324*
Capital: *Des Moines*
State bird: *Eastern goldfinch*
State flower: *Wild rose*

The red, white, and blue honor the colors of France, which twice ruled the area, and of the U.S., which received the area as part of the Louisiana Purchase. An eagle symbolizes protection.

Kansas

Population: *2,688,418*
Capital: *Topeka*
State bird: *Western meadowlark*
State flower: *Native sunflower*

The state seal depicts the Kansas landscape. Thirty-four stars represent Kansas's position as 34th state to join the Union.

27 North America

Kentucky

Population: *4,041,769*
Capital: *Frankfort*
State bird: *Cardinal*
State flower: *Goldenrod*

The flag features the state seal, which shows two men exchanging a handshake. They represent the rural pioneers and the urban population, illustrating the state motto, "United We Stand, Divided We Fall."

Louisiana

Population: *4,468,976*
Capital: *Baton Rouge*
State bird: *Eastern brown pelican*
State flower: *Magnolia*

A pelican mother is depicted sacrificing herself to feed her young, symbolizing the state's commitment to boundless giving.

Maine

Population: *1,274,923*
Capital: *Augusta*
State bird: *Chickadee*
State flower: *White pine cone and tassel*

A coat of arms features a white pine, the official state tree. A farmer, representing the land, and a sailor, representing the sea, support the shield. The North Star represents Maine's northernmost status at the time the crest was chosen.

Maryland

Population: *5,296,486*
Capital: *Annapolis*
State bird: *Baltimore oriole*
State flower: *Black-eyed Susan*

The design features the coat of arms of Maryland's two founding families, the Calverts (the checkered design) and the Crosslands.

Massachusetts

Population: *6,349,097*
Capital: *Boston*
State bird: *Black-capped chickadee*
State flower: *Mayflower*

The coat of arms depicts a Native American, representing peace. The white star symbolizes Massachusetts. An arm wielding a sword corresponds to the state motto, "By the Sword We Seek Peace, but Peace Only Under Liberty."

Michigan

Population: *9,938,444*
Capital: *Lansing*
State bird: *Robin*
State flower: *Apple blossom*

The state seal depicts a peninsula and includes the state motto, which refers to the state's location between the Great Lakes.

Minnesota

Population: *4,919,479*
Capital: *St. Paul*
State bird: *Common loon*
State flower: *Pink and white lady slipper*

The state seal is surrounded by a design of 19 stars, referring to the state's position as the 19th state. Three dates are given: 1819, the arrival of the first colonial settlers; 1858, statehood attained; and 1893, flag adopted.

Mississippi

Population: *2,844,658*
Capital: *Jackson*
State bird: *Mockingbird*
State flower: *Magnolia*

A red, white, and blue design honors U.S. heritage. In the upper corner is a reproduction of the Confederate flag. Thirteen stars represent the original colonies.

27 North America

Missouri

Population: *5,595,211*
Capital: *Jefferson City*
State bird: *Bluebird*
State flower: *White hawthorn blossom*

Twenty-four stars around the state seal represent Missouri's status as 24th state. Roman numerals signifying 1820 on the state seal refer to the year of the Missouri Compromise.

Montana

Population: *902,195*
Capital: *Helena*
State bird: *Western meadowlark*
State flower: *Bitterroot*

The state seal is displayed, which depicts a Montana landscape and includes references to agricultural pursuits of the pioneers. A banner reading "Oro Y Plata," Spanish for "gold and silver," reflects the state's nickname, "The Treasure State."

Nebraska

Population: *1,711,263*
Capital: *Lincoln*
State bird: *Western meadowlark*
State flower: *Goldenrod*

The state seal is shown with the date, March 1, 1867—the date statehood was attained. Other themes include travel and agriculture.

Nevada

Population: *1,998,257*
Capital: *Carson City*
State bird: *Mountain bluebird*
State flower: *Sagebrush*

A crest located in the corner on a cobalt blue background includes branches of sagebrush, the state flower. Also noted are the words "Battle Born," referring to the many struggles in the area during the War of Mexico.

New Hampshire

Population: *1,235,786*
Capital: *Concord*
State bird: *Purple finch*
State flower: *Purple lilac*

The state seal on the flag depicts a frigate and a granite boulder. The granite is a reference to the nickname, "The Granite State." The 1776 date refers to the formation of the U.S., and nine stars interspersed around the seal represent New Hampshire's status as the ninth state.

New Jersey

Population: *8,414,350*
Capital: *Trenton*
State bird: *Eastern goldfinch*
State flower: *Common meadow violet*

The state seal depicts ploughs and a horse's head symbolizing agriculture and a knight's helmet signifying sovereignty. The 1776 date of the signing of the Declaration of Independence is on the scroll. Two female figures personify "Liberty and Prosperity," the state motto. A fruit- and vegetable-filled cornucopia represents the abundance of the land.

New Mexico

Population: *1,819,046*
Capital: *Santa Fe*
State bird: *Roadrunner*
State flower: *Yucca*

A Native American Zia Pueblo sun symbol is depicted. Four sunbursts symbolize the four gifts the Zia people attributed to their divine maker: the seasons, the stages of life, the stages of each day, and the directions.

New York

Population: *18,976,457*
Capital: *Albany*
State bird: *Bluebird*
State flower: *Rose*

The state seal is depicted. Women representing Liberty and Justice are shown above a banner with the state motto, which translates as "Ever Upward," signifying the state's commitment to ongoing self-improvement.

27 North America

North Carolina

Population: *8,049,313*
Capital: *Raleigh*
State bird: *Northern cardinal*
State flower: *Flowering dogwood*

The red, white, and blue represent the U.S. colors. The dates of the Mecklenberg Declaration (1775) and the Halifax Resolve (1776) are noted.

North Dakota

Population: *642,200*
Capital: *Bismarck*
State bird: *Western meadowlark*
State flower: *Wild prairie rose*

An American eagle holding an olive branch and a bundle of arrows is depicted. Thirteen stars above the eagle represent the first 13 states.

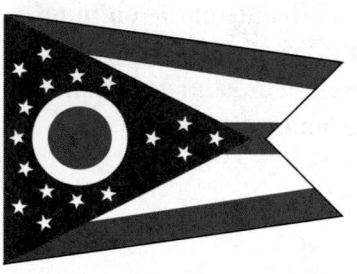

Ohio

Population: *11,353,140*
Capital: *Columbus*
State bird: *Cardinal*
State flower: *Scarlet carnation*

The stripes represent the roads and waterways of the state and the blue represents hills and valleys. The white "O" represents the state's name, as well as its nickname, "The Buckeye State," and its official tree, "the buckeye." Seventeen stars refer to its position as 17th state to enter the Union.

Oklahoma

Population: *3,450,654*
Capital: *Oklahoma City*
State bird: *Scissor-tailed flycatcher*
State flower: *Mistletoe*

A Native American war shield is depicted. A Native American peace pipe and an olive branch form a cross across the shield and represent good will between Native Americans and settlers.

Oregon

Population: *3,421,399*
Capital: *Salem*
State bird: *Western meadowlark*
State flower: *Oregon grape*

The state shield is featured surrounded by 33 stars, representing Oregon's status as the 33rd state. Depicted are two ships, representing trade, and tools, representing farming and mining. An American eagle represents protection and unity.

Pennsylvania

Population: *12,281,054*
Capital: *Harrisburg*
State bird: *Ruffed grouse*
State flower: *Mountain laurel*

The state coat of arms is depicted, with a shield representing aspects of the state. Depicted are bundles of wheat and a plough, representing agriculture, and a ship, representing industry and commerce.

Rhode Island

Population: *1,048,319*
Capital: *Providence*
State bird: *Rhode Island Red chicken*
State flower: *Violet*

The anchor represents the Atlantic Ocean, indicating the importance of the Atlantic to the state's economy and landscape. Thirteen stars represent the original colonies. "Hope" is the state's motto.

South Carolina

Population: *4,012,012*
Capital: *Columbia*
State bird: *Carolina wren*
State flower: *Yellow jessamine*

The design represents South Carolina's troops in the Revolutionary War. The blue in the background is the color of the troop uniforms, the crescent moon was the emblem on the soldiers' caps, and a palmetto tree represents the successful defense of a palmetto log fort on Sullivan's Island.

27 North America

South Dakota

Population: *754,844*
Capital: *Pierre*
State bird: *Chinese ring-necked pheasant*
State flower: *Pasque*

The state seal is featured, depicting a farmer, cattle, and a steamboat. A jagged yellow border surrounding the seal gives the impression of the sun lying behind it, representing the former nickname, "The Sunshine State."

Tennessee

Population *5,689,283*
Capital: *Nashville*
State bird: *Mockingbird*
State flower: *Iris*

The red background symbolizes courage and memorializes bloodshed, honoring the state's volunteers in the War of 1812. Three stars represent the three geographic divisions of the state, united by an encircling white band.

Texas

Population: *20,851,820*
Capital: *Austin*
State bird: *Mockingbird*
State flower: *Bluebonnet*

The colors match those on the national flag. Red represents bravery; white represents purity; blue represents loyalty. The large star represents Texas as "The Lone Star State," its nickname.

Utah

Population: *2,233,169*
Capital: *Salt Lake City*
State bird: *California gull*
State flower: *Sego lily*

The state seal depicts a beehive, representative of the hard-working nature of bees and symbolic of the state motto, "Industry." Sego lilies represent peace. Unity and protection are symbolized by flags of a stars-and-stripes design. Featured dates are 1847, when state founder Brigham Young led Mormon followers to establish a settlement, and 1896, when Utah became the 45th state.

Vermont

Population: *608,827*
Capital: *Montpelier*
State bird: *Hermit thrush*
State flower: *Red clover*

The coat of arms depicts a New England landscape on a shield, alluding to the diverse offerings of the state's outdoors. The scene includes a cow, representative of the dairy industry, and bundles of grain, representing agriculture. A stag's head represents the abundant wildlife.

Virginia

Population: *7,078,515*
Capital: *Richmond*
State bird: *Northern cardinal*
State flower: *American dogwood*

The state seal depicts the results of a battle between the concepts of virtue and tyranny. The personification of virtue stands victorious atop a defeated tyranny. The state motto, which translates as "Thus Always to Tyrants," acknowledges that the virtuous will always overcome the tyrannical.

Washington

Population: *5,894,121*
Capital: *Olympia*
State bird: *Willow goldfinch*
State flower: *Coast rhododendron*

The state seal features a portrait of George Washington and indicates the date, 1889, when the state entered the Union.

West Virginia

Population: *1,808,344*
Capital: *Charleston*
State bird: *Cardinal*
State flower: *Rhododendron*

The state seal features a shield being held by a farmer, representing the agriculture industry, and a miner, representing the mining industry. June 20, 1863, indicates when statehood was attained.

27 North America

Wisconsin

Population: *5,363,675*
Capital: *Madison*
State bird: *Robin*
State flower: *Wood violet*

The state coat of arms depicts a sailor and a miner holding the state shield. The shield features the economic pursuits of agriculture, mining, industry, and navigation.

Wyoming

Population: *493,782*
Capital: *Cheyenne*
State bird: *Meadowlark*
State flower: *Indian paintbrush*

A native bison is featured, on which the state seal is printed, symbolizing the custom of branding cattle. The woman on the seal represents the state motto, "Equal Rights," the men represent ranching and mining. The words Livestock," "Grain," "Oil," and "Mines" represent the state's wealth. The embossed 44 indicates the status as the 44th state. The years 1869, when Wyoming became a territory, and 1890, when it became a state, are shown.

American Samoa

Population: *69,000*
Capital: *Pago Pago*
Bird: *None*
Flower: *None*

A bald eagle clutching a uatogi (war club) and a fue (ritual staff), Samoan symbols of power, represents the protection and partnership of the U.S.

Guam

Population: *161,000*
Capital: *Agana*
Bird: *Tottot*
Flower: *Bougainvillea*

The blue background represents the Pacific Ocean; a red border represents courage. The coconut tree on the seal, growing on a sandy beach, signifies Guam's ability to prosper under any conditions.

Puerto Rico

Population: *3,863,000*
Capital: *San Juan*
Bird: *Reinita*
Flower: *Maga*

Three red stripes symbolize the branches of government; two white stripes, individual freedom and the rights that protect it. A blue triangle represents the government and the white star Puerto Rico itself.

U.S. Virgin Islands

Population: *123,000*
Capital: *Charlotte Amalie*
Bird: *Bananaquit*
Flower: *Yellow elder*

An eagle grasps in one talon three arrows representing the three major islands, St. Croix, St. John, and St. Thomas. The eagle is protected by a shield featuring an American red, white, and blue stars-and-stripes design.

United States of America

Population: *281,421,906*
Capital: *Washington, D.C.*
Bird: *Bald eagle*
Flower: *Rose*

The 13 stripes symbolize the original colonies; the 50 stars represent the states of the Union. Red represents hardiness, valor, and courage; white symbolizes purity and innocence; blue signifies vigilance, perseverance, and justice.

27 North America

Display and Care of the United States Flag

Folding the Flag

Fold the flag in half width-wise twice. Beginning at the striped end, fold up a triangle and repeat until only the end of the union (the blue field of stars) shows. Tuck the last bit into the other folds to secure it. The final folded flag resembles a cocked hat, with only white stars on a blue field showing.

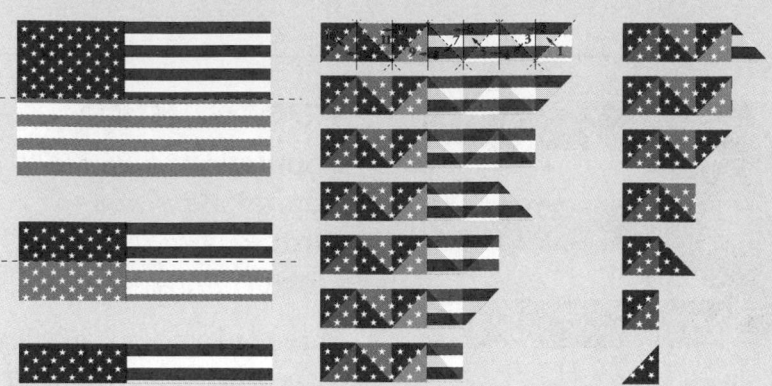

Displaying the Flag

(1) The U.S. flag is flown upside down only as a distress signal. (2) When suspended over a street, the flag should be vertical, with the union to the north in an east-west street or to the east in a north-south street. (3) When displayed in a window, the union should be to the left of an outside observer. (4) When used to cover a casket, the union should be at the head and over the left shoulder. Remove the flag before lowering the casket into the grave.

(5) When flown at half-staff, the flag should be raised to the peak for an instant, then lowered to half-staff. The flag should again be raised to the peak briefly before it is lowered for the day.

(6) When flags or pennants of states, cities, or societies are flown with the U.S. flag on the same halyard, the U.S. flag should fly at the peak, above all others. If flown from adjacent staffs, the U.S. flag is to be hoisted first and lowered last.

(7) When the U.S. flag and the flags of a number of states, cities, or societies are grouped and displayed from staffs, the U.S. flag should be at the center and at the highest point of the grouping.

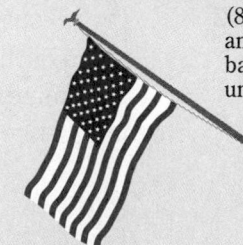

(8) When displayed at an angle from a windowsill, balcony, or building, the union should be placed at the peak (unless the flag is at half-staff).

Caring for the Flag

(1) When the flag is lowered, no part of it should touch the ground or any other object. (2) Be sure the flag is dry before storing it. Outdoor flags should be correctly folded and sealed inside moisture-proof plastic bags and then stored in a cool, dry place. (3) Iron-on patches may be used to repair small tears and holes. The patches are available in many fabric departments. (4) A flag that is worn beyond repair should be burned, beyond recognition as a flag, in a modest but blazing fire. This should be done with dignity and respect. Most American Legion posts regularly conduct dignified flag-burning ceremonies, often on Flag Day (June 14).

United States Flag

The design of the United States flag evolved over a period of roughly 200 years. Today, every American easily recognizes the "stars and bars." Thirteen stripes, which symbolize the thirteen original colonies, lie horizontally; seven are colored red, and six are white. In the upper corner nearest the staff, there is a rectangular blue field (called a "canton") that holds the 50 stars that represent all the states of the Union. Congress has defined the symbolic values of the colors as follows: white represents purity and innocence; red symbolizes hardiness, valor, and courage; blue signifies vigilance, perseverance, and justice.

Most Americans know the legend giving Betsy Ross the distinction of being the first person to produce the American flag. According to the popular myth, which originated with the testimony of William Canby (Ms. Ross's grandson), General George Washington came to her Philadelphia home in the summer of 1776. He requested that the seamstress sew the first flag with the aid of a sketch he brought along. Ms. Ross supposedly followed his design exactly, with only a slight modification—she reduced the number of points on the stars from six to five.

Some still believe the Betsy Ross legend, but it is most likely untrue. General Washington was in Philadelphia at the alleged time, but he was on urgent military business, making the visit unlikely. Historians have attributed the design to other individuals several times without success. Now, it is widely held that the first flag was designed and produced as a group effort.

While the origin of the first flag's design and production is unclear, it is known that Congress passed the First Flag Act on June 14, 1777, shortly after the Declaration of Independence was ratified. It specified that the flag should have 13 stripes, alternately red and white in color, as well as a blue field containing 13 stars to represent a "new constellation." The arrangement of the design, however, was not explicitly worded. Important pieces of information, such as proportions of elements and the direction of stripes, were not included. This ambiguity resulted in considerable diversity among the first flags. The stars appeared in a number of different arrangements, including rows, circles, and stars. The number of points on the stars varied.

Of course, the United States grew from the 13 states that originally formed the Union. As more areas gained statehood, a debate regarding the appropriate number of stripes for the flag ensued. Many people believed that the number of stripes should reflect the number of states, while others argued that the change was superfluous and an unnecessary expense. The controversy officially ended May 1, 1795, when Congress passed the Second Flag Act, which called for 15 stripes and 15 stars to reflect the recent additions of Vermont and Kentucky. This was the second official version of the national flag, but flags continued to be produced differently; uniformity in design was lacking. Incidentally, this design inspired Francis Scott Key to write the "Star-Spangled Banner," which became the national anthem in 1931.

February 4, 1783, marked the end of the Revolutionary War, and the U.S. flag gained recognition throughout the world, lending it new importance. The Union continued to grow, and the old debate over the number of stars and stripes resurfaced. As states joined the Union, flag designs varied even more. Eventually, it was obvious that the stripe-to-state ratio was becoming unmanageable; the stripes were so thin that they were difficult to distinguish from any distance. In 1818, President James Monroe passed the Third Flag Act, which settled the dispute and has directed the flag's design ever since. The new legislation set the number of stripes at the original 13. The second section of the Act allowed for the addition of a star each time a state was admitted to the Union. It also stipulated that the change in number would always take effect on the July 4 following admittance. Unfortunately, the text did not specify the arrangement of the stars, so the flag still lacked a definitive design.

At the time of the Third Flag Act, there were 20 stars. The following year, another star was added to signify the admittance of Illinois. July 4, 1820, saw two more additions, representing Alabama and Maine. The 24th star, representing Missouri, was added two years later. It wasn't until 1836 that another, symbolizing the statehood of Arkansas, was added, followed by another star in 1837 for Michigan. In 1845, a star was added for Florida; in 1846, another was added for Texas. The additions of Iowa and Wisconsin came in 1847 and 1848, respectively. California gained a star in 1851. Minnesota assumed statehood in 1858, and Oregon became the 33rd star in 1859.

Kansas, West Virginia, and Nevada gained stars in 1861, 1863, and 1865, respectively. The Civil War also ended in 1865; notably, despite the secession of a number of states, the number of stars on the official design was not altered. The start of the Reconstruction era saw admittance of Nebraska in 1867. A star was added for Colorado in 1877. Five stars, symbolizing North Dakota, South Dakota, Washington, Idaho, and Montana, were added in 1890, for a total of 43. The 44th star, Wyoming's, was added in 1891, and Utah was added in 1896.

Oklahoma's star came in 1908, while two stars for New Mexico and Arizona were added in 1912. Also in 1912 the flag finally gained specifications for its design. President William Taft's executive order of June 24, 1912, set the flag's width and length, and the measurements of all the design's elements. This order led to a much-needed uniformity in design. In 1959, Alaska was added. Hawaii, the last state to join the Union, added the 50th star in 1960—resulting in the 27th, and most current, design.

Several traditions and customs surround the United States flag; Congress established the definitive guidelines in the 1942 Flag Code. It detailed the conventions for proper display and handling. Generally, the flag should be displayed from sunrise to sunset; if it flies in the dark, appropriate lighting should be provided. The flag should be raised briskly and lowered ceremoniously. In addition, the flag should not be used for advertising purposes nor be embroidered on disposable or inappropriate items (e.g., handkerchiefs or cushions). Finally, the Flag Code provided comprehensive instructions for its display in a variety of scenarios involving the presence of other flags.

Perhaps the most familiar tradition associated with the flag is the Pledge of Allegiance. Francis Bellamy authored the Pledge in 1892; it was written to be repeated by schoolchildren on Columbus Day. It first appeared in a publication called *The Youth's Companion* and was officially recognized by Congress in 1942.

Flag Day is another tradition related to the flag; it marks the anniversary of the First Flag Act. It was first celebrated in Connecticut June 14, 1861. The first nationwide celebration was in 1877, but it was a centennial celebration. Flag Day became an annual tradition in 1949, when it was made a national, legally observed holiday.

Southwest States

The Southwest states are California on the Pacific coast, Arizona and Nevada on California's eastern border, and the chain of Hawaiian Islands in the Pacific, 2,000 miles (3,200 kilometers) southwest of California. The continental Southwest borders the Northwest region to the north and the Mountain states to the east.

Once ignored as a barren desert region, the continental Southwest experienced a population explosion in the 20th century. In 1880 the population was less than 1 million, or about 2 percent of the U.S. total. In 2000 the population was 42.2 million, or about 15 percent of the U.S. total. The growth of California has been the most dramatic: In 1960 it became the most populous state in the country; in 2000 California's population was more than 33 million, or about 12 percent of the U.S. population. California accounts for 80 percent of the population of the entire Southwest region. It continues to add to its population each year, despite a growing movement of residents to less populous states in the West and Midwest. Nevada and Arizona, though much less populous, had the highest growth rates in the country in the 1980s. They again had the nation's highest growth rate in the 1990s.

The land.   Two principal topographical features unite the continental Southwest: the Great Basin plateau and the Colorado River. The Great Basin dominates Nevada and touches both California and Arizona. It is home to some of the major desert areas in the United States, including the Mojave Desert in California and the Sonoran Desert in Arizona.

All three states have borders formed by the Colorado River, the principal freshwater resource in the region. Where it crosses the Great Basin in northern Arizona, the Colorado has created the Grand Canyon, 217 miles (349 kilometers) long and some 1,500 feet (457 meters) deep. Dams along the Colorado are also an important source of hydroelectric power.

The Southwest also includes significant mountain ranges, notably the Sierra Nevadas along the California-Nevada border and the Coastal Ranges along the California coastline. Hawaii, the only state not part of the North American continental landmass, is a geographically remote cluster of volcanic islands.

Climate.   The climate of the continental Southwest varies with distance from the sea and elevation. The coastal regions of northern and central California are cool and damp; the southern part of the state has a moderate year-round "Mediterranean" climate attractive to winter visitors. The Coastal Ranges separate the shore areas from the generally dry and warm interior valleys and plains. Much of the moisture blown inland from the Pacific is trapped by the high Sierra Nevadas along the California-Nevada border. Sierra peaks are snow-covered much of the year, but regions east and south of these mountains are left with the semiarid or desert conditions common in southeastern California, most of Arizona, and all of Nevada.

At low elevations, daytime temperatures in the desert may exceed 110°F (43°C), but nights in these areas are cool. At higher elevations, daytime temperatures in the 80°F (27°C) range may be followed by night temperatures dropping to 40°F (4°C). In the Hawaiian Islands, regions near sea level are dry and warm year-round, but at higher elevations rainfall is greater and temperatures cooler.

History.   The continental Southwest, alone among U.S. regions, was explored and settled from the south and west. California was first visited by a Spanish expedition led by the navigator Juan Rodríguez Cabrillo in 1542, although the first permanent mission, at San Diego, was not established until 1769. Between 1769 and 1823 the Spanish Franciscans established 21 missions in California, but settlement was sparse. Arizona was first explored in 1539 by Spaniards in quest of wealth, and in 1540 Francisco Vásquez de Coronado journeyed into Arizona looking for the mythical "Seven Cities of Cíbola." Nevada, farther inland, waited until the 1820s for its first important exploration, by the Canadian Peter Skene Ogden and Americans Jedediah Smith and Joseph Walker. In 1778 Captain

Southwest States

State	Area (Sq. Mi.)	Population 2000	Population Change 1990–2000 Number	Population Change 1990–2000 Percent	Persons per Sq. Mi.
Arizona	113,642	5,130,632	1,465,404	40.0	45.1
California	155,973	33,871,648	4,111,627	13.8	217.1
Hawaii	6,423	1,211,537	103,308	9.3	188.6
Nevada	109,806	1,998,257	796,424	66.3	18.1
Region Totals	385,844	42,212,074	6,476,763	18.1	109.4

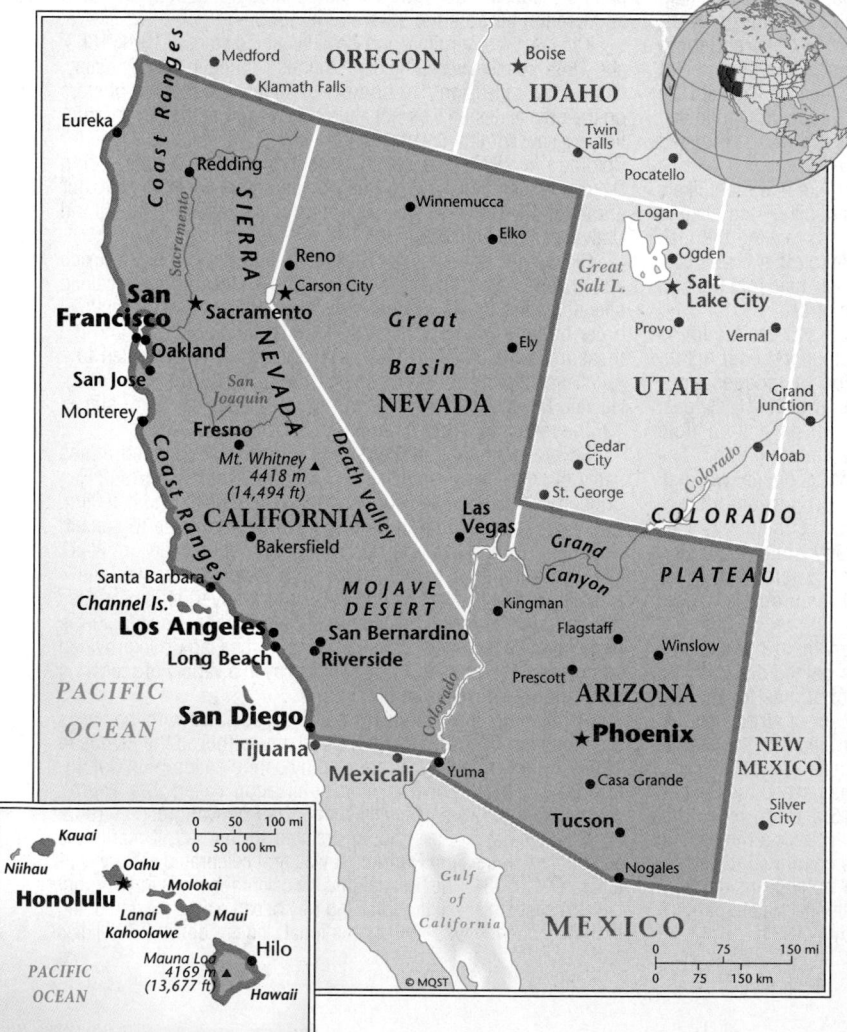

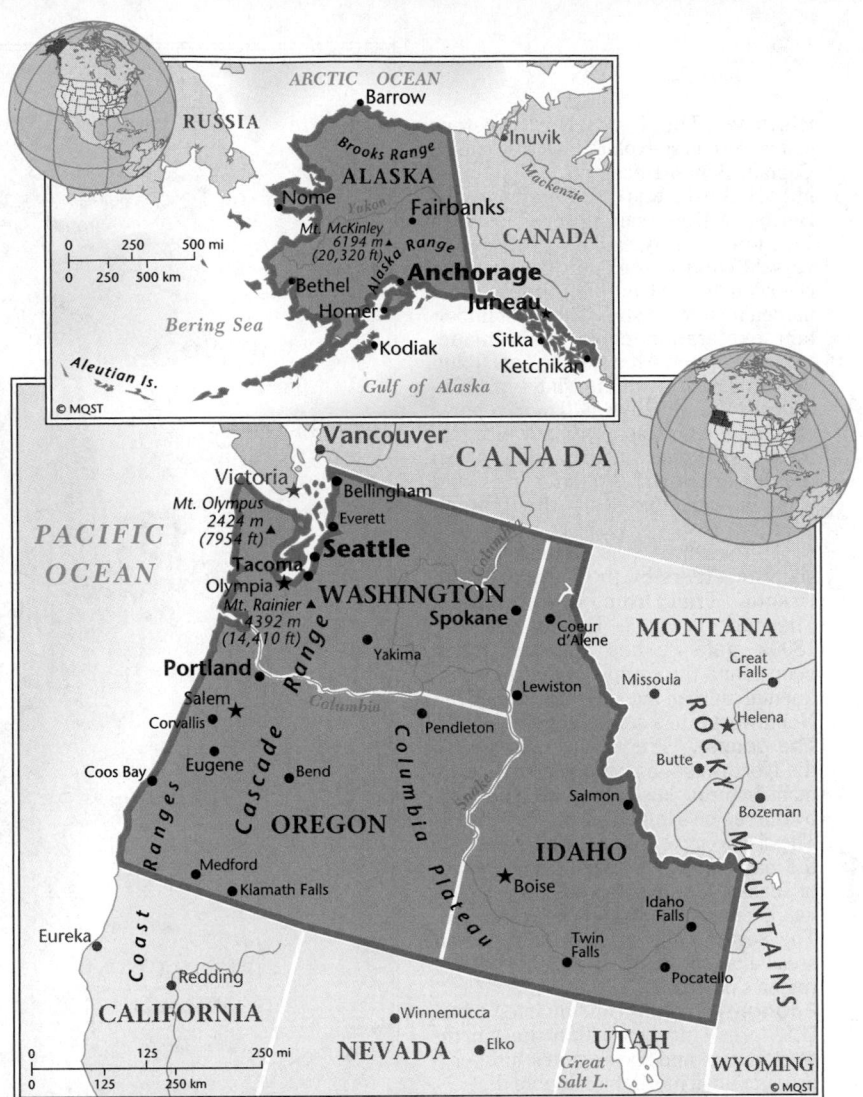

James Cook, from England, discovered the Hawaiian Islands and named them the Sandwich Islands.

Most of the continental Southwest was ceded by Mexico at the end of the Mexican War, in 1848. Immediately after becoming part of the United States, the region attracted a large influx of settlers because of a series of mining bonanzas: gold at Sutter's Mill in California in 1848; silver at the Comstock Lode in Nevada in 1859; then gold again in Tombstone, Arizona, in 1877. California and Nevada became states soon after their mining booms, but Arizona remained a territory until 1912. Hawaii was an independent nation through most of the 1800s. It was annexed by the United States in 1898, then became a U.S. territory in 1900 and a state in 1959.

The people. Today the population of the Southwest is heavily concentrated in urban areas. All of the Southwest states have urban populations far greater than the national average, and the metropolitan regions of Los Angeles, San Francisco, and San Diego in California account for more than half the Southwest's total population.

The population contains high proportions of three ethnic groups: Mexicans, who immigrate across the Mexico-U.S. border; Asians, who began settling in California in gold-rush times; and Native Americans, who are most numerous in California and Arizona. Many residents of the Southwest are recent arrivals. Only a third of those in the region were born in the states in which they now live.

Economy. Because of their varied and dramatic natural features, tourism is the largest industry in two Southwestern states, Hawaii and Nevada. It is also among the largest industries in the other two states. California is also the leading agricultural producer among the 50 states, and it is the national leader in manufacturing as well.

Northwest States

The Northwest states include Oregon and Washington on the Pacific coast, Idaho immediately inland, and Alaska separated by a coastal strip of Canada. Together, these states represent one-fifth of the total land area of the United States, yet the population is less than 4 percent of the U.S. total. The region is growing rapidly, however, and in the 1980s, the rate of population growth was greater than the national average.

The land. The principal topographical features of the Northwest are mountain ranges and powerful rivers. Oregon, Washington, and Alaska have in common coastal ranges that rise from 4,000 to over 10,000 feet (1,219 to 3,048 meters) in altitude. Another mountain range, the Cascades, is shared by Washington and Oregon. These two states are touched by the spurs of the Rocky Mountains that also cover the western half of Idaho. Alaska contains the spectacular Alaska and Brooks ranges. All Northwestern

Northwest States

State	Area (Sq. Mi.)	Population 2000	Population Change 1990–2000 Number	Population Change 1990–2000 Percent	Persons per Sq. Mi.
Alaska	570,374	626,932	76,889	14.0	1.1
Idaho	82,751	1,293,953	287,204	28.5	15.6
Oregon	96,002	3,421,399	579,078	20.4	35.6
Washington	66,581	5,894,121	1,027,429	21.1	88.5
Region Totals	815,708	11,236,405	1,970,600	19.1	13.7

states lie to the west of the Continental Divide, and their principal rivers flow toward the Pacific Ocean. The contiguous northwestern states are dominated by the Columbia River and its inland tributary, the Snake River. Alaska is traversed from east to west by the Yukon River.

The states of Washington, Oregon, and Idaho have in common upper branches of the Great Basin that covers major portions of Nevada and Utah to the south. The striking variety of relief characteristics gives the states a full range of contrasting landmarks. The extremes include the highest mountain in North America, Mt. McKinley (20,320

feet, 6,194 meters); the deepest gorge, Hell's Canyon (7,900 feet, 2,408 meters, deep) on the Snake River at the Idaho-Oregon border; the largest rain forest in the United States, on Olympic Peninsula in Washington; and the extensive, barren lava beds called Craters of the Moon, in Idaho.

Climate. The greatest influence on the climate of the Northwest is the Cascade Range. Areas west of the range along the Pacific have mild climates with heavy rainfall. Areas to the east of the Cascades are dry and have greater seasonal variations in temperature. A similar pattern holds in Alaska.

History. The lower Northwestern states were first explored by the Spanish Captain Bruno Heceta in 1775. Earlier, in 1741, Alaska was discovered by Vitus Bering, a Dane sailing for Russia. In 1792 Robert Gray, captain of the British vessel *Columbia,* sailed up the principal river of "the Oregon Country" and named it after his ship. The most important exploration came from inland, however, when Meriwether Lewis and William Clark spent the winter of 1805–1806 in the Northwest. Their reports encouraged fur trappers to advance into the region. Present boundaries between the lower Northwestern states and Canada were fixed by the Oregon Treaty of 1846.

The Northwest was first made accessible to settlers by the opening of the Oregon Trail from Independence, Missouri, in 1843. During the late 1800s, gold rushes attracted many people, and the completion of transcontinental railroad lines helped change the Northwest into a settled region.

The people. Present-day migration to the Northwest has been encouraged by manufacturing businesses made possible by the region's huge hydroelectric dams. The discovery of enormous oil deposits is the main cause of the rapid recent growth of Alaska. The Northwest's population has become increasingly concentrated. The Seattle and Portland metropolitan areas alone account for one-third of the region's population.

Economy. About one-quarter of all U.S. forestland lies within the Northwest states, and the region's lumber production is more than double that of any other region in the United States. In recent years its rank in agriculture has declined, but the value added by manufacture tripled between 1967 and 1977. Comparable growth continued throughout the 1980s and 1990s.

kilometers
US

kilometres
Brit.

center
US

centre
Brit.

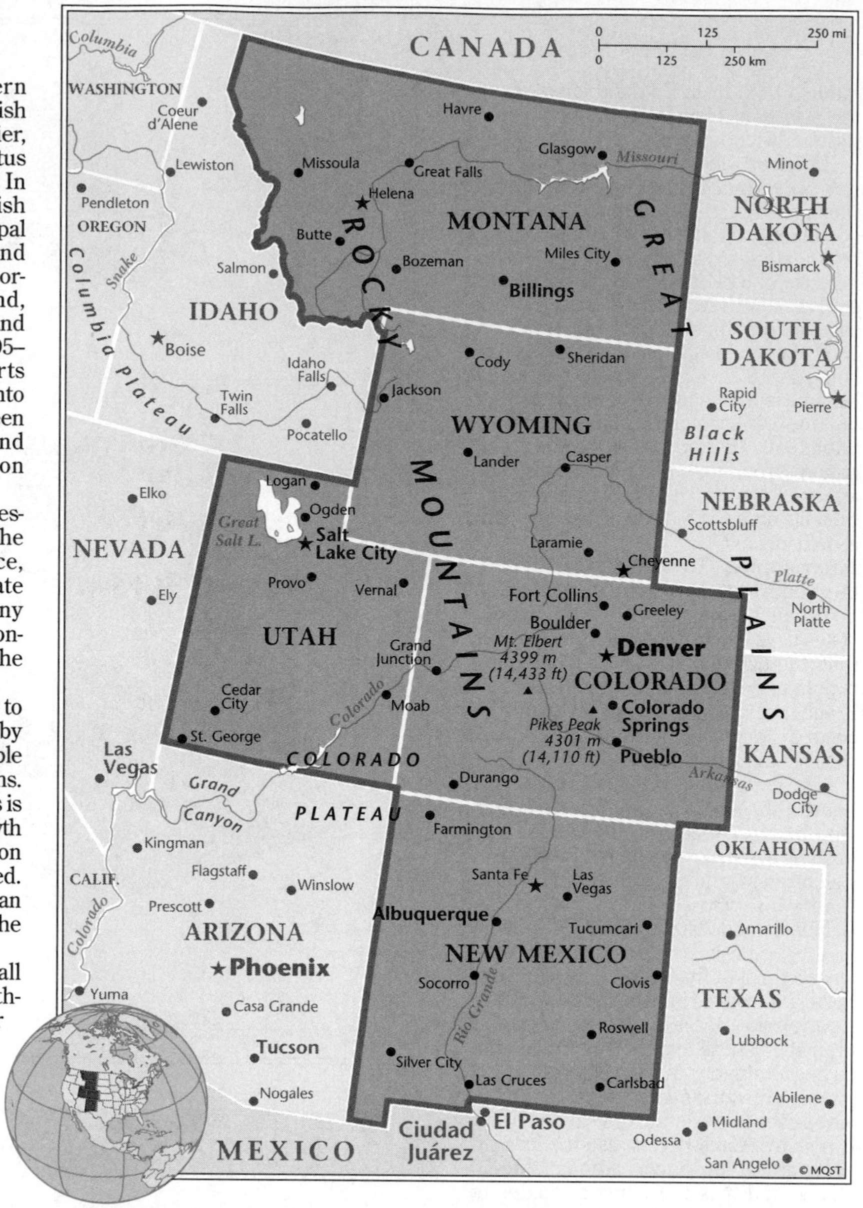

Mountain States

The disinguishing feature of the Mountain States cross the breadth of the American West from Canada 1,200 miles (1,931 kilometers) all the way south to Mexico. The area is bounded by the Northwest and Southwest regions to the west and by the Grain states and Oil states to the east. The central ridge of the Rocky Mountains runs south from western Montana through Wyoming and Colorado and about 100 miles (161 kilometers) into New Mexico. A branch ridge isolated by the Wyoming Basin runs south through Utah.

The region is one of the largest and most sparsely populated in the United States. There are large areas of undisturbed natural beauty in all the states, including mountain scenery, sand dunes, desert, salt flats, geysers, and glaciers. The region is now experiencing strong population growth.

The land. The Rocky Mountains that unite the Mountain states are the highest in the 48 contiguous United States. The three main divisions of the Rockies are all represented in the Mountain states. The Northern Rockies cover western Montana and extend north across Canada to Alaska. The Middle Rockies cover Wyoming, where they are interrupted by the Wyoming Basin and then divide into two ranges: the main chain, which runs southeast through the center of Colorado, and the Wasatch Range, which runs south through much of Utah. These Southern Rockies are the highest in the chain. Colorado contains the highest peaks. To the south the Rockies decline into the Sangre de Cristo Range, which extends 100 miles (161 kilometers) into New Mexico.

The central ridge of the Rocky Mountains forms the great watershed

Mountain States

State	Area (Sq. Mi.)	Population 2000	Population Change 1990–2000		Persons per Sq. Mi.
			Number	Percent	
Colorado	103,730	4,301,261	1,006,867	30.6	41.5
Montana	145,556	902,195	103,130	12.9	6.0
New Mexico	121,364	1,819,046	303,977	20.1	14.9
Utah	82,168	2,233,169	510,319	29.6	27.1
Wyoming	97,105	493,782	40,194	8.9	5.0
Region Totals	549,923	9,749,453	1,964,487	25.2	17.7

called the Continental Divide. Rain falling to the west of this imaginary line will flow west into the Pacific Ocean. Rain falling to the east of it will flow east. Four of the major rivers in the United States have headwaters in the Rockies. The Missouri flows east to the Mississippi, and then to the Gulf of Mexico. The Rio Grande flows southeast directly to the Gulf. The Columbia flows west to the Pacific. And the Colorado flows west and then south to the Gulf of California.

Climate. The climate of the region varies north to south from the harsh winters and hot summers of Montana to the desert climate of warm days and cool nights throughout the year in New Mexico. Precipitation, however, is uniformly low throughout the region. The Mountain states average about 15 inches (38 centimeters) of precipitation per year, with New Mexico significantly lower. Much of it falls as snow in the highest elevations.

History. The Mountain states were the last to be fully opened to settlement. The French Canadians were the first European explorers in Montana and Wyoming, and the Spanish were the first European visitors to Colorado, Utah, and New Mexico. However, the region was not fully explored until well into the 1800s. The Great Salt Lake was not discovered until 1825, only 22 years before Brigham Young led his Mormon followers there. The northern half of the region came into U.S. possession with the Louisiana Purchase of 1803. The southern half was ceded by Mexico after the Mexican War in 1848. Early settlers established huge cattle ranches because most of the land was too dry for farming.

Principal cities. The largest metropolitan area in the region is the Denver area, located near the center of the region. It is also the commercial heart of the Mountain states. Its population of 2.1 million makes it half again as large as any other metropolitan area in the region. Salt Lake City-Ogden, 350 miles (563 kilometers) west of Denver, and Albuquerque, 300 miles (483 kilometers) south of Denver, are other populous cities. These three metropolitan areas account for about 43 percent of the region's population.

The people. The major ethnic groups are Hispanic and Native American. Both groups live in all Mountain states, but Hispanics are especially numerous in Colorado and New Mexico; Native Americans, in Montana and New Mexico.

Economy. All Mountain states have three industries in common: tourism, mining, and ranching. Yellowstone in Wyoming was the first U.S. national park. Along with such natural preserves as Glacier in Montana, Grand Teton in Wyoming, and Rocky Mountain in Colorado, it is the basis of the tourism industry. In recent years, winter sports have become an important business, especially in Colorado.

Wyoming and New Mexico lead the region in mining because of their rich endowments of oil and natural gas. But

Utah's Bingham Canyon copper mine is the world's largest open pit mine; Colorado leads all states in production of the industrially important element molybdenum; and Montana is rich in both coal and copper. Ranching is the traditional business of the region, and profits from cattle and sheep exceed those from crops in the agricultural economies of all Mountain states.

Oil States

The Oil states, Texas, Oklahoma, Louisiana, and Arkansas, are in the south-central United States. In the southwest the region borders Mexico across the Rio Grande, and in the southeast it has a long shoreline on the Gulf of Mexico. The U.S. borders are with the southernmost Mountain state of New Mexico on the west, the Grain states on the north, and the South-Central states across the Mississippi River on the east.

In the 1970s the Oil states grew at twice the national rate. This slowed in the following decades, with only the

growth rate of Texas exceeding the national rate. Part of the attraction of the Oil states is their energy industries, and part is the general population trend away from the Northeast to the South and Southwest area known as the "Sun Belt."

The region had long been the principal oil producer in the United States, but skyrocketing fuel costs during the 1970s greatly increased the income of the oil industry. A decline in oil prices in the 1980s brought economic problems to the region, however. The Oil states also account for most of the country's natural gas, an increasingly valuable fuel. In addition, the region exports drilling machinery and sends drilling experts to oil-rich areas around the world.

The land. The major topographical feature within the region is the Gulf Coastal Plain. The plain extends north from the Gulf itself along the Mississippi embayment, or river valley, narrowing to a point and ending in southern Illinois. Consequently, the Gulf Coastal Plain covers a wide area of southeast Texas, all of Louisiana, and the south and east of Arkansas.

Oil States

State	Area (Sq. Mi.)	Population 2000	Population Change 1990–2000 Number	Population Change 1990–2000 Percent	Persons per Sq. Mi.
Arkansas	52,075	2,673,400	322,675	13.7	51.3
Louisiana	43,566	4,468,976	249,003	5.9	102.5
Oklahoma	68,679	3,450,654	305,069	9.7	50.2
Texas	261,914	20,851,820	3,865,310	22.8	79.6
Region Totals	**426,234**	**31,444,850**	**4,742,057**	**17.8**	**73.8**

Along the region's eastern boundary is a strip of alluvial land built up by Mississippi River silt; in southern Louisiana the Mississippi delta was created by the same process. Eastern Oklahoma and western Arkansas share a portion of interior highland comprising the Ozark Plateau and the Ouachita Mountains. The western panhandle of Oklahoma and western Texas lie within the Great Plains, a treeless tableland reaching 4,000 feet (1,219 meters) above sea level. The highest elevations in the region are found in extreme western Texas, which is a part of the Mexican Highlands.

Climate. The entire region has a moderate climate, with rainfall and temperatures highest along the Gulf Coast. Louisiana experiences temperatures over 70°F (21°C) for much of the year and an annual rainfall of over 50 inches (127 centimeters). Its climate is humid and semitropical. Farther inland, in Oklahoma and west Texas, however, rainfall declines to less than 30 inches (76 centimeters) per year. The weather is dry, and seasonal temperature extremes vary from below freezing in winter to more than 90°F (32°C) in summer.

History. The Oil states were originally explored by the Spanish from Florida and the French from Canada in the first half of the 1500s. Louisiana, Arkansas, and Oklahoma came to the United States as part of the Louisiana Purchase in 1803. Texas was still part of Mexico when that country became independent of Spain in 1821. The American settlers in Texas rebelled in 1836, and Texas entered the Union as a state in 1845 after a period of nine years as a republic. Oklahoma was designated an Indian territory before being opened to homesteaders in the 1890s.

The people. This history has left the region with an unusual mix of people. Texas has one of the highest proportions of Hispanic residents in the country, and Oklahoma contains a large Native American population. Louisiana is unique in its population of Creoles, who are descendants of early Spanish and French peoples, and Cajuns, who are descendants of French Acadians from Canada. The African-American population is proportionally largest in Arkansas, where it represents 16 percent of the total, and Louisiana, where it represents 32.5 percent.

Principal cities. Two out of every three residents of the Oil states live in urban areas. The largest metropolitan areas are Houston-Galveston, near the Texas Gulf Coast, and Dallas-Fort Worth, 200 miles (322 kilometers) north and inland from Houston. Other cities with more than a million metropolitan area residents are New Orleans, Louisiana, and San Antonio, Texas. The major cities in the north are Oklahoma City and Little Rock, Arkansas.

Economy. Houston is the largest city in the region, reflecting its prominence as the seat of the oil industry. The region produces about half of the total U.S. output of crude petroleum and 80 percent of the nation's natural gas. In addition to the mining income that fuels and related industries generate, rapidly expanding manufacturing industries in the Oil states have helped to generate new income and broaden the region's economic base. Although principally known for its fuels, the region is also third in the United States in agriculture. Cattle and irrigated grain crops for feed predominate in relatively dry Texas and Oklahoma, and large crops of soybeans and rice are harvested in Louisiana and Arkansas.

Grain States

The Grain states include the heart of the central plains and prairies, occupying a large part of the north-central United States. The region looks west to the Rocky Mountains and east to the Great Lakes region. The Great Plains themselves run north deep into Canada and south into the Oil states of Oklahoma and Texas.

The Great Plains predominate in the western states of the Grain region, including most of North Dakota, South Dakota, Nebraska, and Kansas. Prairie, plateau, and hilly lands predominate in the eastern states of Minnesota, Iowa, and Missouri. The region is dominated by two great rivers: the Mississippi, which rises in Minnesota and forms most of the region's eastern boundary, and the Missouri, which flows through or touches each

Grain States

State	Area (Sq. Mi.)	Population 2000	Population Change 1990–2000		Persons per Sq. Mi.
			Number	Percent	
Iowa	55,875	2,926,324	149,569	5.4	52.3
Kansas	81,823	2,688,418	210,844	8.5	32.8
Minnesota	79,617	4,919,479	544,380	12.4	61.7
Missouri	68,898	5,595,211	478,138	12.4	81.2
Nebraska	76,878	1,711,263	132,878	8.4	22.2
North Dakota	68,994	642,200	3,400	.5	9.3
South Dakota	75,898	754,844	58,840	8.5	9.9
Region Totals	507,983	19,237,739	1,578,049	8.9	37.8

THE PLAINS of the Grain states spring to life with the modern technology of irrigation.

of the other six states, flowing into the Mississippi near St. Louis, Missouri.

The Grain region contains the geographical center of North America, the geographical center of the United States, and the central point of the U.S. population. The region is also the agricultural center of the nation, with an economy based on grain crops: wheat in Kansas, corn in Iowa, and oats in Minnesota. In addition, it exports enormous quantities of meat and dairy products.

The importance of the Grain states' farm country has been realized since the 1800s, but the region's modern prosperity owes much to farming innovation: hybrid seeds for high yields, chemical fertilizers, and mechanized cultivation.

The land. The eastern Grain states lie in the central lowland drained by the Mississippi River. The plains covering the western Grain states are actually a plateau of this central lowland, rising gradually in elevation from east to west. The dividing line between the areas, known as the Break of the Plains, is a series of steep escarpments running north-south from North Dakota to Kansas. The plains are broken in western areas by mountains such as the Black Hills in South Dakota, where peaks rise more than 3,000 feet (914 meters) above the level of the land.

Climate. The climate of the Grain states is known for dramatic seasonal variations. Arctic storms arrive from the northwest without obstruction, causing bitter cold and drifting snow in winter. In summer, warm moist air from the Gulf of Mexico brings high humidity to eastern parts of the region. The Grain states also have the highest average wind speed of any U.S. region and startling temperature extremes. In North Dakota, for example, record lows are -40°F (-40°C) and record highs exceed 110°F (43°C). The region's normal temperatures range from about 80°F (27°C) in summer to about 10°F (-12°C) in winter, with southern states more moderate in climate than

northern ones. Rainfall averages over 30 inches (76 centimeters) per year near the Mississippi, where crops predominate, but it is significantly lighter on the plains, where cattle grazing is more common and agriculture is only possible with irrigation in some areas. Rapid changes in weather are common in all seasons.

History. The initial exploration of the Grain states was carried out by Francisco de Coronado in 1541, but it was the expeditions south from Canada by Père Jacques Marquette, Louis Jolliet, and Robert Cavelier, Sieur de La Salle in the 1600s that first brought notice to the region. French influence continued until most of this land area came into U.S. hands with the Louisiana Purchase of 1803. In 1804, Meriwether Lewis and William Clark began their exploration of the new territory by following the Missouri River to its source.

The earliest settlers in most of the region were adventurous farmers from eastern territories looking for good farmland. They established homesteads and were followed by a wave of settlers, and also by buffalo hunters, who exterminated the buffalo by the millions for their valuable hides. These two forces were disastrous for the Plains Indians, notably the Sioux, whose entire culture was based on the buffalo hunt. The Indian wars flared from about 1810 until the 1870s, when the Plains Indians were overpowered militarily and starved into submission.

The Grain states grew rapidly from the 1880s to the 1930s, when drought in the western plains and economic depression ruined the agriculture-based economy. It was only after World War II that improvements in farming techniques and increased manufacturing restored the economy.

The people. Most Grain states, particularly those on the western plains, continue to lose residents to migration. The natural population increase accounts exclusively for the region's small population growth.

Principal cities. Despite relatively low growth, the Grain states have several thriving cities, primarily in their eastern half. Kansas City, on the Missouri-Kansas line, is a major business and commercial center. Omaha, on the Nebraska-Iowa border, serves a large central area. Minneapolis-St. Paul, in the north, is the cultural and business capital of the northern plains. St. Louis, near the southeastern corner of the region, serves as a connecting city to the Great Lakes region to the east and to the nearby Southern states.

Economy. The Grain region includes all U.S. states with more than 90 percent of their land area devoted to agriculture: North Dakota, South Dakota, Nebraska, Kansas, and Iowa. The region also includes the nation's leading producers of wheat, corn, oats, soybeans, and several other crops. These crops support large livestock and dairy industries and serve as raw materials for the food processing industry. In addition, the region includes the principal U.S. producer of iron ore, in Minnesota, and of gold, in South Dakota. In 1993 the region and its economy were hard hit by months of record rainfalls that caused the Missouri and upper Mississippi rivers to inundate vast areas along their floodplains.

Great Lakes States

The Great Lakes states are located in the north-central United States. They are separated from the Grain states to the west by the Mississippi River, and from the South-Central states to the south by the Ohio River. Three of the five Great Lakes form the region's northern border, separating the region from the Canadian Province of Ontario. Lake Michigan, the only Great Lake entirely in the United States, touches four of the five states in the region. The state of Michigan has 1,700 miles (2,735 kilometers) of Great Lakes shoreline. The region's eastern boundary is with Pennsylvania.

The Great Lakes states are notable for their network of industrial cities along the southern reaches of the lakes, from Milwaukee and Chicago on Lake Michigan to Detroit and Cleveland on Lake Erie. The lakes themselves, connected to the Atlantic by the St. Lawrence River, form a major transportation system and provide an important source of water for industrial use. Steel plants cluster along the lakefronts near Gary, Indiana, and Youngstown, Ohio. And the automobile industry made Detroit, halfway between Gary and Youngstown, the largest industrial complex in the world. Foreign competition, both in steel production and manufacturing, led to a decline of these industrial cities, which have begun to replace noncompetitive heavy industries with high-technology industries. At the same time, a modest resurgence is taking place in the less industrial North Woods areas of northern Wisconsin and Michigan, attracting people who leave the industrial cities.

27 North America

Great Lakes States

State	Area (Sq. Mi.)	Population 2000	Population Change 1990–2000		Persons per Sq. Mi.
			Number	Percent	
Illinois	55,593	12,419,293	988,691	8.6	223.4
Indiana	35,870	6,080,485	536,326	9.7	169.5
Michigan	56,809	9,938,444	643,147	6.9	174.9
Ohio	40,953	11,353,140	506,025	4.7	277.2
Wisconsin	54,314	5,363,675	471,906	9.6	94.3
Region Totals	243,539	45,155,037	3,146,095	7.5	185.4

meters
US

metres
Brit.

center
US

centre
Brit.

The land. Almost all of the land area of the Great Lakes states lies within the vast Central Lowland, which stretches from the Appalachian Plateau in eastern Ohio to the Mississippi River on the western border. This relatively flat plain, broken by low ranges of moraines, or glacial hills, is fertile and ideally suited to large, mechanized farming. Along the coastlines of the lakes themselves the region also includes strips of Great Lakes Plain, and lower-lying and marshy areas on which most of the region's major cities stand. Northern Wisconsin and the western half of Michigan's Upper Peninsula also share a portion of Superior Upland, a glacial hill area containing the highest elevations in the region, about 1,900 feet (579 meters).
Climate. The Great Lakes states have a consistent climate of cold winters and

hot summers. The normal temperature range throughout the region runs from winter lows of about 10°F (-12°C) to summer highs of about 80°F (27°C). The average precipitation is about 35 inches (89 centimeters) per year, and the snowfall averages between 25 and 35 inches (63.5 and 89 centimeters). In the North Woods area, however, winters are colder and snowfalls average over 100 inches (254 centimeters) per year.
History. The Great Lakes states were first explored by the French explorers Louis Jolliet, Père Jacques Marquette, and Robert Cavelier, Sieur de La Salle in the 1600s. They remained a French territory until 1763, when France ceded the region to Britain. American claims to the region were recognized by the Treaty of Paris in 1783, which ended the American Revolution, and in 1787

the region was organized, along with part of Minnesota, as the Northwest Territory.

Almost immediately, settlers crossed the Appalachians and began to live in Ohio, which entered the Union in 1803. Indiana and Illinois joined before 1820; Michigan and Wisconsin, less suited for agriculture and off the main thoroughfares, gained statehood in 1837 and 1848. When the railroads opened in the 1850s, the industrial cities began to grow, and the population was increased by huge numbers of European immigrants.
Principal cities. The largest metropolitan area in the region is Chicago, which includes almost 9 million residents of Illinois and Indiana. Its diversified economy helped it avoid the decline experienced by other large Great Lakes cities—Detroit, Cleveland, and Milwaukee—in the 1970s. By the 1990s Milwaukee and Detroit were making modest gains, while Cleveland continued to lose population.
The people. The stream of people leaving the region because of the decline of the automobile and steel industries reached enormous proportions in the 1970s. Although all five states increased slightly in population, they nonetheless lost 1.5 million people to other regions. Growth rates in the 1980s and 1990s remained well below the national average. The inner cities today have increasing concentrations of poor African-American residents and decreasing tax bases and employment opportunities. The region also includes significant numbers of Hispanic people.
Economy. The principal industries of the region are the automobile plants in Detroit, Flint, and other Michigan cities, and the steel mills around Gary, Indiana, and Cleveland and Youngstown, Ohio. This economic core has spawned related machinery, shipping, and transportation industries that together make the Great Lakes states the manufacturing center of America. Across the Central Lowland the region also generates significant agricultural income, most of it in dairy farming and crops for cattle feed. Northern Wisconsin and Michigan rely primarily on mining, timber, and tourism.

South-Central States

The South-Central states extend 550 miles (885 kilometers) from the Ohio River south to the Gulf of Mexico and a maximum of 430 miles (692 kilometers) from the Mississippi River east to the Appalachian Mountains. These continental southern states are Mississippi and Alabama along the Gulf Coast, Tennessee along the northern border of Alabama and Mississippi, and Kentucky between Tennessee and the Ohio River.

Until 1970 the South-Central states regularly lost population to employment opportunities in other regions, particularly the Great Lakes states north of the

Ohio River. The following decades, however, brought growth.

The change from net loss to net gain in population has been especially apparent among African-Americans, who traditionally migrated from this region for both economic and social reasons. By 1980 this migration from the region had virtually ceased, and the African-American proportion of the total population (more than 20 percent in 2000) is expected to continue to rise.

Although the primary economic factor in the rise of the so-called "New South" has been its growth in manufacturing, social factors have also been very important. The increase in employment opportunities in the 1970s and 1980s followed the civil rights clashes of the 1950s and '60s.

The land. All the South-Central states have in common portions of the Gulf Coastal Plain, which runs from the southern part of Mississippi and Alabama to a narrow northern extreme in western Kentucky. To the west, along the Mississippi River, lies a narrow strip of swampy silt. To the east lie the highland plateaus, which rise into the Appalachian Mountains. In the north the region includes a portion of the Interior Low Plateau running from the Great Lakes states south across central Kentucky and into the Nashville Basin in central Tennessee.

The lower Mississippi River, which forms the western border of the region, is the great trunk of the central U.S. drainage system. Running from its confluence with the Ohio River at the edge of western Kentucky to its mouth at the Gulf, the river travels 560 air miles (901 kilometers). Its actual route, however, is approximately twice that distance because of wide bends that are especially serpentine, winding and curving, along the Mississippi-Arkansas border.

Climate. The climate of the region ranges from moderate in Kentucky to subtropical along the Gulf Coast. Winter temperatures fall below freezing in the Appalachian Highlands but only to 40°F (4°C) in the south of the region. Summers are warm throughout. Light snows are common in the north, but the Gulf Coast experiences year-round heavy rains surpassing 60 inches (152 centimeters) per year at Mobile in southern Alabama.

History. Most of the region was explored simultaneously during the 1500s by the French from Canada and the Spanish from Florida. Great Britain took possession of the region at the end of the French and Indian War in 1763. Effective settlement was first accomplished from the American colony of Virginia. The major trauma in the region's history was the Civil War. The Convention of Confederate States was convened in Montgomery, Alabama, on February 4, 1861. Alabama and Mississippi entered the Confederacy at this time, but Tennessee joined only after hostilities had begun. Kentucky, although a slave state, remained in the Union. Following the defeat of the Confederate army in 1865, the region entered a period of reconstruction by outsiders that devastated its economy and crippled it politically.

Principal cities. The South-Central states lack the major urban centers created in other regions by massive industrialization. The largest population centers are Nashville, Tennessee, in the central part of the state; Memphis, Tennessee, on the Mississippi River; Louisville, Kentucky, on the Ohio River; and Birmingham, Alabama, in the north-central part of the state. Memphis and Louisville are both located on the periphery of the region, and both include population from states outside the region. Many South-Central residents look toward major cities just outside the region: New Orleans to the southwest, Atlanta to the southeast, and Cincinnati to the north. The largest population center lying entirely within the region is Nashville, ranked only 37th among U.S. urban centers.

Economy. The principal industry in the region is now manufacturing, which tripled in value between 1967 and 1977 and continued to grow during the 1980s and 1990s. Metal products and mineral refining, textiles, chemicals, wood and paper products, machinery, and electrical and electronic equipment are among the main manufactures. The region's fivefold increase in mineral production in the 1970s, and further substantial increases, helped the region's economy to grow.

The principal river ports, such as Memphis and Louisville, and Gulf ports such as Mobile, have also benefited from the importation of raw materials for manufacturers. During this era of industrialization the agricultural sector has continued to thrive, producing some $10 billion annually.

27 North America

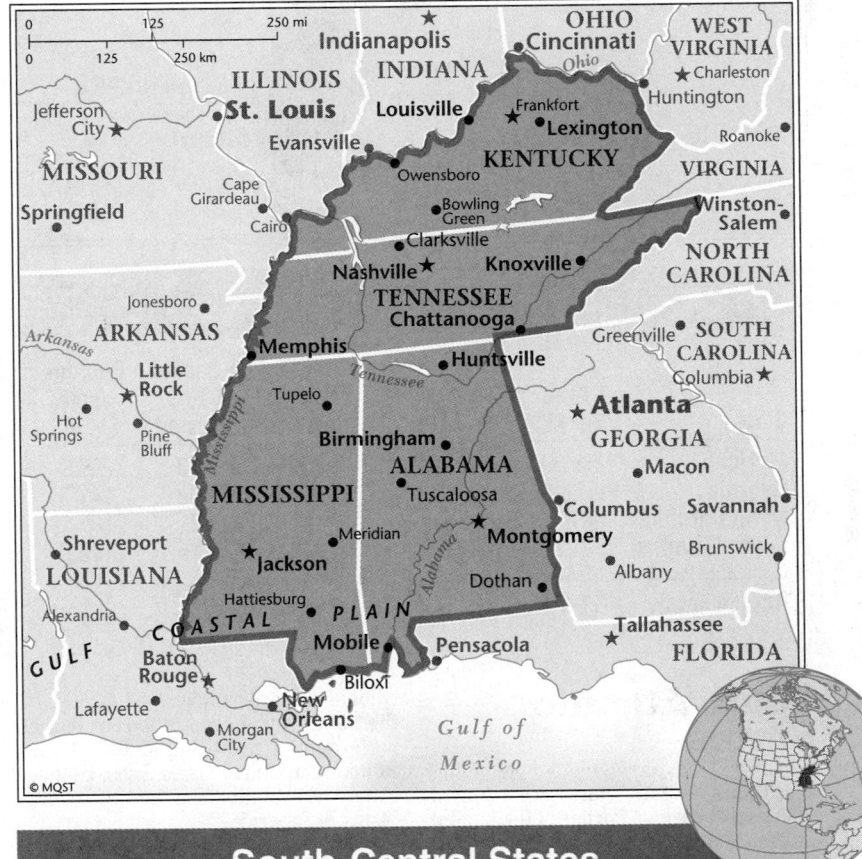

South-Central States

State	Area (Sq. Mi.)	Population 2000	Population Change 1990–2000		Persons per Sq. Mi.
			Number	Percent	
Alabama	50,750	4,447,100	406,513	10.1	87.6
Kentucky	39,732	4,041,769	356,473	9.7	101.7
Mississippi	46,914	2,844,658	271,442	10.5	60.6
Tennessee	41,219	5,689,283	812,098	16.7	138.0
Region Totals	178,615	17,022,810	1,846,526	12.2	95.3

kilometers
US

kilometres
Brit.

center
US

centre
Brit.

South Atlantic States

State	Area (Sq. Mi.)	Population 2000	Population Change 1990–2000		Persons per Sq. Mi.
			Number	Percent	
Florida	53,997	15,982,378	3,044,452	23.5	295.9
Georgia	57,919	8,186,453	1,708,237	26.4	141.3
North Carolina	48,718	8,049,313	1,420,676	21.4	165.2
South Carolina	30,111	4,012,012	525,309	15.1	133.2
Region Totals	190,745	36,230,156	6,698,674	22.7	189.9

South Atlantic States

The South Atlantic states are situated in the southeastern corner of the United States. At the south, a peninsula consisting of most of Florida extends 450 miles (724 kilometers) south between the Atlantic Ocean and the Gulf of Mexico. The other three states—Georgia, South Carolina, and North Carolina—all extend from the Atlantic coast inland to the Appalachian Mountains. The region is bordered on the west by the South-Central states of Alabama and Tennessee, and on the north by the Tidewater state of Virginia.

Spanish settlers established a colony at St. Augustine, Florida, in 1565. This city still bears signs of its Spanish heritage. Other states in the region had long colonial histories under British rule. All the South Atlantic states except Florida were among the original 13 colonies forming the United States. Later, all these states were members of the Confederate States of America.

Today the greatest bond of the South Atlantic states is population growth. These states have the highest growth rate of any region except the Southwest states. New jobs provided by manufacturing and the region's combination of mild climate and recreational attractions are key factors in this growth.

The land. Topographically, the South Atlantic states all share portions of the Atlantic Coastal Plain, a lowland covering most of Florida and the eastern lands of Georgia, South Carolina, and North Carolina. The plain includes swamplands and shifting islands of sand just offshore that are part of the Great Barrier Reef. Along their western boundaries, Georgia, South Carolina, and North Carolina include parts of the Blue Ridge Mountains. The highest peak in the eastern United States is Mount Mitchell (6,684 feet, 2,037 meters) in northwestern North Carolina. Between the mountains and the coastal plain lies the Piedmont Plateau, stretching northward from central Georgia across western South Carolina and central North Carolina. At the point where the rock beds of the plateau drop off to the lower lands of the plain, rivers become rapids. This fall line extends northeast from Columbus, Georgia, through South Carolina to Raleigh, North Carolina, and on into the Tidewater states.

Climate. The climate of the region ranges from subtropical on the islet keys south of Florida to moderate continental in inland North Carolina. In summer normal high temperatures are about 90°F (32°C) throughout the region, and normal winter lows range from 45°F (7°C) in Florida to freezing in the northern states. Precipitation ranges from 60 inches (152 centimeters) in Florida to 42 inches (107 centimeters) in North Carolina. Only the western regions of North and South Carolina receive appreciable snow.

History. The Spanish lost West Florida in 1810 but kept possession of East Florida until 1819, more than 30 years after the establishment of the United States. The original colony of Carolina was divided into North and South in 1729. Georgia was established in 1732. The Carolinas and Georgia approved the U.S. Constitution in 1788 and 1789, and Florida entered the Union in 1845 as a slave state.

The people. Today the South Atlantic states, which were relatively slow-growing in population until World War II, attract immigrants from other U.S. regions. The greatest growth is in Florida, which has become a haven for retired people, particularly from the eastern United States. But the other states of the region also have significant population increases. All of these states include a large proportion of African Americans, and Florida is unique among U.S. states for its large population of Cuban Americans.

Principal cities. The two largest metropolitan areas in the region are Miami, Florida, a center of the tourist and retirement business in Florida; and Atlanta, Georgia, a business and transportation center for the South Atlantic region as well as for nearby sections of northern Alabama and eastern Tennessee. The Carolinas have smaller cities, some of which are clustered into sizable urban regions.

Economy. The importance of agriculture has lessened in the economies of the South Atlantic states. The principal industry in all these states except Florida is now manufacturing, especially of textile products. In Florida, manufacturing ranks second only to tourism, which is an important industry in all South Atlantic states.

Tidewater States

The Tidewater states are situated near the center of the Atlantic Ocean coastline. The region, including Virginia, West Virginia, Maryland, Delaware, and the District of Columbia, is surrounded on its inland borders by Pennsylvania and New Jersey on the north, North Carolina on the south, and Kentucky and Ohio on the west.

The principal natural feature of the region, and the source of its name, is Chesapeake Bay along with its many tidal river estuaries. From its mouth just north of Norfolk, Virginia, the bay extends 180 miles (290 kilometers) north between the Delmarva peninsula and the mainland. The western, or mainland, shore boasts many tidal rivers, including the Potomac and the Susquehanna. The peninsula contains all of the state of Delaware and parts of Maryland and Virginia, giving the Delmarva peninsula its name.

The shelter provided by the bay and its inlets first attracted European settlers to the region. The shipping access it provides continues to support most of the region's industry. The Potomac River estuary between Virginia and Maryland divided the original 13 colonies into northern and southern parts. This led to the location on it of the country's "federal city," the capital, Washington, D.C.

The land. The region has a complex topography. The Allegheny Mountains, part of the great Appalachian chain, run through the western regions of Maryland and West Virginia. To the east of the mountains is a broader strip of the Appalachian ridge and valley region. Beyond the great Appalachian valley are the Blue Ridge Mountains, which run through northwestern Virginia and into Maryland. The land declines gradually toward the sea.

A strip of Piedmont Plateau runs through central Virginia and Maryland. The eastern border of the plateau is the fall line, where streams from the plateau fall in rapids to the coastal plain. This line often marks the highest point to which rivers are navigable; the rapids have also provided industrial power from an early date.

The eastern reaches of the region are part of the Atlantic Coastal Plain. In the geological past, part of the plain fell below sea level. Several river mouths are submerged under Chesapeake Bay, leaving estuaries that are flooded for miles upstream by tidewaters.

Climate. The climate of the Tidewater states is generally moderate, influenced by the states' proximity to the sea and bay. Temperatures range between normal summer highs of 85° to 90°F (29° to 32°C) to normal winter lows of 25°F (-4°C). Annual precipitation is between 40 and 46 inches (102 and 117 centimeters). In the western reaches, winters are more severe, and snowfall is common, averaging 31 inches (79 centimeters) in West Virginia.

Tidewater States

State	Area (Sq. Mi.)	Population 2000	Population Change 1990–2000 Number	Percent	Persons per Sq. Mi.
Delaware	1,995	783,600	137,914	17.6	395.2
District of Columbia	61	572,059	-34,841	-5.7	9,378.0
Maryland	9,775	5,296,486	515,018	10.8	541.8
Virginia	39,598	7,078,515	891,157	14.4	178.7
West Virginia	24,087	1,808,344	14,867	.8	75.0
Region Totals	75,516	15,539,004	1,524,115	10.7	205.8

History. The Tidewater region was principally settled by the British, who built their first permanent establishment in America at Jamestown, Virginia, in 1607, and who sent a party to settle Maryland in the next year. The Dutch first occupied Delaware, and the Swedes established the first permanent settlement there, at Wilmington, in 1664. Until 1861 West Virginia was still part of Virginia. Then its residents, who opposed secession from the Union, requested statehood, which was granted to it in 1863.

Principal cities. Today the Tidewater region is predominantly urban, except for West Virginia. Two metropolitan areas alone, Baltimore, Maryland, and Washington, D.C., include 48 percent of the entire region's population.

The people. The movement of the people is primarily from cities to suburbs within the region. In the 1990s population growth was above the national average in Virginia and Delaware, but West Virginia, Maryland, and the District of Columbia lost population.

Economy. Manufacturing is the major industry of the Tidewater states, and it ranges from food processing throughout the region to heavy machinery manufacturing in Baltimore to chemical production in Delaware. Government employees constitute a large proportion of the workforce both in Washington, D.C., and in nearby parts of Virginia and Maryland.

Tourism is the second most important source of income. Seaside resorts on the Delmarva peninsula and the attractions in the nation's capital draw visitors. Agriculture is of less importance to the area's economy, but all states in the region participate in poultry farming, and West Virginia and Virginia mine a substantial portion of the country's coal.

Mid-Atlantic States

The three Mid-Atlantic states, Pennsylvania, New Jersey, and New York, in the northeastern United States, border the New England states and the Atlantic Ocean on the east; the Tidewater states of Delaware, Maryland, and West Virginia on the south; and the Great Lakes state of Ohio on the west. The region's northern border is with Lake Ontario and the Canadian provinces of Ontario and Quebec.

The Mid-Atlantic states are the second most populous region after the Great Lakes states. The region is the most densely populated in the country, however, including 15 percent of the U.S. population on only 3 percent of its land area. In modern times, people were attracted by prospects of employment in the region's huge industrial complex. Earlier, trade had flourished because of the states' Atlantic harbors and their river and canal transportation. The Erie Canal, which was completed in 1825, connected Lake Erie and the Atlantic by way of the Hudson River, bringing prosperity to New York State. The rivers of Pennsylvania offered access to the west via the Ohio River, and to the Eastern seaboard via the Susquehanna and Delaware rivers. New Jersey, facing harbors both at New York City and Philadelphia, shared in the commercial prosperity. All three states remain among the top seven in manufacturing production.

Like the Great Lakes states to the west, however, the Mid-Atlantic states experienced an economic decline beginning in the 1960s. Increased competition in manufacturing from the Southern states and from overseas, combined with skyrocketing energy costs and difficult economic times in the 1970s, caused many businesses and residents to seek better opportunities elsewhere. The region was the only one to record an outright population decline during the 1970s, and its growth rate continues to be only about one-quarter the national average.

The land. The states in the Mid-Atlantic region all share several topographical features. The Appalachian Mountains run northeast from south-central Pennsylvania through a corner of New Jersey and into New York. To the northwest of the mountains, the lands run down to the Great Lakes Plain beside Lake Erie and to the St. Lawrence and Champlain lowlands in northern New York. To the southeast of the mountains lie valley and upland regions in southeastern Pennsylvania and New York and northern New Jersey. The southern two-thirds of New Jersey and New York's Long Island consist of Atlantic Coastal Plain.

Climate. The climate of the region is cooler and drier in the west than in the east. Along Lake Erie normal summer highs are 80°F (27°C) and winter lows are below 20°F (-7°C). Precipitation in western New York and Pennsylvania averages 36 inches (91 centimeters) per year, including snowfall ranging from 46 inches (117 centimeters) in western Pennsylvania to 92 inches (234 centimeters) at Buffalo in western New York. In the coastal eastern areas, however, normal summer high temperatures average a warmer 85°F (29°C) and winter lows are a milder 25°F (-4°C). These eastern areas average approximately 40 inches (102 centimeters) of precipitation per year, including less than 30 inches (76 centimeters) of snow.

centimeters
US

centimetres
Brit.

centers
US

centres
Brit.

labor
US

labour
Brit.

Mid-Atlantic States

State	Area (Sq. Mi.)	Population 2000	Population Change 1990–2000		Persons per Sq. Mi.
			Number	Percent	
New Jersey	7,419	8,414,350	684,162	8.9	1134.1
New York	47,224	18,976,457	986,002	5.5	401.8
Pennsylvania	44,820	12,281,054	399,411	3.4	274.0
Region Totals	99,463	39,671,861	2,069,575	3.7	398.8

History. The Mid-Atlantic states were explored and settled by the Dutch and the British. The Dutch controlled southern New York, as far up the Hudson River valley as Fort Orange, later called Beverwyck, and parts of New Jersey until 1664, when the British took control; the Dutch city of New Amsterdam became New York, and Beverwyck became Albany. New Jersey was organized as a separate colony one year later, and in 1681 the English Crown granted the Quaker William Penn a charter to Pennsylvania. During the Revolutionary War, the American army under George Washington retreated from New York, leaving it to British control, but it scored important early victories in New Jersey; later in the war the army wintered at Valley Forge, Pennsylvania, near Philadelphia. American forces under General Horatio Gates won a decisive victory at Saratoga, New York. The region was largely untouched during the Civil War except for the monumental battle at Gettysburg in southern Pennsylvania.

Principal cities. Today the region is dominated by the metropolitan centers of Philadelphia and New York City. Both include portions of New Jersey, and together they account for two-thirds of the region's total population. The largest metropolitan areas in the west of the region are Pittsburgh, in west-central Pennsylvania, and Buffalo, on Lake Erie in New York.

The people. All of these metropolitan areas experienced substantial population declines in the 1970s, but the New York City and Philadelphia metropolitan areas made significant gains during the 1980s, as did their core cities. New York was the only state in the nation that recorded a substantial population decline in the 1970s, and did not again surpass its 1970 population until the latter part of the 1990s.

Economy. The leading industry in all Mid-Atlantic states is manufacturing, and the second leading industry is tourism. Coal and steel businesses based near the Great Lakes around Buffalo and Pittsburgh have been the major heavy industries in the region. In the eastern areas, manufactures are more diversified. Tourism earns the three states a total of more than $35 billion per year, most of it derived from summer activities throughout New York and Pennsylvania and from the coastal beaches of New Jersey. The region's agricultural income is lower than that of any other except New England.

New England States

The New England states occupy a comparatively narrow arm of land that extends to the northeast between the Atlantic Ocean and Canada. The region borders New York on the west and southwest. To the north are the Canadian provinces of Quebec and New Brunswick. Five of the region's states have southeastern Atlantic coastlines. Only Vermont is landlocked.

Of the U.S. regions, New England is the smallest in area and, after the Mid-Atlantic states, is the most densely populated. Many of the region's early farmers left their fields and settled in the Midwest, seeking better soil. The textile industry abandoned its plants, seeking cheaper labor and raw materials in other regions. Yet New England has survived its hard times, preserving its picturesque village greens and covered bridges, and developing new businesses to replace the old. New industries include the development and manufacture of electronics equipment. The region also attracts millions of visitors to view its autumn foliage, ski in winter, and participate in summer recreation along its Atlantic seashore and many lakes and streams.

The land.   The topographical feature that joins the states of the region is the New England Upland. This hill and valley area covers all of Connecticut and half of Rhode Island in the south, and it extends northward across central Massachusetts, southeastern Vermont, southern New Hampshire, and central and northern Maine. To the northwest of the upland, the Taconic and Green mountains extend north and east across western Massachusetts and Vermont, and the White Mountains run from northeastern Vermont across New Hampshire and into central Maine. Southeast of the upland, the distinctive New England Seaboard Lowlands, partially submerged in the Atlantic, create a varied coastline with many peninsulas, islands, and deep harbors. Cape Cod, off eastern Massachusetts, is part of the Atlantic Coastal Plain and has a sandy shoreline characteristic of states farther south.

Climate.   New England has a generally cool climate with winters that become harsher in elevated areas distant from the coast. Normal summer highs are in the low 80°F (26°C) range throughout the region, but normal winter lows vary from 22°F (-6°C) in coastal Massachusetts to 8°F (-13°C) in Vermont. Precipitation varies from 43 inches (109 centimeters) per year in coastal areas to only 33 inches (84 centimeters) in Vermont. Snowfall varies from 39 inches (99 centimeters) per year in Rhode Island to 80 inches (203 centimeters) per year in Vermont. In the highest mountain areas of the region, subzero temperatures and annual snowfalls over 100 inches (254 centimeters) are common.

History.   Early explorers to the New England region included Dutch and British visitors to Connecticut and Vermont, but the effective settlement of the region began with the landing of the Pilgrims at Plymouth Rock in 1620. By 1623 the Pilgrims had sent parties to homestead New Hampshire and Maine. Another group of religious dissenters, the Puritans, began to arrive in Massachusetts in the late 1620s. Within ten years, a number of them had left the colony to settle Rhode Island and Connecticut.

Connecticut, Massachusetts, Rhode Island, and New Hampshire were among the original 13 states. Vermont became the 14th in 1791, and Maine, part of Massachusetts, chose separation and statehood in 1819. Both Vermont and Maine have retained their reputations of independence.

The people.   The New England states are the third least populated region of the United States after the Mountain and Northwest states. During the 1990s the states recorded an 8 percent population increase, slightly less than two-thirds the national average. Population in this region has risen steadily since 1950, with the exception of Rhode Island, which showed a slight decrease in the 1970s, before rising again in the 1980s and 1990s.

Massachusetts and Connecticut account for 70 percent of the region's population. These states also have the highest proportion of African-American and Hispanic residents.

Economy.   The economy of the New England states is based on manufacturing and tourism. Manufacturing is the largest industry in all the states, with Connecticut and Massachusetts the leaders. Tourism ranks second in importance in the economy of each state. Tourism has increased in value with the rise in popularity of winter sports, for which the New England states are especially well suited. Agricultural output, chiefly of dairy products and greenhouse vegetables, is limited, but the region is known for special farm products such as cranberries in Massachusetts, shade-grown tobacco in Connecticut, and maple syrup in Vermont.

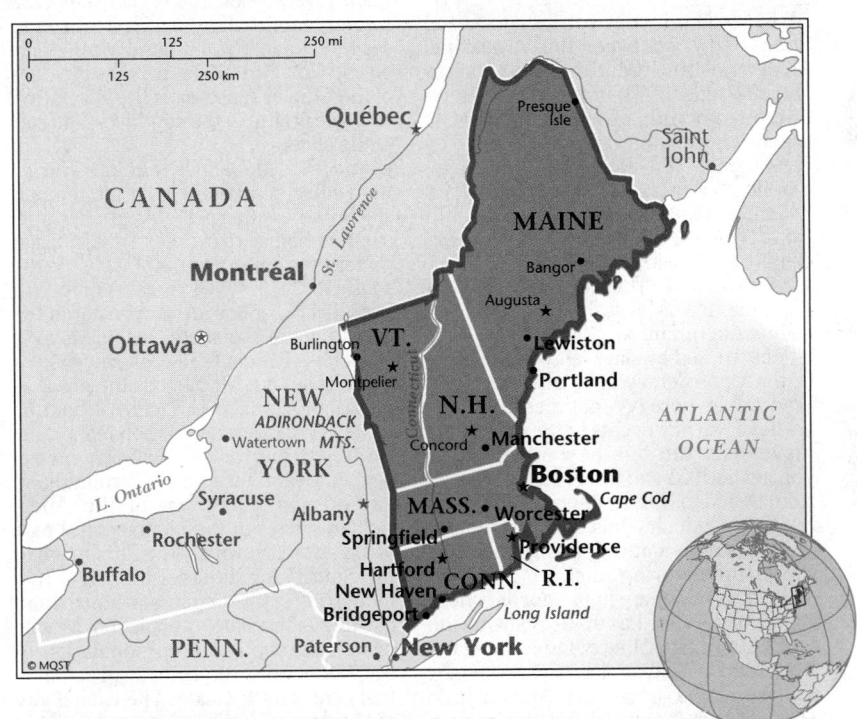

27 North America

New England States

State	Area (Sq. Mi.)	Population 2000	Population Change 1990–2000 Number	Population Change 1990–2000 Percent	Persons per Sq. Mi.
Connecticut	4,845	3,405,565	118,449	3.6	702.9
Maine	30,865	1,274,923	46,995	3.8	41.3
Massachusetts	7,838	6,349,097	332,672	5.5	810.0
New Hampshire	8,969	1,235,786	126,534	11.4	137.7
Rhode Island	1,045	1,048,319	44,855	4.5	1003.1
Vermont	9,249	608,827	46,069	8.2	65.8
Region Totals	62,811	13,922,517	715,574	7.8	221.6

Alabama

Abbreviations: *Ala., AL*
Area: *50,750 sq. mi.,*
    131,443 sq. km.
    Rank (of 50)   28th
Population:
    2000   4,447,100
    Rank (of 50)   23rd
    Change 1995–2000
    +194,100
    Persons per sq. mi.   87.6
Capital: *Montgomery*
Largest city: *Birmingham*
    Pop.   242,820
Entered Union: *Dec. 14, 1819*
    (22nd)
State bird: *Yellowhammer*
State flower: *Camellia*
State tree: *Southern pine*
State map: *Page 97*

THE PRIMARY INDUSTRY in Alabama is the refining of mineral products, such as iron and coal, and related manufacturing processes.

kilometers
US
kilometres
Brit.

centered
US
centred
Brit.

realized
US
realised
Brit.

Alabama lies in the southern United States midway between the Mississippi River and the Atlantic Ocean. It has about 60 miles (97 kilometers) of shoreline on the Gulf of Mexico, but it is otherwise separated from the Gulf by the 50-mile- (80-kilometer-) wide panhandle of Florida. The state stretches 335 miles (539 kilometers) north-south from Tennessee to the Gulf, and its eastern border is with Georgia.

Nicknamed "the Heart of Dixie," Alabama, like Mississippi, was historically an agrarian state with large plantations worked by slaves. It was a symbol of the Confederacy long after the Civil War, and in more recent times it was the scene of two key events in the civil rights movement: the bus boycott in Montgomery in 1955 and the Freedom March from Selma to Montgomery in 1965.

Today industry has supplanted agriculture as the state's leading business; the manufacturing district centered around Birmingham in the north-central region of the state has made Alabama the South's principal heavy-industry state.
The land. Alabama has three major topographical areas: the Appalachian Highlands in the northeast, the interior plateau in the far north, and the Gulf Coastal Plain in the south and west. The Appalachian region is the southernmost extension of the Appalachian mountain range, which runs northeast through the eastern United States and into Canada. The mineral-rich highlands represent more than one-third of Alabama's area. The mountain and valley region is flanked by the Cumberland Plateau on the northwest and the Piedmont Plateau on the southeast. The state's highest point, Cheaha Mountain (2,407 feet, 734 meters) is in the midst of the Appalachian region. The interior plateau in the far north is crossed by the Tennessee River, which enters Alabama at its northeast corner and flows out again at the

northwest corner. The fertile Gulf Coastal Plain rarely rises above 500 feet (152 meters) in elevation, and it declines to sea level swampland around Mobile Bay on the Gulf Coast. The principal feature of the plain in Alabama is the Black Belt of fertile prairie in the southwest quarter of the state.
Climate. Alabama's climate varies from subtropical in the south to temperate in the northern highlands. Normal summer highs are over 90°F (32°C), and winter lows range from 44°F (7°C) in the south to 32°F (0°C) in the northeast. Seasonal variations are far greater in the north than in the south. Rainfall is over 50 inches (127 centimeters) everywhere in the state, but Mobile has the greatest rainfall of all major U.S. cities, about 67 inches (170 centimeters) per year.
Principal cities. The largest metropolitan area in the state is Birmingham, located just northwest of the Appalachian ranges in the north-central part of the state. Known as "the Pittsburgh of the South" for its steel industry, this industrial center includes more than one-fifth of the state's population. Mobile has a metropolitan area population of 540,258 and is the second largest industrial center in the state. The capital city of Montgomery has a metropolitan population of over 300,000. Together these three urban seats account for over 40 percent of the state's population.
The people. The rate of growth in the 1970s was higher than for any decade since 1900 to 1910, and for the first time in 50 years more people moved into the state than out. Hundreds of thousands of African Americans moved from the state between 1930 and 1970, but the exodus ended in the 1970s. Growth in the 1980s was only about two-fifths the national average, but neared the national average in the 1990s. African Americans constitute 26 percent of the total population.
Economy. The principal industry in Alabama is manufacturing. Value added from manufacturing totals more than

$21 billion per year. Iron and coal are both mined in the highlands north of Birmingham, and the local industry is based on refining these products and smelting the pig iron into a variety of major manufactures such as cast-iron pipe. The economy of Mobile is also based on refining mineral products, mostly petroleum and natural gas drilled near the Gulf Coast.

Agriculture is second to manufacturing, and principal products include livestock, dairy products, and poultry. Soybean and peanut production have superseded cotton in importance.
Places of interest. Montgomery preserves the so-called "White House of the South" occupied by Jefferson Davis during the Civil War. Bridgeport, in the highlands at the extreme northeast corner of the state, is the location of the Russell Cave National Monument, which was occupied by American Indians in prehistoric times. Tuskegee Institute, west of Montgomery, is the home of the George Washington Carver Museum.

ALABAMA'S ABUNDANT RAINFALL and warm temperatures allow flowers to flourish.

Alaska

Abbreviations: *Alas., AK*
Area: *570,374 sq. mi.,*
   1,477,268 sq. km.
   Rank (of 50) 1st
Population:
   2000 626,932
   Rank (of 50) 48th
   Change 1995–2000
   +22,932
   Persons per sq. mi. 1.1
Capital: *Juneau*
Largest city: *Anchorage*
   Pop. 260,283
Entered Union: *Jan. 3, 1959*
   (49th)
State bird: *Willow ptarmigan*
State flower: *Forget-me-not*
State tree: *Sitka spruce*
State map: *Page 91*

Alaska, the largest and least populated of U.S. states, is a peninsula extending north and west from Canada's Pacific shore to a point only 56 miles (90 kilometers) from Asia, across the Bering Strait. Alaska has a land border with Canada, and the rest of the state is surrounded by the Arctic Ocean to the north, the Bering Strait to the west, and the Gulf of Alaska to the south. The southern reaches of the state are distinguished by two extremely narrow panhandles: one running southeast along the Pacific coast toward Prince Rupert, Canada, and one reaching southwest toward the Aleutian Island chain. The most westerly island in the Aleutian chain lies farther west than Honolulu and is on the same longitude as New Zealand.

Alaska was purchased from Russia in 1867. Its strategic importance has only recently been realized, however, as its natural resources have increased in value in the world economy.

Alaska, like Hawaii, differs from the contiguous 48 states in its extensive reliance on air and water transportation. The Alaska Highway, completed in the 1940s, connects Anchorage and Fairbanks to the "south 48," running through British Columbia and the Yukon Territory before entering Alaska. But weather conditions, rugged terrain, water barriers, and the difficulties of building on permafrost have encouraged sea and air travel.

The land. The area of Alaska, one-fifth the size of the 49 other states combined, is comprised of the Coastal Ranges, an interior plateau, and the northern Arctic Slope. The mountains running the length of the state's southern shores are a continuation of the coastal ranges found along the entire Pacific coast of the United States. In Alaska, however, the mountains are taller than any in the contiguous 48 states. Many of these mountains are covered by the glaciers that envelop 15,000 square miles (38,835 square kilometers) of the state.

Slightly inland these ranges rise to become part of the spectacular Alaska Range, which includes the highest point in North America, Mt. McKinley (20,320 feet, 6,194 meters). The chain of coastal ranges isolates the central plateau of Alaska from the warmth and rainfall of the Pacific winds; as a result, parts of the interior experience only temporary, superficial thaws in summer. This central plateau, traversed by the Yukon River, extends to the Brooks Range of mountains north of the Arctic Circle. Beyond the Brooks Range lies the Arctic Slope, a barren region of treeless tundra leading to the northernmost point in the United States, Point Barrow.

Coastal Alaska, on the Pacific Rim or "ring of fire," is geologically unstable and prone to volcanic and seismic activity. On March 27, 1964, the strongest earthquake recorded in North America, registering 8.4 on the Richter scale, struck Alaska, causing enormous damage. A resultant tidal wave, or tsunami, caused further destruction.

Climate. Large portions of Alaska enjoy relatively warm weather. The southern and coastal regions benefit from the warm ocean currents. Juneau, the state capital, has average lows of 17°F (-8°C) in January and average highs of 63°F (17°C) in July. Inland, however, the climate is drier and colder, and the limited daylight in such northern latitudes increases the effects of the cold. Summer temperatures in the interior may reach 80°F (27°C), but these brief thaws never completely undo the effects of winter temperatures that may plunge to -60°F (-51°C). At Point Barrow, the mean, or near average, July temperature is 40°F (4°C); the mean winter temperature is -19°F (-28°C).

Principal cities. The largest city in Alaska is Anchorage, located at the center of the southern coast on the inland reaches of the huge Cook Inlet. Anchorage is both the business and transportation center of Alaska. Only Fairbanks (population, 30,224) and Juneau (30,711) have more than 25,000 in population.

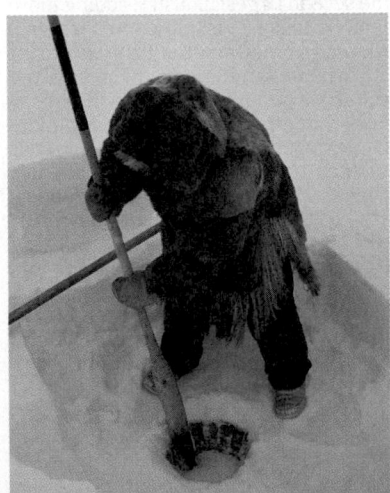

FISHING takes place through holes in the ice for much of the northern reaches of Alaska.

The people. Throughout its history as a territory of Russia, Alaska had a population that remained almost entirely American Indian, Inuit, and Aleut. The gold rush of 1898 brought the first wave of American immigrants to Alaska, and in modern times the discovery of huge oil reserves has brought more workers to "America's last frontier." As a consequence of the oil discoveries, the population today is less than one-fifth Native American, including about 44,000 Inuit, 10,000 Aleuts, and 31,000 American Indians. Alaska has one of the highest per capita incomes in the United States, but this figure must be balanced against its unusually high cost of living.

Economy. Mining of crude oil and of natural gas brings Alaska more than ten times the revenue of any other industry. The principal industrial achievement in the state's recent history was the 1977 opening of the $7.7 billion Alaska pipeline, stretching from Prudhoe Bay on the Arctic Ocean to the Pacific coast. Its presence provided diversification of the state's traditional reliance on government employment and defense spending. Other industries include limited agriculture, commercial fishing, and the processing of food products—principally fish—for export.

Places of interest. The primary attractions in Alaska are unusual natural features such as Mt. McKinley, the Mendenhall Glacier, and the volcanic "Valley of Ten Thousand Smokes." There are also many wildlife preserves and places devoted to Alaska's Inuit, American Indian, and Aleut heritage.

THE $7.7 BILLION Alaska pipeline stretches from Prudhoe Bay on the Arctic Ocean to the Pacific Coast.

27 North America

Arizona

Abbreviations: *Ariz., AZ*
Area: *113,642 sq. mi.,*
294,334 sq. km.
Rank (of 50)   6th
Population:
2000   5,130,632
Rank (of 50)   20th
Change 1995–2000
+912,632
Persons per sq. mi.   45.1
Capital: *Phoenix*
Largest city: *Phoenix*
Pop.   1,321,045
Entered Union: *Feb. 14, 1912*
(48th)
State bird: *Cactus wren*
State flower: *Saguaro cactus*
blossom
State tree: *Paloverde*
State map: *Page 90*

THE GRAND CANYON of the Colorado River in Arizona is one of the great natural wonders of the world.

Arizona is an arid state in the southwest United States bordered to the south by Mexico and to the west by California. Named Arizona from the Indian word meaning "few springs," it was organized as a U.S. territory in 1863, but for many years was considered a desert wasteland populated by hostile American Indians. In modern times, however, the warm, dry climate and improvements in transportation, irrigation, and air-conditioning have brought Arizona a strong and steady rate of population growth.

The land.   Arizona is crossed diagonally from northwest to southeast by mountain ranges collectively known as the Mexican Highlands. North and east of this mountain system lies the Colorado Plateau. The Colorado River enters the state from the north, then turns west, flowing through the highlands in the gigantic cut known as the Grand Canyon. After emerging from this canyon, the river turns south and forms Arizona's border with Nevada and California.

The river is dammed at several points in Arizona for irrigation, hydroelectric power, and water supply. The two largest dams are Hoover on the Nevada border and Glen Canyon on the Utah border.

The region south and west of the highlands is an extension of the western basin and range and is drained by the Gila River and its tributaries.

Climate.   The climate of Arizona varies with elevation. Phoenix, in the south-central region, has average high temperatures of more than 100°F (38°C) in summer. Midwinter temperatures range from highs in the 70s F (20s C) to lows below freezing. Yuma, in the southwest corner of the state, is generally warmer than Phoenix, while Flagstaff, in the highlands to the north, is much cooler. There is an average rainfall of under 8 inches (20 centimeters) in Arizona,

most of it falling in the northern mountains. The state receives the highest percentage of available sunshine, 86 percent, in the United States.

Principal cities.   Phoenix, the business and transportation center of Arizona, contains more than half the state population in its metropolitan area. A former U.S. Cavalry hay camp, incorporated as a city in 1881, Phoenix is now the sixth largest city in the United States. Arizona's second largest city is Tucson, 120 miles (193 kilometers) southeast of Phoenix, with a population of 487,000. Tucson has come to be reknowned as a resort town.

The people.   The population of Arizona doubled in the 20 years before 1960 and then doubled again between 1960 and 1980. The largest single ethnic group is Hispanic, representing 25 percent of the population. Arizona has the third largest Native American population in the United States, 255,879, or more than 5 percent of the total population.

Economy.   Arizona was once dependent on copper, cotton, and cattle, but by 1960 manufacturing had surpassed farming and mining. The chief manufactured goods are electronic equipment and primary and fabricated metals. The total value added by manufacture exceeds $8 billion per year. Tourism is the second largest industry, adding more than $4 billion. Visitors come for warm winter weather and the national parks.

Arizona's mines produce half the country's supply of copper ore, a business valued at more than $4 billion. Large quantities of nonmetallic minerals such as sand, gravel, and lime are also mined. The chief agricultural products are livestock, cotton, grains, and citrus.

U.S. military installations brought significant growth in the 1950s, and today the federal government continues to be the state's largest single employer.

Places of interest.   The main natural attraction in Arizona is the Grand Canyon. Other areas of dramatic desert

scenery include the Painted Desert and the Petrified Forest. The town of Tombstone commemorates the state's cowboy history, and numerous Indian reservations also attract many visitors. Hoover Dam and Lake Mead on the Colorado River are among the premier engineering marvels in the United States.

Arkansas

Abbreviations: *Ark., AR*
Area: *52,075 sq. mi.,*
134,875 sq. km.
Rank (of 50)   27th
Population:
2000   2,673,400
Rank (of 50)   33rd
Change 1995–2000
+189,400
Persons per sq. mi.   51.3
Capital: *Little Rock*
Largest city: *Little Rock*
Pop.   183,133
Entered Union: *June 15, 1836*
(25th)
State bird: *Mockingbird*
State flower: *Apple blossom*
State tree: *Pine*
State map: *Page 93*

Arkansas, in the south-central United States, is situated on the west shore of the Mississippi River between Louisiana to the south and Missouri to the north. The state's principal western border is with Oklahoma.

For most of its history, Arkansas was an agricultural state heavily reliant on the cotton crop grown near the Mississippi River, but more recently the state has focused on mining and manufacturing. The result has been significant economic growth.

centimeters
US
centimetres
Brit.

center
US
centre
Brit.

aluminum
US
aluminium
Brit.

The land. The land of Arkansas falls into two areas of approximately equal size: the coastal plain in the east and south, and the interior highlands in the west and north. The coastal plain consists in part of a 50-mile- (80-kilometer-) wide strip of Mississippi alluvial land running parallel to the river. Only about 150 feet (46 meters) above sea level, this large tract represents the state's finest farmland. The remainder of the coastal plain consists of plains slightly higher in elevation and more heavily forested.

The interior highlands consist of the Ozark Plateau in the north and the Ouachita Mountains to the west, with the Arkansas River valley dividing them. The Ozark region is a plateau averaging over 1,000 feet (305 meters) in elevation and heavily eroded by streams and rivers flowing east. Its northern extent includes the fertile Springfield Plateau; its southern extent rises into the Boston Mountains. The Ouachitas south of the Arkansas River valley are steep and mineral-rich. The Arkansas River valley is 30 to 40 miles (48 to 64 kilometers) wide, and the river falls 300 feet (91 meters) as it flows east to the Mississippi.

Climate. Arkansas has a mild climate, influenced by winds from the Gulf of Mexico. Little Rock, in the center of the state, has winter lows of about 30° F (-1°C) and summer highs of 90°F

The people. After a major population decline of almost 200,000 between 1940 and 1960, Arkansas managed to build an economy in the 1970s that attracted 136,000 immigrants from other states. Urbanization has increased as a result, but the state remains well below the national average in that respect. African Americans, the major ethnic group, represent 16 percent of the total population.

Economy. In 1955, after years of population decline, Arkansas established an Industrial Development Commission to formulate legislation beneficial to business. Today the state has extensive mining and manufacturing businesses. It produces most of the U.S. supply of bauxite, the ore from which aluminum is refined, and major portions of the national bromine and vanadium output. Oil and natural gas are drilled in the southern regions of the state.

Manufacturing, which centers on processing the state's mineral and agricultural output, generates more than $5 billion in income per year. Poultry processing has also become a major business since 1940. The state's agricultural decline was related to its preponderance of small farms and reliance on the cotton crop, but in recent years heavily mechanized farming has converted the cotton fields along the Mississippi River to high-yield crops such as soybeans and rice.

THE OZARK REGION of Arkansas is a plateau, averaging over 100 feet in elevation, that is heavily eroded by streams and rivers flowing east.

(32°C). Portions of the state to the south have warmer winters, but those to the north have only slightly colder ones. The average rainfall in the state is about 50 inches (127 centimeters), most of it falling in winter. Spring and autumn are especially long seasons in Arkansas, and they add to the state's growing season.

Principal cities. Arkansas is a state of small towns and a relatively rural population. The major city is the capital, Little Rock, on the Arkansas River. It is the site of most of the state's manufacturing businesses. Other manufacturing centers on the Arkansas River are Fort Smith (population, 80,268), on the Oklahoma border, and Pine Bluff (55,085), 35 miles (56 kilometers) southeast of Little Rock.

The forestry industry on the west Gulf coastal plains presently produces nearly 2 billion board feet of timber per year. Tourism has become a major industry, generating more than $2 billion of revenue a year.

Places of interest. The major tourist attraction in Arkansas is Hot Springs National Park, 45 miles (72 kilometers) southwest of Little Rock, where mineral waters naturally flow at temperatures up to 147°F (64°C) throughout the year. Blanchard Springs Caverns in the Ozarks, 60 miles (97 kilometers) north of Little Rock, are among the largest in the country, and Ouachita and Ozark national forests cover thousands of acres in western Arkansas.

California

Abbreviations: *Calif., CA*
Area: *155,973 sq. mi.,*
403,970 sq. km.
Rank (of 50)   3rd
Population:
2000   33,871,648
Rank (of 50)   1st
Change 1995–2000
+2,282,648
Persons per sq. mi.   217.1
Capital: *Sacramento*
Largest city: *Los Angeles*
Pop.   3,694,820
Entered Union: *Sept. 9, 1850*
(31st)
State bird: *California valley quail*
State flower: *Golden poppy*
State tree: *California redwood*
State map: *Page 90*

California has an 850-mile (1,368-kilometer) coastline on the Pacific Ocean at the extreme southwest of the contiguous 48 states. It ranks first in population and third in area, after Alaska and Texas. If California were a separate country, it would rank eighth in the world in gross national product. If metropolitan Los Angeles were a separate state, its population would rank ninth in the United States. California's remarkable growth accelerated in the 1980s and continued through the 1990s. Between 1970 and 2000 its population grew by 13.9 million, and the metropolitan regions of southern California (Anaheim, San Diego, Los Angeles, Riverside-San Bernardino) alone gained 4.5 million.

Much of this growth defies common logic. The southern part of the state lacks both water and power resources; the economy after World War II was based too heavily on wartime industries; and the state as a whole is far from other large population centers. Yet California leads the United States in agricultural production, and its manufacturing businesses have managed remarkably successful diversification. For example, "Silicon Valley," near San Francisco, so named for the tiny silicon integrated circuit chips used in microcircuitry, is a major electronics center.

The land. California's topographical pattern is one of contrasts. Along the northern two-thirds of the ocean shore, the mountains of the Coastal Range come almost to the water's edge. Inland from the Coastal Range lies the semiarid Central Valley, stretching some 400 miles (644 kilometers) from north to south. Since the advent of modern irrigation, this low-lying valley has become one of the most productive farm regions in the world. Inland from the Central Valley rise the Sierra Nevada, among the steepest mountains in North America. The range includes Mt. Whitney (14,494

GIANT SEQUOIAS are a major attraction in the redwood forest north of San Francisco.

feet, 4,418 meters), the highest point in the 48 contiguous states; four national parks, Yosemite, Sequoia, Kings Canyon, and Lassen; and Squaw Valley and various other well-known ski resorts.

Along the southern third of the state, the ocean shore alternates between rocky stretches and wide beaches. A ring of mountains surrounds the large coastal plain on which Los Angeles is built and separates it from the great Mojave Desert, which covers 15,000 square miles (38,850 square kilometers) of inland southern California. Here the lowest point in the United States, Death Valley, 282 feet (86 meters) below sea level, lies only 80 miles (129 kilometers) southeast of Mt. Whitney.

Climate. The climates of northern and southern California contrast as much as their topography. The southern coast enjoys year-round sun and warm temperatures, while the northern coast is cooler and damper. Temperatures above 100°F (38°C) are frequent in the southern inland deserts, and heavy snows and intense cold are common in the northern high Sierra.

Principal cities. California's two great metropolitan regions are representative of the contrasts in the state

meters	*US*
metres	*Brit.*
center	*US*
centre	*Brit.*

between north and south. In the north, San Francisco became the state's principal city in the wake of the 1849 gold rush. The city was almost totally destroyed by an earthquake and fire in 1906, but it was soon rebuilt. Another major earthquake hit San Francisco in 1989. Today San Francisco is the center of a large metropolitan region stretching from San Jose, 30 miles (48 kilometers) to the south, to a string of cities, including Oakland and Berkeley, on the inland shores of the bay.

By contrast, Los Angeles, 400 miles (644 kilometers) to the south, experienced no dramatic growth until after 1920. Then, in the 1950s, out-of-state immigrants (many from the Midwest and the South) began arriving at the rate of 1,000 per week. Because of its rapid expansion, Los Angeles today lies sprawled out in all directions, linked by a complex system of freeways. This sprawl has overtaken many formerly separate cities.

The people. California boasts a wide variety of people. One person in three is a member of an ethnic group. About 11 million (32 percent) are of Hispanic, chiefly Mexican, descent; more than 2.2 million (7 percent) are African Americans; and 3.6 million (10 percent) are of Asian descent. Because of its large metropolitan areas, California also has the highest proportion of urban population in the United States.

Economy. Agriculture is the largest industry, chiefly because of production in the Central Valley of a variety of crops ranging from cotton to wine grapes. Citrus fruits declined in importance as residential developments replaced orange groves. The most important farm products are grapes, tomatoes, grain for livestock feed, cotton, lettuce, fruits and nuts, and dairy products.

The state's early reliance on military and aerospace industries has been corrected in part in recent years by the diversification of manufacturing. Manufactures, including food products and fabricated metals, now produce about $150 billion in value added per year. Tourism is another major source of

MOVIE STARS OF YESTERDAY and today are honored on the Walk of Fame in Hollywood.

income, with visitors from both the United States and abroad spending nearly $49 billion per year. The most famous industry in the state is entertainment: the film and television businesses are largely centered in and around Hollywood, a section of Los Angeles.

Places of interest. California offers a wide range of attractions. Among its most spectacular natural landscapes are Yosemite Valley, giant redwood and sequoia forests, and the wide beaches and desert expanses of southern California. Some popular man-made attractions are Disneyland and Hollywood in the south. San Francisco, in the north, is known for its picturesque harbor and its literary and artistic community.

Colorado

Abbreviations: *Colo., CO*

Area: *103,730 sq. mi., 268,660 sq. km.*
Rank (of 50)   8th

Population:
2000   4,301,261
Rank (of 50)   24th
Change 1995–2000 +554,261
Persons per sq. mi.   41.5

Capital: *Denver*

Largest city: *Denver*
Pop.   554,636

Entered Union: *Aug. 1, 1876 (38th)*

State bird: *Lark bunting*

State flower: *Rocky mountain columbine*

State tree: *Colorado blue spruce*

State map: *Page 92*

Colorado is divided roughly in half from north to south by the Rockies, sharing the mountains with its neighboring states to the north, south, and west: Wyoming, New Mexico, and Utah. The most elevated of all U.S. states, Colorado offers some of the most spectacular mountain scenery in the country and includes within its borders both the highest peak in the Rockies, Mt. Elbert (14,433 feet, 4,399 meters), and the highest city in the United States, Leadville (10,200 feet, 3,109 meters). The state is growing at a rapid rate, having gained over 1 million residents in the 1970s and 1980s, and more than 1 million again in the 1990s.

The land. Colorado contains three clearly defined topographical areas: the mountains running north-south through the center of the state; the Great Plains to the east; and the Colorado Plateau to the west. The Southern Rockies include 54 peaks over 10,000 feet (3,048 meters) in elevation within Colorado. They also contain the headwaters of rivers that supply water to six states and Mexico.

THE FOUR CORNERS AREA of Colorado, Utah, Arizona, and New Mexico has a number of long-abandoned sites of the Anasazi culture.

Connecticut

Abbreviations: *Conn., CT*
Area: *4,845 sq. mi., 12,550 sq. km.*
  Rank (of 50) 48th
Population:
  2000 3,405,565
  Rank (of 50) 29th
  Change 1995–2000 +130,565
  Persons per sq. mi. 702.9
Capital: *Hartford*
Largest city: *Bridgeport*
  Pop. 139,529
Entered Union: *Jan. 9, 1788*
  (5th)
State bird: *American robin*
State flower: *Mountain laurel*
State tree: *White oak*
State map: *Page 101*

The entire eastern third of the state is part of the Great Plains, which stretch east over most of neighboring Nebraska and Kansas. Eastern Colorado has poor, arid land, suitable only for grazing. The region is crossed by the South Platte River in the north flowing into Nebraska, and by the Arkansas River in the south flowing into Kansas.

Colorado's western plateau is built of horizontal rock broken by canyons, mesas, and subsidiary plateaus ranging in elevation from 5,000 to 10,000 feet (1,524 to 3,048 meters). The western plateau is drained by a network of waterways that converge to form the Colorado River.

Climate. The climate in Colorado is dry and sunny, with temperatures in Denver, in the eastern foothills of the Rockies, ranging from winter lows below 20°F (-7°C) to summer highs of nearly 90°F (32°C). Alpine conditions prevail in the highest elevations, and both the western plateau and the eastern plains remain warmer than the center of the state. Statewide rainfall is low, averaging about 16 inches (41 centimeters) per year in Denver, but the mountain regions receive heavy snows.

Principal cities. Metropolitan Denver, originally a gold mining camp, contains almost half the state population. It is a manufacturing city and the center of rail, road, and air transport for much of the Mountain states region. Colorado's other major cities lie clustered north and south of Denver along the eastern face of the Rockies. Colorado Springs (population, 360,890), 60 miles (97 kilometers) south of Denver, is a resort and the home of the U.S. Air Force Academy. Pueblo (population, 102,121), another 35 miles (56 kilometers) south, is an industrial city once known as the Pittsburgh of the West for its steel mills. For 50 miles (80 kilometers) north of Denver, along the

same corridor, a chain of towns stretches from nearby Boulder (population, 94,673) to the northern cities of Greeley (76,930) and Fort Collins (118,652).

The people. The population of Colorado is largely urban and is concentrated in cities within 100 miles (161 kilometers) north or south of Denver. People of Spanish origin, chiefly Mexicans, are the only large ethnic group, numbering 735,601, or 17.8 percent of the population. Colorado's growth in recent decades has been due in part to growth of its resort facilities and industries as well as to its natural beauty and recreation areas.

Economy. Manufacturing is the most important sector of the state economy, and the state's manufactured goods are worth more than twice as much as those of any other Mountain state. The principal manufactures are electronic equipment and aerospace products. Mining, primarily of petroleum, natural gas, and coal, is valued at more than $2 billion per year. The agricultural activities of the state are concentrated on livestock. Colorado is second to Montana among Mountain states in forestland and in the production of lumber. Tourism is now a major and growing activity, due largely to Colorado's ski resorts.

Places of interest. Mountains are the main attraction in Colorado, and the prime mountain reserve is Rocky Mountain National Park in the north-central region, within 40 miles (64 kilometers) of Denver. Also of interest are Pike's Peak, near Colorado Springs, and Great Sand Dunes National Monument, south of Pueblo. Colorado Springs, with its combination of mountain scenery, mineral springs, and the U.S. Air Force Academy, is also one of the great attractions in the Rockies. Colorado is rich in ski resorts, the best-known being those at Aspen and Vail.

Connecticut is situated in the southwestern corner of the New England region bordering New York to the west and southwest. Rhode Island is to its east and Massachusetts to the north. The southern boundary is the shoreline facing Long Island Sound, an arm of the Atlantic between Connecticut and Long Island, and a part of New York State. Connecticut is rectangular in shape, with a narrow southwestern extension reaching 15 miles (24 kilometers) toward New York City.

Connecticut was a relatively rural state until after 1945. Then, the development of suburban communities in the southwest part of the state in the New York City metropolitan region sent the population soaring. It reached 2 million in 1950, 2.5 million in 1960, 3 million in 1970, and was approaching 3.5 million in 2000. Suburban growth never reached

THE BEAUTY of the countryside, along with the attraction of winter sports, makes tourism second only to manufacturing in New England.

Delaware

Abbreviations: *Del., DE*
Area: *1,995 sq. mi., 5,163 sq. km.*
    Rank (of 50)   49th
Population:
    2000   783,600
    Rank (of 50)   45th
    Change 1995–2000   +66,000
    Persons per sq. mi.   395.2
Capital: *Dover*
Largest city: *Wilmington*
    Pop.   72,664
Entered Union: *Dec. 7, 1787*
    (1st)
State bird: *Blue hen chicken*
State flower: *Peach blossom*
State tree: *American holly*
State map: *Page 99*

MYSTIC SEAPORT, on the southeastern coast of Connecticut, is a restored 19th-century whaling and shipbuilding village.

center
US

centre
Brit.

meters
US

metres
Brit.

the northern areas, however, and there Connecticut retains its rural New England character, with small farms on rolling hills and solid wood frame houses in small towns facing handsome village greens.

The land. Connecticut consists almost entirely of New England Upland, divided through the center of the state by the lower Connecticut River valley. The uplands are highest to the west of the valley, and in the northwestern corner they reach a portion of the Taconic Mountains. The state high point is located at Mt. Frissell (2,380 feet, 725 meters), near the New York and Massachusetts borders. The uplands to the east of the valley seldom rise more than 1,000 feet (305 meters) above sea level; they are characterized by rolling hills and gentle river valleys. The Connecticut valley between these highlands is narrow in the north, but it broadens into fertile floodplains around Hartford, where most of the land is scarcely above sea level. Along its southern coast, Connecticut also includes a narrow strip of New England Seaboard Lowland, a shoreline that mixes rocky peninsulas and deep bays with sandy beaches.

Climate. The climate of Connecticut is coldest in the elevated northwest and milder in the central valley. Normal winter lows at Hartford average 16°F (-9°C) and summer highs average 84°F (29°C). Statewide precipitation averages 43 inches (109 centimeters) per year, including snowfall of 54 inches (137 centimeters) per year. The northwest receives less total precipitation, but its long winters bring it snowfalls above the state average.

Principal cities. The greatest portion of Connecticut's population resides in a series of southwest coastal metropolitan areas linked to New York City by highway and railroad routes, including the state's largest city, Bridgeport. The eastern limit of this urban region is the New Haven-Meriden metropolitan area (population, 542,149), 100 miles (161 kilometers) from New York City. Another large city is Hartford (population, 121,578), a center for insurance companies, manufacturers, and state government.

The people. Connecticut's growth slowed during the 1970s, when more people moved out of the state than moved in. Since its major growth is so recent, Connecticut has a low proportion of lifelong residents. The resident population is 9 percent African American and 9 percent Hispanic, with the heaviest concentrations of these groups in urban areas. Many other ethnic communities are also represented in Connecticut.

Economy. Since the 1800s, Connecticut's principal industry has been manufacturing. In earlier times hardware was the chief product. This tradition led to large aircraft engine industries around Hartford and a shipbuilding industry around the U.S. submarine base in Groton on the southeast coast. Manufacturing in Connecticut now produces about $24 billion in value added annually.

Another large industry in the state is finance, reflecting the great number of major corporate headquarters in the southwest of the state and large insurance companies in Hartford. Tourism in both coastal and inland areas is the third major industry, accounting for more than $3 billion per year. Connecticut's agriculture is a limited industry, based chiefly on dairy products but also noted for the shade-grown tobacco harvested on the floodplains around Hartford.

Places of interest. The state's Long Island Sound shoreline is its principal natural attraction. Mystic Seaport, along the southeastern coast, is a restored 19th-century whaling and shipbuilding village. Other places of interest include the P. T. Barnum Museum in Bridgeport and the Winchester Gun Museum and Yale University in New Haven.

Delaware is the most northeastern of the Tidewater states, bordered on both the west and the south by Maryland. The state borders Pennsylvania to the north, and its northern half faces New Jersey to the east across the Delaware River. The southern half of the state's eastern border is coastline on Delaware Bay and the Atlantic Ocean.

Delaware, called the "First State" because it ratified the Constitution first, is the second smallest state in the United States in land area and the fourth smallest in population. The northern part of the state, however, is a heavily populated metropolitan area, part of the populous northeastern corridor stretching from Washington, D.C., to Boston.

The land. Virtually all of the state land area lies on the Atlantic Coastal Plain. This portion of the plain is 80 miles (129 kilometers) from north to

MORE THAN HALF the farm income in Delaware is derived from poultry.

south and broadens from 10 miles (16 kilometers) wide in the north to 35 miles (56 kilometers) wide in the south. Its maximum elevation is 60 feet (18 meters) and its small rivers drain both east into Delaware Bay and west into Chesapeake Bay. These two bodies of water are linked in the north of the plain by the Chesapeake-Delaware Canal.

The northern tip of Delaware is a tiny portion of the Piedmont Plateau. There, the rolling pasturelands and wooded slopes include the state high point of 442 feet (135 meters) above sea level near Centerville. The Piedmont Plateau is separated from the Atlantic Coastal Plain by the northeastern route of the Christina River to the Delaware River.

Climate. Delaware's climate is moderated by the surrounding bodies of water. At Wilmington, in the northern part of the state, normal summer high temperatures are 85°F (29°C) and normal winter lows are 25°F (-4°C). Precipitation at Wilmington averages 40 inches (102 centimeters) per year, including an average of 20 inches (51 centimeters) of snow.

Principal cities. The only major urban center in the state is Wilmington, on the Piedmont Plateau at the confluence of the Brandywine, Christina, and Delaware rivers. Wilmington is the heart of a large metropolitan area that includes Newark (population, 28,547) and portions of Pennsylvania and New Jersey. The metropolitan area's Delaware residents represent 75 percent of the total state population. The second largest city in the state is the capital, Dover, which has 32,135 residents.

The people. The state's population was swelled slightly by immigration from other states in the 1970s, but its growth rate was better in the 1980s and 1990s. The general population movement is from cities to suburbs. In the 1970s the city population of Wilmington continued a decline that began in the 1940s. This was followed by slight increases in 1980s and 1990s. The minority populations in the state are 19 percent African American and 4 percent Hispanic.

Economy. The principal industry in Delaware is manufacturing, which accounts for more than $4 billion in value added and generates four times as much income as agriculture. Most of the manufacturing is based in Wilmington, the home of DuPont, a giant chemical company. Other major manufactures include food products, an outgrowth of Delaware's pioneering role in introducing fruit and vegetable canning in the late 1800s.

Half the state's land is farmland, and more than half the farm income in Delaware is from poultry. The principal crops are corn and soybeans for animal feed, and fruits and vegetables for shipment to markets in the Northeast. The state's low taxes and liberal corporate regulations have attracted many businesses and have made banking and finance an important industry. Tourism brings in more than $700 million per year.

Places of interest. Points of interest around Wilmington include the Swedish-American Fort Christina Monument, the Francis du Pont Winterthur Museum, and the Holy Trinity Church, the oldest operating Protestant parish in the United States.

District of Columbia

Abbreviations: *D.C., DC*
Area: *61 sq. mi., 159 sq. km.*
Population:

> 2000   572,059
> *Change 1995–2000   +18,059*
> *Persons per sq. mi.   9,378.0*

Established as capital:

> *June 10, 1800*

District bird: *Wood thrush*
District flower:

> *American beauty rose*

District tree: *Scarlet oak*
Area map: *Page 99*

The District of Columbia is the seat of U.S. government. It is located on a roughly rectangular plot of land on the bank of the Potomac River, surrounded on three sides by Maryland and bordering northern Virginia across the Potomac.

The District was originally a square of land 10 miles (16 kilometers) on a side, through which the Potomac passed. But the land on the Virginia side was returned to that state in 1846. The city of Washington and the District of Columbia have the same boundaries.

A "federal town" had been contemplated by American leaders since 1783, and in 1790 the present site on the Potomac was chosen. The choice was a compromise worked out by Northern and Southern states. Including the original Virginia area, the new federal town would lie between the North and South. Philadelphia remained the U.S. capital until the new city, named for the first president, was ready to be occupied.

The Federal District of Columbia in Washington was designed as a spacious network of promenades and open vistas by Pierre Charles L'Enfant, who had come to America with the Marquis de Lafayette. The city he designed was completed by Andrew Ellicott and Benjamin Banneker. During the War of 1812, the city was captured. A number of buildings were burned by the British in 1814, partly in retaliation for the American burning of the British capital of Upper Canada, York (Toronto), in 1813. The Capitol and the White House were among the buildings burned, but they and other structures were later rebuilt.

Politically, Washington was incorporated as a town in 1802. Much later, it was reorganized, with adjacent Georgetown, to become coextensive with the District of Columbia. In 1974 a new charter was approved that gave Washington residents an elected mayor and a city council for the first time. The U.S. Congress retains veto power over the local government. In 1978 a constitutional amendment to give the District of Columbia full voting representation in the House and the Senate was passed by Congress. It requires, but has not yet received, ratification by 38 states to become law.

THE WHITE HOUSE in the District of Columbia is the home of the president of the United States.

THE SMITHSONIAN INSTITUTION is the national museum of the United States and actually consists of a number of museums in several locations.

27 North America

Washington has experienced serious urban problems. More prosperous professionals and government employees have tended to move to suburbs in Virginia and Maryland, leaving the city with a poor population and a small tax base, since it is unable to tax federal property. The Washington metropolitan area has a population of almost 4 million, but less than one-sixth of its people live in the District itself.

The people. The population of Washington has been predominantly African American since 1960, and in 2000 the population was 60 percent African American. Hispanics represent 8 percent of the total city population. Half of all residents are employed by the government, and the major industry is tourism.

Places of interest. Some popular sights in Washington, D.C., are the Washington Monument, the Lincoln Memorial, the White House, the Capitol Building, the Supreme Court Building, the National Air and Space Museum, the National Gallery of Art, the Smithsonian Institution, and the Vietnam War Memorial.

YEAR-ROUND WARM TEMPERATURES and wide beaches make tourism Florida's principal industry. Miami Beach is a tourism center of the state.

Florida

Abbreviations: *Fla., FL*
Area: *53,997 sq. mi.,*
    139,852 sq. km.
    Rank (of 50) 26th
Population:
    2000 15,982,378
    Rank (of 50) 4th
    Change 1995–2000
    +1,816,378
    Persons per sq. mi. 295.9
Capital: *Tallahassee*
Largest city: *Jacksonville*
    Pop. 735,617
Entered Union: *Mar. 3, 1845*
    (27th)
State bird: *Mockingbird*
State flower: *Orange blossom*
State tree: *Sabal palm*
    (cabbage palmetto)
State map: *Page 98*

kilometer
US
kilometre
Brit.

center
US
centre
Brit.

Florida is situated in the extreme southeast of the continental United States. Most of the state area consists of a 450-mile- (724-kilometer-) long peninsula extending southeast between the Atlantic Ocean and the Gulf of Mexico. The peninsula ends in a string of islets called the Florida Keys, the southernmost part of the contiguous 48 states. Florida also includes a narrow northern panhandle extending 350 miles (563 kilometers) west from the Atlantic and separating Georgia and most of Alabama from the Gulf of Mexico.

The oldest European settlement in North America is the Spanish outpost at St. Augustine on Florida's Atlantic coast. Florida has a long history under Spanish, English, and American control, but its present character is a product of the 20th century. There were fewer than 200,000 people in the state in 1880; the population reached only 1 million in 1930. From 1950 to 1980, the state had a greater numerical population growth than any state except California: 7 million. In the subsequent 20 years, population grew again by more than 6 million. Many are retired people, and the populace is by far the oldest in the United States. People are drawn by the state's beaches and warm sunny climate.

The land. Florida lies entirely within the Atlantic and the Gulf coastal plains. The peninsula is wholly a part of the Atlantic Coastal Plain. Along the Atlantic coast are the barrier beaches separated from the mainland by tidal lagoons. The interior of the peninsula consists of hills and lakes from the northern border south to Lake Okeechobee. The southern third of the peninsula is the great swamp area known as the Everglades.

The northern panhandle is wholly a part of the Gulf Coastal Plain. South of Alabama the panhandle consists of highlands that reach a maximum elevation of 345 feet (105 meters). South of Georgia it consists of the marshy Mariana lowlands and of the Tallahassee Hills in the extreme east.

Climate. Florida has year-round warm temperatures. Normal summer temperatures throughout the state are 90°F (32°C), and winter normal lows range from 45°F (7°C) in Jacksonville in the north to 60°F (16°C) in Miami, 350 miles (563 kilometers) to the south. Precipitation averages 60 inches (152 centimeters) per year in Miami and 55 inches (140 centimeters) in Jacksonville. Snowfall is rare anywhere in the state, but hurricanes are a threat in summer and early fall. In August 1992, for example, Hurricane Andrew swept south Florida, leaving some 250,000 homeless and causing billions of dollars of damage.

Principal cities. The largest population center is Tampa-St. Petersburg (population, 2.4 million), at the center of the peninsula's Gulf Coast. Tampa Bay is the principal deepwater port in the state and the site of its shipping of export goods. The second largest urban center in the state is the 100-mile- (161-kilometer-) long "Gold Coast" of cities surrounding Miami in the southeast. This consolidated metropolitan area includes more than 2 million residents, and it is a tourism center of the state. The major cities in the panhandle and northern Florida are Tallahassee (population, 150,624), the capital, and Jacksonville, also the largest city in land area in the United States.

The people. Nearly 20 percent of the population of Florida is over 65 years of age. The state's rapid population growth is principally from migration. The population is nearly 15 percent African American and 17 percent Hispanic. The state is unique for its large concentration of Cuban residents, especially in Miami. Cuba is less than 100 miles (161 kilometers) from the Florida coast across the Straits of Florida. The Cuban community received a great number of Cuban political refugees in 1980.

Economy. The principal business of Florida is tourism, now a year-round industry that draws over 35 million visitors per year and produces an annual income of more than $16 billion. (A series of killings of foreign tourists in 1993 caused great problems for Florida's tourism industry.) Manufacturing is the second most important sector of the state's economy. Florida's manufacturers concentrate on wood pulp and paper products, food processing, and electronics equipment associated with the aerospace businesses surrounding Cape Canaveral on the Atlantic coast near Orlando. Orlando is also the center of the citrus industry. Citrus fruit is

Florida's most important agricultural product. Other important crops include sugarcane, tobacco, and winter vegetables such as tomatoes. Florida also mines 80 percent of the U.S. production of phosphate rock.

Places of interest. Florida's most popular attractions are the luxury hotels and beach resorts along the Atlantic coast. The islands to the south of Florida, especially Key West, also attract many winter visitors to their tropical climate. Everglades National Park in southern Florida is a 5,000-square-mile (12,945-square-kilometer) preserve of swamplands and unusual wildlife. Places of interest in central Florida include Disney World near Orlando and the John F. Kennedy Space Center at Cape Canaveral.

THIS CIVIL WAR MONUMENT can be seen at Stone Mountain Park near Atlanta, Georgia.

THE EVERGLADES in Florida is home to many varieties of wildlife, such as the great white heron.

Georgia

Abbreviations: *Ga., GA*

Area: *57,919 sq. mi.,*
      150,010 sq. km.
      Rank (of 50)   21st

Population:
      2000   8,186,453
      Rank (of 50)   10th
      Change 1995–2000
      +985,453
      Persons per sq. mi.   141.3

Capital: *Atlanta*

Largest city: *Atlanta*
      Pop.   416,474

Entered Union: *Jan. 2, 1788*
      (4th)

State bird: *Brown thrasher*

State flower: *Cherokee rose*

State tree: *Live oak*

State map: *Page 98*

Georgia is located in the southeast United States to the north of Florida. The state has 100 miles (161 kilometers) of coastline on the Atlantic Ocean, and a long northeastern border with South Carolina formed by the Savannah River. To the west, Georgia borders Alabama, and to the north, Tennessee and North Carolina. Georgia is the largest state in land area east of the Mississippi River.

Georgia has endured a series of social and economic problems since the Civil War, most of them related to racial and economic inequalities. During the first half of the 1900s, thousands of African Americans and poor whites left the state in search of opportunity elsewhere. Since 1950, however, Georgia has grown rapidly, and many state rural residents have moved to the cities. Atlanta has emerged today as the commercial and financial center of the southeastern region.

The land. The land area of Georgia runs from the Appalachian Mountains in the north and west to the Atlantic coast. The northeastern part of the state includes a portion of forested Blue Ridge Mountains with a number of peaks over 4,000 feet (1,219 meters) in elevation. Most of the northern half of the state, however, consists of the Piedmont Plateau, which is the agricultural and population center of the state. The rolling hills of the plateau decline in elevation from about 2,000 feet (610 meters) in the north to about 1,000 feet (305 meters) at the Fall Line Hills running east to west across the center of the state.

South of these hills lie the coastal plains. The western part slopes toward the Gulf of Mexico (only 30 miles, or 48 kilometers, from Georgia's southwest border with Florida), and the eastern half slopes toward the Atlantic Ocean. Water power generated by streams falling from the plateau to the plain made the hills Georgia's early industrial belt. The Atlantic Plain in the south covers more than half the Georgia land area.

Individual features include the Okefenokee Swamp on the Florida border and the Sea Islands, part of the Great Barrier Reef, which is separated from the mainland by narrow tidal lagoons.

Climate. Georgia has a warm, humid climate with a long growing season. Normal summer highs approach 90°F (32°C), and winter temperatures usually remain above freezing. Precipitation throughout the state averages 48 inches (122 centimeters) per year, but the Blue Ridge Mountains in the northeast receive nearly 70 inches (178 centimeters), some of it in the form of snow.

Principal cities. The major urban center of Georgia is Atlanta, on the northwestern portion of the Piedmont Plateau. Atlanta is the model for new cities throughout the South. Its city center has been rebuilt, major businesses have been attracted, and its metropolitan population more than doubled between 1970 and 1998. The other major cities lie on a line running northeast across the center of the state, along the Fall Line Hills. Columbus (population, 186,291) is a textile city straddling the Chattahoochee River. Macon (population, 97,255) is a manufacturing city. Augusta (population, 199,775) is a food processing city on the Savannah River beside South Carolina. The only other major city in the state is Savannah (population, 131,510), a river port on the South Carolina border 20 miles (32 kilometers) from the Atlantic.

The people. Like the rest of the South Atlantic states, Georgia is growing at a rate well above the national average. Its central position in the region and the importance of Atlanta as a transportation and communications center suggest that its growth will continue.

The other population movement over the past few decades has been from farms to cities. In the case of Atlanta, the movement has gone a step further, from cities to outer suburbs. In addition, the exodus of African-American residents

HAWAII
offers diverse
landscapes, from
mountains to active
volcanos and lava
fields to beautiful
beaches.

kilometer
US

kilometre
Brit.

civilization
US

civilisation
Brit.

center
US

centre
Brit.

has ended. This group represents 29 percent of the state population, and Hispanics, the only other sizable minority group, represent 5.3 percent.

Economy.   The chief industry of Georgia is manufacturing, and its principal product is textiles. All major cities in the state produce textiles, ranging from cottons to synthetics. Other major manufactures are paper, other wood products, processed foods, transportation equipment, electrical and electronic equipment, chemicals, and fabricated metals.

Georgia's agriculture was over-dependent on cotton until the 1920s, when the crop was lost to boll weevil infestation. Now the farmland, principally on the Atlantic Coastal Plain, grows peanuts, soybeans, tobacco, corn, and peaches. Livestock generates as much income as crops, primarily because of the state's enormous production of chickens and eggs. Tourism is the third largest industry, generating well over $7 billion per year.

Places of interest.   The Okefenokee National Wildlife Refuge is a 660-square-mile (1,709-square-kilometer) preserve of swamplands on the Florida border. The Atlantic coast is lined with seashore beaches. Historical attractions include the so-called "Little White House" near Columbus, where President Franklin Delano Roosevelt died in 1945, and various memorials to the Confederacy scattered throughout the state.

Hawaii

Abbreviations: *Haw., HI*
Area: *6,423 sq. mi., 16,637 sq. km.*
　　　Rank (of 50)   47th
Population:
　　　2000   1,211,537
　　　Rank (of 50)   42nd
　　　Change 1995–2000
　　　+24,537
　　　Persons per sq. mi.   188.6
Capital: *Honolulu*
Largest city: *Honolulu*
　　　Pop. 371,657
Entered Union: *Aug. 21, 1959*
　　　(50th)
State bird: *Hawaiian goose*
State flower: *Hibiscus*
State tree: *Kukui (candlenut)*
State map: *Page 90*

Hawaii is the 50th state and the only one situated outside continental North America. Located in the Pacific Ocean 2,000 miles (3,218 kilometers) southwest of California, Hawaii is a 1,500-mile-long (2,414-kilometer-long) archipelago of over 100 islands with a total area less than that of New Jersey. The principal islands are clustered in the southeastern end of the chain. They are, in descending order of size, Hawaii, Maui, Oahu, Kauai, Molokai, Lanai, and Niihau. One other significant island, Kahoolawe, is a cattle station with no permanent population.

Despite its small land area and limited population, Hawaii is a remarkably diversified state. In addition to the tropical beaches that most visitors from the mainland expect to see, the state includes cattle ranches, pineapple and coffee plantations, winter skiing on the volcanic cone of Mauna Kea, large suburban neighborhoods, and a citizenry that includes many interesting ethnic backgrounds.

History.   The first European to report on the Hawaiian Islands was Captain James Cook of England. In 1778 he discovered a thriving civilization of Polynesian peoples on the main islands. Hawaii attracted more visitors, including Christian missionaries from the United States, in the next 50 years, but kept its independence. It was recognized as an independent country by the United States in 1842.

U.S. business investments in the islands increased in the late 1800s. In 1894 the Hawaiian monarchy gave way to a republic. In 1898 the United States annexed Hawaii, and in 1900 it became a territory. The Navy base at Pearl Harbor increased in size and strategic importance after World War I. Carrier-launched Japanese war planes attacked the base on December 7, 1941. The next day, the United States entered World War II.

After the war, sentiment for statehood grew rapidly, and in 1959 Hawaii became the 50th state.

The land.   The Hawaiian Islands are volcanic in origin. The largest island, called Hawaii, is the creation of twin volcanic peaks—Mauna Loa (13,680 feet, 4,170 meters) and Mauna Kea (13,796 feet, 4,205 meters)—giving it a total land area of 4,021 square miles (10,414 square kilometers). The second largest island is Maui (728 square miles, 1,886 square kilometers), an agricultural plantation dominated by the volcanic peak that gives Haleakala National Park its name. The island of Oahu (595 square miles, 1,541 square kilometers) is the location of the capital city, Honolulu. The remaining populated islands of Kauai, Molokai, Lanai, and Niihau are all dominated by single volcanic mountains and have coastlines of steep cliff faces broken by small natural harbors.

Climate.   The climate of Hawaii is relatively mild, because the ocean winds moderate temperatures usual in such subtropical latitudes. Temperatures in the most populous areas remain in the 70°F (21°C) range year-round. Rainfall varies greatly, from 15 inches (38 centimeters) per year along the southwestern shores to more than 100 inches (254 centimeters) along northeastern shores and at high altitudes. The higher peaks may be snow-covered during part of the year. Hawaii is vulnerable to damaging hurricanes and typhoons. In September 1992, Hurricane Iniki, the most powerful hurricane to hit Hawaii in a century, devastated the island of Kauai.

Principal cities.   The major city is Honolulu on Oahu. About 72 percent of the state's people live in the metropolitan area. The city is situated southwest of Pearl Harbor, largest natural harbor on the islands. In addition to being the seat of state government, Honolulu is also the tourist capital of Hawaii, with large vacation hotels stretching along the beaches to the east of the older city center.

Other major cities are Kailua (population, 36,513) and Pearl City (30,976), both on Oahu; and Hilo (40,759), the principal port on the island of Hawaii.

The people.   Native Hawaiians are descended from Polynesian peoples who first settled the island during the seventh century. The state's other major ethnic groups are Japanese, Chinese, and Filipino. Intermarriage and influences from the mainland have led to the integration of these ethnic groups, but 60 percent of the population consider themselves of Asian-American or Pacific Islander heritage. The total population of the state is now almost nine-tenths urban and enjoys both a higher per capita income and a lower unemployment rate than the national average.

Economy.   Tourism brings Hawaii over $9 billion per year, far more than any other industry, and provides the principal employment for the workforce. However, Hawaii has long been known for its pineapple, sugarcane, and coffee crops. They are grown and processed on huge corporate plantations that occupy the entire area of some smaller islands. Large herds of cattle are also grazed on isolated islands. Other businesses in the state have increased in recent years, including electronics research sponsored by the U.S. military and businesses associated with trade and shipping.

Places of interest. The major geological places of interest in Hawaii, identified by island, include Hawaii Volcanoes National Park (Hawaii) and Haleakala National Park (Maui). Places associated with the islands' Polynesian heritage include Puuhonua o Honaunau National Historical Park (Hawaii), the Polynesian Cultural Center (Oahu), and Iolani Palace (Oahu), the only royal palace in the United States. Near Honolulu visitors abound at the U.S.S. *Arizona* memorial at Pearl Harbor, Waikiki Beach, and Diamond Head.

Idaho

Abbreviations: *Ida., ID*
Area: *82,751 sq. mi.,*
　　214,325 sq. km.
　　Rank (of 50)　11th
Population:
　　2000　1,293,953
　　Rank (of 50)　39th
　　Change 1995–2000
　　+130,953
　　Persons per sq. mi.　15.6
Capital: *Boise*
Largest city: *Boise*
　　Pop.　185,787
Entered Union: *July 3, 1890*
　　(43rd)
State bird: *Mountain bluebird*
State flower: *Syringa*
State tree: *White pine*
State map: *Page 91*

Idaho is the only landlocked state in the Northwest. Its rectangular southern region is defined by ruler-straight borders with other U.S. states, and its northern region is an irregular panhandle that narrows to a width of only 45 miles (72 kilometers) at the extreme nor-thern border with Canada. A sparsely populated state, Idaho contains natural features as contrasting as lava plateaus, subalpine lakes, desert tablelands, and deep river gorges.

The land. Idaho is situated at the meeting point of three major topographical features. Its northern panhandle is dominated by Rocky Mountain spurs running northwest from Wyoming and Montana. Southeastern Idaho touches the beginning of the Great Basin, which extends south into Nevada and Utah. This plateau is volcanic in origin and includes extensive lava beds in Idaho.

The third distinct feature of the land is the Snake River Plateau, which follows the Snake River across the wide southern part of the state, and then northward along the Oregon border. This plateau is

SKIING IS A MAJOR WINTER SPORT in Idaho, which also attracts many camping, hunting, and fishing enthusiasts throughout the other seasons.

an arm of the Columbia Plateau, which dominates eastern portions of Washington and Oregon, and it includes the finest farmland and open grazing land in Idaho. Almost a dozen national forests protect its natural beauty. The state's numerous hydroelectric plants, many on the Snake River and its tributaries, provide virtually all of Idaho's electrical needs.

Climate. Mountains to the north shelter Idaho from cold arctic air, giving the state a moderate continental climate. July high temperatures at Boise average 91°F (33°C) and January lows average 20°F (-7°C). Like western Oregon and Washington, Idaho has sparse rainfall, averaging 12 inches (30 centimeters) per year.

Principal cities. The only city in Idaho with a population over 100,000 is Boise, in the southwestern plateau. Other cities are Twin Falls, Pocatello, and Idaho Falls. The only large city in the northern reaches of the state is Lewiston, a river port at the confluence of the Snake and Clearwater rivers beside the Washington border.

The people. Among Idaho's earliest settlers were French trappers who gave French names to many of the state's northern areas. Later, the state was settled by large numbers of German, Scandinavian, and Dutch immigrants. Basque shepherds from Spain also settled in Idaho to tend flocks on land too hilly for cattle grazing.

Economy. Profits from livestock now exceed those from crops in Idaho, but the state continues to grow one-quarter of the U.S. potato crop. The principal manufacturing business is food processing, and tourism has become the third most profitable industry. The other chief industries are lumber and mining. The state provides one-third of the U.S. silver output.

Places of interest. Natural places of interest in Idaho include Hell's Canyon on the Snake River, at 7,900 feet (2,408

meters) the deepest canyon in the United States; the volcanic Craters of the Moon National Monument and Lava Hot Springs; and the northern Lake Coeur d'Alene. The state is also known for its ski resort at Sun Valley and for numerous camping, fishing, and hunting areas.

Illinois

Abbreviations: *Ill., IL*
Area: *55,593 sq. mi.,*
　　143,987 sq. km.
　　Rank (of 50)　24th
Population:
　　2000　12,419,293
　　Rank (of 50)　5th
　　Change 1995–2000
　　+589,293
　　Persons per sq. mi.　223.4
Capital: *Springfield*
Largest city: *Chicago*
　　Pop.　2,896,016
Entered Union: *Dec. 3, 1818*
　　(21st)
State bird: *Cardinal*
State flower: *Violet*
State tree: *White oak*
State map: *Page 96*

Illinois is at the southwest corner of the Great Lakes states, separated from Missouri and Iowa by the Mississippi River on the west and from Kentucky by the Ohio River on the south. Its northern border is with Wisconsin, and its eastern border is with Indiana. In the northeast, the state has a 50-mile (80-kilometer) shoreline on Lake Michigan, which is covered by the sprawling Chicago metropolitan area.

THE METROPOLITAN AREA of Chicago, Illinois, is the third largest in the United States.

Illinois has been one of the most prosperous of U.S. states. Millions from other states and European countries have gravitated to Illinois because of immense economic advantages it enjoys. The land is fertile, rich in minerals, and watered by abundant rivers. The state is the geographical connection between north-south traffic on the Mississippi River and east-west traffic through the Great Lakes to the Atlantic Ocean.

In the 1850s, Chicago, which only a few years earlier had been a frontier town of little distinction, rapidly grew into the hub of a great railroad system. In the 1900s it became a similar center for highway and air routes. Northern Illinois is one of the major U.S. manufacturing centers, and southern Illinois is one of the nation's major producers of agricultural goods.

In the 1980s the steady growth and traditional prosperity of Illinois had stalled, resulting in one of the smallest growth rates in the country. This trend changed with an 8.6 percent population increase in the 1990s.

The land. Nine-tenths of the land area of Illinois consists of predominantly flat central lowlands and till plains. This expanse is rich loam covered by a thin layer of sod. The periphery of the state includes small portions of other topographical areas. In the northwest, there is a small section of unglaciated Wisconsin Driftless Plain. In the northeast, along the shore of Lake Michigan, there is a small hill and marsh region known as the Great Lakes Plain. In the far south, Illinois includes strips of Ozark Plateau extending northeast from Missouri; interior low plateau extending northwest from Kentucky; and the northernmost point of the Gulf Coastal Plain.

Climate. Illinois has a temperate continental climate with snowy winters and warm summers. Winter lows average below 20°F (-7°C) in the north but only 30°F (-1°C) in the south. Summer temperatures throughout the state are above 80°F (27°C). Precipitation varies from 44 inches (112 centimeters) per year at the southern point to 33 inches (84 centimeters) per year in Chicago, in the northeast. Snowfall in the north averages 40 inches (102 centimeters) per year.

Principal cities. The Chicago metropolitan area is the third-largest in the United States. It is also part of a consolidated metropolitan area that extends along the southern shore of Lake Michigan to Gary, Indiana; it includes a population of more than 8 million people. Rockford, northwest of Chicago, is the second-largest city (population, 150,115). The third largest city is Aurora (population, 142,990) just west of the Chicago metropolitan area. Illinois shares metropolitan areas with Missouri at St. Louis and with Iowa at the Quad Cities (Davenport, Iowa, and Rock Island, Moline, and East Moline, Illinois).

The people. Illinois attracted major waves of European immigrants throughout the 1800s. First came the Irish, Germans, Scandinavians, and English, and later the Poles, Czechs, and Italians. After World War I, Illinois also attracted a steady stream of African Americans from the southern states. Today the African-American population is about 15 percent of the total, or about 1.8 million, and it is heavily concentrated in major cities. Other significant ethnic groups are Hispanics, who represent 12 percent of the population, and Asians, who represent 3.4 percent.

Economy. Illinois ranks fifth among U.S. states in manufacturing and third in farming. Principal manufactures include farm and earth-moving machinery, electrical goods, and processed food products. Although no longer "hog butcher to the world," Chicago is still an important food-processing center. It is also a banking and financial center.

Illinois is sixth of all the states in the exportation of manufactured goods, first in the production of soybeans, and second only to Iowa in the production of corn. It also mines significant quantities of coal and oil in its southern regions, and it leads all states in the mining of fluorspar, a mineral important to the steel industry.

Places of interest. Various places associated with the life of Abraham Lincoln, around the capital city of Springfield near the center of the state, are preserved. Other places of interest include the Mormon settlement at Nauvoo, on the Mississippi River, and the many cultural attractions of Chicago.

Indiana

Abbreviations: *Ind., IN*
Area: *35,870 sq. mi., 92,904 sq. km.*
    Rank (of 50)   38th
Population:
    2000   6,080,485
    Rank (of 50)   14th
    Change 1995–2000
    +277,485
    Persons per sq. mi.   169.5
Capital: *Indianapolis*
Largest city: *Indianapolis*
    Pop.   791,926
Entered Union: *Dec. 11, 1816*
    (19th)
State bird: *Cardinal*
State flower: *Peony*
State tree: *Tulip tree*
State map: *Page 96*

Indiana is situated between the Great Lakes states of Illinois to the west and Ohio to the east and just south of Michigan. Its southern border with Kentucky is formed by the Ohio River. Like the surrounding Great Lakes states, Indiana has been industrialized for more than a century. The capital city, Indianapolis, was once a crossroads for trails from the American East. This historical role is maintained by the modern interstate highways that converge near the city.

Indiana's three distinct business interests are industry in the north, farming in the central region, and mining and quarrying in the south.

The land. The land of Indiana shows three topographical divisions. A narrow band across the extreme north of the state is part of the Great Lakes Plain. This is a low-lying region with hundreds of lakes and ponds. The shoreline of Lake Michigan in the northwest corner consists of drained swamplands and sand dunes at the water's edge. The larger central region of the state is part of the Central Lowlands, a plain of rich soil characterized by ranges of low hills. In its southern region Indiana includes a

---

center
US

centre
Brit.

centimeters
US

centimetres
Brit.

portion of the Interior Low Plateau, a hilly region of limestone beds eroded by groundwater into caverns and sinkholes.

Climate. The climate of Indiana is one of hot summers and cold winters. At Indianapolis normal winter lows are below 20°F (-7°C) and summer highs are over 80°F (20°C). In the center of the state, precipitation averages 39 inches (99 centimeters) and snowfall averages 20 inches (51 centimeters) per year. The extreme south remains about 10 degrees warmer in both summer and winter than does the north, and snowfall in the north is twice that in the south.

Principal cities. Indianapolis is twice as large in population as any other city in the state. It functions as the commercial center of Indiana's agricultural region and as an industrial center based on the manufacture of automobile and airplane engines. The other major cities are in industrial districts in the north of the state. Fort Wayne in the northeast (population, 205,727) is a principal manufacturer of farm machinery and electronic equipment. The Gary-Hammond metropolitan area beside Lake Michigan is an industrial center that includes 631,361 residents of the greater Chicago metropolitan area. South Bend (population, 107,789), to the east of Gary and near the border of Michigan, is the home of the University of Notre Dame. The principal population centers in central and southern Indiana are Evansville in the southwest (population, 121,582); Bloomington (69,291), in south-central Indiana; Terre Haute (59,614), in west-central Indiana; and New Albany (37,603), across the Ohio River from Louisville, Kentucky.

The people. The population growth rate in Indiana declined from 18.5 percent in the 1950s to less than 6 percent in the 1970s. Between 1970 and 1980, a total of 150,000 state residents migrated to other states. Despite this, Indiana's population recorded a net gain of 295,000, and in the 1980s Indiana's population growth rate, although an extremely weak 1 percent, was second only to that of Wisconsin among Great Lakes states. The growth rate rebounded with a 9.7 percent increase in the 1990s. The present population is 8 percent African American and 3.5 percent Hispanic. Indiana has the lowest proportion of foreign-born residents, about 7 percent, within the Great Lakes region.

Economy. The principal industry of Indiana is manufacturing, and most of the manufacturing centers are located in the north of the state. The most important center is in the Calumet region in the northwest, an area of steel mills and oil refineries where raw materials are imported and finished goods are exported via Great Lakes freighters. The state is also known for its specialty manufacturers, which are concentrated in single towns. For example, musical instruments are made in Elkhart, and Mason jars in Muncie.

The principal farmland is located in central Indiana. Crops, chiefly corn and soybeans, account for more than half the total farm income, and the greatest livestock production is of hogs and sheep. Coal is strip-mined from the Interior Low Plateau in the southwest of the state. Also on the plateau, Indiana quarries more building limestone than does any other state; it also quarries substantial amounts of stone and gravel.

Places of interest. Southern Indiana contains several extensive limestone cavern systems. The Wyandotte Cave, near the Ohio River, is the most noteworthy. Other natural attractions include the Indiana Dunes National Lakeshore, beside Lake Michigan, and the Hoosier National Forest. The principal annual attraction in the state is the Indianapolis 500 automobile race in the state capital, which attracts millions of viewers nationally.

INDIANA quarries more building limestone than any other state, in addition to substantial amounts of stone and gravel.

Iowa

Abbreviations: *Ia., IA*
Area: *55,875 sq. mi.,*
144,716 sq. km.
Rank (of 50) 23rd
Population:
2000 2,926,324
Rank (of 50) 30th
Change 1995–2000
+84,324
Persons per sq. mi. 52.3
Capital: *Des Moines*
Largest city: *Des Moines*
Pop. 198,682
Entered Union: *Dec. 28, 1846*
(29th)
State bird: *Eastern goldfinch*
State flower: *Wild rose*
State tree: *Oak*
State map: *Page 94*

Iowa is an eastern Grain state situated between the Missouri River to the west and the Mississippi River to the east. Its northern and southern borders are formed, respectively, by the Grain states of Minnesota and Missouri.

Iowa falls near the middle of the U.S. range in both population and land area. It is balanced in other ways as well. One of the principal U.S. exporters of food products, it is also the seat of extensive scientific research into plant hybrids and chemical fertilizers, and it is the home of considerable manufacturing. Known as the Corn State, Iowa produces a fifth of the U.S. crop, but it earns more from livestock than from all its crops combined.

The land. Virtually all of Iowa is considered part of the Central Lowland Plain. Two-thirds of the state is nearly level, varying in elevation from 800 to 1,400 feet (244 to 427 meters) across its width of more than 300 miles (483 kilometers). The two significant variations in this topography are the Till Plains in the south, the smoothest and most regular area in the state, and the hillier

COVERED BRIDGES are still an appealing feature of Indiana's landscape. Western Indiana has the largest concentration of covered bridges in the world.

27 North America

IOWA'S PRODUCTION of corn, soybeans, and hogs surpasses that of all other states.

center
US

centre
Brit.

centimeters
US

centimetres
Brit.

Young Drift Plains in the north, a region of recent, or young, glacial soil deposits. The extreme northeast also contains a hilly unglaciated area called the Wisconsin Driftless region. It is now the center of the state's dairy farming.

Climate. Iowa has an extremely changeable climate, with occasional variations in temperature of as much as 50°F (10°C) in a single day. Ordinarily, high temperatures average over 80°F (27°C) in summer, and lows approach 10°F (-12°C) in winter. The rainfall is heaviest in the southeast, where precipitation averages about 40 inches (102 centimeters) per year.

Principal cities. Iowa is relatively rural, even by Grain state standards. Metropolitan Des Moines, with over 15 percent of the state population, is the largest city in the state. It is situated near the center of Iowa on the Des Moines River, and it is known for its insurance companies, farm equipment manufacturers, and publishing enterprises. Davenport, on the Mississippi River, is the largest of the "Quad Cities," a metropolitan area whose other cities are in Illinois. Similarly, Council Bluffs, on the Missouri River at the state's western border, is part of the Omaha, Nebraska, metropolitan area. Most of Iowa's other principal cities—Cedar Rapids (population, 120,758), Waterloo (68,747), and Dubuque (57,686)—are industrial centers located in the eastern third of the state.

The people. Iowa's limited population growth gives it the highest percentage of

lifelong residents (67.4 percent) among the Grain states. Because of the consolidation and mechanization of farms, young people in Iowa tend to migrate to other states. Iowa's population is the oldest in the region, with more than 15 percent aged 65 years and older.

Economy. Iowa ranks second only to California in agricultural produce, and its production of corn, soybeans, and hogs surpasses that of all other states. Corn production is based in the central and northern regions of the state. These businesses have spawned a large food processing industry.

Places of interest. The attractions in Iowa include the Herbert Hoover birthplace and his presidential library at West Branch, near Cedar Rapids; the Effigy Mounds National Monument in the extreme northeast corner of the state, a prehistoric burial site; and the Fort Dodge Stockade and Historical Museum, 70 miles (113 kilometers) up the Des Moines River from the state capital.

Kansas

Abbreviations: *Kan., KS*
Area: *81,823 sq. mi.,*
211,922 sq. km.
Rank (of 50)   13th
Population:
2000   2,688,418
Rank (of 50)   32nd
Change 1995–2000
+123,418
Persons per sq. mi.   32.8
Capital: *Topeka*
Largest city: *Wichita*
Pop.   344,284
Entered Union: *Jan. 29, 1861*
(34th)
State bird: *Western meadowlark*
State flower: *Sunflower*
State tree: *Cottonwood*
State map: *Page 94*

Kansas may be said to be located at the center of North America. The geodetic center, or reference point, for maps of the continent lies in Osborne County in north-central Kansas. Among the U.S. regions it lies in the southwest of the Grain states, bordering Colorado to the west and Oklahoma to the south, with a northeastern corner just brushed by the Missouri River.

Among Grain states, Kansas ranks first in land area and fourth in population. Its history has been a turbulent one, with pre–Civil War confrontations violent enough to give it the name "bleeding Kansas." With the coming of the first railroads, a period of wild cattle drives from Texas to railheads in Kansas made towns like Dodge City symbols of the lawless West. Since those times Kansas has survived droughts and economic depressions to become the wheat state of America, producer of more than one-sixth of the national crop. More recently, diversified manufacturing has superseded agriculture in the state economy.

The land. The topography of Kansas is entirely one of plains, but the surface of the state has significant detail. The elevation of the land rises from less than 1,000 feet (305 meters) in the extreme east to over 4,000 feet (1,219 meters) in the extreme west. Across this rising slope are three distinct areas. The eastern third includes the hilly Osage Plains and the glacial Till Plains, which extend into Kansas from Nebraska. The central third is known as the Plains Border, a level region characterized by isolated low ranges such as the Blue Hills and the Red Hills. The western third is composed of High Plains, a flat, treeless expanse so arid that many of its rivers completely dry up for portions of the year. The agricultural prominence of Kansas is related to its soil's natural growth of grasses, and each of its three regions is associated with a particular growth of grass: tall grass in the east, mixed grasses in the central third, and short grass in the west.

Climate. Like most Grain states, Kansas has a variable climate characterized by seasonal extremes because of

GAS STORAGE TANKS in Kansas serve the gas production industry, an important feature of the state's economy. Kansas ranks fifth nationally in gas production.

the absence of mountains or bodies of water in the surrounding areas. Normal daily highs are above 90° F (32° C) in summer and below 20° F (-7° C) in winter. Rainfall averages about 40 inches (102 centimeters) per year in the southeast and about half that in the west. Sudden changes of weather in Kansas often take the form of hailstorms, thunderstorms, or tornadoes, and winter blizzards are also common.

Principal cities. All of Kansas's large cities are in the state's eastern third. The largest city that stands entirely in Kansas is Wichita, located in the southeast, at the confluence of the Arkansas and Little Arkansas rivers. The principal manufacturer of private aircraft in the United States, Wichita is also the wholesale and retail center for a large area that includes northern Oklahoma as well as Kansas. Kansas City lies in the northeast of the state at the junction of the Kansas and Missouri rivers. Kansas City, Kansas, has a relatively small population of 146,866, but its metropolitan area, which includes Kansas City, Missouri, has a total population of more than 1.7 million. It is also a distribution center for areas beyond the Kansas state borders. The capital city of Topeka (population, 122,377) lies to the west of Kansas City.

The people. Kansas was famous after the Civil War for opening its borders to freed slaves, and it continues to have a high proportion of African Americans (6 percent) for a Grain state. The state was settled by Germans, Russians, and other European nationalities. Like all western Grain states, Kansas experienced a severe population decline during the 1930s. A drought destroyed the farm economy in the west, and thousands left the state.

Economy. Kansas leads all Grain states in farm acreage and produces almost a quarter more wheat than its nearest competitor, North Dakota. Most of the wheat crop is grown in the central third of the state, and huge crops of sorghum grain are grown on irrigated lands in the western third. However, most of the state's farm income is derived from livestock.

Since World War II, Kansas has emerged as a leading manufacturing state. The manufacturing sector, mainly in Wichita, Kansas City, and Topeka, is based on aviation, food processing, and transportation equipment. It employs nearly 20 percent of the state workforce and produces about $13 billion in value added per year. Kansas also ranks 16th among all U.S. states in mining, chiefly because of petroleum and natural gas production. Kansas leads the nation in helium production, which is extracted from natural gas.

Places of interest. The primary attractions in Kansas are Dodge City, with its restored Front Street, in the southwest; the Eisenhower Museum at Abilene, near the center of the state; preserved landmarks of the Santa Fe Trail; and early military outposts.

Kentucky

Abbreviations: *Ky., KY*
Area: *39,732 sq. mi., 102,906 sq. km.*
   Rank (of 50)   36th
Population:
   2000   4,041,769
   Rank (of 50)   25th
   Change 1995–2000 +181,769
   Persons per sq. mi.   101.7
Capital: *Frankfort*
Largest city: *Lexington*
   Pop.   260,512
Entered Union: *June 1, 1792 (15th)*
State bird: *Cardinal*
State flower: *Goldenrod*
State tree: *Coffeetree*
State map: *Page 97*

Kentucky has a straight southern border with Tennessee and a long, irregular northern border formed by the Ohio River, which separates it from the three Great Lakes states of Illinois, Indiana, and Ohio. The state extends 425 miles (684 kilometers) from the Mississippi River on the west to Virginia and West Virginia on the east.

Daniel Boone crossed the Cumberland Gap into eastern Kentucky in 1775 and established Boonesboro, a year after James Harrod established Harrodsburg, the first permanent settlement in Kentucky. After the American Revolution, the first wave of American settlers from Virginia came to the lush bluegrass region of north-central Kentucky. They found the region congenial to the horse farms and cotton and tobacco fields favored in Virginia, and the central area of the state retains some of that character today.

The Ohio River was the traditional border between northern and southern states in the 1800s, but Kentucky has always looked north. Today it shares parts of three metropolitan areas that straddle the river, and its own fortunes are tied to those of the Great Lakes states. Manufacturing and coal mining have become major factors in the state economy.

The land. The surface of Kentucky slopes down from Pine Mountains along its southeast border with Virginia across the Interior Low Plateau in the central region to a small area of Gulf Coastal Plain lying near sea level beside the Mississippi River in the extreme west. The eastern mountain region includes one-quarter of Kentucky's area. It consists of the chain of Pine Mountains, and a portion of the mineral-rich Cumberland Plateau, including the eastern coalfield. The Interior Low Plateau, covering more than half the state area, includes the bluegrass area around the city of Lexington, the Pennyroyal Plateau in the south-central area, and the western coalfield along the Indiana border. In the extreme west of Kentucky there is a small area of Gulf Coastal Plain along the Mississippi River. It is isolated by the Tennessee and Cumberland rivers, which flow north into the Ohio.

Climate. Kentucky has a moderate continental climate, with warm summers and cool winters. Normal summer high temperatures approach 90° F (32°C) and normal winter low temperatures approach 20°F (-7°C). Precipitation across Kentucky averages about 45 inches (114 centimeters) per year, and all regions of the state receive snow in winter.

Principal cities. Lexington, in the midst of the meadowlands and grazing areas of the bluegrass region, is the largest urban center of Kentucky. Louisville, on the Ohio River, is the second largest city, with a population of 256,231. It is an industrial river port, and it includes two counties of Indiana across

THE ATCHAFALAYA RIVER is a feature of the swampy alluvial floodland that comprises much of Louisiana.

kilometers
US

kilometres
Brit.

center
US

centre
Brit.

the river within its metropolitan area. In the far northern corner, part of Kentucky is within the Cincinnati, Ohio, metropolitan region, with a total population of over 1.6 million. It shares smaller metropolitan regions with Evansville, Indiana, in the northwest, and with Huntington, West Virginia, in the northeast.

The people. Kentucky grew more in the 1970s than it had in the previous 30 years, but its growth rate was only slightly above the national average. In the 1980s growth was marginal, followed by a 9.6 percent increase in the 1990s. Traditionally, the state had lost population to industrial employment opportunities in the Great Lakes states. In the 1970s, however, this trend was reversed. About 7 percent of the total population is African American. There is no other large racial or ethnic group. Most of the population live in the central bluegrass region. The mountainous mining regions to the east remain sparsely populated and economically depressed.

Economy. Manufacturing is the major industry in Kentucky. The principal manufactures are refined coal and tobacco products. One special manufacture is whiskey, in which Kentucky leads all states. Kentucky is second to Wyoming in the mining of bituminous (soft) coal, principally from the eastern coalfield on the Cumberland Plateau and from the western coalfield on the Interior Low Plateau.

The bluegrass region contains most of the state's farmland, and agricultural income is equally divided between crops, principally tobacco and cotton, and livestock, including poultry and dairy products. The region is also famous for breeding thoroughbred horses.

Places of interest. The state's greatest attraction is the annual Kentucky Derby horse race run at Churchill Downs in Louisville. The Mammoth Caves beneath the Pennyroyal Plateau are spectacular examples of limestone caverns; and the Land Between the Lakes National Recreation Area is the state's principal water resort. The U.S. gold depository is located at Fort Knox, 12 miles (19 kilometers) southwest of Louisville.

Louisiana

Abbreviations: *La., LA*
Area: *43,566 sq. mi.,*
112,836 sq. km.
Rank (of 50)   33rd
Population:
2000   4,468,976
Rank (of 50)   22nd
Change 1995–2000
+126,976
Persons per sq. mi.   102.5
Capital: *Baton Rouge*
Largest city: *New Orleans*
Pop.   484,674
Entered Union: *April 30, 1812*
(18th)
State bird: *Eastern brown pelican*
State flower: *Magnolia blossom*
State tree: *Bald cypress*
State map: *Page 93*

Louisiana lies in the south-central United States, bordering Texas to the west and Arkansas to the north. Its eastern border with Mississippi is formed by the Mississippi River, except in the south, where the state has a large extension of land to the east of the river that includes New Orleans and Baton Rouge, the two major cities. Its southern boundary is the shore of the Gulf of Mexico, dominated by the Mississippi River delta.

Louisiana is a fascinating combination of European and American influences. Its local governmental units are 64 parishes, so-called rather than counties. Its civil laws were influenced by the legal systems of France and Spain, from which many of its original settlers came. Its population includes large numbers of Creoles, descendants of French and Spanish settlers; and Cajuns, descendants of French settlers who were driven from Nova Scotia in Canada by the British after 1760. French and Spanish influence is most apparent in New

Orleans, with its French Quarter, Mardi Gras celebrations, and Creole cookery.
The land. All of the state area lies within the low Gulf Coastal Plain. Local elevations below sea level are common, and the highest point in the state, Driskill Mountain near Arkansas, has an elevation of only 535 feet (163 meters).

The largest individual feature of the plain is the alluvial floodland west of the Mississippi crossed by the Red, Ouachita, and Atchafalaya rivers. Generally swampy, the floodland is protected—imperfectly, of course—from river waters by an extensive system of levees. Only near the state's northern borders with Arkansas and Mississippi does the plain rise into forested hills.

The southern delta region is a fertile lowland full of bayous, or freshwater inlets from the river, and the entire Gulf Coast is a swampy region where marshes cover extensive mineral deposits.
Climate. Louisiana has a generally subtropical climate influenced more by the Gulf of Mexico than by inland weather patterns. At New Orleans, low temperatures rarely fall below 50°F (10°C), and high temperatures average 65°F (18°C) in winter and 90°F (32°C) in summer. Louisiana is one of the wettest states in the country, with rainfall averaging well over 50 inches (127 centimeters) per year.
Principal cities. Louisiana's major city is New Orleans, situated in the southeast 100 miles (161 kilometers) above the mouth of the Mississippi. Its metropolitan area of well over 1 million represents about 30 percent of the state's population. The city is the export center for most of the Mississippi valley and the second largest port in the country after New York. The capital city of Baton Rouge, 100 miles (161 kilometers) upstream from New Orleans, has a population of 227,818 and it is also a large deepwater port. The only major city in northern Louisiana is Shreveport (population, 200,145), a manufacturing center in the extreme northwest.
The people. Rural northern Louisiana has a population and lifestyle similar to that of other Oil states. Southern Louisiana includes most of the state's Cajun and Creole population and cosmopolitan city centers. One in six state residents speaks French. The French-speaking community is almost entirely located in the southern swamplands and bayous near the Gulf Coast.

The state also has a large African-American population, about 32.5 percent of the state's total population. The major population pattern within the state since World War II has been one of urbanization.
Economy. After 1945 Louisiana was gradually transformed from an agricultural to an industrial state. Virtually all of its industry is located in the southern regions of the state. The oil and petrochemical industries, including both the drilling and refining of crude oil and the processing of petroleum-based products, make up the largest and fastest growing sector of the state economy. Louisiana

is also the nation's largest producer of natural gas, and it ranks third to Texas and Alaska in production of crude oil.

Most oil drilling is located along the Gulf Coast, and in recent years offshore drilling rigs have accounted for 20 percent of the state's production. The principal oil refineries are located south of Baton Rouge, and the 100-mile (161-kilometer) river corridor between Baton Rouge and New Orleans is lined with manufacturers of food products and transportation equipment as well as oil-related industries.

Tourism, principally in New Orleans and the coastal region, is also a major industry. Agricultural businesses continue to produce large soybean, rice, and cotton crops.

Places of interest. The principal attraction in Louisiana is New Orleans, where modern structures such as the Superdome have been added to older sites of historical and cultural interest. Plantations are preserved near New Iberia in the south-central region. The Mississippi delta region includes places of Cajun interest and Chalmette National Historical Park.

GROTESQUE MASKS in a New Orleans shop window await Mardi Gras festivities.

Maine

Abbreviations: *Me., ME*

Area: *30,865 sq. mi., 79,940 sq. km.*
   Rank (of 50)   39th

Population:
   2000   1,274,923
   Rank (of 50)   40th
   Change 1995–2000   +33,923
   Persons per sq. mi.   41.3

Capital: *Augusta*

Largest city: *Portland*
   Pop.   64,249

Entered Union: *Mar. 15, 1820*
   (23rd)

State bird: *Chickadee*

State flower: *White pine cone and tassel*

State tree: *White pine*

State map: *Page 101*

THE RUGGED 230-MILE coastline of Maine, with its many islands and harbors, has several lighthouses still in operation.

Maine is the most northeastern of U.S. states. It is surrounded on three sides by Canada: the Province of Quebec to the northwest and the Province of New Brunswick to the north and east. Its only boundary with another state is the lower western boundary with New Hampshire. The southeastern edge of Maine is an irregular 230-mile (370-kilometer) Atlantic coastline that includes many islands and harbors.

Maine contains a land area nearly equal to that of all the other New England states combined; it is also the most sparsely populated of New England states. After a history of slow growth since voting to separate itself from Massachusetts in 1819, Maine added more residents in the 1970s and 1980s than in any comparable period of its history. The population is concentrated in the southern half of the state.

The land. Maine is uniformly hilly and rocky, sharing three distinct features with the rest of New England. The White Mountains enter the state from the northern part of the New Hampshire border and extend northeast into the center of Maine, where the state high point is located at Mt. Katahdin (5,267 feet, 1,605 meters). To the east and north of the mountains is the New England Upland, a region of rounded glacial "horsebacks," or low ridges. The upland declines in elevation toward the St. John River along the northern Canadian border and toward the southeastern coast. Perhaps the state's most remarkable feature is its varied and beautiful Atlantic coast. The New England Seaboard Lowlands provide a predominantly rocky and highly irregular shoreline. Mount Desert Island, two-thirds of the way from the New Hampshire border to the Canadian border, was the site of an early French settlement in the 1600s. In the early 1900s it was a wealthy seaside resort, and today it is preserved for all to enjoy as Acadia National Park.

Climate. The climate of Maine is one of long, cold winters and cool summers. Normal summer highs are below 80°F (27°C) along the southeast coast, and normal winter lows are 12°F (-11°C). Summer highs may be higher inland, and winter lows are lower, falling below zero in the far north. Precipitation averages 41 inches (104 centimeters) per year, with 75 inches (191 centimeters) of snow per year in Portland and more to the north.

Principal cities. The metropolitan area around Portland has twice the population of any other urban area in the state. The city is located on the large Casco Bay, and its harbor commerce is chiefly the transport of oil brought from Canada by pipeline and commercial fishing. The second largest population hub centers on the adjacent cities of Lewiston (population, 35,690) and Auburn (23,203), located inland 25 miles (40 kilometers) due north of Portland. Bangor, farther north and 25 miles (40 kilometers) inland from the coast on the Penobscot River, has a city population of 31,473. Augusta (population, 18,560) is on the Kennebec River, 25 miles (40 kilometers) northeast of Lewiston.

The people. Maine has the lowest population density and the second lowest proportion of urban residents (after Vermont) in the region. African-American and Hispanic populations both make up less than 1 percent of the total population.

Economy. The economy of Maine is heavily based on manufacturing, which accounts for more income than all other industries combined. The principal manufactures are paper and wood products, textiles, leather goods, and processed foods. Tourism brings the state more than $1 billion per year, particularly along the Atlantic coast and the many inland lakes in southern Maine. The state also contains some 17.7 million acres (7.2 million hectares) of forestland, more than half the New England total.

Maine's agriculture is principally based on dairy and poultry farms, but its crop production is notable for producing the third largest U.S. potato harvest. Commercial fishing generates far less total income than these other industries, but Maine is especially noted for its lobster catch, which represents 80 percent of the U.S. total.

Places of interest. The principal attraction for visitors to Maine is the state's rocky coastline, where Acadia National Park is found in the northern third, and Boothbay Harbor in the southern third. There are also many inland lakes and streams that attract campers and anglers.

kilometers	US
kilometres	Brit.
center	US
centre	Brit.

Maryland

Abbreviations: *Md., MD*
Area: *9,775 sq. mi., 25,317 sq. km.*
   Rank (of 50)   42nd
Population:
   2000   5,296,486
   Rank (of 50)   19th
   Change 1995–2000
   +254,486
   Persons per sq. mi.   541.8
Capital: *Annapolis*
Largest city: *Baltimore*
   Pop.   651,154
Entered Union: *Apr. 28, 1788*
   (7th)
State bird: *Baltimore oriole*
State flower: *Black-eyed Susan*
State tree: *White oak*
State map: *Page 99*

BALTIMORE'S REFURBISHED HARBOR on Chesapeake Bay is an important focus for the state's thriving tourism industry.

the Delmarva peninsula. A square 10 miles (16 kilometers) on a side along the Potomac River was cut out of Maryland in 1790 to serve as the nation's capital; this area is now the separately governed District of Columbia.

Maryland is a diverse state combining social characteristics of different U.S. regions. The far western counties between West Virginia and Pennsylvania are mountainous parts of the Appalachian region. Central Maryland includes the major manufacturing city of Baltimore, and it is part of the heavily populated northeastern corridor that stretches from Washington, D.C., on Maryland's southern boundary, to Philadelphia, just to the north, and on to New York City and Boston. The eastern shore, a largely agricultural region, resembles the states to the south.

The land. Across its nearly 250-mile (402-kilometer) west-to-east extent, Maryland includes parts of three different topographical regions. The narrow western arm lies within the

tidewater estuaries are found on both sides of the bay in Maryland.

Climate. Most of Maryland has a warm and mild climate influenced by the moderating effects of the Atlantic Ocean and Chesapeake Bay. At Baltimore, on the bay in the north-central region of the state, normal summer high temperatures are 85°F (29°C) and winter lows are 25°F (-4°C). Precipitation in Baltimore averages 46 inches (117 centimeters) per year, including 22 inches (56 centimeters) of snow. The eastern shore and Atlantic coast are generally warmer in both winter and summer. Winters in the western Allegheny Mountains are colder, and more snow falls.

Principal cities. The major population center in the state is the Baltimore metropolitan area; 49 percent of the state's residents live in this area. The suburban areas around Baltimore are continuing to grow in population, but the central city population continues a decline that began in the 1970s. Two Maryland counties along the Potomac River lie within the Washington, D.C., metropolitan area, and they account for nearly 30 percent of the total state population. In the northeast, farther along the transportation corridor running from Washington through Baltimore, parts of Maryland lie within the Wilmington, Delaware, metropolitan area.

The people. The state population is concentrated in urban areas in central Maryland, leaving both the western arm of the state and the entire eastern shore sparsely populated. Most growth continues to be in the suburban areas around Baltimore and Washington, and the population increase is primarily among African Americans. This group makes up about 28 percent of the state population. Hispanics and Asians each represent 5 percent.

Economy. Tourism generates more than $4 billion in expenditures per year, making it an important component of the state economy. However, manufacturing is more important, employing some 212,000 persons and accounting for almost $16 billion in value added per year. Baltimore is a center for heavy industries, including steel mills and manufactures of machinery, ships, and aircraft. Along the eastern shore, food processing of fish and vegetables predominates the economy. The state's third major business is agriculture, which produces about $1.3 billion in farm marketings per year. Most farm income is generated by poultry farms on the eastern shore. In the west of the state there is limited dairy farming and some corn and soybean crops intended for feed.

Places of interest. The principal natural attractions in Maryland are the beach resorts around Ocean City on the Atlantic and the Catoctin and Piscataway Mountain parks in the west of the state. Other attractions in central Maryland include Fort McHenry and the USS *Constellation* in Baltimore, and the U.S. Naval Academy in Annapolis.

Maryland lies in the northern tier of Tidewater states. The bulk of its land is along upper Chesapeake Bay, including the mainland north of the Potomac River (the border with Virginia) and the eastern bay shores on the Delmarva peninsula. The northern border with Pennsylvania, a straight line along the 40th parallel, is part of the famous Mason-Dixon line that traditionally has separated the North from the South. To the west, Maryland has a long, irregularly shaped panhandle formed by the approach of the Potomac River to the 40th parallel. At one point, the state narrows to a north-south breadth of only 1.9 miles (3 kilometers).

The state has a long irregular shoreline along Chesapeake Bay and a 30-mile (48-kilometer) stretch of Atlantic shore along the eastern edge of

Appalachian Mountains. The individual features of this mountain region are the Allegheny Mountains in the far west, where the state high point is located at Backbone Mountain (3,360 feet, 1,024 meters); a portion of Appalachian valley at the narrowest point on the western arm; and the Blue Ridge Mountains running north from Virginia.

The central region of the state includes an area on the Piedmont Plateau extending east of the Blue Ridge Mountains nearly to Washington and Baltimore. The fall line at which the plateau drops off to the Atlantic Coastal Plain runs through those cities from southwest to northeast.

Maryland's share of the coastal plain consists of rolling lands west of the Chesapeake Bay and flat, featureless lowlands on the eastern shore. Major

Massachusetts

Abbreviations: *Mass., MA*
Area: *7,838 sq. mi., 20,300 sq. km.*
   Rank (of 50)   45th
Population:
   2000   6,349,097
   Rank (of 50)   13th
   Change 1995–2000   +275,097
   Persons per sq. mi.   810.0
Capital: *Boston*
Largest city: *Boston*
   Pop.   589,141
Entered Union: *Feb. 6, 1788*
   (6th)
State bird: *Chickadee*
State flower: *Mayflower*
State tree: *American elm*
State map: *Page 101*

Massachusetts is the central New England state, with borders on four of the other five states of the region. Two-thirds of the state area is a 50-mile- (80-kilometer-) wide rectangle between Vermont and New Hampshire on the north, and Connecticut and Rhode Island on the south. The state's western border is with New York. The eastern third of Massachusetts extends 90 miles (145 kilometers) from north to south; it has an irregular Atlantic Ocean coastline. The shape of the state is distinctive for the 75-mile- (121-kilometer-) long peninsula of Cape Cod hooking to the north from the eastern coastline.

The commercial and population center of New England, Massachusetts has historical importance that extends beyond the region. Its early settlements, founded by Pilgrims and Puritans after 1620, were among the strongest in North America. In the years before the American Revolution, Massachusetts patriots were outspoken in their opposition to British excesses. The Boston Tea Party became a symbol of American resolve. The war itself began with the battles of Lexington and Concord in 1775.

In the 1800s Massachusetts was home to the preeminent American philosophers and writers of the time. It was also the testing ground for the earliest American manufacturers, and port of entry for waves of Irish immigrants driven from their own country by potato famines. Today it is home to 45 percent of New England's residents and generates almost as much income from manufacturing as all other states of the region combined. It enjoyed consistent growth throughout the early 20th century. That increase virtually stopped in the 1970s, but was followed by steady growth increases throughout the 1980s and 1990s.
The land. The western two-thirds of Massachusetts consists wholly of New England Upland. The far western region

is Appalachian in character, consisting of narrow ranges of the Taconic Mountains entering the state from New York, the Berkshire Hills, and the Green Mountains that extend northward into Vermont. Central Massachusetts is an upland plateau of rolling hills divided by the north-south Connecticut River valley. The eastern third of the state consists of New England Seaboard Lowlands, with an irregular coastline that is generally rocky in the north and sandy in the south. The sandy peninsula of Cape Cod is a small part of the Atlantic Coastal Plain. Two large islands to the south of the cape, Martha's Vineyard and Nantucket, are also part of the plain.
Climate. The climate of Massachusetts is moderate for New England. At Boston on the Atlantic coast, normal summer highs are 81°F (27°C) and winter lows are 22°F (-6°C). Boston receives an average of 43 inches (109 centimeters) of precipitation per year, including 43 inches (109 centimeters) of snow. The winters are harsher, and the snowfalls are greater in the interior regions.

Principal cities. The great metropolitan area is Boston, which has almost 54 percent of the state's population. Boston is the manufacturing and financial center of all of eastern New England and a cultural and educational center of national importance. Its educational institutions include Harvard University, the Massachusetts Institute of Technology, and Boston University.

The third largest city is Springfield (population, 152,082), a manufacturing center 60 miles (96 kilometers) southwest of Boston near the Connecticut border. Worcester, almost equidistant between these two, is the second largest city, with a population of 172,648. There is also a large urban population north of

Boston around the cities of Lawrence, Haverhill, and Lowell, with a combined population of 236,179. Their metropolitan area includes part of New Hampshire.
The people. Massachusetts contains the greatest proportion of lifelong residents in New England. One-third of its people are of foreign birth or parentage, many of them members of the Italian and Irish communities of Boston and Springfield. The state population is 5.4 percent African American and 6.8 percent Hispanic, mostly concentrated in and around Boston and Springfield.
Economy. Manufacturing far exceeds any other industry in value to Massachusetts's economy. The leading manufactures include machinery, electrical and electronic equipment, fabricated metal products, and textiles.

The second largest contributor to the state economy is tourism, particularly from resorts that extend the full range of the state from the Berkshire Hills in the west to Cape Cod in the east. The

BOSTON
is the manufacturing and financial center of eastern New England and a cultural and educational center of national importance.

CRANBERRIES,
which are native to North America, are grown commercially in flooded areas known as bogs.

agricultural businesses of Massachusetts are evenly divided between livestock, chiefly from dairy and poultry farms, and crops, especially greenhouse vegetables and the largest U.S. harvest of cranberries. In addition, Boston is a major center for banking and insurance companies.

Places of interest. Boston is the principal attraction to year-round visitors to Massachusetts; it is the site of the Old North Church and many other historical landmarks, Harvard University, and the John F. Kennedy Library. The summer resorts in both the Berkshire Hills and Cape Cod are noted for their cultural events. In addition to mountain scenery, the Berkshires offer concerts at Tanglewood and the Jacob's Pillow Dance Festival. The summer colonies on Cape Cod's beaches feature artistic exhibits and theatrical performances, especially at Provincetown.

ONE-THIRD OF MICHIGAN'S sizeable manufacturing industry is related to the production of automobiles.

Michigan

Abbreviations: *Mich., MI*
Area: *56,809 sq. mi.,*
    147,135 sq. km.
    Rank (of 50)   22nd
Population:
    2000 9,938,444
    Rank (of 50)   8th
    Change 1995–2000
    +389,444
    Persons per sq. mi.   177.9
Capital: *Lansing*
Largest city: *Detroit*
    Pop.   951,270
Entered Union: *Jan. 26, 1837*
    (26th)
State bird: *Robin*
State flower: *Apple blossom*
State tree: *White pine*
State map: *Page 96*

Michigan is a north-central state composed of two peninsulas with shorelines on four of the five Great Lakes. The Upper, or Northern, Peninsula stretches from its southwestern border with Wisconsin 320 miles (515 kilometers) east between lakes Superior and Michigan toward Ontario, Canada. The Lower Peninsula, which is much larger, is urbanized and industrialized, contains most of the population, and extends north from borders with Indiana and Ohio between Lake Michigan on the west and lakes Huron and Erie on the east. The two peninsulas are separated from each other by the 5-mile- (8-kilometer-) wide Straits of Mackinac that connect lakes Michigan and Huron. The Mackinac Bridge, one of the largest suspension bridges in the world, provides highway connections between the two parts of the state.

Michigan is the only Great Lakes state that has land borders with Canada. Detroit lies just across the Detroit River from Windsor, in the heavily populated southern region of Ontario. And the Upper Peninsula city of Sault Ste. Marie faces the Ontario town of the same name across the St. Mary's River.

The automobile industry, based in Detroit, is the focus of the state's economy. The increasing cost of motor fuel, and competition from foreign manufacturers, brought a severe decline to the industry in the 1970s and 1980s, but the 1990s saw a significant rebound.

The land. The Lower Peninsula of Michigan lies within the Central Lowland region, principally within the Great Lakes Plain. This central plain is characterized by ridges rising from about 1,000 feet (305 meters) in the south to about 1,700 feet (518 meters) in the north, where some tablelands are found.

The Upper Peninsula consists of two topographical regions of equal area. In the east the Great Lakes Plains predominate, and maximum elevations of only 400 feet (122 meters) decline into marshy lands along the lake shores. In the west is the Superior Upland extending into Wisconsin. The state high point lies near Lake Superior.

Climate. The climate differs in the two peninsulas. In southeastern Detroit normal winter lows are 30°F (-1°C) and summer highs above 80°F (27°C). At Sault Ste. Marie, on the Upper Peninsula, winter lows are about 10°F (-12°C) and summer highs 70°F (21°C). Precipitation averages 31 inches (79 centimeters) per year throughout the state, but Sault Ste. Marie receives almost four times as much snow as Detroit—about 112 inches (284 centimeters) per year.

Principal cities. All the large cities of Michigan are located in the Lower Peninsula. The largest is Detroit, situated in the southeast on the Detroit River, part of the link between lakes Erie and Huron. The second largest is Grand Rapids (population, 197,800), an industrial center in the western part of the state 40 miles (64 kilometers) from Lake Michigan. The

third largest is Flint (population, 124,943), about 40 miles (64 kilometers) northwest of Detroit. Flint is the state's second largest automobile manufacturer. These three metropolitan areas combined account for 60 percent of the state's population. Lansing, the capital, and adjacent East Lansing have a combined population of 165,653. Ann Arbor, southwest of Detroit, has a population of 114,024. Marquette (population, 19,661) is the largest town in the Upper Peninsula.

The people. Because of the automobile industry, Michigan grew in population at a rate above the national average from 1910 to 1970. By contrast, growth in the following three decades was well below the national average, and the proportion of people living in urban places actually declined. Over 14 percent of the state population are African Americans. Hispanics are the only other large ethnic group within the population. They represent 3.3 percent of the total.

Economy. Michigan is the sixth largest manufacturing state in the United States, and one-third of its manufactures are related to the automobile industry. In addition to the principal car and truck builders in Detroit and Flint, major manufacturers of automobile parts and accessories exist in cities such as Lansing, Battle Creek, and Kalamazoo.

The second largest business in the Lower Peninsula is agriculture, with equal concentrations of livestock and crops. Most of the cattle are raised on dairy farms, and most of the crops are grown for feed. The principal businesses of the Upper Peninsula are timber, chiefly hardwoods, and mining, chiefly of iron, cement, and natural gas. The northern half of the Lower Peninsula and much of the Upper Peninsula are rich in lakes, streams, and shoreline areas, helping to make tourism a large and significant part of the state economy.

AT AGATE FALLS, the Ontonagon River cascades 80 feet over a series of shelves.

Places of interest. There are many summer resorts along the Great Lakes shorelines of Michigan, including the Pictured Rocks National Lakeshore in the Upper Peninsula and Sleeping Bear Dunes in the northwest Lower Peninsula. Major attractions near Detroit are the automobile plants themselves, the Henry Ford Museum, and the preserved 19th-century Greenfield Village in Dearborn.

Minnesota

Abbreviations: *Minn., MN*
Area: *79,617 sq. mi.,*
206,208 sq. km.
Rank (of 50)   14th
Population:
2000   4,919,479
Rank (of 50)   21st
Change 1995–2000
+309,479
Persons per sq. mi.   61.7
Capital: *St. Paul*
Largest city: *Minneapolis*
Pop.   382,618
Entered Union: *May 11, 1858*
(32nd)
State bird: *Common loon*
State flower: *Pink and white lady's*
slipper
State tree: *Red pine*
State map: *Page 94*

Minnesota is situated near the northern center of the country, with a 350-mile (563-kilometer) border with the Canadian provinces of Manitoba and Ontario. It is the only Grain state with access to the Great Lakes, through Lake Superior, and its eastern border is with Wisconsin. The Dakotas are to the west and Iowa to the south.

Minnesota ranks second among the Grain states in land area (to Kansas) and in population (to Missouri). Its landscape is one of great beauty and variety, including extensive bluff, prairie, and hill formations. It is especially noted for its lakes, which number more than 20,000 and cover 7,326 square miles (18,967 square kilometers). Its northern reaches are heavily wooded and are popular with vacationers. The state also claims enormous iron ore reserves in its northeastern corner and fertile farmland along its southern and western borders. This combination of natural assets gives the state a diversified economy.

The land. Minnesota contains two principal topographical areas of approximately equal size, the superior upland in the north and the central lowlands in the south. The central lowlands are the beginning of the fertile region of rolling hills and river valleys that stretch south along the route of the Mississippi River. In Minnesota the area consists of the Young Drift Plains, a fertile grassland of more recent, or younger, glacial deposits, or drift, than those found to the east or west. The superior upland is characterized by 2,000-foot (610-meter) hills in the east, beside Lake Superior, and a flat clay prairie in the west. Its eastern region, called the Arrowhead for its shape, contains the iron-rich Mesabi Range as well as well-forested ranges. Its western region was once covered by the glacial Lake Agassiz, which left behind fertile flats on which grows the state's large oats crop.

The topography of Minnesota is also notable for its river drainage in three directions: south via the Mississippi, north via the Red River, and east via the Great Lakes.

Climate. Minnesota is a generally cool state, with temperatures declining toward the west and north. In the east-central city of Duluth, normal summer highs are in the 70°F (21°C) range, and winter lows are below zero. The Minneapolis-St. Paul area farther south is milder in both seasons. The state has a relatively light annual rainfall of about 30 inches (76 centimeters), but most of it falls during the growing season.

Principal cities. More than half the population of Minnesota lives in the Minneapolis-St. Paul metropolitan area. These Twin Cities at the junction of the Minnesota and Mississippi rivers process and distribute food products; both have developed modern and diversified manufacturing sectors. The next largest city in Minnesota is Duluth (population, 86,918), at the western reach of Lake Superior. It is from Duluth's giant inland harbor that northern Minnesota's exports of iron ore are shipped.

The people. Many state residents are of Scandinavian descent, but among recent immigrants, people of German extraction outnumber Scandinavians. African Americans, Hispanics, and Asians each account for about 3 percent of the population.

Economy. One of the largest hay crops in the United States is grown in the northeast hills of Minnesota; the northwest prairie grows one of the largest oat crops; and the southern region grows the fourth largest corn crop. Minnesota also ranks third in soybean production and sixth in wheat production. About half of the state's farm income is from livestock. Minnesota ranks third among U.S. states in hog and pig production, eleventh in cattle, and fourth in milk production.

Minnesota also mines 60 percent of the U.S. iron ore yield, principally from open pits in the Mesabi Range. The state's manufacturing businesses generate $10 billion in commerce each year. Tourism and timber are also significant industries.

Places of interest. The principal attractions in Minnesota are outdoor activities, including camping, fishing, and winter sports. Of special interest is Voyageurs National Park at the Canadian border. The Twin Cities have many cultural attractions.

Mississippi

Abbreviations: *Miss., MS*
Area: *46,914 sq. mi.,*
121,507 sq. km.
Rank (of 50)   31st
Population:
2000   2,844,658
Rank (of 50)   31st
Change 1995–2000
+147,658
Persons per sq. mi.   60.6
Capital: *Jackson*
Largest city: *Jackson*
Pop.   184,256
Entered Union: *Dec. 10, 1817*
(20th)
State bird: *Mockingbird*
State flower: *Magnolia*
State tree: *Magnolia*
State map: *Page 97*

Mississippi is a South-Central state on the east bank of the Mississippi River, bordering Louisiana and Arkansas to the west. Its southern border includes 44 miles (71 kilometers) of coastline on the Gulf of Mexico. It is otherwise separated from the Gulf by the 50-mile- (80-kilometer-) wide eastern extension of Louisiana. Mississippi's eastern and northern borders are with Alabama and Tennessee.

MINNESOTA
claims enormous iron ore reserves in its northeastern corner, giving it a diversified economy. Shown here is a mine conveyor.

27 North America

SOYBEANS have replaced cotton in the fields of Mississippi's delta.

kilometer	*US*
kilometre	*Brit.*
center	*US*
centre	*Brit.*
aluminum	*US*
aluminium	*Brit.*

Historically, Mississippi was the heart of the South's plantation society. This heritage continued to dominate the state's social, political, and economic character well into modern times. Until the 1940s African Americans outnumbered whites, and although slavery had long been abolished, the vast majority were poor and powerless. In the next 30 years, thousands of African Americans left to find better conditions in the North. During this time, however, African Americans in Mississippi gained greater economic opportunities and political power, and by 1970 the Northern migration had slowed to a trickle. The state's new businesses brought it a larger population increase in the 1970s than it had seen in the previous 40 years. In the 1980s growth slowed to less than a quarter of the national average, but neared the national average in the 1990s. Today Mississippi remains last among U.S. states in per capita income.

The land.   There are two principal topographical areas in Mississippi: a 200-mile- (322-kilometer-) long stretch of Mississippi delta along the river in the northwest, and a far larger expanse of Gulf Coastal Plain covering the rest of the state area. The delta, ranging from 10 to 85 miles (16 to 137 kilometers) in width, lies between the Mississippi River on the west and the Tallahatchie and Yazoo rivers on the east. It is separated from the rest of the area of Mississippi by a line of rugged loess bluffs that runs north into Tennessee. The Gulf Coastal Plain to the east and south is a hillier region, with many individual relief features. From a sea level elevation along the Gulf Coast, the plain rises to the north. The state's high point is Woodall Mountain (806 feet, 246 meters) in the extreme northeast corner. The plain is broken along Mississippi's eastern border by the Black Belt, a prairie of rich black soil that extends eastward into Alabama.

Climate.   Mississippi has a warm, humid subtropical climate. Normal high temperatures in summer exceed 90°F (32°C), and normal lows in winter remain above 40°F (4°C). Rainfall throughout the state is a heavy 50 inches (127 centimeters) per year, and snows are rare even in the highest northeastern regions.

Principal cities.   Mississippi remains a predominantly rural state. The principal city is the capital, Jackson, near the center of the state on the Pearl River. The second largest population center is Biloxi-Gulfport-Pascagoula (population, 147,971) on the Gulf Coast. Their metropolitan areas account for only 30 percent of the state's population. Several important cities lie near Mississippi's border in adjacent states: Memphis to the north and New Orleans and Mobile to the south.

The people.   Mississippi has one of the most stable populations in the United States. It has the fewest foreign-born residents in the country, and a large majority of the people were born in the state. African Americans represent about 36 percent of the population, the highest proportion of any state.

Economy.   Manufacturing is the principal industry in Mississippi. Diversified manufactures include textiles, food, wood, and electrical goods. In agriculture soybeans have replaced cotton on the fields of the delta. Chickens and cattle account for most of the state's livestock. Other principal industries include timber and petroleum and natural gas drilling along the Gulf Coast.

Places of interest.   Mississippi is rich in Civil War monuments, such as the Vicksburg National Military Park, Brice's Crossroads National Battlefield Site, and the Tupelo National Battlefield. Plantation mansions are preserved at Oxford in the north of the state and at Hattiesburg and Natchez, both in the south. Prehistoric Indian mounds are also preserved along the Natchez Trace National Parkway.

Missouri

Abbreviations: *Mo., MO*
Area: *68,898 sq. mi.,*
       178,446 sq. km.
       Rank (of 50)   18th
Population:
       2000   5,595,211
       Rank (of 50)   17th
       Change 1995–2000
       +271,211
       Persons per sq. mi.   81.2
Capital: *Jefferson City*
Largest city: *Kansas City*
       Pop.   441,545
Entered Union: *Aug. 10, 1821*
       (24th)
State bird: *Bluebird*
State flower: *Hawthorne*
State tree: *Dogwood*
State map: *Page 94*

Missouri, the most southeastern of the Grain states, is situated on the west bank of the Mississippi River. It borders Iowa to the north and Kansas and Nebraska to the west. To the south and east, it touches states of several other regions: the Oil states of Oklahoma and Arkansas, the South-Central states of Tennessee and Kentucky, and the Great Lakes state of Illinois. The Missouri River forms the upper third of the state's western border and then turns east to cross the state and join the Mississippi just north of St. Louis.

In the early 1800s, Missouri became the gateway between the upper and lower reaches of the Mississippi River. St. Louis became the principal city north of New Orleans and prospered from the river trade. Later in the century, Missouri became the "Gateway to the West." The city of Independence, near the western border, became the starting point for generations of settlers taking the Santa Fe or the Oregon trails to the Western lands in the 1840s and 1850s. Independence and neighboring Kansas City later became important depots on the new transcontinental railroads.

MARK TWAIN'S HOMETOWN of Hannibal, Missouri, commemorates his life and works. This statue portrays Tom Sawyer and Huckleberry Finn.

This prominence in commerce and transportation has made Missouri the most populous, urban, and industrial of the Grain states. Its principal cities, St. Louis (population, 348,189) in the east and Kansas City in the west, lie almost 250 miles (402 kilometers) apart. In 1980 the U.S. center of population moved west of the Mississippi River for the first time. In 2000 the U.S. center of population continued its southwestward movement to 3 miles (4.8 kilometers) east of Edgar Springs, Missouri.

Montana

Abbreviations: *Mont., MT*
Area: *145,556 sq. mi.,*
  336,990 sq. km.
  Rank (of 50)   4th
Population:
  2000   902,195
  Rank (of 50)   44th
  Change 1995–2000
  +32,195
  Persons per sq. mi.   6.0
Capital: *Helena*
Largest city: *Billings*
  Pop.   89,847
Entered Union: *Nov. 8, 1889*
  (41st)
State bird: *Western meadowlark*
State flower: *Bitterroot*
State tree: *Ponderosa pine*
State map: *Page 92*

THE AREA OF MISSOURI north of the Missouri River consists of fertile plains. South of the river are the Osage Plains.

The land. The area north of the Missouri River consists of fertile plains such as those in Iowa to the north. South of the Missouri River are the Osage Plains along the western border. The remainder of the land consists of the hillier and more forested Ozark Plateau. The Ozarks region is composed of steep hills and man-made lakes, such as the Lake of the Ozarks near the center of the state. One unusual feature of the Ozarks is the large number of springs, caves, and sinkholes created by groundwater dissolving the limestone bed of the plateau. In the extreme southeast of the state, the "boot heel" region that extends into Arkansas includes a stretch of Mississippi alluvial plain, whose rich soil makes it a fertile farming area.

Climate. Missouri has a mild, humid climate. High summer temperatures average near 90°F (32°C) and winter lows average about 20°F (-7°C). Rainfall averages over 35 inches (89 centimeters) per year, and it is heavier in the east than in the western part of the state.

Principal cities. With a metropolitan area including parts of Illinois, St. Louis is a city of heavy industry, resembling cities in the Great Lakes states. It is second only to Detroit as a producer of automobiles and trucks, and it is the home of a major aerospace manufacturer, the McDonnell-Douglas Corporation. St. Louis ranks tenth in the United States in number of major corporations, and it is noted for its breweries, aluminum plants, and electrical component manufacturers. Kansas City lies in a metropolitan area that includes parts of Kansas. It is a center of the nation's food industry. The major businesses are stockyards and cereal grain mills.

The people. Missouri had a population of over 3 million before 1900. Its growth since then has been gradual, reaching 5 million in 1985. More than two-thirds of the population are lifelong residents of the state. There has been considerable movement within the state, however, as rural population has declined and urban population has increased rapidly. African Americans represent 11 percent of the total population, and they are heavily concentrated in urban areas.

Economy. Missouri is the third largest manufacturing state west of the Mississippi, after California and Texas. Dominated by heavy industry and food processing, which are concentrated in St. Louis and Kansas City respectively, value added from manufacturing amounts to more than $30 billion each year.

Agriculture continues to be a major industry. Missouri grows a variety of crops because of its position between the Corn Belt to the north and the Cotton Belt to the south. Income derived from livestock is twice that which is derived from crops, with cattle grazing concentrated north of the Missouri River and dairy farming to the south of it. There is also a large mining industry operating in the Ozarks. It produces quantities of lead, iron, and zinc. Tourism, principally in the Ozarks, produces some $5 billion per year.

Places of interest. The principal natural attraction of Missouri is the Ozarks, which can be toured along the Ozark National Scenic Riverway. Mark Twain's boyhood hometown of Hannibal is located along the northern part of Missouri's Mississippi shoreline; it includes the Mark Twain Cave and a number of other places related to his life and works. Other notable sights include the magnificent 630-foot (192-meter) Gateway Arch in St. Louis, the Pony Express Museum in St. Joseph, and the Harry S. Truman Library in Independence. St. Louis is also home to an acclaimed zoo.

Montana, the most northern of the Mountain states, stretches more than 650 miles (1,046 kilometers) along the Canadian border between the plains of North Dakota and the mountains of Idaho. Its eastern two-thirds is a precise rectangle, but the western third is a wider and more irregular area defined by the ridges of the Bitterroot Mountains. In surface area, too, the eastern two-thirds is more regular, mostly consisting of the grazing lands of the western Great Plains. The western third, a rugged mountain area, includes the Continental Divide ridge of the Northern Rockies.

Montana contains more U.S. government-defined wilderness areas than any other state. The population is sparse and the cities few, so the residents are inured to long trips for the limited social entertainment found in small towns. Rich in mineral resources, Montana has been the stage for bitter clashes between environmentalists and supporters of industrial and economic development.

The land. The eastern two-thirds of Montana is a vast plain and prairie region crossed by the Missouri River in the north and the Yellowstone River in the south, with the two rivers converging at

MINING IS THE PRINCIPAL INDUSTRY of Montana, but the state has been the stage for bitter clashes between environmentalists and supporters of industrial development.

THE BATTLE-FIELD ON THE LITTLE BIGHORN in Montana was the site of Custer's ignominious last stand in 1876.

center
US

centre
Brit.

kilometers
US

kilometres
Brit.

the North Dakota border. In the western third, the central ridge of the Rockies extends from Yellowstone Park at the Wyoming border in a northwest direction to Glacier National Park on the Canadian border. In the Rockies are found the headwaters of rivers that drain west via the Snake and Columbia rivers into the Pacific, and east and south via the Missouri and Yellowstone rivers to the Mississippi and the Gulf of Mexico.

Climate.   Landlocked in the northern interior of the country, Montana has a harsh climate. At Great Falls, in the center of the state, winter lows fall below zero, and summer highs rise above 80°F (26°C). Daily extremes can vary widely: The record low at Great Falls is -43°F (-42°C), and the record high is 106°F (41°C). Winter storms in the Rockies and along the Canadian border can be especially harsh.

Principal cities.   Montana does not have any metropolitan areas. The largest city is Billings, an agricultural marketplace for northern Wyoming as well as Montana. All other major cities are located in the western, mountainous third of the state. Great Falls (population, 56,690) grew dramatically when the hydroelectric power of the Missouri River was first tapped. The capital city of Helena (population, 25,780) was originally a stockyard town for cattle grazed in the Big Belt Mountains. The Butte-Silver Bow-Anaconda area in the southwest was built on the profits of copper mines and was once the scene of violent battles between union workers and the Anaconda Mining Company.

The people.   The population of Montana, while comparatively small, is among the stablest in the West. Social status is often measured by one's descent from pioneer stock. Most migrations tend to be within state borders. Since the 1960s there has been a significant movement from the agricultural areas of eastern Montana, where farms are being consolidated, to the mining and manufacturing towns of the western mountain region. The state grew slightly faster than the country during the 1970s, but at below the national rate during the 1980s and 1990s.

Economy.   The agriculture of eastern Montana accounts for a large portion of the state's business. The chief agricultural products are wheat, of which Montana is one of the country's largest suppliers, and cattle. Montana leads all Mountain states both in amount of forestland, with 22.5 million acres (9.1 million hectares), and in lumber production, which amounts to about 1.5 billion board feet annually.

The mining industry continues to be the principal support of the Mountain region, where in recent years coal has surpassed copper in importance. Petroleum and natural gas production has outstripped both coal and copper. Tourism is also a substantial industry, with most visitors attracted by the hunting of big game, such as moose, elk, and bear, and the state's natural beauty.

Places of interest.   From Yellowstone north to Glacier National Park, the western region of Montana is full of impressive mountain, lake, cavern, and river landscapes preserved in virtually untouched condition. The plains areas in the eastern two-thirds of Montana include places associated with the early history of the state, such as the Little Bighorn Battlefield National Monument, the Fort Union Trading Post, and the Museum of the Plains Indian.

Nebraska

Abbreviations: *Neb., NE*
Area: *76,878 sq. mi.,*
  199,114 sq. km.
  Rank (of 50)   15th
Population:
  2000   1,711,263
  Rank (of 50)   38th
  Change 1995–2000
  +74,263
Capital: *Lincoln*
Largest city: *Omaha*
  Pop.   390,007
Entered Union: *Mar. 1, 1867*
  (37th)
State bird: *Western meadowlark*
State flower: *Goldenrod*
State tree: *Cottonwood*
State map: *Page 94*

Nebraska lies at the very heart of the U.S. Grain region. Its borders are with South Dakota to the north, Iowa to the east, and Kansas to the south. On the west, it touches the Mountain states of Colorado and Wyoming. Part of its northern border and all of its eastern border are formed by the Missouri River.

Nebraska is one of the principal agricultural states of the United States, second only to North Dakota in percentage of farmland (94.5 percent), and fourth, after Texas, Montana, and Kansas, in total acreage of farmland (47 million acres, 19 million hectares).

Change is apparent, however, in the increasing automation of farms and in the urban growth around Omaha and Lincoln.

The land.   Nebraska has two principal topographical areas, a strip of central lowlands in the extreme east of the state and a huge expanse of the Great Plains covering the rest of its land area. The central lowlands are limited to lands extending about 80 miles (129 kilometers) west from the Missouri River. Although it represents less than one-quarter of the state area, this strip contains most of its population centers and the fertile lands on which grow most of the state's enormous corn crop. The western three-quarters of the state, more than 60,000 square miles (155,340 square kilometers) in area, is crossed from west to east by the Platte River.

Climate.   The climate of Nebraska is known for its sudden changes, with fast-moving meteorological fronts often resulting in hail or thunderstorms. Warm, moist air from the Gulf of Mexico gives Nebraska warm, humid summers, with temperatures above 80°F (27°C). Normal daily lows are about 10°F (-12°C) in winter, but colder local extremes are common in the western regions. The state's average annual precipitation is about 30 inches (76 centimeters).

Principal cities.   The Omaha metropolitan area, on the Missouri River, contains more than one-third of Nebraska's total population. A regional center for portions of Iowa as well as Nebraska, it is one of the major meat-packing cities in the country, a large grain storage depot, and a transportation hub at the intersection of river, rail, and highway routes. The capital city of Lincoln (population, 225,581), 50 miles (80 kilometers) to the southwest, is a center for grain and insurance businesses. Between them, the Omaha and Lincoln metropolitan areas have 51 percent of the state's population.

EAGLE ROCK in Nebraska marks the route of the old Oregon Trail.

The people. The people of Nebraska are for the most part descendants of the European immigrants who settled the state before 1900. The state grew from 28,000 to 1.1 million between 1860 and 1890, but it lost population to migration throughout the 20th century. Birthrates now give the state a small population growth, but the trend of young people moving elsewhere for employment leaves the state with a high proportion of senior citizens: more than 13 percent of Nebraska's population is over 65 years of age.

Economy. Nebraska is one of the great food producers in the country. It ranks third in production of corn, eighth in production of soybeans, and high in production of sorghum grain and oats. Crops, however, account for less than half the state's farm income. On the plains of its central and western regions, Nebraska raises more beef cattle than any state except Texas, and hog production ranks fifth in the United States. Nebraska's manufacturing businesses, chiefly food processing, produce more than $7 billion in value added per year.

Places of interest. Nebraska is home to the Scotts Bluff National Monument and the Chimney Rock National Historic Site, both near the Wyoming border. Also of interest are the Buffalo Bill Ranch and the Oregon Trail, along the North Platte River.

Nevada

Abbreviations: *Nev., NV*
Area: *109,806 sq. mi., 284,398 sq. km.*
   Rank (of 50)   7th
Population:
   2000   1,998,257
   Rank (of 50)   35th
   Change 1995–2000 +468,255
   Persons per sq. mi.   18.1
Capital: *Carson City*
Largest city: *Las Vegas*
   Pop.   478,434
Entered Union: *Oct. 31, 1864 (36th)*
State bird: *Mountain bluebird*
State flower: *Sagebrush*
State tree: *Single-leaf piñon*
State map: *Page 90*

Nevada is a southwestern state situated between the Sierra Nevada and Rocky Mountain ranges, with a long border to the west and southwest with California. The state is mostly desert, yet its limited population is generally prosperous. In 1859 the discovery of the famous Comstock silver lode transformed a barren territory into a mining property of such value that Nevada was admitted to the Union in 1864, during the Civil War, without the required number of

LAS VEGAS is famous for the gambling casinos, nightclubs, and luxury hotels that line "The Strip."

inhabitants. Then, in 1931, gambling was legalized in Nevada and divorce requirements eased. Since then, Nevada's principal cities, Las Vegas and Reno, have grown rapidly by attracting large numbers of visitors, helping to make tourism one of the largest growth industries in the American West.

The land. The largest topographical area in Nevada is the Great Basin, a desert plain more than 3,000 feet (914 meters) above sea level running north-south between the Sierra Nevadas on the west and a spur of the Rocky Mountains on the east. Only near the Colorado River, at Nevada's southern border with Arizona, is its altitude below 1,000 feet (305 meters). Many of Nevada's rivers carry water only after rainfall, and many of its alkaline lakes exist as dry beds, or sinks, for much of the year. The largest body of water in the state is Lake Mead, a man-made lake formed by the construction of the Hoover Dam on the Colorado River.

Climate. Nevada has the lowest annual rainfall of any state, averaging under 7 inches (18 centimeters). Winds from the Pacific drop most of their moisture on California's Sierra Nevadas, leaving very little for Nevada. In most of the state days are hot and nights cold, regardless of the season.

Principal cities. Almost 96 percent of the state's population live in its two metropolitan areas. Nevada's largest city is Las Vegas, in the southern corner of the state near the Colorado River. Originally settled because of its mineral springs, the city began to expand with the legalization of gambling and the construction of nearby Hoover Dam in the 1930s. Since then, a steady stream of tourists has caused huge increases in the resident population. The city is famous for the gambling casinos, nightclubs, and luxury hotels that line its central avenue, "The Strip."

The second largest city is Reno (population, 180,480), more than 300 miles (483 kilometers) northwest at the base of the Sierra Nevadas near the California border. Reno is older and more traditional than Las Vegas, and its casinos and hotels attract tourists from the San Francisco area.

The other cities in the state, all much smaller, include the cattle town of Elko, the mining town of Ely, and Carson City, the capital.

The people. Nevada is sparsely populated. Its growth has been rapid, but the limited base from which it began accounts for its exceptionally high recent growth rate. Less than a quarter of the people residing in Nevada were born in the state, and most newcomers are attracted by the solid economic base that gives the state a lower than average unemployment rate. The population is heavily urban.

Economy. The major industry in Nevada is tourism, which exceeds $9 billion annually. Taxes on gambling alone account for nearly half of Nevada's total tax revenues. Another leading industry is mining, which now far exceeds the production levels of the state's early boom years. In addition to its large production of copper and a variety of other minerals, Nevada accounts for 26 percent of the total U.S. output of gold. Manufacture of electronic equipment and chemical products now constitutes an increasingly important sector of the economy. Livestock and feed provide most of the state's agricultural income.

Places of interest. In addition to the large resorts in Las Vegas and Reno, Nevada has major resort areas near Lake Tahoe, along the California border, and Lake Mead, along the Arizona border. Among the principal attractions associated with the state's desert geography are Carson Hot Springs, Cathedral Gorge State Park, and many preserved fossil beds. Other places of interest include such former boom towns as Virginia City, and the many ghost towns and abandoned mines scattered across the state.

New Hampshire

Abbreviations: *N.H., NH*
Area: *8,969 sq. mi., 23,230 sq. km.*
Rank (of 50) 44th
Population:
2000 1,235,786
Rank (of 50) 41st
Change 1995–2000 +87,786
Persons per sq. mi. 137.7
Capital: *Concord*
Largest city: *Manchester*
Pop. 107,006
Entered Union: *June 21, 1788 (9th)*
State bird: *Purple finch*
State flower: *Purple lilac*
State tree: *White birch*
State map: *Page 101*

New Hampshire is a roughly triangular state situated in the northern tier of the New England region. The state is broadest in the south, where it has a 125-mile (201-kilometer) border with Massachusetts, and is narrowest in the north, where its east-west breadth narrows to less than 20 miles (32 kilometers) at the northern border with the Canadian Province of Quebec. On the west, New Hampshire has an irregular border with Vermont formed by the Connecticut River, and on the east it has a straight border with Maine. A short eastward extension between Maine and Massachusetts gives the state a 15-mile (24-kilometer) Atlantic Ocean coastline.

kilometer *US*
kilometre *Brit.*

centers *US*
centres *Brit.*

In the 1970s New Hampshire had the greatest numerical and proportionate population growth in New England. The state population grew by 100,000 in the 1950s and 1960s, and again in the 1990s, but during the 1970s and 1980s it grew by 371,000, or 50 percent. The growth has been especially striking in southern New Hampshire, where most of the state's people live. Many commuters to Boston have relocated across the New Hampshire border, and companies have made similar moves for tax reasons. Northern New Hampshire remains sparsely populated.

TOWN MEETINGS have historically been the main focus of self-government for New England's small towns and villages.

The land. All of New Hampshire is hilly and forested, but the state lands fall into northern and southern topographical areas. The north is dominated by the White Mountains, which cross the state from Vermont to Maine. The Presidential range within the White Mountains includes Mt. Washington (6,288 feet, 1,917 meters), the highest peak in the entire northeast and the windiest spot in the country, with record gusts well over 200 miles (322 kilometers) per hour. The southern half of the state consists of New England Upland, a region that in New Hampshire averages 1,200 feet (366 meters) in elevation and includes peaks over 3,000 feet (914 meters) high. Along the small southeastern extension between Maine and Massachusetts to the Atlantic Ocean, New Hampshire includes a fringe of New England Seaboard Lowland, with sandy beaches and a major harbor at Portsmouth.

Climate. New Hampshire's climate typically consists of short summers and long, cold winters. At the capital city of Concord in south-central New Hampshire, the normal summer highs are 82°F (28°C) and the winter lows are 10°F (-12°C). However, Concord has recorded temperatures as low as -37°F (-38°C), and subzero temperatures are common in the northern mountains. Precipitation at Concord averages 36 inches (91 centimeters) per year with 66 inches (168 centimeters) of snow, but snowfall is heavier in the north.

Principal cities. The major cities in New Hampshire are all clustered in the southeast, near the Massachusetts border. The largest is Manchester, an industrial city on the Merrimack River less than 20 miles (32 kilometers) from the Massachusetts border. The second largest city is Nashua (population, 86,605), farther down the Merrimack and closer to Massachusetts. Other large cities in the state include the capital of Concord (population, 40,687) and harbor city of Portsmouth (20,784).

The people. Well over half of New Hampshire's total population growth in recent decades has been from immigrants from other states. Most of these new residents settled in southern New Hampshire, which includes two-thirds of the total population. The African-American and the Hispanic populations in the state are each under 2 percent of the total.

Economy. Manufacturing is the principal industry of New Hampshire, producing more than $5.5 billion in value added per year. Because New Hampshire's lands are rocky and hilly, water-powered manufacturing was the traditional business of the state. The first products were leather, textiles, and wood. These eventually declined in economic importance. The major new manufactures include electrical and electronic equipment and machinery, which are produced in the cities in the south of the state. The second leading industry is tourism, based mostly in the northern, less populated, areas of the state. The state's agricultural businesses are principally dairy farms, vegetable greenhouses, and fruit orchards.

Places of interest. The major attractions in New Hampshire are its mountains and more than 1,000 lakes and ponds. Mountain attractions include the hiking trails around Mt. Washington, White Mountains National Forest, and the unusual "Old Man of the Mountain" granite formation in the Franconia range in the northwest of the state. The largest body of water in the state is 70-square-mile (181-square-kilometer) Lake Winnipesaukee in the east-central region; the lake and the Franklin Falls Reservoir both drain into the scenic upper reaches of the Merrimack River.

New Jersey

Abbreviations: *N.J., NJ*
Area: *7,419 sq. mi., 19,215 sq. km.*
Rank (of 50) 46th
Population:
2000 8,414,350
Rank (of 50) 9th
Change 1995–2000 +684,162
Persons per sq. mi. 1,134.1
Capital: *Trenton*
Largest city: *Newark*
Pop. 273,546
Entered Union: *Dec. 18, 1787 (3rd)*
State bird: *Eastern goldfinch*
State flower: *Purple violet*
State tree: *Red oak*
State map: *Page 100*

New Jersey is located between Pennsylvania to the west and New York to the north and northeast. To the southeast, the state has a long Atlantic Ocean shore, and it shares a short water border with Delaware in the extreme south.

Among the top ten states in population and the bottom ten in land area, New Jersey is the most densely populated state in the country. Its population centers are clustered around New York City in the northeast and Philadelphia in the southwest, and along the heavily developed corridor that connects the two cities. Many New Jersey communities are so-called bedroom suburbs for those who work out of state in New York and Philadelphia. The remainder of the state, less heavily populated, includes pastoral hill and farm country in the northwest and sandy pine barrens in the southeast.

The land. New Jersey is divided by a diagonal line running from Trenton on the Delaware River northeast across the narrow center of the state to New York Harbor. To the south of this line lies

ATLANTIC CITY, a historic resort, is at the heart of New Jersey's 127 miles of beaches.

three-fifths of the state area, consisting entirely of Atlantic Coastal Plain, the flat, sandy land that stretches from the Delaware River to the Atlantic Ocean. The interior varies from farmland to sandier barrens of scrub pine, and the coastline is a uniformly sandy one characterized by the built-up sand bars of the Great Barrier Reef that are separated from the mainland by tidal lagoons.

North of the dividing line, the state lands consist of a series of hilly formations running from southwest to northeast. Nearest the dividing line is the northernmost extension of the Piedmont Plateau, a lowland broken by isolated ridges. Northwest of the plateau is a range of higher hills related to the New England Highlands. The northeastern corner of the state is part of the Appalachian valley shared with Pennsylvania and cut by the Delaware River at the Delaware Water Gap, a picturesque canyon near the state's northwest corner.

Climate. The climate of New Jersey is moderate, influenced by the long Atlantic coastline. Normal winter lows throughout the state are above 20°F (-7°C), and normal summer highs are about 85°F (29°C). Precipitation averages 45 inches (114 centimeters) per year, including an average of 16 inches (41 centimeters) of snow per year.

Principal cities. The largest urban area entirely within New Jersey is Newark, a port facility on the New Jersey side of New York Harbor. However, Newark itself is part of the consolidated metropolitan area of New York City, which includes most of the area of New Jersey within a 40-mile (64-kilometer) radius of the harbor. The consolidated metropolitan area of Philadelphia includes major cities in southern New Jersey, such as Trenton (population,

85,403), the capital, and Camden (79,904). Atlantic City (population, 40,517), the only metropolitan area not part of the New York or Philadelphia metropolitan regions, is a seaside resort on the Atlantic coast. Casino gambling was made legal in Atlantic City in 1977, creating a major increase in the tourist business.

The people. Between 1950 and 2000, New Jersey grew rapidly, increasing its population by almost 60 percent. The rate of growth slowed in the 1970s but increased slightly in the 1980s and 1990s. Large cities showed significant population losses in the 1970s, which either slowed or became slight gains in the 1980s and 1990s. During this period some smaller towns continued to grow. The African-American population, concentrated in cities such as Newark, makes up 13 percent of the state population. Hispanics make up 13.3 percent and are concentrated in older manufacturing towns alongside New York Harbor.

Economy. The principal business of New Jersey is manufacturing, which generates many times the income of any other industry. Most of the manufacturers are based in northeastern New Jersey, which produces chemicals, packaged foods, machinery, electrical and electronic equipment, and other goods. The container port of Newark is also a base for large oil-refining companies.

The second leading industry is tourism, which accounts for some $9 billion annually, principally in summer along the Atlantic coast. Crops represent 70 percent of New Jersey's limited agricultural income, most of it from the vegetable produce of southern truck farms. Poultry and dairy products are also important. Despite the small contribution of agriculture to its economy, New Jersey is still sometimes called the Garden State.

Places of interest. The major tourist center in New Jersey is Atlantic City, a historic beach resort with a famous boardwalk. Atlantic City legalized gambling in 1977. It is the heart of the state's 127 miles (204 kilometers) of ocean beaches. Attractions in northern New Jersey include the Thomas Alva Edison Museum, the Grover Cleveland Birthplace, and Princeton University.

New Mexico

Abbreviations: *N.M., NM*
Area: *121,364 sq. mi.,*
314,333 sq. km.
Rank (of 50)   5th
Population:
2000   1,819,046
Rank (of 50)   36th
Change 1995–2000
+134,046
Persons per sq. mi.   14.9
Capital: *Santa Fe*
Largest city: *Albuquerque*
Pop.   448,607
Entered Union: *Jan. 6, 1912*
(47th)
State bird: *Roadrunner*
State flower: *Yucca*
State tree: *Piñon*
State map: *Page 92*

New Mexico, the most southern of the Mountain states, lies directly south of Colorado. It borders Arizona on the west, Texas and Oklahoma on the east, and Texas and Mexico on the south. The southern extreme of the Rocky Mountain chain extends into New Mexico from the north, and it is along the edges of the mountains that most residents of the state have settled.

New Mexico is the most Spanish-influenced of U.S. states, with traditions passed down by Spanish settlers of the 1700s. At the same time it is a center of America's most modern military technology, symbolized by the northern city of Los Alamos, where the early atomic bombs were constructed. The state also has a large Native American population. The area around Santa Fe and Taos attracts many artists and writers.

The state was nearly ruined by a long drought followed by the Depression of the 1930s, but since World War II it has experienced increasing prosperity.

The land. New Mexico's complex topography begins with the foot of the southern Rocky Mountains in the north-central region. The mountains protrude 100 miles (161 kilometers) into the state to a point near Santa Fe and contain the headwaters of the Rio Grande River, which flows south through the center of the state. To the east of the river lie the southern reaches of the Great Plains. This flat tableland, averaging over 4,000 feet (1,219 meters) in elevation, joins the

THIS ADOBE HOUSE in historic Santa Fe is reputed to be the oldest house in the United States.

meters
US

metres
Brit.

center
US

centre
Brit.

theaters
US

theatres
Brit.

high plains of Texas across the state's eastern and southern borders. West of the Rio Grande, New Mexico includes portions of the Colorado Plateau in the north and portions of the intermontane basin and range in the south. The Colorado Plateau is a scenic mesa, butte, and canyon region broken by mountain ranges approaching 10,000 feet (3,048 meters) in elevation. The southwest basin and range region is a semiarid desert characterized by low mountain ranges separated by elongated dry desert floors.

Climate. The climate is one of warm days and cool nights, with winter temperature averages ranging from 55°F (13°C) in the south to 35°F (2°C) in the north and summer temperatures ranging over 80°F (27°C) throughout the state. New Mexico is an exceptionally dry state. In Albuquerque precipitation averages about 8 inches (20 centimeters) annually, although high mountains receive much more rain.

Principal cities. More than a third of the state's population reside in metropolitan Albuquerque, established by the Spanish settlers in 1706. The city is the financial, educational, and industrial center of the state. Santa Fe (population, 62,203), 60 miles (97 kilometers) north at the foot of the Rockies, is the state capital and a popular resort center for artists, musicians, and writers. It was the capital of a Spanish overseas province as early as 1610. Las Cruces (population, 74,267), on the Rio Grande, is only 50 miles (80 kilometers) from El Paso, Texas, and Ciudad Juárez, Mexico.

The people. The population of New Mexico is 42 percent Hispanic, and Spanish is in common use among a third of its residents. New Mexico also contains a population of over 170,000 Native Americans. The major tribes in the state are Zuni, Apache, and Navajo. The state's growth rate from the 1970s through the 1990s averaged 21 percent, far exceeding the national average.

Economy. Mining is the chief industry in New Mexico, accounting for three-fifths of its commerce. The state is the country's leading producer of potash, perlite, and uranium. New Mexico also produces large amounts of energy fuels. New Mexico ranks fourth in the United States in natural gas production and tenth among U.S. states in nonfuel mineral production.

Agricultural production is chiefly of livestock, with some hay and cotton crops. New Mexico produces large quantities of stone, clay, and glass products, but the most important manufactures are electric and transportation equipment associated with the U.S. military.

Places of interest. Among the principal natural features of interest in New Mexico are the Carlsbad Caverns, located in the extreme southeast near the corner of the Texas border; the caverns include the largest cave in the United States. The basin and range region in the southwest is the site of extensive ancient pueblo ruins at the Gila Cliff Dwellings National Monument. The Colorado Plateau in the northwest is the location of Indian reservations as well as places associated with the state's mining and cowboy history.

New York

Abbreviations: *N.Y., NY*
Area: *47,224 sq. mi.,*
122,310 sq. km.
Rank (of 50)   30th
Population:
2000   18,976,457
Rank (of 50)   3rd
Change 1995–2000   +840,457
Persons per sq. mi.   401.8
Capital: *Albany*
Largest city: *New York*
Pop.   8,008,278
Entered Union: *July 26, 1788*
(11th)
State bird: *Bluebird*
State flower: *Rose*
State tree: *Sugar maple*
State map: *Page 100*

NEW YORK CITY (pictured before the September 2001 terrorist attacks) is a world commercial, trade, cultural, and financial center and home to the headquarters of the United Nations.

New York is the northernmost of the Mid-Atlantic states, stretching 325 miles (523 kilometers) from Lake Erie in the west to the New England states and the Atlantic Ocean in the east. Along its eastern edge, the state stretches nearly 300 miles (483 kilometers) north to south, from a boundary with Canada near Montreal, Quebec, to New York Bay. From that bay, the state extends 90 miles (145 kilometers) farther east on Long Island, along the coast of Connecticut. Its southern borders are with Pennsylvania and New Jersey; to the east are Vermont, Massachusetts, and Connecticut. To the west and north, the state borders Lake Erie, the Canadian Province of Ontario across the Niagara River, Lake Ontario, and Canada again, across the St. Lawrence River.

For most of the 20th century, New York was the largest and most influential state in the Union. In the early 1960s, however, California's population exceeded that of New York, and in the succeeding years, New York entered a period of economic decline and state residents began moving to more promising regions. In the 1970s, New York was the only state to record a substantial loss of population. A modest growth rate of 2.5 percent in the 1980s was followed by an increased rate of 5.5 percent in the 1990s.

New York is one of the most diverse of all states, containing the nation's largest city and many other important commercial centers as well as vast rural areas of great beauty.

The land. The topography of New York is complex. More than half its area, along the southern border with Pennsylvania, is part of the Appalachian plateau, a hill and valley region covering all of south and central New York. To the east of the plateau is a lowland along the Hudson and Mohawk rivers, which join at Albany in the east-central part of the state. The Hudson runs south from above Albany, reaching the Atlantic at New York Bay. The Hudson and Mohawk valleys represent a major break in the Appalachian Mountain chain, which stretches both southwest and northeast from the river lowlands. Early settlers recognized the importance of this break, and the Hudson-Mohawk system was connected to Lake Erie by the Erie Canal system, which was completed in 1825. This system, linking Buffalo, Albany, and New York City, was the forerunner of the state's modern rail and highway connections.

North of Albany lie the Adirondack Mountains, which include some of the oldest geologic formations in North America. The state high point is at Mt. Marcy (5,344 feet, 1,629 meters). The northern reaches of the state are lowlands bordering the Great Lakes and the St. Lawrence River. Long Island, in the extreme southeast, is part of the Atlantic Coastal Plain.

Climate. New York has differing climates in the east and west. At New York City in the southeast, normal summer highs are 85°F (29°C), winter lows 25°F (-4°C); precipitation averages 40 inches (102 centimeters) per year, including snowfall of 29 inches (74 centimeters). At Buffalo in the west on Lake Erie, normal temperatures are a cooler 80°F (27°C) in summer and 17°F (-8°C) in winter; precipitation averages 36 inches (91 centimeters), including snowfall of 92 inches (234 centimeters). In the northern Adirondacks winters are colder and bring even more snow.

Principal cities. New York City is the urban center of the state and the surrounding region. Its metropolitan area has a population of more than 9 million. New York City is a world commercial, trade, cultural, and financial center, and it is also the headquarters of the United Nations.

The second largest city in the state is Buffalo (population, 292,648), a Great Lakes steel town that is also the commercial center of western New York. From west to east across the center of the state is a series of large industrial cities: Rochester (population, 219,773), on Lake Ontario; Syracuse (147,306), in the center of the state; and Albany-Schenectady-Troy (206,649), near the Hudson River less than 30 miles (48 kilometers) from the Massachusetts border.

The people. Because of New York City's historical role as the port of entry for successive waves of European immigrants, the population of New York State continues to include the largest proportion of foreign-born residents in the United States. The population also includes large numbers of African Americans (16 percent), Hispanics (15 percent), and Asians (5.5 percent). New York's population also includes some 82,000 Native Americans and a small number of Inuit and Aleut residents, for the second-largest total Native American population east of the Mississippi, after North Carolina. The population is divided almost equally between the New York City region and the rest of the state.

Economy. The leading industry in New York is manufacturing, and the state ranks second only to California in value added by manufacture, more than $85 billion. Virtually all products are represented, from steel in Buffalo to photographic and optical supplies in Rochester to machinery products in Syracuse to 10 percent of the U.S. apparel output in New York City.

Tourism is the second largest industry, with out-of-state visitors attracted both to the cultural landmarks of New York City and to the scenery of upstate New York. Agriculture ranks third in economic importance, with two-thirds of the farm income coming from dairy livestock and cattle. Crops include vegetables, apples, maple syrup, and the fourth-largest harvest of potatoes in the United States. There are also a variety of less important industries in the New York economy, including wine fermenting, timber, mining, and commercial fishing.

Places of interest. The greatest number of visitors to the state come to see the skyscrapers, museums, theaters, stock exchange, and many other attractions of New York City. Natural attractions in upstate New York include Niagara Falls near Buffalo, the Adirondack Mountain resorts, and the Thousand Islands of the St. Lawrence River in the northeast. Special points of interest include West Point, home of the U.S. Military Academy, 60 miles (97 kilometers) up the Hudson River from New York City; Fort Ticonderoga at the southern end of Lake Champlain; and the Baseball Hall of Fame at Cooperstown, 60 miles (97 kilometers) west of Albany.

NEW YORK'S ROCKEFELLER CENTER, with its outdoor ice skating rink, is a major tourist attraction.

27 North America

kilometer
US

kilometre
Brit.

center
US

centre
Brit.

North Carolina

Abbreviations: *N.C., NC*
Area: *48,718 sq. mi.,*
126,180 sq. km.
Rank (of 50)   29th
Population:
2000   8,049,313
Rank (of 50)   11th
Change 1995–2000
+854,313
Persons per sq. mi.   165.2
Capital: *Raleigh*
Largest city: *Charlotte*
Pop.   540,828
Entered Union: *Nov. 21, 1789*
(12th)
State bird: *Cardinal*
State flower: *Dogwood blossom*
State tree: *Pine*
State map: *Page 98*

North Carolina is the most northern of the South Atlantic states. It has a 300-mile (483-kilometer) Atlantic coastline and is situated between Virginia to the north and South Carolina to the south. From the broad coastline the state narrows to a point more than 500 miles (805 kilometers) inland, where it borders Tennessee on the north and Georgia on the south.

The character of North Carolina belies its status as a heavily populated and economically powerful state. North Carolina is only about half urban, yet it ranks tenth in the United States in population. There is no heavy industry in the state, but North Carolina ranks eighth in the United States in value added from manufacturing. The industries in the state are among the oldest in the South, yet North Carolina has attracted numerous high-technology research and development companies. The state's economic power derives from its national leadership in textiles, furniture, and tobacco. These businesses are dispersed across the state, and so is the population.

The land.   The land of North Carolina falls away from mountains in the western interior to sea-level elevations along the coast. The mountain region is the smallest in the state. The Great Smoky Mountains lie along the Tennessee border. Thirty miles (48 kilometers) farther east are the Blue Ridge Mountains, which include the highest peak in the eastern United States at Mt. Mitchell (6,684 feet, 2,037 meters).

Two-fifths of the state land area consists of the Piedmont Plateau to the east of the mountains. This forested plateau ranges between 60 and 75 miles (97 and 121 kilometers) in west-east breadth and declines in elevation from 1,500 feet (457 meters) in the west to 500 feet (152 meters) in the east. At its eastern extent there is a fall line at which the land drops away to the Atlantic Coastal Plain and the rivers pass through rapids and waterfalls. The Atlantic Coastal Plain of fertile sands and silts occupies the eastern two-fifths of the state land area. Along the Atlantic it includes tidewater areas where rivers are flooded into estuaries by the action of the sea. Tidewater areas are especially prevalent in the northeast; they are characterized by shifting banks of sand dunes, such as Cape Hatteras, and low-lying marshes such as the Great Dismal Swamp.

Climate.   The climate of North Carolina is warm and humid except in the mountain region. Average temperatures on the Piedmont Plateau range from normal highs over 85°F (29°C) in summer to normal lows around freezing in winter. Precipitation throughout the state averages 42 inches (107 centimeters) per year, including 5 inches (13 centimeters) of snow. The winters are longer and the snowfalls greater in the mountains.

Principal cities.   All the major cities of North Carolina are located on the inland Piedmont Plateau, and the largest is the manufacturing center of Charlotte near the South Carolina border. Farther north on the plateau, three cities—Winston-Salem, Greensboro, and High Point—form a triangular urban center 30 miles (48 kilometers) wide on a side. These cities are the center of the state's tobacco industry as well as other manufactures. The capital city of Raleigh plus nearby Durham form the third large urban area. These two cities are located on the fall line between plateau and coastal plain. Together with Chapel Hill, the seat of the state university, Raleigh and Durham attracted new electronics and research business to the state in the 1970s and 1980s.

The people.   More than half of the population growth during the 1970s was produced by immigrants from other states drawn to local employment opportunities. Population growth continued to increase steadily through the 1980s and 1990s, and by 2000 was almost two thirds greater than the national rate.

Many African Americans migrated from North Carolina; during the 1970s, however, this traditional loss by migration slowed to a trickle. African-American residents now account for 22 percent of the total population. Hispanics represent 5 percent of the total. The state's Native American residents give North Carolina the highest Native American population of any state east of the Mississippi River.

Economy.   North Carolina's manufactures generate $57 billion in value added each year. Textile, tobacco, and wood products predominate. The state lacks the natural resources required for heavy industry.

In agriculture, the state produces some $4.8 billion in farm marketings each year. The major crops are cotton for textiles and bright leaf tobacco for cigarettes. Poultry farms account for most of the income from livestock. North Carolina also produces a significant amount of timber, principally hardwoods and pine harvested from the Piedmont Plateau. Much of the wood is used in the manufacture of furniture in the region around High Point. Tourism is also an important industry, and visitors to the state spend more than $6 billion per year.

Places of interest.   The Cape Hatteras and Cape Lookout national seashores are the principal natural attractions in North Carolina, although the state shares some Smoky Mountain resorts with Tennessee. Historical sites include Revolutionary War memorials at Guilford Courthouse and Moore's Creek in southeastern North Carolina, and the Wright Brothers Museum at Kitty Hawk on Cape Hatteras.

INTERESTING ROADSIDE STANDS can still be found on the backroads of rural North Carolina.

North Dakota

Abbreviations: *N.D., ND*
Area: *68,994 sq. mi.,*
178,694 sq. km.
Rank (of 50)   17th
Population:
2000   642,200
Rank (of 50)   47th
Change 1995–2000
+1,200
Persons per sq. mi.   9.3
Capital: *Bismarck*
Largest city: *Fargo*
Pop.   90,599
Entered Union: *Nov. 2, 1889*
(39th)
State bird: *Western meadowlark*
State flower: *Wild prairie rose*
State tree: *American elm*
State map: *Page 94*

REMNANTS OF THE GREAT HERDS of bison that once roamed the Dakota plains can still be found in protected areas.

North Dakota borders the Canadian provinces of Saskatchewan and Manitoba on the north and the U.S. state of South Dakota on the south. It lies between the states of Montana to the west and Minnesota to the east, near the center of the Great Plains. The geographic center of North America lies in the north-central part of the state.

North Dakota is one of the most agricultural states in the country, with more than 90 percent of its total acreage given over to farms (principally in the east) and to ranches (in the drier western areas).

The landscape of North Dakota is one of broad horizons and unending grasslands. Consolidation of many small farms into giant holdings more economical to cultivate have led to a gradual population decline. Yet North Dakota today harvests more than 14 percent of the nation's wheat, second only to Kansas.

The land.   The principal topographical features of North Dakota are the central lowlands in the eastern half of the state and the Missouri Plateau in the west. The central lowlands consist of the fertile Red River valley, which forms the state border with Minnesota and, farther west, the Young Drift Plains, where the glaciers of the last ice age deposited rich soils, or "drift." The eastern dry-farming region extends from the Minnesota border to a north-south divide, near the center of the state, called the Missouri escarpment, a chain of hills rising 300 to 400 feet (91 to 122 meters) above ground level.

West of the escarpment lies the Missouri Plateau region of the Great Plains. Crossed by the Missouri River, this plateau, ranging in elevation from 2,000 to 3,000 feet (610 to 914 meters), is covered by only a thin, easily eroded layer of soil. In the southwest, along the Little Missouri River, are the Badlands, an area of chiseled buttes called *mauvaises terres à traverser* (bad lands to cross) by the first French-Canadian explorers.

Climate.   North Dakota's climate is subject to great seasonal extremes. At Fargo, on the state's eastern border, January lows average -3°F (-19°C) and July highs average 84°F (29°C). Average precipitation is only about 16 inches (41 centimeters), but 75 percent of it falls as rain during the growing season. The rest is snow that often blankets the state under blizzard conditions.

Principal cities.   The largest city in North Dakota, the second most rural of Grain states, is Fargo, in the southern portion of the Red River valley. Grand Forks (population, 49,321), also lies in this river valley, farther north. Bismarck (population, 55,532), the capital, is located in the south-central area of the state on the Missouri River.

The people.   Three-quarters of the people in North Dakota are descended from north European and Canadian settlers, and two-thirds of the present population were born in North Dakota. The devastating effects of drought and the Depression caused a population decline of 40,000 in the 1930s. Despite a small population increase due to birthrate, the state lost 17,000 residents to migration in the 1970s. The population reached a peak of 681,000 in 1984, and then began a steady decline.

Economy.   North Dakota's economy is agriculture-based, and two-thirds of farm income is derived from crops grown principally in the eastern half of the state. The state ranks second in the country in the production of wheat and barley. Livestock ranches in the western half of the state generate a fourth of the farm income.

Second to agriculture in the state economy is mining, with 70 percent of its income derived from oil drilling, principally in the Williston Basin in the southwest. The western areas of the state also mine significant quantities of coal, uranium, and clay.

Places of interest.   One unusual attraction in North Dakota is the International Peace Garden, near the center of the state's Canadian border, commemorating friendly relations between the United States and Canada. Theodore Roosevelt National Park, in two parts of the southwest Badlands, preserves the president's ranch and its natural surroundings.

Ohio

Abbreviations: *O., OH*
Area: *40,953 sq. mi.,*
106,067 sq. km.
Rank (of 50)   35th
Population:
2000   11,353,140
Rank (of 50)   7th
Change 1995–2000
+202,140
Persons per sq. mi.   277.2
Capital: *Columbus*
Largest city: *Columbus*
Pop.   711,470
Entered Union: *Mar. 1, 1803*
(17th)
State bird: *Cardinal*
State flower: *Scarlet carnation*
State tree: *Buckeye*
State map: *Page 96*

Ohio is the most eastern of the Great Lakes states. Its northern border is formed by Michigan and by Lake Erie, which separates Ohio from the Canadian Province of Ontario. Its entire southern border is formed by the Ohio River, which separates it from Kentucky in the southwest and West Virginia in the southeast. Ohio stretches about 200 miles (322 kilometers) from Indiana in the west to Pennsylvania in the east.

THE STEEL MILLS of Cleveland's steel industry are supplied with ore by Great Lakes barges. Youngstown, Ohio, is also associated with the steel industry.

centimeters
US

centimetres
Brit.

center
US

centre
Brit.

The first settlement in the Northwest Territory was established at Marietta in 1788 along the Ohio River on the state's southern border. The advent of heavy industry along Lake Erie in the 20th century made the northeast the most populous region of the state. Today Ohio is the most densely populated of Great Lakes states. The state ranks third nationally, after California and New York, in manufacturing yet only thirty-fifth in land area.

The land. Most of the land of Ohio lies within the central lowland that covers its central and western regions. This is a generally flat plain of fertile soils deposited by glacial action.

In the east and the southeast, the state includes portions of the Appalachian Plateau, a hillier region rich in mineral deposits. In the extreme east this Appalachian Plateau includes the beginnings of the rugged Allegheny Mountains, which extend into Pennsylvania. Along its northern border, Ohio includes a strip of Great Lakes Plain. Much of the region once lay beneath Lake Erie; for that reason it remained swampland until drained by modern engineering techniques. West of Lake Erie, the Great Lakes Plain broadens into a fertile farming valley.

Climate. Ohio has a continental climate with seasonal extremes ranging from below 20°F (-7°C) in winter to over 80°F (27°C) in summer. Precipitation averages about 36 inches (91 centimeters) across the state. Winters are longer in Cleveland, on the shore of Lake Erie, than in the rest of the state, and the annual snowfall of more than 50 inches (127 centimeters) in Cleveland is nearly twice that in Columbus, near the geographical center of the state.

Principal cities. Ohio includes three metropolitan areas with more than 1 million residents. The largest is Cleveland, the center of a consolidated metropolitan area extending nearly 30 miles (48 kilometers) south to Akron and including about 2.2 million people. Cincinnati is part of another consolidated metropolitan area, extending north to Dayton and into Indiana and Kentucky; it has 1,646,395 people. Columbus, with a metropolitan population of 1,540,157 is both the state capital and its central city. Other large cities are Toledo (population, 313,619), on the Michigan border in the northwest, and Youngstown (82,026), near the Pennsylvania border in the east. The state's eastern border is only 30 miles (48 kilometers) from Pittsburgh, and its northwestern border is 40 miles (64 kilometers) from Detroit.

The people. Population growth in Ohio virtually ceased during the 1970s, when the rate was only 1.3 percent, and declined further to 0.5 percent in the 1980s. In the 1990s population increased at a more significant rate of 4.7 percent. The state population is almost 12 percent African American and about 2 percent Hispanic. The population is notable for the number of European groups, such as people of Germanic extraction in Cincinnati and Polish extraction in Cleveland, who have retained their ethnic identities.

Economy. Ohio is a major manufacturing state. Cleveland's steel industry is supplied with ore by Great Lakes barges. Cincinnati is a leader in machine tools and electronic equipment. Other cities are associated with particular products: Akron with rubber; Canton with steel bearings; Toledo with glass; and Youngstown with steel.

Ohio ranks 12th among all states in mining, with the principal products being coal, natural gas, and limestone. Ohio ranks 11th in agricultural production. The major crops are soybeans, corn, and greenhouse vegetables. The livestock income, less than that of crops, is derived from hogs, sheep, and dairy products.

Places of interest. All of Ohio's major cities include special cultural attractions, and the smaller towns offer such attractions as the Air and Space Museum at Wapakoneta, the Air Force Museum at Dayton, and the Pro Football Hall of Fame at Canton. Ohio also preserves the homes of and memorials to five U.S. presidents—Hayes, Garfield, McKinley, Taft, and Harding.

THE HORSES AND BUGGIES of the Amish people can still be seen on the rural roads of Ohio.

Oklahoma

Abbreviations: *Okla., OK*
Area: *68,679 sq. mi.,*
177,879 sq. km.
Rank (of 50)   19th
Population:
2000   3,450,654
Rank (of 50)   27th
Change 1995–2000
+172,654
Persons per sq. mi.   50.2
Capital: *Oklahoma City*
Largest city: *Oklahoma City*
Pop.   506,132
Entered Union: *Nov. 16, 1907*
(46th)
State bird: *Scissor-tailed flycatcher*
State flower: *Mistletoe*
State tree: *Redbud*
State map: *Page 93*

Oklahoma is situated in the south-central United States, north of Texas. It also borders Kansas to the north and Arkansas and Missouri to the east. The shape of the otherwise rectangular state is distinguished by the 35-mile- (56-kilometer-) wide panhandle that extends 165 miles (265 kilometers) due west to New Mexico.

Oklahoma was originally set aside by the U.S. government as an Indian territory. In 1889, however, the government decided to open the territory to homesteaders. Ten land rushes ensued in the following decade. Before the dates on which the land rushes were scheduled to begin, homesteaders lined up at the border, ready to rush across and claim their land. Those who sneaked across the border early were called "Sooners," a nickname that is now applied to Oklahoma residents.

During the droughts of the 1930s, Oklahoma turned into a "Dust Bowl." Thousands of Oklahomans, who were referred to, frequently disparagingly, as "Okies," were forced off their land by economic hardship. Most headed west for California in search of a new life. Since that time economic prosperity has returned because of the extensive Arkansas River Navigation Project, soil and water conservation acts, and the construction of huge multipurpose dams. Once a predominantly agricultural state, Oklahoma has broadened its economic base by tapping its mineral resources, especially oil and natural gas.

The land.   The shape of Oklahoma is irregular, sloping gradually upward from an average elevation above sea level of 400 feet (122 meters) in the southeast to nearly 5,000 feet (1,524 meters) in the extreme west.

Rough distinctions can be drawn among three principal topographical areas: the Great Plains of the panhandle, the hills and mountains of the east, and the central lowland between them that covers most of the state area.

The Great Plains cover the three counties in the panhandle, a 4,000-foot- (1,219-meter-) high plateau bisected west to east by the Beaver River. The state high point of Black Mesa (4,973 feet, 1,516 meters) is located in the extreme west. The hills and mountains of the east comprise a 60-mile- (96-kilometer-) wide strip of the Ozark Plateau in the north and the Ouachita Mountains in the south. The Arkansas River valley passes east through these hill regions, and valley streams throughout it have been dammed to create reservoirs. Three-fourths of the state area is included in the central lowland between these extremities. The southern lowland region is characterized by low ranges such as the Arbuckle and Wichita mountains. The northern lowland region is characterized by the Redbud Plains, a tableland crossed by small streams lined by sand dunes.

Climate.   Oklahoma's climate is generally temperate. Summer highs average above 90°F (32°C) and winter lows average just below 32°F (0°C). Rainfall is greatest in the southeast, where it averages over 50 inches (127 centimeters) per year; it declines sharply toward the west to less than 20 inches (51 centimeters) in the panhandle.

Principal cities.   Oklahoma has two large metropolitan areas. The larger one is the capital, Oklahoma City, situated near the center of the state on the Canadian River. The area includes parts of five counties. The hub of a network of interstate highways, Oklahoma City is the state's financial and agricultural business center and is the site of several major electronics components manufacturers. Tulsa (population, 393,049) in the northeast is the center of the state's oil industry and a base for aerospace and airline businesses. The Arkansas River Navigation Project, which was authorized by Congress in 1946 and completed in 1971, has helped make Tulsa an important inland port.

The people.   Oklahoma is populated by members of at least 67 American Indian tribes, many of them transported there by the U.S. government. Between 1890 and 1910, the era of land openings for homesteaders, the population of Oklahoma rose from about 250,000 to more than 1.6 million, a number which the state doubled in the early 1980s before experiencing a decline in the financially troubled late 1980s. Today the state's population is about 8 percent Native American. This population of

OKLAHOMA CITY is the state's financial and agricultural business center.

more than 270,000, the largest of any state and more than one-eighth the total Native American population in the United States, is unique in that Oklahoma has no formal Indian reservations. This has caused hardships for Oklahoma's Native Americans, but it has also encouraged assimilation. The population of the state shrank by 60,000 during the Dust Bowl drought of the 1930s, and it did not return to its 1930 level until nearly 1970. Other than Native Americans, the only significant ethnic group in the state today is the large number of African Americans, who represent more than 7 percent of the population.

Economy.   Oklahoma ranks fifth in the production of crude oil and third in natural gas among U.S. states. Mineral fuels account for 95 percent of the state's mining industry income, which is ranked fourth overall in the United States. The remaining mining products are principally sand, gravel, stone, cement, and gypsum. The largest oil fields are in the state's south-central regions, and the major natural gas fields are in the panhandle. Production of coal, once the state's primary mineral product, has diminished.

27   North America

Manufacturing easily exceeds mining in value, with most of the income from manufacturing derived from machinery, transportation equipment, electrical equipment, and fabricated metal products. Agriculture was the traditional basis of the local economy, and nearly 80 percent of the land area of Oklahoma remains farmland. Two-thirds of the state farm income is derived from livestock, and the principal crops are winter wheat, sorghum, and cotton lint, all of which are grown on irrigated portions of the central lowland.

Places of interest. Oklahoma is rich in places of Indian interest, especially the Fort Gibson Stockade and Cherokee Cultural Center near Muskogee in the Arkansas River valley. Other attractions include the Ouachita National Forest, the National Cowboy Hall of Fame in Oklahoma City, and the Will Rogers Memorial in Claremore, near Tulsa.

CRATER LAKE NATIONAL PARK nestles in the Cascade Mountains in southwest Oregon.

Oregon

Abbreviations: *Ore., OR*
Area: *96,002 sq. mi.,*
248,645 sq. km.
Rank (of 50)   10th
Population:
2000   3,421,399
Rank (of 50)   28th
Change 1995–2000
+280,399
Persons per sq. mi.   35.6
Capital: *Salem*
Largest city: *Portland*
Pop.   529,121
Entered Union: *Feb. 14, 1859*
(33rd)
State bird: *Western meadowlark*
State flower: *Oregon grape*
State tree: *Douglas fir*
State map: *Page 91*

center
US

centre
Brit.

kilometers
US

kilometres
Brit.

Oregon is a Northwestern state on the Pacific Ocean. It borders Washington on the north and California on the south. Second among Northwestern states to Alaska in area and to Washington in population, Oregon is distinguished for the 30 million acres (12,150,000 hectares) of forestland that cover about half its total land area.

The land. The Cascade Mountains run north-south through Oregon about 100 miles (161 kilometers) inland from the ocean. This range defines the state's principal topographical and climatic areas. The Pacific coast is composed of rocky cliffs that rise into coastal ranges such as those found in Washington to the north and California to the south. These ranges reach a maximum elevation of about 4,000 feet (1,219 meters) within the state borders.

Inland from the coastal ranges lies the Willamette Valley, a lowland farming region that now includes most of the

state's population. This valley widens to the north and adjoins the Puget Trough in Washington. The eastern limit of the Willamette Valley is defined by the wall of the Cascades, rugged mountains with several peaks higher than 10,000 feet (3,048 meters).

Inland from the Cascades lies two-thirds of Oregon's area, an immense plateau extending to the Idaho border. In its eastern reaches this plateau is broken by minor mountain ranges into distinct areas related to the Columbia Plateau in Washington, the Snake River Plateau in Idaho, and the Great Basin that covers most of Nevada.

Climate. From the Pacific coast inland to the Cascades, Oregon's climate is moderated by the warming effects of the ocean's Japan Current. Temperatures in this area range from 30° to 50°F (-1° to 10°C) in January and from 50° to 85°F (10° to 29°C) in July, with heavy rains falling in winter. The Cascades block rains from the eastern plateau, however, where precipitation averages about 12 inches (30 centimeters) per year. On the plateau winters are far colder and summers are warmer than in coastal areas.

Principal cities. The state's four largest cities are all clustered in the Willamette Valley. The largest city is Portland, which straddles the Willamette River near its meeting with the Columbia River at the Washington border. The Portland metropolitan area, which includes Vancouver, Washington, is the retail center of a large area of Washington as well as Oregon. The state's other principal population centers, Salem and Eugene-Springfield, both lie south of Portland on the banks of the Willamette River. The remainder of the state is very sparsely populated.

The people. The state waited until the opening of the Oregon Trail in the 1840s for its first significant wave of German, Scandinavian, and English

settlers. Generous land-grant policies attracted hardy farmers in the 1850s. After 1870 the railroads brought another influx of settlers. Many more new residents arrived between 1950 and 1970.

Today the towns of the Willamette Valley attract most of the state's new residents. Only about 13 percent of the population are Hispanic, African American, or Asian.

Economy. The economy of Oregon has been based on agriculture and lumber since the 1800s. The seats of agriculture are the Willamette Valley, where small dairy farms predominate, and the open eastern region, where large consolidated farms produce quantities of wheat, potatoes, cattle, and sheep. The state's huge stands of timber,

SALMON RETURN to the rivers of the Pacific Northwest to spawn. Sport fishing for salmon, once a staple of the Native American diet, is now regulated.

principally Douglas fir, provide more than 7 billion board feet annually, or about one-sixth of the total U.S. output. These two industries support diversified manufacturing businesses based on the processing of food and wood products.

Tourism is also one of the largest industries, with visitors to Oregon's forest and ocean areas spending over $3 billion each year. The largest known lode of nickel ore in the United States has been mined beneath Nickel Mountain in the southwest since 1954. Oregon also mines large quantities of gravel and cement from its eastern plateau.

Places of interest. Natural attractions include volcanic Crater Lake, the deepest lake in the United States; Oregon Dunes National Recreation Area on the Pacific coast near Florence; and Oregon Caves National Monument. Also of interest are Fort Clatsop, where Lewis and Clark spent the winter of 1805–1806, and numerous summer and winter resorts.

Pennsylvania

Abbreviations: *Pa., PA*
Area: *44,820 sq. mi.,*
116,084 sq. km.
Rank (of 50) 32nd
Population:
2000 12,281,054
Rank (of 50) 6th
Change 1995–2000 +209,054
Persons per sq. mi. 274.0
Capital: *Harrisburg*
Largest city: *Philadelphia*
Pop. 1,517,550
Entered Union: *Dec. 12, 1787*
(2nd)
State bird: *Ruffed grouse*
State flower: *Mountain laurel*
State tree: *Hemlock*
State map: *Page 100*

Pennsylvania lies south of New York and west of New Jersey. Its New Jersey border is formed by the Delaware River. Its border with New York follows the 42nd parallel except in the far west, where a 35-mile (56-kilometer) northward extension gives the state a port on Lake Erie. Pennsylvania's western border is with Ohio and West Virginia, and its southern border is with West Virginia, Maryland, and the northern tip of Delaware.

Pennsylvania is one of the most economically diverse states in the country, ranking in the top 10 states in manufacturing and mining and in the top 20 in agriculture. Its 310-mile (499-kilometer) west-east extent includes many sparsely populated mountainous areas.

Pennsylvania resembles the Great Lakes states to the west in that its heavy industries have suffered from foreign competition. Just as the automobile industry has, Pennsylvania's steel and coal industries have declined in importance. The state has struggled to attract enough modern industries to shore up its economy. Despite this effort, total population growth was insignificant in the final decades of the 20th century.

The land. The Appalachian Mountain range runs through the state from southwest to northeast. The Alleghenies are the principal mountain ridge. They enter the state from West Virginia in the south and trace a broad northeastern curve toward the Delaware River, the state's eastern boundary. To the west and to the north of the mountains lies the Appalachian plateau, which covers half the state area. The plateau is a layered rock hill and valley region that declines along the shore of Lake Erie into a small fringe of Great Lakes plain. To the southeast of the mountains lie the Appalachian valley and the Piedmont Plateau. The Appalachian valley is a 40- to 50-mile- (64- to 80-kilometer-) wide strip of parallel ridges that includes the Cumberland and Lebanon valleys. The small and low-lying farmland in the southeast corner of the state is part of the Piedmont Plateau.

Climate. Pennsylvania's climate varies from east to west. In Philadelphia, near the mouth of the Delaware River, normal summer highs are near 90°F (32°C) and winter lows are 25°F (-4°C); there is 40 inches (102 centimeters) of precipitation per year, including 21 inches (53 centimeters) of snow. Pittsburgh, in western Pennsylvania, is cooler in both summer and winter. It receives 4 inches (10 centimeters) less precipitation than Philadelphia but twice as much snow.

Principal cities. The major urban centers in Pennsylvania are Philadelphia and Pittsburgh, which lie 250 miles (402 kilometers) apart at the eastern and western ends of the state. Philadelphia's metropolitan area, including part of New Jersey, has more than 5 million residents. Pittsburgh, where the Allegheny and Monongahela rivers meet to form the Ohio, has a population of 334,563. An old manufacturing city, Pittsburgh's metropolitan area lost almost 300,000 residents between 1970 and 1990. Other large metropolitan areas are in the east of the state: Scranton-Wilkes-Barre-Hazleton (population, 624,726) in the northeast and Allentown-Bethlehem-Easton (637,958) at the center of the state's eastern border. The largest city in western Pennsylvania other than Pittsburgh is Erie, with a population of 103,717, in the northwest on the shore of Lake Erie.

The people. Like other states in its region, Pennsylvania lost a sizable population to migration in recent decades, giving the state a negligible growth rate. African Americans, concentrated in major cities, are 10 percent of the total, and Hispanics make up 3 percent. The rural regions of eastern Pennsylvania were settled in the 1800s by German immigrants popularly known as the Pennsylvania Dutch (a corruption of "Pennsylvania *Deutsche,*" or German). This group is remarkable for having

kept intact its language, religious beliefs, and cultural identity for over a century. A small proportion of these immigrants are Amish people, who resist such modern conveniences as electricity and automobiles on religious grounds. They travel in horse-drawn vehicles and cultivate their farms largely by hand.

Economy. Pennsylvania ranks seventh in the United States in manufacturing, which generates more than six times the income of mining or agriculture. The major manufacturing centers are Philadelphia, a diversified industrial town, and Pittsburgh, famous for coal and steel. Pennsylvania is also a leader among the states in mining, chiefly because of its coal reserves. In western Pennsylvania soft bituminous coal for industrial use is mined, and Pennsylvania ranks fourth among the states in this soft coal production. Northeastern Pennsylvania produces virtually all of the U.S. supply of hard, clean-burning anthracite coal.

Three-quarters of the state farm output is in livestock, principally producing dairy products. Tourism throughout Pennsylvania brings the state more than $8 billion per year, making it second only to manufacturing in the state economy.

Places of interest. Philadelphia, once the U.S. capital, contains historic attractions such as Independence Hall and the Liberty Bell. The National Historic Park at Valley Forge is near the Philadelphia city limits, and the Gettysburg National Military Park is in southeastern Pennsylvania. There are ski resorts in the mountains in central Pennsylvania and many summer fishing and camping areas throughout the state.

PHILADELPHIA'S INDEPENDENCE HALL was the scene of the signing of the Declaration of Independence in 1776.

Rhode Island

Abbreviations: *R.I., RI*
Area: *1,045 sq. mi., 2,707 sq. km.*
   Rank (of 50)   50th
Population:
   2000   1,048,319
   Rank (of 50)   43rd
   Change 1995–2000   +58,319
   Persons per sq. mi.   1,003.1
Capital: *Providence*
Largest city: *Providence*
   Pop.   173,618
Entered Union: *May 29, 1790*
   (13th)
State bird: *Rhode Island Red*
   chicken
State flower: *Violet*
State tree: *Red maple*
State map: *Page 101*

WATER RECREATION is a major attraction of Rhode Island's southern beach areas and the historic resort town of Newport.

kilometers
US

kilometres
Brit.

center
US

centre
Brit.

Rhode Island, the smallest of U.S. states in area, is situated in the southeast portion of the New England region. To the north and east the state borders Massachusetts, and to the west it borders Connecticut. Its southern border is the Atlantic coastline. The eastern part of the state is broken by Narragansett Bay, which extends 25 miles (40 kilometers) inland from the sea. Rhode Island borders the bay on all sides and includes several large islands in its territory, including Rhode Island, for which the state is named. The rest of the southern coast is formed by Block Island Sound, named for an island 10 miles (16 kilometers) offshore that is included in the Rhode Island state lands.

Rhode Island was founded in 1636 when Roger Williams, a minister, led a group of followers south to Providence from the Massachusetts Bay Colony, where they had been persecuted. At the beginning of the American Revolution, the tiny colony was among the first to take up arms against the British, but after the war its citizens were reluctant to ratify the Constitution. They voted it down in 1788, but it was finally ratified by a state convention 2 years later.

The land. Rhode Island's lands include only two major topographical features. The lands surrounding Narragansett Bay in the east of the state consist of New England Seaboard Lowlands. These lands have settled to the extent that the highest elevation in the area is only 200 feet (61 meters) above sea level, and the bay has submerged lands as far as 30 miles (48 kilometers) inland. The seaboard lowland also includes the coast of western Rhode Island, which is sandy and includes shifting Barrier Reef islands just offshore. In the west and north, Rhode Island consists of New England Upland, a hilly region of lakes that rises to a maximum elevation of 812 feet (247 meters) at Jerimoth Hill in the northwest of the state.

Climate. Rhode Island's climate is slightly milder than that of the rest of New England because of its southern coastal location. Normal summer highs are 80°F (27°C) and winter lows are 20°F (-7°C). Precipitation averages 43 inches (109 centimeters) per year, including an average of 30 inches (76 centimeters) of snow.

Principal cities. All points in Rhode Island lie within 30 miles (48 kilometers) of the Providence metropolitan area. This area includes about 90 percent of the state population and is part of the Providence-Warrick-Fall River consolidated metropolitan area, which extends into Massachusetts and has a population of 1,188,613, more than the total population of Rhode Island. Other cities are Woonsocket (population, 43,224) in the northern extreme of the state, and Newport (26,475), in the southeast on the coast.

The people. Rhode Island was the only state other than New York to record a total population decrease in the 1970s, but it gained steadily in the 1980s and 1990s. Rhode Island's resident population is 4 percent African American and 8.7 percent Hispanic.

Economy. It was in the town of Pawtucket, Rhode Island, that the first water-powered mill in the United States was put into operation in 1790.

The state economy today is based on light manufacturing leading the United States in two traditional products, jewelry and silverware; they also produce large quantities of textiles and electronics equipment. The second leading industry is tourism, chiefly in southern beach areas and the historic resort town of Newport. Rhode Island's agricultural produce is chiefly vegetables and potatoes, but some dairy farming is carried out on the hills of the western uplands.

Places of interest. The major attraction for visitors to Rhode Island is Newport, famous since the 19th century as a summer resort for the rich, and notable today for its large seaside mansions and for Touro Synagogue, the oldest synagogue in the United States. Places of interest in Providence include the first Baptist church in America and the Roger Williams National Memorial. In Pawtucket, Samuel Slater's original 1793 water mill has been restored.

South Carolina

Abbreviations: *S.C., SC*
Area: *30,111 sq. mi., 77,987 sq. km.*
   Rank (of 50)   40th
Population:
   2000   4,012,012
   Rank (of 50)   26th
   Change 1995–2000
   +339,012
   Persons per sq. mi.   133.2
Capital: *Columbia*
Largest city: *Columbia*
   Pop.   116,278
Entered Union: *May 23, 1788*
   (8th)
State bird: *Carolina wren*
State flower: *Yellow jessamine*
State tree: *Palmetto*
State map: *Page 98*

South Carolina is a South Atlantic state bordered by North Carolina to the north and Georgia across the Savannah River to the south. The state's 190-mile (306-kilometer) Atlantic coastline is broken by large inlets and sounds and, at its center, a major harbor at Charleston.

South Carolina was the first state to secede at the beginning of the Civil War, and the first battle in the war took place at Fort Sumter, in Charleston Harbor. South Carolinians were so deeply disillusioned by the reconstruction that followed the war that a lingering resentment against government has remained. In fact, voter participation in elections is the lowest in the United States.

The land. South Carolina includes a fringe of the Blue Ridge Mountains in the extreme northwest. From that mountain fringe, the state lands decline in elevation across two major topographical areas. The northwest "up" country consists principally of the heavily forested Piedmont Plateau. The southeastern two-thirds of the area of the state is part of the Atlantic Coastal Plain. This area consists of cleared lands of great agricultural value. The irregular Atlantic coastline includes the Sea Islands barrier reef in the south and an extensive intercoastal waterway in the north.

Climate. The climate of South Carolina is warm and humid. At the capital city of Columbia, near the center of the state, normal summer high temperatures are over 90°F (32°C), and normal winter lows remain above freezing. Precipitation throughout most of the state averages about 46 inches (117 centimeters) per year. Precipitation is significantly higher in the state's Blue Ridge Mountains area, and that area is the only one that receives occasional light snowfalls.

Principal cities. The major city and principal commercial and educational center in South Carolina is Columbia, the state capital. The other major urban areas are clusters of towns with collective populations exceeding that of Columbia. Charleston (population, 96,650) is the state's major shipping port and the commercial center of the "low" country plain. The Greenville-Spartansburg-Anderson area (population, 962,441) is a long cluster of industrial towns in the northwest "up" country.

The people. Population growth in South Carolina was above the national rate in the 1990s. The proportion of African-American population is 30 percent, the highest in the United States after the District of Columbia, Louisiana, and Mississippi. There are no other major ethnic groups.

Economy. Manufacturing accounts for an income many times greater than that from farms. The state's manufacturing businesses employ a full third of the workforce, and value added from manufacturing totals more than $19 billion each year. The state agricultural businesses are concentrated in the "low" country of the coastal plain. Crops produce about a quarter more income than livestock, and the total value of farm marketings is more than $1.2 billion. Tobacco and peaches and new plantings of soybeans have replaced the cotton crop in importance. Tourism is an important industry in the state, generating more than $4 billion per year.

Places of interest. Most of the attractions for out-of-state visitors to South Carolina are found along the Atlantic coast. The shore is lined with beach resorts from Myrtle Beach in the north to Hilton Head Island near the Georgia border. The coast includes some of the state's major historic attractions, such as the Fort Sumter National Monument.

South Dakota

Abbreviations: *S.D., SD*
Area: *75,896 sq. mi.,*
  196,571 sq. km.
  Rank (of 50)   16th
Population:
  2000   754,844
  Rank (of 50)   46th
  Change 1995–2000
  +25,844
  Persons per sq. mi.   9.9
Capital: *Pierre*
Largest city: *Sioux Falls*
  Pop.   123,975
Entered Union: *Nov. 2, 1889*
  (40th)
State bird: *Ring-necked pheasant*
State flower: *Pasqueflower*
State tree: *Black Hills spruce*
State map: *Page 94*

South Dakota is located in the upper Great Plains, bordered by Wyoming and Montana in the west, North Dakota to the north, and Minnesota and Iowa to the east. The state is bisected north-south by the Missouri River, which then turns east to form part of its southern border with Nebraska.

Most of South Dakota's population live east of the Missouri River, but most of the symbols of its identity lie to the west. Along the state's far western border with Wyoming lie the Black Hills, the highest mountains east of the Rockies. Just south and east of the Black Hills is the Badlands National Monument, in a region of strange and desolate rock formations and buttes carved by wind erosion.

The western region is also the home of most of the state's 62,000 Native Americans. A symbol of their presence is found in the west at Wounded Knee, the site of the massacre of Sioux Indians in 1890, the last major conflict in the war against the Plains Indians.

The land. The eastern third of the state is a region known as the Prairie Plains, rolling hills formed by glacial action and dotted by small lakes. The western two-thirds is the unglaciated area of the Missouri Plateau, uplands varying in elevation from 2,000 to 3,000 feet (610 to 914 meters) and crossed by the Missouri River. The river and its tributaries drain nearly all of South Dakota. Along the southwestern border with Wyoming are the Black Hills, an isolated mountain group including the state's high point, Harney Peak (7,242 feet, 2,207 meters). These rocky mountains have been eroded down to their granite cores by centuries of wind action.

Climate. The climate of South Dakota is one of seasonal extremes. Winter lows average near 5°F (-15°C) and summer highs average near 90°F (32°C). The state is also subject to high winds and blizzard conditions in winter. The average precipitation across the state is only 18 inches (46 centimeters) per year, with higher averages in the east and lower in the west.

Principal cities. Only 35 percent of the population of South Dakota live in urban

THE PLANTATION-BASED ECONOMY of South Carolina resulted in its being the first state to secede from the Union. The first shot of the Civil War was fired at Fort Sumter.

areas, making it the most rural of Grain states. The largest city, Sioux Falls, is in the southeastern corner of the state. Its stockyards are the third largest in the United States, and it is near retail and wholesale markets in southern Minnesota, Iowa, and Nebraska. The second largest city in the state, and the principal urban seat of the western region, is Rapid City (population, 59,607).

The people.   South Dakota attained more than 50 percent of its present population by 1900, and it has experienced periodic population declines since then. In the decade following 1930, a period of national economic depression and local drought, the population declined by about 50,000, or more than 7 percent. In the 1970s and 1980s, population increased only slightly followed by an 8.5 percent increase in the 1990s. South Dakota is notable for its high proportion of Native Americans, about 8 percent of the population. There are nine reservations, all in the western region, and the state area includes 5 million acres (2 million hectares) of lands owned by or allotted to the Sioux tribe.

Economy.   Agriculture is carried out on more than 90 percent of South Dakota's land area, and livestock production accounts for roughly two-thirds of the state's farm income. Most of the cattle and hog production is based in the eastern area of the state. The central and northern regions of the state produce most of its crops, principally wheat, rye, and oats. Mining is the principal industry in the state's western region. The town of Lead, near the Wyoming border, is the site of the Homestake Mine, the largest single source of gold in the United States. South Dakota is fourth among the states in gold mining, and it also mines large quantities of crude oil, stone, sand, and gravel.

Places of interest.   The greatest attraction by far in the state is Mount Rushmore, a 6,200-foot (1,890-meter) granite peak with likenesses of Presidents Washington, Jefferson, Theodore Roosevelt, and Lincoln that were carved into its face by Gutzon Borglum. Mount Rushmore is located in the Black Hills, which are themselves a principal tourist attraction that can be toured by car along the famous Needles Highway. Also in the western region are the Crazy Horse Memorial and the George Armstrong Custer State Park.

meter
US

metre
Brit.

center
US

centre
Brit.

aluminum
US

aluminium
Brit.

MOUNT RUSHMORE, with the heads of Presidents Washington, Jefferson, Theodore Roosevelt, and Lincoln sculpted in the rock, is the greatest tourist attraction in South Dakota.

Tennessee

Abbreviations: *Tenn., TN*
Area: *41,219 sq. mi.,*
   106,757 sq. km.
   Rank (of 50)   34th
Population:
   2000   5,689,283
   Rank (of 50)   16th
   Change 1995–2000
   +433,283
   Persons per sq. mi.   138.0
Capital: *Nashville*
Largest city: *Memphis*
   Pop.   650,100
Entered Union: *June 1, 1796*
   (16th)
State bird: *Mockingbird*
State flower: *Iris*
State tree: *Tulip poplar*
State map: *Page 97*

Tennessee has borders on the states of four other regions. It stretches for more than 400 miles (644 kilometers) from its western Mississippi River border with Arkansas and Missouri to its irregular eastern border with North Carolina. Its north-south extent is over 100 miles (161 kilometers) from a northern border with Kentucky and Virginia to a southern border with Mississippi, Alabama, and Georgia.

The Tennessee River passes through Tennessee twice. The upper Tennessee River flows south through the eastern region and then, after a loop through northern Alabama, returns to flow north across the more populated western region to Kentucky and the Ohio River. The river divides Tennessee into eastern, central, and western regions that are distinct in topography, economy, and population. The river has been the most important factor in making Tennessee an industrial state. The Tennessee Valley Authority, established in 1933, created a network of dams and reservoirs that gives the state an abundance of cheap hydroelectric power.

The land.   The traditional division of Tennessee into east, central, and west provides the primary distinctions within its rugged and complex topography. East Tennessee is a mountainous area of the Appalachian Highland. The highest mountains are the Unakas, on the North Carolina border, where the state high point at Clingman's Dome (6,643 feet, 2,025 meters) is located. East of the Unakas lies the Great Appalachian Valley, a 30- to 60-mile- (48- to 97-kilometer-) wide region of parallel ridges that average over 1,000 feet (305 meters) in elevation. The western extent of the Appalachian Highland consists of the Cumberland Plateau, made up of rugged flat-topped hills.

Central Tennessee is part of the Interior Low Plateau and includes the Nashville Basin, farmland ringed in all directions but north by highland rims rising 600 feet (183 meters) from ground level. Western Tennessee is part of the Gulf Coastal Plain, a moderately hilly region extending north from Mississippi and Alabama. In the extreme west of the state, beyond a line of 150-foot (46-meter) bluffs, the Gulf Coastal Plain drops to a narrow strip of Mississippi bottomland.

Climate.   Tennessee has a moderate continental climate. Normal winter lows throughout Tennessee are about 30°F (-1°C), and normal summer highs are near 90°F (27°C). Rainfall throughout the state is about 50 inches (127 centimeters) per year, and substantial snows occur only in the eastern mountains.

Principal cities.   Memphis, Tennessee's largest city, is a Mississippi River port in the southwest whose metropolitan area includes adjacent parts of Arkansas and Mississippi. Nashville (population, 569,891), the state's capital and a major industrial center, is the second largest city. At the edge of the eastern mountains are three growing metropolitan areas: Knoxville (population, 173,890), a mineral refining center; Johnson City-Kingsport-Bristol (125,195), on the northeastern border with Virginia; and Chattanooga (155,554), on the southeastern border with Georgia.

The people.   Tennessee has a growing and increasingly urban population because of the spread of its manufacturing industries. The population was swelled by more than 200,000 immigrants from other states during the

MINNIE PEARL was a beloved icon of the Grand Ole Opry, a leading feature of Nashville's claim to the title "Music City, U.S.A."

1970s. Growth in the 1980s was less than two-thirds the national average, but the 1990s brought a 16.7 percent increase, surpassing the national rate. Most population growth has occurred in the metropolitan areas of the western and central regions. Eastern Tennessee remains, in comparison, an economically depressed Appalachian mining region. The African-American population represents 16 percent of the total.
Economy. Manufacturing has come to exceed agriculture in value. A large portion of the manufacturing industry is devoted to refining the Tennessean mineral and agricultural output, but there are also large manufacturers of transportation and electronic equipment. The mining industry produces large quantities of bituminous coal on the Cumberland Plateau in the east. Tennessee is also a major producer of zinc and aluminum.

Farm income from livestock slightly exceeds that from crops. Cattle ranches and dairy farms predominate in central Tennessee. There is extensive trade in show animals such as Tennessee walking horses. Soybeans now exceed the traditional crops of cotton and tobacco in value.
Places of interest. The principal attraction in eastern Tennessee is Great Smoky Mountains National Park. Reelfoot Lake, formed by an earthquake in 1811, is a major attraction on the far west Mississippi bottomland. There are several places of historical interest in Nashville, including the homes of Presidents Andrew Jackson, James Polk, and Andrew Johnson. Tennessee is also the home of two major American music centers: Memphis, an important jazz center and former home of Elvis Presley, and Nashville, a recording and performance center for country and western music. Knoxville was the host to a world's fair in 1982, attracting millions of visitors.

Texas

Abbreviations: *Tex., TX*
Area: *261,914 sq. mi.,*
678,358 sq. km.
Rank (of 50)   2nd
Population:
2000   20,851,820
Rank (of 50)   2nd
Change 1995–2000
+2,127,820
Persons per sq. mi.   79.6
Capital: *Austin*
Largest city: *Houston*
Pop.   1,953,631
Entered Union: *Dec. 29, 1845*
(28th)
State bird: *Mockingbird*
State flower: *Bluebonnet*
State tree: *Pecan*
State map: *Page 93*

Texas, the largest in area of the 48 contiguous states, is located in the south-central United States between the Red River, which separates it from Oklahoma to the north, and the Rio Grande River, which separates it from Mexico to the south. Three extensions of the state give it its characteristic shape: the Panhandle in the north, the Pecos region extending west between Mexico and New Mexico, and the lower Rio Grande valley to the south.

Once a territory of Mexico, Texas was opened to settlement by Americans in the 1820s. Texans rebelling against Mexican rule established an independent republic for nearly a decade beginning in 1836. Its period of independence and its enormous land area, greater than that of

France, have combined to give Texans a special sense of pride in their state. Until 1900 this pride was associated with rugged ranchers and cowboys, but the discovery of oil at the turn of the century transformed the state's economy and produced oil barons of enormous wealth.
The land. The surface of Texas is generally a series of plains rising in elevation as they extend north and west from the Gulf of Mexico. There are four principal divisions: Coastal Plain, Central Lowland, Great Plains, and Basin and Range. The Coastal Plain covers most of the eastern half of the state from the Red River in the north to the Rio Grande valley in the south. It rises in elevation from sea level at the water's edge to over 500 feet (152 meters) inland. The largest cities are within this region.

The Central Lowland covers north-central Texas from the Oklahoma border almost 200 miles (322 kilometers) south. Ranging in elevation from 1,000 to 2,000 feet (305 to 610 meters), this hilly region is an extension of the Osage Plains in Oklahoma and Kansas. The Great Plains cover a belt from the Panhandle in the

north to the Pecos and Rio Grande rivers in the south. This region includes flat and arid high plains in the north, the steep Central Texas Hills, and limestone escarpments in the south. The western extension of the state is a part of the Mexican Highlands of the Basin and Range region. It includes the highest elevations in the state.
Climate. Summer temperatures are fairly consistent throughout Texas, with highs averaging in the low 90s F (30s C), but the weather is humid near the Gulf Coast and very dry in the west and north. Winters are far colder in the interior, where snow falls, than on the coast, where frost is uncommon. Precipitation ranges from 60 inches (152 centimeters) per year in the far eastern section to only 7 inches (18 centimeters) in the

FIVE TIMES AS MUCH LAND is devoted to livestock as is devoted to agricultural crops in Texas.

extreme west. Winter may bring blizzards to the Panhandle in the north, and in summer the Gulf Coast may experience hurricanes.

Principal cities. Texas includes two of the largest and fastest-growing metropolitan regions in the United States. Houston-Galveston, near the Gulf Coast, includes more than 4 million people and increased by almost 1 million in the 1970s, and almost 2 million in the 1980s and 1990s. Once an uninhabited swampland, the city has become the headquarters of many U.S. oil companies and a center of the aerospace industry. Dallas-Fort Worth, about 200 miles (322 kilometers) north, at the inland edge of the Coastal Plain, includes over 5.2 million people in its metropolitan area. It is a banking and insurance capital. San Antonio, in the south-central region, has a population of 1,144,646. It is the site of the famous fort called the Alamo, where defenders of Texas's independence were wiped out in a siege and assault by the Mexican army in 1836. These three metropolitan areas grew rapidly during the decades following 1970. Other important cities include Amarillo (population, 173,627), in the northern Panhandle; El Paso (563,662), at the state's extreme western border with Mexico and New Mexico; and Austin (656,562), the state capital.

The people. The population of Texas nearly doubled between 1950 and 1980 and increased again by nearly 47 percent between 1980 and 2000, making Texas both the fastest growing and most urban of the Oil states. Texas has one of the highest proportions of Hispanic population in the United States, 32 percent. Most are of Mexican descent. More than 2.4 million, or 12 percent of the population, are African Americans.

Economy. Oil is the historical and present basis of Texas's growth and prosperity. The west Texas oil fields near Lubbock (population, 199,564) are the richest in the state. The second most important mineral resource is natural gas; Texas ranks second only to Louisiana in this resource. Texas is also a U.S. leader in sulfur production.

Next to California, Texas is the largest manufacturing state west of the Mississippi. Petroleum refining and production of drilling equipment are the largest industries. Other products include aerospace equipment, chemicals, and processed food.

Texas is also second to California among all U.S. states in total cash value of farm products. Five times as much land is devoted to livestock as is devoted to crops, and Texas produces twice as many or more beef cattle and sheep as any other state. Although most of its croplands must be irrigated by wells or rivers, Texas produces about half the crops of the Oil states region. It grows more cotton, its most important crop, than any other state in the United States, and it also produces large crops of sorghum, rice, citrus fruits, peanuts, and vegetables.

Places of interest. Padre Island National Seashore, along the southern Gulf Coast, and Big Bend National Park, along the Rio Grande, are among the major tourist attractions of Texas. There are striking examples of desert, mountain, and plains scenery scattered throughout the state, and many cultural and recreational attractions in the major cities. The principal historic attractions are the Alamo in San Antonio, the Lyndon Johnson Birthplace and Presidential Library and Museum 60 miles (97 kilometers) north of San Antonio, and the fascinating border cities of Laredo and El Paso on the Rio Grande.

center
US

centre
Brit.

kilometer
US

kilometre
Brit.

colored
US

coloured
Brit.

Utah

Abbreviations: *U., UT*
Area: *82,168 sq. mi.,*
212,815 sq. km.
Rank (of 50)   12th
Population:
2000   2,233,169
Rank (of 50)   34th
Change 1995–2000
+282,169
Persons per sq. mi.   27.1
Capital: *Salt Lake City*
Largest city: *Salt Lake City*
Pop.   181,743
Entered Union: *Jan. 4, 1896*
(45th)
State bird: *Seagull*
State flower: *Sego lily*
State tree: *Blue spruce*
State map: *Page 92*

Utah is located at the western edge of the Rocky Mountain region, bordered by the Mountain states of Wyoming and Colorado to the east, Idaho to the north, and the Southwestern states of Nevada and Arizona to the west and south.

Nearly three-quarters of Utah's population are members of the Church of Jesus Christ of Latter-Day Saints, commonly called Mormons. The church was founded in New York State in the early 1800s, but persecution both in the East and Midwest prompted Brigham Young to lead the membership to the wilderness of Utah in 1847. Early Mormons practiced polygamy, and the United States refused on that ground to admit Utah as a state. Finally, in 1890, the church abandoned its policy of polygamy, and Utah was accepted as a state in 1896. The Mormon church continues to be an important factor in the state.

The land. The Rocky Mountain range enters Utah from the north and covers most of the northeastern region. Utah's principal cities cluster along the western slope of these mountains, which are called the Wasatch Range.

The eastern and southern regions are parts of the great Colorado Plateau, which extends south into Arizona. The Colorado River enters the state from the east and is soon joined by the Green River, the principal watershed of eastern Utah. Glen Canyon Dam, in northern Arizona, has backed up the waters of the Colorado, creating Lake Powell in southern Utah, which has become a large national recreation area. The Colorado Plateau is a huge area of sedimentary rock upland cut by strikingly colored canyons and occasional lava flows.

The western third of the state is part of the Great Basin, which forms Nevada and parts of neighboring states. It is characterized by smooth desert floors broken by parallel mountain ranges averaging 4,000 feet (1,219 meters) in

PRODUCTION OF CRUDE petroleum is the foundation of Texas's prosperity.

elevation. The Great Salt Lake Desert and the Great Salt Lake lie in the northwest. The lake, with a salt content of 25 percent, is approximately 75 miles (121 kilometers) long and, subject to dramatic variations from evaporation, averages about 1,800 square miles (4,660 square kilometers) in area, about the size of the state of Delaware.

Climate. The northeastern mountains and the eastern plateau are the coolest regions of the state. In Salt Lake City temperatures range from winter lows of 20°F (-7°C) to summer highs of 90°F (32°C). The basin and range region to the west is predominantly desert, warmer in both winter and summer than the rest of the state. As a whole, the state averages less than 15 inches (38 centimeters) of rain per year, but mountain regions receive much more, and extensive desert areas receive less.

Principal cities. Two-thirds of the population of Utah live on the western slope of the Wasatch Range, in the north-central part of the state. Salt Lake City, Provo, and Ogden lie within 75 miles (121 kilometers) of one another. Salt Lake City, situated in a valley surrounded by mountains, is the headquarters of the Mormon church and a warehousing center for the entire U.S. West. Provo, 40 miles (64 kilometers) to the south beside freshwater Utah Lake, is the hub of the state's grain and mining businesses. Ogden, about the same distance north of Salt Lake City, lies at the center of the state's railroad network and is the home of its principal military defense and stockyard industries.

The people. The Mormon church is a stabilizing influence on Utah's population. Almost 70 percent of the residents are Mormons. About half of Utah's citizens are lifelong residents of the state, the highest percentage in the Far West. The population has increased steadily, more than doubling between 1970 and 2000.

Economy. Devastating droughts in the 1930s destroyed the Mormons' hopes for building a farm paradise in the desert. Since then the state economy has shifted to manufacturing. Manufactures such as food products, transportation equipment, primary metals, and aerospace weapons produce about $6 billion in value added per year.

Next in importance is mining. Utah ranks second only to Arizona in copper mining and also produces significant amounts of petroleum, coal, natural gas, gold, and silver. Nearly 80 percent of the state's farm income comes from livestock, notably sheep grazing. Tourism is becoming an increasingly important business.

Places of interest. Utah's greatest natural attraction is the Great Salt Lake. Other sites of rugged scenery include Zion, Canyonlands, and Bryce Canyon national parks, and unusual natural rock formations at the Natural Bridges and Rainbow Bridge national monuments. Despite a reputation for deserts and salt flats, the state also includes 11,000 miles

(17,700 kilometers) of fishing streams and 147,000 acres (59,535 hectares) of freshwater lakes and reservoirs. The principal places associated with the Mormon church surround the Mormon Tabernacle in Salt Lake City.

Vermont

Abbreviations: *Vt., VT*
Area: *9,249 sq. mi., 23,955 sq. km.*
  Rank (of 50)   43rd
Population:
  2000   608,827
  Rank (of 50)   49th
  Change 1995–2000   +23,827
  Persons per sq. mi.   65.8
Capital: *Montpelier*
Largest city: *Burlington*
  Pop.   38,889
Entered Union: *Mar. 4, 1791*
  (14th)
State bird: *Hermit thrush*
State flower: *Red clover*
State tree: *Sugar maple*
State map: *Page 101*

Vermont is the most northwestern of the New England states. To the north it borders the Canadian province of Quebec, and to the west, New York. The northern part of this western border is formed by the narrow north-south extent of Lake Champlain. To the south Vermont has a straight border with Massachusetts; to the east it has an irregular border with New Hampshire formed by the Connecticut River. The state extends about 150 miles (241 kilometers) from north to south; its east-west breadth broadens from about 40 miles (64 kilometers) in the south to about 80 miles (129 kilometers) in the north.

Vermont is well known for its old New England ambience. The increased popularity of winter sports and increased interest in country living have brought recent growth to the state. Vermont had a population of 300,000 as early as 1850 and did not pass 500,000 until the late 1970s. In the 1980s and 1990s its growth rate was second highest in the region, after New Hampshire. Even with this growth, Vermont remains the least populated New England state.

The land. All of Vermont is hilly or mountainous, but the state lands fall into three narrow regions that extend its entire length from Massachusetts to Canada. The western region consists of the Taconic Mountains running north from Massachusetts, and the Champlain valley surrounding the lake, which drains into the St. Lawrence River 80 miles (129 kilometers) north in Canada. Central Vermont is the most mountainous region of the state, with its 20- to 40-mile- (32- to 64-kilometer-) wide range of Green Mountains. Eastern Vermont lies within the New England Upland, a hilly region declining slightly in elevation toward the Connecticut River along the New Hampshire border. In the northeast is one end of the White Mountains, which extend across New Hampshire and into Maine.

Climate. The climate of Vermont is very cold because of the state's elevation and inland location. Normal summer highs for the state are 81°F (27°C), but its winter lows average 8°F (-13°C), and extreme lows in the mountains fall below -30°F (-34°C). Precipitation averages 33 inches (84 centimeters) per year. Winters are long, and the state averages 80 inches (203 centimeters) of snow per year, with heavier snowfalls in the mountains.

Principal cities. Vermont is unique in the eastern United States for its lack of a metropolitan area. The largest city in the state is Burlington, in the northwest on the shore of Lake Champlain.

RUGGED SCENERY and unusual rock formations abound in Utah.

27 North America

Chittendon County, in which Burlington is located, has 146,571 residents, more than twice that of the second largest county. The second largest city is Essex (population 18,626) in the northwest region of the state. The third largest city is Rutland (population 17,292) in the south-central region of the state within the Green Mountains.

The people. Vermont was one of only two states in the Northeast whose growth exceeded the national average in the 1980s and was second among New England states only to New Hampshire in growth in the 1990s. African Americans and Hispanics each represent less than 1 percent of the total population. Vermont has the second lowest number of residents of foreign birth or parentage among New England states, after Maine. The foreign-born population is chiefly Canadian, most of whom live in northern communities near the U.S. border.

Economy. The chief industry of Vermont is manufacturing, mainly of machine tools, electrical equipment, and computers. Tourism is a much more visible industry, although it generates less income. Vermont attracts numerous visitors in both winter and summer, but the winter ski resorts generate most of the income. Mining contributes a small portion of the income of the state economy, but Vermont is the U.S. leader in the quarrying of monument granite and talc. Agricultural businesses produce dairy products, cattle, and eggs. Maple syrup is a specialty of Vermont, which produces greater amounts than any other state.

Places of interest. There are more than 50 ski areas in Vermont, the best-known being Stowe, Killington, Mt. Snow, and Sugarbush. Mountain landscapes and lakes also attract many summer visitors to the state, especially to Green Mountain National Forest and the shores of Lake Champlain. Also of interest are the Shelburne Museum, south of Burlington; the Bennington Battle Monument in the southwest; the Vermont Marble exhibit in Proctor, just northwest of Rutland; and the Maple Grove Museum and Sugar House and the Fairbanks Museum and Planetarium, both at St. Johnsbury in the northeast.

center
US

centre
Brit.

kilometers
US

kilometres
Brit.

NEW ENGLAND has preserved its picturesque villages, some of which still maintain covered bridges.

Virginia

Abbreviations: *Va., VA*
Area: *39,598 sq. mi.,*
102,559 sq. km.
Rank (of 50)   37th
Population:
2000   7,078,515
Rank (of 50)   12th
Change 1995–2000
+460,515
Persons per sq. mi.   178.7
Capital: *Richmond*
Largest city: *Virginia Beach*
Pop.   425,257
Entered Union: *June 25, 1788*
(10th)
State bird: *Cardinal*
State flower: *Dogwood blossom*
State tree: *Flowering dogwood*
State map: *Page 99*

Virginia lies near the center of the Atlantic seaboard. The state is triangular in shape, with a wide southern base that borders North Carolina and Tennessee. To the northwest the borders are with Kentucky and West Virginia, and to the northeast Virginia shares borders with Maryland, the District of Columbia, and Chesapeake Bay. The southern portion of the peninsula separating Chesapeake

Bay from the Atlantic Ocean is also part of Virginia, separated from the rest of the state by water.

America's history is closely tied to events in Virginia. The first permanent English colony in the New World was founded at Jamestown in 1607, and the first Africans were transported there as servants in 1619. Subsequent court rulings and legislation established the practice of slavery. The surrender that ended the American Revolution occurred at Yorktown in 1781, and the Civil War ended with Lee's surrender at Appomattox in 1865. Eight present-day states contain part of Virginia's original territory, and Virginia has produced eight U.S. presidents.

Virginia borders Washington, D.C., and many of its residents are federal government employees. The state economy, however, is based on manufacturing.

The land. The Appalachian Mountains lie along Virginia's northwestern border with West Virginia. This mountain and valley region includes parts of the Allegheny Mountains and the Blue Ridge Mountains. The two ranges are separated by a great valley whose northern reaches are traversed by the Shenandoah River.

The central region of Virginia falls within the Piedmont Plateau, a rolling upland 40 miles (64 kilometers) wide in the extreme north broadening to 160 miles (257 kilometers) in the south. To the east of the plateau lies the Atlantic Coastal Plain, which reaches a maximum east-west breadth of 100 miles (161 kilometers) near the North Carolina border. The principal waterway is the James River, which runs across the state from the Blue Ridge to Chesapeake Bay, passing through Lynchburg and Richmond, and entering the bay at Norfolk-Newport News. From Norfolk north along the bay, river estuaries are flooded to points far inland by the action of the sea. South of Norfolk the land is marshy. The Great Dismal Swamp is located at the North Carolina border.

Climate. Virginia has a mild climate in which temperatures rarely rise above 90°F (32°C) in summer or drop below 25°F (-4°C) in winter except in high elevations. Precipitation at Richmond in the east-central region is 43 inches (109 centimeters) per year, including 13 inches (33 centimeters) of snow. Snowfall is lighter along the coast and is heavier inland.

Principal cities. The largest urban area in Virginia is on the banks of the James River at the mouth of Chesapeake Bay. The Norfolk-Virginia Beach-Chesapeake-Portsmouth area on the south bank of the river, and the Newport News-Hampton area on the north bank, have combined populations of over 3.3 million. They are the state's principal shipbuilding and shipping centers. Norfolk is connected to the end of the Delmarva peninsula by the Chesapeake Bay Bridge-Tunnel, an 18-mile (29-kilometer) complex of trestles, bridges, and underwater tunnels completed in 1964.

MONTICELLO, the beautiful home Thomas Jefferson designed for himself, is open to the public.

Nearly as large are the suburban centers surrounding Washington, D.C., in the northeastern corner of the state. Of almost 5 million in the Washington metropolitan area, more than 2 million live in Virginia, in Arlington, Alexandria, and a host of smaller cities. The Richmond-Petersburg metropolitan area (population, 996,512) is the center of the tobacco processing industry. During the Civil War, Richmond was the capital of the Confederate States. Among the cities farther inland are the Shenandoah Valley manufacturing city of Roanoke (population, 94,911) and Lynchburg (65,269) in the Blue Ridge foothills.

The people. The population of Virginia grew slowly through the early 1900s. But beginning in the 1940s, its rate of growth suddenly increased, thanks in large part to increased federal payrolls during World War II in and around Washington. Businesses supporting the work of the federal government in this area continue to contribute to rapid population growth in the state. In the past, African-American residents tended to move from Virginia, but during the 1970s this trend ended. The African-American population now represents 19 percent of the total, and Hispanic residents make up 4.7 percent.

Economy. Virginia's manufacturing income exceeds that of all the state's other businesses combined, with value added by manufacture exceeding $32 billion per year. With the exception of shipbuilding at Newport News, all of this industry is diversified, light manufacturing. The principal manufactures are chemical products exported from Norfolk, tobacco products processed in Richmond, and food and textile goods produced throughout the state.

Agriculture is important, with farm marketings valued at more than $2 billion per year. Crops exceed livestock in farm value. Virginia ranks fourth in the United States in tobacco production, most of it raised in the south and southeast of the state. The mountain and valley region grows large quantities of grain for feed. Poultry and cattle farms predominate in the region. Other important crops include peanuts, apples, and sweet potatoes.

Mining income is principally derived from coal, which is shipped from inland Virginia to Norfolk and Newport News for export. Tourism exceeds agriculture or mining in value. Visitors spend some $8 billion per year.

Places of interest. Virginia's Atlantic Ocean shoreline, reached from the south by the Chesapeake Bay Bridge-Tunnel from Norfolk, includes beach resorts at Chincoteague and Assateague islands. Near the West Virginia border at the opposite extreme of the state is Shenandoah National Park. Virginia is

ARLINGTON NATIONAL CEMETERY in Virginia near Washington, D.C., is the final resting place of many of the nation's servicemen.

unusually rich in historic monuments and preservations, including restored colonial Williamsburg near Newport News; the homes of Presidents Washington and Jefferson at Mount Vernon and Monticello, respectively; the Arlington National Cemetery near Washington, D.C.; and many Revolutionary and Civil War monuments.

Washington

Abbreviations: *Wash., WA*
Area: *66,581 sq. mi.,*
172,445 sq. km.
Rank (of 50)   20th
Population:
2000   5,894,121
Rank (of 50)   15th
Change 1995–2000
+463,121
Persons per sq. mi.   88.5
Capital: *Olympia*
Largest city: *Seattle*
Pop.   563,374
Entered Union: *Nov. 11, 1889*
(42nd)
State bird: *Willow goldfinch*
State flower: *Rhododendron*
State tree: *Western hemlock*
State map: *Page 90*

Washington is located in the northwest corner of the contiguous 48 states, with borders on the Pacific Ocean and British Columbia, Canada. Its shape is rectangular, except for a notch in the northwest formed by Vancouver Island, a part of Canada that extends south of the 49th parallel. The Strait of Juan de Fuca leads past Vancouver Island and into Puget Sound, which extends 100 miles (161 kilometers) into the state and provides its primary deep-water ports. Washington's southern border is formed primarily by the Columbia River, which flows south through the center of the state before turning at the so-called Big Bend to form the boundary between Washington and Oregon. Its rapid flow and great volume give it huge potential for generating hydroelectric power, and a system of dams along its length makes Washington the largest producer of hydroelectric power in the United States. These water resources, a mild climate, and extensive forestland have combined to make Washington the home of slightly more than half the population of the Northwest states, with a population density slightly greater than the national average.

The land. Washington is characterized by four distinct topographical areas. The farthest west is the peninsula of Olympic Mountains. Isolated by the southern reaches of Puget Sound, surrounded by water, and subject to Pacific westerly winds, the peninsula is the site of the largest rain forest in the United States.

Immediately inland is the lowland Puget Trough, which extends south from Puget Sound toward Oregon. About 100 miles (161 kilometers) farther east, the Cascade Mountains run parallel to the Pacific. An extension of the Sierra Nevadas in California, this spectacular range is the principal topographical division of the state. Its peaks include Mt. Rainier (14,410 feet, 4,392 meters) and Mt. St. Helens (8,365 feet, 2,550 meters), a long-dormant volcano that erupted in spectacular fashion on May 31, 1980.

Inland from the Cascades and covering the southeast quarter of the state is the Columbia Plateau, a semiarid tableland between 500 and 2,000 feet (152 and 610 meters) above sea level. At its northeast corner the state is touched by western spurs of the Rocky Mountains.

Climate.   Washington has two distinct climates, defined by the Cascades. Western Washington has a moderate seasonal variation, with winter mean temperatures of about 30°F (-1°C) and summer temperatures about 60°F (16°C). Rain-

---

kilometers
US

kilometres
Brit.

centers
US

centres
Brit.

Spokane, hub of a metropolitan area including parts of northwestern Idaho, is the center of the aluminum industry and a processor of agricultural and lumber products from Idaho as well as Washington.

The people.   Having lain nearly barren until the opening of railroad links with the east in 1883, Washington developed as the gateway to Alaska, Asia, and the Pacific. The major ethnic groups in those early years were people of German, English, and Norwegian extraction. In recent years, the state has attracted a much wider range of people. Today about 7.5 percent of the population are of Hispanic descent, 3 percent are African Americans, and 5.5 percent are of Asian descent. About 93,301, or 1.6 percent of the state population, are Native Americans, including small Inuit and Aleut populations.

Economy.   Washington's manufacturing businesses have outgrown the traditional industries of timber and agriculture, with the major employer being the Boeing Company, the world-famous producer of civilian and military aircraft.

the state tree, the western hemlock, is a close second.

Places of interest.   The major attractions in Washington are Mount Rainier National Park, North Cascades National Park, and Olympic National Park. Also of interest are the state's Pacific beaches, the Columbia River Gorge, and Grand Coulee Dam.

West Virginia

Abbreviations: *W. Va., WV*
Area: *24,087 sq. mi., 62,385 sq. km.*
    Rank (of 50)   41st
Population:
    2000   1,808,344
    Rank (of 50)   37th
    Change 1995–2000
    -19,656
    Persons per sq. mi.   75
Capital: *Charleston*
Largest city: *Charleston*
    Pop.   53,421
Entered Union: *June 20, 1863*
    (35th)
State bird: *Cardinal*
State flower: *Big rhododendron*
State tree: *Sugar maple*
State map: *Page 99*

West Virginia is extremely irregular in shape. To the south and east it borders Virginia, and to the west it borders Kentucky and Ohio. The northern borders are with Pennsylvania and Maryland. The outline of the state is unusual because of two panhandles. One extends 60 miles (97 kilometers) north between Ohio and Pennsylvania and narrows to a breadth of only 7 miles (11 kilometers). The other stretches 90 miles (145 kilometers) east between the Potomac River border with Maryland on the north and Virginia to the south.

West Virginia was the Trans-Allegheny region of Virginia until 1861. But it chose to remain in the Union during the Civil War. It is distinct from all surrounding states in character, in that it is entirely mountainous and extremely rural. In modern times, the basis of the economy has been coal, and the fortunes of the state have varied with coal's market value. The population grew during the peak mining years between 1930 and 1950. When coal suffered from competition with oil and natural gas fuels in the years that followed, West Virginia experienced the most dramatic population declines in recent U.S. history. Of late, the state has begun to show population growth again.

The land.   West Virginia's average elevation of 1,500 feet (457 meters) is the highest east of the Mississippi. The Allegheny Mountains, part of the vast Appalachian chain, run through the eastern panhandle and all along the state's southeastern border. To the west

---

MOUNT ST. HELENS, long dormant, caused great damage in a spectacular volcanic eruption in May 1980.

fall near the coast is heavy, averaging about 35 inches (89 centimeters) at Seattle and over 100 inches (254 centimeters) on the Olympic peninsula. East of the Cascades, however, rainfall diminishes to about 16 inches (41 centimeters) per year and temperature variations, depending on elevation, increase to the usual continental averages of 70°F (21°C) in summer and below freezing in winter. The Cascade Range itself includes many peaks with elevations great enough to support year-round ice caps.

Principal cities.   Washington's principal urban centers are at either end of the state. The Seattle-Bellevue-Everett and Tacoma metropolitan areas on the east shore of Puget Sound are home to more than 50 percent of the state population. This is also the business center of the Northwest. Across the state,

Seattle is now rated the fourth largest containerized seaport in the United States, primarily because of manufactured exports. Manufacturing industries farther inland have prospered by processing the state's timber and agricultural produce. Another substantial factor in the state economy is the aluminum industry, which has benefited from plentiful hydroelectric power from the Columbia River's dams and which provides one-quarter of the nation's output of raw aluminum.

Washington's agricultural products are stratified into regions: dairy products in the west, apples in the central region, and wheat on the eastern plateau. Lumbering is an important industry; production remains second only to that of Oregon among U.S. states. As in Oregon, the principal harvest is of Douglas fir, but in Washington

THE APPALACHIAN PLATEAU covers 80 percent of West Virginia's land area, which is carved by narrow valleys with river gorges and waterfalls.

Wisconsin

Abbreviations: *Wis., WI*
Area: *54,314 sq. mi.,*
  140,673 sq. km.
  Rank (of 50)   25th
Population:
  2000   5,363,675
  Rank (of 50)   18th
  Change 1995–2000
  +240,675
  Persons per sq. mi.   94.3
Capital: *Madison*
Largest city: *Milwaukee*
  Pop.   596,974
Entered Union: *May 29, 1848*
  (30th)
State bird: *Robin*
State flower: *Wood violet*
State tree: *Sugar maple*
State map: *Page 96*

of the Alleghenies lies the Appalachian plateau, representing 80 percent of the state's land area. This land is cut into narrow valleys notable for river gorges and waterfalls, and it lacks large natural lakes. The state's high point is located at Spruce Knob (4,862 feet, 1,482 meters), near the Virginia border.

Climate. West Virginia has a harsh climate compared with the rest of the region because it is inland and elevated. Normal temperatures at Charleston in the southwest range between 85°F (29°C) in summer and 25°F (-4°C) in winter, but record temperatures of 102°F (39°C) in summer and -12°F (-24°C) in winter have been recorded. Precipitation averages 41 inches (104 centimeters) per year at Charleston, which receives an average of 31 inches (79 centimeters) per year of snow. Winters are colder and snowfalls heavier along the eastern ridge of the Alleghenies.

Principal cities. Charleston, the capital, is the largest metropolitan area lying entirely within West Virginia. The state shares its other metropolitan areas with neighboring states. The Ohio River port of Huntington (population, 51,475) has a metropolitan area that includes Ashland, Kentucky, and suburbs in Ohio. Wheeling, on the Ohio border in the northern panhandle, has a population of 31,419. The metropolitan area populations of these cities, however, are many times larger.

The people. Between 1950 and 1970, West Virginia lost more than 260,000 in population. In the 1970s, the resurgence of coal mining and some diversification of industry brought a healthy increase of 205,000. Subsequent decades showed only declines or insignificant increases. African Americans account for 3 percent

of the population, and there are no other large ethnic or racial groups. West Virginia has traditionally had a low per capita income.

Economy. The principal industry in West Virginia is manufacturing based on the state's mining production. Important products include iron, steel, aluminum, chemicals, machinery, electrical and electronic equipment, and fabricated metals. The largest center of manufacture is in the Kanawha River valley, running northwest from Charleston to the Ohio River, where production is concentrated on chemical products and fabricated metals. The northern panhandle around Wheeling is an industrial region of blast furnaces and steel mills. In the eastern panhandle, manufacturers produce textile goods.

Income from mining nearly equals that from manufacturing, and West Virginia is one of the leading states in total mining production. The principal ore is bituminous coal, which West Virginia produces in greater quantities than any other state except Wyoming and Kentucky, but oil and natural gas are also drilled, and clay and cement are mined in large amounts. The only other large industry is tourism, which accounts for more than $1 billion in income.

Places of interest. West Virginia contains 34 state parks and 9 state forests, as well as resorts at Berkeley Springs which is in the eastern panhandle and White Sulphur Springs in the south-central region. At the extreme of the eastern panhandle is the Harpers Ferry National Historic Park, on the site where John Brown seized the U.S. Armory in a brave but ultimately doomed attempt to spark a popular uprising against slavery in 1859.

Wisconsin is north of Illinois, between the Mississippi River, which forms part of its western border with Minnesota and Iowa, and Lake Michigan to the east. Its northern border is formed by Lake Superior and the Upper Peninsula of Michigan.

Wisconsin is an important manufacturing state despite its small population and relative lack of natural resources. It is also the least populated state in the region. These apparent deficiencies became assets in the 1970s: Wisconsin was the only one of the region's states to gain more new residents from other states than it lost. In addition, the same forests and lakes that attracted residents have made tourism a major industry.

The land. Wisconsin has a complex topography consisting of two major landmasses. The northern half of the state is a portion of the Superior Upland that extends northwest into Minnesota and northeast into the Upper Peninsula of Michigan. The rolling lands and glacial hills here are a part of the enormous Canadian Shield that extends into the far north. In north-central Wisconsin, the state's high point at Timm's Hill (1,952 feet, 595 meters) is found.

Southern Wisconsin lies within the Central Lowland and contains two distinct features. In the southeast, uplands decline into the Great Lakes Plain lying only about 500 feet (152 meters) above sea level. In the southwest, the lowlands include a portion of the Wisconsin Driftless Plain, a hilly region never covered by glacial ice sheets and so lacking the soil, or "drift," they left behind. This plain contains the state's most dramatic relief features, limestone hills as high as 1,700 feet (518 meters) eroded by streams into steep valleys. Close to the Mississippi River this region drops off from the same 500-foot (152-meter) elevations found on the Great Lakes Plain beside Lake Michigan.

27 North America

aluminum
US
aluminium
Brit.

armory
US
armoury
Brit.

DAIRY PRODUCTS generate the most income in Wisconsin's important agricultural businesses.

Climate. Wisconsin's climate is notable for its long frigid winters and short warm summers. At Milwaukee in the southeast, normal winter lows are 10°F (-7°C) and summer highs approach 80°F (27°C). However, record temperatures in other state areas range from -54° to 114°F (-47° to 45°C). Precipitation is a consistent 29 inches (74 centimeters) per year throughout the state, and snows average 46 inches (117 centimeters) per year in Milwaukee and more in the northern regions.

Principal cities. The largest urban center in the state is a consolidated metropolitan area running 20 miles (32 kilometers) along the Lake Michigan shore from Milwaukee to Racine. The Milwaukee metropolitan area, the state's industrial seat, is also an important commercial and transportation center as well as an educational and cultural center. The second largest city in the state is the capital of Madison (population, 208,054), 80 miles (129 kilometers) east of Milwaukee. Madison is an insurance and banking center and the home of the largest campus of the University of Wisconsin. The western and northwestern parts of the state look toward the metropolitan centers of Minneapolis-St. Paul and Duluth, Minnesota.

The people. The population of the state returned in the 1980s to less urbanized levels before moving toward a slight growth in urbanization. The proportion of minority groups in Wisconsin is lower than that in any other Great Lakes state: African Americans represent 6 percent of the total population and Hispanics 3.6 percent.

Economy. Wisconsin's manufacturing businesses generate $26 billion in income per year and rank 12th in the United States. The principal manufactures, mostly coming out of the Milwaukee and Madison areas, are machinery, electrical components, paper goods, and food products (including cheese). More than half of the state is covered by farmland, making Wisconsin's agricultural businesses second only to those of Illinois in the region. Dairy products generate the most income, and the chief crops are feed grains such as corn and oats. Tourism is the state's third largest business, with visitors from

centimeters
US

centimetres
Brit.

center
US

centre
Brit.

colonized
US

colonised
Brit.

out of state spending approximately $2.5 billion per year.

Places of interest. The major attractions in Wisconsin are natural preserves such as the Apostle Islands in Lake Superior; Lake Winnebago near Lake Michigan; and the Dells region in the south-central part of the state, where the Wisconsin River has carved picturesque sandstone canyons.

Wyoming

Abbreviations: *Wyo., WY*
Area: *97,105 sq. mi.,*
251,502 sq. km.
Rank (of 50)　9th
Population:
2000　493,782
Rank (of 50)　50th
Change 1995–2000
+13,782
Persons per sq. mi.　5.0
Capital: *Cheyenne*
Largest city: *Cheyenne*
Pop.　53,011
Entered Union: *July 10, 1890*
(44th)
State bird: *Meadowlark*
State flower: *Paintbrush*
State tree: *Cottonwood*
State map: *Page 92*

Wyoming lies in the heart of the Mountain region; its borders enclose some of the most spectacular Rocky Mountain peaks. The mountains cross the state in isolated ranges from the rugged northwest to the southeast, where the capital city of Cheyenne is located.

The state was explored by John Colter, who first saw the Yellowstone

area in 1807. From the 1840s on, the territory was an important way station on the Oregon and Mormon trails. Forts Laramie in the southeast and Bridger in the southwest were the major outposts.

Wyoming, with the smallest population of any state, to some extent remains a frontier: men outnumber women, and mining sometimes brings sudden wealth. The land wars of the 1890s between ranchers and homesteaders have been replaced by today's less violent environmental battles between mineral developers and environmentalists.

The land. Wyoming is dominated by the Rocky Mountains, and the state's average elevation of 6,700 feet (2,042 meters) is second only to Colorado's.

The ranges in the northwest corner of the state include some of the highest peaks in the United States and two national parks, Yellowstone and Grand Teton. In north-central Wyoming, the Big Horn Mountains rise above 13,000 feet (3,962 meters), and in the southeast, the Laramie Mountains reach 10,000 feet (3,048 meters). These ranges are separated by great arid basins, a wandering extension of the basin and range country to the south and west. Along the state's eastern edge, approaching the foothills of the Laramie and Big Horn ranges, are the western edges of the Great Plains.

Climate. Wyoming's climate is generally cool and dry, but it varies with elevation. The northwestern mountains contain glaciers, and the basin country is predominantly desert. In moderately elevated Cheyenne, in the extreme southeast, temperature averages are 20°F (-7°C) for winter lows, and 80°F (27°C) for summer highs. Precipitation averages about 15 inches (38 centimeters) per year, most of it falling in the mountains and drained by an extensive network of rivers.

GRAND TETON NATIONAL PARK and Yellowstone National Park, just to the north, attract many visitors to Wyoming each year.

Principal cities. Wyoming's cities lie clustered for the most part in the southeastern region. Casper stands on the North Platte River, which pioneer travelers to Oregon and California followed to the Rockies. Casper's modern growth has been encouraged by oil and mining businesses. Cheyenne (population, 53,011) and Laramie (27,204) both lie in the extreme southeast of the state, along the principal transcontinental railway and highway route as it crosses the Laramie Mountains.

The people. Wyoming experienced the highest growth rate among Mountain states in the 1970s, followed by a decline in the 1980s before a return to growth in the 1990s. The major incentives drawing the new population were increasing oil and mining businesses and a surviving frontier spirit.

Economy. Wyoming raises significant amounts of wheat and grazes cattle and sheep on its northeast plains, but the major industry of the state is mining. Wyoming is the chief producer of crude oil among Mountain states and the leading producer of coal west of the Mississippi. In plains and in basin and range areas, large strip mines yield enormous quantities of low-sulfur coal. The state ranks second to New Mexico among Mountain states in its production of natural gas and uranium. Manufacturing is concentrated around Casper, where food products and cattle are processed and some oil is refined. Wyoming has also had a large tourist industry ever since Yellowstone became the first national park, in 1872. Nearby Grand Teton Park and other attractions help bring the state some $1 billion annually.

Places of interest. Wyoming's principal attractions are its mountains and the nearly 10 million acres (4,050,000 hectares) of forestland that cover them. Yellowstone and Grand Teton national parks are found beside each other in the state's northwest mountains, but across the state there are many natural landscapes of different character, such as Devil's Tower National Monument near the South Dakota border. Historic attractions include Fort Laramie, the restored fur-trapping and military outpost; the state historical museum in Cheyenne; and the Buffalo Bill Museum in Cody.

U.S. Territories

The United States retains control of a number of outlying territories in both the Caribbean area and the west and central Pacific. The greatest number are in the Pacific, but many of these are uninhabited coral atolls. The most important territory, and the only one considered to have potential for statehood, is Puerto Rico, between the Caribbean Sea and the Atlantic Ocean to the southeast of Florida. Puerto Rico is presently a commonwealth possession with powers of self-government similar to those of a state, but without voting representation in Congress.

Of the rest, the greatest number of U.S. possessions are unincorporated territories, a status that grants autonomous elections for local governments under the administration of the U.S. Department of Interior.

The Canal Zone, a strip of land in the Central American republic of Panama extending approximately 5 miles (8 kilometers) on either side of the Panama Canal, was controlled by the United States from 1904 to 1979, when, by the provisions of treaties signed in 1977 and 1979, control of the zone was returned to Panama. The Panama Canal was under joint U.S.-Panamanian jurisdiction until the year 2000, when Panama assumed full responsibility for the canal's maintenance and operation.

The political status of the populated U.S. possessions is frequently revised to permit greater self-government while protecting U.S. access to military installations. The many uninhabited U.S. territories, particularly those in the western Pacific, are retained for their strategic importance. In addition to the official U.S. territories, there are some 25 Pacific islands of disputed sovereignty that have been claimed both by the United States and by either Great Britain or New Zealand.

Puerto Rico

Abbreviations: *P.R., PR*
Area: *3,514 sq. mi., 9,104 sq. km.*
Population:
2000   3,863,000
Change 1995–2000 -4,390
Persons per sq. mi.   1111.3
Capital: *San Juan*
Largest city: *San Juan*
Metro. pop.   1,816,300
Declared Commonwealth:
July 25, 1952
Bird: *Reinita*
Flower: *Maga*
Tree: *Ceiba*
Area map: *Page 150*

Puerto Rico is an island located 1,000 miles (1,609 kilometers) southeast of Miami, Florida, in the chain of islands called the Greater Antilles, which stretches east-west between the Atlantic Ocean on the north and the Caribbean Sea on the south. Puerto Rico is the smallest of the major islands in the chain. The chain includes Cuba and the island of Hispaniola, which is shared by Haiti and the Dominican Republic. The island of Puerto Rico is roughly rectangular in shape, averaging 100 miles (161 kilometers) from east to west and 35 miles (56 kilometers) from north to south. The Commonwealth of Puerto Rico includes a number of smaller islands, notably Vieques and Culebra.

Officially known as *Estado Libre Asociado de Puerto Rico,* Puerto Rico was discovered by Christopher Columbus on his second voyage, in 1493, and first colonized in 1508, by Juan Ponce de León. The island's small Taino Indian population was virtually wiped out in the 16th century. The Spaniards fortified the city of San Juan and overcame attacks by the English and the Dutch. In the 19th century a strong movement for self-government arose in Puerto Rico, but although the island gained substantial autonomy, it was ceded by Spain to the United States at the end of the Spanish-American War in 1898. Puerto Ricans became citizens of the United States in 1917, and began to elect their own governor in 1947. Since becoming a commonwealth in 1952, the people have had nonvoting representation in the Congress of the United States.

In 1992 Puerto Ricans favoring statehood over continued commonwealth status or independence elected the pro-statehood candidate Pedro Rosselló governor and gained a number of seats in the legislature, both indications that the statehood movement was gaining strength.

In the 1940s, Puerto Rico had a depressed economy. But an industrialization program known as Operation Bootstrap, combining tax incentives for investment and diversification of manufactures, succeeded in bolstering the local economy. A constant flow of immigrants from Puerto Rico came to the U.S. mainland between 1945 and the late 1960s. New York City was the most popular destination, and it has the largest community of Puerto Ricans outside of Puerto Rico. In the 1970s, however, migration slowed, and the commonwealth, at the peak of a long period of economic growth that had begun in the early 1950s, gained more new residents than it lost in migration to other places.

The land. Three-quarters of the island of Puerto Rico is mountainous. The mountains rise to a maximum elevation of 4,389 feet (1,338 meters) at Cerro de Punta, near the center of the island. From the central Sierra de Luquillo and Cordillera ranges, the land declines to coastal valleys on the east and west and sandy lowland beaches on the north and south.

Climate. The climate of Puerto Rico is warm and humid year-round. Normal winter temperatures along the coast seldom fall below 70°F (21°C), and normal summer temperatures remain above 80°F (27°C). The less populated areas in the central mountains are cooler in both summer and winter. Precipitation ranges from 20 inches (51 centimeters) per year on the southern coast to 200 inches (508 centimeters) per year in some mountain areas, with an average of 60 inches (152 centimeters) per year falling on the capital city of San Juan on the northeastern coast.

Principal cities. The major population center in Puerto Rico is San Juan, which accounts for about one-ninth of the total population. One of the oldest cities in the Americas, San Juan is situated on a penin-

27 **North America**

sula extending northwest from the island; it functions as the island's principal tourist and shipping center. The port of San Juan is one of the Caribbean's busiest and is the center of Caribbean shipping. Other large cities include Ponce, situated near the center of the southern coast and Mayaguez, a port and apparel center on the west coast. Three rapidly growing cities near San Juan are Bayamón, Carolina, and Guaynabo. Caguas is south-southeast of San Juan.

The people. The population of the commonwealth is 99 percent Hispanic, two-thirds of which is urban, and one of the densest in the world. The per capita income has risen dramatically in the last four decades but it remains low in comparison with that of U.S. states.

The common language of the people is Spanish, but most Puerto Ricans are now bilingual to some extent, at least, and official documents are published in both English and Spanish.

Economy. Once almost totally reliant on sugar and tobacco crops for its income, Puerto Rico now generates more than half its domestic income from manufacturing. The principal manufactures are chemicals, plastics, metal products, foods, electrical and electronic equipment, and apparel, but the most famous export is 75 percent of all the rum sold in the United States. Tourism is the second largest industry, which amounted to more than $2.7 billion in 2001. Agriculture accounts for about half the income generated by tourism. The farm industry is based on sugar cane, from which molasses for rum is refined; coffee grown on the western mountains; and tobacco grown on the eastern mountains.

Places of interest. The principal attraction in Puerto Rico is Old San Juan, a walled city surrounded by historic forts at the tip of the San Juan peninsula. The city is also home to a number of museums, the Puerto Rican Botanical Gardens, and a music conservatory famous for the mid-June Pablo Casals Festival. Points of interest inland include the Cordillera Park and El Yunque Rain Forest.

Other Territories in the Americas

The United States has a number of other possessions in the Caribbean area. The major possession is the U.S. Virgin Islands.

The Virgin Islands. The U.S. Virgin Islands is an unincorporated territory 40 miles (64 kilometers) east of Puerto Rico. Great Britain retains possession of three major islands in the chain, but the United States governs St. Croix, St. Thomas, St. John, and about 50 minor islets, with a total area of 134 square miles (347 square kilometers). The three major islands under U.S. control are all volcanic in origin, with steep elevations and little arable land. They have subtropical climates cooled by trade winds, with average year-round temperatures of 78°F (26°C) and annual precipitation of 45 inches (114 centimeters). More

than half of the population lives on St. Croix. Fewer than 3,000 people live on St. John. The capital city of Charlotte Amalie, with a population of 11,000, is on St. Thomas.

The people of the Virgin Islands are English-speaking, and 80 percent are of African descent; they were granted U.S. citizenship in 1927, and in 1970 elected their first governor. The islands lack agricultural lands, and the economy is

THE LUSH TROPICAL AMBIANCE of the U.S. Virgin Islands makes the area a leading tourist destination.

based on tourism and exportation of manufactured goods such as rum, apparel, and costume jewelry.

Other territories. The Corn Islands off the east coast of Nicaragua in Central America are the only other inhabited U.S. possessions in the Caribbean. Great and Little Corn Islands have a combined land area of 4 square miles (10 square kilometers), and the population lives entirely on Great Corn Island. Both islands are leased from Nicaragua.

Quita Sueño Bank, Roncador, and Serrana are uninhabited cays in the Caribbean between Nicaragua and Jamaica. A 1972 treaty to cede them to Colombia has never been ratified by Congress. Navassa is an island of 2 square miles (5 square kilometers) in the Caribbean, between Jamaica and Haiti. It is a navigation point on which stands a U.S. Coast Guard lighthouse.

Pacific territories

Trust Territory of the Pacific Islands. After World War II the United States was given a mandate by the United Nations to administer the islands in the western Pacific known as Micronesia. There are 2,100 identified islands spread over 3 million square miles (7.8 million square kilometers) just north of the island of New Guinea and east of the Philippines. The southern extreme of the island region lies on the equator, and its western boundary is near the international dateline.

The islands were controlled by Spain from 1565 until 1898, when they were sold to Germany. In 1947 they became the UN–mandated Trust Territory of the Pacific Islands. The territory included the Northern Mariana Islands, located due north of Guam; the Federated

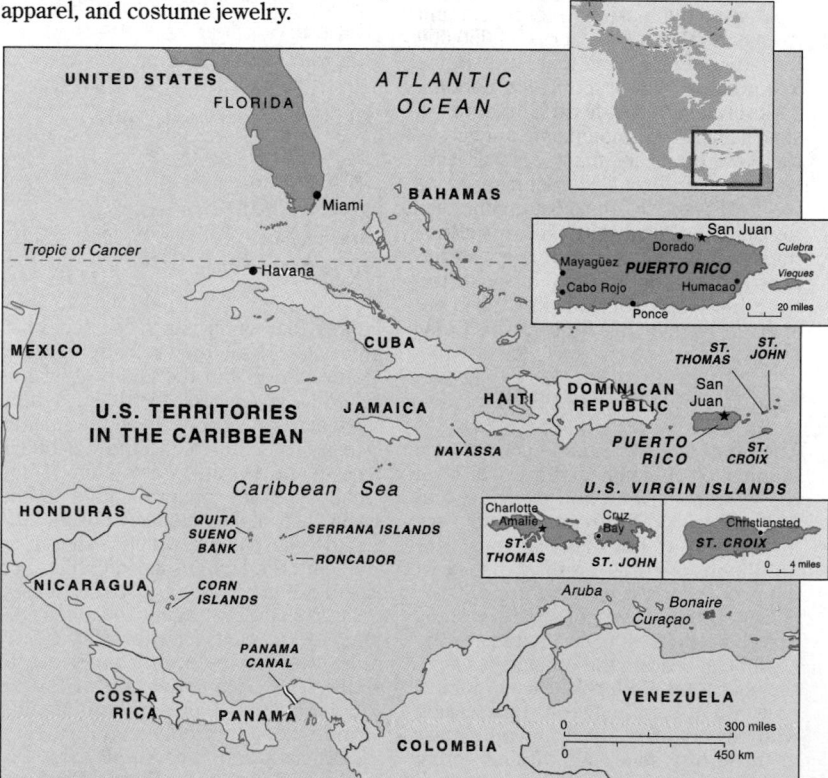

States of Micronesia, located about 3,200 miles (5,149 kilometers) southwest of Hawaii; the Marshall Islands, 2,375 miles (3,821 kilometers) southwest of Hawaii; and Palau, about 530 miles (853 kilometers) southeast of the Philippines.

In 1986 the Northern Marianas achieved commonwealth status and were removed from the Trust Territory. Also in that year, Micronesia became the independent Federated States of Micronesia; the Marshalls became independent as the Republic of the Marshall Islands. These, too, were removed from the Trust Territory.

Both Micronesia and the Marshall Islands have entered into Compacts of Free Association with the United States, by which agreements the United States has authority in military and defense matters, but the countries retain sovereignty in all other matters.

Palau, now the Republic of Palau, negotiated a Compact of Free Association with the United States in 1986. But a provision in Palau's 1980 constitution, establishing the country as a nuclear-free zone, conflicted with the U.S. defense authority under the terms of the compact, and it was never put into effect. In November 1994 the United States notified the United Nations that Palau had voted to become independent, thus ending the function of the Trust Territory.

Guam. Guam was originally part of the larger group of Micronesian islands, but it

AMERICAN SAMOA in the Trust Territory of the Pacific consists of five volcanic islands and two coral atolls, with a total land area of just 76 square miles.

was set apart by the United States as a separate territory in 1950. The island has a land area of 212 square miles (549 square kilometers) and is by far the most populous in Micronesia, with 161,000 people. Guam has considerable internal self-government, but its external affairs are guided by the United States. Of all the South Pacific territories, Guam has the closest relationship with the United States. It sends a representative to the U.S. House of Representatives; the representative has a voice but no vote in Congress.

East Pacific territories. All but one of the remaining Pacific U.S. possessions are east of the international dateline, and most of them are south of the equator.

American Samoa. An unincorporated territory consisting of five volcanic islands and two coral atolls, American Samoa has a land area of 76 square miles (197 square kilometers) and a Polynesian population of 69,000.

Johnston Atoll. Formerly a U.S. nuclear weapons testing site, Johnston Atoll includes Johnston and Sand islands as well as two man-made islands and a chain of coral reefs. The entire population of the islands are U.S. Air Force personnel or employees.

Midway Islands. Consisting of two main islands, Sand and Eastern, and a chain of coral reefs, Midway is a strategic U.S. naval air facility. The Japanese suffered a decisive defeat at Midway during World War II.

Wake Island. An unincorporated territory consisting of three volcanic islands, Wake Island is administered by the U.S. Air Force.

Uninhabited islands. Among the islands north of Samoa, U.S. possessions include Howland, Baker, and Jarvis islands; Kingman Reef; and Palmyra Atoll.

For more information on U.S. territories, see the AUSTRALIA AND OCEANIA volume.

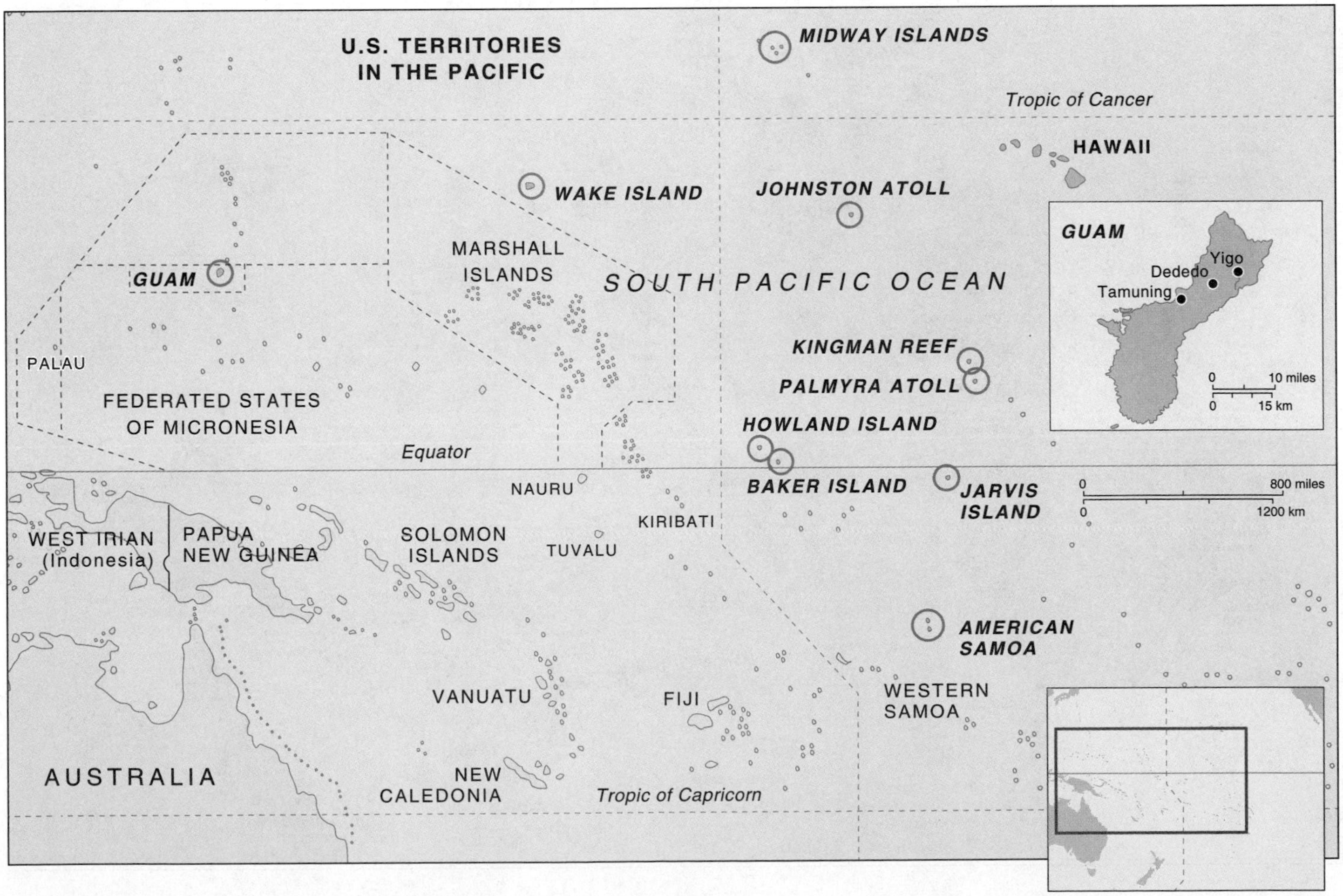

27 North America

U.S. TERRITORIES IN THE PACIFIC

MIDWAY ISLANDS

Tropic of Cancer

HAWAII

WAKE ISLAND

JOHNSTON ATOLL

MARSHALL ISLANDS

SOUTH PACIFIC OCEAN

GUAM

GUAM

Dededo Yigo

Tamuning

0   10 miles
0   15 km

PALAU

FEDERATED STATES OF MICRONESIA

KINGMAN REEF

PALMYRA ATOLL

HOWLAND ISLAND

Equator

NAURU

BAKER ISLAND

JARVIS ISLAND

0   800 miles
0   1200 km

WEST IRIAN (Indonesia)

PAPUA NEW GUINEA

SOLOMON ISLANDS

KIRIBATI

TUVALU

AMERICAN SAMOA

VANUATU

FIJI

WESTERN SAMOA

AUSTRALIA

NEW CALEDONIA

Tropic of Capricorn

Canada

Canada Today

Canada, a nation of some 31 million people, derives its name from an Indian word, *kanata,* meaning village or settlement. The population is made up of descendants of Canada's aboriginal groups, including Indians, Inuit, and Métis (people of mixed Indian and European, particularly French, descent); the descendants of French, British, and other European settlers; and more-recent immigrants, notably from the Caribbean area, South America, and Asia.

Canada has developed in four distinct stages. The first period, characterized largely by French domination, lasted from the early 1600s until 1759, when the British gained control of Canada. The second period, initially one of direct British control, witnessed the emergence of Canada as a self-governing parliamentary democracy. The third period, ending in 1949, saw Canada become politically independent of Great Britain in every respect, and expand from Newfoundland and Labrador in the Atlantic to British Columbia on the Pacific. The last period, continuing to the present, has seen Canada grow into a multicultural society.

The land. The landmass of Canada occupies all of the North American continent north of the United States, except Alaska. Its area is 3,851,792 square miles (9,976,140 square kilometers), making it about 5 percent larger than the United States. In the east, Canada borders the U.S. states of Maine, New Hampshire, Vermont, and New York. From Cornwall, Ontario, the border extends west along the St. Lawrence River, through lakes Ontario, Erie, Huron, and Superior, and along the northern border of the state of Minnesota. From there, it runs along the 49th parallel of latitude to the Pacific Ocean in the west. This boundary is just under 4,000 miles (6,400 kilometers) long. Canada is bordered on the east by the Atlantic Ocean, on the west by the Pacific Ocean, and on the north by the Arctic Ocean. There are many islands belonging to Canada off all three coasts.

Geographic areas. Canada can be divided into five main geographic areas. The first of these is the southeastern region. On Canada's extreme east, the land is an extension of the Appalachian Mountain system running north from the United States. It continues to Quebec's Gaspé peninsula and to the island province of

Canada

Official name: *Canada*
Area: *3,851,792 sq. mi.,*
  9,976,140 sq. km.
Type of government:
  Parliamentary democracy
Population: *31,902,000*
Capital: *Ottawa, Ontario*
  (Pop. 774,072)
Largest city: *Toronto, Ontario*
  (Pop. 2,481,494)
Languages: *English, French*
Literacy: *97%;* **Currency:** *Dollar*
Per capita GDP: *$29,400*
  (Rank: 6th)

Newfoundland and Labrador. The Atlantic coast is quite indented and provides excellent harbors. Beginning at Quebec City, the valley of the St. Lawrence River becomes broader, and there are fertile plains into southeastern Ontario.

The second principal geographic area is the Canadian Shield, which covers more than half of all of Canada and is the dominant physiographic feature of the country. The Shield, shaped like an enormous U, with Hudson Bay in the center, extends from Labrador on the Atlantic coast westward to the prairies, more than halfway across the country. Its western edge slants northwest to the Arctic Ocean. The northern boundary of the Shield is the coast of the continental mainland. In the south it pushes down to the St. Lawrence valley and the Ontario peninsula.

Ice sheets and water have eroded the Canadian Shield for millions of years, so that today it is generally only some 1,000 to 2,000 feet (300 to 600 meters) above sea level. Much of the soil has been carried away, and the erosion has created thousands of lakes, bogs, and rock formations.

The southern part of the Shield is heavily forested, with little land suitable for farming. As one goes north, the trees give way to scrub and then to perpetually frozen, treeless tundra. However, the Shield is rich in natural resources. It has minerals, especially gold and nickel, timber, fur-bearing animals, and great potential for waterpower development. The $15 billion James Bay hydroelectric project, begun in 1975, produces some 20 percent of Canada's total generating capacity. Along the south and west shore of Hudson Bay, in the center of the Shield, are the Hudson Bay Lowlands, a generally marshy area.

West of the Shield and east of the Rocky Mountains lies a third important region, the Canadian prairies. The prairies are a part of the Great Plains, which run from Texas in the south to the Arctic region. In general, it is a high grassland area, sloping upward from east to west, and covering parts of Manitoba, Saskatchewan, Alberta, the Yukon and Northwest Territories, and Nunavut.

Where the climate is favorable, the deep soil is excellent for farming. There are some extremely productive grain-growing areas and many places that are good for livestock grazing.

From the western edge of the prairies to the Pacific Ocean, a distance of about 400 miles (640 kilometers), is the fourth and most mountainous area of the country. It is Canada's portion of the Western Highlands, the mountain system that runs from northern Alaska south through the western United States. These mountains, the result of the uplifting of Earth's crust, run parallel to the coast and are very rugged. On the eastern side of the area are the Rocky Mountains, which extend south into the United States. Some of the Rockies' peaks are over 12,000 feet (3,600 meters) high, and present a barrier to travel.

West of the Rockies lies a region of mountainous plateaus and basins with several small ranges of lower elevation. Then come the Coast Mountains, which extend for about 1,000 miles (1,600 kilometers) in Canada and Alaska. They meet the Cascade Range in southern British Columbia. There are a number of peaks from about 10,000 to 13,000 feet (3,000 to 4,000 meters) high, with Mt. Waddington being the highest of the Coast Mountains at 13,000 feet (3,994 meters). The mountains act as a barrier to keep much of the rainfall from reaching inland.

Finally come the Coastal Ranges, which run from Alaska south to lower California. In Canada they consist of the St. Elias Range in the southwestern Yukon and islands off the coast, such as the Queen Charlotte Islands, where all

kilometers
US

kilometres
Brit.

center
US

centre
Brit.

27 North America

THE CANADIAN ROCKIES
lie on the border between Alberta and British Columbia.

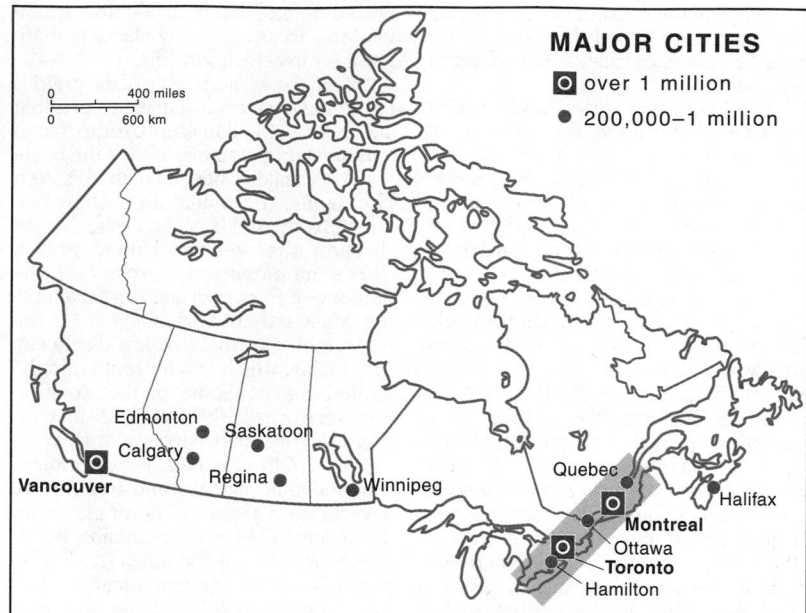

MAJOR CITIES

◎ over 1 million

● 200,000–1 million

0   400 miles
0   600 km

Edmonton
Calgary   Saskatoon
Regina   Winnipeg
Vancouver
Quebec
Halifax
Montreal
Ottawa
Toronto
Hamilton

centimeters
US

centimetres
Brit.

theater
US

theatre
Brit.

emphasize
US

emphasise
Brit.

but the peaks of the mountains have been submerged.

Far to the north, mostly beyond the Arctic Circle, is a fifth distinct geographic region, consisting of the Arctic Ocean, the mainland just south of it, and the Arctic Archipelago, comprising more than 50 large islands.

Climate. Because of its great expanse and its northern location, the climate of Canada shows wide variations, with some of the world's coldest weather in its northern regions. Except for the Pacific coast, winters are cold. Both coasts are more moderate than the interior. The Atlantic is cool because it is open to the north, while the Pacific, more closed to the north, is warmed by ocean currents from the tropics.

The southern sections of Canada have a temperate climate. Along the St. Lawrence and around the Great Lakes, the mean temperature in winter is 23°F (-5°C), and in summer 72°F (22°C). In the prairies, it gets colder to the north, 0°F or about -18°C. The lower regions may be about 10 degrees warmer in winter and much like the eastern temperate region in summer.

The long north-south prairies make it possible for polar air masses to move south and for subtropical air to move north into Canada. The Pacific mountains keep the polar air mass from reaching the coast, while the waters of Hudson Bay and the Great Lakes act to modify somewhat the climate in their areas. In the Arctic region, in the tundra areas, the average temperature of the warmest month is below 50°F (10°C), while in areas permanently covered with ice and snow, the year-round average is below freezing. In a good deal of the far north, the mean daily temperature in January is some -10° to -20°F (-23° to -29°C) and, in certain areas, colder still.

Precipitation varies greatly across Canada. The Arctic areas receive less than 20 inches (51 centimeters) a year,

mostly as snow, but the winds make it seem as though it is constantly snowing. While precipitation along the Pacific coast may reach nearly 100 inches (254 centimeters) a year, the mean annual rainfall in the lower part of the prairies is only 12 to 16 inches (30 to 40 centimeters). The coastal areas of Newfoundland and Labrador and Nova Scotia are on the damp side, with annual precipitation of around 56 inches (142 centimeters). The St. Lawrence-Ontario heartland annually receives 32 to 48 inches (81 to 122 centimeters) of rain.

The people. Canada's population in 2002 was 31,902,000. This is about 11 percent of the population of the neighboring United States.

Until the 1800s, Canada's population grew quite slowly. It did not pass the 1 million mark until about 1840, and it did not cross the 5 million mark until the last decade of the century. For the past hundred years, its population has risen at a more rapid rate, passing 10 million by 1930.

Approximately two-thirds of Canadians, about 18 million, live in the southern part of the country, within 200 miles (322 kilometers) of the U.S. border. In turn, more than half of these people dwell in the southern parts of Ontario and Quebec. In fact, these two provinces account for about 62 percent of Canada's total population, while another 12 percent live on the west coast in British Columbia.

As the population grew, Canada became more industrialized and more urban. Today nearly 80 percent of the people live in urban areas.

Immigration. Canada has depended to a large extent on immigration for its growth in population. The earliest immigrants were from France, and they established a thriving French colony in eastern Canada before 1750. After the British victory in 1759, a new wave of immigration came from Great Britain.

This wave was soon swelled by Loyalists who left the American colonies during and after the American Revolution.

A new surge came after the War of 1812, with the newcomers mostly from Scotland and Ireland. The great period of immigration, though, began in the latter part of the 19th century, and continued until 1914, when World War I began. More than 3 million persons came, and immigrants from continental Europe made up a much larger proportion of the whole than before. After World War II, in a period of just a dozen years, a million and a half people arrived, about one-third of whom came from Britain. Among European immigrants at the time were many southern Italians.

There is still a steady flow of immigrants, but the countries of origin have changed. Of the 1985 arrivals, for example, 46 percent were from Asia, only 5 percent from Great Britain, and 8 percent from the United States. There has also been a steady crossing and recrossing of the border by Americans and Canadians.

The nation today includes people of many ethnic backgrounds and religious beliefs. The largest ethnic group comprises those originally from the British Isles—45 percent. Those of French descent represent 29 percent of the population. Of the slightly more than 6 million people in this group, all but about 1 million live in the Province of Quebec. The other large groups, in descending order, report as their mother tongues Italian, Chinese, German, Portuguese, Polish, Ukrainian, Spanish, Dutch, Greek, and Punjabi.

Religion. Of Canadians claiming religious affiliation, Roman Catholics are in the majority nationally, with the Anglican Church of Canada having the greatest number of adherents in the Protestant group, and the United Church of Canada next. The Jewish religion follows, with Buddhism a close runner-up.

The Indians. When Europeans first made contact with the Indians of Canada, in the 1500s, there probably were about 220,000 Indians and Inuit. Hardly any of the Indians practiced agriculture, except those living along the St. Lawrence and in what became southern Ontario. Many Indians relied chiefly on hunting and fishing.

Among the tribes were, in the east, the Micmac and, especially, the Huron, who allied themselves with the French. Somewhat farther west were the Ottawa and the Cree, the former around Georgian Bay, the latter farther north. In the interior prairie region were the Ojibwa (or Chippewa), the Nipissing, the Assiniboine, the Blackfoot, the Sioux, the Athabascan, and the Gros Ventre.

Far to the north were smaller tribes such as the Dogrib and the Nahani. On the Pacific coast and its islands were such tribes as the Kwakiutl, whose ceremony of potlatch amounted to seeing who could give the most lavish presents; the Nootka, who carved elaborate totem poles; the Tlingit; and the Haida.

The Indians of Canada warred with the Europeans much less than did their compatriots in the United States. Such clashes as occurred were mostly caused by Indians fighting on the side of the French or the English when those nations fought for control of North America.

The Indians did, however, suffer from the coming of the Europeans. They had little resistance to European diseases, so epidemics such as smallpox wiped out half of the members of the tribes.

Today many of Canada's Indians live on government reserves, of which there are 2,242, totaling about 10,000 square miles (25,900 square kilometers).

The Inuit. Except possibly for the Vikings, the first contact between Inuit and Europeans came in the 1500s, all along the coast of Labrador. (Inuit means "the people," and this is the term now officially used in Canada to designate so-called Eskimos. To the Inuit, the white man is "kabloona.") It was the mid-1700s before there was much further contact, mostly with trading posts along the tree line. Because they were so isolated in the north, the Inuit kept more to their own ways than did the Indians. It was the early 20th century before there were settlements where Inuit could conveniently trade and live something like a modern life.

The Inuit along the coastlines were hunters of seal, whale, and walrus, while those in the interior hunted caribou. Contact with the Europeans brought tuberculosis, and the Inuit had little resistance to it. Today the Inuit are partly integrated into the rest of the economy, as fishermen, fur traders, tour guides, and producers of arts and crafts. Of the 100,000 or so Inuit in the world, more than 25,000 live in Canada—in Labrador, the Mackenzie delta, the mainland coast of Nunavut, and the shores of Hudson and Ungava bays.

An important development for the Inuit occurred when Nunavut, which separated from the Northwest Territories in 1999, joined the Confederation. With most of Canada's Inuit population residing in Nunavut, this territorial change brought with it greater governmental representation.

Culture. In Canadian literature, there are inevitably two traditions: one for the Anglophone, the other for the Francophone group. Canada exhibits quite distinct differences between the two language groups, so that, for example, the theater of Quebec is often very different from the theater in other areas.

Well-known novelists, biographers, and other authors of contemporary books or plays often seek to have their work translated from one language to the other; however, they may gain popular recognition in one language but not succeed in the other.

The federal government has taken a positive role over the years in promoting Canadian culture in both language groups. The federal expenditure on culture in 1990–1991, for example, was nearly $3 million—and provincial expenditure approached $2 million. Canada Council grants, which are federally funded, assist various programs in the arts, as well as individual artists.

Literature. By the first quarter of the 20th century, some Canadian novelists began to reach a wide audience outside their own land. *Anne of Green Gables* and its sequels by Lucy Maud Montgomery, and the Jalna series by Mazo de la Roche, were best-sellers in Britain and the United States. Stephen Leacock was a popular essayist/humorist, and the historical novels of Thomas Costain gained a wide audience at home and abroad. In French, Louis Hémon found an international audience with his *Maria Chapdelaine* (1914).

In more recent years, Canadian authors who have gained international recognition include Margaret Atwood, Morley Callaghan, Matt Cohen, Robertson Davies, Margaret Laurence, Hugh MacLennan, Farley Mowat, Alice Munro, Mordecai Richler, Michael Ondaatje, and Carol Shields for English fiction. In French, the works of Canadians Marie-Claire Blais, Anne Hébert, André Langevin, Roger Lemelin, Gabrielle Roy, Yves Thériault, and Michel Tremblay are also well known.

The arts. Inuit artists are noted for their superb work in bone, stone, and ivory carvings of the arctic animal life around them, as well as ceremonial masks. Indians, especially those on the northwest coast, were also carvers, working in wood. The early French-Canadian artists expressed themselves chiefly in woodcarving, often of a religious nature. In the 1800s Canadian painters turned to landscapes and ordinary life for their themes. Paul Kane, after 1845, travelled in fur-trapping areas to paint Indians. Cornelius Krieghoff brought out the picturesque in French-Canadian life. Somewhat later, Horatio Walker, Emily Carr (in British Columbia), and David Milne carried these themes forward. In the 1920s the Group of Seven, led by Tom Thomson, broke from the more international tradition to emphasize Canada's unique natural features in works of landscape that, like those of Emily Carr, have an almost mystical quality. Other well-known Canadian artists include Indian painters Norval Morrisseau and Daphne Odjig, Jack Shadbolt, Jean-Paul Lemieux, Alfred Pellan, Jean-Paul Riopelle, Ken Danby, James W. Morrice, Paul-Emile Borduas, and Alex Colville.

Education. The development of a nationwide system of education at all levels involved the problems of religious and linguistic minorities, as well as the usual ones of cost. With confederation, education was reserved to the provinces, which meant that in Quebec, education was in effect administered by the Roman Catholic Church. Elsewhere, school systems were secular institutions for the most part. There are now some 6 million Canadian children in primary and secondary schools.

Higher education developed slowly, with church-sponsored schools first, and, by the 20th century, six universities established by the provinces. Beginning in the late 1950s, there was a great increase in government support for higher education, and an even greater surge in the number of students. In Ontario alone, nine universities were founded in ten years.

Today there are 65 public universities in Canada, of which 12 are federated with another university.

Canada's library system has also expanded over the years. There are almost 2,800 libraries of all kinds, of which 778 are public.

THE INUIT PRESERVE many of their traditional ways, sometimes in the shadow of modern technology such as the satellite seen here.

27 North America

MCGILL UNIVERSITY in Montreal, chartered in 1821, is one of 65 public universities in Canada.

labor
US

labour
Brit.

kilometers
US

kilometres
Brit.

Communications. To Canada, the coming of the telegraph, the telephone, radio, and television has been a great boon. The telegraph first reached across the country in 1883, and the first telephone exchange opened in 1878. There are now some 15 million telephones in use, and a microwave network is the backbone of a nationwide telecommunications system.

The federal government organized the Canadian Broadcasting Corporation (CBC) in 1936 for radio broadcasting. The CBC (Radio-Canada is its French-language network) is government-owned but controlled by an independent board. It added television to its radio service in 1952. There are also private English and French networks. About 400 privately owned stations are associated with the CBC, and there are another 600 independent radio and TV outlets.

Economy. Canada's economic history is much like that of the United States, only on a smaller scale and developing somewhat later in time.

Canada's gross national product was $760 billion in 2000, making Canada's per capita income among the ten highest in the world.

Ever since its first furs were shipped out, Canada has been a trading nation. Today Canada's main exports are communications and transportation equipment, food and beverage products (about one-third of which is wheat), lumber, newsprint, wood pulp, natural gas, machinery, crude oil, chemicals, and precious metals.

Canada's major imports include transportation and communications equipment, fabricated materials, raw materials, machinery, miscellaneous equipment, and food products.

Canada's extensive forests were among the first of its resources to be exploited. Nearly 10 million tons of newsprint are now produced annually, and almost 90 percent of it is exported.

In addition to autos and paper, Canada manufactures a variety of products, from iron and steel to refrigerators and washing machines, food and beverage products, rubber goods, textiles and clothing, shoes, railroad and subway cars, ships, and tobacco products.

Labor. In 2001 Canada's labor force totalled 16,689,400 persons, of whom 92.3 percent were employed, with 7.7 percent unemployed nationwide. Of those employed, 53.6 percent were men and 46.4 percent were women.

Agriculture is one of the vital parts of the Canadian economy. Canada is a leading world exporter of grains, exporting almost half of the cereal grains grown. Livestock, its products, and dairy products combined are the largest dollar element in agriculture. Wheat is by far the most valuable crop, followed by barley, rapeseed, and vegetables. Wheat is produced at an annual rate of about 900 million bushels.

Commercial fishing, which was once a great economic asset, is no longer so important. Cod and lobster are the principal sea crops in the Atlantic and salmon the main catch off the Pacific coast.

Transportation. Canada's first transcontinental line, the Canadian Pacific Railway, was built between 1880 and 1885. It ran for 2,881 miles (4,636 kilometers) from Montreal to the Pacific coast, and soon acquired 500 miles (805 kilometers) of track to carry it from Montreal to St. John, New Brunswick.

By 1915 two more cross-country railroads had been built, the National Transcontinental and the Canadian National Railway. The latter, with many branches, had 9,362 miles (15,063 kilometers) of track. By this time Canada's total railroad system had expanded to 37,400 miles (60,177 kilometers). The new lines, however, were not successful financially. The government took over and combined the private lines into the Canadian National Railway. Canada's rail trackage reached its peak of 42,600 miles (68,543 kilometers) in 1930.

Canada's most notable achievement in highway construction has been the building of the Trans-Canada Highway, which was completed in 1962. Extending approximately 4,800 miles (7,723 kilometers), it is the longest national highway in the world. Including ferry links on both coasts, it runs from St. John's, Newfoundland and Labrador, to Victoria, British Columbia.

TRANSPORTATION was greatly enhanced in Canada with the construction of the Canadian Pacific Railway, the National Transcontinental, and the Canadian National Railway.

Canadian History

The first human beings to inhabit what is now Canada were the ancestors of the present-day Indians and Inuit. These ancient peoples began arriving by way of northeastern Asia and Alaska nearly 50,000 years ago.

Over the centuries, some of these aborigines, moving south and east, spread themselves sparsely over the huge expanse of northern North America. These people came to constitute the tribes that the Europeans called Indians. The tribes developed distinctive languages, cultures, and ways of making a living.

The ways of life of these people depended largely on the natural resources available to them. Most of the Indians lived by hunting and fishing along the seacoasts and the river valleys. Animals, birds, and fish were plentiful, but the Indians had only crude tools and weapons for catching them. The great forests provided wood for fuel and housing, while animals provided skins for clothing and shelter. The caribou, a large animal that existed in enormous herds, was the chief prize of the hunt for both the Indians and the Inuit.

There was little agriculture, although it was practiced to some extent in the warmer region of southern Ontario and in the valley of the St. Lawrence River. For transportation, the Indian had only feet for walking or the light and reliable canoe. There was a continuing struggle to find enough food to survive, and when different tribes met while on hunting expeditions, armed conflict over choice areas sometimes resulted.

The far northern areas, mostly treeless tundra, were occupied by the Inuit. As was previously stated, *Inuit* means people, or human beings in their own language, and is used today instead of the old term *Eskimos,* a pejorative word of Cree origin that means "eaters of raw meat." The Inuit depend on fish, waterfowl, sea mammals, and the few land animals of the far north, such as bears and caribou, for food and for skins to be used for clothing and shelter. Some, but not all, Inuit live in igloos, domed houses made of snow or ice. The total aboriginal population—Indians and Inuit—was probably only about 220,000 when the Europeans arrived.

The term *Canada* was not applied to any part of the land until it appeared in an account by Jacques Cartier (1491–1557) of his voyage of exploration in 1535. It is a form of a Huron-Iroquois word for village or settlement.

Vikings. It has been claimed that Irish monks, sailing by way of Iceland, settled on Cape Breton Island, northeast of Nova Scotia, about A.D. 875. Legend has it that they were absorbed by the native population, and the settlement died out.

The first European persons of whom it can be said with certainty that they landed on the North American continent were the Vikings, the Scandinavian warriors and traders who were active from the ninth to the twelfth centuries. They were the best shipbuilders and sailors of the time. Eric the Red (fl. 980–1000), a Norwegian explorer who named and settled Greenland, claimed he landed on what is now Baffin Island in 982.

According to the Icelandic sagas, Bjarni Herjulfsson sailed, around 986, along the coast from Newfoundland to Labrador. It was Leif Ericson (fl. c 1000), however, the son of Eric the Red, who sailed to this same region and landed there about 1001. He probably first touched the mainland on the coast of Labrador near Belle Isle. The best evidence indicates that the Vikings spent the winter in a settlement they built at l'Anse aux Meadows on the northern coast of Newfoundland. The remains of two large houses and of primitive ironworks have been uncovered there.

Thorwald Ericson, brother of Leif, spent two winters in Newfoundland, between 1005 and 1008, and was killed there. Beginning about 1010 or 1012, Thorfinn Karlsefni, who married Thorwald's widow, is said to have spent three winters in Newfoundland, but his settlement was abandoned. Thus, the Vikings never established a permanent settlement, and knowledge of the European discovery of the continent was lost for nearly 500 years.

The Northwest Passage. It was almost the end of the 15th century before Europeans returned to Canada. When they did, they were not looking for it but, rather, for a way around it, through the fabled Northwest Passage, to the riches of the Orient and the spice trade. Later, these explorers also nursed the hope that in the interior of North America they would find kingdoms as rich as those the Spaniards were conquering in Mexico and Peru.

The first of the explorers who tried to bypass the northern part of the western hemisphere was John Cabot (1450–1498). An Italian born in Genoa who anglicized his name, Cabot sailed for America under the auspices of Henry VII, king of England. On June 24, 1497, he landed on either the southwest corner of Newfoundland or the northern tip of Cape Breton Island. He took possession of the land in the name of the king; England's first claim to Canada stemmed from this action.

On his return, Cabot, who was sure he had reached Asia, reported that he had sighted fish in great numbers. By the next year English fishermen began to work the area around Newfoundland. They were soon joined by Portuguese, French, and Spanish fishing boats.

Cabot made another voyage, in 1498, this time with five ships. The expedition disappeared, and presumably all were lost. Cabot's son Sebastian (1476?–1557) led a voyage in 1509, also seeking the

Northwest Passage. Whether he discovered Hudson Strait and saw part of Hudson Bay, as some have claimed, is disputable.

Following the early explorations of the Vikings, the first Europeans to establish a colony were the Portuguese, in 1521. Drawn by cod fishing, João Alvarez Fagundes with two ships transported Portuguese families to what is believed to have been Cape Breton Island, where a settlement was established. This enterprise was abandoned for unknown reasons. The significance of the Portuguese effort, however, lies in the excellent work of their cartographers in mapping Nova Scotia and the southern shore of Newfoundland. France's claim to Canada began with the voyages of Jacques Cartier, who was sent out by King Francis I of France in 1534. He saw the Labrador coast, found Prince Edward Island and the Magdalen

MUCH OF THE ECONOMIC MOTIVE behind the efforts to establish settlements in Canada in the 16th century was the desire to trade with the Indians for furs.

SHAMEN OF THE INUIT wore masks such as this one in ceremonies to manipulate the supernatural world or to cure illness.

27 North America

HUDSON'S BAY COMPANY was founded in London in 1670 to establish a fur trade in what is now the Hudson Bay region of Canada. It still ranks today as the world's largest fur-trading firm.

SAMUEL DE CHAMPLAIN'S 1632 MAP of Canada was the most comprehensive produced up to that time. It shows his explorations of the St. Lawrence River basin between 1603 and 1629.

Islands, explored the Gulf of St. Lawrence, and landed on the Gaspé peninsula to take possession for France on July 24 in the presence of a band of Indians.

When Cartier returned to France, he reported that in the New Brunswick region and on the Gaspé peninsula there was fertile soil as well as a suitable climate for agriculture. Until then the region had been thought useful only for the fisheries off Newfoundland and Labrador. The French king sent Cartier back to America.

On this second voyage, in 1535, Cartier discovered the St. Lawrence River and sailed up it to the Indian village of Stadacona, the site of present-day Quebec City. Continuing on, he reached another village, Hochelaga, now the site of Montreal. Indians he met told him of three "kingdoms" farther west. Cartier and his men wintered near Hochelaga and returned to France the next spring. On the return voyage, Cartier determined that Newfoundland was an island. He described this voyage in *Brief Récit et succincte narration* (1545). On Cartier's third and final voyage, in 1541, he went up the St. Lawrence to the Lachine Rapids, built a fort, and wintered at Cap Rouge.

Jean François de la Rocque, sieur de Roberval (c 1500–1561), in April, 1542, sailed for North America with three ships and colonists who planned to found

France's first settlement in Canada. Meanwhile, tired of waiting for Roberval, Cartier started his return voyage to France and met Roberval in Newfoundland. Cartier refused to remain in Canada, having failed to find the Northwest Passage or the riches of the Far East. He had, however, made important geographical discoveries, and they were the basis of French claims to the St. Lawrence River region. At the same time, relationships with the Indians of the region had become strained, a situation that would have ominous consequences. Roberval established his colony near Stadacona, but it lasted only about a year before the colonists returned to France.

The French continued to try—five times in all—to establish settlements during the rest of the century. The economic motive was the discovery of excellent furs, and French merchants wanting to go beyond the confines of an internal supply in Europe jumped at this opportunity.

It was not until the early 17th century that France was able to establish permanent colonies in Canada. This was accomplished under the leadership of Samuel de Champlain (1567–1635), a veteran soldier as well as a naval commander and cartographer. He visited Canada in 1603 and returned the next year as joint leader of an expedition with Pierre du Gua, sieur de Monts

(1558–1630), a wealthy Huguenot. They founded a colony on Saint Croix Island (now a U.S. national monument) off the coast of Maine. In 1605 they moved the colony across the Bay of Fundy to found Port Royal (now Annapolis Royal, Nova Scotia). Port Royal was abandoned for a while in 1607, but in 1608 Champlain set up a fur-trading post at Quebec, and this became the first permanent establishment of France in Canada.

Champlain and the men he sent out began to learn much more about the interior of Canada. For example, Champlain explored the New England coast as far south as Martha's Vineyard. He discovered Lake Champlain in the spring of 1609. There, with French troops and Indian allies, he fought a battle with some Iroquois. The guns of the French easily routed the Iroquois. The following year, Champlain wiped out another Iroquois band near the mouth of the Richelieu River. The military alliances formed with the Algonquins of the Ottawa River, the Montagnais of the St. Lawrence River, and the Hurons, together with these French military victories, were the basis of the long feud between the Iroquois and the French.

In 1615 Champlain, with a party of Hurons, made an expedition to Georgian Bay on Lake Huron. He returned southeastward by way of Lake Ontario. Another time, Champlain accompanied a Huron war party on a raid on an Onondaga village in present-day New York State. He was wounded and had to spend the winter in an Indian village. This ended his activities as an explorer, but in 1634 he sent Jean Nicollet de Belleborne (c 1598–1642) west, and it was he who explored Lake Michigan and went as far as Wisconsin. This was another aspect of the search for an easy route to Asia, but it also helped develop the fur trade, the profits from which were needed to enable exploration to continue.

Champlain had brought Christian missionaries to Canada in 1615. They were four members of the Récollet branch of the Franciscan Order. Inspired by the strong force of the French Counter Reformation in 1639, the Society of Our Lady of Montreal was founded for the conversion of the "savages." With the help of the Jesuits already established at Quebec, they set up a religious settlement on the island of Montreal. The Jesuits had already set up the first college in North America in Quebec in 1635 and went on to become leaders in the work of converting the Indians to Christianity; this lasted until the fall of New France in 1763.

In 1629, when the British seized Quebec, Champlain was captured along with the city. He was taken to England, where he was held for four years. While there he prepared a third edition of his *Voyages de la Nouvelle France* (1632). He had introduced scientific cartography to Canada in 1603 and his map of 1632 was the most comprehensive produced up to that time.

New France

Formal government came to Canada, on October 8, 1612, when Louis XIII, king of France, appointed his nephew Louis de Bourbon, comte de Soissons, governor and lieutenant general of New France. New France consisted at that time of fur traders, trappers, and Catholic missionaries operating along the St. Lawrence River. Louis de Bourbon died on November 12, 1612, before he could take advantage of the trading monopoly and seigniorial rights that also had been granted to him.

Champlain had already been appointed deputy commander and so in effect became the first governor of New France. From 1633 until his death in Quebec City on December 25, 1635, Champlain held the title of commandant and acted as the French king's viceroy in New France.

Many aspects of French law and government were transferred to New France. For example, on February 4, 1623, when Louis Hébert was granted a fief at Sault-au-Matelot, a system akin to feudalism was introduced in the New World. Later, especially after 1627, many such fiefs were granted in order to stimulate settlement of New France. Each seigneur brought in colonists at his own expense. By 1760 there were about 250 such landholdings, amounting to nearly 8 million acres (3.2 million hectares). Most of them were on the St. Lawrence River, extending inland as long narrow strips. Since seigneurs were not actually liege lords of the king, this system was not strictly feudal; nevertheless, these landholders had considerable authority over the lives of their tenants.

In November 1635, the French set up a separate government for Acadia (which today includes part of southeastern Quebec, New Brunswick, Nova Scotia, and Prince Edward Island). Charles de Menou, sieur d'Aulnay-Charisnay, and Charles de Saint-Étienne de la Tour were named joint governors of Acadia. They quarreled to such an extent that civil war broke out, resulting in the recall of la Tour, who was reinstated on February 25, 1651, following de Menou's accidental death by drowning in May 1650.

Much of the power of government was in the hands of those who had been granted monopolistic trading privileges, especially the Company of New France, or One Hundred Associates. It was established in 1627 by Cardinal Richelieu, Louis XIII's chief minister, and granted royal approval on May 6, 1628. This group, which consisted mostly of wealthy nobles, proved incapable of maintaining control over the Iroquois, whose attacks had so destabilized the colony that farms had been abandoned and people were under a constant state of siege. As a result, Louis XIV decreed in May 1663 that New France was henceforth to be a royal province and, by 1674, it would no longer be the property of a trading company, subject to purely commercial concerns. Authority then was vested in the Sovereign Council (after 1703 called the Superior Council). It consisted of a governor, who was the military and political chief and who held the most power; an intendant, responsible for administration and finance; and the bishop of Quebec, the spiritual leader.

The fur trade. In the early 1600s, the French controlled the best routes for trading with the Indians in the interior. It was an especially favorable time for fur trading because of the style then current in Europe for felt hats. Beaver skins, which were plentiful in Canada, provided the best fur.

The trappers, whether European or Indian, spent the winter at their work. In the spring, in Indian canoes, they came east to trade the furs for knives, beads, cloth, firearms, liquor, and other valuable merchandise.

There were three key points for the fur trade along the St. Lawrence River. One was at the mouth of the Saguenay River. Tadoussac was founded there in 1600 by Pierre Chauvin, who built Canada's first trading post, in the form of a fortified stone house (now reconstructed). The other two posts were at Trois-Rivières, Canada's second oldest city (after Quebec), founded in 1634, and on the site of Montreal, established in 1642.

The French fur trade was officially a monopoly of the king, or his viceroy in Canada, or other individuals and groups chartered by the king. A large number of young Frenchmen defied the monopoly laws and took to the fur trade on their own account. They journeyed to the interior, lived like the Indians, and married Indian women. After 1649, when the Huron were badly defeated by the Iroquois, these *coureurs de bois*—runners of the woods—took the place of the Indians as middlemen to deal with the tribes farther west. The descendants of these men and women, called Métis (mixed blood), later provided a large part of the fur trade's personnel.

As the French fur trade prospered, the competition grew. To the south of the French trade routes, Iroquois raided Huron canoes carrying furs. The Dutch and then the English began to give the French strong competition.

The fur trade rivalry also brought Indian tribes into conflict with each other. The Huron, as allies of the French, were a steady source of supply. The Iroquois, with their depleted fur reserves and with the support of the English, who supplied them with guns, moved to seize the fur trade from the Huron. At one point, they blocked the Richelieu River and made the Ottawa River unsafe for Huron trappers.

One center of Indian conflict, which also involved French missionaries, was Huronia, a region dominated by the Huron, which lay in southern Ontario. It was a fertile area about 40 miles (64 kilometers) long and 20 miles (32 kilometers) wide. In 1616 Champlain estimated that 30,000 Huron lived in the various towns and villages there. The Récollet fathers began their missionary work in Huronia in 1615. Later they were assisted by Jesuits. The Iroquois determined to exterminate the Huron in the region and their attacks reached a climax from 1648 to 1649. In the attacks, three Jesuit fathers were killed and the Huron almost wiped out. Between the Iroquois

TRAPPERS, primarily Indians, spent the winter accumulating furs to trade with the French.

attacks and epidemics of smallpox and influenza, only a few hundred survived in Huronia. The Iroquois then went on to destroy their other rivals, the Petun, the Neutral, and the Erie nations. By 1660, Iroquois war parties were striking farms and settlements all over New France.

In the face of the Iroquois threat to New France, Louis XIV moved decisively. For the first time, the resources of the French state's military might were employed when the Carignan-Salières regiment, a battle-hardened unit, was dispatched to Canada. In 1666, the Marquis Prouville de Tracy led his troops to victory over the Iroquois, destroying their villages and crops. The Mohawks and other Iroquois tribes made peace with the French in the next year.

The French answered this competition from the English by making more of an effort to explore the continent, by building trading and military posts, and by claiming large areas for the French king. Fort Frontenac (now Kingston) was founded in 1673 to control the point where Lake Ontario flows into the St. Lawrence. Sieur de la Salle (1643–1687), commandant of Frontenac, established a fort at the mouth of the Niagara River six years later. Among his explorations was the trip that took him to the mouth of the Mississippi River in 1682. Louis Hennepin (1640–1701?), Louis Joliet (1645–1700), and Jacques Marquette (1637–1675) also explored the western Great Lakes and the routes to the south.

French against English. Until the early 1600s, the French and English in America, while they competed for the fur trade and made conflicting territorial claims, had not clashed directly. The French did little to bring in settlers to populate Canada and little to encourage

center
US

centre
Brit.

kilometers
US

kilometres
Brit.

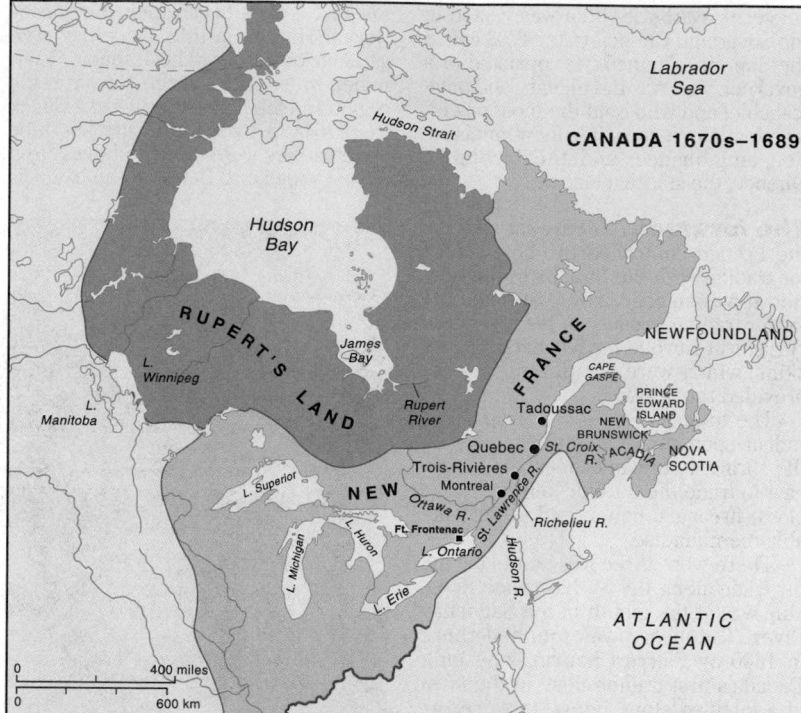

agriculture. The English, on the other hand, were beginning to settle the Atlantic seaboard south of Canada in growing numbers.

France and Britain were also involved in Europe, in the perpetual rivalries of the European nations. In 1621 King James I, disregarding the French claim, granted to a Scotsman—William Alexander, later the Earl of Stirling—the whole of the region from Cape Gaspé to the St. Croix River. Following the outbreak of war between England and France in 1627, an expedition organized by London merchants was launched against Canada. Led by the Kirke brothers, the English force took Quebec in 1629 after the war had ended. As a result, both Quebec and Acadia were returned to the French in the Treaty of Saint-Germain-en-Laye in 1632.

Champlain returned to Quebec in 1633 and would die there in 1635. In over 25 years, his emphasis on settlement had transformed a trading post into a Canadian colony of France and signaled a dramatic change in French involvement in Canada.

During this period, the French did make an attempt to strengthen New France, as they called their Canadian lands. The fur monopoly was taken away from the viceroy and in 1627 it was given to the Company of New France, or One Hundred Associates. They not only took over the monopoly but also were to arrange for 4,000 immigrants to come to Canada. The company granted large estates to men who agreed to bring over these settlers, but most of them did far less than they were supposed to do. By 1663 the population of New France was only about 2,500. Many of the French troops sent over in 1665 remained as settlers.

Such success as the new settlers had was due largely to two energetic men. One was Count Louis de Frontenac (1620–1698), who was governor from 1672 to 1682 and again from 1689 to his death. Frontenac was both an able and a controversial character. He quarreled with the Jesuits and with the intendant, but he established posts and forts in new French territory. By his efforts, he enabled France to withstand English pressure on the colony at a difficult time.

Frontenac attempted to make New France more independent of King Louis XIV and his advisers, but he was always overruled. As a result of the controversies surrounding him, he was recalled in 1682. When his successors were unable to solve the colony's problems, and the Iroquois became more troublesome, he was sent back to New France in 1689 to serve as governor once more.

The other leader, Jean Baptiste Talon (1625?–1694), served as intendant from 1665 to 1668 and 1670 to 1672. Talon sent out prospectors and explorers, but he also encouraged other enterprises.

The most important English explorer of northern North America was Henry Hudson (fl. 1607–1611). His voyages were attempts to find either the Northeast or the Northwest Passage. His first voyage was undertaken in 1607 for the English Muscovy Company, his second in 1608. Both of these attempts to sail east around northern Europe failed in their objective. In 1609 Hudson, making a voyage for the Dutch East India Company, discovered the Hudson River in New York State. His fourth and final voyage, in 1610, was financed by British adventurers. Entering Hudson Strait, between Greenland and Labrador, he discovered Hudson Bay. His ship then went down the east coast of the bay to

James Bay at the mouth of the Rupert River. After wintering there, Hudson wanted to continue the voyage in the spring, certain that he had found the passage to Asia. The crew mutinied, however, seized Hudson and his young son, John, and set them adrift in a small boat with six members of the crew, five of whom were suffering from scurvy. They were never seen again.

Hudson's explorations led to the chartering on May 2, 1670, by Charles II, king of England, of the Hudson's Bay Company. The charter granted to a group of courtiers and merchants all areas drained by the many rivers flowing into Hudson Bay. The company was given the right to trade, settle, and search for the Northwest Passage. The grant was known as Rupert's Land, for the leader of the company, Prince Rupert, who had been a capable general for his uncle, Charles I, in the English Civil War.

Though high-ranking Englishmen were governors of the Hudson's Bay Company, they, like Rupert, never went to Canada. James, duke of York, brother of Charles II, was elected to the post on January 3, 1683, but he resigned on February 6, 1685, when he was installed as James II. York was succeeded on April 2 by John Churchill, later the first duke of Marlborough. Rupert's Land was governed as a commercial company under the control of the governors of the Hudson's Bay Company until 1869.

The English had been encouraged in their enterprise by information they had obtained from two defecting French traders and explorers, Médard Chouat, sieur de Groseilliers (1618–1696?), and Pierre-Esprit Radisson (1640–1710). These Frenchmen believed it would be cheaper and faster to bring in supplies by ship to Hudson Bay and to take furs out by sending these goods down the rivers to the bay rather than via the Great Lakes-St. Lawrence route. They proved their point in 1668 by establishing a post on Hudson Bay and taking a valuable cargo to England. By 1685 the company had built four other posts at the mouths of rivers on Hudson and James bays. The French tried to cut into this operation by intercepting the Indian traders as they went down the rivers to the bay. One peaceful occasion was the signing on November 19, 1686, of the Treaty of Neutrality, which provided for a commission to settle the boundaries of New France and Rupert's Land, as all of western Canada was then known.

A century of wars. The competition between England and France for land, fur, fish, and other commerce now moved to the battlefield. In 1689 there began the first of four wars that ended nearly a century later with the complete defeat of France. In Canada they are known separately as King William's War, Queen Anne's War, King George's War, and the Seven Years' War. In the United States they are known collectively as the French and Indian Wars (1689–1763). They were, in reality, a playing out in the western hemisphere of a worldwide struggle for empire involving opposing coalitions of European nations. In European history the four wars are known as the War of the Grand Alliance, the War of the Spanish Succession, the War of the Austrian Succession, and the Seven Years' War. What the nations agreed on at the end of each war depended more on what had happened in Europe than in North America.

Even before King William's War began in 1689, the French had raided English shipping in Hudson Bay. In 1690 they attacked some of the Hudson's Bay Company posts. For several years posts were captured and recaptured. In 1690 the Count de Frontenac directed raids by the French and their Indian allies on English settlements in Maine, New Hampshire, and New York.

Reacting to these attacks, a force of New England sailors and militiamen, on seven ships, and under the command of Sir William Phipps (1651–1695), a native of Maine, sailed for Port Royal, Nova Scotia, in 1690. The fort was in no shape to defend itself and surrendered. In August Phipps headed a second expedition from Boston, consisting of 31 ships and about 14,000 men. Its objective was to capture Quebec City. Bad weather, fever, and a strong defense left by Frontenac forced Phipps to abandon the siege. On October 9 he gave up and sailed for home. The war ended in 1697 with each side giving back whatever territory or fort it had taken.

Queen Anne's War (1702–1713) was almost as indecisive in North America. Northern English settlements were raided again and New Englanders did the same to settlements in Acadia. In 1708 the French captured St. John's, Newfoundland. After failing twice, New Englanders captured Port Royal in 1710. This time the colonial expedition was led by Francis Nicholson (1655–1728), formerly a British army colonel and colonial administrator. His force was a combination of American and English troops. In 1711 Nicholson also led New England troops and Iroquois warriors in an expedition against Montreal; but, attacked by smallpox, they were forced to return without having made contact.

In Europe, the French lost badly. The Treaty of Utrecht in 1713 put an end to French expansion and indicated the growing power of England. In America, France gave up claims to Hudson Bay, Newfoundland, and most of Acadia.

These losses staggered New France. The immense fur-producing country around Hudson Bay was gone, and the English now had access to the Great Lakes, raising the threat of cutting off the route from Quebec to Louisiana. The loss of Acadia and Newfoundland meant that French control of the Gulf of St. Lawrence and the Atlantic coast was now also threatened.

After two decades of peace, King George's War broke out in 1744; it lasted until 1748. French troops in 1744 failed to retake Port Royal (now named

Annapolis Royal), but British troops the next year successfully assaulted the fortress of Louisbourg on Cape Breton Island. On this expedition the land forces were commanded by Sir William Pepperell (1696–1759), who was an American colonial military leader. The accompanying British fleet was commanded by Sir Peter Warren (1703–1752). The next year a French attempt to retake Louisbourg failed. At the end of the war, Louisbourg, Cape Breton Island, and Prince Edward Island were restored to France.

The Seven Years' War, the decisive conflict for control of North America, began in 1754. The objective of William Pitt (1759–1806), the British prime minister, was to shift the emphasis of the war effort from Europe to the defeat and conquest of the French Empire—and in particular, New France, whose ability to make war swiftly on the richer British colonies marked it as a menace to the British Empire. The campaign began badly for the British. The French routed them at Fort Duquesne (Pittsburgh, Pennsylvania) in 1755. This influenced the Indians of the Northwest to join the French side and left the English frontier settlements of Pennsylvania, Maryland, and Virginia open to attack.

In Acadia, which had a large French population, the British demanded in 1755 that the Acadians swear allegiance to Great Britain. They refused, although they wished to remain neutral in the conflict. In August the British began rounding up Acadians preparatory to deporting them. There was considerable delay and confusion and some families were separated. The British distributed these exiles among the English colonies along the Atlantic coast, and even in the

Caribbean and England. Some ended up in Louisiana, where their descendants, known as Cajuns, still retain a separate culture. Henry Wadsworth Longfellow's poem *Evangeline* (1847) tells of the expulsion in terms of two separated lovers. In all, between 6,000 and 10,000 Acadians were exiled.

In the early part of the war, the French under the leadership of Louis Joseph de Montcalm (1712–1759), a veteran of the War of the Polish Succession, took the initiative and gained some victories. In 1756 French forces captured Fort Oswego, on Lake Ontario, which the British had built in 1727, and destroyed it.

The following year British troops set out to capture Louisbourg. However, they were unable to rendezvous with the supporting fleet because of bad weather. This, combined with the French massing of strong reinforcements at the fort, defeated the plan. Montcalm won another victory for the French when in 1757 he attacked Fort William Henry on Lake George in New York; the fort surrendered after six days of bombardment. Unfortunately, the Indian allies of the French massacred the British prisoners in spite of Montcalm's attempts to control them.

France's fortunes began to decline in 1758 as the British government increased its military strength in America. Although British forces failed in an attempt to capture Fort Carillon (Ticonderoga) in New York, they reduced Louisbourg after a siege of seven weeks. Louisbourg was finally taken by an amphibious assault while a fleet prevented the French from reinforcing the stronghold. Now the French had lost all control of the gulf and Atlantic coast.

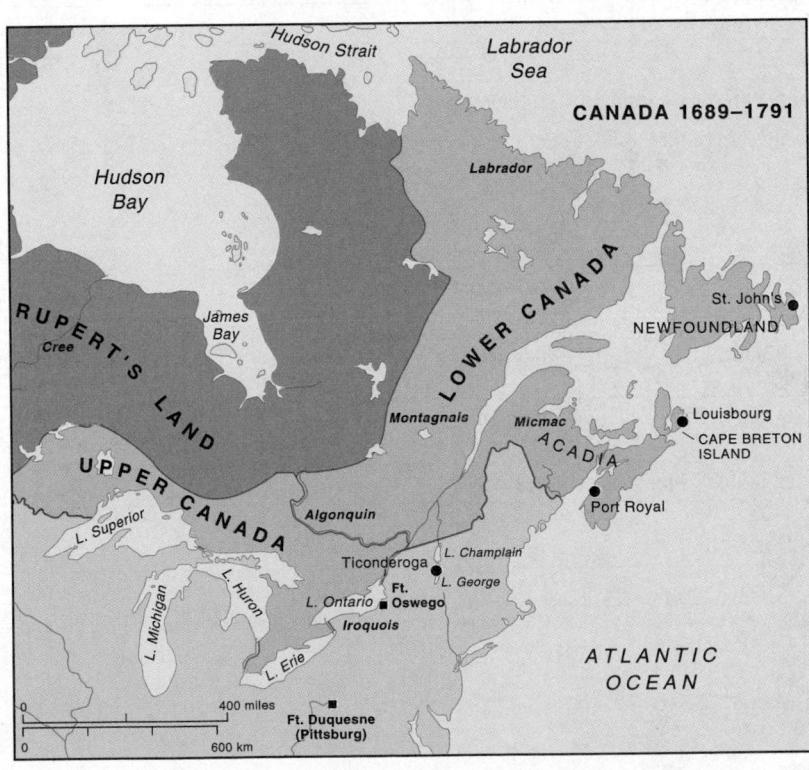

CANADA 1689–1791

Governors and Administrators of New France 1612–1760

The intendant was the administrative officer in charge of commerce, finance, and police in New France. His duties were not clearly defined, so he and the governor often clashed over their jurisdictions.

GOVERNOR OR ADMINISTRATOR	TITLE	SERVED	INTENDANT	SERVED
Samuel de Champlain[1]	Lieutenant to Lieutenants General de Monts and Soissons; Lieutenant to Viceroys Condé Montmorency, Ventadour; Commandant Commander in New France	1612–1629 1633–1635		
Marc-Antoine Bras-de-Fer de Chateaufort	Administrator	1635–1636		
Charles Jacques Huault de Montmagny	Governor	1636–1648		
Louis d'Ailleboust de Coulonge et d'Argentenay	Governor	1648–1651		
Jean de Lauzon	Governor	1651–1656		
Charles de Lauzon	Administrator	1656–1657		
Louis d'Ailleboust de Coulonge et d'Argentenay	Administrator	1657–1658		
Pierre de Voyer d'Argenson	Governor	1658–1661		
Augustin de Saffray de Mezy	Governor	1663–1665	Louis Robert[4]	1663–1665
Jacques Le Neuf de La Potherie	Adminstrator	1665	Jean Baptiste Talon	1665–1668
Daniel de Remy de Courcelle[2]	Governor	1665–1672	Claude de Bouteroue	1668–1670
			Jean Baptiste Talon	1670–1672
Louis de Buade, Comte de Frontenac	Governor	1672–1682	Jacques Duchesneau	1675–1682
Joseph-Antoine Le Febvre de La Barre	Governor	1682–1685	Jacques de Meulles	1682–1686
Jacques-Rene de Brisay, Marquis de Denonville	Governor	1685–1689	Jean Bochart de Champigny	1686–1702
Louis de Buade, Comte de Frontenac	Governor	1689–1698		
Louis-Hector de Callieres	Administrator and Governor	1698–1703	Francois de Beauharnois	1702–1705
Phillippe de Rigaud, Marquis de Vaudreuil	Governor	1703–1725	Jacques Raudot	1705–1710
Claude de Ramezay	Administrator[3]	1714–1716	Michel Begon[5]	1710–1726
Charles Le Moyne, 1st Baron de Longueuil	Administrator	1725–1726		
Charles, Marquis de Beauharnois	Governor	1726–1747	Claude-Thomas Dupuy	1726–1728
			François Clairambault d'Aigremont[6]	1728–1729
			Giles Hocquart	1729–1748
Roland-Michel Barrin, Marquis de La Galissonière	Provisional Governor	1747–1749	Francois Bigot	1748–1760
Jacques-Pierre de Taffanel, Marquis de La Jonquière	Governor	1749–1752		
Charles Le Moyne, 2nd Baron de Longueuil	Administrator	1752		
Ange, Marquis Duquesne de Menneville	Governor	1752–1755		
Pierre de Rigaud, Marquis de Vaudreuil-Cavagnial	Governor	1755–1760		

THE YORK FACTORY TRADING POST on the Hayes River in Manitoba can still be visited.

[1] Quebec was in English hands from July 19, 1629, to July 13, 1632.
[2] From 1666 to 1667, Marquis Prouville de Tracy as Lieutenant General of French America (New France and the West Indies) held supreme command and was above Governor Courcelle.
[3] While Vaudreuil was in France.
[4] Robert never went to New France.
[5] Served as substitute Intendant, 1724–1725.
[6] Served as interim Intendant.

The British were under the command of Lord Jeffrey Amherst (1717–1797), who became after his victory the supreme commander of British forces in America.

While the French defeated a British force under James Grant, near Fort Duquesne in the Ohio valley, the English took Fort Frontenac on the northeast shore of Lake Ontario, thus seizing the gateway to the St. Lawrence River.

The year 1759 was even more disastrous for France. In July Fort Niagara, on the south shore of Lake Ontario at the mouth of the Niagara River, was captured by a force led by Sir William Johnson (1715–1774). At the same time, the French withdrew from Lake George and Lake Champlain, destroying Fort Carillon and Fort Saint-Frédéric (Crown Point). The French had previously retreated from Fort Duquesne in the late fall of 1758.

The military climax to a century of struggle between France and England for control of northern North America came in September 1759, with the fall of Quebec City. The British campaign to take this vital stronghold began with a naval blockade that closed the St. Lawrence River both above and below the city. In June, 9,000 British troops landed opposite Quebec. They were commanded by James Wolfe (1727–1759), a young officer who had been second in command at Louisbourg's capture. Montcalm meanwhile had gathered a force of 10,000 to defend Quebec.

Wolfe's forces poured a heavy bombardment into the city, but the general could at first find no way to assault the French forces. At last his troops reached the Plains of Abraham, outside the walls of the city under cover of darkness on September 12. The next day Montcalm decided to risk a battle. A French attack was quickly repulsed and the British were victorious within 15 minutes. In the battle, however, both commanders were mortally wounded. Quebec was forced to surrender on September 18.

In 1760 the French made a futile attempt to retake Quebec, but they had to retreat to Montreal. In July the French fleet in the St. Lawrence was destroyed and on September 8, 1760, Montreal surrendered. After the final defeat of French forces in Newfoundland in 1762, the power of France in the New World was ended.

This defeat was acknowledged in the Treaty of Paris of 1763. France gave up Canada and ceded western Louisiana to Spain, its ally, to compensate for Florida, which Spain handed over to England. Besides keeping the islands of St. Pierre and Miquelon, south of Newfoundland, France recovered Guadeloupe and Martinique in the West Indies. France ceded Grenada and the Grenadines to Great Britain.

Other terms agreed on between France, Spain, and England, involving other parts of the continent and other parts of the world, showed England to be the leading empire and sea power. France had been too concerned with European wars and too intent on keeping Canada as an enterprise devoted to one economy—the fur trade—to build up a strong colony. Canada's population in 1763 was still only a little more than 60,000.

The government of England now had to decide on important matters of policy affecting Canada. Most of the inhabitants were defeated enemies who spoke a different language and who were French Catholics rather than English Protestants.

British North America

A measure of self-government first came to Canada in 1758 when, on October 2, a legislative assembly met in Halifax as part of the government of Nova Scotia. Its members were popularly elected by property owners. The government also consisted of a governor, who served as the bridge between the British Parliament—the ultimate authority—and the interests of the local population, and a council nominated by the governor, who shared judicial and administrative duties with them. In 1773 Prince Edward Island was granted a similar kind of limited representative government.

On September 8, 1760, after the French surrendered Montreal to British forces, Jeffrey Amherst, the British commander, was appointed governor-general of British North America. Canada was put under a military government reporting to Amherst in New York City. This military government consisted of three commands. Quebec, which had been formed into a British colony on September 3, 1759, was ruled by Brigadier James Murray, who was appointed October 23, 1759. Brigadier Thomas Gage commanded in Montreal, and Colonel Ralph Burton in Trois Rivières, both having been appointed September 22, 1760. After Amherst returned to England in 1763, civil government was again established in Canada under Murray, who was appointed governor on August 10, 1764.

Further changes in government came after the Treaty of Paris of 1763. A British royal proclamation of October 7, 1763, set the boundaries of Quebec and established a governmental system. Quebec now consisted, approximately, of the valley of the St. Lawrence River from Nova Scotia on the east to Lake Nippissing in the west.

A governor appointed by the king ruled Quebec. A council and a general assembly advised him, but only he had the power to summon the assembly. At this time Prince Edward Island and Cape Breton Island were made part of Nova Scotia, and Labrador was annexed to Newfoundland. On June 28, 1769, however, Prince Edward Island again became a separate colony.

Nova Scotia continued to have its own government and royal governor until the unification of Canada in 1867. New Brunswick was separated from Nova Scotia on August 16, 1784, and had its own assembly together with a governor and nominated council until unification in 1867. Cape Breton Island was separated from Nova Scotia in 1764 and had its own government until October 9, 1820, when it was once more attached to Nova Scotia. Prince Edward Island joined Canada in 1873, six years after confederation. By 1867 most of what now constitutes eastern and central Canada had enjoyed some form of representative government for at least 20 years.

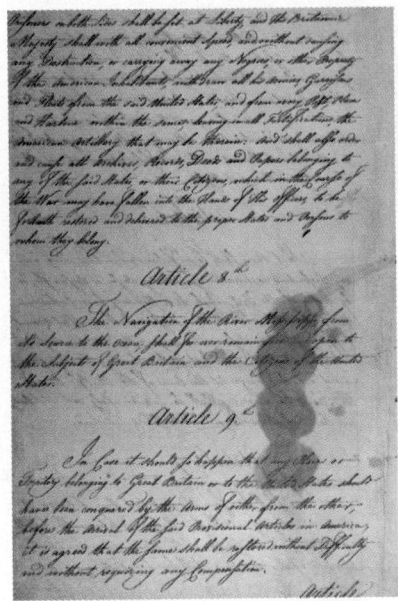

BY THE TREATY OF PARIS, France gave up Canada and ceded western Louisiana to its ally, Spain, to compensate for Florida, which Spain handed over to England.

THE STRUGGLE between the French and British for control of Canada was mounted at such forts as this in Louisbourg, Nova Scotia.

A REENACTMENT
at Ontario's Fort Henry recalls the 1860s, by which time Canada was unified under the Union Jack.

centered
US

centred
Brit.

THIS 1776 MAP
shows Quebec, New England, and New York during the American Revolution.

The Quebec Act. The Quebec Act of June 22, 1774, was a milestone in the history of government in Canada. Made law by the British Parliament, it introduced two important changes. First, it extended the boundaries of Quebec south of Lake Erie to the Ohio River; west to the Mississippi River; east to the Atlantic, including Labrador; and north and west to Rupert's Land, the domain of the Hudson's Bay Company. Secondly, it restored religious freedom to the Catholic population of Quebec and restored French civil law in place of English law. Both changes irritated the American colonies. Many of them claimed, by charter, lands extending west to the Mississippi River. The predominantly Protestant population of the American colonies resented what they saw as favoritism to a religious denomination they hated and feared. The Quebec Act became one of the Intolerable Acts cited by the American colonists against Great Britain and helped bring on the American Revolution. At the same time, though, the act helped keep Quebec loyal to England during that war.

British Rule. The shift from French to British rule brought economic changes as well as changes in the areas of law and government. British merchants followed the invading army and profited by supplying the soldiers and sailors with goods they needed. Some of these tradesmen came from the English colonies to the south. In effect, Canada was now economically dependent on London rather than on Paris.

In one way the change of government meant the replacement of an absolute monarchical and Catholic system by a capitalistic and individualistic system. In turn, this would lead to a serious division in other areas, such as cultural life and religion, between the French and the English. However, most French Canadians were not too disheartened by the change in their status because they benefited from the improvement in economic conditions.

The British victory did not end the dominance of the fur trade in the Canadian economy; for a while, the French continued to be the most important element in this trade. The French traders and trappers had the experience to move confidently through western lands and to deal profitably with the Indian tribes. The tribes still disliked and distrusted the English, whom they had fought, and preferred to deal with the French. Nevertheless, English merchants became involved in the Canadian fur trade because they supplied the needed credit and had the business connections that opened European markets. In fact, the rivalry continued between the Canadian fur trade in the east, the Hudson Bay area to the west, and the trade centered on Albany, New York, to the south.

With the establishment in August 1764 of a new civil government in the province of Quebec, problems arose because of the differences between the French and English legal systems. On the whole, the French establishment was not disturbed. For example, the seigniorial land tenure system was not abolished. The English rule that Catholics could not hold public office caused a problem because there were few Englishmen qualified to fill these positions. Governor Murray therefore allowed French citizens to serve on juries and to practice in the courts.

Murray and the growing merchant class did not get on well. The merchants felt that Murray was arbitrary and his idea of civil government differed little in practice from harsh military rule. Murray in turn thought of the merchants as contentious and unruly, and disliked them, especially because so many of them came from the English colonies to the south. The businessmen asked London to recall Murray, and this was done in 1765.

His successor was Sir Guy Carleton (1724–1808), later Lord Dorchester, a man of high principles. He was a distinguished veteran of the French and Indian Wars, destined to play a leading role in the American Revolution. Carleton, who was hostile to Murray's rule, replaced Murray's officials, and the province enjoyed a relatively peaceful period.

The American Revolution.
When the First Continental Congress of the 13 American colonies met in 1774, a message was sent to Quebec. It invited delegates from Quebec to attend the next congress in 1775. No delegates came. Most of the French Canadians resented the anti-Catholic bigotry of the colonies and preferred to remain neutral. Many of the English inhabitants of Canada, especially in Nova Scotia, reacted the same way, even though most Nova Scotians were originally New Englanders.

The rebellious Americans invaded Canada, partly in hope of changing the people's minds, partly to forestall the use of Canadian ports and strongpoints by the British. The invasion was authorized by the Continental Congress in June 1775 but little progress was made until fall. An expedition moved northward under Richard Montgomery (1736–1775), who had served in the British army in the French and Indian Wars and had then taken up residence in New York. On November 2, 1775, his forces captured St. Johns on the Richelieu River in Quebec, the only remaining strongpoint before Montreal, the objective of the invasion.

Governor Carleton had little with which to defend Montreal, and the French inhabitants did not want to be involved in a siege. As a result, the city surrendered on November 12 and Carleton narrowly escaped to Quebec City. Meanwhile, Benedict Arnold (1741–1801) had been leading another American expedition up the Kennebec River and through the forests of Maine toward Quebec. Montgomery's force joined Arnold's and laid siege to Quebec, but they lacked artillery and Carleton had organized a strong defense. In the

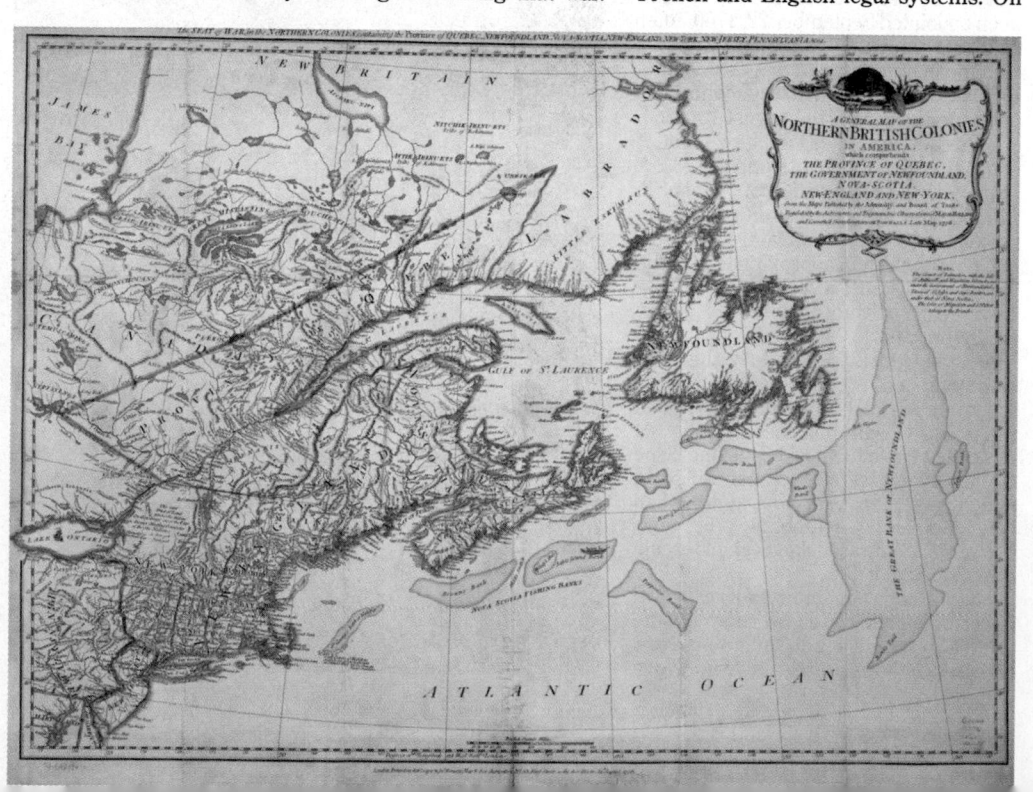

dark of the early morning of December 31, 1775, in a heavy snowstorm, the American forces attacked from two directions, but they were badly beaten and Montgomery was killed. The Americans continued the siege all winter to no avail. In May 1776, a British force of 10,000 men reached Quebec, and the Americans retreated to their own territory.

Carleton had a plan for ending the American rebellion by an invasion from Canada along the Lake Champlain-Hudson River route that would split the colonies in two. When it was later attempted, in 1777, it was not under Carleton's command. The result was a dismal failure. Thereafter, the focus of the war shifted south and Canada was left in relative peace.

After the Revolution. The Treaty of Paris, signed in that city on September 3, 1783, which gave the United States its independence, affected Canada in several ways. It established the boundary line between the two countries in such a way that the area of Quebec was greatly reduced. All the land north of the Ohio River, south of the midpoint of the Great Lakes (except for Lake Michigan), and east of the Mississippi River was now U.S. territory. Merchants in the fur trade protested to London against this surrender of western lands, but they got no satisfaction. The treaty also granted Americans the right to fish off Newfoundland and to cure fish in the uninhabited parts of Labrador and Nova Scotia, but not in Newfoundland.

Canada, with a sparse population, benefited from the American Revolution in one unusual way. In the years during and following the war, about 50,000 Loyalists moved to Canada from the colonies. These were persons who had sided with the British and did not favor independence. They represented a wide and diverse group, from the rich and well educated to the farmer and artisan.

Among the first Loyalists to emigrate were a large number who were taken to Halifax from Boston in 1776 when the British army evacuated that city. Nova Scotia continued to be the haven for most Loyalists. In 1783, when the British evacuated New York City at the end of the war, another large group left for that region. Nova Scotia was conveniently reached by sea and there were large areas of vacant land. It is estimated that by the end of 1783, 35,000 Loyalists had arrived, almost doubling the size of the provincial population.

The government of Nova Scotia was supposed to supply these newcomers with land, tools, and help in the building of houses. However, it lacked the facilities and ability to provide this aid. The situation was worsened because some of the refugees arrived in destitute condition. In addition, many had been town or city dwellers who were not equipped to deal with the demands of farming under pioneer conditions.

Some Loyalists moved on to England or the West Indies, but others settled in southern Ontario. Three districts were laid out where land would be granted them: along the upper St. Lawrence River; from Kingston to the Bay of Quinte; and on the Niagara peninsula. Here, too, there were hardships of the kind suffered in Nova Scotia. In 1789, in fact, there was a near-famine situation. Nevertheless, Loyalists, other settlers from the United States, and a number of German mercenary soldiers who had been disbanded in Canada made up a population of about 10,000.

In 1789 it was officially decreed that Loyalists who had come to Canada before 1783 were to be designated "United Empire Loyalists"; those who came after 1783 were known as "late Loyalists." In fact, some of the latter were simply persons who had come from the United States to acquire land in Canada in the hopes of bettering themselves economically.

Fur trade. In spite of wars and changes of government, the fur trade continued to thrive and to expand westward. The Hudson's Bay Company no longer had French government competition, but it faced yet another rival in 1779 when a group of nine partnerships joined forces and in 1783 became the North West Company. In 1789 the new organization built Fort Chipewyan on Great Slave Lake as its headquarters.

The North West Company contributed a great deal to the exploration and knowledge of the geography of the Canadian Far West. Scottish-born Alexander Mackenzie (1764–1820) was put in charge of the Athabasca district in 1788. In June, 1789, he set out from Fort Chipewyan on his first exploratory trek. He discovered the river named for him and followed it from its source to its mouth on the Arctic Ocean, which he reached on July 12. In 1793 Mackenzie and his party made their way overland to the Pacific coast, becoming the first Europeans to cross North America north of Mexico; however, the route proved too difficult to be of practical value.

Another North West Company explorer, Simon Fraser (1776–1862), was Vermont born and the son of a Loyalist officer. His most important journey, which took him in 1808 along the river named for him, provided a great deal of new geographical information (though Fraser thought mistakenly that he was on the Columbia River). Fraser laid the groundwork for the future settlement of British Columbia by finding sites across the mountains suitable for agriculture. He also set up a series of posts for traders.

Another trader and explorer who helped open up the Canadian Far West was David Thompson (1770–1857), born in England, who first worked for the Hudson's Bay Company in 1797. Among his accomplishments was the building in 1807 of Kootenae House, the first trading post on the Columbia River. In 1811 he descended this river to its mouth, arriving on July 15 only to find some Americans already there. They had arrived by sea and had built Fort Astoria, named for New York's John Jacob Astor, whose Pacific Fur Company carried on the leading U.S. fur trading operation.

When this post was threatened with capture by the North West Company during the War of 1812, Astor sold the fort to its besiegers. Meanwhile, that company and the Hudson's Bay group had been competing fiercely for the fur trade with the Indians. On March 21, 1821, however, to end their ruinous competition, and under pressure to help spread British influence across North America, the two companies merged under the Hudson's Bay Company name.

Pacific coast. In the late 18th century, controversy over territorial rights along the northwestern Pacific coast flared between England and Spain. First to arrive in the area, on March 29, 1778, was Captain James Cook (1728–1779) of the British navy, who claimed possession for Great Britain. He landed on the west coast of Vancouver Island.

Spurred by Cook's reports of furs that could be purchased cheaply from the Indians and sold dearly in the Orient, British traders swarmed to the area. The first was John Meares, who set up a trading post at Nootka Sound in 1788 and later that year launched the *Northwest America,* the first vessel other than the Indian canoe built on those shores.

Because of the Spanish explorers Juan Pérez, who discovered British Columbia in 1774, and Bruno Heceta, who was said to have laid formal claim to much of the region in 1775, Spain claimed prior rights. On May 5, 1789, a Spanish sea captain, Estevan José Martinez, arrived; he seized some British ships, but did not interfere with American ships trading there. Though Pérez

EXPLORER ALEXANDER MACKENZIE left his mark at Bella Coola in British Columbia in 1793. His party became the first to cross North America north of New Mexico.

LOYALISTS WHO FLED THE UNITED STATES after the American Revolution were given new land in Canada. A lottery was held to distribute the land fairly.

THIS MASK was made by the Nootka of the western coast of British Columbia.

except within 10 miles (16 kilometers) of any existing Spanish settlements.

The British sent Captain George Vancouver (1757–1798) to Nootka Sound in 1791 to arrange for the transfer back to English traders of the property the Spaniards had seized. The Spanish delayed matters as long as possible and did not withdraw until 1795. Meanwhile, Vancouver was conducting a survey of the coast. In 1793 he was off the mouth of the Bella Coola River, only a short time before Alexander Mackenzie arrived there on his overland trip.

The Canada Act. An important event in the history of Canadian government occurred on June 10, 1791, when the British Parliament passed the Constitutional Act of 1791, also known as the Canada Act. This legislation was intended to cope with changing political sentiment in Canada. There was a growing demand for more democratic government, stimulated partly by Loyalists who had fled the American colonies during the American Revolution and who were accustomed to more democracy than they found in Canada. Thus, it was felt in England that a more representative government, but one that retained a strong executive authority, would at once keep Canada peaceful and help it continue in the British tradition.

On August 24, 1791, Canada was divided into Lower Canada (roughly present-day Quebec) and Upper Canada

and Heceta apparently did not make landings, Martinez took possession in the name of the Spanish king. Great Britain threatened to go to war with Spain over this incident, but the matter was resolved by the Nootka Sound Convention of October 28, 1790. By its terms, the Pacific coast was declared open to British subjects for trading purposes

(roughly present-day Ontario). In effect, this divided Canada in two: an English-speaking section and a French-speaking section. Though each was provided with a lieutenant governor with veto power, there was a council, with members appointed for life, and an elected assembly. The assembly was called to meet once a year, but it could not continue for more than four years without another election. The governor could dissolve it at will. The position of the governor and his council was greatly strengthened through their control of revenues from Crown land reserves, which allowed them to implement unpopular programs and ignore opposition in the assemblies.

The Canada Act also provided for a land tenure system intended to result in development of a landed aristocracy. This never came about, probably because of lack of interest on the part of Canadians and Britons who had the means to participate in such a system.

Quebec City became the capital of Lower Canada. Newark (now Niagara-on-the-Lake) was the temporary capital of Upper Canada, while York (now Toronto) was being prepared to be the capital city. York, founded in 1793 by British Loyalists, became the capital in 1797. The first legislature of Upper Canada convened on September 17, 1791, and that of Lower Canada on December 17, 1791.

In the end, the Canada Act resulted in political and economic oligarchies in both parts of Canada and caused intercultural conflicts, especially in Lower Canada, where the English governor and council ignored the French-dominated assembly. The first real breach in French-English relations occurred in the early 1800s when Governor Sir James Craig, during the Napoleonic wars, twice dissolved the assembly, and threw its French-Canadian leaders into prison. However, the act did reduce the resentment against England that might have arisen if no form of free government had been permitted.

After the Americans burned the Parliament building at York during the War of 1812, the seat of government of Upper Canada had to be moved to Kingston. Western Canada remained separate, still governed by the Hudson's Bay Company rather than by the British government. After this company and the North West Company merged in 1821, a new governing body was established. A governor and council were to run the overall commercial operation.

Administration was divided into two departments. The northern section was made up of districts called Athabasca, Peace, Mackenzie, New Caledonia, and Columbia. According to its charter, the northern section was outside the limits of Rupert's Land; it was claimed by the North West Company. The southern department included the area between James Bay, at the south end of Hudson Bay, and eastern Canada, including the eastern shore of Hudson Bay.

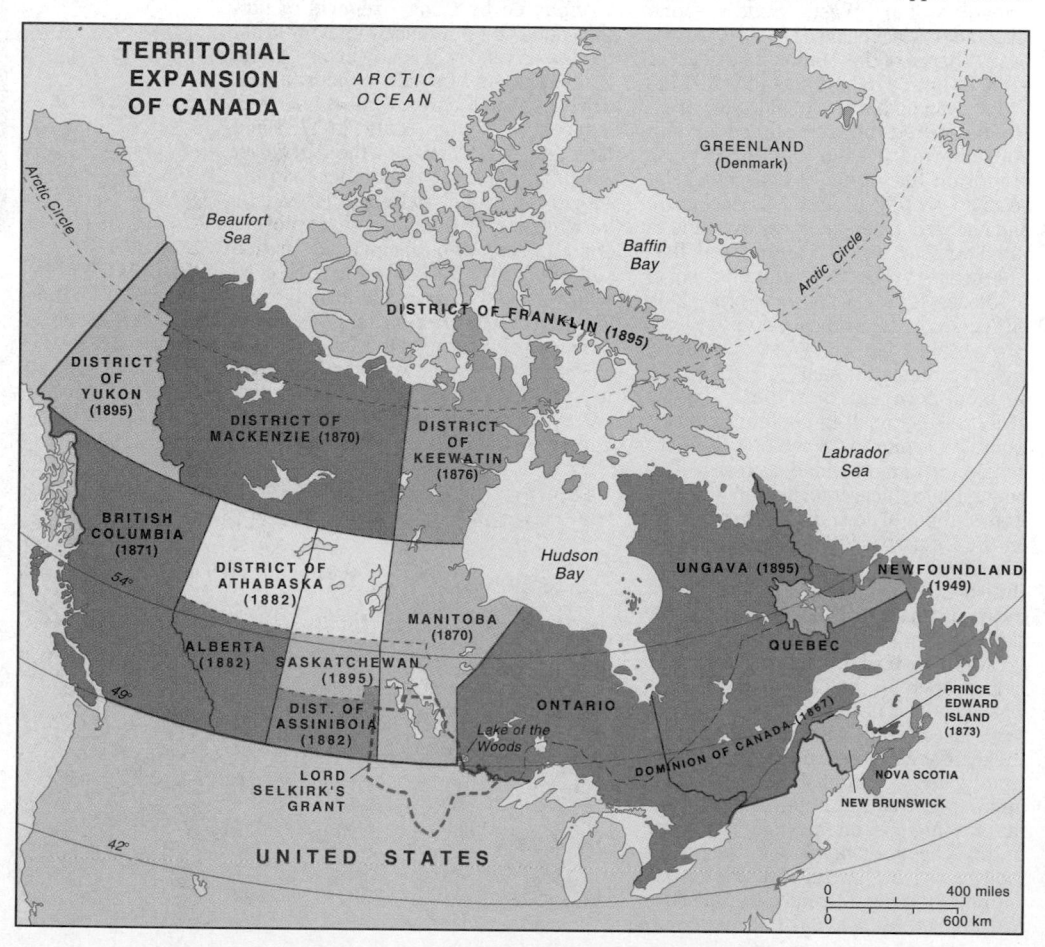

TERRITORIAL EXPANSION OF CANADA

War of 1812.

Important engagements of the War of 1812 between Great Britain and the United States were fought on Canadian soil. In addition, several of the war's battles on American soil involved British forces operating out of Canada. A faction of American members of Congress, the "war hawks" who had agitated for the war, saw it as an excuse for conquering Canada.

War was declared by the United States on June 18, 1812. In July General Isaac Brock (1769–1812), military commander and acting administrator of Upper Canada, declared martial law. Brock moved quickly to attack Detroit, which was defended by American forces under General William Hull (1753–1825). Brock outsmarted and outmaneuvered Hull, who surrendered Detroit on August 16. Hull, who had had an outstanding record in the Revolutionary War, was in this instance incompetent at best. Earlier Hull had rashly invaded Canada, only to have his supply line cut and be forced to retreat. Brock now considered all of the Michigan territory to have been restored to the British Empire.

The Americans tried again to take the initiative on October 13, when troops under the command of General Stephen Van Rensselaer (1764–1839) crossed the Niagara River from New York and soon occupied Queenston Heights, Ontario. Brock's forces defeated the Americans, who retreated to the United States, but Brock was killed in battle. On November 28 the Americans again tried to cross the Niagara River, but they were repulsed.

The English benefited considerably from the help of their Indian allies, especially those led by Tecumseh, the Shawnee chief. British and Canadian forces, along with the Indians, defeated the Americans on January 22, 1813, at Frenchtown, Ohio, but they were unable to dislodge the army of General William Henry Harrison (1773–1841), a future president of the United States, at Fort Meigs, Ohio, May 1 to 9.

Both sides won victories on the Niagara peninsula in 1813. On May 27 the Americans captured Fort George, Ontario, but on June 6 the British and Canadians, with their Indian allies, won the Battle of Stony Creek, while the Indians were victorious at Beaver Dam on June 24. The Americans retired from Fort George on December 10, but not before they had burned Newark (Niagara-on-the-Lake). The British pursued the Americans and on December 18 took Fort Niagara, New York. Their Indian allies, under Phineas Rialls's command, then carried the war farther into New York, burning Lewiston, Manchester, Fort Schlosser, Black Rock, and Buffalo, ending their invasion on December 30.

Farther east, an American force on April 27, 1813, entered the harbor of York (Toronto) and occupied the town. Public buildings, including Parliament and the governor's residence, were burned. It was in retaliation for this deed that the British the next year burned the Capitol, other government buildings, and the White House in Washington, D.C.

On Lake Erie on September 10, 1813, Captain Oliver H. Perry (1785–1819) and his small American armada defeated a British fleet. This made it possible for General Harrison to move on Detroit, and the British evacuated that post. Harrison moved into Ontario and on October 5 forced the British to join battle. The Americans totaled about 3,000 while the British had only 300 regulars and 1,000 Indians under Tecumseh. The British ranks broke under an American attack and Tecumseh was among those killed. This defeat, at the Thames River, put an end to the Indian confederacy that had been formed by Tecumseh.

About the same time, on October 26, an important and decisive victory was won by a Canadian force in Quebec on the Châteauguay River. Charles de Salaberry (1778–1829) and his small army of 460 Canadian Voltigeurs and some Indians defeated a much larger American force, numbering 4,000, under General Wade Hampton (1752?–1835). This victory ended the effort by the Americans to attack Montreal.

The fiercest battle of the war was fought at Lundy's Lane, just west of Niagara Falls, on July 25, 1814. The Americans were attempting to advance into Ontario but they were fought to a standstill, with heavy casualties on both sides. The American force withdrew to Fort Erie, on the Canadian side of the Niagara River, its previous position.

One further military engagement took place before the war ended. On Lake Champlain on September 11, 1814, an American force under Thomas Macdonough (1783–1825) soundly defeated a British fleet near Plattsburgh, New York, thus putting a stop to any plan to invade New York from Canada.

After numerous military and naval engagements, the militarization of the Great Lakes proceeded apace, culminating in the construction of the 120-gun three-decker *St. Lawrence* at Kingston, Ontario, and the laying down of other powerful battleships on each side of Lake Ontario. However, by 1814, exhaustion was setting in on both sides of the border, with no real gains registered.

The war was formally ended by the Treaty of Ghent, signed in Belgium on December 24, 1814. The two nations agreed to restore territory to each other on a prewar basis and to set up four commissions to settle the boundary line between Canada and the United States.

Rush-Bagot and London Conventions.

The arms race on the Great Lakes continued at a rapid pace after the war's end, with growing construction of ships and fortifications. In 1817 the Rush-Bagot Convention brought this expensive militarization to a halt.

The convention took its name from an agreement signed by Richard Rush (1780–1859), acting secretary of state of the United States, and Sir Charles Bagot (1781–1843), the British minister in Washington. Bagot later became governor of the Province of Canada, from

kilometers
US

kilometres
Brit.

AMERICAN FORCES defeated the British at the Battle of Chippewa in 1814, just above Niagara Falls in Ontario.

27 North America

DURING A BATTLE AT FORT MCHENRY with British forces operating from Canada in the War of 1812, Francis Scott Key wrote the United States' national anthem.

Heads of Government 1791–1841

Lower Canada

OFFICIAL	TITLE	SERVED
Sir Alured Clarke	Lieutenant Governor Administrator	Dec. 25, 1791– Oct. 1, 1793
Lord Dorchester (formerly Sir Guy Carleton)	Governor	Oct. 2, 1793– July 9, 1796
Robert Prescott	Lieutenant Governor Administrator Governor	July 12, 1796– Apr. 26, 1797 Apr. 27, 1797– July 29, 1799
Sir Robert Shore Milnes	Lieutenant Governor Administrator	July 30, 1799– Aug. 5, 1805
Thomas Dunn	Administrator	Aug. 12, 1805– Oct. 24, 1807
Sir James Henry Craig	Governor	Oct. 24, 1807– June 19, 1811
Thomas Dunn	Administrator	June 19, 1811– Sept. 14, 1811
Sir George Prevost	Administrator	Sept. 14, 1811– July 15, 1812
	Governor	July 15, 1812– Apr. 3, 1815
Sir Gordon Drummond	Administrator	Apr. 4, 1815– May 21, 1816
John Wilson	Administrator	May 21, 1816– July 12, 1816
Sir John Coape Sherbrooke	Governor	July 12, 1816– July 30, 1818
Duke of Richmond	Governor	July 30, 1818– Aug. 28, 1819
James Monk	Administrator	Sept. 20, 1819– Mar. 17, 1820
Sir Peregrine Maitland	Administrator	Mar. 17, 1820– June 19, 1820
Lord Dalhousie	Governor	June 19, 1820– June 6, 1824
Sir Francis Burton	Lieutenant Governor Administrator	June 7, 1824– Sept. 16, 1825
Lord Dalhousie	Governor	Sept. 17, 1825– Sept. 8, 1828
Sir James Kempt	Administrator	Sept. 8, 1828– Oct. 20, 1830
Lord Aylmer	Administrator Governor	Oct. 20, 1830– Feb. 4, 1831 Feb. 4, 1831– Aug. 24, 1835
Lord Gosford	Governor Commissioner	Aug. 24, 1835– Feb. 27, 1838
Sir John Colborne	Administrator	Feb. 27, 1838– May 29, 1838
Lord Durham	Governor	May 29, 1838– Nov. 1, 1838
Sir John Colborne	Administrator Governor	Nov. 1, 1838– Jan. 17, 1839 Jan. 17, 1839– Oct. 19, 1839
Charles Poulett Thomson (later Lord Sydenham)	Governor	Oct. 19, 1839– Feb. 10, 1841

Upper Canada

OFFICIAL	TITLE	SERVED
John Graves Simcoe	Lieutenant Governor	July 8, 1792– July 20, 1796
Peter Russell	Administrator	July 20, 1796– Aug. 17, 1799
Peter Hunter	Lieutenant Governor	Aug. 17, 1799– Aug. 21, 1805
Alexander Grant	Administrator	Sept. 11, 1805– Aug. 25, 1806
Francis Gore	Lieutenant Governor	Aug. 25, 1806– Oct. 8, 1811
Isaac Brock	Administrator	Oct. 9, 1811– Oct. 13, 1812
Roger Hale Sheaffe	Administrator	Oct. 20, 1812– June 19, 1813
Baron Francis de Rottenburg	Administrator	June 19, 1813– Dec. 13, 1813
Sir Gordon Drummond	Administrator	Dec. 13, 1813– Apr. 25, 1815
Sir Frederick P. Robinson	Provisional Lieutenant Governor	July 1, 1815– Sept. 21, 1815
Francis Gore	Lieutenant Governor	Sept. 21, 1815– June 11, 1817
Samuel Smith	Administrator	June 11, 1817– Aug. 13, 1818
Sir Peregrine Maitland	Lieutenant Governor	Aug. 13, 1818– Nov. 4, 1828
Sir John Colborne	Lieutenant Governor	Nov. 4, 1828– Jan. 25, 1836
Sir Francis Bond Head	Lieutenant Governor	Jan. 25, 1836– Mar. 23, 1838
Sir George Arthur	Lieutentant Governor	Mar. 23, 1838– Feb. 10, 1841

January 1842, to March 1843, when he was also governor-general of all the other colonies of British North America, that is, Nova Scotia and New Brunswick.

Under the convention, each country was to have no more than four warships, not to exceed 100 tons each, on the Great Lakes.

The agreement set a precedent for the settling of Anglo-American differences by negotiation, although in 1864, during the American Civil War, when Canada was accused of harboring Confederate raiders and outfitting Confederate ships, the United States did, in fact, threaten to cancel the agreement. In 1865, however, with the end of the war, the notice of cancellation was withdrawn. Much later, during World War II, both countries agreed to ignore the provision concerning warships.

In 1818 the London Convention was signed by Great Britain and the United States. By its terms, the boundary between the United States and British North America would run from the Lake of the Woods, on the border of the present-day provinces of Ontario and Manitoba and the U.S. state of Minnesota, to the crest of the Rocky Mountains along the 49th parallel. The area west of there, known as the Oregon Territory, would be open to both countries for settlement and trade.

Growth of Canada.

In spite of this agreement, there was considerable anti-American feeling in Canada after the War of 1812. Many Canadians considered that they had been the victims of aggressors who sought to conquer and rule them. Some recent American settlers in Canada were believed to be outright disloyal, while those settlers who had come from the states as Loyalists after the Revolution boasted that it was they who had saved Canada from invasion.

One result of the anti-American feeling was the banning in 1815 of any more land grants to Americans. This inhibited the growth of Canada to some extent; nevertheless, Canada was growing. By 1825 the outlines of the eventual Dominion of Canada were becoming clearer. Canada now consisted of six settled areas: Lower Canada, Upper Canada, Newfoundland, Prince Edward Island, Nova Scotia, and New Brunswick. In the west, the Hudson's Bay Company continued to rule.

As time went on, the flow of emigrants from Europe, chiefly from the British Isles, increased. Most of the immigrants followed the St. Lawrence River route into Lower and Upper Canada, with the number increasing from about 12,000 in 1828 to 66,000 in 1832. By 1838 the population of Upper Canada was almost 400,000 despite its distance from Europe. Settlement in Lower Canada was impeded somewhat by the seigniorial system, left over from French rule. Immigrants also flowed into the maritime provinces. In the decade after 1815, nearly 40,000 arrived in Nova Scotia, the population of which

DEMANDS FOR SELF-GOVERNMENT led in 1837 to armed, though relatively short-lived, rebellions in both Upper and Lower Canada.

was 200,000 by 1838. New Brunswick, with most of its influx coming from Ireland, had an average of 5,000 or more newcomers per year.

This influx was not without its problems. Many of those who came were destitute, or very poor, farmers or artisans; all were ill-equipped to become pioneers. In some areas land was not easy to acquire. Many immigrants found that the more prosperous United States had its attractions. As a result, a good many immigrants who arrived in Canada continued on to the United States, where land was more easily available.

The Red River settlement.

An experiment in settlement in the west in this period brought about clashes between fur-trapping and farming interests. Seeking to do something to benefit impoverished inhabitants of Scotland and Northern Ireland, Thomas Douglas (1771–1820), 5th earl of Selkirk, who had an interest in the Hudson's Bay Company, secured a grant of 116,000 acres (300,000 square kilometers) from the company in 1811. The land lay chiefly in present-day Manitoba, on the Red and

WILLIAM LYON MACKENZIE (left) AND LOUIS-JOSEPH PAPINEAU were leaders of the militant reformers demanding self-government.

Assiniboine rivers, but extended south into parts of the present-day U.S. states of North Dakota, Minnesota, and South Dakota. The North West Company bitterly opposed the Red River Colony, as it was known, because it lay across the company's trade route and deprived it of a source of food supply.

The company incited the Métis, the original inhabitants of the banks of the Red River, to resist new settlers on the grounds that they were encroaching on land that rightfully belonged to the Métis as descendants of Indian forebears. The settlers were driven away to temporary shelter near the north end of Lake Winnipeg, but were brought back in 1815 and reinforced. In March of 1816, the governor of the settlement captured Fort Gibraltar, the stronghold of the North West Company, and found evidence that the company planned the final destruction of the colony that summer.

The burning of the fort in June enraged the Métis, who now banded together in an armed force. Sacking the Hudson's Bay Company's post at Brandon, Manitoba, they then moved against the Red River fort. When the governor, on June 19, 1816, went out to exhort the Métis to halt their violence, a fight ensued at Seven Oaks; the governor and 20 of his men were killed and some of the bodies mutilated. Once more the settlers retired to the area north of Lake Winnipeg.

Lord Selkirk, who had come to Canada late in 1815, now brought a force of former soldiers west. They seized the North West Company's headquarters at Fort William in August of 1816. The provincial governor sent out a commissioner who arranged a peaceful settlement. Again the colonists were brought back, but their troubles were not over. There were floods and a plague of locusts. In the end, though, agriculture flourished on the western plains.

kilometers
US

kilometres
Brit.

DANIEL WEBSTER, pictured here, and Alexander Baring, First Lord Ashburton, representing Great Britain, authored the treaty that set up the boundary between New Brunswick and Maine in 1842.

kilometers
US

kilometres
Brit.

Rebellions of 1837.

During the 1820s and 1830s, increasing unrest in both Lower Canada and Upper Canada led to the Rebellions of 1837. The unrest was both economic and political, stemming from the fact that in both provinces economic and political power were held by a small group of individuals and families. Cooperating with the British-controlled government, those in power were ultraconservative socially, economically, and politically. In Upper Canada, this faction was known as the Family Compact. In Lower Canada, a similar group was known as the Château Clique, the name being derived from the residence of the governor, the Château Saint-Louis.

In the political arena, militant reformers demanded self-government, which was not about to be granted either by the Canadian Tories (Conservatives) or the government in London. In Upper Canada the leader of the reformers was William Lyon Mackenzie (1795–1861), a Scot who emigrated to Canada in 1820 and in 1824 founded a journal, the *Colonial Advocate*. Elected to the House of Assembly in 1828, he was expelled in 1831 for libeling that body. Mackenzie's reform proposals were extreme, although some of them, such as the sale of public lands on easy terms, were adapted from the U.S. system.

In Lower Canada Mackenzie's counterpart was Louis-Joseph Papineau (1786–1871), born in Montreal and a militia officer in the War of 1812. In 1834 Papineau helped draw up the Ninety-two Resolutions. Though the resolutions stated grievances with which many agreed, and though they advocated democratic government, they were also extreme in their bitter attacks on the British and colonial administrations.

Armed rebellion broke out in a minor way on December 7, 1837, near Toronto, where a few hundred militants had gathered. They were attacked by the militia and some were captured; two were later convicted of treason and hanged on April 12, 1838. Mackenzie, however, escaped to the United States and on Navy Island in the Niagara River he optimistically proclaimed a Canadian republic. He was arrested for violating the American neutrality laws and in June, 1839, was sentenced to 18 months in prison. Mackenzie returned to Canada under the Amnesty Act of 1849 and was elected to the House of Assembly in 1851, but he found little support. He retired from politics in 1858.

In Lower Canada, the unrest turned into more serious armed conflict. In the autumn of 1837, armed militants—or Patriotes, as they called themselves—controlled some of the rural areas around Montreal. On November 6 rioting broke out between a Tory club and a Patriote group, the *Fils de la Liberté* (Sons of Freedom). The Patriotes then massed in the Richelieu region and defeated a British force at St.-Denis. However, on November 25, 1837, the British then routed the Patriotes at St.-Charles, killing 56 while suffering 3 dead and 18 wounded. At St.-Eustache on December 14, the Patriotes were again defeated, suffering 71 dead to only 1 killed on the British side. Some of these rebels, Papineau among them, took refuge in the United States. Papineau later went to Paris to live but returned to Canada in 1844.

Other militants participated in incursions into Canada from the United States between February and December 1838.

Further insurrections flared up in Lower Canada in 1838, with battles taking place during November and December; the Patriotes were defeated in all. Martial law was proclaimed and 733 rebels were taken prisoner. Of these, 28 were executed and more than 90 were transported to the penal colony in Australia.

The Aroostook War.

While rebellion was taking place in Canada and spilling over into the United States, a border dispute between the two countries brought about a minor clash that became known as the Aroostook War. The trouble began in 1839 when both Maine and New Brunswick claimed territory along the border where no exact determination of the international boundary had been agreed upon. The area included the valley of the Aroostook River, whose fertile farmlands were of interest to farmers in Maine and also to lumbermen in New Brunswick. When the lumbermen appeared, Maine raised a force to eject them. The lumbermen, however, surprised the Maine force and seized 50 of the Americans.

Both sides armed for further conflict but cooler heads prevailed in March of 1839. Sir John Harvey (1778–1852), a veteran of the War of 1812 and lieutenant governor of New Brunswick, together with General Winfield Scott (1786–1866), who had been sent to command a small U.S. force, agreed on a truce. A final settlement was made by the Ashburton-Webster Treaty (Treaty of Washington), signed on August 9, 1842. It took its name from Daniel Webster (1782–1852), the American secretary of state, and Alexander Baring (1774–1848), 1st Lord Ashburton, representing Great Britain. By its terms, more than 5,000 square miles (13,000 square kilometers) of the territory were given to New Brunswick. The treaty fixed the boundary between New Brunswick and Maine in part along the St. Croix River. Several rivers, including the Saint John, which also formed part of the boundary, were opened to free navigation by both countries. The northern boundaries of the states of Vermont and New York were the subject of some minor adjustments, and the boundary from Lake Huron to Lake of the Woods was defined in it.

The Ashburton-Webster Treaty again demonstrated the desire of Great Britain, representing Canada, to settle differences peacefully.

Union

The Rebellions of 1837 made the British government aware that reform of the Canadian system of government was needed. Those who had rebelled had been extremists, but there was general dissatisfaction in the land. The need to replace the governing cliques with more democratic rule became evident.

The first step toward reform was the appointment of John George Lambton (1792–1840), 1st earl of Durham, as governor-general and high commissioner to British North America. Durham had been an outspoken liberal in the British Parliament from 1813 to 1832 and had played a leading role in the creation of the milestone electoral Reform Bill of 1832. His activities and personality had earned him the nickname of "Radical Jack." He arrived in Lower Canada on May 29, 1838, bringing with him colonial experts to help him determine a course of action that would keep Canada a contented part of the British Empire. Between May and November 1, when he resigned and returned to England, he studied the problems in both Upper and Lower Canada.

Durham wrote his "Report on the Affaires of British North America" and submitted it to the Colonial Office on February 4, 1839. The report contained two significant recommendations: the first, for "responsible government," meant that the government executive would be drawn from the party that held the majority in the elected Assembly; the second held that Upper and Lower

Canada would be united as the Province of Canada, consisting of Canada East (Lower Canada, now Quebec) and Canada West (Upper Canada, now Ontario), thus ensuring the supremacy of the English-speaking majority. On July 23, 1840, this resolution, known as the Act of Union, received royal assent. It became effective in Canada on February 10, 1841.

An elected House of Assembly was provided for, with an equal number of members from each of the two former provinces, as well as an appointed council. All legislative procedures were to be conducted in the English language. The power to impose duties for the regulation of commerce was retained by the British government but those duties, together with such other revenues as fines, land sales, and seigniorial dues, were to be used by the Province of Canada for its budget. Kingston was chosen as the capital on February 10, 1841, but on May 10, 1844, the capital was moved to Montreal, where it would remain for five and a half years.

Durham's report and the Act of Union did not win unanimous praise. The Tories in both England and Canada, and the members of the Family Compact and the Château Clique, opposed the changes. In addition, Durham had been sharply critical of the French Canadians, hoping that the governmental reorganization would officially and in practice make them subordinate to the English-speaking people of the new province. Durham was willing to allow the French to retain their religious rights, but he wanted to wipe out the differences in language and law.

Nevertheless, the former Upper and Lower Canada consented to work within the act, and when the united Reform Party came into power, its liberal approach alleviated many grievances.

Province of Canada. In 1839 Charles Poulett Thomson (1799–1841) was sent to Canada as governor-general of British North America, to secure the consent of Upper and Lower Canada to the proposed union. He did so and was then named 1st Baron, becoming Lord Sydenham, governor-general of the Province of Canada. He had entered Parliament in 1826 as a Whig and was known as a reformer and as an exponent of free trade. At the same time, he wanted Great Britain to maintain strong imperial ties with its colonies.

Sydenham attempted to control the government by keeping the French-speaking region and the reformers in the minority of the new legislature. He was unsuccessful, however, when these two factions agreed to cooperate. Sydenham's administration brought useful changes, especially in municipal institutions and schools.

But Sydenham balked at accepting the idea of responsible government. In parliamentary terms, the phrase "responsible government" means that a governor-general accepts a prime minister and cabinet from the majority group or party of the elected legislature, which controls and manages legislation and so exercises effective governance, subject, in the case of a colony, to the formal approval of the British Crown and its representatives. Sydenham believed that the newly constituted council was simply an advisory body that the governor-general could consult or not, but that he was the one who should make all executive decisions.

Lord Sydenham was killed in September of 1841 when he fell from his horse in Kingston. His successor as governor-general was Sir Charles Bagot (1781–1843). He found that the majority of the members of the elected House of Assembly, known as Reformers, were at odds with the Tory members of the council, or ministry, appointed by Sydenham. Bagot saw a solution in persuading the leaders of the Reformers, Louis-Hippolyte La Fontaine (1807–1864) of Canada East and Robert Baldwin (1804–1858) of Canada West, to join the ministry.

La Fontaine had been elected to the House of Assembly of Lower Canada in 1830, but he did not approve of the Rebellion of 1837. Baldwin was elected to the House of Assembly of Upper Canada in 1829, but was defeated in the following year. He and La Fontaine formed an alliance, and in 1842 accepted Bagot's request that they take over the ministry. But in 1843 Charles Theophilus Metcalfe (1785–1846), who had been governor of Jamaica, succeeded Bagot as governor-general. He had received instructions in England from the colonial secretary to make no concessions regarding responsible government, even though the existing Reform ministry headed by La Fontaine had been based upon that principle. Metcalfe demonstrated his firm belief in his orders by making appointments without the advice of the members of the ministry and by taking other actions that bypassed them. Accordingly, La Fontaine and Baldwin resigned. Metcalfe received a lifetime baronetcy as a reward for his efforts, but he was dying and returned to England in 1845.

The situation was reversed after James Bruce (1811–1863), 8th Earl of Elgin, was commissioned governor-general of Canada on October 1, 1846. A son-in-law of Lord Durham, he arrived in Montreal on January 30, 1847. He carried new instructions from the British government to concede the right to govern. Accordingly, on December 6, 1847, Elgin dissolved the assembly and, in the following election, Reformers won a majority. Baldwin and La Fontaine formed a ministry on March 11, 1848. Their government became known as the Great Ministry because of the reforms it undertook and because its cabinet was the first real parliamentary cabinet in Canada.

The ministry passed a number of laws, some controversial. On August 14, 1848, it repealed the clause in the Act of Union that made English Canada's only official language. This meant that the French language could once again be used at will in legislative proceedings.

The Rebellion Losses Bill of 1849 was intended to repay people in Canada East whose property had been damaged during the Rebellion of 1837. (A previous bill in 1841 had compensated people in Canada West.) Lord Elgin approved the bill. The Tory faction revolted so strenuously that the Parliament buildings in Montreal were burned and Elgin's carriage was stoned. But Elgin did not waver on the issue, thus confirming the status of responsible government and achieving a landmark in Canada's constitutional development.

The Baldwin-La Fontaine ministry also passed the Amnesty Act of 1849, granting immunity to all persons who had fled the country after participating in the Rebellions of 1837. In the same year, it secularized King's College and made it the University of Toronto, strengthened the school system, and provided a guarantee of funds to stimulate the building of railroads.

BRITISH NORTH AMERICA still contained sizeable Indian populations as discussions proceeded with the United States over control of their lands.

Trade Agreement. In Washington, D.C., in June 1854, Lord Elgin and William L. Marcy (1786–1857), the U.S. secretary of state, negotiated an agreement. Free trade in many natural products was established, and the mutual use of fisheries in coastal and inland waters was agreed on. For example, the American market was opened to Canada for export of fur, fish, and timber, and Americans could freely sell in Canada such products as rice, turpentine, and tobacco.

Although the agreement was for a time popular on both sides, the United States abrogated it on March 17, 1866, partly as the result of pressure from manufacturing interests, partly because the British government had favored the South in the U.S. Civil War, which ended in 1865. Though the free trade agreement contributed a great deal to Canadian prosperity, British North America had also benefited from the demand for goods resulting from the Crimean War (1853–1856) in Europe and the American Civil War. A British and Canadian attempt was made in 1869 to renegotiate the agreement, but it failed.

Oregon Territory. In 1818 the southern boundary of this valuable region was the 42nd parallel. That same year, Britain and the United States had agreed on the 49th parallel as the northern boundary, from Lake of the Woods to the Rockies. While the United States was prepared to agree that the 49th parallel should be extended to the Pacific as a boundary, the British held out for the Columbia River. So it was that the two countries agreed to joint occupation of the disputed territory for ten years. In 1827 this was extended indefinitely. However, hawkish elements in the United States tried to insist on a boundary line that would give America the whole area.

"WHAT? YOU YOUNG YANKEE-NOODLE, STRIKE YOUR OWN FATHER!"

THE OREGON TERRITORY controversy with the United States was the subject of this cartoon.

On May 21, 1846, the United States gave England one year's notice that it would end the joint occupation agreement. On June 15, the Oregon Treaty defined the boundary from the Rockies to the Pacific along the 49th parallel, though Great Britain received all of Vancouver Island, a portion of which lies south of the agreed upon line.

Far West. In 1849, concerned by U.S. northward expansion, Britain leased the colony of Vancouver Island to the Hudson's Bay Company for ten years for development as an agricultural settlement. James Douglas (1803–1877) had established the company's first trading post on the island in 1843, calling it Fort Camosun. On December 12 that year, it was renamed Fort Victoria. Douglas became chief factor in 1849. The first governor of the island was

Richard Blanshard (1817?–1894), who arrived in 1850. The following year, he appointed a Legislative Council, which held its first session on August 30. However, Blanshard, clearly unsuited to this post, had already resigned.

On October 30, 1851, Douglas learned that he was to replace Blanshard as governor. As instructed, he established a legislative assembly for the island in 1856.

The population of the island and the adjacent mainland did not increase much for some time, largely because the Hudson's Bay Company was more interested in its fur trade than in bringing in farmers to settle the west. The situation changed in 1858 as the result of the discovery of deposits of gold along the mainland's Lower Fraser River. A throng of miners, mostly from the United States, poured in. This influx of adventurers, some of whom did not stay long, prompted the British Parliament to establish on August 2, 1858, the colony of British Columbia, of which James Douglas was appointed governor, while remaining governor of Vancouver Island.

In 1859 New Westminster was named the capital of British Columbia by Governor Douglas. And on November 19, 1866, Vancouver Island, by an act of Parliament in London, was made part of the colony, although the Hudson's Bay Company continued to manage affairs there until April 3, 1867. Victoria became the capital of the province in 1868.

For his contributions to the development of the province, James Douglas was knighted in 1863. History recognizes him as the father of British Columbia.

New attempts at the Northwest Passage. The first half of the 19th century witnessed a number of expeditions to find the Northwest Passage through the arctic lands and waters of northern North America. The leader of several expeditions, and an eventual tragic victim of the search, was Sir John Franklin (1786–1847) of the British navy, who led expeditions from 1819 to 1822 and 1825 to 1827 to explore the arctic coast.

In 1845 Franklin sailed from England with two ships to seek the Northwest Passage. On July 26 a whaling ship met his ships in Baffin Bay. That was the last that was ever seen of Franklin or any of the members of his expedition. In 1848 three search parties were sent out to seek clues to the fate of the expedition and more than 40 others, looking for remains, followed in later years. It was not until 1854 that John Rae (1813–1893), another explorer, learned from Inuits of Franklin's fate. The two ships had become frozen in the ice between Victoria Island and King William Island, remaining there for more than a year. Franklin had died on June 11, 1847.

The other members of the expedition, scurvy-ridden, abandoned the ships in April 1848, and tried to make their way back to civilization overland, but all perished. Relics and documents of the

THE COLONY OF VANCOUVER ISLAND
was leased to the Hudson's Bay Company in 1849, in response to concern about U.S. northward expansion. Pictured here is a company store in Seattle.

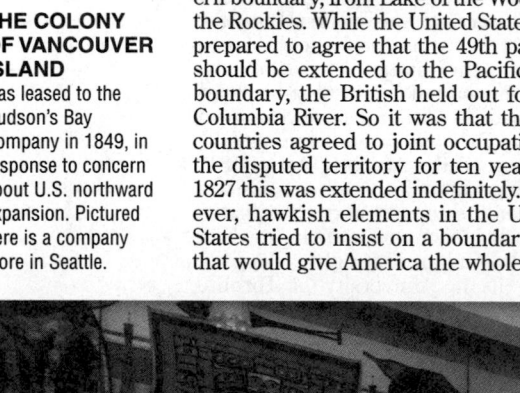

Heads of Government 1841–1867

Province of Canada

Official	Title	Served
Charles Edward Poulett Thomson, 1st Baron Sydenham	Governor-General	Feb. 10, 1841–Sept. 19, 1841
Sir Richard Downes Jackson	Administrator	Sept. 24, 1841–Jan. 12, 1842
Sir Charles Bagot	Governor-General	Jan. 12, 1842–Mar. 30, 1843
Charles Theophilus, Baron Metcalfe	Governor-General	Mar. 30, 1843–Nov. 26, 1845
Charles Murray, 2nd Earl Cathcart	Administrator	Nov. 26, 1845–Apr. 24, 1846
	Governor-General	Apr. 24, 1846–Jan. 30, 1847
James Bruce, 8th Earl of Elgin	Governor-General	Jan. 30, 1847–Dec. 19, 1854
Sir Edmund Walker Head	Governor-General	Dec. 19, 1854–Oct. 24, 1861
Charles Stanley, 1st Baron Monck	Governor-General	Oct. 25, 1861–June 30, 1867

(For a list of governors-general since confederation, see the volume on GOVERNMENT AND LAW.)

ill-fated expedition have turned up as recently as 1984, when an almost perfectly preserved body, that of Petty Officer John Torrington, was discovered in the ice of Beechy Island, Northwest Territories (now part of Nunavut). Examination of these remains has suggested that the men may, in fact, have died of lead poisoning from the canned foods they consumed.

Provincial government. The arrival of the second half of the 19th century was marked by the end of the Baldwin-La Fontaine ministry. In 1851 Francis Hincks (1807–1885), a Reform leader in Canada West and inspector general in the ministry, replaced Baldwin as leader. Augustin-Norbert Morin (1803–1865), who had been speaker of the Assembly of Lower Canada from 1848 to 1851, took La Fontaine's place. Hincks was interested in economic affairs and especially in railroad promotion. In 1852 he secured the incorporation of the Grand Trunk Railway, which became in 1867 the longest rail system in the world, running for 1,100 miles (1,770 kilometers) from Portland, Maine, westward to Sarnia, at the southern end of Lake Huron. Because of its vast distances and scattered population centers, Canada badly needed railroads; their construction and financing played a major role in Canadian politics for many years.

Hincks also began negotiations that led to the Reciprocity Treaty with the United States in 1854. For his part, Morin was an advocate of responsible

government and of the political rights of French Canadians within Canada. The ministry lasted until 1854, when it was brought down by Hincks's involvement in questionable financial transactions connected with the railway.

Morin remained a leader in the next ministry with Sir Allan Napier MacNab (1798–1862), who had served with gallantry in the War of 1812 (he was only 14 years of age at its opening), and had been

elected to the provincial assembly in 1841. He was a leader of the Tory and Conservative groups and when a Liberal-Conservative coalition was formed in 1854, he became its leader. The alliance with Morin, a Reformer, was possible because moderates on both sides, whether French or English, shared the desire for economic development.

Several important pieces of legislation were passed by the MacNab-Morin coalition. One concerned the "clergy reserves." By the Constitutional Act of 1791, an area equal to one-seventh of all land granted to settlers in both Lower and Upper Canada was to be used for the support of a Protestant clergy. This act greatly angered the Catholics of Upper Canada and even some Protestants because the government at first chose to equate Protestantism solely with the Church of England.

In 1819 it was agreed that the Church of Scotland, a Presbyterian sect, should share in the reserved land. Methodists and Baptists, however, did not believe the state should support any denomination, wanting the money derived from the lands used for educational purposes. Finally, in 1854, a bill was passed whereby proceeds from the sale of the reserved lands would be passed to the municipalities, funds being determined in proportion to population. Any obligations already incurred to pay pensions for retired clergymen were allowed to be met.

In the same year, seigneurial tenure rights were terminated. Unlike anything in the English legal system, those who had held these rights had certain judicial powers and were conceded privileges in church affairs. The first of these grants had been made as far back as January 15, 1634. The system, in reality originating in feudalism, favored the well-to-do. In 1854, legislation permitted tenants to claim the rights to their land.

A SATELLITE VIEW OF HUDSON BAY gives evidence of the difficulties experienced by explorers searching for the Northwest Passage in its frozen reaches.

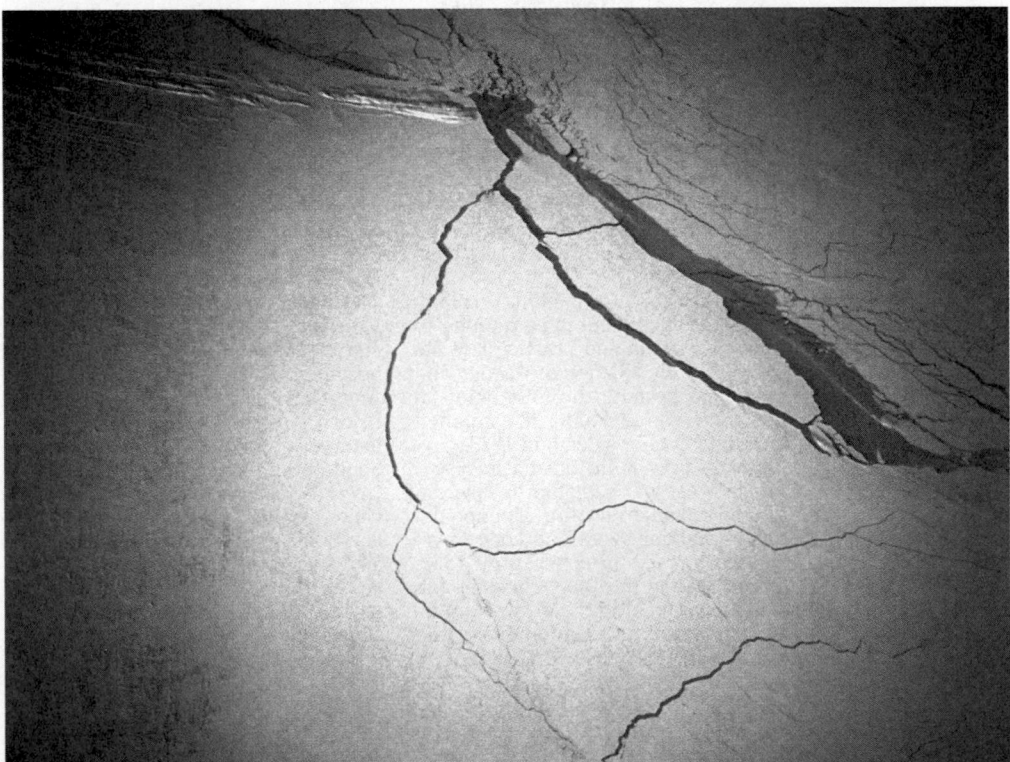

JOHN A. MACDONALD, first elected to the Province of Canada's legislative Assembly as a Tory in 1844, became the first prime minister of the Dominion, after leading the movement for confederation.

Morin was appointed judge of the Superior Court in 1855, and the ministry then became that of MacNab and Etienne-Paschal Taché (1795–1865), who was born in Lower Canada. He had served in the House of Assembly of the Province of Canada from 1841 to 1846, and was a member of the Hincks-Morin ministry.

In 1856 John A. Macdonald (1815–1891), who was born in Scotland and came to Canada in 1820, replaced Mac-Nab. Macdonald had first been elected member of Kingston to the Province of Canada's Legislative Assembly as a Tory in 1844. He now became the leader of the governing Liberal-Conservative coalition.

George-Etienne Cartier (1814–1873) of Lower Canada, who had fought in the Rebellion of 1837, replaced Taché as the leader of the French-Canadian part of the coalition in 1857. Cartier had been banished for his part in the rebellion and took refuge in Burlington, Vermont, but he was successful in petitioning to return to Canada and practice law the next year. This alliance of Cartier and Macdonald became the foundation of the Conservative Party; it remained intact until Cartier's death in 1873.

Liberal groups in Canada East and Canada West were unable to form an effective alliance, so the Macdonald-Cartier coalition, with one very short interruption, was in power until 1862. During its time in office, considerable attention was paid to the growth of railways, industry, and settlement in the west. The Huron district of Canada West

was opened by the construction of roads, while settlement of the hinterlands of Canada East was also encouraged. On August 7, 1858, Cartier included the concept of confederation in the party platform. It was presented to the British colonial secretary in London by a Canadian delegation, but rejected on the grounds of "lack of support" in British North America. In September 1858, a decimal currency became legal tender. A tariff act of 1856 was expanded in 1859, at which time protective duties were placed on goods of British manufacture.

Cartier, who, like Macdonald, would become one of the fathers of confederation, was responsible for persuading most of French Canada that it would be advantageous to unite. He also became the negotiator in London for the transfer of Rupert's Land (the Hudson's Bay Company lands) to the Dominion. He was made a baronet in 1868.

American Civil War. Canada became involved, involuntarily, in the American Civil War (1861–1865). The British government made no secret of its support for the Confederacy in the South, even though most individuals in Great Britain and Canada favored the Union in the North and opposed slavery. Some of England's actions, such as allowing armed ships for the Confederacy to be built in its ports, outraged northern Americans, and they took out some of their resentment on their northern neighbor.

Canada, which was entirely subordinate to Great Britain in the area of foreign relations, could not prevent agents of the South from using its ports as refuges and bases. Although the majority of Canadians deplored the situation, there was a Tory minority of some influence that disliked the democratic North and feared another attempt at invasion. When events reached the point where it seemed that Britain and the United States might go to war over English support of the South, 15,000 British troops were sent to Canada to ward off possible invasion.

Worst of all to American northerners was the extremist element among the Confederates who slipped into Canada to use it as a base for raids into the United States. One plan was to free Confederate prisoners of war held in camps near the border. Another was to incite an uprising in Chicago.

The one raid of any consequence took place in October 1864, when a band of 40 Confederate soldiers, led by Bennett Young, raided St. Albans, Vermont, from Canadian soil. The men set fires, took $200,000 from three banks, killed one man, and wounded another. American anger was further inflamed when a Canadian judge, on technical grounds, ordered the raiders released after they had been captured (although the stolen money was returned to the banks).

In fact, Canada's contribution to the Union cause outweighed the importance of such incidents. Canada had long been the final haven on the Underground Railroad through which abolitionists in the North helped slaves escape from the Southern states. About 40,000 African Americans ended up in Canada. In addition, according to one historian, 53,532 men of British North America served in the Union army. About two-thirds of them were French Canadians, prompted in part to enlist by the lack of economic opportunity in Canada East.

In early June 1866, after the war was over, about 900 members of the Irish Fenian Brotherhood crossed from the United States at the Niagara frontier to seize Fort Erie in Ontario. The brotherhood had been organized in New York City in 1857 with the purpose of securing the independence of Ireland from Great Britain by any means available. At the time of their raid, they were encouraged by the anti-British feeling that had been building up in the North during the Civil War. The Fenians repulsed an attempt by some Canadian volunteers to dislodge them; but when regular army troops showed up, they retreated to American soil, where they were arrested and their arms seized. The Fenians remained a threat for five years, with rumors abounding of raids to take place from Maine to Minnesota. The last raid, into Manitoba in 1871, was a failure.

If the Fenians achieved anything at all, it was to assist the desire for unity among Canadians. They had shown themselves as one more external threat to the developing nation.

Confederation

By the mid-19th century both Canada and England sensed a need to consolidate British North America into a confederation that would eventually include the vast region from coast to coast and from the U.S. boundary to the Arctic north. It was perceived that representation in the Legislative Assembly was inequitable for both Canada East and Canada West and that the number of seats in the legislature should be based on population. There was a movement to bring the land of the Hudson's Bay Company under Canadian government control.

The idea of confederation was not new. A British officer suggested a form of union for defense as early as 1783. A plan for civil government with a central legislature for all of Canada was proposed in 1785 by William Smith (1728–1793), a Loyalist who had been chief justice of the colony of New York and who was named chief justice of Quebec in 1786. He later assisted in writing the Constitutional Act of 1791. Another proposal was made in 1807 by Jonathan Sewell (1766–1839), chief justice of Lower Canada; in 1824 he reformulated the plan with John Beverley Robinson (1791–1863), attorney general of Upper Canada.

Other proposals were also made. In 1826 the attorney general of Nova Scotia, Richard John Uniacke (1753–1830), presented a plan for confederation to the British Colonial Office. During the American Revolution, Uniacke had been jailed in Halifax under suspicion of aiding the colonies.

Lord Durham, the governor-general whose report resulted in the 1841 Act of Union, suggested in the report that confederation of British North America might come about later. As Britain's colonial secretary from 1846 to 1852, Henry George (1802–1894), 3rd Earl Grey, took the initiative when he discussed the idea with the lieutenant governors of the provinces. In the early 1850s there was a move for confederation of the maritime provinces, comprising New Brunswick, Nova Scotia, and Prince Edward Island.

It was not until 1864, however, that a significant meeting was held among provinces to discuss confederation. The three maritime provinces agreed to meet at Charlottetown, Prince Edward Island, and they hastened into action when the Province of Canada asked to send representatives. The conference met on September 1, 1864; when the talks took a favorable turn and the delegates of the provinces said they had a detailed plan to propose, it was agreed to hold another session in Quebec from October 10 to 27. Newfoundland joined this conference, with two delegates.

Presiding over the conference was Sir Etienne-Paschal Taché of Canada East, who had won respect for his work in public life and who had agreed in 1864 to head a coalition ministry pledged to achieve confederation. By October 27, when the conference adjourned, it had adopted 72 resolutions on the matter of confederation.

Yet there remained considerable disagreement over the kind of confederation, or union, that would be best. One difference developed between those who wanted a national government that would leave the provinces with little power and those who wanted to safeguard provincial rights. In the end, the provincial rights advocates prevailed, but only the Province of Canada formally adopted the plan.

British North America Act.

After a final conference in London, with both the Canadians and the British represented, Parliament on March 8, 1867, passed the British North America Act (since 1982, called the Constitution Act, 1867). It received royal assent on March 29 and provided that on July 1, 1867, the Dominion of Canada would be established. At first the intention had been to call the new confederation the Kingdom of Canada, but fears were expressed that there would be a hostile reaction to this designation in the United States.

To begin with, the new Dominion consisted of only four provinces: Ontario (formerly Canada West or Upper Canada), Quebec (formerly Canada East or Lower Canada), New Brunswick, and Nova Scotia. Although the other provinces, Prince Edward Island and Newfoundland, had participated in all the discussions of confederation, they did not join until 1873 and 1949, respectively.

A BURIAL BEARS WITNESS to the fierce loyalty of Canadians who fought for British supremacy in North America. As late as the U.S. Civil War, Canadians were responding to external threats to their developing nation.

British North America Act, 1867

(Now also known as the Constitution Act, 1867)
Some excerpts

Whereas the Provinces of Canada, Nova Scotia, and New Brunswick have expressed their Desire to be federally united into One Dominion under the Crown of the United Kingdom of Great Britain and Ireland, with a Constitution similar in Principle to that of the United Kingdom:

And whereas such a Union would conduce to the Welfare of the Provinces and promote the Interests of the British Empire:

And whereas on the Establishment of Union by Authority of Parliament it is expedient, not only that the Constitution of the Legislative authority in the Dominion be provided for, but also that the Nature of the Executive Government herein be declared:

And whereas it is expedient that Provision be made for the eventual admission into the Union of other Parts of British North America:

Be it therefore enacted and declared by the Queen's most Excellent Majesty, by and with the Advice and Consent of the Lords Spiritual and Temporal, and Commons, in this present Parliament assembled, and by the Authority of the same, as follows: . . .

II. UNION

3. It shall be lawful for the Queen, by and with the advice of Her Majesty's Most Honourable Privy Council, to declare by Proclamation that, on and after a Day therein appointed, not being more than Six Months after the passing of this Act, the Provinces of Canada, Nova Scotia, and New Brunswick shall form and be One Dominion under the Name of Canada; and on and after that day these Three Provinces shall form and be One Dominion under the name accordingly. . . .

Canada shall be divided into Four Provinces, named Ontario, Quebec, Nova Scotia, and New Brunswick.

6. The Parts of the Province of Canada (as it exists at the passing of this Act) which formerly constituted respectively the Provinces of Upper Canada and Lower Canada shall be deemed to be severed, and shall form two separate Provinces. The Part which formerly constituted the Province of Upper Canada shall constitute the Province of Ontario; and the Part which formerly constituted the Province of Lower Canada shall constitute the Province of Quebec. . . .

9. The Executive Government and Authority of and over Canada is hereby declared to continue and be vested in the Queen. . . .

12. All Powers, Authorities, and Functions which under any Act of the Parliament of Great Britain, or of the Parliament of the United Kingdom of Great Britain and Ireland, or of the Legislature of Upper Canada, Lower Canada, Nova Scotia, or New Brunswick, are at the Union vested in or exercisable by the respective Governors or Lieutenant-Governors of those Provinces, with the advice, or with the Advice and Consent, of the respective Executive Councils thereof, or in conjunction with those Councils, or with any Number of Members thereof, or by those Governors or Lieutenant-Governors individually, shall, as far as the same continue in existence and capable of being exercised after the Union in relation to the Government of Canada, be vested in and exercisable by the Governor General, with the Advice or with the Advice and Consent of or in conjunction with the Queen's Privy Council for Canada, or any Members thereof, or by the Governor General individually, as the Case requires, subject nevertheless (except with respect to such as exist under Acts of the Parliament of Great Britain or of the Parliament of the United Kingdom of Great Britain and Ireland) to be abolished or altered by the Parliament of Canada. . . .

17. There shall be One Parliament for Canada, consisting of the Queen, an Upper House styled the Senate, and the House of Commons.

18. The Privileges, Immunities, and Powers to be held, enjoyed and exercised by the Senate and by the House of Commons and by the members thereof respectively shall be such as are from Time to Time defined by Act of the Parliament of Canada, but so that the same shall never exceed those at the passing of this Act held, enjoyed, and exercised by the Commons House of Parliament of the United Kingdom of Great Britain and Ireland and by the Members thereof.

19. The Parliament of Canada shall be called together not later than six Months after the Union.

20. There shall be a Session of the Parliament of Canada once at least in every Year, so that Twelve Months shall not intervene between the last sitting of the Parliament of one Session and its first Sitting in the next Session.

21. The Senate shall, subject to the Provisions of this Act, consist of Seventy-two Members, who shall be styled Senators. . . .

37. The House of Commons shall, subject to the Provisions of this Act, consist of One hundred and eighty-one Members, of whom Eighty-two shall be elected for Ontario, Sixty-five for Quebec, Nineteen for Nova Scotia, and Fifteen for New Brunswick. . . .

58. For each Province there shall be an Officer, styled the Lieutenant-Governor, appointed by the Governor General in Council by Instrument under the Great Seal of Canada. . . . .

91. It shall be lawful for the Queen by and with the Advice and Consent of the Senate and House of Commons, to make Laws for the Peace, Order and good Government of Canada, in relation to all Matters not coming within the Classes of Subjects by this Act assigned exclusively to the Legislatures of the Provinces: . . .

93. In and for each Province the Legislature may exclusively make Laws in relation to Education, . . .

95. In each Province the Legislature may make Laws in relation to Agriculture in the Province, and to Immigration into the Province; and it is hereby declared that the Parliament of Canada may from Time to Time make Laws in relation to Agriculture in all or any of the Provinces, and to Immigration into all or any of the Provinces; and any Law of the Legislature of a Province relative to Agriculture or to Immigration shall have effect in and for the Province as long and as far only as it is not repugnant to any Act of the Parliament of Canada. . . .

102. All Duties and Revenues over which the respective Legislatures of Canada, Nova Scotia, and New Brunswick before and at the Union had and have Power of Appropriation, except such portions thereof as are by this Act reserved to the respective Legislatures of the Provinces, or are raised by them in accordance with the special Powers conferred on them by this act, shall form One Consolidated Revenue Fund, to be appropriated for the public Service of Canada in the Manner and subject to the Charges in this Act provided. . . .

145. Inasmuch as the Provinces of Canada, Nova Scotia, and New Brunswick have joined in a Declartion that the Construction of the Intercolonial Railway is essential to the Consolidation of the Union of British North America, and to the assent thereto of Nova Scotia and New Brunswick, and have consequently agreed that provision should be made for its immediate Construction by the Government of Canada: Therefore, in order to give effect to that Agreement, it shall be the duty of the Government and Parliament of Canada to provide for the Commencement within Six Months after the Union, of a Railway connecting the River St. Lawrence with the City of Halifax in Nova Scotia, and for the Construction thereof without Intermission, and the Completion thereof with all practiable Speed.

146. It shall be lawful for the Queen, by and with the Advice of Her Majesty's Most Honourable Privy Council, on Addresses from the Houses of the Parliament of Canada, and from the Houses of the respective Legislatures of the Colonies or Provinces of Newfoundland, Prince Edward Island, and British Columbia, to admit those Colonies or Provinces, or any of them, into the Union, and on Address from the Houses of Parliament of Canada to admit Rupert's Land and the Northwestern Territory, or either of them, into the Union, on such Terms and Conditions in each case as are in the Addresses expressed and as the Queen thinks fit to approve, subject to the Provisions of this Act; and the Provisions of any Orders of Council in that Behalf shall have effect as if they had been enacted by the Parliament of the United Kingdom of Great Britain and Ireland. . . .

The Dominion of Canada had an upper house, called the Senate, and a House of Commons. The 72 senators were appointed by the governor-general, with 24 each from Ontario and Quebec and 12 each from New Brunswick and Nova Scotia. The House of Commons consisted of 181 members, apportioned on the basis of population so that Ontario would hold 82 seats, Quebec 65, Nova Scotia 19, and New Brunswick 15.

The largest part of the confederation would consist of the Province of Canada, but Nova Scotia and New Brunswick were important parts of the new Dominion. Nova Scotia had been claimed and settled as part of Acadia by the French, but had been a British possession, excluding Cape Breton Island, since the Treaty of Utrecht in 1713. It had first had a legislature in 1759; in 1838 separate legislative and executive councils were formed. Responsible government was granted in 1847 and a Reform ministry took office in 1848. There was considerable opposition to the idea of confederation, but the forces in favor of joining the Dominion prevailed.

What became the Province of New Brunswick had earlier been considered by the French as part of Acadia. After the French were defeated in North America, British and American colonial officers, as well as thousands of Loyalists who had fled the northeastern United States after the Revolution, began to settle the region, causing friction with wealthy landholders of Nova Scotia who had grants there. As a result, in 1784 the British government created the colony of New Brunswick, with its own governor, legislature, and judiciary. The first legislature met in 1786. As in Nova Scotia, there was some opposition to joining the confederation, but in the end New Brunswick became one of the four founding provinces of the Dominion of Canada.

The British North America Act gave Canada internal self-government, but the British Parliament held reserve powers and could change the governmental system if it so desired. Executive authority continued to be vested in the British monarch. In effect, Canada had to ask Great Britain for permission to amend its constitution. Foreign affairs remained in British hands. The division of powers between the federal government and the provinces was spelled out: Each province was to have a lieutenant governor appointed by the governor-general. Although the provincial lieutenant governor had extensive powers, each province had its own legislature. The provinces also had almost unlimited power over educational policy. Independence of judges was safeguarded. Provisions were made for admitting other colonies as provinces of the federal Dominion.

Special provision was also made for "immediate construction" by the federal government of an intercolonial railway.

The city of Ottawa, in southeastern Ontario, just across the Ottawa River from the Province of Quebec, became the capital of the Dominion. It had been selected by Queen Victoria in 1857 as the permanent capital of the Province of Canada and government departments had moved there in mid-November of 1865.

New Dominion. The first prime minister of the Dominion was John A. Macdonald, who in 1864 had become one of the leaders of the Great Coalition, the ministry that had pledged to bring about confederation. The other two leaders were George-Etienne Cartier and George Brown (1818–1880). Brown was a Liberal who resigned in December 1865, because he could no longer work amicably with his Conservative colleagues.

The ministry had played a leading role both in Canada and in England in bringing about confederation. Macdonald was one of the most influential members of the Charlottetown conference in 1864. In that same year, at the Quebec conference, he wrote many of the resolutions approved by that body. He was disappointed, however, that the final confederation did not provide for a stronger union.

Macdonald became prime minister on July 1, 1867, and the first Canadian Parliament met in November. Macdonald was eager to increase the influence of the Dominion, so he started a legislative process for acquiring the land of the Hudson's Bay Company. In 1859 the British government had refused to renew the license of the company, and in 1863 its shares were taken over by the International Financial Society, a group that intended to establish telegraphic communications, among other systems, and to sell land to settlers. On June 22, 1869, this society agreed officially to sell Rupert's Land to the Dominion for £300,000, but it retained the rights to one-twentieth of the land in arable regions. Though most of the land taken over became the Northwest Territories, and later Nunavut, much of the area of Canada's western provinces was carved also out of this vast region.

Manitoba was the first province to be added to the Dominion from land formerly belonging to the Hudson's Bay Company. Established in 1870, it was at first known as the "postage stamp province" because of its shape and extent of only 14,240 square miles (36,882 square kilometers). Enlarged in 1881, in 1912 it reached its present size with its extension to Hudson Bay. Two more portions of the former Rupert's Land eventually became Alberta and Saskatchewan. They were first established as administrative districts in the southwestern part of the Northwest Territories in 1882 and became provinces in 1905.

On the Pacific coast, British Columbia, which had had its own government for some time, joined the confederation in 1871, with the proviso that a transcontinental railroad to link it to the eastern provinces be built within ten years.

Prince Edward Island, which had been claimed by France as early as 1534 and named by the French Ile-Saint-Jean, became British territory in 1763 by the Treaty of Paris, which ended French rule in this region. It was renamed in 1799 in honor of Edward, duke of Kent, commander of British forces in Canada at the time. Representatives of the island's government took part in the conferences that preceded confederation, but they objected to many of the specific proposals for the union. Both a public meeting and the legislature rejected the proposed plan. In 1873, however, the island, which had a weak economy and was badly in debt from the costs of building a railway, joined the Dominion. It asked for and received from England an increase in its annual subsidy.

In 1880 and again in 1895, Great Britain transferred to Canada territory it claimed in North America so that the

kilometers
US

kilometres
Brit.

honor
US

honour
Brit.

27 North America

QUEEN VICTORIA
of England selected Ottawa in southeastern Ontario as the permanent capital of the Province of Canada in 1857, and it later became the capital of the Dominion.

Dominion would include all of North America north of the United States, except for Alaska and Newfoundland, the latter remaining a separate British colony. The Dominion by now stretched well above the Arctic Circle and included the islands of the Arctic Archipelago, which in 1897 were made part of the Northwest Territories (and in 1999 became part of Nunavut).

Red River Rebellion.

The early days of the new Dominion were not entirely peaceful. The move to take over the Hudson's Bay Company land and to establish the new province of Manitoba, which was centered on the Red River settlement, aroused mixed feelings among inhabitants of the area. Retired clerks and traders of the company did not want a change in government; this also applied to the so-called English half-breeds, descendants of Scottish and English traders and their Indian wives, many of whom were now farmers. Even more resistant to change were the Métis, the people of mixed Indian and French blood who were also known as *bois brûlés*. They thought, correctly, that an influx of settlers would bring in people with land titles who opposed their nomadic way of life, which was built around the fur trade and the hunting of buffalo, much in the manner of the Indians of Canada's prairies.

On the other side were newcomers from eastern Canada and a considerable number of Americans who had moved north of the border into the region. Both of these groups were in favor of Dominion rule as opposed to that of the Hudson's Bay Company. Some of the Americans advocated annexing the land to the United States. Actions of the Canadian government increased the fears of the Métis. A company of road builders came to the Red River area in 1868. In

INHABITANTS
of the area that is now Manitoba resisted the efforts of surveyors sent in to lay out townships, seeing it as a threat to their nomadic life and fur trade.

GREAT BRITAIN'S transferral of the last remaining British territories to Canada in 1880 and 1885 was just prior to the discovery of gold in the Yukon. Shown above is Dawson in the gold rush days.

1869 they were followed by surveyors who arrived to lay out townships. Both trespassed on farmland of the Métis.

At this juncture a leader stepped forward for the Métis. He was Louis Riel (1844–1885), who was born in the Red River settlement and educated in Montreal. Returning to the settlement in 1868, he organized resistance to the proposed takeover of Rupert's Land: He believed there was no guarantee of Métis rights. On October 11, 1869, Riel led a group that prevented a surveying party from carrying on its work on Métis land. The group stood on the chains of the surveyors, who withdrew in the face of the confrontation.

The Métis began to organize more formally; by October 24 they had formed a 200-man armed unit that soon grew to about 600 men. On December 1, 1869, William McDougall (1822–1905), representing the Dominion, crossed the border into what had been Rupert's Land and declared Canadian sovereignty. In reply, Riel on December 8 proclaimed an independent provisional government, retroactive to November 24. He and his followers had taken possession of Fort Garry on the site of present-day Winnipeg.

When a pro-Canadian government group raided the fort, they were captured and imprisoned by the Métis. Surveyor Thomas Scott, who had escaped earlier imprisonment at the fort and helped lead this force, was sentenced to death by an improvised court-martial and executed by firing squad on March 4, 1870. Riel's illegal provisional government then sent intermediaries to Ottawa with a list of rights that they demanded be allowed them in any takeover of the land.

In the end, the main features of the list of rights were included in the act that established the Province of Manitoba, in spite of certain opposition over Scott's death. Riel remained at Fort Garry and was prepared to turn over the government to Adams G. Archibald (1814–1892), a lawyer and an advocate of confederation who had been named the first lieutenant governor of Manitoba and the Northwest Territories. However, when a force of British and Canadian troops arrived ahead of Archibald on August 24, Riel fled. The Red River Rebellion—officially—was over.

Riel went to the United States only to return on September 17 to involve himself in a proposal that the Métis assist an invasion of Manitoba from the United States by the Fenian Brotherhood.

He decided against such a plan and, in October 1871, led a Métis group that assembled to repel any such attempt. In 1873 Riel was elected to the House of Commons in a by-election and reconfirmed in the general election of 1874. He went to Ottawa, but was expelled from the House over the Thomas Scott affair, for which his associate, Ambroise Lépine, was sentenced to death (commuted, 1875). Riel then fled once more to the United States. He suffered a mental breakdown and was in institutions in Quebec for two years, from January 1876 to 1878. Riel became an American citizen in 1883, but his career in Canadian affairs was far from over.

This unrest in the west was one reason for the establishment of the North-West Mounted Police in 1873. Their original task was to control the Indians, to protect them from traders who supplied them with whiskey, and to police the new Dominion territory. King Edward VII granted the use of the prefix Royal in 1904, and in 1920 the official name became the Royal Canadian Mounted Police (RCMP). The force now provides provincial police service for all but Ontario and Quebec, which have their own provincial police. Nationally, the RCMP is the force responsible for investigations of organized crime, narcotics, and fraud. In 1993 the RCMP employed 22,312 individuals across Canada, 3,855 of whom were public servants.

Foreign affairs. The fact that Canada, in international affairs, was subordinate to Great Britain was demonstrated when the Treaty of Washington was negotiated in 1871. Prime Minister Macdonald attended the meetings, but

THE PACIFIC SCANDAL, centered around the building of a transcontinental railway, forced the resignation of Prime Minister Macdonald.

only as a member of the British delegation. The negotiations concerned a number of matters that were at issue between the United States and Great Britain, but only two of them directly affected Canada.

One concerned fishing rights for Americans in Canadian waters. The Reciprocity Treaty of 1854 had given the United States certain rights, but these had expired when the United States abrogated the treaty in 1866. Canada then imposed a license fee on American fishermen, which they resented and tried to evade. In Washington, Macdonald made an effort to secure renewal of trade reciprocity in return for granting fishing rights again, but the British did not care to make an issue of this. Accordingly, the Americans were given inshore rights for a 12-year period in exchange for $5 million and free entry of Canadian fish to the U.S. market. The British agreed to reimburse Canadians for losses resulting from the Fenian raids into Canada from the United States.

The other matter of Canadian interest concerned the San Juan boundary dispute, also called the Northwest boundary dispute, between England and the United States over the line to be drawn between British Columbia and the state of Washington. In 1846 the agreement concerning the Oregon Territory had fixed a line through the middle of the channel between Vancouver Island and the mainland and through the middle of Juan de Fuca Strait. The strait, however, has several channels and so there was disagreement as to the ownership of several islands. One of them was San Juan Island, which had been occupied by U.S. troops in 1859. Joint occupation was agreed on, and the new treaty provided that Emperor William I of Germany would arbitrate the issue. In 1872 he decided on a line that gave the island to the United States.

In a gesture that to some extent acknowledged that Canada had an official part to play in such negotiations, the British asked the Canadian Parliament to ratify the treaty. Although there was considerable bitterness over the grant of fishing rights, the legislators did so.

In 1879 Canada began in a small way to have its own diplomatic representatives abroad. With the consent of the British government, Alexander Galt (1817–1893), who had been a member of the Great Coalition cabinet, active in the movement for confederation, and minister of finance in the first federal cabinet, was appointed to negotiate trade agreements with France and Spain. Knighted for his work that led to the fishery settlement in the Treaty of Washington, he became Canada's first high commissioner in London, a post he held from 1880 to 1883. In 1882 Hector Fabre (1834–1910), a journalist and lawyer who was appointed to the Dominion Senate in 1875, was named agent general for Canada in Paris. He held the post until his death.

Pacific scandal. Prime Minister Macdonald's moves to carry out the promise to British Columbia to build a transcontinental railway ended in political disaster for him. Two rival groups of capitalists wanted to secure the contract, and one group included some Americans. They were suspected of joining the enterprise merely to delay matters to protect the Union Pacific Railroad, in which they had an interest. One group of capitalists was centered in Montreal, the other in Toronto, and Macdonald tried to get them to unite their efforts. When this did not come about, the prime minister chartered the Canadian Pacific Railway Company and named men from each of the rival groups as directors.

This charter excluded the Americans, who became so angry that they entered into a conspiracy with some Liberals, Macdonald's political opponents, to destroy Macdonald. Stolen papers revealed that the man at the head of one of the rival groups of capitalists had made contributions to the Conservatives' election campaign in 1872. While some of the contributions seemed to have been given freely, others appeared to have resulted from demands for money. When a committee appointed to investigate the matter brought in a damaging report to Parliament, the Conservative government of Macdonald was forced to resign, on November 5, 1873.

THE NORTHWEST MOUNTED POLICE, formed in 1873 to police the Dominion's newly acquired western territories, still exists today.

THE NORTHWEST REBELLION arose primarily because the inhabitants saw the bison, on which they depended for food, disappearing as a result of farms and railroads in the developing area.

Macdonald was succeeded by Alexander Mackenzie (1822–1892), who was born in Scotland and emigrated to Canada in 1842. He became active in Reform politics in 1851 and was elected to Parliament in 1867 at the time of confederation. In the election of January 22, 1874, Mackenzie and the Liberals won 133 of the 206 seats in the House of Commons. Overly cautious, Mackenzie did not accomplish much. He preferred to have the government, instead of private interests, build the transcontinental railroad, but sufficient public funds for such a large project were not available. Mackenzie proposed, therefore, to build a series of portage roads to connect with the Great Lakes and to construct a short rail line on Vancouver Island. Public opinion in British Columbia was outraged at what appeared to be a failure to keep a promise, and the province threatened to secede.

Macdonald returned to office in 1878 after an election on September 17 in which the Conservatives reversed the results of the previous election and won 142 of the 206 seats in the House. Macdonald held the office of prime minister until his death in 1891. Among the problems he dealt with during that time was the issue of a transcontinental railroad. In 1880 the Canadian Pacific Railway Company was incorporated; the line was completed in 1885.

Northwest Rebellion. In 1885 revolt flared up again with the start of the Northwest Rebellion. As in the earlier Red River Rebellion, Louis Riel was the leader of the Métis (he had arrived in Batoche, Saskatchewan, in July 1884), this time along with two Indian leaders, Big Bear (d. 1888) and Poundmaker (c 1842–1886). Big Bear and Poundmaker were chiefs of the Crees. At this time in the valley between the

North and the South Saskatchewan rivers there was a good deal of discontent on the part of whites, Métis, and Indians. All three groups felt that the government in Ottawa had no understanding of their problems. The Indians and Métis saw the buffalo, on which they largely depended for food, disappearing. Farms and railroads were destroying their way of life. The English population, for its part, wanted representative government and a lowering of tariffs on American agricultural machinery and tools.

A petition setting forth all the grievances was agreed upon and sent to Ottawa on December 16, 1884. The federal government acknowledged it, promising to set up a commission to investigate the issues it raised. But Riel was encountering opposition in Saskatchewan and, by February 1885, talked of forming a provisional, independent government. Apart from local memories of the Thomas Scott affair and Riel's own demands of financial claims against the federal government, which made his political motives suspect, he appeared to be suffering from delusions in that he believed himself to be a prophet, that changes should be made in the Roman Catholic liturgy, and that the local bishop should become the pope of North America. As a result, he soon lost the support of the English-speaking settlers and of many of the Métis.

In March 1885 Riel seized the Batoche parish church. He armed his men and set up a provisional government. He surrendered less than two months later to the North-West Mounted Police.

On March 30 Poundmaker and his Indians overran a settlement, although the residents escaped to safety, but on April 2 Big Bear massacred all the whites at Frog Lake except for three who were taken prisoner and one who escaped.

Riel was condemned to death for treason. Though he was granted three reprieves, and a commission considered the matter of his sanity, he was hanged at Regina on November 16, 1885. The two Indian chiefs were sentenced to prison. Eleven other Indians were sentenced to death, but three had their sentences commuted.

Echoes of the rebellion and its aftermath were heard for some time in the east, where many in Quebec regarded Riel as a hero who had defended French-Canadian rights. To most of Ontario, however, he was a man who had rebelled against the legitimate government twice, taken up arms, and so deserved his fate.

Jesuits' Estates Act. An act of the Quebec provincial legislature in 1888 again raised controversial issues in the French- and the English-speaking sections of Canada, pointing up their differences in matters of religion and culture. This act was passed on July 12, 1888, under the aegis of Honoré Mercier (1840–1894), who had become premier of Quebec in 1886. Its purpose was to compensate the Jesuits for land that belonged to them before Britain awarded it to the Province of Canada in 1831.

The land had been given to the Jesuits to provide funds for education, so in 1832 the revenues were assigned for educational purposes. The Jesuit order was invited in 1842 to take up again its educational work in Quebec. By 1880 there was a growing opinion that the Jesuits should be compensated for their lost land, and other religious orders also claimed compensation. Mercier's act appropriated $400,000 for this purpose and stipulated that the pope would decide how the funds were to be distributed. Ultimately the Jesuits were to receive $160,000 to cover all claims; Université de Laval was to receive $140,000; and $100,000 was to be shared among certain dioceses. The act also granted an additional $60,000 to Protestant institutions of higher learning.

The act was popular in Quebec but it did not please public opinion in Ontario, especially in the Orange Order, a militant Protestant group. This group did not want the pope to be named in an act of a Canadian legislature. Efforts were made to get Prime Minister Macdonald and the Dominion government to cancel the act, but Macdonald refused, believing it to be a matter for the province to decide since it concerned education.

Manitoba Schools Act. Another act of a provincial legislature—the Manitoba Schools Act of March 31, 1890—ignited a similar controversy between the French- and English-speaking people of Canada. When the Province of Manitoba was created 20 years before, the school system was to have both Protestant and Roman Catholic schools. As time went on, however, immigration into Manitoba became predominantly that of English-speaking people. This migration changed the balance in the schools and other institutions. The situation was deliberately aggravated in 1889 by D'Alton McCarthy (1836–1898), a lawyer who served in Parliament from 1876 until his death. He was a conservative Protestant who had voted against the Jesuits' Estates Act. Because he so opposed the use of French outside Quebec, he naturally advocated a monolingual school system in Manitoba.

Anti-Catholic and anti-French feeling built up. The result was the enactment of a strict law that abolished denominational schools and the use of the French language in schools. French Canadians in Manitoba and Quebec were outraged and appealed to the courts. The government in Ottawa was also asked to intervene, although by the terms of confederation, educational matters were to be supervised only by the provinces.

In 1897 a new Liberal ministry in Ottawa worked out an agreement. Any school in Manitoba attended by ten or more students who spoke a language other than English would provide instruction for those pupils in their own language. In the long run, however, this arrangement did not work. After 1900, immigration to Manitoba consisted largely of persons who, when they came, spoke neither English nor French. Multilingual schools then posed a formidable practical problem. The result was an act in 1916 making English the only language to be used in the schools for instructional purposes. It was not until the 1970s that the matter of bilingual instruction in the province's schools was satisfactorily resolved.

Laurier and the Liberals.
Macdonald's death in 1891 resulted in a breakup of the Conservative Party. The election of June 23, 1896, confirmed Liberal strength when the Conservatives won only 88 seats in the House of Commons to the Liberals' 123. Wilfrid Laurier (1841–1919) became the new prime minister, the first Francophone to hold the post under confederation. He had already been active in politics, having held a seat in the Commons from 1874.

Laurier had a national outlook: He saw the Dominion as more important than its parts, and Canada as a nation independent of British Empire interests though solidly loyal to the Crown. He organized a cabinet of like-minded leaders. His decision to expand the railway system, always a controversial subject in Canada, caused a rift in the party, but two new lines were begun, the Grand Trunk Pacific and the National Transcontinental.

Laurier took an active part in Canada's relations with Great Britain. He attended a colonial conference in London in 1897 at the time of Queen Victoria's Diamond Jubilee, and two others in 1902 and 1907. At all of these, Laurier refused to commit Canada to proposals that, he believed, would pledge action in areas where the nation would not have a proper share in deciding on the policies involved, such as imperial defense. In 1907, for example, Laurier refused to allow Canada to contribute to the cost of the British navy, but three years later he proposed, without the full support of the Liberal Party, that Canada build a small naval force of its own. This issue helped lead to Laurier's defeat in 1911.

The problem of relations with Great Britain was especially acute at the outbreak of the Boer War (1899–1902) in South Africa. English Canadians, for the most part, advocated sending troops to support the British cause, while French Canadians opposed this. Laurier's government decided to send a token force of 1,000 infantrymen to join with the British forces. As the British position worsened in South Africa, another 6,000 volunteers readily enlisted, some 7,000 men eventually serving there. Laurier's initial action, however, caused another rift in the Liberal Party because the Quebec branch had opposed helping England.

A long-standing dispute over the boundary between the Alaskan panhandle and British Columbia was settled in 1903 by a commission made up of two Canadians, three Americans, and Lord Chief Justice Alverstone of England. The question of where the boundary should be located had become important in recent years because of the gold rush in the Yukon in 1896. The British representative sided with the Americans, and awarded the United States almost all it claimed. The implication to the Canadians was that Great Britain was so eager to have America on its side in world affairs that it would sacrifice Canadian interests to do so.

In 1911 Canada and the United States negotiated a new reciprocal trade agreement. By its terms, certain Canadian food products could enter the United States free of duty. There was to be reciprocal reduction of tariffs on manufactured goods. At first there was little opposition, although the Canadian Conservative Party was against it. Then Canadian industrialists, who were beginning to build up a substantial market in their own country, voiced opposition, as did the railway interests. The agreement was approved by the American Congress, although more trouble was caused in Canada when one influential congressman said that he saw the pact as a step toward joining Canada to the United States. In Canada 18 Liberals who had close ties to banking and insurance interests abandoned their party on the issue. Consequently, the agreement was not approved by the Canadian Parliament. The issue of reciprocal trade between the two nations then died down for more than half a century.

Laurier felt compelled to resign the prime ministership, and an election was held on September 21, 1911. The Conservative Party was voted into office with 134 seats in the Commons. The new prime minister was Robert L. Borden (1854–1937) of Nova Scotia, who had been elected to Parliament in 1896 and who became the leader of the Conservative Party in 1901.

IN WORLD WAR I, Canada put 628,000 men and women into uniform, about two-thirds of whom saw service overseas. They withstood the first gas attack in the history of warfare in northwest Belgium in 1915.

World War I.
As a dominion within the British Empire, Canada had no official voice in matters of war and peace. Thus, when Great Britain declared war on Germany and Austria-Hungary on August 4, 1914, Canada was at war as well. In fact, the Dominion had no hesitation about doing its part, although many Francophones were less than enthusiastic when it came to serving in the army. They felt that their language was a barrier to promotion; indeed, they were badly underrepresented during the war, especially in the higher ranks.

By the time the war ended in 1918, Canada had put 628,000 men and women in uniform, about two-thirds of whom saw service overseas. Casualties were high, with 59,544 dead or missing (almost identical in terms of lives and expense to that of the United States), and about 175,000 wounded, these falling on a population of only 7.5 million people.

CANADA'S MEMORIAL to its dead in World War I stands on Vimy Ridge in France. The 1917 battle, predominantly a Canadian operation, took the ridge, something that the French had tried to do since 1914.

THE WAR and its aftermath brought broad economic changes. Canadian industry grew with the building of steel mills and shipyards, and the country became a net lender.

One reason for the high toll was the way in which the Canadian troops were used. Their spirit made them crack shock troops. Only two months after they arrived in France, in April 1915, Canadian soldiers withstood the first gas attack in the history of warfare; it was launched by the Germans in the Ypres salient in northwest Belgium. By August 1916, four divisions were in France, constituting a separate Canadian corps. During 1916 Canadians fought in several desperate battles on the Somme, where casualties were overwhelming. It was there that Canadian troops established their reputation.

Canadians exhibited their valor again on April 9 and 10, 1917, at Vimy Ridge in northern France. The battle was predominantly a Canadian operation designed to capture the great ridge overlooking the plain between Lens and Arras and from which German observers

called down deadly artillery fire on Allied troops. The Canadian corps, in a meticulously planned operation, stormed and held the ridge, something that the French had tried to do since 1914. Canada's memorial to its war dead was erected here after the war. Finally, the Canadian corps played a key role in the last great struggles of 1918 when the Hindenburg line was broken. On August 8, at the Battle of Amiens, Canadians were the spearhead of a vital breakthrough.

In the air war, 11 Canadians were among 27 British Empire aces who shot down 30 or more aircraft. Leading them were Lieutenant Colonel W. A. "Billy" Bishop, third highest with 72 victories, and Lieutenant Commander Raymond Colishaw with 60.

On the home front during the war, a bitter political battle arose over the issue of conscription. By 1917 not enough volunteers were coming forward to keep the ranks of the army filled in light of the unexpected length of the war and the heavy casualties. Prime Minister Borden's government felt it necessary to introduce the Military Service Bill in June 1917. The Liberals were split on the issue, while the Conservatives, although on the whole favoring conscription, were not supported by their Quebec associates.

Conscription became law and the struggle over it was a main factor in bringing about a union government. An election on December 17 was fought between the Laurier Liberals, named for the party leader, Wilfrid Laurier, who opposed conscription, and the Unionists led by Borden. The latter triumphed, winning 153 seats in the House of Commons. Riots flared up over conscription in Quebec City in March and April of 1918.

At the Paris Peace Conference in France after the war, Canada had its own representatives. It signed the Versailles

Treaty on June 28, 1919, as a full national state. The important part Canada had played in support of Britain during the war thus paid off in enhanced status internationally. Canada began to expand its own diplomatic service and first exchanged ministers with the United States in 1927.

The war brought broad economic changes to the country. Agriculture expanded with the demand for foodstuffs. Prairie acreage under cultivation, for example, increased by 80 percent between 1913 and 1919. Industry also grew with the building of steel mills and shipyards. Overall, the economy grew by 20 percent in this period, and Canada became a net lender instead of a borrower. On the other hand, a growing demand for goods and debt brought on by the large sums the government had to borrow to finance the war brought about an alarming inflation. The cost of living increased by 60 percent between the start of the war and 1918.

The wartime atmosphere speeded the granting of women's suffrage. The prairie provinces allowed it in 1916 and others followed. The right to vote in Canada-wide elections was granted in all provinces except Quebec by 1922. On April 13, 1925, Newfoundland granted the vote to women, though it did not attain provincial status until 1949. Quebec did not give the vote to women until 1940.

The 1920s. The dominant figure in Canadian politics between the two world wars was William Lyon Mackenzie King (1874–1950), grandson of the 19th-century leader William Lyon Mackenzie. King entered Parliament as a Liberal in 1909 and the next year became a member of the cabinet as minister for labor. He was chosen leader of the Liberal Party in 1919 and rose to be prime minister after the election of December 6, 1921. The Liberals were a seat short of a majority in the House of Commons, but King secured the support of the Progressive Party. This new political group was organized in 1920, chiefly as the voice of western farmers who thought they were neglected by the government in Ottawa. The Progressives won 65 seats in the 1921 election, 15 more than the Conservatives, making them the second largest party in Parliament. A similar new political unit, the United Farmers of Alberta, governed that province from 1921 to 1935.

In the 1925 election the Liberals lost seats, but King was able to stay in power until 1926. At that time he faced a vote of censure against his government because of a scandal in which the minister of customs was involved. Seeking to avoid the vote, King asked Julian Hedworth George (1862–1935), Lord Byng, the governor-general, to dissolve Parliament and call an election. Normally, such a request would not be made until the government had been defeated in Parliament. Byng refused the request, whereupon King resigned without giving time, as was customary, for the governor-

general to arrange for a successor. This was an unprecedented situation in terms of parliamentary procedure.

The crisis that ensued was not resolved until Arthur Meighen (1874–1960), the Conservative leader, King's successor, was defeated in a vote in the House of Commons, making it necessary to hold a general election. The Liberals won, increasing the number of seats they held in Parliament, and King became prime minister again.

Statute of Westminster. More formal recognition of the new status of Canada and the other self-governing British dominions came in 1926 at the Imperial Conference in London. Here Prime Minister King played a leading role in drafting the Balfour Report. Arthur James Balfour (1848–1930) was a former British prime minister. The report defined the dominions as "autonomous communities within the British Empire, equal in status and in no way subordinate one to another in any aspect of domestic or external affairs, though united by a common allegiance to the Crown and freely associated as members of the British Commonwealth of Nations."

The 1926 conference also established a committee to carry out a further study of the relationship of the dominions to the British government and the Crown. In 1929 this committee made its report, which was adopted at the next Imperial Conference in 1930. The end result was the Statute of Westminster, an act of the British Parliament of December 11, 1931. This statute made more legally binding the Balfour Report of 1926 and ensured the dominions of their autonomous standing as full members of the Commonwealth with full control of their foreign and domestic policies.

The dominions could now make their own laws without the British Parliament having to legislate for them or approve their actions. The new statute also repealed some laws that had become obsolete in view of the new relationship between the mother country and the dominions.

The Statute of Westminster applied in part to Australia, New Zealand, South Africa, the Irish Free State, and Newfoundland. It did not contravene the British North America Act of 1867, which remained in effect.

Great Depression. The world-wide depression that began with the crash of the New York stock market in late October 1919 demonstrated, as conditions worsened, that Canada was vulnerable to bad times in other lands. Agriculture was hit especially hard when other countries raised their tariffs on agricultural products, with the export of wheat suffering the most. Wheat production shrank from 567 million bushels in 1928 to 182 million by 1937, while the price of 38 cents a bushel by the end of 1932 did not cover the cost of growing. In addition, drought in 1934 and 1937 ruined many crops.

The depression in agriculture was felt throughout the country. Railroads lost millions of dollars in freight revenues because of the decline in farm production. Demand for manufactured goods slumped drastically, as did construction activity. By 1935 fully one-tenth of the population, both urban and rural, was receiving some kind of relief. With an estimated 23 percent of the labor force out of work by 1933, many Canadians emigrated to the United States, where the situation turned out to be no better.

An election on July 28, 1930, swept into power with a sizable majority the Conservative Party with Richard B. Bennett (1870–1947) as prime minister, showing that the Great Depression and the failure of the Liberal government under King to cope with it had turned Canadian politics around. In 1927 Bennett had succeeded Arthur Meighen as leader of the Conservative Party. Bennett was born in New Brunswick but moved west; in 1911 he was elected to the House of Commons from Alberta.

The new administration promised to end unemployment by raising tariff barriers to eliminate competition from foreign goods of any kind. The general tariff level was raised by as high as 50 percent on 180 items in the hopes that Canada would become self-sufficient through the creation of new jobs. Unfortunately for Canada, other nations had the same idea, especially the United States with its Smoot-Hawley Tariff of 1930. For practical purposes, this tariff barred many of Canada's basic products from entering the United States. The government's action, however, did reduce imports and change a trade deficit into a surplus. It thereby kept unemployment from being as high as it might have been, but it raised costs for both producers and consumers and so did not do much to increase purchasing power.

Bennett also promised to stimulate the economy by building railroads, starting work on the St. Lawrence Seaway, and constructing a national highway.

Parliament, in September 1930, not only raised tariffs but also voted $20 million for unemployment relief. At the Imperial Conference in London in 1930 and again at the Imperial Economic Conference in Ottawa in 1932, Bennett sought to improve matters by advocating a strong system of preference among the nations of the British Commonwealth. Thus, Bennett, for the most part, adhered to conservative policies.

In January 1935, however, Bennett suddenly announced a change of course and advocated legislation similar to that of the New Deal of President Franklin D. Roosevelt in the United States; he called for strong action by the federal government to deal directly with economic problems. Canada's Parliament enacted legislation that established minimum wages, hours of work per week, unemployment insurance, loans and credits for farmers, and control of unfair trade practices. These measures, however, did not remain in effect for long. Faced with court tests in 1937, they were held to be unconstitutional by the Privy Council in England.

As a political leader, Bennett was high-handed and unwilling to consult with his colleagues. For example, he demanded what amounted to a blank check for appropriations dealing with relief. He lost public confidence, resigned from the cabinet, and formed a faction of disgruntled Conservatives. A federal election on October 14, 1935, put the Liberal Party in office with a large majority of the seats in the House of Commons. William Lyon Mackenzie King became prime minister once more, holding the office until November 15, 1948, when he was succeeded by a fellow Liberal, Louis St. Laurent (1882–1973).

The Great Depression brought into being new and radical political groups that began to influence Canadian life. Chief among them was the Social Credit Party, with its center in Alberta. Imported from England, the somewhat vague doctrine of "social credit" called for the redistribution of purchasing power. The

27 North America

labor
US

labour
Brit.

check
US

cheque
Brit.

center
US

centre
Brit.

Statute of Westminster, 1931

An Act to give effect to certain resolutions passed by Imperial Conference
held in the years 1926 and 1930
11th December, 1931.

Whereas the delegates to His Majesty's Governments in the United Kingdom, the Dominion of Canada, the Commonwealth of Australia, the Dominion of New Zealand, the Union of South Africa, the Irish Free State and Newfoundland, at Imperial Conferences holden at Westminster in the years of our Lord nineteen hundred and twenty-six and nineteen hundred and thirty did concur in making the declarations and resolutions set forth in the Reports of the said Conferences:

And whereas it is meet and proper to set out by way of preamble to this Act that, inasmuch as the Crown is the symbol of the free association of the members of the British Commonwealth of Nations, and as they are united by a common allegiance to the Crown, it would be in accord with the established constitutional position of all the members of the Commonwealth in relation to one another that any alteration in the law touching the Succession to the Throne or the Royal Style and Titles shall hereafter require the assent as well of the Parliaments of all the Dominions as of the Parliament of the United Kingdom:

And whereas it is in accord with the established constitutional position that no law hereafter made by the Parliament of the United Kingdom shall extend to any of the said Dominions as part of the law of that Dominion otherwise than at the request and with consent of that Dominion:

And whereas it is necessary for the ratifying, confirming and establishing of certain of the said declarations and resolutions of the said Conferences that a law be made and enacted in due form by authority of the Parliament of the United Kingdom:

And whereas the Dominion of Canada, the Commonwealth of Australia, the Dominion of New Zealand, the Union of South Africa, the Irish Free State and Newfoundland have severally requested and consented to the submission of a measure to the Parliament of the United Kingdom for making such provision with regard to the matters aforesaid as is hereafter in this Act contained:

Now, therefore be it enacted by the King's Most Excellent Majesty by and with the advice and consent of the Lords Spiritual and Temporal, and Commons, in the present Parliament assembled, and by the authority of the same, as follows:

1.   In this Act the expression "Dominion" means any of the following Dominions, that is to say, the Dominion of Canada, the Commonwealth of Australia, the Dominion of New Zealand, the Union of South Africa, the Irish Free State and Newfoundland.

2.   (1) The Colonial Laws Validity Act, 1865, shall not apply to any law made after the commencement of this Act by the Parliament of a Dominion.

(2) No law and no provision of any law made after the commencement of this Act by the Parliament of a Dominion shall be void or inoperative on the ground that it is repugnant to the law of England, or to the provisions of any existing or future Act of Parliament of the United Kingdom, or to any order, rule, or regulation made under any such Act, and the powers of the Parliament of a Dominion shall include the power to repeal or amend any such Act, order, rule or regulation in so far as the same is part of the law of the Dominion.

3.   It is hereby declared and enacted that the Parliament of a Dominion has full power to make laws having extra-territorial operation.

4.   No Act of Parliament of the United Kingdom passed after the commencement of this Act shall extend or be deemed to extend, to a Dominion as part of the law of that Dominion, unless it is expressly declared in that Act that that Dominion has requested, and consented to, the enactment thereof.

5.   Without prejudice to the generality of the foregoing provisions of this Act, sections seven hundred and thirty-five and seven hundred and thirty-six of the Merchant Shipping Act, 1894, shall be construed as though reference therein to the Legislature of a British possession did not include reference to the Parliament of a Dominion.

6.   Without prejudice to a generality of the foregoing provisions of this Act, section four of the Colonial Courts of Admiralty Act, 1890 (which requires certain laws to be reserved for the signification of His Majesty's pleasure or to contain a suspending clause), and so much of section seven of that Act as requires the approval of His Majesty in Council to any rules of Court for regulating the practice and procedure of a Colonial Court of Admiralty, shall cease to have effect in any Dominion as from the commencement of this Act.

7.   (1) Nothing in this Act shall be deemed to apply to the repeal, amendment or alteration of the British North America Acts, 1867 to 1930, or any order, rule or regulation made thereunder.

(2) The provisions of section two of this Act shall extend to laws made by any of the Provinces of Canada and to the Powers of the Legislatures of such Provinces.

(3) The powers conferred by this Act upon the Parliament of Canada or upon the legislatures of the Provinces shall be restricted to the enactment of laws in relation to matters within the competence of the Parliament of Canada or of any of the legislatures of the Provinces respectively.

8.   Nothing in this Act shall be deemed to confer any power to repeal or alter the Constitution or the Constitution Act of the Commonwealth of Australia or the Constitution Act of the Dominion of New Zealand otherwise than in accordance with the law exsiting before the commencement of this Act.

9.   (1) Nothing in this Act shall be deemed to authorize the Parliament of the Commonwealth of Australia to make laws on any matter within the authority of the States of Australia, not being a matter within the authority of the Parliament or Government of the Commonwealth of Australia.

(2) Nothing in this Act shall be deemed to require the concurrence of the Parliament or Government of the Commonwealth of Australia, in any law made by the Parliament of the United Kingdom with respect to any matter within the authority of the States of Australia, not being a matter within the authority of the Parliament or Government of the Commonwealth of Australia, in any case where it would have been in accordance with the constitutional practice existing before the commencement of this Act that the Parliament of the United Kingdom should make that law without such concurrence.

(3) In the application of this Act to the Commonwealth of Australia the request and consent referred to in section four shall mean the request and consent of the Parliament and Government of the Commonwealth.

10.   (1) None of the following sections of this Act, that is to say, sections two, three, four, five and six, shall extend to a Dominion to which this section applies as part of the law of that Dominion unless that section is adopted by the Parliament of the Dominion, and any Act of that Parliament adopting any section of this Act may provide that the adoption shall have effect either from the commencement of this Act or from such later date as is specified in the adopting Act.

(2) The Parliament of any such Dominion as aforesaid may at any time revoke the adoption of any section referred to in subsection (1) of this section.

(3) The Dominions to which this section applies are the Commonwealth of Australia, the Dominion of New Zealand and Newfoundland.

11.   Notwithstanding anything in the Interpretation Act, 1889, the expression "Colony" shall not, in any Act of the Parliament of the United Kingdom passed after the commencement of this Act, include a Dominion or any Province or State forming part of a Dominion.

12.   This Act may be cited as the Statute of Westminster, 1931.

ideas of social credit were picked up by William Aberhart (1878–1943), a Calgary teacher who was also a radio evangelist. One of his proposals was a "social dividend" of $25 a month to every person. Such ideas swept the province and in 1935 the Social Credit Party won control, with Aberhart as premier. That same year, in the general election, the Social Credit Party won 17 seats in the Federal Parliament. It remained in power in Alberta until 1971, although most of the social credit laws passed were declared unconstitutional.

In 1932, in Calgary, the Cooperative Commonwealth Federation (CCF) was founded; it represented farm, labor, and socialist interests. In the 1935 election, the CCF captured 7 seats in the House of Commons; in 1961 it changed its name to the New Democratic Party.

Although a political opponent of Bennett, King now wished to carry out some of the same policies that, when submitted to the Privy Council in England, had been found to conflict with the British North America Act, in that they would have allowed the federal government to do what was reserved to the provinces. On the other hand, the provinces clearly could not cope with the Great Depression.

In 1937 King appointed the Royal Commission on Dominion-Provincial Relations to investigate "the economic and financial basis of Confederation and the distribution of legislative powers in the light of the economic and social developments of the last 70 years." The Rowell-Sirois Report (from the commission's chairmen) of 1940 advocated what amounted to a rewriting of the British North America Act. However, when a provincial-federal conference was held, there was so much opposition from Ontario, Quebec, and British Columbia to the commission's recommendations that the meeting proved fruitless. An amendment to the act did allow the federal government in Ottawa to establish a system of unemployment insurance.

World War II. Such constitutional problems and conflicts of interest between the provinces and the federal government were now overshadowed by World War II. Great Britain declared war on Germany on September 3, 1939, and Canada followed on September 10. Prime Minister King pledged that there would be no conscription for overseas service, which was to be voluntary; but under the National Resources Mobilization Act (June 1940), men could be conscripted for training and service within Canada.

As the war went on, with Germany inflicting crushing defeats on the Allies in 1940 and Japan entering the war in December 1941, public support for conscription was voiced. Accordingly, a plebiscite was held on April 27, 1942, and the nation voted by a large margin to release the government from its no-conscription pledge. In the face of bitter opposition in Quebec, however, King did nothing to implement the vote until December 1944, when his cabinet revolted because he had not acted.

CANADIAN TROOPS evacuated French towns during the fierce fighting in 1944.

At the outbreak of war, Canada's armed forces comprised an army of 4,500 regular soldiers and 60,000 militia reservists, a Royal Canadian Air Force of about 4,500, and a navy made up of 1,800 men and 13 ships. By December 1939, one infantry division had been dispatched to England. Further troops followed so that by late 1942, there were five divisions, two of them armored, in England. In all, Canada put about 1 million men and women into uniform: nearly 700,000 in the ground forces, 220,000 in the air force, and 90,000 in the navy. By the end of the war, 41,700 Canadians had been killed or were missing. Canada's contribution to the Allied air forces was proportionally large because most of the training of pilots and air crews for the British Commonwealth was carried out in Canada, where space was available and facilities could be constructed with comparative ease and speed. In all, more than 131,000 airmen were trained.

In Europe, on August 19, 1942, Canadian troops went into major combat for the first time, in an action that proved disastrous. Two brigades and other units raided Dieppe, France, partly to test the German defenses and partly to keep Nazi forces pinned down. Of the approximately 5,000 men who took part, over 900 were killed and another 900 taken prisoner.

The 1st Division, as part of the British 8th Army, took part in the invasion of Sicily on July 10, 1943, and then engaged in the invasion of Italy. Eventually, Canadians participated in the capture of Rome on May 23, 1944.

The 3rd Canadian Division and the 2nd Armored Brigade took part in the initial assault on the beaches of Normandy on D-Day, June 6, 1944. More Canadians were soon sent across the English Channel, and on July 23 the 1st Canadian Army was activated. These troops captured Caen on July 8–9, were defeated at Verrières Ridge on July 28, but captured Falaise on August 15. From then on, Canadians continued to fight on the left flank of the Allies, capturing the Scheldt area of Belgium against strong German resistance in November. In February 1945, the 1st Army took part in the drive on the Siegfried Line and on into Germany. Some troops remained in Germany until April 1946, as part of the Allied occupation forces.

In 1941, when Hong Kong fell to the Japanese, two Canadian battalions were present; they lost nearly as many men to harsh treatment in prison camps as in the defense of the colony. A squadron of the Royal Canadian Air Force fought in the Battle of Britain in 1940. By the end of the war in Europe, there were 48 squadrons overseas, 14 of which were bombers. The navy had grown to 471 combat ships and was the third largest in the world; its most valuable service was accomplished in convoy operations battling German U-boats. In the invasion of Normandy, the navy contributed 110 ships. In 1943 the Canadian navy took over all convoy duties in the northwest Atlantic Ocean west of the 47th meridian.

Prime Minister King and President Franklin D. Roosevelt, in August 1940, announced a Permanent Joint Board on Defense for their two countries. Canada took part in the crash research program that led to the atomic bomb, and cooperated with the United States in the construction of the 1,523-mile-(2,451-kilometer-) long Alaska Highway, which began at Dawson Creek, British Columbia, and crossed the Yukon Territory to Fairbanks, Alaska.

labor	*US*
labour	*Brit.*
armored	*US*
armoured	*Brit.*
kilometer	*US*
kilometre	*Brit.*

THE ST. LAWRENCE SEAWAY
is a system of canals, locks, and dams that creates a shipping route from the Atlantic Ocean to the western end of the Great Lakes.

Postwar Canada. After the war, both Canada's standing and activity in international affairs increased. In 1945 Canada joined the United Nations and all its specialized agencies. On April 4, 1949, Canada became the first nation to ratify the North Atlantic Treaty. In the Korean War, which began in 1950, Canada furnished an infantry brigade to the United Nations forces. In 1954 Canada became one of three nations to supervise the armistice in Southeast Asia. In 1956 the nation helped form the United Nations peacekeeping force in the Suez area, and in 1964 a similar force on Cyprus. Canada and the United States established a joint air defense command (NORAD, or North American Air Defense Command) in 1958.

Several amendments to the British North America Act, passed by the British Parliament between 1949 and 1960, allowed the federal government to legislate in new areas. The most important amendment was that of December 16, 1949, which enabled the Canadian Parliament to amend the constitution of its own accord in matters that affected the federal government but not the provinces. After that, the only area in which action by the British Parliament was necessary was in matters that affected both the nation and the provinces. However, formal assent of the British Crown was still required. An example was the amendment on May 31, 1951, that approved the Old Age Security Act. Another came when royal assent was given on August 10, 1960, to the passage of the Canadian Bill of Rights.

When King decided to retire in late 1948, he selected as his successor Louis Stephen St. Laurent (1882–1973), a bilingual lawyer who had entered politics in 1942 as minister of justice in the King cabinet. St. Laurent was minister of external affairs from 1946 to 1948, when he became leader of the Liberal Party and prime minister of Canada.

Canada enjoyed an economic boom while St. Laurent headed the government.

As in World War I, Canada's economy expanded greatly during World War II. By the end of the war, the government had invested $1.5 billion in the war industry. During the war, military products valuing more than $10 billion were produced. About two-thirds of these products went to Allied nations. The result of this stimulus to manufacturing was to accelerate the growth of Canada as a fully developed industrial state.

Agriculture suffered during the war because of the closing of many overseas markets, but the grain surpluses built up were badly needed after the end of hostilities. The cost of living was kept under control, considering wartime conditions, but the government had to borrow over $12 billion between 1939 and 1945. Nearly half of this came from private citizens.

He and the Liberals sponsored more social insurance legislation and supported the growth of education facilities. Perhaps the most lasting achievement of the St. Laurent administration was the construction of the St. Lawrence Seaway, although it was not completed until two years after St. Laurent left office.

Built jointly with the United States, the seaway is a system of canals, dams, and locks that creates a shipping route from the Atlantic Ocean to the western end of the Great Lakes that is capable of handling oceangoing vessels. In all, it is some 2,375 miles (3,821 kilometers) long. The Canadian government first approved the start of construction in 1951. Initial cost to Canada was $330 million ($130 million to the United States), but improvements cost another $300 million. The $600 million for a hydroelectric plant—with the cost shared by both countries—has since been recovered through sales of electric power.

The seaway was formally opened by a ceremony at St. Lambert, Quebec, attended by Prime Minister John Diefenbaker, Queen Elizabeth II, and President Dwight D. Eisenhower of the United States on June 26, 1959.

By the second half of the 1950s, the Liberals, who had been in power for two decades, became arrogant. For example, in 1956 they used harsh parliamentary tactics known as closure to shut down debate and force through Parliament a controversial bill that would provide an $80 million loan from the government to Trans-Canada Pipe Lines, a U.S.–owned company, for the construction of a natural gas pipeline from Alberta to Ontario and also to U.S. markets. The bill was passed on June 1, 1956, and received royal assent on June 7.

An election on June 10, 1957, showed that the voters had become disenchanted with the Liberal Party. The Progressive Conservative Party, as the opposition had been called since 1942, won the most seats in Parliament, 112, but not a clear majority. Even so, with

CANADA INITIATED
a program of transcontinental highway construction and cooperated with the United States to complete the Alaska Highway from Dawson Creek, British Columbia, to Fairbanks, Alaska.

the aid of third-party groups, John George Diefenbaker (1895–1979) took office as prime minister. He had first been elected to Parliament in 1940 and was chosen leader of the Progressive Conservative Party the year before he became prime minister.

Diefenbaker was a skillful strategist. Having gained favorable publicity at a Commonwealth ministers meeting in June/July 1957, by promising to shift Canadian trade from the United States to Great Britain, he went on to humiliate Lester B. Pearson, the new leader of the opposition, by lowering taxes, raising the old age pension, and increasing housing loans. He then proceeded to dissolve Parliament and go back to the people, seeking a majority.

Canadian voters approved of Diefenbaker, as shown in the federal election of March 31, 1958, in which they voted into the House of Commons 208 Progressive Conservatives against only 57 candidates of all other parties. The tilt to the right, however, did not last long.

On the positive side of the ledger, the Diefenbaker government helped revitalize agriculture in western Canada through selling wheat to China and other agricultural reform policies. His "northern vision," a term often heard in his 1957 and 1958 election campaigns, led in practice to a certain amount of economic development in the region and increased public awareness of the Far North. He personally regarded the 1960 Canadian Bill of Rights as his greatest achievement. One of its most positive elements was the granting of the federal vote to native peoples. However, the bill disregarded the needs and aspirations of Canada's Francophones, who saw in it a determination to assimilate them. This would cost Diefenbaker dearly in the next two elections.

In the 1962 election campaign, the Liberal Party used to its advantage a controversy over the presence of nuclear weapons on Canadian soil, a perceived economic crisis—the Canadian dollar was trading at only 92.5 cents U.S.—and the government's highly controversial cancellation in 1959 of the Avro Arrow program. The Avro Arrow was the Canadian-designed supersonic fighter, the most advanced aircraft of its day. While the Diefenbaker government retained power in the federal election of June 18, 1962, the 50 seats it had won in Quebec in 1958 were reduced to 14; in the 1963 election, which it would lose, it got only 8 seats in Quebec.

In the election of April 8, 1963, the Liberal Party won more seats than any other party. Although it did not have an absolute majority, it was able to form a government with Lester Bowles Pearson (1897–1972) as prime minister. A veteran of World War I and a former university professor of history, Pearson had had a long and distinguished career as a diplomat. In 1945 he became Canadian ambassador to the United States and was his nation's key representative at the conference in San Francisco that founded the United Nations. He then headed Canada's delegation to the new international body.

In September 1946, Prime Minister King summoned Pearson home to take on the duties of deputy minister of external affairs. Two years later, he would become minister. Pearson's efforts led to Canada's joining NATO in 1949, and he saw to it that Canada contributed troops to the UN army in the Korean War (1950–1953). Serving as president of the UN General Assembly in 1952, he tried unsuccessfully to find a way of solving the Korean dispute; in 1956, however, by proposing a UN peacekeeping force to serve in the Suez, thereby separating Egyptian forces from invading French, British, and Israeli troops, he achieved his shining hour in diplomacy. On October 12, 1957, he was awarded the Nobel Peace Prize.

In January 1958, Lester Pearson was elected leader of the Liberal Party of Canada; on April 22, 1963, he became prime minister.

The legacy of the Pearson government is particularly rich in terms of social welfare: In February 1965, the age of becoming a beneficiary of the Old Age Pension was lowered from 70 to 65 years, and in April of that year, the Canada Pension Plan was established. On December 21, 1966, royal assent was given to the national Medicare Act, effective July 1, 1968, ensuring universal medical care. In addition, the Department of Regional Economic Expansion was set up to oversee the country's disadvantaged regions. And, after much preliminary debate, the new national flag of Canada was raised for the first time on Ottawa's Parliament Hill, on February 15, 1965.

Troubled provinces. The 1960s were a period of agitation because French-speaking Canadians, most of whom reside in Quebec, wanted to protect themselves from what they saw as the danger of being overwhelmed by English-speaking Canada. The Francophones believed they were politically and economically disadvantaged, in part because the rest of Canada refused to adopt bilingualism to any extent. As a result of the unrest, the federal government, in 1963, had established the Royal Commission on Bilingualism and Biculturalism. The commission recommended in 1967 that both English and French be made official languages of the federal government and that in any province where the minority, either French or English, reached 10 percent, both languages should be official. This latter proposal was enacted into law in 1969. A second report in the next year said that children should have the right to be educated in whichever of the official languages they chose.

The 1960s also saw the beginning of what became known as the Quiet Revolution, as Quebec Province emerged from what many Francophones regarded as its economic dark ages under the leadership of the late provincial premier Maurice Duplessis (1890–1959), in office from 1936 to 1939 and again from 1944 to 1959. Most industry at that time was owned by Anglophones—Canadian and American. Although Quebec's population was 80 percent Francophone, there was no Francophone business class as such, just a tiny elite that owed much to inherited wealth. The Quiet Revolution sought to change all that, and one of its prime movers was Jacques Parizeau (1930–), a young politician, fluently bilingual, who held a Ph.D. from the London School of Economics. He became economic adviser to Liberal provincial premier Jean Lesage (1912–1980), the man known as the father of the Quiet Revolution.

LESTER BOWLES PEARSON was the prime minister of Canada from 1963 to 1968. He had been awarded the Nobel Peace Prize in 1957 for his efforts to resolve the Suez Canal crisis.

27 North America

A large number of Francophones in Quebec wanted to go even further and declare that province independent of and separated from the rest of Canada. The situation was exacerbated by President Charles de Gaulle of France when he visited Quebec in July of 1967. In a speech in Montreal, he seemed to promise support for independence, exclaiming, *"Vive le Québec libre"* (Long live a free Quebec).

When Pearson retired in 1968, he was able to pass on the leadership of the Liberal Party and with it the office of prime minister to Pierre Elliott Trudeau (1919–2000). A writer, constitutional lawyer, and law professor at the Université de Montréal, he had been elected to the House of Commons in 1965.

On April 6, 1968, Trudeau was elected leader of the Liberal Party, succeeding Lester B. Pearson. He took office as prime minister of Canada on April 20. Then, in the federal election of June 25, 1968, the Liberals won a decisive victory, with 155 seats in the House of Commons.

Trudeau was a fervent nationalist whose success at the polls was rivaled only by that of Prime Minister King. His tide of popularity was known as "Trudeaumania."

kilometers
US

kilometres
Brit.

The 1970 October Crisis was the most dramatic episode of his early years in office. When a Quebec separatist group, the Front de Libération du Québec (FLQ), carried on terrorist activities, including kidnappings and the murder of a Quebec cabinet minister, Pierre Laporte, Trudeau invoked the War Measures Act and had hundreds of suspects rounded up. This extreme action remains a point of controversy.

Trudeau had to deal not only with the demands of Quebec but also with dissatisfaction from other provinces on other issues. He called a conference of all the provinces in June 1968, at which provincial leaders argued for more tax sharing between the central government and themselves. Little came of the conference.

After the 1972 election, Trudeau had to form a minority government; however, he was returned with a majority in 1974. At this point, he faced an economic crisis and burgeoning inflation. Wage and price controls were enforced in 1975, under much protest, and problems were compounded by the Quebec provincial election the next year.

The Quebec separatist movement scored a victory on its home territory on November 15, 1976, when the Parti Québécois won 89 of the 110 seats in the provincial legislature. The Liberal Party was the big loser. René Lévesque (1922–1987), born on the Gaspé peninsula, the leader of the Quebec nationalists, was the man who became premier of Quebec as the result of the vote. Lévesque had been a war correspondent in World War II and had also served as an interpreter between the American forces and the Free French. In 1967 he was one of the founders of the *Mouvement souveraineté-association*

French Canada, Quebec Separatism, and the Future

Although the French separatist movement in Quebec came into its own during the so-called Quiet Revolution of the 1960s, the origins of the movement can be traced back to the early colonial period of Canada and followed through the nation's history. Because it was colonized by two mother countries—Great Britain and France—Canada inherited two distinct cultures, languages, and civil systems. English and French rivalry in the Americas culminated in the French and Indian War. In 1763 Great Britain gained virtually all of France's possessions east of the Mississippi River and French Canadians were effectively cut off—economically, culturally, and politically—from their country of origin.

An unsuccessful early attempt to assimilate French Canadians into English Canada and the rapid domination of Quebec's economy by an English-speaking business class heightened French-Canadian fears that their way of life was in danger. Friction and conflict arose periodically between English-speaking and French-speaking Canada throughout the 19th and 20th centuries.

The rebuilding of educational and cultural ties with France in the early 1960s augmented the growing belief among many French Canadians that their cultural and economic security could be gained only through separation from Canada. Much positive change has occurred in Quebec in the last 30 years, however, and it is now unclear whether the majority of Quebec's citizens favor independence, autonomy, or some form of special status within Canada.

THE MOVEMENT in Quebec for separation from Canada has been active since the 1960s, with strong support for the issue on both sides, as these signs indicate.

(Sovereignty-association movement) which, the following year, became the Parti Québécois. Now, as premier, he put through the provincial legislative measures intended to improve the status of the French language and culture—notably Bill 101, which made French the official language of Quebec—and other acts to increase the province's power in the fields of education and social welfare. The minister of finance in the Lévesque government, who would be credited with revolutionizing Quebec's economy, was Jacques Parizeau.

The animosity between French- and English-speaking Canada, and between the provinces and Ottawa over other issues, came to a head in 1980. Trudeau proposed a tax on natural gas that would transfer revenue from the provinces to Ottawa. The Western Provinces, where most of the natural gas originates, were against this.

In Quebec, on May 22, 1980, a referendum was held on a proposal to take the province out of Canada politically, although Lévesque had declared he wanted to keep economic relations intact. Even French-speaking citizens rejected this move, however, when about 54 percent of them joined the English-speaking minority (for a total of 60 percent) in voting no. In 1985 the Parti Québécois was voted out of office.

On November 10, 1987, Pierre Marc Johnson (1946–) resigned as leader of the Parti Québécois and gave up his seat in the provincial legislature. After Lévesque resigned in 1985, Johnson stayed on as leader of the opposition. Johnson's resignation was forced by

party militants who wanted to renew the campaign for the independence of Quebec. Johnson had proposed deferring any such action until after the next election in the province, to be held before December 1990. The renewal of the fight for independence seemed to have been fueled by the emotion arising from the death in 1987 of Lévesque.

The Liberal Party government of Quebec, headed by Premier Robert Bourassa (1933–1996) and in power since the December 1985 election, received a high rating in public opinion polls. Bourassa announced his resignation on September 14, 1993, and was succeeded as provincial party leader and premier of Quebec by Daniel Johnson, in January 1994. In parliamentary elections in September 1994, the Liberals were narrowly defeated by the Parti Québécois. The new premier was Parizeau, who had become the leader of the Parti Québécois in 1987.

A New Constitution

In spite of evolution toward complete sovereignty, the fact remained that the Canadian government would not be fully sovereign until it could amend its own constitution without referring the amendments to England for parliamentary approval and royal assent.

A movement to change this situation had begun as far back as 1927, but the federal government and the provinces found it hard to agree on proposed constitutional revisions. Plans drawn up in 1961 and 1964 were withdrawn when the provinces were not unanimous in supporting them.

After Prime Minister Trudeau and the provincial premiers failed once again to agree on constitutional amendments during talks held September 8 to 13, 1980, the federal government began to prepare its own plan in October. A Special Joint Committee of the House of Commons and the Senate began televised hearings on November 6, 1980. On February 13, 1981, the report, advocating 65 constitutional amendments, was tabled, and on February 17, the final round of constitutional debates began in the Commons.

The proposed new constitution was perceived as increasing the power of the federal government. As a result, the western provinces opposed the plan on the grounds that it would give too much control of their natural resources to the central government. Quebec feared that more federal power would bring domination by English-speaking Canada and lead to the decline of French culture.

In the end, these two major points of contention centered on a proposed bill of rights and on the process that Canada would employ to amend its constitution. The proposed rights bill was revised to make explicit the rights of Indians, Inuit, and women. Educational rights of the French-speaking minority outside Quebec and the English-speaking minority inside Quebec were extended.

A complicated system for amending the new constitution was finally agreed on by nine provinces, with Quebec dissenting. If the House of Commons and the Senate propose a constitutional amendment, it must be approved by the legislatures of at least two-thirds of the provinces, representing at least 50 percent of the population of all ten provinces. In effect, this means that at least seven provinces must approve. Another provision, however, allows a province, by a majority vote of its legislature, to dissent. If that occurs, the amendment has no effect in that province. There is also the provision that a province may repeal its dissent.

After 18 months of debate, the House of Commons, on December 2, 1981, approved by a vote of 246 to 24 a resolution, the British North America Act, to patriate Canada's constitution from Great Britain, joining to it this new amending formula and the Charter of Rights. On December 8 the Senate approved the constitutional package by a vote of 59 to 23.

In England, by a 177 to 33 vote, the House of Commons gave its approval on March 8, 1982, the House of Lords on March 25. On the following day, Queen Elizabeth II gave her royal assent.

In April the queen journeyed to Canada. In Ottawa, on April 17, she proclaimed the Constitution Act, incorporating the Charter of Rights and Freedoms, and signed the constitutional document in a formal ceremony. This was 115 years and 19 days after her great-great-grandmother, Queen Victoria, had assented to the British North America Act.

The constitutional package consisted of 30 domestic documents: 18 acts of the British Parliament, 8 acts of the Canadian Parliament, and 4 British orders-in-council. Elizabeth II remained queen of Canada and head of state, and Canada remained in the Commonwealth of Nations.

The 1982 Constitution Act amended and revised existing acts, renaming the British North America Act, 1867, the Constitution Act, 1867. New features of the

1982 Constitution Act are, most importantly, the Canadian Charter of Rights and Freedoms and the previously outlined amendment procedure. It is specific as to the right of all Canadian citizens to "enter, remain in, or leave Canada." Everyone is equal under the law without discrimination based on "race, national or ethnic origin, color, religion, sex, age, or mental or physical disability."

English and French are now the official languages and have equal rights in government. Language rights in some of the provinces are spelled out, and in all of them with regard to educational facilities. The existing aboriginal and treaty rights are affirmed. The term "aboriginal" here applies not only to Indians and Inuit but also to Métis.

(For the full text of the Constitution Act, 1982, see the GOVERNMENT AND LAW volume.)

Recent trends and events.
Pierre Trudeau led the Liberal Party to victory in October 1972, and again in July 1974, but his role as head of government was briefly interrupted in 1979 when an election in May gave the Progressive Conservative Party more seats than the Liberals but not an absolute majority. Charles Joseph Clark (1939–) became prime minister, but only until March 1980. A federal election on February 18 had returned the Liberals to power with an absolute majority (146 seats) in the House of Commons. The New Democratic Party reached its peak to that point, winning 32 seats.

In June 1984 Trudeau stepped down as prime minister. He was succeeded by John N. Turner (1929–), who served as prime minister for a short time. An election on September 4, 1984, gave the Progressive Conservatives an overwhelming mandate, with 211 seats in the House against 40 for the Liberals and 30 for the New Democratic Party. This represented the largest majority won in a federal election in Canadian history.

Quebec. The new prime minister was Brian Mulroney (1939–), who had hitherto not held public office. On July 4, 1986, Prime Minister Mulroney began a drive to persuade Quebec to sign the new constitution. Quebec's government had demanded the right of unilateral veto over amendments, a right no other province would have. Mulroney met on April 30, 1987, with the ten provincial premiers, and the Meech Lake Agreement

A NEW CANADIAN FLAG, without the British Union Jack, was first raised in 1965.

27 North America

centered
US

centred
Brit.

color
US

colour
Brit.

APPROXIMATELY 17,500 INUIT inhabit the new territory of Nunavut.

kilometers
US

kilometres
Brit.

NUNAVUT, separated from the Northwest Territories, became a territory in 1999.

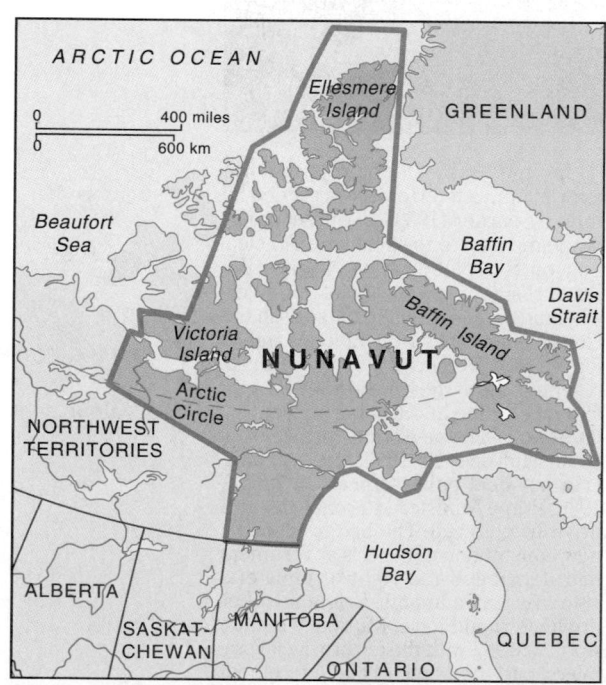

was worked out. It provided that Quebec be labeled a "distinct society," that it have three of the nine judges of the Canadian Supreme Court, and that no changes in federal institutions or provincial boundaries be made without the unanimous consent of the federal government and the provinces. All the provinces would now have the right to nominate members of the Senate and justices of the Supreme Court.

The final agreement, signed on June 3, 1987, further provided that Quebec has the right to pass laws to "preserve and protect" its special identity. On June 23, Quebec became the first province to ratify the agreement. The House of Commons on October 26 voted 242 to 16 to approve the agreement. However,

the requirement that all ten provinces ratify the agreement was not fulfilled, because Manitoba and Newfoundland did not comply.

Continued demands by Quebec for recognition of its special cultural and historical status, and further threats to separate from the rest of Canada, resulted in another attempt to reach a compromise following the failure of the Meech Lake Agreement. As a result, the ten premiers of the provinces and Prime Minister Mulroney worked out a new agreement at Charlottetown, Prince Edward Island, on August 27, 1992. The new draft agreement again called for the amendment of the Canadian constitution to recognize Quebec's distinctness, and to give it and the other provinces more autonomy. Also, a new and elected Senate would replace the current one, whose members are appointed; self-government would be established for indigenous people; the Supreme Court would be realigned so as to adhere both to English common law and the Napoleonic Code of Quebec; and the commitment of Canada to democratic values, sexual and ethnic equality, and respect for human rights would be reaffirmed. However, a national referendum on October 26 that year resulted in rejection of these proposals, with Quebec and the four western provinces voting against the scheme and the Atlantic provinces voting in favor. In all, five of the nine English-speaking provinces voted no.

Trade. Talks began June 17, 1986, with the United States to negotiate a free trade agreement between the two countries. After much difficulty, the talks succeeded, resulting in a treaty that would, by the end of the century, eliminate tariffs and import quotas and end restrictions on investments in one country by businesses located in the other. Trade between the two countries, already amounting to $150 billion a year, was expected to increase.

The agreement required ratification by Parliament, and this became the major issue in the election of November 21, 1988. Mulroney and the Progressive Conservative Party supported the pact, but the Liberal and New Democratic parties denounced the agreement as threatening Canada's sovereignty. They also blamed the Mulroney government for continuing economic problems and a high rate of unemployment. Although 56 percent of the votes were cast against the Progressive Conservatives, they nevertheless retained control of the House of Commons with 170 seats, against 82 seats for the Liberals and 43 for the New Democrats. The U.S.-Canada Free Trade Agreement was ratified by Parliament on December 30 and took effect on January 1, 1989.

On December 17, 1992, Canada joined Mexico and the United States in signing the North American Free Trade Agreement (NAFTA), which was implemented on January 1, 1994. The accord gradually eliminates virtually all import taxes and other trade barriers between the three countries.

Native populations. On September 5, 1988, the government agreed to give to 390,000 Indians, Inuit, and people of mixed ancestry title to 200,000 square miles (518,000 square kilometers) of the arctic region of the nation. The agreement also gave these groups a major role in the development of another 1.1 million

THE OLYMPIC GAMES of 1976 were held in Montreal, Quebec.

square miles (2.8 million square kilometers) in northern Canada. The pact, negotiations for which had been going on for a decade, included a provision for a cash settlement to Indians, Inuit, and people of mixed ancestry of $400 million, to be disbursed over a 20-year period.

In a further agreement, on December 16, 1991, the government said it would grant political rule over 770,000 square miles (1.9 million square kilometers), about a fifth of Canada's total territory, to the 17,500 Inuit who inhabit a region to be carved out of the Northwest Territories, extending north beyond the Arctic Circle. In addition, the Inuit would be paid more than $1 billion over a period of 14 years. This area officially became a territory on April 1, 1999. The territory was named Nunavut, "our land" in the Inuit language.

Foreign affairs. The government announced on February 25, 1992, that it would withdraw all its combat forces from Europe, where they are part of NATO, by the end of 1994. In August 1994, the last Canadian NATO troops in Europe were withdrawn, ending 27 years of Canadian service. It had been stated in September 1991 that the troop contingent would be reduced from 6,600 to 1,100. The change in plans was attributed to the collapse of the Soviet Union and the need to reduce the federal budget deficit. Canada remains an important participant in United Nations peacekeeping efforts.

Contemporary leaders and issues. The failure of both the Meech Lake and Charlottetown accords, as well as the still-simmering Quebec separatist issue, the country's economic woes, and dissatisfaction with the U.S.-Canada Free Trade Agreement—plus the government's implementation on January 1, 1991, of the unpopular Goods and Services Tax (GST), a form of value-added tax—all fueled disenchantment with the Mulroney government, which sank to an all-time low in popularity in national opinion polls.

In February 1991, Brian Mulroney, prompted by clear signs that changes were required if the Conservatives hoped to avoid a severe setback in upcoming federal elections, announced his intention to resign as prime minister and federal Conservative Party leader.

In June that year, Kim Campbell (1947–), who had served as attorney general and minister of justice, then as minister of defense, in Mulroney's cabinet, was elected Conservative Party leader and succeeded Mulroney as prime minister. She was Canada's first female prime minister, but her attempts at a so-called "fresh approach" were neither well organized nor well received and were rejected by voters en masse in the federal election of October 25, 1993—an election that changed the country's political map completely.

The Conservatives won only two seats in Parliament, a humiliating blow to the party that had roared to victory only 9 years earlier, in 1984. The electorate instead returned the Liberal Party to power, with 177 seats in the House of Commons, for a full majority. Only nine New Democratic Party candidates were elected, including party leader Audrey McLaughlin (1936–). The western-based Reform Party (founded 1987), under its leader, Preston Manning (1942–), returned 52 members of Parliament, and the Bloc Québécois (founded 1990), the federal separatist party, under leader Lucien Bouchard (1938–), became the official opposition with 54 seats. One seat was won by an independent candidate.

The new prime minister of Canada, Jean Chrétien (1934–), was sworn in on November 4, 1993. A law graduate of Laval University, Chrétien was first elected to the House of Commons in 1963. He served in the Pearson government as parliamentary secretary to the prime minister (1965), then as minister of finance (1966). As minister of national revenue (1968) in the Trudeau cabinet, Chrétien went on to serve in various other posts, including minister of Indian affairs and northern development, before being named minister of finance in 1977, then in 1980, minister of justice and attorney general of Canada.

Chrétien left public life in 1986, returning after being elected federal Liberal leader in 1990. Reelected to the House of Commons that year, he then became leader of the opposition.

As prime minister, Jean Chrétien took steps to fulfill his pledge of "good government," and his popularity in public opinion polls continued to rise. Nevertheless, solutions to difficult issues remained elusive. The country's high deficit continued to hamper economic growth.

After a decade in office, Chrétien, who had planned to retire in early 2004 before his term expired, stepped down on December 12, 2003 and was replaced as prime minister by the new leader of the Liberal Party, Paul Martin (1938–). Martin, a lawyer and businessman, was first elected to Parliament in 1988. He became finance minister in 1993 and is credited with balancing the budget and eliminating a multibillion-dollar deficit. Martin was introduced to politics early through his father, Paul Sr., who served many years in the House of Commons and was a cabinet minister under four prime ministers.

Martin's plans included the creation of a cabinet-level national security department intended to deal with terrorism and disasters. Another plan called for a committee devoted to improving relations with the United States, which had become strained when Chrétien refused to provide forces to the Iraq war.

The issue of Quebec separatism is seen as a significant factor in the steady decline in the value of the Canadian dollar, despite some post-recession improvement in the nation's economy. NAFTA has produced mixed results and continues to have its critics. The Goods and Services Tax (GST), which the Liberals pledged to eliminate or replace, is still in effect.

—*Frances Hanna*

PAUL MARTIN BECAME PRIME MINISTER when Jean Chrétien retired early.

27 North America

THE POPULAR GAME OF HOCKEY developed in Canada, which still boasts the majority of professional stars today. It was reputed to have been first played by British soldiers in Kingston, Ontario, about 1855.

The Provinces and Territories

The Canadian provinces have governments much like their federal government and have considerable autonomy over their own affairs. Each province controls such matters as education, justice, civil rights, and property rights. The territories have separate governments as well, but with less local control than the provinces have.

In this section, you will find first the flags of the provinces and territories, followed by information on the Canadian national flag. Next you will find a general overview of the provinces, divided into three regions. A general overview of all the regions is presented first, with regional maps showing how the member provinces fit together. The regions are arranged geographically in order of appearance. Then information on each province is presented separately, in alphabetical order. Following that is a regional map of the territories and information on each of them.

Provinces and Territories

Atlantic Provinces
Central Provinces
Western Provinces
Territories

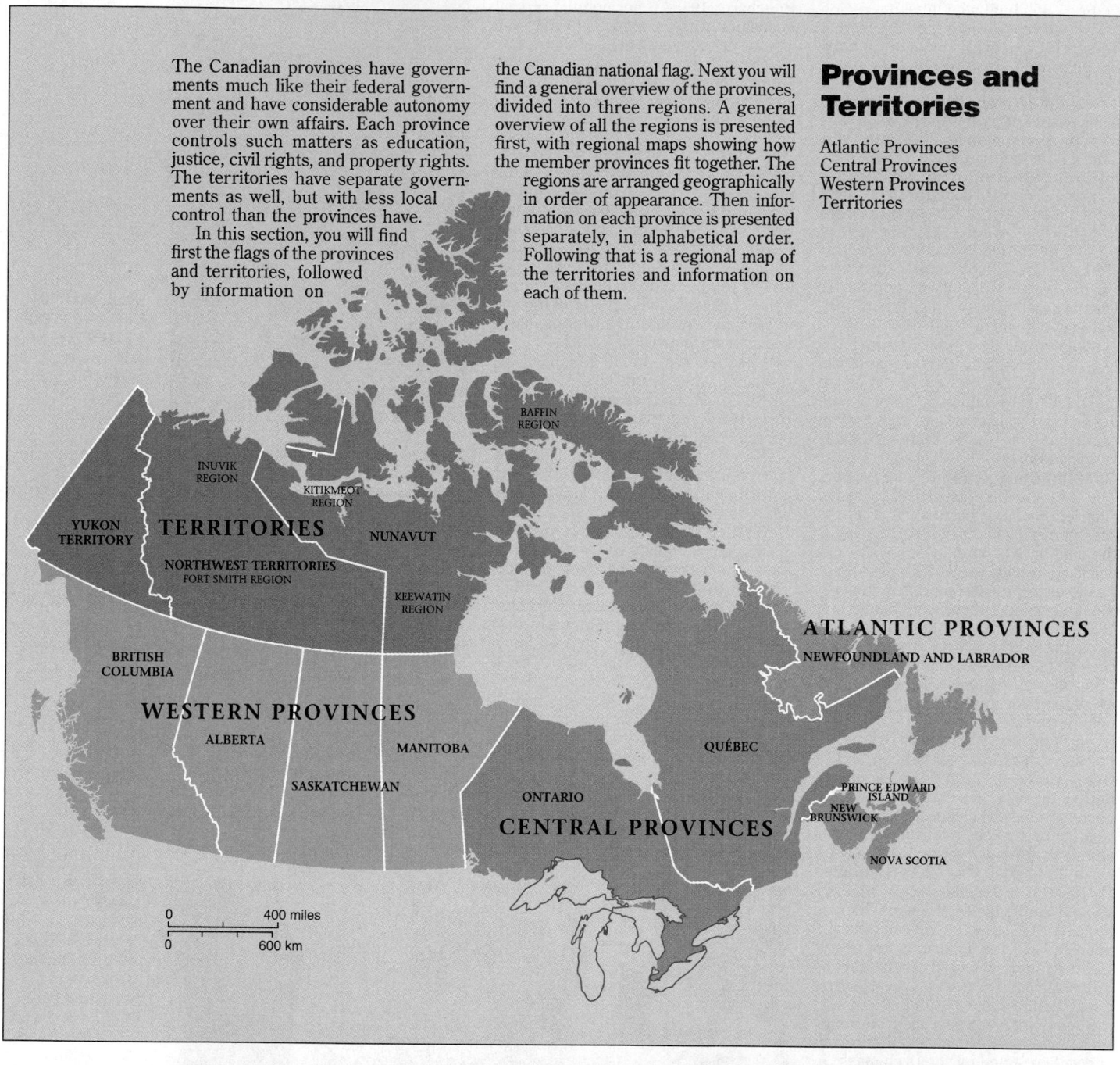

Where To Find Provinces and Territories

Flags of Canada

Alberta

Population: *2,974,807*
Capital: *Edmonton*
Provincial bird: *Great horned owl*
Floral emblem: *Wild rose*

The blue background represents the skies of the prairie. The Cross of St. George is representative of England. Depictions of the mountains, foothills, prairies, and wheat fields represent the landscape.

British Columbia

Population: *3,907,738*
Capital: *Victoria*
Provincial bird: *Steller's Jay*
Floral emblem: *Pacific dogwood*

The Union Jack represents the former status as a British colony. Blue waves symbolize the Pacific Ocean, and the setting sun indicates British Columbia's position as westernmost province.

Manitoba

Population: *1,119,583*
Capital: *Winnipeg*
Provincial bird: *Great gray owl*
Floral emblem: *Prairie crocus*

The Union Jack represents the former status as a British colony, as does the Cross of St. George. The bison represents the thousands of bison that roamed the prairie prior to the arrival of settlers.

New Brunswick

Population: *729,498*
Capital: *Fredericton*
Provincial bird: *Black-capped chickadee*
Floral emblem: *Purple violet*

The golden lion of Britain symbolizes ties to England. A sailing ship indicates the importance of shipbuilding and sailing industries historically.

Newfoundland and Labrador

Population: *512,930*
Capital: *St. John's*
Provincial bird: *Atlantic puffin*
Floral emblem: *Pitcher plant*

White represents snow and ice; blue represents the sea; yellow represents confidence for a bright future. Red triangles symbolize sails of fishing boats, representing the importance of the fishing industry.

Northwest Territories

Population: *37,360*
Capital: *Yellowknife*
Official bird: *Gyrfalcon*
Floral emblem: *Mountain avens*

The blue of the background and on the shield represents water, and the white represents ice. The lower green area on the shield represents southern forests and the upper red area represents northern tundra. Gold bars symbolize minerals and the fox symbolizes fur-bearing animals.

Nova Scotia

Population: *908,007*
Capital: *Halifax*
Provincial bird: *Osprey*
Floral emblem: *Mayflower*

The blue St. Andrew's cross, as well as the royal lion of Scotland on the shield, is representative of Scotland.

Nunavut

Population: *26,745*
Capital: *Iqaluit*
Official bird: *Rock ptarmigan*
Floral emblem: *Purple saxifrage*

The gold and white background represents the land. The stone marker (inuksuk) and the North Star are depicted as guides to assist people in finding their way.

Ontario

Population: *11,410,046*
Capital: *Toronto*
Provincial bird: *Common loon*
Floral emblem: *White trillium*

The Union Jack, as well as the Cross of St. George at the top of the shield, represents England. Green and gold on the shield are official colors of Ontario.

Prince Edward Island

Population: *135,294*
Capital: *Charlottetown*
Provincial bird: *Blue jay*
Floral emblem: *Lady's slipper*

The gold lion comes from Prince Edward's coat of arms, and is the royal lion of England. The large oak tree on the shield represents England, and each smaller one, a county of Prince Edward Island.

Quebec

Population: *7,237,479*
Capital: *Quebec City*
Provincial bird: *Snowy owl*
Floral emblem: *Blue flag iris*

The white cross on the blue background is reminiscent of an ancient French military banner. The fleurs-de-lis symbolize France, as well.

Saskatchewan

Population: *978,933*
Capital: *Regina*
Provincial bird: *Sharp-tailed grouse*
Floral emblem: *Western red lily*

A green background represents northern forests, and the gold represents fields of grain. The Western red lily is the province's floral emblem. The gold lion on the shield is representative of England, and the wheat sheaves symbolize agriculture.

Yukon Territory

Population: *28,674*
Capital: *Whitehorse*
Official bird: *Raven*
Floral emblem: *Fireweed*

Green represents forests; white represents snow; blue represents water. The malamute on the shield symbolizes courage, loyalty, and stamina. A Cross of St. George represents England. Red triangles symbolize the mountains. Gold circles represent minerals, and white lines represent rivers.

Canada

Population: *31,902,000*
Capital: *Ottawa, Ontario*
Official bird: *Common loon*
Floral emblem: *None*

Design is a red flag with a white square completely filling the center half and bearing a stylized red 11-point maple leaf. Red and white are the official colors of Canada, and, since the early days of Canada, the maple leaf has been its traditional emblem.

Display and Care of the National Flag of Canada

Folding the Flag

There is no formal method of folding the National Flag. It is simply folded ready for use the next time. However, the following guidance can afford ease in hoisting a flag on a pole: Fold the flag lengthwise, and again lengthwise, and then fold it three-quarters of the way to the hoist. Roll it on the vertical, and then tie with a light cotton string in such a way that, when the flag is hoisted, a sharp tug on the lower rope will break the string and the flag will unfurl.

1. Fold in half.

2. Fold in half again.

3. Fold.

4. Fold 3/4 from fly to hoist and roll.

5. Tie with lightweight cotton string or equivalent.

A. Method of attachment with Inglefield clips

B. Method of hitching tackline through the string

C. Method of tying with tackline only

DIsplay and Care of the National Flag of Canada

Displaying the Flag

(1) The National Flag always takes precedence over all other national flags flown in Canada. The only flags given precedence are the personal standards of members of the Royal family and Her Majesty's representatives when present. (2) When two, or more than three, flags are flown or displayed together or are in procession, the National Flag should be on the left of observers facing the display, but when three flags are displayed, it is to have the place of honor at the center. (3) When displayed with provincial flags, the Canadian flag takes precedence as follows: in a single line, at the beginning (on the left as seen by spectators) and at the end (if two National Flags available); in a double line, first flag of the left line; in a V-shaped display, at forward apex of the V. (4) When hung vertically, the top of the maple leaf should be pointing left; the maple leaf should be stem down when hung horizontally. (5) When crossed with another flag, the National Flag should be crossed from the right with the staff over that of the other flag. (6) When suspended over a street, the upper part of the leaf should face north in an east-west street and east in a north-south street. (7) When flying the flag at half-mast, first raise the flag to the peak, and then slowly bring it down (at least the width of the flag, but no more than halfway). (8) When displayed at an angle from a building, the top left corner (canton) should be placed at the peak. (9) When used to cover a casket, the canton should be draped over the upper left corner of the casket.

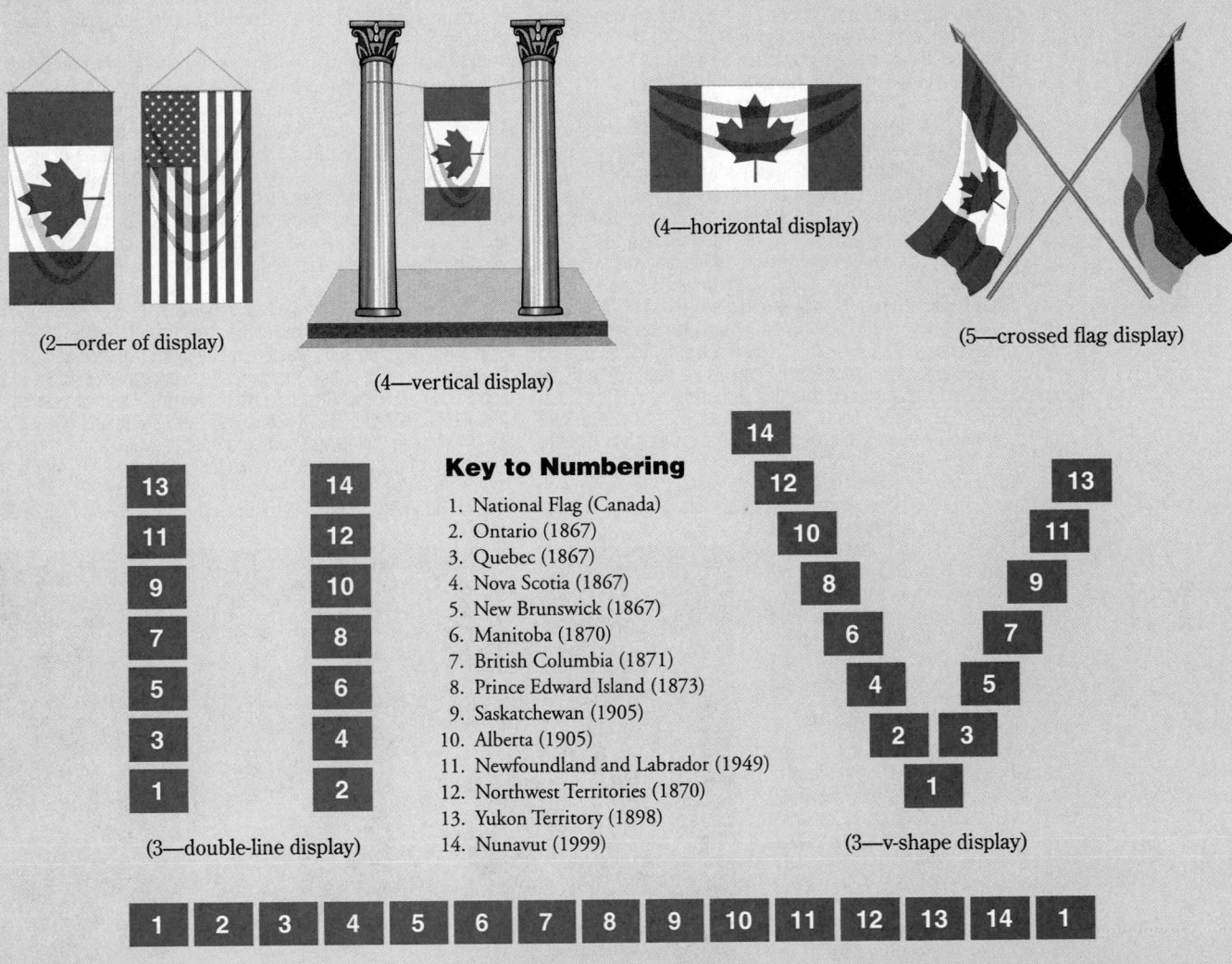

(2—order of display)

(4—vertical display)

(4—horizontal display)

(5—crossed flag display)

Key to Numbering

1. National Flag (Canada)
2. Ontario (1867)
3. Quebec (1867)
4. Nova Scotia (1867)
5. New Brunswick (1867)
6. Manitoba (1870)
7. British Columbia (1871)
8. Prince Edward Island (1873)
9. Saskatchewan (1905)
10. Alberta (1905)
11. Newfoundland and Labrador (1949)
12. Northwest Territories (1870)
13. Yukon Territory (1898)
14. Nunavut (1999)

(3—double-line display)

(3—v-shape display)

(3—single-line display)

North America 27

Caring for the Flag

(1) Although it is not inappropriate to fly the National Flag after sunset, it should, when possible, be taken down every night. (2) The flag should never be stored wet or damp. (3) If in need of cleaning, the flag may be safely washed using soap or non-chlorine detergent. (4) A slightly torn or frayed flag can and should be repaired. (5) If a flag is tattered, faded, or otherwise damaged to the extent that it is no longer fit for display, it should be completely destroyed by burning it privately in a dignified manner.

Canadian Flag

The national flag of Canada is relatively new; it was not officially approved until 1965. It is easily recognizable and features a bold yet straightforward design. The governing aesthetic concept is simplicity; the color scheme consists of only two shades, red and white. Similarly, the design is relatively simple; it consists of three vertical panels. The central panel is white and contains a stylized 11-point maple leaf, which is red. Red panels of equal proportion stand to either side.

The maple leaf began to function as a Canadian symbol as early as 1700; it represents the country's land and people. Red and white have been Canada's official colors since King George V's proclamation of the Royal Arms of Canada in 1921. Notably, an element of the design that does not hold any symbolic significance is the number of points on the maple leaf. Many people have speculated that the 11 points are of some particular importance. More specifically, some speculate that the points represent the governments of the Canadian provinces, but any connections that could be drawn are purely coincidental.

The Canadian flag is not surrounded by as many traditions as the flag of its North American neighbor, the United States. For instance, there is no official pledge for those wishing to salute the Canadian flag. Although there is no governmental legislation specifying a flag code, there is a document in circulation outlining proper flag etiquette, including directions for proper display and handling of the flag.

Canada has had only one official flag, but several other flags have flown there in the last 500 years. The first flag to fly over Canada was the national flag of England, which features the cross of St. George, a red cross on a white background. John Cabot, a 15th century sailor, brought it to the eastern coast of Canada in 1497, where it flew until 1534. In 1534 Jacques Cartier claimed the area for France. The French fleur-de-lis, a gold design printed on a blue background, represented France's sovereignty until the area was ceded to the United Kingdom in the early 1760s.

By this time, England had joined forces with Scotland, and their new flag featured the crosses of the patron saints of both countries, St. George and St. Andrew. The incorporated design featured St. George's emblem imposed over St. Andrew's symbol, which was a white diagonal cross on a blue background. The flag was altered again in 1801, when the Act of Union passed; it ended the Irish Parliament and created the United Kingdom of Great Britain and Ireland. In order to express Ireland's new status, the symbol of St. Patrick, the patron saint of Ireland, was incorporated with the other two crosses on the British flag. St. Patrick's cross, a diagonal red cross on a white background, was integrated by placing the red cross over the white cross of St. Andrew. The Union flag continued to fly over Canada even after Canada's Confederation, up until a new design was chosen in 1965.

An unofficial, yet widely used, flag was the Canadian Red Ensign, which was created in 1707. Its original function was as the flag for the British Merchant Marine. The Red Ensign was red and had Union Jack in the upper left-hand corner (an area on the flag called the "canton"); it also featured a shield with the arms of the various Canadian provinces. The first shield displayed the arms of Ontario, Quebec, Nova Scotia, and New Brunswick, but new province symbols were incorporated as they entered the Confederation. Eventually, the Canadian Coat of Arms replaced the shield in 1924. Although it was originally designed for nautical use, over time it became appropriate to fly on both land and sea. It came to be considered as Canada's flag, even though the title was never officially approved. Despite its lack of an official endorsement, the Red Ensign was often flown alongside the Union Jack until the new design was inaugurated in 1965.

Although the new flag was not approved until the mid-20th century, the process of finding a new design began as early as 1925. At that time, a committee whose task was to find a design for a new Canadian flag was appointed. Their assignment was never fulfilled, and the project was shelved until 1946, when another committee was appointed to the same project. They collected potential designs from a number of sources, and they eventually accepted and considered well over 2,000 submissions. Despite these efforts, they never formally voted on a winner. Once again, the committee dispersed before they succeeded in officiating a design.

In 1964, another committee was formed after Prime Minister Lester Pearson announced that the Canadian government wanted to adopt a new flag; in this case, however, their efforts were not fruitless. Later that year, the committee had narrowed the potential designs to three. The first candidate was red with a fleur-de-lis and a Union Jack, a combination that represented Canada's historical ties to France and Britain. The second nominee, which was put forth by the prime minister, featured three red maple leaves. The final contender, which was eventually chosen as the winning design, is the red and white, single leaf design that flies over Canada today.

The first person to create the Canadian flag was Jane Donovan (later, she married and her last name changed to O'Malley). The story of the first flag's creation was not mythologized like the story of the first American flag; in fact, the seamstress once joked that she never considered herself as the Betsy Ross type. Ms. Donovan sewed the first flag in the fall of 1964. She also created versions of the other two finalists in the design competition; they were to be presented in order for the committee to make their final decision. Afterward, the design was approved by Parliament October 22, 1964, and Queen Elizabeth II officially endorsed it on February 15, 1965.

Western Provinces

The Western Provinces lie side by side and extend from the Pacific Ocean in the west to Hudson Bay in central Canada. Together they make up nearly 30 percent of Canada's land area. They are—from the Pacific—British Columbia, Alberta, Saskatchewan, and Manitoba. The southern border of the region is formed by the 49th parallel, which separates the Canadian provinces from a row of U.S. states extending from Washington in the west to Minnesota in the east. The northern border is formed by the 60th parallel, which separates the provinces from the Yukon and Northwest Territories. In the northwest, British Columbia is separated from the Pacific by the narrow southern panhandle of Alaska.

For much of their history the Western Provinces were the frontier of Canada, known only to fur trappers who worked their way slowly west from Lake Superior. The land itself was claimed at various times by France and Russia, but in 1792 Britain gained undisputed control. In the following year, Sir Alexander Mackenzie pioneered the first land route across the Canadian mainland to the Pacific. Part of the southern border with the United States was disputed until 1846, when Britain and the United States agreed to the 49th parallel by treaty. The Western Provinces were organized as territories after Canada gained independent status in 1867. British Columbia and Manitoba, the westernmost and easternmost of the region's provinces, achieved provincial status in 1871 and 1870, respectively. The territory between them entered the confederation as Alberta and Saskatchewan some 35 years later, in 1905.

Today, the Western Provinces are no longer the dynamic region they once were. Consolidation after the hectic growth from 1971 to 1981 continues as Alberta's major industry, petroleum, adjusts to difficult times.

The 1991 census indicated that British Columbia had the most significant increase in population of the Western Provinces between 1986 and 1991, followed by Alberta. Manitoba had only a slight rise and Saskatchewan showed a decrease during the same time. Results of the 2001 census showed some of the same trends with Manitoba's population increasing only slightly by 0.5 percent and Saskatchewan's decreasing again by 1.1 percent. Alberta showed the greatest increase between 1996 and 2001 with an increase of 10.3 percent; British Columbia's grew by 4.9 percent.

The land. Topographically, Alberta, Saskatchewan, and Manitoba, known as the Prairie Provinces, share the vast plains—called prairies in Canada—that stretch southward from north-central Canada into the central United States. These prairies rise from Manitoba in the east across Saskatchewan to southern Alberta. Beyond the prairies lies the Western Cordillera, a mountain region that covers the western edge of Alberta and nearly all of British Columbia except for the Peace River area in the northeast.

Northern Saskatchewan and the northern two-thirds of Manitoba are part of the Canadian Shield, a vast plateau that runs from the Arctic Ocean in the northwest, around Hudson Bay, all the way to the Atlantic in the northeast. The extreme northeastern fringe of Manitoba lies in the Hudson Bay Lowlands.

Climate. The climate of the region varies from temperate in coastal British Columbia to extreme in the interior and northern regions. Victoria, situated on Vancouver Island, in the southwest corner of the region, has average winter temperatures above freezing and annual precipitation of 26 inches (66 centimeters).

In Regina, Saskatchewan, 100 miles (161 kilometers) north of the U.S. border, winter temperatures average 0°F (-18°C), and annual precipitation averages 11 inches (28 centimeters) of rainfall, with 45 inches (114 centimeters) of snow.

Principal cities. The largest urban centers of the region are found in its southern areas. The port city of Vancouver, with 2 million people in its metropolitan area, is the third largest in Canada. The fastest growing manufacturing cities are Edmonton and Calgary, in Alberta. The agricultural center of the region is Saskatoon, in southern Saskatchewan.

The people. The Western Provinces account for 30 percent of the Canadian population. Alberta and British Columbia, because of their mineral wealth, are the fastest growing provinces in the country, but agriculture-reliant Saskatchewan and Manitoba are among the slowest growing. The region is largely English speaking. The highest percentage of French is spoken in Manitoba, where over 4 percent consider French their mother tongue. The largest ethnic populations are of German and Ukrainian extraction. Canada's second largest concentration of Oriental peoples is in British Columbia.

Economy. The principal industries of the Western Provinces are forestry and manufacturing in the west and agriculture in the eastern prairies. Alberta provides most of Canada's fuel output but all the Western Provinces are rich in mineral deposits. In addition to oil and natural gas, these include copper and coal. Potash is mined in Saskatchewan making Canada a leading producer of the mineral. Saskatchewan and Manitoba supply the region's best farmland. Manufacturing in the region is concentrated in British Columbia and Alberta.

centimeters
US

centimetres
Brit.

centers
US

centres
Brit.

27 North America

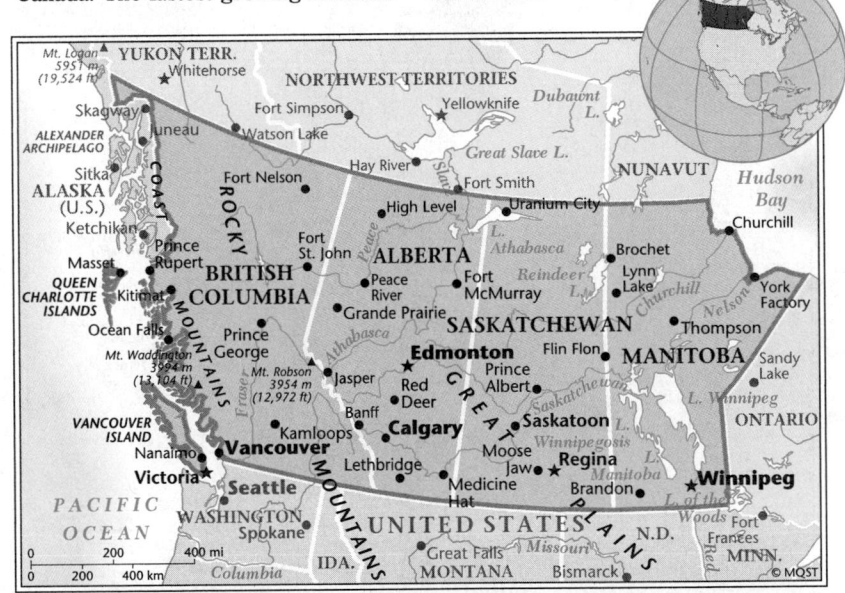

Western Provinces

Province	Area (Sq. Mi.)	Population 2001	Population Change 1996–2001 Number	Percent	Persons per Sq. Mi.
Alberta	255,219	2,974,807	278,000	10.3	11.7
British Columbia	365,851	3,907,738	183,000	4.9	10.7
Manitoba	250,881	1,119,583	6,000	0.5	4.5
Saskatchewan	251,793	978,933	-11,000	-1.1	3.9
Region Totals	1,123,744	8,981,061	456,000	5.1	8.0

Central Provinces

The Central Provinces of Ontario and Quebec, in many ways the heartland of Canada, lie to the east of the Western Provinces and to the west of the Atlantic Provinces. Hudson Bay forms the northern border of Ontario and part of the western border of Quebec. Most of the region's southern limits border the United States.

The first European settlements in Canada were established in this region in the 1500s and 1600s. French settlement predominated in Quebec, which was part of New France, and English settlement in Ontario.

The Central Provinces make up a quarter of Canada's land area. Quebec is the largest province, and Ontario, which is about two-thirds as large as Quebec, is the most populous. The country's political, economic, social, and cultural character radiates from this region.

The land. The mineral-rich Canadian Shield dominates the topography of Ontario and Quebec, rising from the shores of Hudson Bay to a plateau that extends through most of both provinces. Ontario shares four of the five Great Lakes with the United States. In Quebec's southeastern corner the Laurentian Mountains rise on both sides of the St. Lawrence River, which flows northeastward from the Great Lakes to the Atlantic Ocean.

Climate. The climate varies from arctic to subarctic in the north to humid continental in the south. Temperatures and precipitation levels are lowest in the north. The Great Lakes have a moderating influence on winter temperatures in the south.

Principal cities. The southern corridor of the region, from the Great Lakes along the St. Lawrence Seaway to the Gulf of St. Lawrence, includes many of Canada's largest cities, including Ottawa, the nation's capital. Toronto, Ontario, with close to 5 million people, is the largest metropolitan area in the country, followed by Montreal, with more than 3 million people.

The people. The Central Provinces account for about 63 percent of the Canadian population. The rate of population growth in the region is moderate. The majority of Ontario's population is English-speaking, and the majority of Quebec's population is French-speaking.

Economy. The Central Provinces are the economic heartland of Canada. The main economic activities include manufacturing, mining, food processing, agriculture, tourism, and production of wood and wood products and textiles.

Atlantic Provinces

The Atlantic Provinces surround the Gulf of St. Lawrence and separate the gulf from the Atlantic Ocean. To the south are the three Maritime Provinces: New Brunswick to the southwest; the peninsula of Nova Scotia and its Cape Breton Island to the south; and Prince Edward Island, 10 miles (16 kilometers) off the New Brunswick shore in the gulf itself. To the northeast of the gulf and separated from the other provinces by Cabot Strait lies the island of Newfoundland. The province of Newfoundland and Labrador includes this island and Labrador to the north, a large, barren part of the Canadian mainland that faces the North Atlantic Ocean.

The Atlantic Provinces are the four smallest provinces in Canada in terms of land area and population. Perhaps the first lands of what is now Canada that Jacques Cartier saw when he entered the Gulf of St. Lawrence in 1534, they have long histories of settlement. But the region has remained Canada's most rural due to its scarcity of arable land and natural resources. Today the region is a popular vacationland. All of the Atlantic Provinces are known for their dramatic coastal scenery of rugged cliffs interrupted by sandy beaches, their rustic fishing villages in secluded coves, and their unspoiled interior land of forests and small farms.

The land. Newfoundland and Labrador and all of the Maritime Provinces lie within the Canadian topographical area known as the Appalachian Uplands. This is the northern extreme of the mountain belt that runs southwest into the United States. The meeting of such mountain topography with the sea accounts for the coastal cliffs characteristic of much of the region's shoreline. Labrador, farther north, is the most easterly part of the Canadian Shield, the glacially leveled area that covers much of northern and central Canada.

Offshore from the Atlantic Provinces lies an unusually broad continental shelf of submerged banks that extend some 300 miles (483 kilometers) east of the island of Newfoundland. These banks, once teeming with fish, attracted early inhabitants to the region.

Climate. The Atlantic Provinces' climate varies with proximity to the sea. Mainland New Brunswick has relatively low winter temperatures and the highest summer readings. The island of Newfoundland is slightly warmer in winter months and cooler in summer. Since Newfoundland is more northerly, however, it receives more snowfall (an annual average of 140 inches, or 356 centimeters) than New Brunswick. The climate of Labrador is subarctic, both colder and drier than the rest of the region.

---

kilometers
US

kilometres
Brit.

center
US

centre
Brit.

Central Provinces

Province	Area (Sq. Mi.)	Population 2001	Population Change 1996–2001 Number	Population Change 1996–2001 Percent	Persons per Sq. Mi.
Ontario	412,472	11,410,046	656,000	6.1	27.7
Quebec	594,702	7,237,479	98,000	1.4	12.2
Region Totals	1,007,174	18,647,525	754,000	4.0	18.5

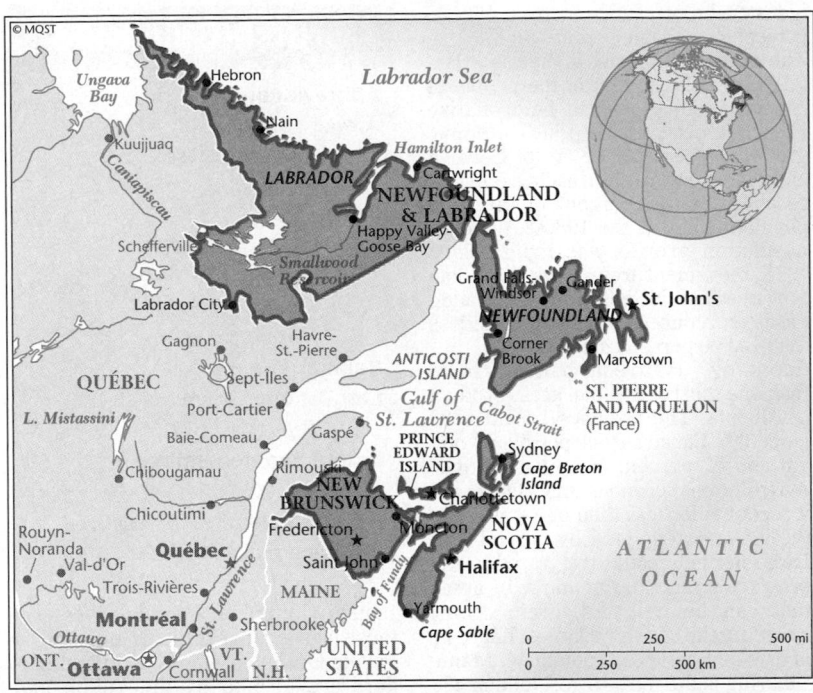

industry; it is chiefly based on the refining and processing of mineral, food, and forest products.

The region's mining industries are chiefly devoted to ores, and its farm produce is chiefly potatoes and fruits. Although it ranks behind these other businesses in contribution to the gross domestic product, commercial fishing is one of the most visible industries throughout the region.

Alberta

Abbreviation: *Alta., AB*
Area: *255,219 sq. mi.,*
   661,190 sq. km.
   Rank 4th
Population:
   2001 2,974,807
   Rank 4th
   Change 1996–2001 +278,000
   Persons per sq. mi. 11.7
Capital: *Edmonton*
Largest city: *Calgary*
   Pop. 878,866
Entered confederation:
   Sept. 1, 1905
Floral emblem: *Wild rose*
Province map: *Page 199*

Alberta, to the east of British Columbia, shares a border running northwest to southeast along the ridge of the Canadian Rockies. It borders the Northwest Territories to the north, Saskatchewan to the east, and has a short southern border with the U.S. state of Montana.

Agriculture—in particular grain and livestock production—remains extremely important to the province, but Alberta owes its strong growth in the last two

Atlantic Provinces

Province	Area (Sq. Mi.)	Population 2001	Population Change 1996–2001 Number	Population Change 1996–2001 Percent	Persons per Sq. Mi.
New Brunswick	28,348	729,498	-9,000	-1.2	25.7
Newfoundland and Labrador	156,608	512,930	-39,000	-7.0	3.3
Nova Scotia	21,419	908,007	-1,000	-0.1	42.4
Prince Edward Island	2,185	135,294	<1,000	0.5	61.9
Region Totals	208,560	2,285,729	-49,000	-2.1	10.98

Principal cities. The largest urban center in the Atlantic Provinces is the city of Halifax, Nova Scotia, a deepwater port with a population of 355,900. Halifax ranks 13th in population among Canadian cities. The only other large metropolitan areas in the region are the ports of St. John's on the island of Newfoundland, with a population of 175,800, and Saint John in southern New Brunswick, with a population of 127,700.

The people. The population of the Atlantic Provinces is the most rural in Canada. The region's growth rate is substantially below that of the national average, and as a unit the Atlantic Provinces experienced a net loss due to migration during the 1970s. A sizable minority of the population is French speaking.

Economy. Because of their spectacular coastal scenery, the Atlantic Provinces rely on tourism for a large proportion of their local economy. Manufacturing is the next most important

SALMON PONDS are a feature of the important salmon protection practices in the Atlantic Provinces.

HELMCKEN FALLS IN Wells Gray Provincial Park is an example of the spectacular scenery in British Columbia.

center
US

centre
Brit.

meters
US

metres
Brit.

decades to the wealth of its mineral reserves. Oil has been extracted near Calgary since 1914 and Edmonton since 1947. Increasing production and the boom in oil prices in the 1970s suddenly made the province the economic center of western Canada. During the 1970s Alberta had the highest growth rate in the country and the second greatest numerical increase in population after the province of Ontario.

The land. Most of Alberta consists of treeless prairies that rise in elevation from east to west. Near the British Columbia border the prairies rise into the Rocky Mountains. The highest point in the province is Mt. Columbia at 12,290 feet (3,746 meters) in Jasper National Park on the southwest border with British Columbia.

Climate. Alberta's climate is one of short, pleasant summers and long, cold winters. In Edmonton winter temperatures average 5°F (-15°C) and summer temperatures average 63°F (17°C), but extreme temperatures of -55°F (-48°C) in winter and 94°F (34°C) in summer have been recorded. Inland and isolated from the Pacific by mountains to the west, Alberta has precipitation that averages 17 inches (43 centimeters) annually, with 53 inches (135 centimeters) of snow. In southern Alberta, irrigation systems dependent on water levels of the South Saskatchewan River are important to agriculture.

Principal cities. Alberta's two major cities, Edmonton and Calgary, account for 64 percent of the province's total population. The capital city of Edmonton on the North Saskatchewan River is the province's administrative center; it grew in population by more than 41 percent between 1971 and 1986. Calgary (population, 878,866), 200 miles (322 kilometers) south of Edmonton, is Alberta's financial center and the hub of its petroleum

industry. Its population increased by 66 percent in the same period.

The people. English is the native language of 80.9 percent of the people of Alberta, with 2 percent being native French speakers. The principal ethnic groups in the province are of German and Chinese extraction; each group represents about 3 percent of the total population. Until the 1980s, Alberta's population growth was rapid. Since 1981, movement from other Canadian provinces has declined and immigration has been reduced by 50 percent to less than 10,000 persons per year.

Economy. Petroleum generates more than one-third of the total gross product of Alberta. The province provides 83 percent of Canada's total petroleum output and 87 percent of its natural gas. Agriculture is second in importance, but it accounts for less than one-quarter of the income generated by oil and gas. Large herds of cattle are grazed in the province's ranching country. In areas that can be irrigated, grain crops, including the country's largest harvests of oats and barley, predominate. Manufacturing is the third largest industry in the province, nearly all of it devoted to refining mineral and food products.

Places of interest. Banff and Jasper national parks are Alberta's best known, and their magnificent mountain scenery is frequently photographed. The province has five national parks, like neighboring British Columbia, and two of them began as sanctuaries for the wildlife reflected in their names: Wood Buffalo National Park, on the province's northern border (Canada's largest national park), and Elk Island National Park, west of Edmonton. Waterton Lakes National Park, on the Canadian/U.S. border, was joined in 1932 with the state of Montana's Glacier National Park, creating the first international peace park in the world. There are over 100 miles (160 kilometers) of hiking trails in the park, linking such attractions as Red Rock Canyon and Cameron Falls.

(For information on Alberta's two major cities, Calgary and Edmonton, see Cities of North America section.)

British Columbia

Abbreviation: *B.C., BC*
Area: *365,851 sq. mi.,*
947,800 sq. km.
Rank   3rd
Population:
2001   3,907,738
Rank   3rd
Change 1996–2001 +183,000
Persons per sq. mi.   10.7
Capital: *Victoria*
Largest city: *Vancouver*
Pop.   545,671
Entered confederation:
July 20, 1871
Floral emblem: *Pacific dogwood*
Province map: *Page 199*

British Columbia, Canada's westernmost province, is the only one with a Pacific Ocean coastline. Its inland borders are formed by the Yukon and Northwest Territories to the north, Alberta to the east, and the U.S. states of Washington, Idaho, and partially Montana to the south. The upper third of its western border is separated from the Pacific by the narrow southern panhandle of Alaska. The lower two-thirds includes many offshore islands, the largest being Vancouver, 288 miles (463 kilometers) long, across Queen Charlotte Strait and paralleling its coast in the extreme southwestern corner.

The third largest of Canadian provinces in area, British Columbia was not settled extensively until after the completion of the Canadian Pacific Railroad in 1885. Since then, however, its valuable forestland, ample natural resources, and hydroelectric power have made it the most populous of the Western Provinces and currently, the fastest growing.

The land. British Columbia lies almost entirely within the Cordillera, the mountain region that extends northward into

THE POSSIBILITY OF SIGHTING orca whales attracts many visitors yearly to the waters off British Columbia.

the Yukon and Alaska, and southward into the contiguous United States. The western third consists of coastal ranges that rise in elevation to the north. The highest peak in the Western Provinces is Mt. Fairweather, at 15,300 feet (4,663 meters), near British Columbia's border with Alaska and the Yukon.

The central third of the province consists of mountain plateaus and large lakes. The eastern third of the province includes the principal ridge of the Canadian Rockies and the Peace River lowland in the northeast.

Climate. Because of the coastal ranges, British Columbia's climate is mild and moist along the coast and cooler and drier farther inland. Average temperatures at Vancouver in the southwest are 37°F (3°C) in winter and 63°F (17°C) in summer, with 40 inches (102 centimeters) of annual total precipitation and little snow. At east-central Prince George, however, average winter temperatures are 10°F (-12°C). Although annual precipitation is lower at 25 inches (64 centimeters), the longer winters bring 95 inches (241 centimeters) of snow per year.

Principal cities. Vancouver, only 15 miles (24 kilometers) from the U.S. border, is the third largest city in Canada and the busiest port in the country. Victoria (population, 74,125), southwest of Vancouver on Vancouver Island, is the capital of the province. Together these two cities account for more than half the population of the province.

The people. British Columbia is the third largest province in Canada, after Ontario and Quebec. In the 1970s it grew faster than either of the others, taking second place only to Alberta. From 1986 to 1996, it showed the highest population growth of any province. Alberta has the highest proportion of native English speakers (80.9 percent). British Columbia has the lowest proportion of native French speakers (1.4 percent). The province has a high proportion of people with one of the Chinese dialects as their mother tongue (6.8 percent). Many of these people live in Vancouver's large Chinatown district.

Economy. Manufacturing, based on wood, paper, food, and fuel products, is the largest industry in British Columbia. Mineral production is an important aspect of the economy and is equally divided between ores such as zinc and copper and fuels such as petroleum and natural gas. Forestry is the major industry in the northern areas. The province's limited agriculture is carried out in the south, where fruits, vegetables, and grains are grown on irrigated lands, and also in the northeastern Peace River country. The commercial fishing industry in British Columbia recorded a seafood harvest with a wholesale worth after processing of $1 billion. This accounted for 25 percent of Canada's seafood exports.

Places of interest. British Columbia is a popular tourist destination year-round for visitors from other parts of Canada, the United States, and overseas. Summertime attractions include boating, swimming, camping, and hiking, as well as fishing and hunting in season. In the winter months, superb skiing locations such as Whistler Mountain attract enthusiasts of the sport. The province's spectacular scenery appeals to photographers, both amateur and professional.

There are four national parks in the mountains of British Columbia: Glacier, Kootenay, Mount Revelstoke, and Yoho. On Vancouver Island, Pacific Rim National Park has the province's longest sand beach. In addition, there are more than 300 provincial parks in British Columbia.

(For information on the province's two major cities, Vancouver and Victoria, see Cities of North America section.)

Manitoba

Abbreviation: *Man., MB*

Area: *250,881 sq. mi.,*
649,950 sq. km.
Rank   5th

Population:
2001   1,119,583
Rank   5th
Change 1996–2001   +6,000
Persons per sq. mi.   4.5

Capital and largest city: *Winnipeg*
Pop.   619,544

Entered confederation:
July 15, 1870

Floral emblem: *Prairie crocus*

Province map: *Page 199*

Manitoba is the easternmost of the Western Provinces. It stretches some 750 miles (1,207 kilometers) from a southern border with the U.S. states of North Dakota and Minnesota to a northern border with Nunavut. The breadth of the province from its western border with Saskatchewan to its eastern border with Ontario varies from about 240 miles (386 kilometers) in the south to a maximum of more than 400 miles (644 kilometers) in the northern third. The northeast border of the province is an irregular shoreline on Hudson Bay.

Most of Manitoba's population live in the lower third of the province, a rolling prairie grassland notable for large lakes, such as Winnipeg, Winnipegosis, and Manitoba. Northern Manitoba is a sparsely populated wilderness of deep forests and scenic rivers draining northeast into Hudson Bay. The province is a popular summer camping, hunting, fishing, and boating site.

The land. The southwestern part of Manitoba, from its southern and western borders to the western shore of Lake Winnipeg, is a region of prairies rising in elevation from southeast to northwest. The two-thirds of the provincial area that lies to the north and east of this division consists of the forested Canadian Shield and the Hudson Bay Lowland in the northeast corner south of the bay.

Climate. Manitoba's cold winters, caused by arctic winds from the north, and dry warm summers reflect its geographical situation at the center of the continental landmass. At the capital city of Winnipeg in south-central Manitoba, normal winter temperatures average -1°F (-17°C) and normal summer temperatures average 67°F (19°C). Extreme temperatures in Winnipeg, however, have ranged from -49°F (-45°C) in winter to 104°F (40°C) in summer. The total rainfall at Winnipeg averages 21 inches (53 centimeters) annually, with 52 inches (132 centimeters) of snow.

Principal cities. The largest city in Manitoba is Winnipeg, which is the seventh largest metropolitan area in the country. Winnipeg is the capital and the principal agricultural marketplace and manufacturing center of the province. The second largest city is Brandon, with a population of 39,716, which is just over 100 miles (161 kilometers) due west of Winnipeg. The only large city in northern Manitoba is Thompson, with a population of 13,256, located 150 miles (241 kilometers) north of Lake Winnipeg.

The people. Manitoba is the least English of the Western Provinces. Some 74 percent of the population are native English speakers, and more than 4 percent are native French speakers. The population also has a high proportion of people of German (6 percent) and Ukrainian (3 percent) extraction. During the 1980s, agriculture-reliant Manitoba experienced above average growth under the influence of an expanding manufacturing sector. Population grew 4.4 percent from 1981 to 1986, but only 2.7 percent from 1986 to 1991, and 0.05 percent between 1996 and 2001.

Economy. The principal business of Manitoba has shifted from agriculture to manufacturing. While farmland on the southern prairies continues to be a significant producer of cereal grains and specialty crops, shipments of manufactured goods are more than triple the cash receipts from farming. Products are primarily in the food, transportation, and farm machinery industries. Mining ranks third in economic importance. Key minerals are nickel, copper, and zinc. Pulpwood is also of economic significance.

Places of interest. Manitoba's large tourist industry is centered on the many lakes of the southern region and on such parks as Riding Mountain National Park in the southwest and Whiteshell Provincial Park on the Ontario border to the southeast. Places of historical interest include Lower Fort Garry, a restoration of the Hudson's Bay Company fort originally built in 1832. It is located just north of Winnipeg.

(For information on Winnipeg, see Cities of North America section.)

New Brunswick

Abbreviation: *N.B., NB*
Area: *28,348 sq. mi., 73,440 sq. km.*
    Rank   8th
Population:
    2001   729,498
    Rank   8th
    Change 1996–2001   -9,000
    Persons per sq. mi.   25.7
Capital: *Fredericton*
Largest city: *Saint John*
    Pop.   69,661
Entered confederation:
    July 1, 1867
Floral emblem: *Purple violet*
Province map: *Page 201*

New Brunswick, the largest in size of the three Maritime Provinces, is situated to the east of the U.S. state of Maine. Its northern border is shared with the province of Quebec. To the east of New Brunswick is the Gulf of St. Lawrence. Prince Edward Island lies some 10 miles (16 kilometers) offshore, on the Northumberland Strait across from the Isthmus of Chignecto, a neck of land that connects New Brunswick to Nova Scotia. To the south, New Brunswick faces the Bay of Fundy, which separates it from the southern reaches of Nova Scotia by 30 to 50 miles (48 to 80 kilometers) of water. The bay, which has the highest tides in the world, opens into the Atlantic Ocean just opposite the New Brunswick-Maine border.

Lacking an abundance of arable land, New Brunswick has developed more slowly than the provinces to the west. The population today is smaller than that of any province except Newfoundland and Labrador and Prince Edward Island. Most of the population lives along the southern coast.

The land.   Nearly all of New Brunswick lies within the Appalachian Uplands, which extend southwest into New England in the United States. In New Brunswick the Appalachian Uplands are highest in the north, with Mt. Carleton (2,690 feet, 820 meters) in the provincial park of the same name being the highest peak. To the east and northeast, New Brunswick also includes a small strip of lowland along the Gulf of St. Lawrence.

Climate.   Because its weather is determined by wind movement from west to east, New Brunswick has a humid continental climate despite its maritime location. At southwestern Saint John, the long winters average 19°F (-7°C), and the short summers average 63°F (17°C). Precipitation in New Brunswick is heavier than in the interior provinces, averaging 56 inches (142 centimeters) per year, with 82 inches (208 centimeters) at Saint John.

Principal cities.   The only metropolitan area in New Brunswick is Saint John.

Located at the mouth of the Saint John River on the Bay of Fundy, it is an ice-free port in winter and a ferry point for transportation to Nova Scotia. The only other large cities are Moncton, 93 miles (150 kilometers) northeast of Saint John, with a population of 61,046, and the capital city of Fredericton, which has a population of 47,560 and is located 66 miles (106 kilometers) northwest of Saint John.

The people.   The population of New Brunswick is the most rural in Canada after that of Prince Edward Island. The population growth rate was only 2 percent between 1986 and 1996, and population decreased by 1.2 percent between 1996 and 2001. The composition of the population by language is 65 percent English and 33 percent French. The equal status of the two official languages is protected by provincial legislation.

Economy.   New Brunswick's leading industry is the manufacture of wood and paper products. Food processing is second in importance, followed by mining. New Brunswick leads Canada in the production of specialized ores such as antimony and bismuth. Agriculture in the south of the province is based on potato crops and dairy products and is significant. Commercial fishing, most of it out of the Bay of Fundy, brings in about a third of the revenues from agriculture.

Places of interest.   Two important historic attractions in New Brunswick are King's Landing, upriver from Fredericton, which recreates Loyalist village life of the early 19th century, and Village Historique Acadien at Caraquet, which recreates French life of a similar period. Fundy and Kouchibouguac national parks are also popular attractions. The villages of inland New Brunswick have many covered bridges, with the world's longest (1,282 feet, 391 meters) spanning the Saint John River at Hartland.

Newfoundland and Labrador

Abbreviation: *Nfld. Lab., NL*
Area: *156,608 sq. mi.,*
    405,720 sq. km.
    Rank   7th
Population:
    2001   512,930
    Rank   9th
    Change 1996–2001   -39,000
    Persons per sq. mi.   3.3
Capital and largest city:
    St. John's
    Pop.   99,182
Entered confederation:
    Mar. 31, 1949
Floral emblem: *Pitcher plant*
Province map: *Page 201*

Newfoundland and Labrador is an Atlantic Province consisting of two

parts, the island of Newfoundland and mainland Labrador. The island accounts for less than one-third of the provincial land area but has 95 percent of the population. Triangular in shape, it forms the eastern limit of the Gulf of St. Lawrence and is separated from Labrador in the north by the narrow Strait of Belle Isle. Labrador is the easternmost point of the Canadian mainland. Also triangular in shape, it is bordered on the west and south by Quebec and on the northeast by the Atlantic Ocean, where its coastline (over 600 miles, or 965 kilometers, long) includes many small offshore islands. The province's name was changed from Newfoundland to Newfoundland and Labrador on December 6, 2001, by constitutional amendment.

Newfoundland was probably one of the first points in North America seen by John Cabot on his 1497 voyage, but rights to the lands were disputed by France until 1763, when the Treaty of Paris restored the territory to Great Britain, with France being granted the small islands of St. Pierre and Miquelon (still belonging to France today). Because most of the province's land area is barren and subject to harsh weather, it was settled very slowly.

Labrador's interior boundary was long the subject of a dispute, but a court decision settled it in 1927. Newfoundland remained a separate dominion of the British Commonwealth until it accepted provincial status in 1949. At that time, its Labrador boundary was confirmed in what is now called the Newfoundland Act, part of the Constitution Act, 1982.

Today the province remains the most sparsely populated in Canada. Remote areas, such as Heart's Content and Come-by-Chance, are still referred to by the names given them by the first settlers. A unique dialect of English influenced by Irish and rural British inflections prevails.

The land.   All of the island of Newfoundland lies within Canada's Appalachian Uplands. Most of its area is a barren central plateau that drops off to the surrounding sea in rocky cliffs, but there is a small region of lowlands on the northernmost peninsula. All of Labrador is part of the Canadian Shield, a forested granite plateau of large lakes. Labrador's northernmost point lies above the tree line and consists of arctic tundra. Like Newfoundland, Labrador has a very irregular and rocky coast, with many fjords, inlets, and bays. Hamilton Inlet/Lake Melville is some 125 miles (200 kilometers) long.

Climate.   Most of Labrador has a subarctic climate, but the island of Newfoundland, home of virtually all of the provincial population, has a cool and stormy climate. At St. John's, at the southeastern tip of the island, normal winter temperatures are on average 25°F (-4°C) and summer temperatures average 60°F (16°C). Precipitation averages 60 inches (152 centimeters) per year, more than anywhere in Canada except parts of British Columbia, and

kilometers
US
kilometres
Brit.

center
US
centre
Brit.

the annual snowfall averages 140 inches (356 centimeters), more than in any other large city in the country.

Principal cities. The only metropolitan area in the province is St. John's, a deepwater port that served as an important military installation during World War II. Corner Brook, 263 miles (423 kilometers) west of St. John's on the island's western coast, has a population of 20,103.

The people. Almost 95 percent of the provincial population live on the island of Newfoundland. Fewer than 30,000 people live in Labrador, with the greatest population concentrated in Labrador City (7,744) in the interior. Most of the smaller settlements are around its southeast coastline. Large areas of Labrador are totally uninhabited. The population of Newfoundland and Labrador by mother tongue is 98 percent English, with a relatively small number of French-speaking people. There are also Inuit living in northern Labrador.

Economy. The major industry in Newfoundland and Labrador is mining, which accounts for three times the income of any other business. The principal product is iron ore. Mines in Labrador account for more than half of Canada's production. In recent years there has been some offshore oil drilling. Newfoundland and Labrador's other industries, ranked in order of importance, are manufacturing and lumber. Tourism is gaining in importance.

Commercial fishing, once ranked after manufacturing in importance, was adversely affected by the serious decline in stocks of northern cod off Newfoundland's east coast in the early 1990s. The problem had mainly to do with ecological factors that also caused a 75 percent decline in the vital spawning stock. Other factors included overfishing and an increase in the seal population since restrictions were placed on seal hunting and killing in the region. The federal government called a 2-year moratorium on the northern cod fishery in 1992, putting many Newfoundlanders out of work, although the government did offer them emergency assistance and retraining programs. In July 1994, however, scientists announced that the spawning stocks had continued to decline and at that point, despite the moratorium, were at only 3 percent of their 1990 level. At that time, landed value in the fishing industry was at $200 million. By the late 1990s a rebound occurred, with the average landed value in the fishing industry above $400 million and, in 2001, up to $489 million.

Places of interest. A paradise for hunting and sport fishing, Newfoundland and Labrador boasts spectacular scenery both on its coasts and in the interior. There are two national parks: Gros Morne, where mountain peaks drop to narrow fjords along Bonne Bay on the island's west coast, and Terra Nova, overlooking Bonavista Bay in the east/central region, some 100 miles (161 kilometers) north of St. John's.

NOVA SCOTIA HAS A LONG SHORELINE with small villages. The fishing industry is second only to that of British Columbia.

Northwest of Terra Nova, on Gander Lake, is Gander International Airport, which opened in 1938. An aviation museum and memorial commemorate the Atlantic Ferry Pilots, whose World War II missions were launched there.

Picturesque little fishing villages, known as "outports," dot the Newfoundland and Labrador coast and are also of interest to the visitor.

Nova Scotia

Abbreviation: *N.S., NS*
Area: *21,419 sq. mi., 55,490 sq. km.*
   Rank   9th
Population:
   2001   908,007
   Rank   7th
   Change 1996–2001   -1,000
   Persons per sq. mi.   42.4
Capital and largest city: *Halifax*
   Pop.   359,111
Entered confederation:
   July 1, 1867
Floral emblem: *Mayflower*
Province map: *Page 201*

Nova Scotia consists of a long peninsula and the smaller Cape Breton Island, just offshore from its most northeastern point. The peninsula extends some 265 miles (426 kilometers) from southwest to northeast and is joined to southeastern New Brunswick by the low-lying Isthmus of Chignecto. Nova Scotia's western arm is separated from New Brunswick by the Bay of Fundy, and its eastern arm extends eastward toward Cape Breton Island. At no point is the peninsula more than 81 miles (130 kilometers) across.

Cape Breton, separated from mainland Nova Scotia by the narrow Strait of Canso, extends 100 miles (161 kilometers) north and east between the Gulf of St. Lawrence and the Atlantic Ocean.

Nova Scotia means New Scotland in Latin, the name given it in the original British charter of 1621. Rights to the land were contested by the French until 1713, when the British gained full control of Nova Scotia under the Treaty of Utrecht. While still under British rule in 1848, Nova Scotia became the first Canadian province with self-governing powers. Although the second smallest in area of all Canadian provinces, after Prince Edward Island, Nova Scotia is today the most developed of the Atlantic Provinces. It is especially noted for dramatic coastal scenery along its long southeastern shoreline with the Atlantic Ocean.

The land. Nova Scotia lies entirely within the region of Appalachian Uplands that cover most of the Atlantic Provinces. From a central spine of low mountains, the land declines in elevation to the north, with the Isthmus of Chignecto characterized by marshlands and bogs. Both the Atlantic coastline and the Bay of Fundy, which records the greatest tidal changes in the world, are irregular and dotted with rocky coves and harbors.

Climate. Owing to the influence of the surrounding bodies of water, Nova Scotia has the mildest climate of the Atlantic Provinces. At Halifax, near the center of the province's Atlantic coast, winter temperatures average 26°F (-3°C) and summer ones average 65°F (18°C). Yearly precipitation averages 55 inches (140 centimeters), with about 85 inches (216 centimeters) of snow.

Principal cities. Halifax is the only large city in Nova Scotia and the only metropolitan area in the province. It is the leading industrial center of the Atlantic Provinces. In recent years it has attracted a large number of diversified scientific research companies. The second largest city in the province and the largest on Cape Breton Island is Sydney (metro. area population, 109,330).

The people. Owing to its small size, Nova Scotia is the second most densely populated province of Canada, after Prince Edward Island. The composition of the population by mother tongue is

THE 19TH-CENTURY RIDEAU CANAL and Locks are located in Ottawa, Ontario.

center
US

centre
Brit.

kilometers
US

kilometres
Brit.

THE COSMOPOLITAN CITY of Toronto is the largest city in Canada, with a population close to 4 million.

93 percent English and 4 percent French. A 10.7 percent rise in population from 1971 to 1986 was largely from natural increase, which countered the effects of a small population loss from net migration to other provinces in the 1970s. There were only slight population increases between 1986 and 1996. A downward trend continued with a 0.1 percent decrease between 1996 and 2001.

Economy. The principal industry of Nova Scotia is manufacturing, which accounts for more than four times the income of any other business. The leading manufactures are paper and wood pulp products; processed foods, including fish; and refined petroleum and coal fuels. Mining is second in importance to the province, and mineral production is equally divided between fuels and structural metals. The majority of the agricultural businesses are dairy farms. Although fishing generates less income than agriculture, Nova Scotia's commercial fishing industry is second only to that of British Columbia among Canadian provinces. Forestry is also an important business.

Places of interest. Tourism is an important industry in Nova Scotia, with large numbers of visitors attracted to the beaches of the Bay of Fundy, the historic Citadel at Halifax, and Kejimkujik National Park in the southwest interior.

Attractions on Cape Breton Island include the scenic Cabot Trail around the island, the restored 18th-century fortress at Louisbourg, and the northern Cape Breton Highlands National Park, where John Cabot may have landed in 1497.

(For information on Halifax and Sydney, see Cities of North America section.)

Ontario

Abbreviation: *Ont., ON*
Area: *412,472 sq. mi.,*
         1,068,580 sq. km.
         Rank   2nd
Population:
         2001   11,410,046
         Rank   1st
         Change 1996–2001
         +656,000
         Persons per sq. mi.   27.7
Capital and largest city: *Toronto*
         Pop.   2,481,494
Entered confederation:
         July 1, 1867
Floral emblem: *White trillium*
Province map: *Page 200*

Ontario is the southernmost of the Canadian provinces. It lies southeast of the geographical center of the country, bordering four of the five Great Lakes. It stretches nearly 1,000 miles (1,600 kilometers) at its widest point from the Ottawa River, which forms much of its eastern border with Quebec, to its western border with Manitoba. To the north the province borders Hudson Bay and its southern extension, James Bay. To the south Ontario has a longer border with the United States than any other province, and it faces six U.S. states across the Great Lakes: Minnesota, Wisconsin, Michigan, Ohio, Pennsylvania, and New York. The border crossings between Windsor and Detroit and into New York State at Niagara Falls are the two busiest between Canada and the United States.

Ontario is known as the Heartland Province because it is the population, government, metropolitan, and economic center of Canada. The province is the home of about 38 percent of the Canadian people, and it has over 4 million more people than the second most populous province, Quebec.

The triangle formed by lakes Huron, Erie, and Ontario contains Canada's largest city, Toronto, and 10 other of the country's 25 largest cities. The area known as the Golden Horseshoe, around the western tip of Lake Ontario from St. Catharines to Oshawa and including the cities of Hamilton and Toronto, is home to almost half of the province's population.

Economically, Ontario is the most industrial of the provinces, accounting for more than half of Canada's manufactured goods; it is also the leader in cash receipts from farms. With its many border crossings into the United States, Ontario is the province most familiar to many Americans and the base for most U.S.–Canadian commerce.

The land. The central and western two-thirds of Ontario's land area consists of the Canadian Shield, a vast expanse of Precambrian sedimentary and volcanic rock leveled by glacial ice sheets to an average elevation of about 1,000 feet (305 meters) above sea level. Along its northern limit, Ontario also includes a strip of Hudson Bay Lowland, where forested land drops off to marshland at the shore of the saltwater bay. Elevation also declines in the extreme southeast, where there is a narrow strip of Great Lakes Lowland and St. Lawrence Lowland. These lowlands contain the most fertile farmland in the province.

Climate. The climate of Ontario varies broadly, partly because of its north-to-south extent, but also because of its location with respect to the Great Lakes. The climate ranges from subarctic in the north near Hudson Bay to humid continental in the south, with clear, cold winters and mild to hot summers. At Toronto, on the north shore of Lake Ontario, normal winter temperatures average 24°F (-4°C), and summer ones average 71°F (22°C). Annual precipitation is 31 inches (79 centimeters), with 52 inches (132 centimeters) of snow. At Thunder Bay, on Lake Superior in the northwest, temperatures average 5°F (-15°C) in winter and 64°F (18°C) in summer, with a lower annual precipitation of 28 inches (71 centimeters) but more of this precipitation falling as snow (84 inches, 213 centimeters).

Principal cities. Ontario is the most urban of Canadian provinces, and it includes a large number of the nation's major cities. Toronto, the provincial capital and one of the most appealing urban centers in North America, is the largest city in the country (and its rapid growth rate of 5.9 percent from 1997 to 2000 brought it close to the 5 million population mark). The Ottawa-Gatineau metropolitan area on the southeastern border with Quebec is second in population in the province, with well over 1 million people (part in Quebec). Ottawa is the nation's capital and center of its federal government. The next

largest cities are Hamilton (population, 490,268), at the western tip of Lake Ontario, and St. Catharines-Niagara Falls (377,009), on the south shore of Lake Ontario near the U.S. border. These two metropolitan areas are old industrial centers whose populations showed slight increases between 1996 and 2001.

The cities of Kitchener (population, 190,399), London (336,539), and Windsor (208,402) are located on the peninsula between Lake Huron and Georgian Bay on the north and lakes Erie and Ontario on the south. Oshawa (on Lake Ontario east of metropolitan Toronto) has 139,051 people. The only large metropolitan areas outside the southern triangle are the cities of Greater Sudbury (155,219), above Georgian Bay, and Thunder Bay (109,016), on the north shore of Lake Superior.

The people. Ontario's indigenous population consisted of the Algonquian tribes of the north and the Iroquois of the south by the time French fur traders came to settle in the area in the early 1600s. The first large population growth occurred in the 1770s and 1780s when British Empire Loyalists moved into the Great Lakes region from the American colonies during the American Revolution. In 1791 an act of the British Parliament established Upper Canada (now the province of Ontario) as a separate political unit from Lower Canada (now the province of Quebec).

The population of Ontario today consists of 72 percent English speakers and 5 percent French speakers. The largest ethnic groups in the province are of Chinese extraction, representing 4.5 percent of the total population, with people of German extraction representing 1.5 percent. Ontario recorded the greatest numerical population increase in the country from 1986 to 1991, and the highest percentage growth of any province between 1991 and 1996. Ontario's population is heavily concentrated in the Ottawa-Toronto-Windsor corridor, where 90 percent of the provincial population live on one-sixth of the land.

Economy. Manufacturing accounts for nearly one-third of the province's gross domestic product. Ontario's manufacturing facilities, like its population, are heavily concentrated in the southeast, where the largest numbers of automobiles, iron and steel products, and food and paper goods are produced. Although Ontario leads the provinces in farm goods, agriculture generates only one-sixth as much income as manufacturing. Two-thirds of the farm income is derived from poultry and livestock, especially cattle, which can be grazed in the rural central region. The chief crops are grains for livestock feed, such as corn and soybeans, and cereals such as wheat and oats. Third in importance to the local economy is mining, with the Canadian Shield regions yielding 51 percent of world nickel production and large amounts of lead, zinc, and copper. Lumber is also an important industry in the north, and tourism has

become a significant economic activity in many parts of the province.

Places of interest. North of the populated corridor, but still in southern Ontario, a land of lakes awaits the traveler. In Algonquin Provincial Park alone, there are some 2,500 lakes. The resort areas of Muskoka, Haliburton, and the Kawartha lakes to the east have long been popular with vacationers. There is boating, fishing, swimming in summer, hunting in season, cross-country skiing, and snowshoeing and snowmobiling in winter. The rugged terrain of northern Ontario attracts truly adventurous campers, hikers, and canoeists.

Niagara Falls is a major attraction for visitors, as is the historic village of Niagara-on-the-Lake, with its annual Shaw Festival featuring performances of the plays of George Bernard Shaw. Stratford, west of Hamilton, houses Canada's world-famous Shakespeare Festival, along with a number of other theatrical attractions (May through November annually).

(For additional information on Ontario's major cities, see Cities of North America section.)

Prince Edward Island

Abbreviation: *P.E.I., PE*
Area: *2,185 sq. mi., 5,660 sq. km.*
    Rank   10th
Population:
    2001   135,294
    Rank   10th
    Change 1996–2001   <1,000
    Persons per sq. mi.   61.9
Capital and largest city:
    Charlottetown
    Pop.   32,245
Entered confederation:
    July 1, 1873
Floral emblem: *Lady's slipper*
Province map: *Page 201*

Prince Edward Island, Canada's smallest province, is located in the southern part of the Gulf of St. Lawrence. It is 120 miles (193 kilometers) across at its greatest east-west extent, and up to 35 miles (56 kilometers) wide. The island lies some 10 miles (16 kilometers) north of the New Brunswick-Nova Scotia mainland.

Prince Edward Island, discovered by the French explorer Jacques Cartier in 1534, was originally called Ille St-Jean. It was formally ceded to England in 1763 under the Treaty of Paris, and named after a son of King George III of England in 1799. It has the nickname the Cradle of Confederation because in Charlottetown, now the provincial capital, the initial Canadian self-rule talks were held in 1864.

Today, in addition to being the smallest in area, Prince Edward Island is the least populous and the most rural of Canadian provinces. It retains an Old

World, pastoral character, one typified by gently rolling fields bordered by low walls and hedges. Its coastal scenery is especially attractive to visitors, who are drawn to the island's extensive sandy beaches and quiet inlets.

The land. Prince Edward Island is a low-lying section of the Appalachian Uplands region notable for its underlying bed of red sandstone. The island's highest elevation is 466 feet (142 meters), and the rolling hills are drained only by small streams. The coastline is sharply indented on all sides and uniformly sandy except for a stretch of low coastal cliffs along the southern shore.

Climate. Prince Edward Island has a slightly sunnier and drier climate than the other Atlantic Provinces. On the southern coast, at Charlottetown, normal winter temperatures average 20°F (-7°C) and normal summer temperatures average 65°F (18°C). Average precipitation is 45 inches (114 centimeters) per year, the lowest in the Atlantic Provinces, but snowfall averages 129 inches (328 centimeters) per year, higher than in any Atlantic province except Newfoundland and Labrador.

Principal cities. The capital city of Charlottetown is the largest on Prince Edward Island, the hub of island life, the principal tourist center, and the major port. Ferry service connects Prince Edward Island with New Brunswick and Nova Scotia from the towns of Borden and Wood Islands, approximately equidistant from Charlottetown to the west and southeast respectively. Confederation Bridge, a bridge connecting the province with the mainland, was completed and opened in the spring of 1997.

The people. Because of its limited land area, Prince Edward Island's population is the densest in Canada; there are no uninhabited places on the predominantly rural island. The proportions of the population by mother tongue are

COMMERCIAL FISHING is an important element of the economy on Prince Edward Island, ranking just behind manufacturing.

27 North America

PRINCE EDWARD ISLAND is the most rural of the Canadian provinces, retaining an Old World flavor with its pastoral character and rolling fields.

kilometers
US
kilometres
Brit.

94 percent English and 4 percent French. The population is very stable.

Economy. Tourism, the island's leading industry, employs nearly one-third of the workforce. Agriculture is second in importance, with the field crops being potatoes and grain and the livestock chiefly dairy cattle. Manufacturing ranks next, followed by commercial fishing.

Places of interest. Prince Edward Island is small enough to be toured conveniently in its entirety. Its 1,000 miles (1,609 kilometers) of shoreline include many harbor villages and campgrounds. Places of historic interest include the Province House, Fort Amherst National Historic Site, and the restored Micmac Indian village, all in Charlottetown.

Internationally, the island is probably best known for the Anne of Green Gables series of books by Lucy Maud Montgomery (1874–1942). Tourists come in the thousands every year from as far away as Japan to view the old farmhouse, Green Gables, at Cavendish, immortalized in the books. It was the home of friends of the author, and visitors may also see the white cottage with green trim at New London where Montgomery was born. At Park Corner, 6 miles (10 kilometers) away, stands Silver Bush House, where Montgomery later married and lived.

(For information on Charlottetown, see Cities of North America section.)

Quebec is the largest in area of the provinces of Canada, occupying well over half a million square miles (over 1.5 million square kilometers) of the country's eastern mainland. The province's greatest north-south extent, well over 1,100 miles (1,770 kilometers), is along its western border, which is formed by Ontario in the south and west, James Bay in the west-central area, and the larger Hudson Bay in the northwest. The northern limit is defined by Hudson Strait and Ungava Bay, across which Quebec faces Baffin Island, of Nunavut. In the northeast Quebec extends to the border of Labrador, the mainland region of the province of Newfoundland and Labrador, and in the east to the Gulf of St. Lawrence, both north and south of the gulf. In the southeast, Quebec borders the province of New Brunswick and the U.S. state of Maine; in the south it borders the states of New Hampshire, Vermont, and New York.

Although larger in area, Quebec ranks second to Ontario in population and economic importance. It is unique, however, in the sense of being the most French of all the provinces.

Quebec is sometimes called the cradle of Canada because it was in the southeastern St. Lawrence area that Jacques Cartier landed in 1534 and named the region New France. Samuel de Champlain founded the original settlement at Quebec City in 1608. The province has remained thoroughly French in language and culture ever since. In recent years, Francophone supporters of Quebec's Parti Québécois have begun to agitate for separation from the Canadian confederation as a means of resolving their differences with the federal government.

The land. Fully 90 percent of the Quebec land area lies within the topographical region called the Canadian Shield, the vast plateau that arcs around Hudson Bay. The Shield reaches as far south as the Laurentian Mountains, some 75 miles (121 kilometers) northwest of Montreal. It is poor farmland, with exposed Precambrian bedrock stripped of soil by glacial ice sheets, but it is rich in minerals and, in the south, well forested. Canada's tree line, however, crosses Quebec from James Bay in the west to the northeastern border with Labrador; above this line the frozen tundra supports only scrub vegetation.

The remaining 10 percent of the land area consists of the St. Lawrence Lowlands, which surround the river in the southeast, and the Appalachian Uplands, between the river and the U.S. border. The St. Lawrence Lowlands contain the most valuable farmland in the province, and the Appalachian Uplands include the mountains of the Gaspé peninsula south of the river and north of New Brunswick.

Climate. Quebec's climate ranges from subarctic above the tree line to humid and continental in the south. At Fort Chimo on Ungava Bay in the north, temperatures average -10°F (-23°C) in winter and 53°F (12°C) in summer, with an annual precipitation of 20 inches (51 centimeters), including 96 inches (244 centimeters) of snow. Most of the people live in the south, where the climate is one of cold winters and brief but warm summers. At Montreal, in the extreme south of the province, normal winter temperatures average 16°F (-9°C), normal summer temperatures average 70°F (21°C), and there is an annual average precipitation of 40 inches (102 centimeters), with 97 inches (246 centimeters) of snow.

Quebec

Abbreviation: *Que., QC*
Area: *594,702 sq. mi.,*
  1,540,680 sq. km.
  Rank   1st
Population:
  2001   7,237,479
  Rank   2nd
  Change 1996–2001   +98,000
  Persons per sq. mi.   12.2
Capital: *Quebec*
Largest city: *Montreal*
  Pop.   1,039,534
Entered confederation:
  July 1, 1867
Floral emblem: *Blue flag iris*
Province map: *Page 200*

QUEBEC IS HOME to the Canadian Museum, one of the many museums in Canada.

Principal cities. Montreal is the second largest city in Canada, after Toronto, and also the second largest French-speaking city in the world, after Paris. The metropolitan area includes over 45 percent of the population of Quebec. For much of Canada's history, Montreal was the largest and most important city, being surpassed by Toronto only in the early 1970s.

Quebec City (population, 682,757), the province's second largest metropolitan area, is located 169 miles (272 kilometers) northeast of Montreal on the St. Lawrence River. Quebec City is especially French in character, and it is the only walled city in North America outside of Mexico. The only other metropolitan areas in the province are Chicoutimi-Jonquière (population, 154,938), northeast of Quebec City on the Saguenay River; Trois-Rivières (137,507), on the St. Lawrence River between Montreal and Quebec City; and Ottawa-Gatineau, on the Ontario border (of 1,063,664 people, about a third live in Quebec). There are no large cities in the northern nine-tenths of the province.

The people. In population Quebec is both the second largest and the second most urban of the Canadian provinces after Ontario. As in Ontario, the overwhelming majority of Quebec's population is concentrated in the limited area of the southern lowlands. The population growth rate in Quebec, however, is only about half that of Ontario. In Quebec 81 percent of the population claim French as their mother tongue, and only 8 percent claim English. The largest ethnic group is of Italian extraction, representing about 2 percent of the total population. A small number of Inuit live in the far northern regions of the province.

Economy. Quebec's largest industry is manufacturing, which generates almost a third of its gross domestic product. Manufacturing in Quebec is based along the river systems of the southern region. Since 1960 it has been given a boost by the availability of hydroelectric power generated by the St. Lawrence Seaway, a joint Canadian–U.S. project that created an oceangoing ship route from the Atlantic to the Great Lakes and, subsequently, by the enormous capacity of the James Bay hydroelectric generating complex. The principal manufactures are processed foods, textiles, and paper goods. Mining and agriculture are the most important industries after manufacturing. Quebec's northern mines produce large quantities of asbestos and structural metals, and its farms are equally divided between livestock, chiefly dairy cattle, and crops such as oats, corn, and potatoes.

Places of interest. Like neighboring northern Ontario, the northern region of Quebec appeals to wilderness enthusiasts, and there are numerous hunting and fishing camps that can be reached only by air.

Farther south, the Laurentian Mountains have long been a popular resort area in both summer and winter, with excellent downhill and cross-country skiing facilities. The first ski tow in Canada was built there in 1932, at Prévost. Mont-Tremblant Provincial Park (founded in 1894 as a forest reserve) is the province's oldest, and includes about 1,000 lakes.

On the north shore of the St. Lawrence River, where it meets the Saguenay River, whale watching tours to spot belugas can be joined at Tadoussac, a locale known also for sand skiing in the summer.

The scenic Gaspé peninsula, south of the St. Lawrence, is another popular tourist destination.

(For information on Montreal and Quebec City, see Cities of North America section.)

Saskatchewan

Abbreviation: *Sask., SK*
Area: *251,793 sq. mi.,*
  652,330 sq. km.
  Rank   5th
Population:
  2001   978,933
  Rank   6th
  Change 1996–2001   -11,000
  Persons per sq. mi.   3.9
Capital: *Regina*
Largest city: *Saskatoon*
  Pop.   196,811
Entered confederation:
  Sept. 1, 1905
Floral emblem: *Western red lily*
Province map: *Page 199*

Saskatchewan is almost rectangular in shape, stretching 766 miles (1,225 kilometers) from north to south, and up to 394 miles (630 kilometers) from east to west. It borders Alberta in the west and Manitoba in the east. Its northern border is with the Northwest Territories, and its southern border is with the U.S. states of Montana and North Dakota.

Most of Saskatchewan lies within the prairie region that extends south and east into the Great Plains of the U.S. grain states. The province is the major breadbasket of Canada. Saskatchewan includes more than half the improved farmland in Canada, typified by the rolling wheat fields of the south. It is the least populous of the Western Provinces; during the 1980s, growth resumed, with a population gain of 4.3 percent from 1981 to 1986. In the period between 1986 and 1994, however, there was practically no growth.

The land. The southern two-thirds of Saskatchewan consists of grassland prairies that rise from an average of 1,000 feet (305 meters) in the southeast to an average of 3,000 feet (914 meters) in the southwest. The northern third of the province is part of the Canadian Shield, a glacial plateau characterized by large lakes, such as Lake Athabasca on the northwestern Alberta border and Reindeer Lake on the northeastern Manitoba border. The division between the two regions is formed by the Churchill River and a series of small lakes that are its headwaters.

Climate. At the capital city of Regina in the south-central region of the province, winter temperatures average -1°F (-18°C) and summer temperatures average 66°F (19°C). Precipitation at Regina averages 11 inches (28 centimeters) annually, with 45 inches (114 centimeters) of snow. Northern Saskatchewan is both colder and drier than Regina.

Principal cities. Nearly 42 percent of the provincial population live in Saskatchewan's only large cities, Regina and Saskatoon. Regina (population, 178,225), 100 miles (161 kilometers) from the U.S. border, is the principal

REGINA, seen here from Wascana Park, is the principal processing point for Saskatchewan's agricultural products.

kilometers
US

kilometres
Brit.

center
US

centre
Brit.

GRAIN DELIVERY is part of Saskatchewan's important agricultural sector. The province supplies almost 60 percent of Canada's enormous wheat harvest.

processing point for the province's agricultural products. Saskatoon, standing 160 miles (257 kilometers) to the northwest, is the province's manufacturing center and the processing point for its mineral products.

The people. The population of Saskatchewan is 84 percent native English speakers and 1.8 percent native French speakers. The major ethnic groups are of German and Ukrainian extraction, and native peoples, including Indians and Métis, people of mixed Indian and European descent. The province lost population to migration in the 1970s, and again in the 1986 to 1991 period. By 2001 population was showing a decrease of 1.1 percent. Because its leading businesses are agricultural, Saskatchewan's population is the least urban among the Western Provinces.

Economy. Agriculture is still Saskatchewan's most important economic activity. The province supplies almost 60 percent of the enormous Canadian wheat harvest; it also raises more beef cattle than any western province except

Alberta. Manufacturing is Saskatchewan's second largest economic activity, concentrated largely in the processing of food and mineral products. Mining ranks third in economic value, with production of fuels and minerals, particularly potash and uranium, being of equal importance.

Places of interest. Tourist attractions in central Saskatchewan include Prince Albert National Park, 125 miles (201 kilometers) north of Saskatoon. Lac la Ronge, Saskatchewan's largest provincial park, is almost one-third

water, thus forming a popular fishing location where trout, walleye, and northern pike are caught. Crossing the park's northern boundary is the Churchill River, with its many lakes joined by spectacular white water and rapids. It is Canada's only wilderness river that is readily accessible to the average tourist.

(For information on the province's two major cities, Regina and Saskatoon, see Cities of North America section.)

Territories

The Northwest Territories, the Yukon Territory, and Nunavut occupy nearly the entire Canadian mainland north of 60° north latitude; they include the numerous Arctic islands. A portion of Quebec's Ungava peninsula and the northern tip of Labrador are the only other Canadian lands above 60°. The total expanse of almost 1.5 million square miles (almost 4 million square kilometers) represents 39 percent of the Canadian land area and is the home of only a fraction of 1 percent of the total population. Along with the U.S. state of Alaska, which forms its western

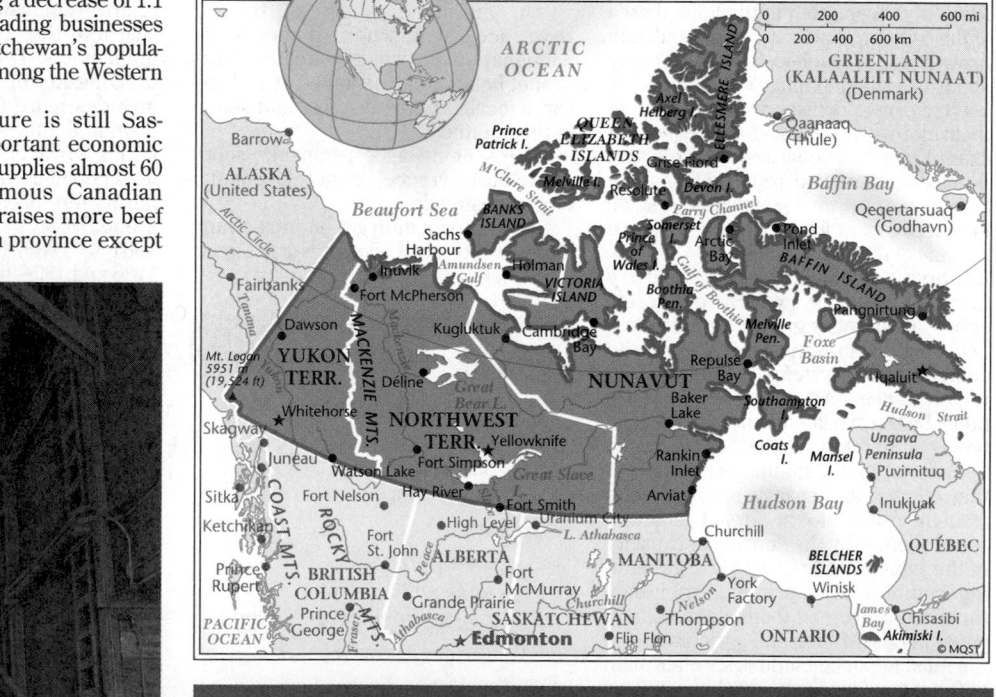

Territories

Territory	Area (Sq. Mi.)	Population 2001	Population Change 1996–2001 Number	Population Change 1996–2001 Percent	Persons per Sq. Mi.
Northwest	501,574	37,360	-3,000	-5.8	0.07
Nunavut	769,888	26,745	2,000	8.1	0.03
Yukon	186,607	28,674	-2,000	-6.8	0.14
Region Totals	1,458,069	92,779	-3,000	-3.2	0.06

boundary, this territorial area is the last great unexplored wilderness of North America.

The land. The land of the territories consists of the Canadian Shield, which covers the eastern two-thirds, and the northern expanse of the Western Cordillera, a mountain region that covers the western third. The Canadian Shield is a vast plateau that averages between 600 and 1,200 feet (183 and 366 meters) above sea level. Once mountainous in character, it was leveled by glacial ice sheets into rounded hills and depressed lake valleys. It is crossed from northwest to southeast by the timberline, north of which the frozen tundra cannot support forests. The Cordillera in this region consists of the St. Elias Mountains, a coastal range in the southwest Yukon that is the highest in Canada, and the Mackenzie Mountains, in the western Northwest Territories, the northern end of the Rocky Mountain chain. Between these ranges lies a large mountain plateau that covers most of the Yukon Territory.

Climate. The climate of the territories varies from subarctic below the timberline to arctic above it. Winter temperatures are subzero in either case, but the subarctic area experiences mild summers while the arctic region never has a complete thaw. Precipitation is low throughout the area, dropping to extremes of less than 10 inches (25 centimeters) per year far inland.

History. Possibly the first European visitors to North America were Norse sailors who landed on Baffin Island in Nunavut. After a party from the British vessel *Nonsuch,* including the intrepid explorer Sieur des Groseilliers, wintered at James Bay in 1668–1669, returning to England on October 10, 1669, with a substantial cargo of furs, the British established the Hudson's Bay Company for trapping. The date of its charter is May 2, 1670.

The company owned the northern land area, called Rupert's Land, and explored westward to the Yukon Territory in the 1840s. In 1870 Canada purchased Rupert's Land from the company for £300,000. The company retained one-twentieth of the fertile land area for new settlement as well as all lands on which it had built trading posts.

In 1898, the year of the great Klondike gold rush, the Yukon was set off from the Northwest Territories and admitted to Confederation. Gold had been discovered there on August 17, 1896, and that date is still observed as a holiday (Discovery Day) in the Yukon.

The Northwest Territories were admitted to Confederation in 1870.

Nunavut, created from the Northwest Territories, was admitted to the Confederation in April 1999, after years of negotiations between the Inuit people and the Canadian and Northwest Territories governments.

The people. The population of the territories is predominantly English-speaking, but it is notable for its large proportion of Inuit and Indians. The Northwest Territories and Nunavut include 75 percent of Canada's Inuit. The Inuit are relatively unaffected by modernization because of the remoteness of the Arctic homelands. The Indian population is concentrated in the forested land south of the timberline. It includes a distinct group of mixed Indian and non-Indian ancestry called Métis.

Government. The governments of both the Northwest Territories and the Yukon Territory are headed by a commissioner who is federally appointed, plus an elected body. The commissioner must report directly to the federal minister of Indian Affairs and Northern Development. Lands, natural resources, taxation, and native rights claims are controlled by Ottawa. As the result of a land claim agreement prior to admittance to the Confederation, the government of Nunavut has more decision-making power than that of the other territories. An elected 19-member assembly appoints a speaker, premier, and cabinet. The Yukon Territory elects one representative to Parliament; the Northwest Territories and Nunavut elect two.

Northwest Territories

Abbreviation: *N.W.T., NT*

Area: *501,574 sq. mi.,*
1,299,070 sq. km.

Population:

2001   37,360

Change 1996–2001   -3,000

Persons per sq. mi.   0.07

Capital and largest city:

Yellowknife

Pop.   16,541

Entered confederation:

July 15, 1870

Floral emblem: *Mountain avens*

Territory map: *Page 210*

The Northwest Territories include all of the Canadian land area north of the Western Provinces of Alberta, Saskatchewan, and part of British Columbia between the Yukon Territory on the west and Nunavut on the east. The Northwest Territories are divided into two regions for purposes of administration: Inuvik Region and Fort Smith Region.

The land. Much of the Northwest Territories consist of the glacially leveled hills of the Canadian Shield. The timberline, north of which this plateau is barren tundra, runs from Mackenzie Bay in the extreme northwest to the border with Nunavut. In the far west, the territories include the Mackenzie and Franklin mountains. The extreme north lies within the Arctic Lowlands.

Climate. South of the timberline the territories are subarctic in climate. At Fort Simpson in the southwest, average temperatures are -18°F (-27°C) in winter and 60°F (16°C) in summer, with a total precipitation of 14 inches (36 centimeters) per year and 59 inches (150 centimeters) of snow. Arctic climates in which the permafrost never thaws prevail north of the tree line.

Principal cities. The only city in the entire Northwest Territories is Yellowknife, the seat of territorial government. All other settlements, such as Hay River, Inuvik, and Fort Smith, fall below 5,000 in population.

The people. With the separation of Nunavut from the territory, the population is now almost equally divided between those of French and English decent and those of native decent. Of the native population, almost 29 percent is Indian and 11 percent is Inuit.

Economy. Mining is the only large industry of the Northwest Territories, though tourism is becoming important. Oil and gold were the earliest mineral products. Mining income is divided almost equally between gold and zinc.

Places of interest. The many natural attractions of the Northwest Territories

CANADA ENACTED LAWS to protect the almost-extinct musk ox in 1917, and today large herds again roam the Northwest Territories of arctic Canada.

KLUANE LAKE, in Kluane National Park in the Yukon Territory, is a spectacularly beautiful wintertime sight.

meters
US

metres
Brit.

center
US

centre
Brit.

theaters
US

theatres
Brit.

include Wood Buffalo National Park, which straddles the Alberta border, and Nahanni National Park, along the South Nahanni River in the southwest—a UNESCO World Heritage site.

Yellowknife, the capital, is of interest for its gold-rush heritage and its promotion of the arts. In May 1984 the Globe Theatre of the Northern Arts and Cultural Centre opened there.

Nunavut

Abbreviation: *Nvt., NU*
Area: *769,888 sq. mi.*
            1,994,000 sq. km.
Population:
            2001   26,745
            Change 1996–2001   +2,000
            Persons per sq. mi.   0.03
Capital and largest city: *Iqaluit*
            Pop.   5,236
Entered confederation:
            April 1, 1999
Floral emblem: *Purple saxifrage*
Territory map: *Page 210*

Nunavut, meaning "our land" in Inuktitut, the Inuit language, separated from the Northwest Territories as the outcome of more than 30 years of negotiation and a land claims agreement between the Inuit people and the Canadian government. The Nunavut government is being established transitionally, and a 19-member elected assembly will assume all governing powers by 2009. The new territory encompasses almost 20 percent of Canada and was formed from the central and eastern portions of the Northwest Territories. Nunavut contains three regions: Kitikmeot, Kilvalliq, and Qikiqtani (formerly Baffin).
The land. The territory is surrounded by Baffin Bay and the Labrador Sea to

the east, Manitoba and Saskatchewan to the south, and the Northwest Territories to the west, and includes an extensive archipelago of islands in the north. Baffin Island is the largest and Ellesmere Island is the most northerly point in Canada. Primarily tundra, the majority of the area is frozen and snow-covered for more than half the year.
Climate. The vast area encompasses regional variations of arctic climate, from flat barren lands to fiords and mountain ranges and icebergs. Nunavut lies almost entirely north of the tree line. The northernmost city of Grise Ford, which lies north of the Arctic Circle, ranges in temperature from -40°F (-40°C) in winter to 5°F (-15°C) in summer. The overall average territorial temperatures are: midwinter, -30°F (-34°C), with an average of three hours of sunlight each day; and midsummer, 50°F (10°C), with over 22 hours of sunlight daily. At Iqaluit, at the southeastern point of Baffin Island, temperatures average -15°F (-26°C) in winter and 46°F (8°C) in summer.
Principal cities. Iqaluit (formerly Frobisher Bay), population 5,236, is the largest city and the capital. Most of the remaining population resides in small widespread communities.
The people. The majority of the population, 83 percent, is Inuit and has continuously inhabited the region for over 5,000 years. Most live in one of 26 small communities and depend on trapping and mining for their livelihood. This population is the youngest in Canada, with 60 percent of the residents under the age of 25.
Economy. In Nunavut there is a mixed land-based and wage economy. Employment in the government accounts for 39 percent of jobs in the wage economy. Since joining the confederation, Nunavut has had a significant growth in mining and construction, and tourism is expected to become increasingly more important. Arts and crafts are seen as a supplemental income to many. The land-based econ-

omy is a significant contribution, valued in the $40 to $60 million range. Only 60 percent of the adult Inuit population participate in the wage-based economy.
Places of interest. Nearly 39 percent of tourists visit the national or territorial parks, including Auyuittuq National Park, above the Arctic Circle on Baffin Island's Cumberland peninsula. Quittinirqaaq National Park on Ellesmere Island, the northernmost national park in North America, is mostly polar desert and contains most of the major ice shelves in North America.

Yukon Territory

Abbreviation: *Y.T., YT*
Area: *186,607 sq. mi.,*
            483,450 sq. km.
Population:
            2001   28,674
            Change 1996–2001   -2,000
            Persons per sq. mi.   0.14
Capital and largest city:
            Whitehorse
            Pop.   19,058
Entered confederation:
            June 13, 1898
Floral emblem: *Fireweed*
Territory map: *Page 210*

The Yukon Territory is located in the extreme northwest of Canada. It is triangular in shape, with a straight western border and jagged southwest corner on the U.S. state of Alaska. Its straight southern border is with the province of British Columbia. The Yukon's irregular eastern border with the Northwest Territories roughly approximates the ridge of the Mackenzie Mountains, with the Richardson Mountains at the northern extremity.

The Yukon Territory remains an unspoiled wilderness that is notable for its spectacular glaciers, even in its southernmost regions. A large portion of its dramatic mountain scenery has been accessible to visitors since the opening of the Alaska Highway in 1942. The Dempster Highway, from Dawson to Inuvik (Northwest Territories) in the Mackenzie River Delta, was completed in 1979, thereby helping to open up the northern Yukon and attract tourism to that area.
The land. The Yukon Territory lies entirely within the Western Cordillera, or mountain region, of western Canada. The highest mountain peaks are located in the southwest, where the St. Elias Mountains, part of the Pacific coastal ranges, include the highest point in Canada at Mt. Logan (19,850 feet, 6,050 meters).

The interior of the Yukon is a mountain plateau that occupies more than half of the territorial area. Along the northeastern border the Yukon includes several individual ranges of the Mackenzie Mountains—notably, the Selwyns and the Richardsons—a northern extension of the Rockies.

Climate. Because of its mountainous surface, the Yukon has a varied climate. At Dawson, near the center of the territory's western border, temperatures average -20°F (-29°C) in winter and 60°F (16°C) in summer, with a total precipitation of 12 inches (30 centimeters) per year, and 55 inches (140 centimeters) of snow. To the east and southeast, the Yukon's inland plateau is far drier, with some places averaging under 10 inches (25 centimeters) of precipitation per year, and colder, with temperatures that have dropped to the Canadian record low of -81°F (-63°C).

Principal cities. The only city in the Yukon Territory is Whitehorse, which replaced Dawson as the territorial capital in 1951. Including surrounding towns, the city accounts for almost two-thirds of the total population. There is no other settlement with a permanent population of more than 2,000.

The people. Most of the territorial population is English speaking. Nearly one-fifth of the population is accounted for by Indians of the Athabasca tribe and Métis, who are of mixed Indian and non-Indian ancestry.

Economy. One-third of the Yukon's gross domestic product is derived from mining, principally of ores including copper, lead, zinc, gold, and silver. Manufacturing has increased steadily in importance, however, especially in the areas of furniture, clothing, and handicrafts. The only other significant industries are forestry and tourism.

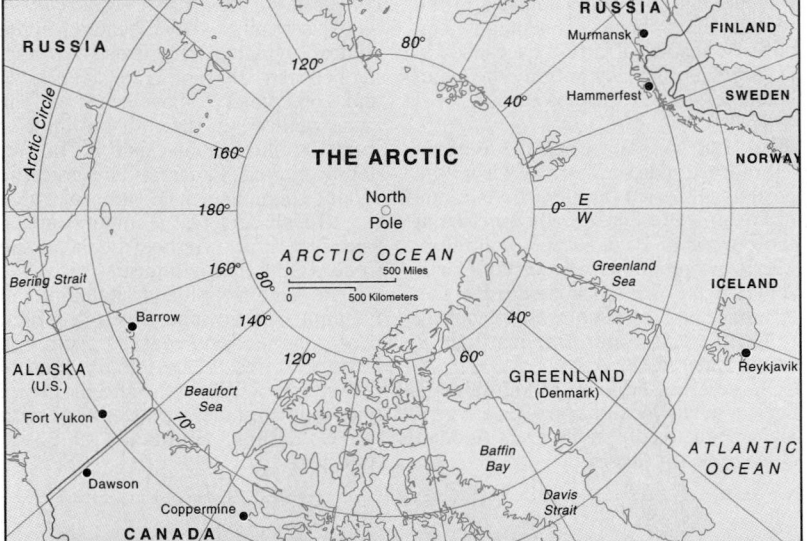

Places of interest. Mount Logan, Canada's highest peak, towers over the Yukon's Kluane National Park. There are over 2,000 glaciers in the park, more than half of which is under ice and snow. In addition to the breathtaking beauty of the region, which appeals to all those who love the great outdoors, the Yukon's gold rush history is a notable attraction. The Klondike Gold Rush International Historical Park at Dawson is a joint cooperative venture between the United States and Canadian national park services. Reconstructions of saloons, dance halls, and theaters from the town's heyday (1897–1898) are a significant tourist draw.

Whitehorse, the territory's principal city and capital, is also of historical interest, especially for its beginnings in the heady days of gold fever.

MOUNT ASGARD, on Baffin Island, is part of a mountainous landscape of fjords, glaciers, a large ice cap, and many species of wildlife.

The Far North

Not until the 1500s did the North interest the people of Europe. Then, in a race to find a Northwest Passage to the Orient, a succession of explorers risked their lives in the cold, ice, and fog.

The fate of the 1847 expedition led by the English explorer Sir John Franklin pointed up the dangers of arctic exploration. Franklin's ship was trapped in the ice and he and all his company perished. Even so, it took several other expeditions to learn what had happened to the Franklin party. The lesson was clear however: The arctic could become, without warning, a hostile environment, and any miscalculation could bring the highest penalty.

The fabled Northwest Passage was not discovered until the late 1800s, and it never proved practical for transportation or trade, but by then, a new breed of explorers were in a race to be the first to the North Pole. The first party to reach the Pole was led by Admiral Robert E. Peary of the United States, who attained his goal on April 6, 1909, after several failed attempts. In 1926 U.S. Admiral Richard E. Byrd and American aviator Floyd Bennett became the first to fly over the North Pole. On August 3, 1958, the world's first nuclear submarine, the U.S.S. *Nautilus*, became the first ship to sail beneath the North Pole, on a cruise from the Pacific to the Atlantic oceans.

By the 1950s, the Arctic regions had gained economic and strategic importance. Large deposits of iron, nickel, uranium, and other metals were found in northern Canada and the Soviet Union, and deposits of oil on the arctic slope of Alaska and in the sea north of Norway have added to the world's fuel supply. Both the Americans and the Soviets, fearful of attack from the other, set up monitoring stations around the edges of the arctic region. These stations provided not only defense security during the Cold War but also much valuable scientific data.

The region itself is bounded by the Arctic Circle, an imaginary line that marks the southernmost point where the sun never rises above the horizon on the shortest day of the year (about December 21). The circle is about 1,600 miles (2,575 kilometers) from the North Pole at 66.5 degrees north latitude.

Most of the arctic is occupied by the Arctic Ocean, which has an area of more than 5 million square miles (13 million square kilometers). Much of the ocean is covered year-round with ice, but near the Arctic Circle, its waters are navigable in the late summer. On land, although trees do not grow, a surprising variety of vegetation, including many kinds of flowers, springs up during the short warm season. A large variety of land and sea animals, including caribou, reindeer, bears, seals, and walruses, live in the area.

Small groups of people have also lived in or near the arctic for centuries. Along its western shores from Greenland to Alaska, the Inuit have mastered the art of hunting arctic animals and fishing the icy waters. On the European shores, Lapps, Finns, and many isolated Siberian tribes still live. Many have abandoned their earlier patterns of life, however, and now rely on modern conveniences.

Intense scientific research conducted in the arctic by a number of nations during the International Geophysical Year (IGY) of 1957–1958 advanced the world's understanding of the arctic region as not just a vast cold wasteland, but as a fragile and threatened ecosystem and an extremely valuable repository of information about Earth's environmental processes. Concern for the preservation of the arctic environment and for the protection of the culture and way of life of the Inuit of Canada were major considerations that prompted the Canadian government to establish the new Inuit homeland Nunavut.

Mexico and Central America

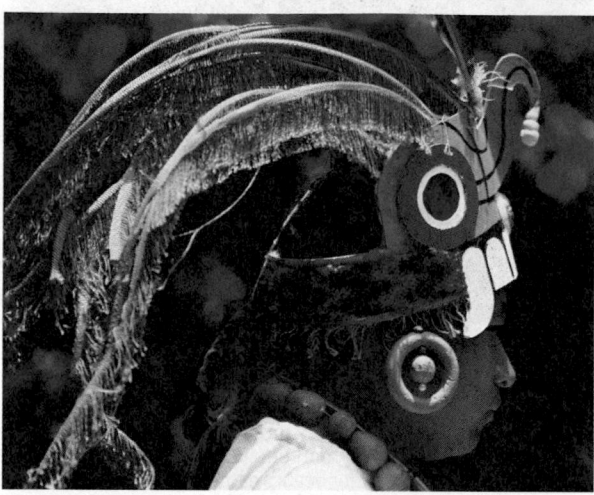

PRESENT-DAY DESCENDANTS of the Mayan people of the Yucatan Peninsula retain many of the characteristics still seen in the paintings in the archaeological sites preserved there.

This area includes Mexico and the smaller countries in the isthmus south of Mexico and north of the South American mainland.

Central America has often been grouped with Latin America, since most of the countries in the area derive their modern civilizations from Spain and Portugal, the countries that colonized them following discovery of the Americas by Europeans beginning in A.D 1492.

The small republics of Guyana and Suriname and the French possession of French Guiana on the northern coast of South America are exceptions.

The population of Mexico and Central America is approximately 150 million. Until the end of the 19th century the population of the region was relatively low. However, the rate of population growth increased sharply in the late 19th and early 20th centuries, peaking from the 1950s to the 1970s; it remains high in many countries in the region. The problems of unemployment, poverty, and social unrest are caused in part by their inability to bring the population growth rate under control.

The land. The Central American isthmus extends southeasterly from the border of Mexico through the isthmus of Panama and joins South America at the border of Panama and Colombia. Mexico is geographically part of North America, but cultural and historical factors have tied the country more closely to Central and South America than to North America.

Central America is a mountainous region, but its mountain groups are geologically distinct from the great Andean chain of South America.

Mexico has two major mountain ranges—the Sierra Madre Oriental in the east and the Sierra Madre Occidental in the west. They run parallel to each other on either side of the main interior region of the country, the Mexican Plateau. There are narrow lowland strips along the coasts, and most of the Yucatán peninsula is lowland.

South of Mexico, the Central American isthmus consists of narrow coastal lowlands dominated by mountainous central highlands that are volcanically and seismically active. Elevations in the central highlands vary greatly, averaging between 4,000 and 12,000 feet (1,220 and 3,660 meters) above sea level. Volcanic ranges run through the interior from the Nicaraguan-Costa Rican border to central Panama. The volcanic Mount Tajumulco, in Guatemala, which rises 13,846 feet (4,220 meters) above sea level, is the highest peak on the Central American isthmus.

The central highland chain ends in Panama in a lowland through which the Panama Canal passes from the Caribbean Sea to the Pacific. East of the canal, another mountain group rises and continues east to merge with the Colombian Highlands of South America.

civilizations
US

civilisations
Brit.

colonized
US

colonised
Brit.

meters
US

metres
Brit.

Rivers. Rivers are not a significant feature of Central America. Most are relatively small and shallow and are navigable only by small craft.

The major rivers in Mexico are the Rio Bravo (the Rio Grande in the United States), which forms part of the border between the United States and Mexico; the Yaqui, in northwestern Mexico; the Rio Conchos, in the north; the Rio Grande de Santiago, in west central Mexico; the Pánuco, in east-central Mexico; and the Rio Balsas in the southwest.

Central America has several large lakes, including lakes Managua and Nicaragua, both in Nicaragua's Pacific lowland region and the largest lakes in the region; lakes Atitlán and Izabal in Guatemala; and Lake Chapala located in Mexico.

Climate. The climate of Central America varies generally with elevation and with proximity to moisture-laden Caribbean air masses.

Rainfall is heavy on the eastern coast of Mexico and the Central American isthmus. The lowlands in these areas are hot and humid. The Pacific coast plains are also hot, but they are much drier because the mountain ranges of the central highlands block the Caribbean currents. The interior plateau of Mexico is also quite dry.

Vegetation. Much of the Central American isthmus and the Caribbean coast of Mexico are covered by dense tropical forests. The Mexican interior receives little rainfall and therefore has sparse vegetation.

The people. South and Central America share a similar variety of ethnic and cultural backgrounds. The predominant ethnic groups are American Indian (or, perhaps more properly, Native American), European, and African. These groups have, through intermarriage, produced two new groups: mestizos, persons of combined European and Indian ancestry, and mulattoes, persons of combined European and African ancestry.

Native Americans inhabited Central America for many centuries before the arrival of European explorers at the close of the 15th century. It is believed that the original Americans crossed from Asia to North America by way of a land bridge connecting Siberia with Alaska, then migrated over time south and east throughout the hemisphere. Evidence suggests that coastal fishing may have played an important role in this migration.

The great variety of Indian cultures that arose in Central America was caused at least in part by geographic factors that tended to isolate the cultures from one another. Among the most advanced of these cultures were those of the Aztecs of central Mexico and the Mayas of the Central American isthmus. However, hundreds of distinct Indian groups flourished throughout Central America. Many of these American cultures were based on agriculture and had advanced social and political structures.

The Spanish conquest of Central America was a devastating blow to the Native American cultures. Many Indian groups were virtually wiped out in warfare against the European conquerors. Others were decimated by European diseases to which they had no immunity. Of those Indians who survived the wars and diseases, many were forced into slave labor.

During the European colonial period, shortages of manpower developed in several areas. The Indian population that remained could not provide the great pool of cheap labor required by the colonial economies. As a result, millions of Africans were brought to work as slaves in Central and South America. Today the population of Mexico and the Central American isthmus is largely mestizo.

Languages. The common language of Central American nations is Spanish. English is spoken in Belize.

Religion. Roman Catholicism is the predominant religion in Central America, although Protestantism has grown rapidly in recent years. Two factors have played an important role in the growth of Protestantism in the region. The first is the vitality and commitment of the evangelical Christian movement in the region. The second is the perception in many places of the Roman Catholic Church as a reactionary institution, and as part of the ruling class. The church has been slow to change this perception, yet in Nicaragua, El Salvador, and other places it has taken positions favoring the bulk of the population and clearly antagonistic to the established powers.

Economy. For centuries the Latin American economy was centered on colonial agriculture and the exploitation of raw materials. Agricultural products and raw materials were sent to the mother country, and finished goods were received from the mother country. It was a system that benefited only the mother country and a very small group of colonial landowners, merchants, and administrators.

In most countries, significant industrial development did not occur until the late 19th or 20th centuries. This delay was caused in part by geographic problems. Development of roads and railways across mountain ranges and through tropical jungles, a prerequisite for large-scale industrial growth, was an enormous task, often beyond the scope of relatively unstable national governments. Financing new industry was another problem, as was the securing of stable markets for products.

Agriculture. Despite the move toward diversification in many countries, agriculture remains the main economic activity in much of Central America.

Export crops in Central America include bananas, coffee, cotton, sugar cane, and cacao. Beef production and fishing are also important.

Export crops are grown mainly on large tracts owned by a small group of wealthy citizens or by international corporations. However, in some countries the state has stepped in to reorganize the agricultural system. In Mexico, the government has for decades followed a policy of acquiring large estates, redistributing the land as small holdings, and establishing farm collectives operated by the farmers.

Natural resources. Central America has a number of important mineral deposits, including nickel, bauxite, silver, gold, copper, iron ore, petroleum, and natural gas.

Much of the Central American isthmus is richly forested, and Mexico has vast tracts of forest. Forestry on the isthmus, however, is largely undeveloped. In Mexico, forestry is controlled by the government.

There is an abundance of marine life off the Pacific coast of Mexico and in the Caribbean, and fishing is a growing but still small sector of the Central American economy.

Industry. Mexico is by far the most industrialized nation of Central America. The Mexican industries produce metals, chemicals, plastics, petrochemicals, pharmaceuticals, machinery, automobiles, electronic equipment, and a large variety of consumer products. Mexico's leading industry, petroleum, is strictly controlled by the government. An increasingly important sector of Mexican industry is light manufacturing and assembly for re-export.

Elsewhere in Central America, the growth of industry has been very slow. Countries are encouraging the establishment of small, export-oriented industries as a way to promote economic stability

labor
US

labour
Brit.

centered
US

centred
Brit.

PYRAMIDS OF THE SUN AND MOON at Teotihuacan outside of Mexico City bear witness to the height of civilization reached by native populations prior to western exploration.

THE GROWTH OF INDUSTRY has been slow in Central America, which still depends for stability on small export-oriented industries such as the weaving of rugs and textiles.

and growth. The economic downturn of the early 1980s, however, has slowed industrial development in the region.

Most of Central America's exports go to the United States and Europe, but a growing percentage of trade is among the Central American nations and with the nations of South America.

Transportation and trade. In the second half of the 20th century, the nations of South America improved their air and road transportation systems, the most important modes of travel on the continent. Railroads are also important, particularly for freight transport. Improved transportation, by motor vehicles particularly, has helped increase commerce among the South American nations. However, most trade is intercontinental, mainly with the United States and Europe.

Trade barriers between the nations of Central and South America have restricted the development of intracontinental commerce. However, in the 1960s, several initiatives were made to establish closer economic cooperation. Chief among these was the Latin American Free Trade Association (LAFTA), which was established in 1960 and included Mexico and the South American nations of Argentina, Brazil, Chile, Paraguay, Peru, and Uruguay.

LAFTA sought the eventual elimination of trade barriers among member nations, along the lines of the program established by the European Community, but it made little progress toward the continent's economic integration. One problem was the great disparity between the highly industrialized nations, such as Mexico and Brazil, and the much less industrialized countries, such as Paraguay. Complete elimination of tariffs proved unworkable because of inequities. In August 1980 Mexico became the only Central American country to join the Latin American Integration Association (ALADI), a new trade structure.

In Central America growth of trade is influenced in part by geography, since the rugged, mountainous terrain of the Central American isthmus presents numerous obstacles to overland transportation. However, Mexico and its southern neighbors are linked by the Pan-American Highway. In addition, several railroads connect the Atlantic and Pacific coasts, and airlines link most of the major urban centers. Sea transport is important throughout the isthmus.

The development of adequate transportation throughout Central America has played and will continue to play an important role in the region's economic

growth. Another factor has been the rise of regional economic cooperation.

In 1958 the nations of Costa Rica, El Salvador, Guatemala, Honduras, and Nicaragua formed the Central American Common Market (CACM) to equalize tariffs and to foster economic development among members. The success of the organization has been limited by political events in the region as well as by international economic factors, however.

Chief among the political factors was the 1979 Sandinista revolution in Nicaragua, which was the focus of considerable economic and political dislocation in the 1980s. In El Salvador, a long and bloody civil war has sapped that nation's ability to foster desperately needed economic growth.

Economic factors affecting CACM include the rise in oil prices in 1973–1974, 1979, and 1990. These price increases fostered inflation and international indebtedness, crippled growth, and promoted political instability.

Hidden economy. One of the results of unfavorable economic pressures is the growth of economic activity outside the mainstream—the so-called black market or illegal economy. Black market trading in Central America has grown in part due to government policies such as wage and price controls, taxes, and tariffs, but also due to external factors such as price fluctuations on international markets.

Hidden economies generally have been small in relation to overall national economies in the region. However, the drug economy of Latin countries has proven to be a startling exception.

In the 1970s and 1980s an enormous demand for cocaine grew in the United

A PAINTING BY MEXICAN ARTIST Diego Rivera depicts the Aztecs of central Mexico bringing gifts of fruits, tobacco, cocoa, and vanilla for the emperor.

States. The concept of using military and police force to curb the drug traffic was dealt a further blow in 1989, when the United States invaded Panama and toppled the regime of General Manuel Antonio Noriega. He had gained control of the drug trade in Panama and greatly expanded it. It was hoped that with his downfall drug traffic in Panama would be severely curtailed. However, one year after the invasion, the drug trade was still thriving. It became clear that substantial additional resources would have to be committed to locate processing centers, identify transportation routes, and find and seize drug shipments.

Economic trends. Throughout the last several decades, the economic focus of South and Central America has been on industrial development and diversification to broaden the economic base, produce new jobs, and encourage growth and long-term stability.

Rapid industrial growth was financed largely through deficit spending and large-scale borrowing by countries of the region. Although rapid growth was achieved in the short term, the cost of servicing a large foreign debt was a burden on the economies. In addition, the development of nonexport industries, while intended to reduce imports, also had the effect of drawing labor and capital from export industries, further weakening the economies. Extensive government involvement frequently meant the expenditure of resources to maintain businesses that were not run efficiently and could not compete on the international market.

The efficiency of government-controlled economies seemed to be unrelated to the political philosophy espoused by a government.

In the late 1980s many countries introduced bitter but necessary austerity programs intended to control consumption and reduce inflation, increase exports, reduce international debt, and restore investor confidence. Governments began to close or sell off unprofitable businesses and reduce spending, measures that were strongly opposed by organized labor.

Although the austerity measures produced great hardships and sometimes provoked violent disturbances and deep political turmoil, they averted total economic collapse. However, it was clear that continued progress toward economic stabilization depended in part on the world economy, the availability of ample investment funds, and the growth of foreign markets for Central American products.

Government. Prior to the early 19th century, all of Central America was under European colonial rule. Mexico and most of the Central American isthmus were controlled by Spain.

The 19th century saw the end of colonialism in much of the region and the establishment of a number of independent republics. In many of the new states, political forces were divided into conservative and liberal factions.

SAN MIGUEL DE ALLENDE in central Mexico is a cultural center. Its major artists' colony and colonial atmosphere attract many tourists.

Early attempts at political confederation in the region proved unsuccessful. The dream of Simón Bolívar to establish a United States of South America did not become a reality. On the Central American isthmus, the short-lived United Provinces of Central America gave way to the independent and sometimes democratic republics of Guatemala, Honduras, El Salvador, Nicaragua, and Costa Rica.

In many countries the division between conservatives and liberals was the dominant political factor well into the 20th century. The often bitter rivalry between these factions has been complicated by the involvement of the military in political affairs. Military coups, dictatorships, and civil conflicts have slowed the development of stable political institutions.

In the 20th century, two factors played particularly important roles in changing the dynamics of Central American politics. The rapid rate of population growth and a surge in economic development produced two new forces for change. The increasing population created a strong demand for more equitable redistribution of land and wealth, traditionally controlled by a few aristocratic families in many countries. Industrial and commercial growth and the growth of urban centers was accompanied by the rise of strong urban middle and working classes. Their interests have brought them into competition with the landed aristocracy in both the political and economic spheres.

In some countries, such as Mexico, the forces of change were institutionalized and achieved varying degrees of success. In Mexico, significant land redistribution and rapid industrial growth have transformed the country during the 20th century.

A number of countries in the region have been centers of violence associated with Cold War politics, including Nicaragua, El Salvador, and Guatemala. In the 1980s the United States supported forces opposing the Marxist-dominated Sandinista revolutionary government in Nicaragua, which had overthrown the dictator Anastasio Somoza in 1979. The United States has also opposed leftist guerrilla activities in Guatemala, El Salvador, and other countries.

Despite the numerous and continuing economic, social, and political problems facing the nations of Central America, there has been a significant trend away from armed conflict and military rule and toward the growth of democratic institutions and traditions. Continued progress, however, requires regional and international cooperation in solving the region's major problems.

The United States has been involved in Central American affairs since the 19th century, when its economic interests in the region increased significantly. Frequently, its policy in the region took the form of military intervention, which did little to secure the respect or friendship of Central Americans. The inauguration of the Alliance for Progress by the United States in the 1960s signaled a significant shift toward economic and political cooperation in an attempt to finally achieve regional peace, growth, and unity.

Perhaps the most important organization advancing regional unity is the Organization of American States (OAS), whose members now include all 35 nations of North, Central, and South America. Founded in 1948, the OAS has worked to promote collective security, peaceful resolution of disputes, and economic, social, and cultural development.

With the end of the Cold War and the dramatic shift of the global economy toward greater integration, it is likely that in the 21st century new economic and political ties will bring all the nations of the western hemisphere closer together.

27 North America

VANILLA
has been cultivated
in Mexico for
hundreds of years.

Countries of Mexico and Central America

Belize

Official name: *Belize*
Area: *8,863 sq. mi., 22,960 sq. km.*
Type of government:
Parliamentary democracy
Population: *260,000*
Capital: *Belmopan*
(Pop., 8,000)
Largest city: *Belize City*
(Pop., 49,000)
Languages: *English (official),*
Spanish, Mayan, Garifuna
Literacy: *70%;* **Currency:** *Dollar*
Per capita GDP: *$3,250*
(Rank: 111th)

The land. The southern half of Belize is dominated by the Maya Mountains; the highest point, Victoria Peak, reaches 3,681 feet (1,122 meters). The northern part of the country is mostly lowland, much of which is swamp. The vegetation throughout most of the country is tropical jungle. About 15 miles (24 kilometers) off Belize's long Caribbean coastline lies the second largest barrier reef in the world.

The people. About 50 percent of the population is of African or part African descent. Mestizos and Indians make up the next largest groups. There are also small minorities of East Indians and Europeans. The largest cities are Belmopan, the capital, and Belize City (population, 49,000), the former capital. The site for the city of Belmopan was located 50 miles (80 kilometers) inland following a hurricane in 1961 that devastated Belize City. Work on Belmopan was begun in 1967; it became the new capital of Belize, supplanting Belize City, in 1970.

Economy. Agriculture is the most important sector of the Belizean economy, accounting for about 25 percent of gross domestic product. Major crops include sugar, citrus fruits, and bananas. Manufacturing is dominated by the clothing, beverage, construction materials, and tobacco industries. Fishing, largely for domestic consumption, is also a significant commercial activity. Tourism has become an important component of the nation's economy. Belize's major trading partners are the United States, Great Britain, and Canada.

MEXICO
Corozal
Progresso
Orange Walk
Neustadt · Maskall · Ambergris Cay
Hill Bank · Belize City
Belmopan · Turneffe Islands
San Ignacio · Dangriga · Caribbean Sea
Victoria Pk. 1122 m (3681 ft) · Glovers Reef
Maya Mts. · Placentia
San Antonio · Punta Gorda
0   30 mi
0   30 km
Sarstoon
GUATEMALA   HONDURAS
© MQST

Government. The British monarch, represented by a governor-general, is the head of state. The head of government is a prime minister. Legislative power is held by a bicameral National Assembly, made up of a popularly elected House of Representatives with 29 members and a Senate with 12 appointed members. Six are appointed by the governor-general on the advice of the prime minister, three on the advice of the opposition leader, and one each on the advice of three particular church and business organizations.

History. The first recorded European settlement was begun in 1638 by shipwrecked English sailors. Over the next several hundred years, more English settlements were established.

Until 1798 the history of Belize was dominated by the struggle between the English settlers and the nearby Spanish colonists. In that year the English defeated the Spanish in the battle of St. George's Cay. By the early 19th century, Great Britain had established its control over the territory.

In 1862 the region became the colony of British Honduras. In 1871 it became a crown colony, subordinate to Jamaica. In 1884 it was separated from Jamaica and made an independent crown colony.

In the period just before World War I, British Honduras enjoyed a time of prosperity, but the colony remained undeveloped. In 1964 it received a new constitution that gave the colony internal autonomy.

In 1973 British Honduras became known as Belize. It became independent in 1981, and a new constitution was promulgated. Relations with neighboring Guatemala are strained because of Guatemalan claims to a large part of Belize. Guatemala severed diplomatic ties with Great Britain upon the independence of Belize and refused to recognize the new nation until 1992. Negotiations between Belize and Guatemala to resolve the longstanding dispute continue.

Costa Rica

Official name: *Republic of Costa Rica*
Area: *19,725 sq. mi., 51,100 sq. km.*
Type of government: *Democratic republic*
Population: *3,835,000*
Capital and largest city: *San José*
(Pop., 344,000)
Language: *Spanish (official),*
English
Literacy: *96%;* **Currency:** *Colon*
Per capita GDP: *$8,500*
(Rank: 60th)

The land. The Republic of Costa Rica, a small country in Central America, has three major regions: a Caribbean coastal plain, a mountainous central area, and a Pacific coastal plain.

The Caribbean coast is rainy and covered with tropical evergreen forests and swamps. The central region, which has a temperate climate, consists of high flat basins formed by three mountain ranges—the Cordillera de Guanacaste, the Cordillera Central, and the Cordillera de Talamanca. The *Meseta Central,* or central plateau, the largest basin of the region, lies between the Cordillera de Guanacaste and the Cordillera de Talamanca. The bulk of Costa Rica's population lives in the Meseta Central.

The Pacific coastal plain, a region of tropical forests and savanna, has alternating wet and dry seasons. Average rainfall for the entire country is about

meters
US

metres
Brit.

center
US

centre
Brit.

labor
US

labour
Brit.

ARENAL
is an active volcano in the Cordillera Central of Costa Rica. It has a height of about 5,360 feet.

100 inches (254 centimeters), with the Caribbean coastal plain receiving more rainfall than the Pacific coastal plain or interior highlands.

The people. With the exception of a relatively small black population concentrated in the Caribbean coastal area, Costa Ricans are almost all of European, largely Spanish, descent. Most live in the Meseta Central, the site of San José, the industrial and cultural center as well as the capital of the country.

Costa Rica has a high population growth rate, although it is considerably lower than it was in the 1960s.

Nearly two-thirds of the people live in rural areas. About one-third of the labor force is occupied by agriculture, and another 25 percent by industry and commerce.

Major cities include the capital, San José; Alajuela (population, 188,000), in the sugar- and coffee-growing region of the country; Cartago (129,000), just southeast of San José; Limón (84,000), a major port; and Puntarenas (109,000), a seaport on the Pacific coast.

Economy. Costa Rica is one of the most prosperous and industrialized countries of Central America, and its prosperity is more evenly distributed than most. Since 1960, manufacturing has been rapidly developed; it now contributes about one-fifth of the gross national product, while agriculture contributes slightly more.

Most manufacturing involves the processing of agricultural products—food, cotton, and wood. Gold, silver, mercury, and manganese are the most important minerals produced, and a substantial deposit of bauxite is just beginning to be exploited. Membership in the Central American Common Market (beginning in 1963) has opened up new markets for the nation, which began to produce pharmaceuticals, textiles, tires, and other consumer items after its entry.

Hydroelectric power, which is the main domestic source of energy, has developed gradually. A huge facility at Arenal opened in 1979. It has added greatly to the nation's power reserves. Hydroelectric power accounts for about 80 percent of Costa Rica's electricity production.

The main source of national income is still agriculture, which accounts for about 60 percent of export value. Coffee and bananas are the main cash crops, followed by cacao and sugar. Fruits, vegetables, cereals, and cotton arc also grown, and livestock production has increased as part of Costa Rica's plan for economic diversification.

Most trade is conducted with other Latin American states, the United States, Germany, and Japan. Imports consist of manufactured goods, machinery, chemicals, and petroleum. Coffee, bananas, cacao, cotton, and cattle and beef are the major agricultural exports. Other significant exports are fish, lumber, gold, and manganese.

Costa Rica's economic progress is heavily dependent on foreign aid and investment. Through the Alliance for Progress the United States has helped significantly to finance Costa Rica's efforts to industrialize and diversify its economy.

Government. Costa Rica has a presidential form of government. The head of state and chief executive is the president, who is popularly elected to a four-year term. There are two vice presidents; neither they nor the president are permitted multiple terms. Legislative powers rest with the unicameral Legislative Assembly, whose 57 deputies are popularly elected to four-year terms. Judicial powers rest with the Supreme Court of Justice, with 22 members elected to eight-year terms.

Costa Rica is divided into seven provinces. Provincial governors are appointed by the president.

History. Columbus first discovered Costa Rica in 1502 on his last voyage to America. Expecting to find gold, he named the land *Costa Rica,* or rich coast. Disappointed treasure hunters who followed him stayed only long enough to pillage the land. The Indians of Costa Rica, who were not numerous, fiercely resisted the Spanish advance. Most died in combat or from epidemics introduced by the Europeans.

The first permanent European settlement was established in 1564 at Cartago, on the Meseta Central, by Francisco Vásquez de Coronado.

Costa Rica was part of the Spanish colonial province ruled by the captain-general of Guatemala. When Agustín de Iturbide proclaimed Mexico's independence from Spain in 1821, the captain-general, Gabino Gaínza, declared Central America independent. In 1822 Gaínza was overthrown and the region was annexed to Mexico.

Iturbide fell in 1823, and Costa Rica joined Guatemala, El Salvador, Honduras, and Nicaragua to form the United Provinces of Central America. Dissatisfaction with Guatemala's domination of the union soon developed, and in 1838 Costa Rica withdrew from the federation and became a separate nation.

Independence. Braulio Carrillo, a dynamic president who served from 1834 to 1837 and again from 1838 to 1842, promoted the cultivation of coffee, which became a major export, and subdivided many large estates, thus increasing the number of small landholders.

In 1842 Carrillo's government was toppled by a revolt under the leadership of Francisco Morazán. Morazán was himself shortly overthrown, and a period of anarchy followed. Order was finally restored in 1849.

In 1870 Tomás Guardia overthrew the government and dominated national affairs until his death in 1882. He modernized the economy and increased unity, partly through a large program of railroad construction.

Under President Bernardo Soto (1885–1890), free compulsory education was established, and in 1889 what has been called the first open and honest

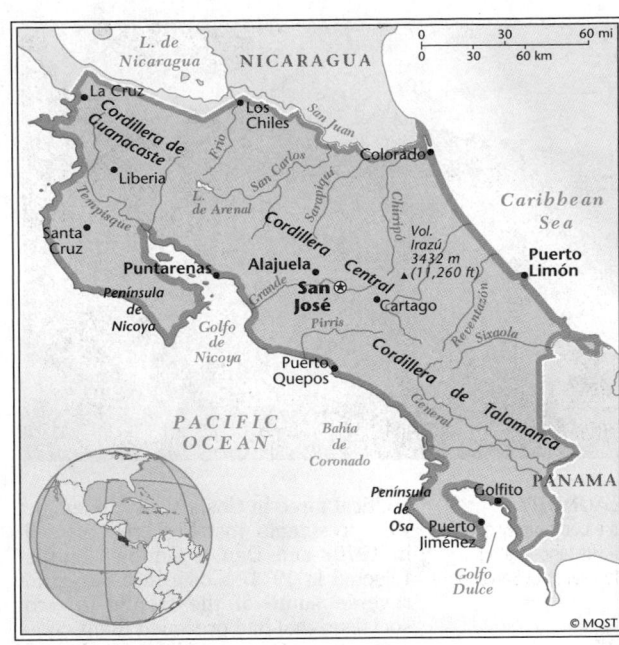

election in Costa Rican history was held. Costa Rican support of democratic principles was expressed in public hostility to a coup in 1917 led by Federico Tinoco Granados. His regime lasted for less than two years.

Conflict with Panama over Coto, a border region on the Pacific coast, dominated Costa Rica's foreign affairs during the 1920s and 1930s. Costa Rica occupied the disputed territory in 1921, after the United States pressured Panama to accept Costa Rican control of Coto. The issue was finally settled in 1941, when both countries agreed to redefine their common boundary.

Contemporary Costa Rica. A fraudulent presidential election in 1948 prompted a revolution led by José Figuéres. The revolt claimed between 1,500 and 2,000 lives and became the bloodiest event in the country's history. The Figuéres victory was followed by 18 months of rule by a junta. In 1949 the junta introduced a new constitution that enacted many progressive social reforms into law. Otilio Ulate Blanco, the victorious moderate president and the actual winner in the aborted 1948 election, was inaugurated in 1950 after civilian rule was restored.

In 1953 Figuéres was elected president. A liberal, Figuéres was a severe critic of Latin American dictators, in particular of President Anastasio Somoza of Nicaragua. Early in 1955 a Nicaraguan-instigated rebellion broke out, but the rebels were crushed.

Francisco Orlich Bolmarich, a supporter and friend of Figuéres, was defeated in the 1958 election by Mario Echandi Jiménez, a conservative. In 1962, however, Orlich Bolmarich won the presidency and, a year later, brought Costa Rica into the Central American Common Market. The resulting economic progress led to greater political stability and unity.

Since 1966 the National Liberation Party (PLN) has become the dominant

LAUNDRY
is a community chore
in the lagoon at El
Jocolal in El Salvador.

centimeters
US

centimetres
Brit.

centers
US

centres
Brit.

political force in Costa Rica. Under the PLN presidents, José Figuéres (elected in 1970) and Daniel Oduber Quirós (elected in 1974), Costa Rica began to reverse some of the trends toward socialism that had preceded them.

Rodrigo Carazo Odio was elected president in 1978 as head of the new Social Christian Unity Party (PUSC). He supported the Sandinista movement to overthrow the Somoza dictatorship in Nicaragua, but the subsequent Sandinista policy of supporting guerrilla activity in other countries of Central America led to a break in relations between Nicaragua and Costa Rica. In addition, severe economic problems beset Costa Rica in the early 1980s.

The National Liberation Party returned to power in 1982 with the election of Luis Alberto Monge; it remained in power with the election of Oscar Arias Sanchez in 1986.

In 1987 Arias won the Nobel Peace Prize for his regional peace plan, aimed mainly at ending fighting in Nicaragua, Guatemala, and El Salvador.

In 1990 Rafael Calderon, Jr., a critic of the Arias plan and a proponent of less government control in economic affairs, was elected president. Abel Pacheco became president in 2002, in an election with the lowest voter turnout in 50 years.

El Salvador

Official name: *Republic of El Salvador*
Area: *8,121 sq. mi., 21,040 sq. km.*
Type of government: *Republic*
Population: *6,354,000*
Capital and largest city:
San Salvador (Pop., 473,000)
Languages: *Spanish (official), Nahua*
Literacy: *72%;* **Currency:** *Colon*
Per capita GDP: *$4,600*
(Rank: 91st)

The land. The Republic of El Salvador is the smallest and most densely populated of the Central American states. The backbone of El Salvador is formed by two volcanic mountain ranges that run parallel to the Pacific coast. Between the two ranges is a large, high plateau with rich volcanic soil. The plateau is the most densely populated region of the country. There is a narrow plain along the Pacific coast. The Río Lempa cuts El Salvador in two and provides hydroelectric power and much-needed water that is required for irrigation.

The climate of El Salvador is tropical, but the heat is modified by elevation. Rainfall is heavy from May to October and slight from November to April. Annual rainfall in San Salvador is about 71 inches (178 centimeters). In the mountains the annual precipitation is higher. There are frequent earthquakes and volcanic eruptions.

The people. Most of the people are mestizo, of mixed European and Indian origin, but there are white and Indian minorities. The population is growing at a rapid rate and this has led to dramatic growth of the country's urban centers, as most of El Salvador's agricultural land is already populated and under cultivation. The major cities include San Salvador, the capital; Santa Ana (population, 245,000), a center of the coffee industry; and San Miguel (233,000).

Economy. El Salvador suffers from a grossly unequal distribution of land and wealth. Most farmers live like peasants, while nearly all of the best farmland is owned by only a handful of rich people. Social reform is traditionally scorned as being communistic, with the result that the country has been devastated by a brutal civil war.

Agriculture, which employs about 50 percent of the nation's work force, is El Salvador's main source of income and the source of most of the country's exports. Coffee, cotton, sesame, and balsam are grown for export, and corn, sorghum, beans, rice, sugar cane, and fruits are raised largely for domestic consumption. Cattle raising is also important, and fishing is becoming an important, but still quite small, part of El Salvador's export trade.

Mineral resources include modest amounts of gold and silver. Major manufactured products include textiles, footwear, clothing, pharmaceuticals, and machinery.

In recent years El Salvador's exports have dropped substantially below imports, in large part due to the effect of the civil war on coffee production. Part of the deficit has been offset by financial aid from the United States, which is El Salvador's main trading partner. El Salvador also conducts substantial trade with the European Community and with co-members of the Central American Common Market.

Coffee, sugar, and cotton are the major exports. The chief imports include machinery, chemicals, and petroleum products.

Government. El Salvador is a republic, with a new constitution that was adopted on December 20, 1983. Executive power is vested in a president, who is popularly elected to a 5-year term and who cannot succeed himself or herself. Legislative power rests with the unicameral Legislative Assembly, consisting of 84 members popularly elected to 3-year terms. Judicial authority rests with the Supreme Court, whose members are elected by the assembly to 3-year terms.

El Salvador is divided into 14 departments, whose governors are appointed.

History. In 1524 Pedro Alvarado led an expedition from Guatemala southeast into El Salvador to continue the Spanish conquest of the area. In 1525 Alvarado founded San Salvador de Cuscatlán.

As a Spanish colony, El Salvador was part of a province under the control of the captain-general of Guatemala. The whole province, including El Salvador, declared its independence from Spain on September 15, 1821.

Soon after, Augustín de Iturbide, who had been crowned emperor of Mexico, sent troops to El Salvador and incorporated the country into his empire. In 1822, however, the government in El Salvador petitioned to be included in the United States as a state, but the U.S. Congress quickly rejected the appeal.

In 1823 Iturbide's empire fell and El Salvador joined the other Central American states to form the United Provinces of Central America. In 1838 the federation was dissolved and El Salvador, even though it continued to champion the cause of a Central American federation, became an independent state.

Independence. The history of the republic has been turbulent. During the 1800s there were frequent presidential successions and revolutions that reflected the factional strife between liberals and conservatives. Internal unrest was complicated by foreign aggression and the country's participation in numerous wars. The period from 1900 to 1930 was relatively peaceful, however. The coffee industry grew and the country prospered.

In 1931 General Maximiliano Hernández Martínez seized power, ruling until 1944. Although he instituted one of the

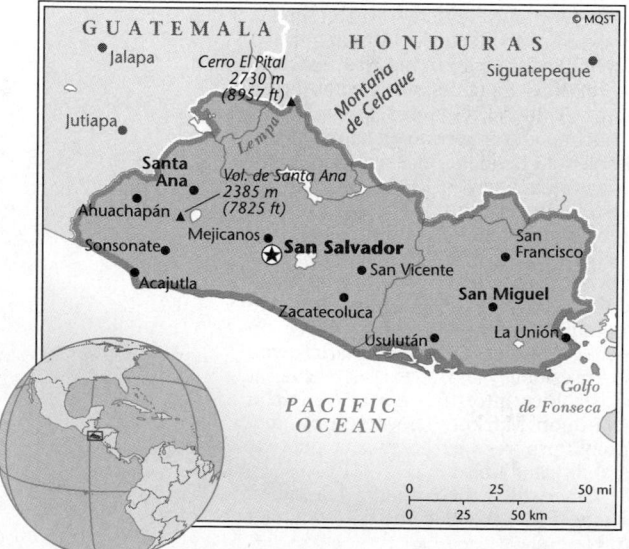

GUATEMALA
Jalapa
Cerro El Pital
2730 m
(8957 ft)
Jutiapa
HONDURAS
Siguatepeque
Montaña de Celaque
Santa Ana
Vol. de Santa Ana
2385 m
(7825 ft)
Ahuachapán
Sonsonate
Mejicanos
San Salvador
San Vicente
San Francisco
Acajutla
Zacatecoluca
San Miguel
Usulután
La Unión
Golfo de Fonseca
PACIFIC OCEAN
© MQST
0   25   50 mi
0   25   50 km

most brutal regimes in the country's history, the period was one of the most prosperous for El Salvador.

Contemporary El Salvador. The final overthrow of Martínez in 1944 was followed by a new period of political instability. In 1945 General Salvador Castañeda Castro became president. Castro was removed from office at the expiration of his term in 1948, however, when he tried to alter the constitution to retain power indefinitely as a dictator.

Castro was replaced by a junta, and in 1950 Major Oscar Osorio, a member of the junta, was elected president. His administration grew increasingly autocratic, and in 1956 a follower of his, Lieutenant Colonel José Mariá Lemus, was chosen president.

Lemus ruled until 1960, when he was deposed by a junta. In 1961 a military directorate seized control and Colonel Julio Adalberto Rivera became president.

In 1969 the first of several bloody clashes erupted between El Salvador and Honduras in what came to be known as the Soccer War. The cause of the conflict was the influx over a decade of about 300,000 Salvadorans into the Honduran border region. Constant unregulated travel across the border, coupled with Honduran fears that El Salvador would attempt to seize the territory, led to the armed clash. After several weeks of fighting, the Organization of American States negotiated a truce. In 1976 the two countries agreed to permit third-party mediation of any future border conflicts.

When General Carlos Humberto Romero won the disputed presidential election of 1977, the country was upset by a stream of violent protests from both right and left extremists. Romero was deposed on October 15, 1979, and a revolutionary junta took control.

In 1980 the junta appointed José Napoleón Duarte, a moderate, as president. Despite attempts at agricultural reform, violence by both right- and left-wing extremists escalated into full-scale civil war. At the end of 1980 the left-wing guerrilla organizations formed the Farabundo Marti National Liberation Front (FMLN) and its political arm, the Democratic Revolutionary Front (FDR).

A high turnout in elections in 1982 brought a right-wing coalition to power, with Alvaro Alfredo Magana as president. The new government's first act was to suspend the land redistribution laws enacted in 1980.

A new election in May 1984 brought Duarte, leader of the moderate Christian Democrats, back to the presidency. He had the difficult task of keeping the country on a moderate course to ensure that the United States continued to provide military and economic aid.

In 1989 Alfredo Cristiani, leader of the right-wing Nationalist Republican Party (ARENA), was elected president. The defeat of the Christian Democrats in the election was viewed by some as evidence of further polarization in the country. After years of negotiations between the government and FMLN leaders, the civil war, which claimed more than 70,000 lives, was ended by a peace treaty on January 16, 1992.

Francisco Flores became president in 1999, and in 2000 joined with the leaders of Guatemala and Honduras in signing a free trade agreement with Mexico to stimulate the economy.

Guatemala

Official name: *Republic of Guatemala*

Area: *42,032 sq. mi., 108,890 sq. km.*

Type of government: *Republic*

Population: *13,542,000*

Capital and largest city: *Guatemala City (Pop., 1,007,000)*

Languages: *Spanish, Indian dialects*

Literacy: *64%*

Currency: *Quetzal*

Per capita GDP: *$3,700 (Rank: 103rd)*

The land. Guatemala, the third largest country in Central America, is a mountainous land. The Central American Cordillera, which lies parallel to the Pacific coast, includes the highest peak in Central America, the volcanic Mount Tajumulco, which rises 13,812 feet (4,210 meters) above sea level.

A narrow plain borders the Pacific coast. Inland are the central highlands, which include about one-fifth of the country's land area. In the southeast are the Caribbean lowlands. In the north is the Petén district, a sparsely settled forest region containing about one-third of the country's area.

The Caribbean lowlands are hot and rainy. The Pacific coast has dry winters and wet summers. The central highlands have a cool, dry climate. Annual rainfall in Guatemala City is about 52 inches (132 centimeters), but the Caribbean slopes of the interior highlands can receive upward of 100 inches (254 centimeters) or more.

The people. Most of Guatemala's people are American Indian descendants of the Mayas, or are *ladino,* or mestizo, of mixed Indian and European background. Most of the people live in the highlands, where Guatemala City is located.

Nearly two-thirds of the residents live in rural areas. Major cities include Guatemala City, the capital; Puerto Barrios (population, 67,000), Guatemala's main Caribbean port; and Quetzaltenango (109,000). Guatemala has a high rate of population growth and is the most populous country in Central America.

THE PORTABLE HAND LOOM is used to create many of the beautiful textiles found in Central America.

Economy. The economy is based on agriculture, which provides a fairly high standard of living for farm owners, and which is supported by relatively advanced technology and cheap labor. About half of Guatemala's labor force is employed in agriculture. Most Indians work for poverty wages on prosperous plantations, and land distribution is grossly unequal.

Coffee is the most important crop, accounting for more than 40 percent of the value of all exports. Sugar, cotton, and bananas are also important agricultural exports. A program of diversification has helped boost production of tobacco, meat, and other agricultural commodities. About 55 percent of the country is forested, but Guatemala's lumber industry remains small. Guatemala is one of the world's leading producers of chicle, a base for chewing gum.

Agriculture is concentrated in the central highland valleys and the narrow coastal plains. The major food crops include corn, rice, wheat, and beans. Livestock include cattle, sheep, and pigs. Mineral resources include antimony, chromium, lead, and zinc.

Industry has grown steadily in recent years, particularly since Guatemala joined the Central American Common Market (CACM) in the 1960s; it now employs about 15 percent of the labor force. Textiles, chemicals, and tires are the newer industries, and food processing is traditionally important.

27 North America

labor
US

labour
Brit.

MEXICO

Paxbán

Belize City

L. Petén-Itzá

Tikal

Belmopán

BELIZE

Flores

La Libertad

Comitán

San Luis

Gulf of Honduras

Chinajá

Puerto Barrios

Santo Tomás de Castilla

Cobán

San Pedro Sula

Vol. Tacaná 4093 m (13,428 ft)

Huehuetenango

Salamá

HONDURAS

Vol. Tajumulco 4220 m (13,845 ft)

Zacapa

Quetzaltenango

Guatemala City

Antigua Guatemala

Champerico

L. de Atitlán

Sierra Madre

Jutiapa

Escuintla

Santa Ana

San José

San Salvador

EL SALVADOR

PACIFIC OCEAN

0   45   90 mi
0   45   90 km

© MQST

MODERN TRANSPORT is developing gradually in Central America, but much travel is still done on foot.

civilization *US*

civilisation *Brit.*

CACM co-members are significant trading partners, but most of Guatemala's trade is with the United States. After coffee, cotton, meat, sugar, bananas, chicle, and essential oils, such as citronella, are valuable exports. Manufactured goods are of growing importance. Imports include machinery and manufactured goods, petroleum products, chemicals, and foodstuffs.

Government. Guatemala has a tradition of political upheaval and dictatorial rule. A new constitution was drawn up in 1985 and put into effect in 1986.

Executive powers are vested in a president who is popularly elected to a four-year term. The president cannot be reelected. Legislative powers rest with a unicameral, 113-member Legislative Assembly that serves a four-year term. If no presidential candidate wins a majority in a popular election, a runoff election is held between the two candidates who receive the most votes. Judicial powers rest with a 13-member Supreme Court.

The country is divided into 22 departments, whose governors are appointed by the president.

History. Long before the Spanish conquest of Central America in the 1500s, most of present-day Guatemala was part of the great Mayan civilization that flourished in the area between 300 B.C. and A.D. 900. Mayan civilization declined as a result of internal dissension, and in 1524 Spanish forces led by Pedro de Alvarado conquered the area.

The region became part of the Spanish colonial captaincy-general of Guatemala, which included much of Central America. In 1543 the capital of the captaincy was established at Antigua, a city near present-day Guatemala City. Antigua was destroyed by an earthquake in 1773, and soon after Guatemala City became the capital.

Independence. On September 15, 1821, following Mexico's successful independence struggle, Guatemala was peacefully separated from Spain and joined to the Mexican empire of Augustín de Iturbide. Quickly dissatisfied with Mexican control, Guatemala joined with other states of Central America to form the United Provinces of Central America. The United Provinces were torn by internal conflicts, however, and in 1838 the confederation collapsed.

Guatemala became a sovereign state in 1839 under the leadership of Rafael Carrera, who remained the country's strongman until his death in 1865. Carrera had the complete support of the Indians, and his conservative policies won the support of the upper classes and the army. He made Guatemala a republic in 1847, and in 1851 he was elected president. He assumed the presidency for life in 1854. Conservatives remained in power until a liberal revolt in 1871.

Guatemala was ruled by a liberal dictator, Justo Rufino Barrios, from 1873 to 1885. His administration was characterized by great progress in railroad construction, educational reforms, and encouragement of foreign investment. In an attempt to reestablish the Central American Federation under his leadership, Barrios launched a war against Guatemala's neighbors and was killed in battle.

Manuel Estrada Cabrera gained control of the country in 1898. During his administration, the United Fruit Company, a U.S. firm, entered Guatemala and began to play an influential role in Guatemalan politics. Estrada Cabrera was toppled from power in 1920.

Jorge Ubico Castañeda ruled Guatemala from 1931 to 1944. He led the country through the world economic depression of the 1930s, but his despotic rule provoked widespread dissatisfaction. He was removed from power by the military, which attempted to replace him with Federico Ponce. But student riots and a general strike in 1944 forced the military to allow free elections and grant a new constitution.

Guatemala in recent times. The success of the October uprising raised the hopes of many Guatemalans for a new era of social reform. Serious inequalities in the distribution of wealth and income plagued the country. A small number of wealthy people controlled economic and political life, and the masses had little land and lived in poverty.

In December 1944 Dr. Juan José Arévelo was overwhelmingly elected president. He launched a program that included support for trade unions and the introduction of social security programs. Although opposition from the privileged minority threatened his administration, he became one of the few presidents to complete his term. In 1951 he was peacefully succeeded by Colonel Jacobo Arbenz Guzmán.

Arbenz Guzmán attempted to continue and expand the reforms. He initiated an extensive land reform program and restricted the activities of the United Fruit Company and other foreign corporations in Guatemalan affairs. His administration was charged with being communist dominated, and in 1954 an armed force led by Colonel Carlos Castillo Armas, and supported by the United States, invaded Guatemala from Honduras and toppled Arbenz Guzmán.

Castillo Armas took control and promulgated a new constitution in 1956. He was assassinated in 1957, and in 1958 General Miguel Ydígoras Fuentes became president. Attempts at moderate reform won Ydígoras Fuentes the enmity of the conservatives, who thought his programs were too liberal, and of those on the left, who felt his programs were too conservative.

In 1963 the military overthrew Ydígoras Fuentes, and Colonel Enrique Peralta Azurdía was placed in power. Peralta Azurdía's administration abrogated the 1956 constitution. Considerable economic growth was achieved under Peralta Azurdía's rule, and in 1964, bowing to popular pressure, a constituent assembly was convened to draw up a new constitution. The new basic law, promulgated in 1965, outlawed communist and other totalitarian groups.

Elections were held in 1966, but the military split into two major factions and a civilian candidate, Julio César Méndez Montenegro, led the *Partido Revolucionario,* or the Revolutionary Party, to victory. During his term of office, killings by leftist guerrillas and right-wing terrorist groups increased dramatically.

Carlos Arana Osorio was elected president in 1970. He was succeeded by Kjell Laugerud Garcia in 1974.

In 1975 the Guerrilla Army of the Poor was founded. Its terrorist activities on behalf of the oppressed Indians underscored the vast gulf existing between the poor and virtually powerless majority and the wealthy minority.

General Romeo Lucas Garcia was elected president in 1978. Once again, violence from both the left and right arose, reaching the proportions of a full-scale civil war.

In 1982, following presidential elections that were widely believed to be fraudulent, a group of junior military officers led a coup and established a junta. The junta, headed by General Efrain Rios Montt, immediately annulled the election, suspended the constitution, and banned the activities of all political parties. A year later, Rios Montt was overthrown. His successor was General Oscar Humberto Mejia Victores.

In 1985 the military permitted new elections and Marco Vinicio Cerezo Arévalo, candidate of the Christian Democrat Party, was chosen president. He failed to negotiate a settlement with the leftist guerrillas or halt a rapidly growing drug trade.

In 1991 Jorge Serrano Elias, a former aide to Rios Montt, was elected president. He continued negotiations to end the civil war, which had been marked by the government's brutal human rights violations. In May 1993 Serrano attempted to dissolve the congress and suspend the constitution, but he was removed by the military, which had initially supported him. Ramiro de Leon Carpio, the nation's attorney general of human rights, was sworn in to complete Serrano's term of office.

Honduras

Official name: *Republic of Honduras*

Area: *43,267 sq. mi., 112,090 sq. km.*

Type of government: *Republic*

Population: *6,514,000*

Capital and largest city:
*Tegucigalpa
(Pop., 835,000)*

Language: *Spanish, Indian dialects*

Literacy: *74%*

Currency: *Lempira*

Per capita GDP: *$2,600
(Rank: 121st)*

The land. Honduras, the second largest of the Central American republics, is a mountainous country. The Central American Andes dominate the landscape, running from northwest to southeast. The highlands are cut by fertile river valleys, the largest of which is the valley of the Río Ulúa.

A fertile, well-watered plain stretches inland from the Caribbean coast. The plain is narrow in the west, near the border with Guatemala, and broad in the east, along the border with Nicaragua. The eastern part of the plain is known as the Mosquito Coast. There is another, smaller lowland region along the Pacific coast. The Bay Islands, or Islas de la Bahía, which lie off the north coast, are also part of Honduras.

The Caribbean lowlands have a hot, humid tropical climate. The Pacific coastal region has wet summers and dry winters. The uplands have a pleasant temperate climate.

The people. Most Hondurans are mestizo, of mixed Indian and European origin. There are also small groups of African, European, and Indian descent.

The population of Honduras is increasing at a rapid rate. This places heavy strains on the economy to provide food, housing, and jobs.

The majority of the population is rural. The main urban centers include Tegucigalpa, the capital; San Pedro Sula (population, 445,000); La Ceiba (117,000); El Progreso (157,000); and Choluteca (122,000).

Economy. Honduras has an agricultural economy. About 62 percent of the work force is engaged in agriculture, which accounts for 65 percent of all exports. The chief agricultural products raised for export are bananas, coffee, and beef. Shellfish fishing is also an important economic activity. Before 1960 bananas accounted for three-quarters of the country's total exports, but banana production has dropped off with crop failures and diversification of the economy. Nonetheless, bananas still account for 40 percent of exports. Sugar cane, corn, sorghum, beans, and rice are grown for local food needs.

Honduras has rich forest resources, and lumbering is an important economic activity. The country also has considerable mineral resources, including gold, silver, lead, and zinc. But there is little manufacturing, and the major products of Honduran industry are goods for home consumption.

Despite attempts to diversify the economy, transportation remains poor, there is a lack of skilled labor, and actual growth has been very slow. The country's vast potential hydroelectric power is still largely untapped, although Honduras is a net exporter of electric power.

Exports consist almost entirely of agricultural products and raw materials; they include bananas, coffee, cotton, wood, and minerals. Imports consist largely of manufactured goods, and of machinery, transportation equipment, chemicals, and foodstuffs.

Honduras's main trading partner is the United States. Other leading trading partners are Germany, Japan, Mexico, Guatemala, and Brazil.

Government. Honduras is a republic with democratic institutions. But there is a strong tradition of political instability and of military interference in government.

In 1982 a new constitution was adopted. Executive power is vested in a president who is popularly elected to a 4-year term. Legislative power is held by a 128-member unicameral National Congress. Judicial power is held by the Supreme Court, whose members are elected by the congress.

Honduras is divided into 18 departments. The departments are headed by governors appointed by the president.

History. Christopher Columbus discovered the area of Honduras in 1502, on his final voyage to the New World. But it was not until 1524 that the first Spanish colony was established. The American Indian inhabitants fiercely resisted the Spanish conquest, and the Indian chief Lempira is regarded as a national hero for his bravery in the struggle against the Spanish.

In 1539 Honduras was included in Spain's captaincy-general of Guatemala. Silver was discovered in the 1570s, and an influx of prospectors led to the founding of Tegucigalpa.

Independence. Following achievement of independence by Mexico in 1821, the Central American region proclaimed its independence from Spanish rule. The area was annexed to Augustín de Iturbide's Mexican empire, but after Iturbide's fall in 1823 it regained its freedom. Honduras then formed part of the United Provinces of Central America, which also included Costa Rica, El Salvador, Guatemala, and Nicaragua.

By the late 1830s the federation was divided by bitter rivalries among its members as well as by divisions within the member states. In 1838 Honduras withdrew to become a separate nation. In 1841 Francisco Ferrara became the country's first constitutional president.

During the late 1800s and early 1900s, Honduras struggled to remain independent in the face of threats posed by its neighbors, particularly Guatemala and Nicaragua.

In 1841 Great Britain gained control of the Bay Islands, withdrawing only in 1859. From 1871 to 1874 Honduras fought a war with Guatemala and El Salvador, and in 1906 Honduras and El Salvador fought Guatemala.

By 1912 the troubled political situation led President William Howard Taft to send troops to protect U.S. business interests, mainly the United Fruit Company. U.S. forces intervened again in 1919 and in 1924.

Contemporary Honduras. Tiburcio Carías Andino ruled from 1933 to 1948. He improved the economy, built roads, and opened schools and hospitals.

In 1948 Carías Andino was succeeded in the presidency by Juan Marval Gálvez, who permitted organization of trade unions, a free press, and political debate. He retired in 1954, which was a year marked by a ten-week strike against the United Fruit Company.

No candidate won a majority of the votes in 1954 elections, although the Liberal candidate, Ramon Villeda Morales, won 48 percent of the popular vote. The political deadlock ended when Gálvez's vice president, Julio Lozano Díaz, assumed the presidency. He was overthrown in 1956 and an army-supported junta took power.

The junta held elections for a constituent assembly in 1957. The assembly drafted a constitution and chose Villeda Morales president. Villeda brought Honduras into the Central American Common Market and instituted programs of agrarian and educational reform. He was

centers
US

centres
Brit.

labor
US

labour
Brit.

27 North America

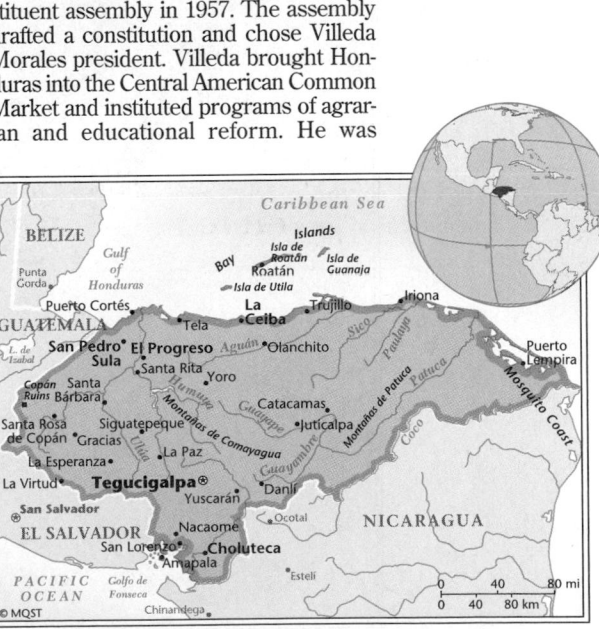

overthrown by a military coup in 1963 led by Oswaldo López Arellano, who was elected president by a new constituent assembly in 1965.

Elections were held in 1971 and Ramón Ernest Cruz was chosen president. But one year later, following another coup, López Arellano regained the presidency. In 1975 he was deposed after his involvement in a bribery scandal with U.S. businessmen.

In 1978 there was another change of leadership as a new military government deposed President Juan Melgar (1975–1978), who was too slow in effecting promised social and economic reforms.

In new elections held in 1981, the right-of-center Liberal Party candidate Roberto Suazo Cordova was elected president. His party gained an absolute majority in the National Congress. A new constitution went into effect in 1982.

Honduras has a standing border dispute with neighboring El Salvador. A short war broke out in 1969, and several clashes since prompted an agreement in 1976 that any future border disputes would be mediated by a third party.

Tensions between the countries of Honduras and Nicaragua heightened during the 1980s because of the civil war between the Sandinista government in Nicaragua and the anti-Sandinista contra guerrilla units, some of whom were known to have established bases and supply areas in Honduras.

meters
US

metres
Brit.

In addition to being plagued by unemployment, inflation, and an economic dependency on bananas and coffee, Honduras endured a devastating hurricane in 1998 and a severe drought in 2000. To help stimulate the economy, Honduras joined with El Salvador and Guatemala in a trade agreement with Mexico.

Mexico

Official name: *United Mexican States*

Area: *761,404 sq. mi., 1,972,550 sq. km.*

Type of government: *Federal republic*

Population: *103,400,000*

Capital and largest city: *Mexico City (Pop., 8,605,000)*

Language: *Spanish, Indian dialects*

Literacy: *90%;* **Currency:** *Peso*

Per capita GDP: *$9,000 (Rank: 55th)*

The land. The physical geography of Mexico is complex, partly because Mexico is formed by both North American and Central American land structures. North American landforms end in the volcanic region south of Mexico City. The mountains of Oaxaca, which lie

west of the Isthmus of Tehuantepec, together with all the highlands to the south, are Central American.

Eastern Mexico, north of Oaxaca, consists of a coastal plain. This plain is broad near the U.S. border, where it forms a continuation of the Texas Gulf coastal plain, but it narrows sharply south of Veracruz, where the Tabasco coastal lowlands and marshes begin.

West of the coastal plain are the eroded valleys and peaks of the Sierra Madre Oriental, whose elevations exceed 13,000 feet (3,962 meters) above sea level. The Sierra Madre Oriental forms the eastern border of the Central Plateau, which is subdivided into two regions by the Sierra de Zacatecas. The southern region of the Central Plateau contains Mexico City and most of the country's people.

The Sierra Madre Occidental forms a barrier of chasms, canyons, and arid pocket valleys between the Central Plateau and the narrow Pacific coastal plain. These mountains are so rugged that in Jalisco the land plunges 5,000 feet (1,524 meters) into the Pacific within a distance of only 275 miles (442 kilometers). Only one pass through this range is used extensively for transportation, and Guadalajara, Mexico's second largest city, is located there.

A cordillera of volcanic mountains, the Sierra Volcánica Transversal, extends from east to west across Mexico south of

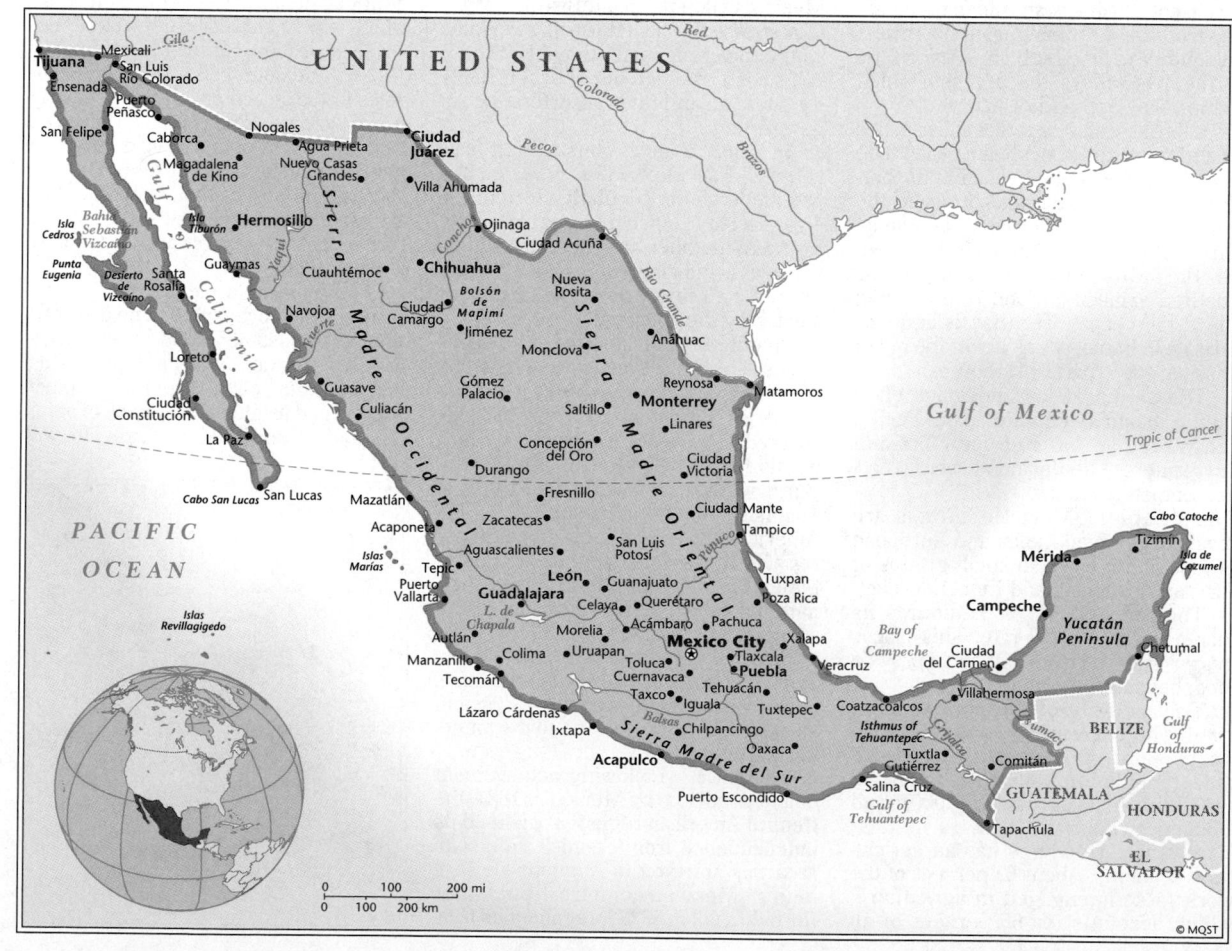

© MQST

Mexico City. Peaks like Popocatépetl, over 17,880 feet (5,450 meters), and Iztaccíhuatl, over 17,340 feet (5,285 meters), are scenically striking, but they form a barrier that isolates the southern plateau region from the Balsas Valley to the south. Volcanic activity continues in this and other regions of Mexico. In 1943 an eruption in Michoacán state, to the west of Mexico City, produced the volcanic mountain Paricutín, which rises 9,213 feet (2,808 meters).

The Sierra Madre del Sur, to the southwest, forms a barrier between the Balsas Valley and the very narrow Pacific coastal plain. This range runs eastward into Oaxaca and forms a tangled mountain knot west of the Isthmus of Tehuantepec.

The Central American portion of Mexico includes the Tabasco lowlands, the limestone plateau of the Yucatán peninsula, and the mountain and plateau system of Chiapas, which extends into Mexico from Guatemala.

The peninsula of Baja California is an extension of the coastal range of California and lies across the Gulf of California from northern Mexico.

Climate. As the surface features of Mexico are exceedingly varied and complex, so is the climate, which changes with altitude, latitude, and the wind pattern. Mountain slopes facing the prevailing winds receive more rainfall than the leeward slopes. The highlands are cooler and have less variation in temperature than the lowlands. Precipitation is generally lower in the north than in the south.

Along the western coast of the peninsula of Baja California are cold, upwelling Pacific waters that chill the air masses passing over them, inhibiting their ability to carry moisture landward. Thus, much of the north and northwest of Mexico is desert. The eastern coastal plain, on the other hand, receives much moisture south of Tamaulipas, where the trade winds encounter the Sierra Madre Oriental and drop their rain.

The people. Most of the people of Mexico are mestizo, of mixed European and Indian ancestry, or of Indian descent. The remainder of the population is of European—largely Spanish—and other descent.

Spanish is the official language, but more than 2 million Mexicans speak Indian languages. These fall into more than 30 major linguistic groups and range from Nahautl, or Aztec, and Otomi, which are spoken by large groups of people, to tribal languages spoken by only a few family groups.

The overall Mexican population density is not overwhelming, but more than 50 percent of the people live within the Central Plateau, which represents only 14 percent of the national territory. Mexico's population is increasing at a rapid rate. Its growth from about 20 million to over 100 million people between 1940 and 2000 has been one of the world's largest population increases. About two-thirds of the population live in urban areas.

THE ARCHAEOLOGICAL SITE of Palenque provided major breakthroughs in deciphering Mayan hieroglyphics and was the first evidence that Mayan pyramids served as funerary structures.

The capital, Mexico City, is the country's largest urban center. Unlike most major cities in the western hemisphere, it is located inland, with no river access to the ocean.

After Mexico City, Mexico's major cities include Guadalajara (population, 1,646,000); Monterrey (1,111,000); and Puebla de Zaragoza (1,272,000). Veracruz (457,000) and Tampico (295,000), on the Gulf of Mexico, are the principal seaports. Mazatlán (328,000) is the most important seaport on the Pacific coast.

Economy. Mexico has a well-balanced and growing economy, due in part to a rate of growth between the mid-1950s and early 1970s that averaged 6.5 percent a year. Industrial development and oil exploitation are chiefly responsible for the growth of the economy since World War II. However, in the 1980s a combination of falling oil prices and large foreign debt caused severe economic difficulties.

Natural resources. Mexico is rich in natural resources. It is one of the world's leading producers of silver and ranks high in the production of antimony, graphite, sulfur, mercury, lead, zinc, copper, and gold. The country also mines quantities of iron ore, cadmium, molybdenum, tungsten, manganese, arsenic, and bismuth.

Mexico has an abundance of oil and ranks fifth among the world's oil producers. However, oil production was limited during the 1980s due to low world oil prices. The oil industry is controlled by the government agency Petróleos Mexicanos (PEMEX). Coal and natural gas are plentiful.

Mining employs about 1.3 percent of the labor force and it was the country's greatest source of wealth until the development of the petroleum industry.

Agriculture. About 26 percent of Mexico's labor force is engaged in agriculture, which accounts for a small percentage of exports. Only 10 percent of the land is arable, and a considerable quantity of the food is imported. Nonetheless, production has increased significantly since 1960, despite natural setbacks and economic difficulties. This increased production is largely the result of government irrigation and soil improvement projects.

A major share of Mexican farming is devoted to the production of basic food crops such as corn, wheat, beans, and rice. Commercial crops include sugar cane, cotton, coffee, and henequen, a fiber plant.

Industry. Industry has grown rapidly since World War II. Hydroelectric power is well developed and the geothermal plant at Baja California is the largest in the western hemisphere. Nuclear power is also being developed.

Oil refining is rising steadily in importance, and in recent years the government has made a concerted effort to develop the manufacture of chemicals, synthetic fibers, plastics, industrial machinery,

THE BASILICA OF GUADALOUPE in Mexico City is evidence of the strong heritage of Catholicism bequeathed to the area by Spanish colonists.

27 North America

HERNÁN CORTÉS
undertook the conquest of Mexico in 1519 with fewer than 600 men, succeeding primarily by the skillful use of horses and firearms, and by trading on the Aztecs' expectations for the return of a god.

civilizations
US

civilisations
Brit.

centered
US

centred
Brit.

BEAUTIFUL POTTERY,
such as this urn, or brazier, in the shape of a priest, is a hallmark of the Mayan culture.

and automobiles. Privatization of many industries that had been nationalized has helped restore the importance of the private sector in economic growth. Manufacturers that import raw materials or components for processing or assembly and reexport the products duty-free have become a significant part of the Mexican economy. Most of these so-called in-bond companies are located in northern Mexico and most of the trade flows between the United States and Mexico.

In spite of major advances in these areas, Mexico's most important industries are textiles, food processing, and beverages. The country also produces cement, iron and steel, and a variety of consumer goods.

Trade. Despite its severe economic problems in the 1980s, Mexico maintained a favorable balance of trade, exporting more than it imported. It was able to reduce its foreign debt significantly. The country's chief exports include oil, manufactured goods, much machinery, chemicals, metals, and agricultural products. Principal imports are machinery, food, appliances, transportation equipment, and chemicals. About two-thirds of Mexico's trade is with the United States.

Government. Mexico is a federal republic composed of 31 states and a federal district in which the capital, Mexico City, is located. Each state has its own governor and popularly elected legislature.

The head of state and chief executive is the president, who is directly elected by popular vote to a six-year term and may not serve more than one term. The president is assisted by a cabinet appointed by him or her.

Legislative power is vested in the Congress, which consists of the Senate and the Chamber of Deputies. The Senate has 128 members, who are elected to six-year terms. The members of the 500-member Chamber of Deputies serve three-year terms. Half of the senators and 300 deputies are directly elected, while the rest are chosen on a proportional basis according to each party's popular vote. Senators and deputies may not serve multiple terms.

History. Before Columbus discovered the New World in 1492, Mexico was the site of two of the greatest Indian civilizations on the North American continent.

The civilization of the Mayas, which was at its height from about 300 B.C. to A.D. 900, was centered in Guatemala and southern Mexico. The Mayas built great cities and were skilled at astronomy and mathematics. They also developed a calendar that was more accurate than the one used in Europe at the time, and they had a well-developed system of writing.

In the 800s the Mayas, for unknown reasons, abandoned their cities and reestablished themselves in the Yucatán peninsula. Gradually, the Mayas were weakened by attacks by the Toltec Indians of the Central Plateau to the north. By the 1400s Mayan civilization was in decline.

The Toltecs, whose capital was in the Valley of Mexico in the Central Plateau, were subjugated in the early 1400s by the Aztecs, whose original homeland is unknown.

The Aztecs built an empire ruled from their capital, Tenochtitlán, founded in 1325 on the site of present-day Mexico City. Nearly impregnable, Tenochtitlán was constructed on a group of islands in the middle of Lake Texcoco and connected to the mainland by a series of causeways.

In 1517–1518 the Spanish governor of Cuba sent two expeditions to investigate rumors of the existence of mainland civilizations rich in gold. Both expeditions retreated to Cuba after brief and bloody encounters with the Indians. In 1519 Hernán Cortés, undaunted by the failures of his predecessors, undertook the conquest of Mexico with fewer than 600 men.

The conquest of the Aztecs was accomplished primarily by the skillful use of horses and guns, which terrified the Indians, who had never seen them before, and by the use of allied Indian warriors to supplement Cortés's small military force. In addition, the Aztecs believed that the light-skinned, bearded Spaniards riding on horses were gods, and Cortés was allowed to enter Tenochtitlán. He captured Montezuma, the Aztec emperor, but warfare between the Spaniards and the Aztecs led to Montezuma's death and Cortés's retreat. In 1521 Cortés subdued the Aztec forces and recaptured the city. By the mid-1500s, all Mexico had been won.

Spanish rule. Following the Spanish conquest, the Indians were reduced to the level of slaves. They were forced to work in the mines or on the estates of the Spaniards. Gold and silver were taken from the land with unceasing zeal.

In 1535 Mexico City became the capital of the viceroyalty of New Spain, which included a large part of Central America as well as Mexico. The immediate subordinates of its governor, or viceroy, were the *peninsulares,* the Spaniards born in Spain. Native-born Spaniards, known as Creoles, were not permitted to hold high government office.

During the colonial period the Creoles grew to resent the privileged position of the *peninsulares.* Discontent also surged among the rapidly growing population of mestizos, those of mixed Spanish and Indian parentage. The successful American and French revolutions of the late 1700s further increased native resentment of Spanish injustice and exploitation.

In 1808 Napoleon Bonaparte of France conquered Spain and imprisoned Spain's king, Ferdinand VII, thus leaving Mexico without a legitimate ruler.

Struggle for independence. On September 16, 1810, a Creole priest in the town of Dolores, Miguel Hidalgo y Costilla, issued the famous "Cry of Dolores," in which he denounced the injustices of the Spanish government and cried out for social reform. With Indian support, Hidalgo and his followers were able to dominate southern Mexico for a short time.

However, a majority of the Creoles would not support Hidalgo's social revolution, which threatened their own position. Without Creole support, the revolt could not succeed. Hidalgo was defeated and executed in 1811. The struggle was renewed by another priest, José María Morelos, a mestizo, but he, too, was eventually defeated and executed, in 1815. The revolutionary standard then passed to Vicente Guerrero, whose small army pressed a guerrilla war that harassed but could not challenge the colonial forces.

Hope for independence lay dormant until 1820, when Ferdinand VII, who had been restored to the Spanish throne after Napoleon's armies were expelled from Spain, was forced by internal pressures to approve a new liberal constitution. Mexican Creoles feared that the liberal reforms would weaken their position in Mexico and they aligned themselves with the struggle for independence.

ACTIVITY AT THE STOCK EXCHANGE in Mexico City is evidence of steps taken in recent decades to participate in world trade networks, reduce foreign debt, and broaden economic reforms.

Independence. Then, in 1821, General Augustín de Iturbide, who had suppressed the Hidalgo and Morelos uprisings, joined forces with Guerrero and issued the Plan of Igualo, which called for the establishment of an independent Mexican empire. Other military commanders joined the movement, and in July 1821, the last viceroy of Mexico signed the Treaty of Córdoba, acknowledging Mexican independence. Iturbide had himself crowned Emperor Augustin I. However, he proved an inept ruler. In 1823 he was overthrown by Antonio López de Santa Anna, another ambitious general. A new constitution, adopted in 1824, established Mexico as a federal republic.

Santa Anna remained the dominant political figure in the new republic until 1855. For most of those years, he was either president or dictator, although he was intermittently overthrown.

In 1836, the territory of Texas, which had been settled largely by people from the United States, declared its independence. Santa Anna attempted to prevent the secession, but after defeating the Texans at the Alamo, he was decisively defeated at the Battle of San Jacinto in April 1836. The United States annexed Texas in 1845, an act that angered the Mexicans, who had never recognized the independence of Texas.

War broke out between Mexico and the United States in 1846. Mexico was defeated, and under the terms of the Treaty of Guadalupe Hidalgo (1848), Mexico was forced to cede a large section of land north of the Río Grande to the United States. The land lost included New Mexico and California as well as Texas. In 1853 Santa Anna, short of government funds, sold the Mesilla Valley to the United States in the Gadsden Purchase. This final loss of territory gravely hurt Mexico.

Revolution and reform. Shortly afterward, bands of guerrillas gathered in the mountains and stormed the capital, demanding liberal reforms. Led by Juan Álvarez and Benito Juárez, the rebels declared their intention to institute many reforms for the good of the people. They planned to assert civilian control over the church and the military; to eliminate sharp class distinctions by breaking up large estates and distributing land among the peasants; and to unite the country to prevent further losses to the United States.

In 1855 Santa Anna was overthrown by the rebels and Álvarez became acting president. Various edicts outlining the reforms were issued from Mexico City, and in 1857 a new constitution, which provided for a more liberal and democratic government, was adopted. The liberals were staunchly opposed by the army, the church, and the upper classes. The ultimate result was the War of the Reform, a civil war that lasted from 1858 to 1860 and that was won at great cost by liberal forces led by Benito Juárez.

Over the years Mexico had become deeply indebted to Spain, Great Britain, and France. In 1861 Juárez, faced with national bankruptcy, suspended payment on these debts. A combined army of French, Spanish, and British troops invaded Mexico in December 1861 to occupy Veracruz and force payment. Napoleon III of France seized this opportunity to conquer the entire country. Upon discovery of Napoleon's ambitions, Spain and Great Britain withdrew their forces from Mexico. A Mexican victory at the Battle of Puebla in May 1862 only temporarily halted the French advance, and with reinforcements the French won control in 1863.

In 1864 Napoleon declared Maximilian, archduke of Austria, the new emperor of Mexico. In 1867, under strong diplomatic pressure from the United States, which objected to French intervention, France withdrew its last troops. Maximilian, under the erroneous impression that he could overcome the liberal forces that still supported Juárez, remained in Mexico. He was defeated, captured, tried, and shot. Juárez returned as president and held office until 1872.

Díaz era. Juárez and his successor, Sebastián Lerdo de Tejada, attempted to enact liberal reforms, but in 1876 the government was overthrown by Porfirio Díaz, who earlier had helped restore Juárez to the presidency. Díaz ruled as

THIS POTTER IN GUADALAJARA practices an ancient art, thus preserving the traditional crafts of Mexico.

labor
US

labour
Brit.

ECONOMIC GROWTH
brings problems as well as advances. The traffic and pollution in Mexico City have introduced new dilemmas.

dictator from 1876 to 1911. Under his rule the upper class again enjoyed prosperity, foreign investments multiplied, and the government budget was balanced. The Indians and the growing working class were neglected, however. The slogan, "Mexico, mother of foreigners, stepmother of Mexicans," expressed the growing popular resentment.

Discontent with Díaz's rule culminated in revolution in 1910. In an interview with a U.S. news correspondent two years earlier, Díaz expressed the view that Mexico was prepared for a truly democratic election and welcomed the idea of an opposition candidate. Although his comments were intended to be read only in the United States, translations of his statement reached Mexico. Francisco Madero, a Creole from northern Mexico, challenged Díaz to hold free elections, and Díaz was forced to uphold the declaration he had made.

The elections were rigged, however, and Madero was imprisoned, remaining behind bars until after his official defeat by Díaz. Resentment surged throughout the country, and the people revolted. In the north, Francisco "Pancho" Villa and Pascual Orozco led armies of peasants in rebellion. In the south, Emiliano Zapata and an army of Indians raided large estates. In May 1911 Díaz was forced to flee from the country.

Civil strife. Madero was elected to the presidency in an open election. He was sworn in as president in November 1911. His term of office brought some extension of democratic institutions, but no sorely needed economic and social reforms. The Indians and workers remained dissatisfied and once again revolted. In 1913 Madero unwisely enlisted the support of General Victoriano Huerta, who betrayed Madero, had him assassinated, and established himself as dictator. Huerta found no support for his regime from the United States, however, a factor that helped lead to his downfall.

In 1914 a wave of violent revolutionary movements erupted throughout Mexico. Venustiano Carranza, Alvaro Obregón, and Pancho Villa led the revolutionary movements in the north. In the south, an army of peasants was again led by Emiliano Zapata. Huerta's army was defeated and he fled to the United States.

Peace was not restored to Mexico, however, for the victorious troops then fought among themselves for control of the government. Villa and Zapata seized Mexico City, while Carranza and Obregón held Veracruz. With promises of extensive liberal reforms, the Obregón forces triumphed. In 1917 Carranza became president and a liberal constitution was drawn up. However, Zapata continued to resist Carranza in the south, and Villa resisted in the north.

Reform era. The new constitution protected labor, limited church authority, and provided for the division of large estates into the ancient Indian communal land system known as the *ejido*. The constitution was not implemented, however, and when Carranza tried to choose his own successor, he was overthrown by Obregón. In September 1920 Obregón was elected president. During his four-year term a modest program of reforms was initiated.

In 1924 General Plutarco Elías Calles, who had participated in the overthrow of Carranza, was elected president. Disputes with the church and with foreign investors plagued his administration. In 1928 Obregón was elected again, but he was assassinated before taking office. From 1928 to 1934 a series of puppet presidents, under the control of Calles, ruled Mexico. During this period the strongly reformist party, *Partido Nacional Revolucionario* (PNR), or National Revolutionary Party, was formed. It came to dominate Mexican politics and was later renamed the Institutional Revolutionary Party (PRI).

In elections held in 1934, the PNR candidate, Lázaro Cárdenas, was elected to the presidency. Under the Cárdenas administration, reforms demanded during the revolution were enacted. Millions of acres of land were distributed to the *ejidos,* and schools, hospitals, and roads were constructed. In 1938 the foreign-owned oil industries were nationalized.

Contemporary Mexico. In 1940 Manuel Avila Camacho was elected president. Although Avila Camacho made no innovations during his own term of office, he consolidated the gains that had already been made. In 1942, after German submarines had sunk Mexican tankers, Mexico declared war on the Axis Powers. Mexico contributed strategic raw materials to the war effort. Mexicans enlisted in the United States armed forces, and a squadron of the Mexican air force was sent to the Pacific. In 1945 Mexico became a charter member of the United Nations.

Postwar administrations basically followed the domestic reform policies of Avila Camacho and focused on increasing food production and developing transportation. President Adolfo Ruiz Cortines (1952–1958) greatly extended Mexico's farmland through irrigation projects. Under Adolfo López Mateos (1958–1964), Mexico's educational system was expanded.

In 1964 Gustavo Díaz Ordaz was elected president. On October 28, 1967, during his administration, Mexico signed a treaty with the United States that settled a century-old border dispute caused by the shifting course of the Rio Grande.

Also during the administration of Díaz Ordaz, Mexico enjoyed great prosperity. There were huge increases in industrial production and in the national income. But the wealth was unevenly distributed, and in the 1960s Mexico experienced a rise in social unrest and political violence. The growing demands for social reform began to be addressed by President Luis Echeverría (1970–1976), who oversaw the government's increasing role in economic affairs.

The new president initiated land redistribution and firmly restricted foreign investments. Relations with the Communist world were improved.

José López Portillo, elected in 1976, immediately began to reverse the leftist policies of his predecessor. He sought to regain the government's support from the privileged and middle classes. Under López Portillo, Mexico pledged policies of neutrality, international nonintervention, and economic independence. In 1982 Miguel de la Madrid Hurtado was elected president. He instituted austerity measures to deal with high inflation, crippling foreign debt, and widespread unemployment. In 1985 two earthquakes caused severe damage to Mexico City, with 7,000 killed and 50,000 left homeless.

In 1988 Carlos Salinas de Gortari was elected president in the closest election in PRI history. The party instituted some democratic reforms to regain political support. Salinas reduced Mexico's foreign debt and championed the North American Free Trade Agreement (NAFTA) with the United States and Canada.

In January 1994, Indians in Chiapas launched a guerrilla uprising to bring attention to the plight of Mexico's poor and to demand broad democratic and economic reforms. Under President Vicente Fox, elected in 2000, Mexico has somewhat recovered economically.

Nicaragua

Official name: *Republic of Nicaragua*
Area: *49,985 sq. mi.,*
 129,494 sq. km.
Type of government: *Republic*
Population: *5,024,000*
Capital and largest city: *Managua*
 (Pop., 903,000)
Language: *Spanish (official),*
 English
Literacy: *68%*
Currency: *Cordoba*
Per capita GDP: *$2,500*
 (Rank: 123rd)

The land. Nicaragua is the largest of the Central American republics. Most of Nicaragua is occupied by the Central American Cordillera of the Andes, which forms a mountainous highland region that extends through the center of the country. The highlands are crossed by several mountain ranges, which extend roughly in an east to west direction. The highland region separates a wide Caribbean coastal plain, known as the Mosquito Coast, from a narrow Pacific coastal plain.

A long, narrow depression runs diagonally across Nicaragua from the Gulf of Fonseca in the northwest into Costa Rica. This depression contains two large lakes, Lake Nicaragua and Lake Managua. Lake Nicaragua, about 100 miles (161 kilometers) long and 45 miles (72 kilometers) wide, is one of the largest bodies of fresh water in Central America.

The mountains to the west of the depression are actively volcanic, and eruptions and earthquakes are a constant hazard.

Nicaragua has a hot climate. Temperatures seldom drop below 75°F (24°C), although it is generally cooler in the central mountain region. Rainfall is moderate on the Pacific coast and in the mountains. It is extremely heavy, however, along the Caribbean coast, where some places receive as much as 200 inches (508 centimeters) a year. The average annual rainfall is 45 inches (114 centimeters).

The people. Most of the people of Nicaragua are mestizo, of mixed Indian and European ancestry. The remainder of the population is of European, African, or indigenous Mosquito (or Miskito) Indian descent.

Much of Nicaragua is thinly settled. The Mosquito Indians and most of the blacks live on the Caribbean coastal plain. The bulk of the population is concentrated along the Pacific coast and in the area around Lake Nicaragua and Lake Managua. Three of Nicaragua's four largest cities—Managua, León (population, 162,000), and Granada (97,000)—are located in this area. About 40 percent of the population live in urban areas.

A PAINTING of peasants was done by the well-known Mexican artist Diego Rivera in 1932.

Economy. Nicaragua is mostly an agricultural nation, although the government has been attempting to diversify the economy. Agriculture accounts for more than two-thirds of Nicaragua's exports. About 25 percent of Nicaragua's land is arable.

Although Nicaragua has great natural potential, it has remained basically undeveloped. Mining is confined to gold, silver, and copper, but deposits of tungsten, lead, and zinc exist.

About half of Nicaragua is covered with forests; timber, including mahogany, pine, cedar, rosewood, and balsa, is an important export. Rubber is also an important forest product.

Agriculture. Agriculture employs about 40 percent of the labor force. A major share of the country's crops are raised in the west, where extensive tracts of fertile soil are ideal for use with mechanized farming. However, a fairly large percentage of Nicaragua's arable land still is not cultivated.

Corn, beans, rice, and sugar cane are raised for domestic consumption. Cotton and coffee are the leading commercial crops. Meat, sugar, and bananas are also important Nicaraguan agricultural products.

Industry. Nicaraguan industry employs about 15 percent of the labor force and is centered on food processing and the manufacturing of a few consumer items for local consumption. The largest industry is sugar refining. Factories produce cement, insecticides, cigarettes, soap, liquor, and clothing.

Trade. Nicaragua's main trading partners are the European Union, Japan, the United States, and the Central American Common Market. Major exports are cotton, coffee, sugar, meat, and timber. Principal imports include machinery, equipment for transportation, chemicals, textiles, and foodstuffs.

Government. Nicaragua is a republic headed by a president who is directly elected to a 6-year term. The president was vested with broad executive powers by

center
US

centre
Brit.

kilometers
US

kilometres
Brit.

27 North America

THE HIGHLY ACTIVE leftist guerrilla force known as the Sandinist National Liberation Front, or Sandinistas, has been behind much of the political unrest in Nicaragua since the 1970s.

centered
US

centred
Brit.

the 1987 constitution; however, a 1995 revision limited these powers and provided for a more powerful legislative branch. Legislative power rests with a unicameral National Assembly consisting of 93 members directly elected by proportional representation.

Judicial authority is vested in the Supreme Court.

Nicaragua is administratively divided into 15 departments and 2 autonomous regions.

History. Nicaragua was discovered in 1502 by Christopher Columbus on his last voyage to the New World, but it was not explored until 1522, when Gil González Dávila led an expedition from Panama. In 1523 and 1524 the Spanish founded the cities of León and Granada in the western lowlands, and except for sporadic raids by English pirates during the latter half of the 1600s, the colonial period in Nicaragua was peaceful.

Independence from Spain was won in 1821, but Nicaragua was annexed to the Mexican empire. When the Mexican empire collapsed in 1823, Nicaragua joined the United Provinces of Central America, which included El Salvador, Honduras, Guatemala, and Costa Rica. In 1838 Nicaragua left the United Provinces and declared itself independent.

Sovereignty. As a sovereign nation, Nicaragua suffered from intense rivalry between liberals, centered in León, and conservatives, in Granada, who battled for political control of the country. In 1855, when the conservatives gained power and attempted to establish a strong, stable government, the liberals

invited an adventurer from the United States, William Walker, to help oust the conservative administration.

With a following of about 60 men, Walker captured control of Nicaragua. In 1856 he installed himself as president. U.S. financier Cornelius Vanderbilt, who had helped Walker's expedition, soon became Walker's opponent when Walker seized property belonging to the Accessory Transit Company, which was controlled by Vanderbilt.

Vanderbilt helped organize an invading army recruited in neighboring countries, and after only one year in office, Walker was forced to flee. In 1860 he was captured in Honduras and executed. Following Walker's death, tension between liberals and conservatives was temporarily abated and Nicaragua enjoyed peace and prosperity under several consecutive conservative administrations.

Zelaya era. A revolution by liberal forces in 1893 brought José Santos Zelaya to power. Zelaya moved the capital from León to Managua, promoted railroad construction, brought the Indians of the east coast under the government's jurisdiction, and promoted agricultural development. Zelaya also involved Nicaragua in revolutions in nearby Central American countries.

In 1909 Zelaya executed two U.S. engineers, whom he maintained were implicated in a plot to overthrow his government. The United States severed diplomatic relations with Nicaragua, weakening the prestige of the Zelaya administration. The conservatives rebelled, forcing Zelaya to resign.

U.S. intervention. For several years political and economic conditions in Nicaragua were in a chaotic state. In 1912 the United States sent marines to restore order at the request of provisional President Adolfo Díaz.

In the same year, Díaz was elected president, and in 1914 Nicaragua signed the Bryan-Chamorro Treaty with the United States. The treaty gave the United States the right to construct a trans-isthmian canal through Nicaragua and to establish military bases on both coasts. The treaty sparked widespread anger and resentment in Nicaragua and other countries in Central America. Liberals in Nicaragua, frozen out of political life by the United States-backed conservatives, forged an alliance with a growing agrarian guerrilla movement. The liberal leader, Augusto Sandino, became the head of the movement. His success led the United States to create a Nicaraguan-armed force, the National Guard, headed by Anastasio Somoza Garcia.

United States forces were withdrawn in 1933 and Sandino began peace negotiations with President Juan Bautista Sacasa. In 1934 Sandino was assassinated by National Guards on Somoza's order.

Contemporary Nicaragua. In 1936 Somoza established himself in the presidency and assumed dictatorial powers.

His administration was characterized by economic development and political repression. During World War II Somoza actively cooperated with the United States.

In 1947 Leonardo Arguello was elected president, but Somoza had him removed from office and governed through less independent presidents until 1950, when Somoza again became president. Somoza was assassinated in September 1956, and his son, Luis Somoza Debayle, was appointed acting president for the duration of his father's term. The next year he was elected president.

Luis Somoza's administration, contrary to expectations, proved to be less oppressive than that of his father. Civil liberties, freedom of the press, and political opposition were now permitted to a limited extent.

In 1963 René Schick Gutiérrez was elected president. Schick died in 1966, and Congress then elected Lorenzo Guerrero Gutiérrez to finish Schick's term. In 1967 General Anastasio Somoza Debayle, the brother of Luis Somoza, was elected president amid charges of election fraud. He was reelected, however, in 1974.

During General Somoza's rule the Sandinist National Liberation Front (FSLN) became a highly active guerrilla force. A socialist coalition, it was dedicated to ending the Somoza family's domination of Nicaragua. It sought to redistribute the country's land more evenly, to relieve the miserable living conditions of the peasantry, and to end the severe political repression imposed by the Somozas.

In 1972 a major earthquake struck Nicaragua, devastating the capital. Somoza and his associates took advantage of the disaster to enrich themselves once again at the expense of the Nicaraguan people. This was a major boost to the FSLN, which stepped up activities against the Somoza dictatorship.

General Somoza countered FSLN attacks by imposing strict martial law in 1975. His regime lost prestige after reports of torture and gross violations of human, as well as civil, rights.

When one of Somoza's foes—publisher Pedro Joaquín Chamorro—was murdered in 1978, the nation erupted into civil war. In 1979 Somoza fled the country and the FSLN took power.

Soon the Marxist element of the FSLN leadership took control of the Nicaraguan revolution. Many former Sandinista officials left the government, and some took up arms against the regime of President Daniel Ortega Saavedra.

Relations between the United States and the Sandinista government worsened steadily through the first half of the 1980s. Accusing the Sandinistas of supporting leftist guerrillas in El Salvador, the United States gave support to anti-Sandinista rebels, and the situation deteriorated into civil war. In 1985 President Reagan ordered an embargo on U.S. trade with Nicaragua.

By the late 1980s the Nicaraguan economy was a shambles. Ortega agreed to hold open elections, and in February 1990 the U.S.-backed opposition coalition, UNO, swept the Sandinistas from power. Violetta Barrios de Chamorro, widow of Pedro Joaquín Chamorro, became president, vowing to unify the country and restore civil and economic order. The Sandinistas retained control of the military and continued to apply political pressure on the new government. Ortega remains in the political arena.

Panama

Official name: *Republic of Panama*
Area: *30,185 sq. mi., 78,200 sq. km.*
Type of government:
  Constitutional republic
Population: *2,920,000*
Capital and largest city:
  Panama City
  (Pop., 416,000)
Languages: *Spanish (official),*
  English
Literacy: *91%;* **Currency:** *Balboa*
Per capita GDP: *$5,900*
  (Rank: 79th)

The land. Panama's land surface is mostly hilly and mountainous. The highest mountains rise in the west, near the Costa Rican border, and are volcanic. The highest peak is Chiriquí Volcano, 11,401 feet (3,775 meters) above sea level. These mountains gradually slope down toward a hilly central lowland, which separates them from a second range of mountains in the east. It is through this central lowland that the Panama Canal runs.

The only other significant lowlands are plains along the Caribbean and Pacific coasts. The Caribbean plain, along the north coast, is extremely rainy. Tropical evergreen rain forests predominate. The Pacific plain, along the south coast, has a wet and a dry season, producing semi-deciduous forest mingled with savanna.

The climate varies with elevation. The lowlands have a tropical climate—the average annual temperature there is about 80°F (27°C). Temperatures in the mountains range from 50°F to 66°F (10°C to 19°C). Precipitation on the Caribbean coast is heavier than on the Pacific coast. The Caribbean side of the isthmus receives up to 120 inches (305 centimeters) of rain each year. The Pacific side receives about 65 inches (165 centimeters) annually. It is the heavy rainfall on the northern, Caribbean side of Panama that provides the water to operate the Panama Canal locks.

The people. The inhabitants of Panama are largely mestizo, of mixed European and Indian parentage. About one-seventh of the population is of African descent, most being the descendants of West Indians who came to Panama to build the canal. There also are groups of whites and Indians.

More than half the population is urban. The major seaports and urban centers are Panama City, the capital, and Colón (population, 42,000), near the northern end of the canal. Outlying areas are sparsely settled, especially the region east of the Canal Zone.

Economy. The economy of Panama is largely based on providing goods and services related to the operation and maintenance of the Panama Canal. In recent years the government has sought to lessen Panama's dependence on the canal and diversify the economy by increasing agricultural production and expanding industry.

Panama has rich natural resources, but they are mostly unexploited. Only small quantites of gold, silver, and manganese are mined, although large copper reserves have been found. Limestone is quarried and it supplies the cement industry. Panama also has valuable timber and an abundance of fish in its coastal waters. Shrimp exports have increased significantly in recent years.

Only a fraction of Panama's arable land is cultivated, and farms traditionally are small and primitive. Rice and corn are the basic food crops, but a variety of fruits and vegetables are also grown. Bananas are by far the most important commercial crop. Sugar cane and coffee are also significant. About 27 percent of the labor force is employed in agriculture.

The rising importance of international banking and industry spurred a period of economic expansion since 1960, and banking has become a major component of the Panamanian economy. Development of industry has centered on small manufacturing operations. While these industries are still the most important ones, chemical and

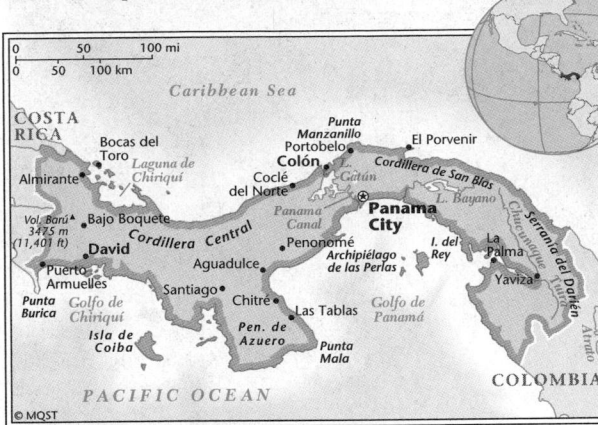

plastic manufacturing and oil refining are growing in importance. A new oil pipeline crossing Panama from Puerto Armuelles on the Pacific coast to Chiriqui Grande on the Caribbean coast has a capacity of 830,000 barrels a day.

Small factories produce cement, shoes, soap, soft drinks, alcoholic beverages, furniture, and clothing. There is also some food processing and a variety of home handicraft industries. Mining and industry employ about 10 percent of the Panamanian work force.

Trade. Panama's traditionally poor balance of trade is compensated for by income from the Panama Canal, fees from the registry of foreign vessels under the Panamanian flag, and income from financial services.

Panama's chief exports are bananas, petroleum products, shrimp, sugar, and coffee. Principal imports include petroleum, machinery, motor vehicles, textiles, chemicals, and foodstuffs. The bulk of Panama's trade is with the United States.
Government. Panama's president, who is directly elected to a term of 5 years, is the head of state and chief executive. Legislative power is vested in the unicameral Legislative Assembly, whose 71 members are elected from regions throughout the country. Judicial authority is vested in a nine-member Supreme Court.

Panama is divided administratively into nine provinces and one territory.
History. Panama was discovered in 1501 by Rodrigo de Bastidas. In 1502 Christopher Columbus explored the Caribbean coast and claimed the territory for Spain. In 1513 Vasco Núñez de Balboa crossed the isthmus and discovered the Pacific Ocean, thereby putting the western coast within Spanish reach.

In 1519 the small village of Panamá, on the Pacific coast, was made the capital of the isthmus. The Spanish explorer Francisco Pizarro used Panama as the base for expeditions to Peru in 1531. The cities of Nombre de Dios and, later,

27 North America

meters	*US*
metres	*Brit.*
labor	*US*
labour	*Brit.*

LA GRANAJA is one of the Caribbean islands off the coast of Central America.

THE TROPICAL evergreen rain forests of the Caribbean plain, along the north coast of Panama, are home to many exotic plant species, such as this fern and heliconia.

kilometers
US

kilometres
Brit.

Portobelo became the ports through which gold and silver were shipped to Spain.

During the late 1600s and the 1700s, Spain entered a period of political and economic decline and the importance of Panama began to wane. In 1717 Panama lost its autonomy and became part of the viceroyalty of New Granada, which included present-day Colombia.

In 1821 Panama gained independence from Spain and joined with Colombia, Ecuador, and Venezuela to form the republic of Gran Colombia. Gran Colombia was dissolved in 1830, but Panama remained part of Colombia. A spirit of Panamanian nationalism began to grow, however, and political relations with Colombia deteriorated. In 1855 Panama was granted self-rule as a state of Colombia, but in 1885 the Colombian government reasserted its authority over Panama, fueling new separatist and nationalist sentiment. In addition, Panamanians took the Colombian government to task for its failure to advance construction of a canal across the isthmus. A French company under Ferdinand de Lesseps had begun construction in 1880 but had gone bankrupt in 1889.

Independence. In 1903 the Colombian government refused to ratify the Hay-Herrán Treaty, which would have authorized the United States to build a canal across the isthmus. Fearing that the United States would build the canal through Nicaragua instead of Panama,

the Panamanians revolted and declared their independence from Colombia. U.S. President Theodore Roosevelt ensured the success of the revolt when he ordered a U.S. warship to prevent Colombian troops from entering the isthmus.

On November 6, 1903, three days after the revolution began, the United States recognized an independent Panamanian government. Panama's newly formed government leased the Canal Zone, a strip of territory across the isthmus about 10 miles (16 kilometers) wide, to the United States in perpetuity for a payment of $10 million and an annual payment of $250,000.

Work was resumed on the canal project, which soon came to be the largest and most complicated engineering feat ever undertaken. In 1914 the canal was opened to traffic.

Panama became prosperous as a result of the Panama Canal, but political unrest developed during the world economic depression of the 1930s. Panama sided with the Allies in World War II and in 1945 became a charter member of the United Nations.

Contemporary Panama. During the mid-1950s opposition to U.S. sovereignty over the Canal Zone began to grow. In November 1959, anti-United States demonstrations broke out in Panama and Colombia. In January 1964, Panamanian students led violent anti-United States riots. The two countries agreed to negotiate their differences, and in 1967 a new treaty was drafted providing for Panamanian sovereignty over the Canal Zone and a joint board to govern the canal itself. In 1974 the United States and Panama agreed that the United States would operate the canal for a certain period, with Panama sharing the revenues.

In 1977 the two countries proposed a plan for Panama's gradual takeover of the canal, which was completed in 1999. In 1978 the U.S. Senate approved the plan, which included a guarantee of the

canal's neutrality. In 1979 the Canal Zone was transferred to Panama. In 1980 Japan and Panama together began to study the construction of a second canal in Panama—one that could accommodate full-size tankers.

A breakdown of order in 1968 resulted in a military coup on October 1. The National Assembly was dissolved and the constitution was suspended. In 1969 Brigadier General Omar Torrijos Herrera took command of the junta. By 1972 he had assumed virtual dictatorial powers, had given the country a new constitution, and had promised to restore civilian rule by 1978. He brought an era of stability to Panama and championed causes for the underprivileged classes.

In 1982 General Manuel Antonio Noriega became commander of the Panamanian Defense Forces (PDF). Noriega virtually controlled the civilian government. He was also implicated in Panama's drug trafficking. In 1988 Noriega was indicted in the United States on charges of drug trafficking. This action led to the further deterioration of relations between the United States and Panama. In March, President Eric Arturo Delvalle attempted to remove Noriega as head of the PDF but was himself overthrown by Noriega.

In May 1989 Guillermo Endara, the anti-Noriega coalition's candidate, claimed victory in a presidential election that was subsequently nullified. Endara and other opposition leaders were attacked and beaten by Noriega's thugs, and the situation in Panama became even more uncertain.

In December 1989, U.S. troops invaded Panama. The constitutionally elected leaders from the 1989 elections were installed in the government and Noriega was arrested and flown to the United States for trial. Panama City suffered enormous damage in the invasion. The constitution was amended in October 1994 to abolish the country's military.

STRAINED RELATIONS between the U.S. and Colombia, of which Panama was originally a part, caused the Panamanians to revolt to avoid having the canal built through Nicaragua.

West Indies

The West Indies is a chain of islands that form the northern edge of the Caribbean Sea, separating it from the Atlantic Ocean. They extend for about 2,000 miles, from near the southern tip of Florida to the northern coast of Venezuela. The West Indies are made up of three major island groups. The northernmost group is the Bahamas, with about 3,000 small islands and reefs. The central group is made up of larger islands, including the Greater Antilles, which include Cuba, Jamaica, Puerto Rico, and Hispaniola, which is divided into the Dominican Republic and Haiti. The smaller southeastern islands are the Lesser Antilles, which are divided into the Leeward and Windward Islands.

Christopher Columbus was the first European to reach the islands. When he landed there in 1492, he called them the Indies because he thought that they were the East Indies of Asia, for which he was searching. When it was discovered that they were part of a heretofore unknown continent, they were given the name of West Indies. Other European countries later colonized many of the islands. Although many of them have since become independent nations, others are still associated with the United States, France, the Netherlands, and the British Commonwealth.

The land.   The West Indies are composed of a combined land mass of about 90,000 square miles spread over an arc of 2,000 miles of ocean. They consist of the tops of an isthmian mountain system that extends eastward from North America to South America. Some of the islands were formed by uplifting sedimentary layers, particularly limestone, or were built up by coral or by a combination of volcanic action and coral construction. Several of the volcanoes are still active, including Mont Pelée on Martinique, and two volcanoes called Soufrière, one on Saint Vincent and one on Basse-Terre in Guadeloupe.

Most of the islands have only narrow strips of lowlands that, typically, lie along the coastlines. Cuba has larger coastal lowlands as well as a large interior plains region flanked by mountains to the east and west. Many of the Caribbean islands have navigable harbors, bays, and inlets.

Rivers.   Rivers are not a significant feature of the West Indian islands, although many of the islands have small rivers, most of which are navigable only by small boats.

Climate and vegetation.   The islands have a warm and sunny tropical climate. Temperatures are mild most of the year, with average temperatures varying as little as 5 degrees. The predominant seasonal change consists of the alternate dry and wet seasons, with the annual rainfall up to as much as 200 inches. Much of the surface consists of lush tropical vegetation and rain forests, with many flowering plants.

The people.   The population of the West Indies is mixed, consisting of an intermingling of the native groups, the European colonizers and the peoples brought in to work in agriculture. The original Indian inhabitants were the Caribs and Arawaks, few of whom still exist as separate populations, although there is a small group of Carib Indians on Dominica. The majority of the people are descendants of black Africans who were brought to the islands to work on sugar cane plantations. Other agricultural workers included the Chinese and East Indians who came after slavery was abolished in the 1800s. European populations include people of Portuguese, Spanish, British, Dutch, and French ancestry.

colonized
US

colonised
Brit.

27   North America

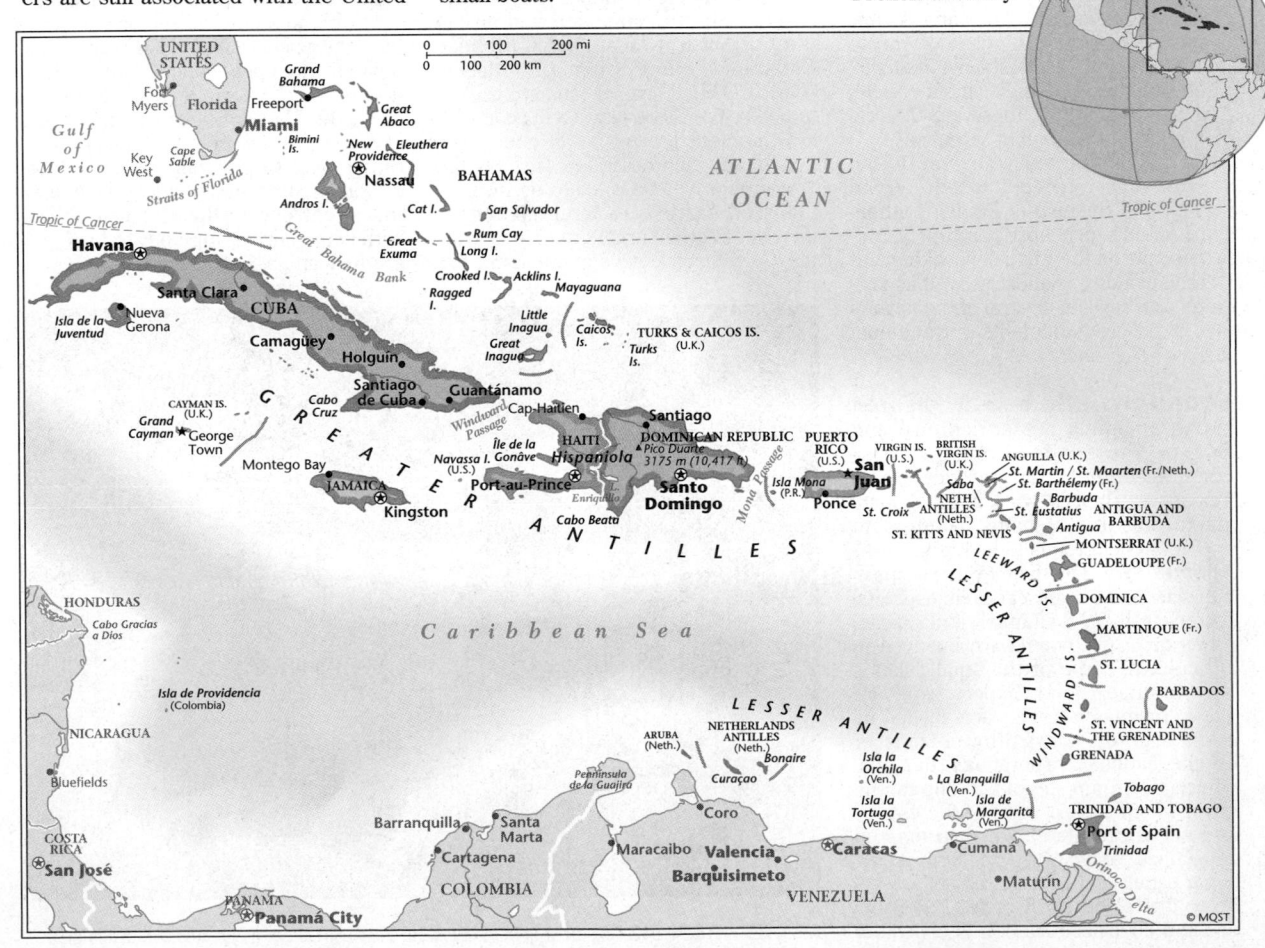

CHRISTOPHER COLUMBUS came ashore on one of the islands at the time he discovered the New World in 1492. Columbus called the island San Salvador, or Holy Savior.

Languages. These European groups that colonized the West Indies have left their imprint on the islands in the form of language. French, for example, is prevalent in Haiti, Martinique, and Guadeloupe. Dutch is the main language of the Netherlands Antilles and Aruba. Spanish is the chief language of Puerto Rico, Cuba, and the Dominican Republic. The rest of the West Indies mainly speak English. In addition, there are dialects that are a combination of languages.

Religion. The main religion on the islands that were colonized by the French and Spanish is Roman Catholicism. There are both Catholics and Protestants on the English-speaking and Dutch-speaking islands, as well as religious practices on several of the islands that incorporate elements of traditional African religions.

Economy. The bases for the West Indian economy are agriculture and tourism. These, with government positions, account for 80 percent of the workforce. The rest work in trade, manufacturing, mining, and fishing, but unemployment tends to be high.

Agriculture. The main export crops in the islands are sugar cane, citrus fruits, coffee, spices, bananas, and cacao. Although many people are involved in agriculture, some of the small islands have to import food. Export crops are grown mainly on large tracts owned by a small group of wealthy citizens or by international corporations. In Cuba, where the main export is sugar, the government took control of the estates and organized state-owned farms and collectives for growing and processing sugar cane.

Transportation and trade. Reliable sea and air transportation is crucial to

colonized
US

colonised
Brit.

the nations of the West Indies because of their heavy reliance on agricultural exports and tourism to provide earnings and a favorable balance of trade.

Economic trends. In 1973, a number of West Indies nations joined with several South American nations in the Caribbean to form the Caribbean Community and Common Market (CARICOM). The organization promoted regional cooperation in economic development as well as in education, health, and cultural affairs. In 1988, the 13 member nations voted to remove virtually all barriers to trade among its members. Other organizations such as the Caribbean Development Bank are

working to stimulate industrial growth in the islands.

Many of the island nations faced austerity measures in the late 1980s in order to control consumption, reduce inflation, increase exports, reduce international debt, and restore investor confidence. Some governments closed or sold off unprofitable businesses.

One nation stood alone against the regional trend toward economic privatization. Cuba, which for three decades had been building its economy on the socialist model provided by the Soviet Union and Eastern Europe, in the 1990s found itself virtually alone. The Cuban economy relied heavily on subsidies from the Soviet Union and on favorable trade agreements with East Block countries. However, with the collapse of communism in the former Soviet Union and Eastern Europe, Cuba has had to endure several years of extreme economic stress as it tries to adapt to modern economic realities while attempting to maintain its authoritarian socialist political system.

Government. Between the 1492 discovery of the islands and the 1800s, various European countries established colonies in the West Indies, including the Spanish, English, French, Dutch, and Danes. The 1800s saw several movements for independence, led by Haiti and the Dominican Republic. The United States entered the area in 1898 with the Spanish-American War, resulting in the independence of Cuba and the acquisition of Puerto Rico as a colony. In 1917, the United States purchased the U.S. Virgin Islands from Denmark. Since that time, many islands have either become independent or gained more control over their internal affairs, with some joining together to form federations and associations.

SPICES ARE A BIG export crop in the West Indies. At left is nutmeg that is sorted and graded.

Countries of the West Indies

Antigua and Barbuda

Official name: *Antigua and Barbuda*

Area: *170 sq. mi., 440 sq. km.*

Type of government:
Parliamentary monarchy

Population: *67,000*

Capital and largest city: *St. John's*
(Pop., 22,000)

Language: *English, local dialects*

Literacy: *89%*

Currency: *East Caribbean dollar*

Per capita GDP: *$10,000*
(Rank: 49th)

The land. Antigua and Barbuda is comprised of the islands of Antigua, Barbuda, and Redonda. The islands are located in the eastern Caribbean, about 250 miles (402 kilometers) southeast of Puerto Rico. They are part of the Lesser Antilles. Antigua is a low-lying island of mixed volcanic and coral construction. Generally flat in the north, the island has hills in the south and west. The highest point on Antigua is Boggy Peak, with an elevation of 1,330 feet (405 meters). Its irregular coastline provides several natural harbors, including St. John's, English, and Parham. Barbuda is a flat, wooded coral island. Antigua and Barbuda has a dry, tropical climate.

The people. The people of Antigua and Barbuda are mostly of African descent. There is a small number of Europeans and mixed minorities. Almost 40 percent of the population live in urban areas. The largest city is St. John's, on Antigua. The great majority of the population live on Antigua. The tiny island of Redonda is uninhabited.

Economy. The economy of Antigua and Barbuda is dominated by the tourist

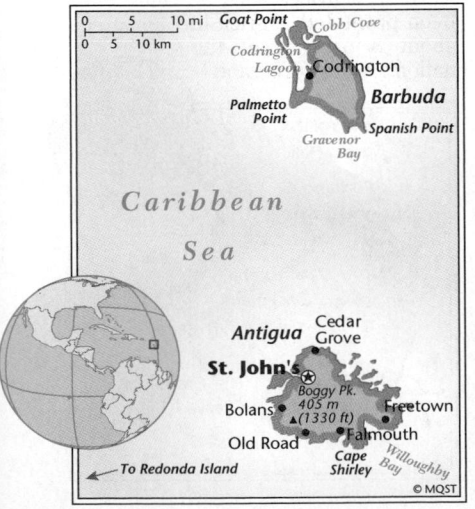

TROPICAL STORMS called hurricanes, with winds of up to 150 miles an hour, are spawned in the Caribbean. Hurricane Andrew caused much damage in the Bahamas in 1992.

industry, which accounts for 40 percent of the gross domestic product and employs 60 percent of the population. Also important are cotton, fruit, and sugar cane cultivation. Most manufacturing has to do with the processing of agricultural products.

Antigua and Barbuda posted a significant increase in gross domestic product in the late 1980s. Most of the growth was due to tourism.

The islands' exports include clothing, fruit, and rum, while imports consist primarily of fuel, food, and machinery.

Government. The head of state of Antigua and Barbuda is the queen of England, who is represented by a governor-general. The head of government is a prime minister. Legislative power rests with a bicameral Parliament, made up of a House of Representatives and a Senate, each with 17 members.

History. The earliest known inhabitants were Arawak and Carib Indians. Antigua was discovered by Columbus in 1493, but the earliest attempts at colonization by the Spanish were unsuccessful. Englishmen from St. Kitts settled there in 1632, introducing sugar cane cultivation and eventually importing slaves from Africa to work on the sugar plantations. Barbuda, settled by colonists from Antigua, was owned by the Codrington family from 1680 to 1872. Its only town is named Codrington.

From 1871 to 1956, Antigua was administered as part of the Federation of the Leeward Islands. In 1967 the islands became an associated state of Great Britain, and enjoyed total internal autonomy.

Independence came on November 1, 1981, though some problems were encountered with the emergence of a strong separatist movement on Barbuda. The political life of the islands has been dominated by the Antigua Labour Party. Its leader, Vere C. Bird, became prime

minister upon independence. He was succeeded in 1994 by his son, Lester. The Antigua Labour Party remained the leading party throughout the 1990s.

Bahamas

Official name: *Commonwealth of The Bahamas*

Area: *5,381 sq. mi., 13,940 sq. km.*

Type of government:
Commonwealth

Population: *295,000*

Capital and largest city: *Nassau*
(Pop., metro. area, 211,000)

Language: *English (official), Creole*

Literacy: *98%;* **Currency:** *Dollar*

Per capita GDP: *$16,800*
(Rank: 37th)

The land. The Bahamas form an archipelago in the Atlantic Ocean off the southeastern tip of Florida. The 700 islands and islets of the archipelago have low, rocky, flat, or rolling terrain and are ringed with coral reefs. The archipelago also includes some 2,000 small, barren rock formations, cays, and reefs. About 30 of the islands are inhabited. The climate is warm throughout the year. About 50 inches (127 centimeters) of rain fall each year.

The people. About 85 percent of the Bahamian people are of African descent; the rest are of European or mixed descent. About 75 percent live in urban areas, mostly in the capital, Nassau, on New Providence Island. Only 5 percent of the labor force is occupied by agriculture; most of the workers are employed in government and in the trade and service industries, especially tourism.

27 North America

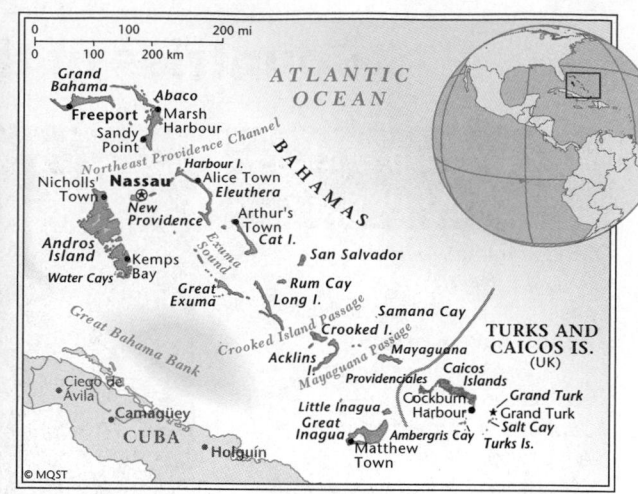

MILD TRADE WINDS
and beautiful white beaches along the western and southwestern coasts of Barbados have led to the development of a thriving tourist industry, the island's main support.

center
US

centre
Brit.

kilometers
US

kilometres
Brit.

labor
US

labour
Brit.

Economy. Tourism is the prime factor in the economy, but agriculture, primarily for local consumption, is conducted on most of the islands. Bananas, citrus fruits, and vegetables are grown. Attempts to increase agricultural production have met with only moderate success, in part because of the limited amount of arable land on the islands. Forestry, rum, salt production, pharmaceutical production, petroleum refining, and oil transshipment constitute the main industrial activities.

Since 1960 government programs have sought to persuade businesses to make their headquarters on the islands. This has helped to make the Bahamas an important financial and banking center. The poor balance of trade caused by the need to import necessities is partially offset by the expenditures of tourists.

Most of the Bahamas' small-volume trade is carried on with the United States, the United Kingdom and other members of the European Communities, and Canada.

Government. According to the democratic constitution of 1973, the Bahamas is governed by an elected prime minister and a bicameral legislature. The General Assembly consists of a 16-member appointed Senate and a 40-member elected House of Assembly. The British monarch, Queen Elizabeth II, is the head of state, represented by a governor-general.

History. The Bahamas were discovered in 1492 by Christopher Columbus, who is believed to have made the first landfall in the New World on the island of San Salvador. However, the first settlements in the Bahamas were established by the English in the 1600s, on New Providence and Eleuthera islands. The settlements were only marginally successful despite the importation of African slaves. The settlers faced Spanish raids and trouble from Carribean pirates, who used the islands as a base. During the American Revolution, Nassau was occupied by American forces. Many loyalists came to the Bahamas from Florida when the islands became a colony in 1783. The islands became a British colony in 1783.

The Bahamas was a center of blockade-running activity during the U.S. Civil War. During the era of Prohibition, it was a center of rum-running to the United States.

The Bahamas remained a British colony until 1964, when self-government was granted. In 1967 the islands' first black prime minister, Lynden O. Pindling, head of the Progressive Liberal Party, took office and began to move the colony toward independence from Britain.

Pindling led the nation to independence in 1973; he was succeeded by Hubert Ingraham in 1992.

Barbados

Official name: *Barbados*
Area: *166 sq. mi., 430 sq. km.*
Type of government:
Parliamentary democracy
Population: *276,000*
Capital and largest city:
Bridgetown
(Pop., 6,000)
Language: *English*
Literacy: *97%*
Currency: *Dollar*
Per capita GDP: *$14,500*
(Rank: 41st)

The land. Barbados, a small island nation at the extreme eastern end of the Windward Islands in the Lesser Antilles, West Indies, lies about 300 miles (483 kilometers) north of Guyana, on the South American mainland. Barbados is a triangular-shaped island about 20 miles (32 kilometers) long and 14 miles (22.5 kilometers) across at its widest point. The island is composed of coral atop a base of sedimentary rock. Most of the island is a low-lying plateau, but there is a small highland area in the northeast. There are beautiful white beaches along the western and southwestern coasts that are produced by the weathering of the coral. The highest point on the island is Mount Hillaby, with an elevation of 1,104 feet (336 meters).

Barbados has an adequate supply of fresh water, but there is little natural vegetation, because about half of the island's total area is under cultivation. The climate is comfortable. Temperatures range between 70°F (21°C) and 87°F (30.6°C), and the trade winds blow across the island all year. Average annual rainfall is about 60 inches (152 centimeters), with more rain falling in the higher elevations inland than on the coasts.

The people. Most of the island's people are of African origin. Persons of mixed African and European background make up about 16 percent of the total, and those of European origin represent about 4 percent.

The island is densely populated, and population growth creates serious economic and social problems. There are over 1,500 people per square mile, one of the highest population densities in the world. Over half of these people live in rural areas. About 40 percent live in St. Michael parish, which includes Bridgetown, the nation's chief port and capital.

Economy. The economy of Barbados has only recently been successfully diversified. Traditionally based on sugar production, the economy has developed a thriving tourist industry that is now considered to be the main support of the island. Light industry has been growing, and other activities, such as fishing, have been promoted. Agriculture occupies about 8 percent of the nation's work force and accounts for about 7.2 percent of the gross domestic product. About 36 percent of the work force is engaged in industry and commerce. About 37 percent is employed in government and service industries.

Sugar cane is grown on about 80 percent of the cultivatable land, and sugar and sugar products—rum and molasses—account for approximately 80 percent of export earnings. Yams, peas, beans, and corn are grown for local food needs.

Major imports include machinery and manufactured goods. Major exports include sugar and sugar products, electronic components, and clothing. Most trade is carried on with the United States, members of the Caribbean Community (CARICOM), and Great Britain.

Government. The head of state is the British monarch, represented on the island by a governor-general. Actual executive powers are exercised by a prime minister and a cabinet. The prime minister is normally the leader of the majority party in the legislature.

The legislature has two houses, the Senate and the House of Assembly. The 21 members of the Senate are appointed by the governor-general. Twelve are named on the advice of the prime minister, two on the advice of the leader of the opposition party, and seven at the governor-general's discretion to represent religious, economic, and other interest groups. The 27 members of the House of Assembly are popularly elected every 5 years.

History. The island was known to Spanish and Portuguese sailors in the 16th century. Arawak Indians lived on Barbados until about 100 years before the arrival of the first British settlers in 1627. An English merchant group had won control of the island by 1629, but during the English civil wars of the 1600s, the English government took direct control. In doing so, the British granted the islanders the Charter of Barbados, providing for government by a governor, council, and elected assembly, and taxes levied only with the express consent of the inhabitants.

British rule. Barbados was a prosperous island. Coffee, tobacco, cotton, and other crops were grown for export, and cassava and corn were raised for local needs. In the late 1600s sugar became the major crop, and large numbers of African slaves were brought to work on sugar plantations.

The abolition of slavery in 1834 had little effect on the island's economic, social, or political life. Prosperity continued until the late 1800s, when home-grown sugar beets began to meet Europe's sugar needs and the world price of sugar dropped.

The economy revived in the early 1900s as a result of British financial aid, improvements in sugar production, and the beginnings of the export of labor. Many Barbadians went to Central America to work on the construction of the Panama Canal.

Federation. Political progress was rapid after World War II, and universal suffrage was introduced in 1951. Political parties formed during the post-war years; elections held in 1951 were won by the Barbados Labour Party (BLP), led by Grantley Adams, who became the colony's first prime minister in 1954.

In 1958 Barbados joined the short-lived Federation of the West Indies, which united ten of Britain's West Indian and Caribbean territories; Adams was the federation's prime minister. Adams's BLP lost the 1961 elections in Barbados. The victor was the Democratic Labour Party (DLP), led by Errol Barrow, which had been formed in 1955 by dissident BLP members.

Independence. The Federation of the West Indies began to break up in 1962, when Jamaica and Trinidad withdrew to become independent nations. In 1965 Barbados decided to seek independence from Great Britain and achieved it on November 30, 1966.

Prime Minister Barrow moved quickly to bring the new country into the United Nations and the Commonwealth of Nations. In 1967 Barbados became a member of the Organization of American States (OAS). Later, it led in developing Caribbean economic and cultural organizations.

In 1976 the BLP returned to power, led by John Adams and later by Bernard St. John. In 1986 the DLP won 24 of the 27 seats in the House of Assembly, and Barrow was returned to the post of prime minister. The DLP retained power until 1994, when the BLP again won a legislative majority. Its candidate and party chairman, Owen Seymour Arthur, has served since 1994 as prime minister.

Cuba

Official name: *Republic of Cuba*
Area: *42,792 sq. mi.,*
110,860 sq. km.
Type of government: *Communist*
Population: *11,224,000*
Capital and largest city: *Havana*
(Pop., 2,192,000)
Language: *Spanish*
Literacy: *96%;* **Currency:** *Peso*
Per capita GDP: *$2,300*
(Rank: 130th)

The land. Cuba, the largest island in the Greater Antilles, occupies a strategic position dominating the sea lanes that link the Atlantic Ocean, the Caribbean Sea, and the Gulf of Mexico. The island lies about 100 miles (160 kilometers) southeast of the United States, from which it is separated by the Straits of Florida.

Made up largely of level or rolling land, Cuba has only three small mountain areas. The Sierra Maestra and associated highlands lie in the extreme southeast and reach a maximum elevation of about 6,500 feet (1,980 meters).

The heavily eroded, limestone Sierra de los Organos, with a maximum elevation of some 2,500 feet (762 meters), is in the dry and barren northwest. The Trinidad Mountains, rising less than 4,000 feet (1,219 meters), are in the center of the island, east of Cienfuegos.

The island has two seasons, a rainy season from May to October and a dry season from November to April. The climate is subtropical and the temperature varies little owing to the moderating influence of the Caribbean. Annual rainfall is about 54 inches (137 centimeters). Hurricanes frequently occur from August through October.

FIDEL CASTRO instituted a dictatorship in Cuba in 1959, with himself as prime minister and first secretary of the Communist Party of Cuba.

The people. The people of Cuba are largely of Spanish, African, and mixed origins. More than half the population live in urban areas. The major cities include Havana, the capital; Santiago de Cuba (population, 440,000), a major port; Camaguey (304,000), a center of the sugar industry; Holguin (256,000); Guantánamo (207,000); and Santa Clara (210,000).

The rate of population increase is high, but it has dropped since 1970 owing largely to a decrease in the birthrate. In addition, there has been heavy emigration since the early 1960s, when the Castro government launched a Communist program. Many of the émigrés settled in the United States, and especially in Miami, opposite Cuba. They included large numbers of professional people, managerial personnel, and technicians.

Economy. Cuba is a rich country and it is among the most economically developed nations of Latin America. The island has fertile soil and considerable mineral wealth. There are abundant deposits of iron ore, chromite, manganese, nickel, cobalt, and copper ore. There is also petroleum, although not enough to meet the country's needs. There is a good transportation system, with an excellent road and rail network and a number of well-equipped ports.

Cuba has long been one of the world's leading producers of sugar; it is also known for its tobacco, which is grown in the region east of the Sierra de los Organos. Coffee is produced in the southeastern region. Other important crops include sweet potatoes, citrus fruits, vegetables, and pineapple. About 30 percent

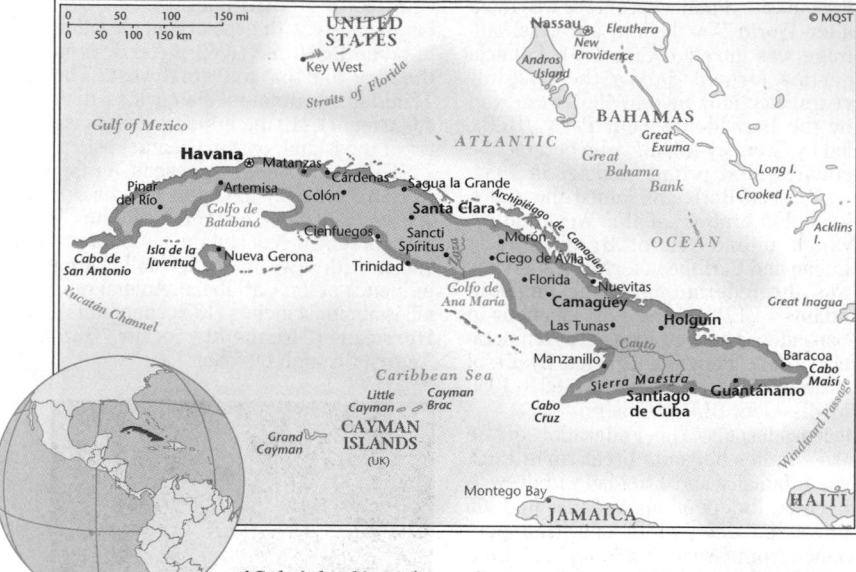

of Cuba's land is under cultivation. Agricultural products account for up to 80 percent of Cuba's export earnings.

Manufacturing has grown rapidly, and it now accounts for over 40 percent of the gross national product. It occupies about 20 percent of the labor force. Sugar processing is the most important activity, but Cuba is also on a par with several European countries in the production of several manufactured goods—synthetic fibers, for example. Steel and power consumption are also high. But industry has been hampered by a shortage of technicians and parts since the Castro revolution.

Sugar represents about 75 percent of export earnings. Ores, especially nickel, as well as fish, tobacco, and chemicals, are also significant exports. Imports consist largely of machinery and transportation equipment, foodstuffs, and manufactured goods.

Beginning in the early 1960s, the Soviet Union and Eastern Europe became Cuba's main trading partners, but the collapse of communism in those countries in the late 1980s has caused enormous economic problems for Cuba. China and other Communist or former Communist countries are major trading partners, and Cuba is making progress on new economic agreements with Russia, its leading creditor.

Government. Cuba traditionally has been a republic with democratic institutions. But the country has experienced long periods of dictatorship. The constitution of 1940, which was suspended in 1959, provided for an elected president and a legislature of two houses. The upper house included 54 members and the lower house had 140 members.

Castro instituted a dictatorship under his personal control. The head of state was still nominally the president, but power rested in Castro's hands as prime minister and first secretary of the Communist Party of Cuba, or PCC.

The United Party of the Cuban Socialist Revolution (PURSC), formed in 1962 by the merger of Cuba's old Communist Party with Castro's Integrated Revolutionary Organizations (ORI), was renamed the Communist Party of Cuba in 1965. Castro's followers remained the dominant group. In 1967 Castro promised that Cuba would have a new, "socialist," constitution by 1970. It was finally granted by 1976.

According to the new constitution, there is now a unicameral National Assembly of People's Power. Its 609 deputies are directly elected to 5-year terms. The real power remains, however, with Castro, who as prime minister, commander in chief of the armed forces, and head of the Cuban Communist Party, is the virtual dictator of Cuba.

History. When Christopher Columbus claimed the island of Cuba for Spain in 1492, on his first voyage to the New World, the island was inhabited by Arawak Indians. The Arawak had been weakened by raids by the warlike Carib Indians, and they were soon enslaved by the Spanish.

Spanish rule. Under the leadership of Governor Diego Velázquez, Cuba became an important base for Spanish exploration and conquest of the American mainland. By 1515 Velázquez had founded seven towns, including Havana and Santiago de Cuba. Soon slaves were brought from Africa to replace the fast-disappearing Arawak as a source of labor. The island developed a thriving sugar and tobacco trade. It was the object of pirate raids during the 1500s and 1600s. During a war with Spain in the 1700s, the British briefly gained control of Havana.

Cuba remained aloof from the general struggle for independence from Spanish rule that occupied the mainland during the early 1800s. Although in 1812 a slave revolt was led by José Aponte, Spanish rule remained secure, based on capable administrators, loyal troops, and an aristocracy that feared the loss of its wealth should relations with Spain be changed. In 1844 another slave revolt was ruthlessly suppressed. Resentment against Spain developed by the mid-1800s, as Spanish rule became increasingly corrupt.

The first serious attempt to organize an independence movement was begun in 1848 by Narcisco López, a veteran of the mainland independence struggles. López was captured and executed in 1851, after making three unsuccessful attempts to liberate the island, but his death served to strengthen Cuban nationalism. The United States offered to purchase Cuba from Spain several times, but in each instance was quickly rebuffed.

In 1868 a group of Cuban patriots, including Carlos Manuel de Céspedes, drew up the *Grito de Yara,* or "Cry of Yara," a call for independence. The new movement fought a bitter ten-year struggle, the Ten Years' War (1868–1878), which ended in a truce. Although they had failed to secure independence, the Cubans won several important concessions from the Spanish government, including a promise to abolish slavery. Slavery was, in fact, ended in 1886, but autocratic and corrupt rule continued unabated.

Resentment against Spanish rule intensified in the early 1890s, when the island was struck by an economic

labor
US

labour
Brit.

fibers
US

fibres
Brit.

CUBA HAS LONG BEEN known as one of the world's leading producers of sugar, which represents about 75 percent of the island's export earnings.

depression and North American tariff restrictions were raised against Cuban tobacco and sugar exports. In 1895 a new rebellion broke out, sparked by the poet and journalist José Martí, Cuba's national hero.

The rebel forces were led by Máximo Gómez, Antonio Maceo, and Calixto García. The Spanish colonial troops were commanded by General Valeriano Weyler. Within a short time, Weyler had the rebellion under control. He launched a bitter campaign of repression, during which many thousands of Cubans died of mistreatment.

U.S. rule. The Spanish repression kindled demands in the United States for support of the Cubans, and in 1898 war broke out between the United States and Spain after the U.S. battleship *Maine* was blown up in Havana harbor. The Spanish-American War lasted but 100 days. Spain gave up Cuba, but instead of granting Cuba independence immediately, U.S. forces remained on the island and a military government was established pending the formation of a civilian government under United States trusteeship.

During the U.S. occupation, Cuba benefited from improved sanitary conditions and extended public education. Yellow fever was wiped out through the efforts of a Cuban doctor, Carlos Finlay, who had proposed that the disease is carried by a mosquito, and U.S. Army personnel supervised by Major Walter Reed. But Cuban resentment grew as the United States continued for years to refuse to withdraw its troops.

The United States set as a condition for withdrawal the inclusion in the Cuban constitution of the Platt Amendment. The amendment provided the United States with naval bases in Cuba, including a naval base which is still an American presence at Guantanamo Bay, on the eastern tip of the island, and allowed the United States to intervene if it felt Cuban sovereignty to be threatened.

Independence. The Cuban constitution was promulgated in 1901, and in 1902 a conservative, Tomás Estrada Palma, became Cuba's first president. Liberal opposition and popular unrest led to the resignation of Estrada Palma in 1906, and U.S. forces were again landed in Cuba.

In 1909 José Gómez, a liberal, was elected president. Instability continued, and in 1917 U.S. troops again returned. In 1925 General Gerardo Machado won the presidency and changed the constitution to keep himself in power. Machado instituted an era of tyranny that lasted until 1933, when he was toppled by a general strike. His successor, Dr. Carlos Manuel de Céspedes, was in turn toppled by an army revolt led by Sergeant Fulgencio Batista. Although a series of presidents were sworn into office in the years that followed, Batista really controlled the Cuban government with military support.

In 1940 Batista supported the drafting of a new, democratic constitution, and in the ensuing election won the presidency.

MANY REFUGEES HAVE FLED CUBA during Castro's dictatorship. In 1980, when he allowed a massive emigration, an estimated 125,000 people left Cuba, most of them going to the United States.

He continued in control of Cuba until 1944, when Dr. Ramón Grau San Martín, once an associate of Batista, but by then a bitter political foe, was elected president. Grau San Martín was succeeded in 1948 by Carlos Prío Socarrás. In 1952 Batista again seized power and gradually instituted a repressive regime that became increasingly unpopular.

Castro revolution. In 1953 a young law school student, Fidel Castro, and his brother, Raúl, led a revolt against Batista. On July 26 the rebels unsuccessfully tried to seize the Moncado army base in Santiago. Captured, but later pardoned in a general amnesty, the Castros went into exile.

In 1956 Castro returned with a small band of followers that included an Argentinian, Ernesto "Che" Guevara. They succeeded in reaching the rugged range of the Sierra Maestra; gradually their strength grew as students and peasants from Oriente Province joined them. Other anti-Batista organizations joined in the effort to topple the dictator. Large-scale fighting broke out in 1958, and on January 1, 1959, Batista fled the country.

Castro seized the initiative afforded by Batista's departure and took power on a wave of popular support, but his popularity quickly waned at home and abroad. Former associates broke with him over Communist domination in the new government, and in 1960 a socialist program was launched resulting in the nationalization of much of the economy. Hundreds of thousands of Cubans fled, most of them finding refuge in the United States.

U.S. property was among that seized, and the United States retaliated by ordering an embargo on sugar imports from the island. In 1961 Cuba signed a trade agreement with the Soviet Union, and Castro announced his acceptance of Marxist-Leninist doctrine.

U.S. diplomatic relations with Cuba were severed in 1961. In that year the United States sponsored an invasion of Cuba by a force of Cuban exiles. The force landed at the Bay of Pigs, and, in the absence of direct U.S. military support, was soon destroyed. In 1962 Castro exchanged the survivors of the invasion for needed foodstuffs and medical supplies from the United States.

A new crisis in Cuban-U.S. relations occurred in 1962, when U.S. President John F. Kennedy announced that Soviet missiles were being installed in Cuba. A blockade of Cuba was put into force by the United States, and preparations for military action were made. In the face of a potential nuclear war, the Soviet Union agreed to dismantle the missile bases in return for the promise that the United States would not invade Cuba.

Castro attempted to spread his form of revolution throughout Latin America, and Cuban-supported insurrections broke out in many countries. In 1962 the Organization of American States (OAS), under pressure from the United States, suspended Cuba's participation in the work of the organization. Prominent among the Cuban revolutionaries active in promoting Castro-type revolutions in other countries was Che Guevara, who was killed in Bolivia in 1967. Cuba has also played an active role in support of Communist revolutionary groups in Africa, sending troops to Angola in 1976 and to Ethiopia in 1978.

In 1979 the United States learned that Soviet combat troops were based in Cuba, but the Soviets insisted that their mission was strictly advisory.

In 1977 the United States and Cuba agreed to exchange diplomats. In 1980 Castro allowed massive emigration from Cuba in what came to be called the Mariel Boatlift, after the Cuban port from which the refugees left the island. An estimated 125,000 people left Cuba, most of them going to the United States.

The emigrations were instigated in part by the repressive nature of the

TOURISM IS A small but growing sector of Dominica's economy. The tropical climate and sports such as scuba diving are major attractions.

Cuban system and also by the failure of the Castro revolution to bring economic stability to Cuba. A disastrous industrialization program in the 1960s was replaced by an equally disastrous attempt to increase sugar production. Only massive Soviet economic aid enabled Cuba to weather the loss of U.S. markets and trade. The political and economic reforms that swept eastern Europe and the Soviet Union, and the continuing U.S. trade embargo, have devastated Cuba's economy. Although Cuba has increased its income from tourism and has introduced minor free-market reforms, it has failed to make changes necessary to attract foreign investment. To recover from a hurricane's devastation, Cuba in 2002 purchased emergency food supplies from the U.S.

centimeters
US

centimetres
Brit.

labor
US

labour
Brit.

Dominica

Official name: *Commonwealth of Dominica*

Area: *290 sq. mi., 750 sq. km.*

Type of government: *Parliamentary democracy*

Population: *70,000*

Capital and largest city: *Roseau (Pop., 16,000)*

Languages: *English (official), French patois*

Literacy: *94%*

Currency: *East Caribbean dollar*

Per capita GDP: *$3,700 (Rank: 107th)*

The land. Dominica is one of the Windward Islands of the Lesser Antilles, lying between the Caribbean Sea and the

Atlantic Ocean. It lies south of Guadeloupe and north of Martinique.

Dominica has a rugged, densely forested, and mountainous terrain. The climate is hot throughout the year, and rainfall is heavy, particularly in the mountainous interior, where the annual precipitation can reach 200 inches (508 centimeters).

The people. Dominica's population is of mixed African, European, and Carib Indian descent. Most of the population is of African descent, 2 percent is European, and a small minority is Carib. English is the official language of Dominica, but French patois is also commonly spoken.

Economy. Agricultural activity employs about 37 percent of the labor force and fuels the economy. Banana production, accounting for almost two-thirds of Dominica's total export earnings, dominates the economy.

In addition to bananas, limes and other citrus fruits, cacao, vanilla, and coconuts are the chief crops. Industry and commerce employ about 21 percent of the labor force. Industry has grown and diversified somewhat in recent years, but most industries are still geared toward the processing of agricultural products. Tourism is a growing but still small sector of the economy.

Exports of bananas, soap, copra, and lime juice are outweighed by imports of foodstuffs, machinery, and other necessities. Most trade is with the United Kingdom, the United States, and other islands of the West Indies. Although Dominica continues to suffer a negative balance of trade, in the late 1980s its exports increased substantially, inflation and unemployment decreased dramatically, and construction and development boomed.

Government. According to its democratic constitution of 1978, Dominica is ruled by a powerful prime minister, although there is also a president. The legislature is the unicameral House of Assembly, which has 21 elected representatives and 9 appointed senators. Elections, by universal adult suffrage, must be held every 5 years, but the prime minister may call elections before that time.

History. The island was inhabited by Carib Indians when it was discovered by Christopher Columbus on November 3, 1493. The Caribs had arrived on the island in the 1300s and had wiped out the indigenous Arawak Indians. The Caribs repulsed all attempts at colonization in the 1500s. Between the 1600s and the 1800s, the island was settled by colonists from several European countries. They developed plantations worked by imported African slaves.

In 1763, by the Treaty of Paris, Dominica became a British possession. It was part of the Leeward Islands colony until 1771, when it became a separate colony. In 1833 it was again attached to the Leeward Islands, and was so governed until 1940, when it became a separate colony administered under the Windward Islands group. In 1967 Dominica gained self-government as a state in association with Great Britain. It soon joined the West Indies Associated States.

In 1978 Dominica attained independence. A devastating hurricane in 1979 was followed by another in 1980. French, British, and U.S. aid has helped restore the economy somewhat.

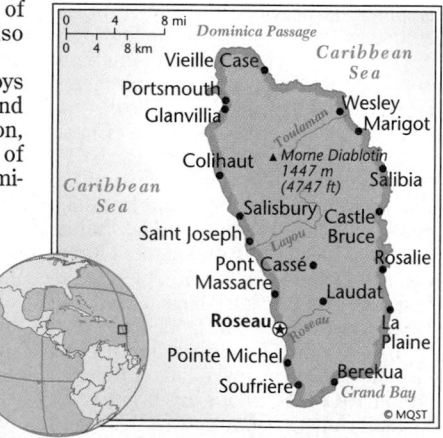

Civil unrest has been chronic since independence. Nationwide strikes were waged in 1979 to protest government suppression of political opposition. This resulted in the resignation of Prime Minister Patrick John. Mary Eugenia Charles and her antisocialistic Dominica Freedom Party won a landslide victory in 1980. The first female prime minister of a Caribbean nation, she retained the post in 1985 and 1990. In 2000 Pierre Charles attained the position. On his death in 2004, Roosevelt Skerritt was appointed to the post.

Dominican Republic

Official name: *Dominican Republic*
Area: *18,810 sq. mi., 48,730 sq. km.*
Type of government: *Republic*
Population: *8,596,000*
Capital and largest city:
    Santo Domingo
    (Pop., 2,677,000)
Language: *Spanish*
Literacy: *83%*
Currency: *Peso*
Per capita GDP: *$5,800*
    (Rank: 80th)

The land. The Dominican Republic occupies the eastern two-thirds of the Caribbean island of Hispaniola. The western third of the island is occupied by Haiti.

The Dominican Republic has four mountain ranges, which lie roughly parallel to each other. The narrow Cordillera Septentrional is the northernmost range. The Cordillera Central, with peaks over 10,000 feet (3,048 meters), is the backbone of the country; it includes Pico Duarte, the highest peak in the Caribbean, with an elevation of 10,206 feet (3,110 meters). To the south are the Sierra de Neiba and the Sierra de Bahoruco.

The Cibao Plain, the largest lowland in the republic, separates the Cordillera Septentrional from the Cordillera Central. In the eastern part of the plain is the humid and rich Vega Real, which is drained by the Río Yuna in the east and by the Río Yaque del Norte in the northwest. Southwest of the Cordillera Central is the San Juan Valley, and south of the Sierra de Neiba lies the Cul de Sac, a semiarid lowland area watered by Lake Enriquillo. A broad Caribbean coastal plain in the south contains Santo Domingo, which was founded in 1496 by Bartholomew Columbus and is the oldest permanent European settlement in the western hemisphere.

The climate of the Dominican Republic is generally subtropical. Extremes in temperature do not often occur, and rain is abundant in most areas. The higher inland regions, however, are cooler, and rainfall is greatest on the slopes facing northeast, toward the trade winds. Annual rainfall averages 60 inches (152 centimeters).

The people. Most Dominicans are mulatto, of mixed European and African origin, but there are white and black minorities. The Vega Real and the Caribbean coastal plain are the most heavily populated regions. About 50 percent of the population is urban. The main urban centers include Santo Domingo, the capital; Santiago (population, 837,000), a trade center; San Pedro de Macoris (146,000), a seaport; and San Francisco de Macoris (267,000), in the country's northern agricultural belt.

Economy. Fertile soil and a favorable climate have made agriculture and stock raising the principal economic activities. Sugar, cacao, coffee, tobacco, and bananas are grown for export. Meat and dairy products are also exported. Farming methods in the dominican Republic are backward, and agricultural production is inefficient. Approximately 21 percent of the labor force works in commerce and industry, 45 percent in agriculture.

There is a great variety of mineral resources, and gold, silver, copper, iron, and bauxite are mined for export. Textiles and lumber are manufactured mainly for domestic use.

The Dominican Republic has an unfavorable balance of trade, with the service payments on its foreign debt significantly higher than the value of its annual exports. The United States is its leading trade partner, followed by Switzerland, The Netherlands, Puerto Rico, and Venezuela. Sugar and sugar products make up about 70 percent of all exports. The major imports are machinery, textiles, and petroleum products.

Government. The head of the government is the president, who is popularly elected to a four-year term and is assisted by a cabinet, whose members are appointed by him or her. Legislative power rests with the 30-member Senate and 149-member Chamber of Deputies. All legislators are popularly elected to 4-year terms.

The Dominican Republic is divided into 29 provinces and the National District of Santo Domingo, each of which sends one senator to the National Congress. The governors of the provinces are appointed by the president. Judicial power rests with the Supreme Court of Justice, whose members are appointed by the Senate.

History. Columbus discovered the island of Hispaniola in 1492 and claimed it for Spain. In 1697 Spain ceded the western third to France, and in 1795 it also surrendered the eastern two-thirds of the island, which had been named Santo Domingo. Spain regained Santo Domingo in 1809 with British and Dominican help.

Independence. In 1821 the middle class rebelled against Spain and proclaimed the country's independence. But in 1822 Haitian forces occupied Santo Domingo, and for 22 years Dominicans suffered under oppressive Haitian rule. In 1844 the Dominicans expelled the Haitians and established the Dominican Republic, with Pedro Santana as president.

During the following years, a power struggle between Santana and Buenaventura Báez and the continued fear of Haitian aggression threatened the republic. To protect the state and maintain himself in office, Santana, in 1861, proclaimed the reannexation of the Dominican Republic to Spain, with himself as governor-general. Spanish forces occupied the country, but a popular uprising, called the War of Restoration, forced the withdrawal of Spanish troops in 1865.

Under Báez's intermittent rule, from 1865 until 1878, the country continued to be poor and backward and accumulated large foreign debts. In 1869 Báez negotiated a treaty of annexation with the United States. Although the measure was supported by President Grant, it was rejected by the Senate.

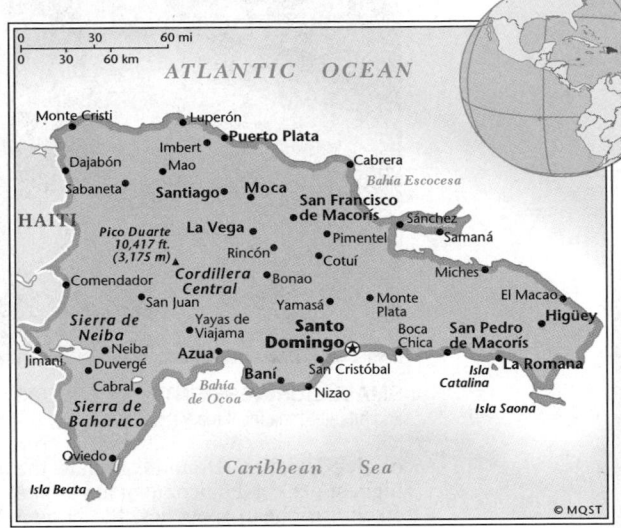

In 1882 Ulises Heureaux gained the presidency and ruled until he was assassinated in 1899. Although he increased foreign debt, he maintained internal peace, launched public works, and developed industry.

U.S. role. With the death of Heureaux, violence and disorder erupted. In 1905 President Roosevelt, fearing aggression by foreign nations demanding repayment of loans, agreed to place Dominican customs duties under control of U.S. collectors, who would use the revenues to pay the foreign debts. In addition, U.S. loans reassured both foreign creditors and Dominicans.

Political instability continued, however, and in 1911 President Ramón Cáceres was assassinated and a military government installed. Peace was temporarily restored, in 1912 by a U.S. mission and in 1914 by U.S. supervision of elections.

Further difficulties in 1916 led President Woodrow Wilson to send troops to establish a U.S. military government in the Dominican Republic. Although material improvements were made during the occupation, Dominicans resented foreign rule. The occupation forces were withdrawn in 1924, but U.S. control of Dominican customs continued until the 1940s.

Trujillo regime. Horacio Vásquez was elected president of the republic in 1924. Vásquez secured a constitutional amendment extending his term to 1930, but when he attempted to remain in power indefinitely, his government was overthrown in 1930 by Rafael Leonidas Trujillo Molina. Trujillo ruled the country, directly or indirectly, with an iron hand, until he was assassinated in 1961.

Trujillo achieved political stability and economic progress at the expense

27 North America

centers
US

centres
Brit.

SMALL-BUSINESS ENTREPRENEURS abound, and almost any item produced in the Dominican Republic can be found in the colorful hustle and bustle of the local markets.

emphasized *US*	
emphasised *Brit.*	
centimeters *US*	
centimetres *Brit.*	
center *US*	
centre *Brit.*	
labor *US*	
labour *Brit.*	

of civil liberties. Dominicans had the highest per capita income of any of the small Caribbean republics, the budget was balanced, and foreign debts were paid. Expansion of industry and public works broadened the economy and raised the standard of living.

Nonetheless, opposition was not tolerated and Trujillo, supported by the army, ruled by terror. In 1960 the Trujillo regime was censured by the Organization of American States (OAS) for trying unsuccessfully to assassinate President Romulo Bétancourt of Venezuela.

Trujillo was assassinated on May 26, 1961. The army and the bureaucracy, both controlled by the Trujillo family and their supporters, attempted to restore the Trujillo family to power. But they were forced out when the United States threatened to intervene.

Search for stability. A provisional council of state governed until 1962, when elections were held. Juan Bosch, a popular intellectual and a member of the Dominican Revolutionary Party (DRP), became president.

Seven months later the military deposed Bosch and established an army-backed civilian triumvirate, headed by Donald Reid Cabral, which initiated economic reforms. On April 24, 1965, however, civil war broke out between government forces led by General Elías Wessin y Wessin and Bosch supporters under Colonel Francisco Caamaño Deñó.

U.S. President Lyndon B. Johnson, fearing Communist infiltration of the pro-Bosch faction, sent troops to the Dominican Republic. After bitter fighting, a military occupation of U.S. and OAS forces was established. Despite the condemnation by some Latin American countries for this violation of the nonintervention provisions of the OAS charter, an OAS-sponsored provisional government headed by Héctor García-Godoy was formed.

Elections were held in June 1966, and Joaquín Balaguer Ricardo, a former puppet president under Trujillo, defeated former president Bosch. The U.S. and OAS forces were withdrawn by September, and the country set about restoring its economy and developing democratic processes. Balaguer, reelected in 1970 and again in 1974, succeeded in establishing a period of relative peace and stability for the republic.

The economy improved as the world price for sugar rose, and foreign investment returned. However, a serious drop in sugar prices caused renewed economic problems.

Antonio Guzmán Fernández, a moderate, defeated Balaguer in the 1978 elections. Guzmán concentrated on agricultural development and the improvement of human rights. Despite these efforts, the economy received a severe blow in 1979 when Hurricane David devastated the nation. U.S. aid was given during the crisis.

In 1982 Guzmán declined to run for a second term, and was succeeded by a member of his own party, Jorge Blanco. Blanco instituted several economic recovery programs, including an austerity program that led to rioting in 1984 and 1985.

In 1986 Balaguer was again elected; he emphasized the need for economic diversification. Balaguer faced continuing economic problems, including a steep rise in inflation in 1988 and a dispute with the mining company Falconbridge Dominicana over a special duty on its nickel exports. Despite these and other setbacks, the economy improved owing to increased tourism and larger exports of sugar and nickel. Balaguer remained in office until 1996. The late 1990s saw privatization of some industry. In 2000, Hipólito Mejía the DRP candidate, was elected president. He is known for promoting rural agricultural development and technification.

Grenada

Official name: *Grenada*
Area: *131 sq. mi., 340 sq. km.*
Type of government:
    Parliamentary democracy
Population: *89,000*
Capital and largest city:
    St. George's (Pop., 4,600)
Languages: *English (official),*
    French patois
Literacy: *98%*
Currency: *East Caribbean dollar*
Per capita GDP: *$4,750*
    (Rank: 88th)

The land. The island nation of Grenada consists of Grenada Island, the southernmost of the Windward Islands, and the islands and islets of the southern Grenadines, including Carriacou Island and Petit Martinique. Volcanic in origin, the islands have few rivers and a mountainous terrain. The climate is hot throughout the year and rainfall is heavy. Annual precipitation on Grenada Island varies from about 60 inches (153 centimeters) along the coast to 150

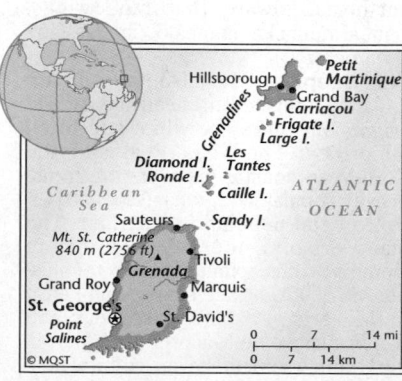

inches (381 centimeters) or more in the mountainous interior.

The people. The great majority of Grenada's population live on Grenada Island, and about 30 percent live in and around the capital.

Economy. Grenada's economy is based on agriculture. Cacao, nutmeg, mace, and bananas are the chief crops. Agriculture employs about one-third of the Grenadian work force and accounts for about 90 percent of domestic exports. Processing agricultural products constitutes the main industry. There is ongoing exploration for offshore oil and gas.

In recent years tourism has become significant. Point Salines International Airport, opened in 1984, and improved ports, roads, hotels, and other construction, have all contributed to the growing tourist industry. It now rivals agriculture as the country's economic mainstay.

Grenada's farming is done mostly at a subsistence level, and production is insufficient to meet domestic demand. Grenada must therefore import considerable amounts of food and various consumer goods. Its exports go mainly to Great Britain, Germany, and the countries of the Caribbean. Imports of food, fuel, machinery, and manufactured goods come mainly from Caribbean countries, the United States, and Great Britain.

Government. Grenada has a parliamentary system of government based on the British model. The British monarch, represented by a governor-general, is the head of state. The prime minister is the most powerful executive figure. There is a 15-seat elected House of Representatives and a 13-seat appointed Senate.

History. The island was inhabited by Carib Indians when discovered by Columbus in 1498. Colonists from several European countries, beginning with the French in 1650, settled in Grenada in the 1600s and 1700s. They wiped out the indigenous population and established plantations worked by slaves brought from Africa. The British captured Grenada from the French in 1762, and it was formally ceded a year later. The French recaptured it in 1779 but relinquished it to Great Britain in 1783. Grenada was governed as a unit with the other Windward Island colonies until 1967, when it gained self-government as a state in association with Great Britain.

Following independence on February 7, 1974, Grenada became the scene of political turmoil. Prime Minister Eric Gairy, accused of abusing his power in dictatorial fashion, responded by establishing a reactionary regime backed by a secret police unit. Nonetheless, he was reelected in 1976.

On March 13, 1979, Maurice Bishop, head of an organization called the New Jewel Movement, led a military overthrow of the government, which he replaced with the radical socialist People's Revolutionary Government. He sought close ties with Cuba and the Soviet bloc.

In October 1983 Bishop was overthrown in a coup led by Vice Minister Bernard Coard. Bishop and a number of other Grenadians were subsequently executed, and the political situation deteriorated. The new regime had been in place for about a week when a force made up of troops from other Caribbean nations and the United States invaded Grenada with the announced intention of protecting Americans and other non-Grenadians and restoring peace, security, and stable government to Grenada. Following elections in 1984, Herbert Blaize became prime minister. Dr. Keith Mitchell, a former math professor at Howard University, became prime minister in 1995 and was reelected in 1999.

Haiti

Official name: *Republic of Haiti*
Area: *10,712 sq. mi.,*
27,750 sq. km.
Type of government: *Republic*
Population: *7,405,000*
Capital and largest city:
Port-au-Prince
(Pop., 991,000)
Languages: *French (official),*
Creole (majority)
Literacy: *45%;* **Currency:** *Gourde*
Per capita GDP: *$1,700*
(Rank: 144th)

The land. The Republic of Haiti occupies the western third of the island of Hispaniola in the Greater Antilles. The Dominican Republic occupies the eastern two-thirds of the island.

Haiti is a mountainous country. The principal ranges are the Massif du Nord in the north; the Montagnes Noires in the center; the Montagnes du Trou d'Eau, the Chaine des Matheux, and the Massif de la Selle in the southeast; and the Massif de la Hotte in the south.

Between the mountains is a system of plains and valleys. Among the most important are the Cul-de-Sac in the south, where Port-au-Prince is situated; the Plaine du Nord which is in the northeast; the Plaine de l'Artibonite in the center; and the Plaine Centrale in the east. Haiti's most important river is the Artibonite.

Haiti has a tropical climate, but temperatures are modified by altitude, rainfall, and sea winds. Annual precipitation ranges from about 20 inches (51 centimeters) to more than 100 inches (254 centimeters).

The people. Haiti's people are mainly of African origin, and only a small percentage are mulatto, of mixed African and European background. The mulattoes dominated the political, economic, and social life of Haiti for many years, however.

Most of the population lives in the mountain valleys, but transportation facilities through the mountains are poor and the cities lie along the coasts. Major urban centers include Port-au-Prince, the capital; Les Cayes, on the southern coast of Haiti's long southern peninsula; Cap-Haïtien, on the northern coast; and Gonaïves, on Haiti's western coast.

Three-quarters of the nation's people live in rural areas. Haiti is one of the most densely populated countries of Latin America. There is heavy emigration into both the Bahamas and the Dominican Republic.

Most of Haiti's black population is illiterate, while the mulattoes are relatively well educated. Roman Catholicism is the chief religion, but it is commonly blended with primitive voodoo practices.

Economy. Agriculture, the mainstay of the economy, accounts for about 40 percent of Haiti's export earnings and is the largest sector of the Haitian economy. Agriculture employs about three-fourths of the labor force. The importance of tourism has risen significantly in the last two decades, and it now represents a significant sector of the Haitian economy. Haiti's only significant mineral resource is bauxite, and the only bauxite mining operation closed down in the 1980s. Industry, which accounts for about 16 percent of Haiti's gross national product, includes a number of light manufacturing and assembly plants located mostly around Port-au-Prince.

Most farmers work at subsistence levels on very small plots of land in the mountain valleys. The leading cash crops are coffee, cacao, essential oils, mangoes, and sugar cane. Sisal and castor beans are also important export crops. Cotton, bananas, tobacco, fruits, and rice are grown as well.

Manufacturing industries produce cotton textiles, soap, pharmaceuticals, sisal rope, plastics, furniture, building materials, foodstuffs, and molasses and rum.

Haiti's major exports are coffee, light manufactured goods, cocoa, mangoes, essential oils, and sugar. Imports include machinery, vehicles, petroleum products, and manufactured goods. The United States is Haiti's chief trading partner.

A major barrier to economic development is the increasing pressure of people on the

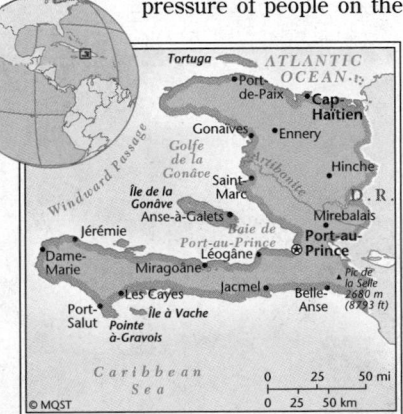

land. Only about one-third of the country's land can be cultivated, and it is estimated that there are some 1,500 persons per square mile in the agricultural areas. Although the government has instituted programs to encourage industrial development and increase food production, Haiti's poor infrastructure, large foreign debt, and continuing political turmoil have severely curtailed the country's development. Haiti remains one of the world's poorest and most underdeveloped nations.

Government. In 1987 a new constitution instituted a democratic form of government in Haiti. A system of checks and balances was introduced and local and national elections were organized. However, military governments effectively ruled Haiti from early 1986 until March 1990, when an interim advisory Council of State was installed.

Under the 1987 constitution, executive power is vested in a popularly elected president and his or her cabinet of ministers. The directly elected bicameral legislature consists of an 83-member Chamber of Deputies and a 27-member Senate. Judicial power is vested in a Supreme Court.

Haiti is divided into nine departments, whose prefects are appointed by the central government.

History. Christopher Columbus discovered the island of Hispaniola in 1492 during his first voyage to the New World. The Arawak Indian inhabitants called the island Haiti, "land of mountains," but Columbus named it Española. It later was known as Hispaniola.

Columbus described the Arawak in a letter to the Spanish monarchs as "timid, full of fear, and lovable." Nonetheless, the Indians were soon subjected to severe exploitation by Spanish colonists, and by the end of the

IN HAITI, as in most countries in which Catholicism is the main religion, the carnival festivals before Lent are popular occasions.

1500s the Arawak had been almost completely exterminated.

Although Spain claimed the entire island, the Spanish settlements were concentrated in the east, and French and English pirates were able to establish themselves on the island of Tortuga, off the island's northwestern coast, and on the western third of the island. The French eventually drove out the English, and French settlers soon began colonizing the western portion of Hispaniola. In 1697 Spain ceded the western end of the island to France, which called it St. Dominique.

French rule. The French established sugar and tobacco plantations, importing slaves to work the land. They gradually built a flourishing colony in which many mulattoes prospered

and became slaveholders themselves. But social class rivalry was intense, and the slaves were kept in atrocious conditions.

In 1791, sparked by the French Revolution in Europe, civil war broke out in Haiti. Toussaint L'Ouverture, a former slave, led a victorious revolt. In 1795 Toussaint joined French forces against invading British forces and became a general. By 1801 he had subdued all external forces on Hispaniola and established an autonomous government with himself as president for life. However, in 1802 he was captured and sent to prison in France, where he died.

Independence. Jean Jacques Dessalines, another former slave, assumed leadership of the struggle and ultimately led a black army to victory. Independence was declared on January 1, 1804, and Dessalines proclaimed himself governor-general of the island, which was renamed Haiti, for life. He was later crowned Emperor Jacques I. His despotic rule over a war-ravaged country ended with his murder in 1806.

Two states emerged in Haiti following Dessalines' death, and there began a struggle for power between Henri Christophe in the north and Alexandre Pétion in the south. Christophe ruled as a benevolent despot from 1811 to 1820, and the north made considerable economic progress. Pétion's rule in the south had disastrous results.

North and south were reunited in 1820 under the rule of Jean Pierre Boyer, who had succeeded Pétion in the south in 1818 and then extended his rule to the north when Christophe committed suicide. Boyer ruled ineffectively until 1843, when he was exiled. In 1844 the Spanish-speaking inhabitants of Santo Domingo broke away and established the Dominican Republic.

U.S. intervention. The next 70 years were a time of almost constant misrule, misery, and revolution. Dictators rapidly succeeded each other, and Haiti fell into

PUBLIC TRANSPORT is very public and, though reasonably convenient, probably is not very comfortable, in the much utilized bus system of Haiti.

a state of chaos. By 1915 Haiti's political situation had approached a state of anarchy, and its international financial obligations had opened up the possibility of French or German intervention. In July 1915, under the direction of President Woodrow Wilson, U.S. marines landed in Haiti.

Although considerable progress in stabilizing Haitian political and financial affairs was made during the occupation, Haitians expressed continued resentment of the often harsh foreign interference. A U.S. commission met with leading Haitian citizens to discuss withdrawal of U.S. troops; by 1934 withdrawal of the marines was completed.

Contemporary Haiti. Following the end of the U.S. occupation, several mulatto leaders ruled Haiti. In 1946 the blacks revolted and a military junta took power, ordered new elections, and oversaw the election of a new legislature. The new government elected Dumarsais Estimé the first black president of Haiti since 1915.

The government changed hands often during the next several years, and disorder and misery increased. Then, in 1957, François Duvalier, a physician, was elected president.

"Papa Doc," as Duvalier became known, established an oppressive dictatorship. Duvalier's rule rested in large part on his secret police, popularly called the *Tontons Macoutes* (Haitian Creole for "bogeymen").

Duvalier died in 1971. He had designated his son, Jean-Claude "Baby Doc," to succeed him as president.

After assuming the presidency, Jean-Claude Duvalier increasingly showed himself to be a harsh ruler. Like his father, Duvalier maintained control with the Tontons Macoutes.

Though the national economy improved marginally, Haiti remained the poorest country in the western hemisphere. Large numbers of impoverished Haitians fled the country, many going to the United States.

In early 1986, in the face of rising demonstrations and riots, Duvalier fled the country, leaving power to a five-man military junta led by Lieutenant General Henri Namphy. In 1987 a new constitution was approved. It ensured a change to a democratic form of government. In June 1988, six months after Leslie F. Manigat was elected president, Namphy ousted Manigat and declared himself president.

In September 1988 Lieutenant General Prosper Avril was declared president after a coup overthrew Namphy. In March 1990 a provisional council of state, headed by Ertha Pascal-Trouillot, was established. In December 1990 Jean-Bertrand Aristide, a Roman Catholic priest and political outsider, was elected president. He was overthrown by a military coup in 1991, prompting an international trade embargo that crippled Haiti's economy and led thousands to flee by boat to the United States. A 1993 agreement providing for the restoration of Aristide collapsed and

sanctions were reimposed. In 1994, under the threat of a U.S. invasion, the military leadership resigned and Aristide was returned to power. He was reelected in 2000, although many groups protested the legitimacy of the election.

Haiti's government remains in continual jeopardy from attempted coups, due to its ineffectuality and the country's poor economy. UN peacekeepers retain a presence in the country.

Jamaica

Official name: *Jamaica*
Area: *4,242 sq. mi., 10,990 sq. km.*
Type of government:
 Parliamentary democracy
Population: *2,680,000*
Capital and largest city: *Kingston*
 (Pop., metro. area, 578,000)
Languages: *English (official),*
 Creole
Literacy: *85%;* **Currency:** *Dollar*
Per capita GDP: *$3,700*
 (Rank: 104th)

The land. Jamaica is a mountainous island. A central mountain axis runs from west to east, reaching elevations above 7,000 feet (2,134 meters) in the Blue Mountains in the east. There is a narrow coastal plain in the north and a wider coastal plain in the south, where Kingston, the capital and chief port, is located.

The climate varies with elevation. Temperatures throughout the year average in the low 80s F (20s C) in the plains, but it is much cooler in the mountain areas. The mountains also affect the distribution of rain. The slopes facing northeast receive the heaviest rainfall, about 200 inches (508 centimeters) a year. The southern coast is blocked off from rain-bearing winds and receives little rain. The average annual precipitation is 77 inches (196 centimeters).

The people. Most Jamaicans are of African or mixed African and European descent. There are also people of Chinese, East Indian, European, and Near Eastern origins.

Jamaica is a densely populated island. In the cultivable

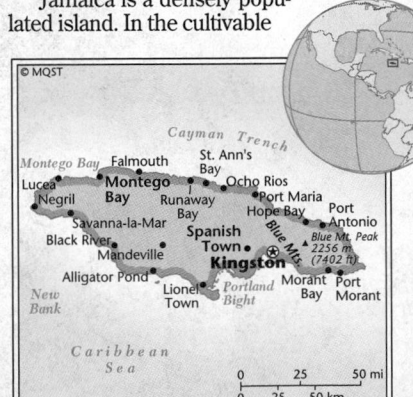

areas, there is an average of more than 2,000 people per square mile. Many Jamaicans have migrated to other countries, particularly to the United States and Great Britain, in search of work.

Immigration restrictions, however, have reduced the possibilities for employment abroad. Thus, the country constantly must find more jobs for its growing population.

More than half of the population live in rural areas. The main urban centers are Kingston, the capital; Spanish Town (population, 131,000); and Montego Bay (82,000).

Economy. Agriculture, mining, and tourism are the mainstays of the Jamaican economy, and they form the basis for the island's developing industry. The country has rich soils and produces valuable tropical crops. Jamaica is one of the world's major sources of bauxite, from which aluminum is made. The island earns a great deal of money from tourism, drawing more than a million visitors a year, mostly from the United States. Resorts such as Montego Bay, on the northwest coast, are popular.

The most valuable export crops are sugar cane and bananas, but sweet potatoes, rice, and corn also are important food crops. Other crops include coffee, citrus fruits, cacao, ginger, pimento, cassava, and tobacco.

Jamaica's mineral resources include gypsum, but bauxite is the most valuable product of the island.

Industry and construction have grown rapidly since the mid-1970s. They now contribute about one-quarter of the gross national product, compared with about 10 percent each contributed by the important mining and agricultural industries.

Industry is based on processing agricultural and mineral products. Sugar and sugar products, alumina (enriched bauxite ore), and cement are all produced as well, and oil refining is also an important activity.

The major exports are bauxite and alumina, which account for about half of all export earnings, and foodstuffs, especially sugar and sugar products—rum and molasses. Jamaica trades mainly with the United States, Great Britain, and Canada.

Government. Jamaica has a parliamentary system of government patterned on that of Great Britain. The head of state is the British monarch, who is represented by a governor-general. Executive powers are wielded by a prime minister and cabinet responsible to the Parliament. The prime minister is normally the leader of the majority party in the Parliament.

The Parliament has two houses, a 21-member Senate and a 60-member House of Representatives. Senators are appointed by the governor-general—13 on the advice of the prime minister and 8 on the advice of the leader of the opposition party. House members are popularly elected to a term of 5 years. Judicial power is vested in the Supreme Court.

27 North America

meters
US

metres
Brit.

centers
US

centres
Brit.

aluminum
US

aluminium
Brit.

MOURNERS PARTICIPATE in a Nine Nights Celebration after a death in Jamaica.

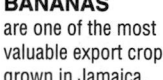

labor
US

labour
Brit.

center
US

centre
Brit.

meters
US

metres
Brit.

BANANAS
are one of the most valuable export crops grown in Jamaica.

Jamaica is administratively divided into 14 parishes, governed by elected parish councils with limited powers.

History. It was Christopher Columbus who claimed Jamaica for Spain in 1494, during his second voyage to the New World. The island, called Xaymaca by its Arawak Indian inhabitants, became a Spanish colony in 1509. Under Spanish rule, the Arawak were exterminated and slaves were brought from Africa to provide labor for the colony in their place.

Great Britain captured Jamaica in 1655. During the British conquest, many of the slaves fled to the mountains, where they developed a distinct culture. Known as Maroons, they successfully fought off the British for more than a hundred years. Jamaica had become a haven for pirates, but piracy was suppressed after

1670, when British control was officially recognized in the Treaty of Madrid.

British rule. Jamaica became a prosperous colony as the major slave market of the western hemisphere and as a producer of tropical produce, especially sugar and coffee. The center of the slave trade, and of all other commercial activity, was Port Royal, the base of Henry Morgan and other Caribbean buccaneers. In 1692 Port Royal was destroyed by a severe earthquake, prompting construction of Kingston nearby.

The slave trade was abolished in 1807, and slavery itself was ended in 1838, after a serious revolt. Before the island could recover from the loss of slave labor, Britain, in 1846, removed its protective colonial tariff and the plantation economy was ruined.

Economic hardship and misgovernment combined in 1865 to provoke a black uprising at Morant Bay. The rebellion quickly spread throughout the island and was suppressed only after a bitter struggle marked by violent excesses on both sides.

In 1866 Jamaica was made a Crown colony and Sir John Peter Grant was sent from Britain as governor. He initiated political, economic, and social reforms and promoted the cultivation of bananas, which soon became an important export. The colonial administration lasted into the 1900s.

Self-government. World War II led to an economic depression. The conflict cut Jamaica's trade and almost eliminated tourism. But political progress was rapid. In 1944 the island received virtual self-rule, and in 1945 universal suffrage was introduced.

Jamaican politics had come to be dominated by two figures—Alexander Bustamante, leader of the Jamaica Labour Party (JLP), and Norman Manley, leader of the People's National Party (PNP). Both parties rested on trade union support. Bustamante won elections held in 1945 and in 1949, but Manley was victorious in 1955.

In 1958 Manley brought Jamaica into the Federation of the West Indies, which united several British Caribbean and West Indian territories. Jamaicans voted in 1961 to withdraw from the federation, and in 1962 general elections were held.

Independence. Bustamante returned to power in April, and on August 6, 1962, he led the island to independence. The Labour Party remained in power under Bustamante (1962–1967) and Hugh Shearer (1967–1972). It was defeated in the 1972 elections by Michael N. Manley, son of Norman Manley, and the People's National Party, marking the beginning of strides toward socialism.

Manley forged ties with the Marxist regime in Cuba and attacked U.S. policies in the region.

Manley's government permitted private enterprise, but only for businesses owned by Jamaicans. Reelected in 1976, Manley oversaw the government purchase of controlling interests in the foreign-owned mining companies and nationalization of many plantations and industries. He initiated welfare programs and made a determined effort to increase industry and tourism.

The results of Manley's program, though, were dismal. The new socialist policies scared off foreign investors as well as tourists. Production dropped as emigration reached new heights. Manley repressed political dissent and sought economic aid from other socialist countries.

In 1980 Manley was defeated by Edward P. G. Seaga, a conservative who reversed Manley's policies and helped restore international confidence in Jamaica. Through the 1980s, investment increased, as did tourism, which had been curtailed by the unattractive political climate.

In September 1988, Hurricane Gilbert struck Jamaica, killing 45 people and causing severe damage to the country and its economy.

In 1989 Manley and the PNP were voted back into power. Manley resigned in March 1992. He was succeeded by former deputy prime minister P. J. Patterson, amid deepening economic troubles and rising political violence.

St. Kitts and Nevis

Official name: *Federation of St. Kitts and Nevis*
Area: *104 sq. mi., 269 sq. km.*
Type of government:
Constitutional monarchy
Population: *39,000*
Capital and largest city:
Basseterre
(Pop., 13,000)
Language: *English*
Literacy: *97%*
Currency: *East Caribbean dollar*
Per capita GDP: *$8,700*
(Rank: 59th)

The land. The topography of St. Kitts is dominated by a volcanic ridge that occupies the center of the island. The highest point on the island, and in the country, is Mount Misery, which is 3,711 feet (1,131 meters) above sea level. Nevis, which lies about two miles from St. Kitts, has an area of about 36 square miles (93 square kilometers) and is also volcanic in origin. The islands have a tropical climate with an average yearly rainfall of 55

inches (140 centimeters) and a mean temperature of about 79°F (26°C).

The people. The majority of the islands' inhabitants are of African or African-European descent. More than a third of the population is urban, and most live in the two main cities, Basseterre, the capital, and Charlestown (population, 1,400), on Nevis.

Economy. The sugar industry is the mainstay of the islands' economy. It is the largest employer and sugar products are the largest export. Cotton and pineapples are also cultivated. The manufacturing sector has grown in importance. Manufactured products include clothing, shoes, furniture, and electronics. As with many other Caribbean islands, tourism is becoming an increasingly important part of the economy. The country's main trading partners are the United States and Great Britain.

Government. St. Kitts and Nevis has a parliamentary form of government, with a prime minister as the head of government and a governor-general, representing the British monarch, as head of state. Dr. Denzil Douglas became prime minister in 1995. The prime minister presides over a cabinet. The legislative body is the 14-member House of Assembly, consisting of eleven elected and three appointed members. Judicial power is vested in the Supreme Court.

The country is administratively divided into 14 parishes.

History. St. Kitts and Nevis were both discovered in 1493 by Christopher Columbus, who named the larger island St. Christopher. The islands were settled in 1623 and 1628, respectively, by English settlers, who then renamed the larger of the islands St. Kitts. The French also established a colony, and possession of the islands was disputed until 1783, when it was settled in favor of the British through the Treaty of Versailles.

St. Kitts and Nevis, along with the nearby island of Anguilla, were granted internal self-government as an associated state of the United Kingdom in February of 1967. Anguilla withdrew from the association later that year. St. Kitts and Nevis became an independent country on September 19, 1983.

St. Lucia

Official name: *St. Lucia*
Area: *239 sq. mi., 620 sq. km.*
Type of government:
Parliamentary democracy
Population: *160,000*
Capital and largest city: *Castries*
(Pop., 11,000)
Languages: *English (official), French patois*
Literacy: *67%*
Currency: *East Caribbean dollar*
Per capita GDP: *$4,400*
(Rank: 95th)

The land. Volcanic in origin, the island of St. Lucia has a rugged, mountainous terrain. The highest point on St. Lucia is the peak of Morne Gimie, in the southwestern part of the island, with an elevation of 3,117 feet (950 meters). The capital, Castries, has an excellent harbor.

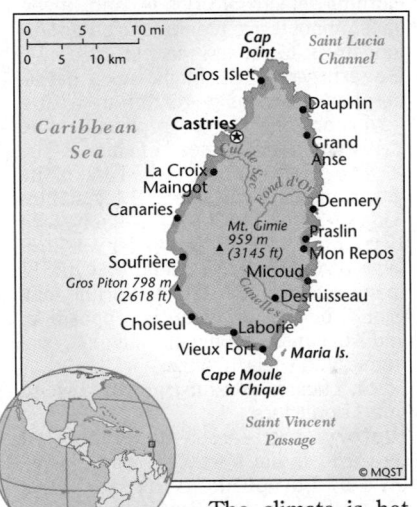

The climate is hot and dry throughout the year, and rainfall is abundant, particularly in the interior, where annual precipitation is about 140 inches (356 centimeters).

The people. The population is of mixed African, European, and Indian origin. Most of the people are of African or mixed descent. English is the official language, but a French patois is in common use.

Castries is the only sizable city, and over one-third of the population reside there. The next largest urban center is the port town of Vieux Fort (population, 13,000).

Economy. Agriculture is the mainstay of the economy, and bananas, copra, cocoa, and spices are the chief crops.

Industry and tourism are rising rapidly in economic importance. About one-third of the labor force is now employed in industry, just slightly less than in agriculture. Tourism has become the nation's largest single source of income. There is considerable manufacturing growth, although food processing remains of prime importance.

NET FISHING is a community occupation in the Caribbean.

labor
US

labour
Brit.

kilometers
US

kilometres
Brit.

center
US

centre
Brit.

A major oil transshipment port and free trade zone have also helped to improve St. Lucia's economy. St. Lucia's main trading partners are Great Britain, the United States, and other Caribbean nations. Main exports include bananas, clothing, electronic goods, and beverages. Imports are manufactured goods, foodstuffs, fuels, and machinery.

Government. St. Lucia has a parliamentary form of government with a governor-general who represents the British monarch as head of state.

The prime minister is the head of the government. The bicameral legislature consists of the House of Assembly, with 17 members elected by popular vote to 5-year terms, and the Senate, with 11 members—6 selected by the prime minister, 3 by the leader of the opposition, and 2 in consultation with religious, economic, and social groups.

St. Lucia is administratively divided into 11 quarters.

History. St. Lucia was inhabited by Carib Indians when it was discovered by Europeans in the late 1400s and settled by colonists in the 1600s. During the 1700s, slaves were brought from Africa to work on plantations. From the mid-1600s to 1814, the French and British competed for control of the island, which changed possession numerous times. In 1814 St. Lucia became a British colony by the Treaty of Paris. It gained self-government in 1967.

After 1967, the United Workers Party (UWP), led by Prime Minister John Compton, became the chief political force. Compton pushed for independence and closer economic ties with other CARICOM nations and oil-rich Venezuela.

In February 1979 the island won its independence. The socialist-oriented Labor Party won two-thirds of the new nation's assembly seats, and Allan Louisy became prime minister.

In 1982 Compton became prime minister and the UWP regained control of parliament. Compton was returned in 1987 and 1992. Labor Party candidate Kenneth Anthony became prime minister in 1997.

St. Vincent and the Grenadines

Official name: *St. Vincent and the Grenadines*

Area: *131 sq. mi., 340 sq. km.*

Type of government: *Constitutional monarchy*

Population: *116,000*

Capital and largest city: *Kingstown (Pop., 15,000)*

Languages: *English (official), French patois*

Literacy: *96%*

Currency: *East Caribbean dollar*

Per capita GDP: *$2,900 (Rank: 118th)*

The land. St. Vincent and the northern islets of the Grenadines are part of the Windward Islands of the Lesser Antilles. St. Vincent is the main island of the group. Its total area is 133 square miles (345 square kilometers); the total area of the Grenadines is 17 square miles (43 square kilometers). St. Vincent consists of a heavily forested spine of mountains flanked by coastal plains. In the north is the imposing Soufrière volcano, rising to an elevation of 4,048 feet (1,234 meters), the country's highest point. The volcano had a violent and destructive eruption in 1902 and a smaller eruption in 1979. The climate is tropical, with a mean temperature of about 80°F (27°C). Annual rainfall varies from about 60 inches (152 centimeters) on the coast to about 150 inches (381 centimeters) inland.

The people. The population is mostly of African or mixed African, European, and Indian origin. Kingstown, the capital and main urban center, is also the country's principal port.

Economy. Agriculture and tourism are the basis of the economy. Bananas, arrowroot, copra, cotton, fruits, spices,

and yams are the chief crops.

Manufacturing, mainly processing agricultural products, has grown since 1970.

Farm products are the main exports, and foodstuffs, manufactured goods, fuels, and machinery are the main imports Most trade is conducted with Great Britain, neighboring islands, and the United States.

Government. St. Vincent and the Grenadines has a parliamentary form of government, with a governor-general representing the British monarch as head of state. The prime minister is the head of government. A unicameral legislature—the House of Assembly—has 15 members elected to 5-year terms, plus six senators appointed by the governor-general. Judicial power is vested in a high court.

History. Inhabited by Carib Indians when discovered by Christopher Columbus in the 1490s, St. Vincent and the Grenadines were settled in the 1700s by Europeans from several countries. They established plantations worked by slaves brought from Africa. Control of the islands was contested by Great Britain and France. In 1783 the islands were ceded to Great Britain by the Treaty of Versailles. In 1795 the French aided the Caribs in a bloody uprising that was crushed the following year. Most of the Indians were deported to an island off Honduras in 1797. St. Vincent and the Grenadines were governed with the other Windward Islands until gaining self-government in 1967.

Milton Cato and his moderately socialist Labor Party came to power in 1974. The party remained the chief political force in the islands for many years. The islands achieved independence on October 27, 1979, and Cato was reelected prime minister on December 5. Two days later, Union and Palm islands, in the Grenadines, rebelled. The secessionist movement was put down, although a state of emergency remained in effect for half a year. In 1984

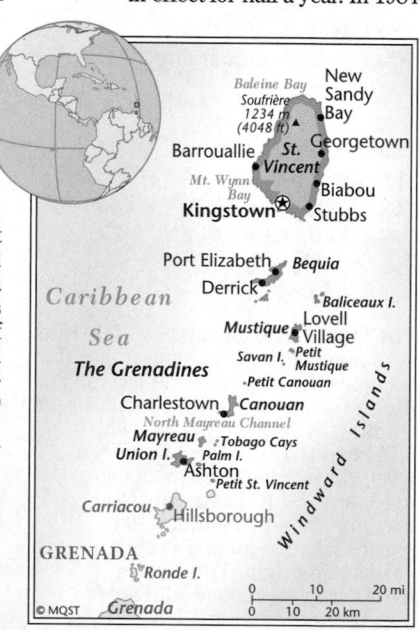

James Mitchell was elected prime minister and the National Democratic Party (NDP) became the majority party. Mitchell and the NDP were returned to office in 1989. Unity Labor Party leader Dr. Ralph Gonsalves, who received his doctoral degree in government studies, became prime minister in 2001.

The eruption of Mount Soufrière on April 13, 1979, devastated the nation's banana crop, and emergency foreign aid (mostly from Great Britain) was needed to sustain the economy. This along with chronic high unemployment slowed the nation's economic growth in the 1980s. The economy began to rebound in the 1990s with a growth in tourism.

Trinidad and Tobago

Official name: *Republic of Trinidad and Tobago*

Area: *1,980 sq. mi., 5,130 sq. km.*

Type of government:
Parliamentary democracy

Population: *1,112,000*

Capital and largest city:
Port of Spain
(Pop., 48,000)

Languages: *English (official), Hindi, French, Spanish*

Literacy: *94%*

Currency: *Dollar*

Per capita GDP: *$9,000*
(Rank: 56th)

The land. Trinidad and Tobago, an independent island country in the West Indies, consists of two islands: Trinidad, the second largest island in the West Indies, 1,864 square miles (4,826 square kilometers) in area; and Tobago, some 20 miles (32 kilometers) northeast of Trinidad, 116 square miles (300 square kilometers) in area; and some tiny islets.

Trinidad is crossed in an east-to-west direction by three mountain ranges—the Central, Southern, and Northern ranges. The mountains of the Northern range rise to a peak of more

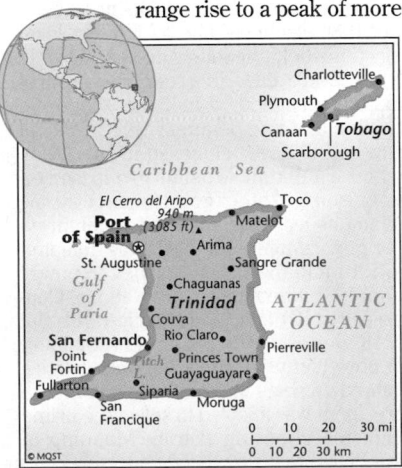

CACAO, second in importance only to sugar cane as a commercial crop, is raised mainly on Tobago and in the wetter regions of Trinidad.

than 3,000 feet (914 meters). The three highland ranges are separated by lowlands. Tropical forests cover about one-half of Trinidad. There are many small streams, and the east-central coast is swampy.

Tobago's terrain is rugged. A central core of volcanic hills rises over 1,800 feet (549 meters) and drops sharply to the sea in the northeast. Except for some isolated coastal plains, flatland is limited to the southwestern tip of Tobago.

The climate of the islands is tropical, with temperatures averaging 77°F (25°C) throughout the year. Rainfall ranges from about 120 inches (305 centimeters) a year on Tobago and northern Trinidad to about 50 inches (127 centimeters) a year in southwestern Trinidad.

The people. Most of Trinidad and Tobago's people are of African, East Indian, or mixed European and African descent. English is the official language, but a dialect that combines English with French, Spanish, and other tongues is widely spoken.

About 90 percent of the country's population live on Trinidad. About one-third of the population live in urban areas. The main urban centers are Port-of-Spain, the nation's capital; San Fernando (population, 29,000); and Arima (28,000).

Trinidad and Tobago's population has increased rapidly, resulting in high rates of unemployment and emigration to Great Britain and the United States.

Economy. The economy of Trinidad and Tobago is based on international trade, tourism, and the exploitation of its rich natural resources, especially petroleum and asphalt.

Industry. The nation's economy is dominated by the oil and asphalt industries, which account for about three-fourths of export value. Trinidad and Tobago is a

leading producer of asphalt, which is extracted from Pitch Lake, on the southwestern coast of Trinidad. Natural gas reserves are an important source of energy for domestic use, as is electricity.

Oil production declined in the 1980s after a decade of rapid growth. As production declined, the country moved to diversify its industries to include petrochemical production, iron and steel, plastics, electronics assembly, and clothing manufacture. Rum, a product of the sugar industry, is also produced.

Tourism is an important sector of the nation's economy, providing a valuable source of foreign exchange.

Agriculture. Arable land is limited in Trinidad and Tobago, but agriculture employs about 12 percent of the labor force and provides important exports.

Sugar cane is the most important commercial crop; it is grown in western Trinidad. Cacao, second in importance, is raised mainly on Tobago and in the wetter regions of Trinidad. Coffee, citrus fruits, and vegetables are grown for local consumption.

Trinidad and Tobago's chief exports are petroleum and petroleum products, chemical fertilizers, sugar, and manufactured goods. Principal imports are crude petroleum, food, machinery, and transportation equipment.

The country's main trading partners are the United States and the nations of the Caribbean Community.

Government. Trinidad and Tobago is a republic with a parliamentary system of government. The head of state is the president, who is elected by the parliament. Actual executive powers are wielded by a prime minister and cabinet responsible to the bicameral parliament, which consists of an appointed Senate of 31 members and a popularly elected

THE TROPICAL ISLAND nation of Trinidad and Tobago consists of two main islands, one of which lies just seven miles off the coast of Venezuela.

labor
US

labour
Brit.

kilometers
US

kilometres
Brit.

House of Representatives of 36 members, all of whom serve five-year terms. Tobago has limited self-government and has a 15-member House of Assembly.

Judicial power is vested in the Court of Appeal, but the final court of appeal is the Privy Council in London. Trinidad is divided administratively into eight counties and three municipalities.

History. Both Trinidad and Tobago were visited by Christopher Columbus on his third voyage to the New World, in 1498. Trinidad was at that time inhabited by Arawak Indians. Tobago was uninhabited when Dutch settlers arrived in 1632.

Trinidad was settled by Spain, which made it a colony about 1550. The island was subject to constant raids by French, Dutch, and British privateers, and the Spanish maintained their control only with difficulty. Cocoa crop failures in the early 1700s led to the abandonment of most settlements on the island.

The colony revived after 1783, when the Spanish government asked Roman Catholics from other countries to settle in Trinidad. Many French settlers moved to the island, bringing with them sugar cane, cotton, coffee, and new types of cocoa. Plantation agriculture prospered, based on the labor of slaves imported from Africa.

British rule. In 1798 Great Britain captured Trinidad and its control was recognized in 1802 by the Treaty of Amiens. The treaty gave Tobago to France, but the French ceded the island to Great Britain in 1814. The sugar and cocoa industries prospered and were expanded under British colonial rule.

In the 1830s the slaves were freed, and a critical labor shortage in the sec-

ond half of the 1800s led to contract workers being brought from India. Oil was discovered in the early 1900s and soon played a key role in the economy.

The islands had been made a single colony in 1889, and they began to move toward independence in 1925, when popular representatives were first elected to the governing council. Public participation in government gradually increased. In 1958 the colony entered the Federation of the West Indies, which united a number of Great Britain's West Indian and Caribbean colonies, but it withdrew in 1961 when Jamaica left the federation.

Independence. In 1962, a year after complete internal self-government had been granted, Trinidad and Tobago became independent. Dr. Eric Williams, leader of the People's National Movement (PNM), was chosen as the first prime minister.

Williams was consistently reelected and the PNM remained the country's dominant political force for 30 years following its founding in 1956. The PNM, which draws its strongest support from black citizens, was opposed by the Democratic Labour Party, which chiefly represented the East Indians, and by the United Labor Front, which mostly represented the leftist trade unions. In the 1976 elections the United Labor Front made a strong showing, winning about one-third of the legislative seats.

Unemployment was a chronic problem for Williams and the PNM. Following labor strikes and civil riots in 1970, a state of emergency was declared. The economy did not improve until

1974, when the quadrupling of world oil prices brought a windfall to the nation. Between 1974 and 1982, when world oil prices began to drop, Trinidad and Tobago was able to invest in industrial and social programs to diversify the economy and help ease the nation's 20 percent unemployment rate.

Williams's family planning programs to reduce overpopulation and unemployment were only partially successful. He also sought to attract foreign investment to help develop his country, but there is still a deficiency of working capital. Williams died in 1981 but the PNM remained in power, holding a large majority in parliament.

In 1986 several political parties merged to form a new entity, the National Alliance for Reconstruction (NAR). Its leader, A. N. R. Robinson, became prime minister after the NAR won 33 of the 36 House seats in December 1986 elections. The NAR swept local elections held the following year, as well.

A severe austerity program was introduced but failed to halt the economic decline that had begun in 1982. Political and social unrest climaxed in July 1990, when a militant Muslim group seized Robinson and other government officials in an unsuccessful attempt to overthrow the government. The NAR was defeated in 1991 and the PNM returned to power until 1995 when the United National Congress (UNC) formed a coalition with the NAR, defeating the PNM and remaining in power until 2001. When both parties gained 18 seats in the 2001 election, the president was allowed to select the prime minister, choosing Patrick Manning of the PNM.

Dependencies in North America

British Dependencies

Anguilla (35 square miles, 91 square kilometers), one of the Leeward Islands of the Lesser Antilles chain, between the Caribbean Sea and the Atlantic Ocean, northwest of St. Kitts (Christopher) and near St. Martin. Its population (12,000) is mostly of African origin, although there is a small white minority. The capital is The Valley. Sheep and goat herding and lobster fishing are the island's main economic activities.

In 1967, St. Christopher-Nevis-Anguilla became a federated state, but Anguilla seceded later that year. The British took possession of the island again in 1969, and it officially became a separate dependency in 1980.

Bermuda (19 square miles, 50 square kilometers), an archipelago of 20 inhabited islands and numerous uninhabited islets in the Atlantic Ocean, some 600 miles (965 kilometers) east of the United States. Two-thirds of the population (64,000) of Bermuda is of African descent, with the remainder of British descent. Hamilton (population, 4,700) is the capital. Tourism, farming, and international business transactions constitute the mainstay of the economy.

Believed to have been discovered in 1503 by a Spanish expedition led by Juan de Bermudez, it was first settled by the British in the early 1600s. It soon became a thriving plantation colony as thousands of Africans were brought to the islands for slave labor. In the 1900s Bermuda became a popular resort for the wealthy. A new constitution, which went into effect in 1968, gave Bermuda domestic self-rule. Bermuda's governor is appointed by the British Crown. Racial hostility flared in the early 1970s following the assassination of the colony's governor and several other high officials. British troops were called in to restore peace.

The British Virgin Islands (58 square miles, 150 square kilometers) lie in the northern Lesser Antilles in the eastern Caribbean. The colony consists of three large islands and over 30 islets. The population (21,000) lives on 16 of the islands, and is almost entirely of African descent. Road Town on Tortola is the capital. Agriculture and tourism are the economic mainstays.

Discovered by Christopher Columbus in 1493, the islands were a base for pirates until the early 1700s, when plantations, worked by African slaves, first appeared. The islands became a British colony in 1774.

Cayman Islands (100 square miles, 260 square kilometers)—Grand Cayman, Little Cayman, and Cayman Brac—lie in the Caribbean Sea some 100 miles (161 kilometers) northwest of Jamaica and about 100 miles south of Cuba. The population (41,000) includes people of European, African, and mixed origins. Since becoming a tax-free haven for foreign funds in the early 1970s, the islands have developed a thriving commercial, banking, and tourist economy. George Town (population, 20,000) is the capital.

Discovered by Christopher Columbus in 1503, the islands passed into British possession in 1670 and were part of the British colony of Jamaica. First inhabited by British Jamaicans in the 1700s, the Caymans did not gain independence from Jamaica until 1962.

Montserrat (39 square miles, 100 square kilometers), north of Guadeloupe, is one of the Leeward Islands of the Lesser Antilles, which lie between the Atlantic Ocean and the Caribbean Sea. The population (8,400) is of mixed African and European origin. Agriculture, formerly the mainstay of the economy, now accounts for about 16 percent of exports. Manufacturing now supplies the bulk of export earnings. Plymouth, the capital, and southern and central areas were abandoned in 1997 due to volcanic activity, which continues.

Discovered by Columbus in 1493, Montserrat was settled by Irish colonists in 1632. A British possession since 1783, it was granted self-rule in 1962 but has chosen to remain a British colony. In 1989 Hurricane Hugo devastated Montserrat, damaging or destroying almost every building on the island.

Turks and Caicos Islands (166 square miles, 430 square kilometers), numerous small islands of the Bahama Archipelago, lie in the Atlantic Ocean about 100 miles (161 kilometers) north of the island of Hispaniola.

The population (19,000) is mainly of African origin. Fishing and tourism are the main economic activities. Cockburn Town, on Grand Turk Island, is the capital.

The islands were incorporated into the British colony of Jamaica in 1873. When Jamaica became independent in 1962, the Turks and Caicos were made a separate colony.

French Departments

Guadeloupe (687 square miles, 1,780 square kilometers) is one of the Windward Islands of the Lesser Antilles, which lie between the Caribbean Sea and the Atlantic Ocean. It consists of two adjacent islands, Basse-Terre and Grande-Terre, and many smaller islands to the south and east. Guadeloupe's population (436,000), comprised mostly of the black descendants of slaves and of mulattoes, is growing rapidly.

Basse-Terre (on Basse-Terre Island) is the capital. Pointe à Pitre (population, 26,000) is the second largest city. Guadeloupe has fertile land. Agriculture is the main economic activity, and bananas, sugar, and rum are the main exports. Guadeloupe's main trading partner is France. Tourism is also an important industry.

THE BRITISH FLAVOR of Bermuda is reflected in the citizens' enthusiasm for cricket.

kilometers
US

kilometres
Brit.

labor
US

labour
Brit.

centers
US

centres
Brit.

LIVING AND TRAVEL on the water is not uncommon on the French island of Martinique, the birthplace of Napoleon's empress, Josephine.

Discovered by Columbus in 1493, Guadeloupe was first settled by the French in 1635. In 1674 France annexed the islands and developed plantation agriculture, employing slaves imported from Africa. Slavery was abolished in the 1800s. In 1946 Guadeloupe was made an overseas department of France. In 1983 Guadeloupe was granted limited self-rule.

Martinique (425 square miles, 1,100 square kilometers) is one of the Windward Islands of the Lesser Antilles. It lies 130 miles (209 kilometers) south of Guadeloupe, between Dominica and St. Lucia. The population (422,000) is of mixed African, European, and Carib descent. The island is of volcanic origin, with a generally chilly or mountainous terrain. In 1902 Mount Pelée erupted, burying the city of St. Pierre in volcanic ash and lava.

The capital, Fort-de-France (population, 100,000), has nearly one-fourth of the island's total population. Agriculture is the mainstay of the economy, and bananas, rum, sugar, and pineapples are the leading agricultural exports. Tourism is also very important. Close economic ties with France are maintained and French aid is significant in the economy. Industry, including petroleum refining, cement, and plastics, is a small but important part of the economy, and its growth is being encouraged.

Discovered by Columbus in 1493, Martinique was first settled in 1635 by the French; it was annexed by France in 1674 and became a thriving plantation colony before slavery was abolished in the 1800s. In 1946 the island was made an overseas department of France. Napoleon's empress, Josephine, was born in Martinique in the 1700s.

Martinique's high population density has contributed to its chronic unemployment. National labor strikes in 1980, resulting in violence and chaos, were blamed on Cuban interference. In 1983 Martinique was granted limited self-rule.

Netherlands Dependencies

Aruba (75 square miles, 193 square kilometers) is an island located just off the northeast coast of Venezuela.

More than half the population (70,000) is descended from the island's original Arawak Indian inhabitants. The remainder is of Dutch, Spanish, or mixed descent. The main urban centers are Oranjestad (population, 20,000), the capital, and Sint Nicolaas (14,000), the site of an oil refinery that was closed in 1985. The refinery provided about one-third of Aruba's income. Tourism is now the main economic activity.

Aruba was discovered in 1499 by the Spanish explorer Alonzo de Ojeda. Acquired by the Dutch in 1634, it became part of the Dutch West Indies in 1828 and part of the Netherlands Antilles in 1845. In 1986 it was separated from the Netherlands Antilles. Aruba was scheduled to become fully independent in 1996 but elected to remain a dependency.

The Netherlands Antilles (371 square miles, 960 square kilometers) consists of five islands in the Caribbean Sea. The islands of Bonaire and Curaçao lie off the northwest coast of Venezuela. They are part of the Leeward Islands. Saba, St. Eustacious, and St. Maarten, the last of which is divided between the Netherlands and France, are in the Windwards, some 200 miles (322 kilometers) east of Puerto Rico.

The population (214,000) is mostly of mixed African and Indian origin, although there are also European descendants. More than half of the people live in the capital city of Willemstad (population, 123,000) on Curaçao.

Curaçao is the most important island and has most of the islands' population and prosperity. Its residents enjoy a high standard of living, the result of Curaçao's oil refining industry, which is operated by Venezuela. Tourism is also important, while agriculture is the mainstay on the other four islands.

The islands were taken by the Dutch in 1815 after being claimed and occupied by Spain (in the early 1500s) and then by Portugal and Great Britain. In 1828 the islands, along with Aruba, became part of the Dutch West Indies; they were reorganized as the Netherlands Antilles in 1845. Curaçao was an important center for the Caribbean slave trade between 1700 and 1860. The Netherlands Antilles attained self-rule in 1954, and Aruba seceded in 1986.

PETROGLYPHS on the Netherlands dependency of Aruba are evidence of the Arawak Indians, from whom more than half the present-day population is descended.

United States Dependencies

Navassa (2 square miles, 5 square kilometers) is a Caribbean island that lies between Jamaica and Haiti. A U.S. possession since 1865, it is uninhabited except for workers at a U.S. Coast Guard lighthouse that was established on the island in 1916.

Puerto Rico (3,514 square miles, 9,104 square kilometers) is an island lying between the Atlantic Ocean and the Caribbean Sea, about 1,000 miles (1,609 kilometers) southeast of the United States. Puerto Rico's population (3,863,000) is almost totally Hispanic. With nearly 1,000 people per square mile (386 per square kilometer), it is very densely populated. Two-thirds of the people live in urban areas. San Juan (population, metro. area, 1,816,300), the capital, is the island's largest city. Roman Catholicism is the chief religion and English and Spanish are commonly spoken.

Puerto Rico has one of the highest standards of living in all of South and Central America. For centuries its economy was based on one crop—sugar cane. Since World War II, however—aided by the U.S.-initiated "Operation Bootstrap" program—Puerto Rico has been rapidly industrialized. Both heavy and light industries now form the leading economic activities, employing one-fifth of the labor force. Tourism is also very important.

Discovered by Christopher Columbus in 1493, Puerto Rico was conquered by the Spaniard, Ponce de León, in 1508. It flourished as a plantation colony following the introduction of sugar cane in 1515 and African slaves in 1518. Plantation society deteriorated after slavery was abolished in 1873.

U.S. troops occupied the island in 1898 during the Spanish-American War, making it a U.S. possession. Self-rule began in 1900 (U.S. Foraker Act), and

THE YACHT CLUB in Virgin Gorda in the British Virgin Islands attracts boaters from all over the world to its warm waters.

U.S. citizenship was granted in 1917 (U.S. Organic Act). Luis Muñoz Marin was the first governor popularly elected by Puerto Ricans. He served from 1948 to 1964.

Puerto Rico attained commonwealth status in 1952, and by popular referendum in 1967 and 1993 the people chose to maintain that status. A Puerto Rican independence movement has been active on the island for many years, but it enjoys only limited support.

U.S. Virgin Islands (136 square miles, 352 square kilometers) are located 35 miles (56 kilometers) east of Puerto Rico, between the Caribbean Sea and the Atlantic Ocean, in the western part of the Lesser Antilles. Their population (123,000) is mostly of African origin, with about 15 percent being white. English is the chief language. Although there are some 100 islands in the group, most of the people live on St. John, St. Croix, and St. Thomas. With over 750 people per square mile (290 per square kilometer), the islands are crowded. Charlotte Amalie (population, 11,000) on St.

Thomas has one of the best Caribbean harbors, and it is the capital.

The Virgin Islands have a pleasant, low-humidity, subtropical climate; this helped make tourism the chief source of income. Agriculture, mainly sugar production, was the main economic activity before World War II. Since then, sugar production has ended and oil refining and bauxite processing have become the leading exports. Tourism is now the prime sector of the economy. The main trading partner is the United States.

Discovered by Columbus in 1493, the Virgin Islands were settled by English and Dutch planters. Briefly held by the French, the islands passed under Danish control in the early 1700s. Plantations worked by African slaves formed the economic and social base of the islands during the colonial period. In 1917, during World War I, the United States bought the islands from Denmark for defense purposes. U.S. citizenship was granted to the inhabitants in 1927, and the islands began electing their own governors in 1970.

EL MORRO FORTRESS in the old Spanish colony in Puerto Rico guards the Bay of San Juan.

Cities of North America

Acapulco, seaport in southwestern Mexico, on the Pacific Ocean. It is a resort with lavish facilities for recreation. It is the shipping point for cotton, sugar, coffee, and other agricultural products. Pop., 621,000.

center
US

centre
Brit.

theater
US

theatre
Brit.

Anchorage, the largest city in the U.S. state of Alaska, located at the head of Cook Inlet on the southern coast of the state. It is an important port, international and regional air transportation center, and defense center. Tourism and oil-related industry are important to the city's economy. Institutions of higher learning include Alaska Pacific University and the University of Alaska at Anchorage. Pop., 260,283.

Atlanta, the capital and largest city of Georgia, and one of the leading commercial, transportation, and financial centers of the southeastern United States. A major rail center of the Confederacy during the Civil War, it was captured by Union forces under Sherman in 1864 and largely destroyed by fire. Modern Atlanta has a diversified economy and is the headquarters of many corporations. Its Hartsfield International Airport is one of the busiest in the country. Among Atlanta's institutions of higher learning are Emory University, Atlanta University, Georgia State University, and the Georgia Institute of Technology. The city's leading cultural institution is the Robert W. Woodruff Arts Center, home of the Atlanta Symphony Orchestra and the Alliance Theater. Other points of interest include the Martin Luther King, Jr., National Historic Site and the Jimmy Carter Library. Pop., 416,474.

Baltimore, the largest city in Maryland and the 14th largest city in the United States, situated on the Patapsco River estuary, part of Chesapeake Bay. Excellent road, rail, canal, and air facilities link the city's busy port with a large manufacturing and industrial region. Production of steel and chemicals and shipbuilding and repair are the largest industries. The city's leading institution of higher learning is Johns Hopkins University. Its many cultural institutions include the Enoch Pratt Free Library, the Walters Art Gallery, the Peale Museum, and the Baltimore Museum of Art. Among the numerous points of interest is Fort McHenry, whose bombardment in the War of 1812 inspired Francis Scott Key to write "The Star-Spangled Banner." Pop., 651,154.

Basseterre, capital of St. Kitts and Nevis, in the Leeward Islands group in the eastern Caribbean. The city lies on the southwest coast of St. Kitts island. Pop., 13,000.

Basse-Terre, capital of the overseas department Guadeloupe in the French West Indies, on the southwest coast of Basse-Terre Island. It is commercially underdeveloped. Pop., 14,000.

Belmopan, capital city of Belize since 1970. It is situated inland, southwest of the former capital, Belize City, which was devastated by a hurricane in 1961. Pop., 8,100.

Boston, the capital and largest city in Massachusetts and center of the tenth largest metropolitan area in the United States. Boston was founded by Puritan settlers in 1630. By the time of the American Revolution it was the largest city in the American colonies and had the busiest port. Its growth in the 19th century was exceeded by that of New York and Philadelphia, but its population was fed by waves of immigrants, including Irish, Italians, French Canadians, and African Americans. The decline of Boston's importance as a port and manufacturing city in the 20th century has been offset in part by its growth as a financial, corporate, educational, and medical center. Among its many educational institutions are Boston University and Northeastern University and, across the Charles River in adjacent Cambridge, Harvard University and the Massachusetts Institute of Technology. Its abundant cultural institutions include the Boston Public Library, the Boston Symphony Orchestra, and the New England Conservatory of Music. Other points of interest include historical sites from the American Revolutionary period, among them the Old State House, the Old North Church, and the Paul Revere House. Pop., 589,141.

Bridgetown, capital, largest city, and chief port of Barbados, in the West Indies. The city is located on the southwest coast of the island, on Carlisle Bay. Bridgetown is a railroad terminus and the financial and commercial center of Barbados. Exports include sugar, molasses, and rum. Pop., 5,900.

Calgary, Canada's sixth largest city, located on the Bow River, where the prairie meets the eastern foothills of the Rockies in southern Alberta. It is at the heart of a booming gas- and oil-producing region, and is a major supplier of machinery and other goods to the gas and oil industries. There are some 900 industrial plants, and construction is also a major industry. In addition, Calgary acts as the processing, distributing, and service center for the bulk of Alberta's agricultural regions. Calgary was founded as a Northwest Mounted Police post in 1875. The Calgary stampede, held each July, attracts visitors from all over the world. The city's Heritage Park is an attractive reconstructed pioneer community, and Calgary houses Canada's second largest zoo. Other points of interest include the Calgary Centre for the Performing Arts and the Glenbow Museum, which houses over 20,000 works of art and is one of Canada's most important museums for western history. Pop., 878,866.

Castries, capital, largest city, and chief port of St. Lucia, in the West Indies. Castries has a fine, landlocked harbor. Chief exports are bananas, cocoa, copra, and coconut oil. Castries is also the tourist center of St. Lucia. Pop., 11,000.

Charleston, the second largest city in South Carolina and a major coastal port and transportation and commercial center. Its manufactures include wood and paper products, petroleum products, metal and rubber products, and textiles. The firing on Fort Sumter in Charleston Harbor in 1861 marked the beginning of

BALTIMORE has rejuvenated its harbor on the Patapsco River estuary, which is part of the Chesapeake Bay.

HISTORIC HOMES line Charleston's Battery Street.

the American Civil War. The fort is now Fort Sumter National Monument. Charleston's numerous historic buildings and sites and its beautiful gardens attract many tourists. The city is also host to an annual arts festival, Spoleto Festival, U.S.A. Pop., 96,650.

Charlotte Amalie, capital, largest city, and chief port of the Virgin Islands of the United States. The city is located on the south-central coast of St. Thomas Island, about 40 miles (64 km.) east of Puerto Rico. It was formerly called St. Thomas. The city is the chief commercial and tourist center of the Virgin Islands. Pop., 11,000.

Charlottetown, capital of Prince Edward Island, Canada, located on the island's south-central coast where its wide harbor opens into the Northumberland Strait. Once an important center for shipbuilding, the city today depends mainly on tourism, though it does have food processing plants and some light industry. Incorporated in 1855, the city is known as the Cradle of Confederation for the Charlottetown conference of 1864 that led to Canada's confederation three years later. The only city in Canada's smallest province, it is a peaceful place with fine Victorian homes and tree-lined squares. Points of interest include the Confederation Centre for the Arts, an impressive modern complex and a national memorial to the fathers of confederation, and Province House, where the articles that led to confederation were signed. Pop., 32,245.

Chicago, the most populous city in Illinois and the third most populous city in the United States. Situated on the shore of Lake Michigan, it is one of the country's leading transportation, manufacturing, trade, and financial centers. The city grew up on the site of Fort Dearborn, a military outpost established in 1803. Development of its harbor and rail facilities from the 1830s to the 1850s spurred rapid growth. Although Chicago was virtually destroyed by fire in 1871, it was quickly rebuilt. The new, improved city hosted the celebrated 1893 World's Fair, or Columbian Exposition, and became a cultural and literary center in

the early 20th century. Trading at the Chicago Mercantile Exchange and the Chicago Board of Trade is an important component of the city's economy, as is manufacturing. Products include steel, fabricated metals, machinery, chemicals, food products, and electronic equipment. Chicago is also a major printing and publishing center. Its O'Hare International Airport is the busiest in the world. The city's institutions of higher learning include the University of Chicago, Northwestern University (whose main campus is located in nearby Evanston), the University of Illinois at Chicago, Loyola University, and DePaul University. Chicago's cultural institutions include the Chicago Symphony Orchestra, the Art Institute of Chicago, the Field Museum of Natural History, and the Museum of Science and Industry. Chicago has North America's tallest building, the Sears Tower. Pop., 2,896,106

Cincinnati, the third largest city in Ohio, on the Ohio River in the southwestern part of the state. An important U.S. port and commercial and industrial city, Cincinnati produces a variety of items, including soap products, meat products, cosmetics, chemicals, machine tools, and playing cards. Also important are printing and publishing.

Institutions of higher learning include the University of Cincinnati, Xavier University, and Hebrew Union College —Jewish Institute of Religion. Its cultural institutions include the celebrated Cincinnati Symphony Orchestra and the Cincinnati Art Museum. Pop., 331,285.

Cleveland, the second largest city in Ohio, located on Lake Erie. A leading U.S. industrial port on the St. Lawrence Seaway, it produces steel, fabricated metals, machinery, electrical equipment, motor vehicles, and chemicals. Numerous industrial and medical research facilities are located in and around Cleveland, including NASA's Lewis Research Center. Among Cleveland's many institutions of higher learning is Case Western Reserve University. The city is home to the internationally renowned Cleveland Orchestra. Pop., 478,403.

Columbus, the capital and largest city in the U.S. state of Ohio, on the Scioto River in the center of the state. Government, business and financial services, and education are the foundations of the city's economy, although manufacturing is also important. Leading manufactures include aircraft, machinery, fabricated metals, and transportation equipment. The city's institutions of higher learning include Ohio State University, Franklin University, and Capital University. Pop., 711,470.

Dallas, the second largest city in Texas and seventh largest city in the United States. Along with nearby Fort Worth (population, 454,000), it is the center of the eighth largest metropolitan area in the country. Located on the Trinity River in northeastern Texas, Dallas is a major financial, commercial, and cultural center. Manufacturing is a rapidly growing sector of the economy, and major products include apparel, electronic equipment, aerospace components, petroleum products, and processed foods. The Dallas-Fort Worth Airport is

THE DALLAS metropolitan area is the eighth largest in the country, with a rapidly growing manufacturing sector, and is a financial, commercial, and cultural center.

256

256

DENVER,
the Mile High City, is located near the Rocky Mountains. It is a center for popular winter sports.

centers
US

centres
Brit.

kilometers
US

kilometres
Brit.

theater
US

theatre
Brit.

honoring
US

honouring
Brit.

CHRISTMAS LIGHTS
in Guadalajara display both the Latin reverence for the religious holiday and the love of festival.

one of the busiest in the country. The city's institutions of higher learning include Southern Methodist University, the University of Dallas, and the University of Texas at Dallas. Its cultural institutions include the Dallas Symphony Orchestra, the Dallas Opera, and the Dallas Museum of Art. Pop., 1,188,580.

Denver, the capital of Colorado and one of the leading transportation and commercial centers in the southwestern United States. Situated on the South Platte River at the eastern foot of the Rocky Mountains, Denver has an elevation of about 1 mile (1.6 kilometers), hence its nickname, the Mile High City. It is located in one of the most popular winter sports regions in the country. Manufacturing and the processing of agricultural products from the region around Denver are important. Denver's new airport, which opened in 1995, is a

major transportation hub. Its institutions of higher learning include the University of Denver and the University of Colorado Medical Center. Other points of interest include the Denver branch of the United States Mint, the Denver Art Museum, and the Colorado State Historical Museum. Pop., 554,636.

Detroit, the largest city in Michigan and ninth largest city in the United States, on the Detroit River. It is nicknamed Motor City because it is the center of the American automobile industry. Much of its economy is based on the production of automobiles and associated products and materials. Detroit's cultural institutions include the Detroit Symphony Orchestra, the Detroit Institute of Arts, and the Detroit Historical Museum. Its institutions of higher learning include Wayne State University, the University of Detroit, and the Dearborn campus of the University of Michigan. Pop., 951,270.

Edmonton, the largest city and capital of the Province of Alberta, Canada, nearly in the center of the province, on the North Saskatchewan River. It is also in the heart of a growing oil-, gas-, and coal-producing region. Edmonton has many manufacturing plants, most importantly of products for energy companies. Food and beverage production represents the second largest economic activity. Edmonton is also an important transportation center for western and northern Canada. Edmonton houses the Provincial Museum, the provincial government's Legislative Building, the University of Alberta, and Canada's Aviation Hall of Fame. Edmonton has a symphony orchestra, an opera company, and an eclectic range of theater. Each July, Edmonton holds a jamboree called Klondike Days, inspired by the gold rush of 1898. Pop., 666,104.

Fort-de-France, capital and largest city of Martinique, French West Indies. Located on the Bay of Fort-de-France,

on the southwest coast of the island, the city has a large, landlocked harbor. Its exports include sugar, rum, and bananas. Pop., 100,000.

Fredericton, capital of New Brunswick, Canada, situated in the middle of the province on the Saint John River. First named Frederick's Town (1783) after Prince Frederick of Osnaburg, the city eventually became a headquarters of the British military. It was incorporated in 1848 with its present name. The city's economy is dominated by its provincial government role and by education—specifically the University of New Brunswick and St. Thomas University. Canada's first astronomical observatory, dating from 1851, and its first school of engineering (1854) were founded here. Points of interest include the Beaverbrook Art Gallery, which has a particularly fine collection of British and

EDMONTON SKATERS enjoy this glass-roofed ice rink.

CITIES

Canadian art; Christ Church Cathedral; and, on the University of New Brunswick campus, a memorial honoring New Brunswick authors Bliss Carman, Sir Charles G. D. Roberts, and Francis Joseph Sherman. Pop., 47,560.

Guadalajara, second largest city in Mexico and capital of the state of Jalisco, located about 280 miles (450 km.) northwest of Mexico City. Guadalajara is the commercial center for a rich agricultural and mining region and is an important rail and highway hub. Its industries produce flour, textiles, leather goods, pottery, and glassware. Pop., 1,646,000.

Guatemala City, capital and largest city of Guatemala. It is located in the central highlands, at an altitude of about 5,000 feet (1,525 m.) about 75 miles (120 km.) from the Pacific Ocean. It is the commercial, cultural, educational, financial, and political center of the country. Manufactures include textiles, soap, cement, and furniture. Pop., 1,007,000.

Halifax, on the south coast of Nova Scotia, Canada, one of the most important ports on the Atlantic seaboard. Because of its ice-free harbor, the port is busiest in winter, when ports on the St. Lawrence are closed. It is also a center of commercial fisheries. In manufacturing, food and beverages account for the largest single sector. The city is also the center of retail trade for the province. It was the first town in Canada settled primarily by the English. In Fleming Park, also known as the Dingle, is a memorial tower commemorating Canada's first legislative assembly—held October 2, 1758, in Halifax. Other points of interest include the Citadel fortress, which houses maritime and military exhibits as well as the Centennial Art Gallery of Nova Scotia, and Halifax North Memorial Library. Of four major universities, Dalhousie is the best known. Pop., 359,111.

Hamilton, at the western end of Lake Ontario, a producer of more than half the steel made in Canada. It has 800 industries in all, and major products include machinery, food, and beverages. Hamilton has a large harbor that handles some 900 ships a year. It was first settled in 1778 by Loyalists from the United States, during the American Revolution. Points of interest include Dundurn Castle, a restored mansion with a museum that portrays Hamilton's early history; the Art Gallery of Hamilton, which houses works by many prominent Canadian artists; the Canadian Football Hall of Fame, which depicts the history of the sport in Canada; and the Royal Botanical Gardens, just outside the city. Pop., 490,268.

Hamilton, free port and the capital of Bermuda, on Bermuda Island. It is a bustling tourist center with important fisheries. Pop., 4,700.

Havana, capital and chief commercial city of Cuba, located on the island's northwestern coast. Havana is Cuba's major port and exports the island's chief commercial crops, sugar and tobacco. Cigars, cigarettes, consumer goods, and heavy machinery are manufactured in the city. Havana is also Cuba's cultural center. It has universities, libraries, museums, and other cultural amenities. Pop., 2,192,000.

Holguín, a city in north-central Oriente Province, eastern Cuba. The city is a transportation and commercial center in a rich agricultural area that produces cattle, coffee, tobacco, and sugar cane. It is served by the port of Gibara, about 19 miles (30 km.) to the north. Pop., 256,000.

Honolulu, the capital, largest city, and main port of Hawaii, on the southeastern coast of the island of Oahu. Honolulu is an important center for shipping between the mainland United States and the countries of Asia and the Pacific. Processing of pineapple and sugar, diversified manufacturing, and tourism are the foundations of the city's economy. Also important are federal expenditures for the military installations located around adjacent Pearl Harbor. Honolulu International Airport is one of the country's busiest airports. The city is also a major resort center. Points of interest include Iolani Palace, the former residence of Hawaii's monarchs, and the Bishop Museum, which has exhibits illuminating Polynesian history and culture. Pop., 371,657.

IN HAVANA revolutionary celebrations are part of the extreme patriotism encouraged by Fidel Castro, with the motto *Patria o Muerte, Venceremos,* or "Fatherland or Death, We Shall Conquer."

HONOLULU is an important shipping center as well as a major resort center, popular for its beautiful weather and beaches.

HOUSTON, in Texas, is founded on the petroleum industry, for which it utilizes its port on Galveston Bay and the Gulf of Mexico.

Houston, the largest city in Texas and fourth largest city in the United States. One of the country's major ports, Houston is connected with Galveston Bay and the Gulf of Mexico by the 50-mile-(80-kilometer-) long Houston Ship Channel. The city was the capital of Texas from 1836 to 1839. The petroleum industry is the foundation of Houston's economy. Grain, cotton, cattle, and diversified manufacturing are also important. Pop., 1,953,631.

Juárez, or Ciudad Juárez, in northern Mexico, opposite El Paso, Texas, on the Rio Grande. It is the marketing and processing center for a large cotton-growing area and an important highway and railroad terminus. It handles extensive trade with the United States. Pop., 1,187,000.

Kansas City, the largest city in the U.S. state of Missouri. It is located on the east bank of the Missouri River; on the west bank is Kansas City, Kansas, the second largest city in that state. The two cities form the center of a large metropolitan area that is one of the economic and transportation centers of the Midwest. Central to its economy is the processing and shipping of the region's agricultural products. Industry is also important, and the chief products include automobiles, transportation equipment, metal products, machines, petroleum products, and chemicals. Pop., Kansas City, Missouri, 441,545; Kansas City, Kansas, 146,866.

Kingston, capital and chief port of Jamaica, located on the southeastern coast of the island in the western Caribbean Sea. It exports Jamaica's rum, sugar, molasses, bananas, bauxite, and alumina. Pop., metro. area, 578,000.

kilometer
US

kilometre
Brit.

center
US

centre
Brit.

theater
US

theatre
Brit.

Kingstown, the capital and seaport of St. Vincent and the Grenadines, in the Windward Islands, located on the southern coast of St. Vincent Island. Pop., 15,000.

Kitchener and Waterloo, twin cities in southwestern Ontario, Canada. They make up a busy commercial, industrial, and insurance center. Important also are meat packing, distilling, furniture making, and the manufacture of metal and rubber goods. The boyhood home of William Lyon Mackenzie King is now Woodside National Historic Park, situated between the two cities. The area was first settled about 1800 by Mennonites emigrating from Pennsylvania. Kitchener's nine-day Oktoberfest is its main annual event. Other attractions include the city's Saturday-morning Farmers' Market, which features Mennonite and Amish specialties, notably beautiful handmade quilts, and Doon Pioneer Village, a reconstruction of an 1860s settlement. There is a Kitchener-Waterloo Symphony Orchestra, and theater can be seen at Kitchener's Centre-in-the-Square. The University of Waterloo and Wilfrid Laurier University, both at Waterloo, are affiliated with the University of Western Ontario. Pop., 276,942.

León, in central Mexico, on the Turbio River. The city is located in a fertile river plain and was once subject to frequent floods; it is now protected by a dam. It is an agricultural, commercial, and industrial center whose manufactures include shoes, textiles, flour, and leather goods. Local artisans produce knives, metal goods, and distinctive gold and silver embroideries. Pop., 1,021,000.

London, Canada's tenth largest city, in southwestern Ontario, on the Thames River. Situated in a rich agricultural region, it is a commercial, manufacturing, and regional financial center. The first European settlers in the region, in 1783, were Loyalists who left the United States at the end of the American Revolution. The site of the city was first occupied in 1830. London hosts the Western Fair, the oldest fall fair in Ontario. The city has a number of cultural attractions, including the Ridout Street Restoration, featuring restored Victorian houses, and St. Paul's Cathedral (1846). The University of Western Ontario is located in London. Pop., 336,539.

Los Angeles, on the Pacific coast in southern California, the second most populous city in the United States. It was founded in 1781 as a Spanish mission settlement. By the 1830s it had become an important trading port for American ships, and in 1846 it was captured by U.S. forces during the Mexican War. The city flourished during the 1849 California gold rush and expanded rapidly in the late 19th and early 20th centuries. Los Angeles is a major manufacturing, transportation, and financial center. Its manufactures include electronic equipment, building supplies, metal products, apparel, and processed foods. Los Angeles International Airport is one of the world's busiest airports. Hollywood, a district of Los Angeles, has been called the motion picture capital of the world, and many movie and television personalities

TOPIARY TREES surround a fountain and bandstand in León, Mexico's, Jardin de los Martires.

VISITORS TO Managua can see this monument to Nicaraguan poet Ruben Dario.

live in the Los Angeles metropolitan area. Writers, artists, and composers have also made their homes in and around the city, which is one of California's leading cultural and educational centers. Its institutions of higher learning include the University of Southern California and the University of California at Los Angeles. Cultural attractions include the Los Angeles Public Library; the Southwest Museum, which contains collections and exhibits of Native American art, culture, and history; the California Museum of Science and Technology; the Henry E. Huntington Library and Art Gallery in nearby San Marino; and the Music Center of Los Angeles County, home of the Los Angeles Philharmonic Orchestra. Pop., 3,694,820.

Managua, capital and largest city of Nicaragua, situated on the southern shore of Lake Managua. It lies on the main rail and road transportation routes and is the economic and cultural center of the country. It has food processing plants, textile mills, and pharmaceutical factories, as well as other industries. Pop., 903,000.

Memphis, the largest city in the U.S. state of Tennessee, on the Mississippi River in the southwestern corner of the state. An important commercial and industrial center, Memphis is one of the country's largest cotton and hardwood lumber markets. Its major manufactures include wood products, chemicals, textiles, farm equipment, and pharmaceuticals. The city is celebrated as the birthplace of the music known as the blues. The composer W. C. Handy immortalized Memphis in such songs as "Memphis Blues" and "Beale Street Blues." Graceland, the home and burial place of Elvis Presley, is one of the city's best-known points of interest. Pop., 650,100.

Mexico City, capital and largest city of Mexico, located in the southern part of the Central Plateau. Mexico City is one of the oldest cities in North America. The Aztecs built their capital, Tenochtitlán, on the site. Today the largest city in the western hemisphere, Mexico City is a major cultural, commercial, and industrial center. Its manufactures include steel, petroleum, textiles, machinery, chemicals, and food products. Mexico City's many fine buildings, sites of historical interest, beautiful location, and pleasant climate attract many tourists from all over the world. Pop., 8,605,000.

Milwaukee, a port city on Lake Michigan, the largest city in the U.S. state of Wisconsin, and a leading industrial and manufacturing center. Its major products include engines, electrical machinery, agricultural equipment, metal products, automotive parts, motorcycles, beer, and foodstuffs. Milwaukee's institutions of higher learning include Marquette University and the University of Wisconsin at Milwaukee. The city is the home of the Milwaukee Symphony Orchestra and also has opera and theater companies. It is noted for its spacious and beautiful parks. Pop., 596,974.

Minneapolis, the largest city in the U.S. state of Minnesota and, with the adjacent city of St. Paul, part of what is known as the Twin Cities metropolitan area. Located at the Falls of St. Anthony, at the head of navigation on the Mississippi River, the city is known for its numerous lakes and beautiful parks as well as its importance as a business, financial, transportation, and manufacturing center. The Minneapolis Grain Exchange is one of the largest in the world. Manufacturing and service industries have gained importance, and among the city's chief products are electronic equipment, transportation equipment, machinery, fabricated metals, apparel, and processed foods. Publishing and printing are also major industries. The main campus of the University of Minnesota is located in Minneapolis. The city's cultural institutions include the Tyrone Guthrie Theater and the Minneapolis Institute of Arts. A site of special interest is Minnehaha Falls, immortalized by Henry Wadsworth Longfellow in the poem *The Song of Hiawatha.* Pop., 382,618.

Moncton, named in the 1860s for Robert Monckton, a British commander who became lieutenant governor of Nova Scotia, located in eastern New Brunswick, Canada, on the Petitcodiac River. Once a prosperous shipbuilding center, Moncton lost this trade when wooden ships lost favor. The railway put the town on its feet again, and today it is still referred to as the Hub of the Maritimes, because all railway lines in and out of the area pass through it. Moncton's population is more than one-third

Francophone. Université de Moncton is the province's only French-language university. Points of interest include the Free Meeting House (c 1821), Moncton's oldest building; the Civic Museum; the Acadian Museum; Bore View Park, where a tidal bore races up the Petitcodiac River twice a day; and Magnetic Hill, where cars appear to coast uphill. Pop., 61,046.

Monterrey, one of Mexico's largest cities, the capital of Nuevo León State, located about 440 miles (710 km.) north of Mexico City. Second only to Mexico City as an industrial center, Monterrey produces iron and steel, refined nonferrous metals, cement, flour, textiles, and beverages. The city is an important financial center and the rail and highway hub of northern Mexico. It is the site of the University of Nuevo León. Pop., 1,111,000.

Montreal, Canada's second largest metropolitan area and also the second largest French-speaking city in the world, located on Ile de Montreal in the St. Lawrence River in southwestern Quebec. A cosmopolitan city with much evidence of French culture, it is also by virtue of its location on the St. Lawrence Seaway the chief gateway to the North American heartland. Montreal is an important transportation, banking,

MINNEAPOLIS receives an average of 49 inches of snowfall per year.

center
US

centre
Brit.

theaters
US

theatres
Brit.

kilometers
US

kilometres
Brit.

MONTREAL, the second largest metropolitan area in Canada, is also the second largest French-speaking city in the world and the French-language book publishing capital of Canada.

Nashville, the capital of the U.S. state of Tennessee, on the Cumberland River in the north-central part of the state. An industrial and transportation center, Nashville is also an important printing and publishing, financial, educational, and music center. The country music capital of the world, it is a center of the U.S. recording industry and the site of the Country Music Hall of Fame and of the Grand Ole Opry. A number of Nashville's public and institutional buildings are constructed in the Greek architectural style, and the city is often called the Athens of the South. An exact replica of the Parthenon stands in Centennial Park. Nashville is the headquarters of a number of religious organizations. The city's institutions of higher learning include Vanderbilt University, Fisk University, and Tennessee State University. Points of interest include the tomb of James K. Polk on the Capitol grounds and The Hermitage, the home of Andrew Jackson, about 12 miles (19 kilometers) east of the city. Pop., 569,891.

Nassau, port and capital of the Bahamas, on the northeast coast of New Providence Island. Tourism is the leading industry. Pop., metro. area, 211,000.

Newark, the largest city in New Jersey and a major U.S. port, situated on Newark Bay, just west of the southern tip of New York City. Dominating northeastern New Jersey, the state's main industrial and manufacturing region, Newark produces a wide variety of goods and materials, including chemicals, electronic equipment, plastics, machinery, and foodstuffs. The city is also an important financial and transportation center. Newark International Airport is a major hub of the U.S. air transportation system. Pop., 273,546.

financial, and manufacturing center, as well as the French-language book publishing capital of Canada. Of the total population, about 64 percent are of French descent. The site of Montreal was one of the earliest to be used by the French explorers, who found an Indian village there in 1535. The city's many attractions include Mount Royal Park, which rises behind the city; Old Montreal, which was declared a historic district in 1963; the city hall (Hôtel de Ville), an elaborate example of French Renaissance architecture; Place des Arts, a complex with three theaters, including Salle Wilfred-Pelletier, base of the world-famous Montreal Symphony Orchestra; the Montreal Museum of Fine Arts, Canada's oldest art museum; and the basilica of St. Joseph's Oratory, Canada's largest church. Montreal has an excellent Métro (subway system) with access to the city's underground network of shops and restaurants. The Montreal Botanical Gardens is the world's third largest. Montreal's institutions of higher learning include McGill University and the Université de Montréal. Pop., 1,039,534.

NASHVILLE'S EXACT REPLICA of the Parthenon, with its 40-foot statue of Athena, is the icon for its claim as the Athens of the South. It is also known as the home of country music and is a center for the recording industry.

NEW YORK CITY'S Lincoln Center is home to 12 resident companies, including the Juilliard School.

New Orleans, the largest city in Louisiana and one of the busiest ports in the United States, located on the Mississippi River about 110 miles (177 kilometers) from where the river empties into the Gulf of Mexico. The city's economy is centered on port trade. Major exports include petroleum products, grain, cotton, steel, and fabricated metals. Manufactures include chemicals, paint, processed foods, and paper products. Founded in 1718, the city reflects in its cosmopolitan population its varied history as a French colony, Spanish colony, Southern city, and American city. Its French quarter, or Vieux Carré (literally, "Old Square"), is the original site of New Orleans and a favorite attraction of the many tourists who visit each year. The leading tourist event is the famous Mardi Gras festival. New Orleans was the birthplace of jazz music, and the city holds an annual Dixieland jazz festival. Its institutions of higher learning include Tulane University, Loyola University, and the University of New Orleans. Pop., 484,674.

New York, the most populous city in the United States and one of the great metropolitan centers of the world. Situated at the mouth of the Hudson River, it was founded by the Dutch in 1624 as the settlement of New Amsterdam. By the time it passed under British control in 1664 and was renamed New York, it had become a center of trade and commerce. The U.S. Congress met in New York from 1785 to 1790 and George Washington, the first president under the Constitution, was inaugurated there in 1789. In the early 19th century, New York passed Boston and Philadelphia to become the shipping, manufacturing, and financial center of the country. New York was the port of arrival for millions of European immigrants in the late 19th and early 20th centuries. The city is served by two major airports, La Guardia and John F. Kennedy International. New York is a world center for finance, trade, transportation, communications, fashion, entertainment, and the arts, so it is fitting that it is also the home of the United Nations. The city's many cultural institutions include Lincoln Center for the Performing Arts, home of the New York Philharmonic, New York City Ballet, New York City Opera, and Metropolitan Opera; Carnegie Hall; the Museum of Modern Art; the Metropolitan Museum of Art; the Solomon R. Guggenheim Museum; the Whitney Museum; the American Museum of Natural History; the New York Public Library; and the Pierpont Morgan Library. Its institutions of higher learning include Columbia University, New York University, Fordham University, Rockefeller University, and the City University of New York. Among points of interest are the Broadway theater district, Statue of Liberty, Empire State Building, and the site where the World Trade Center Towers once stood. Pop., 8,008,278.

Niagara Falls. *See* St. Catharines and Niagara Falls.

Ottawa, the capital of Canada, situated on the Ottawa River at Ontario's eastern border. Across the river in Quebec is the city of Gatineau. Lumbering was the first major industry of the area, but today the main business of the city is that of government. Manufacturing is also important, and there is a growing high-technology sector. Ottawa was first known as Bytown, for Colonel John By who, with British army engineers, arrived in 1826 to build the Rideau Canal. Ottawa's skyline is still dominated by Canada's Parliament buildings, three large Victorian Gothic structures that were built from 1859 to 1865. The Centre Block houses the House of Commons and the Senate; the East Block, the prime minister's, governor-general's, and Privy Council's offices, and the cabinet chamber; the West Block, offices and committee rooms. The Peace Tower, with its 53-bell carillon, rises 285 feet (87 meters) above the Centre Block. Visitors are permitted to watch proceedings from the House of Commons gallery.

Major museums and galleries in Ottawa include the new National Gallery of Canada, the Museum of Man (across the river in Hull), the fine National Aeronautical Collection, the National Postal Museum, and the museum of the Royal Canadian Mint. Visitors may also tour the mint itself. The Rideau Canal runs through the heart of the city and provides a popular skating area in winter. Ottawa's institutions of higher learning include the University of Ottawa, Canada's oldest bilingual university, and Carleton University. Pop., 774,072.

THE COPPER SPIRE of Peace Tower at the Parliament buildings rises over the Ottawa River.

center
US

centre
Brit.

colored
US

coloured
Brit.

Panama City, capital city of Panama, situated at the Pacific Ocean end of the Panama Canal. The city is a transportation and commercial center with an important tourist industry. Its manufactures include food products, metal products, furniture, beer, and clothing. The city is the seat of two universities. Pop., 416,000.

Philadelphia, the largest city in Pennsylvania and fifth largest city in the United States. Situated on the Delaware River in southeastern Pennsylvania, it was founded by William Penn in 1681. In the 1700s Philadelphia became the financial center of the American colonies and a major trading port. It was the meeting place of the first and second Continental Congresses during the American Revolution, the site of the Constitutional Convention of 1787, and the capital of the United States from 1790 to 1800. Today service industries make up the largest component of the city's economy. Wholesale and retail trade and manufacturing are also important. The city is a known educational center. Its institutions of higher learning include the University of Pennsylvania, Temple University, Drexel University, and La Salle University. Its Independence National Historical Park includes Carpenters Hall, seat of the First Continental Congress; Independence Hall, seat of the Second Continental Congress; Congress Hall, seat of Congress from 1790 to 1800; and Liberty Bell Pavilion, where the original Liberty Bell is on display. Pop., 1,517,550.

Port-au-Prince, capital and chief port of Haiti, situated on the west coast of Hispaniola, on the Caribbean Sea. The chief exports of Port-au-Prince include coffee, sugar, textiles, and sisal. Pop., metro. area, 991,000.

Portland, the largest city in the U.S. state of Oregon, on the Willamette River near its confluence with the Columbia River. Its port can accommodate oceangoing vessels. Major commodities passing through the port include wood and wood products, agricultural products, and ores. Portland produces a variety of manufactured goods, including machinery and electronic equipment. Pop., 529,121

Port of Spain, or Port-of-Spain, seaport and capital of Trinidad and Tobago, on the northwest coast of the island of Trinidad. It is the commercial and industrial center of the country and one of the principal shipping centers for the

REGINA'S Legislative and Executive Building, begun in 1908, was completed and opened in 1912.

RAMONA FALLS, near Portland, drops 120 feet over a basalt cliff.

Pittsburgh, the second largest city in Pennsylvania, formerly one of the most important steel-producing centers in the United States. Its location, in coal-rich southwestern Pennsylvania, where the Monongahela and Allegheny rivers join to form the Ohio River, was ideal for the growth of the steel industry. Steel production declined in the 1970s and has been replaced by manufacturing, service, and research and development industries. Pittsburgh is a transportation hub and an important educational center. Its institutions of higher learning include Carnegie Mellon University, the University of Pittsburgh, and Duquesne University. Its cultural institutions include the Pittsburgh Symphony Orchestra and the Frick Art Museum. Pop., 334,563.

Pointe à Pitre, capital and chief city of Guadeloupe, in the West Indies. The city is a seaport that exports food products, especially sugar, rum, cacao, coffee, and bananas. Pop., 26,000.

Caribbean. Its exports include oil, citrus fruits, rum, plastics, lumber, and textiles. Pop., 48,000.

Puebla, or Puebla de Zaragoza, in east-central Mexico, about 75 miles (120 km.) southeast of Mexico City. The city is an agricultural, commercial, and industrial center noted for its onyx work, glazed colored tiles, textiles, pottery, and glass. It is also a popular tourist center. Pop., 1,272,000.

Quebec City, the capital of the Province of Quebec, Canada, on the St. Lawrence River, where the St. Charles River flows into it. It is a center of government administration as well as a commercial and industrial city and a popular place for tourists. Food products, textiles, clothing, machinery, autos, and lumber are included in its output. Only about 4 percent of the population come from an English background. An Indian village was on the site in 1535 when Jacques

THE HISTORIC CITY OF QUEBEC, founded by Samuel de Champlain in 1608, is Canada's oldest city and headquarters of the provincial government.

Cartier arrived. Canada's oldest city, founded by Samuel de Champlain in 1608, Quebec has much of historical interest to offer. National Battlefields Park commemorates the Battle of the Plains of Abraham (September 13, 1759), probably the most decisive battle in Canadian history. The Basilica of Notre Dame, begun in 1647, is the church of Canada's oldest parish (from 1659). Place Royale features restorations of some 80 houses from the 17th and 18th centuries. In 1688 Jean Talon, the "Great Intendant," had Canada's first commercial brewery built there. Today Talon's Vaults house a museum of 17th-century artifacts beneath a modern brewery.

The National Assembly (which was completed in 1886), is the provincial government's headquarters. Quebec is North America's only walled city (outside of Mexico), and the fortifications—3.5 miles (5.6 kilometers) long—are accessible to visitors. Quebec's leading festival is its Winter Carnival, called Carnaval, a pre-Lent celebration that lasts for ten days in January or February and usually doubles the city's population. University Laval was founded in 1852. Its campus is at Ste-Foy, southeast of Quebec City. Pop., 169,076.

Regina, capital and second largest city of the Province of Saskatchewan, Canada, founded at a site called Wascana ("pile of bones") by the Indians of the region. It is located south and slightly east of center in the province, 100 miles (161 kilometers) north of the U.S. border. In 1882 Wascana was renamed Regina (for Queen Victoria) and became the capital of the then Northwest Territories, until Saskatchewan was made a province in 1905. With its economy dependent on the rich wheat-growing region that surrounds it, Regina is the headquarters of the Saskatchewan Wheat Pool, the largest grain-handling cooperative in the world. The provincial government is also an important employer. Metal fabricating industries are significant, as are industries producing plastic, petroleum, and coal products. The city is southern Saskatchewan's main retail and service center. Wascana Center, in the heart of

Regina, is an attractive park and the site of the provincial Legislative Building, the Saskatchewan Centre of the Arts, and the University of Regina. The Royal Canadian Mounted Police Museum (Regina is the training center for the force) tells the story of Canada's famous Mounties. Pop., 178,225.

Roseau, capital and largest city of Dominica in the Windward Islands. The city is located on the Caribbean Sea. Primarily a port, Roseau exports the island's limes, lime juice, bananas, and spices. Pop., 16,000.

St. Catharines and Niagara Falls, the two largest of the 12 municipalities that make up the Niagara peninsula, a wedge of land between Lake Ontario and Lake Erie. It is bounded on the east by the United States and on the west by the Hamilton, Ontario, region. St. Catharines, on the Welland Canal, is in the heart of Canada's wine country, and half of the fruit grown in Ontario comes from the immediate area. It also has

nearly 250 manufacturing establishments, the main product being transportation equipment. St. Catharines was founded after the American Revolution by Loyalists who came north. The first families on the site of Niagara Falls arrived in 1782. Millions of people from all over the world visit Niagara Falls every year. A fleet of little boats, all called *Maid of the Mist,* transport sightseers to the base of Canada's Horseshoe Falls, and an aerocar crosses the Niagara Gorge, affording a fine view of the whirlpool there. Niagara-on-the-Lake was burned by American troops in 1813, but rebuilt thereafter. Today it is notable as one of the finest preservations/restorations of an early 19th-century town in North America. Other attractions include nearby Fort George National Historic Park, and Niagara-on-the-Lake's annual Shaw Festival, featuring performances of the works of George Bernard Shaw. Brock University was founded at St. Catharines in 1964. Pop., metro. area, 377,009.

St. George's, capital and principal town of Grenada, in the Caribbean Sea. The town, on the island's southwestern coast, has a deep natural harbor. Its economy relies heavily on shipping and tourism. Its exports include cocoa, bananas, and spices. Pop., 4,600.

Saint John, largest city of New Brunswick, Canada, situated at the mouth of the Saint John River, 66 miles (106 kilometers) southeast of Fredericton. It is one of North America's oldest cities. Samuel de Champlain anchored in the harbor there in 1604. In 1631 Charles de la Tour set up a fortified trading post. While 1762 marks the date of the first permanent English settlement, the arrival of a few thousand Loyalists from the United States in the summer of 1783 was a settlement landmark. In the 19th century, the city was noted for

kilometers
US

kilometres
Brit.

27 North America

THE CAPITAL CITY of Grenada, St. George's, has a deep natural harbor that plays an important role in both shipping and tourism, the mainstays of its economy.

THE FAMOUS GATEWAY ARCH in St. Louis was designed by Eero Saarinen to commemorate the role of the city as the settlers' Gateway to the West.

kilometers
US

kilometres
Brit.

centers
US

centres
Brit.

commerce in lumber and shipbuilding, but its fortunes declined as the use of wooden ships did. Saint John remains an important port, with pulp and paper a significant industry—along with tourism. A monument commemorates Champlain's naming of the Saint John River on June 24, 1604—June 24 being the saint's name day. Loyalist Days, an annual, five-day celebration of the Loyalists' arrival by sea in May, 1783, is held in late July. Saint John is also the site of the world-famous Reversing Falls, which can be seen in action twice a day. Pop., 69,661.

St. John's, the capital of Newfoundland and Labrador, Canada, and its principal city, situated at the northeast tip of the Avalon peninsula. Legend says John Cabot discovered Newfoundland on June 24, 1497, and named the St. John's site for John the Baptist. In 1583 the island was formally claimed for Elizabeth I by Sir Humphrey Gilbert, thus becoming England's oldest colony. In 1762 the Battle of Signal Hill was the last clash between French and English troops in North America. In 1832, when England granted Newfoundland a colonial legislature, St. John's became the seat of government. A vital port during both world wars, St. John's Harbor is to this day frequented by ships of all nations. With the decline of the east coast fishery, government jobs have helped to stabilize the city's economy. Cabot Tower, on Signal Hill high above St. John's Harbor, was built to

commemorate John Cabot's discovery of Newfoundland; it is also of interest as the place where Guglielmo Marconi received the first transatlantic wireless message on December 12, 1901. Cape Spear, a scenic promontory 6.25 miles (10 kilometers) southeast of St. John's is North America's most easterly point. The Newfoundland Museum contains a significant collection of Beothuk Indian artifacts and other exhibits from the island's history. Memorial University of Newfoundland is the province's only university. Pop., 99,182.

St. Louis, the largest city in Missouri and a major inland port of the United States. Situated on the Mississippi River, it was founded in 1764 as a French fur-trading post. In the mid-19th century, St. Louis was the jumping-off point for many settlers moving west, and it became known as the Gateway to the West. Contemporary St. Louis is one of the country's leading commercial and transportation centers. Its broadly diversified manufactures include automobiles, transportation equipment, chemicals, electronics, paper products, beer, and processed foods. Its cultural institutions include the prestigious St. Louis Symphony Orchestra and the St. Louis Art Museum. Of special interest is the Jefferson National Expansion Memorial, dominated by the spectacular

630-foot (192-meter) stainless steel Gateway Arch, designed by the architect Eero Saarinen. Pop., 348,189.

St. Paul, the capital of Minnesota, forming with Minneapolis the Twin Cities, one of the largest metropolitan areas in the United States. Its leading products include electronic equipment, appliances, automobiles, processed foods, and beer. Printing and publishing are important industries. Major attractions include the St. Paul Arts and Science Center, the Minnesota Museum of Art, and the Gibbs Farm Museum. The annual St. Paul Winter Carnival, held for ten days each January, attracts many visitors. Pop., 287,151.

San Diego, a city in southwestern California, the sixth largest city in the United States. It is a major port and site of several U.S. military facilities. The area was first settled in 1769, when a Spanish fort and mission were built. San Diego grew rapidly in the late 1800s and early 1900s and became an important military base and a center for the fledgling aviation industry. Its major products include aerospace components, electronics, marine supplies, apparel, and agricultural products from the surrounding farm region. San Diego has a number of institutions of higher learning, including San Diego State Uni-

THE STEEP STREETS of San Francisco lend a roller coaster atmosphere to its trolley rides.

San José, capital and largest city of Costa Rica, situated on the Rio Grande near the center of the country. It is on international air and rail routes and is the commercial center for a coffee-growing region. Pop., 344,000.

San Juan, seaport and the capital of Puerto Rico, on the island's northeast coast. It has an excellent harbor and is an export center for agricultural goods such as sugar, tobacco, and fruit. Manufactures include petroleum products, chemicals, pharmaceuticals, and cement. It was first settled in 1509 by Spaniards commanded by Ponce de León. Pop., metro. area, 2,450,292.

San Salvador, capital and largest city of El Salvador, situated in the mountains in the west-central portion of the country. It is a cultural, transportation, and commercial center whose manufactures

by members of the Temperance Colonization Society. Places of interest include Fort Carlton Historic Park, a reconstruction of an important fur trade fort; the Ukrainian Museum of Arts and Crafts; the Western Development Museum (with other branches at Yorkton and Moose Jaw), which features an indoor pioneer village; the Mendel Art Gallery; and the Civic Conservatory. The University of Saskatchewan has an observatory that is open to the public. Pop., 196,811.

Seattle, the largest city in the state of Washington and one of the centers of the U.S. aerospace industry. Located on Puget Sound, Seattle is an important port for trade with Asia and the Pacific and a gateway to Alaska and western Canada. It is the home of the Boeing aircraft company. Diversified manufacturing, shipbuilding, containerized

A BRIDGE leads to the entrance of the King's Bastion at Louisbourg Fortress, near Sydney.

versity, the University of San Diego, and the Scripps Institution of Oceanography, which is a part of the University of California at San Diego. Other points of interest include the restored Mission San Diego de Alcalá and the world-famous San Diego Zoo. Pop., 1,223,400.

San Francisco, one of the most celebrated cities of the United States, situated on the Pacific coast in northern California. Located on the northern tip of a peninsula between the Pacific Ocean and San Francisco Bay, it is one of the finest harbors in the world. In 1776 a Spanish mission and military post were established on the peninsula. In 1835 a second settlement, Yerba Buena, rose nearby. In 1847 this settlement was renamed San Francisco. The California gold rush of 1849 turned the settlement into a boom town, marking the beginning of its rise as the financial, business, and cultural center of northern California. In 1906 San Francisco was virtually destroyed by an earthquake and subsequent fire, but it was speedily rebuilt. The city was struck by another major earthquake in 1989. San Francisco's population includes many diverse ethnic groups, including Chinese, Japanese, Hispanic, Filipino, African-American, Italian, and Russian communities. Modern San Francisco is one of the leading financial and trade centers of the United States. Its manufactures include textiles, fabricated metals, electrical equipment, and paper products. The city's major cultural institutions include the San Francisco Symphony Orchestra and the San Francisco Opera. Its institutions of higher learning include the University of San Francisco and the University of California, San Francisco. Among points of interest are the Golden Gate Bridge, which links the city with its northern suburbs, and Golden Gate Park. Pop., 776,733.

include textiles, clothing, leather goods, liquor, and tobacco products. The city has frequently been badly damaged by severe earthquakes. Pop., 473,000.

Santo Domingo, capital and largest city of the Dominican Republic. Its refineries and distilleries process locally grown sugar cane. Other industries include textiles, chemicals, plastics, and food processing. The city is the chief port of the country. Founded in 1496, it has been continuously inhabited longer than any other city in the western hemisphere. Pop., 2,677,000.

Saskatoon, located in south-central Saskatchewan, Canada, on the South Saskatchewan River. Now the province's largest city, its 210 manufacturing establishments produce a variety of goods, and the city has benefited from increased production of potash, uranium, and oil. It is also a processing and distributing center for agricultural products. Saskatoon was first settled in 1882

shipping, fishing, food processing, and financial services are important economic activities. Seattle's institutions of higher learning include the University of Washington and Seattle University. Pop., 563,374.

Sydney, situated at the east end of Cape Breton Island, Canada, the second-largest city in Nova Scotia. Coal mining and steelmaking dominate the city's economy, just as the steel mill itself dominates most of the city's outer harbor. The mill is one of the largest of its kind in North America. The city is the home of the University College of Cape Breton. About 19 miles (30 kilometers) south of Sydney, the magnificent Fortress of Louisbourg, Canada's largest historical reconstruction, is the focal point of Fortress of Louisbourg National Historic Park (20 square miles, 51 square kilometers). The French began construction of the fortress in 1720, and the original plans and drawings may be seen at its museum. Pop., metro. area, 109,330.

THE NAME OF SAN JUAN, the capital of Puerto Rico, is derived from San Juan Bautista, or St. John the Baptist, the name given the entire island by Christopher Columbus in 1493.

27 North America

Tegucigalpa, capital and largest city of Honduras, situated in the south-central part of the country. It produces textiles, clothing, chemicals, cigarettes, plywood, and plastics. Pop., 835,000.

Tijuana, in Baja California, northwestern Mexico, just south of the U.S. border. The city is a popular tourist resort, with casinos, racetracks, and bullfights. It is a principal point of entry on the U.S.-Mexico border. It is the center of a region that produces wheat, barley, and grapes. Pop., 1,149,000.

Toronto, located on the northwestern shore of Lake Ontario, the capital of the Province of Ontario and Canada's largest metropolitan area. It is a cosmopolitan city of commerce, industry, and retail trade, and is the financial center of Canada. Its varied manufactures include metal, electrical, rubber, plastic, chemical, paper, and printing products, food, and beverages. Toronto is the English-language book publishing capital of Canada. The French built a fort on the city's site in 1749, and the British formally named the locality York in 1793. The name was changed to Toronto in 1834. Toronto's Roy Thomson Hall, Massey Hall, O'Keefe Center, and Royal Alexandra Theatre are the city's major

TOTEM POLES such as these in Vancouver's Stanley Park are symbols of the area's indigenous peoples.

musical and theatrical showplaces, but there are also many experimental and fringe theaters. Toronto has a symphony orchestra that is well known, and it is the base of the National Ballet of Canada and its National Ballet School, as well as of the Canadian Opera Company. The Royal Ontario Museum and the Art Gallery of Ontario are both located in the heart of the city and have major collections. The CN Tower is the world's tallest free-standing structure at 1,815.4 feet (553.3 meters). It rises to the Space Deck, from which visitors can see the U.S. shore of Lake Ontario on a very clear day. It is some 33 miles (53 kilometers) away.

The city's Chinatown, along with three suburban versions, is now Canada's largest in population and area. The University of Toronto, founded in 1827, is Canada's largest university. York University is located north of the city. In the northeast of the city is the Ontario Science Centre. Located on the grounds of the Canadian National Exhibition are the Hockey Hall of Fame and the Canadian Sports Hall of Fame. Pop., 2,481,494.

Vancouver, a port city situated on a peninsula in southwestern British Columbia, Canada, some 15 miles (24 kilometers) north of the U.S. border. Vancouver is Canada's third largest metropolitan area. It is also Canada's gateway to Asia and the Pacific, and one of North America's busiest ports. Vancouver is a cosmopolitan city with a varied ethnic population. The city has a vibrant Chinatown that was until recently the largest in Canada. An appealing downtown restoration called Gastown (Vancouver's original name) features shops with indigenous handicrafts, galleries, and restaurants. Scenic Stanley Park is a favorite destination for visitors, as is the Public Aquarium. Other points of interest include the Vancouver Art Gallery and the Vancouver Playhouse (1962), adjoining the larger Queen Elizabeth Theatre. The city is noted for its lively theater scene and for its symphony orchestra. The University of British Columbia has its campus west of the city, and Simon Fraser University is at Burnaby, to the northeast. Pop., 545,671.

FOUNDED BY THE HUDSON'S BAY COMPANY as a trading outpost, the beautiful city of Victoria on Vancouver Island is reputed to be "more English than England."

Victoria, the capital of British Columbia, Canada, at the southeastern end of Vancouver Island, about 63 miles (100 kilometers) south of mainland Vancouver. Tourism is the city's major business, followed by government, labor, and commercial fisheries. Reputed to be "more English than England," Victoria began in 1843 as a Hudson's Bay Company post known as Fort Camosun, but the name was soon changed to Fort Victoria. It became the capital of the Crown colony of Vancouver Island in 1862 and part of British Columbia in 1866. The Art Gallery of Greater Victoria has a fine collection of European and Canadian art, including works by Emily Carr, who was born in Victoria. Other points of interest include the British Columbia Provincial Parliament Buildings; the Provincial Museum and Archives; Thunderbird Park, where a magnificent collection of totem poles is on display, carved c 1850 to 1890 by members of Pacific coast Indian tribes; and Butchart Gardens, north of the city, which has a superb botanical display. The University of Victoria was founded in 1963. The city has a symphony orchestra, and its Bastion Theatre is well known. Pop., 74,125.

A SCENIC PATH winds through a flower garden in a Windsor park.

Washington, D.C., the capital of the United States. Situated on the east bank of the Potomac River, the city is the center of the sixth largest metropolitan area in the country. Founded in 1791 as the seat of U.S. government, the city was named after George Washington. It is coextensive with the federal District of Columbia. Government is the chief employer, and tourism is the second most important component of the city's economy. Washington has many points of interest, including the Capitol, seat of the U.S. Congress; the White House, official residence of the president; the Lincoln Memorial; the Washington Monument; the Jefferson Memorial; the National Archives; the Library of Congress; the National Air and Space Museum; the National Gallery of Art; the Smithsonian Institution; and the Vietnam War Memorial. The John F. Kennedy Center for the Performing Arts is the home of the American Ballet Theater and

NICKNAMED "THE NATION'S ATTIC," the Smithsonian Institution is the world's largest museum.

National Symphony Orchestra. The city's institutions of higher education include Georgetown University, George Washington University, Howard University, American University, and Gallaudet University, which was founded for the education of the deaf. Pop., 572,059.

Waterloo. *See* the entry for Kitchener and Waterloo.

Windsor, Canada's southernmost city and largest city on the U.S. border. In Ontario on the Detroit River, opposite Detroit, Michigan, Windsor is Canada's busiest port of entry. Auto manufacturing is the largest single enterprise. Located in a region favorable to agriculture, Windsor is also a large producer of foods and beverages. The city was founded by French trappers in 1749. After the American Revolution many Loyalists arrived. The Art Gallery of Windsor has a particularly fine Canadian collection, including Inuit prints and carvings. The city has a symphony orchestra, and the Windsor Light Opera Company is also a popular attraction. Cleary Auditorium and Convention Centre is the city's performing arts complex. The cities of Detroit and Windsor hold an annual, weeklong International Freedom Festival to coincide with Canada Day (July 1) and U.S. Independence Day (July 4). Windsor's two riverfront parks, Dieppe and Centennial, offer excellent views of Detroit's skyline across the river and are popular attractions. The city is the home of the prestigious University of Windsor. Pop., 208,402.

Winnipeg, in southern Manitoba, Canada, where the Assiniboine River joins the Red River, the province's capital and largest city. It is located close to the geographical center of the North American continent, and it is the chief market center of one of the world's largest grain-producing areas.

Winnipeg's varied industries make it the most diversified secondary manufacturing city in Canada, and it is also important as the financial, distribution, and transportation center of western Canada. The first settlement here was a fort that was built by the French in 1783. Later, the English also built forts. In 1873 the city was incorporated as Winnipeg. Places of historical interest include Lower Fort Garry, a restoration of the Hudson's Bay Company fort, originally built in 1832. It is located just north of Winnipeg. The city is home to the world-famous Royal Winnipeg Ballet; the Manitoba Theater Centre; and the Winnipeg Art Gallery, which has one of the world's largest collections of Inuit art. The University of Manitoba and the University of Winnipeg are both located here. Pop., 619,544.

WINNIPEG is one of the world's largest wheat markets.

Glossary of North America

Alcalde. The title used in the Iberian peninsula since the 1000s, and later in the Spanish colonies, to designate a local official. The term, derived from the Arabic *al qadi,* the judge, was also part of many government titles indicating some judicial authority.

Aleutian Islands. A chain of about 70 volcanic islands extending some 1,200 miles (1,931 kilometers) in a broad southwestern arc from the Alaska peninsula, on the south-central coast of the U.S. state of Alaska. An extension of the Aleutian Range on mainland Alaska, the island chain has a number of active volcanoes. The land area of the Aleutians is 6,821 square miles (17,666 square kilometers). The islands, which separate the Pacific Ocean from the Bering Sea, include five island groups; in order from the mainland they are the Fox, Islands of the Mountains, Andreanof, Rat, and Near islands. During the second World War, Attu and Agattu islands in the Near Islands and Kiska Island in the Rat Islands were occupied from 1942 to 1943 by Japanese forces.

Alliance for Progress. A pan-American program initiated in 1961 by U.S. President John F. Kennedy. It called on the Americas to unite in their attempts to install and protect democratic governments while working toward economic prosperity. This enthusiastic and idealistic program called for labor and agrarian reforms to ensure that all people would share equitably in the resulting progress.

Antilles. A large archipelago between North and South America lying partly in the Caribbean Sea and partly in the Atlantic Ocean. The Greater Antilles, at

kilometers
US
kilometres
Brit.

labor
US
labour
Brit.

center
US
centre
Brit.

BAFFIN ISLAND in the Arctic Archipelago is home to many species of wildlife, including polar bears.

THE APPALACHIAN TRAIL is a footpath that extends about 2,000 miles (3,200 kilometers) from Maine to Georgia, following the Appalachian Mountains. Serious hikers walk its entire length in about six months.

the northwestern end of the curving chain, includes the large islands of Cuba, Jamaica, Hispaniola, and Puerto Rico. The Lesser Antilles, the southern and eastern portions of the archipelago, includes the many small islands off the coast of Venezuela and the islands of the Windward and Leeward groups. Many of the Antilles are volcanic in origin, and most are mountainous.

Appalachian Mountains. A mountain system running roughly parallel to the Atlantic coast of North America, a distance of about 1,200 miles (1,931 kilometers) from Newfoundland in Canada, to the U.S. state of Alabama. The Appalachians vary in width from about 80 miles (129 kilometers) to about 200 miles (322 kilometers), widening in the central and southern regions. Elevation ranges from several hundred feet to 6,684 feet (2,037 meters) at Mount Mitchell, in the Blue Ridge Mountains in west-central North Carolina. The Appalachians were formed between 1 billion and 250 million years ago, making them among the oldest land features on Earth; they have been worn down considerably over time.

Article 123. A revolutionary provision of Mexico's constitution of 1917 that granted political recognition of the country's labor groups. It guaranteed wage controls, an 8-hour workday, an end to

child labor, occupational safety provisions, and the right of labor to organize. It is often called the Magna Carta of Mexican labor.

Athabasca. The fourth largest lake situated entirely within Canada, covering about 3,064 square miles (7,936 square kilometers). It is about 200 miles (322 kilometers) long and from 5 miles (8 kilometers) to 35 miles (56 kilometers) wide. Lying in northeast Alberta and northwest Saskatchewan, the lake is part of the Mackenzie River system and drains north into Great Slave Lake by way of the Slave River.

Athabasca River. A body of water that rises in the Columbia Icefield in Canada, along the British Columbia/Alberta border, flows north through Jasper National Park, and then northeast and north to Lake Athabasca. About 769 miles (1,237 kilometers) long, it is the most southerly tributary of the Mackenzie River. Near its headwaters is Athabasca Pass, elevation 5,733 feet (1,747 meters), which leads across the Continental Divide to the Columbia River.

Audiencia. A Spanish royal court of appeal that came into existence in Spain in the 1200s. The institution was carried to Spain's colonial possessions beginning in the 1500s. The first audiencia in the Americas was established in 1511 on the island of Santo Domingo (Hispaniola). The audiencia had judicial and administrative functions. In the Americas these bodies came to function as councils of state, often acting as checks on the exercise of arbitrary power by the Spanish governor. A total of 13 audiencias were established in the New World.

Baffin Island. The largest island in the Arctic Archipelago, northeast of Hudson Bay, Canada. Its area is 195,928 square miles (507,454 square kilometers). It is about 1,000 miles (1,600 kilometers) long and 125 to 440 miles (200 to 700 kilometers) wide. On the west it is mostly covered with tundra, while to the east mountains rise to about 8,000 feet (2,438 meters). The coastline is deeply indented and has many fjords. In the southeastern Cumberland peninsula, Auyuittuq National Park (13,438 square miles, 21,500 square kilometers) is Canada's first national park north of the Arctic Circle.

Baja California. Or Lower California, a long, narrow peninsula about 750 miles (1,208 kilometers) long in western Mexico south of California. The Pacific Ocean lies to its west, and the Gulf of

California to the east separates it from the rest of Mexico. Mountain ridges occupy the eastern and central portions of the peninsula. Most of the land is desert or arid plain.

Banff National Park. Created in 1887, Canada's oldest national park. Situated 78 miles (126 kilometers) west of Calgary, it is 2,590 square miles (6,708 square kilometers) in area. In the midst of the Rockies, stretching along the eastern slope of the Continental Divide, the park has several peaks that approach 12,000 feet (3,658 meters) in elevation. Natural features of the park include hot mineral springs, ice fields, and spectacular mountain lakes, of which Lake Louise, discovered in 1882 and named for a daughter of Queen Victoria, is probably the best known. The town of Banff, on the Bow River, is noted for its fine resorts. Banff is Canada's most widely visited national park.

Caribbean Sea. A body of water between North and South America, and east of Central America, at the western edge of the Atlantic Ocean. On the north and east it is ringed by the islands of the Greater and Lesser Antilles. The Caribbean Sea is approximately 1 million square miles (2.6 million square kilometers) in area.

Caudillos. Leaders that rose to power in the early 1800s in most of the South and Central American republics, notably Brazil, Venezuela, Colombia, Bolivia, and Mexico. They were usually powerful military figures who gained political control through violence and maintained it with repression and terrorism.

Colorado. One of the major rivers of the southwestern United States, rising in the Rocky Mountains in northcentral Colorado. It flows some 1,450 miles (2,333 kilometers) generally southwestward through Colorado, Utah, and Arizona, then turns south, forming part of Arizona's border with Nevada and Mexico and all of its border with California. The river then crosses Mexico for a short distance before emptying into the Gulf of California. Its tributaries include the Green, San Juan, Little Colorado, and Gila rivers. A number of dams, including Imperial, Hoover, and Glen Canyon, have largely controlled the wide seasonal variation in the Colorado River's volume and have created large reservoirs for municipal, agricultural, and recreational use. The river has cut deep canyons along its course, the best known being Grand Canyon.

Columbia. A river rising in southeastern British Columbia, Canada, and flowing some 1,243 miles (2,000 kilometers) to the Pacific Ocean. The river first flows northwestward, then turns south through British Columbia and enters the northeastern portion of the U.S. state of Washington. It turns west, then south, then west again and forms part of

Washington's border with Oregon. Its main tributary is the Snake River; others include the Kootenay, Okanogan, and Willamette rivers. The main population center on the river is Portland, Oregon. The Columbia's numerous dams, including the Bonneville, John Day, Rock Island, and Grand Coulee, produce an enormous supply of electric power. However, the dams have greatly decreased the salmon runs along the river and have damaged both commercial and sport fishing. The lakes and

reservoirs along the Columbia's length are important sources of drinking and irrigation water and are also very popular as recreational sites. The Columbia has the greatest volume of any river in North America flowing into the Pacific.

Creoles. The second highest class of citizens (behind the *peninsulares,* born in Spain) in colonial Spanish America. They were Spaniards or Europeans but were American-born. The Creoles were important landholders and artisans, but they were generally passed over in favor of *peninsulares* for high positions in both church and government, a fact that led them to play a major role in the independence movement of the early 1800s.

Cumberland. One of the main tributaries of the Ohio River, formed by the confluence of the Poor and Clover forks in the southeastern part of the U.S. state of Kentucky. It is 687 miles (1,105 kilometers) long and flows generally southwest into Tennessee, then turns northwest at Nashville to reenter Kentucky. It parallels the Tennessee River to the west, and empties into the Ohio at Smithland, Kentucky.

During the American Civil War, control of the Cumberland and Tennessee river valleys was important to both the Union and the South. In 1862 Union troops under General Ulysses S. Grant moved south along the rivers and opened an invasion route into the Confederacy. Dams on the Cumberland built by the

Tennessee Valley Authority have created several long lakes, including Lake Cumberland in south-central Kentucky and Kentucky Lake in southwestern Kentucky and northwestern Tennessee.

Cumberland Gap. A natural pass through the Cumberland Mountains in the southeastern United States, at the junction of the states of Virginia, Kentucky, and Tennessee. The gap, discovered in 1750, was the route of the Wilderness Road that was blazed by

Daniel Boone in 1775. It became the main route for westward migration to Kentucky and the Ohio River valley.

Death Valley. An arid desert depression in the southeastern part of the U.S. state of California, situated between the Amargosa Range on the east and the Panamint Mountains on the west. About 140 miles (225 kilometers) long and 5 to 15 miles (8 to 24 kilometers) wide, it was named by pioneers of the gold rush of 1849 in memory of the many emigrants who died there. Its flattest point, 282 feet (86 meters) below sea level, is the lowest elevation in the western hemisphere. The highest temperature in North America, 134° F (57° C), was recorded there in 1913.

Erie. Smallest of the Great Lakes by volume, also the shallowest. At 9,940 square miles (25,745 square kilometers) it ranks fourth in area. Of the lake's total area, 4,992 square miles (12,929 square kilometers), approximately half, lie in Canada. Lake Erie is mainly fed via the Detroit River from Lake Huron, and its outflow via the Niagara River at Fort Erie creates Niagara Falls, with a 176-foot (54-meter) drop. The Welland Canal joins Lake Erie to Lake Ontario, forming a crucial part of the St. Lawrence Seaway system. Point Pelee National Park, a peninsula 11 miles (18 kilometers) long on the lake's northwest shore, is the most southerly point of Canada's mainland. The park is considered a superb bird-watching site.

ELK AND OTHER WILDLIFE are protected in Banff National Park, Canada's oldest and most widely visited national park.

27 North America

Everglades. An extensive marshland located at the southern end of the U.S. state of Florida. It originally extended from Lake Okeechobee in south-central Florida to the Gulf of Mexico, but water diversion and reclamation have turned areas in the north into farmland. In 1947 most of the southern part became Everglades National Park. Rich in mangrove, cypress, shrubs, and sawgrass, as well as a wide variety of birds and other animals, the Everglades are threatened by the diversion of water, which has caused seawater to intrude into the marsh, and by fertilizer pollution, which promotes the growth of algae and other undesirable plant life.

Five Civilized Tribes. The collective name given five Native American tribes of the southeastern United States: Cherokee, Chickasaw, Choctaw, Creek, and Seminole. The tribes were so called because of their adoption of European ways. Many built European-style homes and copied European dress, took up farming and crafts, and converted to European religions. Despite this, they were forcibly removed from their lands in the 1830s to the Indian Territory, in what is now the state of Oklahoma.

Fraser. A river in Canada about 850 miles (1,368 kilometers) long, rising near Yellowhead Pass in the Rockies. It flows northwest, then bends south at Prince George, British Columbia, to flow west to the Strait of Georgia at Vancouver. The Fraser River Canyon, with walls more than 3,000 feet (914 meters) high, is noted for its scenery. The river was discovered in 1793 by Alexander Mackenzie. Simon Fraser, for whom it was named, first followed it to its mouth in 1808.

kilometers
US

kilometres
Brit.

colorations
US

colourations
Brit.

centered
US

centred
Brit.

THE SPECTACULAR GRAND CANYON in northwest Arizona was formed by erosion from the Colorado River, a process that began about 6 million years ago.

THE MARSHY EVERGLADES in Florida, home to many birds and plants, is an ecosystem that is threatened by the diversion of water and the subsequent intrusion of sea water.

Fundy. A bay of the Atlantic Ocean between New Brunswick and Nova Scotia, Canada. It is about 170 miles (274 kilometers) long and ranges from 30 to 50 miles (48 to 80 kilometers) wide. The bay is famous for its tides, the highest in the world, which reach a maximum of about 52 feet (16 meters). The tide creates the unusual Reversing Falls in the city of Saint John, where twice a day the river of the same name is thrown back by the sea.

Gaspé. A peninsula in eastern Quebec, Canada, between the St. Lawrence River and Chaleur Bay. It extends eastward into the Gulf of St. Lawrence, with Forillon National Park at its tip. It is about 150 miles (241 kilometers) long and 60 to 90 miles (97 to 145 kilometers) wide. The backbone of the Gaspé is part of the Appalachian Mountain system; the Chic-Chocs Mountains, the highest part, are tallest in eastern Canada.

Grand Canyon. The deepest and most impressive canyon carved by the Colorado River, located in the northwestern part of the U.S. state of Arizona. It is 217 miles (349 kilometers) long and from 4 to 18 miles (6 to 29 kilometers) wide. The walls of the canyon reveal the successive layers of sedimentary and igneous rock that were deposited in the region over time. These strata take on different colorations at different times of day. About half of the canyon is part of Grand Canyon National Park, which was established in 1919.

Great Bear. The fourth largest lake in North America, bigger than Erie or Ontario, and the largest lake entirely within Canada. Its area is 12,096 square miles (31,329 square kilometers), and it is 200 miles (322 kilometers) long, and up to 109 miles (175 kilometers) wide. Its maximum depth is 1,356 feet (413 meters). The lake lies on the Arctic Circle between the Inuvik and Fort Smith regions of the Northwest Territories, and is on the edge of the Canadian Shield. It is drained by the Great Bear River into the Mackenzie River.

Great Salt Lake. A saline inland sea located in the northwestern part of the U.S. state of Utah, between the Wasatch Mountains on the east and the Great Salt Lake Desert on the west. It is fed by the Jordan, Bear, and Weber rivers but it has no outlet. The lake is several times more saline than ocean water, and salt extraction is an important industry. Its level and surface area fluctuate broadly due to the diversion of water from its tributaries and the rate of evaporation. The lake has varied in size from about 950 square miles (2,460 square kilometers) to 2,400 square miles (6,216 square kilometers). Salt Lake City (population, 166,000), the capital of Utah and world headquarters of the Church of Jesus Christ of Latter-Day Saints (Mormon Church), is located near the southeastern shore of the lake.

Great Slave. The second largest lake entirely within Canada and fifth largest on the North American continent, covering 11,031 square miles (28,570 square kilometers). It drains into the Mackenzie River. The lake is 300 miles (483 kilometers) long and is the deepest in North America at 2,014 feet (614 meters). It is frozen over during eight months of the year. At its southern and eastern shores lie the Canadian Shield; to the north and west is tundra.

Gulf of California. An arm of the Pacific Ocean extending northwest for about 750 miles (1,208 kilometers) between Baja California and the Mexican mainland.

Gulf of Tehuantepec. An inlet of the Pacific Ocean on the coast of the Isthmus of Tehuantepec, in southern Mexico. Its irregular coastline is backed by steep mountains.

Hay-Pauncefote treaties. Agreements negotiated in 1899 and 1901 between the United States and Great Britain, giving exclusive rights to the United States for construction, ownership, operation, and defense of the Panama Canal. They included an abrogation of the Clayton-Bulwer Treaty (1850), which had previously provided for U.S.-British joint control of the projected canal.

Hispaniola. A large island of the West Indies between the Caribbean Sea and the Atlantic Ocean. Its two mountain ranges are separated by a deep valley and ringed by narrow coastal plains. The climate is tropical and the vegetation is lush. Hispaniola is shared by Haiti and the Dominican Republic.

Hudson Bay. An enormous inland sea of about 317,500 square miles (822,325 square kilometers) in east-central Canada. It is part of the Northwest Territories, but Manitoba, Ontario, and Quebec have shorelines on the bay. Its greatest dimensions are 938 miles (1,509 kilometers) in length by 519 miles (835 kilometers) in width. There is too much ice for navigation from October until July. The rivers flowing into the bay drain an area of 1.4 million square miles (almost 4 million square kilometers). Hudson Bay is connected to the Atlantic Ocean by Hudson Strait, which extends northwest from northern Labrador about 450 miles (724 kilometers), and to the Arctic Ocean by means of Foxe Channel.

Huron. Second largest of the Great Lakes, fifth largest lake in the world. With an area of 23,010 square miles (59,596 square kilometers), of which about half is in Canada, and a maximum depth of 748 feet (228 meters), it measures 208 miles (335 kilometers) long by 184 miles (296 kilometers) wide. The north and east shores of the lake, the latter around Georgian Bay, are particularly scenic and a popular resort area, with fishing and hunting in season. Georgian Bay Islands National Park (founded 1929) consists of 50 islands off the bay's southeast shore, of which Beausoleil is the largest. Manitoulin Island, near the lake's north shore, is the world's largest island in a freshwater lake (1,068 square miles, 2,766 square kilometers).

Jasper. The second largest of Canada's scenic national parks, covering about 4,200 square miles (10,878 square kilometers). Located in the Rockies, in western Alberta on the British Columbia border, it was established in 1907. There are many high peaks, part of the Columbia Icefield, hot springs, game reserves, rivers, and lakes. Among the lakes are Jasper and Maligne.

Klondike. An area of Yukon Territory, Canada, just east of the border with the U.S. state of Alaska. The area is centered on the Klondike River and is about 100 miles (161 kilometers) in length. The river flows into the Yukon River at Dawson. In August 1896, gold was found in a tributary of the Klondike, and when news of it reached the outside world the next year, a stampede began. By 1898 there were 25,000 people where hardly any had been before. The rush soon died down and by 1920 fewer than 1,000 persons lived in Dawson.

Kluane. A national park covering 13,750 square miles (35,613 square kilometers). It is located in the southwest corner of the Yukon Territory, Canada. Mount Logan, Canada's highest peak (see below), is situated here, as are huge ice fields, the Lowell Glacier, and numerous spectacular lakes and alpine meadows. The wildlife in the park is abundant and varied, and includes more than 170 species of birds. Hiking and climbing are popular sports in Kluane, as is fishing from June to August. In the winter, camping facilities are available for enthusiasts of cross-country skiing and ice fishing.

Laurentian Highlands. Mountains in southern Quebec, Canada, north of the St. Lawrence River, stretching from the Gatineau River in the west to the Saguenay in the east. They form the watershed between Hudson Bay and the St. Lawrence. Mont Tremblant, at 3,175 feet (968 meters), is situated in the provincial park that bears its name. The Laurentians are a year-round recreation area, especially noted for skiing in the winter months.

Logan. The highest peak in Canada, the second highest in North America. It is 19,850 feet (6,050 meters) high and rises in the St. Elias Mountains in Kluane National Park. It stands at the center of the largest glacial expanse on the continent.

Mackenzie. A river in Canada about 1,120 miles (1,802 kilometers) long, but with the rivers and lakes that flow into it, a system of about 2,600 miles (4,200 kilometers). It is exceeded in North America only by the Mississippi-Missouri system. The Mackenzie begins in the western part of the Northwest Territories, flows out of the west arm of Great Slave Lake, and northwest into the Beaufort Sea. There is a large delta at its mouth. The system includes the Finlay, Parsnip, Peace, Liard, Athabasca, and Slave rivers, and Great Bear Lake. It is navigable from June to

October over almost 2,000 miles (3,200 kilometers) of its length, with only one portage. The region historically was important for fur trapping, but became dominated by mining until the recession of the 1980s. At the north end, the Beaufort Sea has much potential for development, as does the Athabasca Tar Sands (oil and natural gas) to the south.

The river is named for the explorer Sir Alexander Mackenzie, who first followed it to its mouth in 1789. It is flanked on the east by the Canadian Shield and on the west by the Mackenzie Mountains (which were named after the Canadian prime minister Alexander Mackenzie), part of the Rockies. The mountains extend for about 500 miles (805 kilometers), with Mt. Sir James MacBrien (9,066 feet, 2,764 meters) the highest in the Northwest Territories. In the southern part of the range is Nahanni National Park, opened in 1972.

Managua. A lake in western Nicaragua with an area of about 400 square miles (1,036 square kilometers).

Manitoba. A lake in south-central Manitoba, Canada, about 125 miles (201 kilometers) long and 28 miles (45 kilometers) wide, covering 1,817 square miles (4,659 square kilometers). It drains into Lake Winnipeg. The two lakes are part of the remains of Lake Agassiz, the vast body of water formed 10,000 years ago when the continental ice sheet melted.

FORTS ON HUDSON BAY played an important part in the development of the Canadian frontier.

MOUNT MCKINLEY in south-central Alaska is the highest point in North America. Native Americans know it as Denali, or "the high one."

kilometers
US

kilometres
Brit.

honor
US

honour
Brit.

centering
US

centring
Brit.

Mason-Dixon line. Originally the boundary surveyed from 1765 to 1768 by two Englishmen, Charles Mason and Jeremiah Dixon, to settle a border dispute between the English colonies of Pennsylvania and Maryland. The line was later extended to establish part of Pennsylvania's border with the colony of Virginia (now West Virginia). In 1820, during the debates in the U.S. Congress on the Missouri Compromise, the line was used to establish a boundary between the slave states of the South and the free states of the North. For purposes of the Compromise, the line of division was extended west to the Ohio River; it then followed the Ohio to the Mississippi, and the eastern, northern, and southern borders of Missouri, which was admitted as a slave state. The line continued west at 36° 30′ north latitude. The term Mason-Dixon line came to be used in a more general sense as the dividing line between the North and the South.

McKinley (Denali). A mountain in the Alaska Range in south-central Alaska, about 140 miles (225 kilometers) north of Anchorage, Alaska. The highest of its two peaks, South Peak, rises 20,320 feet (6,194 meters) above sea level and is the highest point in North America. The upper two-thirds of the mountain is permanently covered with snow. Called Denali, "the high one," by Native Americans of the region, the mountain was named McKinley in 1896 in honor of William McKinley, who soon after became president of the United States. Mount McKinley National Park, established in 1917, was renamed Denali National Park in 1980.

Mestizos. The mixed Indian-Spanish populace in Spanish America. As a group, the mestizos have generally been rejected by both Indians and Spaniards, who look upon them with distrust. They are middle-class citizens, working as merchants and artisans.

Michigan. The only one of the Great Lakes which is entirely within the United States. It has a surface area of 22,178 square miles (57,441 square kilo-

meters) and a shoreline of more than 1,600 miles. The Straits of Mackinac connect it with Lake Huron and the Illinois Waterway links it to the Mississippi River. Indiana Dunes National Lakeshore runs 25 miles along its southern shore. The eastern shore has a moderate climate and is a popular resort area. The northern shorelines include many bays, Green Bay being one of the largest. The southwest shore is an urbanized area which includes the cities of Chicago, Illinois; Gary, Indiana; and Milwaukee, Wisconsin.

Mississippi. The longest river in the United States. Rising at Lake Itasca in northern Minnesota, at an elevation of about 1,680 feet (512 meters), the Mississippi flows south some 2,340 miles (3,765 kilometers) to the Gulf of Mexico. The river's exact length changes, as it periodically cuts through bends and makes a new watercourse. Also, the enormous amount of silt it carries is deposited at the large delta at the Gulf of Mexico, continuously extending the delta into the gulf and increasing the river's length. The Mississippi's main tributaries are the Missouri and Ohio rivers. Other major tributaries include the Wisconsin, Des Moines, Illinois, Arkansas, Yazoo, and Red rivers. These rivers and other arms form the largest drainage basin on the North American continent.

The Mississippi forms the southeastern border of Minnesota and the southwestern border of Wisconsin; the eastern borders of Iowa, Missouri, Arkansas, and most of Louisiana; and the western borders of Illinois, Kentucky, Tennessee, and most of Mississippi. Major cities along the river are Minneapolis and Saint Paul, Minnesota; St. Louis, Missouri; Memphis, Tennessee; Vicksburg, Mississippi; and Baton Rouge and New Orleans, Louisiana. The combined Missouri-Mississippi-Red Rock river system, which flows some 3,710 miles (5,969 kilometers) from Montana to the Gulf of Mexico, is the fourth longest river system in the world.

Missouri. The second longest river in the United States, after the Mississippi. Rising at the confluence of the Jefferson, Madison, and Gallatin rivers in southwestern Montana, the Missouri flows generally southeast some 2,315 miles (3,725 kilometers) to its junction with the Mississippi River just north of St. Louis, Missouri. Its main tributaries are the Milk, Yellowstone, Cheyenne, James, Platte, and Kansas rivers. Major cities on the Missouri include Bismarck, North Dakota; Pierre, South Dakota; Sioux City and Council Bluffs, Iowa; Omaha, Nebraska; and St. Joseph and Kansas City, Missouri.

Mojave. A desert in the southeastern part of the U.S. state of California, extending also into Arizona and Nevada. Situated between the Colorado River to the east, the Tehachapi Mountains to the west, and Death Valley to the north, it covers about 25,000 square miles (64,750 square kilometers). Its terrain consists largely of salt flats, low worn mountains, and sandy basins. Vegetation is sparse, mostly creosote bushes and burroweed. Annual precipitation is about 5 to 7 inches (13 to 18 centimeters), and temperatures in summer rise in places to about 125° F (52° C). Joshua trees grow in a protected area that was designated in 1936 as Joshua Tree National Monument. The desert is

THE DISTINCTIVE JOSHUA TREE is found in the Mojave Desert, which rises from 2,000 to 5,000 feet above sea level in southeastern California.

the site of several military installations, including Edwards Air Force Base. Mining is an important commercial activity in the Mojave, which has significant deposits of borax, potash, salt, silver, gold, and tungsten.

Nelson. A river flowing about 400 miles (644 kilometers) from the northeastern tip of Lake Winnipeg in Canada to Hudson Bay at Port Nelson. With the rivers that flow into the lake, the Nelson is the last part of the 1,600-mile (2,574-kilometer) Saskatchewan River system from western Alberta to Hudson Bay. The river was a significant fur trade route. A trading post at its mouth, York Factory, was operated from 1684 by the Hudson's Bay Company for 273 years.

New France. The name given the portion of North America claimed by France from 1534 to 1763. At its greatest, the region extended west from Acadia, or present-day Nova Scotia, in eastern Canada, through the Great Lakes, then south through the Mississippi River valley to the Gulf of Mexico. The Mississippi region was given the name Louisiana.

New Netherland. The name given the portion of North America claimed by the Dutch between 1621 and 1664. Centering on the settlement of New Amsterdam (later named New York), at the mouth of the Hudson River, the colony extended north along the Hudson valley to present-day Albany, and included parts of present-day Connecticut, New Jersey, and Delaware.

New Spain. The name given the viceroyalty established by Spain in 1535 to administer its possessions in the New World. It initially included present-day California and much of the southwestern United States, Florida, Mexico, Central America, and possessions in the Caribbean. Later the Philippine Islands were added to the viceroyalty. It was overthrown in 1821.

Niagara Falls. In the Niagara River, between lakes Erie and Ontario, shared by Canada and the United States. On the Canadian side is the Horseshoe, or Canadian, Falls, 176 feet (54 meters) high and 2,214 feet (675 meters) wide. The falls were formed about 10,000 years ago, when the Ice Age ended and the Niagara escarpment was exposed. This allowed water to flow north from Lake Erie over the escarpment.

Nicaragua. The largest lake in Central America, with an area of 3,100 square miles (8,260 square kilometers). It is located in southwestern Nicaragua. The lake, believed to have been part of an ocean bay, is fed by some 40 rivers and streams, the most important being the Tipitapa River. Lake Nicaragua is drained by the San Juan River, which flows southeast from the lake some 120 miles (193 kilometers) to the Caribbean.

Northwest Passage. A water route through the northern part of North America, sought as a shorter and safer route from Europe to Asia than the passages around the southern tips of Africa or South America. Expeditions to find such a route began in the 1500s, but the first successful one was led by the Norwegian explorer Roald Amundsen, who sailed from Oslo, Norway, in 1903, and arrived in San Francisco, California, in 1906. Other ships have since completed the passage, but the route is not commercially practical.

Ohio. One of the two main tributaries of the Mississippi River, located in the east-central part of the United States. Formed by the confluence of the Allegheny and Monongahela rivers at Pittsburgh, Pennsylvania, the Ohio flows generally southwest some 981 miles (1,578 kilometers) to the Mississippi at Cairo, Illinois. It forms portions of the borders of Ohio, West Virginia, Indiana, Illinois, and Kentucky. Major cities on the river include Pittsburgh, Pennsylvania; Wheeling, West Virginia; Cincinnati, Ohio; Evansville, Indiana; and Louisville, Kentucky. Tributaries of the Ohio include the Tennessee, Cumberland, Kentucky, Green, Miami, Wabash, Scioto, and Muskingum rivers. The Ohio River valley is a rich industrial and agricultural region, and the river has been improved with canals and locks to accommodate barge and ship traffic. Possession of the Ohio valley was contested by the British and French in the early 1700s, and the region passed to British control in 1763 at the end of the French and Indian War. When the area was opened to settlement, the Ohio River became the main route of travel for pioneer settlers.

Okeechobee. A lake in south-central Florida and one of the largest freshwater lakes in the United States. The lake is about 40 miles (64 kilometers) long and 25 miles (40 kilometers) wide and covers 700 square miles (1,813 square kilometers). It is fed by the Kissimmee River and drains through the Everglades to the Gulf of Mexico.

Okefenokee. A swamp in the southeastern part of the U.S. state of Georgia and the northeastern part of Florida. About 40 miles (64 kilometers) long and 25 miles (40 kilometers) wide, it covers an area of about 700 square miles (1,813 square kilometers). The swamp is drained by the Suwanee River, which flows across northern Florida to the Gulf of Mexico, and the St. Mary's River, which flows to the Atlantic Ocean. In 1937 most of the swamp was designated the Okefenokee National Wildlife Refuge.

Ontario. The smallest of the Great Lakes in surface area (194 by 53 miles, 312 by 85 kilometers), covering 7,606 square miles (19,700 square kilometers), of which slightly over half are in Canada. It is North America's eighth-largest lake, and thoroughly urbanized from the city of St. Catharines in the southwest around its western tip and all the way to Oshawa, east of Toronto. The Canadian side of the lake then gives way to smaller cities and towns interspersed with rolling farmland. Much of the Niagara peninsula, between lakes Erie and Ontario, is fertile farmland where the relatively mild climate is conducive to growing much of Canada's soft fruit crop, including grapes for the local wine industry.

MUCH OF OKEFENOKEE SWAMP has been designated the Okefenokee National Wildlife Refuge in an effort to preserve the plant and animal species found there.

LAKE ONTARIO is connected to the Atlantic Ocean through the St. Lawrence River and to the Hudson River and New York City by the Erie Canal.

Oregon Trail. The main route taken by pioneer settlers travelling to the Oregon Territory in the 1840s and 1850s. Beginning at Independence, Missouri, it extended some 2,000 miles (3,200 kilometers) to the fertile Willamette River valley, in present-day Oregon, and to Astoria, on the Pacific coast of what is now Washington State. The trail followed the Platte and North Platte river valleys to Fort Laramie in southeastern Wyoming, then turned north across the North Platte, and looped south again to cross the Sweetwater. It continued west through South Pass, a gap in the Rocky Mountains, and followed a difficult course through the mountains to Fort Bridger in southwestern Wyoming. From there the trail continued northwest to Fort Hall, on the Snake River in southeastern Idaho, then west and north along the Snake. In western Idaho the trail left the Snake River valley and crossed through the Blue Mountains, then continued northwest to the Columbia River, then west along the Columbia to Fort Vancouver, on the site of present-day Vancouver, Washington. From there, settlers could travel south into the Willamette River valley or west to Astoria, on the Pacific coast of Oregon.

Organization of American States (OAS). An organization of 31 countries in the western hemisphere. The OAS was established in 1948 to promote mutual assistance between the nations of Latin America and the United States.

In 1889 the International Union of the American Republics was established, with both the United States and Latin American nations participating. The International Union was reorganized in 1910 as the Pan American Union.

Despite the existence of the Pan American Union, relations between the United States and Latin America deteriorated during the first two decades of the 1900s, and under the administration of President Theodore Roosevelt, the United States asserted its right to intervene in the internal affairs of Latin American countries, which made the Pan American Union virtually useless.

During the 1930s, the good neighbor policy was instituted under U.S.

president Franklin Roosevelt, and attempts were made to revive the pan-American movement. A conference in Lima, Peru, in 1938 established the principle of nonintervention.

The outbreak of World War II tightened the bonds between the nations of the western hemisphere. In an attempt to provide for mutual defense, most of the Latin American countries joined the United States in declaring war on the Axis powers. Only Argentina and Chile remained on friendly terms with the Axis through most of the war.

In 1945, after the war had come to an end, the members of the Pan American Union signed a mutual security treaty known as the Act of Chapultepec. In 1947 the Inter-American Treaty of Reciprocal Assistance was signed in Rio de Janeiro, Brazil. In 1948, at a meeting held in Bogotá, Colombia, the OAS was established.

The OAS is recognized as a regional organization under the UN Charter. It was formed to consolidate the policies and treaties of the pan-American organizations that preceded it. Its charter members were the United States and the then 20 sovereign nations of Latin America. Subsequently, independent nations Jamaica, Trinidad and Tobago, Barbados, and Grenada joined the organization. In 1962, following the missile crisis, Cuba was excluded from all organizational activities; however, its membership was not rescinded, although a diplomatic and commercial embargo was invoked.

Orizaba, Pico de. Or Citlaltépetl, a volcanic peak in southeastern Mexico, southwest of Veracruz. Rising to an elevation of 18,700 feet (5,700 meters) above sea level, it is the highest peak in Mexico.

Ottawa. A river 790 miles (1,271 kilometers) long, rising in the Laurentian Highlands of southwestern Quebec, Canada. For much of its length it forms the boundary between Quebec and Ontario, passing Canada's capital city of Ottawa and emptying into the St. Lawrence near Montreal. There are large hydroelectric developments on the river. From Ottawa there is a connection by the 125-mile- (200-kilometer-) long Rideau Canal (completed in 1832) to Kingston on Lake Ontario. Built but never used for military purposes, the canal system today is a popular recreation route.

Panama, Isthmus of. A narrow S-shaped neck of land between Costa Rica and Colombia separating the Caribbean Sea from the Gulf of Panama. An arm of the Pacific Ocean, it is occupied by Panama.

Parícutin. A volcano 200 miles (320 kilometers) west of Mexico City that erupted out of a cornfield in 1943 and now reaches 7,451 feet (2,271 meters) in height.

Peninsulares. New World Spaniards in the colonial period who had been born in Spain, located on the Iberian peninsula. They were considered first-class citizens in Spanish America and generally held the highest government and church positions.

Platt Amendment. U.S. legislation that rejected the idea of U.S. intervention in Cuban affairs while declaring its duty to "protect" Cuba. Sponsored in 1901 by U.S. Senator Orville H. Platt as a rider to an Army appropriations bill, the amendment proved cumbersome and unpopular as the distinction between protection and interference became more difficult to decipher. It was abrogated in 1934 under President Franklin Roosevelt's good neighbor policy.

Platte. A river located in the U.S. state of Nebraska. Formed at North Platte, Nebraska, by the confluence of the North Platte and South Platte rivers, both of which rise in Colorado, the Platte flows eastward some 310 miles (500 kilometers) to join the Missouri River just south of Omaha. The Platte is very shallow and its width varies greatly with seasonal changes. Its broad valley was an ideal route for westward-travelling pioneers in the mid-19th century. Part of the Oregon Trail followed the upper Platte and North Platte valleys. In the 1860s the Union Pacific Railroad, which had contracted to build the eastern portion of the first transcontinental railroad, routed its track from Omaha along the Platte valley.

Popocatépetl. A volcano in south central Mexico. It is perpetually snow-capped and rises to a height of 17,887 feet (5,452 meters). It is the second-highest mountain in Mexico.

RIDEAU CANAL'S skateway is the world's longest maintained skating rink (7.8 kilometers).

A CHURCH built before 1943 is buried by lava flows from Parícutin volcano, which erupted out of a cornfield that year and now reaches 7,451 feet (2,271 meters) in height.

Powhatan Confederacy. An alliance of about 30 Native American tribes in eastern Virginia and southern Maryland in the early 17th century. It was so named after its leader, Powhatan, who expanded the confederacy from its original six tribes. The confederacy maintained generally peaceful relations with the colonists until Powhatan's death in 1618. In 1622 his successor began a long period of intermittent warfare that culminated, in 1644, with the destruction of the confederacy.

Repartimiento. Practice whereby the Spanish conquerors of the New World enslaved native Indians and forced them to labor on public projects and private plantations. Indian family members were often separated from each other by this system, and entire villages were often converted into virtual labor camps.

Rio Pact. Or Inter-American Treaty of Reciprocal Assistance, a treaty signed in 1947 stating that an attack on any member would be considered by the others as an attack on them, and that collective steps would be taken to repel the aggression. Originally there were 22 members, including the United States, but in 1964 Cuba was suspended.

Rocky Mountains. A chain of related mountain ranges extending some 3000 miles (4,827 kilometers) in a general north-south direction through most of the western part of North America, from British Columbia, Canada, to the U.S. state of New Mexico. The Rockies vary in width from about 70 miles (113 kilometers) to about 400 miles (644 kilometers). Elevation ranges from about 5,000 feet (1,524 meters) to 14,433 feet (4,399 meters) at Mt. Elbert, in the Sawatch Range in central Colorado. At their southern extent, the Rockies are 1,000 miles (1,609 kilometers) inland from the Pacific Ocean.

St. Lawrence. A river and prime commercial route since the earliest days of fur trapping. It flows from the northeast end of Lake Ontario and runs northeast some 744 miles (1,197 kilometers) to the Gulf of St. Lawrence. Combined with the Great Lakes, all of which it drains, the St. Lawrence is part of a system of about 2,300 miles (3,680 kilometers). The first 114 miles (183 kilometers) form the border between Canada and the United States. In a stretch of about 50 miles (80 kilometers) between Brockville and Kingston, Ontario, is the scenic Thousand Islands region, site of St. Lawrence Islands National Park.

Saskatchewan. A river in Canada formed where the North and South Saskatchewan rivers merge, some 31 miles (50 kilometers) east of Prince Albert. About 1,212 miles (1,950 kilometers) long, it flows 375 miles (600 kilometers) east into Lake Winnipeg. The North and South Saskatchewan rivers both start in the Rockies of

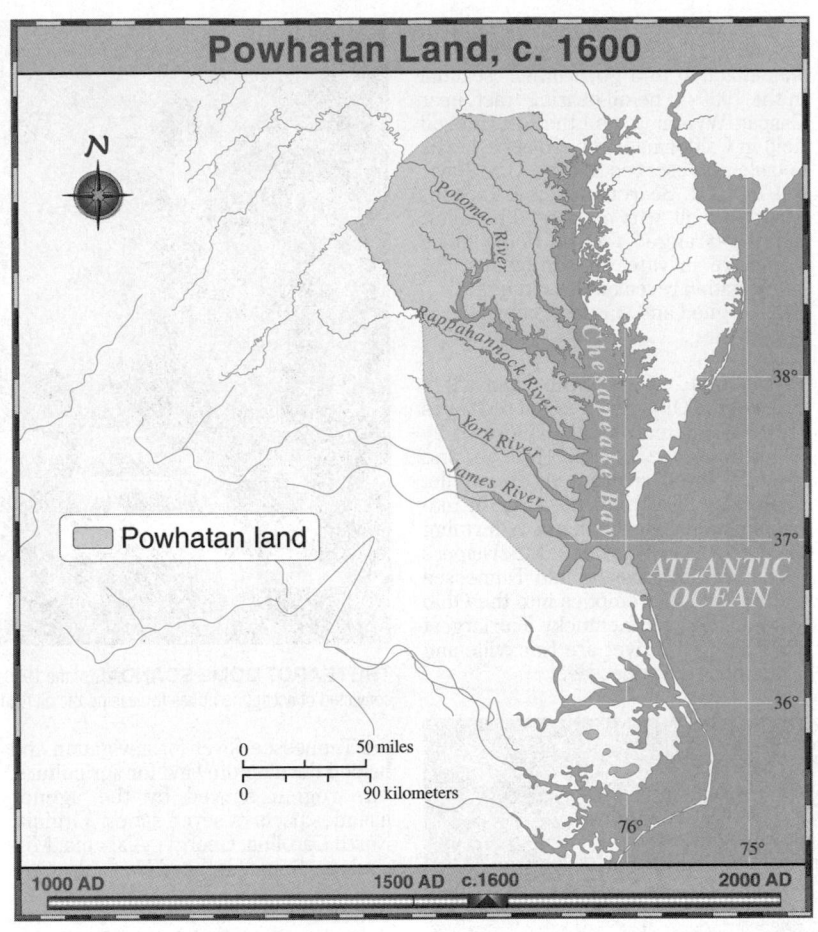

Powhatan Land, c. 1600

Potomac River
Rappahannock River
York River
James River
Chesapeake Bay
ATLANTIC OCEAN

☐ Powhatan land

0   50 miles
0   90 kilometers

38°
37°
36°
76°
75°

1000 AD   1500 AD   c.1600   2000 AD

27 North America

western Alberta. The former is about 804 miles (1,294 kilometers) long and the latter 870 miles (1,400 kilometers). The Saskatchewan system drains most of the prairie region. On the South Saskatchewan, near Outlook, is Gardiner Dam, of rolled-earth fill, one of the largest dams of its kind in the world. Officially opened in 1967, it created Lake Diefenbaker reservoir, serving to irrigate and bring hydroelectricity to the southwestern part of the Province of Saskatchewan.

Shenandoah Valley. A long, narrow, fertile valley in northern Virginia, United States. Bordered by the Blue Ridge Mountains on the east and the Allegheny Mountains on the west, it is noted for its scenic views and many lush orchards. During the American Civil War it was an important source of food and supplies for the Confederate army and the site of a string of Confederate victories in 1862. In 1863 General Robert E. Lee advanced through the valley en route to Gettysburg, Pennsylvania. In 1864 Union forces under General Philip H. Sheridan swept through the valley, destroying everything in their path.

Sierra Madre. Three high mountain ranges that dominate the landscape of Mexico. The Sierra Madre Oriental runs from north to south in eastern Mexico. The Sierra Madre Occidental lies in the west. The Sierra Madre del Sur is in the southwest. All three have

peaks above 10,000 feet (3,050 meters). The combined ranges extend some 1,500 miles (2,415 kilometers) from north to south.

Superior. The largest freshwater lake in the world, 31,820 square miles (82,414 square kilometers) in area, with 11,212 square miles (29,039 square kilometers) on the Canadian side. Its maximum depth is 1,329 feet (405 meters), and its dimensions are 352 by 161 miles (563 by 259 kilometers). Of its two large islands, Michipicoten is in Canadian waters, with Isle Royale being a U.S. national park. Pukaskwa National Park, which was established in 1971, is a rugged patch of Canadian Shield country on Superior's northeast shore. This spectacular, austere landscape, where more than 200 rivers feed the most northwesterly of the Great Lakes, offers a challenge to any outdoors enthusiast.

Takakkawa. The highest falls in Canada, descending some 1,246 feet (380 meters) in three drops. It is a major attraction of Yoho National Park. The park, 507 square miles (1,313 square kilometers) in area, lies in the Rockies in British Columbia, on the Alberta border, bounded by Banff and Kootenay national parks to the east and south. The Trans-Canada Highway passes through Yoho, affording excellent views of the park's 30 peaks that are over 9,480 feet (2,890 meters) in elevation.

Teapot Dome. A tract of land in Wyoming, United States, whose name was attached to a government scandal in the 1920s. The oil-bearing tract, near Caspar, Wyoming, and the Elk Hills oil field in California had been set aside as petroleum reserves for the U.S. Navy, but in 1922, Secretary of the Interior Albert B. Fall, who opposed this policy, quietly arranged for the fields to be leased to private oil companies. An investigation revealed the arrangement. Fall resigned and was later convicted of bribe-taking.

THE SCENIC YELLOWSTONE RIVER
rises in northern Wyoming and flows 671 miles, through Yellowstone National Park into Montana and northeast to its junction with the Missouri River in western North Dakota.

Tennessee. One of the main tributaries of the Ohio River. About 652 miles (1,049 kilometers) long, it is formed by the confluence of the Holston and French Broad rivers near Knoxville, Tennessee. The river flows south into Alabama, then west and north, forming the northeastern corner of Mississippi's border before crossing into Tennessee and Kentucky. It empties into the Ohio River at Paducah, Kentucky. The largest cities along the river are Knoxville and Chattanooga, Tennessee.

THE TEAPOT DOME SCANDAL of the 1920s resulted when Secretary of the Interior Albert Fall was convicted of accepting bribes for leasing the oil fields of that Wyoming area to private oil companies.

Tennessee Valley Authority (TVA). A U.S. federal agency established in 1933 to improve the region of the Tennessee River and its tributaries. The TVA constructed numerous dams to control flooding and produce abundant, inexpensive electricity and encourage business and industry. It also improved the Tennessee River for navigation and helped develop the land for agriculture. The region served by the agency includes parts of seven states: Virginia, North Carolina, Georgia, Alabama, Mississippi, Tennessee, and Kentucky.

Vancouver. An island of British Columbia, Canada, lying in the Pacific off the southwest coast of the mainland. It covers 12,200 square miles (31,598 square kilometers) and is some 288 miles (464 kilometers) long by 30 to 50 miles (48 to 80 kilometers) wide. The island is a partially submerged section of the Coast Ranges and is separated from the Canadian mainland by Georgia, Queen Charlotte, and Johnstone straits. The greatest amount of precipitation in North America falls on the island's western side. Pacific Rim National Park extends for 66 miles (106 kilometers) along the rugged west coast. It has a number of islands, a 45-mile (72-kilometer) hiking trail, and an offshore boundary extending to the 10-fathom line. This is in the interest of protecting the marine environment.

Victoria. Canada's second largest island, in the Arctic Archipelago, north of Queen Maud and Coronation gulfs. It covers nearly 84,000 square miles (217,560 square kilometers) and has an irregular, deeply indented coastline. Prince Albert Sound is a deep inlet on the west coast.

Winnipeg. A lake about 9,417 square miles (24,390 square kilometers) in extent, the third largest entirely within Canada. It is about 264 miles (425 kilometers) long by 25 to 68 miles (40 to 109 kilometers) wide. Lake Winnipeg is in south-central Manitoba and the Red, Winnipeg, and Saskatchewan rivers drain into it. It is drained by the Nelson River. It is marshy at the southern end, with sandy bays in among granite outcroppings along its eastern shore. High clay cliffs surround its northwestern shore.

Yellowstone. One of the longest and most scenic rivers in the northwestern United States and a principal tributary of the Missouri River. It rises in northern Wyoming and flows north to Yellowstone Lake, in what is now Yellowstone National Park, then drops 417 feet (127 meters) over two falls into a spectacular 24-mile- (39-kilometer-) long canyon, one of the most impressive features of the park. The Yellowstone then crosses into Montana and flows generally northeast to its junction with the Missouri River in western North Dakota, completing a course of 671 miles (1,080 kilometers). Its main tributaries include the Bighorn River and Powder River.

Yucatán. A large peninsula off Mexico's southeastern coast. It lies between Campeche Bay and the Caribbean Sea and is separated from Cuba, to the northeast, by the Yucatán Channel. The terrain is barren and consists largely of swamps and semidesert. Nevertheless, Yucatán was the site of such Mayan cities as Chichén Itzá and Uxmal.

Yukon. A river that rises in Tagish Lake in northwest British Columbia, Canada, the fifth longest in North America. It flows northwest, past Dawson, Yukon Territory, into Alaska, and eventually into the Bering Sea, a total distance of about 2,000 miles (3,218 kilometers). It is navigable for three months of the year as far as Whitehorse, in the southern Yukon.

THE HELP DESK

➤ **Take** a younger sibling or friend to visit historic sites in your community. Point out buildings that are old. Tell them about things that were happening about the time the buildings were under construction.

➤ **Talk** about your family history by sharing stories of your own childhood to help develop a sense of past, present, and future.

➤ **Document** your family's ethnic heritage. What country did your forebears come from? When did they come? Why? Who came? What famous people share your background? Older relatives would be a good source of information.

➤ **As** you read about different historical places, use current maps to find modern locations with the same names, for example, Troy, N.Y.; Rome, Ga.; etc.

➤ **Look** at maps and globes with a child. Help the child learn directions—start with up, down, right, and left, and progress to north, south, east, and west. Help the child tell the difference between land and water on a globe and identify the continents and major countries by name.

➤ **Make** simple maps and diagrams, such as a floor plan of your house, the block you live on, school, or playground.

➤ **Imagine** a route you travel frequently, for example, home to school or home to mall. Write instructions to lead someone unfamiliar with the route. Include directions, distances, landmarks, etc. Test your skill by having someone follow your instructions.

➤ **Draw** a map illustrating the above instructions. Be sure it uses standard mapping guidelines with North at the top and a rough distance indication if possible.

➤ **When** riding in a car, keep a list of the out-of-state license plates you see, then locate each state on a map and learn its capital city.

➤ **Help** plan the next family vacation.
- Where would you like to go?
- What would you like to do?
- Write to tourist bureaus and chambers of commerce (the library can help find addresses and give you other ideas). Use the information to plot routes and fun places to see.

➤ **Keep** a journal of a vacation trip. What would you do again? What do you wish you hadn't done?

➤ **Study** the continental map. Pay particular attention to the locator inset map that will help you locate the portion of the globe the continent occupies. Is it in the Northern or Southern Hemisphere? In the Eastern or Western Hemisphere? Is it north or south of the equator? What are the major physical features—any large rivers, mountains, deserts? Make a list of the names of those features.

➤ **Study** the individual country maps. Use the locator inset map to pinpoint the country and then turn to the continent map to confirm the location. Look at the list of physical features you made as you studied the continental map. Do any of those features appear in the country

you are studying? How do you think the presence of that feature affects the country?

➤ **Look** at the participation of different groups at different times in that country's history, for example, women in the Revolutionary War or African Americans in the Civil War.

➤ **Make** a map of play dough or salt clay that shows mountains, lakes, rivers, plains, peninsulas, etc. Just for practice, your first map can be an imaginary place with many features. Then select a continent, country, state, or other real place to make.

➤ **When** studying any individual country or group of countries, be sure to include as many of the following areas of interest as possible:

- Review the historical background of the countries. Do they date back thousands or hundreds of years, or are they much younger?

- Write a short report noting major events in the country's history in chronological order.

- Now compare the events in the countries to each other. Is there any similarity? Are they friends or enemies? Do the people speak the same language?

- What are other similarities or differences that you have detected?

- Don't forget to use the History of the World volume for related information.

- Make a list of people important in the development of the country. As you note events in your historical report, watch for names of people associated with those events.

- Read the newspapers and listen to news reports to add current names to your list of people. See if you can find pictures of current rulers or other important people, and try to determine why they are important to that country.

- See if the people on your list appear in other volumes of the *Volume Library* by checking the Index.

- Make a list of the largest cities. How does the size of those cities compare with cities that you are familiar with? Why do you think people began to live in that area and continued to live there?

- Look at the photographs of a country. What can you learn about the climate, geographical features, and the people?

- Test yourself. As you read the newspapers and listen to the news, and you hear the names of countries or regions, can you visualize the area so that the information is more meaningful to you?

➤ **What** is the first thought that comes to your mind when the name of a state or province is mentioned? Do you have a mental map that lets you think: "mountains," "ocean," "snow," "near _____ ?" Can you relate the state or province to a significant historical happening or group, e.g., Pilgrims? Civil War? Gold Rush? Quebec's Separatist Movement?

➤ **When** traveling across time zones, practice thinking, "If it is _____ o'clock in Los Angeles, then it must be _____ o'clock in Miami."

➤ **For** a list of helpful references, go to the *customers* section of www.southwestern.com.

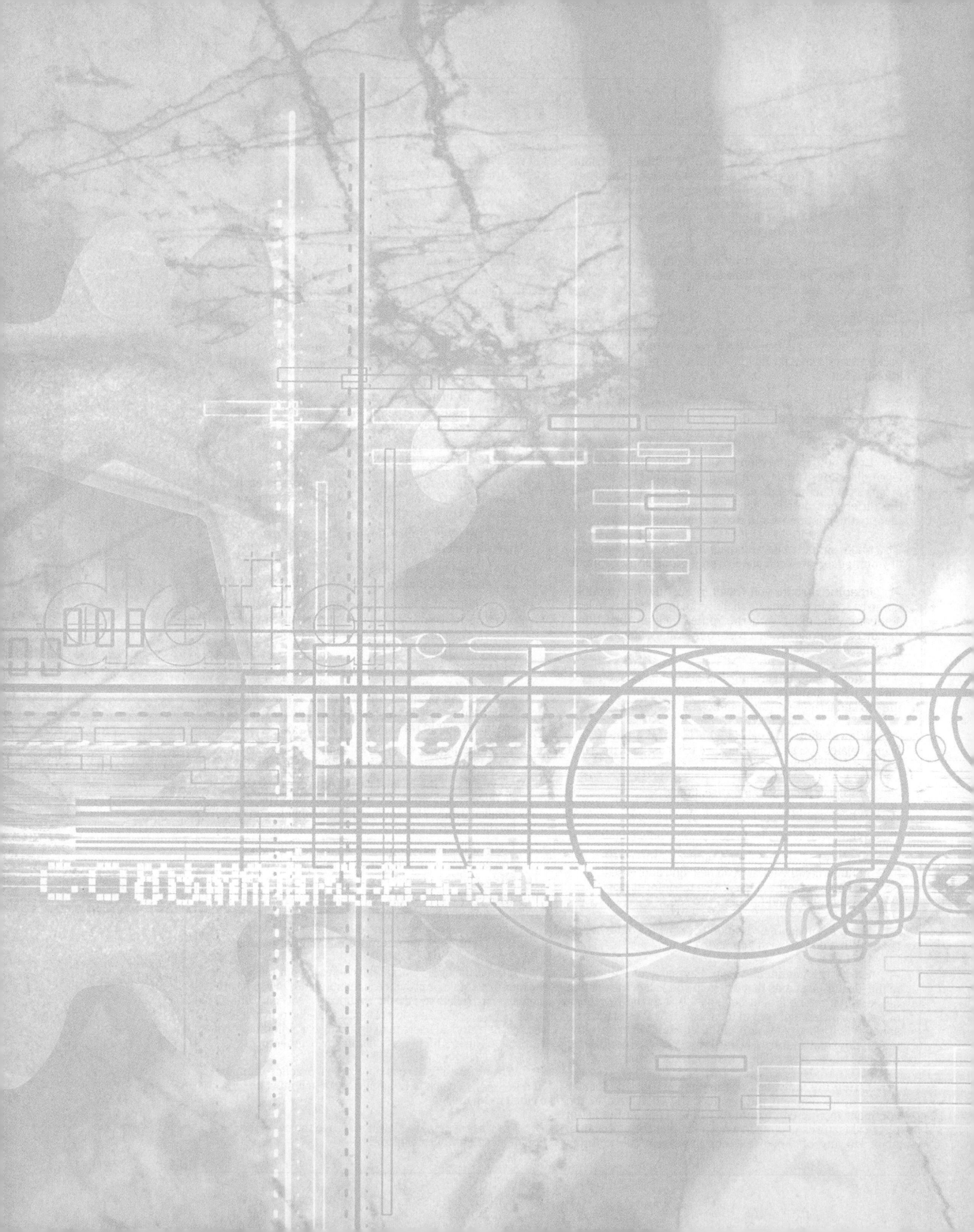

28

South
America

28 South America

Contents

South America

A Note about Spellings

As with any language that is written in a script other than the Roman alphabet, Arabic is, at times, difficult to transliterate into English, and there is no single universally accepted system for doing so. This difficulty also arises with words from other languages that are, or have been in the past, written in the Arabic script, such as Farsi and Turkish. When rendering Arabic words into English, this publication follows standard modern international practice, avoiding, for example, the use of diacritics, which some systems of transliteration employ.

Note on the Country Listings

Most of the information included in the following section is self-explanatory; however, some of the recurring statistical information requires a word of explanation about its importance.

Literacy

The literacy rate, that is, the percentage of people in a country who can read out of the total population, gives an important indication of the level of education in that country.

Per capita GDP

This figure represents the gross domestic product of the country divided by the total population; it provides an indication of the standard of living in each country. This figure is of necessity given as an estimate. (Each country's current world rank is also provided.)

Population

Population estimates are based on the most recent data available. Whenever possible, they are based on census or other official figures.

civilizations
US

civilisations
Brit.

colonized
US

colonised
Brit.

kilometers
US

kilometres
Brit.

center
US

centre
Brit.

This region comprises the vast area of the Americas south of the Central American countries, which are discussed in the NORTH AMERICA volume in *The Volume Library*.

South and Central America have often been called Latin America, since most of the countries derive their modern civilizations from Spain and Portugal, the countries that colonized them following discovery of the Americas by Europeans beginning in A.D. 1492.

Although most of the nations in South America are Latin, there are exceptions, notably the small republics of Guyana and Suriname and the French possession of French Guiana on the northern coast of South America.

The population of South America is approximately 360 million. Until the end of the 19th century, the population of the region was relatively low. However, the rate of population growth increased sharply in the late 19th and early 20th centuries, peaking from the 1950s to the 1970s; it remains high in many countries in the region. The problems of unemployment, poverty, and social unrest are caused in part by their inability to bring the population growth rate under control.

The land. South America, the fourth largest continent, is located in the southern part of the western hemisphere. Roughly triangular in shape, it extends from north of the equator to the subantarctic region. South America has an area of 6.9 million square miles (17.8 million square kilometers). It is bordered on the north by the Caribbean Sea; on the northeast, east, and southeast by the Atlantic Ocean; on the south by the Drake Passage; and on the west by the Pacific Ocean.

The South American coastline is relatively even, and the continent has a few good natural harbors. Among the best harbors are those located at Valparaiso in Chile, Guayaquil in Ecuador, and Rio de Janeiro in Brazil.

Mountains. South America may be generally divided into three geographic regions, two of which are highland and mountain zones. The two upland zones are the Andes mountain system, in the west, and the eastern highlands, which extend from eastern Venezuela along the northeastern and eastern edges of the continent.

Extending along the entire western edge of South America is the great system of mountain ranges known as the Andes. The rugged, high, and relatively young Andes Mountains tower over the narrow Pacific coastal plain in the west, isolating it from the interior lowlands. Mount Aconcagua, in the Argentine Andes, is the highest peak in the western hemisphere, rising 22,834 feet (6,960 meters) above sea level. The Andes Mountains were formed by folding and uplifting of crustal rock that was accompanied by extensive volcanism. The system continues to the present to be the center of often devastating seismic and volcanic activity.

The Andes Mountains are frequently interspersed with deep river valleys and plateau regions. Over the ages the numerous volcanic eruptions deposited over the adjacent plateaus and valleys a deep layer of lava, which over time was transformed into extremely fertile soil.

The Pacific slope of the Andes and the narrow strip of land between the mountains and the ocean receive little rainfall. The Atacama Desert of Chile is one of Earth's most arid and desolate regions.

South America's eastern highlands zone consists of several uplifted plateau regions. Chief among these is the Brazilian Highlands, or Brazilian Shield, which contains the oldest rock formations on the continent located beneath layers of younger sedimentary deposits. The Brazilian Highlands rises rapidly along the Atlantic coast to an average elevation of about 3,000 feet (914 meters), then slopes gradually to the north and west.

The Guiana Highlands, which extend from eastern Venezuela through Guyana, Suriname, and French Guiana and into northern Brazil, are higher and more rugged than the Brazilian Highlands. They reach their greatest elevations in southern Venezuela and Guyana. To the east the hills gradually slope down to the Amazon basin.

At the southern tip of the continent, east of the Andes, is the Patagonian Plateau, a vast flatland that rises abruptly out of the Atlantic to an elevation of 1,000 feet (305 meters) and slopes upward to an elevation of about 5,000 feet (1,524 meters) at the base of the eastern Andes. A number of deep canyons cut through the Patagonian Plateau. The third major natural region of South America is the interior lowlands region, which varies from tropical and densely forested land in the north to swampy or arid in the south.

Rivers. The lowlands include the basins of the continent's three major river systems—the Orinoco, Amazon, and Paraná-Paraguay. The Orinoco lowlands, or Ilanos, extend through Venezuela from the base of the Andes to the Guiana Highlands. The Amazon basin is one of the world's most extensive lowlands. The Paraná-Paraguay plains slope down from the Andes to form the Gran Chaco plains of northern Argentina, western Paraguay, and southern Bolivia; the La Plata plains along the Argentine-Uruguayan border; and the pampas lowlands of Argentina, north of the Patagonian Plateau.

Climate. South America's climate is extremely varied. The major factors influencing climate in South America are latitude, elevation, and ocean currents and associated air masses.

Temperature generally decreases toward the south and in the higher elevations. Freezing temperatures occur only in the upper elevations of the Andes and on the extreme southern tip of the continent.

The warm Brazilian Current that flows off the continent's Atlantic coast, coupled with warm steady breezes, provides heavy rainfall to the Amazon basin region, which has a tropical climate year-round. The Pacific coasts of Colombia, northern Peru, and southern Chile also receive heavy rainfall, but the cold Humboldt Current flowing off the continent's central Pacific coast creates a cool stable air mass that provides little precipitation for the rest of South America's Pacific coast. The Patagonian region of southern Argentina is also extremely dry, as are parts of Venezuela's Caribbean coast.

Vegetation. South America is famous for its rich natural vegetation, particularly in the tropical rain forests of the Amazon basin. The Amazon basin may

be contrasted, however, with Chile's Atacama Desert, one of the most barren places on Earth. The central plains are characterized by mixed forests and grasslands in the north, changing into broad grasslands that extend southward from central Brazil to east-central Argentina.

The people. South and Central America share a similar variety of ethnic and cultural backgrounds. The predominant ethnic groups are American Indian (or, perhaps more properly, Native American), European, and African. These groups have, through intermarriage, produced two new groups: mestizos, persons of combined European and Indian ancestry; and mulattoes, persons of combined European and African ancestry.

Native Americans inhabited South America for many centuries before the arrival of European explorers at the close of the 15th century. It is believed that the original Americans crossed from Asia to North America by way of a land bridge connecting Siberia with Alaska, then migrated over time south and east throughout the hemisphere. Evidence suggests that coastal fishing may have played an important role in this migration.

The great variety of Indian cultures that arose in South America was caused at least in part by geographic factors that tended to isolate the cultures from one another. Among the most advanced of these cultures was that of the Incas of Peru. However, hundreds of distinct Indian groups flourished throughout South America, including the Chibchas of the Colombian Andes, and the Araucanans of the southern Andes. Many of these American cultures were based on agriculture and had advanced social and political structures. Others were essentially nomadic hunting societies. Many were warlike.

The Spanish and Portuguese conquest of South America was a devastating blow to the Native American cultures. Many Indian groups were virtually wiped out in warfare against the European conquerors. Others were decimated by European diseases to which they had no immunity. Of those Indians who survived the wars and diseases, many were forced into slave labor. The most fortunate of the Indian groups were those in the South American interior, which for many centuries was left largely untouched and unexplored by the Europeans.

During the European colonial period, shortages of manpower developed in several areas. The Indian population that remained could not provide the great pool of cheap labor required by the colonial economies. As a result, millions of Africans were brought to work as slaves in South America, particularly in Brazil.

Today a majority of the population of Peru, Ecuador, and Bolivia is Indian. The populations of Chile, Argentina, and Uruguay are largely of European ancestry. Brazil has a broad ethnic mix.

Nearly all the peoples of South America live in highlands or plateau regions. In South America these regions rarely extend over 200 miles (320 kilometers) from the coastlines. The bulk of the population lives along South America's Atlantic coast and in the Andean highlands. The continent's interior is sparsely populated.

Languages. The common language of the majority of South American nations is Spanish. Notable exceptions include Brazil, where the common language is Portuguese, and Suriname, where Dutch is spoken. In addition, nearly a hundred Indian dialects have survived.

Religion. Roman Catholicism is the predominant religion in South America, although Protestantism has grown rapidly in recent years. Two factors have played an important role in the growth of Protestantism in the region. The first is the vitality and commitment of the evangelical Christian movement in the region. The second is the perception in many places of the Roman Catholic Church as a reactionary institution and as part of the ruling class.

TYPICAL DRESS of South American Indians in the 1800s

centered
US

centred
Brit.

lead, zinc, manganese, gold, emeralds, petroleum, and natural gas. The continent is poor in coal, and this has slowed its industrial development. South America has vast hydroelectric potential, however.

The coastal waters of South America are rich in fish, particularly off the western coast. Fishing is important in Chile, Peru, and Ecuador, and other countries are rapidly expanding their fishing industries.

The continent has vast forest tracts, particularly in the rain forest of the Amazon basin and in the Andes. The many varieties of wood that are available constitute an important resource that has yet to be developed fully.

The destruction of the Amazon rain forest represents the depletion of one of South America's greatest resources. The rain forest, which plays an important role in regulating world climate, is also the habitat of countless species of flora and fauna, many of which have yet to be studied and classified. It has been estimated that by early this century, only 5 to 10 percent of the Amazon rain forest will remain. The cutting down of the rain forest to provide charcoal for industry and low-grade farmland for Brazil's growing population, as well as to promote exploitation of Brazil's substantial mineral wealth, is seen by scientists as an ecological disaster of enormous magnitude.

Industry. Although agriculture and the exploitation of raw materials remain key factors in the South American economy, several nations have developed thriving industrial and manufacturing sectors. The processing of agricultural products remains the key industrial activity. However, the manufacture of such things as metals, chemicals, plastics, textiles, automobiles, electrical goods, machinery, and consumer goods has expanded rapidly in the last three decades. Most industries are located in or near the major urban centers.

Transportation and trade. In the second half of the 20th century, the nations of South America improved their air and road transportation systems, the most important modes of travel on the continent. Railroads are also important, particularly for freight transport. Improved transportation, by motor vehicles particularly, has helped increase commerce among the South American nations. However, most trade is intercontinental, mainly with the United States and Europe.

Trade barriers between the nations of South America have restricted the development of intracontinental commerce. However, in the 1960s, several initiatives were made to establish closer economic cooperation. Chief among these was the Latin American Free Trade Association (LAFTA), which was established in 1960 and included Mexico and the South American nations of Argentina, Brazil, Chile, Paraguay, Peru, and Uruguay. Another association, the Andean Group, including

A WOMAN OF BAHIA in Brazil displays her festival finery.

Bolivia, Chile, Colombia, Ecuador, and Peru, was established in 1967 to promote economic cooperation and development among member nations. The members of the Andean Group became associated with LAFTA, but Chile withdrew in 1976.

LAFTA sought the eventual elimination of trade barriers among member nations, along the lines of the program established by the European Community (now the European Union), but it made little progress toward the continent's economic integration. One problem was the great disparity between the highly industrialized nations, such as Mexico and Brazil, and the much less industrialized countries, such as Paraguay. Complete elimination of tariffs proved unworkable because of inequities.

In August 1980, the 11 member nations signed the Montevideo Treaty, which established a new trade structure, the Latin American Integration Association (known by its Spanish acronym as ALADI), which came into force in March 1981. The new organization established three economic tiers for its members: one for the highly industrialized nations (Argentina, Brazil, and Mexico); one for the moderately industrialized nations (Chile, Colombia, Peru, Uruguay, and Venezuela); and one for the least industrialized nations (Bolivia, Ecuador, and Paraguay).

ALADI has sought to address tariff and trade issues on an individual basis, taking into account the economic needs and levels of development of member countries. The organization's increased flexibility in dealing with trade issues

Economy. For centuries the South American economy was centered on colonial agriculture and the exploitation of raw materials. Agricultural products and raw materials were sent to the mother country, and finished goods were received from the mother country. It was a system that benefitted only the mother country and a very small group of colonial landowners, merchants, and administrators.

In most countries, significant industrial development did not occur until the late 19th and 20th centuries. This delay was caused in part by the geographic problems faced by the South American nations. Development of roads and railways across mountain ranges and through tropical jungles, a prerequisite for large-scale industrial growth, was an enormous task, often beyond the scope of relatively unstable national governments. Financing new industry was another problem, as was the securing of stable markets for South American products, particularly among the South American nations themselves.

Agriculture. Despite the move toward diversification in many countries, agriculture remains the main economic activity in much of South America. Brazil and Argentina are among the world's leading food producers. Specifically, southern Brazil and northern Argentina constitute one of the world's top agricultural regions. Argentina exports wheat, corn, beef, wool, and mutton. Brazil exports coffee, cotton, bananas, and cacao. The temperate climate and rich volcanic soils of the Andean highlands helped Colombia and Ecuador become major exporters of coffee, bananas, and cacao. Colombia, attempting to diversify from its main cash crop, coffee, has developed a thriving flower industry and is now an important exporter of cut flowers.

Natural resources. South America has an abundance of mineral resources, including iron ore, bauxite, copper, tin,

promises to promote greater cooperation among the member nations, but the ideal of a Latin American common market free of internal trade barriers remains thus far an elusive goal.

Hidden economy.   One of the results of unfavorable economic pressures is the growth of economic activity outside the mainstream—the so-called black market or illegal economy. Black market trading in South and Central America has grown in part due to government policies, such as wage and price controls, taxes, and tariffs, but also due to external factors, such as price fluctuations on international markets.

Hidden economies generally have been small in relation to overall national economies in the region. However, the drug economy of Colombia and neighboring countries has proven to be a startling exception.

In the 1970s and 1980s, an enormous demand for cocaine grew in the United States. Andean farmers in Peru, Bolivia, and Colombia planted increasingly large crops of coca, the plant from which cocaine is processed. The coca was transported to chemical laboratories in the Colombian jungles for processing. These drug factories produced about 80 percent of all the cocaine shipped to the United States.

The enormous profits enjoyed by the leaders of the drug cartels that organized and operated the flourishing drug industry caused severe problems for the nations of the region. The vast wealth led to political and police corruption in many countries. In Colombia, where the drug lords were often considered by the rural and urban poor as modern Robin Hoods, an alliance formed between the leftist guerrilla movement and the drug cartels. Drug profits helped the local economies of Colombia, Peru, and Bolivia. In addition, vast amounts of money were sent to foreign banks willing to overlook and even help obscure their source. Panama became a major center for drug transshipment and money laundering.

In Colombia drug violence reached a peak in the late 1980s. This impelled the Colombian government to inaugurate a campaign to break the power of the most violent cartels.

The United States, facing an unprecedented level of drug-related crime, offered aid for police and military action to break up the drug trade and eliminate cultivation of coca. However, the offer of this form of aid was not warmly received by the South American nations.

This reluctance was caused in part by the perception that the core of the problem is U.S. demand for cocaine. The South American nations argued that if demand was curbed in the United States, the drug trade and drug violence in South and Central America would be much easier to control. In addition, eradication of coca crops would be disastrous for the hundreds of thousands of farmers who rely on coca for income.

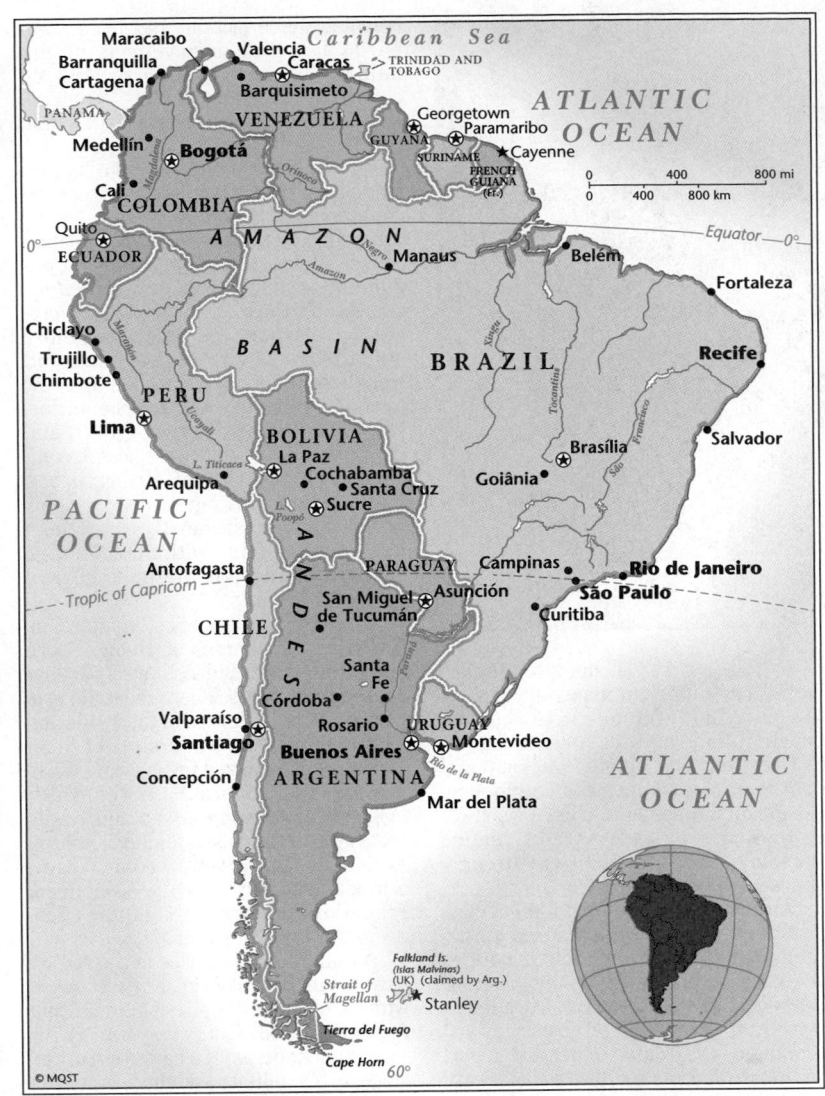

Instead, they proposed a comprehensive program to encourage farmers to grow alternative crops that are legal and equally or more profitable than coca.

Economic trends.   Throughout the last several decades, the economic focus of South America has been on industrial development and diversification as a means to broaden the economic base, produce new jobs, and encourage growth and long-term stability.

Rapid industrial growth was financed largely through deficit spending and large-scale borrowing by countries of the region. Although rapid growth was achieved in the short term, the cost of servicing a large foreign debt was a burden on the economies. In addition, the development of nonexport industries, while intended to reduce imports, also had the effect of drawing labor and capital from export industries, further weakening the economies. Extensive government involvement frequently meant the expenditure of resources to maintain businesses that were not run efficiently and could not compete on the international market.

The efficiency of government-controlled economies seemed to be unrelated to the political philosophy espoused by a government. For example, the Marxist-oriented program of Salvador Allende in Chile produced generally undesirable results in the Chilean economy. However, after Allende's overthrow, the military government of General Augusto Pinochet relied on heavy borrowing and increased government control of the economy, with ultimately disastrous results.

Another example of the inability of central government controls and policies to promote growth in the economy occurred in Peru in the 1980s. The government of Alan Garcia interrupted interest payments on Peru's large foreign debt and introduced domestic economic policies that led to considerably increased imports, a drop in exports, and a rate of inflation that defied comprehension.

Many nations in South America experienced major economic problems in the early 1980s, as growth slowed or declined, imports increased, and the value of exports failed to keep pace with growing foreign debt. Inflation rates reached three-, four-, and even five-digit levels.

28 South America

labor
US

labour
Brit.

CHILDREN DON'T GO FAR from their mothers on market day in Cajamarca, Peru.

In the late 1980s, many countries introduced bitter but necessary austerity programs intended to control consumption and reduce inflation, increase exports, reduce international debt, and restore investor confidence. Governments began to close or sell off unprofitable businesses and reduce spending, measures that were strongly opposed by organized labor.

Although the austerity measures produced great hardships and sometimes provoked violent disturbances and deep political turmoil, they averted total economic collapse. However, it was clear that continued progress toward economic stabilization depended in part on the world economy, the availability of ample investment funds, and the growth of foreign markets for South American products.

Government. Prior to the early 19th century, all of Central and South America was under European colonial rule. Mexico, most of the Central American isthmus, and South America, and many islands in the West Indies were controlled by Spain. Portugal dominated the region that today is Brazil. The English, French, and Dutch established colonies on the Caribbean coast of South America and also in the West Indies.

The 19th century saw the end of colonialism in much of the region and the establishment of a number of independent republics. In many of the new states, political forces were divided into conservative and liberal factions.

Early attempts at political confederation in the region proved unsuccessful. The dream of Simón Bolívar to establish a United States of South America did not become a reality.

In many countries the division between conservatives and liberals was the dominant political factor well into the 20th century. The often bitter rivalry

centers *US*

centres *Brit.*

between these factions has been complicated by the involvement of the military in political affairs. Military coups, dictatorships, and civil conflicts have slowed the development of stable political institutions.

In the 20th century, two factors played particularly important roles in changing the dynamics of South American politics. The rapid rate of population growth and a surge in economic development produced two new forces for change. The increasing population created a strong demand for more equitable redistribution of land and wealth, traditionally controlled by a few aristocratic families in many countries. Industrial and commercial growth and the growth of urban centers was accompanied by the rise of strong urban middle and working classes. Their needs and interests have brought them into competition with the landed aristocracy in both the political and economic spheres.

In some countries, such as Argentina, the forces of change were institutionalized and achieved varying degrees of success. There the rapid economic growth occurred in the 1940s and 1950s under the leadership of Juan Perón, who mobilized the growing working class as a political base with which to push forward ambitious and costly programs of industrial and agricultural modernization. However, continued government involvement in the economy of Argentina eventually brought the country to the brink of bankruptcy.

A number of countries in the region have been centers of violence associated with Cold War politics, including Argentina and Chile. In the 1970s Argentina underwent a paroxysm of violence as the military sought to eradicate

leftist and Marxist political activity in the country. In 1973 Chile's elected Marxist government was overthrown in a bloody coup.

Despite the numerous and continuing economic, social, and political problems facing the nations of South America, there has been a significant trend away from armed conflict and military rule and toward the growth of democratic institutions and traditions. Continued progress, however, requires regional and international cooperation in solving the region's major problems.

The United States has been involved in South American affairs since the 19th century, when its economic interests in the region increased significantly. Frequently, its policy in the region took the form of military intervention, which did little to secure the respect or friendship of South Americans. The inauguration of the Alliance for Progress by the United States in the 1960s signaled a significant shift toward economic and political cooperation in an attempt to finally achieve regional peace, growth, and unity.

Perhaps the most important organization advancing regional unity is the Organization of American States (OAS), whose members now include all 35 nations of North, Central, and South America. Founded in 1948, the OAS has worked to promote collective security, the peaceful resolution of disputes, and economic, social, and cultural development of those countries.

With the end of the Cold War and the dramatic shift of the global economy toward greater integration, it is likely that new economic and political ties will bring all the nations of the western hemisphere closer together during this century.

SEVERAL VOLCANOS in South America are still active. Osorno Volcano overlooks the town of Puerto Varas in Chile.

Countries of South America

Argentina

Official name: *Argentine Republic*
Area: *1,068,020 sq. mi.,*
2,766,890 sq. km.
Type of government: *Republic*
Population: *38,331,000*
Capital and largest city:
Buenos Aires
Pop. 2,965,000
Language: *Spanish (official),*
English, Italian, German,
French
Literacy: *96%,* **Currency:** *Peso*
Per capita GDP: *$10,200*
(Rank: 48th)

The land. Argentina, in the southern part of South America, is the second largest Latin American country in area. It contians four major land regions: the pampas, the north, the Andes, and Patagonia.

The pampas, great level plains, are divided into the Humid Pampa, in the east of Argentina's central region, and the Dry Pampa, in the west. The rich, black soil of the Humid Pampa makes it one of the most fertile agricultural areas in the world.

The pampas form the economic, political, and social heartland of the nation. The half circle around Buenos Aires, with a radius of 250 miles (402 kilometers), includes only 24 percent of Argentina's total area, but it contains some 75 percent of the country's total population.

The north contains the semiarid, forested plains of the Chaco, the rolling hills and the floodplains of a region called Mesopotamia, which lies between the Paraná and Uruguay rivers and the Paraná Plateau.

The Andes region includes the "Monte," or foothill zone, with elevations below 2,500 feet (762 meters), and the Andes cordillera (range). In the northwest the cordillera reaches a height of 22,834 feet (6,960 meters) at Mount Aconcagua, the highest point in the western hemisphere.

Patagonia is a dry, windswept plateau south of the Rio Colorado. Rainfall ranges between 20 inches (51 centimeters) a year near the Andes and less than 8 inches (20 centimeters) along the Atlantic coast. Patagonia's dryness is an obstacle to both farming and grazing, and as a result it is sparsely populated.

Annual rainfall in Argentina varies widely, decreasing generally from north to south and east to west. Misiones Province in the northeast corner of Argentina receives the greatest rainfall. About 80 inches (203 centimeters) fall there annually.

The people. About nine out of every ten of Argentina's people are of European descent, and approximately one out of five Argentinians was born in Europe. During the 1800s, large numbers of Europeans, primarily Italians and Spaniards, emigrated to Argentina; their influence has made the country in many ways more European than Latin American. The dwindling indigenous population consists of small groups of Guaraní Indians in the north and Patagonian Indians in the south.

One-third of the people of Argentina live in the metropolitan area of Buenos Aires, the capital.

Argentina's leading cities include: Córdoba (population, 1,158,000), an educational and commercial center in the heart of the country that has become important in manufacturing; Rosario (908,000), the country's wheat-exporting center, about 200 miles (322 kilometers) from Buenos Aires on the Río Paraná; La Plata (522,000), located southeast of Buenos Aires; and San Miguel de Tucumán (471,000), the major metropolis of northwestern Argentina and the heart of the sugar-growing area.

Economy. Industry contributes over one-third of the gross national product and employs one-quarter of the labor force. Agriculture employs about 20 percent of the labor force, but contributes only about 10 percent of the gross national product. Before World War II, the *estancieros,* ranch and farm owners whose wealth derived from the old colonial economy, formed the dominant economic and social class in Argentina. Since that time, however, middle-class urban-based industrialists have made broad economic gains. They have replaced the *estancieros* as the dominant economic force, although the latter have retained much of their traditional social and political power.

Most farming occurs in the Humid Pampa, where corn, wheat, oats, barley, and potatoes are grown. Argentina is a world leader in wheat, corn, and cotton production. Beef cattle are raised in the pampas, and sheep are raised in arid Patagonia. Argentina is one of the world's leading beef producers and a major supplier of sheep, pigs, and horses. About 41 percent of the land in Argentina is used for pasture.

Since the early 1960s, Argentina's fishing industry has grown rapidly, reflecting a trend in the Argentine diet away from beef consumption.

About 23 percent of Argentina is woodland. Argentina is the world's leading producer of tannin, which is obtained from the quebracho tree and is used in the tanning of leather and in other industrial applications.

Mining had been limited mainly to copper, lead, and zinc in the northwestern Andes and coal in the Río Turbio area. Petroleum and natural gas, however, have now become Argentina's main mineral resources; 23 million metric tons of crude oil were produced in 1988.

After World War II, Argentina made an effort to broaden the base of its economy. Industrial development has increased gradually since then. However, Argentine industry is largely confined to the processing of food and agricultural products. Meat packing, flour milling, sugar refining, and wine making each play an important role. Argentina has encouraged the development of heavy industry in recent years. It now manufactures automobiles, machinery, chemicals, and iron and steel. Aluminum production, which began in 1970, is becoming quite important as well.

The country's main exports are agricultural goods, such as grains, meat, wool, and vegetable and linseed oils. Imports consist mostly of manufactured goods, including machinery and wood products.

Argentina imports mainly from the United States, Brazil, Germany, and the People's Republic of China. Exports go primarily to Brazil, the United States, Chile, and Spain.

kilometers
US
kilometres
Brit.

labor
US
labour
Brit.

aluminum
US
aluminium
Brit.

SHEEP ARE HERDED on the arid Patagonian plateau of southern Argentina.

28 South America

Government.

Argentina has been called a republic since 1853, when its first constitution was drawn up. But democratic processes have frequently been disrupted by the military.

Under the terms of a 1994 revision to the constitution, Argentina is headed by a president with a vice president who is elected by direct popular vote to a four-year term. They are limited to two consecutive terms, but can run for a third term after a term interval.

Legislative power rests with a 72-member Senate, whose members are now mandated to be elected by direct popular vote, and with a 257-member Chamber of Deputies, elected by universal suffrage. Argentina is organized into 23 provinces, the capital, Buenos Aires, and one national territory.

History.

In the 1400s the Inca Empire extended into the northern corner of what is now Argentina. Its drive south, however, was permanently halted by Argentina's more primitive Indians, who were largely nomadic.

The first European to explore Argentina was the Spaniard Juan Díaz de Solís, who discovered the Río de la Plata in 1516. In 1526 Sebastian Cabot, an Italian navigator sailing for Spain,

explored the Río de la Plata and the Paraná and Paraguay rivers. In 1536 an expedition headed by Pedro de Mendoza built a village on the site of present-day Buenos Aires, but difficulties in supplying the settlement and hostilities with the Indians led to the outpost's abandonment a few years later. A majority of the early settlers of Argentina were Spanish colonists who crossed the Andes from Chile and Peru in the late 1500s.

The hostility of the Indians and the relative lack of precious metals at first made Argentina a neglected and sparsely settled part of the Spanish empire. It was not until the late 1700s that the colony acquired major economic importance as an exporter of cattle products, principally hides. In 1776 its capital, Buenos Aires, became the seat of the Spanish colonial viceroyalty of Río de la Plata, which also included modern-day Bolivia, Paraguay, and Uruguay.

Independence.

The Argentinians acquired a new sense of their own power and importance in 1806, during the Napoleonic wars, when a colonial army expelled a British force that had seized Buenos Aires. Four years later, on May 25, 1810, the Argentinians established an autonomous junta to rule during the captivity in France of Spain's King Ferdinand VII. Although independence was not formally declared until 1816, in practice the Argentinians had been self-governing since 1810.

Within Argentina a strong rivalry had developed between Buenos Aires and the inland provinces. The capital favored a centralized government and was receptive to liberal reforms; the interior desired a federal system that would provide almost complete local autonomy and tend to be very politically conservative.

In the early 1820s, the liberal and centralist faction, the Unitarios, consoli-

dated its control of the city and surrounding province of Buenos Aires under the leadership of Bernardino Rivadavia. The Unitarios encouraged immigration and investment, reformed the tax system, and restricted the influence of the Roman Catholic Church.

But they were unsuccessful when they tried to establish a centralized government over the entire country. The move provoked bitter federalist resistance, which coincided with a war fought against Brazil over control of Uruguay (1825–1828).

Rosas era.

In 1829 the Unitarios lost even Buenos Aires, which came under the control of the wealthy rancher and federalist leader, Juan Manuel de Rosas. Rosas ruled the Buenos Aires province as dictator from 1829 to 1832 and from 1835 to 1852. He brutally suppressed political opponents, repealed many of the reforms of the Unitarios, and governed in the interest of his own class of great ranchers.

Rosas fought a brief war with Bolivia in 1837–1838 and continually intervened in Uruguay's affairs. He also engaged in disputes with France and Britain, which resulted in a hostile blockade of the Argentine coast from 1845 to 1848.

The European powers failed to humble Rosas, but eventually some of his own collaborators in the interior provinces turned against him. One of these, General Justo José de Urquiza, formed a coalition with the Unitarios and in 1852, with aid from Brazil, drove Rosas from power.

Federalism.

Urquiza sought to reorganize the government of Argentina, and in 1853 a new constitution providing for a federal system was adopted. Urquiza became the first president of the new Argentine Republic. The province of Buenos Aires at first remained outside the union, but it agreed to join after being defeated militarily by combined forces of the other provinces in 1859. In

IGUAÇU FALLS forms part of the boundary between Argentina and Brazil. It is about 2 miles (3 kilometers) wide and falls 240 feet (72 meters).

1862 its governor, Bartolomé Mitre, became the first president of a fully united Argentina, serving from 1862 to 1868. During his administration, Argentina joined Brazil and Uruguay in the War of the Triple Alliance against Paraguay between 1865 and 1870, when Paraguayan troops ignored Mitre's refusal to allow them to cross Argentine territory.

Domingo F. Sarmiento, president from 1868 to 1874, was an ardent admirer of the United States and especially of U.S. educational methods. With the aid of the progressive educator Horace Mann, whom he had met on a visit to the United States, Sarmiento established a public school system that became the best in Latin America. Moreover, the nation experienced a period of rapid economic expansion during the latter 1800s and early 1900s. Argentina built up an elaborate railway network, attracted a flood of European immigrants, and became a major world supplier of meat and wheat.

The small but wealthy and powerful ruling class that arose in Argentina was in many respects able and progressive, but it frequently stayed in power by irregular election practices and the use of arbitrary federal intervention in provincial affairs. The result was a gradual increase in political unrest, which found its most important expression in the Radical Party, organized in the 1890s. The Radicals had special appeal for the middle class.

Enactment of an electoral reform law in 1912 finally opened the way for the Radicals to elect a president, Hipólito Irigoyen, in 1916. The Radicals did not introduce any fundamental changes in social and economic policy, and Irigoyen, the first Argentine president ever chosen in a truly democratic election, was best known outside Argentina for his course of strict neutrality in World War I.

Irigoyen resigned in 1922 but was reelected in 1928. He was overthrown by a military coup in 1930, however, amid the crisis of the world economic depression.

This first revolutionary change of government in almost 70 years was followed in 1932 by the resumption of an outwardly constitutional government under a wealthy oligarchy similar to the one that had ruled prior to 1916. Another revolt occurred in June, 1943, however, and led to the establishment of a military regime under General Pedro Ramírez and later under General Edelmoir Farrell. General Juan Domingo Perón ultimately emerged as the leading figure of this regime.

Perón dictatorship. The new regime was politically repressive, but through Perón's inspiration it gained working class support by expanding social security and other benefits. During World War II it continued the neutral policy that it had inherited from the preceding administration, but with pro-Axis overtones. In March 1945, however, when

BUENOS AIRES, one of the largest metropolitan areas in the world, is a center of government, commerce, manufacturing, and culture.

the conflict was almost over, Argentina declared war on Germany and Japan.

Perón was briefly stripped of power in October 1945, but he was returned to power in the face of a massive popular movement. Perón scored an impressive victory early in 1946 in a free election and became president.

As president, Perón expanded his labor policy into a doctrine called *justicialismo,* which claimed to be a middle course of true social justice between the extremes of communism and capitalism. Workers received a stream of wage increases and benefits. Perón's wife, Eva, a former actress whom he had married in 1945, took effective control of the organized labor movement and played a major role in cementing support for Perón among the people of Argentina. Eva Perón's death in 1952 was mourned by many staunch followers throughout Argentina.

Perón also gave special encouragement to industry. His extravagant spending and economic favoritism, however, damaged grazing and agriculture and produced severe inflation. In addition, he quarreled with the Roman Catholic Church and alienated the army. Dissatisfaction with his policies steadily increased. He was finally overthrown by a military coup on September 19, 1955.

Contemporary Argentina. A series of provisional military governments ruled from 1955 until 1958. Then, in the first free elections held in 12 years, Dr. Arturo Frondizi was elected president. However, he soon lost popular and military support in his efforts to stabilize the economy, and he was overthrown in a coup in 1962.

None of the governments since Frondizi's has gained lasting popular support owing to economic difficulties.

Civilian government was restored when President Alejandro Lanusse called for national elections in 1973. Hector Campora, a Perón supporter, was elected president. He subsequently resigned and, after 18 years in exile, Juan Perón was elected again. He was in office only 9 months when he died in 1974. His third wife, Isabel, succeeded him. Economic failures continued to plague the country, and when her administration's policies faltered, she was replaced by a military regime in 1976. The regime, under President Jorge Videla, immediately took up the chore of suppressing the Marxist and Perónist guerrilla activities that sought to undermine it. In its attack on political opposition, the junta was responsible for countless executions, torture, and wanton incarcerations. In the late 1970s, groups of Argentine women began gathering weekly in the main square in Buenos Aires to demand a government accounting for relatives who had disappeared during the junta's terror campaign. It had been estimated that some 20,000 to 30,000 Argentinians disappeared, presumably with the tacit or active support of the government and the military. The situation became so bloody and arbitrary that the 1980 Inter-American Human Rights Commission issued a scathing declaration of condemnation against Argentina's government.

In 1982 Argentina invaded the British colony of the Falkland Islands, which it has claimed since 1833. After more than a month of fighting, Britain recaptured the islands, serving up a political and military defeat to the junta.

In 1983 the junta allowed elections to be held. The Perónist Party, for the first time in almost 40 years, was defeated by the Radical Civic Union Party and its presidential candidate, Raúl Alfonsín. One of Alfonsín's first actions was to order an investigation into human rights abuses by the junta.

The country's economy declined rapidly during the 1980s. Inflation reached phenomenal levels in 1989, causing looting and riots.

Perónist Carlos Saúl Menem was elected president in 1989. He moved to control Argentina's soaring inflation, reduce its international debt, privatize government businesses, and stimulate the economy. In 1998, however, Argentina entered a recession, which continued into 2001. The International Monetary Fund provided emergency aid to no avail, as Argentina neared economic collapse. Argentina defaulted on foreign debt payments and president Eduardo Duhalde devalued the peso causing crisis in the banking industry. Economic woes persist under president Néstor Kirchner who took office in 2003.

labor
US

labour
Brit.

28 South America

Bolivia

Official name: *Republic of Bolivia*
Area: *424,052 sq. mi.,*
1,098,580 sq. km.
Type of government: *Republic*
Population: *8,445,000*
Capital: *Sucre*
Pop. 216,000
Largest city: *La Paz*
Pop., metro. area, 1,484,000
Languages: *Spanish, Quechua,*
Aymara (all official)
Literacy: *83%*
Currency: *Boliviano*
Per capita GDP: *$2,600*
(Rank: 120th)

centimeters
US
centimetres
Brit.

centers
US
centres
Brit.

civilization
US
civilisation
Brit.

The land. Bolivia, a landlocked country in west-central South America, ranks fifth in size among the nations of South America. The basic natural division of the country is between lowland Bolivia and mountainous Bolivia. The lowlands, or Oriente, in the east, occupy about 70 percent of the country. Mountainous Bolivia includes four regions—the Altiplano, the Western Cordillera, the Northeastern Cordillera and Yunga Zone, and the Eastern Bolivia Highland.

Lowland Bolivia. The eastern lowlands are sparsely inhabited, although pioneer activity begun in the 1950s has attracted a number of people from the overpopulated upland areas. The humid, tropical condition of the north, situated within the southern part of the Amazon basin, contrasts with the southeastern Chaco, which has frost as well as temperatures

of over 100°F (37.8°C). Rainfall can vary as much as 25 inches (62.5 centimeters) a year from an average of 38 inches (95 centimeters).

Mountainous Bolivia. The heartland of mountainous Bolivia is the vast central plateau of the Bolivian Andes, the Altiplano (literally, "high flat area"). The Altiplano, averaging 12,000 to 13,000 feet (3,658 to 3,962 meters) above sea level, is composed of a series of high and gently rolling basins surmounted here and there by snowcapped mountains. The region is cool and dry in the south but more humid in the north. Annual rainfall varies widely, from 28 inches (71 centimeters) around Lake Titicaca to about 5 inches (12.7 centimeters) or less in the south.

The Western Cordillera, separating Bolivia from Chile, is a long series of dry slopes among which are several extinct volcanoes. The Northeastern Cordillera forms the edge of the Altiplano. Its streams have carved steep valleys in the course of their descent to the Beni River system, which empties into the Amazon River. The Altiplano has a large population and supplies food to the highland communities.

The remaining area of mountainous Bolivia is the Eastern Bolivia Highland, or the Puna, a sloping region connecting the Northeastern Cordillera with the plains. The important regional centers of Cochabamba, Sucre, and Tarija provide markets for the corn, wine, and fruit grown in the area.

The people. Over half of the people of Bolivia are Indians. A small percentage of the population is of European, primarily Spanish, descent. The remainder of the people are mestizo, of mixed Indian and European origin.

The Indians in the Lake Titicaca area speak Quechua, the Inca language, but the majority of the Andean Indians speak Aymara. Most of the mestizo and white populations are found in the eastern valley towns of the Yungas and in the south.

La Paz, lying more than 12,000 feet (3,658 meters) above sea level, is the social, political, and economic center of the country. It is the political and administrative capital, a position formerly held by Sucre, which remains Bolivia's judicial capital.

Bolivia's largest cities are: La Paz; Santa Cruz (population, 1,136,000), capital of the Santa Cruz Department in the eastern lowlands; and Cochabamba (517,000), the focus of the road and rail routes that link mountainous Bolivia with the lowlands. It is also the center of a populous farming area.

Economy. Bolivia's economy is based on the export of raw materials and its industry is centered on mining. The country depends on the export of its mineral resources to earn the foreign exchange necessary to import essential goods. Bolivia is the second largest tin-producing country in the world, and for many years tin represented its most valuable commodity. There are also

large deposits of zinc, lead, copper, silver, oil, and natural gas. Natural gas exports account for more than a third of Bolivia's total exports.

Approximately one of every two Bolivian workers is engaged in agriculture, but farm production has been unable to keep ahead of Bolivia's rapid population growth. Consequently, domestic food production meets only about 75 percent of Bolivia's food needs. The Altiplano, where most of the people live, is ill-suited for agriculture. Nevertheless, some barley, wheat, corn, beans, and potatoes are grown there. Coffee is a major crop and sugar cane is also grown.

Industry is limited and mainly produces simple consumer goods for domestic needs. La Paz is the country's manufacturing center. The lack of an adequate transportation system has been a major obstacle to economic growth, as has Bolivia's extremely low per capita income, which severely limits the domestic market for all but essential manufactured goods.

Bolivian exports of illegal raw coca and partially refined cocaine have contributed hundreds of millions of dollars to the Bolivian economy. For this and other reasons, the joint U.S.-Bolivian program to reduce drug traffic has proved largely ineffective. Some success in encouraging Bolivian farmers to grow legal crops has been achieved, however.

Bolivia usually imports more than it exports, and the deficit has been met by foreign economic aid, principally from the United States. However, Bolivia has secured funding for a national gas pipeline to the Brazilian border. This project will include the construction of a power-generating plant and two petrochemical plants. It is expected that these projects will bring major new revenues to the Bolivian economy in the coming decades.

Foodstuffs and manufactured goods make up the bulk of imports. Bolivia exports primarily to the United States and Great Britain. Most imports come from the United States, Japan, and Brazil.

Government. Bolivia is a republic with a strong executive branch headed by a president. Legislative power is vested in a bicameral congress consisting of a 27-member Senate and a 130-member Chamber of Deputies. Each of Bolivia's nine regional departments elects three senators, but departmental officials are appointed by the central government.

History. The Andean portion of what is now Bolivia was long a center of advanced Indian civilization. It formed part of the Inca Empire from the 15th to the 16th century. The Empire was overthrown by the Spanish in 1533, and in 1538 an expedition led by Gonzalo and Hernando Pizarro conquered Bolivia.

In 1559 Bolivia became part of the Spanish colonial viceroyalty of Peru and was known as Upper Peru. It became

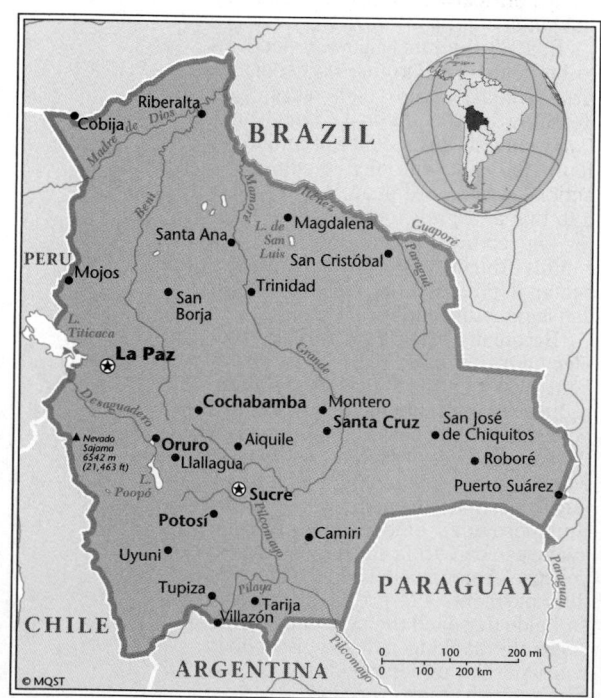

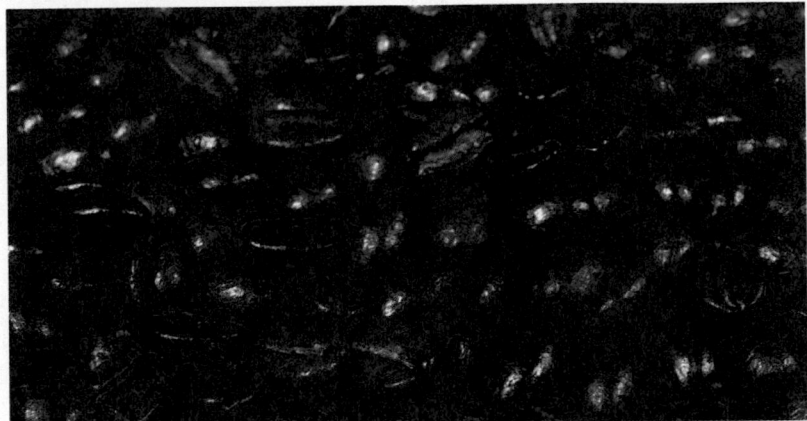

GREEN COFFEE BEANS acquire their tempting color and aroma only after roasting. They are grown on the Altiplano in Bolivia.

important to Spain as a supplier of precious metals, especially silver. Spanish rule was harsh, and from 1661 to 1780 there were many Indian uprisings.

Independence. In 1809, after Napoleon had conquered Spain, the people of the city of La Paz deposed the Spanish authorities. A junta led by Pedro Domingo Murillo was soon overthrown by the Spanish, and Argentine patriots were unsuccessful at liberating Bolivia from the south.

In December 1824, Simón Bolívar's forces, under the command of Antonio José de Sucre, won a decisive victory at Ayacucho, Peru, that set the stage for the final defeat of the Spanish in Bolivia the following year. Bolivians were then faced with the alternatives of joining Argentina, joining Peru, or becoming a separate nation. An assembly in 1825 chose independence and adopted the name Bolivia in honor of Bolívar.

The early republic. Antonio José de Sucre was elected Bolivia's first president in 1826. His administration was enlightened but brief. Unrest among his own troops combined with an invasion by Peru forced him from power in 1828. Sucre was succeeded by Andrés Santa Cruz, one of the leaders of the struggle for Bolivian independence. Santa Cruz remained in office for the next ten years. In 1836 he formed a confederation of Bolivia and Peru that led to conflict with Chile. Santa Cruz was defeated and exiled in 1839 and the confederation collapsed. For roughly the next 40 years, government consisted largely of a rapid succession of dictatorships.

Bolivia again fought Chile in the War of the Pacific (1879–1884), which resulted from Chilean designs on the nitrate deposits controlled by Bolivia and Peru in the Atacama Desert along the Pacific coast. Bolivia was defeated and lost its portion of the desert, which included Bolivia's only outlet to the sea. The loss was a severe blow to the Bolivian economy. Efforts to regain the lost territory were unsuccessful, and in 1904 Bolivia signed a treaty ceding the territory to Chile. In return, Chile agreed to grant free access to the port of Arica and to build a railroad from Arica to La Paz.

Modernization. Bolivia began to modernize rapidly in the early 1900s under presidents Ismael Montes (1904–1909; 1913–1917) and Eleodoro Villazón (1909–1913). Railroads were constructed, industries developed, and tin mining greatly expanded. During World War I Bolivia remained neutral until 1917, when it broke off diplomatic relations with Germany.

In the late 1920s, an old boundary dispute with Paraguay over the Chaco region was renewed following the discovery of petroleum reserves. What came to be known as the Chaco War broke out in 1932, and in 1935 Bolivia was defeated. The final settlement, negotiated in 1938, gave three-fourths of the disputed territory to Paraguay. The defeat, coupled with heavy casualties suffered by the Bolivian army and a serious decline in the Bolivian economy, helped to bring about a wave of political and social unrest.

New political parties arose with programs aimed at modernizing the country and improving the condition of the masses. One of these parties, the National Revolutionary Movement (MNR), took power in 1943 and instituted a program calling for sweeping economic and social reforms.

Contemporary Bolivia. The MNR was overthrown in 1946, before it could accomplish a great deal, but it was returned to power in 1952 by a popular uprising after the party's leader, Victor Paz Estenssoro, had been cheated of his victory in a presidential election. The MNR managed to consolidate its position and carry out a series of reforms that included nationalization of tin mines and distribution of private estates among the Indians.

The MNR incurred huge deficits in operating the tin industry, and the drastic land reforms resulted in a sharp drop in agricultural production. Severe food shortages in the cities followed. Only massive U.S. aid kept the Bolivian economy functioning. Nevertheless, some progress was made in expanding education and in developing the fertile but sparsely populated eastern lowlands.

Paz Estenssoro remained in power from 1952 to 1956, when he resigned in favor of a party colleague, but he returned as president in 1960. After a period of strikes and rioting, especially in the tin mining region, he was overthrown in 1964 by the military.

This was the first in a series of coups. The government changed its leadership seven times before Hugo Banzer Suarez took over in August of 1971. At that time an alliance of political parties, the armed forces, and several middle-class social organizations overthrew the regime of Juan Jose Torres.

Under Banzer, Bolivia enjoyed 7 years of improved economic conditions and relative political stability. In 1978 he permitted presidential elections, but the election results were ruled invalid. There followed several years of governmental chaos, military coups, and political repression. Civilian rule was restored in 1982.

In 1985 Victor Paz Estenssoro was chosen president by the congress after a popular election was declared inconclusive, as was Jaime Paz Zamora in 1989 and Gonzalo Sánchez de Lozada in 1993. In 1997 former dictator Banzer became the elected president. He was replaced again by Sanchez de Losada, but after little more than a year in office, and months of rioting, he was forced to resign.

honor
US

honour
Brit.

28 South America

LAKE TITICACA is the world's highest lake at 12,500 feet (3,810 meters).

Brazil

Official name: *Federative Republic of Brazil*

Area: *3,311,154 sq. mi., 8,511,965 sq. km.*

Type of government: *Federal republic*

Population: *179,914,000*

Capital: *Brasília*
Pop. 2,043,000

Largest city: *São Paulo*
Pop. 10,406,000

Language: *Portuguese (official), Spanish, English, French*

Literacy: *83%*

Currency: *Real*

Per capita GDP: *$7,400 (Rank: 68th)*

center
US

centre
Brit.

meters
US

metres
Brit.

The land. Brazil, South America's only Portuguese-speaking nation, covers almost half of the South American continent and contains nearly half its people. Brazil borders every country in South America except for Chile and Ecuador.

Brazil has a widely varied landscape, but there are two major types of terrain: the broad lowlands of the northern third of the country, which include the Amazon River basin, and the Brazilian Highlands, which consist of low plateaus and mountains.

Brazil's land surface is unusual in that the highest areas lie just behind the Atlantic coast, and most of the rivers flow toward the interior, where they empty into the Amazon River or the Paraná-Paraguay river systems.

The north, which includes more than half the nation's land area, has less than 10 percent of its total population. The area's few inhabitants live mainly within the floodplains of the Amazon River and its numerous tributaries. Since the 1950s, the exploitation of jute, cacao, tropical hardwoods, medicinal plants, oil-bearing nuts, and black pepper, as well as mining and ranching, has improved the economic situation of the north. In addition, a number of Japanese immigrants have settled in this area.

The northeast is a region of great physical diversity. A wet, tropical, coastal plain is separated from desert, or *sertão,* by a dry forest area, the *agreste,* which forms a narrow zone between the two. Droughts have always afflicted the desert, and it is only within the last several decades that the building of reservoirs and the development of drought-resistant forage plants for cattle have lessened the effects of the dry periods.

The northeast is the poorest area of Brazil. Few farmers own land and the general level of productivity is extremely low. Modern agricultural techniques are still alien to the traditional thinking of most farmers of the area. In the 1960s the Brazilian government inaugurated a large-scale development program in the northeast.

The eastern region contains the states of Minas Gerais and Bahia. Minas Gerais is agricultural in the south and west and pastoral in the north. The areas near the city of Rio de Janeiro are devoted to dairy production. The region's western area is one of Brazil's principal food-producing zones, supplying both Rio de Janeiro and São Paulo, the country's largest cities. Belo Horizonte, the capital of Minas Gerais, is a leading manufacturing center and has numerous metallurgical industries.

The south contains over one-third of the nation's population although it constitutes only 10 percent of Brazil's total area. It is Brazil's richest and most productive region and received the major portion of European immigrants. The south is composed of a series of plateaus that rise abruptly from the sea and dip slightly in the west to the lower basin of the Paraná River. It is the center of coffee production and is also important for its forests, which provide softwoods.

The central west, the fifth region, includes almost 22 percent of the total area, but it is occupied by only 3 percent of the country's population. It is an area of grassland with scattered trees known as *campo cerrado,* or savanna. These *cerrados* occupy high plateaus at elevations of between 2,000 and 3,000 feet (610 and 915 meters) and are dry for most of the year.

In the south, it snows during the winter months in the highest areas, but usually the snow does not stay on the ground for more than a day. The vast western central interior of Brazil experiences sporadic showers three to four months a year from November through March or April, followed by a dry season during which the scrub vegetation turns brown. Annual rainfall ranges from about 80 inches (203 centimeters) in the Amazon basin to about 20 inches (50.8 centimeters) in the northeast.

The people. Brazil's population is composed of three main stocks: Indians, descendants of the original inhabitants; Caucasians, descended from Portuguese and other European colonists; and blacks, brought as slaves from Africa by the Portuguese in the 1500s.

The bulk of the population is concentrated along the coast in a strip extending approximately 250 miles (402 kilometers) inland. The few remaining pure-blooded Indians live within the remote interior, particularly in the Amazon basin. Blacks live primarily in the northeast, especially near the coast,

MOST BRAZILIANS LIVE in villages in a strip of land about 250 miles deep along the coast.

where once there were many sugar plantations.

The major cities of Brazil are on or near the coast. The largest city is São Paulo. Rio de Janeiro (population, 5,851,000), the capital of Brazil until 1960, is the country's second largest city. Rio is the artistic and cultural center of the country, but it has been superseded in economic importance by São Paulo. Other cities include Salvador (population 2,441,000); Belo Horizonte (2,230,000); Fortaleza (2,138,000); Recife (1,422,000); and Curitiba (1,587,000).

The capital, Brasília, in the central west, is a model of modern architecture and city planning. It is designed to link the heavily populated coast with the still underdeveloped interior.

Economy. Historically, Brazil's economy has depended heavily on the export of one commodity or group of commodities at a time. Sugar was the mainstay in the 1500s and 1600s; minerals, gold, and diamonds in the 1700s. In the mid-1800s, coffee became Brazil's most important product. Although the coffee boom declined, the country remains the largest coffee producer in the world and has continued to rely heavily on the export of coffee for foreign exchange.

In recent years Brazil has developed a more diversified economy. It is now the leading industrial state of South America and easily has the largest gross national product. Although agriculture occupies about 35 percent of the labor force, it accounts for less than 10 percent of the gross national product. Industry occupies only one-fourth of the labor force, but contributes nearly 40 percent of the gross national product.

Nonetheless, agricultural output has increased markedly in the last decade, although not as much as industrial output. Agricultural products account for 40 percent of all exports, and food processing is a major industry.

In addition to coffee, Brazil produces much of the world's cacao and considerable amounts of sugar, soybeans and soy products, orange juice, and tobacco. Brazil is also a world leader in cotton production.

Brazil is rich in natural resources, including a vast largely untouched supply of minerals, and it has one of the largest hydroelectric capacities in the world. Oil is produced on a small scale even though domestic production has doubled in the last few years. Most of Brazil's oil must be imported. To offset this expense, Brazil has been rapidly developing hydroelectric facilities. It is beginning to develop nuclear energy as well, although economic considerations have forced Brazil to scale back its nuclear power program. In addition, Brazil has increased production of sugar cane used to produce fuel alcohol for domestic automotive use. This has also helped reduce Brazil's imports of costly petroleum.

Mining has changed from the production of gold and diamonds to the exploitation of iron ore and bauxite. Coal is mined in southern Brazil, principally in Santa Catarina, but it is of poor quality. The iron ore and coal are consumed in the various iron and steel mills located at Volta Redonda, on the route between Rio de Janeiro and São Paulo, and in Minas Gerais.

Since World War II there has been an accelerated growth of both light and heavy industry, centered primarily in the state of São Paulo. The major Brazilian industries produce textiles, iron, steel, motor vehicles, and foodstuffs.

Transportation. The transportation situation in Brazil has changed markedly since World War II. The physical integration of the country is being accomplished by building roads to the cities of the interior. Airlines have also come to serve the entire country. As a result, physical isolation, one of the primary barriers to development, is rapidly being overcome.

Trade. Industrial and manufactured goods represent about 60 percent of the value of Brazil's exports. Coffee normally makes up about 10 percent of the value of Brazil's exports. Other major exports include soybeans and soy products, cacao, sugar, pinewood, iron and bauxite ores, and cotton. Brazil imports large quantities of manufactured goods, machinery, fuels, vehicles, industrial raw materials, and foodstuffs.

Brazil exports chiefly to the United States, Germany, the Netherlands, Japan, and the Middle East. Imports come largely from the United States, the Middle East, Germany, and Japan.

Government. Brazil was proclaimed a republic in 1889, but democratic processes often have been disrupted. The military overthrew the constitutional government in 1964 and instituted a new constitution in 1967.

The 1967 constitution strengthened the central government considerably, changing Brazil from a federal union of states into a centralized republic. It vested executive powers in the president, no longer elected by popular vote but chosen indirectly by the congress. The president was given strong powers that were increased even more in 1969 when the constitution was further revised.

In 1988 a new constitution was drafted; it is gradually introducing many changes to the government. Presidential elections were reinstituted and the first popular presidential election since 1960 was held in 1989. In addition, the president can no longer issue laws by decree. Many social and economic changes were also enacted, including new benefits for workers and incentives for Brazilian companies to develop.

The legislature, the National Congress, consists of the Senate and the Chamber of Deputies. The 81 senators serve terms of 8 years and the 513 deputies serve terms of 4 years. Elections are based on a system of proportional representation which favors states large in area, but small in population. Brazil is divided into 26 states and the federal district of Brasília.

History. In 1494 Spain and Portugal, rivals in the establishment of colonies in the New World, signed the Treaty of Tordesillas. This treaty granted Portugal all the territory east of a north-south line that extended from the mouth of the Amazon River to the São Paulo coast, neither of which had then been discovered. Thus, in 1500, when the Portuguese explorer Pedro Alvares Cabral claimed Brazil for the Portuguese crown, the claim was incontestable. Subsequent treaties in 1750 and 1777 extended the Brazilian border far to the west of the original line of demarcation.

Brazil was at first overshadowed by Portugal's Asian and African possessions. It had no great Indian civilization or readily apparent mineral wealth, and early Portuguese contacts consisted mainly of sporadic expeditions to obtain dyewood and to trade with the Indians. Other Europeans, however, especially the French, began frequenting the Brazilian coast for the same reasons, and the rivalry spurred Portugal into taking more effective possession of the vast land.

TROPICAL RAIN FORESTS along the Amazon River are still home to several Indian tribes.

labor
US

labour
Brit.

civilization
US

civilisation
Brit.

28 South America

THE IMPRESSIVE STATUE of Christ atop Corcovado is a famous landmark in Rio de Janeiro.

Colonial administration. In the 1530s Portugal carved Brazil into a series of "captaincies" under proprietary governors called captains donatary, who were authorized to colonize and rule in the name of the king. In 1549 Portugal also sent out a royal governor-general to the city of Salvador, on Brazil's northeast coast, to exercise general jurisdiction over the entire colony.

Gradually, from the mid-1500s through the 1600s, sugar plantations worked by African slaves took root in the northeastern coastal belt. The export of sugar yielded huge profits and became the backbone of Brazil's economy. It was basically sugar that enticed the Dutch to carve out a short-lived colony in northeastern Brazil in the second quarter of the 1600s. Farther south, there arose a more varied agricultural and grazing economy that relied on Indians and mestizos rather than on African slaves for labor.

MANY SPECIES, such as this Amazon Monkey, are losing their habitat as the rain forests are cut down.

At the same time, some settlers, especially those of São Paulo, ranged far and wide through the interior, seizing Indians to work as slaves and searching for gold. In the process they pushed the boundaries of the colony far to the west of the zone allotted to Portugal by the Treaty of Tordesillas. In the late 1600s they found gold and diamonds in the region of Minas Gerais.

In the 1700s population growth and the increased importance of the south with its gold and diamond deposits brought a number of administrative changes. The last vestiges of the powers of the captains donatary, already largely superseded by royal officials, were eliminated, and in 1763 the capital was transferred from Salvador to Rio de Janeiro. Soon, agitation for independence, which drew inspiration from the revolutions in the United States and France, began to occur.

In 1789 in Minas Gerais, a militia subaltern called Tiradentes, meaning "toothpuller," headed a conspiracy against the government. The Tiradentes conspiracy was easily suppressed, but it set a precedent for later attempts.

Brazil's status was altered without a struggle early in 1808, when Prince Regent Dom João and the Portuguese court arrived on Brazilian soil in flight from the armies of Napoleon. Rio de Janeiro became the temporary capital of

THE CUTTING OF BRAZIL'S rain forests, home to many species and important to world climate, is seen by many scientists as an ecological disaster.

the Portuguese empire. In 1815 João elevated Brazil to coequal status with Portugal by establishing the United Kingdom of Portugal, Brazil, and the Algarves, and Brazil obtained many of the advantages of independence. Moreover, Dom João lingered in Brazil even after Portugal was evacuated by Napoleon's forces. When he did return to Portugal in 1821, he left his eldest son, Pedro, in Brazil as regent, and advised him to become an independent monarch if a final separation of the two countries should prove unavoidable.

The empire. The eventuality feared by Dom João became a reality in 1822, when the Portuguese government recalled Pedro in an apparent attempt to return Brazil to a subordinate position within the empire. A resistance movement developed, and on September 7, 1822, Pedro declared Brazil independent. On December 1, 1822, he was crowned Emperor Pedro I of Brazil.

Although Brazil was organized as a limited constitutional monarchy, Pedro I was unable to work smoothly with the Parliament. His government's popularity also suffered because of an unsuccessful war with Argentina over control of the region that ultimately became Uruguay and a general dislike of Pedro's numerous Portuguese advisers. In 1831 the emperor was forced to abdicate in favor of his five-year-old son, Pedro II. From then until 1840, Brazil was governed by a series of regencies chosen by Parliament.

The regency period was marked by outbreaks of republicanism, regional separatism, and general political turmoil, but the monarchy survived. Demands for regional autonomy were partially met by the Additional Act of 1834, which granted limited self-government to the provinces.

Pedro II. In 1840 Pedro II was declared of age, and he began performing his duties personally. During his reign of almost 50 years, Brazil attained a high degree of political freedom and stability. Brazil's two political parties, the Conservatives and the Liberals, peacefully alternated in power under prime ministers who were chosen from first one

and then the other party.

Pedro II wielded substantial personal power, but civil liberties were guaranteed even to the small republican minority. However, the monarchy was slow to deal with the problem of slavery. The slave trade had been outlawed by a treaty signed with Great Britain in 1827, but it continued in practice until the mid-1800s.

Slavery itself was completely ended in 1888, without compensation, alienating the slave-owning aristocracy. By that time the monarchy had also begun to weaken in other ways.

In the 1870s a serious clash with the Roman Catholic Church had occurred as a result of government interference with a strong anti-Masonic campaign launched by a group of bishops. Brazil's participation in the War of the Triple Alliance against Paraguay (1865–1870), although it ended in victory, added little to the empire's prestige.

After the war the army aspired to a greater role in Brazilian life, and thus came into conflict with the civilian-minded emperor and his ministers. Finally, republicanism increased steadily after 1870. The aging Pedro II still retained great personal popularity, but there was no serious resistance on his behalf when a military coup led by Marshal Manoel Deodoro da Fonseca overthrew the monarchy in 1889.

The republic. In 1891 the new Brazilian republic adopted a federal constitution modeled after that of the United States. The initial two presidents, however, were military officers, and both showed arbitrary tendencies that provoked wide unrest. The first president to serve a full term was a civilian from São Paulo, Prudente José de Moraes Barros (1894–1898). His administration was harassed by military upheavals and by a revolt in the back country of northeastern Brazil led by a religious fanatic, Antônio Conselheiro. But when Barros left office, the republic appeared to be firmly established.

Subsequent administrations until 1930 were mostly controlled by a narrow oligarchy representing the large and wealthy states of São Paulo and

Minas Gerais. Nonetheless, constitutional and democratic forms were generally maintained.

During the mid-1800s, coffee had replaced sugar as Brazil's chief crop and major export. Coffee production steadily increased until the early 1900s, when serious overproduction and falling world prices sparked an economic crisis. The government then began to restrict coffee planting and later to buy up surplus stocks, hoping to support coffee prices. Meanwhile, a great rubber boom had swept the Amazon basin, only to collapse on the eve of World War I in the face of Asian competition.

The economy recovered with the wartime and early postwar demand for Brazilian products, but slumped with the later return to normal conditions. The 1920s were characterized by serious social and economic unrest.

The world economic depression of the 1930s caught Brazil in a highly vulnerable position because of its heavy dependence on coffee as an export. The government was unable to halt a disastrous drop in coffee prices. Moreover, the economic crisis coincided with an attempt in 1930 by the outgoing president, Washington Luís Pereira de Souza, to assure the election of Julio Prestes as his successor. Prestes won, but a revolution by the military installed the more popular opposition candidate, Getulio Vargas, in the presidency.

The Vargas era. Although he had condemned undemocratic practices of the previous regime, Vargas himself ruled by decree, which provoked demands for a return to constitutional procedures and an uprising in São Paulo in 1932. The revolt failed, however, and Vargas remained in power as dictator.

From the beginning, Vargas recognized the need for social and economic reforms. On assuming office, he initiated labor legislation, supported labor unions, and expanded educational facilities and social services in the larger towns and cities. He also encouraged industrialization in an attempt to diversify the economy and, with foreign financial assistance, began the creation of a Brazilian steel industry.

In World War II, Vargas sided with the Allies and sent Brazilian troops to fight in Italy. Toward the end of the war, Vargas found himself subject to increasing public pressure to observe in Brazil the democratic principles for which Brazilians were fighting and dying abroad. He therefore began to modify his dictatorship and promised free presidential elections in 1945.

Fearing that Vargas would go back on his word, the military removed him from office in October 1945. The 1945 elections were won by Enrico Gaspar Dutra, who took office on January 1, 1946. In September a new constitution was adopted, completing the restoration of political freedom and representative government.

In 1951 Vargas returned to the presidency in a popular election, but his new administration was soon characterized by blatant corruption and demagoguery. Vargas did create a government petroleum monopoly, which was designed to save Brazil from exploitation by foreign oil interests. Nonetheless, Vargas was generally unable to solve Brazil's difficult postwar economic problems.

An attempt by men close to the president to assassinate an opposition publisher brought forth a new move by the military to oust Vargas. Rather than resign as demanded, he committed suicide in August 1954.

Contemporary Brazil. Following a period of much political confusion, Juscelino Kubitschek took office as president for the next full term (1956–1961). Kubitschek's main accomplishments were the creation of a new capital city, Brasília, located near the geographic center of the country, and the building of highways and hydroelectric works.

To finance these and other expenditures, Kubitschek issued vast amounts of paper money. By doing so he added to an inflationary spiral that had begun before his presidency. Economic growth nonetheless continued.

Jânio da Silva Quadros was elected president in 1960. His government resumed diplomatic relations with the Soviet Union and decorated the Argentine-born Cuban guerrilla expert Ernesto "Che" Guevara. In general, Quadros proved to be a highly erratic leader, and he resigned in less than a year. The military unsuccessfully tried to prevent Vice President Joâo Goulart from succeeding him because of Goulart's strong leftist leanings.

During the Goulart administration (1961–1964), inflation rapidly increased. Much was said about fundamental social reforms, including agrarian reform, but little was done. In March 1964, a new military coup ousted Goulart.

A provisional military government conducted a widespread purge of prominent politicians and gained control of the congress by barring opponents. General Humberto Castello Branco was elected president by the purged congress on April 11, 1964. Castello Branco introduced measures to reduce inflation, promote political stability, and encourage foreign investment.

In December 1966, Castello Branco pushed through the congress a new constitution providing for the consolidation of federal power and the election of the president, with semidictatorial powers. This constitution, extensively amended in 1969, provided for the election of the president to a six-year term by an electoral college composed of members of the congress and representatives of the state legislatures.

CARNIVAL IN BRAZIL, particularly in Rio de Janeiro, is celebrated by thousands of people, such as those in the Escola de Samba seen here.

center
US

centre
Brit.

CONDOMBLÉ CEREMONIES are a syncretism of Roman Catholicism and traditional religions brought from Africa.

From 1968 to 1973, Brazil's economy grew at an annual rate of about 11 percent, driven by austere domestic policies and an enormous influx of foreign capital. The steep rise in oil prices in the 1970s caused the Brazilian economy to slow down.

The succession of military governments following Castello Branco's regime used severe tactics in quieting political opposition. The abrogation of human rights led to deteriorating relations with the United States, which publicly condemned the government in 1977.

Democratic reforms were begun in 1979. In that year, General João Baptista Figueiredo was elected president by an electoral college in the country's first true multiparty election since Goulart's deposition in 1964. Baptista introduced some democratic reforms.

In 1985 Brazil received its first civilian president in 21 years when an electoral college chose Tancredo Neves as president. Neves died before being sworn in, and his vice president, José Sarney, became president. Sarney was unable to halt the economic deterioration of the early 1980s. By 1988 inflation had risen to an annual rate of 683 percent.

In 1989 Fernando Collor de Mello was elected president in the first direct presidential election in 29 years. Collor faced the problems of restructuring Brazil's huge foreign debt and halting destruction of the Amazon rain forest. In 1992 Collor was impeached by the congress on charges of corruption. He resigned and was succeeded by Vice President Itamar Franco. In 1994 Fernando Henrique Cardoso, a former finance minister who had led Brazil's economic recovery in the 1990s, was elected president. In 2003 Luiz Inacio Lula da Silva, leader of the country's only socialist party, became Brazil's first working-class president.

Chile

Official name: *Republic of Chile*
Area: *292,183 sq. mi.,*
756,950 sq. km.
Type of government: *Republic*
Population: *15,499,000*
Capital and largest city: *Santiago*
Pop., metro. area, 4,647,000
Language: *Spanish*
Literacy: *95%,* **Currency:** *Peso*
Per capita GDP: *$10,000*
(Rank: 50th)

The land. Chile is a long, narrow country on the western coast of South America. It stretches about 2,650 miles (4,264 kilometers) from north to south, but averages only 100 miles (161 kilometers) in width. The country has imposing natural boundaries. On the north the Atacama Desert separates Chile from Peru; on the northeast and east, the Andes separate the country from Bolivia and Argentina; on the south the Drake Passage separates Chile from Antarctica; and on the west is the Pacific Ocean.

The highest mountain in the western hemisphere, Mount Aconcagua, with an elevation of 22,834 feet (6,960 meters), lies on the Chile-Argentina border. The highest elevation within Chile is Mount Ojos del Salado, with an elevation of 22,539 feet (6,870 meters). The Chilean Andes form a single mountain range in the east, and there is a low coastal mountain range in the west. A central valley nearly 500 miles (805 kilometers) long nestles between the two parallel ranges.

Northern Chile, the desert region, is very dry, and there are weather stations that have no record of rain ever having fallen. The region has rich mineral resources. The central valley has a mild climate, with a winter rainy season and summer drought. It is the heartland of the country. Almost 90 percent of the people live there, and it produces most of the country's domestic food supply.

Southern Chile is wet and heavily forested. The land is said to resemble Switzerland because of its high, snow-capped mountains and glacial lakes. Temperatures average in the low 50°s F (10°s C). In the extreme south, at the end of the continent, are Patagonia and Tierra del Fuego, inhabited by extremely primitive natives who were of great interest to Charles Darwin when he visited the southern tip of the continent on the *Beagle*. The area has steep slopes, heavy rainfall, mild winter temperatures, and cool summer temperatures, and high winds. It is sparsely populated.

The people. Approximately 25 percent of Chile's population is of Spanish or other European descent. Most of the rest is mestizo, of mixed Spanish and Indian heritage.

About 100,000 Araucanian Indians live in the forests of south-central Chile. Changos live along the northeastern frontier and are employed in the mines. Groups of nomadic Fuegians inhabit Tierra del Fuego.

A dominant trend in Chile is the movement of people from the rural areas to the urban centers, which now contain more than 82 percent of the population. The metropolitan area around Santiago, the capital, contains nearly one-third of the country's people. Concepción (population, 215,000), which is located in the center of Chile on the Bio Bio River, is the largest city, followed by Viña del Mar (299,000), and Valparaiso (270,000), the country's principal seaport. Talcahuano (249,000), Punta Arenas (121,000), the most southerly city, and Puerto Montt (175,000) are also important ports.

Economy. Chile is largely dependent on the exploitation of its mineral resources, which are found primarily in the north within the Atacama Desert.

Copper, iron ore, and nitrates make up three-fifths of the total value of Chilean exports.

Chile has long been a world leader in copper and nitrate production. Copper accounts for almost half of the value of Chile's exports. Because of the price

kilometers
US
kilometres
Brit.

centers
US
centres
Brit.

labor
US
labour
Brit.

instability of copper in the world market, Chile has made an effort to increase industrial, manufacturing, and agricultural exports in order to reduce the effects of market fluctuations on the Chilean economy.

Chile produces the world's total supply of natural sodium nitrate, and most of the world's supply of iodine, a byproduct of nitrate.

Agreements with foreign mining companies provide for a portion of the profits to remain in Chile, and the income has aided the development of the entire economy. All of Chile's mines were nationalized in 1971, but many of them were returned to private ownership in 1975. The government controls and operates the four largest copper mines, accounting for some 70 percent of Chile's copper reserves.

Mining employs a small percentage of the nation's labor force, but accounts for a large part of its international trade and over 10 percent of its gross national product. Agriculture employs about 14 percent of the labor force, but provides a substantial and increasing portion of Chile's exports. In fact, fruit production accounts for about 10 percent of Chile's export earnings.

Only a fraction of Chile's total land area is suitable for cultivation, and only a small part of that is used. Chile's Central Valley is the main agricultural region. The principal crops are fruits, wheat, barley, and oats. Livestock raising is also important, but neither cattle nor crop production is adequate for Chile's needs, and foodstuffs must be imported.

Chile is one of the most industrialized nations of South America. Industry employs 27 percent of the labor force and provides for over one-fifth of the gross national product. The Huachipato steel plant, inaugurated in 1951, meets almost all of Chile's requirements. Chile also manufactures a variety of consumer goods for domestic consumption, including textiles, medicines, shoes, paper, and cement. The major industries are located in the provinces of Santiago, Valparaiso, and Concepción.

Major exports are copper, iron ore, nitrates and iodine, petrochemicals, metals, plastics, processed foods, fruits, fish meal, beans, lentils, wool, and paper. Principal imports include industrial raw materials, industrial and agricultural machinery and equipment, vehicles, petroleum, and consumer goods.

Most exports go to the United States, Great Britain, Germany, the Netherlands, and Japan. Imports come largely from the United States, Japan, Brazil, Argentina, Germany, and Venezuela.

Government. Chile is a republic with a strong tradition of constitutional government. After a 1973 coup, however, it was ruled by a four-man military junta headed by a president and the legislature was dissolved. A new constitution was approved in 1980, but the country

THE STATUE of the Immaculate Conception stands in Santiago, Chile.

remained under military rule until 1989, when a civilian president was elected to office in an open election. Constitutional reforms approved in 1988 provided for an increase in the number of directly elected senators, an important step forward in the country's return to democratic government. The congress now consists of the 49-seat Senate and the 120-seat Chamber of Deputies.

History. During the 1400s, the northern part of Chile had come under the influence of the Inca Empire. The extent of Inca control is not known, but it did not extend to the warlike Araucanian Indians who lived in the southern forest region. The Spaniards first explored Chile in 1535, when an expedition under Diego de Almagro attempted unsuccessfully to defeat the Araucanians. Spanish forces under Pedro de Valdivia conquered Chile in 1541 but they, too, were unable to defeat the Araucanians, who were not subdued until the late 1800s.

In the more open central portion of Chile, Spain created a stable agricultural colony, and Chile was part of the viceroyalty of Peru until the 1800s.

The first move toward independence was made on September 18, 1810, when Chileans established an autonomous junta to rule during the absence of the Spanish king, Ferdinand VII, who had been dethroned and made a prisoner by Napoleon in 1808. The patriot regime was suppressed in 1814 by loyalist forces from Peru.

The Spanish were finally defeated in 1817–1818 by the army of José de San Martin, which crossed the Andes from Argentina. San Martin's Chilean comrade in arms, Bernardo O'Higgins, was made provisional ruler of Chile with the title of supreme director.

Independence. O'Higgins gave Chile a generally sound and progressive administration. Nonetheless, he antagonized Chile's powerful class of wealthy landowners by his efforts at mild social reform and his concentration of authority in his own hands. In 1823 he was forced to resign. Chile was then plunged into a brief period of turmoil, during

which rival political factions battled for control.

In 1830 the conservatives came to power under the leadership of Diego Portales. Although he never assumed the presidency, Portales nonetheless created a strong centralized government while holding various cabinet posts. His views on government were the major influence in the writing of the constitution of 1833, which remained in force for nearly a century. Portales was assassinated in 1837 while organizing a military campaign against a confederation of Peru and Bolivia, which he believed posed a threat to Chile. Chile won the war and broke the confederation in 1839.

Era of growth. From the 1840s through the 1880s, Chile made notable social and material progress, although those who benefitted most were the upper and middle classes. Educational facilities were expanded, and religious toleration and the abolition of entailed estates were peacefully achieved. Economic development was aided by the extension of railway and coastal steam navigation, and by the final subjugation of the Araucanian Indians.

From 1879 to 1883, Chile fought Bolivia and Peru in the War of the Pacific, which began as a dispute over Bolivia's treatment of Chilean nitrate interests in the Atacama region. Chile won the war and annexed the nitrate-producing provinces of Peru and Bolivia. A boom in Chilean nitrate production followed and lasted until the development of synthetic nitrates during World War I.

Commerce, manufacturing, and coal and copper mining grew during the same period. This progress was accompanied by the rapid growth of an urban and mining proletariat whose poor working conditions led to serious unrest in the early 1900s.

EASTER ISLAND, a Chilean territory 2,300 miles (3,700 kilometers) west of the mainland, is famous for its huge carved stone heads.

28 South America

labor
US

labour
Brit.

vigorous
US

vigourous
Brit.

meters
US

metres
Brit.

Reforms. Chile had moved toward a system of constitutional rule in which the legislative branch established its supremacy over the executive. This trend was ensured in 1891 when an attempt by President José Manuel Balmaceda to reassert presidential authority led to civil war. The forces supporting the congress defeated those supporting the president, who committed suicide. Subsequent to the civil war, the congress was controlled by parties representing the landed aristocracy and the allied urban upper class, and little was done to improve the conditions of Chilean labor.

Chile remained neutral during World War I. The economy was stimulated by the wartime need for nitrates in the manufacturing of explosives, but it was badly hurt when prices dropped after peace was declared. Social and political dissatisfaction on the part of the middle and working classes increased and resulted in the election in 1920 of Arturo Alessandri Palma, who had run on an ambitious reform platform. Once in office, however, Alessandri Palma had little success in carrying out his program and was forced to resign in 1924.

From 1924 to 1932, constitutional government was severely shaken. In 1925 Alessandri Palma was returned to power and presided over the establishment of a new constitution. There

CHILE
has long been a world leader in copper and nitrate production.

remained instability in the national administration and a partial dictatorship was instituted from 1927 to 1931 under reform-minded General Cárlos Ibanez. Nevertheless, Chile emerged from this period of turmoil with a start in labor legislation and a constitution designed to end congressional domination of the executive.

Alessandri Palma, allied with both conservatives and liberals, returned to the presidency in 1932 and successfully restored the pattern of constitutional government. He was succeeded in 1938 by Pedro Aguirre Cedra, whose Popular Front administration drew support from

both Socialists and Communists, although Aguirre himself was from the generally moderate Radical Party.

The Popular Front sponsored additional benefits for labor, including government medical programs and low-cost housing. It collapsed during World War II, and for the following 20 years, Chile was ruled by a succession of middle-of-the-road and right-of-center administrations.

Contemporary Chile. Despite a high degree of political freedom and stability and a seemingly impressive body of social legislation, Chile still had serious economic and social problems. Almost nothing had been done for the landless rural masses, and the standard of living of the growing mass of urban workers did not keep pace with overall national economic gains.

Persistent inflation became a major problem, and in the late 1950s, a vigorous Socialist-Communist alliance showed signs of growing political strength. This was counterbalanced by the rise of the Christian Democratic Party, which gained power in 1964 when its leader, Eduardo Frei Montalva, was elected president. He initiated government acquisition of controlling interest in Chile's copper mines and instituted a program of agrarian reform.

In 1970 a coalition of Socialists, Communists, radicals, and dissident former Christian Democrats backed Dr. Salvador Allende Gossens of the Socialist Party to a narrow presidential victory. Abrupt economic changes, recurring strikes, and general social unrest thwarted his programs for nationalizing the copper mines and taking over foreign-owned industries and banks. A drop in the world price for copper, declining agricultural production, and rising inflation also helped stall Allende's program to turn Chile into a socialist state. Allende was overthrown by a military coup in September of 1973.

The ruling military junta—headed by President Augusto Pinochet Ugarte—that succeeded Allende suspended the congress and instituted a vigorous anti-Communist program that can only be characterized as repressive and dictatorial. The United States, which played a role in the 1973 coup, joined world criticism of the regime's disregard for human rights.

Since 1973 Chile has benefitted from an influx of foreign (chiefly U.S.) investment, which had declined during the Allende years.

In 1980 a new constitution was adopted and Pinochet became president. In 1988 Chileans voted against an extension of Pinochet's rule, and in 1989 Patricio Aylwin was elected president of a civilian government.

In 1993 Eduardo Frei Ruiz-Tagle was elected president. Frei sought to continue the economic and social reforms advanced by Aylwin and to reduce the continuing influence of the military in Chilean politics. Socialist Ricardo Lagos was elected president in 2000.

Colombia

Official name: *Republic of Colombia*
Area: *439,619 sq. mi.,*
1,138,910 sq. km.
Type of government: *Republic*
Population: *41,008,000*
Capital and largest city: *Bogotá*
Pop. 6,422,000
Language: *Spanish*
Literacy: *91%*
Currency: *Peso*
Per capita GDP: *$6,300*
(Rank: 76th)

The land. Colombia is unique among the South American nations in that it faces both the Caribbean Sea and the Pacific Ocean.

The western third of the country is crossed by three distinct ranges of the Andes, which create substantial barriers. Most of the country's people and economically important areas lie in scattered valleys in this region, separated by the Andes, by climate, and by different ways of life.

Physical regions. Colombia has two main land regions—the Andes in the west and the lowlands in the east. The Andean region is a continuation of the broad Andes mountain system, which runs almost the entire length of the western side of the South American continent. The Colombian Andes fan out in the southwest direction to form three distinct ranges: the Cordillera Occidental, the Cordillera Central, and the Cordillera Oriental.

The Cordillera Central has peaks that rise more than 18,000 feet (5,486 meters) above sea level. The cordilleras Occidental and Oriental are somewhat lower. The Cordillera Oriental widens in the north and forms a narrow plateau in the vicinity of Bogotá. The Magdalena River separates the Cordillera Oriental from the Cordillera Central, and the Cauca River separates the Cordillera Central from the Cordillera Occidental. Both rivers flow northward and empty into the Caribbean Sea.

The eastern lowlands drain into the Amazon and Orinoco river systems. The southern section of the region is tropical rain forest and sparsely populated. The northern section consists of savannas, or *llanos.* Although flooded for a large portion of the year, it is suitable for livestock raising.

Climatic zones. Climate in Colombia varies with altitude. The lower areas, from sea level to about 3,000 feet (915 meters), comprise the *tierra caliente,* or hot country. It has average temperatures of 75° to 85°F (24° to 29°C), and tropical crops, such as rice and bananas, are grown there.

The *tierra templada,* or temperate country, lies between 3,000 and 6,500 feet (915 and 1,980 meters) above sea level. It has year-round temperatures of

65° to 70°F (18° to 21°C), and coffee flourishes on the Andean slopes.

The third level is the *tierra fría,* or cold country, between 6,500 and 10,000 (1,980 and 3,048 meters) feet above sea level. Wheat, maize, and fruit are grown there. Above 10,000 feet but below the 15,000-foot (4,572-meter) snow line, the land is unsuitable for cultivation and so is devoted to pasturing livestock.

The people. About 72 percent of the Colombian population is mestizo, of mixed Spanish and Indian descent, and mulatto, of mixed black and white descent. Whites constitute about 20 percent of the total and are concentrated in the major cities. Blacks make up about 4 percent of the population and live mainly along the Caribbean and Pacific coasts. Indians represent only about 1 percent of the total population, while Colombians of mixed black and Indian heritage represent an additional 3 percent.

Nearly three-quarters of the people live in urban areas, particularly in the Andean valleys. Bogotá, the capital, lies more than 8,500 feet (2,591 meters) above sea level. Medellín (population, 1,885,000), in the Cordillera Central, is the commercial center of the coffee and textile industries. Cali (2,129,000), in the fertile Cauca valley, is a marketplace for agricultural products and an industrial center.

Barranquilla (1,549,000), on the Caribbean coast, is the country's largest port. Cartagena (829,000), one of the oldest South American cities, is Colombia's foremost tourist center. It is also the shipping point for petroleum and petroleum products from a large local refinery.

Economy. Agriculture is the most important part of Colombia's economy. Although only 5 percent of the nation's total land area is cultivated, almost one half of the population is employed in agriculture. Coffee is the chief crop and Colombia is the second leading coffee exporter, after Brazil, in the world. Colombia relies heavily on its export to

THE PUTAMAYO RIVER AREA in Colombia is home to the Cofan Indians.

earn foreign exchange. Other major commercial crops are bananas, flowers, sugar cane, tobacco, cotton, and cacao. Cattle are also important and are raised on the *llanos,* or plains, of the country's eastern lowlands.

Colombia is rich in mineral resources. Mining plays an important role and is the fastest growing sector of the economy. However, processing and transportation of Colombia's mineral wealth remain serious obstacles. Petroleum is the country's second most valuable export. Colombia is the second leading producer in South America of gold and platinum and is the world's leading source of emeralds. In addition, Colombia produces significant quantities of silver and iron ore, and possesses large reserves of high-grade coal.

Although industry is not highly developed, it has been growing. It now contributes about 20 percent of the gross national product, just slightly less than agriculture, and employs about one-fifth of the labor force. Manufacturing is largely devoted to textiles and food processing, but beverages, shoes, steel, and a variety of chemicals are also produced. The growth of both industry and mining, however, is hampered by a lack of capital for investment, poor transportation facilities, a small domestic market, and political instability.

Coffee accounts for about 37 percent of the value of all exports. Other exports include petroleum, bananas, tobacco, textiles, flowers, and sugar. Chemicals, machinery, steel products, paper, and vehicles are the country's main imports. Colombia's major trading partner is the United States. Other trading partners are Germany and Japan.

Government. Colombia is a constitutional republic. The chief executive and head of state is the president, who is popularly elected to a term of four years and cannot be reelected. The president appoints and is assisted by a Cabinet, whose members are answerable to the congress.

The congress is composed of the 102-member Senate and the 166-member House of Representatives.

Senators and representatives are elected by popular vote to four-year terms and may serve any number of consecutive terms.

Colombia is divided into 32 departments headed by governors who are directly elected by popular vote. In addition, there is the special Capital District of Bogotá.

History. Before the Spanish conquest in the 1500s, the high Andean region of Colombia stretching northeastward from Bogotá was the home of the Chibchas, an American Indian people who had a stable agricultural society and who were highly skilled at goldwork. They were easily subdued by the Spaniards, who had begun exploring the Caribbean coast as early as 1500.

THE ANDES of Colombia and Ecuador are home to populations that retain much of their Indian heritage.

center
US

centre
Brit.

labor
US

labour
Brit.

Spanish era. The first permanent Spanish communities were established at Santa Marta in 1525 and Cartagena in 1533. Santa Marta later served as the base for an expedition under Gonzalo Jiménez de Quesada that moved inland to conquer the Chibchas and resulted in the founding of Santa Fé de Bogotá in 1538. Bogotá eventually became the administrative center of what Quesada named the New Kingdom of Granada, a region including Colombia and, at various times, lands that later became Ecuador, Venezuela, and Panama.

To the west, the Spaniards discovered what was to become the chief gold-producing area of their empire. Cartagena, on the Caribbean coast, became the principal naval base of the Spanish fleet. Nonetheless, most of Colombia remained virtually uninhabited throughout the Spanish colonial period. Its few people were engaged chiefly in raising cattle and growing crops for local consumption.

Colombia's struggle for independence began in 1810, when local leaders deposed the Spanish authorities and established a number of juntas, ostensibly to rule in the absence of Spain's King Ferdinand VII, who had been removed from the Spanish throne and was held captive by Napoleon. Some areas of New Granada declared their independence of the Spanish crown, but most retained allegiance to Spain. However, this brief period of self-rule set the stage for conflict when, in 1814, Ferdinand regained the throne and moved to reestablish direct Spanish rule of New Granada. His armies reoccupied many regions of the country in 1815–1816, but in 1819 Simón Bolívar routed Spanish forces at Boyacá.

Independence. In the same year, 1819, the viceroyalty of New Granada was organized by the leaders of the independence movement into the republic of Grán Colombia. Bolívar was elected president, but he had to leave to continue the war against Spain and turned over the government to his vice president, Francisco de Paula Santander.

Santander proved an able administrator, but was harassed by separatist movements in Venezuela and Ecuador. Not even the return of Bolívar could prevent the final dissolution of the republic of Grán Colombia, and Venezuela and Ecuador withdrew from the republic shortly after Bolívar's death in 1830.

In 1831 the territory of modern Colombia and Panama was established as the Republic of New Granada. Santander became its first elected chief executive in 1832. Soon, however, a long and violent struggle began between liberals and conservatives over church policy and constitutional organization. **Era of conflict.** During the 1850s and 1860s, the liberals established freedom of worship and separation of church and state, but they also aroused conservative antagonisms by seizing church lands, abolishing monastic orders, and placing restrictions on the Roman Catholic clergy. Politically, they carried the concept of states' rights to such extremes that the national government itself was often rendered ineffective.

The liberals' extreme approach to local autonomy and their church policy produced the inevitable conservative reaction in the 1880s. Although originally a liberal, President Rafael Núñez joined forces with the conservatives to adopt a rigorously centralist constitution in 1886 and to remove the major restrictions placed on the church.

The policies of Núñez did not end internal strife. Liberals fought to undo his work by launching civil wars, the longest and bloodiest of which raged from 1899 to 1902 and claimed some 100,000 lives. This war, plus the secession of Panama in 1903, shocked the leaders of both factions into laying aside some of their bitterness or directing it at the United States, which had played a crucial role in securing Panamanian independence.

Civil wars abruptly ceased and, for nearly 50 years, Colombia enjoyed relative stability and constitutional government with economic growth. The production of coffee increased. New commodities, such as bananas and petroleum, and the beginnings of light manufacturing, especially of textiles, did a great deal to broaden the economic base. But it was not enough to insulate Colombia from the international depression that began in 1929.

Reforms. Until the liberal administration of Alfonso López (1934–1938), however, neither party had given much attention to the great majority of Colombians, who remained illiterate, impoverished, and beyond the reach of modern health facilities and social services. To deal with this problem, López launched a program that included labor and land reform as well as social welfare legislation.

Although his program was generally moderate, it aroused strong opposition from wealthy, conservative Colombians. At the same time, it instilled among the working class hopes that could be only partially satisfied. Colombia thus faced a new period of strife that came to be known as *la violencia:* Inherited political rivalries were aggravated by new social and economic conflicts.

Tensions reached a climax on April 9, 1948, when the leftist liberal leader Jorge E. Gaitán was assassinated in Bogotá and his followers rioted in protest. A year later, interparty relations broke down entirely, and violence began to spread to large areas of Colombia. Beginning as a struggle between liberals and conservatives, the conflict often degenerated into banditry.

Contemporary Colombia. A dictatorship led by General Gustavo Rojas Pinilla, from 1953 to 1957, brought a slight decline in civil strife but failed to stop the violence, which in the two decades following Gaitán's death claimed a quarter of a million lives.

The violence of the 1950s and the growing unpopularity of the Rojas Pinilla regime led liberals and conservatives to cooperate once again. After joining to overthrow the dictator in May 1957, the two factions created a National Front coalition government with terms that provided for the alternation of liberals and conservatives in the presidency and the division of other offices on a fifty-fifty basis for a 16-year period.

A new approach to the nation's fundamental social and economic problems included efforts at agrarian reform. But Colombia's difficulties were compounded by an extremely high rate of population increase, large scale migration to the cities, and a sharp drop in the world price of coffee, which limited the financial resources available for reform programs.

The last president to serve under the National Front system was Misael Pastrana, a conservative elected in 1970.

Since 1970 the left-wing Movement of April 19 (M-19) has increased its guerrilla and terrorist activities as the government has lagged in effecting adequate social and land reform.

In 1974 Alfonso López Michelson, the Liberal Party candidate, was elected president. Despite growing social and economic problems, the Liberals retained the presidency in 1978. However, in 1982 the Conservative candidate, Belisario Betancur, was elected president. He attempted to neutralize the growing guerrilla movement and to eradicate the burgeoning traffic in cocaine. However, guerrilla leaders and drug lords joined forces and the effort stalled. In 1986 the Liberal candidate, Virgilio Barco Vargas, became president.

Colombia has been troubled by high inflation, high unemployment, and an illegal drug traffic that reached monumental levels in the 1980s. In 1989, following a dramatic rise in violence by the drug cartels, notably the Medellín group, the Colombian government began a major new drug crackdown by seizing the cartels' property and confiscating their drugs. This battle continued despite violent retaliations.

In 1990 César Gaviria Trujillo was elected president, following a campaign in which three other candidates were murdered. He worked to reduce drug-related and political violence through negotiation. In 1991 a new constitution was approved and legislative elections were held. Successive presidents have pledged to make inroads against corruption and drug trafficking, but these issues continue to plague the country.

Ecuador

Official name: *Republic of Ecuador*
Area: *109,454 sq. mi.,*
283,560 sq. km.
Type of government: *Republic*
Population: *13,447,000*
Capital: *Quito*
Pop. 1,616,000
Largest city: *Guayaquil*
Pop. 2,118,000
Languages: *Spanish (official),*
Indian dialects
Literacy: *90%*
Currency: *Sucre*
Per capita GDP: *$3,000*
(Rank: 115th)

The land. Ecuador has three major zones: the coastal lowlands in the west, the Andes, and the eastern lowlands. Ecuador's territory also includes the Galapagos Islands, 600 miles (965 kilometers) off the mainland.

The Andes in Ecuador form two parallel chains: the Cordillera Occidental and the Cordillera Oriental. The mountains of these ranges, which have elevations between 10,000 and 20,000 feet (3,000 and 6,000 meters) above sea level, are the site of considerable volcanic and seismic activity. Many of the mountains are of volcanic origin. The ranges are highest in the north, where there are three towering volcanic peaks—Chimborazo, whose peak, at 20,702 feet (6,310 meters), is the highest point in Ecuador; Cotopaxi, with an elevation of 19,347 feet (5,897 meters); and Cayambe, with an elevation of 18,996 feet (5,790 meters).

Between the ranges is nestled a long trough with an elevation between 6,000 and 9,000 feet (1,829 and 2,743 meters). This trough is composed of a series of interconnected mountain basins cut by rivers flowing west to the Pacific or east to the Amazon. About half of the population live within this central valley region, and about half live in the coastal lowlands. Livestock, poultry, grains, and vegetables are produced in the highland region, mainly for local consumption. Cotton and sugar cane are also cultivated in the lower basins.

The Cordillera Occidental descends abruptly to a warm coastal plain that averages about 50 miles (80 kilometers) wide. The northern part of the plain is well watered and forested, but the southern region is semiarid and grades into the desert of the Peruvian coast.

The coastal plain is crossed by rivers; the most important is the Guayas, which flows south and empties into the Gulf of Guayaquil. It is in this region that Ecuador's banana, coffee, and cacao plantations are found.

The eastern lowlands form a humid, tropical area that is almost uninhabited except for the Jivaro Indians.

The Galapagos archipelago consists of five large and nine small islands that are known for their numerous unique species of flora and fauna.

The people. Most of the people of Ecuador are Indian or mestizo, of mixed Indian and European origin. The Indians live mainly in the Andes; the mestizos are concentrated in the Andes and in the coastal areas. Ecuadoreans of European, largely Spanish, descent, live primarily in the large cities, particularly Quito and Guayaquil. Those of African descent live mainly along the coast.

The capital, Quito, lies about 9,500 feet (2,896 meters) above sea level. The chief commercial center and largest city, Guayaquil, located on the warm coastal plain, sends out about 75 percent of Ecuador's exports and receives about 90 percent of all imports. It is linked with Quito by rail, highway, and air transportation.

Economy. The economy has been revolutionized since the discovery of oil in eastern Ecuador in the 1960s. Isolated from the coast by the Andes Mountains, oil was not effectively incorporated into the economy until after 1972, when the construction of a trans-Andean pipeline was completed. It is estimated that at the current rate of extraction, deposits will be largely depleted by the turn of the century.

kilometers
US

kilometres
Brit.

Oil is Ecuador's leading export, replacing the traditional agricultural products and accounting for about 45 percent of exports. Shrimp and bananas, the second and third main exports, account for 18 and 14 percent of exports respectively. In the 1970s Ecuador's economic growth more than doubled the 1960s rate. By the late 1980s, however, Ecuador faced economic stagnation as world prices for oil and other commodities declined. An increased emphasis on oil refining has resulted in increased industrial output, although food processing is still the leading manufacture. The government has nationalized over 60 percent of the oil industry and has embarked on major development of its vast hydroelectric potential.

PEOPLE CARRYING LOADS
such as this are a common sight in a country with few beasts of burden and limited means of transportation.

28 South America

COTOPAXI, in the Andes in Ecuador, has an elevation of 19,347 feet (5,897 meters).

MARKET DAY is important to both the economic and social structures in the Ecuadorean Andes.

Agriculture, previously the most important sector of the economy, employs about one-third of the country's labor force. Bananas, coffee, and cacao are the chief crops.

Ecuador remains largely underdeveloped. Most farming is on a subsistence level and it lacks, as does industry, technological sophistication. Land distribution is grossly unequal, causing considerable social and political tensions.

Ecuador's leading trading partner is the United States, but Japan and Germany are also important. After oil, fish and fish products, and bananas, other important exports are coffee, cacao, rice, sugar, and balsa wood. Ecuador's imports consist primarily of manufactured goods—machinery, motor vehicles, chemicals, textiles, and paper.

Government. Ecuador is a republic with a long tradition of political upheaval and frequent coups.

According to Ecuador's constitution, executive power is held by the president, who is popularly elected to a four-year term and who appoints the twelve-member cabinet. Legislative power is held by the unicameral, 123-member National Congress, whose members are elected to four-year terms. Twenty are elected on a national level and 103 are elected on a provincial level. Judicial power rests with the Supreme Court and provincial courts. The country of Ecuador is divided into 22 provinces.

labor
US

labour
Brit.

History. Present-day Ecuador was originally the Indian kingdom of Quito. The Incas, however, conquered Quito and incorporated it into their empire. After the Spanish conquest of Peru by Francisco Pizarro in 1533, an army led by one of his captains, Sebastián de Belalcázar, conquered Ecuador and in 1534 established the city of San Francisco de Quito on the site of the ancient Indian capital. At first Ecuador was part of the Spanish colonial viceroyalty of Peru, but for a time, from 1717 to 1723, it was administered by New Granada. After 1740 it again belonged to the viceroyalty of New Granada.

During the Spanish American struggle for independence in the early 1800s, Quito was one of the first cities to establish an autonomous government, or junta (in August 1809). This junta was quickly suppressed by forces loyal to Spain.

A second patriot government, created in October 1810, was also suppressed. In 1820, however, the port of Guayaquil threw off Spanish rule. Two years later, the rest of Ecuador was liberated with the help of one of Simón Bolívar's lieutenants, Antonio José de Sucre, who decisively defeated the Spaniards at the Battle of Pichincha on May 24, 1822.

Independence. After gaining its freedom, Ecuador joined with Venezuela and Colombia to form the republic of Gran Colombia. But separatist feeling was strong, and in 1830, with the dissolution of Gran Colombia, Ecuador became independent.

Ecuador's first president was General Juan José Flores, another of Bolívar's lieutenants and a Venezuelan by birth. Flores remained a dominant figure until 1845, serving twice as president (1830–1835, 1839–1845) and keeping control of the army even during the four years he was out of office. His late administration was followed by 15 years of political instability, during which time the exiled Flores attempted unsuccessfully to mount expeditions against Ecuador. During this period, however, some attention was given to liberal reforms—slavery, for example, was abolished in 1854.

A new era began in 1860 with the election of Gabriel García Moreno as president. He exercised firm control over Ecuador until 1875. García Moreno launched an ambitious public works program and expanded the school system, but his rule is remembered chiefly for its generally conservative policies, notably its close alliance with the Roman Catholic Church, to which García Moreno gave wide control over both education and culture.

García Moreno was assassinated in 1875, and during the following two decades political anarchy reigned. In 1895 Ecuadorean Liberals, led by General Eloy Alfaro, gained control of the government. Over the next few years they attempted to weaken the influence of the church and enacted a series of

laws that included the legalization of divorce and the granting of religious freedom. In addition, the completion in 1908 of a railroad from Guayaquil to Quito was a major step toward modernization of the country.

Various factions of the Liberal Party generally remained in control until the mid-1940s, despite numerous coups and periods of political chaos. During the period from 1925 to 1948, for example, Ecuador had more than 20 presidents or chiefs of state, and none completed a normal term of office.

Contemporary Ecuador. An undeclared border war with Peru broke out in 1941. The Ecuadorean army was no match for the invading Peruvian forces. The conflict was settled by the Rio de Janeiro Protocol of 1942. Under its terms Ecuador was forced to give up most of its claims to territory in the Amazon basin, Ecuador's Eastern Region, constituting about half of Ecuador's entire area. In 1961 Ecuador unilaterally denounced the 1942 Rio agreement, however, and renewed its claims.

In 1960 José María Velasco Ibarra, an independent, was elected president. This was his fourth term, having previously been elected to the presidency in 1934, 1944, and 1952. In 1961, owing to violent demonstrations, Velasco Ibarra resigned in favor of Vice President Carlos Julio Arosemena Monroy.

Arosemena Monroy was overthrown in 1963. A military junta ruled until widespread civil protest, beginning in 1966, led to the temporary restoration of civil rule in 1968, when Velasco Ibarra was elected president again.

In 1970 Velasco Ibarra assumed full dictatorial powers. He was ousted in 1972. A new military junta ruled until 1979, when it provided for a return to civilian rule. In 1979 Jaime Roldós Aguilera won a disputed presidential election, but he was killed in an airplane crash in 1981. Osvaldo Hurtado, who was vice

THIS FAMILY is typical of the sturdy population produced by the rugged terrain and harsh climate of the Andes.

president, became president. His plans for economic development were often obstructed by financial problems.

Leon Febres Cordero, a Social Christian, was elected president in 1984. He encountered many conflicts with the opposition-dominated congress and saw the rise of two leftist guerrilla groups. His attempts to deal with the subsequent political violence led to charges of human rights abuses.

The late 1980s saw a presidential attempt to bring inflation, unemployment, and massive foreign debt under control. In the early 1990s the president sought to increase privatization, reduce bureaucracy, and encourage growth in the private sector. Regardless, economic crises (damage resulting from El Niño, a plunge in oil prices, high inflation) in the late 1990s saw the government near bankruptcy. This led to a military coup in 2000 and the restructuring of foreign debt. Within 2 years the economy had rebounded.

Guyana

Official name: *Co-Operative Republic of Guyana*

Area: *83,978 sq. mi., 214,970 sq. km.*

Type of government: *Republic*

Population: *700,000*

Capital and largest city:
*Georgetown
Pop. 72,000*

Language: *English, Amerindian dialects*

Literacy: *98%*

Currency: *Dollar*

Per capita GDP: *$3,600 (Rank: 106th)*

The land. Guyana's land surface consists of a low coastal plain that rises gradually into the heavily faulted Guiana Highlands. The coastal plain, from 10 to 40 miles (16 to 65 kilometers) in width, represents only 3½ percent of Guyana's total land area, yet it is the home of 90 percent of the population. The coastal plain is the only area suitable for agriculture, and the country's two main crops, sugar cane and rice, are raised there.

South of the coastal plain is an inland forest region that covers 86 percent of Guyana. The inland forest contains great quantities of commercially valuable wood, but transportation is poor and the region has remained largely unexploited. Guyana also has about 8,000 square miles (20,700 square kilometers) of grassland savannas, located primarily in the southwestern interior.

Guyana has four major rivers—the Essequibo, Demerara, Berbice, and Courantyne—as well as a number of small rivers, but they are generally navigable only from about 40 to 100 miles

(65 to 160 kilometers) upstream. Farther inland the irregularity of the highland terrain creates numerous falls and rapids, which have hindered access to the interior.

Guyana has a humid, tropical climate. The coastal plain is cooled by the northeast trade winds and has an average temperature of 80°F (26.7°C), but the savannas and inland forest have somewhat higher temperatures. Annual rainfall ranges from about 80 inches (203 centimeters) on the coast to about 100 inches (254 centimeters) in the interior. The coast has two rainy seasons, from April to August and from November to January.

The people. About half of the population is descended from East Indian laborers who came to work on the sugar plantations in the mid-1800s. About one-third is descended from African slaves. The remainder consists of people of mixed African and Indian descent, indigenous American Indians, and Chinese, Portuguese, and other Europeans.

The diversity of Guyana's peoples is reflected in their religious beliefs. Some 35 percent of the population is Hindu, 10 percent Muslim, 35 percent Protestant, and 15 percent Roman Catholic. Two-thirds of the population lives in rural areas.

Economy. Guyana's economy is based on agriculture and mining. About 34 percent of the labor force is employed in agriculture and about 45 percent in industry and commerce. The government has sought to decrease its dependence on sugar, the chief agricultural product. Rice has also become an important crop. Coconuts, coffee, cocoa, citrus, and other fruits are grown largely for domestic consumption. Although only about 1 percent of Guyana's land is under cultivation, increased land cultivation is a major goal of the country's economic planning.

Guyana's most important mineral is bauxite, from which aluminum is made. Manganese has been discovered in the northwest, at Matthews Ridge, and large-scale mining operations began in 1960. Small amounts of gold and diamonds are also mined. Guyana has some oil reserves, but the country still is dependent on oil imports. In the 1980s Guyana began a program to develop its considerable hydroelectric capacity.

Most of Guyana's industry is based on bauxite production and food processing. The country seeks to increase the output of consumer goods to reduce imports of those items.

Bauxite is the leading export. Other exports include sugar, rice, fish, uncut diamonds, manganese ore, rum, and wood. Principal imports are petroleum products, machinery, transportation equipment, textiles, most iron and steel products, and most chemicals. Guyana trades primarily with Great Britain, Canada, the United States, and Trinidad and Tobago.

Government. Guyana has a modified parliamentary system of government.

ALMOST 85 PERCENT OF GUYANA is covered by commercially valuable forest, but access is limited to waterways.

The country became a republic in 1970. In 1980 a new constitution was introduced. The president is elected by the National Assembly. Executive power is exercised by the president and his appointed cabinet, including a prime minister, who must be a member of the National Assembly. The president is normally the person who is leader of the majority party in the legislature.

Legislative power is vested in the 68-member, unicameral National Assembly. Sixty-five of the members are elected by popular vote, one is an elected Speaker of the National Assembly, and two are appointed by the president and do not vote. The president may dissolve the assembly and call for new elections.

kilometers
US

kilometres
Brit.

aluminum
US

aluminium
Brit.

History. The coast of Guyana was one of the first parts of South America to be discovered by Europeans. There was no immediate attempt at colonization, but the legend of the golden land of El Dorado and tales of fabulous riches to be found farther inland led to the exploration of the interior by Sir Walter Raleigh, who led expeditions in 1595 and 1617.

During the 1600s the Dutch, French, and British established small settlements along the coast. For 200 years different parts of the Guianas passed back and forth among the three powers, and it was not until the Congress of Vienna in 1814–1815 that the Guianas were formally divided into British, French, and Dutch areas. In 1831 the British holdings were consolidated to form the colony of British Guiana.

British rule. The economy of British Guiana was based on sugar, which was grown on large plantations worked by African slaves. During the early 1800s there was a great deal of unrest among the slaves, partly fostered by abolitionists in England. Slavery was abolished in 1833, and the economy suffered when the former slaves drifted off into the unsettled backlands and established themselves as small farmers.

Efforts were made to find an alternative labor force, and East Indians were eventually brought to work on the sugar plantations under a system of indentured labor. By 1883 they constituted one-fourth of the population. Sugar production rose in step with East Indian immigration, but friction began to develop among groups of different backgrounds.

The British kept the colony under tight political control and allowed only a few wealthy Guyanese to have some voice in its government. Serious discontent, however, did not become evident until the 1900s. There was some minor labor unrest as a result of the world economic depression of the 1930s, but it did not reach major proportions until after World War II.

In 1949 Cheddi Jagan, of East Indian origin, and Forbes Burnham, of African descent, established the People's Progressive Party (PPP) to work for social and economic reforms and to aim toward self-government. Great Britain granted the colony a constitution providing for a good deal of domestic autonomy in 1953. The PPP won elections held in April 1953, under the new constitution, but in October Britain suspended the constitution, charging that the PPP was operating under strong Communist influence.

In 1955 the PPP split along ethnic lines. Forbes Burnham led most of the black members into a new party, the People's National Congress (PNC). New elections were held in 1961 under a new constitution, and the PPP returned to power. But communal violence and fear of Jagan's left-wing connections led the British to intervene once more in 1962 and 1963.

Independence. Elections were conducted under a system of proportional representation in 1964, and the PNC gained control of the government. Guyana achieved full independence on May 26, 1966, and Forbes Burnham became the country's first prime minister. Burnham was returned to power in 1968, 1973, and 1978.

As the executive authority of South America's only Marxist socialist state, Burnham initiated a program of broad nationalization in the mid-1970s. The government now owns all of the bauxite industry and most of the commercial enterprises. Burnham died in 1985. His prime minister, Desmond Hoyte, succeeded to the presidency. In 1992 Cheddi Jagan defeated Hoyte in the presidential election.

In November 1978 some 900 members of a religious community at Jonestown were victims of a mass murder-suicide engineered by their leader, Jim Jones. Jones, leader of the People's Temple of Disciples of Christ (based in San Francisco, California), ordered the mass poisoning after his aides had assassinated five members of an investigative committee from the United States.

Intensified border disputes with Venezuela and Suriname, as well as continuing racial tensions, are issues of current concern in Guyana.

THE MISSION OF TRINIDAD in Paraguay echoes the country's strong historical ties with the Jesuit Order.

Climate. Because of its location within the interior of the continent, Paraguay experiences wider temperature fluctuations than almost any other part of South America. Summer temperatures average about 80°F (27°C), but temperatures over 100°F (38°C) are fairly common. Winter temperatures average 55°F (13°C).

Annual rainfall varies, although it is generally quite dry in the west and becomes progressively wetter toward the east. The average annual rainfall at Asunción, on the Paraguay River, is 62 inches (157 centimeters), but near the Brazilian border it increases to about 80 inches (203 centimeters).

The people. The overwhelming majority of the people are of mixed Guaraní Indian and Spanish ancestry. There are few pure-blooded Indians left in Paraguay; they mostly inhabit the remoter regions of the Chaco. There are also small numbers of foreigners who have settled mostly in agricultural communities. These include Germans, Japanese, Italians, Brazilians, Argentines, and Canadian Mennonites. The official language is Spanish but Guaraní is also spoken almost universally.

About 45 percent of the labor force is employed in agriculture, with about 15 percent in manufacturing. Paraguay is very sparsely populated, and nearly two-thirds of the people live in rural areas. The major urban centers include Asunción, the capital; San Lorenzo (population, 203,000), just southeast of Asunción; Encarnación (70,000); and Pedro Juan Caballero (64,000).

Economy. Paraguay is one of the least developed nations in South America. The government owns many of the nation's public utilities but encourages private enterprise and depends heavily on foreign investment.

Paraguay

Official name: *Republic of Paraguay*

Area: *157,006 sq. mi., 406,750 sq. km.*

Type of government: *Republic*

Population: *5,884,000*

Capital and largest city: *Asunción Pop. 513,000*

Languages: *Spanish (official), Guaraní*

Literacy: *92%*

Currency: *Guaraní*

Per capita GDP: *$4,600 (Rank: 92nd)*

The land. The Paraguay River, which flows down from Brazil and joins the Paraná River in the southwestern corner, at the Argentine border, divides Paraguay into two contrasting regions. The western region, the Gran Chaco, is a hot, parched wasteland partially covered with scrub forest. The eastern region consists of many fertile plains, grasslands, and dense forests.

In the extreme east is the heavily forested Paraná Plateau, which ranges in altitude from 1,000 to 2,000 feet (305 to 610 meters) above sea level. In the northern part of the plateau the forests give way to grasslands or savannas. West of the plateau are rolling, grassy plains.

The economy is based on agriculture and forestry, which account for almost all the country's exports.

Paraguay has deposits of manganese, iron, copper, and other minerals, but the only two minerals mined are limestone and salt. The country's most important natural resource is its forests, which yield valuable hardwoods and a variety of other products. Two important forest products are tannin, used in tanning, dyeing, ink, and medicine, and yerba maté, from which a tealike beverage is made.

Hydroelectric production on the Paraná River has stimulated economic growth since the 1970s. The facility, built through a joint effort with Brazil, is the largest in the world, and a second is scheduled to be built.

Agriculture. Although almost half of the people are engaged in agriculture, only a fraction of Paraguay's arable land is cultivated. Farming methods are primitive and most farmers raise only enough to feed their own families.

Food crops include manioc, corn, sugar cane, sweet potatoes, rice, and citrus and other fruits. The country's most important commercial crops are cotton and soybeans.

Cattle have long been an important source of income, and meat products are among Paraguay's most valuable exports. Cattle are raised chiefly in the area between the Paraguay and Paraná rivers, in Concepción near the northwestern border, and in the Chaco.

Industry. Paraguay is one of the least industrialized countries in South America. The nation's few industries are limited to the processing of its agricultural products and the manufacture of a small number of consumer goods and construction materials, such as soap, matches, glass, cement, and bricks.

Trade. Paraguay's major exports are cotton, soybeans, meat, lumber, and coconut and other oils. Imports include machinery, wheat, iron and steel products, transportation equipment, fuel oil, and chemicals.

Brazil, Argentina, Uruguay, the countries of the European Union, and the United States are Paraguay's chief trading partners.

Government. Paraguay is a republic. The head of state and chief executive is the president, who is directly elected to a term of five years. He is assisted by a cabinet, which he appoints.

Legislative power rests with a bicameral legislature consisting of a 45-member Senate and an 80-member Chamber of Deputies. Members of both houses are popularly elected to five-year terms.

Judicial power is vested in a nine-member Supreme Court of Justice, whose judges are chosen by the senate and president on the recommendation of a constitutionally created Council of Magistrates. Paraguay is divided administratively into 17 departments and the capital district. Department heads are elected by popular vote.

History. The area that came to be known as Paraguay was populated by the Guarani Indians when it was discovered by Spanish and Portuguese explorers in the early 1500s. The explorers were searching for a route across the continent to the fabled gold and silver treasures of the Inca Empire on the western coast. In 1537, Juan de Ayolas ventured up the Paraguay and Paraná Rivers, and his men built a permanent settlement in Asunción. This settlement became the seat of government for all of Spain's colonies in southeastern South America.

Spanish rule. In 1609 the Jesuits arrived in Paraguay to convert the Guaraní Indians. The Jesuits were highly successful in their missionary work and they founded more than 30 *reducciones,* self-sufficient, autonomous mission communities, exporting cotton, tobacco, hides, and wood. Between 150,000 and 200,000 Indians lived and worked within this system.

The Jesuits were not popular with the Spanish colonists, who wanted the Indians to work for them and resented competition from mission agricultural produce. In 1767 Spain expelled the Jesuits from South America, and the *reducciones* collapsed.

In 1776 Paraguay was incorporated into the newly formed viceroyalty of Río de la Plata, which included present-day Argentina and was governed from Buenos Aires. In 1810 the Argentinians rebelled against Spain and set up a junta, or government council, at Buenos Aires. Paraguayans refused to recognize this government. In May of 1811 Paraguayan independence was proclaimed and a government was established at Asunción.

Independence. In 1814 one of the members of the original Paraguayan junta, José Gaspar Rodríguez de Francia, took over the government and became president. Francia exercised strong autocratic control, aided both by an internal spy network and by the reverence that he managed to inspire in the common people. He followed a policy of political isolation, which protected Paraguay from outside pressures, particularly from Argentina, and encouraged economic self-sufficiency.

Francia died in 1840, and in 1844, after a brief period of transition, his nephew, Carlos Antonio López, became president. López made education free and compulsory, built roads, created a powerful army, and loosened Francia's policy of isolation. But whereas Francia had been personally honest, López and his family profiteered at the nation's expense. When López died in 1862, his son Francisco Solano López became president.

THE ITAIPU HYDROELECTRIC DAM on the border between Paraguay and Brazil is the largest in the world.

The central feature of the regime of Francisco Solano López was the War of the Triple Alliance, which pitted Paraguay against Argentina, Brazil, and Uruguay. In 1864 López attacked Brazil, ostensibly because of Brazil's interference in the affairs of Uruguay. Also at stake was López's ambition to expand Paraguayan influence and territory at the expense of Argentina and Brazil, with which Paraguay had long-standing territorial disputes.

In 1865 the conflict expanded into a general war. Paraguay was victorious at first, but the overwhelmingly superior resources of the allies assured Paraguay's eventual defeat. In 1870 López was killed and the war ended. The devastation from the war was tremendous. Paraguay's population had fallen from approximately 1 million to about 220,000, of whom fewer than 30,000 were adult males. Paraguay also lost some territory and suffered military occupation, but rivalry between Argentina and Brazil prevented Paraguay's complete dismemberment.

Contemporary Paraguay. Recovery was slow and political conditions unstable. Between 1870 and 1932, Paraguay had 29 presidents. Nonetheless, Paraguay made economic progress in these years. Foreign capital and enterprise, much of it from Argentina, assisted the nation's development, and colonies of immigrants were established.

In 1932 Paraguay fought a war with Bolivia over the Gran Chaco, the semi-wasteland stretching across western Paraguay and into eastern Bolivia. Paraguay defeated Bolivia because of superior leadership and shorter lines of communication. A truce was declared in 1935, and a 1938 treaty allotted Paraguay three-fourths of the disputed territory.

General José Félix Estigarribia, the commander of Paraguay's forces during the Chaco War, became president in 1939. He was killed in an airplane accident and was succeeded by Higinio Morínigo. Morínigo was forced out of office by a revolt in 1948.

In 1954, following a period of political and civil chaos and a series of short-lived governments, the army, under General Alfredo Stroessner, took over the government. Running without opposition, Stroessner was elected to the presidency later that year.

Stroessner established a rigid dictatorship. He gave the country stability and relative prosperity but was accused of severe oppression. He ruled Paraguay for 35 years, until a coup led by General Andrés Rodríguez ousted him in February 1989.

Rodríguez was confirmed as president in an election held in 1989. He vowed to support human rights and lead Paraguay toward democracy. In May 1993 Juan Carlos Wasmosy of the ruling Colorado Party was elected president. Despite some indications of fraud, the election was termed the first free democratic balloting in Paraguay's history.

Peru

Official name: *Republic of Peru*
Area: *496,099 sq. mi.,*
1,285,220 sq. km.
Type of government: *Republic*
Population: *27,950,000*
Capital and largest city: *Lima*
Pop., metro. area, 6,988,000
Languages: *Spanish, Quechua*
(both official), Aymara
Literacy: *88%*
Currency: *Nuevo sol*
Per capita GDP: *$4,800*
(Rank: 87th)

The land. Peru is a country of striking diversity. Within its borders are humid tropical lowlands in the east, ice-covered peaks in the Andes, and rainless coastal desert in the west. The country has three main geographic regions: the coastal desert, or *costa;* the Andean highlands, or *sierra;* and the eastern Andean slopes and Amazon lowlands, or *montaña.*

The coastal zone extends from Ecuador to Chile and is generally less than 30 miles (48 kilometers) wide. It is extremely dry. Winds blowing in from the ocean are chilled by the cold Peru, or Humboldt, Current and yield no moisture. The only oases are the valleys of 50 or 60 seasonal rivers that drain the western slopes of the Andes.

The Andean highlands consist of a broad altiplano, or plateau, between 10,000 and 15,000 feet (3,048 and 4,572 meters) above sea level, that is surmounted by mountain peaks. The grassland vegetation of the altiplano, known as *puna,* provides pasturage for livestock, and the mountain valleys contain Peru's most fertile land.

THE ANDES MOUNTAINS in Peru offer some of the world's most spectacular vistas.

The *montaña* is part of the Amazon basin and is covered with tropical forests and jungle. Although it constitutes 60 percent of the nation's territory, it is very thinly populated. Development of the area has been impeded by its physical isolation.

Climate varies from region to region. The climate on the coast is dry and temperate. Temperatures in the *sierra* vary with altitude from temperate to frigid, and most of the area is fairly dry. The *montaña* is hot and humid, with temperatures in the 70°s and 80°s F (20°s C). Rainfall in this region often exceeds 100 inches (254 centimeters) a year. This is in sharp contrast to the climate of Lima, on the coast, where 2 inches (5 centimeters) or less of rain fall each year.

The people. About half of the people of Peru are Indian; most of the other half are mestizo, of mixed Indian and Spanish ancestry. Spanish, the official language, is spoken by only about half of the population. The Andean Indians speak either Quechua or Aymara, and the Amazon tribes of the *montaña* have their own Indian languages.

Peru's principal city is Lima, the capital, which is the largest and most important city on the Pacific coast of South America. Other major urban centers of Peru are Trujillo (population, 273,000); Callao (787,000); Chiclayo (275,000); Cuzco (101,000); and Arequipa (94,000).

Since 1960 the population has shifted toward urban centers, where nearly two out of every three people now live. Two-fifths of the people live on the Pacific coast, which consists of just over 10 percent of Peru's total area.

Economy. Peru's economy is based largely on agriculture and mining, and the Peruvian Andes are rich in minerals. Although the country has deposits of a wide variety of minerals from which it could prosper, copper, gold, zinc, lead, silver, and oil are the mainstays of the mining industry. Mining earns half of Peru's export revenues.

Fish abound in Peru's offshore waters, and as recently as the late 1960s, the country had the world's largest catch. By the 1970s, however, overexploitation and shifting marine conditions had resulted in a large drop in fish production. Improved conditions and careful planning have restored the Pacific fisheries and Peru is once again a world leader in fish exports.

The forests of the *montaña* cover more than half the country's territory. Although still largely unexploited, they produce valuable quantities of cedar, mahogany, and other tropical hardwoods, as well as rubber, leche caspi (used in making chewing gum), jute, and a variety of medicinal plants.

Agriculture. Agriculture employs approximately two-fifths of the labor force and is an important part of the Peruvian economy. Agricultural production is slowed down by a lack of well-watered arable land. Farming methods are often inefficient. As a result,

COUNTRIES

Peru cannot raise enough food for its own use and foodstuffs must be imported.

Potatoes and corn are the major food crops. They are raised in the *sierra,* which has 60 percent of the country's cultivated land. Large quantities of rice and beans are also grown. The leading commercial crops are sugar cane and cotton, which are grown in the coastal valleys and in the *montaña.* The *montaña* also produces coffee, tobacco, cacao, fruit, and nuts.

Peru has very few cattle, and meat and dairy products must be imported. Sheep, vicuñas, and alpacas are raised in the southern Andes and their wool is exported.

Industry. Peruvian industry is limited largely to the processing of agricultural products, smelting and refining, and the manufacture of a variety of domestic consumer goods. Most important of these are textiles, beverages, footwear, leather goods, construction materials, paper and cardboard, chemicals, and motor vehicles.

Trade. Peru's major exports are manufactured goods, copper, oil, zinc, lead, silver, fishmeal, coffee, and cotton. Peru's principal imports include machinery and transport equipment as well as foodstuffs, chemicals, and pharmaceuticals. Major trade partners are the United States, Japan, and the European Community.

Government. Peru is a republic. Executive power is vested in a popularly elected president who serves a five-year term. He is assisted by the Council of Ministers, which he appoints. Legislative power is vested in a unicameral congress, the 120-member Congress of the Republic. All legislators are also elected to five-year terms. Judicial authority rests with a 16-member Supreme Court.

Peru is divided administratively into 24 departments and one constitutional province headed by prefects who are appointed by the central government.

History. Before Christopher Columbus reached the New World in 1492, Peru was the center of a great American Indian civilization, that of the Incas. In about 1100 the Incas began to move from their original homeland in the southern Peruvian Andes to subjugate neighboring Indian peoples living in the highlands and on the coast.

By the late 1400s, the Incas had established an empire that stretched along the western coast of South America from Ecuador to Chile. The various regions of this vast empire were linked by an intricate network of roads. It was ruled from the city of Cuzco, high in the Andes of southern Peru.

In 1531 a small army of Spaniards led by Francisco Pizarro invaded Peru. Despite their small numbers, the Spanish easily conquered the Incas, who were weakened and divided by civil war and terrified by the guns and horses of the Spaniards.

Spanish rule. In 1542 the Spaniards transformed what had been the Inca Empire into the viceroyalty of Peru, ruled from Lima, which Pizarro had founded as Ciudad de los Reyes in 1535. Rich deposits of precious metals, particularly silver, made Peru for many years the most prized of Spain's American colonies.

In the 1700s Peru's importance was diminished by the creation of the viceroyalties of New Granada, in 1717, and Río de la Plata, in 1776. Between 1780 and 1815 internal tranquility was shaken by a number of Indian uprisings, the most serious being that of Tupac Amaru in 1780. Nevertheless, during the first years of the 1800s, when Spain's other South American colonies were seeking independence, Peru remained a loyalist stronghold.

It was not until 1820, when the Argentine leader José de San Martín, who had already defeated the Spaniards in Chile, landed with an Argentine-Chilean army of liberation, that the Peruvian struggle for independence began in earnest. San Martín captured Lima and a year later, on July 28, 1821, declared Peru independent. But Spain's power was not finally broken until December 9, 1824, when the forces of Simón Bolívar, who had replaced San Martín, routed the Spanish at the Battle of Ayacucho. The independence of Peru marked the end of Spain's empire in South America.

Independence. For nearly 20 years after gaining independence, Peru was controlled by a succession of military dictators, or *caudillos,* including Luis José Orbegosa. He drew Peru into a short-lived confederation with Bolivia, from 1836 to 1839.

In 1845 the presidency was assumed by General Ramón Castilla, who, except for a brief interval from 1851 to 1854, ruled the country until 1862. Castilla brought about the abolition of black slavery and a reduction in the special privileges of the church. He also promoted the exploitation of Peru's guano deposits, valued for their nitrate content, and provided the country with a measure of political and economic stability.

EXCAVATIONS AT SIPÁN on the north coast of Peru have revealed an administrative and ceremonial center of the Moche culture.

civilization
US

civilisation
Brit.

MACHU PICCHU probably served as a royal estate for the ruling families of the Inca Empire.

The 10 years following Castilla's regime were marked by growing public debt, political corruption, and internal disorder, all of which were intensified in 1865–1866 by a brief war with Spain. Chile, Ecuador, and Bolivia came to the aid of Peru, and the Spanish ultimately withdrew.

Dissatisfaction with the military in Peruvian politics increased. As a result, in 1872 Manuel Pardo, who represented a coalition of landed aristocrats and financial and commercial interests, was elected Peru's first civilian president. Pardo aided higher education, sought to reduce the size and influence of the army, and tried to improve the economy. He was hindered in his efforts by a decline in the important guano industry, which was only partially offset by increased nitrate production in the southern coastal province of Tarapacá.

Through an alliance that Pardo had made with Bolivia in 1873, Peru became involved in the War of the Pacific, from 1879 to 1883, which resulted from a dispute between Bolivia and Chile over the Atacama nitrate fields. Chile was victorious, and under the terms of the peace treaty Peru was forced to yield its province of Tarapacá as well as to permit Chilean occupation of the adjoining provinces of Arica and Tacna. Peru was left bankrupt and exhausted.

Contemporary Peru. Peru did not fully recover until the early 1900s. Progress was especially notable during the second administration of Augusto B. Leguía y Salcedo, which stretched from 1919 to 1930. Leguía managed to bolster the economy by securing foreign loans and investments. He also supported large-scale public works.

Leguía was relatively popular, despite his autocratic rule and the widespread corruption of his government, until 1930, when the world economic depression cut off the flow of foreign capital and reduced the earnings of Peruvian exports. He was then overthrown by Colonel Luis Sánchez Cerro, who remained in power until 1933. Under his successor, Oscar Benavides, in office until 1939, Peru gradually recovered from the depression.

Nevertheless, the Indian population of the Andean region received little benefit from the progress that had taken place. Control of Peruvian society remained in the hands of a small, wealthy minority and protest movements arose. One of these protest movements was the *Alianza Popular Revolucionaria Americana* (APRA—American Popular Revolutionary Alliance), which had been founded in 1924 by Victor Raúl Haya de la Torre.

APRA's original program was pro-Indian, socialistic, and extremely hostile to foreign capital. During the 1930s, APRA became the strongest political movement in Peru, but it was distrusted by the military and repeatedly frustrated in its efforts to gain power. During the rule of Sánchez Cerro, the struggle between APRA and the ruling powers broke out into open warfare, and APRA was suppressed. In 1933 an APRA supporter assassinated Sánchez Cerro. APRA continued agitation against the government and was outlawed for long periods.

The moderately leftist and prodemocratic *Partido de Acción Popular* (PAP—Popular Action Party), founded and led by Fernando Belaúnde Terry, had more success. Belaúnde was elected president in 1963. He sponsored agrarian reforms and supported measures beneficial to the Indians, policies long championed by APRA, and sought to involve more people in the government. In 1968 President Belaúnde was overthrown by an army coup and General Juan Velasco Alvarado became head of a new government.

The new military government insisted that it would not relinquish power until its reforms were irreversible. Its program was to implement a social democracy with full popular participation and to formulate a nationalist approach to industrialization.

Velasco's regime, however, became authoritarian and intolerant, and he was deposed by his military commanders in 1975. They placed General Francisco Morales Bermudez in the presidency. He vowed not to change the revolutionary process of Velasco, and asserted that all Peruvians would be permitted to take part in forming a "new society."

The sweeping social and agrarian reforms for which Velasco was responsible remained in effect, but inflation, unemployment, and severe food shortages became worse. Stringent austerity programs were begun by Morales Bermudez to counter foreign debt.

Elections were held in 1978 for the first time in 15 years. A constitutional assembly was elected to draw up a new democratic constitution and pave the way for a return to civilian rule. These plans became a reality in 1980, and Fernando Belaúnde Terry, deposed in 1968, was reelected to the presidency. Severe economic and social problems and an increase in terrorist acts by two Peruvian leftist guerrilla movements decreased Belaúnde's popularity.

In 1985 Alan García Pérez was elected president. García moved to tackle the economic problems by limiting payments on Peru's foreign debt, but inflation continued to rise. In 1989 inflation rose to 3,100 percent.

In 1990 Alberto Fujimori, the son of Japanese immigrants, was elected to the presidency. He introduced a severe austerity plan that sparked riots and looting as well as numerous terrorist attacks.

In April 1992 Fujimori, backed by the army, suspended the constitution and dissolved Peru's congress and courts. He declared a Government of National Reconstruction and began new efforts to deal with government corruption, drug traffickers, the leftist Shining Path guerrilla movement, and the economy. A new constitution was approved in 1993. Fujimori was reelected in 2000, but in response to evidence of corruption he declared he would step down after new elections. Instead, he resigned while on a trip to Japan; he could not be extradited due to his secretly held Japanese citizenship. In 2001, centrist Alejandro Toledo was elected president.

Suriname

Official name: *Republic of Suriname*

Area: *63,022 sq. mi., 163,270 sq. km.*

Type of government: *Republic*

Population: *434,000*

Capital and largest city: *Paramaribo Pop. 219,000*

Languages: *Dutch (official), English, Sranang Tongo, Hindustani, Javanese*

Literacy: *93%*

Currency: *Guilder*

Per capita GDP: *$3,500 (Rank: 108th)*

The land. Suriname has a flat, narrow, fertile coastal plain and a hilly, forested interior, from which flow many rivers. The majority of the population lives on the coastal plain, which extends only about 50 miles (80 kilometers) inland. The climate is warm and damp. Annual rainfall is about 89 inches (223 centimeters), and the temperature ranges year round from about 70° to 90°F (21° to 32°C).

The people. The population is of varied origins, but most of the people are of East Indian, Indonesian, African, and mixed descent. A Creole group is the most politically significant.

Almost half of Suriname's people live in and around Paramaribo, the nation's capital, chief port, and major city.

The population rose at an extremely rapid rate in the 1960s, but since independence was attained in 1975,

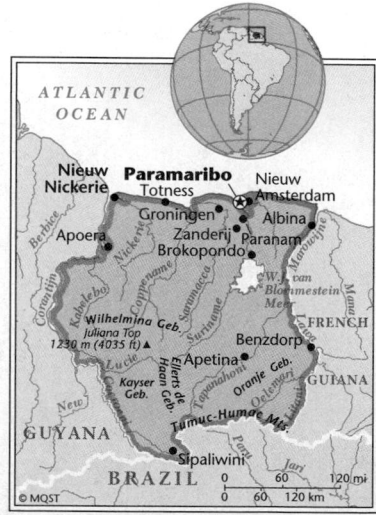

mass emigration has reduced the population by nearly one-third. The East Indians emigrated more than other groups because they resented a Creole-dominated government and economy; most went to the Netherlands.

Dutch and Sranan Tongo, a local dialect, are the chief languages. Religious life is diverse, and there are substantial numbers of Hindus, Muslims, Protestants, and Roman Catholics.

Economy. Suriname possesses rich deposits of bauxite, the ore from which aluminum is made. It also has an abundance of excellent timber resources. Farming is important, and rice, sugar, cacao, fruits, and coffee are raised. Mining and forestry are thus far the only important industries.

Nearly one-third of the labor force is engaged in agriculture along the coastal plains, but the backbone of the economy is the production of bauxite and aluminum, which accounts for about 80 percent of the country's export value. Suriname produces 10 percent of the world's supply of bauxite, most of it mined at Moenga and Paranam. Gold is also mined.

There are great potential water-power resources in the country. Most of it is undeveloped, however, and industrial production is backward. For example, a 500-megawatt hydroelectric project on the Kabalebo River in the western highlands, which would double Suriname's power-generating capacity, has been slowed due to the country's economic difficulties.

Main exports include bauxite and aluminum, bananas, timber and wood products, palm oil, rice, and shrimp. Leading imports include machinery, oil, and raw materials. Suriname's chief trading partners are the United States, the Netherlands, and other nations of the European Union.

Government. Upon independence in 1975, Suriname enjoyed a parliamentary form of government. In 1980 a National Military Council overthrew the government. A new constitution was approved by referendum in 1987, and a 51-member National Assembly and a State Council were installed. Democracy was restored in 1988. The president is elected to a 5-year term by the National Assembly. The military is still involved in the government.

Suriname is divided administratively into 10 districts.

History. Suriname was first visited in the 1500s by Spaniards in search of gold. They abandoned the territory, and during the 1600s and 1700s, Suriname changed hands among Great Britain, the Netherlands, and France.

In 1815 the area was ceded to the Netherlands by the Treaty of Paris. The Dutch established plantations and began extensive mining and timber operations in the late 1800s and early 1900s, when they brought Indian and Indonesian laborers to Suriname.

During the 1900s Suriname gained an increasing measure of popular gov-

ernment, and in 1954 it became a self-governing part of the Kingdom of The Netherlands. Suriname faced severe economic and social problems because of its rapid rate of population growth and the variety of ethnic groups constituting its population. In the 1950s and 1960s the government concentrated on expanding industry and improving agriculture.

Led by Prime Minister Henck Arron (1973–1980) and the National Party Coalition, Suriname became independent on November 25, 1975. The East Indians who, along with the blacks, had strongly opposed independence, left the country in great numbers, many emigrating to the Netherlands. A large number remain abroad. The economy was severely damaged by the loss of many people from this highly educated and skilled group.

Additional economic problems have arisen because of heavy migrations of people from the farms to urban areas, as well as fluctuations in the world price of aluminum, Suriname's main source of income.

In 1980 an army coup ended the democratic government, and the coup leader, Desi Bouterse, became head of the government. In 1987 Bouterse allowed free national elections, but a coup by the army in 1990 again brought down the democratic government. New elections in May 1991 were won by a coalition seeking civilian control of the military and stronger ties with the Netherlands. In April 1992 work was begun on a new constitution, and in November Bouterse, accused of corruption, resigned as head of the military.

BAUXITE MINING and forestry are the only important industries in Suriname.

CHILDREN OF THE DJUKA TRIBE play in front of a house with ornamentation typical of the people.

Uruguay

Official name: *Oriental Republic of Uruguay*

Area: *68,038 sq. mi., 176,220 sq. km.*

Type of government: *Republic*

Population: 3,387,000

Capital and largest city: *Montevideo* Pop. 1,303,000

Language: *Spanish*

Literacy: 97%, **Currency:** *Peso*

Per capita GDP: *$9,200*

(Rank: 53rd)

---

centimeters
US

centimetres
Brit.

centers
US

centres
Brit.

labor
US

labour
Brit.

colonized
US

colonised
Brit.

The land. Most of Uruguay consists of low, gently rolling plains. There are two long ranges of hills known as *cuchillas,* or "knives"—the Cuchilla de Haedo in the west and the Cuchilla Grande in the east. The eastern coast is edged by tidal lakes, lagoons, and sand dunes. The southern coast is characterized by wide, sandy beaches.

The climate of Uruguay is temperate. The summers are warm and winter temperatures are generally above freezing. Rainfall is fairly evenly distributed throughout the year and averages about 35 inches (89 centimeters).

The people. The people of Uruguay are mostly of Italian and Spanish descent. The native Churrúa Indians were almost completely driven out during the Spanish colonial period, and today only a small percentage of the population can be classified as Indian or mestizo.

Uruguay's rate of population increase is one of the lowest in South America. This is due in part to a low birthrate and to a steady emigration of Uruguayans to other countries, notably Argentina and Brazil. Over 80 percent of the people live in urban areas. Nearly half the people live in the capital city of Montevideo. Other major

urban centers are Salto (population, 93,000); Paysandú (75,000); Rivera (63,000); and Melo (47,000).

Economy. Uruguay is fairly well developed, with a relatively high standard of living and little subsistence farming. Only about 14 percent of the labor force is employed in agriculture, which produces about four-fifths of the nation's export earnings. About 16 percent of the labor force is employed in industry. There are rich fish reserves, and Uruguay's fishing industry is developing rapidly. Uruguay has some mineral resources, but these are largely unexploited.

Agriculture. The economy is based on agriculture. About 70 percent of the country's land is devoted to the raising of cattle and sheep, and almost half of Uruguay's exports consist of wool, hides, meat, and various important meat products.

About 11 percent of the total land area is under cultivation. Wheat is the principal crop but rice, oats, corn, and barley are grown in large quantities. Sunflower seeds and linseed are also major crops.

Industry. Uruguay's industry—largely government owned and operated—is almost totally dependent on imported oil, although domestic electric capacity is being rapidly increased. The country's industry includes meat packing, textiles and clothing, leather and hides, food processing, and a growing manufacturing sector. Manufactured products include textiles, glass, rubber, paper, cement, ceramics, beverages, and tobacco.

Uruguay's principal exports are wool, meat, and hides. Major imports include oil, motor vehicles and parts, machinery, chemicals, pharmaceuticals, metals, food, plastics, and paper.

Uruguay's main trading partners are the United States, Argentina, Brazil, and Germany.

Government. Uruguay is a republic. Executive authority is vested in a president who is popularly elected to a 5-year term. Legislative powers are vested in a bicameral General Assembly with a 30-member Senate and a 99-member Chamber of Representatives. Judicial power is exercised by a Supreme Court whose members serve for 10 years. Uruguay is divided administratively into 19 departments.

History. Uruguay was discovered by the Spanish navigator Juan Diaz de Solís in 1516 and further explored in 1520 by the Portuguese captain Ferdinand Magellan. It was not colonized until 1680, however, when Portugal built a fort at Colonia. Uruguay's location between Brazil and what is now Argentina made it a bone of contention between the Portuguese and Spanish empires during the 1700s.

Spain had the stronger claim to Uruguay, however. Furthermore, Uruguay was too close to the Spanish military and administrative center of Buenos Aires for Spain to allow it to

remain in Portuguese hands. In 1776 Spain included Uruguay in the newly formed viceroyalty of Río de la Plata, and in 1777 seized control of the Portuguese settlement at Colonia.

In 1810 Argentina began its struggle for independence from Spain, and in 1811 Uruguay followed suit under the leadership of José Gervasio Artigas. Artigas favored the formation of a loose confederation with Argentina, but Argentina was unwilling to accept this solution.

A complex struggle soon developed among the forces of Artigas, Argentina, and Spain, as well as Portugal, which took advantage of the general confusion to revive its earlier claim to the country. The Portuguese were successful, and when Brazil gained its independence in 1822, Uruguay became a Brazilian province.

Independence. In 1825 a new group of Uruguayan revolutionaries, called the "Thirty-three Immortals," led by Juan Antonio Lavalleja, rose up against Brazil and declared Uruguay annexed to Argentina. The result was a war between Argentina and Brazil that ended in a military stalemate. In 1828 British mediation brought about a peace treaty that provided for Uruguay's independence. But its independence was precarious. It did not mark the end of foreign intervention in Uruguayan internal affairs.

Uruguay soon developed two political parties, the conservative Blancos and the liberal Colorados, and Argentina, Brazil, and Paraguay frequently intervened in the struggles for power between the two. In 1865 the 5-year War of the Triple Alliance broke out, in which Uruguay was allied with Argentina and Brazil against Paraguay.

During the last two decades of the 1800s, Uruguay began to achieve a degree of stability. Educational facilities were expanded, agricultural production increased, and large-scale European immigration took place.

Batlle era. It was not until the early 1900s, however, under José Batlle y Ordóñez, that Uruguay made major social and economic progress. Batlle twice served as president (1903–1907, 1911–1915) and exerted a strong influence over the country until his death in 1929.

Batlle helped make Uruguay a model of democratic government and encouraged such necessary social and economic reforms as workers' accident compensation and a minimum wage. He also initiated government enterprises in banking and meat packing, and championed the establishment of a nine-member Council of State to share powers and responsibilities with the president. Six members were chosen from the party in power and three from the opposition party.

Contemporary Uruguay. Some democratic procedures and institutions, including the Council of State, were suspended during the world economic depression of the 1930s under the administration of Gabriel Terra (1931–1938), but many were reinstated later in the 1930s and 1940s. In 1942 Uruguay broke diplomatic relations with the Axis powers and in February 1945 declared war on them. Later that year Uruguay became a charter member of the United Nations.

In 1951 Uruguay adopted a new constitution, which replaced the president with a nine-member executive council. This idea had been proposed originally by José Batlle, but the first Council of State had not replaced the presidency. Rather, it had attempted to function as a complement to the presidency.

In the late 1950s, the country began to suffer from serious economic difficulties, caused in part by a decline in foreign trade and the heavy financial burden imposed by extensive social welfare programs.

The executive council proved unable to provide the leadership necessary to deal effectively with these and other problems, and in November 1966 a new constitution reinstating the presidential system was approved in a popular referendum.

Oscar Gestido was elected president in 1966. Gestido initiated an austerity program and took strong fiscal measures that slowly began to improve the country's economic situation.

Gestido died in December 1967 and was replaced by Jorge Pacheco Areco. Pacheco turned to repressive tactics when faced with massive labor strikes, and he could do nothing about the skyrocketing price of imported oil, which led to inflation and a decline in the Uruguayan standard of living.

In the early 1970s, a left-wing urban terrorist group known as the Tupamaros, consisting largely of young people from middle- and upper-class families, stepped up guerrilla activity. Juan Maria Bordaberry became president in 1971, but by 1973 he was forced to accept military rule over his government.

Relations with the United States were damaged by reports of government repression and disregard for human rights. The economy continued to decline, however. In 1984 Julio Maria Sanguinetti of the Colorado Party was elected to the presidency. Democratic civilian rule was returned to Uruguay in February 1985. In 1989 the return to democracy was reinforced with the election of Luis Alberto Lacalle of the centrist National Party to the presidency. Lacalle initiated a program to reduce the government's role in the economy by ending state monopolies of some industries and by selling inefficient state-owned enterprises in whole or in part to private companies. However, his program faced strong resistance from leftist organizations and from Uruguay's strong organized labor movement. Sanguinetti, again representing the Colorado Party, was re-elected in the 1994 election.

Venezuela

Official name: *Bolivarian Republic of Venezuela*
Area: *352,051 sq. mi., 912,050 sq. km.*
Type of government: *Republic*
Population: *24,288,000*
Capital and largest city: *Caracas Pop. 1,836,000*
Languages: *Spanish (official), Indian dialects*
Literacy: *91%*
Currency: *Bolivar*
Per capita GDP: *$6,100 (Rank: 77th)*

The land. Venezuela has four major geographic regions—the northern highlands, the Maracaibo lowlands, the Orinoco *llanos,* or plains, and the Guiana highlands. The northern highlands, part of the Andes mountain system, extend from the Colombian border to the Paria peninsula in the northeastern part of the country.

The mountainous highland area has five subdivisions: the Sierra de Perijá in the extreme west; the Sierra Nevada de Mérida in the southwest; the Segovia highlands, which run eastward from the Sierra Nevada de Mérida along the coast; the central highlands, which run parallel to the coast; and the northeastern highlands, in the Araya and Paria peninsulas.

Although the northern highlands cover only about 12 percent of Venezuela's land area, they contain three-fifths of the population and constitute the economic, political, and cultural core of the country.

The Maracaibo lowlands lie to the northwest of the northern highlands. In the center of this region is Lake Maracaibo, which has an area of 6,300 square miles (16,311 square kilometers) and is the largest lake in South America. The world's largest known deposits of petroleum lie in the Maracaibo Basin.

The Orinoco *llanos* extend from the northern highlands south to the Orinoco River. This region is a rolling savanna, or grassland, dotted with a few scattered trees and bushes and crossed by the numerous streams that feed the Orinoco. These streams swell enormously during the rainy season, and large areas in the *llanos* are flooded for almost half the year.

The Guiana highlands lie to the south of the Orinoco and cover roughly half of the country's territory. This area is a high, jungle-covered tableland with elevations ranging between 3,000 and 6,000 feet (914 and 1,829 meters) above sea level. It is not easily accessible and parts of the area have not been thoroughly explored.

The country's major river is the

Orinoco, which rises in the south and flows northeast for about 1,500 miles (2,414 kilometers) before emptying into the Atlantic Ocean. The Orinoco and its many tributaries provide Venezuela with excellent water transportation routes.

ABOUT 90 PERCENT of the population of Venezuela lives in urban areas, such as the capital, Caracas.

THIS OIL STORAGE PLATFORM on Lake Maracaibo is part of Venezuela's vast oil production industry.

meters
US

metres
Brit.

labor
US

labour
Brit.

aluminum
US

aluminium
Brit.

Climate. Venezuela lies entirely within the tropics, but its climate varies widely according to altitude. The lowlands are hot and humid, and Maracaibo has an annual average temperature of 86°F (30°C), the highest registered in South America. The capital, Caracas, in the central highlands at an altitude of about 3,000 feet (914 meters), has an annual average temperature of 71°F (21.7°C). Temperatures, of course, become lower as the elevation increases.

Venezuela has a wet summer season from May to November and a dry winter season from December to April. Rainfall is generally heavier at higher altitudes. It ranges from about 17 inches (43 centimeters) a year at Maracaibo on the coast to over 70 inches (178 centimeters) at Mérida in the northern highlands.

The people. Most of Venezuela's population is mestizo, of mixed Indian and European descent. Pure-blooded Indians are few in number and live in the more remote parts of the Guiana highlands, the Orinoco delta, and the western Maracaibo lowlands. Venezuelans of European descent are mainly concentrated in the larger cities. Venezuelans of African or mixed descent live largely along the coast.

Although Venezuela still is sparsely populated, its growth rate has been one of the highest in South America. Most of the population is concentrated in the northern highlands and along the coast. About 86 percent of the population live in urban areas.

Venezuela's major cities include Caracas, the capital and leading city; Maracaibo (population, 1,220,000); Valencia (742,000); Barquisimeto (896,000); and Maracay (396,000).

Economy. The Venezuelan economy depends heavily on petroleum. The country's proven oil reserves were conservatively estimated at 58 billion barrels as of 1988. At current production rates, this should last well into the next century. In addition, large new reserves have been located off the coast, and a major heavy oil reserve is located near the Orinoco.

In recent years the government has made an attempt to diversify the economy by reducing its dependence on oil-derived income, expanding industry, particularly the export industry, and strengthening agriculture through agrarian reform measures.

Venezuela's most important natural resource is its petroleum deposits. The country also has extremely valuable iron ore deposits at El Pao and Cerro Bolívar in the Guiana highlands. Iron ore ranks as the second largest export. Gold, diamonds, natural gas, asbestos, bauxite, sulfur, copper, gypsum, limestone, and salt are also mined.

Hydroelectric power is an abundant resource in Venezuela. A large portion of this power comes from the huge Guri Dam on the Caroni River.

Agriculture. Agriculture employs about 13 percent of the labor force. Food production has increased over 70 percent since 1960, despite generally poor development in technology. A 10-year plan for improved irrigation begun in 1984, coupled with programs for land improvement and crop rotation, has led to increased agricultural output and a reduction in food imports. Nonetheless, Venezuela remains a net importer of agricultural products.

The major crops are sugar cane, corn, bananas, and rice. Coffee and cacao are the two important commercial crops. Beans, sesame, cotton, cassava, sisal, potatoes, and tobacco are also raised in large quantities.

Cattle are raised in the Orinoco *llanos,* but they are generally of poor quality. The government has been working to improve the breed and to upgrade the pastureland to provide better grazing conditions.

Industry. Venezuelan industry has expanded rapidly since World War II. In recent years oil refining has become one of the most important industries. Aluminum production—totally supplied by Venezuelan bauxite—is rapidly increasing in importance. Iron and steel production are also rising steadily. Manufacturing and construction now employ more than one-fourth of the labor force.

Venezuela's major industries include cotton and wool textiles, leather goods, cement, petrochemicals, and automobile assembly. Other industries are food processing, meat packing, construction materials, fats and oils, tires, automobile parts, soap, matches, and liquor.

The greatest industrial area in the country is Ciudad Guayana, along the Caroni River, 300 miles (483 kilometers) southeast of Caracas.

Trade. Venezuela's major exports include petroleum and petroleum products, aluminum, iron and steel, coffee, and cocoa. Major imports are machinery and transport equipment, manufactured goods, chemicals and raw materials, and foodstuffs.

Venezuela exports primarily to the United States, Brazil, Colombia, Italy, and Spain. Imports come from the United States, Germany, Japan, Italy, Brazil, and Colombia.

Government. Venezuela is a republic. The head of state and chief executive is the president, who is popularly elected to a 5-year term. Legislative power is vested in a 165-member unicameral National Assembly elected by popular vote.

Two senators are elected from each of Venezuela's 20 states and from its federal district, Caracas. Additional senators are appointed to represent minorities. There is one seat in the Chamber of Deputies for every 50,000 inhabitants. Senators and deputies are elected to 5-year terms.

Judicial power is vested in a Supreme Tribunal of Justice. Each magistrate is elected to a single 12-year term by the National Assembly.

Venezuela is divided administratively into 23 states, one federal district, and one federal dependency consisting of 72 Caribbean islands. State governors are appointed by the president.

History. Venezuela was discovered in 1498 by Christopher Columbus on his third voyage to the New World. The first permanent settlement was made by Spain in 1523 at Cumaná, on the Caribbean coast. In 1528 Charles I of Spain (Charles V of the Holy Roman Empire) granted a contract to settle Venezuela to the Welser mercantile firm of Augsburg, Germany. The Welsers were ruthless administrators, and in 1546 the contract was cancelled.

In 1546 the original colony of Venezuela was placed under the jurisdiction of the Audiencia of Santo Domingo. Later it was included in the viceroyalty of New Granada (Colombia). In 1777 Venezuela became the Captaincy-General of the United Provinces of Venezuela, and in 1786 the Audiencia of Caracas was created. In the last half of the 1700s, Venezuela became prosperous from plantation agriculture and a flourishing cattle industry.

Struggle for independence. In 1806 a Venezuelan patriot, Francisco de Miranda, and a group of volunteers attempted to free the country from Spain. But most Venezuelans remained loyal to Spain, and the attempt failed. In 1808 Napoleon Bonaparte of France deposed Spain's King Ferdinand VII and placed his brother Joseph Bonaparte on the throne. In 1810 a successful revolt took place at Caracas; it deposed the Spanish captain-general of Venezuela and installed a junta, or ruling council.

In 1811 Venezuela declared its independence from Spain, and for several years control passed back and forth between Venezuelan patriots and forces loyal to Spain. Leadership of the struggle passed to Simón Bolívar.

In 1819 Bolívar defeated the Spanish at the Battle of Boyacá, in what is now Colombia. He subsequently formed the Republic of Gran Colombia, which included the territories of Venezuela, Colombia, Panama, and Ecuador. In 1821 Bolívar virtually completed the struggle for independence with a decisive victory at the Battle of Carabobo.

Independence. In 1830, under the leadership of General José Antonio Páez, Venezuela seceded from the Republic of Gran Colombia. Páez, an outstanding military leader during the struggle for independence, governed Venezuela from 1830 to 1846. He gave the country stability without resorting to oppression, but those who benefitted most were the members of a small elite of the educated and well-to-do.

During the 1850s and 1860s, the government was often dictatorial, and the political scene was marked by confusion and instability. Nonetheless, a few constructive measures were undertaken, including the abolition of slavery in 1854.

In 1870 Antonio Guzmán Blanco seized power and ruled the country for 18 years. During his dictatorship there was relative peace, and although he was corrupt and autocratic, Guzmán Blanco did much to extend public education and to stimulate economic development. In 1889 an uprising in Caracas against Guzmán Blanco's absolute control of the country led to his overthrow and repudiation. His elimination from the political scene prompted a subsequent period of turmoil.

During 1895 and 1896, Venezuela engaged in a dispute with Great Britain over the border with British Guiana, the present-day republic of Guyana. In 1902–1903 the country was blockaded by Great Britain, Germany, and Italy as the result of financial claims of their citizens against the Venezuelan government. The United States intervened to promote a settlement.

Domestic peace returned following the seizure of the presidency in 1908 by Juan Vicente Gómez, who ruled the country with a heavy hand for 26 years. Gómez encouraged the rapid growth of the petroleum industry through liberal concessions to British and U.S. companies. He used the oil revenues to pay off Venezuela's large national debt, and also for personal gain, military expenses, and showy public works. However, little money or effort was expended on Venezuela's other needs, such as education, public welfare, or development.

Reform and reaction. Gómez died in 1935 and his immediate successors gradually dismantled the apparatus of dictatorship and devoted attention to social and labor legislation. Nevertheless, many Venezuelans were dissatisfied with the pace of change. In 1945 a popular uprising brought the leftist Acción Democrática Party, led by Rómulo Betancourt, to power.

The new regime's most notable achievement was an agreement with the oil companies that stipulated that half their profits were to go to the Venezuelan government, which hoped to use this income for a far-reaching program of social betterment. Presidential elections were held in 1947, and Rómulo Gallegos, the Acción Democrática candidate, was elected.

In November 1948, the government was overthrown by the army, which set up a military junta. In 1952, after an interlude of confusion, Marcos Pérez Jiménez, the key figure in the military regime, was declared the provisional president. He soon established a dictatorship that was in many ways a repetition of the Gómez regime.

Public opposition to the dictatorship was strong, and in 1958 Pérez Jiménez was forced to resign. A brief provisional government restored political liberty, increased the government's share of oil industry profits, and in December 1958, held free elections. The elections returned Betancourt and the Acción Democrática to power.

Betancourt launched a program of agrarian reform, agricultural and industrial development, and educational expansion. He was bitterly opposed by supporters of Pérez Jiménez and harassed by both right-wing and left-wing extremists and by an attempt by Cuban dictator Fidel Castro to foment a leftist guerrilla war in Venezuela. Despite these pressures, the country held to its democratic course.

Carlos Andrés Pérez was elected president in 1974. The Pérez administration emphasized industrial development, but agricultural production was allowed to drop. In 1977, unfortunately, there were severe food shortages and in 1978 Luis Herrera Campins was elected president.

During Herrera's term the boom in oil prices sparked earlier in the 1970s began to subside. Lower oil revenues caused a serious rise in the nation's foreign debt.

The elections in 1983 declared Jaime Lusinchi president. In 1985 he refinanced Venezuela's $25 billion debt.

In 1988 Carlos Andrés Pérez was reelected president. He instituted austerity measures that in 1989 sparked rioting and looting that left some 300 dead. In 1992, despite strong economic growth, Venezuela was rocked by two bloody coup attempts, in February and November. Banking collapse, falling oil prices, and inflation marked the 1990s.

Leftist Hugo Chavez became president in 1999 and replaced the elected Congress with his own allies. In 2002 his increasing authoritarianism prompted protests, strikes, calls for his resignation, and a coup attempt. A 2003 petition for a recall referendum was deemed invalid, but attempts to constitutionally remove Chavez by opposition groups continue, as both sides seem entrenched in their views.

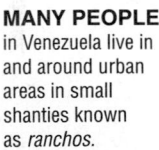

emphasized
US

emphasised
Brit.

MANY PEOPLE in Venezuela live in and around urban areas in small shanties known as *ranchos.*

28 South America

Dependencies in South America

British Dependencies

kilometers
US

kilometres
Brit.

center
US

centre
Brit.

EMPEROR PENGUINS are just one of six kinds of penguins that thrive in the Antarctic.

British Antarctic Territory (660,000 square miles, or 1,708,700 square kilometers) consists of the South Orkney and the South Shetland islands, in the South Atlantic Ocean off the southern tip of South America; Palmer Land and Graham Land, on the Antarctic peninsula; Coats Land and Caird coast, along the Antarctic's Weddell coast; and the Filchner and Ronne ice shelves.

A separate colony since 1962, it is uninhabited. Research stations are located on the islands, which are also claimed by Argentina.

Falkland Islands (4,699 square miles, or 12,170 square kilometers), consisting of East Falkland Island, West Falkland Island, and several small islands, lie in the South Atlantic Ocean off the southeastern coast of Argentina. The population of 2,900 is mostly of British origin. Sheep raising and wool manufacturing are the main economic activities. Stanley on East Falkland is the capital.

First settled by the French and British in the 1760s, the islands were abandoned and then resettled in the 1820s by Argentina and in the 1830s by Great Britain. Argentina continues to claim the Falkland Islands. In 1982, angered at the failure to negotiate a transfer of the islands, Argentina seized the Falklands. The British retaliated by sending a force to the islands. After a bloody war that lasted for more than two months, Great Britain was able to regain the islands.

St. Helena (158 square miles, or 410 square kilometers) and its two dependencies, Ascension and Tristan de Cunha, are located between South America and Africa, in the South Atlantic Ocean. Its population of 7,000 is mostly of European origin. A U.S. satellite tracking center is on Ascension. St. Helena Island is mostly agricultural. Jamestown (population, 5,600) is the capital.

Claimed by the British in 1673, St. Helena was the place of Napoleon's exile between 1815 and 1821. Ascension was the site of a vital Allied air base during World War II. Tristan de Cunha was devastated by a volcanic eruption in 1961.

Chilean Dependencies

Chilean Antarctic Territory (482,502 square miles, or 1,249,200 square kilometers) is located in Antarctica between 59° and 67° west. It is uninhabited.

Juan Fernández (69 square miles, or 179 square kilometers) is an island group in the Pacific Ocean, 360 miles (579 kilometers) off the coast of Chile. Its two main islands are Robinson Crusoe and Alejandro Selkirk. The islands have a population of 629. Lobstering is the main economic activity. The islands, which were discovered in 1572, are best known for Daniel Defoe's 18th century classic, *Robinson Crusoe,* which used an island of the same name for its setting.

San Ambrosio Island and San Felix Island (1.3 square miles, or 3.4 square kilometers) are uninhabited islands located in the Pacific Ocean, 600 miles (965 kilometers) off the coast of Chile. They were discovered in 1574.

French Departments

French Guiana (35,126 square miles, or 91,000 square kilometers), on the northeastern coast of South America, is bordered on the north by the Atlantic Ocean, on the east and south by Brazil, and on the west by Suriname. The population of 182,000 consists mostly of people of mixed African and European descent. Guiana has substantial deposits of bauxite, but these have not been exploited. Gold mining, logging, and shrimp fishing are the main industries. French aid and investment are also important.

The capital, Cayenne (population, 41,200), has about one-fourth of the population of French Guiana, which includes the Îles du Salut island group.

Guiana was sighted by Christopher Columbus in 1498, and in the early 1600s Frenchmen established a settlement at present-day Cayenne. Captain Alfred Dreyfus was incarcerated there between 1894 and 1899 at the famous prison colony on Devil's Island in French Guiana.

FRANCE conducts test launches for its space program in French Guiana.

Cities of South America

Arequipa, in southern Peru, on the Chili River. It is a commercial center whose manufactures include textiles, leather goods, processed foods, and plastics. Pop., 94,000.

Asunción, capital of Paraguay and a port on the Paraguay River about 630 miles (1,014 km.) north of Buenos Aires. It is the country's chief city.

Paraguay has no seacoast and Asunción's river port handles most of the country's trade. Its industries consist mostly of food processing and the manufacture of textiles and footwear. Pop., 513,000.

Barranquilla, seaport in northern Colombia, on the Magdalena River, 10 miles (16 km.) from its mouth. It is Colombia's chief port. Its industries include shipbuilding, sugar refining, brewing, textile mills, and publishing. Pop., 1,549,000.

Belem, or Pará, seaport and the capital of Pará State, Brazil, located on the Pará River, about 90 miles (145 km.) inland from the Atlantic Ocean. The city lies at the mouth of the Amazon River system and is a transshipment point for river traffic. It is linked by highway and railroad with Brasília. Belem's exports include nuts, pepper, cocoa, timber, and jute. Pop., 1,280,000.

Belo Horizonte, in southeastern Brazil, the capital of Minas Gerais State. The first planned city in South America, it was inaugurated in 1897. Belo Horizonte produces iron and steel and processes manganese, gold, and precious stones mined in the state. Other industries include food processing, meat packing, and the manufacture of textiles. The city has several universities and is the educational center of Minas Gerais. Pop., 2,230,000.

Bogotá, capital of Colombia, located in the central part of the country on a fertile plateau 8,660 feet (2640 meters) above sea level. The city is the political, economic, and cultural center of Colombia. Industries produce a variety of goods for domestic consumption. Bogotá is the seat of the National University and has a number of other educational institutions. Pop., 6,422,000.

Brasília, capital of Brazil, located in the interior of the country, about 600 miles (965 km.) northwest of Rio de Janeiro. Brasília is a planned city that was built in the late 1950s and inaugurated as the capital in April of 1960. It was designed by Lucio Costa and Oscar Niemeyer.

The city is linked by highways and air routes to the rest of Brazil. Pop., 2,043,000.

Buenos Aires, capital of Argentina and the largest city in South America, located on the Río de la Plata. The city is the financial, commercial, and industrial center of Argentina. The chief industries are meat packing, tanning, flour milling, and the manufacture of textiles, chemicals, automobiles, metal and paper products, wool, and foodstuffs. Buenos Aires has one of the world's largest and busiest ports and is an important rail and air center. The city has many libraries, museums, and theaters. It is the seat of the University of Buenos Aires. Pop., 2,965,000.

Cali, in western Colombia, on the Cali River, is an industrial and commercial center that ships farm products, timber, and minerals. Its chief manufactures, many in small family-operated plants, are textiles, chemicals, building materials, and paper. It is also a tourist center and the seat of two universities. Pop., 2,129,000.

Callao, chief seaport of Peru, on the Pacific Ocean, 8 miles (13 km.) west of Lima. The city exports minerals, refined metals, wool, lumber, fish meal, and fish oil. Its main industries include breweries, textile mills, sugar refineries, and shipbuilding. Pop., 787,000.

Caracas, capital and largest city of Venezuela, in a mountain basin more than 3,000 feet (915 meters) above sea level. The city is linked by superhighway with nearby La Guaira, its port on the Caribbean. Earnings from the nation's oil industry have financed extensive development. Central University and Simón Bolívar University are in the city. Manufactures include chemicals, pharmaceuticals, textiles, glass, and cement. Pop., 1,836,000.

Cartagena, seaport on the northwest coast of Colombia, 60 miles (96 km.) southwest of Barranquilla. Its principal industries are the manufacture of textiles, leather products, sugar, petrochemicals, and tobacco. It is also a tourist center with many old landmarks and beaches that attract swimmers and sunseekers. Pop., 829,000.

Cayenne, the capital and principal port of French Guiana, on an island near the mouth of the Cayenne River. Nearby Devil's Island was the site of a French penal colony from 1851 to 1945. Exports include tropical woods, rosewood essence, sugar, rum, and gold. Its most famous product is Cayenne pepper. Pop., 50,000.

Concepción, in south-central Chile, on the banks of the Bío Bío River. Concepción is Chile's largest city and an industrial and commercial center. Its port, Talcahuano, lies nearby, to the northwest. Its industries produce coal, petroleum products, chemicals, textiles, timber, steel, sugar, and processed foods. Pop., 215,000.

theaters
US

theatres
Brit.

BOGOTA
in Colombia is home to the government, much of the country's industry, and the National University.

28 South America

LIMA, PERU, was founded as Ciudad de los Reyes in 1535 by Francisco Pizarro.

Córdoba, city in central Argentina, on the Primero River. It is a cultural and commercial center for an agricultural region. It exports cattle, wheat, and minerals, and its manufactures include leather goods, textiles, automobiles, processed foods, and glass. The city has several museums, two universities, and an astronomical observatory. Pop., 1,158,000.

Curitiba, in southern Brazil, on a plateau near the Igue Iguaçú River, about 65 miles (105 km.) west of Paranagua, its port on the Atlantic Ocean. Curitiba is the capital of the state of Paraná and an important transportation, trade, and industrial center. The city's products include textiles, paper, furniture, automobiles, cement, timber, coffee, maté, and cattle. Pop., 1,587,000.

Cuzco, in southern Peru, about 350 miles (563 km.) southeast of Lima. It lies at an altitude of about 11,000 feet (3,353 meters) above sea level in the Andes. Cuzco, the capital of the Inca Empire, was captured by the Spanish in 1533. The city's Inca ruins and Spanish colonial buildings attract many tourists. Cuzco is also a transportation and commercial center. Pop., 101,000.

center
US

centre
Brit.

Fortaleza, on the northeast coast of Brazil, about 270 miles (435 km.) northwest of Natal. Fortaleza is a port and the capital of the state of Ceara. The city manufactures textiles and processes agricultural products. Coffee, sugar, and cotton are exported. Pop., 2,138,000.

Georgetown, capital, largest city, and chief port of Guyana, located on the northeastern coast of South America. Georgetown is positioned at the mouth of the Demerara River, on the Atlantic Ocean. It is a railroad terminus and Guyana's communications and transportation center. Chief exports are sugar, bauxite, gold, timber, and rice. Pop., 72,000.

Guayaquil, in western Ecuador, on the Guayas River, about 40 miles (65 km.) from the Pacific Ocean. It is the major seaport and largest city in Ecuador and its economic and commercial center. It exports bananas, cacao, cattle, sugar, and coffee, and its industries manufacture textiles, iron, leather goods, machinery, wood products, and cement. It is the seat of two universities. Pop., 2,118,000.

La Paz, administrative capital and largest city of Bolivia, in west-central South America. Situated at an altitude of more than 11,000 feet (3,355 meters) on the high plateau of western Bolivia, La Paz is the world's highest capital city. It is also the industrial, commercial, political, and cultural center of Bolivia. Sucre is the legal capital and seat of the judiciary. Manufactures include processed foods, textiles, glass, and furniture. Pop., metro. area, 1,484,000.

La Plata, seaport and capital of Buenos Aires Province, about 35 miles (56 km.) southeast of Buenos Aires, Argentina. It has a large, artificial harbor and exports grain, meat, and oil. Its industries include oil refining, chemicals, and electrical goods. La Plata is also a major cultural center, with museums and colleges. Pop., 522,000.

Lima, capital and largest city of Peru, on the Rimac River, about 8 miles (13 km.) inland from the Pacific Ocean and its port, Callao. The city is the political, economic, and cultural center of Peru. Its diverse industries include textiles, chemicals, plastics, food processing, leather goods, foundries, and oil refineries. Founded in 1535 by Francisco Pizarro, Lima retains many buildings from its colonial past and the oldest university in South America. It is connected by rail and road to Callao and other cities in Peru. Pop., metro. area, 6,988,000.

THE FESTIVAL OF FLOWERS in Medellin annually celebrates this important Colombian export.

Maracaibo, seaport in northwestern Venezuela, on the western shore of a channel connecting Lake Maracaibo and the Gulf of Venezuela. It is a commercial and industrial center and the oil capital of South America. In addition to oil, its exports include sugar, cacao, coffee, and timber, and its manufactures include textiles, rope, and soap. Pop., 1,220,000.

Medellín, in Colombia, in a mountain valley at an altitude of about 5,000 feet (1,524 meters) above sea level. Medellín is the capital of the department of Antioquia and the second largest city of Colombia. It is an educational center and the nation's chief industrial city. Principal products include steel, textiles, chemicals, foodstuffs, rubber products, sugar, and coffee. An annual event is the Festival of Flowers. Pop., 1,885,000.

Mendoza, in west-central Argentina, 60 miles (96 km.) southeast of Aconcagua. The city is the center of an extensive wine-producing area irrigated by the Mendoza River. Wine and fruit are important, and petrochemicals are also produced. Pop., 122,000.

Montevideo, capital, largest city, and chief port of Uruguay. It is located on the north shore of the Rio de la Plata, about 135 miles (215 km.) east of Buenos Aires, Argentina. Montevideo is the industrial, commercial, and cultural center of Uruguay. The city's leading industry is meat packing. Chief exports are wool, meat, hides, textiles, and fish. Pop., 1,303,000.

Nova Iguaçu, (formerly Maxambamba), municipality northwest of Rio de Janeiro, in the Sarapui River valley, Brazil. Its manufactures include chemicals, pharmaceuticals, soft drinks, and canned foods. Pop., 915,000.

Paramaribo, capital of Suriname, situated in northeastern South America. The city is a port that has good rail and road connections with the interior. Its exports include bauxite, coffee, timber, and citrus fruits. Pop., 219,000.

Pôrto Alegre, seaport in southeastern Brazil, on an inlet at the northern end of the Lagoa dos Patos. It is a major industrial and commercial center of Brazil and exports the products of a rich agricultural region. Pôrto Alegre's manufactures include leather goods, textiles, metal products, and chemicals. It has shipyards, meat-packing plants, and foundries. It is also a cultural and educational center. Pop., 1,360,000.

Quito, capital and second largest city of Ecuador, located on a plateau in the Andes near the equator. An important city in the empire of the Inca Indians, it still has a large Indian population. Quito is primarily an administrative center. Pop., 1,616,000.

Recife, capital of Pernambuco State, in northeastern Brazil, located at the mouths of the Capibaribe and Beberibe rivers on the Atlantic Ocean. The city's economy is based on processing and exporting the agricultural products of the interior, including coffee, cotton, sugar, and hides. A rail and road network links Recife with other parts of Brazil. The city has two universities and many fine churches, some of which date from the colonial period. Pop., 1,422,000.

Rio de Janeiro, second largest city in Brazil and capital of Rio de Janeiro state, located on Guanabara Bay, on the Atlantic Ocean. It served as the capital of the country from 1763 to 1960. Rio de Janeiro is Brazil's cultural center and a major port, ranking second only to São Paulo. It has three universities and several museums. Its varied industries produce footwear, clothing, furniture, drugs, chemicals, and processed foods. It is also a popular tourist center, particularly during Carnival. Pop., 5,851,000.

cultural, and commercial heart of Chile, it manufactures iron and steel, chemicals, textiles, paper, and other products. Pop., metro. area, 4,647,000.

São Paulo, capital of São Paulo state in southeastern Brazil. It is the largest city and principal commercial and industrial center of Brazil, with oil refineries, chemical plants, and factories manufacturing heavy machinery and vehicles, pharmaceuticals, electrical devices, and textiles. The city is a cultural and educational center with extensive libraries, museums, and four universities. It is the location of the famous Butantan Institute, where snake serums are produced. Pop., 10,406,000.

Sucre, legal capital of Bolivia and seat of the judiciary, situated in a high Andean valley in the south-central part of the country. Although Sucre is the site of the national university and many government buildings, La Paz is the administrative capital. Sucre is impor-

theaters
US

theatres
Brit.

28 South America

Rosario, river port in east-central Argentina, on the Paraná River. It is the second largest city of Argentina and a commercial center. Its industries include sugar refining, meat processing, flour milling, petroleum refining, steel production, and machinery manufacture. Pop., 908,000.

Santa Cruz, in central Bolivia, on the Piray River. The second largest city in Bolivia, Santa Cruz is a trade, commercial, and processing center for oil and natural gas, metal ores, coffee, rice, cattle, and timber. It is connected by rail to both the Pacific and Atlantic oceans. Pop., 1,136,000.

Santiago, capital of Chile, situated in a high valley near the center of the country. In addition to being the political,

tant mainly as a commercial center for an agricultural and mining region. Pop., 216,000.

Valparaíso, principal seaport of Chile, on the west-central coast. The city is the entry point for most of the imports and is also an industrial center that manufactures textiles, paint, shoes, leather goods, and chemicals. Pop., 270,000.

Viña del Mar, seaside resort on the central coast of Chile, about 6 miles (10 km.) northeast of Valparaíso. It has a pleasant summer climate and many hotels, clubs, public gardens, and fine beaches, along with museums and theaters. The city's industries include oil refining, textiles, food processing, and sugar refining. Pop., 299,000.

THE INHABITANTS of Rio de Janeiro reside in the valleys nestled between the mountains that overlook the city.

Glossary of South America

Aconcagua. A mountain in the Andes chain of South America, situated on the Chile-Argentina border. Aconcagua is the highest mountain in the western hemisphere, rising to 22,834 feet (6,965 meters) above sea level.

Alcalde. The title used in the Iberian peninsula since the 1000s, and later in the Spanish colonies, to designate a local official. The term, derived from the Arabic *al qadi,* the judge, was also part of many government titles indicating some judicial authority.

Alliance for Progress. A pan-American program initiated in 1961 by U.S. President John F. Kennedy. It called on the Americas to unite in their attempts to install and protect democratic governments while working toward economic prosperity. This enthusiastic and idealistic program called for labor and agrarian reforms to ensure that all people would share equitably in the resulting progress.

DEVIL'S ISLAND, off the coast of French Guiana, was the site of a famous French penal colony.

Altiplano. In Spanish, a high flat area or plain, especially a high South American plateau in Peru and Bolivia. The plateau has an average altitude of about 12,000 feet (3,660 meters) above sea level and a gently rolling surface. The eastern edge, or *montaña* zone, is deeply cut by rivers. Its climate is cool and dry. The altiplano was the heartland of the Inca Empire.

Amazon. A South American river, the largest in the world in volume and catchment area, and second in length. It extends about 4,000 miles (6,440 kilometers) across Brazil and Peru, and its tributaries form a basin of some 2.7 million square miles (7 million square kilometers) in central South America. Its basin includes a floodplain, or *varzea,* which is fertile following rains between November and May, and unflooded areas, or *terra firme,* which have sterile soils.

Andes. A massive mountain system of western South America. The Andes stretch for more than 4,000 miles (6,440 kilometers) in a great crescent from northeastern Venezuela westward and then southward to the southernmost tip of the continent. Elevations range generally from 10,000 to 20,000 feet (3,050 to 6,100 meters), but there are several peaks that rise over 20,000 feet, including Aconcagua.

Angel Falls. The highest waterfall in the world, located in southeastern Venezuela on a tributary of the Caroni River. Actually a series of falls, it drops a total of 3,212 feet (980 meters); its highest fall is 2,650 feet (808 meters).

Atacama. A desert region that extends for about 600 miles (965 kilometers) in northern Chile. It lies between the Pacific coastal range on the west and the Andean piedmont on the east. The desert proper, with an elevation of about 2,000 feet (610 meters), is a series of dry salt basins rich in nitrates.

Audiencia. A Spanish royal court of appeal that came into existence in Spain in the 1200s. The institution sustained and was carried to Spain's colonial possessions beginning in the 1500s. The first audiencia in the Americas was established in 1511 on the island of Santo Domingo (Hispaniola).

The audiencia had judicial and administrative functions. In the Americas these bodies came to function as councils of state, often acting as checks on the exercise of arbitrary power by the Spanish governor. A total of 13 audiencias were established in the New World.

Bandeirantes. Profit-seeking slave catchers in the colonial Portuguese empire in Brazil. They pushed into the Brazilian frontier regions in search of new groups of Indians that could be sold into slavery on the coastal plantations. The slave-catching expeditions, called *bandeiras,* were well-organized and helped open the Brazilian interior for settlement. However, their main objective and activity brought them into conflict with Jesuit missionaries in the region.

Cape Horn. The southernmost point of South America, on Horn Island in the Tierra del Fuego archipelago.

Caudillos. Leaders that rose to power in the early 1800s in most of the South and Central American republics, notably Brazil, Venezuela, Colombia, Bolivia, and Mexico. They were usually powerful military figures who gained political control through violence and maintained it with repression and terrorism.

Colorado. A river 530 miles (853 kilometers) long in southeastern South America. It rises in the Andes near the Chilean border and flows southeast across south-central Argentina to the Atlantic Ocean.

Creoles. The second highest class of citizens (behind the *peninsulares,* born in Spain) in colonial Spanish America. They were Spaniards or Europeans but were American-born. The Creoles were important landholders and artisans, but they were generally passed over in favor of *peninsulares* for high positions in both church and government, a fact that led the Creoles to play a major role in the independence movement of the early 1800s.

Cuquenán Falls. Or Kukenaam, a waterfall in eastern Venezuela, northwest of Mount Roraima. Dropping some 2,000 feet (610 meters), it is one of the world's highest waterfalls.

Devil's Island. An island in the Atlantic about 6 miles (10 kilometers) off the northern coast of French Guiana. It was the site of a famous penal colony. France stopped sending prisoners to the island in 1938, and the last prisoners were repatriated in 1951.

Donatários. The recipients of *capitanias,* or captaincies, large land grants that carried economic and political privileges in the colonial Portuguese empire in Brazil. The donatário enjoyed more privileges than a feudal lord, including tax exemptions and the right to use Indian slaves. He was, in return, obliged to improve his grant by settling on and developing the land. Overall, the donatários were inefficient, and the system was ended by the mid-1700s.

Drake Passage. A channel separating the southern tip of South America from the Antarctic peninsula, joining the Pacific and the Atlantic oceans.

Gran Chaco. A lowland plain, about 300,000 square miles (777,000 square kilometers) in area, of south-central South America. Gran Chaco is divided among Argentina, Bolivia, and Paraguay. Much of the region is arid, but there are swampy areas. The climate is hot in the north and more temperate in the south. Rainfall is heaviest in the east. The area is sparsely populated and is generally unsuitable for intensive agriculture. Cattle grazing is the main economic activity.

Japurá. A river that rises in southwestern Colombia and flows southeast for about 1,750 miles (2,816 kilometers) across the Brazilian border into the Amazon.

Juruá. A river flowing from the Andes in east-central Peru across northwestern Brazil for more than 2,000 miles (3,200 kilometers) into the upper course of the Amazon.

Lagoa dos Patos. A shallow lagoon in southern Brazil covering an area of about 4,000 square miles (10,360 square kilometers) and separated from the Atlantic by a sandy peninsula about 15 miles (24 kilometers) wide. Porto Alegre lies at its northern end. The port of Río Grande at its southern end is linked to the Atlantic by a narrow opening.

Llanos. Low-lying plains of South America, in eastern Colombia and the Orinoco basin of Venezuela. The area is about 220,000 square miles (570,000 square kilometers). Most of the region is grassland.

Madeira. A river in central South America formed from the union on the Bolivia-Brazil border of the Beni and the Mamoré rivers, which rise in Bolivia. The Madeira, from the headwaters of the Mamoré, is 2,082 miles (3,352 kilometers) long and flows north and east to join the Amazon.

Magdalena. A river that flows northward for 956 miles (1,540 kilometers) through Colombia into the Caribbean Sea. It lies between the massive Cordillera Central to the west and the Cordillera Oriental to the east. It is joined near its mouth by the Cauca.

Maracaibo. A large lake, 130 miles (209 kilometers) long and 75 miles (120 kilometers) wide, in northwestern Venezuela. It is a major petroleum-producing area.

Marañón. A river rising in the Andes in west central Peru and flowing north-

west and then east for about 1,000 miles (1,600 kilometers) to combine with the Ucayali to form the Amazon.

Mestizos. The mixed Indian-Spanish populace in Spanish America. As a group, the mestizos have generally been rejected by both Indians and Spaniards, who look upon them with distrust. They are middle-class citizens, working as merchants and artisans.

Organization of American States (OAS). An organization of 31 countries in the western hemisphere. The OAS was established in 1948 to promote mutual assistance between the nations of Latin America and the United States.

In 1889 the International Union of the American Republics was established, with both the United States and Latin American nations participating. The International Union was reorganized in 1910 as the Pan American Union.

Despite the existence of the Pan American Union, relations between the United States and Latin America deteriorated during the first two decades of the 1900s, and under the administration of President Theodore Roosevelt, the United States asserted its right to intervene in the internal affairs of Latin American countries. This policy made the Pan American Union virtually useless.

In the 1930s, the good neighbor policy was put forth under U.S. President Franklin Roosevelt, and attempts were made to revive the Pan-American movement. A conference in Lima, Peru, in 1938 established the principle of nonintervention.

The outbreak of World War II tightened the bonds between the nations of the western hemisphere. In an attempt to provide for mutual defense, most of the Latin American countries joined the United States in declaring war on the Axis powers. Only Argentina and Chile remained on friendly terms with the Axis through most of the war.

In 1945, after the war had ended, the members of the Pan American Union signed a mutual security treaty known as the Act of Chapultepec. In 1947 the Inter-American Treaty of Reciprocal Assistance was signed in Rio de Janeiro, Brazil. A year later in 1948, at a meeting in Bogotá, Colombia, the OAS was established.

The OAS is recognized as a regional organization under the UN Charter. It was formed to consolidate the policies and treaties of the Pan-American organizations that preceded it. Its charter members were the United States and the then 20 sovereign nations of Latin America. Subsequently, independent Jamaica, Trinidad and Tobago, Barbados, and Grenada joined the organization. In 1962, following the missile crisis, Cuba was excluded from all organizational activities; however, its membership was not rescinded, although a diplomatic and commercial embargo was invoked.

Orinoco. A river of South America that flows for some 1,600 miles (2,575 kilometers) from the Parima Mountains of Venezuela west, then north along the Venezuela-Colombia border, and then northeast through central Venezuela to the Atlantic Ocean. The Orinoco forms a wide delta at its mouth. Because of the heavy volume of sediment carried by the river, the delta is growing rapidly. The Orinoco River basin is sparsely populated and largely undeveloped despite large deposits of iron ore, bauxite, and petroleum.

Pampas. Or Pampa, the grassy treeless plains of South America. The pampas extend some 1,000 miles (1,600 kilometers) through central Argentina from the lower Paraná River south to the Colorado River. The Pampas is about 295,000 square miles (765,000 square kilometers) in area. The western part, the Dry Pampas, is mostly barren. The eastern part, the Humid Pampas, is the heart of Argentina's agricultural area.

THE WIDE DELTA of the Orinoco River is growing rapidly because of the heavy volume of sediment carried by the river.

LAKE NORGENSKJOLD lies in the rugged Patagonia region of southern Argentina.

Pará. A 200-mile (320-kilometer) river in northeastern Brazil forming the estuary of the Tocantins River. It is a navigable mouth of the Amazon and flows into the Atlantic Ocean to the south and east of Marajó Island.

Paraguay. A river of South America, rising in southwestern Brazil and flowing generally south for some 1,585 miles (2,550 kilometers). The Paraguay River forms parts of the boundaries between Brazil and Bolivia, Brazil and Paraguay, and Paraguay and Argentina before it empties into the Paraná River in the southwestern corner of Paraguay.

Paraná. The second longest river in South America. Formed by the junction of the Grande and Paranaíba rivers in south-central Brazil, it flows generally southwest for some 2,500 miles (4,025 kilometers).

The river forms part of the boundary between Brazil and Paraguay and between Paraguay and Argentina. It continues south through northeastern Argentina to the Río de la Plata.

Patagonia. A barren tableland of southern Argentina lying between the Andes and the Atlantic Ocean. It extends south of the Negro River to the Strait of Magellan. The region has an area of about 260,000 square miles (673,000 square kilometers).

Peninsulares. New World Spaniards in the colonial period who had been born in Spain. They were considered first-class citizens in Spanish America and generally held the highest government and church positions.

Putumayo. A river rising in southwestern Colombia that flows southeastward for about 1,151 miles (1,853 kilometers) into the Amazon. It forms a great part of the border between Colombia, Ecuador, and Peru before entering Brazil, where it is called the Içá.

Repartimiento. Practice whereby the Spanish conquerors of the New World enslaved native Indians and forced them to labor on public projects and private plantations. Indian family members were often separated from each other by this system, and entire villages were frequently converted into virtual labor camps.

Río de la Plata. An estuary on the southeast coast of South America. It forms part of the border between Uruguay and Argentina, stretching some 250 miles (400 kilometers) from the Atlantic Ocean to the mouths of the Paraná and Uruguay rivers.

Rio Pact. Or Inter-American Treaty of Reciprocal Assistance, a treaty signed in 1947 stating that an attack on any member would be considered by the others as an attack on them and that collective steps would be taken to repel the aggression. Originally there were 22 members, including the United States, but in 1964 Cuba was suspended.

Strait of Magellan. A passage at the southern tip of South America, winding between the mainland and Tierra del Fuego. It is 350 miles (564 kilometers) long and connects the South Pacific and South Atlantic oceans.

Tierra del Fuego. An archipelago at the southern tip of South America comprising all the islands south of the Strait of Magellan. The western two-thirds of the island group is controlled by Chile, and the eastern third is controlled by Argentina. The total area of the archipelago is about 28,470 square miles (73,750 square kilometers).

Titicaca. A lake in South America on the border of Peru and Bolivia. It lies 12,500 feet (3,810 meters) above sea level in the altiplano of the central Andes. Lake Titicaca is about 120 miles (193 kilometers) long, 45 miles (73 kilometers) wide, and 920 feet (280 meters) at its greatest depth.

Tocantins. A river rising in south central Brazil and flowing north for about 1,700 miles (2,740 kilometers) into the Pará River.

Uruguay. A 1,000-mile-long (1,610-kilometer-long) river of southeastern South America. It rises in the Serra do Mar of southern Brazil and flows west, southwest, and then south into the Río de la Plata.

---

kilometer
US

kilometre
Brit.

labor
US

labour
Brit.

THE HELP DESK

➤ **Make** a list of great civilizations—Mayan, Incan, etc. Locate the area and arrange in the order of their height of power. Arrange in order of length of power.

➤ **Study** the maps that show where the ancient civilizations developed. Note that most sprang up around rivers. Why do you think that happened?

➤ **Spend** some time each day locating countries and cities that are in the news on a map or globe.

➤ **As** you study South America, try to analyze the manner in which people adapted to their environment.

➤ **Make** a list of the largest cities. How does the size of those cities compare with cities that you are familiar with? Why do you think that people began to live in that area and continued to live there?

➤ **Study** the information box for each country. What can you determine from each set of facts? Is the country large or small? Rich or poor? Heavily or sparsely populated? Is it an industrial nation or an agricultural one? Are the people well educated?

➤ **Make** a list of important people in the development of the country. As you note events in your historical report, watch for people associated with those events. Read the newspapers and listen to news reports to add current names to your list of people. Find pictures of current rulers or other important people; try to determine why they are important to the country. See if the people on your list appear in other volumes of the Volume Library by checking the Index.

➤ **Review** the historical background of the country. Does it date back thousands or hundreds of years, or is it much younger? Write a short report noting major events in the history in chronological order. Now compare the events in the country to events in countries nearby. Is there any similarity? Are they friends or enemies? Do the people speak the same language? What are other similarities or differences that you have detected? Don't forget to use the HISTORY OF THE WORLD volume for related information.

➤ **For** a list of helpful references, go to the *customers* section of www.southwestern.com.

Index

Index

How to Use the Index

This index is a quick, easy guide to the information in *The Volume Library*.

Book 1 includes chapters 1-14; **Book 2** includes chapters 15-28 and the Index. Each entry contains the chapter number and page number for locating that topic. For example, the entry **abacus 2:57** means that a reference to abacus can be found on page 57 of chapter 2.

Page numbers are followed by a letter indicating the column on the page: *a* refers to the first column; *b* to the second; *c* to the third. This will help you pinpoint information quickly and easily.

All entries are placed in alphabetical order in a letter-by-letter system. That is, all entries, regardless of punctuation, are in precise alphabetical order.

Port Elizabeth (South Africa)
Porter, Cole
  biography
Porter, George
Porter, Katherine Anne
  biography
Porter, William Sidney *see* Henry, O.
Port Etienne (Mauritania)

There are no alphabetical priorities for persons with like names. In the case of persons of rank, such as kings and emperors, all the firsts (I) are listed together, then the seconds (II), thirds (III), and so forth. Descriptive material identifying such persons follows the name in parentheses.

Henry I (King of Germany)
Henry I (King of England)
Henry II (Duke of Silesia)
Henry II (King of England)
Henry III (King of England)
Henry III (King of France)
Henry IV (Holy Rom. Emp.)

Names beginning with Mac or Mc are also arranged in strict alphabetical order. Mac is located among the general *mac* listings and Mc among the *mc* listings. Spanish and French names preceded by an article, such as *La, Les,* or *Los,* are listed under the article, since the article is part of the name. Arabic names beginning with *ibn* (son of), as ibn Saud, are under *i*. However, Burmese names preceded by the honorary term *U,* such as U Thant, are indexed under the surname.

Names beginning with prepositions such as *von, van,* or *de* are indexed according to the traditional use of the name. For example, the names De Gaulle and D'Annunzio are indexed under the letter *d;* Van Gogh is listed under *v*. But Honoré de Balzac, Simone de Beauvoir, and St. Thomas à Becket are all indexed under *b;* Alexis de Tocqueville is listed under *t*. Handy cross-references are used whenever a listing may be ambiguous.

References to prominent works of art, books, plays, and so forth are listed under the name of the author (except in the case of anonymous works, which have their own listings).

Wagner, Richard
  biography
  Die Meistersinger
  Lohengrin
  Ring of the Nibelungs

Famous works are cross-referenced to their authors: **Iliad** *see* Homer; **Little Women** *see* Alcott, Louisa May; **Importance of Being Ernest** *see* Wilde, Oscar.

Abbreviations

Afgh.	Afghanistan	Eur.	Europe	Mich.	Michigan	print.	printing
Afr.	Africa, African	fin.	finance	mineral.	mineralogy	pseud.	pseudonym
Ala.	Alabama	Fla.	Florida	Minn.	Minnesota	psych.	psychology
Am.	America, American	form.	former, formerly	Miss.	Mississippi	R.I.	Rhode Island
anat.	anatomy	Fr.	France, French	Mo.	Missouri	Rom.	Roman
anc.	ancient	Ga.	Georgia	mod.	modern	S. Afr.	South Africa
anthro.	anthropology	geog.	geography	Mont.	Montana	S. Am.	South American
arch.	architecture	geol.	geology	myth.	mythology	S.C.	South Carolina
Arg.	Argentina	Ger.	Germany	N. Am.	North American	Scan.	Scandinavian
Ariz.	Arizona	govt.	government	N.C.	North Carolina	sci.	science
Ark.	Arkansas	Gr.	Greece	N. Dak.	North Dakota	Scot.	Scotland
astro.	astronautics	il.	illustration	Neb.	Nebraska	sculp.	sculpture
astron.	astronomy	Ill.	Illinois	Neth.	Netherlands	S. Dak.	South Dakota
bib.	biblical	Ind.	Indian, Indiana	Nev.	Nevada	St.	Saint
biol.	biology	Ire.	Ireland	N.H.	New Hampshire	Switz.	Switzerland
bot.	botanical, botany	is.	island, islands	N.J.	New Jersey	tab.	table
bus.	business	It.	Italian	N. Mex.	New Mexico	Tenn.	Tennessee
Calif.	California	Kan.	Kansas	N.Y.	New York	Tex.	Texas
cer.	ceramics	Ky.	Kentucky	oceanog.	oceanography	U.K.	United Kingdom
chem.	chemistry	La.	Louisiana	Okla.	Oklahoma	U.S.	United States
co.	company	lang.	language	Oreg.	Oregon	Va.	Virginia
Colo.	Colorado	Leb.	Lebanon	Pak.	Pakistan	Venez.	Venezuela
comp.	computers	leg.	legend, legendary	Para.	Paraguay	Vt.	Vermont
Conn.	Connecticut	lit.	literature	Penn.	Pennsylvania	Wash.	Washington
Czech.	Czechoslovakia	Lux.	Luxembourg	philos.	philosophy	Wis.	Wisconsin
Del.	Delaware	Mass.	Massachusetts	physiol.	physiology	W. Va.	West Virginia
econ.	economics	math.	mathematics	Port.	Portugal,	Wyo.	Wyoming
Emp.	Emperor, Empress	Md.	Maryland		Portuguese	Yugo.	Yugoslavia
Eng.	England	meteorol.	meteorology	P.R.	Puerto Rico	zool.	zoology

Index

Index

Index

Anouilh, Jean 20:41b
  Becket 20:57b
  biography 14:43b
Ansar brotherhood 22:62a
Anschluss 26:17a
Ansky, S. (Solomon Rapoport)
  The Dybbuk 20:70b
ant *il* 4:41, 4:40c-41a
  white *see* termite
Antaeus (myth.) 20:53a-b
Antananarivo (Madagascar)
  22:42b, 22:71a
Antarctica
  see also South Pole
  Adelie Land 25:20c
  Australian Antarctic Territory
  25:20a
  greenhouse effect 9:26b
  nature reserve 9:44a
  ozone layer 9:28b-c
  Scott expeditions 14:156b
Antarctic Treaty 9:44a
anteater *il* 4:41, 4:41a
antecedent (lang.) 16:11c
antelope 4:35c, 4:41a-b
Anthemius 19:17c
anther 11:19b
anthology 20:53b
Anthony, Kenneth 27:248a
Anthony, Saint
  biography 14:43b
Anthony, Susan Brownell
  biography 14:43b
anthropology and archaeology
  15:40a-54c
  Benedict biography 14:49b
  Boas biography 14:52c
  cultural 15:47a-54c
  Leakey biography 14:113a
  Mead biography 14:125b
  physical 15:40a-45c
  prehistory and protohistory
  see prehistory
  Schliemann biography
  14:155b
  Westernization 15:52c-53c
antibiotics 2:9a, 6:76c
antibodies 6:31a-32c, 6:76c
anticline 8:42b, *il* 8:44
anticoagulant 6:76c
antidiuretic hormone (ADH)
  4:27a
Antietam, Battle of 27:40b
antigens 6:76c
Antigone (drama) *see* Sophocles
Antigonids 21:13a
Antigonus 21:13a, 26:68b
Antigua and Barbuda 27:235a
  economy 27:235a
  government 27:235b
  history 27:235b
  land 27:235a
  map 27:235
  people 27:235a
antihistamine 2:9a
Antilles Islands 27:252c, 27:268a
Anti-Masonic Party (U.S.)
  27:33b
antimatter 10:57a
antimony 7:30a-c
  metallic 2:5c
antineutrinos 10:40c
antioxidant 6:77a
antiparticles *see* particles, atomic
antipoverty programs *see* social
  welfare

antiprotons 10:40c
antiseptics
  Lister's work 14:116b
  Semmelweis's work 14:157a
antitrust laws 12:26a-b, 13:103b
  see also Clayton Act; Sherman
  Antitrust Act
  Justice Department 13:72b
antivirus program 1:30c
Antonescu, Ion 26:82a
Antonius, Marcus *see* Antony,
  Mark
Antony, Mark 14:45b
  biography 14:43b
  Cleopatra biography 14:64b
Antony and Cleopatra *see*
  Shakespeare, William
antonyms *tab* 16:19
Antwerp, Truce of 21:41b
Antwerp (Belgium) 26:143a
anvil (anat.) *see* ear, anvil
anvil top (meteorol.) 8:76a
anxiety (psych.) 15:22b-c
Anyang (China) 19:68b
ANZUS Pact 13:20a, 25:8c,
  25:11c
A-1 Diamant (satellite) 5:50c
Aono, So
  Nights of a Fool 20:37c
Aoun, Michel 24:16b
Apache (N. Am. Ind.)
  Cochise biography 14:65a
apartheid *see* South Africa
apatosaurus *see* brontosaurus
ape 4:34b, 4:41b, 15:41a-42a,
  15:48c
  see also baboon; chimpanzee;
  gibbon; gorilla; orangutan;
  siamang
Apennine Mountains (Italy)
  26:5c, 26:150b
Apennine Tunnel (Italy)
  tab 2:12
aperture 5:58b
aphelion 5:58b
aphid 4:41b
aphorism 20:53c
aphotic 8:76a
Aphrodite (myth.) 20:53c
Apia (Western Samoa) 25:19c,
  25:22a
Apianus, Petrus 5:24b-c
apical dominance *il* 5:26,
  11:25c-26a
apical meristem 11:15a, 11:16a-
  17b
Apithy, Sourou-Migan 22:17b
APL (computer language) 1:24a-c
Apocrypha *see* Bible
apogee 5:58b
Apollo (Phoebus: myth.) 19:17b,
  20:54a, 20:99b, 20:102b
  Delphic Oracle *il* 26:152,
  26:152b-c
Apollo (spacecraft program)
  5:47b-c, 27:62c
  Apollo 1 5:51a
  Apollo 5 5:51a
  Apollo 7 5:51a
  Apollo 9 5:51b
  Apollo 10 5:51b
  Apollo 11 2:8b, 5:47b, 5:51b,
  14:44a
  Apollo 12 5:47b, 5:51b
  Apollo 13 5:47c

Apollo 14 5:51b
Apollo 15 5:51b
Apollo 16 5:51b
Apollo 17 2:8b, 5:51c
Apollo 18 5:51c
moon landing 5:47b-c
Apollonius of Rhodes 20:51c
  Argonautica 20:5c
Apology *see* Socrates
apology (lit.) 20:54a
Aponte, Jose 27:238c
apoplexy *see* stroke
apostrophe 17:143, *tab* 17:146-
  147
apothecaries' system 3:75b-c
Appalachian Mountains 8:26c,
  27:99a, 27:100a, 27:137b,
  27:144c, 27:146c, 27:268b
Appalachian Plateau 8:46a,
  27:134a
Appalachian region 8:46a
Appalachian Uplands (Canada)
  27:200c, 27:204c, 27:208c
apparel *see* textiles
apparent magnitude 5:28c-29b,
  5:38b, 5:60c
appeals court *see* court, appeals
Appelfeld, A. 20:38c
appendix (anat.) 2:5a, 6:77a
Appert, Nicholas 2:7c
Appian Way (Italy) 2:4a
apple 11:37a
Apple Computers, Inc. 1:8a-c,
  1:24c, 2:9b
Appleseed, Johnny *see*
  Chapman, John
Appleton, Sir Edward
  biography 14:43b
  Nobel Prize 14:191a
application software 1:8a-c,
  1:24b, 1:29a-30c, 1:46b
appositive (lang.) 17:142, 17:148
appreciation (fin.) 12:73a
apricot *il* 11:37, 11:37a-b
Apuleius
  Golden Ass 20:10a, 20:76b,
  20:92a, 20:105b
Aqaba, Gulf of 22:30b, 24:12b,
  24:13a, 24:28a
Aqi 20:38a
Aqua Alsientina aqueduct 2:4a
Aqua Appia aqueduct 2:4a
aquaculture 9:59b-c
aqua fortis *see* nitric acid
aqua regia 2:5c
aquatic environments *see* water,
  environments
Aqua Virgo aqueduct 2:4a
aqueduct 2:10c-11a
  Roman 2:4a, 19:15c
  Samos 2:4a
aquifer 8:65c, 9:55c-56b, 9:60a
Aquilo (myth.) 20:59c
Aquinas, St. Thomas 20:9a,
  21:31b
  biography 14:43b-c
  Maritain's work 14:122b
Aquino, Benigno 23:53a
Aquino, Corazon 23:53a
Arabi, Ahmad 22:30a
Arabia, 24:28a
Arabian Desert 22:28c, 24:3a
Arabian Nights'
  Entertainments
  (Thousand and One
  Nights) 20:9a

Index

Index

Index

Index

Index

Index

Index

economy 26:22b-c
government 26:10c, 26:22c, 26:23b-c
Greece 26:23b
history 26:22c-23c
  Balkan wars 26:23b, 26:150b-c
  Communist rule 26:23b-c
  independence 26:23a-b
  Ottoman rule 26:23a
land 26:22a
Macedonia 26:68c
map 26:22
people 26:22a-b
Soviet Union 26:23b-c
trade 26:22c
Yugoslavia 26:23b-c, 26:139a, 26:140c
Bulgars (people) 26:23a, 26:68b
Bulge, Battle of the 27:58c
bulimia 6:25a, 6:78a
bull (zool.) *see* cattle
bulletin board systems 1:34c-35a
bullfinch *see* finch
bullfrog *il* 4:19, 4:56a
bullhead (fish) 4:47b
bullhead (insect) *see* mosquito
bull market 12:74a
Bull Moose Party *see* Progressive Party
Bull Run, Battles of 27:39b-c, 27:40b
bullrush *see* papryus (bot.)
bulrush 11:41a
Bunche, Ralph *il* 14:57, *il* 14:189
  biography 14:57a-b
  Nobel Prize 14:190a
Bunin, Ivan A. 20:39a
  Nobel Prize 14:191c
Bunker Hill, Battle of 27:23b
Bunsen, Robert Wilhelm von
  biography 14:57b
Bunyan, John 20:23a
  biography 14:57b
  Pilgrim's Progress il 20:23, 20:23a, 20:52a, 20:103a
Bunyan, Paul *see* Paul Bunyan
Bunyoro (Bantu state) 21:52c
Buonarroti, Michelangelo *see* Michelangelo
Buoninsegna, Duccio di *see* Duccio di Buoninsegna
Burbank, Luther
  biography 14:57b
Burchfield, Robert 18:14c
burdock 11:41a-b
bureaucracy 13:5b, 13:46c-47a, *tab* 13:47, 15:27a
Bureau of the Census *see* Census, Bureau of the
Burebistas (Dacian leader) 26:81a
Burger, Warren 13:38c, *il* 13:39, 27:70a
Burgess, Ernest W. 15:24c
Burghley (Burleigh), 1st Baron *see* Cecil, William
burglary 13:120b
Burgoyne, John 27:24a
  biography 14:57b
Burke, Edmund 13:94c, 20:25b, 20:32a
  biography 14:57b-c
Burkina Faso 22:18c-19b

agriculture 22:18c
climate 22:18c
economy 22:18c-19a
government 22:19a
history 22:19a-b
  French rule 22:19a
  independence 22:19a-b
land 22:18c
map 22:19
people 22:18c
trade 22:18c-19a
Burleigh, Lord *see* Cecil, William
Burlington (Vt.) 27:143c
Burlusconi, Silvio 26:64a
Burma *see* Myanmar
Burmans (people) 23:45a-46a
Burmese language 18:6a
Burnet, Sir Frank Macfariane 14:192b
Burnham, Forbes 28:26a-b
Burns, Robert 20:28a
  biography 14:57c
  Poems, Chiefly in the Scottish Dialect 20:28a, 20:103c
  "Tam O'Shanter" 20:115b
Burns, Tommy 14:104a
Burnside, Ambrose E. 27:40b
bur oak 11:60b
Burr, Aaron
  biography 14:57c
  Hamilton 14:90b
burro *see* donkey
Burroughs, William 20:48b
bursitis 6:78a
Burton, Ralph 27:163b
Burton, Robert
  Anatomy of Melancholy 20:22a, 20:82b
Burundi 22:19b-20b
  agriculture 22:19c
  climate 22:19b
  economy 22:19c
  government 22:19c
  history 22:19c-20b
  land 22:19b
  map 22:19
  people 22:19b-c
  trade 22:19c
bus (comp.) 1:12c-13a
bus (vehicle)
  see also busing
  diesel-powered 2:23a-b
Bush, George H. *il* 13:33, *tab* 13:53, *tab* 13:56-57, *il* 13:57, *il* 14:57, 14:201a-b
  biography 14:57c-58a
  domestic legislation 27:70b
  election of 1980 27:68c
  election of 1988 27:69c
  election of 1992 27:71a-b
  foreign policy 27:70b-71a
  Iran-Contra scandal 27:69b-c
  Iraq 21:80c-81b
  savings and loan associations 27:69c-70a
  Strategic Arms Reduction Treaty 27:70c
Bush, George W. *il* 13:46, *tab* 13:53, *tab* 13:56-57, *il* 14:201, 21:84a, 21:88c
  biography 14:201a-b
Bush, Laura *il* 14:201, 14:201a
Bush, Vannevar 2:7b
bushido 21:38b, 23:70b

bushmaster (snake) 4:69c
Bushmen
  Namibia 22:50c
  southern Africa 21:53a
  Zimbabwe 22:69b
Bushnell, David 2:24b-c
business 12:6a-52c
  see also economics; industry
  Canada 12:47a-52c
  corporation *see* corporation
  definition 12:12a, 12:74a
  financing 12:7a-9c
  forms of 12:12a-19a
  Galbraith's views 12:69a-c
  glossary of terms 12:73a-12:79c
  informal organization structure 12:20c
  Internet and 12:12a-b
  lobbying 13:48b-49c
  management *see* management
  marketing *see* marketing
  small *see* small business
  tight money and 12:53c-54a
  U.K. 12:34a-46c
    financial system 12:39a-46c
    international role 12:46a-c
  U.S. 12:7a-33c
    Coolidge era 27:53c
    history of 27:45a
  writing 17:91-108
business law *see* law, commercial
business letter 17:92-93, 17:95, 17:97-98
busing 15:28b
Bustamante, Alexander 27:246c
Buster, John 2:9a
Bustillo, Maria 2:9a
butane 7:24b-c
Butcher, Harvey 5:42c
Butenandt, Adolf Friedrich Johann 14:191b
Butler, Nicholas Murray 14:188a
Butler, Robert N. 20:127c
Butler, Robert Olen 20:126c
Butler, Samuel 20:29a
  biography 14:58a
  Erewhon 14:58a, 20:71c
  realism 20:106b-c
  The Way of All Flesh 14:58a, 20:29a, 20:122a
butterball (duck) *see* bufflehead
butterbur *il* 11:41, 11:41b
buttercup 11:41b
butterfly *il* 4:45, 4:45c, 4:47b
  metamorphosis 4:23b-c
butterfly shell *see* coquina (shell)
butternut 11:77b
butterwort 11:41b
button mangrove 11:57a
butylated hydroxyanisole (BHA) 6:78a
buyer's market *il* 12:74, 12:74a
Buyoya, Pierre 22:20a
buzzard *see* vulture
By, John 27:261c
Byelrussia *see* Belarus
Byng (Lord) 13:75b-c, *tab* 13:79, 27:182c
Byrd, Richard Evelyn
  biography 14:58a
Byron, George (Lord) 20:28b
  biography 14:58a

Index

Index

Index

Index

Chrétien de Troyes 20:11c, 20:55a

Christ, Jesus *see* Jesus Christ

Christian IV (King of Denmark and Norway) 26:74c

Christian X (King of Denmark) 26:28b

Christian Frederick (King of Norway) 26:74c

Christianity 20:66b, 21:23-26a-c
  Africa 22:11a
  architecture 19:17c
  Armenia 26:14c
  art 19:17a-18c, 19:19b-20b, 19:27a, 19:39c, 19:40b, 19:45b-c, 19:72c
  Australasia 25:7a
  bestiary 20:58a
  Bible *see* Bible
  Byzantine Empire 21:28c
  catacombs 19:17b
  Chad 22:23b
  chanson de geste 20:62a
  Christ *see* Jesus Christ
  churches 19:17c, 19:72c
  Constantine biography 14:66a-b
  Croatia 26:24b
  Crusades *see* Crusades
  Eastern Orthodox Church 21:24c
  Ethiopia 21:34b
  Europe 26:7c-8a
  Germany 13:12c
  Ireland 26:58c
  Japan 21:49b-c
  Jesus *see* Jesus Christ
  Lebanon 24:15b-16a
  literature 20:7a-c, 20:10a-c, 20:11b, 20:12a-b, 20:21c, 20:22c-23a
  manuscripts 19:17c, 19:19b-c
  medieval 21:31a-b
  Middle East 24:4b
  philosophy 20:9a, 20:10a-b
  Protestant Church 21:25-26c
  psalms 19:20a-b
  Roman Catholic Church 21:23c-24b
  Roman Empire 19:17a-18c, *il* 21:16, 21:16c, 26:7c
  St. Paul biography 14:137b
  sculpture 19:17c, 19:20c
  Spain 20:9a, 26:98c-99a
  Sweden 26:101b
  symbolism 19:17b-c, 19:18c
  Syria 24:20b
  Uganda 22:67a-c
  U.S. 27:8a

Christian Science
  Eddy biography 14:75b-c

Christie, Agatha
  biography 14:63b, 26:128a

Christmas 15:57b

Christmas cactus *see* cactus family

Christmas Carol *see* Dickens, Charles John Huffam

Christmas Island 25:9a, 25:20a

Christophe, Henri (King of Haiti) 27:244c

chromatic aberration 5:8b, 5:58c

chromatids 6:48b-49a

chromatin 6:38c, 6:48c, 6:79b

chromium 7:32a-c
  body requirement *tab* 6:22
  discovery 2:5c

chromophores (chem.) 7:12b-c

chromoplast 11:14c

chromosome 6:10a-b, 6:79b, 11:25a
  abormalities 6:58b-c
  crossover 6:50b
  diploid 6:80c
  DNA *il* 6:50, 6:54a
  environmental hazards 9:10b
  genes 6:48a
  karyotyping *il* 6:58
  mapping 6:50a-b
  meiosis 6:48c-49a
  mitosis 6:48b-c
  unraveling *il* 6:50
  X chromosome 6:49a-c, 15:17c, 15:31c
  Y chromosome 6:49a-c, 15:17c, 15:31c

chromosphere 5:26c

chrysalis 4:23c

chrysanthemum *il* 11:43, 11:43c-44a

Chuang-tse 20:3a

Chu Hsi 21:37a

Chulalongkorn (King of Thailand) 23:59c-60b

Chun Doo Hwan 23:38c

Chungyang Mountains (Taiwan) 23:55c

Chunnel (English Channel) 2:8a, *il* 2:12, 2:13a, 26:136b-c

Church, Frederick 19:62c

churches *see* religion; specific churches

Churchill, John *see* Marlborough, Duke of

Churchill, Sir Winston Leonard Spencer *il* 13:3, 20:46a, 26:131c-134a
  Atlantic Charter 21:90a, 27:56c
  biography 14:63b-c
  "iron curtain" phrase 27:60b
  Nobel Prize 14:191c
  World War II *il* 26:130, 26:130a-131a, 27:57c, 27:58b
  Yalta Conference 21:66b, *il* 21:67, 27:58c

Churchill River (Canada) 27:210c

Church of England (Anglican Church) 26:119b, 26:122a
  Cranmer biography 14:67c-68a
  creation of 26:115a-b
  James II 26:122c
  Puritans 27:17b-c

Church of Jesus Christ of the Latter-day Saints *see* Mormon Church

Church of Rome *see* Roman Catholic Church

Church of St. Nicholas (Novgorod, Russia) 2:4a

Church of the Nativity (Bethlehem) 24:27a

Chu River 23:39a

Churrua (S. Am. Ind.) 28:32a

Chu, Steven 14:196c

Chu Yüan-chang 21:37b, 23:20a

chyme 6:8c, 6:79b

C.I.A. *see* Central Intelligence Agency

Ciampi, Carlo Azeglio 26:64a

cicada 4:48b-c

Cicero, Marcus Tullius 21:15a, 21:15c
  biography 14:63c
  literature 20:6b

Cid, El 20:63a
  biography 14:63c

Cid, Le *see* Corneille, Pierre

Cid, Song of the 20:63a, 20:71b

Cierva, Juan de la 2:6b

cigarettes *see* tobacco

cilia 4:17b, 6:79b, 11:9b

cinchona 11:44a

Cincinnati (Ohio) 27:134b-c, 27:255b

cinematography
  Lumière process 14:118b-c
  story lines 19:75a-b
  sound recording 19:75b

cinnamon 11:44a

cinnamon rose 11:69c

Cintra, Pedro da 22:57a

circadian rhythms 4:29a

Circe (myth.) 20:123b

circle 3:87c-90c, *il* 3:108, 3:108a, 3:108b, 3:109a
  arc and angle measurement 3:89b-90c
  arc degrees 5:6a
  area 3:79a
  circumscribed 3:154c
  great 5:6a, 5:60a
  hour 5:6b
  radian 3:76b
  tangent to 3:159a
  verticle 5:6a

circuit (electric) *see* electric circuit

circuit boards *il* 1:12, 1:12b-c
  printed 1:46a

circulatory system 2:5a, *il* 6:6, 6:6a-7a
  see also artery; blood; capillary; vein (human)
  animal *il* 4:25, 4:25b-26a
  cephalopod 4:18a
  closed 4:25c
  Harvey's work 4:13a
  hormones 4:26c
  open 4:25b-c

circus 14:148b
  Barnum biography 14:47a-b

cirque 8:38b

cirrhosis *see* liver

cirrus cloud *il* 8:52, 8:53a

citizenship 13:40b

city 15:35c-36c, 15:49a, 15:61c, 15:63a
  see also specific cities
  Industrial Revolution 21:45c
  urban renewal 15:36c
  U.S. 15:36b
    government 27:47b-c
    growth of 27:46c
    health standards 27:47b
    major 27:13a
    manager 27:47c
    map 27:12
    poverty in 27:47b

City of God *see* Augustine, St.

city-state *see* Greece, city-state

Civilian Conservation Corps (CCC) *tab* 27:55, 27:55b

Index

Cockcroft, J. Douglas 2:8b, 10:3b-c, 10:38a, 14:177a
   Nobel Prize 14:191a
Cockcroft-Walton accelerator 2:8b, 10:3b-c, 10:38a
Cockerell, Christopher 2:8b
cockroach 4:49b
cocoa
   see also cacao
   Africa 22:11b
   beans 11:44b
coconut 11:62a
cocoon 4:23c
Cocos Islands (Keeling Islands) 25:9a, 25:20a
Cocteau, Jean 20:41b
cod 4:49b-c
code (comp.) 1:43a
Code Napoléon 13:97a, 13:114a, 26:36c
Code of Hammurabi *see* Hammurabi, Code
Code of Justinian *see* Justinian, law code
codon 6:79b
Codrington (Barbuda) 27:235b
Cody, William Frederick (Buffalo Bill) *il* 14:65
   biography 14:65a-b
coelacanth *il* 4:9, 4:9a
coelenterate 4:16a, 4:16c, 4:22b
coelom 4:16b, 4:17c, 4:18b
coelostat 5:9c
coercevate droplet 6:34c-35a, 6:79b
Coercive Acts 27:22b
coexistence (zool.) 4:38c
coffee 11:44b-c, *il* 28:13
   Africa 22:11b
   Bolivia *il* 28:13
   Brazil 28:15a, 28:15b, 28:17a
   Colombia 28:21a-b, 28:22c
   Côte d' Ivoire 22:27b-c
   Ethiopia 22:32b-c
cogeneration 9:8b-c
cognitive ethology 4:34a
Cohen, Stanley 14:196b
Cohen-Tannoudji 14:196c
Cohong *see* Hong
coho salmon 4:72b
coin, coinage *see* money
Coit, Margaret L. 20:126a
coke *see* coal
Coke, Sir Edward
   biography 14:65b
col 8:38c
COLA *see* cost of living adjustment
Colbert, Jean Baptiste 19:42c, 21:43b, 26:35a-b
cold *see* climate; weather
cold, common 6:79c
cold-blooded animals 4:27b
cold front *il* 8:54, 8:54b-c
Cold War 21:66a-b, 21:68a, 26:10c, 26:91c
   Africa 21:73b-c
   China 21:69a
   Europe 21:66c
   Latin America 21:74c, 21:75b, 28:8b-c
   Soviet Union 26:91c
   U.S. 27:60a-c
   Vietnam 21:70c
Cole, Thomas 19:62c
Coleman, James 15:28c, 15:39a

Coleridge, Samuel Taylor 20:28a-b, 20:29b, 20:86a
   biography 14:65b
   "Christabel" 20:123b
   "Kubla Khan" 20:85c
   Lyrical Ballads 20:117a
   "Rime of the Ancient Mariner" 20:56c, 20:89a, *il* 20:107, 20:108a
   romanticism 20:109b
   Wordsworth 14:183a-b
Coles, Robert 20:127c
Colet, John 20:18a
Colette, Sidonie Gabrielle 20:41b
   Cheri 20:41b
   Gigi 20:41b
   The Innocent Wife 20:41b
Colfax, Schuyler 27:46c
coliform index 9:60c
Colishaw, Raymond 27:182b
colitis 6:79b
collagen 6:37b-c, 6:79b-c, 7:27b
collard 11:59a
collateral 12:8a
collective bargaining 12:32b-33a, 12:74b
   Labor-Management Services Administration 13:73a
colleges and universities 13:24a
   see also names of specific schools
   finances *tab* 13:27
   state and land-grant 13:28a
collenchyma *see* tissue (bot.)
Collett, Camilla
   Governor's Daughters 20:34c
Collins, Michael 27:62c
Collins, William 20:25c
Collodi *see* Lorenzini, Carlo (Collodi)
colloid 6:79c, 7:47a
Collor de Mello, Fernando 28:18a
Cologne (Ger.) 26:144c-145a
Colombia 28:20c-22c
   agriculture 28:6c, 28:21a
   climate 28:20c-21a
   contemporary 28:22c
   drug trade 28:7a, 28:22c
   economy 28:21a, 28:22c
   government 28:21b-c
   history 21:63b, 28:21c-22c
     era of conflict 28:22b
     independence 28:22a-b
     Panama Canal 27:50b-c
     reforms 28:22b-c
     Spanish era 28:22a
   land 28:20c-21a
   map 28:21
   Panama 27:232a
   people 28:21a
   religion 28:22b
   trade 28:21b
   U.S. 21:63b, 27:50b-c
Colombo (Sri Lanka) 23:66a
Colombo Plan 25:23a, 23:71a
colon (anatomy)
   cancer 6:12b-c, 6:14b
   sigmoidoscopy 6:91b
colon (lang.) 16:16a, 17:143, *tab* 17:146-147
Colón (Panama) 27:205b, 27:231b
colonial (bot.) 11:9b
colonoscopy 6:79c

color 10:34c-35a
   see also light; spectrum
   additive process *il* 10:34, 10:34c-35a
   mineral 8:10c
   photosynthesis and 11:22b
   subtractive process *il* 10:34, 10:35a
   television *see* television
Colorado 27:106a-107b
   cities 27:107a
   climate 27:107a
   economy 27:93a, 27:107b
   flag 27:75
   land 27:106a
   map 27:92
   people 27:107b
   places of interest 27:107b
Colorado Plateau 8:46c, 27:106a, 27:130a, 27:142c
Colorado River 27:6b, 27:90c, 27:104a, 27:269a, 27:270c, 28:40c
Colorado Springs (Colo.) 27:107a-b
Colosseum *see* Rome (Italy), Colosseum
Colossus of Rhodes 21:5
colostomy 6:79c
Colter, John 27:148b
Columbia, Mt. (Canada) 27:202a
Columbia (S.C.) 27:139a
Columbia (space shuttle) 5:47c, 5:52a, 5:53c, 5:56a-b
Columbia Broadcasting System (CBS) 27:54a
Columbia Plateau 8:46b-c
Columbia River 27:91b, 27:145a, 27:146b, 27:165b, 27:269a
Columbia University
   anthropology department 15:48a
columbine 11:44c
Columbus, Bartholomew 27:241a
Columbus, Christopher *il* 14:65, *il* 27:234
   biography 14:65b-c
   discoveries and explorations 20:17a, 27:15c-16a
     Bahamas 27:16a, 27:236a
     Costa Rica 27:219b
     Cuba 27:238c
     Dominica 27:240c
     Dominican Republic 27:241b
     Grenada 27:243a
     Hispaniola 27:16a, 27:244a
     Honduras 27:223b
     Jamaica 27:246a
     Nicaragua 27:230a
     Panama 27:231c
     Puerto Rico 27:149c
     St. Kitts and Nevis 27:247b
     St. Vincent and the Grenadines 27:248c
     Trinidad and Tobago 27:250a
     Venezuela 28:34c
   literature 20:17b
   New World 21:42b
   Spain 26:99a
Columbus (Ohio) 27:134b, 27:255c
coma (astron.) 5:58c
Come Back, Little Sheba *see* Inge, William

Index

bugs and debugging 1:27b-c, 1:42b
flowcharts 1:25a-c, 1:26b
pulsars 5:33a
RAM *see* memory *above*
ROM *see* memory *above*
schoolwork and 1:7a-10c
science and 1:9a-c
security 1:41b-c
social studies and 1:9c-10c
software 1:23a-25c, 1:46b
applications 1:25b-c, 1:29a-40c
educational 1:10b-c
graphics 1:32c-33c
operating system 1:24a-25a, 1:45c
translation 1:25a-b
spreadsheet 1:46c, 2:9b
storage devices 1:20a-21c
magnetic 1:20a-21b
optical 1:21b-c, 1:45c
supercomputers 1:22c
large-scale integrated circuits 2:40c-41a
tapes 1:21a-b
viruses 1:30c, 1:41b, 1:47b
weather forecasting *il* 1:35, 8:59b-c
word processing *see* word processing
Comstock Lode (Nev.) 27:35b, 27:91a, 27:127a
Comte, Auguste 15:24b, 15:38b-c
Conakry (Guinea) 22:36c, 22:72a
Conan Doyle, Sir Arthur *see* Doyle, Sir Arthur Conan
concentration 16:36a-37a
Concepción (Chile) 28:18b, 28:37c
conch 4:49c
conchoidal fracture 8:11a
Concord (Mass.) 27:22c
Concorde *il* 10:60
concrete *il* 2:45
dams 2:10a-b
definition 2:44c-45a
Roman Empire 19:15c
condensation 8:51c
Condition Humaine, La *see* Malraux, André
conditioning *see* learning, animal
condor *il* 4:49, 4:49c
Condorcet, Marie Jean 20:21b, 20:102b
conduction (heat) 10:14b-c, 10:57c
conduction band 10:26a
conductor (electric) 10:21c-22b
see also electrode; semiconductor
cone (anat.) *see* retina
cone (math.) 3:80b, 3:93c-94a
section *il* 3:108, 3:108a-111c
coneflower 11:44c
Confederacy (Confederate States of America) *see* Civil War
Confederation Bridge (Canada) 2:8a, *il* 27:207
Confederation of the Rhine 26:44b
Confessions *see* Augustine, St.; Rousseau, Jean Jacques

Confessions of an English Opium-Eater *see* De Quincey, Thomas
confrontation (zool.) *il* 4:31, 4:31c-32a
Confucianism 20:3a, 20:7c-8a, 23:18a, 23:19c
Asia 23:8a
China 21:18c-19b, 21:36c
Four Books 23:71b
Korea 23:37c
Confucius (K'ung Fu'tzu) *il* 14:66, 20:3a-b, 21:19a, 23:19a
art 19:69a
biography 14:65c-66a
Five Classics 20:3a, 23:71b
conger eel 4:53c
conglomerate *il* 12:15, 12:15b
conglomerate rock 8:14c, 8:76b
conglomerates 12:49c
Congo, Democratic Republic of the (formerly Zaire) 22:24c-26a
ancient calendar 5:4a
Belgium 26:20a-c
Cold War competition 21:73b-c
economy 22:24c-25a
government 22:25a
history 22:25a-26a
colonial rule 22:25b
independence 22:25b-26a
land 22:24c
map 22:25
people 22:24c
trade 22:25a
Tshombe biography 14:172a
Congo, Republic of 22:26a-27a
economy 22:26b, 22:27a
government 22:26b, 22:27a
history 22:26a-27a
French rule 22:26c-27a
independence 22:27a
land 22:26a
map 22:26
people 22:26b
Congo River 22:8c, 22:77b
Congress (U.S.) *see* United States—Government
Congress of Berlin 13:96b
Congress of Industrial Organizations (CIO) 12:31b, 14:125b
see also American Federation of Labor-Congress of Industrial Organizations
Murray biography 14:131b
Congress of Vienna 21:45a-b, 21:46a, 26:36c
Belgium 26:19c
France 21:45a-b, 21:46b
Germany 26:44b
Italy 26:62b
Luxembourg 26:67c
Netherlands 26:72c
Poland 26:77a
Switzerland 26:104a
Congreve, William 20:107a
biography 14:66a
drama 20:23a
Way of the World 20:122b
coniferous forests *see* forests, coniferous
conifers 11:11b-12c
conjugation (biol.) 6:79c

conjunction (astron.) 5:58c
conjunction (lang.) 16:13b-c, 17:134, 17:137
Connaught, Duke of 13:79a
Connecticut 27:107a-108b
cities 27:108a
climate 27:108a
economy 27:108b
flag 27:75
history 27:101b
early 27:18a
land 27:108a
map 27:101
people 27:107c, 27:108b
places of interest 27:108c
connective tissue 4:20c
Connell, J.H. 4:36b
conquistador 21:42b
Conrad, Joseph 20:32b
biography 14:66a
Heart of Darkness 20:32b, 20:78b
Lord Jim 20:88c
Nostromo 20:32b
Conrad IV (Holy Rom. Emp.) 14:97a
Conrad of Rothenburg 14:96c
consciousness 15:10a-12c
conscription and draft *see* United States, armed forces
Conselheiro, Antônio 28:16c
conservation 9:59c, 15:36a-b
see also air pollution; water, public health and pollution
Conservation Congress (1908) 27:48b-c
forest 9:43a-c
fuel 9:27b-c
Interior Department 13:71c-72b
Justice Department 13:72c
Muir's work 14:131b
resource 9:6a-9c
soil *see* soil conservation
water 9:58c-59c
laws 9:59a
conservation of energy 7:14b, 10:15b-16b
conservation of momentum 10:9a-b
conservation tillage 11:35a
consonants *tab* 16:30
Constable, John 19:50c, 19:52a
constant (physics) 10:57c
Constantine I (King of Greece) 26:52c
Constantine I (Rom. Emp.) 19:17a-c, 21:28a
biography 14:66a-b
Constantine II (King of Greece) 26:53b
Constantine XI (Byzantine Emp.) 21:29c
Constantinople *see* Istanbul
constellation *il* 5:3, *il* 5:6, 5:6b-c
see also galaxy; zodiac
definition 5:59a
zodiac *il* 5:3
Constitution (U.S.) 13:3a-b, 13:5c, 13:22c, 13:31a, 13:58a-68c
amendments *tab* 13:40, 13:40a-c, 13:64a-68c
Congress 13:35b, 13:37b, 13:39c, 13:58a-61a, 13:62a-c

Index

Cosimo I (Grand Duke of Florence) 14:125c
cosine 3:114c-115a
Cos lettuce 11:55a-b
Cosmic Background Explorer (COBE) 5:43a
cosmic background radiation
  see cosmic rays, background radiation
cosmic rays 5:37b-c, 5:59a, 9:19a
  background radiation 5:42c, 5:59a
    black body radiation 5:42c-43a
  origin of 5:37c
cosmic strings 5:43b-c
cosmogony 5:14c, 5:59a
cosmology 5:13b, 5:41a-43c
  age of universe 5:42b-c
  ancient 5:4b-c
  big bang theory 5:4b, 5:42a-b, 5:58b
    primeval atom 5:61c
  closed universe theory 5:41c, *il* 5:42
  cosmic background radiation 5:42c, 5:59a
    black body radiation 5:42c-43a
  definition 5:59a
  extraterrestrial intelligence 5:44a-c
  flat universe 5:41b-c, 5:43b
  geometry of universe 5:42a
    hidden mass 5:42a
  Greek 5:4c
  inflationary universe 5:43a-b
  models 5:4b, 5:41b-c, 5:43b
  modern 5:41b-c
  Olber's paradox 5:41a-b
  open universe theory 5:41c, *il* 5:42
  steady state theory 5:62c
  structure of universe 5:43b-c
Cossacks 26:105a, 26:152a
cost
  fixed 12:76a
  indirect 12:76b
  marginal 12:77a
  production 12:17b-c
  variable 12:79c
Costain, Thomas 27:136b
COSTAR (Corrective Optics Space Telescope Axial Replacement) 5:9b
Costa Rica 27:218c-220a
  agriculture 27:219a
  climate 27:218c
  contemporary 27:219c-220a
  economy 27:219a
  forests 9:43b
  government 27:219b
  history 27:219b-220a
    independence 27:219b
  land 27:218c
  map 27:219
  Nicaragua 27:220a
  Organization of Central American States 13:21b
  Panama 27:219c
  people 27:219a
  trade 27:219a
cost of living adjustment (COLA) 12:32c-33a, 12:74c

cost-push inflation 12:54b, 12:66b
cotangent 3:115a
Côte d'Ivoire 22:27a-c
  climate 22:27b
  economy 22:27b-c
  government 22:27b
  history 22:27b-c
    French rule 22:27b-c
    independence 22:27c
  land 22:27a-b
  map 22:27
  people 22:27b
Coto (Costa Rica) 27:219c
Cotonou (Benin) 22:17b
Cotopaxi, Mt. *il* 28:23
Cotrell, F. 2:6b
cottage tulip 11:76a
cotton *il* 11:45, 11:45a-b
  gin 27:30c
    Whitney biography 14:180b
  U.K. *il* 12:34
  U.S.
    history in South 27:30c-31a
Cotton, Charles
  Compleat Angler 20:63c
cottongum 11:76b
cottonmouth moccasin 4:69c
cottonseed oil 11:45a
cottontail *il* 6:64
cottonwood 11:67a
cotyledons 11:26c
cough, bronchial 6:7b-8b
coulomb 10:21b, 10:22b-c
Coulomb, Charles Augustin de 10:21b, 10:22c
  biography 14:67b
Coulomb's law 10:21b
coumarin 2:7c, 2:9a
Council Bluffs (Iowa) 27:116a
Council of Economic Advisers
  see Economic Advisers, Council of
Council of Europe 13:21a, 26:152a
  founding 21:66c
counterglow *see* Gegenschein
Counter Reformation 19:38a-c, 19:39b-40b, 21:41b
  see also Diet of Worms; Edict of Nantes
  Paul III biography 14:137b
counting 3:3a-c, 3:95a-97c
Count of Monte Cristo
  see Dumas, Alexandre (pere)
Country Wife *see* Wycherley, William
couplet *see* poetry
Courbet, Gustave 19:50c, 19:52a, 19:53a
  The Stone Breakers 19:50c
Cournand, André Frédéric 14:192b
court 13:37b-39a, 13:62a-c, 13:119a-127c
  see also jury
  appeals 13:115b, 13:116b
  attorney *see* lawyers
  civil 13:113a, 13:114a
    procedure 13:118a-c
  criminal 13:113a, 13:114a
    procedure 13:116c-117c
  Darrow biography 14:69c
  district 13:116a, 13:122c

  evidence *see* evidence
  federal 13:37b-39a, 13:40a, 13:113a, 13:114c, 13:116a-c
    appeals 13:116b
    district 13:116a
  international *see* Hague, The
  judges 13:36c, 13:37c-38a, 13:39c
  small claims 13:126c
  state 13:113a, 13:114a, 13:115a-c
    general trial courts 13:115a-c
    jurisdiction 13:115a
    minor courts 13:115a
    supreme courts 13:115c
  suit *see* suit
  Supreme Court *see* United States—Government, Supreme Court
  United Kingdom 13:93b
Courtenay, Tom *il* 20:39
courtly love 20:64b-c
Courtois, Bernard 2:7c
courtship (zool.) *il* 4:32, 4:32a-b
Cousteau, Jacques-Yves *il* 14:67
  biography 14:67b
covalent network solids 7:15c-16a
cover cropping (green manuring) 9:45b, 9:47a, 9:61c
Coverdale, Miles
  biography 14:67b
Coverley, Sir Roger de *see* Addison, Joseph, *Spectator*; Steele, Richard, *Spectator*
cow *see* cattle; dairy
Cowan, Clyde 10:40c
Coward, Noel 20:46a
  biography 14:67c
cowbird 4:50b
cow lily 11:77c
cowslip *il* 11:45, 11:45b
Cox, Archibald 27:67a-b
coyote 4:37a, *il* 4:50, 4:50b
Cozzens, James Gould 20:127a
CPI *see* consumer price index
CPU *see* central processing unit
crab 4:8c, *il* 4:50, 4:50b-c
  see also horseshoe crab
crab apple 11:37a
crab louse 4:63c
Crab nebula 5:32b-c
Crab pulsar 5:12c
crab shell pesticide 9:48a-b
Cracow *see* Kraków
Craig, Sir James 27:166c
Cram, Donald J. 14:197a
Cranach, Lucas 19:36c
cranberry 11:45b-c
Crane, Hart 20:47a, 20:48c, 20:89a
  biography 14:67c
  "The Bridge" 20:60a
Crane, Stephen 20:31b
  biography 14:67c
  Maggie: A Girl of the Streets 20:31b
  Red Badge of Courage 14:67c, 20:31b, 20:106c
crane (zool.) 4:50c, *il* 4:51
cranesbill (bot.) 11:49b
Cranmer, Thomas
  biography 14:67c
crash (comp.) 1:43b

Index

Index

Index

Index

factors of production 12:62a-63a, 12:75c
Friedman, Milton 12:66c, *il* 12:67, 12:68c-69a
Galbraith 12:69a-c
glossary of terms 12:73a-79c
Great Depression *see* depression (econ.), 1930s
gross national product *see* gross national product
income *see* income
inflation *see* inflation
Keynesian 12:66c, 12:68a-b, 14:108a-b
macroeconomics 12:63a-b
Malthusian 12:68b-c, 14:121a
Marxian 12:67c
microeconomics 12:63b-c
Myrdal biography 14:132a-b
Nobel Prizes 14:186-199
objectives 12:64a-c
price stability 12:65b-66c
production *see* production
Smith, Adam 12:66c-67b, *il* 12:67, 12:71a, 12:72a, 14:160b
systems 12:69c-72c
taxation *see* tax
theory 12:66c-69c
trade *see* international trade
unemployment *see* employment
wage-price controls *see* price; wages
economies of scale 12:17b, 12:75b
ecosystem 4:35a, *il* 6:65, 6:81a, 9:4a-c, 9:61a
biomes 4:35a-36b, 11:28a-30c
clasifications 6:64c-66c
consumers 9:4b
decomposers 9:4b
ecological units 6:61a-64b
energy flow 6:62b-c
food chains *il* 6:62, 6:62c-63c
people and 9:4b-c
plant 11:27a-28a, *il* 11:28
biomes 11:28a-30c
classification of 11:28a
producers 9:4b
ultraviolet radiation 9:29c-30a
Ecuador 28:23a-24c
agriculture 28:24a
contemporary 28:24c
economy 28:23b-24a, 28:24c
government 28:24a-b, 28:24c
history 28:24b-c
independence 28:24b-c
land 28:23a-b
map 28:23
people 28:23b
trade 28:23c-24a
Eddas (Scan. lit.) 20:70b
Eddington, Sir Arthur
biography 14:75b
Eddy, Mary Baker
biography 14:75b-c
Eddystone Lighthouse (Eng.) 2:4a
Edel, Leon 20:126a
Edelman, Gerald M. 14:194b
edelweiss *il* 11:47, 11:47b
edema (dropsy) 2:5a, 6:11a, 6:81a
Eden, Garden of (bib.) 20:70b-c

Eden, Sir Anthony 26:134a-b
biography 14:75c
Edgeworth, Maria 20:28c
Castle Rackrent 20:28c
Ediacran Hills (Australia) 8:22c
Edict of Nantes 21:41b, 26:34c, 26:35b
Edinburgh (Scot.) 26:145a
architecture 19:54c
Edison, Thomas Alva 15:18c
biography 14:75c
electric generation station 2:6b
incandescent lamp 2:6b, 27:45b
microphone 27:45b
phonograph 27:45b
telegraph 27:45a
Edmonton (Canada) 27:199c, 27:202a, 27:256b
Edmund (Crouchback; Earl of Lancaster) 26:114b
Edmund (Earl of Richmond) 26:115a
Edmund of Langley 26:115a
Edo *see* Tokyo
EDSAC (comp.) 2:9b
education 13:23c-24a, 13:28a, 13:31a
see also colleges and universities; Head Start
Canada 27:155c
computers *see* computers, schoolwork and
grammar *see* grammar
Mann 14:121a
Montessori 14:129b
prayer *tab* 13:39
reading *see* reading
segregation *tab* 13:39, 15:28b-c, 15:60c
teachers
NEA 12:31b
U.K. 12:45a-b
U.S. 15:28a-c, 15:59a-60b, 27:13b
Education Department 13:70c-71a
writing *see* writing
Education, Department of (U.S.) 13:70c-71a
Edward I (King of England) 13:85b, 26:113a, 26:117b
Edward II (King of England) 13:93b, 26:125a-b
Edward III (King of England) 26:34b, 26:114b, 26:115a, 26:117b-118b
Edward IV (King of England) 26:114b, 26:115a, 26:119a
Edward V (King of England) 26:115a
Edward VI (King of England and Ireland) 26:115a, 26:119b
Edward VII (King of England and Ireland) 26:116b, 26:125a-b, 26:127a
biography 14:75c
Edward VIII (King of England) *see* Windsor, Duke of
Edwards, Jonathan
biography 14:75c-76a
Edward the Confessor (King of England) 26:111b-c
Westminster Abbey 2:4a

EEC *see* European Economic Community
eel 4:53b-c, *il* 4:53
lamprey *see* lamprey
efficiency 10:58a, 12:62b-c, 12:64c
effluent 9:61a-b
EFTA *see* European Free Trade Association
Egbert of Wessex 26:111a
egg (ovum) *il* 6:33
eggs
cholesterol 6:15a
egret 4:59b, *il* 6:60
Egypt 22:28c-30b
agriculture 22:29a
Alexander the Great 19:9a
ancient 15:46a, 21:5b-6c, 22:29b-c
gold figure *il* 2:5
hieroglyphics 21:5c, *il* 21:6
Ikhnaton biography 14:100c-101a
Khufu biography 14:108c
Middle Kingdom 21:6b
New Kingdom 21:6c
Old Kingdom 21:6a-b
Palestine 24:11b-c
religion 21:5c-6a
Tutankhamen biography 14:172c
unification 21:5b-6a
architecture 19:7c-9a, 19:15c, 21:6b
art 19:7a-9a, 19:11a, 19:17c, 19:21a, 21:6b
Assyria 19:9a
astronomy 5:3a-5c
Byzantine Empire 19:9a
calendar 5:4a-b
climate 22:29a
contemporary 22:30b
cosmology 5:4b-c
economy 21:52b, 22:29a-b, 22:30a-b
Faruk I biography 14:79b
government 13:7c, 22:29b
history 21:52b, 21:62c, 22:29b-30b
ancient *see* ancient *above*
European influence 22:29c-30a
Islam 21:88a, 22:29c
kingdom of Kush 21:34a-b
republic 22:30a
United Arab Republic 22:30a-b
Islamic civilization 19:9a
Israel 13:20c, 21:71b-72b, 22:30a-b, 24:12b-c
see also Israeli-Arab conflict
Camp David accords 21:72b, 21:90c, 27:68b
land 22:28c-29a
language 18:6a
Libya 22:42a
literature 20:3a, 21:6b
map 22:29
mathematics 3:71c
Mubarak biography 14:204b
mummies 19:7c
Nasser biography 14:133a
people 22:29a
Persia 19:9a, 19:10c
pharaohs 19:7c, 18:8c, *il* 19:9, 19:9a, *il* 13:7, 13:7c

Index

Index

Index

Index

Index

Index

Index

Index

Index

H

Index

Index

Index

human development *see* adult development; children and youth; infancy
Human Genome Project 6:54a-b, 7:26c
humanism
  psychology 15:5c
  Renaissance 21:40a-b
human rights 13:21a
  see also specific countries, subhead government
Humayun (Mongol chieftain) 23:26c
Humbert II (King of Italy) 26:63c
Humboldt, Alexander 15:46b
  biography 14:99b
Humboldt, Wilhelm 14:99b
Humboldt Current 28:5a
Hume, Allan Octavian 23:27b
Hume, David 20:22a, 20:25b, 20:26b, 20:102b
  biography 14:99b
  History of England 20:25b
Hume, John 14:196a
humid continental climate
  il 8:63, 8:64b-c
humidity
  definition 8:52a
  measurement of 8:52a-b
  relative 8:52a
humid subtropical climate 8:63c-64a
hummingbird *il* 4:60, 4:60b-c
humor *see* comedy
humoral immunity 6:84a
humours 20:82b
Humperdinck, Engelbert
  Hansel and Gretel 20:78a-b
Humphrey, Hubert Horatio
  il 14:99, 27:62a, 27:63c, 27:65c
  biography 14:99c-100a
humus 8:77b, 9:44c
Hunchback of Notre Dame *see* Hugo, Victor
Hundred Days *see* Napoleon I
Hundred Years' War 21:92b, 26:114b, 26:115a, 26:117c
  Battle of Agincourt 21:90a
  France 26:34b
  Joan of Arc 14:103b
Hungarian language 18:6b, 20:33c
Hungarian Plain 26:95a
Hungary 26:53c-56c
  agriculture 26:54b
  climate 26:54a
  Croatia 26:24b-25a
  Czechoslovakia 26:25b-c
  Dual Monarchy 26:55c-56a
  economy 13:12a, 26:54b, 26:56b
  industry 26:54b
  government 13:12a, 21:67c, 26:54b-c
  history 26:54c-56c
    see also Austro-Hungarian Empire
    Austrian rule 26:55b-c
    Communist rule 26:56b-c
    Franz Josef biography 14:81b-c
    Hapsburgs 14:91b
    Hunyadi, János 26:55a
    kingdom 26:54c

  liberalism and nationalism 21:46b-c
  Ottoman era 26:55a-b
  regency 26:56a-b
  Soviet Union 21:67a-b, 26:92b
  land 26:53c-54a
  literature 20:34a, 20:40b-c
  map 26:53
  natural resources 26:54b
  people 26:54a-b
  Slovakia 26:95b-96a
  trade 26:54b
  World War I 26:55c
  World War II 26:56a-b
  Yugoslavia 26:140c
Hunley (ship) 2:24c
Huns
  China 21:19b-c
  Germany 26:42b
  India 21:18c, 21:36a, 23:26b
  Roman Empire 19:19a, 21:16c
Hunt, Leigh 14:106c
  biography 14:99b-c
Hunt, Timothy 14:198b
hunting
  endangered species 9:6c
  hunter-gatherer societies 15:48c, *il* 15:49
Hunyadi, János 26:55a
Huron, Lake 27:271a
Huron (N. Am. Ind.)
  Canada 27:135c, 27:158c, 27:159b-c
Huronia (Canada) 27:159c
hurricane 8:55b-56c, *il* 8:56, *tab* 8:58
  eye 8:55b-c
  names 8:56c
  power of 8:56b-c
  stages 8:56a-b
Hurricane David 27:242b
Hurricane Gilbert 27:247a
Hurtado, Osvaldo 28:24c
Hus, John 20:15a, 26:25c
  biography 14:99c
Husak, Gustav 26:27a
Husayn, Abdullah ibn al- (Emir) 24:13b-c
Husayn, Sharif 24:19a
Husaynid dynasty 22:66b
husbandry *see* agriculture; animals, breeding
Hu Shih 20:37c
Hussein, Haja Muhammad 22:58a
Hussein, Saddam 21:76b-85c, *il* 21:77, *il* 21:85, 24:10a-b
  biography 14:203a
Hussein (King of Jordan) *il* 24:13, 24:13c-14a
  biography 14:99c-100a
Hussites 26:95b, 26:154b
Hutchinson, Anne
  biography 14:100a
Hutchinson, Millar 2:7a
Hutton, James 4:14a-b, 8:3c, 8:16b-c
Hutu (people) 22:19b-20a, 22:53c, 22:75c
  Rwanda 22:54a
Huxley, Aldous
  biography 14:100a
  Brave New World 20:60a
  Point Counter Point 20:104a
Huxley, Andrew Fielding 14:192b

Huxley, Sir Julian
  biography 14:100a
Huxley, Thomas Henry *il* 14:100
  biography 14:100a-b
Huygens, Christiaan 10:3b-c
  biography 14:100b
  pendulum clock 2:5b
  Saturn's moon 5:22c
  Saturn's rings 5:22a-b
Hwang He River *see* Huang He River
hyacinth 11:52a
Hyades (constellation) 5:30a, 5:36c
Hyatt, John Wesley 2:39a
hybrid (zool.) *see* animals, breeding
  plant 11:34b-c, 11:35c
Hyde, Edward (Earl of Clarendon) 20:22a
  History of the Rebellion 20:22a
hydrangea 11:52a
hydration 2:38c, 8:34a
hydraulic action 8:35b-c
hydrocarbon 7:24a-26c, 9:19c, 9:21c, 9:61c
hydrocephalus 6:84a
hydrochloric acid (muriatic acid) 2:5c
hydrochlorofluorocarbons (HCFCs) 9:30a
hydroelectric power 2:16a-c, 9:9a
  Canada *il* 12:51, 12:51c-52a, 27:153b, 27:186c
  Costa Rica 27:192a-b
  Nigeria 22:52c
  Norway 26:73c
  turbines and waterwheels 2:16a
  Uganda 22:67b
  U.S.
    first dam to produce 2:6b
    TVA *see* Tennessee Valley Authority
    Washington State 27:145c
hydrofoil 2:6b
hydrogen 6:84a, 7:34a-c
  atmosphere 6:34b-c
  atomic reactions 7:15c-16c
  atomic structure *il* 7:10, 10:37a
  discovery of 2:5c
  exosphere 8:50b
  fuel cells 2:19a-b, 7:22b-c
  manufacture 2:7c
  nuclear fusion 2:15b-c
hydrogenation 2:38b
hydrogen bomb 2:8b, 2:15b-c, 27:61c
  Teller biography 14:167c
hydrologic cycle *il* 6:63, 8:51b-53c
hydrolysis 8:34b-c
hydronephrosis 6:84b
hydropathy 2:7a
hydrophobia *see* rabies
hydroponics *il* 11:35, 11:35a
hydrosphere 8:31a-b, 8:65a-75c
  groundwater 8:65a-66b
  lakes 8:66b-67a
  oceans *see* ocean
  streams 8:66b
hydrotropism 11:24a
hydroxyl radical 7:47b

Index

Index

Index

Index

Index

L

Index

Index

Index

Index

Index

Index

metallurgy
Renaissance 19:26b
metalmark (butterfly) 4:45c
metamorphic rock *il* 8:15, 8:15a-16b, *il* 8:16
dating 8:18b
foliated 8:15b
nonfoliated 8:15b
metamorphism (geol.) 8:15a, 8:15b-16b, 8:47c-48a
Metamorphoses *see* Ovid (Publius Ovidius Naso)
Metamorphosis (story) *see* Kafka, Franz
metamorphosis (zool.) 4:9b, *il* 4:22, 4:22c-23b
metastasis 6:86a
Metaxas, Ioannes 26:53a
Metcalfe, Charles Theophilus 27:171a
Metchnikoff, Elie 14:186b
meteor 5:25b-c
definition 5:60b
showers 5:25a
meteorite 5:25b-c, 5:60b
mass extinction theory 4:11a
meteoroid 5:25b-c, 5:60b
meteorology *see* weather forecasting
methane 7:24b, 7:25c, 9:25b-c, 9:62a
methanol 9:21c
Methodism
Wesley biographies 14:179b-c
Métis 27:152a, 27:159b, 27:169c, 27:178b-c, 27:180a, 27:213b
metric system *see* measurement, metric
metropolitan areas *see* city
Metternich, Clemens Wenzel Nepomuk 21:45b, 21:46b, 26:16b
biography 14:126b-c
Germany 26:44b
Meung, Jean de
Roman de la Rose 20:11c
Meuse River (Belgium) 26:155b, 27:52b
Meuse River valley (Belgium) 9:10c
Mexican War 21:55b, 27:34c-35a
Mexico 27:224b-228c
see also Aztecs; Maya civilization
agriculture 27:215c, 27:225b-c
climate 27:215a, 27:225a
contemporary 27:228b-c
economy 21:74c-75a, 27:225b-226b, 27:228c
industry 27:215c, 27:225c-226a
forests 27:215a
government 27:226b, 27:227b-c
history 21:54c-55c, 27:226b-228c
civil strife 27:228a-b
Cortés biography 14:67a-b
Diaz 14:72a-b, 27:227c-228a
Hidalgo y Costilla biography 14:95a
independence 27:226c-227b
Iturbide biography 14:101b
Juárez biography 14:105c
Maximilian biography 14:124a

Montezuma II biography 14:129b
Olmecs 21:35a
Pancho Villa biography 14:175b-c
reform 27:227a-b, 27:228a
Santa Anna biography 14:154b
Spanish rule 21:54c, 27:226c
Zapata biography 14:185a
labor 21:64a
Article 123 27:268b-c
land 21:64a, 27:214b-c, 27:224b-225a
ejido system 27:228b
languages 27:224b
map 27:224
natural resources 27:225b
people 27:225a-b
revolution 27:227b-c
rivers 27:215a
trade 27:9a-b, 27:226b-c, 27:228c
free trade agreement 27:71a
U.S. 27:50c-51a, 27:227a-b
see also Mexican War
Gadsden Purchase 27:37b-c
Texas 27:34b-c
Wilmot Proviso 27:36b
World War I 27:51b
World War II 27:228c
Mexico City (Mexico) 27:225b, 27:226b, 27:259b
climate 8:60a
Meyer, Lothar
periodic table 7:7c
Meyerhof, Otto Fritz 14:188b
Miami (Fla.) 27:110c
waste disposal 9:36c
mica
properties 8:12c, *tab* 8:13
Michael (King of Romania) 26:82a
Michael III (Byzantine Emp.) 21:29a-b
Michael VIII (Byzantine Emp.) 14:29c
Michael Romanov (Czar of Russia) 14:150a, 26:86c
Michael the Brave 26:81a
Michel, Hartmut 14:197a
Michel, Helen 4:11a
Michelangelo (Buonarroti) *il* 14:126, 19:31a-32b, 19:36c, 19:39c-40a, 19:41b, 19:55b-c, 21:40a
biography 14:126b-127a
David il 19:31, 19:31a-b, 19:39b
literature 20:16b
Pietà 19:31a
St. Peter's 2:4a, 19:32a, *il* 19:38
Sistine Chapel 14:126c-127a, *il* 19:32, 19:31c-32a, 19:40a, 21:40b
Michelson, Albert Abraham 14:187a
speed of light 10:29c
Michener, Daniel Roland *tab* 13:75
Michener, James 20:127a
biography 14:127a
Michigan 27:122a-123a
cities 27:122b-c
climate 27:122b

economy 27:122c
flag 27:79
land 27:122b
map 27:96
people 27:122c
places of interest 27:123a
Michigan
Lake 27:272b
Mickiewicz, Adam 20:33c
MICR (magnetic ink character reader) 1:17a
microbe 6:86a
microbiology *tab* 6:51
microcomputer *see* computers, microcomputer
microdose digital radiography (DR) 6:27a-c, 6:86a
microeconomics *see* economics, microeconomics
microelectronics *see* computers, microcomputer
microelements 11:21b
microfilament 6:40b
microfilm and microfiche 2:36c, 17:47
micrometer 2:5b
Micronesia 25:6a, 25:13b-14a, 27:150c-151a
economy 25:14a
government 25:14a
history 21:51a, 25:14a
land 25:13b-c
map 25:13
people 25:13c
microorganism 4:7c, 6:86a
spontaneous generation theory 6:33a-c
microphone 27:45b
microprocessor *see* computers, microcomputer
microscope 6:86a
achromatic 2:7a
compound 2:5a
early uses 4:13a-b
electron 2:8b, *il* 6:36, 10:25c
light *il* 6:36
Microsoft Corporation 12:14a-b, 14:202b
microsurgery *see* surgery
microtubule 6:40b
Microwave Observing Project 5:44c
microwaves
see also maser
radio 2:32a-b
relay system 2:33c-34a
telephone 2:34a
television 2:33a, 2:34a
Midas (myth.) 20:92b
mid-Atlantic ridge 8:7b, 8:78a-b
Mid-Atlantic states 27:100a-c
cities 27:100b-c
climate 27:100a
economy 27:100c
history 27:100b
land 27:100a
map 27:100
people 27:100c
mid-channel bar 8:36c
Middle Ages 21:28a
see also Anglo-Saxons; Crusades
art 19:19a-24c
Byzantine Empire 21:28a-29c
cities 19:22c-23a

Index

Index

Morrison, Toni 20:49a, 20:127a
  biography 14:204b
  Nobel Prize 14:197b
Morrison formation 8:28b-c
Morse, Samuel Finley Breese
  il 14:130
  biography 14:130b
  telegraph 2:7b, 27:45a
mortar 8:47a-b
Morte d'Arthur *see* Malory,
  Thomas
mortgage 12:53c, 13:115a
  bonds 12:8c
  definition 12:77b
  loans 12:8c
  types of 12:78b-c
Mortimer's Cross, Battle of
  26:114b
mosaics
  Byzantine 19:18b-c, 19:20c,
    19:25a
  Christian 19:17b-c, 19:18b-c
Moscow (Russia) 14:101b,
  26:83a, 26:147a
  history 21:43c, 26:85c-86a
  industry 26:85a
  population 26:83b
  St. Basil's Cathedral *il* 26:83
Moscow Art Theater 14:162b
Mosel, Tad
  All the Way Home 20:66a
Moseley, Henry Gwyn-Jeffreys
  biography 14:130b-c
Moses 21:9c, 21:32b
  bulrushes 11:41a
Moses, Grandma *il* 14:130
  biography 14:130c
Moshoeshoe II (King of
  Lesotho) 22:39b
Moslem League *see* Muslim
  League
Moslems *see* Islam; Islamic
  civilization
Mosquito (Central Am. Ind.)
  27:229a
mosquito (zool.) 4:65b-c
  diseases spread by 2:7a, 4:65c
moss *il* 11:10, 11:10a
  club *see* club moss
  early 11:4c
  Spanish *see* Spanish moss
Mossadegh, Mohammad 24:8c
Mössbauer, Rudolf Ludwig
  14:193a
Mossi (people) 22:18c-19a
moss verbena 11:76c
Mostar (Bosnia and
  Herzegovina) 26:21a
most-favored-nation clause
  12:77b
moth 4:46a, 4:47b, 4:65c
motherboard *il* 1:12, 1:12b-c,
  il 10:26
Mother Carey's chickens *see*
  stormy petrel
**Mother Courage and Her
  Children** *see* Brecht,
  Bertolt
Mother Goose's Melody
  20:94a
Mother Teresa
  biography 14:206b
  Nobel Prize 14:194a
motion, laws of *il* 10:5
  first (inertia) 10:5b
  second (force) 10:5b-c

  third (action and reaction)
    10:5c-6a
motion pictures
  see cinematography; names of
    actors, actresses, and
    directors
  Coppola biography 14:201c
  Disney biography 14:72c-73a
  Griffith biography 14:88b-c
  Lee, Spike, biography 14:203c
  Spielberg biography 14:206b
motor, electric 2:22a-c, 2:45b
  see also generator, electric
  alternating-current *il* 2:22,
    2:22c
    basic 2:22c
    induction 2:22c
  direct-current *il* 2:22,
    2:22a-c
    compound 2:22b-c
    series 2:22b-c
    shunt 2:22b
    universal 2:22c
  invention 2:6b
motor oil 9:36b
Motorola (co.) 2:9b
motor vehicles *see* automobiles;
  bus; trucks
Mott, John Raleigh 14:190a
Mott, Nevill F. 14:194c
Mottelson, Ben 14:194c
mount *see* names inverted, e.g.,
  Everest, Mount
Mount, William Sidney 19:63a
mountain 8:42c-45b
  see also specific mountains
  Africa 22:8b-c
  climate 8:61c, *il* 8:62
  fault-block 8:44b-45a
  folded 8:45b, *il* 8:47
  Middle East 24:3b
  oceanic 8:45a-b
  undersea *see* guyot; seamount
  volcanic 8:43a-44b, *il* 8:44,
    il 8:45
mountain ash 11:58b
mountain bluebird 4:44c
mountain cranberry 11:45c
mountain dogwood 11:47b
mountain gorilla 4:57b
mountain laurel 11:58b
mountain lion 4:46c
mountain quail 4:71a
mountain sheep *see* bighorn
Mountain states 27:92a-93b
  cities 27:93a
  climate 27:93a
  economy 27:93a-b
  history 27:93a
  land 27:92a-93a
  map 27:92
  people 27:93a
mountain zebra 4:80c
Mountbatten, Louis; 1st Earl of
  Burma 14:130c
Mountbatten, Louis Alexander;
  1st Marquess of Milford
  Haven 14:130c
Mountbatten (family) 14:130c
Mourning Becomes Electra
  see O'Neill, Eugene
  Gladstone
mourning dove 4:69b
mouse (comp.) *il* 1:15, 1:15b-c,
  1:45b
mouse (zool.) *il* 4:65, 4:65c-66a

movement
  animal 4:7b, *il* 4:21
    air 4:22a-b
    land 4:22a
    multicellular organisms 4:7c
    water 4:21b-c
    friction 4:21b
movies *see* cinematography;
  motion pictures
Mowat, Farley
  Canada North 9:15a
Moynihan, Daniel Patrick
  il 15:62, 15:62b
Mozambique 22:48c-50a
  agriculture 22:49a
  climate 22:49a
  economy 22:49a-b
  forced labor 22:49c-50a
  government 22:49b
  history 22:49b-50a
  land 22:48c-49a
  map 22:49
  people 22:49a
  slavery 21:49a
  trade 22:49a-b
Mozart, Wolfgang Amadeus
  il 14:131
  biography 14:131a
  Don Giovanni 20:20a, 20:68c
  Figaro 20:90c
Mphahlele, Ezekiel 20:46c
Mrs. Dalloway *see* Woolf, Virginia
MS-DOS (operating system)
  1:24c, 12:14a-b
Mswati (Swazi chief) 22:63b
Mswati III (King of Swaziland)
  22:63b
Muang Swa (Laos) 23:40c
Muawed, Rene 24:16b
Mubarak, Hosni 21:72b, 22:30b
  biography 14:204b
Much Ado About Nothing *see*
  Shakespeare, William
muckrakers 20:94a
mucus 6:86b
mud dauber *see* wasp
mudflow *il* 8:41, 8:41c-42a,
  il 8:42
mud hen 4:50a
mud turtle 4:78c
Mueller, Karl Alex 14:196c
Mugabe, Robert 22:69c
Mughals *see* Moguls
Muhammad, Dost 23:12a-b
Muhammad (Mohammed)
  19:72b, 21:32b-c, 21:27a-c,
  24:18c
  see also Islam
  biography 14:131a
  Hegira 21:32c
  Koran *see* Koran
Muhammad II (Ottoman Emp.)
  21:29c
Muhammad V (Muhammad bin
  Yusuf; King of Morocco)
  22:48b-c
Muhammad Ali (boxer) *see* Ali,
  Muhammad
Muhammad Ali (Egyptian
  Muslim) 22:29c
**Muhammad Reza Shah
  Pahlevi** *see* Pahlevi,
  Mohammed Riza (Shah
  of Iran)
Mühlenberg, Henry
  biography 14:131a-b

Index

Index

Index

Index

olfaction *see* smell
oligopoly 12:77b
Olitski, Jules 19:59b
olive 11:60b-c
    see also jasmine; lilac
Olive Branch Petition 27:23b
Oliver Twist *see* Dickens,
    Charles John Huffam
olivine 8:13a
Olmec (S. Am. Ind.) 21:35a
Olmsted, Frederick Law
    biography 14:135b
Olson, Charles 20:48c
Olympic Games 26:50-51
    Greece 19:12a
        satellite 2:35b
    Thorpe biography 14:169a-b
Olympic peninsula (Wash.
        state) 11:28c
    plant life 11:28c, 11:32b
    rain forest 11:28c, 11:32b
Olympio, Sylvanus 22:65b
Olympus, Mount (Gr.) 26:156a
    mythology 20:99a
Olympus Mountains (Cyprus)
        24:6c-7a
Olympus Mountains (Gr.) 26:156a
Omaha (Nebr.) 27:126c
Oman 24:16b-17a
    agriculture 24:16c
    economy 24:16b-c
    government 24:16c
    history 24:16c-17a
    land 24:16b
    map 24:16
    people 24:16b
    trade 24:16c
Omar Khayyám
    biography 14:135b
    Rubáiyát of Omar Khayyám
        il 20:9, 20:9b, 20:109b,
        21:33c
OMB *see* Office of Management
        and Budget
ommatidia 4:28b
omnivores 4:38a
Omo River (Ethiopia) 22:32a
onager 4:41c
oncogenes *see* cancer, oncogenes
oncology *tab* 6:53
One Day in the Life of Ivan
        Denisovich *see*
        Solzhenitsyn, Alexander
One Hundred Associates
        27:159a
onion *il* 11:60, 11:60c
on-line 1:45c
O'Neill, Eugene Gladstone
    biography 14:135b-c
    The Iceman Cometh
        20:47c-48a, *il* 20:82, 20:82c
    Long Day's Journey into
        Night 20:48a, 20:88b
    Mourning Becomes Electra
        20:81c
    Nobel Prize 14:191c, 20:47a
O'Neill, Hugh 26:59b
Onizuka, Ellison S. 5:48b
On Liberty *see* Mill, John Stuart
Onnes, Kamerling 2:7c, 10:28b
    Nobel Prize 14:187a
Onsager, Lars 14:193b
Ontario, Lake 27:273c
Ontario (Canada) 27:206b-207b
    climate 27:200b, 27:206c
    economy 27:200b-c, 27:207a

flag 27:195
government 13:76b,
    13:77c-78c
    seats in Parliament 13:77a
history 27:165b, 27:175c
land 27:200a, 27:206c
map 27:200
people 27:154b, 27:200b,
    27:207a
On the Road *see* Kerouac, Jack
Oort, Jan Hendrik 5:35b
OPACs *see* online public access
        catalogues
Oparin, Alexander I.
    theory of origin of life
        6:34a-c
Oparin-Haldane hypothesis
        6:34a-b
OPEC *see* Organization of
        Petroleum Exporting
        Countries
open corporation 12:14c
open-door policy 21:48c, 21:93c,
        23:73c
open growth (bot.) 11:15a
open-hearth process *see* iron
        and steel
open-market operations
        12:61b, 12:77b-c
opera
    see also names of composers;
        names of singers
    Chinese 20:8a
    German 20:27b
    Italian 20:42a-b
    Paris Opera 19:54c
operant conditioning *see*
        learning
operating system (comp.)
        1:8a-c, *il* 1:24, 1:24a-25a,
        1:45c
ophthalmology *tab* 6:53
ophthalmoscope 2:7a
opinion polls *see* public opinion
Opitz, Martin 20:14c
opium 2:5a, 11:67a-b, 15:12b
    China 23:21a
Opium War 21:48b-c, 21:93c,
        23:21a, 23:73c-74a
Oporto (Port.) *see* Porto
opossum 4:66c, *il* 4:67
Oppenheimer, J. Robert 14:167c
    biography 14:135c
opposite arrangement (bot.)
        11:18a
optical character reader (OCR)
        1:16c, 1:17a
optical disk 1:21b-c, 1:45c
optical interferometer *see*
        interferometer
optical pumping 10:36a-c,
        10:61a-b
optic nerve 2:5a
optics 10:3b, *il* 10:30, *il* 10:31
    see also fiber optics; light
    color 10:34c-35a
    diffraction 10:32c-33a
    dispersion 10:31a
    geometrical 10:30a-32c
    interference *il* 10:32, 10:32c
    laser *see* laser
    lens *see* lens (optics)
    physical 10:32c-35a
    polarization 10:33a-c
    prism *see* prism (optics)
    reflection 10:30a-b

refraction 10:30b-c
Renaissance 19:26b
units 10:33c-34c
optometry *tab* 6:53
oracle (myth.) 20:99b
orange (bot.) *il* 11:61, 11:61a
Orange Free State (S. Afr.)
        21:53b, 22:39b, 22:60b
Orange Order 27:180c
Orange River (S. Afr.)
        22:59a
orangutan 4:34b, 4:41b,
        il 4:67, 4:66c-67a
Orbegosa, Luis José 28:29c
orbit (astron.) 5:61a
    see also planet, orbit; specific
        celestial bodies
    revolution 5:62a
orbit (chem.)
    electrons 7:10b-11b
orchestra *see* music, orchestra
Orchidaceae *see* orchid
        family
orchid family 11:13a, 11:16c,
        il 11:61, 11:61a-b
orchis 11:61b
Ordeal of Richard Feverel *see*
        Meredith, George
order (bot.) 11:8b
order (zool.) 4:15b, 4:16a
order of magnitude 3:158b
Order of the Garter 26:121a-b
ordinance (law) 13:125c
Ordinance of Nullification
        (S.C.) 27:32c
Ordinance of 1787 *see*
        Northwest Ordinance
ordinate (math.) 3:63c
Ordovician period 8:20b,
        il 8:23, 8:23a-c
    fossils 8:23b-c
ore
    see also mining
    metal 8:45c-47a
    smelting and casting 2:4b
Oregon 27:136a-137a
    agriculture 27:136c
    cities 27:136b
    climate 27:136b
    economy 27:136c-137a
    flag 27:83
    history 27:92a, 27:136b-c
    land 27:91a-c, 27:136a-b
    map 27:91
    people 27:136b-c
    places of interest 27:137a
Oregon Territory 27:34a-b,
        27:172a-b, 27:179b
Oregon Trail 27:34a, 27:92a,
        27:136b, 27:274a
Oregon Treaty (1846) 27:34b
Oresteia (drama) *see* Aeschylus
organ (zool.) 4:20c
organelle 4:20a, 6:87a,
        11:14b-c
organic chemistry 7:24a-26c,
        tab 7:25
organic farming 9:48a
organic waste 9:36c
organism 6:34c-35c, 6:87a
    see also microorganism
    classification of 6:43a
organizational theory 12:20a-b
Organization of African Unity
        (OAU) 13:20b-c, 22:13b-c,
        22:76b

Index

P

Index

Index

Index

Index

China 21:47c, 21:48c
climate 26:78b
colonies and dependencies
21:42b, 21:42c, 21:54a,
21:54c, 21:94c, 22:70b
Africa 21:73a-b
Angola *see* Angola *above*
Cape Verde *see* Cape Verde
above
Macao 23:67a
EC membership 13:21a
economy 26:78b-c
EEC 13:67a
Ethiopia 22:32c
exploration 13:42a-b, 26:79a
government 13:67a, 26:78c
Guinea-Bissau 22:37b-c
history 26:78c-80a
Avis dynasty 26:79a
Bragança dynasty 26:79a-b
early exploration 27:15c
republic 26:79b-80a
Japan *il* 21:48, 21:49b
land 26:78a-b
literature 20:12c, 20:17b,
20:20b, 20:42c
map 26:78
Mozambique 22:49b-50a
people 26:78b
Salazar biography 14:153c
São Tomé and Principe 22:54c
Seven Years' War *see* Seven
Years' War
Southeast Asia 21:50c
Spain 26:99a-b
Tanzania 22:64b-c
trade 21:42a-b, 26:78c
World War I 26:79b
Portuguese Guinea *see* Guinea-
Bissau
Portuguese man-of-war
(zool.) 4:16c, 4:70b
Poseidon (myth.) 20:104c
positron 7:48a
**positron emission
tomography** (PET) 2:27c-
28a, *il* 6:88, 6:88c
possessive adjectives 16:13a,
17:134
possessives (lang.) 16:12b-13a,
17:134
plural 16:12c
singular 16:12b-c
possum *see* opossum
Post, Emily *il* 14:143
biography 14:143a
Post, Wiley
biography 14:143a-b
postal service 13:35a
abbreviations *tab* 16:20
Postel, Sandra 9:50b
postmortem 2:5a
Postojna Caves 26:96b
Postum Company 2:9c
posture 6:5a
potassium 6:88c, 7:37a-c, 8:47b
body requirement *tab* 6:22
discovery 2:7c
potato 11:67b
see also sweet potato
carbohydrates 6:14a
potato family *see* belladonna;
jimsonweed; mandrake;
nightshade; petunia;
potato
pot marigold 11:57c

Potok, Chaim 20:49b
Potsdam Conference 27:58c
Germany 26:46c
pottery *see* ceramics
Pott's disease 6:88c
Poulenc, Francis
biography 14:143b
poultry
cholesterol 6:15b
Pound, Ezra 20:32b, 20:45a-b,
20:47a
biography 14:143b
Cantos 20:61a
Personae 20:32b
Poundmaker (Ind. chief)
27:180a
Poussin, Nicolas 19:43a-b
Burial of Phocian il 19:43,
19:43a-b
poverty 15:33a-b, 15:61b-63c
Powell, Anthony 20:46b
Powell, Cecil Frank 14:191a
Powell, Colin Luther *il* 14:205
biography 14:205a
Powell, Lake 27:142c
Powell, Lewis F., Jr. 27:70a
Powell vs. Alabama *tab* 13:39
power (math.) *see* exponent
power (mechanics) 10:8b
electric *see* electricity
nuclear *see* nuclear power
Power and the Glory, The *see*
Greene, Graham
Power, Samantha 19:127c
Powers, Francis Gary 27:61c
power train 2:23b-c, *il* 2:46,
2:46c
Powhatan (Ind. chief) 27:20a,
27:275a
biography 14:143b
Powhatan Confederacy 27:20a,
27:275a
Pozzo, Andrea dal 19:39c
Prague (Czech Republic)
26:25b-c, *il* 26:26, 26:26c-
27a, 26:147c
Praha (Czech Republic) *see*
Prague
Praia (Cape Verde) 22:74a
prairie 11:32c
prairie dog 4:32c, *il* 4:70,
4:70b, 9:6c-7a
prairie falcon 4:54b
Prakrit language
literature 20:9b
praseodymium 2:7c, 7:37a-c
prawn *see* shrimp
Praxiteles 19:14c, 19:27b
prayer *tab* 13:39
praying mantis *il* 4:70, 4:70b-c
Precambrian eon 8:20b, 8:20c-
22c
fossils 8:22a-c
paleobotany 11:4a
rocks 8:20c-22a
precedent (law) 13:126a
precious stone *see* gemstone;
jewelry; names of stones
precipitation 8:52c
see also rain
cloud seeding 8:59c
forms of 8:53a-c
orographic 8:78b
runoff 8:35a
salinity 8:68b
precognition *see* parapsychology

predation 4:37a, 4:37c-38b
predicate (lang.) 16:8c, 16:21b-c,
17:132-133
see also verbs
subject agreement 17:148-149
predicate adjective 16:8c,
17:133
predicate noun 17:133
preemptive right 12:77c
preferred stock 12:9a
prefixes (lang.) *see* vocabulary
Pregl, Fritz 14:189b
pregnancy
amniocentesis *see*
amniocentesis
embryo 2:9a, 6:9c, 6:81a
fetus 6:9c-10b, 6:82a
surgery 2:9a
tests 6:88c
ultrasound 6:10b
Pregnancy Discrimination Act
(1978) 12:27b
prehistory 15:40a-44c
see also Paleolithic period
fossil *see* fossil
Neanderthals *see*
Neanderthals
reptiles *see* dinosaur
rock art *see* rock art
Prelog, Vladimir 14:195a
Prempeh I (King of Ashanti)
22:35a
prepositional phrase 16:13a-b,
17:136
prepositions 16:13a-b, 17:136
Pre-Raphaelite Brotherhood
20:104c
prereading 16:35a
Prescott, William 15:46b
presentment (law) 13:126a
present participle 16:9c, 17:150
president *see* United States—
Government, President;
names of presidents
Presley, Elvis
biography 14:143b
Prespa, Lake 26:68a
press *see* journalism; news
pressure (physics) 10:9c, 10:14a-b
Prestes, Julio 28:17a
prestige *il* 12:23, 12:23c
Pretoria (S. Afr.) 22:59b, 22:74a
Pretorius, Andries
biography 14:143b
Pretorius, Marthinus 14:143b
prevailing westerlies 8:78b
Priam (myth.) 20:104c
price
see also consumer price index
inflation *see* inflation
stability 12:65b-66c
wages and 12:67a-b, 12:68b
price-earnings ratio 12:77c
price-support program 12:77c
prickly-pear (cactus family)
il 11:41, 11:42a
Pride and Prejudice *see*
Austen, Jane
Priessnitz, Vincenz 2:7a
Priestley, Joseph
biography 14:143b-c
oxygen discovered by 2:5c,
7:3a
plants and oxygen 11:6b
Prigogine, Ilya 14:195a
primary (astron.) 5:61b

Index

Index

R

Index

Index

Index

S

Index

Index

Index

Index

sonar 2:46c-47a
  invention 2:7b
Sondheim, Stephen Joshua
  14:206a
Songhai, kingdom of 22:36b
  Mali 22:45a
  Niger 22:51c
Song of Roland *see* Chanson de
  Roland
Song of the Nibelungs *see*
  Nibelungenlied
Songs of Innocence *see* Blake,
  William
song sparrow 4:75a
Sonnets from the Portuguese
  see Browning, Elizabeth
  Barrett
Sonni Ali 21:34c
Sons and Lovers *see* Lawrence,
  David Herbert
Sons of Liberty 27:21b,
  27:22a
Sontag, Susan 14:161a, 20:49a
Sony (co.) 2:9b
Sophocles
  biography 14:161a-b
  drama 21:12c
   Ajax 20:51b
   Antigone 20:5a, *il* 20:53,
    20:53b
   Electra 20:81c
   Oedipus at Colonus 20:5a
   Oedipus Rex 20:5a, 20:53b,
    20:98a
   Philoctetes 20:5a, 20:102a
sorghum 11:72b
  see also broomcorn
Sorrows of Young Werther *see*
  Goethe, Johann Wolfgang
  von
Sosigenes 2:5b
Sostrastos of Cnidos 2:4a
Sotatsu 19:72a
  Poem Scroll with Bamboo
   il 19:71, 19:72a
Sotho (people) 21:53a
  Botswana 22:18b
  Lesotho 22:39b
  South Africa 22:59a
  southern Africa 21:53a
Soto, Bernardo 27:219b
Soto, Hernando (Fernando) de
  see De Soto, Hernando
Soudan *see* Mali
Soufflot, Jacques Germain
  Pantheon 19:48a
Soufrière, Mount 27:249a
sound 10:17a-20c
  acoustics *see* acoustics
  breaking of sound barrier 2:8b
  hearing *see* hearing
  intensity *tab* 10:17, 10:17b-18a
  pitch 10:18a
  reverberation *il* 10:19
  ultrasound *see* ultrasonics
  velocity *tab* 10:17, 10:18a-b
Sound and the Fury, The *see*
  Faulkner, William
sound boards 1:20b-c
sound card (comp.) 1:46b-c
sound recording
  compact disk 2:9b
  digital 10:19b
  Dolby sound 2:9b
  electroacoustics 10:18c-19b
  long-playing record 2:9b

phonograph
  Edison 27:45b
  stereophonic 10:19a-b
  tape recorder 2:7b
sound wave *il* 10:17, 10:17a-18b
  resonance *il* 10:18, 10:18b
sour cherry *see* cherry
Sousa, John Philip *il* 14:161
  biography 14:161b
Souter, David *il* 13:38, 27:70a
  biography 14:206a
South (U.S.)
  agricultural history 27:30c-31a
  Civil War *see* Civil War
  economic history 27:30c-31a
  Reconstruction 27:42b-44c
   economic conditions 27:44b-c
  secession 27:38c-39a
  slavery *see* slavery
  tariff opposition 27:32c
South Africa 13:20c, 22:58c-61a
  agriculture 22:59b-c
  Angola 22:51a-b
  apartheid 21:63a, 21:74b,
   22:44b, 22:60c-61a, 22:75a-b
   end of 22:13c
  Boer War *see* Boer War
  Botha biography 14:54a
  climate of 22:59a
  economy 22:59b-60a
  government 22:60a
  history 22:60b-61a
   British-Boer conflict
    22:60b-c
   Pretorius biography 14:143b
   republic 22:60c-61a
   Rhodes biography 14:147a-b
   Smuts biography 14:160b-c
   union 22:60c
  land 22:58c-59a
  literature
   Paton biography 14:137a
  Luthuli biography 14:118c
  Malawi 22:44b
  Mandela biography 14:204a
  map 22:59
  mining and manufacturing
   22:59c-60a
  Namibia 22:51a-b
  people 22:59a-b
  Swaziland 22:63b-c
  trade 22:60a
  Transvaal *see* Transvaal
  Tutu biography 14:206c
  U.K. 21:63a
South African War *see* Boer War
South America *see* Latin
  America; specific countries
South Asian Association for
  Regional Cooperation
  (SAARC) 23:74b
South Atlantic states 27:98a-c
  cities 27:98c
  climate 27:98c
  economy 27:98c
  history 27:98a, 27:98c
  land 27:98b-c
  map 27:98
  people 27:98c
South Australia 25:9a
South Carolina 27:138c-139b
  cities 27:139a
  climate 27:139a
  economy 27:139a
  flag 27:83
  history 27:98c

  Civil War 27:38c, 27:139a
   early 27:18b-c
  land 27:139a
  map 27:98
  people 27:139a
  places of interest 27:139b
  tariff opposition 27:32c
South-Central states 27:96c-97c
  cities 27:97b-c
  climate 27:97a
  economy 27:07c
  history 27:97a-b
  land 27:97a
  map 27:97
  people 27:96c-97a
South Dakota 27:139b-140b
  agriculture 27:140a
  cities 27:139c-140a
  climate 27:139c
  economy 27:140a
  flag 27:84
  land 27:139c
  map 27:94
  people 27:140a
  places of interest 27:140a-b
Southeast Asia *see* Asia; specific
  countries
Southeast Asian Nations,
  Association of (ASEAN)
  13:20a-b, 21:71a, 23:8b,
  23:10a, 23:70a-b
Southern Colonies (U.S.)
  27:18b-19a
  American Revolution 27:26a-b
  economy 27:20a
  Indian wars 27:20a-b
  slavery 27:20a
Southern Forest (U.S.)
  11:32b
Southern New England
  Telephone Company
  2:34c
Southern Rockies 8:46b
Southern Yemen *see* Yemen
Southey, Robert 14:86a
  biography 14:161b
South Island (New Zealand)
  25:14c-15c, 25:16a
South Korea *see* Korea, South
South Orkney Island *see* British
  Antarctic Territory
South Pacific Commission
  (SPC) 13:20b
South Pacific Forum *il* 13:20,
  13:20b, 25:23b-c
South Pole 8:31b
  Amundsen biography 14:43a
  latitude 8:32c
  magnetic field reversal 8:10a
  Scott expeditions 14:156b
South Shetland Islands *see*
  British Antarctic Territory
South-West Africa *see* Namibia
Southwest states 27:90a-91a
  climate 27:90c
  economy 27:91a
  history 27:90c-91a
  Indians 27:15b
  land 27:90c
  map 27:90
  people 27:90a-b, 27:91a
Souza, Washington Luís Pereira
  de 28:17a
Soviet Union 20:37a
  see also Russia; specific
   former republics

Index

Index

storm *tab* 8:58
  cold front 8:54b-c
  hurricane *see* hurricane
  severe 8:55a-57c
  thunderstorm *see*
    thunderstorm
  tornado *see* tornado
Stormer, Horst L. 14:196c
stormy petrel 4:68c
story writing *il* 16:25, 16:25a-c
Stout, Rex
  biography 14:164a
Stowe, Harriet Elizabeth
  Beecher 20:31b
  biography 14:164a
  Uncle Tom's Cabin 20:31b,
    il 20:119, 20:119c, 27:37a
Strachey, Lytton 20:45c,
  20:59c
  biography 14:164a
  Eminent Victorians 20:59a
  Queen Victoria 20:59a
Stradivari, Antonio
  biography 14:164a
Strait of Magellan 28:42c
Stranger, The *see* Camus, Albert
Strategic Arms Limitation
  Talks (SALT) 13:68a,
  26:92b-c, 27:66c
Strategic Arms Reduction
  Treaty (START) 26:11c,
  26:93a-c, 26:105c, 27:70c
Stratford-on-Avon (Eng.)
  20:114a
stratification (sociology) *see*
  sociology, stratification
stratified drift 8:78c
stratosphere 8:49c
stratus cloud *il* 8:52, 8:53a
Strauss, Johann
  biography 14:164a
Strauss, Richard
  biography 14:164b
Stravinsky, Igor *il* 14:164
  biography 14:164b
streak (mineral.) 8:10c-11a
streak lightning 8:57b
stream 8:66b
  deposition 8:36b-37a
  erosion 8:35b-c
  meanders 8:36c
  transport 8:36a-b
  velocity 8:36c
stream of consciousness (lit.)
  20:114a
Streetcar Named Desire *see*
  Williams, Tennessee
streptococcus 6:92b
streptomycin 2:9a
Stresemann, Gustav
  biography 14:164b
  Nobel Prize 14:188a
stress (physiol.) 4:27b, 4:37b
Stribling, T. S. 20:127a
stress (psych.) 6:26a-c, *il* 15:21,
  15:21a-22a
strike (labor) *il* 12:33, 12:33a-b,
  27:46b-c
  see also Taft-Hartley Act;
    specific industries
Strindberg, Johan August
  il 20:34, 20:34c, 20:43b,
    20:44a
  biography 14:164b-c
  Dance of Death 20:65c
  Dream Play 20:35a, 20:69b

The Father 20:35a
Ghost Sonata 20:35a, 20:75b
Miss Julie 20:35a, 20:93b
Red Room 20:35a
strip cropping 9:45b
striped hyena 4:60c
strip mining 9:62c
Stroessner, Alfredo 28:28a
Strohmeyer, Friederich 2:7c
stroke (apoplexy) 6:15a, *il* 6:92,
  6:92b
stroma tissue 4:20b
stromatolite 8:22b, 8:23a
strong force 10:41b-c
strontium 2:7c, 7:38a-c, 9:10a
Strowger, Almon Brown 2:7b
structural unemployment
  12:65b, 12:78c
struthiomimus *il* 4:10
Strutt, John William 14:187a
Strymon River 26:68a
Stuart, Charles Edward *see*
  Stewart, Charles Edward
  (Bonnie Prince Charlie)
Stuart, Gilbert 19:62b-c
  biography 14:164c
  George Washington 19:62c
  Mrs. Richard Yates il 19:62,
    19:62b
Stuart, House of 26:114a,
  26:115b, 26:116a, 26:158a
Stuart, James Ewell Brown (Jeb)
  27:39a
  biography 14:164c
Stubbs, George 19:46b-c, 19:50a
  Lion Attacking a Horse 19:46c,
    19:50a
Studs Lonigan *see* Farrell,
  James T.
Stúr, Ľudovít 20:33c
sturgeon 4:75c-76a
Sturluson, Snorri *see* Snorri
  Sturluson
Sturm und Drang *see* Germany,
  literature
stuttering 17:114
Stuyvesant, Peter 27:18b
  biography 14:164c
style (bot.) 11:19c
stylus (comp.) 1:46c
style (writing) *see* writing
Styron, William 20:127a
  Confessions of Nat Turner
    20:64a
Styx (myth.) 20:114c
Suazo Cordova, Roberto
  27:224a
subarctic climate 8:64c
subatomic particle *see* meson;
  positron
subchapter S corporation
  12:13c
subduction 8:7c, 8:78c
subduction zone 8:7c
suberin 11:15b
subject (lang.) 16:21b-c, 17:3
  noun as 16:8b
  predicate agreement 16:9a,
    17:148-149
  simple 16:22a, 17:132
sublittoral region 8:75b-c
submarine *il* 2:24
  battery-powered 2:24c
  diesel-powered 2:24c-25a
  first to sink ship 2:24c
  first used for war 2:24b

  modern design 2:24c-25a
  nuclear-powered 2:24c-25a
    first 2:8b
  safety 2:24c
  steam-powered 2:24c
submersible 2:24b-25a
  see also submarine
subordinating conjunctions
  17:134, 17:137
subpoena 13:127a
subsidence 8:78c, 9:26b-c
subsidiary 12:15a-b, 12:78c
subsidy 12:78c
subsurface water *see*
  groundwater; water
subtraction *see* algebra;
  arithmetic; decimal
  system; fractions
subtrahend (math.) 3:9a
subtropical high-pressure
  belts 8:79a
suburbs 13:26c
succession (bot.) 11:31c-32a
succory *see* chicory
succulents (bot.) 11:29a
succulent stems 11:17c
Suckling, John 20:61c
Sucre, Antonio José de 28:13a
  biography 14:164c
  Ecuador 28:24b
Sucre (Bolivia) 28:39c
sucrose *see* sugar
Sudan 22:61a-62b
  agriculture 22:61b-c
  climate 22:61b
  economy 22:61b-c
  Egypt 22:61c-62a
  food shortages 22:10a,
    22:62b
  government 22:61c
  history 21:52b, 22:61c-62b
    condominium 22:62a-b
    independence 22:62b
  Islamists 21:88a
  land 22:61a-b
  map 22:61
  people 22:61b
  trade 22:61c
Sudanic languages 22:10c
Sudbury (Ontario, Canada)
  9:24b-c
Sudermann, Hermann 20:27b
Sudetanland 21:64c
Sudra (caste) 23:70c
Suetonius
  Lives of the Caesars 20:58c-59a
Suez Canal 2:6a, 21:52b, 21:72a,
  22:29a, 22:30a, 24:12b
  Great Britain 26:134a-b
  Lesseps biography 14:114c
  Syria 24:20c
suffixes (lang.) *see* vocabulary
suffrage *see* blacks, voting
  rights; elections; women,
  voting rights
sugar *see also* glucose; glycogen
  Brazil 28:15a, 28:16a
  Mauritius 22:46c-47a
  photosynthesis 11:22c-23a
Sugar Act 27:21a
sugar cane *il* 11:73, 11:73c
sugar maple 11:57b
sugar pear 11:63c
sugar pine 11:65b
Suger (abbot) 2:4a, 19:23a
Suharto 23:31a

Index

T

Index

Index

Index

Index

Index

Index

V

Index

Index

Index

Index

X

Y

Index